PENGUIN BOOKS

TOTAL TELEVISION

Alex McNeil was born in Washington, D.C., in 1948. Having earned his bachelor's degree in history at Yale, he graduated cum laude from Boston College Law School in 1973. He is employed by the Massachusetts Appeals Court as the administrative assistant to the Chief Justice. Since the publication of the first edition of *Total Television* in 1980, he has taught, lectured and written about various aspects of broadcasting. He served as a special consultant to Boston's Museum of Afro-American History on the history of blacks in television and as a special consultant to AP Radio on television and popular music. In 1988 he landed a day's work as an extra on "The Kennedys of Massachusetts," a miniseries telecast on ABC in 1990. His second television appearance was as a contestant on *Jeopardy!* in 1995. He lists as his hobbies record collecting and, of course, television watching, for which he long ago developed the interest that led him to write *Total Television*. He is also a member of the Shakespeare Oxford Society.

✦✦✦ TOTAL TELEVISION

THE COMPREHENSIVE GUIDE TO PROGRAMMING FROM 1948 TO THE PRESENT

FOURTH EDITION

Alex McNeil

PENGUIN BOOKS

PENGUIN BOOKS
Published by the Penguin Group
Penguin Group (USA) Inc., 375 Hudson Street, New York, New York 10014, U.S.A.
Penguin Books Ltd, 80 Strand, London WC2R 0RL, England
Penguin Books Australia Ltd, 250 Camberwell Road, Camberwell, Victoria 3124, Australia
Penguin Books Canada Ltd, 10 Alcorn Avenue, Toronto, Ontario, Canada M4V 3B2
Penguin Books India (P) Ltd, 11 Community Centre, Panchsheel Park, New Delhi – 110 017, India
Penguin Books (N.Z.) Ltd, Cnr Rosedale and Airborne Roads, Albany, Auckland, New Zealand
Penguin Books (South Africa) (Pty) Ltd, 24 Sturdee Avenue,
Rosebank, Johannesburg 2196, South Africa

Penguin Books Ltd, Registered Offices: 80 Strand, London WC2R 0RL, England

First published in the United States of America in Penguin Books 1980
First updated and revised edition published 1984
Second updated and revised edition published 1991
This third updated and revised edition published 1996

10   9   8

Copyright © Alexander M. McNeil, 1980, 1984, 1991, 1996
All rights reserved

LIBRARY OF CONGRESS CATALOGING IN PUBLICATION DATA
McNeil, Alex, 1948–
Total television: a comprehensive guide to programming from 1948
to the present/Alex McNeil.—4th ed.
p.   cm.
Includes index.
ISBN 0 14 02.4916 8
1. Television programs—United States—Encyclopedias.   I. Title.
PN1992.3.U5M3   1996
791.45'75'0973—dc20   95-48224

Printed in the United States of America
Set in Times Roman and Spectra

CONTENTS

This is a book for the TV fan—particularly for the person who, like me, is fascinated by the parade of television series that passes each year and who enjoys watching the shows come and go as much as watching the shows themselves. More than half of the population alive today have never known life without television. We've woken up with Dave Garroway and Captain Kangaroo and gone to bed with Jack Paar and Johnny Carson. In between we've laughed at Lucy and Archie and Uncle Miltie, wept with Kunta Kinte, and screamed at Elvis and the Beatles. We've seen a young President buried, a war in living color, an Eagle land on the moon, and a baby trapped in a well. We've seen a lot.

For the past twenty-seven years I have collected information on more than 5,400 series, network and syndicated, prime time and daytime. The series are listed alphabetically in Part I, which takes up most of this book. More detailed information on the scope of that part may be found in the explanatory notes preceding Part I.

To give a fuller picture of television programming, other material is also included:

Part II is a chronological list of special programs and broadcasts (the list is entirely subjective).

Part III is a set of charts showing the prime-time fall schedules for the major commercial networks.

Part IV is a list of Emmy and Peabody Award winners.

Part V is a list of the top-rated series for each season.

Finally, there is an index of people who are mentioned in this book. Information has been gathered from many sources: from watching the series themselves, from the networks, and from a number of periodicals and books. Among the most useful periodicals were: *TV Guide,* which assumed its present format in April 1953; *Variety,* which covers the television industry and reviews almost every new series; *The New York Times;* and the *New York Herald Tribune,* which ceased publication in 1966.

Though I have tried to insure that the information included here is accurate and up to date, I am sure that I have not been completely successful and I would appreciate any additions, corrections, comments, or suggestions.

Finally, I offer my very special thanks to several people who have helped me a lot: David and Jane Otte, Kathryn Court and Caroline White at Penguin Books, Jamie Canning at ABC, and Barbara Abseck at CBS. Extra credit goes to my wife, Jill McNeil, who has tolerated this pastime for twenty-six years, and to my children, Joanna and Jeffrey McNeil, who have patiently explained some of the intricacies of Saturday morning television to their father.

PREFACE TO THE FOURTH EDITION

In this edition all of the sections have been updated through late 1995. In Part I, about six hundred new entries have been added. Additionally, many entries appearing in the 1991 edition have been extensively revised, and a number of corrections have been made. I extend my thanks to everyone who wrote in with corrections and useful comments.

The growth of cable television has been a major development during the past decade. It would be impossible, however, to chronicle in a single volume all television series which have originated on the networks, in domestic syndication, and on cable. Although the primary focus of this book remains on network and "over-the-air" broadcasting, I have included in this edition a number of series which originated on cable services. Of particular interest have been those like *The Paper Chase* and *SCTV Network,* which moved from network to cable, and those like *Remote Control* and *It's Garry Shandling's Show,* which moved from cable to over-the-air.

PART I

ON AND OFF

Explanatory notes: It is difficult, if not impossible, to define a "series." Included here are open-ended, regularly scheduled programs, regardless of their duration; thus, *Turn-On,* a 1969 show which was canceled after only one showing, is included, while *Project 20,* the overall title for a large number of irregularly scheduled news and cultural documentaries on NBC, is not included (significant *Project 20* specials are noted in Part II of this book, however). A show like *Hallmark Hall of Fame* falls somewhere in between—it was regularly scheduled during its first seasons and is now seen a few times a year on an irregular basis; such a show is included in this part.

Also included are closed-end, multiple-episode programs, commonly known as "miniseries," such as *Roots, America,* and *The Six Wives of Henry VIII.* These programs have been included if the program contained four or more episodes or segments as originally telecast and if the episodes or segments were scheduled at regular intervals.

Shows which were broadcast during or after the fall of 1948 are included. Though network broadcasting existed prior to that time, the fall of 1948 was chosen as a starting date for several reasons: there was a tremendous growth in the number of broadcasting stations and the number of television sets during that year; television's first big stars—Milton Berle, Ed Sullivan, and Arthur Godfrey—all came to the medium during the 1948–1949 season; seven-days-a-week, four-network broadcasting began in New York in August 1948; and broadcasting took on a true national character during the 1948–1949 season, as coaxial cables linking the East with the Midwest in January 1949 made simultaneous broadcasting to different areas of the country a reality.

Series are listed alphabetically, by the titles by which they were most commonly known rather than by their exact titles. Thus, *The Adventures of Ozzie and Harriet* is listed under *Ozzie and Harriet,* and *The Many Loves of Dobie Gillis* is listed under *Dobie Gillis.*

Following the title appears the broadcast network or cable service affiliation (if any). The networks are:

ABC—the American Broadcasting Company, which numbered only fourteen affiliates in 1953, when a new corporate structure was established, but which had become equally competitive with the other networks by the 1970s

CBS—the Columbia Broadcasting System (now simply CBS, Inc.), founded in 1927, and which (with NBC) was one of the two major networks during television's early years

DUMONT—a small network established by Allen B. DuMont Laboratories in 1946; with few primary affiliates, the network never made money and perished in 1955

FOX—the Fox Broadcasting Company, organized in 1986 and financially successful by the end of the decade, becoming the first viable fourth network since the demise of Du-Mont three decades earlier

NBC—the National Broadcasting Company, a subsidiary of RCA; founded in 1926, it became the first network to begin regular television broadcasting (April 1939), and together with CBS was a major network from the outset

NET—National Educational Television; in a sense, NET was less a true network than a distributor of programs to individual educational stations throughout the country; it was not until late 1966 that simultaneous broadcasting began on educational outlets

PBS—Public Broadcasting Service, the successor to NET;

established in 1969, it distributes programs (both by simultaneous transmission and by physical delivery) to
educational stations

UPN—the United Paramount Network, which began prime-time
broadcasting on a limited basis in January 1995

WB—the WB Television Network, owned by Warner Bros.,
which also began broadcasting in prime time on a limited
basis in 1995

The principal cable services listed in this book include:

A&E—The Arts & Entertainment Cable Network, established
in February 1984

CINEMAX—A companion service of HBO, established in August
1980

CNN—The Cable News Network, established in June 1980

COM—Comedy Central, which resulted from the merger of two
comedy cable networks in 1991

DISC—The Discovery Channel, launched in June 1985

DISNEY—The Disney Channel, begun in April 1983

E!—Entertainment Television, begun in 1990

FAM—The Family Channel; formerly known as the Christian
Broadcasting Network, it was established as a cable service in April 1977

HBO—Established in 1972 as Home Box Office

LIFETIME—Established in February 1984 with the merger of two
other services, Cable Health Network and Daytime

MTV—Music Television, begun in August 1981

NICK—Nickelodeon, launched in April 1979

SHOWTIME—Premiered in July 1976

TBS—An Atlanta-based station carried on many local cable
outlets; though its call letters are WTBS, it is also known
as Superstation TBS

TNN—The Nashville Network, which began telecasting in 1983

TNT—Turner Network Television, established in 1988

USA—USA Network, which emerged from the Madison Square
Garden Sports Network in April 1980

Not all series are carried by a network or cable system, however. Many are offered
directly to individual stations or jointly owned groups of stations; that method of
distribution is known as syndication, and the word "syndicated" appears following
the title of series so distributed.

[Special note: a few programs are listed in Part II of this book, "Special Occa-
sions," with the notation "PPV," which stands for "Pay Per View." This is not a
separate cable network, but rather an ad hoc system of syndication whereby viewers
who desire to watch such a program pay their cable operator separately for it.]

The network, cable, or syndication affiliation applies only to first-run episodes or
segments of a series. If a series was rerun on another network, or if its reruns were
offered in syndication, no such affiliation is indicated. It should be noted that virtually all successful network programs are eventually offered in syndication (as reruns)
following the completion of their original network runs.

Following the network, cable, or syndication affiliation, the running dates are
listed. For network or cable series, the dates are those of the original network or
cable run. If a series returned to a network in reruns (as did *I Love Lucy,* both in
prime time and in daytime), or if a series ran simultaneously in first runs and in
reruns (as did *Gunsmoke,* reruns of which were shown under the title *Marshal Dillon*
for several seasons on CBS), the dates of the reruns are not included. Dates listed are
those for the New York City affiliates of the networks, unless otherwise indicated

(generally speaking, most CBS and NBC series were carried at the same time by all affiliates, as have been most ABC series since the early 1960s; several ABC series of the 1940s and 1950s, and most DuMont series, were not broadcast simultaneously by most network affiliates). Exact dates for some NET series are not included, as most NET programs were distributed by mail or messenger, at least until late 1966. Similarly, exact dates for syndicated series are not given, for individual stations which broadcast a syndicated series may air it whenever they choose; unless otherwise noted, the dates listed for a syndicated series are the dates when it was in production. A few syndicated series, notably *Fernwood 2-Night* and *America 2Night,* were offered to most stations for broadcast on the same dates; in those instances, exact dates are indicated.

Following the dates is a description of the series and a list of its cast. The cast includes players who were "regulars"; that is, those who appeared often enough to be considered regular performers. The list is intended to be reasonably complete, but for certain series (especially serials) it is impossible to include every performer who appeared on more than one episode. If a cast member left a series while it was still in production, the dates of his or her participation (where known) are noted. Notable guest appearances are also included where appropriate.

Certain kinds of shows are not contained here: series which consist entirely of motion pictures (such as NBC's *Saturday Night at the Movies* or *The ABC Tuesday Movie of the Week*); motion picture shorts or serials subsequently distributed to television stations (such as the *Our Gang* or *Little Rascals* comedies, *The Three Stooges* or *Renfrew of the Mounted*); shows which consisted entirely of reruns of other series (such as *Royal Playhouse,* which consisted of *Fireside Theatre* reruns); shows which consisted entirely of unsold pilot films (such shows occasionally surfaced on network TV during the summer, under a title such as *Comedy Spot*); irregularly scheduled sports broadcasts; nonnetwork shows of less than ten minutes' length; and regionally and locally televised programs.

Lastly, it should be noted that series are listed alphabetically by the first *word;* thus, for example, *All in the Family* precedes *Allen Ludden's Gallery.* A series whose title begins with a single letter will be found at the beginning of that letter; thus, *M*A*S*H, The M & M Candy Carnival, M-G-M Parade, M Squad* and *M.V.P.* all appear at the beginning of the "M" listings. Series beginning with *Dr.* or *Mr.* are listed as though the first words were spelled out in full, and hyphenated words are deemed to be one word for purposes of alphabetizing.

ABC AFTERNOON PLAYBREAK
ABC

31 OCTOBER 1973–14 AUGUST 1975   Irregularly scheduled ninety-minute dramatic specials for the afternoon-viewing audience. Presentations included: "The Things I Never Said," with Diana Hyland and Joseph Campanella (31 October 1973); "The Last Bride of Salem," with Bradford Dillman (who won an Emmy for his performance) and Lois Nettleton (8 May 1974); "Heart in Hiding," with Kay Lenz (Emmy) and Clu Gulager (14 November 1974); "Oh! Baby, Baby, Baby. . ." with Bert Convy and Judy Carne (5 December 1974); and "The Girl Who Couldn't Lose," with Julie Kavner and Jack Carter (13 February 1975; Emmys for outstanding daytime drama and for director Mort Lachman).

ABC AFTERSCHOOL SPECIALS
ABC

4 OCTOBER 1972–   Sixty-minute specials, both dramatic and documentary, for young people. Broadcast on occasional weekday afternoons. Presentations included: "Last of the Curlews," an ecology-oriented cartoon from Hanna-Barbera studios (4 October 1972); "Rookie of the Year," an Emmy award winner starring Jodie Foster (3 October 1973); "Cyrano," a Hanna-Barbera cartoon with the voices of José Ferrer (recreating his 1950 film role), Joan Van Ark, and Kurt Kasznar (6 March 1974); "Winning and Losing," a documentary about the 1974 South Dakota Senate race (6 November 1974); "Santiago's America," with Ruben Figueroa, filmed in Spanish Harlem (19 February 1975); "The Secret Life of T. K. Dearing," with Jodie Foster (23 April 1975); and "Me & Dad's New Wife," with Kristy McNichol (18 February

1976); "Mighty Moose and the Quarterback Kid," with Brandon Cruz and Dave Madden (1 December 1976); "My Mom's Having a Baby," with Dr. Lendon Smith and Shane Sinutko (16 February 1977); "Schoolboy Father," with Rob Lowe (14 October 1980); "Stoned," with Scott Baio (12 November 1980); "The Woman Who Willed a Miracle," with Cloris Leachman and Leif Green (9 February 1983); "I Want to Go Home," with Lindsay Crouse, Seth Greene and Maddie Corman (13 February 1985); "Just a Regular Kid: An AIDS Story," with Christian Hoff (9 September 1987); "Taking a Stand," with Timothy Collins (19 January 1989); "All That Glitters," with Marc Price (25 January 1990); "It's Only Rock & Roll," with Carole King and Davy Jones (21 March 1991); "Shades of a Single Protein," a look at race, moderated by Oprah Winfrey (28 January 1993); "Love Hurts," with Holly Shaw (16 September 1993); "I Hate the Way I Look," moderated by Oprah Winfrey (21 March 1994); "Boys Will Be Boys," with Ami Dolenz, David Lipper, and Joan Van Ark (15 September 1994); and "Bonnie Raitt Has Something to Talk About," in which singer Raitt was interviewed by Whoopi Goldberg (16 March 1995).

ABC ALBUM (PLYMOUTH PLAYHOUSE)   ABC
12 APRIL 1953–5 JULY 1953   Thirteen-week half-hour dramatic anthology series, seen on Sunday evenings. Presentations included: "Justice," with Paul Douglas and Lee Grant (12 April, the pilot for the series of the same title); "Jamie," with Brandon DeWilde and Ernest Truex (26 April, the pilot for that series); Charles Dickens's "A Tale of Two Cities," with Wendell Corey, Wanda Hendrix, and Judith Evelyn (3 May and 10 May); and Daphne du Maurier's "The Split Second," with Geraldine Fitzgerald (7 June).

THE ABC COMEDY HOUR   ABC
12 JANUARY 1972–5 APRIL 1972   Seven segments of this thirteen-week comedy-variety series brought together a group of highly talented impressionists calling themselves The Kopykats: Rich Little, Frank Gorshin, George Kirby, Marilyn Michaels, Charlie Callas, Joe Baker, and Fred Travalena (last four segments). Those segments were later syndicated under the title *The Kopykats*. Guest hosts included Steve Lawrence (19 January), Orson Welles with Ron Moody (26 January), Ed Sullivan with Will Jordan (9 February), Raymond Burr (23 February), Robert Young (8 March), Debbie Reynolds (22 March), and Tony Curtis (5 April). The other six segments of the series included two Alan King specials, a Friars Club roast of Sammy Davis, Jr., and a revival of "Hellzapoppin" with Jack Cassidy and Ronnie Schell.

THE ABC MONDAY MYSTERY MOVIE   ABC
6 FEBRUARY 1989–22 MAY 1989   This was the umbrella title for the three two-hour mystery series introduced by ABC early in 1989: *Columbo, Gideon Oliver* and *B. L. Stryker* (see individual titles for details). In August 1989 the series returned as *The ABC Saturday Mystery Movie*.

ABC MONDAY SPORTSNITE   ABC
1 JUNE 1987–31 AUGUST 1987   Al Trautwig hosted this sports wrap-up, which was telecast after *ABC News Nightline* on Monday evenings. The show, which sometimes featured celebrity guests, took an irreverent look at the sporting news of the preceding week.

ABC NEWS   ABC
12 OCTOBER 1953–   For many years ABC ran a distant third to CBS and NBC in news and public affairs programming. Although the network offered an evening newscast as early as 1948, few affiliates chose to carry it. In the fall of 1952 a new, more ambitious effort was attempted (see *All-Star News*), but by January of 1953 that series was seen only once a week. It was not until the fall of 1953 that Monday-through-Friday newscasts were resumed, with John Daly as the anchorman (except on Tuesdays during the 1953–1954 season, when Taylor Grant filled in). Daly, who had been a CBS radio correspondent from 1937 to 1949, had been with ABC for four

years before being named vice president in charge of news, special events, and public affairs. For the remainder of the 1950s Daly was the virtual personification of ABC News. The network scrapped the evening broadcasts during the 1957–1958 season, but returned in the fall of 1958 with a new idea—early-evening and late-evening newscasts. Don Goddard handled the early broadcast, while John Daly anchored the late one, which, though unsuccessful, is significant in that it was network television's first regularly scheduled late-night newscast.

Daly left ABC News late in 1960 (his last broadcast was on 16 December; he would continue to host *What's My Line?* on CBS for another six years), and was succeeded as head of ABC News by James C. Hagerty, who had been President Eisenhower's press secretary. Following Daly's departure the parade of anchormen and -women, most of them refugees from other networks, got under way; from 1961 to 1984 ABC put at least ten people behind its anchor desks, while CBS relied on just three and NBC five. ABC first employed John Cameron Swayze, who had anchored NBC's *Camel News Caravan* from 1948 to 1956, then Bill Shadel. On 26 March 1962, Ron Cochran, formerly of CBS, came aboard and remained until 29 January 1965 (in 1962 ABC hired reporter Mal Goode, becoming the first TV network to a hire a black reporter full-time). On 1 February 1965, Peter Jennings, a twenty-six-year-old Canadian, took over. It was during Jennings's tenure that ABC's evening newscasts expanded to thirty minutes nightly; again, ABC was the third network to lengthen its early-evening newscast. Jennings departed on 29 December 1967, and, as 1968 began, Bob Young was at the anchor desk.

Young lasted only until 24 May; Frank Reynolds succeeded him on 27 May. Reynolds, who had previously worked at ABC's Chicago affiliate, was the lone anchorman for a year, until he was joined by Howard K. Smith on 26 May 1969. Smith, a former CBS Washington correspondent, had been with ABC for seven years. ABC now seemed committed to the dual anchor concept popularized by Chet Huntley and David Brinkley at NBC. After Reynolds departed on 4 December 1970, he was succeeded the following Monday by Harry Reasoner, another CBS alumnus. The Smith-Reasoner team stayed together until 12 September 1975, after which Reasoner remained behind the desk while Smith did commentary and analysis.

In a bold move consummated in the spring of 1976, ABC lured NBC's Barbara Walters away from the *Today* show. A multiyear, multimillion-dollar contract, the opportunity to produce several specials, and the distinction of being television's first anchorwoman were offers that Walters could not refuse. She joined Reasoner at ABC's anchor desk on 4 October 1976; though the ratings for ABC's evening newscast rose slightly, the network remained third in the news race. When ABC Sports chief Roone Arledge became head of ABC News and Sports in 1977, Reasoner's future was rumored to be in doubt.

Under Arledge's aegis major changes were made in the summer of 1978. Reasoner was released from his contract and returned to CBS News. ABC elected to deemphasize the anchor concept, at least temporarily, and in July of 1978 *ABC World News Tonight* was introduced. The new format featured not one desk, but four, staffed by Frank Reynolds in Washington, Peter Jennings in London, Max Robinson in Chicago, and Barbara Walters in New York; Howard K. Smith continued to provide commentary. Barbara Walters soon left her New York anchor desk to concentrate almost exclusively on interviewing newsmakers and celebrities; most of these interviews have been put together as network specials. In March 1980 the network, which had attempted a late-night newscast in 1958, successfully reintroduced the concept (see *ABC News Nightline*).

On 20 April 1983 Frank Reynolds, seriously ill with hepatitis and cancer, gave his last broadcast; he died three months later. In September 1983 Peter Jennings, who had relocated to New York, was named sole anchor of *ABC World News Tonight*. (Max Robinson's future at ABC had been cloudy after he accused the network of alleged racism in a 1981 speech; he died of AIDS in 1988). Under Jennings's stewardship, *ABC World News Tonight* gradually climbed to the top spot by late 1989 in the three-network evening news race. Although the ratings of all three network newscasts declined during the 1990s, ABC managed to hold on to the top spot without serious opposition from CBS or NBC.

ABC NEWS NIGHTLINE

ABC

24 MARCH 1980–   The most successful of the networks' late-night newscasts began in the aftermath of the seizure of the American embassy in Iran early in November 1979. Shortly after the embassy takeover, ABC began televising a nightly update on the situation, from 11:30 to 11:45 P.M. Titled *The Iran Crisis: America Held Hostage,* the program was originally hosted by Frank Reynolds, one of the anchormen on the network's regular early-evening newscast, *ABC World News Tonight.* On 29 November 1979, ABC diplomatic correspondent Ted Koppel filled in for Reynolds and soon became the program's regular host.

The ratings of *The Iran Crisis* (which ran against the first fifteen minutes of the *Tonight* show on NBC) were significantly higher than expected and led ABC news executives to believe that a regular late-evening newscast could attract an audience. Thus emerged *ABC News Nightline* on 24 March 1980; with Koppel at anchor, *Nightline* was scheduled from 11:30 to 11:50 P.M. Mondays through Thursdays; on 5 January 1981 it was lengthened to thirty minutes, and on 3 April 1981 it expanded to include Friday nights. With the Iranian crisis showing no sign of imminent resolution, *Nightline* shifted its focus to other matters. Most programs were devoted to a single topic, and the show was widely praised for its in-depth analysis of issues.

The success of *Nightline* prompted CBS and NBC also to inaugurate late-night newscasts (see *CBS News Nightwatch* and *NBC News Overnight*) and led ABC to introduce follow-ups to *Nightline;* both of these experiments, *The Last Word* and *One on One,* were unsuccessful. On 25 April 1983 *Nightline* was expanded to an hour; multiple topics were often covered on these longer telecasts. One of the more noteworthy presentations was "The Crisis Game" (22–25 November 1983), in which a war game was simulated; former Secretary of State Edmund Muskie appeared as the president. *Nightline* returned to a half-hour format on 20 February 1984.

Among the series's many notable programs have been those from South Africa during the week of 18 March 1985 (one of which featured foreign minister R. F. Botha and Bishop Desmond Tutu appearing together), one from Ho Chi Minh City in Vietnam (29 April 1985), an April 1987 interview with Los Angeles Dodgers executive Al Campanis that cost him his job for his remarks that black ballplayers lacked "some of the necessities" to become successful managers, an April 1988 roundtable discussion commemorating the twentieth anniversary of Martin Luther King's death, the "town meeting" in Israel featuring Jews and Palestinians (26 April 1988), and a November 1988 interview with Democratic presidential candidate Michael Dukakis (perhaps best remembered for Koppel's remark to an obviously weary Dukakis, "You just don't get it, do you, Governor?"). The series celebrated its tenth anniversary with a prime-time retrospective special on 24 April 1990. Its regular starting time was moved from 11:30 to 11:35 P.M. beginning in April 1993, in order to give local stations more time to sell commercials during their 11 P.M. newscasts.

ABC ROCKS

ABC

22 JUNE 1984–2 AUGUST 1985   This half-hour pastiche of music videos was ABC's attempt to compete with NBC's *Friday Night Videos.* The attempt met with only limited success, as had *Fridays,* ABC's previous effort at cloning an NBC late-night program.

THE ABC SATURDAY MYSTERY MOVIE

ABC

19 AUGUST 1989–4 AUGUST 1990   This was the umbrella title for four two-hour mystery series. Two of them—*Columbo* and *B. L. Stryker*—had been part of the lineup on the network's spring 1989 series, *The ABC Monday Mystery Movie;* the other two—*Kojak* and *Christine Cromwell*—were new to ABC: see individual titles for details.

ABC SCOPE

ABC

11 NOVEMBER 1964–27 JANUARY 1968   A news analysis program hosted by Howard K. Smith. The series focused mainly on the war in Vietnam.

ABC SHOWCASE
22 JUNE 1950–26 JULY 1950 Allyn Edwards hosted this prime-time grab-bag of audience participation games and short comedy and dramatic sketches.

ABC SPORTS REVIEW
21 AUGUST 1948–26 APRIL 1949   One of the network's first sports programs, *ABC Sports Review* was a fifteen-minute roundup of the week's sports news, hosted by Joe Hasel.

ABC STAGE 67
14 SEPTEMBER 1966–11 MAY 1967   Among the few high points of this sixty-minute dramatic anthology series were appearances by John Gielgud in "The Love Song of Barney Kempinski" (14 September); Olivia de Havilland in "Noon Wine" (23 November, her first TV dramatic appearance); and Ingrid Bergman in "The Human Voice" (4 May). Hubbell Robinson was the executive producer of the series.

THE ABC WEEKEND SPECIAL
10 SEPTEMBER 1977–   Weekend daytime series for children which presented some first-run dramas and some reruns of shows originally aired on *The ABC Afterschool Specials*.

ABC WORLD NEWS NOW
5 JANUARY 1992–   ABC inagurated its overnight news service early in 1992. The broadcast was originally coanchored by Lisa McRee and Aaron Brown. By mid-1993 Thalia Assuras and Brian Rooney were the coanchors; Boyd Matson succeeded Rooney in late 1993, and Kevin Newman became Assuras's coanchor in late 1994. See also *ABC World News This Morning*.

ABC WORLD NEWS THIS MORNING
5 JULY 1982–   ABC inaugurated its early-morning news service with this series, scheduled weekdays at 6:00 A.M. Steve Bell and Kathleen Sullivan were the original coanchors of the broadcast. After Kathleen Sullivan left in May 1985, Jeanne Meserve coanchored with Bell. Jed Duvall took over as sole anchor early in 1987; Edie Magnus became his coanchor in June of that year, and the team stayed together until late 1988. In early 1989 Forrest Sawyer (who had earlier coanchored CBS's early-morning newscast) and Paula Zahn were teamed up; Mike Schneider succeeded Sawyer in September 1989. When Zahn left for *CBS This Morning* in February 1990, Schneider remained as sole anchor. After Schneider's departure in early 1993, the anchors of ABC's overnight news service, *ABC World News Now*, served as the anchors of the early morning newscast as well.

ABC'S WIDE WORLD OF ENTERTAINMENT
1 JANUARY 1973–5 SEPTEMBER 1975   The umbrella title for ABC's late-night programming after it became clear that *The Dick Cavett Show* would never overtake NBC's *Tonight* show. During 1973 *The Dick Cavett Show,* which had been shown nightly for three years, was cut back to one week per month. Jack Paar was lured back to network television, and thus *Jack Paar Tonite* occupied another week each month. The remaining evenings consisted of made-for-TV movies, variety programs, and a rock-music series produced by Dick Clark called *In Concert* (usually broadcast Fridays).

ABC'S WIDE WORLD OF SPORTS
29 APRIL 1961–   The brainchild of Roone Arledge, this durable "athletic anthology" series has captured the thrill of victory and the agony of defeat in virtually every known sporting event from every corner of the globe. Host Jim McKay (formerly host of *The Verdict Is Yours*) was with the series from the beginning, and served as its anchor for many seasons. Principal commentators over the years have included Howard Cosell, Frank Gifford, Bill Flemming, Chris Schenkel, Keith Jackson, Bud Palmer, Bob Beattie, and Warner Wolf. The premiere telecast presented the Drake

Relays from Des Moines and the Penn Relays from Philadelphia. The series celebrated its twenty-fifth anniversary with a two-hour prime-time special on 26 April 1986, featuring clips from past shows and a special appearance by former Yugoslavian ski jumper Vinko Bogataj, whose spectacular fall epitomized "the agony of defeat" in the show's opening sequence. Gifford succeeded McKay as anchor in the late 1980s. In January 1994 Julie Moran was named anchor, and served in that capacity until mid-1995, when she left to become the weekend coanchor of *Entertainment Tonight*.

A.D. NBC
31 MARCH 1985–4 APRIL 1985   The arrival of Christianity in ancient Rome was depicted in this twelve-hour, five-night miniseries. Featured were Denis Quilley as Peter; James Mason as Tiberius; Amanda Pays as Sarah, a Jewish slave; John McEnery as Caligula; Philip Sayer as Saul; Neil Dickson as Valerius, a Roman soldier; John Houseman as Gamaliel; Richard Kiley as Claudius; Anthony Andrews as Nero; Ava Gardner as Agrippina; and Jennifer O'Neill as Messalina, Claudius's wife.

A.E.S. HUDSON STREET ABC
23 MARCH 1978–20 APRIL 1978   Created by the crew responsible for *Barney Miller*, *A.E.S. Hudson Street* was a half-hour hospital sitcom which bore more than a superficial resemblance to *Barney Miller*. Set in the Emergency Service section of a large New York hospital, it starred Gregory Sierra (a *Barney Miller* alumnus) as Dr. Tony Menzies, chief resident. Also featured were Stefan Gierasch as Mr. Karbo, the administrator; Rosana Soto as Rosa, a nurse pregnant with her eighth child; Allan Miller as Dr. Glick, a psychiatrist; Susan Peretz as Foshko, a paramedic; Ralph Manza as Stanky, an ambulance driver; Ray Stewart as Newton, a gay nurse; and Bill Cort as Dr. Jerry Mackler, an intern. Danny Arnold, Tony Sheehan, and Chris Hayward created the series. See also *Stat*.

AG-U.S.A. (AG-DAY) SYNDICATED
1974–   Half-hour series on agricultural topics, hosted first by John Stearns, later by Al Pell.

a.k.a. PABLO ABC
6 MARCH 1984–17 APRIL 1984   Norman Lear, whose sitcoms had changed the face of television in the 1970s, teamed with Rick Mitz to create this short-flight series about a Mexican-American stand-up comic whose growing success generated problems with his family at home in East Los Angeles. The large cast featured Paul Rodriguez as Pablo (Paul) Rivera, the comic; Joe Santos as his father, Domingo, a gardener; Katy Jurado as his mother, Rosa Maria; Alma Cuervo as his sister Sylvia, who worked at a K-Mart; Martha Velez as his sister Lucia, a maid; Bert Rosario as his brother, Manuel, a bricklayer; Arnaldo Santana as Hector del Gato, Lucia's husband; Maria Richwine as Carmen, Manuel's wife; Edie Marie Rubio as Linda, Manuel and Carmen's daughter; Antonio Torres as Nicholas, Manuel and Carmen's son; Martha Gonzales as Susana del Gato, Hector and Sylvia's daughter; Mario Lopez as their son Tomas; Michelle Smith as their daughter Elena; Beto Lovato as their son Mario; Claudia Gonzales as their daughter Anna Maria; and Hector Elizondo as Paul's agent, Jose Sanchez, who called himself Jose Shapiro.

A.M. AMERICA ABC
6 JANUARY 1975–31 OCTOBER 1975   ABC's entry into early-morning programming. Bill Beutel was the host of the two-hour Monday-to-Friday show which, like NBC's *Today*, combined news, interviews, and features. Stephanie Edwards served as cohost until May. Peter Jennings read the news. Semiregular contributors included columnist Jack Anderson, naturalist Roger Caras, former senator Sam Ervin, former mayor John Lindsay, Boston physician Dr. Timothy Johnson, civil rights activist Reverend Jesse Jackson, and Ralph Story (who also served as West Coast cohost). The show failed to catch on and was replaced by *Good Morning, America*.

A.M. WEATHER

1979–   A comprehensive fifteen-minute national weather forecast, broadcast by satellite from the Maryland Center for Public Broadcasting. Dale Bryan, Barry Richwein, and Carl Weiss were the original meteorologists.

THE A TEAM
NBC

23 JANUARY 1983–30 DECEMBER 1986; 31 MAY 1987–14 JUNE 1987   Introduced in midyear, this tongue-in-cheek adventure show proved to be NBC's most popular series of the 1982–1983 season (indeed, it was the only NBC series to crack Nielsen's Top Twenty). The A Team consisted of four Vietnam veterans whose services were available to anyone who could afford them. The A Team also tried to stay a step ahead of the U.S. Army, which suspected the vets of misappropriating the proceeds of a raid on the Bank of Hanoi. Featured were George Peppard as the leader, Colonel John "Hannibal" Smith; Mr. T as B. A. Barracus, strongman and ace mechanic (born Laurence Turcaud, T changed his name legally, bedecked himself with jewelry, and adopted a Mandinkan haircut before breaking into showbiz); Dirk Benedict as Templeton "Face" Peck, a skilled imposter; Dwight Schultz as H.M. "Howlin' Mad" Murdock, a slightly deranged pilot; Melinda Culea (1983) as Amy Amanda Allen, the reporter who joined them in the premiere; and William Lucking (1983) as Colonel Lynch, the commander of the Fort Bragg military prison who grimly pursued the team. In the fall of 1983 the pursuit-by-the-army story line was deemphasized, and Melinda Culea left the show; Marla Heasley was selected as her replacement, Tawnia Baker. Heasley left at the end of the 1983–1984 season. Lance LeGault was occasionally seen as the Team's new pursuer, Colonel Decker, between 1984 and 1986. In the fall of 1986 three new regulars were added: Robert Vaughn as General Stockwell, who finally succeeded in capturing the Team and forced them to become government agents; Judy Ledford as Carla, Stockwell's secretary; and Eddie Velez as Dishpan Frankie Santana, the newest member of the Team. A total of 128 episodes were produced. Stephen J. Cannell and Frank Lupo created the series, and were its executive producers. Mike Post and Pete Carpenter provided the music. See also *Mister T.*

AARON'S WAY
NBC

9 MARCH 1988–25 MAY 1988   This hour family drama told the unlikely story of an Amish family who moved to California's wine country following the death of their son there. Featured were Merlin Olsen as Aaron Miller, the patriarch; Belinda Montgomery as his wife, Sarah Miller; Samantha Mathis as their daughter Roseanne; Scott Curtis as their son, Frank; Erin Chase as their daughter Martha; Kathleen York as Susannah Lo Verde, who, as the series began, was pregnant with the late son's child; Jessica Walter as Susannah's divorced mother, Connie Lo Verde; and Christopher Gartin as Connie's teenage son, Mickey. Twelve episodes were shown. William Blinn and Jerry Thorpe were executive producers.

THE ABBOTT AND COSTELLO SHOW
SYNDICATED

1952   One of America's most popular comedy teams, Bud Abbott (the irascible straight man) and Lou Costello (the fat funny man) made fifty-two half-hour films for television. The shows incorporated many of their best burlesque routines. Their supporting cast included Sid Fields (as their cigar-chomping landlord), Hillary Brooke (as Lou's girlfriend, who lived across the hall in the rooming house), Bobby Barber, Joe Besser (as Lou's pal Stinky), Gordon Jones (as Mike the Cop), Joe Kirk (Costello's real-life brother-in-law, as Mr. Bacigalupe), Joan Shawlee, and Milt Bronson. Besser, Brooke, Kirk, and Shawlee appeared only in the first twenty-six episodes. Alex Gottlieb, the series's original producer, was succeeded by Pat Costello, Lou's brother. Jean Yarborough directed. After the TV series Abbott and Costello made two or three more motion pictures before splitting up. Costello died in 1959.

THE ABBOTT AND COSTELLO SHOW
SYNDICATED

1966   Hanna-Barbera Productions produced an animated cartoon series based on the characters of Bud Abbott and Lou Costello; it was one of the first cartoon series based on real people. Abbott supplied his own voice, and Stan Irwin provided Costello's.

ABE BURROWS' ALMANAC   CBS
4 JANUARY 1950–29 MARCH 1950   A half hour of comedy and conversation on Wednesday nights, hosted by humorist Abe Burrows. Abe's guests on the premiere included songwriters Adolph Green and Betty Comden.

ABOUT FACES   ABC
4 JANUARY 1960–30 JUNE 1961   A daytime game show hosted by Ben Alexander which, like *Place the Face,* featured pairs of contestants whose paths had crossed previously; the first contestant to recall their association won a prize.

ABSOLUTELY FABULOUS   COM
24 JULY 1994–   Made in England, this politically incorrect sitcom quickly acquired a cult following in the U.S. after its introduction on the Comedy Central cable network. It starred Jennifer Saunders (who created and wrote the show's eighteen episodes) as Edina Monsoon, a public relations executive, and Joanna Lumley as her fashion editor pal, Patsy Stone. The two chain-smoking, booze-guzzling ladies sloshed their way through life, careening from one trendy fixation to the next. Also featured were Julia Sawalha as Edina's levelheaded daughter, Saffron, June Whitfield as her mother, and Jane Horrocks as her assistant, Bubble. The American rights to the series were obtained by Roseanne, although at least two other *AbFab*-inspired series managed to hit the air in 1995: see *Cybill* and *High Society*.

ACADEMY THEATER   NBC
25 JULY 1949–12 SEPTEMBER 1949   A summer replacement for *Tele-Theatre, Academy Theater* was a Monday-night dramatic anthology series.

ACAPULCO   NBC
27 FEBRUARY 1961–24 APRIL 1961   An attempt to salvage the *Klondike* series by moving its stars down the Pacific Coast and ahead a century. The two *Klondike* costars, Ralph Taeger (now Patrick Malone) and James Coburn (now Gregg Miles), were cast as adventurer beach bums. Also featured were Allison Hayes as Chloe, a nightclub entertainer, and Telly Savalas as Carver, a lawyer. Like most midseason format changes (e.g., *Headmaster/The New Andy Griffith Show; The John Forsythe Show*), this one was unsuccessful.

ACAPULCO H.E.A.T.   SYNDICATED
1993–1994   Hour adventures series about a group of special agents who comprised the H.E.A.T.—the Hemisphere Emergency Action Team—which operated out of an Acapulco hotel. The cast included Catherine Oxenberg as Ashley Hunter-Coddington; Alison Armitage as former cat burglar Marie Claire "Cat" Pascal; Brendan Kelly as Michael Savage; Spencer Rochfort as Brett Richards; Holly Floria as Krissie Valentine; Michael Worth as Tommy Chase; Randy Vasquez as Marcos Guettierez; Graham Heywood as Arthur Small; Fabio as Claudio, the hotel owner; and John Vernon as the boss, Mr. Smith, who communicated with the team via a video screen. The series was filmed on location at Puerto Vallarta, Mexico.

ACCENT   CBS
26 FEBRUARY 1961–6 SEPTEMBER 1962   This wide-ranging documentary and cultural series was seen on Sundays for most of its run. It was hosted by James Fleming (spring 1961), Winston Burdett (summer 1961), John Ciardi (fall 1961–1962). During the summer of 1962 it was telecast in prime time on Thursdays as *Accent on an American Summer*. The premiere telecast, a tribute to poet Robert Frost, featured an appearance by President John F. Kennedy.

ACCIDENTAL FAMILY   NBC

15 SEPTEMBER 1967–5 JANUARY 1968   Situation comedy about a Las Vegas comic, recently widowed, who owned a farm in California where dwelt a divorcée and her young daughter, who agreed to care for the comic's young son while he was on the job. With Jerry Van Dyke as comic Jerry Webster; Lois Nettleton as divorcée Susannah Kramer; Ben Blue as Susannah's uncle, Ben McGrath, the handyman; Teddy Quinn as Jerry's son Sandy; Susan Benjamin as Susannah's daughter Tracy; and Larry D. Mann as Jerry's manager, Marty.

ACCUSED   ABC

3 DECEMBER 1958–30 SEPTEMBER 1959   A midseason replacement consisting of half-hour courtroom dramas, broadcast on Wednesdays. With Edgar Allan Jones, Jr. (a law professor in real life) as the presiding judge.

ACE CRAWFORD, PRIVATE EYE   CBS

15 MARCH 1983–12 APRIL 1983   Another unsuccessful sitcom for Tim Conway, who this time starred as bumbling gumshoe Ace Crawford (Conway had previously played a bumbling ensign on *McHale's Navy,* a bumbling Texas Ranger on *Rango,* and a bumbling pilot on *The Tim Conway Show*). Also featured were Joe Regalbuto as Toomey, Crawford's accountant and part-time assistant (Toomey also provided the voiceover narration on the show); Billy Barty as Inch, the bartender at Crawford's favorite nightspot; Bill Henderson as Mello, the club's blind pianist; and Shera Danese as Ace's girlfriend Luana, the singer at the club.

ACROBAT RANCH   ABC

19 AUGUST 1950–12 MAY 1951   One of the first network children's shows to be aired on Saturday mornings, *Acrobat Ranch* was an audience participation show in which kids competed in games and stunts. Broadcast live from Chicago, the half-hour show was hosted by Jack Stillwell and featured Billy and Valerie Alberts.

ACROSS THE BOARD   ABC

1 JUNE 1959–9 OCTOBER 1959   A crossword game show, hosted daily by Ted Brown.

ACROSS THE SEVEN SEAS   SYNDICATED

1962   Travelogue, hosted by Jack Douglas.

ACT IT OUT   NBC

20 FEBRUARY 1949–7 AUGUST 1949   Bill Cullen hosted this early game show on which a group of actors acted out a scene; a telephone call was then placed to a home viewer, who could win a prize if he or she could describe, in a single word, the nature of the scene performed.

ACTION AUTOGRAPHS   ABC

24 APRIL 1949–8 JANUARY 1950   This series of interviews with celebrities and human-interest films was hosted first by Jack Brand, later by Ed Prentiss.

ACTION IN THE AFTERNOON   CBS

2 FEBRUARY 1953–29 JANUARY 1954   Television's only live western was broadcast on weekday afternoons from suburban Philadelphia, though the action was set in the town of Huberle, Montana. Jack Valentine starred in the half-hour show which also featured Mary Elaine Watts and Barry Cassell. Blake Ritter was the narrator. For most of its run, the show employed a team of four writers, each of whom wrote for a week at a time. One of the crew, Hugh Best, later recalled that the program's prime ingredient was "violence—that's what it was all about—drowning, stoning, trampling, hanging, burning, impaling, and so on. It was an aptly titled show."

ACTORS HOTEL   ABC

25 SEPTEMBER 1951–13 MAY 1952   A situation comedy set at a boardinghouse, with William Edmunds as Carlo Corelli and Alan Dale as Uncle Antonio.

ACTORS' STUDIO   ABC/CBS

26 SEPTEMBER 1948–26 OCTOBER 1949 (ABC); 1 NOVEMBER 1949–31 JANUARY 1950
(CBS)   One of television's earliest dramatic anthology series, *Actors' Studio* was
broadcast live from New York. Twenty-four-year-old Marlon Brando made an ex-
tremely rare TV appearance on 9 January 1949, when he starred in "I'm No Hero."
Other notable guest appearances on the half-hour show included those by Jessica
Tandy ("Portrait of a Madonna," 26 September 1948); Jocelyn Brando (Marlon's
sister, who starred in "The Thousand Dollar Bill" on 17 October 1948, and "A Day in
Town" on 2 January 1949); Kim Hunter ("Ropes," 7 November 1948; "The Return to
Kansas City," 1 November 1949); Tom Ewell ("Ropes" and "A Reputation," 7 April
1949); and Henry Jones ("The Timid Guy," 24 January 1950). See also *The Play's the
Thing*.

ADAM SMITH'S MONEY WORLD (ADAM SMITH)   PBS

1984–   Half-hour weekly series which explored the top economic story of the
week. The host was George J. W. Goodman, who had long used the pseudonym
Adam Smith (the name of an eighteenth-century economist) in his writings. The title
was shortened to *Adam Smith* in 1991.

THE ADAMS CHRONICLES   PBS

20 JANUARY 1976–13 APRIL 1976   Thirteen-part hour-long dramatic series depicting
the lives of the Massachusetts Adams family from 1750 to 1900; the Adams Papers—
journals and other writings of the principals—were the primary source for the screen-
plays, which were written by nine veteran playwrights. The cast included George
Grizzard as John Adams; Kathryn Walker and Leora Dana as Abigail Adams; W. B.
Brydon as Samuel Adams; David Birney and William Daniels as John Quincy Ad-
ams; David Hooks as George Washington; Robert Symonds as Ben Franklin; Curt
Dawson as John Hancock; John Houseman as Jeremiah Gridley; Peter Brandon as
Henry Adams; John Beal as Charles Francis Adams; Nicholas Pryor as John Quincy
Adams II; Charles Siebert as Charles Francis Adams II; and Charles Tenney as
Brooks Adams. Executive producer: Jac Venza for WNET, New York.

ADAM'S RIB   ABC

14 SEPTEMBER 1973–28 DECEMBER 1973   A short-lived version of the 1949 Spencer
Tracy–Katharine Hepburn movie comedy about two newlyweds, both lawyers. With
Ken Howard as Adam Bonner, an assistant district attorney; Blythe Danner as
Amanda Bonner, an associate at Kipple, Kipple & Smith; Ron Rifkin as Roy Mendel-
sohn, another assistant D.A.; Edward Winter as lawyer Kip Kipple; Dena Dietrich
as Amanda's secretary, Grace Peterson. Most of the episodes dealt with women's
rights; one hour-long special episode, adapted directly from the movie, pitted Adam
and Amanda against each other in the courtroom: he prosecuting a woman who shot
her wayward husband, she defending her.

ADAM-12   NBC

21 SEPTEMBER 1968–26 AUGUST 1975   Jack Webb developed this successful series
about two Los Angeles police officers; their patrol car identification was Adam-12.
Like Webb's own *Dragnet* series, this one stressed authenticity, even in such details as
police radio broadcasts. Typically, the officers responded to several calls during each
half-hour episode, rather than dealing with just one crime (that technique would later
be used to advantage in Webb's *Emergency!*). Starring television veteran Martin
Milner as veteran officer Pete Malloy and Kent McCord (né Kent McWhirter when
he was featured as one of Rick Nelson's frat pals on *Ozzie and Harriet*) as his rookie
partner, Jim Reed. With William Boyett as Sergeant MacDonald, their commanding
officer; Gary Crosby as Officer Wells; and Fred Stromsoe as Officer Woods. Created
by Jack Webb and Robert A. Cinader; produced by Tom Williams. Milner and
McCord were reunited in a 1989 TV-movie, "Nashville Beat," the first original film
broadcast on The Nashville Network. In 1990 a new version of the series appeared in
syndication: see *The New Adam 12*.

THE ADDAMS FAMILY   ABC

18 SEPTEMBER 1964–2 SEPTEMBER 1966   A situation comedy based on the bizarre
cartoon characters created by Charles Addams. For television, Addams provided his
motley characters with names (they'd never had any in his cartoons), and the producers made it clear that they were basically a nuclear family. With Carolyn Jones as
Morticia Addams, the macabre matriarch; John Astin as her husband, lawyer Gomez
Addams; Ken Weatherwax as son Pugsley; Lisa Loring as daughter Wednesday;
Jackie Coogan (sans hair and eyebrows) as Morticia's kindly Uncle Fester; six-foot-
nine Ted Cassidy as the laconic Lurch, their butler, and as Thing, the hand that
popped out of a box for various errands; Blossom Rock as Grandmama, Gomez's
mom; Felix Silla as the amorphous Cousin Itt. Produced by David Levy and Nat
Perrin. In retrospect ABC's *The Addams Family* seems a bit better than CBS's *The
Munsters,* another 1964 sitcom about a family of eccentrics, although both shows
lasted only two seasons. Excessive gimmickry probably helped kill them both off.
Most of the cast was reassembled for a TV-movie sequel, "Halloween with the
Addams Family," broadcast 30 October 1977 on NBC. Two popular theatrical films
were produced in the mid-1990s, starring Raul Julia and Angelica Houston as Gomez
and Morticia.

THE ADDAMS FAMILY   NBC/ABC

8 SEPTEMBER 1973–30 AUGUST 1975 (NBC); 12 SEPTEMBER 1992–7 JANUARY 1995
(ABC)   Two animated versions of the 1964 series were shown on Saturday mornings. The voices of Ted Cassidy and Jackie Coogan from the original cast were used in
the first, which was aired in the 1970s. Produced by Hanna-Barbera studios, the
animation was actually done in England. The second season consisted entirely of
reruns. The popularity of the motion picture inspired the second animated version,
which aired on ABC from 1992 to 1995.

ADDERLY   CBS

24 SEPTEMBER 1986–3 AUGUST 1988   One of several series made in Canada for CBS's
late-night schedule, this one starred Winston Rekert as V. H. Adderly, a spy assigned
to his agency's "Miscellaneous Affairs" bureau after an injury to his left hand. Oddly
enough, the low-priority assignments given to Adderly always turned out to be major
cases. Also on hand were Jonathan Welsh as his officious boss, Melville Greenspan;
Dixie Seatle as Greenspan's secretary, Mona Ellerbee; and Ken Pogue as Major
Clack. Elliott Baker created the series.

ADLAI STEVENSON REPORTS   ABC

1 OCTOBER 1961–26 MAY 1963   One of the few television programs "starring" a top
government official (*Meet the Veep* was another), this Sunday-afternoon series focused on international issues and on the United Nations in particular; Adlai Stevenson was the United States representative to the UN at the time. Arnold Michaelis,
who coproduced the Peabody Award–winning series with Stanley A. Frankel, served
as host.

THE AD-LIBBERS   CBS

3 AUGUST 1951–1 SEPTEMBER 1951   A five-week summer replacement for *Mama,* on
which a celebrity panel ad-libbed to suggestions supplied by home viewers. Hosted
by Peter Donald, the celebrity panel included Jack Lemmon and Cynthia Stone, who
would later star together in *Heavens to Betsy.*

THE ADMIRAL BROADWAY REVUE   NBC and DUMONT

28 JANUARY 1949–3 JUNE 1949   A Friday-night variety hour, *The Admiral Broadway
Revue* held the exceedingly rare distinction of having been broadcast on two networks simultaneously. More importantly, it was the start of the television career of a
twenty-seven-year-old comedian named Sid Caesar. The show was produced by Max
Liebman, who had previously worked with Caesar and who would later produce
Caesar's *Your Show of Shows.* Other regulars on *The Admiral Broadway Revue*
included Imogene Coca, Mary McCarty, Marge and Gower Champion, Bobby Van,

and Tom Avera. Charles Sanford conducted the orchestra. The format of the show was similar to that of *Your Show of Shows,* relying heavily on monologues and satires of movies and plays. Its sponsor, Admiral, was a major manufacturer of television sets. See also *Your Show of Shows.*

ADVENTURE CBS
10 MAY 1953–8 JULY 1956   An educational series for children produced by CBS in conjunction with the American Museum of Natural History in New York. It was hosted first by Mike Wallace, later by Charles Collingwood. Produced by Perry Wolff.

ADVENTURE PBS
1987–1991   Hour series of independently produced documentaries on modern-day explorers and globetrotters. The series premiered with an account of Dodge Morgan's solo sail around the world, and later took viewers on such adventures as a walk across Antarctica, the search for the yeti, and a recreation of Captain Bligh's voyage after being thrown off H. M. S. *Bounty.*

ADVENTURE AT SCOTT ISLAND
See HARBOURMASTER

ADVENTURE CALLS SYNDICATED
1966   Richard Simmons (better known as TV's Sergeant Preston) hosted this nonfiction series about modern-day adventurers.

ADVENTURE THEATRE NBC
16 JUNE 1956–1 SEPTEMBER 1956   A summer replacement for *Your Hit Parade,* it consisted of half-hour dramas filmed in England. Hosted by Paul Douglas, the series was rerun the following summer.

THE ADVENTURER SYNDICATED
1972   In this half-hour series filmed in Europe, Gene Barry starred as Steve Bradley, an international movie star who moonlights as a spy. With Barry Morse as Parminter, Bradley's contact man.

THE ADVENTURERS SYNDICATED
1966   European import about two journalists, with Edward Meeks and Yves Renier.

ADVENTURES IN JAZZ CBS
22 JANUARY 1949–24 JUNE 1949   Prime-time jazz music program, hosted by Fred Robbins. Robert L. Bach was the producer, Ralph Levy the director.

ADVENTURES IN PARADISE ABC
5 OCTOBER 1959–1 APRIL 1962   Handsome Gardner McKay, a virtual unknown (he'd done the syndicated *Boots and Saddles*), sailed to stardom as Adam Troy in this 20th Century-Fox adventure hour set in the South Pacific and based very loosely on James Michener's book. Troy was captain of the *Tiki,* an 85-foot schooner which plied the warm waters of the South Pacific. Assisting him from time to time were James Holden as Clay Baker, Troy's first mate for the first two seasons (Baker got a job at the Bali Maki Hotel as the third season began); Guy Stockwell (1961–1962) as Chris Parker, the new first mate; Linda Lawson (1959–1960) as Renée, owner of Renée's Bar in Tahiti; Weaver Levy (1959–1960) as Oliver Kee; Henry Slate (1959–1960) as Bulldog Lovey; George Tobias (1959–1961) as Penrose; Sondi Sodsai, Miss Thailand of 1960 (1960–1961), as Sondi; Marcel Hillaire (1960–1962) as Inspector Bouchard; and Lani Kai (1960–1962) as Kelly. Barbara Steele, who starred in several European horror films during the 1960s, made a rare American TV appearance on one episode, "Daughter of Illusion," broadcast 12 December 1960. The first network show set in the South Pacific, *Adventures in Paradise* was one of the few successful series set

outside the United States. Its success seems to have done little for Gardner McKay, however, whose television appearances since 1962 have been infrequent; McKay has since turned his talents to writing.

THE ADVENTURES OF BLACK BEAUTY   SYNDICATED
1972   Anna Sewell's classic book was the basis for a story made into a limited series of half-hour programs, produced in Great Britain. With Judi Bowker as Vicky Gordon; Roderick Shaw as her brother Kevin; William Lucas as their father James Gordon; and Tom Maidea as Albert.

THE ADVENTURES OF BRISCO COUNTY, JR.   FOX
27 AUGUST 1993—28 AUGUST 1994   Bruce Campbell played the title role in this lighthearted hour western. Brisco was a Harvard-educated bounty hunter tracking down the bad guys who had killed his dad, Brisco County, Sr. Also on hand were Christian Clemenson as Brisco's sometime sidekick, attorney Socrates Poole; Julius Carry as fellow bounty hunter Lord Bowler; John Astin as the wacky inventor, Professor Wickwire; Kelly Rutherford as comely saloon girl Dixie Cousins; Billy Drago as villain John Bly; and John Pyper-Ferguson as Pete Hutter. Although the series was critically hailed, it never found a sizable audience in its usual Friday night slot.

THE ADVENTURES OF CHAMPION   CBS
30 SEPTEMBER 1955–3 FEBRUARY 1956   This half-hour children's western was produced by Gene Autry's Flying A Productions, and its central character was Champion, Autry's horse. The human parts were played by Barry Curtis as twelve-year-old Ricky North and Jim Bannon as Uncle Sandy; a German shepherd named Rebel was also featured. The series, which was scheduled opposite ABC's *Rin Tin Tin,* was replaced in midseason by another kids' horse opera, *My Friend Flicka.*

THE ADVENTURES OF FALCON   SYNDICATED
1955   A television version of the espionage series which began on radio in 1945. Charles McGraw starred as Mike Waring, an American agent whose code name was The Falcon.

THE ADVENTURES OF FU MANCHU
See DR. FU MANCHU

THE ADVENTURES OF GULLIVER
See GULLIVER

THE ADVENTURES OF HIRAM HOLLIDAY
See HIRAM HOLLIDAY

THE ADVENTURES OF HYPERMAN   CBS
14 OCTOBER 1995–10 FEBRUARY 1996   The title character of this half-hour Saturday morning cartoon show was a not-too-bright superhero from another galaxy who tried to thwart the efforts of the evil Entrobe to take over the world by contaminating its environment. Hyperman was assisted by his dog, Studd Puppy, and by a teen physics whiz, Emma C. Squared.

THE ADVENTURES OF JIM BOWIE
See JIM BOWIE

THE ADVENTURES OF JONNY QUEST
See JONNY QUEST

THE ADVENTURES OF KIT CARSON
See KIT CARSON

THE ADVENTURES OF MARK & BRIAN   NBC
9 SEPTEMBER 1991–17 NOVEMBER 1991   Another of the many series which was slotted
in a "black hole" in NBC's schedule—Sundays at 7, opposite CBS's perennial powerhouse *60 Minutes*—this one gave well-known Los Angeles deejays Mark Thompson
and Brian Phelps the opportunity to live out some of their fantasies, such as
firefighting, broadcasting a pro football game, arranging someone else's wedding, or
performing onstage with the Temptations. After eleven weeks on TV, Mark and
Brian were back on radio.

THE ADVENTURES OF OZZIE AND HARRIET
See OZZIE AND HARRIET

THE ADVENTURES OF RAGGEDY ANN AND ANDY   CBS
17 SEPTEMBER 1988–1 SEPTEMBER 1990; 3 AUGUST 1991–7 SEPTEMBER 1991   Seventy
years after their literary creation, Raggedy Ann and her pals came to Saturday-
morning television in cartoon form. Joining Ann were Raggedy Andy, Raggedy Cat,
Raggedy Dog, The Camel with Wrinkled Knees, Kracklin the Wizard, and others,
who left Marcella's bedroom to go on various adventures. Reruns were hastily inserted in the summer of 1991 following the sudden cancellation of *Pee-Wee's Playhouse*.

THE ADVENTURES OF RIN TIN TIN
See RIN TIN TIN

THE ADVENTURES OF ROBIN HOOD
See ROBIN HOOD

THE ADVENTURES OF SIR FRANCIS DRAKE
See SIR FRANCIS DRAKE

THE ADVENTURES OF SIR LANCELOT
See SIR LANCELOT

THE ADVENTURES OF SUPERMAN
See SUPERMAN

ADVENTURES OF THE GUMMI BEARS
See THE GUMMI BEARS

THE ADVENTURES OF THE SEA HAWK   SYNDICATED
1961   Caribbean adventure series starring John Howard as John Hawk, skipper of
the *Sea Hawk*.

THE ADVENTURES OF THE SEASPRAY   SYNDICATED
1968   South Pacific adventure series starring Walter Brown as freelance writer John
Wells, skipper of the *Seaspray*. With Gary Gray as son Mike; Rodney Pearlman as
son Noah; and Susanne Haworth as daughter Susan. Produced in Australia.

THE ADVENTURES OF T-REX   SYNDICATED
1992   No doubt inspired by the success of the crime-fighting foursome in *Teenage
Mutant Ninja Turtles*, this show featured a crime-fighting quintet of dinosaurs: brothers Bernie, Bruno, Bubba, Buck, and Bugsy.

THE ADVENTURES OF WILLIAM TELL
See WILLIAM TELL

THE ADVOCATES   PBS
5 OCTOBER 1969–23 MAY 1974; 26 JANUARY 1978–9 SEPTEMBER 1979   One of PBS's
most popular public affairs programs, *The Advocates* was essentially a series of

debates (usually live) on topical issues. Each week two speakers, espousing opposite points of view, presented their respective "cases" for or against the proposition at issue and could call "witnesses" to "testify" on their behalf. On many shows during the early 1970s the two sides were taken by Howard Miller, a law professor of liberal bent, and William Rusher, a conservative associated with the *National Review*. Michael Dukakis, who was elected governor of Massachusetts in 1974 and would run for president in 1988, frequently moderated the series in its first years. The show was the brainchild of Roger Fisher, a professor of international law at Harvard, and was seen locally in Boston before going network in 1969. It was produced by both KCET, Los Angeles, and WGBH, Boston. Early in 1978 the show returned on a biweekly basis with Marilyn Berger as moderator.

THE AFFAIRS OF CHINA SMITH
See CHINA SMITH

AFRICAN PATROL   SYNDICATED
1959   John Bentley starred as Inspector Paul Derek of the African Patrol, a modern-day police force, in this adventure series filmed on location in Kenya.

THE AFRICANS   PBS
7 OCTOBER 1986–2 DECEMBER 1986   A nine-part exploration of African cultures and institutions, hosted by Kenyan-born political scientist Ali A. Mazrui.

AFTER HOURS   SYNDICATED
1989–1990   A fast-paced half-hour daily magazine show, intended for late-night access time slots. Heidi Bohay (late of *Hotel*) and John Majhor were the principal correspondents.

AfterMASH   CBS
26 SEPTEMBER 1983–18 DECEMBER 1984   Described in the credits as "a continuation of *M*A*S*H*," this half-hour sitcom followed three members of the *M*A*S*H* crew—Colonel Potter, Corporal Klinger, and Father Mulcahy—as they returned to the United States after the Korean War. All three joined the staff of General John J. Pershing Veterans Memorial Hospital (better known as General General) in River Bend, Missouri. Repeating their *M*A*S*H* roles were: Harry Morgan as Colonel Sherman Potter, who became chief of staff; Jamie Farr as Max Klinger, who quit the army but signed on as Potter's administrative assistant; and William Christopher as Father Francis Mulcahy, who became the hospital chaplain. Other regulars included Rosalind Chao (who had appeared in the last episodes of *M*A*S*H*) as Max's Korean wife, Soon-Lee Klinger, doing her best to adjust to the American life-style; Barbara Townsend (1983–1984) and Anne Pitoniak (fall 1984) as Sherman's wife, Mildred Potter; Jay O. Sanders (to January 1984) as Dr. Gene Pfeiffer, a surgical resident; John Chappell as Mike D'Angelo, General General's glory-hunting administrator; Brandis Kemp as Mike's assistant (and Klinger's nemesis), officious Alma Cox; Wendy Schaal as Alma's secretary, Bonnie Hornback; and David Ackroyd (January 1984–   ) as Dr. Boyer. *AfterMASH* got off to an excellent start in the fall of 1983; it was the first series premiere since *Laverne and Shirley* to top the ratings in its first week. The series ranked fifteenth overall in the 1983–1984 ratings race, and was renewed. Second-season ratings proved disappointing, however, and the show was one of the first casualties of the 1984–1985 season.

AGAINST ALL ODDS   NBC
19 APRIL 1992–19 JULY 1992   Lindsay Wagner and Everett McGill cohosted this reality-based prime-time series, which documented persons, and occasionally animals, who had triumphed over adversity.

AGAINST THE GRAIN   NBC
1 OCTOBER 1993–12 NOVEMBER 1993; 17 DECEMBER 1993–24 DECEMBER 1993; 15 JULY 1994   Sumpter, Texas—a town where people took their high school football

seriously—was the backdrop for this hour continuing drama. The cast included John Terry as Ed Clemons, the former star quarterback who was named coach of the Mustangs when his predecessor suddenly departed; Donna Bullock as his wife, Maggie Clemons; Ben Affleck as their sixteen-year-old son, Joe Willie; Robyn Lively as their college age daughter, Jill; Vanessa Lee Evigan as their eleven-year-old daughter, Jenny; Stephen Tobolowsky as auto dealer and Booster Club head Niles Hardeman; Jeanine Jackson as his wife, Mindy Hardeman; Michael Cudlitz as their son, Bud; Derek McGrath as Abel; and Wayne Knight as Froggy Wilson.

AGAINST THE LAW FOX
23 SEPTEMBER 1990–12 APRIL 1991   Hour crime show, filmed on location in Boston, starring Michael O'Keefe as maverick attorney Simon MacHeath, who left a stodgy firm to set up his own practice. With Elizabeth Ruscio as his secretary, Elizabeth Verhagen; Suzzanne Douglas as his assistant, Yvette; M. C. Gainey as "Miggsy" Meigs, who lived on a fishing boat and was MacHeath's occasional leg man; and Barbara Williams as Phoebe, Simon's ex-wife.

AN AGE OF KINGS SYNDICATED
1961   A limited series of William Shakespeare's historical plays (e.g., *Richard II, Richard III, Henry IV, Henry V,* and *Henry VI*), which were produced in England and performed by the BBC Repertory Company. Introductions for the American telecasts were presented by Dr. Frank Baxter. The series won a Peabody Award in 1962.

AGRONSKY & CO. SYNDICATED
1976–1988   Veteran newsman Martin Agronsky hosted this weekly news program after anchoring *Martin Agronsky: Evening Edition.* The series was aired on the Post-Newsweek commercial stations as well as on many PBS outlets. See also *Inside Washington.*

AIR POWER CBS
11 NOVEMBER 1956–5 MAY 1957   CBS's answer to NBC's successful documentary series *Victory at Sea, Air Power* was a twenty-six-week series of documentaries about aviation. Because producers Perry Wolff and Jim Faichney were able to obtain rare German and captured Japanese film, there was emphasis on aerial warfare during World War II. Walter Cronkite was the principal narrator; Winston Churchill and Michael Redgrave served as guest narrators for the "Battle of Britain" segment. The series was rerun in 1958 as a summer replacement for *The Twentieth Century.*

AIR TIME '57 ABC
27 DECEMBER 1956–4 APRIL 1957   Half-hour Thursday-night musical series hosted by Vaughn Monroe. Sponsored by the United States Air Force Reserve.

AIRFLYTE THEATRE (NASH AIRFLYTE THEATRE) CBS
21 SEPTEMBER 1950–15 MARCH 1951   Undistinguished half-hour dramatic anthology series, seen on Thursdays. Typical episodes included: "A Double-Eyed Deceiver," with Van Heflin (21 September); "Waltz Dream," with Kitty Carlisle (4 January); and "Peggy," with Joan Bennett (8 February). William Gaxton was the host.

AIRWOLF CBS/USA
22 JANUARY 1984–23 JULY 1986 (CBS); 29 SEPTEMBER 1986–2 OCTOBER 1988 (USA)
One of two 1984 dramatic series about helicopters (see also *Blue Thunder*), this one starred Jan-Michael Vincent as Stringfellow Hawke, a cello-playing loner who was persuaded by the government to leave his mountain home and recapture the *Airwolf,* a superhelicopter that had been spirited to Libya by its demented designer; Hawke succeeded in his mission, but refused to turn *Airwolf* back to the government, forcing the latter to keep its promise to find the whereabouts of Hawke's brother, missing in action in Vietnam. Also featured were Alex Cord as Michael Archangel, the government liaison, and Ernest Borgnine as Hawke's old pal and copilot, Dominic Santini. The *Airwolf,* which Hawke took out of hiding occasionally to perform a mission for

the government, carried an array of fourteen weapons systems and could fly at the speed of sound. Occasionally featured was Deborah Pratt as Marella, an agent of The Firm, the government agency that enlisted Hawke's services (Pratt was married to series creator Donald Bellisario). In the fall of 1984 Jean Bruce Scott joined the cast as helicopter pilot Caitlin O'Shanessy.

The USA Cable Network acquired the series in 1986 and introduced new episodes, with an entirely new cast, beginning in January 1987. Stringfellow Hawke and Dominic Santini had been killed off; replacing them were Barry Van Dyke as Stringfellow's long-lost brother, St. John Hawke, and Michele Scarabelli as Dominic's niece, Jo Santini. Other new regulars included Anthony Sherwood as Jason Locke, the new government liaison, and Geraint Wyn Davies as Major Mike Rivers.

THE AL CAPP SHOW SYNDICATED
1968   Conservative cartoonist Al Capp, creator of Li'l Abner and Fearless Fosdick, briefly hosted his own ninety-minute talk show.

THE AL HIRT SHOW
See FANFARE; MAKE YOUR OWN KIND OF MUSIC

THE AL MORGAN SHOW DUMONT
5 SEPTEMBER 1949–30 AUGUST 1951   Half-hour musical variety series with pianist Al Morgan and the Billy Chandler Trio. Broadcast from Chicago, the show was directed by Don Cook.

THE AL PEARCE SHOW CBS
Daytime: 11 FEBRUARY 1952–9 MAY 1952; 30 JUNE 1952–26 SEPTEMBER 1952; *Nighttime:* 3 JULY 1952–4 SEPTEMBER 1952   Comedian Al Pearce's first television show was a forty-five-minute daytime variety series, which was broadcast live from Hollywood. His second daytime series and his prime-time half-hour show, which replaced *The Burns and Allen Show* for the summer, both originated from New York. Pearce's best-remembered character is probably Elmer Blurt, the bumbling door-to-door salesman.

ALADDIN CBS/SYNDICATED
17 SEPTEMBER 1994–   (CBS); 1994–   (SYNDICATED) Based on the popular Disney animated feature film, this cartoon series featured Aladdin, The Genie, Princess Jasmine, the monkey Abu, and the parrot Iago. It could be seen on CBS's Saturday morning schedule and in first-run syndication on weekdays, where it was part of the two-hour *Disney Afternoon* cartoon block.

THE ALAN BURKE SHOW SYNDICATED
1966   Talk show with the accent on the sensational, presided over by the acerbic Alan Burke. Burke and Joe Pyne were probably the best-known practitioners of this peculiar talk show subcategory, which relied more on a steady flow of crackpots (who were of course subject to vicious personal attack by the host) for its guests than on showbiz personalities. See also *The Joe Pyne Show.* Two decades later the confrontational cudgel was again taken up in the talk show format: see *The Morton Downey, Jr., Show.* Burke surfaced in 1988 on an episode of *Wiseguy,* playing a controversial talk show host who was murdered.

THE ALAN YOUNG SHOW CBS
6 APRIL 1950–27 MARCH 1952; 15 FEBRUARY 1953–21 JUNE 1953   One of television's earliest stars, comedian and mime Alan Young first hosted a Thursday-night variety show that featured Polly Bergen. Early in 1953 he returned in a Sunday-night slot, which he shared biweekly with Ken Murray. This effort was a situation comedy which featured Mabel Paige. After doing a British variety series in 1958, Young resurfaced in 1961 with *Mister Ed.* When *Mister Ed* folded in 1965, Young left show business to become active in the Christian Science church; he returned to television in the late 1980s: see *Coming of Age* and *Ducktales.*

THE ALASKANS   ABC
4 OCTOBER 1959–25 SEPTEMBER 1960   One of the many Warner Brothers adventure series, this was set in Alaska during the Gold Rush of 1898 (as the theme song went, "Got the fever, got the fever—gold fever!"). With Roger Moore as Silky Harris; Dorothy Provine as Rocky Shaw; and Jeff York (he'd played Mike Fink on the Davy Crockett episodes of *Disneyland*) as Reno McKee.

THE ALCOA HOUR/ALCOA THEATRE   NBC
14 OCTOBER 1955–19 SEPTEMBER 1960   This dramatic anthology series alternated with *Goodyear Theatre* during its five-season run. Four Star Films produced both series. *The Alcoa Hour,* the first of several dramatic series sponsored by the aluminum company, was shown on Sunday nights during the 1955–1956 and 1956–1957 seasons. In 1957 a thirty-minute format was adopted, and *Alcoa Theatre* was seen on Mondays for the next three seasons. Among the major stars who appeared were Laurence Harvey (in his first major TV role, "The Small Servant," 30 October 1955), Charles Boyer (three appearances), Jack Lemmon (four), David Niven (four), Jane Powell (two), and Robert Ryan (four).

ALCOA PREMIERE   ABC
10 OCTOBER 1961–12 SEPTEMBER 1963   Dramatic anthology series hosted by Fred Astaire. Most segments were one hour, although there were some half-hour shows. Episodes included: "People Need People," with Arthur Kennedy and Lee Marvin (10 October 1961); "The Jail," with John Gavin (his first major TV role, 6 February 1962); and "The Voice of Charlie Pont," with Diana Hyland and Robert Redford (25 October 1962; Redford's only Emmy nomination was for this performance).

ALCOA PRESENTS
See ONE STEP BEYOND

THE ALDRICH FAMILY   NBC
2 OCTOBER 1949–29 MAY 1953   A favorite on radio since the late 1930s, *The Aldrich Family* was NBC's first successful television sitcom. Five actors played typical American teenager Henry Aldrich on TV: Bob Casey (1949–1950), Richard Tyler (1950–1951), Henry Girard (1951–1952), Kenneth Nelson (spring 1952), and Bobby Ellis (1952–1953). Also featured were House Jameson (the only member of the original radio cast to make the transition to TV) as his father, Sam; Lois Wilson (1949–1950), Nancy Carroll (1950–1951), Lois Wilson (again), and Barbara Robbins (1951–1953) as his mother, Alice ("Henry! Henry Aldrich!"); Charita Bauer (1949–1950), Mary Malone (1950–1952), and June Dayton (1952–1953) as his sister, Mary; Jackie Kelk (1949–1951), Robert Barry (1951–1952), and Jackie Grimes (1952–1953) as his best friend, Homer Brown; and Loretta Leversee (1952–1953) as his girlfriend, Eleanor. Paul Newman, in one of his earliest TV roles, also appeared occasionally during the 1952–1953 season. The series was created and written by Clifford Goldsmith (the characters first appeared in his play, *What A Life!*), produced and directed by Roger Kay.

ALF   NBC
22 SEPTEMBER 1986–18 JUNE 1990   NBC had tried a sitcom with a talking orangutan three years earlier; *Mr. Smith* was a bomb. Three years later it introduced a sitcom with a talking alien; *ALF* became a hit. ALF—an acronym for Alien Life Form—was a wisecracking, fur-covered, diminutive 229-year-old from the planet Melmac (where he was known as Gordon Shumway) who, like filmdom's E. T., crashed into a suburban garage and was taken in by a suburban family. Always trying to gobble up his hosts' pet cat, ALF settled into a life of domesticity, commenting wryly on American culture. The human roles were played by Max Wright as Willie Tanner; Anne Schedeen as his wife, Kate; Andrea Elson as their daughter, Lynn; Benji Gregory as their son, Brian; and John LaMotta and Liz Sheridan as next-door neighbors Trevor and Raquel Ochmonek. Josh Blake was seen during the 1988–1989 season as the Tanners' cousin, Jake; at the end of the season the Tanner family

celebrated a new arrival, baby Eric (played by J. R. and Charles Nickerson). Occasionally featured during the 1989–1990 season was Jm J. Bullock as Willie's brother, Neal. Paul Fusco, who created the series with Tom Patchett, provided ALF's voice. The show's producers attempted to keep secret the means by which ALF moved, but it was revealed that a midget, Michu Meszaros, donned the ALF costume for walking scenes; stationary scenes were performed by a puppet.

In the last first-run show of the 1989–1990 season (24 March), which was taped before the producers knew of the series's fate for the next season, ALF was invited to join two of his Melmackian cohorts, Skip and Rhonda, and to colonize another planet (Melmac having been destroyed). On his way to rendezvous with their spacecraft, after an emotional farewell to the Tanner clan, ALF was captured by a federal military investigative unit.

The series spawned not one, but two, Saturday morning cartoon series, *ALF* and *ALF Tales*. See below.

ALF   NBC
26 SEPTEMBER 1987–25 AUGUST 1990
ALF TALES   NBC
16 SEPTEMBER 1989–25 AUGUST 1990   After one season in prime time, ALF came to NBC's Saturday morning lineup in cartoon form. The animated series focused on the earlier years of ALF's life on his home planet, Melmac; known there as Gordon Shumway, he was a 193-year-old high school graduate who lived at home with his folks, Flo and Bob, his brother, Curtis, and his kid sister, Augie. In the fall of 1988 the series expanded to an hour and added a new segment, "ALF Tales," which featured spoofs of fairy tales, movies, and other works. In the fall of 1989 *ALF Tales* became a separate series.

ALFRED HITCHCOCK PRESENTS/THE ALFRED HITCHCOCK HOUR   CBS/NBC
2 OCTOBER 1955–25 SEPTEMBER 1960 (CBS); 27 SEPTEMBER 1960–18 SEPTEMBER 1962 (NBC); 20 SEPTEMBER 1962–18 SEPTEMBER 1964 (CBS); 5 OCTOBER 1964–6 SEPTEMBER 1965 (NBC)   Alfred Hitchcock, who had been directing films for three decades by 1955, entered television that fall as host of a half-hour anthology series of mysteries and melodramas. At the beginning of each episode Hitchcock's silhouette was seen filling the famous line drawing of his profile. The camera would then pan to Hitchcock himself, who would introduce the evening's story with a few well-chosen witty remarks; the set on which he appeared either bore a connection to the plot or was a spoof of a popular commercial. The opening remarks (which were filmed in French and German as well as English) typically ended with a barb at the sponsor; all were written by James Allardice. After the inevitable commercial, the episode ran. Suspense and surprise endings were the trademarks of the series. Hitchcock reappeared at the end of each show, sometimes to tie up loose ends, sometimes to assure viewers that the killer had been apprehended ("a necessary gesture to morality," as Hitchcock told *TV Guide*). In 1962 the show returned to CBS, expanded to one hour, and was retitled *The Alfred Hitchcock Hour*. Although Hitchcock hosted every episode, he directed only twenty of the several hundred shows. Between 1957 and 1959 several episodes were directed by Robert Altman, who went on to direct such notable films as *M*A*S*H* and *Nashville*. Among the many stars who made multiple appearances over the ten-year run of the series were Barbara Baxley (six appearances), Barbara Bel Geddes (four), Pat Collinge (six), Mildred Dunnock (four), Robert H. Harris (eight), Paul Hartman (five), Robert Horton (five), Henry Jones (four), Brian Keith (five), Hugh Marlowe (four), Ralph Meeker (four), Gary Merrill (seven), Claude Rains (four), Gena Rowlands (four), Phyllis Thaxter (eight), Cara Williams (four), and Dick York (five). Other notable guest appearances included those by Cloris Leachman ("Premonition," 9 October 1955), Joanne Woodward ("Momentum," 24 May 1956), Steve McQueen ("Human Interest Story," 24 May 1959; Peter Lorre ("Man from the South," 3 January 1960), Michael J. Pollard ("Anniversary Gift," 1 November 1959, his first major TV role), Dick Van Dyke ("Craig's Will," 6 March 1960), Judy Canova ("Party Line," 29 May 1960, her first TV dramatic appearance), Robert Redford ("The Right Kind of Medicine," 19

December 1961; "A Piece of the Action," 20 September 1962), Katharine Ross ("The Dividing Wall," 6 December 1963), and Peter Fonda ("The Return of Verge Likens," 5 October 1964). One episode, "The Sorcerer's Apprentice," included in the syndicated package of reruns, was never shown on network television. It featured Brandon De Wilde as a retarded youngster who, after watching a magician, accidentally sawed someone in half; the network felt that Hitchcock's concluding remarks were insufficient to "save" the show.

ALFRED HITCHCOCK PRESENTS NBC/USA
29 SEPTEMBER 1985–20 JULY 1986 (NBC); 1987–1988 (USA)   Surely Alfred Hitchcock would have been morbidly pleased to know that, five years after his death, he would return to television. On this half-hour mystery anthology series colorized versions of Hitchcock's introductions and conclusions from his old series were now wrapped around new stories, some of which were remakes of original Hitchcock shows. The show was given the go-ahead following the 5 May 1985 telecast on NBC of a two-hour telefilm which presented four updated classic Hitchcock episodes (together with a colorized Hitchcock): "Incident in a Small Jail," with Ned Beatty; "The Man from the South," with John Huston, Tippi Hedren (star of Hitchcock's *The Birds*), and Melanie Griffith (Hedren's daughter); "Bang! You're Dead," with Bianca Rose and Billy Mumy (who had played the lead in the original telecast); and "An Unlocked Window," with Annette O'Toole. New episodes were produced for the USA Cable Network during the 1987–1988 season; reruns were shown on USA through September 1991.

ALIAS SMITH AND JONES ABC
21 JANUARY 1971–13 JANUARY 1973   A breezy western featuring two outlaws who tried to earn amnesty for themselves by assuming new identities and going straight for a year ("Only you and me and the governor'll know!"). With Peter Duel (he'd spelled his last name Deuel on *Love on a Rooftop*) as Hannibal Heyes, alias Joshua Smith; Ben Murphy as Kid Curry, alias Thaddeus Jones. On 30 December 1971, Duel shot and killed himself after watching the show at his home. He was replaced by Roger Davis on 3 February 1972.

ALICE CBS
29 SEPTEMBER 1976–10 NOVEMBER 1982; 9 JANUARY 1983–19 MARCH 1985; 18 JUNE–2 JULY 1985   Based on the 1975 movie *Alice Doesn't Live Here Any More,* this half-hour sitcom proved to be one of the most durable programs of its time. Set in Phoenix, it starred Linda Lavin as Alice Hyatt, a recently widowed woman who settled there with her twelve-year-old son. Hoping to become a singer, she took a "temporary" job as a waitress at a diner. Also featured were Vic Tayback (repeating his film role) as her boss, crusty Mel Sharples, owner of Mel's Diner; Philip McKeon as Alice's son, Tommy Hyatt; Beth Howland as Vera Gorman, a mousy, scatter-brained waitress; and Marvin Kaplan (1978–1985) as one of Mel's regular customers, Henry Beesmyer, a telephone lineman. Polly Holliday (1976–1980) was featured as Florence Jean "Flo" Castleberry, a brassy, man-hungry waitress, but in the spring of 1980 she left to star in a spinoff (see *Flo*), and Diane Ladd joined the cast; ironically, Ladd had played Flo in the movie, but on TV she appeared as Belle Dupree, another brassy blonde Southerner hired by Mel to wait on tables. By the time Ladd left the series in the spring of 1981, Celia Weston had been added as the *new* new waitress, Jolene Hunnicutt. Dave Madden also began to appear regularly as Earl Hicks, Alice's sometime boyfriend and young Tommy's basketball coach. In the fall of 1982 Martha Raye, who had guest-starred previously, became a regular as Mel's mother, Carrie. In the fall of 1983 Vera met and married Elliot Novak (played by Charles Levin), a cop who had cited her for jaywalking. For the series's final season (1984–1985), Michael Durrell joined the cast as Alice's new beau, Nicholas Stone. In *Alice*'s 202nd–and final–episode, Mel sold the diner as Alice, after waitressing "temporarily" for nine years, finally found a gig as a singer.

THE ALICE PEARCE SHOW   ABC
28 JANUARY 1949–11 MARCH 1949   Alice Pearce, who would later become famous as
Gladys Kravitz, the suspicious neighbor on *Bewitched,* broke into television with her
own fifteen-minute musical show, broadcast 9:45 on Friday evenings. Accompanied
by pianist and songwriter Mark Lawrence, she sang such novelty numbers as "I'm in
Love with a Coaxial Cable." (The coaxial cable, of course, was the principal means
by which television signals were then transmitted from city to city.)

ALIEN NATION   FOX
18 SEPTEMBER 1989–17 SEPTEMBER 1990   Based on the 1988 motion picture, this hour
cop show was set in Los Angeles in 1995, where a cop was teamed up with a new
partner: a refugee from another galaxy, one of 300,000 newly arrived aliens trying to
assimilate themselves into American society while coping with the prejudice they
encountered; the allegory to contemporary race relations was obvious. Though the
aliens were of human form, they were easy to spot because of their bald heads and
mottled, elongated skulls; they also required three for sex, and found sour milk
intoxicating. The cast included Gary Graham as the human cop, Matthew Sikes; Eric
Pierpoint as his new partner, George Francisco; Michele Scarabelli as George's wife,
Susan; Lauren Woodland as their daughter, Emily; Sean Six as their son, Buck; and
Terri Treas as Matthew's alien neighbor Cathy, a biochemist with whom he became
involved. Fox reran the series during the summer of 1991, and broadcast a TV-movie
featuring many of the series regulars, "Alien Nation: Dark Horizon," on 25 October
1994.

ALIVE FROM OFF-CENTER   PBS
1 JULY 1985–   The umbrella title for a wide-ranging series of performances,
veering toward the avant-garde. The series is broadcast during the summer. It was
retitled *Alive TV* in 1992.

ALKALI IKE   CBS
17 APRIL 1950–11 MAY 1950   A fifteen-minute puppet show with a western theme,
Alkali Ike was seen after the evening news once or twice a week. Ventriloquist Al
Robinson was assisted by Beverly Fite and the Slim Jackson Quartet. Barry Wood
produced the series.

ALL ABOARD   CBS
19 OCTOBER 1952–11 JANUARY 1953   Fifteen-minute interview show hosted by Skeets
Minton.

ALL ABOUT FACES   SYNDICATED
1971   Richard Hayes hosted this lackluster game show, similar in format to Gene
Rayburn's *The Amateur's Guide to Love* and similar in title to Ben Alexander's
About Faces. On this one, celebrity pairs were shown brief film sequences and tried
to predict their outcome.

ALL AROUND THE TOWN   CBS
18 JUNE 1951–7 AUGUST 1952   Hosted by Mike Wallace and Buff Cobb (his then
wife), this half-hour series examined goings-on in New York City. Originally seen
three afternoons a week, the show moved to prime time in November 1951.

ALL CREATURES GREAT AND SMALL   PBS/A&E
1979 (PBS); 4 FEBRUARY 1988–7 APRIL 1988 (A&E); 11 JUNE 1989–27 AUGUST 1989
(A&E)   This series was based on James Herriot's delightful tale of his life as a
veterinarian in Yorkshire. Christopher Timothy portrayed Herriot on the series,
which was produced in England by the BBC.

ALL IN THE FAMILY (ARCHIE BUNKER'S PLACE)   CBS
12 JANUARY 1971–21 SEPTEMBER 1983   Because of its impact on American audiences
and on the style of television comedy, *All in the Family* is perhaps the single most

influential program in the history of broadcasting. In terms of production techniques, the series added nothing new; in some ways it represented a return to the old days of television: one basic set, a small cast, and little reliance on guest stars. *I Love Lucy,* TV's first smash hit sitcom, was the first to be filmed before a live audience; *All in the Family* was the first sitcom to be videotaped, and, unlike the vast majority of sitcoms of the 1960s, it was performed before a live audience.

It was in story development and character treatment that *All in the Family* broke new ground. It was the first situation comedy to deal openly with bigotry, prejudice, and politics. "Hot" issues such as abortion, birth control, mate-swapping, menopause, and homosexuality were handled successfully on the show. "Taboo" words, such as "spic," "hebe," and "spade" were uttered. And throughout it all, audiences laughed. The show's immense popularity with all segments of the population demonstrated that it had broad appeal and indicated that American audiences of the 1970s were sophisticated enough to appreciate well-produced, well-written, and well-acted topical comedy. Studies showed that, by 1973, the face of central character Archie Bunker was the most widely recognized in America; phrases such as "Stifle yourself!" "Dingbat!" and "Meathead!" were part of the American vocabulary.

The men responsible for *All in the Family* were Norman Lear and his partner Alan "Bud" Yorkin, two motion picture producer-directors with considerable television experience. Lear had been a comedy writer in the early 1950s, then a director, and later a producer ("The TV Guide Awards Show" in 1962, "Henry Fonda and the Family" in 1963, *The Andy Williams Show* in 1965–1966); Yorkin had directed many shows at NBC (including *The Colgate Comedy Hour, The Dinah Shore Show, The Tony Martin Show, Tennessee Ernie Ford,* and *The George Gobel Show*) and directed and produced Fred Astaire's 1958 and 1959 specials. Together or separately during the 1960s they made such films as *Come Blow Your Horn* (Lear producer, Yorkin director), *Never Too Late* (Yorkin director), *Divorce American Style* (Lear producer, Yorkin director), and *The Night They Raided Minsky's* (Lear producer).

All in the Family was on the drawing board as early as 1968, shortly after Lear learned of a hit series on British television, *Till Death Us Do Part.* Created by Johnny Speight, it told of a British family of modest means, with bigoted father and live-in son-in-law. Lear bought the American rights to the series, wrote a script, and convinced ABC to finance a pilot. With Carroll O'Connor and Jean Stapleton in the lead roles, a pilot was made; the show was called *Those Were the Days.* But ABC, unhappy with the concept even after a second pilot, let its option lapse. CBS executives then saw the pilot, and the network grabbed the series. Rob Reiner and Sally Struthers were brought in for the supporting roles as production began. At 9:30 P.M. (EST) on Tuesday, January 12, 1971, the show premiered. It was prefaced by an announcement: "The program you are about to see is *All in the Family.* It seeks to throw a humorous spotlight on our frailties, prejudices, and concerns. By making them a source of laughter we hope to show—in a mature fashion—just how absurd they are."

Those who watched the premiere (it was fifty-fourth in the weekly Nielsen ratings) apparently liked what they saw and told their friends. By summer, the show was number one. In the fall it was moved to Saturdays at 8 P.M., the slot it occupied for the next four seasons. It was there that America learned to love the people of *All in the Family.*

Carroll O'Connor, a character actor of much experience but little previous recognition, caught Lear's eye when he appeared in a 1968 film, *What Did You Do in the War, Daddy?* Lear was certain that O'Connor would be just right for the role of Archie Bunker, a bigoted, right-wing, lower-middle-class, high-school-educated, white Protestant with a tendency to run off at the mouth. Archie lived in Queens (704 Hauser Street) with his wife, daughter, and son-in-law, and until 1976 worked as a loading dock foreman at Prendergast Tool and Die Company. As O'Connor explained his role to *TV Guide,* "Archie's dilemma is coping with a world that is changing in front of him. . . . But he won't get to the root of the problem because the root of the problem is himself, and he doesn't know it."

Jean Stapleton, also a relatively unheralded character player, was well known to Lear and Yorkin. As Archie's devoted wife, Edith Bunker, she was patient, tolerant, even-tempered, and honest, though perhaps a bit confused at times. Unlike Archie, Edith was able to cope with the changes that life brings.

Two virtual unknowns filled out the main cast. Sally Struthers, with brief TV comedy experience from the Smothers Brothers' 1970 summer show and Tim Conway's 1970 fall series, played the Bunkers' only child, Gloria, who, though liberal in outlook, loved her parents. She worked part-time as a salesclerk to help support her husband, Mike Stivic. Rob Reiner, son of Carl Reiner, one of television's most creative funny people, played Mike, a student with a big appetite and a big mouth. Vocally liberal, he enjoyed baiting Archie. As the series progressed, Mike finally finished college and got a job as an instructor. He and Gloria then moved next door and had a baby; little Joey Stivic (played by Jason Draeger, and later by Cory Miller) was born in January 1976 (a 1976 episode caused some consternation at the network when it showed Archie changing a naked baby boy).

Other principal characters over the seasons included: Michael Evans (to January 1975) as Lionel Jefferson, Mike and Gloria's black friend; Isabel Sanford (who first appeared on 2 March 1971 and became a regular in 1972) as Louise Jefferson, Lionel's mom; Mel Stewart (1972–1974) as Henry Jefferson, Lionel's uncle; and Sherman Hemsley (1974–January 1975) as George Jefferson, Lionel's dad. In January 1975 the Jeffersons, who had become the Bunkers' next-door neighbors, moved out of the neighborhood and into their own series. In 1973 Betty Garrett and Vincent Gardenia joined the cast as Irene and Frank Lorenzo, the Bunkers' other next-door neighbors. Gardenia left after one season, Garrett after three. In the fall of 1976 the Bunkers rented out their now spare bedroom (the kids having moved into the Jeffersons' old house) for the season to Teresa Betancourt (played by Liz Torres), a Puerto Rican hospital worker. In the fall of 1977, a year after his promotion to a dispatcher's job at the plant, Archie quit his job to become his own boss: he bought Kelsey's, his favorite local watering hole, and renamed it Archie's Place. Added to the cast were Jason Wingreen as Harry Snowden, the bartender; Allan Melvin as Archie's neighbor, Barney Hefner; and Danny Dayton as Archie's pal Hank Pivnik.

Both Rob Reiner and Sally Struthers announced their plans to leave the show at the end of the 1977–1978 season; in the season finale viewers learned that Mike Stivic had landed a teaching job at a distant university, forcing the Stivics to move away. As *All in the Family*'s ninth season began in the fall of 1978, Archie and Edith found themselves alone together, but only temporarily, as Danielle Brisebois (who had been in the cast of *Annie* on Broadway) was introduced as Stephanie Mills, a distant niece of Edith's who was dropped off—indefinitely—at the Bunkers' by her vagabond father.

More changes occurred in the fall of 1979. The show's title was changed to *Archie Bunker's Place,* as the action shifted from the Bunker household to Archie's bar. O'Connor, Brisebois, Melvin, and Dayton remained as regulars, with Stapleton scheduled to make a number of guest appearances during the season. Martin Balsam joined the cast as Archie's new business partner, Murray Klein; Bill Quinn appeared regularly as the blind Mr. Van Ranseleer, a regular customer; Anne Meara was the new chef, Veronica Rooney; Guerin Barry and Dino Scofield played her nephew Fred, the waiter; and Abraham Alvarez played Jose, the cook.

Jean Stapleton left the show entirely at the end of the 1979–1980 season, and *Archie Bunker's* producers decided to "kill off" her character, Edith Bunker. The 1980–1981 season began with a deeply moving episode, "Edith's Death," in which Archie finally came to grips with the loss of his wife; Carroll O'Connor won a Peabody Award for this performance. Joining the cast that season were Janet MacLachlan as the black next-door neighbor, Polly Swanson; Mel Bryant as her husband, Ed Swanson; Barbara Meek as Ed's sister, Ellen Canby, who became Archie's housekeeper; Heidi Hagman (daughter of Carroll O'Connor's good friend Larry Hagman of *Dallas*) as Linda, a waitress; and Joe Rosario as Raoul, the busboy.

Martin Balsam departed in the spring of 1981 after two seasons as Archie's business partner. Denise Miller signed on that fall as Archie's niece, Billie Bunker, daughter of his late brother. Steven Hendrickson also appeared as Archie's young accountant, Roger Abbott, who took an interest in Billie. In the last of the personnel changes, Anne Meara quit the show in 1982, and Barry Gordon was added as Archie's new accountant, Gary Rabinowitz.

In 1983 *All in the Family/Archie Bunker's Place* left the prime-time airwaves, although its reruns continued to be widely distributed. Its twelve-and-a-half-season run was second only to that of *Ozzie and Harriet* among television sitcoms.

The show's opening theme song, "Those Were the Days" (which was to have been the program's title), was composed by Lee Adams and Charles Strouse. It was sung by O'Connor and Stapleton until 1980, when an instrumental version was used. The closing theme, "Remembering You," was written by Roger Kellaway; lyrics (not used on the show) were written by Carroll O'Connor. Two series were spun off from *All in the Family: Maude* (1972–1978; *Maude*'s star, Beatrice Arthur, appeared as Edith's cousin on 11 December 1971) and *The Jeffersons* (1975–1985). A sequel of sorts appeared in 1982 when Sally Struthers returned as Archie Bunker's daughter in *Gloria*. The Bunkers' old house was the setting of a 1994 effort, *704 Hauser*. Among the other notable series developed by Norman Lear and/or Bud Yorkin were *All That Glitters, All's Fair, Good Times, Grady, Hot L Baltimore, Mary Hartman, Mary Hartman, One Day at a Time,* and *Sanford and Son.* CBS telecast a ninety-minute retrospective of *All in the Family* on 16 February 1991. The network aired a few reruns in prime time during the summer of 1991 (following Lear's new series, *Sunday Dinner*), and again in January 1992.

ALL IS FORGIVEN   NBC

20 MARCH 1986–12 JUNE 1986   Bess Armstrong starred in this half-hour sitcom as Paula Winters, who landed a new job on the morning, and got married in the evening, of her "lucky day": March 29th. The job she landed was as producer of a TV soap opera, "All Is Forgiven," and the marriage was to a divorced donut entrepreneur, Matt Russell (played by Terence Knox, late of *St. Elsewhere*). Also aboard were Shawnee Smith as Matt's 16-year-old daughter, Sonia; David Alan Grier as Oliver Royce, one of the soap's writers; Bill Wiley as Wendell, the director; Judith-Marie Bergan as Cecile Porter-Lindsey, the star; Debi Richter as Sherry Levy; Valerie Landsburg as receptionist Lorraine Elder; and Carol Kane as Nicolette Bingham, the head writer. After two showings on Thursday evenings, *All Is Forgiven* actually moved to Saturdays on March 29th, Paula's "lucky day," but to little avail; the series faded away quietly after nine showings.

ALL MY CHILDREN   ABC

5 JANUARY 1970–   Created by veteran serial writer Agnes Nixon (who had worked on *Search for Tomorrow, Another World,* and *One Life to Live,* among others), *All My Children* became TV's top-rated soap opera in 1978–1979; for much of the following decade it ran second to *General Hospital.* The program is set in Pine Valley, a town not far from New York City. Originally, it centered on two families—the Tylers and the Martins—but most of the Martin clan was written out by the end of the first decade.

Principal players have included: Hugh Franklin as Dr. Charles Tyler, a prominent physician; Ruth Warrick as his status-conscious wife, Phoebe Tyler (Phoebe and Charles were subsequently divorced); James Karen, Paul Dumont, Nicholas Pryor, and Peter White as their son, Lincoln; Diana De Vegh, Joanna Miles, and Judith Barcroft as their daughter, Ann (Ann was committed to a mental institution as the character was written out; she returned to Pine Valley three years later, played by Gwyn Gilliss); Jack Stauffer, Chris Hubbell, Gregory Chase, and Richard Van Vleet as Charles's grandson (by a former marriage), Dr. Chuck Tyler, who had been orphaned as an infant; Rosemary Prinz (1970) as Lincoln's wife, Amy, who left him after the news was spread that she had had an illegitimate child; Susan Lucci as the woman who spread that news, the self-centered Erica Kane, who would later pursue a quest for celebrity and would be married eleven times to eight men in 24 years (Erica became one of daytime TV's most popular characters, and Lucci one of its most popular performers; unfortunately, Lucci had not won an Emmy for her role by 1995, despite having been nominated fifteen times); Larry Keith as Nick Davis, the man with whom Amy had had an affair; Richard Hatch and Nick Benedict as Phillip

Brent, son of Amy and Nick; Mary Fickett as Amy's sister, Ruth Brent, who raised young Phillip; Mark Dawson as Ruth's husband, Ted Brent, who was killed in a car crash; Karen Gorney, Stephanie Braxton, Karen Gorney (again), Nancy Frangione, and Mary Lynn Blanks as Tara Martin, Phil's girlfriend, who was abandoned by Phil after he contracted amnesia and left town (Phil returned, thoughtlessly interrupting Tara and Chuck's wedding); Ray MacDonnell as Tara's father, Dr. Joseph Martin, a prominent physician who married Ruth Brent; Deborah Solomon as Sydney Scott, who opened a boutique with Ann Tyler; Charles Frank, Christopher Wines, Robert Perault, James O'Sullivan, Jeffrey Byron, and John Tripp as Jeff Martin, Tara's brother, who was ensnared by Erica Kane (Erica subsequently underwent the first legal abortion on a TV soap opera); Ken Rabat and William Mooney as Joe Martin's brother, lawyer Paul Martin, who married Ann Tyler after her marriage to Nick Davis; Ian Miller Washam and Brian Lima as Phillip Tyler, son of Tara and Phil, who was raised by Tara and Chuck; Tom Rosqui and John Devlin as modeling agent Jason Maxwell, who caused Erica to divorce Jeff Martin and was later murdered; Jacqueline Boslow and Susan Blanchard as nurse Mary Kennicott, Jeff's second wife, who was killed by burglars; Frances Heflin as Erica's mother, Mona Kane, who had murdered Jason Maxwell (Mona later married Charles Tyler after his divorce from Phoebe); Francesca James as Kitty Shea, who married Nick Davis (James later appeared as Kitty's twin sister, Kelly Cole); Eileen Letchworth as Margo Flax, who married Paul Martin after his divorce from Ann; Dan Hamilton as drug dealer Hal Short, Kitty's ex-husband; Paulette Breen and Susan Plantt-Winston as Margo's daughter, Claudette Montgomery; Eileen Herlie as Myrtle Lum (later known as Myrtle Fargate), a woman hired by Phoebe to pose as Kitty's long-lost mother; Paul Gleason as ex-doctor David Thornton, with whom Ruth Martin fell in love; Don Blakely and John Danelle as Dr. Franklin Grant, a black physician; Avis MacArthur and Lisa Wilkinson as his wife, Nancy Grant (Franklin and Nancy were divorced, and remarried; Franklin died in 1983); Pat Dixon as nurse Carolyn Murray, who was wed to Franklin Grant between his two marriages to Nancy; Francesca Poston and Candice Earley as Donna Beck, a prostitute who was rehabilitated by Chuck Tyler and married him (they were later divorced); Christine Thomas, Kate Harrington, and Kay Campbell as Kate Martin, mother of Joe and Paul Martin; Marilyn Chris as Edie Hoffman; Michael Shannon as Bill Hoffman; Maureen Mooney as Stacy Coles; Bruce Gray as Wyatt Coles; Daren Kelly as Danny Kennicott; Elissa Leeds, Harriet Hall, and Julia Barr as Brooke English; Matthew Anton, John E. Dunn, and Michael E. Knight as Tad Gardner, who was adopted by the Martins; Reuben Green as Clay Watson; Dawn Marie Boyle and Tasia Valenza as Dottie Thornton; Matthew Cowles as Billy Clyde Tuggle, a crook; Larry Fleischman and Vasili Bogazianos as Benny Sago; Sandy Gabriel as Edna Thornton Ferguson; William Griffis as Harlan Tucker, who married Mona Kane; John K. Carroll and Steven James as Carl Blair; Mark LaMura as Erica's brother, Mark Dalton, who became addicted to crack cocaine (and later kicked the habit); Kathleen Noone as Ellen Shepherd, who married Mark; Tricia Pursley (also known as Tricia P. Hawkins) as Devon Shepherd; Gil Rogers as Ray Gardner; Richard Shoberg as Tom Cudahy, who married Erica, then married Brooke English; Robin Strasser as Dr. Christina Karras; Paula Trueman as Maggie Flanagan.

Other comings and goings included those of Kathleen Dezina as Estelle LaTour, who married Benny Sago; Jack Magee, Nigel Reed, and Patrick Skelton as Wally McFadden, who married Devon Shepherd; Ross Petty and Warren Burton as Eddie Dorrance; Bob Hover as Adrian Shepherd; Harry Boda as Mel Jacobi; David Pendleton as Dr. Russ Anderson; Fred Porcelli as Freddy; Judith Roberts as Lettie Jean; Linda Gibboney as nurse Sybil Thorne; Louis Edmonds as con artist Lenny Vlasic, better known as Langley Wallingford, who married Phoebe Tyler after her divorce from Charles; James Mitchell as business executive Palmer Cortlandt, who married Donna Beck Tyler; Gillian Spencer as Daisy Cortlandt, Palmer's ex-wife (Daisy was also known as Monique Jonvil); Taylor Miller, Heather Stanford, and Barbara Kearns as Palmer and Daisy's daughter, Nina Cortlandt; Elizabeth Lawrence as Daisy's mother (and Palmer's housekeeper), Myra Murdock; Peter Bergman as Dr. Cliff Warner, who married Nina; Matthew McNamara and Chris Mazura as Bobby Warner,

Cliff's son (by nurse Sybil Thorne); Carla Dragoni as Betsy Kennicott; Tracey Fitzpatrick as Suzanne Robbins; Lizabeth MacKay as Leora Sanders; Bill Ferriter as Curt Sanders; Alan Dysert as Sean Cudahy; Paul Falzone as Jim Jefferson; Andrea Moar as Carrie Sanders, who married Chuck Tyler; Carol McCluer and Paige Turco as Melanie Sawyer Cortlandt; William Cain as Hughes; Frances Foster as Bessie; Mike Minor as Brandon Kingsley, a cosmetics executive who employed Erica as a model, and had an affair with her; Tudi Wiggins as Sarah Kingsley, Brandon's wife; Kathy Kamhi and Kathleen Rowe McAllen as Pamela Kingsley, daughter of Brandon and Sarah; Michael Woods and Lee Godart as Kent Bogard, owner of Sensuelle Cosmetics, for whom Erica later modeled (Kent was accidentally shot by Erica); William Blankenship, Robert Milli, and Jack Betts as Lars Bogard, Kent's father; Deborah Goodrich as Connie Wilkes, who posed as Erica's sister, Silver Kane; Dack Rambo as lawyer Steve Jacobi; Dorothy Lyman and Jill Larson as the consummately tacky Opal Gardner, ex-wife of Ray Gardner, who took a job as the Wallingfords' housekeeper and later started a chain of beauty parlors; Kim Delaney as Opal's teenage daughter, Jenny Gardner; Laurence Lau as Greg Nelson, Jenny's boyfriend; Natalie Ross as Enid Nelson, Greg's mother; Marcy Walker and Alice Haining as Jenny's bitchy classmate, Liza Colby; Darnell Williams as Jesse Hubbard, nephew of Franklin Grant; Debbi Morgan and Saundra Quarterman as Angie Baxter, who secretly married Jesse; Lee Chamberlin as Angie's mother, Pat Baxter; Antonio Fargas as Les Baxter, Angie's father; Lynne Thigpen as Flora Baxter, Angie's aunt; Amanda Bearse as Amanda Cousins; Ronald Drake as Jasper Sloane; Jason Kincaid as Sam Brady; Michael Scalera and Michael Brainard as Joey Martin; Bill Timoney as Alfred Vanderpoole; Charles Weldon and Robert Lupone as Zach Johnson; Alan Campbell as Evan; Mel Boudrot as Father Tierney; Portia Nelson as Mrs. Gurney; Brent Barrett as Tony Barclay; Barbara Hooyman as Ethel; Jennifer Bassey as Marian Colby; Joseph Warren as Larry Colby; Peg Murray as Olga Svenson, sister of Lars Bogard; Donna Pescow as child psychologist Lynn Carson, a lesbian; Robert Gentry as Ross Chandler; Steve McNaughton as Gil Barrett; Melissa Leo as Linda Warner; Carmen Thomas as Hillary Wilson; Jennifer Leigh Warren as Karen Smith; and Nicolas Surovy and Hugo Napier as Mike Roy.

Also: David Canary as twins Adam and Stuart Chandler; Elizabeth Forsyth as Candy Brown; Jane Elliot as Cynthia Preston; Steve Caffrey as Andrew Preston/ Andrew Cortlandt; Tom Wright as Eugene Hubbard; Carole Shelley as June Hagen; Marie Reynolds as Micki Barlow; Meg Myles as Joanna Yaeger; Vanessa Bell as Yvonne Caldwell; Jean LeClerc as mysterious Jeremy Hunter (the character, along with others from *AMC*, later moved to *Loving*, an ABC soap created by Agnes Nixon); Kate Collins and Melody Anderson as Natalie Hunter, who married Palmer Cortlandt (Collins also played a second role, Janet); Mary Kane as Coral; Michael Tylo as Matt Connolly; Stephanie Winters and Lauren Holly as Julie Cortlandt Chandler; Rosa Langschwadt (later known as Rosa Nevin) as Cecily Davidson; Lisa Howard as Syd Weber; Susan Pratt as Barbara Montgomery; Larkin Malloy and Daniel Hugh-Kelly as Travis Montgomery, who became Erica's fifth husband (and the father of her daughter, Bianca; a special two-part episode, told entirely from Erica's point of view before the baby's birth, reunited many of the men from Erica's life); Antoinette Byron and Robin Christopher as Skye Patterson, who married Tom Cudahy in 1987; Brian Fitzpatrick as Mitch Beck; Catherine Christianson as Dr. Amy Stone; Christopher Holder as Wade Matthews; Rosalind Ingledew and Claire Beckman as Noelle Keaton (who turned out to be the real Silver Kane, Erica's sister); Louise Shaffer as Constance Keaton, also known as Goldie Kane; Lisa Eichhorn as Elizabeth Carlyle; Deborah Morehart as Robin McCall; Charles Keating as Damon Lazare; Laura San Giacomo and Maria Strova as Luisa; Ann Flood as Bitsy Davidson; Walt Willey as Jackson Montgomery; Jack Couch as Dabney Paine; Mark McCoy as Roy Cramer; Robbie Duncan McNeill, Charles Van Eman, and Christopher Lawford as Charlie Brent; Jo Henderson and Dena Dietrich as Wilma Marlowe; James Horan as Creed Kelly; Maurice Benard as Nico Kelly; Ellen Wheeler as AIDS victim Cindy Parker; Teri Eoff as Pilar; Roberta Maxwell as Nanny Judith; Robert Swan as Jeb Tidwell; Stan Albers as Josh Waleski; Kari Gibson and Cady McClain as Dixie Cooney, who married Adam Chandler in 1989; Lonnie Quinn as Will Cooney;

Eddie Earl Hatch as John Remington; Nicholas Carter as Steven Andrews; Nicole Orth-Pallavicini and Nancy Addison as Marissa; Trent Bushey as David Rampal, son of Jeremy Hunter; Alice Webb as Mrs. Valentine, a maid; Matt Servitto as Trask; David Jordan and James Kiberd as Trevor Dillon; Liz Vassey as Emily Ann Sago; Eugene Anthony as Stanley "Uli" Ulatowski; Philip Amelio and Shane McDermott as Scott Chandler; Tichina Arnold as Sharla Valentine; Count Stovall as Cal Cummings; Z. Wright as Frankie Hubbard; Albert Stratton as Eric Kane; Genie Francis as Ceara Connor, Myrtle Fargate's niece; Kelly Ripa as Hayley Vaughn, niece of Trevor Dillon; William Christian as Derek Frye; Gregory Gordon, Matt Borlenghi, and Brian Green as Brian Bodine; Tommy J. Michaels as Timmy Hunter; Patrick Stuart (later known as James Patrick Stuart as Will Cortlandt; and Jessica Falborn, Carolyn Wilde, Lacey Chabert, and Gina Gallagher as Bianca Montgomery, Erica's daughter (born on the show in 1988, the precocious child was six years old in 1989).

By 1991 five members of the original cast remained: Mary Fickett, Frances Heflin, Susan Lucci, Ray MacDonnell, and Ruth Warrick. New faces for the 1990s included the following: Shari Headley as police officer Mimi Reed; Greta Lind as Katie Kennicott; Tonya Pinkins as Livia Frye Cudahy; Bethel Leslie as Claudia Connor, Ceara's mother; Stephen Joyce as George Connor; Scott Thompson Baker as Craig Lawson; Michael Nader as Dimitri Marick, who became Erica's tenth and eleventh husbands; Season Hubley as Angelique Marick; Fritz Weaver as Hugo Marick; Susan Willis as Helga, Dimitri's housekeeper; David L. King as Keith Gordon; Andrew Jackson as Dr. Steve Hamill; Akili Prince and Dondre T. Whitfield as Terrence Frye; Richard Lawson as Terrence's father, Lucas Barnes; Irene Ng and Lindsay Price as An-Li Chen; Marlo Marron as Sabrina; Teresa Blake as Gloria Marsh Chandler; Courtney Gibbs Eplin and Karen Person as district attorney Galen Henderson; John Callahan as Edmund Grey; Steven Keats as Alfred Gresham, Edmund's father; Ingrid Rogers and Kelli Taylor as Taylor Roxbury-Cannon; John-Wesley Shipp as Carter Jones; Jennifer Van Dyck as Marta Jones, Carter's sister; Andrea McArdle as Cookie; Christine Belford as Elena Lazlo; Lois Robbins as Dr. Anna Tolan; Margaret Sophie Stein as Corvina Lang; Larry Pine as Max Jeffries; Barbara Rush as Nola Orsini; Charles Cioffi as lawyer Lionel Glynn; Morgana King as Mrs. Manganaro; Anne Meara as Peggy Moody; Sarah Michelle Gellar as Kendall Hart; Kristen Jensen and Felicity LaFortune as Laurel Banning Montgomery; Eva LaRue as Dr. Maria Santos; Sydney Penny as Julia Santos; Grant Aleksander as Alex McIntyre; Kale Brown as Denny Benton; Rudolf Martin as Anton Lang; Gregg Edelman as Irv Star; Franc Luz as prosecutor Seth Tanner; Robin Mattson as Janet Green; Jeffrey DeMunn as Ben Logan; Cynthia Harris as Judge Patricia Hale; Kathleen Chalfant as Rae Ella; James Harris Wiggins III and Amir Williams as Jamal Johnson; Winsor Harmon as Del Henry (also known as Del Hunkle); Steve Kanaly as Del's father, Seabone Hunkle; Tina Louise as Tish Pridmore; Keith Hamilton Cobb as Noah Keefer; Kim Hawthorne as Belinda Keefer; Daniel von Bargen as Lieutenant Cody; Tony Roberts as Dr. Rosenstein; Kimberly Foster as Liz Sloan; Lisa D. Brenner as Allison Sloan; Sean Marquette as young Jamie Martin; Kip Niven as Matt Callaway; James Garde as Justin Carrier; Joyce Van Patten as Helen Marsh; Chris Bruno as Michael Delaney; Cecilia DeWolf as Sophie; Kevin Alexander as Adam Chandler, Jr.; Cheryl Hulteen as Winifred; and Michelle Trachtenberg as Lily Banning.

In an unusual guest appearance, Carol Burnett turned up as a hospital patient, Mrs. Johnson, on 16 March 1976; *All My Children* is her favorite soap opera. Burnett returned in 1983 as a regular character, Verla Grubbs, the long-lost daughter of Lenny Vlasic/Langley Wallingford. Elizabeth Taylor (who had appeared in *General Hospital*) also appeared in an uncredited walk-on role, chatting with Verla in a restaurant scene. *All My Children* was the first daytime serial to go on location for storyline purposes, taping scenes in St. Croix in 1978. Most of the other serials soon followed suit. On 25 April 1977 *All My Children* expanded to sixty minutes. Like most daytime serials, *All My Children* has its legion of celebrity viewers. One of them is pro basketball star Charles Barkley, who showed up late for a daytime game in January 1987 because he had been watching the show. The show celebrated its twenty-fifth anniversary in January 1995 with a week's worth of special episodes.

ALL THAT GLITTERS   SYNDICATED

18 APRIL 1977–15 JULY 1977   The success of *Mary Hartman, Mary Hartman*
prompted Norman Lear to develop a second soap opera which, like *Mary Hartman,*
was shown in most markets in a late-night time slot. The setting of the short-lived
effort was the Globatron Corporation, a conglomerate in which all the key positions
were held by women and the secretarial slots were filled by men. The cast included:
Lois Nettleton as executive Christina Stockwood; Chuck McCann as her stay-at-
home spouse, Bert Stockwood; Anita Gillette as Nancy Bankston; Wes Parker as
Glen Bankston, an aspiring actor; Barbara Baxley as L. W. Carruthers, the chair-
woman of the board; Vanessa Brown as Peggy Horner; Louise Shaffer as Andrea
Martin; David Haskell as Michael McFarland; Linda Gray as model Linda
Murkland, a transsexual; Jessica Walter as agent Joan Hamlyn; Eileen Brennan as
Ma Packer; Marte Boyle Slout as Grace Smith; and Gary Sandy as Dan Kincaid, the
secretary with "the cutest little buns in the corporation." Stephanie Stills was the
executive producer, Viva Knight the producer.

ALLAKAZAM
See THE MAGIC LAND OF ALLAKAZAM

ALL-AMERICAN GIRL   ABC

14 SEPTEMBER 1994–22 MARCH 1995; 16 AUGUST 1995–23 AUGUST 1995   One of the
few network shows to feature a mostly Asian cast, this half-hour sitcom starred
standup comic Margaret Cho as Margaret Kim, a thoroughly westernized Korean-
American woman who worked part-time in a department store, attended college and
lived at home, where she battled her tradition-bound mother and her middle-of-the-
road father. Also featured were Jodi Long as Mom, who was always trying to fix
Margaret up with an eligible Korean man; Clyde Kusatsu as Dad, who, together with
Mom, owned a bookstore; Amy Hill as Grandma; J. B. Quon as Margaret's little
brother, Eric; B. D. Wong as Margaret's older brother, Stuart, a cardiologist; and
Maddie Corman and Judy Gold as Margaret's co-workers, Ruthie and Gloria.

ALLEN LUDDEN'S GALLERY   SYNDICATED

1969   Allen Ludden was one of a number of game show hosts who took a stab at the
talk show format during the late 1960s. After a brief run, Ludden returned to the
quizmaster's desk.

THE ALL-NEW SUPERFRIENDS HOUR
See THE SUPER FRIENDS

ALL'S FAIR   CBS

20 SEPTEMBER 1976–15 AUGUST 1977   Unlike most of Norman Lear's earlier comedies, *All's Fair* was set neither in a typical town nor in a typical household. Here, in
Washington, D.C., a conservative political columnist, forty-nine, fell in love with a
feminist freelance photographer, twenty-three. Their differences in age and outlook
provided the tension; the Washington setting provided the topicality. With Richard
Crenna (a sitcom veteran who had made only a few TV appearances after 1966) as
syndicated columnist Richard Barrington; Bernadette Peters (in her first series role)
as photographer Charlotte (Charley) Drake; J. A. Preston as Al Brooks, Barrington's black but equally conservative assistant; Judy Kahan as Ginger Livingston,
Charley's roommate (when Charley was not at Richard's), a secretary; Lee Chamberlin as Lucy Daniels, a CBS-TV newswoman and Al's female companion (they got
married early in 1977); Jack Dodson as bumbling Senator Wayne Joplin (constituency
unspecified), a friend of Barrington's; Michael Keaton as Lanny Wolfe, a presidential joke writer.

ALL-STAR ANYTHING GOES
See ALMOST ANYTHING GOES

ALL-STAR BLITZ   ABC
8 APRIL 1985–20 DECEMBER 1985   Peter Marshall hosted this daytime game show, which was reminiscent of Marshall's earlier series, *Hollywood Squares*. Here, two contestants faced a panel of four celebrities, and could agree or disagree with the answers provided by the celebs to questions; successful contestants were thus able to view a portion of a mystery phrase hidden behind a grid of six boxes.

ALL-STAR GOLF   ABC/NBC
12 OCTOBER 1957–29 APRIL 1961 (ABC); 4 OCTOBER 1961–23 MARCH 1963 (NBC)   A weekend series of head-to-head golf matches, hosted for most of its run by Jimmy Demaret, and filmed at the Apple Valley Country Club in California.

ALL-STAR NEWS   ABC
9 OCTOBER 1952–30 AUGUST 1953   ABC's innovative news show began as a five-nights-a-week effort, with a full hour of news (compared with the fifteen-minute newscasts on NBC and CBS) on four of those evenings. By January of 1953, however, *All-Star News* had been trimmed to just one hour on Sunday nights. The show relied not on a single anchorman, but rather on live reports from ABC correspondents all over the country. Regular news broadcasts resumed on ABC in the fall of 1953: see *ABC News*.

ALL-STAR REVUE   NBC
8 SEPTEMBER 1951–18 APRIL 1953   A variety hour that preceded *Your Show of Shows* on Saturday nights for two seasons. There were many guest hosts, but those who appeared with regularity included Ezio Pinza, Jimmy Durante, Ed Wynn, Danny Thomas, George Jessel, Tallulah Bankhead (who made five appearances during the second season), and finally, Martha Raye.In the fall of 1953 Martha Raye's monthly replacements for *Your Show of Shows* were entitled *All-Star Revue* before the title was changed to *The Martha Raye Show* in December. See also *Four Star Revue*.

ALL STAR SECRETS   NBC
8 JANUARY 1979–10 AUGUST 1979   A straightforward daytime game show hosted by Bob Eubanks, *All Star Secrets* featured three contestants and a panel of five guest celebrities. At the outset of each round the host revealed a "secret" held by one of the celebs; contestants won money by correctly guessing the holder of the secret.

ALMOST ANYTHING GOES   ABC
31 JULY 1975–28 AUGUST 1975; 24 JANUARY 1976–9 MAY 1976
ALL-STAR ANYTHING GOES   SYNDICATED
1977   A raucous hour game show, *Almost Anything Goes* was modeled after a British series, *It's a Knockout*. In the American version teams from three small towns, selected by local civic groups, competed in various zany stunts (such as negotiating obstacle courses, or trying to carry loaves of bread across a greased beam suspended over a pool of water). Each show was shot on location at one of the competing towns. No prizes were awarded to the competitors; civic pride, and the chance to appear on nationwide TV, motivated the participants. Reporting the festivities were Charlie Jones and Lynn Shackleford; the on-the-field correspondents were Dick Whittington (1975) and Regis Philbin (1976). Bob Banner and Beryl Vertue were the executive producers. *All-Star Anything Goes,* which was introduced a year later, was played similarly, except that the teams were composed of celebrities; the half-hour show was hosted by Bill Boggs. Bill Healy handled the play-by-play, and Judy Abercrombie kept score. See also *Junior Almost Anything Goes*.

ALMOST GROWN   CBS
27 NOVEMBER 1988–27 FEBRUARY 1989   An ambitious failure, *Almost Grown* tracked, through extensive flashback sequences laced with period rock music, the relationship of its two main characters as it grew from high school romance in the 1960s through living together, marriage, parenthood, and divorce. The cast included Timothy Daly as Norman Long; Eve Gordon as Suzie Long; Raffi DiBlasio as their

son, Jackson; Ocean Hellman as their daughter, Anya; Anita Gillette as Suzie's mother, Vi; Richard Schaal as Suzie's father, Dick; Albert Macklin as Suzie's brother, Joey; Rita Taggart as Norman's mother, Joan; and Malcolm Stewart as Dr. Bob Keyes, a plastic surgeon whom Suzie planned to marry after her divorce from Norman.

ALMOST HOME   NBC
6 FEBRUARY 1993–3 JULY 1993   A reworked version of the 1991–1992 sitcom *The Torkelsons*. This time Millicent Torkelson and three of her kids moved from Oklahoma to Seattle, where Millicent became the housekeeper for a widower and his two kids. With Connie Ray as Millicent; Olivia Burnette as her daughter Dorothy Jane; Lee Norris as her son Chuckie Lee; Rachel Duncan as her daughter Mary Sue; Perry King as the widower, Brian Morgan; Brittany Murphy as his daughter, Molly; and Jason Marsden as his son, Gregory.

ALMOST PERFECT   CBS
17 SEPTEMBER 1995–   Half-hour sitcom about two busy single professionals who met at a Los Angeles bar and began a romance. With Nancy Travis as Kim Cooper, the newly promoted executive producer of "Blue Justice," a TV cop show; Kevin Kilner as Mike Ryan, prosecutor in the major crimes unit of the D.A.'s office; Chip Zien as Gary, one of the "Blue Justice" writers, who had expected to get the producer's job; Matthew Letscher as Rob, the junior "Blue Justice" writer; and David Clennon as Neal Luder, the strangest of the writers.

ALOHA PARADISE   ABC
25 FEBRUARY 1981–29 APRIL 1981   Set at Paradise Village, an exclusive Hawaiian resort for the romantically inclined, *Aloha Paradise* resembled a land-based Love Boat. The crew included Debbie Reynolds as Sydney Chase, the general manager; Bill Daily as assistant manager Curtis Shaw; Stephen Shortridge as lifeguard Richard Dean; Pat Klous as social director Fran Linhart; Mokihana as Evelyn, the bartender; and Charles Fleischer as Everett, the gardener. Steve Lawrence sang the title song.

ALUMNI FUN   ABC/CBS
20 JANUARY 1963–28 APRIL 1963 (ABC); 12 JANUARY 1964–5 APRIL 1965 (CBS); 10 JANUARY 1965–28 MARCH 1965 (CBS); 23 JANUARY 1966–7 MAY 1966 (CBS)   This weekly game show, an earlier version of which had been on radio, featured two teams, each composed of famous alumni from the same college or university. The winning team would return the following week to face a new team of challengers. The show was usually seen on Sunday afternoons, following the completion of the professional football season. John K. M. McCaffery hosted during the first season; Peter Lind Hayes was the host during the other seasons.

ALVIN AND THE CHIPMUNKS (THE CHIPMUNKS)   NBC
17 SEPTEMBER 1983–7 SEPTEMBER 1991   This Saturday-morning cartoon show was a sequel to *The Alvin Show* (see also that title). In the new show the three high-voiced chipmunks—Alvin, Simon, and Theodore—attended the Thomas Edison Elementary School, lived at home with David Seville, and made music together as a rock and roll trio. The series was retitled *Chipmunks* in the fall of 1988, as the male trio was joined by the Chippettes—Brittany, Eleanor, and Jeannette—and a puppy named Lily. In the fall of 1990 the show was retitled *Chipmunks Go to the Movies* as Alvin and his pals parodied famous motion pictures.

THE ALVIN SHOW   CBS
4 OCTOBER 1961–12 SEPTEMBER 1962   ABC introduced prime-time cartoon programs in 1960 with *Bugs Bunny* and *The Flintstones*. CBS followed suit in 1961 with this effort, which featured three singing chipmunks (known as The Chipmunks, oddly enough) and their songwriter-manager, David Seville. The Chipmunks had gained real-life fame in 1958 when songwriter Ross Bagdasarian (who used the name David Seville and wrote such hits as "The Witch Doctor") wrote a novelty Christmas

number and recorded it for Liberty records. As a gimmick Bagdasarian used three speeded-up vocal tracks and named his high-pitched hitmakers The Chipmunks. The record was a smash. In the song the three characters were named Alvin, Simon, and Theodore. In his book, *Rock On,* Norm Nite notes that Bagdasarian named them after Liberty executives Al Bennett and Si Warnoker and recording engineer Ted Keep. When the series came to television Bagdasarian continued to supply the main characters' voices; an additional segment featured the adventures of inventor Clyde Crashcup, with voice supplied by Shepard Menken. Though the series fared poorly on prime time (it was opposite *Wagon Train*), it lasted three seasons (1962–1965) on Saturday mornings. The series returned, in reruns, to NBC's Saturday morning schedule in March of 1979. See also *Alvin and the Chipmunks*.

AMANDA'S ABC
10 FEBRUARY 1983–24 MARCH 1983 An uninspired adaptation of the British sitcom *Fawlty Towers*, with Beatrice Arthur as Amanda Cartwright, proprietor of Amanda's-by-the-Sea, a quaint coastal inn; Fred McCarren as Marty, her son; Simone Griffeth as Arlene, Marty's wife; Tony Rosato as Aldo, the bellhop; Rick Hurst as Earl, the cook; and Michael Constantine as Amanda's main competitor, Krinsky, the owner of Casa Krinsky.

THE AMATEUR HOUR
See TED MACK'S ORIGINAL AMATEUR HOUR

THE AMATEUR'S GUIDE TO LOVE CBS
27 MARCH 1972–23 JUNE 1972 Gene Rayburn hosted this daytime game show which involved a panel of three celebrities, two studio contestants, and a videotaped sequence. First, the celebs ("The Guidebook Panel") watched part of the videotaped sequence, in which the contestants became involved in a sexy or amorous situation. The tape was stopped prior to its conclusion and the Guidebook Panel voted on how the contestants should have reacted to the situation. The tape was then resumed; if the contestants reacted as the panel predicted, they won money. The show's credits carried the following disclaimer: "Studio interviews are discussed with panel and guests in advance."

THE AMAZING CHAN AND THE CHAN CLAN CBS
9 SEPTEMBER 1972–22 SEPTEMBER 1974 Charlie Chan's second television incarnation was in cartoon form, produced by Hanna-Barbera, shown on Saturdays during the first season and Sundays during the second. The inscrutable detective was assisted by his ten children. The voice of Charlie was supplied by Keye Luke, who had played number-one son (to Warner Oland's Charlie) in the Chan films of the 1930s. See also *Charlie Chan*.

AMAZING GRACE NBC
1 APRIL 1995–22 APRIL 1995 Patty Duke starred in this hour dramatic series as a newly ordained minister whose name was not Grace, but rather Hannah Miller (presumably no relation to the Hannah Miller of the ABC sitcom *Anything But Love*). A divorcée, Hannah had been a nurse and had become addicted to pills; after a near-death experience she decided to leave nursing for the ministry, though she continued to serve as the chaplain at her old hospital. Also featured were Marguerite Moreau as her teenage daughter, Jenny; Justin Garms as her preteen son, Brian; Joe Spano as Detective Dominick Corso, a tough cop with whom Hannah tangled; Lorraine Toussaint as Yvonne, a nurse and former coworker of Hannah's; Robin Gammell as Arthur Sutherland, president of the church board which had selected Hannah (despite Sutherland's reservations); Gavin Harrison as Linc, a laconic teen whom Jenny met in a park; and Dan Lauria as Hannah's friend, lawyer Harry Kramer. The series was NBC's lowest-rated program of the 1994–1995 season.

THE AMAZING LIVE SEA MONKEYS CBS

19 SEPTEMBER 1992–4 SEPTEMBER 1993   Howie Mandel created, and starred in, this half-hour Saturday morning series. Mandel played a wacky professor who enlarged a trio of sea monkeys—Aquarius, Bill, and Dave—to human size, and helped guide them through life on dry land.

THE AMAZING MR. MALONE ABC

24 SEPTEMBER 1951–10 MARCH 1952   A short-lived television version of the radio series that premiered in 1948. Lee Tracy starred as John J. Malone, a Chicago criminal defense lawyer.

THE AMAZING POLGAR CBS

16 SEPTEMBER 1949–28 OCTOBER 1949   This ten-minute show, seen Fridays after the evening news, was probably television's first show to deal with hypnotism. Each week Dr. Franz Polgar demonstrated his hypnotic prowess upon selected members of the studio audience. Chuck Lewin produced the series.

THE AMAZING SPIDER-MAN CBS

5 APRIL 1978–3 MAY 1978   Like *The Incredible Hulk* and *Wonder Woman, The Amazing Spider-Man* was an hour adventure series based on a comic book character. The series starred Nicholas Hammond as Peter Parker, a reporter for the New York *Bugle* who, as the result of a mysterious spider bite, could transform himself into Spider-Man; Spider-Man's arachnid powers include the ability to walk along walls and ceilings, and to cast ropelike lines between buildings. Also featured were Robert F. Simon as his boss, Mr. Jameson; Chip Fields as Rita, another newspaper employee; and Michael Pataki as Captain Barbera of the New York Police Department. Charles Fries and Dan Goodman were the executive producers of the series, a single episode of which was introduced in the fall of 1977. After a five-week trial run in the spring of 1978, it was seen on an irregular basis, and a new character was added: Ellen Bry as Julie, a photographer.

AMAZING STORIES NBC

29 SEPTEMBER 1985–15 MAY 1987   To entice filmmaker Steven Spielberg into television series production, NBC offered a two-season, forty-four-episode commitment (with lavish license fees per program) and full creative control to Spielberg. Unfortunately, the resulting half-hour anthology series neither measured up to expectations nor found a large audience; the anthology format itself had fallen out of favor years earlier, and efforts to revive it (including two other 1985 efforts, the remakes of *Alfred Hitchcock Presents* and *The Twilight Zone*) had failed. Nevertheless, there were a few interesting presentations on *Amazing Stories,* such as "Mummy, Daddy," with Bronson Pinchot (27 October 1985), "The Amazing Falsworth," with Gregory Hines (5 November 1985), and "Mr. Magic," with Sid Caesar (17 November 1985). Some stories were directed by Spielberg himself, while others were directed by such notables as Clint Eastwood and Martin Scorsese.

THE AMAZING TALES OF HANS CHRISTIAN ANDERSEN SYNDICATED

1954   A series for children, based on the writings of the Danish fabulist. Hosted by George and Gene Bernard.

THE AMAZING THREE SYNDICATED

1967   Cartoon series in which three intergalactic beings were sent to Earth to determine whether it should be destroyed. Upon their arrival they assumed the identities of a rabbit, a duck, and a horse and befriended young Kenny Carter.

THE AMAZING WORLD OF KRESKIN SYNDICATED

1971   Demonstrations of apparent mind-reading and ESP by the amazing Kreskin, a self-described "mentalist" and frequent talk show guest. Like Dunninger, the leading TV mentalist of the 1950s, Kreskin used just one name and never divulged his secrets.

AMEN   NBC

27 SEPTEMBER 1986–25 AUGUST 1990; 1 DECEMBER 1990–27 JULY 1991   One year after the demise of *The Jeffersons,* Sherman Hemsley returned to television to star in another hit sitcom. Here he played Ernest Frye, a lawyer and the scheming deacon of the First Community Church of Philadelphia. Clifton Davis costarred as Reuben Gregory, the church's newly hired minister (in real life, Davis had actually left show business to study divinity, and had become an ordained minister). Also featured were Anna Maria Horsford as Thelma, Ernest's daughter, who had her eyes on Reuben (they were finally married in February 1990); Barbara Montgomery (1986–1990) and Roz Ryan as sisters Casietta and Amelia Hetebrink, faithful churchgoers and members of its governing board; and Jester Hairston as elderly Rolly Forbes, also a board member. Franklyn Seales was seen occasionally during the first two seasons as choir director Lorenzo Hollingsworth; Rosetta LeNoire was seen during the 1987–1988 season as Rolly's wife, Leola. Elsa Raven appeared during the 1988–1989 season as Inga, the Frycs' housekeeper. Bumper Robinson joined the cast in 1990 as Clarence, a neighborhood teenager. Frye became a judge for *Amen*'s final season, and soul singers James Brown and Lloyd Price appeared on the last first-run episode (11 May 1991).

AMERICA   NBC/PBS

14 NOVEMBER 1972–15 MAY 1973 (NBC); 17 SEPTEMBER 1974–18 MARCH 1975 (PBS) Alistair Cooke's highly acclaimed "personal history" of the United States was produced by Michael Gill for BBC and Time-Life Films. It was originally telecast as thirteen hours, each focusing on a given topic, on alternate Tuesdays. In 1974, it was presented on PBS as a series of twenty-six half hours, with new introductions and conclusions by host Cooke.

AMERICA   SYNDICATED

1985–1986   A one-hour daily magazine show, hosted by Sarah Purcell, McLean Stevenson, and Stuart Damon.

AMERICA ALIVE!   NBC

24 JULY 1978–4 JANUARY 1979   Broadcast live, this hour daytime magazine show was hosted by Jack Linkletter, who had hosted a similar show eighteen years earlier (see *On the Go*). Linkletter's traveling cohosts included Pat Mitchell, Bruce Jenner, and Janet Langhart. Other regular contributors included David Sheehan (films), Virginia Graham (gossip and interviews), David Horowitz (consumer affairs), Dick Orkin and Bert Berdis (comedy), and Dr. William H. Masters and Virginia Johnson (sex and health). Woody Fraser was the executive producer.

AMERICA BY DESIGN   PBS

28 SEPTEMBER 1987–26 OCTOBER 1987   A five-part look at American architecture, hosted by Spiro Kostof.

AMERICA SPEAKS   NBC

2 JULY 1951–24 AUGUST 1951   A summer replacement for *The Bert Parks Show,* this daytime documentary series examined the American economy.

AMERICA 2NIGHT
See FERNWOOD 2-NIGHT

AMERICA TONIGHT   CBS

1 OCTOBER 1990–29 MARCH 1991   CBS's entry into the late-night news market was a half-hour program at 11:30 P.M. Veteran correspondents Charles Kuralt and Lesley Stahl coanchored the show Mondays through Thursdays, while Robert Krulwich and Edie Magnus did the Friday shows. The show became a regular program after a half-dozen late-night specials had been aired during the 1990 Persian Gulf crisis. The series was to have been canceled on 18 January 1991 to make room for CBS's new

late-night lineup, but when war erupted in the Persian Gulf the network postponed its plans and kept *America Tonight* on the air.

AMERICA TONIGHT
NBC

1 JUNE 1994–10 AUGUST 1994   Prime-time magazine series, cohosted by Deborah Norville and Dana King.

THE AMERICAN ADVENTURE
SYNDICATED

1960   A series of thirteen 15-minute films on American government and patriotism.

AMERICAN ALMANAC
NBC

6 AUGUST 1985–30 NOVEMBER 1985   Roger Mudd was the host of this hour news-magazine series, NBC's umpteenth attempt to establish a successful series in that genre. *American Almanac* was introduced as a monthly show, with the expectation that it would land a weekly berth on NBC's prime-time schedule sometime in midseason; it never did, and vanished after four outings.

AMERICAN BANDSTAND
ABC/SYNDICATED/USA

5 AUGUST 1957–5 SEPTEMBER 1987 (ABC); 1987–1989 (SYNDICATED); 8 APRIL 1989–7 OCTOBER 1989 (USA)   ABC's long-running series actually began as a local show in Philadelphia in 1952. Then called *Bandstand,* it was hosted by Bob Horn. The set resembled a record shop, and the show featured records, film clips of popular singers, and a live audience of local teenagers who danced while the records played. Dick Clark, then a disc jockey on a Philadelphia radio station, took over as sole host in 1956. The show soon attracted network attention, as it was the highest-rated program in its time slot in the Philadelphia area. Sixty-seven ABC affiliates carried the show starting in the summer of 1957; some carried it for the full ninety minutes, others for only thirty or sixty minutes. For the next six years the show was telecast weekday afternoons from the studios of WFIL-TV in Philadelphia. A prime-time version also surfaced for thirteen weeks in the fall of 1957. Clark, who was twenty-six when the show first went network, kept the format simple: The new set contained little but a set of bleachers for the kids to sit on when they weren't dancing, a raised podium for the host, an autograph table for guest stars, and a signboard listing the week's top ten hits.

Kids (and quite a few adults) watched the show to see other kids dance; many of the 200 or so teenagers who filled the studio each day were regulars, and some received considerable fan mail. The show also provided the chance for performers to do their newest hits. Over the years almost every major rock star appeared at least once (two notable exceptions were Elvis Presley and Rick Nelson). On the 1957 Thanksgiving show, for example, two New York teenagers who called themselves Tom and Jerry sang their hit record, "Hey, Schoolgirl." They are better known today as Paul Simon and Art Garfunkel. Because the show was broadcast from Philadelphia during those years, Philadelphia artists showed up frequently: Frankie Avalon, Bobby Rydell, Chubby Checker, Fabian, and James Darren all guested dozens of times.

Clark was a shrewd businessman, and by the end of 1957 he had invested in various music publishing and record distributing ventures. He later put together road shows—the *Dick Clark Caravan of Stars* toured the country (by bus) many times. Clark's involvement in such activities, though profitable, almost cut short his career as a TV personality, as the "payola" scandal broke in 1959. A Congressional subcommittee investigating "payola"—the payment of money or other favors to get a new record played on radio—called Clark to testify in 1960. By that time, Clark, at network insistence, had divested himself of his interests in music publishing and record distributing outfits. He steadfastly denied ever having received payment to play a song on *American Bandstand* and also tried to show that certain songs in which he had a financial interest were not played disproportionately often on the show. Clark emerged from the hearings relatively unscathed and, unlike many less fortunate disc jockeys, continued to host his show. *Bandstand* continued to run weekday afternoons until 30 August 1963, when it was switched to Saturday afternoons. In the spring of 1964 the show moved to Los Angeles, where it remained. There Clark established Dick Clark Productions, successfully promoted many concerts, and also developed such TV series as *Where the Action Is* and *It's Happening.* On 30 October 1981 *American Bandstand* celebrated its thirtieth anniversary a few months early with a prime-time retrospective. On 1 December 1985 "American Bandstand's 33 1/3 Celebration," another prime-time special, aired, again on ABC. A fortieth anniversary prime-time special was aired 13 May 1992 on ABC.

In the fall of 1987 Clark and ABC parted company after thirty years. The network had offered Clark a three-year extension but wanted to trim the series to thirty minutes. Clark preferred to retain the hour format, and he introduced the show in syndication two weeks after its farewell telecast on ABC (for the record, the last performer to appear on the ABC version was Laura Branigan, who sang "Shattered Glass"). After eighteen months in syndication, *American Bandstand* switched to the USA Cable Network, again in a Saturday afternoon time slot, but with a new host: Dick Clark turned over the microphone to David Hirsch, who, at 26, was the same age as Clark was when the show began its network run in 1957. USA dropped the show after twenty-six weeks.

American Bandstand should be noted not only as one of television's longest-running musical series, but also as the first network series devoted exclusively to rock-and-roll music.

AMERICAN CHRONICLES   FOX
8 SEPTEMBER 1990–15 DECEMBER 1990   *Twin Peaks* collaborators Mark Frost and David Lynch were the executive producers of this arty and offbeat half-hour documentary series which examined facets of American culture. New Orleans at Mardi Gras was the subject of the premiere telecast, while later shows looked at such topics as New York City nightlife, America's obsession with automobiles, and the Miss Texas beauty pageant. Richard Dreyfuss narrated.

AMERICAN CINEMA   PBS
23 JANUARY 1995–27 FEBRUARY 1995   A ten-part look at the history of American films, arranged by genre. John Lithgow hosted.

AMERICAN DETECTIVE   ABC
2 MAY 1991–20 JULY 1992; 9 NOVEMBER 1993–26 JUNE 1993   One of several reality-based series which followed in the wake of Fox's *Cops*, this one tracked real-life police officers on and off the job. A real-life cop, Oregon's John Bunnell, became the series's host in January 1992.

AMERICAN DREAM   ABC
26 APRIL 1981–10 JUNE 1981   An hour-long dramatic series about a family of six who decide to move into Chicago from suburban Arlington Heights. With Stephen Macht as Danny Novak, who worked at the Marshall Field department store; Karen Carlson as his wife, Donna Novak; Tim Waldrip as their son Casey; Michael Hershewe as their son Todd; Andrea Smith as their daughter, Jenny; John McIntire as Sam, Donna's father; Hans Conried as Berlowitz, the realtor; and Helen Rubio as neighbor Paula Navarro. A fascinating account of this series's creation, development, and ultimate demise may be found in Todd Gitlin's 1984 book, *Inside Prime Time.*

AMERICAN DREAMER   NBC
20 SEPTEMBER 1990–22 DECEMBER 1990; 25 MAY 1991–22 JUNE 1991   Robert Urich starred in this half-hour sitcom as Tom Nash, a former TV reporter who now wrote human interest stories for a Chicago newspaper; Nash and his two children had recently settled in a small Wisconsin town after Nash's wife—also a journalist—had been killed in Lebanon while covering a story there. From time to time Nash spoke directly to the camera, as characters from his past or present appeared behind him on a minimally set stage. Other regulars included Carol Kane as Lillian Abernathy, Nash's ditzy assistant; Chay Lentin as his teenage daughter, Rachel; Johnny Galecki as his son, Danny; Margaret Welsh as Holly, proprietor of the town café; and Jeffrey

Tambor as Nash's editor, Joe Baines. Susan Seeger created the series, and, with Gary David Goldberg, was its executive producer.

THE AMERICAN EXPERIENCE   PBS
4 OCTOBER 1988–   A look at selected events in American history, hosted by David McCullough, utilizing contemporary film footage whenever possible. Among the presentations were "The Great San Francisco Earthquake" (4 October 1988); "Kennedy v. Wallace: A Crisis Up Close" (15 November 1988); "The Great Air Race of 1924" (3 October 1989); "Roots of Resistance: A Story of the Underground Railroad" (16 January 1990); "G-Men: The Rise of J. Edgar Hoover" (18 November 1991); "The Quiz Show Scandal" (6 January 1992), and Ric Burns's six-hour examination of the treatment of American Indians during the nineteenth century, "The Way West" (8 and 9 May 1995). In 1994 the series received three Peabody Awards (the most ever awarded to a series in a single year) for its presentations of "FDR," a four-and-one-half-hour biography, "The Battle of the Bulge," and "Malcolm X: Make It Plain."

AN AMERICAN FAMILY   PBS
11 JANUARY 1973–29 MARCH 1973   A controversial documentary series chronicling the lives of the members of the Loud family of Santa Barbara, California, *An American Family* was shown in twelve hour-long installments. Producer Craig Gilbert and his two assistants spent seven months with the Louds in 1971 and shot some 300 hours of film of the seven Louds—husband Bill, president of American Western Foundries, his wife Pat, and their five children, Lance, Kevin, Grant, Delilah, and Michele. The footage that finally emerged on television was sometimes banal, sometimes boring, and sometimes riveting. In the second episode, viewers saw Pat meeting Lance in New York's Greenwich Village and learning of his involvement in the local homosexual scene. The eighth and ninth episodes concerned the breakup of the Louds' marriage, as Pat decided to file for a divorce, and Bill moved out of the house (the two were divorced in 1972). The Louds themselves criticized the series, maintaining that selective editing of 300 hours into twelve-hour segments had painted a grossly distorted picture of their lives. Producer Gilbert's two assistants, Alan and Susan Raymond, produced a sequel ten years later; "American Family Revisited" was shown on the HBO cable network 9 August 1983. A 1988 news report found Pat selling antiques in England, Bill enduring the breakup of his second marriage, Lance peddling adult postcards in Los Angeles, Grant studying acting, Kevin living in Houston, Michele designing clothes in New York, and Delilah working as a publicist in L.A. Craig Gilbert reflected on his creation: "The series was about a land of plenty that produces mindless people, who talked all the time, but not about the things that were troubling them. . . . In some ways, all American families resemble the Louds."

THE AMERICAN FORUM OF THE AIR   NBC
4 FEBRUARY 1950–15 SEPTEMBER 1957   This Sunday-afternoon public affairs program featured debates on topical issues. Theodore Granik, who introduced the series on radio in 1937, moderated until 1953, when Stephen McCormick succeeded him. Toward the end of its run the series alternated with *Youth Wants to Know.*

THE AMERICAN GIRLS   CBS
23 SEPTEMBER 1978–10 NOVEMBER 1978   Hour-long dramatic series about two field researchers for *The American Report,* a television newsmagazine. With Priscilla Barnes as Becky Tomkins, a veteran staffer; Debra Clinger as her new partner, Amy Waddell, a former college reporter who landed the job because she had once obtained an interview with President Nixon; David Spielberg as Francis X. Casey, their producer. Harve Bennett and Harris Katleman were the executive producers. The series was a vain attempt to cash in on the popularity of *Charlie's Angels.*

AMERICAN GLADIATORS   SYNDICATED
1989–   Another entry in the genre known as "trashsport," *American Gladiators* was an hour syndicated entry in which male and female contestants competed in

various physical endeavors not directly against one another, but rather against one (or more) of the show's in-house staff of challengers. The contests included jousting (with padded pugil sticks), wall-climbing, stuffing balls into containers, and the like. The show's male challengers bore names like Gemini, Titan, and Nitro, while their female counterparts included Blaze, Gold, and Lace, among others. Mike Adamle cohosted the series, first with Joe Theismann, then with Todd Christensen, Larry Csonka, and Lisa Malosky. A kid's version appeared in 1994: see *Gladiators 2000*.

AMERICAN GOTHIC   CBS
22 SEPTEMBER 1995–31 JANUARY 1996   The first TV series set in South Carolina, *American Gothic* was an hour continuing drama in which the forces of good and evil confronted each other against a backdrop of the supernatural. The goings-on were centered in the small town of Trinity, which was ruled by an utterly evil sheriff. As the series unfolded, the sheriff murdered a teenage girl, imprisoned and killed her father, and then plotted to gain custody of the slain girl's younger brother (the sheriff had apparently killed the child's mother some years earlier). The cast included Gary Cole as Sheriff Lucas Buck; Lucas Black as the young orphan, Caleb Temple; Paige Turco as Caleb's cousin, Gail Emory, a reporter who returned to Trinity to thwart the sheriff's custody attempts, and began to unravel the mystery of her own parents' deaths; Jake Weber as Dr. Matt Crowder, an enemy of the sheriff's; Brenda Bakke as schoolteacher Selena Coombs, who had been corrupted by the sheriff; Nick Searcy as the sheriff's powerless deputy, Ben Healy; and Sarah Paulson as Caleb's sister, murder victim Merlyn Temple, who appeared to Caleb in visions and tried to help him. Shaun Cassidy was one of the co-creators.

AMERICAN HORSE AND HORSEMAN   SYNDICATED
1973   Dale Robertson hosted this equestrian documentary series.

THE AMERICAN HOUR
See THE MOTOROLA TV HOUR

AMERICAN INVENTORY   NBC
1 JULY 1951–16 JANUARY 1955   Panel discussions and documentary films were the staples of this public affairs program, which was seen Sunday afternoons for most of its run.

AMERICAN JOURNAL   SYNDICATED
1993–   Half-hour daily investigative report program, anchored by Nancy Glass.

AMERICAN LIFESTYLE   SYNDICATED
1972   E. G. Marshall narrated this documentary series, which often presented biographies of famous Americans.

AMERICAN MASTERS   PBS
14 JULY 1986–   A summertime series of documentary films on American artists, writers, and musicians. Among those who have been profiled are Billie Holiday (4 August 1986), Isaac Bashevis Singer (6 July 1987), Aretha Franklin (22 August 1988), Charlie Parker (17 July 1989), Neil Simon (21 August 1989), Edward R. Murrow (30 July and 6 August 1990), Helen Hayes (1 July 1991), Ray Charles (3 January 1992), D. W. Griffith (24 March 1993), and Tennessee Williams (19 December 1994).

THE AMERICAN PARADE (CROSSROADS)   CBS
27 MARCH 1984–5 SEPTEMBER 1984   This prime-time magazine series was first hosted by Charles Kuralt. Humorist Art Buchwald was to have been a regular contributor, but was dropped after the second week. The series itself, which garnered low ratings opposite *The A Team* on NBC, was taken off the air in May for an extensive overhaul. When it returned in June, retitled *Crossroads*, Bill Moyers had joined Kuralt as cohost.

AMERICAN PLAYHOUSE   PBS

12 JANUARY 1982–   Among the noteworthy presentations on this dramatic anthology series were an original teleplay by John Cheever (his first), "The Shady Hill Kidnapping," with George Grizzard and Polly Holliday (12 January 1982); a seven-part biography, "Oppenheimer," starring Sam Waterston as controversial physicist J. Robert Oppenheimer (the first episode was aired 11 May 1982; ironically, the programs were produced in England by the BBC); Thornton Wilder's "The Skin of Our Teeth," with Blair Brown, Sada Thompson, Harold Gould, and Rue McClanahan (broadcast live from San Diego's Old Globe Theatre, 18 January 1983); "Family Business," with Milton Berle in a rare dramatic role (1 February 1983); Lanford Wilson's "The Fifth of July," with Richard Thomas and Swoosie Kurtz (10 May 1983); James Baldwin's "Go Tell It on the Mountain," with Paul Winfield, Olivia Cole, Rosalind Cash, and James Bond III (14 January 1985); "Three Sovereigns for Sarah," with Vanessa Redgrave, Kim Hunter, Phyllis Thaxter, and Patrick McGoohan (27 May, 3 and 10 June 1985); Mark Twain's "The Adventures of Huckleberry Finn," with Patrick Day and Samm-Art Williams (10 February 1986, the first of four parts); "Sunday in the Park with George," with Mandy Patinkin (16 June 1986, originally aired on Showtime); "Smooth Talk," with Laura Dern and Treat Williams (9 February 1987); "Story of a Marriage," with Hallie Foote, William Converse-Roberts, and Matthew Broderick (6 April 1987, the first of five parts); Eugene O'Neill's "Strange Interlude," with Ken Howard and Glenda Jackson (18 January 1988); "Suspicion," with Jane Curtin and Anthony Andrews (20 April 1988); "The Trial of Bernhard Goetz," with Peter Crombie, Richard Libertini, Andrew Robinson, and Dann Florek (11 May 1988, using excerpts from the trial transcripts); "I Never Sang for My Father," with Daniel J. Travanti and Harold Gould (15 June 1988); "A Raisin in the Sun," with Danny Glover and Esther Rolle (1 February 1989); "Zora Is My Name," with Ruby Dee (14 February 1990); "Into the Woods," with Bernadette Peters, Chip Zien, and Joanna Gleason (20 March 1991); and "Tru," with Robert Morse as Truman Capote (23 November 1992). *American Playhouse*'s most controversial offering was the three-night, six-hour presentation of "Armistead Maupin's Tales of the City" (10–12 January 1994), adapted from Maupin's fictional serialized newspaper stories about life—straight and gay—in San Francisco during the 1970s. Starring Olympia Dukakis, Chloe Webb, Paul Gross, and Marcus D'Amico, it was produced by England's Channel 4, where it was first televised in 1993. *American Playhouse* offered it to PBS stations in two versions, one uncut and one without the four-letter words and the shots of bare female breasts; both versions, however, retained images of pot smoking and of men kissing men. Although "Tales" was highly praised (and won a Peabody Award that year), plans for a sequel were scuttled when PBS withdrew a commitment to fund it.

In January 1990 *American Playhouse* became the first national series to use Descriptive Video Service (DVS), in which an audio channel is used to supply additional information about the program for the benefit of the visually impaired.

AMERICAN RELIGIOUS TOWN HALL   ABC/SYNDICATED

9 OCTOBER 1955–9 JUNE 1957 (ABC); 1970–   (SYNDICATED)   Religious and moral topics are debated on this panel show. The ABC version, which was seen Sunday afternoons, was moderated by James A. Pike, rector of the Cathedral of St. John the Divine in New York. The syndicated version, based in Dallas, is moderated by Bishop A. A. Leisky.

AMERICAN SONG   NBC

15 APRIL 1948–21 FEBRUARY 1949   A twenty-minute musical series broadcast once or twice a week before the evening newsreel, *American Song* featured singer Paul Arnold and dancers Nellie Fisher and Ray Harrison.

THE AMERICAN SPORTSMAN   ABC

31 JANUARY 1965–24 JUNE 1984   Curt Gowdy hosted this outdoor series, on which celebrities and athletes went hunting and fishing. Executive producer: Roone

Arledge. Produced by Curt Gowdy, Neil Cunningham, and Pat Smith. The program surfaced again, in 1989 and in 1990, as one-shot special telecasts.

THE AMERICAN WEEK   CBS
4 APRIL 1954–10 OCTOBER 1954   Sunday-afternoon news review with Eric Sevareid.

THE AMERICAN WEST   SYNDICATED
1966   Travelogue hosted by Jack Smith.

AMERICANA
See BEN GRAUER'S AMERICANA QUIZ

THE AMERICANS   NBC
23 JANUARY 1961–11 SEPTEMBER 1961   The story of two brothers, Virginia farmers, fighting on opposite sides during the Civil War. With Darryl Hickman as Corporal Ben Canfield, fighting for the Union, and Dick Davalos as Corporal Jeff Canfield, fighting for the Confederacy. Robert Redford guest starred in one episode, "The Coward" (8 May). A midseason replacement for *Riverboat*.

AMERICA'S GREATEST BANDS   CBS
25 JUNE 1955–24 SEPTEMBER 1955   Bandleader Paul Whiteman reintroduced the Big Band era of the 1930s on this Saturday-night hour, a summer replacement for *The Jackie Gleason Show*. Most of the bands which had survived the era guested on the show.

AMERICA'S CENTURY   PBS
24 OCTOBER 1989–28 NOVEMBER 1989   A six-part examination of American foreign policy, hosted by Lewis Lapham, editor of *Harper's Magazine*.

AMERICA'S FUNNIEST HOME VIDEOS   ABC
14 JANUARY 1990–   This half-hour show zoomed to instant popularity following its midseason premiere as a regular weekly series. The format was disarmingly simple: thirty minutes of home video snippets, culled by the show's production staff from submissions solicited from viewers. Dancing animals, collapsing backyard pools, and tumbling toddlers were all typical fodder for the show. Comedian Bob Saget (who continued to costar in ABC's sitcom *Full House*) provided the introductions and the occasional voiceovers. At the end of each program, the studio audience was asked to vote for the evening's funniest video, choosing among three entries preselected by the producers; the winning segment won $10,000, and the opportunity for a seasonal grand prize of $100,000.
    The idea for the series came to producer Vin DiBona at an international television fair, where he spotted "Fun with Ken and Kaito Chen," a popular segment of a Japanese variety show which employed an analogous format. Curiously, a somewhat similar program had appeared on American television as early as 1963: see *Your Funny, Funny Films*. See also *America's Funniest People*. In the fall of 1994 reruns were paired with new programs to fill an hour time slot on Sunday nights.

AMERICA'S FUNNIEST PEOPLE   ABC
8 SEPTEMBER 1990–28 AUGUST 1994   This half-hour sequel to ABC's huge hit *America's Funniest Home Videos* consisted of more of the same—videos of folks telling jokes, doing impressions, or performing stunts. David Coulier (who, like Bob Saget of *America's Funniest Home Videos*, was also a regular on ABC's sitcom *Full House*) cohosted the show with Arleen Sorkin for the first two seasons; Tawny Kitaen succeeded Sorkin in the fall of 1992. The pilot for the series was telecast as a special on 13 May 1990.

AMERICA'S HEALTH   ABC
20 AUGUST 1951–6 MARCH 1952   A series of public-interest films on health and medicine.

AMERICA'S MOST WANTED   FOX
7 FEBRUARY 1988–   This half-hour series became one of the most popular and durable shows on the fledgling Fox network. It was first aired on Fox's several owned-and-operated stations, and was offered to all affiliates on 10 April 1988. It presented information on wanted fugitives, and incorporated photographs, interviews, and reenactments of crimes. By 1992 more than 200 persons who had been profiled on the series had been apprehended; a few of those "captured" were already in prison at the time, serving sentences under another name on unrelated charges. John Walsh was the host; the kidnapping and murder of his young son had been the subject of a 1983 TV-movie, "Adam." In 1995 a companion series was introduced. Also hosted by Walsh, *America's Most Wanted: Final Justice* focused on those persons who had been apprehended after their crimes had been depicted on *America's Most Wanted*. On 16 July 1989 the series became the first Fox program to rank first in its time slot. The format of *America's Most Wanted* was not new to television. CBS had carried a similar series more than thirty years earlier: see *Wanted*.

AMERICA'S TOP 10   SYNDICATED
1980–1990   Announcer/disc jockey Casey Kasem hosted this half-hour musical series, which highlights the week's Top Ten records as appearing on *Billboard* magazine's pop singles chart. Shadoe Stevens took over from Kasem as host in 1988.

AMERICA'S TOWN MEETING   ABC
5 OCTOBER 1948–8 MARCH 1949; 27 JANUARY 1952–6 JULY 1952   Public affairs discussion program which featured guest speakers and audience debate. George V. Denny, who originated the show on radio in 1935, hosted the series in 1948 and 1952, John Daly in 1949.

AMERIKA   ABC
15 FEBRUARY 1987–22 FEBRUARY 1987   A heavy-handed, seven-part, fourteen-and-a-half-hour miniseries set in 1997, when the United States has fallen, without bloodshed, under Soviet domination. Featured were Kris Kristofferson as Vietnam veteran Devin Milford; Wendy Hughes as his ex-wife, Marion; Armin Mueller-Stahl as General Samanov; Robert Urich as Peter Bradford, the governor-general of Heartland, the new American government; Cindy Pickett as Amanda, his wife; Sam Neill as Colonel Andrei Denisov; and Mariel Hemingway as Kimberly Ballard.

THE AMES BROTHERS SHOW   SYNDICATED
1955   Fifteen-minute musical series starring the Ames Brothers (Joe, Gene, Vic, and Ed), who began recording in 1949. Youngest brother Ed went on to record as a solo artist and later appeared as Mingo in *Daniel Boone*.

THE AMOS AND ANDY SHOW   CBS
28 JUNE 1951–11 JUNE 1953   Amos and Andy, the immensely popular black characters created on radio in 1928 by white dialecticians Freeman Gosden and Charles Correll, were brought to television in 1951. CBS is reported to have paid Gosden and Correll $1 million each for the rights to the series. All the television roles were filled by black performers: Tim Moore as George (Kingfish) Stevens, a scheming con man and president of the Mystic Knights of the Sea, a fraternal order; Spencer Williams as Andrew H. Brown, Kingfish's trusting friend and usual mark; Alvin Childress as Amos Jones, a level-headed cabdriver (for the Fresh Air Cab Co.); Ernestine Wade as Sapphire Stevens, the Kingfish's nagging wife; Amanda Randolph as Mama, Sapphire's mother; Johnny Lee as Algonquin J. Calhoun, a fast-talking lawyer; Nick O'Demus as Lightnin', the janitor at the lodge. Jester Hairston was seen occasionally, playing two roles: Leroy, Sapphire's brother, and snooty Henry Van Horne. Theme: "The Perfect Song." Gosden and Correll supervised the production; Charles Barton directed most of the episodes. Many of the scripts were written by Joe Connelly and Bob Mosher, who went on to greater fame as the creators of *Leave It to Beaver*.

Although the series lasted only two seasons, it was widely syndicated until 1966, when pressure from civil rights groups prompted CBS to withdraw the series from syndication. The basis of their complaints was that the characterizations were stereotyped and only served to reinforce the feelings of prejudice harbored by white Americans. Whether the characterizations presented a more objectionable stereotype than those of *Sanford and Son* is for the sociologists to debate. Its historical significance should not be overlooked: It was the first television dramatic series with an all-black cast, and the only one until *Sanford and Son* in 1971. Indeed, it was not until 1965 that a black performer (Bill Cosby) costarred as a regular in a dramatic series, *I Spy*.

In the fall of 1983, after a seventeen-year hiatus, reruns of *Amos and Andy* popped up on an independent station in Atlanta. A San Diego attorney, Michael Avery, also produced a documentary about the series, "Amos 'n' Andy, Anatomy of a Controversy"; the program was hosted by George Kirby and featured interviews with surviving cast members and with civil rights leaders, as well as highlights from the series.

AMOS BURKE, SECRET AGENT
See BURKE'S LAW

AMY PRENTISS NBC
1 DECEMBER 1974–6 JULY 1975   One segment of the *NBC Sunday Mystery Movie*, alternating with *McCloud, Columbo,* and *McMillan and Wife.* Jessica Walter starred as widow Amy Prentiss, chief of detectives for the San Francisco police department; Art Metrano costarred as Detective Roy Pena; Steve Sandor as Sergeant Tony Russell; and Gwenn Mitchell as Joan Carter, her secretary. Produced by Cy Chermak for Universal Television.

AND EVERYTHING NICE DUMONT
8 MARCH 1949–9 JANUARY 1950   Maxine Barratt hosted this weekly talk show for women.

AND HERE'S THE SHOW NBC
9 JULY 1955–24 SEPTEMBER 1955   A summer replacement for *The George Gobel Show,* this half-hour variety series was a showcase for new talent. Hosted by Ransom Sherman, it featured a young comedian named Jonathan Winters, and the Double-Daters: Stephanie Antie, Kay O'Grady, Tommy Knox, and Ted Canterbury.

THE ANDROS TARGETS CBS
31 JANUARY 1977–9 JULY 1977   Hour adventure series about a team of investigative journalists working for the New York *Forum,* a great metropolitan daily newspaper. With James Sutorius as Mike Andros; Pamela Reed as Sandi Farrell; Roy Poole as Chet Reynolds; and Ted Beniades as Wayne Hillman. Bob Sweeney and Larry Rosen were the executive producers.

ANDY
See THE ANDY WILLIAMS SHOW

THE ANDY GRIFFITH SHOW CBS
3 OCTOBER 1960–16 SEPTEMBER 1968   The first, and probably the best, of the rural-oriented comedies brought to TV by James T. Aubrey, then president of CBS-TV. Its success engendered later hits such as *The Beverly Hillbillies, Petticoat Junction,* and *Green Acres,* as well as *Gomer Pyle, U.S.M.C.,* a spinoff. It starred Andy Griffith, a low-key comedian from North Carolina who had starred in "No Time for Sergeants" on *The U.S. Steel Hour* and later on Broadway. Here, Griffith played widower Andy Taylor, sheriff of Mayberry, North Carolina. Regulars included Don Knotts (1960–1965) as his cousin Barney Fife, the zealous but inept deputy sheriff; six-year-old Ronny Howard as Opie, Andy's son; Frances Bavier as Andy's aunt, Bee Taylor, who lived in and helped care for Opie. The townspeople included Jim Nabors (1963–1964) as Gomer Pyle, gas pump jockey; Howard McNear as Floyd Lawson, the barber; Paul Hartman as Emmet Clark, a handyman; Jack Dodson as Howard Sprague, the town clerk; Elinor Donahue (1960–1961) as Elly Walker, drugstore

salesclerk; Betty Lynn as Thelma Lou, Barney's girlfriend; Aneta Corsaut (1964–1967) as schoolteacher Helen Crump, Andy's girlfriend; Hal Smith as Otis Campbell, the town drunk.

When Nabors left in 1964 for his own series (*Gomer Pyle*), George Lindsey joined the cast as Goober Pyle, Gomer's cousin. In 1965, Knotts, who won five Emmys for his portrayal of Deputy Fife, left the series; it was explained that Fife became a detective in Raleigh. Replacing him as deputy was Warren Ferguson, played by Jack Burns. By 1968 Griffith, too, had decided to leave the series. During the last season Andy Taylor married Helen Crump. Joining the cast were Ken Berry as farmer and town councilman Sam Jones, and Arlene Golonka as Millie Hutchins. After Griffith's departure the series continued for three more seasons as *Mayberry, R.F.D.* (see that title). *The Andy Griffith Show* was syndicated as *Andy of Mayberry*.

Most of the cast (except for Frances Bavier, who was ill) was reunited in "Return to Mayberry," an NBC TV-movie broadcast 13 April 1986. Directed by Bob Sweeney (who had directed some 100 of the series's 249 episodes), it was one of the better TV sequels. It was also the top-rated TV-movie of the 1985–1986 season. CBS broadcast a retrospective, "The Andy Griffith Show Reunion," on 10 February 1993.

THE ANDY WILLIAMS SHOW
NBC/ABC/CBS/SYNDICATED

2 JULY 1957–5 SEPTEMBER 1957 (NBC); 3 JULY 1958–25 SEPTEMBER 1958 (ABC); 7 JULY 1959–22 SEPTEMBER 1959 (CBS); 27 SEPTEMBER 1962–3 SEPTEMBER 1967 (NBC); 20 SEPTEMBER 1969–17 JULY 1971 (NBC); 1976 (SYNDICATED)   Singer Andy Williams began his musical career in his teens as one of the Four Williams Brothers, who sang behind Kay Thompson. The group disbanded in 1952, and in 1954 Williams became a featured vocalist on the *Tonight* show, joining Steve Lawrence and Eydie Gormé. In 1957 he appeared in the first of several shows that bear his name; *The Andy Williams-June Valli Show* was a twice-weekly, fifteen-minute series, a summer replacement for *The Jonathan Winters Show* and *The Dinah Shore Show*. June Valli, Williams's cohost, had been a winner on Arthur Godfrey's *Talent Scouts* and had been featured on *Your Hit Parade* and *Stop the Music;* she and Williams had appeared together in "Five Stars for Springtime," a 1957 NBC special.

In 1958 Williams's show, titled *The Chevy Showroom*, was a summer replacement for *The Pat Boone Show;* Dick Van Dyke and the Bob Hamilton Trio were regulars. In 1959 Williams moved to his third network and his third summer series, a replacement for *The Garry Moore Show*. In 1962, Williams was finally given a fall series on NBC; the hour show lasted five seasons and featured The New Christy Minstrels and the Osmond Brothers. His third NBC series, which premiered in 1969, featured comics Charlie Callas and Irwin Corey, along with Janos Prohaska (as the Cookie Bear); the hour show lasted another two seasons. In an effort to make this Saturday-night series appealing to younger audiences, Mike Post was hired as musical director; Post had produced Mason Williams's gigantic instrumental hit, "Classical Gas," a year earlier. One of Post's first ideas was to prerecord the band arrangements in a recording studio, rather than record them on stage simultaneously with the actual taping of the program. This innovation, then unheard of, soon became the norm for most television variety shows. Post went on to compose (often in collaboration with Pete Carpenter) the music for many TV series, including *Toma, The Rockford Files, The Greatest American Hero,* and *Hill Street Blues*. In 1976 Williams hosted a syndicated series, entitled *Andy*. The half-hour show featured puppeteer Wayland Flowers; Pierre Cossette was the executive producer.

ANDY'S GANG
NBC

20 AUGUST 1955–31 DECEMBER 1960   *Andy's Gang* was the successor to *Smilin' Ed's Gang* and was so retitled when gravel-voiced Andy Devine took over as host following the death of Smilin' Ed McConnell. The rest of the gang remained with the show, including Midnight the Cat, Squeaky the Mouse, and the mischievous Froggy the Gremlin ("Plunk your magic twanger, Froggy!"). Filmed sequences were also part of the program; the adventures of Gunga Ram, an Indian boy, were often shown, starring Nino Marcel as Gunga.

ANGEL   CBS
6 OCTOBER 1960–20 SEPTEMBER 1961   Domestic sitcom about an American architect
married to a Frenchwoman. With Marshall Thompson as Johnny Smith; Annie Farge
as Angel Smith; Doris Singleton as neighbor Susie; and Don Keefer as Susie's
husband George. Produced by Jess Oppenheimer.

ANGEL FALLS   CBS
26 AUGUST 1993–30 SEPTEMBER 1993   A small town in Montana was the setting of
this short-lived hour prime-time serial. With Chelsea Field as Rae Dawn Snow, who
took over the Red Eye Pool Hall in Angel Falls after her father's death; Jeremy
London as Sonny, her son; Brian Kerwin as her old boyfriend, Eli Harrison; Kim
Cattrall as Eli's wife, Genna; Peggy Lipton as Hadley Larson; James Brolin as her
husband, Luke, the school basketball coach; Jean Simmons as Luke's mother, Irene
Larson; Cassidy Rae as Molly Harrison; Robert Rusler as Toby; Marlee Shelton as
Brandi; Shirley Knight as Eddie Wren; Shannon Wilcox as Rowena; Grace Zabriskie
as Cuema; and William Frankfather as Sheriff Bailey.

ANGEL STREET   CBS
15 SEPTEMBER 1992–3 OCTOBER 1992   The first casualty of the 1992–1993 season,
Angel Street was placed on hiatus after three episodes and never returned. The hour
cop show starred Robin Givens and Pamela Gidley as Officers Anita King and
Dorothy Paretsky, the only women assigned to a Chicago homicide unit. Also featured were Ron Dean as Detective Kenny Branigan and Joe Guzaldo as Sergeant
Ciamacco. Originally to have been titled *Polish Hill*, its troubles began long before it
hit the airwaves. The show had to be extensively reworked after rival producer Barry
Levinson claimed that it had borrowed too heavily from the book *Homicide*, which
was the inspiration for his 1993 crime show, *Homicide: Life on the Street*.

ANGIE   ABC
8 FEBRUARY 1979–23 OCTOBER 1980   Half-hour sitcom about a Philadelphia waitress
who met and married a wealthy pediatrician. With Donna Pescow as Angie Falco, a
waitress at the Liberty Coffee Shop; Robert Hays as Dr. Brad Benson; Sharon
Spelman as Joyce Benson, Brad's thrice-divorced and insufferable older sister;
Tammy Lauren (spring 1979) as Hillary, Joyce's daughter; Debralee Scott as Marie
Falco, Angie's younger sister; Diane Robin as waitress DiDi Malloy; and Doris
Roberts as Angie's mother, Theresa Falco, a newsstand operator. Executive produc-
ers: Dale McRaven and Bob Ellison for Paramount TV.

ANIMAL CLINIC   ABC
19 AUGUST 1950–13 JANUARY 1951   This early Saturday morning series focused on
animal care and behavior. Broadcast from Chicago, it was hosted by a veterinarian,
Dr. Wesley A. Young, who was assisted by trainer Oscar Franzen and Don Driscoll.

ANIMAL CRACK-UPS   ABC
8 AUGUST 1987–1 SEPTEMBER 1990   Alan Thicke hosted this panel show, on which
celebrity panelists attempted to answer questions about animals and their behavior.
The actual answers were supplied in video footage acquired from the Tokyo Broadcasting System. The series was introduced in prime time in August 1987, but moved
to ABC's Saturday-morning lineup on 12 September 1987; early in 1990 it moved
briefly to Sunday mornings.

ANIMAL SECRETS   NBC
15 OCTOBER 1966–8 APRIL 1967   Half-hour documentary series on animal behavior,
hosted by Loren C. Eisley.

ANIMAL WORLD (ANIMAL KINGDOM)   NBC/CBS/ABC/SYNDICATED
16 JUNE 1968–1 SEPTEMBER 1968 (NBC); 8 MAY 1969–18 SEPTEMBER 1969 (CBS); 30
APRIL 1970–17 SEPTEMBER 1970 (ABC); 11 JULY 1971–12 SEPTEMBER 1971 (CBS);
1973–1980 (SYNDICATED)   Narrated by Bill Burrud, *Animal World* was a series

of half-hour wildlife documentaries which frequently found its way onto network schedules as a summer replacement. From 1973 to 1980 the show was available in syndication. Charles Sutton was the executive producer for Bill Burrud Productions, Inc.

ANIMALS, ANIMALS, ANIMALS ABC
12 SEPTEMBER 1976–8 NOVEMBER 1981   This Sunday-morning show about animals was narrated by Hal Linden, star of *Barney Miller*.

ANIMANIACS (STEVEN SPIELBERG PRESENTS ANIMANIACS) FOX/WB
13 SEPTEMBER 1993–2 SEPTEMBER 1995 (FOX); 9 SEPTEMBER 1995– (WB)   Half-hour cartoon show whose central characters were the Warner Brothers—Yakko and Wakko—and their sister, Dot. The zany trio had escaped from the Warner Bros. lot, and often battled a psychiatrist named Dr. Scratchansniff.

ANN JILLIAN NBC
30 NOVEMBER 1989–20 JANUARY 1990; 5 AUGUST 1990–1 SEPTEMBER 1990   Ann Jillian, star of the sitcom *It's a Living* and of the 1988 TV-movie that dramatized her battle with breast cancer, briefly headlined in this half-hour sitcom. Jillian played Ann McNeil, a widow who moved from New York City to Marvel, California, with her teenage daughter. Also featured were Lisa Rieffel as her daughter, Lucy; Cynthia Harris as Sheila, owner of the cafe where Ann found work; Amy Lynne as Sheila's assistant, Robin Winkle; Noble Willingham as Ann's neighbor, Duke Sumner; Zachary Rosenkrantz as Duke's grandson, Kaz Sumner; and Chantel Rivera Batisse as stuck-up Melissa Santos, whom Kaz had a crush on. The series ran in prime time during the winter of 1989–1990 and again in August 1990, ending its run with a brief stop on NBC's Saturday-morning schedule.

THE ANN SOTHERN SHOW CBS
6 OCTOBER 1958–25 SEPTEMBER 1961   A new format for Ann Sothern, last seen as Susie, a private secretary. In this sitcom Sothern played Kathleen (Katy) O'Connor, assistant manager of the Bartley House, a New York hotel. The original cast included Ernest Truex as Jason McCauley, the manager; Ann Tyrrell as Olive Smith, Katy's secretary; Jack Mullaney as Johnny Wallace, the bellhop; Jacques Scott as Paul Martine, the desk clerk; and Reta Shaw as Flora McCauley. In March 1959 all the cast members except for Tyrrell were jettisoned, and virtually the entire cast from the old *Private Secretary* series was brought in: Don Porter as James Devery, the manager; Ken Berry as Woody, the bellhop; Louis Nye (1960–1961) as Dr. Delbert Gray, the hotel dentist; and Jesse White as Oscar Pudney, the newsstand operator.

ANNA AND THE KING CBS
17 SEPTEMBER 1972–31 DECEMBER 1972   Anna Leonowens's true-life adventures in nineteenth-century Siam were the subject of a book, a play, and two films before this television series. Despite lavish sets (including backdrops from the 1956 film, *The King and I*) and the presence of Yul Brynner (recreating his film role), the show went nowhere. With Yul Brynner as the King of Siam; Samantha Eggar as Anna Owens, the American schoolteacher hired by the King to educate his children; Keye Luke as Kralahome, the King's officious aide; Eric Shea as Louis, Anna's son; Brian Tochi as Prince Chula, the crown prince; and Lisa Lu as Lady Thiang, the King's number-one wife.

ANNIE McGUIRE CBS
26 OCTOBER 1988–28 DECEMBER 1988   Mary Tyler Moore's 1988 sitcom lasted just eight episodes after changing titles (it was to have been called *Mary Tyler Moore*) and leading men just weeks before the premiere date. Moore played Annie McGuire, a community relations coordinator in New York who had recently remarried. Denis Arndt played her husband (replacing Edward J. Moore), Nick McGuire. Other regulars included Adrien Brody as Nick's fourteen-year-old son, Lenny; Cynthia Marie King as Nick's nine-year-old daughter, Debbie; Bradley Warden as Annie's

twelve-year-old son, Lewis; Eileen Heckart as Emma, Annie's ultraliberal mother; and John Randolph as Red, Nick's ultraconservative father.

ANNIE OAKLEY   SYNDICATED
1952–1956   Children's western, set in the town of Diablo. With Gail Davis as Annie Oakley, gun-toting rancher; Brad Johnson as Sheriff Lofty Craig; and Jimmy Hawkins as Tagg, Annie's kid brother. Shelley Fabares, later to star in *The Donna Reed Show,* appeared occasionally. Davis, a skilled rider (her horse was called Target) and a crack shot, did most of her own stunt work. The series, the first western to star a woman, was produced by Gene Autry's Flying A Productions.

THE ANNIVERSARY GAME   SYNDICATED
1970   Al Hamel hosted this game show which featured three married couples. Most of the games involved one person attempting to predict whether his or her spouse would successfully perform a stunt.

ANOTHER DAY   CBS
8 APRIL 1978–29 APRIL 1978   Domestic sitcom about a married couple, both of whom held down full-time jobs, their two children, and her mother-in-law. With David Groh as Don Gardner, an advertising executive; Joan Hackett as Ginny Gardner, who worked at an insurance company; Hope Summers as Don's live-in mother, Olive Gardner; Lisa Lindgren as their daughter, Kelly; and Al Eisenmann as their son, Mark. Created by James Komack, the half-hour series was produced by Paul Mason. Paul Williams composed and sang the show's theme.

ANOTHER LIFE   SYNDICATED
1981–1984   Produced by the Christian Broadcasting Network, this daily half-hour serial dealt, as do other soap operas, with such topics as adultery, divorce, and alcoholism. Unlike the others, however, it conveyed a message: that all crises can be resolved (according to CBN) "through the application of Judeo-Christian principles." The series was set in the town of Kingsley, and its principal players included: Mary Jean Feton as recently widowed Terry Davidson, a nurse; Jeannette Larson and Debbie McLeod as her daughter, Lori; Darrel Campbell as her son, Peter; Matt Williams as Dr. Ben Martin, who married Lori; Edye Byrde as Ione Redlon; Eddie Hailey as her son, reporter Gene Redlon; Kari Page and Elain Graham as Gene's wife, Carla Redlon; Randy Kraft, Jr., as businessman Charles Carpenter; Suzanne Granfield as his wife, Helen Carpenter; Ginger Burgett as their daughter, Miriam; Robert Bendall as Miriam's husband (and later ex-husband), Paul Mason; Tom Urich as Dr. David Phillips, a reformed alcoholic; Dorothy Stinette (formerly of *Somerset* and *The Edge of Night*) as his former wife, Kate Phillips, who was murdered; Karen Chapman as their daughter Stacey; Peggy Woody as their daughter Amber; Chris Roland as Russ Weaver; Susan Scannell as Becky Huette, who married Russ; Michael Ryan as Russ's father, mobster Vince Cardello; Nick Benedict (formerly of *All My Children*) as Vince's murderer, Ronnie Washington; Kelly Gwin as Hugo Lancelot; Chandler Harben (formerly of *Love of Life* and *The Doctors*) as Blue Nobles; Paul Gleason and Jim Williams as politician Lee Carothers; Julie Jenny as Babs Farley; Alan Sader as Harold Webster; Nancy Mulvey as Nancy Lawson; Jerry Timm and Michael Hunter as Gil Prescott; Renee Crawford-McCullah as Marianne Prescott; Tom McGowan as Jeff Cummings; Carolyn Lenz as Liz Cummings; Kathryn King and Annamarie Smith as Vicki Lang; Dee Dee Bridgewater as Samantha Marshall; Ray Owens as Mitch Dunbar; Bob Turnbull as Tab Baron; Kim Strong as Dan Myers; Bob Burchette as Alex Greeley; and Rick Warner as John Brewbaker. Robert Aaron was the original executive producer, and Roy Winsor (who created *Search for Tomorrow* and *The Secret Storm*) the first story consultant, of the series, which was taped at CBN's Virginia Beach facilities.

ANOTHER WORLD   NBC
4 MAY 1964–   Another of the successful daytime serials created by Irna Phillips, *Another World* has made soap opera history: it was the first serial to engender a

spinoff (*Somerset*, which bore little resemblance to the parent; a second spinoff, *Texas*, premiered in 1980), the first to expand to a full hour (on 6 January 1975; many other soaps followed suit), and the first to expand again to ninety minutes (from 5 March 1979 to 1 August 1980, when it was cut back to an hour to make room for *Texas*). *Another World*'s story lines have emphasized psychological themes; as Irna Phillips explained in an interview, the serial is supposed to depict the difference between "the world of events we live in and the world of feelings and dreams that we strive for." The series was the number-two-ranked soap opera for most of the 1970s, before slipping to the middle of the daytime pack during the 1980s. Irna Phillips, who created the series with William Bell, left it during the late 1960s; among her successors as head writers have been James Lipton, Agnes Nixon, Robert Cenedella, Harding Lemay, Tom King and Robert Soderberg, L. Virginia Browne, Corinne Jacker, Soderberg and Dorothy Ann Purser, Richard Culliton, Gary Tomlin, Samuel Ratcliffe, Gillian Spencer, Sam Hall, Donna Swajeski, Peggy Sloane, and Carolyn Culliton. Procter and Gamble owns the series.

Another World is set in Bay City. The cast has included: John Beal, Leon Janney, Shepperd Strudwick, and Hugh Marlowe as accountant Jim Matthews, husband of Mary and father of three children; Virginia Dwyer as his wife, Mary Matthews (Mary and Jim were both written out by the end of the 1970s); Susan Trustman and Beverly Penberthy as their elder daughter, Pat Matthews; Joey Trent, Sam Groom, Bob Hover, and David Bailey as their son, Dr. Russ Matthews; Jacqueline Courtney, Susan Harney, Wesley Ann Pfenning, Vana Tribbey, Linda Borgeson, and Jacqueline Courtney (again) as their younger daughter, Alice Matthews; Sara Cunningham, Audra Lindley, Nancy Wickwire, and Irene Dailey as Jim and Mary's sister-in-law, Liz Matthews (in the very first scene on the 1964 premiere, Liz, whose husband had just died, was in tears); Joe Gallison as Liz's son, lawyer Bill Matthews, who drowned in 1968; Liza Chapman as Liz's daughter Janet Matthews; Fran Sharon, Roni Dengel, Lisa Cameron, and Lynn Milgrim as Liz's daughter Susan Matthews; Vera Allen as Grandma Matthews; Nicholas Pryor as Pat's boyfriend, Tom Baxter, who talked Pat into having an abortion and was later killed by her; William Prince as Ken Baxter; Michael Ryan as lawyer John Randolph, who defended Pat and later married her (they were then divorced); Jeanne Beirne, Lora McDonald, Tracey Brown, Loriann Ruger, Jill Turnball, Tiberia Mitri, Ariane Munker, Adrienne Wallace, and Beth Collins as Marianne Randolph, daughter of John and Pat; Gaye Huston and Barbara Rodell as John's daughter from a previous marriage, Lee Randolph, who got into LSD and died in a car crash; Carol Roux as Melinda Palmer, who was accused of murder and was defended by Bill Matthews, who later married her; Antony Ponzini as Melinda's ex-husband, Danny Fargo, a crook; Constance Ford as Ada Davis Downs Hobson (Ford played the role from 1967 until her death in 1993); Jordan Charney as Ada's brother, Sam Lucas; Ann Wedgeworth as Lahoma Vane, who married Sam (Lahoma and Sam later moved to *Somerset*); Robin Strasser, Margaret Impert, and Victoria Wyndham as Ada's daughter, Rachel Davis, who married Russ Matthews and later divorced him (after Wyndham took over the role, Rachel became one of the series's major characters; Wyndham also played a second role, Justine, in 1994); George Reinholt as Steven Frame, who married Alice Matthews, then Rachel Davis, and then Alice again before his supposed death in a helicopter accident (thought to have been killed, he miraculously reappeared a few years later, played by David Canary; Steven finally died in a car crash on his way to remarry Rachel); Victoria Thompson and Christine Jones as evil Janice Frame, Steven's sister; John Fitzpatrick and Leon Russom as Willis Frame, Steven's brother; Charles Baxter as Fred Douglas, who married Susan Matthews; Robert Milli as Wayne Addison; Val Dufour as District Attorney Walter Curtin, who killed Wayne; Judith Barcroft and Susan Sullivan as Lenore Moore Curtin, Walter's wife, who was indicted for Wayne's murder; Scott Firestone and Dennis McKiernan as Wally Curtin, son of Walter and Lenore; Muriel Williams as Helen Moore, Lenore's mother; Janice Young as Bernice Addison; Seth Holzlein, Aiden McNulty, Tyler Mead, Brad Bedford, Bobby Doran, Tim Holcum, Richard Bekins, Stephen Yates, Laurence Lau, and Russell Todd as James (Jamie) Frame, son of Rachel and Steve; Stephen Bolster as Ted Clark, who became Rachel's second husband; Leonie Norton as nurse

Cindy Clark, Ted's sister, who married Russ Matthews on her deathbed; Walter Matthews as Gerald Davis, Rachel's father; Janet Ward as Belle Clark; Beverly Owen as Dr. Paula McCrae; Joe Hannaham and James Douglas as writer Eliot Carrington; Beverlee McKinsey as Iris Carrington, his estranged wife; Michael Hammett and Jim Poyner as Iris's son, Dennis Carrington (Iris and Dennis Carrington left Bay City in 1980 for *Texas*; the characters later returned to *Another World*, with Carmen Duncan as Iris and Chris Bruno as Dennis); Donald Madden as Dr. Kurt Landis, Iris's boyfriend; Anne Meacham as Iris's secretary, Louise Goddard; Nick Coster as architect Robert Delaney, who married Lenore Curtin, then Iris Carrington; Robert Emhardt and Douglass Watson as Mac Cory, Iris's father, who became Rachel Davis's fourth husband (they would subsequently divorce twice and remarry twice); Charles Durning and Dolph Sweet as Lieutenant Gil McGowan, who married Rachel's mother, Ada; Chris Allport as Tim McGowan; Doris Belack as Madge Murray, a friend of Ada's; Ann Sheridan as Cathryn Corning, Melinda Palmer's mother; Colgate Salisbury as David Thornton, a friend of Lee Randolph's; Beverlee McKinsey (who would later play Iris) and Tresa Hughes as Emmy Ordway, Steven Frame's older sister; Jeanne Lange as architect Carol Lamont; John Getz as Carol's co-worker, Neil Johnson; John Considine, Jr., as lawyer Vic Hastings; Roberta Maxwell and Kathryn Walker as lawyer Barbara Weaver; Cathy Greene, Julie Philips, Jennifer Runyon, Dawn Benz, Mary Page Keller, and Taylor Miller as Sally Spencer, adopted daughter of the widowed Alice Matthews Frame; Jacqueline Brookes as Sally's grandmother, Beatrice Gordon, housekeeper for Mac and Rachel Cory; Ted Shackelford and Gary Carpenter as Beatrice's son, Raymond Gordon, who fell in love with Alice Frame; David Ackroyd as Dr. David Gilchrist; Gail Brown as Clarice Hobson; Ralph Camargo as Judge Merrill; Toni Kalem and Maeve Kinkead as Angie Perini; Dennis Sullivan, John Sullivan, Christopher Corwin, Tim Nissen, Tom Ruger, Tom Sabota, Jr., Glenn Zachar, Christopher J. Brown and Lionel Johnston as Michael Randolph; Robert Kya-Hill as Frank Chadwick; Micki Grant as Peggy Nolan; Andrew Jarkowsky as Mark Venable; Vera Moore as Linda Metcalf; Rosetta LeNoire as Mrs. Metcalf; James Preston as Ray Scott; Terry Alexander as Zach Richards; Jane Alice Brandon as Harriet Sullivan; William Roerick as Dr. Richard Gavin; James Luisi as Phil Wainwright; John Braden as Rocky Olson; Maia Danziger as Glenda Toland; Michael Goodwin and Paul Tulley as Scott Bradley; Rob Gibbons as Mel Lafferty; Elaine Kerr as Loretta Simpson; Laurie Heineman and Anna Holbrook as Sharlene Watts Matthews (Holbrook also played Kate Baker); Caroline McWilliams and Janice Lynde as Tracy DeWitt; Kelly Monaghan as Ken Palmer; Anna Shaler as Phyllis; Karin Wolfe as Pam Sloan; Dorothy Blackburn as Louella Watson; Jennifer Leak as Olive Gordon; Rolanda Mendels as Molly Ordway; Roberts Blossom as Sven Petersen; Pamela Brook as Corinne Seton; Danielle Jean Burns and Jane Cameron as Nancy McGowan, Rachel's half-sister; Richard Dunne as Darryl Stevens; Dan Hamilton as Jeff Stone; Carol Mayo Jenkins as Vera Finley; Barry Jenner as Evan Webster; Dorothy Lyman as Gwen Parrish; John Horton and John Tillenger as Leonard Brooks, who married Louise Goddard; Eric Roberts, Richard Backus, and Luke Reilly as Ted Bancroft; Paul Stevens and Luke Reilly as Brian Bancroft; Joe Hindy and William Russ as Burt McGowan; Helen Stenborg as Helga Lindemann; Barbara Eda-Young as Regine Lindemann; Patricia Estrin as Joan Barnard; Ned Schmidtke as Greg Barnard; Jay Ingram as Cal Zimmerman; Arthur E. Jones as Claude Kelley; Lynn Mowry as Doris Bennett; Jay Morran as Vince (Otis) Frame; Christina Pickles and Maeve McGuire as Countess Elena DePoulignac; Susan Keith and Nancy Frangione as Elena's stepdaughter, Cecile, who married James Frame and Sandy Cory; Tom Rolfing as Cliff Tanner; Fred J. Scollay as Charlie Hobson; Peter Ratray as Quentin Ames; Vicky Dawson as Eileen Sampson; Paul Perry and Ray Liotta as Joey Perini; Kathleen Widdoes as Rose Perini; Laurie Bartram as Karen Campbell; Eric Conger as Buzz Winslow; Leora Dana as Sylvie Kosloff; Robert Gibson as Ray Barry; Trish Hawkins as Mimi; Laura Malone and Judy Dewey as Blaine Ewing, who married James Frame; John Cunningham and Brian Murray as Dan Shearer; Gretchen Oehler as Vivian Gorrow (who also left for *Texas*); and Rick Porter as Blaine's brother, police officer Larry Ewing, who married Clarice Hobson.

Regulars in recent years have also included: Lee Patterson as Dr. Kevin Cooke; Geraldine Court as June Laverty; William Gray Espy as Mitch Blake; Chris Knight as Leigh Hobson; Ann McCarthy as Samantha; Linda Dano as novelist Felicia Gallant; Michael Garfield, Kevin Conroy, and Paul Tinder as Jerry Grove, who was married to Blaine Ewing; Warren Burton as Jason Dunlap; Judith McConnell as Miranda Bishop; Carla Borelli as Reena Cooke; Bradley Bliss as Kit Farrell; Curt Dawson as Zachary Colton; Robert Gentry as Philip Lyons; Deborah Hobart as Amy Dudley; Michael Stone as Craig Caldwell; Christopher Marcantel as Peter Shea; Anne Rose Brooks as Peter's wife, Diana Shea; Ed Power as Peter's father, Harry Shea; Taro Meyer as Melissa Needham; Chris Rich and Stephen Bogardus as Sandy (Alexander) Cory, Mac Cory's illegitimate son, who married Cecile DePoulignac, then Blaine Ewing; Alexander Parker, Daniel Dale, and Matthew Crane as Matthew Cory, son of Rachel Cory (by Mitch Blake); Nicole Schrank, Kitlin Roark, Nicole Catalanotto, Dana Klaboe, Sandra Reinhardt, Sandra Ferguson, and Christine Tucci as Amanda Cory, daughter of Mac and Rachel Cory (born on the show in 1978, the child celebrated her eighteenth birthday in 1987); Ron Harper as Taylor Holloway; Stephen Joyce as Paul Connolly; Pamela Payton-Wright as Hazel Parker; Joel Simon as Rudy Enright; Judy Cassmore as Margo Grove; Tony Cummings as Rick Holloway; Dee Ann Sexton as Cindy Lee; Paul Katz as Dooley; J. Kenneth Campbell as Jordan Scott; Jack Betts as Louis St. George, father of Cecile DePoulignac; Kyra Sedgwick, Jonna Lee and Faith Ford as Julia Shearer; Carmine Grey (also known as Carmine Rizzo) as Cory McGowan, Clarice's son; Robert Christian as Bob Morgan; Michelle Shay as his wife, caterer Henrietta Morgan; Reggie Rock Blythewood as their daughter, R.J. Morgan; Petronia Paley as Quinn Harding; Tracy Brooks Swope as actress Christine Wylie; Ben Masters as film director Vic Strang; David Oliver as Perry Hutchins; Terry Davis and Hilary Edson as Stacey Winthrop; Morgan Freeman as Roy Bingham; John Hutton, Christopher Holder, and Marcus Smythe as Peter Love; Anna Stuart and Philece Sampler as Donna Love; Kim Morgan Greene, Laurie Landry, and Anne Howard as cocaine addict Nicole Love; Joe Morton as Dr. Abel Marsh; Stephen Schnetzer as Cass Winthrop; Sheila Spencer and Pamela G. Kay as Thomasina Harding; Tom Wiggin as Gil Fenton; Drew Coburn as Barry Durrell; Tisha Ford as Mary Sue Morgan; Melissa Luciano as Jeanne Ewing; Ann Kerry as Janet Singleton; Robin Thomas as Mark Singleton; Jackee Harry as Lily Mason; Elizabeth Franz as Alma Rudder; Lenka Peterson as Marie Fenton; John Seitz as Zack Hill; David Combs as Bill Gorman; Patricia Hodges as Maisie Watkins; Sofia Landon as Jennifer Thatcher; Lewis Arlt as David Thatcher and as Ken Jordan; Trevor Richards as Kevin Thatcher; Evalyn Baron as Miss Devon; Charles Keating as Carl Hutchins; Thomas Ian Griffith as Catlin Ewing; and Kathleen Layman and Sally Spencer as M. J. McKinnon.

Also, Sharon Gabet as Brittany Peterson, who married Peter Love and was tried for his attempted murder (the show advertised nationally for viewers to serve on camera as jurors, and the writers agreed to be bound by the jury's verdict); Brent Collins as Wallingford; Patrick Tovatt as Zane Lindquist, who married Felicia Gallant in 1986; Hank Cheyne as Scott LaSalle; Ellen Wheeler, Rhonda Lewin, Anne Heche, and Jensen Buchanan as twins Victoria Love and Marley McKinnon; Kristen Marie as Cheryl McKinnon; Tom Eplin as Jake McKinnon; Jack Ryland, Duke Stroud, and Robert Hogan as Vince McKinnon; Denise Alexander as Mary McKinnon; John Considine (in his second role) as Reginald Love; Barbara Berjer as maid Bridget Connell; Missy Hughes as Sara Montaigne; Kale Brown as Michael Hudson, who married Donna Love in 1986; Ed Fry as Adam Cory; Anita Gillette as Loretta Shea; Richard Burgi as Chad Rollo; Barbara Bush (no relation to the First Lady) as Dawn Rollo; Joanna Going as Lisa Grady; John Brennan as Tony Carlyle; David Forsyth as John Hudson; Rebecca Hall as Peggy Lazarus; David O'Brien as psychiatrist and murderer Dr. Alan Glaser; Chris Cousins as Greg Houston; Robert Kelker-Kelly, Thomas Gibson, Danny Markel, and Brian Green as Sam Fowler, who married Amanda Cory in 1988; Rosemary Murphy as Loretta Fowler; James Pickens, Jr., as Zack Edwards; Tara Wilson as Julie Edwards; Alexandra Wilson and Amy Carlson as Josie Watts; Chris Robinson as Jason Frame; John Anderson and Benjamin Alexander as young Michael Spencer Hudson; Charles Grant (formerly known as Charles Flohe) and Eric Scott Woods as Evan Bates; Rick Gianese and Thom Zimerle as Rick Graham; Joy Bell as Caroline Stafford; B. J. Jefferson as Veronica Lawrence; Clayton Prince as her brother, Reuben Lawrence; Dondre Whitfield as Jesse Lawrence; Kevin Carrigan as Derek Dane; James Kiberd as Dustin Marlowe; Alice Barrett as Mary Frances "Frankie" Frame Winthrope; Allison Hossack as Olivia Matthews; John Aprea as Lucas; Denny Albee as Drew Marston; Rose Alaio as Arianna; Dack Rambo and Mark Pinter as Grant Harrison; Cali Timmins and Judi Evans (later known as Judi Evans Luciano) as Paulina Cory; Kate Wilkinson as Clara Hudson; Paul Michael Valley as Ryan Harrison, brother of Grant; Christine Andreas as Dr. Taylor Benson; Alla Korot as Jenna Norris; Julie Osburn as Kathleen McKinnon Winthrop; Ricky Paull Goldin as Dean Frame; and Valarie Pettiford as Courtney Walker. Later cast members included David Hedison as Spencer Harrison, father of Ryan and Grant; Alicia Coppola and Robin Christopher as Lorna Devon; James Goodwin as Kevin Anderson; Mitch Longley as attorney Byron Pierce; Jennifer Lien as Hannah Moore; Kaitlin Hopkins as Kelsey Harrison; Sarah Malin as Stefanie Preston; Geoffrey Pierson as Roger Jackson; Lenka Peterson (in her second role) as Helen D'Angelo; Bok Yun Chon as Lily Tran; Patti D'Arbanville as Christy Carson; Peter Galman as Christy's husband, Douglas Carson; Cassandra Creech and Michelle Hurd as Dana Kramer; Colleen Dion as Brett Gardner; Carlos Sanz as Victor Rodriguez; Julian McMahon as Ian Rain; Robyn Griggs and Jodi Lyn O'Keefe as Maggie Cory; Darlene Love, Saundra McClain, and Kim Sykes as Judy Burrell, Felicia Gallant's AA sponsor; Grayson McCouch as Morgan Winthrop; Robert Floyd as Kyle Berkley; Diego Serrano as Tomas Rivera; John Bolger as Dr. Alton Spencer; Frank Runyeon as Ed McClain; Reed Birney as Walter Trask; Blaise Garza as Gregory Hudson; Terrence McCrossan as Trent Forbes; Randy Brooks as Marshall Lincoln Kramer III; Mark Krassenbaum as Jerry Hoch; Kristen Wilson and Mary Teresa as Lyla Dawson; Angela Pietropinto as Connie Corelli; Brandy Brown as Angela Corelli; Steve Barton and Tom Ligon as Bailey Thompson; Joseph Barbara as Joe Carlino; Lisa Eichhorn as Apple Annie; Marcia McCabe as Eberhardt, a hitwoman; Timothy Gibbs as Gary Sinclair; Ilene Kristen as Madeline Thompson; Justin W. Chambers and Kevin McClatchy as Nick Terry; Tony Montero as Eddie Carlino; Eric LaRay Harvey as Darryl; David King as Billy Cooper; Steve Fletcher as Hank Kent; and Cory Lee Rogers as Tommy Kent.

ANSWER YES OR NO   NBC
30 APRIL 1950–23 JULY 1950   Playwright Moss Hart hosted this Sunday-night game show on which a celebrity panel tried to predict whether contestants would answer yes or no to getting involved in a hypothetical situation.

ANSWERS FOR AMERICANS   ABC
11 NOVEMBER 1953–24 FEBRUARY 1954   Wednesday-evening public affairs show, moderated by Deven Garrity. The panel included General Frank Howley, Professor John K. Norton, and Hardy Burt.

THE ANTAGONISTS   CBS
26 MARCH 1991–30 MAY 1991   Hour crime show about a young prosecutor, a young defense attorney, and their on-again, off-again personal relationship. With Lauren Holly as the prosecutor, Kate Ward; David Andrews as the defense lawyer, Jack Scarlett; Matt Roth as Jack's law student assistant, Clark Munsinger; Lisa Jane Persky as Kate's friend and co-worker, Joanie Rutledge; and Brent Jennings as their supervisor, assistant D.A. Marvin Thompson. Nine episodes were televised.

ANYBODY CAN PLAY (ANYONE CAN PLAY)   ABC
6 JULY 1958–8 DECEMBER 1958   George Fenneman hosted this nighttime game show on which four contestants sought to identify a hidden object. The show was originally entitled *Anybody Can Play* and, for reasons unknown, was retitled *Anyone Can Play*.

ANYONE CAN WIN CBS

14 JULY 1953–1 SEPTEMBER 1953   Al Capp hosted this prime-time game show, which was seen biweekly for most of its short run. On each show four celebrity panelists competed in a question-and-answer segment; three of the celebs were fully visible to viewers, while the fourth wore the mask of a Capp cartoon character, Hairless Joe. Members of the studio audience could back any of the celebrities; those who backed the panelist who correctly answered the most questions split $2,000 among themselves. Periodically through the show, calls were placed to home viewers, who were given the opportunity to identify the masked panelist.

ANYTHING BUT LOVE ABC

7 MARCH 1989–11 APRIL 1989; 15 AUGUST 1989–29 AUGUST 1989; 27 SEPTEMBER 1989–28 MARCH 1990; 18 JULY 1990–5 SEPTEMBER 1990; 6 FEBRUARY 1991–5 JUNE 1991; 7 AUGUST 1991–12 FEBRUARY 1992; 27 MAY 1992–10 JUNE 1992   A witty sitcom, set at the offices of a Chicago magazine. It starred Jamie Lee Curtis as Hannah Miller, a former teacher and aspiring writer who was originally hired as a researcher, and Richard Lewis as Marty Gold, an established writer. Hannah and Marty started out in a purely platonic relationship, but gradually they realized they were attracted to each other, and consummated their relationship in March 1991. In the spring of 1989, the setting was the *Chicago Weekly,* and the supporting cast included Sandy Faison as Pamela Peyton-Finch; Richard Frank as Jules Kramer; Bruce Kirby as Leo Miller, Hannah's father; Louis Giambalvo as Norman Kiel; and Robin Frates as Debbie. When the show returned in the fall of 1989, most of the supporting cast had been replaced, the magazine was now the *Chicago Monthly,* and Hannah became a writer. Featured were Ann Magnuson as the new editor, the trendy and hyper Catherine Hughes; Richard Frank as her assistant, now named Jules Bennett; Joseph Maher (1989–1990) as writer Brian Alquist; and Holly Fulger as Robin Dulitski, a school chum of Hannah's who owned the duplex in which Hannah lived. Bruce Weitz joined the cast in 1991, as writer Mike Urbanek, and John Ritter appeared occasionally as dashing photographer Patric Serreau. Wendy Kout created the series, and served as its executive producer and head writer during its spring 1989 run, but left the show due to "creative differences" with Curtis and Lewis. *Anything But Love* constantly disappeared and reappeared on ABC's schedule during its three-year run, which made it difficult to build a loyal audience. In the spring of 1992 the production company, rather than the network, announced it was halting production.

ANYTHING FOR MONEY SYNDICATED

1984–1985   This game show borrowed an element from *Candid Camera,* as two contestants watched videos of unsuspecting persons being approached by the show's staffers, who would ask them to do something ridiculous (such as ride a rowboat through a carwash) for money (up to $300 per stunt). The tapes were stopped before the subjects announced their decisions, and the contestants tried to predict whether the subjects would agree to do the stunt. Impressionist Fred Travalena presided over the merriment.

ANYWHERE, U.S.A. ABC

9 NOVEMBER 1952–14 DECEMBER 1952   A lighthearted look at health and nutrition, hosted by Eddie Dowling.

APPLE PIE ABC

23 SEPTEMBER 1978–7 OCTOBER 1978   Half-hour sitcom, set in 1933 in Kansas City, about a woman who put together a "family" by placing classified ads in the newspaper. With Rue McClanahan as Ginger-Nell Hollyhock, a hairdresser; Jack Gilford as the blind and feisty Grandpa; Caitlin O'Heaney as the daughter, Anna Marie; Derrel Maury as the son, Junior; and Dabney Coleman as Eddie Murtaugh, the man of the house. Charlie Hauck produced this short-lived show for Norman Lear's T. A. T. Communications.

APPLE'S WAY   CBS
10 FEBRUARY 1974–12 JANUARY 1975   A Los Angeles architect returns to his home-
town (Appleton, Iowa) with his family. With Ronny Cox as George Apple; Frances
Lee McCain as Barbara Apple; Vincent Van Patten as son Paul; Patti Cohoon as
daughter Cathy; Franny Michel (February 1974–September 1974) and Kristy
McNichol (September 1974–January 1975) as daughter Patricia; Eric Olson as son
Steven; and Malcolm Atterbury as Grandpa (Alden Apple). Created by Earl
Hamner, the series was supposed to be a contemporary version of *The Waltons*.
Executive producers: Lee Rich and Earl Hamner.

APPOINTMENT WITH ADVENTURE   CBS
3 APRIL 1955–1 APRIL 1956   Half-hour dramatic anthology series.

THE AQUANAUTS   CBS
14 SEPTEMBER 1960–22 FEBRUARY 1961   Ivan Tors, producer of *Sea Hunt,* produced
this hour-long adventure series which featured not one, but two divers. Originally
featured were Keith Larsen as Drake Andrews and Jeremy Slate as Larry Lahr. A
sinus operation necessitated Larsen's withdrawal from the show in midseason, and he
was replaced by Ron Ely, as Mike Madison, on 25 January. It was explained that
Drake Andrews had decided to rejoin the Navy. Charles Thompson was occasionally
featured as the Captain. In March the show's format and title were changed (see
Malibu Run).

ARA'S SPORTS WORLD   SYNDICATED
1976   Sports series hosted by Ara Parseghian, former football coach at Notre
Dame.

ARCHER   NBC
30 JANUARY 1975–13 MARCH 1975   Brian Keith starred as Lew Archer, the private
eye created by Ross Macdonald. With John P. Ryan as Lieutenant Barney Brighton.
Executive producer: David Carp. Produced by Jack Miller and Leonard B. Kaufman.
The pilot for the series, "The Underground Man," was televised 6 May 1974 on NBC.

THE ARCHIE SHOW   CBS
14 SEPTEMBER 1968–30 AUGUST 1969
THE ARCHIE COMEDY HOUR   CBS
6 SEPTEMBER 1969–5 SEPTEMBER 1970
ARCHIE'S FUNHOUSE   CBS
12 SEPTEMBER 1970–4 SEPTEMBER 1971
ARCHIE'S TV FUNNIES   CBS
11 SEPTEMBER 1971–1 SEPTEMBER 1973
EVERYTHING'S ARCHIE   CBS
8 SEPTEMBER 1973–26 JANUARY 1974
THE U.S. OF ARCHIE   CBS
7 SEPTEMBER 1974–5 SEPTEMBER 1976
NEW ARCHIE SABRINA HOUR   NBC
10 SEPTEMBER 1977–12 NOVEMBER 1977
THE BANG-SHANG LALAPALOOZA SHOW   NBC
19 NOVEMBER 1977–28 JANUARY 1978
THE NEW ARCHIES   NBC
12 SEPTEMBER 1987–3 SEPTEMBER 1988; 5 NOVEMBER 1988–4 FEBRUARY 1989   Bob
Montana's cartoon high schoolers were a fixture on Saturday-morning TV for a
decade, though the gang—including Archie Andrews, Jughead Jones, Veronica
Lodge, Betty Cooper, Reggie Mantle, and all the rest—have been featured in a
different format almost every season. The early years of the series emphasized music,
and the Archies (as the assemblage of anonymous studio musicians was called)
released several records; one, "Sugar, Sugar," was a monster hit. After one season
The Archie Show, a half-hour vehicle that introduced the Riverdale revelers to television, gave way to *The Archie Comedy Hour.* Archie and his pals now shared space

with Sabrina, the teenage witch. (In later years, Sabrina would be featured in her own shows, and even later would be reunited with Archie in a joint hour.) In 1970, *Archie's Funhouse,* back to a half hour, premiered (Sabrina had gone off to her own show with the Groovie Goolies). A year later came *Archie's TV Funnies,* a half-hour show in which Archie and the crew ran a television station. This was the first format which lasted more than one season. It was replaced by *Everything's Archie,* which in turn was replaced by *The U.S. of Archie* in 1974, as the group prepared for the Bicentennial. After a season's absence (1976–1977), Archie returned in 1977 on NBC, in *The New Archie Sabrina Hour.* Archie and Sabrina parted company again after only a few weeks, as the hour was broken into two half-hour shows, *The Bang-Shang Lalapalooza Show* (featuring the Archie gang) and *Super Witch* (featuring Sabrina). Both were dropped in midseason. After a nine-year hiatus, Archie and his pals returned to NBC's Saturday morning lineup as junior high schoolers in *The New Archies.* A TV-movie surfaced in 1990, marking the first time that the characters had appeared in live-action form. A grown-up Archie and his pals returned for their high school reunion in "Archie, To Riverdale and Back," which aired on NBC 6 May 1990.

ARCHIE BUNKER'S PLACE
See ALL IN THE FAMILY

ARE YOU POSITIVE   NBC
6 JULY 1952–24 AUGUST 1952   Bill Stern first hosted this Sunday game show, on which sports personalities tried to guess the identities of other famous athletes from blown-up negatives. Stern was succeeded by Frank Coniff late in July.

ARK II   CBS
11 SEPTEMBER 1976–13 NOVEMBER 1977; 16 SEPTEMBER 1978–25 AUGUST 1979   Week-end daytime series for children, set in the twenty-fifth century, in which the Ark II, a traveling repository of scientific knowledge, and its youthful crew attempted to save a civilization ravaged by global war and ecological plunder. Its mission: "To bring the hope of a new future to mankind." With Terry Lester as Jonah, the captain; Jean Marie Hon as Ruth; José Flores as Samuel, and Adam the talking chimp.

THE ARLENE FRANCIS SHOW   NBC
12 AUGUST 1957–21 FEBRUARY 1958   The successor to *Home,* the ambitious magazine of the air hosted by Arlene Francis. This thirty-minute daytime show was a blend of chitchat and features.

ARMCHAIR DETECTIVE   CBS
6 JULY 1949–28 SEPTEMBER 1949   John Milton Kennedy hosted this early game show in which studio contestants tried to solve mysteries acted out on stage.

THE ARMED FORCES HOUR   NBC/DUMONT
30 OCTOBER 1949–11 JUNE 1950 (NBC); 4 FEBRUARY 1951–6 MAY 1951 (DUMONT)
One of the first television series supplied by the United States government, *The Armed Forces Hour* was produced by the Department of Defense. Broadcast from Washington, it emphasized the process of the unification of the separate service branches. Segments were culled from the estimated 500 million feet of film already on hand. Production of the series (which, despite its title, was only a thirty-minute show) was supervised by Major Robert P. Keim (USAF) and Lieutenant Benjamin S. Greenberg (USNR) of the Public Information Office of the Department of Defense.

ARMSTRONG CIRCLE THEATER (CIRCLE THEATER)   NBC/CBS
6 JUNE 1950–25 JUNE 1957 (NBC); 2 OCTOBER 1957–28 AUGUST 1963 (CBS)   This high-quality anthology series specialized in dramatizations of actual events, but a few documentaries were also broadcast. It began as a half-hour weekly series and was more commonly known as the *Circle Theater.* In 1955, a one-hour format was adopted, and the series began a biweekly run, alternating with *Playwrights '56* (1955–

1956), *The Kaiser Aluminum Hour* (1956–1957), and on CBS, *The U.S. Steel Hour* (1957–1963). John Cameron Swayze hosted the show on NBC, Douglas Edwards, Ron Cochran, and Henry Hamilton on CBS. David Susskind served as executive producer for several seasons. Many stars played their first major television dramatic roles in this series, including John Cassavetes ("Ladder of Lies," 1 February 1955); Robert Duvall ("The Jailbreak," 14 October 1959); Anne Jackson ("Johnny Pickup," 28 August 1951); and Telly Savalas ("House of Cards," 18 February 1959).

ARNIE   CBS
19 SEPTEMBER 1970–9 SEPTEMBER 1972   The story of a loading dock foreman who is suddenly named Director of Product Improvement at Continental Flange became a run-of-the-mill sitcom that barely lasted two seasons. With Herschel Bernardi as new executive Arnie Nuvo; Sue Ane Langdon as Lillian, his wife; Stephanie Steele as teenage daughter Andrea; Del Russel as teenage son Richard; Roger Bowen as Hamilton Majors, Jr., top banana at Continental Flange; Herb Voland as Neil Oglivie, company VP; Olan Soule as executive Fred Springer; Tom Pedi as Julius, Arnie's pal from the loading dock; and Charles Nelson Reilly (1971–1972) as next-door neighbor Randy Robinson (TV's "Giddyap Gourmet").

AROUND THE TOWN   NBC
7 JANUARY 1950–18 FEBRUARY 1950   Not to be confused with CBS's *All Around the Town,* this Saturday-night series was emceed by Bob Stanton and was broadcast from various locations in New York City.

AROUND THE WORLD IN 80 DAYS   NBC
9 SEPTEMBER 1972–1 SEPTEMBER 1973   Saturday-morning cartoon show based loosely on the Jules Verne novel. Produced in Australia.

ARREST AND TRIAL   ABC
15 SEPTEMBER 1963–6 SEPTEMBER 1964   A ninety-minute crime show, with half the show spent catching the crook and half spent convicting him. With Ben Gazzara as Sergeant Nick Anderson; Chuck Connors as Public Defender John Egan; John Larch as Prosecutor Jerry Miller; Roger Perry as Detective Kirby; Noah Keen as Detective Bone; Joe Higgins as Jake Shakespeare; and Don Galloway as Harris. The concept was revived in 1990 on NBC's *Law & Order.*

ARRESTING BEHAVIOR   ABC
18 AUGUST 1992–9 SEPTEMBER 1992   This half-hour sitcom about a police officer was made to look like a documentary. The cast included Leo Burmester as Officer Bill Ruskin of the Vista Valley police department; Ron Eldard as his partner, Officer Donny Walsh; Chris Mulkey as Donny's divorced brother, Officer Pete Walsh; Lee Garlington as Bill's wife, Connie Ruskin, a dog groomer; Amy Hathaway as their daughter, Rhonda; Eric Balfour as their elder son, Bill Jr.; and Joey Simmrin as their younger son, Seth.

THE ARROW SHOW   NBC
17 DECEMBER 1948–19 MAY 1949   Phil Silvers first hosted this Thursday-night half-hour variety show, until he landed a starring role in the Broadway musical *High Button Shoes.* Hank Ladd succeeded Silvers as host. Rod Erickson produced the series.

THE ARSENIO HALL SHOW   SYNDICATED
3 JANUARY 1989–9 SEPTEMBER 1994   In 1989 Arsenio Hall became the first black to host a successful late-night talk show. It was a lifelong dream of Hall's, who admitted that, as a teenager, he had performed monologues and interviewed imaginary guests in his bedroom. Earlier in the decade, Hall had appeared on television as a standup comedian, and had been a regular on such short-lived variety and talk shows as *The 1/2 Hour Comedy Hour, Motown Revue,* and *Thicke of the Night.* In mid-1987 Hall took over as the regular host of Fox's *The Late Show,* following the departure of Joan

Rivers. Ratings improved under Hall's tenure, but Fox replaced *The Late Show* with the ill-fated *Wilton North Report.* Fox later invited Hall to return, but by that time he was at Paramount, making a film (*Coming to America*) with his pal Eddie Murphy. Paramount succeeded in signing Hall for this hour series, which became one of the more pleasant surprises of the 1988–1989 season. Televised in a late-night slot in most markets, the show was able to attract a younger audience than *The Tonight Show Starring Johnny Carson,* and effectively blunted the impact of CBS's 1989 late-night entry, *The Pat Sajak Show.* Although his format was similar to other talk shows, Hall succeeded in booking guests—particularly soul and rap music acts—who were rarely seen on other talk shows. Presidential candidate Bill Clinton appeared on the show, and played the saxophone, during the fall 1992 campaign. In June 1990 *TV Guide* named Hall its first "TV Person of the Year." Hall's show was the principal casualty of the Jay Leno-David Letterman talk show war. When Letterman's *Late Show* moved into its 11:30 P.M. time slot on CBS in September 1993, Hall's ratings began to slip badly. The last first-run program aired on 27 May 1994. By that time viewers had been treated to the sight of guest Bobcat Goldthwait spray-painting "Paramount sucks" on the set, and of Hall himself telling his bosses to "kiss my black ass."

THE ART FORD SHOW (IN RECORD TIME)   NBC
4 AUGUST 1951–15 SEPTEMBER 1951   On this summer replacement for *One Man's Family,* a celebrity quiz was sandwiched around musical numbers. New York disc jockey Art Ford hosted the series.

THE ART LINKLETTER SHOW   NBC
18 FEBRUARY 1963–16 SEPTEMBER 1963   Half-hour prime-time show hosted by Art Linkletter on which celebrity guests attempted to predict the outcome of a situation shown on film, performed either by unsuspecting participants or by the Art Linkletter Players. Some segments involved audience participation. Linkletter was one of the few personalities to have hosted series simultaneously on two networks: Both this series and Linkletter's earlier *People Are Funny* were seen on NBC, while *Art Linkletter's House Party* enjoyed a long run on CBS.

ART LINKLETTER'S HOUSE PARTY (THE LINKLETTER SHOW)   CBS
1 SEPTEMBER 1952–5 SEPTEMBER 1969   Television's longest-running daytime variety show began on radio in 1944. When the easygoing Linkletter first brought his blend of talk and audience participation to television, it was aired at 2:45 P.M. (EST). By February 1953, it had been moved back to the 2:30 P.M. slot, where it remained for fifteen years. In 1968 the show was retitled *The Linkletter Show* and given a morning slot. During its first TV season the sound portion was replayed on CBS radio immediately following the telecast. The most memorable feature of the series was the daily interview with four young schoolchildren, who were seated on a raised platform. Their "unrehearsed" remarks were the fodder for a series of books by Linkletter, the first of which was *Kids Say the Darndest Things.* The format, and part of the title, were revived in 1990; see *House Party with Steve Doocy.*

ART OF THE WESTERN WORLD   PBS
2 OCTOBER 1989–27 NOVEMBER 1989   A nine-part survey of European and American art, historical and modern, hosted by Michael Wood.

ARTHUR GODFREY AND HIS FRIENDS   CBS
12 JANUARY 1949–26 JUNE 1957
ARTHUR GODFREY AND HIS UKULELE   CBS
4 APRIL 1950–30 JUNE 1950
ARTHUR GODFREY TIME   CBS
7 JANUARY 1952–24 APRIL 1959
THE ARTHUR GODFREY SHOW   CBS
23 SEPTEMBER 1958–28 APRIL 1959   Born in 1903, Arthur Godfrey began his broadcasting career on radio in 1930 at the CBS affiliate in Washington, D.C. Before long he was working for CBS radio in New York. During those years he developed his

easygoing, straightforward, low-key style; his show, a blend of musical numbers and relaxed comedy, was a perennial hit. Godfrey had little discernible talent; though he could pluck the ukulele a bit, he was neither an accomplished singer nor a skilled actor. But he was a shrewd judge of commercial talent, a superb salesman, and a hard worker; these qualities helped make him an effective catalyst on the air.

In 1948 Godfrey entered television as the host of *Talent Scouts,* a long-running Monday-night showcase for amateur and professional talent. He soon became one of the most popular—and ubiquitous—personalities on television. Early in 1949 he could also be seen on Wednesday nights, hosting *Arthur Godfrey and His Friends,* an hour-long variety series which lasted eight seasons. For a brief period in 1950 Godfrey hosted a third prime-time series, *Arthur Godfrey and His Ukulele,* a fifteen-minute show seen after the news on Tuesday evenings. During the entire period the seemingly inexhaustible Godfrey continued to do a daytime radio show.

Beginning in 1952 the hour-long Monday-through-Thursday daytime radio show—*Arthur Godfrey Time*—was televised. Godfrey was again hosting three television series. Though he maintained that hectic pace for several seasons, Godfrey was often in great pain. A 1931 auto accident left him with injuries from which he never fully recovered: a broken pelvis, two broken kneecaps, one broken hip, and one permanently damaged hip. Godfrey's bouts with pain and depression have been cited as a cause of his mercurial temperament and as a reason for the fact that few of his stage "Friends" remained with the show for long, other than announcer Tony Marvin.

A large number of "Friends" shared the stage with Godfrey over the years: Carmel Quinn, Janette Davis, Bill Lawrence, Julius LaRosa, Marion Marlowe, Frank Parker, LuAnn Simms, Haleloke, The McGuire Sisters (Phyllis, Christine, and Dorothy), The Chordettes, The Mariners (one of the few integrated vocal groups that regularly appeared on TV), Pat Boone, Anita Bryant, and Johnny Nash, to name only a few. Many, like Boone, Nash, and the McGuire Sisters, were discovered on *Talent Scouts* and later joined the Godfrey troupe (the regulars appeared on both *Arthur Godfrey and His Friends* and on *Arthur Godfrey Time*). Several left voluntarily to pursue solo careers; some were quietly fired by the boss. But only one—LaRosa—was fired publicly, in what was one of the most widely publicized incidents in television history.

Julius LaRosa, a kid who could sing, was in the Navy when Godfrey heard him during a visit to Pensacola, Florida. Impressed with LaRosa, Godfrey arranged for him to come to New York in the fall of 1951. After LaRosa's second appearance on the show (Christmas 1951), Godfrey announced to his viewers that when "Julie" left the Navy, he could go to work for Godfrey. By the spring of 1952 LaRosa was a regular, and a popular one. His television exposure helped launch a recording career: His first record, "Anywhere I Wander," released in January 1953, sold 750,000 copies. By the middle of 1953 LaRosa's fan mail outstripped Godfrey's.

Meanwhile, Godfrey was sidelined with a hip operation. When he returned to the show in the fall, he detected an aura of laziness and cockiness among some of his regulars. The first of the last straws came when LaRosa missed a ballet rehearsal (upon his return, Godfrey had ordered ballet lessons for the cast); Godfrey abruptly yanked LaRosa from the next day's broadcast. LaRosa, understandably upset and unable to reach Godfrey directly, deepened his own grave by hiring an agent (Godfrey didn't deal with agents).

On Monday, October 19, 1953, the boom was lowered on an unsuspecting LaRosa. Godfrey brought LaRosa on for the last spot on the morning show. After innocuously asking whether LaRosa thought doing the show "was a pain in the neck," he bade him do his song. At the conclusion of the number, Godfrey announced, "That, folks, was Julie's swan song," and closed the show. LaRosa is reported to have been unaware that he'd just been fired, because he didn't know what "swan song" meant. Later that week, Godfrey also fired his musical director, Archie Bleyer, who was a partner with LaRosa in a record company. Bleyer was replaced by Paul Farber.

At that time Godfrey's popularity was probably at its zenith. In his book *CBS: Reflections in a Bloodshot Eye,* Robert Metz states that the Godfrey shows generated 12 percent of CBS's television revenues. After the LaRosa incident, however, Godfrey's popularity began to slip. The press had a field day; at a press conference

Godfrey said that LaRosa had shown "a lack of humility," a statement Godfrey later regretted.

Godfrey continued his three shows until 1957, when competition from ABC's *Disneyland* knocked off *Arthur Godfrey and His Friends. Talent Scouts* lasted one more season, while *Arthur Godfrey Time* continued during the day. In the fall of 1958 Godfrey returned with a half-hour Tuesday offering, *The Arthur Godfrey Show.* In 1959 Godfrey decided to leave television when he learned he had lung cancer. In a tearful farewell to his daytime audience, Godfrey explained that he didn't want viewers to see him waste away. The operation proved successful (a lung was removed), and Godfrey returned briefly in 1960 as cohost of *Candid Camera.* He died in 1983. See also *Candid Camera; Talent Scouts; Your All-American College Show.*

THE ARTHUR MURRAY PARTY   ABC/DUMONT/CBS/NBC
20 JULY 1950–7 SEPTEMBER 1950 (ABC); 15 OCTOBER 1950–11 MARCH 1951 (DU-MONT); 2 APRIL 1951–25 JUNE 1951 (ABC); 19 SEPTEMBER 1951–11 MAY 1952 (ABC); 11 JULY 1952–29 AUGUST 1952 (CBS); 12 OCTOBER 1952–26 APRIL 1953 (DUMONT); 28 JUNE 1953–4 OCTOBER 1953 (CBS); 12 OCTOBER 1953–12 APRIL 1954 (NBC); 15 JUNE 1954–14 SEPTEMBER 1954 (NBC); 28 JUNE 1955–13 SEPTEMBER 1955 (NBC); 5 APRIL 1956–27 SEPTEMBER 1956 (CBS); 9 APRIL 1957–16 SEPTEMBER 1957 (NBC); 29 SEPTEMBER 1958–6 SEPTEMBER 1960 (NBC)   One of the handful of shows broadcast over all four major commercial networks of the 1950s, *The Arthur Murray Party* most often surfaced as a summer replacement series, sometimes as a half-hour show and sometimes as a full hour. Ballroom dancing was the subject of the show, which was hosted by Kathryn Murray, wife of Arthur Murray, founder of the dancing schools which bear his name. Most shows featured songs, comedy sketches, and dance contests.

ARTS & ENTERTAINMENT REVUE   A&E
4 MAY 1990–10 JULY 1992   Hour magazine show on the performing arts, hosted first by Eric Burns, then by Jack Perkins, later by Robert Klein.

AS THE WORLD TURNS   CBS
2 APRIL 1956–   *As the World Turns* and *The Edge of Night,* which premiered the same day, were daytime television's first thirty-minute serials. *ATWT* was created by Irna Phillips, the prolific writer whose career began in radio and who was responsible for *The Guiding Light, The Brighter Day,* and many other soaps. From 1959 to 1978 *ATWT* was the highest-rated daytime show; its daytime success spawned a short-lived prime-time serial, *Our Private World* (1965), which failed to catch on as ABC's *Peyton Place* had a year earlier. On 1 December 1975 *ATWT* expanded to a full hour, but ratings, which had begun to decline in 1972, did not improve substantially. Early in the 1980s many new characters were introduced in an effort to attract a younger audience. Producers have included Ted Corday, Joe Willmore, Mary-Ellis Bunim, Laurence Caso, and John Valente. Irna Phillips was the original head writer, first with Agnes Nixon and later with William J. Bell (both Nixon and Bell would go on to create daytime dramas of their own). Subsequent head writers have included Joe Kane and Winnifred Wolfe, Katherine Phillips (Irna's daughter), Robert Soderberg and Edith Sommer, Ralph Ellis and Eugenie Hunt, Douglas Marland (twice), Jerome and Bridget Dobson (twice), K. C. Collier and Tom King, Caroline Franz and John Saffron, Tom King and Millee Taggart, Cynthia Benjamin and Susan Bedsow Horgan, Richard Backus and Juliet Packer, and Richard Culliton. By the late 1980s, *As the World Turns*'s ratings had stabilized, usually placing it among the top six daytime dramas; the series won the Emmy for outstanding daytime dramatic series in 1986–1987 and again in 1990–1991. The show celebrated its 10,000th telecast on 12 May 1995.

Set in the Midwestern town of Oakdale, *ATWT* originally contrasted two families, the middle-class Hugheses and the upwardly mobile Lowells. The Lowells were gradually written out, but several members of the Hughes clan have remained in Oakdale. As *ATWT* premiered in 1956, viewers were introduced to the main characters: Chris and Nancy Hughes and their three children (Don, Penny, and Bob); Jim and Claire Lowell and their daughter, Ellen, best friend of Penny Hughes. Featured were Don MacLaughlin as lawyer Chris Hughes and Helen Wagner as his wife, Nancy (after 25 years, Wagner was written out of the show in 1981, leaving MacLaughlin as the only original cast member; Wagner subsequently returned to the series, and Don MacLaughlin died shortly after the show's thirtieth anniversary telecast in April 1986). Also featured were Hal Studer, Richard Holland, Jim Noble, Peter Brandon, Martin West and Conrad Fowkes as Don Hughes; Rosemary Prinz and Phoebe Dorin as Penny Hughes; Bobby Alford, Ronnie Welch, and Don Hastings (formerly the Video Ranger on *Captain Video*) as Bob Hughes. Hastings was still on the show in 1995. Santos Ortega, who succeeded William Lee, played Grandpa Hughes until his death in 1976.

As the story began, the Hugheses learned that Chris's law partner, Jim Lowell (played by Les Damon), was having an affair with Chris's sister, Edith Hughes (Ruth Warrick). Jim died in 1957, and Edith later married Dr. George Frye (George Petrie). Jim's widow, Claire Lowell (played by Anne Burr, Gertrude Warner, Nancy Wickwire, Jone Allison, and Barbara Berjer), subsequently married Dr. Doug Cassen (Nat Polen) and was again widowed. Her third marriage—to Dr. Michael Shea—ended in divorce, and Claire herself died in a car crash in 1968.

Wendy Drew and Pat Bruder played the Lowells' daughter, Ellen (Bruder was still going strong in 1995, after 35 years in the role). Ellen had an affair with Dr. Tim Cole (William Redfield), who died of a blood disease in 1964; custody of their child had been awarded to Dr. David Stewart (Henderson Forsythe) and his wife, Betty (Pat Benoit). Ellen was briefly imprisoned for killing the Stewarts' housekeeper, Franny Brennan (Toni Darnay); by the time of her release, Ellen could marry Dr. Stewart, for Betty had died. Ellen and David raised Ellen's son, Dan Stewart (played by Paul O'Keefe, Doug Chapin, Jeff Rowland, John Colenback, John Reilly, and again by John Colenback), David's son by a previous marriage, Paul Stewart (played by Alan Howard, Edmund Gaynes, Steve Mines, Michael Hawkins, Garson DeBramenio, Marco St. John, and Dean Santoro), and a child of their own: Annie (played by Jean Mazza, Barbara Jean Ehrhardt, Ariane Munker, Shelley Spurlock, Martina Deignan, Julie Ridley, Randall Edwards, and Mary Lynn Blanks).

Young Dan Stewart grew up to become a doctor. After learning that Dan had had an affair with an Englishwoman, Elizabeth Talbot (Jane House and Judith McGilligan), Dan's wife Susan (Connie Scott, Diana Walker, Jada Rowland, Leslie Perkins, Judith Barcroft, and Marie Masters) refused to give him a divorce. Elizabeth married Dan's stepbrother, Paul, who died of a brain tumor shortly afterward. Dan finally succeeded in getting a divorce, but his marriage to the now widowed Elizabeth was brief, for she died after a fall down the stairs at home. Dan, despondent, later left Oakdale with his two daughters: Emily (nicknamed Emmy, she was his daughter by Susan and has been played by Jenny Harris, Colleen McDermott, Melanie Smith, and Kelley Menighan) and Betsy (his daughter by Elizabeth and played by Tiberia Mitri, Maurine Trainor, Patricia McGuiness, Suzanne Davidson, Lisa Denton, Meg Ryan, and Jordan Baker, who had previously played FBI agent Brianne Hunt).

Penny Hughes was first widowed in 1959, when her husband Jeff Baker (Mark Rydell) was killed in an auto accident. Sadly, Penny's second husband, a nonpracticing physician named Neil Wade (Michael Lipton), also died in a car crash. Penny eventually moved to England and adopted a Eurasian girl, Amy (played by Irene Yah-Ling Sun).

In 1960, Eileen Fulton joined the series as Lisa Miller, one of soapdom's most hated villainesses. Her first target was Bob Hughes, whom she met at college. Lisa married Bob and bore him a son, Tom. Lisa had an affair with Bruce Elliott (James Pritchett), was divorced from Bob, and left town. When she returned to Oakdale, it was learned that she had married a wealthy oldster and had been widowed. Lisa then married Dr. Michael Shea (former husband of Claire Lowell, and played by Jay Lanin and Roy Shuman) and bore him a son, Chuck (played by Pip Sarser, Willie Rook, and David Perkins). When Michael Shea was found murdered, Tom Hughes, Lisa's son by her first marriage, was implicated but proved to be innocent. Lisa, now widowed, tried unsuccessfully to win back Bob Hughes, her first husband, and later married lawyer Grant Colman, an associate of Chris Hughes (Colman was played by Konrad Matthaei and James Douglas). In 1980 Fulton also portrayed the corpse of her lookalike, Ruth Hadley. In 1983, dissatisfied with the dimensions of the Lisa character, Fulton temporarily left *ATWT;* she was replaced by Betsy von Furstenburg (Jane Powell filled in for Fulton briefly in 1990). By this time, Lisa had acquired yet another husband, Whit McColl (played by Robert Horton of *Wagon Train* fame). Lisa then fell for Whit's son, lawyer Brian McColl (played by Robert Burton, Frank Telfer, and Mark Pinter).

Tom Hughes, son of Bob and Lisa, has been played by James Madden, Jerry Schaffer, Frankie Michaels, Richard Thomas, Paul O'Keefe, Peter Link, Peter Galman, C. David Colson, Tom Tammi, Justin Deas, Jason Kincaid, Gregg Marx, and Scott Holmes. Tom was briefly interested in Meredith Halliday (Nina Hart) but married Carol Demming (played by Rita McLaughlin, later known as Rita McLaughlin Walter). After that marriage ended in divorce, Tom wed Natalie Bannon (Judith Chapman and Janet Zarish).

Tom's father, Bob Hughes, kept active after his divorce from Lisa Miller. He married Sandy McGuire (played by Dagne Crane, Jill Andre, Ronnie Carrol, and Barbara Rucker), whom Ellen Lowell had met while in prison. After a second divorce, Bob married Jennifer Ryan (played by Geraldine Court and Gillian Spencer), a widow, in 1972. Jennifer's son by her earlier marriage, Dr. Rick Ryan (Con Roche and Gary Hudson), resented the presence of Bob and was responsible for Jennifer leaving Bob. Jennifer returned when she learned she was pregnant; their daughter was named Franny (played by Kelly Campbell, Maura Gilligan, Tracy O'Neill, Helene Udy, Terri VandenBosch, Julianne Moore [who also played Franny's lookalike half-sister and cousin Sabrina Fullerton], and Mary Ellen Stuart; Claire Beckman later played Sabrina). In the meantime, Jennifer's sister, Kim Reynolds (played by Kathryn Hays and temporarily by Patty McCormack), came to town, had an affair with Bob, married villainous Dr. John Dixon (Larry Bryggman), then married restaurateur Nick Andropolous (Michael Forest) and, later, Bob Hughes.

Others who have appeared over the years have included: William Johnstone as Judge Lowell, Jim Lowell's father and founder of Chris Hughes's law firm; Martin Rudy and Anna Minot as Sandy McGuire's parents, Carl and Martha Wilson; Michael Nader and Max Brown as Kevin Thompson, whom Sandy later married; Jerry Lacy as Simon Gilbey, Meredith Halliday's guardian; Charles Siebert as Wally Matthews, a onetime boyfriend of Lisa's; Dennis Cooney as Jay Stallings, another boyfriend of Lisa's who married Carol Demming after her divorce from Tom Hughes; Joyce Van Patten and Virginia Dwyer as Janice Turner, who fell in love with Don Hughes before marrying Carl Whipple (Rod Colbin); Barbara Rodell as Joyce Colman, ex-wife of Grant Colman who later married Don Hughes; Grace Matthews as Grace Baker, mother of Jeff Baker, Penny's first husband; Hal Hamilton and Charles Baxter as Tom Pope, a lawyer in Chris Hughes's firm; Geoffrey Lumb as lawyer Mitchell Drew; Millette Alexander as nurse Sylvia Hill; George Rose as Dr. Prescott; Ben Hayes as Dr. Bruce Baxter; John Swearingen as Dr. Bill Jenkins; Addison Powell as Dr. Flynn; Joan Anderson as nurse Mary Mitchell; Bernie McInerney as Jerry Butler; Ethel Remey and Dorothy Blackburn as Alma Miller, Lisa's mother; Ed Kemmer as lawyer Dick Martin; Bob Hover and Kelly Wood as Brian and Mary Ellison, adoptive parents of Grant Colman; Stephen Bolster and Anthony Herrera as Mark Galloway (Herrera later returned in another role, as James Stenbeck); Fran Carlon as Julia Burke; Donna Wandrey and Colleen Zenk (also known as Colleen Zenk Pinter) as Barbara Ryan, who married James Stenbeck; Lisa Cameron as Peggy Reagan; Peter Stuart and Curt Dawson as Ron Talbot; Carmine Stipo and Jill Harmon as Tony and Maria Moreno; Michael Lombardo as Lieutenant Joe Fernando; Michael Finn as Richard Taylor; Christopher Hastings as Peter Burton; and Ted Agress as Luke Peters.

Other additions to the cast have included: Clarice Blackburn as Marion Connelly; Keith Charles as Ralph Mitchell; Jon Cypher as Dr. Alexander Keith; Laurel Delmar as Laurie Keaton; Jason Ferguson, Sean Anthony, and Scott DeFreitas as Andrew Dixon; Wayne Hudgins as Beau Spencer; Georgann Johnson as Jane Spencer; Simone Schachter, Jean Mazza (who had previously played Annie Stewart), Glynnis O'Connor, Marcia McClain, Heather Cunningham, Jacqueline Schultz, Vicky Dawson, and Alexandra Neil as Dawn (Dee) Stewart; Judith McConnell as Valerie Conway; Ariane Munker (in her second role) as Melinda Gray; Biff Warren as Mark Lewis; Tommy Baudo and T. R. Hill as Teddy Ellison; Doug Travis as Nick Conway; Leslie Denniston as Karen Peters; Kipp Whitman as Hank Robinson; Rebecca Hollen as Tina Cornell; Rachel Kelly as Kate; Robert Lipton as Dr. Jeff Ward, who married Annie Stewart; and Dennis Romer as Dr. Doug Campbell.

Also: Lisa Loring (who had been a regular on *The Addams Family* as a child) as Cricket Montgomery; Margaret Colin, Hillary Bailey (later known as Hillary Bailey Smith), Ellen Dolan, and Glynnis O'Connor as her sister, Margo Montgomery, who married Tom Hughes; Scott Bryce as their brother, Craig Montgomery, who married Betsy Stewart; Velekka Gray and Ann Sward as their mother, Lyla Montgomery; Mary Linda Rapelye as Maggie Crawford, Lyla's sister; Martha Lambert as Sheila Winston; Maureen McNamara as Tiffany; Peter Brouwer as Brad Hollister; Peter Reckell as Eric Hollister; Elden Ratliff, Daniel Pintauro, C. B. Barnes, and Andrew Kavovit as Paul Stenbeck; Hugo Napier as Gunnar Stenbeck, James's cousin; Anthony Inneo as Johanssen; Frank Runyeon as Steve Andropolous, Nick's brother, who married Carol Hughes; Deborah Hobart as Dana McFarland; Lee Meredith as Charmane McColl; Chris LeBlanc as Kirk McColl; Kim Ulrich as Diana McColl; Judith Blazer as Ariel Aldrin, who married Dr. John Dixon; Linda Dano as Cynthia Stewart; Kathy McNeil as Karen Haines, Cynthia's unstable daughter; Robin Thomas as Dr. Matt Butler, a psychiatrist; W.T. Martin as private eye Stan Holder; Elaine Princi as Miranda Marlowe; Kathleen Rowe McAllen as Bilan Marlowe, Miranda's daughter; Betsy Palmer as Suz Becker; J. Marshall Watson as Ernie Ross; Jay Acovone as Cliff Matson, a cop; Ron Foster as Lincoln Foster; Eddie Earl Hatch as Tucker Foster; Brian Bloom as Dustin Donovan; David Forsyth as Burke Donovan; Juanita Mahone and Brooke Alexander as Samantha Jones; Einar Perry Scott as Nels Anderson; Patricia Mauceri as Andrea Korackes; Jacques Perreault as Frank Andropolous; Breck Jamison as Jay Connors; Nancy Pinkerton-Peabody as Dorothy Connors; Tonya Pinkins as Heather Dalton; Elizabeth Hubbard as Lucinda Walsh; and Tracy Kolis as Juliet Spear.

More new faces included: Lucy Deakins, Martha Byrne, and Heather Rattray as Lily Walsh; Finn Carter as Sierra Esteban; Peter Boynton as Tonio Reyes, who married Sierra in 1986; Margaret Reed as Shannon O'Hara; Kathleen Widdoes as Emma Snyder; Lisa Brown as Iva Snyder; Jon Hensley as Holden Snyder; Jennifer Ashe as Meg Snyder; Michael Swan as Duncan McKechnie; Ashley Crow as Beatrice McKechnie; Benjamin Hendrickson as detective Hal Munson; John Wesley Shipp as murderous Doug Cummings; Colleen Broomall, Kristanna Loken, and Ashley Williams as Danielle Andropolous; Bill Shanks as Dr. Casey Peretti; Gloria Pagano as Marsha Talbot; Steve Bassett as Seth Snyder; William Fichtner as Josh Snyder/Rod Landry; Charles Cioffi as Henry Lansing; Maggie Baird as Dr. Taylor Baldwin; Robin Morse as Pam Wagner; Tamara Tunie (also known as Tamara Tunie Bouquett) and JoAnna Rhinehart as Jessica Griffin; Steven Weber as Kevin Gibson; Count Stovall as Roy Franklin; Julie Ann Lowery as Monica Lawrence; Neil Maffin as Beau Farrell; Carolyn Ann Clark as Laura Simmons; Michael David Morrison and Graham Winton as Caleb Snyder; Brian Starcher as Hank Eliot, daytime TV's first gay male character; Ming-Na Wen as Lien Truong; Sarah Botsford as Lilith; Tom Wiggin as Kirk Anderson; Farley Granger as Earl Mitchell, who became Lisa McColl's seventh husband; Richard Burgi as Glenn Harrington; Jeff Hayenga as Colin Crowley; Renee Props as Ellie Snyder; Patrick Tovatt as Cal Stricklyn; Paul Hartel as Matthew, Lucinda Walsh's servant; Christopher Durham as Mark Harrington; Michael Louden as Ian "Duke" Cramer; Greg Beecroft as Brock Lombard; Cynthia Dozier as Olivia Hyland; Thomas Gibson as Derek Mason; Burke Moses as Sean Baxter; Peter Francis James as Blake; Ryan Reed as Jeff Dolan; Dan Frazer as Dan McCloskey, who married Nancy Hughes after Chris's death; Joris Stuyck and Mark Tymchyshyn as Gavin Kruger; Ed Fry as Larry McDermott; Jonathan Hogan as Jason Benedict; Rex Smith as Darryl Crawford; Leslie Denniston (in her second role) as Carolyn Crawford, Darryl's wife; Hayley Barr as Courtney Baxter; Garland Hunter as April O'Shea; Allyson Rice-Taylor as Connor Walsh; and James Wlcek and Lonnie McCullough as Linc Rafferty.

Joining the series during the 1990s were: Susan Marie Snyder as Julie Snyder;

Parker Posey as Tess Shelby, niece of Hal Munson; Alice Haining as Angel Snyder; Judson Mills as Hutch Hutchinson; Dan Ziskie as Woody Hutchinson; Kathleen McKenny and Jill Powell as Marcy Breen; Kim Stanton as Katherine Johnson; Michael Levin as John Eldridge; Richard Backus as John's brother, Karl Eldridge; Ann Shropshire as their mother, Ann Eldridge; Joe Breen as Scott Eldridge; Frank Converse as Ned Simon; John Cunningham as lawyer Emerson Gallagher; Ann Flood as Ruth Mansfield; Greg Watkins as Evan Walsh; Christian Baskous as Greg Noble; Yvonne Perry as Rosanna Cabot; Margaret Klenck as Kitty Fielding; Terry Lester as Royce Keller; Mary Kay Adams as Neal Alcott; Richard Bekins as Michael, Neal's ex-husband; Sharon Case as Debbie Simon; Kim Snyder as Leslie; Nick Ullett as Graham Hawkins; Paolo Seganti as Damian Grimaldi; Nicolas Coster as Eduardo Grimaldi; Claire Bloom and Lynn Milgrim as Orlena Grimaldi; Tovah Feldshuh as Dr. Bethany Rose; Lisby Larson as Mary Campbell; Shawn Christian as Mike Kasnoff; Darnell Williams as Jack Derbin; Gerrit Vooren as Hans, a terrorist; Holly Cate as Janice Maxwell; Ken Garito as Dave Egan; Malcolm Gets as Ron Gillette; Jack Gwaltney as Dr. Bradley Wyndham; Courtney Sherman as Dr. Lynn Michaels; Sarah Knowlton as Tracey Donely; Dane Leach as R. J. Donely, Tracey's son; Mark Kevin Lewis as Gregory Varner; Matt Servitto as Cesare; Paul Hecht as Alexander Cabot; Jason Biggs as Pete Wendall; Robert Vaughn as lawyer Rick Hamlin; Maura West as Carly Tenney; Sam Rovin and John Dauer as Jeremy Wheeler; Jordana Brewster as Nikki; Karina Arroyave as Bianca Walsh; Mason Boccardo as Aaron Snyder; Michael Genet as Lamar Griffin; Damian Leake as Joel Higgins; Jenny O'Hara as Thelma Dailey; Christian Seifert as Christopher Hughes; Michael Zderko as Adam Hughes; and Dick Latessa as Ambrose.

THE ASCENT OF MAN
PBS

7 JANUARY 1975–1 APRIL 1975   Highbrow series which focused on the development of humankind and how certain scientific discoveries shaped the growth of civilization. Hosted by Dr. Jacob Bronowski, a Polish-born scientist who headed the Council for Biology in Human Affairs at the Salk Institute in California. Jointly produced by Time-Life Films and the BBC, the series was broadcast in England during the 1972–1973 season. Bronowski died shortly before the program premiered in the United States.

ASK DR. RUTH
SYNDICATED

1987   A talk show about sex, hosted by irrepressible psychologist Dr. Ruth Westheimer, with celebrity guests. Westheimer had hosted similar shows on the Lifetime cable service, but the syndicated version, which was less explicit than the cable programs, lasted only thirteen weeks.

ASK WASHINGTON
NBC

11 JANUARY 1954–26 FEBRUARY 1954   Monday-through-Friday public affairs program on which a panel of Washington journalists answered questions sent in by viewers. Replaced by *Home*.

THE ASPHALT JUNGLE
ABC

2 APRIL 1961–24 SEPTEMBER 1961   TV version of the 1950 film, based on the novel by W. R. Burnett. Set in New York. With Jack Warden as Deputy Police Commissioner Matt Gower; Arch Johnson as Captain Gus Honochek; and Bill Smith (later known as William Smith on *Laredo*) as Sergeant Dan Keller. Theme music for the hour series was composed by Duke Ellington.

ASSIGNMENT FOREIGN LEGION
CBS

1 OCTOBER 1957–24 DECEMBER 1957   Anthology series depicting the exploits of the French Foreign Legion during World War II. Appearing as a war correspondent, Merle Oberon also hosted the series.

ASSIGNMENT MANHUNT NBC

14 JULY 1951–1 SEPTEMBER 1951; 5 JULY 1952–23 AUGUST 1952   Produced by Julian Claman, this half-hour crime show starred John Baragrey and was a summer replacement for *Your Hit Parade*.

ASSIGNMENT UNDERWATER SYNDICATED

1960   Maritime adventure starring Bill Williams as Bill Greer, diver and skipper of *The Lively Lady*. With Diane Mountford as his daughter Patty.

ASSIGNMENT: VIENNA ABC

28 SEPTEMBER 1972–9 JUNE 1973   This segment of ABC's adventure trilogy, *The Men* (see also *The Delphi Bureau* and *Jigsaw*), starred Robert Conrad as Jake Webster, American undercover agent and owner of a Viennese nightspot; Charles Cioffi as Major Bernard Caldwell, his contact man; and Anton Diffring as Inspector Hoffman of the Austrian police.

THE ASSOCIATES ABC

23 SEPTEMBER 1979–28 OCTOBER 1979   Half-hour sitcom set at Bass & Marshall, a prestigious Manhattan law firm. With Wilfrid Hyde-White as Emerson Marshall, the highly respected but slightly dotty senior partner; Martin Short as Tucker Kerwin, an idealistic new associate; Alley Mills as wholesome Leslie Dunn, Tucker's office mate; Joe Regalbuto as obnoxious Eliot Streeter, a newly named partner; Shelley Smith as sophisticated Sara James, another new associate; and Tim Thomerson as Johnny Danko, the macho office boy. The series was created by the group responsible for the 1978 hit *Taxi:* Jim Brooks, Stan Daniels, Charlie Hauck and Ed. Weinberger. The show's musical theme, "The Wall Street Blues," was sung by B. B. King.

ASTRO BOY SYNDICATED

1963   A cartoon series about a robotic youngster, *Astro Boy* was the first Japanese-produced television series exported to the United States. The character was created in comic book form in 1952 by Osamu Tezuka and was originally known as *Tetsuwan Atomu* (Mighty Atom). The TV title character was created by a scientist as a robotic replacement of his son, Astor Boynton, who had been killed in a traffic accident. Astro Boy's mission was to prove his ultimate reality to his father by serving humanity. Before his 193-episode run was completed, Astro Boy was joined by a robotic sister, Astro Girl. Billie Lou Watt provided the English-language voice of Astro Boy.

AT EASE ABC

4 MARCH 1983–15 JULY 1983   A pale imitation of *You'll Never Get Rich*, TV's archetypal service sitcom, *At Ease* was set at Camp Tar Creek, Texas, home of the 5033rd Personnel Administrative Center. Stationed there were Jimmie Walker as scheming Sergeant Tyrone Valentine; David Naughton as his partner in hijinks, Private Tony Baker; Roger Bowen as befuddled Colonel Clapp, the commanding officer; Richard Jaeckel as zealous Major Hawkins; George Wyner as Hawkins's lackey, "Weasel" Wessel; Jourdan Fremin as Corporal Lola Grey, Clapp's secretary; Joshua Mostel as Private Maxwell; and John Vargas as Private Cardinel. Hy Averback, the veteran producer whose credits included *Ensign O'Toole, F Troop*, and *Mrs. G Goes to College*, produced this one with Jim Mulligan.

AT HOME AND HOW ABC

1 JANUARY 1949–27 APRIL 1949   Tips on home improvement were given on this half-hour prime-time show.

THE AT HOME SHOW

See THE MASLAND AT HOME SHOW

AT ISSUE ABC

12 JULY 1953–24 FEBRUARY 1954   Martin Agronsky hosted this fifteen-minute public affairs program on which he interviewed guests.

AT RONA'S   NBC

6 MARCH 1989–17 MARCH 1989   Hollywood gossip columnist Rona Barrett was given a two-week tryout in a morning talk-show format. The half-hour program was set in her dining room, with Barrett interviewing celebrity guests over a meal prepared by a Hollywood chef. One segment, in which Barrett quizzed Meredith Baxter Birney about her then troubled marriage, was axed at Birney's insistence.

AT THE MOVIES   SYNDICATED

1982–1990   Chicago film critics Roger Ebert and Gene Siskel left PBS's *Sneak Previews* to cohost this half-hour weekly series. In 1986 the pair left for their third such effort (see *Siskel & Ebert & The Movies*), and were succeeded by critics Rex Reed and Bill Harris; Harris in turn was succeeded by Dixie Whatley in 1988. The formats of all three programs were similar: Each week the two critics screened clips of recently released films and discussed them. See also *Sneak Previews*.

THE ATOM ANT SHOW   NBC
2 OCTOBER 1965–2 SEPTEMBER 1967
THE ATOM ANT/SECRET SQUIRREL SHOW   NBC

9 SEPTEMBER 1967–31 AUGUST 1968   A super-powered insect was the star of this Hanna-Barbera cartoon show. In 1967, Ant joined forces with Secret Squirrel, the daring rodent who had had his own show for two seasons. Other cartoon segments included "Precious Pupp" and "The Hillbilly Bears."

ATOM SQUAD   NBC

6 JULY 1953–22 JANUARY 1954   Science fiction for the kids. Bob Hastings starred as Steve Elliot, head of the Atom Squad, a top-secret planetary defense organization. Bob Courtleigh played Elliott's assistant. The fifteen-minute show was televised live from Philadelphia weekdays at 5 P.M.

ATTACK OF THE KILLER TOMATOES   FOX

8 SEPTEMBER 1990–22 AUGUST 1992   This half-hour Saturday morning cartoon show was derived from the 1980 sci-fi film spoof of the same name and its 1988 sequel, *Return of the Killer Tomatoes!* It was set in the town of San Zucchini, where a mad scientist, Dr. Putrid T. Gangreen, had discovered a way to excite ordinary tomatoes by a combination of sounds; as a consequence of his experiments, the federal government had since outlawed tomatoes, but Gangreen still had control over a secret stash of the forbidden fruits. Battling the evil scientist were two teenagers, Chad and Tara, and a good tomato, F. T., who masqueraded as a dog. John Astin (who had starred in the film sequel) provided the voice of Gangreen.

AUCTION-AIRE   ABC

30 SEPTEMBER 1949–23 JUNE 1950   Home viewers bid labels of the sponsors' products, not cash, to win merchandise on this Friday-night game show. Jack Gregson, a licensed auctioneer, hosted the series, assisted by Charlotte "Rebel" Randall. *Variety* noted in 1949 that an irate viewer telephoned in a bid of "30,000 labels if you'll take the show off the air." The offer was not accepted, as *Auction-Aire* stayed on for another eight months.

AUDUBON WILDLIFE THEATRE   SYNDICATED
1971   Wildlife films.

AUSTIN CITY LIMITS   PBS

1976–   Country-and-western music is the staple of this series, produced at KLRN-TV, Austin/San Antonio. Most programs feature a single guest performer.

THE AUTHOR MEETS THE CRITICS   NBC/ABC/DUMONT

21 SEPTEMBER 1947–24 JULY 1949 (NBC); 3 OCTOBER 1949–25 SEPTEMBER 1950 (ABC); 10 JANUARY 1952–10 OCTOBER 1954 (DUMONT)   This panel show began on radio in 1946 and came to television a year later. Each week two critics discussed a recently

published book during the first segment of the show; one of the critics assailed the book, while the other praised it. During the latter segment the author was given the chance to defend the criticisms or acknowledge the kudos. Martin Stone produced the half-hour show; John K. M. McCaffery was the moderator for most of the show's run, though James Michener and Virgilia Peterson appeared as moderators in 1954.

AUTOMAN ABC
15 DECEMBER 1983–2 APRIL 1984   The central character in this hour fantasy/cop show was a computer-generated creature who assisted the police department. The series starred Desi Arnaz, Jr., as Walter Nebicher, a bumbling cop who was assigned to the department's computer room. After programming vast amounts of information into the computer, Nebicher discovered that he had created a humanlike being, which he named Automan. Chuck Wagner costarred as Automan, the creature who inhabited (as he put it) "a world of space and energy, not of substance." Because of the large quantities of energy that it required to function, Automan only emerged from the computer late at night (when the city's energy use was low), when he could put his formidable physical and mental powers to work in helping the Department. Accompanying Automan was "Cursor," a miniature holograph, which could be instructed to create cars, airplanes, or almost anything, on the spot. Also featured were Heather McNair as Roxanne, Walter's girlfriend, who also worked for the police department; Gerald S. O'Loughlin as Walter's gruff commanding officer, Captain Boyd; and Robert Lansing as Lieutenant Jack Curtis.

THE AVENGERS ABC
28 MARCH 1966–15 SEPTEMBER 1969
THE NEW AVENGERS CBS
15 SEPTEMBER 1978–23 MARCH 1979   This whimsical British spy series began in 1961 as a more straightforward adventure show: the search by a husband for his wife's killers. The husband was joined in his search by John Steed (Patrick Macnee), an urbane and sophisticated bon vivant. By 1962 the bereaved husband was gone (he never found the killers), having been replaced by Cathy Gale (Honor Blackman— she played Pussy Galore in *Goldfinger*). By this time Steed and his partner had become government agents.

The early *Avengers* shows would not be shown in the United States for another twenty-five years, however. American viewers of the mid-sixties saw only the next incarnation of the series, the adventures of Steed and Mrs. Emma Peel. Played by Diana Rigg, Mrs. Peel was not a secret agent, but rather a talented amateur with a thirst for adventure. She was also one of the most liberated women characters on television during the 1960s. It was established that she was the widow of a test pilot, but her relationship with Steed was never really explained. Though hampered by a limited variety of plots, the show was generally well-written and well-acted. More importantly, it embodied a certain element of style all too infrequent on adventure series: Steed, typically in a three-piece suit and bowler, and Mrs. Peel, often in boots and leather, relentlessly pursued an assortment of psychopaths, robots, and human-eating monsters.

Some fifty-one Steed-Peel episodes were filmed; the last twenty-five were in color. Five of the black-and-white episodes were never shown by ABC, as the network considered them too racy for American audiences (all five were included when the reruns went into syndication). For example, in one famous episode, "Honey for the Prince," Mrs. Peel joins the harem of an Arabian potentate and displays her navel in a dance sequence. In "The Forget-Me-Knot" (shown here 20 March 1968), Mrs. Peel learned that her husband had been found alive and decided to rejoin him. Steed then joined forces with agent Tara King. King, played by twenty-year-old Linda Thorson, lacked the appeal of Mrs. Peel, and the Rigg episodes are generally considered to be far superior to the Thorson episodes.

Also appearing was Patrick Newell (1967–1969) as "Mother," Steed's wheelchair-bound boss. Among the many guest stars who appeared were Christopher Lee ("The Cybernauts"), Gordon Jackson ("Castle De'Ath"), Ron Moody ("The Bird Who

Knew Too Much"), Donald Sutherland ("The Superlative Seven"), and Peter Cushing ("Return of the Cybernauts"). Produced by Brian Clemens and Albert Fennell.

In the fall of 1978 *The New Avengers* first appeared on American television. Filmed in England in 1977, the hour series again featured Patrick Macnee as British agent John Steed, along with Joanna Lumley as Purdey and Gareth Hunt as Mike Gambit. It was also produced by Brian Clemens and Albert Fennell.

In the fall of 1990, the Arts & Entertainment cable network reran the Rigg episodes and, finally, provided American viewers with their first glimpses of the Blackman episodes.

AWAY WE GO
CBS

3 JUNE 1967–2 SEPTEMBER 1967   A summer replacement hour for *The Jackie Gleason Show,* featuring George Carlin, Buddy Greco, and the Buddy Rich Band.

B.A.D. CATS
ABC

4 JANUARY 1980–8 FEBRUARY 1980   An hour of car chases with the Burglary Auto Detail of the Los Angeles Police Department. With Asher Brauner as Nick Donovan; Steve Hanks as his partner and roommate, Ocee James; Michelle Pfeiffer as their associate, Samantha; LaWanda Page as Ma, owner of a local rib joint; Vic Morrow as Captain Nathan; and Jimmie Walker as Rodney Washington, a goodnatured car thief.

B.J. AND THE BEAR
NBC

10 FEBRUARY 1979–1 AUGUST 1981   Hour adventure series starring Greg Evigan as B.J. (Billie Joe) McKay, an independent trucker who rode the roads with his simian sidekick, a chimp named The Bear. During the spring of 1979 Claude Akins was occasionally featured as McKay's nemesis, Sheriff Lobo, but in the fall of 1979 Lobo sidled off into his own series (see *The Misadventures of Sheriff Lobo*). Joining the cast were Slim Pickens as Sergeant Beauregard Wiley; Richard Deacon as Sheriff Masters; Conchata Ferrell as Wilhelmina Johnson (better known as The Fox), a state cop sent to check up on Wiley and Masters's operation; Janet Louise Johnson as B.J.'s friend, Tommy; and Joshua Shelley as Bullets, operator of the Country Comfort Truck Stop. All of the regulars except for Evigan and the ape were gone when the show returned in January 1981 for its final season. B.J. had finally settled down in California, where he started his own trucking company, Bear Enterprises, and found a new foe: Captain Rutherford T. Grant (played by Murray Hamilton), the corrupt head of S.C.A.T. (Special Crimes Action Team). Grant owned a piece of a trucking company himself, and ruthlessly sought to eliminate all opposition. Meanwhile, B.J. took on a bevy of female truckers as his employees: twins Candi and Randi Brough as twins Teri and Geri Garrison; Sheila DeWindt as Angie Cartwright; Barbara Horan as Sam; Judy Landers as Stacks; Linda McCullough as Callie Smith; and Sherilyn Wolter as Cindy Grant, Rutherford's daughter. Also featured were Eric Server as Lieutenant Jim Steiger, Grant's aide, and John Dullaghan as Nick the bartender. Executive producers: Glen A. Larson and Michael Sloan for Glen A. Larson Productions in association with Universal TV.

B. L. STRYKER
ABC

13 FEBRUARY 1989–4 AUGUST 1990   One segment of the two-hour *ABC Monday Mystery Movie* (which became *The ABC Saturday Mystery Movie* in the fall of 1989), with Burt Reynolds as B. L. (Buddy Lee) Stryker, a retired New Orleans cop who moved back to a houseboat in Palm Beach, Florida, where he hoped to relax, but soon found himself called upon to solve crimes; Ossie Davis as his pal Oz Jackson, a former boxer; Michael O. Smith as Chief McGee of the Palm Beach Police Department; Rita Moreno as Kimberly Baskin, B. L.'s ex-wife; Alfie Wise as wealthy computer whiz Oliver Wardell, who owned the houseboat that B. L. lived on, and who frequently assisted B. L.; and Dana Kaminski as aspiring actress Lyynda Lynnox, who was temporarily serving as B. L.'s office manager. Tom Selleck was executive producer, Reynolds the co-executive producer.

BAA BAA BLACK SHEEP (BLACK SHEEP SQUADRON) NBC

21 SEPTEMBER 1976–30 AUGUST 1977; 14 DECEMBER 1977–1 SEPTEMBER 1978   Set in the Pacific, this hour-long adventure series was based on the real-life exploits of Marine Corps Major Gregory "Pappy" Boyington, World War II flying ace, who put together a squadron of misfits and castoffs from other service outfits and nicknamed it "The Black Sheep." Featured were Robert Conrad as Major Boyington; Dana Elcar as his commanding officer, Colonel Lard; Simon Oakland as General Moore; James Whitmore, Jr., as Captain Gutterman; Robert Ginty as Lieutenant T. J. Wiley; Dirk Blocker (son of the late Dan Blocker) as Lieutenant Jerry Bragg; W. K. Stratton as Lieutenant Larry Casey; John Larroquette as Lieutenant Bob Anderson; Red West as Sergeant Andy Micklin; Joey Aresco as Hutch; Jeff Mackay as French; and Larry Manetti as Boyle. *Baa Baa Black Sheep* was canceled by NBC after one season but was revived in December, thanks to the lobbying efforts of Robert Conrad and executive producer Stephen Cannell. When it returned, it was titled *Black Sheep Squadron*. Several new regulars were added in February of 1978: Jeb Adams (son of the late Nick Adams) as Lieutenant Jeb Pruitt; Denise DuBarry as nurse Samantha Green; Nancy Conrad (daughter of Robert) as Nancy, a nurse; Kathy McCullem as Ellie, a nurse; and Brianne Leary as Susan, also a nurse (the four nurses were temporarily assigned to duty at the Squadron's Solomon Islands headquarters).

BABES FOX

13 SEPTEMBER 1990–10 AUGUST 1991   Half-hour sitcom about three overweight sisters who lived together in a cramped Manhattan apartment. With Wendie Jo Sperber as Charlene Gilbert; Susan Peretz as her older sister, Darlene, who moved in after her marriage collapsed; Lesley Boone as her younger sister, Marlene, who moved in after losing her job; and Rick Overton as Charlene's boyfriend, Ronnie.

BABY BOOM NBC

10 SEPTEMBER 1988; 2 NOVEMBER 1988–4 JANUARY 1989; 13 JULY 1989–10 SEPTEMBER 1989   Based on the 1987 motion picture, this half-hour sitcom suffered from erratic scheduling: there was a gap of almost eight weeks between the premiere and the second episode, and, during its brief fall run, it was never telecast for more than three consecutive weeks at a time. Kate Jackson starred in the TV version as J. C. Wiatt, a high-powered single female executive who inherited a baby from a deceased relative. Repeating his film role, Sam Wanamaker co-starred as Wiatt's boss, Fritz Curtis. Also on hand were Susie Essman as Wiatt's secretary, Charlotte; twins Michelle and Kristina Kennedy as the baby, Elizabeth; Daniel Bardol as Wiatt's enthusiastic assistant, Ken Arrenberg; and Robyn Peterson as Arlene. Charles Shyer and Nancy Meyers, who wrote the film version (Shyer also directed it) were executive producers.

THE BABY GAME ABC

1 JANUARY 1968–12 JULY 1968   Daytime game show on which three couples demonstrated their knowledge of infant behavior by predicting the outcome of previously filmed sequences involving youngsters. Hosted by Richard Hayes.

BABY, I'M BACK CBS

30 JANUARY 1978–12 AUGUST 1978   Situation comedy about a black man who returns home to his wife and family in Washington, D.C., after a seven-year absence. With Demond Wilson as Ray Ellis; Denise Nicholas as his wife, Olivia; Tony Holmes as their son, Jordan; Kim Fields as their daughter, Angie; Helen Martin as Olivia's mother, Luzelle Carter; and Ed Hall as Olivia's new suitor, Colonel Wallace Dickey, an Army public relations officer. Lila Garrett and Charlie Fries were the executive producers; Garrett and Mort Lachman created the series. Sandy Krinski and Chet Dowling were the producers.

BABY MAKES FIVE ABC

1 APRIL 1983–29 APRIL 1983   A short-flight sitcom about a couple with three kids who then have twins. With Peter Scolari as accountant Eddie Riddle; Louise Williams as his wife, Jennie Riddle; Andre Gower as their son, Michael; Emily Moultrie

as daughter Laura; Brandy Gold as daughter Annie; Priscilla Morrill as Edna, Jennie's mother; and Janis Paige as Blanche, Eddie's mother.

BABY TALK
ABC

8 MARCH 1991–12 APRIL 1991; 16 AUGUST 1991; 20 SEPTEMBER 1991– 26 JUNE 1992
Troubled sitcom about a baby whose thoughts were uttered by an adult voice, based on the hit 1989 movie *Look Who's Talking*. The series was to have premiered in the fall of 1990, with Connie Sellecca starring, but Sellecca quit the show. When it finally debuted in March 1991 it starred Julia Duffy as Maggie Campbell, an accountant and single mom who had moved into a not-quite-finished Manhattan apartment building. Also featured were George Clooney as Joe, the contractor; William Hickey as Fogarty, the painter; Lenny Wolpe as Howard, the electrician; Tom Alan Robbins as Dr. Eliot Fleisher, the pediatrician; twins Paul and Ryan Jessup as Maggie's young son, Mickey; and Tony Danza as the voice of Mickey. When the show returned in the fall of 1991 it sported an entirely new cast, except for the Jessup twins and Danza. Mary Page Keller (late of *Duet*) played Maggie, who now lived in Brooklyn. Also featured were Scott Baio as James Holbrook, the building handyman, with whom Maggie began a relationship; Francesca P. Roberts as neighbor Anita Craig; Alicia and Cecilia Johnson as Anita's baby daughter, Danielle, whose thoughts were also vocalized; Vernee Watson-Johnson as the voice of Danielle; Polly Bergen as Doris Campbell, Maggie's mom; and Jessica Lundy as Susan, Maggie's office pal. Talking babies had surfaced on TV three decades earlier: see *Happy*.

BABYLON 5
SYNDICATED

1994–   One of several syndicated space shows introduced in the mid-1990s, this one was set in the year 2258 at a remote space station at which ambassadors of various alien races congregated. The cast included Michael O'Hare (spring 1994) as Commander Jeffrey Sinclair; Bruce Boxleitner (fall 1994–) as Captain John Sheridan; Claudia Christian as Commander Susan Ivanova; Jerry Doyle as security chief Michael Garibaldi; Andrea Thompson as the telepathic Talia Winters; Peter Jurasik as Londo Mollari, the ambassador from Centauri; Stephen Furst as Londo's henchcreature, Vir; Andreas Katsulas as G'Kar, the ambassador from Narn; Mira Furlan as Delenn, the ambassador from Minbari; Bill Mumy as Lennier, an alien from Minbari; and Richard Biggs as Doctor Franklin. J. Michael Straczynski created the series, which was introduced in early 1993 as a syndicated two-hour TV-movie; Straczynski envisioned the series' basic story unfolding over five seasons.

BACHELOR FATHER
CBS/NBC/ABC

15 SEPTEMBER 1957–7 JUNE 1959 (CBS); 18 JUNE 1959–21 SEPTEMBER 1961 (NBC); 3 OCTOBER 1961–25 SEPTEMBER 1962 (ABC)   One of the few situation comedies to have run on all three networks, *Bachelor Father* told the story of an unmarried Beverly Hills attorney whose carefree bachelor life is disrupted when his newly orphaned thirteen-year-old niece comes to live with him. With John Forsythe as lawyer Bentley Gregg; Noreen Corcoran as niece Kelly Gregg, daughter of Bentley's sister; Sammee Tong as Peter Tong, the butler; Jimmy Boyd (1958–1962) as Kelly's boyfriend, Howard Meachum; Bernadette Withers as Kelly's girlfriend, Ginger (she was Ginger Farrell on CBS, Ginger Loomis on NBC, and Ginger Mitchell on ABC); Whit Bissell (1959–1961) as Ginger's father, Bert Loomis; Alice Backes (1957–1959) as Bentley's secretary, Vicki; Sue Ane Langdon (1959–1961) as Bentley's secretary, Kitty Marsh; Victor Sen Yung as Peter's cousin, Charlie Fong; and Jasper, a neighborhood dog who adopted the Greggs. During its CBS years, *Bachelor Father* alternated on Sundays with *The Jack Benny Program*. It was produced at Revue-Universal studios. The pilot for the series, "A New Girl in His Life," was shown on *General Electric Theater* 26 May 1957. A teenaged Linda Evans (then known as Linda Evanstad) made one of her earliest TV appearances in one episode, "A Crush on Bentley," which was aired 13 October 1960; Evans and Forsythe would be reunited more than two decades later on *Dynasty*.

THE BACHELORS
See IT'S A GREAT LIFE

BACK THAT FACT ABC
22 OCTOBER 1953–26 NOVEMBER 1953   Comic Joey Adams was the host of this
Thursday-night game show, developed by Jack Barry and Dan Enright. Adams interviewed contestants, who were periodically interrupted by an offstage voice (supplied
by Carl Caruso) asking them to "back that fact"—to provide proof of any assertion
made by them. A contestant who succeeded in providing the documentation won a
prize. Contestants were escorted onstage by Hope Lange, who would later star in
The Ghost and Mrs. Muir. Double-talk comic Al Kelly was also featured on the half-
hour show.

BACK TO THE FUTURE CBS
14 SEPTEMBER 1991–4 SEPTEMBER 1993   Saturday morning cartoon show, based on
the motion picture trilogy, about a zany scientist and a young man who traveled
through time. Michael J. Fox and Christopher Lloyd, who had starred in the movies,
provided the voices of Marty McFly and Emmet "Doc" Brown. Lloyd also appeared
in live-action wraparounds between animated segments.

BACKGROUND NBC
16 AUGUST 1954–26 JUNE 1955   Joseph C. Harsch produced and hosted this news
analysis program.

BACKSTAGE WITH BARRY WOOD CBS
1 MARCH 1949–24 MAY 1949   Fifteen-minute variety show featuring new talent,
hosted by Barry Wood.

BACKSTAIRS AT THE WHITE HOUSE NBC
29 JANUARY 1979–19 FEBRUARY 1979   Four-part miniseries based on the book by
Lillian Rogers Parks and Frances Spatz Leighton, drawn from the careers of Maggie
Rogers and Lillian Rogers Parks on the White House staff. With Olivia Cole as
Maggie Rogers, hairdresser and maid; Tania Johnson and Leslie Uggams as her
daughter, seamstress Lillian Rogers; Louis Gossett, Jr., as Levi, butler and footman;
Leslie Nielsen as Ike Hoover, one of their supervisors; Cloris Leachman as Mrs.
Jaffray, another of their supervisors; Victor Buono as President Taft; Julie Harris as
Nellie Taft; Robert Vaughn as President Wilson; Kim Hunter as Ellen Wilson; Claire
Bloom as Edith Galt Wilson; George Kennedy as President Harding; Celeste Holm
as Florence Harding; Ed Flanders as President Coolidge; Lee Grant as Grace Coo-
lidge; Larry Gates as President Hoover; Jan Sterling as Lou Hoover; Richard Ander-
son as President Roosevelt; Eileen Heckart as Eleanor Roosevelt; Harry Morgan as
President Truman; Estelle Parsons as Bess Truman; Andrew Duggan as President
Eisenhower; and Barbara Barrie as Mamie Eisenhower. Ed Friendly was the executive producer of the nine-hour program for Ed Friendly Productions.

THE BAD NEWS BEARS CBS
24 MARCH 1979–6 OCTOBER 1979; 7 JUNE 1980–28 JUNE 1980   Half-hour sitcom based
on the *Bad News Bears* films, which starred Walter Matthau. The video version
featured Jack Warden as Morris Buttermaker, a swimming-pool cleaner who agreed
to coach baseball at a school for problem youngsters as an alternative to a prison
term; Catherine Hicks as Dr. Emily Rappant, principal of the W. Wendell Weaver
School, to which Buttermaker was assigned; J. Brennan Smith as Mike Engelberg,
the porcine catcher; Tricia Cast as Amanda Wurlitzer, the star pitcher; Billy Jacoby
as Rudi Stein; Corey Feldman as Regi; Sparky Marcus as Ogilvie, the team's manager; Meeno Peluce as Tanner; Shane Butterworth as Lupus; Christoff St. John as
Ahmad Abdul Rahim; Gregg Forrest as Kelly; Rad Daly (fall 1979) as Josh; Phillip
R. Allen as Roy Turner, coach of the rival Lions. Executive producers: Arthur Silver
and Bob Brunner. Producers: John Boni and Norman Stiles. After a shaky start in the

fall of 1979, *The Bad News Bears* left the air in October, returning briefly the following summer.

BAFFLE   NBC
26 MARCH 1973–5 OCTOBER 1973
ALL-STAR BAFFLE   NBC
8 OCTOBER 1973–29 MARCH 1974   Dick Enberg hosted this daytime game show on which players attempted to guess words and phrases from successive one-letter clues. The format was almost identical to that of *PDQ,* an earlier game show. *Baffle* featured two teams, each consisting of a celebrity and a contestant; *All-Star Baffle* featured teams consisting of two celebrities.

BAGDAD CAFE   CBS
30 MARCH 1990–11 MAY 1990; 28 SEPTEMBER 1990–23 NOVEMBER 1990; 27 JULY 1991
Half-hour sitcom based on the offbeat 1988 German film. The TV version featured Whoopi Goldberg as Brenda, the black proprietor of the Bagdad Cafe, a tiny restaurant-motel located in the middle of the California desert, miles from nowhere; Jean Stapleton as Jasmine, a white woman who wandered in (on foot) after her husband left; Monica Calhoun as Debbie, Brenda's sixteen-year-old daughter; Scott Lawrence (spring 1990) as Juney, Brenda's piano-playing son; James Gammon as Rudy, one of the cafe's few regulars and Jasmine's would-be suitor; Sam Whipple (fall 1990) as Rudy's nephew, Dewey Kunkle, the cafe's short-order cook; and Cleavon Little as Sal, Brenda's philandering husband. Whoopi Goldberg abruptly left the show after the first nine episodes of the fall 1990 season, and the show immediately sputtered to a halt.

BAGGY PANTS & THE NITWITS   NBC
10 SEPTEMBER 1977–28 OCTOBER 1978   Two segments were presented on this Saturday-morning cartoon show: *Baggy Pants,* the adventures of a Chaplinesque cat (this segment featured no dialogue) and *The Nitwits,* the adventures of Tyrone, a secret agent who came out of retirement, and his wife, Gladys (the two characters were based on those created by Arte Johnson and Ruth Buzzi on *Laugh-In*).

BAILEY'S COMETS   CBS
8 SEPTEMBER 1973–31 AUGUST 1975   Children's cartoon show with an unusual format: a teenage roller-skating team competing in a global roller derby. The second season consisted entirely of reruns. Produced by David H. DePatie and Friz Freleng.

THE BAILEYS OF BALBOA   CBS
24 SEPTEMBER 1964–1 APRIL 1965   Feeble sitcom about a couple of inept charter-boat operators. With Paul Ford as Sam Bailey, skipper of the *Island Princess;* Sterling Holloway as first mate Buck Singleton; John Dehner as Commodore Cecil Wyntoon, their nemesis; Judy Carne as Barbara Wyntoon, his daughter; Les Brown, Jr., as Jim Bailey, Sam's son. Clobbered in the ratings race by *Peyton Place* (ABC) and *Hazel* (NBC), *The Baileys of Balboa* was one of three series developed by actor Keefe Brasselle and sold to CBS without a pilot. See also *The Cara Williams Show* and *The Reporter.*

BAKER'S DOZEN   CBS
17 MARCH 1982–21 APRIL 1982   A New York Police Department anti-crime unit, headed by a woman, was the focus of this half-hour comedy-drama. Featured were Doris Belack as Captain Florence Baker; Ron Silver as Detective Mike Locasale; Cindy Weintraub as Detective Terry Munson, Mike's lover; Alan Weeks as Detective Otis "O.K." Kelly; Sam McMurray as Detective Harve Schondorf; Thomas Quinn as Martin; and John Del Regno as Jeff Diggins, a knowledgeable street source.

BAKERSFIELD P.D.   FOX
14 SEPTEMBER 1993–4 JANUARY 1994; 7 JULY 1994–25 AUGUST 1994   Offbeat sitcom about the men of the Bakersfield, California, police department. With Giancarlo

Esposito as Paul Gigante, a half-black, half-Italian cop who left a big city force to work in Bakersfield; Ron Eldard as his partner, Detective Wade Preston; Chris Mulkey as Officer Denny Boyer; Tony Plana as his partner, Officer Luke Ramirez; Jack Hallett as indecisive Captain Stiles; and Brian Doyle-Murray as Sergeant Phil Hampton.

BALANCE YOUR BUDGET   CBS
18 OCTOBER 1952–2 MAY 1953   Bert Parks hosted this prime-time game show on which female contestants competed by trying to solve household budget problems; the winning contestant won the right to choose a key which would open a treasure chest. The biweekly series was produced by Peter Arnell and directed by Sherman Marks; Bert Parks was assisted by Lynn Connor.

BALL FOUR   CBS
22 SEPTEMBER 1976–27 OCTOBER 1976   Situation comedy developed by Jim Bouton, ex-major leaguer and New York sportscaster whose book, *Ball Four,* provided an inside view of professional baseball. Most of the action on the series seemed to take place in the locker room; perhaps that explains why *Ball Four* was the first casualty of the 1976–1977 season. Bouton starred as Jim Barton, pitcher for the hapless Washington Americans. With Ben Davidson as Ben (Rhino) Rhinelander, catcher; Jack Somack as manager John (Cappy) Capogrosso; Jack McCutcheon as coach Harold (Pinky) Pinkney; Sam Wright as outfielder Travis; Jaime Tirelli as utility man Orlando Lopez; Marco St. John as pitcher Ray Plunkett; David-James Carroll as rookie Westlake; Lenny Schultz as pitcher Birdman. The "Ball Four" theme was composed and sung by Harry Chapin.

BANACEK   NBC
13 SEPTEMBER 1972–3 SEPTEMBER 1974   One segment of *The NBC Wednesday Movie.* Starring George Peppard as Banacek, an independent insurance investigator of Polish descent who works for the Boston Casualty Company on a contingent fee basis. With Murray Matheson as Felix Mullholland, owner of Mullholland's Rare Book and Print Shop, and confidante of Banacek; Ralph Manza as Jay Drury, Banacek's chauffeur; and Christine Belford (1973–1974) as insurance investigator Carlie Kirkland.

THE BANANA SPLITS ADVENTURE HOUR   NBC
7 SEPTEMBER 1968–5 SEPTEMBER 1970   Saturday-morning fare from Hanna-Barbera Studios, presenting both cartoons and live action. The live characters were the Banana Splits, a rock-and-roll band made up of four animals (Drooper, Snorky, Bingo, and Fleegle).

BAND OF AMERICA   NBC
17 OCTOBER 1949–9 JANUARY 1950   Hosted by Paul Lavalle, this Monday-night variety show was simulcast on NBC Radio.

BANDSTAND   NBC
30 JULY 1956–23 NOVEMBER 1956   Bert Parks hosted this live half-hour daytime variety show. Developed by Billy Goodheart, it featured appearances by guest bands.

THE BANG-SHANG LALAPALOOZA SHOW
See THE ARCHIE SHOW

BANK ON THE STARS   CBS/NBC
20 JUNE 1953–5 SEPTEMBER 1953 (CBS); 15 MAY 1954–21 AUGUST 1954 (NBC)   On this Saturday-night game show contestants were quizzed after viewing clips from newly released movies. Jack Paar hosted in 1953; Bill Cullen was the first host in 1954, and was succeeded by Jimmy Nelson in July.

BANYON NBC
15 SEPTEMBER 1972–12 JANUARY 1973   Private eye series, set in Los Angeles during the 1930s. With Robert Forster as Miles Banyon; Joan Blondell as Peggy Revere, who ran the secretarial school which supplied Banyon with temporary help; Richard Jaeckel as Lieutenant Pete McNeil; and Julie Gregg as friend and singer Abby Graham. The pilot for the series was telecast 15 March 1971.

BARBAPAPA SYNDICATED
1978   The stars of this Dutch-produced cartoon series were a family of Shmoo-like creatures who could change themselves into any shape or size. The group included Barbapapa, Barbabravo, Barbazoo, Barbabright, Barbalala, and Irving the dog.

BARBARA DeANGELIS CBS
14 JANUARY 1991–26 APRIL 1991   Psychologist and author Barbara DeAngelis dispensed advice on personal problems to a studio audience on this half-hour daytime series.

BARBARA MANDRELL & THE MANDRELL SISTERS NBC
18 NOVEMBER 1980–26 JUNE 1982   An hour of music and comedy starring country-and-western singer Barbara Mandrell, assisted by her two sisters, Louise and Irlene, and the Krofft Puppets.

THE BARBARA McNAIR SHOW SYNDICATED
1969–1970   Variety hour with little talk and lots of music, hosted by Barbara McNair. One of the few series hosted by a black woman.

THE BARBARA STANWYCK SHOW NBC
19 SEPTEMBER 1960–11 SEPTEMBER 1961   Half-hour dramatic anthology series hosted by, and frequently starring, Barbara Stanwyck. The success of *The Loretta Young Show* apparently prompted NBC to introduce this series. Like *The Loretta Young Show, The Barbara Stanwyck Show* was given a late-evening time slot (10:00 P.M. Mondays), but even against only moderate competition (*Adventures in Paradise* and *Hennesey*) the show was not a success. Stanwyck, however, reappeared in 1965 in a more successful vehicle: *Big Valley*.

BARBARY COAST ABC
8 SEPTEMBER 1975–9 JANUARY 1976   Limpid western set in San Francisco. Starring William Shatner as Jeff Cable, undercover agent for the governor of California; and Doug McClure as Cash Conover, owner of the Golden Gate Casino. With seven-foot-two Richard Kiel as Moose Moran, useful employee at the casino; Dave Turner as Thumbs, another employee. Created by Douglas Heyes. Executive producer: Cy Chermak. The series pilot (starring Shatner and Dennis Cole) was aired on 4 May 1975.

THE BARBOUR REPORT ABC
10 MARCH 1986–21 MARCH 1986   John Barbour (late of *Real People*) was given a two-week tryout as host of a talk and comedy show. The thirty-five-minute program was broadcast at midnight after *Nightline*.

BARE ESSENCE NBC
15 FEBRUARY 1983–13 JUNE 1983   Introduced as a two-part made-for-TV movie on CBS in October 1982, *Bare Essence* surfaced as a series a few months later on NBC. Its basic story line centered on the perfume industry. The cast included Genie Francis (late of *General Hospital*) as Patricia "Tyger" Hayes, who married into the Marshall family (unfortunately, her husband died under mysterious circumstances in the first episode); Jennifer O'Neill as Lady Bobbi Rowan, Tyger's mother; Ian McShane as Greek tycoon Niko Theopolous, who wooed Lady Bobbi; John Dehner as Hadden Marshall, Tyger's father-in-law; Jessica Walter as Hadden's sister-in-law, evil Ava Marshall; Jonathan Frakes as Ava's weak son, Marcus; Jaime Lyn Bauer (late of *The*

Young and the Restless) as account executive Barbara Fisher; Susan French as Margaret; Michael Woods as Sean, Margaret's illegitimate son; Wendy Fulton as Muffin; Morgan Stevens as filmmaker Larry Levito; and Penny Fuller as Laura Parker.

BAREFOOT IN THE PARK ABC
24 SEPTEMBER 1970–14 JANUARY 1971   The play, written by Neil Simon, was a hit. The movie, starring Jane Fonda and Robert Redford, was also a success. But the television series was a flop. It told the story of a black couple, newlyweds, living in a tiny top-floor apartment in lower Manhattan. With Scoey Mitchlll as lawyer Paul Bratter, an associate at Kendricks, Keene & Klein; Tracy Reed as his wife, Corie Bratter; Thelma Carpenter as Corie's mother, Mabel Bates, a domestic for a Park Avenue family; Nipsey Russell as friend Honey Robinson, proprietor of Honey Robinson's Pool & Billiard Emporium; Harry Holcombe as Arthur Kendricks, Paul's boss. The series was beset with production problems from the beginning and folded when Scoey Mitchlll was fired after thirteen episodes.

BARETTA ABC
17 JANUARY 1975–1 JUNE 1978   After *Toma's* Tony Musante announced that he would not return to that series for a second season, the surprised producers subsequently signed Robert Blake to star in a "new" series. Blake, a former child actor whose best-known film role was the psychopathic killer of *In Cold Blood,* starred as Tony Baretta, an unorthodox big city cop who lived in a run-down hotel with his pet cockatoo, Fred, and who was constantly getting in hot water with his superiors. Also featured were Tom Ewell as Billy Truman, desk clerk at the King Edward, Baretta's seedy residence; Dana Elcar (to July 1975) as Lieutenant Shiller, his commanding officer; Edward Grover (1975–1978) as Lieutenant Hal Brubaker, his new commanding officer; Michael D. Roberts as Rooster, his streetwise informant; and Chino Williams as Fats, a gravel-voiced street source. Blake often took an active interest in the production of the series, sometimes to the consternation of the people in charge. Bernard L. Kowalski was executive producer; Jo Swerling, Jr., was the first producer and was succeeded by Ed Waters as supervising producer.

BARGAIN HUNTERS ABC
6 JULY 1987–4 SEPTEMBER 1987   Peter Tomarken hosted this short-lived daytime game show on which contestants tried to find bargains among merchandise on display, then competed in a "super-savers" round. Home viewers could also pick up merchandise by dialing an 800 number.

BARKER BILL'S CARTOON SHOW CBS
18 NOVEMBER 1953–25 NOVEMBER 1956   Animator Paul Terry's black-and-white cartoons, known as Terrytoons, were broadcast on this series. Some of the features, such as "Farmer Al Falfa," dated back to the silent era. The program was seen as a fifteen-minute series, two afternoons a week, in some markets; in other areas it was carried as a half-hour Saturday-morning show.

THE BARKLEYS NBC
9 SEPTEMBER 1972–1 SEPTEMBER 1973   Saturday-morning cartoon series about a lower-middle-class family of dogs, patterned on the Bunkers of *All in the Family.*

BARNABY JONES CBS
28 JANUARY 1973–4 SEPTEMBER 1980   After a year layoff following the cancellation of *The Beverly Hillbillies* in 1971, Buddy Ebsen returned to television as Barnaby Jones, a soft-spoken, milk-drinking private eye who usually worked for insurance companies. Jones had come out of semiretirement when his son was murdered. With Lee Meriwether as Betty Jones, his widowed daughter-in-law and assistant; John Carter as Lieutenant Biddle; Mark Shera (1976–1980) as Jedediah Jones, Barnaby's cousin once removed, who came to work for Barnaby after his father was murdered. Executive producer: Quinn Martin. 177 episodes were produced.

BARNEY & FRIENDS   PBS

6 APRIL 1992– Hugely popular with two- and three-year-olds, this half-hour daily show starred a giant purple dinosaur named Barney. The character was created in 1988 by Sheryl Leach, who had been looking for a home video to keep her young son amused. She wrote three scripts in which a teddy bear came to life, but changed the character to a dinosaur after noticing her son's interest in dinosaurs. With money borrowed from her father-in-law, a book publisher, Leach produced three "Barney & the Backyard Gang" videos starring Sandy Duncan. Marketed mainly through day care centers and video stores, they caught the attention of a PBS executive in Connecticut, who in 1991 secured a grant from the Corporation for Public Broadcasting for the production of the series. The first group of thirty episodes premiered on PBS in April 1992 and featured a multi-ethnic group of children who were able to make a small stuffed dinosaur come to life as a huggable and bubbly six-foot-four-inch creature. The gang sang songs, played games, and learned simple lessons about getting along with each other. David Joyner played Barney, while Bob West supplied the voice; Jeff Ayers played Barney's younger dinosaur pal, Baby Bop, with Carol Farabee providing its voice. Lambasted by some observers as an "infomercial for a stuffed animal," the series caught on quickly with the pre-*Sesame Street* set. By 1993 some four million "Barney" home videos had been sold, together with other Barney merchandise estimated at $300 million. Barney and Company came to commercial television in 1994, with a prime time special, "Bedtime with Barney: Imagination Island" (NBC, 24 April).

BARNEY GOOGLE   SYNDICATED

1963 A cartoon series based on the popular comic strip created by Billy DeBeck in the 1920s. His backwoods characters included Barney Google, Snuffy Smith, Loweezy, and Jughead.

BARNEY MILLER   ABC

23 JANUARY 1975–9 SEPTEMBER 1982 This half-hour situation comedy about a New York City precinct captain and his multiethnic band of officers starred Hal Linden as Captain Barney Miller of the Twelfth Precinct; Barbara Barrie (1975–1976) as his wife, Elizabeth Miller; Abe Vigoda (1975–1977) as deadpan Detective Phil Fish; Max Gail as Sergeant Stan Wojehowicz (Wojo); Gregory Sierra (1975–1976) as Sergeant Chano Amengual; Jack Soo (1975–1979) as Sergeant Nick Yemana; Ron Glass as Detective Ron Harris; James Gregory as Inspector Frank Luger, the man from headquarters; Steve Landesberg (January 1977–1982) as Detective Arthur Dietrich; Ron Carey (1977–1982) as Officer Carl Levitt; Florence Stanley (1975–1977) as Bernice Fish, Phil's wife. Early episodes also featured Michael Tessier and Anne Wyndham as the Millers' children, David and Rachel. Created by Danny Arnold and Theodore J. Flicker, the series was produced by Chris Hayward and Arne Sultan. There were 170 episodes. See also *Fish*.

THE BARON   ABC

20 JANUARY 1966–14 JULY 1966 Steve Forrest starred as John Mannering, suave American art dealer involved in international intrigue. With Sue Lloyd as his assistant Cordelia; Paul Ferris as his assistant David Marlowe; and Colin Gordon as Mr. Templeton-Green. This hour-long series, a midseason replacement for *The Long Hot Summer,* was produced in England. It was based on the short stories by John Creasey.

BARRIER REEF   NBC

11 SEPTEMBER 1971–2 SEPTEMBER 1972 Saturday-morning live-action adventure series, filmed in Australia. With Joe James as Captain Chet King, skipper of the windjammer *Endeavor;* Richard Melkle as marine biologist Joe Francis; and Ken James as Kip, Chet's young son.

BASEBALL PBS

18 SEPTEMBER 1994–28 SEPTEMBER 1994   A painstaking look at America's national pastime, produced by Ken Burns, using still photographs, films, and reminiscences of players and other key figures. The eighteen-and-one-half-hour series was divided into nine telecasts, each labeled an inning. John Chancellor was the series narrator.

THE BASEBALL CORNER ABC

1 JUNE 1958–27 AUGUST 1958   Half-hour series on which host Buddy Blattner interviewed baseball stars and introduced film clips.

BAT MASTERSON NBC

8 OCTOBER 1958–21 SEPTEMBER 1961   Gene Barry starred as Bat Masterson, dapper ex-lawman who roamed the West. Masterson's gimmick was a goldtipped cane that disguised a sword; he also carried a gun, of course. In real life William Bartley Masterson had been a deputy of Wyatt Earp. Notable guest stars included Dyan Cannon (in her first prime-time appearance, "Lady Luck," 5 November 1959) and William Conrad ("Stampede at Tent City," 29 October 1958, his first TV dramatic appearance). Andy White and Frank Pittman produced the half-hour series for United Artists TV. Gene Barry returned to TV as Bat Masterson in an episode of *Paradise* in 1989.

BATMAN ABC

12 JANUARY 1966–14 MARCH 1968   *Batman*, the cartoon crimefighter created by Bob Kane in 1939, came to television with a big splash (and lots of publicity) early in 1966. Originally scheduled as a fall 1966 entry, the show was rushed into production late in 1965 as a midseason replacement. Broadcast twice a week, *Batman* was an immediate hit—both half hours cracked Nielsen's top ten that season, and millions of dollars of *Batman* merchandise was sold to children and adults. But by the fall of 1966 the ratings had already begun to fall off. In the fall of 1967 the show was cut back to once a week, and it passed away quietly in midseason. Unlike *Superman, Batman* was written and played for laughs—it was "camp." Visually, it should be remembered for its comic book look, achieved by the use of bright colors, slanted camera angles and by the use of such words as "Pow!" and "Smash!" that were flashed on the screen during fight scenes. The show starred Adam West, a handsome, athletic type who had been featured on *The Detectives,* as Bruce Wayne, a Gotham City millionaire whose secret identity was Batman, a masked, caped crusader who used sophisticated paraphernalia to capture crooks (unlike Superman, Batman was a mere mortal and possessed no super powers). Burt Ward costarred as Dick Grayson, Wayne's teen-aged ward, whose secret identity was Robin (the Boy Wonder), similarly masked and caped. Together, the Dynamic Duo assisted the usually impotent police force and helped keep Gotham City's streets safe for the citizenry. Also featured were Alan Napier as Alfred Pennyworth, Wayne's butler, the only other person who knew of their secret identities; Madge Blake as Dick's aunt, Harriet Cooper; Neil Hamilton as Police Commissioner Gordon, the city official who often dialed the Caped Crusaders on the Batphone; and Stafford Repp as Chief O'Hara. In the fall of 1967 Yvonne Craig joined the cast as Barbara Gordon (daughter of the Commissioner), whose secret identity was Batgirl. She often assisted the Dynamic Duo, though she never learned the identities of Batman and Robin and they never learned hers. Among the many "guest villains" who appeared were Burgess Meredith as The Penguin; Frank Gorshin as The Riddler; Julie Newmar, Lee Meriwether, and Eartha Kitt as Catwoman; George Sanders, Otto Preminger, and Eli Wallach as Mr. Freeze; Victor Buono as King Tut; Cesar Romero as The Joker; Liberace as Chandell; Vincent Price as Egghead; Milton Berle as Louie the Lilac; Tallulah Bankhead as The Black Widow; Ethel Merman as Lola Lasagne; and Pierre Salinger (former press secretary to President Kennedy) as Lucky Pierre. Several of the guest villains appeared more than once—the only character ever killed off on *Batman* was Molly, one of The Riddler's henchpeople, who was played by Jill St. John. Production of the series was supervised by William Dozier (who also provided the narration) for 20th Century-Fox; Howie Horwitz was the line producer. The *Batman* theme was composed by

Neal Hefti. The 120 episodes of the series remained reasonably popular in reruns, but received a big boost in 1989 with the release of the theatrical film *Batman,* starring Michael Keaton as the Caped Crusader and Jack Nicholson as The Joker.

BATMAN   CBS/NBC
14 SEPTEMBER 1968–6 SEPTEMBER 1970 (CBS); 12 FEBRUARY 1977–2 SEPTEMBER 1978 (CBS); 27 SEPTEMBER 1980–5 SEPTEMBER 1981 (NBC)   Like many other cartoon characters, Batman and Robin appeared in a bewildering array of weekend cartoon shows, headlining some and costarring in others. The popularity of the live-action prime-time series (see above) led to the initial animated series, *The Batman/ Superman Hour,* which ran for a single season on CBS; Bud Collyer provided Batman's voice, and Casey Kasem supplied Robin's. Reruns were seen on Sunday mornings during the 1969–1970 season under the title *The Adventures of Batman.* New episodes were made in 1977 and were shown on Saturday mornings under the title *The New Adventures of Batman;* on these shows, Adam West and Burt Ward, who had starred in the prime-time series, provided the voices of the caped crusaders. Batman and Robin were assisted by Batgirl and by a new character, Bat-Mite, who replaced Alfred the butler. Reruns of *The New Adventures of Batman* were seen on CBS as part of *The Batman/Tarzan Adventure Hour* during the 1977–1978 season, as part of *Tarzan and the Super 7* (see also that title) during the next two seasons, and surfaced the following season on a new network—NBC—as *Batman and the Super 7.* To make matters even more complicated, Batman and Robin also appeared as regular characters on ABC's long-running cartoon series *Superfriends* (see also that title) during the 1970s.

BATMAN: THE ANIMATED SERIES   FOX
Daytime: 5 SEPTEMBER 1992–   *Nighttime*: 13 DECEMBER 1992–14 MARCH 1993   An animated version of *Batman* first surfaced on the Fox network in the fall of 1992; it was previewed twice on Saturday mornings, and ran weekday afternoons from 7 September 1992 through 2 September 1994. In the fall of 1994 it shifted to Saturday mornings, and was retitled *The Adventures of Batman & Robin*. It also aired in a Sunday night slot for three months during the 1992–1993 season. Principal voices were supplied by Kevin Conroy (Batman), Loren Lester (Robin), and Efrem Zimbalist, Jr. (Alfred the butler).

BATTLE LINE   SYNDICATED
1963   Author Jim Bishop narrated World War II film footage on this documentary series.

BATTLE OF THE AGES   DUMONT/CBS
1 JANUARY 1952–17 JUNE 1952 (DUMONT); 6 SEPTEMBER 1952–29 NOVEMBER 1952 (CBS)   This prime-time game show was a talent contest between a team of children and a team of adult celebrities. John Reed King hosted the DuMont version; Morey Amsterdam the CBS version; and Norman Brokenshire and Arthur Van Horn were the announcers. The studio audience voted for the more talented team at the end of the show. If the adults won, their winnings were donated to the Actors Fund of America. If the kids won, their winnings went to the Professional Childrens' School. In a rare TV appearance, composer W. C. Handy ("The St. Louis Blues") performed on the DuMont premiere.

BATTLE OF THE PLANETS   SYNDICATED
1978   A science fiction cartoon series, *Battle of the Planets* pitted the G Force, a team of five orphans headquartered at a secret base beneath the Pacific, against invaders from alien galaxies. The series was made in Japan in 1972 and was televised there under the title *Gatchaman*.

BATTLE REPORT   NBC

13 AUGUST 1950–20 APRIL 1952   A weekly report on the Korean conflict, broadcast live from Washington, D.C. Produced by Ted Ayers, the show was originally seen Sunday evenings, and was shifted to Sunday afternoons in 1951.

BATTLESTAR GALACTICA   ABC

17 SEPTEMBER 1978–4 AUGUST 1979   An expensive and elaborate science fiction series, *Battlestar Galactica* was obviously inspired by the colossal film *Star Wars* (one of Galactica's producers was John Dykstra, who was responsible for the special effects in *Star Wars*). Hurtling through space in a huge convoy of spacecraft, Galactica's inhabitants were heading toward Earth, trying to avoid annihilation by the Cylons, a mechanical race of beings out to destroy all humanoid forms of civilization. The cast included: Lorne Greene as Adama, commander of the fleet; Richard Hatch as Apollo; Dirk Benedict as Starbuck; Herb Jefferson, Jr., as Boomer; Maren Jensen as Athena; Noah Hathaway as Boxey; Tony Swartz as Jolly; Laurette Spang as Cassiopeia; and Terry Carter as Tigh. Glen A. Larson was the executive producer for Universal TV in association with Glen Larson Productions. The show, normally an hour program, kicked off with a three-hour premiere, which, at $3 million, was reported to be the most costly premiere telecast in TV history. See also *Galactica 1980*.

BATTLESTARS   NBC

26 OCTOBER 1981–23 APRIL 1982; 4 APRIL 1983–1 JULY 1983   Alex Trebek hosted this daytime game show on which two contestants and a panel of six celebrities appeared; the game was similar to *Hollywood Squares,* except that the celebs were seated in a grid of triangles rather than squares. The contestant who won three triangles (by guessing whether the celebs' answers to questions were correct) got the chance to identify a partially covered photo of another celebrity for a top prize of $5,000.

THE BAXTERS   SYNDICATED

1979–1981   An unusual half-hour series, *The Baxters* was created by Hubert Jessup and televised locally for several years on WCVB-TV in Boston before Norman Lear acquired the series in 1979. The first part of the program was an eleven-minute dramatic vignette highlighting a particular problem, which was then the subject of discussion by a studio audience for the remainder of the half hour. The 1979 cast of the nationally syndicated version included Anita Gillette as Nancy Baxter; Larry Keith as her husband, Fred Baxter; Derin Altay as daughter Naomi; Terri Lynn Wood as daughter Rachel; and Chris Petersen as son Jonah. Local stations which broadcast *The Baxters* were encouraged to provide their own audiences and moderators, although the audience-discussion portion taped in Los Angeles (where the vignettes were also taped) was made available to stations which chose not to provide a local studio audience. In 1980 production was shifted to Toronto, and a new cast was assembled: Terry Tweed as Susan, the mother; Sean McCann as Jim, the father; Marianne McIsaac as daughter Allison; Sammy Snyders as son Gregg; and Megan Follows as daughter Lucy.

BAY CITY BLUES   NBC

25 OCTOBER 1983–15 NOVEMBER 1983   This hour dramatic series followed the ups and downs of a minor-league baseball team, the Bay City (California) Bluebirds of the AA Western League, two notches below the majors. It was created by one of the cocreators of *Hill Street Blues,* Steven Bochco, and one of *Hill Street*'s producers, Jeffrey Lewis. Like *Hill Street,* it featured a large cast of regulars (several of whom had guest-starred on *Hill Street*) and continuing storylines. The regulars included Michael Nouri as the young manager, Joe Rohner, who hoped eventually to manage in the big leagues; Pat Corley as used-car dealer Ray Holtz, the owner; Perry Lang as pitcher John "Frenchy" Nuckles, a big-league prospect; Michele Greene as his wife, Judy Nuckles; Patrick Cassidy as Terry St. Marie, an outstanding athlete who was also a bedwetter; Sharon Stone as his patient wife, Cathy St. Marie; Dennis Franz as coach Angelo Carbone; Ken Olin as womanizing Rocky Padillo; Jeff McCracken as

Vic Kresky; Larry Flash Jenkins as Linwood "Linoleum" Scott; Tony Spiridakis as catcher Lee Jacoby; Mykel T. Williamson as Dee Jay Cunningham; Peter Jurasik as radio-TV announcer Mitch Klein; Bernie Casey as aging player-coach Thomas "Ozzie" Peoples; Kelly Harmon as Sunny Hayward, who began an affair with Joe; Kevin McCarthy as her husband, banker George Hayward; and Marco Rodriguez as "Bird," the team mascot. A major disappointment in the ratings, *Bay City Blues* was pulled from NBC's schedule after just four episodes.

THE BAY CITY ROLLERS SHOW   NBC
4 NOVEMBER 1978–27 JANUARY 1979   A popular recording group from Scotland, the Bay City Rollers hosted *The Krofft Superstar Hour* from September to late October of 1978, when the series was trimmed to thirty minutes and retitled. The group included Derek Longmuir, Alan Longmuir, Stuart Wood, Eric Faulkner, and Leslie McKeown. Also featured on the live-action show were Billie Hayes, Billy Barty, and Jay Robinson.

BAYWATCH   NBC/SYNDICATED
22 SEPTEMBER 1989–26 AUGUST 1990 (NBC); 1991– (SYNDICATED)   A perfect excuse to show plenty of bare-chested young men and bikini-clad young women, *Baywatch* was an hour adventure series about the lifeguards who patrolled the beaches of greater Los Angeles. Canceled after one lackluster season on NBC, *Baywatch* was revived for first-run syndication in 1991, where it soon became an international hit. The network cast included David Hasselhoff as Mitch Buchannon, newly promoted lieutenant; Parker Stevenson as his best friend, lawyer and part-time lifeguard Craig Pomeroy; Shawn Weatherly as Jill Riley, who was killed off (by a shark) in midseason; Billy Warlock as rookie lifeguard Eddie Kramer; Erika Eleniak as rookie Shauni McClain; Peter Phelps as rookie Trevor Cole; Gregory Alan-Williams as Sergeant Garner Ellerbee; Monte Markham as Mitch's boss, Captain Don Thorpe; Holly Gagnier as Gina Pomeroy, Craig's wife; Brandon Call as Hobie Buchannon, Mitch's young son; and John Allen Nelson as John D. Cort, who ran Sam's Surf & Dive, a beachfront rental shop. For the syndicated version, Hasselhoff, Warlock, Eleniak, Alan-Williams, and Markham remained from the network cast. Jeremy Jackson replaced Brandon Call as Hobie, and two new characters were added: Tom McTigue as lifeguard Harvey Miller, and Richard Jaeckel as Captain Ben Edwards. McTigue, Warlock, and Eleniak left in 1992, as several newcomers appeared: Alexandra Paul as Mitch's ex-girlfriend, Lieutenant Stephanie Holden; Pamela Anderson (later known as Pamela Lee) as lifeguard C. J. Parker; David Charvet as lifeguard Matt Brody; Nicole Eggert as junior lifeguard Summer Quinn; Kelly Slater as surfer Jimmy Slade; and Susan Anton as Summer's mother, Jackie Quinn. Markham, Jaeckel, Eggert, Slater, and Anton departed in 1994, while Yasmine Bleeth was added as Caroline Holden, Stephanie's younger sister, and Jaason Simmons joined as Logan Fowler, an Australian lifeguard who had moved to Los Angeles. Hasselhoff's wife, Pamela Bach, appeared occasionally during the first two syndicated seasons as Kay Morgan, Mitch's love interest. Gena Lee Nolin was added in 1995 as Neely Capshaw.

Filmed mostly on location at Will Rogers State Park in Los Angeles, the syndicated version was widely distributed overseas, reaching a weekly audience estimated as high as one billion by 1994. A made-for-video feature, "Baywatch the Movie: Forbidden Paradise," was released in 1995. A second series, *Baywatch Nights*, was scheduled to appear in late 1995. The series pilot, *Baywatch: Panic at Malibu Pier*, was telecast 23 April 1989 as a TV-movie on NBC.

BAYWATCH NIGHTS   SYNDICATED
1995–   In this spinoff from the hugely successful *Baywatch*, two characters from the parent series moonlighted as private eyes. The hour show starred *Baywatch* veterans David Hasselhoff and GregAlan Williams as Mitch Buchannon and Garner Ellerbee, and featured Angie Harmon as their boss, Ryan McBride, owner of the detective agency; Lisa Stahl as Destiny, a tarot reader; and Lou Rawls as Lou Raymond, owner of the nightspot located beneath the detective office.

BE OUR GUEST CBS

27 JANUARY 1960–JUNE 1960   Hour-long variety series, hosted first by George DeWitt and Mary Ann Mobley (Miss America of 1958), later by Keefe Brasselle and Mobley. Music by the Burt Farber orchestra. A midseason replacement for *The Lineup.*

THE BEACHCOMBER SYNDICATED

1961   Cameron Mitchell starred as John Lackland, a San Francisco adman who forsakes a successful career for the tranquility of a South Pacific island called Amura. With Don Megowan as Captain Huckabee; Sebastian Cabot as Commissioner Crippen; and Joan Staley as Linda.

BEACON HILL CBS

25 AUGUST 1975–4 NOVEMBER 1975   The biggest flop of the 1975–1976 season, *Beacon Hill* was an expensive, cumbersome and much-ballyhooed attempt to Americanize *Upstairs Downstairs,* the British export which had proven popular on PBS. Set in Boston's fashionable Beacon Hill in 1918, it told the story of a large, wealthy Irish family and their company of servants. The cast was so large that it was often difficult for viewers to keep track of the many characters. Some Bostonians noted also that the series was historically inaccurate, as few Irish families lived on Beacon Hill at that time, even fewer had so many servants, and no house on the Hill was as large as the Lassiters' seemed to be. Though thirteen episodes were taped, two were never televised as CBS decided to cut its losses after only eleven weeks.

Regulars included Stephen Elliott as Benjamin Lassiter, the hardnosed head of the clan; Nancy Marchand as his wife, Mary Lassiter, the grande dame; David Dukes as their embittered son Robert, who lost an arm in World War I; Kathryn Walker as Fawn, their arty-Bohemian daughter; Maeve McGuire as their daughter Maude Palmer; Edward Herrmann as Richard, Maude's boring husband; DeAnn Mears as the Lassiters' daughter Emily Bullock; Roy Cooper as Trevor, Emily's husband; Linda Purl as Betsy, Trevor and Emily's eighteen-year-old daughter; Kitty Winn as Rosamund Lassiter, the Lassiters' youngest daughter; Michael Nouri as Giorgio Balanci, Fawn's voice teacher and lover; George Rose as Mr. Hacker, the family butler and head of the servant staff; Beatrice Straight as his wife, Emmaline Hacker; Paul Rudd as Brian Mallory, the young chauffeur; David Rounds as Terence O'Hara, Hacker's assistant; Richard Ward as William Piper, the black cook; Don Blakely as his son Grant, also a veteran of World War I; Barry Snider as Harry Emmet, a former servant; Holland Taylor as Marilyn Gardiner, Mrs. Lassiter's secretary; Sydney Swire as Eleanor, a maid; Susan Blanchard as Maureen Mahaffey, a maid; and Lisa Pelikan as Maureen's sister, Kate Mahaffey, also a maid. Executive producer: Beryl Vertue. Produced by Jacqueline Babbin. Music by Marvin Hamlisch.

THE BEAGLES CBS/ABC

10 SEPTEMBER 1966–2 SEPTEMBER 1967 (CBS); 9 SEPTEMBER 1967–7 SEPTEMBER 1968 (ABC)   Saturday-morning cartoon series about a pair of rock-and-rolling dogs. (Not to be confused with *The Beatles.*)

BEAKMAN'S WORLD SYNDICATED/TLC/CBS

1992–1993 (SYNDICATED); 30 SEPTEMBER 1992–   (TLC); 18 SEPTEMBER 1993– (CBS)   Half-hour series explaining science to kids, with Paul Zaloom as nerdy scientist Beakman, with assistance from Alanna Ubach (as Josie), Mark Ritts (Lester), and Eliza Schneider (Liza). Derived from the comic strip "You Can with Beakman," created by Jok Church, the series debuted in 1992, with different episodes available on The Learning Channel and in first-run syndication. CBS added the series to its Saturday morning schedule in 1993, while the show continued its run on TLC.

BEANY AND CECIL

See TIME FOR BEANY

BEARCATS!   CBS

16 SEPTEMBER 1971–30 DECEMBER 1971   Forgettable adventure series about two
troubleshooters roaming the West, circa 1914, in their Stutz Bearcat. With Rod
Taylor as Hank Brackett; Dennis Cole as Johnny Reach. The show fared poorly
against NBC's *The Flip Wilson Show.*

BEAT THE CLOCK   CBS/ABC/SYNDICATED

23 MARCH 1950–12 SEPTEMBER 1958 (CBS); 13 OCTOBER 1958–30 JANUARY 1961 (ABC);
1969–1974 (SYNDICATED); 17 SEPTEMBER 1979–1 FEBRUARY 1980 (CBS)   One of
the earliest and most successful game shows from the fertile minds of Mark Goodson
and Bill Todman. On *Beat the Clock* couples (usually married couples) were required
to perform various stunts within certain time periods (usually less than sixty seconds).
The winning couple was given the chance to try a special stunt for a large prize; the
stunt was quite difficult and would be attempted weekly until someone was able to
perform it. Bud Collyer hosted the network versions, which were seen on prime time
over CBS and daily over CBS and ABC; for many seasons he was assisted by an
attractive blonde known as Roxanne (her real name was Dolores Rosedale). The
stunts were devised by Frank Wayne and Bob Howard and were always pretested by
members of the show's staff; in 1952 a young, unemployed actor got his first job in
TV testing stunts and warming up audiences. His name was James Dean.
   A syndicated version of the series appeared in 1969; it was hosted first by Jack
Narz, later by Gene Wood. It was substantially identical to the network version,
except that guest celebrities were on hand to aid the contestants, and there was no
special stunt for the winners to attempt. Monty Hall hosted the 1979 daytime revival
on CBS, on which two couples competed.

THE BEATLES   ABC

25 SEPTEMBER 1965–20 APRIL 1969   Saturday cartoon series starring animated versions of the enormously popular British rock group, The Beatles (John Lennon, Paul
McCartney, George Harrison, and Ringo Starr). Two Beatles songs were usually
"performed" on each episode; the Beatles' speaking voices were supplied by Paul
Frees (John and George) and Lance Percival (Paul and Ringo). One of the few series
which featured cartoon characterizations of real-life people.

THE BEAUTIFUL PHYLLIS DILLER SHOW   NBC

15 SEPTEMBER 1968–22 DECEMBER 1968   Variety hour hosted by Phyllis Diller, featuring Norm Crosby and Rip Taylor.

BEAUTY AND THE BEAST   CBS

25 SEPTEMBER 1987–25 AUGUST 1989; 12 DECEMBER 1989–24 JANUARY 1990; 9 JUNE
1990–4 AUGUST 1990   One of television's truly romantic series, *Beauty and the
Beast* was an updated version of the fairy tale. With its handsome sets and poetic
dialogue, it acquired an almost instant cult following, but the audience never widened enough to satisfy the network. Linda Hamilton starred as Catherine Chandler,
a Manhattan corporate attorney who was beaten and left for dead in Central Park.
Ron Perlman costarred as Vincent, the furry-faced, leonine man-beast who found
her and carried her to a labrynthine city beneath the city, where he healed her
wounds. Catherine eventually returned to the "real" New York and joined the
district attorney's office, but realized that she and Vincent had fallen in love.
Vincent, whose extranormal powers included the ability to sense Catherine's feelings, came to the same realization.
   Over the next two years their relationship deepened (they didn't even kiss until the
end of the first season). Catherine and Vincent recited poetry to each other, at least
whenever Vincent wasn't rescuing her from danger. Catherine learned more about
Vincent and the closed community under the city where he dwelled. Vincent had
been abandoned as an infant and found by one of the underground people, who lived
in a subterranean world of steam pipes, sewer lines, unused subway tunnels, and
abandoned basements. Other regulars included Roy Dotrice as Father, the unofficial
leader of the community, who had raised Vincent; Jay Acovone as Catherine's boss,

Deputy District Attorney Joe Maxwell; Ren Woods as computer operator Edie, who worked for Catherine; and Cory Danziger and David Greenlee (1988–1990) as Kipper and Mouse, two of the underground people.

Beauty and the Beast finished a mediocre 40th for the 1987–1988 season, and 55th in 1988–1989. Linda Hamilton announced her intention to leave the show. She appeared in the two-hour premiere of the abortive third season. At that time, Catherine was about to give birth to Vincent's child, but was kidnapped by a wealthy and well-connected criminal, who took the baby and killed Catherine. Jo Anderson joined the cast for the last few episodes as Diana Bennett, an investigator for the New York Police Department, who met Vincent. But the magic of the series had already died, and it expired quietly in January 1990.

BEAVIS AND BUTT-HEAD   MTV
8 MARCH 1993–   The MTV cartoon series about a pair of inarticulate, moronic teenage boys is perhaps best summarized by an on-screen promo clip: "Beavis and Butt-head are dumb, crude, thoughtless, ugly, sexist, self-destructive fools. But for some reason, the little wienerheads make us laugh." Their creator, Mike Judge, had begun making cartoons at home while taking graduate courses in the late 1980s; by 1990 he had conceived the pair. Butt-head, the dominant force, had brown hair, wore an AC/DC T-shirt, sported braces and had prominent gums; Beavis, his inseparable pal, was blonde with a huge lower jaw and wore a Metallica T-shirt. Both had annoying nervous laughs (Judge provided the voices of both characters). Their first feature, "Frog Baseball," found the lads using a live frog for batting practice. Entered in an animation festival, it was spotted by an MTV executive and was picked up on the cable channel's experimental animation series, *Liquid Television*. By late 1992 some 65 episodes had been commissioned, and the series premiered under its own name early in 1993.

Originally telecast at 7 P.M., the series soon generated controversy because of the characters' propensities for cruelty to small animals and for starting small fires. After a report surfaced that a five-year-old Ohio boy had set fire to his mobile home, killing his younger sister, the series was moved to a late-night timeslot and the stars' excesses were curbed: Beavis and Butt-head refrained from torturing animals and no longer carried lighters; they did, however, continue to torment humans (as well as take some brutal beatings themselves).

Fortunately, the toned-down *Beavis and Butt-head* was just as humorous. Each cartoon ran only six or seven minutes; the stories were punctuated by the characters' constant channel-surfing (with running commentary) through an endless parade of music videos (MTV made its immense video library available for use on the series). Beavis and Butt-head's artistic criterion was a simple one: what they liked was "cool," and what they didn't like "sucked." The boys were especially fond of heavy metal bands (particularly ones whose videos featured "cool chicks"), and the sales of records by bands such as White Zombie and Babes in Toyland soared after exposure on the series. In 1994 a Beavis and Butt-head record was released, in 1995 several volumes of cartoons were packaged for home video release, and other merchandise has also appeared.

Judge's crude animation style harmonized perfectly with the title characters' limited attention spans and vocabularies. He succeeded in creating two of television's most utterly hopeless figures, in the tradition of such human sitcom characters as Chester A. Riley, Ralph Kramden, and Al Bundy.

BEDROOM BUDDIES   SYNDICATED
1992   Half-hour game show in which three couples were quizzed on how well they knew each other. The winning couple was awarded a "bedroom fantasy" trip. Bobby Rivers presided over the festivities.

BEETHOVEN   CBS
17 SEPTEMBER 1994–2 SEPTEMBER 1995   This Saturday morning cartoon show was based not on the life of the famous composer, but instead on a dog, the mischievous

Saint Bernard who had been the title character in a popular 1992 live-action motion picture and its 1993 sequel.

BEETLEJUICE ABC
9 SEPTEMBER 1989–5 SEPTEMBER 1992 Half-hour Saturday morning cartoon series inspired by the 1988 film. Here, a fun-loving ghost named Beetlejuice befriended a little girl, Lydia Deetze, while delighting in playing tricks on her parents, Charles and Delia.

BEFORE HOURS NBC
2 MARCH 1987–16 SEPTEMBER 1988 Fifteen-minute early-morning weekday business report, hosted by Bob Jamieson.

BEHIND CLOSED DOORS NBC
2 OCTOBER 1958–9 APRIL 1959 Stories on this half-hour anthology series were adapted from the files of Rear Admiral Ellis M. Zacharias, deputy chief of naval intelligence during World War II. Bruce Gordon, as Commander Matson, hosted the show.

BEHIND THE LINES PBS
1971–1976 Half-hour news analysis show, hosted by Harrison E. Salisbury of *The New York Times*, produced at WNET in New York.

BEHIND THE NEWS CBS
11 JANUARY 1959–27 SEPTEMBER 1959 CBS newsman Howard K. Smith hosted this Sunday-afternoon news analysis program; William Weston produced it. Smith, who was CBS's Washington correspondent at the time, had joined the network in 1941; in 1961, following a dispute with CBS concerning on-the-air editorializing, Smith left for ABC News.

BEHIND THE SCENES PBS
1992 Guerrilla magicians Penn and Teller hosted this ten-part series exploring the creative arts and aimed at children.

BEHIND THE SCREEN CBS
9 OCTOBER 1981–8 JANUARY 1982 A short-lived late-night (11:30 P.M.) serial, *Behind the Screen* told the story of the cast and crew of a fictional daytime soap opera called "Generations" (the serial-within-a-serial idea was hardly new, having been tried thirty-two years earlier in one of TV's very first soaps, *A Woman to Remember*). Featured were Mel Ferrer as Evan Hammer, producer and starmaker; Janine Turner as starlet Janie-Claire Willow, Evan's cousin; Joshua Bryant as the producer, Gerry Holmby; Loyita Chapel as Gerry's wife, Dory, an aspiring writer; Michael Sabatino as Gerry's son, Brian; Debbi Morgan as Lynette Porter, another starlet; Bruce Fairbairn as Bobby; Joanne Linville as Zina; Catherine Parks as Sally; Erica Yohn as Joyce; and Mark Pinter as Karl. Because the show was not scheduled in prime time, it ran for thirty-five minutes, thereby permitting the insertion of five extra minutes of commercials.

BELIEVE IT OR NOT NBC
1 MARCH 1949–5 OCTOBER 1950 This half-hour series usually presented dramatizations of some of the amazing incidents depicted by cartoonist Robert L. Ripley in his "Believe It or Not" newspaper strip. Ripley, who died in 1949, hosted the show for many years on radio and also hosted the first few telecasts. Robert St. John succeeded Ripley as host. In 1982 ABC introduced a remake of the series (see *Ripley's Believe It or Not*).

THE BELL TELEPHONE HOUR NBC
12 JANUARY 1959–14 JUNE 1968 This musical series ran semiregularly for almost ten seasons—sometimes weekly, sometimes biweekly, and sometimes as irregularly

scheduled specials. All types of music were presented on the hour series; Donald Voorhees conducted the Bell Telephone Orchestra.

BEN CASEY ABC
2 OCTOBER 1961–21 MARCH 1966   "Man, woman, birth, death, infinity." So began the introduction to *Ben Casey,* which, together with NBC's *Dr. Kildare,* ushered in a new era of doctor shows. Both series lasted five seasons. Vince Edwards starred as Ben Casey, resident neurosurgeon at County General Hospital, seemingly an expert in every known area of medicine. Edwards's good looks and surly disposition (on-camera, anyway) helped make him a heartthrob among the female fans. Other regulars included Sam Jaffe (1961–1965) as Dr. David Zorba, chief of neurosurgery; Bettye Ackerman (Jaffe's wife) as anesthesiologist Dr. Maggie Graham; Harry Landers as Dr. Ted Hoffman; Nick Dennis as orderly Nick Kanavaras; Jeanne Bates as Nurse Wills; and Franchot Tone (1965–1966) as Dr. Freeland, Zorba's replacement as chief of neurosurgery. Created by James Moser (who also created *Medic*); produced by Matthew Rapf for Bing Crosby Productions. Edwards reprised the role in a two-hour 1988 TV-movie, *The Return of Ben Casey.*

BEN GRAUER'S AMERICANA QUIZ NBC
8 DECEMBER 1947–4 JULY 1949   Ben Grauer hosted this prime-time half-hour game show on which contestants were quizzed about American history.

BEN JERROD NBC
1 APRIL 1963–28 JUNE 1963   This daytime serial told the story of two small-town attorneys. With Michael Ryan as young lawyer Ben Jerrod; Addison Richards as his older partner, John Abbott, a former judge; Regina Gleason as Janet Donelli, who became a defendant in a murder case; Jeanne Baird as Agnes, Abbott's daughter; Ken Scott as Jim O'Hara, Janet's boyfriend; William Phipps as Coroner Engle; John Napier as Dan Joplin, the D.A.; Lyle Talbot as Lieutenant Choates; Peter Hansen as druggist Pete Morrison; and Martine Bartlett as Lil Morrison, Pete's wife. *Ben Jerrod* was one of television's shortest-running soap operas; ironically, two other serials that premiered the same day—*The Doctors* and *General Hospital*—proved exceptionally durable.

THE BEN STILLER SHOW FOX
27 SEPTEMBER 1992–31 JANUARY 1993   Half-hour filmed comedy sketch show, starring Ben Stiller (son of comedian-actors Jerry Stiller and Anne Meara), with Andy Dick, Janeane Garofalo, Bob Odenkirk, and occasional guest stars. The Sunday program, which was critically acclaimed and won a posthumous writing Emmy, was the lowest rated prime-time series of the season, finishing 109th in the Nielsen parade.

BEN VEREEN—COMIN' AT YA NBC
7 AUGUST 1975–28 AUGUST 1975   This four-week summer variety hour showcased the multitalented Ben Vereen, star of the Broadway hit *Pippin*. Vereen later achieved wider fame in television for his portrayal of Chicken George in *Roots*. Other regulars included singer Lola Falana and comedians Arte Johnson, Avery Schreiber, and Liz Torres. Produced by Jaime Rogers and Gene McAvoy.

BENJI, ZAX & THE ALIEN PRINCE CBS
17 SEPTEMBER 1983–25 AUGUST 1984   This half-hour series was the only live-action program on the commercial networks' Saturday-morning schedules during the 1983–1984 season. It starred a mutt named Benji (described in the credits as "America's most huggable hero"), who had been featured in several motion pictures. In the series Benji befriended Prince Yubi (played by Chris Burton), who, with his talking robot, Zax, had escaped to Earth from a faraway planet. The three creatures tried to keep one step ahead of two emissaries of the alien planet's evil ruler, who sought to recapture the child prince. Rig Spiegel provided Zax's voice. The program was videotaped in Dallas.

THE BENNETTS (THE BENNETT STORY)   NBC
6 JULY 1953–8 JANUARY 1954   Another short-lived soap opera about a small-town attorney, this one featured Don Gibson as lawyer Wayne Bennett and Paula Houston as his wife, Nancy. Also featured were Jerry Harvey and Kay Westfall. The setting was the town of Kingsport.

THE BENNY HILL SHOW   SYNDICATED
1979–1989   A half-hour series of comedy skits featuring bawdy British comic Benny Hill and an assortment of scantily clad females. The American programs were edited versions of the one-hour specials that Hill did for Thames Television between 1969 and 1989. The British shows contained considerably more nudity.

THE BENNY RUBIN SHOW   NBC
29 APRIL 1949–1 JULY 1949   Comedian Benny Rubin, whose career began in vaudeville, starred as a talent agent in this comedy-variety show, which also featured Vinnie Monte as the office boy. Jerry Rosen was the producer.

BENSON   ABC
13 SEPTEMBER 1979–30 AUGUST 1986   A spinoff from *Soap,* starring Robert Guillaume as Benson, who left his employ at the Tate residence to manage the household of the state's governor. With James Noble as Governor Gene Gatling, a widower, a cousin of *Soap*'s Jessica Tate; Inga Swenson as Gretchen Kraus, the Teutonic housekeeper at the governor's mansion; Caroline McWilliams as Marcy Hill, the governor's secretary; Missy Gold as Katie, the governor's precocious daughter; Lewis J. Stadlen (1979–1980) as Taylor, the governor's aide. The half-hour show was created by Susan Harris. In the fall of 1980 two new cast members were added: Rene Auberjonois as Clayton Endicott, the governor's officious chief of staff, and Ethan Phillips as Pete Downey, the governor's press secretary. In one of his earliest TV appearances, Jerry Seinfeld appeared in a few episodes that year as Frankie, the governor's joke writer. Later that season Marcy met and married TV producer Dan Slater (played by Ted Danson); Caroline McWilliams, who played Marcy, left the show early in the 1981–1982 season. That fall Benson acquired a new job— budget director for the governor—and his last name was finally revealed: Dubois. Didi Conn also joined the series as Benson's secretary, Denise Stevens. Denise and Pete were married in the fall of 1983, and departed the series in the middle of the next season. Benson was elected lieutenant governor in the fall of 1984, and chose Kraus as his executive aide. In the series's final season, Benson fell for a legislator, Diane Hartford (played by Donna LaBrie), and, ultimately, decided to run for governor against Gatling; the election took place on the last first-run episode. The producers filmed four different endings—Benson winning, Gatling winning, a third candidate upsetting them both, and Benson and Gatling watching the returns with no winner announced—and chose to air the last one.

THE BERENSTAIN BEARS   CBS
14 SEPTEMBER 1985–5 SEPTEMBER 1987   The central characters on this Saturday morning cartoon show were the four members of the Bear family—Mama, Papa, Brother, and Sister. The show was based on the popular series of children's books written by Stan and Jan Berenstain.

BERNSTEIN/BEETHOVEN   PBS
25 JANUARY 1982–12 APRIL 1982   An eleven-week series of concerts, in which Beethoven's nine symphonies (as well as other of his works) were presented. Leonard Bernstein (who received top billing on the show) conducted the Vienna Philharmonic Orchestra. Maximilian Schell provided the commentary.

BERRENGER'S   NBC
5 JANUARY 1985–9 MARCH 1985   A posh New York City department store was the centerpiece of this ill-fated hour prime-time serial. With Sam Wanamaker as Simon Berrenger, chairman of the board; Ben Murphy as his eldest son, Paul Berrenger, the

store president; Anita Morris as Babs, Simon's daughter; Robin Strand as Billy Berrenger, Simon's black sheep son; Art Hindle as Todd Hughes, Babs's husband; Claudia Christian as Melody, their daughter; Andrea Marcovicci as Gloria, Paul's estranged wife; Yvette Mimieux as Shane Bradley, vice president of merchandising, who was hot for Paul; Laura Ashton as model Laurel Hayes; Jonelle Allen as Stacy Russell, a department manager, Laurel's roommate; Jeff Conaway as John Higgins, office lothario; Leslie Hope as new employee Cammie Springer; Eddie Velez as aspiring clothes designer Julio Morales; Donna Dixon as executive trainee Allison Harris; and Jack Scalia as Danny Krucek. Diana Gould created the series.

BERT D'ANGELO-SUPERSTAR ABC
21 FEBRUARY 1976–10 JULY 1976   Paul Sorvino starred as Bert D'Angelo, a former New York City police detective who worked in San Francisco. With Robert Pine as Inspector Larry Johnson; Dennis Patrick as Captain Jack Breen. Produced by Mort Fine for Quinn Martin Productions. Filmed on location.

THE BERT PARKS SHOW NBC/CBS
1 NOVEMBER 1950–11 JANUARY 1952 (NBC); 14 JANUARY 1952–26 JUNE 1952 (CBS)
Although Bert Parks hosted many TV series, this daytime variety show—originally aired three times weekly, later daily—was the only one which bore his name. Other regulars included vocalist Betty Ann Grove, Harold Lang, the Heathertones, and the Bobby Sherwood Quintet.

THE BERTICE BERRY SHOW SYNDICATED
1993–1994   Low-rated daytime talk show hosted by Bertice Berry, a black woman who had previously been a standup comic and had also earned a doctorate in sociology.

THE BEST IN MYSTERY NBC
13 JULY 1956–31 AUGUST 1956   Rebroadcasts of the several episodes of *Four Star Playhouse* in which Dick Powell starred as Willie Dante, an ex-gambler who owned Dante's Inferno, a San Francisco nightclub. With Alan Mowbray as Jackson; Herb Vigran as Monte; and Regis Toomey as Lieutenant Waldo. Willie Dante reappeared in 1960, and was played by Howard Duff; see *Dante*. Reruns culled from other series were also broadcast under the title *The Best in Mystery* on CBS during the summers of 1954 and 1955.

THE BEST OF BROADWAY CBS
15 SEPTEMBER 1954–4 MAY 1955   Martin Manulis produced this series of specials, which replaced *Pabst Blue Ribbon Bouts* every fourth Wednesday for one season. Presentations included: "The Royal Family," with Claudette Colbert (making her TV debut), Helen Hayes and Fredric March (15 September); "The Man Who Came to Dinner," with Buster Keaton, Margaret Hamilton, Joan Bennett, Bert Lahr, and Monty Woolley (13 October); "The Philadelphia Story," with Mary Astor and John Payne (8 December); "Arsenic and Old Lace," with Pat Breslin and Orson Bean (5 January); "The Guardsman," with Margaret Hamilton and Mary Boland (2 March); "Stage Door," with Rhonda Fleming (in her first major TV role, 6 April); and "Broadway," with Martha Hyer (4 May).

THE BEST OF EVERYTHING ABC
30 MARCH 1970–25 SEPTEMBER 1970   Daytime serial based on the 1959 film about three young career women, all working at Key Publishing Company, trying to make it in New York City. With Susan Sullivan and Julie Mannix as April Morrison; Patty McCormack as Linda Warren; Geraldine Fitzgerald as Violet Jordan; and Gale Sondergaard as Amanda Key.

THE BEST OF SATURDAY NIGHT LIVE
See NBC'S SATURDAY NIGHT LIVE

THE BEST OF THE POST   SYNDICATED
1957   Dramatic anthology series; episodes were based on stories from the *Saturday Evening Post*. Produced by MGM.

BEST OF THE WEST   ABC
10 SEPTEMBER 1981–28 JANUARY 1982; 7 JUNE 1982–23 AUGUST 1982   Joel Higgins starred in this comedy-western as Sam Best, a Philadelphian who bought a general store in the seamy western town of Copper Creek; upon his arrival there, he became the new marshal. With Carlene Watkins as his addled wife, Elvira; Meeno Peluce as his homesick son, Daniel; Leonard Frey as Parker Tillman, the town boss; Tracey Walter as Frog, Tillman's lamebrained lackey; Tom Ewell as Doc Jerome Kullens; and Valri Bromfield as mountain woman Laney Gibbs. Earl Pomerantz created the series, which was well received by the critics, but, like most other comedy-westerns, failed to score in the ratings.

THE BEST OF THE WORST   FOX
17 AUGUST 1991–24 JANUARY 1992   Greg Kinnear emceed this weekly variety show, which highlighted "the worst" in the media and the arts. The series lived up to its title, finishing in a tie with *Charlie Hoover* as the lowest-rated prime-time series of the season.

BEST SELLERS   NBC
30 SEPTEMBER 1976–25 APRIL 1977   The umbrella title for an anthology series made up of several serialized novels. Presentations included: (1) "Captains and the Kings," Taylor Caldwell's story of three generations of an influential Irish Catholic family, shown in eight parts. The large cast included Richard Jordan (Joseph Armagh), Patty Duke Astin (Bernadette Armagh, Joseph's wife), Charles Durning (Ed Healey), Henry Fonda (Senator Enfield Bassett), Perry King (Joseph's son Rory), Celeste Holm (Sister Angela), John Houseman (Judge Chisholm), Harvey Jason (Harry Zeff), Vic Morrow (Tom Hennessey), Barbara Parkins (Martinique), Joanna Pettet (Katherine Hennessey), Ann Sothern (Mrs. Finch), and Robert Vaughn (Charles Desmond). (2) "Once an Eagle," Anton Meyer's tale of two soldiers and two wars, shown in seven parts, with Sam Elliott (Sergeant Sam Damon), Cliff Potts (Lieutenant Courtney Massengale), Darleen Carr (Tommy Caldwell Damon, Sam's wife), Amy Irving (Emily Massengale, Courtney's wife), Glenn Ford (Major Caldwell), Gary Grimes (Jack Devlin), Clu Gulager (Lieutenant Merrick), John Saxon (Captain Townshend), and William Windom (General Pulleyne). (3) "Seventh Avenue," Norman Bogner's saga of New York's garment industry, shown in three two-hour segments, featuring Steven Keats (Jay Blackman), Dori Brenner (Rhoda Gold Blackman, his wife), Anne Archer (Myrna Gold, Rhoda's sister), Herschel Bernardi (Joe Vitelli), Jack Gilford (Finkelstein), Alan King (Harry Lee), Ray Milland (Fredericks), Paul Sorvino (Dave Shaw), Kristoffer Tabori (Al Blackman), and William Windom (John Meyers). (4) "The Rhinemann Exchange," a three-part, five-hour adaptation of Robert Ludlum's World War II spy thriller, with Stephen Collins (David Spaulding), Lauren Hutton (Leslie Hawkewood), José Ferrer (Rhinemann), John Huston (Ambassador Granville), and Roddy McDowall (Bobby Ballard). Although "Captains and the Kings" fared well in the ratings, the other serializations did not, and the umbrella concept was scrapped in the spring of 1977.

THE BEST TIMES   NBC
19 APRIL 1985–7 JUNE 1985   This hour dramatic series focused on the lives of the students and faculty at John F. Kennedy High School, located in a Southern California beach community. With Beth Ehlers as student Mia Braithwaite; Janet Eilber as her mother, Joanne Braithwaite, who landed a job as substitute English teacher there; Jim Metzler as science teacher Dan Bragen; David Packer as Neil "Trout" Troutman; K. C. Martel as Dale, Trout's younger brother; Melora Hardin as Joy, Trout's girlfriend; Darren Dalton as ex-dropout Chris Henson; Liane Curtis as Annette; Tammy Lauren as Giselle; Jay Baker as Tony; and LaSaundra J. Hall as Dionne.

BETTER DAYS   CBS

1 OCTOBER 1986–29 OCTOBER 1986   Raphael Sbarge starred in this half-hour sitcom
as Brian McGuire, a teenager who moved from Beverly Hills to Brooklyn to live with
his grandfather following his parents' separation. Also featured were Dick O'Neill as
the grandfather, Harry Clooney; Chip McAllister as Luther Kane and Guy Killum as
Anthony "Snake" Johnson, two of Brian's basketball-playing pals at Buckner High;
Randall Batinkoff as Terence Dean; and Randee Heller as homeroom teacher Harriet Winters. The first announced cancellation of the 1986 fall season, *Better Days*
was lifted after only four showings.

THE BETTER HOME SHOW   ABC

5 MAY 1951–26 APRIL 1952   Home repair was the focus of this Saturday evening
series, hosted by Norman Brokenshire, with help from Dick and Doreen Wilson,
who played Brokenshire's neighbors.

BETTER LIVING TELEVISION THEATER   ABC/DUMONT

21 JUNE 1953–16 AUGUST 1953 (ABC); 21 APRIL 1954–29 AUGUST 1954 (DUMONT)
Like *Enterprise U.S.A.* and *Industry on Parade, Better Living Television Theater* was
a series of documentaries designed to promote American industry. Fischer Black
hosted the half-hour series. Typical of the presentations was the 1954 DuMont premiere, "A Is for Atom: The Story of Nuclear Power."

THE BETTER SEX   ABC

18 JULY 1977–13 JANUARY 1978   A Goodson-Todman daytime game show in which a
team of six men faced a team of six women. One player was given a question, then
handed a card which indicated the correct answer and an incorrect answer; the player
read one of those answers to members of the opposite team. Two members of the
opposite team had to agree on whether the announced answer was the correct one; if
their response was correct, two members of the first team were eliminated. If their
response was incorrect, they were eliminated. The first team to eliminate all the
members of the opposite team was the winner and split $1,000. The winning team
then played against thirty audience members of the opposite sex in a similar format
for the chance to win $5,000. Former country and western singer Bill Anderson
served as cohost with Sarah Purcell; Purcell was the first woman to emcee a game
show in more than twenty years.

THE BETTY CROCKER STAR MATINEE   ABC

3 NOVEMBER 1951–26 APRIL 1952   Saturday noontime potpourri of variety, talk and
short dramas, hosted by Adelaide Hawley.

THE BETTY FURNESS SHOW
See BY-LINE and PENTHOUSE PARTY

THE BETTY HUTTON SHOW   CBS

1 OCTOBER 1959–30 JUNE 1960   One of the most popular film stars of the 1940s (*The
Fleet's In, The Miracle of Morgan's Creek,* and *Annie Get Your Gun*), Betty Hutton
was unable to make a successful transition to television. Her dramatic debut, "Satins
and Spurs" (NBC, 12 September 1954), spurred little excitement. In 1959, she and
her former husband, Charles O'Curran, put together this unsuccessful situation comedy in which Hutton played Goldie Appleby, a former showgirl, now a manicurist,
who is unexpectedly named executrix of a millionaire's estate and guardian of the
three children. Also featured were Richard Miles as Nicky Strickland, Gigi Perreau
as Patricia Strickland, and Dennis Joel as Roy Strickland, Goldie's wards; Joan
Shawlee as Goldie's friend, Lorna; Jean Carson as Rosemary, Goldie's roommate;
Tom Conway as Howard Seaton, attorney for the estate; and Gavin Muir as
Hollister, the butler. Slated against ABC's *The Donna Reed Show* and NBC's *Bat
Masterson,* the series perished quietly. Hutton then made a few television appear-
ances (the most recent was a 1965 *Gunsmoke*) and vanished from Hollywood. Early

in the 1970s she was discovered washing dishes in a Portsmouth, Rhode Island, rectory.

THE BETTY WHITE SHOW   NBC/ABC
8 FEBRUARY 1954–31 DECEMBER 1954 (NBC); 5 FEBRUARY 1958–30 APRIL 1958 (ABC)
Betty White hosted two shows during the 1950s. The first was a daytime talk show; it was broadcast at lunchtime except during the summer, when it was aired late afternoons. Early in 1958 she returned as host of a prime-time comedy-variety show; regulars included John Dehner, Reta Shaw, Peter Leeds, Johnny Jacobs, and Frank DeVol's orchestra. In 1977 she starred in her own sitcom: see below.

THE BETTY WHITE SHOW   CBS
12 SEPTEMBER 1977–9 JANUARY 1978   After achieving her greatest fame as the delightfully catty Sue Ann Nivens on *The Mary Tyler Moore Show,* Betty White was given her own sitcom in 1977. She starred as Joyce Whitman, the not-too-talented star of TV's *Undercover Woman,* a purely fictional series that bore some resemblance to NBC's *Police Woman.* Also featured were John Hillerman as unemotional John Elliot, Joyce's ex-husband and *Undercover Woman*'s director; Georgia Engel (another *Mary Tyler Moore* alumna) as Joyce's roommate, Mitzi Maloney, recently laid off from her job at the unemployment office; Caren Kaye as voluptuous Tracy Garrett, Joyce's costar; Barney Phillips as timid Fletcher Huff, who played the police chief; Charles Cyphers as Hugo Muncy, Joyce's burly double; Alex Henteloff as Doug Porterfield, a network vice president who oversaw the production of *Undercover Woman.* Executive producer: Bob Ellison. Produced by Charles Raymond and Dale McRaven for MTM Enterprises.

BETWEEN THE WARS   SYNDICATED
1978   Sixteen half-hour documentaries on American diplomacy, 1919–1941, narrated by Eric Sevareid. Produced by Alan Landsburg Productions.

BEULAH   ABC
3 OCTOBER 1950–22 SEPTEMBER 1953   The first TV dramatic series to star a black performer, *Beulah* told the story of a maid with a heart of gold. The character had been created by a white actor, Marlin Hurt, who played the part on the *Fibber McGee and Molly* radio series and on the first radio version of *Beulah,* which premiered in 1945 (the character was later played by a second white performer, Bob Corley, before Hattie McDaniel took over the radio role). Television's first Beulah was Ethel Waters, a blues singer and Oscar nominee (for *Pinky*); Hattie McDaniel was scheduled to replace Waters in 1951, but was unable to do so; Louise Beavers took over the role in April 1952 (McDaniel filled in for Beavers for six episodes during the summer of 1952). Other regulars included William Post, Jr. (1950–1952) and David Bruce (1952–1953) as Beulah's employer, New York lawyer Harry Henderson; Ginger Jones (1950–1952) and June Frazee (1952–1953) as Alice Henderson, his wife; Clifford Sales (1950–1952) and Stuffy Singer (1952–1953) as Donnie, their son; Percy (Bud) Harris (1950–1952) and Dooley Wilson (1952–1953; he played Sam in *Casablanca*) as Bill Jackson, Beulah's boyfriend; Butterfly McQueen as Beulah's friend and confidante, Oriole, also a domestic.

THE BEVERLY HILLBILLIES   CBS
26 SEPTEMBER 1962–7 SEPTEMBER 1971   Together with *The Andy Griffith Show, The Beverly Hillbillies* was the most successful of the "rural" situation comedies brought to television under the aegis of James T. Aubrey, then president of CBS-TV. Universally blasted by the critics upon its premiere, *Hillbillies* climbed to the number-one spot in the Nielsens by January and remained there through 1964. It was the story of a backwoods family who suddenly became rich beyond description when oil was discovered on their property (located somewhere in Appalachia); they immediately packed their belongings in their decrepit car and headed for California. With Buddy Ebsen (song-and-dance man of the 1930s, and Davy Crockett's sidekick on *Disneyland*) as widower Jed Clampett; Irene Ryan (former vaudevillian) as Granny (Daisy Moses),

his crusty mother-in-law; Donna Douglas as Jed's daughter, Elly May; Max Baer, Jr., son of the former heavyweight champion, as Jethro Bodine, Jed's dimwitted nephew; Raymond Bailey as Milburn Drysdale, president of the Commerce Bank of Beverly Hills, custodian of the Clampett funds and neighbor of the Clampetts; Nancy Kulp as Jane Hathaway, Drysdale's officious aide-de-camp; Harriet MacGibbon as Margaret Drysdale, Milburn's snooty wife; Shug Fisher (1969–1971) as Shorty, Elly May's boyfriend; Roger Torrey (1970–1971) as Mark Templeton, another boyfriend; and Stretch as Duke, the Clampett bloodhound. The "Beverly Hillbillies Theme" was played by Lester Flatt and Earl Scruggs, who occasionally appeared as themselves, and sung by Jerry Scoggins. Also appearing during the 1963–1964 season was Sharon Tate, as bank secretary Janet Trego, in one of her first professional roles. In 1963 *Petticoat Junction* was spun off, and in 1965 *Green Acres* appeared; its premise was the converse of the *Hillbillies*—a city family moves to the hinterlands. On 6 October 1981 a made-for-TV-movie sequel was broadcast; "The Return of the Beverly Hillbillies" reunited Buddy Ebsen, Nancy Kulp, and Donna Douglas (Max Baer, Jr., the other surviving principal, refused to recreate his role).

During its network run the series set some ratings records that have never been equalled. According to the A. C. Nielsen Company, the eight most widely watched half-hour programs of all time are all episodes of *The Beverly Hillbillies*. Perhaps even more interesting is the fact that all eight episodes were aired during the first three months of 1964, as the nation tried to recover from the shock of the assassination of President Kennedy. A total of 274 episodes were produced, the first 106 of which were in black and white; the show was aired in color starting in the fall of 1965.

.A theatrical film was released in 1993, featuring Jim Varney (Jed), Cloris Leachman (Granny), Erika Eleniak (Elly May), Diedrich Bader (Jethro), Dabney Coleman (Drysdale), and Lily Tomlin (Miss Hathaway). Buddy Ebsen had a cameo role—as Barnaby Jones.

BEVERLY HILLS BUNTZ   NBC
5 NOVEMBER 1987–22 APRIL 1988   *Beverly Hills Buntz* was one of two 1987 series starring alumni of *Hill Street Blues* (*Mama's Boy* was the other) and intended by NBC to serve as "designated hitter" series—shows that could be quickly summoned to replace faltering programs. The idea never caught on, mainly because both were scheduled so erratically that there was no chance for either to build an audience. On this series, played mostly for laughs, Dennis Franz continued his *Hill Street* role as Norman Buntz, now an ex-cop, who decided to set up shop as a private eye in Beverly Hills. Accompanying Buntz was his snitch from *Hill Street,* greasy Sid Thurston (played by Peter Jurasik). Dana Wheeler-Nicholson was seen as writer Rebecca Griswold, whose office was near Buntz's, and Guy Boyd played Lieutenant Pugh.

BEVERLY HILLS 90210   FOX
4 OCTOBER 1990–   TV's first series with a zip code in its title was an hour dramatic series about a pair of sixteen-year-old twins whose family moved from Minnesota to Beverly Hills; the twins enrolled at West Beverly High, and tried to fit in with the new crowd. The series quickly became popular with teenagers, because the stories dealt with sensitive topics such as teen sex, alcohol, and drugs. The cast included Jason Priestley as twin Brandon Walsh; Shannen Doherty (1990–1994) as twin Brenda Walsh; Carol Potter (1990–1995) as their mom, Cindy, who could usually be found at home; James Eckhouse (1990–1995) as their dad, Jim, an accountant who was transferred from Minneapolis; Jennie Garth as Kelly Taylor, daughter of a recovering alcoholic mother; Ian Ziering as Steve Sanders, adopted son of a television star; Gabrielle Carteris (1990–1995) as brainy Andrea Zuckerman, editor of the school paper; Brian Austin Green as David Silver; Luke Perry as brooding Dylan McKay; Tori Spelling (real life daughter of executive producer Aaron Spelling) as dyslexic Donna Martin; and Douglas Emerson (1990–fall 1991) as Scott Scanlon, who was accidentally killed in a handgun mishap. During the first season Brenda became involved with Dylan; they had sex in a hotel room on their prom night, after which Brenda worried that she might be pregnant (she wasn't). In a clever programming move, the series started its second season in the summer of 1991 (it also dropped the

comma from its title). The strategy worked, as teens continued to follow the show. Occasional new regulars included Christine Elise as Emily Valentine; Nicholle Tom as Sue Scanlon, Scott's sister; Joe E. Tata as Nat, owner of the Peach Pit, a restaurant where the gang hung out (and where Brandon found work); Ann Gillespie as Kelly's mother, Jackie; and Dana Barron as Nikki. David and Kelly found themselves stepsiblings for a while, as David's father, Mel (played by Matthew Laurance) married Jackie Taylor in the spring of 1992 (they later divorced after having a daughter). Grant Show was introduced late in the season as Jake Hanson, Kelly's boyfriend; he then headed to *90210*'s spinoff series, *Melrose Place*. *90210* again aired first-run episodes during the summer, as a lead-in to *Melrose Place* on Wednesdays, while summer reruns continued to run on Thursdays. In the fall of 1992 Cory Tyler joined the cast as Herbert, the first black regular on the series. The gang graduated from high school in the spring of 1993, and headed for college that fall. Andrea met and married law student Jesse Vasquez (played by Mark Damon Espinoza); they had a baby in the spring of 1994.

Amid much publicity, Shannen Doherty left the series at the end of the 1993–1994 season (it was explained that Brenda was studying in England). Three new regulars were added in the fall of 1994: Kathleen Robertson as Clare Arnold; Jamie Walters as musician Ray Pruit; and Tiffani-Amber Thiessen as unwholesome Valerie Malone, the daughter of friends of the Walshes from Minnesota, who moved into Brenda's old room.

As the series' sixth season began in 1995, Jim and Cindy Walsh had gone to Hong Kong; leaving Brandon as the only Walsh still living in Beverly Hills. New additions included Rebecca Gayheart as Antonia Marchette, Dylan's love interest; Emma Caulfield as Susan Keats, Brandon's love interest; and Jason Wiles as Colin. Luke Perry left the series in the middle of the 1995–1996 season.

BEWITCHED   ABC

17 SEPTEMBER 1964–1 JULY 1972   Situation comedy in which a winsome witch, married to a mere mortal, tried to curb her supernatural powers. With Elizabeth Montgomery (daughter of Robert Montgomery) as Samantha Stephens; Dick York (1964–1969) and Dick Sargent (1969–1972) as her husband, Darrin, an account executive at McMahon and Tate, a New York advertising agency; Agnes Moorehead as Endora, Samantha's meddlesome mother; David White as Larry Tate, Darrin's boss; Alice Pearce (1964–1966) and Sandra Gould (1966–1972) as Gladys Kravitz, a nosy neighbor; George Tobias as her husband, Abner Kravitz; Irene Vernon (1964–1966) and Kasey Rogers (1966–1972) as Louise Tate, Larry's wife; Maurice Evans as Maurice, Samantha's warlock father; Marion Lorne (1964–1968) as Samantha's daffy Aunt Clara; Paul Lynde (1965–1966) as Samantha's Uncle Arthur; and Alice Ghostley (1968–1970) as Esmeralda, also a witch. In 1965 the Stephens' first child, Tabitha, was born; she too had supernatural powers. The part was played by three sets of twins: first, Heidi and Laura Gentry; second, Tamar and Julie Young; third (1966–1972), Diane and Erin Murphy (the part was credited to Erin). In 1970 son Adam was born, played by twins David and Greg Lawrence. In the later seasons, Elizabeth Montgomery also played the part of Serena, Samantha's free-spirited cousin; the part was credited to "Pandora Sparks." One of ABC's longest-running sitcoms (252 episodes), the series was created by Sol Saks and produced by William Asher, Montgomery's husband, for Screen Gems. See also *Tabitha*.

BEYOND TOMORROW   FOX

10 SEPTEMBER 1988–16 DECEMBER 1989   Science and technology were the subjects of this Saturday-night documentary series. Regular correspondents included Gary Cubberly, Randy Meier, Susan Hunt, and Richard Wiese. The series was produced in Australia and was based on a show that had originated there.

BEYOND WESTWORLD   CBS

5 MARCH 1980–19 MARCH 1980   Hour fantasy series about a mad scientist hoping to take over the world with his crew of remarkably humanlike robots, and the security agent assigned to thwart him. With Jim McMullan as John Moore, security agent for

the Delos Corporation; James Wainwright as Simon Quaid, the mad scientist; Judith Chapman as Laura Garvey, Moore's partner; William Jordan as Professor Joseph Oppenheimer, who created the robots, only to have them fall into Quaid's evil clutches; Stewart Moss and Severn Darden as Foley, one of Quaid's assistants; Ann McCurry as Roberta, another of Quaid's assistants; and Connie Sellecca as Pam. The series was based on Michael Crichton's novel *Westworld,* and was developed for television by Lou Shaw. John Meredyth Lucas was the producer.

BID 'N' BUY   CBS
1 JULY 1958–23 SEPTEMBER 1958   Bert Parks hosted this Tuesday-night auction game show, a summer replacement for *The $64,000 Question.*

BIFF BAKER, U.S.A.   CBS
6 NOVEMBER 1952–26 MARCH 1953   Cold War espionage series starring Alan Hale, Jr., and Randy Stuart as Biff and Louise Baker, husband-and-wife spy team posing as American importers behind the Iron Curtain. Produced at Revue Studios by Alan Miller.

THE BIG ATTACK
See CITIZEN SOLDIER

THE BIG BANDS   SYNDICATED
1966   Half-hour series showcasing some of the big bands that had survived from the 1930s and 1940s.

BIG BATTLES   SYNDICATED
1974   A warfare documentary series.

BIG BLUE MARBLE   SYNDICATED
1974–1983   Ambitious children's series underwritten by the ITT Corporation. A magazine for kids, with filmed segments showing children around the world at work and at play. Created and first produced by Harry Fownes, the show was so titled because the Earth, when seen from a satellite, resembles "a big blue marble."

THE BIG BREAK   SYNDICATED
1990–1991   A one-hour talent contest series, hosted by Natalie Cole.

BIG EDDIE   CBS
23 AUGUST 1975–7 NOVEMBER 1975   Abysmal situation comedy about an ex-gangster who went straight as the owner of the Big E sports arena. With Sheldon Leonard as Big Eddie Smith; Sheree North as Honey, his new wife, a former showgirl; Quinn Cummings as Ginger, his perky granddaughter; Alan Oppenheimer as Jesse, his younger brother; Billy Sands as Monte (Bang Bang) Valentine, an ex-jockey, now the cook; and Ralph Wilcox as Raymond McKay, Eddie's black business associate. Created by Bill Persky and Sam Denoff.

THE BIG EVENT   NBC
26 SEPTEMBER 1976–26 JULY 1981   The umbrella title for assorted movies and specials broadcast frequently throughout the year. Presentations included movies such as *Earthquake* and *Gone with the Wind* (which was the highest-rated single program in TV history at the time), made-for-TV features such as "Sybil," the story of a multiple personality with Sally Field and Joanne Woodward, and "The Moneychangers," and documentaries such as "The Search for the Loch Ness Monster—An Adventure," and "Life Goes to the Movies."
    By far the most noteworthy presentation of the 1977–1978 season was "Holocaust," a four-part, nine-and-one-half-hour dramatization of the persecution and extermination of European Jews by the Nazis during World War II. Written by Gerald Green, the drama centered on the lives of the Weiss family, who lived in Berlin. Principal players included Fritz Weaver as Dr. Josef Weiss; Rosemary Harris

as his wife, Berta Weiss; James Woods as their elder son, Karl; Meryl Streep as Karl's Christian wife, Inga; Joseph Bottoms as their younger son, Rudi; Blanche Baker as their daughter, Anna; Sam Wanamaker as Josef's brother, Moses; and Michael Moriarty as Erik Dorf, an ambitious Nazi officer. "Holocaust" won eight Emmys in 1978.

The chief "Big Event" of the 1978–1979 season was "Centennial," a twenty-five-hour, $25 million adaptation of James Michener's hefty saga of the West, starring Robert Conrad (Pasquinel), Richard Chamberlain (McKeag), Clint Walker (Joe Bean), Raymond Burr (Bockweiss), Sally Kellerman (Lise), Barbara Carrera (Clay Basket), Richard Crenna (Colonel Skimmerhorn), Chad Everett (Maxwell Mercy), and Alex Karras (Hans Brumbaugh). John Wilder was the producer.

BIG GAME
NBC

13 JUNE 1958–12 SEPTEMBER 1958   On this Friday-night game show two contestants played a game similar to "Battleships," in which each sought to locate his opponent's game animals on a hidden board. This was the first of several game shows hosted by Tom Kennedy, younger brother of television quizmaster Jack Narz.

BIG HAWAII
NBC

21 SEPTEMBER 1977–30 NOVEMBER 1977   An early casualty of the 1977–1978 season, *Big Hawaii* told the story of modern-day cattle ranchers in the fiftieth state. With Cliff Potts as Mitch Fears; John Dehner as Barrett Fears, his father, the ranch owner; Lucia Stralser as Keke, Barrett's niece; Bill Lucking as Oscar, the foreman; Elizabeth Smith as Lulu (Auntie Lu), the housekeeper; Moe Keale as Garfield; Remi Abellira as Kimo; and Josie Over as Asita. Created by William Wood, with Perry Lafferty as executive producer and William Finnegan as supervising producer. Only seven episodes were telecast.

THE BIG IDEA
DUMONT

15 DECEMBER 1952–22 OCTOBER 1953   Half-hour documentary series on recent inventions. Donn Bennett was the host.

THE BIG ISSUE
See KEEP POSTED

BIG JOHN, LITTLE JOHN
NBC

11 SEPTEMBER 1976–3 SEPTEMBER 1977   Saturday-morning sitcom about a forty-five-year-old science teacher, who, after drinking from a "fountain of youth," changes into a twelve-year-old (and back again) at inopportune times. With Herb Edelman as the adult John Martin (Big John); Robbie Rist as the young John Martin (Little John); Joyce Bulifant as his wife, Marjorie; Mike Darnell as their son, Ricky; and Olive Dunbar as Miss Bertha Bottomly, the school principal. Created by Sherwood Schwartz and Lloyd J. Schwartz.

THE BIG MOMENT
NBC

5 JULY 1957–13 SEPTEMBER 1957   Great moments in sports history were relived on this half-hour series, hosted by former Princeton football star Bud Palmer.

THE BIG PARTY
CBS

8 OCTOBER 1959–31 DECEMBER 1959   *The Big Party* was planned as a series of fifteen variety extravaganzas which would alternate with *Playhouse 90* on Thursdays. The set for each show was a living room, with a party going on. Making his television debut, a nervous Rock Hudson hosted the premiere, which also featured a rare TV appearance by Tallulah Bankhead. The entire concept was scrapped after the New Year's Eve "Big Party" and replaced by a series of variety shows entitled *The Revlon Revue*.

THE BIG PAYOFF
NBC/CBS

Daytime: 31 DECEMBER 1951–27 MARCH 1953 (NBC); 30 MARCH 1953–23 OCTOBER 1959 (CBS) *Nighttime:* 29 JUNE 1952–14 SEPTEMBER 1952 (NBC); 21 JUNE 1953–27 SEPTEM-

BER 1953 (NBC)   This long-running game show had several hosts, including Bert Parks, Randy Merriman, Mort Lawrence, and Robert Paige; the principal prizes given away were furs, which were modeled for several seasons by Bess Myerson. Vocalist Betty Ann Grove was later featured on the show, as were Denise Lor and Susan Sayers. In addition to its eight-year daytime run, *The Big Payoff* also surfaced as a prime-time show for two summers, and during the summer of 1953 it became one of the few series to have been carried by two networks at the same time.

THE BIG PICTURE   SYNDICATED
1951–1964   Probably the most widely televised public service program in history, *The Big Picture* was the story of the United States Army, as told by the United States Army. Most of the several hundred half-hour shows were assembled from documentary footage filmed over the years by the Army Signal Corps; occasional scenes, however, were dramatized. The first series of thirteen programs was organized by Lt. Carl Bruton and offered to just one station in Washington, D.C. The experiment proved popular, and production continued under the supervision of William Brown of the Army Pictorial Center. By 1957 the show was carried by more than 350 stations in the United States—it seemed to fill the odd nooks and crannies of practically every station's program schedule. The series was also picked up by the ABC network off and on from 1953 to 1959. See also *Flight; Uncommon Valor.*

THE BIG QUESTION   CBS
9 SEPTEMBER 1951–9 MARCH 1952   This Sunday series featured debates on current issues among leading journalists and other experts. Charles Collingwood acted as moderator. The series moved from evenings to afternoons in October.

THE BIG RECORD   CBS
18 SEPTEMBER 1957–11 JUNE 1958   Popular recording artists stopped by to sing their hits on this musical variety series, hosted by Patti Page and featuring the Vic Schoen orchestra. The show's one-hour format was cut to a half hour beginning 26 March 1958.

BIG SHAMUS, LITTLE SHAMUS   CBS
29 SEPTEMBER 1979–6 OCTOBER 1979   An early casualty of the 1979–1980 season, *Big Shamus, Little Shamus* was an hour crime show about a father-and-son detective team. With Brian Dennehy as Arnie Sutter, house dick at the Hotel Ansonia in Atlantic City; Doug McKeon as Max Sutter, his 13-year-old son; George Wyner as Mr. Korman, the security chief; Kathryn Leigh Scott as Stephanie Marsh; Cynthia Sikes as Jingles, a waitress; Ty Henderson as Jerry, another hotel employee. Terry Hotchner created the series; Lee Rich and Sam H. Rolfe were the executive producers for Lorimar Productions. Canceled after just two episodes, *Big Shamus, Little Shamus* was the lowest-rated prime-time series of the 1979–1980 season.

THE BIG SHOW
See THE BIG PARTY

THE BIG SHOW   NBC
4 MARCH 1980–3 JUNE 1980   Ninety-minute variety series, with regulars Graham Chapman, Mimi Kennedy, Charlie Hill, Owen Sullivan, Edie McClurg, Paul Grimm, Joe Baker, and a dancing group known as Shabba-Doo.

THE BIG SHOWDOWN   ABC
23 DECEMBER 1974–4 JULY 1975   Jim Peck hosted this daytime game show on which contestants won points by answering questions. The highest scorer then rolled a special pair of dice for cash. If the dice came up "Show" and "Down," the contestant won the $10,000 top prize. Executive producers: Don Lipp and Ron Greenberg.

THE BIG STORY   NBC/SYNDICATED

16 SEPTEMBER 1949–28 JUNE 1957 (NBC); 1957 (SYNDICATED)   This half-hour anthology series presented stories about courageous journalists. It was hosted first by William Sloane, then by Norman Rose, Ben Grauer, finally by Burgess Meredith.

THE BIG SURPRISE (THE $100,000 BIG SURPRISE)   NBC

8 OCTOBER 1955–2 APRIL 1957   This nighttime game show began as a giveaway show, rewarding good Samaritans with valuable prizes. As big-money game shows began to gain popularity, however, the show changed to a question-and-answer format with a $100,000 top prize. The good Samaritans were replaced by contestants with areas of specialized knowledge; silent film star Francis X. Bushman, for example, won $30,000 as an expert in poetry. Jack Barry was the first host but was fired during the second season; he was replaced by Mike Wallace. Executive producer: Steve Carlin.

BIG TOP   CBS

1 JULY 1950–21 SEPTEMBER 1957   Circus program for kids, broadcast weekends from Camden, New Jersey, by WCAU-TV in Philadelphia. Jack Sterling was the ringmaster; regulars included Ed McMahon (in his first national television appearance) as a clown and strongman Dan Luri. Charles Vanda was the producer.

BIG TOWN   CBS/NBC

5 OCTOBER 1950–16 SEPTEMBER 1954 (CBS); 11 OCTOBER 1954–2 OCTOBER 1956 (NBC) This popular crime show, which began on radio in 1937 (and, for a time, featured Edward G. Robinson), was set in Big Town, U.S.A., home of the *Illustrated Press*, a crusading daily paper. It first starred Patrick McVey as reporter Steve Wilson, with Mary K. Wells as society columnist Lorelei Kilbourne; Wells was succeeded in 1951 by Julie Stevens, then by Jane Nigh, Beverly Tyler, and, late in 1954, by Trudy Wroe. In the fall of 1954 the series switched networks. Mark Stevens, who had starred in another crime show—*Martin Kane*—during the previous season, took over, not only as the star but also as producer and director. Stevens upgraded Steve Wilson from reporter to managing editor. Barry Kelley was also featured as city editor Charlie Anderson, and in the fall of 1955 Doe Avedon was added as reporter Diane Walker, replacing Lorelei Kilbourne. Grace Kelly was the guest star on the 1950 CBS premiere, entitled "The Pay-Off." *Big Town* was widely syndicated during the 1950s under several titles, including *Byline: Steve Wilson, City Assignment,* and *Heart of the City.* It was telecast live until the spring of 1952.

THE BIG VALLEY   ABC

15 SEPTEMBER 1965–19 MAY 1969   ABC's answer to *Bonanza, The Big Valley* told the story of the Barkley family, trying to make a go of it on their 30,000-acre ranch in California's San Joaquin Valley. While the Barkley ranch may not have been as large as the Ponderosa, it boasted a mine, a vineyard, an orange grove, and a black servant. With Barbara Stanwyck as the widowed Victoria Barkley, iron-willed head of the clan; Richard Long as level-headed number one son Jarrod, a lawyer; Peter Breck as hot-headed number two son Nick; Lee Majors as feisty number three son Heath (actually, Heath was the illegitimate half-Indian son of Victoria's husband); Charles Briles (1965–1966) as introspective number four son Eugene; Linda Evans as beautiful daughter Audra; and Napoleon Whiting as servant Silas.

BIG WAVE DAVE'S   CBS

9 AUGUST 1993–13 SEPTEMBER 1993   Half-hour sitcom about a Chicago stockbroker who persuaded his two pals to leave the Windy City with him to open a surf shop in Hawaii. With David Morse as the stockbroker, Dave Bell; Adam Arkin as lawyer Marshall Fisher; Patrick Breen as typing teacher Richie Lamonica; Jane Kaczmarek as Marshall's wife, Karen; and Kurtwood Smith as local guy Jack Lord. Ken Levine and David Isaacs created the series and were the executive producers.

THE BIGELOW SHOW　　　　　　　　　　　　　　　　　　NBC/CBS
14 OCTOBER 1948–7 JULY 1949 (NBC); 5 OCTOBER 1949–28 DECEMBER 1949 (CBS)
Mentalist Joseph Dunninger was featured on this half-hour variety show hosted by
ventriloquist Paul Winchell and his star dummy, Jerry Mahoney.

BIGELOW THEATER　　　　　　　　　　　　　　　　　　　　CBS
10 DECEMBER 1950–3 JUNE 1951
BIGELOW-SANFORD THEATER　　　　　　　　　　　　　DUMONT
6 SEPTEMBER 1951–27 DECEMBER 1951　　This half-hour dramatic anthology series was
seen Sundays on CBS, Thursdays on DuMont. Presentations included: "Charming
Billy," with Spring Byington (3 June); "A Man's First Debt," with Lloyd Bridges (27
September); and "TKO," with Richard Jaeckel (25 October, his first major television
role).

BIGFOOT AND WILDBOY　　　　　　　　　　　　　　　　　　ABC
2 JUNE 1979–18 AUGUST 1979　　A Saturday-morning adventure series set in the
Pacific Northwest, *Bigfoot and Wildboy* was first seen during the 1977–78 season as
one segment of *The Krofft Supershow.* It starred Ray Young as the anthropomorphic
Bigfoot and Joe Butcher as Wildboy, a human teenager who had been raised by
Bigfoot. Also featured was Yvonne Regalado as their friend, Cindy.

BIKER MICE FROM MARS　　　　　　　　　　　　　　SYNDICATED
1993–1994　　The central characters in this daily cartoon show were three Martian
mice—Modo, Throttle, and Vinnie—who escaped to Earth after their home planet
was taken over by the evil Plutarkians.

THE BIL BAIRD SHOW　　　　　　　　　　　　　　　　　　CBS
4 AUGUST 1953–29 OCTOBER 1953　　This fifteen-minute puppet show, featuring the
creations of Bil and Cora Baird, was seen on Tuesday and Thursday mornings.

BILL & TED'S EXCELLENT ADVENTURE　　　　　　　　　　FOX
28 JUNE 1992–20 SEPTEMBER 1992　　The live-action series based on the two movies
had a brief prime-time run. It featured Evan Richards as Bill S. Preston; Christopher
Kennedy as Ted Logan; Danny Breen as Mr. Keilson, who ran the hardware store
where Bill and Ted sometimes worked; Ron Lake as Bill's father, Mr. Preston;
Matthew Sanders as Ted's father, Mr. Logan; and Rick Overton as Rufus. Set in San
Dimas, California, the half-hour show was produced in Vancouver.

BILL & TED'S EXCELLENT ADVENTURES　　　　　　　　CBS/FOX
15 SEPTEMBER 1990–31 AUGUST 1991 (CBS); 14 SEPTEMBER 1991–5 SEPTEMBER 1992
(FOX)　　Saturday-morning cartoon show based on the 1989 film *Bill & Ted's Excellent Adventure,* about two Southern California teen dudes who, assisted by a holographic mentor known as Rufus, travel through time to meet various historical figures. Keanu Reeves, Alex Winter, and George Carlin, who had starred in the film,
supplied the voices of their cartoon characters. When the series moved to Fox in
1991, it was titled *Bill & Ted's Excellent Adventure.* In the summer of 1992 the live-
action version debuted: see above.

THE BILL ANDERSON SHOW　　　　　　　　　　　SYNDICATED
1966　　Country-and-western music, hosted by singer Bill Anderson.

THE BILL COSBY SHOW　　　　　　　　　　　　　　　　　NBC
14 SEPTEMBER 1969–31 AUGUST 1971　　Bill Cosby, the first black actor to costar in an
adventure series (*I Spy*), returned to TV after a year's absence in this low-key
situation comedy. In so doing, he became the first black man to star in a comedy
series since *Amos and Andy* ceased production in 1953. Cosby played Chet Kincaid,
a gym teacher at Richard Allen Holmes High School. Also featured were Lillian
Randolph (1969–1970) and Beah Richards (1970–1971) as his mother, Rose; Lee
Weaver as his brother Brian, a garbage collector; De De Young (1969) and Olga

James (1969–1971) as Brian's wife, Verna; Donald Livingston as Roger, Brian and Verna's young son; Joyce Bulifant as Mrs. Marsha Patterson, the school guidance counselor; Sid McCoy as Mr. Langford; and Joseph Perry as Max.

THE BILL CULLEN SHOW   CBS
12 FEBRUARY 1953–14 MAY 1953   A fifteen-minute Thursday-morning variety show, hosted by Bill Cullen, with Betty Brewer and the Milton DeLugg Trio.

THE BILL DANA SHOW   NBC
22 SEPTEMBER 1963–17 JANUARY 1965   Bill Dana's many appearances on *The Steve Allen Show* as José Jiminez, the easily confused Latin American, led him to his own series. On this Sunday-evening sitcom he continued to play Jiminez, now employed as a bellhop at a New York hotel. Also featured were comic Don Adams (in his first continuing TV role) as Byron Glick, the house dick; Jonathan Harris as the persnickety Mr. Phillips, hotel manager; Gary Crosby as Eddie, a fellow bellhop; and Maggie Peterson as Susie, a waitress in the coffee shop.

THE BILL GOODWIN SHOW   NBC
11 SEPTEMBER 1951–27 MARCH 1952   Bill Goodwin left his job as announcer on *The Burns and Allen Show* to host his own half-hour variety show, broadcast Tuesday and Thursday afternoons at 3:30. Regulars included Eileen Barton, Roger Dann, and the Joe Bushkin Trio. Produced and directed by Sherman Marks.

THE BILL GWINN SHOW   ABC
5 FEBRUARY 1951–21 APRIL 1952   Hosted by Bill Gwinn, this series began under the title *It Could Happen to You,* on which couples from the studio audience acted out scenes suggested by songs. In April of 1951 the show was retitled *The Bill Gwinn Show.*

BILL MOYERS' JOURNAL   PBS
14 NOVEMBER 1972–16 APRIL 1976; 5 FEBRUARY 1979–21 JUNE 1981   Magazine series hosted by Bill Moyers, who served as President Johnson's press secretary during the 1960s. During the 1972–1973 and 1975–1976 seasons Moyers's programs focused on life in America; during the 1974–1975 season Moyers reported on international issues. After a two-and-one-half-year stint with CBS, Moyers returned to PBS in 1979. See also *This Week.*

BILL MOYERS' WORLD OF IDEAS   PBS
12 SEPTEMBER 1988–18 NOVEMBER 1988   Wide-ranging half-hour interview series with writers, philosophers, historians, scientists, and other intellectuals, hosted by Bill Moyers. On most programs Moyers discussed a single topic with a single guest.

BILL NYE, THE SCIENCE GUY   SYNDICATED
1993–   Half-hour educational series for children on which Bill Nye, a former engineer at Boeing, explained the mysteries of science. Despite its use of sound effects, slapstick demonstrations, and music video-style sequences, the show was less comedic and more straightforward than its contemporary, *Beakman's World.*

BILLY   CBS
26 FEBRUARY 1979–28 APRIL 1979   Half-hour sitcom hastily scheduled by CBS to replace *Co-Ed Fever,* which the network shelved after just one showing. With Steve Guttenberg as Billy Fisher, a nineteen-year-old who fantasized a lot; James Gallery as George Fisher, his father; Peggy Pope as Alice Fisher, his mother; Paula Trueman as Gran, his grandmother; Michael Alaimo as Norville Shadrack, Billy's employer, a funeral director; and Bruce Talkington as Arthur Milliken, Billy's coworker. *Billy* was supplied by John Rich Productions.

BILLY   ABC
31 JANUARY 1992–4 JULY 1992   The second series with this title starred Scottish
comedian Billy Connolly as Billy MacGregor, the role he had played a season earlier
on *Head of the Class*. This time Billy was a college teacher who married a divorced
student so that he could remain in the country; the marriage was strictly on paper, as
Billy lived in the basement apartment in his wife's house. Also featured were Marie
Marshall as the student he married, Mary Springer; Johnny Galecki as her fourteen-
year-old, David; Natanya Ross as her ten-year-old, Laura, a violinist; Clara Bryant
as her five-year-old, Annie, a pianist; Kathy Wagner as Giselle; and Mary Gross as
Phoebe.

BILLY BOONE AND COUSIN KIB   CBS
9 JULY 1950–27 AUGUST 1950   A summer replacement for *Mr. I. Magination,* this
half-hour children's show starred Carroll "Kib" Colby and Patti Milligan. *Billy
Boone* was an animated figure whose adventures were drawn by Colby. Judy Dupuy
produced the series.

THE BILLY CRYSTAL COMEDY HOUR   NBC
30 JANUARY 1982–27 FEBRUARY 1982   Another unsuccessful attempt by NBC to fill
its 10:00 P.M. time slot on Saturdays. Fresh from *Soap,* Billy Crystal hosted the series,
with help from Jane Anderson, Monica Ganas, Tino Insana, and Phyllis Katz. Music
was provided by Van Dyke Parks.

THE BILLY DANIELS SHOW   ABC
5 OCTOBER 1952–28 DECEMBER 1952   One of few blacks to host a variety series, singer
Billy Daniels ("That Old Black Magic") emceed his own fifteen-minute show on
Sunday evenings. Benny Payne and Jimmy Blaine were also featured.

BILLY GRAHAM CRUSADES (HOUR OF DECISION)   ABC/SYNDICATED
30 SEPTEMBER 1951–21 FEBRUARY 1954 (ABC); 1954– (SYNDICATED)   One of
the first evangelists to utilize television, Billy Graham first appeared on a fifteen-
minute series entitled *Hour of Decision*. Since that time, the *Billy Graham Crusades,*
taped at cities throughout the world, have been widely telecast, usually as specials.

BILLY JAMES HARGIS AND HIS ALL-AMERICAN KIDS   SYNDICATED
1972   Religious show, featuring the Reverend Billy James Hargis and several of his
youthful followers, known as the All-American Kids.

BILLY ROSE'S PLAYBILL   ABC
3 OCTOBER 1950–27 MARCH 1951   Theatrical producer Billy Rose hosted this half-
hour dramatic anthology series.

THE BING CROSBY SHOW   ABC
14 SEPTEMBER 1964–14 JUNE 1965   An established recording and motion picture star,
Bing Crosby had made few forays into television before taking the big plunge with
this 1964 sitcom. In it he played Bing Collins, an architectural designer. Also featured
were Beverly Garland as his wife, Ellie; Diane Sherry as their daughter Janice; Carol
Faylen as their daughter Joyce; and Frank McHugh as the handyman, Willie Walters.
The cast usually performed one or two musical numbers each week. The series was
produced by Steven Gethers for Bing Crosby Productions and was telecast Mondays
immediately preceding *Ben Casey,* another Bing Crosby Productions venture.

BIOGRAPHY   SYNDICATED
1962   Mike Wallace hosted this self-explanatory documentary series on which the
lives of notables were presented through the use of film clips and interviews.

BIOGRAPHY   A&E
5 JANUARY 1988–   The second series of this title was similar to the first, presenting
filmed biographies of notable people, usually in an hour format. Peter Graves and

Jack Perkins hosted. The series began in 1988 as a weekly program, without a continuing title; each week's presentation bore the name of its subject. By 1992 the *Biography* title had stuck, and in May 1994 it became a nightly series.

THE BIONIC SIX   SYNDICATED
1987   The six members of the Bennett family, who possessed bionic powers, battled Dr. Scarab on this cartoon series.

THE BIONIC WOMAN   ABC/NBC
14 JANUARY 1976–4 MAY 1977 (ABC); 10 SEPTEMBER 1977–2 SEPTEMBER 1978 (NBC)
A spinoff from *The Six Million Dollar Man, The Bionic Woman* starred Lindsay Wagner, a newcomer to television, as Jaime Somers. Severely injured in a skydiving mishap, Jaime was outfitted with bionic legs, a bionic right arm, and a bionic right ear. Employed as an OSI operative, she had the cover occupation of a schoolteacher at the Ventura Air Force Base school. Also featured were Richard Anderson as OSI topsider Oscar Goldman; Martin E. Brooks as Dr. Rudy Wells, OSI physician; Sam Chew, Jr., as Mark Russell, another OSI employee; Ford Rainey as Jim; and Martha Scott as Helen. In 1977, the series was dropped by ABC and picked up by NBC; it was one of the few shows to switch networks during the 1970s. As a result of the switch costars Richard Anderson and Martin E. Brooks, who continued to appear on *The Six Million Dollar Man* over at ABC, became two of the very few (if not the only two) performers ever to play the same role simultaneously on two series aired by different networks. Added to the cast in the fall of 1977 was Maximillian, the bionic German shepherd. The series was created by Kenneth Johnson, and its executive producer was Harve Bennett for Universal Television. Wagner returned in several made-for-TV movies: *The Return of the Six Million Dollar Man and the Bionic Woman,* with Lee Majors and Richard Anderson (17 May 1987, NBC), *Bionic Showdown: The Six Million Dollar Man and the Bionic Woman,* with Majors, Anderson, and Brooks (30 April 1989, NBC); and *Bionic Ever After?* with Majors, Anderson, and Brooks (29 November 1994, CBS).

BIRDLAND   ABC
5 JANUARY 1994–9 FEBRUARY 1994; 14 APRIL 1994–21 APRIL 1994   Hour dramatic series set at Riverside Hospital in Oakland, California. With Brian Dennehy as Dr. Brian McKenzie, the caring, accessible and sensitive chief of psychiatry; Lindsay Frost as Dr. Jesse Lane, who was also McKenzie's love interest; John Rothman as Dr. Alan Bergman, hospital administrator; Leslie Mann as Mary, a shy nurse; C. C. H. Pounder as Lucy, a psychiatric nurse; Jeff Williams as Dr. Lewis Niles; Kevin J. O'Connor as psychiatric patient Steve Horner; David Packer as Zuchetti; and Julio Oscar Mechoso as Hector, a gay man who was the head orderly (Mechoso had also played an orderly named Hector on the 1991 sitcom, *Stat*). Walter F. Parkes and Scott Frank created the series.

BIRDMAN AND THE GALAXY TRIO   NBC
9 SEPTEMBER 1967–28 DECEMBER 1968   Saturday-morning cartoon series produced by Hanna-Barbera, featuring the adventures of Ray Randall (alias Birdman), who was endowed with the usual array of super powers by Ra, the Egyptian sun god, and fought evildoers. The series's second segment, "The Galaxy Trio," followed three superheroes—Vapor Man, Galaxy Girl, and Meteor Man—as they traveled through space aboard the Condor I.

BISHOP SHEEN
See LIFE IS WORTH LIVING

THE BISKITTS   CBS
17 SEPTEMBER 1983–1 SEPTEMBER 1984; 30 MARCH 1985–7 SEPTEMBER 1985   In this Saturday-morning cartoon series, set at Biskitt Island, a group of miniature dogs—the Biskitts—were the guardians of the crown jewels of their late king; the clever

canines thwarted the efforts of the king's brother, Max, and his dimwitted jester, Shecky, to seize the jewels.

BIZARRE SHOWTIME

1980–1985   Half-hour series of comedy sketches, hosted by John Byner, and later packaged (without the racier segments) for broadcast syndication.

BLACK JOURNAL PBS

1968–1976   Long-running public affairs program focusing on issues of concern to black Americans. Produced and hosted after 1970 by Tony Brown at New York's WNET, the show was aired in both an hour and a half-hour format. It was one of the few programs on which controversial black leaders such as Angela Davis, Bobby Seale, and Malcolm X were able to appear. Early in 1976 the program experimented with a talk-show format; after the program was dropped by PBS, Brown decided to syndicate the program commercially (see *Tony Brown's Journal*).

BLACK OMNIBUS SYNDICATED

1973   Talent showcase for black performers, hosted by James Earl Jones.

BLACK PERSPECTIVE ON THE NEWS PBS

1973–1979   Black journalists interviewed newsmakers on this educational series produced by Acel Moore and Reginald Bryant (who also served as moderator) for Philadelphia's WHYY-TV.

THE BLACK ROBE NBC

18 MAY 1949–6 APRIL 1950   Created by Phillips Lord (creator of *Gangbusters*), this series recreated court cases. In its early weeks, it was entitled *Police Night Court*. To achieve realism, nonprofessionals were used as witnesses and attorneys. Frankie Thomas, Sr., appeared as the judge, and John Green played the court clerk. The live series was usually seen Thursdays.

BLACK SADDLE NBC/ABC

10 JANUARY 1959–5 SEPTEMBER 1959 (NBC); 2 OCTOBER 1959–30 SEPTEMBER 1960 (ABC)   Half-hour western starring Peter Breck as Clay Culhane, a former gunfighter who is now a frontier lawyer. With Russell Johnson as Marshal Gib Scott; Anna Lisa as widow Nora Travers, proprietor of the Marathon Hotel. Set in Latigo, a town in New Mexico Territory. Antony Ellis was the producer.

BLACK SHEEP SQUADRON

See BAA BAA BLACK SHEEP

BLACK TIE AFFAIR NBC

29 MAY 1993–19 JUNE 1993   Short-lived, quirky sitcom created by Jay Tarses (*Buffalo Bill, The 'Slap' Maxwell Story, The Days and Nights of Molly Dodd*). Tarses, who was given a thirteen-episode commitment and creative control by NBC in 1992, intended his show to examine contemporary adult relationships in a film noirish milieu; he titled it *Smoldering Lust*. The cast included Bradley Whitford as Dave Brodsky, a part-time private eye who ran a used record store on the side; Kate Capshaw as Margo Cody, who hired Brodsky to watch her philandering husband; John Calvin as the husband, Christopher Cody; and Alison Elliott as Eve Saskatchewan, in whom Chris Cody was interested. Although production was completed by September 1992, the network waited eight more months before deciding to run it. The series debuted in a highly inauspicious time slot—10 P.M. on the Saturday night of Memorial Day weekend—and with a few changes: NBC had rechristened it *Black Tie Affair* (its original working title) and had stripped the lyrics from the show's theme song. Hardly surprised when the series was canceled after five telecasts, an infuriated Tarses vowed never to work for NBC again. The series's evolution and evaporation was chronicled by Vance Muse in his 1994 book, *We Bombed in Burbank*.

THE BLACK TULIP   SYNDICATED

1972   Dumas's story, set in seventeenth-century France and Holland, was told in a six-part miniseries produced in England and aired as part of *Family Classics Theatre*. It starred Simon Ward as Cornelius von Baerle, a young Dutchman trying to cultivate the legendary black tulip.

BLACKADDER   A&E

3 JANUARY 1987–7 DECEMBER 1989   A satiric look at British history, starring Rowan Atkinson as Edmund, the Black Adder, and Tony Robinson as his faithful servant, Baldrick. Produced in England, the series was shown in four parts: *The Black Adder* was set during the War of the Roses in the late fifteenth century, *Blackadder II* during Elizabethan times, *Blackadder the Third* during the eighteenth century, and *Blackadder Goes Forth* in World War I.

BLACKE'S MAGIC   NBC

5 JANUARY 1986–11 JUNE 1986; 29 JULY 1988–9 SEPTEMBER 1988   An hour crime show from the team responsible for *Murder, She Wrote:* Peter Fischer, Richard Levinson, and William Link. Here, Hal Linden and Harry Morgan starred as a son-and-father detective duo, Alexander Blacke (a former magician) and his dad, Leonard, a semi-retired con artist. Reruns were shown during the summer of 1988.

BLACKOUT   CBS

4 JANUARY 1988–1 APRIL 1988   Bob Goen hosted this daytime game show on which two celebrity-and-contestant teams competed. One member of the team was given twenty seconds to describe a word missing from a phrase; when that twenty-second playback was provided to the teammate, the other team could activate its "blackout" button to delete up to seven seconds of the description. The winning team had the opportunity to play a bonus round for a top prize of $10,000.

BLACKSTAR   CBS

12 SEPTEMBER 1981–11 SEPTEMBER 1982   Saturday-morning cartoon series about the adventures of John Blackstar, an astronaut who, while in space, slipped through a black hole to a planet ruled by a tyrant; he then sought to organize a rebellion there.

THE BLAIR & RAITT SHOW (THE CHEVY SHOW)   NBC

7 JUNE 1959–20 SEPTEMBER 1959   Janet Blair and John Raitt cohosted this musical variety hour, a summer replacement for *The Dinah Shore Show*.

BLANK CHECK   NBC

6 JANUARY 1975–4 JULY 1975   A dull daytime game show on which panelists tried to outguess each other in selecting digits that form the sum of a "blank check." Executive producer: Jack Barry. Hosted by Art James.

BLANKETY BLANKS   ABC

21 APRIL 1975–27 JUNE 1975   Bill Cullen hosted this short-lived daytime game show on which panelists tried to guess puns. Executive producer: Bob Stewart.

BLANSKY'S BEAUTIES   ABC

12 FEBRUARY 1977–27 JUNE 1977   Following the cancellation of her eponymous series, Nancy Walker was immediately cast in a new sitcom, which was in turn canceled; she thus earned the dubious distinction of starring in two unsuccessful series in a single season. In *Blansky's Beauties* she played Nancy Blansky, the manager and den mother of a troupe of Las Vegas showgirls. Featured were Eddie Mekka (also of *Laverne and Shirley*) as her nephew, Joey DeLuca, the troupe's dance instructor; Scott Baio as Anthony DeLuca, her worldwise twelve-year-old nephew; Lynda Goodfriend as Sunshine (Ethel Akalino), the klutzy showgirl; Caren Kaye as Bambi Benton, the daffy one; Rhonda Bates as Arkansas, the tall one; Taaffe O'Connell as Hillary Prentiss, the one who knew the boss; Bond Gideon as Lovely Carson; Gerri Reddick as Jackie Outlaw; Elaine Bolton as Bridget Muldoon; Jill Owens as

Misty Karamazov; Shirley Kirkes as Cochise (Gladys Littlefeather); Antonette Yuskis as Sylvia Silver; George Pentecost as Horace (Stubs) Wilmington, manager of the Oasis Hotel; Pat Morita (on loan from *Happy Days*) as Arnold; and Blackjack the Great Dane. Garry K. Marshall, Bob Brunner, and Arthur Silver created the series; Marshall, Edward K. Milkis, and Thomas L. Miller were the executive producers. Three members of the show's cast turned up in a 1978 sitcom which was also set in Las Vegas: see *Who's Watching the Kids.*

BLESS THIS HOUSE CBS
11 SEPTEMBER 1995–17 JANUARY 1996   Obviously inspired by *The Honeymooners*, this half-hour sitcom starred Andrew Clay (the raunchy standup comic formerly known as Andrew Dice Clay) as postal worker Burt Clayton, who lived in a cramped New York apartment with his wife and two children; Cathy Moriarty as wife Alice Clayton, who worked as a cashier; Raegan Kotz as twelve-year-old daughter Danny; Sam Gifaldi as young son Sean; Don Stark as Lenny, Burt's co-worker and neighbor; Molly Price as Lenny's wife, Phyllis, Alice's best friend; Wren T. Brown as Cuba, another postal worker; Patricia Healy as neighbor Vicki Shetski, a single mother; and Kimberly Cullum as Vicki's daughter, Jane, who hung out at the Claytons' apartment.

BLIND AMBITION CBS
20 MAY 1977–23 MAY 1979   A four-part, eight-hour docudrama on Watergate, based on the books *Blind Ambition* by former White House counsel John Dean and *Mo* by Maureen Dean, his wife. Principal players included: Martin Sheen as John Dean; Theresa Russell as Maureen Dean; Rip Torn as Richard Nixon; Lawrence Pressman as H. R. Haldeman; Graham Jarvis as John Ehrlichman; John Randolph as John Mitchell; Christopher Guest as Jeb Magruder; Michael Callan as Chuck Colson; Ed Flanders as Dean's lawyer, Charlie Shaffer. The scenes in the Oval Office between Dean and Nixon were all verbatim extracts from the official White House tapes. George Schaefer and Renée Valente produced the series.

BLIND DATE ABC/NBC/DUMONT
5 MAY 1949–20 SEPTEMBER 1951 (ABC); 7 JUNE 1952–19 JULY 1952 (NBC); 9 JUNE 1953–15 SEPTEMBER 1953 (DUMONT)   A precursor of *The Dating Game, Blind Date* began on radio in 1943. It was the first TV game show to be hosted by a woman: Arlene Francis (Jan Murray hosted the version in 1953). The format was similar to that of *The Dating Game;* two eligible college men talked with a model, who could not see her hopeful suitors. She then chose one of the men to be her date.

BLOCKBUSTERS NBC
27 OCTOBER 1980–23 APRIL 1982; 5 JANUARY 1987–1 MAY 1987   On this daytime game show, a solo player competed against two persons from the same family; by answering questions, each side tried to connect a chain of boxes on a grid. The winner(s) then played a "Gold Rush" round for extra cash. Bill Cullen hosted the 1982 version, Bill Rafferty the 1987 version.

BLONDIE NBC
4 JANUARY 1957–27 SEPTEMBER 1957   The first of two short-running adaptations of Chic Young's long-running comic strip. With Pamela Britton as Blondie Bumstead, hard-working housewife; Arthur Lake as Dagwood Bumstead, her bumbling husband (Lake had played Dagwood to Penny Singleton's Blondie in a score of movies during the 1940s), an architect; Stuffy Singer as teenage son Alexander; Ann Barnes as preteen daughter Cookie; Florenz Ames as J. C. Dithers, Bumstead's blustery boss, president of Dithers Construction Company; and Hal Peary as next-door neighbor Herb Woodley.

BLONDIE CBS
26 SEPTEMBER 1968–9 JANUARY 1969   The second attempt at turning the comic strip into a successful series also failed. This effort featured Patricia Harty as Blondie

Bumstead; Will Hutchins as Dagwood; Peter Robbins as son Alexander; Pamelyn Ferdin as daughter Cookie; Jim Backus as boss J. C. Dithers; Henny Backus (Jim's real-life wife) as Cora Dithers; Bryan O'Byrne as neighbor Herb Woodley; and Bobbi Jordan as Tootsie Woodley.

BLOSSOM
NBC

3 JANUARY 1991–20 MARCH 1995; 22 MAY 1995–6 JUNE 1995   Half-hour sitcom, starring Mayim Bialik as fourteen-year-old Blossom Russo, who lived with her divorced father and her two older brothers; Ted Wass as her dad, musician Nick Russo; Joey Lawrence as brother Joey; Michael Stoyanov as brother Anthony, a recovering substance abuser; Jenna Von Oy as Blossom's fast-talking best friend, Six LeMeure; Barnard Hughes (1991–1994) as Blossom's maternal grandfather, Buzz Richman; David Lascher (1992–1994) as Blossom's boyfriend, Vinnie; Samaria Graham (1993–1995) as Shelly, who married Anthony; Finola Hughes (1993–1995) as Nick's new girlfriend, Carol (they were married in the fall of 1994); and Courtney Chase (1993–1995) as Carol's precocious young daughter, Kennedy. During the early seasons the series employed fantasy sequences (many featuring guest stars), but this device was downplayed in later years. *Blossom* became especially popular with teen and preteen girls, many of whom identified with the title character; other fans helped make Joey Lawrence a teen idol and recording star. Don Reo created the series, and Bill Bixby directed many of the episodes in 1991 and 1992 before his death from cancer in 1993.

THE BLUE ANGEL
CBS

6 JULY 1954–12 OCTOBER 1954   This Tuesday-night variety series was a summer replacement for *See It Now.* Orson Bean and Polly Bergen hosted the series, set at a posh New York nightclub.

THE BLUE ANGELS
SYNDICATED

1960   The adventures of the Blue Angels, a precision squadron of four U.S. Navy flyers who tour the country giving exhibitions. With Dennis Cross as Commander Arthur Richards, head of the squadron; Warner Jones as Captain Wilbur Scott; Don Gordon as Lieutenant Hank Bertelli; Mike Galloway as Lieutenant Russ MacDonald; Robert Knapp as crewman Zeke Powers; and Ross Elliott as crewman Cort Ryker. Simeon G. Gallu, Jr., produced the half-hour show.

BLUE JEAN NETWORK
SYNDICATED

1981   Another hour of rock music.

THE BLUE KNIGHT
CBS

17 DECEMBER 1975–27 OCTOBER 1976   Joseph Wambaugh's novel about a veteran cop on the beat was first telecast as an eight-hour mini-series in 1973 (shown on four consecutive nights, 13 November–16 November), starring William Holden as patrolman Bumper Morgan. It was Holden's first serious dramatic role on television (he'd played himself on an *I Love Lucy* episode some eighteen years earlier). Holden was not interested in doing a series, however. George Kennedy was then signed for the part. The series pilot was aired 9 May 1975, and the series itself was selected as a midseason replacement for *Kate McShane.* Although the series was renewed in 1976, competition from ABC's *Charlie's Angels* proved too strong. Also appearing (in the last three episodes) was Barbara Rhoades as Carrie Williams, Bumper's lady friend. Executive producers: Lee Rich and Philip Capice.

BLUE LIGHT
ABC

12 JANUARY 1966–31 AUGUST 1966   This half-hour adventure series starred Robert Goulet as David March, a double agent working for the U.S.A. in the intelligence unit of the Third Reich. March's code name was "Blue Light." With Christine Carere as Suzanne Duchard, his confidante.

BLUE SKIES   CBS

13 JUNE 1988–1 AUGUST 1988   Hour family drama, with Tom Wopat as newly remarried widower Frank Cobb, who left his advertising job in San Francisco and returned to his Oregon home town to join his father at the family's woodworking mill; Season Hubley as his new wife, Annie Cobb; Alyson Croft as Frank's twelve-year-old daughter, Sarah; Kim Hauser as Annie's twelve-year-old daughter, Zoe; Danny Gerard as Frank's ten-year-old son, Charley; and Pat Hingle as Frank's father, Henry.

BLUE SKIES   ABC

12 SEPTEMBER 1994–31 OCTOBER 1994   The second series with this title was a sitcom set at the Cambridge, Massachusetts, headquarters of the Blue Skies Trading Company, a mail-order catalog business. In the cast were Corey Parker as co-owner Joel Goodman; Matt Roth as co-owner Russell Evans; Julia Campbell as Ellie Baskin, a Harvard MBA taken on by Joel and Russell as a partner; Richard Kind as Kenny, the crooked accountant; Stephen Tobolowsky as Oak, the products tester; and Adilah Barnes as Eve, the secretary. John Peaslee and Judd Pillot created the series, which was axed after seven weeks. Peaslee and Pillot then cast Campbell, Kind, and Tobolowsky in *Blue Skies*'s eventual replacement, *A Whole New Ballgame*.

BLUE THUNDER   ABC

6 JANUARY 1984–7 SEPTEMBER 1984   Based on the 1983 movie, this hour crime show focused on the Blue Thunder Unit, a Los Angeles police unit which operated a special helicopter equipped with (among other things) an electric cannon, night sensors, airborne video gear, laser tracking systems, and a "whisper mode" that enabled it to run almost noiselessly. James Farentino starred as its pilot, gutsy Frank Chaney. Also featured were Dana Carvey as his observer, Clinton "Jafo" Wonderlove ("Jafo" is the acronym for "Just Another Frustrated Observer"); Sandy McPeak as Captain Ed Braddock, the unit commander; Dick Butkus and Bubba Smith as the ground support team, Officers "Ski" Butowski and "Bubba" Kelsey; and Ann Cooper as Officer J. J. Douglas. See also *Airwolf*.

BLUES BY BARGY   CBS

24 JANUARY 1949–6 JULY 1950   Singer-pianist Jeane Bargy was the star of this durable musical show. It was usually broadcast several times a week, sometimes in a fifteen-minute format, other times in a thirty-minute format.

BOB   CBS

18 SEPTEMBER 1992–31 MAY 1993; 22 OCTOBER 1993–12 NOVEMBER 1993; 27 DECEMBER 1993   Bob Newhart starred in his third sitcom as Bob McKay, who had created a comic book, *Mad Dog*, which had lasted for twelve issues in the 1950s; the title character was a veterinarian with the adrenal glands of a Doberman pinscher. After years of designing greeting cards, McKay was asked to bring back his cartoon superhero. Also featured were Carlene Watkins as Bob's wife, Kaye; Cynthia Stevenson as their myopic daughter, Trisha; Ruth Kobart as animator Iris Frankel; Timothy Fall as inker Chad Pfefferle; Andrew Bilgore as rookie employee Albie Strauss; John Cygan as story writer (or "graphic novelist") Harlan Stone, who wanted Mad Dog to become a bloodthirsty vigilante rather than a good guy; and Michael Cumpsty as the voice of Chuck Terhorst, head of the parent company (American Canadian Transcontinental Communications Co.), who insisted that Bob and Harlan work together. Lisa Kudrow joined the cast in the spring of 1993 as Trisha's roommate, Kathy. *Bob* finished the 1992–1993 season in a disappointing 62nd place among prime-time series. It was revived for a few episodes in the fall of 1993, with a different format: Mad Dog had died again, and Bob was asked to head up the greeting card company he had previously worked for. Newhart, Watkins, and Stevenson were retained from the old cast, and four new regulars were added: Betty White as Sylvia Schmidt, the owner; Jere Burns as her son, Pete; Eric Allan Kramer as Whitney van de Bunt; and Megan Cavanaugh as Chris Szelinski.

BOB AND CAROL AND TED AND ALICE   ABC

26 SEPTEMBER 1973–7 NOVEMBER 1973   This pale adaptation of the 1969 film comedy about mate swapping was the first fatality of the 1973–1974 season. With Robert Urich as film director Bob Sanders; Anne Archer as his wife, Carol; David Spielberg as attorney Ted Henderson; Anita Gillette as his wife, Alice; Jodie Foster as Elizabeth, Ted and Alice's preteen daughter; and Brad Savage as Sean, Bob and Carol's young son.

THE BOB AND RAY SHOW   NBC

26 NOVEMBER 1951–1 FEBRUARY 1952; 12 JULY 1952–16 AUGUST 1952; 7 OCTOBER 1952–23 JUNE 1953; 27 APRIL 1953–28 SEPTEMBER 1953   Bob (Elliott) and Ray (Goulding), two low-key satirists, first joined forces on a Boston radio station in the late 1940s. Though they made several forays into television (they also did a Broadway show, *The Two and Only,* in 1972), their unique brand of humor seemed best suited to radio. Their first TV program, a fifteen-minute affair, was seen Mondays through Fridays at 7:15 P.M. and featured Audrey Meadows. During the summer of 1952 they hosted a half-hour show on Saturdays, which featured Cloris Leachman. In the fall of that year, they were again seen in a fifteen-minute format; this show, also known as *Club Embassy* or *Club Time,* featured Audrey Meadows (again) and singer Mindy Carson, who replaced Bob and Ray as host in midseason. In late April of 1953 they began a second fifteen-minute show, which was seen Mondays at 7:30 P.M. Bob and Ray later cohosted a game show, *The Name's the Same,* in 1955, and were regulars on *Happy Days,* a 1970 summer series. Goulding died in 1989.

THE BOB CONSIDINE SHOW   NBC/ABC

20 JANUARY 1951–19 JANUARY 1954 (NBC); 11 JULY 1954–29 AUGUST 1954 (ABC)   Syndicated columnist Bob Considine had two network shows of his own. The first, a fifteen-minute weekly show, featured comments and interviews with guests; it was also known as *On the Line with Considine.* The second show was seen once a week as a summer replacement for *The Walter Winchell Show.* Considine was later one of the regulars on *Tonight! America After Dark,* the short-lived NBC late-night show that replaced Steve Allen's *Tonight* show in 1957.

THE BOB CRANE SHOW   NBC

6 MARCH 1975–19 JUNE 1975   Insipid sitcom about a middle-aged man who decided to go to medical school. With Bob Crane as Bob Wilcox; Trisha Hart as his wife, Ellie Wilcox; Erica Petal as daughter Pam; Ronny Graham as Ernest Busso, their eccentric landlord, an inventor; Jack Fletcher as Lyle Ingersoll, dean of the medical school; Todd Susman as fellow student Marvin Susman; and James Sutorius as student Jerry Mallory. The half-hour show was produced by Norman S. Powell and Martin Cohan for MTM Enterprises. Bob Crane, a one-time disc jockey who had been featured on *The Donna Reed Show* and had starred in *Hogan's Heroes,* was found murdered in an Arizona hotel room in June of 1978.

THE BOB CROSBY SHOW   CBS/NBC

14 SEPTEMBER 1953–30 AUGUST 1957 (CBS); 14 JUNE 1958–6 SEPTEMBER 1958 (NBC)   Bing's younger brother was a popular bandleader during the 1930s and 1940s; Bob Crosby's Bobcats even appeared on television in 1939. Crosby later hosted several radio shows, including *The Crosby Music Shop* and *The Crosby Night Shift.* The first of the two television series he hosted was a half-hour daytime show, broadcast Monday through Friday; it featured the Modernaires (who had sung with Crosby on radio), Joan O'Brien, Jack Narz, and (in later seasons) Bob's daughter Cathy Crosby. Bob's second series was an hour-long prime-time effort, a summer replacement for *The Perry Como Show;* it featured singer Gretchen Wyler, the Peter Gennaro dancers, the Clay Warnick singers, The Carl Hoff orchestra, and (at the opening and closing) clown Emmett Kelly. Produced by Louis DaPron.

THE BOB CUMMINGS SHOW
See LOVE THAT BOB

THE BOB CUMMINGS SHOW   CBS

5 OCTOBER 1961–1 MARCH 1962   Shortly after the demise of *Love That Bob,* Bob Cummings returned in another situation comedy strikingly similar to the earlier one. This time Bob played Bob Carson, a wealthy girl-crazy adventurer who owned three airplanes (including one that converted into an automobile) and lived near a desert hotel with a private airstrip. Murvyn Vye costarred as Bob's sidekick, Lionel, and Roberta Shore played "Hank" Geogerty, the daughter of the hotel owner. Broadcast on Thursday nights, the show was clobbered in the ratings by *Dr. Kildare.*

BOB HOPE PRESENTS THE CHRYSLER THEATER   NBC

4 OCTOBER 1963–6 SEPTEMBER 1967   Hour-long dramatic anthology series hosted by Bob Hope. Interspersed throughout each season were *The Bob Hope Specials,* musical or variety hours with Hope and guest stars. Dramatic presentations on the anthology series included Aleksandr Solzhenitzyn's "One Day in the Live of Ivan Denisovich" (8 November 1963); "Double Jeopardy," with a rare television appearance by Lauren Bacall (8 January 1965); "The War and Eric Kurtz," with David Carradine (his first major TV role, 5 March 1965); and "Blind Man's Bluff," with Susan Clark (her first major TV role, 8 February 1967).

THE BOB HOPE SHOW   NBC

12 OCTOBER 1953–22 MAY 1956   One of the world's best-known personalities and America's premier comedian, Bob Hope's regular appearances on television during the 1950s were on a monthly basis. During the 1952–1953 season he hosted *The Colgate Comedy Hour* on Sundays every four weeks; during the 1953–1954 and 1954–1955 seasons he was seen once a month on Tuesdays, replacing Milton Berle; during the 1955–1956 season he was also seen on Tuesdays, alternating with Milton Berle, Martha Raye, and Dinah Shore. Hope's famous theme song, "Thanks for the Memory," was written by Ralph Rainger and Leo Robin.

THE BOB NEWHART SHOW   NBC

11 OCTOBER 1961–13 JUNE 1962   Bob Newhart, a onetime accountant, was one of the most successful of the "new wave" of stand-up comics who appeared on television in the late 1950s. Newhart's trademark was a telephone; many of his monologues were done as telephone conversations. Nicknamed the "button-down comedian" (because of his button-down shirts), he headlined a thirty-minute variety series in 1961. It was adored by the critics, if not by a large viewing audience, and won both an Emmy and a Peabody award in 1962. Other regulars included Jackie Joseph, Kay Westfall, Jack Grinnage, Mickey Manners, Pearl Shear, June Ericson, Andy Albin, and announcer Dan Sorkin.

THE BOB NEWHART SHOW   CBS

16 SEPTEMBER 1972–2 SEPTEMBER 1978   Bob Newhart's second eponymous series, his first situation comedy, was a clear success. In it he played Bob Hartley, a Chicago psychologist. With Suzanne Pleshette as his wife Emily, a third-grade teacher; Bill Daily as divorced neighbor Howard Borden, a 747 navigator; Peter Bonerz as orthodontist Jerry Robinson, whose office is on the same floor as Bob's; Marcia Wallace as their receptionist Carol (Kester) Bondurant; Patricia Smith (1972–1973) as Margaret Hoover, the Hartleys' neighbor; Pat Finley (1974–1976) as Ellen, Bob's sister; Will MacKenzie (1975–1978) as travel agent Larry Bondurant, who married Carol. For several seasons Bob's therapy group included Jack Riley as paranoid Elliott Carlin; Florida Friebus as kindly Mrs. Bakerman; John Fiedler as timid Mr. Peterson; Renee Lippin as shy Michelle; and Noam Pitlik and Daniel J. Travanti as obnoxious Mr. Gianelli. Created by David Davis and Lorenzo Music. Executive producers (and script supervisors): Tom Patchett and Jay Tarses (a former comedy team). The show's 142 episodes were produced by MTM Enterprises. CBS aired a series retrospective, "The Bob Newhart 20th 19th Anniversary Special," on 23 March 1991. Marcia Wallace reprised her role in an episode of *Murphy Brown,* which aired 14 March 1994.

THE BOB SMITH SHOW
See THE GULF ROAD SHOW

BOBBIE GENTRY'S HAPPINESS HOUR   CBS
5 JUNE 1974–26 JUNE 1974   A four-week summer replacement for *The Sonny and Cher Comedy Hour,* hosted by singer Bobbie Gentry, who is best known for her 1967 record, "Ode to Billy Joe."

THE BOBBY DARIN AMUSEMENT CO.   NBC
27 JULY 1972–7 SEPTEMBER 1972; 19 JANUARY 1973–27 APRIL 1973   Born Walden Robert Cassotto, Bobby Darin burst on the entertainment scene in 1958 with a hit record: "Splish Splash." After several more hits (including "Mack the Knife"), a marriage to Sandra Dee, and a string of movies, he disappeared from show business in 1967. He returned early in the 1970s and was given his own series in 1972, a summer replacement for *The Dean Martin Show.* The series was revived that winter as a midseason replacement. Regulars included Dick Bakalyan, Steve Landesberg, and Rip Taylor. Stricken as a child with rheumatic fever, Darin had had two artificial valves inserted in his heart in 1971; following open heart surgery to correct a malfunctioning valve, Darin died on December 20, 1973, at the age of thirty-seven.

THE BOBBY GOLDSBORO SHOW   SYNDICATED
1972   Half-hour variety series hosted by pop singer Bobby Goldsboro. The announcer was a frog puppet named Calvin Calaveras. Goldsboro's musical career began as a guitarist for Roy Orbison; his hits have included "See the Funny Little Clown," "Little Things," and "Honey."

THE BOBBY LORD SHOW   SYNDICATED
1966   A half hour of country-and-western music, hosted by Bobby Lord.

THE BOBBY VINTON SHOW   SYNDICATED
1975–1976   Hosted by singer Bobby Vinton, this half-hour musical variety series was produced in Toronto. Vinton began his recording career as a clarinetist and bandleader but is best known as a vocalist. His hits (dating back to 1962) have included "Roses Are Red," "Blue on Blue," "Blue Velvet," and "My Melody of Love." Executive producers: Allan Blye and Chris Bearde.

BOBBY'S WORLD   FOX
8 SEPTEMBER 1990–   Fox's first entry in the Saturday-morning cartoon arena, *Bobby's World* looked at life through the eyes of four-year-old Bobby Generic, who lived in suburbia with his parents, older brother and sister, and dog Roger. Bobby was based on a character created by actor/comedian Howie Mandel, who supplied the voice and who appeared in live form at the beginning and end of each program. John Tesh (of *Entertainment Tonight*) composed the theme music. In the fall of 1994 the series moved to Fox's weekday schedule.

BOBO THE HOBO   SYNDICATED
1956   A filmed color anthology series for children, starring a repertory company of puppets. The puppets' limbs were manually controlled, but their jaws and lips were operated by a person wearing a special helmet which electronically transmitted the wearer's jaw and lip movements to the puppets. Samuel H. Evans invented the helmet device and co-produced the series with Lorraine Lester. Brett Morrison supplied the voice of Bobo, leader of the puppet troupe.

BODIES OF EVIDENCE   CBS
18 JUNE 1992–27 AUGUST 1992; 30 MARCH 1993–28 MAY 1993   Hour crime show focusing on the homicide squad of the Metropolitan Police Force. With Lee Horsley as Lt. Ben Carroll; George Clooney as Det. Ryan Walker; Kate McNeil as new member Det. Nora Houghton; Al Fann as Det. Walt Stratton; Francis X. McCarthy as Nora's father, Sgt. Tim Houghton; Michele Scarabelli as TV reporter Holly Ben-

nett; Lorraine Toussaint as pathologist Dr. Mary Rocket; and Leslie Jordan as Lemar the lab man.

BODY BY JAKE   SYNDICATED
1988–1990   An exercise program with Jake Steinfeld, bodybuilder to the stars, who charged up to $200 per half hour for private workouts.

THE BODY IN QUESTION   PBS
1980   Author-actor-director-physician Jonathan Miller hosted this British-produced series on human anatomy and physiology.

BODY LANGUAGE   CBS
4 JUNE 1984–3 JANUARY 1986   Tom Kennedy hosted this daytime game show on which two celebrity-and-contestant teams competed. In the "body language" segment, one member tried to pantomime a series of words to his or her partner; all such words correctly guessed were inserted into the blanks of a sentence, which formed a puzzle for the player to solve. If the player was unable to solve the puzzle, a member of the opposing team was given a chance to solve it.

THE BOLD AND THE BEAUTIFUL   CBS
23 MARCH 1987–   A half-hour daytime serial created by William Bell and Lee Phillip Bell, the pair responsible for *The Young and the Restless*. Their son, Bradley Bell, has been its supervising producer and head writer. The series is set in the fashion business of Los Angeles, and its two central families are the Forresters and the Logans. The cast has included: John McCook as Eric Forrester, head of the family clothing business; Susan Flannery as his wife, Stephanie Forrester; Clayton Norcross and Jeff Trachta as son Thorne Forrester; Ronn Moss as son Ridge Forrester; Teri Ann Linn as daughter Kristen Forrester; Colleen Dion as daughter Felicia Forrester; Robert Pine as Steve Logan; Judith Baldwin and Nancy Burnett as his wife, Beth Logan; Nancy Sloan as daughter Katie Logan; Carrie Mitchum (granddaughter of Robert Mitchum) as daughter Donna Logan; Ethan Wayne (son of John Wayne) and Brian Patrick Clarke as son Storm Logan; Katherine Kelly Lang as daughter Brooke Logan; Lesley Woods as Grandma Logan; Joanna Johnson as Caroline Spencer, who married Thorne Forrester (Johnson also appeared as Caroline's twin, Karen, and as their cousin, Faith); Jim Storm as her father, Bill Spencer; Lauren Koslow as Eric Forrester's assistant, Margo Lynley; Bryan Genesse as Rocco Carner; Ron Deacon as Greg Wrangler; Allan Hayes as Nick Preston; Daniel McVicar as Clarke Garrison, who married Kristen Forrester; Judith Borne as Angela Forrester; Darlene Conley as Sally Spectra; Bobbie Eakes as her daughter, Macy Spectra; Jeff Conaway as Kristen's ex-boyfriend, Mick Savage; Michael Fox as Saul Feinstein; Schae Harrison as Darla; Jane Rogers as Julie DeLorian; Tippi Hedren as Helen MacClaine; John Brandon as Ben MacClaine; Todd McKee as Jake MacClaine; Hunter Tylo as Dr. Taylor Hayes; Chris Robinson as Jack Hamilton, Taylor's father; Michael Watson as Zach Hamilton; Dorothy Lyman as Bonnie Roberts; Kimberlin Brown as Sheila Carter Grainger (who had also appeared on *The Young and the Restless*); Brent Jasmer as Sly Donovan; Alex Kubik as Ganz; Brett Stimely as Dr. Jay Garvin; Marnie Mosiman as Dr. Tracy Peters; Scott Thompson Baker as Connor Davis; Perry Stephens as Steve Crown; Ken LaRon as bartender Keith Anderson; Keith Jones as Keith's brother, Kevin Anderson; Robert Gentry as Elliott Parker; Ian Buchanan as Dr. James Warwick; Peter Brown as Blake Hayes; Michael Sabatino as Anthony Armando; James Doohan as Damon Warwick; Maitland Ward as Jessica Forrester; Monika Schnarre as Ivana; Roya Megnot as Imane; Dylan Neal as Dylan Shaw; Olivia Virgil White as district attorney Teresa Emerson; Krista Allen as Shelley; Jeremy Snyder as Eric Forrester, Jr.; Rita Gomez as Maria; Lindsay Price as Michael Lai; and Lark Voorhies as Jasmine.

BOLD JOURNEY   ABC/SYNDICATED
16 JULY 1956–31 AUGUST 1959 (ABC); 1959 (SYNDICATED)   Amateur adventurers narrated films of their daring deeds on this documentary series hosted by John Stephenson (1956–1957) and Jack Douglas (1957–1959).

THE BOLD ONES   NBC

14 SEPTEMBER 1969–9 JANUARY 1973   The umbrella title for four different series, each with its own producer: (1) *The Doctors*—the only one of the four to last for the duration—starred E. G. Marshall as Dr. David Craig, founder of the David Craig Institute of Medicine; David Hartman as Dr. Paul Hunter; John Saxon as Dr. Ted Stuart; Julie Adams (1970–1971) as Mrs. David Craig. (2) *The Lawyers* (1969–1972)—Nichols, Darrell & Darrell—with Burl Ives as sly senior partner Walter Nichols; Joseph Campanella as tweedy junior partner Brian Darrell; James Farentino as Brian's swinging brother, Neil Darrell. (3) *The Law Enforcers* (1969–1970) with Leslie Nielsen as Deputy Police Chief Sam Danforth; Hari Rhodes as black District Attorney William Washburn. (4) *The Senator* (1970–1971)—with Hal Holbrook as the idealistic Senator Hays Stowe; Michael Tolan as his aide, Jordan Boyle; Sharon Acker as Erin Stowe, the senator's wife; and Cindy Eilbacher as Norma, their young daughter.

BOLD VENTURE   SYNDICATED

1959   Dane Clark starred as adventurer Slate Shannon, skipper of *The Bold Venture,* in this half-hour adventure series set in the Caribbean. With Joan Marshall as Sailor Duval, Shannon's ward and companion, and Bernie Gozier as calypso singer King Moses. The series was based on the 1950 radio series which had starred Humphrey Bogart and Lauren Bacall.

BON VOYAGE
See TREASURE QUEST

BONANZA   NBC

12 SEPTEMBER 1959–16 JANUARY 1973   Second only to *Gunsmoke* among long-running westerns, *Bonanza* was the archetype of the "property" western that dominated the genre during the 1960s. Set in Virginia City, Nevada, it told the story of the Cartwrights, owners of a nearby 600,000-acre (give or take a few) ranch—The Ponderosa (named because of the ponderosa pines growing there). Hardworking, resourceful, and independent, the Cartwrights seemed to devote little time to running the ranch, despite the fact that their hired help never numbered more than four; obviously, the Cartwrights knew good labor when they saw it. With Canadian actor Lorne Greene as Ben Cartwright, a three-time widower; Pernell Roberts (1959–1965) as eldest son Adam; big Dan Blocker (1959–1972) as son Hoss; Michael Landon (star of the 1957 film, *I Was a Teenage Werewolf*) as youngest son, Little Joe; Victor Sen Yung as Hop Sing, the cook; Ray Teal as Sheriff Roy Coffee, the Virginia City lawman who frequently called on the Cartwrights for assistance; David Canary (1968–1970; 1972–1973) as foreman Mr. Canaday (Candy); Mitch Vogel (1970–1972) as Jamie Hunter, a young runaway taken in by the Cartwrights; and Tim Matheson (1972–1973) as ranch hand Griff King, an ex-con.

Each of the Cartwright sons was a half-brother to the other two; the story of Ben Cartwright's three marriages was told in flashbacks. Adam, born in New England, was the son of Ben's first wife Elizabeth. Hoss was the son of second wife Inger, a woman of Scandinavian extraction who was killed by Indians; Hoss's real name is Eric (*hoss* is Norwegian for "good luck"). Little Joe, the youngest, was the son of Marie, whom Ben met in New Orleans; Marie died as the result of a fall from her horse.

During its first two seasons, *Bonanza* was seen on Saturdays and failed to outdraw CBS's *Perry Mason*. In the fall of 1961, it was scheduled on Sundays at 9 P.M. It remained there for eleven years, ranking consistently among the Top Ten, eventually knocking off *Perry Mason* in 1965–1966. Even after Pernell Roberts quit the series in 1965 (explaining he'd grown tired of the role), the show continued to do well. But two calamitous events in 1972 led to *Bonanza's* cancellation halfway through its fourteenth season: the sudden death of Dan Blocker during the summer and a scheduling change to Tuesdays.

In 1988 a TV-movie was made for syndication, intended as a pilot for a possible sequel series. Titled "Bonanza: The Next Generation," it starred John Ireland as

Aaron Cartwright, brother of the deceased Ben (Lorne Greene had been signed to reappear as Ben, but died before filming began), and featured Gillian Greene (Lorne's daughter) as Jennifer Sills and Michael Landon, Jr., as Hoss's son, Benj. Michael Landon, Jr., and Dirk Blocker (son of Dan Blocker) teamed up in two subsequent TV-movies: "Bonanza: The Return" (28 November 1993, NBC), and "Bonanza: Under Attack" (15 January 1995, NBC).

BONINO NBC
12 SEPTEMBER 1953–26 DECEMBER 1953 An early ethnic situation comedy about an Italian-American opera singer, a widower with several children, who decides to spend more time with his family. With Italian-American opera singer Ezio Pinza as Babbo Bonino; Mary Wickes as Martha, the maid; David Opatoshu as Walter Rogers, Bonino's manager; Conrad Janis as eldest son Edward; Lenka Peterson as daughter Doris; Chet Allen as son Terry; Oliver Andes as son Carlo; Gaye Huston as daughter Francesca; and Van Dyke Parks as son Andrew. Parks grew up to be a rock-music producer and composer and cowrote (with Brian Wilson) the Beach Boys' hits "Heroes and Villains" and "Surf's Up."

BONKERS SYNDICATED
1978 Comedy-variety half hour starring the Hudson Brothers—Bill, Brett, and Mark—with Bob Monkhouse and the Bonkettes. Produced by Jack Burns for ITC.

BONKERS SYNDICATED
1993– A wacky bobcat was the title character in this half-hour cartoon series. He was introduced in 1992 on Saturday mornings in *Disney's Raw Toonage*; a season later *Bonkers* became one segment of the daily two-hour cartoon block, *Disney Afternoon*.

THE BONNIE HUNT SHOW CBS
22 SEPTEMBER 1995–27 OCTOBER 1995; 10 MARCH 1996– Half-hour sitcom, partially unscripted, set mostly in the newsroom of Chicago TV station WBDR. With Bonnie Hunt as newly hired reporter Bonnie Kelly; Mark Derwin as news director William Kirkland; Janet Carroll as Kirkland's officious assistant, Diane Fulton; Richard Gant as assignment editor Joe Briggs; Brian Howe as Sammy Sinatra, who ran the food cart; Tom Virtue as cameraman Tom Vandoozer; Eamonn Roche as news editor Andrew Wiggins; Holly Wortell as Bonnie's friend and neighbor, Holly Jankovsky, who was also a makeup artist at the station; and Don Lake as Bonnie and Holly's neighbor, Keith Jetzek, a limousine driver. The series returned in midseason as *Bonnie*.

THE BONNIE PRUDDEN SHOW SYNDICATED
1968 Half-hour exercise show, hosted by physical fitness expert Bonnie Prudden.

BOOK BEAT PBS
1965–1978 Hardy half-hour series hosted by Robert Cromie of the Chicago *Tribune,* featuring interviews with authors.

THE BOOK OF LISTS CBS
4 MAY 1982–25 MAY 1982 A lightweight hour of trivial information and dramatizations of matters appearing in the popular *Book of Lists* books. Bill Bixby hosted the show.

BOOKER FOX
24 SEPTEMBER 1989–26 AUGUST 1990 In this spinoff from *21 Jump Street,* Richard Grieco starred as Dennis Booker, who was now an investigator for the Teshima Corporation of America. Joining him were Katie Rich (fall 1989) as his assistant, Elaine Grazzo; Carmen Argenziano as Chick Sterling; and Marcia Strassman as Alicia Rudd, Teshima's vice president of acquisitions. Lori Petty joined the cast early

in 1990 as Booker's new assistant, Diane Dunne. Rocker Billy Idol composed and sang the show's theme.

BOOKMARK   PBS
1989–1991   Half-hour series of book reviews and discussions with authors, hosted by Lewis Lapham.

BOONE   NBC
26 SEPTEMBER 1983–12 DECEMBER 1983; 28 JULY 1984–11 AUGUST 1984   Created by Earl (*The Waltons*) Hamner, this hour dramatic series was set in 1953 in Trinity, Tennessee. It starred Tom Byrd as Boone Sawyer, a young man who sang and played the guitar, and dreamed of making it big as an entertainer. Also featured were Barry Corbin as his father, Merit, a mechanic who hoped Boone would join him in the garage business; Elizabeth Huddle as his mother, Faye, who hoped Boone would become a preacher; Kitty Moffatt as his teenaged sister, Susannah; Amanda Peterson as his little sister, Squirt; Greg Webb as Boone's fellow musician, Rome Hawley; Ronnie Claire Edwards and William Edward Phipps as Boone's Aunt Dolly and Uncle Linc Sawyer, who ran Linc's Orchid Lounge, where Boone and Rome frequently performed.

BOOTS AND SADDLES   SYNDICATED
1957–1959   The adventures of the Fifth Cavalry. With Jack Pickard as Captain Shank Adams, Patrick McVey as Lieutenant Colonel Hays; Gardner McKay as Lieutenant Kelly; David Willock as Lieutenant Binning; John Alderson as Sergeant Bullock; and Michael Hinn as scout Luke Cummings. Thirty-nine half-hour episodes were filmed by California National Productions.

BORDER PATROL   SYNDICATED
1959   Modern-day adventure series starring Richard Webb (*Captain Midnight*) as Don Jagger, Deputy Chief of the United States Border Patrol.

BORDERTOWN   FAM
7 JANUARY 1989–   Jointly produced in Canada by The Family Channel (formerly the Christian Broadcasting Network) and Global TV, Bordertown was a western—a northwestern, to be precise—set during the 1890s in a town that straddled the U.S.–Canada border. John Brennan and Richard Comar costarred as Corporal Clive Bennett of the North West Mounted Police and United States Marshal Jack Craddock, the two lawmen whose jurisdiction and temperament clashed there. Also featured was Sophie Barjac as Dr. Marie Dumont, the town's physician, in whom both lawmen were interested. A total of 78 episodes were produced between 1988 and 1990; the series continued in reruns on The Family Channel.

BORN FREE   NBC
9 SEPTEMBER 1974–30 DECEMBER 1974   Conservation-minded adventure series set in Kenya. With Gary Collins as game warden George Adamson; Diana Muldaur as Joy Adamson; Hal Frederick as Makedde, their scout and assistant. The series was based on Joy Adamson's best-selling books, *Born Free* and *Living Free,* which told of the Adamsons' adventures with Elsa the lioness. Created for television by Carl Forman. Executive producer: David Gerber.

BOSOM BUDDIES   ABC
27 NOVEMBER 1980–12 AUGUST 1982   A well-crafted sitcom, *Bosom Buddies* borrowed its original gimmick—two guys in drag—from the Tony Curtis–Jack Lemmon–Marilyn Monroe film *Some Like It Hot.* The series starred Tom Hanks and Peter Scolari as Kip Wilson and Henry Desmond, two young men whose cheap New York apartment was demolished; desperate, they moved into the Susan B. Anthony, a hotel for women, where they masqueraded as their own "sisters," Buffy and Hildegarde. Also featured were Donna Dixon as Sonny Lumet, their naive and voluptuous hallmate (and Kip's girlfriend); Holland Taylor as Ruth Dunbar, Kip and

Henry's boss at a Manhattan ad agency; Wendie Jo Sperber as Amy Cassidy, their co-worker and hallmate, who pursued Henry and who was the only person who knew of their charade; Telma Hopkins as hallmate Isabel Hammond; and Lucille Benson (1980–1981) as crusty Lily Sinclair, the hotel manager. During the second season, Kip revealed his dual identity to Sonny, and the boys-in-drag storyline was deemphasized as Kip and Henry opened their own production outfit, 60 Seconds Street, with financial help from Ruth and Amy. NBC reran a few episodes of the series during the summer of 1984.

BOSS LADY   NBC
1 JULY 1952–23 SEPTEMBER 1952   Lynn Bari, who began her film career in 1933 at age eighteen, starred as Gwen Allen, the boss of a construction company, Hillendale Homes, Inc., in this summer replacement for *Fireside Theatre*. Also featured were Nicholas Joy as Gwen's father, Glen Langan as her boyfriend, Jeff, and Lee Patrick as Aggie, the secretary.

BOSTON BLACKIE   SYNDICATED
1951   Boston Blackie, the criminal-cum-detective made famous in films by Chester Morris, was played on television by veteran character actor Kent Taylor. With Lois Collier as his lady friend, Mary Wesley; Frank Orth as Inspector Faraday. The half-hour series was set in Los Angeles, not Boston. Produced by Ziv TV; directed by Eddie Davis, Sobey Martin, and George M. Cahan.

BOTH SIDES   ABC
15 MARCH 1953–7 JUNE 1953   A series of debates on public policy issues, moderated by Quincy Howe.

BOURBON STREET BEAT   ABC
5 OCTOBER 1959–26 SEPTEMBER 1960   New Orleans was the setting for this Warner Brothers hour-long detective series. It starred Richard Long as Rex Randolph and Andrew Duggan as Cal Calhoun, the owners of Randolph and Calhoun, Special Services. Also featured were Arlene Howell as their receptionist, Melody Lee Mercer; Van Williams as their young assistant, Kenny Madison; and Eddie Cole as "The Baron," a local pianist. After *Bourbon Street Beat* expired, Rex Randolph moved West to join *77 Sunset Strip,* while Kenny Madison headed southeast to Warner Brothers' new detective series, *SurfSide 6.*
    Although the series was shot in Hollywood on the set of the film *A Streetcar Named Desire,* ABC desired to give the series a look of local authenticity. The network bought a half-interest in a real New Orleans restaurant, The Absinthe House, and set the offices of Randolph and Calhoun above it.

BOWLING HEADLINERS   ABC/DUMONT
26 DECEMBER 1948–30 OCTOBER 1949 (ABC); 13 NOVEMBER 1949–9 APRIL 1950 (DU-MONT)   One of network television's first bowling shows, this half-hour series was hosted by Jimmy Powers during its first season and by Al Cirillo (who also produced it) during its second season.

BOWLING STARS   ABC/NBC
22 SEPTEMBER 1957–29 DECEMBER 1957 (ABC); 1 OCTOBER 1960–6 MAY 1961 (NBC) A series of head-to-head matches between professional bowlers. The ABC version, which ran in prime time, was hosted by "Whispering Joe" Wilson (so named because he spoke softly to avoid disturbing the keglers' concentration). The NBC version, a weekend feature, was hosted by Bud Palmer. See also *National Bowling Champions.*

BOY MEETS WORLD   ABC
24 SEPTEMBER 1993–   Half-hour sitcom starring Ben Savage (younger brother of *The Wonder Years'* Fred Savage) as eleven-year-old Cory Matthews, whose next-door neighbor also happened to be his teacher. William Daniels costarred as the teacher, the ever-watchful George Feeny. Also featured were William Russ as Cory's

father, Alan, a supermarket manager; Betsy Randle as Cory's mother, Amy; Will Friedle as his older brother, Eric; Lily Nicksay as his younger sister, Morgan; Rider Strong as his best friend, Shawn Turner; Lee Norris (1993–1994) as his nerdy class-mate, Minkus; and Danielle Fishel as classmate Topanga. For the series' second season, Cory and his pals left elementary school and started middle school; unfortu-nately for them, Mr. Feeny joined them, too, as the new vice principal. Added to the cast were Anthony Tyler Quinn as Jonathan Turner, Shawn's father; Sydney Bennett as Desiree; Danny McNulty as school bully Harley Kiner; Ethan Suplee as Frankie; and Blake Soper as Joey. Alex Desert joined the cast in the fall of 1995 as student Eli Williams.

THE BOYS   CBS
20 AUGUST 1993–17 SEPTEMBER 1993   In this half-hour sitcom, a young horror novelist moved into a house whose former owner, an elderly man, had died, and became friends with the former owner's cronies. With Christopher Meloni as the novelist, Doug Kirkfield; Isabella Hofmann as his live-in girlfriend, Molly; Ned Beatty as nextdoor neighbor Bert Greenblatt; Doris Roberts as Bert's wife, Doris; Richard Venture as Al, who worked in a tar plant; and John Harkins as Harlan, a retired firefighter.

THE BOYS ARE BACK   CBS
11 SEPTEMBER 1994–28 JANUARY 1995   Half-hour sitcom about a middle-aged couple whose plans for a peaceful life together were thrown asunder when their two grown sons, daughter-in-law, and three grandchildren suddenly moved back home. With Hal Linden as Fred Hansen; Suzanne Pleshette as Jackie Hansen; George Newbern as son Mike, who had lost his job; Kevin Crowley as son Rick, a police officer; Bess Meyer as Mike's wife, Judy; Ryan O'Donohue as Mike and Judy's son Peter; Kelsey Mulrooney as their daughter, Sarah; and Justin Cooper as their son Nicky.

THE BOYS OF TWILIGHT   CBS
29 FEBRUARY 1992–21 MARCH 1992   This four-episode modern-day western, about the two elderly lawmen in the town of Twilight, starred Richard Farnsworth as Sheriff Cody McPherson; Wilford Brimley as Deputy Bill Huntoon; Louise Fletcher as Cody's wife, Geneva; Ben Browder as the young deputy, Tyler Clare; and Amanda McBroom as Mayor Troxell.

BOYS WILL BE BOYS
see SECOND CHANCE (1987 version)

BOZO THE CLOWN (BOZO'S BIG TOP)   SYNDICATED
1956–   Not exactly a national series, *Bozo the Clown* is essentially a television "franchise" controlled by Larry Harmon. Bozo was originally the star of dozens of children's records released by Capitol. In 1956 Harmon bought the TV rights to the character and developed the idea of a live Bozo (each local station supplying its own) introducing Bozo cartoons. The idea caught on; by 1966 Bozo could be seen on more than 240 stations in over forty countries. By that time several dozen stations featured the same Bozo on videotape: Frank Avruch, Boston's Bozo. Willard Scott of the *Today* show also served as a local Bozo in Washington, D.C. The durable character carried on through the 1970s and 1980s, and was still being carried in a number of markets in 1990. *Variety* reported in 1992 that Chicago superstation WGN had re-newed the show through 1997, and that the waiting list for tickets had dropped from ten years to five.

BRACKEN'S WORLD   NBC
19 SEPTEMBER 1969–25 DECEMBER 1970   Life at Hollywood Century Studios. With Peter Haskell as producer Kevin Grant; Madlyn Rhue as his wife, Marjorie; Eliza-beth Allen as Laura Deane, who runs a talent school; Dennis Cole as young leading man David Evans; Karen Jensen as starlet Rachel Holt; Steven Oliver as Brando-type Tom Huston; Laraine Stephens as young leading lady Diane Waring; Linda

Harrison as shy young actress Paulette Douglas; Jeanne Cooper as Mrs. Douglas, Paulette's overbearing mother; and Eleanor Parker as Sylvia Caldwell, executive secretary to studio boss John Bracken. During the 1969–1970 season Bracken was unseen; for the second season (Cole and Oliver having left the series) Leslie Nielsen was added to play the now-visible Bracken. The hour show was produced by 20th Century-Fox.

THE BRADBURY CHRONICLES
see RAY BRADBURY THEATER

THE BRADY BRIDES   NBC
6 FEBRUARY 1981–17 APRIL 1981   This sequel to *The Brady Bunch* was made as a two-hour made-for-TV movie, titled "The Brady Girls Get Married." Shortly before its scheduled broadcast, however, the network decided to air it in three parts, and subsequently ordered a few additional episodes. For the movie, the original *Brady Bunch* cast was reassembled for the double wedding of the two older Brady girls, Marcia and Jan: Marcia married Wally Logan (played by Jerry Houser) and Jan wed Phillip Covington III (Ron Kuhlman). After the wedding, the two couples bought a house together, forcing the easygoing Wally and the uptight Phillip to co-exist. Also featured in the latter episodes was Keland Love as Harry, a neighborhood kid; Florence Henderson and Ann B. Davis (from the original *Brady Bunch*) also appeared occasionally.

THE BRADY BUNCH   ABC
26 SEPTEMBER 1969–30 AUGUST 1974   Harmless sitcom about a widower with three sons who married a widow with three daughters. Featuring Robert Reed as architect Mike Brady; Florence Henderson as Carol Brady; Ann B. Davis as Alice Nelson, their harried housekeeper; Maureen McCormick as Marcia; Barry Williams as Greg; Eve Plumb as Jan; Christopher Knight as Peter; Susan Olsen as Cindy; and Michael Lookinland as Bobby. Robbie Rist was also featured in the last six episodes as Carol's eight-year-old nephew, Oliver, who stayed with the Bradys while his parents were away. Sherwood Schwartz created the series and was its executive producer. The Bunch also turned up in animated form (see *The Brady Kids*), in a variety format (see *The Brady Bunch Hour*), in a 1981 sequel (see *The Brady Brides*), in a 1988 TV-movie ("A Very Brady Christmas"), and a 1990 sequel (see *The Bradys*). By the 1990s the series had achieved cult status among the late and post-baby boomers. Several books were written about the series, including Barry Williams's autobiography, *Growing Up Brady*. Verbatim versions of some episodes were produced on stage in several cities under the title "The Real Live Brady Bunch." Florence Henderson hosted an ABC prime-time special, "Bradymania," on 19 May 1993, and a motion picture based on the series emerged in 1995. "The Brady Bunch Movie" featured cameo appearances by original cast members Henderson, Davis, Williams, and Knight. To the disappointment of some fans, Robert Reed expressed utter disdain for the series before his untimely death in 1992.

THE BRADY BUNCH HOUR   ABC
23 JANUARY 1977–25 MAY 1977   A variety hour with some running sketches broadcast irregularly during 1977. With Florence Henderson (Carol), Robert Reed (Mike), Maureen McCormick (Marcia), Barry Williams (Greg), Geri Reischl (Jan), Chris Knight (Peter), Susan Olsen (Cindy), and Michael Lookinland (Bobby).

THE BRADY KIDS   ABC
16 SEPTEMBER 1972–31 AUGUST 1974   A Saturday-morning cartoon series. The voices of the six *Brady Bunch* children (McCormick, Williams, Plumb, Knight, Olsen, and Lookinland) were used.

THE BRADYS   CBS
9 FEBRUARY 1990–9 MARCH 1990   Most of the original cast of *The Brady Bunch* reassembled for this hour comedy-drama sequel to the original 1969–1974 sitcom;

CBS thoughtfully scheduled the show in the same time slot (Fridays at 8 P.M.) that *The Brady Bunch* had had for its last three seasons. This time, however, there were not two generations of Bradys, but three; Mike and Carol now had four grandchildren. They still didn't have the house to themselves, however, as daughter Marcia and her family moved in with Mike and Carol after her husband lost his job. Returning from the old cast were Robert Reed as Mike Brady, who ran for city council (and won); Florence Henderson as Carol Brady, who now sold real estate; Ann B. Davis as Alice Franklin, who had finally married Sam the butcher and was no longer the Bradys' housekeeper; Barry Williams as son Greg, now an obstetrician; Christopher Knight as son Peter, an environmental activist; Mike Lookinland as son Bobby, who had been paralyzed in an auto racing mishap; Eve Plumb as daughter Jan Covington, an architect like her father; and Susan Olsen as Cindy, a disc jockey. Leah Ayres played the sixth Brady child, oldest daughter Marcia. Other cast members included Caryn Richman as Greg's wife, Nora; MTV vee-jay Martha Quinn as Bobby's wife, Tracy; Ron Kuhlman as Jan's husband, Philip; Jerry Houser as Marcia's hapless husband, Wally Logan; Ken Michelman as Cindy's boss, Greg Greenberg; Jonathan Weiss as Greg and Nora's son, Kevin; Valerie Ick as Jan and Phillip's adopted daughter, Patty; Jaclyn Bernstein as Marcia and Wally's daughter, Jessica; and Michael Melby as Marcia and Wally's son, Mickey. The series was liberally laced with clips from the original *Brady Bunch,* as the various members of the clan took to reminiscing pretty often.

THE BRAIN   PBS
10 OCTOBER 1984–5 DECEMBER 1984   Highly acclaimed eight-part series on the workings of the human brain. Among the topics examined were stress, vision, learning, the brain's two hemispheres, and states of mind. In 1988 a sequel series was produced: see *The Mind.*

BRAINS AND BRAWN   NBC
13 SEPTEMBER 1958–27 DECEMBER 1958   Bifurcated prime-time game show featuring a contest between two teams, each composed of one athlete and one celebrity. Fred Davis hosted the Brain portion, a general knowledge quiz; Jack Lescoulie hosted the Brawn portion, which involved physical exertion.

BRAINS & BRAWN   NBC
10 JULY 1993–16 OCTOBER 1993   The second game show with this title was for kids. Mark-Paul Gosselaar, star of *Saved by the Bell*, hosted the Saturday morning series on which two teams of three young contestants, each captained by a young celebrity, competed in tests of mental and physical ability. Danielle Harris was the cohost.

BRANDED   NBC
24 JANUARY 1965–4 SEPTEMBER 1966   A midseason replacement for *The Bill Dana Show.* Starring Chuck Connors as Jason McCord, an Army officer wrongfully court-martialed after the Battle of Bitter Creek (he was the only known survivor) and dishonorably discharged. Forty-eight half hours were made.

BRAVE EAGLE   CBS
28 SEPTEMBER 1955–6 JUNE 1956   One of the few westerns told from the Indians' point of view. With Keith Larsen as Brave Eagle, a Cheyenne chief; Kim Winona as Morning Star; Keena Nomkeena (a real Indian) as Keena, Brave Eagle's adopted son; and Bert Wheeler as halfbreed Smokey Joe.

BREAK THE BANK   ABC/NBC/CBS/SYNDICATED
22 OCTOBER 1948–23 SEPTEMBER 1949 (ABC); 5 OCTOBER 1949–9 JANUARY 1952 (NBC); 13 JANUARY 1952–1 FEBRUARY 1953 (CBS); 30 MARCH 1953–18 SEPTEMBER 1953 (NBC); 31 JANUARY 1954–20 JUNE 1956 (ABC); 12 APRIL 1976–23 JULY 1976 (ABC); 1976 (SYNDICATED); 1985 (SYNDICATED)

BREAK THE $250,000 BANK   NBC

9 OCTOBER 1956–29 JANUARY 1957   This durable game show, whose network peregrinations have sometimes been difficult to follow, began on radio in 1945. From 1948 until 1956, it was seen in prime time, except for a brief daytime run on NBC in 1953. Bert Parks hosted the ABC and NBC versions of the show, and Bud Collyer emceed the CBS version. It employed a straightforward question-and-answer format; contestants were quizzed in their chosen areas of specialized knowledge and could answer up to eight questions. Those who answered the first eight questions (one wrong answer was permitted) could then opt to answer a ninth question to "break the bank." Winners were paid on the spot—in cash for small amounts and by check for larger sums. In the fall of 1956 the show returned to NBC, with Parks as host, and was retitled *Break the $250,000 Bank*. On this version contestants were permitted to have their families with them and could call upon one family member to answer one question if the contestant had previously missed it. Joseph Nathan Kane, who wrote the questions used on the show, also served as judge, and Janice Gilbert was featured as the paying teller. In 1976 *Break the Bank* again returned, after an absence of almost two decades. The new format featured a panel of nine celebrities and two contestants. When a question was asked, one celebrity provided the correct answer for it, and one provided a false answer; contestants won money by choosing the one who had answered correctly. Tom Kennedy hosted the short-lived daytime network version, and Jack Barry (whose longtime partner, Dan Enright, produced it) hosted the syndicated version. The show surfaced again in 1985, hosted first by Gene Rayburn, then by Joe Farago.

BREAKAWAY   SYNDICATED

19 SEPTEMBER 1983–7 SEPTEMBER 1984   This hour talk show was broadcast live from New York on weekday afternoons. Monte Markham and Martha Lambert were the original cohosts; Markham was succeeded by Norman Mark.

BREAKFAST IN HOLLYWOOD   NBC

11 JANUARY 1954–5 FEBRUARY 1954   Short-lived morning show broadcast live from Hollywood. Johnny Dugan hosted the festivities, which included songs, chitchat, and audience-participation features.

BREAKFAST PARTY   NBC

7 JANUARY 1952–23 MAY 1952   Mel Martin hosted this half-hour morning variety show, which was broadcast live from Cincinnati.

BREAKING AWAY   ABC

29 NOVEMBER 1980–10 JANUARY 1981   Based on the 1979 movie, this refreshing series unfortunately never got off the ground. Set in Bloomington, Indiana (but actually filmed in Athens, Georgia), it told the story of four teenage boys growing up in a college town; the locals, many of whose fathers had worked at the nearby quarries, were derogatorily known as "cutters" to the college kids. Featured were Shaun Cassidy as Dave Stohler, an idealistic youngster obsessed by the European sport of cycling; Tom Wiggin as jockish Mike Carnahan; Jackie Earle Haley as rebellious Moocher; Thom Bray as cerebral Cyril; Vincent Gardenia as Dave's father, Ray Stohler, a used-car dealer; Barbara Barrie as Dave's mother, Evelyn Stohler; and Shelby Brammer as Nancy, Moocher's girlfriend. Two members of the TV cast—Haley and Barrie—had also appeared in the film. Though the show was canceled in January 1981, a few episodes were later televised on Mondays to fill the gap in programming caused by the baseball players' strike.

BREAKING POINT   ABC

16 SEPTEMBER 1963–7 SEPTEMBER 1964   The success of *Ben Casey* led to a proliferation of medical shows; this one (like NBC's *Eleventh Hour*) featured two psychiatrists. With Paul Richards as Dr. McKinley Thompson, resident in psychiatry at York Hospital; Eduard Franz as Dr. Edward Raymer, clinic director. Produced by Bing Crosby Productions (which also produced *Ben Casey*). Robert Redford made one of his last TV appearances in one episode, "Bird and Snake" (7 October).

BRENNER CBS

6 JUNE 1959–10 OCTOBER 1959; 10 MAY 1964–13 SEPTEMBER 1964   This half-hour cop show starred Edward Binns and James Broderick as Roy and Ernie Brenner, father and son police officers. Roy was a lieutenant assigned to the Confidential Squad, an internal investigative unit, while Ernie was a rookie plainclothesman. The series was based on "The Blue Men," a police drama broadcast on *Playhouse 90*. After its 1959 summer run, *Brenner* was rerun on CBS in 1961 and 1962; the 1964 run led óff with a number of newly made episodes.

BRET MAVERICK NBC

1 DECEMBER 1981–24 AUGUST 1982   James Garner returned to the role he had created two dozen years earlier in this hour western. However, like virtually all sequels in television history, *Bret Maverick* was not nearly as popular as its predecessor. As the sequel opened, Maverick won himself the Red Ox Saloon in a card game, and finally decided to settle down in the town of Sweetwater, Arizona. Also on hand were Darleen Carr as photographer M. L. (Mary Lou) Springer; John Shearin as Sheriff Mitchel Dowd; Ed Bruce as Maverick's partner, former sheriff Tom Guthrie; David Knell as Rodney, M. L.'s Assistant; Stuart Margolin (co-starring in his third series with Garner) as Philo Sandine; Ramon Bieri as Mr. Crow, the banker; and Richard Hamilton as Cy Whitaker, the chief hand at Maverick's Lazy Ace Ranch. Ed Bruce, better known as a country-and-western singer than as an actor, co-wrote (with Patsy Bruce and Glenn Ray) and sang the show's theme. NBC reran the series during the summer of 1990. See also *Maverick; Young Maverick*.

BREWSTER PLACE ABC

1 MAY 1990–11 JULY 1990   Oprah Winfrey produced and starred in this half-hour dramatic series, derived from the two-part TV-movie *The Women of Brewster Place* (ABC, 19–20 March 1989), which in turn was based on Gloria Naylor's novel. The series depicted life in the black community of a large city in the mid-1960s. Winfrey reprised her role as Mattie Michael, who lost her job as a hairdresser and bought a restaurant with her best friend. Brenda Pressley played Etta Mae Johnson, Mattie's friend and partner in the new venture, La Scala. Olivia Cole (who had also been in the telefilm) played Miss Sophie, the officious and opinionated woman who owned the neighborhood grocery. The rest of the cast included Oscar Brown, Jr., as Jesse, Sophie's husband; John Cothran, Jr., as Ralph Thomas, who had just moved to the city from Arkansas; Steven Crump as Matthew, Ralph's older son; DeLeon Richards as Margaret, Ralph's daughter; Jason Weaver as Miles, Ralph's younger son; Rachael Crawford as Kiswana; Kelly Neal as her boyfriend, Abshu; and John Speredakos as Mickey, the white cook at La Scala. Oprah Winfrey was executive producer, together with Earl Hamner and Donald Sipes.

THE BRIAN KEITH SHOW
See THE LITTLE PEOPLE

BRIDE AND GROOM CBS/NBC

25 JANUARY 1951–9 OCTOBER 1953 (CBS); 7 DECEMBER 1953–27 AUGUST 1954 (NBC); 1 JULY 1957–10 JANUARY 1958 (NBC)   Couples were married before a live coast-to-coast audience on this daytime show broadcast from New York. John Nelson was the first host of the show; Robert Paige and Byron Palmer cohosted the 1957–1958 version (Palmer was later replaced by Frank Parker).

BRIDESHEAD REVISITED
See GREAT PERFORMANCES

BRIDGES TO CROSS CBS

24 APRIL 1986–12 JUNE 1986   Half-hour sitcom about two divorcés who were journalists on *World Week*, a Washington, D.C., newsmagazine. With Suzanne Pleshette as Tracy Bridges; Nicolas Surovy as her ex, Peter Cross; Roddy McDowall as Norman Parks, Tracy's secretary; Jose Ferrer as Morris Cane, the editor; Barry Sobel as

Aaron, the office boy; and Eva Gabor as Washington socialite Maria Talbot. Tracy and Peter often wrote the "Bridges to Cross" column for the magazine, in which they took opposite points of view.

BRIDGET LOVES BERNIE CBS

16 SEPTEMBER 1972–8 SEPTEMBER 1973 An updated video version of the long-running Broadway hit, *Abie's Irish Rose,* about a rich Irish girl who marries a poor Jewish boy. Starring Meredith Baxter as Bridget Theresa Mary Coleen Fitzgerald, a young schoolteacher, and David Birney as Bernie Steinberg, an aspiring writer and part-time cabbie. As luck would have it, Baxter and Birney actually did fall in love and were married in 1973 (they were later divorced). Also featured were David Doyle as Walter Fitzgerald, Bridget's wealthy father, an executive; Audra Lindley as Amy Fitzgerald, Bridget's pompous mother; Harold J. Stone as delicatessen owner Sam Steinberg, Bernie's folksy father; Bibi Osterwald as Sophie Steinberg, Bernie's stereotypically Jewish mother; Robert Sampson as Bridget's brother Mike, a priest; Ned Glass as Bernie's uncle, Moe Plotnick; and William Elliott as Bernie's black friend, Otis Foster. Aired at 8:30 P.M. on Saturdays, between CBS's monster hits *All in the Family* and *The Mary Tyler Moore Show, Bridget Loves Bernie* was one of the highest-rated shows ever to be cancelled after one season. It was widely reported that many Jewish groups had pressured CBS to axe the series, but the network's official explanation was that the show's ratings were not high enough. Too many viewers, it said, were switching away from CBS after *All in the Family* and returning for *The Mary Tyler Moore Show.*

BRIGHT PROMISE NBC

29 SEPTEMBER 1969–31 MARCH 1972 A soap opera apparently aimed at a youthful audience, *Bright Promise* was set at Bancroft College, a small Midwestern institution. It featured Dana Andrews as college president Thomas Boswell; Paul Lukather as Professor William Ferguson; Susan Brown as Martha Ferguson; Dabney Coleman as Dr. Tracy Brown; Coleen Gray and Gail Kobe as Ann (Boyd) Jones; Mark Miller as Howard Jones; Pamela Murphy as Sandy Jones Pierce, dropout, adulteress and accused murderer; David Lewis as Henry Pierce; Peter Ratray as Stuart Pierce; Sherry Alberoni as Jody Harper; Richard Eastham as Red Wilson; Anthony Eisley as Charles Diedrich; Regina Gleason as Sylvia Bancroft; and June Vincent as Dr. Amanda Winninger.

THE BRIGHTER DAY CBS

4 JANUARY 1954–28 SEPTEMBER 1962 Another successful soap opera created by Irna Phillips ("The Queen of the Soaps"), *The Brighter Day* began on radio in 1948, where it remained until 1956; from 1954 to 1956, the radio broadcast was an audio repeat of the day's television episode. The serial's central characters were the members of the Dennis family, who had just moved from Three Rivers to New Hope as the video version began. Featured were William Smith (1954–1955) and Blair Davies (1955–1962) as the Reverend Richard Dennis, a widower with five children (the eldest of the children, Liz, was never seen on TV; she had been institutionalized earlier in the series); Brooke Byron and Jayne Heller as Althea Dennis Bigby, second eldest, recently widowed; Hal Holbrook and James Noble as son Grayling Dennis; Lois Nettleton and June Dayton as teenage daughter Patsy Dennis; Mary Linn Beller and Nancy Malone as youngest daughter Barbara (Babby) Dennis; Larry Ward as Doctor Randy Hamilton, who married Patsy; Gloria Hoye and Mary K. Wells as Sandra Talbot, who married Grayling; Mona Bruns as Aunt Emily (Potter), Richard's sister; Paul Langton as Uncle Walter, Richard's brother; Herb Nelson as the Reverend Max Canfield; Muriel Williams as Lydia Herrick; Lori March as Lydia's sister, Lenore; Mark Daniels as Robert Ralston; and Joe Sirola as Peter Nino. Also featured were Patty Duke, John Heath, Harriet MacGibbon, Peter Donat, and Anne Meacham. *The Brighter Day* was televised from New York until 1961, when it moved to Hollywood. On 18 June 1962 it expanded from fifteen minutes daily to twenty-five, and moved from a late afternoon to a late morning time slot. Leonard Blair was the producer.

BRING 'EM BACK ALIVE   CBS

24 SEPTEMBER 1982–21 JUNE 1983   One of several 1982 series that tried to capitalize on the phenomenal success of the movie *Raiders of the Lost Ark* (see also *The Quest* and *Tales of the Gold Monkey*), this silly show was ostensibly based on the adventures of Frank Buck, the real-life explorer and big-game hunter of the 1930s whose motto was the show's title. The television Buck grappled not with animals, but rather with assorted smugglers and spies. Bruce Boxleitner starred as Frank Buck, with Cindy Morgan as Gloria Marlowe, who worked for the American consulate in Singapore; Clyde Kusatsu as Ali, Buck's "number one boy"; Ron O'Neal as H. H., the Sultan of Johore, Buck's buddy; Sean McClory as Myles Delaney, who ran Singapore's Raffles Hotel; John Zee as dastardly G. B. von Turgo; and Harvey Jason as Bhundi.

BRINGING UP BUDDY   CBS

10 OCTOBER 1960–25 SEPTEMBER 1961   Situation comedy about a young bachelor who boards with his two spinster aunts. With Frank Aletter as stockbroker Buddy Flower; Enid Markey as Aunt Violet Flower; and Doro Merande as Aunt Iris Flower.

BRINGING UP JACK   ABC

27 MAY 1995–24 JUNE 1995   Formulaic domestic sitcom, with Jack Gallagher as Jack McMahon, host of "The Locker Room," a sports-related radio talk show in Philadelphia, who had recently married a woman with two kids; Harley Jane Kozak as his wife, Ellen McMahon, who was pregnant with Jack's child; Matthew Lawrence as Ellen's teenage son, Ryan; Kathryn Zaremba as Ellen's preteen daughter, Molly; Jeff Garlin as Jack's cohost, Artie Hudson, a single guy who hung around at the McMahons house a lot; and Ralph Manza as Lou, Jack's producer. The series was to have premiered in March 1995, but was abruptly postponed; it then debuted in a throwaway time slot — Saturday evening of Memorial Day weekend.

BROADSIDE   ABC

20 SEPTEMBER 1964–5 SEPTEMBER 1965   Essentially a *McHale's Navy* with women, *Broadside* featured four WAVES mechanics assigned to duty at New Caledonia in the South Pacific during World War II. With Kathy Nolan as Lieutenant Anne Morgan, the commanding officer; Joan Staley as Private Roberta Love; Lois Roberts as Private Molly McGuire; Sheila James as Private Selma Kowalski; Edward Andrews as Commander Adrian, the stuffy supervisor of the New Caledonia outpost; Dick Sargent as Lieutenant Maxwell Trotter, Anne Morgan's boyfriend; George Furth as Lieutenant Beasley, Adrian's assistant; Arnold Stang as Stanley Stubbs, the cook; Jimmy Boyd as Marion Butnick, a GI mistakenly assigned to the WAVES. In the fall of 1977 ABC dusted off the format: see *Operation Petticoat*.

BROADWAY GOES LATIN   SYNDICATED

1962   Bandleader Edmundo Ros hosted this musical variety series syndicated by ITC.

BROADWAY OPEN HOUSE   NBC

29 MAY 1950–24 AUGUST 1951   Network television's first regularly scheduled late-night program was conceived by Sylvester "Pat" Weaver, the NBC VP whose ideas in programming (such as *Today, Ding Dong School, Home,* and *Wide Wide World*) helped shape American television. *Broadway Open House* bore little resemblance to the talk shows which succeeded it; the show was a heavy-handed mixture of vaudeville routines, songs, dances, and sight gags. It was to have been hosted by comedian Don "Creesh" Hornsby (so nicknamed because he yelled "Creesh!" a lot), but Hornsby died of polio two weeks before the premiere. Two veteran comedians were quickly signed up to share the hosting duties: Jerry Lester, "The Heckler of Hecklers," and Morey Amsterdam, a walking repository of jokes who also played the cello. Lester emceed the show three nights each week, Amsterdam the other two nights. Assisting them were announcer Wayne Howell, singers Andy Roberts, Jane

Harvey, and David Street, accordionist Milton DeLugg, tap dancer Ray Malone, and a buxom blonde named Jennie Lewis, but better known as Dagmar, who played it dumb. The show went through many changes of personnel, and was trimmed to three nights a week in May of 1951. Its fifteen-month week-night run demonstrated at least that there was an audience for late-night TV. Weaver refined his ideas and in 1954 introduced the *Tonight* show (see also that title).

BROADWAY SCRAPBOOK
See SHOW BUSINESS, INC.

BROADWAY TELEVISION THEATER (BROADWAY THEATER)   SYNDICATED
1952–1954   Adaptations of Broadway plays comprised this hour-long dramatic anthology series.

BROADWAY TO HOLLYWOOD   DUMONT
20 JULY 1949–15 JULY 1954   This half-hour series was one of the most durable shows aired on the DuMont network. It began in 1949 as an all-purpose show and was titled *Broadway to Hollywood Headline Clues.* Hosted by George F. Putnam, it consisted of thirty minutes of news, gossip, celebrity interviews, and a quiz for home viewers. By the fall of 1949, however, *Headline Clues* was made a separate daytime game show, while *Broadway to Hollywood* continued as a prime-time variety show. Bill Slater later hosted the series.

BROKEN ARROW   ABC
25 SEPTEMBER 1956–23 SEPTEMBER 1958   Half-hour western starring Michael Ansara as Cochise, Chief of the Apaches, and John Lupton as Indian Agent Tom Jeffords, a blood brother of Cochise. Filmed at 20th Century-Fox Studios, the series was syndicated under the title *Cochise.* Although *Broken Arrow* was one of the few westerns to show American Indians in a positive light, Michael Ansara was less than thrilled with the role: In a 1960 *TV Guide* interview, he recalled that in the series, "Cochise could do one of two things—stand with his arms folded, looking noble; or stand with arms at his sides, looking noble."

BROKEN BADGES   CBS
24 NOVEMBER 1990–22 DECEMBER 1990; 6 JUNE 1991–20 JUNE 1991   Short-lived crime show from Stephen J. Cannell Productions, starring Miguel Ferrer as Beau Jack Bowman, a New Orleans cop sent on an assignment to Bay City, California, where he decided to set up a "nonspecific undercover unit" comprised of Bay City officers who were considered misfits by their department. Bowman's team included Eileen Davidson as sexually aggressive J. J. "Bullet" Tingreedies; Ernie Hudson as forensic specialist (and kleptomanic) Toby Baker; and Jay Johnstone as ventriloquist Stanley Jones. Charlotte Lewis was featured as department psychiatrist Dr. Priscilla Mathers.

BRONCO   ABC
20 OCTOBER 1959–13 SEPTEMBER 1960   This hour-long western from Warner Brothers starred Ty Hardin as Bronco Layne, a loner who drifted across the Texas plains after the Civil War. Though *Bronco* existed as a separate series only during the 1959–1960 season, when it alternated with *Sugarfoot,* the character was seen for several seasons on *Cheyenne,* another Warner Brothers western. During the 1958–1959 season, when Clint Walker did not appear on *Cheyenne* because of a contractual dispute, a season of *Bronco* episodes was shown under the *Cheyenne* title. During the 1960–1961 season, *Cheyenne, Bronco,* and *Sugarfoot* episodes were all shown under the *Cheyenne* title (Clint Walker had returned to the show in 1959), and during the 1961–1962 season, *Bronco* and *Cheyenne* shows were aired under the *Cheyenne* banner. See also *Cheyenne; Sugarfoot.*

BRONK   CBS
21 SEPTEMBER 1975–18 JULY 1976   Jack Palance starred as Lieutenant Alexander (Bronk) Bronkov, a police detective specially assigned to the mayor of Ocean City,

California. With Joseph Mascolo as Mayor Pete Santori; Henry Beckman as former cop Harry Mark; Tony King as Sergeant John Webber, Bronk's assistant; and Dina Ousley as Ellen, Bronk's crippled daughter. Executive producer: Bruce Geller, for MGM Television. Palance apparently thought little of the series, characterizing it as "stupid" in a 1982 interview.

THE BRONX ZOO   NBC
19 MARCH 1987–6 MAY 1987; 19 AUGUST 1987–9 SEPTEMBER 1987; 9 DECEMBER 1987–20 JANUARY 1988; 30 MARCH 1988–20 APRIL 1988; 1 JUNE 1988–29 JUNE 1988   Benjamin Harrison High School, in the heart of a tough (but unnamed) inner city, was the setting for this gritty hour dramatic series that focused more on the lives of the faculty than on the students. With Edward Asner as principal Joe Danzig; Kathryn Harrold as English teacher Sara Newhouse; Nicholas Pryor as vice principal Jack Felspar; Kathleen Beller as art and drama teacher Mary Caitlin Callahan; David Wilson as history teacher Harry Barnes; Mykel T. Williamson as science teacher and basketball coach Gus Butterfield; Jerry Levine as math teacher Matthew Lippman; and Janet Carroll as Danzig's wife, Carol, who died unexpectedly on the episode of 8 June 1988. The series bounced in and out of NBC's Wednesday schedule for fifteen months, but was never aired long enough in any one time slot to find an audience.

BROOKLYN BRIDGE   CBS
20 SEPTEMBER 1991–14 NOVEMBER 1992; 10 APRIL 1993–24 APRIL 1993; 16 JULY 1993–6 AUGUST 1993   Gary David Goldberg drew on his own childhood experiences to create this sitcom about a Jewish family living in Brooklyn in 1956. The cast included Danny Gerard as fourteen-year-old Alan Silver; Marion Ross and Louis Zorich as his grandparents, Sophie and Jules Berger, who had emigrated from Russia years earlier; Amy Aquino as their daughter, and Alan's mother, Phyllis; Peter Friedman as Phyllis's husband, and Alan's father, George Silver; Matthew Louis Siegel as Alan's nine-year-old brother, Nathaniel; Jenny Lewis as Alan's sometime girlfriend, Katie Monahan; Aeryk Egan as Warren Butcher; Jake Jundef as Benny Belinsky; David Wohl as Sid Elgart; and Adam LaVorgna as Nicholas Scamperelli. Art Garfunkel composed and sang the show's theme.

BROTHERLY LOVE   NBC
16 SEPTEMBER 1995–1 APRIL 1996   Real life brothers Joey, Matthew, and Andrew Lawrence teamed up in this half-hour sitcom. Eldest brother Joey Lawrence headlined as twenty-year-old Joe Roman, who returned home after his father's death to help his stepmother run the family auto customizing business. Matthew Lawrence was Joe's fifteen-year-old half-brother, Matt, and Andrew Lawrence was seven-year-old half-brother Andy, who loved to wear disguises and costumes. Rounding out the cast were Melinda Culea as Joe's stepmother (and Matt and Andy's mom), Claire Roman; and Michael McShane and Liz Vassey as Lloyd and Lou, the two employees.

THE BROTHERS   CBS
2 OCTOBER 1956–26 MARCH 1957   CBS had high hopes for this situation comedy, which went nowhere. It starred Gale Gordon and Bob Sweeney as brothers Harvey and Gilmore (Gilly) Box, who operated a photography studio in San Francisco. With Nancy Hadley as Marilee Dorf, Gilly's girlfriend; Oliver Blake as her father, Carl Dorf; Barbara Billingsley as Barbara, Harvey's girlfriend; Ann Morris as Dr. Margaret Kleeb; and Frank Orth as Captain Sam Box, the brothers' father.

BROTHERS   SHOWTIME
13 JULY 1984–25 JULY 1989   A groundbreaking show, *Brothers* was the first original sitcom produced for pay-cable TV. It was also among the first shows on which a major character was homosexual. It starred Robert Walden as Joe Waters, a former pro football player who now ran a restaurant; Brandon Maggart as his older brother, Lou, a conservative construction worker; and Paul Regina as his younger brother, Clifford, who, as the series began, announced to his siblings that he was gay. Also featured were Philip Charles MacKenzie as Clifford's friend, Donald Maltby, a ste-

reotypically effeminate gay man; Hallie Todd as Joe's daughter, Penny; Robin Riker as Kelly, a waitress at Joe's restaurant; and Mary Ann Pascal as Samantha, who married Joe in 1988.

During its lengthy (115-episode) run, *Brothers* dealt with such topics as AIDS, gay-bashing, and coming out of the closet; it also allowed men to kiss men and dared to use the word *faggot*. It is therefore no surprise that the series had been turned down by both ABC and NBC before finding a home on Showtime. Greg Antonacci and Gary Nardino were the executive producers.

BROTHERS AND SISTERS NBC
21 JANUARY 1979–6 APRIL 1979   Half-hour sitcom set at Larry Krandall College, home of the Pi Nu fraternity and the Gamma Iota sorority. With Chris Lemmon (son of Jack Lemmon) as Checko; Randy Brooks as Ronald Holmes, Pi Nu's token black; Jon Cutler as the irrepressible Stanley Zipper; Larry Anderson as Harlan Ramsey, beleaguered president of the frat; Amy Johnston as Mary Lee, Harlan's girlfriend; Mary Crosby (daughter of Bing Crosby) as Suzi Cooper; and Roy Teicher as Seymour, frat brother with a ravenous appetite. Producers: Bob Brunner and Arthur Silver for Universal TV.

THE BROTHERS BRANNAGAN SYNDICATED
1960   This low-budget half-hour crime show was set in Phoenix and starred Steve Dunne and Mark Roberts as private eyes Mike and Bob Brannagan, who were based at the Mountain Shadows Resort Inn.

THE BUCCANEERS CBS
22 SEPTEMBER 1956–14 SEPTEMBER 1957   Set in the Caribbean island of New Providence in 1720, this half-hour adventure series featured Robert Shaw as Captain Dan Tempest, an ex-pirate turned commander of the *Sultana,* who fought evildoers; Peter Hammond as Lieutenant Beamish, the island's newly appointed governor; Paul Hansard as crewman Taffy; Brian Rawlinson as crewman Gaff; Hugh David as crewman Benjy; and Wilfrid Downing as Dickon, Tempest's cabin boy. Tempest's pet monkey was called Captain Morgan. The show was filmed at Falmouth, England; the *Sultana* had formerly served as the *Pequod* in the 1956 film *Moby Dick.*

BUCK JAMES ABC
27 SEPTEMBER 1987–10 JANUARY 1988; 10 MARCH 1988–5 MAY 1988   Dennis Weaver starred in this hour medical drama as Dr. Buck James, head of the trauma unit at the Holloman Trauma Center in Texas, who headed back to his ranch when he was off duty. With Alberta Watson as chief resident Rebecca Meyer, newly arrived from New York, whose urban manner contrasted with Buck's homespun style; Elena Stiteler as his daughter, Dinah; Jon Maynard Pennell as his son, Clint, a wrangler; Shannon Wilcox as Jenny, his ex-wife (Wilcox was well suited for the role, for in real life she was the ex-wife of a surgeon); Dehl Berti as Vittorio, the ranch foreman; and John Cullum as Henry Carliner. The lead character was based loosely on a real-life Texas surgeon/rancher, Dr. Red Duke, who had been profiled on NBC's *Lifeline* in 1978.

THE BUCK OWENS SHOW SYNDICATED
1972   A half hour of country-and-western music, hosted by Buck Owens.

BUCK ROGERS ABC
15 APRIL 1950–30 JANUARY 1951   Better known as a radio serial, *Buck Rogers* enjoyed a brief television run. It starred Kem Dibbs and Robert Pastene as Buck Rogers, an ordinary American who woke up to find himself in the year 2430; from a cave hidden behind Niagara Falls, he battled intergalactic troublemakers. Also featured were Lou Prentis as Lieutenant Wilma Deering; Harry Southern as Doctor Huer; and Harry Kingston as the evil Black Barney Wade. Babette Henry produced and directed.

BUCK ROGERS IN THE 25TH CENTURY   NBC

27 SEPTEMBER 1979–16 APRIL 1981   The second television incarnation of *Buck Rogers* was a prime-time hour, which starred Gil Gerard as Captain William "Buck" Rogers, a twentieth-century astronaut who was caught in a time warp and returned to Earth 500 years later, where he assisted the Defense Directorate. Other regulars during the 1979–1980 season were Erin Gray as Colonel Wilma Deering, commander of Earth's defense systems and Buck's romantic interest; Felix Silla as Twiki, Buck's favorite robot; and Tim O'Connor as Dr. Elias Huer, head of the Defense Directorate. Buster Crabbe, who had starred in the 1939 Buck Rogers theatrical serial, made a cameo appearance in the premiere episode, "Planet of the Slave Girls."

When the show returned in January 1981 for its brief second season, the format had changed: Buck and Wilma were aboard the *Searcher,* a space ship attempting to find the "lost tribes" of Earth who had fled the planet after a nuclear war. Tim O'Connor had left the series, and new regulars included: Thom Christopher as Hawk, a bird-man creature from the planet Throm, who was searching for others of his species; Jay Garner as Admiral Asimov, commander of the *Searcher;* Wilfrid Hyde-White as Dr. Goodfellow, the ship's scientist; and Crichton, a haughty robot who refused to believe that Dr. Goodfellow had built him. William Conrad narrated the series, which was created by Glen Larson.

BUCKAROO 500   SYNDICATED

1964   Children's variety program, hosted by Buck Weaver.

BUCKSKIN   NBC

3 JULY 1958–14 SEPTEMBER 1959   Set in the town of Buckskin, Montana, during the 1880s, this half-hour western was told from the point of view of a ten-year-old boy. It starred Tommy Nolan as young Jody O'Connell and also featured Sallie Brophy as Annie O'Connell, his widowed mother; Mike Road as Sheriff Tom Sellers; Michael Lipton as Ben Newcomb, the town schoolteacher; and Marjorie Bennett and Shirley Knight as Mrs. Newcomb. In 1958 *Buckskin* was introduced as a summer replacement for *The Tennessee Ernie Ford Show* (Ford owned an interest in the series) and was given its own berth in NBC's fall schedule.

BUFFALO BILL   NBC

1 JUNE 1983–17 AUGUST 1983; 15 DECEMBER 1983–5 APRIL 1984   Creators Tom Patchett and Jay Tarses intentionally violated one of the cardinal rules of sitcoms in this unusual half-hour series—the central character was a thoroughly unlikable soul who had almost no redeeming virtues. Dabney Coleman starred as "Buffalo Bill" Bittinger, the self-centered, self-infatuated host of a talk show on WBFL-TV in Buffalo. Also featured were Joanna Cassidy as his director, Jo-Jo White, with whom he had an affair; Max Wright as Karl Shub, WBFL's Milquetoast station manager; John Fiedler as stage manager Woody Deschler, the only person who genuinely liked Bill; Charles Robinson as Newdell, the brooding black makeup man; Geena Davis as Wendy Killian, the naive researcher; Meshach Taylor as assistant director Tony Fitipaldi; and Pippa Pearthree as prop person Melanie Bittinger Wayne, Bill's homely daughter.

BUFFALO BILL, JR.   SYNDICATED

1955   Children's western featuring Dick Jones as Buffalo Bill, Jr., an orphan adopted by a judge and subsequently named marshal of Wileyville, Texas; Nancy Gilbert as Calamity, Bill's younger sister; and Harry Cheshire as Judge Ben Wiley, their guardian, founder of Wileyville. The half-hour series was produced by Gene Autry's Flying A Productions.

THE BUFFALO BILLY SHOW   CBS

22 OCTOBER 1950–14 JANUARY 1951   Buffalo Billy was the main character in this half-hour Sunday-afternoon puppet show, set in the old West.

BUFORD AND THE GALLOPING GHOST   NBC

3 FEBRUARY 1979–1 SEPTEMBER 1979   Formerly part of *Yogi's Space Race,* Buford the lethargic bloodhound was given his own half-hour cartoon series in midseason. Buford was a crime-solving mutt who starred in "The Buford Files" segment of the show; "The Galloping Ghost" was a horse who haunted a dude ranch.

THE BUGALOOS   NBC

12 SEPTEMBER 1970–2 SEPTEMBER 1972   Live-action Saturday-morning series set in the Tranquility Forest, where a witch sought to destroy a four-insect singing group, the Bugaloos. With Martha Raye as Benita Bizarre, the witch; Carolyn Ellis as Joy; John Philpott as Courage; John McIndoe as I.Q.; Wayne Laryea as Harmony; and Billy Barty as Sparky the firefly, the Bugaloos' pal. Created by Sid and Marty Krofft.

THE BUGS BUNNY SHOW   ABC/CBS

11 OCTOBER 1960–2 SEPTEMBER 1967 (ABC); 11 SEPTEMBER 1971–1 SEPTEMBER 1973 (CBS); 8 SEPTEMBER 1973–30 AUGUST 1975 (ABC)

THE BUGS BUNNY/ROAD RUNNER HOUR   CBS

14 SEPTEMBER 1968–4 SEPTEMBER 1971; 6 SEPTEMBER 1975–7 SEPTEMBER 1985

THE BUGS BUNNY/LOONEY TUNES COMEDY HOUR   ABC

7 SEPTEMBER 1985–6 SEPTEMBER 1986

THE BUGS BUNNY & TWEETY SHOW   ABC

13 SEPTEMBER 1986–   One of the world's most popular cartoon characters, Bugs Bunny hopped into prime-time television in 1960 after a long career in animated films. His half-hour show remained in prime time for two seasons and began as a Saturday-morning series in April 1962. Bugs and his Warner Brothers cartoon pals— including Daffy Duck, Sylvester and Tweety, Elmer Fudd, and Yosemite Sam—have appeared in various half-hour, hour, and ninety-minute formats. Bugs has shared top billing with the Road Runner, the resourceful bird who always outwits his pursuer, Wile E. Coyote, and with Tweety, the diminutive household pet who always outwits his feline nemesis, Sylvester. The voice of Bugs Bunny (and of many other Warner Brothers cartoon characters) was, until his death in 1989, supplied by Mel Blanc.

THE BUICK-BERLE SHOW

See THE MILTON BERLE SHOW

THE BUICK CIRCUS HOUR   NBC

7 OCTOBER 1952–16 JUNE 1953   A musical variety hour that replaced Milton Berle's *The Texaco Star Theater* every fourth week. Regulars included Joe E. Brown, Dolores Gray, and John Raitt.

THE BUILDING   CBS

20 AUGUST 1993–17 SEPTEMBER 1993   Half-hour sitcom starring Bonnie Hunt as Bonnie Kennedy, an actress who returned to her old Chicago apartment house after her wedding plans fell through. Also on hand were Michael G. Hagerty as Finley, a firefighter and bartender; Richard Kuhlman as the foul-mouthed hoodlum, Big Tony (whose expletives were bleeped out on the show's soundtrack); Holly Wortell as Holly; Don Lake as Brad, a newspaper columnist; and Tom Virtue as Brad's roommate, actor Stanley Michaels. Bonnie Hunt created the series, and was the executive producer with David Letterman. Hunt, Wortell, Lake, and Virtue were reunited two years later on *The Bonnie Hunt Show*.

BULLSEYE   SYNDICATED

1980   Jim (*The Dating Game*) Lange hosted this question-and-answer game show, which employed a pair of contestants and a game board with three wheels; each player tried to fulfill a "contract" by answering a particular number of questions, as determined by the spin of the wheels.

THE BULLWINKLE SHOW NBC/ABC
24 SEPTEMBER 1961–12 SEPTEMBER 1964 (NBC); 20 SEPTEMBER 1964–2 SEPTEMBER 1973
(ABC)   Bullwinkle the moose, faithful companion of Rocky the flying squirrel on
Rocky and His Friends, hosted and starred in his own animated spinoff series; the
half-hour show was seen Sunday evenings on NBC for one season, before beginning
a long run on weekend mornings, first on NBC, later on ABC. Bill Scott provided
the voice of Bullwinkle, and William Conrad narrated the series. Jay Ward was the
producer. CBS reran an episode in prime time on 29 May 1991. See also *Rocky and
His Friends.*

BUMP IN THE NIGHT ABC
10 SEPTEMBER 1994–   Sophisticated animation techniques were employed in this
Saturday morning cartoon series in which a group of toys, who lived under the bed in
a little boy's room, came alive. Mr. Bumpy, a small green toad-like creature, was the
leader of the group, which also included a blue animal named Squishington and a doll
named Mollycoddle. Voices were supplied by Jim Cummings (Bumpy), Rob Paulsen
(Squishy), and Gail Matthius (Molly). The series expanded to an hour for a few
weeks during the summer of 1995.

BUMPER STUMPERS USA
29 JUNE 1987–28 DECEMBER 1990   Daytime game show, hosted by Al Dubois, on
which contestants tried to decipher the sometimes cryptic clues suggested by various
hypothetical vanity license plates.

BURKE'S LAW ABC
20 SEPTEMBER 1963–31 AUGUST 1965
AMOS BURKE, SECRET AGENT ABC
15 SEPTEMBER 1965–12 JANUARY 1966   Gene Barry starred as Amos Burke in both of
these adventure series. The character, however, was introduced on the premiere
telecast of *The Dick Powell Show*, "Who killed Julie Greer?" (26 September 1961).
Dick Powell played Burke; Ronald Reagan also appeared on the program. In
Burke's Law, Burke was the debonair homocide chief of Los Angeles. A swinging
bachelor, he was independently wealthy and traveled around town in a chauffeured
Rolls Royce. Also featured were Regis Toomey as Detective Lester Hart ("old
cop"); Gary Conway as Detective Tim Tilson ("young cop"); Eileen O'Neill as
Sergeant Ames; and Leon Lontoc as Henry, Burke's chauffeur. Most episodes were
entitled "Who Killed _____?" Many featured cameo appearances by film stars such
as William Bendix (30 September 1964, his last TV appearance), Rhonda Fleming
("Who Killed 711?" 9 December 1964, her last appearance to date), Jack Haley
("Who Killed Beau Sparrow?" 27 December 1963), Buster Keaton (8 May 1964, his
last TV appearance), Jayne Mansfield (27 March 1964, her last dramatic appear-
ance), ZaSu Pitts (20 September 1963, her last appearance), Frank Sinatra ("Who
Killed Wade Walker?" 15 November 1963), and Terry Thomas ("Who Killed Julian
Buck?" 18 October 1963, his first American appearance).
    In the fall of 1965 the show's producers decided to make Burke a secret agent
(apparently to cash in on the success of NBC's 1964 smash, *The Man from
U.N.C.L.E*). All the regulars except for Barry were dropped, and Carl Benton
Reid was added as The Man, Burke's superior. The show perished opposite NBC's
new hit, *I Spy*. Twenty-eight years later *Burke's Law* returned: see below.

BURKE'S LAW CBS
7 JANUARY 1994–9 SEPTEMBER 1994; 21 MARCH 1995–3 AUGUST 1995   The remake of
the 1963–1965 series was remarkably similar to the original. Gene Barry returned as
Amos Burke, who was still the chief of the homicide squad, who was still driven
around town in a chauffeured Rolls Royce, and who still uttered vacuous platitudes
together with the catchphrase "Burke's law." Joining Barry were Peter Barton as
Amos's handsome and eligible son, Peter Burke, also a homicide detective; Danny
Kamekona as Henry, Amos's cheerful chauffeur and butler; Dom DeLuise as
Amos's friend Vinnie, a restaurateur who often found himself at the crime scenes;

and Bever-Leigh Banfield (1995) as Lily Morgan, the homicide squad's forensics specialist. The new version continued the series' tradition of featuring stars of yesteryear in guest roles. Among them was Anne Francis, who appeared as Honey West on 21 January 1994; she had, of course, starred in the 1965–1966 series *Honey West*.

BURNING QUESTIONS ABC

13 APRIL 1989–1 JUNE 1989 This was the title of a series of prime-time documentaries on ABC, several of which were broadcast as specials before the series was given a weekly berth in April 1989. Among the topics covered were job safety ("Working in America: Hazardous Duty"), public education ("America's Kids: Teaching Them How to Think"), and honesty ("Lying, Cheating and Stealing in America"). Some programs were shown under the umbrella title *Burning Questions,* while others were aired as *ABC News Specials.*

THE BURNS AND ALLEN SHOW CBS

12 OCTOBER 1950–22 SEPTEMBER 1958 This long-running comedy series is probably best remembered for the vaudeville routines performed at the end of each show by its stars, George Burns and Gracie Allen ("Say goodnight, Gracie!"). Burns and Allen played themselves on the show, though Burns would frequently talk directly to the camera, to comment on the plot, to analyze Gracie's scatterbrained antics, or to tell a few jokes. Ronnie Burns, their son, also played himself on the show. Also featured were Bea Benaderet as Gracie's friend and neighbor, Blanche Morton. Blanche's husband (and George's accountant), Harry Morton, was originally played by Hal March, then by John Brown, until he was blacklisted by the "red scare" of the early 1950s. The part was later played by Fred Clark and Larry Keating (on the episode when Keating took over the role, Burns candidly explained to the viewing audience that Clark had asked for too big a raise and had been replaced). Bill Goodwin was the show's first announcer, but he left in 1951 to host his own series; Harry Von Zell was brought in to replace him. Ralph Levy produced and directed the half-hour show, which was done live for the first two seasons (all but the first six shows were done in Hollywood). Among the show's writers were Paul Henning (who later developed *The Beverly Hillbillies*), Sid Dorfman, Harvey Helm, and William Burns. In 1958 Gracie Allen retired from show business. George Burns tried a second comedy series, which was unsuccessful: see *The George Burns Show.* Burns also hosted a comedy anthology series in 1985: see *George Burns' Comedy Week.*

Burns's technique of talking directly to the camera—known as "breaking the fourth wall"—would not again be employed effectively until the mid-1980s. See *It's Garry Shandling's Show.*

THE BURNS AND SCHREIBER COMEDY HOUR ABC

30 JUNE 1973–1 SEPTEMBER 1973 Summer variety series cohosted by comedy duo Jack Burns and Avery Schreiber.

BURTON HOLMES TRAVELOG SYNDICATED

1949 A series of fifteen-minute travelogues filmed in America, sponsored by the Santa Fe Railroad. Burton Holmes was the host and narrator.

BUS STOP ABC

1 OCTOBER 1961–25 MARCH 1962 This drama series bore little resemblance to William Inge's play or the 1956 film which had starred Marilyn Monroe. It was billed as a dramatic anthology series with continuing characters. The guest stars, passing through Grace's Diner (located in Sunrise, Colorado) were supposed to provide the drama and the regulars the continuity. The Sherwood was the town's bus depot as well. Featured were Marilyn Maxwell as Grace Sherwood, the diner owner; Rhodes Reason as Sheriff Will Mayberry; Richard Anderson as District Attorney Glenn Wagner; and Joan Freeman as waitress Emma Gahringer. Robert Redford guest-starred in one episode, "The Covering Darkness" (22 October). The most noteworthy episode, however, was titled "A Lion Walks Among Us," broadcast 3 December. Several ABC affiliates refused to carry the episode, which attracted much publicity

before it was shown and even more afterward. Universally excoriated for its excessive violence (such as guest star Fabian going after an old man with an axe), it precipitated a congressional inquiry into violence on television.

BUSINESS WORLD ABC
5 OCTOBER 1986–28 MARCH 1993   A weekly business report, hosted by Sander Vanocur and broadcast Sunday mornings. Stephen Aug succeeded Vanocur early in 1992.

BUSTIN' LOOSE SYNDICATED
1987   Based on the 1981 motion picture, this half-hour sitcom starred Jimmie Walker (of *Good Times* fame) as Sonny Barnes, a streetwise con artist who, after one of his frequent run-ins with the law, was assigned to help out a home for foster children. Vonetta McGee played Mimi Shaw, the social worker who ran the home. The four kids included: Larry Williams as Rudey; Tyren Perry as Trish; Aaron Lohr as Nikky; and Marie Lynn Wise as Sue Anne.

BUSTING LOOSE CBS
17 JANUARY 1977–16 NOVEMBER 1977   Situation comedy about a twenty-four-year-old who left his overprotective Jewish parents to start out on his own. With Adam Arkin (son of Alan Arkin) as Lenny Markowitz; Pat Carroll as his mother, Pearl Markowitz; Jack Kruschen as his father, Sam Markowitz; Danny Goldman as his friend Lester Bellman; Greg Antonacci as his pal Vinnie Mortabito; Stephen Nathan as his pal Allan Simmonds; Paul Sylvan as his pal Woody Warshaw; Barbara Rhoades as his voluptuous neighbor, Melody Feebeck; Ralph Wilcox as Raymond St. Williams, Lenny's coworker; and Paul B. Price as Ralph Cabell, Lenny's boss, owner of the Wearwell Shoe Store. Executive producers: Mark Rothman and Lowell Ganz. Producer: John Thomas Lenox.

BUTCH CASSIDY AND THE SUNDANCE KIDS NBC
8 SEPTEMBER 1973–31 AUGUST 1974   Saturday-morning cartoon series about a bunch of young government agents posing as a rock-and-roll group.

BUZZY WUZZY ABC
17 NOVEMBER 1948–8 DECEMBER 1948   Fifteen-minute comedy series starring Jerry Bergen.

BWANA MICHAEL
See THE MICHAELS IN AFRICA

BY POPULAR DEMAND CBS
2 JULY 1950–22 SEPTEMBER 1950   This half-hour variety series, a summer replacement for *This Is Show Business,* was hosted first by Robert Alda, later by Arlene Francis. It was a Mark Goodson–Bill Todman Production.

BY-LINE ABC
20 OCTOBER 1951–16 DECEMBER 1951   Half-hour mystery series, starring Betty Furness as reporter Harriet Hildebrand. The show premiered in a Saturday daytime slot as *Newsgal*, but soon shifted to prime time.

BYLINE
See BIG TOWN

THE BYRDS OF PARADISE ABC
3 MARCH 1994–5 MAY 1994; 16 JUNEO 1994–23 JUNE 1994   Hour dramatic series about a Yale professor who, with his three kids, left New Haven after his wife's death to take a job as headmaster of a private school in Hawaii. The cast included Timothy Busfield as widower Sam Byrd; Seth Green as his sixteen-year-old, Harry; Jennifer Love Hewitt as his fifteen-year-old, Franny; Ryan O'Donohue as his eleven-year-

old, Zeke; Elizabeth Lindsey as Healani Douglas, dean of students at the Palmer School; Andy Bumatai as teacher Tony Argabrita; Alani Apio as English teacher Alan Akana; Elsa Awaya as Crystal; Robert Kekaula and Lani Opunui-Ancheta as the Byrds' housekeepers, Sonny and Manu; and folksinger Arlo Guthrie as aging hippie Alan Moon. Charles H. Eglee and Channing Gibson created the series.

THE BYRON ALLEN SHOW SYNDICATED
1989–1992   The success of *The Arsenio Hall Show* no doubt led to the creation of this weekly hour talk show, hosted by black comedian Byron Allen.

C.B. BEARS NBC
10 SEPTEMBER 1977–28 JANUARY 1978   Saturday-morning cartoon show featuring a bunch of bears who used citizens' band radios.

CBS CARTOON THEATER CBS
13 JUNE 1956–5 SEPTEMBER 1956   This little heralded summer show was network television's first prime-time cartoon show, antedating *The Flintstones* by four years. It was hosted by Dick Van Dyke, who introduced "Terrytoons," the animated adventures of such creatures as Heckle and Jeckle (who later got a show of their own), Little Roquefort, Dinky Duck, and Gandy Goose.

THE CBS CHILDREN'S FILM FESTIVAL CBS
11 SEPTEMBER 1971–25 AUGUST 1984   This Saturday-afternoon series was first introduced in 1967 on an irregular basis and was given a permanent slot four years later. Each week films from around the world of interest to youngsters were aired. The series was hosted by Fran Allison and her puppet friends, Kukla and Ollie (see also *Kukla, Fran and Ollie*).

CBS EARLY MORNING NEWS CBS
4 OCTOBER 1982–   CBS introduced its early-morning newscast three months after its competitors introduced theirs (see also *ABC World News This Morning* and *Early Today*). Broadcast weekday mornings at 6:00 A.M., it was coanchored by Bill Kurtis and Diane Sawyer, who also coanchored *The CBS Morning News* an hour later. Sawyer left in the fall of 1984, and was briefly succeeded by Jane Wallace. Thereafter Kurtis anchored the newscast alone until March 1985, when Faith Daniels succeeded him. Daniels would stay with the program for five years, sometimes as sole anchor and sometimes as coanchor. She was teamed up with Forrest Sawyer from mid-1985 to early 1986, and again from January to September of 1987; during the latter period, when CBS's ill-fated *The Morning Program* was introduced, the early morning newscast expanded to ninety minutes and was retitled *The CBS Morning News*. In late November 1987, following the cancellation of *The Morning Program,* the newscast reverted to sixty minutes, and Charles Osgood became Daniels's coanchor. The Daniels–Osgood team remained intact until the spring of 1990, when Daniels moved to NBC to anchor that network's early morning newscast. Victoria Corderi became Osgood's new coanchor. Victoria Corderi was succeeded by Giselle Fernandez in August 1991; she and Osgood coanchored until February 1992, when Meredith Vieira replaced Fernandez. John Roberts replaced Charles Osgood in June 1992; he and Vieira were paired until March 1993, when Vieira left. Roberts served as sole anchor until late August 1993, when Monica Gayle was named coanchor. Roberts departed in late 1994, leaving Gayle as the sole anchor until the spring of 1995, when Jane Robelot and Troy Roberts became the new coanchors.

CBS EVENING NEWS CBS
3 MAY 1948–   CBS has relied on just four anchors for its evening newscasts: Douglas Edwards, Walter Cronkite, Dan Rather, and Connie Chung. Edwards, who had worked with CBS radio, hosted local television newscasts in 1947 (Larry LeSueur had preceded him) and continued in that position for fifteen years; Edwards also hosted *Armstrong Circle Theater* from 1957 to 1961. For most of its run the fifteen-minute newscast was officially titled *Douglas Edwards with the News*. On 30 Novem-

ber 1956, it became the first network news show to be videotaped for rebroadcast in the western time zones.

In April of 1962 Walter Cronkite succeeded Edwards as CBS's evening newscaster (Edwards continued to do a five-minute daytime newscast until 1 April 1988). A seasoned journalist, Cronkite had worked for radio station KCMO in Kansas City before joining the United Press in 1939. Cronkite covered World War II from several locations in Europe, and on D-Day, June 6, 1944, he was chosen (by lot) to be the only reporter to cover the Normandy invasion from the air. After the war he was UP's chief correspondent at the Nuremberg trials; he then worked in Moscow before returning to the United States in 1948. He left UP to become a radio correspondent for a group of ten midwestern radio stations, and in 1950 he joined CBS News. For a time he anchored the newscasts on CBS's Washington affiliate, and in 1952 he was named the network's anchorman for the political conventions (he anchored every subsequent convention through 1980, except for the 1964 Democratic convention, when the network experimented with Roger Mudd and Robert Trout in a vain attempt to outdraw NBC's Huntley–Brinkley combination). Cronkite hosted and narrated several CBS public affairs shows during the 1950s and early 1960s, including *You Are There, The Morning Show, Air Power,* and *The Twentieth Century.* He also hosted several news specials, including in-depth interviews with former President Dwight Eisenhower and with political columnist Walter Lippmann.

Cronkite was not only the anchorman for the network newscast, but also served as its "managing editor." The dual position gave him considerable latitude in the selection, timing, and arrangement of the day's news items. It was during Cronkite's early days at anchor that the nightly broadcasts expanded from fifteen to thirty minutes. The first half-hour show was aired 2 September 1963 (a week ahead of NBC's first expanded newscast) and featured a special interview with President John Kennedy. Less than twelve weeks later Cronkite anchored the network's marathon coverage of Kennedy's death and funeral (CBS was the first of the television networks to report the shooting, interrupting *As the World Turns* at 1:40 P.M. on 22 November 1963, but it was the last to confirm his death an hour later). Cronkite also anchored the coverage of almost all of America's space missions of the 1960s and 1970s, as well as CBS's day-long coverage of America's bicentennial observance on 4 July 1976. Perhaps his most significant television reportage were his broadcasts from Vietnam following the 1968 Tet offensive, in which he sadly concluded that Americans had been misled about the course of the conflict and (much to the chagrin of President Johnson) advocated a negotiated withdrawal.

Color broadcasts of the evening news began early in 1966, about two months after NBC's. By the end of the decade, the *CBS Evening News* had recaptured the ratings lead from NBC's *Huntley-Brinkley Report.* According to a poll taken in 1974, Cronkite was America's most trusted newscaster.

From the late 1960s until his retirement in 1977, Eric Sevareid commentated on the evening news. A native North Dakotan, Sevareid joined CBS News at Edward R. Murrow's invitation in 1939 and covered World War II from several locations. From 1946 until 1959 he worked mostly in Washington, where for a time he was CBS's bureau chief. From 1961 until 1964 he hosted a series of CBS News specials entitled "The Roots of Freedom." Later in 1964 he was named national correspondent for CBS News. Cronkite's conscientious efforts to maintain objectivity and to separate news reporting from news advocacy were epitomized by the show's closing during the Sevareid years. Cronkite's familiar benediction, "And that's the way it is. . ." was deliberately omitted on those evenings when Sevareid's commentary was scheduled as the final item of the *CBS Evening News*.

Cronkite reached CBS's semi-mandatory retirement age of sixty-five in 1981 and anchored the newscast for the last time on 6 March of that year. He was succeeded on 9 March by Dan Rather, one of the two CBS correspondents who had most frequently filled in for Cronkite during the latter's vacations (the other one, Roger Mudd, soon left CBS for NBC and became that network's coanchor in 1982). A native Texan, Rather joined the network in 1962 after working in local radio and television in Houston. Shortly after joining CBS he was named the chief of its new domestic bureau in Dallas (the bureau subsequently became headquartered in New

Orleans). Rather was on the scene in Dallas at the time of President Kennedy's assassination in 1963 and anchored CBS's coverage from there. In 1964 he covered the Johnson administration at the White House. After tours of duty in London and Vietnam, he returned to the White House during the Nixon administration. His exchange of words with President Nixon at the latter's March 1974 press conference in Houston has become legendary. After recognizing Rather, Nixon quipped, "Are you running for something?" Rather immediately responded, "No sir, Mr. President, are you?" Rather left the White House beat in 1974 and joined the *60 Minutes* staff in 1975; he also hosted the irregularly scheduled *CBS Reports* documentaries.

The 1980s were turbulent years for *The CBS Evening News* and for CBS in general, as the news division coped with sagging ratings, shrinking budgets, and the alienation and loss of many of the "old guard" at CBS News (one group of the old guard, headed by *60 Minutes* executive producer Don Hewitt, even considered buying CBS News from the network). Dan Rather, the beneficiary of a ten-year, $22 million contract, saw the ratings of *The CBS Evening News* plummet to third place by the fall of 1981, when Van Gordon Sauter was named president of CBS News. Sauter, who had not come up through the division ranks, dared to redesign the newscast. He, his top assistant, Ed Joyce, and *Evening News* producer Howard Stringer (both of whom would later be news division presidents) changed not only the set, the camera angles, and Rather's wardrobe (even putting him in a sweater at one time), but also the tone of the stories. Human interest stories received more coverage. Reports of government policy decisions from Capitol Hill hearing rooms were deemphasized in favor of reports depicting the effects of those policies on individuals. Sauter characterized the new approach as "moments" television. As a direct result, many veteran reporters found themselves getting fewer stories on the broadcast, as a carefully selected list of favored correspondents, generally younger and more telegenic, was cultivated. Although many staffers from the Murrow–Cronkite era were horrified by the changes, *The CBS Evening News* climbed out of third place in 1982 and recaptured the top spot, where it remained for the next four years.

However, CBS News was no longer insulated from economic pressures, as it had been during the Murrow–Cronkite era. CBS's top executives ordered reductions in the news division's budgets, which resulted in three series of layoffs between the fall of 1985 and the spring of 1987. The latter prompted a critical op-ed piece in the *New York Times* by CBS News producer Richard Cohen (joined by Dan Rather), which the newspaper ran under the now-famous headline "From Murrow to Mediocrity." By the summer of 1987 *The CBS Evening News* had sunk again to third place in the ratings; its June 1987 figures were the lowest in twenty-five years.

Unusual things happened on the air as well. *The CBS Evening News* was to have originated from Miami on 11 September 1987, covering the pope's visit to the city. Shortly before airtime it appeared that a semifinal match of the US Open tennis tournament, which CBS Sports was carrying, would run late and would delay the start of the newscast. Dan Rather insisted that the newscast begin at 6:30 P.M. as scheduled, and, when it did not, walked off the set. When the tennis coverage ended moments later, Rather could not be located, and the network went "dark" for six minutes until the anchorman agreed to return to the desk. The Miami incident came back to haunt Rather four months later during a live interview with then vice president George Bush. As Rather attempted to pin Bush down about his alleged involvement in Iran-Contra activities, Bush countered by asking Rather if he would like to have his entire career judged by the six-minute hiatus in Miami.

Another insult to CBS News was dealt in the fall of 1988, this time by the network's own "flagship" station in New York, which opted to move *The CBS Evening News* back from 7 P.M. to 6:30 P.M. in order to run a game show in the competitive 7:00 slot. By the end of the decade, the CBS evening newscast found itself in second place most of the time, having surrendered the top spot to ABC.

In August 1990 Rather scored a major journalistic coup when he secured an exclusive interview with Iraqi leader Saddam Hussein in Baghdad, following Iraq's invasion of Kuwait.

On 1 June 1993, with *The CBS Evening News* still running second to ABC, Dan Rather was paired with a coanchor: Connie Chung. Chung had been a local reporter

131

in Washington, D.C., and a local anchor in Los Angeles before joining NBC News in the early 1980s; by 1989 she had moved over to CBS News, where she anchored weekend newscasts and hosted two magazine shows, *Saturday Night with Connie Chung* (later known as *Face to Face with Connie Chung*) and *Eye to Eye with Connie Chung*.

The pairing did nothing to improve the newscast's ratings, which soon sank to third place behind ABC and NBC. There was little on-air chemistry between Rather and Chung; indeed, the two appeared together in the New York studio on only 210 of the 513 newscasts during the two-year dual anchor period. Chung was criticized for her *Eye to Eye* interview with Kathleen Gingrich in January 1995, at which she persuaded Gingrich to confide to her that her son, Speaker of the House Newt Gingrich, thought Hillary Rodham Clinton was a "bitch." Chung was also criticized for her field reporting from Oklahoma City following the April 1995 bombing in that city. On 18 May 1995 Chung was relieved of her coanchor duties (she was also removed from *Eye to Eye*). On 22 May 1995 the newscast was retitled *The CBS Evening News with Dan Rather*, and, at the end of the program, Rather wished his former colleague "good luck and Godspeed."

THE CBS MORNING NEWS   CBS

2 SEPTEMBER 1963– CBS has tried since 1954 to compete successfully with NBC's *Today* show. First came *The Morning Show,* which ran from 1954 to 1957. Then the network experimented briefly with an early-morning variety show hosted by Jimmy Dean (see *The Jimmy Dean Show*). In 1963 the network made yet another attempt. From 1963 until 1969 it aired a twenty-five-minute morning news show which was anchored for several seasons by veteran newsman Mike Wallace. In the fall of 1966 Wallace was succeeded by Joseph Benti, who remained until 28 August 1970. It was during Benti's tenure (on 31 March 1969) that the program was expanded to a full hour. On 31 August 1970, John Hart, who had previously been featured on the show, took over the anchor desk and remained there for almost three years. In an effort to boost ratings the network teamed up a man and a woman in August 1973: Hughes Rudd, gravel-voiced former bureau chief of CBS's Moscow office, and Sally Quinn, a former reporter for the *Washington Post,* who had had no television experience. Quinn's lack of experience was apparent, and by January 1974, she was on her way back to the *Post.* (The full story of her television career, gaffes and all, is told in her book, *We're Going to Make You a Star,* which she dedicated to Hughes Rudd.) Rudd continued at the anchor desk and was soon joined by CBS correspondent Bruce Morton in Washington. Morton and Rudd both left in the fall of 1977 and were replaced by Richard Threlkeld and Lesley Stahl; Rudd continued to appear occasionally as a wry commentator. The show emphasized hard news, eschewing the lighter features characteristic of its competitors, *Today* and *Good Morning America.*

On 28 January 1979 CBS expanded its morning show to six days a week, Sundays through Fridays. The new shows were titled *Sunday Morning, Monday Morning,* etc. Bob Schieffer took over as the anchor of the weekday programs, replacing Threlkeld and Stahl; Charles Kuralt, CBS's "on the road" correspondent, was named to host the new Sunday show. To make room for the latter program, which ran ninety minutes, the network dropped three venerable but little watched Sunday series— *Camera Three, Lamp unto My Feet,* and *Look Up and Live*—each of which had been on the air for at least twenty-three years. In the fall of 1980 the titles were all shortened to *Morning,* and Charles Kuralt took over as the daily host. On 28 September 1981 the weekday telecasts expanded to ninety minutes (at the expense of *Captain Kangaroo*), and Diane Sawyer became Kuralt's cohost. On 18 January 1982 the weekday programs again expanded (again at the expense of *Captain Kangaroo*), this time to two hours, the same length as *Today* and *Good Morning America.* Kuralt left the weekday broadcasts in March of that year, and was succeeded as cohost by Bill Kurtis. Sawyer in turn left the show (for *60 Minutes*) in the fall of 1984.

To find a replacement for Sawyer, the network passed over an in-house candidate, Jane Wallace, and settled instead on Phyllis George, a former Miss America who had previously hosted *The New Candid Camera, The Challenge of the Sexes,* and *People,* but who had no news experience. George was given a three-year, multimillon-dollar contract, but proved to be a disaster. Her cohost, Bill Kurtis, quoted as expressing his disappointment that the show was now a clone of ABC's *Good Morning America,* left the program in July 1985, and was temporarily replaced by Bob Schieffer. Phyllis George herself was taken off the air in September 1985, after just eight months on the job. Another Sawyer then came aboard as cohost—Forrest Sawyer (no relation to Diane), who shared the job with Maria Shriver. Their stay lasted less than a year; both left in August 1986, when the network announced that the show would be taken away from CBS News and put under CBS Entertainment. Bruce Morton and Faith Daniels were named temporary cohosts until the new format was ready.

On 12 January 1987 *The Morning Program* made its debut. It was a ninety-minute show, produced by CBS Entertainment and hosted by actress Mariette Hartley. Rolland Smith handled the news and served as cohost, while Mark McEwen did the weather and Bob Saget did comedy; a studio audience was present. Clearly, the shift had been made from news to entertainment. To be sure, *The CBS Morning News* still existed, with Faith Daniels and Forrest Sawyer, but it was now a ninety-minute program that ran from 6:00 A.M., too early to attract more than a minuscule audience. Unfortunately, *The Morning Program* didn't attract much of an audience either, and the format was aborted after ten and a half months.

With the time slot now back in the hands of CBS News, *CBS This Morning* made its debut on 30 November 1987, with cohosts Kathleen Sullivan (formerly of *Good Morning America*) and Harry Smith. Sullivan and Smith stayed together for a little over two years; after remarking on *Donahue* that she felt an "ax hanging" over her head, and after being quoted as referring to CBS as the "Cheap Broadcasting System," Sullivan left the show in February 1990. She was succeeded by Paula Zahn (formerly of *ABC World News This Morning*); at last, all three network morning shows were cohosted by a man and a blonde woman. Greg Gumbel (brother of the *Today* show's Bryant Gumbel) became the show's sports anchor in 1989. The Smith-Zahn team remained a stable one well into the 1990s, although the ratings of *CBS This Morning* never seriously challenged those of *Good Morning America* or *Today*. In October 1995 the program acquired a new set and regained a live format.

Amid all the turmoil on the weekday show, Charles Kuralt's *CBS News Sunday Morning* managed to hang on, relatively undisturbed, through the entire decade. Kuralt bade farewell to the Sunday show on 3 April 1994; he was succeeded by Charles Osgood.

CBS NEWS NIGHTWATCH · CBS

3 OCTOBER 1982–26 MARCH 1992   CBS began providing its overnight news service about three months after NBC started its late-late-night newscast (see also *NBC News Overnight*). CBS's effort was more ambitious, offering four hours of coverage from 2:00 to 6:00 A.M., Sunday through Thursday nights. Principal correspondents were Christopher Glenn, Felicia Jeter, Harold Dow, Karen Stone, and Mary Jo West. In the summer of 1983 network-imposed budget cuts led to staffing reductions, and service was trimmed to two hours live; the second two hours was simply a rebroadcast of the first two. Charlie Rose and Lark McCarthy were the coanchors in 1984. McCarthy left in the spring of 1985, and Rose carried on as sole anchor until his departure in May 1990. The program carried on for two more years without permanent anchor until it was revamped in March 1992: see *Up to the Minute*.

CBS REPORTS · CBS

27 OCTOBER 1959–   *CBS Reports* is the umbrella title for most of the documentaries produced by CBS News. Though *CBS Reports* has sometimes been scheduled regularly (e.g., during the 1961–1962 and 1970–1971 seasons), the documentaries have usually been telecast as specials. Fred Friendly, longtime associate of Edward R. Murrow, produced the series for the first several years. The premiere telecast, "Biography of a Missile," was narrated by Murrow. Recent offerings have included "The Best Congress Money Can Buy" (a report on political campaign financing anchored by Dan Rather, broadcast 31 January 1975), "The Guns of Autumn" (a report on hunting and firearms anchored by Rather, 5 September 1975), "The American Assassins" (a four-part series, also hosted by Rather, which examined the Ken-

nedy, King, and Wallace incidents, broadcast between November 1975 and January 1976), "The Selling of the F-14" (a report on the marketing of a fighter plane to Iran, anchored by Jay L. McMullen and Bill McLaughlin, broadcast 27 August 1976), "Honor, Duty and a War Called Vietnam" (with Walter Cronkite returning to Vietnam, broadcast 25 April 1985), "Hiroshima Plus 40 Years . . . and Still Counting" (31 July 1985, also with Cronkite), "Four Days in November: The Assassination of President Kennedy" (a look back at the events of November 22–25, 1963, broadcast 17 November 1988); "CBS Reports: Who Killed JFK—The Final Chapter?" (19 November 1993), hosted by Dan Rather; "Space: Last Frontier or Lost Frontier" (14 July 1994), with Connie Chung, an examination of America's space program twenty-five years after the moon landing; and "Legacy of Shame" (20 July 1995), a follow-up to 1960's "Harvest of Shame" which examined the plight of America's migrant workers a generation later.

CBS SPORTS SPECTACULAR   CBS
3 JANUARY 1960–   The original umbrella title for CBS's long-running weekend sports anthology series; in its early seasons the show was titled *Sunday Sports Spectacular.* The Harlem Globetrotters were featured on the premiere. Later the series was titled *CBS Sports Saturday* or *CBS Sports Sunday.* On 17 April 1994 the network introduced *Eye on Sports*, a weekend sports anthology cohosted by Greg Gumbel and Andrea Joyce. Michele Tafoya succeeded Joyce in 1995.

CBS STORYBREAK   CBS
30 MARCH 1985–4 JANUARY 1986; 3 JANUARY 1987–   Cartoon adaptations of works of children's literature were presented on this Saturday morning anthology show, hosted for several seasons by Bob Keeshan, who is better known to viewers as *Captain Kangaroo*. Malcolm-Jamal Warner later hosted.

CBS SUMMER PLAYHOUSE   CBS
12 JUNE 1987–18 SEPTEMBER 1987; 21 JUNE 1988–6 SEPTEMBER 1988   This hour series presented "busted pilots"—pilot episodes of series commissioned by the network, but never ordered into further production. Some shows presented a one-hour pilot, while others consisted of two half-hour pilots. The 1987 version was hosted by Tim Reid and his wife, Daphne Maxwell Reid, and featured a "900" toll number on which viewers could indicate their preferences; although one pilot, "Doctors Wilde" (17 July), with Joseph Bottoms and Jennifer Hetrick as husband-and-wife veterinarians, received more than 100,000 affirmative calls, none of the programs ever made it onto CBS's permanent lineup. Other programs from the 1987 run included a new version of "The Saint" (12 June, with Andrew Clarke), and "Kung Ku: The Next Generation" (19 June, with David Darlow and Brandon Lee). The 1988 version of the show featured neither a host nor a telephone number.

CBS TELEVISION WORKSHOP   CBS
24 JANUARY 1960–1 MAY 1960; 2 OCTOBER 1960–25 DECEMBER 1960   Broadcast at noon on Sundays, this was an experimental anthology series. Among the presentations were "Tessie Malfitano," with Maureen Stapleton (3 April); "Afterthought," by Guy Parent, described as "a play without actors or dialogue" (1 May); "The Dirtiest Word in the English Language," with Uta Hagen and Ben Piazza (2 October); and "A Pattern of Words and Music," featuring Joan Baez, John Sebastian, and Lightnin' Hopkins.

CBS THIS MORNING
see CBS MORNING NEWS

CE NEWS MAGAZINE   PBS
13 OCTOBER 1988–12 JANUARY 1989   "CE" stood for Children's Express on this half-hour weekly newsmagazine show on which all of the contributors were fourteen or under.

C. EVERETT KOOP, M.D.
4 JUNE 1991–7 JULY 1991   This series of six informational hours about medical topics was hosted by former Surgeon General C. Everett Koop.

CHiPs
NBC
15 SEPTEMBER 1977–17 JULY 1983   Popular with young viewers, this hour action series showed the officers of the California Highway Patrol (CHiPs, for short) at work and at play. From 1977 to 1982 Erik Estrada and Larry Wilcox starred as Officers Francis "Ponch" Poncherello and Jonathan Baker, motorcycle-riding partners. Personal differences between the two stars led to Wilcox's departure after five seasons, and Estrada carried on with new partners for the show's final year. Other regulars included: Robert Pine as the commanding officer, Sergeant Joe Getraer; Paul Linke as Officer Grossman; Brodie Greer (1977–1982) as Officer Barickza; Lou Wagner (1978–1983) as Harlan, the police mechanic; Brianne Leary (1978–1979) as Officer Sindy Cahill; Randi Oakes (1979–1982) as Officer Bonnie Clark; Michael Dorn (1980–1981) as Officer Turner; Bruce Jenner (1981–1982) as Officer Steve McLeish (the former Olympic decathloner was hired to fill in for Estrada, who refused to report for work during part of the fifth season); Tom Reilly (1982–1983) as Officer Bobby "Hot Dog" Nelson; Bruce Penhall (1982–1983) as his half-brother, Officer Bruce Nelson; and Tina Gayle (1982–1983) as Officer Kathy Linahan. *CHiPs* offered its audiences lots of action, especially crashes and car chases; Estrada himself was seriously injured in a 1979 motorcycle mishap. 138 episodes were filmed.

C.P.O. SHARKEY
NBC
1 DECEMBER 1976–28 JULY 1978   Service sitcom starring Don Rickles as C.P.O. (Chief Petty Officer) Otto Sharkey, a Navy drill instructor with twenty-four years of experience. Also featured were Harrison Page as C.P.O. Robinson, Sharkey's black colleague; Elizabeth Allen (1976–1977) as Captain Quinlan, his commanding officer; tall Peter Isacksen as Seaman Pruitt; Jeff Hollis as Daniels; David Landsberg as Skolnick; Tom Ruben as Kowalski; Richard Beauchamp as Rodriguez; Phillip Sims as Apodaca; and Barry Pearl as Mignone. In the fall of 1977 two new cast members were added: Richard X. Slattery as Captain Buckner, the new commanding officer; Jonathan Daly as Whipple, his aide. The series was created by Aaron Ruben, who also served as its executive producer; Arnie Rosen was the supervising producer. Though *C.P.O. Sharkey* was not on NBC's 1977 fall schedule, it was quickly resuscitated to replace the faltering *Sanford Arms* in October.

CADE'S COUNTY
CBS
19 SEPTEMBER 1971–4 SEPTEMBER 1972   Glenn Ford starred as Sam Cade, sheriff of Madrid County, in this hour-long adventure series set in the modern-day Southwest. With Edgar Buchanan as Senior Deputy J. J. Jackson; Taylor Lacher as Deputy Arlo Pritchard; Victor Campos as Deputy Rudy Davillo; Peter Ford (Glenn's son) as Pete; and Betty Ann Carr as Betty Ann Sundown, the dispatcher.

CADILLACS AND DINOSAURS
CBS
18 SEPTEMBER 1993–26 MARCH 1994   This Saturday morning cartoon show was based on Mark Schultz's comic books. Its central characters, ecologist Jack Tenrec and scientist Hannah Dundee, traveled through a dinosaur-riddled world in a special Cadillac.

CAESAR'S CHALLENGE
NBC
14 JUNE 1993–14 JANUARY 1994   Sportscaster Ahmad Rashad hosted this short-lived daytime game show, taped at Caesar's Palace in Las Vegas. Each day three contestants tried to unscramble seven-, eight-, and nine-letter combinations to form words. Assisting Rashad was toga-clad Dan Doherty.

CAESAR'S HOUR
NBC
27 SEPTEMBER 1954–25 MAY 1957   After the ninety-minute *Your Show of Shows* left the air in 1954, Sid Caesar returned that fall in a sixty-minute format with most of the

old gang. Regulars included Nanette Fabray (1954–1956) and Janet Blair (1956–1957), who played Sid's wife in many sketches; Carl Reiner; Howard Morris; Pat Carroll (who often played Reiner's wife); Shirl Conway; Sandra Deel; Ellen Parker; singer Bill Lewis; and pianist Earl Wild. Although the show won five Emmys in 1957, it was canceled because it could not top *The Lawrence Welk Show* in the ratings race.

CAFÉ AMERICAIN   NBC
18 SEPTEMBER 1993–8 FEBRUARY 1994; 28 MAY 1994   Valerie Bertinelli starred in this half-hour sitcom as Holly Aldrich, a divorcée from Minneapolis who moved to Paris and landed a job at the Café Americain. Also featured were Lila Kaye as the owner, Margaret Hunt; Sofia Milos as model Fabiana Borelli; Peter Spears as Mark; Maurice Godin as Marcel, a mineral water executive; Graham Beckel as Steve Sullivan; and Jodi Long as Madame Ybarra, the deposed former first lady of an unnamed Asian government.

CAFE DePARIS   DUMONT
17 JANUARY 1949–4 MARCH 1949   Sylvie St. Clair hosted this fifteen-minute musical series, which was seen on Mondays, Wednesdays, and Fridays. The show, which featured Jacques Aubuchon and the Stan Free Trio, was set in a Paris bistro which St. Clair had inherited.

CAGNEY & LACEY   CBS
25 MARCH 1982–25 APRIL 1982; 25 OCTOBER 1982–12 SEPTEMBER 1983; 19 MARCH 1984–25 AUGUST 1988   *Cagney & Lacey* was the first TV crime show in which the two central characters were female. Executive producer Barney Rosenzweig had formerly worked on *Charlie's Angels,* and was not interested in doing a show like that one; after reading Molly Haskell's history of the treatment of women in films, *From Reverence to Rape,* Rosenzweig conceived of a series in which the two female leads would have a Butch Cassidy–Sundance Kid relationship. The series was based on a made-for-TV movie, aired 8 October 1981, which had starred Loretta Swit and Tyne Daly as New York police officers Chris Cagney and Mary Beth Lacey. Swit was unable to appear in a series because of her commitment to *M*A*S*H,* so Meg Foster was signed to play Cagney in the spring 1982 episodes. When the series was picked up for the following season, Foster had been dropped; *TV Guide* quoted an unnamed CBS executive as saying that Foster's character was "too tough, too hard and not feminine." Another network executive said that audience testing revealed that the "world perceived them as too masculine." Foster was replaced in the fall of 1982 by Sharon Gless (ironically, Gless had replaced the costar of another CBS series, *House Calls,* a season earlier). The new combination worked: Daly's Lacey was a solid, earthy wife and mother, while Gless's Cagney was spontaneous, beautiful, and single. Between them, Daly and Gless won six consecutive Emmys for Outstanding Lead Actress in a Drama Series. A fine supporting cast was also on hand, including: Al Waxman as the boss, Lieutenant Bert Samuels; Carl Lumbly as Detective Marcus Petrie; Martin Kove as macho Detective Victor Isbecki; Sidney Clute (1982–1985) as Detective Paul LaGuardia; John Karlen as Mary Beth's patient husband, Harvey Lacey, a contractor; Tony La Torre as their older son, Harvey Jr.; Troy Slaten as their younger son, Michael; Dana and Paige Bardolph (1985–1987) and Michelle Sepe (1987–1988) as their baby daughter, Alice; Harvey Atkin as Desk Sergeant Ronald Colman, who kept his first name secret for several seasons; Barry Primus (1984–1985) as Cagney's one-time boyfriend, Sergeant Dory McKenna, who had a drug problem; Dan Shor (1985–1986) as Detective Jonah Newman; Stephen Macht (1985–1988) as Cagney's later boyfriend, lawyer David Keeler; Dick O'Neill (1983–1987) as Cagney's alcoholic father, Charlie Cagney, a retired cop; Robert Hegyes (1986–1988) as Detective Manny Esposito; Paul Mantee (1986–1988) as Detective Al Corassa; Merry Clayton (1987–1988) as Detective Verna Dee Jordan; and Carl Weintraub (1987–1988) as plumber Nick Amatucci. Producer Rosenzweig himself appeared in one episode as a Broadway producer, while his mother-in-law, Jo Corday, was seen frequently as Josie the bag lady. *Cagney & Lacey* narrowly escaped cancellation after its first full season; CBS had decided not to renew the series at the end of the 1982–

1983 season, but complaints from viewers helped the network to change its mind. Seven episodes were ordered as midseason replacement fare, and the series returned to the air in March 1984, enjoying its highest ratings that spring.

Gless and Daly reprised their roles in several two-hour made-for-TV movies, including "Cagney & Lacey: The Return" (6 November 1994, CBS) and "Cagney & Lacey: Together Again" (2 May 1995, CBS).

CAIN'S HUNDRED NBC
19 SEPTEMBER 1961–11 SEPTEMBER 1962 Mark Richman starred as Nick Cain, a former syndicate lawyer who decided to fight crime; his mission was to apprehend the nation's 100 most dangerous underworld figures. Paul Monash was the creator and executive producer.

CALENDAR CBS
2 OCTOBER 1961–30 AUGUST 1963 A daytime series, aimed at housewives, which emphasized news and current events. Hosted by Harry Reasoner and Mary Fickett.

CALIFORNIA DREAMS NBC
12 SEPTEMBER 1992– Live-action Saturday morning series about a multi-ethnic bunch of high schoolers who formed a rock band known as California Dreams. With Brent Gore (1992–1993) as guitarist and songwriter Matt Garrison; Heidi Noelle Lenhart (1992–1993) as Matt's sister, Jennifer, the keyboardist; Kelly Packard as Tiffany Smith, who played bass and sang; William James Jones as drummer Tony Wicks; Michael Cade as the group's youthful manager, Sylvester "Sly" Winkle; Ryan O'Neill (1992–1993) as Matt and Jennifer's little brother, Dennis; Jay Anthony Franke (1993–) as the new guitarist and singer, Jake Sommers; Jennie Kwan (1993–) as the new keyboardist, Samantha Woo; Diana Uribe (1994–) as rich kid Lorena Costa; and Aaron Jackson (1994–) as Sly's cousin, Mark Winkle.

CALIFORNIA FEVER CBS
25 SEPTEMBER 1979–11 DECEMBER 1979 Hour adventure series about four carefree California teenagers. With Jimmy McNichol as Vince Butler; Marc McClure as Ross Whitman; Michele Tobin as Laurie; and Lorenzo Lamas as Rick, the proprietor of Rick's Place, a Sunset Beach hangout. The series, which was titled *We're Cruisin'* before it reached the air, was created by Dan Polier, Jr., for Warner Brothers TV and Lou-Step Productions.

THE CALIFORNIA RAISIN SHOW CBS
16 SEPTEMBER 1989–1 SEPTEMBER 1990 Saturday-morning cartoon series featuring the characters originally created in claymation form by Will Vinton Productions in 1986 for a series of commercials promoting the raisin industry. The four singing and dancing raisins were Stretch, Beebop, A. C., and Red; all the other characters on the show were fruits, vegetables, or other food products.

THE CALIFORNIANS NBC
24 SEPTEMBER 1957–10 SEPTEMBER 1959 This half-hour western was set in San Francisco during the 1850s. The original stars were Adam Kennedy as Dion Patrick and Sean McClory as Jack McGivern. Dion Patrick was an Irish immigrant who headed west to pan for gold; instead, he ended up in San Francisco and became a vigilante along with Jack McGivern, who ran a general store. By midseason, however, pressure from the show's sponsors, who were uneasy about glorifying vigilantes, caused the producers to drop Adam Kennedy and to introduce a new star. Richard Coogan joined the show in March 1958 as Matt Wayne, a newcomer to San Francisco who bought a saloon and soon became the town's marshal. Sean McClory lasted out the first season but was dropped thereafter; also featured during the first season was Nan Leslie as Mrs. McGivern. Two new regulars were added for the second season: Arthur Fleming (who would later host *Jeopardy*) as Jeremy Pitt, a young lawyer, and Carole Matthews as the widowed Wilma Fansler, who ran a

casino. Robert Bassler produced the show until January 1958, when he was replaced by Felix Feist.

CALL MR. D
See RICHARD DIAMOND, PRIVATE DETECTIVE

CALL MY BLUFF   NBC
29 MARCH 1965–24 SEPTEMBER 1965   Bill Leyden hosted this daytime game show on which contestants tried to guess which of three proffered definitions of an esoteric word was the correct one. A Mark Goodson–Bill Todman Production.

CALL TO GLORY   ABC
13 AUGUST 1984–12 FEBRUARY 1985   An ambitious idea, *Call to Glory* was envisioned as a journey through the turbulent 1960s, as seen through the eyes of a conservative Air Force family. To help achieve realism, vintage TV news clips and actual sixties music were incorporated into the story lines. Featured were Craig T. Nelson as Colonel Raynor Sarnac, Air Force pilot; Cindy Pickett as his wife, Vanessa; Elisabeth Shue as their teenaged daughter, Jackie; Gabriel Damon as their young son, R.H., who was so traumatized by fear of his father's flying that he could speak only to his sister; David Hollander as Raynor's nephew, Wesley, who lived with the Sarnacs; Keenan Wynn as Raynor's father, Carl Sarnac; J. D. Cannon as General Hampton; and David Lain Baker as Tom Bonelli, a young Air Force pilot who was interested in Jackie.

Call to Glory was originally intended to be a limited-run series, but in May 1984 ABC decided not only to make it a regular series, but also to premiere it in August, immediately after the conclusion of the 1984 Summer Olympics. The network extensively promoted the upcoming series throughout its Olympics coverage, and the two-hour premiere on 13 August (which focused on the 1962 Cuban missile crisis) drew an impressive 24.8 rating and 44 share. Audiences soon began turning away, however, and the network suggested to co-executive producers Steve Tisch and Jon Avnet that more of the scripts should center around the Sarnac family rather than on historical events. The shift in focus begat further production problems, especially with star Craig T. Nelson, and the series sputtered off the air early in 1985. Scenes from unaired episodes were subsequently pieced together for a two-hour program, "Call to Glory: JFK," set in November 1963 and aired 30 June 1985 as a TV-movie.

CALUCCI'S DEPT.   CBS
14 SEPTEMBER 1973–28 DECEMBER 1973   A half-hour situation comedy created by Renée Taylor and Joseph Bologna. Scheduled at 8:00 P.M. on Fridays, opposite NBC's *Sanford and Son,* it went nowhere. James Coco starred as Joe Calucci, supervisor of a state unemployment office in New York City, who tried to manage a motley crew of nincompoops and deadbeats. With José Perez as Ramon Gonzales; Candy Azzara as Shirley Balukis, Joe's secretary and girlfriend; Peggy Pope as Elaine Fusco; Jack Fletcher as claims adjuster Oscar Cosgrove; Bill Lazarus as Jack Woods; and Bernard Wexler as Walter Frohler.

CALVIN AND THE COLONEL   ABC
3 OCTOBER 1961–22 SEPTEMBER 1962   Freeman Gosden and Charles Correll, who created *Amos and Andy* on radio, provided the voices for this prime-time cartoon series about a bear (Calvin) and a fox (The Colonel) afoot in a big city. Other voices included those of Beatrice Kay as Sister Sue; Virginia Gregg as Maggie Belle; and Paul Frees as Oliver Wendell Clutch.

THE CAMEL CARAVAN (THE VAUGHN MONROE SHOW)   CBS
10 OCTOBER 1950–3 JULY 1951   Singer-bandleader Vaughn Monroe ("Ghost Riders in the Sky") hosted this Tuesday-night musical variety series, sponsored by Camel cigarettes.

CAMEL NEWS CARAVAN
See NBC NEWS

CAMEO THEATER NBC

14 JUNE 1950–27 SEPTEMBER 1950; 18 JUNE 1951–6 AUGUST 1951; 6 JANUARY 1952–13 APRIL 1952; 3 JULY 1955–21 AUGUST 1955   This dramatic anthology series was aired three times as a summer replacement and in 1952 was a midseason replacement for *Leave It to the Girls* on Sundays. The emphasis was on the story; no props, scenery, or fancy costumes were used in the productions.

CAMERA THREE CBS/PBS

22 JANUARY 1956–21 JANUARY 1979 (CBS); 4 OCTOBER 1979–10 JULY 1980 (PBS) A Sunday-morning fixture for more than twenty years, *Camera Three* had perhaps the loosest format of any television series: anything in the arts or sciences was fair game. Concerts, dramas, and interviews were all featured regularly. Developed by Robert Herridge, the series was broadcast locally in New York beginning in 1953. In the fall of 1979 *Camera Three* moved to prime time on PBS.

CAMOUFLAGE ABC/SYNDICATED

9 JANUARY 1961–16 NOVEMBER 1962 (ABC); 1980 (SYNDICATED)   Daytime game show on which contestants sought to trace the outline of a described object camouflaged within a larger scene on the game board. When a contestant answered a question correctly, a portion of the camouflage was electronically removed from the board. Don Morrow hosted the network version, Tom Campbell the syndicated.

CAMP CANDY NBC

9 SEPTEMBER 1989–7 SEPTEMBER 1991   John Candy, one of the stars of *SCTV,* went on to make a number of motion pictures in the late 1980s that proved popular with young audiences. In the fall of 1989 he lent his name and voice to this Saturday morning cartoon series, in which he played the chief counselor at a kids' summer camp located on the shores of Lake Cacciatore. Helped by his friends, campers Rick, Robin, Alex, Binky, Vanessa, and Iggy, and pursued by amorous Nurse Molly, he went on various adventures and spun various tall tales; some stories involved Candy's archenemy, Rex de Forrest, who plotted with his henchman Chester to buy the camp and turn it into condos.

CAMP RUNAMUCK NBC

17 SEPTEMBER 1965–2 SEPTEMBER 1966   Situation comedy about two summer camps across the lake from each other: Camp Runamuck (for boys) and Camp Divine (for girls). With Arch Johnson as Commander Wivenhoe, child-hating boss of Runamuck; Dave Ketchum as Spiffy, his second in command; Dave Madden as Counselor Pruett; Alice Nunn as Mahalia May Gruenecker, chief counselor at Divine; Nina Wayne (older sister of Carol Wayne) as voluptuous counselor Caprice Yeudleman; Hermione Baddeley as Eulalia Divine, owner of the girls' camp; Frank DeVol and Leonard Stone as Doc; and Mike Wagner as Malden, the cook.

CAMP WILDER ABC

18 SEPTEMBER 1992–26 FEBRUARY 1993   Half-hour sitcom about a divorced nurse who, with her young daughter, moved back home to care for her teenage brother and sister after their parents' death. With Mary Page Keller as nurse Ricky Wilder; Tina Marjorino as Ricky's young daughter, Sophie; Jerry O'Connell as Ricky's brother, Brody; Meghann Haldeman as Ricky's sister, Melissa; Margaret Langrick as Beth, a neighbor; Jay Mohr as Dorkman, a neighbor; and Hilary Swank as Danielle, another neighbor.

CAMPAIGN PBS

3 OCTOBER 1988–7 NOVEMBER 1988   Six-part documentary series that examined various aspects of the 1988 presidential campaign.

CAMPBELL PLAYHOUSE
NBC

6 JUNE 1952–29 AUGUST 1952   This dramatic anthology series was a summer replacement for *The Aldrich Family*. See also *TV Soundstage*.

THE CAMPBELLS
FAM

4 JANUARY 1986–31 DECEMBER 1989   Half-hour dramatic series about a Scottish family that emigrated to the Canadian frontier in the 1830s. With Malcolm Stoddard as physician James Campbell; Amber-Lea Weston as Emma Campbell; Eric Richards as John Campbell; and Cedric Smith as Captain Simms.

CAMPY'S CORNER
SYNDICATED

1960   Half-hour sports talk show, hosted by former Brooklyn Dodgers catcher Roy Campanella and sportscasters Chris Schenkel and Don Dunphy.

CAN DO
NBC

26 NOVEMBER 1956–31 DECEMBER 1956   Robert Alda hosted this Monday-night game show on which contestants tried to predict whether celebrity guests could successfully perform prescribed stunts.

CAN WE SHOP?
SYNDICATED

17 JANUARY 1994–15 JULY 1994   Following the demise of her daytime talk show, Joan Rivers experimented with her own daytime home shopping program for six months. Each day Rivers and guests hawked products, which viewers could purchase by dialing an 800 number. Local stations which aired the show received a percentage of net sales in their respective markets. Rivers had previously marketed successfully a line of jewelry on the QVC cable service.

CAN YOU TOP THIS
ABC/SYNDICATED

3 OCTOBER 1950–26 MARCH 1951 (ABC); 1970 (SYNDICATED)   This show was derived from the radio program of the same title. Jokes sent in by home viewers were read to the audience, and a celebrity panel then tried to "top" the response to that joke by telling a funnier joke on the same subject. Ward Wilson hosted the 1950–1951 network version; Wink Martindale first hosted the syndicated version but was replaced by Dennis James. Morey Amsterdam was a permanent panelist.

CANDID CAMERA
ABC/NBC/CBS/SYNDICATED

10 AUGUST 1948–3 DECEMBER 1948 (ABC); 29 MAY 1949–18 AUGUST 1949 (NBC); 12 SEPTEMBER 1949–25 SEPTEMBER 1950 (CBS); 27 AUGUST 1951–23 MAY 1952 (ABC); 2 JUNE 1953–5 AUGUST 1953 (NBC); 2 OCTOBER 1960–3 SEPTEMBER 1967 (CBS); 4 MAY 1990–31 AUGUST 1990 (CBS); 1991–1992 (SYNDICATED)

THE NEW CANDID CAMERA
SYNDICATED

1974–1978   Allen Funt created and hosted this unique, and often hilarious, human interest show on which people were filmed by a hidden camera and were "caught in the act of being themselves." The idea originated when Funt was in the armed services; he surreptitiously recorded servicemen's gripes and broadcast them on Armed Forces Radio. In 1947 Funt took the idea to network radio, and the show appeared as *Candid Microphone*. The filmed version, at first titled *Candid Microphone,* followed one year later. Many of the situations were staged by Funt and his stooges (such as driving a car with no engine into a service station, or posting a guard at the Pennsylvania-Delaware border to inform motorists that Delaware was closed for the day), but other situations were not contrived at all (such as filming a traffic cop at work, or teenage boys combing their hair). Some sequences were edited and set to music. On the early years of *Candid Camera,* Funt was assisted by Jerry Lester. When the show returned in 1960, Funt's cohost was Arthur Godfrey; Godfrey left after one season and was replaced by Durward Kirby for the next five seasons. Bess Myerson was the cohost for the 1966–1967 season. In 1974 Funt returned to television with *The New Candid Camera,* which included not only new segments, but also highlights of the old shows. Phyllis George cohosted the show from 1974 until 1976, when Jo Ann Pflug succeeded her. On 14 February 1983 the show marked its thirty-fifth anniversary with a prime-time retrospective on NBC; the hour special was cohosted by Allen Funt and Loni Anderson. Other specials have subsequently popped up in prime time; on one, titled "On Wheels" and broadcast 17 May 1989 on CBS, all the stunts involved automobiles. The series spawned a few competitors over the years: see *People Do the Craziest Things* and *Totally Hidden Video*. Funt filed suit against the latter, but did not prevail. In May 1990, in the wake of the sudden popularity of *America's Funniest Home Videos*, *Candid Camera* surfaced briefly on CBS's weekly lineup, with Allen Funt, his son Peter, and celebrity guest hosts. A daily syndicated version appeared in 1991, hosted by Dom DeLuise. This version, which was licensed by the Funt family to King World, was criticized by Peter Funt in *Variety*, who called it "not a good show—and not very funny."

CANNON   CBS
14 SEPTEMBER 1971–19 SEPTEMBER 1976   This successful crime show starred William Conrad as Frank Cannon, a former cop turned private eye. Though television viewers may not have recognized Conrad's hefty frame before this series, his voice certainly should have been familiar: Conrad was radio's Matt Dillon on *Gunsmoke*, and narrated several television series, including *Rocky and His Friends*, and *The Fugitive*. A Quinn Martin production, *Cannon* was one of the few series of the 1970s with only one regular; 124 episodes were made. The character came out of retirement in a made-for-TV movie, "The Return of Frank Cannon," telecast 1 November 1980.

CANNONBALL   SYNDICATED
1958   A half-hour adventure series about a couple of long-distance truckers (NBC exhumed this concept for its 1974 series, *Movin' On*). With Paul Birch as Mike Malone and William Campbell as his partner, Jerry Austin. Robert Maxwell was the producer.

CAN'T HURRY LOVE   CBS
18 SEPTEMBER 1995–26 FEBRUARY 1996   Nancy McKeon starred in this half-hour sitcom as Annie O'Donnell, a young single woman who lived in a New York apartment, worked for an employment agency, and tried to find true love. With Mariska Hargitay as Annie's hedonistic neighbor, Didi Edelstein; Louis Mandylor as Roger Carlucci, Annie's oversexed coworker at People Pleasers; and Kevin Crowley as Elliot Tenney, Annie's married coworker.

CAPITAL NEWS   ABC
9 APRIL 1990–30 APRIL 1990   *The Washington Capital,* a great metropolitan daily newspaper, was the centerpiece of this hour dramatic series. The ensemble cast included Lloyd Bridges as Jonathan "Jo Jo" Turner, the editor; Mark Blum as national editor Edison King; Christian Clemenson as mild-mannered reporter Todd Lunden; Kurt Fuller as Miles Plato, flamboyant syndicated gossip columnist; Wendell Pierce as Conrad White, a black reporter assigned to the local desk; William Russ as maverick local reporter Redmond Dunne; Helen Slater as rookie reporter Anne McKenna, also assigned to the local desk; Michael Woods as local editor Clay Gibson; Jenny Wright as local reporter Doreen Duncan; Chelsea Field as national reporter Cassy Swann; and Charles Levin as business editor Vinnie DiSalvo. David Milch, who had previously worked on *Hill Street Blues,* created the series with Christian Williams.

CAPITOL   CBS
29 MARCH 1982–20 MARCH 1987   Washington, D.C., with its trappings of politics and power, was the locale for this half-hour daytime serial. The original storyline centered on two powerful, feuding families, the McCandlesses and the Cleggs; borrowing a plot from *Romeo and Juliet, Capitol*'s writers arranged to have a McCandless son fall in love with a Clegg daughter. The cast included: Rory Calhoun as Judge Judson Tyler, head of the McCandless clan; Constance Towers as his daughter, Clarissa McCandless, mother of four; David Mason Daniels and Dane Witherspoon as son Tyler, a politician; Brian-Robert Taylor and Michael Catlin as crippled son Thomas, a doctor; Bill Beyers as son Wally, a gambler; Shea Farrell and Chris

Durham as son Matt, a jock; Kelly Palzis as daughter Gillian, a college student (Gillian was actually a distant relative adopted by Clarissa); Carolyn Jones (who died in August 1983), Marla Adams, and Marj Dusay as Myrna Clegg, head of the Clegg clan; Nicholas Walker as Myrna's stepson, Samuel "Trey" Clegg III, a congressman; Leslie Graves, Ashley Laurence, and Karen Kelly as Myrna's daughter, Brenda; Todd Curtis as Myrna's son, Jordy (after Curtis sustained facial scars in an auto accident, his character met the same fate); Kimberly Beck-Hilton and Catherine Hickland as Myrna's daughter (and Jordy's twin sister), Julie Clegg, who fell for Tyler McCandless and married him in September 1983 (Hickland also played Jenny Diamond); Ed Nelson as Myrna's friend, Senator Mark Denning; Julie Adams as Mark's wife, Paula Denning; Deborah Mullowney (later known as Debrah Farentino) as Mark's daughter, Sloane Denning, a reporter who married Trey Clegg; Anthony Eisley as Philip Dade; Corinne Michaels as his wife, Joan Dade; Jeff Chamberlain as Lawrence Barrington, a spy; Robert Sampson and Richard Egan as Samuel Clegg II, Trey's father; Wolf Muser as Kurt Voightlander; Rodney Saulsberry as Jeff Johnson; Tonja Walker as Lizbeth Bachman; Carol Cooke as Sugar Laine; Kimberly Ross as Amy; Lana Wood as Amy's mother, Fran Burke; Victor Brandt and Eddie Zammit as Danny Donato; Dawn Parrish as Veronica Angelo; Julie Parrish as Maggie Brady; Todd Starks as Roje Avery; Bradley Lockerman as Zed Diamond; Jim McKrell as Dr. Yale Parker; Jane Daly Gamble and Jess Walton as former prostitute Shelly Granger, later known as Kelly Harper; Walter Malet as Hal Dayton; Billy Warlock as Ricky Driscoll; Becca C. Ashley as Cheetah; Lindsey Richardson as Chip Landry; Lara Parker as Linda Vandenburg; Valarie Reynolds as Vera Sweet; Joey Aresco as Nino Vincent; Beth Windsor as Frankie Bridges; Paul Comi as Victor Markham; Christine Kellogg as Leanne Foster; Ron Harper as Jarrettt Morgan/Baxter Mc-Candless, who married Clarissa in 1986; Grant Aleksander as D. J. Phillips; Cheryl-Ann Wilson as Kate Wells; Peter Lochran as Prince Ali; Alisha Das as Princess Yasmeen, who married Ali in 1986; Teri Hatcher as Angelica, who married Trey Clegg in 1986; Mitch Brown as Dylan Ross; and Malachi Pearson as Scotty Harper, Kelly's son. Among the celebrities who made guest appearances were Michael Reagan (three shows in 1986), Lola Falana as Charity Blake, and Tammy Wynette, who appeared as waitress Darlene Stenkowski.

Capitol was the first daytime serial to be introduced during prime time; a special one-hour preview was aired on Friday, 26 March 1982, three days before the series's daytime premiere (ABC would follow the same practice with its 1983 soap, *Loving*). John Conboy (of *The Young and the Restless*) was the executive producer of the series, which encountered strong competition from ABC's *One Life to Live*. *Capitol* went through three sets of head writers in its first eighteen months: Stephen and Elinor Karpf were succeeded by Joyce and John William Carrington, who were in turn succeeded by Peggy O'Shea. Henry Slesar later served as head writer. The series never enjoyed high ratings, and vanished after a modest five-year run. Although most canceled daytime serials have tied up loose ends on their final episodes, *Capitol* did not: the program terminated with reporter Sloan Denning facing a firing squad in the Mideast nation of Baracq.

CAPITOL CAPERS   NBC
1 AUGUST 1949–7 SEPTEMBER 1949   A fifteen-minute musical variety show, broadcast twice a week before the evening news from Washington, D.C. The show featured singer Gene Archer and was also known as *The Gene Archer Show*.

CAPITOL CLOAKROOM   CBS
14 OCTOBER 1949–15 SEPTEMBER 1950   Friday-night public affairs program, with Eric Sevareid, Willard (Bill) Shadel, Griffing Bancroft, and a guest panelist. The show was broadcast live from Washington, D.C. Explanatory notes

CAPITOL CRITTERS   ABC
28 JANUARY 1992–29 FEBRUARY 1992   Steven Bochco created this prime-time animated sitcom set at the White House. Its central characters were the vermin—rats, mice, and roaches—who lived there. Among the many characters were Max, a

mouse from Nebraska; Moze the cockroach; Berkeley, a hippie mouse; and Muggle, an escaped lab rat. Neil Patrick Harris supplied Max's voice, Bobcat Goldthwait supplied Muggle's.

THE CAPTAIN & TENNILLE ABC
20 SEPTEMBER 1976–14 MARCH 1977   ABC's answer to Sonny and Cher, The Captain (Daryl Dragon) and Tennille (Toni Tennille, his wife) were given their own musical variety series after a string of hit records, the biggest of which was "Love Will Keep Us Together" (written by Neil Sedaka). The laconic Captain and the toothsome Tennille were both talented musicians (each had worked at one time with the Beach Boys), but neither seemed at ease with the labored comedy sketches which often dominated the series.

CAPTAIN BILLY'S MISSISSIPPI MUSIC HALL CBS
24 SEPTEMBER 1948–3 DECEMBER 1948   This half-hour musical variety show was set aboard a nineteenth-century riverboat and was hosted by Ralph Dumke as Captain Billy Bryant. Also on board were Johnny Downs, Bibi Osterwald, and Juanita Hall. The series was produced by Paul Killiam and actually premiered (as *Captain Billy's Showboat*) on 16 August 1948, though it was not broadcast weekly until late September.

CAPTAIN CAVEMAN AND THE TEEN ANGELS ABC
8 MARCH 1980–21 JUNE 1980   The central character in this Saturday-morning cartoon series was Captain Caveman, a prehistoric creature who had been frozen in a glacier; after thawing out, he teamed up with a trio of teenage girls—Brenda, Dee Dee, and Taffy—and helped them solve mysteries. The cartoons were originally shown in 1977 as part of *Scooby's All-Star Laff-a-Lympics* and were subsequently seen in 1980 on *The Flintstones Comedy Show*.

CAPTAIN DAVID GRIEF SYNDICATED
1955   These adaptations of the Jack London stories starred Maxwell Reed as South Seas sailor Captain David Grief and Maureen Hingart as Anura, his permanent passenger aboard the *Rattler*.

CAPTAIN GALLANT OF THE FOREIGN LEGION NBC
13 FEBRUARY 1955–7 DECEMBER 1957   This half-hour adventure series for children starred Buster Crabbe as Captain Michael Gallant, commander of the North African headquarters of the French Foreign Legion. Also featured were Cullen Crabbe (Buster's son) as Cuffy Sanders, an orphan taken in by Captain Gallant after the death of his Legionnaire father; Al "Fuzzy" Knight as Private Fuzzy Knight; and Gilles Queant as Sergeant Du Val. Produced by Serge Glykson, the series was filmed on location from 1954 until 1956, when production was shifted to the politically safer climate of Northern Italy. Syndicated reruns were shown under the title *Foreign Legionnaire*.

CAPTAIN HARTZ AND HIS PETS SYNDICATED
1954   Ned Locke starred in this children's series as Captain Hartz, an airline pilot who brought back unusual pets from his travels; Jerry Garvey was also featured as his teenage pal.

CAPTAIN KANGAROO CBS
3 OCTOBER 1955–8 DECEMBER 1984   Television's longest-running network children's series. Its star, Bob Keeshan, began his show business career as Clarabell on *Howdy Doody*. After hosting two local shows in New York (*Time for Fun* and *Tinker's Workshop*), he brought this show on the air in 1955, playing Captain Kangaroo, a gentle man so named because of the large pockets of his jacket (the show premiered on the same day as *The Mickey Mouse Club*). In three decades the show changed little. Stressing gentleness, with a touch of morality and religion, Keeshan managed to keep its tone calm and its pace even. The show was geared to the individual child

watching at home—no children appeared in the studio (though some were occasionally featured in filmed segments). But the Captain was not alone; Hugh (Lumpy) Brannum, as Mr. Green Jeans, was with the show from its early days. Mr. Green Jeans was apparently a farmer (and an amateur inventor); several times a week he introduced animals on the show. For many seasons Cosmo Allegretti was featured as Dennis, the bumbling apprentice. Allegretti and Brannum also appeared in other roles on the show; in addition, Allegretti was the show's chief puppeteer and was thus responsible for such characters as the mischievous Mr. Moose, the introspective Bunny Rabbit, the curious Miss Frog, the quiet Mr. Whispers, and the erudite Word Bird. Cartoons were also featured but never predominated in the show; one of the most popular segments during the 1950s was "Tom Terrific," the serialized adventures of Tom Terrific, a little boy who could change himself into anything, and his canine sidekick, Mighty Manfred the Wonder Dog. During most of the 1970s two other humans were also featured: Larry Wall as Mr. Baxter and Debby Weems as Debby. Bill Cosby became a regular contributor in the fall of 1980, and shortly thereafter a character known as Slim Goodbody began to appear; played by John Burstein, Slim wore a costume showing the parts of the body and sang "Top 40 Health Hits." Additionally, many guest stars have appeared on *Captain Kangaroo,* including Alan Arkin, Pearl Bailey, Carol Channing, Imogene Coca, Doug Henning, Earl Monroe, Dick Shawn, Marlo Thomas, Edward Villella, and Eli Wallach.

For the first three months of its run, *Captain Kangaroo* was seen on weekday mornings. On 7 January 1956 a Saturday telecast was added, and the show could be seen six days a week until 7 September 1968, except during the 1964–1965 season when Keeshan hosted a separate series on Saturdays (see *Mister Mayor*). Occasionally the show was aired in a forty-five-minute format, but for most of its run between 1955 and 1981 it occupied a full hour. During the 1970s, about 120 new programs were made each year and were mixed in with reruns.

In the fall of 1981 *Captain Kangaroo*'s 8:00 A.M. time slot was changed to make room for the expanding *CBS Morning News.* On 28 September it was moved back to 7:00 A.M., trimmed to thirty minutes, and retitled *Wake Up with the Captain.* Less than four months later, on 18 January 1982, when *CBS Morning News* expanded to two hours, *Wake Up* was moved back again, to 6:30 A.M., an hour when very few children (or grownups) were even awake. On 18 September 1982, after a twenty-seven-year weekday run, the program was moved to weekends, where it was seen at 7:00 A.M. on Saturdays and 8:00 A.M. Sundays (the Saturday shows were new ones, the Sunday shows were reruns from the previous season). *Captain Kangaroo*'s departure from the weekday schedule marked the end of an era. By 1982 it was the only weekday program on any of the three commercial networks aimed specifically at children. In the fall of 1984 the show was reduced to a half-hour, and left the network, after a twenty-nine-year run, in December of that year. Keeshan later turned up on CBS's Saturday morning schedule as the host of *CBS Storybreak.* In 1991 and 1992 edited excerpts from the series, blended with some newly produced segments, were made available to public television stations.

Bob Keeshan has long been aware of the impact of commercials on young viewers. No cast members delivered commercials on the show, and all advertisements were approved by program executives. Keeshan was among the first people to insert "bumpers"—announcements separating the program from the commercials—a practice later implemented by all the networks (and most local stations) on their child-oriented shows.

CAPTAIN MIDNIGHT   CBS

4 SEPTEMBER 1954–12 MAY 1956   A half-hour adventure series for children, *Captain Midnight* began on radio in 1940 and ran for thirteen years. On TV, Richard Webb starred as Captain Midnight, head of the Secret Squadron, an omnibus crime-fighting agency (according to the radio story, Captain Midnight was really Captain Albright, a brave and daring World War I flying ace who returned to his home base after a particularly hazardous mission precisely at the stroke of midnight). Also featured were Sid Melton as Ichabod (Ikky) Mudd, Midnight's none-too-bright assistant, and Olan Soule as Tut (Aristotle Jones), an eccentric scientist who worked for the Secret

Squadron. The network version of the series was sponsored by Ovaltine, which had also sponsored the radio show. Because Ovaltine owned the rights to the name "Captain Midnight," when the reruns of the series went into syndication (without Ovaltine's sponsorship) they were seen under the title *Jet Jackson, Flying Commando;* all references in the dialogues to "Captain Midnight" were crudely over-dubbed with the words "Jet Jackson."

CAPTAIN N: THE GAME MASTER   NBC

9 SEPTEMBER 1989–25 JULY 1992   Saturday morning hour cartoon series about a young boy, Kevin, and his dog, Duke, who crossed over through their home video screen into the world of Videoland. There the boy, known as Captain N, went on various adventures (some of which were based on Nintendo video games) with Duke and their new friends, Megaman the robot, Princess Lana, self-infatuated Simon Belmont, and Dr. Wilcy. The group's chief foe was the evil Motherbrain. The main title sequence used live action; Dorian Barag appeared as Kevin and Louie played Duke.

In the fall of 1990 another Nintendo-based segment was added, as the show was retitled *Captain N and the Adventures of Super Mario Bros. 3.* In the new segment, brothers Mario and Luigi (who were also featured on the syndicated *Super Mario Bros. Super Show*) battled King Coopa and his seven kids, and tried to help Princess Toadstool. In the fall of 1991 the series was retitled *Captain N and the New Super Mario World.*

CAPTAIN NICE   NBC

9 JANUARY 1967–28 AUGUST 1967   An imitation *Batman, Captain Nice* was set in Big Town. With William Daniels as Carter Nash, a police chemist who devised a secret formula, one swallow of which turned him into Captain Nice, crimefighter; Alice Ghostley as his mother, Mrs. Nash; and Ann Prentiss as Sergeant Candy Kane, his admirer. (*Captain Nice* should not be confused with *Mr. Terrific,* the CBS imitation *Batman,* which premiered and closed on the same dates as *Captain Nice.*)

CAPTAIN PLANET AND THE PLANETEERS   TNT/SYNDICATED

16 SEPTEMBER 1990– (TNT); 1990– (SYNDICATED)   Half-hour cartoon series in which Captain Planet and his five-kid Planeteer force battled environmental villains around the world.

CAPTAIN POWER AND THE SOLDIERS OF THE FUTURE   SYNDICATED

1987–1988   Although many kids' shows of the 1980s were based on toys, this one went one step further: kids who owned Mattel's Powerjet XT-7 or Phantom Striker could actually play along and attempt to zap characters onscreen. This form of "interactive" television had not been seen since the days of *Winky Dink and You* three decades earlier. *Captain Power and the Soldiers of the Future* combined live action and computer animation; each episode contained a five-minute "interactive" segment. The half-hour daily series was set in the year 2146, when the good guys—Captain Power and his cohorts—battled the baddies, led by Lord Dread. Tim Dunigan starred as Captain Jonathan Power. David Hemblen appeared as Lord Dread; Sven-Ole Thorsen played Tank; Peter MacNeil was Hawk; Maurice Dean Wint was Scott; and Jessica Steen was The Pilot.

CAPTAIN SCARLET AND THE MYSTERONS   SYNDICATED

1967   Created by Gerry and Sylvia Anderson, this British children's series was filmed in "Supermarionation," a technique using plastic models operated by very fine wires. Captain Scarlet led the forces of Spectrum, an international planetary defense force, against the Mysterons, unseen invaders from Mars.

CAPTAIN VIDEO   DUMONT/SYNDICATED

27 JUNE 1949–1 APRIL 1955 (DUMONT); 1953–1955 (SYNDICATED); 1956 (SYN-DICATED)   Television's best-known space serial began in 1949 with Richard Coogan as Captain Video, the ordinary human who led the Video Rangers, a squad

of loyal agents which fought terrestrial and extraterrestrial villains during the twenty-second century. Coogan was replaced later in 1949 by Al Hodge, who continued in the role for seven years. Also featured were Don Hastings (who would go on to greater fame in *As the World Turns*) as a teenager, The Video Ranger, the Captain's main assistant; Hal Conklin as Dr. Pauli, the Captain's arch-enemy; and Tobor the robot ("Tobor" is "robot" spelled backwards), originally a foe but later an ally of the Captain. Guest villains over the years included Ernest Borgnine (as Nargola, one of his first TV roles), Jack Klugman, and Tony Randall.

A scientific genius, Captain Video invented dozens of fantastic gadgets in his secret mountain headquarters, such as the Remote Tele-Carrier, the Cosmic Vibrator, the Opticon Scillometer, and the Astra-Viewer. His first spaceship— the *X-9*—crashed; Video replaced it with the *Galaxy*. Broadcast live from New York for its first six years, *Captain Video* started out as a half-hour show four nights a week; by the fall of 1949 it was on every weeknight. To fill the half hour, clips from old western moviews were spliced in; it was explained that the good guys were allies of Captain Video. In the fall of 1953 the daily version was cut back to fifteen minutes, and it was finally dropped in 1955. In 1953, however, a second *Captain Video* series had begun, titled *The Secret Files of Captain Video*, which appeared in a half-hour, noncontinuing form. In 1956 Al Hodge returned as the host of a syndicated cartoon show, *Captain Video's Cartoons*. After *Captain Video* left the air, Al Hodge appeared only rarely on television. In March of 1979 he died alone in a New York hotel room.

Written by M. C. Brook, the original *Captain Video* was the first and longest-running of the several TV space shows; it spawned a host of competitors, including *Atom Squad, Captain Midnight* (which was not actually set in outer space), *Commando Cody, Rocky Jones, Space Ranger, Rod Brown of the Rocket Rangers, Space Patrol*, and *Tom Corbett, Space Cadet*.

CAPTAIN Z-RO   SYNDICATED
1955   Children's fantasy series written by and starring Roy Steffens as Captain Z-Ro, inventor of a combination rocket ship and time machine. This device enabled him to travel anywhere in the past, present, or future. The show, which began as a local show in Los Angeles in 1952, also featured Bobby Trumbull as Jet, his teenage assistant.

CAPTURED
See GANGBUSTERS

CAR 54, WHERE ARE YOU?   NBC
17 SEPTEMBER 1961–8 SEPTEMBER 1963   Created by Nat Hiken, who also created *You'll Never Get Rich, Car 54* was the first situation comedy about police officers. It was also one of the few series of its time to feature a black performer (Nipsey Russell) as a regular. The large cast included Joe E. Ross (he played Ritzik on *You'll Never Get Rich*) as Officer Gunther Toody; Fred Gwynne as his partner, Officer Francis Muldoon; Beatrice Pons as Lucille Toody, Gunther's wife (Pons had played Ritzik's wife on *You'll Never Get Rich;* Ross and Pons thus became the first actor-actress team to play two different married couples on two sitcoms); Al Lewis as Schnauzer; Charlotte Rae as Mrs. Schnauzer; Paul Reed as Captain Block; Nipsey Russell as Officer Dave Anderson; Fred O'Neal as Officer Wallace; Mickey Deems as Officer Fleisher; Al Henderson as Officer O'Hara; Duke Farley as Officer Riley; Hank Garrett as Officer Nicholson; Shelley Burton as Officer Murdock; Jerry Guardino as Officer Antonnucci; Jim Gormley as Officer Nelson; and Joe Warren as Officer Steinmetz. Sixty episodes were produced. A theatrical movie was released in 1994, with David Johansen and John C. McGinley as Toody and Muldoon; Nipsey Russell and Al Lewis reprised their roles.

THE CARA WILLIAMS SHOW   CBS
23 SEPTEMBER 1964–10 SEPTEMBER 1965   Half-hour sitcom about a pair of newlyweds who worked for a company where marriage between employees was forbidden. With Cara Williams as Cara Bridges; Frank Aletter as her husband, Frank Bridges; Jack

Sheldon as their neighbor, jazz trumpeter Fletcher Kincaid; Paul Reed as their boss, Damon Burkhardt; Reta Shaw as Mrs. Burkhardt; and Jeanne Arnold as Mary, Burkhardt's secretary. The series was developed by Keefe Brasselle.

CARD SHARKS   NBC/SYNDICATED/CBS
24 APRIL 1978–23 OCTOBER 1981 (NBC); 1982 (SYNDICATED); 1986 (SYNDI-CATED); 6 JANUARY 1986–31 MARCH 1989 (CBS)   The basic format of this game show was one of the simplest ever devised: contestants tried to predict whether the value of the next playing card would be higher or lower than the preceding one. Jim Perry presided over the NBC daytime and 1982 syndicated versions. The show surfaced again in 1986, with an added wrinkle: contestants had to first predict how a group of one hundred persons had answered a question before they could tackle the cards. Bob Eubanks hosted the CBS daytime version, while Bill Rafferty emceed the syndicated one.

THE CARE BEARS FAMILY   ABC/SYNDICATED
13 SEPTEMBER 1986–23 JANUARY 1988 (ABC); 1988–1990 (SYNDICATED)   A car-toon show based on the line of toys and books, and the 1985 motion picture, about the Care Bears Family, each member of whom depicted a human emotion, who left their home on Carealot each week to help youngsters learn about their emotions, and to battle the evil Dark Heart, who sought to rid the world of feelings. The series ran on ABC's Saturday morning schedule for a season and a half, before going into syndication.

CARIBE   ABC
17 FEBRUARY 1975–11 AUGUST 1975   Standard crime show about a two-man police unit (Caribe Force), operating out of Miami, whose territory spanned the Caribbean. With Stacy Keach as Lieutenant Ben Logan; Carl Franklin as Sergeant Mark Walters; and Robert Mandan as Police Commissioner Ed Rawlings. This Quinn Martin production was filmed on location.

THE CARLTON FREDERICKS SHOW   SYNDICATED
1967   Health and diet were the subjects discussed on this half-hour talk show hosted by nutrition expert Carlton Fredericks.

THE CARMEL MYERS SHOW   ABC
26 JUNE 1951–21 FEBRUARY 1952   Fifteen-minute Tuesday-night interview show, hosted by former silent film star Carmel Myers.

CARNIE   SYNDICATED
1995–1996   Hour daytime talk show, broadcast from New York and hosted by Carnie Wilson. Wilson, the daughter of Beach Boy Brian Wilson, was herself one-third of the pop group Wilson Phillips.

CAROL & COMPANY   NBC
31 MARCH 1990–20 JULY 1991   Carol Burnett returned to series television in an unusual format: a comedy anthology series. Each week Burnett and her repertory company (sometimes augmented by guest stars) performed a single comedy skit. The repertory players included Anita Barone, Meagen Fay, Richard Kind, Terry Kiser, Peter Krause, and Jeremy Piven.

CAROL BURNETT & COMPANY   ABC
18 AUGUST 1979–8 SEPTEMBER 1979   A four-week comedy-variety hour with Carol Burnett, Tim Conway, Vicki Lawrence, Craig Richard Nelson, and Kenneth Mars.

THE CAROL BURNETT SHOW   CBS
11 SEPTEMBER 1967–9 AUGUST 1978   Popular variety hour hosted by Carol Burnett, a physical comedienne who became familiar to audiences during her three seasons on *The Garry Moore Show*. By the fall of 1975, *The Carol Burnett Show* was the second-

oldest prime-time series on the air (*Walt Disney* was first). A California native, Burnett moved to New York in the mid-1950s, where she landed a role on Buddy Hackett's 1956 sitcom, *Stanley*. She then guested on several variety shows, including *The Garry Moore Show* (daytime version) and Jack Paar's *Tonight* show, where she brought down the house singing a novelty number, "I Made a Fool of Myself over John Foster Dulles." In 1959 she became a regular on the nighttime version of *The Garry Moore Show;* it was there that she met her husband and future producer, Joe Hamilton. After leaving the Moore show in 1962, she appeared in several specials and also hosted *The Entertainers* in 1964. On her own show she brought together a group of talented supporting players: Harvey Korman, a versatile funny man who had previously been featured on *The Danny Kaye Show;* handsome Lyle Waggoner; and a newcomer named Vicki Lawrence, whose resemblance to Burnett led her to be cast as Burnett's younger sister in many sketches. In 1974 Waggoner left the series; a year later Tim Conway (who had guested frequently on the show) joined as a regular. Korman left in 1977 and was replaced by Dick Van Dyke, who announced his "resignation" from the series in December 1977. In later seasons, the show did not emphasize guest stars, relying instead on the talents of the regulars. Spoofs of movies, especially musicals, had become a staple; other recurring segments included "As the Stomach Turns," a soap opera parody, and "The Family," a group of rural folks who constantly bickered with one another. Most shows began with questions from the studio audience and ended with Burnett tugging her ear. Music was supplied by the Peter Matz Orchestra, with choreography by Ernest Flatt and costumes by Bob Mackie. See also *Carol & Company; Mama's Family.* Two retrospectives were produced: "The Carol Burnett Show: A Reunion" (10 January 1993, CBS), and "Carol Burnett: The Special Years" (20 May 1994, CBS).

THE CAROL BURNETT SHOW   CBS
1 NOVEMBER 1991–20 DECEMBER 1991   Carol Burnett's fourth prime-time series, which lasted only seven weeks, was an hour of sketch comedy. Assisting Burnett were Rick Aviles, Chris Barnes, Meagen Fay, Roger Kabler, Jann Karam, Richard Kind, and Jessica Lundy.

CAROLINE IN THE CITY   NBC
21 SEPTEMBER 1995–   Half-hour sitcom about a single woman coping with life in New York. It featured Lea Thompson as cartoonist Caroline Duffy, who made a living designing greeting cards and drawing the "Caroline in the City" comic strip; Eric Lutes as Del Cassidy, Caroline's boyfriend and the head of the greeting card company; Malcolm Gets as Richard Karinsky, a quirky, starving painter who took a job as Caroline's illustrator; Amy Pietz as Caroline's TriBeCa neighbor, Annie Spidara; Andy Lauer as Charlie, one of Del's goofy employees; and Tom La Grua as Remo, proprietor of Remo's, Caroline and Del's favorite restaurant.

THE CAROLYN GILBERT SHOW   ABC
15 FEBRUARY 1950–23 JULY 1950   A fifteen-minute musical variety show hosted by singer Carolyn Gilbert.

CARRASCOLENDAS   PBS
1972–1978   An educational series for children, presented partly in Spanish and partly in English, set in the village of Carrascolendas. With Harry Frank Porter as Agapito, the Lion; Mike Gomez as Campamocha, the handyman; Dyana Elizondo as Dyana, the Doll; Lizanne Brazell as Pepper, the detective; Agapito Leal as Carrascoles, owner of the village café. Produced under a federal grant at KLRN-TV, San Antonio–Austin, for the Southwest Texas Public Broadcasting Council. Executive producer: Aida Barrera.

CARTER COUNTRY   ABC
15 SEPTEMBER 1977–23 AUGUST 1979   The first situation comedy to use the name of a current President in its title, *Carter Country* was set in Clinton Corners, a medium-sized town somewhere in the deep South. With Victor French as Roy Mobey, the white

police chief; Kene Holliday as Curtis Baker, his black deputy; Richard Paul as Ted Burnside, the town's spineless mayor; Vernée Watson as Lucille Banks, Burnside's black secretary; Barbara Cason as Cloris, the town's policewoman; Guich Koock as Officer Harley Puckett; Harvey Vernon as Officer DeWitt; and Melanie Griffith (1978–1979) as Tracy. Created by Phil Doran and Douglas Arango. Executive producers: Bud Yorkin, Saul Turteltaub, and Bernie Orenstein.

CARTOON TELETALES   ABC
11 AUGUST 1948–24 SEPTEMBER 1950   One of the first children's programs to incorporate the philosophy that television can be a participatory medium, rather than a passive one for its viewers, *Cartoon Teletales* was a Sunday-evening feature which encouraged children to sketch along with artist Chuck Luchsinger as he drew illustrations to accompany stories narrated by his brother, Jack Luchsinger. Featured characters included Pinto the Pony, Cletus the Caterpillar, and Alice the Alligator. The series premiered locally in Philadelphia in May 1948.

CARTOONIES   ABC
13 APRIL 1963–28 SEPTEMBER 1963   Known as *Cartoonsville* in its early weeks, this half-hour Saturday-morning cartoon show was hosted by Paul Winchell and his dummies, Jerry Mahoney and Knucklehead Smith.

CASABLANCA   ABC
27 SEPTEMBER 1955–24 APRIL 1956   One segment of *Warner Brothers Presents, Casablanca* alternated with *Cheyenne* and *King's Row* for one season. It was a pale adaptation of the 1941 classic film which had starred Humphrey Bogart and Ingrid Bergman. On television Charles McGraw starred as Rick Blaine, the American expatriate who ran a night spot in Casablanca at the outbreak of World War II.

CASABLANCA   NBC
10 APRIL 1983–24 APRIL 1983; 27 AUGUST 1983–3 SEPTEMBER 1983   The second TV version of the movie was no more successful than the first had been twenty-eight years before. In this incarnation, which employed some of the props from the movie, the action was supposed to be taking place slightly before that in the film. The cast included David Soul as American café owner Rick Blaine; Scatman Crothers as Sam, the club pianist; Ray Liotta as Sacha, the bartender; Arthur Malet as Carl, the maitre'd; Reuven Bar-Yotam as the mysterious Ferrari; Hector Elizondo as the beleaguered gendarme, Captain Renault; Patrick Horgan as Major Strasser of the German forces; and Kai Wulff as Strasser's adjutant, Lieutenant Heinz. David Wolper was the executive producer, and Charles Fitsimons the producer, of the hour series.

THE CASE OF THE DANGEROUS ROBIN
See DANGEROUS ROBIN

THE CASES OF EDDIE DRAKE   DUMONT
6 MARCH 1952–29 MAY 1952   Don Haggerty starred in this half-hour crime show as New York private eye Eddie Drake. Nine episodes were filmed by CBS in 1949, but were never shown on that network. DuMont bought them and filmed four more in 1952, adding Patricia Morrison as Karen Gayle, a criminal psychologist who assisted Drake.

CASEY JONES   SYNDICATED
1958   Half-hour adventure series for children, based on the life of the legendary engineer. Alan Hale, Jr., starred as Casey Jones, engineer on the Cannonball Express for the Midwest and Central Railroad. Also featured were Mary Lawrence as his wife, Alice, and Bobby Clark as their son, Casey Jr.

CASPER AND THE ANGELS   NBC

22 SEPTEMBER 1979–3 MAY 1980   Half-hour Saturday-morning cartoon show starring Casper the Friendly Ghost. This one was set in the future, with Casper helping out two space officers, Mini and Maxi, and another ghost, Harry Scary.

CASPER, THE FRIENDLY GHOST   ABC

5 OCTOBER 1963–27 DECEMBER 1969   Casper, a childlike ghost who tried to help people rather than scare them, was the star of a series of theatrical cartoons produced by Paramount in the 1940s. His half-hour TV series was a mainstay of ABC's Saturday-morning schedule for most of the 1960s. Other characters who appeared with Casper were "Nightmare the Galloping Ghost," "Wendy the Good Little Witch," and "The Ghostly Trio."

CASSIE & CO.   NBC

29 JANUARY 1982–19 FEBRUARY 1982; 15 JUNE 1982–20 AUGUST 1982   Angie Dickinson starred in this predictable hour crime show as Cassie Holland, a divorced former cop who bought a private detective agency. Costarring were John Ireland as "Shack" Shackleford, who sold her the business; Dori Brenner as Meryl, a paroled shoplifter who worked as Cassie's office assistant; A Martinez as Benny Silva, who ran a nearby gym; and Alex Cord as Mike, Cassie's ex-husband. Jazz saxophonist Grover Washington, Jr., wrote the series's opening theme, which accompanied footage of Dickinson's legs.

THE CATHOLIC HOUR (GUIDELINE)   NBC

4 JANUARY 1953–30 AUGUST 1970   This long-running religious series shared a time slot with *Frontiers of Faith* and *The Eternal Light*. It was produced by NBC in cooperation with the National Council of Catholic Men.

CATS & DOGS   PBS

1 FEBRUARY 1986–2 AUGUST 1986   Twenty-six-week half-hour series on the care of cats and dogs, hosted by veterinarian Anita Migday.

CATTANOOGA CATS   ABC

6 SEPTEMBER 1969–5 SEPTEMBER 1971   In this Hanna-Barbera production, the Cattanooga Cats were live-action figures who introduced three cartoon segments: "Around the World in 79 Days," "It's the Wolf," and "Autocat and Motormouse." In 1970 Motor Mouse was given his own series.

CATWALK   SYNDICATED

1992   An hour dramatic series about six young adults who formed Catwalk, a rock band. With Karam Malicki-Sanchez as Johnny, the guitarist; Lisa Butler as Sierra, the vocalist; Neve Campbell as Johnny's girlfriend, Daisy, the keyboardist; Christopher Lee Clements as Atlas; Kelli Taylor as Mary, the bassist; Paul Popowich as Jesse, the drummer; and Joel Wyner as club owner Billy K. A few new episodes surfaced on MTV in 1994, without Malicki-Sanchez and Campbell.

CAVALCADE OF AMERICA (CAVALCADE THEATER)   NBC/ABC

1 OCTOBER 1952–24 JUNE 1953 (NBC); 29 SEPTEMBER 1953–23 OCTOBER 1956 (ABC) Presentations on this half-hour anthology series focused on incidents in American history. During the 1952–1953 season the show alternated biweekly with *The Scott Music Hall,* and during the 1955–1956 season it was known as *DuPont Cavalcade Theater.*

CAVALCADE OF BANDS   DUMONT

17 JANUARY 1950–25 SEPTEMBER 1951   This Tuesday-night musical series featuring the Big Bands was hosted first by Fred Robbins, then by Warren Hull, singer Ted Steele, and finally by Buddy Rogers.

CAVALCADE OF STARS DUMONT

4 JUNE 1949–26 SEPTEMBER 1952   One of the longest-running series on the short-lived DuMont network, *Cavalcade of Stars* was an hour of variety. It was hosted by Jack Carter (1949–1950), Jackie Gleason (1950–1952), and Larry Storch (summer 1952). It was here that the first episodes of *The Honeymooners* were broadcast, with Pert Kelton as Alice Kramden. See also *The Jackie Gleason Show.*

CAVALCADE THEATER

See CAVALCADE OF AMERICA

THE CAVANAUGHS CBS

1 DECEMBER 1986–9 MARCH 1987; 8 AUGUST 1988–3 OCTOBER 1988; 29 JUNE 1989–27 JULY 1989   The members of a South Boston Irish Catholic family were the central characters of this half-hour sitcom. With Barnard Hughes as the cantankerous widower patriarch, Francis Cavanaugh; Christine Ebersole as his worldly daughter, Kit, an ex-dancer who returned home; Peter Michael Goetz as his son Chuck, also a widower; John Short as Chuck's eldest son, Father Chuck, a priest; Mary Tanner as Chuck's daughter, Mary Margaret; and Danny Cooksey and Parker Jacobs as Chuck's young twin boys, Kevin and John. Art Carney appeared occasionally as Francis's brother, James.

CELANESE THEATRE ABC

3 OCTOBER 1951–25 JUNE 1952   Alex Segal directed this dramatic anthology series. Presentations included: "Ah! Wilderness," with Thomas Mitchell (3 October); "Susan and God," with Wendell Corey (his first major TV role, 17 October); "Anna Christie," with June Havoc (23 January); "The Petrified Forest," with Kim Hunter (20 February); "Brief Moment," with Veronica Lake (6 February); "On Borrowed Time," with Ralph Morgan, Mildred Dunnock, and Billy Gray (25 June; Gray later played Bud in *Father Knows Best*).

CELEBRITY BILLIARDS SYNDICATED

1967   Celebrity guests challenged America's best known pool player, Minnesota Fats (né Rudolph Wanderone, Jr.), on this half-hour series.

CELEBRITY BOWLING SYNDICATED

1971–1978; 1987   Two two-celebrity teams competed on the lanes in this sports series. Originally, the show was hosted by Jed Allan and Sherry Kominsky and later by Allan alone. An attempt to revive the series in 1987, with Allan hosting *The New Celebrity Bowling,* was unsuccessful. Produced by Joe Siegman and Don Gregory.

CELEBRITY CHALLENGE OF THE SEXES CBS

31 JANUARY 1978–28 FEBRUARY 1978   Lightweight half-hour prime-time series featuring head-to-head competition between male and female celebrities in selected athletic endeavors. Taped at Mission Viejo, California, the series was hosted by CBS sportscaster Tom Brookshier, a one-time defensive back with the Philadelphia Eagles. Also on hand were McLean Stevenson and Barbara Rhoades, who served as "coaches" for their respective genders. Mel Ferber produced the show; Bernie Hoffman directed it.

CELEBRITY CHARADES SYNDICATED

1979   Assisted by his dummy, Squeaky, ventriloquist Jay Johnson hosted this half-hour game show on which two four-member celebrity teams played charades; the prize money was donated to the team captains' favorite charities.

CELEBRITY COOKS SYNDICATED

1978   Half-hour series from Canada on which celebrities dropped by to cook and chat with host Bruno Gerussi. Derek Smith was the executive producer.

THE CELEBRITY GAME   CBS
5 APRIL 1964–13 SEPTEMBER 1964; 8 APRIL 1965–9 SEPTEMBER 1965   Carl Reiner
hosted this prime-time game show, which, like *The Hollywood Squares,* involved two
contestants and a panel of nine celebrities. A Merrill Heatter–Bob Quigley Production, the show replaced *The Judy Garland Show* in 1964 and *The Baileys of Balboa* in
1965.

CELEBRITY GOLF   NBC
25 SEPTEMBER 1960–28 MAY 1961   Half-hour sports show on which Sam Snead teed
off against a celebrity challenger, who was given a handicap. Harry Von Zell handled
the play-by-play.

CELEBRITY QUIZ
See CELEBRITY TIME

CELEBRITY REVUE   SYNDICATED
1976   A variety hour with no regulars, produced in Vancouver.

CELEBRITY SWEEPSTAKES   NBC/SYNDICATED
1 APRIL 1974–1 OCTOBER 1976 (NBC); 1974–1977 (SYNDICATED)   A game show
involving two contestants, six celebrities, and the studio audience. First, host Jim
McKrell asked a question; the members of the audience then set the "odds" for each
celebrity by voting electronically for the one they thought was most likely to answer
correctly. Once the odds were established and posted, one contestant could wager on
any of the celebrities; if that celebrity answered correctly, the contestant won money.
At the end of the show each contestant could wager "all or none" of his or her
winnings on one celebrity. Frequently seen on the celebrity panel were Carol Wayne,
Buddy Hackett, Dick Martin, and Joey Bishop. The NBC daytime version ran for
two-and-one-half years, spawning a nighttime syndicated version. Executive producer: Ralph Andrews.

CELEBRITY TALENT SCOUTS
See TALENT SCOUTS

CELEBRITY TENNIS   SYNDICATED
1974–1978   Hosted by Tony Trabert and Bobby Riggs, this series featured four
guest celebrities playing doubles.

CELEBRITY TIME (CELEBRITY QUIZ)   ABC/CBS
3 APRIL 1949–26 MARCH 1950 (ABC); 2 APRIL 1950–21 SEPTEMBER 1952 (CBS) This
prime-time series was part game show and part talk show. Conrad Nagel presided over
the panel, which often included Ilka Chase, Kyle MacDonnell, and Kitty Carlisle.

CENTENNIAL
See THE BIG EVENT

CENTER STAGE   ABC
1 JUNE 1954–21 SEPTEMBER 1954   A biweekly dramatic anthology series.

CENTRAL PARK WEST   CBS
13 SEPTEMBER 1995–15 NOVEMBER 1995   Darren Star, creator of the popular Fox
prime-time serials *Beverly Hills 90210* and *Melrose Place,* cooked up this hour drama
set not in trendy L.A., but in gritty New York City. The ensemble cast included
Mariel Hemingway as Stephanie Welles, who had just moved from Seattle to edit
Communique magazine; Madchen Amick as bad girl Carrie Fairchild, who wrote the
magazine's column on downtown nightlife; Lauren Hutton as Carrie's mother,
Linda; John Barrowman as Carrie's handsome brother, Peter, an assistant district
attorney; Melissa Errico as Alex Bartoli, reporter for the tabloid *New York Globe;*
Justin Lazard as stockbroker Gil Chase; Michael Michele as art gallery owner Nikki

Sheridan; Tom Verica as Stephanie's husband, writer Mark Merrill; Kylie Travis as fashion writer Rachel Dennis; and Ron Leibman as *Communique*'s publisher, Allen Rush, who was also Linda's husband and Carrie's stepfather. A ratings disappointment, the series was lifted in November and scheduled to return later in the season.

CHAIN LETTER NBC
4 JULY 1966–14 OCTOBER 1966   Jan Murray hosted this daytime game show. It featured two celebrity-and-contestant teams. Each team was given a category, then required to name one-word elements of that category; each word so named had to begin with the final letter of the previous word.

CHAIN REACTION NBC/USA
14 JANUARY 1980–20 JUNE 1980 (NBC); 1985–1991 (USA)   Half-hour daytime game show first hosted by Bill Cullen, on which two teams of three players (each with two celebrities and a contestant) competed. The teams were shown the first and last words in a "chain" of eight words, and tried to win points by guessing the six missing words. Geoff Edwards emceed the USA version, which featured two contestants, competing individually.

CHALLENGE GOLF ABC
12 JANUARY 1963–7 APRIL 1963   Thirteen-week series of golf matches in which Arnold Palmer and Gary Player teamed up against a pair of challengers.

CHALLENGE OF THE GOBOTS SYNDICATED
1984–1985   A half-hour cartoon show based on the popular Tonka Toys characters, a group of robots who could transform themselves into vehicles. The Gobots hailed from the planet Gobotron, where, led by Leader-1, they battled the evil Cy-Kill and his evildoers.

THE CHALLENGE OF THE SEXES CBS
10 JANUARY 1976–20 MARCH 1976; 16 JANUARY 1977–3 APRIL 1977; 8 JANUARY 1978–9 APRIL 1978; 14 JANUARY 1979–15 APRIL 1979   A sports show on which top male and female athletes compete against each other. Hosts have included Vin Scully, Suzy Chaffee, and Phyllis George. See also *Celebrity Challenge of The Sexes*.

THE CHALLENGERS SYNDICATED
3 SEPTEMBER 1990–13 SEPTEMBER 1991   Dick Clark hosted this daily quiz show on which three contestants competed for cash by answering questions based on current events and on general knowledge.

THE CHALLENGING SEAS SYNDICATED
1969   Bill Burrud hosted this nautical documentary series.

CHAMPAGNE AND ORCHIDS DUMONT
6 SEPTEMBER 1948–10 JANUARY 1949   Fifteen-minute Monday-night musical show, hosted by Adrienne.

THE CHAMPIONS NBC
10 JUNE 1968–9 SEPTEMBER 1968   This British spy series combined *The Lost Horizon* with *The Man from U.N.C.L.E.* It featured three secret agents, operatives of Nemesis, a Swiss-based law-and-order outfit. On a mission to China, the three were shot down in the Himalayas. There they were taken by an old man to a lost city and endowed with superior sensory and extrasensory powers. With Stuart Damon as Craig Stirling; Alexandra Bastedo as Sharon Macready; William Gaunt as Richard Barrett; and Anthony Nichols as W. L. Tremayne, their boss.

CHAMPIONSHIP BRIDGE WITH CHARLES GOREN ABC/SYNDICATED
18 OCTOBER 1959–10 APRIL 1960 (ABC); 1960–1962 (SYNDICATED)   Each week four expert bridge players (all of them Life Masters) played two or three hands of

bridge. Charles Goren, America's best-known bridge expert, preselected the hands and analyzed the play from a soundproof booth; Alex Dreier provided the card-by-card commentary. The series, which was seen Sunday afternoons in most areas, was filmed in Chicago.

CHAMPIONSHIP DEBATE   NBC
3 FEBRUARY 1962–19 MAY 1962   Broadcast live on Saturday afternoons, this half-hour series featured debates between two two-member teams representing American colleges and universities. Dr. James H. McBath was the moderator.

CHANCE FOR ROMANCE   ABC
13 OCTOBER 1958–5 DECEMBER 1958   This daytime show was an early version of *The Dating Game*. John Cameron Swayze hosted.

CHANCE OF A LIFETIME   ABC/DUMONT
20 SEPTEMBER 1950–20 AUGUST 1953 (ABC); 11 SEPTEMBER 1953–17 JUNE 1955 (DUMONT); 3 JULY 1955–23 JUNE 1956 (ABC)   John Reed King (who also hosted the radio version of the show) was the first host of this lighthearted guessing game; when Dennis James succeeded him in the spring of 1952, the format switched to a talent contest for professional acts. See also *The $1,000,000 Chance of a Lifetime*.

THE CHANGING EARTH   SYNDICATED
1964   Geology was the subject of this educational series, hosted by Jim McClurg of the University of Michigan.

CHANNING   ABC
18 SEPTEMBER 1963–8 APRIL 1964   This dramatic series was set at Channing College and starred Jason Evers as Joseph Howe, professor of English, and Henry Jones as Fred Baker, the dean. Jack Laird was the producer.

CHARADE QUIZ   DUMONT
27 NOVEMBER 1947–23 JUNE 1949   One of television's first game shows, *Charade Quiz* was the forerunner of *Pantomime Quiz*. Bill Slater hosted the show, on which a celebrity panel acted out charades submitted by home viewers.

CHARGE ACCOUNT
See THE JAN MURRAY SHOW

CHARLES BOYER THEATER   SYNDICATED
1953   Charles Boyer hosted this half-hour dramatic anthology series.

THE CHARLES FARRELL SHOW   CBS
2 JULY 1956–24 SEPTEMBER 1956   A summer replacement for *I Love Lucy*, this sitcom starred Charlie Farrell (playing himself) as the proprietor of the Racquet Club in Palm Springs, California. With Charles Winninger as Dad, Charlie's crusty father; Richard Deacon as Sherman Hull, club director; Ann Lee as Doris Mayfield, Charlie's girlfriend; Kathryn Card as Mrs. Papernow; and Jeff Silver as Rodney.

CHARLES IN CHARGE   CBS/SYNDICATED
3 OCTOBER 1984–27 APRIL 1985; 5 JUNE 1985–24 JULY 1985 (CBS); 1987–1990 (SYNDICATED)   Fresh from his role as Chachi on *Happy Days,* Scott Baio starred in this sitcom as Charles, a college student who agreed to help care for a family's three kids in exchange for room and board. Also featured in the network version were: Julie Cobb and James Widdoes as his employers, Jill and Stan Pembroke; Jonathan Ward as twelve-year-old Douglas; April Lerman as fourteen-year-old Lila; Michael Pearlman as ten-year-old Jason; Willie Aames as Charles's pal, Buddy Lembeck; and Jennifer Runyon as Gwendolyn Pierce, the girl Charles pursued (usually in vain). After its network cancellation, production resumed for syndication, but only Baio and Aames remained from the cast, as the Pembrokes sold their house to the Powell

family. Joining the cast were Sandra Kerns as the mother, Ellen Powell; James Callahan as the grandfather, Walter Powell (the father was at sea); Nicole Eggert as the fourteen-year-old Jamie; Josie Davis as thirteen-year-old Sarah; and Alexander Polinský as twelve-year-old Adam. Also seen occasionally was Ellen Travolta as Charles's mother, Lillian.

CHARLES PEREZ SYNDICATED
1995–1996   Hour daytime talk show, hosted by Charles Perez.

THE CHARLES RUGGLES SHOW
See THE RUGGLES

THE CHARLEY WEAVER SHOW (CHARLEY WEAVER'S HOBBY LOBBY)   ABC
30 SEPTEMBER 1959–23 MARCH 1960   This prime-time series began with an unusual format: host Cliff Arquette (as beloved bumpkin Charley Weaver) interviewed celebrity guests about their hobbies. By midseason that idea had been scrapped, and a standard comedy-variety format was adopted.

CHARLIE & CO. CBS
18 SEPTEMBER 1985–28 JANUARY 1986; 25 APRIL 1986–23 JULY 1986   In the wake of *The Cosby Show*'s sudden popularity, CBS came up with its version of a black family sitcom. Set in Chicago, it featured Flip Wilson as Charlie Richmond, who worked for the city highway department; Gladys Knight (better known as a singer than as an actress) as his wife, Diana, a teacher; Kristoff St. John as elder son Charlie Jr.; Fran Robinson as teen daughter Lauren; Jaleel White as younger son Robert; Della Reese as Aunt Rachel, who moved in with the Richmonds; Ray Girardin as Charlie's boss, Walter Simpson; and Richard Karron, Terry McGovern, Eddie Velez, and Kip King as Charlie's ethnically diverse coworkers, Milton Bieberman, Jim Coyle, Miguel Santana, and Ronald Sandler, respectively.

THE CHARLIE BROWN AND SNOOPY SHOW CBS
17 SEPTEMBER 1983–3 AUGUST 1986   Although Charles Schulz's *Peanuts* cartoon characters had appeared in prime-time specials since 1965 ("A Charlie Brown Christmas" was the first), they did not come to Saturday morning television until 1983. The half-hour series featured all the popular *Peanuts* characters—Charlie Brown, Lucy Van Pelt, Linus, Peppermint Patty, Snoopy, Woodstock, and others. As in the comic strip and the prime-time specials, adults were never pictured; on the Saturday morning show, adult voices were supplied by musical instruments. Lee Mendelson and Bill Melendez, who produced the prime-time programs, also produced this series.

CHARLIE CHAN SYNDICATED
1958   Earl Derr Biggers's fictional sleuth first came to television in this half-hour series starring J. Carrol Naish as Charlie Chan and James Hong as number-one son, Barry. In 1972 the Oriental detective reappeared in cartoon form. See *The Amazing Chan and the Chan Clan*. The Chan character was based on a Honolulu police detective, Chang Apana.

CHARLIE GRACE ABC
14 SEPTEMBER 1995–19 OCTOBER 1995   Predictable crime show starring Mark Harmon as Charlie Grace, a none-too-successful private eye who kept an office at the back of a bar in Los Angeles. Divorced, Charlie struggled to help raise his daughter while assisting his clients. Also featured were Cindy Katz as lawyer Leslie Loeb; Leelee Sobieski as Charlie's twelve-year-old daughter, Jenny; and Robert Costanzo as Artie Crawford, a fellow p.i. who, like Charlie, had also been an L.A. cop.

CHARLIE HOOVER FOX
9 NOVEMBER 1991–2 FEBRUARY 1992   Domestic sitcom about a mild-mannered accountant whose diminutive alter ego appears on his fortieth birthday. With Tim

Matheson as Charlie Hoover; Sam Kinison as Hugh, who could be seen and heard only by Charlie; Lucy Webb as Charlie's wife, Helen; Michael Manasseri as their son, Paul; Leslie Engel as their daughter, Emily; Julie Hayden as Charlie's secretary, Doris; and Kevin McCarthy as Charlie's boss, Mr. Culberton. The half-hour series tied with *The Best of the Worst* as the lowest-rated prime-time series of the season.

CHARLIE ROSE PBS
4 JANUARY 1993– Late-night talk show, hosted by lawyer and former newscaster Charlie Rose, usually featuring a single guest each evening. The series was produced at WNET in New York, and was originally aired on The Learning Channel from January to September 1992.

CHARLIE WILD, PRIVATE DETECTIVE CBS/ABC/DUMONT
22 DECEMBER 1950–27 JUNE 1951 (CBS); 11 SEPTEMBER 1951–4 MARCH 1952 (ABC); 13 MARCH 1952–19 JUNE 1952 (DUMONT) Half-hour crime show starring Kevin O'Morrison, then John McQuade as New York private eye Charlie Wild, with Cloris Leachman as Effie Perrine, his woman Friday. Herbert Brodkin produced the series, and Leonard Valenta directed it.

CHARLIE'S ANGELS ABC
22 SEPTEMBER 1976–19 AUGUST 1981 By far the most popular new show of the 1976–1977 season, *Charlie's Angels* was an hour crime show with enormous visual appeal: three stunning young women who often went braless. The three "Angels" were all police academy graduates who signed on with Charles Townsend Associates, a private detective agency. Featured were Kate Jackson (late of *The Rookies*) as Sabrina Duncan; former Wella Balsam model Farrah Fawcett-Majors (1976–1977) as Jill Munroe; former Breck girl Jaclyn Smith as Kelly Garrett; David Doyle as John Bosley, their avuncular associate; and John Forsythe as the voice of Charlie Townsend, the Angels' unseen boss, who usually communicated by telephone. In 1977 Farrah Fawcett-Majors decided to leave the series, even though another year remained on her contract. She was replaced by Cheryl Ladd (the then wife of actor David Ladd, she was formerly known as Cheryl Stoppelmoor when she was featured on *Search*) as Jill's younger sister, Kris Munroe, also a police academy graduate. Cheryl Ladd proved every bit as popular with viewers as Farrah Fawcett-Majors had been; some three million posters of Ladd were sold during the 1977–1978 season. In the spring of 1978 Fawcett-Majors settled her dispute with Aaron Spelling and Leonard Goldberg, the executive producers of the show, by agreeing to appear in six episodes during the 1978–1979 season. Kate Jackson left the show after the third season, and was succeeded by Shelley Hack as Tiffany Welles. Hack lasted only one season herself; Tanya Roberts became the new third Angel, Julie Rogers, in the fall of 1980, the series's final season. A total of 115 episodes were produced. In 1988 Aaron Spelling produced a pilot for an updated version of the series for the Fox network, but the series never made it to the air. *Angels '88*, as the show was known, would have had four females, rather than three.

THE CHARMINGS ABC
20 MARCH 1987–24 APRIL 1987; 6 AUGUST 1987–11 FEBRUARY 1988 In this fantasy sitcom, the fairy tale characters Snow White and Prince Charming awoke from a spell to find themselves living in modern-day suburbia. Featured were Caitlin O'Heaney (spring 1987) and Carol Huston (August 1987–February 1988) as Snow White; Christopher Rich as her husband, Prince Eric Charming; Judy Parfitt as Snow's wicked stepmother, Queen Lillian, who still managed to cast a mean spell; Cork Hubbert as Luther the dwarf, Snow and Eric's servant, who attended college; Garette Ratliffe as their son Corey; Brandon Call as their son Thomas; Paul Winfield as The Mirror, who talked back to Queen Lillian whenever she consulted him; Paul Eiding as the Charmings' next-door neighbor, carpet salesman Don Miler; and Dori Brenner as Don's wife, Sally. As a promotional gimmick, the producers of *The Charmings* sent hand-held mirrors to TV critics late in the summer of 1987, heralding the series's

upcoming new season; unfortunately, as *TV Guide* reported, many of the mirrors arrived cracked.

CHASE
NBC

11 SEPTEMBER 1973–28 AUGUST 1974   Jack Webb produced this crime show around a special police unit that handled "the tough ones, the ones nobody wants." With Mitchell Ryan as Captain Chase Reddick, head of the unit; Wayne Maunder as Detective Sergeant Sam MacCray; Reid Smith as Officer Norm Hamilton, helicopter ace; Michael Richardson as Officer Steve Baker, hot-rodder; and Brian Fong as Fred Sing, motorcycle man. In January, Smith, Richardson, and Fong were dropped. Added to the cast were Gary Crosby as Officer Ed Rice; Craig Gardner as Officer Tom Wilson; and Albert Reed as Officer Frank Dawson.

THE CHEAP SHOW
SYNDICATED

1978   Raucous game show combining *Truth or Consequences* with *Liars Club*. Hosted by Dick Martin, the game involved two competing couples and a pair of celebrities. Martin asked a question of the celebrities, one of whom answered correctly, one incorrectly. One member of one couple team then tried to guess which celeb had answered correctly; if the guess proved incorrect, the player's partner was then "punished" with a hosing, pie in the face, or other surefire laugh-getter. Cheap prizes were also given away from time to time by Polly the Prize Lady, and the grand prize award was determined by a rat, Oscar the Wonder Rodent. Chris Bearde and Robert D. Wood were the executive producers.

THE CHEATERS
SYNDICATED

1961   John Ireland starred as John Hunter, insurance fraud investigator for the Eastern Insurance Company, in this half-hour adventure series filmed in England. Also featured was Robert Ayres as his associate, Walter Allen.

CHECK IT OUT!
USA/SYNDICATED

2 OCTOBER 1985–15 MARCH 1986 (USA); 1986–1988 (SYNDICATED)   A weak half-hour sitcom, based on the British series *Tripper's Day*. With Don Adams as Howard Bannister, manager of Cobb's Supermarket; Jeff Pustil as assistant manager Jack Christian; Dinah Christie as Howard's secretary, Edna Moseley; Kathleen Laskey as checker Marlene; Henry Beckman (1985–1987) as Alf, the security guard; Aaron Schwartz as checker Leslie; Tonya Williams (1985–1987) as checker Jennifer; Simon Reynolds (1985–1987) as stockboy Murray; Jason Warren (1985–1986) as stockboy Marvin; Barbara Hamilton (1985–1986) as Mrs. Cobb; Gordon Clapp (1986–1988) as handyman Viker; and Elizabeth Hanna (1987–1988) as T. C. Collingwood, one of the new owners of the store. Filmed in Toronto, the series was originally seen on Canada's CTV before coming to the United States.

CHECKING IN
CBS

9 APRIL 1981–30 APRIL 1981   In this spinoff from *The Jeffersons,* Marla Gibbs starred as Florence Johnston, who left her position as the Jeffersons' maid to become the executive housekeeper at New York's St. Frederick Hotel. Also featured were Larry Linville as Lyle Block, the manager; Liz Torres as Elena, Florence's assistant; Patrick Collins as Earl, the dimwitted house detective; Robert Costanzo as Hank, the maintenance man; Ruth Brown as Betty, the maid; and Charles Fleischer as Dennis, the bellhop. After a four-week spring tryout, the series was not renewed, and Florence returned to the Jeffersons' employ the next season.

CHECKMATE
CBS

17 SEPTEMBER 1960–19 SEPTEMBER 1962   The private eyes who comprised Checkmate, Inc., tried not only to solve crimes but also to prevent them. The hour-long series starred Tony George as Don Corey; Doug McClure as young Jed Sills; Sebastian Cabot as Dr. Carl Hyatt, theoretician and criminologist; and Frank Betts (1961–1962) as Chris Devlin. Notable guest appearances included those by Charles

Laughton (in "Terror from the East," 7 January 1961, his last TV role) and Cyd Charisse (in "Dance of Death," 22 April 1961, her first TV dramatic role). *Checkmate*'s distinctive title sequence, which featured swirling liquid shapes, was accompanied by theme music composed by John Williams. Williams, of course, was later to score such colossal motion pictures as *Star Wars, The Empire Strikes Back,* and *E.T.*

CHEER TELEVISION THEATRE   NBC
30 MAY 1954–27 JUNE 1954   This half-hour filmed dramatic anthology series was produced by MCA-TV and sponsored by Procter & Gamble. It was seen only on the West Coast for a time before going coast-to-coast.

CHEERS   NBC
30 SEPTEMBER 1982–19 AUGUST 1993   Cheers, a Beacon Street bar in downtown Boston, was the setting for this popular half-hour sitcom. Featured were Ted Danson as its owner, Sam "Mayday" Malone, a former Red Sox pitcher, a reformed alcoholic, and a womanizer; Shelley Long (1982–1987) as Diane Chambers, an overeducated intellectual who took a "temporary" job as a barmaid and gradually got involved with Sam; Nicholas Colasanto (1982–1985) as "Coach" Ernie Pantusso, the thick-skulled ex-Red Sox coach who worked the bar; Rhea Perlman as the acid-tongued waitress Carla Tortelli; George Wendt as beefy Norm Peterson, a beer-guzzling regular; and John Ratzenberger as Cliff Clavin, a postal employee who was also a regular customer. Later additions to the cast included Kelsey Grammer (1984–1993) as Dr. Frasier Crane, a stuffy psychiatrist who dated Diane for a while; Woody Harrelson (1985–1993) as Woody Boyd, the naive new bartender who replaced Coach (Nicholas Colasanto had died in February 1985); and Bebe Neuwirth (1986–1992) as Frasier's new love interest, icy psychiatrist Dr. Lilith Sternin (Sternin and Crane were later married, had a son, and were separated). By the fall of 1987 Diane had finally jilted Sam to pursue her writing career; Sam sold the bar to a conglomerate and started to sail around the world. Unfortunately, his boat sank, and Sam returned to Cheers, this time as just a bartender. Kirstie Alley joined the cast as the new manager, Rebecca Howe, and she and Sam embarked upon a new relationship. Tom Skerritt appeared occasionally during the 1987–1988 season as Rebecca's boss, Evan Drake, for whom Rebecca swooned, and Roger Rees signed on in 1988 as ultrawealthy corporate raider Robin Colcord, who also captured Rebecca's attention; unfortunately, Colcord himself was captured—by federal authorities—and imprisoned for stock-market crimes. By the fall of 1990 Sam had regained ownership of the bar, and Rebecca now worked for him. In the meantime, Carla had married—again. Jay Thomas was occasionally featured between 1987 and 1989 as her ne'er-do-well spouse, Eddie LeBec, a former hockey player who was run over by a Zamboni machine. Woody also got himself a girlfriend; Jackie Swanson joined the cast in 1989 as wealthy Kelly Gaines. She and Woody were married in the spring of 1992.

Cheers narrowly escaped cancellation after its first season. Fortunately, it was allowed to remain on Thursday nights. When *The Cosby Show* premiered in 1984, the network soon found itself with a powerhouse Thursday lineup. *Cheers* first entered Nielsen's top five in its fourth season; it remained there for six more years, reaching number one during the 1990–1991 season. In 1992 Ted Danson (who was then earning an estimated $450,000 per episode) announced he would leave the show after the 1992–1993 season. The producers decided not to continue the show without him. The final first-run episode of *Cheers* was a ninety-six-minute program, aired 20 May 1993, following a twenty-four-minute series retrospective; after a six-year absence, Shelley Long returned for the finale. It was the highest-rated entertainment program of the season. Later that evening most of the cast (many of whom had already been celebrating for a few hours) appeared on the *Tonight* show, which was broadcast live from the Bull and Finch Pub in Boston, the real-life bar which had inspired the series.

The series was created by Glen Charles, Les Charles, and James Burrows, who had also worked together on *Taxi.* Its theme, "Where Everybody Knows Your Name," was recorded by Gary Portnoy, who wrote it with Judy Hart Angelo; the song was nominated for an Emmy in 1983. See also *Frasier.*

CHER   CBS

16 FEBRUARY 1975–4 JANUARY 1976   After the divorce and the demise of *The Sonny and Cher Comedy Hour* in 1974, Sonny (Bono) was the first to return to television. His ABC series, *The Sonny Comedy Revue,* was gone in thirteen weeks. A few weeks later, Cher returned to host this musical variety series; it did well enough to be renewed. Cher kicked off her new series with a special preview broadcast on 12 February; her guests included Elton John, Flip Wilson, and Bette Midler. In January 1976 Cher left the air, returning a month later with Sonny in *The Sonny and Cher Show* (see that title). Also featured on the *Cher* show was Gailard Sartain. Executive producer: George Schlatter; producers: Lee Miller, Alan Katz, and Don Reo.

CHESTER THE PUP   ABC

7 OCTOBER 1950–30 SEPTEMBER 1951   On this kids' show the adventures of Chester the Pup and his friend Drizzlepuss were sketched onscreen by Sid Stone, as they were narrated by Art Whitefield. The show was originally seen Saturday mornings but switched to Sundays in January.

THE CHESTERFIELD SUPPER CLUB
See THE PERRY COMO SHOW

CHET HUNTLEY REPORTING   NBC

26 OCTOBER 1958–17 SEPTEMBER 1963   For one season, each half of NBC's Huntley–Brinkley news team had his own prime-time news analysis series. *David Brinkley's Journal* premiered in 1961, and its relative success led to the rescheduling of this series from Sunday afternoons to prime time.

CHEVROLET ON BROADWAY
See TELE-THEATRE

CHEVROLET SHOWROOM   ABC

25 SEPTEMBER 1953–12 FEBRUARY 1954   Cesar Romero hosted this half-hour variety show, which featured appearances by guest stars and by the 1954 Chevrolets.

THE CHEVY CHASE SHOW   FOX

7 SEPTEMBER 1993–15 OCTOBER 1993   One of the season's biggest debacles, Chevy Chase's one-hour late-night talk show mercifully was axed after only six weeks. Simply put, Chase was not right for the job; the comedy bits were unfunny, and the interviews were awkward. The show was Fox's fourth attempt to establish itself in the late-night arena; the previous efforts—*The Late Show Starring Joan Rivers, The Late Show,* and *The Wilton North Report*—had all failed. Following its cancellation, Fox televised reruns of *Code 3* and *In Living Color* for a few weeks before returning the time slot to its local affiliates.

CHEYENNE   ABC

20 SEPTEMBER 1955–13 SEPTEMBER 1963   One of the first series for TV by Warner Brothers, *Cheyenne* was introduced during the 1955–1956 season as one segment of *Warner Brothers Presents.* The hour-long western starred Clint Walker as Cheyenne Bodie, a laconic drifter of mixed descent. During the first season L. Q. Jones was also featured as Smitty, an itinerant mapmaker who accompanied Bodie. *Cheyenne* was the only one of the *Warner Brothers Presents* segments to be renewed; during the 1956–1957 season it alternated with *Conflict,* an anthology series. In its third season (1957–1958) *Cheyenne* alternated with *Sugarfoot,* a new Warner Brothers western, and its subsequent history is closely entwined with that of *Sugarfoot* and a third Warner Brothers western, *Bronco.* In 1958 Walker walked out of the series, but the show continued; Ty Hardin, as Bronco Layne, starred in the series during the 1958–1959 season, as *Cheyenne* again alternated with *Sugarfoot.* By mid-1959 Walker had agreed to return to *Cheyenne;* meanwhile, Hardin had proved popular enough as Bronco to merit his own series. The problem was solved by making *Bronco* a separate series, which alternated with *Sugarfoot* during the 1959–1960 season. During the

1960–1961 season, episodes of *Cheyenne, Bronco,* and *Sugarfoot* were all shown under the *Cheyenne* title, and during the 1961–1962 season *Cheyenne* and *Bronco* shows were both aired under the *Cheyenne* banner. *Cheyenne,* with Walker alone in the saddle, continued on for another season, leaving the air early in 1963; reruns popped up later that year. See also *Bronco; Sugarfoot.*

CHICAGO HOPE   CBS
18 SEPTEMBER 1994–   Created by David E. Kelley, this hour medical drama was originally scheduled on Thursdays, directly opposite NBC's new medical drama, *ER* (which was also set in Chicago). *Chicago Hope* blinked first, moving to an earlier Thursday timeslot in October, then to a Monday slot in midseason. The series was set at Chicago Hope Hospital, a busy urban medical center. The cast included Adam Arkin as surgeon Aaron Shutt; Roxanne Hart as his wife, nurse Camille Shutt (the marriage was on the ropes); Mandy Patinkin (1994–1995) as Dr. Jeffrey Geiger; E. G. Marshall (1994–1995) as Dr. Arthur Thurmond, whose skills were beginning to deteriorate; Hector Elizondo as chief surgeon Phillip Watters; Peter MacNicol (1994–Fall 1995) as hospital lawyer Alan Birch; Roma Maffia as Angela; Thomas Gibson as Dr. Daniel Nyland; Robyn Lively as nurse Maggie Atkisson; Diane Venora as Dr. Infante; Peter Berg (January 1995–   ) as Dr. Billy Kronk; and Vondie Curtis-Hall (February 1995–   ) as Dr. Dennis Hancock (coincidentally, Curtis-Hall had guested earlier in the season on *ER*).
    Mandy Patinkin left the series early in the second season. Two new regulars were added: Christine Lahti as Dr. Kathryn Austin, a surgeon, and Jamey Sheridan as Dr. John Sutton, an obstetrician.

CHICAGO JAZZ   NBC
26 NOVEMBER 1949–31 DECEMBER 1949   A short-lived program of jazz music, broadcast live from Chicago. The series was also titled *Sessions.*

CHICAGO STORY   NBC
6 MARCH 1982–27 AUGUST 1982   Filmed on location, this ninety-minute series focused on a group of doctors, police officers, and lawyers working in the Windy City. It featured Maud Adams as Dr. Judith Bergstrom; Vincent Baggetta as public defender Lou Pellegrino; Molly Cheek as defense attorney Megan Powers; Dennis Franz as street cop Joe Gilland; Daniel Hugh-Kelly as plainclothes officer Frank Wajorski; Richard Lawson as Wajorski's partner, O. Z. Tate; Craig T. Nelson as state's attorney Kenneth A. Dutton; and Kristoffer Tabori as Dr. Max Carson.

THE CHICAGO SYMPHONY CHAMBER ORCHESTRA   ABC
25 SEPTEMBER 1951–18 MARCH 1952   A half-hour program of classical music.

THE CHICAGO TEDDY BEARS   CBS
17 SEPTEMBER 1971–17 DECEMBER 1971   Set at Linc & Latzi's Speakeasy in Chicago during the 1920s, this sitcom was gone in thirteen weeks. With Dean Jones as Linc McCray; John Banner as Uncle Latzi, his partner; Art Metrano as Big Nick Marr, Linc's cousin, a gangster; Huntz Hall (one of the original Bowery Boys) as Dutch, Nick's henchman; Jamie Farr as henchman Duke; Mickey Shaughnessy as henchman Lefty; Mike Mazurki as Julie, Linc's bouncer; and Marvin Kaplan as Marvin, Linc's accountant.

THE CHICAGOLAND MYSTERY PLAYERS (THE CHICAGOLAND PLAYERS)   DUMONT
11 SEPTEMBER 1949–23 JULY 1950   Broadcast live from Chicago, this series began as a crime drama, with Gordon Urquhart as criminologist Jeff Hall and Bob Smith as Sergeant Holland. In midseason, the crime format was dropped, and the show became a dramatic anthology series.

CHICKEN SOUP

12 SEPTEMBER 1989–7 NOVEMBER 1989   One of the highest-rated new series ever to be canceled in midseason, *Chicken Soup* was dropped because its ratings weren't high enough. Scheduled immediately after the powerhouse sitcom *Roseanne,* it couldn't retain enough of its lead-in's viewers—most likely because of its markedly East Coast urban ethnicity; and was canned after only eight airings. The sitcom starred standup comic (and star of the one-man Broadway show *The World According to Me*) Jackie Mason as New Yorker Jackie Fisher, who quit his job as a pajama salesman after falling in love with an Irish Catholic divorcee. Lynn Redgrave costarred as his love interest, Maddie Peerce, who lived next door and owned his townhouse. Also featured were Rita Karin as Jackie's mom, Bea Fisher; Johnny Pinto as Maddie's son, Donnie; Alisan Porter as Maddie's daughter Molly; Katherine Erbe as Maddie's daughter Patty; and Brandon Maggart as Maddie's brother, Mike.

CHICO AND THE MAN

13 SEPTEMBER 1974–21 JULY 1978   A situation comedy set in the barrio of East Los Angeles, *Chico and the Man* told the story of a salty white garage owner and his Mexican-American employee. It starred Jack Albertson, a former vaudevillian, as cantankerous Ed Brown, the last WASP left in the neighborhood, and young Freddie Prinze as Chico Rodriguez, the optimistic, fast-talking Chicano who convinced Ed to hire him. Although the show was the first series set in a Mexican-American neighborhood, it was criticized by many Chicano organizations because there were no Chicanos in the cast (indeed, few Mexican-Americans were involved in any aspect of television production, despite the fact that the large majority of programs are produced in Los Angeles). Freddie Prinze was of Puerto Rican and Hungarian extraction (a "Hungarican," as he described himself), and José Feliciano, who composed and sang the show's theme, was also of Puerto Rican origin. Additionally, the name "Chico" was considered a derogatory nickname to many Chicanos. To rectify matters, executive producer James Komack soon expanded the cast, adding four new members, including two Mexican-Americans: Isaac Ruiz as Ramon (Mando), Chico's friend, and Rodolfo Hoyos as Rudy, Ed's pal. Also added were Scatman Crothers, a black trouper with fifty years of experience, as Louie Wilson, the garbage collector ("I'm the man who empties your can"), and Bonnie Boland as Mabel, the letter carrier. All but Crothers were gone by the end of the second season. Ronny Graham was seen in 1975–1976 as Reverend Bemis and Della Reese was added in 1976 as Della Rogers, Ed's landlady (she also operated a traveling snack wagon).

Freddie Prinze committed suicide in January 1977, at the age of twenty-two. The young performer had been an overnight success—a high school dropout who first appeared on TV late in 1973, Prinze was the star of a smash hit series less than a year later. Though he played a happy-go-lucky character, Prinze was a troubled young man offstage. In nightclub appearances Prinze often emulated Lenny Bruce, the so-called "sick" comic whose troubles with the law precipitated his death from a drug overdose in 1966. Prinze was briefly engaged to the comic's daughter, Kitty Bruce. Prinze, too, was involved with drugs and was also fascinated by guns. He had remarked to several friends that he did not expect to live to be an old man. On 27 January 1977, a despondent Prinze shot himself in the head; he died two days later.

Despite the tragic death of Prinze, NBC elected to continue the series. In the fall of 1977, twelve-year-old Gabriel Melgar joined the cast as Raul Garcia, a Mexican youngster who sneaked into the trunk of Louie's car when Ed and Louie went fishing in Mexico. Ed proceeded to adopt the boy. Also joining the show was Charo, as Aunt Charo. James Komack, creator of the series, served as its executive producer. Produced by Alan Sacks (1974–1975); Michael Morris (1975–1976) and Ed Scharlach (1975–1976); Jerry Ross (1976–1978) and Charles Stewart (1976–1978).

THE CHICO MARX SHOW
See THE COLLEGE BOWL

CHILDHOOD   PBS

14 OCTOBER 1991–2 DECEMBER 1991   Alex Chadwick and Lynn Neary narrated this seven-part series which examined the experience of childhood in different cultures.

THE CHILDREN'S CORNER   NBC

20 AUGUST 1955–28 APRIL 1956   This Saturday-morning puppet show for children was cohosted by Josie Carey and Fred Rogers, who later emceed *Mister Rogers' Neighborhood* on PBS. Featured puppets included King Friday and Daniel S. Tiger. In addition to its eight-month network run, the show was seen locally in Pittsburgh for several years.

CHILDREN'S SKETCH BOOK   NBC

12 MARCH 1949–4 FEBRUARY 1950   Edith Skinner told stories for young viewers on this half-hour series.

CHILD'S PLAY   CBS

20 SEPTEMBER 1982–16 SEPTEMBER 1983   Bill Cullen was the host of this daytime game show, on which contestants tried to identify words from "definitions" given by children.

CHILD'S WORLD   ABC

1 NOVEMBER 1948–27 APRIL 1949   Helen Parkhurst hosted this fifteen-minute discussion show, on which groups of children talked about their feelings and problems.

CHINA BEACH   ABC

26 APRIL 1988–8 JUNE 1988; 24 AUGUST 1988–15 DECEMBER 1990; 4 JUNE 1991–22 JULY 1991   *China Beach* was the second dramatic series of the 1987–1988 season set during the Vietnam War (CBS's *Tour of Duty* had premiered in September). Creators William Broyles, Jr., and John Sacret Young chose to look at the war through the eyes of the American women who were there. The result was a well-crafted, evocative, and emotional drama. The setting, China Beach, was a U.S. Armed Forces hospital and recreational facility at Da Nang. The cast included Dana Delany as Lieutenant Colleen McMurphy, a nurse; Michael Boatman as Samuel Beckett; Nancy Giles as Armed Forces Radio DJ Frankie Bunsen; Jeff Kober as Dodger; Robert Picardo as Dr. Dick Richard; Concetta Tomei as Major Lila Garreau of Special Services; Brian Wimmer as Boonie Lanier, a lifeguard; Marg Helgenberger as K.C., a self-employed civilian working girl; Chloe Webb (spring 1988) as USO entertainer Laurette Barber; Nan Woods (spring 1988–1989) as Red Cross volunteer Cherry White; Megan Gallagher (fall 1988–1989) as reporter Wayloo Marie Holmes; Ned Vaughn (1989–1990) as Jeff Hyers; and Ricki Lake (1989–1990) as Red Cross volunteer Holly Pelegrino. The series incorporated much period music from the late 1960s: the Supremes' hit "Reflections," was used as the theme. Nancy Sinatra even made a cameo appearance on 8 June 1988, singing her 1966 hit, "These Boots Are Made for Walking." Another effective episode, aired 15 March 1989, incorporated the reminiscences of actual Vietnam veterans around the dramatic scenes. The final episode, set as a 1988 reunion of the characters, incorporated a visit to the Vietnam Veterans Memorial in Washington, D.C.

CHINA SMITH (THE AFFAIRS OF CHINA SMITH) (THE NEW ADVENTURES OF CHINA SMITH)   SYNDICATED

1953   This half-hour filmed series starred Dan Duryea as China Smith, an opportunistic American adventurer living in Singapore. Smith's services were available to the highest bidder.

CHIP & PEPPER'S CARTOON MADNESS   NBC

14 SEPTEMBER 1991–25 JULY 1992   Twins Chip and Pepper Foster introduced vintage cartoons on this Saturday morning kids' show.

CHIP 'N' DALE'S RESCUE RANGERS　　　　　　　　　　　SYNDICATED

1989–1993　　Chip and Dale, Walt Disney's two chipmunks, headlined their own weekday cartoon series. Assisted by their friends Monterrey Jack, Gadget, and Zipper, they helped other critters in distress. The series rated highly in most markets, and was often shown back-to-back with Disney's other first-run animated program, *DuckTales*. It was later part of the two-hour *Disney Afternoon* cartoon block.

CHIPMUNKS GO TO THE MOVIES
See ALVIN AND THE CHIPMUNKS

THE CHISHOLMS　　　　　　　　　　　　　　　　　　　CBS

29 MARCH 1979–19 APRIL 1979; 19 JANUARY 1980–15 MARCH 1980　　During the initial four-week run of this western series, viewers saw the Chisholm family begin their journey west from Virginia to Wyoming; when the series returned in 1980, the Chisholms resumed their trip and headed for California. The cast included Robert Preston as Hadley Chisholm, head of the clan (Hadley died early in the 1980 season); Rosemary Harris as Minerva Chisholm, his wife; Ben Murphy as son Will; Brian Kerwin (1979) and Brett Cullen (1980) as son Gideon; Jimmy Van Patten as son Bo; Stacey Nelkin (1979) and Delta Burke (1980) as daughter Bonnie Sue; Susan Swift (1979) as daughter Annabel, who was killed by Indians (Susan Swift returned to the series in 1980 as Mercy Hopwell, who joined the wagon train); Charles Frank (1979) and Reid Smith (1980) as guide Lester Hackett; Victoria Racimo as Kewedinok, an Indian woman who married Will; and Mitchell Ryan (1980) as wagon master Cooper Hawkins. The series was created by David Dortort and developed by Evan Hunter.

CHOOSE UP SIDES　　　　　　　　　　　　　　　　　NBC

7 JANUARY 1956–31 MARCH 1956　　This kids' game show was hosted by Gene Rayburn (who was also the announcer on Steve Allen's *Tonight* show at the same time). Produced by Mark Goodson and Bill Todman, it began in 1953 as a local show in New York, hosted by Dean Miller (later of *December Bride*).

CHOPPER ONE　　　　　　　　　　　　　　　　　　　ABC

17 JANUARY 1974–11 JULY 1974　　A half hour of cops and choppers, this series was essentially an updated version of *The Whirlybirds*, TV's first helicopter series. It starred Jim McMullan as Officer Don Burdick and Dirk Benedict as Officer Gil Foley, the two pilots of the Chopper One unit. With Ted Hartley as Captain Ted McKeegan, their commanding officer, and Lew Frizzell as Mitch, the mechanic.

CHRISTIAN LIFESTYLE MAGAZINE
see FAITH FOR TODAY

CHRISTINE CROMWELL　　　　　　　　　　　　　　　ABC

11 NOVEMBER 1989–24 MARCH 1990　　One segment of *The ABC Saturday Mystery Movie*, starring Jaclyn Smith as Christine Cromwell, an attorney and financial adviser who solved crimes involving the rich and famous. Also featured were Celeste Holm as her mother, Samantha; Ralph Bellamy as Cyrus, who owned the investment firm for which Christine worked; and Rebecca Cross as Sarah.

THE CHRISTOPHERS (CHRISTOPHER CLOSEUP)　　　SYNDICATED

1952–1987　　This long-running religious program was brought to television by the Reverend James Keller, founder of the Christophers, a Catholic religious group. By the 1970s the show was entitled *Christopher Closeup*. It usually featured interviews and was cohosted by the Reverend Richard Armstrong and Jeanne Glynn, who also served as its executive producer and producer respectively.

CHRISTY　　　　　　　　　　　　　　　　　　　　　CBS

3 APRIL 1994–5 MAY 1994; 17 AUGUST 1994–7 SEPTEMBER 1994; 15 APRIL 1995–22 APRIL 1995; 14 JUNE 1995–2 AUGUST 1995　　Hour family drama set in 1912. With Kellie Martin as nineteen-year-old Christy Huddleston, the new schoolteacher in Cutter

Gap, Tennessee, a backwoods mountain community; Tyne Daly as Miss Alice Henderson; Randall Batinkoff as Reverend David Grantland, who courted Christy; Tess Harper as Fairlight Spencer; Annabella Price (1994–April 1995) as David's sister, Miss Ida Grantland, who married and moved to California; Stewart Finlay-McLennan as Scots immigrant Dr. McNeil; Emily Schulman as Ruby Mae; and Trip Cogburn as Isaac McHone. Based on Catherine Marshall's 1967 novel, the series was filmed in Townsend, Tennessee.

CHRONICLE   CBS
2 OCTOBER 1963–25 MARCH 1964   This hour documentary series shared a Wednesday time slot with *CBS Reports*. Richard Siemanowski was the executive producer of the show, which focused on the arts and sciences.

CHRONOLOG   NBC
22 OCTOBER 1971–28 JULY 1972   This monthly newsmagazine was the successor to *First Tuesday;* it was telecast on the fourth Friday of each month. Garrick Utley hosted the two-hour show. In 1974 NBC again revived the concept: see *Weekend*.

CHRYSLER THEATER
See BOB HOPE PRESENTS THE CHRYSLER THEATER

THE CHUCK BARRIS RAH-RAH SHOW   NBC
28 FEBRUARY 1978–11 APRIL 1978   A prime-time variety hour hosted by game show magnate Chuck Barris. The show featured celebrity guest stars as well as acts originally seen on *The Gong Show,* the daytime game show created and hosted by Barris.

CHUCK NORRIS KARATE COMMANDOS   SYNDICATED
1986   Half-hour cartoon series featuring characters inspired by those played by actor Chuck Norris in various action films.

THE CHUCK WOOLERY SHOW   SYNDICATED
1991–1992 Already familiar to daytime audiences as the host of *Love Connection*, Chuck Woolery also hosted this short-lived hour talk show from Group W Prods.

CIMARRON CITY   NBC
11 OCTOBER 1958–26 SEPTEMBER 1959   This hour-long western battled CBS's *Have Gun Will Travel* and *Gunsmoke* for one season. It featured George Montgomery as cattleman Matt Rockford, ex-mayor of Cimarron City, Oklahoma; Audrey Totter as Beth Purcell, proprietor of a boardinghouse; and John Smith as blacksmith and Deputy Sheriff Lane Temple. Montgomery's wife—Dinah Shore—guest-starred in one episode ("Cimarron Holiday," 20 December). Norman Jolley and Richard Bartlett were the producers.

CIMARRON STRIP   CBS
7 SEPTEMBER 1967–19 SEPTEMBER 1968   Television's third ninety-minute western (following *The Virginian* and *Wagon Train*) was the second western set in Oklahoma's Cimarron country. This time there was a range war brewing. With Stuart Whitman as Marshal Jim Crown; Randy Boone as Francis Wilde, a young photographer and part-time deputy; Percy Herbert as MacGregor, another deputy; and Jill Townsend as Dulcey Coopersmith, café owner.

CIRCLE   SYNDICATED
1960   Singer Lonnie Sattin hosted this half-hour musical variety series.

CIRCLE OF FEAR   NBC
5 JANUARY 1973–22 JUNE 1973   *Circle of Fear* was the new title given to NBC's *Ghost Story*, following Sebastian Cabot's departure as its host.

CIRCLE THEATER
See ARMSTRONG CIRCLE THEATER

THE CIRCUIT RIDER ABC
5 MARCH 1951–7 MAY 1951   A filmed religious show presented by America for Christ, Inc., *The Circuit Rider* featured guests, biographies of evangelists and musical selections. Franklyn W. Dyson produced the series.

CIRCUS! SYNDICATED
1971   Bert Parks hosted this half-hour series, which, like *International Showtime,* presented European circus acts. The series was filmed on location.

CIRCUS BOY NBC/ABC
23 SEPTEMBER 1956–8 SEPTEMBER 1957 (NBC); 19 SEPTEMBER 1957–11 SEPTEMBER 1958 (ABC)   Children's western from Screen Gems, starring Mickey Braddock as Corky, a youngster whose parents were killed in a high-wire accident; Robert Lowery as Big Tim Champion, the new owner of the circus, and guardian of Corky; Noah Beery, Jr., as Uncle Joey, one of the clowns; and Guinn Williams as Pete, a roustabout. Braddock, later known as Mickey Dolenz (his real name), achieved stardom as one of the Monkees on the show of that title.

CIRCUS TIME ABC
4 OCTOBER 1956–27 JUNE 1957   Circus and novelty acts were featured on this Thursday-night hour-long series hosted by ventriloquist Paul Winchell and his dummy, Jerry Mahoney.

THE CISCO KID SYNDICATED
1950–1955   One of the most durable of television's early westerns, *The Cisco Kid* began on radio in 1943. The TV version, from Ziv TV, starred Duncan Renaldo as Cisco and Leo Carillo as his jovial sidekick, Pancho. In the eyes of the law, Cisco and Pancho were desperadoes, wanted for unspecified crimes; in the eyes of the poor and downtrodden, the two were do-gooders who often acted where inept and unscrupulous lawmen would not. The producers' decision to film the series in color proved to be a wise one, for Cisco and Pancho were widely seen well into the 1970s. The characters reappeared in a TV-movie which aired 6 February 1994 on TNT; Jimmy Smits played Cisco and Cheech Marin was Pancho.

CITIZEN SOLDIER (THE BIG ATTACK) SYNDICATED
1958   Half-hour anthology series which dramatized true-life incidents during World War II and the Korean conflict. Each episode was narrated by the individual whose exploits were the subject of the drama. Ron Alcorn produced the thirty-nine episodes, which were filmed on location in Germany and used G.I.'s as actors and extras.

CITY CBS
29 JANUARY 1990–16 APRIL 1990; 12 MAY 1990–8 JUNE 1990   Half-hour sitcom starring Valerie Harper as Liz Gianni, city manager of a large but unnamed metropolis, with Lu Anne Ponce as Penny, her nineteen-year-old daughter, Stephen Lee as Ken Resnick, the sleazy deputy mayor; Todd Susman as Roger Barnett, Liz's assistant; Mary Jo Keenen as Gloria, the city's social coordinator; Sam Lloyd as snoopy stenographer Lance Armstrong; Tyra Farrell as Wanda, Liz's secretary; James Lorinz as police officer Victor Sloboda; and Liz Torres as Anna Maria. The series was originally scheduled on Mondays, directly opposite NBC's *The Hogan Family,* which had started life in 1986 as *Valerie,* starring none other than Valerie Harper. Coincidentally, the scheduling setup also meant that *City* costar Lu Anne Ponce was appearing directly opposite her brother Danny Ponce, who played one of the kids on *The Hogan Family.*

THE CITY
See LOVING

CITY DETECTIVE   SYNDICATED
1953   Rod Cameron starred as Lieutenant Bart Grant, tough New York cop, in this half-hour crime show. Late in 1953 *Variety* noted that the series had been sold to 171 stations, a record at the time.

CITY HOSPITAL   ABC/CBS
3 NOVEMBER 1951–19 APRIL 1952 (ABC); 25 MARCH 1952–1 OCTOBER 1953   One of TV's first medical shows, *City Hospital* starred Melville Ruick as Dr. Barton Crane, New York City physician. A real-life drama forced the cancellation of one episode, scheduled for 30 June 1953. During rehearsal that afternoon a man burst into the studio, stabbed a camera operator, and shattered a pitcher over the head of one of the actors. The half-hour series was telecast biweekly. On ABC it was seen Saturday afternoons, on CBS in prime time.

CITY OF ANGELS   NBC
3 FEBRUARY 1976–10 AUGUST 1976   Inspired by the film *Chinatown,* this private eye series was set in Los Angeles during the 1930s. It featured Wayne Rogers (formerly of *M*A*S*H*) as Jake Axminster; Clifton Jones as Lieutenant Murray Quint; Elaine Joyce as Marsha, Jake's secretary; Timmie Rogers as Lester; and Philip Sterling as Michael Brimm. Executive producer: Jo Swerling, Jr. Produced by Philip DeGuere, Jr., and William F. Phillips.

CITYKIDS   ABC
18 SEPTEMBER 1993–12 FEBRUARY 1994   On this live action Saturday morning program from Jim Henson Productions, a multi-ethnic septet of youths, assisted by two Muppets named Trish and Toya, embarked on various urban adventures. The cast included Brad Stoll as David; Cynthia Cartagena as Angelica; Renoly Santiago as Tito; Hassan Elgendi as Chris or "Snoopy"; Diana Smith as Nikki; Anne Ho as Susan; and Dule Hill as John.

THE CIVIL WAR   PBS
23 SEPTEMBER 1990–27 SEPTEMBER 1990   Ken Burns's moving documentary on the American Civil War proved to be the highest-rated series in PBS's history. Burns skillfully wove contemporary still photographs, modern-day cinematography, new recordings of period music, sound effects, and readings into an eleven-hour saga, which PBS shrewdly decided to air on consecutive nights. David McCullough narrated the series. Other voices included those of Sam Waterston (as Abraham Lincoln), Morgan Freeman (Frederick Douglass), Jason Robards (U. S. Grant), and Julie Harris (Mary Chesnut).

CIVIL WARS   ABC
20 NOVEMBER 1991–2 MARCH 1993; 3 AUGUST 1993–10 AUGUST 1993   Hour dramatic series about domestic relations attorneys, created by William M. Finkelstein for Steven Bochco Productions. The cast included Mariel Hemingway as Sydney Guilford; Peter Onorati as her new law partner, Charlie Howell; Alan Rosenberg as her former partner, Eli Levinson; and Debi Mazar as the secretary, Denise Iannello. The series attracted some notoriety for one episode, "Grin and Bare It" (30 September 1992), in which Guilford agreed to pose nude for a photographer; the viewing audience saw most of Mariel Hemingway's backside. In the fall of 1993, following *Civil Wars*'s cancellation, Rosenberg and Mazar (and their characters) moved to *L.A. Law.*

CLASS OF '96   FOX
19 JANUARY 1993–25 MAY 1993   The campus of Havenhurst College was the setting of this dramatic series. With Jason Gedrick as David Morrissey, the track star; Perry Moore as the black student, Antonio Hopkins; Brandon Douglas as the rich guy,

Whitney Reed; Megan Ward as Patty Horvath, the dramatic hopeful; Kari Wuhrer as her slutty roommate, Robin Farr; Lisa Dean Ryan as the third roommate, Jessica Cohen, the rich girl; and Gale Hansen as Sam (Stroke) Dexter, the computer nerd. The hour show was filmed in Toronto.

CLASSIC CONCENTRATION
see CONCENTRATION

CLAUDIA (CLAUDIA, THE STORY OF A MARRIAGE)   NBC/CBS
6 JANUARY 1952–23 MARCH 1952 (NBC); 31 MARCH 1952–30 JUNE 1952 (CBS) This situation comedy was based on Rose Franken's stories about a young woman and her romance. With Joan McCracken as newlywed Claudia Naughton; Hugh Reilly as her husband, David Naughton, an architect; and Margaret Wycherly as Mrs. Brown, Claudia's mother.

THE CLEAR HORIZON   CBS
11 JULY 1960–10 MARCH 1961; 26 FEBRUARY 1962–11 JUNE 1962   This soap opera attempted to capitalize on the topicality of the space age; it told the story of astronauts and their families. *The Clear Horizon* was the first daytime serial to originate from Hollywood and was also one of the few programs to reappear after its original cancellation. The cast included Ed Kemmer as Captain Roy Selby; Phyllis Avery as his wife, Ann; Craig Curtis; Denise Alexander as Lois; Jimmy Carter (the actor, not the president); Lee Meriwether; Ted Knight; William Roerick as Colonel Adams; Rusty Lane as Sergeant Moseby; and William Allyn as Frank.

CLEGHORNE!   WB
10 SEPTEMBER 1995–24 DECEMBER 1995   Half-hour sitcom starring Ellen Cleghorne (late of *Saturday Night Live*) as Ellen Carlson, a single mom who was co-owner of a small TV commercial production business; to her consternation, her parents moved into a neighboring apartment in Ellen's New York neighborhood. The cast also included Garrett Morris as Ellen's father, Sidney, a postal worker; Alaina Reed Hall as her mother, Lena; Steve Bean as her business partner, Brad; Cerita Monet Bickelmann as her young daughter, Akeyla; Michael Ralph as her ex-husband, Tyrell; and Sherri Shepherd as her empty-headed sister, Victoria.

THE CLIENT   CBS
17 SEPTEMBER 1995–   Set in Atlanta, this hour dramatic show was inspired by John Grisham's best-selling novel (the series' full title was *John Grisham's The Client*) which was made into a 1994 movie. JoBeth Williams starred as lawyer Regina "Reggie" Love, whose specialty was family law and whose own family life was a shambles; a recovering alcoholic, she was embroiled in a bitter custody dispute with her ex-husband. Also featured were John Heard as district attorney Roy Fortrigg; Polly Holliday as Momma Love, with whom Reggie lived; David Barry Gray as Clint McGuire, Reggie's young assistant; and Ossie Davis (who also appeared in the movie) as Judge Harry Roosevelt. Occasionally featured was William Converse-Roberts as Reggie's ex, Gus Cardoni, a physician.

THE CLIFF EDWARDS SHOW   CBS
23 MAY 1949–19 SEPTEMBER 1949   Cliff "Ukulele Ike" Edwards hosted this fifteen-minute musical series seen on Mondays, Wednesdays, and Fridays after the network news (sometimes the show was only ten minutes long, preceding the five-minute *Ruthie on the Telephone*). Edwards is better known to the public as the voice of Jiminy Cricket in Walt Disney films.

CLIFFHANGERS   NBC
27 FEBRUARY 1979–1 MAY 1979   An unusual prime-time program, *Cliffhangers* presented chapters from three continuing serials each week. The first (and only) three offerings were: "Stop Susan Williams," with Susan Anton as Susan Williams, a news photographer investigating the mysterious death of her brother; "The Secret Em-

pire," a science fiction western with Geoffrey Scott as Marshal Jim Donner, a frontier lawman who accidentally stumbles on a futuristic subterranean society, and Diane Markoff and Stepfanie Kramer as Tara, leader of the secret empire; "The Curse of Dracula," with Michael Nouri as the five-hundred-year-old vampire who turns up teaching night courses in history at South Bay College in California, Stephen Johnson as Kurt von Helsing, and Carol Baxter as Mary. Executive producer: Kenneth Johnson for Universal TV.

CLIMAX
CBS

7 OCTOBER 1954–26 JUNE 1958   This hour-long dramatic anthology series began as a live show but soon switched to film. It was cohosted by William Lundigan and Mary Costa. Presentations included: Raymond Chandler's "The Long Goodbye," with Dick Powell (as Philip Marlowe), Cesar Romero, and Teresa Wright (7 October 1954); Ian Fleming's "Casino Royale," with Barry Nelson (the first person to play James Bond), Linda Christian, and Peter Lorre (21 October 1954); "The Great Impersonation," with Zsa Zsa Gabor (10 March 1955; her first TV dramatic role); "Fear Strikes Out," with Tab Hunter (as baseball player Jimmy Pearsall; 18 August 1955); "Edge of Terror" with Tom Laughlin (11 September 1955; the first major TV role for Laughlin, later the star of the *Billy Jack* films). *Climax* shared a time slot with *Shower of Stars,* which was seen every fourth week (see also that title).

THE CLOCK
NBC/ABC

16 MAY 1949–31 AUGUST 1951 (NBC); 17 OCTOBER 1951–9 JANUARY 1952 (ABC)   An anthology series of half-hour suspense dramas, *The Clock* was seen sporadically for three seasons. It was derived from the radio show which began in 1946.

A CLOSER LOOK
NBC

28 JANUARY 1991–19 MARCH 1993   A rarity in modern daytime television, *A Closer Look* was a half-hour public affairs series that examined topical issues. Faith Daniels hosted, and other NBC news personnel contributed.

CLOSEUP
See THE TEX AND JINX SHOW

CLUB EMBASSY
See THE BOB AND RAY SHOW

CLUB MTV
MTV

31 AUGUST 1987–14 MARCH 1992   Weekday dance show, broadcast from the Palladium in New York City, hosted by MTV veejay Julie Brown. The series shifted to weekends in 1991.

CLUB OASIS
NBC

28 SEPTEMBER 1957–6 SEPTEMBER 1958   This biweekly variety series, set in a nightclub, alternated with *The Polly Bergen Show.* Each program was hosted by a different guest star until 7 June, when bandleader Spike Jones took over as permanent host. Other summer regulars included Helen Grayco, Doodles Weaver, Phil Gray, George Rock, Gil Bernal, and Jad Paul.

CLUB SEVEN
ABC

12 AUGUST 1948–17 MARCH 1949; 11 SEPTEMBER 1950–28 SEPTEMBER 1951   One of the first programs broadcast from ABC's New York studios, *Club Seven* was a weekly half-hour variety show during the 1948–1949 season, when it was hosted by Johnny Thompson (the show was titled *Thompson's Talent Show* during its early weeks). Tony Bavaar took over as host when the show was revived as a Monday-through-Friday-evening entry during the 1950–1951 season.

CLUB 60　　　　　　　　　　　　　　　　　　　　　　　　　NBC

18 FEBRUARY 1957–27 SEPTEMBER 1957

THE HOWARD MILLER SHOW　　　　　　　　　　　　　　　　NBC

30 SEPTEMBER 1957–10 JANUARY 1958　　A daytime variety hour broadcast live and in color from Chicago, *Club 60* featured vocalists Mike Douglas, Nancy Wright, and the Mello-Larks. Don Sherwood was the first host, but he was succeeded in March by Dennis James. By late summer Howard Miller took over as host, and late in September the show's title was changed to *The Howard Miller Show.* Music on both programs was supplied by the NBC Orchestra, conducted by Joseph Gallicchio.

CLUB TIME

See THE BOB AND RAY SHOW

CLUE CLUB　　　　　　　　　　　　　　　　　　　　　　　CBS

14 AUGUST 1976–3 SEPTEMBER 1977; 10 SEPTEMBER 1978–21 JANUARY 1979 Two bloodhounds, Woofer and Wimper, and a group of teenage sleuths—D.D., Dotty, Larry, and Pepper—were the main characters on this Hanna-Barbera cartoon show.

COACH　　　　　　　　　　　　　　　　　　　　　　　　　ABC

28 FEBRUARY 1989–7 JUNE 1989; 21 NOVEMBER 1989–　　　　Half-hour sitcom starring Craig T. Nelson as divorcé Hayden Fox, the football coach at Minnesota State University; Jerry Van Dyke as Luther Van Dam, assistant coach of the Screaming Eagles; Clare Carey as Hayden's daughter, Kelly, whom he hadn't seen for sixteen years until she enrolled at MSU; Shelley Fabares as Hayden's lady friend, newscaster Christine Armstrong; Bill Fagerbakke as student assistant Dauber Dybinski; and Kris Kamm (1989–fall 1991) as Stuart Rosebrock, who married Kelly in the fall of 1989 (they were divorced in 1991). After a successful trial run in the spring of 1989, *Coach* returned to ABC's schedule as a replacement for *Chicken Soup.* After an on-again, off-again romance, a lengthy courtship, and aborted wedding ceremonies, Hayden and Christine finally got married in 1993. That fall Christine became host of a local TV talk show, and Kelly landed a job in New York (Clare Carey no longer appeared regularly on the series). Ken Kimmins, who had been featured occasionally in previous seasons, had become a regular as athletic director Howard Burleigh. Other semi-regulars included Pam Stone (1989–1994) as women's basketball coach Judy Watkins, who became Dauber's girlfriend; Georgia Engel as Howard's wife, Shirley; and Rita Taggart (1994–1995) as Luther's girlfriend, Ruthanne. In the fall of 1995 Hayden, Christine, Luther, and Dauber left Minnesota for Florida, where Hayden became the coach of the Orlando Breakers, a new pro team. Katherine Helmond joined the cast as Doris, the team's owner.

CODE R　　　　　　　　　　　　　　　　　　　　　　　　　CBS

21 JANUARY 1977–10 JUNE 1977　　An unimaginative imitation of NBC's *Emergency!,* *Code R* was a midseason replacement for *Spencer's Pilots,* the unlucky occupant of CBS's least successful time slot, Fridays at 8:00 P.M. *Code R* featured James Houghton as Rick Wilson, chief of the Channel Island fire and rescue unit; Marty Kove as George Baker, unit member; Tom Simcox as Walt Robinson, the island police chief; Susanne Reed as Suzy, the dispatcher and office manager; W. T. Zacha as Harry; Ben Davidson as Ted Milbank; and Robbie Rundle as Bobby Robinson, Walt's young son. Edwin Self produced the hour series for Warner Brothers.

CODE RED　　　　　　　　　　　　　　　　　　　　　　　ABC

1 NOVEMBER 1981–28 MARCH 1982　　An hour adventure series about a family of firefighters. With Lorne Greene as arson investigator Joe Rorchek; Julie Adams as his wife, Ann Rorchek; Andrew Stevens as their son Ted, a firefighter; Sam J. Jones as their son Chris, a helicopter pilot; Martina Deignan as Haley Green; Adam Rich as young Danny Blake; and Jack Lindine as Al Martelli. Broadcast Sundays at 7 P.M., the series was aimed mainly at children, and failed to dent the ratings of its CBS competitor, *60 Minutes.*

CODE 3 SYNDICATED

1957 This half-hour crime show was ostensibly based on actual case histories. It was hosted by Richard Travis, who appeared as Assistant Sheriff Barnett; as Barrett explained, "Code 3" meant "get there fast." Additional authenticity was imparted to the series by the appearance of Eugene W. Biscailuz, then sheriff of Los Angeles County, at the conclusion of most episodes.

CODE 3 FOX

11 APRIL 1992–23 JULY 1993 The second series of this title was a reality-based show hosted by Gil Gerard. Boasting that it used "no actors [and] no reenactments,"-it presented video footage of actual rescue attempts.

CODENAME: FOXFIRE NBC

27 JANUARY 1985–22 MARCH 1985 This hour action series featuring a trio of female agents who took their orders from a male boss was obviously inspired by *Charlie's Angels:* even NBC admitted as much, advertising the trio in its promos as "the hottest team of hellcats since you-know-who!" The show starred Joanna Cassidy as Liz "Foxfire" Towne, a former CIA agent who formed the trio to undertake special assignments from the U.S. government; Sheryl Lee Ralph as Maggie Bryan, safe-cracker and combat expert; Robin Johnson as Danny O'Toole, the trio's designated driver; and John McCook as their boss, Larry Hutchins, the president's brother. Sheryl Lee Ralph attempted to downplay the inevitable comparisons to *Charlie's Angels* in a *TV Guide* interview, explaining that "We're trying to make it more believable and real." Following a two-hour TV-movie premiere, six episodes were televised.

CO-ED FEVER CBS

4 FEBRUARY 1979 A hapless half-hour sitcom, *Co-Ed Fever* was pulled from CBS's schedule after its only showing, a special preview following the telecast of the movie *Rocky.* Set at Baxter College, an Eastern women's school which recently admitted men, it featured David Keith as Tucker Davis; Alexa Kenin as Maria (Mousie); Christopher S. Nelson as Doug, a wealthy chap; Cathryn O'Neil as Elizabeth; Michael Pasternak as the zany Gobo; Tacey Philips as Hope; Heather Thomas as Sandi; and Jane Rose as Mrs. Selby, the housemother at Brewster House. Martin Ransohoff was the executive producer for Ransohoff Productions. CBS chose a new sitcom, *Billy,* to replace *Co-Ed Fever* in its midseason lineup.

COKE TIME NBC

29 APRIL 1953–22 FEBRUARY 1957 Eddie Fisher, a pop star of the early 1950s who later made headlines when he married Debbie Reynolds, then Elizabeth Taylor, hosted this fifteen-minute musical series which was seen Wednesdays and Fridays before the news. Singer Jaye P. Morgan appeared frequently. Fisher's backup group was known as the Echoes: Ralph Brewster, Marilyn Jackson, Norma Zimmer, and Don Williams (Zimmer was later a featured vocalist on *The Lawrence Welk Show*). Coca-Cola sponsored the series.

THE COLBYS ABC

20 NOVEMBER 1985–26 MARCH 1987 Trying to match the success of *Dallas* in generating a popular spinoff serial (*Knots Landing*), the producers of *Dynasty* spawned this series, which was formally titled *Dynasty II: The Colbys* in its early weeks. The major characters were introduced on the first few episodes of *Dynasty* during the fall of 1985, after which *The Colbys* went its own way as a separate series. Set in Los Angeles, its central characters were the members of the family of one of *Dynasty's* main characters, Jeff Colby. Principal players included: Charlton Heston as corporate magnate Jason Colby, Jeff's father (by an out-of-wedlock union); Stephanie Beacham as his wife, Sable Scott Colby; Katharine Ross as Francesca, Sable's sister (and Jeff's mother); Barbara Stanwyck (1985–1986) as Jason's sister, Constance Colby; Tracy Scoggins as Jason and Sable's older daughter, Monica; Maxwell Caulfield as their son, Miles; Claire Yarlett as their younger daughter, Bliss; Emma Samms as Fallon

Carrington, who married Miles, and later, Jeff Colby (Fallon was thought to have been killed on *Dynasty,* but was resurrected for this series); Ken Howard (1985–1986) as Garrett Boydston; Joseph Campanella (1985–1986) as Hutch Corrigan; Ricardo Montalban as Zachary Powers; Charles Van Eman (1985–1986) as Sean McAlister; Kim Morgan Greene (1986–1987) as Channing Carter; James Houghton (1986–1987) as Senator Cash Cassidy; Shanna Reed (1986–1987) as Adrienne Cassidy; and Michael Parks as Jason's brother, Phillip Colby. In one of the most implausible cliffhangers ever concocted on any of the prime-time serials, *The Colbys* wrapped up its second, and final, season, with Fallon being abducted by a UFO. Fortunately for *Dynasty* fans, she showed up safe and sound on the latter series in the fall. Although it had been expected that there would be interaction between the main characters of *Dynasty* and *The Colbys,* in fact there was little, except for the characters of Jeff and Fallon. Joan Collins (*Dynasty*'s Alexis) was particularly perturbed by the existence of the new series, and, according to *TV Guide,* urged her cohorts to have nothing to do with it.

THE COLGATE COMEDY HOUR NBC
10 SEPTEMBER 1950–25 DECEMBER 1955   This Sunday-evening variety hour competed successfully with *The Ed Sullivan Show* for its first four seasons. Most shows were comedy-variety hours with guest hosts—Dean Martin and Jerry Lewis appeared dozens of times, and Eddie Cantor, Bob Hope, Donald O'Connor, Jimmy Durante, and Fred Allen also appeared frequently. A few comedy plays and musicals were also televised, such as "Roberta," with Gordon MacRae (10 April 1955). In the fall of 1955 the show was retitled *The Colgate Variety Hour;* when Colgate dropped its sponsorship in midseason, the show continued as *The NBC Comedy Hour* (see also that title).

COLGATE THEATER NBC
3 JANUARY 1949–25 JUNE 1950   Half-hour dramatic anthology series.

COLISEUM CBS
26 JANUARY 1967–1 JUNE 1967   A compendium of European and American circus acts, *Coliseum* was hosted by a different guest star each week. The series was a midseason replacement for *Jericho.*

THE COLLEGE BOWL ABC
2 OCTOBER 1950–26 MARCH 1951   This little-known half-hour variety series was hosted by Chico Marx, who appeared as the operator of the College Bowl, a campus hangout. Andy Williams was also featured on the series.

COLLEGE BOWL CBS/NBC/DISNEY
4 JANUARY 1959–16 JUNE 1963 (CBS); 22 SEPTEMBER 1963–14 JUNE 1970 (NBC); 13 SEPTEMBER 1987–20 DECEMBER 1987 (DISNEY)   Each week two four-member teams from America's colleges and universities competed on this fast-paced quiz show; by answering "toss-up" and multiple-part questions the teams amassed points. The winning school was awarded $1,500 in scholarship funds (and the right to return the following week), the losing school $500 in funds. General Electric sponsored the series, which was hosted by Allen Ludden (1959–1962) and Robert Earle (1962–1970); Jack Cleary was the producer. On 23 May 1984 NBC aired a prime-time special "The 30th Anniversary College Bowl National Championship," hosted by Pat Sajak. Dick Cavett hosted the Disney version, which was titled *College Bowl '87.*

COLLEGE MAD HOUSE SYNDICATED
1989–1990   *College Bowl* it wasn't. This half-hour weekly series pitted two four-member teams from different colleges against each other in a battle of stunts and games. The winning team then tried to tackle an obstacle course. Greg Kinnear was the host, Donna Wilson and Richard McGregor the referees.

COLLEGE OF MUSICAL KNOWLEDGE (KAY KYSER'S KOLLEGE OF MUSICAL KNOWLEDGE) NBC

1 DECEMBER 1949–28 DECEMBER 1950; 4 JULY 1954–12 SEPTEMBER 1954   This popular radio giveaway program came twice to television. The first version was hosted by Kay Kyser ("The Old Perfesser"), who began the show on radio in 1938. Attired in cap and gown, Kyser required contestants to identify songs played by the band and to answer true-false questions incorrectly ("That's wrong, you're right!"). Assisting Kyser was mop-topped Mervyn Bogue, better known to audiences as Ish Kabibble; Mike Douglas was one of the show's featured vocalists. After a four-year absence, the show reappeared in the summer of 1954 with Tennessee Ernie Ford as host; it was then called simply *College of Musical Knowledge*. Assisting Ford were three "cheerleaders": Donna Brown, Spring Mitchell, and Maureen Cassidy.

COLLEGE PRESS CONFERENCE ABC

11 OCTOBER 1954–20 NOVEMBER 1960   Ruth Geri Hagy moderated this half-hour public affairs program on which a panel of college students questioned a newsmaker. During its first season the show was seen Monday nights; thereafter, it was relegated to Sunday afternoons.

COLONEL HUMPHREY FLACK (THE FABULOUS FRAUD) DUMONT/SYNDICATED

7 OCTOBER 1953–2 JULY 1954 (DUMONT); 1958–1959 (SYNDICATED)   This half-hour situation comedy was based on the stories by Everett Rhodes Castle about a modern-day Robin Hood whose specialty was swindling swindlers. The pilot for the series was shown on *Plymouth Playhouse*. Alan Mowbray starred as Colonel Humphrey Flack, and Frank Jenks was featured as his sidekick, Uthas P. (Patsy) Garvey. A similar story line was later used in such series as *The Rogues* and *Switch*. The thirty-nine stories were produced twice: once for DuMont, where most episodes were done live, and once for syndication five years later, when all were filmed.

COLONEL MARCH SYNDICATED

1954   This British detective series starred Boris Karloff as Colonel March, a Scotland Yard sleuth who wore an eyepatch.

COLT .45 ABC

18 OCTOBER 1957–20 SEPTEMBER 1960   Half-hour western starring Wayde Preston as government agent Christopher Colt, son of the inventor of the famous Colt revolver. Donald May replaced Preston as Christopher's cousin, Sam Colt, Jr., and was in turn replaced when Preston returned to the series early in 1960.

COLUMBO NBC/ABC

15 SEPTEMBER 1971–1 SEPTEMBER 1978 (NBC); 6 FEBRUARY 1989–28 JULY 1990 (ABC) Peter Falk starred as Columbo, a nonviolent police lieutenant with no first name, in this popular segment of *The NBC Mystery Movie*. Most shows followed the same formula. The crime (usually murder most foul) was committed at the outset, and the viewing audience learned the identity of the culprit. The fun came from watching Columbo pursue his investigation; his beguilingly inept manner and disheveled appearance often led the villain to underestimate his adversary. It was clear from the questions he asked that Columbo was nobody's fool; by the conclusion of each ninety-minute or two-hour episode, he had snared his quarry. By 1975 Falk was reportedly earning $125,000 per episode, thus ranking him as one of the highest-paid regular performers on television. No new *Columbo*s were shown during the 1976–1977 season, but four were scheduled for the 1977–1978 season. Created by Richard Levinson and William Link, the character first appeared in one segment of *The Sunday Mystery Hour*, a summer anthology series aired in 1960 and 1961. In that segment, broadcast 13 August 1961 and titled "Enough Rope," Lieutenant Columbo was played by Bert Freed. Levinson and Link subsequently incorporated the character into a play, "Prescription: Murder," which featured Thomas Mitchell as Columbo. The script was then submitted to Universal Studios, which expressed interest in it. Lee J. Cobb and Bing Crosby were considered for the role, but were

unavailable, and Falk was finally selected. The TV version of "Prescription: Murder" was shown on 20 February 1968; a second TV movie, "Ransom for a Dead Man," was aired 1 March 1971. Levinson and Link noted in their entertaining book, *Stay Tuned*, that Falk wore the same suit, shirt, tie, and shoes for the entire run of the series, thereby keeping the star's wardrobe costs to an almost absolute minimum. After a decade-long hiatus, Peter Falk returned as Columbo in 1990; the new episodes, now two hours in length, were shown as one segment of *The ABC Monday Mystery Movie* (later *The ABC Saturday Mystery Movie*). A few *Columbo* shows were telecast irregularly thereafter. In the fall of 1992 Columbo actually acquired a new raincoat, his first in almost twenty-five years. The garment, however, had been carefully weathered to resemble the old one. See also *Kate Loves a Mystery*.

COMBAT   ABC
2 OCTOBER 1962–29 AUGUST 1967   The longest-running of the several World War II dramas of the 1960s, *Combat* outlived such rivals as *The Gallant Men, The Rat Patrol, Twelve O'Clock High, Jericho, Convoy,* and *Garrison's Gorillas.* Set in Europe, it told the story of one platoon and featured Vic Morrow as Sergeant Chip Saunders; Rick Jason as Lieutenant Gil Hanley; Dick Peabody as Littlejohn; Pierre Jalbert as Caje; Steven Rogers (1962–1963) and Conlan Carter (1963–1967) as Doc; Jack Hogan as "Wild Man" Kirby; and Tom Lowell (1963–1967) as Nelson. Gene Levitt produced the series.

COMBAT SERGEANT   ABC
29 JUNE 1956–27 SEPTEMBER 1956   One of the first series set during World War II, *Combat Sergeant* blended actual footage from the North African campaign with dramatic action. Featured were Michael Thomas as Sergeant Nelson; Cliff Clark as General Harrison; Bill Slack as Lieutenant Kruger; and Mara Corday as Corporal Harbin of the WACs.

COME CLOSER   ABC
20 SEPTEMBER 1954–13 DECEMBER 1954   Half-hour game show, played for laughs. Ventriloquist Jimmy Nelson was the host, assisted by his puppets Danny O'Day, Humphrey Higby, and Farful. The series was not carried regularly by the network's New York affiliate.

COMEBACK   SYNDICATED
1979   Like *The Comeback Story,* ABC's 1953 series, this half-hour show presented biographies of people who had faced and overcome great adversities in their lives. James Whitmore was the host.

THE COMEBACK STORY   ABC
2 OCTOBER 1953–5 FEBRUARY 1954   George Jessel first hosted this series which resembled *This Is Your Life. The Comeback Story* highlighted dramatic moments from the lives of its guests, all of whom were once-famous personalities. Arlene Francis later hosted the show.

COMEDY BREAK   SYNDICATED
1985   Half-hour potpourri of skits, monologues, and interviews with comedians and other funny people, cohosted by Mack Dryden and Jamie Alcroft.

THE COMEDY FACTORY   ABC
21 JUNE 1985–9 AUGUST 1985   On this half-hour summer series, a resident repertory company, working with a different guest star each week, presented a sitcom. Seven of the eight scripts were from unsold pilot series. The repertory players included Geoff Bowes, Susan Hogan, Mary Long, Mary Ann McDonald, Derek McGrath, and Denis Simpson.

THE COMEDY SHOP   SYNDICATED
1978–1980   Norm Crosby hosted this half-hour series, a showcase for standup comics, known and unknown. Paul Roth was the executive producer.

COMEDY THEATRE   ABC
11 OCTOBER 1949–20 NOVEMBER 1949   An experimental anthology series of six comedies produced by Arch Oboler, the playwright and writer who was active in radio. The series was first seen locally on 23 September over KECA-TV, Los Angeles.

COMEDY TONIGHT   CBS
5 JULY 1970–23 AUGUST 1970   A summer replacement for *The Glen Campbell Goodtime Hour,* this hour comedy-variety series was hosted by Robert Klein and produced in part by Shelley Berman, a prominent stand-up comic of the early 1960s. Regulars included Marty Barris, Peter Boyle, Barbara Cason, MacIntyre Dixon, Boni Enten, Judy Graubart, Laura Greene, Madeline Kahn, Jerry Lacy, and Lynn Lipton.

COMEDY TONIGHT   SYNDICATED
1985   A half hour of stand-up comics, hosted (and coproduced) by Bill Boggs.

COMEDY ZONE   CBS
17 AUGUST 1984–7 SEPTEMBER 1984   A short-lived, New York-based summer comedy hour consisting of skits performed by guest stars and the regulars: Joe Mantegna, Audrie J. Neenan, Bob Gunton, Bill Randolph, and Mark Linn-Baker.

COMEDYWORLD (DEAN MARTIN'S COMEDYWORLD)   NBC
6 JUNE 1974–15 AUGUST 1974   *Comedyworld*, a summer replacement for *The Dean Martin Comedy Hour,* was a showcase for comics, known and unknown. Most segments were videotaped on location in various clubs. Jackie Cooper hosted the hour show, which also featured Nipsey Russell and Barbara Feldon as roving "Comedy Correspondents."

COMIC STRIP LIVE (COMIC STRIP LATE NIGHT) (THE SUNDAY COMICS)   FOX
12 AUGUST 1989–15 JANUARY 1994   An hour of standup comedy, taped at the Comic Strip in Los Angeles, and hosted by John Mulrooney (1989), then by Gary Kroeger. The program began as a local show in Los Angeles in July 1988. It was offered to Fox's owned-and-operated stations in the fall of that year, before going to all of Fox's affiliates a year later. When Fox added a second hour of prime-time standup comedy in November 1990, *Comic Strip Live* moved from Saturday to Sunday nights; it was now taped on location across the country, and featured a guest host each week. The Sunday program was retitled *Comic Strip Prime Time* early in 1991, and ran until 21 April of that year. The Kroeger-hosted broadcasts continued on Saturdays, but with a new title, *Comic Strip Late Night.* Wayne Kotter succeeded Kroeger as host in January 1991, and on 27 April of that year the Saturday show resumed use of the *Comic Strip Live* title. On 28 April a new Sunday comedy hour appeared, replacing *Comic Strip Prime Time.* Entitled *The Sunday Comics,* it featured standup acts as well as other comedy presentations. It was hosted briefly by Jeff Altman, then by Lenny Clarke, and then by various guest hosts through 29 March 1992.

COMING OF AGE   CBS
15 MARCH 1988–29 MARCH 1988; 24 OCTOBER 1988–21 NOVEMBER 1988; 29 JUNE 1989– 27 JULY 1989   An Arizona retirement community, The Dunes, was the setting of this half-hour sitcom, with Paul Dooley and Phyllis Newman as Dick and Ginny Hale, a Pittsburgh couple who had just moved in; Alan Young and Glynis Johns as Ed and Trudie Pepper, who loved the place; Kevin Pollak as the director, Brian Brinker; Pearl Shear as Marvel; Lenore Woodward as Wilma, Brinker's assistant; and Ruta Lee as Pauline, who still had eyes for the male residents of The Dunes. Nada Despotovich was occasionally seen as the Hales' adult daughter, Cindy. The

comedy team of Bob (Elliott) and Ray (Goulding), in one of their last TV appearances together, guested on 14 November 1988.

COMMAND POST   CBS
14 FEBRUARY 1950–4 APRIL 1950   Of the many shows which did battle with NBC's Milton Berle on Tuesday nights, *Command Post* was among the most unusual—the hour-long show was an experiment conducted by the United States Army to train reservists.

COMMANDO CODY   NBC
16 JULY 1955–8 OCTOBER 1955   This Saturday-morning outer space show starred Judd Holdren as Commando Cody, Sky Marshal of the Universe, and Aline Towne as Joan Albright, his assistant. Cody usually did battle with the Ruler (played by Gregory Gay), whose home base was on Saturn. Commando Cody should not be confused with Commander Corry of *Space Patrol* (see also that title).

COMMENT   NBC
14 JUNE 1954–9 AUGUST 1954; 13 APRIL 1958–10 AUGUST 1958; 24 JANUARY 1971–10 SEPTEMBER 1972   *Comment* first surfaced during the summer of 1954 as a Monday-night series on which NBC news reporters commented on topical issues. The 1958 version of the series was more erudite, featuring discussions with luminaries such as Arnold J. Toynbee and Aldous Huxley (the 1958 dates listed above are those of *Comment*'s Sunday-afternoon run; the show had previously been aired as a "filler" program after the conclusion of NBC's Friday-night boxing telecasts). The 1971–1972 version of *Comment* was again seen on Sundays; hosted by Edwin Newman, it featured interviews with newsmakers.

THE COMMISH   ABC
28 SEPTEMBER 1991–20 MAY 1995   Michael Chiklis starred in this hour crime show as Tony Scali, the unorthodox, hands-on police commissioner of Eastbridge, New York. Other regulars included Theresa Saldana as his wife, Rachel; Kaj-Erik Eriksen as their teenage son, David (Tony and Rachel had a baby, Sarah, in late 1992); Geoffrey Nauffts (1991–1994) as Detective Stan Kelly, who was killed in action; Alex Bruhanski (1991–1992) as Irv Wallerstein, chief of detectives; Nicholas Lea (1991–1993) as Officer Ricky Caruso; Gina Belafonte (1991–1993) as Officer Carmela Pagan, Caruso's partner; David Paymer (1991–1992) as Tony's live-in brother-in-law, Arnie Metzger; Phil Peters (1991–1992; he was Theresa Saldana's husband in real life) as Sergeant William Frawley; John Cygan (1991–1992; 1994–1995) as Detective Paulie Pentangeli; Melinda McGraw (1992–1994) as Detective Cyd Madison; Jason Schombing (1994–1995) as Detective Lopez; and Ian Tracey (1994–1995) as Detective Hibbs. Created by Stephen J. Cannell and Stephen Kronish, the series was filmed in Vancouver; the Scali character was based loosely on the experiences of Tony Schembri, the police chief of Rye, New York.

COMPASS   ABC
23 OCTOBER 1954–11 AUGUST 1957   Half-hour travelogue, broadcast irregularly over a three-year period.

THE COMPLETELY MENTAL MISADVENTURES OF ED GRIMLEY   NBC
10 SEPTEMBER 1988–2 SEPTEMBER 1989   Ed Grimley, the quintessential nerd character created by Martin Short at Toronto's Second City, and popularized by him on *Saturday Night Live,* got his own Saturday morning series for a season. The half hour combined cartoons with some live-action sequences, and featured the voices of Short, Andrea Martin, Catherine O'Hara, and Jonathan Winters.

CONAN AND THE YOUNG WARRIORS   CBS
5 MARCH 1994–27 AUGUST 1994   On this Saturday morning cartoon series, Conan the Barbarian found himself protecting three young warriors, each with special powers, who were destined to rule a mythical kingdom.

CONCENTRATION   NBC/SYNDICATED
28 JULY 1958–23 MARCH 1973 (NBC); 1973–1979 (SYNDICATED)
CLASSIC CONCENTRATION   NBC
4 MAY 1987–14 JANUARY 1994   *Concentration* enjoyed one of the longest continuous runs of any network daytime game show; it also enjoyed brief nighttime runs in the fall of 1958 and the spring of 1961. The TV game was based on the card game and featured two contestants each day, seated opposite a board containing thirty numbered squares. Behind each numbered square was the name of a prize, and behind that was a portion of a rebus puzzle; each prize was listed twice on the board. Contestants took turns naming pairs of numbers, which were then turned to reveal the prizes. If the prizes matched, the two portions of the rebus puzzle were uncovered. The first contestant to solve the rebus won all the prizes he or she had accumulated. Hugh Downs was the first host of the series. During his tenure as host, Downs also continued to appear on the *Tonight* show (until Jack Paar's departure in 1962), and later on the *Today* show (which Downs hosted from 1962 to 1971). Downs relinquished his duties as *Concentration*'s host in 1965, and a string of hosts followed: Jack Barry, Art James, Bill Mazer, Ed McMahon, and finally Bob Clayton (26 September 1969–1973). The syndicated version of the show, substantially identical to the network version, first appeared in 1973 and was hosted by Jack Narz. In 1987 the series returned to NBC's daytime schedule after a fourteen-year absence. With occasional interruptions, it ran for another six years, sometimes in reruns. Titled *Classic Concentration* and hosted by Alex Trebek, it featured a grid of twenty-five boxes that no longer needed to be turned manually; the prize or puzzle piece was now revealed electronically.

CONCERNING MISS MARLOWE   NBC
5 JULY 1954–1 JULY 1955   Another of NBC's unsuccessful daytime serials, *Concerning Miss Marlowe* concerned a forty-year-old actress who lived in New York. Louise Allbritton played Maggie Marlowe until April 1955, when Helen Shields replaced her. Other regulars included John Raby as Bill; Efrem Zimbalist, Jr. (in his first TV role) as Jim Gavin; Jane Seymour as "Hat"; and Ross Martin as Bojalian.

CONCERT TONIGHT   DUMONT
30 DECEMBER 1953–31 MARCH 1954; 15 SEPTEMBER 1954–6 APRIL 1955   An hour of classical music broadcast from Chicago, featuring the Chicago Symphony.

CONCRETE COWBOYS   CBS
7 FEBRUARY 1981–21 MARCH 1981   A light hour adventure series starring Jerry Reed as J. D. Reed and Geoffrey Scott as Will Ewbanks, two guys who liked to drive. Each week found them looking for excitement in a new city.

CONDO   ABC
10 FEBRUARY 1983–16 JUNE 1983   On this half-hour sitcom a WASP family and a Hispanic family each bought adjacent condominiums in a Southern California development, much to the consternation of the two patriarchs. The series managed to borrow a storyline from *Romeo and Juliet,* as the WASP son fell in love with (and married) the Hispanic daughter. Featured were McLean Stevenson (in his sixth sitcom in fifteen years) as James Kirkridge; Brooke Alderson as his wife, Margaret "Kiki" Kirkridge; Mark Schubb as their older son, Scott; Marc Price as their younger son, Billy; Luis Avalos as Jesus "Jessie" Rodriguez, who had started his own landscaping business; Yvonne Wilder as his wife, Maria Rodriguez; Julie Carmen as their daughter, Linda, who fell for Scott; and James Victor as José Montoya, Maria's father.

CONFESSION   ABC
19 JUNE 1958–13 JANUARY 1959   Jack Wyatt hosted this unusual half-hour interview show: Wyatt's guests were convicted criminals, who talked about the crimes they had committed. Law enforcement personnel were also featured on the videotaped show, which originated from Dallas.

CONFIDENTIAL FILE   SYNDICATED
1955–1957   Paul Coates narrated this half-hour series, which presented interviews with guests as well as dramatic adaptations of topical subjects, particularly crime and show business.

CONFIDENTIAL FOR WOMEN   ABC
28 MARCH 1966–8 JULY 1966   A daytime series that, like NBC's *Modern Romances,* presented a new five-part story each week. Jane Wyatt (formerly of *Father Knows Best*) narrated and psychiatrist Theodore Isaac Rubin provided daily commentary.

CONFLICT   ABC
18 SEPTEMBER 1956–3 SEPTEMBER 1957   Warner Brothers supplied this biweekly anthology series, which alternated with *Cheyenne.* A few *Conflict* segments had been seen during the preceding season on *Warner Brothers Presents.* Personal conflicts were the subjects of the episodes; the series was produced by Jack Barry in cooperation with the National Association for Mental Health. Will Hutchins, later star of *Sugarfoot,* made his television debut in "Stranger on the Road," broadcast 11 December.

CONFLICTS   PBS
21 NOVEMBER 1973–16 JANUARY 1974   Dramatic anthology series presented by the Hollywood Television Theatre. Among the presentations were "Me," a two-act play by Gardner McKay (former star of *Adventures in Paradise*) with Richard Dreyfuss and Alison Rose, and "Double Solitaire," a drama with Richard Crenna and Susan Clark.

CONGRESSIONAL REPORT   NBC
13 APRIL 1969–31 AUGUST 1969   Bill Monroe was the moderator of this Sunday public-interest series on which groups of four members of Congress discussed current issues.

CONNECTIONS   PBS
30 SEPTEMBER 1979–2 DECEMBER 1979   A ten-week hour series on the history of technology, hosted by James Burke, and produced by BBC-TV and Time-Life Television. A successor series, *Connections²,* aired on The Learning Channel in 1994.

CONRAD NAGEL THEATER   SYNDICATED
1955   Actor Conrad Nagel, whose film career began in 1919, hosted this half-hour dramatic anthology series.

THE CONSTITUTION: THAT DELICATE BALANCE   PBS
18 SEPTEMBER 1984–11 DECEMBER 1984   A thirteen-part hour discussion series on constitutional topics. Among the issues discussed were executive privilege (with former President Gerald Ford), elections, criminal justice, and national security. The genesis of the series was a fall 1983 seminar on war powers, in which Ford also participated.

CONSULT DR. BROTHERS
See DR. JOYCE BROTHERS

CONSUMER BUYLINE   SYNDICATED
1978   David Horowitz hosted this informational show for consumers, which had been featured on local television in Los Angeles before going national. Lloyd Thaxton, host of several game shows and rock music programs of the 1960s, produced the show.

CONSUMER SURVIVAL KIT   PBS

1975–1979   Educational series for consumers on products and services, presented with a light touch. Hosted by Lary Lewman, the show was produced by the Maryland Center for Public Broadcasting.

THE CONTENDER   CBS

3 APRIL 1980–1 MAY 1980   Five-part miniseries about an amateur boxer who left his native Oregon to train for the Olympics. With Marc Singer as Johnny Captor; Moses Gunn as ex-fighter Beifus, his trainer, who envisioned Johnny as the next "great white hope"; Katherine Cannon as Johnny's girlfriend, Jill; Louise Latham as his mother, Alma Captor; Tina Andrews as Missy Dinwittie; and Alan Stock as Brian.

CONTEST CARNIVAL   CBS

3 JANUARY 1954–18 DECEMBER 1955   Telecast on Sunday mornings from Philadelphia, this talent contest for aspiring young circus performers was hosted by Gene Crane. Also on hand were three clowns—Kernel, Puff, and Carney—and Dave Stephen's band.

THE CONTINENTAL   CBS

22 JANUARY 1952–17 APRIL 1952   This unusual series starred Renzo Cesana as a suave bachelor (The Continental), who wooed the ladies watching at home; the set featured a table for two, a bottle of champagne, and a rose. The show was aired live on Tuesdays and Thursdays at 11:15 P.M. Cesana later hosted a similar series. See *First Date*.

CONTINENTAL CLASSROOM   NBC

6 OCTOBER 1958–18 DECEMBER 1964   Like CBS's *Sunrise Semester, Continental Classroom* was an early-morning educational series for adults. The first offering was a course on physics taught by Dr. Harvey E. White of the University of California at Berkeley. The half-hour show was produced by NBC in cooperation with the American Association of Colleges for Teacher Education.

CONTINENTAL SHOWCASE   CBS

11 JUNE 1966–10 SEPTEMBER 1966   CBS put together this circus show by reediting tapes of European circus acts supplied by Bavarian Television in Munich. Jim Backus was then added as "host," to introduce the acts and provide a measure of continuity.

CONVERSATIONS WITH ERIC SEVAREID   CBS

13 JULY 1975–7 SEPTEMBER 1975   Public affairs series on which Eric Sevareid conversed with notables such as West German Chancellor Willy Brandt, former ambassador George Kennan, and others.

CONVOY   NBC

17 SEPTEMBER 1965–10 DECEMBER 1965   One of the lesser known World War II series, *Convoy* told the story of a group of 200 American ships heading across the North Atlantic. With John Gavin as Commander Dan Talbot, skipper of the fleet's escort destroyer, a naval officer longing for more action; John Larch as Ben Foster, merchant captain of the fleet's flagship; Linden Chiles as Chief Officer Steve Kirkland; and James Callahan as Lieutenant O'Connell. One of the last NBC shows filmed in black and white, *Convoy* was shot down after thirteen weeks.

COOL McCOOL   NBC

10 SEPTEMBER 1966–31 AUGUST 1968; 17 MAY 1969–30 AUGUST 1969   Saturday-morning cartoon series about a secret agent, Cool McCool, who took his orders from an unseen boss, Number One, and who battled such villains as the Rattler, the Owl and the Pussycat, and Jack-in-the-Box. Another regular segment of the series was "Harry McCool," Cool's father, a bumbling policeman.

COOL MILLION   NBC

25 OCTOBER 1972–11 JULY 1973   One segment of *The NBC Mystery Movie, Cool Million* alternated with *Banacek* and *Madigan*. It starred James Farentino as private eye Jefferson Keyes, who charged a cool $1 million per assignment, with results guaranteed. Also featured was Adele Mara as Elena, the woman who ran Keyes's answering service.

THE COP AND THE KID   NBC

4 DECEMBER 1975–4 MARCH 1976   In this situation comedy a white bachelor cop became the foster father of a black orphan. With Charles Durning as Officer Frank Murphy; Tierre Turner as young Lucas Adams, his ward; Patsy Kelly as Brigid Murphy, Frank's mother; Sharon Spelman as Mary Goodhew, the school principal; Curtiz Willis as Shortstuff, Lucas's pal; and Eric Laneuville as Mouse, another of Lucas's pals. Jerry Davis created the series and was also its executive producer. Produced by Ben Joelson and Art Baer.

COP ROCK   ABC

26 SEPTEMBER 1990–26 DECEMBER 1990   Steven Bochco and William M. Finkelstein created this unusual series, the first to mix music into a crime show format. Each week four or five original songs were blended into the story line. Randy Newman composed the show's theme, "Under the Gun," and the other songs used on the premiere; others composed music for the subsequent episodes, under the direction of veteran TV composer Mike Post. Most of the performances were actually sung live during the filming by the actors themselves. The cast included: Ronny Cox as Chief Roger Kendrick, a Wild West buff; Larry Joshua as Captain John Hollander; Peter Onorati as Detective Vincent LaRusso; Mick Murray as Detective Joseph Gaines; Ron McLarty as Detective Ralph Ruskin; Anne Bobby as Ruskin's wife, Officer Vicki Quinn; David Gianopoulos as Officer Andy Campo, Vicki's partner; James McDaniel as Officer Franklin Rose; and Barbara Bosson as Louise Plank, mayor of Los Angeles, where the action took place.

The show was reportedly one of the most expensive hour series ever produced for television, at an estimated cost of $1.8 million per episode.

COPS   FOX

7 JANUARY 1989–   An interesting, video-verité look at real law enforcement officers on and off the job. Camera crews followed their subjects in the office, on stakeouts, on raids, and, to a lesser extent, at home. The results were often fascinating. The series focused first on the men and women of the Broward County (Fla.) Sheriff's Department, then moved to other locations, mostly in the United States. One special sixty-minute program, broadcast 15 July 1989, was produced on location in Moscow and Leningrad. The success of this series, with its relatively low production costs, led to a proliferation of similar programs: see *American Detective, FBI: The Untold Stories, Real Stories of the Highway Patrol, Secret Service,* and *True Detectives.*

THE CORAL JUNGLE   SYNDICATED

1976   A series of marine documentaries filmed at and around the Great Barrier Reef off the coast of Australia; narrated by Leonard Nimoy.

THE CORNER BAR   ABC

21 JUNE 1972–23 AUGUST 1972; 3 AUGUST 1973–7 SEPTEMBER 1973   Shown during two summers, this sitcom was set in a New York bar. In 1972 the bar was known as Grant's Toomb; in 1973 it was simply The Corner Bar. The 1972 cast included Gabriel Dell as Harry Grant, the owner of Grant's Toomb; J. J. Barry as cabbie Fred Costello, token bigot; Bill Fiore as Phil Bracken, token drunk; Joe Keyes as Joe the cook, token black; Vincent Schiavelli as Peter Panama, token homosexual; and Shimen Ruskin as waiter Meyer Shapiro, token Jew. The 1973 cast featured Barry, Fiore, and Ruskin from the 1972 crew and newcomers Anne Meara as Mae, the widowed co-owner of The Corner Bar; Eugene Roche as Mae's partner, Frank

Flynn; and Ron Carey as actor Donald Hooten. Comedian Alan King was the executive producer, and comedian Howard Morris (one of the second bananas on *Your Show of Shows*) was the producer.

CORONADO 9 SYNDICATED
1959 Rod Cameron, who had played cops on *City Detective* and *State Trooper*, played a private eye—Dan Adams—in this half-hour series set in San Diego. Beverly Garland was also featured. Coronado 9 was Adams's telephone exchange.

CORONET BLUE CBS
29 MAY 1967–4 SEPTEMBER 1967 This offbeat hour-long series featured an amnesiac searching for his identity. Frank Converse starred as Michael Alden, a young man who lost his memory following an attempt on his life. Fearful that his assailants may still be pursuing him, Alden's only clue to his past were the words "coronet blue." Also featured were Joe Silver as his new friend, Max, and Brian Bedford as Brother Anthony, a monk who tried to help him. Eleven episodes were filmed in 1965, but CBS decided not to air the show at that time. Although the show proved fairly popular in 1967, production could not have continued because Converse had been signed for a fall series, *N.Y.P.D.*. Several prominent guest stars appeared on the program, including Susan Hampshire ("A Time to Be Born," 29 May), Candice Bergen ("The Rebel," her first dramatic role on American television, 19 June), Hal Holbrook (10 July), Alan Alda ("Six Months to Live," 14 August), and disc jockeys Murray the K and Dick Clark ("The Flip Side of Tommy Devon," 4 September). Filmed on location in New York, the series was produced by Herbert Brodkin and directed by Paul Bogart.

COS ABC
19 SEPTEMBER 1976–31 OCTOBER 1976 An unsuccessful Sunday-evening variety hour aimed principally at children, hosted by Bill Cosby, with help from Charlie Callas, Jeff Altman, Buzzy Linhart, Timothy Thomerson, Marion Ramsey, Mauricio Jarrin, Willie Bobo, and Rod Hull. Chris Bearde was the producer.

THE COSBY MYSTERIES NBC
21 SEPTEMBER 1994–12 APRIL 1995 Bill Cosby returned to network television after a two-year absence in this hour crime show as Guy Hanks, a criminologist who came out of retirement to assist the New York City police on selected cases. Also featured were James Naughton as Detective Sully; Rita Moreno as Guy's housekeeper, Angie Corea; Dante Beze as Dante, Guy's occasional assistant; and Lynn Whitfield as Guy's girlfriend, Barbara Lorenz. William Link and David Black were the executive producers of the series, which was filmed in New York.

THE COSBY SHOW NBC
20 SEPTEMBER 1984–17 SEPTEMBER 1992 Considered to be the most popular series of the 1980s, *The Cosby Show* was the principal cause of NBC's rise to prime-time ratings supremacy. Introduced in 1984, at a time when some analysts predicted that the age of the sitcom had passed, the program finished second in the ratings in 1984–1985, and topped the charts (sometimes by huge margins) for the next four seasons. Its phenomenal success ushered in a new era of sitcoms, many of them based on the traditional family; by the end of the decade there were more sitcoms on the network prime-time schedules than at any other time in television history.

The series was created by Bill Cosby, Ed. Weinberger, and Michael Leeson for the Carsey-Werner Company, whose principals, Marcy Carsey and Tom Werner, had been programming executives at ABC. Cosby was well known as a comedian and performer; in 1965 he had made TV history by becoming the first black performer to star in a network dramatic series. He won three Emmys for his portrayal of Alexander Scott on *I Spy*. After that groundbreaking series, however, his prime-time record was unimpressive: a low-key sitcom (*The Bill Cosby Show*) and two failed variety series (*The New Bill Cosby Show* and *Cos*). His biggest TV success was the long-running Saturday morning cartoon series, *Fat Albert and the Cosby Kids,* based loosely on his childhood days in Philadelphia.

For his 1984 show, Cosby had in mind a family sitcom, with two working parents and several children. He was actively involved in almost every aspect of the show (his name would appear up to six times in the credits during some seasons), and was able to insist that it be taped in New York, rather than in Hollywood. Originally, Cosby proposed that the parents should have blue collar jobs—the father a limousine driver, the mother a plumber. But by the time NBC had picked up the show (ABC, Carsey and Werner's old network, having passed on an earlier version), the parents were both professional people; indeed, the show was beginning to resemble Cosby's own life. Cosby played Dr. Cliff (short for Heathcliff) Huxtable, an obstetrician living in a Brooklyn townhouse. His wife, Clair, an attorney, was played by Phylicia Ayers-Allen (later known as Phylicia Rashad after her marriage to NBC sportscaster Ahmad Rashad, who proposed to her on the air during *NFL Live!* in 1985). As the series progressed, the parents' professional lives gradually became less significant as more of the stories centered on family life.

For the show's first few weeks the Huxtable household had only four children. Playing them were Lisa Bonet as daughter Denise; Malcolm-Jamal Warner as son Theodore (Theo); Tempestt Bledsoe as daughter Vanessa; and Keshia Knight Pulliam as daughter Rudy. A fifth child had been mentioned in some of the early episodes (although in the pilot episode Clair had asked Cliff, "Why do we have four children?"), and on 24 November 1984 Sabrina LeBeauf was introduced as the oldest daughter, Sondra, a student at Princeton. The Huxtable household now mirrored Cosby's own: each had four daughters and a son. Occasionally appearing were: Earle Hyman as Cliff's father, Russell Huxtable; Clarice Taylor as Cliff's mother, Anna Huxtable; Peter Costa (1985–1989) as Rudy's quiet pal, Peter Chiara; Deon Richmond (1986–1992) as Rudy's pal Kenny; and Carl Anthony Payne (1986–1987) as Theo's friend Cockroach.

Geoffrey Owens joined the cast in 1986 as Sondra's boyfriend, Elvin Tibideaux; Elvin and Sondra were married in 1987 and their twins, Nelson and Winnie, were born in November 1988. Also in 1986 daughter Denise graduated from high school and started college at Hillman, alma mater of her father and grandfather; in the fall of 1987 this story line evolved into a spinoff series, *A Different World.* Lisa Bonet, however, lasted only one season on the new series, returning to *The Cosby Show* in the fall of 1988 (although not on a regular basis that season, due to her real-life pregnancy). In the fall of 1989 the character returned full time; Denise was now married to Lieutenant Martin Kendall (played by Joseph C. Phillips, who had previously appeared on the show as a suitor of Sondra's), and was the stepmother of Martin's three-year-old daughter, Olivia (played by Raven-Symone). In the fall of 1990 Erika Alexander joined the cast as Pam Turner, Clair's second cousin once removed, who came from the tough Bedford-Stuyvesant neighborhood of Brooklyn. Also appearing occasionally for the last two seasons were Mushond Lee as Pam's friend Slide, Karen Malina White as Pam's friend Charmaine, and Allen Payne as Pam's friend Lance. By the fall of 1991, *The Cosby Show's* eighth and final season, Lisa Bonet had been dropped from the show. Jessica Vaughn and Gary Gray appeared as Elvin and Sondra's twins, Winnie and Nelson, and William Thomas, Jr., played Vanessa's boyfriend, Dabnis Brickley. The series' last first-run episode (30 April 1992) was an hour program celebrating Theo's graduation from college. In the final scene Cliff and Clair "broke the fourth wall," as they sauntered off the set, past the studio audience and out a studio door.

The rerun rights to *The Cosby Show* were sold to local stations in 1988 at the peak of the show's popularity, grossing an estimated $500 million for the distributor, Viacom, and for the principals, Cosby, Carsey, and Werner. In some markets the price charged per episode was more than twice the amount ever charged for any previous program. Inevitably, some local stations were disappointed when local rerun ratings failed to justify the enormous cost.

The Cosby Show engendered much discussion among critics and academics, particularly for its treatment of race and class. The "blackness" of the show was simply a given. While it was not overtly stressed, it was always present in subtle ways: anti-apartheid posters and portraits of Martin Luther King, Jr., and Frederick Douglass on the kids' walls, references to predominantly black colleges (including the mythical Hillman College), and Cliff's reminiscing about "conking" his hair to impress a girl. Some have criticized the obvious affluence of the Huxtable family, noting that few black American households are headed by two working professionals. But almost everyone has praised the series for its wholehearted endorsement of family values.

COSMOPOLITAN THEATER   DUMONT
2 OCTOBER 1951–25 DECEMBER 1951   This hour-long filmed dramatic anthology series was seen on Tuesday nights. The stories were adapted from those appearing in *Cosmopolitan* magazine.

COSMOS   PBS
1980   Cornell astronomer Carl Sagan was the host of this lavishly produced and highly acclaimed multipart series on astronomy. The production crew made good use of special effects to help bring the subject matter alive.

COUCH POTATOES   SYNDICATED
1989   Television itself was the subject of this game show, hosted by Marc Summers. Two teams of three players each competed, winning "ratings points" by answering TV trivia questions. The winning team was given the opportunity to try for a top prize of $5000.

THE COUNT OF MONTE CRISTO   SYNDICATED
1955   George Dolenz starred as Edmond Dantes, the French patriot who escaped from prison and fled to the isle of Monte Cristo, where he set up shop to battle evildoers; Faith Domergue was also featured as Princess Anne. Hal Roach, Jr., was the executive producer of the half-hour adventure series, which was filmed in Hollywood, using the sets from the 1940 film of the same title, and later in England.

COUNTERATTACK: CRIME IN AMERICA   ABC
2 MAY 1982–23 MAY 1982   George Kennedy hosted this hour documentary series on crime. Each show was a potpourri of dramatic reenactments of various crimes, descriptions of assorted fugitives, and advice on crime prevention. Scheduled on Sundays opposite CBS's *60 Minutes,* it vanished quickly.

COUNTRY CARNIVAL   SYNDICATED
1969   Half-hour country-and-western music show, hosted by singer Del Reeves.

COUNTRY MUSIC CARAVAN   SYNDICATED
1966   Half-hour musical show.

COUNTRY MUSIC JUBILEE
See OZARK JUBILEE

COUNTRY STYLE   DUMONT
29 JULY 1950–25 NOVEMBER 1950   One of network television's first country-music programs, *Country Style* was seen for an hour on Saturday nights and was hosted by Peggy Anne Ellis.

COUNTRY STYLE U.S.A.   SYNDICATED
1959   Fifteen-minute country-and-western musical show hosted by singing serviceman Charlie Applewhite, who had been featured on *The Milton Berle Show* in 1953.

COUNTY FAIR   NBC
22 SEPTEMBER 1958–25 SEPTEMBER 1959   Bert Parks hosted this daytime variety half hour, which was set at a county fair.

A COUPLE OF JOES   ABC
5 AUGUST 1949–12 JULY 1950   This half-hour variety series was cohosted by Joe Bushkin and Joe Rosenfield and featured Warren Hull, Joan Barton, Allyn Edwards, the Milton DeLugg Orchestra (1949), and Mike Reilly's Orchestra (1950), and Morgan the basset hound, owned by producer Richard Gordon.

COUPLES   SYNDICATED
1982   On this half-hour "reality show," pairs of people—husbands and wives, parents and children, brothers and sisters, or whatever—were persuaded to pour out their most intimate problems to psychologist Dr. Walter Brackelmanns and, of course, to a nationwide viewing audience.

COURT MARTIAL   ABC
8 APRIL 1966–2 SEPTEMBER 1966   Another World War II series, this one focused on the United States Army Judge Advocate General Corps. With Bradford Dillman as Captain David Young; Peter Graves as Major Frank Whittaker; Kenneth J. Warren as their aide, Sergeant MacCaskey; and Diene Clare as their secretary, Wendy.

COURT OF CURRENT ISSUES   DUMONT
9 FEBRUARY 1948–26 JUNE 1951   This early public affairs program featured debates on topical issues. It was not widely watched because for most of its run it was slotted opposite Milton Berle's *The Texaco Star Theater*.

THE COURT OF HUMAN RELATIONS   NBC
22 JUNE 1959–21 AUGUST 1959   On this unusual daytime program a panel of three experts gave advice on interpersonal problems presented to them by guests. The moderator, A. L. Alexander, had hosted a similar program on radio.

THE COURT OF LAST RESORT   NBC
4 OCTOBER 1957–11 APRIL 1958   This half-hour series dramatized the work of the Court of Last Resort, a real-life organization, founded in 1948, which was not a court of law but rather a group of seven criminal law experts. Its purpose was to aid defendants whom it believed had been convicted unjustly. The series starred Lyle Bettger as investigator Sam Larsen; Paul Birch appeared occasionally as defense attorney Erle Stanley Gardner (Gardner, of course, is better known as the creator of *Perry Mason*). Jules Goldstone was the producer. The series was rerun on ABC during the 1959–1960 season.

COURT TV: INSIDE AMERICA'S COURTS   SYNDICATED
1993–   A weekly half hour of highlights of trials from the Court TV cable network. Cynthia McFadden and Gregg Jarrett were the anchors. The cable service, which was launched in July 1991, saw its ratings escalate in 1995 because of widespread public interest in the murder trial of O. J. Simpson.

COURTHOUSE   CBS
13 SEPTEMBER 1995–15 NOVEMBER 1995   Hour prime time drama set at the courthouse in Clark County, an urban center in an unspecified state. With Patricia Wettig as Presiding Judge Justine Parkes; Annabeth Gish as assistant district attorney Lenore Laderman; Robin Givens as investigator Susanne Graham; Bob Gunton as unmerciful Judge Homer Conklin; Brad Johnson as hunky Judge Wyatt Earp Jackson, newly arrived from Montana; Michael Lerner as Judge Myron Winkleman, head of the family court; Jennifer Lewis as family court Judge Rosetta Reide, a gay woman; Nia Peeples as idealistic public defender Veronica Gilbert; and Jeffrey D. Sams as assistant district attorney Ed Moore.

COURTROOM U.S.A.   SYNDICATED
1960   Actual court cases were dramatized on this series, which starred Jay Jostyn.

THE COURTSHIP OF EDDIE'S FATHER   ABC

17 SEPTEMBER 1969–14 JUNE 1972   In this sitcom, a widower was constantly getting entangled with women, thanks to the persistent match-making efforts of his young son. Nevertheless, the two were (in the words of the show's theme song) "best friends." With Bill Bixby as Tom Corbett, editor of *Tomorrow* magazine; Brandon Cruz as son Eddie; Miyoshi Umeki as their Japanese housekeeper, Mrs. Livingston; James Komack as Tom's friend Norman Tinker, the magazine's art director; Kristina Holland as Tina Rickles, Tom's secretary; and Jodie Foster (1970–1972) as Joey Kelly, a schoolmate of Eddie's. Costar Komack also produced the series for MGM-TV (he later created *Chico and the Man* and *Sugar Time!*).

COVER TO COVER   NBC

29 JULY 1991–25 OCTOBER 1991   Daytime magazine series aimed at women, co-hosted by Gayle King and Robin Wagner. King had been a local news anchor in Hartford and Baltimore; Wagner had anchored local newscasts in Cleveland.

COVER UP   CBS

22 SEPTEMBER 1984–6 JULY 1985   This ill-fated adventure series was an updated version of *I Spy*. Originally, it starred Jennifer O'Neill as Dani Reynolds and Jon-Erik Hexum as Mac Harper, two American secret agents who, operating undercover as a fashion photographer and her male model, traveled all over the world to help Americans in trouble overseas. Also featured were Richard Anderson as their boss, Henry Towler; Mykel T. Williamson as Dani's assistant, Rick; and Ingrid Anderson, Irena Ferris, Dana Sparks, and Kimberly Foster as models Gretchen, Billie, Ashley, and Kim. Sadly, on 12 October 1984 Hexum, while reloading blanks into a prop gun, accidentally shot himself in the head. The force of the shot proved fatal, and Hexum died a few days later; his heart was transplanted into a critically needy recipient. (The series carried a tribute to Hexum at the end of the next televised episode, read by costar Richard Anderson, but unfortunately Hexum's name was misspelled.) Following Hexum's death, the producers frantically searched for a replacement, and ultimately came up with Australian actor Antony Hamilton as Jack Striker, who was introduced on 24 November. Glen A. Larson created the series.

COVINGTON CROSS   ABC

25 AUGUST 1992–31 OCTOBER 1992   The first prime-time dramatic series in three decades to be set during the Middle Ages, *Covington Cross* can perhaps be described as *Dallas* with armor. Created by Gil Grant and filmed on location in England, the continuing drama's central characters were a widowed lord and his five children. The cast included Nigel Terry as Sir Thomas Gray, the patriarch; Jonathan Firth as son Richard, a knight; Ben Porter as son William, also a knight; Glenn Quinn as son Cedric, headed for the clergy; Tim Killick as son Armus, who was off on a crusade; Ione Skye as daughter Eleanor, a medieval feminist; Cherie Lunghi as Lady Elizabeth, a potential love interest for Sir Thomas; and James Faulkner as the evil John Mullens.

COWBOY G-MEN   SYNDICATED

1952   This low-budget western starred Russell Hayden and Jackie Coogan as Pat Gallagher and Stoney Crockett, two nineteenth-century government agents. Lesley Selander directed the series.

COWBOY IN AFRICA   ABC

11 SEPTEMBER 1967–16 SEPTEMBER 1968   This adventure series starred Chuck Connors as Jim Sinclair, an American rodeo star who goes to Kenya to assist in an ambitious wildlife management project. With Tom Nardini as John Henry, a Navajo who accompanies Jim; Ronald Howard as Wing Commander Hayes, the wealthy rancher who recruited their services; and Gerald B. Edwards as Samson, a young Kenyan boy who makes friends with the two Americans. The series was filmed largely at Africa, U.S.A., near Los Angeles.

COWBOY THEATRE   NBC
15 SEPTEMBER 1956–15 SEPTEMBER 1957   Monty Hall, better known as the host of *Let's Make a Deal,* emceed this weekend series of western films.

THE COWBOYS   ABC
6 FEBRUARY 1974–14 AUGUST 1974   Adapted from the 1972 film starring John Wayne, *The Cowboys* was a half-hour western about seven homeless boys who go to work on a ranch owned by a widow. With Jim Davis as Marshal Bill Winter; Diana Douglas as widow Kate Andersen; Moses Gunn as Nightlinger, the black cook and overseer of the boys; Robert Carradine as Slim; A Martinez as Cimarron; Sean Kelly as Jimmy; Kerry MacLane as Homer; Clint Howard as Steve; Mitch Brown as Hardy; and Clay O'Brien as Weedy. Four of the youngsters—Carradine, Martinez, Kelly, and O'Brien—had appeared in the film (Carradine and Martinez repeated their film roles on television; Kelly had played Bob and O'Brien had played Hardy in the movie).

COWTOWN RODEO   ABC
23 JUNE 1958–8 SEPTEMBER 1958   Half-hour rodeo show, with commentary by Marty Glickman, broadcast from New Jersey.

CRAFTS WITH KATY   SYNDICATED
1971   A half-hour of macrame and decoupage and the like, demonstrated by Katy Dacus.

CRAIG KENNEDY, CRIMINOLOGIST   SYNDICATED
1952   Donald Woods starred as criminologist Craig Kennedy in this little-noted half-hour series. Adrian Weiss produced and directed.

CRASH CORRIGAN'S RANCH   ABC
15 JULY 1950–29 SEPTEMBER 1950   Ray "Crash" Corrigan hosted this summer variety series for children. Corrigan's real-life "ranch," located near Hollywood, was widely used for location filming by many TV western series.

CRAZY LIKE A FOX   CBS
30 DECEMBER 1984–4 SEPTEMBER 1986   This lighthearted detective show starred Jack Warden as rumpled private eye Harry Fox and John Rubinstein as his son, attorney Harrison Fox, Harry's reluctant crime-solving partner. Penny Peyser played Harrison's wife, Cindy, and Robby Kiger their son, Josh. Also around were Lydia Lei (1984–1985) and Patricia Ayame Thomson (1985–1986) as Harrison's secretary, Allison Ling, and Robert Hanley as Lieutenant Walker of the San Francisco Police Department. Thirty-seven episodes were made. The cast was reunited for a TV-movie, "Still Crazy Like a Fox," filmed in England and broadcast 5 April 1987.

CREATIVE COOKERY   NBC/ABC
10 OCTOBER 1953–3 APRIL 1954 (NBC); 30 AUGUST 1954–25 FEBRUARY 1955 (ABC)
A cooking instruction program broadcast from Chicago, hosted by chef François Pope and his sons, Frank and Robert Pope. The NBC version was seen for an hour on Saturday mornings, while the ABC version ran for 55 minutes on weekdays. Elina Fahrenholz was the producer, Phil Bodwell the director.

CREATIVITY WITH BILL MOYERS   PBS
8 JANUARY 1982–21 MAY 1982   In an effort to examine the creative process, host Bill Moyers interviewed poets, playwrights, entrepreneurs, and scientists on this half-hour series.

THE CREW   FOX
31 AUGUST 1995–25 JANUARY 1996   Predictable sitcom about a flight crew based in Miami and employed by Regency Airlines. With Rose Jackson as Jess Jameson; Kristin Bauer as Maggie Reynolds (Jess and Maggie not only worked together, but

also shared an apartment); David Burke as Paul Steadman, a gay man; Charles Esten as Randy Anderson, a randy womanizer; Christine Estabrook as flight crew supervisor Lenora Zwick; Lane Davies as pilot Captain Rex Parker; and Dondre T. Whitfield as Mac, who worked at the Mambo Lambo, the crew's favorite hangout when they weren't airborne.

CRIME AND PUNISHMENT SYNDICATED
1961 Like *Confession,* this series featured interviews with convicted criminals as well as with law and corrections officials. The program was hosted by Clete Roberts, with additional commentary provided by criminologist Robert A. McGee. Collier Young was the producer.

CRIME & PUNISHMENT NBC
3 MARCH 1993–6 APRIL 1993 The cops on this hour crime show tried to think like criminals in order to catch them. Featured were Jon Tenney as Detective Ken O'Donnell; Rachel Ticotin as his partner, Detective Annette Rey; Carmen Argenziano as the boss, Lieutenant Bartoli; James Sloyan as the voice of the unseen interrogator, who pushed the detectives to "get inside the criminal mind"; Maria Celedonio as Annette's young daughter, Tanya; and Lisa Darr as O'Donnell's girlfriend, Jan. Dick Wolf created the series and was its executive producer.

CRIME PHOTOGRAPHER CBS
19 APRIL 1951–5 JUNE 1952 The television version of the radio program originally starred Richard Carlyle as Casey, the gutsy photographer for the *Morning Express,* a New York daily. Carlyle was later replaced by Darren McGavin (in his first starring role on television; McGavin would later play a similar role in *The Night Stalker*). Also featured were Jan Miner as Annie Williams, Casey's girlfriend (Miner had played the role on radio but is better known to modern viewers as Madge the Manicurist in commercials for Palmolive); John Gibson as Ethelbert, bartender at the Blue Note Café, Casey's favorite hangout (Gibson, too, had played the role on radio); and Bernard Lenrow as Inspector Logan of the New York Police Department, Casey's nemesis. George Harmon Coxe created Casey in a series of novels. Martin Manulis produced the TV series.

CRIME STOPPERS 800 SYNDICATED
1990–1991 A clone of *America's Most Wanted,* except that some of the crime depicted and fugitives sought were international, rather than domestic. Edwin Hart was the principal reporter.

CRIME STORY NBC
18 SEPTEMBER 1986–13 MARCH 1987; 12 JUNE 1987–10 MAY 1988 To its credit, NBC gave this ambitious cop show two full seasons to catch on, but it was never able to capture a large audience. The action started in Chicago in 1963, where Lieutenant Mike Torello (played by Dennis Farina, who had been a Chicago cop in real life) waged a vendetta against mobster Ray Luca (played by Anthony Denison). Torello headed the Major Crime Unit of the police department, which also included Sergeant Danny Krychek (Bill Smitrovich), Detective Nate Grossman (Steve Ryan), Detective Joey Indelli (Bill Campbell), and Detective Walter Clemmons (Paul Butler). Stephen Lang played prosecutor David Abrams, and John Santucci (who had been a criminal in real life) played Luca's loyal but dimwitted henchman, Paul (Paulie) Taglia. Darlanne Flugel was seen in the earliest episodes as Torello's wife, Julie (they were divorced by midseason). By the middle of the season Luca and Taglia had left Chicago for Las Vegas, and Torello and his squad followed, becoming agents of a federal strike force in the process. Others who appeared from time to time as "guest mobsters" included Joseph Wiseman (he'd had the title role in *Dr. No*) as Manny Weisbrod, Jon Polito as Phil Bartoli, and comedian Andrew Dice Clay as Max Goldman. The first season ended with an unusual cliffhanger: escaping from the Feds, Paulie drove Luca to what appeared to be a "safe house" in the Nevada desert. Unfortunately, it was the site of an imminent nuclear bomb test. Miraculously, the

two escaped without serious injury to enjoy a second season of cops and robbers. Later in the season Luca fled to a Latin American country, where he was eventually tracked down by Torello. Del Shannon sang the series's theme, "Runaway," updating the lyrics to his 1961 hit. Michael Mann, executive producer of *Miami Vice,* created the series.

CRIME SYNDICATED CBS
18 SEPTEMBER 1951–23 JUNE 1953 This anthology series of crime dramas, supposedly based on true stories, was hosted and narrated by Rudolph Halley, an investigator for the congressional crime committee chaired by Senator Estes Kefauver. It was produced by Jerry Danzig and directed by John Peyser. The half-hour series began as a weekly effort, then alternated biweekly with *City Hospital* beginning in March 1952.

CRIME TIME AFTER PRIME TIME CBS
8 APRIL 1991–4 JANUARY 1995 *Crime Time After Prime Time* was the umbrella title of CBS's late-night group of crime shows. They were telecast weeknights at 11:30 P.M. from 1991 through 26 August 1993; *Late Night with David Letterman* took over the slot on 30 August 1993. In the meantime, a second nightly telecast of *Crime Time After Prime Time,* scheduled at 12:30 A.M., was inaugurated early in 1993; it followed *Late Night* until 4 January 1995 (although the comedy show *The Kids in the Hall* usually aired on Friday evenings). *The Late Late Show with Tom Snyder* inherited the time slot the following week.
   Nine separate series were aired on *Crime Time After Prime Time: Dangerous Curves, Dark Justice, The Exile, Fly by Night, Forever Knight, Scene of the Crime, Silk Stalkings, Sweating Bullets,* and *Urban Angel.* See individual titles for details.

CRIME WITH FATHER ABC
31 AUGUST 1951–25 JANUARY 1952 Comedy-mystery starring Rusty Lane and Peggy Lobbin as a father-daughter detective team, Jim and Chris Riland.

CRIMEWATCH TONIGHT SYNDICATED
1989–1990 A half-hour show, best described in its own words: "a daily report on America's war against crime." It presented segments on wanted fugitives, news of recent crimes, and tips on crime prevention. Former CBS News reporter Ike Pappas was the host.

CRISIS NBC
5 OCTOBER 1949–28 DECEMBER 1949 Arthur Peterson hosted this unusual half-hour dramatic anthology series, which was broadcast from Chicago. Each week a group of actors reenacted three events from the life of a guest; periodically through the show, host Peterson checked with the guest to see if the dramatizations accurately reflected the incidents.

CRISIS TO CRISIS WITH BARBARA JORDAN PBS
23 JULY 1982–8 OCTOBER 1982 Former Congresswoman Barbara Jordan hosted this ten-week series of independently produced documentaries.

THE CRITIC ABC/FOX
26 JANUARY 1994–2 MARCH 1994 (ABC); 1 JUNE 1994–20 JULY 1994 (ABC); 5 MARCH 1995–30 JULY 1995 (FOX) The central figure in this half-hour animated series was nerdy film critic Jay Sherman, a fat, balding divorcé with a young son, Marty. Jay hosted a film review program, "Coming Attractions," on cable television. Jon Lovitz provided the character's voice. Other voices were supplied by Nancy Cartwright, Christine Cavanaugh, Gerrit Graham, Doris Grau, Judith Ivey, Nick Jameson, Maurice LaMarche, Charles Napier, and Kath Soucie. Al Jean and Mike Reiss, two veterans of *The Simpsons,* created the series; its show-within-a-show format provided ample opportunities to satirize current films and TV shows.

CRITIC AT LARGE   ABC
18 AUGUST 1948–27 APRIL 1949   John Mason Brown was the host of this half-hour series, on which he chatted with guest critics about the arts.

CRO   ABC
18 SEPTEMBER 1993–15 JULY 1995   Inspired by the book "The Way Things Work," this semi-educational Saturday morning cartoon series was set in prehistoric times. The title character, Cro, was an orphaned cave boy who was able to show his less intelligent contemporaries the basic principles of science. In the fall of 1994 Cro acquired a girlfriend, Sooli. The episodes were introduced by Cro's pal Phil, a mammoth who had been frozen in a glacier and was thawed out in the twentieth century. Max Casella provided the voice of Cro.

CROCKETT'S VICTORY GARDEN
See VICTORY GARDEN

CROOK AND CHASE   SYNDICATED/TNN
1986–1989 (SYNDICATED); 1989–1993 (TNN)   Nashville's equivalent of *Entertainment Tonight, Crook and Chase* was a half-hour weekday entertainment magazine show cohosted by Lorrianne Crook and Charlie Chase and broadcast from Nashville. A weekend wrap-up, *Weekend with Crook and Chase,* was also nationally syndicated between 1987 and 1993. By 1992 *Crook and Chase* had expanded to an hour nightly on TNN, and in October 1993 the duo began hosting *Music City Tonight* on TNN; the latter series was originally a ninety-minute program, but was later trimmed to sixty minutes.

CROSS CURRENT
See FOREIGN INTRIGUE

CROSSFIRE   CNN
1982–   Half-hour nightly debate series on newsworthy topics, with Patrick Buchanan representing the conservative viewpoint, and Tom Braden (to 1989) and Michael Kinsley (1989–1995) espousing the liberal side. Columnist Robert Novak filled in for Buchanan when the latter served as White House director of communications in 1987. Former White House chief-of-staff John Sununu succeeded Buchanan in 1992.

CROSSROADS   ABC
7 OCTOBER 1955–27 SEPTEMBER 1957   This half-hour dramatic anthology series depicted the work of clergymen.

CROSSROADS
See THE AMERICAN PARADE

CROSSROADS   ABC
14 SEPTEMBER 1992–31 OCTOBER 1992; 10 JUNE 1993–15 JULY 1993   Robert Urich starred in this hour dramatic series as Johnny Hawkins, a Manhattan prosecutor who quit his job after being reunited with his troubled sixteen-year-old son; they decided to hit the road together. Dalton James costarred as the son, Dylan, who was released to his father's custody after getting in trouble with the law.

THE CROSS-WITS   SYNDICATED
1976–1980; 1986–1987   On this half-hour game show two teams, each consisting of two celebrities and a noncelebrity captain, scored points by filling in words on a giant crossword puzzle. Jack Clark hosted the first version of the series; David Sparks presided over the latter version, which was officially titled *The New Cross-Wits*. Ralph Edwards was executive producer.

CROWN THEATRE
See THE GLORIA SWANSON SHOW

CRUNCH AND DES   SYNDICATED
1955   This half-hour adventure series, set in the Bahamas, featured Forrest Tucker as Crunch Adams, owner of the Crunch Adams Charter Boat Service and skipper of the *Poseidon,* and Sandy Kenyon as his partner, Des (short for "Desperate") Smith. The series was based on stories by Philip Wylie.

CRUSADE IN EUROPE   ABC
5 MAY 1949–27 OCTOBER 1949   One of the first documentary series filmed especially for television, *Crusade in Europe* was a series of twenty-six half hours based on Dwight Eisenhower's book about the American effort in Europe during World War II. Sponsored by Time, Inc., the series was produced by Richard de Rochemont and narrated by Westbrook Van Voorhis.

THE CRUSADER   CBS
7 OCTOBER 1955–28 DECEMBER 1956   Brian Keith starred as Matt Anders, a freelance writer who helped persons escape from Communist nations, in this little-remembered adventure series. Dick Lewis was the producer.

CRUSADER RABBIT   SYNDICATED
1949–1957   One of the first cartoon series made especially for television, *Crusader Rabbit* was the brainchild of Jay Ward and his partner, Alexander Anderson. The witty, five-minute segments were produced in color and were in serial form; some stations thus ran a single cartoon each day, while other combined several into a longer show. The stars of the series were Crusader Rabbit, a small but noble adventurer, and Rags the Tiger, his somewhat less intelligent partner. The first set of cartoons was produced between 1948 and 1951; NBC was offered the series in 1949 but declined it. A second set of cartoons was made in 1956; by that time Jay Ward had sold his interest in the show and had begun to develop a new series for television, *Rocky and His Friends* (Rocky and Bullwinkle closely resembled Crusader and Rags). The voices of Crusader and Rags were supplied by Lucille Blass and Verne Loudin respectively.

THE CRUSADERS   SYNDICATED
1993–1994   An hour weekly investigative show with five correspondents: Mark Hyman, Carla Wohl, William LaJeunesse, Howard Thompson, and Ted Wayman.

CURIOSITY SHOP   ABC
11 SEPTEMBER 1971–2 SEPTEMBER 1973   This educational show for children was a mix of cartoons, filmed segments, and interviews; each hour was devoted to one theme, such as "Tools," "Rules," or "Flight." With Pamelyn Ferdin as Pam; Kerry MacLane as Ralph; John Levin as Gerard; Jerrelyn Fields as Cindy; and Barbara Minkus as Gittel the Witch. Seen on Sunday mornings, the series was created and produced by Chuck Jones.

A CURRENT AFFAIR   SYNDICATED
1987–   This half-hour, five-day-a-week series that has been described as "tabloid television" offered a regular dose of sensational stories on lurid crimes, sex, and celebrities. Maury Povich was the chief correspondent. The series was originally seen only on the several stations owned by the Fox network before being made available for national syndication in 1987. In the fall of 1990 a weekend edition was introduced; titled *A Current Affair Extra,* it was hosted by Maureen O'Boyle, who also took over as the weekday host that fall. Penny Daniels succeeded O'Boyle in 1994. In June 1995 longtime chief reporter Steve Dunleavy was let go as new producers took over the series. Jon Scott was named anchor in the fall of 1995.

CURTAIN CALL NBC

20 JUNE 1952–26 SEPTEMBER 1952   This half-hour dramatic anthology series was a summer replacement for *The Dennis Day Show*. Telecasts included: "The Promise," with Carol Bruce (20 June); "The Soul of the Great Bell," with Boris Karloff (27 June); and "Season of Divorce," with Richard Kiley (8 August).

CUSTER (THE LEGEND OF CUSTER) ABC

6 SEPTEMBER 1967–27 DECEMBER 1967   *Custer* was an unsuccessful attempt to tell the story of America's best-known Calvary officer, a flamboyant twenty-eight-year-old who had risen to the rank of major general and was demoted for dereliction of duty; ordered reinstated, he was put in command of the Seventh Regiment of the United States Cavalry, which was stationed at Fort Hays, Kansas. The series was canceled long before the men of the Seventh would have reached the Little Big Horn. With Wayne Maunder as Lieutenant Colonel George A. Custer; Michael Dante as Sioux chief Crazy Horse; Slim Pickens as scout California Joe Milner; Peter Palmer as Sergeant James Bustard, a former Confederate soldier; Robert F. Simon as General A. H. Terry; and Grant Woods as Captain Myles Keogh. Created by Samuel Peeples and David Weisbart.

CUT DUMONT

4 JUNE 1949–18 JUNE 1949   Hosted by Carl Caruso, this hour-long game show featured phone calls to home viewers. If the viewer could identify the subject of the scene being acted out by a group of players on stage, the viewer could try to identify a photograph of a famous personality as it spun on a wheel. After just three weeks the format was modified, and the show was retitled *Spin the Picture* (see that title). Jerry Layton and Wilbur Stark produced the series, and the Alan Logan Trio provided the music.

CUTTER TO HOUSTON CBS

1 OCTOBER 1983–31 DECEMBER 1983   This hour medical show was set at Cutter Community Hospital in Cutter, Texas, a small rural town about an hour's flight from Houston. The series focused on three physicians who worked there, and starred Jim Metzler as Dr. Andy Fenton, a general practitioner who had grown up in Cutter; Alec Baldwin as internist Dr. Hal Wexler, who had agreed to serve there after his implication in a big-city prescription-forging scandal; and Shelley Hack as surgeon Dr. Beth Gilbert, who had been advised to work at Cutter by her Houston superiors in order "to learn more about taking responsibility." Also featured were K Callan as Connie, a nurse; Susan Styles as Patty, another nurse; and Noble Willingham as Cutter's Mayor Jarvis. The program was CBS's lowest rated series of the 1983–1984 season.

CUTTERS CBS

11 JUNE 1993–9 JULY 1993   Unfunny sitcom about a father and son who decided to knock down the wall between their barber shop and the mother-and-daughter beauty parlor next door. With Robert Hays as barber Joe Polachuk; Dakin Mathews as his irascible dad, Harry Polachuk, an Archie Bunker clone; Margaret Whitton as Adrienne St. John, co-owner of the beauty parlor; Julia Campbell as her stepdaughter and business partner, Lynn Fletcher, who had an on-again, off-again romance with Joe; Julius Carry as their gay black hairdresser, Troy King, a former Olympic champion; Robin Tunney as Deborah, who also worked in the beauty shop; and Ray Buktenica as Chad, one of the barber shop regulars. The short-lived series was set in Buffalo, New York.

CYBER C.O.P.S. CBS

20 MARCH 1993–4 SEPTEMBER 1993   Set in the future, this Saturday morning cartoon series featured a team of superpowered crimefighters known as the Cyber C.O.P.S.— the Central Organization of Police Specialists.

CYBILL   CBS

2 JANUARY 1995–   Half-hour sitcom starring Cybill Shepherd as Cybill Sheridan, a Hollywood actress with two ex-husbands and two daughters, who began to find it increasingly harder to get work as middle age loomed. Other regulars included Christine Baranski as Cybill's booze-guzzling best friend, Maryann Thorpe, also divorced; Tom Wopat as Cybill's first ex, Jeff, a stuntman; Alan Rosenberg as Cybill's second ex, Ira, a writer; Dedee Pfeiffer as Cybill and Jeff's 22-year-old daughter, Rachel Blanders; and Alicia Witt as Cybill and Ira's 16-year-old daughter, Zoey. Marilu Henner appeared occasionally as Terry, Jeff's other ex-wife.

THE D.A.   NBC

17 SEPTEMBER 1971–7 JANUARY 1972   Jack Webb produced this half-hour series in which most of the action took place in the courtroom. With Robert Conrad as Paul Ryan, deputy district attorney in Los Angeles; Harry Morgan as H. M. "Staff" Stafford, chief deputy D.A.; Ned Romero as investigator Bob Ramirez; and Julie Cobb as Katy Benson, deputy public defender.

THE D.A.'S MAN   NBC

3 JANUARY 1959–29 AUGUST 1959   John Compton starred as private detective Shannon, the man whom the New York district attorney called on for help when he needed it, in this half-hour crime show. Also featured was Ralph Manza as Al Bonacorsi, Shannon's contact man in the D.A.'s office. Based on the book by James B. Horan and Harold Danforth, the series was produced by Jack Webb's Mark VII, Ltd.

D. C. FOLLIES   SYNDICATED

1987–1989   Political satire was the thread of this half-hour comedy show, set at a Washington, D.C., bar. Fred Willard played the bartender, and the other characters were all puppets designed, by Sid and Marty Krofft, as caricatures of prominent politicians and showbiz people. The show was no doubt inspired by the popular British show *Spitting Image,* which also employed puppets.

DEA   FOX

7 SEPTEMBER 1990–16 NOVEMBER 1990; 19 APRIL 1991–7 JUNE 1991   An hour crime show, shot in video verité style, about the efforts of five agents of the federal Drug Enforcement Agency. With Tom Mason as Bill Stadler; Byron Keith Minns as Jimmy Sanders; Chris Stanley as Nick Biaggi; David Wohl as Phil Jacobs; and Jenny Gago as Teresa Robles. When the series returned to the air in April 1991 it was retitled *DEA: Special Task Force.* Richard DiLello created the series and was its executive producer.

DADDY DEAREST   FOX

5 SEPTEMBER 1993–12 DECEMBER 1993   Richard Lewis teamed up with Don Rickles in this predictable sitcom about a single guy whose father moved in with him. Lewis played the son, psychologist Steven Mitchell, Rickles the dad, Al Mitchell, whose wife had thrown him out of their house. Also on board were Renee Taylor as Helen, Al's wife and Steven's mother; Carey Eidel as Steven's brother, Larry; Jeffrey Bomberger as Steven's son, Danny (Jonathan Gibby played the role on the premiere); Sydney Walsh as Steven's office partner, therapist Christine Winters; and Alice Carter as Lisa, their receptionist.

DADDY'S GIRLS   CBS

21 SEPTEMBER 1994–12 OCTOBER 1994   This short-lived sitcom was Dudley Moore's second flop on CBS in eighteen months (see also *Dudley*). This time he starred as Dudley Walker, the head of a New York fashion business, whose wife had run off with his best friend and business partner. Assisting him were Harvey Fierstein as his gay designer, Dennis Sinclair; Meredith Scott Lynn as middle daughter Samantha, who worked in the office; Stacy Galina as eldest daughter Amy; Keri Russell as youngest daughter Phoebe; Alan Ruck as Lenny, Amy's dull husband, an optometrist; and Eugene Roche as Seymour, one of Dudley's employees.

DADS   ABC

5 DECEMBER 1986–6 FEBRUARY 1987; 6 JUNE 1987–27 JUNE 1987   This half-hour sitcom could be described as *The Odd Couple . . . with Children.* It starred Barry Bostwick and Carl Weintraub as best friends (and single fathers) Rick Armstrong and Louie Mangiotti, who shared a Philadelphia house with their three teenaged kids: Kelly Armstrong (played by Skye Bassett), Allan Mangiotti (Eddie Castrodad), and Kenny Mangiotti (Jason Naylor).

THE DAFFY DUCK SHOW   NBC

4 NOVEMBER 1978–11 SEPTEMBER 1982   Half-hour Saturday-morning cartoon show starring the Warner Brothers character. In the fall of 1981 the show was retitled *The Daffy–Speedy Show,* as Speedy Gonzales, the fastest mouse in Mexico, became Daffy's costar. Other Warner Brothers cartoons were also shown, including Tweety and Sylvester, Yosemite Sam, Elmer Fudd, and Foghorn Leghorn. In the fall of 1982 Daffy and Company moved to CBS (see *Sylvester and Tweety*).

DAGMAR'S CANTEEN   NBC

22 MARCH 1952–14 JUNE 1952   Broadcast at 12:15 A.M. on Saturday nights, this short-lived fifteen-minute variety series was hosted by Dagmar (Jennie Lewis), late of *Broadway Open House,* and presented talent culled from the armed forces. Ray Malone and Milton DeLugg were also featured.

THE DAKOTAS   ABC

7 JANUARY 1963–9 SEPTEMBER 1963   Set in the Dakota Territory, this Warner Brothers western replaced *Cheyenne.* With Larry Ward as Marshal Frank Ragan; Chad Everett as Deputy Del Stark; Jack Elam as Deputy J. D. Smith, a former gunslinger; and Michael Green as Deputy Vance Porter.

DAKTARI   CBS

11 JANUARY 1966–15 JANUARY 1969   This African adventure series was set at the Wameru Study Center for Animal Behavior. It featured Marshall Thompson as Dr. Marsh Tracy, a veterinarian and conservationist (*daktari* is the Swahili word for "doctor"); Cheryl Miller as Paula, his daughter; Yale Summers as conservationist Jack Dane; Hari Rhodes as Mike, an African conservationist; Hedley Mattingly as District Officer Hedley, local game warden; Ross Hagen (1968–1969) as hunter Bart Jason; and Erin Moran (1968–1969) as six-year-old Jenny Jones, an orphan taken in by Dr. Tracy. The show's two animal stars—Clarence the cross-eyed lion and Judy the chimp—were as popular as its human stars. Like *Cowboy in Africa, Daktari* was filmed at California's Africa, U.S.A., the home for some 500 beasts established by Ralph Helfer and Ivan Tors. Tors, the producer of *Daktari,* had produced the 1965 film, *Clarence the Cross-Eyed Lion* (which featured Thompson and Miller), from which the series was derived.

DALLAS   CBS

2 APRIL 1978–30 APRIL 1978; 23 SEPTEMBER 1978–3 MAY 1991   The first popular prime-time serial since *Peyton Place* in the late 1960s, *Dallas* emerged as one of the most popular series of its, or any other, era. When *Dallas* finished first in the 1980–1981 seasonal ratings (by a wide margin), it became only the second dramatic series ever to do so (*Marcus Welby, M.D.* was the first). *Dallas* also enjoyed enormous popularity abroad; it became a runaway hit in almost every nation where it was shown, with the lone exception of Japan.

Created by David Jacobs for Lorimar Productions, *Dallas* was introduced in the spring of 1978 for a five-week trial run. It introduced the two generations of the Ewing family, whose huge fortunes had been made in the oil business; all of the Ewings lived at South Fork, the family's sprawling ranch in Braddock County outside of Dallas. Also introduced were the two generations of the Barnes family, the Ewings' bitter adversaries. The basic story line of the spring tryout was borrowed from *Romeo and Juliet*—the youngest Ewing son fell for the Barnes daughter, and married her. The original cast included: Jim Davis as John "Jock" Ewing, the head of Ewing

Oil, a rough-hewn, self-made man; Barbara Bel Geddes as his stolid wife, Eleanor ("Miss Ellie") Southworth Ewing; Larry Hagman as the eldest son, John Ross (J. R.) Ewing, an unprincipled philanderer; Linda Gray as Sue Ellen (Shepard) Ewing, J. R.'s beautiful but troubled wife; Patrick Duffy as the youngest son, Bobby Ewing, considerably more honest and principled than J. R.; Victoria Principal as Bobby's beautiful (but less troubled) wife, Pamela (Barnes) Ewing; Ken Kercheval as Pamela's brother, lawyer Cliff Barnes; David Wayne as their father, Willard "Digger" Barnes, whose one-time partnership with Jock Ewing had long since disintegrated into bitter enmity (Keenan Wynn succeeded Wayne in the fall of 1978; Digger died in 1980); Charlene Tilton as Jock's granddaughter, Lucy Ewing (she was the daughter of the middle son, seldom-seen Gary); and Steve Kanaly as Ray Krebbs, the ranch foreman.

Dallas was renewed for the 1978–1979 season, and performed adequately in the 10:00 P.M. Saturday time slot. Its popularity zoomed, however, later in the season when it was moved to Fridays at 10:00 P.M. The Ewing-Barnes rivalry remained a major story line; after Digger's death, his son Cliff waged an incessant, but unsuccessful, campaign to destroy Ewing Oil. Other story lines also began to develop, particularly those involving the Ewings themselves: J. R. Ewing became one of fiction's most dastardly villains as he schemed to destroy his enemies, betray his friends, outmaneuver his brothers, and even to institutionalize his wife. The stormy marriage between J. R. and Sue Ellen would dissolve, only to be reestablished. Bobby and Pamela's marriage would also crumble, with some behind-the-scenes assistance from J. R. The family would be shocked at Jock's revelation that Ray Krebbs was his illegitmate son. The family would later learn of Jock's death in South America (in real life, Jim Davis had died in March 1981).

Dallas's most effective ploy, however, was the introduction of a cliffhanger ending to each season, one which was designed to keep the audience in suspense during six long months of reruns. The most famous of these climaxed the 1979–1980 season; at the end of the final episode, J. R., working late at the office, was shot in the chest. The "Who Shot J. R.?" mystery generated worldwide publicity, and was resolved during the first five weeks of the 1980–1981 season. J. R., it turned out, had been wounded, but not killed; his wife, Sue Ellen, became the prime suspect. However, it was revealed on the fifth show that Sue Ellen's younger sister, Kristin (played by Mary Crosby), who had had an affair with J. R., had fired the gun. That episode, telecast 21 November 1980, was then the most widely watched TV program of all time (it would later be topped by the finale of *M*A*S*H* in 1983). To help insure secrecy up to the last minute, at least five alternate endings were filmed—Kristin, Sue Ellen, Cliff, Ellie, and Jock were all filmed shooting J. R.—and the one with Kristin was delivered to the network on the day of the broadcast.

Subsequent seasons ended with other cliffhangers, but none proved quite as exciting as the first one. The 1980–1981 season ended with Cliff Barnes's discovery of a body floating in the Ewings' pool (it was Kristin's). The 1981–1982 season was capped with Cliff's attempted suicide (he recovered), and the 1982–1983 season came to a close with J. R., Sue Ellen, their son, and Ray Krebbs trapped in the burning South Fork mansion (all were safely rescued). The 1983–1984 season cliffhanger offered a variation of the "Who Shot J. R.?" ploy, as an unidentified assailant stalked J. R. in his office and fired a gun through his chair; unfortunately, Bobby Ewing was seated in his brother's chair at the time. Bobby survived, but in the fall it was revealed that it was he, not J. R., who had been stalked; his wife's half-sister, Katherine Wentworth (played by Morgan Brittany from 1982 to 1984) was the culprit.

Other members of the original cast began to depart. In the fall of 1984 Donna Reed succeeded Barbara Bel Geddes as Miss Ellie; Bel Geddes had been ill, and wished to leave the series. However, the substitution never really worked, and Bel Geddes was persuaded to return to her role in the fall of 1985 (Reed later sued for breach of contract, and the case was settled for an undisclosed seven-figure sum).

Patrick Duffy announced his departure from *Dallas* in 1985; at the end of the season, he was apparently killed while trying to save Pam from a hit-and-run driver (again, Katherine Wentworth was at the wheel). Charlene Tilton also left the show at that time, though she would return for two more seasons beginning in 1988. It became obvious during the 1985–1986 season that *Dallas* just wasn't the same without the two Ewing brothers; the show's ratings began to decline, as the series slipped from second to sixth place. Larry Hagman and the show's producers convinced Duffy to return for the 1986–1987 season. With Duffy back in the fold, they then faced the even more challenging problem of explaining his return. The solution, divulged in the fall 1986 opener, was one of the most disappointing in television history: Pamela discovers Bobby happily showering, and realizes that the entire preceding season had been only her dream.

Perhaps Pamela was never able to recover from the dream, as Victoria Principal exited the show in the spring of 1987. Two other longtime regulars followed her—Steve Kanaly in the fall of 1988 and Linda Gray in the spring of 1989. As the 1989–1990 season—*Dallas*'s thirteenth—dawned, Larry Hagman (who by now wore the executive producer's hat as well as J.R.'s Stetson) and Ken Kercheval were the only continuously serving members of the original cast. No exteriors were filmed in Dallas that year, although the series had previously made jaunts to Europe and the Soviet Union. The series finished the season in 43rd place.

Other regulars have included: Susan Howard (1979–1987) as Donna Culver, who married Ray Krebbs; Leigh McCloskey (1979–1981) as Mitch Cooper, an idealistic medical student who married Lucy but who couldn't accept her wealth; Jared Martin (1979–1982 and 1985–1987) as Steven "Dusty" Farlow, a cowboy who had an affair with Sue Ellen (thought to have died, he returned as a bitter paraplegic); Randolph Powell (1979–1980) as Alan Beam; Susan Flannery (1980–1982) as public relations agent Leslie Stewart; Tyler Banks (1980–1983) and Omri Katz (1983–1991) as J. R. and Sue Ellen's son, John Ross Ewing; David Ackroyd (1979–1980) and Gary Shackelford (1980–1981) as Gary Ewing, J. R. and Bobby's brother; Joan Van Ark (1979–1981) as Gary's wife, Valene Ewing (Gary and Valene, of course, went west to California and their own spinoff, *Knots Landing*); Howard Keel (1981–1991) as Dusty's father, Clayton Farlow, who married Ellie Ewing in 1984; Audrey Landers (1981–1984) as Mitch's sister, singer Afton Cooper; Priscilla Pointer (1981–1983) as Rebecca Wentworth, mother of Cliff and Pamela; Timothy Patrick Murphy (1982–1983) as Ray Krebbs's nephew, Mickey Trotter; Lois Chiles (1982–1983) as Holly Harwood, owner of a rival oil company; John Beck (1983–1984 and 1985–1986) as Mark Graison, who fell for Pamela after her divorce from Bobby; Deborah Tranelli as Bobby's secretary, Phyllis; Debbie Rennard as J. R.'s secretary, Sly; Christopher Atkins (1983–1984) as Peter Richards, a psychology student who had been John Ross's camp counselor; Priscilla Beaulieu Presley (1983–1988) as Bobby's old flame, Jenna Wade (the part had previously been played by Morgan Fairchild and Francine Tacker); Shalane McCall (1983–1988) as Jenna's daughter, Charlie Wade; Deborah Shelton (1984–1987) as Mandy Winger; Jennilee Harrison (1984–1986) as cousin Jamie Ewing, who married Cliff Barnes; Dack Rambo (1985–1987) as Jamie's brother, Jack Ewing; Joshua Harris (1984–1991) as Christopher Ewing, son of Bobby and Pam; Barbara Carrera (1985–1986) as shipping magnate Angelica Nero; Sheree J. Wilson (1986–1990) as April Stevens, ex-wife of Jack, who married Bobby and was later killed; Steve Forrest (1986–1987) as Ben Stivers (also known as Wes Parmalee, who claimed to be Jock Ewing); Jack Scalia (1987–1988) as banker Nicholas Pearce, who had an affair with Sue Ellen; Bert Remsen (1987–1988) as wildcatter Harrison "Dandy" Dandridge; Leigh Taylor-Young (1987–1988) as Kimberly Cryder; Amy Stock (1987–1988) as Lisa Alden, who claimed to be the mother of Christopher Ewing; Andrew Stevens (1987–1989) as Casey Denault; Michele Scarabelli (1987–1988) as Connie Hall; Karen Kopins (1987–1988) as Kay Lloyd; Sherril Lynn Rettino as Jackie, Cliff Barnes's secretary; George Kennedy (1988–1991) as Carter McKay, who bought Ray Krebbs's ranch; Kimberly Foster (1989–1991) as Michelle Stevens, April's younger sister; Cathy Podewell (1989–1991) as Cally Harper, who married J. R.; Sasha Mitchell (1989–1991) as James Richard Beaumont, who turned out to be J.R.'s long-lost son; and Michael Wilding as Alex Barton.

Barbara Bel Geddes ceased appearing as a regular after the 1989–1990 season. Added to the cast the following fall were Susan Lucci (in her first prime-time series role) as Sheila Foley; Deidre Imershein as Sheila's daughter, Jory; Gayle Hunnicutt as James's mother, Vanessa; Barbara Eden (Larry Hagman's former costar on *I Dream of Jeannie*) as oil baroness LeeAnn de la Vega, who had been impregnated by J. R. many years earlier and now schemed to gain control of Ewing Oil; Paul Ganus as Derrick; Jeri Gaile as Rose McKay, Carter's wife; and Padraic Duffy (son of Patrick Duffy) as Mark Harris.

In addition to the spinoff, *Knots Landing, Dallas* also produced a host of imitators (in the fall of 1983 the three networks scheduled seven prime-time serials), and even a spoof (see *Filthy Rich*). A two-hour movie, "Dallas: The Early Years" (23 March 1986, CBS), set in the 1930s, filled in much of the "backstory" of the series, and starred Dale Midkiff and Molly Hagan as the young Jock and Ellie Ewing.

DALTON'S CODE OF VENGEANCE   NBC
27 JULY 1986–24 AUGUST 1986   This four-week summer show can barely be called a series. It was derived from two TV-movies that starred Charles Taylor as drifter David Dalton, a Vietnam veteran: "Code of Vengeance," telecast 30 June 1985, and "Dalton: Code of Vengeance II," shown 11 May 1986. The former film was cut in half to make two hour episodes; two more hour shows were filmed, and the four resulting programs were shown on Sundays late in the summer of 1986.

DAMON RUNYON THEATRE   CBS
16 APRIL 1955–30 JUNE 1956   Some of the episodes on this Saturday-night dramatic anthology series were based on the stories of 1920s and 1930s New York written by Damon Runyon (1884–1946).

DAN AUGUST   ABC
23 SEPTEMBER 1970–26 AUGUST 1971   Set in Santa Luisa, California, this hour-long crime show starred Burt Reynolds as Detective Lieutenant Dan August, a tough young cop. With Norman Fell as Detective Sergeant Charles Wilentz; Richard Anderson as Chief George Untermeyer; Ned Romero as Detective Joe Rivera; and Ena Hartman as Katy Grant, department secretary. A Quinn Martin Production, the series was re-broadcast on CBS during the summers of 1973 and 1975, after Reynolds had become a major film star (he did *Deliverance* after *Dan August* ceased production).

DAN RAVEN   NBC
23 JANUARY 1960–6 JANUARY 1961   Former child film star Skip Homeier was featured as Hollywood cop Lieutenant Dan Raven in this crime show; also featured was Dan Barton as Sergeant Burke, his assistant, and Quinn Redeker as photographer Perry Levitt. The series began as a half-hour show and was expanded to a full hour in the fall of 1960. Bobby Darin guest-starred on the fall premiere.

DANCE FEVER   SYNDICATED
1979–1987   Dance contest on which couples competed for a grand prize of $25,000. The half-hour series, which originated from Los Angeles, was first hosted by Deney Terrio, and featured a panel of three guest celebrities, who judged the contestants. Freeman King was the announcer during the first season. From 1979 to 1981 couples competed in disco dancing, but as disco music began to wane, *Dance Fever* broadened its base and permitted couples to choose any style of dancing. Deney Terrio was succeeded as host in 1985 by Adrian Zmed (who had costarred in *T. J. Hooker*). By that time the grand prize had been doubled to $50,000.

DANCE PARTY
See SATURDAY NIGHT DANCE PARTY

DANCE PARTY USA   USA
30 JUNE 1986–28 JUNE 1991   A modern incarnation of *American Bandstand, Dance Party USA* was a weekday music show for young people, with a studio audience of teenagers dancing to recorded music. The show expanded from thirty to sixty minutes early in 1988.

DANCIN' TO THE HITS
SYNDICATED

1986   Half-hour rock music series, hosted by Lorenzo Lamas, featuring a resident dance troupe (Sweet Dreams) and guest appearances by rock artists.

DANGER
CBS

26 SEPTEMBER 1950–31 MAY 1955   A suspense-filled dramatic anthology series. Notable guest appearances included those by Steve Allen ("Five Minutes to Die," 15 September 1953; "Flamingo," 10 November 1953); Carroll Baker ("Season for Murder," 29 March 1955); Mildred Dunnock and James Dean ("Padlocks," 9 November 1954); Lee Grant (three appearances in 1952); Grace Kelly ("Prelude to Death," 5 February 1952); Jack Lemmon ("Sparrow Cop," 24 July 1951); Paul Newman ("Knife in the Dark," 7 December 1954); and Jacqueline Susann ("A Day's Pay," 24 August 1954). The live series originated from New York. The aura of suspense even permeated the commercial breaks, as announcer Richard Stark habitually appeared visibly shaken by the drama when he delivered the commercials. *Danger* was one of the first television dramatic series to make effective use of background music. Jazz guitarist Tony Mottola was hired to compose the program's haunting theme and to score each episode. Several of these compositions later appeared on what is believed to be television's first soundtrack album.

DANGER BAY
DISNEY

1985–1992   Half-hour adventure series for children, produced in Canada and set in the Canadian Northwest, with Donnelly Rhodes as biologist Grant "Doc" Roberts, and Cristopher Crabb and Ocean Hellman as his children, Jonah and Nicole.

DANGER IS MY BUSINESS
SYNDICATED

1958   People with dangerous occupations were the subjects of this documentary series produced by Lieutenant Colonel John D. Craig (whose 1938 book of the same name inspired the series) and hosted by Jack Douglas.

DANGER MAN
CBS

5 APRIL 1961–13 SEPTEMBER 1961   Patrick McGoohan starred as NATO agent John Drake in this half-hour British import; in 1965, McGoohan returned as Drake. See *Secret Agent.*

DANGER THEATRE
FOX

11 JULY 1993–22 AUGUST 1993   Robert Vaughn, appearing as the unnamed Attorney General of the United States, was the host of this half-hour series which spoofed adventure shows. Each program contained mini-episodes of "The Searcher," which starred Diedrich Bader as The Searcher, a motorcycle-riding dimwit who offered his services to persons in trouble, and "Tropical Punch," with Adam West as clueless Captain Mike Morgan, head of a special police unit in Hawaii, Billy Morrissette as Detective Tom McCormick, and Peter Navy Tuiasosopo as Detective Al Hamoki.

DANGEROUS ASSIGNMENT
SYNDICATED

1952   Brian Donlevy starred as Steve Mitchell, government agent, in this half-hour adventure series; Donlevy originated the role on radio in 1940. Harold Knox was the producer.

DANGEROUS CURVES
CBS

26 FEBRUARY 1992–15 DECEMBER 1993   One installment of CBS's late-night adventure umbrella series, *Crime Time After Prime Time,* this one was filmed on location in Dallas. It starred Lise Cutter and Michael Michele as Gina McKay and Holly Williams, two private security operatives, with Gregory McKinney as Ozzie Bird, their friend on the police force. The hour series was made available in foreign markets with more nudity than the American version.

DANGEROUS ROBIN (THE CASE OF THE DANGEROUS ROBIN)   SYNDICATED

1960   Rick Jason starred as insurance investigator Robin Scott in this half-hour crime show. A karate expert, Scott eschewed firearms. Also featured was Jean Blake as Phyllis Collier, his assistant.

DANGEROUS WOMEN   SYNDICATED

1991   Continuing drama set at a women's prison. With Kelli Van Londerself as Holly, a teenager convicted of murder; Maria Rangel as Maria Trent, who had killed her husband; Melanie Vincz as prostitute Crystal Fox; Lynn Hamilton as Cissie Johnson; Valerie Wildman as Faith Cronin; Katherine Justice as Rita; Stephen Liska as Officer Jack Fisher; and Randy Mancuso as the electrician, Randy Carter. The series was marketed to local stations as a weekly hour series or as two half-hours.

DANIEL BOONE   NBC

24 SEPTEMBER 1964–27 AUGUST 1970   A surprisingly successful series based loosely on the life of the American pioneer who was instrumental in the settlement of Kentucky during the 1770s. Fess Parker, who owned an interest in the show, starred as Daniel Boone; a decade earlier Parker had skyrocketed to stardom in *Disneyland* as Davy Crockett, another American folk hero. Also featured were Ed Ames (1964–1968) as Mingo, Boone's friend, a college-educated Cherokee; Pat Blair as Rebecca Boone, Daniel's wife; Albert Salmi (1964–1965) as Yadkin, Boone's companion; Jimmy Dean (March 1967–1969) as his companion Josh Clements; Roosevelt Grier (1969–1970) as his companion Gabe Cooper, a runaway slave; Darby Hinton as Boone's son, Israel; Veronica Cartwright as Boone's daughter, Jemima; and Dallas McKennon (1968–1970) as his friend Cincinnatus. In the fall of 1977, CBS made an unsuccessful attempt to revive the character: see *Young Dan'l Boone*.

DANNY!   SYNDICATED

1995   Hour daytime talk show hosted by Danny Bonaduce, who had achieved fame a quarter century earlier as Danny Partridge of *The Partridge Family*.

THE DANNY KAYE SHOW   CBS

25 SEPTEMBER 1963–7 JUNE 1967   Danny Kaye, an all-around entertainer perhaps best known for his work on behalf of UNICEF, hosted his own Wednesday-night variety hour for four seasons. Regulars included Harvey Korman, four-year-old Victoria Meyerink (1963–1964), youngster Laurie Ichino, the Earl Brown Singers, the Tony Charmoli Dancers, and the Paul Weston Orchestra.

THE DANNY THOMAS HOUR   NBC

11 SEPTEMBER 1967–10 JUNE 1968   An all-purpose hour hosted by Danny Thomas. Presentations included musical programs, comedy and variety hours, and filmed dramas. Several of the latter were noteworthy because they featured appearances by stars seldom seen on American television, such as Geraldine Chaplin ("The Scene," her only American dramatic appearance, 25 September), Horst Buchholz and May Britt ("Fear Is the Chain," 19 February), and Olivia de Havilland ("The Last Hunters," 29 January).

THE DANNY THOMAS SHOW

See FOUR STAR REVUE; MAKE ROOM FOR DADDY

DANTE   NBC

3 OCTOBER 1960–10 APRIL 1961   This adventure series starred Howard Duff as Willie Dante, the ex-gambler who ran Dante's Inferno, a San Francisco nightspot. With Alan Mowbray as Stewart Styles, the maitre'd; Tom D'Andrea as Biff, Dante's man Friday; Mort Mills as Lieutenant Bob Malone. Dick Powell had previously played Dante on several episodes of *Four Star Playhouse*, which were later rebroadcast under the title *The Best in Mystery* (Alan Mowbray was also featured). This series, however, was clobbered by its competition, *The Andy Griffith Show* and *Adventures in Paradise*.

197

DARK ADVENTURE ABC

5 JANUARY 1953–1 JUNE 1953   This half-hour dramatic anthology series was seen on Monday nights; some of the presentations were rebroadcasts of shows aired on other anthologies.

DARK JUSTICE CBS

5 APRIL 1991–14 APRIL 1994   One element of the CBS late-night *Crime Time After Prime Time* umbrella, this one was reminiscent of the 1983–1986 ABC series *Hardcastle and McCormick*. *Dark Justice* starred Ramy Zada (1991–1993) and Bruce Abbott (1993–1994) as Nicholas Marshall, who served as a judge by day and a motorcycle-riding vigilante by night; Marshall's second career began after his wife and daughter were killed and the perpetrators escaped unpunished. Marshall had three accomplices: Clayton Prince as Jericho "Gibs" Gibson, Dick O'Neill as Arnold "Moon" Willis, and Begona Plaza (1991) as Cat Duran, who also ran a day-care center. After Cat was killed, Viviane Vives joined the group as Maria Marti; she was succeeded in 1993 by Janet Gunn as Kelly Cochran. Also featured were Carrie Anne Moss as Marshall's secretary, Tara McDonald, and Kit Kincannon as prosecutor Ken Horton. An American-Spanish coproduction, the hour show was filmed in Barcelona. It ran steadily on CBS for two and a half years, and popped up occasionally on CBS's late-night schedule in 1994.

DARK OF NIGHT DUMONT

3 OCTOBER 1952–1 MAY 1953   This half-hour mystery anthology series was seen on Friday nights. Broadcast live and on location from New York, it was produced and directed by Frank Bunetta.

DARK SHADOWS ABC

27 JUNE 1966–2 APRIL 1971   This soap opera was a radical departure from other daytime serials: it featured vampires, ghosts, haunted houses, werewolves, and other assorted Gothic surprises. Telecast in a late afternoon time slot, it was especially popular with teenagers. Set at brooding Collins House in Collinsport, Maine (exteriors were actually filmed in Newport, Rhode Island), it told the story of the Collins family. Principal players included Alexandra Moltke as Victoria Winters, a governess sent to take care of young David Collins; Louis Edmonds as Roger Collins, David's father; David Hennessy as David; Joan Bennett as Elizabeth Collins, Roger's sister; Jonathan Frid as Barnabas Collins, a 200-year-old vampire; Grayson Hall as Dr. Julia Hoffman, the physician sent to cure Barnabas who ended up falling in love with him; David Selby as Quentin Collins; Kate Jackson as Daphne Harridge; Lara Parker as Angelique; and Jerry Lacy as Reverend Trask. Toward the end of the show's five-year run the plot grew even thicker as action shifted back and forth between the 1800s and the 1960s; many performers played two roles. Dan Curtis created the serial and produced it with Robert Costello. Early in 1990 NBC announced plans to make a TV-movie and new episodes for the 1990–1991 season. See below.

DARK SHADOWS NBC

13 JANUARY 1991–22 MARCH 1991   The prime-time remake of the cult 1960s serial was considerably gorier, and more sexually explicit, than its predecessor. Dan Curtis, who had created the original series, returned as executive producer. The new cast included: Ben Cross as 200-year-old vampire Barnabas Collins; Joanna Going as the governess, Victoria Winters (Going also appeared as Josette in the flashbacks to the 1790s); Jean Simmons as Barnabas's cousin, Elizabeth Collins Stoddard (and as Naomi); Jim Fyfe as Willie Loomis, the simple-minded caretaker of Collinsport (and as Ben); Roy Thinnes as Roger Collins, Elizabeth's brother (and as Reverend Trask); Joseph Gordon-Levitt as Roger's son, David (and as Daniel Collins); former horror-movie queen Barbara Steele as Dr. Julia Hoffman (and as Countess Natalie Dupre); Ely Pouget as Roger's lover, Maggie Evans; Barbara Blackburn as Carolyn, Elizabeth's daughter, Veronica Lauren as Sarah; Lysette Anthony as Angelique; and Michael Cavanaugh as Sheriff George Patterson.

DARKROOM ABC

27 NOVEMBER 1981–15 JANUARY 1982; 24 JUNE 1982–22 JULY 1982   James Coburn was the host of this undistinguished hour anthology series of supernatural tales.

DARKWING DUCK ABC/SYNDICATED

7 SEPTEMBER 1991–11 SEPTEMBER 1993 (ABC); 1991–1993 (SYNDICATED)   The hero of this cartoon from Walt Disney Television Animation was Drake Mallard, a duck who fought crime under the *nom de quack* of Darkwing Duck. Assisted by his daughter, Gosalyn, her pal Honker Muddlefoot, and pilot Launchpad McQuack, Darkwing kept the town of St. Canard safe from evildoers.

DASTARDLY AND MUTTLEY IN THEIR FLYING MACHINES CBS

13 SEPTEMBER 1969–4 SEPTEMBER 1971   A Saturday-morning cartoon series from Hanna-Barbera about a pair of World War I era aerial racers: Dick Dastardly and his snickering canine companion, Muttley. The main characters had been introduced in 1968 on *The Wacky Races.*

A DATE WITH JUDY ABC

2 JUNE 1951–23 FEBRUARY 1952; 15 JULY 1952–2 OCTOBER 1952; 7 JANUARY 1953–30 SEPTEMBER 1953   *A Date with Judy* began on radio in 1941, was made into a movie in 1948 (with Elizabeth Taylor) and twice came to television. The 1951 version featured Patricia Crowley (who later starred in *Please Don't Eat the Daisies*) as Judy Foster, all-American teenager; Jimmie Sommer as her goofy boyfriend, Ogden "Oogie" Pringle; Gene O'Donnell as her father, Melvin Foster; Anna Lee as her mother, Dora Foster; and Judson Rees as her kid brother, Randolph. The summer 1952 and 1953 versions featured an entirely new cast, except for Jimmie Sommer: Mary Linn Beller as Judy; John Gibson as Melvin; Flora Campbell as Dora; and Peter Avramo as Randolph. Both versions of the half-hour sitcom were produced and written by Aleen Leslie.

A DATE WITH LIFE NBC

10 OCTOBER 1955–29 JUNE 1956   Bay City was the setting of this fifteen-minute daytime serial, on which a new story was presented every few weeks. Logan Field appeared as newspaper editor Jim Bradley, who appeared in the stories and served as narrator; Mark Roberts later served a similar function, playing Jim's brother, Tom.

A DATE WITH THE ANGELS ABC

10 MAY 1957–29 JANUARY 1958   This domestic sitcom starred Betty White as Vickie Angel and Bill Williams as her husband, Gus Angel, an insurance agent. Burt Mustin was also featured as their elderly neighbor, Mr. Finley. Produced by Don Fedderson.

DATELINE: EUROPE

See FOREIGN INTRIGUE

DATELINE: HOLLYWOOD ABC

3 APRIL 1967–29 SEPTEMBER 1967   Joanna Barnes interviewed celebrities on this daytime series. The show was twenty-five minutes long and was followed by a five-minute series, *Children's Doctor,* with pediatrician Lendon Smith.

DATELINE NBC NBC

31 MARCH 1992–   After countless attempts through the 1970s and 1980s, NBC finally put together a newsmagazine series that lasted more than a season. Indeed, *Dateline NBC* proved so successful that a second weekly telecast was added in June 1994, followed by a third one in September 1994. Jane Pauley and Stone Phillips were the busy coanchors. The series generated much controversy for a November 1992 segment, "Waiting to Explode?" In an effort to show that design defects of certain GM pickup trucks caused the fuel tanks to explode in accidents, explosive charges were detonated under the trucks while a collision was filmed. General Motors ex-

posed the fakery, and Stone Phillips later apologized on camera. The incident eventually led to the departure of NBC News president Michael Gartner.

THE DATING GAME   ABC
20 DECEMBER 1965–6 JULY 1973
THE NEW DATING GAME   SYNDICATED
1973; 1977–1980; 1986; 1988   Jim Lange hosted the network incarnations of this game show, which typically featured one young woman (the "bachelorette") and three young men seated behind a screen, hidden from her view. By asking questions of the men, the bachelorette chose the one she'd most like to go out with. The lucky couple was then sent on a date—with a chaperone, of course. Occasionally the tables were turned: one bachelor would quiz three hopeful young women. The series enjoyed a seven-year daytime run and was also seen during prime time from 1966 to 1970. The syndicated version appeared in 1973, 1977, 1986, and 1988. Jim Lange hosted the first two versions. Elaine Joyce emceed the 1986 version, and Jeff MacGregor the 1988 version, which was titled *The All-New Dating Game*. *The Dating Game* was the first of several game shows developed by Chuck Barris, the best known of which would include *The Newlywed Game* and *The Gong Show*.

DAVE AND CHARLEY   ·   NBC
7 JANUARY 1952–28 MARCH 1952   This fifteen-minute daytime comedy series featured Cliff Arquette (as Charley Weaver) and Dave Willock (as himself).

DAVE ELMAN'S CURIOSITY SHOP   SYNDICATED
1952   Dave Elman hosted this half-hour human interest series, which was essentially a video version of his popular radio show, *Hobby Lobby,* on which people with unusual hobbies or talents demonstrated them. See also *Charley Weaver's Hobby Lobby.*

THE DAVE GARROWAY SHOW   NBC
2 OCTOBER 1953–25 JUNE 1954   In addition to hosting the *Today* show, Dave Garroway also found time to host this Friday-night half-hour variety series. Regulars included Jack Haskell, Jill Corey, Shirley Harmer, Cliff Norton, and dancers Ken Spaulding and Diane Sinclair; Haskell and Norton had worked previously with Garroway on his first series, *Garroway at Large.*

THE DAVE KING SHOW   NBC
27 MAY 1959–23 SEPTEMBER 1959   British singer Dave King hosted this summer replacement for *The Perry Como Show.*

THE DAVE THOMAS COMEDY SHOW   CBS
29 MAY 1990–25 JUNE 1990   *SCTV* alumnus Dave Thomas was given his own half-hour show on Mondays, comprised mostly of short skits. Anson Downes, Fran Ryan, and Teresa Ganzel were also featured.

DAVE'S WORLD   CBS
20 SEPTEMBER 1993–   This half-hour sitcom set in Miami was based loosely on the life of columnist Dave Barry, whose humorous observations on life were nationally syndicated. With Harry Anderson as Dave Barry; DeLane Matthews as his wife, Beth; Zane Carney as their older son, Tommy; Andrew Ducote as their younger son, Willie; Shadoe Stevens as Dave's friend and editor, Kenny Becket; Meshach Taylor as Dave's newly divorced pal, plastic surgeon Sheldon Baylor; J. C. Wendel as Dave's assistant, Mia; and Tammy Lauren (1994–   ) as Beth's sister, Julie. Patrick Warburton joined the cast in 1995 as Eric, Mia's boyfriend.

DAVEY AND GOLIATH   SYNDICATED
1960–1965   A long-running series of fifteen-minute morality lessons for children. The central characters are young Davey Hanson and Goliath, his talking dog. *Davey and Goliath* was one of the few series which employed "pixillation," the process by

which small models appear to move by themselves; this is usually accomplished by shooting a few frames of film, physically moving each model a fraction of an inch, then shooting a few more frames, and so on.

DAVID BRINKLEY'S JOURNAL NBC
11 OCTOBER 1961–26 AUGUST 1963   This highly acclaimed public affairs program won both an Emmy and a Peabody Award in 1962. NBC newscaster David Brinkley covered a wide variety of topics, heavy and light, during its two-season run. Brinkley himself appeared live, though filmed segments were regularly featured. One of the show's researchers was Marya McLaughlin, who later became an on-camera correspondent for CBS News.

DAVID CASSIDY—MAN UNDERCOVER NBC
2 NOVEMBER 1978–18 JANUARY 1979   Hour crime show starring David Cassidy as Officer Dan Shay, an undercover police officer in Los Angeles, with Wendy Rastatter as his wife, Joanne Shay; Elizabeth Reddin as their young daughter, Cindy; Simon Oakland as his commanding officer, Lieutenant Abrams; and Ray Vitte as T. J. Epps. David Gerber was the executive producer for David Gerber Productions in association with Columbia Pictures TV. A few episodes were telecast during the summer of 1979.

THE DAVID FROST REVUE SYNDICATED
1971   A half hour of satirical comedy with host David Frost and regulars Jack Gilford, Marcia Rodd, and George S. Irving.

THE DAVID FROST SHOW SYNDICATED
7 JULY 1969–14 JULY 1972   A ninety-minute talk show hosted by David Frost, the British television star who became familiar to American audiences on *That Was the Week That Was*. As host, Frost chose not to sit behind a desk, relying instead on a clipboard to hold his notes. Seemingly able to concentrate totally on each guest, he appeared to be equally fascinated by all of them. During the three-year run of his American talk show, Frost continued to appear regularly on London Weekend Television. To accommodate his hectic schedule, the show was taped in New York Mondays through Thursdays (two shows were taped each Wednesday). Frost was then free to commute back to London each weekend. About 750 American shows were taped; among the most famous guests were Elizabeth Taylor and Richard Burton, and Johnny Carson. Music was provided by the Billy Taylor Orchestra; the show's theme was composed by George Martin. The series was syndicated by Westinghouse. After the show ceased production in 1972, Frost was seldom seen on American TV until 1977, when his multipart series of interviews with former President Richard Nixon was shown on many stations.

THE DAVID LETTERMAN SHOW NBC
23 JUNE 1980–24 OCTOBER 1980   Freewheeling comedian David Letterman, who had frequently substituted for Johnny Carson on the *Tonight* show, was turned loose in his own daytime show, which by most accounts was a disaster. It was a live show with no fixed format, one which mixed typical talk-show celebrity interviews with intentionally boring satirical interviews. Letterman also involved (some would say exploited) the studio audience; he once sent a hapless visitor out for sandwiches and coffee, and on another occasion persuaded a woman to come onstage to host the show while he departed. A large crew of regulars was also on hand: Valri Bromfield, Edie McClurg, Bob Sarlatte, Wil Shriner, Paul Raley, and Mark Goldstein. Other contributors included Edwin Newman, Senator William Proxmire, Jimmy Breslin, Jon-Michael Reed, and Karen Blaker.

The series lasted only four months. It began as a ninety-minute program, but was cut to sixty minutes as of 4 August. As various network affiliates began to drop the show, and as the ratings slipped below those of the game shows it had replaced, NBC pulled the plug on *The David Letterman Show* (ironically, Letterman and his writers won two Emmys that season). Fortunately, the network didn't give up completely on the comedian. He returned early in 1982 at the other end of the broadcast day (see *Late Night with David Letterman*).

THE DAVID MCLEAN SHOW   SYNDICATED
1970   A short-lived talk show, hosted by David McLean.

THE DAVID NIVEN SHOW   NBC
7 APRIL 1959–15 SEPTEMBER 1959   A half-hour dramatic anthology series, hosted by (and occasionally starring) David Niven. Vincent Fennelly was the producer.

DAVID NIVEN'S WORLD   SYNDICATED
1976   On this documentary series adventurers tried to set records in various fields of endeavor. Hosted by David Niven, the series's executive producer was Aubrey Buxton.

THE DAVID STEINBERG SHOW   CBS
19 JULY 1972–16 AUGUST 1972   A five-week summer variety hour, hosted by comedian David Steinberg. Born in Manitoba, Steinberg was a member of the Second City comedy troupe in Chicago and frequently appeared on the *Tonight* show during the late 1960s. In 1969 he hosted *The Music Scene*.

THE DAVID SUSSKIND SHOW (OPEN END)   SYNDICATED
1958–1987   This long-running New York–based talk show was hosted by theatrical and television producer David Susskind. Typically, each show centered around one topic and featured four to seven guests, who often seemed to spend much of their time interrupting each other. In 1960 Soviet premier Nikita Khrushchev appeared on the program as the sole guest; the interview was generally criticized as dull. The show was originally titled *Open End* because it had no fixed time limit: guests could chatter on as long as they (or Susskind) wished. By the early 1960s a two-hour format was established; this was subsequently reduced to one hour and later expanded to ninety minutes. The show was seen on educational outlets in many markets.

DAVIS RULES   ABC/CBS
27 JANUARY 1991–9 APRIL 1991; 7 AUGUST 1991–11 SEPTEMBER 1991 (ABC); 30 DECEMBER 1991–8 JULY 1992 (CBS)   A 90s version of *My Three Sons,* this sitcom starred Randy Quaid as grammar-school principal Dwight Davis, a widower trying to raise his three boys with the help of his father. Also featured were Jonathan Winters as his wacky dad, Gunny Davis, a former Marine; Trevor Bullock as eldest son, Robbie; Luke Edwards as son Charlie; Nathan Watt as son Ben; Patricia Clarkson as Dwight's colleague and lady friend, Cosmo Yergin; Tamayo Otsuki as Mrs. Elaine Yamagami, the assistant principal of the Pomahac School; and Rigoberto Jiminez as Robbie's pal Rigo. When the series shifted networks the following season there were a few changes. Quaid, Winters, Edwards, and Watt were retained from the former cast. Dwight Davis now had only two sons of his own to care for, but the teenage son of some college pals moved into the Davis household. Vonni Ribisi played the new arrival, Skinner. Bonnie Hunt was added as Dwight's sister, Gwen, who helped him care for the brood, and Kelly Rutherford was seen occasionally as Dwight's love interest, Erika. Danny Jacobson and Norma Safford Vela created the series.

DAVY CROCKETT
See WALT DISNEY

DAY & DATE   SYNDICATED
1995–   Hour newsmagazine series, aimed at late afternoon time slots. Dana King and Patrick VanHorn were the coanchors.

DAY AT NIGHT   PBS
1974–1975   Half-hour interview series hosted by James Day, former president of New York's educational outlet, WNET.

DAY BY DAY   NBC
29 FEBRUARY 1988–10 MAY 1988; 30 OCTOBER 1988–25 JUNE 1989   On this half-hour
sitcom a yuppie St. Louis couple quit their jobs to open a home day-care center. With
Doug Sheehan as Brian Harper, ex-stockbroker; Linda Kelsey as Karen Harper, ex-
lawyer; C. B. Barnes as their teenaged son, Ross; Courtney Thorne-Smith as Kristin
Carlson, the Harpers' day-care aide, whom Ross fell for; and Julia Louis-Dreyfus as
Eileen Swift, a former colleague of Brian's. Appearing as the Harpers' preschool
charges were Chris Finefrock as Justin O'Donnell; Christine Healey as Nina; Jack
Blessing as Kevin; Thora as Molly; Garrett Taylor as Blake; Sara and Erin Leonard
as Emily; and J. P. Dizon as Dana.

DAY IN COURT   ABC
13 OCTOBER 1958–24 JUNE 1965   On this half-hour daytime series of courtroom
dramas, each case was based on a real case from which the show's writers developed
an outline. The actual dialogue was largely improvised by the participants: professional actors portrayed the litigants and witnesses, while real attorneys appeared as
the lawyers. The presiding judges were played by Edgar Allan Jones, Jr. (a law
professor at UCLA) and by William Gwinn (a former law professor). Created by
Selig J. Seligman, the show was televised locally in Los Angeles before going network
in 1958.

DAY ONE   ABC
7 MARCH 1993–11 JULY 1994; 5 JANUARY 1995–21 SEPTEMBER 1995   Hour newsmagazine show, so named because it was originally televised on Sunday evenings. Forrest
Sawyer was the original anchor. When the series returned in early 1995 in a Thursday
slot, Forrest Sawyer was joined by a coanchor, Diane Sawyer (no relation).

THE DAY THE UNIVERSE CHANGED   PBS
13 OCTOBER 1986–15 DECEMBER 1986   Host James Burke examined the relationship
between major scientific advancements and social events on this ten-week series.
Burke had previously hosted *Connections,* a 1979 series on technology.

DAYDREAMING WITH LARAINE
See THE LARAINE DAY SHOW

THE DAYS AND NIGHTS OF MOLLY DODD   NBC/LIFETIME
21 MAY 1987–13 AUGUST 1987; 24 MARCH 1988–29 JUNE 1988 (NBC); 27 FEBRUARY
1989–8 AUGUST 1991 (LIFETIME)   Jay Tarses, cocreator of *Buffalo Bill,* again
came up with a series that was a critical success but a commercial disappointment.
Certainly, it was one of the best of the sub-genre of late 80s TV known as
"dramadies," which attempted to combine dramatic and sitcom elements. Blair
Brown starred as Molly Dodd, a divorced New Yorker hoping to find Mr. Right while
coping with her mother's well-intended intrusions. Allyn Ann McLerie played
Molly's meddlesome mom, Florence Bickford; William Converse-Roberts dropped
in and out as Molly's ex, jazz musician Fred Dodd; and James Greene was Davey
McQuinn, the advice-dispensing elevator man in Molly's apartment building who was
never able to land his car even with the floor. Occasionally featured were Sandy
Faison (1987–1988) as Molly's sister, Mamie; Victor Garber (1987–1988) as realtor
Dennis Widmer, Molly's one-time boss and lover, and David Strathairn (1988–1990)
as bookseller Moss Goodman, Molly's next boss. Following its NBC cancellation,
Molly Dodd moved to the Lifetime cable network, where reruns and new episodes
were shown. In the spring of 1990 Molly discovered that she was pregnant, but didn't
know whether the father was Moss (with whom she'd been stranded in an elevator)
or her new boyfriend, Detective Nathaniel Hawthorne (played by Richard Lawson).
Her plans to marry Hawthorne were thwarted by the character's sudden death early
in 1991. The baby, Emily, turned out to be Hawthorne's. By that time Molly had
acquired new neighbors, Ron and Ramona Luchesse (John Pankow and J. Smith-
Cameron), and the services of Davey's son, Jimmy (James Gleason), who was learning the fine points of the doorman business from his dad.

DAY'S END

6 MARCH 1989–2 JUNE 1989   Another of ABC's attempts to find a late-night series to schedule after *Nightline*, this one was a sixty-minute magazine show cohosted by Spencer Christian and Ross Shafer; Shafer had previously hosted *The Late Show* on the Fox network.

DAYS OF OUR LIVES

8 NOVEMBER 1965–   "Like sands through the hourglass, so are the days of our lives. . . ." So begins this popular daytime serial, created in 1965 by Ted Corday, Irna Phillips, and Allan Chase. Ted Corday died shortly after the show began; his wife, Betty Corday, then became the executive producer. Subsequent executive producers have included H. Wesley Kenney, Jack Herzberg, Al Rabin, and Ken Corday. Among the numerous head writers have been Peggy Phillips and Kenneth Rosen, William Bell, Pat Falken Smith, Ann Marcus, Elizabeth Harrower, Ruth Brook Flippen, Nina Laemmle, Gary Tomlin and Michele Poteet-Lisanti, Smith (again), Margaret DePriest, Sheri Anderson, Leah Laiman, Anne Howard Bailey, Gene Palumbo, Richard Allen and Beth Millstein, and James Reilly. The series enjoyed its peak popularity in the early 1970s. *Days of Our Lives* began as a half-hour show; in April 1975 it became TV's second soap opera to expand to a full hour. The late United States Supreme Court Justice Thurgood Marshall was said to be among *Days'* biggest fans.

Set in the town of Salem, the serial was built around the Horton family—Tom and Alice, their five children, assorted grandchildren, and (as children often grow up faster on soaps than on real life) assorted great- and great-great-grandchildren. The large cast has included: Macdonald Carey as Dr. Tom Horton, chief of internal medicine at University Hospital (Carey played the role until his death in March 1994; his voice continued to be used for the series' introduction, however); Frances Reid as his wife, Alice; John Lupton as their eldest son, Dr. Tommy Horton, who was believed missing in action in Korea but turned up in town having undergone plastic surgery (Tommy seems simply to have disappeared from the story; writer De Priest confessed that Tommy is the "legendary character who went upstairs and never came down"); Pat Huston and Patricia Barry as their daughter Addie Olson, who died; John Clarke as their son, Mickey, a lawyer; Maree Cheatham as their daughter Marie Horton (Marie decided to become a nun and was written out; several years later she returned, played first by Kate Woodville, later by Lanna Saunders); Paul Carr and Ed Mallory as their youngest son, Dr. Bill Horton (Bill was written out in the major shakeup that took place in 1979–1980; the character briefly returned a few years later, played by Christopher Stone); Floy Dean, Susan Flannery, Susan Oliver, Rosemary Forsyth, and Jaime Lyn Bauer as psychiatrist Dr. Laura Spencer, who married Mickey Horton; Steven Mines and Clive Clerk as David Martin; Denise Alexander and Bennye Gatteys as Susan Martin, who killed David; Regina Gleason as Kitty Horton, who married Tommy; Heather North, Martha Smith, and Pamela Roylance as Sandy Horton, daughter of Tommy and Kitty; Dick Colla, Don Briscoe, and Ron Husmann as Tony Merritt, Marie Horton's boyfriend; Robert Knapp as Ben Olson, Addie's husband; Charla Doherty, Catherine Dunn, Cathy Ferrar, and Susan Seaforth as Julie Olson, daughter of Addie and Ben; Robert Carraway, Mike Farrell, Robert Hogan, and Ryan MacDonald as Julie's first husband, Scott Banning, who died in a construction accident; Mark Tapscott as Bob Anderson, Julie's second husband; Nancy Wickwire (who died in 1973) and Corinne Conley as Bob's former wife, Phyllis Anderson; Brigid Bazlen, Karin Wolfe, Carla Borelli, Nancy Stephens, Barbara Stanger, Susan Keller, and Melinda Fee as Bob and Phyllis's daughter, Mary Anderson.

In 1970 Bill Hayes joined the cast as former nightclub singer Doug Williams. Doug married Addie (Horton) Olson, who became ill with leukemia, and was later killed trying to save their baby from the path of an oncoming truck. After Addie's death Doug fell for her daughter, Julie Olson. Following a long courtship, Doug became her third husband in one of TV's biggest weddings on 1 October 1976 (in real life Bill Hayes and Susan Seaforth were married in October 1974). After Doug and Julie were divorced in 1979, Doug married his brother's widow, Lee Carmichael (played by Brenda Benet, who committed suicide in 1982). Doug and Julie later remarried. Bill Hayes also appeared as his brother, Byron, though the part was credited to George Spelvin, in deference to theatrical tradition. On the show, Doug became the proprietor of Doug's Place, where he occasionally sang a few numbers. Featured there were Marty Davich as Marty, the pianist, and Don Frabotta as Dave, the bartender. Hayes and Seaforth left the show in April 1984 (Susan Seaforth Hayes returned later).

Other regulars have included: Joyce Easton as Janet Banning, Scott Banning's first wife; Bobby Eilbacher, Eddie Rayden, Stuart Lee, Alan Decker, John Amour, Dick DeCoit, Wesley Eure, Paul Coufos, and Michael Weiss as Michael Horton, son of Mickey and Laura Horton; Flip Mark, James Carroll Jordan, and Stephen Schnetzer as Steve Olson, Julie's brother; Natasha Ryan, Tammy Taylor, and Kristian Alfonso as Hope Williams, daughter of Addie and Doug Williams (Alfonso later returned as Gina, an amnesiac); Stanley Kamel as Eric Peters; Peter Brown as Eric's brother, Dr. Greg Peters; Jeanne Bates as Anne Peters; Herb Nelson as Phil Peters; Margaret Mason and Elaine Princi as Linda Anderson, Mickey Horton's secretary and lover; Victor Holchak as lawyer Jim Phillips, who eventually wed Linda; Coleen Gray as Diane Hunter; Jed Allan as lawyer Don Craig; Suzanne Rogers (also known as Suzanne Rogers Groom) as Maggie Simmons, who married Mickey Horton in 1986 (Rogers's bout with the debilitating muscular disease myasthenia gravis was incorporated into the story line); Kaye Stevens as Jeri Clayton, a singer at Doug's Place; Patty Weaver as Trish Clayton, Jeri's daughter; Joe Gallison as Dr. Neal Curtis; Mary Frann as Amanda (Howard) Peters; Jan Jordan as Helen Cantrell, Jim Phillips's secretary; Jeffrey Williams, Steve Doubet, Richard Guthrie, and Gregg Marx as David Martin Banning, Julie's illegitimate son (by David Martin), who married Trish Clayton; Burt Douglas as Sam Monroe; Helen Funai as Kim Douglas; Robert Brubaker as John Martin; K. T. Stevens as Helen Martin; Mark Miller as Howard Jones; Robert Clary as Robert LeClair; Garry Marshall as Bert Atwater; Jack Denbo as Jack Clayton; Brooke Bundy as Rebecca North; Joan Van Ark as Janene Whitney; John Aniston as Dr. Eric Richard; John Howard as Cliff Peterson; Eloise Hardt as Rita Beacon; Maidie Norman as Gracie Jones; Graham Brown as Jeffrey Jones; Susan Adams as Meredith Marshall; Tina Andrews, Rose Fonseca, and Diane Sommerfield as Valerie Grant; Ketty Lester as Helen Grant; Michael Dwight-Smith and Roger Aaron Brown as Danny Grant, manager of Shenaningans, a nightspot; Lawrence Cook as Paul Grant; Paul Henry Itkin as Johnny Collins; Mike Warren as Jerry Davis; Fred Beir as Larry Atwood; John Lombardo as Fred Barton; Jocelyn Somers as Jean Barton; Chip Fields as Toni Johnson; Tom Scott as Jim Bradley; Josh Taylor as Chris Kositchek; Deidre Hall as Dr. Marlena Evans (in 1992, a spinoff soap starring Hall was considered; in 1994 Marlena found herself possessed by the devil); Andrea Hall Lovell (Deidre's twin sister) as Samantha Evans, Marlena's twin sister; Fran Ryan as Rosie Carlson; Jenny Sherman as Betty Worth; William H. Bassett as Dr. Walter Griffin; Cindy Fisher as Patti Griffin; Stephen Manley as Billy Barton; Ken Sansom as Dr. Powell; Martha Nix and Elizabeth Storm as Janice Horton; Kim Durso, Debbie Lytton, Lisa Trusel, and Camilla Scott as Melissa Anderson, daughter of Jim and Linda Phillips, who was adopted by Linda's second husband, Bob Anderson; Frederic Downs as Hank; Paul Savior as Sam; Tom Brown as Nathaniel Curtis; Dee Carroll as Adele Hamilton; Pauline Myers as Mrs. Jackson; Sid Conrad as Ribitz; Ben DiTosti as Ben; Myron Natwick as Rick; Peter Brandon as Dr. Cunningham; Peter MacLean as Dr. Paul Whitman; Gary McGurrin as Roy Hazeltine; Francine York as Lorraine Temple; Elizabeth MacRae as Phyllis Curtis; Tracey E. Bregman as Donna Craig; Diana Douglas as Mrs. Evans; Corinne Michaels as Joann Barnes; Elizabeth Brooks as Theresa Harper; Gail Johnson as Mimi; Amanda Jones as Dora; Adrienne LaRussa and Eileen Barnett as Brooke Hamilton (Barnett also appeared as Stephanie Woodruff); Meegan King as Pete Curtis; Robin Pohle as Amy Kositchek; Suzanne Zenor as Margo Horton.

Also: Quinn Redeker as evil Alex Marshall; John McCann as Tony Kingman; George McDaniel as Dr. Jordan Barr; Jennifer Peterson, Melissa Brennan, and Melissa Reeves as Jennifer Rose Horton, daughter of Bill and Laura Horton; Robert Pickering as Dr. Goddard; John Stevenson as Terry Gilbert; Dianne Harper as Leslie

James, Chris Kositchek's girlfriend; Jack Coleman as "The Salem Strangler" (who turned out to be Chris's brother, Jake); Brett Williams, Paul Keenan, and David Wallace as Todd Chandler; Deborah Dalton as Cassie Burns; Barbara Crampton as Trista Evans; Tyler Murray as Carol Welles; Hal Riddle and Charles Bateman as Max Jarvis; William Joyce as Kellam Chandler; Jean Bruce Scott as Jessica Blake, daughter of Alex Marshall and Marie Horton; Howard Sylvester as Warren Heywood; Richard Hill as Kyle McCullough; Stephen Brooks and Scott Palmer as Joshua Fallon; Wayne Northrop and Drake Hogestyn as police officer Roman Brady, who married Marlena Evans (when Northrop returned to the show, the producers decided to keep Hogestyn also; it developed that Hogestyn's Roman Brady was really an impostor, and that his true identity was John Black); Lane Caudell as singer Woody King; Erick Petersen, Dick Billingsley, and Rick Hearst as Scotty Banning, son of David Banning and Trish Clayton; Gloria Loring as Liz Chandler DiMera; Joe Mascolo as Stephano DiMera; Thaao Penghlis as Stephano's son, Anthony DiMera; Philece Sampler as Stephano's daughter (and Anthony's half-sister), Renee Dumonde; James Reynolds as detective Abe Carver; Anne Marie Martin (formerly known as Eddie Benton) as lawyer Gwen Davies; Catherine Mary Stewart and Mary Beth Evans as Roman's sister, nurse Kayla Brady; John deLancie as Eugene Bradford, a psychic; Andrea Barber, Christie Clark, and Tracy Middendorf as Carrie Brady; Jason Bernard as Preston Wade; Kim Hamilton as Penelope Wade; Shirley Deburgh as Delia Abernathy; Leann Hunley as Anna Brady DiMera; Perry Bullington and Richard Bergman as Anna's brother, Brett Fredericks; Dorothy James as Esther Kensington; Renee Jones as Nikki Wade; Katie Krell, Aimee Brooks, Shana Lane-Block, and Alli Brown as Sarah Horton, Maggie's daughter (by artificial insemination); Shawn Stevens as Oliver Martin; H. M. Wynant as Orby Jansen; Christina Maisano as Noel Curtis; Madlyn Rhue as Daphne DiMera; Meg Wyllie as Mrs. Chisholm; Sheila DeWindt as Joan Hopkins; Michael Leon as Pete Jannings; Melonie Mazman as Tess Jannings; Lenore Kasdorf as Dr. Victoria Kimball; Tom Hallick as Max Hathaway; and Don Diamont as Carlo Forenza.

Later additions to the cast have included: Peter Reckell and Robert Kelker-Kelly as Bo Brady, who had a long-running romance with Hope Williams and married her in 1985; Dana Kimmel, Cindy Fisher, and DeAnna Robbins as Diane Parker; Andrew Masset as Larry Welch; Jane Windsor as Emma Donovan; Shannon Tweed as Savannah Wilder; Derya Ruggles as Robin Jacobs; Marilyn McCoo as Tamara Price; Stephen Nichols as Steve "Patch" Johnson, who became one of the series's most popular characters, and would marry Kayla Brady in 1988 (though usually seen with his trademark eyepatch, Patch was seen without it in fantasy sequences and when on an undercover assignment); Peggy McCay and Barbara Beckley as Caroline Brady; Rob Estes as Glenn Gallagher; Gregory Mortensen and Robert S. Woods as Paul Stewart; Arleen Sorkin as wacky Calliope Jones, who married Eugene Bradford in 1986; John Aniston as crime boss Victor Kiriakis; Wally Kurth as Justin Kiriakis; Judi Evans as Adrienne Johnson, who married Justin in 1987; Joy Garrett and Marilyn McIntyre as Jo Johnson; Charles Shaughnessy as Shane Donovan; Joseph Campanella as Senator Harper Deveraux; Frank Parker and Lew Brown as Shawn Brady; twins Carey More and Camilla More as Grace Forrester (Camilla More had previously played Grace's murderous twin, Gillian Forrester); Genie Francis as Diana Colville, who married Roman Brady in 1989; Jane Elliot, Shelley Taylor Morgan and Judith Chapman as Anjelica Deveraux; Harrison Douglas and Darby Hinton as Ian Griffith; Joseph Adams, James Acheson, Matthew Ashford, and Mark Valley as Jack Deveraux, who married Kayla in 1987; George DeLoy as Orpheus; Billy Warlock as young Frankie Brady, who romanced Jennifer Rose Horton; Ken Jezek as Lars Englund; S. Marc Jordan as Eli Jacobs; Elizabeth Burr as Barbara Stewart; George Jenesky as reformed pimp Nick Corelli; Richard Biggs as Dr. Marcus Hunter; Charlotte Ross as Eve Donovan; Joyce Little as Vanessa Walker; Jay Robinson as Monty Dolan; Billy Hufsey as Emilio Ramirez; Michael Bays as Julio Ramirez; Lisa Howard as April Ramirez; Karen Moncrieff as Gabrielle Pascal; Sandy McPeak as Orion; Darrell Utley as Benjy, a deaf child; Silvana Gallardo as Rosa; Joe Colligan as Ethan Reilly; Cindy Gossett, Angelique Francis, and Renee Jones (in her second role) as Lexie Brooks; Jason Culp as Jerry Pulaski; Wortham Krimmer and Joseph Bottoms as Cal Winters; Patrice Chanel as Carlson; Randy Reinholz as Adam Scott; James Hampton as evangelist Saul Taylor;

Mindy Clarke (daughter of longtime cast member John Clarke) as Saul's daughter, Faith; Steve Eastin as Jericho; James Luisi as Earl; Bumper Robinson and Thyme Lewis as Jonah Carver; Staci Greason as Isabella Toscano; Ryan Brennan as Max Brady; Pamela Jean Sanders and Claire Yarlett as Dr. Whitney Baker; Robert Mailhouse as Brian Scofield; Avery Schreiber as Leopold von Leuschner; Anne Howard, Patsy Pease, and Ariana Chase (formerly known as Ariane Munker) as Kimberly Donovan; Pamela Kosh as Lavinia Peach; Michael Easton as Tanner Scofield; Antony Alda as Johnny; Crystal Chappell as Carly Manning; Charles Cioffi as Ernesto Toscano; and Michael Sabatino as Lawrence Alamain.

More recent cast additions included: Felecea M. Bell as district attorney Glynnis Turner; Susan Diol as Emmy Borden; Jamie Bozian as Dylan; J. Eddie Peck as Hawk Hawkins; Roberta Leighton as Ginger Dawson; Shannon Sturges as Molly Brinker; Bonnie Burroughs as Gretchen; Deborah Moore as Danielle Stevens; Lynn Herring as Lisanne Gardener; Louise Sorel as Vivian Alamain; Ivan G'Vera as Ivan Marias, Vivian's servant; Erik von Detten as Nicky Alamain; Tony Rhodes as Jesse Lombard; Mark Drexler as Roger Lombard; Elaine Bromka as Stella Lombard; Charley Lang and Robert Duncan as Rob Stemkowski; Patrick Muldoon and Austin Peck as Austin Reed; Lisa Rinna as Billie Reed; Richard Burgi as Phillip Collier; J. Cynthia Brooks as Taylor McCall; Marnie McPhail as Hayley; Justin Deas as Frank Cooper, Sr.; Dani Minnick as Rebecca Morrison; Alison Sweeney as Sami Brady; Deborah Adair as Kate Roberts Kiriakis; Bryan Dattilo as Lucas Roberts, Kate's son; Lark Voorhies and Tammy Townsend as Wendy Reardon; Eileen Davidson as Kristen Blake; Jason Brooks as Peter Blake, Kristen's brother; Miriam Parrish as Jamie Caldwell; Vaughn Armstrong as David Caldwell; Nicholas Benedict as Curtis Reed; Paul Kerasey as Alan Harris; Rosemary Lord as Mary, the Kiriakis's maid; Stan Ivar as Daniel Scott; Jocelyn Seagrave as Tanya Hampstead; Tanya Boyd as Celeste; Meghan and Michael Ryan, and Paige and Ryanne Kettner as young Abby Deveraux; Evan Hansen as Tyrone; Tara Reid as Ashley; Scott Groff as Shawn Douglas Brady; Wayne Heffley as Vern Scofield; and Alex and Max Lucero as Brady Victor Black.

DEAD AT 21   MTV
9 JUNE 1994–24 DECEMBER 1994   MTV's first adventure series, punctuated by quick cuts and a throbbing music score, starred Jack Noseworthy as twenty-year-old Ed Bellamy, who learned that he was a "neurocybernaut": a microchip had been placed in his brain at birth as part of a government plan to create smarter humans. He further learned that the plan had not worked as intended, and that most neurocybernauts died by the age of twenty-one. Ed's mission was to find other neurocybernauts and their creator, Victor Heisenberg. The half-hour series also featured Lisa Dean Ryan as Maria, who assisted him on his quest, and Whip Hubley as Major Winston, a government agent who tried to track him down.

DEADLINE   SYNDICATED
1959   An anthology series about journalists, hosted and narrated by Paul Stewart.

DEADLINE FOR ACTION   ABC
8 FEBRUARY 1959–13 SEPTEMBER 1959   Rebroadcasts of those episodes of *Wire Service* which starred Dane Clark as reporter Dan Miller. See *Wire Service*.

DEADLY GAMES   UPN
5 SEPTEMBER 1995–10 JANUARY 1996   In this hour sci-fi series a video game designer's villains came to life, and challenged him in a series of adventures as they sought to conquer the world. With James Calvert as the designer, Gus Lloyd; Christopher Lloyd as the arch villainous Sebastian Jackal; Cynthia Gibb as Lauren Ashborne, Gus's ex-wife and not-too-willing partner in battling Jackal; Stephen T. Kay as Gus's nerdy assistant, Peter Rucker; and Page Leong as Dr. Judy Chang.

DEALER'S CHOICE   SYNDICATED
1973   An audience-participation game show broadcast from Las Vegas. Hosted first by Bob Hastings, later by Jack Clark.

THE DEAN JONES VARIETY HOUR
See WHAT'S IT ALL ABOUT, WORLD?

THE DEAN MARTIN COMEDY HOUR
See THE DEAN MARTIN SHOW

DEAN MARTIN PRESENTS MUSIC COUNTRY
See MUSIC COUNTRY

DEAN MARTIN PRESENTS THE GOLDDIGGERS
See THE GOLDDIGGERS

THE DEAN MARTIN SHOW (THE DEAN MARTIN COMEDY HOUR)   NBC
16 SEPTEMBER 1965–24 MAY 1974   A variety hour hosted by Dean Martin. Few
would have predicted that when the comedy team of Dean Martin and Jerry Lewis
broke up in 1956, it would be Martin who would have the more successful solo career.
Martin demonstrated, however, that he could not only do comedy but could also sing
and act; he appeared in more than thirty films after splitting with Lewis. By not
taking himself too seriously, Martin became an enormously popular television personality. In 1970 it was reported that he and NBC negotiated the largest contract in
history between a network and a star. The TV show itself required little of Martin: he
usually spent only one day a week rehearsing and taping. It was obvious to viewers
that Martin was reading from cue cards (as do most stars on variety shows), but it was
equally obvious that he was having a good time doing the show. Several of the shows
were celebrity "roasts," set at a banquet table, in which the guest of honor was
showered with insults by other celebs. Regulars on the series included pianist Ken
Lane (1965–1972), Kay Medford, Lou Jacobi, The Golddiggers, Marian Mercer
(1971–1972), Tom Bosley (1971–1972), Rodney Dangerfield (1972–1973), Dom
DeLuise (1972–1973), and Nipsey Russell (1972–1974). Among the several attractive young women who assisted Martin in various comedy sketches were Kathi King,
Diana Lee, Betty Rosebrock, Diane Shatz, and Melissa Stafford. Music was provided by Les Brown and his Band of Renown. Greg Garrison produced the series,
which was entitled *The Dean Martin Comedy Hour* during its final season.

DEAN MARTIN'S COMEDYWORLD
See COMEDYWORLD

DEAR DETECTIVE   CBS
28 MARCH 1979–18 APRIL 1979   Four-week miniseries based on the French film
Tendre Poulet. With Brenda Vaccaro as Sergeant Kate Hudson, a detective with the
Los Angeles Police Department; Arlen Dean Snyder as Richard Wayland, her boyfriend, a professor of Greek philosophy; Ron Silver as Sergeant Schwartz; Michael
MacRae as Sergeant Brock; John Dennis Johnston as Sergeant Clay; Jack L. Ging as
Sergeant Chuck Morris; Lesley Woods as Mrs. Hudson, Kate's mother; Jet Yardum
as Lisa, Kate's daughter by a previous marriage. Dean Hargrove and Roland Kibbee
were the producers.

DEAR JOHN . . .   NBC
6 OCTOBER 1988–22 JULY 1992   Half-hour sitcom starring Judd Hirsch as John Lacey,
who moved into an apartment and joined a singles group after his wife left him a
"Dear John" letter. Appearing as the other members of the One-Two-One Club at
the Rego Park (N.Y.) Community Center were: Jane Carr as Louise Mercer, the
British moderator; Jere Burns as self-proclaimed macho stud Kirk Morris; Isabella
Hofmann as the seemingly well-adjusted Kate McCarron; Harry Groener (1988–
1991) as the terminally shy Ralph Drang; and Billie Bird as the sex-crazed biddy,
Mrs. Philbert. Susan Walters joined the cast in the spring of 1990 as Mary Beth
Sutton, a new member of the club. Tom Willett also appeared as Mrs. Philbert's quiet
boyfriend, Tom. Olivia Brown signed on early in 1991 as Denise, and William

O'Leary was seen as Ben, the janitor. Ed Weinberger, Hal Cooper, and Rod Parker were the executive producers.

DEAR PHOEBE   NBC
10 SEPTEMBER 1954–2 SEPTEMBER 1955   A situation comedy about a former psychology professor who got a job writing the advice-to-the-lovelorn column (under the name Phoebe Goodheart) for a Los Angeles newspaper. With Peter Lawford as Bill Hastings; Marcia Henderson as sports columnist Mickey Riley, his girlfriend; Charles Lane as Mr. Fosdick, the editor; and Joe Corey as Humphrey, the copyboy.

DEATH VALLEY DAYS   SYNDICATED
1952–1970; 1974   This long-running series began on radio in 1930; it was one of television's few western anthology series. Approximately twenty new episodes were filmed each year; several were filmed on location at Death Valley. The series was hosted by Stanley Andrews from 1952 to 1965 (as the Old Ranger). Ronald Reagan succeeded him and when Reagan left for politics in 1966, he was replaced by Robert Taylor. In 1968 Taylor was succeeded by Dale Robertson (star of two previous westerns, *Wells Fargo* and *The Iron Horse*). Merle Haggard hosted the short-lived revival in 1974. The show was sponsored for many years by Twenty Mule Team Borax. It was originally produced by Darrell McGowan for Gene Autry's Flying A Productions; early episodes were directed by Stuart McGowan.

THE DEBBIE REYNOLDS SHOW   NBC
16 SEPTEMBER 1969–1 SEPTEMBER 1970   This unsuccessful situation comedy was NBC's attempt to rival CBS's 1968 hit, *The Doris Day Show*. Like Doris Day, Debbie Reynolds was a popular and talented film star, and like Day she had not appeared in a dramatic role on television before. Created by Jess Oppenheimer (*I Love Lucy*), the show featured Reynolds as Debbie Thompson, a housewife who longed to become a newspaperwoman; Don Chastain as her husband, Jim Thompson, a sportswriter (note the parallel between this show and *I Love Lucy*—in each the housewife wanted to break into her husband's line of work); Tom Bosley as accountant Bob Landers, their neighbor and Debbie's brother-in-law; Patricia Smith as Bob's wife, Charlotte Landers, Debbie's sister; Bobby Riha as Bruce Landers, Bob and Charlotte's young son; and Billy DeWolfe as accountant Delbert Deloy. Reynolds, who owned a 50 percent interest in the show, had originally been guaranteed a two-year run by NBC. Infuriated by the fact that the show was sponsored by a cigarette manufacturer, she relinquished the second-season guarantee in exchange for the network's agreement to drop the cigarette sponsorship.

DECEMBER BRIDE   CBS
4 OCTOBER 1954–24 SEPTEMBER 1959   This domestic sitcom starred Spring Byington as Lily Ruskin, a widow who lived with her daughter and son-in-law; Frances Rafferty as Ruth Henshaw, her daughter; Dean Miller as architect Matt Henshaw, Ruth's husband; Harry Morgan as next-door neighbor Pete Porter, an insurance agent who constantly wisecracked about his wife, Gladys (who was never seen in the flesh); Verna Felton as Lily's comrade, Hilda Crocker. Occasionally featured was Arnold Stang, as Private Marvin Fisher, Pete's brother-in-law. Filmed at Desilu Studios before a live audience, most of the "action" in *December Bride* took place in the Henshaw's living room. Joel Grey guest-starred as Lily's nephew (7 December 1957 and 14 December 1957). Parke Levy created the series; Lily Ruskin was based on his own mother-in-law. In 1960 a spinoff appeared: see *Pete and Gladys*.

DECISION   NBC
6 JULY 1958–28 SEPTEMBER 1958   This half-hour dramatic anthology series was a summer replacement for *The Loretta Young Show*. The premiere telecast, "The Virginian," starring James Drury, became a series in 1962.

DECISION: THE CONFLICTS OF HARRY S TRUMAN   SYNDICATED
1964   Truman's presidency (1945–1953) was the subject of this half-hour documentary series.

DECOY (POLICEWOMAN DECOY)   SYNDICATED
1957   Beverly Garland starred as New York policewoman Casey Jones in this half-hour crime show, apparently the first series to feature a female cop.

THE DEFENDERS   CBS
16 SEPTEMBER 1961–9 SEPTEMBER 1965   This high-quality series about a father-and-son defense team attracted much controversy, as well as much critical acclaim during its four-year run. The show regularly dealt with such sensitive issues as euthanasia, abortion, blacklisting, and civil disobedience. Even more atypical was the fact that the defenders occasionally lost a case. The show starred E. G. Marshall as Lawrence Preston: It was the first continuing role for Marshall, one of the most frequently seen performers on television during the 1950s. Robert Reed costarred as his Ivy League son, Kenneth Preston. Also featured were Polly Rowles (1961–1962) as their secretary, Helen Donaldson, and Joan Hackett (1961–1963) as Ken's girlfriend, social worker Joan Miller. Among the many guest stars who appeared were Gene Hackman ("Quality of Mercy," 16 September 1961; "Judgment Eve," 20 April 1963), Martin Sheen ("The Attack," 9 December 1961, his first major TV role), James Farentino ("The Last Illusion," 9 March 1963, his first major TV role), Jon Voight ("The Brother Killers," 25 May 1963, a rare TV appearance), Ossie Davis (seven appearances), James Earl Jones ("The Non-Violent," 6 June 1964), Robert Redford ("The Siege," 3 December 1964, his last TV dramatic role), and Dustin Hoffman ("A Matter of Law and Disorder," 8 April 1965). The series was created by Reginald Rose, who wrote several of the scripts, including the two-part genesis of the series for *Studio One,* which was entitled "The Defenders" (with Ralph Bellamy and William Shatner, 25 February and 4 March 1957). Other regular writers included Ernest Kinoy and Robert Crean. Produced by Herbert Brodkin, the series was filmed in New York.

DEFENDERS OF THE EARTH   SYNDICATED
1986   Flash Gordon, Mandrake, Lothar, and the Phantom teamed up to protect the planet on this half-hour cartoon series. The four veteran superheroes were assisted by a quartet of youngsters: Flash's son Rick, Lothar Jr. (known as L.J.), the Phantom's daughter Jedda, and an orphan named Kshin.

DEGRASSI JUNIOR HIGH (DEGRASSI HIGH)   PBS
1987–1991   This half-hour dramatic series depicted life with all its problems at a modern urban junior high school. The series, which evolved from a 1979 Canadian production (*The Kids of DeGrassi Street*), was produced in Toronto and was televised in Canada beginning in 1986; within two years it was aired in forty countries. Most of the fifty-odd roles were filled by the members of the Playing with Time repertory company. Among the regulars: Pat Mastroianni as Joey Jeremiah; Stefan Brogren as Snake; Duncan Wangh as Arthur; Amanda Stepto as Spike; Anais Granofsky as Lucy; Neil Hope as Wheels; Maureen Deiseach as Heather; Michael Carry as Simon; Irene Courakos as Alexa; Sara Ballingall as Melanie; Rebecca Haines as Kathleen; Jacey Hunter as Amy; and Siluck Saysanasy as Yick. In 1989 the teens all moved up to Degrassi High, and the show was retitled.

DELLA   SYNDICATED
1969   A talk show hosted by singer-actress Della Reese, who began her professional career as a gospel singer and became a pop artist in 1957.

THE DELPHI BUREAU   ABC
5 OCTOBER 1972–1 SEPTEMBER 1973   Part of ABC's trilogy *The Men,* this segment alternated with *Assignment: Vienna* and *Jigsaw.* It featured Laurence Luckinbill as

Glenn Garth Gregory, a secret agent who possessed total recall, and Anne Jeffreys (infrequently seen since *Topper*) as his assistant, Sybil Van Loween.

DELTA   ABC
15 SEPTEMBER 1992–17 DECEMBER 1992; 6 APRIL 1993–27 APRIL 1993; 21 JULY 1993–25 AUGUST 1993   Following her well-publicized departure from *Designing Women,* Delta Burke returned in this sitcom as Delta Bishop, a blonde aspiring country and western singer who moved to Nashville and got a job in a small bar. Also featured were Earl Holliman as her employer, Darden Towe, owner of the Green Lantern; Gigi Rice as Delta's cousin, Lavonne Overton, with whom she stayed; Beth Grant as hairstylist Thelma Wainwright; Nancy Giles as Connie; and Bill Engvall as Buck. The series was pulled from ABC's schedule after thirteen weeks. When it returned in April with four new episodes, it had two new cast members (Joe Urla as Delta's agent, Sandy Scott, and Elizabeth Wilson as Delta's mom, Rosalind Dupree), and Delta had become a brunette.

DELTA HOUSE   ABC
18 JANUARY 1979–28 APRIL 1979   Half-hour sitcom based on *National Lampoon's Animal House,* one of the most successful films of 1978. Students at Pennsylvania's Faber College in 1962, its central characters resided at Delta House, the campus's most hedonistic and socially undesirable fraternity, where they managed to thwart the efforts of the dean (and the upright lads of Omega House) to expel them. With John Vernon as Dean Vernon Wormer; Stephen Furst as Kent (Flounder) Dorfman; Bruce McGill as Daniel (D-Day) Day; Jamie Widdoes as Bob Hoover, Delta's president; Josh Mostel (son of Zero Mostel) as Jim (Blotto) Blutarski, a transfer student, the younger brother of Bluto Blutarski (played by John Belushi in the film); Peter Fox as Eric "Otter" Stratton; Richard Seer as Larry (Pinto) Kroger; Gary Cookson as Doug Niedermeyer of Omega House; Brian Patrick Clarke as Greg Marmalarde of Omega House; Susanna Dalton as Mandy Peppridge; Wendy Goldman as Muffy Jones, Pinto's girlfriend; Peter Kastner as Professor Jennings; Lee Wilkof as Einswin; and Michelle Pfeiffer as Bombshell. Vernon, Furst, McGill, and Widdoes had been featured in the motion picture. Executive producers: Matty Simmons and Ivan Reitman for Universal TV in association with Matty Simmons–Ivan Reitman Productions.

DELVECCHIO   CBS
9 SEPTEMBER 1976–17 JULY 1977   This crime show starred Judd Hirsch as Sergeant Dominick Delvecchio, a tough but fair-minded cop who graduated from law school but flunked the bar exam. With Charles Haid as Officer Paul Shonski, his eager-beaver assistant; Michael Conrad as Lieutenant Macavan, his commanding officer; and Mario Gallo as Tomaso Delvecchio, Dom's father, a barber. William Sackheim was the executive producer.

DEMI-TASSE TALES   SYNDICATED
1953   A half-hour dramatic anthology series of little note.

DEMPSEY & MAKEPEACE   SYNDICATED
1985   British-made hour crime show about an American cop who teamed up with a Scotland Yard officer. With Michael Brandon as Lieutenant James Dempsey, late of Brooklyn; Glynnis Barber as Det. Sgt. Harriet Makepeace (Brandon and Barber later married in real life); and Ray Smith as their boss, Det. Supt. Spikings.

THE DENNIS DAY SHOW (THE RCA VICTOR SHOW STARRING DENNIS DAY)   NBC
8 FEBRUARY 1952–2 AUGUST 1954   Dennis Day, the singer-actor who worked with Jack Benny for many years, also hosted his own comedy-variety series. Regulars included Cliff Arquette (fall 1952–1954, as Charley Weaver), Hal March (fall 1952–1953), and Jeri Lou James. During the spring of 1952 the show was seen biweekly, alternating with *The Ezio Pinza Show,* also sponsored by RCA. Paul Henning, who later developed *The Beverly Hillbillies,* was the producer.

THE DENNIS JAMES SHOW   ABC

24 SEPTEMBER 1951–15 FEBRUARY 1952   One of television's most ubiquitous performers (he was seen regularly as early as 1938), Dennis James hosted this half-hour
daytime variety show as well as countless other programs. It was produced by Aaron
Steiner and directed by Lou Sposa (James's brother).

THE DENNIS MILLER SHOW   SYNDICATED

20 JANUARY 1992–10 SEPTEMBER 1992   After leaving *Saturday Night Live,* the acerbic
Dennis Miller entered the talk show arena with this nightly hour produced by Tribune Entertainment. Despite revamping in March, the program never found a large
audience and was dropped after eight months. Miller then found a more suitable
niche on HBO, hosting *Dennis Miller Live* starting in 1994.

THE DENNIS O'KEEFE SHOW   CBS

22 SEPTEMBER 1959–14 JUNE 1960   This half-hour sitcom featured Dennis O'Keefe
as newspaper columnist Hal Towne, a widower who lived in a Manhattan penthouse
with his young son and a housekeeper; Rickey Kelman as the son, Randy; Hope
Emerson as Amelia "Sarge" Sargent, the formidable housekeeper; and Eloise Hardt
as Karen, Hal's sometime girlfriend. Les Hafner produced the series, which was
subtitled "All Around Towne," the title of Hal's newspaper column.

THE DENNIS PRAGER SHOW   SYNDICATED

1994   Half-hour daily talk show.

DENNIS THE MENACE   CBS

4 OCTOBER 1959–22 SEPTEMBER 1963   Hank Ketcham's mischievous cartoon character made a successful transition to television in this prime-time series. There were
146 half-hour episodes filmed, with Jay North as young Dennis Mitchell; Herbert
Anderson as his father, Henry; Gloria Henry as his mother, Alice; Joseph Kearns
(1959–1962) as next-door neighbor George Wilson, the object of many of Dennis's
well-intentioned escapades; Sylvia Field (1959–1962) as Martha Wilson, Mr. Wilson's kindly wife; Billy Booth as Dennis's friend Tommy Anderson; Gil Smith as
Dennis's friend Joey MacDonald; and Jeannie Russell as Dennis's sometime friend
Margaret Wade. After Kearns's death Gale Gordon joined the cast in the spring of
1962 as Mr. Wilson's brother (and the Mitchells' neighbor), John Wilson, and Sara
Seegar was added as his wife, Eloise, that fall. In real life cartoonist Ketcham has a
son named Dennis; the inspiration for the comic strip came one day when Ketcham's
wife remarked, "Our son, Dennis, is a menace." Harry Ackerman was the executive
producer.

   In 1993 a theatrical film was released, starring Mason Gamble as Dennis and
Walter Matthau as Mr. Wilson.

DENNIS THE MENACE   SYNDICATED

1987–1988   Not to be confused with the live-action sitcom (see above), this animated version of the comic strip was supplied by DIC Enterprises. See also *The New
Dennis the Menace.*

DENVER THE LAST DINOSAUR   SYNDICATED

1989–1990   Half-hour cartoon series about Denver, a modern-day dinosaur who
was befriended by a group of teenagers: Mario, Shades, Jeremy, and Wally.

THE DEPUTY   NBC

12 SEPTEMBER 1959–16 SEPTEMBER 1961   Henry Fonda, who had starred in many a
movie western, had top billing in this half-hour TV western, set in Silver City,
Arizona Territory. Fonda played Chief Marshal Simon Fry, whose district included
several nearby towns as well. Allen Case costarred in the title role, as Deputy Clay
McCord, a storekeeper who bore arms with great reluctance. Also featured during
the first season were Wallace Ford as Silver City's elderly marshal, Herk Lamson,
and Betty Lou Keim as Clay's sister, Fran McCord. Read Morgan joined the show

for the second season as Sergeant Tasker (Sarge), the one-eyed cavalry officer stationed in town. Although Henry Fonda may have had top billing, he starred in only about a dozen episodes, and appeared only briefly (sometimes only to introduce the program) in the others. Robert Redford made his television debut on one episode ("The Last Gunfight," 30 April 1960).

DEPUTY DAWG   SYNDICATED/NBC
1961 (SYNDICATED); 11 SEPTEMBER 1971–2 SEPTEMBER 1972 (NBC)   A cartoon show about a fumbling canine law enforcement officer.

THE DES O'CONNOR SHOW (KRAFT MUSIC HALL)   NBC
20 MAY 1970–2 SEPTEMBER 1970; 2 JUNE 1971–1 SEPTEMBER 1971   A summer variety series taped in London, starring singer Des O'Connor. Other regulars included Jack Douglas, the MacGregor Brothers (1970), and Connie Stevens (1971).

DESIGNING WOMEN   CBS
29 SEPTEMBER 1986–24 MAY 1993   Like *The Golden Girls, Designing Women* was a sitcom in which all of the stars were female. *Designing Women* focused on the four women who ran Sugarbakers, an interior design business in Atlanta. It starred Dixie Carter as widowed Julia Sugarbaker; Delta Burke (1986–1991) as her younger sister, the thrice-divorced former beauty queen Suzanne Sugarbaker; Annie Potts as divorced mother Mary Jo Shively; and Jean Smart (1986–fall 1991) as the (initially) single Charlene Frazier. Meshach Taylor costarred as their man Friday, ex-con Anthony Bouvier. Occasionally seen were Hal Holbrook (who was married to Dixie Carter) as Julia's suitor, Reese Watson; Richard Gilliland (who was married to Jean Smart) as Mary Jo's beau, J. D. Shackleford; Alice Ghostley as Bernice Clifton; Olivia Brown (1989–1990) as Vanessa, Anthony's girlfriend; and Priscilla Weems and Brian Lando as Mary Jo's kids, Claudia and Quinton. In another much-publicized real-life romance, Delta Burke fell in love with Gerald McRaney on the set of *Designing Women* and eventually married him; McRaney had been hired to appear as Dash Goff, the second of Suzanne's ex-husbands. Burke's conspicuous weight gain was also addressed on the series, in an episode in which Suzanne, apprehensive about attending her high school reunion because of her weight, decides to go and makes no apologies. At the end of the 1988–1989 season Charlene married Bill Stillfield (played by Doug Barr), and on 1 January 1990 their baby, Olivia, was born (again, art imitated life, as Jean Smart had had a baby boy in October). The series's executive producers were the husband-and-wife team of Harry Thomason and Linda Bloodworth-Thomason; Bloodworth had previously worked with Burke and Carter on the 1982 sitcom *Filthy Rich*. *Designing Women*'s theme, "Georgia on My Mind," was performed by Doc Severinsen for the first five seasons.

Numerous changes occurred in the fall of 1991. The theme was now performed by Ray Charles, while two cast members departed. Following a lengthy and well-publicized feud with the producers, Delta Burke's contract was not renewed, and Jean Smart ceased appearing as a regular after the fall 1991 premiere. Two new cast members were added: Julia Duffy as Julia's whiny cousin, Alison Sugarbaker, and Jan Hooks as Carlene Dobber, Charlene's younger sister, fresh from the country. Duffy left after one season. Judith Ivey joined the cast in the fall of 1992 as Bonnie Jean (B. J.) Poteet, a Texas customer of Sugarbakers who bought Alison's interest. Also joining for the final season was Sheryl Lee Ralph as Etienne Toussant, who married Anthony.

The off-network reruns of *Designing Women* were sold to 200 different U.S. stations in 1992, a then record for distribution. The feud between Burke and the Thomasons was eventually settled, as Burke headlined the Thomason-produced sitcom *Women of the House* in 1995.

DESILU PLAYHOUSE   CBS
6 OCTOBER 1958–10 JUNE 1960   Desi Arnaz was the host and occasional star of this hour dramatic anthology series, filmed at Desilu Studios. Some episodes of *The Lucy-Desi Comedy Hour* were shown during this time slot (see also *I Love Lucy*).

DESTRY   ABC

14 FEBRUARY 1964–11 SEPTEMBER 1964   This little-watched western replaced 77 *Sunset Strip* on Friday nights; it starred John Gavin as Harrison Destry, a loner who sought to prove himself innocent of a trumped-up robbery charge.

DETECTIVE SCHOOL   ABC

31 JULY 1979–24 NOVEMBER 1979   Introduced for a four-week trial run in the summer of 1979, *Detective School* (then titled *Detective School—One Flight Up*) proved popular enough to warrant a spot on ABC's fall schedule. The half-hour sitcom starred James Gregory as Nick Hannigan, veteran private eye, now the sole instructor at a low-budget school for fledgling gumshoes. Hannigan's class included Randolph Mantooth as Eddie Dawkins; LaWanda Page as Charlene Jenkins; Jo Ann Harris (summer 1979) as Teresa; Melinda Naud (fall 1979) as Maggie; Douglas V. Fowley as Robert Redford; Pat Proft as Leo; and Taylor Negron as Silvio. Executive producers were Bernie Kukoff and Jeff Harris for the Kukoff-Harris Partnership.

DETECTIVE IN THE HOUSE   CBS

1 MARCH 1985–19 APRIL 1985   Six-episode hour detective show starring Judd Hirsch as Press Wyman, who abandoned his engineering career to become an apprentice to a famous private detective. With Cassie Yates as his wife, Diane, a teacher; Jack Elam as his mentor, Nick Turner; and Meeno Peluce, Mandy Ingber, and R. J. Williams as the Wymans' kids, Todd, Deborah, and Dunc.

THE DETECTIVES (ROBERT TAYLOR'S DETECTIVES)   ABC/NBC

16 OCTOBER 1959–22 SEPTEMBER 1961 (ABC); 29 SEPTEMBER 1961–21 SEPTEMBER 1962 (NBC)   This straightforward crime show was set in New York. With Robert Taylor as Captain Matt Holbrook; Tige Andrews as Lieutenant Johnny Russo; Lee Farr (1959–1960) as Lieutenant Jim Conway; Russell Thorsen (1959–1961) as Lieutenant Otto Lindstrom; Mark Goddard (1960–1962) as Sergeant Chris Ballard; and Adam West (1961–1962) as Sergeant Steve Nelson. The series expanded from a half hour to an hour when it shifted networks in 1961.

DETECTIVE'S DIARY
See MARK SABER

DETECTIVE'S WIFE   CBS

7 JULY 1950–6 OCTOBER 1950   Broadcast live from New York, this comedy-mystery was a summer replacement for *Man Against Crime*. It starred Lynn Bari as Connie Conway, who tried to help her private-eye husband solve his cases, and Donald Curtis as her husband, Adam Conway.

DEVLIN   ABC

7 SEPTEMBER 1974–15 FEBRUARY 1976   Kids' cartoon show about three orphans (Ernie, Tod, and Sandy) who decide to become motorcycle stunt drivers. The Hanna-Barbera production was seen Saturdays during its first season; reruns were shown on Sundays during the second season.

THE DEVLIN CONNECTION   NBC

2 OCTOBER 1982–25 DECEMBER 1982   Rock Hudson starred in this hour detective show as Brian Devlin, a former military intelligence officer who ran the Los Angeles Performing Arts Center; Brian then met Nick Corsello (played by Jack Scalia), a young private investigator who was also the racquetball pro at a local health club. Oddly enough, Nick turned out to be Brian's son—the son he never knew he had. Brian soon found himself helping Nick on his cases. Filling out the cast were Leigh Taylor-Young as Lauren, Brian's secretary, and Louis Giambalvo as Lt. Earl Borden of the Los Angeles police. The series had been scheduled for the 1981–1982 season, but Rock Hudson underwent heart surgery, forcing its postponement.

DIAGNOSIS MURDER   CBS

29 OCTOBER 1993–8 SEPTEMBER 1995; 8 DECEMBER 1995–   Dick Van Dyke starred in this hour crime show as Dr. Mark Sloan, a physician at Community General Hospital who dabbled in crime solving. Also on hand were Scott Baio (1993–1995) as Dr. Jack Stewart; Victoria Rowell as Amanda Bentley; Delores Hall as Mark's secretary, Delores; Barry Van Dyke (Dick's real-life son) as Mark's son, Steve Sloan, a cop; and Michael Tucci as hospital administrator Norman Briggs. Dick Van Dyke's character first appeared in an episode of *Jake and the Fatman* on 20 March 1991, and later in a made-for-TV movie, "Diagnosis of Murder" (5 January 1992, CBS).

DIAGNOSIS: UNKNOWN   CBS

5 JULY 1960–20 SEPTEMBER 1960   A summer replacement for *The Garry Moore Show, Diagnosis: Unknown* starred Patrick O'Neal as New York police pathologist Dr. Daniel Coffee. Also featured were Chester Morris as Detective Ritter; Phyllis Newman as lab assistant Doris Hudson; Cal Bellini as Dr. Motilal Mookerji, a visiting physician from India; and Martin Huston as Link, the teenage lab assistant.

THE DIAHANN CARROLL SHOW   CBS

14 AUGUST 1976–4 SEPTEMBER 1976   This four-week variety series was a summer replacement for *The Carol Burnett Show*. Diahann Carroll, formerly the star of *Julia*, hosted the show. Executive producers: Robert DeLeon and Max Youngstein.

DIAL 999   SYNDICATED

1959   Set at Scotland Yard, this crime show starred Robert Beatty as Inspector Michael Maguire, a Canadian police officer sent to London to learn advanced methods of detection.

THE DIAMOND HEAD GAME   SYNDICATED

1975   Bob Eubanks hosted this game show, taped at Oahu's Kuilima Hotel. Through a series of questions, the field of contestants was gradually reduced until only one remained. That contestant was then placed in a plastic booth ("The Diamond Head Treasure Vault"), where dollar bills of various denominations were blown about. The contestant was given fifteen seconds to fill a "treasure bag" with dollar bills; afterward, Eubanks pulled out up to ten bills from the bag. Those bills were then awarded to the contestant, unless a $1-bill was drawn, in which case the contestant lost everything.

DIAMONDS   CBS/USA

22 SEPTEMBER 1987–13 SEPTEMBER 1988 (CBS); 9 OCTOBER 1988–25 MARCH 1990 (USA) Another of the several Canadian-produced shows that dotted CBS's late-night schedule (see also *Adderly* and *Night Heat*), *Diamonds* starred Nick Campbell and Peggy Smithhart as Mike Devitt and Christina Towne, who, when married, had starred in a private-eye show called *Diamonds;* now divorced, they teamed up again, this time as real private eyes. Also featured were Tony Rosato as Lieutenant Gianetti and Alan Feiman as their assistant, Darryl. After a one-year run on CBS, the series remained in production and was picked up by the USA Cable Network.

DIANA   NBC

10 SEPTEMBER 1973–7 JANUARY 1974   *Diana* was an unsuccessful vehicle for Diana Rigg, the former star of *The Avengers*. In this comedy she starred as Diana Smythe, a recent divorcée who left London for New York, where she moved into the apartment of her brother, Roger (he was out of the country) and got a job as a fashion coordinator at Buckley's Department Store. Also featured were David Sheiner as Norman Brodnik, her boss; Barbara Barrie as Norman's wife, Norma Brodnik, head of the merchandising department; Richard B. Shull as coworker Howard Tolbrook, a copywriter; Robert Moore as window dresser Marshall Tyler; and Carol Androsky as Diana's neighbor, Holly Green, a model. Executive producer: Leonard Stern.

DICK AND THE DUCHESS   CBS

28 SEPTEMBER 1957–16 MAY 1958   This comedy-mystery was set in London. With
Patrick O'Neal as insurance investigator Dick Starrett; Hazel Court as his British
wife, Jane Starrett, a duchess; Richard Wattis as Dick's boss, Peter Jamison; and
Ronnie Stevens as Rodney, a young man who also worked in Dick's office.

THE DICK CAVETT SHOW   ABC/CBS/PBS/USA

4 MARCH 1968–24 JANUARY 1969; 26 MAY 1969–19 SEPTEMBER 1969; 29 DECEMBER 1969–
1 JANUARY 1975 (ABC); 16 AUGUST 1975–6 SEPTEMBER 1975 (CBS);1977–1981 (PBS);
30 SEPTEMBER 1985–23 SEPTEMBER 1986 (USA); 23 SEPTEMBER 1986–30 DECEMBER 1986
(ABC)   Though Dick Cavett has hosted several series, he is best known as the host
of ABC's late-night show, a noble attempt to compete with Johnny Carson of NBC.
Like Carson, Cavett was raised in Nebraska and was interested in magic as a teenager. After graduating from Yale, Cavett went to New York, hoping to get a job as a
writer; he thrust some material into Jack Paar's hand in an NBC corridor and was
subsequently hired by Paar. After writing for others, he became a stand-up comic for
a while and continued to do summer stock. During the mid-1960s he was occasionally
seen as a game show panelist. In 1968 he was given his first series on ABC. It was a
daytime talk show and was originally titled *This Morning* before it was changed to
The Dick Cavett Show. In the summer of 1969 he hosted a thrice-weekly prime-time
series on ABC, and later that year he succeeded Joey Bishop as host of the network's
late-night talk show. Cavett brought with him the announcer and the bandleader who
had worked with him on the earlier shows—Fred Foy (better known as the announcer on *The Lone Ranger*) and drummer Bobby Rosengarten. The show was
originally seen five nights a week but was gradually cut back over the years as
Cavett's ratings failed to dent Carson's. By January of 1973 the show was seen one
week a month, as part of *ABC's Wide World of Entertainment;* by late 1974 the show
was seen only twice a month and disappeared altogether on New Year's Day 1975.
Perhaps because of Cavett's Yale background and because of his interest in language,
he has acquired the image of an "intellectual" host (an image which Cavett himself
disputes), and because of it the show probably failed to attract more viewers. Nevertheless, there were some fine moments on the show, such as Lester Maddox's sudden
departure after getting into an argument with Cavett, and a verbal brawl between
Norman Mailer and Gore Vidal, with Cavett and Janet Flanner caught in the middle.
Cavett also made effective use of the one-guest show, managing to lure such elusive
talk show guests as Marlon Brando, Katharine Hepburn, and John Lennon and Yoko
Ono. In the summer of 1975 Cavett switched networks, hosting a four-week variety
series on CBS. Regulars included Leigh French and Marshall Efron; the show was
produced by Carole Hart and Bruce Hart. In the fall of 1977 he appeared on PBS in a
half-hour talk show on which he returned to his strong suit: one-guest interviews. The
show was produced by Cavett's former Yale roommate, Christopher Porterfield. In
the fall of 1985 Cavett hosted a one-hour prime-time talk show on the USA Cable
Network, and in the fall of 1986 he returned briefly to ABC late-night television as
host of an hour talk show, which followed *ABC News Nightline* on Tuesday and
Wednesday nights. See also *Jimmy Breslin's People.*

DICK CLARK PRESENTS THE ROCK AND ROLL YEARS   ABC

28 NOVEMBER 1973–9 JANUARY 1974   On this half-hour series, host Dick Clark
reminisced with live guests and introduced film clips of rock performances from the
fifties and sixties.

**THE DICK CLARK SHOW (THE DICK CLARK SATURDAY NIGHT
BEECHNUT SHOW)**   ABC

15 FEBRUARY 1958–10 SEPTEMBER 1960   Dick Clark, who was already hosting *American Bandstand* weekdays, commuted to New York from Philadelphia on weekends to
host this half-hour rock-and-roll show, broadcast live from the Little Theater. Dick's
guests on the premiere included Pat Boone, Connie Francis, Jerry Lee Lewis,
Johnnie Ray, Chuck Willis, and the Royal Teens. Sponsored by Beechnut Foods.

DICK CLARK'S LIVE WEDNESDAY   NBC
20 SEPTEMBER 1978–27 DECEMBER 1978   The only live prime-time entertainment show of the 1978–1979 season, this hour variety series was hosted by Dick Clark, who also served as its executive producer. The show was seen live only in the East and Midwest and was shown on tape in areas farther west.

DICK CLARK'S NITETIME   SYNDICATED
1985   An hour of rock music, hosted by the ubiquitous Dick Clark, consisting of in-studio appearances by artists, videos, and dancing.

DICK CLARK'S WORLD OF TALENT   ABC
27 SEPTEMBER 1959–20 DECEMBER 1959   Dick Clark, one of ABC's most ubiquitous personalities of the time, hosted this half-hour series on which aspiring performers were rated by a celebrity panel; regular panelists included Jack E. Leonard and Zsa Zsa Gabor.

THE DICK POWELL SHOW   NBC
26 SEPTEMBER 1961–17 SEPTEMBER 1963   Dick Powell hosted and occasionally starred in some episodes of this hour-long dramatic anthology series. These were the last appearances of Powell, who died in January 1963 (after his death, various guest stars hosted the program). The most widely acclaimed drama was probably "The Price of Tomatoes" (16 January 1962), Richard Alan Simmons's story of a truck driver (Peter Falk) who picked up a pregnant hitchhiker (Inger Stevens); Falk won an Emmy for his performance.

DICK POWELL'S ZANE GREY THEATER
See ZANE GREY THEATER

DICK TRACY   ABC
13 SEPTEMBER 1950–12 FEBRUARY 1951   One of fiction's most famous cops, Dick Tracy first appeared in the comic strip drawn by Chester Gould. In 1935 he went to radio, and in 1937 a fifteen-chapter movie serial was made starring Ralph Byrd. Byrd played Tracy in several more films before making this television series; his death in 1952 terminated plans to continue production beyond the twenty-six programs already filmed. Also featured were Joe Devlin as Tracy's partner, Sam Catchem, and Angela Greene as Tracy's wife, Tess Trueheart. The Dick Tracy character reappeared on television in cartoon form in 1961 and in 1971 (where he could be seen on *The Archie Show*). In 1990 a feature film was released that starred Warren Beatty and Madonna and was directed by Beatty.

THE DICK VAN DYKE SHOW   CBS
3 OCTOBER 1961–7 SEPTEMBER 1966   After a shaky first season (the series didn't crack Nielsen's top thirty-five shows), this popular situation comedy became a solid hit. It was one of the first series in which the central characters worked for a television series; both Van Dyke and costar Mary Tyler Moore employed a similar format on their later series (*The New Dick Van Dyke Show* and *The Mary Tyler Moore Show*). With Dick Van Dyke as Rob Petrie, head writer for *The Alan Brady Show,* a variety series; Mary Tyler Moore as his wife, Laura Petrie, a former dancer; Morey Amsterdam as Buddy Sorrell, wisecracking comedy writer; Rose Marie as Sally Rogers, husband-hunting comedy writer; Richard Deacon as Mel Cooley, producer of *The Alan Brady Show* (and brother-in-law of Alan Brady), the target of many of Buddy's barbs; Carl Reiner as Alan Brady, the vain star; Jerry Paris (who also directed many episodes) as dentist Jerry Helper, the Petries' next-door neighbor in New Rochelle; Ann Morgan Guilbert as Millie Helper, Jerry's wife; Larry Matthews as Richie Petrie, Rob and Laura's young son. Occasionally appearing were Jerry Van Dyke (Dick's brother) as Rob's brother, Stacy Petrie; Peter Oliphant as Freddy Helper, Jerry and Millie's son and Richie's pal; Joan Shawlee as Buddy's wife, Viona (Pickles) Sorrell; Tom Tully and J. Pat O'Malley as Rob's father, Sam Petrie; and Isabel Randolph and Mabel Albertson as Rob's mother, Clara Petrie. Created by Carl

Reiner, the pilot for the series, "Head of the Family" (with Reiner as Rob and Barbara Britton as Laura), was broadcast 19 July 1960. Production of the series was supervised by Sheldon Leonard; many of the 158 episodes were written by Bill Persky and Sam Denoff, who later produced the show. CBS aired a retrospective, "The Dick Van Dyke Show Remembered," on 23 May 1994. Carl Reiner reprised his role as Alan Brady on a February 1995 episode of *Mad About You.*

A DIFFERENT WORLD   NBC
24 SEPTEMBER 1987–9 JULY 1993   In this spinoff from enormously popular sitcom *The Cosby Show,* second daughter Denise Huxtable found herself going away to the predominantly black Hillman College, alma mater of her father and grandfather, where she moved into Gilbert Hall. During the first season the cast included Lisa Bonet as Denise; Marisa Tomei as her white roommate, Maggie Lawton; Dawnn Lewis as her black roommate, Jaleesa Vinson, who was twenty-six and divorced; Jasmine Guy as wealthy and obnoxious dormmate Whitley Gilbert; Loretta Devine as dorm director Stevie Rollins; Amir Williams as Stevie's young son, J. T.; Kadeem Hardison as ladies' man Dwayne Wayne; Darryl Bell as Ronald Johnson; and Marie-Alise Recasner as Millie. Mary Alice succeeded Devine in midseason as the new dorm director, Lettie Bostic, and Sinbad also joined the cast as coach Walter Oakes (a standup comic, Sinbad had actually been hired to warm up the studio audience at tapings of the program; impressed with his work, the producers gave him a regular role).

During that first season *A Different World* featured a catchy theme (sung by Phoebe Snow over a snappy title sequence), but not much else. Had it not had the benefit of a great time slot (in the "hammock" between *The Cosby Show* and *Cheers*), the treacly show would almost surely have been canceled. *TV Guide* noted in May 1988 that it was "the worst sitcom in recent memory to do so well in the ratings," finishing second to *The Cosby Show*. Fortunately, the quality of the show improved in its second year, as Debbie Allen took over as producer-director. Lisa Bonet (who was pregnant) left the series and returned to *The Cosby Show*. Lewis, Guy, Hardison, Bell, Alice, and Sinbad returned from the previous season, and three new members were added: Charnele Brown as Kim Reese; Cree Summer as Freddie Brooks; and Glynn Turman as the no-nonsense math professor Colonel Clayton ("Dr. War") Taylor. The series's theme was now sung by Aretha Franklin, who was married to Turman. Mary Alice left at the end of the season. In the fall of 1989, Gilbert Hall had become a coed dorm, and Coach Oakes was the new dorm director; Jaleesa, who had a budding romance with Oakes, was now a resident adviser. Occasionally featured was Lou Myers as Vernon Gaines, chef at the campus hangout, The Pit. Cory Tyler was occasionally featured as the Colonel's son, Terrence. Jada Pinkett joined the cast in the fall of 1991 as freshman Lena James. Joe Morton was added in February 1992 as Senator Byron Douglas III, a Hillman alumnus who almost married Whitley before she realized that Dwayne was her true love. The newlyweds were the focus of the series' sixth and final season, which also featured Patrick Y. Malone as Terrell and Karen Malina White as Charmaine, a refugee from *The Cosby Show*.

DIFF'RENT STROKES   NBC/ABC
3 NOVEMBER 1978–31 AUGUST 1985 (NBC); 27 SEPTEMBER 1985–21 MARCH 1986 (ABC); 14 JUNE 1986–30 AUGUST 1986 (ABC)   A half-hour sitcom about a white Park Avenue millionaire who adopted two black kids, *Diff'rent Strokes* was developed by Norman Lear's Tandem Productions especially for its young star, Gary Coleman. A natural comedic talent with an impeccable sense of timing, Coleman looked younger than his true age due to a congenital kidney condition that affected his growth. His big break came after a successful guest role as a wisecracking youngster on *Good Times,* another Norman Lear sitcom. On *Diff'rent Strokes,* Coleman starred as eight-year-old Arnold Jackson, who, with his thirteen-year-old brother, Willis (played by Todd Bridges), came downtown to live with wealthy widower Philip Drummond (played by Conrad Bain) after the death of their mother, who had been Drummond's housekeeper. Sullen and distrustful at first, the boys gradually came to love Drummond and were adopted by him. Also featured on the series were Dana

Plato (1978–1984) as Drummond's natural daughter, the teenaged Kimberly; Charlotte Rae (1978–1980) as the housekeeper, Mrs. Edna Garrett, who left after her spinoff series, *The Facts of Life,* was renewed; Nedra Volz (1980–1982) as the next housekeeper, Adelaide Brubaker; Dody Goodman (1981–1982) as Drummond's daffy sister, Aunt Sophia; Mary Jo Catlett (1982–1986) as the last housekeeper, Pearl Gallagher; Shavar Ross (1981–1986) as Arnold's best friend, Dudley Ramsey; Nikki Swasey (1982–1986) as Arnold's classroom nemesis, the stuck-up Lisa Hayes; Janet Jackson (1981–1982) as Willis's girlfriend, Charlene Dupree. In January 1984 Dixie Carter joined the cast as Maggie McKinney, whom Drummond married later that season; Danny Cooksey also came aboard, as Maggie's young son, Sam. When the series changed networks in the fall of 1985, Carter was replaced by Mary Ann Mobley as Maggie. Arnold was permitted to grow up from age thirteen to age fifteen, and to begin getting interested in girls (in real life, Gary Coleman had turned seventeen by then).

During its 189-episode run, *Diff'rent Strokes* deftly addressed some sensitive topics, such as child molesting (in an episode featuring guest star Gordon Jump) and drug abuse (in a 1983 episode featuring a special appearance by Nancy Reagan). Jeff Harris and Bernie Kukoff were the creators of the series. All three of the child stars made headlines after the series had run its course: Dana Plato posed for *Playboy,* Gary Coleman filed suit against his parents and a former manager (claiming they had mishandled his earnings), and Todd Bridges was arrested for attempted murder in a drug-related shooting incident (he was later acquitted).

DINAH!   SYNDICATED
1974–1980   Ninety-minute talk show hosted by Dinah Shore. Featuring a set resembling a living room, the program was seen during the daytime in most markets. Executive producers: Henry Jaffe and Carolyn Raskin. In 1979 the show was retitled *Dinah! & Friends,* as Dinah employed a weekly cohost.

DINAH AND HER NEW BEST FRIENDS   CBS
5 JUNE 1976–31 JULY 1976   This summer replacement for *The Carol Burnett Show* starred Dinah Shore and a group of young professionals: Diana Canova, Bruce Kimmel, Gary Mule Deer, Mike Neun, Leland Palmer, Michael Preminger, Avelio Falana, and Dee Dee Rescher. Executive producer: Henry Jaffe. Producer: Carolyn Raskin.

THE DINAH SHORE SHOW   NBC
27 NOVEMBER 1951–18 JULY 1957; 20 OCTOBER 1957–1 JUNE 1962
DINAH'S PLACE   NBC
3 AUGUST 1970–26 JULY 1974   One of the few females to host a successful television variety series, Dinah Shore came to TV in 1951 with several years experience in show business; she had experimented in television in 1936, had had her own radio series in 1939 (at the age of twenty-two), and had begun making records in 1941. From 1951 until 1957 she hosted a fifteen-minute musical show, which was seen once or twice a week before the evening news. For several seasons the show was sponsored by Chevrolet and was known officially as *The Dinah Shore Chevy Show;* Shore's backup group during the latter seasons was the Skylarks, who included George Becker, Earl Brown, Joe Hamilton, Lee Lombard, and Gilda Maiken. During the 1956–1957 season, in addition to her fifteen-minute show, Shore starred in a number of specials, which were also sponsored by Chevrolet and were scheduled on Sunday evenings. These specials were the genesis of her second series, an hour variety show which ran from 1957 to 1962, and was again sponsored by Chevrolet; for most of these five seasons Shore hosted the series three out of every four weeks, with guest hosts filling in every fourth week. In 1970, after an eight-year absence, Shore returned to host *Dinah's Place,* a daytime half-hour talk show. After the cancellation of that show in 1974, she continued to host a talk show: see *Dinah!*

DING DONG SCHOOL   NBC/SYNDICATED

22 DECEMBER 1952–28 DECEMBER 1956 (NBC); 1959 (SYNDICATED)   One of the
first educational series for young children, *Ding Dong School* was seen Mondays
through Fridays on NBC. It was presided over by Dr. Frances Horwich, head of the
education department at Roosevelt College in Chicago; she was better known to
viewers, of course, as Miss Frances. The show was given its title by the three-year-old
daughter of producer Reinald Werrenrath after she watched a test broadcast of the
opening sequence (a hand ringing a small bell). In 1959 a syndicated version appeared.

DINK, THE LITTLE DINOSAUR   CBS

16 SEPTEMBER 1989–31 AUGUST 1991   Saturday morning cartoon show about a young
brontosaurus, Dink, and his prehistoric pals Crusty, Scat, Flapper, and Shyler.

DINNER AT JULIA'S   PBS

1983   Public television's most famous chef, Julia Child, returned to PBS to host her
third series. Unlike her previous shows, *The French Chef* and *Julia Child & Company, Dinner at Julia's* emphasized American cuisine.

DINNER DATE   DUMONT

28 JANUARY 1950–29 JULY 1950   Saturday-evening musical show, broadcast from the
Grill Room at New York's Hotel Taft, featuring Vincent Lopez and his orchestra,
Ann Warren, and Lee Russell.

DINOSAURS   ABC

26 APRIL 1991–3 SEPTEMBER 1993; 1 JUNE 1994–20 JULY 1994   A collaboration of
Walt Disney Television, Michael Jacobs Productions, and Jim Henson Productions,
this half-hour sitcom was set during the age of dinosaurs—in the year 60,000,003
B.C., to be exact. The premise was that the dinosaurs lived mundane lives much like
their modern human counterparts, and were thoughtlessly bringing about their own
extinction. The series was a live-action program, shot on film. The elaborately constructed characters were operated from within by human performers, and their facial
expressions were created by a process called audio animatronics. Voices were supplied by Stuart Pankin as Earl Sinclair, a megalosaurus; Jessica Walter as his wife,
Fran; Jason Willinger as their fourteen-year-old, Robbie; Sally Struthers as their
twelve-year-old, Charlene; Kevin Clash as their baby, Baby; Florence Stanley as
Fran's mother, Grandma Ethyl; Sam McMurray as Earl's best friend, Roy Hess; and
Sherman Hemsley as B. D. Richfield, Earl's boss at the Wesayso Development
Company. The last names of the characters—Sinclair, Hess, and Richfield—were
deliberately chosen: all are extinct gasoline brands.

DIONE LUCAS' COOKING SHOW   CBS

25 FEBRUARY 1948–29 DECEMBER 1949   One of television's first cooking shows, this
prime-time series, hosted by Dione Lucas, was titled *To the Queen's Taste* in its early
weeks.

THE DIPSY DOODLE SHOW   SYNDICATED

1974   An hour-long children's show produced at WJW-TV in Cleveland. Its central
character was an animated figure, Dipsy Doodle; also featured were live performers
Karen League Barrett, Sandy Faison, Jon Freeman, Michael McGee, Harry Gold,
Emil Herrera, and Helene Leonard. Executive producer: Bob Huber.

DIRECTIONS   ABC

13 NOVEMBER 1960–25 MARCH 1984   Sunday-morning religious program produced by
the News Public Affairs department of ABC. Executive producer: Sid Darion.

DIRTY DANCING   CBS

29 OCTOBER 1988–14 JANUARY 1989   An unsuccessful sitcom based on the 1987 hit
movie. Set in 1963 at Kellerman's Mountain Resort in New York's Catskills, it
featured Patrick Cassidy as Johnny Castle, the streetwise dance instructor; Melora

Hardin as the owner's daughter, Frances "Baby" Kellerman, the new talent coordinator (a job Johnny had had); McLean Stevenson as Baby's father, Max Kellerman; Constance Marie as Penny, Johnny's dancing partner; and Mandy Ingber as Baby's buddy, Robin.

DIRTY DOZEN: THE SERIES FOX
30 APRIL 1988–30 JULY 1988   A low-budget action series, based on the 1967 World War II film about a group of military convicts formed into a special unit, and its three made-for-TV sequels: "The Dirty Dozen: The Next Mission" (1985), "The Dirty Dozen: The Deadly Mission" (1987) and "The Dirty Dozen: The Fatal Mission" (1988). The TV series featured Ben Murphy as Lieutenant Danko; John DiAquino as Lebec, demolition expert; John Slattery as Leeds, a forger; Jon Tenney as Feke, intelligence ace; John Bradley as Farrell, the actor; Mike Jolly as Vern; Glenn Withrow as Roy; and Barry Cullison as Cutter. The Fox network had ordered thirteen episodes from the supplier, MGM/UA Television, but, apparently disappointed with the show and its lack of ratings, only aired seven, and repeated six of them.

DIRTY SALLY CBS
11 JANUARY 1974–19 JULY 1974   This light western starred Jeanette Nolan as crusty Sally Fergus, a wandering junk collector, and Dack Rambo as Cyrus Pike, the ex-outlaw with whom she teamed up. Nolan had first appeared as Sally on an episode of *Gunsmoke.*

DISCO MAGIC SYNDICATED
1978   Half-hour disco music show, taped in Fort Lauderdale and hosted by Evelyn "Champagne" King.

DISCO '77 SYNDICATED
1977   Los Angeles-based disco music series.

THE DISCOPHONIC SCENE SYNDICATED
1966   Disc jockey Jerry Blavat hosted this hour of rock music. For many years Blavat was the only white DJ on Philadelphia soul station WHAT, where he was known as "The Geater with the Heater."

DISCOVERY ABC
1 OCTOBER 1962–5 SEPTEMBER 1971   This highbrow series for children, bankrolled by a large investment from ABC, began as a twenty-five-minute weekday series but was unable to attract enough affiliates in that format. In 1963 it switched to Sunday mornings, where it remained for the duration of its run. Historical and cultural themes were emphasized on the program, which was cohosted by Frank Buxton and Virginia Gibson, later by Bill Owen and Gibson. The exact title of the series included the last two digits of the current year (*Discovery '63,* etc.)

DISNEY AFTERNOON SYNDICATED
1990–   *Disney Afternoon* was the umbrella title given to Disney's two-hour block of daily cartoon programming. During the first season the four components were *The Gummi Bears, Ducktales, Chip 'n' Dale's Rescue Rangers*—all of which had been launched previously—and a new series, *Tale Spin.* In 1991 the components were *Ducktales, Chip 'n' Dale's Rescue Rangers, Tale Spin,* and *Darkwing Duck.* In 1992 *Goof Troop* was substituted for *Duck Tales;* in 1993 *Bonkers* replaced *Chip 'n' Dale,* and in 1994 *Aladdin* replaced *Tale Spin.* See individual titles for details.

DISNEYLAND
See WALT DISNEY

DISNEY'S ADVENTURES OF THE GUMMI BEARS
See THE GUMMI BEARS

DISNEY'S RAW TOONAGE   CBS

19 SEPTEMBER 1992–28 AUGUST 1993   Saturday morning cartoon series from Disney.
A different Disney character hosted each program. Among the newly introduced
characters were Marsupilami, a long-tailed monkeylike creature, and Bonkers, a
bobcat, each of whom later had his own cartoon series. Also included in each program were "Totally Tasteless Videos," which spoofed commercials and other TV
programs.

DIVORCE COURT   SYNDICATED

1957–1969; 1986–1991   This long-running courtroom drama presented a new case
each day. The purpose of the show (according to the announcer, anyway) was "to
help stem the rising tide of divorces." In the earlier version actor Voltaire Perkins
played the judge, while Bill Walsh and Colin Male were the courtroom-based narrators. When the series was remade in the late 1980s, William B. Keene (who, like
Judge Wapner of *The People's Court,* was a retired California Superior Court judge)
presided, with Jim Peck as the host-narrator.

DIVORCE HEARING   SYNDICATED

1958   This unusual documentary series was filmed in Los Angeles; on each program
couples discussed marital problems with marriage counselor Dr. Paul Popenoe (the
participants were identified by first names or by initials). Dave Walpert produced and
directed the half-hour show.

DO IT YOURSELF   NBC

26 JUNE 1955–18 SEPTEMBER 1955   A light approach to home repair was taken on
this series, cohosted by Dave Willock and Cliff Arquette (as Charley Weaver). The
two had previously been seen on *Dave and Charley.* This Sunday-night series replaced *Mr. Peepers.*

DO YOU KNOW?   CBS

12 OCTOBER 1963–25 APRIL 1964   On this Saturday-afternoon game show for kids,
children were quizzed about books they had been assigned to read. Afterward they
discussed the books with their authors and with host Robert Maxwell.

DO YOU TRUST YOUR WIFE?
See WHO DO YOU TRUST?

DOBIE GILLIS (THE MANY LOVES OF DOBIE GILLIS)   CBS

29 SEPTEMBER 1959–18 SEPTEMBER 1963   This situation comedy about a girl-crazy
teenager was ahead of its time. Its central characters would have felt equally at home in
the late sixties: Dobie Gillis, the confused romantic who could never figure out what he
wanted from life, and Maynard G. Krebs, his carefree beatnik friend, television's
primordial hippie. During the show's four-year run, Dobie and Maynard finished high
school, enlisted in the army, and eventually went to junior college. Dwayne Hickman
starred as Dobie Gillis; his hair was lightened for the series, apparently to make him
look younger (it grew darker as time wore on). When Dobie wasn't at the malt shop
trying to impress some sweet young thing, he could be found seated beneath a replica
of Rodin's "The Thinker," trying to explain his thoughts to the audience. Bob Denver
costarred as Dobie's good buddy, Maynard G. Krebs, a goateed and sweatshirted free
spirit who shuddered whenever the word "work" was uttered. Also featured were
Frank Faylen as Dobie's father, Herbert T. Gillis, who owned the grocery store over
which the Gillises dwelt and whose unrealized dream was that Dobie would come to his
senses and take over the business; Florida Friebus as Dobie's mother, Winnifred Gillis,
who seemed to understand Dobie and often interceded between father and son; Stephen Franken as Dobie's wealthy classmate, Chatsworth Osborne, Jr., who found the
Gillises boorishly amusing; Doris Packer as Mrs. Chatsworth Osborne, the equally
insufferable mother of Chatsworth; Sheila James as classmate Zelda Gilroy, who,
confident that she and Dobie were meant for each other, pursued him in vain; William
Schallert as Mr. Pomfritt, Dobie's English teacher (both at Central High and at S.

Peter Pryor Junior College); Tuesday Weld (1959–1960) as Thalia Menninger, the unattainable object of Dobie's affections who put him off with an armada of excuses. In the earliest episodes Warren Beatty was seen as Milton Armitage, the boy whom Thalia preferred. Darryl Hickman (Dwayne's brother) appeared occasionally as Dobie's brother Davey Gillis. Michael J. Pollard also appeared briefly as Maynard's cousin; when Denver was drafted in 1960, Pollard was under consideration to replace him, but Denver flunked his physical. Robert Diamond (formerly of *Fury*) appeared as Dobie's cousin Duncan during the show's final season. Ryan O'Neal made his TV debut on one episode, "The Hunger Strike," which also featured Marlo Thomas (26 January 1960). Created by Max Shulman, the series was produced by Rod Amateau. Some members of the cast reassembled for two TV sequels. The first, "Whatever Happened to Dobie Gillis?" was aired in 1977. In the second, "Bring Me the Head of Dobie Gillis," telecast 21 February 1988, Dwayne Hickman, Bob Denver, Sheila James, Stephen Franken, and William Schallert all reprised their roles, and Connie Stevens played Thalia Menninger. Dobie ran Gillis's Market and Pharmacy, had married Zelda, and had a young son.

DOC   CBS
13 SEPTEMBER 1975–30 OCTOBER 1976   In this situation comedy about a dedicated New York physician, Barnard Hughes starred as Dr. Joe Bogert. During the first season Bogert was a private practitioner with eight grown children. The cast included: Elizabeth Wilson as his wife, Annie Bogert; Mary Wickes as his nurse, Mrs. Beatrice Tully; comic Irwin Corey as cabbie Happy Miller, a frequent patient; Judy Kahan as Laurie Fenner, Joe and Annie's daughter; John Harkins as Fred Fenner, her pompous husband; and Herbie Faye as Mr. Goldman, another patient. For the second season, Bogert (now widowed) worked at the Westside Community Clinic. The 1975–1976 cast was jettisoned (Mary Wickes appeared on the season premiere), and the new regulars included: Audra Lindley as Janet Scott, R.N.; Ray Vitte as lab technician Woody Henderson; Lisa Mordente as receptionist Teresa Ortega; and David Ogden Stiers as clinic director Stanley R. Moss. The series was created by Ed. Weinberger and Stan Daniels, who also served as its executive producers. Produced by Norman Barasch, Carroll Moore, and Paul Wayne for MTM Enterprises, Inc.

DOC CORKLE   NBC
5 OCTOBER 1952–19 OCTOBER 1952   In this situation comedy about a dentist, Eddie Mayehoff starred as Doc Corkle; also featured were Connie Marshall as his daughter, Chester Conklin as his father, Arnold Stang, Hope Emerson, and Billie Burke. The first fatality of the 1952–1953 season, *Doc Corkle* was replaced after three episodes by a series which had proved popular that summer: *Mr. Peepers*. Lou Place was the producer, Dick Bare the director.

DOC ELLIOT   ABC
10 OCTOBER 1973–14 AUGUST 1974   A dramatic series about a doctor who gave up his lucrative New York practice for life in rural Colorado. With James Franciscus as Dr. Ben Elliot; Neva Patterson as "Mags" Brimble, his landlady; Noah Beery as store owner Barney Weeks; and Bo Hopkins as pilot Eldred McCoy. The series began as a once-a-month replacement for *Owen Marshall* and went weekly in January.

THE DOCTOR   NBC
24 AUGUST 1952–28 JUNE 1953   Warner Anderson hosted this half-hour medical anthology series, which was produced by Marion Parsonnet. Charles Bronson played one of his first major TV roles on one episode, "Take the Odds," seen 18 January 1953.

DR. CHRISTIAN   SYNDICATED
1956   This medical show was based on the film and radio series, which had starred Jean Hersholt. On TV Macdonald Carey starred as small-town physician Dr. Mark Christian, nephew of Hersholt's character, Dr. Paul Christian; Hersholt himself actually appeared in the first two TV episodes.

DR. DEAN   NBC
15 JUNE 1992–15 JANUARY 1993   On this half-hour daytime series, Dr. Dean Edell
dispensed advice on medical matters and health care.

DOCTOR, DOCTOR   CBS
12 JUNE 1989–24 JULY 1989; 13 NOVEMBER 1989–26 JANUARY 1990; 20 AUGUST 1990–3
JANUARY 1991; 8 JUNE 1991–6 JULY 1991   This half-hour sitcom was the first televi-
sion series set in Rhode Island. It starred Matt Frewer (late of *Max Headroom*) as
Dr. Mike Stratford, an unconventional practitioner at Northeast Medical Partners in
Providence; Beau Gravitte as Dr. Grant Linowitz; Julius Carry III as Dr. Abe
Butterfield; Maureen Mueller as Dr. Dierdre Bennett; Audrie J. Neenan as Nurse
Faye Barylski; and Sarah Abrell as Pia Bismarck, anchor of the local TV show *Wake
Up Providence*, on which Mike landed a regular spot as medical correspondent.
Occasionally featured were Dakin Matthews as Mike's father, Harold; Inga Swenson
as Mike's mother, Connie; and Tony Carreiro as Mike's gay brother, Richard. In the
fall of 1990 Anne Elizabeth Ramsay joined the group as Grant's sister, Dr. Leona
Linowitz. Norman Steinberg created the series.

DR. DOOLITTLE   NBC
12 SEPTEMBER 1970–2 SEPTEMBER 1972   A Saturday-morning cartoon series about a
kindly veterinarian who could talk to the animals, based on the stories by Hugh
Lofting and inspired by the 1967 film starring Rex Harrison.

DR. FIX-UM   ABC
3 MAY 1949–6 AUGUST 1950   Host Arthur Youngquist presented tips on home repair
on this prime-time show.

DR. FU MANCHU (THE ADVENTURES OF FU MANCHU)   SYNDICATED
1956   The inscrutable Oriental mastermind created by Sax Rohmer almost came to
television in 1952; that year a pilot film was made at Fox Movietone Studios in New
York with John Carradine as Fu Manchu and Sir Cedric Hardwicke as Detective
Nayland Smith, his adversary. In 1956 Fu reappeared, played by Glen Gordon, with
Lester Stevens as Nayland Smith.

DR. HUDSON'S SECRET JOURNAL   SYNDICATED
1955–1957   The character of Dr. Wayne Hudson appeared in two novels by Lloyd
C. Douglas, *Magnificent Obsession* and *Dr. Hudson's Secret Journal*. The television
series, a syndicated half-hour serial, starred John Howard as the widowed Dr. Hudson, a neurosurgeon at Center Hospital. Also featured were Olive Blakeney as his
housekeeper, Mrs. Grady; Cheryl Gallaway as his daughter, Kathy; Jack Kelly (who
would soon move to *Maverick*) as Dr. Bennett. The seventy-eight episodes were
produced by Eugene Solow and Brewster Morgan.

DR. I.Q.   ABC
4 NOVEMBER 1953–10 OCTOBER 1954; 15 DECEMBER 1958–23 MARCH 1959   Neither of
the television adaptations of this popular radio quiz show fared well. Jay Owen was
the first host of the 1953–1954 version. As Dr. I.Q., the Mental Banker, he awarded
twenty silver dollars for each question answered correctly by contestants from the
studio audience. An Episcopalian minister, James McClain, succeeded Owen during
the 1953–1954 season, and Tom Kennedy hosted the show when it was revived four
years later as a midseason replacement for *Anybody Can Play*.

DOCTOR IN THE HOUSE   SYNDICATED
1971–1974   This British comedy about a group of medical students studying at St.
Swithin's Teaching Hospital in London was based on the stories by Richard Gordon
(which in turn had formed the basis for the 1953 film). With Barry Evans (1971–
1973) as Michael A. Upton; Ernest Clark as Professor Loftus, anatomy instructor;
Robin Nedwell (1971–1972; 1973–1974) as Duncan Waring; George Layton as Paul
Collier; Jeffrey Davies as Dick Stuart-Clark; Martin Shaw as Huw Evans; Simon Cuff

(1971–1972) as David Briddock; Ralph Michael (1971–1972) as The Dean; and Richard O'Sullivan (1972–1974) as Dr. Lawrence Bingham. Filmed between 1969 and 1972, the series was not made available to American markets until 1971. The students had earned their degrees by the second season and left St. Swithin's, only to return (as interns) a year later; it was explained that Upton had gone away to sea.

DOCTOR JOYCE BROTHERS (CONSULT DR. BROTHERS) (TELL ME, DR. BROTHERS) (LIVING EASY WITH DR. JOYCE BROTHERS)   SYNDICATED

1961; 1964; 1972   Doctor Joyce Brothers, the psychologist who was the first woman to win the top prize on *The $64,000 Question* (her category was boxing), hosted several syndicated series. The first two—*Consult Dr. Brothers* (1961) and *Tell Me, Dr. Brothers* (1964)—focused on human relationships; the third—*Living Easy with Dr. Joyce Brothers* (1972)—was basically a talk show, featuring celebrity guests.

DR. KATZ: PROFESSIONAL THERAPIST   COM

28 MAY 1995–   Comedian Jonathan Katz lent his name and voice to this half-hour prime time cartoon series about a psychologist and his teen son, Ben. Other voices were provided by Katz's fellow comedians including Rita Rudner and Steven Wright.

DR. KILDARE   NBC

28 SEPTEMBER 1961–30 AUGUST 1966   This popular medical series, like ABC's *Ben Casey*, enjoyed a five-year run. NBC sealed its doom in 1965 by breaking up the show into two half-hour segments. Richard Chamberlain starred as Dr. James Kildare, an intern at Blair General Hospital. Raymond Massey costarred as Dr. Leonard Gillespie, the paternal senior staff physician who guided him. Also featured were Jud Taylor as Dr. Gerson; Steven Bell (1965–1966) as Dr. Lowry; Lee Kurty (1965–1966) as Nurse Lawton; and Jean Inness (1965–1966) as Nurse Fain. Norman Felton was the executive producer of the series, which was produced at MGM studios. The *Doctor Kildare* short stories were written by Frederick Schiller Faust, who commonly used the pen name of Max Brand; the inspiration for the stories came from Dr. George Winthrop Fish (1895–1977), a prominent urologist. Several films were made, beginning in 1938, and a radio series appeared in 1939. A second TV series was made in 1972: see *Young Dr. Kildare*. In 1989 Chamberlain returned to TV as a physician: see *Island Son*.

DR. QUINN, MEDICINE WOMAN   CBS

1 JANUARY 1993–   To the surprise of almost everyone, this hour family drama series, set in the 1860s, found an audience in its Saturday night time slot. It starred Jane Seymour as Dr. Michaela "Mike" Quinn, a single female physician who moved from Boston to Colorado Springs, where she set up a practice in the rough-and-tumble frontier town; she also became mother to three children who were orphaned when one of her patients died. Also featured were Chad Allen as Matthew Cooper, eldest of the three children; Erika Flores (1993–January 1995) and Jessica Bowman (January 1995–   ) as Colleen Cooper; Shawn Toovey as Brian Cooper; Joe Lando as Byron Sully, the moody and handsome young widower who kept a pet wolf and rented his homestead to Mike and the kids; Guy Boyd (pilot program) and Orson Bean as storekeeper Loren Bray; Colm Meaney (pilot) and Jim Knobeloch as barber Jake Slicker; Geoffrey Lower as Reverend Johnson; William Shockley as Hank the bartender; and Helene Udy as Myra the saloon girl. Mike married Sully at the end of the 1994–1995 season, and in the fall of 1995 she became pregnant.

DR. RUTH WESTHEIMER   LIFETIME

27 AUGUST 1984–1 JANUARY 1988; 2 APRIL 1988–14 JANUARY 1989; 4 AUGUST 1989–1 JUNE 1991   Sex therapist Ruth Westheimer has hosted several discussion shows on the Lifetime Cable Channel (formerly known as the Cable Health Network). On the first series, originally titled *Good Sex! With Dr. Ruth Westheimer* (and later simply titled *Dr. Ruth*), she dispensed advice to actors who appeared as patients. Her subsequent shows, *The All New Dr. Ruth Show*, *What's Up, Dr. Ruth?* and *On the Air*

with Dr. Ruth, featured call-ins and interviews with physicians and celebrities. See also *Ask Dr. Ruth.*

DOCTOR SIMON LOCKE   SYNDICATED
1971   A half-hour medical drama, filmed in Canada. With Jack Albertson as Dr. Andrew Sellers, a general practitioner in the small town of Dixon Mills; Sam Groom as Dr. Simon Locke, the young associate who joined him in the practice; Nuala Fitzgerald as their housekeeper and nurse, Mrs. Louise Winn; and Len Birman as Dan Palmer, local police chief. After one season Doctor Locke left Dixon Mills for the big city: see *Police Surgeon.*

DR. SNUGGLES   SYNDICATED
1981   A Dutch-produced cartoon series featuring Dr. Snuggles, a lovable inventor, and Miss Nettles, his housekeeper. Principal voices were supplied by Peter Ustinov.

DR. SPOCK   NBC
9 OCTOBER 1955–9 AUGUST 1956   Dr. Benjamin Spock, America's most famous pediatrician, advised parents on child care on this Sunday-afternoon series. The show was broadcast from KYW-TV in Cleveland; Spock taught at the Western Reserve University College of Medicine.

DOCTOR WHO   SYNDICATED
1978–1989   This low-budget but highly entertaining science fiction series acquired cult status in many of the one hundred countries in which it was televised. Produced in England, it began in 1963, though it was not widely seen in this country until 1978. Its central character was the Doctor, a 750-year-old native of the planet Gallifrey who traveled through the universe; though not precisely human, the Doctor found it convenient to use a human form. The title role was played by more than half a dozen actors: William Hartnell, Patrick Troughton, Jon Pertwee, Tom Baker, Peter Davison, Colin Baker, Sylvester McCoy, and Paul McGann; additionally, Richard Hurndall played the first Doctor in a special twentieth-anniversary episode in 1983.

THE DOCTORS   NBC
1 APRIL 1963–31 DECEMBER 1982   Created by Orin Tovrov, who had written the radio serial *Ma Perkins* for many years, *The Doctors* was set in and around Hope Memorial Hospital. It began not as a continuing drama, but rather as a daily anthology series in which one of four main characters was featured: Jock Gaynor as Dr. William Scott; Margot Moser as Dr. Elizabeth Hayes; Richard Roat as Dr. Jerry Chandler; and Fred J. Scollay as Sam Shafer, the chaplain. *The Doctors* experimented with a weekly anthology format later in 1963, and became a continuing serial early in 1964. In 1972 it became the first daytime serial to win an Emmy. Its producers included Allen Potter, Joseph Stuart, Jeff Young, Doris Quinlan, and Gerry Straub. Head writers included Eileen Pollack and Robert Mason Pollack, Margaret DePriest, and Douglas Marland. By the early 1980s, however, *The Doctors* had become television's lowest-rated soap opera, and the show expired quietly at the end of 1982.
   When *The Doctors* changed formats in 1964 Richard Roat and Fred J. Scollay were retained for a time, but were eventually written out as new characters took over. Principal players included: James Pritchett as Dr. Matt Powers, the head of Hope Memorial (Pritchett had appeared on the show in 1963, as a corporate president in a single episode), who was a widower; Ann Williams, Bethel Leslie, and Lydia Bruce as Dr. Maggie Fielding, who married Matt in 1968; Adam Kennedy as Brock Hayden, who was murdered; Ellen McRae (later known as Ellen Burstyn) as Dr. Kate Bartok; Elizabeth Hubbard as Dr. Althea Davis (Hubbard was replaced briefly by Virginia Vestoff in 1969, but returned to the role); Gerald O'Loughlin as Pete Banas, hospital custodian; Karl Light as Dave Davis, Althea's ex-husband; Dorothy Blackburn as Nurse Brown; Katherine Meskill as Faith Collins; and Court Benson as Willard Walling.
   Additional players have included: Charles Braswell and Joseph Campanella as Alec Fielding, Maggie's first husband; Byron Sanders as Kurt Van Allen, Maggie's

second husband; Harry Packwood, Peter Burnell, Michael Landrum, Armand Assante, John Shearin, and Stephen Burleigh as Dr. Mike Powers, Matt's son by his first marriage; Pamela Toll as Liz Wilson, Mike's girlfriend; Morgan Sterne as Keith Wilson, Liz's father; Meg Myles as Harriet Wilson, Liz's mother; Julia Duffy as Penny Davis, daughter of Althea and Dave Davis (their other child, Buddy, died of spinal meningitis); Gerald Gordon as Dr. Nick Bellini, a brain surgeon who was briefly married to Althea; Eileen Kearney, Jennifer Houlton, and Gracie Harrison as Greta Van Allen, daughter of Kurt and Maggie, who was adopted by Matt Powers when he married Maggie; Terry Kiser as Dr. John Rice; Nancy Donohue as nurse Nancy Bennett; James Shannon as Paul Bennett, Nancy's missing husband; Conrad Roberts as Dr. Simon Harris; Zeida Coles as Anna Ford; Ginger Gerlach as Julie Forrest, who died after a fall down the stairs (not long afterward, Gerlach herself died of a drug overdose); Carolee Campbell and Jada Rowland as nurse Carolee Simpson; Richard Higgs as Dr. Dan Allison, who married Carolee and later committed suicide (though he tried to make it look like murder); David O'Brien as Dr. Steve Aldrich, who was implicated in Dan's death but later married Carolee; Laryssa Lauret as Dr. Karen Werner, Steve's lover, killed in a plane crash; Keith Blanchard and Thor Fields as Erich Aldrich, illegitimate son of Steve and Karen; Bobby Hennessy, David Elliott, Shawn Campbell, and Alec Baldwin as Billy Allison Aldrich, son of Dan and Carolee, later adopted by Carolee and Steve; Patrick Horgan as psychiatrist Dr. John Morrison, who was murdered; Carol Pfander, Nancy Barrett, and Holly Peters as nurse Kathy Ryker, who committed suicide; Anna Stuart as lab technician Toni Ferra, who married Mike Powers and was later killed in a plane crash; Nancy Franklin (who also wrote for the series) as Toni's mother, Barbara Ferra; Paul Henry Itkin as Dr. Vito McCray; Palmer Deane as Dr. Hank Iverson, a black physician; Marie Thomas as Lauri James, Hank's girlfriend; Katherine Squire as Carolee's mother, Emma Simpson; Sally Gracie as Martha Allen; Tara Baker, Bridget Breen, and Gloria Mattioli as Stephanie Aldrich, daughter of Steve and Carolee; Meg Mundy as Mona Aldrich Croft, Steve's mother; Glenn Corbett as Jason Aldrich; Geraldine Court as Dr. Ann Larimer, ex-wife of Steve Aldrich; Gil Gerard as Dr. Alan Stewart, Matt Powers's nephew; Mary Denham as Margo Stewart; Leslie Ann Ray as Stacy Wells; Lloyd Bremseth as Andy Anderson; Lauren White and Kathy Glass as Mary Jane (M.J.) Match; Alex Sheafe as lawyer Luke McAlister; Dino Narizzano as Dr. Kevin MacIntyre; Chandler Hill Harben as Dr. Rico Bellini; Jess Adams as Webb Sutherland; Thomas Connolly as Dr. Clifford DeSales; Edmund Lyndeck as Dr. Carl Hendryx; Toni Darnay as Vivian Hendryx; Anthony Cannon as Dr. Tom Barrett; Roni Dengel as Dawn Eddington; George Smith as Detective Ernie Cadman; Tammy McDonald as Iris Fonteyne; Matthew Tobin as Rex Everlee; Robert Coppes as Reverend Joe Turner; George Coe as Scott Conrad; Peter Lombard as Dr. Robert Wilson; Lois Smith as Eleanor Conrad; Fanny Speiss and Kathy Eckles as Wendy Conrad; Alan Koss as Alvin Ing; Dale Robinette as Dr. Gil Lawford; Paul Carr as Dr. Paul Sommers; Kathryn Harrold, Kathleen Turner, and Kim Zimmer as Nola Dancy Aldrich; Jonathan Hogan as Jerry Dancy; Frank Telfer as Luke Dancy; Elizabeth Lawrence as Virginia Dancy; Jonathan Frakes as Tom Carroll; Jason Matzner as Ricky Manero; Petronia Paley as Dr. Jesse Rawlings; Larry Weber as Barney Dancy; Pamela Lincoln as Doreen Aldrich; Philip English as Colin Wakefield; Melissa Sherman as Judy; Peggy Cass as Sweeney; Dorothy Fielding as Sara Dancy; Martin Shakar as Dr. Speer; John Downes as Michael Paul Powers; Jane Fleiss as Kim; John Newton as Dr. Cummings; Dorian LoPinto as Missy Roberts, who was killed by terrorists; Heywood Hale Broun as Cappy Randall; Patricia Hayling as Mrs. Chambers; and Count Stovall as Hank Chambers.

Other regulars during *The Doctors'* later years included: Amanda Treyz and Jeannine Costigan as Lee Ann Aldrich, young daughter of Billy Allison Aldrich and Greta Van Allen; Doris Belack as Claudia Howard; Richard Borg as Alan Ross; Nancy Pinkerton as Viveca Strand; Laurie Klatscher and Jane Badler as Natalie Dancy, Luke's wife; Chris Calloway as singer Ivie Gooding; Rex Robbins as Dr. Murray Glover; John Pankow as Danny Martin; Hillary Bailey as nurse Kit McCormack; Michael Stark as Dr. Jeff Manning; James Douglas as Jeff's father, banker

Phillip Manning; Nancy Stafford as Adrienne Hunt; Mark Goddard as Lieutenant Paul Reed, a cop; Valerie Mahaffey as Ashley Bennett; Franc Luz as Dr. John Bennett; Ben Thomas as Jack Garner; David Canary as Warner; Carolyn Byrd as Dr. Terri Foster; Diane Kirksey as Bobby; Nana Tucker as Darcy Collins; Laurie Kussold as Jessica; Elaine Lee as Mildred Turnbull; Larry Riley as Calvin Barnes; Nicholas Walker as Brad Huntington; Bea Winde as Lillian Foster; and Augusta Dabney as Theodora Van Allen.

THE DOCTORS AND THE NURSES
See THE NURSES

DOCTORS HOSPITAL NBC
10 SEPTEMBER 1975–14 JANUARY 1976   Hour-long medical series set at Lowell Memorial Hospital. With George Peppard as Dr. Jake Goodwin, chief of neurosurgery; Zohra Lampert as Dr. Noah Purcell; Victor Campos as Dr. Felipe Ortega; and Albert Paulsen as Dr. Janos Varga. Executive producer: Matthew Rapf. Produced by Jack Laird.

DOCTORS' PRIVATE LIVES ABC
5 APRIL 1979–26 APRIL 1979   Four-week medical miniseries. With Ed Nelson as Dr. Michael Wise, chief of surgery; John Gavin as Dr. Jeff Latimer, head of the hospital cardiovascular unit; Randolph Powell as Dr. Rick Calder, a young surgeon; Phil Levien as Kenny Wise, Michael's son; Gwen Humble as med student Sheila Castle, a friend of Michael's; Eddie Benton as nurse Diane Curtis; William Smithers as Dr. Trilling; Elinor Donahue as Mona, Michael's ex-wife. James Henerson created the series; David Gerber was the executive producer, Matthew Rapf the producer.

DOG AND CAT ABC
5 MARCH 1977–14 MAY 1977   Crime drama about a woman police officer assigned to work with a male officer who, at least initially, doubted her abilities. With Kim Basinger as Officer J. Z. Kane; Lou Antonio as Sergeant Jack Ramsey; and Matt Clark as Lieutenant Kipling. Walter Hill created the series; Lawrence Gordon was the executive producer.

DOG CITY FOX
26 SEPTEMBER 1992–28 JANUARY 1995   This Saturday morning kids' series, created by Jim Henson Productions, combined puppetry with animation. Its central character was Eliot Shag, a canine muppet who had created a cartoon series about a canine private eye named Ace Hart.

DOLLAR A SECOND DUMONT/NBC/ABC
20 SEPTEMBER 1953–14 JUNE 1954 (DUMONT); 4 JULY 1954–22 AUGUST 1954 (NBC); 1 OCTOBER 1954–24 JUNE 1955 (ABC); 5 JULY 1955–23 AUGUST 1955 (NBC); 2 SEPTEMBER 1955–31 AUGUST 1956 (ABC); 22 JUNE 1957–28 SEPTEMBER 1957 (NBC)   Jan Murray hosted this prime-time game show, which was not unlike *Truth or Consequences*. Contestants earned $1 for each second during which they could answer questions correctly; if they answered incorrectly or were interrupted by the host, they were required to perform a stunt. The show was based on a French radio program, *Cent Francs par Seconde,* created by Jean-Pierre Bloudeau.

THE $1.98 BEAUTY CONTEST SYNDICATED
1978   This half-hour game show bore the unmistakable marks of a Chuck Barris Production. Hosted by comic Rip Taylor, it was similar to *The Gong Show;* three celebrity panelists watched a group of contestants compete—in talent and swimsuit segments—for the daily prize, $1.98 in cash and a tacky tiara.

DOLLY SYNDICATED
1976–1977   A half hour of country and western music, hosted by Dolly Parton, one of the most popular country and western stars of the decade.

DOLLY   ABC

27 SEPTEMBER 1987–7 MAY 1988   In the hope of finding someone who could host a successful network variety show (a feat undone since the demise of *The Carol Burnett Show*), ABC made a two-season, $44 million commitment to country music star Dolly Parton. Unfortunately, the glitzy, big-budget hour finished 47th in the ratings for its first season, and the second season never materialized. Parton's considerable talents were probably overutilized on the show; she seemed to appear in virtually every segment, singing with the musical guests and performing in skits with the acting guests. Except for a four-man vocal group called A Cappella, there were no other regulars besides Parton. Nevertheless there were some memorable musical highlights, such as the appearance of Linda Ronstadt and Emmylou Harris (with whom Parton had recorded the album *Trio*) on 11 October.

DOLPHIN COVE   CBS

21 JANUARY 1989–11 MARCH 1989   Hour adventure series about a widowed scientist who moved to Australia with his kids to study dolphins. With Frank Converse as Michael Larson; Trey Ames as son David; Karron Graves as daughter Katie, who hadn't spoken since her mother's death; Virginia Hey as Allison, Katie's speech therapist; Antony Richards as Kevin; Ernie Dingo as Didge, a local aborigine; and Nick Tate as Trent. The series was filmed on location.

THE DOM DeLUISE SHOW   CBS

1 MAY 1968–18 SEPTEMBER 1968   Comedian Dom DeLuise hosted this variety hour, a summer replacement for *The Jackie Gleason Show* (though it was televised in a different time slot). Regulars included Carol Arthur (Dom's wife), Marian Mercer, Bill McCutcheon, Paul Dooley, B. S. Pulley, the Gentry Brothers, Dick Lynn, the June Taylor Dancers, and the Sammy Spear Orchestra. Taped in Miami Beach, the show was produced by Ronnie Wayne.

THE DOM DeLUISE SHOW   SYNDICATED

1987–1989   In this half-hour sitcom Dom Deluise starred as Dom, a widower who operated a barber shop across the street from a Hollywood film studio. George Wallace (the black actor, not the former governor) played his partner, George Wallace. With Maureen Murphy as Maureen the manicurist; Lauren Woodland as Dom's daughter, Rosa; Lois Foraker as Dom's romantic interest, Blanche; Angela Aames as Penny; and Michael Chambers as Michael.

DOMESTIC LIFE   CBS

4 JANUARY 1984–31 JULY 1984   Half-hour sitcom about the home life of a local television personality. With Martin Mull as Martin Crane, who delivered commentaries on "Domestic Life" over station KMRT in Seattle; Judith-Marie Bergan as his wife, Candy Crane; Christian Brackett-Zika as their precocious young son, Harold; Megan Follows as their teenage daughter, Didi; Robert Ridgely as Cliff, coanchor of the KMRT newscast; and Mie Hunt as Jane, the other coanchor.

DON ADAMS' SCREEN TEST   SYNDICATED

1975   Half-hour game show on which preselected contestants acted out scenes from various motion pictures with celebrity partners. At the end of the show a guest judge (usually a producer or director) selected the best amateur, who was then promised a small role in an upcoming film or television series. Don Adams was host and executive producer. Producer: Marty Pasetta.

DON AMECHE PLAYHOUSE (DON'S MUSICAL PLAYHOUSE)   ABC

5 JULY 1951–4 OCTOBER 1951   Half-hour musical comedy series hosted by Don Ameche; it replaced the very similar *Holiday Hotel* on Thursdays.

THE DON HO SHOW   ABC

25 OCTOBER 1976–4 MARCH 1977   Half-hour daytime variety series broadcast from various sites in Hawaii and hosted by singer Don Ho.

DON KIRSHNER'S ROCK CONCERT   SYNDICATED
1973–1982   Film clips of various rock-and-roll stars introduced by Don Kirshner, the music publisher and rock impresario responsible for the success of such groups as the Monkees and the Archies. Kirshner also served as executive producer of the series; it was produced by David Yarnell.

THE DON KNOTTS SHOW   NBC
15 SEPTEMBER 1970–6 JULY 1971   After years as a supporting player on *The Steve Allen Show* and *The Andy Griffith Show,* Don Knotts took a stab at headlining a variety series. Also featured were Elaine Joyce, Frank Welker, John Dehner, Kenneth Mars, Eddy Carroll, Francis DeSales, Mickey Deems, Brad Logan, Fay DeWitt, Gary Burghoff, and Bob Williams and his dog, Louis. Executive producer: Nick Vanoff. Producer: Bill Harbach. Director: Norman Abbott.

THE DON LANE SHOW   SYNDICATED
1980   An hour talk show, hosted by Don Lane and broadcast from Australia. Lane, a native New Yorker, hosted the Sydney-based show from 1974 to 1983.

DON McNEILL'S TV CLUB   ABC
13 SEPTEMBER 1950–19 DECEMBER 1951
THE BREAKFAST CLUB   ABC
22 FEBRUARY 1954–25 FEBRUARY 1955   Don McNeill hosted one of America's longest-running radio shows: *The Breakfast Club* ran from 1933 to 1968. It was a spontaneous, low-key blend of music, interviews, comedy, and audience participation broadcast weekday mornings from Chicago. In 1950 McNeill brought his show to prime-time television, where it was titled *Don McNeill's TV Club.* Regulars included Fran Allison (of *Kukla, Fran and Ollie* fame), Johnny Desmond, Eileen Parker, Patsy Lee, Sam Cowling, and Eddie Ballantine and his orchestra. The show was produced by George M. Cahan and directed by Grover J. Allen. In 1954 McNeill again tried television, this time on weekday mornings. The show, called *The Breakfast Club,* was simulcast with the radio show.

THE DON RICKLES SHOW   ABC
27 SEPTEMBER 1968–31 JANUARY 1969   An ill-conceived half-hour series, part game show and part variety show. Host Don Rickles, known to most audiences strictly as an insult comic (his sobriquet, "The Merchant of Venom," was well deserved), spent most of the show trading insults with celebrity guests. Occasionally he found time to quiz—and insult—contestants from the studio audience. Rickles's considerable talents as a dramatic actor never surfaced on the series, unfortunately. Also featured was Pat McCormick, king-sized comic (and the show's head writer). The show was a Mark Goodson–Bill Todman Production.

THE DON RICKLES SHOW   CBS
14 JANUARY 1972–26 MAY 1972   Don Rickles's second series was a sitcom in which Rickles was cast as Don Robinson, a high-strung executive with Kingston, Cohen & Vanderpool, a New York advertising agency. With Louise Sorel as Barbara Robinson, Don's wife; Erin Moran as Janie, their daughter; Robert Hogan as Don's friend and coworker, Tyler Benedict; Joyce Van Patten as Jean Benedict, Tyler's wife and Barbara's best friend; Barry Gordon as Conrad Musk, aggressive young adman. Executive producer: Sheldon Leonard. Director: Hy Averback.

DONAHUE
See THE PHIL DONAHUE SHOW

THE DONALD O'CONNOR SHOW   NBC
9 OCTOBER 1954–10 SEPTEMBER 1955   This half-hour filmed variety series was seen biweekly, alternating with *The Jimmy Durante Show* on Saturdays. It was hosted by singer-dancer Donald O'Connor, who had earlier hosted *The Colgate Comedy Hour.*

THE DONALD O'CONNOR SHOW   SYNDICATED

1968   Donald O'Connor, the star of countless musical comedies during the 1940s and 1950s, made few appearances on TV after his earlier show left the air in 1955. He returned briefly in 1968 to host this syndicated talk show.

THE DONNA FARGO SHOW   SYNDICATED

1978   Half-hour country-and-western music show hosted by singer Donna Fargo.

THE DONNA REED SHOW   ABC

24 SEPTEMBER 1958–3 SEPTEMBER 1966   One of the most wholesome sitcoms ever made, *The Donna Reed Show* barely escaped cancellation after its first season. It was moved to Thursdays in 1959, where it remained for seven more seasons; by the end of its run in 1966 it was ABC's third oldest prime-time series. Donna Reed, who won an Academy Award for her performance in *From Here to Eternity* (1955), starred as Donna Stone, all-American housewife and mother. Also featured were Carl Betz as her husband, Alex Stone, a small-town pediatrician; Shelley Fabares (1958–1963) as Mary, their teenage daughter; Paul Petersen as Jeff, their son (he was eleven when the show started and had been one of the original Mouseketeers on *The Mickey Mouse Club*). In 1963 Patty Petersen (Paul's real-life sister) joined the cast as Trisha, an orphan taken in by the Stones. Other regulars included Kathleen Freeman (1958–1960) as Mrs. Wilgus, their nosy neighbor; Harvey Grant as Jeff's pal, Philip; Darryl Richard as Jeff's friend, Smitty; Jimmy Hawkins as Scotty Simpson; Candy Moore (1964–1966) as Bebe Barnes, Jeff's girlfriend; Bob Crane (1963–1965) as Dr. Dave Kelsey, their neighbor; and Ann McCrea (1963–1966) as Midge Kelsey, Dave's wife and Donna's best friend. Both Shelley Fabares and Paul Petersen attempted to launch recording careers on the strength of their popularity; each had a hit or two (Fabares's "Johnny Angel," Petersen's "My Dad" and "She Can't Find Her Keys"), but neither approached the phenomenal success achieved by Rick Nelson of ABC's other long-running sitcom, *Ozzie and Harriet*. *The Donna Reed Show* was produced by Reed's husband, Tony Owen. Among the guest stars who made their first major TV appearances on the series were John Astin ("Mouse at Play," 5 October 1961), James Darren ("April Fool," 1 April 1959), and George Hamilton ("Have Fun," 4 February 1959). Margaret Dumont made a rare television appearance on the show ("Miss Lovelace Comes to Tea," 12 May 1959) as did Buster Keaton ("A Very Merry Christmas," 24 December 1958).

DONNY AND MARIE   ABC

23 JANUARY 1976–19 JANUARY 1979   The first variety hour hosted by a brother-and-sister team: Donny and Marie Osmond, two of the nine talented Osmond children. Both are excellent singers (she, "a little bit country," he, "a little bit rock and roll") as well as competent ice skaters; many routines were done on ice, and the dancing Ice Vanities were regular performers (the ice routines were dropped in the fall of 1978). Additional regulars included Jim Connell and Hank Garcia. The other Osmond siblings appeared frequently on the show (Donny had sung with his older brothers in the Osmonds). In the fall of 1977 designer Bob Mackie was hired to help dress up Marie's image and plans were undertaken to shift production of the series from Hollywood to Utah, the Osmonds' home state. Executive producer: Raymond Katz. Producers: Sid and Marty Krofft. See also *Marie; The Osmond Family Show*.

DON'T CALL ME CHARLIE   NBC

21 SEPTEMBER 1962–25 JANUARY 1963   Forgettable sitcom about an Iowa veterinarian who was drafted and ended up assigned to the Army in Paris. With Josh Peine as Private Judson McKay; John Hubbard as Colonel U. Charles ("Don't call me Charlie!") Barker; Alan Napier as General Steele; Cully Richards as Sergeant Wozniak; Arte Johnson as Corporal Lefkowitz; Louise Glenn as secretary Selma Yossarian; Linda Lawson as Pat Perry, the general's secretary; and Penny Santon as Madame Fatime.

THE DOODLES WEAVER SHOW NBC

9 JUNE 1951–1 SEPTEMBER 1951   A half hour of sight gags, costumery, and sound effects hosted by Doodles Weaver and featuring Lois Weaver (his wife) and Red Marshall. Weaver, whose real first name was Winstead, was the brother of NBC executive Sylvester "Pat" Weaver, the creative genius responsible for such shows as *Today* and *Tonight*. This series was a summer replacement for *Your Show of Shows*.

DOOGIE HOWSER, M.D. ABC

19 SEPTEMBER 1989–21 JULY 1993   Half-hour comedy-drama series from Steven Bochco (who created the series with David Kelley) about a child prodigy, with Neil Patrick Harris as sixteen-year-old Douglas "Doogie" Howser, the youngest physician in the country, a second-year resident at Eastman Medical Center; James B. Sikking as his father, Dr. David Howser; Belinda Montgomery as his mother, Katherine; Max Casella as Doogie's hormone-driven pal, Vinnie Delpino; Lawrence Pressman as chief of staff Dr. Canfield; Mitchell Anderson (1989–1991) as Dr. Jack McGuire; Kathryn Layng as Nurse Curly Spaulding; Lisa Dean Ryan (1989–1992) as Doogie's girlfriend, Wanda Plenn; Lucy Boryer as Vinnie's girlfriend, Jeannine; and Rif Hutton as Dr. Welch. In the fall of 1990 Markus Redmond joined the cast as Raymond Alexander, who became a hospital orderly; the character had appeared in an episode during the first season as the robber of a convenience store. As the series progressed, Doogie eventually moved out of his parents' house and into his own place, as Wanda went away to college. Appearing occasionally during the final season was Robyn Lively as Doogie's new girlfriend, Michele, a nurse.

THE DOOR WITH NO NAME NBC

6 JULY 1951–17 AUGUST 1951   A summer replacement for *Big Story,* this half-hour spy show starred Grant Richards as an American intelligence agent, Doug Carter, and Melville Ruick as his boss. Westbrook Van Voorhis narrated the series. See also *Doorway to Danger.*

DOORWAY TO DANGER NBC

4 JULY 1952–22 AUGUST 1952; 3 JULY 1953–28 AUGUST 1953   This half-hour spy series was twice a summer replacement for *Big Story.* It starred Roland Winters as secret agent John Randolph and Stacy Harris as agent Doug Carter. See also *The Door with No Name.*

DOORWAY TO FAME DUMONT

7 MARCH 1949–4 JULY 1949   This half-hour dramatic anthology series was significant because of a technical innovation it utilized: the actors performed in front of a simple black backdrop, while a second camera was trained on miniature sets or on painted backdrops. The two images were then blended in the control room to create the desired illusion.

THE DORIS DAY SHOW CBS

24 SEPTEMBER 1968–3 SEPTEMBER 1973   Doris Day was one of the few film stars whose initial entry into television proved successful; her situation comedy lasted five seasons and weathered four formats. Doris Day starred as Doris Martin in each of them. The first format found Doris, recently widowed, settling down on her uncle's farm with her two young sons. It featured Denver Pyle (1968–1970) as her uncle, Buck Webb; Tod Starke (1968–1971) as son Toby; Philip Brown (1968–1971) as son Billy; James Hampton (1968–1969) as Leroy B. Simpson, Buck's handyman; Fran Ryan (1968) as Aggie, the first housekeeper; Naomi Stevens (1969) as Juanita, the second housekeeper. As the second season began, Doris found work as an executive secretary for *Today's World* magazine. Pyle, Starke, and Brown remained and new additions to the cast included McLean Stevenson (1969–1971) as her boss, Michael Nicholson; Rose Marie (1969–1971) as coworker Myrna Gibbons; Paul Smith (1969–1971) as Ron Harvey, associate editor; Billy DeWolfe as fussy Willard Jarvis, Doris's neighbor. For the third season, Doris left the farm (and Denver Pyle left the series) and moved into an apartment over an Italian restaurant; joining the series were Kaye

Ballard (1970–1971) as Angie Palucci and Bernie Kopell (1970–1971) as Louie Palucci, the proprietors of the eatery. The fourth season saw the most dramatic change in format: Doris became a swinging single. Gone were the kids, as well as Stevenson and Marie. The final format lasted two seasons, longer than any of the others. It featured John Dehner (1971–1973) as editor Sy Bennett and Jackie Joseph (1971–1973) as his secretary, Jackie Parker (Doris had finally become a reporter). Occasionally appearing was Peter Lawford as her boyfriend, Dr. Peter Lawrence. Day's son, Terry Melcher, was executive producer of the series.

DOROTHY CBS
8 AUGUST 1979–29 AUGUST 1979   A four-episode half-hour sitcom set at the Hannah Huntley School for Girls. With Dorothy Loudon as the divorced music and drama teacher, Dorothy Banks; Russell Nype as Mr. Foley, the headmaster (and grandson of the founder); Priscilla Morrill as Lorna Cathcart, the French teacher; Kenneth Gilman as T. Jack Landis, the biology teacher; Linda Manz as fresh Frankie Sumter, a scholarship student; Elissa Leeds as Cissy; Susan Brecht as Meredith; and Michele Greene as Margo. Created by Nick Arnold, Madelyn Davis, and Bob Carroll, Jr., *Dorothy* should not be confused with NBC's *The Facts of Life,* another 1979 sitcom set at a girl's boarding school.

DO'S AND DONT'S ABC
3 JULY 1952–18 SEPTEMBER 1952   Hints on safety were dispensed on this half-hour public service series.

DOTTO CBS/NBC
Daytime: 6 JANUARY 1958–15 AUGUST 1958 (CBS); *Nighttime:* 1 JULY 1958–19 AUGUST 1958 (NBC)   Jack Narz hosted this game show which, like the parlor game, required contestants to identify a figure outlined in dots; by answering questions correctly, contestants saw the lines connecting the dots. *Dotto* is probably better remembered as one of the first series implicated in the quiz show scandals. In August 1958, a standby contestant accidentally happened upon some notes left by another contestant; the notes contained the answers to the questions asked that day. The discovery led to an investigation of game shows by the New York District Attorney and precipitated the cancellation of several series, including *Dotto*.

THE DOTTY MACK SHOW DUMONT/ABC
16 FEBRUARY 1953–25 AUGUST 1953 (DUMONT); 3 SEPTEMBER 1953–3 SEPTEMBER 1956 (ABC)   The regulars on this variety series, broadcast from Cincinnati, performed pantomime routines to popular recordings. Surprisingly, the show lasted three years. Assisting former model Dotty Mack were Colin Male and Bob Braun. The DuMont series was originally titled *Girl Alone.*

DOUBLE DARE CBS
13 DECEMBER 1976–29 APRIL 1977   Alex Trebek hosted this daytime game show on which two contestants sought to identify subjects from descriptive clues; the first contestant to identify the subject could then "dare" the opponent to identify the subject from subsequent clues. If the opponent then missed, the first contestant won extra money. The first contestant to win $500 faced "The Spoilers," a panel of three Ph.D.s. If two of the spoilers failed to identify a subject after four clues, the contestant was awarded $5,000. The show was a Mark Goodson–Bill Todman Production.

DOUBLE DARE CBS
10 APRIL 1985–22 MAY 1985   The second of the three series of this title was an hour crime show about a suave San Francisco thief who, to avoid prosecution, agreed to help out the cops if they would agree to let him team up with his ex-partner, now in jail. With Billy Dee Williams as the thief, Billy Diamond; Ken Wahl as his ex-con partner, Ken Sisko; Joseph Maher as Sylvester, Billy's butler; and Janet Carroll as Lieutenant Samantha Warner (Jennifer Warren played the part in the pilot). Garry

Michael White created the series, of which six episodes were aired. Costar Ken Wahl went on to star in the more successful *Wiseguy* in 1987.

DOUBLE DARE   NICK/SYNDICATED
6 OCTOBER 1986– (NICKELODEON); 1989–1991 (SYNDICATED)
FAMILY DOUBLE DARE   FOX
3 APRIL 1988–23 JULY 1988   The third series titled *Double Dare* was an updated version of the venerable game show *Beat the Clock,* aimed at kids. Marc Summers hosted the program, on which two pairs of children competed first in a quiz segment. If one team did not know the answer to a question, it could "dare" the other team to answer; that team could elect to answer or could "double dare" the first team. The first team could then choose either to answer the question or to take the "physical challenge," i.e., perform a stunt of some kind, which usually involved making a mess. The winning team was given the opportunity to negotiate an obstacle course within a specified time limit for a series of prizes. During part of its Nickelodeon run the show was known as *Super Sloppy Double Dare.* In 1988 a second version was introduced on the Fox network, *Family Double Dare,* in which groups of parents and children competed in a similar format. Both variants were also aired on Nickelodeon.

DOUBLE EXPOSURE   CBS
13 MARCH 1961–29 SEPTEMBER 1961   Steve Dunne hosted this daytime game show on which contestants sought to identify a picture hidden beneath a large jigsaw puzzle.

THE DOUBLE LIFE OF HENRY PHYFE   ABC
13 JANUARY 1966–1 SEPTEMBER 1966   This situation comedy—a midseason replacement for *O.K. Crackerby!*—was a pale imitation of *Get Smart.* Red Buttons, whose TV appearances had been infrequent since the cancellation of his own series in 1954, starred as Henry Phyfe, a bumbling accountant hired by American intelligence to impersonate a deceased enemy agent known as U-31. Also featured were Fred Clark as Chief Hannahan, his immediate superior; Parley Baer as Mr. Hamble, Phyfe's boss at the accounting firm; Zeme North as Judy, Phyfe's girlfriend, who was unaware of his double life; and Marge Redmond as Phyfe's landlady, Florence.

DOUBLE OR NOTHING   CBS/NBC
6 OCTOBER 1952–2 JULY 1954 (CBS) 5 JUNE 1953–3 JULY 1953 (NBC)   One of the many game shows hosted by Bert Parks, *Double or Nothing* began on radio in 1940. Each show featured five contestants in a question-and-answer format; contestants jointly agreed whether to try to double their winnings on the "Double or Nothing" round, and split their earnings evenly. The CBS version was a daytime entry; the NBC version was a prime-time program.

DOUBLE PLAY   SYNDICATED
1953   Sports personalities were interviewed by Leo Durocher and his then wife, Laraine Day, on this series.

DOUBLE RUSH   CBS
4 JANUARY 1995–12 APRIL 1995   After several seasons as Eldin the painter on *Murphy Brown,* Robert Pastorelli was given his own sitcom. This one was set at a Manhattan bicycle courier service, and Pastorelli played its owner, Johnny Verona, a former rock musician. Also featured were David Arquette, the madman bike messenger; Corinne Bohrer as Zoe Fuller, a down-on-her-luck Harvard Business School graduate, who stumbled into a job as the bookkeeper; Adam Goldberg as Leo; D. L. Hughley as Marlon; Phil Leeds as the ancient messenger known simply as Kid, who didn't use a bike; and Sam Lloyd as Barkley, the dispatcher. Stephen Nathan and Diane English created the series.

DOUBLE TALK (CELEBRITY DOUBLE TALK)   ABC
18 AUGUST 1986–19 DECEMBER 1986   On this daytime game show two two-member teams, each with a celebrity and a contestant, tried to solve word puzzles by decipher-

ing the "double talk" (e.g., a clue like "Freezing Dollars") into plain English ("Cold Cash"). Henry Polic II, who was a regular on *Webster* at the time, hosted. By mid-September the show had been retitled *Celebrity Double Talk*.

DOUBLE TROUBLE   NBC
4 APRIL 1984–5 SEPTEMBER 1984; 1 DECEMBER 1984–21 AUGUST 1985   This innocuous sitcom about twin high-schoolers—one zany, the other serious—was reminiscent of *The Patty Duke Show* some two decades earlier. There were two principal differences, however: in *Double Trouble* real-life twins played the leading roles (while Patty Duke had played both roles herself), and *The Patty Duke Show* lasted three times longer. When the show premiered in the spring of 1984, it was set in Des Moines, with the twins in high school. Jean Sagal played Kate Foster, the headstrong, impulsive twin; and Liz Sagal played Allison, the studious, sensible one. Also featured were Donnelly Rhodes as their widowed father, Art; and Pat Richardson as Art's woman friend, Beth McConnell. When the show returned in the winter of 1984, the twins had moved to New York City to live with their aunt, with Allison studying fashion design and Kate hoping to become an actress. Rhodes and Richardson were gone. Joining the cast were Barbara Barrie as the girls' aunt, Margo Foster, author of the "Bongo Bear" kids' books; James Vallely as Charles Kincaid, and Jonathan Schmock as Billy Batalato, two actors who also lived in Margo's townhouse; and Michael D. Roberts as Mr. Arrechia, Allison's pompous fashion instructor. In real life the Sagal twins were the daughters of the late film director Boris Sagal and the younger sisters of Katey Sagal of *Married . . . with Children.*.

DOUBLE UP   NBC
12 SEPTEMBER 1992–24 OCTOBER 1992   J. D. Roth hosted this Saturday morning kids' game show on which a brother and sister tried to choose the ideal date for each other by quizzing panels of three girls or three boys.

DOUG   NICK
11 AUGUST 1991–   The central character in this half-hour cartoon series was eleven-year-old Doug Funnie, who hung around with his pal Skeeter and his dog, Porkchop.

DOUGH RE MI   NBC
24 FEBRUARY 1958–30 DECEMBER 1960   Hosted by Gene Rayburn, this daytime game show was similar to *Name That Tune:* Contestants tried to identify songs after hearing a limited number of notes.

DOUGLAS FAIRBANKS PRESENTS   SYNDICATED
1953–1956   Dramatic anthology series hosted by, and occasionally starring, Douglas Fairbanks, Jr. Buster Keaton's first dramatic appearance was on this show ("The Awakening"); Christopher Lee, star of countless British horror films, made his American TV debut in an episode entitled "Destination Milan." In some areas, the show was known by another title, such as the name of the sponsor; in New York, for example, the series was called *Rheingold Theatre*.

DOWN AND OUT IN BEVERLY HILLS   FOX
25 JULY 1987–12 SEPTEMBER 1987   An unsuccessful sitcom based on the 1986 film of the same title, which itself was a remake of Jean Renoir's 1932 film, *Boudu Saved from Drowning*. The TV version starred Hector Elizondo as Dave Whiteman, a successful clothes hanger manufacturer who lived in Beverly Hills; Anita Morris as his wife, Barbara; Evan Richards (repeating his film role) as their son, Max; Eileen Seeley as their daughter, Jenny; Tim Thomerson as Jerry Baskin, a down and out drifter who moved into the Whitemans' mansion after Dave pulled him from the swimming pool; and April Ortiz as Carmen, the Whitemans' maid. Mike the Dog also repeated his film role as Matisse. The half-hour series had a special preview on 26 April, but did not begin weekly telecasts until July.

DOWN HOME   NBC

12 APRIL 1990–12 MAY 1990; 28 FEBRUARY 1991   Half-hour sitcom starring Judith
Ivey as Kate McCrorey, a successful Manhattan executive who returned home to
Hadley Cove, Texas, to help save her father's business. With Dakin Matthews as her
dad, Walt, owner of McCrorey's Landing, a fishing pier with an attached café; Eric
Allan Kramer as her dim-witted brother, Drew, who worked for Walt; Gedde
Watanabe as Tran Van Din, an Asian immigrant who also worked for Walt; Ray
Baker as Kate's old boyfriend, Wade Prescott, a successful local businessman who
hoped to develop McCrorey's Landing; and Tim Scott as Grover, the mayor of
Hadley Cove. Barton Dean created the series, which NBC scheduled as a backup
series on its 1990–1991 roster.

DOWN THE SHORE   FOX

21 JUNE 1992–13 SEPTEMBER 1992; 3 DECEMBER 1992–5 AUGUST 1993   A Belmar, New
Jersey, beach house was the setting of this sitcom, where six young New Yorkers
gathered. With Louis Mandylor as Aldo, the ladies' man; Anna Gunn as Arden; Lew
Schneider as the nice guy, Zack, a teacher; Pamela Segall (summer 1992) as Miranda;
Cathryn de Prume as Donna Shipko; Tom McGowan as Eddie, the girth-enhanced
virgin; and Nancy Sorel (December 1992–1993) as the new roomie, Sammy.

DOWN YOU GO   DUMONT/CBS/ABC/NBC

30 MAY 1951–27 MAY 1955 (DUMONT); 18 JUNE 1955–3 SEPTEMBER 1955 (CBS); 15
SEPTEMBER 1955–14 JUNE 1956 (ABC); 16 JUNE 1956–8 SEPTEMBER 1956 (NBC)   One
of the few programs broadcast over all four commercial networks, *Down You Go* was
a prime-time game show hosted by Dr. Bergen Evans. The game, played by a panel
of celebrities, was similar to "Hangman." The object was to guess a mystery word or
phrase. The panel was shown a row of blanks representing the number of letters in
the secret word or phrase; panelists then took turns suggesting a letter of the alphabet. A panelist who suggested an incorrect letter was eliminated from the game.
Among the many panelists who appeared over the years were Carmelita Pope, Toni
Gilman, Robert Breen, Francis Coughlin, Georgann Johnson, William Williams,
Patricia Cutts, and Arthur Treacher.

DOWNTOWN   CBS

27 SEPTEMBER 1986–27 DECEMBER 1986; 22 AUGUST 1987–5 SEPTEMBER 1987   A lame
crime show about a Los Angeles cop who was asked to supervise a diverse group of
four parolees, who sometimes tried to assist him with his cases. With Michael Nouri as
Detective John Forney; Blair Underwood (later of *L.A. Law* fame) as Terry Corsaro, a
runaway; Millicent Martin as swindler Harriet Conover, in whose mansion the parolees all lived; Mariska Hargitay (daughter of Jayne Mansfield) as troubled teen Jesse
Smith; Robert Englund (better recognized as Freddy Krueger in the *Nightmare on Elm
Street* films) as imposter Dennis Shotoffer; Virginia Capers as social worker Delia
Bonner; and David Paymer as Captain Kiner, Forney's supervisor.

DRACULA—THE SERIES   SYNDICATED

1990–1991   A modern-day adaptation of the classic vampire legend. With Geordie
Johnson as Alexander Lucard, Dracula's latest incarnation, a wealthy industrialist who
lived in a European castle (the name "A. Lucard," of course, is "Dracula" spelled
backwards; a similar name, "Alucard," was used in the 1943 film *Son of Dracula*);
Jacob Tierney and Joe Roncetti as young brothers Max and Chris Townsend, who were
sent by their globetrotting mother to live with their European uncle, and quickly
learned of Lucard's identity; Bernard Behrens as the uncle, Gustav Helsing, a fourth-
generation vampire hunter; Geraint Wyn Davies as Gustav's son, Klaus, a vampire
(Davies would go on to play a vampire again in *Forever Knight*); and Mia Kirshner as
Sophie Metternich, a student who boarded with Gustav.

DRAGNET   NBC

16 DECEMBER 1951–6 SEPTEMBER 1959; 12 JANUARY 1967–10 SEPTEMBER 1970 One of
the most famous (and often lampooned) crime shows in television history, *Dragnet*

began on radio in 1949. It starred Jack Webb as Sergeant Joe Friday, a hardworking Los Angeles cop who seemed to have no personal life and no interests other than police work. Civil but not quite courteous (everyone was "ma'am" or "sir"), tireless but not quite overzealous ("It's my job. I'm a cop."), Friday pursued every lead, interviewed every witness ("Just the facts, ma'am"), and eventually apprehended the wrongdoer. Webb, who owned an interest in the series, directed most episodes, and also served as narrator, stressed realism in *Dragnet:* police jargon, paperwork, and intensive investigation characterized the show. Episodes were supposedly based on actual cases; as announcers Hal Gibney and (later) George Fenneman stated at the end of each show: "The story you have just seen is true. The names have been changed to protect the innocent." The emphasis on authenticity also characterized most of the shows which Webb later produced, such as *Adam-12* and *Emergency!*

When *Dragnet* came to TV in 1951, Barton Yarborough was featured as Friday's partner, Sergeant Ben Romero. Yarborough died after three episodes were filmed; for the rest of the first season Barney Phillips was seen as Friday's partner, Sergeant Ed Jacobs. In the fall of 1952 Ben Alexander (a former child star in several Cecil B. DeMille films) replaced Phillips as Friday's sidekick, Officer Frank Smith; Smith's character gave the show a touch of comic relief, offering counterpoint to Friday's matter-of-fact character. By the time *Dragnet* left the air in 1959, Friday and Smith had earned promotions to lieutenant and sergeant respectively. Occasionally a female character was introduced as a romantic interest for Friday, though no serious relationship ever developed. Dorothy Abbott appeared as Ann Baker in the fall of 1954, and Marjie Millar was seen as Sharon Maxwell, a civilian who worked in the Records Bureau, during the spring of 1956.

Eight years later a new version of *Dragnet* returned to NBC as a midseason replacement for *The Hero.* It was titled *Dragnet '67* (and later *Dragnet '68,* etc.). Webb again starred as Sergeant Joe Friday (how he lost his former rank was never explained). Harry Morgan was featured as his partner, Officer Bill Gannon (Webb and Morgan had appeared together in a 1950 film, *Dark City*). Many of the shows dealt with topical issues, especially student dissidence and drug use. The show seemed a bit heavy-handed in its second incarnation but lasted two and a half seasons nevertheless. The little details that helped fashion *Dragnet*'s unique style will long be remembered: Walter Schumann's suspenseful theme, the epilog relating the fate of the evening's evildoers, and the chiseling of "Mark VII" (the name of Webb's production company) in stone at the show's conclusion.

In 1987 *Saturday Night Live* alumnus Dan Aykroyd paid comic respect to the series in a theatrical film; Aykroyd starred as Joe Friday's nephew, Tom Hanks played his partner, and Harry Morgan appeared as their supervisor, Captain Gannon.

In the fall of 1990 a new version of the TV series appeared: see *The New Dragnet.*

DRAGON'S LAIR   ABC
8 SEPTEMBER 1984–27 APRIL 1985   A Saturday-morning cartoon series based on the popular video game, featuring Dirk the Daring, his horse, Bert, The King, and Princess Daphne.

THE DRAK PACK   CBS
6 SEPTEMBER 1980–5 SEPTEMBER 1981   Saturday-morning cartoon show about the Drak Pack, a trio of teenagers (Frankie, Howler, and Drak, Jr., all descended from famous monsters) who did battle with OGRE (Organization of Generally Rotten Enterprises), headed by the sinister Doctor Dread.

DRAW ME A LAUGH   ABC
15 JANUARY 1949–5 FEBRUARY 1949   This short-lived series was part variety show and part game show. The object of the game portion was for cartoonist Mel Casson, a regular, to sketch a cartoon from an idea submitted by a viewer. Simultaneously, a studio contestant attempted to sketch a cartoon, having been given the gag line of the cartoon. A panel then chose the funnier cartoon. The game portion was interspersed with music from folksinger Oscar Brand.

DRAW TO WIN   CBS
22 APRIL 1952–10 JUNE 1952   A Tuesday-night game show which briefly replaced *See It Now.* Henry Morgan hosted the series, on which a panel of four cartoonists tried to identify subjects drawn by home viewers.

DRAWING POWER   NBC
11 OCTOBER 1980–16 MAY 1981   This Saturday-afternoon series combined live action with cartoons. Set at an animation studio, it featured Bob Kaliban, Kari Page, and Lenny Schultz. Regular segments included "Superperson U.," "Pet Peeves," "Turkey of the Week," and "Bus Stop."

DREAM GIRL OF '67   ABC
19 DECEMBER 1966–29 DECEMBER 1967   This daytime game show was a yearlong beauty pageant. Each day four young women competed for the "Dream Girl of the Day" title. The four daily winners competed for the weekly title on Fridays; the weekly winners all competed at year's end. Dick Stewart hosted the series until September, when he was replaced by Paul Petersen (formerly of *The Donna Reed Show*). See also *Dream Girl U.S.A.*

DREAM GIRL U.S.A.   SYNDICATED
1986   Ken Howard hosted this updated version of *Dream Girl of '67,* on which a panel of four celebrities judged groups of four aspirants in the typical beauty contest categories.

DREAM HOUSE   ABC/NBC
Nighttime: 27 MARCH 1968–19 SEPTEMBER 1968 (ABC); *Daytime:* 1 APRIL 1968–2 JANUARY 1970 (ABC); 4 APRIL 1983–29 JUNE 1984 (NBC)   Couples had the chance to win a house on this game show. On the ABC versions, which were hosted by Mike Darrow, three couples competed in a question-and-answer format, and the winning couple won the furnishings for one room of a house. If a couple won seven times, they were awarded the grand prize, a "dream house" valued at up to $40,000, built for them on the site of their choice. On the NBC version, hosted by Bob Eubanks some thirteen years later, two couples competed and the winning pair again won a room of furnishings; however, a couple needed to win only five times in order to obtain the house.

DREAM ON   HBO/FOX
8 JULY 1990–27 MARCH 1996 (HBO); 8 JANUARY 1995–16 APRIL 1995 (FOX); 19 JUNE 1995–3 JULY 1995 (FOX)   Short clips from vintage films and TV series (all from MCA's archives) punctuated this adult sitcom about a divorced thirty-six-year-old book editor. Brian Benben starred as Martin Tupper, who tried to get a love life off the ground as he struggled in his thankless job. Also featured were Wendie Malick as his ex-wife, Judith; Chris Demetral as their teenage son, Jeremy; Denny Dillon as Martin's abrasive secretary, Toby Pedalbee; and Jeff Joseph (1990–1991) and Dorien Wilson (1991–1996) as Martin's best friend, Eddie Charles, host of a New York talk show. Michael McKean joined the cast in 1991, and was occasionally seen as Gibby Fisk, Martin's overbearing boss. Brief movie and TV clips were deftly inserted throughout the episodes, to amplify Martin's thoughts or to complement the storyline. The HBO version included four-letter words and bare breasts; bowdlerized alternate takes were produced as well, for later use on broadcast outlets such as Fox, which aired selected reruns in 1995.

DREAM STREET   NBC
13 APRIL 1989–19 MAY 1989   An hour dramatic series from Ed Zwick and Marshall Herskovitz, the creators of *thirtysomething.* Set in Hoboken, N. J., it featured Dale Midkiff as Denis Debeau, who took over the family refrigeration business from his ill father; Peter Frechette as Denis's older brother, Harry; David Barry Gray as Denis's younger brother, Eric; Tom Signorelli as their father, Peter; Thomas Calabro as Denis's childhood friend, Joey Coltrera, now a mobster; Cecil Hoffmann as Joey's

girlfriend, Joni Goldstein; Jo Anderson as Denis's girlfriend, Marianne McKinney; Victor Argo as Anthony Coltrera; and Debra Mooney as Lillian Debeau.

DREAMS   CBS
3 OCTOBER 1984–31 OCTOBER 1984   This short-lived sitcom attempted to cash in on the music video craze by telling the story of Dreams, an aspiring Philadelphia rock band; performance videos were incorporated into each episode. With John Stamos as guitarist Gino Manelli; Cain Devore as bassist Phil Taylor (Gino and Phil worked as machinists by day); Jami Gertz as vocalist Martha Spino; Albert Macklin as keyboardist Moe Weiner; Valerie Stevenson as the newest band member, vocalist Lisa Copley; David Logeman as Angie, the drummer (oddly, he was the only band member not identified in the show's opening credits); Ron Karabatsos as Frank Franconi, owner of Club Frank, where Dreams performed; and Sandy Freeman as Louise, Frank's wife. A "soundtrack" LP from the band was released after the show had left the air.

DREXELL'S CLASS   FOX
19 SEPTEMBER 1991–25 JUNE 1992   Dabney Coleman starred in this sitcom as cantankerous Otis Drexell, a tax cheat forced to take a job teaching fifth grade in order to satisfy his obligation to the IRS. Also featured were Dakin Matthews as Roscoe Davis, the other fifth grade teacher, whom Drexell couldn't stand; A. J. Langer as Drexell's daughter Melissa; Brittany Murphy as Drexell's daughter Brenda; Jason Biggs as student Willie Trankis; Damian Cagnolatti as student Kenny; Heidi Zeigler as student Nicole; Randy Graff (1991) as Francine Itkin, principal of the Grantwood Elementary School; and Edie McClurg (1992) as Marilyn Ridge, the new principal.

THE DREW CAREY SHOW   ABC
13 SEPTEMBER 1995–   Following a stint on the short-lived sitcom *The Good Life,* standup comic Drew Carey headlined his own series. Here he played Drew Carey, the assistant director of personnel at a Cleveland department store, who lived by himself and hung out with three friends. The supporting cast included Diedrich Bader as Oswald, a disc jockey; Christa Miller as Kate; and Ryan Stiles as Lewis, a janitor at a pharmaceutical ccompany. Kathy Kinney was occasionally seen as coworker Mimi, and Katy Selverstone appeared as Drew's girlfriend, Lisa.

THE DREW PEARSON SHOW   ABC/DUMONT
4 MAY 1952–9 NOVEMBER 1952 (ABC); 24 DECEMBER 1952–18 MARCH 1953 (DUMONT)   A half hour of commentary by Washington political columnist Drew Pearson. See also *Washington Merry-Go-Round.*

DROIDS: THE ADVENTURES OF R2D2 and C3PO   ABC
7 SEPTEMBER 1985–22 FEBRUARY 1986   The popular androids from the movie *Star Wars* were the principal characters in this Saturday-morning cartoon series. In March 1986 the series was combined with *Ewoks* to form *The Ewoks and Droids Adventure Hour.* See also *Ewoks.*

DROODLES   NBC
21 JUNE 1954–24 SEPTEMBER 1954   Roger Price hosted this lighthearted game show on which celebrity panelists tried to think of captions for line drawings submitted by home viewers or sketched by Price himself. The panel included playwright Marc Connelly, Denise Lor, and Carl Reiner. The show was scheduled irregularly during the summer of 1954.

DROOPY, MASTER DETECTIVE   FOX
2 OCTOBER 1993–1 JANUARY 1994   Droopy, the laconic basset hound created by Chuck Jones, came to television in this half-hour Saturday morning cartoon show. He was a private detective, and was assisted by his faithful son, Dripple.

THE DUCK FACTORY   NBC
12 APRIL 1984–11 JULY 1984   A small, struggling Hollywood cartoon studio was the
setting for this half-hour sitcom from MTM Enterprises. Featured were: Jim Carrey
as Skip Tarkenton, who arrived in Los Angeles and landed a job at Buddy Winkler
Productions just after the death of its founder; Jack Gilford as veteran animator
Brooks Carmichael; Don Messick (the real-life voice of such cartoon characters as
Boo Boo of *Yogi Bear,* Ruff of *Ruff and Reddy,* and Scooby-Doo, to name a few) as
voice man Wally Wooster; Jay Tarses as writer Marty Fenneman; Teresa Ganzel as
Winkler's dippy widow, Sheree; Julie Payne as Aggie Aylesworth, the martinet busi-
ness manager; Nancy Lane as Andrea, the film editor; and Clarence Gilyard, Jr., as
Roland Cope, another animator. Allan Burns and Herbert Klynn created the series.

DUCKTALES   SYNDICATED
1987–1992   A new series of cartoons from Disney Studios (the studio's first daily
TV animated series), starring Scrooge McDuck as an adventurer trotting around the
globe with his three grand-nephews (Huey, Dewey, and Louie), a girl duck (Webby),
and his trusty pilot (Launchpad). Alan Young supplied the voice of Scrooge.

DUDLEY   CBS
16 APRIL 1993–14 MAY 1993   Half-hour sitcom starring Dudley Moore as New York
nightclub pianist Dudley Bristol, a divorced father who reluctantly agreed to take in
his teenage son. Harley Cross played the son, Fred, and Joanna Cassidy was Dudley's
ex, Laraine. Also featured were Max Wright as Paul, Dudley's manager; Lupe
Ontiveros as his housekeeper, Marta; and Joel Brooks as Harold Krowten, owner of
Liaisons, the nightspot where Dudley performed. Not long after the quick demise of
this series, Moore returned to CBS for an equally brief stint: see *Daddy's Girls.*

THE DUDLEY DO-RIGHT SHOW   ABC
27 APRIL 1969–6 SEPTEMBER 1970   Sunday-morning cartoon series featuring Dudley
Do-Right, the inept Mountie who loved Nell Fenwick, daughter of Inspector Ray K.
Fenwick, Dudley's boss. Alas, Dudley's love was unrequited, for Nell was in love
with Dudley's horse, Horse. Jay Ward's cartoon characters originally appeared on
The Bullwinkle Show.

DUE SOUTH   CBS
22 SEPTEMBER 1994–7 JULY 1995; 8 DECEMBER 1995–   On this light hour crime show
a straight-as-an-arrow Canadian Mountie was teamed up with a streetwise Chicago
detective. With Paul Gross as the Mountie, Benton Fraser; David Marciano as
Detective Ray Vecchio; Beau Starr as the boss, Lieutenant Walsh; Daniel Kash as
Detective Louis Guardino; Tony Craig as Detective Jack Huey; and Catherine
Bruhier as Elaine, a civilian aide at the police precinct. The pilot for the series was ·
telecast as a made-for-TV movie on 23 April 1994, and was rerun on 15 September, a
week before the series premiere. Paul Haggis was the creator.

DUET   FOX
19 APRIL 1987–20 AUGUST 1989   This half-hour sitcom changed considerably during
its two-and-a-half-year run. It started as the chronicle of two 30-ish singles who met
and fell in love, and ended when one of the supporting characters was given her own
series. At the outset, the two central characters were Ben Coleman (played by
Matthew Laurance), an aspiring mystery writer, and Laura Kelly (Mary Page Keller), a caterer. Their relationship unfolded against the backdrop of Ben's best friend
and his wife, yuppies Richard (Chris Lemmon), a patio furniture salesman, and
Linda Phillips (Alison LaPlaca), a film studio executive. Also around were Laura's
wacky younger sister, Jane (Jodi Thelen); the Phillips' maid, Geneva (Arleen
Sorkin); Linda's boss, Hayden Cooper (Larry Poindexter); and Ben's dog, Reuben
(Bo). During the next season and a half, Ben and Laura were married, Ben's first
novel had been published, Richard had quit his job to become a cocktail pianist, and
he and Linda had a baby.
    In the fall of 1988 the action had been moved up: Ben and Laura had returned

from a two-year honeymoon trip, which explained why the Phillips' baby had become a talking preschooler. Ginger Orsi joined the cast as little Amanda Phillips. After Ben and Laura's return, however, little was seen of them as the episodes focused increasingly on the Phillipses, particularly on Linda, whose delightfully bitchy character had become popular with viewers. By the end of the season Linda had found a new job as a realtor. At the end of the summer the show's title was changed, as Matthew Laurance and Jodi Thelen were dropped. See *Open House*.

DUFFY'S TAVERN   SYNDICATED
1954   An unsuccessful attempt to bring a popular radio program to television. Ed Gardner created the series, which ran on radio from 1941 to 1951. Gardner starred as Archie, the manager of Duffy's Tavern, a seedy bar and grille on New York's Third Avenue; Duffy, the owner, was never seen. Also featured were Pattee Chapman as Miss Duffy, Duffy's husband-hunting daughter; Alan Reed as Archie's slow-witted comrade, Charlie Finnegan. The radio series had been as much a showcase for guest stars (such as Bing Crosby and Clifton Fadiman) as a situation comedy; the TV adaptation was merely the latter.

THE DUKE   NBC
2 JULY 1954–10 SEPTEMBER 1954   This summer sitcom had a fairly interesting story line: a boxer with a penchant for the arts suddenly quit the fight game to open a night club. With Paul Gilbert as Duke Zenlee; Allen Jenkins as Johnny, his former trainer; Phyllis Coates (formerly featured on *Superman*) as Gloria, his girlfriend; and Rudy Cromwell as Claude Stroud, his partner in the club.

THE DUKE   NBC
5 APRIL 1979–18 MAY 1979   Miniseries about an aging Chicago boxer who decided to become a private eye. With Robert Conrad (who actually fought professionally in his younger days) as Duke Ramsey; Larry Manetti as Joe Cadillac, a promoter of less than impeccable integrity; Red West as Sergeant Mick O'Brien; Patricia Conwell as Duke's friend, Dedra, a wealthy socialite. Stephen J. Cannell was the executive producer for Stephen J. Cannell Productions in association with Universal TV.

THE DUKES   CBS
5 FEBRUARY 1983–5 NOVEMBER 1983   In this animated Saturday-morning spinoff from *The Dukes of Hazzard,* the characters were involved in an automobile race around the world.

THE DUKES OF HAZZARD   CBS
26 JANUARY 1979–16 AUGUST 1985   An hour comedy-adventure series, *The Dukes of Hazzard* told the tale of the fast-driving, fun-loving cousins of the Duke clan, who lived in southern Hazzard County and who spent their time outwitting Hazzard's buffoonish political boss and his inept lawmen. The program was popular, especially with children, because of its emphasis on action mixed with slapstick.

The cast included Tom Wopat as Luke Duke; John Schneider as Bo Duke; Catherine Bach as Daisy Duke (Daisy, Bo, and Luke were all cousins); Denver Pyle as sage Uncle Jesse; Sorrell Booke as potbellied Jefferson Davis "Boss" Hogg, Hazzard County's thoroughly corrupt boss; James Best as Sheriff Rosco Coltrane, Hogg's dim-witted aide; Sonny Shroyer (1979–1980; 1982–1985) as Deputy Enos Strate; Ben Jones as Cooter; Rick Hurst (1980–   ) as Deputy Cletus; and Waylon Jennings (who wrote and sang the show's theme, "Good Ol' Boys") as The Balladeer, who provided the offscreen narration. The *real* star of the show, at least to the kids, was the Dukes' car, a 1969 Dodge Charger known as the General Lee; car chases and automotive acrobatics were an integral part of every episode. On the average, three General Lees were used each week. Wear and tear was so great (particularly from jumps) that few, if any, of them could be used again; thus, the *Dukes* staff was constantly in the market to acquire '69 Chargers for use on the program.

Scheduled on Fridays as the lead-in to *Dallas, The Dukes of Hazzard* ranked in the top ten prime-time shows for three seasons, from 1979 to 1982. The popularity of the program led to the licensing and manufacture of millions of dollars worth of *Dukes*-related merchandise. In 1982 costars Wopat and Schneider claimed to be owed substantial sums from the sale of that merchandise; they also claimed to be dissatisfied with the quality of the scripts. Suits and countersuits followed, and Wopat and Schneider sat out the 1982–1983 season. On the show, Bo and Luke were said to have left Hazzard County to race on the NASCAR circuit, and two new Duke cousins suddenly appeared: Byron Cherry as Coy, and Christopher Mayer as Vance. As the show's ratings plummeted during the season, the lawsuits were settled, and Wopat and Schneider returned to their roles in late February 1983; Mayer and Cherry lasted out the season but did not return thereafter.

Supplied by Warner Brothers Television, *The Dukes of Hazzard* lasted for 143 episodes, and sired two spinoffs: *Enos,* a prime-time series starring Sonny Shroyer, and *The Dukes,* a Saturday-morning cartoon show.

DUMB AND DUMBER   ABC
28 OCTOBER 1995–   Half-hour Saturday morning cartoon show, based on the 1994 hit movie of the same title. The central characters were two intellectually challenged pals, Harry and Lloyd.

THE DUMPLINGS   NBC
28 JANUARY 1976–31 MARCH 1976   One of Norman Lear's most forgettable ventures, this sitcom told the story of a happily married couple who ran a luncheonette (Dudley's Take-Out) in a New York skyscraper. With James Coco as Joe Dumpling; Geraldine Brooks as Angela Dumpling; George S. Irving as Charles Sweetzer, executive vice president of the Bristol Oil Company, located upstairs; Jane Connell as Norah McKenna, Sweetzer's secretary; George Furth as Frederic Steele; Marcia Rodd as Stephanie, Angela's sister; and Mort Marshall as Cully, the Dumplings' employee. The show was produced by Don Nicholl, Michael Ross, and Bernie West.

DUNDEE AND THE CULHANE   CBS
6 SEPTEMBER 1967–13 DECEMBER 1967   The most interesting feature of this western was probably its title. It starred John Mills as Dundee, a British lawyer who roamed the West with a feisty young American lawyer, The Culhane (played by Sean Garrison). Mike Dann, chief of CBS programming during the 1960s, disclosed in a 1968 *TV Guide* interview that the network had decided to cancel the show before it premiered. Network officials had been pleased with the pilot, but were disappointed after reviewing the scripts for the next several episodes; the decision was made in September to replace it with *The Jonathan Winters Show* in December.

DUNGEONS & DRAGONS   CBS
17 SEPTEMBER 1983–30 AUGUST 1986; 20 JUNE 1987–5 SEPTEMBER 1987   This half-hour Saturday-morning cartoon show was inspired by Dungeons and Dragons, the role-playing fantasy game that achieved popularity in the 1970s. The central characters in the series were six youngsters who find themselves trapped in a mysterious fantasy land; they were searching for a way to get back to Earth.

THE DUNNINGER SHOW   NBC/ABC
25 JUNE 1955–10 SEPTEMBER 1955 (NBC); 9 MAY 1956–10 OCTOBER 1956 (ABC)
Master mentalist Joseph Dunninger, who had cohosted *The Bigelow Show* with Paul Winchell some years earlier, hosted two summer shows on which he demonstrated his mind-reading prowess. A reward of $10,000 was offered each week to anyone who could prove that Dunninger was a fake; it was never claimed.

THE DuPONT SHOW STARRING JUNE ALLYSON
See THE JUNE ALLYSON SHOW

DuPONT THEATER   ABC
30 OCTOBER 1956–4 JUNE 1957

THE DuPONT SHOW OF THE MONTH   **CBS**
29 SEPTEMBER 1957–21 MARCH 1961
THE DuPONT SHOW OF THE WEEK   **NBC**
17 SEPTEMBER 1961–6 SEPTEMBER 1964   DuPont sponsored an anthology series on
each of the three major commercial networks. The first, on ABC, ran for one season
in a half-hour weekly format. The second, which lasted four seasons on CBS, was a
series of ninety-minute monthly specials. Most of those presentations were of well
known novels and plays, including: "A Tale of Two Cities," with Denholm Elliott,
Gracie Fields, and George C. Scott (in his first major TV role, 27 March 1958); "The
Red Mill," with Harpo Marx, Mike Nichols and Elaine May, and Donald O'Connor
(19 April 1958); "Wuthering Heights," with Richard Burton (in his American TV
dramatic debut, 9 May 1958); "The Count of Monte Cristo," with Colleen Dewhurst
and Hurd Hatfield (28 October 1958); "The Browning Version," with Sir John Gielgud (in his American TV debut, 23 April 1959); "I, Don Quixote," with Lee J. Cobb
(from which the musical *Man of La Mancha* was adapted, 9 November 1959); "Arrowsmith," with Diane Baker, Ivan Dixon, and Oscar Homolka (17 January 1960);
and "Ethan Frome," with Sterling Hayden (18 February 1960). In 1961 DuPont
switched its sponsorship to NBC and inaugurated a weekly hour-long format; most of
the presentations on this series were dramatizations of real-life incidents, though
some documentaries were also shown.

DUSTY'S TRAIL   **SYNDICATED**
1973   Abysmal sitcom about a Conestoga wagon separated from the rest of the
train somewhere in the old West. With Bob Denver as Dusty, the bumbling scout;
Forrest Tucker as Callahan, the bumbling wagonmaster; Ivor Francis as Carson
Brookhaven, stuffy Bostonian passenger; Lynn Wood as Mrs. Brookhaven, his stuffy
wife; Jeannine Riley as Lulu, an aspiring showgirl; Lori Saunders as Betsy, an aspiring schoolteacher (Riley and Saunders were both alumnae of *Petticoat Junction*); and
Bill Cort as Andy, a regular guy. Produced by Sherwood Schwartz, the man responsible for Denver's previous venture, *Gilligan's Island*.

DUSTY'S TREEHOUSE   **SYNDICATED**
1976   Stu Rosen hosted this all-purpose children's show, which consisted of skits,
songs, and demonstrations.

DWEEBS   **CBS**
22 SEPTEMBER 1995–27 OCTOBER 1995   Half-hour sitcom about a technophobic
woman hired as the office manager of Cyberbyte Software, a small high-tech
company with an all-male, ultra-nerdy staff. With Farrah Forke as the office
manager, Carey Garrett, whose most difficult job was to humanize the guys; Peter
Scolari as Cyberbyte's brilliant but uncommunicative founder, Warren Mosby; Stephen Tobolowsky as Karl; Corey Feldman as Vic; David Kaufman as Morley;
Adam Biesk as Todd, the gopher; and Holly Fulger as Carey's pal, Noreen. The
show's dismal performance on Friday evenings led to a quick cancellation.

DYNASTY   **ABC**
12 JANUARY 1981–11 MAY 1989   Of the many prime-time serials that followed in the
wake of *Dallas, Dynasty* proved to be the most popular. Like *Dallas,* it focused on a
super-rich family living in the West (Denver), whose fortune was made in the oil
business. It also flaunted lavish sets and costumes; its weekly wardrobe budget of
$10,000 was the highest in television.
   Principals included John Forsythe as Blake Carrington, the head of the family and
the business empire (George Peppard had played him in the pilot but was considered
too likable); Linda Evans as beautiful Krystle Jennings, a divorcée who married
Blake in the premiere episode; Pamela Sue Martin (1981–1984) and Emma Samms
(1984–1985 and 1986–1989) as Blake's devious and outspoken daughter, Fallon Carrington; Al Corley (1981–1982) and Jack Coleman (1983–1989) as Blake's idealistic,
bisexual son, Steven Carrington (the character had actually been "killed off" in an oil
rig explosion after Corley complained about the show; when it was decided to recast

the role, it was explained that Steven hadn't died, but had been badly burned and had undergone plastic surgery); John James as Jeff Colby, a young politician who married Fallon (they were later divorced); Lloyd Bochner (1981–1982) as Jeff's uncle, Cecil Colby, a rival oil magnate; Bo Hopkins (spring 1981) as Matthew Blaisdel, a Carrington geologist and an ex-boyfriend of Krystle; Pamela Bellwood (1981–1986) as his unstable wife, Claudia Blaisdel; Katy Kurtzman (spring 1981 and 1986–1987) as their teenage daughter, Lindsay (Matthew and Lindsay were killed off); Lee Bergere (1981–1983) as the Carrington butler, Joseph Anders; Wayne Northrop (spring 1981) as the Carrington chauffeur, Michael Culhane; Peter Mark Richman (1981–1982) as Blake's attorney, Andy Laird; and Dale Robertson (spring 1981) as feisty wildcatter Walter Lankershim.

In the fall of 1981 English actress Joan Collins joined the cast as Blake's former wife (and Fallon and Steven's mother), Alexis Carrington. A thoroughly despicable villainess, Alexis managed to move into the Carrington guest house for a time and to make life miserable for Krystle while she plotted to win Blake back. Alexis became *Dynasty*'s most popular character; whether defending herself for murder, luring a man into her bedroom, or engaging in one of her annual catfights with Krystle, Collins always played her role to the hilt and thoroughly seemed to enjoy herself in the process. Other new regulars were James Farentino (1981–1982) as Dr. Nick Toscanni, a psychiatrist who treated Claudia Blaisdel; and Heather Locklear as Krystle's niece, Sammy Jo Dean, who married Steven Carrington but was paid by Alexis to leave him (Steven subsequently married Claudia Blaisdel).

Four new regulars were added in the fall of 1982: Gordon Thomson as Adam Carrington, the long-lost son of Blake and Alexis (he had been kidnapped at a young age); Kathleen Beller (1982–1984) as Kirby Anders, the butler's daughter, who married Jeff Colby after his divorce from Fallon; Geoffrey Scott (1982–1984) as Krystle's ex-husband, tennis pro Mark Jennings, who saved Krystle and Alexis from a burning cabin; and Paul Burke as Congressman Neil McVane. Added in 1983 were Deborah Adair as Tracy Kendall, and Michael Nader as Dex Dexter. At the end of the 1983–1984 season Diahann Carroll joined the cast as Dominique Deveraux, who turned out to be the illegitimate offspring of Blake's father.

Dynasty reached the peak of its popularity during the 1984–1985 season, when it topped the prime-time ratings. Among the new faces seen that year were Catherine Oxenberg (1984–1986) as Alexis's daughter Amanda (Karen Cellini succeeded Oxenberg for the 1986–1987 season); Billy Dee Williams (1984–1985) as Dominique's husband, Brady Lloyd; William Campbell (1984–1985) as Steven's lover, Luke Fuller; and Rock Hudson (1984–1985, in his last TV role) as Daniel Reece, who had an affair with Krystle. The season ended with the famous "Moldavian massacre": the regulars had gathered for Amanda's wedding in the European kingdom of Moldavia, but the wedding was interrupted by machine-gun toting terrorists who gunned down the entire party.

As the 1985–1986 season unfolded, everyone had survived the wedding, but *Dynasty*'s slippage had begun. A spinoff serial, *The Colbys*, was introduced that fall, and *Dynasty* regulars John James and Emma Samms departed for the new show. Joan Collins was embroiled in a salary dispute, and did not appear in the early episodes, necessitating rewrites of those stories (the producers had planned for her to become queen of Moldavia, but the entire Moldavian story line was dropped in midseason). Another odd story line was introduced as Krystle was kidnapped and a lookalike actress was hired to masquerade as Krystle (Linda Evans, of course, played Rita, the lookalike). Joining the cast during that season were George Hamilton (1985–1986) as Joel Abrigore, who masterminded the kidnapping plot with Sammy Jo; Christopher Cazenove (1985–1987) as Blake's brother, Ben Carrington; Kate O'Mara (spring 1986) as Alexis's sister, Caress, an author (in real life, Joan Collins's sister Jackie was a best-selling author); Richard Anderson (spring 1986–1987) as Senator Buck Fallmont; Pat Crowley (spring 1986) as his wife, Emily; and Ted McGinley (spring 1986–1987) as their son, Clay, who married Sammy Jo.

The inexorable ratings decline continued. The series, which had finished seventh in 1985–1986, sagged to 24th in 1986–1987. By the latter season, Alexis had managed to evict Blake and Krystle from the Carrington mansion at 173 Essex Drive in

Denver. New to the cast were Leann Hunley (1986–1988) as Dana Waring, who married Adam Carrington; Richard Lawson (1986–1987) as Nick Kimball; Terri Garber (spring 1987–1988) as Leslie Carrington; and Cassie Yates (spring 1987–1988) as Sarah Curtis. *Dynasty* dropped to 33rd place in 1987–1988, adding James Healey (1987–1988) as mysterious Sean Rowan, who turned out to be the son of the Carringtons' old butler; Jessica Player as Krystina, young daughter of Blake and Krystle; and Stephanie Dunnam (1987–1988) as Karen Atkinson. For its final season, the series fell to 57th place, ending its nine-year run quietly in May 1989, without tying up loose story lines (there had been rumors that a two-hour finale might be produced for the 1989–1990 season, but it did not come to pass until 20 and 22 October 1991). Stephanie Beacham joined the cast as Sable, reprising the role she had played on *The Colbys*. Also featured during the final season were Stella Hall as Claire; Liza Morrow as Virginia; Ray Abruzzo as Sergeant Zorelli; Kenneth Tigar as Heath; Kim Terry-Costin as Joanna; Tracy Scoggins as Monica; and Lezlie Deane as Phoenix.

Dynasty was created by Richard and Esther Shapiro. Nolan Miller designed the costumes.

DYNOMUTT   ABC
3 JUNE 1978–2 SEPTEMBER 1978   Dynomutt, the bionic dog introduced on *The Scooby-Doo/Dynomutt Hour* in 1976, had his own half-hour cartoon show for a few weeks in 1978. Dynomutt accompanied another superhero, a bird known as the Blue Falcon.

E.A.R.T.H. FORCE   CBS
16 SEPTEMBER 1990–29 SEPTEMBER 1990   The premise for this hour adventure series was an unlikely one: a dying executive assembled a group of scientists to battle threats to the planet's environment; the newly formed unit was known as E.A.R.T.H.—Earth Alert Research Tactical Headquarters. Regulars included Gil Gerard as Dr. John Harding; Clyton Rohner as physicist Carl Dana; Tiffany Lamb as marine biologist Catherine Romano; Stewart Finlay-McLennan as mercenary Charles Dillon; and Joanna Pacula as the director, Diana Randall. The series was the first cancellation of the 1990–1991 season, lasting only three episodes.

E.D.J.
See PERSONALITIES

E/R   CBS
16 SEPTEMBER 1984–27 APRIL 1985; 5 JUNE 1985–24 JULY 1985   Elliott Gould starred in this half-hour sitcom as Dr. Howard Sheinfeld, a Chicago ear-nose-and-throat specialist who had to moonlight in the Emergency Room (E/R) of Clark Street Hospital in order to maintain the alimony payments to his ex-wives. Other regulars included Mary McDonnell as Dr. Eve Sheridan, the E/R supervisor (Marcia Strassman played the part in the pilot); Conchata Ferrell as head nurse Joan Thor; Lynne Moody as Nurse Julie Williams (the character was the niece of George Jefferson of *The Jeffersons*); Shuko Akune as Maria, the receptionist; Bruce A. Young as police officer Fred Burdock, Maria's boyfriend; Corinne Bohrer as Nurse Cory Smith; Luis Avalos as Dr. Thomas Esquivel; William Schilling as Richard, the orderly; Jeff Doucette as Bert, the paramedic; George Clooney as Thor's nephew, Ace; and Jason Alexander as hospital administrator Harold Stickley.

ER   NBC
19 SEPTEMBER 1994—   Created by novelist (and medical school graduate) Michael Crichton, this hour dramatic series premiered opposite CBS's *Chicago Hope*, a new medical drama also set at a Chicago hospital. *ER* quickly won the time slot battle, forcing a rescheduling of Hope, and went on to finish second in the seasonal Nielsen ratings, the best rating ever for a first-year dramatic series and the highest ranking for any TV drama in ten years. The series was set in the Emergency Room of Cook County General Hospital, where the beleaguered staff did its best to cope with a

stunning array of crises, both personal and medical. The ensemble cast featured Anthony Edwards as chief resident Dr. Mark Greene; George Clooney as womanizing pediatrician Dr. Douglas Ross (Clooney, who had also appeared in the 1984 sitcom *E/R*, thus became the first actor to be a regular in two different series with the same title); Sherry Stringfield as Dr. Susan Lewis; Noah Wyle as intern Dr. John Carter; Eriq La Salle as resident surgeon Dr. Peter Barton; Julianna Margulies as head nurse Carole Hathaway; William H. Macy as Dr. David Morgenstern; Christina Harnos as Jennifer Greene, Mark's wife; CCH Pounder as Dr. Angela Hicks; Rick Rossovich as Dr. John Taglieri, who almost married Carole; Ming-Na Wen (1994–1995) as Dr. Deb Chen; Abraham Benrubi as Jerry, the orderly; Gloria Reuben as Jeanie Bouler; Christine Elise (1995–   ) as third-year medical student Harper Tracy; and Laura Innes (1995–   ) as new chief resident Kerry Weaver (Greene had received a promotion).

E.S.P.   ABC
11 JULY 1958–22 AUGUST 1958   Vincent Price hosted this short-lived series, which explored the phenomenon of extrasensory perception. Guests related personal experiences and also participated in various tests calculated to demonstrate their putative abilities.

THE EARL WRIGHTSON SHOW
See THE MASLAND AT HOME SHOW

EARLY TODAY   NBC
5 JULY 1982–29 JULY 1983   NBC's first early-early-morning news show was conceived as a lead-in to its long-running *Today* show. Broadcast weekday mornings from 6:00 to 7:00 A.M., immediately preceding *Today,* the program was designed so that local stations could carry either the full hour or one of the two half hours. *Early Today*'s hosts were the same trio who presided over *Today:* Bryant Gumbel, Jane Pauley, and jovial Willard Scott. Eventually, network executives concluded that *Early Today* bore too close a resemblance to *Today,* and the early-early-morning news concept was reworked (see *NBC News at Sunrise*). See also *ABC World News This Morning* (which premiered the same day as *Early Today*) and *CBS Early Morning News.*

EARN YOUR VACATION   CBS
23 MAY 1954–5 SEPTEMBER 1954   On this prime-time game show contestants competed for the chance to win a vacation to the spot of their choice. The show had been on radio in 1951. The host of the TV version was a twenty-seven-year old comedian who had had his own local show in Los Angeles: Johnny Carson.

EARTH 2   NBC
6 NOVEMBER 1994–4 JUNE 1995   Expensive sci-fi series set in the year 2192, when Earth had become uninhabitable and its people were forced to live in space stations. A small band of Earthlings left a space station and crash landed on the planet they hoped to colonize, where they encountered various other life forms such as the humanoid Terrians, the small Kobas, and the Grendlers. The cast included Debrah Farentino as Devon Adair, leader of the expedition; Joey Zimmerman as her young son, Ulysses, who suffered from "the syndrome" (caused by an absence of fresh air and water; Devon hoped that an organic environment might cure him); Clancy Brown as Danziger, the mechanic; J. Madison Wright as True, Danziger's young daughter; Jessica Steen as Dr. Heller; Antonio Sabato, Jr., as Alonzo Solace, the pilot; Sullivan Walker as Yale; John Gegenhuber as Morgan; Rebecca Gayheart as Bess; Terry O'Quinn as Reilly; and Tim Curry as Gaal, a human who already lived there (the planet had been a penal colony). If the colonists' new habitat looked remarkably terrestrial, it was because the series was filmed in the Jemez Mountains of New Mexico.

EARTHLAB   SYNDICATED
1971   A science series for kids, hosted by Rex Trailer. Produced at WBZ-TV in Boston.

EARTHWORM JIM   WB
9 SEPTEMBER 1995–   Saturday morning cartoon show based on the video game about a worm who became a superhero after donning a special "supersuit" which had fallen on him from outer space. Jim was accompanied by Peter, his faithful canine companion.

EAST SIDE, WEST SIDE   CBS
23 SEPTEMBER 1963–14 SEPTEMBER 1964   A dramatic series about social workers. Because of its treatment of many controversial issues, especially race relations, CBS was never able to sell the entire hour to sponsors, and the show barely lasted a season. Network executives were never enthusiastic about the series. A scene from one episode, which showed the white star (George C. Scott) dancing with a black woman, was deleted at network insistence. In retrospect, *East Side, West Side* was probably ahead of its time; TV audiences of 1963 just weren't ready for a hard-hitting series focusing on social problems, especially one in which most of the problems remained unsolved at the hour's end. The show starred George C. Scott as Neil Brock, social worker for the Community Welfare Service, a private agency located in Manhattan; Elizabeth Wilson as Frieda (Hecky) Hechlinger, his boss; Cicely Tyson as the secretary, Jane Porter (Tyson was the first black performer cast in a regular role on a noncomedy series and was also the first to feature an Afro hair style). In midseason the format was changed slightly but ratings failed to improve—Brock went to work for a New York congressman; Linden Chiles appeared as Representative Hanson. David Susskind was the executive producer of the series, which was shot on location in New York.

EASY ACES   DUMONT
14 DECEMBER 1949–7 JUNE 1950   A television version of the popular radio comedy show which began in 1930. Goodman Ace and his wife, Jane Sherwood Ace, starred as themselves, and Betty Garde was featured. Goodman Ace was one of radio's foremost comedy writers and later wrote for several television shows, including Milton Berle's *The Texaco Star Theater* and *The Perry Como Show.* Jane Ace was famous for her malaprops. Much of each fifteen-minute program was ad-libbed.

EASY DOES IT   CBS
25 AUGUST 1976–15 SEPTEMBER 1976   A four-week summer variety series starring Frankie Avalon, the Philadelphia rock-and-roller who catapulted to stardom in 1958 with such hits as "De De Dinah" and "Venus." Dick Clark, who had featured Avalon frequently on *American Bandstand,* was the executive producer of this half-hour effort. Avalon's special guest star on the premiere was Annette Funicello, his costar in several "beach" films of the early 1960s.

EASY STREET   NBC
13 SEPTEMBER 1986–27 MAY 1987   Half-hour sitcom starring Loni Anderson as L. K. McGuire, an ex-showgirl who inherited a mansion from her late husband; she invited her down-and-out uncle, Alvin "Bully" Stevenson (played by Jack Elam), and his black roommate, Ricardo Williams (Lee Weaver), to leave the Shady Grove Retirement Home in Los Angeles and move in with her; unfortunately, the three had to share the property with L. K.'s insufferable sister-in-law, Eleanor Stander (played by Dana Ivey), and her husband, Quentin (James Cromwell), who were contesting the will. Also featured was Arthur Malet as Bobby the butler.

EBONY/JET SHOWCASE   SYNDICATED
1983; 1985–1993   Half-hour weekly magazine show, aimed at black audiences. Hosts have included Greg Gumbel (brother of *Today* show's Bryant Gumbel), Tom Joyner, Darryl Dennard, Debra Crable, and Elliott Francis.

ED ALLEN TIME   SYNDICATED
1964   Half-hour exercise show with Ed Allen and his dog, Alice.

THE ED NELSON SHOW   SYNDICATED
1969   A ninety-minute talk show hosted by actor Ed Nelson.

THE ED SULLIVAN SHOW (TOAST OF THE TOWN)   CBS
20 JUNE 1948–6 JUNE 1971   Television's longest-running variety show ran on Sunday
nights for twenty-three years. Its host, Ed Sullivan, couldn't sing or dance, but he
knew who could, and he signed them for his show. A syndicated newspaper columnist, Sullivan had hosted two radio shows before agreeing to try television in 1948.
On camera Sullivan always seemed ill at ease; he regularly fluffed introductions, and
his habit of wandering around the stage during the broadcasts was a continual challenge to the show's technical crew. Ironically, Sullivan's mannerisms probably helped
launch the careers of many impressionists. Fortunately for those comics, Sullivan was
not too vain to poke fun at himself; Frank Fontaine lampooned him as early as 1949.
But when Sullivan shared the stage with the most accomplished Sullivan impersonator of all—Will Jordan—the effect was eerily hilarious.
   The show began inauspiciously. Although eight acts appeared on the 1948 premiere, the total talent budget was only $475, with headliners Dean Martin and Jerry
Lewis (making their TV debut) splitting $200; composers Richard Rodgers and Oscar
Hammerstein 2nd also appeared on that broadcast. From the beginning, Ray Bloch
and his orchestra provided the music; the June Taylor Dancers also began appearing
regularly that summer. It was reported that during the early months of the series CBS
offered the show to sponsors with or without Sullivan as emcee; fortunately for the
network, none of the sponsors opted against "Old Stone Face," as Sullivan had been
described by reviewers.
   The format for the show was soon established and was changed very little during
the next two decades. Sullivan tried to present something to please everyone each
week. Thus a typical evening's fare might include an acrobatic act, a couple of
comics, a recording star, an aria by an operatic performer, a film star plugging a new
movie, and the introduction of a few notables "in our studio audience" by Sullivan.
Occasionally an entire program would be devoted to a single event, such as a biography of playwright Josh Logan, or the appearance of the Moiseyev Dancers, a folk
troupe from the Soviet Union. In 1959 Sullivan took a group of American performers
to the USSR.
   It would take a small book just to catalog the thousands of performers who
appeared, ranging from Bob Hope (who made his East Coast TV debut on 26
September 1948) to Albert Schweitzer (filmed playing the organ at his African mission). Other notables who made their television debuts on *The Ed Sullivan Show* (it
was officially titled *Toast of the Town* until 1955) were Irving Berlin (15 August 1948),
Victor Borge (25 September 1949), Hedy Lamarr (17 September 1950), Walt Disney
(8 February 1953), and Fred Astaire and Jane Powell (14 February 1954). Two acts,
however, deserve special mention, for they attracted some of the largest television
audiences of the time: Elvis Presley and the Beatles.
   In the summer of 1956 Presley was signed for three appearances at the unheard-of
fee of $50,000. The twenty-one-year-old recording artist had signed with RCA Rec-
ords earlier that year, and his career was already skyrocketing by that time. For the
record, Presley first appeared on 9 September 1956 and performed "Don't Be
Cruel," "Love Me Tender," "Reddy Teddy," and "Hound Dog." Charles Laughton
was the substitute host that evening. On 28 October, Presley again appeared, singing
"Don't Be Cruel," "Love Me Tender," "Love Me," and "Hound Dog." Presley's
final appearance was 6 January 1957, when he performed seven numbers: "Hound
Dog," "Love Me Tender," "Heartbreak Hotel," "Don't Be Cruel," "Peace in the
Valley," "Too Much," and "When My Blue Moon Turns to Gold Again." Two popu-
lar misconceptions about the Presley appearances should be dispelled. First, Presley
did not make his TV debut on Sullivan's show—he had appeared several times on the
Dorsey Brothers' *Stage Show,* as well as on *The Milton Berle Show* and *The Steve
Allen Show* (it was reported that Sullivan signed Presley after noting the ratings from

his appearance on the Allen show; this act exacerbated the feud between the two men, whose shows were in direct competition with one another). Second, Presley was not photographed only from the waist up; his "lascivious" posturings (which had been the subject of a *TV Guide* editorial during the week of 7 July 1956) were seen in full on the first two Sullivan shows. It was only for the third show, after much furor, that the decision was made to photograph Presley in tight close-ups. After the third appearance, Presley had had enough of television. By that time his film career had begun to look promising, and, except for a brief appearance on a Frank Sinatra special in May 1960, eleven years would pass before he again appeared on TV.

In the fall of 1963 Sullivan signed the Beatles for two appearances for $25,000. At that time the group was a sensation in England and was gaining a sizable reputation throughout Europe. Their first American singles, however, had gone nowhere. By the time of their first appearance on the Sullivan show, all that had changed, thanks in large part to a publicity blitz by Capitol Records. On 9 February 1964 most Americans saw the quartet for the first time (Jack Paar had shown film clips of them on 3 January, and they had also been covered by the network news) as they performed "All My Loving," "She Loves You," "I Saw Her Standing There," "I Want to Hold Your Hand," and "Till There Was You." Beatlemania was officially under way on this side of the ocean. After concerts in New York and Washington, they returned a week later to perform six songs in a segment broadcast live from the Deauville Hotel in Miami Beach. A third appearance, taped on 9 February, was aired 23 February. The Beatles' appearances opened the floodgates for a torrent of British rock groups; more important, rock acts became a regular feature of the show for the remainder of its run.

One of the few musical giants of the 1960s who did not appear was Bob Dylan, but not because he wasn't asked. Dylan had been signed for an appearance in 1963 and indicated he intended to perform "Talkin' John Birch Society Blues," a humorous number about a man who begins to look for Communists everywhere. Reportedly Sullivan liked the song when he heard it during rehearsal and voiced no objection. He subsequently informed Dylan that the network brass, fearful of a lawsuit, had vetoed the number. Dylan understandably refused to compromise and declined to appear on the program.

Sullivan's ratings, which had remained fairly steady during the 1950s and 1960s, began to slip in 1968, as *The F.B.I.* and *Walt Disney* made inroads. In 1971 his show was canceled as part of CBS's attempt to acquire a new image as the network for youthful audiences. Sullivan, who had coproduced the show (first with Marlo Lewis, later with his son-in-law, Bob Precht), appeared in a few specials and also hosted one episode of *The ABC Comedy Hour (The Kopykats)*. He died in 1974. In 1990 Andrew Solt purchased the rights to the show from the Sullivan estate, and CBS telecast a two-hour retrospective on the series on 17 February 1991. Edited segments from the series were packaged for syndication in the fall of 1992.

THE ED WYNN SHOW   CBS
6 OCTOBER 1949–4 JULY 1950   CBS's first Los Angeles-based variety show starred Ed Wynn, a trouper who began his career in vaudeville in 1904 and appeared on radio as early as 1922, where he starred in such comedy series as *The Perfect Fool* and *The Fire Chief*. Wynn's guests on television included Leon Errol, Charles Laughton, Andy Devine, and Dinah Shore. Produced by Harlan Thompson and directed by Ralph Levy, the show was seen via kinescopes on the East Coast.

THE ED WYNN SHOW   NBC
25 SEPTEMBER 1958–1 JANUARY 1959   During the mid-1950s Ed Wynn was not often seen on television; he made a triumphant return in 1956, however, on *Playhouse 90*'s "Requiem for a Heavyweight." That performance established him, after fifty years in show business, as a character actor. In this half-hour sitcom he starred as John Beamer, a retired man trying to raise two granddaughters in a small college town. Also featured were Jacklyn O'Donnell as granddaughter Laurie; Sherry Alberoni as granddaughter Midge; and Herb Vigran as Beamer's friend, lawyer Ernie Hinshaw. Ben Feiner, Jr., produced the series and William Russell directed it.

THE EDDIE ALBERT SHOW   CBS

2 MARCH 1953–8 MAY 1953   For nine weeks in 1953 Eddie Albert hosted his own half-hour daytime variety show. Also featured were Ellen Hanley and Norman Paris's band.

THE EDDIE CANTOR COMEDY THEATER   SYNDICATED

1955   An anthology series that sometimes featured variety acts and sometimes presented half-hour comedies. Eddie Cantor was the host and occasional star.

THE EDDIE CAPRA MYSTERIES   NBC

8 SEPTEMBER 1978–12 JANUARY 1979   A typical crime show starring Vincent Baggetta as lawyer-sleuth Eddie Capra. With Ken Swofford as his senior partner, J. J. Devlin; Wendy Phillips as his friend and secretary, Lacey Brown; Michael Horton as Capra's junior investigator, Harvey Winchell; and Seven Ann McDonald as Lacey's young daughter, Jennie. Peter S. Fischer was executive producer, James McAdams producer for Universal TV. CBS reran some episodes during the summer of 1990.

THE EDDIE CONDON PROGRAM
See FLOOR SHOW

EDDIE DODD   ABC

12 MARCH 1991–2 APRIL 1991; 29 MAY 1991–5 JUNE 1991   Based on the 1989 movie "True Believer," this hour crime show starred Treat Williams as Eddie Dodd, a streetwise New York defense attorney, and featured Corey Parker as his young associate, Roger Baron; Sydney Walsh as his investigator, Kitty Greer; and Annabelle Gurwitch as the secretary/office manager, Billie.

THE EDDIE FISHER SHOW   NBC

1 OCTOBER 1957–17 MARCH 1959   After *Coke Time* left the air in February of 1957; Eddie Fisher returned as host of an hour-long variety series that alternated biweekly with *The George Gobel Show*. During the 1957–1958 season Gobel was "permanent guest star" on Fisher's show, and Fisher reciprocated on Gobel's program. Debbie Reynolds, Fisher's wife at the time, also appeared occasionally. Music was provided by the Buddy Bregman Orchestra. Fisher's theme song was "As Long As There's Music," by Sammy Kahn and Jule Styne.

THE EDDY ARNOLD SHOW   CBS/NBC/SYNDICATED/ABC

14 JULY 1952–22 AUGUST 1952 (CBS); 7 JULY 1953–1 OCTOBER 1953 (NBC); 1954–1956 (SYNDICATED); 26 APRIL 1956–26 SEPTEMBER 1956 (ABC)   A popular country-and-western singer for several decades, Eddy Arnold made his television debut on Milton Berle's *Texaco Star Theater* in 1949. In 1952 he hosted the first of his several TV series, a summer replacement for *The Perry Como Show* on CBS which was seen three nights a week after the news. In the summer of 1953 he substituted for Dinah Shore twice a week on NBC. A year later he began a syndicated show, *Eddy Arnold Time,* which originated from Springfield, Missouri. Produced and directed by Ben Park, it featured Betty Johnson, the Gordonaires, Hank Garland, and Roy Wiggins. In 1956 he hosted a live half-hour series on ABC, which featured the Paul Mitchell Quartet and guitarist Chet Atkins.

THE EDGE   FOX

19 SEPTEMBER 1992–18 JULY 1993   Half-hour comedy sketch show, with Julie Brown, Jennifer Aniston, Tom Kenney, Wayne Knight, Carol Rosenthal, James Stephens III, and Jill Talley.

THE EDGE OF NIGHT   CBS/ABC

2 APRIL 1956–28 NOVEMBER 1975 (CBS); 1 DECEMBER 1975–28 DECEMBER 1984 (ABC)   CBS introduced television's first thirty-minute daytime serials, *As the World Turns* and *The Edge of Night,* on the same day; both proved extremely successful. *The Edge of Night,* so titled because of its late afternoon (4:30 P.M., originally) time slot, was

created by Irving Vendig, and, for the first few years, emphasized crime stories and courtroom drama; gradually, however, its story lines drifted away from crime toward the romantic and sexual themes common to most soap operas. The show's time slot has drifted as well since 1963, when it was first shifted back an hour. In 1975, after two or three years of declining ratings on CBS, *The Edge of Night* became the first daytime serial to shift networks. ABC restored the show to a late-afternoon time slot, but by the early 1980s a number of affiliates had dropped the show, substituting syndicated talk shows for the serial. After twenty-eight and a half years, and 7,420 episodes, *The Edge of Night* departed on 28 December 1984. The show was produced for Procter and Gamble, first by Werner Michel, later by Don Wallace, Charles Fisher, and Erwin Nicholson. Henry Slesar was the head writer from 1968 to 1983; Lee Sheldon succeeded him.

Principal players over the years included: John Larkin (1956–1962; Larkin had previously played Perry Mason on radio), Larry Hugo (1962–1971), and Forrest Compton (1971–1984) as lawyer Mike Karr, who began as an assistant district attorney in Monticello, where *Edge* was set, but later switched to private practice; and Teal Ames (1956–1961) as Sarah Lane, who married Mike and was killed while saving the life of their daughter. (Sarah's demise was one of the first deaths of a major TV soap opera character; CBS received so many calls after the broadcast that John Larkin and Teal Ames appeared at the end of the next day's program to assure viewers that only the character, and not Teal Ames, had died); Don Hastings (1956–1960) as Jack Lane, Sarah's brother; Mary Alice Moore as Betty Jean Lane, Jack's wife; Betty Garde, Peggy Allenby, and Katherine Meskill as Mattie Lane, Sarah and Jack's mother; Walter Greaza as Winston Grimsley, a widower who married Mattie; Carl Frank and Mandel Kramer as Bill Marceau, Monticello's police chief; Joan Harvey as Judy Marceau, Bill's daughter; Teri Keane (1965–1975) as Martha, Bill's secretary and eventual wife; Heidi Vaughn, Renne Jarrett, Laurie Kennedy, and Johanna Leister as Phoebe Smith, a troubled teenager adopted by Bill and Martha; Ann Flood (1962–1984) as Nancy Pollock, who became Mike Karr's second wife; Ronnie Welch, Sam Groom, and Tony Roberts as Lee Pollock, Nancy's brother; June Carter and Fran Sharon as Cookie Pollock, Nancy's sister; Ed Kemmer as Malcolm Thomas, who married Cookie and was later murdered; Burt Douglas as Ron Christopher, Cookie's next husband; John Gibson and Allen Nourse as Joe Pollock, Nancy's father; Ruth Matteson, Frances Reid, Kay Campbell, and Virginia Kaye as Rose Pollock, Nancy's mother; Millette Alexander as Gail Armstrong, Laura Hillyer, and Julie Jamison (Alexander played the three roles at different times—Gail Armstrong was a commercial artist, Laura Hillyer was killed in a car crash, and Julie Jamison was Laura's lookalike, who showed up shortly after Laura's death); Wesley Addy as Hugh Campbell; Ed Holmes as Detective Willie Bryan; Larry Hagman as lawyer Ed Gibson; Karen Thorsell as Margie Gibson, Ed's sister; Maxine Stuart as Grace O'Leary; Ray MacDonnell as Phil Capice; Lisa Howard and Mary K. Wells as Louise Capice, Phil's wife, daughter of Winston Grimsley; Conrad Fowkes as Steve Prentiss; Liz Hubbard as Carol Kramer; Val Dufour as André Lazar; Lauren Gilbert as Harry Lane; Lester Rawlins as Orin Hillyer (who was married first to Laura Hillyer, and then to Julie Jamison; both roles were played by the aforementioned Millette Alexander); Alberta Grant as Liz Hillyer, Orin's daughter; Penny Fuller, Joanna Miles, and Millee Taggart as Gerry McGrath, who married Pollock; Keith Charles as disc jockey Rick Oliver, who was murdered by Laura Hillyer; Barry Newman as lawyer John Barnes, a young associate of Mike Karr's; Donald May (1967–1977) as Adam Drake, Mike Karr's law partner; Maeve McGuire, Jayne Bentzen, and Lisa Sloan as Nicole Travis, who married Drake in 1973; Bibi Besch as Susan Forbes, Nicole's onetime partner in a dress shop; William Prince and Cec Linder as Nicole's father, Ben Travis, a crook; Alice Hirson as murder victim Stephanie Martin; Irene Dailey as Pamela Stewart; Richard Clarke as Duane Stewart; Alan Feinstein as Dr. Jim Fields, who married Liz Hillyer; Victoria Larkin, Kathleen Bracken, Kathy Cody, Emily Prager, Jeannie Ruskin, and Linda Cook as Laurie Ann Karr, daughter of Mike and Sarah Karr; Ted Tinling as Vic Lamont, Laurie's first husband; John LaGioia as nightclub owner Johnny Dallas, Laurie's second husband; Pat Conwell as Tracey Dallas, Johnny's sister; Alan Gifford as former Senator Gordon Whitney; Lois Kibbee (who would later write for the series) as his wife, Geraldine Whitney; Anthony Call as their son, Collin Whitney; Lucy Martin as Collin's wife, Tiffany; Bruce Martin as Gordon and Geraldine's other son, Keith Whitney (a split personality, Keith was also known as Jonah Lockwood); George Hall as John, the Whitney butler; Mary Hayden as Trudy, the Whitney maid; Hugh Reilly as Simon Jessup; Fred J. Scollay as Lobo Haines; Francine Beers as Nurse Lillian Hubbell; Jay Gregory as Morlock; Elizabeth Farley as Kate Reynolds; Nick Pryor and Paul Henry Itkin as Joel Gantry; Ward Costello as Jake Berman; Dorothy Lyman as Elly Jo Jamison; Dick Shoberg and John Driver as Kevin Jamison, who would marry Raven Alexander; Dixie Carter as assistant district attorney Olivia Brandeis "Brandy" Henderson; Michael Stroka as Brandy's brother, Dr. Quentin Henderson; Lou Criscuolo as Danny Micelli, who married Tracey Dallas; Louise Shaffer as Nicole Travis's cousin, Serena Faraday (another split personality, Serena was also known as Josie); Doug McKeon as Serena's son, Timmy; Dick Latessa as Noel Douglas; Niles McMaster as Dr. Clay Jordan; Brooks Rogers as Dr. Hugh Lacey; Helena Carroll, Jane Hoffman, and Laurinda Barrett as Molly O'Connor; Herb Davis as Lieutenant Luke Chandler; and Tony Craig as Draper Scott.

Later additions to the cast included: Juanin Clay and Sharon Gabet as Charlotte "Raven" Alexander (Jamison)(Swift)(Whitney)(Devereaux) Whitney; Louis Turrene as Tony Saxon; Frances Fisher as Deborah Saxon; Denny Albee as Steve Guthrie; Polly Adams as Carol Barclay; Joel Crothers as Dr. Miles Cavanaugh, who married Nicole Travis; Holland Taylor as Denise Cavanaugh; Terry Davis as April Cavanaugh Scott; Robin Groves as Maggie; Joe Lambie and Tom Tammi as Logan Swift, who was Raven's second husband; Irving Lee as Calvin Stoner; Yahee as Star Stoner, Calvin's wife; Kiel Martin as Raney Cooper; Marilyn Randall as Theresa; Dick Callinan as Ray Harper; Micki Grant as Ada Chandler; Dennis Marino as Packy Dietrich; Gwynn Press as Inez Johnson; Dorothy Stinette as Nadine Scott; Eileen Finley as Joannie Collier; Lee Godart as Elliot Dorn, leader of the "Children of the Earth" cult; Dan Hamilton as Wade Meecham; Michael Longfield as Tank Jarvis; Ann Williams as Margo Huntington; Susan Yusen as Diana Selkirk; Lori Cardille and Stephanie Braxton as Winter Austen; Mel Cobb as Ben Everett; and Wyman Pendleton as Dr. Norwood.

Also, Lori Loughlin and Karrie Emerson as Nicole's sister, Jody Travis; Sonia Petrovna as ballerina Martine Duval; Joey Alan Phipps and Allen Fawcett as Kelly McGrath; Bruce Gray as Owen Madison; Dennis Parker as Derek Mallory, who succeeded Bill Marceau as Monticello's police chief; Shirley Stoler as Frankie; Mark Arnold as dancer Gavin Wylie; Kim Hunter as Nola Madison; Ernie Townsend as lawyer Cliff Nelson; Larkin Malloy as Schuyler Whitney, who was Raven's third and fifth husband (Raven had also been married to Jeff Brown, a man posing as the real Schuyler Whitney; Malloy also played Jeff Brown); Lela Ivey as Mitzi Martin; Mariann Aalda as lawyer Di Di Bannister; George D. Wallace as Dr. Leo Gault; Patricia DeRosa as Julia; James Noseworthy as Jamie; Paul Tinder as Larry Watts; Mark Andrews as artist Chad Sutherland; Ray Serra as gangster Eddie Lormer; Karen Needle as Eddie's secretary, Poppy Johnson; Chris Jarrett as detective Damian Tyler; Victor Arnold as Joe Bulmer, one of Eddie's henchmen; Leah Ayres as Valerie Bryson; David Brooks as Jim Dedrickson; Richard Borg as Schuyler Whitney's brother, Spencer Varney; David Froman as Gunther Wagner, Schuyler's chauffeur (Froman also played Gunther's twin brother, Bruno); Catherine Bruns as Nora Fulton; Meg Myles as tavernkeeper Sid Brennan; Alan Coates as Raven's fourth husband, Ian Devereaux; Charles Flohe as John "Preacher" Emerson; Mary Layne as Camilia Devereaux; Norman Parker as David Cameron; Pat Stanley as Mrs. Goodman; Willie Aames as Robbie Hamlin; Michael Stark as Barry Gillette; Ronn Carroll as Stan Hathaway; Derek Evans as Marty Stillwater; Steven Flynn as Davey Oakes; Pamela Shoemaker as Shelley Franklyn; Chris Weatherfield as Alicia Van Dine; Sandy Faison as Dr. Beth Correll; Jerry Zacks as Louis Van Dine; Cyd Quilling as Claire Daye; Ralph Byers as Donald Hext; Jason Zimbler as Jamey Swift, son of Logan and Raven; Ken Campbell as Russ Powell; A. C. Weary as Gary Shaw; Kerry Armstrong as Tess McAdams; Kelly Patterson as Hollace Dinneen; John Allen Nelson as Jack Boyd; Julianne Moore as Carmen Engler; Bob Gerringer as Del Emerson; Pamela Shoemaker as Shelley Franklyn; Christopher Holder as Mark Hamilton; Jennifer Taylor as Chris Egan; and Amanda Blake as Dr. Juliana Stanhower.

THE EDIE ADAMS SHOW
See HERE'S EDIE

EDITOR'S CHOICE   ABC
18 JUNE 1961–24 SEPTEMBER 1961; 14 JANUARY 1962–6 JANUARY 1963 Public affairs show on which host Fendall Yerxa and others interviewed newsmakers. The show was seen Sunday evenings in 1961 and on Sunday afternoons thereafter.

EDWARD & MRS. SIMPSON   SYNDICATED
1980   Six-part historical drama about England's King Edward VIII. The king, known as David to his family and friends, abdicated after a brief reign to marry "the woman I love." With Edward Fox as Edward; Cynthia Harris as Wallis Warfield Simpson, the American socialite whom Edward married in 1937; Marius Goring as Edward's father, King George V; and Peggy Ashcroft as Edward's mother, Queen Mary. The series was produced in England by Thames Television, and was hosted by Robert MacNeil.

EDWARD ARNOLD THEATER   SYNDICATED
1954   Half-hour dramatic anthology series hosted by portly character actor Edward Arnold.

EDWARD THE KING   SYNDICATED
1979   A thirteen-part miniseries based on the life of Edward VII, the son and successor of Queen Victoria. Produced in England in 1975, the American versions of the hour programs were hosted by Robert MacNeil and sponsored by Mobil Oil. With Charles Sturridge and Timothy West as the teenage and adult Edward; Annette Crosbie as Victoria; Robert Hardy as Prince Albert, Edward's father; Deborah Grant and Helen Ryan as Alexandra, Edward's Danish wife; and John Gielgud as Benjamin Disraeli.

EDWIN NEWMAN REPORTING   NBC
5 JUNE 1960–4 SEPTEMBER 1960   Also titled *Time: Present,* this half-hour Sunday series was hosted by Edwin Newman, who was then NBC's Paris correspondent. Newman was subsequently featured on the *Today* show.

EEK! THE CAT   FOX
12 SEPTEMBER 1992–   Saturday morning cartoon series about the adventures of a wisecracking housecat. During the second season a second cartoon segment was added and the series was retitled *Eek! the Cat and the Terrible Thunderlizards.* The Thunderlizards were a group of dinosaurs trying to eliminate the upstart human race, led by Scooter and Bill, and their monster pal Huckleberry. By 1995 the series had been retitled *Eek!Stravaganza.* The series moved to Fox's weekday schedule in January 1996.

EERIE INDIANA   NBC
15 SEPTEMBER 1991–12 APRIL 1992   Quirky sitcom about a fifteen-year-old who moved with his family from New Jersey to Eerie, Indiana, an aptly named town where unusual things happened. The cast included Omri Katz as Marshall Teller; Justin Shenkarow as his pal, nine-year-old Simon Holmes; Mary-Margaret Humes as Marshall's mother, Marilyn; Francis Guinan as his father, Edgar, an inventor; and Julie Condra as his older sister, Syndi. John Astin was added in midseason as the owner of one of Eerie's stores, The World of Stuff. Created by Karl Schaefer and Jose Rivera, the program was scheduled Sundays opposite *60 Minutes* on CBS, and, unfortunately, proved to be NBC's lowest-rated series of the 1991–1992 season.

THE EGG AND I CBS

3 SEPTEMBER 1951–1 AUGUST 1952 Television's first comedy serial, *The Egg and I* told the story of a young woman from New York City who married a chicken farmer from upstate. It was based on Betty MacDonald's book, which had been made into a movie in 1947 starring Claudette Colbert. The fifteen-minute series ran five days a week at noon and starred Pat Kirkland as Betty MacDonald and John Craven as Bob MacDonald.

EIGHT IS ENOUGH ABC

15 MARCH 1977–29 AUGUST 1981 A comedy-drama from the producers of *The Waltons, Eight Is Enough* was based on the autobiography of Washington columnist Tom Braden. Set in Sacramento, the hour series starred Dick Van Patten as Tom Bradford, a columnist for the Sacramento *Register*. Diana Hyland costarred as his wife, Joan Bradford; Hyland died of cancer in 1977 after five shows had been filmed, and the series continued with Tom as a widower. The eight Bradford children were played by: Grant Goodeve as David; Lani O'Grady as Mary; Laurie Walters as Joannie; Susan Richardson as Susan; Dianne Kay as Nancy; Willie Aames as Tommy; Connie Newton (known as Connie Needham after her 1979 marriage to a former *Eight Is Enough* set decorator) as Elizabeth; and Adam Rich as Nicholas. In the fall of 1977 Betty Buckley joined the cast as Abby Abbott, a widow hired as a tutor; Abby and Tom were married on 9 November. In the fall of 1979 a double wedding was celebrated: David married Janet McArthur (played by Joan Prather) and Susan married minor-league baseball pitcher Merle Stockwell (played by Brian Patrick Clarke). Ralph Macchio was added in 1980 as Jeremy, Abby's troubled nephew. Also featured were James Karen as Tom's boss, Eliot Randolph; Jennifer Darling as Tom's secretary, Donna; Michael Thoma as Dr. Maxwell; Virginia Vincent as Daisy Maxwell; and John Louie (1980–1981) as Nicholas's pal, Melvin. Lee Rich and Philip Capice created the series for Lorimar Productions, which churned out 112 episodes. Most of the gang was reunited for Tom's fiftieth birthday on "Eight is Enough: A Family Reunion," shown 18 October 1987 on NBC; Van Patten and all eight kids returned, while Mary Frann appeared as Abby. The clan gathered again, to celebrate eldest son David's second marriage, on "An Eight Is Enough Wedding" (15 October 1989, also NBC); this time, Sandy Faison played Abby.

EIGHTH MAN SYNDICATED

1965 Japanese cartoon series about Tobor the Eighth Man, a robot imbued with the spirit of a slain police officer.

87TH PRECINCT NBC

25 SEPTEMBER 1961–10 SEPTEMBER 1962 Standard New York cop show. With Robert Lansing as Detective Steve Carella; Norman Fell as Detective Meyer Meyer; Gregory Wolcott as Detective Roger Havilland; Ron Harper as Detective Bert Kling; and Gena Rowlands, who was occasionally featured as Carella's wife, Teddy, a deaf-mute. Executive producer: Hubbell Robinson. The characters were based on those created by Ed McBain. A TV-movie, "Ed McBain's 87th Precinct" (NBC, 19 March 1995), starred Randy Quaid as Carella.

EISCHIED NBC

21 SEPTEMBER 1979–27 JANUARY 1980 Hour crime show starring Joe Don Baker as Earl Eischied, the unorthodox chief of detectives of the New York City Police Department, with Alan Oppenheimer as Finnerty; Alan Fudge as Kimbrough; Eddie Egan (a former cop in real life) as Chief Ed Parks; Suzanne Lederer as Carol Wright; Vincent Bufano as Alessi; Joe Cirillo as Malfitano; and Waldo Kitty as P. C., Eischied's cat. The executive producer was David Gerber for David Gerber Productions and Columbia Pictures TV. Buried in the ratings by CBS's *Dallas, Eischied* was exhumed in the summer of 1983, when reruns were aired by NBC on Fridays.

EISENHOWER & LUTZ   CBS

14 MARCH 1988–20 JUNE 1988   Allan Burns created this sitcom about a Palm Springs lawyer struggling to get by. With Scott Bakula as Barnett M. "Bud" Lutz, Jr., who hung out his shingle at a small shopping mall (although he was a solo practitioner, he thought it more impressive to make it seem that he had a partner); Rose Portillo as his secretary, Millie Zamora; DeLane Matthews as his girlfriend, Megan O'Malley, a waitress; Patricia Richardson as his ex-girlfriend, Kay Dunne, a successful attorney; Leo Geter as Dwayne Spitler, a sushi delivery boy and pre-law student who volunteered at Lutz's office; and Henderson Forsythe as Bud's dad, Big Bud, a local sign painter.

ELDER MICHAUX   DUMONT

17 OCTOBER 1948–9 JANUARY 1949   Probably the first black evangelist to appear regularly on network television, Solomon Lightfoot Michaux hosted his own half-hour religious show, which was broadcast from Washington, D.C.

THE ELECTRIC COMPANY   PBS

1971–1976   Aimed principally at seven- to ten-year-olds, *The Electric Company* emphasized the development of reading skills. Produced by the Children's Television Workshop, its format was similar to that of *Sesame Street,* CTW's notable series for preschoolers. Regulars included Bill Cosby, Rita Moreno, Lee Chamberlin, Jim Boyd, Morgan Freeman, Hattie Winston, Luis Avalos, Judy Graubart, Skip Hinnant, and Danny Seagren.

THE ELEVENTH HOUR   NBC

3 OCTOBER 1962–9 SEPTEMBER 1964   NBC followed up its 1961 smash, *Dr. Kildare,* with a second medical series that focused on mental problems. It starred Wendell Corey (1962–1963) as Dr. Theodore Bassett, a court-appointed psychiatrist, and Jack Ging as Dr. Paul Graham, a clinical psychologist. In the fall of 1963 Corey was replaced by Ralph Bellamy, who played psychiatrist Dr. Richard Starke. Norman Felton was the executive producer for MGM.

THE ELGIN HOUR   ABC

5 OCTOBER 1954–14 JUNE 1955   This undistinguished hour-long dramatic anthology series alternated on Tuesdays with *The U.S. Steel Hour.* The premiere telecast, "Flood," starred Robert Cummings and Dorothy Gish.

ELLEN (THESE FRIENDS OF MINE)   ABC

29 MARCH 1994–4 MAY 1994; 2 AUGUST 1994–   Half-hour sitcom often compared to NBC's *Seinfeld* because of its focus on life's little problems and small satisfactions. Starring standup comic Ellen DeGeneres as bookstore/cafe owner Ellen Morgan, the series premiered in the spring of 1994 as *These Friends of Mine.* It also featured Arye Gross as Ellen's roommate, Adam Greene; Holly Fulger as Ellen's friend, Holly; and Maggie Wheeler as Adam's girlfriend, Anita. The show scored impressive ratings during its brief tryout, finishing fifth in the seasonal Nielsen ratings. When the series returned in August (with reruns of the spring episodes), it was retitled *Ellen,* and the season's new episodes no longer featured Fulger and Wheeler. David Anthony Higgins joined the cast as Joe, who worked for Ellen at Buy the Book, and Joely Fisher was added as Ellen's friend, Paige Clark. Clea Lewis joined the cast in the spring of 1995 as Audrey Penney, Ellen's annoying neighbor. In the fall of 1995 Arye Gross left the series (his character moved to London), and Jeremy Piven was added as Ellen's cousin and new roommate, Spence Kovak.

THE ELLEN BURSTYN SHOW   ABC

20 SEPTEMBER 1986–15 NOVEMBER 1986; 8 AUGUST 1987–12 SEPTEMBER 1987   Half-hour sitcom about four generations living under one roof in a Baltimore townhouse. With Ellen Burstyn as Ellen Brewer, a widowed writer and professor of creative writing at a nearby college; Megan Mullally as her daughter, Molly Ross, a divorcée; Jesse Tendler as Molly's five-year-old, Nick; Elaine Stritch as Ellen's mom, Sydney

Brewer; and Barry Sobel as Tom Heinz, a college student who boarded with the Brewers. The series was scheduled on Saturdays following Lucille Ball's new series, *Life with Lucy;* both failed.

ELLERY QUEEN   DUMONT/ABC/SYNDICATED/NBC
19 OCTOBER 1950–6 DECEMBER 1951 (DUMONT); 16 DECEMBER 1951–26 NOVEMBER 1952 (ABC); 1954 (SYNDICATED); 26 SEPTEMBER 1958–4 SEPTEMBER 1959 (NBC); 11 SEPTEMBER 1975–19 SEPTEMBER 1976 (NBC)   Ellery Queen, the fictional detective created by two cousins, Frederic Dannay and Manfred Lee, has been played by six actors in five television series. Each series employed the device of having Queen address the home audience at the show's climax, to see if they had been as skillful as he in identifying the real murderer. The first effort—*The Adventures of Ellery Queen*—was seen originally on the DuMont network and later switched to ABC. Richard Hart was TV's first *Ellery Queen;* he was succeeded in 1951 by Lee Bowman. The 1954 version starred Hugh Marlowe, who had played the part on radio. Florenz Ames was also featured in the first three versions as Ellery's father, Inspector Richard Queen of the New York Police Department. Irving and Norman Pincus produced the half-hour series. In the fall of 1958 the character returned in a sixty-minute format, *The Further Adventures of Ellery Queen;* it lasted one season. George Nader played Ellery Queen until March 1959, when he was replaced by Lee Philips. Televised in color, the show was originally broadcast live from Hollywood and later became one of the first dramatic series to be videotaped. In 1971 Peter Lawford played the character in a TV-movie. In 1975 NBC revived the character again; the new series, entitled simply *Ellery Queen,* was set in 1947, and the cast included: Jim Hutton as Ellery Queen; David Wayne as his father, Inspector Richard Queen; Tom Reese as Sergeant Velie; John Hillerman as criminologist Simon Brimmer; and Ken Swofford as reporter Frank "Front Page" Flannigan. The 1975 edition was produced by Peter S. Fischer and Michael Rhodes; Richard Levinson and William Link were the executive producers.

ELVIS   ABC
6 FEBRUARY 1990–18 MARCH 1990; 5 MAY 1990–19 MAY 1990   A loving look at the early years of Elvis Presley's musical career, beginning in 1954 in Memphis. With Michael St. Gerard as Elvis Presley; Jesse Dabson as guitarist Scotty Moore; Blake Gibbons as bassist Bill Black; Jordan Williams as Sam Phillips, owner of Sun Records, where Elvis cut his first recordings; Billy Green Bush as Elvis's father, Vernon; and Millie Perkins as Elvis's mother, Gladys. Created by Rick Husky, the half-hour series was produced with the cooperation of Presley's widow, Priscilla (who provided the voiceover narration), and his estate. Presley's singing voice was supplied by Ronnie McDowell. Michael St. Gerard had previously played Elvis in the 1989 film about singer Jerry Lee Lewis, *Great Balls of Fire!*

EMERALD POINT N.A.S.   CBS
26 SEPTEMBER 1983–12 MARCH 1984   One of two 1983 prime-time serials with a military background (*For Love and Honor* was the other), this one was set at Emerald Point Naval Air Station, somewhere on the American coastline. Principals included: Dennis Weaver as the chief officer, Rear Admiral Thomas Mallory, a widower with three grown daughters; Susan Dey as his oldest daughter, Celia Warren, wife of a Navy lawyer; Stephanie Dunnam as the middle daughter, Kay; Doran Clark as the youngest daughter, Leslie, an Annapolis graduate; Charles Frank as Celia's husband, Commander Jack Warren; Andrew Stevens as Lieutenant Glenn Matthews, who was implicated in a murder; Sela Ward as Glenn's fiancée, Hilary Adams, best friend of Kay Mallory; Patrick O'Neal and Robert Vaughn as Hilary's manipulative father, Harlan Adams; Richard Dean Anderson as Hilary's half-brother, Simon Adams, a Navy pilot; Maud Adams as Maggie Farrell, who was employed by the city's Military Affairs Council and whose husband had been missing in action for ten years; Jill St. John as Tom Mallory's sister-in-law, Deanna Kincaid; and Robert Loggia as Soviet Admiral Yuri Bukharin. The hour series was created by Richard and Esther Shapiro, who had created *Dynasty* in 1981.

EMERGENCY! NBC
22 JANUARY 1972–3 SEPTEMBER 1977   When this series was introduced as a midseason replacement for *The Partners* and *The Good Life,* few people would have predicted that it could withstand the competition from CBS's *All in the Family. Emergency!* lasted, however, because it appealed to a different audience; for several seasons it was the most popular prime-time program among viewers aged two to eleven. It was a fast-moving show which depicted the efforts of a team of paramedics assigned to Squad 51 of the Los Angeles County Fire Department; the paramedical team was also associated with nearby Ramparts General Hospital. With Robert Fuller as Dr. Kelly Brackett of the hospital staff; Bobby Troup as Dr. Joe Early of the hospital staff; Julie London (Bobby Troup's wife) as Nurse Dixie McCall; Randolph Mantooth as paramedic John Gage; Kevin Tighe as paramedic Roy DeSoto; Dick Hammer as Captain Henderson; Mike Stoker as fireman-engineer Stoker; Tim Donnelly as fireman Chet Kelly; Marco Lopez as fireman Marco Lopez; Michael Norrell as Captain Stanley; Ron Pinkard as Dr. Morton; and Deidre Hall as Sally. Executive producer: Robert A. Cinader for Jack Webb's Mark VII Productions. On 31 December 1978 a two-hour *Emergency!* was aired on NBC, which consisted mainly of flashbacks.

EMERGENCY +4 NBC
8 SEPTEMBER 1973–4 SEPTEMBER 1976   Saturday-morning cartoon series based on *Emergency!* Paramedics DeSoto and Gage from the prime-time series were assisted by four kids: Sally, Randy, Jason, and Matt. The third season consisted entirely of reruns. Produced by Fred Calvert.

EMPIRE (REDIGO) NBC/ABC
25 SEPTEMBER 1962–31 DECEMBER 1963 (NBC); 22 MARCH 1964–6 SEPTEMBER 1964 (ABC)   *Empire* was an hour-long dramatic series set in modern New Mexico. It featured Richard Egan as Jim Redigo, foreman of the Garrett ranch; Anne Seymour as Lucia Garrett, the owner; Terry Moore as her daughter, Connie; Ryan O'Neal as her son, Tal; Warren Vanders as Chuck Davis; Charles Bronson joined the cast in February 1963 as ranch hand Paul Moreno. In the fall of 1963 the format was changed, shortened to a half hour, and retitled *Redigo.* Egan remained as Jim Redigo, who now owned his own spread. The rest of the *Empire* cast was jettisoned; the new regulars included Roger Davis as ranch hand Mike; Rudy Solari as ranch hand Frank; and Elena Verdugo as Gerry, assistant manager of the local hotel. In 1964 ABC reran some of the *Empire* episodes.

EMPIRE CBS
4 JANUARY 1984–1 FEBRUARY 1984   Half-hour sitcom about skullduggery and intrigue at a large conglomerate. With Dennis Dugan as Ben Christian, the newly appointed, idealistic vice-president; Patrick Macnee as Calvin Cromwell, the chairman of the board; Maureen Arthur as Peg, Ben's secretary; Richard Masur as Jack Willow; Christine Belford as Jack's wife, Jackie Willow; Caren Kaye as Meredith Blake, head of public relations; Michael McGuire as senior vice-president Everett Roland; Dick O'Neill as v.p. Arthur Broderick; Edward Winter as v.p. Howard Daniels; and Howard Platt as lawyer Roger Martinson.

EMPTY NEST NBC
8 OCTOBER 1988–29 APRIL 1995; 10 JUNE 1995–8 JULY 1995   This half-hour sitcom was spun off from *The Golden Girls.* It featured Richard Mulligan as Harry Weston, a widowed pediatrician living in Miami; Dinah Manoff as his eldest daughter, Carol, a divorcee; Kristy McNichol (1988–fall 1992) as middle daughter Barbara, a cop (a third daughter, Emily, was away at college); David Leisure (already well known as commercial spokesman Joe Isuzu) as Charley Dietz, Harry's obnoxious freeloading neighbor; Park Overall as LaVerne Todd, Harry's very Southern nurse; and Bear as Dreyfuss, Harry's enormous dog. McNichol left the series in the fall of 1992 to seek treatment for a manic depressive condition (it was explained that her character, Barbara, had moved to Tucson). Lisa Rieffel joined the cast early in 1993, as the

hitherto unseen third daughter, Emily, who had returned home from college. Paul Provenza also appeared occasionally as Carol's boyfriend, Patrick Arcola. In the fall of 1993 Rieffel had left, and two new regulars were added: Marsha Warfield as Dr. Maxine Douglas, Harry's wisecracking new partner; and Estelle Getty as Sophia Petrillo, a wisecracking oldster (a role she had originated on *The Golden Girls*). Carol became a pregnant that season, and gave birth to a son, Scotty (later played occasionally by Caston Holmes). Created by Susan Harris, the series had originally been conceived for the fall of 1987, and was to have starred Paul Dooley and Rita Moreno as a married couple. After a surprisingly lengthy seven-season run, *Empty Nest* wrapped up on 29 April 1995 (though a few episodes were televised later) with a double wedding at LaVerne's Arkansas home: LaVerne married Matt (Stephen Nichols) and Carol wed Kevin Millen (D. David Morin). Kristy McNichol returned for the final episode, and Harry decided to leave Miami for a teaching position in Vermont.

ENCOUNTER ABC
5 OCTOBER 1958–2 NOVEMBER 1958   *Encounter* was an experimental dramatic anthology series; broadcast live from Toronto, the hour-long show was also carried by the Canadian Broadcasting Corporation.

ENCOUNTERS: THE HIDDEN TRUTH FOX
24 JUNE 1994–22 JULY 1994; 9 OCTOBER 1994–21 AUGUST 1995   John Marshall hosted this hour show which focused on supernatural and unexplained phenomena. The series had a brief run during the summer of 1994 and was revived in October to replace *Fortune Hunter*.

THE END OF THE RAINBOW NBC
11 JANUARY 1958–15 FEBRUARY 1958   On this Saturday-night game show contestants were given the chance to realize a lifetime ambition. The short-lived series was a midseason replacement for another game show, *What's It For?* Art Baker, the first host, was succeeded in February by Bob Barker.

THE ENGELBERT HUMPERDINCK SHOW ABC
21 JANUARY 1970–19 SEPTEMBER 1970   An hour-long variety series taped in London and hosted by British pop star Engelbert Humperdinck. Known previously by his real name—Arnold Dorsey—he had enjoyed little success until his manager, Gordon Mills, decided on the name change (the real Engelbert Humperdinck was a nineteenth-century German composer). In 1967, Humperdinck was voted Show Business Personality of the Year in Great Britain.

ENOS CBS
12 NOVEMBER 1980–19 SEPTEMBER 1981   In this hour spinoff from *The Dukes of Hazzard,* Sonny Shroyer starred as Enos Strate. After apprehending some wanted criminals in Hazzard County, the naive deputy was invited by Los Angeles police officials to join that city's new Metro Special Branch. Also on board were Samuel E. Wright as Enos's partner, Turk Adams; John Dehner as their boss, Lieutenant Broggi; John Milford as Captain Dempsey; and Leo V. Gordon as Sergeant Kick. Enos subsequently returned to Hazzard County after his own show was canceled.

ENSIGN O'TOOLE NBC
23 SEPTEMBER 1962–15 SEPTEMBER 1963   Military sitcom, set aboard the destroyer *Appleby* in the Pacific. With Dean Jones as easygoing Ensign O'Toole; Jay C. Flippen as cantankerous Captain Homer Nelson; Jack Albertson as Lieutenant Commander Virgil Stoner; Jack Mullaney as Lieutenant Rex St. John; Harvey Lembeck as Seaman Gabby DiJulio; Beau Bridges as Seaman Spicer; and Robert Sorrells as Seaman White. Hy Averback produced and directed for Four Star Films.

ENTERPRISE   PBS

1981–1984   Eric Sevareid was the host and narrator of this series on American business. Each segment was produced by a different PBS affiliate.

ENTERPRISE U.S.A.   ABC

19 OCTOBER 1952–8 MARCH 1953; 6 OCTOBER 1954–26 JANUARY 1955   A series of half-hour documentaries on American industry, produced by ABC News and Public Affairs. Though *Enterprise U.S.A.* was a network offering, ABC's New York affiliate did not carry it regularly. The series popped up later on ABC's schedule as a "filler" program.

THE ENTERTAINERS   CBS

25 SEPTEMBER 1964–27 MARCH 1965   An unsuccessful variety series. Originally, the idea was to have three rotating hosts: Carol Burnett, Bob Newhart, and Caterina Valente. After the first few weeks, however, the three cohosts usually appeared together. Other regulars included Dom DeLuise, John Davidson, Ruth Buzzi, Don Crichton, and columnist Art Buchwald.

ENTERTAINMENT TONIGHT   SYNDICATED

14 SEPTEMBER 1981–   One of the few successful syndicated shows of the 1980s, *Entertainment Tonight* was also one of the first programs to utilize satellites for its distribution; the half-hour roundup of news and features from the showbiz world is fed from Los Angeles each weekday to local stations by Earth-orbiting satellites; each station tapes the satellite feed and may broadcast it at any time that day. The series was originally hosted by Tom Hallick (a former soap opera performer), Marjorie Wallace, and Ron Hendren (a former San Francisco TV critic who had been a regular contributor on the *Today show*). Hallick and Wallace were quickly dumped, and Hendren became the co-host with Dixie Whatley in November 1981. Whatley was in turn replaced by Mary Hart in August 1982. Hendren left the show in September 1984, and was succeeded as cohost by Robb Weller, who was in turn replaced by John Tesh in the fall of 1986. Thereafter, a new set was constructed, designed to minimize the height difference between Hart and Tesh and to highlight Hart's legs. The Hart-Tesh pairing worked well, as Entertainment Tonight was never seriously challenged by rival showbiz magazine series (see *Extra—The Entertainment Magazine* and *Personalities*). By the mid-1990s Tesh had become known as a composer as well, having recorded several CDs of instrumental music (he also composed the theme to the Saturday morning cartoon show *Bobby's World*). Julie Moran succeeded Leeza Gibbons as weekend coanchor, with Bob Goen, in mid-1995.

A companion show, *Entertainment This Week,* a weekly recap of showbiz news intended for weekend broadcast, has also been offered since 1981. It was emceed by the *ET* weeknight cohosts until the fall of 1982, when Dixie Whatley and Steve Edwards took over; Alan Arthur succeeded Edwards in 1983. Both cohosts were replaced in 1984, as Robb Weller and Leeza Gibbons took over. Weller in turn was replaced by weekday cohost John Tesh in 1989.

EQUAL JUSTICE   ABC

27 MARCH 1990–27 JUNE 1990; 15 AUGUST 1990–29 AUGUST 1990; 9 JANUARY 1991–10 APRIL 1991; 19 JUNE 1991–24 JULY 1991   The men and women of the Pittsburgh district attorney's office were the subjects of this hour dramatic series. The ensemble cast included George DiCenzo as District Attorney Arnold Bach; Cotter Smith as his chief deputy, Gene Rogan; Joe Morton as Michael James; Debrah Farentino as Julie Janovich; Barry Miller as male chauvinist Peter "Briggs" Brigman; Jane Kaczmarek as Linda Bauer, head of the sex crime unit; James Wilder as Christopher Searls; Jon Tenney as Peter Bauer; Sarah Jessica Parker as rookie prosecutor Jo Ann Harris; Kathleen Lloyd as Jessie Rogan, Gene's wife; and Lynn Whitfield as local TV anchor Maggie Mayfield.

THE EQUALIZER   CBS

18 SEPTEMBER 1985–7 SEPTEMBER 1989   A modern-day version of the classic TV western *Have Gun Will Travel,* this hour adventure series was set in New York, and starred British actor Edward Woodward as Robert McCall, a former government agent who made his services available, through a newspaper advertisement, to persons who faced adverse situations; McCall's presence was intended to "equalize" the situation. Also featured were Robert Lansing as Control, McCall's former supervisor at the federal agency; William Zabka as McCall's teenage son, Scott; Steven Williams (1985–1986) as Lieutenant Burnett of the N.Y.P.D.; Ron O'Neal (1986–1987) as Lieutenant Smalls; Chad Redding (1987–1989) as Sergeant Alice Shepard; and Keith Szarabajka (1986–1989) as McCall's young assistant, Mickey Kostmayer. In the summer of 1987 Woodward suffered a heart attack, and had to curtail his schedule; Richard Jordan was signed to take up some of the slack, appearing that season as Harley Gage, a former federal colleague. Maureen Anderman joined the cast in December 1987 as Pete O'Phelan, another former colleague who now operated a Manhattan cafe.

THE ERN WESTMORE SHOW   SYNDICATED/ABC

1953 (SYNDICATED); 7 AUGUST 1955–11 SEPTEMBER 1955 (ABC)   Advice on make-up for women from beauty consultant Ern Westmore. Westmore's wife, Betty, also appeared on the series, which was seen Sundays over ABC.

ERNIE KOVACS   NBC/CBS

14 MAY 1951–29 JUNE 1951 (NBC); 2 JULY 1951–24 AUGUST 1951 (NBC); 4 JANUARY 1952–28 MARCH 1952 (NBC); 30 DECEMBER 1952–14 APRIL 1953 (CBS); 12 DECEMBER 1955–27 JULY 1956 (NBC); 2 JULY 1956–10 SEPTEMBER 1956 (NBC)   A brilliant and iconoclastic comedian, Ernie Kovacs pioneered the use of blackouts and trick photography in television comedy. He frequently satirized TV programs and commercials, and introduced his audiences to a host of Kovacsian characters, such as lisping poet Percy Dovetonsils, German disc jockey Wolfgang Sauerbraten, Chinese songwriter Irving Wong, as well as J. Walter Puppybreath and Uncle Gruesome. Many of his shows also featured The Nairobi Trio, a motley group of three instrumentalists dressed in ape suits.

Kovacs grew up in Trenton, New Jersey, but honed his unique skills in Philadelphia, where at one time he found himself hosting three local shows simultaneously: *Three to Get Ready,* a two-hour daily morning show on Philadelphia's channel 3; *Deadline for Dinner,* a lighthearted afternoon cooking show; and *Pick Your Ideal,* a weekly fashion show. His work on *Three to Get Ready,* most of which was improvised, caught the attention of network executives, and in May of 1951 he hosted his first NBC series, *It's Time for Ernie,* a fifteen-minute afternoon effort. In July Kovacs was given a weekday evening slot as a summer replacement for *Kukla, Fran and Ollie;* the thirty-minute show was titled *Ernie in Kovacsland.* Early in 1952 he reappeared on daytime TV as the host of a morning show, *Kovacs on the Korner,* the last of his shows to originate from Philadelphia.

In April of 1952 Kovacs moved to New York to host a local daytime show on WCBS-TV, *Kovacs Unlimited,* which ran until January 1954. In December 1952 the CBS network gave him a prime-time hour series, *The Ernie Kovacs Show.* Billed as "the shortest hour in television," the program was unfortunately scheduled opposite Milton Berle's *Texaco Star Theater* on NBC, and, like most of Berle's competition in those years, folded quickly.

In the spring of 1954 Kovacs moved over to WABD-TV, New York's DuMont outlet, where he hosted a late-night local show for about a year. Late in 1955 he returned to NBC, where he hosted another daytime series; shortly before the daytime show ended its seven-month run, Kovacs began hosting a Monday-night variety hour, which replaced *Caesar's Hour* for the summer.

All of Kovacs's network shows (except *It's Time for Ernie*) featured singer Edie Adams. One of Kovacs's staffers had spotted her on Arthur Godfrey's *Talent Scouts,* where she was an unsuccessful contestant, and recommended her to Kovacs; they were married in 1954. Other regulars on Kovacs's early shows included Andy McKay,

Trigger Lund, and Eddie Hatrak. Regulars on the 1956 summer series included Barbara Loden, Peter Hanley, Bill Wendell, Al Kelly, and the Bob Hamilton Dancers.

In addition to the several series mentioned here, Kovacs also filled in twice a week for Steve Allen on the *Tonight* show during the fall of 1956, hosted a game show (see *Take a Good Look*), a motion picture anthology series (see *Silents Please*), and starred in several television specials. The first, and most unusual, of these was a half-hour special broadcast by NBC on 19 January 1957 which featured not a single word of dialogue. Kovacs's final television work was a series of monthly specials carried by the ABC network during 1961 and 1962; these programs, which were videotaped, demonstrated his mastery of the medium. A technical perfectionist, Kovacs conceived a wide array of special effects and thought nothing of spending thousands of dollars on a three- or four-second sequence.

The last Kovacs special was televised 23 January 1962, barely a week after his tragic death in an auto accident while returning home from a party in Beverly Hills. In 1977 excerpts from several of Kovacs's shows were packaged for educational television under the title *The Best of Ernie Kovacs*. On 14 May 1984 ABC aired a made-for-TV movie, "Ernie Kovacs: Between the Laughter," which dramatized Kovacs's desperate efforts to locate the two daughters from his first marriage. Jeff Goldblum and Melody Anderson starred as Kovacs and Adams; Edie Adams herself made a cameo appearance as Mae West.

THE ERROL FLYNN THEATRE   SYNDICATED
1957   Half-hour dramatic anthology series hosted by Errol Flynn, the swashbuckling star of dozens of adventure films.

ESCAPE   CBS
5 JANUARY 1950–30 MARCH 1950   This Thursday-night anthology series—usually of thrillers—was derived from the radio show which ran from 1947 to 1954; it was narrated by William Conrad, and produced and directed by Wyllis Cooper.

ESCAPE   NBC
11 FEBRUARY 1973–1 APRIL 1973   Jack Webb produced and narrated this dramatic anthology series purportedly based on true stories of persons enmeshed in do-or-die situations.

ESPECIALLY FOR YOU
See THE ROBERTA QUINLAN SHOW

ESPIONAGE   NBC
2 OCTOBER 1963–2 SEPTEMBER 1964   Produced in England, this anthology series presented spy stories. Herbert Brodkin produced.

ETHEL AND ALBERT   NBC/CBS/ABC
25 APRIL 1953–25 DECEMBER 1954 (NBC); 20 JUNE 1955–26 SEPTEMBER 1955 (CBS); 14 OCTOBER 1955–6 JULY 1956 (ABC)   A low-key situation comedy, *Ethel and Albert* starred Peg Lynch and Alan Bunce as Ethel and Albert Arbuckle, a middle-aged married couple who lived in the town of Sandy Harbor. Lynch created and wrote the series, which began on radio over a local station in Minnesota in 1938 and went network in 1944 (Lynch's radio costar for several years was Richard Widmark). *Ethel and Albert*'s first television exposure was during the 1952–1953 season, when it was telecast as a regular fifteen-minute segment of *The Kate Smith Hour;* in April of 1953 it was given its own half-hour slot on Saturday nights. In 1955 it was carried by CBS as a summer replacement for *December Bride,* and in the fall of 1955 ABC broadcast the show on Fridays. By the spring of 1956, it had become the last live sitcom regularly broadcast on network television. The practice was revived briefly in 1959 on *Too Young to Go Steady,* and not again until 1992 on *Roc.*

ETHEL BARRYMORE THEATER SYNDICATED

1953 Half-hour dramatic anthology series hosted by seventy-seven-year-old Ethel Barrymore, star of stage and screen, and sister of John and Lionel Barrymore.

ETHICS IN AMERICA PBS

31 JANUARY 1989–11 APRIL 1989 Hour panel discussion series on which hypothetical ethical questions were discussed and analyzed. Fred W. Friendly was the producer.

EUREEKA'S CASTLE NICKELODEON

4 SEPTEMBER 1989– An hour daytime potpourri of puppetry, live action, and animated segments, aimed at young viewers.

EVANS AND NOVAK SYNDICATED

1976 This hour-long series examined political issues in depth. Syndicated columnists Rowland Evans and Robert Novak hosted the show, which was produced in Washington by Gordon Hyatt.

THE EVE ARDEN SHOW CBS

17 SEPTEMBER 1957–25 MARCH 1958 After the cancellation of *Our Miss Brooks,* Eve Arden returned a year later in this unsuccessful situation comedy, based on Emily Kimbrough's autobiography. Arden starred as Liza Hammond, a widow who made her living as a traveling lecturer. Also featured were Allyn Joslyn as George Howell, her agent; Karen Greene as Mary, her thirteen-year-old, the nonidentical twin sister of Jenny, played by Gail Stone; and Frances Bavier as Nora, the housekeeper who tended the twins while Liza was on the road. Produced by Robert Sparks and Edmund Hartmann, the series was directed by John Rich.

THE EVE HUNTER SHOW NBC

10 OCTOBER 1951–28 MARCH 1952 Eve Hunter hosted this daily hour interview show for six months during the 1951–1952 season. Because the show was broadcast at one o'clock, few NBC affiliates carried it, choosing instead to carry local programs at that hour. It was not until the late 1970s that NBC again carried a regular network show at one o'clock.

EVENING AT POPS PBS

12 JULY 1970– A recurring summer series, *Evening at Pops* presents the Boston Pops Orchestra, under the direction of Arthur Fiedler (until his death in 1979), together with guest artists. The series continued under the Pops' new director, John Williams. Though he is best known as a composer of film scores (including *Star Wars, The Empire Strikes Back, E.T.,* and many others), Williams also worked extensively in television; he composed themes for such series as *Bachelor Father, Alcoa Premiere, Checkmate, Wide Country, The Time Tunnel,* and *Lost in Space,* and won Emmys for his scores of "Heidi" (1968) and "Jane Eyre" (1971). Keith Lockhart was named to replace Williams in 1995.

EVENING AT SYMPHONY PBS

6 OCTOBER 1974–20 DECEMBER 1979 An hour of classical music, taped at Symphony Hall in Boston, with the Boston Symphony Orchestra.

AN EVENING AT THE IMPROV SYNDICATED/A&E

1981–1983 (SYNDICATED); 5 OCTOBER 1985– (A&E) An hour program of stand-up comedy, taped at the Improv in Los Angeles, a popular showcase for up-and-coming funny people. The series ceased production in 1994, but continued to be aired on A&E.

EVENING MAGAZINE
See P.M. MAGAZINE

EVENING SHADE CBS

21 SEPTEMBER 1990–4 JULY 1994   The first network series set in Arkansas, this sitcom was created by Linda (*Designing Women*) Bloodworth-Thomason. It was set in Evening Shade, a sleepy town peopled largely by eccentrics, and starred Burt Reynolds as Wood Newton, coach of Evening Shade's hapless high school football team. Also on board were Marilu Henner as Wood's wife, Ava, candidate for local prosecuting attorney; Jay R. Ferguson as their older son, Taylor; Melissa Renee Martin (1990–1991) and Candace Hutson (1991–1994) as their daughter, Molly; Jacob Parker as their younger son, Will; Hal Holbrook as Ava's father, Evan Evans, publisher of the *Evening Shade Argus;* Linda Gehringer as stripper Fontana Beausoleil, who married Evan in the fall of 1991; Elizabeth Ashley as Evan's sister, Freida Evans; Charles Durning as Harlan Elldridge, the town doctor; Ann Wedgeworth as his wife, Merleen; Ossie Davis as Ponder Blue, owner of the local rib joint; Michael Jeter as Wood's inexperienced assistant coach, math teacher Herman Stiles; and Charlie Dell as the addled adult paper boy, Nub Oliver. In the spring of 1991 Wood and Ava had a fourth child, Emily (played in later seasons by Alexa Vega).

AN EVENING WITH SYNDICATED

1966   An anthology variety series that showcased a different performer each week. There were no regulars.

THE EVERGLADES SYNDICATED

1961   In this half-hour adventure series Ron Hayes starred as Lincoln Vail, officer of Florida's Everglades County Patrol. Gordon Cosell costarred as Chief Anderson, Vail's commanding officer.

THE EVERLY BROTHERS SHOW ABC

8 JULY 1970–16 SEPTEMBER 1970   A summer replacement for *The Johnny Cash Show.* The cohosts, Don and Phil Everly, began making records in 1957; their sound, which blended elements of country and rock music, influenced many artists, including the Beatles. Regulars on the series included Ruth McDevitt and Joe Higgins.

EVERYBODY'S TALKING ABC

6 FEBRUARY 1967–29 DECEMBER 1967   Daytime game show on which contestants, after watching film clips of people talking, tried to guess what they were talking about. A celebrity panel was on hand to help the players. Lloyd Thaxton hosted the show. A very similar concept was employed in the 1973 game show, *Hollywood's Talking.*

EVERYDAY SYNDICATED

1978–1979   A daily hour variety-talk show with two cohosts—Stephanie Edwards and John Bennett Perry—and five other regulars: Anne Bloom, Tom Chapin, Robert Corff, Judy Gibson, and Murray Langston (formerly *The Gong Show*'s "Unknown Comic"). David Salzman was the executive producer for Group W Productions.

EVERYDAY WITH JOAN LUNDEN SYNDICATED

1989–1990   A five-day-a-week talk show emceed by busy Joan Lunden, who simultaneously cohosted *Good Morning America* on ABC. The show was available to local stations in either a thirty- or sixty-minute format.

EVERYTHING GOES SYNDICATED

1973   Variety show produced in Canada, cohosted by comedians Norm Crosby and Tom O'Malley.

EVERYTHING'S ARCHIE
See THE ARCHIE SHOW

EVERYTHING'S RELATIVE   SYNDICATED

1965   Jim Hutton hosted this game show, which pitted two families against each other. Individual family members were called on to answer a question or perform a task; the remaining family members then predicted whether the other one would be able to answer or perform correctly.

EVERYTHING'S RELATIVE   CBS

3 OCTOBER 1987–7 NOVEMBER 1987   Only six episodes of this sitcom were broadcast. It told the story of two brothers, one white collar and one blue collar, who shared a Manhattan loft, and their meddlesome mom. With Jason Alexander as Julian Beeby, the white collar, who was co-owner of a products testing company; John Bolger as Scott Beeby, the blue collar, who was a construction worker; Anne Jackson as their mother, Rae; Tony Deacon Nittoli as their pal Mickey; and Gina Hecht as Julian's partner, Emily Cabot.

EVERYWHERE I GO   CBS

7 OCTOBER 1952–6 JANUARY 1953   Dan Seymour hosted this human interest series, which was seen Tuesday and Thursday afternoons. It was one of the first daytime shows to employ production techniques such as backscreen projection, so that a housewife on stage would appear to be standing in her kitchen at home; producer Irv Gitlin described the effect as a "studio without walls." Lloyd Gross directed.

THE EVIL TOUCH   SYNDICATED

1973   An anthology series of half-hour melodramas, hosted by Anthony Quayle. Produced in Canada.

EWOKS   ABC

7 SEPTEMBER 1985–5 SEPTEMBER 1987   The furry creatures from the movie *Return of the Jedi* were the stars of this Saturday-morning cartoon show. From 1 March to 6 September 1986 *Ewoks* combined forces with *Droids,* another cartoon show based on characters from the *Star Wars* films; the resulting hour was titled *The Ewoks and Droids Adventure Hour.* In the fall of 1986 the series was titled *The All-New Ewoks.*

EXCLUSIVE   SYNDICATED

1960   The stories on this half-hour dramatic anthology series were all written by members of the Overseas Press Club of America.

EXCURSION   NBC

13 SEPTEMBER 1953–21 MARCH 1954   Burgess Meredith hosted this wide-ranging Sunday-afternoon documentary series. Some programs were devoted to the arts, some examined foreign cultures, and some featured interviews with such guests as former President Harry S. Truman. The show was produced first by Jerry Bragg, and later by Pete Barnum, for the Ford Foundation TV Workshop; Dan Petrie directed.

EXECUTIVE SUITE   CBS

20 SEPTEMBER 1976–11 FEBRUARY 1977   A continuing drama set at the Cardway Corporation, a large conglomerate headquartered in Los Angeles. The large cast included Mitchell Ryan as Dan Walling, concerned corporate president; Sharon Acker as Helen Walling, his wife; Leigh McCloskey as Brian Walling, their prodigal son; Wendy Phillips as Stacey Walling, their radical daughter; Stephen Elliott as Howell Rutledge, reactionary senior vice president; Gwyda DonHowe as Astrid Rutledge, his scheming wife; Byron Morrow as Pearce Newberry, alcoholic VP; Madlyn Rhue as Hilary Madison, the only woman on the board of directors; Percy Rodriguez as Malcolm Gibson, the only black board member; William Smithers as Anderson Galt, philandering VP; Patricia Smith as Leona Galt, his troubled wife; Joan Prather as Glory Dalessio, Anderson Galt's secretary and after-hours companion; Paul Lambert as Tom Dalessio, Glory's father, the plant manager; Brenda Sykes as Summer Johnson, Glory's black roommate who fell in love with Brian Walling; Richard Cox as Mark Desmond, hotshot young executive; Trisha Noble as Yvonne

Holland, the woman who purported to be Mark's wife; Carl Weintraub as Harry Ragin, shop steward; and Scott Marlowe as Nick Coslo, an industrial spy. Based loosely on the novel by Cameron Hawley, the show was produced by Don Brinkley and later by Buck Houghton; its executive producers were Norman Felton and Stanley Rubin.

THE EXILE   CBS
2 APRIL 1991–21 DECEMBER 1994   One segment of CBS's late-night umbrella, *Crime Time After Prime Time*, this one was filmed in Paris. It starred Jeffrey Meek as John Stone, an American spy in East Germany who had been framed for murder; he was given a new identity—John Phillips—by friends in the intelligence service so that he could elude capture while continuing to search for the people who had framed him. Christian Burgess costarred as Charles Cabot, Paris bureau chief of the DCS intelligence agency. Also featured were Patrick Floershim as French intelligence agent Danny Montreau, and Jacquie Decaux as Stone's landlady, Nadia. In the series' final episode Stone learned that it was Cabot himself who had framed him. *The Exile* was scheduled regularly through the fall of 1991, and then popped up on *Crime Time After Prime Time* only occasionally.

EXPEDITION!   ABC
20 SEPTEMBER 1960–23 APRIL 1962   Documentary series that presented modern-day geographical adventures. Hosted by Colonel John D. Craig.

EXPLORING   NBC
13 OCTOBER 1962–17 APRIL 1965; 8 JANUARY 1966–9 APRIL 1966   An educational series for children that explored language, music, mathematics, social studies, and science. Televised Saturdays, the show was hosted by Dr. Albert R. Hibbs, who was assisted by the Ritts Puppets: Magnolia the Ostrich, Albert the Chipmunk and Sir Godfrey Turtle.

EXPLORING GOD'S WORLD   CBS
4 JULY 1954–26 SEPTEMBER 1954   This Sunday-morning series for children presented films about natural history. Carrie McCord was the host, and was assisted by youngsters Lydia Jean Shaffer and Glenn Walken.

EXPOSÉ   NBC
6 JANUARY 1991–1 NOVEMBER 1991   Half-hour prime-time investigative news program, anchored by Tom Brokaw, with reports from Brian Ross. The show was seen approximately three times a month; on the fourth week, *Real Life with Jane Pauley* expanded to a full hour to fill the gap.

EXTRA—THE ENTERTAINMENT MAGAZINE   SYNDICATED
1994–   A clone of *Entertainment Tonight*, this half-hour daily series presented news and other features from the world of entertainment. Dave Nemeth and Arthel Neville were the weekday anchors, Maureen O'Boyle the weekend anchor.

THE EXTRAORDINARY   SYNDICATED
1994–   Hour weekly series comprised mainly of videotaped interviews with persons who claimed to have experienced extraordinary events—such as premonitions, encounters with aliens, etc.—and reenactments of those events. A cigar smoking Corbin Bernsen hosted the series and provided the overblown introductions to the segments.

EXTREME   ABC
29 JANUARY 1995–6 APRIL 1995   Hour adventure series set in the Colorado Rockies, and filmed on location. The central characters were the handsome men and women of Extreme Mountain Rescue, who were likely to be found in bed with one another when they weren't on the slopes rescuing the unfortunate. James Brolin played the boss, Reese Wheeler, and was joined by Cameron Bancroft as new member Kyle

Hansen (Reese had climbed with Kyle's father); Brooke Langton as Sarah Bowen; Justin Lazard as Lance Monroe; Julie Bowen as Amanda "Andie" McDermott; Tom Wright as pilot Farley Potts; Micah Dyer as Sarah's teen brother, "Bones" Bowen; Danny Masterson as Bones's snowboarding pal, Skeeter; and Elizabeth Gracen as scheming businesswoman Callie Manners.

EYE GUESS NBC
3 JANUARY 1966–26 SEPTEMBER 1969   This daytime game show tested contestants' abilities to memorize. After observing a board containing the answers to eight upcoming questions for eight seconds, the contestants had to choose the location of the correct answer when the corresponding questions were asked by host Bill Cullen.

EYE ON HOLLYWOOD ABC
4 AUGUST 1983–1 SEPTEMBER 1983; 21 FEBRUARY 1984–18 JULY 1986   Like *Entertainment Tonight,* this series presented short features mainly about showbiz. During the summer of 1983 it was seen in prime time, and was hosted by Chuck Henry, Johnny Mountain, and Tawny Schneider. In February 1984 it returned to the air, scheduled weeknights at midnight, with cohosts Tawny Schneider and Paul Moyer. Jann Carl took over as host in 1985.

EYE ON NEW YORK CBS
25 DECEMBER 1955–4 NOVEMBER 1956; 9 JUNE 1957–1 SEPTEMBER 1957; 2 MARCH 1958–31 AUGUST 1958; 28 DECEMBER 1958–6 SEPTEMBER 1959   A wide-ranging Sunday-morning documentary series, *Eye on New York* examined the problems, the politics, and the cultural life of New York City. Bill Leonard hosted the half-hour show, which shared a time slot with *The U.N. in Action.*

EYE ON SPORTS
See CBS SPORTS SPECTACULAR

EYE TO EYE ABC
21 MARCH 1985–2 MAY 1985   Hour crime series based on the 1977 film *The Late Show,* about an aging private eye who teamed up with the daughter of his ex-partner after the latter's murder. With Charles Durning as Oscar Poole and Stephanie Faracy as Tracy Doyle. Six episodes were produced; the premiere was televised twice during the show's brief run.

EYE TO EYE WITH CONNIE CHUNG CBS
17 JUNE 1993–13 APRIL 1995; 25 MAY 1995–31 AUGUST 1995   Connie Chung's third CBS news or interview series (see also *Face to Face with Connie Chung* and *Saturday Night with Connie Chung*) was an hour of interviews and reported stories, anchored by Chung. The series' most noteworthy moment occurred on a January 1995 broadcast, when Chung persuaded interviewee Kathleen Gingrich, mother of newly elected speaker of the house Newt Gingrich, to whisper to Chung that her son thought First Lady Hillary Rodham Clinton was a "bitch." The elder Gingrich, a stranger to the ways of broadcast journalism, thought that her remark was a private one and would not be aired. In mid-May 1995 Chung was relieved of her duties as coanchor of *The CBS Evening News* and as regular anchor of *Eye to Eye.*

EYE WITNESS NBC
30 MARCH 1953–29 JUNE 1953   A half-hour mystery anthology series, broadcast live from New York, *Eye Witness* presented stories about people who had witnessed crimes. Richard Carlson was the first host and was succeeded by Lee Bowman.

THE EYES HAVE IT NBC
20 NOVEMBER 1948–19 JUNE 1949   Ralph McNair hosted this half-hour game show on which contestants sought to identify photographs.

EYES ON THE PRIZE   PBS
21 JANUARY 1987–25 FEBRUARY 1987
EYES ON THE PRIZE II   PBS
15 JANUARY 1990–5 MARCH 1990   An absorbing look at America's struggle for civil
rights, brilliantly put together by Henry Hampton. The series relied almost exclusively on newsreel footage and interviews with participants, and avoided analysis by
academics and journalists. The first series, narrated by Julian Bond and televised in
six hour-long segments, spanned the period from 1954 to 1965 and focused mainly on
desegregation efforts in the South. The second series, in eight hour-long installments,
moved from the turbulent years of the late 1960s up to the mid-1980s.

EYEWITNESS TO HISTORY   CBS
30 SEPTEMBER 1960–26 JULY 1963   Charles Kuralt hosted this Friday-night public
affairs program on which the most significant news story (or stories) was reviewed.
The show's title was shortened to *Eyewitness* in its last season.

THE EZIO PINZA SHOW (THE RCA VICTOR SHOW
STARRING EZIO PINZA)   NBC
23 NOVEMBER 1951–13 JUNE 1952   Ezio Pinza, the Italian-American opera singer
who starred in *South Pacific* on Broadway, made his TV debut in September 1951 as
host of *All-Star Revue*. The reaction was so favorable that he was given his own
variety series later that fall. The half-hour show was seen weekly until February,
when it began alternating bi-weekly with *The Dennis Day Show*. In the fall of 1953,
Pinza returned to star in an ethnic sitcom: see *Bonino*.

THE F.B.I.   ABC
19 SEPTEMBER 1965–8 SEPTEMBER 1974   ABC's longest-running crime show was
produced with the cooperation of J. Edgar Hoover, director of the Federal Bureau of
Investigation. It starred Efrem Zimbalist, Jr., as Inspector Lewis Erskine, a man of
impeccable integrity and little humor; Philip Abbott as Agent Arthur Ward; Stephen
Brooks (1965–1967) as Agent Jim Rhodes, boyfriend of Erskine's daughter; Lynn
Loring (1965–1966) as Barbara Erskine, Lew's daughter; William Reynolds (1967–
1974) as Agent Tom Colby; and Shelly Novack (1973–1974) as Agent Chris Daniels.
At the conclusion of some episodes, Zimbalist appeared to broadcast the photograph
and description of certain real-life fugitives sought by the FBI. An attempt was made
in 1981 to update the series: see *Today's F.B.I.*

FBI: THE UNTOLD STORIES   ABC
26 SEPTEMBER 1991–26 JUNE 1993   Pernell Roberts hosted this reality-based series
on which exploits of FBI agents were re-enacted.

F.D.R.   ABC
8 JANUARY 1965–10 SEPTEMBER 1965   A series of twenty-seven half-hour documentaries on the life of Franklin Delano Roosevelt. Arthur Kennedy served as host and
narrator; Charlton Heston read excerpts from Roosevelt's writings. Robert D. Graff
and Ben Feiner, Jr., produced the series.

FM   NBC
17 AUGUST 1989–6 SEPTEMBER 1989; 28 MARCH 1990–9 JUNE 1990   A Washington,
D. C., public radio station was the setting for this sitcom. With Robert Hays as Ted
Costas, the program director of WGEO-FM; Patricia Richardson as Ted's ex-wife,
Lee-Ann Plunkett, a reporter; Lynne Thigpen as Naomi; DeLane Matthews as
Gretchen Schreck, a writer; Leo Geter as Jay Edgar, the station's all-purpose production staffer who shared an apartment with Gretchen; Nicole Huntington as Nicole,
Ted and Lee-Ann's fifteen-year-old daughter; Fred Applegate as conservative on-
the-air personality Harrison Green, who cohosted the *Toe to Toe* program with
liberal Lee-Ann; James Avery as Quentin Lamoreaux, host of the classical music
show; John Kassir as Don Topsuni, host of the *Capital Punishment* comedy show; and

Rainbow Harvest as Daryl, the computer technician. Richardson, Matthews, and Geter had all costarred in the short-lived 1988 sitcom *Eisenhower & Lutz*.

FTV   SYNDICATED
1985   The cable network MTV was the target of this syndicated series, which presented parodies of popular music videos. It was hosted by Don Felder, formerly of the Eagles. Other regulars included Khandi Alexander, John Paragon, Stephen Bishop, Pat Matterson, Mark McCollum, and Vic Dunlop.

F TROOP   ABC
14 SEPTEMBER 1965–31 AUGUST 1967   A farcical western that featured a crew of bumbling cavalrymen and a complement of inept Indians. With Ken Berry as Captain Wilton Parmenter, assigned to a command at Fort Courage as a promotion following his unintentional instigation of a Union victory during the Civil War; Forrest Tucker as scheming Sergeant Morgan O'Rourke (the Sergeant Bilko of his day); Larry Storch as Corporal Randolph Agarn, O'Rourke's main henchman; Melody Patterson (who was only sixteen when the series began) as Wrangler Jane, the young woman who ran the post store; Edward Everett Horton as Roaring Chicken, medicine man of the Hekawi tribe; and Frank DeKova as Wild Eagle, Hekawi chief. Produced by Hy Averback.

F.Y.I.   CBS
3 JANUARY 1960–25 SEPTEMBER 1960   This series of half-hour documentaries on various subjects was shown Sunday mornings; *F.Y.I.* was an acronym for "For Your Information."

FABIAN OF SCOTLAND YARD   SYNDICATED
1955   Half-hour crime show starring Bruce Seton as Inspector Fabian. The series was also known as *Patrol Car*.

THE FABULOUS FRAUD
See COLONEL HUMPHREY FLACK

THE FABULOUS FUNNIES   NBC
9 SEPTEMBER 1978–1 SEPTEMBER 1979   On this Saturday-morning children's show, serious topics such as safety and health care were dealt with by characters from the newspaper comic strips such as Alley Oop, Broom Hilda, The Katzenjammer Kids, Nancy and Sluggo, and Shoe. The executive producers of the half-hour series were Norm Prescott and Lou Scheimer.

THE FACE IS FAMILIAR   CBS
7 MAY 1966–3 SEPTEMBER 1966   This Saturday-night game show involved two teams, each consisting of a celebrity and a contestant. The object of the game was to identify the photograph of a famous person; the photo had been cut up into large pieces, scrambled, and covered. By answering questions correctly, contestants were shown the pieces, one by one, and given the chance to identify the subject. The show was hosted by Jack Whitaker, a former weather forecaster for WCAU-TV in Philadelphia, later a CBS network sportscaster.

FACE THE FACTS   CBS
13 MARCH 1961–29 SEPTEMBER 1961   Red Rowe hosted this daytime game show on which contestants tried to predict the outcome of previously filmed dramatizations of criminal trials.

FACE THE MUSIC   CBS
3 MAY 1948–10 DECEMBER 1948   This fifteen-minute musical show was usually seen three nights a week. Featured were singers Johnny Desmond and Shaye Cogan (who was later replaced by Sandra Deel) and the Tony Mottola Trio. Ace Ochs produced the series and Worthington "Tony" Miner directed it.

FACE THE MUSIC   SYNDICATED

1980   Half-hour game show hosted by Ron Ely (formerly the star of the TV series *Tarzan*) on which three contestants tried to identify song titles and associate them with photographs of celebrities.

FACE THE NATION   CBS

7 NOVEMBER 1954–20 APRIL 1961; 15 SEPTEMBER 1963–   *Face the Nation* is the CBS counterpart of NBC's *Meet the Press:* Newsmakers are interviewed by a panel. CBS correspondent George Herman moderated the program from 1969 until September 1983, when correspondent Lesley Stahl succeeded him. At that time the composition of the panels was expanded to include experts as well as journalists. Bob Schieffer took over as moderator in May 1991. The program usually originates from Washington but has been produced at other locations; Soviet Premier Nikita Khrushchev, for example, was interviewed in Moscow in May 1957. Senator Joseph McCarthy was the guest on the 1954 premiere. The series was produced for many years by Mary O. Yates.

FACE TO FACE WITH CONNIE CHUNG   CBS

23 JULY 1990–10 SEPTEMBER 1990   Connie Chung's previous newsmagazine effort, *Saturday Night with Connie Chung*, had struggled in its weekend time slot, but two special Monday telecasts earned respectable ratings and convinced CBS to move the series. *Face to Face* focused less on news stories and more on celebrity interviews.

Shortly after her new series' premiere, Chung surprised her bosses by asking for time off so that she and her husband (Maury Povich of *A Current Affair*) could try to have a child. The series was not scheduled regularly after 1990.

In 1993 Chung returned with a similar series: see *Eye to Eye with Connie Chung*.

FACES OF JAPAN   PBS

1986; 1987   A look at modern Japanese life and culture, hosted by Dick Cavett.

THE FACTS OF LIFE   NBC

24 AUGUST 1979–14 SEPTEMBER 1979; 14 MARCH 1980–10 SEPTEMBER 1988   This durable sitcom, spun off from *Diff'rent Strokes*, went through several changes of format during its nine seasons; only three regulars stayed with the series for its entire run. Originally, it starred Charlotte Rae as Mrs. Edna Garrett, who left the Drummonds' employ on *Diff'rent Strokes* to become a housemother at the Eastland School, a prestigious girls' boarding academy near Peekskill, New York. The original cast also featured John Lawlor (1979–1980) as Steven Bradley, the headmaster; Jenny O'Hara (1979) as Miss Mahoney; Lisa Whelchel as wealthy, self-infatuated Blair Warner; Mindy Cohn as chubby Natalie Green; Kim Fields as Dorothy "Tootie" Ramsey, the black kid; Felice Schachter (1979–1980) as Nancy Olson; Julie Piekarski (1979–1980) as Sue Ann Weaver; Julie Anne Haddock (1979–1980) as Cindy Webster; and Molly Ringwald (1979–1980) as Molly Parker. In the fall of 1980, however, the cast was trimmed to include Rae and just four girls, Whelchel, Cohn, and Fields, and a newcomer: Nancy McKeon as Jo Polniazek, a streetwise kid attending Eastland on a scholarship (the new character was suggested by NBC chief Fred Silverman after he had seen the film *Little Darlings*). From 1981 to 1984 comedienne Geri Jewell was occasionally seen as Blair's cousin, Jeri (Jewell, who had cerebral palsy, was one of the few disabled persons ever to have a regular role on a series).

At the end of the 1982–1983 season Blair and Jo graduated from Eastland. That fall Mrs. Garrett left the school and opened Edna's Edibles, a gourmet food shop in Peekskill; Blair and Jo, now enrolled at nearby Langley College, lived above the store and worked there part-time, as did Tootie and Natalie. Pam Segall was featured during the 1983–1984 season as Kelly Alfonato, a local kid. In the fall of 1985 Edna's Edibles burned to the ground, and Mrs. Garrett opened a new store, a novelty shop called Over Our Heads; again, all four girls worked there. Added to the cast were George Clooney (1985–1986) as handyman George Burnett and Mackenzie Astin (1985–1988) as delivery boy Andy Moffett. In the fall of 1986 (by this time, *The Facts of Life* was NBC's oldest prime-time series) Mrs. Garrett remarried and moved to

Africa with her new husband. Cloris Leachman came aboard as her sister, Beverly Ann Stickle, who took over the store. By the spring of 1987 all four girls were ready to leave the nest: Tootie pursued an acting career, Jo had a job offer in California, Blair planned to go to law school (and eventually bought the Eastland School), and Natalie hoped to become a writer. Over Our Heads closed in the fall of 1987. Joining the cast for the series' final season were Sherrie Krenn as Pippa McKenna, an Australian exchange student; Paul Provenza as Casey Clark; Robert Romanus as Natalie's boyfriend, "Snake" Robinson (Natalie was the first of the girls to have sex); Todd Hollowell as Tootie's fiancé, Jeff Williams; and Scott Bryce as musician Rick Bonner, who married Jo.

FAERIE TALE THEATER SHOWTIME
1982–1987 An engaging hour series of adaptations of classic children's fairy tales. Actress Shelley Duvall served as executive producer, host, and occasional star; she succeeded in attracting some of the industry's top stars and directors, even though her budget was limited. Only twenty-seven programs were made. Among them were "The Tale of the Frog Prince," with Robin Williams and Teri Garr; "Pinocchio," with Pee-wee Herman; and "Rip Van Winkle," with Harry Dean Stanton (directed by Francis Ford Coppola). Duvall went on to develop a second series for Showtime: see *Tall Tales*.

FAIR EXCHANGE CBS
21 SEPTEMBER 1962–28 DECEMBER 1962; 28 MARCH 1963–19 SEPTEMBER 1963 Situation comedy about an American family and a British family who exchanged their teenage daughters for a year. The Yankee family included Eddie Foy, Jr., as Eddie Walker, owner of a New York ticket agency; Audrey Christie as his wife, Dorothy; Lynn Loring as their daughter, Patty; and Flip Mark as their son, Larry. The British family included Victor Maddern as Thomas Finch, owner of a sporting goods store; Diane Chesney as his wife, Sybil; Judy Carne as their daughter, Heather; and Dennis Waterman as their son, Neville. Also featured was Maurice Dallimore as Tom's friend, Willie Shorthouse. Filmed in England and in Hollywood, *Fair Exchange* was one of TV's first hour-long sitcoms. That format proved unwieldy, and the show was canceled in December 1962. Three months later it returned in a half-hour format.

FAIRMEADOWS, U.S.A. NBC
4 NOVEMBER 1951–27 APRIL 1952 *Fairmeadows, U.S.A.* began as a Sunday-afternoon serial about life in a small town. It featured Howard St. John as John Olcott, a businessman who suffered a setback and returned to his hometown, where he opened a general store; Ruth Matteson as his wife, Alice Olcott; Hazel Dawn, Jr., as their older daughter, Mary; Tom Taylor as their son, Jim; Mimi Strongin as their younger daughter, Evvie. In the fall of 1952 the series reappeared with several changes: a new title (*The House in the Garden*), a new time slot (weekday afternoons, as the third quarter hour of *The Kate Smith Hour*), and several new faces, including Lauren Gilbert as John Olcott; Monica Lovett as the older daughter; James Vickery as the older daughter's boyfriend (Ruth Matteson and Tom Taylor were retained). Agnes Ridgeway wrote the series, and Alan Neuman directed it.

FAITH BALDWIN ROMANCE THEATER ABC
20 JANUARY 1951–20 OCTOBER 1951 This dramatic anthology series, hosted by Faith Baldwin, was shown on Saturday afternoons, usually on a biweekly basis.

FAITH FOR TODAY ABC/SYNDICATED
1950–1955 (ABC); 1955–1981 (SYNDICATED); 1984– (SYNDICATED) This long-running religious series, produced in cooperation with the Seventh Day Adventist Church, was hosted for many years by the Reverend William A. Fagal, often assisted by his wife, Virginia. The half-hour program was centered around a dramatic vignette, usually followed by a short "sermonette" from Reverend Fagal. In the show's early years, members of Fagal's home church played the dramatic parts; later on, professional actors took over the roles. In 1971, the show's format shifted to a

filmed anthology series set at a hospital. Regulars included Robert Clarke as Dr. Jeff Mason; Gordon DeVol as Dr. Wes Gallagher; Laura Wallace as Nurse Penny Peters; and Sarina Grant as Nurse Kitty Williams. Reverend Fagal occasionally appeared as the hospital chaplain. In most areas the show was then known as *Westbrook Hospital,* although in some markets it retained the *Faith for Today* title.

Production of the anthology series ceased in 1981; Reverend Fagal also died that year. In 1984 a new talk-show format was introduced. The new series, titled *Christian Lifestyle Magazine,* was hosted by Dan Matthews; Lena Nozizwe joined him as cohost from 1987 to 1991. In that year the series focused on health, and shortened its title to *Lifestyle Magazine.*

THE FALCON
See THE ADVENTURES OF THE FALCON

FALCON CREST CBS
4 DECEMBER 1981–17 MAY 1990 The wine country of northern California was the locale for this prime-time hour serial, created by Earl (*The Waltons*) Hamner. Scheduled at 10:00 p.m. on Fridays for its first three seasons, the show benefited from an exceptionally strong lead-in, *Dallas.* The basic storyline of *Falcon Crest* centered on the efforts of strong-willed Angela Channing to gain complete and exclusive control of the Falcon Crest vineyard and winery. The cast included: Jane Wyman as Angela Channing, the ruthless, calculating co-owner; Robert Foxworth (1981–1987) as her nephew, Chase Gioberti, who came to claim his share of Falcon Crest after the mysterious death of his father, Angela's brother; Abby Dalton (1981–1986) as Julia Cumson, Angela's divorced daughter; Lorenzo Lamas as Julia's son, Lance Cumson, Angela's frequent co-conspirator; Margaret Ladd as Emma Channing, Angela's unbalanced daughter; Susan Sullivan (1981–1989) as Chase's wife, writer Maggie Gioberti; Jamie Rose (1981–1983) as their daughter, Victoria; Billy R. Moses (1981–1986) as their son, Cole; Chao-Li Chi as Chao-Li Chi, the Channings' butler; Nick Ramus (1981–1982) as Gus Nunoz, a vineyard worker; Mario Marcelino (1981–1982) as Gus's son, Mario; Stephen Elliott (1981–1982) as Angela's ex-husband, San Francisco publisher Douglas Channing; Ana Alicia (1982–1988) as the scheming Melissa Agretti, who married Lance Cumson; Carlos Romero (1982–1983) as Melissa's father, rival vintner Carlo Agretti, who was murdered by Julia; David Selby (1982–1990) as Richard Channing, Douglas's illegitimate son (and his successor as publisher of the San Francisco *Globe*), who became Angela's chief rival and who married Maggie Gioberti after Chase's death; Shannon Tweed (1982–1983) as Richard's assistant, Diana Hunter; Sarah Douglas (1983–1985) as Richard's next assistant, Pamela Lynch; Mel Ferrer (1982–1984) as lawyer Philip Erikson, who married Angela; Roy Thinnes (1982–1983) as Nick Hogan, who married Victoria Gioberti; Cliff Robertson (1983–1984) as Chase's cousin, neurosurgeon Michael Ranson; Mary Kate McGeehan (1982–1984) as Linda, who married Cole Gioberti; and Laura Johnson (1983–1986) as Maggie's sister, Terry Hartford. Lana Turner also appeared occasionally as Chase's mother, Jacqueline Perrault, who was killed at the end of the 1982–1983 season as her son tried to wrestle a gun from Julia Cumson. After Turner's departure, *Falcon Crest* continued the practice of signing up major stars who rarely appeared on television.

The series' popularity peaked during the 1983–1984 season, when it finished seventh in the Nielsens. The biggest addition to the cast during the 1984–1985 season was Gina Lollobrigida, who played Francesca Gioberti, Angela's half-sister, for a season. Also added were Kate Vernon (1984–1985) as Lorraine Prescott; Parker Stevenson (1984–1985) as Joel McCarthy; J. Paul Freeman (1984–1985) as neo-Nazi Gustav Riebmann; Simon MacCorkindale (1984–1986) as Greg Reardon; and Anne Archer (spring 1985) as Cassandra Wilder. Another half dozen major characters were added for the 1985–1986 season: former rocker Apollonia Kotero (1985–1986) as Apollonia (Kotero ordered seventy-two items of lingerie for the show); Cesar Romero (1985–1987) as Peter Stavros, who married Angela Channing; Morgan Fairchild (1985–1986) as Jordan Roberts; Ken Olin (1985–1986) as Father Christopher;

Daniel Greene (1985–1986) as Wayne Cooley; and Barbara Howard (1985–1986) as Robin Agretti. The season climaxed when an earthquake struck the area.

Joining the cast for the 1986–1987 season were Kim Novak (1986–1987) as mysterious Kit Marlowe; Jill Jacobson (fall 1986) as Erin Jones; Jane Badler (1986–1987) as Erin's sister, Meredith Braxton; Jeff Kober (1986–1987) as Guy Stafford; Robin Greer (1986–1987) as Dina Wells; Dana Sparks (1986–1988) as Chase and Maggie's daughter, Vickie (Jamie Rose had originally played the role in the show's early years); John Callahan (1986–1988) as Eric Stavros, who married Vickie; Laurel Schaefer (1986–1988) as Mrs. Whitaker; and Brett Cullen (1986–1988) as drifter Dan Fixx.

By the 1987–1988 season the stories began to drift away from the vineyard and toward crime, as the mysterious Thirteen organization went after Richard Channing. The new emphasis did little good, as the series slipped from 23rd place in 1986–1987 to 34th in 1987–1988. New cast members included John David Carson (1987–1988) as Jay Spence; Mariska Hargitay (1987–1989) as Carly Fixx, sister of Dan; Mary Ann Mobley (1987–1988) as psychiatrist Beth Everdene; Cindy Morgan (1987–1988) as Gabrielle Short; and Maggie Cooper as Allison.

Joining for the 1988–1989 season were Kristian Alfonso (former star of the daytime soap *Days of Our Lives*) as Pilar Ortega, who married Lance Cumson (Ana Alicia, who played Lance's first wife, Melissa, until 1988, made a guest appearance on the series' 200th episode that season, as a Melissa lookalike); David Beecroft (1988–1989) as Nick Agretti; Brandon Douglas (1988–1989) as Ben Agretti; Dan Ferro (1988–1989) as Tommy Ortega; Castulo Guerra (1988–1989) as Cesar Ortega; Danny Nucci (1988–1989) as Gabriel Ortega; and Allan Royal (1988–1989) as R. D. Young, Emma's boyfriend.

After a 47th place finish in 1988–1989, *Falcon Crest* limped along for one final season, dropping to 63rd place in 1989–1990; the show was unceremoniously moved to a new time slot on Thursdays for its last few episodes. Jane Wyman made few appearances during the final season, and the final group of new regulars included Gregory Harrison as Michael Sharpe; David Sheinkopf as his son, Danny; Wendy Phillips as Lauren; Andrea Thompson as Genele; Mark Lindsay Chapman as Charley, Emma's new boyfriend; and Frank Runyeon as Jovan. The series' finale was a happy one, as Richard, who now owned the vineyard, married Lauren, and agreed to return Falcon Crest to Angela; Angela, in turn, agreed to give control of the vineyard to Lance, on condition that he remain there as the vineyard manager.

Exteriors for the series were filmed at the Spring Mountain Vineyards in St. Helena, California. Life imitated art in 1982, as Spring Mountain marketed two wines bearing the "Falcon Crest" label.

THE FALL GUY   ABC
4 NOVEMBER 1981–2 MAY 1986   Lee Majors starred in this hour adventure series as Colt Seavers, a Hollywood stuntman who supplemented his income by working as a modern-day bounty hunter, tracking down persons who jumped bail. Also featured were Douglas Barr as Colt's cousin, Howie Munson, an aspiring stuntman; Heather Thomas as stuntwoman Jody Banks; Jo Ann Pflug (1981–1982) as "Big Jack," Markie Post (1982–1985) as Terri Michaels, and Nedra Volz as Pearl Sperling, the bail bondswomen who hired Colt and Company. Glen A. Larson created the series. Lee Majors also sang the show's theme, "Unknown Stuntman." The series performed well in a Wednesday night time slot during its first three seasons. In its fourth year (1984–1985) it was hurt by an unlikely competitor on NBC, *Highway to Heaven*. A move to a Thursday slot in the fall of 1985 was of no avail. A total of 111 episodes were produced.

FAME   NBC/SYNDICATED
7 JANUARY 1982–4 AUGUST 1983 (NBC); 1983–1987 (SYNDICATED)   This hour dramatic series was based on the hit movie about life at New York's High School of Performing Arts, the city's specialized school for hopeful actors, dancers, and musicians. Four members of the movie cast repeated their roles for television: Debbie Allen as dance teacher Lydia Grant; Albert Hague as venerable music instructor

Benjamin Shorofsky (in real life, Hague was better known as a composer and acting teacher); Lee Curreri as musically gifted student Bruno Martelli; and Gene Anthony Ray as talented dancing student Leroy Johnson. Other regulars included Erica Gimpel as singer-dancer Coco Hernandez; Carol Mayo Jenkins as no-nonsense English teacher Elizabeth Sherwood; P.R. Paul (1982) as Montgomery, a student; Lori Singer as cellist Julie Miller; Valerie Landsburg as acting student Doris Schwartz; Carlo Imperato as embryonic comic Danny Amatullo; Michael Thoma (1982) as Mr. Crandall, the drama teacher (Thoma died in September of 1982); Morgan Stevens as David Reardon, the new drama teacher; and Carmine Caridi (1982–1983) as Bruno's father, cabbie Angelo Martelli. Each episode of *Fame* introduced one or two original musical numbers (some of them written by Lee Curreri) and elaborate dance sequences (choreographed by Debbie Allen); two phonograph records of the material were released, together with a live recording of "The Kids from Fame," staged in England, where the show became enormously popular. Unfortunately, the series was not a ratings success in the United States, although it was almost universally praised by the critics. Following its network cancellation, *Fame*'s coproducers, MGM and United Artists, announced plans to continue production of the series for domestic (and foreign) syndication. The new episodes featured most of the members of the network cast (except for Lori Singer), as well as three new regulars: Ken Swofford (1983–1985) as vice-principal Quentin Morloch; Cynthia Gibb as Holly Laird; and Billy Hufsey as Christopher Donlon. Later arrivals included Janet Jackson (1984–1986) as Cleo Hewitt; Jesse Borrego (1984–1987) as Jesse Velasquez; Nia Peeples (1984–1987) as Nicole Chapman; Dick Miller (1985–1987) as Mr. Mackie; Loretta Chandler (1985–1987) as Dusty Chandler; Graham Jarvis (1985–1987) as the new principal, Mr. Dyrenforth; Carrie Hamilton (daughter of Carol Burnett) (1986–1987) as Reggie Higgins; Page Hannah (1986–1987) as Kate Riley; Elisa Heinsohn (1986–1987) as Jillian Beckett; Robert Romanus (1986–1987) as Miltie Horowitz; and Eric Pierpoint (1986–1987) as Mr. Seeger, the new drama teacher. One of the many young performers who auditioned usuccessfully for *Fame* was Madonna.

FAME, FORTUNE & ROMANCE ABC
16 JUNE 1986–27 JUNE 1986; 8 SEPTEMBER 1986–29 MAY 1987 Another of the several celebrity-worshipping shows hosted by Robin Leach, this one was shown in a late-morning time slot. According to Leach, it emphasized love and romance, rather than material acquisitions. See also *Lifestyles of the Rich and Famous; Runaway with the Rich and Famous.*

FAMILY ABC
9 MARCH 1976–13 APRIL 1976; 28 SEPTEMBER 1976–27 APRIL 1979; 24 DECEMBER 1979–25 JUNE 1980 The story of a family of five living in Pasadena, *Family* first appeared as a six-part miniseries in the spring of 1976; it proved popular enough to merit a slot in ABC's fall lineup. Generally well written, and always well acted, the show managed to avoid much of the mawkishness characteristic of other family dramas of the 1970s. *Family* featured Sada Thompson as strong but sensitive Kate Lawrence, the mother of three; James Broderick as her husband, Douglas Lawrence, a lawyer; Elaine Heilveil (spring 1976) and Meredith Baxter Birney (fall 1976–1980) as their spoiled daughter, Nancy Maitland, who was divorced in 1976 and lived in the family's guest house with her young son Timmy while attending law school; Gary Frank as their son Willie, a headstrong youth who quit school and hoped to become a writer; Kristy McNichol as their younger daughter, Buddy (Letitia), an honest and open young teenager adjusting to adolescence; Michael David Shackelford as Timmy, Nancy's toddler. Occasionally featured was John Rubinstein as Nancy's former husband, Jeff Maitland; Rubinstein also composed the show's theme music. The series was created by Jay Presson Allen, and its executive producers were Mike Nichols, Aaron Spelling, and Leonard Goldberg. In the fall of 1978 Quinn Cummings joined the cast as Andrea (Annie) Cooper, an orphan adopted by the Lawrences; Nancy moved into her own apartment, and Willie took over the guest house.

FAMILY AFFAIR   CBS

12 SEPTEMBER 1966–9 SEPTEMBER 1971   This saccharine sitcom was salvaged by the cuteness of its two youthful costars. It starred Brian Keith as Manhattan bachelor Bill Davis, an industrial designer who suddenly finds himself guardian of his nephew and his two nieces (the three children had been raised in separate homes after their parents' deaths); Sebastian Cabot as Davis's manservant, Giles French, a formal Briton with neither the interest nor the inclination to look after small children; Cathy Garver as Bill's teenage niece, Cissy; Johnny Whitaker as his nephew, Jody; and Anissa Jones as his niece, Buffy, Jody's twin sister. Also featured were John Williams as Mr. French's brother, Nigel, who filled in for Giles in the latter's absence; Nancy Walker (1970–1971) as Emily Turner, the cleaning lady; Gregg Fedderson as Gregg Bartlett, Cissy's occasional boyfriend. Young Fedderson was the son of Don Fedderson, executive producer of the series. Following the cancellation of the show in 1971 (after 138 episodes), Johnny Whitaker continued to be seen regularly on TV; he was a regular on *Sigmund and the Sea Monsters* and was featured in several Walt Disney productions. His costar, Anissa Jones, appeared rarely on television; in 1976, she was found dead (from drug-related causes) in her California home.

FAMILY ALBUM   CBS

24 SEPTEMBER 1993–12 NOVEMBER 1993   Half-hour sitcom about a family from California who relocated to Philadelphia to be near their aging parents. With Peter Scolari as Jonathan Lerner, a physician; Pamela Reed as his wife, Denise Lerner; Phillip Van Dyke as teen son Max; Ashlee Levitch as teen daughter Nicki; Chris Miranda as preteen son Jeffrey; Doris Belack as Jonathan's mother, Lillian; Alan North as Jonathan's father, Sid Lerner, also a physician (Jonathan joined his practice); Rhoda Gemignani as Denise's mother, Ruby DeMattis, a beautician; Nancy Cassaro as Denise's sister, Sheila; and Giovanni Ribisi as Sheila's son, Elvis.

FAMILY CLASSICS THEATER

The umbrella title of a group of three miniseries. See: *The Black Tulip, Ivanhoe,* and *Little Women.*

FAMILY DOG   CBS

23 JUNE 1993–28 JULY 1993   One of the biggest disappointments of the season, this prime time animated series looked at family life from the dog's point of view. Unfortunately, it wasn't a very amusing perspective. No one in the family seemed to care for the poor dog, who didn't even have a name. The series's pedigree was impressive: Steven Spielberg and Tim Burton were its executive producers. The character first appeared in an episode of Spielberg's 1985–1987 series, *Amazing Stories*. Episodes were ready in early 1991, but Spielberg and Burton were not satisfied with them, and the show was shelved for two more years. Voices were supplied by Martin Mull as Skip Binford, Molly Cheek as his wife, Bev Binford, Zak Huxtable Epstein as son Billy, and Cassie Cole as daughter Buffy.

FAMILY DOUBLE DARE

See DOUBLE DARE (1986 version)

THE FAMILY FEUD   ABC/SYNDICATED/CBS

12 JULY 1976–14 JUNE 1985 (ABC); 1977–1983 (SYNDICATED); 1988– (SYNDICATED); 4 JULY 1988–24 MAY 1991 (CBS); 29 JUNE 1992–10 SEPTEMBER 1993 (CBS)   This popular game show from Mark Goodson–Bill Todman Productions pitted two families against each other in an effort to match responses to questions previously given to groups of 100 persons. Each family unit consisted of five persons. Richard Dawson hosted the ABC daytime version and the first syndicated version. Ray Combs was the new host when the show returned, in both network daytime and syndicated formats, in 1988. The 1992–1993 network daytime version was an hour in length, and was titled *The New Family Feud Challenge*. The syndicated version expanded to an hour in 1994, when Richard Dawson resumed the hosting chores.

Some special shows have been telecast pitting casts of TV shows, or members of sports teams, against one another.

A FAMILY FOR JOE   NBC
24 MARCH 1990–5 MAY 1990; 5 AUGUST 1990–19 AUGUST 1990   This half-hour sitcom starred Robert Mitchum in an unlikely role, as Joe Whitaker, a homeless oldster who was persuaded to act as a surrogate grandfather for four orphaned children in order to prevent the children from being split up; suddenly, Joe found himself off the streets and into the kids' house, coping with a new life of domesticity. Appearing as the four kids were David Mascher as Nick Bankston; Juliette Lewis as Holly; Ben Savage (younger brother of *Wonder Years*'s Fred Savage) as Chris; and Jessica Player as Mary. Also featured were Barry Gordon as neighbor Roger, and Leon the dog. The series pilot, a two-hour telefilm, was broadcast 25 February 1990.

THE FAMILY GAME   ABC
19 JUNE 1967–15 DECEMBER 1967   Bob Barker hosted this daytime game show on which three families competed; each family consisted of two parents and two children. The children were asked questions before the telecast; the parents then tried to determine which answers had been given by their respective children.

THE FAMILY GENIUS   DUMONT
9 SEPTEMBER 1949–30 SEPTEMBER 1949   Short-lived sitcom about a child prodigy. With Jack Diamond as Tommy Howard, Phyllis Lowe as his mother, and Arthur Edwards as his father. James L. Caddigan and Elwood Hoffman produced the series.

THE FAMILY HOLVAK   NBC
7 SEPTEMBER 1975–27 OCTOBER 1975   Glenn Ford's second TV series proved even less successful than his first (*Cade's County*). Presumably inspired by *The Waltons,* it was based on Jack Ferris's novel, *Ramey,* and told the story of a preacher and his family living in the South during the 1930s. Ford starred as the Reverend Tom Holvak; Julie Harris as his wife, Elizabeth; Lance Kerwin as their son, Ramey; Elizabeth Cheshire as their daughter, Julie Mae; Ted Gehring as storekeeper Chester Purdle; Cynthia Hayward as Ida, his helper; and William McKinney as police deputy Jim Shanks. Executive producers: Roland Kibbee and Dean Hargrove. A few episodes were broadcast over CBS during the summer of 1977.

FAMILY MAN   ABC
18 MARCH 1988–29 APRIL 1988   Half-hour sitcom focusing on the domestic life of a comedy writer. With Richard Libertini as Shelley Tobin; Mimi Kennedy as his wife, Andrea; Alison Sweeney as Andrea's daughter, Rosie; Whitby Hertford as Andrea's son, Josh; and Keeley Mari Gallagher as Shelley and Andrea's daughter, Sarah. The seven-episode series was produced by Universal Television, and was originally intended for the Fox network, which never picked it up.

THE FAMILY MAN   CBS
11 SEPTEMBER 1990–1 DECEMBER 1990; 10 JUNE 1991–17 JULY 1991   Half-hour sitcom starring Gregory Harrison as recently widowed Jack Taylor, a firefighter trying to raise his four kids. With Al Molinaro as Joe Alberghetti, Jack's father-in-law, who moved in to help out; John Buchanan as eldest son Jeff, sixteen; Scott Weinger as number two son Steve, fourteen; Matthew Brooks as number three son Brian, eleven; Ashleigh Blair Sterling as adorable daughter Allison, five; and Josh Byrn as Allison's best friend, Patrick Kozak.

FAMILY MATTERS   ABC
22 SEPTEMBER 1989–   Created by William Bickley and Michael Warren, this half-hour sitcom about a contemporary black family was spun off from *Perfect Strangers*. With JoMarie Payton-France as Harriette Winslow, who had been the elevator operator at the newspaper on *Perfect Strangers;* Reginald VelJohnson as her husband, Carl Winslow, a Chicago cop; Rosetta LeNoire as Estelle Winslow, Carl's live-in mom;

Darius McCrary as Carl and Harriette's fifteen-year-old, Eddie; Kellie Shanygne Williams as their thirteen-year-old, Laura; Jaimee Foxworth (1989–1993) as their nine-year-old, Judy; Telma Hopkins (1989–1993) as Harriette's widowed sister, Rachel; Joseph and Julius Wright (1989–1990) and Bryton McClure (1990–) as Rachel's young son, Richie; Randy Josselyn as Eddie's pal Rodney; and Shawn Harrison as Eddie's pal, Waldo Faldo. Jaleel White first appeared in the ninth episode of the first season as the ultranerdy Steve Urkel, a neighborhood lad whose crush on Laura was unrequited. The character became extremely popular, and by the show's third season most of the stories centered on Urkel. Though superbly played by White (whose talents enabled him to portray other characters from time to time, such as the ultra-suave Stefan Urquelle), the character was one of the most cartoonish, and least truly human, figures ever concocted for a sitcom. Other changes affected the series as well. Much like Chuck, the older brother on *Happy Days*, the character of younger daughter Judy was written out of the show after four seasons. Telma Hopkins left the series during the 1992–1993 season to star in another sitcom, *Getting By*. Her character's young son, however, remained in the Winslow household. Hopkins returned for a few episodes during the 1994–1995 season.

FAMILY SECRETS   NBC
22 MARCH 1993–11 JUNE 1993   Bob Eubanks hosted this short-lived daytime game show on which two families competed; children were asked questions about their parents, and vice versa. Each family was seated in chairs on a mock front porch. The family group with the higher point total then played for the chance to win a vacation.

FAMILY TIES   NBC
22 SEPTEMBER 1982–17 SEPTEMBER 1989   One of the most popular family sitcoms of the 1980s, *Family Ties* was created by Gary David Goldberg. It was originally intended to focus on the generation gap between the parents and their children: mom and dad were caring liberals who traced their ideology to the turbulent sixties (the original opening title sequence, with its flashback photos, illustrated the point), while the kids were either conservative or apathetically materialistic. The dichotomy was downplayed, however, after network research indicated that viewers were more interested in the children. The result was that one of the kids, Michael J. Fox, became a superstar; ironically, NBC executives had originally balked at Goldberg's suggestion of Fox for the role.

The series was set in Columbus, Ohio. Appearing as the Keaton family were: Meredith Baxter Birney as Elyse, an architect; Michael Gross as Steven, manager of WKS-TV, the local public TV station; Michael J. Fox as eldest child Alex, a whiz kid who worshipped Richard Nixon, William Buckley, and *The Wall Street Journal;* Justine Bateman as elder daughter Mallory, an unscholastic teen who loved shopping; and Tina Yothers as younger daughter Jennifer. On 31 January 1985 a fourth Keaton kid appeared, as Elyse gave birth to baby Andrew, who grew up to worship his older brother (in real life, Meredith Baxter Birney had had twins the previous fall); Tyler and Grant Merriman appeared as baby Andrew, but Brian Bonsall took over the role in the fall of 1986 (this meant that Andy grew from baby to preschooler virtually over the summer). Creator Goldberg revealed in 1987 that his inspiration for the Alex character came from the stepson of a newspaper editor friend, while that of Jennifer came from his own daughter, Shana. Marc Price was featured as neighbor Irwin "Skippy" Handleman, a hopeless nerd who had a crush on Mallory.

In the fall of 1984 Alex left Harding High for Leland College, where a year later he met his first regular girlfriend, Ellen Reed (played by Tracy Pollan). Ellen left for Paris at the beginning of the 1986–1987 season; later that season Alex met Lauren Miller (played by Courteney Cox). In real life, however, Michael J. Fox married Tracy Pollan. Meanwhile, Mallory began dating junk sculptor Nick Moore (played by Scott Valentine), much to the chagrin of her parents and her older brother.

Though most episodes were played for laughs, *Family Ties* also had its share of serious programs, including a three-parter dealing with Steven's heart attack and a poignant one-man show starring Fox, on which Alex comes to grips with the death of a friend. The series was also paid an unusual tribute by PBS, which on 15 October

1988 broadcast a one-hour special about the preparation of a single episode. *Family Ties* enjoyed its peak popularity between 1984 and 1987, when it followed *The Cosby Show* on NBC's Thursday night schedule. In the fall of 1987 it was moved to Sunday nights opposite CBS's *Murder, She Wrote,* and ratings began to slip. The last first-run episode, in which Alex left home, was aired 14 May 1989.

THE FAMILY TREE NBC
22 JANUARY 1983–26 FEBRUARY 1983   An hour dramatic series about two divorced parents who married each other. With Anne Archer as Annie Benjamin Nichols, a realtor; Frank Converse as Kevin Nichols, owner of a building supply company; James Spader as Kevin's son, Jake; Martin Hewitt as Annie's older son, Sam; Melora Hardin as Annie's daughter, Tess; and Jonathan Hall Kovacs as Annie's younger son, Toby, who was deaf (Kovacs himself was also deaf). Carol Evan McKeand, who had produced *Family,* created the show.

THE FAMOUS ADVENTURES OF MR. MAGOO
See MR. MAGOO

FAMOUS FIGHTS FROM MADISON SQUARE GARDEN DUMONT
15 SEPTEMBER 1952–22 DECEMBER 1952   Highlights of famous boxing matches were telecast on this fifteen-minute filmed series.

FAMOUS JURY TRIALS DUMONT
12 OCTOBER 1949–12 MARCH 1952   Most, but not all, of the action in this dramatic series took place in the courtroom; flashbacks were also used to flesh out the stories. Jim Bender played the prosecuting attorney, and Truman Smith played the defense attorney.

THE FAMOUS TEDDY Z CBS
18 SEPTEMBER 1989–15 JANUARY 1990; 12 MAY 1990–19 MAY 1990   A Hollywood talent agency was the setting for this half-hour sitcom. With Jon Cryer as young Teddy Zakalokis, who started in the mailroom at the Unlimited Talent Agency but soon became an agent after impressing a "difficult" UTA client with his no-nonsense attitude; Alex Rocco as Al Floss, UTA's most high-powered heavyweight agent; Milton Selzer as Abe Werkfinder, the top UTA executive; Jane Sibbett as Laurie Parr, another mailroom minion who taunted Teddy until he made her his assistant; Nick Segal as Marty Kane; Tom La Grua as Richie Herby, Teddy's old boss at the mailroom; and Erica Yohn as Deena, Teddy's Greek grandmother, who was bewildered by Teddy's job. The series was picked by many critics to be a big hit, but never found an audience, perhaps because most viewers were as bewildered as Teddy's grandmother about what Hollywood agents really *do* do. Hugh Wilson created the series.

FAN CLUB SYNDICATED
1987   Half-hour "infotainment" show for teens, hosted by Olympic gymnast Mitch Gaylord.

THE FANELLI BOYS NBC
8 SEPTEMBER 1990–16 FEBRUARY 1991   Sitcom about four Italian brothers who moved back to their widowed mother's house in Brooklyn. With Joe Pantoliano as Dominic Fanelli, a hustler; Ned Eisenberg as Anthony Fanelli, a funeral director; Christopher Meloni as Frank Fanelli, a jock; Andy Hirsch as Ronnie Fanelli, a college student; Ann Guilbert as their mother, Theresa; Richard Libertini as Theresa's brother, Father Angelo Lombardi; and Vera Lockwood as Theresa's fortune-telling friend, Philamena.

FANFARE CBS
19 JUNE 1965–11 SEPTEMBER 1965   Trumpeter Al Hirt hosted this variety hour, a summer replacement for *Jackie Gleason and His American Scene Magazine.*

FANGFACE ABC

9 SEPTEMBER 1978–8 SEPTEMBER 1979   Saturday-morning cartoon show about the adventures of four teenagers, one of whom, Sherman Fangsworth, could turn into a werewolf (Fangface). Joe Ruby and Ken Spears were the executive producers for Filmways. See also *The Plasticman Comedy/Adventure Show.*

FANTASTIC FACTS CBS

9 AUGUST 1991–13 SEPTEMBER 1991   Based on the Time-Life book series "Library of Curious and Unusual Facts," this half-hour non-fiction series consisted mainly of short film clips of supposedly interesting items and events, as well as in-studio features. Merlin Olsen hosted the show.

THE FANTASTIC FOUR ABC/NBC

9 SEPTEMBER 1967–15 MARCH 1970 (ABC); 9 SEPTEMBER 1978–1 SEPTEMBER 1979 (NBC)   Based on the comic book, *The Fantastic Four* premiered in 1967 as a Hanna-Barbera Production. Each of the four characters had acquired a special power after their rocket ship encountered a radioactive field: Reed Richards could be stretched infinitely, his wife Sue Richards could become invisible, Johnny Storm ("The Human Torch") could ignite himself, and Ben Grimm ("The Thing") was extraordinarily strong. The series returned in 1978, with new producers (David H. DePatie and Friz Freleng) and a new member— Johnny Storm had been replaced by a robot named HER-B.

THE FANTASTIC JOURNEY NBC

3 FEBRUARY 1977–16 JUNE 1977   In this science fiction series, an expedition investigating the Bermuda Triangle found itself mysteriously transported to what appeared to be another world. In their quest to return to their own time, the three expedition members encountered others who, for various reasons, also wished to join them. Featured were Jared Martin as Varian, expedition leader; Carl Franklin as Dr. Fred Walters, medical expert; Ike Eisenmann as Scott Jordan, a youngster who could read minds; Katie Saylor as Liana, a mysterious woman who joined them in the first episode; and Roddy McDowall as Jonathan Willoway, a scientist who joined up in the third episode. Bruce Lansbury was the executive producer for Bruce Lansbury Productions, Ltd., in association with Columbia Pictures Television and NBC.

FANTASTIC VOYAGE ABC

14 SEPTEMBER 1968–6 SEPTEMBER 1970   This weekend cartoon series about four people who could be miniaturized was based loosely on the 1966 film that starred Raquel Welch.

FANTASY NBC

13 SEPTEMBER 1982–28 OCTOBER 1983   Peter Marshall and Leslie Uggams cohosted this hour daytime game show, on which people were rewarded with gifts, or had the chance to make their dreams come true; most of the recipients were nominated by friends or relatives. Some persons received relatively mundane gifts, such as new tools or a newly repaired automobile, while others received more elaborate surprises, such as the opportunity to go "wingwalking" on a moving airplane or a free vacation. Recipients did not have to be present in the studio audience, either; a camera crew traveled the country with roving reporters Chris Lemmon and Meredith MacRae to surprise people all over the country.

FANTASY ISLAND ABC

28 JANUARY 1978–18 AUGUST 1984   This escapist adventure hour starred Ricardo Montalban as Mr. Roarke, proprietor of Fantasy Island, a tropical resort where guests could live out their wildest dreams; Herve Villechaize (1978–1983) was featured as Roarke's diminutive assistant, Tattoo. During the 1981–1982 season, Wendy Schaal appeared as Julie, Mr. Roarke's goddaughter, and in 1983 Christopher Hewett was added as Mr. Roarke's new assistant, Lawrence, replacing Herve Villechaize. Usually, two stories were presented each week, with the action shifting back and

forth from fantasy to fantasy. Production of the weekly series was begun after two fairly successful pilot films had been televised. Aaron Spelling and Leonard Goldberg were the executive producers; 130 episodes were filmed.

FAR OUT SPACE NUTS CBS
6 SEPTEMBER 1975–4 SEPTEMBER 1976   This live-action sitcom was seen on Saturday mornings. It starred Bob Denver as Junior and Chuck McCann as Barney, two space-center employees who accidentally blasted off while loading food onto a rocket. Also featured were Patty Maloney as Honk, their space pal, and Al Checco. Produced by Sid and Marty Krofft and Al Schwartz.

FARADAY AND COMPANY NBC
26 SEPTEMBER 1973–13 AUGUST 1974   One segment of *The NBC Wednesday Mystery Movie, Faraday and Company* alternated with *Banacek, The Snoop Sisters,* and *Tenafly.* It featured Dan Dailey as Frank Faraday, a private eye who escaped to the United States after spending twenty-eight years in a Caribbean prison (he'd been framed, of course); James Naughton as Steve Faraday, Frank's new partner, the son Frank had never seen; Geraldine Brooks as Lou Carson, Frank's former secretary and Steve's mother, the woman Frank had intended to marry twenty-eight years before; and Sharon Gless as Holly Barrett, their current secretary and Steve's girlfriend. This appears to have been the first series other than a soap opera in which a parent and an illegitimate child were regular characters.

THE FARMER'S DAUGHTER ABC
20 SEPTEMBER 1963–2 SEPTEMBER 1966   Sitcom based on the 1947 film about a young woman from Minnesota who becomes the housekeeper for a widowed Congressman in Washington, D.C. With Inger Stevens as Katy Holstrum; William Windom as Congressman Glen Morley; Cathleen Nesbitt as Glen's mother, Agatha Morley, herself the widow of a Congressman; Mickey Sholdar as Glen's son Steve; Rory O'Brien as Glen's son Danny; and Philip Coolidge as Glen's brother, Cooper. Occasionally featured were Walter Sande as Papa Holstrum, Alice Frost as Mama Holstrum, and Nancy DeCarl as Steve's girlfriend, Pam. During the fall of 1965 (1 November), Katy and Glen finally got married. The event was even celebrated in real-life Washington, where Perle Mesta threw a party for 300 guests (including Stevens and Windom).

FASHION MAGIC CBS
10 NOVEMBER 1950–15 JUNE 1951   Beauty and wardrobe were the topics discussed on this daytime series, which was usually broadcast twice a week. Hosted by Ilka Chase through 20 April, then by Arlene Francis.

FASHION STORY ABC
4 NOVEMBER 1948–22 FEBRUARY 1949   Host Marilyn Day presented news from the world of fashion on this Thursday-night series. Carl Reiner also appeared.

FASHIONS ON PARADE DUMONT/ABC
5 FEBRUARY 1948–24 APRIL 1949 (DUMONT); 27 APRIL 1949–29 JUNE 1949 (ABC)
One of television's first fashion programs, *Fashions on Parade* was hosted by Adelaide Hawley. Leon Roth and Charles Caplin produced the series, which was also broadcast under the titles *Television Fashions* and *Fashion Parade*.

FAST DRAW SYNDICATED
1968   Johnny Gilbert hosted this game show played by two teams, each consisting of a celebrity and a contestant. One partner tried to guess a phrase from sketches drawn by the other partner.

FAST TIMES CBS
5 MARCH 1986–23 APRIL 1986   One of several 80s series set at a high school (see also *The Best of Times, Better Days, The Bronx Zoo,* and *Square Pegs,* to name a few),

Fast Times was based on the 1982 film *Fast Times at Ridgemont High.* The TV version featured Dean Cameron as Jeff Spicoli, typical Valley dude; Ray Walston as Mr. Arnold Hand, the history teacher; Patrick Dempsey as Mike Damone; Courtney Thorne-Smith as Stacy Hamilton; James Nardini as Stacy's brother, Brad Hamilton; Claudia Wells as Stacy's pal, Linda Barrett; Moon Zappa as Barbara DeVille; Wally Ward as Mark Ratner; Jason Hervey as Curtis Spicoli, Jeff's kid brother (Hervey would soon play the older brother on *The Wonder Years*); Kit McDonough as Ms. Leslie Mallon, the life science teacher; and Vincent Schiavelli as Mr. Hector Vargas, also a science teacher. Walston and Schiavelli had also appeared in the film.

FAT ALBERT AND THE COSBY KIDS　　　　　　　CBS/SYNDICATED/NBC
9 SEPTEMBER 1972–25 AUGUST 1984 (CBS); 1984 (SYNDICATED) 11 FEBRUARY 1989– 2 SEPTEMBER 1989 (NBC)　　Bill Cosby hosted this Saturday cartoon series with a humanitarian message. Its central characters—such as Fat Albert, Weird Harold, Mush Mouth, and Donald—were based on the boyhood friends of Cosby, who grew up in Philadelphia. Produced by Norm Prescott and Lou Scheimer; Cosby served as executive producer. The show was retitled *The New Fat Albert Show* in the fall of 1979.

FATHER DOWLING MYSTERIES　　　　　　　　　　　　NBC/ABC
20 JANUARY 1989–10 MARCH 1989 (NBC); 4 JANUARY 1990–5 SEPTEMBER 1991 (ABC) An hour mystery series, based on the Father Dowling books by Ralph McInerny. With Tom Bosley as Father Frank Dowling, pastor of St. Michael's Parish in Chicago, who solved crimes in his spare time; Tracy Nelson as his assistant, Sister Stephanie ("Steve" for short); Mary Wickes as Marie Gillespie, the housekeeper; and James Stephens as Father Philip Prestwick, a priest dispatched by the bishop to keep an eye on Father Dowling. The pilot for the series, "Fatal Confession: A Father Dowling Mystery," was shown 30 November 1987 on NBC.

FATHER KNOWS BEST　　　　　　　　　　　　　　　　CBS/NBC
3 OCTOBER 1954–27 MARCH 1955 (CBS); 31 AUGUST 1955–17 SEPTEMBER 1958 (NBC); 22 SEPTEMBER 1958–17 SEPTEMBER 1962 (CBS)　　This durable sitcom began on radio in 1949, starring Robert Young as Jim Anderson, an insurance agent who lived in the town of Springfield with his wife and three children. Originally, Father was somewhat of a bumbler, but by the end of the show's run on radio, he had become wiser and more paternal. Young was the only member of the radio cast to make the transition to television. Joining him on camera were Jane Wyatt as Margaret Anderson, his wife; Elinor Donahue as Betty (or "Princess" to Father), their eldest child; Billy Gray as teenager Bud (Jim, Jr.); Lauren Chapin as Kathy ("Kitten" to Father), the youngest. Natividad Vacio occasionally appeared as gardener Frank Smith ("Fronk"), a newly naturalized American citizen. The show was produced by Eugene B. Rodney, who owned the series together with Young. Despite critical acclaim, the series was dropped after its first twenty-six weeks; one reason for its initial lack of success may have been that few children saw it—it was scheduled at 10:00 on Sundays. The following season it found a new sponsor, a new time, and a new network and became a solid hit. Between 1954 and 1960, there were 203 episodes filmed; reruns were broadcast on CBS for two more seasons and subsequently on ABC. After *Father Knows Best* ceased production, Young, Wyatt, and Donahue continued to appear frequently on television; Young, of course, starred in *Marcus Welby, M.D.* for seven seasons. Gray and Chapin, however, made few TV appearances. On 15 May 1977 the five appeared together in "The Father Knows Best Reunion," on NBC; the slow-moving hour-long special proved disappointing.

FATHER MURPHY　　　　　　　　　　　　　　　　　　　NBC
3 NOVEMBER 1981–28 DECEMBER 1982　　Merlin Olsen starred in this hour dramatic show as John Michael Murphy, who arrived in the mining town of Jackson after the Civil War. When the town was destroyed, Murphy posed as a priest in order to save the orphaned youngsters from the workhouse. Also featured were Moses Gunn as Murphy's friend and partner, Moses Gage; Katherine Cannon as schoolteacher Mae Wood-

ward, who married Murphy at the end of the first season; Timothy Gibbs as orphan Will Adams; Lisa Trusel as the orphan Lizette Winkler; Scott Mellini as Ephram, Lizette's brother; Charles Tyner as grim Howard Rodman, the man from the workhouse; Ivy Bethune as grim Miss Tuttle, Rodman's associate; Burr DeBenning as evil Mr. Garrett; Richard Bergman (1981–1982) as Father Parker; and Ted Markland (1981–1982) as Frank. Michael Landon was the executive producer of the series; Olsen had previously been a regular on Landon's *Little House on the Prairie*. Reruns of *Father Murphy* surfaced briefly in the spring of 1984 as a replacement for NBC's ill-fated *First Camera*.

FATHER OF THE BRIDE   CBS
29 SEPTEMBER 1961–14 SEPTEMBER 1962   This domestic sitcom was based on the book by Edward Streeter and the 1950 film. The TV version featured Leon Ames as lawyer Stanley Banks, the father of the bride; Ruth Warrick as Ellie Banks, the mother of the bride; Myrna Fahey as Kay Banks, the bride; Rickie Sorensen as Tommy Banks, the bride's kid brother; Burt Metcalfe as Buckley Dunston, Kay's intended; Ransom Sherman as Buckley's father, Herbert Dunston; Lurene Tuttle as Buckley's mother, Doris Dunston. Kay and Buckley became engaged in the premiere episode and were married in midseason. Robert Maxwell was the executive producer.

FATHERS AND SONS   NBC
6 APRIL 1986–4 MAY 1986   A half-hour sitcom, broadcast during the "family viewing hour" (7–8 P.M.) on Sundays. With former pro footballer Merlin Olsen as Buddy Landau; Kelly Sanders as his wife, Ellen; Jason Late as their son, Lanny; Andre Gower as Lanny's pal Sean Flynn; Ian Fried as Lanny's pal Ricky Bolen; Hakeem as Lanny's pal Brandon Russo; and Nicholas Guest as Ricky's father, Dr. Richard Bolen. Rick Nelson appeared in the pilot episode as Sean's father, Michael Flynn.

FAVORITE STORY
See MY FAVORITE STORY

FAWLTY TOWERS   SYNDICATED
1980   Half-hour sitcom starring John Cleese (of *Monty Python's Flying Circus*) as Basil Fawlty, who tried to manage a country hotel, and Prunella Scales as his wife, Sybil. Also featured were Connie Booth (who wrote the series with Cleese) as housekeeper Polly Sherman; Andrew Sachs as Manuel, the Barcelonan bellhop; and Ballard Berkeley as daft Major Gowen. The series premiered in England in 1975 and new episodes appeared in 1979; in the U.S., the series was seen on many PBS stations. It also spawned a feeble American version in 1983 (see *Amanda's*).

FAY   NBC
4 SEPTEMBER 1975–23 OCTOBER 1975   A remarkably unsuccessful situation comedy about a forty-three-year-old divorcée who got a job as a secretary in a San Francisco law office. With Lee Grant as Fay Stewart; Joe Silver as Jack Stewart, her ex; Margaret Willock as Linda Baines, Fay's conservative daughter; Stewart Moss as Dr. Elliott Baines, Linda's stuffy husband; Audra Lindley as Lillian, Fay's tactless neighbor; Bill Gerber as lawyer Danny Messina, Fay's boss; Norman Alden as Al Cassidy, Danny's law partner; and Lillian Lehman as Letty Gilmore, Al's black secretary. Created by Susan Harris. Executive producer: Paul Younger Witt. Produced by Jerry Mayer. *Fay*'s theme song was sung by Jaye P. Morgan. Susan Harris later blamed the show's failure on the fact that it had been intended as a sophisticated, adult comedy but had been scheduled by NBC at 8:30 P.M. on Thursdays, smack in the middle of the "family viewing hour." As a result of the scheduling decision, the network ordered many changes in dialogue and characterization, which seriously weakened the show's import.

FAYE AND SKITCH   NBC

26 OCTOBER 1953–22 OCTOBER 1954   Faye Emerson and Skitch Henderson (who
were married to each other at the time) cohosted this fifteen-minute nightly series of
music and chitchat. Johnny Stearns produced and directed it.

THE FAYE EMERSON SHOW   CBS/NBC

13 MARCH 1950–9 JULY 1950 (CBS); 22 APRIL 1950–30 AUGUST 1950 (NBC); 26 SEPTEM-
BER 1950–23 DECEMBER 1950 (CBS)   One of network television's first female interviewers, Faye Emerson attracted much attention—and a large number of male
viewers—because of the low-cut gowns she wore. She began hosting a local show in
New York, which went network in March of 1950; a month later she began a second
series, *Fifteen with Faye,* on NBC, thus becoming one of the few performers to
appear on two networks simultaneously. Each of her first two series was seen once a
week; in the fall of 1950, however, her CBS show was seen three evenings a week. In
1951 she hosted another local show in New York, before returning to network TV
with *Faye Emerson's Wonderful Town* (see below).

FAYE EMERSON'S WONDERFUL TOWN
(WONDERFUL TOWN, U.S.A.)   CBS

16 JUNE 1951–19 APRIL 1952   Faye Emerson returned to CBS in this half-hour
variety series that replaced part of *The Frank Sinatra Show.* Skitch Henderson also
appeared on the show, which was broadcast live from a different city each week;
Boston was the site of the premiere telecast.

FEAR AND FANCY   ABC

13 MAY 1953–2 SEPTEMBER 1953   Half-hour filmed dramatic anthology series that
usually featured supernatural stories.

FEARLESS FOSDICK   NBC

1 JUNE 1952–28 SEPTEMBER 1952   Fearless Fosdick, the bumbling cartoon detective
created by Al Capp, was the star of this short-lived filmed puppet show. Other
characters included Schmoozer and The Chief. John Griggs provided the voice of
Fosdick.

THE FEATHER AND FATHER GANG   ABC

7 MARCH 1977–6 AUGUST 1977   A pale imitation of CBS's *Switch,* this hour-long
adventure series featured a female lawyer and her dad, an ex-con man, who combined forces to outwit assorted evildoers. With Stefanie Powers as Toni "Feather"
Danton; Harold Gould as her father, Harry Danton. The "Gang," all of them
Harry's henchpeople, included Frank Delfino as the midget Enzo; Monte Landis as
Michael; Joan Shawlee as Margo; and Lewis Charles as Lou. Bill Driskill created the
series, and Larry White was the executive producer.

FEATHER YOUR NEST   NBC

4 OCTOBER 1954–27 JULY 1956   Bud Collyer hosted this daytime game show on
which couples had the chance to win home furnishings; questions were written on
feathers that were hidden among the merchandise. Assisting Collyer at various times
were Lou Prentis, Janis Carter, and Jean Williams.

FEELIN' GOOD   PBS

1974   Produced by the Children's Television Workshop, *Feelin' Good* attempted to
educate adults on matters of health care. Two formats were tried: The first, a sixty-
minute sitcom-variety, was set at a club known as Mac's Place. It featured Tex
Everhart as Mac; Priscilla Lopez as Rita; Marjorie Barnes as Melba; Joe Morton as
Jason; Ethel Shutta as Mrs. Stebbins; and Ben Slack as Hank. That format was
scrapped after eleven weeks, and Dick Cavett was brought in to host a half-hour
narrative program.

FELONY SQUAD   ABC

12 SEPTEMBER 1966–31 JANUARY 1969   Half-hour crime show set in Los Angeles.
With Howard Duff as Detective (and later Sergeant) Sam Stone; Ben Alexander as
Sergeant Dan Briggs; Dennis Cole as Detective Jim Briggs, Dan's son; Frank Max-
well (1966–1967) as Captain Nye; and Barney Phillips (1967–1969) as Captain Ed
Franks. The series was supplied by 20th Century-Fox TV.

FERNWOOD 2-NIGHT   SYNDICATED
4 JULY 1977–30 SEPTEMBER 1977
AMERICA 2NIGHT   SYNDICATED
10 APRIL 1978–18 AUGUST 1978   A satire of talk shows, *Fernwood 2-Night* was
developed by Norman Lear to fill the summer gap between *Mary Hartman, Mary
Hartman* and *Forever Fernwood*. Set at the studios of Channel 2 in Fernwood, Ohio,
it starred Martin Mull as host Barth Gimble, Fred Willard as his half-witted sidekick,
Jerry Hubard, and Frank DeVol as Happy Kyne, leader of the show's four-man band,
the Mirthmakers. Host Gimble was the twin brother of Garth Gimble, a wife-beater
who had impaled himself on an aluminum Christmas tree on *Mary Hartman, Mary
Hartman*. Second banana Hubard was the brother-in-law of the station owner, while
bandleader Kyne supplemented his income by running a chain of fast-food outlets
known as Bun 'n' Run. In real life, Frank DeVol was a talented musician and
composer of many TV theme songs, including the song in *Family Affair*. Most of the
guests on *Fernwood 2-Night* were purely fictional (such as Fernwood's high school
principal, who demonstrated the proper technique for spanking the bottom of a
shapely sixteen-year-old), but a few celebrities, such as singer Tom Waits and journalist Harry Shearer, played themselves. *America 2Night* was introduced in the spring of
1978 and was similar in format to its predecessor, except that it was broadcast from
Alta Coma, California, "the unfinished furniture capital of the world." Many of
America 2Night's guests appeared as themselves; Charlton Heston, for example, was
a guest on the premiere. Bill Kirchenbauer frequently appeared as hugely untalented
lounge singer Tony Roletti on both *Fernwood* and *America 2Night*. Robin Williams
and Paul Reubens (who later became famous as Pee-wee Herman) also made ap-
pearences on *America 2Night,* Williams as the operator of an escort service and
Reubens as a dancing Indian.

FERRIS BUELLER   NBC
23 AUGUST 1990–16 DECEMBER 1990; 11 AUGUST 1991   Half-hour sitcom, based on the
1986 film *Ferris Bueller's Day Off*. With Charlie Schlatter as sixteen-year-old Ferris
Bueller, a student at California's Ocean Park High School who always succeeded in
outwitting the administration; Richard Riehle as Bueller's nemesis, principal Ed
Rooney; Jennifer Aniston as Ferris's older sister, Jeannie, a senior; Cristine Rose as
their mother, Barbara; Sam Freed as their father, Bill; Brandon Douglas as Ferris's
best friend, Cameron Frye; Ami Dolenz (daughter of former Monkee Mickey
Dolenz) as transfer student and love interest Sloan Peterson; Judith Kahan as
Rooney's assistant, Grace; and Jeff Maynard as Arthur Petrelli.

FESTIVAL OF STARS   NBC
2 JULY 1957–17 SEPTEMBER 1957   Jim Ameche hosted this Tuesday-night series of
rebroadcasts from *The Loretta Young Show*. The episodes that were shown did not
feature Young.

FIBBER McGEE AND MOLLY   NBC
15 SEPTEMBER 1959–5 JANUARY 1960   A short-lived version of the popular radio
comedy that starred Jim Jordan (who created the show with Don Quinn) and his
wife, Marian Jordan. On television Bob Sweeney starred as Fibber McGee, teller of
tall tales, and Cathy Lewis played his long-suffering wife, Molly. Also featured were
Hal Peary (who originated The Great Gildersleeve on the radio version of *Fibber
McGee*) as Mayor Charles LaTrivia, a bombastic politician; Addison Richards as
Doctor Gamble; Paul Smith as next-door neighbor Roy Norris; Elisabeth Fraser as

his wife, Hazel; and Barbara Beaird as Teeny, their daughter (the McGees, of course, resided at 79 Wistful Vista).

FIEVEL'S AMERICAN TAILS   CBS
12 SEPTEMBER 1992–11 SEPTEMBER 1993   This Saturday morning cartoon series, based on the feature films *An American Tail* and its sequel *An American Tail: Fievel Goes West*, found the immigrant rodent Fievel Mousekiwitz living in town of Green River in the Old West.

THE FIFTH CORNER   NBC
17 APRIL 1992–24 APRIL 1992   Axed after just two telecasts, this adventure series starred Alex McArthur as intelligence agent Richard Braun, who woke up with amnesia one morning in a Latin American country (and with a dead woman in his bed); Braun soon discovered that he had five identities, and struggled to determine which of the five was the real one. Also featured were J. E. Freeman as Boone; Kim Delaney as Erica, a journalist; Christoph Ort as Rolf; Anthony Valentine as The Hat; and James Coburn as billionaire Mr. Grandwell.

50 GRAND SLAM   NBC
4 OCTOBER 1976–31 DECEMBER 1976   Tom Kennedy hosted this daytime game show on which contestants could earn up to $50,000. The format was somewhat similar to that of *Twenty-One:* Pairs of contestants competed in areas of specialized knowledge or in games. The winner of the first round (which paid $200) could elect to risk his or her winnings on the next round against a new challenger; each new challenger began at the $200 level, while the champion competed for ever-increasing amounts up to the $50,000 top prize.

54TH STREET REVUE   CBS
5 MAY 1949–25 MARCH 1950   This Thursday-night variety hour, broadcast live from a theater on 54th Street in New York, was a showcase for up-and-coming professionals. The first few shows were hosted by comic Al Bernie; other regulars included Carl Reiner, Jack Sterling, Mort Marshall, Wynn Murray, and dancer Bob Fosse. Reiner, of course, went on to *Your Show of Shows* and later created *The Dick Van Dyke Show;* Fosse choreographed many Broadway hits and later directed the film *Cabaret.* Barry Wood was the executive producer of the series. Ralph Levy, who directed it, later produced and directed *The Burns and Allen Show* and served as executive producer of *The Jack Benny Program.* Original music and lyrics were supplied by Al Selden, who later wrote *Man of La Mancha;* Bill Scudder also provided musical material for the series. Writers included Max Wilk, George Axelrod, and Allan Sherman. The last few shows were hosted by Billy Vine.

FIGHT BACK! WITH DAVID HOROWITZ   SYNDICATED
1980–1992   Consumer advocate David Horowitz tested products and exposed consumer ripoffs on this half-hour weekly series. Horowitz had previously hosted a similar series, *Consumer Buyline.*

THE FIGHT OF THE WEEK   ABC
24 JANUARY 1953–11 SEPTEMBER 1964   ABC's weekly boxing series, which ran continuously for eleven years, was aired under several different titles. From 1953 to 1955 it was known as *The Saturday Night Fights.* In the summer of 1955 it moved to a new day and became *The Wednesday Night Fights.* In the fall of 1960 the series moved back to Saturdays and was retitled *The Fight of the Week;* that title was retained when the show switched to Fridays for its final season. Jack Drees announced the bouts during the early seasons, Don Dunphy during the later ones. The popularity of boxing on television (and in the arenas) took a significant down-turn during the early 1960s. One reason for this decline may have been *The Fight of the Week* of 24 March 1962, when Emile Griffith defeated Benny "Kid" Paret for the welterweight championship. Paret was carried unconscious from the ring and later died of his injuries.

THE FILES OF JEFFREY JONES   SYNDICATED

1954   This half-hour crime show starred Don Haggerty as New York private eye Jeffrey Jones and Gloria Henry as reporter "Mike" Malone, his girlfriend. Produced by Lindsley Parsons; directed by Lew Landers.

FILTHY RICH   CBS

9 AUGUST 1982–23 AUGUST 1982; 6 OCTOBER 1982–10 NOVEMBER 1982; 17 JANUARY 1983–14 FEBRUARY 1983; 8 JUNE 1983–15 JUNE 1983   A broadly played spoof of *Dallas,* in which the members of a Memphis family tried to live by the dictates of the recently deceased head of the clan, who thoughtfully had videotaped his will. With Slim Pickens (who was succeeded by Forrest Tucker) as Big Guy Beck, the decedent; Delta Burke as Cathleen, his widow; Dixie Carter as his daughter-in-law, Carlotta; Michael Lombard as his son Marshall, Carlotta's husband; Charles Frank as his son Stanley; Jerry Hardin as his illegitimate son, Wild Bill Winchester; Ann Wedgeworth as Bill's wife, Bootsie, an aspiring singer; and Nedra Volz as Mother B, Big Guy's first wife, the mother of Marshall and Stanley. Though the show fared well in the ratings during its summer tryout, it did poorly in the fall and was quickly yanked from the schedule, only to resurface (twice) later in the season.

FINAL APPEAL: FROM THE FILES OF UNSOLVED MYSTERIES   NBC

18 SEPTEMBER 1992–16 OCTOBER 1992   This half-hour reality show was created by the producers of *Unsolved Mysteries*, and was hosted by *Unsolved*'s Robert Stack. Each week the show examined the case of a convicted felon—from the defendant's and prosecution's side—to determine whether the defendant's case should be reopened.

FINDER OF LOST LOVES   ABC

22 SEPTEMBER 1984–24 AUGUST 1985   This hour dramatic series starred Tony Franciosa as widower Cary Maxwell, who ran an agency that tried to reunite separated loved ones, or to locate old flames for would-be suitors. Working for Maxwell were Deborah Adair as Daisy Lloyd, his late wife's sister; Anne Jeffreys (seldom seen on TV since *Topper*) as office manager Rita Hargrove; Richard Kantor as Brian Fletcher; and Larry Flash Jenkins (1985) as gofer and chauffeur Lyman Whittaker. Dionne Warwick sang the show's theme. Series creator Gail Parent got her inspiration for the show after reading about a real-life "finder" on an airplane flight.

A FINE ROMANCE   ABC

18 JANUARY 1989–16 MARCH 1989   Promoted as a throwback to the "screwball" film comedies of the 1940s, this ambitious hour comedy-adventure series lasted only eight weeks, and finished 122nd out of 126 prime-time series in the seasonal ratings. Filmed on location in Europe, it starred Margaret Whitton and Christopher Cazenove as Louisa Phillips and Michael Trent, a divorced couple who cohosted a TV travel show (Anthony Andrews had played Trent in the pilot, which never aired). Also featured were Dinah Lenney as Friday; Kevin Moore as Miles; and Ernie Sabella as George. Although the series garnered good reviews, it was scheduled opposite NBC's *The Cosby Show* on Thursdays, and it vanished quietly.

FIREBALL FUN FOR ALL   NBC

28 JUNE 1949–27 OCTOBER 1949   Ole Olsen and Chic Johnson, the veteran comedy team who starred in *Hellzapoppin* on Broadway, hosted this hour of slapstick and sight gags. Broadcast from the Center Theater in New York, it began as a summer replacement for Milton Berle's *The Texaco Star Theater* on Tuesdays and later shifted to Thursdays before its cancellation. Produced and directed by Ezra Stone, its writers included Arnold Horwitt, Lew Lipton, Mike Stewart (who later wrote *Hello, Dolly*), and Max Wilk. Also in the cast were June Johnson, Marty May, Bill Hayes, and J. C. Olsen.

FIREBALL XL-5   NBC

5 OCTOBER 1963–25 SEPTEMBER 1965   This Saturday-morning series was one of the first to use Supermarionation, a technique utilizing fine wires and plastic models developed

by Gerry Anderson; the technique was refined in Anderson's later series (*Captain Scarlet and the Mysterons, The Thunderbirds,* etc.). This series was set in Space City; its central character was Colonel Steve Zodiac, who piloted his spacecraft—*Fireball XL-5*—throughout the galaxy.

FIREHOUSE
ABC

17 JANUARY 1974–1 AUGUST 1974   This half-hour adventure series was apparently inspired by NBC's *Emergency!* It told the story of the fearless firefighters of Engine Company 23 in Los Angeles. With James Drury as Captain Spike Ryerson; Richard Jaeckel as number two man Hank Myers; Mike DeLano as firefighter Sonny Capito, who doubled as the company cook; Bill Overton as firefighter Cal Dakin, token black; Scott Smith as firefighter Scotty Smith; and Brad David as rookie firefighter Billy DelZell.

FIRESIDE THEATRE
NBC

5 APRIL 1949–23 AUGUST 1955   Produced and directed by Frank Wisbar, *Fireside Theatre* was a low-budget half-hour filmed anthology series, and a fixture at 9:00 P.M. on Tuesdays. During the first season two 15-minute films were presented each week; thereafter, the series offered thirty-minute dramas. One notable presentation, "The Reign of Amelika Jo" (12 October 1954), featured a largely black and Asian cast (James Edwards, Nick Stewart, Johnny Lee, and Keye Luke) in a fact-based story set in the South Pacific during World War II. *TV Guide* noted that it was "probably the first all-Negro show ever to go out over a network." Gene Raymond hosted the show for several seasons; in 1955 Jane Wyman took over as host, and the show's title was changed. See *Jane Wyman Theatre.*

FIRING LINE
SYNDICATED/PBS

1966–1971 (SYNDICATED); 1971– (PBS)   William F. Buckley, Jr., the erudite conservative columnist, hosts this durable political discussion program.

1ST & TEN
HBO

2 DECEMBER 1984–30 AUGUST 1991   The world of professional football was the setting for this half-hour sitcom, which incorporated female toplessness and four-letter words into almost every episode. The cast included: Delta Burke (1984–1988) as Diane Barrow, new owner of the California Bulls, who acquired the team in a divorce settlement (after her husband had run off with a lineman); Reid Shelton as Coach Ernie Denardo; O. J. Simpson (1985–1991) as T.D. Parker, who became the general manager; John Matuszak (1984–1990) as John Manzak; Don Gibb as "Dr. Death" Crunchner; John Kassir as Bulgarian-born placekicker Zagreb Shkenusky; Jason Beghe as quarterback Tom Yinessa; Prince Hughes as lineman Bubba Kincaid; Cliff Frazier as Jethro Snell; Tony Longo as "Mad Dog" Smears; Jay Kerr as quarterback Mac Daniels; Jeff Hochendonner as linebacker Elvin Putts; Keith Amos (1990–1991) as receiver "Miracle Miles" Coolidge; and Shannon Tweed (1989–1991) as Kristy Fulbright, who succeeded Diane as the team's owner. Simpson and Matuszak had, of course, been professional football players; many other pro players, past and present, made guest appearances on the show.

Beginning with the second season, the series bore a new subtitle each year: *Training Camp: The Bulls Are Back, The Championship, Going for Broke, The Bulls Mean Business, Do It Again,* and *In Your Face!*

FIRST CAMERA
See MONITOR

FIRST DATE
SYNDICATED

1952   Renzo Cesana, formerly the host of *The Continental,* presided over this unusual program on which he greeted couples who were on their first date together.

THE FIRST EDEN   PBS

2 NOVEMBER 1987–23 NOVEMBER 1987   A four-part look at life—human and animal—in the Mediterranean basin, the area described by host David Attenborough as the birthplace of western civilization.

THE FIRST HUNDRED YEARS   CBS

4 DECEMBER 1950–27 JUNE 1952   CBS's first television soap opera, *The First Hundred Years* accentuated the lighter side of married life. It starred Jimmy Lydon and Olive Stacey as newlyweds Chris and Connie Thayer; Stacey was later replaced by Anne Sargent. Also featured were Dan Tobin and Valerie Cossart as Chris's parents, Mr. and Mrs. Thayer; Robert Armstrong and Nana Bryant as Connie's parents, Mr. and Mrs. Martin; and Nancy Malone as Connie's sister, Margie. In 1952 CBS replaced the show with a more successful serial: *The Guiding Light.*

FIRST IMPRESSIONS   CBS

27 AUGUST 1988–1 OCTOBER 1988   The most notable thing about this short-lived sitcom was that it was the first network series to be set in Nebraska. It starred Brad Garrett as Frank Dutton, a producer of commercial jingles in Omaha who was suddenly left to raise his child after his wife walked out. Also in the cast were Brandy Gold as his nine-year-old daughter, Lindsay; Thom Sharp as Frank's business partner at Media of Omaha, Dave Poole; James Noble as recording engineer Raymond Voss; and Sarah Abrell as receptionist Donna Patterson. The six-foot, nine-inch Garrett had won the "Best Comedian of 1984" award on *Star Search.* Unfazed by the unfavorable ratings of this sitcom, CBS introduced another series with an almost identical format barely a month later: see *Raising Miranda.*

FIRST LOOK   NBC

16 OCTOBER 1965–9 APRIL 1966   An educational series for children hosted by singer Oscar Brand and featuring youngsters Sally Sheffield, Jackie Washington, and Neil Jones.

FIRST LOVE   NBC

5 JULY 1954–30 DECEMBER 1955   This soap opera also centered on newlyweds. With Val Dufour and Tod Andrews as jet engineer Zach James; Patricia Barry as Laurie James; Rosemary Prinz as Amy; Bob Courtleigh as David; Joe Warren as Phil Gordon; Henrietta Moore as Peggy; Jay Barney as Bruce McKee; Peter Cookson as Tony Morgan; and Frederic Downs as Andrews. The fifteen-minute show was aired live from Philadelphia.

FIRST PERSON PLAYHOUSE (FIRST PERSON SINGULAR)   NBC

3 JULY 1953–11 SEPTEMBER 1953   In this half-hour dramatic anthology series, a summer replacement for *The Life of Riley,* the camera was the principal character.

FIRST TIME OUT   WB

10 SEPTEMBER 1995–17 DECEMBER 1995   Half-hour sitcom about three young women who shared an apartment in Los Angeles. With Jackie Guerra as Jackie, who worked at a Beverly Hills beauty salon; Mia Cottet as Susan, a therapist; Leah Remini as Dominique, who worked for a record company; Craig Anton as Nathan, Jackie's nerdy friend; Tracy Vilar as Rosa; and Roxanne Beckford as Madeleine.

FIRST TUESDAY   NBC

7 JANUARY 1969–7 SEPTEMBER 1971; 3 OCTOBER 1972–7 AUGUST 1973   Eliot Frankel produced this news magazine series, televised on the first Tuesday of each month. Sander Vanocur was the original host, but was succeeded by Garrick Utley. From 1969 to 1971 *First Tuesday* was a two-hour series; when it returned to NBC's schedule in the fall of 1972, however, it was trimmed to sixty minutes. The network continued to experiment with the concept of a monthly magazine series during the 1970s: see also *Chronolog* and *Weekend.*

FISH   ABC

5 FEBRUARY 1977–8 JUNE 1978   This half-hour sitcom was a spinoff from *Barney Miller*. Abe Vigoda starred as Phil Fish, who retired from the New York Police Department to run a home for juvenile delinquents. Also featuring Florence Stanley as his devoted wife, Bernice; Barry Gordon as live-in counselor Charlie. The lovable young troublemakers included Lenny Bari as Mike, Denise Miller as Jilly, Todd Bridges as Loomis, Sarah Natoli as Diane Pulaski, and John Cassisi as Victor. Executive producer: Danny Arnold. Produced by Norman Barasch and Roy Kammerman.

FISH POLICE   CBS

28 FEBRUARY 1992–13 MARCH 1992   This half-hour prime-time animated series was set in Fish City, and all the characters were marine life. Principal voices were supplied by John Ritter as Inspector Gil; Edward Asner as Chief Abalone; JoBeth Williams as Angel; and Megan Mullally as Pearl the waitress. Other voices were provided by Hector Elizondo, Georgia Brown, Jonathan Winters, Buddy Hackett, Robert Guillaume, and Tim Curry. Produced by Hanna-Barbera Productions, the series was paired with *Scorch* on CBS's Friday schedule; both shows were dropped after three episodes.

FISHING AND HUNTING CLUB   DUMONT

7 OCTOBER 1949–31 MARCH 1950   Half-hour panel show on which the panelists answered questions about outdoor activities submitted by viewers. Bill Slater was the host, and the panel included former Olympian Gail Borden, author Jeff Bryant, the New York *Mirror* outdoor editor Jim Hurley, and Dave Newell, a former editor of *Field and Stream*. The show was later titled *Sports for All*.

FITZ AND BONES   NBC

24 OCTOBER 1981–21 NOVEMBER 1981   Tom and Dick Smothers starred in this hour dramatic series, but they did not portray brothers. The action took place at KSFB-TV in San Francisco, with Dick as news reporter Ryan Fitzpatrick, and Tom as Edsel-driving ENG technician Bones Howard. Also featured were Diana Muldaur as news director Terri Seymour; Mike Kellin as station manager Robert Whitmore; Lynnette Mettey as Bones's ex-wife, Lt. Rosie Cochran; Roger C. Carmel as Lawrence Brody, reporter for a rival station; and Doug Hale as anchorman Mel Bishop. NBC scheduled the show on Saturdays at 10:00, one of its weakest time slots; the series had the unfortunate distinction of being the lowest-rated prime-time series of the 1981–1982 season.

THE FITZPATRICKS   CBS

5 SEPTEMBER 1977–10 JANUARY 1978   One of the plethora of family dramas presented during the 1977–1978 season, *The Fitzpatricks* were a middle-class family who lived in Flint, Michigan. With Bert Kramer as steelworker Mike Fitzpatrick; Mariclare Costello as Maggie Fitzpatrick, pregnant with their fifth child; Clark Brandon as son Sean, sixteen; James Vincent McNichol (brother of Kristy McNichol of ABC's *Family*) as son Jack, fifteen; Michele Tobin as daughter Maureen, fourteen; Sean Marshall as son Max, ten; Derek Wells as R. J., Max's best friend, a black; Helen Hunt as teenager Kerry, a neighbor; and Detroit, the family dog. Created by John Sacret Young. Executive producer: Philip Mandelker. Produced by John Cutts.

FIVE FINGERS   NBC

3 OCTOBER 1959–9 JANUARY 1960   Cold War spy drama set in Europe; it was based on the 1952 film starring James Mason. With David Hedison (who starred in the 1958 horror film, *The Fly*) as Victor Sebastian, American counterintelligence agent; Luciana Paluzzi as Simone Genet, his gal Friday; and Paul Burke as Robertson, Sebastian's contact man. Herbert Bayard Swope, Jr., was the producer.

THE FIVE MRS. BUCHANANS   CBS

24 SEPTEMBER 1994–15 APRIL 1995   Half-hour sitcom set in Mercy, Indiana, the home of the title characters: the four women who had married brothers, and their

crusty mother-in-law. With Judith Ivey as Alex, a Jew from New York who ran a store and was married to Roy; Beth Broderick as Delilah, a former cocktail waitress who was married to Charles; Harriet Sansom Harris as Vivian, who was married to Ed and had twins; Charlotte Ross as Bree, the newest Mrs. B., who was wed to Jesse; and Eileen Heckart as gravel-voiced and acid-tongued Mother Buchanan.

FIVE STAR JUBILEE NBC
17 MARCH 1961–22 SEPTEMBER 1961   Broadcast live from Springfield, Missouri, *Five Star Jubilee* was a half-hour country-and-western music series similar to *Ozark Jubilee*. Five stars shared the hosting chores on an alternating basis: Rex Allen, Snooky Lanson, Tex Ritter, Carl Smith, and Jimmy Wakely. Other regulars included Slim Wilson and His Jubilee Band, the Promenaders, and the Jubilaires.

FIVE-STAR COMEDY ABC
18 MAY 1957–15 JUNE 1957   A five-week comedy show for kids, shown on Saturday afternoons. Guest hosts included Paul Winchell and Jerry Mahoney, Jerry Colonna, and Señor Wences.

FLAMBARDS PBS
11 JULY 1980–26 SEPTEMBER 1980   Twelve-part series produced in England by Yorkshire Television. Set at the beginning of World War I, it told the story of a teenage orphan who came to live with her tyrannical uncle at his Essex estate, Flambards. With Christine McKenna as Christina Parsons; Edward Judd as Uncle Russell; Steven Grives as his son Mark; Alan Parnaby as his son William, a flyer; and Sebastian Abineri as Dick. The series was based on the trilogy by K. M. Peyton.

FLAME IN THE WIND
See A TIME FOR US

FLAMINGO ROAD NBC
6 JANUARY 1981–13 JULY 1982   Based on a 1949 motion picture of the same name, *Flamingo Road* was introduced as a made-for-TV movie in May 1980. When it was brought back the following season as a prime-time serial, it picked up where the movie had left off. Set in the steamy Southern town of Truro, it featured Howard Duff as Sheriff Titus Semple, a political boss; Morgan Fairchild as his bitchy daughter, Constance Semple; Mark Harmon as Fielding Carlyle, who married Constance; John Beck as contractor Sam Curtis; Woody Brown as Skipper Weldon; Kevin McCarthy as Claude Weldon; Cristina Raines as singer Lane Ballou, who married Sam; Barbara Rush as Eudora Weldon, Claude's wife; Stella Stevens as Lute-Mae Sanders, the local madam; and Cynthia Sikes as Sandy Swanson. The series was produced by Lorimar (together with MF Productions), TV's principal supplier of prime-time serial fare.

THE FLASH CBS
20 SEPTEMBER 1990–19 JULY 1991   Hour adventure series based on the DC comic book character. Set in Central City, it starred John Wesley Shipp as police scientist Barry Allen, who was doused with chemicals and then struck by lightning; the accident irreversibly accelerated Allen's metabolism, making him extra-strong and extra-fast. Also featured were Amanda Pays as fellow scientist Tina McGee; Alex Desert as lab technician Julio Mendez; Richard Belzer as TV reporter Joe Klein; Biff Manard as Officer Michael Francis Murphy; Mike Genovese as Lieutenant Garfield; and Vito D'Ambrosio as Officer Bellows.

FLASH GORDON SYNDICATED
1953   The television adaptation of the popular movie serial was produced in Europe. It starred Steve Holland as Flash Gordon; Irene Champlin as his assistant, Dale Arden; and Joe Nash as Dr. Alexis Zarkov. The trio worked for the Galaxy Bureau of Investigation. The thirty-nine episodes were filmed in West Berlin and in Marseilles.

FLASH GORDON   NBC
8 SEPTEMBER 1979–20 SEPTEMBER 1980; 18 SEPTEMBER 1982–10 SEPTEMBER 1983   Half-hour Saturday-morning cartoon version of the story of Flash Gordon, the astronaut who sought to save Earth from the evildoings of Ming the Merciless. Lou Scheimer and Norm Prescott were the executive producers.

FLATBUSH   CBS
26 FEBRUARY 1979–12 MARCH 1979   Half-hour sitcom about the five fun-loving members of a Brooklyn gang known as the Flatbush Fungos. With Joseph Cali as Presto; Adrian Zmed as Socks; Vincent Bufano as Turtle; Randy Stumpf as Joey D; Sandy Helberg as Figgy; Antony Ponzini as Esposito, owner of the pool hall where the boys hung out; and Helen Verbit as Mrs. Fortunato, neighborhood busybody. The series was created by David Epstein for Lorimar Productions. Producers: Philip Capice and Gary Adelson.

FLESH 'N BLOOD   NBC
19 SEPTEMBER 1991–15 NOVEMBER 1991   In this half-hour sitcom set in Baltimore, a young single assistant district attorney was reunited with her newly discovered hill-billy brother (the two had been put up for adoption as young children). With Lisa Darr as assistant D.A. Rachel Brennan; David Keith as her unsophisticated brother, Arlo Weed; Meghan Andrews as Arlo's teen daughter, Beauty; Chris Stacy as Arlo's son, King; Perry Anzilotti as Rachel's much shorter co-worker, Marty Travers; and Peri Gilpin as Rachel's secretary, Irene, who lusted for Arlo.

FLICK-OUT   PBS
5 OCTOBER 1970–27 SEPTEMBER 1971   A showcase for young independent filmmakers.

FLIGHT   SYNDICATED
1958   The saga of the United States Air Force, which was hosted by General George C. Kenney. Al Simon was the executive producer for California National Productions.

FLIGHT NUMBER 7   ABC
5 SEPTEMBER 1954–10 SEPTEMBER 1955   A travelogue hosted by Robert McKenzie, *Flight Number 7* relied heavily on aerial photography. The half-hour series was not carried regularly by ABC's New York affiliate.

FLIGHT TO ADVENTURE   SYNDICATED
1960   A series of thirty-nine real-life adventure films, which were shot all over the world. Host: Bill Burrud.

FLIGHT TO RHYTHM   DUMONT
10 MARCH 1949–22 SEPTEMBER 1949   Musical series hosted by Delora Bueno. The show premiered as a fifteen-minute series under the title *The Delora Bueno Show;* it was retitled when it expanded to thirty minutes in May, and became a musical serial.

THE FLINTSTONES   ABC/NBC
30 SEPTEMBER 1960–2 SEPTEMBER 1966 (ABC); 4 OCTOBER 1981–18 OCTOBER 1981 (NBC)   Produced by William Hanna and Joseph Barbera, *The Flintstones* was the first prime-time cartoon series made especially for television; remarkably, it enjoyed a six-year run, far longer than any of the other prime-time cartoon shows. Set in the Stone Age, *The Flintstones* was little more than an animated version of *The Honeymooners*—the voices of the characters were similar to the *Honeymooners,* and the Flintstones' cave even resembled the Kramdens' apartment. The voices were provided by: Alan Reed as Fred Flintstone, quarry worker; Jean vander Pyl as Wilma Flintstone, his wife; Mel Blanc as Barney Rubble, Fred's best friend; Bea Benaderet and Gerry Johnson as Betty Rubble, Barney's wife. Before the series had

run its course, Fred and Wilma had a daughter, and Barney and Betty had a son (credit for the Flintstone and Rubble children should be given to Sheila Barbera, wife of cocreator Joe Barbera, who suggested the idea to her husband). The two children—Pebbles and Bamm Bamm—were later featured in their own Saturday-morning cartoon series. In the fall of 1962 *The Flintstones* and another ABC cartoon series, *Beany and Cecil,* became the first ABC prime-time shows to be regularly broadcast in color. *The Flintstones* was rerun on Saturday mornings over NBC from 1967 to 1970, and new episodes were aired in 1972 (see *The Flintstones Comedy Hour*). Additionally, *Flintstones* segments were later combined with other Hanna-Barbera properties (such as *The Jetsons, The Banana Splits,* and *Top Cat*) and syndicated under the title *Fred Flintstone and Friends.* After an absence of fifteen seasons, *The Flintstones* returned briefly to prime time in the fall of 1981; the show was hastily added to NBC's Sunday night schedule (at 7:00 p.m.) when *The Powers of Matthew Star,* which had been slotted there, was forced to suspend production after injuries to its two stars. A prime-time special was aired 20 May 1986 on CBS: "The Flintstones 25th Anniversary Celebration" featured the cartoon characters, as well as such real-life luminaries as Harvey Korman, Tim Conway, Vanna White, and Joseph Barbera. ABC aired two prime-time specials in 1993: "I Yabba-Dabba Do!" (7 February) in which Pebbles wed Bamm-Bamm, and "A Flintstone Family Christmas" (18 December). A moderately successful live-action theatrical film followed in 1994, starring John Goodman (Fred), Elizabeth Perkins (Wilma), Rick Moranis (Barney), and Rosie O'Donnell (Betty). A short clip from the TV series's 1960 pilot, "The Flagstones," surfaced on The Cartoon Network 7 May 1994. The title was subsequently changed to *The Flintstones* when it was learned that a *Flagstones* comic strip already existed.

THE FLINTSTONES COMEDY HOUR CBS
9 SEPTEMBER 1972–1 SEPTEMBER 1973
THE FLINTSTONES SHOW CBS
8 SEPTEMBER 1973–26 JANUARY 1974
THE NEW FRED AND BARNEY SHOW NBC
3 FEBRUARY 1979–15 SEPTEMBER 1979
FRED AND BARNEY MEET THE THING NBC
22 SEPTEMBER 1979–1 DECEMBER 1979
FRED AND BARNEY MEET THE SHMOO NBC
8 DECEMBER 1979–15 NOVEMBER 1980
FLINTSTONE COMEDY SHOW NBC
22 NOVEMBER 1980–11 SEPTEMBER 1982
FLINTSTONE FUNNIES NBC
18 SEPTEMBER 1982–8 SEPTEMBER 1984
THE FLINTSTONE KIDS ABC
13 SEPTEMBER 1986–3 SEPTEMBER 1988; 6 JANUARY 1990–SEPTEMBER 1990   Episodes of *The Flintstones* and *Pebbles and Bamm Bamm* were shown Saturday mornings on CBS for a season and a half as *The Flintstones Comedy Hour* and *The Flintstones Show.* NBC acquired the program in 1979; its first offering, *The New Fred and Barney Show,* was not new—it consisted of some of the original cartoons with new voices (Henry Corden as Fred, and Gay Autterson as Betty). *Fred and Barney Meet the Thing* was an hour program, with "Flintstones" segments alternating with "The Thing," the adventures of Benjy Grimm, a high school student who could turn into a behemoth. That show expanded to ninety minutes in December 1979 and was retitled *Fred and Barney Meet the Shmoo,* with the addition of "The New Shmoo," a series which had been introduced in September 1979 (see also that title). In 1980 the Flintstones acquired new neighbors, the Frankenstones, on *Flintstone Comedy Show.* The Flintstone clan moved back to ABC's Saturday morning lineup in the fall of 1986. The new series, *The Flintstone Kids,* put the characters in a slightly more prehistoric setting: as ten-year-olds in Bedrock, with Dino the dinosaur as a mere pup. Another regular feature on the latter series was "Captain Caveman," the world's first superhero.

FLIP!   CBS
17 SEPTEMBER 1988–22 OCTOBER 1988   A short-lived, low-budget Saturday morning series that combined music videos, comedy blackouts, celebrity interviews, and unseen voices that quibbled with each other between segments.

THE FLIP WILSON SHOW   NBC
17 SEPTEMBER 1970–27 JUNE 1974   A successful variety hour hosted by a talented black comedian, Flip Wilson. Wilson, whose real first name is Clerow, created and popularized such characters as Geraldine Jones ("What you see is what you get!"), Reverend Leroy (pastor of the Church of What's Happenin' Now), and Freddie Johnson, Wilson's Everyman.

FLIPPER   NBC
19 SEPTEMBER 1964–2 SEPTEMBER 1967   Another aquatic adventure series created by Ivan Tors (*Sea Hunt, The Aquanauts,* etc.). The star of the show was Flipper, a dolphin who was the seagoing equivalent of Lassie. The human roles were filled by Brian Kelly as Porter Ricks, the Chief Ranger at Coral Key Park, a marine refuge in Florida; Luke Halpin as his son Sandy; Tommy Norden as his son Bud; and Ulla Stromstedt (1965–1966) as Ulla Norstrand, a visiting biochemist. Though Flipper was supposed to be a male dolphin, he was played by a female named Susie.

FLIPPER   SYNDICATED
1995–   On this updated, sixty-minute version of the 1964–1967 network series, young Bud Ricks, inspired by spending three years with Flipper, had grown up to become a marine biologist who ran a research institute in the Florida Keys. It starred Brian Wimmer as Bud, who now preferred to be called Dr. Keith Ricks; Colleen Flynn as Dr. Pam Blondell, a Navy researcher assigned to the institute; Payton Haas as Mike, Pam's troubled thirteen-year-old son; and Jessica Marie Alba as Maya, a local girl.

FLIPSIDE   SYNDICATED
1973   A showcase for rock-and-roll performers with no regulars.

FLO   CBS
24 MARCH 1980–28 APRIL 1980; 21 JULY 1980–2 MAY 1981   In this spinoff from *Alice,* Polly Holliday starred as Flo Castleberry. Heading east to a new job in Houston, Flo stopped off at her hometown (Cowtown, Texas), bought the local café, and renamed it Flo's Yellow Rose. Also featured were Geoffrey Lewis as Earl Tucker, the bartender; Jim B. Baker as Farley Waters, the former owner (and Flo's creditor); Sudie Bond as Flo's mother, Velma Elmore; Joyce Bulifant as Flo's childhood friend, Miriam; Leo Burmester as Randy, the gas jockey; Stephen Keep as Les Kincaid, the piano player; and Lucy Lee Flippin as Fran, Flo's forlorn sister. Hoyt Axton sang the show's theme song.

FLOOR SHOW   NBC/CBS
1 JANUARY 1949–1 OCTOBER 1949 (NBC); 13 MAY 1950–24 JUNE 1950 (CBS)   One of the first TV programs to feature jazz musicians, *Floor Show* was hosted by guitarist Eddie Condon. The half-hour show was seen on Saturday nights.

THE FLORIAN ZaBACH SHOW   SYNDICATED
1954   Half-hour musical show hosted by fleet-fingered violinist Florian ZaBach.

FLY BY NIGHT   CBS
4 APRIL 1991–4 JANUARY 1995   Part of CBS's late-night *Crime Time After Prime Time,* this one was filmed in Vancouver. It starred Shannon Tweed as Sally "Slick" Monroe, who bought an airplane and founded Slick Air, a charter service which barely kept itself aloft. Flying the plane were David Elliott as the pilot, Mack Sheppard, and Francois Guetary as the copilot, Jean-Phillippe Pasteur. *Fly by Night* was a

regular part of *Crime Time After Prime Time* until the fall of 1991, then resurfaced occasionally in reruns.

FLYING BLIND   FOX
13 SEPTEMBER 1992–18 JULY 1993   Half-hour sitcom about an uptight young New York and the wild woman he met at a Manhattan restaurant. With Corey Parker as Neil Barash, a recent college grad who worked at his father's company; Tea Leoni as Alicia, the uninhibited woman who entered his life; Marcus Giamatti as Neil's ambitious coworker, Ted Sharperson; Michael Tucci as Neil's father, Jeremy Barash, head of Hochman Foods; Clea Lewis and Robert Bauer as Megan and Jordan, Alicia's roommates; and Cristine Rose as Ellen.

THE FLYING DOCTOR   SYNDICATED
1959   Richard Denning starred in this half-hour series as an American physician who served the Australian outback by airplane; Jill Adams costarred as his nurse. Donald Hyde was executive producer for Associated British Pictures Corporation; Gross-Krasne Productions distributed the series.

THE FLYING FISHERMAN
See GADABOUT GADDIS

FLYING HIGH   CBS
29 SEPTEMBER 1978–23 JANUARY 1979   Hour comedy-drama about a trio of flight attendants working for Sunwest Airlines. With Pat Klous as Marcy Bower; Connie Sellecca as Lisa Benton; Kathryn Witt as Pam Bellagio; and Howard Platt as their pilot, Captain Douglas March. Mark Carliner was the executive producer.

THE FLYING NUN   ABC
7 SEPTEMBER 1967–18 SEPTEMBER 1970   Situation comedy about a novice nun who discovers she could fly. Sally Field starred as Elsie Ethrington, a young woman who joined the Convent San Tanco in Puerto Rico where she was ordained as Sister Bertrille. Because of the trade winds, her light weight, and the lofty coronets worn by members of her order, Sister Bertrille developed the ability to leave the ground. Also featured were Madeline Sherwood as Reverend Mother Plaseato; Marge Redmond as Sister Jacqueline; Shelley Morrison as Sister Sixto; Alejandro Rey as Carlos Ramirez, owner of a nearby nightspot; and Vito Scotti as Gaspar Formento, local police captain. The half-hour series, of which 82 episodes were made, was a Screen Gems production.

FOCUS ON AMERICA   ABC
27 JUNE 1961–12 SEPTEMBER 1961; 11 JULY 1962–12 SEPTEMBER 1962; 9 JULY 1963–10 SEPTEMBER 1963   This three-time summer-replacement series was comprised of half-hour documentaries produced by various ABC affiliates throughout the country. ABC newsman Bill Shadel served as the program's host during the 1962 season.

FOLEY SQUARE   CBS
11 DECEMBER 1985–8 APRIL 1986; 11 JUNE 1986–23 JULY 1986   Half-hour sitcom set at the Manhattan District Attorney's Office. With Margaret Colin as assistant district attorney Alex Harrigan; Michael Lembeck as her neighbor, Peter Newman; Cathy Silvers as assistant D.A. Molly Dobbs; Sanford Jensen as assistant D.A. Carter deVries; Vernee Watson-Johnson as Alex's secretary, Denise Willums; Israel Juarbe as messenger Angel Gomez; Richard C. Safarian as Spiro, owner of a nearby coffee shop; and Hector Elizondo as the boss, district attorney Jesse Steinberg. Coincidentally, series regulars Cathy Silvers and Michael Lembeck were the second generation of their respective families to costar in a sitcom; their fathers, Phil Silvers and Harvey Lembeck, appeared together in the classic fifties comedy *The Phil Silvers Show*. *Foley Square* was created and produced by Diane English, who sought to have the show represent the "women's viewpoint."

FOLLOW THAT MAN
See MAN AGAINST CRIME

FOLLOW THE LEADER   CBS
7 JULY 1953–18 AUGUST 1953   On this prime-time game show studio contestants
tried to reenact scenes demonstrated by the "leader"—hostess Vera Vague.

FOLLOW THE SUN   ABC
17 SEPTEMBER 1961–9 SEPTEMBER 1962   This hour-long adventure series was set in
Honolulu; thus, for one season, ABC carried two shows with Hawaiian locales (the
other was *Hawaiian Eye*). On this effort, the heroes were freelance writers rather
than detectives. With Barry Coe as Ben Gregory; Brett Halsey as Paul Templin;
Gary Lockwood as boatsman Eric Jason; Gigi Perreau as their secretary, Katherine
Ann Richards; and Jay Lanin as Lieutenant Frank Roper, Honolulu cop.

FOLLOW YOUR HEART   NBC
3 AUGUST 1953–8 JANUARY 1954   A short-lived serial set on Philadelphia's Main
Line, *Follow Your Heart* told the story of a society girl who didn't want to marry the
man her mother had in mind for her. Created by Elaine Carrington, the series was
inspired by Carrington's popular radio serial, *When A Girl Marries*. It starred Sallie
Brophy as Julie Fielding; Nancy Sheridan as her mother, Mrs. Fielding; and Grant
Williams as Julie's boyfriend, Peter Davis, an FBI agent.

THE FONZ AND THE HAPPY DAYS GANG   ABC
8 NOVEMBER 1980–18 SEPTEMBER 1982   This Saturday-morning cartoon show borrowed three characters from *Happy Days:* Fonzie, Richie, and Ralph. Together with
their friend Cupcake and their dog, Mr. Cool, they traveled throughout history in a
time machine, trying to get back to 1957. In the fall of 1982 the cartoon Fonz hooked
up with the cartoon Laverne and Shirley (see *The Mork & Mindy/Laverne & Shirley/
Fonz Hour*).

FOOD FOR THOUGHT   SYNDICATED
1956–1961   A daytime talk show hosted by Virginia Graham.

FOODINI THE GREAT   ABC
25 AUGUST 1951–29 DECEMBER 1951   A filmed puppet show created by Hope and
Morey Bunin. Its star puppets, a bumbling magician named Foodini and his assistant
(Pinhead), first appeared on the Bunins' earlier show, *Lucky Pup*. Foodini had been
created by the Bunins in 1932, originally as an organ grinder. His favorite expression
was "Gadzooks!" Lou Prentis was the series' human hostess.

FOOFUR   NBC
13 SEPTEMBER 1986–3 SEPTEMBER 1988   Hanna-Barbera Saturday-morning cartoon
program about a dog who inherited the mansion of his late owner.

FOOT IN THE DOOR   CBS
28 MARCH 1983–2 MAY 1983   An American version of the British sitcom *Tom, Dick
and Harriet,* with Harold Gould as Jonah Foot, a widower who left his home in sleepy
Pitts Ferry, New Hampshire, to live with his son and daughter-in-law in their Manhattan co-op and to enjoy the New York night life. Also featured were Kenneth Gilman
as the son, James Foot; Diana Canova as the daughter-in-law, Harriet Foot; and
Marian Mercer as Mrs. Griffin, the manager of the co-op.

FOOTBALL SIDELINES   DUMONT
6 OCTOBER 1952–22 DECEMBER 1952   Sportscaster Harry Wismer narrated highlights
of the preceding weekend's football games on this fifteen-minute Monday-night
series.

FOOTLIGHTS THEATER CBS

4 JULY 1952–26 SEPTEMBER 1952; 3 JULY 1953–25 SEPTEMBER 1953   This half-hour dramatic anthology series was seen on Friday nights. In 1953, it was a summer replacement for *Our Miss Brooks.*

FOR ADULTS ONLY SYNDICATED

1971   Talk show cohosted by Barbara Howar and Joyce Susskind.

FOR BETTER OR WORSE CBS

29 JUNE 1959–24 JUNE 1960   A daytime serial that focused on problems in marriages; stories generally lasted one or two weeks. Dr. James A. Peterson, a professional marriage counselor, served as host and commentator. Dyan Cannon made her television debut on this series.

FOR LOVE AND HONOR NBC

23 SEPTEMBER 1983–27 DECEMBER 1983   Presumably inspired by the film *An Officer and a Gentleman,* this hour serial was set at an Army post. Principal players included Cliff Potts as First Sergeant Gene Allard; Shelley Smith as Captain Carolyn Engel, a doctor; Gary Grubbs as the ambitious and humorless Captain Steven Wiecek; Yaphet Kotto as Sergeant China Bell, a Vietnam veteran who left a wife and child in that country; Rachel Ticotin as Corporal Grace Pavlik; Keenen Ivory Wayans as Private Duke Johnson; Pete Kowanko as Private Chris Dolan; Tony Becker as Private Andy "Utah" Wilson; John Mengatti as Private Dominick Trezo; Shanna Reed as Steven's wife, Phyllis Wiecek; Amy Steel as Sharon, Dolan's girlfriend; and Kelly Preston as Mary Lee, a general's daughter. Though the series garnered some critical praise, it was scheduled on Fridays opposite ABC's *Matt Houston* and another serial, CBS's *Falcon Crest.* After the first two or three low-rated episodes were broadcast, NBC ordered executive producer David Gerber to "redesign" the series so that it would more closely resemble other prime-time soap operas.

FOR LOVE OR MONEY CBS

30 JUNE 1958–2 JANUARY 1959   Bill Nimmo hosted this question-and-answer daytime game show.

FOR RICHER, FOR POORER NBC

6 DECEMBER 1977–29 SEPTEMBER 1978   Set in suburban Chicago, *For Richer, For Poorer* was a revamped version of *Lovers and Friends,* which had left the air seven months earlier. Both serials were created by Harding Lemay; Paul Rauch was the executive producer of both. The cast included most of the principals of *Lovers and Friends,* plus a few new faces: Darlene Parks as Megan Cushing; Tom Happer as Bill Saxton, whom Megan was about to marry as the show began; Cynthia Bostick as Connie Ferguson Saxton; Rod Arrants as Megan's brother, Austin Cushing; Laurinda Barrett as the widowed Edith Cushing, mother of Megan and Austin; Albert Stratton as Lester Saxton, Bill's alcoholic father; Patricia Englund as Lester's wife, Josie Saxton; Flora Plumb as their daughter, Eleanor Saxton Kimball; Richard Backus as their son, Jason Saxton; David Abbott as their son, Bentley Saxton; Breon Gorman as their daughter, Tessa Saxton; Stephen Joyce as Eleanor's husband, lawyer George Kimball; Christine Jones as the Saxtons' cousin, Amy Gifford Cushing, wife of Austin; Charles Bateman as investment banker Roger Hamilton; David Knapp as his son, lawyer Desmond Hamilton; Julia MacKenzie as Laurie Brewster Hamilton, Desmond's wife; Robert (Skip) Burton as Lee Ferguson, Connie's brother; Patricia Barry as Viola Brewster; Anthony Call as Fred Ballard; Michael Goodwin as Stan Hillmer; Lynne MacLaren as Barbara Manners; Roy Poole as Ira Ferguson; Sloane Shelton as Mildred Quinn; David Laden as Turk; Chu Chu Mulave as Paco; Stephen Burleigh as Frank Damico; Connie LoCurto as Wendy Prescott; Dennis Romer as Dr. Ray White; and Nancy Snyder as Colleen Griffin.

FOR THE PEOPLE CBS
31 JANUARY 1965–9 MAY 1965   Herbert Brodkin produced this series about an assistant district attorney in New York City. With William Shatner as David Koster; Howard Da Silva as his boss, Anthony Celese; Anthony Celese; Jessica Walter as his wife, Phyllis; and Lonny Chapman as Frank Malloy, an investigator for the D.A.'s office. Fortunately for *Star Trek* fans, *For the People* was canceled (though it was highly acclaimed); had the show been renewed for the 1965–1966 season, Shatner would not have been available to begin work on *Star Trek*.

FOR YOU, BLACK WOMAN SYNDICATED
1977–1978   Public affairs program from Gerber/Carter Productions, hosted by Alice Travis, former cohost of *A.M. New York,* a local show.

FOR YOUR PLEASURE
See GIRL ABOUT TOWN

FORD FESTIVAL (THE JAMES MELTON SHOW) NBC
5 APRIL 1951–26 JUNE 1952   Singer James Melton hosted this hour-long variety series, which replaced *The Ford Star Revue* on Thursdays.

FORD STAR JUBILEE CBS
24 SEPTEMBER 1955–3 NOVEMBER 1956   Ford Motor Company sponsored this lavish series of monthly specials, all of which were broadcast in color. Presentations included: "The Judy Garland Show," a variety special which marked her television debut (24 September 1955); "The Caine Mutiny Court-Martial," with Lloyd Nolan, Barry Sullivan, and Frank Lovejoy (19 November; directed by Franklin Schaffner); Noel Coward's "Blithe Spirit," with Lauren Bacall and Noel Coward (in his American TV debut; 14 January); "The Day Lincoln was Shot," with Raymond Massey, Lillian Gish, and Jack Lemmon as John Wilkes Booth (11 February; directed by Delbert Mann); "High Tor," a musical version of the play by Maxwell Anderson, with Bing Crosby and Julie Andrews (in her TV debut; 10 March); "Twentieth Century," with Betty Grable and Orson Welles (7 April); Noel Coward's "This Happy Breed," with Coward and Edna Best (5 May); the first television showing of the 1939 film, *The Wizard of Oz* (3 November 1956).

FORD STAR REVUE NBC
6 JULY 1950–28 SEPTEMBER 1950; 4 JANUARY 1951–29 MARCH 1951   This hour-long variety series began as a summer replacement for *Kay Kyser's Kollege of Musical Knowledge* and replaced it again that winter. Jack Haley hosted the show, which also featured singer Mindy Carson.

FORD STARTIME NBC
6 OCTOBER 1959–31 MAY 1960   An anthology series of dramatic and variety shows. Presentations included: "The Turn of the Screw," with Ingrid Bergman (her first dramatic role on television, 20 October); "The Wicked Scheme of Jebal Deeks," with Alec Guinness (his American TV dramatic debut, 10 November); "Dear Arthur," with Rex Harrison (a rare television appearance, 22 March); "The Young Juggler," with Tony Curtis (29 March); "Sing Along with Mitch," the first of Mitch Miller's sing-along specials (24 May). Sponsored by the Ford Motor Company, all presentations were done in color.

FORD THEATER (THE FORD TELEVISION THEATER) CBS/NBC/ABC
17 OCTOBER 1948–29 JUNE 1951 (CBS); 2 OCTOBER 1952–27 SEPTEMBER 1956 (NBC); 3 OCTOBER 1956–26 JUNE 1957 (ABC)   *The Ford Television Theater* was CBS's first sponsored dramatic anthology series, beginning in 1948 as a once-a-month effort. By the end of its run the show had been aired over all three major networks, sometimes as a half hour and sometimes as an hour, sometimes live and sometimes filmed. Marc Daniels produced and directed the series when it was aired on CBS; Jules Bricken later produced and directed it during its NBC run. Among the many stars who played

their first major TV roles on the series were Ernest Borgnine ("Night Visitor," 29 April 1954), Michael Connors ("Yours for a Dream," 8 April 1954), Vince Edwards ("Garrity's Sons," 24 March 1955), Barbara Hale ("The Divided Heart," 27 November 1952), Judy Holliday ("She Loves Me Not," 4 November 1949), Robert Horton ("Portrait of Lydia," 16 December 1954), Tab Hunter ("While We're Young," 28 April 1955), Peter Lawford ("The Son-In-Law," 30 April 1953), Donna Reed ("Portrait of Lydia"), Gilbert Roland ("The Arden Woodsman," 14 January 1954), Ann Sheridan ("Malaya Incident," 18 June 1953), Roger Smith ("Never Lend Money to a Woman," 19 January 1956), Barry Sullivan ("As the Flame Dies," 19 November 1953), Claire Trevor ("Alias Nora Hale," 31 December 1953), James Whitmore ("For Value Received," 18 February 1954), Shelley Winters ("Mantrap," 28 January 1954), and Robert Young ("Keep It in the Family," 27 May 1954).

FOREIGN INTRIGUE   SYNDICATED
1951–1955   Sheldon Reynolds produced this half-hour adventure series, which was filmed in Europe. From 1951 to 1953 the show starred Jerome Thor and Sydna Scott as Robert Cannon and Helen Davis, reporters for the *Consolidated News*. During the 1953–1954 season James Daly and Ann Preville starred as Mike Powers and Pat Bennett, reporters for the *Associated News*. The third, and final, version of the series starred Gerald Mohr as Chris Storm, the American owner of a Vienna hotel. Each of the three shows was later syndicated under a different title: Those with Thor and Scott were titled *Dateline: Europe,* those with Daly and Preville as *Overseas Adventures,* and those with Mohr as *Cross Current. Foreign Intrigue* also holds the distinction of being the first American series televised in Canada when broadcasting began in that country in 1952.

THE FOREST RANGERS   SYNDICATED
1964   A half-hour adventure series produced in Canada. With Graydon Gould as Ranger George Keeley of the Forest Rangers; Michael Zenon as Joe Two Rivers, an Indian; Gordon Pinsent as Sergeant Scott; and Rolland Bedard as Uncle Raoul. Also featured were the Junior Rangers, a group of youngsters who helped out the Rangers: Ralph Endersby as Chub; Rex Hagon as Peter; Peter Tully as Mike; George Allen as Ted; Susan Conway as Kathy; and Barbara Pierce as Denise.

FOREVER FERNWOOD   SYNDICATED
1977–1978   Following the departure of Louise Lasser from *Mary Hartman, Mary Hartman,* production of the serial resumed, after a summer hiatus, under this title. Most of the gang from *MH2* returned: Greg Mullavey as Tom Hartman, Mary Kay Place as Loretta Haggers, Graham Jarvis as Charlie Haggers, Dody Goodman as Martha Shumway, Debralee Scott as Cathy Shumway, Claudia Lamb as Heather Hartman, Victor Kilian as Grandpa Larkin, Marian Mercer as Wanda, and Dabney Coleman as Merle Jeeter. Tab Hunter, seldom seen on TV since the early 1960s, replaced Philip Bruns as George Shumway; it was explained that George had accidentally fallen into a chemical vat at work and had undergone plastic surgery. Other cast members included: Shelley Fabares as Eleanor Major; Judy Kahan as Penny; Richard Hatch as T'Harmon; Dennis Burkley as Mac; Severn Darden as Popesco, a balloonist; Joe Penny as Sal; Randall Carver as Jeffrey DeVito; Shelley Berman as Mel Beach; Renée Taylor as Annabelle; Orson Bean as Reverend Brim, Archbishop of Ohio; Skip Young (formerly of *Ozzie and Harriet*) as Freddie Friesen; and James Staley as Dr. Szymon.

FOREVER KNIGHT   CBS/SYNDICATED
5 MAY 1992–23 AUGUST 1994 (CBS); 1994–   (SYNDICATED)   Originally broadcast as part of CBS's late-night umbrella, *Crime Time After Prime Time*, *Forever Knight* starred Geraint Wyn Davies as Nick Knight, a 700-year-old vampire who desired to return to mortality. He stopped drinking human blood and joined a big city police force (working only the night shift, of course) where he battled not only criminals, but also other vampires who disapproved of his new lifestyle. Also on hand were Catherine Disher as police pathologist Dr. Natalie Lambert, the only mortal

who knew Nick's secret; John Kapelos as Nick's wisecracking partner, Don Schanke; Nigel Bennett as Lacroix, Nick's vampire mentor; Deborah Duchene as the vampire Janette, Nick's former love interest; Gary Farmer (1992–1993) as Nick's boss, Captain Stonetree; and Natsuko Ohama (1994–) as the new boss, Captain Amanda Cohen. The hour series was broadcast regularly from May 1992 to August 1993, and popped up occasionally on CBS's late-night schedule in 1994. New episodes were made for first-run syndication in the fall of 1994. In the fall of 1995 new episodes were shown first in syndication and shortly thereafter on the USA Cable Network. The show was filmed in Toronto.

THE FORSYTE SAGA   NET
5 OCTOBER 1969–29 MARCH 1970   A twenty-six-part adaptation of John Galsworthy's series of novels, *The Forsyte Saga* was produced in England (in black and white) by the BBC in 1967. Spanning the period from 1879 to 1926, it chronicled the lives of the members of a moderately wealthy English family against a backdrop of Victorian and Edwardian life. Principal players included: Kenneth More as Jolyon (Jo) Forsyte, the heir apparent; Eric Porter as lawyer Soames Forsyte; Nyree Dawn Porter as Irene; Susan Hampshire as Fleur; Margaret Tyzack as Winnifred; Nicholas Pennell as Michael Mont; Joseph O'Connor as Jolyon, Sr. (Old Jolyon); Fay Compton as Aunt Ann; Lana Morris as Helene; Martin Jarvis as Jon Forsyte; Ursula Howells as Frances; and George Woodbridge as Swithin. Donald Wilson was the producer, David Giles and James Cellan Jones the directors.

FORTUNE DANE   ABC
15 FEBRUARY 1986–27 MARCH 1986   Carl Weathers had the title role in this hour crime show; he played an ex-cop who moved from Twin Rivers to Bay City, where he became a special agent for the mayor. Also featured were Alberta Watson as assistant district attorney Amy Steiner; Penny Fuller as the mayor, Amanda Harding; Daphne Ashbrook as Speed Davenport, another special agent; Joe Dallesandro as "Perfect" Tommy Nicautri, a Bay City cop who worked with Fortune and Speed; and Morgan Upton as Chief Bukowski.

FORTUNE HUNTER   FOX
4 SEPTEMBER 1994–2 OCTOBER 1994   An early casualty of the 1994-1995 season, *Fortune Hunter* was an hour spy show. It starred Mark Frankel as Carlton Dial, a former government agent now working for Intercept. Dial had been fitted with a micro-camera the size of a contact lens, which enabled a "monitor partner" at headquarters to see and hear what Dial did. John Robert Hoffman appeared as Harry Flack, the monitor partner, and Anne Francis was the boss, Mrs. Brady. Steven Aspis created the series.

48 HOURS   CBS
19 JANUARY 1988–   Each week on this prime-time news program, a forty-eight-hour slice of a single topic was distilled into a single broadcast hour. Topics ranged from the serious (drugs, the 1988 New Hampshire primary, the Israeli army) to the light (dogs, compulsive shoppers, and, in a rare ninety-minute program, rock star Paul McCartney). Dan Rather was the anchor, Bernard Goldberg the principal correspondent. The arrival of *48 Hours* gave CBS News its third hour of prime time (together with *60 Minutes* and *West 57th*), a noteworthy achievement.

FOUL PLAY   ABC
26 JANUARY 1981–23 FEBRUARY 1981   A light crime show, based on the movie about a bumbling cop and his librarian girlfriend. With Barry Bostwick as Sergeant Tucker Pendleton of the San Francisco Police; Deborah Raffin as Gloria Mundy; Richard Romanus as Pendleton's boss, Captain Lombardi; Mary Jo Catlett as Stella, Gloria's co-worker; and twins Greg and John Rice as Gloria's diminutive landlords, Ben and Beau.

FOUL-UPS, BLEEPS & BLUNDERS   ABC

10 JANUARY 1984–16 OCTOBER 1984   Like NBC's *TV's Bloopers & Practical Jokes,* this series presented clips of "outtakes" and tapes of practical jokes played on celebrities. The half-hour show was hosted by Steve Lawrence and Don Rickles.

FOUR JUST MEN   SYNDICATED

1959   Half-hour adventure series filmed largely in Europe. The Four Just Men were former comrades during World War II and later joined forces to combat crime on an international scale; each episode featured just one of the Four Just Men. With Dan Dailey as Tim Collier, an American reporter; Jack Hawkins as Ben Manfred, a British detective; Richard Conte as Jeff Ryder, an American attorney living in Paris; and Vittorio DeSica as Rico Poccari, an Italian hotelier with connections. Jack Wrather produced the series in association with the J. Arthur Rank Organisation.

THE FOUR SEASONS   CBS

29 JANUARY 1984–5 AUGUST 1984   Created by Alan Alda, this half-hour sitcom was a continuation of Alda's 1981 film about adult friendships. As the TV series unfolded, Danny and Claudia Zimmer had left Manhattan to join their friends in Southern California. Featured were Jack Weston (repeating his film role) as neurotic dentist Danny Zimmer; Marcia Rodd as his wife, Claudia Zimmer; Tony Roberts as Ted Callan, who dabbled in real estate; Joanna Kerns as Ted's girlfriend, Pat, a stuntwoman; Allan Arbus as Boris, a lawyer who gave up his practice to open a bike shop; Barbara Babcock as Boris's wife, Lorraine, an orthopedist; Beatrice Alda as Ted's daughter, Lisa Callan; and Elizabeth Alda as Beth Burroughs, who headed west with Lisa hoping to find a job as a writer. Beatrice and Elizabeth Alda had also appeared in the film; they are the real-life daughters of Alan Alda, who appeared occasionally in the series as lawyer Jack Burroughs.

FOUR STAR PLAYHOUSE   CBS

25 SEPTEMBER 1952–27 SEPTEMBER 1956   This half-hour dramatic anthology series originally featured appearances by the actors who founded Four Star Films: Dick Powell, Charles Boyer, Joel McCrea, and Rosalind Russell. McCrea and Russell left shortly after the inception of the project and were replaced by David Niven and Ida Lupino. Several episodes starred Dick Powell as Willie Dante, operator of Dante's Inferno, a San Francisco nightspot; these episodes were rebroadcast in 1956 as *The Best in Mystery* (see also that title). Other notable appearances included those by Nigel Bruce (in "A String of Beads," his only U.S. TV role, 21 January 1954), Ronald Colman (in "The Lost Silk Hat," his first TV dramatic appearance, 23 October 1952), and Joan Fontaine (in "The Girl on the Park Bench," her first major dramatic role on television, 3 December 1953).

FOUR STAR REVUE   NBC

4 OCTOBER 1950–18 JULY 1951   This Wednesday-night variety hour featured four rotating hosts: Danny Thomas, Jack Carson, Jimmy Durante, and Ed Wynn. In the fall of 1951, more hosts were added, and the show was retitled *All-Star Revue* (see also that title).

FOUR-IN-ONE   NBC

16 SEPTEMBER 1970–8 SEPTEMBER 1971   The umbrella title for four miniseries introduced by NBC. See: *McCloud; Night Gallery; The Psychiatrist; San Francisco International Airport.*

FOURSQUARE COURT   ABC

16 MARCH 1952–22 JUNE 1952   Norman Brokenshire hosted this unusual panel show on which convicted criminals, all wearing masks, discussed their bad deeds. Other experts in the area of criminal law also participated in the panel discussions. David Lown and Albert T. Knudsen were the producers.

THE FOURTH R   NBC
28 MARCH 1954–26 MAY 1957   The fourth "R" stood for "religion" in this Sunday-morning series, which was produced by several different religious organizations.

THE FOX CUBHOUSE   FOX
3 OCTOBER 1994–   Fox's weekday morning children's show consisted of three segments. In "Jim Henson's Animal Show with Stinky and Jake," shown twice a week, muppets Stinky (a skunk) and Jake (a polar bear) introduced films about real animals and interviewed muppet guest creatures. In "Johnson and Friends," also shown twice a week, the toys in a boy's bedroom (including a pink elephant named Johnson) came to life. In "Rimba's Island," a live-action segment shown once a week, a group of multi-colored animals lived together on an island. All three segments were introduced by a young woman known as Rosie (played by Nancy Mura).

FRACTURED FLICKERS   SYNDICATED
1963   Silent films from Hollywood's early days were embellished with "funny" dialogue on this half-hour series hosted by Hans Conried.

FRACTURED PHRASES   NBC
27 SEPTEMBER 1965–31 DECEMBER 1965   Art James hosted this daytime game show on which contestants tried to decipher sayings or titles of books and songs after seeing them spelled phonetically.

FRAGGLE ROCK   HBO
10 JANUARY 1983–28 MARCH 1988   HBO's first original children's series was supplied by Jim Henson. The live-action puppet show was set in the rock beneath the house of a scientist named Doc, where dwelt three groups of creatures: the fun-loving Fraggles, the small, tower-building Doozers, and the large Gorgs. In 1987 a cartoon series based on the characters premiered on network TV: see below.

FRAGGLE ROCK   NBC
12 SEPTEMBER 1987–3 SEPTEMBER 1988   Saturday-morning cartoon version of the Jim Henson-produced puppet show that previously ran on the HBO cable service.

THE FRANCES LANGFORD-DON AMECHE SHOW   ABC
10 SEPTEMBER 1951–14 MARCH 1952   Frances Langford and Don Ameche, who played *The Bickersons* on radio, hosted this daytime variety hour. A regular feature of the show was "The Couple Next Door," with Jack Lemmon and Cynthia Stone (Lemmon's wife at the time) as young marrieds; this sketch formed the basis of their 1952 series, *Heaven for Betsy.* Also featured on the Langford-Ameche show were Neil Hamilton and the Tony Romano Orchestra. Produced by Ward Byron.

THE FRANK LEAHY SHOW   ABC
27 SEPTEMBER 1953–6 DECEMBER 1953   Fifteen-minute Sunday-night sports show, hosted by football coach Frank Leahy.

FRANK McGEE: HERE AND NOW   NBC
29 SEPTEMBER 1961–29 DECEMBER 1961   Friday-night news analysis and commentary with NBC correspondent Frank McGee. Chet Hagan produced the series.

THE FRANK SINATRA SHOW   CBS
7 OCTOBER 1950–1 APRIL 1952   Frank Sinatra's first series, a musical variety show, inexplicably failed to catch on during its first season; for the 1951–1952 season, it was cut from an hour to a half hour and scheduled opposite Milton Berle's *The Texaco Star Theater,* where, like virtually all of Berle's competition, it perished. Regulars on the show included Erin O'Brien and comic Ben Blue.

THE FRANK SINATRA SHOW ABC

18 OCTOBER 1957–27 JUNE 1958   Frank Sinatra's second attempt at a series proved as unsuccessful as the first. This time he was given free reign (and a reported $3 million) by ABC. The series was a mixed bag—a combination of dramatic shows (some of which starred Sinatra, the rest of which were introduced by him), musical programs, and one or two live half hours. Despite unimposing competition (CBS's *Mr. Adams and Eve* and NBC's *M Squad*), the show was canceled after one season.

FRANKENSTEIN JR. AND THE IMPOSSIBLES CBS

10 SEPTEMBER 1966–7 SEPTEMBER 1968   Saturday-morning cartoon show from the Hanna-Barbera Studios; Frankenstein Jr. was a giant robot activated by Buzz Conroy, and the Impossibles were a team of super-powered government agents (Coil Man, Multi Man, and Fluid Man) masquerading as a rock and roll trio. The series was rerun in 1976–1977.

THE FRANKIE CARLE SHOW NBC

7 AUGUST 1956–29 OCTOBER 1956   Frankie Carle hosted this fifteen-minute musical series, which preceded the network news. It was first seen on Tuesdays, later on Mondays, and was officially titled *The Golden Touch of Frankie Carle*.

FRANKIE LAINE TIME (THE FRANKIE LAINE SHOW) CBS/SYNDICATED

20 JULY 1955–7 SEPTEMBER 1955; 1 AUGUST 1956–19 SEPTEMBER 1956 (CBS); 1955–1957 (SYNDICATED)   One of America's most popular singers during the pre-rock-and-roll years, Frankie Laine twice hosted a summer replacement series for *Arthur Godfrey and His Friends* on Wednesday nights entitled *Frankie Laine Time*. In 1957 he hosted a syndicated half-hour variety program, *The Frankie Laine Show*. Laine is perhaps best remembered by television audiences as the vocalist of the *Rawhide* theme.

FRANK'S PLACE CBS

14 SEPTEMBER 1987–17 MARCH 1988; 16 JULY 1988–1 OCTOBER 1988   One of the most critically acclaimed shows of the 1987–1988 season, *Frank's Place* offered a rare look at contemporary black culture in an urban black community; unfortunately, the series never found its audience (or perhaps vice versa) and was canceled after one season. The brainchild of Hugh (*WKRP in Cincinnati*) Wilson, it starred Tim Reid (also of *WKRP*) as Frank Parrish, a Boston professor of Italian Renaissance history who inherited a New Orleans restaurant from his estranged father; leaving the white academic world, Parrish moved into his late father's apartment above the restaurant and gradually rediscovered his cultural heritage. Wilson and Reid, who were also the executive producers, wisely set the restaurant not in the touristy French Quarter, but squarely in the city's black community (after making several visits to New Orleans), they patterned their restaurant, Chez Louisiane, after the real Chez Helene, run by Austin Leslie). *Frank's Place* had more in common with the "dramadies" of the late 1980s (shows like *Hooperman, The "Slap" Maxwell Story,* and *The Days and Nights of Molly Dodd*) than with the traditional sitcoms: it was filmed with a single camera, with no studio audience and no laugh track. It also dealt with some serious issues, including drug use and suicide. Oddly, it was originally scheduled Mondays at 8 P.M., a poor slot considering its look and lack of appeal to young viewers. During its one-year run it was moved four more times, a frustrating pattern that effectively prevented it from building a regular audience.

In addition to Reid (who won a 1988 NAACP Image Award for his portrayal), the predominantly black ensemble cast included: Daphne Maxwell Reid (Tim Reid's real-life wife) as mortician Hanna Griffin, a Chez Louisiane regular who became Parrish's love interest; Robert Harper as Si "Bubba" Weisberger, one of the few white patrons; Francesca P. Roberts as waitress Anna-May; Tony Burton as Big Arthur, the chef; Frances E. Williams as waitress Miss Marie Walker; Don Yesso as assistant chef Shorty LaRoux; Charles Lampkin as bartender Tiger Shepin; Lincoln Kilpatrick as Reverend Deal; William Thomas, Jr., as Cool Charles, part-time bartender and handyman; and Virginia Capers as Hanna's mother, Bertha Griffin-

Lamour, also a mortician. As its theme music the series employed Louis Armstrong's "Do You Know What It Means to Miss New Orleans."

FRANNIE'S TURN — CBS

13 SEPTEMBER 1992–10 OCTOBER 1992   Half-hour sitcom about an overworked New York seamstress. With Miriam Margolyn as Frannie Escobar; Tomas Milian as her Cuban-American husband, Joseph; Alice Drummond as her bedridden live-in mother-in-law, Rosa; Phoebe Augustine as her daughter, Olivia; Stivi Paskoski as her son, Eddie; LaTanya Richardson as her co-worker, Vivian; and Taylor Negron as her boss, Armando, a fashion designer.

FRASIER — NBC

16 SEPTEMBER 1993–   Successful sitcom on which Kelsey Grammer continued the role of psychiatrist Frasier Crane, which he had originated on *Cheers*. As the new series unfolded, Dr. Crane moved from Boston to Seattle to host a radio call-in show; upon his arrival, his irascible father moved in with him. The cast also included John Mahoney as Frasier's widowed father, Martin, an ex-cop; David Hyde Pierce as Frasier's younger but equally high strung brother, Niles (also a psychiatrist); Jane Leeves as Daphne Moon, Martin's home health care aide; Peri Gilpin as Frasier's producer, Roz Doyle; and Dan Butler as Bulldog Briscoe, the womanizing host of the radio station's sports call-in show. Mercedes Ruehl joined the cast in 1995 as station manager Kate Costas. Almost as popular as the human regulars was a Jack Russell terrier known as Moose, who played Eddie, Martin's dog.

FREAKAZOID! — WB

9 SEPTEMBER 1995–   The central character in this Saturday morning cartoon show was a mild-mannered teenager named Dexter Douglas, whose alter ego was teen superhero Freakazoid!

FRED AND BARNEY MEET THE THING

See THE FLINTSTONES COMEDY HOUR

THE FRED WARING SHOW — CBS

17 APRIL 1949–30 MAY 1954; 22 JULY 1957–30 AUGUST 1957   Fred Waring organized his first band in 1920; by 1932 he and his group, the Pennsylvanians, had their own radio show. Waring's assemblage usually numbered about sixty-five musicians and singers. Among the featured performers were Joanne Wheatley, Daisy Bernier, Joe Marino, Keith and Sylvia Textor, Virginia and Livingston Gearhart, and Hugh Brannum, who later played Mr. Green Jeans on *Captain Kangaroo*. Waring's first TV series was a half-hour show, which ran on Sunday nights for most of its run; it was produced and directed by Bob Banner. Waring's 1957 series was a daytime show, a six-week summer replacement for *The Garry Moore Show* broadcast from Waring's Pennsylvania resort, Shawnee-on-the-Delaware.

THE FREDDY MARTIN SHOW (THE HAZEL BISHOP SHOW) — NBC

12 JULY 1951–5 DECEMBER 1951   This half-hour musical series, sponsored by Hazel Bishop cosmetics, was introduced as a summer replacement for *Martin Kane, Private Eye* and was later given another time slot. Bandleader Freddy Martin hosted the series; one of its featured vocalists was Merv Griffin.

FREDDY'S NIGHTMARES — SYNDICATED

1988–1990   A gory hour anthology series based on the *Nightmare on Elm Street* films. Robert Englund reprised his movie role as Freddy Krueger, who wore a glove with long, straight-edge razors for nails and could insert himself into teenagers' dreams. In some cities where the show was aired in an early time slot, complaints were received that the show was causing real nightmares in younger viewers; the distributor dutifully advised its clients to run the show later at night. In a further effort to reassure the viewing public, the producers issued a statement that "no one under the age of 18 will be murdered on this show." Nevertheless, the National

Coalition on Television Violence named the series (together with *Friday the 13th*) TV's "most violent" in 1989.

FREE COUNTRY ABC
24 JUNE 1978–22 JULY 1978   Half-hour comedy-drama starring Rob Reiner and Judy Kahan as Joseph and Anna Bresner, Lithuanian immigrants who came to America in 1906 and 1909 respectively. The five-part series spanned almost seventy years, and each show was "hosted" by Reiner as the eighty-nine-year-old Joseph. Reiner and Phil Mishkin created the series and were its executive producers; Gareth Davies was the producer. Also featured were Larry Gelman and Renée Lippin as the Bresners' friends, Leo and Ida Gewurtzman.

FREE SPIRIT ABC
22 SEPTEMBER 1989–21 JANUARY 1990   An updated version of the 1970 sitcom, *Nanny and the Professor,* this one starred Corinne Bohrer as Winnie Goodwinn, a winsome witch who was hired as a housekeeper for a motherless family; Franc Luz as the father, attorney Thomas J. Harper, the only member of the family who didn't know of Winnie's true identity; Paul Scherrer as son Robb, fifteen; Alyson Hannigan as daughter Jessie, thirteen; and Edan Gross as son Gene, ten. The family was originally to have been called the Haggartys, but the surname was changed to Harper after production had started. The switch thus gave ABC the odd distinction of having *two* new sitcoms on its fall schedule with families named Harper (*Homeroom,* featuring a black Harper family, was the other); both flopped.

FREE TO CHOOSE PBS
11 JANUARY 1980–14 MARCH 1980   Ten-part series on capitalism and free enterprise, hosted by economist Milton Friedman.

FREE WILLY ABC
24 SEPTEMBER 1994–   Saturday morning cartoon series based on the popular movie of the same title. On the TV version Willy the whale had been freed, and could communicate with a twelve-year-old boy named Jesse.

FREEBIE AND THE BEAN CBS
6 DECEMBER 1980–24 JANUARY 1981   An early casualty of the 1980–1981 season, *Freebie and the Bean* was an hour crime show derived from the motion picture of the same title. It starred Hector Elizondo as Don "the Bean" Delgado, and Tom Mason as Tim "Freebie" Walker, a pair of plainclothes cops assigned to the District Attorney. William Daniels costarred as Walter Cruikshack, the D.A., and Mel Stewart was featured as "Axle," the police mechanic.

FREEDOM RINGS CBS
3 MARCH 1953–27 AUGUST 1953   John Beal hosted this audience participation show, on which contestants acted out household problems with members of the show's cast—Alice Ghostley, Malcolm Broderick, Joy Hilton, Chuck Taylor, and Ted Tiller. Applause from the studio audience determined the prizewinning contestants. Lloyd Gross produced the half-hour show, which was seen Tuesday and Thursday afternoons.

THE FRENCH CHEF NET-PBS
1962–1973   Half-hour series on French cooking. Thanks to its host, the irrepressible Julia Child, the show was enjoyed by those not interested in French cuisine as well as by gastronomes. See also *Julia Child & Company.*

THE FRESH PRINCE OF BEL-AIR NBC
10 SEPTEMBER 1990–   Rap musician Will Smith (latter half of the duo D. J. Jazzy Jeff and The Fresh Prince) starred in this half-hour sitcom as, appropriately, Will Smith, a streetwise West Philadelphia teenager who was sent to live with rich relatives in ritzy Bel Air, California. Costarring were James Avery as Will's uncle, lawyer

Phillip Banks; Janet Hubert as Philip's wife, Vivian Banks; Alfonso Ribeiro as their preppy son, Carlton, who worshipped Bryant Gumbel; Karyn Parsons as their narcissistic teen daughter, Hilary; Tatyana M. Ali as their younger daughter, Ashley, Will's closest friend in his new home; and Joseph Marcell as the Banks's officious butler, Geoffrey Butler. Occasionally featured was Jeffrey A. Townes as Jazzy Jeff, Will's pal (in real life, of course, Townes was the former half of rap duo D. J. Jazzy Jeff and the Fresh Prince).

In the spring of 1993 Phillip (who had become a judge) and Vivian had a baby boy, Nicholas. Janet Hubert (by now known as Janet Hubert-Whitten) left the series at the end of the 1992–1993 season (she later filed suit against NBC and Smith for defamatory statements allegedly made by Smith about her departure). She was replaced by Daphne Maxwell Reid. In the fall 1993 premiere, one character—Jazzy Jeff— alluded to the personnel change. Jazz himself was married in 1993; Karen Malina White appeared occasionally as his wife, Jewel. Will and Carlton were now attending college at the University of Los Angeles. In the fall of 1994 young Nicky, who had been born only eighteen months earlier, was now played by a five-year-old, Ross Bagley. Once again, Jazz noted the difference as he stared incredulously at the new Nicky (attentive viewers would also have heard him ask Will, "Who's playing the mother this year?"). In the spring of 1995, Will and his girlfriend, Lisa Wilkes (played by Nia Long) headed for the altar, but did not tie the knot.

FRESHMAN DORM   CBS

11 AUGUST 1992–9 SEPTEMBER 1992   Hour dramatic series about seven new arrivals at a southern California college. With Paige French as Lulu Abercrombie, the rich kid; Arlene Taylor as Kamala Consuelo Richardo, the poor kid who told her new friends that her name was K. C. Richards; Robyn Lively as Molly Flynn, the wholesome kid from Milwaukee; Matthew Fox as Danny Foley, Molly's boyfriend; Kevin Mambo as Alex Woods, the black guy; Casper Van Dien as Alex's roommate, Zack Taylor, the surfer; Justin Lazard as Joe Ellis; Lisa Fuller as Cynthia; and Robin Thomas as Sydney.

FRESNO   CBS

16 NOVEMBER 1986–20 NOVEMBER 1986   *Fresno* was a rarity in television programming: a comedy miniseries. The five-part, six-hour, $12-million production was an effective spoof of prime-time soap operas. Set in Fresno, California, it told the tale of two warring raisin dynasties, the Kensingtons and the Canes. The large cast included Carol Burnett as Charlotte Kensington; Dabney Coleman as Tyler Cane; Charles Grodin as Charlotte's son, Cane Kensington; Teri Garr as Cane's wife, Talon; Gregory Harrison as Torch; Teresa Ganzel as Bobbi Jo Bobb; Valerie Mahaffey as Tiffany Kensington; and Pat Corley as Earl Duke. Barry Kemp created the miniseries, which was rerun on CBS in July 1989.

FRIDAY NIGHT VIDEOS   NBC

29 JULY 1983–   The surprising popularity of MTV, the twenty-four-hour all-music cable service, led to the creation of this late-night (12:30 A.M. Fridays) series. Like MTV's service, the program consists mainly of short video clips of rock and roll groups, either performing their material or appearing in visual dramatizations of the songs. Also featured are occasional interviews and vintage clips of yesterday's rockers. The offscreen announcer was Nick Michaels, but in November of 1983 the program began to be hosted each week by a celebrity guest. Among the more unusual celebrity pairings were sex adviser Dr. Ruth Westheimer and rocker Ozzy Osbourne, who cohosted on 2 May 1986. In 1985 Scott Muni took over as announcer. In June of 1987 the show's late-night time slot was moved back another hour (to 1:30 A.M.) in order to make room for the Friday telecast of *Late Night with David Letterman*. New York disc jockey Frankie Crocker became the anouncer in 1990, and began appearing on camera in 1991, when Tom Kenny was named permanent host. Tonight show bandleader Branford Marsalis was named host in April 1993, and served until 1994, when comedian Henry Cho took over. In January 1994 the series' title was shortened to *Friday Night*; by now it presented in-studio performances by

musical acts, movie reviews, and other segments, in addition to its stable of rock videos.

FRIDAY THE 13TH: THE SERIES   SYNDICATED

1987–1990   This Canadian-produced hour fantasy series borrowed the title, and nothing else, from the film series. The TV show told the tale of two young cousins who traveled around, trying to recover the hexed antiques that had been sold from their late uncle's shop; each of the sought-for items had caused, or would soon cause, evil to its owner. With Robey as Micki Foster; John D. LeMay (1987–1989) as Ryan Dallion; Steven Monarque (1989–1990) as Johnny Ventura, who replaced Ryan as Micki's sleuthing partner; and Chris Wiggins as Jack Marshak, a retired magician who sometimes helped the duo.

FRIDAYS   ABC

11 APRIL 1980–22 OCTOBER 1982   This seventy-minute late-night comedy-variety series was broadcast, not surprisingly, on Friday nights. Originally criticized as a clone of *NBC's Saturday Night Live,* the show slowly acquired its own identity; after a two-and-a-half-year run, it was dropped from ABC's schedule as *ABC News Nightline* expanded from four nights a week to five. *Fridays'* resident company included Mark Blankfield, Maryedith Burrell, Melanie Chartoff, Larry David, Darrow Igus, Brandis Kemp, Bruce Mahler, Michael Richards, and John Roarke. Veteran comedy writer Jack Burns headed up the writing staff and also served as the announcer.

FRIENDS   ABC

25 MARCH 1979–22 APRIL 1979   Wholesome hour miniseries about three suburban sixth graders. With Charles Aiken as Pete Richards; Jill Whelan as Nancy Wilks; Jarrod Johnson as Randy Summerfield; Andy Romano and Karen Morrow as Pete's parents, Mr. and Mrs. Richards; Roger Robinson and Janet MacLachlan as Randy's parents, Warren and Jane Summerfield; Dennis Redfield as Nancy's divorced father, Mr. Wilks; Charles Lampkin as Randy's grandfather; Alicia Fleer as Cynthia, Pete's sixteen-year-old sister. A. J. Carothers created the series, and Aaron Spelling and Douglas S. Cramer were the executive producers.

FRIENDS   NBC

22 SEPTEMBER 1994–   Created by David Crane and Marta Kauffman, this ensemble comedy was the most popular new sitcom of the 1994–1995 season, finishing eighth in the Nielsen ratings. Its central characters were six twenty-somethings who lived in New York and hung out at a neighborhood coffee bar, the Central Perk Cafe. Featured were Jennifer Aniston as waitress Rachel Green; Courteney Cox as her roommate, Monica Geller, an assistant chef; Lisa Kudrow as Phoebe Buffay (and occasionally as her twin sister Ursula, who originally appeared on *Mad About You*); Matt LeBlanc as aspiring actor Joey Tribbiani; Matthew Perry as Joey's roommate, Chandler Bing (their place was across the hall from Rachel and Monica's); and David Schwimmer as Monica's recently divorced brother, Ross Geller. Ross and Rachel became more than friends, though Ross also had another girlfriend (Julie, played by Heather Tom). He also became a father during the first season, as his ex-wife (who had left him for another woman) gave birth to their child.

The success of *Friends* spawned a host of similar sitcoms in the fall of 1995. See, for example, *Can't Hurry Love, The Crew, The Drew Carey Show, First Time Out, Misery Loves Company, Partners,* and *The Single Guy.*

FRIENDS AND LOVERS   CBS

14 SEPTEMBER 1974–4 JANUARY 1975   Set in Boston, this situation comedy starred Paul Sand as Robert Dreyfuss, a young man who wins a job as bass violinist with the Boston Symphony Orchestra (the show's official title was *Paul Sand in Friends and Lovers*). Also featured were Michael Pataki as his brother, Charlie Dreyfuss; Penny Marshall as Charlie's wife, Janice; Dick Wesson as Jack Reardon, orchestra manager; Steve Landesberg as Robert's friend, Fred Meyerbach, a violinist; and Craig Richard Nelson as Mason Woodruff, the young conductor. Henry Winkler guest-starred in the

premiere episode. Like *Bridget Loves Bernie*, *Friends and Lovers* was scheduled between two blockbusters (*All in the Family* and *The Mary Tyler Moore Show*) and was canceled when it failed to win large enough ratings. Executive producers: James L. Brooks and Allan Burns. Produced by Steve Pritzker for MTM Enterprises.

FRIENDS OF MAN   SYNDICATED
1974   Animals were the subject of this half-hour documentary series narrated by Glenn Ford. Executive producer: John Must. Produced by Tony Bond, Henning Jacobsen, and Rupert McNee.

FROM A BIRD'S EYE VIEW   NBC
29 MARCH 1971–16 AUGUST 1971   This comedy, imported from England, centered around two stewardesses employed by International Airlines. With Millicent Martin as Millie Grover, the British one; Patte Finley as Maggie Ralston, the American one; Peter Jones as Mr. Clyde Beauchamp, their supervisor; and Robert Cawdron as Uncle Bert, Millie's uncle.

FROM HERE TO ETERNITY   NBC
10 MARCH 1980–9 APRIL 1980; 3 AUGUST 1980–16 AUGUST 1980   A prime-time serial set in wartime Hawaii following the attack on Pearl Harbor, *From Here to Eternity* picked up where James Jones's novel left off. Principal players included William Devane as Sergeant Milt Warden; Barbara Hershey as Karen Holmes, who had an affair with Warden; Roy Thinnes as Major Dana Holmes, her husband; Don Johnson as Jeff Prewitt; Kim Basinger as prostitute Lorene Rogers; Lacey Neuhaus as Emily Austin; and Daniel Spielberg as Captain Ross. The hour series was introduced on *NBC Movies for Television* in 1979.

FROM JUMPSTREET   PBS
1980–1981   A thirteen-week series on the history of black music, hosted by Oscar Brown, Jr.

FROM THESE ROOTS   NBC
30 JUNE 1958–29 DECEMBER 1961   This daytime serial is fondly remembered by soap opera fans as a high quality show; it was also the spawning ground for a number of performers who went on to play major roles in other soaps. Created by Frank Provo, the series was produced by Paul Lammers and directed by Don Wallace. The cast included: Rod Henrickson and Joseph Macauley as Ben Fraser, editor of the Strathfield *Record*; Ann Flood as Liz Fraser, his daughter, a fiction writer; Helen Shields as his daughter, Emily Fraser Benson; Frank Marth as Ben Fraser, Jr.; Julie Bovasso and Tresa Hughes as Rose Corelli Fraser, his wife; Len Wayland and Tom Shirley as Dr. Buck Weaver; Billie Lou Watt as Maggie Barker Weaver, his wife; Robert Mandan as playwright David Allen, who married Liz Fraser; Barbara Berjer as Lynn Franklin; Audra Lindley as Laura Tompkins; Millette Alexander as Gloria Saxon; Henderson Forsythe as Jim Benson, Emily's husband; Craig Huebing as Tom Jennings; David Sanders as Bruce Crawford; and Vera Allen as Kass, Ben Sr.'s maid. The serial wrapped up its 915 episodes by tying up its loose ends happily.

THE FRONT PAGE   CBS
29 SEPTEMBER 1949–26 JANUARY 1950   Franklin Heller directed this Thursday-night series, which was based on the film of the same title. John Daly starred as editor Walter Burns; Richard Boone also appeared as a regular. One week after the show's cancellation, Daly and Heller moved on to a new game show created by Mark Goodson and Bill Todman called *What's My Line?*

FRONT PAGE   FOX
26 JUNE 1993–26 APRIL 1994   Prime time weekly investigative series, with five young reporters: Ron Reagan, Josh Mankiewicz, Andria Hall, Tony Harris, and Vicki Liviakis.

FRONT PAGE DETECTIVE   DUMONT

16 MARCH 1951–19 SEPTEMBER 1952; 16 OCTOOBER 1953–13 NOVEMBER 1953   Edmund Lowe starred as reporter David Chase in this half-hour series. Paula Drew costarred as his girlfriend, a fashion designer, and Pamela Duncan played his secretary, Dorabelle. Jerry Fairbanks produced the show, which was filmed in Los Angeles.

FRONT ROW CENTER   DUMONT

25 MARCH 1949–2 APRIL 1950   Regulars on this musical variety series included Phil Leeds, Hal Loman, Joan Fields, and Bibi Osterwald.

FRONT ROW CENTER   CBS

1 JUNE 1955–21 SEPTEMBER 1955; 8 JANUARY 1956–22 APRIL 1956   This dramatic anthology hour, produced and directed by Fletcher Markle, alternated with *The U.S. Steel Hour* during the summer of 1955, then reappeared on Sunday afternoons early in 1956. Presentations included: "Dinner at Eight," with Mary Astor, Everett Sloane, Pat O'Brien, and Mary Beth Hughes (1 June); "Ah, Wilderness!" with Leon Ames and Lillian Hellman (15 June); and "The Human Touch," with Lisa Kirk (15 April).

FRONTIER   NBC

25 SEPTEMBER 1955–9 SEPTEMBER 1956   Worthington Miner produced this half-hour western anthology series in which gunplay was deemphasized. Walter Coy served as narrator, and starred in occasional episodes; the stories were said to have been based on fact.

FRONTIER CIRCUS   CBS

5 OCTOBER 1961–20 SEPTEMBER 1962   The T & T Circus provided the backdrop for this hour-long western, which featured Chill Wills as Colonel Casey Thompson and John Derek as Ben Travis, co-owners of the circus, and Richard Jaeckel as their scout, Tony Gentry.

FRONTIER DOCTOR   SYNDICATED

1958   Rex Allen, star of countless "B" western movies, starred as Dr. Bill Baxter, a frontier physician in the Arizona Territory.

FRONTIER JUSTICE   CBS

14 JULY 1958–29 SEPTEMBER 1958; 6 JULY 1959–21 SEPTEMBER 1959   This series of rebroadcasts of *Zane Grey Theater* episodes was seen as a summer replacement for *December Bride* in 1958 and for *Make Room for Daddy* in 1959. Lew Ayres hosted in 1958, Melvyn Douglas in 1959.

FRONTIERS OF FAITH   NBC

7 OCTOBER 1951–19 JULY 1970   This long-running religious series was sponsored by the National Council of Churches. For many years it shared a time slot with two other religious programs: *The Catholic Hour* (later known as *Guideline*) and *The Eternal Light*.

FRONTLINE   PBS

17 JANUARY 1983–   Jessica Savitch first hosted this hour series of independently produced documentaries. The premiere telecast, "An Unauthorized History of the NFL," which examined gambling in professional football, attracted much controversy and criticism, but most of the other presentations—including programs on abortion clinics, Soviet émigrés, and life in the poorer neighborhoods of Washington, D.C.—were solid. Savitch was to have hosted a second season of *Frontline* but was killed in an automobile accident in the fall of 1983. Judy Woodruff (who, like Savitch, had also worked for NBC News) was selected to replace her. A small sample of the programs offered over the years would include: "Crisis in Central America" (9–12 April 1985); "Memories of the Camps" (7 May 1985); "AIDS: A National Inquiry" (a live two-hour broadcast, 25 March 1986); "Holy War, Holy Terror" (3 June 1986);

"Praise the Lord" (26 January 1988, which replaced a 1987 program on TV evangelists that was shelved); "Guns, Drugs and the CIA" (17 May 1988); "The Real Life of Ronald Reagan" (18 January 1989); "The Noriega Connection" (30 January 1990); "High Crimes and Misdemeanors" (23 April 1991), hosted by Bill Moyers; "Innocence Lost" (7 May 1991), a two-hour program questioning allegations of child abuse at a North Carolina day care center (a follow-up report was televised in July 1993); "The Secret File on J. Edgar Hoover" (9 February 1993); "Who Was Lee Harvey Oswald?" (16 November 1993); and "Does TV Kill?" (10 January 1995), an examination of violence on television.

FROSTY FROLICS   ABC
19 SEPTEMBER 1951–10 OCTOBER 1951   This four-week series appears to have been the first ice revue series on television; it was produced and directed by Klaus Landsberg. The idea was later employed on such series as *Music on Ice* and *Ice Palace,* and to a limited extent on *Donny and Marie.*

THE FRUGAL GOURMET   PBS
1983–   On this half-hour series chef Jeff Smith emphasizes the efficient preparation and use of food. The show ran locally in Tacoma, Washington, from 1973 to 1977 before going national (from Chicago) six years later.

FUDGE   ABC
14 JANUARY 1995–   Live-action Saturday morning sitcom for kids, based on the series of books by Judy Blume. With Luke Tarsitano as Farley Drexel "Fudge" Hatcher, a four-year-old who lived with his family in a Manhattan apartment; Jake Richardson as his older brother, Peter, from whose point of view the stories were told; Eve Plumb as their mother, Ann; Forrest Witt as their father, Warren; Nassira Nicola as Sheila, the girl who lived next door; Alex Burrall as Peter's best friend, Jimmy; and Rob Monroe as Henry, the building superintendent. The TV series was introduced by a prime-time made-for-TV movie, "Fudge-A-Mania," on 7 January.

THE FUGITIVE   ABC
17 SEPTEMBER 1963–29 AUGUST 1967   Quinn Martin produced this popular adventure series, which starred David Janssen as Dr. Richard Kimble and Barry Morse as Lieutenant Philip Gerard. Wrongly convicted for the murder of his wife and sentenced to death, Kimble escaped from custody in a train wreck while being transported to prison. He spent the next four years searching for the mysterious one-armed man whom he had seen running from the house the night his wife was murdered. Complicating his search was the fact that he was being relentlessly (if unsuccessfully) pursued by Lieutenant Gerard. The series climaxed in a two-parter shown after the summer reruns in 1967. After learning that the one-armed man had been captured in Los Angeles, Kimble surrendered. Shortly thereafter, the one-armed man escaped from custody; Kimble prevailed upon Gerard to let him track the man down. Kimble found him in a deserted amusement park and chased him to the top of a water tower; there, the one-armed man confessed to the killing just as he was about to throw Kimble from the tower. At that moment, Gerard arrived below and, apparently convinced of Kimble's innocence, shot the one-armed man. The final episode (29 August 1967) was the highest-rated single television program ever broadcast, and would not be surpassed in the ratings until 1976. Also featured on the series were Bill Raisch as Fred Johnson, the one-armed man, and (in the openings and in flashbacks) Diane Brewster as Helen Kimble. William Conrad served as narrator. A popular theatrical film based on the series was released in 1993, starring Harrison Ford as Kimble and Tommy Lee Jones as Gerard (his first name was now Sam). David Janssen's mother, Berniece Janssen, appeared in a courtroom scene as an extra. Capitalizing on the film's popularity, NBC dusted off three hours from the original series, rerunning the sixth episode (which showed Helen Kimble's murder) on 18 August 1993 and the two-part finale on 19 and 21 August; the latter telecast won its timeslot.

FULL CIRCLE   CBS

27 JUNE 1960–10 MARCH 1961   Bill Barrett wrote this little-known daytime serial, which featured Robert Fortier as Gary Donovan, a romantic drifter, and Dyan Cannon as Lisa Crowder, the young widow with whom he got involved. Also featured were Bill Lundmark as songwriter David Talton; Amzie Strickland as Beth Perce; Jean Byron as Dr. Kit Aldrich; and Byron Foulger as Carter Talton.

FULL HOUSE   ABC

22 SEPTEMBER 1987–29 AUGUST 1995   Half-hour sitcom about a widowed San Francisco sportscaster who enlisted his best friend and his brother-in-law to move in and help him raise the kids. With Bob Saget as widower Danny Tanner; Dave Coulier as his friend, standup comic Joey Gladstone; John Stamos as his brother-in-law, exterminator (and part-time rocker) Jesse Katsopolous (the character was originally named Jesse Cochran, but Jesse decided to change his last name after his Greek grandparents visited); Candace Cameron as eldest daughter D. J. (Donna Jo); Jodie Sweetin as middle daughter Stephanie; twins Mary-Kate and Ashley Fuller Olsen as baby Michelle; and Andrea Barber as D.J.'s pal, Kimmy Gibler. In the fall of 1988 Danny became the cohost of a local talk show, and Jesse landed a job writing commercial jingles. Lori Loughlin joined the cast as Danny's cohost, Rebecca Donaldson, whom Jesse fell for. Rebecca and Jesse were married in February 1991. In the fall of 1991 Jesse and Rebecca had twin sons, Nicholas and Alexander; they were played first by Daniel and Kevin Renteria, later by Dylan and Blake Tuomy-Wilhoit. Gail Edwards was featured from 1991 to late 1993 as Vicky, Danny's girlfriend; the two made plans to marry, but did not go through with it. Scott Weinger played D. J.'s boyfriend, Steve Hale, from 1992 to 1994. Jeff Franklin created the series.

THE FUN FACTORY   NBC

14 JUNE 1976–1 OCTOBER 1976   Bobby Van hosted this daytime show, which combined audience-participation games with songs and sketches performed by the regulars: Jane Nelson, Betty Thomas, Deborah Harmon, Doug Steckler, and Dick Blasucci. Executive producers: Ed Fishman and Randall Freer. Produced by David Fishman.

FUN FOR THE MONEY   ABC

17 JUNE 1949–9 DECEMBER 1949   Johnny Olson hosted this Chicago-based game show on which teams of women and men competed against each other. James Saphier produced the half-hour series, and Ed Skotch directed it.

FUN HOUSE (FOX'S FUN HOUSE)   SYNDICATED/FOX

1989–1990 (SYNDICATED); 8 SEPTEMBER 1990–13 APRIL 1991 (FOX)   This kids' game show began life as a five-day-a-week syndicated series; after one season it shifted to Fox's new Saturday morning lineup. J. D. Roth was the emcee of both versions, on which kids performed various physical stunts.

THE FUNKY PHANTOM   ABC

11 SEPTEMBER 1971–1 SEPTEMBER 1973   Saturday-morning cartoon show about three kids—April, Augie, and Skip—and their pal Jonathan Muddlemore, a two-hundred-year-old chap who had locked himself in a grandfather clock in 1776.

FUNNY BONERS   NBC

27 NOVEMBER 1954–9 JULY 1955   A game show for children, which was seen on Saturday mornings and hosted by ventriloquist Jimmy Weldon and his dummy duck, Webster Webfoot. Broadcast from Hollywood.

FUNNY FACE   CBS

18 SEPTEMBER 1971–11 DECEMBER 1971   This half-hour sitcom starred Sandy Duncan as Sandy Stockton, a student teacher who also did commercials for an ad agency. Also featured were Valorie Armstrong as her friend and neighbor, Alice McCraven, and (in the first few episodes only) Henry Beckman and Kathleen Freeman as Pat

and Kate Harwell, Sandy's landlords. Production of the series was discontinued in 1971 when Duncan required eye surgery; she returned to television in 1972 in a slightly different format. See *The Sandy Duncan Show*.

FUNNY MANNS SYNDICATED
1960 Cliff Norton hosted this series of silent film comedy shorts. Between segments, Norton appeared as any one of several "Mann" characters, such as Mail Mann, Police Mann, or Trash Mann.

FUNNY PEOPLE (GEORGE SCHLATTER'S FUNNY PEOPLE) NBC
27 JULY 1988–7 SEPTEMBER 1988 Comedy was the subject of this hour variety series, which blended standup routines, visits with comics, and reports on humorous goings-on around the country. Among the hosts were Leeza Gibbons, Blake Clark, Scott Blakeman, and Rita Rudner; Dave Spector was a regular contributor. George Schlatter, the creator of the series, was the father of the seminal *Laugh-In* series twenty years earlier and of *Real People* a decade earlier.

THE FUNNY SIDE NBC
14 SEPTEMBER 1971–7 DECEMBER 1971 On this hour-long comedy series, a repertory company of five couples explored the funny side of a particular subject each week. Gene Kelly hosted most of the episodes. The players included: Burt Mustin and Queenie Smith as the old couple; Dick Clair and Jenna McMahon as the sophisticated couple; John Amos and Teresa Graves as the black couple; Warren Berlinger and Pat Finley as the blue-collar couple; and Michael Lembeck and Cindy Williams as the young couple. Bill Persky and Sam Denoff were the producers.

FUNNY YOU SHOULD ASK ABC
28 OCTOBER 1968–27 JUNE 1969 Lloyd Thaxton hosted this daytime game show on which contestants tried to match answers with the celebrities who had supplied them.

THE FURTHER ADVENTURES OF ELLERY QUEEN
See ELLERY QUEEN

FURY NBC
15 OCTOBER 1955–3 SEPTEMBER 1966 This popular show about a boy and his horse was a Saturday staple for several seasons. Bobby Diamond starred as Joey Newton, a city orphan who was taken into custody after a street fight and was permitted to live on a ranch owned by a man who had recently lost his wife and children; Peter Graves costarred as Jim Newton, the rancher who eventually adopted Joey. Also featured were William Fawcett as Pete, the chief hand at the Broken Wheel Ranch; Roger Mobley as Joey's friend, Packy; and Jimmy Baird as Joey's friend, Pee Wee (Rodney Jenkins). Fury, the black horse given to Joey by Jim, was owned and trained by Ralph McCutcheon. There were 114 episodes filmed between 1955 and 1960 and rerun by the network until 1966. The series was syndicated under the title of *Brave Stallion*.

FUTURE COP ABC
5 MARCH 1977–6 AUGUST 1977 An irregularly scheduled crime show, *Future Cop* starred Ernest Borgnine as Officer Joe Cleaver and John Amos as his partner, Officer Bill Bundy. The two veterans were assigned to break in a rookie officer, a robot supposedly programmed to be the perfect cop. The android, Officer Haven, was played by Michael Shannon. Anthony Wilson and Gary Damsker were the executive producers of the hour series.

THE G.E. COLLEGE BOWL
See COLLEGE BOWL

G.E. THEATER
See GENERAL ELECTRIC THEATER

G.E. TRUE   CBS

30 SEPTEMBER 1962–22 SEPTEMBER 1963   Jack Webb served as host and narrator of
this half-hour anthology series; the episodes were based on stories from *True* magazine. Sponsored by General Electric, the show occupied the same Sunday slot that
General Electric Theater held down for many seasons.

G. I. JOE: A GREAT AMERICAN HERO   SYNDICATED

1985; 1990–1992   Five-day-a-week cartoon series based on the line of action figures
produced by Hasbro Toys. Introduced in 1964, the toy character was named by a
Hasbro executive after watching the 1945 movie "The Story of G.I. Joe." Production
was halted in 1978, and resumed in 1982 with a smaller figure. Production was again
suspended in mid-1994.

THE GABBY HAYES SHOW   NBC/ABC

11 DECEMBER 1950–1 JANUARY 1954 (NBC); 12 MAY 1956–14 JULY 1956 (ABC)
George "Gabby" Hayes, the grizzled character actor who appeared in countless
western films, showed clips from the old westerns on both his series. The first was a
fifteen-minute show that immediately preceded *Howdy Doody* weekdays; the second
was a half-hour show seen on Saturday mornings.

GABRIELLE   SYNDICATED

1995–1996   Hour daytime talk show, hosted by Gabrielle Carteris. A regular on
Beverly Hills 90210 for the previous five seasons, Carteris tested the talk show waters
during the spring of 1995 with a series of ten syndicated talk specials.

GABRIEL'S FIRE   ABC

12 SEPTEMBER 1990–22 AUGUST 1991   James Earl Jones starred in this hour dramatic
series as Gabriel Bird, a former police officer who was convicted of killing his white
partner in 1969 and was sentenced to life imprisonment. Twenty years later, Bird met
a high-powered criminal attorney who was investigating the death of a fellow inmate;
she took an interest in Bird's case, and managed to get him freed from prison. Bird
agreed to become her investigator. Laila Robbins costarred as the attorney, Victoria
Heller. Also featured were Dylan Walsh as Louis Kline, Victoria's assistant; Madge
Sinclair as Bird's old friend, Empress Josephine Austin, who now ran a soul food
restaurant; Brian Grant as Jamil Duke, son of the inmate whose death Heller was
investigating; and Chelcie Ross (fall 1990) as police captain Jack O'Neil, brother of
the cop allegedly killed by Bird, who was determined to send Bird back to prison.
Jones and Sinclair took their roles into a lighter series in the fall of 1991: see *Pros &
Cons*.

GADABOUT GADDIS   SYNDICATED

1950–1965   Roscoe Vernon, better known as Gadabout Gaddis, hosted this long-
running series about fishing.

THE GALAXY GOOF-UPS
See YOGI'S SPACE RACE

THE GALE STORM SHOW
See OH! SUSANNA

GALACTICA 1980   ABC

16 MARCH 1980–4 MAY 1980   In this short-lived sequel to *Battlestar Galactica,* the
action took place on Earth, where the planet was threatened by the evil Cylons.
Lorne Greene (as Captain Adama) and Herb Jefferson, Jr., (as Boomer), were the
only members of the *Battlestar* cast who remained. The new cast included Kent
McCord as Captain Troy; Barry Van Dyke as Lieutenant Dillon; Robyn Douglass as
newscaster Jamie Hamilton; Allan Miller as Colonel Sydell; Patrick Stuart as Dr.
Zee. The series was introduced in a special broadcast in January 1980 and began its
weekly schedule in March; it was rerun during the summer.

GALAXY HIGH SCHOOL   CBS

13 SEPTEMBER 1986–5 SEPTEMBER 1987; 2 JANUARY 1988–27 AUGUST 1988   An interplanetary high school, with its astronomically diverse group of students, was the
setting for this Saturday-morning cartoon show.

THE GALLANT MEN   ABC

5 OCTOBER 1962–14 SEPTEMBER 1963   *The Gallant Men* and *Combat* ushered in a
wave of World War II dramas beginning in 1962. This one focused on the American
campaign in Italy, as seen through the eyes of a war correspondent. With William
Reynolds as Captain James Benedict; Robert McQueeney as correspondent Conley
Wright; Robert Ridgely as Kimbro; Eddie Fontane as D'Angelo; Richard X. Slattery
as McKenna; Roland LaStarza as Lucavich; Roger Davis as Gibson; and Robert
Gothie as Hanson.

THE GALLERY OF MADAME LIU-TSONG   DUMONT

27 AUGUST 1951–21 NOVEMBER 1951   Anna May Wong starred as Madame Liu-
Tsong, owner of an art gallery, in this little-noted half-hour adventure series (Miss
Wong's real name was, in fact, Wong Liu-Tsong).

THE GALLOPING GOURMET   SYNDICATED

1968–1971   Graham Kerr, with a glass of wine in hand, presided over this freewheeling half hour on which gourmet dishes sometimes came out right and sometimes
didn't. The show was produced by Treena Kerr (his wife) at CJOH-TV, Ottawa. In
the 1970s the Kerrs reportedly found religion and gave up wine, even for cooking. In
1990 Kerr returned with a new half-hour series, *Graham Kerr,* which emphasized
low-fat, low-cholesterol cooking.

GAMBIT   CBS

4 SEPTEMBER 1972–10 DECEMBER 1976
LAS VEGAS GAMBIT   NBC

27 OCTOBER 1980–27 NOVEMBER 1980   Couples played blackjack with oversize cards
on this daytime game show, both versions of which were hosted by Wink Martindale.
Elaine Stewart dealt the cards on the CBS version, Beverly Malden on the NBC
version; the latter program was taped at the Tropicana Hotel in Las Vegas. Merrill
Heatter and Bob Quigley were the executive producers.

GAMBLE ON LOVE   DUMONT

16 JULY 1954–20 AUGUST 1954   This prime-time quiz show for married couples was
originally hosted by Denise Darcel. Ernie Kovacs took over early in August, and
shortly thereafter, the show's title and format were changed: see *Time Will Tell.*

THE GAME GAME   SYNDICATED

1969   Jim McKrell hosted this game show on which contestants tested their knowledge of psychology against a panel of three celebrities.

GAMES PEOPLE PLAY   NBC

21 AUGUST 1980–25 DECEMBER 1980   This hour program was hastily concocted in the
face of the 1980 actors' strike—so-called "reality shows" like these were not affected
by the work stoppage. Bryant Gumbel (who would later move to the *Today* show)
was the host of the hour series, which examined America at play; most of the
contests, however, were staged specifically for the program. Viewers could thus
watch such exciting events as belly-bucking, jeep racing, and the "Toughest Bouncer"
contest. The latter event was won by Chicago's Mr. T, who went on to greater fame in
movies (*Rocky III*) and television (*The A Team*). Assisting Gumbel with his reporting duties were Cyndy Garvey, Johnny Bench, Mike Adamle, Donna de Varona,
Arte Johnson, Ian Woolridge, and announcer Gary Owens. The show left the air
after the actors' strike was settled, but was rerun during the summer of 1981.

GANGBUSTERS NBC

20 MARCH 1952–25 DECEMBER 1952   A crime anthology series, *Gangbusters* was created by Phillips Lord and enjoyed a far longer run on radio (1935–1957) than it did on TV. The stories were based on fact, and the show featured interviews with law enforcement officials. The half-hour show alternated with *Dragnet* on Thursdays. Reruns, together with a few new programs, were syndicated under the title *Captured* and were hosted by Chester Morris.

THE GANGSTER CHRONICLES: AN AMERICAN STORY NBC

12 FEBRUARY 1981–8 MAY 1981   Described by the network as "a fact-based dramatization of the development of organized crime in America," *Gangster Chronicles* was presumably inspired by Francis Ford Coppola's *Godfather* movies, which had proven popular in theaters and on television. The series spanned the first three dozen years of the twentieth century. Two of its three main characters—Salvatore "Lucky" Luciano (played by Michael Nouri) and Benny "Bugsy" Siegel (Joe Penny)—were based on real persons, while the third—Michael Lasker (Brian Benben) was described as a "composite." Also featured were Kathleen Lloyd as Stella Siegel, Bugsy's wife; Chad Redding as Joy Osler, Lucky's mistress; Madeline Stowe as Ruth Lasker, Mike's wife; Allan Arbus as Goodman; Richard Castellano as Joe "the Boss" Masseria; Joseph Mascolo as Maranzano; and Markie Post as prostitute Chris Brandon. E. G. Marshall narrated the series, which was supplied by Universal TV.

GARFIELD AND FRIENDS CBS

17 SEPTEMBER 1988–7 OCTOBER 1995   Garfield, the lazy feline gourmand created by cartoonist Jim Davis in 1978, headlined the first of several prime-time animated specials in 1982. It was not until 1988, however, that he made his debut on CBS's Saturday morning lineup, appearing in various domestic adventures with his owner, Jon Arbuckle, and Arbuckle's hapless canine pet, Odie. It was no coincidence that Garfield's voice sounded like that of Carlton the Doorman on *Rhoda:* both were supplied by Lorenzo Music. The series also featured "U. S. Acres" cartoons, based on another Davis comic strip featuring various barnyard animals such as Orson Pig, Wade the Duck, Roy Rooster, Bo Sheep, Booker the Chick, and Sheldon the Egg. *Garfield and Friends* began as a half-hour show, expanding to an hour in the fall of 1989. In the fall of 1994 it was separated into two half hours.

THE GARLUND TOUCH

See MR. GARLUND

GARRISON'S GORILLAS ABC

5 SEPTEMBER 1967–17 SEPTEMBER 1968   This World War II drama was inspired by the film *The Dirty Dozen.* It starred Ron Harper as Lieutenant Craig Garrison, an Army officer who put together a squad of four men, all of whom were serving time in federal prisons; the men were promised pardons in exchange for their cooperation. With Chris Cary as Goniff, a pickpocket; Rudy Solari as Casino, a thief; Brendon Boone as Chief, a knife-wielding Indian; and Cesare Danova as Actor, a con man. Executive producer: Selig J. Seligman. Produced by Richard Caffey. The series was one of the first American programs purchased by the People's Republic of China for broadcast there; *TV Guide* reported in 1981, however, that *Garrison's Gorillas* had been canceled in China because of its "adverse effects" on Chinese youth.

GARROWAY AT LARGE NBC

18 JUNE 1949–24 JUNE 1951   This prime-time half-hour musical variety series, broadcast live from Chicago, introduced Dave Garroway to national television audiences. Other regulars included Jack Haskell, Cliff Norton, Connie Russell, Betty Chappel, Jimmy Russell, and Aura Vainio. The show's trademarks were its spare sets (necessitated by a low budget) and humorous endings (such as Garroway announcing that the show was broadcast from Chicago, "the friendliest city in the world," then turning around to show a knife stuck in his back). Ted Mills produced the series, and

Charlie Andrews wrote it. Garroway's theme song, "Sentimental Journey," was later used on the *Today* show.

THE GARRY MOORE SHOW   CBS
26 JUNE 1950–27 JUNE 1958; 30 SEPTEMBER 1958–14 JUNE 1964; 11 SEPTEMBER 1966–8 JANUARY 1967

THE GARRY MOORE EVENING SHOW   CBS
18 OCTOBER 1951–27 DECEMBER 1951   Before coming to television in 1950, Garry Moore had worked on several radio shows, including *Club Matinee, Take It Or Leave It,* and *The Jimmy Durante-Garry Moore Show.* It was on *Club Matinee* that he first teamed up with Durward Kirby, who would be his sidekick for many years; it was also on *Club Matinee* that a contest to choose Garry Moore's stage name was held (until then he was known by his real name, Thomas Garrison Morfit).

The first of his several television series began in June 1950; it was originally telecast five evenings per week but moved to weekday afternoons in October. Moore again hosted an evening show in the fall of 1951; lasting only a few weeks, it alternated biweekly with *The Burns and Allen Show.* The daytime show, however, proved durable: It lasted eight years, blending songs and chatter in a low-key, straightforward manner. Moore was neither a singer nor a comedian, but rather a relaxed and congenial host who surrounded himself with a crew of talented performers. In addition to sidekick Kirby, regulars on the daytime show included singers Ken Carson (who had worked with Moore on the *Durante-Moore Show*) and Denise Lor (whom Moore had spotted on *Broadway Open House*). Comedians were regularly featured; among the funny people who made some of their earliest appearances on the show were Don Adams, Kaye Ballard, Wally Cox, George Gobel, Milt Kamen, Don Knotts, Roger Price and his "Droodles" cartoons, Jonathan Winters, and the comedy team of Mickey Ross and Bernie West (Ross and West were later two of the producers of *All in the Family*). Other young performers who appeared on the show included singers Leslie Uggams and Peter Marshall (with his then partner, Tommy Farrell), and a twelve-year-old blonde named Tuesday Weld. Another newcomer was, of course, Carol Burnett, who first appeared on the daytime show in the fall of 1956 and later became a regular on Moore's prime-time series. One of the most notable guests to appear was Frank Lloyd Wright, who, at the age eighty-seven, did two shows in 1956.

Not all of Moore's guests were human: Naturalists Ivan Sanderson and Lorraine D'Essen frequently brought unusual animals to the program. The home audience also had the opportunity to "participate" in the show from time to time. In a contest held in 1954, one lucky Ohio family won Durward Kirby for a weekend. On another 1954 broadcast, Moore asked viewers to send one member of the studio audience (a Michigan housewife) a nickel. Within two days the woman had received 48,000 letters, and it was reported that she eventually received more than $12,000 in nickels.

In 1958, Moore announced that he had grown "tired" of the daytime grind and would leave the show. Moore's last regular appearance was on 16 May; Dick Van Dyke and Durward Kirby cohosted the final six weeks. It is small wonder that Moore was tired: In addition to hosting more than 2,000 shows, he had also been hosting *I've Got a Secret* for six years. Apparently, a summer's rest did him a world of good, for he returned to television that fall to host a prime-time variety series. That show held down a Tuesday-night slot for six seasons. Regulars included Durward Kirby, Ken Carson, Denise Lor, Carol Burnett (1959–62), and Marion Lorne; a regular feature each week was a musical salute to "That Wonderful Year 19—." Moore grew tired of that series (and of *I've Got a Secret,* which he had continued to host) in 1964, and briefly retired from show business.

In the fall of 1966 he returned to host a Sunday-night variety series which fared poorly against NBC's *Bonanza.* Moore's regulars included Durward Kirby, John Byner, Jackie Vernon, Pete Barbutti, and Patsy Elliott.

Moore's daytime series was produced by Herb Sanford and directed for many seasons by Clarence Schimmel. Among the show's writers were Bill Demling, Vinnie Bogert, Marsha Durant, Harold Flender, Chuck Horner, Hank Miles, Charlie Slocum, Aaron Ruben, Roland Scott, and Allan Sherman. Moore's 1958–1964 series was produced by Joe Hamilton and Bob Banner, and the executive producer of the 1966 series was Sylvester "Pat" Weaver.

THE GARY COLEMAN SHOW NBC
18 SEPTEMBER 1982–10 SEPTEMBER 1983   Gary Coleman, star of NBC's prime-time hit *Diff'rent Strokes,* was also the star of this Saturday-morning cartoon show. The half-hour series was based on Coleman's made-for-TV movie "The Kid with the Broken Halo," and featured Coleman as Andy LeBeau, an apprentice angel who was dispatched back to Earth to earn his wings by helping others.

GAVILAN NBC
26 OCTOBER 1982–28 DECEMBER 1982   Robert Urich starred in this hour adventure series as Robert Gavilan, an ex-CIA agent who became an oceanographer but still accepted assignments from his former employers. Featured were Patrick Macnee as actor Milo Bentley, Gavilan's housemate, and Kate Reid as Marion "Jaws" Jaworski, dean of the DeWitt Institute of Oceanography. *Gavilan* was the first announced cancellation of the 1982–1983 season.

GAY NINETIES REVUE ABC
11 AUGUST 1948–14 JANUARY 1949   This musical variety series recreated the early days of vaudeville. It was hosted by eighty-one-year-old Joe Howard, a trouper whose career actually went back to the 1890s; Howard had previously hosted the show on radio.

THE GAYELORD HAUSER SHOW ABC
31 OCTOBER 1951–25 APRIL 1952   Health and nutrition were the subjects discussed on this daytime show hosted by Gayelord Hauser; it was seen Wednesday and Friday afternoons.

GEMINI MAN NBC
23 SEPTEMBER 1976–28 OCTOBER 1976   This hour-long adventure series featured a think-tank employee who could become invisible for up to fifteen minutes a day. With Ben Murphy as Sam Casey; Katherine Crawford as Dr. Abby Lawrence; and William Sylvester as Leonard Driscoll, director of Intersect, the think tank. Produced by Harve Bennett, the show was little more than a rewarmed version of *The Invisible Man,* a 1975 NBC series that folded after eleven episodes.

THE GENE AUTRY SHOW CBS
23 JULY 1950–7 AUGUST 1956   One of the first western film stars to begin filming a series especially for television, Gene Autry formed his own production company (Flying A Productions) and made 104 half-hour episodes. He played himself; his sidekick was Pat Buttram. Autry was not a lawman, but often assisted the men with the badges in bringing outlaws to justice. His series proved so successful that it led to a pair of spinoffs: One featured TV's first female western hero (*Annie Oakley*), and the other featured Autry's horse (*The Adventures of Champion*).

GENERAL ELECTRIC GUEST HOUSE
See GUEST HOUSE

GENERAL ELECTRIC SUMMER ORIGINALS ABC
3 JULY 1956–18 SEPTEMBER 1956   Half-hour filmed anthology series. Vivian Blaine starred in the premiere, a musical comedy titled "It's Sunny Again."

GENERAL ELECTRIC THEATER CBS
1 FEBRUARY 1953–16 SEPTEMBER 1962   This popular half-hour dramatic anthology series was seen on Sunday nights; Ronald Reagan hosted the show from 1954 to 1962. Among the major stars who made their television dramatic debuts on the series were Joseph Cotten ("The High Green Wall," 3 October 1954), Alan Ladd ("Committed," 5 December 1954), Fred MacMurray ("Bachelor's Pride," 20 February

1955), James Stewart ("The Windmill," 24 April 1955), Myrna Loy ("It Gives Me Great Pleasure," 3 April 1955), Bette Davis ("With Malice Toward None," 10 March 1957), Anne Baxter ("Bitter Choice," 21 April 1957), Tony Curtis ("Cornada," 10 November 1957), Fred Astaire ("Imp on a Cobweb Leash," 1 December 1957), Sammy Davis, Jr. ("Auf Wiedersehen," 5 October 1958), Peggy Lee ("So Deadly, So Evil," 13 March 1960), and Gene Tierney ("Journey to a Wedding," 27 November 1960). Other notable appearances included those by Joan Crawford ("The Road to Edinburgh," 31 October 1954), Harry Belafonte ("Winner by Decision," 6 November 1955), Rosalind Russell ("The Night Goes On," 18 March 1956), Ernie Kovacs ("The World's Greatest Quarterback," 19 October 1958), Harpo and Chico Marx ("The Incredible Jewel Robbery," 8 March 1959), Groucho Marx ("The Holdout," 14 January 1962), and Nancy Davis Reagan, who appeared with her husband in "A Turkey for the President" (23 November 1958), in which the Reagans played an American Indian couple.

GENERAL HOSPITAL   ABC
1 APRIL 1963–   One of daytime television's biggest success stories, *General Hospital* was created by Doris and Frank Hursley. It began as a half-hour show (and premiered the same day as another medically oriented serial, *The Doctors*), then expanded twice: to forty-five minutes on 26 July 1976 and to sixty minutes on 16 January 1978. Under the stewardship of Gloria Monty, who took over as producer in the late 1970s, ratings climbed steadily. By 1980 *General Hospital* had become TV's top-rated soap opera, and one of its episodes—the November 1981 wedding of Luke and Laura (Anthony Geary and Genie Francis), with Helena Cassadine (Elizabeth Taylor) lurking in the background—attracted the largest audience ever to watch a daytime dramatic series. Ratings began to dip after Genie Francis's departure (she returned briefly in 1983) and after a fling with some absurd story lines—such as an attempt by a villain to freeze Port Charles, *General Hospital*'s hometown—that were more appropriate to *Batman* than to a daytime serial. The show quickly dropped the sci-fi stuff and went back to more conventional plots in a successful effort to retain its audience. The show was TV's top-rated daytime drama from 1979 through 1987.

With the death in May 1996 of John Beradino (a former major-league baseball player) who played Steve Hardy, director of medicine at General Hospital, the show lost its last original cast member. Emily McLaughlin played nurse Jessie Brewer, his close friend and confidante, from April 1963 until her death in 1991. Lucille Wall joined the series in July 1963 as head nurse Lucille March (she left in 1976). Rachel Ames came in 1964, as Lucille's sister, nurse Audrey March, who married Steve Hardy (they were later divorced and remarried). Another long-time cast member was Peter Hansen, who replaced Ross Elliott in 1965 as lawyer Lee Baldwin and remained for thirty years. Other principal players over the years have included: Roy Thinnes, Rick Falk, Robert Hogan, Craig Huebing, and Martin West as Jessie's husband, Dr. Phil Brewer (Phil was thought to have been killed in a car crash, but surfaced later under the name of Harold Williamson; Phil was finally murdered in 1974); Carolyn Craig as Phil's girlfriend, Cynthia Allison; K. T. Stevens as Steve Hardy's onetime romantic interest, Peggy Mercer; Allison Hayes as Priscilla Longworth, who was also interested in Steve; Patricia Breslin and Elizabeth MacRae as widowed nurse Meg Bentley, who married Lee Baldwin, and later suffered a nervous breakdown and died; Adrienne Hayes and Indus Arthur as Meg's stepdaughter, Brooke Clinton, who was murdered; Dean Harens as Noll Clinton, Brooke's husband; Paul Savior and Don Chastain as Dr. Tom Baldwin, brother of Lee Baldwin; Barry Atwater as Dr. John Prentice, who married Jessie Brewer and was later murdered; Catherine Ferrar and Jennifer Billingsley as his daughter (and murderer), Polly Prentice, who was killed in the car crash that also involved Phil Brewer; Ed Platt as Dr. Miller (Platt returned to the show several years later to play another role, Wyatt Chamberlain); Peggy McCay as nurse Iris Fairchild; Shelby Hiatt as nurse Jane Harland; Ray Girardin as Howie Dawson, who married Jane; Maxine Stuart and Phyllis Hill as Howie's mother, Mrs. Dawson; Julie Adams as Howie's girlfriend, Denise Wilton; Jim McKrell as Denise's boyfriend, Bruce Andrews; Kim Hamilton as Dr. Tracy Adams; Robin Blake as nurse Judy Clampett; Adolph Caesar as Douglas Burke, a blind patient who fell for

Judy (his eyesight was subsequently restored); Paul Carr and Craig Huebing as psychiatrist Dr. Peter Taylor, who was married briefly to Jessie Brewer (their marriage was annulled when Phil Brewer returned to Port Charles); Valerie Starrett and Brooke Bundy as Diana Maynard, Peter Taylor's next wife; Sharon DeBord as nurse Sharon McGillis; Peter Kilman as Dr. Henry Pinkham, who married Sharon; Susan Bernard as student nurse Beverly Cleveland, who had an affair with Howie Dawson; Tom Brown as Al Weeks of the hospital maintenance staff, who married head nurse Lucille March in 1972; Doug Lambert and Craig Curtis as Al's son, Eddie Weeks; Jana Taylor as Eddie's girlfriend, Angie Costello; Anne Helm as nurse Mary Briggs; Tom Simcox as Mary's husband, Wade Collins, an ex-con; Denise Alexander (who came to *General Hospital* in 1973 after several years on *Days of Our Lives*) as Dr. Lesley Williams; Don Matheson as Cameron Faulkner, who married Lesley; Stacy Baldwin and Genie (Ann) Francis as Lesley's illegitimate daughter, Laura Vining; Judy Lewis as Laura's foster mother, Barbara Vining; Jonathan Carter as Laura's foster father, Jason Vining; Deanna Lund as Cameron Faulkner's secretary, Peggy Lowell; Anne Collings as Florence Gray, a patient of Lesley's; Howard Sherman and Eric Server as her husband, Gordon Gray; James Sikking as Dr. James Hobart; Judith McConnell as nurse Augusta McLeod, killer of Phil Brewer; Barry Coe and Rod McCary as Dr. Joel Stratton; Linda Cooper as nurse Linda Cooper (a rare instance in which the actress and the role share the same name); Jenny Sherman as Sally Grimes; Augusta Dabney as Caroline Chandler; Ted Eccles as Caroline's son, Bobby Chandler; Kimberly Beck and Marla Pennington as nurse Samantha Livingston, who married Bobby; Michelle Conaway as Beth Maynard, sister of Diana Maynard Taylor; Daniel Black as Dr. Kyle Bradley, Beth's boyfriend; Victoria Shaw as Kira Faulkner; Tony Campo, Don Clarke, Johnny Jensen, and Kin Shriner as Scotty Baldwin, son of the late Meg Baldwin; John Gabriel and James Westmoreland as newspaper reporter Teddy Holmes; Anne Wyndham as Jessie Brewer's niece and ward, Carol Murray; Mark Hamill as Jessie's nephew and ward, Kent Murray; Monica Gayle as Jessie's niece, Kate Marshall; George Chandler as Walter Douglas; Georgia Schmidt as Amy Douglas; Kevin Matthews as Dr. Duncan Stewart; Maida Stevens as Mrs. Andrews; Virginia Ann Lee as Mai Lin, a visiting dancer from the People's Republic of China; Nathan Jung as Won Chu; George Chiang as Ling Wang; Ivan Bonar as Chase Murdock; Betty Ann Rees as Margaret Colson; Jennifer Peters as Martha Taylor; Mark Travis as Felix Buchanan; Mark Miller as Randy Washburn; Louise Fitch as Mrs. Taylor; William Mims as Gus Wheeler; Don Hammer as Lieutenant Adams; Laura Campbell as Pat Lambert; Joseph DiSante as Dr. Gerald Henderson; Richard Eastham as Mr. Livingston; and Burt Douglas as Mac.

Other additions to the cast have included: Richard Dean Anderson as Dr. Jeff Webber; Jerry Ayres as David Hamilton, who was killed by Laura (Laura's mother confessed to protect her daughter); Susan Brown as Dr. Gail Adamson, who married Lee Baldwin; George E. Carey and William Bryant as Lamont Corbin; Steve Carlson as Dr. Gary Lansing; Angela Cheyne as Dorrie Fleming; David Comfort, Bradley Green, David Walker, David Wallace, and Matthew Ashford as Tommy Baldwin Hardy; Stuart Damon as Alan Quartermaine; Jane Elliot as Tracy Quartermaine; David Lewis and John Ingle as Edward Quartermaine; Anna Lee as Lila Quartermaine; Dennis Dinster as Mike Mallon; Camila Ashland and Lieux Dressler as Alice Grant; Gerald Gordon as Dr. Mark Dante; Michael Gregory and Chris Robinson as Dr. Rick Webber, who married Lesley Williams; Brett Halsey as Dr. Adam Streeter; Janice Heiden as Lisa Holbrook, a split personality; Bobbi Jordan as Terri Arnett; Georganne LaPiere (sister of Cher), Mary O'Brien and Robin Mattson as Heather Grant Webber, who accidentally overdosed on LSD; Maria Perschy as Maria Schuller; Patsy Rahn and Leslie Charleson as Dr. Monica Bard, who married Jeff Webber; William Schreiner as Darren Blythe; Anna Stuart, Brenda Scott, and Donna Bacalla as Dr. Gina Dante; Maggie Sullivan as Katie Corbin, Lamont's wife; Richard Venture as Herbert Behrman; Lee Warrick as Mary Ellen Dante; Lesley Woods as Edna Hadley; Jackie Zeman as Barbara (Bobbi) Spencer; Todd Davis as Dr. Bryan Phillips; Jay Gerber as Jim Richardson; Bob Hastings as police chief Burt Ramsey; Gail Rae Carlson as Susan Moore; Frank Maxwell as hospital administrator Dan Rooney; Richard Sarradet as Howard Lansing; Joan Tompkins as Mrs. Maynard; Christopher Stafford Nelson as Chris; Joyce Jameson as Colleen Middleton; Craig Littler as Dr. Todd Levine; Susan O'Hanlon and Susan Pratt as Ann Logan; Chris Pennock as Mitch Williams; and David Mendenhall as Mike Webber.

In 1978 Anthony Geary joined the cast as Luke Spencer, Bobbi's brother. Geary soon became one of daytime TV's most popular actors, and Luke's romance with Laura one of its most popular story lines. Geary accurately described Luke as an "antihero." Shortly after arriving in Port Charles, Luke forced himself on Laura, who eventually dropped her husband, Scotty Baldwin, and ran off with Luke. After their return to town, Luke turned a boat into a nightclub, got into trouble with gangsters, and finally married Laura in November 1981. Shortly afterward, Laura was lost in a boating accident and was presumed drowned (it would later be learned that she had been kidnapped). Luke, too, was presumed to have been killed in an avalanche, but miraculously survived. Eventually he became the mayor of Port Charles; in the fall of 1983 he was reunited with Laura.

Later comings and goings have included those of: Tristan Rogers as Robert Scorpio, an ex-secret agent who became Luke's friend; Sharon Wyatt as actress Tiffany Hill, who fell for Scorpio; Emma Samms as Holly Sutton, who became Luke's new love interest after Laura's first departure, but who eventually married Scorpio; Demi Moore as reporter Jackie Templeton; Janine Turner as Jackie's sister, Laura Templeton; Miles McNamara as boxer Johnny Morrissey; Leonard Stone as Johnny's manager, Packy Moore; Eddie Ryder as cabbie Slick Jones; Chuck Wagner as Randall Thompson; Merrie Lynn Ross as Emma Lutz; John Stamos as Blackie Parrish; George Gaynes and Mitchell Ryan as gangster Frank Smith; Richard Caine as Smith's associate, Bill Watson; Peter Miller as Lieutenant Stoddard; Warren Reed as Greg Talmidge; Wayne Sherman as Don Carr; Renee Anderson as Alexandria Quartermaine; Eric Kroh, Abraham Geary, Justin Whalin, Christopher Nelson, Gerald Hopkins, and Sean Kanan as Alan Quartermaine, Jr.; Milton Selzer as Pop Snyder; Dawn Jeffory as Jo Anne Eden; Philip Tanzini as Jeremy Hewitt Logan, adopted son of Ann Logan; Bianca Ferguson as Claudia Johnson, who married Bryan Phillips; Sarah Simmons as Zelda Bernstein; Lisa Marie as Jennifer Smith; Antony Ponzini and Michael Baselon as Dr. Tony Perelli; Robert Betzel as P. J. Taylor; Norma Connolly as Ruby Anderson, a one-time madam who became a nurses' aide; Jeff Donnell as Stella Fields; Louise Hoven as Beverly DeFreest; Vanessa Brown as Mrs. DeFreest; Cari Ann Warder and Shell Kepler as Amy Vining, adopted daughter of Rick and Lesley Webber; Frank Parker as Paddy Kelly; Douglas Sheehan as Joe Kelly; exercise guru Richard Simmons as himself; rock and roller Rick Springfield as Dr. Noah Drake; Rick Moses as Jefferson Smith "Hutch" Hutchins, a hit man who stalked Luke and Laura; Christopher Morley as Max, another hit man who stalked Luke and Laura (Max also disguised himself as Sally, a hit woman); John Colicos as evil Mikos Cassadine, who plotted to freeze Port Charles, among other dastardly deeds; Elizabeth Taylor as his wife, Helena Cassadine, who arranged to have Laura kidnapped; Andre Landzaat as Tony Cassadine; Thaao Penghlis as Victor Cassadine; Sam Behrens as Jake Meyer; Loanne Bishop as Rose Kelly, stepmother of Joe Kelly; Mark Roberts as Charles Sutton; Jeanna Michaels as Constance Atkins (also known as Constance Townley), Scorpio's former love; Billie Hayes as O'Riley, a spy; Melinda Cordell as Natalie Dearborn; Ron Hajek as Derek; Eileen Dietz as Sarah; Joe Lambie as Russian pianist Gregory Malko; Roberta Leighton as Shirley Pickett, a friend of Luke's; Steve Bond as Jimmy Lee Holt; Brian Patrick Clarke as Dr. Grant Putnam/Grant Andrews; Brioni Farrel as Martha; Lisa Figus as Georgia; Booth Colman as Hector Jerrold; David Groh as D. L. Brock; Danielle Von Zerneck as Louisa Swenson; Sherilyn Wolter as Celia Quartermaine; Kabir Bedi as Lord Rama; John Martinuzzi as Stavros Cassadine, who had married the kidnapped Laura; Elissa Leeds as Steffie Brand; Jack Wagner as rock singer Frisco Jones; Judith Chapman as Ginny Blake; Shelley Taylor Morgan as Lorena Sharpe; Will Macmillan as Boris Raskov; Hilary Edson as his daughter, Tania; Brad Maule as Dr. Anthony Jones; Marcella Markham as Beatrice LeSeuer; James McNichol as Josh Clayton; and John Callahan as Leo Russell.

Also: Kristina Malandro (also known as Kristina Wagner) as Felicia Cummings, who married Frisco Jones in 1986; John Reilly as Sean Donely, who wed Tiffany Hill in 1988; Finola Hughes and Camilla More as Anna Devane; Anne Jeffreys as Amanda Barrington; Mark Goddard as Derek Barrington; Robyn Bernard as Terry Brock; Kevin Bernhardt as Kevin O'Connor, who married Terry in 1986; Tia Carrere as Jade Soong; Mae Hi as nurse Sarah Braddock; Patrick Bishop as Yank Se Chung; Gloria Carlin as Charity Gatlin, who married Jimmy Lee Holt in 1987; Yvette Nipar as Sandy Stryker; Don Galloway as Dr. Buzz Stryker; Lynn Herring as Lucy Coe, who married Tony Jones in 1987; Ian Buchanan as Duke Lavery, who married Anna Devane in 1987; Guy Mack as Patrick O'Connor; Kimberly McCullough as Robin (Soltini) Scorpio, Robert Scorpio's daughter; Argentina Brunetti as Filomena; Dawn Merrick as Samantha Welles; Joe diReda as Angel Moran; Maria Rangel as Rosa; Kristina Wayborn as Gretta Ingstrom; John Denos as Malcolm Rutledge; George Lyter as Corey Blythe; Liz Keifer as ex-nun Camellia McKay; Guy Doleman as Angus McKay; Laura Carrington, Stephanie Williams, and Felecea Bell as Simone Ravelle, who married Tom Hardy in 1988 (it was an interracial romance, a rarity for daytime TV); Shaun Cassidy as singer Dusty Walker; Ami Dolenz (daughter of Mickey Dolenz of *The Monkees*) as Melissa McKee; paraplegic actress Nancy Becker Kennedy as Martha McKee; Ron Mychal Hayes as Andy Matthews; Ebonie Smith as Susie Matthews; Maree Cheatham as Charlene Simpson; Jaime McEnnan as Skeeter; Will Hunt as Herbert Quartermaine; Allan Miller as Quentin Quartermain; Linda Sanders as Autumn Clayton; Jennifer Anglin as Cheryl Stansbury; Scott Thompson Baker as Colton Shore; Corey Young as Dr. Walt Benson; Tonja Walker as Olivia St. John; Kati Powell as Louise Knotts; John Preston and Alan Feinstein as Gregory Howard; Diane McBain as Claire Howard; Amy Gibson as Collette Francoise; Linda Cristal as Dimitra; Jane Higginson as Arielle Ashton; Hugo Napier as Larry Ashton; Michael Tylo as Charlie Prince/Lord Charles Ashton; Kurt Robin McKinney and Wallace Kurth as Ned Ashton; Jack Axelrod as Victor Jerome; Jason Culp as Julian Jerome; Edie Lehmann as pianist Katherine Delafield; Mary Jo Catlett as her maid, Mary Finnegan; Kevin Best as Dr. Harrison Davis; Joe Burke as Paul Devore; Kaye Kittrell as Hillary Bates; Keely Shaye Smith as Valerie Freeman; Kim Valentine, Sharon Case, Lisa Fuller and Jennifer Guthrie as Dawn Winthrop; Lydie Denier as Yasmine Bernoudi; Joe Mascolo as Domino/Nicholas Van Buren; Frank Killmond and Stephen T. Kay as Reginald Jennings, the Quartermaines' servant; Dwan Smith as Irma Foster; Curt Lowens as Claude; Chantal Contouri as Prunella Witherspoon; Don Dolan as police chief Guy Lewis; Beulah Quo as Olin; Brighton Hertford as Barbara Jean (B. J.) Jones; Janis Paige as Iona; Alexia Robinson and Lisa Canning as Meg Lawson; Michael Watson as Decker; Pierrino Mascarino as Drago; John Vargas as Rico; Mark St. James as Evan "Edge" Jerome; Kim Terry as Rita; Robert Fontaine as Frankie Greco; and Laura Herring as Carla Greco. In early 1991, after a seven-year absence from the series, Anthony Geary returned to *General Hospital,* first as Luke Spencer's cousin, Bill Eckert, later as Luke Spencer himself (Geary briefly played both roles). After stints on *All My Children* and *Loving,* Genie Francis returned to *General Hospital* in 1993, reuniting Luke and Laura.

Other cast changes during the early 1990s included Bradley Lockerman as one of soapdom's most unusual characters, Casey, an alien visitng from the planet Lumina; Crystal Carson as Julia Barrett; Michael Cole as Harlan Barrett; Stacey Cortez as Sheila Cantillon; Charles Lucia as Leopold Taub; Tawny Fere Ellis and Shell Danielson as Dominique Taub Baldwin; James Morrison as Joey Moscini; Carol Lawrence as Angela Eckert; Cheryl Richardson as Jenny Eckert, Bill's sister; Keith Washington as Keith; Patricia Allison as Evelyn Hornsby; Paul Satterfield as Paul Hornsby, Evelyn's son; Irina Cashen as Susan Hornsby, Paul's daughter; Frank Aletter as Mayor Richmond; Sheila MacRae as the mayor's wife, Madelyn Richmond; Steve Burton as Jason Quartermaine; Camille Cooper as Nikki Langton; Jeff Pomerantz as David Langton; Peter Kelleghan as Barry Durbin; Antonio Sabato, Jr., as John "Jagger" Cates; Nikki Cox as Gina, Jagger's sister; Michael Sutton as Stone Case; Cari Shayne as Karen Wexler; Scott Lincoln as Joseph Atkins; Jon Lindstrom as twins Kevin Collins and Ryan Chamberlain; Vanessa Marcil as Brenda Barrett; Randolph Mantooth as Richard Halifax; Terri Garber as Victoria Parker; Mary Beth Evans as Katherine Bell; Stephen Burleigh as Ray Conway; Frank Runyeon as Simon Romero; Michael Lynch as Connor Olivera; Elaine and Melanie Silver and

Robyn Richards as Maxie Jones, Felicia's daughter; Maurice Benard as Sonny Corinthos; John Martin as Jon Russell; Robin Christopher as Abby Mitchell; Leigh McCloskey as Damian Smith; Jonathan Jackson as Lucky Spencer, son of Luke and Laura; Rena Sofer as Lois Cerullo; Ellen Travolta as Gloria Cerullo; Rosalind Cash as Mary Mae Ward; Joseph C. Phillips as Justus Ward; Senait Ashenafi as Keesha Ward; Ricky Martin as Miguel Morez; Lilly Melgar as Lily; Valentino Moreno as Juan, son of Miguel and Lily; Chuckie and Kenny Gravino and Jay Sacane as Lucas Jones; Brynn Thayer as Kylie Quinlan; Chase Masterson as Ivy Lief; Ismael Carlo as Hernando Rivera; Ron Hale as Michael Corbin; Paul Carr as Milton Stanis; Starr Andreeff as Jessica; Glenn Walker Harris, Jr., as Sly Eckert; Amy Benedict as Connie Cooper; Robert Miano as Joe Scully; Riley Steiner as Page Bowen; Amber Tamblyn as Emily, Page's daughter; Denise Galik-Furey as Rhonda Wexler; and John J. York as Mac Scorpio.

Gloria Monty, who had guided the show as executive producer for ten years, left in 1987, and was succeeded by H. Wesley Kenney; Kenney was in turn succeeded by Joseph Hardy late in 1989. Gloria Monty returned in late 1990 as executive producer, and was succeeded in early 1992 by Wendy Riche. Among the many head writers have been Theodore and Mathilde Ferro, Frank and Doris Hursley (the show's creators), Bridget and Jerome Dobson, Richard and Suzanne Holland, Eileen and Robert Mason Pollack, Irving and Tex Elman, Douglas Marland, Pat Falken Smith, Robert J. Shaw, Joyce and John William Corrington, Anne Howard Bailey, Smith and Norma Monty, Maralyn Thoma, Norma Monty (again), Bill Levinson, and Claire Labine.

THE GENERATION GAP   ABC
7 FEBRUARY 1969–23 MAY 1969   A team of three adults faced a team of three juveniles on this convoluted prime-time game show; each team had to predict whether the other team would be able to answer questions about the opposite generation. Dennis Wholey first hosted the series and was replaced by Jack Barry.

GENERATIONS   NBC
27 MARCH 1989–25 JANUARY 1991   Created by Sally Sussman, *Generations* was the first daytime serial in which one of the two major families was black. The series was set in Chicago, and explored the relationships between the Marshalls and the Whitmores. The cast included Lynn Hamilton as Vivian Potter, who many years earlier had been a maid for the Whitmores; Joan Pringle as her daughter, Ruth Marshall; Taurean Blacque and James Reynolds as Ruth's husband, Henry Marshall, owner of a chain of ice cream shops; Sharon Brown and Debbi Morgan as Chantal Marshall, an attorney; Jonelle Allen as Doreen Jackson; Kristoff St. John as college student Adam Marshall; Patricia Crowley as Rebecca Whitmore, matriarch of that clan; Gail Ramsey as Laura Whitmore McCallum; Gerard Prendergast as J. D. Whitmore; Kelly Rutherford as Sam Whitmore; Andrew Masset as ad executive Trevor McCallum; Barbara Rhoades and Linda Gibboney as Jessica Gardner; Tony Addabbo as Jason Gardner; George Deloy as Rob Donnelly; Rick Fitts as Martin Jackson; Nancy Sorel as Monique McCallum; Myles Thoroughgood as Wally; Christopher Duncan as Adam's pal, Gordon Williams; Tom Hermann as Cory McCallum; George Duke as Johnny, owner of a local club; Ronald Allen as Lloyd Bradfield; Mark Goodman as Wolf; Amy Yasbeck as Carla; John J. Dalesandro as Mr. Trask, Monique's boss; Bernie White and Dean Devlin as Chris Mendoza; Bruce Gray as Philip Webb, Rebecca's boss; Ron Marquette and David Ciminello as Mitch; Marla Adams as Helen Mullin; Robin Dearden as Kate Wilson; Vivica A. Fox as Maya; Victor Gardell as Sidney; Rick Lohman as Joel Resnick; Antony Ponzini as Corelli; Richard Roundtree as Dr. Daniel Reubens; George Shannon as Jordan Hale; Robert Torti as Kyle Masters; Stacey Nelkin as Christy Russell; Ron Harper as Peter Whitmore; Gina Gallego as Melina; Butch Hartman as Sean Masters; Randy Brooks as Eric Royal; Paul Carr as Alex Hawkins; Ian Ogilvy as Reginald Hewitt; Robert Gentry as Jordan Hale; and Dorothy Lyman as Rebecca Whitmore. Following *Generations'* cancellation by NBC, its 470 episodes were purchased by BET Cable Network.

The title *Generations* had previously been used in another serial. CBS's ill-fated

1981 late-night soap opera, *Behind the Screen,* used a soap-within-a-soap format; *Generations* was the name of the fictional serial on which many of the characters worked.

GENTLE BEN   CBS
10 SEPTEMBER 1967–31 AUGUST 1969   The adventures of a boy and his pet bear (Ben). With Clint Howard as young Mark Wedloe; Dennis Weaver as his father, Tom Wedloe, a game warden in the Florida Everglades; Beth Brickell as his mother, Ellen Wedloe; Jack Morley as Tom's friend, Spencer; and Angelo Rutherford (1968–1969) as Mark's friend, Willie. Ben, the bear, was played by Bruno and trained by Monty Cox. Ivan Tors produced the series; it was filmed on location in Florida.

GEORGE   ABC
5 NOVEMBER 1993–19 JANUARY 1994   Half-hour sitcom starring semi-retired boxer George Foreman as retired boxer George Foster, who decided to lend a helping hand to the kids at his wife's middle school. Sheryl Lee Ralph costarred as his wife, Maggie Foster, a guidance counselor. Also featured were Lauren Robinson as George and Maggie's daughter, Virginia (nicknamed Vee); Tony T. Johnson as George and Maggie's son, George Jr. (nicknamed Bubba); Anne Haney as Juanita; Larry Gilliard, Jr., as Lathan; Doniell Spencer as Shasta; and Cleandre Norman as Daniel.

THE GEORGE & ALANA SHOW   SYNDICATED
1995–1996   A divorced couple—George Hamilton and Alana Stewart—cohosted this daytime hour talk/celebrity interview show.

THE GEORGE BURNS AND GRACIE ALLEN SHOW
See THE BURNS AND ALLEN SHOW

GEORGE BURNS COMEDY WEEK   CBS
18 SEPTEMBER 1985–25 DECEMBER 1985   Venerable George Burns became the oldest person ever to host a television show when he agreed to emcee this half-hour comedy anthology series: he turned ninety less than a month after the program's cancellation. One of the programs, "The Couch," directed by Steve Martin and starring Harvey Korman and Valerie Perrine (with Carrie Fisher and Bronson Pinchot in smaller roles), so impressed network executives at a screening that they ordered a series based on it: see *Leo & Liz in Beverly Hills.*

THE GEORGE BURNS SHOW   NBC
21 OCTOBER 1958–14 APRIL 1959   After Gracie Allen retired from show business, George Burns continued the situation comedy, this time on NBC. He continued to play himself, though he now cast himself as a television producer. Most of the old gang from *The Burns and Allen Show* remained: Bea Benaderet as Blanche Morton, his secretary; Larry Keating as Harry Morton, his accountant; Ronnie Burns (as himself); and Harry Von Zell as his announcer, always eager to land a dramatic role.

THE GEORGE CARLIN SHOW   FOX
16 JANUARY 1994–28 AUGUST 1994; 16 OCTOBER 1994–1 JANUARY 1995; 2 JULY 1995–3 SEPTEMBER 1995   Half-hour sitcom set mostly at The Moylan Tavern, a neighborhood watering hole in New York, and starring George Carlin as grumpy George O'Grady, a cabbie. Also with Alex Rocco as Broadway Harry Rosetti, a bookie; Paige French as waitress Sydney Paris; Anthony Starke as bartender Jack Donahue; Christopher Rich as plastic surgeon Neal Beck; Susan Sullivan as George's sometime lady friend, Kathleen Rachowski, who owned a pet shop; and Matt Landers as Larry Pinkerton. After a seven-month run in 1994, the series returned to Fox's Sunday night schedule as a replacement for *Wild Oats.*

THE GEORGE GOBEL SHOW   NBC/CBS
2 OCTOBER 1954–10 MARCH 1959 (NBC); 11 OCTOBER 1959–5 JUNE 1960 (CBS) A casual, folksy, down-home comedian, George Gobel hosted a half-hour comedy-

variety series on Saturday nights beginning in 1954; regulars included singer Peggy King and Jeff Donnell, who played his wife, Alice, in many sketches. In the fall of 1957, he moved to Tuesday nights, where he hosted a biweekly hour-long series that alternated with *The Eddie Fisher Show;* Fisher was the "permanent guest star" on the Gobel shows, and Gobel reciprocated on the Fisher broadcasts. Gobel's other regulars included Jeff Donnell (1957–1958), Phyllis Avery (1958–1959, who replaced Donnell as Alice), Shirley Harmer, and the Johnny Mann Singers. The telecast of 21 October 1958 was presented in stereo; one audio channel was carried on the regular TV signal, while the other was broadcast simultaneously on selected radio stations throughout the country. In the fall of 1959 Gobel moved to CBS, where he hosted a half-hour variety series that alternated with *The Jack Benny Program* on Sundays; regulars there included Joe Flynn, Anita Bryant, and Harry Von Zell. Gobel's theme song, "Gobelues," was composed by his longtime bandleader, John Scott Trotter.

THE GEORGE HAMILTON IV SHOW   ABC
13 APRIL 1959–29 MAY 1959   Country and western singer George Hamilton IV ("A Rose and a Baby Ruth") hosted this half-hour musical series, which was seen weekdays at noon. Originating from Washington, D.C., it featured Roy Clark and Mary Klick.

THE GEORGE JESSEL SHOW   ABC
13 SEPTEMBER 1953–11 APRIL 1954   One of several major stars signed up by ABC in 1953, George Jessel, America's "Toastmaster General," hosted a half-hour variety series on Sunday evenings. Hal Sawyer was also featured on the show that was produced by Mannie Manheim. Making one of his earliest television appearances, Buddy Hackett guest-starred on the premiere.

THE GEORGE MICHAEL SPORTS MACHINE   SYNDICATED
1984–   Sunday night sports wrapup, hosted by sportscaster George Michael. The program began in Washington, D. C., in 1980 as a local show, *George Michael's Sports Final*.

GEORGE OF THE JUNGLE   ABC
9 SEPTEMBER 1967–5 SEPTEMBER 1970   Jay Ward created this fairly sophisticated Saturday-morning cartoon show. Segments included: "George of the Jungle," with George, a clumsy Tarzan type, Ape, an erudite gorilla, and Shep, George's trusty elephant; "Super Chicken," the story of Henry Cabot Henhouse III, an ordinary fowl who turned into Super Chicken after a swig of Super Sauce, and his pal, Fred the lion; and "Tom Slick," an auto racer who always played fair. Reruns of the series resurfaced briefly on ABC in the early fall of 1995.

THE GEORGE RAFT CASEBOOK
See I AM THE LAW

GEORGE SANDERS MYSTERY THEATRE   NBC
22 JUNE 1957–14 SEPTEMBER 1957   Suave British actor George Sanders hosted this half-hour anthology series.

THE GEORGE WENDT SHOW   CBS
8 MARCH 1995–12 APRIL 1995   Half-hour sitcom set in Madison, Wisconsin, where two brothers operated a garage and hosted a radio call-in show on cars and car repair. With George Wendt as older brother George Coleman; Pat Finn as younger brother Dan Coleman; Mark Christopher Lawrence as garage employee Fletcher; Kate Hodge as garage employee Libby; and Brian Doyle-Murray as garage employee Finnie. The series was inspired by "Car Talk," a nationally syndicated radio show.

GEORGE SCHLATTER'S FUNNY PEOPLE
See FUNNY PEOPLE

GEORGETOWN UNIVERSITY FORUM   DUMONT
3 JULY 1951–11 OCTOBER 1953   An early public affairs series, produced at Georgetown University in Washington, D.C.

GEORGIA GIBBS' MILLION RECORD SHOW   NBC
1 JULY 1957–2 SEPTEMBER 1957   "Her Nibs," Georgia Gibbs, hosted this musical series on which million-sellers were performed. The fifteen-minute show was seen Mondays preceding the news.

THE GERALD McBOING-BOING SHOW   CBS
16 DECEMBER 1956–10 MARCH 1957; 30 MAY 1958–3 OCTOBER 1958   Gerald McBoing-Boing, the star of several U.P.A. cartoon shorts who was familiar to moviegoers, first came to television late in 1956 in a Sunday-afternoon slot. The lad spoke only in sounds, not words; the voice of Bill Goodwin was employed to interpret McBoing-Boing's utterings. Also featured were two other cartoon segments: "The Twirliger Twins" and "Dusty of the Circus." When the show was rerun in a Friday-night slot during the summer of 1958, it became one of television's first prime-time cartoon series, antedating *The Flintstones* by two seasons.

GERALDO   SYNDICATED
1987–   An hour daytime talk show hosted by former ABC correspondent Geraldo Rivera. Like those of his main competitors (Oprah Winfrey, Phil Donahue, and Sally Jessy Raphael), Rivera's show featured a studio audience and was centered on a single topic each day. Generally considered somewhat harder edged than the others, *Geraldo*'s most infamous program was no doubt the 1988 show in which the host's nose was broken in a fight that erupted between black activist Roy Innis and a group of white supremacists. Another program was taped at a topless donut shop in Colorado. By January 1990, even the host had had enough; "I'm embarrassing myself," Rivera told *TV Guide,* promising to be "more prudent in my topic selection." Whether he recalled the remark is questionable, however. A sample of topics aired during May 1995 included "Girls Who Will Commit Crimes for Their Men," "Family of Prostitutes," "Bisexuality," "Ménages à Trois," and "Couples Who Detest Each Other."
   Rivera, who had been a regular on ABC's *20/20,* left the network after protesting the decision to axe a *20/20* segment on the personal life of Marilyn Monroe. On 21 April 1986 he hosted a live syndicated program, "The Mystery of Al Capone's Vaults." Although nothing of value was uncovered on the show, it became the highest-rated syndicated special in history and eventually led to the development of his talk show. Early in 1991 it was announced that *Geraldo* would be dubbed into Russian and would become the first American daytime television series to be regularly televised in the Soviet Union. In the fall of 1991 Rivera embarked upon a second daily syndicated series: see *Now It Can Be Told.*

THE GERTRUDE BERG SHOW
See MRS. G. GOES TO COLLEGE

GET A LIFE   FOX
23 SEPTEMBER 1990–14 JUNE 1992   Half-hour sitcom starring Chris Elliott as Chris Peterson, a guy who never grew up; at thirty years of age, he lived above his parents' garage and was still employed as a paperboy. Also featured were Bob Elliott (Chris's real-life father and half of the famed comedy duo Bob and Ray) as his bathrobed father, Fred; Elinor Donahue as his mother, Gladys; Sam Robards (1990–1991) as Chris's best friend from childhood, Larry Potter, now an executive; Robin Riker as Larry's un-understanding wife, Sharon; and Taylor Fry and Brady Bluhm as their two kids, Amy and Bobby Potter. In the fall of 1991 Chris moved out of folks' garage and into someone else's. Brian Doyle-Murray played his new landlord, short-tempered Gus Borden.

THE GET ALONG GANG

CBS

15 SEPTEMBER 1984–28 JUNE 1986   The central characters of this Saturday-morning cartoon show were six animal pals—Zipper, Portia, Woolma, Dotty, Montgomery, and Bingo—who lived together in a caboose.

GET CHRISTIE LOVE!

ABC

11 SEPTEMBER 1974–18 JULY 1975   *Laugh-In* alumna Teresa Graves starred as TV's first black policewoman, Christie Love, in this hour-long crime show. The series was originally produced by Paul Mason and featured Charles Cioffi as her boss, Lieutenant Matt Reardon of the Special Investigations Unit of the Los Angeles Police Department; Dennis Rucker as Lieutenant Steve Belmont; and Andy Romano as Lieutenant Joe Caruso. In January some changes were made: Glen A. Larson and Ron Satlof replaced Mason as producers, and Cioffi and Romano were dropped from the cast. Joining the series were Jack Kelly as her new boss, Captain Arthur P. Ryan; Michael Pataki as Officer Pete Gallagher; and Scott Peters as Officer Valencia. In one episode (aired 5 February), six members of the *Laugh-In* crew guest-starred: Arte Johnson, Henry Gibson, Jo Anne Worley, Judy Carne, Johnny Brown, and Gary Owens.

GET IT TOGETHER

ABC

3 JANUARY 1970–5 SEPTEMBER 1970   This half-hour rock music show was usually seen on Saturday mornings. It was hosted by Cass Elliott (formerly of The Mamas and the Papas) and Sam Riddle.

GET SET, GO!

SYNDICATED

1958   Half-hour variety show, with Chuck Richardson and Sue Ane Langdon.

GET SMART

NBC/CBS

18 SEPTEMBER 1965–13 SEPTEMBER 1969 (NBC); 26 SEPTEMBER 1969–11 SEPTEMBER 1970 (CBS)   Mel Brooks and Leonard Stern created this spoof of spy shows, one of few successful sitcoms (138 episodes) not centered around a family. It starred Don Adams as Maxwell Smart, Agent 86 for CONTROL, a Washington-based counterintelligence agency. An inept secret agent, Smart could barely operate the telephone implanted in his shoe; nevertheless, he and his cohorts usually succeeded in thwarting the operations of KAOS, an organization dedicated to evil. Barbara Feldon, a former winner on *The $64,000 Question,* costarred as Smart's partner, Agent 99 (she used the name Susan Hilton in one episode), an intelligent and resourceful agent. In the fall of 1968, she and Smart became engaged and were married on 16 November; the Smarts had twins during the 1969–1970 season. Character actor Edward Platt played their boss, known simply as The Chief. Also featured from time to time were Robert Karvelas as Agent Larraby; Dick Gautier as Hymie, a robot; and Dave Ketchum as Agent 13. Co-creator Leonard Stern also served as executive producer. Don Adams again played Smart in a 1980 film, *The Nude Bomb.* The film (which was a bomb in the theaters) was televised by NBC on 23 May 1982 under the title "The Return of Maxwell Smart." Adams later supplied the voice of a similarly inept cartoon character, *Inspector Gadget* (see also that title). On 26 February 1989 ABC aired a TV-movie, "Get Smart, Again," with Adams, Feldon, Karvelas, Gautier, and Ketchum. A new version of the series surfaced briefly in 1995: see below.

GET SMART

FOX

8 JANUARY 1995–19 FEBRUARY 1995   The short-lived revival of the 1965–1970 sitcom reunited Don Adams and Barbara Feldon. Adams's Maxwell Smart had now become the Chief of CONTROL, and Feldon's 99 had become a Congresswoman. Andy Dick costarred as their bumbling son, Zach, who had just been promoted by his dad from research to full agent status. Elaine Hendrix played Agent 66, his talented partner, and Markus Redmond was featured as Duane, the lab man.

GET THE MESSAGE   ABC
31 MARCH 1964–25 DECEMBER 1964   Frank Buxton hosted this Goodson-Todman daytime game show on which contestants, each teamed with two celebrities, tried to identify a secret word or phrase from clues supplied by the celebs.

GETTING BY   ABC/NBC
5 MARCH 1993–21 MAY 1993 (ABC); 21 SEPTEMBER 1993–12 FEBRUARY 1994 (NBC); 28 MAY 1994–18 JUNE 1994 (NBC)   Half-hour sitcom about a pair of Chicago social workers, one black with two sons and one white with two daughters, who decided to save money by sharing a house. With Cindy Williams as Cathy Hale, who was separated from her husband; Telma Hopkins as Dolores Nixon, who was widowed; Nicki Vannice as Cathy's teenager, Nikki; Ashleigh Blair Sterling as Cathy's nine-year-old, Julie; Merlin Santana as Dolores's fifteen-year-old, Marcus; and Deon Richmond as Dolores's fourteen-year-old, Darren. Telma Hopkins had previously appeared in *Family Matters*, which was created by the same duo: William Bickley and Michael Warren.

GETTING IN TOUCH   SYNDICATED
1987   Psychiatrist David Viscott conducted actual counseling sessions with patients and also interviewed celebrities about psychological topics on this half-hour daily series.

GETTING TOGETHER   ABC
18 SEPTEMBER 1971–8 JANUARY 1972   This half-hour sitcom about a couple of young songwriters featured onetime teen idol Bobby Sherman as Bobby Conway; Wes Stern as his partner Lionel Poindexter; Pat Carroll as their landlady, Rita Simon; Jack Burns as Rita's boyfriend, Rudy Colchek, a cop; and Susan Neher as Jenny, Bobby's kid sister.

THE GHOST AND MRS. MUIR   NBC/ABC
21 SEPTEMBER 1968–6 SEPTEMBER 1969 (NBC); 18 SEPTEMBER 1969–18 SEPTEMBER 1970 (ABC)   This half-hour sitcom starred Hope Lange as Carolyn Muir, a recently widowed writer who moved with her two children to the town of Schooner Bay in New England and settled into Gull Cottage, a house that turned out to be haunted by the ghost of an old ship captain; Edward Mulhare as Captain Daniel Gregg, the ghost who proceeded to look out for the best interests of the Muirs after his initial protests; Charles Nelson Reilly as Claymore Gregg, the Captain's mortal nephew; Harlen Carraher as Jonathan Muir, Carolyn's son; Kellie Flanagan as Candy Muir, Carolyn's daughter; Reta Shaw as Martha Grant, their housekeeper; Guy Raymond as Peavey, Martha's friend; and Scruffy, the family dog. Produced by Howard Leeds for 20th Century-Fox TV, the series was based on the 1947 film which starred Rex Harrison and Gene Tierney.

THE GHOST BUSTERS   CBS
6 SEPTEMBER 1975–4 SEPTEMBER 1976   This live-action Saturday-morning series starred Larry Storch as Eddie Spenser and Forrest Tucker as Kong, the "ghost busters" who fought the ghosts of historical villains. Also featured was Bob Burns as Tracy, their gorilla. Created by Mark Richards. Executive producers: Lou Scheimer and Norm Prescott. Produced and directed by Norman Abbott. See also *Ghostbusters*.

GHOST STORY   NBC
15 SEPTEMBER 1972–22 DECEMBER 1972   This anthology of supernatural tales was hosted by Sebastian Cabot, who appeared as Winston Essex, a wealthy gentleman who owned and operated the Mansfield House, his former mansion that had been turned into a hotel. When Cabot departed in 1972, the series continued under the title *Circle of Fear*.

GHOSTBUSTERS SYNDICATED

1986–1987   Despite its title, this animated series from Filmation was not based on the 1984 motion picture, but rather on the 1975–1976 live-action TV series *The Ghost Busters* (see above). The two lead characters, Jake and Eddie, assisted by Tracy the gorilla, Jessica the reporter, and Futura the sorceress, battled ghosts from fairy tales as well as present-day phantoms. See also *The Real Ghostbusters*.

GHOSTWRITER PBS

4 OCTOBER 1992–   This hour children's series was aimed at 7-to-10-year-olds, and was intended to spark their interest in reading and writing. It featured a multi-ethnic cast of youngsters who became involved in solving mysteries; they were assisted by a spirit known as Ghostwriter, who provided them with written clues, often on a computer screen. The cast included Sheldon Turnipseed, Blaze Berdahl, David Lopez, Tram-Anh Tran, Mayteana Morales (1992–1993), Lateaka Vinson, William Hernandez, and Melissa Gonzalez (1994–).

THE GIANT STEP (TAKE A GIANT STEP) CBS

7 NOVEMBER 1956–29 MAY 1957   Bert Parks hosted this prime-time game show for young people.

GIBBSVILLE NBC

11 NOVEMBER 1976–30 DECEMBER 1976   This little noticed hour-long dramatic series was based on John O'Hara's short stories about Gibbsville, a Pennsylvania mining town. The action—what there was of it—took place during the 1940s. Featured were Gig Young as reporter Ray Whitehead; John Savage as young reporter Jim Malloy; Biff McGuire as Jim's father, Dr. Malloy; Peggy McCay as Jim's mother, Mrs. Malloy; and Bert Remsen as Mr. Pell. The series was originally on NBC's 1976 fall schedule but was displaced at the last minute. It finally surfaced in November, replacing *Gemini Man* in NBC's reshuffled Thursday lineup. David Gerber was the executive producer.

GIDEON OLIVER ABC

20 FEBRUARY 1989–2 SEPTEMBER 1989   One segment of *The ABC Monday Mystery Movie,* this one starred Louis Gossett, Jr., as Gideon Oliver, an anthropology professor at Columbia University who used his knowledge of other cultures to solve baffling crimes, and featured Shari Headley as his daughter and assistant, Zina. *Gideon Oliver* was the only segment of the *Mystery Movie* not renewed for the 1989–1990 season; only five episodes were made.

GIDGET ABC

15 SEPTEMBER 1965–1 SEPTEMBER 1966   Based on the film series, this sitcom starred Sally Field as California teenager Frances "Gidget" Lawrence. Also featured were Don Porter as her father, Russell Lawrence, a widower; Betty Connor as her older sister, Anne; Peter Deuel as Anne's husband, John Cooper, a psychologist; and Lynette Winter as Gidget's friend, Larue. Richard Dreyfuss was seen occasionally as Norman Durfner, one of Gidget's pals at Westside High. The half-hour show was a Screen Gems production. In 1986 a new version surfaced, featuring an adult Gidget: see *The New Gidget*.

GIGANTOR SYNDICATED

1966   Produced in Japan, this cartoon series featured a huge robot (Gigantor) who was controlled by twelve-year-old Jimmy Sparks. New episodes were produced in 1993 and televised on the Sci-Fi Channel.

THE GILLETTE CAVALCADE OF SPORTS NBC

4 SEPTEMBER 1948–24 JUNE 1960   NBC's Friday-night boxing telecast was sponsored by Gillette for most of its run, and the ringside commentary was usually provided by Jimmy Powers. In the early years the fights were broadcast from St. Nicholas Arena in New York, but from the mid-1950s the matches were telecast from anywhere in the

country. If the featured fight failed to go the full distance, the remainder of the hour was filled with features, of variable lengths, such as *Greatest Fights of the Century, Great Moments in Sports,* or *Red Barber's Corner.* Summer broadcasts usually consisted of filmed bouts.

GILLIGAN'S ISLAND
26 SEPTEMBER 1964–4 SEPTEMBER 1967   Situation comedy about seven people left stranded on an uncharted isle in the Pacific after their boat, the *Minnow,* ran aground in a storm. With Bob Denver as Gilligan, the inept first mate; Alan Hale, Jr., as The Skipper (Jonas Grumby); Jim Backus as billionaire Thurston Howell III; Natalie Schafer as his wife, Lovey Howell; Tina Louise as movie star Ginger Grant; Russell Johnson as The Professor (Roy Hinkley); and Dawn Wells as farm girl Mary Ann Summers. Created and produced by Sherwood Schwartz, the show was generally criticized as inane, but its 98 episodes have proven extremely popular in syndication, especially among young viewers. In 1974 a cartoon version appeared: see *The New Adventures of Gilligan.* Most of the cast was reassembled for three made-for-TV-movies, all broadcast on NBC: "Rescue from Gilligan's Island" (1978); "The Castaways on Gilligan's Island" (1979); and "The Harlem Globetrotters on Gilligan's Island" (1981). In 1982 a second cartoon series appeared (see *Gilligan's Planet*). Superstation WTBS aired the never-before broadcast pilot of *Gilligan's Island* on 16 October 1992.

GILLIGAN'S PLANET
18 SEPTEMBER 1982–3 SEPTEMBER 1983   The second Saturday cartoon series based on *Gilligan's Island* (*The New Adventures of Gilligan* was the first), this one found the castaways stuck on a distant planet, trying to get back to Earth.

GIMME A BREAK!
29 OCTOBER 1981–12 MAY 1987   Nell Carter starred in this half-hour sitcom as Nell Harper, housekeeper for a crusty but lovable cop and his three daughters (in flashbacks, it was established that Nell had agreed to take the job as a favor to her old friend, the cop's dying wife). Dolph Sweet costarred (until his death in 1985) as Carl Kanisky, the chief of police in Glenlawn, California. Other regulars included: Kari Michaelsen as Katie, the eldest daughter; Lauri Hendler as the middle daughter, Julie; Lara Jill Miller as the youngest daughter, Samantha; Alvernette Jiminez (1981–1982) as Nell's ditsy friend, Angie; and Howard Morton as Carl's dimwitted subordinate, Officer Ralph Simpson. In 1982 John Hoyt joined the cast as Carl's equally crusty father, Stanley Kanisky; Jane Dulo was seen during the 1982–1983 season as Carl's mother, Mildred. Pete Schrum was seen occasionally as Carl's brother, mortician Ed Kanisky. In 1983 young Joey Lawrence was added as Joey Donovan, a six-year-old orphan who came to live with the Kaniskys. Telma Hopkins signed on in 1984 as Nell's childhood friend, Dr. Addy Wilson, now an educator (the addition of Hopkins, a former member of Tony Orlando and Dawn, made it easy to incorporate musical numbers into the series, taking advantage of Nell Carter's considerable talents). In the fall of 1985, with Dolph Sweet having died, the Kanisky household also came to grips with Carl's death. By that time middle daughter Julie had married Jonathan Maxwell (played by Jonathan Silverman), and the two newlyweds had moved into the Kanisky house. Major changes occurred in the fall of 1986: Katie had moved to San Francisco; Julie, Jonathan, and their baby, Nell, had moved to San Jose; and Samantha headed off to Littlefield College in New Jersey. When Addy Wilson landed a job in New York, Nell and Joey decided to join her there, as did Grandpa Stanley; Nell landed a job at a publishing house. They were joined by Joey's little brother, Matthew (played by Joey Lawrence's real-life brother, Matthew Lawrence). Other new regulars included Paul Sand as building manager Marty; Rosetta LeNoire as Maybelle Harper, Nell's mother; and Rosie O'Donnell as Maggie O'Brien. In a rare prime-time event, the episode of 23 February 1985 was broadcast live. Mort Lachman and Sy Rosen were the creators of the series.

GIRL ABOUT TOWN (FOR YOUR PLEASURE)
(THE KYLE MacDONNELL SHOW)   NBC
15 APRIL 1948–10 SEPTEMBER 1949   Singer Kyle MacDonnell appeared frequently in television's early days, and hosted several series. Her first show was originally seen on Thursdays, and was titled *For Your Pleasure;* by the summer of 1948, however, it had shifted to Wednesdays, and in September it was retitled *Girl About Town;* the twenty-minute series moved to Sundays in February 1949. That summer the show expanded to thirty minutes, moved to Saturday nights, and again assumed the title *For Your Pleasure.*

GIRL ALONE
See THE DOTTY MACK SHOW

THE GIRL FROM U.N.C.L.E.   NBC
13 SEPTEMBER 1966–29 AUGUST 1967   This hour-long adventure series was an unsuccessful spinoff from *The Man from U.N.C.L.E.* It starred Stefanie Powers as agent April Dancer; Noel Harrison (son of Rex Harrison) as agent Mark Slate; Leo G. Carroll (duplicating his *Man from U.N.C.L.E.* role) as U.N.C.L.E. chief Alexander Waverly; and Randy Kirby as U.N.C.L.E. trainee Randy Kovacs. Produced by Douglas Benton.

THE GIRL IN MY LIFE   ABC
9 JULY 1973–20 DECEMBER 1974   Fred Holliday presided over this half-hour daytime show on which women who had done nice things for people were rewarded. Executive producer: Bill Carruthers. Produced by Brad Lachman.

GIRL OF THE WEEK   NBC
9 SEPTEMBER 1948–2 DECEMBER 1948   Sarah Palfrey Cooke hosted this five-minute show, broadcast before the news on Thursday nights, which honored a different woman each week. By November of 1948, however, the show's focus had shifted to honoring only female athletes, and its title was changed to *Sportswoman of the Week.*

GIRL TALK   SYNDICATED
1963–1970   This talk show for women was hosted for most of its run by Virginia Graham; Betsy Palmer took over the hosting duties in 1969. The show was produced and directed by Monty Morgan.

THE GIRL WITH SOMETHING EXTRA   NBC
14 SEPTEMBER 1973–24 MAY 1974   This sitcom was not unlike *Bewitched*—it featured two newlyweds, one of whom (she) possessed ESP. With Sally Field as Sally Burton; John Davidson as lawyer John Burton; Jack Sheldon as Jerry, John's brother; and Zohra Lampert as Anne, Sally's best friend. Produced by Bob Claver and Bernie Slade.

THE GIRLS
See YOUNG AND GAY

THE GISELE MacKENZIE SHOW   NBC
28 SEPTEMBER 1957–29 MARCH 1958   Singer Gisele MacKenzie left *Your Hit Parade* in 1957 to host this half-hour musical variety series, which was produced by Jack Benny's J & M Productions.

GIVE AND TAKE   CBS
20 MARCH 1952–12 JUNE 1952   This unheralded game show, not to be confused with CBS's 1975 show, *Give-N-Take,* was seen on Thursday afternoons for thirteen weeks. Jack Carney produced the question-and-answer program, which is notable chiefly because it was the first network TV show in which Bill Cullen, who cohosted it with John Reed King, appeared regularly.

GIVE-N-TAKE   CBS

8 SEPTEMBER 1975–28 NOVEMBER 1975   This half-hour daytime game show was the successor to *Spin-Off.* Four contestants competed for a top prize of $5,000 on the series that was hosted by Jim Lange and produced by Bill Carruthers and Joel Stein.

GLADIATORS 2000   SYNDICATED

1994–   A junior version of the popular syndicated series *American Gladiators*, this one involved two teams, each comprised of a boy and a girl and coached by one of the *American Gladiators* regulars, in physical challenges and in quizzes on health and nutrition. Ryan Sechrist and Maria Santos cohosted.

GLADYS KNIGHT AND THE PIPS   NBC

10 JULY 1975–31 JULY 1975   This four-week summer variety series was hosted by recording group Gladys Knight and the Pips (Edward Patten, William Guest, and Merald "Bubba" Knight, Gladys's brother). The group got together in the 1950s and began making records in 1961, although their first big hit was not until 1967 ("I Heard It Through the Grapevine"). Bob Henry produced the series.

GLAMOUR GIRL   NBC

6 JULY 1953–8 JANUARY 1954   Harry Babbitt hosted this daytime audience-participation show; each day four women from the studio audience told why they wanted to be the day's "Glamour Girl"; the winner was given a twenty-four-hour beauty treatment, an assortment of gifts, and a vacation trip. Jack McCoy was the executive producer.

THE GLEN CAMPBELL GOODTIME HOUR   CBS

29 JANUARY 1969–13 JUNE 1972

THE SUMMER BROTHERS SMOTHERS SHOW   CBS

23 JUNE 1968–8 SEPTEMBER 1968   Glen Campbell came to Hollywood from Arkansas in the early 1960s and for several years made his living as a guitarist on recording sessions; in 1965 he toured briefly as a guitarist with the Beach Boys. In 1967 he began appearing regularly on *The Smothers Brothers Comedy Hour,* and in 1968 he hosted their summer replacement series, *The Summer Brothers Smothers Show.* Regulars on that show included Pat Paulsen, Leigh French, singer John Hartford (composer of "Gentle on My Mind," one of Campbell's biggest records), the Louis DaPron dancers, the Jimmy Joyce singers, the Nelson Riddle orchestra, and announcer Bill Thompson. In 1969 he returned to TV as host of *The Glen Campbell Goodtime Hour;* his regulars included Pat Paulsen (1969–1970), Jack Burns (1969–1970), John Hartford, Jerry Reed, Larry McNeeley, the Mike Curb Congregation (1971–1972), the Ray Charles Singers, the Ron Poindexter dancers, the Marty Paich orchestra, and announcer Eddie Mayehoff. Among the show's writers was comedian Steve Martin.

GLENCANNON   SYNDICATED

1959   This comedy-adventure series was set in the Caribbean and starred Thomas Mitchell as Captain Colin Glencannon, skipper of a freighter, *The Inchcliffe Castle,* and Patrick Allen as Bos'n Hughes. Based on the stories by Guy Gilpatric, the series was produced in England by Gross-Krasne, Ltd.

GLENN MILLER TIME   CBS

10 JULY 1961–11 SEPTEMBER 1961   Vocalist Johnny Desmond and bandleader Ray McKinley (who was the drummer in Glenn Miller's orchestra) cohosted this live, half-hour musical series, which sought to recreate the Big Band Era of the 1940s. Also featured were singers Patty Clark and the Castle Sisters. The show was a summer replacement for *Hennesey.*

THE GLENN REEVES SHOW   SYNDICATED

1966   Country and western singer Glenn Reeves hosted this half-hour musical series.

GLITTER   ABC
13 SEPTEMBER 1984–25 DECEMBER 1984; 13 DECEMBER 1985–27 DECEMBER 1985   An
hour dramatic series set at the offices of *Glitter,* a trendy magazine. The cast included
Arthur Hill as Charles Hardwick, the publisher; David Birney as reporter Sam
Dillon; Morgan Brittany as reporter Kate Simpson, Hardwick's daughter; Christopher Mayer as reporter Pete Bozak; Dianne Kay as reporter Jennifer Douglas; Timothy Patrick Murphy as Chip, the gofer; Tracy Nelson as Angela, the receptionist;
Arte Johnson as photographer Clive Richlin; Barbara Sharma as Shelley Sealy; and
Millie Slavin as Ellen, Hardwick's secretary. The series began as an uneven mix of
comedy (including office romances) and drama; producer Duane Poole described the
early episodes as "schizophrenic," and promised a harder edge to subsequent stories.
The changes were to no avail, as *Glitter* finished 94th out of 97 series in the prime-
time seasonal Nielsens and was yanked on Christmas night. Seven previously unaired
episodes were later seen in a late-night slot on ABC a year later.

GLOBAL ZOBEL   SYNDICATED
1961   Myron Zobel hosted this half-hour travelogue.

GLORIA   CBS
26 SEPTEMBER 1982–10 APRIL 1983; 29 JUNE 1983–21 SEPTEMBER 1983   Sally
Struthers, who had played Archie Bunker's daughter on *All in the Family* from 1971
to 1978, returned to that role four years later. In this sequel, Gloria Stivic, now
divorced, landed in upstate New York with her young son and found a job as a
veterinarian's assistant. Also featured were Burgess Meredith as the crusty vet, Dr.
Willard Adams; Jo de Winter as Willard's partner, Dr. Maggie Lawrence; Lou Richards as Clark Uhley, Gloria's fellow assistant; and Christian Jacobs as Gloria's son,
Joey Stivic.

THE GLORIA SWANSON SHOW
(CROWN THEATRE WITH GLORIA SWANSON)   SYNDICATED
1954   This half-hour dramatic anthology series, hosted by (and occasionally starring) Gloria Swanson, was produced by Bing Crosby Enterprises.

GLORY DAYS   FOX
25 JULY 1990–27 SEPTEMBER 1990   This hour dramatic series traced the lives of four
friends who had recently graduated from high school. It featured Spike Alexander as
Dave Rutecki, a rookie cop; Evan Mirand as Fopiano, a fraternity pledge; Nicholas
Kallsen as Peter "T-Bone" Trigg, a rock-and-roll fan; Brad Pitt as Walker Lovejoy, a
college dropout and aspiring newspaper writer; Robert Costanzo as Rutecki's boss,
Lieutenant V. T. Krantz; Beth Broderick as Lovejoy's editor, Sheila Jackson; Freder-
ick Coffin as Lovejoy's father, Jim; and Sam Jenkins as Lovejoy's girlfriend, Sherry
Jensen.

GLYNIS   CBS
25 SEPTEMBER 1963–18 DECEMBER 1963   This sitcom was one of the early fatalities of
the 1963–1964 season. It starred Glynis Johns as Glynis Granville, a novelist and
amateur detective; Keith Andes as her husband, Keith Granville; George Mathews
as Chick Rogers, a retired policeman who occasionally assisted Glynis.

GO (GO-U.S.A.)   NBC
8 SEPTEMBER 1973–4 SEPTEMBER 1976   *Go,* the TV series with the shortest title (until
NBC's *V* in 1984), was aimed at children. It began in 1973 as a series that explored
occupations; in 1975 its title was lengthened (to *Go-U.S.A.*) and its emphasis was
shifted to America's bicentennial observance. The Saturday series' executive producer was George A. Heinemann.

GO!   NBC

3 OCTOBER 1983–20 JANUARY 1984   The second TV series with this short title was a
daytime game show on which two five-member teams sought to identify a word or a
phrase from clues supplied by team members. Kevin O'Connell was the host.

GO LUCKY   CBS

15 JULY 1951–2 SEPTEMBER 1951   Jan Murray hosted this game show, a summer
replacement for *This Is Show Business,* on which guest celebrities acted out charades
for contestants.

THE GODZILLA POWER HOUR   NBC

8 SEPTEMBER 1978–5 SEPTEMBER 1981   A Saturday-morning cartoon series from
Hanna-Barbera Productions, *The Godzilla Power Hour* began as a sixty-minute show
featuring segments of "Godzilla" (who was now a friendly monster from the depths
of the ocean who helped out his friends, a group of research scientists stationed
aboard the *Calico*) and "Jana of the Jungle" (a female Tarzan). In November of 1978
the show expanded to ninety minutes and was retitled *Godzilla Super 90,* adding on
segments of *Jonny Quest,* another Hanna-Barbera series. In the fall of 1979 the series
was reduced to thirty minutes and titled *The Godzilla Show;* it later became *The
Godzilla Globetrotters Hour.* During the 1979–1980 and 1980–1981 seasons, Godzilla
headlined two Saturday-morning series simultaneously. *The Godzilla Show,* a half-
hour program, ran during both seasons; it was coupled with *The Godzilla/ Globetrotters Adventure Hour* in 1979–1980, with *The Godzilla/Dynomutt Hour,* from September to November 1980, and with *The Godzilla/Hong Kong Phooey Hour,* from
November 1980 to May 1981.

THE GO-GO GLOBETROTTERS

See THE HARLEM GLOBETROTTERS

THE GO-GO GOPHERS   CBS

14 SEPTEMBER 1968–6 SEPTEMBER 1969   This Saturday-morning cartoon series was
set in the old West and featured two gophers who tried to fight off the advances of Kit
Coyote of the Cavalry.

GOING BANANAS   NBC

15 SEPTEMBER 1984–1 DECEMBER 1984   Live-action Saturday morning series about an
orangutan (Roxanna) and her two human pals, James (played by Tim Topper) and
his sister Louise (Emily Moultrie).

GOING MY WAY   ABC

3 OCTOBER 1962–11 SEPTEMBER 1963   Based on the 1944 film, this situation comedy
starred Gene Kelly as Father Charles O'Malley, a priest assigned to St. Dominic's
Parish in Manhattan; Leo G. Carroll as Father Fitzgibbon, the parish pastor; Dick
York as Tom Colwell, the progressive director of the local community center; and
Nydia Westman as Mrs. Featherstone.

GOING PLACES   ABC

3 JUNE 1956–26 AUGUST 1956   This weekend variety series was broadcast each week
from a different city in Florida. Jack Gregson hosted the first few shows and was
replaced by Merv Griffin.

GOING PLACES   ABC

21 SEPTEMBER 1990–8 MARCH 1991; 31 MAY 1991–5 JULY 1991   Mindless sitcom about
four young staffers on a fictional TV series who shared a house. With Alan Ruck as
Charlie Davis; Jerry Levine as his brother, Jack Davis; Hallie Todd as Kate Griffin;
Heather Locklear as Alex Burton; Holland Taylor as Dawn St. Claire, who produced
the series, a *Candid Camera*-type show titled *Here's Looking at You* for National
Studios, and who also owned the house where the four lived; and Staci Keanan as
their teenage neighbor, Lindsay Bowen. In January 1991 *Here's Looking at You* was

canceled, and the four found work on a new National Studios series, *The Dick Roberts Show*. Holland Taylor ceased appearing as a regular, and three new regulars were added: Steve Vinovich as Dick Roberts, the insufferable talk-show host; Philip Charles MacKenzie as Dick's long-suffering producer, Arnie Ross; and J. D. Daniels as Kate's eight-year-old nephew, Nick.

GOING TO EXTREMES   ABC
1 SEPTEMBER 1992–27 JANUARY 1993   Filmed on location in Jamaica, this hour dramatic series was set at a medical school on the Caribbean island of Jantique. The cast included Roy Dotrice as Dr. Henry Croft, the school's founder; Carl Lumbly as the dean, Dr. Michael Norris, an American-educated Jantique native; June Chadwick as internal medicine professor Dr. Alice Davis; Charles Keating as anatomy instructor Dr. Jack Van De Weghe; Erika Alexander as student Cheryl Carter; Camilo Gallardo as Australian student Kim Selby; Joanna Going as student Kathleen McDermott; Daniel Jenkins as student Alex Lauren; Andrew Lauer as student Charlie Moran; and Robert Duncan McNeill as second-year-student Colin Mitford. Joshua Brand, John Falsey, and Frank South created the series.

THE GOLDBERGS   CBS/NBC/DUMONT/SYNDICATED
17 JANUARY 1949–18 JUNE 1951 (CBS); 4 FEBRUARY 1952–14 JULY 1952; 3 JULY 1953–25 SEPTEMBER 1953 (NBC); 13 APRIL 1954–19 OCTOBER 1954 (DUMONT); 1954–1955 (SYNDICATED)   Created by Gertrude Berg in 1929, the hit radio show became one of TV's first popular sitcoms. In addition to writing and producing the show, Gertrude Berg also starred as Molly Goldberg, the lovable Jewish mother who lived with her family at 1038 East Tremont Avenue in the Bronx. Philip Loeb first played her husband, Jake, a tailor, but was blacklisted during the "Red Scare" of the early 1950s (Loeb committed suicide in 1955); Harold J. Stone took over the role in 1952, and Robert H. Harris (who had previously played Jake's partner, Mendel) played the part from 1953 through 1955. Also featured were Arlene McQuade as their daughter Rosalie; Larry Robinson (1949–1952) and Tom Taylor (1953–1955) as their son Sammy; Eli Mintz (1949–1952 and 1954–1955) and Menasha Skulnik (1953) as Uncle David, Molly's brother. From 1949 to 1951 the show was seen on Monday nights. In 1952 it was seen Monday, Wednesday, and Friday evenings in a fifteen-minute format. In 1953 it reverted to a half-hour format. The 1954–1955 syndicated version was also a half-hour series; the Goldbergs, however, had left the Bronx and moved to Haverville, a suburban community. Arnold Stang was featured in the latter version as Seymour, Jake's shipping clerk.

THE GOLDDIGGERS   NBC/SYNDICATED
20 JUNE 1968–5 SEPTEMBER 1968; 17 JULY 1969–11 SEPTEMBER 1969; 16 JULY 1970–10 SEPTEMBER 1970 (NBC); 1971 (SYNDICATED)   The Golddiggers were a group of attractive young women put together by producer Greg Garrison. Their show was a summer replacement for *The Dean Martin Show* in 1968, 1969, and 1970; in 1971 they hosted a syndicated series. The show was entitled *Dean Martin Presents the Golddiggers* in 1968 and 1969. The 1968 show was set in the 1930s, and regulars included cohosts Frank Sinatra, Jr., and Joey Heatherton, and Paul Lynde, Barbara Heller, Stanley Myron Handelman, Stu Gilliam, The Times Square Two, Skiles and Henderson, and the Les Brown Orchestra. In 1969 the series was hosted by Lou Rawls, Gail Martin (Dean's daughter), and Paul Lynde; other regulars included Stanley Myron Handelman, Tommy Tune, Albert Brooks, Danny Lockin, Allison McKay, Darleen Carr, and Fiore and Eldridge. The 1970 series was taped in England and titled *The Golddiggers in London;* regulars included Charles Nelson Reilly (the host), Marty Feldman, Tommy Tune, and Julian Chagrin. The 1971 series was entitled simply *The Golddiggers* and featured Charles Nelson Reilly, Jackie Vernon, Barbara Heller, and Alice Ghostley; unlike the summer series, it was only a half hour in length. The composition of the ten-to-twelve member Golddiggers troupe changed from time to time. In 1970 the group consisted of Pauline Antony, Wanda Bailey, Jackie Chidsey, Paula Cinko, Rosetta Cox, Michelle della Fave, Tara Leigh, Susan Lund, Micki McGlone, and Patricia Mickey. A year later, only Chidsey and Lund

remained: New arrivals included Jimmi Cannon, Loyita Chapel, Lee Crawford, Liz Kelley, Francie Mendenhall, Nancy Reichert, and Janice Whitby.

THE GOLDEN GIRLS
NBC

14 SEPTEMBER 1985–12 SEPTEMBER 1992   The most popular new series of the 1985–1986 season, *The Golden Girls* was the first successful modern sitcom in which all of the stars were female. Even more surprising was that all were well over age fifty. Its central characters were four mature women living together in Miami: Bea Arthur as teacher Dorothy Zbornak, a divorcée; Betty White as the naive grief counselor Rose Nylund; Rue McClanahan as sex-obsessed museum worker Blanche Devereaux, who owned the house where the four ladies lived; and Estelle Getty as Dorothy's acid-tongued mother, Sophia Petrillo, who moved in after her retirement home burned down. Unlike most of TV's earlier "older ladies," the *Golden Girls* characters never abandoned their hopes for romance and their interest in sex. On the final first-run episode (9 May 1992), Dorothy married Blanche's Uncle Lucas (played by Leslie Nielsen). The other three golden girls carried on with a new series on a new network: see *The Golden Palace*.

Created by Susan Harris, *The Golden Girls* finished in Nielsen's top ten in each of its first five seasons.

THE GOLDEN PALACE
CBS

18 SEPTEMBER 1992–6 AUGUST 1993   Three of the principals of *The Golden Girls* carried on for another season, on a new network, in this sequel series. Here, they were the new owners of a South Miami Beach hotel, The Golden Palace. Featured were Betty White as Rose Nylund; Rue McClanahan as Blanche Devereaux; Estelle Getty as Sophia Petrillo; Don Cheadle as Roland, the hotel manager; Billy L. Sullivan as Oliver, Roland's foster son; and Cheech Marin as Chuy Castillos, the chef.

GOLDEN WINDOWS
NBC

5 JULY 1954–8 APRIL 1955   This fifteen-minute afternoon serial told the story of a young woman who left Capstan Island, Maine, to pursue a singing career in New York. Along the way she became involved with a man who was in trouble with the law. Featured were Leila Martin as Julie Goodwin; Herb Patterson as her boyfriend, Tom Anderson; Eric Dressler as her father, Charles Goodwin; Grant Sullivan as John Brandon; Millicent Brower as Ellen, Tom's former fiancée; Joe DeSantis as Carl Grant; Phillip Pine as Paul; Frank Hammerton as vocal teacher Joseph Kindler; Barbara Cook as Hazel; Vicki Cummings as Jane Talbert; and E. A. Krumschmidt as Streicher.

GOLDEN YEARS (STEPHEN KING'S GOLDEN YEARS)
CBS

16 JULY 1991–22 AUGUST 1991   Stephen King created this continuing series about a seventy-year-old janitor, injured in a lab explosion, who found himself growing younger. With Keith Szarabajka as the not-so-senior citizen, Harlan Williams; Frances Sternhagen as his wife, Gina; Felicity Huffman as Terry Spann, the security director at the lab, a government research facility called Falco Plains; Ed Lauter as General Louis Crewes; R. D. Call as Jude Andrews, an intelligence agent pursuing Williams; and Bill Raymond as Dr. Richard Todhunter, the scientist whose experiments caused Williams's predicament. King himself appeared in the fourth of the seven episodes as a bus driver.

GOLDIE
See THE BETTY HUTTON SHOW

GOLDIE GOLD AND ACTION JACK
ABC

12 SEPTEMBER 1981–18 SEPTEMBER 1982   Goldie Gold, the world's richest girl, was the star of this Saturday-morning cartoon show; Action Jack was the ace reporter for Goldie's newspaper, the *Goldstreet Journal*.

GOLF FOR SWINGERS
See LEE TREVINO'S GOLF FOR SWINGERS

GOMER PYLE, U.S.M.C. CBS
25 SEPTEMBER 1964–19 SEPTEMBER 1969   This military sitcom was a spinoff from *The Andy Griffith Show.* It starred Jim Nabors as Gomer Pyle, the naive and trusting gas pump jockey from Mayberry, North Carolina, who decided to join the Marines. Assigned to Camp Henderson in California, he served a five-year enlistment as a private. Also featured were Frank Sutton as the irascible Sergeant Vince Carter, his platoon leader; Forrest Compton as Colonel Gray, the commanding officer; Ronnie Schell as his buddy, Private Duke Slater; Ted Bessell (1964–1966) as pal Frankie Lombardi, also a private; Ray Stuart as Corporal Boyle, Carter's aide; Allan Melvin (1967–1969) as Sergeant Hacker; and Elizabeth MacRae (1967–1969) as Gomer's girlfriend, Lou Ann Poovie, an aspiring singer. Executive producers: Aaron Ruben and Sheldon Leonard. 150 episodes were produced.

THE GONG SHOW NBC/SYNDICATED
14 JUNE 1976–21 JULY 1978 (NBC); 1976–1980 (SYNDICATED); 1988 (SYNDICATED)   This popular game show took *Ted Mack's Original Amateur Hour* one step further: A panel of three celebrities judged unusual amateur (and professional) talent acts, and any member of the panel could, by banging a large gong, terminate any act before completion. Completed acts were then rated on a one-to-ten scale, and the winning act received a cash award—$516.32 on the day show, $712.05 (or sometimes $1,000) on the syndicated version. The show was a magnet for unusual acts: nose-whistlers, sink players, and singing dogs were all commonplace. Chuck Barris, who created the show with coproducer Chris Bearde, chose to host the festivities (John Barbour, later of *Real People,* was to have been the host, but was replaced before the premiere). It was the first time in front of the microphone for Barris, the man responsible for *The Dating Game, The Newlywed Game,* and *How's Your Mother-in-Law* (before that, he'd written "Palisades Park" for singer Freddy Cannon). The syndicated version was hosted for one season by Gary Owens before Barris assumed those chores as well. Among the celebrities who frequented the panel were Jaye P. Morgan, Rex Reed, Arte Johnson, Michele Lee, and Jamie Farr. Siv Aberg kept score. Don Bleu hosted the short-lived 1988 version.

GOOBER AND THE GHOST CHASERS ABC
8 SEPTEMBER 1973–31 AUGUST 1975   On this weekend cartoon show a dog who could become invisible teamed up with some magazine staffers to chase ghosts. Some of the voices were supplied by Paul Winchell (as Goober, the dog), Ronnie Schell, and several members of *The Partridge Family:* Susan Dey, Danny Bonaduce, Brian Forster, and Suzanne Crough. Iwao Takamoto produced the series for Hanna-Barbera Productions, Inc. The second season consisted entirely of reruns.

GOOD ADVICE CBS
2 APRIL 1993–7 MAY 1993; 23 MAY 1994–10 AUGUST 1994   Disappointing sitcom about a marriage counselor and a divorce lawyer who shared an office suite. With Shelley Long as the counselor, Susan De Ruzza; Treat Williams as the lawyer, Jack Harold; George Wyner as chiropractor Artie Cohen, who also shared the offices; Estelle Harris as Artie's mother, Ronnie, the receptionist; Chris McDonald (1993) as Susan's husband, Joey De Ruzza; Ross Malinger as their young son, Michael; and Lightfield Lewis as the office boy, Sean. When the series returned in 1994, Harris and McDonald were gone from the cast (it was explained that Susan had kicked her husband out), and two new cast members were added: Henriette Mantel as Henriette, Susan's housekeeper; and Teri Garr as Susan's sister, Paige, who became the new receptionist. Norma Safford Vela and Danny Jacobson created the series.

GOOD AND EVIL ABC
25 SEPTEMBER 1991–30 OCTOBER 1991   Susan Harris created this continuing sitcom, much like her groundbreaking effort, *Soap*. Its central characters were two sisters

living in Seattle, one good and one bad. The cast included Teri Garr as bitchy businesswoman Denise Sandler; Margaret Whitton as the saintly Genny, a widowed biochemist; Marian Seldes as their mother, Charlotte; Brooke Theiss as Genny's daughter, Caroline, who had been mute since her father's death (she broke her silence on the final telecast); Marius Weyers as Denise's long-lost husband, recently thawed out after being frozen in a glacier on Mount Everest; Mark Blankfield as George, a blind psychiatrist who lusted for Genny; Lane Davies as Dr. Eric Haan, Genny's suitor; Lane Smith as Harlan Shell, Charlotte's suitor; Mary Gillis as Mary, Denise's secretary; Seth Green as David, Denise's teenage son; Sherman Howard as Roger, Denise's corporate assistant; and William Shockley as Sonny.

GOOD COMPANY ABC
7 SEPTEMBER 1967–21 DECEMBER 1967   Noted trial lawyer F. Lee Bailey (whose clients have included Dr. Sam Sheppard, Patty Hearst, and O.J. Simpson) hosted this series in which celebrities were interviewed at their homes. Its resemblance to *Person to Person* may have been more than coincidental: John Aaron produced both series.

GOOD GRIEF FOX
30 SEPTEMBER 1990–17 MARCH 1991   Half-hour sitcom set at the Sincerity Mortuary, run by two brothers-in-law. With Howie Mandel as brash Ernie Lapidus, who had recently joined the sixty-year-old family business; Joel Brooks as his staid partner, Warren Pepper; Wendy Schaal as Ernie's wife, and Warren's sister, Debbie; Sheldon Feldner as Raoul, Ernie's eccentric assistant; and Tom Poston as Ringo Prowley, an old friend of Ernie's late father who showed up hoping Ernie would give him a job. Stu Silver created the series.

THE GOOD GUYS CBS
25 SEPTEMBER 1968–23 JANUARY 1970   This low-key sitcom was one of the few shows of the 1960s filmed before a live audience. It starred Herb Edelman as Bert Gramus and Bob Denver as Rufus Butterworth, two childhood friends who buy a diner (Bert's Place) together (Rufus also drove a cab part-time), and Joyce Van Patten as Claudia Gramus, Bert's wife. Also featured was Ron Masak as Andy, their friend and patron. The half-hour show was produced by David Susskind's Talent Associates.

GOOD HEAVENS ABC
29 FEBRUARY 1976–26 JUNE 1976   This irregularly scheduled situation comedy starred Carl Reiner as Mr. Angel, a representative from the afterlife who returns to Earth to grant wishes to deserving people. Created by Bernard Slade, the series was produced by Austin Kalish and Irma Kalish. Carl Reiner also served as executive producer.

THE GOOD LIFE NBC
18 SEPTEMBER 1971–8 JANUARY 1972   In this sitcom a middle-class couple decided to hire themselves out as a butler and maid to a wealthy family. With Larry Hagman as Albert Miller; Donna Mills as Jane Miller, his wife; David Wayne as their wealthy employer, Charles Dutton; Hermione Baddeley as Grace Dutton, Charles's sister; and Danny Goldman as Nick, Charles's son.

THE GOOD LIFE NBC
3 JANUARY 1994–12 APRIL 1994   Another in the string of 90s sitcoms starring standup comics, this one cast John Caponera as a warehouse manager named John Bowman. John had a wife, kids, and some zany coworkers at the warehouse. Also on hand were Eve Gordon as his wife, Maureen; Shay Astar as teen daughter Melissa; Jake Patellis as teen son Paul; Justin Berfield as subteen son Bob; Drew Carey (also a standup comic) as coworker Drew; and Monty Hoffman as coworker Tommy. Carey received his own series in the fall of 1995: See *The Drew Carey Show*.

GOOD MORNING!
See THE MORNING SHOW

GOOD MORNING AMERICA   ABC

3 NOVEMBER 1975–   The first program to compete seriously against NBC's *Today* show, *Good Morning America* is a revamped version of *A.M. America,* ABC's first early-morning effort. Its format is similar to *Today's*—a two-hour blend of news, interviews, and features—but *GMA's* basic set is a living room rather than a newsroom. David Hartman (who had been a regular on *The Virginian, The Bold Ones,* and *Lucas Tanner*) was the show's host from 1975 to 1987. His first cohost was actress Nancy Dussault, who left in April 1977. She was succeeded by Sandy Hill, who held the position for three years. Joan Lunden was named Hill's permanent replacement in August of 1980. *GMA* has also featured a number of regular contributors over the years; this group has included columnists Jack Anderson, Erma Bombeck, and Rona Barrett, former New York mayor John Lindsay, comedian Jonathan Winters, ABC newsman Geraldo Rivera, editor Helen Gurley Brown, former Olympian Bruce Jenner and his wife, Chrystie, and physicians Dr. Timothy Johnson and Dr. Lendon Smith. Charles Gibson succeeded Hartman as cohost in February 1987.

   Good Morning America's ratings climbed slowly but steadily. During the week of 4 May 1979 it overtook *Today* for the first time; three months later it repeated the success. By early 1982 *GMA* had begun to pull ahead of *Today* consistently. In July of that year ABC inaugurated an even earlier newscast (see *ABC World News This Morning*). The Lunden-Gibson partnership proved to be both successful and durable, as *GMA's* ratings generally stayed ahead of *Today's* through the mid-1990s. On 3 January 1993 GMA launched a Sunday edition. The one-hour *Good Morning America/Sunday* was originally cohosted by Dana King and Bill Ritter. King left at the end of 1993, and Ritter was succeeded by cohosts Willow Bay and Antonio Mora in March 1994.

GOOD MORNING WORLD   CBS

5 SEPTEMBER 1967–17 SEPTEMBER 1968   This sitcom was the first to be set at a radio station. It starred Joby Baker as Dave Lewis and Ronnie Schell as Larry Clarke, two Los Angeles disc jockeys who cohosted an early-morning show ("The Lewis and Clarke Show"). Also featured were Julie Parrish as Linda Lewis, Dave's wife; Billy DeWolfe as station manager Roland B. Hutton, Jr.; Goldie Hawn as Sandy, a neighbor of the Lewises who was interested in Larry. The series was developed by the team responsible for *The Dick Van Dyke Show:* Carl Reiner, Sheldon Leonard, Bill Persky, and Sam Denoff.

GOOD SEX! WITH DR. RUTH WESTHEIMER

See DR. RUTH WESTHEIMER

GOOD SPORTS   CBS

10 JANUARY 1991–13 JULY 1991   Half-hour sitcom starring Farrah Fawcett and Ryan O'Neal (who lived together in real life) as Gayle Roberts and "Downtown" Bobby Tannen. Roberts, an ex-model turned sportscaster, suddenly found herself teamed up on the air with Tannen, a dimwitted, down-and-out former football star who, twenty years earlier, had spent a passionate weekend with her but now only barely remembered their tryst. Also featured were Lane Smith as Rappaport, the folksy owner of Rappaport Broadcasting System, parent company of the All-Sports Cable Network for whom Gayle and Bobby worked; Brian Doyle-Murray as Mack MacKinney, their producer; Cleavant Derricks as Jeff Musberger; Paul Feig as Leash, the gofer; Christine Dunford as Missy; and Lois Smith as Mrs. Tannen, Bobby's mother. Alan Zweibel created the series; Al Green sang the theme.

GOOD TIME HARRY   NBC

19 JULY 1980–13 SEPTEMBER 1980   Half-hour sitcom starring Ted Bessell as swinging bachelor Harry Jenkins, who returned to his job as a sportswriter for the San Francisco *Herald.* With Eugene Roche as Jimmy Hughes, the sports editor; Marcia Strassman as fellow sportswriter Carol Younger; Ruth Manning as Sally, Harry's secretary; Jesse Wells as Billie, a cocktail waitress; Richard Karron as Lenny, Harry's favorite bartender; and Barry Gordon as Harry's neighbor Stan.

GOOD TIMES   CBS

8 FEBRUARY 1974–3 JANUARY 1979; 23 MAY 1979–1 AUGUST 1979   *Good Times* was
the first spinoff of a spinoff: it was descended from *All in the Family* by way of
Maude. Set in Chicago, it told the story of a lower-class black family— an often-
unemployed father and a mother trying hard to make ends meet, both hoping to
build a better future for their three children. The show starred Esther Rolle (1974–
1977) as Florida Evans, formerly the maid on *Maude;* John Amos (1974–1976) as
James, her husband; Jimmie Walker as J. J. (James, Jr.), their jive-talking eldest son;
BernNadette Stanis as Thelma, their teenage daughter; Ralph Carter as Michael,
their serious-minded younger son; Ja'net DuBois as their friend and neighbor,
Willona Woods; Johnny Brown as Mr. Bookman, the much-despised building janitor.
Amos left the series at the end of the 1975–1976 season; in the 1976 fall premiere it
was explained that he had found work in Mississippi but had been killed in an auto
accident. Later that season Moses Gunn joined the cast as Carl Dixon, Florida's new
romantic interest. When Esther Rolle decided to leave the series as production began
for the 1977–1978 season, it was explained that she and Carl had gotten married and
had gone to Arizona for Carl's health; the three children remained in Chicago to take
care of themselves (with a little help from Willona); Janet Jackson joined the cast as
Penny, a battered child who was adopted by Willona. In the fall of 1978 Esther Rolle
returned to the show, and Ben Powers joined the cast as former football star Keith
Anderson, who married Thelma. *Good Times* was created by Eric Monte and Michael Evans (of *The Jeffersons*); 133 episodes were televised. Executive producers
included Norman Lear (1974–1975), Allan Manings (1975–1976), Austin and Irma
Kalish (1976–1978), and Norman Paul (1978–1979). Producers included Allan
Manings (1974–1975), Jack Elinson and Norman Paul (1975–1976), Gordon Mitchell
and Lloyd Turner (1976–1978), and Sid Dorfman (1978–1979). The series' theme was
written by Marilyn and Alan Bergman and Dave Grusin.

GOODNIGHT BEANTOWN   CBS

3 APRIL 1983–1 MAY 1983; 28 AUGUST 1983–15 JANUARY 1984; 22 JULY 1984–2 SEPTEM-
BER 1984   Half-hour sitcom about a pair of news anchorpeople at a Boston TV
station. With Bill Bixby as Matt Cassidy, who had been the sole anchor at WYN,
channel 11; Mariette Hartley as Jennifer Barnes, who came to Boston to be Matt's
coanchor, and who ended up living across the hall from him in the same apartment
building; Tracey Gold as Susan, Jennifer's daughter; George Coe (spring 1983) as the
news director, Dick Novak; Louis Giambalvo (spring 1983) as Gus; Gary Bayer
(spring 1983) as Jake; G. W. Bailey (fall 1983–1984) as Albert, the new news director; Jim Staahl (fall 1983–1984) as sportscaster Frank Fletcher; and Stephanie Faracy
(fall 1983–1984) as reporter Valerie Wood.

GOODTIME GIRLS   ABC

22 JANUARY 1980–12 FEBRUARY 1980; 12 APRIL 1980–26 APRIL 1980; 1 AUGUST 1980–29
AUGUST 1980   Wartime Washington, D.C., was the setting for this half-hour sitcom
about four young women who shared an attic room in a boardinghouse in 1942.
Featured were Annie Potts as Edith Bedelmyer; Lorna Patterson as Betty Crandall;
Francine Tacker as photographer Camille Rittenhouse; Georgia Engel as war bride
Loretta Smoot; Marcia Lewis as the landlady, Irma Coolidge; Merwin Goldsmith as
her husband, George Coolidge, the landlord; Adrian Zmed as cabbie Frankie
Malardo, who also lived in the house; and Peter Scolari (summer 1980) as Benny
Loman. Leonora Thuna, Thomas L. Miller and Robert Boyett created the show.

GOODYEAR PLAYHOUSE   NBC

14 OCTOBER 1951–22 SEPTEMBER 1957   Produced by Fred Coe, *Goodyear Playhouse*
was an hour-long dramatic anthology series which, together with several other high-
quality shows, comprised television's so-called "Golden Age," an era of original
teleplays, usually broadcast live. *Goodyear Playhouse* came to the air in 1951 and
shared a Sunday slot first with *Philco Television Playhouse* (until 1955), then with *The
Alcoa Hour.* During the 1956–1957 season, *Goodyear* and *Alcoa* also alternated with
The Dinah Shore Show and *The Bob Hope Show.* Among the many noteworthy

presentations were: "October Story," with Julie Harris and Leslie Nielsen (14 October 1951); "Raymond Schindler, Case One," with Rod Steiger (20 January 1952, his first major TV role); Paddy Chayefsky's "Marty," with Rod Steiger and Nancy Marchand (directed by Delbert Mann, 24 May 1953); "Catch a Falling Star," with Susan Strasberg (28 June 1953, her first major TV role); "The Huntress," with Judy Holliday (14 February 1954, a rare TV appearance); "Guilty Is the Stranger," with Paul Newman (26 September 1954); "The Chivington Raid," with Steve McQueen (27 March 1955); Gore Vidal's "Visit to a Small Planet," with Cyril Ritchard and Dick York (8 May 1955); Paddy Chayefsky's "The Catered Affair," with Thelma Ritter (22 May 1955); Robert Anderson's "All Summer Long," with Raymond Massey and William Shatner (in his first major TV role, 28 October 1956). After this series left the air in 1957, Goodyear sponsored another anthology series: see *Goodyear Theatre*. See also *Philco Television Playhouse*.

GOODYEAR THEATRE   NBC
14 OCTOBER 1957–12 SEPTEMBER 1960   This half-hour filmed dramatic anthology series alternated with *Alcoa Theatre;* both were produced by Four Star Films. Jack Lemmon appeared in four shows during the 1957–1958 season: "Lost and Found," 14 October; "Voice in the Fog," 11 November; "The Victim," 6 January; and "Disappearance," 9 June.

GOOF TROOP   ABC/SYNDICATED
12 SEPTEMBER 1992–11 SEPTEMBER 1993 (ABC); 1991–   (SYNDICATED)
Disney's classic cartoon dog had become a father on this half-hour animated program: Goofy was raising his son, Max, in the town of Spoonerville. The series premiered simultaneously in 1991 on ABC's Saturday morning schedule and in weekday syndication, with different episodes on each version. In 1992 it became part of *Disney Afternoon*, a two-hour cartoon block.

THE GORDON ELLIOTT SHOW   SYNDICATED
1994–   Hour daytime talk show hosted by Gordon Elliott, a six-foot-seven Australian.

THE GORDON MacRAE SHOW   NBC
5 MARCH 1956–27 AUGUST 1956   Musical comedy star Gordon MacRae hosted this fifteen-minute musical show, broadcast Monday before the evening news; a vocal group known as The Cheerleaders backed him up.

GOVERNMENT STORY   SYNDICATED
1969   A series of forty half-hour documentaries which examined various aspects of the United States Government. Stephen Horn hosted the series, which was produced by Group W. Paul Long and E. G. Marshall supplied the narration.

THE GOVERNOR AND J.J.   CBS
23 SEPTEMBER 1969–30 DECEMBER 1970   This half-hour sitcom starred Dan Dailey as Governor William Drinkwater, a widower, and Julie Sommars as his daughter, J. J. (Jennifer Jo), who served as his official hostess when she was not working at the zoo. Also featured were James Callahan as Drinkwater's press secretary, George Callison; Neva Patterson as his personal secretary, Maggie McLeod; Nora Marlowe as Sarah, the housekeeper; and Guv, the basset hound. The series was one of the few sixties sitcoms filmed before a live audience.

GRACE UNDER FIRE   ABC
29 SEPTEMBER 1993–   An immediate hit, this sitcom starred standup comic Brett Butler as Grace Kelly, a single mom raising three youngsters and working in an oil refinery in Victory, Missouri. Also featured were Jon Paul Steuer as her older son, Quentin (Noah Sagan played the role in the premiere); Kaitlin Cullum as her daughter, Libby; twins Dylan and Cole Sprouse as her baby son, Patrick; Julie White as Nadine Swoboda, Grace's high school pal and next-door neighbor; Casey Sander as Wade, Nadine's current husband (her fourth); Dave Thomas as Russell Norton, a dull pharmacist whose relationship with Grace never quite kindled; Walter Olkewicz

as Grace's co-worker, Dougie; Dave Florek as co-worker Vic; Charles Hallahan (1993–1994) as Bill, the foreman; and Paul Dooley (1994–) as John, the foreman. Valri Bromfield appeared occasionally as Grace's sister, Faith. In the fall of 1995 Tom Poston became a regular as Russell's father, Floyd, and Alan Autry appeared as Rick, an executive who became interested in Grace. Chuck Lorre created the series, and served briefly as its executive producer; he departed in the middle of the first season after "creative differences" with Butler. The series finished sixth in the Nielsen ratings during its first season (narrowly nosed out by *These Friends of Mine* as the year's most popular new series), and rose to fourth during its second season. In 1995 it became the first American-made sitcom to be telecast regularly in Russia.

GRADY   NBC
4 DECEMBER 1975–4 MARCH 1976   In this spinoff from *Sanford and Son,* Whitman Mayo starred as Grady Wilson, who left the Sanfords' Los Angeles neighborhood to move in with his daughter and son-in-law in Santa Monica. With Carol Cole as Ellie Marshall, his daughter; Joe Morton as her husband, Hal, a schoolteacher; Rosanne Katon as Laurie, their daughter; and Haywood Nelson as Haywood, their son. Executive producers: Saul Turteltaub and Bernie Orenstein. Produced by Howard Leeds and Jerry Ross for Bud Yorkin Productions.

GRAHAM KERR
See THE GALLOPING GOURMET

GRAND   NBC
18 JANUARY 1990–12 APRIL 1990; 12 JULY 1990–27 DECEMBER 1990   Half-hour sitcom set in the small town of Grand, Pennsylvania. With John Randolph as Harris Weldon, owner of the local piano factory, Grand's chief employer; Michael McKean (to April 1990) as Tom Smithson; Bonnie Hunt as Tom's wife, and Harris's niece, Carol Anne; Pamela Reed as Janice Pasetti, who lived in a trailer and cleaned homes for a living; Sara Rue as Janice's teenage daughter, Edda; John Neville as Harris's trusty servant, Desmond; Jackey Vinson as Tom's son (by a prior marriage), Dylan; Andrew Lauer as local cop Wayne Kasmurski; and Joel Murray as Harris's gadabout son, Norris. Michael Leeson created the series, which was scheduled Thursdays at 9:30 P.M., following *Cheers*. Ratings were consistently disappointing, and it was abruptly pulled from NBC's schedule before its three-episode finale had concluded.

GRAND CHANCE ROUNDUP   CBS
17 FEBRUARY 1951–4 AUGUST 1951   A talent contest for young people, *Grand Chance Roundup* was set at a Western ranch, though it was broadcast Saturday mornings from Philadelphia. Gene Crane and Richard Caulk cohosted the show, and Thomas Freebairn-Smith produced it.

THE GRAND JURY   SYNDICATED
1959   This half-hour crime show starred Lyle Bettger as Harry Driscoll and Harold J. Stone as John Kennedy, two grand jury investigators.

THE GRAND OLE OPRY (STARS OF THE GRAND OLE OPRY)   SYNDICATED/ABC
1955–1957 (SYNDICATED); 15 OCTOBER 1955–15 SEPTEMBER 1956 (ABC)   This country-and-western musical series was filmed at Opryland in Nashville; the show began on radio in 1925 and is still broadcast on WSM every Saturday night. The ABC version was broadcast as a once-a-month replacement for *Ozark Jubilee.*

GRAND SLAM   CBS
27 JANUARY 1990–14 MARCH 1990   Short-lived hour adventure series about two rival bounty hunters in San Diego who decided to join forces. Featured were Paul Rodriguez as Pedro Gomez; John Schneider as his new partner, Dennis "Hardball" Bakelenekoff; Larry Gelman as Irv Schlosser; and Abel Franco as Al Ramirez. The series premiered in the treasured time slot immediately after the 1990 Super Bowl

telecast, and ranked 15th for the week. Audiences fled in droves by the following week, as the series fell to 68th place, and never recovered.

GRANDPA GOES TO WASHINGTON   NBC
7 SEPTEMBER 1978–16 JANUARY 1979   An hour-long comedy-drama about a recently retired college professor who was asked to run for the United States Senate, did so, and won. With Jack Albertson as the irascible but principled new Senator, Josephus (Joe) Kelley; Larry Linville as his son, Kevin Kelley, a two-star general at the Pentagon with whose family Joe moved in; Sue Ane Langdon as Kevin's wife, Rosie Kelley, a health-food fanatic; Michele Tobin as their daughter, Cathleen; Sparky Marcus as their son, Kevin Jr.; and Madge Sinclair as Madge, Joe's secretary. The show was produced by Paramount TV.

GRAPEVINE   CBS
15 JUNE 1992–27 JULY 1992   Sex was the subject of this sitcom whose central characters were three young adults living in Miami. With Jonathan Penner as David, a restaurateur; Lynn Clark as David's girlfriend, Susan, a cruise line executive; and Steven Eckholdt as David's brother, Thumper, a sportscaster. Created by David Frankel, the series was shot in a pseudo-documentary style using inserts in which the characters commented on the action.

GRAVEDALE HIGH   NBC
8 SEPTEMBER 1990–7 SEPTEMBER 1991   This half-hour Saturday-morning cartoon show was officially titled *Rick Moranis in Gravedale High*. Moranis provided the voice of lead character Mr. Schneider, the new teacher of a class of young monsters: Sid, Cleofatra, J. P., Blanche, Frankentyke, Vinnie Stoker, Gill Waterman, and Duzer. Ms. Crone was the headmistress.

THE GRAY GHOST   SYNDICATED
1957   This Civil War series starred Tod Andrews as Major John Mosby, a daring Confederate soldier. The character was based on fact: John Mosby was a young lawyer who joined the Forty-Third Battalion of the First Virginia Cavalry and organized an effective guerilla unit. Created and produced by Lindsley Parsons, the series was distributed by CBS Film Sales.

THE GREAT ADVENTURE   CBS
27 SEPTEMBER 1963–18 SEPTEMBER 1964   Van Heflin hosted this American historical anthology series, which was produced by John Houseman.

THE GREAT AMERICAN DREAM MACHINE   PBS
6 JANUARY 1971–9 FEBRUARY 1972   This unusual, and often irreverent, magazine series incorporated a little bit of everything: interviews, short filmed segments, satirical features, and musical numbers. Regular contributors included Marshall Efron, Andrew Rooney, Nicholas von Hoffman, Ken Shapiro and Chevy Chase (the two heads who pantomimed to music at the beginning of each show), and author Studs Terkel (who was usually seen conversing with a few folks at a Chicago bar). A. H. Perlmutter and Jack Willis were the executive producers of the show, which was first seen in a ninety-minute format; in the fall of 1971 it was trimmed to sixty minutes.

GREAT CIRCUSES OF THE WORLD   ABC
26 FEBRUARY 1989–16 APRIL 1989   Mary Hart hosted this series, which, as its title suggests, was taped on location at various circuses all over the world. A similar series had aired in prime time a quarter century earlier: see *International Showtime*.

THE GREAT DEFENDER   FOX
5 MARCH 1995; 10 JULY 1995–31 JULY 1995   A member of the small fraternity of TV series to be canceled after just one showing (though it would later be briefly revived), *The Great Defender* told the story of Lou Frischetti, a streetsmart Boston lawyer who advertised his services on television (with a vocal group singing "The Great Defender"

to the tune of "The Great Pretender") before being asked to join a snooty Beacon Hill law firm. The cast included Michael Rispoli as Lou Frischetti; Peter Krause as Crosby Caulfield, a young associate at the firm; Kelly Rutherford as Lou's investigator, Frankie Collet; Rhoda Gemignani as Lou's mother, Pearl, who ran the office out of her son's apartment and who accompanied him to his new job; Richard Kiley as Jason DeWitt, senior partner at Osbourne, Merritt and DeWitt, and Caulfield's grandfather; and Carlos Sanz as assistant district attorney Jerry Perez. Although set in Boston, the series was filmed in Toronto. Following a disastrously low-rated premiere the series was placed on hiatus.

GREAT ESCAPES NBC
27 AUGUST 1993–15 OCTOBER 1993   Umbrella title for two Friday night miniseries: "Trade Winds," a six-hour romantic saga set on the Caribbean island of St. Martin, with Michael Michele as Maxine Philips and Michael McLafferty as Ocean Sommers, two young people from rival families who fell in love (the sixth hour was preempted by the network); and "The Secrets of Lake Success," a four-hour potboiler about the quarreling heirs of pharmaceutical magnate Stuart Atkins III (played by Brian Keith), with Liz Vassey as daughter Suzy, Ryan Phillipe as son Stew, and Valerie Perrine as Honey Potts Atkins, their mother.

GREAT GHOST TALES NBC
6 JULY 1961–21 SEPTEMBER 1961   Frank Gallop hosted this half-hour color anthology series, which appears to have been the last live dramatic series on commercial television. Richard Thomas (of *The Waltons*) made one of his earliest TV appearances on 24 August in Saki's "Sredni Vashtar," costarring with Judith Evelyn.

THE GREAT GILDERSLEEVE SYNDICATED
1955   Throckmorton P. Gildersleeve was created by Harold Peary on radio's *Fibber McGee and Molly.* In 1941, the bombastic politician won his own series; this was one of radio's first spinoffs. Peary played the role until 1950 when Willard Waterman took over. When the series came to television in 1955, Waterman continued to play the role of Gildersleeve, the water commissioner of Summerfield. Also featured were Stephanie Griffin as his niece (and ward), Marjorie Forrester; Ronald Keith as his nephew (and ward), Leroy Forrester; Lillian Randolph as their housekeeper, Birdie Lee Coggins (she had originated the role on radio); Willis Bouchey as Mayor Terwilliger, Gildy's boss; Forrest Lewis as Mr. Peavey, the town druggist; Barbara Stuart as Bessie, Gildy's secretary; and Shirley Mitchell as Leila Ransom.

THE GREAT GRAPE APE
See TOM AND JERRY

GREAT MYSTERIES SYNDICATED
1973   An undistinguished half-hour anthology series.

GREAT PERFORMANCES PBS
1974–   Classical music and dance programs are the primary components of this series produced by Jac Venza at New York's WNET, but some dramatic presentations are also included, such as "Jennie: Lady Randolph Churchill," a seven-parter starring Lee Remick and written by Julian Mitchell. By far the most popular (and most highly acclaimed) presentation was *Brideshead Revisited,* an eleven-part adaptation of Evelyn Waugh's novel chronicling a young man's involvement with an aristocratic British family during the 1920s and 1930s. Featured were Jeremy Irons as Charles Ryder (from whose point of view the story was told); Anthony Andrews as his friend, Sebastian Flyte; Laurence Olivier as Lord Marchmain, Sebastian's father; Claire Bloom as Lady Marchmain, Sebastian's mother; Diana Quick as Julia, Sebastian's sister; John Gielgud as Edward Ryder; and Nickolas Grace as Anthony Blanche. The program was produced in England (with exteriors filmed at Castle Howard in Yorkshire) by Granada Television. Waugh's novel was adapted by John Mortimer. The series premiered on *Great Performances* 18 January 1982 and was subsequently rerun.

Other notable performances have included "Big Blonde," with Sally Kellerman, an adaptation of Dorothy Parker's story (30 November 1980); "Judy Garland: The Concert Years" (22 March 1985); "Irving Berlin's America," with Diana Ross, Willie Nelson, and others (7 March 1986); "The Ebony Tower," with Laurence Olivier and Roger Rees (6 February 1987); "Monsignor Quixote," with Alec Guinness and Leo McKern (13 February 1987); John O'Hara's "Natica Jackson," with Michelle Pfeiffer and Brian Kerwin (6 November 1987); "The Mikado," directed by Jonathan Miller (28 October 1988); "Baryshnikov Dances Balanchine" (13 January 1989); and "Mozart in Salzburg" (9 March 1990); "Hamlet," with Kevin Kline (2 November 1990); "The Marriage of Figaro," directed by Peter Sellars (14 December 1990); Paul McCartney's "Liverpool Oratorio," with Kiri Te Kanawa and Jerry Hadley (30 October 1991); "Suddenly Last Summer," with Maggie Smith and Natasha Richardson (6 January 1993); "The Mother," by Paddy Chayefsky, with Anne Bancroft, Anne Meara, and Joan Cusack (24 October 1994; the original version of Chayefsky's story aired on *Philco Television Playhouse* in 1954); and "The Music of Kurt Weill: September Songs" (25 January 1995).

GREAT ROADS OF AMERICA   SYNDICATED
1973   Andy Griffith narrated this half-hour documentary series, which focused on American highways and byways.

GREAT SCOTT!   FOX
4 OCTOBER 1992–29 NOVEMBER 1992   Half-hour sitcom about a suburban teenager with an overactive imagination. The stories were laced with Scott's fantasies as he coped with the crises of adolescence. With Tobey Maguire as Taft High School student Scott Melrod; Nancy Lenehan as his mother, Beverly; Ray Baker as his father, Walt; Sarah Koskoff as his sister, Nina; and Kevin Connolly as his friend, Larry. The Sunday night series perished quickly opposite CBS's *60 Minutes* and ABC's *Life Goes On*.

THE GREAT SPACE COASTER   SYNDICATED
1981–1986   A half-hour series of songs and stories for children, presented by three humans and several life-sized animal figures. With Emily Bindiger as Francine; Chris Gifford as Danny; Ray Stephens as Roy; Kevin J. Clash as Goriddle Gorilla; John Lovelady as Knock Knock the bird and Edison the Elephant; Jim Martin as Gary Gnu and M.T. Promises.

THE GREAT TALENT HUNT
See HENRY MORGAN'S GREAT TALENT HUNT

THE GREAT WAR   SYNDICATED
1964   Michael Redgrave narrated this documentary of World War II.

GREAT WEEKEND   SYNDICATED
1988   Weekend magazine series cohosted by Bob Goen and Dale Harimoto.

THE GREATEST AMERICAN HERO   ABC
18 MARCH 1981–27 MAY 1981; 26 AUGUST 1981–19 NOVEMBER 1982; 6 JANUARY 1983–3 FEBRUARY 1983   Stephen J. Cannell created this tongue-in-cheek fantasy series about a high school teacher who encountered an alien spacecraft in the California desert and was given a red suit, which, when worn, endowed him with superhuman powers. Unfortunately, he immediately lost the instruction book which had come with it, and was forced to learn his new powers of flight, invisibility, and X-ray vision through trial and error. William Katt (the son of Bill Williams and Barbara Hale of *Kit Carson* and *Perry Mason,* respectively) starred as the teacher, Ralph Hinkley. Robert Culp costarred as Bill Maxwell, a zealous FBI agent who had observed the alien encounter and who persuaded Ralph to use his powers on Maxwell's cases. Connie Sellecca also costarred as attorney Pam Davidson, Ralph's girlfriend (they were married in January 1983). Brandon Williams appeared in the spring 1981 epi-

sodes as Kevin, the young son of the divorced Hinkley, and Simone Griffeth was seen occasionally as his ex-wife, Alicia. Also featured during the first season were four of Hinkley's students at Whitney High: Michael Pare as Tony; Faye Grant as Rhonda Harris; Don Cervantes as Rodriguez; and Jesse D. Goins as Cyler.

Less than two weeks after the show's premiere, John Hinckley attempted to assassinate President Reagan (the former host of *Death Valley Days* and *General Electric Theater*). Shortly afterward, ABC announced that in episodes yet to be filmed, Katt's character would be known simply as "Mr. H." In the one or two shows that had been filmed but not yet televised, references to "Hinkley" were overdubbed "Hanley." When the series returned to the air in August 1981, however, Hinkley's surname had been restored.

The Greatest American Hero's opening theme, "Believe It or Not," was composed by Mike Post and Stephen Geyer, and sung by Joey Scarbury; it was released as a record in the summer of 1981 and became a number-one hit. Reruns of the series were seen on ABC during the summer of 1984.

THE GREATEST GIFT   NBC

30 AUGUST 1954–1 JULY 1955   Broadcast live from Philadelphia, this daytime serial was one of the first to center around physicians. It starred Phillip Foster as Dr. Phil Stone, who had returned to his home town of Ridgeton after the Korean War to take over the practice of his late uncle; and Anne Burr as Dr. Eve Allen (apparently TV's first woman doctor), Phil's romantic interest. Also featured were Janet Ward (as Eve's sister, Fran), Gene Peterson (as Ned), Henry Barnard, Joe Draper, Marion Russell, and Jack Klugman.

THE GREATEST MAN ON EARTH   ABC

3 DECEMBER 1952–19 FEBRUARY 1953   Ted Brown hosted this prime-time game show on which five male contestants competed; each man had been "nominated" by a woman, who was also present on stage. The game consisted of several rounds, in which the men went on a scavenger hunt, played charades, or tried to fashion a dress from a few yards of material. One contestant was eliminated after each round, and the man who remained was crowned "The Greatest Man on Earth." The half-hour series was produced by Walt Framer.

THE GREATEST SHOW ON EARTH   ABC

17 SEPTEMBER 1963–8 SEPTEMBER 1964   This hour-long adventure series was based on Cecil B. DeMille's 1952 film. The TV version starred Jack Palance as Johnny Slate, the circus boss, and Stu Erwin as Otto King, the business manager. Among the guest stars who appeared were Brenda Vaccaro (in "Don't Look Down, Don't Look Back," 8 October, her first major TV role), Ruby Keeler (in "The Show Must Go On—To Orange City," 28 January, a rare TV appearance), and Buster Keaton (in "You're All Right, Ivy," 28 April, also a rare TV appearance). Stanley Colbert produced the series.

GREATEST SPORTS LEGENDS   SYNDICATED

1973–1983   Athletes are the subject of this film and interview series, hosted by Paul Hornung (1973–1976), Reggie Jackson (1976–1977), Tom Seaver (1977–1979), George Plimpton (1979–1981), Ken Howard (1981–1982), and Jayne Kennedy (1982–1983). Produced by Berl Rotfeld, the program was originally headquartered in Philadelphia, but later moved to the La Costa Resort at Carlsbad, California.

GREEN ACRES   CBS

15 SEPTEMBER 1965–7 SEPTEMBER 1971   The format of this situation comedy, another of the several CBS "rural" shows, was the converse of *The Beverly Hillbillies:* A wealthy couple left the big city to live in the hinterlands. Like *Petticoat Junction,* *Green Acres* was set in Hooterville, and many members of the *Junction* cast occasionally appeared on *Acres* as well. Principals included: Eddie Albert as Oliver Douglas, a New York lawyer who had always longed for the country life; Eva Gabor as his fashionable wife, Lisa Douglas, who reluctantly agreed to accompany him; Pat

Buttram as Mr. Haney, a fast-talking local who tried to sell the Douglases everything; Tom Lester as Eb Dawson, the Douglases' handyman; Frank Cady as storekeeper Sam Drucker; Alvy Moore as Hank Kimball, the local agricultural agent; Hank Patterson as pig farmer Fred Ziffel, owner of Arnold Ziffel, the smartest pig in town (Arnold was really owned and trained by Frank Inn); Sid Melton as carpenter Alf Monroe; and Mary Grace Canfield as Alf's sister, and partner in the business, Ralph Monroe. Jay Sommers produced the show. Most of the cast was reassembled for a TV-movie sequel, "Return to Green Acres," broadcast on CBS 18 May 1990.

THE GREEN HORNET
ABC

9 SEPTEMBER 1966–14 JULY 1967   Created by George Trendle, *The Green Hornet* first appeared on radio in 1936. His secret identity was that of Britt Reid, editor and publisher of the *Daily Sentinel;* as the masked Green Hornet, he was a dedicated crimefighter. He was also the grandnephew of the Lone Ranger (Trendle also created that masked crimefighter). Reid's secret identity was known only by three people: Kato, his houseboy; Lenore Case, his secretary; and Frank Scanlon, the district attorney. On television Van Williams starred as Britt Reid/The Green Hornet. Also featured were Bruce Lee (later star of countless martial arts films) as Kato; Wende Wagner as Lenore Case (Casey); Walter Brooke as Frank Scanlon; and Lloyd Gough as Mike Axford, a former cop who is now the paper's police reporter. The series, which tried to capitalize on the popularity of *Batman* (another masked crimefighter), was produced by Richard Bluel.

GRIFF
ABC

29 SEPTEMBER 1973–5 JANUARY 1974   This lackluster crime show starred Lorne Greene (late of *Bonanza*) as Wade Griffin, a former cop who became a private eye. With Ben Murphy as his young partner, Mike Murdock; Vic Tayback as Captain Barney Marcus of the Los Angeles Police Department; and Patricia Stich as Gracie Newcombe, Griff and Mike's secretary.

GRIMMY

See MOTHER GOOSE AND GRIMM

GRINDL
NBC

15 SEPTEMBER 1963–13 SEPTEMBER 1964   Imogene Coca starred as Grindl, a house-maid employed by Mrs. Foster's Domestic Agency, in this half-hour sitcom. James Millhollin was featured as Mr. Anson Foster, her boss at the agency.

THE GROOVIE GOOLIES
CBS/ABC

12 SEPTEMBER 1971–17 SEPTEMBER 1972 (CBS); 25 OCTOBER 1975–5 SEPTEMBER 1976 (ABC)   This weekend cartoon series featured a bunch of musical monsters who resided in Horrible Hall. Executive producers: Lou Scheimer and Norm Prescott. The Goolies had first appeared during the 1970–1971 season on *Sabrina and the Groovie Goolies* (see also *Sabrina, the Teenage Witch*).

GROUP ONE MEDICAL
SYNDICATED

1988–1989   On this unusual half-hour daily series, real patients with real medical problems consulted real physicians—on camera. Former CBS News president Van Gordon Sauter produced the show for MGM Television.

GROWING PAINS
ABC

24 SEPTEMBER 1985–27 AUGUST 1992   A durable half-hour family sitcom, with Alan Thicke as psychiatrist Jason Seaver, who shifted his practice to his Long Island home in order to spend more time with his family; Joanna Kerns as his wife, Maggie, who went to work as a newspaper reporter; Kirk Cameron as their elder son, Mike; Tracey Gold as their daughter, Carol; and Jeremy Miller as younger son Ben. As the series started Mike and Carol were high school students. In the fall of 1988 Mike entered junior college, where he became interested in acting, and moved into a room over the Seavers' garage; in the fall of 1989 Carol, who had hoped to attend Colum-

bia, took a job with a publishing company. Meanwhile, Mom had been busy, too; Maggie became a TV reporter in the fall of 1987, and in October 1988 gave birth to a baby girl, Chrissy. Soon afterward Julie McCullough joined the cast as Julie, the nanny who fell in love with Mike; the 1988–1989 season ended with Mike's proposal of marriage, but the two decided not to get married. Other regulars included Josh Koenig as Mike's buddy Richard "Boner" Stabone; K. C. Martel as Mike's buddy Eddie; Chelsea Noble (spring 1990–1992) as Mike's new girlfriend, Kate McDonnell; and Bill Kirchenbauer (1987–1988) as Coach Lubbock, who was spun off into his own series (see *Just the Ten of Us*). By the fall of 1990 Mike had moved from home to New York City to study acting, and Carol was enrolled at Columbia. Ashley Johnson joined the cast as youngster Chrissy, replacing Kristen and Kelsey Dohring. For the series's final season, Mike moved back home, into an apartment above the garage. He brought back with him Luke Brower (Leonardo DiCaprio), a homeless 15-year-old he had befriended. Tracey Gold, who had become severely anorexic, was suspended from the show; it was explained that her character, Carol, had gone to study in London.

THE GROWING PAYNES   DUMONT
20 OCTOBER 1948–3 AUGUST 1949   This early domestic sitcom starred Elaine Stritch and Ed Holmes, and featured David Anderson as their son.

THE GRUDGE MATCH   SYNDICATED
1991 *The People's Court* met *American Gladiators* on this one. People with disputes faced off against each other in a series of three one-minute rounds, using a choice of "weapons" such as oversize boxing gloves, paint, or food. The audience then determined the winner. Steve Albert and pro wrestler Jesse "the Body" Ventura were the commentators, Paula McClure interviewed the combatants, and Michael Buffer was the ring announcer.

GRUEN GUILD PLAYHOUSE   ABC/DUMONT
27 SEPTEMBER 1951–13 DECEMBER 1951 (ABC); 17 JANUARY 1952–7 AUGUST 1952 (DU-MONT)   This half-hour dramatic anthology series was produced by Leon Fromkess.

GUESS AGAIN   CBS
14 JUNE 1951–21 JUNE 1951   Short-lived prime-time game show hosted by Mike Wallace, on which contestants tried to answer questions based on a routine acted out by a celebrity panel. Al Span produced the half-hour show, which was replaced by *Amos and Andy*.

GUESS WHAT?   DUMONT
8 JULY 1952–26 AUGUST 1952   Dick Kollmar hosted this Tuesday-night game show on which a celebrity panel tried to identify subjects from clues supplied by the host.

GUESS WHAT HAPPENED   NBC
7 AUGUST 1952–21 AUGUST 1952   This Thursday-night current events quiz was hosted by NBC newscaster John Cameron Swayze.

GUEST HOUSE (GENERAL ELECTRIC GUEST HOUSE)   CBS
1 JULY 1951–2 SEPTEMBER 1951   A summer replacement for *The Fred Waring Show*, this series blended a celebrity quiz with comedy and music. Oscar Levant and Durward Kirby cohosted the show.

A GUEST IN YOUR HOME   NBC
5 MARCH 1951–30 MARCH 1951   This short-lived fifteen-minute daytime series featured poet Edgar Guest and was directed by Frank Jacoby.

GUESTWARD HO!   ABC
29 SEPTEMBER 1960–21 SEPTEMBER 1961   Based on the book by Patrick Dennis and Barbara Hooton, this situation comedy told the story of a couple who left New York

to buy a dude ranch in New Mexico. With Joanne Dru (sister of *Hollywood Squares'* Peter Marshall) as Babs Hooton; Mark Miller as her husband, Bill; Flip Mark as their son, Brook; J. Carrol Naish as Hawkeye, the local Indian chief; Earle Hodgins as Lonesome, the Hootons' foreman; Jolene Brand as Pink Cloud, Hawkeye's assistant at the trading post; and Tony Montenaro, Jr., as Rocky.

GUIDE RIGHT   DUMONT
25 FEBRUARY 1952–5 FEBRUARY 1954   This variety program was produced in cooperation with the United States Army and Air Force recruiting offices. Each show was hosted by a different guest celebrity, and music was provided by the Eastern Air Defense Command Band. Barry Shear directed the show.

GUIDELINE
See THE CATHOLIC HOUR

THE GUIDING LIGHT   CBS
30 JUNE 1952–   *The Guiding Light* began on radio in 1937 and came to television fifteen years later; it was the only radio serial to make a really successful transition to the new medium. Created by Irna Phillips, it went through several changes of leading characters and locations before settling down in the late 1940s to concentrate on the Bauer family, a close-knit German-American family who settled in the town of Springfield. Agnes Nixon (who later created *One Life to Live* and *All My Children*) succeeded Irna Phillips as head writer when Phillips left the show to create *As the World Turns*. Jerome and Bridget Dobson, who had written for *General Hospital*, were the head writers during much of the 1970s; Pamela Long Hammer (later known as Pamela Long after her divorce from *Guiding Light* cast member Charles Jay Hammer) was head writer during much of the 1980s. David Lesan was the original producer of the TV incarnation of the series, but was soon succeeded by Lucy Rittenberg, who held the job for more than twenty years. Allen Potter later became the executive producer, as did Gail Kobe. Joe Willmore later became executive producer, and was succeeded by Robert Calhoun in 1989.

The Guiding Light and *Search for Tomorrow* were the last television serials to expand from fifteen to thirty minutes a day (both did so in September 1968); *The Guiding Light* expanded to a full hour on 7 November 1977. In 1978 it officially dropped the word *The* from its title. When *Search for Tomorrow* left the air at the end of 1986, *Guiding Light* took its place as TV's longest-running daytime drama. The show celebrated its fiftieth anniversary in broadcasting in mid-1987. It marked its fortieth anniversary on television with a prime time special on 12 June 1992. *Guiding Light* won Emmys as outstanding daytime drama series in 1979–1980 and in 1981–1982. Through the 1980s its ratings placed it near the middle of the daytime pack.

As the action began in 1952, the central characters were the several members of the Bauer clan, and the cast in the early years included: Theo Goetz as Fred (Papa) Bauer, a widower with three grown children (Goetz played the role from 1949 until his death in 1973); Lyle Sudrow (1952–1959) and Ed Bryce (1959–1969) as his son, Bill Bauer, who was believed killed in an air crash (he showed up again in 1979); Charita Bauer as Bill's wife, Bertha (Charita Bauer was the only member of the original television cast still on the show in 1984; following her death in 1985, cast member Jerry ver Dorn delivered an on-the-air tribute to her); Jone Allison (1952) and Ellen Demming as Papa's daughter, Meta (Bauer) (White) Roberts; Helen Wagner and Lisa Howard as Papa's daughter, Trudy, who moved away to New York with her husband shortly after the TV series began; Ron Walken (later known as Christopher Walken), Michael Allen, Paul Prokop, Gary Pillar, Bob Pickering, and Don Stewart as lawyer Michael Bauer, son of Bill and Bertha; Pat Collins, Bob Gentry, Mart Hulswit, Richard van Vleet, and Peter Simon as Dr. Ed Bauer, son of Bill and Bertha; Herb Nelson as Joe Roberts, Meta Bauer's second husband; Les Damon, Barnard Hughes, Sydney Walker, and William Roerick as Dr. Bruce Banning, Meta's third husband; Susan Douglas as Kathy Roberts Lang, Joe Roberts's daughter by a prior marriage, who was killed in a car crash in 1958; James Lipton

(1953–1962) as Dr. Dick Grant, Kathy's second husband; Whit Connor as Mark Holden, who also married Kathy; Zina Bethune (to 1959), Judy Robinson, Abigail Kellogg (1959–1961), Nancy Malone (1961–1964), Ellen Weston, and Gillian Spencer as Kathy's daughter, Robin Lang Holden, who was killed by a truck; Ernest Graves as Alex Bowden, Robin's first husband; Bernie Grant (1957–1971) as Dr. Paul Fletcher, who married Robin after he accidentally shot his first wife; Joan Gray and Elizabeth Hubbard as Anne Fletcher, Paul's unfortunate first wife; Joyce Holden and Lynne Rogers (1958–1962) as Marie Wallace, who married Dick Grant; Sandy Dennis, Diane Genter, and Lin Pierson as Alice Holden; Virginia Dwyer and Louise Platt as Ruth Jennings, who later married Mark Holden; Tarry Green as Joey Roberts, Kathy's younger brother; Joseph Campanella as artist Joe Turino; Kay Campbell as Helene Benedict, mother of Anne Fletcher; John Gibson, John Buloff, Paul McGrath, and Lester Rawlins as Henry Benedict, father of Ann Fletcher; Sandy Smith as Julie Conrad, who became Michael Bauer's first wife.

Among the principal players during the 1960s and early 1970s were: Pamela King and Chase Crosley as Jane Fletcher, Paul Fletcher's half-sister; Phil Sterling as George Hayes, who married Jane; Bernard Kates as Ben Scott; June Graham as Maggie Scott, his wife and Bill Bauer's secretary; Fran Myers as their daughter Peggy Scott Thorpe; Sheldon Golomb, Daniel Fortas, Donald Melvin, Don Scardino, and Erik Howell as Johnny Fletcher, son of Paul Fletcher, who was murdered in 1968 (Peggy was tried for the crime, but was acquitted); Lynne Adams, Kathryn Hays, Barbara Rodell, and Lynne Adams (again) as Leslie Jackson, who married Ed Bauer in 1967, divorced him in 1970, and married Ed's brother Mike in 1971; Stefan Schnabel as Dr. Stephen Jackson, Leslie's father; Jennifer Kirschner, Paula Schwartz, Elissa Leeds, Tisch Raye, Robin Mattson, Katherine Justice, and Elvera Roussel as Hope Bauer, daughter of Mike and Julie; Caroline McWilliams as Janet Mason; Millette Alexander as Dr. Sara McIntyre, a sex therapist; Ray Fulmer as Lee Gantry, who married Sara; Jan Sterling as Mildred Foss; Victoria Wyndham and Melinda Fee as Charlotte Waring, who was briefly married to Michael Bauer; Michael Higgins and William Smithers as Stanley Norris, who married Leslie Bauer and was later murdered; Augusta Dabney and Barbara Berjer as Barbara Norris, Stanley's ex-wife; Lynn Deerfield and Maureen Garrett as Holly Norris, daughter of Barbara and Stanley, who married Ed Bauer, and would later marry Roger Thorpe; Roger Newman as Ken Norris, Barbara and Stanley's son, who married Janet Mason; Ben Hayes, Berkeley Harris, Ed Zimmerman, and Anthony Call as Dr. Joe Werner, who married Sara McIntyre; Nancy Addison as Kit Vestid; Peter D. Greene and Dan Hamilton as David Vestid; David Pendleton as Gil Mehron; Olivia Cole as Deborah Mehron; Mike Durrell as Peter Wexler; Paul Carpinelli as Flip Malone; Grace Matthews as Claudia Dillman; Roger Morden as Dr. Carey; William Beaudine as Dr. King; Billy Dee Williams and James Earl Jones as Dr. Jim Frazier; Carol Teitel as Mrs. Ballinger; Jeanne Arnold as Ellen Mason; Chris Sarandon as Tom Halverson; Christina Pickles as Linell Conway; Lois Holmes and Kate Harrington as Marion Conway; Tudi Wiggins as Karen Martin; and Rosetta LeNoire as Mrs. Herbert.

Also, Michael Zaslow as Roger Thorpe, a crook who married Holly Norris and was supposedly killed falling off a cliff in Santo Domingo (the body was never seen, and the character resurfaced in Springfield in 1988); Robert Gerringer and Robert Milli as his father, Adam Thorpe; Jordan Clarke as Dr. Tim Ryan (Clarke also played Billy Lewis); Maureen Silliman as Pam Chandler; Lenore Kasdorf as Rita Stapleton, who married Ed Bauer in 1978; Maureen Mooney as Ann Jeffers; T. J. Hargrave, Christopher Marcantel, Kevin Bacon, and Nigel Reed as T. J. (later known as Tim), a runaway taken in and later adopted by Joe and Sara Werner; Everett McGill as Chad Richards; Albert Zungallo, Gary Hannoch, Robbie Berridge, Phil MacGregor, and Michael O'Leary as Freddie Bauer (later known as Rick Bauer), son of Ed and Leslie; Lee Richardson as Captain Jim Swanson; Larry Gates as Ira Newton; Graham Jarvis as Charles Eiler; Madeline Sherwood as Betty Eiler; Barney McFadden and Ted Leplat as Andy Norris; Gina Foy and Cheryl Lynn Brown as Christina Bauer; Tom Aldredge as Victor Kincaid; Laryssa Lauret as Simone Morey Kincaid; Linda McCullough and Marsha Clark as Hilary Kincaid Bauer, half-sister of Ed and Mike; Ed Bryce (who had once played Bill Bauer) as William Morey; Chris Bernau,

Daniel Pilon, and Ron Raines as Alan Spaulding; Ben Hammer as Max Chapman; Delphi Harrington as Georgene Granger; Sudie Bond and Kate Wilkinson as Viola Stapleton; Frank Latimore as Emmet Scott; Shane Nickerson and Dai Stockton as Billy Fletcher; Denise Pence as Katie Parker; Stephen Yates as Ben McFarren; Janet Gray as Eve Stapleton, who married Ben in 1978; Tom O'Rourke as Dr. Justin Marler, who married Elizabeth Spaulding in 1979; Cindy Pickett and Carrie Mowery as Jacqueline Marler; Curt Dawson as Peter Chapman; Mark Travis as Jerry McFarren; Sofia Landon as Diane Ballard; Gordon Rigsby as Dean Blackford; Sandy Faison and JoBeth Williams as Brandy Sheloo; Nicholas Kepros as Wilbur Morrison; Kathleen Cullen as Amanda Wexler; Rita Lloyd as Lucille Wexler, who stabbed herself in a quarrel with her housekeeper; Burton Cooper as Dr. Mark Hamilton; Marcus Smythe as Gordon Middleton; Mark Pinter as Mark Evans; and Jane Elliot as split personality Carrie Todd.

Other regulars have included: Gregory Beecroft as Tony Reardon; Lisa Brown as his sister, Nola Reardon; Ellen Dolan and Ellen Parker as their sister, Maureen Reardon, who married Ed Bauer; Lee Lawson as their mother, Bea Reardon; Rebecca Hollen as Trish Lewis; Robert Newman as Trish's brother, Josh Lewis, who managed a singer; Tom Nielsen as the singer, Floyd Parker, Katie Parker's brother; Carolyn Ann Clark as nurse Leslie Ann Monroe, who contracted a fatal disease after being bitten by a mouse; Michael Tylo as mysterious Quint McCord (later known as Quentin Chamberlain); Beulah Garrick as Violet Renfield, Quint's housekeeper; Rose Alaio as Helena Manzini; Anna Stuart and Maeve Kinkead as Vanessa Chamberlain; William Roerick (in his second role) as her father, Henry Chamberlain; Lori Shelle as Gracie Middleton; Deborah May as Ivy Pierce; David Greenan as Dr. Greg Fairbanks; Kathleen Kellaigh as Lainie Marler; Kristen Vigard and Jennifer Cook as Morgan Richards; Geraldine Court as Morgan's mother, Jennifer Richards, Lucille Wexler's housekeeper; John Wesley Shipp as Kelly Nelson, who married Morgan; Jerry ver Dorn as Ross Marler, a lawyer; Michael J. Stark as Joe Bradley; Bill Herndon as Jennifer's brother, Chet Stafford; Harley Venton as lawyer Derek Colby; Eileen Dietz as Lynette; Giancarlo Esposito as Clark Tynan; Micki Grant as Helen Tynan; Leslie O'Hara as Rebecca Cartwright/Mona Enright (Deborah Eckols appeared as Rebecca in flashback sequences, before the character had had plastic surgery); Krista Tesreau, Kimberly Simms, Ann Hamilton, and Barbara Crampton as Mindy Lewis; Judi Evans and Beth Chamberlin as Beth Raines; Harley Kozak as Annabelle Sims; Lori Putnam as Susannah; Susan Pratt as Dr. Claire Ramsey; Warren Burton as Warren Andrews; Jim Rebhorn as Bradley Raines; Tina Sloan as Lillian Raines; Benjamin Hendrickson as Silas Crocker; Mary D. Lepera as Kelly Louise, Nola's daughter; Jessica Zutterman, Carl Tye Evans, and Rick Hearst as Alan Michael Spaulding, son of Alan and Hope Spaulding (born in 1981, the lad had become a teenager by 1987); Stephen Joyce as Eli Sims; Larry Gates as H. B. Lewis; Jarrod Ross, Grant Aleksander, and John Bolger as Philip Spaulding; Beverlee McKinsey and Marj Dusay as his sister, Baroness Alexandra von Halkein; Kim Zimmer as Reva Shayne Lewis; Michael Woods as Dr. Jim Reardon; Vincent Irrizarry as Lujack Luvonaczek, and as his twin, Nick McHenry; and Damion Scheller as Jonathan Brooks.

Other additions have included: Charles Jay Hammer (also known as Jay Hammer) as Fletcher Reade; Leslie Denniston as Maeve Stoddard Sampson, who married Fletcher in 1988; Larkin Malloy as Kyle Sampson; Jordan Clarke and Geoffrey Scott as Billy Lewis; Kristi Ferrell as Roxie Shayne, Reva's sister; Michael Wilding as Jackson Freemont; Kimi Parks as Dorie; Rebecca Staab as Jessie Matthews; Shawn Thompson as Simon Hall; Kassie Wesley as Chelsea Reardon; Lisby Larson as Calla; Terrell Anthony as Rusty Shayne; Ariane Munker as Christine; Jennifer Gatti, Paige Turco, and Wendy Moriz as Dinah Morgan; Jack Betts as John Cutler; Audrey Peters as Sarah Shayne; Gil Rogers as Hawk Shayne, who married Sarah in 1989; Robin Ward as Paul Valere; James M. Goodwin as Johnny Bauer, who successfully battled cancer; Ian Ziering as Cameron Stewart; Joe Lambie as Cameron's father, George Stewart; Nicolette Goulet as Meredith Reade, who married Rick Bauer in 1988; Geri Betzler as Lacey Bauer; Joseph Breen as Will Jeffries, who married Mindy Lewis in 1988; Frank Dicopoulos as Frank Cooper; Beth Ehlers as Harley Davidson Cooper, who married Alan-Michael Spaulding in 1989; Michelle Forbes as Sonni Lewis; W. T. Martin as Mick Sutton; Alexandra Neil as Rose McLerin; Mariann Aalda as Grace Battles; Elizabeth Dennehy, Sherry Stringfield, and Liz Keifer as Blake Lindsey; Jean Carol as Nadine Cooper; Maureen Garrett as Holly Thorpe; Suzy Cote as Samantha Marler; Morgan Englund as Dylan Lewis; Vince Williams as Hampton Speakes; Ashley Peldon and Kimberly J. Brown as Marah Shayne Lewis; Katel Pleven as Dana Jones; Carey Cromelin as Wanda Hite; Allison Daugherty as Rae Rooney; Patrick O'Connell as Neil Everest; William Bell Sullivan as Gary Swanson; Mark Derwin as A. C. Mallet; David Bishins as Daniel St. John; Amelia Marshall as Gilly Grant Speakes; and Christopher Pennock as Justin.

More recently, Jeff Gendelman as Matt Weiss; Melina Kanakaredes and Jennifer Roszell as Eleni Andros Cooper; Eugene Troobnick as Stavros Kouperakis; Melissa Hayden as Bridget Reardon; Jocelyn Seagrave as Julie Camaletti; Jeff Phillips, Leonard Stabb, and Sean McDermott as Hart Jessup; Mary Kay Adams as India von Halkein; Christine Langner as Tracy; Rachel Miner as Michelle Bauer, daughter of Ed and Maureen; Fiona Hutchinson as Jenna Bradshaw; Christopher Norris as Rebecca Nash; Monti Sharp and Russell Curry as David Grant; Hilary Edson as Eve Guthrie; Joe Lando (who was also appearing in *Dr. Quinn, Medicine Woman* in prime time) as Macauley West; Nia Long as Kat Speakes; Maeve McGuire as Selena; Justin Deas as Buzz Cooper; Sonia Satra as Lucy Cooper, Buzz's daughter; Marcy Walker as Tangie Hill; Sherilyn Wolter as George; Kelly Neal as Sidney Dickerson; Will Lyman as Carroll; Elizabeth Lawrence as Bess Lowell; John deVries and Larry Pine as Davis; Mark Margolis as Harry; Scott Hoxby as Patrick Cutter; Tammy Lang and Allison Janney as Donna and Ginger, the Spauldings' maids; Ron Foster and David Wolos-Fonteno as Dr. Charles Grant; Cynthia Watros as nurse Annie Dutton; Bill Martin as Sean Reardon; Bret Cooper as Shayne Lewis; Brian Buffinton as Bill Lewis; Gregory Burke as Ben Reade; Margaret Gwenver as Margaret Sedwick; Petronia Paley as Vivian Grant; Casey Rosenhaus as Marina Cooper; and Stuart Ward as Levy.

In an unusual switch to prime time, six *Guiding Light* cast members reprised their daytime roles in a TV-movie, "The Cradle Will Fall," telecast 24 May 1983 on CBS. Charita Bauer, Carolyn Ann Clark, Joe Ponazecki, Elvera Roussel, Peter Simon, and Jerry ver Dorn were all featured.

THE GUINNESS GAME SYNDICATED
1979   An unusual game show on which three contestants tried to predict whether a challenger would succeed in an endeavor to break one of the records listed in *The Guinness Book of World Records*. Don Galloway hosted the half-hour show. See also *The Spectacular World of Guinness Records*.

GULF PLAYHOUSE NBC
3 OCTOBER 1952–26 DECEMBER 1952   This half-hour dramatic anthology series was seen on Friday nights.

THE GULF ROAD SHOW NBC
2 SEPTEMBER 1948–30 JUNE 1949   This half-hour variety show was hosted for most of its run by Bob Smith, who was better known as the emcee of *Howdy Doody;* Dan Seymour also hosted the series for several weeks in 1949.

GULLIVER (THE ADVENTURES OF GULLIVER) ABC
14 SEPTEMBER 1968–5 SEPTEMBER 1970   The adventures of Gary Gulliver, son of Lemuel Gulliver (*the* Gulliver), were chronicled in this Saturday-morning cartoon show; searching for his father, Gary sailed to Lilliput and there befriended the little people.

THE GUMBY SHOW NBC/SYNDICATED
16 MARCH 1957–16 NOVEMBER 1957 (NBC); 1966 (SYNDICATED); 1988 (SYNDICATED)   This kids' show was spun off from *Howdy Doody:* Gumby was first introduced on that show in 1956. Gumby and his horse, Pokey, were movable clay

figures; their adventures, like those of *Davey and Goliath,* were filmed via the process of "pixillation"—shooting a few frames at a time, moving the figures slightly, and shooting a few more frames. *The Gumby Show* was first hosted by Bobby Nicholson, who had played both Clarabell and Cornelius Cobb on *Howdy Doody,* and later by Pinky Lee. Art Clokey created the series. The network was seen on Saturday mornings; two sets of new episodes were produced for syndication, one in 1966, the other in 1988.

THE GUMMI BEARS   NBC
14 SEPTEMBER 1985–2 SEPTEMBER 1989
DISNEY'S GUMMI BEARS/WINNIE THE POOH HOUR   ABC
9 SEPTEMBER 1989–1 SEPTEMBER 1990   The first network Saturday-morning cartoon series from Disney studios featured the Gummi Bears, a sextet of bears who tried to protect their human friends in the kingdom of Dunwyn, Princess Calla and Cavin the page, from evil forces. After a four-year run on NBC, the series switched to ABC, where it merged with another Disney cartoon show, *The New Adventures of Winnie the Pooh,* in a single hour program (see also that title). See also *Disney Afternoon.*

GUN SHY   CBS
15 MARCH 1983–19 APRIL 1983   Half-hour comedy-western based on the Disney Studios' *Apple Dumpling Gang* films. Set in Quake City, California, the show featured Barry Van Dyke (son of Dick Van Dyke) as Russell Donovan, a gambler saddled with two kids he won in a card game; Keith Mitchell and Adam Rich as Clovis, one of the two kids; Bridgette Anderson as Celia, the other kid; Geoffrey Lewis as Amos, one of the lamebrained townspeople; Tim Thomerson as Theodore, a buddy of Amos's; Henry Jones as Homer McCoy, Quake City's barber and sheriff; and Pat McCormick as Mound.

GUNG HO   ABC
5 DECEMBER 1986–6 FEBRUARY 1986; 6 JUNE 1987–27 JUNE 1987   Culture clash was the theme of this short-lived sitcom, based on the 1986 motion picture. ABC executives were so excited about the movie that they ordered the TV series pilot before the motion picture had even been released. *Gung Ho* was set in Hadleyville, Pa., where a Japanese automobile manufacturer had reopened a closed American plant. Featured were Gedde Watanabe as Kaz Kazuhiro, the manager; Scott Bakula as Hunt Stevenson, labor-management liaison; Sab Shimono as Saito, Kaz's assistant; Patti Yasutake as Kaz's wife, Umeki; Emily K. Kuroda as Saito's wife, Yukiko; Stephen Lee as Buster; Clint Howard as Googie; Rodney Kageyama as Ito; Heidi Banks as Randi; and Scott Atari as Kenji. Watanabe, Shimono, and Howard had all appeared in the film. *Gung Ho* is perhaps notable for having the largest number of Asian actors as regulars of any American TV series. The producers also retained a Japanese-American consulting firm to help ensure that the characterizations were not offensive to Asians or Asian-Americans.

GUNS OF PARADISE
See PARADISE

THE GUNS OF WILL SONNETT   ABC
8 SEPTEMBER 1967–15 SEPTEMBER 1969   This half-hour western starred Walter Brennan as Will Sonnett, a former Cavalry scout who raised his grandson after the boy's father, Jim Sonnett, ran off and became a gunfighter. Dack Rambo costarred as the grandson, Jeff Sonnett, who now wants to find his father. Together, Will and Jeff roamed the West looking for Jim. Jason Evers appeared occasionally as the wayward Jim. Fifty episodes were produced, all under the supervision of Aaron Spelling.

GUNSLINGER   CBS
9 FEBRUARY 1961–14 SEPTEMBER 1961   This hour-long western, a midseason replacement for *The Witness,* starred Tony Young as Cord, an agent for the U.S. Cavalry whose cover was that of a dangerous gunslinger. Also featured were Preston Foster

as Captain Zachary Wingate, commanding officer of the post to which Cord was assigned, Fort Scott in New Mexico Territory; John Pickard as Sergeant Major Murdock; Midge Ware as Amber (Amby) Hollister; Charles Gray as Pico McGuire; and Dee Pollock as Billy. Produced by Charles M. Warren.

GUNSMOKE CBS

10 SEPTEMBER 1955–1 SEPTEMBER 1975   Not only was *Gunsmoke* television's longest-running western, it was also television's longest-running prime-time series with continuing characters. The show began on radio in 1952, with William Conrad (later TV's *Cannon*) as Marshal Matt Dillon, tough lawman of Dodge City, Kansas; the show's producer, Norman Macdonnell, saw Dillon as a fallible antihero, and the show has been described as one of radio's most violent westerns. By 1955 Macdonnell and his associates John Meston and Charles Marquis Warren had decided to bring the show to television. John Wayne was offered the starring role but turned it down; he recommended a tall, relatively unknown actor for the part—James Arness. Arness, brother of Peter Graves (who began co-starring in *Fury* that season), had appeared in several movies, perhaps most notably in the title role of *The Thing* in 1950. Arness was hired, and three other performers were selected to fill out the cast: Amanda Blake as Kitty Russell, owner of the Long Branch saloon, whose relationship with Dillon was close, though never precisely delineated; Dennis Weaver as Chester B. Goode, Dillon's gimpy-legged deputy; and Milburn Stone as Doc Adams (his first name was Galen), the town's crusty but trusty physician. Stone remained with the show for its entire run (except when sidelined by a heart attack), Blake for nineteen seasons. The show began in 1955 as a half-hour series; John Wayne introduced the premiere episode, explaining to viewers that they were about to see a new kind of western.

The opening sequence that season featured Matt Dillon standing in "Boot Hill," Dodge City's graveyard, where he briefly introduced each episode. In 1956, a new opening sequence was shot, which featured Dillon and an unidentified badman squaring off in Dodge's Main Street (Dillon managed to outdraw the outlaw). The sequence was reshot over the years in part to reflect the expansion of Dodge City. By the 1970s, the gunfight sequence had been replaced by a new opening that featured shots of Dillon riding across the plains.

Gunsmoke became the number-one-rated series in its third season (1957–1958) and remained in that position for four seasons. In the fall of 1961 it expanded from a half hour to an hour, and its ratings declined over the next six years. The first changes in the cast were also made during the early 1960s. Dennis Weaver had made it clear by 1962 that he intended to leave the show; he made two pilots for new series, neither of which sold, and twice returned to *Gunsmoke*. In 1964, his third pilot—*Kentucky Jones*—sold, and he left the show for good that year. Ken Curtis was added that fall as Festus Haggen, a backwoodsman who became the new deputy and who provided the comic relief formerly supplied by Chester (Curtis, who had sung with Tommy Dorsey's orchestra at one time, had appeared as Festus in one or two episodes before becoming a regular).

Meanwhile, the producers had decided to add a fifth central character—a rugged male—in 1962. The role was first filled by Burt Reynolds as Quint Asper, a half-breed blacksmith; Reynolds lasted three seasons. In 1965, Roger Ewing joined the cast as Thad Greenwood, a young townsman; he left after two seasons. In the fall of 1967, Buck Taylor (son of character actor Dub Taylor) was added as gunsmith Newly O'Brian; Taylor, who first played a killer in a two-part episode, stayed with the show. A number of other people were occasionally seen as Dodge City's townsfolk. This group included: James Nusser as Louie Pheeters, the town drunk; Dabbs Greer (1956–1964) as Wilbur Jonas, a storekeeper; Charles Seel as Barney, the telegraph agent; Hank Patterson as Hank, the stableman; Howard Culver as Howie, the hotel clerk at the Dodge House; Sarah Selby (1962–1975) as Ma Smalley, boardinghouse owner; Woody Chamblis as Mr. Lathrop, a storekeeper; Roy Roberts as Mr. Bodkin, the banker; Tom Brown as rancher Ed O'Connor; Ted Jordan (1964–1975) as Nathan Burke, the freight agent; Charles Wagenheim as Halligan, another rancher; John

Harper as Percy Crump, the undertaker. Glenn Strange also appeared for many seasons as Sam, the bartender at the Long Branch.

Norman Macdonnell produced the series from 1955 until 1964, when differences with the show's other principals—including Arness—led to his departure. Arness gradually acquired more and more influence over the show, although the degree of his dominance is hard to ascertain because Arness almost never spoke to the press and loathed publicity; it is known, however, that the show's production schedule was arranged so that Arness rarely had to work more than three days a week. Macdonnell was succeeded as producer by Philip Leacock, who was in turn succeeded by John Mantley in 1967.

Gunsmoke's ratings had smoldered considerably by the end of the 1966–1967 season, and CBS programmers had decided to cancel it. CBS President William Paley interceded, however, and the decision was made to change its time slot from Saturday to Monday; that decision proved to be a wise one, for *Gunsmoke* zoomed back into Nielsen's top ten in 1967–1968, and remained there for six seasons. In all, 233 half-hour episodes were filmed, and more than 400 hour segments were made (the series was broadcast in color beginning with the 1966–1967 season); from 1961 to 1964, reruns of the half-hour shows were broadcast Tuesdays on CBS (and were titled *Marshal Dillon*), while the hour version ran Saturdays. Two made-for-TV movie sequels appeared in the late 1980s: in "Gunsmoke: Return to Dodge" (26 September 1987, with Arness, Blake, and Buck Taylor), Dillon had become a Colorado trapper and Miss Kitty had moved to New Orleans; in "Gunsmoke: The Last Apache" (18 March 1990, with only Arness from the old cast), Dillon learned he had fathered a daughter many years earlier. Three more made-for-TV movies, all starring Arness, aired between 1992 and 1994.

THE GUY LOMBARDO SHOW   SYNDICATED
1954   Half-hour musical series with Guy Lombardo and His Royal Canadians.

GUY LOMBARDO'S DIAMOND JUBILEE   CBS
6 MARCH 1956–12 JUNE 1956   In addition to hosting New Year's Eve festivities for decades, Guy Lombardo and His Royal Canadians were also featured on this half-hour musical series, which replaced *Meet Millie* in 1956; Lombardo's brothers—Carmen, Lebert, and Victor—joined him on the show. One of the regular features was the "Song of Your Life" contest, in which viewers were invited to write, describing how a particular song had affected their lives. Winning contestants appeared on the show and, in addition to winning $1,000, heard the orchestra play their song.

THE GUY MITCHELL SHOW   ABC
7 OCTOBER 1957–13 JANUARY 1958   Guy Mitchell, a popular recording artist of the early 1950s, hosted this Monday-night half-hour musical show, produced in Hollywood; the Van Alexander Orchestra accompanied him. Rock-and-roller Chuck Berry appeared on the show on 16 December.

GUYS NEXT DOOR   NBC
27 AUGUST 1990–13 AUGUST 1991   This Saturday-morning live-action show was a blatant attempt to capitalize on the success of the teen singing group New Kids on the Block (who also had their own Saturday show during the same season). The five Guys—Chris Wolf, Eddie Garcia, Damon Sharpe, Patrick Dancy, and Bobby Leslie—appeared in various comedy skits and performance videos. The series premiered in prime time before switching to Saturdays in September.

GYPSY   SYNDICATED
1965

THE GYPSY ROSE LEE SHOW   SYNDICATED
1958   One of America's foremost burlesque queens, Gypsy Rose Lee hosted two talk shows. The 1958 show was ninety minutes, the 1965 show thirty minutes.

HBO COMEDY SHOWCASE SYNDICATED

1992– Hour weekly series of standup comedy performances, taped at various locations. Produced by HBO for first-run syndication, the programs included reruns of performances originally broadcast on HBO plus all-new presentations taped especially for the series.

H.E.L.P. ABC

3 MARCH 1990–14 APRIL 1990 The initials stoood for Harlem Eastside Lifesaving Program, an experimental unit of New York City cops, firefighters, and paramedics working together under a single command. With John Mahoney as the leader, Captain Patrick Meacham, who sought to keep the unit functioning despite internecine warfare from other city departments; Tom Breznahan as rookie firefighter Jimmy Ryan; David Caruso as police officer Frank Sordoni; Lance Edwards as medic Mike Pappas; Kay Tong Lim as medic Danny Tran; Wesley Snipes as police officer Lou Barton; Marjorie Monaghan as E. Jean Ballentry; Kim Flowers as Rodriguez; Joe Urla as Alba; and Fionnula Flanagan as Kathleen Meacham, Patrick's wife. The hour series, created by Dick Wolf and Christopher Crowe, was filmed on location.

H. R. PUFNSTUF NBC

6 SEPTEMBER 1969–4 SEPTEMBER 1971 A children's fantasy series set at Living Island, with Jack Wild (the Artful Dodger in the film *Oliver!*) as Jimmy, Billie Hayes as Witchiepoo, and the Sid and Marty Krofft Puppets (one of whom was H. R. Pufnstuf, the island's mayor, who tried to help Jimmy get back home). The series spawned a 1970 theatrical film.

HAGEN CBS

1 MARCH 1980–24 MARCH 1980 Hour crime show starring Chad Everett as Paul Hagen, an expert animal tracker who became an investigator for a San Francisco attorney. With Arthur Hill as lawyer Carl Palmer, and Carmen Zapata as Palmer's housekeeper, Mrs. Chavez. Frank Glicksman, the executive producer, created the series with Charles Larson.

HAGGIS BAGGIS NBC

Nighttime: 30 JUNE 1958–29 SEPTEMBER 1958; *Daytime:* 30 JUNE 1958–19 JUNE 1959
Players won merchandise on this game show by identifying photos; each photo was gradually uncovered as questions were answered correctly. The winner could choose either a "haggis" or a "baggis" prize—the "haggis" category was comprised of luxury prizes, while the "baggis" group was utilitarian. Twenty-year-old Jack Linkletter, son of Art Linkletter, hosted the nighttime show, a summer replacement for *The Price Is Right*. The daytime version was hosted first by Fred Robbins, later by Dennis James.

HAIL THE CHAMP ABC

22 DECEMBER 1951–14 JUNE 1952; 27 DECEMBER 1952–20 MAY 1953 Saturday game show for children, on which two teams of youngsters competed in various stunts. Broadcast from Chicago, the show was hosted first by Herb Allen, and later by Howard Roberts with Angel Casey.

HAIL TO THE CHIEF ABC

9 APRIL 1985–21 MAY 1985; 18 JUNE 1985–30 JULY 1985 An unfunny sitcom about the first female president. The large cast included Patty Duke as President Julia Mansfield; Ted Bessell as her unfaithful husband, General Oliver Mansfield, a former astronaut; Ricky Paull Goldin as her son Doug; Quinn Cummings as her daughter, Lucy; Taliesin Jaffe as her son Willy; Maxine Stuart as Julia's swinging mother, Lenore; Joel Brooks as her gay Secret Service agent, Randy; Herschel Bernardi as national security adviser Helmut Luger; Glynn Turman as Secretary of Defense LaRue Hawkes; John Vernon as General Hannibal Stryker, chairman of the Joint Chiefs of Staff; Murray Hamilton as Senator Sam Cotton; Alexa Hamilton as Oliver's mistress, Darlene, a Soviet spy; Richard Paul as Reverend Billy Joe Bickerstaff; and Chick Vennera as Raoul, the White House butler. Raechel Donahue was the

announcer. Susan Harris created the show, which was intended to resemble her earlier hit sitcom, *Soap*. Harris blamed the series' demise on network interference; she told *TV Guide* that the finished product was "a bad show" that "should have been canceled."

THE 1/2 HOUR COMEDY HOUR ABC
5 JULY 1983–9 AUGUST 1983   The title of this fast-paced thirty-minute series is self-explanatory. Arsenio Hall and Thom Sharp were the cohosts; assisting them were fast-talking John Moschitta, Jr., John Paragon, Peter Isacksen, Vic Dunlop, Jan Hooks, Victoria Jackson, Barry Diamond, and Rod Hull and his puppet, Emu.

HALF-NELSON NBC
24 MARCH 1985–10 MAY 1985   A lighthearted crime show about a short private eye. With Joe Pesci as Rocky Nelson, a former New York cop who moved west to become an actor and went to work for a private security agency. Also with Victoria Jackson as Annie O'Hara, the office secretary; Fred Williamson as Chester Long, Rocky's boss at the Beverly Hills Patrol; Gary Grubbs as Lieutenant Hamill of the Beverly Hills police; Dick Butkus and Bubba Smith as Beau and Kurt, two of Rocky's co-workers; Dean Martin as Mr. Martin; and Tony as Hunk, the bull terrier. Former pro-footballers Butkus and Smith had previously appeared together on the 1984 crime show *Blue Thunder*.

HALF THE GEORGE KIRBY COMEDY HOUR SYNDICATED
1972   Impressionist George Kirby hosted this Toronto-based variety half hour. Among the regulars was Steve Martin.

HALLMARK HALL OF FAME NBC/CBS/PBS/ABC
6 JANUARY 1952–   One of television's best known dramatic anthology series, *Hallmark Hall of Fame* was a weekly series from 1952 until 1955; since that time it has been seen as a series of specials, with five or six presentations scheduled each season. Sponsored by Hallmark Cards ("When you care enough to send the very best. . ."), it was titled *Hallmark Television Playhouse* during its first two seasons, when it was a half-hour series. Sarah Churchill was the host, and occasional star, from 1952 until 1955. Mildred Freed Alberg produced the show for many seasons; George Schaefer succeeded her. A small sample of the many programs presented would include: "Hamlet," with Maurice Evans and Ruth Chatterton (26 April 1953); "Moby Dick," with Victor Jory (16 May 1954); "Macbeth," with Maurice Evans, Dame Judith Anderson, and House Jameson (28 November 1954); "Alice in Wonderland," with Eva Le Gallienne, Elsa Lanchester, and Reginald Gardiner (23 October 1955); "The Taming of the Shrew," with Maurice Evans and Diane Cilento (18 March 1956); "Born Yesterday," with Mary Martin and Arthur Hill (28 October 1956); "Man and Superman," with Maurice Evans (25 November 1956); "The Green Pastures," with Frederick O'Neal and Eddie "Rochester" Anderson (first broadcast 17 October 1957, it was restaged 23 May 1959); "Twelfth Night," with Maurice Evans, Rosemary Harris, and Piper Laurie (15 December 1957); "Hans Brinker," with Tab Hunter and Basil Rathbone (9 February 1958); "Winterset," with Martin Balsam, George C. Scott, and Piper Laurie (26 October 1959); "A Doll's House," with Julie Harris, Hume Cronyn, Eileen Heckart, and Christopher Plummer (15 November 1959); "The Tempest," with Maurice Evans, Richard Burton, and Lee Remick (3 February 1960); "Captain Brassbound's Conversion," with Christopher Plummer and Robert Redford (2 May 1960); "Give Us Barabbas," with James Daly, Kim Hunter, and Dennis King (26 March 1961); "Victoria Regina," with Julie Harris (30 November 1961); "Cyrano de Bergerac," with Christopher Plummer and Hope Lange (6 December 1962); "Little Moon of Alban," with Julie Harris, Dirk Bogarde, Christopher Plummer, and George Peppard (18 March 1964); "The Fantasticks," with John Davidson and Bert Lahr (18 October 1964); "The Magnificent Yankee," with Alfred Lunt and Lynn Fontanne (28 January 1965); "Anastasia," with Julie Harris (17 March 1967); "The Man Who Came to Dinner," with Orson Welles, Lee Remick, and Don Knotts (29 November 1972); "The Borrowers," with Eddie Albert, Judith Anderson,

and Tammy Grimes (14 December 1973); "Brief Encounter," with Richard Burton and Sophia Loren (12 November 1974); "Caesar and Cleopatra," with Alec Guinness and Genevieve Bujold (1 February 1976); "Beauty and the Beast," with George C. Scott and Trish Van Devere (3 December 1976); "The Last Hurrah," with Carroll O'Connor (16 November 1977); "Return Engagement," with Elizabeth Taylor (17 November 1978). Another important television event which was sponsored by Hallmark Cards (though it was not part of the *Hallmark Hall of Fame* series) was the premiere of Gian-Carlo Menotti's Christmas opera, "Amahl and the Night Visitors," 24 December 1951. *Hallmark Hall of Fame* presentations were televised exclusively by NBC from 1952 to 1978; in 1979, however, Hallmark Cards stated that its subsequent presentations would be broadcast by other networks. Among these presentations were: "Mister Lincoln," a one-man show with Roy Dotrice (PBS, 9 February 1981); "Casey Stengel," with Charles Durning (PBS, 6 May 1981); "Witness for the Prosecution," with Ralph Richardson, Diana Rigg, Beau Bridges, and Deborah Kerr (CBS, 4 December 1982); John Steinbeck's "The Winter of Our Discontent," with Donald Sutherland, E. G. Marshall, Richard Masur, Teri Garr, and Tuesday Weld (CBS, 6 December 1983); "Promise," with James Garner and James Woods (CBS, 14 December 1986); "The Secret Garden," with Gennie James and Jadrien Steele (CBS, 30 November 1987); "Foxfire," with Hume Cronyn and Jessica Tandy (CBS, 13 December 1987); "April Morning," with Tommy Lee Jones, Rip Torn, and Chad Lowe (CBS, 25 April 1988); "My Name Is Bill W.," with James Garner and James Woods (ABC, 30 April 1989); "Sarah, Plain and Tall," with Glenn Close and Christopher Walken (CBS, 3 February 1991); "O, Pioneers!" (CBS, 2 February 1992), with Jessica Lange; "Skylark" (CBS, 7 February 1993), a sequel to "Sarah, Plain and Tall," with Glenn Close and Christopher Walken; "To Dance with the White Dog" (CBS, 5 December 1993), with Hume Cronyn and Jessica Tandy (the top-rated TV-movie of the 1993–1994 season); "Breathing Lessons" (CBS, 6 February 1994), with James Garner and Joanne Woodward; and "The Piano Lesson" (CBS, 5 February 1995), with Charles S. Dutton, Carl Gordon, and Alfre Woodard.

THE HALLS OF IVY   CBS
19 OCTOBER 1954–13 OCTOBER 1955   The television version of the radio sitcom was also set at Ivy College in Ivy, U.S.A. It starred Ronald Colman as Dr. William Todhunter Hall, president of the college; Benita Hume (Colman's wife) as Victoria Cromwell (Vicky) Hall, his wife, former star of the British stage; Herb Butterfield as Dr. Clarence Wellman, chairman of the trustees; Mary Wickes as Alice, the Halls' housekeeper; and Ray Collins as Professor Merriweather. Occasionally seen as Ivy students were John Lupton, Jerry Paris, Richard Tyler, and Bob Sands. Created by Don Quinn.

HAMMERMAN   ABC
7 SEPTEMBER 1991–5 SEPTEMBER 1992   Real-life rap artist Hammer (whose real name is Stanley Burrell) was an animated superhero on this Saturday morning cartoon show. Ordinary citizen Stanley Kirk Burrell became the hero Hammerman whenever he put on his "Magic Dancin' Shoes."

THE HAMPTONS   ABC
27 JULY 1983–24 AUGUST 1983   This prime-time hour serial was set in a ritzy Long Island suburb of New York. The cast included Bibi Besch as department store heiress Adrienne Duncan-Mortimer; John Riley as her husband, Jay Mortimer, an executive at the Duncan-Chadway store; Michael Goodwin as Peter Chadway, the store's managing director; Leigh Taylor-Young as Lee Chadway, Peter's wife; Craig Sheffer as Brian Chadway, Peter and Lee's son; Holly Roberts as Tracy Mortimer, Adrienne's daughter and Brian's fiancée; Kate Dezina as Cheryl Ashcroft; Daniel Pilon as Nick Atwater; Philip Casnoff as David Landau; Martha Byrne as Miranda Chadway; Jada Rowland as Penny Drake, the store's personnel director; and Frances Carlon as Ada, the Chadways' housekeeper. Gloria Monty, the guiding light behind the daytime serial *General Hospital,* was the executive producer.

HANDLE WITH CARE
See THE MAIL STORY

HANDS OF MURDER   DUMONT
24 AUGUST 1949–11 DECEMBER 1951   This half-hour mystery anthology series was
first titled *Hands of Murder.* In April 1950, the Friday-night show became known as
Hands of Destiny; from January through April of 1951, it was called *Hands of
Mystery* and was again known as *Hands of Destiny* for the last months of its run.
James L. Caddigan was the producer, Lawrence Menkin the director.

HANDYMAN   SYNDICATED
1955   Norman Brokenshire hosted this home repair show.

HANG TIME   NBC
9 SEPTEMBER 1995–   This live-action Saturday morning series was set in Deering,
Indiana, where the high school boys' basketball team became the first in the state to
take on a girl player. With former NBA star Reggie Theus as Bill Fuller, coach of the
Deering Tornados; Daniella Deutscher as the athletically gifted but shy star, Julie
Connor; David Hanson as team captain Chris Atwater; Chad Gabriel as Danny
Mellon; Megan Parlen as cheerleader Mary Beth Pepperton; Hillary Tuck as Julie's
best friend, Sam, the team manager; Christian Belnavis as transfer student Michael
Maxwell; and Robert Michael Ryan as Earl.

HANGIN' IN   SYNDICATED
1986   Canadian-produced half-hour sitcom, with Lally Cadeau as Kate Brown, head
of a youth counseling center; David Eisner as Mike; and Ruth Springford as Webster.

HANGIN' WITH MR. COOPER   ABC
22 SEPTEMBER 1992–   Standup comic Mark Curry headlined this sitcom as Mark
Cooper, a substitute teacher in the Oakland, California, school system. During the
first season Cooper shared a house with two single women: his childhood friend
Robin (played by Dawnn Lewis), a music teacher, and her friend Vanessa (played by
Holly Robinson, later known as Holly Robinson Peete), on whom Mark had a crush.
By the fall of 1993 Robin had moved out (and Dawnn Lewis left the series), and
Mark and Vanessa acquired two new housemates: Mark's cousin Geneva (played by
Saundra Quarterman) and her daughter, Nicole (played by Raven-Symone). Nell
Carter also joined the cast as P.J., principal of the school where Mark taught. Also
featured were Marquise Wilson as Tyler, a neighborhood boy, and Omar Gooding as
wisecracking Earvin Rodman, one of Mark's students. *Hangin' with Mr. Cooper*
finished its first season tied with *The Jackie Thomas Show* for fourteenth place in the
seasonal ratings, the highest-rated new series of the year.

HANGING IN   CBS
8 AUGUST 1979–29 AUGUST 1979   Four-week summer sitcom set at Braddock University, a Southern college. With Bill Macy as Lou Harper, the new president; Dennis
Burkley as Sam Diggs, the hefty dean of admissions; Barbara Rhoades as Maggie
Gallagher, the dean of faculty; and Nedra Volz as Pinky Nolan, Harper's saucy
housekeeper. The half-hour show was a reworked version of *Mr. Dugan,* a sitcom
from Norman Lear's T.A.T. Communications about a black Congressman, which
Lear had decided not to air.

HANK   NBC
17 SEPTEMBER 1965–2 SEPTEMBER 1966   Dick Kallman starred as Hank Dearborn, a
youngster who was forced to quit school when his parents died, leaving him to care
for his kid sister; Hank got a job running an ice cream truck near the campus of
Western State University and tried to sneak into college classes and other official
activities. Also featured were Howard St. John as Dr. Lewis Royal, the registrar,
Hank's nemesis; Lloyd Corrigan as Professor McKillup; Linda Foster as Doris
Royal, Hank's girlfriend, the registrar's daughter; Katie Sweet as Tina, Hank's sis-

ter; Dabbs Greer as the athletic coach, Ossie Weiss; and Dorothy Nuemann as Miss Mittleman.

THE HANK McCUNE SHOW   NBC/SYNDICATED
9 SEPTEMBER 1950–9 DECEMBER 1950 (NBC); 1953 (SYNDICATED)   Half-hour sitcom starring Hank McCune as the host of a television show, and featuring Larry Keating, Arthur Q. Bryan, Frank Nelson, Sara Berner, Charles Maxwell, and Tammy Kiper. Written by Mort Lachman and Cy Rose, the show had been seen locally in New York in 1949. The syndicated version featured McCune, Hanley Stafford, and Florence Bates.

THE HANNA-BARBERA HAPPY HOUR   NBC
18 APRIL 1978–4 MAY 1978   This hour-long, prime-time variety series from Hanna-Barbera Productions, the prolific supplier of animated series, was similar in format to *The Muppet Show*. It was hosted by two puppets, Honey and Sis, and featured celebrity guest stars. The life-sized puppets were operated from behind by wands, and through the use of the chroma-key process, the puppets' images were superimposed upon appropriate backgrounds. Joseph Barbera was the executive producer.

HAPPENING '68   ABC
6 JANUARY 1968–20 SEPTEMBER 1969   A Saturday-afternoon rock music show, hosted by Mark Lindsay and Paul Revere and the Raiders. The show was known simply as *Happening* in 1969. See also *It's Happening*.

HAPPY   NBC
8 JUNE 1960–28 SEPTEMBER 1960; 13 JANUARY 1961–8 SEPTEMBER 1961   This trivial sitcom borrowed one idea from *The Peoples' Choice*—instead of a dog who could think out loud, this one featured a baby who could think out loud. With Ronnie Burns as Chris Day, manager of a Palm Springs motel; Yvonne Lime as his wife, Sally; twins David and Steven Born as Happy (Christopher Hapgood Day), their gifted child; Lloyd Corrigan as Uncle Charlie, Sally's uncle; Doris Packer as Clara Mason, a woman who pursued Charlie; Burt Metcalfe as their friend, Joe Brigham; and Wanda Shannon as Joe's wife, Terry. Leone Ledoux supplied the voice of Happy. The idea of a talking infant was revived in the popular 1989 film, *Look Who's Talking*, for which Bruce Willis did the voiceover.

HAPPY DAYS   CBS
24 JUNE 1970–27 AUGUST 1970   An hour of nostalgia, hosted by Louis Nye, with Chuck McCann, Bob (Elliott) and Ray (Goulding), and assorted bandleaders from the 1930s.

HAPPY DAYS   ABC
15 JANUARY 1974–12 JULY 1984   A sitcom set in the nostalgic 1950s, *Happy Days* was one of the cornerstones of ABC's dramatic rise to the top of the ratings heap during the mid-1970s. After a season and a half of unspectacular ratings, *Happy Days* cracked Nielsen's Top Ten in its third season (1975–1976); a year later it climbed to the very top and engendered a spinoff, *Laverne and Shirley,* which also fared well. By the 1983–1984 season, *Happy Days* was the oldest prime-time sitcom then on the air.
   Happy Days was created by Garry Marshall, a veteran comedy writer who had worked on *The Dick Van Dyke Show* and *The Lucy Show,* and who had produced *The Odd Couple.* Marshall produced a pilot for ABC in 1971, titled "New Family in Town." The network was not interested, and the pilot later surfaced as a segment of *Love, American Style.* Aired 25 February 1972, it was titled "Love and the Happy Day," and featured Ron Howard, Marion Ross, Harold Gould, and Susan Neher as a 1950s family getting their first TV set. In the meantime, however, film director George Lucas had seen the pilot, and used it as the inspiration for his tremendously popular film *American Graffiti.* After the success of the movie ABC's interest in Garry Marshall's pilot was rekindled.
   Happy Days was set in Milwaukee in the late 1950s. Its central family was the

Cunninghams: Ron Howard (1974–1980) as typical teenager Richie, who attended Jefferson High and worried about girls; Tom Bosley as his father, Howard, who owned a hardware store; Marion Ross as his mother, Marion; Erin Moran (1974–1982; 1983–1984) as his little sister, Joanie; and Gavan O'Herlihy (spring 1974) and Randolph Roberts (fall 1974) as his jockish older brother, Chuck (the character was written out by 1975). Richie had three close friends: Anson Williams as Warren "Potsie" Webber, his best friend; Donny Most (1974–1980) as loudmouth Ralph Malph; and Henry Winkler as Arthur "Fonzie" Fonzarelli, the leather-jacketed, motorcycle-riding epitome of "cool," an expert on cars and girls.

Fonzie was originally intended to be a minor character, but proved to be extremely popular with the audience (especially with the studio audience, which *Happy Days* began to utilize in the fall of 1974). Noting Fonzie's popularity, ABC programming chief Fred Silverman, newly arrived from CBS, shrewdly decided to emphasize the role; in 1975 Fonzie moved into the apartment above the Cunninghams' garage. This plot device enabled him to retain his cherished independence but also to become involved in almost any situation with the Cunninghams. Garry Marshall noted that Fonzie was to have been named "Marscharelli," which was Marshall's real name, but that he compromised on the issue with his partner, Bob Brunner. Marshall also observed that if ABC had had its way in 1974, Fonzie might not have been so recognizable. The network had decreed that Fonzie should wear a cloth jacket rather than the "threatening" leather one. Marshall suggested a compromise, which was accepted—that Fonzie be permitted to wear the leather jacket when he rode or worked on his motorcycle. Marshall then gradually cut back on the use of the motorcycle, while keeping Fonzie in the leather jacket.

Between 1974 and 1977, other regulars included: Misty Rowe (fall 1974–1975) as Wendy, a waitress at Arnold's, the local hangout; Pat Morita (1975–1976; 1982–1983) as Arnold (Mitsuo Takahashi), the proprietor; and Al Molinaro (1976–1982; 1983–1984) as Al DelVecchio, the new proprietor of Arnold's.

In the fall of 1977 Richie, Potsie, and Ralph all began college at the University of Wisconsin in Milwaukee (Garry Marshall was insistent that the *Happy Days* characters evolve as the show continued). Joining the cast that season were Scott Baio (1977–1982; 1983–1984) as Fonzie's enterprising young cousin, Charles "Chachi" Arcola, who became Joanie's boyfriend; and Lynda Goodfriend (1977–1982) as Richie's girlfriend, Lori Beth Allen.

In the summer of 1980 Ron Howard announced that he had signed a contract with NBC, and abruptly left *Happy Days;* Donny Most also left the series in 1980. On the show it was arranged that Richie and Ralph had joined the Army; in May of 1981 Richie (then stationed in Greenland) married Lori Beth (in Milwaukee) by proxy. Their baby, Richie, Jr., was born in the fall of 1981. Meanwhile, Fonzie had become a teacher of auto mechanics at good old Jefferson High. Joining the cast were Ted McGinley (1980–1984) as Marion's Yale-educated nephew, Roger Phillips, who became Jefferson's new basketball coach and English teacher; and Cathy Silvers (1980–1983), daughter of comedian Phil Silvers, as Joanie's boy-crazy girlfriend, Jenny Piccalo.

In the fall of 1982 Fonzie (who by this time had become a managing partner in Arnold's) found himself falling in love with a divorcée. Linda Purl appeared during the 1982–1983 season as the divorcée, Ashley Pfister; Purl had appeared in six 1974 episodes as Richie's girlfriend, Gloria. Also appearing during the 1982–1983 season were Heather O'Rourke as Ashley's young daughter, Heather; and Crystal Bernard as Howard's niece, K. C., who lived with the Cunninghams. One reason for this addition was that Joanie Cunningham was not at home, having moved to her own spinoff, *Joanie Loves Chachi.*

By the fall of 1983, in what would be *Happy Days*'s final season, Fonzie had become the dean of boys, and Roger the principal, at George S. Patton Vocational High. Joanie and Chachi, whose spinoff had flopped, came back to Milwaukee, and plans were made for their wedding. Also returning were Richie and Ralph, who showed up in a special two-part episode.

In addition to *Laverne and Shirley* and *Joanie Loves Chachi, Happy Days* spawned a Saturday-morning cartoon show, *The Fonz and the Happy Days Gang.* Also, the

1978 sitcom *Mork and Mindy* was based on an episode of *Happy Days*. Most of the gang showed up for a series retrospective, "Happy Days Reunion," which was seen on ABC 3 March 1992.

HAPPY FELTON'S SPOTLIGHT CLUB NBC
4 DECEMBER 1954–26 FEBRUARY 1955 Seen on Saturday mornings, this half-hour audience participation show for children was hosted by Happy Felton.

HAPPY'S PARTY DUMONT
6 SEPTEMBER 1952–9 MAY 1953 Ida Mae Maher hosted this Saturday-morning children's show. Broadcast from Pittsburgh, the series was sponsored by the Florida Citrus Commission.

HARBOR COMMAND SYNDICATED
1957 A half-hour adventure series from Ziv TV, starring Wendell Corey as Captain Ralph Baxter of the United States Coast Guard Harbor Police Command.

HARBOURMASTER (ADVENTURE AT SCOTT ISLAND) CBS/ABC
26 SEPTEMBER 1957–26 DECEMBER 1957 (CBS); 5 JANUARY 1958–29 JUNE 1958 (ABC)
Set in New England, *Harbourmaster* was dropped by CBS in midseason; ABC then picked up the program, airing it under the title *Adventure at Scott Island*. With Barry Sullivan as Captain David Scott, the harbormaster, who ran a boat repair business on Scott Island, a tightly knit island community settled by his forebears; Paul Burke as Jeff Kittredge, Scott's partner; Nina Wilcox as Anna Morrison, proprietor of the Dolphin restaurant; Michael Keene as Cap'n Dan, a local oldtimer; and Evan Elliott as Danny, Cap'n Dan's grandson. Suzanne Pleshette made her TV debut in one episode, "Night Rescue," aired 5 December. Exteriors were filmed at Rockport, Mass.

HARD COPY CBS
25 JANUARY 1987–3 JULY 1987 *The Morning Post,* a big-city newspaper, was the setting for this dramatic series. With Michael Murphy as reporter Andy Omart; Dean Devlin as rookie reporter David Delvalle; Wendy Crewson as city wire-service reporter Blake Calisher; E. Erich Anderson as Lieutenant Packer; Fionnula Flanagan as Lieutenant Guyla Cook; Jeffrey Kramer as John Freed; Charles Cooper as William Boot; and Jim McDonnell as TV anchorman Larry Coverson.

HARD COPY SYNDICATED
1989– A thirty-minute daily investigative series, hosted by Allan Frio and Terry Murphy. Barry Nolan succeeded Frio in 1991. One of several "tabloid" series of the late 1980s and 1990s, *Hard Copy* was distributed by Paramount Television. In the fall of 1994 it was reported that the series had assigned thirty staffers to cover the O. J. Simpson murder case. A weekend edition of the series focused on showbiz topics. Known as *HCTV*, it was hosted by Diane Dimond.

HARD TIME ON PLANET EARTH CBS
1 MARCH 1989–5 JULY 1989 Hour sci-fi series starring Martin Kove as Jesse, an alien warrior sentenced by an intergalactic tribunal to exile on Earth; he was accompanied by his parole officer, an orb-shaped "correctional unit" named Control, who decided that Jesse should settle in Los Angeles, where he would blend in "as quietly as possible." Danny Mann provided the voice of Control (Charles Fleischer supplied it in the pilot).

HARDBALL NBC
21 SEPTEMBER 1989–1 DECEMBER 1989; 20 APRIL 1990–29 JUNE 1990 On this hour crime show the old cop/young cop theme was again explored. With John Ashton as Charlie Battles, almost forty-five; Richard Tyson as his newly assigned partner, Joe "Kaz" Kaczierowski, a long-haired, motorcycle-riding, mid-twentyish cop; and Sean McCann as the boss, Captain Briggs. *Hardball* left the air in December 1989 for

"retooling." When it returned in April it was advertised as "faster, wilder [and] sexier," but the only discernible difference was that Tyson's hair was somewhat shorter.

HARDBALL
FOX

4 SEPTEMBER 1994–23 OCTOBER 1994   The Pioneers, a hapless baseball team, were the central characters in this short-lived sitcom. With Rose Marie as Mitzi Balzer, the Pioneers' crusty owner; Dann Florek as the newly hired manager, Ernest "Happy" Talbot; Bruce Greenwood as pitcher Dave Logan; Mike Starr as catcher Mike Widmer; Joe Rogan as Frank Valente, the $6 million per year centerfielder; Alexandra Wentworth as Lee Emory, the team's p. r. director; Phill Lewis as Arnold Nixon; Steve Hytner as Brad Coolidge, the general manager; Chris Browning as pitcher Lloyd Macomb; Eddie Velez as Diego Escobar; Charles Cyphers as Chuck; and Christopher B. Duncan as Palmer.

HARDCASTLE AND McCORMICK
ABC

18 SEPTEMBER 1983–23 JULY 1986   Stephen J. Cannell (who created *The Greatest American Hero* and *The A Team,* among other shows) created this hour series with Patrick Hasburgh. It starred Brian Keith as Milton C. Hardcastle, a newly retired judge; known on the bench as "Hardcase" because of his tough attitude toward lawbreakers, Hardcastle decided to go after, and bring to justice, criminals who managed to evade the judicial system (such as those whose cases were thrown out of court on legal technicalities). To accomplish this goal, Hardcastle arranged to have his last defendant released in his custody; the pair then teamed up on Hardcastle's quest. Daniel Hugh-Kelly costarred as the defendant, ex-con Mark "Skid" McCormick, whose driving skills were legendary, and whose feelings about teaming up with the judge were mixed. Mary Jackson was also featured in early episodes as Sara, housekeeper for the widowed Hardcastle. John Hancock was seen during the 1984–1985 season as Lieutenant Michael Delaney, Hardcastle's police contact; Joe Santos filled a similar role the following season as Lieutenant Frank Harper. Sixty-seven episodes were produced. This is not the first series to feature a judge named Hardcastle. Such a character was a regular on the 1977 series *Rosetti and Ryan.*

THE HARDY BOYS
ABC

6 SEPTEMBER 1969–5 SEPTEMBER 1970; 2 JANUARY 1971–4 SEPTEMBER 1971   In this Saturday-morning cartoon series, Franklin W. Dixon's youthful sleuths were part of a rock group known as the Hardy Boys.

THE HARDY BOYS/NANCY DREW MYSTERIES
ABC

30 JANUARY 1977–21 JANUARY 1979   *The Hardy Boys Mysteries* and *The Nancy Drew Mysteries* started out as two separate series, alternating biweekly in the same time slot. Early in 1978 the casts merged for the remainder of the season, and in the fall of 1978 *The Hardy Boys Mysteries* continued on alone. Both the Hardy Boys and Nancy Drew were created in 1927 by Edward Stratemeyer, using the pen names Franklin W. Dixon for the Hardy Boys stories and Carolyn Keene for the Nancy Drew stories; his daughter, Harriet Stratemeyer Adams, continued writing the books after his death. *The Hardy Boys* cast included: Parker Stevenson as Frank Hardy; Shaun Cassidy (brother of David Cassidy of *The Partridge Family*) as Joe Hardy; Edmund Gilbert as their father, Fenton Hardy, a private eye; Edith Atwater (to September 1978) as Aunt Gertrude; Lisa Eilbacher (to September 1978) as the boys' friend, Callie Shaw; and Gary Springer (to September 1978) as Chet Morton. The *Nancy Drew* cast included Pamela Sue Martin and Janet Louise Johnson as Nancy Drew (Martin had balked at the idea of merging the two shows and was replaced when the decision to merge was final); William Schallert as Nancy's father, Carson Drew, a criminal lawyer; George O'Hanlon as Ned Nickerson; and Jean Rasey as George Fayne. Glen A. Larson was the executive producer for Glen A. Larson Productions in association with Universal Television.

THE HARLEM GLOBETROTTERS CBS/NBC

12 SEPTEMBER 1970–2 SEPTEMBER 1972 (CBS); 4 FEBRUARY 1978–2 SEPTEMBER 1978 (NBC)   The world famous basketball tricksters came to Saturday-morning television in a Hanna-Barbera cartoon series. Scatman Crothers provided the voice for the Globetrotters star, Meadowlark Lemon. In 1978 reruns were shown on NBC under the title *The Go-Go Globetrotters,* a two-hour program which also included segments of *CB Bears, The Herculoids,* and *Space Ghost.* See also *The Super Globetrotters.*

THE HARLEM GLOBETROTTERS POPCORN MACHINE CBS

7 SEPTEMBER 1974–5 SEPTEMBER 1976   The Harlem Globetrotters again came to weekend television, this time in a live-action format. Several members of the team were featured: Meadowlark Lemon, Curley Neal, Geese Ausbie, Tex Harrison, Bobby Joe Mason, Marques Haynes, John Smith, Theodis Lee, and Nate Brown. Also featured were young Rodney Allen Rippy and Avery Schreiber (as Mister Evil). Executive producers: Frank Peppiatt and John Aylesworth. Produced by Norman Baer.

HARPER VALLEY P.T.A. (HARPER VALLEY) NBC

16 JANUARY 1981–14 AUGUST 1982   Tom T. Hall's song about small-town hypocrisy, recorded in 1968 by Jeannie C. Riley, was a big hit; a decade later it was the inspiration for a film which starred Barbara (*I Dream of Jeannie*) Eden. When the film was first broadcast on television (24 February 1980) its ratings were impressive, and the network ordered a sitcom based on the movie; the series was originally planned as a sixty-minute sitcom, but was trimmed to thirty minutes before its 1981 premiere. Barbara Eden repeated her film role as widow Stella Johnson, a rugged individualist who served on the P.T.A. (Parent-Teacher Association) of the stuffy Ohio town. Also featured were Jenn Thompson as Stella's teenage daughter, Dee; Fannie Flagg as Stella's friend and ally, beautician Cassie Bowman; Anne Francine as snobbish Flora Simpson Reilly, head of the P.T.A.; Bridget Hanley as Flora's equally snobbish daughter, Wanda Reilly Taylor, also a P.T.A. member; Rod McCary as lawyer Bobby Taylor, Wanda's husband; Suzi Dean as Scarlett, their teenage daughter; and George Gobel as Mayor Otis Harper. During the spring of 1981 the other members of the P.T.A. included Vic Dunlop as George Kelly; Mari Gorman as Vivian Washburn; Gary Allen as Norman Clayton; Edie McClurg as Willamae Jones, its secretary; and Robert Gray as Cliff Willoughby. When the series returned in the fall of 1981, the P.T.A. storyline was dropped (as were the last five cast members) and the show was retitled *Harper Valley.* Mills Watson joined the cast as Stella's Uncle Buster.

HARRIGAN AND SON ABC

14 OCTOBER 1960–29 SEPTEMBER 1961   Situation comedy about two lawyers, father and son. With Pat O'Brien as Jim Harrigan; Roger Perry as Jim Harrigan, Jr.; Georgine Darcy as Gypsy, Jim Sr.'s secretary; Helen Kleeb as Miss Claridge, Jim Jr.'s secretary.

HARRIS AGAINST THE WORLD NBC

5 OCTOBER 1964–4 JANUARY 1965   Part Two of NBC's *90 Bristol Court, Harris Against the World* was sandwiched between *Tom, Dick and Mary* and *Karen:* only *Karen* survived the midseason purge. *Harris* featured Jack Klugman as Alan Harris, a businessman constantly battling life's frustrations; Patricia Barry as Kate Harris, his wife; David Macklin as Billy, their son; Claire Wilcox as Dee Dee, their daughter; Fay DeWitt as Helen Miller, their friend; Sheldon Allman as Norm, Helen's husband; and Guy Raymond as Cliff Murdock, the building handyman.

HARRIS & COMPANY NBC

15 MARCH 1979–5 APRIL 1979   Four-episode dramatic miniseries about a contemporary black family. With Bernie Casey as Mike Harris, a widower who, with his five kids, moved from Detroit to Los Angeles; David Hubbard as son David; Lia Jackson as daughter J.P.; Renee Brown as daughter Liz; Eddie Singleton as son Tommy; Dain

Turner as son Richard Allen; Stu Gilliam as Uncle Charlie; and Carol Tillery Banks as Charlie's wife, Angie. Scheduled on Thursdays opposite ABC's *Mork & Mindy* and CBS's *The Waltons*, *Harris & Company* attracted a minuscule audience. It was replaced by two equally unsuccessful shows, *Highcliffe Manor* and *Whodunnit?*

HARRY   ABC
4 MARCH 1987–25 MARCH 1987   Ninth Street Community General Hospital was the setting for this short-lived sitcom. With Alan Arkin as Harry Porschak, who worked in the purchasing department; Holland Taylor as Nurse Ida Duckett; Thom Bray as expediter Lawrence Pendleton; Matt Craven as Bobby Kratz; Barbara Dana (Arkin's wife in real life) as psychiatrist Dr. Sandy Clifton; Kurt Knudson as hospital administrator Wyatt Lockhart; and Richard Lewis as Richard Breskin.

HARRY AND THE HENDERSONS   SYNDICATED
1990–1992   Half-hour sitcom, based on the 1987 movie, about a suburban family who took in a Bigfoot-like creature and named the gentle giant Harry. With Kevin Peter Hall (who died in April 1991) and Dawan Scott as Harry; Bruce Davison as George Henderson; Molly Cheek as Nancy Henderson; Zachary Bostrom as their son, Ernie; Carol-Ann Plante as their daughter, Sarah; Gigi Rice (1990–1991) as next-door neighbor Samantha Glick, a television personality; Cassie Cole (1990–1991) as Samantha's daughter, Tiffany; David Coburn (1990–1991) as biologist Walter Potter; Noah Blake (1991–1992) as Nancy's brother, Bret Douglas, who moved in with the Hendersons; and Courtney Peldon (1991–1992) as Darcy Paine, who was crazy about Ernie Henderson.

HARRY O   ABC
12 SEPTEMBER 1974–12 AUGUST 1976   This crime show starred David Janssen as Harry Orwell, a cop who became a private eye after he was shot in the back. Orwell was a low-paid, low-key private eye who often had to take the bus to pursue criminals when his car was laid up and rarely got the better of the bad guy in a fight. Also featured were Henry Darrow (1974–January 1975) as Detective Manny Quinlan of the San Diego police; Anthony Zerbe (January 1975–1976) as Lieutenant K. C. Trench of the Los Angeles police; Paul Tulley (1975–1976) as Sergeant Don Roberts. In the middle of the first season Orwell moved from San Diego to Los Angeles. The first pilot for the series was shown 11 March 1973. Created by Howard Rodman. Executive producer: Jerry Thorpe. Producer: E. Thompson (for Warner Brothers).

HARRY'S GIRLS   NBC
13 SEPTEMBER 1963–3 JANUARY 1964   This situation comedy about an American vaudeville act touring Europe was filmed in southern France. With Larry Blyden as Harry Burns; Dawn Nickerson as Lois; Susan Silo as Rusty; and Diahn Williams as Terry. It was replaced in midseason by *That Was the Week That Was*.

HART TO HART   ABC
22 SEPTEMBER 1979–31 JULY 1984   Breezy hour adventure series, starring Robert Wagner and Stefanie Powers as Jonathan and Jennifer Hart, husband-and-wife amateur sleuths in their spare time. (Professionally, Jonathan ran a conglomerate and Jennifer was an author.) Also featured was Lionel Stander as Max, their chauffeur and aide. Aaron Spelling and Leonard Goldberg were the executive producers; the show enjoyed a 112-episode run. Wagner, Powers, and Stander returned to their roles for a series of three made-for-TV films telecast on NBC during the 1993–1994 season.

THE HARTMANS (THE HARTMANS AT HOME)   NBC
27 FEBRUARY 1949–22 MAY 1949   This Sunday-night sitcom starred Grace and Paul Hartman as themselves.

HARTS OF THE WEST   CBS

25 SEPTEMBER 1993–29 JANUARY 1994; 4 JUNE 1994–18 JUNE 1994   Beau Bridges
starred in this hour comedy-drama as Dave Hart, an underwear salesman who, after
a heart attack scare, quit his job and headed to the part of America he loved: the
West. As his family struggled to adapt to life in the middle of nowhere—Sholo,
Nevada—Dave tried to revive the defunct Flying Tumbleweed Dude Ranch. The rest
of the cast included: Harley Jane Kozak as Dave's understanding wife, Alison Hart;
Meghann Haldeman as their teen daughter, L'Amour; Sean Murray as their son
Zane; Nathan Watt as their son John "Duke" Wayne; Saginaw Grant as Augie,
Sholo's savvy Native American storekeeper; O-Lan Jones as Rose McLaughlin, the
waitress; Sterling Macer, Jr., as lawyer and would-be cowboy Marcus St. Cloud;
Stephen Root as R. O. Moon, the sheriff; Talisa Soto as Augie's granddaughter,
Cassie Velasquez; Dennis Fimple as Garral; and Lloyd Bridges as flinty old cowpoke
Jake Terrel, who had worked on the Flying Tumbleweed and took Dave under his
wing.

THE HARVEY KORMAN SHOW   ABC

4 APRIL 1978–3 AUGUST 1978   After a onetime telecast on 31 January 1978, *The
Harvey Korman Show* began its regular schedule in April. Harvey Korman, who had
been featured on *The Carol Burnett Show* for ten years, starred in the the half-hour
sitcom as actor Harvey Kavanaugh. Also featured were Christine Lahti as his daughter, Maggie, an employee of the Friendly Community Bank; Barry Van Dyke as
Maggie's boyfriend and coworker, Stuart Stafford; Milton Selzer as Jake, Harvey's
agent. Hal Dresner was the executive producer of the series, and Don Van Atta
produced it.

THE HAT SQUAD   CBS

16 SEPTEMBER 1992–23 JANUARY 1993   Implausible hour crime show about a three-
man squad of modern-day vigilantes who sported fedoras while tracking their quarry;
the three had been orphaned as children and had been raised by an ex-cop. With
James Tolkan as Mike "Rags" Ragland, the ex-cop; Nestor Serrano as Rafael Martinez; Billy Warlock as Matt Mathesson; and Don Michael Paul as Buddy Capatosa.
The inspiration for the series may have been an L.A.P.D. unit of the 1940s whose
members wore fedoras. Stephen J. Cannell created the series.

THE HATHAWAYS   ABC

6 OCTOBER 1961–31 AUGUST 1962   Situation comedy about a couple who agree to
take in a family of performing chimps. With Jack Weston as real estate agent Walter
Hathaway; Peggy Cass as his wife, Eleanor; Harvey Lembeck as the chimps' agent,
Jerry Roper; and the Marquis Chimps. The half-hour show was a Screen Gems
production.

HAVE A HEART   DUMONT

3 MAY 1955–14 JUNE 1955   John Reed King hosted this prime-time game show on
which two four-member teams, each from a different city or town, competed; all
winnings were awarded to charity.

HAVE FAITH   ABC

18 APRIL 1989–23 JULY 1989   Half-hour sitcom about four Chicago priests. With Joel
Higgins as Monsignor Mac Mackenzie; Frank Hamilton as Father Tuttle; Ron Carey
as Father Vincent Paglia; and Stephen Furst as Father Gabriel Podmaninsky.

HAVE GUN WILL TRAVEL   CBS

14 SEPTEMBER 1957–21 SEPTEMBER 1963   This half-hour western starred Richard
Boone as Paladin, a loner who was based at the Hotel Carlton in San Francisco; his
professional services—as detective, bodyguard, courier, or whatever—were available to those who requested them. Paladin's business card, which bore the image of a
chess knight, read: "Have Gun, Will Travel. Wire Paladin, San Francisco." Kam
Tong was also featured as Paladin's servant, Hey Boy, except during the fall of 1959

(when Tong costarred in *Mr. Garlund*) and during the 1960–1961 season, when Lisa Lu was featured as Hey Girl. Boone exercised considerable control over the show; in 1961 *TV Guide* reported that Boone not only had directed several episodes but also exercised script and casting approval. Whatever the case, Boone's judgments seem to have been right, for the show was a solid hit, ranking in Nielsen's top five during each of its first four seasons. The show was extremely popular and was widely syndicated during the 1960s; in 1974, however, a federal magistrate ruled that a Rhode Island radio performer, Victor De Costa, had actually created the character in the 1940s and was entitled to an accounting of the profits realized from the show.

HAVING BABIES (JULIE FARR, M.D.) ABC

7 MARCH 1978–18 APRIL 1978   *Having Babies* was introduced as an hour-long series after three made-for-TV movies had been telecast; midway through its limited run the show's title was changed to *Julie Farr, M.D.* as the emphasis shifted from specialized to generalized medical drama. Featured were Susan Sullivan as obstetrician Dr. Julie Farr; Mitchell Ryan as surgeon Dr. Blake Simmons; Dennis Howard as intern Dr. Ron Danvers; and Beverly Todd as Kelly. A few additional episodes were televised during the summer of 1979.

HAWAII FIVE-O CBS

26 SEPTEMBER 1968–26 APRIL 1980   TV's longest-running crime show embodied the right mixture of scenery (it was filmed entirely on location) and action. Created by Leonard Freeman (who served as executive producer until his death in 1973), it starred Jack Lord as Steve McGarrett, the no-nonsense head of Five-O, a special investigative unit directly responsible to the governor of Hawaii. Almost all the stories were straight-ahead crime dramas; McGarrett's personal life was rarely explored beyond the fact that he was a bachelor who enjoyed sailing. Among those featured were James MacArthur (1968–1979) as Danny ("Dano") Williams, McGarrett's number-one assistant; Kam Fong as Chin Ho Kelly, who was killed off at the end of the 1977–1978 season; Zulu (1968–1972) as Kono; Richard Denning (appearing occasionally) as The Governor (Keith Jameson); Maggi Parker (1968–1969) as May, Steve's secretary; Peggy Ryan (1969–1976) as Jenny Sherman, Steve's secretary; Al Eben as Doc Bergman, the pathologist; Harry Endo as lab expert Che Fong; Al Harrington (1972–1977) as Ben Kokua; Herman Wedemeyer (1972–1980) as Duke Lakela; Douglas Mossman (1974–1975) as Frank Kemana; and Glenn Cannon (1976–1978) as Attorney General John Manicote. Also appearing occasionally was Khigh Dhiegh as Wo Fat, a mysterious Oriental criminal who was McGarrett's archenemy. In the fall of 1979 three new regulars were added: Bill Smith as James (Kimo) Carew; Sharon Farrell as Lori Wilson; and Moe Keale as Tom (Truck) Kealoha. In the final first-run episode (5 April 1980), McGarrett finally apprehended his archenemy, Wo Fat. Following producer Freeman's death, Bill Finnegan and Bob Sweeney took over as producers; they were replaced in 1975 by Philip Leacock and Richard Newton, who were in turn succeeded by Douglas Green and B. W. Sandefur. It was no secret, however, that Jack Lord was actively involved in most aspects of the show's production.

HAWAIIAN EYE ABC

7 OCTOBER 1959–10 SEPTEMBER 1963   Set in Honolulu, this Warner Brothers detective show was cast in the same mold as *77 Sunset Strip,* the first of Warners' private eye shows. *Hawaiian Eye* originally featured Anthony Eisley as Tracy Steele, a former Honolulu cop; Robert Conrad as Thomas Jefferson (Tom) Lopaka, his partner in Hawaiian Eye; Connie Stevens as Cricket Blake, singer at the Shell Bar of the nearby Hawaiian Village Hotel (Cricket usually sang one or two songs in most episodes); Poncie Ponce as Kazuo Kim (Kim), a cabbie; Mel Prestidge as Lieutenant Quon of the Honolulu police. In 1961, Grant Williams joined the cast as Gregg Mackenzie, Tracy and Tom's new partner. Eisley left the series in 1962; for the final season Troy Donahue (late of *Surfside 6*) was added as Phil Barton, social director of the hotel, and Doug Mossman joined the cast as Moke. Sharp-eyed viewers could have noted Chad Everett in his TV debut ("The Kahuna Curtain," 9 November 1960)

and an early appearance by Jack Nicholson ("Total Eclipse," 21 February 1962). William T. Orr was the executive producer of the series.

HAWAIIAN HEAT ABC
14 SEPTEMBER 1984–21 DECEMBER 1984   The fall 1984 season saw two new crime shows set in exotic American locales; only one of them—*Miami Vice*—succeeded, while this one fell by the wayside after thirteen weeks. It starred Robert Ginty and Jeff McCracken as Mac Riley and Andy Senkowski, two Chicago cops who left the Windy City for Hawaii after Mac's father (also a cop) was convicted of taking a bribe. Also featured were Mako as their new boss, Major Oshira of the Honolulu Police Department; Branscombe Richmond as Harker; and Tracy Scoggins as helicopter pilot Irene Gorley, who was usually seen with a macaw perched on her shoulder.

HAWK ABC
8 SEPTEMBER 1966–29 DECEMBER 1966   An hour-long crime show starring Burt Reynolds as Detective Lieutenant John Hawk, an Iroquois Indian police officer assigned to the New York City district attorney's office. Also featured were Wayne Grice as Detective Carter, his sometime partner; Leon Janney as Gorten, a newsdealer who doubled as Hawk's street source. Reruns were shown on NBC during the summer of 1976.

HAWKEYE (HAWKEYE AND THE LAST OF THE MOHICANS) SYNDICATED
1957   Produced in Canada, this adventure series was based loosely on James Fenimore Cooper's book. With John Hart as Hawkeye, a white trapper and scout; Lon Chaney, Jr., as Chingachgook, a Mohican, Hawkeye's blood brother.

HAWKEYE SYNDICATED
1994–1995   The second TV version of the literary classic starred Lee Horsley as Hawkeye; Lynda Carter as Elizabeth Shields, who was searching for her husband, William, who had been abducted by the Huron Indians; Rodney A. Grant as Chingachgook; Garwin Sanford as Captain Taylor Shields, William's brother and Elizabeth's former suitor. Michael Berry appeared occasionally as William. The hour series was filmed in British Columbia.

HAWKINS CBS
2 OCTOBER 1973–3 SEPTEMBER 1974   James Stewart starred as Billy Jim Hawkins, a plain ol' country lawyer from Beauville, West Virginia, in this hour-long crime show. Veteran character actor Strother Martin costarred as his cousin, R. J. Hawkins, who occasionally did some investigating for Billy Jim. Though the format of the show seemed ideally suited for Stewart's talents (unlike his first series, *The Jimmy Stewart Show*), the series failed to catch on. The show was produced by Arena Productions in association with M-G-M TV.

HAWKINS FALLS NBC
Nighttime: 17 JUNE 1950–19 AUGUST 1950; *Daytime:* 2 APRIL 1951–1 JULY 1955   The official title of this serial, in its early days, was *Hawkins Falls, Pop. 6200*. The evening version was broadcast from Chicago and was seen Saturdays; the following spring it began a daytime run which lasted four years. It told of life in a small town (exterior sequences were filmed at Woodstock, Illinois). The cast included: Bernadine Flynn as Lona Drewer Carcy; Michael Golda as Dr. Floyd Carey, the man she married; Win Stracke as Laif Flaigle; Ros Twohey as Millie Flaigle; Helen Bernie as Betty Sawtel; Russ Reed as Spec Bassett; and Elmira Roessler as Elmira Cleebe. The show was seen locally in Chicago in 1946.

HAYWIRE FOX
1 SEPTEMBER 1990–26 JANUARY 1991   Intended as a companion program to Fox's *Totally Hidden Video, Haywire* featured skits, stunts, *Candid Camera*-type scenes, parodies of television series, and new dialog added to clips from old films. The show was emceed by a guest host most weeks, assisted by a gang of regulars which included

David Jackson, Eric Lyons, David Nathan, Nathanal Peterson, Raymond Pounds, Michelle Rudy, Danial Sawyer, Pat Cashman, and Darrel Suto.

HAZEL NBC/CBS

28 SEPTEMBER 1961–9 SEPTEMBER 1965 (NBC); 13 SEPTEMBER 1965–5 SEPTEMBER 1966 (CBS)   One of the few successful TV series based on a comic strip, *Hazel* came to television in 1961, about nineteen years after her creation by Ted Key (the cartoons were published in *The Saturday Evening Post*). Shirley Booth, a stage actress who had done little television previously, starred as Hazel Burke, a domestic with a penchant for getting involved in other people's business. For the first four years of the series, Hazel was employed by the George Baxter family. Appearing as the Baxters were Don Defore as George Baxter, a lawyer; Whitney Blake as his wife, Dorothy Baxter; and Bobby Buntrock as their son, Harold. Occasionally appearing were Cathy Lewis as George's sister, Deirdre Thompson; Robert P. Lieb as Harry Thompson, Deirdre's henpecked husband; Maudie Prickett as Hazel's friend Rosie, also a domestic; Howard Smith as Harvey Griffin, one of George's clients; Norma Varden as next-door neighbor Harriet Johnson; and Donald Foster as Harriet's husband, Herbert Johnson. When the series shifted networks in 1965, Hazel was given new employers—the Steve (younger brother of George) Baxter family. It was explained that George Baxter had been sent to Saudi Arabia on business, and Dorothy had gone with him, but that young Harold had stayed in town to finish school. Defore and Blake, as well as most of the semiregulars, left the cast, though Buntrock remained. Added to the cast were Ray Fulmer as Steve Baxter, a real estate agent; Lynn Borden as Barbara Baxter, his wife; and Julia Benjamin as Susie, their daughter (Harold, their nephew, lived with them while his parents were away). Also added were Mala Powers as Mona Williams, a friend of Barbara's; Ann Jillian as Millie, Steve's secretary. The series, which cracked Nielsen's top ten in its first season, was produced by James Fonda for Screen Gems.

THE HAZEL BISHOP SHOW
See THE FREDDY MARTIN SHOW

THE HAZEL SCOTT SHOW DUMONT
3 JULY 1950–29 SEPTEMBER 1950   Pianist Hazel Scott hosted this fifteen-minute musical series, which was seen Mondays, Wednesdays, and Fridays. It was the first network series hosted by a black woman.

HE & SHE CBS
6 SEPTEMBER 1967–18 SEPTEMBER 1968   This unsuccessful sitcom brought together a talented group of players: Richard Benjamin as Dick Hollister, a cartoonist, the creator of "Jetman"; Paula Prentiss (who was married to Benjamin) as Paula Hollister, Dick's wife, who worked for Travelers' Aid in New York; Hamilton Camp as Andrew Hummel, the superintendent of their apartment building; Jack Cassidy as Oscar North, the actor who played Dick's "Jetman" on TV; Kenneth Mars as the Hollisters' neighbor, Harry, a fireman; and Harold Gould as Norman Nugent, Dick's boss. Though the series was scheduled in a good time slot (9:30 Wednesdays, following *The Beverly Hillbillies* and *Green Acres*), audiences seemed to stay away in droves. Created by Leonard Stern, the half-hour show was produced by Talent Associates.

HE SAID, SHE SAID SYNDICATED
1969   Developed by Mark Goodson and Bill Todman, this game show featured celebrity couples. Husbands and wives were separated, and one set of spouses was asked a question. The object of the game was for the other set of spouses to determine which answers had been given by their respective mates. Joe Garagiola hosted the series.

HEAD OF THE CLASS   ABC
17 SEPTEMBER 1986–15 JANUARY 1991; 28 MAY 1991–25 JUNE 1991   Half-hour sitcom
starring Howard Hesseman (1986–1990) as Charlie Moore, a substitute teacher at
New York's Millard Fillmore High School who was hired to take over the IHP
(Individual Honors Program) class. Moore soon realized that, although his charges
were brainy, they needed a lot of lessons about life itself. Also featured were William
G. Schilling as the meddling principal, Dr. Harold Samuels, who wanted to make
sure that the IHP kids would win the city's Academic Olympics contests; Jeannetta
Arnette as assistant principal Bernadette Meara; Leslie Bega (1986–1989) as the
grade-obsessed Maria Borges, who transferred to a performing arts high school; Dan
Frischman as prototypical nerd Arvid Engen; Robin Givens as preppy Darlene
Merriman; Khrystyne Haje as literary Simone Foster; Jory Husain (1986–1989) as
Indian student Jawarhalal Shoudhury; Tony O'Dell as preppy Alan Pinkard; Brian
Robbins as intelligent hood Eric Mardian; Kimberly Russell as artistic Sarah Nevins;
Dan Schneider as hefty science jock Dennis Blunden; Tannis Vallely (1986–1989) as
twelve-year-old prodigy Janice Lazorotto, who entered Harvard after three years;
Rain Pryor (1988–1991) as T. J.; Michael DeLorenzo (1989–1991) as Alex Torres, a
transfer from an all-boys school; Lara Piper (1989–1991) as Viki Amory; De'Voreaux
White (1989–1991) as artistic Aristotle McKenzie; and Jonathan Ke Quan (spring
1990–1991) as new Asian student Jasper Kwong.
   Howard Hesseman left the show after four seasons (it was explained that his
character had landed an acting job). Scottish-born comedian Billy Connolly succeeded him as the new teacher, Billy MacGregor. *Head of the Class* had been scheduled as a "backup" series for 1990–1991, meaning that it would be available to
replace a faltering fall series, but it was hastily added to ABC's fall 1990 schedule to
replace the problem-beset new series *Baby Talk*. After *Head of the Class* left the air
for good, Connolly returned as MacGregor in the 1992 sitcom *Billy*.
   In 1988 *Head of the Class* became the first American prime-time series to film an
episode in the Soviet Union; the one-hour program aired 2 November. The series was
created by Michael Elias and Rich Eustis; Elias had actually served as a substitute
teacher in the New York City school system while struggling to make it as an actor.

HEADLINE CHASERS   SYNDICATED
1985   Daily game show, hosted by Wink Martindale, on which contestants tried to
fill in the missing words in various hypothetical news headlines.

HEADLINE CLEWS
See BROADWAY TO HOLLYWOOD

HEADLINERS WITH DAVID FROST   NBC
31 MAY 1978–5 JULY 1978   David Frost was the host and the executive producer of
this hour-long interview series; almost all of the segments were taped, though the
introductions and other material were presented live. Frost's guests on the premiere
included John Travolta, the Bee Gees, and former CIA director Richard Helms.

HEADMASTER   CBS
18 SEPTEMBER 1970–1 JANUARY 1971   Andy Griffith returned to television in this
low-key comedy-drama. He played Andy Thompson, headmaster of a coeducational
prep school in California. Also featured were Claudette Nevins as his wife, Margaret
Thompson, who also taught there; Jerry Van Dyke as athletic coach Jerry Brownell;
and Parker Fennelly as Mr. Purdy, the custodian. Aaron Ruben produced the series;
the format was scrapped in midseason, and the show was retitled. See *The New Andy
Griffith Show*. *Headmaster*'s theme, "Only a Man," was sung by a then little-known
vocalist named Linda Ronstadt.

HEALTH AND THE MIND WITH BILL MOYERS   PBS
22 FEBRUARY 1993–24 FEBRUARY 1993   Bill Moyers examined the interrelationship
between the body and the mind in this three-night, five-hour presentation.

THE HEALTH SHOW   ABC
17 JANUARY 1987–4 NOVEMBER 1990   Half-hour weekend informational series on
health issues, produced by ABC News. Hosts have included Kathleen Sullivan, Edie
Magnus, Paula Zahn, and Karen Stone.

HEALTHBEAT   SYNDICATED
1982   A half-hour series on health care, hosted by Boston physician Timothy
Johnson.

HEART OF THE CITY
See BIG TOWN

HEART OF THE CITY   ABC
20 SEPTEMBER 1986–10 JANUARY 1987; 4 JUNE 1987–2 JULY 1987   This hour crime
show focused on the home life as well as the professional life of its main character.
Robert Desiderio starred as Los Angeles police detective Wes Kennedy, who was
suddenly left to care for his two teenagers after his wife was murdered; Kennedy
moved to the night shift in order to spend more time with his kids. Also featured
were Jonathan Ward as fifteen-year-old Kevin; Christina Applegate (who would
achieve greater fame in *Married . . .With Children*) as fourteen-year-old Robin;
Dick Anthony Williams as watch commander Ed Van Duzer; Kario Salem as Detective Rick Arno; Branscombe Richmond as Sergeant Luke Halui; and Robert Alan
Browne as Detective Stanley.

THE HEART OF THE DRAGON   PBS
6 MAY 1985–20 JULY 1985   A twelve-part look at twenty-two centuries of Chinese
culture. The British-produced series was narrated by Anthony Quayle.

HEARTBEAT   ABC
23 MARCH 1988–21 APRIL 1988; 3 JANUARY 1989–6 APRIL 1989   Two female physicians
established the Women's Medical Arts Clinic in this hour medical show. With Kate
Mulgrew as cofounder Dr. Joanne Springsteen, a gynecologist; Laura Johnson as
cofounder Dr. Eve Autrey, a surgeon; Gail Strickland as Marilyn McGrath, a nurse-
practitioner who was gay; Ben Masters as Dr. Leo Rosetti, a pediatrician; Ray Baker
as psychiatrist Dr. Stan Gorshalk; Lynn Whitfield as obstetrician-gynecologist Dr.
Cory Banks; Darrell Larson as fertility specialist Dr. Paul Jared; and Claudette
Sutherland as receptionist Robin Flowers. Following a six-episode trial run in the
spring of 1988, the series returned early in 1989 for another thirteen weeks. At that
time Mulgrew's character had been renamed Dr. Joanne Holloran, and Laura Johnson's, Dr. Eve Calvert. Carmen Argenziano joined the cast as the new shrink, Dr.
Nathan Solt, replacing Ray Baker.

HEARTLAND   CBS
20 MARCH 1989–31 JULY 1989   CBS's second comedy of the 1988–1989 season to be
set in Nebraska (see also *First Impressions*), *Heartland* told the story of a family
trying to hang on to their farm. Featured were Richard Gilliland as Tom Stafford;
Kathleen Layman as his wife, Casey Stafford; Brian Keith as her crusty dad, B. L.
McCutcheon; Jason Kristopher as teen son Johnny; Devin Ratray as younger son
Gus; and Daisy Keith as daughter Kim.

HEARTS AFIRE   CBS
14 SEPTEMBER 1992–1 FEBRUARY 1995   Linda Bloodworth-Thomason created this
sitcom, which was set in Washington, D. C., during its first season. It starred John
Ritter as John Hartman, a senatorial chief of staff and single parent, and Markie Post
as Georgiann Lahti, who was hired by Hartman as the senator's press secretary and
moved into Hartman's house, where a romance between the two began. Also in the
cast were Justin Burnette as John's son Elliott; Clark Duke as John's son Ben; Billy
Bob Thornton as senatorial aide Billy Bob Davis; Wendie Jo Sperber (1992–1993) as
Billy B ob's wife, Mavis Davis, also a senatorial aide (Billy Bob and Mavis were

having marital troubles); Doren Fein as their young daughter, Carson Lee; Beth Broderick (1992–1993) as the ditzy but stunning receptionist, Didi Starr; Adam Carl (1992–1993) as Adam; George Gaynes (1992–1993) as the addled senator, Strobe Smithers; and Beah Richards (1992–1993) as Miss Lula, Georgiann's childhood nanny, who also moved into John's house and helped care for the kids. Occasionally featured was Ed Asner as Georgiann's father, George. The relationship between Hartman and Lahti blossomed, and the two were married in February 1993. In the fall of 1993 the setting shifted from Washington to John's hometown, somewhere in the South, where John and Georgiann settled and bought a newspaper. Burnette, Duke, Thornton, and Fein also made the move, and several new faces were seen: Conchata Ferrell as their friend Madeleine; Beth Broderick (in a new role) as Didi's sister, Lee Ann Folsom; Mark Harelik as Lee Ann's loud and rich husband, Reed Folsom; and Leslie Jordan as Lonnie Garr. Broderick and Harelik departed after the 1993–1994 season, and J. Skylar Testa replaced Justin Burnette as Elliott in the fall of 1994.

HEARTS ARE WILD — CBS

10 JANUARY 1992–13 MARCH 1992   Caesar's Palace in Las Vegas was the setting of this hour dramatic series; most episodes focused on the lives of the resort's guests, few of whom ever seemed to lose at the gaming tables. The regulars were David Beecroft as owner Jack Thorpe; Catherine Mary Stewart as the guest relations director, Kyle Hubbard; and Jon Polito as the casino manager, Leon "Pepe" Pepperman. Eric Roth created the series.

HEATHCLIFF AND DINGBAT — ABC

4 OCTOBER 1980–5 SEPTEMBER 1981

HEATHCLIFF AND MARMADUKE — ABC

12 SEPTEMBER 1981–18 SEPTEMBER 1982   This Saturday-morning cartoon series consisted of segments featuring Heathcliff, a cat, and Dingbat, a dog who also happened to be a vampire. After a season Heathcliff hooked up with Marmaduke, the oversized Great Dane of comic strip fame.

HEAVEN FOR BETSY — CBS

30 SEPTEMBER 1952–25 DECEMBER 1952   This fifteen-minute sitcom was seen on Tuesdays and Thursdays following the network news. It starred Jack Lemmon and Cynthia Stone (Lemmon's wife at the time) as newlyweds Pete and Betsy Bell. Lemmon and Stone previously played newlyweds on a 1951–1952 daytime series, *The Frances Langford-Don Ameche Show.*

HEAVEN HELP US — SYNDICATED

1994   Hour dramatic series from Spelling Entertainment in which a honeymooning couple killed in a plane crash became apprentice angels, and were sent back to Earth to help persons in need. With John Schneider and Melinda Clarke as Doug and Lexy Monroe, and Ricardo Montalban as their angelic guide, Mr. Shepherd.

HEC RAMSEY — NBC

8 OCTOBER 1972–25 AUGUST 1974   This segment of *The NBC Sunday Mystery Movie* starred Richard Boone as Hec Ramsey, a deputy police officer in New Prospect, Oklahoma, at the turn of the century; a former gunslinger, Ramsey now used modern scientific methods to solve cases. Also featured were Rick Lenz as the young police chief, Oliver B. Stamp; Harry Morgan as Doc Coogan, New Prospect's ad hoc physician. Douglas Benton produced the series for Jack Webb's Mark VII Productions.

HECKLE AND JECKLE — SYNDICATED/CBS/NBC

1955 (SYNDICATED); 14 OCTOBER 1956–24 SEPTEMBER 1960 (CBS); 25 SEPTEMBER 1965–3 SEPTEMBER 1966 (CBS); 6 SEPTEMBER 1969–4 SEPTEMBER 1971   (NBC)
Heckle and Jeckle, a pair of fast-talking magpies were created by Paul Terry and starred in hundreds of theatrical cartoons before coming to television in 1955. Other Terrytoon characters who appeared on the durable TV show were Gandy Goose,

Dinky Duck, Little Roquefort, and The Terry Bears. See also *The New Adventures of Mighty Mouse and Heckle and Jeckle*.

THE HECTOR HEATHCOTE SHOW   NBC
5 OCTOBER 1963–25 SEPTEMBER 1965   Saturday-morning cartoon series about a scientist and his time machine. Assisting Heathcote were Hashimoto, a judo-trained mouse, and Sidney, an elephant.

HEE HAW   CBS/SYNDICATED
15 JUNE 1969–7 SEPTEMBER 1969; 17 DECEMBER 1969–13 JULY 1971 (CBS); 1971–1992 (SYNDICATED)   Best described as the country-and-western version of *Laugh-In*, *Hee Haw* was a fast-paced mixture of songs, skits, blackouts, and corny jokes. It began as a summer series and attracted decent enough ratings to warrant its return that winter. Though it was blasted by the critics, there was no doubt that it had wide appeal; it ranked a respectable sixteenth when CBS canceled it in 1971 along with rest of the network's rural shows (*The Beverly Hillbillies, Green Acres*, and *The Jim Nabors Show*). A syndicated version of the show appeared that fall and soon was carried by more stations than when it ran on CBS; by 1977 it was the nation's number-one-rated non-network show.
    From the beginning, the show was taped in Nashville, first at the studios of WLAC-TV, later at WTVF. The show was taped in assembly-line style during periods lasting several weeks. The segments were then cut, edited, and spliced together to comprise the hour-long programs. The show was the brainchild of two Canadians, Frank Peppiatt and John Aylesworth, who served as its executive producers (Sam Lovullo was the producer). The series was cohosted by Buck Owens and Roy Clark (by the late 1980s, Owens and Clark appeared only occasionally, having made room for various guest hosts). A large stable of regular performers was featured, including Louis M. ("Grandpa") Jones, Junior Samples, Jeannine Riley, Lulu Roman, David Akeman ("Stringbean"), Sherry Miles, Lisa Todd, Minnie Pearl, Gordie Tapp, Diana Scott, Cathy Baker, unicyclist Zella Lehr, The Hagers, and Barbi Benton. In later years the nucleus of regulars included Jones, Samples, The Hagers, Roman, Todd, Pearl, Archie Campbell, Roni Stoneham, George Lindsey, Gunilla Hutton, Harry Cole, Don Harron (as Charlie Farquharson), Misty Rowe, Gailard Sartain, Mackenzie Colt, Irlene Mandrell, Dub Taylor, and Jeff Smith.

THE HEE HAW HONEYS   SYNDICATED
1978–1979   A half-hour sitcom set at Honey's Club, a small restaurant in Nashville, this series was spun off from *Hee Haw*. With Kenny Price and Lulu Roman as the proprietors, Kenny and Lulu Honey; Misty Rowe and Kathie Lee Johnson as their daughters, Misty and Kathie, who waited on tables and also sang there; and Gailard Sartain as their son, Willy Billy, the cook. A regular feature of the show was the appearance of guest stars from the world of country-and-western music, who stopped by to sing a number or two at the club. Sam Lovullo was the executive producer.

THE HEIGHTS   FOX
27 AUGUST 1992–26 NOVEMBER 1992   Another unsuccessful series about a rock band (see also *Catwalk* and *Dreams*). With Shawn Thompson as J.T. Banks, the lead singer; Cheryl Pollak as Rita, the sax player; Charlotte Ross as Hope, the guitarist; Alex Desert as Stan Lee, the bassist; Zachary Throne as Lenny, the keyboardist; Ken Garito as Dizzy, the drummer; James Walters as Alex; Ray Aranha as Stan's dad, Mike Lee, who owned a pool hall; and Tasia Valenza as Jodie Abramowitz, Dizzy's girlfriend. Although the TV series was a flop, the show's theme, "How Do You Talk to an Angel?" became a number one record.

THE HELEN O'CONNELL SHOW   NBC
29 MAY 1957–6 SEPTEMBER 1957   Helen O'Connell, who sang with several big bands during the 1940s, hosted this fifteen-minute series, which was seen Wednesdays and Fridays before the evening news.

THE HELEN REDDY SHOW   NBC

28 JUNE 1973–16 AUGUST 1973   Australian-born singer Helen Reddy, who won a Grammy for "I Am Woman," hosted this variety hour, a summer replacement for *The Flip Wilson Show.* Carolyn Raskin produced the series.

HELL TOWN   NBC

11 SEPTEMBER 1985–25 DECEMBER 1985   After his cop show *Baretta* left the air in 1978, Robert Blake starred in three *Joe Dancer* TV-movies and played Jimmy Hoffa in the TV-movie "Blood Feud." He then came up with the idea of playing a priest in a tough East Los Angeles parish. He fought hard to get a pilot film made, and, once made, to get it scheduled; eventually, NBC accommodated him, and the *Hell Town* pilot was aired 6 March 1985, opposite *Dynasty* on ABC. When it turned out that the film had scored NBC's highest rating of the season in that time slot, the series was ordered. It starred Blake as Father Noah "Hardstep" Rivers, who had become a priest after spending time in prison, and vowed to keep his parish (St. Dominic's) clean (Rivers was nicknamed Hardstep because he had been abandoned as an infant on a hard step in a rainstorm). An assortment of odd characters was on hand to help out Fr. Hardstep: Whitman Mayo as pool-playing One Ball; Jeff Corey as atheist attorney Lawyer Sam; Natalie Cole as Mother Maggie; Vonetta McGee as Sister Indigo; Isabel Grandin as Sister Angel Cakes; Rhonda Dodson as Sister Daisy; Tony Longo as Stump; Zitto Karzann as Crazy Horse; and Eddie Quillan as Poco Loco. The sixteen episodes were filmed mostly on location; Blake insisted on using real street people as extras.

HELLO KITTY'S FURRY TALE THEATER   CBS

19 SEPTEMBER 1987–10 SEPTEMBER 1988   Adaptations of nursery rhymes and children's stories were presented on this Saturday-morning cartoon show; all the parts were played by cartoon cats.

HELLO, LARRY   NBC

26 JANUARY 1979–30 APRIL 1980   Half-hour sitcom about a radio talk-show host who moved from Los Angeles to Portland, Oregon, with his two teenage daughters following the breakup of his marriage. With McLean Stevenson as Larry Alder; Donna Wilkes (spring 1979) and Krista Errickson (fall 1979–1980) as daughter Diane; Kim Richards as daughter Ruthie; Joanna Gleason as Morgan Winslow, Larry's producer; and George Memmoli as Earl, Larry's corpulent engineer. In the fall of 1979 Meadowlark Lemon, formerly of the Harlem Globetrotters, joined the cast (as himself), and John Femia was added as Tommy. It is no coincidence that *Hello, Larry* bore more than a passing resemblance to *One Day at a Time,* for *Larry's* executive producers—Dick Bensfield and Perry Grant (for Norman Lear's TAT Communications)—had also worked on *One Day at a Time.* From time to time efforts were made to shore up *Larry's* ratings by cross-pollinating it with *Diff'rent Strokes; Strokes's* Philip Drummond, it turned out, was an old Army buddy of Larry's, facilitating the appearances of the cast members on each other's series.

HELP! IT'S THE HAIR BEAR BUNCH   CBS

11 SEPTEMBER 1971–2 SEPTEMBER 1972; 9 SEPTEMBER 1973–31 AUGUST 1974   Saturday-morning cartoon show from Hanna-Barbera about a bunch of bears living in a zoo, where they tried to improve their living conditions. Reruns were syndicated under the title *The Yo Yo Bears.*

HE-MAN AND THE MASTERS OF THE UNIVERSE   SYNDICATED

1983   Half-hour cartoon series produced by Filmation and underwritten by Mattel Toys. The central characters were He-Man and his alter ego, Prince Adam of Eternia. See also *She-Ra: Princess of Power.*

HENNESEY   CBS

28 SEPTEMBER 1959–17 SEPTEMBER 1962   Situation comedy about a Navy doctor stationed in San Diego. With Jackie Cooper as Lieutenant Charles "Chick" Hennesey;

Abby Dalton as his girlfriend, Nurse Martha Hale; Roscoe Karns as his commanding officer, Captain Walter Shafer; James Komack as Navy dentist Harvey Spencer Blair III; and Henry Kulky as Max Bronsky, an orderly who read Spinoza. In the fall of 1961 promotions were handed out: Hennesey became a lieutenant commander, Hale a lieutenant, Shafer an admiral, and Bronsky a chief petty officer. Hennesey and Hale also got married that season. Don McGuire wrote and coproduced the series with Jackie Cooper. *Hennesey* was one of the very few sitcoms of its time that did not employ a laugh track.

THE HENNY AND ROCKY SHOW   ABC
1 JUNE 1955–31 AUGUST 1955   *The Henny and Rocky Show* was a series of variable length—it was designed to fill out the rest of the hour if and when ABC's Wednesday-night boxing matches ran short. Comedian Henny Youngman and boxer-actor Rocky Graziano cohosted the show, which also featured singer Marion Colby.

HENRY FONDA PRESENTS THE STAR AND THE STORY   SYNDICATED
1955   Half-hour dramatic anthology series hosted by Henry Fonda.

THE HENRY MORGAN SHOW   ABC/NBC
18 APRIL 1948–16 MAY 1948 (ABC); 13 MARCH 1949–22 APRIL 1949 (NBC); 26 JANUARY 1951–15 JUNE 1951 (NBC)   Though comedian Henry Morgan is remembered today mainly as a panelist on game shows such as *I've Got a Secret,* he hosted several shows in television's early days. His 1948 show, titled *On the Corner,* was seen Sunday nights on the ABC network (though it was carried by the DuMont affiliate in New York). In 1949 he moved to NBC, where he was first given a half hour on Sunday nights; that slot was soon shifted to a fifteen-minute slot on Mondays, Wednesdays, and Fridays, before disappearing altogether in April of that year. Early in 1951 he tried a second series for NBC, a Friday-night half hour called *Henry Morgan's Great Talent Hunt.* A forerunner of *The Gong Show,* the series featured people with un-usual talents; assisting Morgan were Arnold Stang and Kaye Ballard. In April 1951 the talent format was scrapped, and Morgan hosted a half-hour comedy-variety show for a few more weeks, which featured Arnold Stang, Pert Kelton, and Art Carney. The principal reason that all of Morgan's series were short-lived was his apparently incurable habit of ridiculing his sponsors; *TV Guide* reported that one advertiser, Life Savers, dropped its sponsorship after one week, following Morgan's tongue-in-cheek accusation that the company was cheating the public by drilling holes in its product.

HERB SHRINER TIME   ABC
11 OCTOBER 1951–3 APRIL 1952
THE HERB SHRINER SHOW   CBS
2 OCTOBER 1956–4 DECEMBER 1956   Indiana comedian Herb Shriner was first seen on television in 1949, when he hosted a thrice-weekly five-minute show on CBS. In 1951 he hosted his first prime-time variety series, seen Thursdays over ABC. He then hosted a game show, *Two for The Money,* before trying a second variety series in 1956 on CBS.

HERBIE, THE LOVE BUG   CBS
17 MARCH 1982–14 APRIL 1982   This hour comedy series was derived from the Disney films about Herbie, a Volkswagen with a mind of its own. In addition to the car, the series featured Dean Jones as Jim Douglas, owner of the Famous Driving School; Patricia Harty as Susan MacLane, a divorcée whom Herbie was trying to match Jim up with; Larry Linville as Susan's stuffy boyfriend, Randy Bigelow; Clau-dia Wells as Susan's daughter, Julie; Nicky Katt as Susan's son Matthew; Douglas Emerson as Susan's son Robbie; and Richard Paul as Bo Phillips, one of Jim's employees. The series was produced by Kevin Corcoran, who had appeared in several Disney films as a child.

HERCULES—THE LEGENDARY JOURNEYS   SYNDICATED
1995–   Greek mythology has rarely been the basis of a TV series. This one starred
Kevin Sorbo as the half-god, half-human Hercules, whose prodigious strength established him as the Superman of the Hellenistic age. Joining him during the first season
was Lucy Lawless as Xena, who got her own spinoff series in the fall of 1995: See also
Xena: Warrior Princess. Anthony Quinn occasionally appeared as Zeus. Filmed in
New Zealand, the hour series followed several made-for-TV movies which had been
telecast in 1994.

THE HERCULOIDS   CBS
9 SEPTEMBER 1967–6 SEPTEMBER 1969   Saturday-morning cartoon show from Hanna-
Barbera featuring several super-powered characters—Zok the dragon, Tundro the
Tremendous, Iago, and Gloop and Gleep—who lived on the planet Quasar in another galaxy.

HERE AND NOW   NBC
19 SEPTEMBER 1992–2 JANUARY 1993   Shortly after *The Cosby Show* left the air,
Malcolm-Jamal Warner returned to star in this sitcom. Here he played Alexander
"A.J." James, a graduate student who worked with youngsters at the Manhattan
Youth Center in New York. Also featured were Charles Brown as Uncle Sydney (who
was not really A.J.'s uncle, but a friend of A.J.'s father), a hotel doorman with whom
A.J. lived; Rachael Crawford as Sydney's daughter, Danielle; Daryl "Chill" Mitchell
as A.J.'s friend T, who also worked at the Center; Brenda Pressley (premiere epi-
sode) and S. Epatha Merkerson as the Center's director, Claudia St. Marth; Pee Wee
Love as Randall; Michael Alexander Jackson as Malik; Shaun Weiss as William;
Amir Williams as Everett; Afi McClendon as Shonna; and Victoria Williams as
Rahina.

HERE COME THE BRIDES   ABC
25 SEPTEMBER 1968–18 SEPTEMBER 1970   Based on the film *Seven Brides for Seven
Brothers,* this Screen Gems sitcom was set at a Washington logging camp in the
1870s, where the men arranged to import 100 available women from New Bedford,
Massachusetts. With Robert Brown as Jason Bolt, unofficial leader of the camp;
David Soul as Joshua Bolt, his brother; Bobby Sherman as Jeremy Bolt, their younger brother; Mark Lenard as Aaron Stempel, operator of the local sawmill; Henry
Beckman as Clancey, the boat captain; Joan Blondell as Lottie Hatfield, proprietor
of the camp saloon; Bridget Hanley as Candy Pruitt, an eligible bride; Susan Tolsky
as Biddie Cloom; Mitzi Hoag as Essie, the schoolteacher; Hoke Howell as Ben
Jenkins; Bo Svenson as Big Swede, camp foreman; Eric Chase (1969–1970) as Christopher, Candy's little brother; and Patti Cohoon (1969–1970) as Molly, Candy's little
sister.

HERE COME THE DOUBLE-DECKERS   ABC
12 SEPTEMBER 1970–17 SEPTEMBER 1972   A British import about a group of youngsters who lived in a reconverted double-decker bus, this half-hour series was seen on
weekend mornings. With Michael Auderson as Brains; Gillian Bailey as Billie; Bruce
Clark as Sticks; Peter Firth as Scooper; Brinsley Forde as Spring; Debbie Russ as
Tiger; and Douglas Simmonds as Doughnut. Also appearing was Melvyn Hayes as
their grownup pal, Albert.

HERE COMES THE GRUMP   NBC
6 SEPTEMBER 1969–4 SEPTEMBER 1971   Saturday-morning cartoon series reminiscent
of *The Wizard of Oz.* Here, a boy (Terry) and his dog (Bib) found themselves in a
fantasy land and were commissioned by Princess Dawn to find a magic key secreted
by The Grump.

HERE WE GO AGAIN   ABC
20 JANUARY 1973–23 JUNE 1973   This situation comedy about divorce failed to make
a dent in the ratings of its CBS competitor, *All in the Family.* With Larry Hagman as

Richard Evans, a divorced architect who remarried; Diane Baker as Susan Standish, the divorcée whom he married; Dick Gautier as Jerry Standish, Susan's ex, a restaurateur who lived nearby; Nita Talbot as Judy Evans, Richard's ex, who edited a movie magazine; Chris Beaumont as Jeff, Richard and Judy's teenage son (he lived with Judy after the divorce); Leslie Graves and Kim Richards as Cindy and Jan, Jerry and Susan's young daughters (they lived with Richard and Susan). Created by Bob Kaufman; produced by Steve Pritzker for Metromedia.

HERE'S BARBARA　　　　　　　　　　　　　　　　　SYNDICATED
1969　　Barbara Coleman hosted this Washington-based half-hour talk show.

HERE'S BOOMER　　　　　　　　　　　　　　　　　　　　NBC
14 MARCH 1980–14 AUGUST 1982　　A remake of *The Littlest Hobo,* this half-hour comedy-drama told the story of Boomer, a lovable mutt who helped out people in distress. Plans were announced to have Boomer (the sole regular on the show) voice his thoughts (as had Cleo the dog on *The People's Choice*), but were abandoned after a single attempt in late 1980. *Here's Boomer* was developed by Dan Balluck and A. C. Lyles. Boomer was owned and trained by Ray Berwick.

HERE'S EDIE　　　　　　　　　　　　　　　　　　　　　ABC
26 SEPTEMBER 1963–19 MARCH 1964　　This half-hour variety series alternated with *The Sid Caesar Show* on Thursdays. It was hosted by singer-comedienne Edie Adams, widow of Ernie Kovacs. Don Chastain was also featured on the show.

HERE'S HOLLYWOOD　　　　　　　　　　　　　　　　　　NBC
26 SEPTEMBER 1960–28 DECEMBER 1962　　Celebrity interviews comprised this daytime half-hour show, cohosted by Dean Miller and Jo-ann Jordan; Helen O'Connell later replaced Jordan.

HERE'S LOOKING AT YOU
See THE RICHARD WILLIS SHOW

HERE'S LUCY　　　　　　　　　　　　　　　　　　　　　CBS
23 SEPTEMBER 1968–2 SEPTEMBER 1974　　*Here's Lucy* was the direct successor to *The Lucy Show,* with a slight change in format. It starred Lucille Ball as Lucille Carter, a secretary at her brother-in-law's employment agency; Gale Gordon as Harrison Carter, her brother-in-law and boss, head of the Unique Employment Agency; Lucie Arnaz as her daughter, Kim; Desi Arnaz, Jr. (1968–1971) as her son, Craig; Mary Jane Croft as Mary Jane Lewis, Lucy's friend. Many prominent stars appeared on the series, including Johnny Carson (1 December 1969), Ann-Margret (2 February 1970), Richard Burton and Elizabeth Taylor (14 September 1970), Flip Wilson (13 September 1971 and 6 March 1972), Ginger Rogers (8 November 1971), David Frost (29 November 1971), and Joe Namath (9 October 1972).

HERITAGE: CIVILIZATION AND THE JEWS　　　　　　　　　PBS
1 OCTOBER 1984–19 NOVEMBER 1984　　A nine-week documentary series on Jewish history and culture, hosted by Abba Eban. The series won a prestigious Peabody Award in 1984.

THE HERMAN HICKMAN SHOW　　　　　　　　　　　　　　NBC
3 OCTOBER 1952–27 MARCH 1953　　Fifteen-minute Friday-night sports show hosted by Herman Hickman, who had formerly coached football at Yale.

HERMAN'S HEAD　　　　　　　　　　　　　　　　　　　FOX
8 SEPTEMBER 1991–16 JUNE 1994　　Half-hour sitcom with an interesting premise: the audience got to see what was happening inside the protagonist's brain as the four sides of his personality battled one another for control. With William Ragsdale as Herman Brooks, a young man who moved to New York and found work as a magazine researcher; Ken Hudson Campbell as Animal, the lusty slob who personified

Herman's baser desires; Rick Lawless as Wimp, who tried to imbue Herman with guilt and apprehension; Peter MacKenzie as Genius, the sensible side of Herman; Molly Hagan as Angel, Herman's altruistic aspect; Hank Azaria as Jay Nichols, Herman's skirt-chasing coworker; Jane Sibbett as icy coworker Heddy Newman; Jason Bernard as Herman's formidable boss, Paul Bracken; and Yeardley Smith (who is perhaps better recognized as the voice of Lisa on *The Simpsons*) as Bracken's secretary, Louise Fitzer. Julia Campbell appeared occasionally during the second season as Herman's girlfriend, Elizabeth.

THE HERO   NBC
8 SEPTEMBER 1966–5 JANUARY 1967   An early casualty of the 1966–1967 season, *The Hero* featured a series-within-a-series format. It starred Richard Mulligan as Sam Garret, star of "Jed Clayton—U.S. Marshal," a hit western, but a clumsy bloke offscreen. Also featured were Mariette Hartley as his wife, Ruth Garret; Bobby Horan as their son, Paul; Victor French as neighbor Fred Gilman; Joey Baio as Fred's son, Burton; and Marc London as Dewey. Leonard Stern created the series and served as its executive producer; Jay Sandrich produced it for Talent Associates.

HE'S THE MAYOR   ABC
10 JANUARY 1986–21 MARCH 1986   Winston Moss and Bob Peete created this sitcom about a twenty-five-year-old black man who was elected mayor of a large city. With Kevin Hooks as Mayor Carl Burke; Al Fann as his father, Alvin Burke, a city hall janitor; David Graf as city council president Harlan Nash; Wesley Thompson as Carl's cousin and chauffeur, Wardell Halsey; Mari Gorman as Carl's secretary, Paula Hendricks; Stanley Brock as neighbor Ivan Bronski; and Pat Corley as Police Chief Walter Padget.

HEY, JEANNIE   CBS
8 SEPTEMBER 1956–4 MAY 1957   Half-hour sitcom about a Scotswoman who emigrated to New York City. With Jeannie Carson as Jeannie MacLennan; Allen Jenkins as her sponsor, Al Murray, a Brooklyn cabbie; and Jane Dulo as Liz Murray, Al's sister. After arriving in New York, Jeannie moved in with Al and Liz and got a job as a waitress in a donut shop.

HEY LANDLORD   NBC
11 SEPTEMBER 1966–14 MAY 1967   Half-hour sitcom about two young bachelors who own an apartment building. With Will Hutchins as Woody Banner, a would-be writer; Sandy Baron as Chuck Hookstratten, a would-be comic; Pamela Rodgers as tenant Timothy Morgan, a weather forecaster; Michael Constantine as tenant Jack Ellenhorn, a photographer; and Ann Morgan Guilbert as tenant Mrs. Henderson, a fussbudget. Produced by Lee Rich.

HEY MULLIGAN
See THE MICKEY ROONEY SHOW

HEY, VERN, IT'S ERNEST!   CBS/FAM
17 SEPTEMBER 1988–2 SEPTEMBER 1989 (CBS); 5 SEPTEMBER 1992–27 MARCH 1994 (FAM)   Half-hour live-action Saturday-morning kids' show, starring Jim Varney as Ernest P. Worrell. Varney had created the inept hayseed character for a series of soft drink commercials, and played him in a 1987 movie, *Ernest Goes to Camp* (two other films followed). Varney also played other characters on the series, including Dr. Otto, a crazed scientist. Mark Goldman and Denice Hicks were also featured. The "Vern" character was the camera, whom Ernest addressed when introducing his various escapades.

HI HONEY, I'M HOME   ABC/NICK
19 JULY 1991–23 AUGUST 1991 (ABC); 21 JULY 1991–8 NOVEMBER 1992 (NICK)   The first sitcom to be introduced simultaneously on network and cable television, this series's central characters were the Nielsen family. The Nielsens had been the stars of

an old sitcom, "Hi Honey, I'm Home"; after its cancellation they had been moved by the SRP (Sitcom Relocation Program) from peaceful Springfield in TV-land to New Jersey to await the return of their series to the airwaves. Recognized by the kid next door, they confided their secret to him. The cast included Charlotte Booker as perfect housewife and mother Honey Nielsen; Stephen Bradbury as her husband, Lloyd Nielsen; Julie Benz as their teen daughter, Babs; Danny Gura as preteen son Chuckie; Pete Benson as Mike Duff, the next-door teen who had been a fan of their show; Eric Kushnick as his nasty little brother, Sidney "Skunk" Duff; and Susan Cella as their divorced mother, Elaine. When modern life became too much for the Nielsens to cope with, they could activate their Turnerizer, a device which turned things into black and white. Sitcom stars of the 1950s and 1960s regularly appeared as guests on the series, which ran for two full seasons on Nickelodeon.

HIDDEN FACES   NBC
30 DECEMBER 1968–27 JUNE 1969   Short-lived daytime serial which NBC scheduled opposite CBS's *As the World Turns*. Soap opera buffs generally agree that it was well written and well acted, but that failure was inevitable against such strong competition. With Conrad Fowkes as lawyer Arthur Adams; Gretchen Walther as Dr. Katherine Walker, a surgeon who left medicine after accidentally killing a patient during an operation, and who eventually fell in love with Adams. Also featured were Stephen Joyce, Rita Gam, Tony LoBianco, and Nat Polen.

THE HIGH CHAPARRAL   NBC
10 SEPTEMBER 1967–10 SEPTEMBER 1971   This fairly successful western was produced by David Dortort, who also produced *Bonanza*. Like *Bonanza, The High Chaparral* was a "property" western: the two central families—the Cannons and the Montoyas—were both large landowners in the Arizona Territory. With Leif Erickson as John Cannon, owner of the High Chapparal Ranch; Linda Cristal as his wife, Victoria Cannon, daughter of the Montoyas; Cameron Mitchell as Buck Cannon, John's brother; Mark Slade as Blue Cannon, John's son and Victoria's stepson; Frank Silvera (1967–1970) as Don Sebastian Montoya, owner of the Montoya Ranch and father of Victoria Cannon; Gilbert Roland (1970–1971) as his brother, Don Domingo de Montoya; and Henry Darrow as Manolito, Don Sebastian's son. The several ranch hands on the two ranches included Bob Hoy as Joe, Roberto Conteras as Pedro, Rudy Ramos as Wind, and Rodolfo Acosta as Vasquero. Ninety-eight episodes were produced.

HIGH FINANCE   CBS
7 JULY 1956–15 DECEMBER 1956   The top prize was $75,000 on this prime-time current events quiz show, hosted by Dennis James. In September 1956 former boxing champ Joe Louis and his wife Rose appeared, trying to earn money to defray a hefty federal tax bill.

HIGH HOPES   SYNDICATED
1978   A half-hour serial set in the small college town of Cambridge. With Bruce Gray as family counselor Neal Chapman; Marianne McIsaac as Jessie Chapman, his possessive daughter; Nuala Fitzgerald as Paula Myles, sister of Neal's ex-wife; Barbara Kyle as Trudy Bowen, hostess of a local talk show; Colin Fox as Walter Telford; Gina Dick as Amy Sperry; Jayne Eastwood as Louise Bates; Jan Muszinski as Dr. Dan Gerard; Vivian Reis as Norma Stewart; Michael Tait as Michael Stewart; Gordon Thompson as Mike Stewart, Jr.; Deborah Turnbull as Mrs. Telford; Candace O'Connor as Helen; and Doris Petrie as Meg Chapman, Neal's mother. Taped in Toronto, the series was written by Winnifred Wolfe and Mort Forer. Dick Cox was the executive producer.

HIGH LOW QUIZ   NBC
4 JULY 1957–12 SEPTEMBER 1957   Contestants battled a panel of experts on this prime-time game show, a summer replacement for *The* (Tennessee Ernie) *Ford Show,*

hosted by Jack Barry. Contestants earned money by matching answers with either the expert with the most correct answers or the expert with the fewest correct answers.

HIGH MOUNTAIN RANGERS   CBS
2 JANUARY 1988–9 JULY 1988   Robert Conrad returned to TV in his ninth series, bringing two of his sons with him (his daughter Joan served as the executive producer). The elder Conrad played Jesse Hawkes, founder of the High Mountain Rangers, an elite rescue squad in the Sierra Nevadas; Christian Conrad played Jesse's older son, Matt, who now ran the squad; Shane Conrad was Jesse's younger son, Cody, who lived with his father (now semiretired) in a nearby mountain cabin. Also featured were Tony Acierto as ranger Frank Avila; Russell Todd as ranger Cutler; Eric Eugene Williams as ranger Hart; P. A. Christian as ranger Robin Kelly; Timothy Erwin (husband of Joan Conrad) as new ranger Izzy Flowers; Med Flory as Sheriff McBride; and Robyn Peterson as Jesse's estranged wife, Jackie. Following the cancellation of *High Mountain Rangers,* the Conrads stayed in character and headed off to still another series: see *Jesse Hawkes.* The pilot for *High Mountain Rangers* was televised 19 April 1987. Conrad dusted off the concept for a similar series in 1995: see *High Sierra Search and Rescue.*

HIGH PERFORMANCE   ABC
2 MARCH 1983–23 MARCH 1983   An hour crime show about a team of crack security agents, based at High Performance, an ultramodern training school for security people. With Mitchell Ryan as Brennan Flannery, H.P.'s founder; Lisa Hartman as his daughter, martial arts expert Kate Flannery; Jack Scalia as Blue Stratton; Rick Edwards as skilled driver Shane Adams; and Jason Bernard as computer ace Fletch. Scalia, who had costarred in *The Devlin Connection* a few months earlier, became one of the few TV performers to appear in two flop series in a single season.

HIGH RISK   CBS
4 OCTOBER 1988–15 NOVEMBER 1988   Wayne Rogers hosted this hour "reality show," which profiled persons who took risks, either at work or at play: wingwalkers, roller coaster testers, and paraplegic water skiers might all be seen on a typical program. The short-term series was ordered into production because of the 1988 writers' strike, which delayed the production of many fiction-format series.

HIGH ROAD (JOHN GUNTHER'S HIGH ROAD)   ABC
7 SEPTEMBER 1959–1 OCTOBER 1960   Prime-time travelogue, hosted by John Gunther.

HIGH ROAD TO DANGER   SYNDICATED
1958   Steve Brodie narrated this half-hour series of films about modern-day adventurers.

HIGH ROLLERS   NBC/SYNDICATED
1 JULY 1974–11 JUNE 1976 (NBC); 1975 (SYNDICATED); 24 APRIL 1978–20 JUNE 1980 (NBC); 1987 (SYNDICATED)   By answering questions correctly, contestants on this game show earned the chance to acquire prizes in accordance with the roll of a pair of giant dice. Alex Trebek hosted the show, which began as a daytime series on NBC; Ruta Lee rolled the dice on the network version, while Elaine Stewart handled the chore on the 1975 syndicated version. When the series returned to NBC's daytime schedule in 1978, it was titled *The New High Rollers.* Wink Martindale hosted the 1987 syndicated version, assisted by Crystal Owens and K. C. Winkler. Merrill Heatter and Bob Quigley were the executive producers.

HIGH SIERRA SEARCH AND RESCUE   NBC
11 JUNE 1995–26 JULY 1995   Robert Conrad starred as Tooter Campbell, a helicopter pilot who led a volunteer rescue team in Bear Lake, California, nestled in California's Sierra Nevada Mountains. Also on hand were Dee Wallace Stone as Morgan Duffy, owner of the general store; LaVelda Fann as Lisa Peterson, who ran a gas station; Alistair MacDougall as the eligible young sheriff, Ty Cooper; Ramon Franco

as schoolteacher Enrique Cruz; Brittney Powell as Kaja Wilson, who worked in Morgan's store; and Jason Lewis as ski instructor Flynn Norstedt. The pilot for the series was a two-hour TV-movie, "Search and Rescue," televised on NBC 27 March 1994. The series, Conrad's eleventh, was remarkably similar to *High Mountain Rangers,* Conrad's ninth, which also centered on a rescue unit in the Sierras.

HIGH SOCIETY   CBS
30 OCTOBER 1995–26 FEBRUARY 1996   Sitcom inspired by the cult British comedy series *Absolutely Fabulous. High Society* starred Jean Smart as narcissistic novelist Ellie Walker and Mary McDonnell as her best friend and publisher, Dott Emerson; both women spent much of their time smoking and drinking. Also on board were Faith Prince as Val, a hopelessly square college chum of Dott's whose marriage was on the rocks and who (to Ellie's chagrin) moved into Dott's Manhattan apartment; David Rasche as Peter, who held the minority interest in Dott's publishing company; Luigi Amodeo as Dott's trendy assistant, Stephano; Dan O'Donahue as Dott's seventeen-year-old son, Brendan; and Jayne Meadows as Dott's mother, Mrs. Morgan.

HIGHLANDER: THE SERIES   SYNDICATED
1992–   Based on the 1986 motion picture *Highlander* and its sequels, the TV version starred Adrian Paul as Duncan MacLeod, a 400-year-old Scotsman who was one of a small number of Immortals living on Earth. Not all the Immortals were good, however, and they battled among themselves, killing one another by ritual beheading. Ultimately, only one Immortal would be left alive, and if it were an evil being the world would know "an eternity of darkness." Also featured were Alexandra Vandernoot (1992–1994) as MacLeod's girlfriend, Tessa Noel, who ran an antique shop with him and was killed off during the second season; Stan Kirsch (1992–1993; 1994–) as Richie Ryan, a youngster who discovered that he too was an Immortal; Jim Byrnes (1993–) as Joe Dawson, one of a group of mortals known as the Watchers, who tracked the Immortals; and Lisa Howard (1994–) as MacLeod's new love interest, surgeon Anne Lindsey. The hour series was filmed in the Pacific Northwest and in France.

HIGHCLIFFE MANOR   NBC
12 APRIL 1979–3 MAY 1979   Comedy melodrama set at a mysterious island, the headquarters of the Blacke Foundation, a research outfit. With Shelley Fabares as Helen Blacke, widow of the foundation's founder; Stephen McHattie as Reverend Glenville; Eugenie Ross-Leming as Frances; Gerald Gordon as Dr. Felix Morger; Audrey Landers as Wendy, secretary to the late Berkeley Blacke; Jenny O'Hara as Rebecca, the housekeeper; Christian Marlowe as Bram Shelley; David Byrd as Dr. Lester; Luis Avalos as Dr. Sanchez; Ernie Hudson as Smythe, valet to the late Mr. Blacke; Harold Sakata as Cheng. Robert Blees created the half-hour series.

HIGHWAY PATROL   SYNDICATED
1955–1959   Very popular crime show produced by Ziv TV, depicting the work of the Highway Patrol, a law enforcement agency analogous to the State Police. Broderick Crawford starred as Captain Dan Matthews, the gravel-voiced chief who seemed to spend most of his time barking "10–4! 10–4!" over the police radio. Narrator: Art Gilmore. The *Highway Patrol* theme was composed by Ray Llewellyn. The show should not be confused with the similarly-titled 1993 documentary series, *Real Stories of the Highway Patrol.*

HIGHWAY TO HEAVEN   NBC
19 SEPTEMBER 1984–29 JUNE 1988   Michael Landon starred in his third successful prime-time series, this time as Jonathan Smith, an angel who was sent back to Earth to help people. Victor French (who had worked on Landon's previous series, *Little House on the Prairie*) played Smith's terrestrial sidekick, Mark Gordon, an ex-cop. Few people expected the series to do well, given its lack of car chases and beautiful women; NBC, desperate to find a "family" show for 8:00 on Wednesday, opposite ABC's popular hit, *The Fall Guy,* bought Landon's concept, though not without

misgivings. To everyone's surprise, *Highway* knocked *Fall Guy* out of Nielsen's Top Twenty and into another time slot. The series was seen weekly until June 1988; a few additional shows were broadcast sporadically during the 1988–1989 season, however.

THE HIGHWAYMAN NBC

4 MARCH 1988–6 MAY 1988   This Friday-night hour adventure series was aimed principally at the kids. Its real star was a massive eighteen-wheeler truck armed with various high-tech devices, piloted by two men who worked under the auspices of the government: The Highwayman (played by Sam Jones) and his Australian sidekick, Jetto (played by Jacko). In the background were the boss, Ms. Tania Winthrop (Jane Badler) and the mechanic, D. C. Montana (Tim Russ). The pilot for the series was telecast 20 September 1987, and featured Jones, G. Gordon Liddy, Jimmy Smits (of *L. A. Law*) and wrestler "Rowdy" Roddy Piper.

THE HILARIOUS HOUSE OF FRIGHTENSTEIN SYNDICATED

1975   Videotaped children's series hosted by Billy Van.

HILL STREET BLUES NBC

15 JANUARY 1981–19 MAY 1987   Not just another crime show, *Hill Street Blues* stood apart from the pack for several reasons: its large cast of interesting characters, its skillful blending of humor with tragedy, and its cinematically realistic look.

The series was germinated in 1980, when Fred Silverman, then president of NBC Television, approached two producers from MTM Enterprises, Michael Kozoll and Steven Bochco. Silverman suggested that they consider doing a cop show that would emphasize the personal lives and relationships of the characters. Kozoll and Bochco agreed to the proposal, but only on the condition that they be given complete artistic control over the development of the show; somewhat to their surprise, NBC acceded. Kozoll and Bochco proceeded to cast the series with a group of actors who were experienced but who, for the most part, were hardly household names. They also decided that *Hill Street* would indeed emphasize its characters rather than its cases—not all crimes would be solved in a single episode, and some would never be solved at all.

Hill Street was set in a decaying area of a large (but unnamed) American city. The grim reality of life in an urban ghetto was frequently offset by unexpected humor. A realistic look was achieved through the use of such techniques as underlit interiors, crowded frames, and background noise. Mike Post's poignant theme music also helped set the series' tone.

The ensemble cast included: Daniel J. Travanti as Captain Frank Furillo, the dedicated and responsible commanding officer of the Hill Street Station; Veronica Hamel as coolly professional public defender Joyce Davenport, who dated Furillo (they were married in March of 1983; Davenport worked briefly as a prosecutor during the 1984–1985 season, but soon returned to defense work); Michael Conrad (who died in November 1983) as the polysyllabic Sergeant Phil Esterhaus, the officer who gave the daily briefing at roll call ("let's be careful out there!"); Bruce Weitz as scruffy Detective Mick Belker, who sometimes resorted to biting the felons he apprehended; James B. Sikking as reactionary Lieutenant Howard Hunter, head of the precinct SWAT team; Joe Spano as compassionate detective Henry Goldblume; Taurean Blacque as streetwise plainclothes detective Neal Washington; Kiel Martin as Washington's hedonistic partner, Johnny (J.D.) LaRue; Rene Enriquez (1981–1986) as sensitive Lieutenant Ray Calletano, the precinct's Hispanic officer; Michael Warren as level-headed Officer Bobby Hill; Charles Haid as Hill's partner, Officer Andy Renko, an urban cowboy; Betty Thomas as Officer Lucy Bates, a woman trying to do her job as a cop (Bates was promoted to sergeant, and succeeded Esterhaus in 1984); Ed Marinaro (fall 1981–1986) as her partner, Officer Joe Coffey; Barbara Bosson (1981–1986) as Fay Furillo, Frank's crisis-laden ex-wife; Barbara Babcock (1981–1982) as Grace Gardener, Esterhaus's ravenously passionate lover; Robert Hirschfeld as desk officer Leo Schnitz; Jon Cypher as Fletcher Daniels, the politically ambitious chief of police; Trinidad Silva as Jesus Martinez, leader of the Diablos, one of the local gangs; George Wyner (1982–1987) as prosecutor Irwin

Bernstein; Lisa Sutton (1983–1987) as Officer Robin Tataglia, who married Belker; Ken Olin (spring 1984–1985) as Detective Harry Garibaldi; Mimi Kuzyk (1984–1985) as Detective Patsy Mayo; Robert Prosky (1984–1987) as Sergeant Stan Jablonski, who took over the morning roll call from Bates; Debi Richter (spring 1984–1987) as Daryl Ann Renko, Andy's wife (Richter and Haid were also married in real life as were Barbara Bosson and Steven Bochco); Dennis Franz (1985–1987) as street-smart Lieutenant Norman Buntz (Franz had previously guest starred as Detective Sal Benedetto, who had been killed); Peter Jurasik (1985–1987) as seedy Sid "the Snitch" Thurston, Buntz's main contact; Robert Clohessy (1986–1987) as Officer Pat Flaherty; and Megan Gallagher (1986–1987) as Officer Tina Russo. Several members of the *Hill Street* cast had previously appeared on the 1979 cop show *Paris,* which Steven Bochco had created and produced for MTM Enterprises (which also supplied *Hill Street*): Mike Warren had been a regular on *Paris,* and Barbara Babcock, Taurean Blacque, Michael Conrad, James B. Sikking, and Bruce Weitz had all made guest appearances. Also, Conrad and Charles Haid had been regulars on *Delvecchio,* a 1976 cop show.

Hill Street premiered to rave reviews from the critics but to meager ratings. Several time-slot changes throughout the spring of 1981 did nothing to attract more viewers. Nevertheless, NBC decided to renew the series for the 1981–1982 season. The decision paid off, as *Hill Street* won eight Emmys (a single-season record for a series) and a Peabody Award in 1981. During its second season, *Hill Street* began to attract a larger audience, which, if not huge by industry standards, was loyal and enthusiastic. After a respectable seven-season run the series called it quits. Franz and Jurasik, as Buntz and Sid the Snitch, turned up in the fall of 1987 on the ill-fated *Beverly Hills Buntz.*

HIPPODROME   CBS
5 JULY 1966–6 SEPTEMBER 1966   European circus acts were presented on this hour-long series; guest hosts included Woody Allen, Eddie Albert, Trini Lopez, and Tony Randall, among others. This Tuesday-night series should not be confused with *Continental Showcase,* another European circus show aired by CBS that summer on Saturdays.

HIRAM HOLLIDAY (THE ADVENTURES OF HIRAM HOLLIDAY)   NBC
3 OCTOBER 1956–27 FEBRUARY 1957   Half-hour filmed sitcom based on the short stories by Paul Gallico. Wally Cox (formerly of *Mr. Peepers*) starred as Hiram Holliday, a newspaper proofreader who was rewarded with a trip around the world by his employer when he corrected an error in an article, thereby preventing a lawsuit against the paper. Also featured was Ainslie Pryor as his companion, Joel Smith, a reporter sent along with Holliday. Most of the stories involved cases of mistaken identity, or the innocent involvement of mild-mannered Holliday in international intrigue. Sharp-eyed viewers may have noticed a beardless Sebastian Cabot, who appeared in four episodes as M. Cerveaux, "The Brain of the Underworld."

HIS & HERS   CBS
5 MARCH 1990–23 APRIL 1990; 2 JULY 1990–22 AUGUST 1990   Half-hour sitcom about a pair of newlywed marriage counselors who practiced together. With Martin Mull as Dr. Doug Lambert; Stephanie Faracy as his wife, Dr. Reggie Hewitt; Richard Kline as Doug's pal, lawyer Jeff Spector; Lisa Picotte as Mandy, Doug and Reggie's receptionist; Blake Soper as Doug's laconic teenage son, Noah, who lived with the newlyweds; and Blair Tefkin as Doug's teenage daughter, who lived with his ex-wife. Patricia Jones and Donald Reiker were the creators.

HIS HONOR, HOMER BELL
See HOMER BELL

THE HISTORY OF ROCK 'N' ROLL   SYNDICATED
1995   This ten-part documentary series on the evolution of rock and roll music was narrated by Gary Busey. See also *Rock & Roll.*

HIT MAN   NBC

3 JANUARY 1983–1 APRIL 1983   Peter Tomarken hosted this complicated daytime
game show, on which three contestants competed for the chance to take on the
preceding day's champion. After the first round, a quiz based on a photo feature, the
low-scoring contestant was eliminated; the remaining two players then faced the
champion, and each was given a prescribed number of "hit men." Whenever a
question was answered, one of the players lost a "hit man"—the last player left thus
became the winner, and had the chance to play a special round for a top prize of
$10,000.

THE HITCHHIKER   HBO/USA

23 NOVEMBER 1983–21 DECEMBER 1988 (HBO); 6 JANUARY 1989–28 MARCH 1993
(USA)   An often lurid anthology series of suspense tales, laced with graphic violence and (on the HBO episodes) female nudity. Nicholas Campbell and Page
Fletcher appeared as the Hitchhiker, who introduced the episodes and provided
commentary.

THE HOGAN FAMILY   NBC/CBS

1 MARCH 1986–18 JUNE 1990 (NBC); 15 SEPTEMBER 1990–1 DECEMBER 1990 (CBS); 10
JULY 1991–20 JULY 1991 (CBS)   This durable sitcom began life in 1986 as *Valerie,*
starring Valerie Harper as Valerie Hogan, a mother coping with three boys while her
airplane pilot husband was frequently out of town. After the 1986–1987 season
Harper was fired as the result of a contract dispute, and the show carried on as
Valerie's Family for one season before changing its title again, to *The Hogan Family,*
in June 1988. Aside from Harper, the remainder of the cast has remained fairly
stable: Josh Taylor as pilot Michael Hogan; Jason Bateman as eldest son David;
Danny Ponce and Jeremy Licht as fraternal twins Willie and Mark; and Sandy Duncan (1987–1991) as Michael's divorced sister, school counselor Sandy Hogan, who
moved into her brother's household to help raise the boys (it was explained that
sister-in-law Valerie had died). Also featured were Edie McClurg as neighbor Patty
Poole; Christine Ebersole (1986) as Valerie's pal Barbara Goodwin; Steve Witting as
David's pal Burt Weems; and (occasionally) Willard Scott (of the *Today* show) as
Patty's husband, Peter. In the fall of 1988 son David started college at Northwestern,
but continued to live at home; by 1989 he had become active in the school's communications department. Lisa Rinna joined the cast early in 1990 as Annie, David's
girlfriend. John Hillerman was featured during the 1990–1991 season as Michael and
Sandy's father, Lloyd. The series is believed to be the first sitcom in which the word
"condom" was used; the subject was discussed in a February 1987 episode, "Bad
Timing."

    After four and a half seasons on NBC, *The Hogan Family* switched to CBS in the
fall of 1990. See also *City.*

HOGAN'S HEROES   CBS

17 SEPTEMBER 1965–4 JULY 1971   Set during World War II, this popular sitcom
proved that a prisoner-of-war camp was as good a site as any for laughs. Featured
were Bob Crane as Colonel Robert Hogan, the ranking American officer at Stalag
13, a German POW camp; Werner Klemperer as Colonel Wilhelm Klink, its inept
commandant; John Banner as Sergeant Hans Schultz, Klink's chief aide; Robert
Clary as Corporal Louis LeBeau, a French prisoner; Richard Dawson as Corporal
Peter Newkirk, a British prisoner; Ivan Dixon (1965–1970) as Corporal James
Kinchloe; Larry Hovis as Sergeant Andrew Carter; Kenneth Washington (1970–
1971) as Corporal Richard Baker; Cynthia Lynn (1965–1966) as Klink's secretary,
Helga; and Sigrid Valdis (1966–1970) as Klink's secretary, Hilda. Bernard Fein and
Albert S. Ruddy created the series, and Ed Feldman produced it, for Bing Crosby
Productions; there were 168 episodes. Ironically, John Banner, who played the Nazi
Schultz, was actually Jewish, and Robert Clary, who played the imprisoned LeBeau,
had been interned in Nazi concentration camps as a child.

HOLD 'ER NEWT   ABC
11 SEPTEMBER 1950–13 OCTOBER 1950; 26 JANUARY 1952–17 MAY 1952   A puppet
show for kids, *Hold 'Er Newt* was first broadcast locally in June 1950 over WENR-
TV in Chicago. In the fall of 1950 it enjoyed a brief Monday-through-Friday network
run, and in 1952 it surfaced again on the network's Saturday morning schedule. Don
Tennant wrote the show and provided the voice of Newton Figg, who ran a general
store in a small town, Figg Center.

HOLD IT PLEASE   CBS
8 MAY 1949–22 MAY 1949   Short-lived prime-time game show incorporating both
charades and telephone calls to home viewers. The charades were performed by a
panel of celebrities, which included Cloris Leachman, Mort Marshall, Bill McGraw,
Max Showalter, and Evelyn Ward. Viewers who were telephoned could win a prize if
they were able to identify a celebrity's picture which was partially covered. The series
was hosted by Gil Fates, who was later the executive producer of several Goodson-
Todman game shows, including *What's My Line?* and *To Tell the Truth.*

HOLD THAT NOTE   NBC
22 JANUARY 1957–2 APRIL 1957   Bert Parks hosted this Tuesday-night musical quiz
show, a midseason replacement for Parks's previous game show, *Break the $250,000
Bank.*

HOLIDAY HANDBOOK   ABC
4 APRIL 1958–20 JUNE 1958   Half-hour travelogue.

HOLIDAY HOTEL   ABC
23 MARCH 1950–28 JUNE 1951   A musical revue set at the Holiday Hotel in New
York. Edward Everett Horton was the first host of the series and was succeeded by
Don Ameche (both appeared as the hotel manager). Other regulars included Bill
Harrington, Betty Brewer, June Graham, Don Sadler, Bob Dixon, the Bernie Green
Orchestra, and the Charles Tate Dancers. See also *Don Ameche Playhouse.*

HOLIDAY LODGE   CBS
27 JUNE 1961–8 OCTOBER 1961   This summer replacement for *The Jack Benny
Program* starred a pair of Canadian comics, Johnny Wayne and Frank Shuster, as
Johnny Miller and Frank Boone, recreation directors at the Holiday Lodge, some-
where in New York's Catskills. Also featured were Maureen Arthur as Dorothy
Jackson, the desk clerk; Justice Watson as J. W. Harrington, the boss; and Charles
Smith as Woodrow, the bellhop.

HOLLYWOOD A GO GO   SYNDICATED
1965   One of the raft of rock music shows in the style of *Hullabaloo, Hollywood A
Go Go* was hosted by Sam Riddle.

HOLLYWOOD AND THE STARS   NBC
30 SEPTEMBER 1963–28 SEPTEMBER 1964   Joseph Cotten hosted and narrated this
documentary series about American movies.

HOLLYWOOD BACKSTAGE
See THE ERN WESTMORE SHOW; HOLLYWOOD TODAY

HOLLYWOOD BEAT   ABC
21 SEPTEMBER 1985–23 NOVEMBER 1985   Standard hour crime show from Aaron
Spelling Productions, about a pair of undercover cops who frequently used disguises
to trap their quarry. With Jack Scalia as Nick McCarren; Jay Acovone as Jack Rado;
Edward Winter as the boss, Captain Wes Biddle; and John Matuszak as gay bar-
keeper George Grinsky, out of whose tavern Nick and Jack sometimes operated.

HOLLYWOOD CONNECTION   SYNDICATED
1977   Game show hosted by Jim Lange on which studio contestants tried to predict how a panel of celebrities would answer questions.

THE HOLLYWOOD GAME   CBS
19 JUNE 1992–10 JULY 1992   Bob Goen hosted this prime time game show on which two two-person teams answered questions about movies and television for a top prize of $25,000.

HOLLYWOOD HOUSE   ABC
4 DECEMBER 1949–26 FEBRUARY 1950   Half-hour variety show starring Jim Backus and Dick Wesson. Set at a hotel, the series was broadcast from Los Angeles and was produced by Joe Bigelow.

HOLLYWOOD JUNIOR CIRCUS   NBC/ABC
25 MARCH 1951–1 JULY 1951 (NBC); 8 SEPTEMBER 1951–19 JANUARY 1952 (ABC)   This circus show for kids was broadcast from Chicago, not Hollywood; the series was seen Sunday afternoons on NBC and Saturday mornings on ABC. Paul Barnes was the ringmaster. Produced by Bill Hyer; directed by George Byrne.

HOLLYWOOD OFF BEAT   SYNDICATED/DUMONT/CBS
1952 (SYNDICATED); 7 NOVEMBER 1952–30 JANUARY 1953 (DUMONT); 16 JUNE 1953–11 AUGUST 1953 (CBS)   Half-hour crime show starring Melvyn Douglas as Steve Randall, a former World War II intelligence agent who became a private eye after he was wrongfully disbarred from the practice of law. Marion Parsonnet produced and directed the series, which was also titled *Steve Randall.*

HOLLYWOOD OPENING NIGHT   CBS/NBC
13 JULY 1951–28 MARCH 1952 (CBS); 6 OCTOBER 1952–23 MARCH 1953 (NBC)   Half-hour dramatic anthology series. Among the stars who made their TV dramatic debuts on this West Coast series were Dorothy Lamour ("The Singing Years," 24 November 1952), Ethel Barrymore ("Mysterious Ways," 8 December 1952), and Gloria Swanson ("The Pattern," 16 February 1953).

THE HOLLYWOOD PALACE   ABC
4 JANUARY 1964–7 FEBRUARY 1970   This hour-long variety series was a midseason replacement for *The Jerry Lewis Show.* The show was videotaped at the El Capitan Theater in Los Angeles, which was renamed The Hollywood Palace. Each week a different guest host introduced several acts. Bing Crosby hosted the premiere telecast; his guests included Bob Newhart, Bobby Van, Nancy Wilson, Mickey Rooney, and Gary Crosby. Other notable guest appearances included those by the Rolling Stones (in their first American TV appearance, 13 June 1964; Dean Martin hosted the show), Groucho Marx and Margaret Dumont (in her last TV appearance, 17 April 1965), and Fred Astaire and Rudolf Nureyev (2 October 1965). Executive producer: Nick Vanoff. Producer: Bill Harbach. Director: Grey Lockwood. Music: the Mitchell Ayres Orchestra (the show's theme was "Put on a Happy Face"). Raquel Welch was featured as the holder of the cards introducing the acts. Two series retrospectives were aired on ABC during the 1992–1993 season.

HOLLYWOOD PREVIEW   SYNDICATED
1955   Conrad Nagel hosted this series on which previews of recently released motion pictures were shown.

HOLLYWOOD SCREEN TEST   ABC
15 AUGUST 1948–18 MAY 1953   One of the first shows on the ABC network, *Hollywood Screen Test* offered young performers the chance to further their careers by appearing in dramatic stories with well-known stars. Neil Hamilton hosted the series during most of its run; Hurd Hatfield hosted during the 1950–1951 season. The show premiered on 15 April 1948 in Philadelphia.

THE HOLLYWOOD SQUARES NBC/SYNDICATED
17 OCTOBER 1966–20 JUNE 1980 (NBC); 1972–1980; 1986–1989 (SYNDICATED)
Durable game show featuring two contestants and a panel of nine celebrities. The contestants played tic-tac-toe, earning their Xs and Os by stating whether a given celebrity had correctly answered a question (the celebrities were seated in a three-tiered box). Regular panelists over the years included Paul Lynde (occupant of the center square), Rose Marie, Cliff Arquette (as Charley Weaver), Wally Cox, John Davidson, George Gobel, and many others. The daytime version of the series began in 1966; a nighttime network version was seen in the spring of 1968 and the summer of 1969, and the syndicated version (televised evenings in most markets) premiered in 1972. Executive producers: Merrill Heatter and Bob Quigley. Announcer: Kenny Williams. The program reappeared on NBC in 1983 (see *The Match Game/Hollywood Squares Hour*). Peter Marshall hosted all the incarnations of the show between 1966 and 1983. In 1986 a new version was produced, which remained in production for three years. Hosted by John Davidson, it originally sported Joan Rivers in the center square; Shadoe Stevens took over the center spot in 1988.

HOLLYWOOD SUMMER THEATRE CBS
3 AUGUST 1956–28 SEPTEMBER 1956   Half-hour filmed dramatic anthology series, hosted by Gene Raymond.

HOLLYWOOD TALENT SCOUTS
See TALENT SCOUTS

HOLLYWOOD TEEN SYNDICATED
1978   Half-hour talk show hosted by teenager Jimmy McNichol, brother of *Family's* Kristy McNichol.

HOLLYWOOD TELEVISION THEATRE PBS
1970–1978   Dramatic anthology series which presented original plays as well as established dramas. Executive producer: Norman Lloyd for KCET, Los Angeles.

HOLLYWOOD THEATER TIME ABC
8 OCTOBER 1950–6 OCTOBER 1951   One of the first dramatic anthology series to originate from the West Coast, this half-hour series was seen via kinescopes in the East. The half-hour show was produced by George M. Cahan and Thomas W. Sarnoff.

HOLLYWOOD TODAY NBC
3 JANUARY 1955–23 SEPTEMBER 1955   *Hollywood Today* began as a daily fifteen-minute show hosted by columnist Sheilah Graham; each week a guest celebrity was featured as her cohost. In the summer of 1955 the show was expanded to thirty minutes and was retitled *Hollywood Backstage;* late in the summer Ern Westmore took over as the show's host (see also *The Search for Beauty*).

HOLLYWOOD'S TALKING CBS
26 MARCH 1973–22 JUNE 1973   Daytime game show hosted by Geoff Edwards on which three contestants, after watching videotaped sequences in which celebrities spoke a line or two about a subject, tried to guess the subject.

HOLMES AND YOYO ABC
25 SEPTEMBER 1976–11 DECEMBER 1976   Hapless sitcom about a police detective and his partner, a human-looking robot. With Richard B. Shull as Detective Alexander Holmes; John Schuck as Gregory Yoyonovich, his mechanical partner; Andrea Howard as policewoman Maxine Moon; and Bruce Kirby as Captain Harry Sedford. Created by Jack Sher and Lee Hewitt, the series' executive producer was Leonard Stern, and its producer was Arne Sultan.

HOLOCAUST
See THE BIG EVENT

HOME   NBC
1 MARCH 1954–9 AUGUST 1957   Styled as a "women's magazine of the air," *Home* was an ambitious weekday series developed by Sylvester "Pat" Weaver and intended to be a logical extension of NBC's early-morning show, *Today*. It was also one of the first NBC programs to be broadcast in color (though not every day). Arlene Francis hosted the series, and, in keeping with *Home*'s magazine format, was billed as editor in chief. In 1955 the group of contributing "editors" included Natalie Cole (fashion and beauty), Katherine Kinne (food), Will Peigelbeck (gardening and home repair), Dr. Ashley Montagu (family affairs), Dorsey Connors (Chicago editor), Esther von Waggoner Tutty (Washington editor), Dr. Leona Baumgartner (health), and Nancyanne Graham (home decorating). At other times the group included Eve Hunter (fashion and beauty), Poppy Cannon (food), Dr. Rose Franzblau (family affairs), and Sydney Smith (home decorating). Also appearing were announcer and sidekick Hugh Downs and singer Johnny Johnston. By 1956 a regular feature of the series, entitled "Hometown U.S.A.," was presented once each week and featured a remote pickup from the town so designated. At that time Fred Freed had become the show's supervising writer or "managing editor." See also *The Arlene Francis Show; The Home Show.*

HOME AGAIN WITH BOB VILA   SYNDICATED
1990–   After his involuntary departure from PBS's *This Old House,* Bob Vila became the host of this series on home remodeling and renovation. The half-hour series was later retitled *Bob Vila's Home Again.*

THE HOME COURT   NBC
30 SEPTEMBER 1995–   Unimaginative sitcom about a Chicago family court judge who was a single mom and attempted to preside over her four children. With Pamela Reed as Judge Sydney J. Solomon; Breckin Meyer as eldest son Mike, who recently quit college and returned home; Meghann Haldeman as daughter Neal; Robert Hy Gorman as middle son Marshall, who spent most of his time at his computer, surfing on the Internet; Phillip Van Dyke as youngest son Ellis, who had Attention Deficit Disorder; Charles Rocket as Sydney's goofy colleague, Judge Gil Fitzpatrick; and Meagen Fay as Sydney's worldly sister, Greer.

HOME FIRES   NBC
24 JUNE 1992–18 JULY 1992   Bruce Paltrow, Tom Fontana, and John Tinker created this half-hour family sitcom, each episode of which began with a therapy session. With Michael Brandon as Ted Kramer; Kate Burton as Anne Kramer; Nicole Eggert as their eighteen-year-old, Libby; Jarrad Paul as their fourteen-year-old, Jessie; Alice Hirson as Nana, Anne's mother; and Norman Lloyd as the therapist.

HOME FREE   ABC
31 MARCH 1993–28 APRIL 1993   Half-hour sitcom about a single mother and her kids who moved back in with mom. With Marian Mercer as Grace Bailey; Diana Canova as Grace's newly divorced daughter, Vanessa; Matthew Perry as Grace's son, Matthew, a reporter; Anndi McAfee as Vanessa's daughter, Abby; Scott McAfee as Vanessa's son, Lucas; Dan Schneider as Matthew's coworker, Walter Peters; Alan Oppenheimer as the editor, Mr. Brookstone; and Brooke Theiss as Laura, the photographer.

HOME IMPROVEMENT   ABC
17 SEPTEMBER 1991–   The most popular new show of the 1991–1992 season, *Home Improvement* was another of the many sitcoms which starred a standup comic. Tim Allen starred as Tim Taylor, a husband and father of three boys who hosted *Tool Time*, a home improvement program on a Detroit TV station. Taylor's solution to home repair problems was a simple one: "More power!" He believed that a souped-up appliance was always superior to a regular model, and that the biggest tools were meant to serve even the smallest jobs. At home Taylor fancied himself an expert on

the sexes also, but in reality he didn't understand women; fortunately, his wife understood *him*. The rest of the cast included Patricia Richardson as Jill Taylor, Tim's wife, the one who really ran the house (she also worked part-time); Zachery Ty Bryan as eldest son Brad; Jonathan Taylor Thomas as middle son Randy; Taran Smith as youngest son Mark; Earl Hindman as Wilson, the wise next-door neighbor who offered sage advice to Tim on the battle between the sexes (in a clever gimmick, Wilson's full face was never seen; he was usually seen obscured by the stockade fence which separated his yard from the Taylors'; Wilson's first name was revealed also to be Wilson in a 1995 episode); Richard Karn as flannel-shirted Al Borland, Tim's burly assistant on *Tool Time*, the one who actually knew how to make home improvements but who was usually overshadowed by Taylor; Pamela Anderson (1991–1993) as Lisa, the "Tool Time Girl," who added glamor (and little else) to Taylor's show; and Debbe Dunning (1993–) as Heidi, the new "Tool Time Girl." Charlie Robinson was added in the fall of 1995 as Tim's new boss, Bud Harper. *Home Improvement* made innovative use of optical wipes, using computer techniques to create humorous transitions between scenes.

The Taylor character was based on Tim Allen's standup comedy. After serving a brief federal prison sentence following a drug conviction in the 1970s, Allen resumed his comedy career. He began incorporating comments on men's passion for tools and motors into his routine. In 1989 Michael Eisner, head of Disney Studios, saw Allen's act and signed him. Allen headlined a Showtime comedy special, "Men Are Pigs," in 1990, and *Home Improvement* followed a year later. The series ended its first season at fifth place in the Nielsen ratings; it rose to third the following season, and to first place in 1993–1994. Reruns of the show were sold to local stations for broadcast in the fall of 1995; in an unusual programming move, the producers announced that some new episodes would be televised first among the rerun packages before airing on ABC.

HOME RUN DERBY   SYNDICATED
1959–1961   Mark Scott hosted this half-hour filmed athletic contest. Each week two big league ballplayers competed head-to-head to see who could hit more home runs. Reruns of the series were resurrected briefly in the late 1980s by the ESPN cable network.

THE HOME SHOPPING GAME SHOW   SYNDICATED
15 JUNE 1987–11 SEPTEMBER 1987   Bob Goen was the host of this short-lived attempt to combine a game show with the popular pastime of home shopping; viewers could participate by dialing an 800 number.

THE HOME SHOW   ABC
18 JANUARY 1988–8 APRIL 1994   The title of NBC's pioneering daytime show was resurrected thirty years later for this daytime magazine-talk show. Originally a half-hour series, it expanded to a full hour as of 16 January 1989, when *Ryan's Hope* left ABC's lineup. Sandy Hill and Robb Weller were the original hosts; Weller later became the sole host. Gary Collins (who had hosted the similar *Hour Magazine*) succeeded Weller late in 1989, and in April 1990 Dana Fleming was named Collins's cohost. Like the old NBC show, the new version featured various "experts" who contributed regularly on such topics as home decorating, health, fitness, and the arts. Fleming was succeeded by Beth Ruyak in 1991, who was in turn succeeded by Sarah Purcell a year later. Cohosts Purcell and Collins received an unexpected scare on a September 1993 program, when a physician demonstrating immunizations accidentally used the same syringe on both of them.

HOMEFRONT   ABC
24 SEPTEMBER 1991–17 SEPTEMBER 1992; 9 MARCH 1993–26 APRIL 1993   Critically acclaimed hour dramatic series set in the town of River Run, Ohio, at the end of World War II. The continuing stories focused on the town's returning soldiers and their efforts to readjust to life at home. The large cast included Ken Jenkins as factory owner Mike Sloan, Sr.; Mimi Kennedy as his wife, Ruth Sloan; Giuliana

Santini as their daughter-in-law, Gina, the Italian war bride of their son who had been killed; Wendy Phillips as Ann Metcalf, who contracted polio; David Newsom as her son, Hank Metcalf; Kyle Chandler as Hank's younger brother, Jeff; Alexandra Wilson as Sarah Brewer, Hank's girlfriend, who had flirted with Jeff while Hank was overseas (Hank eventually married Sarah); Tammy Lauren as Ginger Szabo, Jeff's new girlfriend; Jessica Steen as Linda Metcalf, Hank and Jeff's sister; Harry O'Reilly as Charlie Hailey; Sammi Davis-Voss as his English war bride, Caroline Hailey; Sterling Macer, Jr., as black veteran Robert Davis; Dick Anthony Williams as his father, Abe Davis, the Sloan family's chauffeur; Hattie Winston as his mother, Gloria Davis, the Sloan family's maid; Montrose Hagins as Grandmother Davis; John Slattery as Al Kahn, who married Ann Metcalf; Robert Duncan McNeill as Bill Caswell; Kelly Rutherford as barmaid Judy Owen; John DiSanti as Sam; William G. Schilling (1993) as Barzizza, a sportswriter; and Jack Knight (1993) as Nadolski, a reporter.

HOMER BELL — SYNDICATED
1955   Half-hour comedy-western, starring Gene Lockhart as Judge Homer Bell of Spring City. Also featured were Jane Moultric as Maude, the housekeeper, and Mary Lee Dearring as Casey Bell, Homer's daughter.

HOMEROOM — ABC
16 SEPTEMBER 1989–17 DECEMBER 1989   A black cast was featured in this half-hour sitcom. With Darryl Sivad as Darryl Harper, fourth-grade teacher at an inner-city school; Penny Johnson as his wife, Virginia, a med student; Bill Cobbs as Virginia's dad (and the Harpers' landlord), Phil Drexler, a bus supervisor; Trent Cameron as Sam; Jahary Bennett as Devon; Billy Dee Willis as Donald; Claude Brooks as Anthony; and Daphne Lyn Jones as Lisa.

HOMETIME — PBS
1987–   Half-hour weekly show on home renovation and repair, cohosted by Dean Johnson with JoAnne Liebeler (1987–1991), Susanne Egli (1991–1993), and Robin Hartl (1993–).

HOMETOWN — CBS
22 AUGUST 1985–15 OCTOBER 1985   The 1983 film *The Big Chill* was the inspiration for this hour dramatic series about the lives of seven adults, all of whom had been college chums. With Jane Kaczmarek as Mary Newell Abbott, a former dancer; Franc Luz as bookstore owner Ben Abbott (Mary and Ben were married on the first episode, after living together for thirteen years); Andrew Rubin as rock star Christopher Springer; Margaret Whitton as Barbara Donnelly, an alcoholic divorcée just back from New York; John Bedford-Lloyd as college professor Peter Kinkaid; Christine Estabrook as Dr. Jane Parnell, a political scientist; Daniel Stern as Joey Nathan, a cook; Mickey Viso as Joey's son Dylan; Donna Vivino as Ben and Mary's daughter Tess; and Erin Leigh Peck as their daughter Jennifer. Like *The Big Chill*, *Hometown* also used original versions of 1960s pop music hits as background music. Created by Julie and Dinah Kirgo, the show suffered a steep ratings decline after its August premiere and vanished after eight weeks.

HOMEWOOD — PBS
7 OCTOBER 1970–6 JANUARY 1971   Thirteen-week musical series, hosted by Charles Champlin.

HOMICIDE: LIFE ON THE STREET — NBC
31 JANUARY 1993–31 MARCH 1993; 6 JANUARY 1994–27 JANUARY 1994; 14 OCTOBER 1994–   Set in Baltimore, this gritty hour crime show was based on reporter David Simon's book, *Homicide: A Year on the Killing Streets*. It marked the first foray into television for film director Barry Levinson, who served as executive producer with Tom Fontana. Filmed largely on location, the show relied heavily on handheld camera work. The cast included Ned Beatty (1993–1995) as Detective Stanley Bolander;

Richard Belzer as Detective John Munch; Yaphet Kotto as the boss, Lieutenant Al Giardello; Melissa Leo as Detective Kay Howard; Daniel Baldwin (1993–1995) as Detective Beau Felton; Andre Braugher as Detective Frank Pembleton; Clark Johnson as Detective Meldrick Lewis; Jon Polito (1993–1994) as Detective Steve Crosetti; Kyle Secor as rookie Detective Tim Bayliss; and Isabella Hofmann (1994–) as Lieutenant Megan Russert. Reed Diamond was added in the fall of 1995 as Detective Mike Kellerman, and Harlee McBride appeared as assistant medical examiner Alyssa Dyer.

HONDO ABC

8 SEPTEMBER 1967–29 DECEMBER 1967   This Friday-night hour-long western perished opposite NBC's *Star Trek*. Set in the Arizona Territory in 1869, it starred Ralph Taeger as Hondo Lane, an agent for the U.S. Army; Noah Beery, Jr., as Buffalo Baker, his sidekick; Gary Clarke as Captain Richards, Hondo's commanding officer; Kathie Browne as Angie Dow, a widow (Hondo killed her husband); Buddy Foster as Johnny, Angie's young son; and Michael Pate as Vittoro, an Apache chief. Based on the 1953 film starring John Wayne, the television series was produced by Andrew Fenady.

HONESTLY, CELESTE! CBS

10 OCTOBER 1954–5 DECEMBER 1954   This half-hour sitcom was one of the first casualties of the 1954–1955 season. It starred Celeste Holm as Celeste Anders, a journalism teacher from a Midwestern college who decided to get a job as a reporter with a New York newspaper. Also featured were Scott McKay as her friend, Bob Wallace; Geoffrey Lumb as Bob's father, Mr. Wallace, editor of the paper; Mary Finney as Mary, Mr. Wallace's secretary; and Mike Kellin as Celeste's friend, Marty Gordon, an ex-gangster. When it became apparent early in the fall that the show was in trouble, a young writer named Norman Lear was called in to help out, but his efforts proved unsuccessful. One of the people Lear succeeded was another young writer, Larry Gelbart, who would later develop *M*A*S*H* for television.

HONEY WEST ABC

17 SEPTEMBER 1965–2 SEPTEMBER 1966   Half-hour crime show starring Anne Francis as Honey West, a private eye who took over the business after her father's death. Also featured were John Ericson as her assistant, Sam Bolt; Irene Hervey as her Aunt Meg; and Bruce, her pet ocelot. Francis first appeared as Honey West in an episode of *Burke's Law* aired 21 April 1965. The series was produced by Four Star Films.

THE HONEYMOON RACE ABC

17 JULY 1967–1 DECEMBER 1967   Bill Malone hosted this daytime game show, produced in Florida, in which three couples went on a scavenger hunt in a supermarket. The show was a revamped version of *Supermarket Sweep* (see also that title).

THE HONEYMOONERS

See THE JACKIE GLEASON SHOW

HONG KONG ABC

28 SEPTEMBER 1960–20 SEPTEMBER 1961   A 20th Century-Fox adventure series set in the Far East. With Rod Taylor as Glenn Evans, an American journalist based in Hong Kong; Lloyd Bochner as Neil Campbell, Hong Kong's chief of police; Jerald Jann as Ling, Glenn's houseboy; Jack Kruschen as Tully, owner of The Golden Dragon, where Glenn hung out. In January 1961 Mai Tai Sing (who in real life was co-owner of a San Francisco lounge) joined the cast as Ching Mei, hostess at The Golden Dragon. Twenty-six episodes were filmed.

HONG KONG PHOOEY ABC/NBC

7 SEPTEMBER 1974–4 SEPTEMBER 1976 (ABC); 4 FEBRUARY 1978–2 SEPTEMBER 1978 (NBC); 8 SEPTEMBER 1979–3 NOVEMBER 1979 (NBC); 23 MAY 1981–5 SEPTEMBER 1981

(NBC)   Hanna-Barbera cartoon series about a crime-fighting dog, Penrod Pooch, whose secret identity was that of Hong Kong Phooey. The voice of the lead character was supplied by Scatman Crothers. The series' second season on ABC consisted entirely of reruns, and reruns were again shown when the show popped up on NBC. Reruns were also seen on *The Godzilla/Hong Kong Phooey Hour* from November 1980 to May 1981.

HOOPERMAN   ABC
23 SEPTEMBER 1987–22 MARCH 1989; 14 JUNE 1989–6 SEPTEMBER 1989   Half-hour dramedy from Steven Bochco and Terry Louise Fisher about a San Francisco cop who owned an apartment building and a dog, Bijoux, both of which he had inherited from his landlady who was murdered in the first episode. With John Ritter as Detective Harry Hooperman; Barbara Bosson (who was married to Bochco in real life) as Captain C. Z. Stern; Clarence Felder as Inspector Bobo Pritzger; Felton Perry as Inspector Clarence McNeil; Joseph Gian as gay cop Rick Silardi; Sydney Walsh as Officer Mo DeMott, who constantly tried to seduce Silardi; Alix Elias as dispatcher Betty Bushkin; and Debrah Farentino as Susan Smith, the handyperson at Hooperman's apartment building with whom he had a relationship. In the fall of 1988 Susan became pregnant by Hooperman, but left town (and the series) after a miscarriage. Dan Lauria was occasionally seen as Lou Stern, C. Z.'s ex-husband. Bijoux, a Jack Russell terrier, was played by Britches.

HOOTENANNY   ABC
6 APRIL 1963–12 SEPTEMBER 1964   Jack Linkletter hosted television's first folk music series, broadcast from a different college campus each week. Most of the "folk" music featured was of the commercial type, such as that of the Limeliters and the Chad Mitchell Trio; more controversial folk artists, such as Bob Dylan or Joan Baez, did not appear. According to Pete Seeger's book, *The Incompleat Folksinger,* the word "hootenanny" was coined by Woody Guthrie sometime in the 1940s.

HOPALONG CASSIDY   NBC/SYNDICATED
24 JUNE 1949–23 DECEMBER 1951 (NBC); 1952–1954 (SYNDICATED)   William Boyd first starred as Hopalong Cassidy, a western hero who dressed in black and rode a white horse, in sixty-six movie features filmed between 1935 and 1948. Boyd himself acquired the television rights to the films and edited the features into thirty- and sixty-minute segments; thus, he was in a position to offer a readily available source of action programming to the rapidly expanding postwar television station market. The films proved so popular that Boyd filmed an additional fifty-two episodes especially for TV in 1951–1952. Veteran character actor Edgar Buchanan costarred in these as Hoppy's sidekick, Red Connors.

HOPE & GLORIA   NBC
9 MARCH 1995–   A *Kate & Allie* for the mid-1990s, *Hope & Gloria* told the story of two neighbors in a Pittsburgh apartment building who became friends. With Cynthia Stevenson as newly separated Hope Davidson, the mild-mannered producer of a local TV talk show; Jessica Lundy as Gloria Utz, a brassy hairdresser divorced twice from the same man (and now working on the TV show, thanks to Hope); Enrico Colantoni as Gloria's first and second ex, Louis Utz; Alan Thicke as Dennis Dupree, thickheaded host of Hope's TV show; Robert Garrova as Sonny, son of Louis and Gloria; and JoNell Kennedy as Sheryl, another staffer on the TV show.

HOPPITY HOOPER   ABC
12 SEPTEMBER 1964–2 SEPTEMBER 1967   Cartoon series with a frog (Hoppity Hooper), a bear (Fillmore), and a fox (Uncle Waldo).

THE HORACE HEIDT SHOW   CBS
2 OCTOBER 1950–24 SEPTEMBER 1951   Bandleader Horace Heidt, who hosted several radio programs featuring talented amateurs and young professionals, brought the

same concept to television in this Monday-night variety series. Heidt returned in 1955 to host another series: see *Show Wagon*.

HORIZONS   ABC
2 DECEMBER 1951–30 DECEMBER 1951; 18 MAY 1952–29 JUNE 1952; 12 DECEMBER 1954–6 MARCH 1955   The 1951 and 1952 editions of *Horizons* were half-hour lectures on selected topics; each lecture was titled "The Future of..." The 1954–1955 version of *Horizons* was a fifteen-minute series which focused on medicine. See also *Medical Horizons*.

HOT CITY   SYNDICATED
1978   Los Angeles-based disco dance show, hosted by Shadoe Stevens, with celebrity guest hosts. Ed Warren was the executive producer of the hour series, Kip Walton the producer and director.

HOT COUNTRY NIGHTS   NBC
24 NOVEMBER 1991–8 MARCH 1992   Prime time country music show from Dick Clark Productions, with no regular host.

HOT DOG   NBC
12 SEPTEMBER 1970–4 SEPTEMBER 1971   A highly acclaimed Saturday show for kids which explained how things are made; Jonathan Winters, Woody Allen, and Jo Anne Worley did the explaining. Created by Frank Buxton, *Hot Dog* had Lee Mendelson as executive producer. The show won a Peabody Award in 1971.

HOT FUDGE SHOW   SYNDICATED
1976–1980   Educational series for children featuring puppets and live actors. Produced by Barry Hurd and Bob Elnicky; distributed by Lexington Broadcast Services.

HOT HERO SANDWICH   NBC
10 NOVEMBER 1979–5 APRIL 1980   Hour variety series for children, broadcast at noon on Saturdays; interviews, sketches, and musical selections were the principal components of the show. Regulars include Paul O'Keefe, Denny Dillon, Matt McCoy, Jarett SmithWrick, L. Michael Craig, Nan-Lynn Nelson, and Vicky Dawson. Bruce Hart and Carole Hart created the show and are its executive producers.

HOT HITVIDEO   SYNDICATED
1984–1985   One of several prepackaged series that presented contemporary rock videos.

HOT L BALTIMORE   ABC
24 JANUARY 1975–6 JUNE 1975   The first Norman Lear series that ABC picked up was an unsuccessful one. Based on the play by Lanford Wilson, it was set in a rundown hotel and featured an assortment of seedy characters: Conchata Ferrell as April Green, hooker with a heart of gold; Jeannie Linero as Suzy Marta Rocket, hooker with a heart of silver; James Cromwell as Bill Lewis, the desk clerk; Richard Masur as Clifford Ainsley, the manager; Al Freeman, Jr., as Charles Bingham; Lee Bergere as George, an apparent homosexual; Henry Calvert as Gordon, his roommate; Gloria LeRoy as Millie, a waitress; Stan Gottlieb as Mr. Morse, a mean old man; Robin Wilson as Jackie; and Charlotte Rae as Mrs. Bellotti. Executive producer: Rod Parker. Producers: Ron Clark and Gene Marcione.

HOT OFF THE WIRE
See THE JIM BACKUS SHOW

HOT POTATO   NBC
23 JANUARY 1984–29 JUNE 1984   Another of the many daytime game shows hosted by Bill Cullen, this one was similar in format to *Family Feud*. It featured two teams of

three, each competing to name the most popular responses to a question previously asked of a group of people.

HOT PURSUIT · NBC
22 SEPTEMBER 1984–28 DECEMBER 1984   This hour adventure series could perhaps have been dubbed *Mr. and Mrs. Fugitive.* It starred Kerrie Keane and Eric Pierpoint as auto engineer Kate Wyler and her husband, veterinarian Jim Wyler. Kate was designing a new auto for her employer, Victor Modrian; jealous of the attention Victor was lavishing on Kate, Victor's wife Estelle (played by Dina Merrill) killed him, but hired a double of Kate (also played by Kerrie Keane) in order to frame Kate. Jim freed Kate on her way to prison, and together they searched for the imposter, while being pursued by Estelle's henchman, Alec Shaw (Mike Preston). Having lost an eye in a fight with Jim, Alec had his own reason to track the Wylers down. He never succeeded, however, nor did Jim and Kate find the imposter. *Hot Pursuit* was pulled in midseason and was NBC's lowest-rated prime-time series of the 1984–1985 season.

THE HOT SEAT · ABC
18 APRIL 1952–29 DECEMBER 1952   Stuart Scheftel interviewed newsmakers on this half-hour series. James A. Farley and Harold Stassen were Scheftel's guests on the fall premiere.

THE HOT SEAT · ABC
12 JULY 1976–22 OCTOBER 1976   Jim Peck hosted this daytime game show, which involved a type of lie detector. Two married couples competed; one spouse was hooked up to a machine that measured chemical changes in the skin as he or she responded to questions. The other spouse tried to predict the nature of the forthcoming response. Developed by Merrill Heatter and Bob Quigley, the show's executive producer was Robert Noah.

HOT SHOTS · CBS
23 SEPTEMBER 1986–23 DECEMBER 1986; 29 JULY 1987–9 SEPTEMBER 1987   Another of the Canadian-produced shows that dotted CBS's late-night schedule, *Hot Shots* chronicled the adventures of two reporters for *Crime World* magazine. With Dorothy Parke as Amanda Reed; Booth Savage as Jason West; Paul Burke as former police commissioner Nicholas Broderick, now the publisher; Heather Smith as Cleo, Broderick's secretary; Clark Johnson as researcher Al Pendleton; and Mung Ling as the receptionist.

HOT STREAK · ABC
6 JANUARY 1986–4 APRIL 1986   On this daytime game show, two teams attempted to communicate secret words to each other for a top prize that could reach $60,000. Bruce Forsythe was the host.

HOT WHEELS · ABC
6 SEPTEMBER 1969–4 SEPTEMBER 1971   Saturday-morning cartoon show about a group of teenage racers who, it was emphasized, were "responsible" young drivers.

HOTEL · ABC
21 SEPTEMBER 1983–6 AUGUST 1988   One of the early hits of the 1983–1984 season, *Hotel* was essentially a land-based *Love Boat,* with the stories of several guests at San Francisco's opulent St. Gregory Hotel threaded together each week. Bette Davis had been signed to play her first TV series role, owner Laura Trent, but, because of illness, appeared only in the premiere. Anne Baxter (who, ironically, costarred with Davis in the 1950 film *All About Eve*) took over as her sister-in-law, Victoria Cabot, who ran the St. Gregory in her absence. James Brolin played Peter McDermott, the manager; Connie Sellecca was Christine Francis, the assistant manager, who gradually became romantically involved with McDermott. Other regulars included Shea Farrell (1983–1986) as Mark Danning, director of guest relations; Nathan Cook as

ex-con Billy Griffin, chief of security; Heidi Bohay (1983–1987) as desk clerk Megan Kendall; Michael Spound (1983–1987) as her new husband, bellhop Dave Kendall (Bohay and Spound themselves were married in 1988); and Shari Belafonte-Harper (daughter of Harry Belafonte) as Julie Gillette, manager of hotel information. Anne Baxter died in December 1985; as a tribute, a portrait of her character was hung in the St. Gregory lobby. It was revealed that Victoria Cabot left a 51% share of the hotel to McDermott, who named Christine Francis manager and Megan Kendall assistant manager, and 49% to Cabot's family. Stories on the 1986–1987 focused on the resulting power struggle, and featured Efrem Zimbalist, Jr., (fall 1986) as Charles Cabot, and Michelle Phillips (fall 1986) as Elizabeth Bradshaw Cabot, the new concierge. Three new regulars joined for the series' final season in the fall of 1987: Valerie Landsburg as desk clerk Cheryl Dolan; Susan Walters as desk clerk Ryan Thomas; and Ty Miller as bellhop Eric Lloyd. The series was based on Arthur Hailey's popular novel, which had been made into a movie in 1967. Aaron Spelling and Douglas S. Cramer were the executive producers of the series; Henry Mancini composed the theme. Exteriors were filmed at San Francisco's Fairmont Hotel.

HOTEL BROADWAY   DUMONT
20 JANUARY 1949–17 MARCH 1949   Half-hour variety series hosted by Jeri Blanchard, produced and directed by Harvey Marlowe.

HOTEL COSMOPOLITAN   CBS
19 AUGUST 1957–11 APRIL 1958   This daytime serial replaced *Valiant Lady*. Set in a New York hotel (The Cosmopolitan), it presented episodic, rather than continuing, dramas. Donald Woods (appearing as himself) hosted the series.

HOTEL DE PAREE   CBS
2 OCTOBER 1959–23 SEPTEMBER 1960   In this unlikely titled western, Earl Holliman starred as Sundance, a man recently released from prison who became a partner in a hotel in Georgetown, Colorado. The principal gimmick in the show involved Sundance's hat: the hatband was decorated with shiny oval discs that Sundance could use to temporarily blind his adversaries. Also featured were Jeanette Nolan as Annette Devereaux, his partner in the hotel; Judi Meredith as Monique Devereaux, her niece and Sundance's romantic interest; and Strother Martin as Sundance's pal, Aaron.

HOTEL MALIBU   CBS
4 AUGUST 1994–8 SEPTEMBER 1994   Hour continuing drama about a family-owned hotel. The cast included Joanna Cassidy as Ellie Mayfield, the widowed owner of the hotel; Cheryl Pollak as her daughter, Stevie, who returned home after quitting her job; John Dye as Ellie's son, Jack, who was plotting to sell the property; Harry O'Reilly as bartender Harry Radzimski; Romy Whitehall as Nancy, Harry's scheming sister; Jennifer Lopez as new bartender Melinda Lopez; and Pepe Serna as Melinda's strict father, Sal. See also *Second Chances*.

HOTHOUSE   ABC
30 JUNE 1988–25 AUGUST 1988   An hour dramatic series set at the Garrison Medical Center, a New England psychiatric clinic nicknamed the "Hothouse." The cast included Josef Sommer as Dr. Sam Garrison, head of the facility; Tony Soper as his son, Matt; Alexis Smith as Lily Shannon, Sam's ex-wife; Susan Diol as Claudia, Matt's wife; Art Malik as Dr. Ved Lahari; Michael Learned as Dr. Marie Teller; Ann-Sara Matthews as Abby; Michael Jeter as Art; and Katherine Borowitz as Sam's daughter, Dr. Issy Schrader. Jay Presson Allen created the series, which came and went with little fanfare; ABC, reportedly dissatisfied with the show after two pilots and five episodes, decided to run it Thursdays at 10 P.M., opposite NBC's *L. A. Law*.

THE HOUNDCATS   NBC
9 SEPTEMBER 1972–1 SEPTEMBER 1973   Saturday-morning cartoon show about a cat-and-dog team of secret agents.

HOUR MAGAZINE   SYNDICATED

1980–1988   This hour informational series was cohosted by Gary Collins and Pat Mitchell during its first two seasons, by Collins and Bonnie Strauss until 1985, and thereafter by Collins and celebrity guest hosts.

HOUR OF POWER   SYNDICATED

1970–   Religious series videotaped at the Garden Grove Community Church in California. Four ministers originally appeared: Raymond Beckering, Calvin Rynbrandt, Robert H. Schuller, and Kenneth Van Wyk. Schuller eventually took over as the sole minister, and the show was broadcast from his opulent Crystal Cathedral in Garden Grove.

THE HOUR OF ST. FRANCIS   SYNDICATED

1961   Half-hour religious show that featured dramatizations of moral questions. It was produced in Los Angeles by four Franciscan fathers: Fr. Hugh Noonan, Fr. Edward Henriques, Fr. Terence Cronin, and Fr. Carl Holtsnider.

HOUSE CALLS   CBS

17 DECEMBER 1979–13 SEPTEMBER 1982   Kensington General Hospital was the site of this half-hour sitcom, with Wayne Rogers as Dr. Charley Michaels, a free-spirited physician; Lynn Redgrave (1979–1981) as Ann Anderson, the new assistant administrator, with whom Charley became involved; David Wayne as Dr. Amos Wetherby, the semi-senile chief of surgery; Ray Buktenica as Dr. Norman Solomon; Aneta Corsaut as Head Nurse Bradley; Deedy Peters as dotty Mrs. Phipps, the "gray lady" volunteer; and Mark L. Taylor as Conrad Peckler, Kensington's humorless administrator. Lynn Redgrave appeared in the first eight episodes of the 1981–1982 season, during which Charley proposed to Ann (all eight programs were filmed before a 1981 writers' strike). Redgrave then locked horns with *House Calls'*s producers. The principal dispute was about money, but a minor squabble erupted over Redgrave's desire to breastfeed her baby on the set. In any event, Redgrave was dropped from the show (she showed up in another sitcom, *Teachers Only*, later that season). Sharon Gless replaced her, as assistant administrator Jane Jeffreys, on 4 January 1982.

THE HOUSE IN THE GARDEN

See FAIRMEADOWS, U.S.A.; THE KATE SMITH SHOW

HOUSE OF BUGGIN'   FOX

8 JANUARY 1995–26 FEBRUARY 1995; 9 APRIL 1995–23 APRIL 1995   Short-lived half-hour comedy sketch show, starring Latin comedian John Leguizamo, with Jorge Luis Abreu, Waleska Coindet, Tammi Cubilette, Yelba Osorio, Sixto Ramos, and Luis Guzman. Leguizamo had previously turned his one-man stage show into a comedy special, "Spic-O-Rama," broadcast 15 May 1993 on HBO.

THE HOUSE ON HIGH STREET   NBC

28 SEPTEMBER 1959–5 FEBRUARY 1960   One of the first daytime serials to be videotaped, *The House on High Street* presented three- to five-part stories about divorce and juvenile delinquency, ostensibly based on actual case histories. Continuity was provided by Philip Abbott, who played caseworker John Collier. Produced in New York, the series was directed by Lela Swift and written under the supervision of Jim Elward.

HOUSE PARTY

See ART LINKLETTER'S HOUSE PARTY

HOUSE PARTY WITH STEVE DOOCY   SYNDICATED

1990   An updated version of the long-running daytime series *Art Linkletter's House Party*. Steve Doocy hosted the hour daily show, assisted by a number of regular contributors, most of whom were featured once a week. The new show retained the most memorable segment of Linkletter's show, the interviews with young schoolchildren.

HOUSTON KNIGHTS   CBS
11 MARCH 1987–29 APRIL 1987; 29 JULY 1987–6 JUNE 1988   An hour crime show, set in Houston. With Michael Pare as Sergeant Joey LaFiamma, former Chicago cop; Michael Beck as his laid-back partner, Sergeant LeVon Lundy; Robyn Douglass as the boss, Lieutenant Joanne Beaumont; John Hancock as Chicken, who ran a roadside restaurant where Joey and LeVon hung out; James Crittenden as Sergeant Joe-Bill McCandless; Brian Mitchell as Sergeant Nat Holliday; Efrain Figuerroa as Sergeant Estaban Gutierrez; Madlyn Rhue as Annie Hartung, a wheelchair-bound officer who had been injured on duty (in real life, Rhue had multiple sclerosis); Nancy Everhard as Carol, a leggy officer; D. Franki Horner as LeVon's love interest, widow Jamie Kincaid; and Dana Young as Jamie's son, Eric.

HOW DID THEY GET THAT WAY?
See WHAT'S ON YOUR MIND

HOW DO YOU RATE   CBS
31 MARCH 1958–26 JUNE 1958   Tom Reddy hosted this daytime game show on which a male and a female contestant competed against each other in tests of intelligence and problem solving. A machine called an "Aptigraph" was also used during the contest. The show was seen Monday through Thursday; on Friday the hour-long *Garry Moore Show* took over the time slot.

HOW THE WEST WAS WON   ABC
12 FEBRUARY 1978–23 APRIL 1979   This ambitious western, based loosely on the 1962 M-G-M film, began as a made-for-TV movie entitled *The Macahans,* which was aired 19 January 1976. In 1977 a six-hour sequel, entitled *How the West Was Won,* was broadcast, and in 1978 twenty more hours were presented. The series told the saga of the Macahan clan, several generations of hardy pioneers. Principal players in the 1978 edition included James Arness as Zeb Macahan, former Cavalry scout; Bruce Boxleitner as Luke Macahan, his nephew, an army deserter; Kathryn Holcomb as Laura Macahan; Fionnula Flanagan as Molly Culhane, sister of Zeb's late wife; William Kirby Cullen as Jed Macahan; and Vicki Schreck as Jessie Macahan. John Mantley, who had previously worked with Arness as *Gunsmoke's* last executive producer, was executive producer of *The Macahans* and *How the West Was Won.* The 1978 series was produced by John G. Stephens and directed by Vincent and Bernard McEveety.

HOW TO   CBS
12 JULY 1951–27 AUGUST 1951   A satire on panel shows, *How To* was hosted by humorist Roger Price. The panel—Anita Martell, Stanley Andrews, and Leonard Stern—suggested unusual solutions to problems posed by contestants. Dick Linkroum and Larry Berns produced the half-hour prime-time show.

HOW TO MARRY A MILLIONAIRE   SYNDICATED
1958–1959   Situation comedy based on the 1953 film (which had starred Marilyn Monroe, Betty Grable, and Lauren Bacall) about three New York career girls, each looking for a wealthy and eligible man. The TV version starred Barbara Eden as Loco Jones, a model; Merry Anders as Michelle (Mike) Page, a secretary; Lori Nelson (1958) as Greta Lindquist, secretary to a stockbroker; and Lisa Gaye (1959) as Gwen Laurel, also a secretary. Produced by 20th Century-Fox.

HOW TO SURVIVE A MARRIAGE   NBC
7 JANUARY 1974–18 APRIL 1975   This fairly controversial daytime serial stressed the problems of coping with divorce and widowhood. It premiered with a ninety-minute episode which featured an explicit bedroom scene between a husband and his mistress. Principal players included: Jennifer Harmon as Chris Kirby, whose marriage

was on the rocks; Michael Landrum and Ken Kercheval as Larry Kirby, her philandering husband; Lynn Lowry as Sandra Henderson, Larry's mistress; Rosemary Prinz as Dr. Julie Franklin, a liberated psychiatrist who advised many of the other characters; Fran Brill as Fran Bachman, who became a widow; Allan Miller as her husband, David Bachman; Joan Copeland as Monica Courtland; Peter Brandon as Terry Courtland; Steve Elmore and Berkeley Harris as lawyer Peter Willis; Tricia O'Neil as Joan Willis; Suzanne Davidson as Lori Kirby; Paul Vincent as Dr. Charles Maynard; Armand Assante as Johnny McGhee; and Lauren White as Maria McGhee. The series was created by Anne Howard Bailey, though NBC daytime programming chief Lin Bolen also helped formulate it. Allen Potter was the first producer; he was succeeded by Peter Andrews.

HOWARD COSELL: SPEAKING OF EVERYTHING   SYNDICATED
24 JANUARY 1988–5 JUNE 1988   The irrepressible Howard Cosell took a turn at hosting an hour talk show, on which a wide range of topics was addressed.

HOWARD COSELL SPORTS MAGAZINE   ABC
7 JANUARY 1972–27 APRIL 1975   Fifteen-minute sports show presented during the winter months, hosted by Howard Cosell.

HOWARD K. SMITH NEWS AND COMMENT   ABC
14 FEBRUARY 1962–16 JUNE 1963   Half-hour news analysis show, hosted by Howard K. Smith, the former CBS correspondent who joined ABC News in 1961.

THE HOWARD MILLER SHOW
See CLUB 60

HOW'D THEY DO THAT?   CBS
10 MARCH 1993–12 MAY 1993   Pat O'Brien and Dorothy Lucey cohosted this light non-fiction prime-time series which resembled such older reality shows as NBC's *Real People*. The series featured a studio audience and presented short segments on interesting persons and other topics. Following its departure from CBS's schedule in May 1993, the series popped up sporadically to fill holes in the network lineup.

HOWDY DOODY   NBC/SYNDICATED
27 DECEMBER 1947–30 SEPTEMBER 1960 (NBC); 1976 (SYNDICATED)   Television's first popular kids' show premiered late in 1947 and exited thirteen years—and 2,343 performances—later. It was brought to TV by Bob Smith, a onetime singer who began hosting a kids' radio show, *Triple B Ranch*, in New York in 1945. One of the characters Smith created on that show, Elmer, regularly introduced himself with the phrase, "Well, howdy doody!" The character was popular with Smith's young listeners, and when Smith convinced NBC to introduce a puppet show on television, the newly created marionette was named Howdy Doody. The original puppet, crafted by Frank Paris, bore little resemblance to the freckled, plaid-shirted Howdy that most viewers fondly recall. The first Howdy, together with his maker, departed from the show after only a few weeks when puppeteer Paris became enmeshed in contractual difficulties with NBC. Some months later a new Howdy, designed by two artists who had worked at Walt Disney Studios, appeared; it was explained that Howdy, who was then running for the office of president of All the Boys and Girls (1948 was, after all, a Presidential election year), had undergone "plastic" surgery.

At first Howdy and his friends were seen only once a week for an hour; the show was then titled *Puppet Playhouse*. After experimenting with a thrice-weekly format, the show was seen Mondays through Fridays for a half hour beginning 15 August 1948. From the outset the show was set in Doodyville, a circus town populated by an assortment of puppets and people (the circus setting obviously enabled characters to come and go with relative ease). Each day an audience of children sat in the bleachers, an area known as the "Peanut Gallery." A typical day's activities might have included a silent film short, a song or two, some chitchat, and a running story involving the citizens of Doodyville. By 1948 Bob Smith, who had previously been called "Mr. Smith" by the other characters, became known as "Buffalo Bob"; he was so named by the Sycapoose Indians, a friendly tribe which lived near town (in real life, Smith had been born in Buffalo, N.Y.). Buffalo Bob's principal assistant, and sometime nemesis, was a voiceless clown named Clarabell, who honked a horn attached to his belt and carried a seltzer bottle. Clarabell was first played by Bob Keeshan, an NBC staffer whose jobs included handing props to Buffalo Bob; it was decided that since Keeshan appeared on camera, he should be costumed, and thus the Clarabell character was created. For a short time Keeshan also played Oscar, a professorial chap; when Keeshan left the series in 1953 to host his own local show (in 1955 he returned to network TV as Captain Kangaroo), he was replaced by Bobby Nicholson. Nicholson later switched roles to play Cornelius Cobb, Doodyville's store-keeper, and Lew Anderson took over as Clarabell. Other humans included: Chief Thunderthud, an Indian chief who frequently shouted "Kowabunga!" (played by Bill LeCornec); Princess Summerfall Winterspring, a beautiful Indian princess (the character first appeared as a puppet), played by Judy Tyler (who died in an auto accident in 1957) and briefly by Linda Marsh; Bison Bill, who filled in for Buffalo Bob when the latter was ill or on vacation, played by Ted Brown; and Ugly Sam, a wrestler, played by Dayton Allen.

Howdy Doody, of course, was the star puppet, but he had many wooden costars: Phineas T. Bluster, the misanthropic mayor of Doodyville who instigated most of the sinister plots on the show; Dilly Dally, a lame-brained carpenter who was usually duped by Mr. Bluster into doing his dirty work; Flub-a-Dub, a creature made up of parts of eight different animals; Captain Scuttlebutt, a salty seaman who piloted an old scow; John J. Fadoozle, a private eye; Don José Bluster and Hector Hamhock Bluster, Phineas's triplet brothers; Double Doody, Howdy's twin brother; and Heidi Doody, Howdy's sister. Voices were provided by Bob Smith (who prerecorded Howdy's voice and thus could sing duets with the puppet), Dayton Allen (Mr. Bluster), Bill LeCornec (Dilly Dally), and Alan Swift, among others.

The series continued to run five days a week until 1 June 1956. On 16 June 1956, it moved to Saturdays, where it remained for another four years. During that time other characters were added, including the puppet Sandra, a witch. The filmed adventures of Gumby, a movable clay figure, were also incorporated; in 1957 Gumby was given his own series (see *The Gumby Show*). *Howdy Doody* was one of the first regularly scheduled NBC shows to be shown in color; experimental broadcasts were conducted in the summer of 1953, and regular color-casting began 12 September 1955. Robert Muir was the producer of the series; Edward Kean wrote most of the shows between 1947 and 1955, and also wrote the lyrics to "It's Howdy Doody Time" and Clarabell's theme song. Rufus Rose was the chief puppeteer, assisted by Rhoda Mann and Dayton Allen. At the end of the final telecast, Clarabell sadly broke his series-long silence to say, "Goodbye, kids."

In 1970 Buffalo Bob toured the nostalgia circuit, appearing at colleges and universities. In 1976 he returned to host a new version of *Howdy Doody,* which failed to catch on with the children of the 1970s the way its predecessor had with another generation of youngsters almost thirty years earlier. The 1976 version also featured Bill LeCornec (who now played Nicholson Muir) and Marilyn Patch (as Happy Harmony). In November 1987 a two-hour syndicated special was telecast to celebrate Howdy's fortieth birthday.

HOWIE   CBS
1 JULY 1992–22 JULY 1992   Four-week prime time potpourri of standup comedy and sketches starring Howie Mandel, and taped at the Celebrity Theater in Anaheim, California.

HOW'S YOUR MOTHER-IN-LAW?   ABC
4 DECEMBER 1967–1 MARCH 1968   Chuck Barris created this daytime game show which featured three contestants—each of whom was a mother-in-law—and a panel of three comedians, each of whom joked about his or her mother-in-law; at the end of the show the panel tried to decide which of the contestants was the "best" mother-in-law. Wink Martindale presided over the festivities.

THE HUCKLEBERRY HOUND SHOW   SYNDICATED

1958–1962   One of the first television cartoon series developed by William Hanna and Joseph Barbera, the founders of Hanna-Barbera Productions, *Huckleberry Hound* featured a lovable mutt who would try anything once. In addition to the title character, other segments included "Yogi Bear," the smarter-than-average Ursine-American who lived in Jellystone Park, and "Pixie and Dixie," a pair of mice pursued by the luckless feline Mr. Jinx. After Yogi Bear got his own series, a new segment was added: "Hokey Wolf," the adventures of a scheming lupine. The success of this series led to the creation of dozens of cartoon characters by Hanna-Barbera, the best known of which include Yogi Bear, Quickdraw McGraw, and the Flintstones. In 1960 *Huckleberry Hound* became the first TV cartoon series to win an Emmy Award.

THE HUDSON BROTHERS RAZZLE DAZZLE SHOW   CBS

7 SEPTEMBER 1974–30 AUGUST 1975   After hosting their own prime-time summer series, the Hudson Brothers—Bill (the eldest), Mark, and Brett (the youngest)—next turned up as hosts of a live-action Saturday-morning show for kids. Joining them were Ted Zeigler, Billy Van, Peter Cullen, and Rod Hull. Produced by Chris Bearde and Allan Blye.

THE HUDSON BROTHERS SHOW   CBS

31 JULY 1974–28 AUGUST 1974   This five-week variety series was a summer replacement for *The Sonny and Cher Comedy Hour;* it was hosted by three musical brothers from Oregon—Bill, Mark, and Brett Hudson. Also featured were Ronny Graham, Gary Owens, Ron Hull, and Stephanie Edwards. Sonny and Cher's producers, Chris Bearde and Allan Blye, also produced this show.

HUDSON STREET   ABC

19 SEPTEMBER 1995–17 FEBRUARY 1996   Half-hour sitcom in which a divorced Hoboken cop started a romance with a liberal newspaper reporter. With Tony Danza as the cop, Tony Canetti (Danza had previously played characters named Tony in *Taxi* and *Who's the Boss*); Lori Loughlin as the reporter, Melanie Clifford, who had recently been assigned the police beat; Jerry Adler as Tony's boss, Lieutenant Al Teischer; Christine Dunford as Officer Kirby McIntire; Tom Gallop as Officer Regelski; Jeffrey Anderson-Gunter as Winston, the Jamaican waiter at the restaurant frequented by Tony and Melanie, who subsequently became an undercover cop; Frankie J. Galasso as Mickey, Tony's son; and Shareen Mitchell as Tony's ex-wife, Lucy. Loughlin left the series in midseason.

HULK HOGAN'S ROCK 'N' WRESTLING!   CBS

14 SEPTEMBER 1985–13 JUNE 1987   Pro wrestler Hulk Hogan appeared in live and animated form on this hour Saturday morning show. In addition to the cartoons, the series featured live-action "comedic" wrestling segments.

HULL HIGH   NBC

20 AUGUST 1990–14 OCTOBER 1990; 23 DECEMBER 1990–30 DECEMBER 1990   One of 1990's two musical series (*Cop Rock* was the other), this one was set at Cordell Hull High School. The cast included Nancy Valen as the curvaceous new English teacher, Donna Breedlove; Will Lyman as teacher John Deerborn; Mark Ballou as Mark Fuller; Cheryl Pollak as Camilla; Harold Pruett as new student Cody Rome; Kristin Dattilo as D. J.; Marty Belafsky as Louis Plumb; Gary Grubbs as Mr. Brawley; George Martin as the principal, Emery Dobosh; and Marshall Bell as Mr. Fancher. Trey Parker, Carl Anthony Payne, Bryan Anthony, and Phillip DeMarks appeared as the singing and dancing Hull High Devils. The series was directed by Kenny Ortega, who had choreographed the film *Dirty Dancing*. Stanley Clarke composed the original score.

HULLABALOO   NBC

12 JANUARY 1965–29 AUGUST 1966   The relative success of ABC's *Shindig* prompted NBC to introduce its own rock-and-roll series in midseason. During the spring and

summer of 1965, it was an hour-long show; in the fall it moved from Tuesday to Monday and was cut to a half hour. A different guest host was featured each week, together with several acts; a regular feature during the spring of 1965 was a filmed segment (in black and white, unlike the rest of the show) hosted by Brian Epstein, manager of the Beatles, who usually introduced a British act. Movement was supplied by the Hullabaloo Dancers, the best known of which was Lada Edmund, Jr. Gary Smith produced the series; David Winters was the choreographer. Additional music was supplied by the Peter Matz Orchestra.

THE HUMAN FACTOR
CBS

16 APRIL 1992–28 MAY 1992   On this hour dramatic series a group of medical students learned about the intangible "human factor" in a course taught by a wise physician. With John Mahoney as sage Doctor Alec McMurtry; Kurt Deutsch as Matt Robbin; Eriq LaSalle as Michael Stoven; Melinda McGraw as Rebecca Travis; Matthew Ryan as Joe Murphy; Loryn Locklin as Gwen Byrne; and Larry Joshua as Dr. Binder.

THE HUMAN JUNGLE
SYNDICATED

1964   This British import starred Herbert Lom as a psychiatrist, Dr. Roger Corder, and featured Michael Johnson as his assistant, Davis.

HUMAN TARGET
ABC

20 JULY 1992–29 AUGUST 1992   Fanciful hour crime show starring Rick Springfield as Christopher Chance, a former Special Forces agent who became the "human target": he traded places with persons whose lives were in danger in order to capture their would-be killers. Chance used a high-tech airplane known as Blackwing in his work. Assisting him were Kirk Baltz as Philo Marsden; SaMi Chester as Jeff Carlyle; and Signy Coleman as Libby Page.

THE HUNTER
CBS/NBC

3 JULY 1952–24 SEPTEMBER 1952 (CBS); 26 SEPTEMBER 1954–26 DECEMBER 1954 (NBC) Half-hour Cold War spy series. Barry Nelson starred as Bart Adams, American undercover agent, in the CBS version, and Keith Larsen played the role in the NBC version two years later. Filmed in New York, the series was produced by Ed Montagne and directed by Oscar Rudolph.

HUNTER
CBS

18 FEBRUARY 1977–27 MAY 1977   A pallid adventure series which replaced *Executive Suite*. With James Franciscus as James Hunter, a man who ran a bookstore before being selected to be a member of a special team of government operatives; Linda Evans as Marty Shaw, his frequent partner; and Ralph Bellamy as Mr. Baker, his seldom-seen boss. Created by William Blinn.

HUNTER
NBC

18 SEPTEMBER 1984–30 AUGUST 1991   The third series of this title was a cop show from Stephen J. Cannell Productions. Originally scheduled on Fridays opposite CBS's *Dallas,* it performed poorly and barely escaped cancellation. After a switch to a Saturday time slot ratings began to improve; a change of producers and other refinements helped solidify *Hunter*'s success. The series starred former pro footballer Fred Dryer and Stepfanie Kramer as Sergeant Rick Hunter and Sergeant Dee Dee McCall, partners at the Los Angeles Police Department; originally, Hunter was a tough, unorthodox cop who was the son of a mobster, and McCall, nicknamed "The Brass Cupcake," was his equally tough compatriot. During the first season, they worked mainly in gritty downtown L.A. For the second season, however, under new executive producer Roy Huggins (for whom Stephen Cannell had worked on *The Rockford Files*), the gangster backstory was abandoned, the setting was moved "uptown," and the relationship between Hunter and McCall was broadened; both became less tough. After six seasons, Kramer announced her decision to leave the series in 1990, in part to pursue a musical career; in a two-part finale at the end of the

season, McCall married and left the force. Darlanne Flugel, as Officer Joanne Malinski, became Hunter's new partner in the fall of 1990, as Hunter transferred to the Metro Division. Malinski was killed off in midseason, and Lauren Lane and Courtney Barilla joined the cast as Sergeant Chris Novak and her young daughter, Allison.

Other regulars included Arthur Rosenberg (fall 1984) as the boss, Captain Lester Cain; John Amos (1984–1985) as the next boss, Captain Dolan; Bruce Davison (1985–1986) as boss Captain Wyler; Charles Hallahan (1986–1991) as boss Captain Charlie Devane; James Whitmore, Jr., (1984–1986) as Sergeant Bernie Terwilliger; and Garrett Morris (1986–1991) as streetwise informant Sporty James. Dryer and Hallahan reprised their roles in a made-for-TV movie, "The Return of Hunter" (NBC, 30 April 1995).

HUSBANDS, WIVES & LOVERS   CBS
10 MARCH 1978–30 JUNE 1978   Southern California was the setting for this hour-long comedy series about five contemporary couples. The series had a continuing story line, which began with the announcement by one of the couples (the Willises) of their impending separation. Featured were Cynthia Harris as Paula Zuckerman; Stephen Pearlman as her husband, Murray Zuckerman, a traveling salesman; Lynne Marie Stewart as Joy Bellini; Eddie Barth as her formerly married husband, Harry Bellini, a sanitation removal magnate; Ron Rifkin as Ron Willis, a dentist; Jesse Welles as his wife, Helene Willis; Charles Siebert as lawyer Dixon Fielding; Claudette Nevins as his wife, Courtney Fielding; Mark Lonow as Harry's younger brother, Lennie Bellini; and Randee Heller as Rita, the woman who lived with Lennie and managed "Lennie's Denim Boutique" with him. Hal Dresner was the executive producer, and Don Van Atta the producer for 20th Century-Fox Television.

THE HY GARDNER SHOW   SYNDICATED
1965   Ninety-minute talk show, hosted by columnist Hy Gardner.

I AM THE GREATEST: THE ADVENTURES OF MUHAMMAD ALI   NBC
10 SEPTEMBER 1977–28 JANUARY 1978   Saturday-morning cartoon show featuring the voice of the talkative boxing champ. Executive producer: Fred Calvert. Producer: Janis Diamond.

I AM THE LAW   SYNDICATED
1953   Low-budget cop show, starring George Raft (who usually played gangsters in the movies) as Lieutenant George Kirby of the New York Police Department. Executive producer: Pat Costello (brother of Lou Costello). Produced and directed by Jean Yarborough.

I BELIEVE IN MIRACLES   SYNDICATED
1966–1976   Half-hour religious program hosted by faith healer Kathryn Kuhlman. Most of the guests were persons who had been cured by Kuhlman. Singer Jimmy McDonald was also a regular.

I COVER TIMES SQUARE   ABC
5 OCTOBER 1950–11 JANUARY 1951   Half-hour crime show, starring Harold Huber as newspaper columnist Johnny Warren.

I DREAM OF JEANNIE   NBC
18 SEPTEMBER 1965–1 SEPTEMBER 1970   Half-hour sitcom about an Air Force astronaut who, after a crash landing on an uninhabited island, uncorked a bottle and thereby released a beautiful genie named Jeannie. Though popular during its original run and later in syndication, the show was sexist when judged by current standards— Jeannie was always the "slave," and the astronaut the "master." The series starred Barbara Eden as Jeannie (and, occasionally, as Jeannie's mischievous sister); Larry Hagman as Captain (later Major) Tony Nelson, the lucky astronaut; Bill Daily as Captain Roger Healey, Tony's friend, who also knew of Jeannie's existence and

magical powers; Hayden Rorke as Colonel Alfred Bellows, a NASA psychiatrist; Emmaline Henry as his wife, Amanda Bellows; and Barton MacLane as General Martin Peterson. During the series' first three seasons, Jeannie and Tony apparently enjoyed a platonic relationship; in the fall of 1969 they were married. In a few of the later episodes Farrah Fawcett could be seen—these were among her first TV appearances. Sidney Sheldon was the creator and executive producer of the series for Screen Gems. The first season's episodes were filmed in black and white; the remainder of the 139 shows were broadcast in color. In 1973 a cartoon sequel appeared on Saturday mornings (see *Jeannie*), and in 1983 another prime-time sitcom was introduced with a genie as its central character (see *Just Our Luck*). A TV-movie sequel surfaced on 20 October 1985. "I Dream of Jeannie: Fifteen Years Later" reunited Barbara Eden and Bill Daily from the original cast; Wayne Rogers played Tony (it would have been incongruous for Larry Hagman, now famous as *Dallas*'s J. R. Ewing, to have returned). For the first time ever, viewers were able to see Jeannie's navel, which had always been covered by high-waisted harem pants in the series. Eden and Daily teamed up for a second TV-movie, "I Still Dream of Jeannie," which ran on NBC 20 October 1991.

I HAD THREE WIVES   CBS
14 AUGUST 1985–13 SEPTEMBER 1985   A light detective series about a private eye who enlisted the help of his three ex-wives on his cases. With Victor Garber as Jackson Beaudine; Maggie Cooper as ex number one, Mary Parker, an attorney; Shanna Reed as ex number two, Liz, a journalist; Teri Copley as ex number three, Sam, an actress and stuntwoman; David Faustino as Andrew Beaudine, son of Victor and Mary; and Luis Avalos as Lieutenant Gomez.

I LED THREE LIVES   SYNDICATED
1953–1956   This well-known counterespionage series was based on the real-life adventures of Herbert A. Philbrick, who wrote a best-selling book about his life as a Boston advertising executive by day, as a member of the American Communist Party by night, and as an undercover agent for the FBI after hours. Richard Carlson starred as Philbrick, with Virginia Stefan as his wife, Ann.

I LOVE LUCY   CBS
15 OCTOBER 1951–24 JUNE 1957
THE LUCY-DESI COMEDY HOUR   CBS
6 NOVEMBER 1957–1 APRIL 1960   Television's first smash hit situation comedy, *I Love Lucy* was the most consistently popular program in TV history: during its six seasons it ranked first for four years, second once, and third once. It was also the first sitcom to be filmed before a live audience; the decision to film the show was fortuitous, not only for its principals (the stars, Desi Arnaz and Lucille Ball, owned the show through their production company, Desilu), but also for subsequent generations of viewers, as *I Love Lucy* has proven virtually indestructible in reruns. A classic comedy about a bandleader, his wife, and their frumpy neighbors, *I Love Lucy* clicked simply because it was well written and well played.

Desi Arnaz emigrated to Miami from his native Cuba in 1933, the same year that Lucille Ball headed toward Hollywood after a luckless stay in New York. Arnaz drifted into music, landed a job with Xavier Cugat's orchestra, and led his own band before going to Hollywood in 1940 to repeat his stage role in the filmed version of *Too Many Girls*. He met Lucille Ball on the set of the film, and the two were married a few months later. Arnaz appeared in one or two more films before resuming his career as a bandleader, while Lucille Ball continued her film career. By the end of the decade she was starring in a radio sitcom, *My Favorite Husband,* opposite Richard Denning. Its sponsor wanted to take the show to television with the same cast, but Lucy wanted Desi to be her TV costar. The two decided to produce a pilot film, which was the beginning of the *I Love Lucy* series.

The film was made early in 1951. It was directed by Ralph Levy and written by Jess Oppenheimer (*My Favorite Husband*'s head writer and producer), and Madelyn Pugh and Bob Carroll (*My Favorite Husband*'s writers). Thought to have been lost, the pilot film surfaced forty years later in the hands of the widow of Pepito the clown, who had been featured in it; CBS broadcast it as part of a special program on 30 April 1990. In the film Lucy and Desi played Lucy and Larry Lopez; he was a bandleader, she a housewife who ended up on stage with her husband. There were no neighbors on the show. The script incorporated some of the vaudeville routines that the two had worked up during the preceding year. The Milton Biow advertising agency showed interest in the concept while Oppenheimer, Pugh, and Carroll began to refine it: Desi would now play Ricky Ricardo, a not-too-successful bandleader working in New York, and Lucy would be Lucy Ricardo, a talentless housewife ever hopeful of breaking into showbiz. The Ricardos would live in a small apartment on East 68th Street, above Fred and Ethel Mertz, their friends (and their landlords). Lucy had originally wanted Gale Gordon and Bea Benaderet, both of whom had been featured on *My Favorite Husband,* to play the Mertzes; Desi, however, decided to hire William Frawley, a sixty-four-year-old character actor with a reputation as a two-fisted drinker, after Frawley suggested himself for the part of Fred. Vivian Vance, a character actress with vaudeville, Broadway, and movie experience, was suggested for the Ethel part by Marc Daniels, who would direct the first season's shows. The casting was inspired; though Frawley cared little for Vance, the two seemed perfect as the down-to-earth Mertzes—Frawley as Ricky's irascible but loyal comrade in the battle of the sexes, and Vance as Lucy's frequent conspirator in her incessant attempts to get on stage.

The new concept for *I Love Lucy* was sold to a sponsor, Philip Morris, and was scheduled on CBS. As neither Lucy nor Desi was willing to relocate in New York and as CBS refused to permit the show to be televised live from Hollywood (because Eastern viewers would thus have to watch poor quality kinescopes of the broadcasts, as there were not yet any coast-to-coast transmission lines), it was decided that the show would be filmed; that way, audiences throughout the country would be assured of high quality reception. The show would be produced by Desilu, the production company that Lucy and Desi had formed in 1950; Jess Oppenheimer was named producer and head writer, Pugh and Carroll the writers. Several mammoth production problems were overcome during the summer of 1951: a soundstage was located, leased, and remodeled to accommodate a studio audience, and, under the guidance of cinematographer Karl Freund, the stage itself was redesigned and the four-camera filming system was developed. A more personal preproduction uncertainty was resolved on 17 July 1951, when Lucy gave birth to their first child, Lucie Arnaz. Filming of *I Love Lucy* began in September. *I Love Lucy* premiered on 15 October 1951, to overwhelmingly favorable reviews (the premiere episode, "The Girls Want to Go to a Nightclub," was not the first filmed). By the end of the season it was a smash; the American Research Bureau announced in April 1952 that it had become the first TV program to have been seen in 10 million homes. In May of that year the show made the cover of *Time* magazine. *I Love Lucy* ended its first season third in the seasonal Nielsen ratings.

Production of the second season's show began earlier than usual because Lucy discovered that she was again expecting a child. Desi and Jess Oppenheimer convinced the sponsor to incorporate Lucy's pregnancy into the *I Love Lucy* story line (though the subject of pregnancy had been treated on other TV shows, such as *One Man's Family,* this was the first time that a pregnant woman had played a mother-to-be). Seven of the season's episodes would deal with Lucy's pregnancy; at CBS's insistence, however, the word "pregnant" was forbidden, though the word "expecting" was deemed acceptable. The episode concerning the birth of the baby (to be filmed in November) would be shown on 19 January 1953, and it was decided that the Ricardos' child would be a boy. Arnaz explained that the decision was made mainly for the benefit of little Lucie Arnaz. Her parents felt that Lucie might have been confused if the Ricardos' first child was, like her, a little girl.

The story line proved immensely popular, as *I Love Lucy* became television's top-ranked show, toppling Arthur Godfrey's *Talent Scouts*. As luck would have it, the Ricardos' baby boy (Little Ricky) was born on TV the same day that Lucille Ball gave birth to a son, Desi Arnaz IV (he would later be known as Desi Arnaz, Jr.). News of the events dominated the headlines, crowding out other stories such as the inauguration of President Eisenhower. In April of 1953 young Desi graced the cover of the first issue of *TV Guide*.

I Love Lucy remained the number-one show during its third and fourth seasons, surviving a brief brouhaha in the fall of 1953 when Walter Winchell broadcast the news that in 1936 Lucy had publicly announced her intention to vote Communist (she explained that she had made the statement solely to please her grandfather, and was exonerated by the House Un-American Activities Committee). The episodes of the second, third, and fourth seasons were all directed by William Asher, who would later produce *Bewitched*. Two casting changes occured: twins Michael and Joseph Mayer played Little Ricky from the fall of 1953 until the spring of 1956, replacing twins Richard and Ronald Simmons, and Jerry Hausner, who had occasionally played Ricky's agent, Jerry, left after the 1953–1954 season.

The series broadened its story line for the fourth season, as Ricky Ricardo landed a part in a movie; twenty-seven episodes of the 1954–1955 season chronicled the Ricardos' and Mertzes' move West. This story line lent itself to the use of big-name guest stars, a device not previously employed on the show. Among the big names who appeared that season were: Tennessee Ernie Ford (who first appeared at the end of the third season, and returned 24 January 1955 as the Ricardos began their trip), William Holden (7 February), Hedda Hopper (14 March), Rock Hudson (25 April), Harpo Marx (9 May, featuring a superb "mirror" scene with Lucy), and Richard Widmark (30 May).

For its fifth season, *I Love Lucy* acquired a new sponsor (General Foods), a new director (James V. Kern), and a second pair of writers (Bob Schiller and Bob Weiskopf). The use of guest stars continued, starting with John Wayne (in his TV dramatic debut, 10 October 1955). Half-way through the season, the Ricardos and the Mertzes were on the move again, this time to Europe. In the ratings race, the show finally slipped to second place, behind *The $64,000 Question*.

Producer Jess Oppenheimer left after the fifth season, and the series' final season began with the Ricardos and the Mertzes back in New York, where Ricky now owned his own nitery. Keith Thibodeaux, a six-year-old drummer whose professional name was Richard Keith, joined the cast as Little Ricky, replacing the Mayer twins. Bob Hope appeared as a guest star (1 October 1956), followed by Orson Welles (15 October) and Elsa Lanchester (12 November). William Asher returned to direct the final thirteen episodes, which depicted the Ricardos' move to suburban Connecticut (Mary Jane Croft and Frank Nelson were seen as their New England neighbors, Betty and Ralph Ramsey). In the last episode of *I Love Lucy*, "The Ricardos Dedicate a Statue," Lucie and Desi Arnaz, Jr., made their only appearances on the show. During its last season *I Love Lucy* reclaimed its number-one ranking (*I Love Lucy* and *The Andy Griffith Show* have been the only TV series to cease production after finishing first in the ratings; however, *The Andy Griffith Show* continued, without Griffith, as *Mayberry R.F.D.*). A total of 180 half-hour episodes were produced, though only 179 were made available for syndication; in his book, *The Story of I Love Lucy*, Bart Andrews noted that the episode of 24 December 1956, in which Fred bought a Christmas tree for Little Ricky, had never been rebroadcast. After a thirty-three-year hiatus, CBS located a print and aired the "lost episode" on 18 December 1989; it had not been put in the syndication package because of its Christmas theme and because it included several flashbacks to previous episodes.

From 1957 to 1960, thirteen hour-long shows were filmed, which were shown as *The Lucy-Desi Comedy Hour* and *The Lucille Ball-Desi Arnaz Show*. The first five were telecast as specials during the 1957–1958 season, and the others were broadcast during the *Desilu Playhouse* time slot. The first of these, "Lucy Takes a Cruise to Havana," ran seventy-five minutes, but Desi Arnaz persuaded the sponsor of the succeeding program, *The U.S. Steel Hour*, to permit a fifteen-minute incursion. The last of the thirteen, "Lucy Meets the Moustache," featured Ernie Kovacs and Edie Adams, and was televised 1 April 1960. It was especially poignant, not because it signified the end of the Ricardos and the Mertzes, but because it was filmed after Lucy and Desi had agreed to get divorced.

After their divorce Lucy became the head of Desilu Studios, buying out Desi's interest in 1962; in 1967 the operation was sold to Paramount. Desilu had expanded considerably from a one-show company since it was founded in 1950; Desilu produced many series during the 1950s and 1960s, including *Our Miss Brooks, December Bride, Willy, Those Whiting Girls, It's Always Jan, The Whirlybirds, The Untouchables, Fair Exchange,* and *Glynis.* Desi Arnaz made few TV appearances since 1960, though he was occasionally featured on *The Mothers-in-Law,* a sitcom he produced. Lucille Ball, who married Gary Morton in 1961, went on to star in a pair of similar sitcoms, *The Lucy Show* and *Here's Lucy,* which together lasted twelve seasons. (A fourth series, *Life with Lucy,* lasted only two months in 1986.) On 28 November 1976, CBS broadcast a two-hour tribute to her three shows, "CBS Salutes Lucy— The First 25 Years," which included a rare television appearance by CBS's chief executive, William Paley. Desi Arnaz died in 1986, Lucille Ball in 1989. On 10 February 1991, CBS aired a made-for-TV movie about the couple's life before *I Love Lucy.* "Lucy and Desi: Before the Laughter," with Frances Fisher and Maurice Benard, was hotly criticized by Lucie Arnaz and Desi Arnaz, Jr., as an inaccurate portrait of their parents' lives.

I MARRIED DORA   ABC
22 SEPTEMBER 1987–8 JANUARY 1988; 27 MAY 1988–19 AUGUST 1988   A witless sitcom about a single parent who married his Latin American housekeeper to save her from deportation. With Daniel Hugh-Kelly as architect Peter Farrell, whose wife had disappeared five years earlier in an airplane hijacking; Elizabeth Peña as the housekeeper, Dora Calderon; Juliette Lewis as Peter's daughter, Kate; Jason Horst as Peter's son, Will; Henry Jones as Peter's boss, Hughes Whitney Lennox; and Sanford Jensen as Peter's co-worker, Dolf Menninger. Perhaps the most interesting feature of the show was that it announced its own cancellation on the last first-run episode.

I MARRIED JOAN   NBC
15 OCTOBER 1952–6 APRIL 1955   Domestic sitcom starring Joan Davis as Joan Stevens and Jim Backus as her husband, Judge Bradley Stevens. Also featured as the Stevens's friends and neighbors over the years were Hal Smith and Geraldine Carr as Charlie and Mabel; Dan Tobin and Sheila Bromley as Kerwin and Janet; Wally Brown and Sally Kelly as Wally and Sally; and Sandra Gould as Mildred Webster. Bing Crosby made a rare guest appearance on the show (25 February 1953), as did oldtime cowboy star Hoot Gibson (16 March 1955). The series was owned by Davis's production company and was produced by Dick Mack and directed by Hal Walker. Ninety-eight half-hour episodes were filmed.

I.N.N. NEWS   SYNDICATED
1980–1990   A rarity in television, *I.N.N. News* was a nationally syndicated news broadcast; it gave independent local stations a chance to compete with the three network news broadcasts. Principal correspondents included Pat Harper, Bill Jorgensen, Steve Bausch, Brad Holbrook, Morton Dean, and Carl Rowan. In 1981 a midday edition was launched, coanchored by Marvin Scott and Claire Carter. *I.N.N.,* which stood for Independent Network News, was headquartered at WPIX in New York. In 1987 the evening newscast was retitled *USA Tonight.*

I REMEMBER MAMA
Scc MAMA

I SEARCH FOR ADVENTURE   SYNDICATED
1954   Another of the several documentary series produced and hosted by John D. Craig, this half-hour series featured films taken by modern-day adventurers.

I SPY   SYNDICATED
1956   The first of the two series by this title was an anthology of spy dramas, historical and modern, hosted by Raymond Massey (who appeared as Anton the Spymaster).

I SPY   NBC

15 SEPTEMBER 1965–2 SEPTEMBER 1968   The second series which bore this title told the story of two American undercover agents who traveled around the world on various assignments. More significantly, it was the first noncomedy series to star a black actor—Bill Cosby, who played Alexander Scott (better known as Scotty), a Temple graduate, a Rhodes Scholar, and a spy whose cover was that of the trainer of a tennis pro. Cosby's white costar was Robert Culp, who played Kelly Robinson, a Princeton-educated secret agent who masqueraded as the tennis pro. Filmed largely on location all over the world, *I Spy* was produced by Sheldon Leonard, Mort Fine, and David Friedkin. The two stars were reunited in a 1994 TV-movie, "I Spy Returns" (3 February, CBS).

I WITNESS VIDEO   NBC

23 FEBRUARY 1992–19 AUGUST 1994   *I Witness Video* presented videos of actual crimes, calamities, and other catastrophes, usually taken by amateurs. The premiere telecast generated a storm of controversy for its footage of two killings: a Texas constable's murder by three gunmen (taped by a camera mounted in his car), and a Denver criminal suspect's killing during a police chase (taped by a helicopter pilot). Patrick VanHorn hosted the program from 1992 until the fall of 1993, when John Forsythe took over.

THE ICE PALACE   CBS

23 MAY 1971–25 JULY 1971   A variety hour with guest hosts, guest acts, and a group of talented skaters which included Billy Chappell, Linda Carbonetto, Tim Wood, and the Bob Turk Ice Dancers.

ICHABOD AND ME   CBS

26 SEPTEMBER 1961–18 SEPTEMBER 1962   Low-key sitcom created by Joe Connelly and Bob Mosher. With Robert Sterling as Bob Major, a New Yorker who purchased a New England newspaper and moved to Phippsboro with his son; George Chandler as Ichabod Adams, the man from whom Major bought the paper; Jimmy Mathers (younger brother of *Leave It to Beaver*'s Jerry Mathers) as Benjie, Bob's young son; Christine White as Abigail Adams, Ichabod's daughter, Bob's girlfriend; Reta Shaw as Livvy, Bob's housekeeper; and Guy Raymond as Martin, a typically taciturn New England townsman. The pilot for the series, entitled "Adams' Apples," was shown on *General Electric Theater* 24 April 1960.

I'D LIKE TO SEE   NBC

5 NOVEMBER 1948–29 MARCH 1949   Host Ray Morgan introduced film shorts on subjects suggested by home viewers on this Tuesday-night half-hour series.

IDENTIFY   ABC

14 FEBRUARY 1949–9 MAY 1949   Bob Elson hosted this prime-time sports quiz show.

IF NOT FOR YOU   CBS

18 SEPTEMBER 1995–9 OCTOBER 1995   Half-hour sitcom in which two people dumped their respective fiancés and fell in love with each other. With Elizabeth McGovern as Jessie Kent, who produced books on tape; Hank Azaria as recording studio owner Craig Schaeffer, who bumped into Jessie at a restaurant before meeting her at his studio; Debra Jo Rupp as Eileen Mott, who was employed by Craig to record the voices for canned announcements; Jim Turner as Cal, Craig's chief engineer; Reno Wilson as Bobby, a songwriter; Peter Krause as Jessie's fiancé, Elliot; and Jane Sibbett as Craig's fiancée, Melanie. Lifted from CBS's Monday schedule after four airings, *If Not for You* was the first casualty of the 1995–1996 season.

IF YOU HAD A MILLION
See THE MILLIONAIRE

THE IGOR CASSINI SHOW DUMONT

25 OCTOBER 1953–28 FEBRUARY 1954   Columnist Igor Cassini (who wrote under the name of Cholly Knickerbocker) hosted this Sunday-night celebrity-interview series.

THE ILKA CHASE SHOW CBS

16 FEBRUARY 1950–10 AUGUST 1950   Fifteen-minute Thursday-night series hosted by fashionable Ilka Chase. It was also titled *Glamour-Go-Round*.

I'LL BET NBC

29 MARCH 1965–24 SEPTEMBER 1965   On this daytime game show hosted by Jack Narz, one spouse tried to predict whether the other spouse would be able to answer a question correctly. In 1971 a syndicated version of the show appeared under the title *It's Your Bet* (see that title).

I'LL BUY THAT CBS

15 JUNE 1953–17 DECEMBER 1953   Mike Wallace hosted this twice-weekly daytime game show on which studio contestants tried to identify items sent in by home viewers. A celebrity panel was on hand to assist the contestants.

I'LL FLY AWAY NBC

7 OCTOBER 1991–5 FEBRUARY 1993; 11 APRIL 1993   Highly acclaimed but little watched, this hour series was set in the South at the dawn of the civil rights movement in the early 1960s. With Sam Waterston as Forrest Bedford, the noble prosecutor of Bryland County (he became a United States Attorney a season later); Regina Taylor as his Negro housekeeper, Lily Harper (was it a coincidence that the name was close to that of Harper Lee, author of *To Kill a Mockingbird*?); Jeremy London as Forrest's older son, Nathan; Ashlee Levitch as his daughter, Francie; John Aaron Bennett as his younger son, John Morgan; Kathryn Harrold as lawyer Christina LeKatzis, a potential love interest for Forrest, whose wife had been institutionalized following a nervous breakdown; Bill Cobbs as Lily's father, Lewis; Zelda Harris as Lily's daughter, Adelaide; and Brad Sullivan as high school wrestling coach Zollicofer Weed. Joshua Brand and John Falsey created the series, which was filmed in Atlanta. Following its cancellation by NBC, the series' 38 episodes were purchased by PBS and were rerun during the 1993–1994 season. The reruns were prefaced by a 90-minute sequel featuring most of the cast (except for Jeremy London, who was then working on *Angel Falls*; his twin brother, Jason London, appeared as Nathan).

I'LL TAKE MANHATTAN CBS

1 MARCH 1987–4 MARCH 1987   Four-part adaptation of the Judith Krantz novel about a young woman who takes over the family's fashion magazine publishing business. With Valerie Bertinelli as Maxi Amberville; Barry Bostwick as her father, Zachary Amberville; Perry King as her uncle, Cutter Amberville; Jane Kaczmarek as Zachary's mistress, Nina Stern; Francesca Annis as Maxi's mother, Lily Amberville; and Jack Scalia as art director Rocco Cipriani, who married Maxi. The miniseries was filmed mostly in Toronto.

THE ILONA MASSEY SHOW DUMONT

1 NOVEMBER 1954–3 JANUARY 1955   Half-hour variety show, hosted by Hungarian-born actress Ilona Massey.

I'M A BIG GIRL NOW ABC

31 OCTOBER 1980–24 JULY 1981   Half-hour sitcom starring Danny Thomas as dentist Ben Douglas and Diana Canova as his daughter, Diana Cassidy; after learning that his wife had run off with his partner, Ben moved in with the recently divorced Diana and tried to restrain himself from meddling in her life. Also featured were Rori King as Becky, Diana's precocious seven-year-old; Sheree North as Edie McKendrick, Diana's boss at Cramer Research and Testing Group, a Washington think-tank; Michael Durrell as Walter Douglas, Diana's brother; Joan Welles as Polly, Walter's wife; Martin Short as Neal, one of Diana's co-workers; and Deborah Baltzell as Karen, another

co-worker. Inexplicably, during the last few episodes of the series, Diana and her cohorts were all working for a newspaper rather than for the think-tank.

I'M DICKENS, HE'S FENSTER   ABC
28 SEPTEMBER 1962–13 SEPTEMBER 1963   A pair of zany carpenters were the central characters in this sitcom. With John Astin as Harry Dickens; Marty Ingels as Arch Fenster; Emmaline Henry as Kate Dickens, Harry's wife; Dave Ketchum as Mel Warshaw, their occasional helper; Harry Beckman as Mulligan, another helper; Frank DeVol as Mr. Bannister, their boss; and Noam Pitlik as Bentley. Leonard Stern was the producer.

I'M TELLING   NBC
12 SEPTEMBER 1987–3 SEPTEMBER 1988   On this Saturday-morning kids' game show, teams of siblings were quizzed about each other; although most programs featured ordinary contestants, some shows pitted youthful stars of various NBC series, together with their real-life brothers and sisters, against each other. Laurie Faso emceed.

THE IMMORTAL   ABC
24 SEPTEMBER 1970–14 JANUARY 1971; 12 MAY 1971–8 SEPTEMBER 1971   An hour-long adventure series starring Chris George as Ben Richards, an automobile test driver who discovered that his blood contained certain miraculous antibodies that could make him live forever. Ben searched for his long-lost brother, Jason, in the hope that he, too, had the same kind of blood. Also featured were David Brian as Arthur Maitland, a rich old man who, having once refused a transfusion of Richards's blood, pursued Richards; Don Knight as Fletcher, the man Maitland hired to track Richards down. Tony Wilson was the executive producer of the series, which was based loosely on James Gunn's novel, *The Immortals.* Canceled in midseason, reruns were broadcast later in 1971, replacing *The Johnny Cash Show.*

THE IMOGENE COCA SHOW   NBC
2 OCTOBER 1954–25 JUNE 1955   After several seasons as second banana to Sid Caesar on *Your Show of Shows,* Imogene Coca was given her own half-hour comedy show in 1954 (Sid Caesar having gone on to *Caesar's Hour*), which lasted a season. Regulars included David Burns, Billy DeWolfe, Ruth Donnelly, Hal March, and Bibi Osterwald.

IMUS, PLUS   SYNDICATED
1978   Ninety-minute talk show hosted by New York disc jockey Don Imus. Henri Bollinger and Robert Yamin were the executive producers, Hal Parets the producer.

IN CONCERT   ABC
7 JUNE 1991–   ABC had televised rock concerts under the "In Concert" title during the mid-1970s as part of ABC's *Wide World of Entertainment.* The network brought back the idea in 1991 with this hour series, broadcast late on Fridays. Segments were taped on location. The show had no permanent host until early 1995, when Vanessa Marcil assumed the job.

IN LIVING COLOR   FOX
15 APRIL 1990–25 AUGUST 1994   An innovative half-hour comedy series created by filmmaker Keenen Ivory Wayans (*I'm Gonna Git You Sucka*), inspired by *Saturday Night Live* and featuring a mostly black company of regulars performing various skits. Regulars included Wayans, his brother Damon Wayans, his sister Kim Wayans, James Carrey, Tommy Davidson, David Alan Grier, T'Keyah "Crystal" Keymah, Kelly Coffield, and Kim Coles (1990). The dancers were known as Keenen's Fly Girls. Another Wayans clan member, younger brother Shawn, appeared as S. W. 1, the show's deejay. Among the show's regularly featured bits were mirthless funmaker "Homey the Clown," the effeminate cohosts of "Men on Film," and "Hey Mon," the adventures of a hardworking West Indian family. Shawn Wayans joined the regular cast in the fall of 1991, and two new members were added: Jamie Foxx and Asian comic

Steve Park. Another Wayans brother, Marlon Wayans, joined in 1992, as did Alexandra Wentworth. The Wayans clan abruptly left the series in the middle of the 1992–1993 season, following a dispute between Keenen Ivory Wayans and Fox over the latter's decision to air reruns of *In Living Color* to replace a canceled program; Wayans felt that the extra exposure diminished the value of the series in the syndication market. The series carried on for another full season, however, with Carrey, Davidson, Foxx, Grier, Neymah, and Wentworth, and newcomers Anne-Marie Johnson (formerly of *In the Heat of the Night*), Jay Leggett, Carol Rosenthal, and Marc Wilmore. Following the demise of the show, several of the regulars went on to have successful movie careers, including, most notably, Carrey (now going by Jim).

IN PERFORMANCE AT WOLF TRAP   PBS
1974–1979   Videotaped performances of artists (mainly musicians and dancers) performing at Wolf Trap Farm Park in Arlington, Virginia. Produced at WETA-TV, Washington.

IN RECORD TIME
See THE ART FORD SHOW

IN SEARCH OF   SYNDICATED
1976–1982   Half-hour documentary series which explored strange phenomena, lost civilizations, and the like, narrated by *Star Trek*'s Leonard Nimoy. Jim McGinn and Alan Landsburg were the executive producers, Robert L. Long the series producer.

IN SESSION   SYNDICATED
1974   Musical series on which assorted rockers rapped and rocked. Phil Everly, the younger half of the Everly Brothers, hosted.

IN SPORT   SYNDICATED
1989–1991   Half-hour weekly sports magazine show, cohosted by Ahmad Rashad and Robin Swoboda.

IN THE BEGINNING   CBS
20 SEPTEMBER 1978–18 OCTOBER 1978   Half-hour sitcom about a conservative Irish priest who was teamed up with a streetwise nun and assigned to open a storefront mission in a tough inner-city neighorhood. With McLean Stevenson as Father Daniel M. Cleary; Priscilla Lopez as his coworker, Sister Agnes; Priscilla Morrill as Sister Lillian; Olivia Barash as Willie; Bobby Ellerbee as Jerome Rockefeller; and Jack Dodson as Monsignor Barlow. Mort Lachman was the executive producer for Norman Lear's T.A.T. Communications.

IN THE FIRST PERSON   CBS
29 JANUARY 1949–10 OCTOBER 1950   Fifteen-minute interview and commentary series hosted by journalist Quincy Howe.

IN THE HEAT OF THE NIGHT   NBC/CBS
6 MARCH 1988–3 MAY 1988 (NBC); 26 JULY 1988–21 JULY 1992 (NBC); 28 OCTOBER 1992–4 MAY 1994 (CBS)   Hour crime show based on the 1967 film about a white Mississippi police chief who teams up with a black detective from the north; in the TV version, set in the present time, there was no racial animosity between the two principal characters. The cast included Carroll O'Connor as Bill Gillespie, Chief of the Sparta, Mississippi, Police Department; Howard Rollins (1988–1993) as chief of detectives Virgil Tibbs, who was born in Sparta but had worked in Philadelphia; Alan Autry as Lieutenant Bubba Skinner; Anne-Marie Johnson (1988–1993) as Virgil's wife, Althea Tibbs; David Hart as Deputy Parker Williams; Hugh O'Connor (son of Carroll O'Connor) as Deputy Lonnie Jamison; Christian LeBlanc (1988–1989) as Deputy Junior Abernathy; Geoffrey Thorne (1988–1992) as Deputy Willson Sweet; and Crystal Fox (1989–1994) as dispatcher Lu Ann Corman. When Carroll O'Connor was sidelined because of heart surgery at the end of the 1988–1989 season, Joe

Don Baker filled in for him as Tom Dugan, a police captain who came out of retirement.

The spring 1988 episodes were filmed on location in Louisiana; production moved to Georgia in the fall of 1988. In the fall of 1992 the series switched networks, lasting another two seasons on CBS. Gillespie was voted out of office in the fall of 1993 and became sheriff, and Carl Weathers joined the cast as Sparta's new chief, Hampton Forbes. During the final season, Gillespie's romance with black city councilor Harriet DeLong (played by Denise Nicholas) heated up, and the two were married on the finale. Occasionally featured during the latter seasons were Dee Shaw as Sergeant Dee Sheppard; Harvey E. Lee, Jr., as Officer Ken Covey; and Mark Johnson as Officer Luke Everett. One or two two-hour *In the Heat of the Night* movies were telecast during the 1994–1995 season.

IN THE HOUSE NBC

10 APRIL 1995–15 MAY 1995; 10 JULY 1995–   Half-hour sitcom about a divorced black woman with two kids. It starred Debbie Allen as Jackie Warren, who landed a job as a legal secretary and moved into a rented house, only to find that her landlord would be sharing their kitchen. With rapper LL Cool J as the landlord, Marion Hill, a pro football player sidelined by an injury whose own place was being renovated (he lived in the garage apartment and agreed to look after the kids while Jackie worked); Lisa Arrindell Anderson as Jackie's snooty boss, attorney Heather Comstock; Maia Campbell as Jackie's teen daughter, Tiffany; and Jeffery Wood as Jackie's precocious young son, Austin. John Amos appeared occasionally as Marion's trainer, Sam.

IN THE MORGAN MANNER ABC

1 MARCH 1950–23 JULY 1950   Bandleader Russ Morgan hosted his own half-hour musical variety series, which was usually seen Sunday afternoons. In the summer of 1956 Morgan hosted a second series: see *The Russ Morgan Show.*

IN THE PARK CBS

9 DECEMBER 1951–31 MAY 1953   This children's show was seen Sunday mornings. It was hosted by Bill Sears and his puppet friends: Calvin the Crow, Sir Geoffrey the Giraffe, Magnolia the Ostrich, and Albert the Chipmunk. Paul Ritts and Mary Holliday handled the puppets.

THE INA RAY HUTTON SHOW NBC

4 JULY 1956–5 SEPTEMBER 1956   No male guests or regulars appeared on this half-hour musical variety series, hosted by Ina Ray Hutton. Hutton, who put together her first "all-girl" band in 1935, assembled a new crew in the early 1950s for her local show in Los Angeles. Purex sponsored the show nationally for one summer. Some of Hutton's musicians included Mickey Anderson (clarinet), Deedie Ball (piano), Harriet Blackburn, Lois Cronin (trombone), Janie Davis, Peggy Fairbanks, Helen Hammond (trumpet), Evie Howeth, Margaret Rinker (drums), Helen Smith, Judy Van Euer, Zoe Ann Willy, and Helen Wooley.

INCH HIGH, PRIVATE EYE NBC

8 SEPTEMBER 1973–31 AUGUST 1974   Saturday-morning cartoon series about a very small detective, Inch High, who was assisted by his niece, Lori, her boyfriend, Gator, and Braveheart the dog.

THE INCREDIBLE HULK CBS

10 MARCH 1978–13 NOVEMBER 1981; 5 MAY 1982–19 MAY 1982   After two popular made-for-TV movies, *The Incredible Hulk* was given a weekly spot in March 1978. The series, based on the Marvel Comics character, starred Bill Bixby as Dr. David Banner, a research scientist who was accidentally exposed to an overdose of gamma rays; as a result, Banner found himself transformed into a green-skinned, white-eyed behemoth (The Incredible Hulk) whenever he became enraged. Also featured were former Mr. America Lou Ferrigno as Banner's awesome but inarticulate alter ego, and Jack Colvin as Jack McGee, a reporter for the *National Register* who was out to

expose the Hulk. Kenneth Johnson was the executive producer, and James D. Parriott and Chuck Bowman the producers, for Universal Television. A cartoon version of the character twice came to television: in 1966, as one segment of the syndicated *Marvel Superheroes* (see that title), and in 1982, as half of *The Incredible Hulk and the Amazing Spider-Man* (see *Spiderman*). Bixby and Ferrigno reprised their roles in three made-for-TV movies, all shown on NBC: "The Incredible Hulk Returns" (22 May 1988); "The Trial of the Incredible Hulk" (7 May 1989); and "The Death of the Incredible Hulk" (18 February 1990).

INCREDIBLE SUNDAY · ABC
9 OCTOBER 1988–17 SEPTEMBER 1989   John Davidson, who had cohosted *That's Incredible!* earlier in the decade, hosted this second "incredible" series with Cristina Ferrare. Slated opposite *60 Minutes* on CBS, the hour show focused on unusual people and events. Woody Fraser, who had produced *That's Incredible!*, was executive producer.

INDAY · SYNDICATED
1985   *Inday* was the umbrella for four half-hour programs that were made available to local stations as a two-hour block or individually: a newscast, *Inday News*; a look at trends, *What's Hot! What's Not?*; a video adaptation of *Us* magazine, *All About Us*; and an interview show aimed at older viewers, *It's a Great Life,* cohosted by Robert and Rosemarie Stack.

INDUSTRY ON PARADE · SYNDICATED
1950–1958   Long-running series of fifteen-minute films on American industry, produced by the National Association of Manufacturers. The series won a Peabody Award in 1954.

INFATUATION · SYNDICATED
1992   Bob Eubanks hosted this half-hour weekly program on which guests were brought face to face with people who were, or had been, the objects of their infatuations, such as old flames and lost loves.

THE INFINITE VOYAGE · PBS
1987–1992   A series of hour documentaries on scientific subjects.

INFORMATION PLEASE · CBS
29 JUNE 1952–21 SEPTEMBER 1952   Created by Dan Golenpaul, *Information Please* ran on radio from 1938 to 1948; its television run was considerably shorter, replacing *The Fred Waring Show* for one summer. The format of the game show remained unchanged when it came to television: Viewers were invited to submit questions and won prizes if they succeeded in stumping the celebrity panel. Clifton Fadiman, the show's host on radio, continued as the moderator; permanent panelists included Franklin P. Adams, New York newspaper columnist, and John Kieran, sportswriter for *The New York Times*. Two guest celebrities completed the panel.

THE INNER FLAME
See PORTIA FACES LIFE

THE INNER SANCTUM · SYNDICATED
1954   *The Inner Sanctum*, an anthology series of creepy tales, began on radio in 1941. Its trademark, on radio and television, was a squeaking door, the entrance to the "inner sanctum." Paul McGrath, who had hosted the show for several years on radio, was heard (but not seen) as the host, Mr. Raymond.

INNER SPACE · SYNDICATED
1974   The underwater photography of Ron and Valerie Taylor was featured on this documentary series hosted by William Shatner.

THE INQUIRING MIND SYNDICATED
1965   An educational series produced at the University of Michigan; research work of Michigan scientists was examined. John Arthur Hanson hosted the program.

INSIDE AMERICA ABC
4 APRIL 1982–25 APRIL 1982   Forgettable series which focused on American lifestyles. Dick Clark hosted the hour show, which was scheduled on Sundays opposite *60 Minutes*.

INSIDE DECTIVE
See ROCKY KING, DETECTIVE

INSIDE EDITION SYNDICATED
1988–   Half-hour daily "tabloid" informational show, hosted by Bill O'Reilly and distributed by King World. Deborah Norville succeeded O'Reilly in March 1995.

INSIDE REPORT SYNDICATED
1989–1990   Half-hour daily informational show, hosted by Penny Daniels.

INSIDE STORY PBS
1981–1984   Hodding Carter III (a State Department spokesman during the Carter administration) hosted this half-hour series, which focused on journalism and the coverage of current events by the media.

INSIDE U.S.A. WITH CHEVROLET CBS
29 SEPTEMBER 1949–16 MARCH 1950   This half-hour variety show, cohosted by Peter Lind Hayes and Mary Healy (his wife), was seen biweekly on Thursdays. It alternated first with *Sugar Hill Times,* then with *Romance.*

INSIDE VIDEO THIS WEEK SYNDICATED
1989–1990   Clips from newly released commercial videos—motion pictures, music videos, and informational programs—were showcased on this half-hour weekly series, cohosted by two former *Entertainment Tonight* reporters, Eric Burns and Paula McClure.

INSIDE WASHINGTON SYNDICATED
1988–   This weekly news analysis program, hosted by Gordon Peterson, was the successor to *Agronsky & Co.* Regular panelists have included Carl Rowan, Elizabeth Drew, Strobe Talbott, James Kilpatrick, Hugh Sidey, and Charles Krauthammer. The series was also shown on many PBS stations.

THE INSIDERS ABC
25 SEPTEMBER 1985–8 JANUARY 1986; 2 JUNE 1986–23 JUNE 1986   A *Miami Vice* clone, The Insiders were a pair of young investigative reporters—one white, one black—for *Newspoint* magazine. Featured were Nicholas Campbell as Nick Fox; Stoney Jackson as his partner, James Mackey (better known simply as Mackey), an ex-con; and Gail Strickland as their boss, Alice West. Like *Miami Vice*'s Crockett and Tubbs, Nick and Mackey frequently went undercover and performed their exploits against a rock music soundtrack.

INSIGHT SYNDICATED
1961–1991   Widely syndicated religious program that presented modern-day morality lessons, often with well-known actors. Ellwood E. Kieser, a Paulist priest, was its host and executive producer.

INSPECTOR GADGET SYNDICATED
1983–1985   Inspector Gadget, the bumbling cartoon sleuth, was reminiscent of two earlier law enforcement officers: Inspector Clouseau of *The Pink Panther* films, and Maxwell Smart of *Get Smart.* Don Adams, who had played Smart, provided in early

episodes the voice of Gadget, who was assisted in his investigations by his niece, Penny, and his dog, Brain; Gadget's usual nemesis was the evil Claw (a villain of the same name had also been featured on *Get Smart*). Adams also supplied the title voice for a network holiday animated feature, "Inspector Gadget Saves Christmas" (4 December 1992, NBC).

INSTANT RECALL   SYNDICATED
1990–1991   Half-hour daily archival series that looked at events of the last fifty years. John Palmer was the host.

INTERFACE   PBS
1969–1975   Half-hour public affairs series hosted and produced by Tony Batten for WETA-TV, Washington.

INTERNATIONAL DETECTIVE   SYNDICATED
1959   Stories on this half-hour crime show were supposedly adapted from the files of the William J. Burns Agency. Arthur Fleming starred as Ken Franklin, a Burns Agent. Fleming later shortened his first name to Art and became famous as the host of *Jeopardy*. Filmed in England, the series was produced by Eddie Sutherland for Official Films.

INTERNATIONAL PLAYHOUSE   DUMONT
30 MAY 1951–14 NOVEMBER 1951   Dramatic anthology series that presented short foreign films and other foreign-made dramatic stories.

INTERNATIONAL SHOWTIME   NBC
15 SEPTEMBER 1961–10 SEPTEMBER 1965   European circuses were showcased on this Friday-night series, hosted by Don Ameche. The idea was revived in 1989: see *Great Circuses of the World*.

INTERNATIONAL ZONE   SYNDICATED
1962   Alistair Cooke hosted this half-hour informational series about the United Nations, produced by United Nations Television.

THE INTERNS   CBS
18 SEPTEMBER 1970–10 SEPTEMBER 1971   Based on the movie of the same title, *The Interns* was an undistinguished medical series about a group of young doctors and a crusty hospital director—all of whom worked at New North Hospital. With Broderick Crawford as Peter Goldstone, the director; Mike Farrell as Sam Marsh; Elaine Giftos as Bobbe Marsh, his wife (a nonphysician); Christopher Stone as Jim "Pooch" Hardin; Sandra Smith as Lydia Thorpe; Hal Frederick as Cal Baron; and Stephen Brooks as Greg Pettit.

INTERPOL CALLING   SYNDICATED
1959   Charles Korvin starred as Inspector Duval of Interpol, an international law enforcement organization, in this British import. Jack Wrather produced the half-hour series in association with the J. Arthur Rank Organisation.

INTO THE NIGHT STARRING RICK DEES   ABC
16 JULY 1990–14 NOVEMBER 1991   A midnight talk show, aimed at younger viewers, hosted by Los Angeles disc jockey Rick Dees. Billy Vera and the Beaters were the house band, Lisa Canning the announcer. Greg Binkley also appeared regularly in comedy bits, and Bob Perlow was the self-appointed "correspondent of chaos." Another regular feature was a group of four female senior citizens, known as "The Committee," who chatted with Dees on various topics in taped interviews. Dees departed in July 1991, and the show's title was shortened to *Into the Night* as guest hosts took over. The title was shortened again to *Studio 59* in October 1991, and the series faded quietly away.

THE INVADERS   ABC

10 JANUARY 1967–17 SEPTEMBER 1968   An imaginative adventure series about visitors from space. Roy Thinnes starred as David Vincent, an architect who, having taken a wrong turn on the highway, witnessed the landing of a spacecraft. Returning to the spot the following morning, he found no clues, but subsequent attempts on his life convinced him that somebody—or something—was after him. Gradually, Vincent learned that the Earth had indeed been visited by aliens, creatures capable of assuming human form; their native world was dying, and they were searching for new areas to colonize. Thereafter, Vincent spent most of his time trying to convince other people of the aliens' existence and trying to ferret out the aliens; some aliens were easy to spot because their little fingers were splayed, and all aliens when killed simply dematerialized into red dust. In December of 1967, Kent Smith joined the series as Edgar Scoville, another true believer. A total of forty-three episodes, all in color, were made. Executive producer: Quinn Martin. Creator: Larry Cohen. Producer: Alan A. Armer. A two-part TV-movie, "The Invaders," was aired on Fox 12 and 14 November 1995. Thinnes again played Vincent, but Scott Bakula starred as the principal alien-hunter. See also *The X-Files.*

THE INVESTIGATOR   NBC

3 JUNE 1958–2 SEPTEMBER 1958   This live, color adventure series was a summer replacement for *The George Gobel–Eddie Fisher Show.* It starred Lonny Chapman as Jeff Prior, New York private eye, and Howard St. John as Lloyd Prior, his father, a former reporter.

THE INVESTIGATORS   CBS

5 OCTOBER 1961–28 DECEMBER 1961   Insurance investigators were the central characters in this crime show. With James Franciscus as Russ Andrews; James Philbrook as Steve Banks; Mary Murphy as Maggie Peters; Al Austin as Bill Davis; and June Kenney as Polly, the secretary.

THE INVISIBLE MAN   CBS

4 NOVEMBER 1958–27 JANUARY 1959   H. G. Wells's classic tale of a young scientist who accidentally ingested a formula which made him invisible was the basis of this British import. The scientist's name was Peter Brady, but the name of the actor who portrayed him (his voice was audible and his clothing was, of course, visible) was never disclosed. Also featured were Lisa Daniely as Diane, his sister; Deborah Watling as Sally, his niece; and Ernest Clark as Sir Charles, a member of the British Cabinet. Thirteen half-hour episodes were seen over CBS. Ralph Smart produced the show for Official Films in cooperation with CBS-TV.

THE INVISIBLE MAN   NBC

8 SEPTEMBER 1975–19 JANUARY 1976   The second TV version of H. G. Wells's story was made in America. It starred David McCallum as Dr. Daniel Westin, a research scientist for the Klae Corporation, a West Coast think-tank, who cooked up a formula that rendered him invisible. Westin was outfitted with a special plastic mask that was a replica of his old face; thus, McCallum was quite visible to viewers. Also featured were Melinda Fee as Kate Westin, his wife; Craig Stevens as Walter Carlson, his boss. Harve Bennett was the executive producer of the series, Leslie Stevens its producer. Though the show failed to catch on, NBC apparently thought there was merit in the concept, for they introduced the very similar *Gemini Man* the following season. Undaunted when the show was canceled in midseason, NBC brought on *The Man from Atlantis* in 1977; it, too, proved unsuccessful.

IRELAND: A TELEVISION HISTORY   SYNDICATED

1982   Thirteen-part documentary series on the history of Ireland, written and narrated by Robert Kee. The show was carried by many PBS stations.

IRON HORSE   ABC

12 SEPTEMBER 1966–6 JANUARY 1968   This hour-long western focused on the construction of the Buffalo Pass & Scalplock Railroad. It featured Dale Robertson as Ben Calhoun, the owner; Gary Collins as Dave Tarrant, the engineer; Bob Random as Barnabas Rogers; Roger Torrey as Nils Torvald; and Ellen McRae (1966–1967) as Julie Parsons. Produced by Screen Gems.

IRONSIDE   NBC

14 SEPTEMBER 1967–16 JANUARY 1975   Raymond Burr returned to television one year after the demise of *Perry Mason* in another successful crime show. This time he played Robert T. Ironside, Chief of Detectives for the San Francisco Police Department, who was paralyzed from the waist down by a would-be assassin's bullet. Assisting him were Don Galloway as Lieutenant Ed Brown; Barbara Anderson (1967–1971) as Policewoman Eve Whitfield; Don Mitchell as Mark Sanger, Ironside's personal assistant, an ex-con attending law school; Gene Lyons as Commissioner Dennis Randall; Elizabeth Baur (1971–1975) as Officer Fran Belding; and Joan Pringle (1974–1975) as Diana Sanger, Mark's wife. Executive producer: Joel Rogosin. Burr, Anderson, Galloway, and Mitchell were reunited in a TV-movie, "The Return of Ironside" (4 May 1993, NBC).

ISIS   CBS

6 SEPTEMBER 1975–2 SEPTEMBER 1978   *Isis,* a live-action Saturday-morning show, was introduced in 1975 as one half of *The Shazam!/Isis Hour,* where it remained for two seasons. When *Shazam!* left the air in 1977, *Isis* continued under the title *The Secrets of Isis.* The half-hour adventure series starred JoAnna Cameron as Andrea Thomas, a mild-mannered high school science teacher who learned the secrets of Isis, an Egyptian goddess, and could transform herself into the super-powered Isis. Also featured were Brian Cutler as schoolteacher Rick Mason and Joanna Pang as student Cindy Lee. Lou Scheimer and Norm Prescott were the executive producers of the series. See also *Shazam!*

ISLAND SON   CBS

19 SEPTEMBER 1989–29 MARCH 1990   Richard Chamberlain, who had starred as TV's *Dr. Kildare* in the early 1960s, returned as a TV physician in this hour medical show set in Hawaii. This time, he played Dr. Daniel Kulani, a holistic practitioner who worked at the Kamehameha Medical Center in Honolulu. Also appearing were Kwan Hi Lim and Betty Carvalho as his adoptive parents, Tutu and Nana Kulani; Ray Bumatai as his brother, James; Brynn Thayer as Maggie Judd, the hospital administrator; Clyde Kusatsu as Dr. Kenji Fushida; Timothy Carhart as resident Dr. Anthony Metzger; Carol Huston as Dr. Caitlin McGrath; Michael Adamschick as Dr. Paul Brody; and William McNamara as Daniel's teenage son, Sam.

THE ISLANDERS   ABC

2 OCTOBER 1960–26 MARCH 1961   Intended as a companion series to *Adventures in Paradise,* this M-G-M adventure show was also set in the South Pacific. It starred William Reynolds and James Philbrook as Sandy Wade and Zack Malloy, co-owners of a one-plane airline service. Also featured were Diane Brewster as Willy Vandeveer, the office manager; Roy Wright as Shipwreck Callahan, an island personality; and Daria Massey as Naja. The series was replaced in midseason by *The Asphalt Jungle.*

ISSUES AND ANSWERS   ABC

27 NOVEMBER 1960–8 NOVEMBER 1981   Newsmakers were interviewed by journalists on this public affairs program, ABC's counterpart of CBS's *Face the Nation* and NBC's venerable *Meet the Press.* In its earliest weeks the series was entitled *ABC Press Conference.* The series was produced by Peggy Whedon.

IT COULD BE YOU   NBC

4 JUNE 1956–29 DECEMBER 1961   Bill Leyden hosted this audience participation show. A regular feature involved three members of the audience, one of whom would

be reunited with a long-lost friend or loved one. Wendell Niles was the announcer on the series, which enjoyed a five-year daytime run and was also seen evenings during the summers of 1958 and 1961 and during the entire 1959–1960 season. Ralph Edwards created the show.

IT HAD TO BE YOU CBS
19 SEPTEMBER 1993–15 OCTOBER 1993   Another short-lived sitcom, and another flop for Robert Urich, this one told the story of a haughty Boston publisher who met a widowed carpenter with three sons. It starred Faye Dunaway (in her TV series debut) as publisher Laura Scofield; Robert Urich as carpenter Mitch Quinn; Justin Whalin as oldest son David; Will Estes as middle son Christopher; Justin Jon Ross as youngest son Sebastian; and Robin Bartlett as Laura's assistant, Eve. It was axed after four episodes.

IT HAPPENED IN SPORTS NBC
3 JULY 1953–19 JANUARY 1954   Fifteen-minute sports documentary series.

IT IS WRITTEN SYNDICATED
1975–1986   Half-hour religious discussion show, hosted by George Vandeman and produced by the Seventh Day Adventist Church.

IT PAYS TO BE IGNORANT CBS/NBC/SYNDICATED
6 JUNE 1949–19 SEPTEMBER 1949 (CBS); 5 JULY 1951–27 SEPTEMBER 1951 (NBC); 1973 (SYNDICATED)   *It Pays to Be Ignorant* was a spoof of game shows and was popular on radio during the 1940s. The celebrity panel tried to avoid answering such stumpers as "What beverage is made from tea leaves?" On television the show first surfaced as a summer replacement for Arthur Godfrey's *Talent Scouts* in 1949 and was seen in 1951 as a summer replacement for Groucho Marx's *You Bet Your Life*. The radio and television versions were hosted by Tom Howard, the father-in-law of the show's creator, Bob Howell. The panel, also carried over from radio, consisted of veteran troupers Harry McNaughton, Lulu McConnell, and George Shelton (Shelton and Howard had been partners in vaudeville). In 1973 a revamped syndicated version appeared, featuring host Joe Flynn and panelists Jo Anne Worley, Charles Nelson Reilly, and Billy Baxter.

IT PAYS TO BE MARRIED NBC
4 JULY 1955–28 OCTOBER 1955   Married couples competed for cash on this question-and-answer daytime game show, hosted by Bill Goodwin. It was replaced by *Matinee Theater*. Stefan Hatos (who later produced *Let's Make a Deal* with Monty Hall) created the show with Henry Hoople.

IT SEEMS LIKE YESTERDAY SYNDICATED
1953   Radio newscaster H. V. Kaltenborn narrated old newsreels on this documentary series.

IT TAKES A THIEF ABC
9 JANUARY 1968–14 SEPTEMBER 1970   Light adventure series starring Robert Wagner as Alexander Mundy, a suave thief who was released from prison on condition that he undertake certain sensitive missions requiring his skills for the government. Malachi Throne costarred as Noah Bain, chief of the S.I.A., the government agency which hired Mundy. Fred Astaire appeared occasionally as Alex's father, Alistair Mundy, a master thief. The show was produced by Universal TV.

IT TAKES TWO NBC
31 MARCH 1969–31 JULY 1970   Daytime game show hosted by Vin Scully, featuring three celebrities and their spouses. Questions that called for mathematical answers were asked. The object of the game was for selected members of the studio audience to determine which couple's answers came the closest to the correct answer.

IT TAKES TWO   ABC
14 OCTOBER 1982–1 SEPTEMBER 1983   Half-hour sitcom starring Patty Duke Astin
and Richard Crenna as Molly and Sam Quinn. Sam, a successful surgeon, was
beginning to have second thoughts about his wife's emergence as a career woman—
Molly had gone to law school after their kids had grown up and now worked as an
assistant district attorney. Other regulars included Anthony Edwards as their teenage
son, Andy; Helen Hunt as their teenage daughter, Lisa; Billie Bird as Mama, Molly's
dotty mother; Della Reese as Judge Caroline Philips, a friend of Molly's; and Richard McKenzie as Walter, a psychiatrist colleague of Sam's.

IT WAS A VERY GOOD YEAR   ABC
10 MAY 1971–30 AUGUST 1971   Mel Tormé hosted this nostalgic look at selected
years from the twentieth century; each week a different year was highlighted through
the use of film clips and songs.

IT'S A BUSINESS   DUMONT
19 MARCH 1952–21 MAY 1952   A situation comedy with a Tin Pan Alley setting, *It's a
Business* starred Bob Haymes and Leo DeLyon as song publishers and Dorothy
Loudon as their secretary. The half-hour series was produced by Paul Rosen, directed by Frank Bunetta, and written by Bob Weiskopf (who later produced *Maude*).

IT'S A GREAT LIFE   NBC
7 SEPTEMBER 1954–3 JUNE 1956   Situation comedy about two ex-GI's who moved to
California and took a furnished apartment. With William Bishop as Denny Davis;
Michael O'Shea as Steve Connors; Frances Bavier as Mrs. Amy Morgan, their landlady; James Dunn as Amy's Uncle Earl; and Harry Harvey as Mr. Russell, a neighbor. The show was written and produced by Ray Singer and Dick Chevillat; it was
syndicated under the title *The Bachelors*.

IT'S A HIT   CBS
1 JUNE 1957–21 SEPTEMBER 1957   Happy Felton hosted this Saturday-morning quiz
show for children. Each week two teams of youngsters competed; each squad was
managed by a sports personality.

IT'S A LIVING   ABC/SYNDICATED
30 OCTOBER 1980–29 JANUARY 1981; 21 JULY 1981–4 AUGUST 1981 (ABC); 1985–1989
(SYNDICATED)
MAKING A LIVING   ABC
24 OCTOBER 1981–9 JANUARY 1982; 4 JUNE 1982–10 SEPTEMBER 1982   Half-hour
sitcom about a group of waitresses working at a fancy Los Angeles restaurant. With
Marian Mercer as Nancy Beebe, the martinet manager; Susan Sullivan (1980–1981)
as Lois Adams, the experienced one; Wendy Schaal (1980–1981) as Vicki Allen, the
innocent one; Ann Jillian as Cassie Cranston, the worldly one; Gail Edwards as Dot
Higgins, an aspiring actress; Barrie Youngfellow as Jan Hoffmeyer, a student and
mother; Paul Kreppel as obnoxious Sonny Mann, the pianist; Bert Remsen (1980–
1981) as Mario, the chef. Louise Lasser joined the cast at the end of the first season,
as waitress Maggie McBerney. For its second season, the show was retitled *Making a
Living,* and Earl Boen was added as Dennis, the new chef. In 1985 the show, again
titled *It's a Living,* resurfaced in first-run syndication. Mercer, Jillian, Edwards,
Youngfellow, and Kreppel all returned from the network cast (Jillian left after the
1985–1986 season); new regulars included Richard Stahl as Howard Miller, the chef;
Robyn Peterson as Frisco, the bartender; Crystal Bernard (1985–1989) as Amy
Tompkins; and Sheryl Lee Ralph (1986–1989) as Ginger St. James. Nancy and How-
ard were married in 1987.

IT'S A MAN'S WORLD   NBC
17 SEPTEMBER 1962–28 JANUARY 1963   Half-hour sitcom about three male college
students living together on a houseboat moored on the Ohio River. With Ted Bessell
as Tom (Tom-Tom) DeWitt; Glenn Corbett as Wes Macauley; Randy Boone as Vern

Hodges; Mike Burns as Howie, Wes's orphaned kid brother who also lived with them; Jan Norris as Irene; Kate Murtagh as Mrs. Dodson; Jeanine Cashell as Alma Jean; Ann Schuler as Nora; and Harry Harvey, Sr., as Mr. Stott, owner of the gas station where Wes worked.

IT'S A PROBLEM   NBC
16 OCTOBER 1951–13 OCTOBER 1952   A daytime panel show, hosted by Ben Grauer. Each day a single topic relating to family life was discussed. Fannie Hurst and Helen Parkhurst were permanent panelists; in August of 1952 Parkhurst was succeeded by Alice Thompson, editor-publisher of *Seventeen* magazine. Broadcast live from New York, the half-hour series was originally titled *What's Your Problem?*.

IT'S A SMALL WORLD   DUMONT
27 JUNE 1953–27 JULY 1953   Half-hour travelogue.

IT'S A WONDERFUL WORLD   SYNDICATED
1963   Half-hour travelogue hosted by John Cameron Swayze.

IT'S ABOUT TIME   ABC
4 MARCH 1954–25 MARCH 1954   Short-lived prime-time game show hosted by Dr. Bergen Evans. Studio contestants were quizzed on historical events.

IT'S ABOUT TIME   CBS
11 SEPTEMBER 1966–27 AUGUST 1967   This sitcom took its stars on a journey to the Stone Age and back again. It starred Frank Aletter as Captain Glenn McDivitt (Mac) and Jack Mullaney as Hector, two astronauts who broke through the time barrier and landed in a prehistoric world where they met and befriended a Stone Age family; in midseason they brought the family with them into the modern era. The Stone Agers included Imogene Coca as Shad; Joe E. Ross as Gronk, her mate; Pat Cardi as Breer, their son; Mary Grace as Mlor, their daughter; Cliff Norton as Boss, the unfriendly leader of the cave people; Kathleen Freeman as Mrs. Boss; Mike Mazurki as Clon, Boss's henchman. Frank Wilcox joined the cast in midseason as General Morley, Mac and Hector's commanding officer.

IT'S ACADEMIC   SYNDICATED
1961–1966   A game show for high-schoolers, not unlike *College Bowl*. The show was essentially a franchised series, like *Bozo the Clown* or *Romper Room;* each participating station selected its own emcee and scheduled meets between local schools. Each week three four-member high school teams competed.

IT'S ALEC TEMPLETON TIME   DUMONT
3 JUNE 1955–26 AUGUST 1955   Half-hour musical series hosted by Alec Templeton, the blind, British-born pianist who specialized in playing popular tunes in the style of classical composers.

IT'S ALWAYS JAN   CBS
10 SEPTEMBER 1955–30 JUNE 1956   Situation comedy about three New York career girls, presumably inspired by the film *How to Marry a Millionaire*. With Janis Paige as Jan Stewart, nightclub singer; Patricia Bright as Pat Murphy, a secretary; Merry Anders as Val Marlowe, a model; Jeri Lou James as Josie Stewart, Jan's daughter (Jan was a war widow); Arte Johnson as Stanley Schreiber, delivery boy for the local delicatessen; and Sid Melton as Harry Cooper, Jan's agent. Merry Anders went on to appear in the TV version of *How to Marry a Millionaire*.

IT'S ANYBODY'S GUESS   NBC
13 JUNE 1977–30 SEPTEMBER 1977   Daytime game show hosted by Monty Hall. Two contestants tried to predict whether a panel of five members of the studio audience would supply a preselected answer to a particular question. If the contestant predicted correctly, he or she won one point; if the guess was incorrect, the contestant's

opponent won the point. If one of the five panelists gave the preselected answer, he or she also won a prize. The show was a Stefan Hatos-Monty Hall Production. Jay Stewart, Hall's longtime sidekick on *Let's Make a Deal,* was the announcer.

IT'S FUN TO KNOW   CBS
23 APRIL 1951–22 JUNE 1951   A Monday-through-Friday educational series for children, hosted by Dorothy Engel Clark. Mondays were devoted to history, Tuesdays to crafts, Wednesdays to science, Thursdays to drawing, and Fridays to dancing. The half-hour show was produced by Frederick Kugel.

IT'S GARRY SHANDLING'S SHOW   SHOWTIME/FOX
10 SEPTEMBER 1986–8 JUNE 1990 (SHOWTIME); 6 MARCH 1988–18 MARCH 1990 (FOX)   Standup comic Garry Shandling and former *Saturday Night Live* writer Alan Zweibel borrowed from one of TV's earliest sitcoms to create one of the freshest shows of the 1980s. Their inspiration was *The Burns and Allen Show*: The central character played himself as the star of the TV show, lived at home, and frequently addressed the audience directly. The latter device, known as "breaking the fourth wall," had been seldom utilized in series television since the demise of *Burns and Allen* in 1958, but Shandling used it as effectively as had Burns to comment on the plot, to update the story, or to interject a joke.

Shandling played himself, a standup comic and star of a TV show, which was telecast from his fictional Sherman Oaks condominium. Joining him were: Molly Cheek as his friend and neighbor, Nancy Bancroft; Michael Tucci as neighbor Pete Schumaker; Bernadette Birkett as Pete's wife, Jackie; Scott Nemes as their son, Grant; Paul Willson as condo manager Leonard Smith; and Barbara Cason as Garry's mother, Ruth Shandling. All of the characters knew they were on TV; some even complained onstage about not being featured in a particular episode. Guest stars also dropped by from time to time (usually playing themselves), including Red Buttons, Zsa Zsa Gabor, rock star Tom Petty, and Gilda Radner (29 April 1988, one of her last TV appearances). Some episodes involved the studio audience; others parodied TV shows such as *Lassie* and *The Fugitive.* One program was aired live on Showtime: an election special (8 November 1988), with *Soul Train*'s Don Cornelius as guest political analyst. In the fall of 1989 Shandling acquired a regular girlfriend, Phoebe Bass (played by Jessica Harper); they were married on the show (with Bert Convy, Ned Beatty, and Connie Stevens in attendance) early in 1990.

The genesis of the series was a sketch on NBC's *Michael Nesmith in Television Parts* in which Shandling, on a date with Miss Maryland, narrated the event to the camera. The series was originally pitched to the commercial broadcast networks, but was rejected. The Showtime cable network, for which Shandling had done two well-received specials (1984's "Garry Shandling: Alone in Vegas" and 1986's "The Garry Shandling Show: 25th Anniversary Special"), then picked it up late in 1986. The Fox network began broadcasting the Showtime series in 1988, gradually shortening the gap between the Showtime and Fox telecasts; by early 1990, when Fox dropped the series, the episodes were aired only a month apart. Showtime continued to run new episodes (seventy-two were made in all) after Fox's cancellation.

IT'S HAPPENING   ABC
15 JULY 1968–25 OCTOBER 1968   This short-lived daytime musical series replaced the short-lived game show, *Wedding Party.* It was hosted by Mark Lindsay and his band (Paul Revere and the Raiders), and featured guest appearances by rock stars. A weekend version also appeared: see *Happening '68.*

IT'S MAGIC   CBS
31 JULY 1955–4 SEPTEMBER 1955   A summer replacement for *Lassie, It's Magic* featured guest prestidigitators each week. Paul Tripp (formerly of *Mr. I. Magination*) hosted the series.

IT'S NEWS TO ME   CBS
2 JULY 1951–27 AUGUST 1954   The format of this prime-time game show was similar
to that of *Liars Club*—contestants had to choose which of four celebrity panelists was
telling the truth. The subject of the game was current events; after being shown a clue
to a recent news story, three of the panelists suggested the wrong event, while one
named the correct event associated with the clue. The show was seen sporadically for
three years and was hosted at various times by newsmen John Daly, Walter Cronkite,
and Quincy Howe.

IT'S NOT EASY   ABC
29 SEPTEMBER 1983–20 OCTOBER 1983   This domestic sitcom told the tale of a
divorced couple who lived across the street from one another, in order to simplify the
problems of child custody. Featured were Carlene Watkins as Sharon Townsend; Ken
Howard as Jack Long, her ex-husband; Bert Convy as Neal Townsend, her current
husband; Rachel Jacobs as Sharon and Jack's eleven-year-old daughter, Carol; Evan
Cohen as Sharon and Jack's nine-year-old son, Johnny; Billy Jacoby as Matthew,
Neal's son (by a former marriage); and Jayne Meadows as Jack's live-in mother,
Ruth. It was not easy for *It's Not Easy* to survive; the half-hour series perished
opposite *Simon & Simon* and *Cheers;* it was the first announced cancellation of the
1983–1984 season.

IT'S POLKA TIME   ABC
13 JULY 1956–24 SEPTEMBER 1957   Polka music and dancing from Chicago, hosted by
Bruno "Junior" Zielinski, with Stan Wolowic's Band, The Polka Chips (singers),
Carolyn DeZurik, and the Kanal Siodmy Dancers.

IT'S PUNKY BREWSTER   NBC
14 SEPTEMBER 1985–5 SEPTEMBER 1987; 5 NOVEMBER 1988–2 SEPTEMBER 1989
Saturday-morning cartoon series based on the prime-time series *Punky Brewster*. The
cartoon Punky traveled all over the world, accompanied by her gremlin-like friend,
Glomer.

IT'S SHOWTIME AT THE APOLLO   SYNDICATED
1987–   Hour variety series, taped at Harlem's Apollo Theatre following its $15
million renovation. Over the years the series had employed both guest hosts and
regular hosts. Among the latter were Rick Aviles (1987–1988), Sinbad (1989–1991),
and Steve Harvey (1994–   ). Regularly featured on the program were the "Amateur
Night" segments, hosted by Kiki Shepard; legendary dancer Howard "Sandman"
Sims made his entrance whenever unsuccessful amateur contestants were hissed off
stage by the studio audience.

IT'S YOUR BET   SYNDICATED
1970–1972   This game show was the descendant of *I'll Bet;* the show featured two
celebrities and their spouses, and the object was for one spouse to predict whether
the other would be able to answer a question correctly. The several hosts included
Hal March (seldom seen on TV after the demise of *The $64,000 Question*), Tom
Kennedy, Dick Gautier, and Lyle Waggoner.

IT'S YOUR BUSINESS   SYNDICATED
1979–   A series of half-hour debates on public-policy issues, originally moderated
by Karna Small, and broadcast from Washington, D.C., under the auspices of the
U.S. Chamber of Commerce. Small left the show late in 1980 to join President
Reagan's press staff; she was succeeded by Meryl Comer.

IT'S YOUR MOVE   NBC
26 SEPTEMBER 1984–16 MARCH 1985; 1 JUNE 1985–10 AUGUST 1985   This half-hour
sitcom was created for Jason Bateman (brother of *Family Ties*'s Justine Bateman),
who had been a regular on *Silver Spoons*. Here he played Matthew Burton, a teenaged con artist who lived in an apartment with his widowed mother. Caren Kaye

played his patient mom, Eileen, a legal secretary who began to date a struggling writer, Norman Lamb (played by David Garrison), who had just moved into their building from Chicago; much to Matthew's chagrin, Norman proved to be every bit as crafty as Matthew. Also on hand were Tricia Cast as Julie Burton, Matthew's older sister; Adam Sadowski as Eli, Matthew's pal; and Ernie Sabella as Lou Donatelli, the building manager. After the cancellation of *It's Your Move,* Jason Bateman went on to greater fame in *Valerie* (later known as *The Hogan Family*).

IVAN THE TERRIBLE   CBS
21 AUGUST 1976–18 SEPTEMBER 1976   Forgettable five-week summer sitcom about a group of nine Muscovites living in a small apartment. With Lou Jacobi as Ivan Petrovsky; Maria Karnilova as Olga Petrovsky, his wife; Phil Leeds as Vladimir, Olga's former husband; Matthew Barry as Sascha, Ivan's son; Despo as Tatiana; Alan Cauldwell as Nikolai; Caroline Kava as Sonya; Christopher Hewett as Federov; Nana Tucker as Svetlana, Ivan's mother-in-law; and Manuel Martinez as Raoul. Alan King was the executive producer.

IVANHOE   SYNDICATED
1958   This British adventure series, based on Sir Walter Scott's novel, starred Roger Moore as Ivanhoe, a youthful and noble knight and crusader.

IVANHOE   SYNDICATED
1972   The second incarnation of Sir Walter Scott's novel was serialized in ten chapters as part of *Family Classics Theater* and starred Eric Flynn (son of Errol Flynn) as Ivanhoe.

I'VE GOT A SECRET   CBS/SYNDICATED
19 JUNE 1952–3 APRIL 1967 (CBS); 1972 (SYNDICATED); 15 JUNE 1976– 6 JULY 1976 (CBS)   On this popular prime-time game show the celebrity panelists tried to guess the guests' secrets. The guest whispered his secret to the host, and the secret was superimposed on the screen for the home audience. Top prize on the 1952–1967 network version was only $80 (and a carton of Winstons), so the show was played mainly for laughs; each week a celebrity guest also came on to try to stump the panel. Garry Moore hosted the show from 1952 until 1964, when he was succeeded by Steve Allen. Often seen on the celebrity panel were Bill Cullen, Betsy Palmer, Henry Morgan, Bess Myerson, Steve Allen, and Jayne Meadows. Steve Allen also hosted the 1972 syndicated version; Bill Cullen emceed the 1976 network version. The show was a Mark Goodson-Bill Todman Production. Allan Sherman, who created the show with Howard Merrill, was on the production staff from 1952 to 1956 and devised many of the celebrity "secrets" used on the show during that period; Sherman became more famous in 1963 with his hit record "My Son the Folk Singer." Gil Fates, who was the producer of Goodson-Todman's other popular game show, *What's My Line?*, served as executive producer. In his autobiography Fates recalled that the original set for *Secret* was a courtroom, but it proved to be so unworkable that it was burned after the 1952 premiere.

J. J. STARBUCK   NBC
26 SEPTEMBER 1987–27 FEBRUARY 1988; 28 JUNE 1988–17 AUGUST 1988   Dale Robertson had the title role in this unsuccessful hour adventure series from Stephen J. Cannell Productions. As Jerome Jeremiah Starbuck, homespun San Antonio billionaire and founder of Marklee Industries, he drove around the country in his vintage Lincoln Continental convertible helping out people in need. Jimmy Dean played Starbuck's executive assistant, Charlie Bullets (David Huddleston played the role in the premiere). Occasionally featured was Shawn Weatherly as Jill, J. J.'s niece. In February 1988 Ben Vereen joined the cast as Starbuck's sidekick, E. L. "Tenspeed" Turner; Vereen had played the same character in the 1980 Stephen J. Cannell series *Tenspeed and Brown Shoe*. Although the series was set in San Antonio, it was actually filmed in Vancouver.

JABBERJAW
ABC

11 SEPTEMBER 1976–3 SEPTEMBER 1978   Weekend cartoon series set in 2076 about a giant shark (Jabberjaw) who was the drummer for a rock group known as the Neptunes: Biff, Bubbles, Clam-Head, and Shelly. The creature was later featured on *Yogi's Space Race:* see *Yogi Bear.*

JACK AND MIKE
ABC

16 SEPTEMBER 1986–28 MAY 1987   A Yuppie Chicago couple was the centerpiece of this hour comedy-drama. Shelley Hack and Tom Mason starred as Jackie ("Jack") Shea, a syndicated columnist for the Chicago *Mirror,* and Mike Brennan, a successful restaurateur. Also on hand were Jacqueline Brookes as Nora Adler, Jackie's editor; Kevin Dunn as Anthony, another reporter; Holly Fulger as Carol, a waitress at Mike's newest eatery; Noelle Bou-sliman as Belinda; and Mills Watson as Max.

THE JACK BENNY PROGRAM
CBS/NBC

28 OCTOBER 1950–15 SEPTEMBER 1964 (CBS); 25 SEPTEMBER 1964–10 SEPTEMBER 1965 (NBC)   One of America's best-loved comedians, Jack Benny proved almost as durable on television as he had on radio. His half-hour show transcended the boundary between variety and situation comedy—some shows featured guest stars who sang or danced, and other shows consisted of just one sketch, performed by Benny and his company of regulars.

Benny entered television cautiously, testing the waters with four shows spread out during the 1950–1951 season; the following season he appeared six times, and gradually increased his appearances to twenty in 1954–1955, and to thirty-nine by 1960–1961. Benny succeeded in landing many top stars on his shows; guests during the first season included Ken Murray (28 October 1950), Frank Sinatra (28 January 1951), Claudette Colbert and Basil Rathbone (1 April 1951). A young comedian named Johnny Carson, newly arrived in Los Angeles, made one of his earliest national appearances in 1952. Marilyn Monroe and Humphrey Bogart made their TV debuts during the 1953–1954 season, and it is reported that Benny came close to signing the elusive Clark Gable for a guest shot.

From the beginning Benny relied heavily on a group of supporting players, many of whom had been with him for years on radio. The group included Eddie Anderson as his gravel-voiced valet, Rochester Van Jones; hefty Don Wilson as his announcer; singer Dennis Day; Mel Blanc (the voice of Bugs Bunny) as his violin teacher; Mary Livingstone (Benny's wife); and Frank Nelson as the man who said "Yeeeesssss!" Occasionally seen were Hy Averback, Bea Benaderet, Barry Gordon (as the boyhood Jack Benny), Sandra Gould, Burt Mustin (as the guard of Benny's vaults), Benny Rubin, Herb Vigran, and Dale White (as Don Wilson's son, Harlow).

For most of its run on CBS the show was seen on Sundays, alternating with *This Is Show Business* through January 1953; from February 1953 through 1957 it alternated with Ann Sothern's sitcom, *Private Secretary.* It then shared a slot with *Bachelor Father* for two seasons and with *The George Gobel Show* for one season. In the fall of 1960 it first appeared as a weekly series and moved to Tuesdays in 1962. When CBS dropped the show in 1964, NBC, the network that had lost Benny to CBS in 1949, picked it up and scheduled it on Fridays; the show did poorly and was canceled after one season. Thereafter Benny headlined several specials and frequently appeared on talk shows. The executive producer of his show (for the first several seasons) was Ralph Levy, and its producer was Hilliard Marks, Benny's brother-in-law. Principal writers included Sam Perrin, George Balzer, Hal Goldman, and Al Gordon.

THE JACK CARSON SHOW
NBC

22 OCTOBER 1954–11 MARCH 1955   Comedian Jack Carson, who often hosted such variety hours as *The Colgate Comedy Hour* and *All-Star Revue,* also had his own half-hour series in 1954, which was scheduled as an occasional replacement for *The Red Buttons Show* on Fridays.

JACK CARTER AND COMPANY   ABC
12 MARCH 1949–21 APRIL 1949   This half-hour variety show featured comedian Jack
Carter, comedienne Elaine Stritch, Sonny King, and Rowena Rollin. Kenny Lyons
was the producer and Sean Dillon the director.

THE JACK CARTER SHOW
See ALL-STAR REVUE

THE JACK LA LANNE SHOW   SYNDICATED
1956–1970   America's foremost physical fitness enthusiast, Jack La Lanne hosted a
long-running exercise program, aimed principally at women viewers. He had hosted
a local exercise show in San Francisco for five years before moving to Los Angeles in
1956.

JACK LONDON STORIES
See CAPTAIN DAVID GRIEF

THE JACK PAAR SHOW   CBS
13 NOVEMBER 1953–2 JULY 1954; 17 JULY 1954–4 SEPTEMBER 1954; 4 JULY 1955–25 MAY
1956   Before succeeding Steve Allen as host of the *Tonight* show in 1957, Jack Paar
had gained considerable experience as host of several daytime shows (he also emceed
a quiz show, *Bank on the Stars*). The first of the daytime series was seen Friday
mornings as a weekly replacement for *Arthur Godfrey Time*. It featured singers Edith
Adams (later known as Edie Adams), Richard Hayes, and Jack Haskell, pianist José
Melis (an old Army buddy of Paar's), and the Pupi Campo Orchestra. In July of 1954
he and his crew moved to a Saturday-evening slot, and in August Paar moved to an
earlier time slot, succeeding Walter Cronkite as host of *The Morning Show* (see also
that title), CBS's answer to the *Today* show. After a year on that show, Paar surfaced
in an afternoon slot, hosting a Monday-through-Friday half hour. It featured Adams,
Haskell, Melis, and announcer Hal Simms.

THE JACK PAAR SHOW (THE JACK PAAR PROGRAM)   NBC
21 SEPTEMBER 1962–10 SEPTEMBER 1965   After leaving the daily grind of the *Tonight*
show in March, 1962, Jack Paar returned that fall as host of a Friday-night variety
series. Frequent guests included British humorist Alexander King and American
comedian Jonathan Winters; music was provided by the José Melis Orchestra. Paar's
program was the first American variety show to present the Beatles—film clips of the
foursome were shown on 3 January 1964, more than a month before the group's
famous "debut" on *The Ed Sullivan Show*.

JACK PAAR TONITE   ABC
8 JANUARY 1973–16 NOVEMBER 1973   Jack Paar returned to late night TV after an
eleven-year absence on a one-week-per-month basis; his ninety-minute talk show was
part of ABC's umbrella series, *ABC's Wide World of Entertainment*. Peggy Cass was
Paar's announcer and sidekick. Freddie Prinze, the future star of *Chico and the Man*,
made his TV debut on 18 October.

JACK THE RIPPER   SYNDICATED
1974   This British miniseries was a fictional reopening of the series of murders that
shocked London in the 1880s; two modern-day detectives, using the sophisticated
techniques of twentieth-century criminology, tried to solve the crimes. Sebastian
Cabot hosted the series, which featured Alan Stratford-Johns as Detective Chief
Superintendent Barlow and Frank Windsor as Detective Chief Superintendent Watt.

THE JACKIE GLEASON SHOW (THE HONEYMOONERS)   CBS
(JACKIE GLEASON AND HIS AMERICAN SCENE MAGAZINE)
20 SEPTEMBER 1952–22 JUNE 1957; 3 OCTOBER 1958–2 JANUARY 1959; 3 FEBRUARY 1961–
24 MARCH 1961; 29 SEPTEMBER 1962–12 SEPTEMBER 1970   Jackie Gleason, television's
rotund showman, was a fixture on CBS for most of two decades. His series-within-a-

series, *The Honeymooners,* was one of TV's all-time classic comedies, and its syndicated reruns thrive today. With experience in vaudeville, Broadway, and films already under his considerable belt, Gleason entered television in 1949 in the first version of *The Life of Riley* (dropped by NBC after twenty-six weeks, it reappeared in 1953 with William Bendix). The following season he began to appear regularly on *Cavalcade of Stars,* a variety hour broadcast on the DuMont network. There Gleason introduced to television audiences many of the characters he had developed: the insufferably wealthy Reggie Van Gleason III, The Poor Soul, Joe the Bartender, Charley the Loudmouth, Rudy the Repairman, Pedro the Mexican, Stanley R. Sogg, Fenwick Babbit, Father and Son, The Ham, and Rum Dum. He also introduced a running sketch entitled "The Honeymooners," which was an immediate hit with viewers. *Cavalcade of Stars* soon became one of the most popular shows on the limited DuMont network, and Gleason attracted the attention of CBS. In 1952 he accepted CBS's offer to star in his own variety hour. The network originally planned to schedule Gleason either on Tuesdays opposite Milton Berle on NBC or on Saturdays opposite Sid Caesar's *Your Show of Shows.* Shortly before the start of the 1952 season, however, the network decided to put the show into an earlier slot on Saturdays, where it remained for the next five years. From 1952 until 1955, the show ran a full hour; each one started with a production number staged by the June Taylor Dancers, following which "The Great One" (Gleason) made his entrance. During his short monologue Gleason managed to interject some of his favorite phrases—"How sweet it is," "And away we go," or "A little traveling music, please."

The main event of the evening filled the second half hour—the *Honeymooners* sketch. These were usually done with little rehearsal (Gleason was well known as a quick study), but the chemistry among the players was strong enough to overcome any difficulty that might arise on stage. Gleason played Ralph Kramden, a New York bus driver living in a small apartment with his wife of fifteen years. Audrey Meadows costarred as his weary wife, Alice (the part was first played by Pert Kelton on *Cavalcade of Stars*). Art Carney, a comic and character actor with some television experience, provided the perfect foil for Kramden as Ralph's friend and upstairs neighbor, Ed Norton, a city sewer worker. Norton's apparent dimwittedness was balanced by a certain grace and imperturbability, and these qualities offset Kramden's impatience and hot temper. Joyce Randolph rounded out the foursome as Norton's doting wife, and Alice's best friend, Trixie Norton.

Almost all of the action took place on a sparsely furnished set: the Kramdens' living room contained little more than a bureau, table and chairs, sink, stove, and icebox. Rarely did additional characters appear (Joyce Randolph did not even appear in some sketches), and rarely were any needed; the timing and interaction of the regulars worked almost magically.

During the 1955–1956 season thirty-nine *Honeymooners* were filmed before a live audience. These thirty-nine half hours, produced at the rate of two a week, were scheduled Saturdays at 8:30. The show returned to an hour variety format (with a *Honeymooners* sketch) in the fall of 1956. The show finally left the air in June of 1957 (Gleason himself missed the last three shows). In the fall of 1958 he returned in a live half-hour series scheduled on Fridays. That effort, which also featured Buddy Hackett, vanished in midseason. Gleason was again seen Friday nights in 1961 as host of a game show, *You're in the Picture.* One of the biggest flops in TV history, the show was axed—by Gleason—after a single week. Gleason appeared the following week and apologized to viewers for "that bomb." Early in February the show was retitled *The Jackie Gleason Show* and continued for a few weeks as a half-hour talk show.

In the fall of 1962 Gleason was back to a Saturday slot, which he occupied for another eight seasons. From 1962 to 1966 it was called *Jackie Gleason and His American Scene Magazine,* and featured topical comedy sketches as well as musical numbers. One of Gleason's characters, Joe the Bartender, appeared regularly. Addressing the camera as his patron, ("Hiya, Mr. Dunahy!"), Joe told a few jokes before calling out the tipsy Crazy Guggenham from the back room. Guggenham, played by Frank Fontaine, traded quips with Joe and then sang a song. Sue Ane Langdon, later to costar in *Arnie,* was also featured regularly, and singer Wayne Newton made some of his earliest television appearances on the show.

In 1966 Gleason moved the operation to Miami Beach (where he could indulge in his favorite pastime, golf, all year round). The "magazine" concept was dropped, and the show was retitled *The Jackie Gleason Show*. For the first time in almost a decade, production of *The Honeymooners* was resumed. Gleason was reunited with Art Carney; Sheila MacRae and Jane Kean were added to play Alice and Trixie. Many of these later *Honeymooners* sketches ran a full hour, and the accent was now on music. Lyn Duddy and Jerry Bresler composed several original numbers a week for the show, many of which were performed by the *Honeymooners* crew. Jack Philbin was executive producer of the series, and Ronald Wayne produced it. Frank Bunetta was the director.

Gleason made few TV appearances since 1970, though some *Honeymooners* episodes were rerun on CBS during the winter of 1970–1971. On 2 February 1976, he was again reunited with Art Carney, Audrey Meadows, and Jane Kean in an ABC special, "The Honeymooners—The Second Honeymoon," celebrating the Kramdens' twenty-fifth television anniversary. The thirty-nine filmed Honeymooners episodes from the 1955–1956 season were among the most popular, and most exhaustively rerun, programs of all time. Early in 1985, to the delight of legions of *Honeymooners* fans, Gleason announced the "discovery" of scores of old *Honeymooners* sketches; the latter batch had been performed live between 1952 and 1957 and were of varying lengths. They were packaged into half hours; fifty programs were licensed first to the Showtime cable network and were subsequently made available in sydication (together with another twenty-five half hours). To promote the "new" shows, Gleason and Audrey Meadows hosted "The Honeymooners Reunion" on 13 May 1985 (NBC), introducing clips from these long-lost programs. The even older episodes, with Pert Kelton, finally resurfaced on television 26 May 1994, when The Disney Channel aired "The Honeymooners Really Lost Debut Episodes".

After Gleason's death in 1988, CBS televised a prime-time tribute, "Jackie Gleason: The Great One," on 17 September of that year.

THE JACKIE THOMAS SHOW   ABC
1 DECEMBER 1992–30 MARCH 1993   Much-publicized, and ultimately unsuccessful, sitcom created for Tom Arnold, the onetime meatpacker and standup comic who was married to Roseanne (Barr) (Arnold) at the time. Employing the show-within-a-show format, it starred Arnold as Jackie Thomas, the thoughtless, egotistical star of a highly rated sitcom, "The Jackie Thomas Show" (in which Jackie played a butcher). Also featured were Dennis Boutsikaris as Jerry Harper, the newest in a succession of head writers for the show; Alison LaPlaca as Jerry's assistant, Laura Miller; Paul Feig as Bobby Wynn, the young writer; Michael Boatman as writer Grant Watson; Maryedith Burrell as writer Nancy Mincher-Bates; Martin Mull as Doug Talbot, the network liaison; Jeannetta Arnette as actress Sophie Ford, who played Jackie's wife; and Breckin Meyer as actor Chas Walker, who played Jackie's teenage son. *The Jackie Thomas Show* ranked 14th in the 1992–1993 prime time Nielsen ratings; except for *Cheers,* it was the highest rated series not to be renewed. Instead, Arnold (and costar LaPlaca) moved to CBS, where he headlined a second unsuccessful sitcom: see *Tom.*

JACKPOT   NBC
7 JANUARY 1974–26 SEPTEMBER 1975   Daytime game show on which fifteen contestants, chosen from the studio audience, competed for a top prize of $50,000 by trying to answer riddles. Geoff Edwards was the host, and Bob Stewart was the executive producer.

JACKPOT BOWLING STARRING MILTON BERLE   NBC
19 SEPTEMBER 1960–13 MARCH 1961   Having signed a thirty-year contract with NBC in 1951, Milton Berle starred in two series after *The Milton Berle Show* left the air in 1956. The first was the *Kraft Music Hall* in 1958, and the second was this half-hour sports series, broadcast live from Legion Lanes in Hollywood. Each week competitors bowled in two nine-frame matches, with a cash bonus for hitting six consecutive strikes. Veteran sportscaster Chick Hearn handled the play by play, and Berle sand-

wiched comedy bits between frames. Produced by Buddy Arnold and directed by Dave Brown, the show was dropped after twenty-six weeks.

JACK'S PLACE ABC

26 MAY 1992–7 JULY 1992; 14 JANUARY 1993–11 FEBRUARY 1993; 8 JUNE 1993–13 JULY 1993   Hour dramatic series about an ex-musician who opened a restaurant. With Hal Linden as Jack Evans; Finola Hughes as waitress Chelsea Duffy; John Dye as bartender Greg Toback; and Amanda Peterson as Greg's girlfriend, Elodie.

THE JACKSON 5IVE ABC

11 SEPTEMBER 1971–1 SEPTEMBER 1973   Saturday-morning cartoon series about the Jackson Five, a real-life rock group from Gary, Indiana, discovered in 1968 (legend has it by Diana Ross). The voices of the five Jackson brothers—Michael, Marlon, Jackie, Tito, and Jermaine—were used.

THE JACKSONS CBS

16 JUNE 1976–7 JULY 1976; 26 JANUARY 1977–9 MARCH 1977   The Jacksons, several of whom had previously been seen in cartoon form on TV, hosted a half-hour variety series which first appeared during the summer of 1976 and resurfaced briefly early in 1977. Eight of the nine Jackson children appeared on the show—brothers Michael, Marlon, Jackie, Tito, and Randy, and sisters Maureen (Rebie), La Toya, and Janet; brother Jermaine, an original member of The Jackson Five, had left the group previously to pursue a solo recording career. Additional regulars included Jim Samuels and Marty Cohen on the 1976 show, and Johnny Dark on the 1977 show. The Jacksons danced at least as well as they sang—choreography was handled by Anita Mann. Their father, Joe Jackson, was executive producer of the series with Richard Arons.

THE JACOBS BROTHERS SYNDICATED

1975   Religious music with a country flavor, performed by the Jacobs Brothers Quartet.

JACQUELINE SUSANN'S OPEN DOOR DUMONT

7 MAY 1951–18 JUNE 1951   Though Jacqueline Susann is best remembered for her novels, she also appeared frequently on television in its early days; she was married to producer Irving Mansfield and was a regular on *The Morey Amsterdam Show* in 1948. In 1951 she hosted her own show, *Jacqueline Susann's Open Door,* a late-night weekly program on which she interviewed celebrities and also introduced persons who were looking for jobs. George Scheck produced the series. In 1952 she was featured on a daytime game show, *Your Surprise Store,* and in 1953 she hosted a local talk show in New York.

JACQUES FRAY'S MUSIC ROOM ABC

19 FEBRUARY 1949–9 OCTOBER 1949   Sunday-night half-hour musical series, hosted by Jacques Fray.

JAG NBC

23 SEPTEMBER 1995–   Hour dramatic series starring David James Elliott as Lt. Harmon Rabb, Jr., and Tracey Needham as Lt. Meg Austin, two lawyers assigned to the United States Navy Judge Advocate General's Office. The JAG lawyers were subject to assignment anywhere in the world. Andrea Parker played the role of Rabb's partner, Lt. Kate Pike, in the series' two-hour pilot episode, but was replaced by Needham thereafter.

JAKE AND THE FATMAN CBS

26 SEPTEMBER 1987–7 SEPTEMBER 1988; 15 MARCH 1989–22 AUGUST 1992   Hour crime show starring William Conrad as a portly prosecutor, Jason (J. L.) McCabe, and Joe Penny as his investigator, Jake Styles, with Alan Campbell as Derek Mitchell, a rookie D.A. who assisted McCabe. McCabe also had a pet bulldog, Max, who rather

resembled him. During the 1987–1988 season the show was set in California and also featured Lu Leonard as Gertrude, McCabe's secretary. The show was renewed as a "backup" series for the following season. When it resurfaced in March 1989 production had moved to Hawaii; McCabe became a prosecutor in that state and brought Styles and Mitchell with him. Olga Russell joined the cast as McCabe's secretary, Lisbeth Berkeley-Smythe. Production was again shifted back to California in the fall of 1990.

JAMBO   NBC
6 SEPTEMBER 1969–4 SEPTEMBER 1971   Saturday-morning series of animal films and stories, hosted and narrated by Marshall Thompson, formerly the star of *Daktari;* assisting Thompson was another *Daktari* alumna, Judy the chimp.

JAMES AT 15 (JAMES AT 16)   NBC
27 OCTOBER 1977–27 JULY 1978   Family drama about a teenager who moved from Oregon to suburban Boston with his family. With Lance Kerwin as James Hunter; Linden Chiles as his father, Paul, a college professor; Lynn Carlin as his mother, Joan; David Hubbard as Sly (Ludwig Hazeltine), James's jive-talking black friend; Susan Myers as Marlene, James's intellectual friend; Kim Richards as James's sister, Sandy; and Deirdre Berthrong as James's sister Kathy. The show's first executive producers, Martin Manulis and Joe Hardy, were replaced in December 1977 by Ron Rubin. Its head writer, novelist Dan Wakefield, quit the show in a dispute with the network on the treatment of the show aired 9 February 1978 (on that date the title was changed to *James at 16*), in which young James had a love affair with a Swedish exchange student. NBC's Broadcast Standards department refused to allow the word *responsible* (Wakefield's carefully chosen euphemism for birth control) to be used.

JAMES BEARD   SYNDICATED
1963   Cooking show hosted by chef James Beard.

THE JAMES MASON SHOW   SYNDICATED
1956   A half hour of dramatic readings performed by James Mason, Pamela Mason (his wife at the time), and Richard Burton.

THE JAMES MELTON SHOW
See FORD FESTIVAL

JAMIE   ABC
5 OCTOBER 1953–4 OCTOBER 1954   Brandon De Wilde, the child actor who was featured in the movie *Shane* in 1953, starred as eleven-year-old Jamie McHummer in this family sitcom. Young Jamie had just moved in with relatives as the show began—his parents had been killed. Also featured were Ernest Truex as Grandpa McHummer; Polly Rowles as Aunt Laurie, a widow; and Kathy Nolan as Cousin Liz, Laurie's daughter. Julian Claman was the producer.

THE JAN MURRAY SHOW (CHARGE ACCOUNT)   NBC
5 SEPTEMBER 1960–28 SEPTEMBER 1962   On this daytime game show, hosted by Jan Murray, players competed for the right to purchase prizes by forming words out of a group of sixteen letters.

JANE FROMAN'S U.S.A. CANTEEN (THE JANE FROMAN SHOW)   CBS
18 OCTOBER 1952–23 JUNE 1955   *Jane Froman's U.S.A. Canteen* was first seen as a half-hour series on Saturdays; talented members of the armed services appeared with Froman, who was billed as "The Sweetheart of the Armed Forces." The Saturday show lasted about two months. Beginning 30 December 1952, the show was trimmed to fifteen minutes and shown Tuesdays and Thursdays following the network news. By late 1953 the series had been retitled *The Jane Froman Show,* and by the end of its run in 1955 it was seen only on Thursdays.

THE JANE PICKENS SHOW   ABC

31 JANUARY 1954–5 SEPTEMBER 1954   Fifteen-minute Sunday-night musical series hosted by singer Jane Pickens, who had been a featured vocalist on such radio programs as *Ben Bernie, The Old Maestro*, and *The Chamber Music Society of Lower Basin Street*.

THE JANE WHITNEY SHOW (NIGHTTALK WITH JANE WHITNEY) SYNDICATED/NBC

1992–1993 (SYNDICATED); 18 JANUARY 1994–14 OCTOBER 1994 (NBC)   Jane Whitney had hosted a local talk show in Philadelphia before going national with this effort, which was produced in Boston in 1992 and moved to New York in 1993. In markets where the 1992–1993 syndicated program was aired during a late-night time slot it was titled *Nighttalk with Jane Whitney;* in markets where it found a daytime niche, and during its 1994 daytime run on NBC, it was known as *The Jane Whitney Show*.

JANE WYMAN THEATER   NBC
(JANE WYMAN PRESENTS THE FIRESIDE THEATRE)

30 AUGUST 1955–29 MAY 1958   Actress Jane Wyman made a successful transition to television, taking over as host of *Fireside Theatre* in 1955; Wyman also starred in about one-half of the episodes that season and coproduced the show with William Asher. She co-owned the production company, Lewman Productions, with Music Corporation of America. By the second season the title was shortened to *Jane Wyman Theater*. During the summer of 1957 Wyman hosted *Jane Wyman's Summer Playhouse* on NBC, an anthology series which consisted of rebroadcasts from other anthology series.

JANET DEAN, REGISTERED NURSE   SYNDICATED

1954   The first TV series about a nurse starred Ella Raines as Janet Dean, a New York practitioner. The thirty-nine half hours were produced by Joan Mary Harrison.

JASON OF STAR COMMAND   CBS

15 SEPTEMBER 1979–29 AUGUST 1981   Originally broadcast as one segment of *Tarzan and the Super 7* during the 1978–1979 season, *Jason of Star Command* became a separate Saturday-morning show a season later. Set in the twenty-second century, it featured Craig Littler as Jason, a space explorer; James Doohan and John Russell as The Commander; Charlie Dell as Professor E. J. Parsafoot, an inventor; Tamara Dobson as Samantha; Susan O'Hanlon as Nicole Davidoff; Sid Haig as Dragos, the villain; and Peepo the robot. Arthur H. Nadel created, produced, and directed the series for Filmation.

JAYCE AND THE WHEELED WARRIORS   SYNDICATED

1985   The central character of this cartoon series was a youngster named Jayce, who roamed the universe searching for his father, battling the Monster Minds along the way. Like many other cartoon shows of the mid-1980s, this one was based on a line of toys.

THE JAYE P. MORGAN SHOW   NBC

13 JUNE 1956–31 AUGUST 1956   Singer Jaye P. Morgan hosted her own fifteen-minute musical series, a summer replacement for Eddie Fisher's *Coke Time* on Wednesdays and Fridays. Assisting her were her four brothers—Bob, Charlie, Dick, and Duke—with whom she had sung as a teenager.

JAZZ SCENE, U.S.A.   SYNDICATED

1963   Half-hour series on American jazz, featuring performances by and interviews with jazz artists. Oscar Brown, Jr., hosted the series.

THE JEAN ARTHUR SHOW   CBS

12 SEPTEMBER 1966–5 DECEMBER 1966   The star of many motion picture comedies during the 1930s and 1940s, Jean Arthur came out of retirement to do this short-lived

sitcom about a pair of lawyers, mother and son. She played Patricia Marshall, a widow. Also featured were Ron Harper as her son, Paul Marshall; Richard Conte as Richie Wells, an ex-gangster interested in the elder Marshall; and Leonard Stone as Morton. Producer: Richard Quine.

THE JEAN CARROLL SHOW ABC
4 NOVEMBER 1953–6 JANUARY 1954   This half-hour sitcom starred Jean Carroll as a New York housewife, Lynn Loring as her daughter, Alan Carney as her husband, and Alice Pearce as their neighbor. The series, which was also known as *Take It from Me,* was produced and directed by Alan Dinehart and written by Coleman Jacoby and Arnie Rosen.

JEAN SHEPHERD'S AMERICA PBS
1971   Thirteen-part series of whimsical essays on aspects of American culture and life-style, hosted by Jean Shepherd. Produced by Fred Barzyk for WGBH-TV, Boston.

JEANNE WOLF WITH... PBS
1974–1975   Half-hour talk show, produced and hosted by Jeanne Wolf at WPBT-TV, Miami.

JEANNIE CBS
8 SEPTEMBER 1973–30 AUGUST 1975   A Saturday-morning cartoon spinoff from *I Dream of Jeannie;* the animated Jeannie was discovered not by an astronaut, but by a high school student, Corey Anders. From Hanna-Barbera Productions.

THE JEFF FOXWORTHY SHOW ABC
12 SEPTEMBER 1995–   Standup comic Jeff Foxworthy, a Southerner whose act consisted of telling "Redneck" jokes, was given his own sitcom in 1995. He played Jeff Foxworthy, a down-to-earth Southern family man who lived in Bloomington, Indiana, where he ran a heating and air conditioning business. Also featured were Anita Barone as his wife, Karen, a nurse; Haley Joel Osment as their young son, Matt; Matt Clark as Walt Bacon, who worked for Jeff; Matt Borlenghi as Russ Francis, who also worked for Jeff; Sue Murphy as Karen's best friend and co-worker, Sandi; Steve Hytner as the Foxworthys' snooty neighbor, Craig Lesco; Dakin Matthews as Karen's father, Elliot; and Bibi Besch as Karen's mother, Lois.

JEFFERSON DRUM NBC
25 APRIL 1958–23 APRIL 1959   Half-hour western about a crusading newspaper editor. With Jeff Richards as Jefferson Drum, a man who headed for San Francisco after his wife was murdered and his newspaper destroyed in another town; on his way west Drum stopped in the town of Jubilee and decided to take over its paper when he learned that the former publisher had been murdered. Also featured were Eugene Martin as his young son, Joey; Cyril Delevanti as the old typesetter, Lucius Coin; and Robert J. Stevenson as Big Ed, Drum's friend. *Jefferson Drum* was one of the few dramatic series put together by game show producers Mark Goodson and Bill Todman.

THE JEFFERSONS CBS
18 JANUARY 1975–23 JULY 1985   In this spinoff from *All in the Family,* the Bunkers' black neighbors—the Jeffersons—moved from Queens to Manhattan's East Side. The half-hour sitcom starred Sherman Hemsley as George Jefferson, owner of a chain of successful cleaning stores, and a short-tempered, know-it-all bigot, and Isabel Sanford as Louise Jefferson, his tolerant and forgiving wife. Mike Evans played their son, Lionel, until September of 1975, when he was succeeded by Damon Evans (no relation); and Zara Cully played George's doting mother, Mama Jefferson, until her death early in 1978. Also featured were Franklin Cover and Roxie Roker as Tom and Helen Willis, the Jeffersons' neighbors (the Willises were the first racially mixed married couple to be featured on a prime-time series); Berlinda

Tolbert as Jenny Willis, their daughter; Paul Benedict (1975–1981; 1983–1985) as Harry Bentley, an eccentric neighbor employed as a United Nations translator; Marla Gibbs (1976–1985) as Florence Johnston, the Jeffersons' sassy maid; Ned Wertimer (1976–1985) as Ralph Hart, the obsequious doorman; Ernest Harden, Jr., (1977–1978) as Marcus Wilson, a young man employed at one of George's stores; and Jay Hammer (1978–1979) as Allan Willis, Tom's son. In December of 1976 Lionel and Jenny were married; though Damon Evans left the show in the fall of 1978, Berlinda Tolbert continued to appear. Mike Evans returned to play Lionel in the fall of 1979. Lionel and Jenny's baby, Jessica, was born in the spring of 1980. In the spring of 1981 Marla Gibbs starred in a short-lived spinoff, *Checking In.* Lionel and Jenny were separated in 1981, and Mike Evans no longer appeared as a regular. In 1984 Ebonie Smith joined the cast as their daughter, Jessica, now a school-age youngster. *The Jeffersons* was created by Don Nicholl, Michael Ross, and Bernie West, and developed by Norman Lear.

JEM   SYNDICATED
1986–1987   Half-hour cartoon series based on the Hasbro doll line and underwritten by the toy company. The main character was a young woman named Jerica, who could transform herself into Jem, a super-powered rock star. Assisted by her back-up singers, the Holograms, Jem battled the Misfits, an evil rock group led by Pizzazz. Britta Phillips provided the voice of Jem, Ellen Bernfeld that of Pizzazz.

JENNIFER SLEPT HERE   NBC
21 OCTOBER 1983–29 AUGUST 1984   This half-hour sitcom was reminiscent of *Topper,* the classic 1950s series. As in *Topper,* a family moved into a house that was still occupied by the ghost of its former owner; again as in *Topper,* the ghost could be seen and heard by only one member of the new family. Ann Jillian starred as the ghost, Jennifer Farrell, an actress who had died in her prime about five years previously; she revealed herself to a fourteen-year-old boy, Joey Elliot (played by John P. Navin, Jr.), and used her influence to help the lad through puberty; Brandon Maggart played Joey's father, George Elliot, the lawyer for Farrell's estate; Georgia Engel played Joey's mother, Susan Elliot; Mya Akerling played Joey's little sister, Marilyn; and Glenn Scarpelli (late of *One Day at a Time*) appeared as the next-door neighbor, Marc, a teenaged hustler.

JENNY JONES   SYNDICATED
1991–   Hour daytime talk show taped in Chicago and hosted by effervescent Jenny Jones, a former standup comic, former game show contestant, former backup singer for Wayne Newton, and former winner on *Star Search.* The show made headlines in March 1995 when, after the taping of a program on "secret admirers," one guest allegedly killed another. After learning—onstage—that his secret admirer was a man, Jonathan Schmitz allegedly drove to the house of the admirer, Scott Amedure, three days later and killed him. In a rare display of good taste, the producers opted not to televise the program. A sample of fare from April and May 1995 included topics such as "Exotic Dancers Quarrel," "Women Who Stick with Their Cheating Men," "Sexy Twins," "Aspiring Male Dancers," and "Overweight Mothers' Fashion Faux Pas."

JEOPARDY!   NBC/SYNDICATED/ABC
30 MARCH 1964–3 JANUARY 1975 (NBC); 1974 (SYNDICATED); 2 OCTOBER 1978–2 MARCH 1979 (NBC); 1984–   (SYNDICATED); 16 JUNE 1990–8 SEPTEMBER 1990 (ABC)   This "answer and question" game show enjoyed a long daytime run on NBC. Art Fleming hosted the series, on which three contestants competed for cash by supplying the correct questions to answers uncovered on a board of thirty squares, containing five answers in each of six categories. At the end of the show ("Final Jeopardy"), contestants could wager up to all of their winnings on one answer. The series was developed by Merv Griffin and produced by his production company. The 1978 version of the series was similar to the earlier version; three contestants competed in the first round, but only two contestants moved on to the second round. The

"final jeopardy" round was also modified so that only one player participated. When the series returned in 1984, with Alex Trebek as host, it had reverted to its original format; by the end of the decade it had become one of the most popular first-run syndicated series. The 1990 network prime-time version titled *Super Jeopardy!* and also hosted by Trebek, was a twelve-week invitational tournament pitting big-money champions from the 1984–1990 syndication years. The grand prize winner took home $250,000.

JERICHO   CBS
15 SEPTEMBER 1966–19 JANUARY 1967   One of the lesser-known World War II dramas, *Jericho* featured a trio of Allied agents who usually worked behind German lines. With Don Francks as Franklin Shepard, an American who was an expert in psychological warfare; John Leyton as Nicholas Gage, a Britisher whose specialty was demolition; and Marino Mase as Jean-Gaston André, a Frenchman whose forte was munitions. Dan Melnick and Norman Felton produced the hour-long series.

THE JERRY COLONNA SHOW   ABC
28 MAY 1951–17 NOVEMBER 1951   Half-hour variety series hosted by Jerry Colonna, a mustachioed comic who had worked with Bob Hope on the latter's radio series.

JERRY FALWELL   SYNDICATED
1971–   Evangelist Jerry Falwell, the founder and president of Moral Majority, hosts this half-hour religious program, usually taped at one of his revival meetings. Although the show has been shown on as many as 370 stations, it has had financial problems. *The New York Times* noted in 1980 that Falwell had asked his audience (by letter) for $5 million to sustain the show. In its early seasons the show was titled *The Old-Time Gospel Hour.* Falwell was untouched by the scandals that plagued other televangelists such as Jim Bakker and Jimmy Swaggart. Indeed, after resigning from *The P.T.L. Club,* Jim Bakker asked Falwell to take over the organization. Falwell examined the P.T.L. books, and Bakker was soon indicted.

THE JERRY LESTER SHOW   ABC
28 SEPTEMBER 1953–14 MAY 1954   Jerry Lester, the comedian who had hosted *Broadway Open House,* later hosted his own daytime show. Also featured were singer and violinist Leon Belasco, and vocalists Lorenzo Fuller, Kathy Collin, and Ellie Russell. The hour-long show was produced by Vernon Becker and Milton Stanson.

THE JERRY LEWIS SHOW   ABC/NBC
21 SEPTEMBER 1963–21 DECEMBER 1963 (ABC); 12 SEPTEMBER 1967–27 MAY 1969 (NBC)   After breaking up with partner Dean Martin in 1956, Jerry Lewis appeared little on TV for the next seven years, concentrating instead on films. In 1963 it was reported that he had signed a five-year, $35-million deal with ABC; that fall he hosted a live, two-hour variety-talk show, which proved to be an enormous failure. In 1967 he returned to host an hour-long variety show on NBC, which was somewhat more successful; Bob Finkel produced it.

THE JERRY REED WHEN YOU'RE HOT YOU'RE HOT HOUR   CBS
20 JUNE 1972–25 JULY 1972   A summer replacement for *The Glen Campbell Goodtime Hour,* hosted by country-and-western singer Jerry Reed, whose record, "When You're Hot, You're Hot," was a hit a year earlier. Other regulars included John Twomey, Spencer Quinn, Cal Wilson, Norman Andrews, and eighty-three-year-old Merie Earle.

JERRY SPRINGER   SYNDICATED
1992–   Hour daytime talk show hosted by Jerry Springer, the former mayor of Cincinnati. Among the topics presented during April and May 1995 were "Strip Club Denizens," "Mate Swappers," "Pimps and Prostitutes," "Twins," and "Judge Ito Look-Alike."

JERRY VISITS   SYNDICATED
1971–1973   Celebrities were interviewed in their homes by Jerry Dunphy on this half-hour talk show.

JESSE HAWKES   CBS
26 APRIL 1989–27 MAY 1989   Three of the stars of the 1988 adventure series *High Mountain Rangers* left the high Sierras for San Francisco in this short-lived crime show. With Robert Conrad as Jesse Hawkes; Christian Conrad as his son Matt Hawkes; and Shane Conrad as his son Cody Hawkes.

THE JESSE JACKSON SHOW   SYNDICATED/CNN
1990–1991 (SYNDICATED); 4 JANUARY 1992–25 SEPTEMBER 1993 (CNN)   Politician Jesse Jackson was the host of a syndicated weekly, issue-oriented hour talk show. In 1992 he presided over a similar half-hour on CNN, *Both Sides with Jesse Jackson*.

JESSICA NOVAK   CBS
5 NOVEMBER 1981–3 DECEMBER 1981   An early fatality of the 1981–1982 season, this hour dramatic series starred Helen Shaver as TV news reporter Jessica Novak, and featured David Spielberg as her boss, Maxwell Kenyon, the news director at KLA-TV in Los Angeles; Andrew Rubin as Phil Bonelli, her camera operator; Eric Kilpatrick as Ricky Duran, her sound recordist; and Nina Wilcox as Audrey Stiles, her editor.

JESSIE   ABC
18 SEPTEMBER 1984–13 NOVEMBER 1984   Only seven episodes of this ill-fated police show were broadcast. It starred Lindsay Wagner as Dr. Jessie Hayden, a psychiatrist assigned to a city police department, and featured Tony Lo Bianco as Lieutenant Alex Ascoli; Celeste Holm as her mother, Molly Hayden; James David Hinton as Phil; Renee Jones as Ellie; and Tom Nolan as Hubbell. Production of the series was temporarily halted at MGM/UA after four episodes had been produced, and a new production crew, headed by David Gerber, was brought in. Resuscitation efforts proved to be in vain, however.

JET JACKSON
See CAPTAIN MIDNIGHT

THE JETSONS   ABC/CBS/NBC/SYNDICATED
Nighttime: 23 SEPTEMBER 1962–8 SEPTEMBER 1963 (ABC); *Daytime:* 21 SEPTEMBER 1963–18 APRIL 1964 (ABC); 26 SEPTEMBER 1964–18 SEPTEMBER 1965 (CBS); 2 OCTOBER 1965–2 SEPTEMBER 1967 (NBC); 13 SEPTEMBER 1969–4 SEPTEMBER 1971 (CBS); 11 SEPTEMBER 1971–4 SEPTEMBER 1976 (NBC); 3 FEBRUARY 1979–5 SEPTEMBER 1981 (NBC); 18 SEPTEMBER 1982–2 APRIL 1983 (NBC); 1985 (SYNDICATED); 1987 (SYNDICATED)   This durable cartoon series was the Space Age counterpart of Hanna-Barbera's Stone Age smash, *The Flintstones;* the Jetsons—George, Jane, Judy, and Elroy—lived in the ultramodern world of the twenty-first century. The series was seen in prime time on ABC for one season and on Saturday mornings over all three networks for many seasons thereafter. The voices of the Jetsons were provided by the Hanna-Barbera regulars: George O'Hanlon as George, Penny Singleton as Jane, Janet Waldo as Judy, Daws Butler as Elroy, Don Messick as Astro, the family dog, and Mel Blanc as Cosmo Spacely, George's boss at Spacely Space Age Sprockets. In 1985 and in 1987 new episodes were produced to supplement the batch made twenty-three years previously; a new pet, Orbitty, joined the Jetsons.

In the summer of 1990 the space-age family made their motion picture debut in *Jetsons: The Movie.*

JEWELER'S SHOWCASE (YOUR JEWELER'S SHOWCASE)   SYNDICATED
1952   This half-hour dramatic anthology series was sponsored by the International Silver Company and the Hamilton Watch Company.

JIGSAW   ABC
21 SEPTEMBER 1972–11 AUGUST 1973   One segment of ABC's adventure trilogy, *The Men, Jigsaw* alternated with *Assignment: Vienna* and *The Delphi Bureau.* It starred James Wainwright as Lieutenant Frank Dain, an investigator for the California bureau of missing persons.

JIGSAW JOHN   NBC
2 FEBRUARY 1976–13 SEPTEMBER 1976   Crime show based on the exploits of real-life police investigator John St. John. With Jack Warden as John St. John, Los Angeles cop; Alan Feinstein as Sam Donner, his partner; Pippa Scott as Maggie Hearn, John's friend, a schoolteacher; Marjorie Bennett as Mrs. Cooley; and James Hong as Frank Chen. The hour-long series was created by Al Martinez, and produced by Ronald Austin and James Buchanan.

THE JIM BACKUS SHOW (HOT OFF THE WIRE)   SYNDICATED
1960   Situation comedy starring Jim Backus as John Michael (Mike) O'Toole, editor of a newspaper struggling to keep afloat; Nita Talbot as Dora, his gal Friday; and Bobs Watson as Sidney, the office boy.

JIM BOWIE (THE ADVENTURES OF JIM BOWIE)   ABC
7 SEPTEMBER 1956–29 AUGUST 1958   Half-hour western starring Scott Forbes as Jim Bowie, the nineteenth-century American adventurer who invented the knife that bears his name. Criticism of the frequent use of the knife on the series led to a cutback of violence on *Jim Bowie.* Though Forbes (who was British by birth) was the only regular on the show, he did not appear in all the episodes. Louis Edelman produced the series.

THE JIM HENSON HOUR   NBC
14 APRIL 1989–30 JULY 1989   Puppeteer extraordinaire Jim Henson created this hour prime-time series, which consisted of two discrete half-hour segments: the first resembled *The Muppet Show,* presenting skits and songs featuring the Muppets and guest stars, while the second presented a story, with live actors, narrated by John Hurt.

JIM HENSON'S MUPPET BABIES
see MUPPET BABIES

THE JIM NABORS HOUR   CBS
25 SEPTEMBER 1969–20 MAY 1971   Hour-long variety series hosted by Jim Nabors, the singer-comedian who got his start on *The Andy Griffith Show* and later starred in a spinoff, *Gomer Pyle, U.S.M.C.* Nabors brought with him a couple of his *Gomer Pyle* costars, Frank Sutton and Ronnie Schell. Also on hand were Karen Morrow and the Nabors Kids. Richard O. Linke was the executive producer.

THE JIM NABORS SHOW   SYNDICATED
1978   Talk show hosted by Jim Nabors. Executive producers: Carolyn Raskin and Larry Thompson. Producers: Ken Harris and Charles Colarusso.

THE JIM STAFFORD SHOW   ABC
30 JULY 1975–3 SEPTEMBER 1975   Six-week summer variety series starring Jim Stafford, a country singer who had had a minor hit with "My Girl Bill." Other regulars included Valerie Curtin, Tom Biener, Deborah Allen, Richard Stahl, Phil MacKenzie, Jeanne Sheffield, and Cyndi Wood. Executive producers: Phil Gernhard and Tony Scotti. Producers: Rich Eustis and Al Rogers.

JIM THOMAS OUTDOORS   SYNDICATED
1976   A series for sportsmen, with emphasis on hunting and fishing, hosted by Jim Thomas.

THE JIMMIE RODGERS SHOW   NBC/CBS
31 MARCH 1959–8 SEPTEMBER 1959 (NBC); 16 JUNE 1969–1 SEPTEMBER 1969 (CBS)
Country and western singer Jimmie Rodgers ("Honeycomb" was his biggest hit, recorded in 1957) hosted two variety series. The first was a half-hour show, which featured Connie Francis, the Kirby Stone Four, The Clay Warnick Singers, and the Buddy Morrow Orchestra. The second, an hour-long series, was a summer replacement for *The Carol Burnett Show,* and featured *Burnett* regulars Vicki Lawrence and Lyle Waggoner, plus Don Crichton, Bill Fanning, Nancy Austin, the Burgundy Street Singers, and the Frank Comstock Orchestra.

JIMMY BRESLIN'S PEOPLE   ABC
25 SEPTEMBER 1986–2 JANUARY 1987   Syndicated columnist Jimmy Breslin tried his hand at a late-night talk show, shown after *Nightline* two nights a week.

THE JIMMY DEAN SHOW   CBS/ABC/SYNDICATED
Daytime: 8 APRIL 1957–26 JUNE 1959 (CBS); *Nighttime:* 22 JUNE 1957–14 SEPTEMBER 1957 (CBS); 19 SEPTEMBER 1963–1 APRIL 1966 (ABC); 1974 (SYNDICATED)
Country and western singer Jimmy Dean first hosted a local show on WTOP-TV in Washington, D.C. He attracted network attention and was given a daytime spot in the spring of 1957—the early-morning show originated from Washington and was aired six days a week for part of its two-year run. During the summer of 1957 Dean hosted a Saturday-night variety show, returning to the daytime grind that fall. Assisting him were Jan Crockett, Mary Klick, Jo Davis, ventriloquist Alex Houston, the Texas Wildcats, the Country Lads, the Noteworthies, and the Joel Herron Orchestra. In 1963 Dean hosted a prime-time hour variety series on ABC, which lasted three seasons. Regulars included Karen Morrow, Molly Bee, Chuck McCann, the Chuck Cassey Singers, and Rowlf the Muppet, the first of the puppet creations of Jim Henson to be featured on national TV (Rowlf was operated by Jim Henson and Frank Oznowicz).

JIMMY DURANTE PRESENTS THE LENNON SISTERS HOUR   ABC
26 SEPTEMBER 1969–4 JULY 1970   Hour-long variety series starring seventy-six-year-old Jimmy Durante and the singing Lennon Sisters (Dianne, Janet, Kathy, and Peggy), who were featured on *The Lawrence Welk Show* for many years. Executive producer: Harold Cohen. Producers: Bernie Kukoff and Jeff Harris.

THE JIMMY DURANTE SHOW   NBC
2 OCTOBER 1954–23 JUNE 1956   This half-hour variety show was seen on Saturday nights; during its first season it alternated with *The Donald O'Connor Show.* Joining "The Schnozz" were three of his longtime compatriots—Eddie Jackson, his former vaudeville partner (together with the late Lou Clayton), pianist Jules Buffano, and drummer Jack Roth. The show was set at the Club Durant, and also featured the Durante Girls.

JIMMY HUGHES, ROOKIE COP   DUMONT
8 MAY 1953–3 JULY 1953   Half-hour crime show starring William Redfield as Jimmy Hughes, a young Korean War veteran who joined the New York police force, hoping to find the slayers of his father, also a cop. The cast also included Rusty Lane as Inspector Ferguson, Jimmy's mentor, and Wendy Drew as Jimmy's sister. Barry Shear directed the series.

THE JIMMY STEWART SHOW   NBC
19 SEPTEMBER 1971–27 AUGUST 1972   Situation comedy starring Jimmy Stewart as Jim Howard, professor of anthropology at Josiah Kessel College, a man caught in the generation gap. Also featured were Julie Adams as his wife, Martha Howard; Jonathan Daly as P. J. Howard, their twenty-nine-year-old son; Ellen Geer as Wendy, P. J.'s wife; Kirby Furlong as Jake, P. J. and Wendy's eight-year-old son; Dennis Larson as Teddy, Jim and Martha's eight-year-old son and Jake's uncle; and John McGiver as Luther Quince, a faculty colleague of Jim's. Like many other major film

stars, Jimmy Stewart seemed unable to find the right vehicle for himself on TV; neither this show nor his second series—*Hawkins*—caught on with viewers. Warner Brothers produced the series.

JIMMY SWAGGART   SYNDICATED
1977–   Half-hour religious show hosted by evangelist Jimmy Swaggart and produced by the Jimmy Swaggart Evangelistic Association, first in Baton Rouge, Louisiana, later in New Orleans. Swaggart played a major role in the ouster of rival televangelist Jim Bakker and his *P.T.L. Club*. Earlier, Swaggart had forced Marvin Gorman, a local New Orleans TV evangelist, to resign his ministry after revealing Gorman's adultery. Gorman turned the tables on Swaggart early in 1988 by arranging to have photos taken of Swaggart and a New Orleans prostitute. A tearful Swaggart announced to his congregation in February, "I have sinned," and stepped down from his ministry. Three months later he returned, however, but by that time his TV show had lost many of its affiliates.

THE JO STAFFORD SHOW   CBS/SYNDICATED
2 FEBRUARY 1954–28 JUNE 1955 (CBS); 1962 (SYNDICATED)   Jo Stafford, whose recording career began in 1944 (her biggest hit was probably "You Belong to Me" in 1952), hosted a fifteen-minute musical show seen Tuesdays after the network news. She was backed up by the Starlighters, and music was provided by the orchestra led by her husband, Paul Weston. In 1962 she hosted a second musical series, taped in London, and distributed by ITC.

THE JOAN EDWARDS SHOW   DUMONT
4 JULY 1950–24 OCTOBER 1950   A twice-weekly, fifteen-minute musical series hosted by Joan Edwards. Martin Goodman was the producer, Dick Sandwick the director.

THE JOAN RIVERS SHOW (THAT SHOW)   SYNDICATED
1969   Half-hour talk show hosted by comedienne Joan Rivers; typically, each show featured a celebrity guest and someone with an unusual hobby or talent.

THE JOAN RIVERS SHOW   SYNDICATED
1989–1993   Two and a half years after the demise of her late-night talk show on the Fox network, Joan Rivers returned to the airwaves as the host of an hour talk show, intended for morning time slots. As of 30 April 1990 the show was offered live to affiliated stations; Rivers's guest on the first live broadcast was fellow daytime talkmaster Phil Donahue. Following the demise of her talk show, Rivers tested the home-shopping arena: see *Can We Shop?*

JOANIE LOVES CHACHI   ABC
23 MARCH 1982–13 APRIL 1982; 2 SEPTEMBER 1982–23 DECEMBER 1982; 17 MAY 1983–13 SEPTEMBER 1983   In this spinoff from *Happy Days,* Joanie Cunningham and her boyfriend, Charles "Chachi" Arcola, left Milwaukee for Chicago (where they would live with his mom and her new husband) and started a rock and roll band. Leaving *Happy Days* were Erin Moran as Joanie, and Scott Baio as Chachi; also leaving was Al Molinaro as Al Delvecchio, who married Chachi's mother, Louisa (played by Ellen Travolta), and opened an Italian restaurant with her in Chicago. Art Metrano costarred as Louisa's unsavory relative, Uncle Rico. Featured in Joanie and Chachi's band were Derrel Maury as Mario; Winifred Freedman as Annette; and Robert Peirce as Bingo, the drummer. *Joanie Loves Chachi* is a good example of the lack of correlation between a popular spring tryout and a popular full-season show. When the series was introduced for four weeks in the spring of 1982, it was immensely popular, finishing in a tie for fourth in the 1981–1982 seasonal Nielsens (it should be noted that its competition at that time was mainly reruns). When it returned in the fall of 1982, it flopped, ranking a dismal 68th in the 1982–1983 ratings, and was lifted from the network's schedule in December. Moran, Baio, and Molinaro returned to *Happy Days* the following season.

JOANNE CARSON'S V.I.P.'S SYNDICATED

1973   Half-hour talk show set in a kitchen, hosted by Joanne Carson, the second wife (and second ex-wife) of America's foremost talk show host, Johnny Carson.

JOE AND MABEL CBS

20 SEPTEMBER 1955–25 SEPTEMBER 1956   Half-hour filmed sitcom about a New York cabbie and his marriage-minded girlfriend. With Larry Blyden as Joe Sparton; Nita Talbot as Mabel Stooler, a manicurist; Luella Gear as Mrs. Stooler, Mabel's mother; Michael Mann as Sherman Stooler, Mabel's brother; and Shirl Conway as Dolly, a friend of Mabel's. Alex Gottlieb was producer and head writer of the show, which was directed by Ezra Stone (he'd played Henry Aldrich on radio) and packaged by David Susskind. The show was seen for only a few weeks during the fall of 1955, returning to the air 26 June 1956.

JOE AND SONS CBS

9 SEPTEMBER 1975–13 JANUARY 1976   The only TV series set in Hoboken, N.J., *Joe and Sons* was a situation comedy about a widower and his two sons. With Richard Castellano as Joe Vitale, who ran a screw press; Barry Miller as Mark, the older son; Jimmy Baio as Nick, the younger son; Jerry Stiller as Gus Duzik, Joe's buddy; Bobbi Jordan as Estelle, Joe's neighbor; and Florence Stanley as Josephine, Joe's sister. Executive producer: Douglas S. Cramer. Producers: Bernie Kukoff and Jeff Harris.

JOE AND VALERIE NBC

24 APRIL 1978–10 MAY 1978; 5 JANUARY 1979–19 JANUARY 1979   A half-hour sitcom, *Joe and Valerie* surfaced for two short runs. The 1978 version took its cue from the film *Saturday Night Fever* and featured disco sequences; the 1979 version abandoned the disco element and concentrated on the wedding plans of the two principals. With Paul Regina as Joe Pizo, a young Brooklynite; Char Fontane as Valerie Sweetzer, his dancing partner and fiancée; David Elliott as Joe's pal Paulie, a hearse driver; Bill Beyers (1978) and Lloyd Alann (1979) as Joe's friend Frank; Robert Costanzo as Joe's widowed father, Vince Pizo, a plumber; Pat Benson (1978) and Arlene Golonka (1979) as Valerie's divorced mother, Stella Sweetzer; and Donna Ponterotto as Valerie's friend, Thelma. Linda Hope (daughter of Bob Hope) was the executive producer.

JOE BASH ABC

28 MARCH 1986–10 MAY 1986   Danny Arnold's dark comedy about a cynical old cop bore little resemblance to his earlier police sitcom, *Barney Miller*. Here, Peter Boyle played Joe Bash, a streetwise cop from New York's 33rd Precinct who was nearing retirement when he was assigned an eager young partner, Willie Smith (played by Andrew Rubin).

JOE FORRESTER NBC

9 SEPTEMBER 1975–30 AUGUST 1976   An hour-long cop show which, like CBS's *The Blue Knight,* told the story of a veteran patrolman. With Lloyd Bridges as Officer Joe Forrester; Eddie Egan (a former New York cop) as Sergeant Bernie Vincent; Pat Crowley as Georgia Cameron, Joe's romantic interest; Dwan Smith as Jolene Jackson, one of Joe's street informants; and Taylor Lacher as Detective Will Carson. On 6 May 1975, the pilot for the series, "The Return of Joe Forrester," was shown on *Police Story*. David Gerber was executive producer of the series, which was produced by Mark Rodgers and James H. Brown.

JOE GARAGIOLA'S MEMORY GAME NBC

15 FEBRUARY 1971–30 JULY 1971   Daytime game show on which the five contestants were shown lists of questions and answers, and then quizzed by host Joe Garagiola.

THE JOE NAMATH SHOW SYNDICATED

1969   Short-lived talk show cohosted by Joe Namath (then quarterback for the New York Jets) and sportswriter Dick Schaap.

THE JOE PALOOKA STORY   SYNDICATED

1954   Ham Fisher's cartoon pugilist came to life briefly on television in this low-budget syndicated series. It featured Joe Kirkwood, Jr., as Joe Palooka, the honest and upright, if not quick-witted, boxing champ; Cathy Downs as Ann Howe, his girlfriend; Sid Tomack and Luis Van Rooten as his manager, Knobby Walsh; and "Slapsie" Maxie Rosenbloom as his trainer, Clyde.

THE JOE PYNE SHOW   SYNDICATED

1965–1967   Characterized by its host as a "fist-in-the-mouth" talk show, *The Joe Pyne Show* was a two-hour parade of eccentrics, crackpots, and controversial guests. Chain-smoking Joe Pyne delighted in insulting most of his guests, as well as members of the studio audience, who were given the chance to state their views at the outset of each show. Pyne began his show locally in Los Angeles on KTTV and attracted attention from the beginning. During the Watts riots of 1965, a black militant guested; Pyne opened his desk drawer to reveal a revolver, whereupon the guest drew back his coat to show that he, too, was armed. Another guest, wanted by the police, was arrested on camera. George Lincoln Rockwell, head of the American Nazi Party, and Marguerite Oswald, mother of Lee Harvey Oswald, also appeared on the show. Robert Hayward was the producer. For a later version of the "fist-in-the-mouth" genre, see *The Morton Downey, Jr., Show.*

JOE'S LIFE   ABC

29 SEPTEMBER 1993–15 DECEMBER 1993   Half-hour sitcom about a laid-off defense worker who ran the household while his wife worked as a temp. With Peter Onorati as Joe Gennaro; Mary Page Keller as Sandy Gennaro; Spencer Klein as son Scott; Robert Hy Gorman as son Paul; Morgan Nagler as daughter Amy; George DiCenzo as Stan, Joe's brother, who ran a restaurant where Joe worked evenings; Mimi Kennedy as Stan's wife, Barb; Danny Masterson as Stan and Barb's teenage son, Leo; and Marshall Jones as Ray Wharton, who worked for Stan.

JOE'S WORLD   NBC

28 JANUARY 1979–2 JANUARY 1980; 10 MAY 1980–26 JULY 1980   Ramon Bieri starred in this half-hour sitcom as Joe Wabash, the foreman of a union painting crew in Detroit. Also featured were K Callan as his wife, Katie Wabash; Christopher Knight as their son, Steve, one of Joe's crew; Melissa Sherman as teenage daughter Maggie; Michael Sharrett as son Jimmy; Missy Francis as daughter Linda; Ari Zeltzer as son Rick; Russ Banham as Brad, another crew member, who dated Maggie; and Misty Rowe as Judy, also a crew member.

JOEY AND DAD   CBS

6 JULY 1975–27 JULY 1975   A four-week summer replacement for *Cher,* starring singer-dancer Joey Heatherton and her father, Ray Heatherton, who was better known to many New Yorkers as host of a 1950s kids' show, *The Merry Mailman.* Other regulars included Henny Youngman, Pat Paulsen, and Pat Proft. Executive producers: Allan Blye and Bob Einstein. Producers: Bob Arnott, Coslough Johnson, and Stan Jacobson.

THE JOEY BISHOP SHOW   NBC/CBS

20 SEPTEMBER 1961–5 SEPTEMBER 1964 (NBC); 27 SEPTEMBER 1964–7 SEPTEMBER 1965 (CBS)   This situation comedy, produced by Danny Thomas's Bellmar Productions, changed both formats and networks during its four-year run. The pilot for the series, "Everything Happens to Me," was aired on Thomas's *Make Room for Daddy* on 27 March 1961. During the 1961–1962 season Joey played Joey Barnes, a publicist; he was unmarried. Also featured were Joe Flynn as Frank, his brother-in-law; Marlo Thomas (in her first continuing role) as Stella, Joey's sister, an aspiring actress; Virginia Vincent as his sister Betty; Warren Berlinger as his brother, Larry; Madge Blake as his mother, the widowed Mrs. Barnes; John Griggs as J. R. Willoughby, his boss; and Nancy Hadley as Barbara, Joey's girlfriend. A new format was adopted for the second season, and the show was retitled *The New Joey Bishop Show.* Bishop

continued to play Joey Barnes, but Barnes was now a married man, employed as a nightclub comedian and host of a TV show. Gone were all the old regulars, and joining the cast were Abby Dalton as his wife, Ellie; Guy Marks (1962–1963) as his manager, Freddy; Corbett Monica (1963–1965) as Larry, his next manager; Joe Besser as Mr. Jillson, his landlord; and Mary Treen (1962–1965) as Hilda, the maid and nanny for Joey and Ellie's baby boy, Joey Jr. (played by Matthew David Smith). The second format lasted three seasons—two on NBC and one on CBS.

THE JOEY BISHOP SHOW ABC
17 APRIL 1967–26 DECEMBER 1969   Comedian Joey Bishop took over the host's chair on ABC's late night talk show in 1967; the chair had first been occupied by Les Crane (when the show was known as *The Les Crane Show*), and later by a succession of guest hosts (when it was called *Nightlife*). Though Bishop had had considerable experience as a talk show host, having substituted many times for NBC's Johnny Carson, he was unable to lure enough viewers away from the *Tonight* show; late in 1969 Bishop was succeeded by Dick Cavett. Bishop's sidekick for the two-and-a-half-year run was Regis Philbin, with music provided by Johnny Mann and His Merry Men.

JOHN & LEEZA
See LEEZA

THE JOHN BYNER COMEDY HOUR CBS
1 AUGUST 1972–29 AUGUST 1972   Five-week summer variety hour hosted by comedian John Byner, featuring Patti Deutsch, R. G. Brown, Linda Sublette, Gary Miller, and Dennis Flannigan.

THE JOHN DAVIDSON SHOW NBC/ABC
(THE KRAFT SUMMER MUSIC HALL)
6 JUNE 1966–29 AUGUST 1966 (NBC); 30 MAY 1969–5 SEPTEMBER 1969 (ABC); 24 MAY 1976–14 JUNE 1976 (NBC)   Singer John Davidson has hosted three prime-time variety hours. The first was titled *The Kraft Summer Music Hall* and featured George Carlin, the Lively Set, the 5 King Cousins, and Jackie and Gayle. The latter two shows were both known as *The John Davidson Show*. The 1969 show was taped in London and featured Rich Little, Mireille Mathieu, and Amy McDonald. The 1976 show featured comedian Pete Barbutti; its executive producers were Alan Bernard and Dick Clark.

THE JOHN DAVIDSON SHOW SYNDICATED
1980–1982   Group W Broadcasting abruptly dropped Mike Douglas as the host of its syndicated talk show, *The Mike Douglas Show,* and replaced him with John Davidson, retitling the show, of course.

THE JOHN FORSYTHE SHOW NBC
13 SEPTEMBER 1965–29 AUGUST 1966   *The John Forsythe Show* began as a situation comedy, starring John Forsythe as Major John Foster, an Air Force veteran who inherited the Foster School for Girls from his late Aunt Victoria. Also featured were Elsa Lanchester as Miss Culver, the principal; Ann B. Davis as Miss Wilson, the gym teacher; Guy Marks as Ed Robbins, John's aide, formerly a sergeant. The students included Pamelyn Ferdin as Pamela; Darleen Carr as Kathy; Page Forsythe (John's daughter) as Marcia; Brook Forsythe (also John's daughter) as Norma Jean; Peggy Lipton (later of *Mod Squad*) as Joanna; Tracy Stratford as Susan; and Sara Ballantine as Janice: In midseason that format was scrapped, and the show changed from a sitcom to a spy show. It was explained that Major Foster had been "recalled" to active duty and had become a secret agent; all the regulars except for John Forsythe and Guy Marks were dropped. Peter Kortner produced the series.

THE JOHN GARY SHOW   CBS/SYNDICATED

22 JUNE 1966–7 SEPTEMBER 1966 (CBS); 1968 (SYNDICATED)   The first of pop
singer John Gary's variety hours was a summer replacement for *The Danny Kaye
Show* and featured the Mitchell Ayres Orchestra, the Jimmy Joyce Singers, and the
Jack Regas Dancers. The second show was a syndicated effort and featured Sammy
Spear's Orchestra.

JOHN GRISHAM'S THE CLIENT
See THE CLIENT

THE JOHN LARROQUETTE SHOW   NBC

2 SEPTEMBER 1993–   A year after completing nine seasons on *Night Court,* John
Larroquette returned to star in his own sitcom. This time he played John Hemingway,
a recovering alcoholic who landed a job as night manager of the Crossroads Bus
Terminal in St. Louis, frequented by a motley assortment of people (Larroquette
himself was also a recovering alcoholic). Also aboard were Liz Torres as Mahalia
Sanchez, the assistant manager; Gigi Rice as Carly Watkins, the friendly hooker;
Daryl "Chill" Mitchell as Dexter, the angry young black man who ran the snack bar;
Chi McBride as Heavy Gene, the janitor; Lenny Clarke as Officer Hampton, the
cop; Elizabeth Berridge as Hampton's partner, Officer Eggers; Bill Morey as Oscar,
a demented homeless person who hung around the terminal; David Shawn Michaels
(1993–1994) as Teddi, the transvestite; Glenn Shadix (1993–1994) as Walker, the
cynical bartender who was pessimistic about John's ability to stay sober; and David
Crosby (1993–1994) as Chester, John's AA sponsor. Occasionally featured were
Donna Mills as Carol, one of John's ex-wives, and Omri Katz as Tony, John's son.
The series was scheduled on Wednesdays opposite ABC's *Roseanne* during its first
season, and scored reasonably well enough in the ratings to warrant renewal. Unfortunately, it faced even tougher competition during its second season opposite ABC's
Home Improvement on Tuesdays. Alison LaPlaca joined the cast in the fall of 1994 as
nurse Catherine Merrick, John's neighbor and love interest, and Carly quit the
world's oldest profession to purchase the bus terminal's bar. In the fall of 1995
Mayim Bialik (late of *Blossom*) became a regular as John's daughter, Rachel, and the
series acquired a lighter look when the crew moved from the night shift to the day
shift.

JOHNNY B. ON THE LOOSE   SYNDICATED

1991   Short-lived comedy-talk show from Chicago, hosted by disc jockey Jonathon
Brandmeier.

JOHNNY BAGO   CBS

25 JUNE 1993–6 AUGUST 1993   Lighthearted hour series about an ex-con framed for
murder who jumped into a Winnebago camper and drove off, pursued by the mob
and by his ex-wife, who was also his parole officer. It starred Peter Dobson as Johnny
Tenuti (aka Johnny Bago) and Rose Abdoo as his pursuer, Beverly Florio. The series
was aired during prime time on the dates shown above, and also on CBS's late-night
schedule between 30 June and 18 August.

THE JOHNNY CARSON SHOW   CBS

30 JUNE 1955–29 MARCH 1956; 28 MAY 1956–28 SEPTEMBER 1956   Johnny Carson, who
later became famous as the host of the *Tonight* show, also hosted two game shows
(*Earn Your Vacation* and *Who Do You Trust*) as well as these two variety shows. The
first show, a Thursday-night half-hour series, featured Jill Corey, Virginia Gibson,
and Barbara Ruick. Broadcast from Hollywood, it went through several changes of
directors and writers before expiring after thirty-nine weeks. Carson, aged thirty,
then hosted a daytime half-hour show which replaced *The Robert Q. Lewis Show.*
Also featured were Glenn Turnbull, Betty Holt, Tommy Leonetti, and the New
Yorkers. Both programs showcased the young comedian's puckish style and frequently featured parodies of current films and commercials.

THE JOHNNY CASH SHOW   ABC

7 JUNE 1969–27 SEPTEMBER 1969; 21 JANUARY 1970–5 MAY 1971

JOHNNY CASH AND FRIENDS   CBS

29 AUGUST 1976–19 SEPTEMBER 1976   Both of Johnny Cash's variety series were taped at the Grand Ole Opry in Nashville. The first—*The Johnny Cash Show*—was introduced as a summer series and returned later as a midseason replacement. In addition to Cash it featured June Carter Cash (his wife), Carl Perkins, The Carter Family, the Statler Brothers, and the Tennessee Three. The second show—*Johnny Cash and Friends*—was a summer series and featured Cash, June Carter Cash, Steve Martin, Jim Varney, and Howard Mann. It was produced by Joseph Cates.

THE JOHNNY DUGAN SHOW   NBC

19 MAY 1952–5 SEPTEMBER 1952   Daytime variety half-hour, broadcast from Holly-wood, featuring singers Johnny Dugan, Barbara Logan, and Arch Presby.

THE JOHNNY JOHNSTON SHOW   CBS

22 JANUARY 1951–9 FEBRUARY 1951   Short-lived, forty-five-minute daytime variety show with singers Johnny Johnston and Rosemary Clooney.

JOHNNY JUPITER   DUMONT/ABC

21 MARCH 1953–13 JUNE 1953 (DUMONT); 5 SEPTEMBER 1953–29 MAY 1954 (ABC)

On this imaginative kids' show an Earthling was able to communicate with the inhabitants of Jupiter. On the DuMont version, Vaughn Taylor starred as Ernest P. Duckweather, a television studio janitor who stumbled upon interplanetary TV. On the ABC version Wright King played Duckweather, who was then employed as a store clerk whose hobby was electronics. Jerry Coopersmith wrote and produced the series; Frank Bunetta directed. The Jupiterians were all puppets: Johnny Jupiter, B-12, and Major Domo, B-12's robot. Carl Harms was the puppeteer, and Gilbert Mack supplied the voices. Also featured on the latter version were Pat Peardon as Duckweather's girlfriend, and Cliff Hall as her father, Duckweather's boss.

JOHNNY MIDNIGHT   SYNDICATED

1960   Standard crime show starring Edmond O'Brien as New York private eye, and ex-actor, Johnny Midnight. Also featured were Arthur Batanides as Sergeant Oli-vera; Barney Phillips as Lieutenant Geller; and Yuki Shimoda as Aki, Midnight's manservant. Jack Chertok produced the series.

JOHNNY OLSON'S RUMPUS ROOM   DUMONT

17 JANUARY 1949–4 JULY 1952   Daytime variety and audience participation show hosted by Johnny Olson. Olson is better remembered as the announcer on numerous game shows, including *What's My Line?* and *I've Got a Secret.*

JOHNNY RINGO   CBS

1 OCTOBER 1959–29 SEPTEMBER 1960   Half-hour western starring Don Durant as Johnny Ringo, an ex-gunslinger who became the sheriff of Velardi, Arizona. Ringo kept a lid on trouble with the help of his trusty firearm, a LeMat Special with two barrels—one fired six .45 caliber rounds, and the other held a shotgun shell. Durant himself wrote and sang the show's theme. Also featured were Mark Goddard as his young deputy, Cully; Karen Sharpe as Ringo's girlfriend, Laura Thomas; and Ter-ence de Marney as oldtimer Case Thomas, Laura's father, owner of the general store (Sharpe and de Marney were dropped from the cast in March 1960). Aaron Spelling produced the series for Four Star Films.

JOHNNY STACCATO

See STACCATO

THE JOHNS HOPKINS SCIENCE REVIEW   DUMONT

3 OCTOBER 1950–20 APRIL 1953

JOHNS HOPKINS FILE 7   SYNDICATED

1956–1958   Lynn Poole, faculty member of Johns Hopkins University, hosted both of these public affairs shows, which were produced at WAAM-TV in Baltimore.

JOKEBOOK   NBC

23 APRIL 1982–7 MAY 1982   A rare prime-time cartoon series, *Jokebook* consisted of several animated skits put together by Hanna-Barbera Studios. Among the regular segments were "The Nerd," "Eve and Adam," "WindUps," and "Treeman."

THE JOKER'S WILD   CBS/SYNDICATED

4 SEPTEMBER 1972–13 JUNE 1975 (CBS); 1976–1986; 1990–1991 (SYNDICATED) Jack Barry originally hosted this game show on which two contestants took turns spinning devices that resembled slot machines for the chance to answer questions worth $50, $100, or $150. The first player to win $500 then had the chance to go for as much as $25,000. Barry's longtime partner, Dan Enright, was the executive producer of the series, which had a three-year daytime run on CBS before going into syndication. In 1980 a children's version appeared in syndication, titled *Joker! Joker!! Joker!!!* After Barry's death in May 1984, Bill Cullen took over as the host of *The Joker's Wild.* Pat Finn emceed the 1990 revival.

THE JON STEWART SHOW   SYNDICATED

1994–1995   Hour daily talk show, intended for late-night time slots and hosted by Jon Stewart, with sidekick Howard Feller. Stewart had previously hosted two series on MTV: *You Wrote It, You Watch It,* and a talk show similar to this one, also titled *The Jon Stewart Show.*

THE JONATHAN WINTERS SHOW   NBC/CBS

2 OCTOBER 1956–25 JUNE 1957 (NBC); 27 DECEMBER 1967–22 MAY 1969 (CBS)   Jonathan Winters, an inventive and improvisational funny man, appeared on many variety shows during the early 1950s, including *The Garry Moore Show* and *Tonight.* In 1955 he was a regular on a summer variety series, *And Here's the Show.* In the fall of 1956 he was given his own fifteen-minute show on Tuesdays before the evening news; this was the first network entertainment series to use videotape regularly. Late in 1967 he returned as host of a Wednesday-night variety hour, which replaced *Dundee and the Culhane.* Joining him were Abby Dalton (who often played his wife in sketches), Cliff Arquette (as Charley Weaver), Pamela Rodgers, Alice Ghostley, and Paul Lynde. Winters later starred in a syndicated show: see *The Wacky World of Jonathan Winters.*

JONES & JURY   SYNDICATED

1994–1995   Half-hour daily talk show hosted by Star Jones. The studio audience served as the show's "jury," voting on how best to settle disputes between the parties who appeared on the program.

JONNY QUEST (THE ADVENTURES OF JONNY QUEST)   ABC/CBS/NBC

18 SEPTEMBER 1964–9 SEPTEMBER 1965 (ABC); 9 SEPTEMBER 1967–5 SEPTEMBER 1970 (CBS); 13 SEPTEMBER 1970–2 SEPTEMBER 1972 (ABC); 8 SEPTEMBER 1979–3 NOVEMBER 1979 (NBC); 12 APRIL 1980–6 SEPTEMBER 1981 (NBC)   Hanna-Barbera cartoon series about a young boy—Jonny Quest—who accompanied his father, Dr. Benton Quest, a famous detective, on global adventures, along with pilot Race Bannon and Hadji. Tim Matheson provided the voice of Jonny; John Stephenson and, later, Don Messick, were the voice of Benton. Like several other Hanna-Barbera shows (*The Jetsons, Top Cat,* etc.), *Jonny Quest* was seen in prime time on ABC, and on weekend mornings over the other networks. The characters returned to television in an animated TV-movie, "Jonny's Golden Quest" (4 April 1993, USA).

JOSEPH CAMPBELL AND THE POWER OF MYTH   PBS

1 JULY 1988–5 AUGUST 1988   Though public television is often criticized for its boring documentary fare, this remarkable six-hour series demonstrated that "talking

heads" television can indeed be exciting. Here, in a series of discussions edited into one-hour segments, Bill Moyers explored the meaning of mythology and its relevance in modern society with scholar Joseph Campbell, who died shortly after the taping was completed.

THE JOSEPH COTTEN SHOW
See ON TRIAL

JOSEPH SCHILDKRAUT PRESENTS   DUMONT
28 OCTOBER 1953–21 JANUARY 1954   Half-hour filmed dramatic anthology series hosted by, and occasionally starring, Austrian-born actor Joseph Schildkraut. Ray Benson produced the show and Barry Shear directed it.

JOSIE AND THE PUSSYCATS   CBS/NBC
(JOSIE AND THE PUSSYCATS IN OUTER SPACE)
12 SEPTEMBER 1970–31 AUGUST 1974 (CBS); 6 SEPTEMBER 1975–4 SEPTEMBER 1976 (NBC)   Hanna-Barbera Saturday-morning cartoon show about an all-female rock group. The trio, Josie, Melody, and Valerie (who was probably TV's first black female cartoon character) were managed by Alexander Cabot III. From 1972 to 1974, the show was known as *Josie and the Pussycats in Outer Space*—in which the group accidentally blasted off into space.

JOURNEY THROUGH LIFE   CBS
30 MARCH 1953–2 APRIL 1954   Tom Reddy hosted this daytime show on which married couples talked about their lives together.

JOURNEY TO ADVENTURE   SYNDICATED
1954–1991   Gunther Less hosted this long-running half-hour travelogue. The series was produced by Sheridan-Elson Communications, using film from around the world. The Arts & Entertainment cable network began airing the series in 1987.

JOURNEY TO THE CENTER OF THE EARTH   ABC
9 SEPTEMBER 1967–30 AUGUST 1969   Saturday-morning cartoon show derived from Jules Verne's inner space novel.

JOURNEY TO THE UNKNOWN   ABC
26 SEPTEMBER 1968–30 JANUARY 1969   Undistinguished science fiction anthology hour, produced in England.

THE JOY OF PAINTING   PBS
1983–1995   Half-hour instructional series on landscape oil painting, hosted by Bob Ross, and taped at WIPB-TV in Muncie, Indiana. Ross, who died in 1995, was known as much for his soothing manner as for his remarkable ability to create a complete, original painting in under thirty minutes.

JUBILEE U.S.A.
See OZARK JUBILEE

JUDD FOR THE DEFENSE   ABC
8 SEPTEMBER 1967–19 SEPTEMBER 1969   Standard courtroom drama, starring Carl Betz as lawyer Clinton Judd and Stephen Young as his associate, Ben Caldwell. Executive producer: Paul Monash.

THE JUDGE   SYNDICATED
1986–1992   One of several courtroom dramas created in the wake of *The People's Court,* this one starred Bob Shield as Judge Robert Franklin, who presided over a variety of controversies, all of them fictionalized.

JUDGE FOR YOURSELF (THE FRED ALLEN SHOW)   NBC

18 AUGUST 1953–11 MAY 1954   Prime-time game show that began with Fred Allen as host and featured a panel of three celebrities and three members of the studio audience which judged talent acts; during its early weeks it was also known as *The Fred Allen Show*. In January the format was changed as Dennis James took over the hosting duties: The panel rated songs, which were performed by Kitty Kallen and Bob Carroll and the Skylarks. The series was a Mark Goodson-Bill Todman Production.

JUDGE FOR YOURSELF   SYNDICATED

1994–1995   Attorney Bill Handel hosted this hour daily talk show. Its gimmick was that a "jury" was selected from the studio audience, and cast its votes on either side of the day's topic of discussion.

JUDGE ROY BEAN   SYNDICATED

1956   Half-hour western set in Langtry, Texas, a town named for actress Lillie Langtry. Starring Edgar Buchanan as Judge Roy Bean, "the law west of the Pecos." With Jack Beutel as Jeff Taggert, his right-hand man; Jackie Loughery as Letty, his niece; and Russell Hayden as Steve, a Texas ranger. Judge Bean, a real-life character, was later the subject of a 1972 motion picture, *The Life and Times of Judge Roy Bean*, starring Paul Newman.

THE JUDY GARLAND SHOW   CBS

29 SEPTEMBER 1963–29 MARCH 1964   CBS had high hopes for this musical hour, but backstage problems and competition from NBC's *Bonanza* (the number-two-rated show that season) combined to ensure its doom. Much was done to keep the star happy—Judy Garland's dressing room even had a yellow brick road painted on it. Taping began in June 1963 with George Schlatter as executive producer; network officials, however, were unhappy after watching previews of the first shows, and Schlatter was replaced after five hours had been completed (the shows were not broadcast in the order in which they had been taped). Norman Jewison, who had produced and directed many musical-comedy specials, became the new executive producer and Gary Smith the new producer. Mort Lindsey lasted through the entire season as musical director, but Mel Tormé, an old friend of Garland's who had been hired to do her vocal arrangements, left in the winter after Bobby Cole had been brought aboard. Despite the production problems, there were several noteworthy shows, including one that featured Ethel Merman and Barbra Streisand, another with Danny Kaye, one with Garland's two daughters (Lorna Luft and Liza Minnelli), and one or two solo concerts. Mel Tormé also appeared occasionally, and Jerry Van Dyke was featured as a regular.

THE JUDY LYNN SHOW   SYNDICATED

1969–1971   Half-hour country-and-western music show, hosted by singer Judy Lynn.

JUDY SPLINTERS   NBC

13 JUNE 1949–30 JUNE 1950   This weekday puppet show originated from Los Angeles, where it began locally in 1948. The puppeteer, Shirley Dinsdale, was TV's first Emmy winner.

JUKE-BOX   SYNDICATED

1978–1980   Half-hour rock music show hosted first by Twiggy, the famous fashion model of the 1960s, and later by Britt Ekland.

JUKEBOX JURY   ABC/SYNDICATED

13 SEPTEMBER 1953–28 MARCH 1954 (ABC); 1959 (SYNDICATED)   Peter Potter hosted this game show on which a celebrity panel rated new records and predicted whether each recording would be a hit or a miss. For many years the show was seen locally in Los Angeles.

JULIA   **NBC**

17 SEPTEMBER 1968–25 MAY 1971   The first TV series since *Beulah* to star a black woman, *Julia* was a half-hour situation comedy about a widowed nurse trying to raise her young son. Diahann Carroll, a singer with motion picture experience, starred as Julia Baker; her husband, an Air Force pilot, had been killed in Vietnam, and she took a job as a nurse at an aerospace company in Los Angeles. Also featured were Marc Copage (who was six when the show began) as her son, Corey; Lloyd Nolan as Dr. Morton Chegley, her boss; Lurene Tuttle as Hannah Yarby, chief nurse at the plant; Michael Link as Earl J. Waggedorn, Corey's best friend; Betty Beaird as Marie Waggedorn, Earl's mom; Hank Brandt as Leonard Waggedorn, Earl's dad; Eddie Quillan as Eddie Edwards, a plant employee; Mary Wickes as Melba Chegley, Dr. Chegley's wife; Ned Glass as Julia's landlord, Sol Cooper; Alison Mills (1968–1969) as Carol Deering, a mother's helper who assisted Julia; Virginia Capers (1968–1969) as Mrs. Deering, Carol's mother; Paul Winfield (1969–1970) as Julia's occasional boyfriend, Paul Cameron; Fred Williamson (1970–1971) as Julia's boyfriend, Steve Bruce, a widower; Stephanie James as Kim, Steve's four-year-old daughter; Janear Hines (1970–1971) as babysitter Roberta; and Richard Steele (1970–1971) as Richard, a friend of Corey's. Produced by Hal Kanter for 20th Century-Fox.

JULIA CHILD & COMPANY   **PBS**

1978–1979   Half-hour cooking show, hosted by Julia Child, the star of *The French Chef.*

JULIE   **ABC**

30 MAY 1992–4 JULY 1992   Half-hour sitcom about a TV star who moved her show to Sioux City, Iowa, so that she could be with her new husband. With Julie Andrews as the star, Julie Carlisle; James Farentino as the husband, Dr. Sam McGuire, a veterinarian; Hayley Tyrie as Sam's fourteen-year-old daughter, Alley; Rider Strong as Sam's ten-year-old son, Adam; Eugene Roche as Julie's producer, I. F. "Wooley" Woolstein; Laurel Cronin as Bernie, the housekeeper; and Kevin Scannell as Dickie Duncan, an employee of the local TV station.

THE JULIE ANDREWS HOUR   **ABC**

13 SEPTEMBER 1972–28 APRIL 1973   Unsuccessful variety hour hosted by musical comedy star Julie Andrews and featuring Alice Ghostley and Rich Little. Produced by Nick Vanoff, the show was packaged by British impresario Sir Lew Grade's ITC operation.

THE JULIUS LaROSA SHOW   **CBS/NBC**

27 JUNE 1955–23 SEPTEMBER 1955 (CBS); 14 JULY 1956–4 AUGUST 1956; 15 JUNE 1957–7 SEPTEMBER 1957 (NBC)   After his dismissal from *Arthur Godfrey Time,* singer Julius LaRosa made guest appearances on many shows and hosted his own variety shows for three summers. In 1955 he was seen for fifteen minutes on Mondays, Wednesdays, and Fridays following the network news, backed by the Debutones. In 1956 and 1957, he replaced Perry Como for the summer.

THE JUNE ALLYSON SHOW   **CBS**
(THE DuPONT SHOW STARRING JUNE ALLYSON)

21 SEPTEMBER 1959–12 JUNE 1961   Half-hour dramatic anthology series hosted by, and occasionally featuring, June Allyson. The series was filmed at Four Star Films, a studio founded by Allyson's husband, Dick Powell, and others. Notable guest appearances included those by Ginger Rogers ("The Tender Shoot," 19 October 1959) and Harpo Marx ("Silent Panic," 22 December 1960, one of his last TV appearances).

THE JUNE HAVOC SHOW   **SYNDICATED**

1964   Hour-long talk show hosted by June Havoc (sister of Gypsy Rose Lee).

JUNGLE BOY (ADVENTURES OF A JUNGLE BOY)   SYNDICATED

1958   Filmed on location in Kenya, this children's adventure series starred fourteen-year-old Michael Carr Hartley as Boy, the only survivor of a plane crash in Africa, who generally fended for himself in the wilds. Also on hand was Ronald Adam as Dr. Laurence, a research scientist.

JUNGLE JIM   SYNDICATED

1955   Not to be confused with *Ramar of the Jungle*, *Jungle Jim* was based on the comic strip and starred former Olympian Johnny Weissmuller as an African guide. Also featured were Martin Huston as Skipper, his son; Norman Fredric as Kassim, his aide (Fredric was later known as Dean Fredericks and starred in *Steve Canyon*); and Tamba the chimp.

JUNGLE MACABRE   SYNDICATED

1953   A series of fifteen-minute wildlife films.

JUNIOR ALMOST ANYTHING GOES   ABC

11 SEPTEMBER 1976–4 SEPTEMBER 1977   Kids' game show, based on *Almost Anything Goes*, featuring teams of children representing different localities. Hosted by Soupy Sales.

JUNIOR HI-JINX   CBS

2 MARCH 1952–25 MAY 1952   Sunday-morning children's show hosted by Warren Wright and his puppet, Willie the Worm. The show was seen locally in Philadelphia for several seasons in addition to its brief network run.

JUNIOR PRESS CONFERENCE   ABC

23 NOVEMBER 1952–8 NOVEMBER 1953   A public affairs program for young people on which newsmakers were quizzed by a panel of children. Similar shows were also presented by the other networks: see, for example, *The New York Times Youth Forum* and *Youth Wants to Know*.

JUST FRIENDS   CBS

4 MARCH 1979–11 AUGUST 1979   Officially titled *Stockard Channing in Just Friends*, this half-hour sitcom starred Stockard Channing as Susan Hughes, a woman who left her husband in Boston to find a new life for herself in Los Angeles. Also featured were Mimi Kennedy as her sister, Victoria; Gerrit Graham as Leonard Scribner, her new neighbor; Lou Criscuolo as Milt D'Angelo, owner of the Beverly Hills Fountain of Youth Health Spa, where Susan got a job; Albert Insinnia as Angelo D'Angelo, Milt's son; and Sydney Goldsmith as Coral, a co-worker at the health spa. Executive producer: David Debin for Little Bear Productions. Though *Just Friends* left the air in August 1979, it remained in production as a potential midseason replacement. See also *The Stockard Channing Show*.

THE JUST GENERATION   PBS

1 OCTOBER 1972–24 DECEMBER 1972   Thirteen-part informational series on the law, hosted by Howard Miller, with help from the Ace Trucking Company.

JUST IN TIME   ABC

6 APRIL 1988–18 MAY 1988   A six-episode half-hour sitcom set at the offices of a magazine, *West Coast Review*, where the new editor and the top columnist found themselves at odds professionally, but attracted to each other personally. With Tim Matheson as editor Harry Stadlin; Patricia Kalember as political columnist Joanna Farrell; Kevin Scannell as sports columnist Jack Manning; Alan Blumenfeld as Steven Birnbaum, Harry's assistant; Ronnie Claire Edwards as secretary Carly Hightower; and Nada Despotovich as the rookie office assistant Isabel Miller. Fred Barron created the series. ABC would have better luck a year later with a sitcom set at a magazine: see *Anything But Love*.

JUST MEN!   NBC
3 JANUARY 1983–1 APRIL 1983   Betty White hosted this daytime game show, on which two female contestants tried to win money by predicting the answers of a panel of seven male celebrities.

JUST OUR LUCK   ABC
20 SEPTEMBER 1983–27 DECEMBER 1983   In this half-hour sitcom a bumbling TV weather forecaster bought an old bottle at a flea market; when he got it home, the bottle opened and out popped Shabu, a black genie, unleashed after 196 years in the bottle. The cast included T. K. Carter as the hip genie, Shabu, who swore allegiance to the weatherman; Richard Gilliland as the KPOX-TV weatherman, Keith Burrows; Ellen Maxted as Keith's superior, program director Meagan Huxley; Rod McCary as Meagan's fiance, Nelson Marriott, manager of the station; Hamilton Camp as Professor Bob, another on-the-air personality; Leonard Simon as Jim Dexter, the news anchorman; and Richard Schaal as Keith's neighbor, Chuck. Lawrence Gordon and Charles Gordon created the series, which was assailed by many civil rights organizations for its characterization of a black as the thankful servant of a white. The N.A.A.C.P. announced in October that it had won some changes in the show's content, including the addition of Leonard Simon (a black) to the cast, the assignment of some scripts to black writers, the deletion of the words "master" and "servant" from the dialogue, and less "jive talk" from Shabu.

JUST THE TEN OF US   ABC
26 APRIL 1988–17 MAY 1988; 23 SEPTEMBER 1988–26 JULY 1990   In this sitcom, spun off from *Growing Pains,* Bill Kirchenbauer starred as Coach Graham T. Lubbock, who, with his large family, left Long Island for Eureka, California, and a position at St. Augustine Academy for Boys. Also featured were Deborah Harmon as his wife, Elizabeth; Heather Langenkamp as daughter Marie; Brooke Theiss as daughter Wendy; Jamie Luner as daughter Cindy; Jo Ann Willette as daughter Constance; Heidi Zeigler as daughter Sherry; Matt Shakman as son Graham Jr.; Jeremy and Jason Korstjens as Toddler Harvey (Baby Melissa was the tenth Lubbock); and Frank Bonner as Father Hargis. By special arrangement, Lubbock was able to have his daughters attend the all-boys school. By the end of the 1988–1989 season the four oldest daughters had formed a singing group, the Lubbock Babes, who performed frequently on the show.

JUSTICE   NBC
8 APRIL 1954–25 MARCH 1956   Half-hour dramatic series about lawyers for the Legal Aid Society of New York. With Dane Clark (1954–1955) and William Prince (1955–1956) as Richard Adams; and Gary Merrill (1954–1955) as Jason Tyler.

JUVENILE JURY   NBC/CBS/SYNDICATED
3 APRIL 1947–28 SEPTEMBER 1953 (NBC); 11 OCTOBER 1953–14 SEPTEMBER 1954 (CBS); 2 JANUARY 1955–27 MARCH 1955 (NBC); 1970 (SYNDICATED)   A panel of youngsters dispensed unrehearsed advice to questions sent in by viewers. Jack Barry, who created the series and brought it to radio in 1946, hosted the several television versions and produced it with his partner, Dan Enright. The duo later went into game shows, producing such programs as *Twenty-One, Tic Tac Dough,* and *The Joker's Wild.* Barry also hosted a popular children's show during the 1950s: see *Winky Dink and You.* In 1983 a new version of *Juvenile Jury,* with Nipsey Russell as host, was produced for the Black Entertainment Television cable service.

THE KAISER ALUMINUM HOUR   NBC
3 JULY 1956–18 JUNE 1957   This hour-long dramatic anthology series alternated with *Armstrong Circle Theater* on Tuesdays and is one of the several dramatic shows which comprised TV's so-called "Golden Age." During its one-season run, it employed the directing talents of men such as Worthington Miner, Franklin Schaffner, Fielder Cook, and George Roy Hill. Notable presentations included: "The Army Game," with Paul Newman, Philip Abbott, and George Grizzard (3 July); a modern version

of "Antigone," with Claude Rains and Marisa Pavan (11 September); Steven Gethers's "The Rag Jungle," with Paul Newman (20 November); and "The Deadly
Silence," with Harry Guardino (21 May).

KALEIDOSCOPE   SYNDICATED
1953   John Kieran hosted this fifteen-minute series of films about science and
nature.

KALEIDOSCOPE   NBC
2 NOVEMBER 1958–17 MAY 1959   This wide-ranging Sunday-afternoon series was
described by the network as "an ambitious new experimental series." Some shows
were produced by the NBC news department, others by the program department.
Former *Twenty-One* winner Charles Van Doren hosted the series, which alternated
biweekly with *Omnibus.*

THE KALLIKAKS   NBC
3 AUGUST 1977–31 AUGUST 1977   Uninspired sitcom about a family which moved
from Appalachia to California. With David Huddleston as J. T. Kallikak, gas station
proprietor; Edie McClurg as Venus, his wife; Patrick J. Petersen as Junior, their son;
Bonnie Ebsen as Bobbi Lou, their daughter, who worked at a nearby fried chicken
stand; and Peter Palmer as Oscar, J. T.'s employee. Created by Roger Price and
Stanley Ralph Ross, the series was produced by George Yanok.

THE KARATE KID   NBC
9 SEPTEMBER 1989–1 SEPTEMBER 1990   Half-hour Saturday-morning cartoon show
based on the trilogy of films about a youngster who learns the martial arts and self-
confidence from a Japanese mentor. In the TV series, the boy, Daniel, and his
mentor, Mr. Miyagi, were accompanied by a girl, Taki.

KAREN   NBC
5 OCTOBER 1964–30 AUGUST 1965   *Karen* began as one segment of *90 Bristol Court,* a
troika of sitcoms all set at the same apartment complex. *Karen's* two cotenants—
Harris Against the World and *Tom, Dick and Mary*—were both evicted by the network in midseason, and *Karen* continued alone for the remainder of the year. The
show featured Debbie Watson as typical teenager Karen Scott; Richard Denning as
her dad, Steve; Mary LaRoche as her mom, Barbara; Gina Gillespie as her little
sister, Mimi; Bernadette Withers as her friend Janis; Trudi Ames as her friend
Candy; Teddy Quinn as her friend Peter; and Murray MacLeod as her friend Spider.
Guy Raymond, as Cliff Murdock, the building handyman, was featured in all three
segments of *90 Bristol Court.* Richard Dreyfuss, later to star in such colossal films as
American Graffiti, Jaws, and *Close Encounters of the Third Kind,* was also featured
occasionally as David, another of Karen's many friends. The *Karen* theme was sung
by the Beach Boys.

KAREN   ABC
30 JANUARY 1975–19 JUNE 1975   Topical sitcom, set in Washington, D.C. With
Karen Valentine as Karen Angelo, a young lobbyist for Open America, a progressive
citizens' lobby; Dena Dietrich as Dena Madison, one of her co-workers; Charles
Lane as irascible Dale Busch, the head of Open America (Denver Pyle played Busch
in the premiere episode); Will Seltzer as Adam Cooperman, the office boy; Aldine
King as Karen's roommate, Cissy Peterson, an FBI agent; Oliver Clark as Jerry
Siegel, a neighbor; Alix Elias as Cheryl Siegel, Jerry's wife; and Joseph Stern as
Ernie Stone, a friend of Karen's. Executive producers: Gene Reynolds and Larry
Gelbart (producers of *M*A*S*H*) for 20th Century-Fox.

KAREN'S SONG   FOX
18 JULY 1987–12 SEPTEMBER 1987   Linda Marsh and Margie Peters created this half-
hour sitcom about a divorced literary agent, nearing her fortieth birthday, who
landed a new job with a publishing company, moved into a new condo, and fell in

love with a man twelve years her junior. With Patty Duke as Karen Matthews; Lewis Smith as twenty-eight-year-old caterer Steven Forman; Teri Hatcher as her eighteen-year-old daughter, Laura; Lainie Kazan as Claire Steiner, Karen's best friend; Charles Levin as neighbor Michael Brand; and Granville Van Dusen as Karen's ex, Zach Matthews.

KATE & ALLIE CBS

19 MARCH 1984–7 MAY 1984; 27 AUGUST 1984–12 SEPTEMBER 1988; 11 DECEMBER 1988–11 SEPTEMBER 1989   A sitcom about two women who had been friends in high school and who, after their respective divorces, shared a Greenwich Village apartment with their children. Featured were Susan Saint James as Kate McArdle; Jane Curtin as Allie Lowell; Ari Meyers (1984–1988) as Kate's daughter, Emma; Allison Smith as Allie's daughter, Jennie; and Frederick Koehler as Allie's son, Chip. Occasionally appearing were John Heard and Harley Venton as Kate's ex, Max McArdle, and Paul Hecht as Allie's ex, Charles Lowell. Kate soon found an occasional boyfriend, plumber Ted Bartelo (played by Gregory Salata), and in December 1986 Allie met sportscaster Bob Barsky (played by Sam Freed, who had previously played two other roles on the show). After a lengthy courtship, Allie and Bob were married in 1988, and invited Kate to move in with them in their new condo. By that time, the two daughters, Emma and Jennie, had enrolled at Columbia University, and Kate and Allie had started a catering business together. Peter Onorati joined the cast in 1988 as Lou Corello, superintendent of the building where Kate and Allie and Bob (who now commuted to his job in Washington) lived.

The series was created by Sherry Koben, who got her inspiration while attending her tenth high school reunion, at which she encountered a large number of divorced women with children.

KATE LOVES A MYSTERY (MRS. COLUMBO) NBC

26 FEBRUARY 1979–29 MARCH 1979; 9 AUGUST 1979–6 SEPTEMBER 1979; 18 OCTOBER 1979–6 DECEMBER 1979   An hour crime show starring Kate Mulgrew as Kate Columbo, wife of Lieutenant Columbo (the character played by Peter Falk on *Columbo;* Columbo's wife was never seen on his series, and he was never seen on hers), a part-time reporter for the *Weekly Advertiser* and an amateur sleuth. The show premiered under the title *Mrs. Columbo* in February 1979, and underwent several changes of title between September and October. It was first changed to *Kate Columbo,* then to *Kate the Detective,* before *Kate Loves a Mystery* was selected just before the October return date. Also featured were Lili Haydn as Jenny, the Columbos' young daughter; Henry Jones as Mr. Alden, publisher of the newspaper; and Don Stroud (fall 1979) as Sergeant Varick. The series was produced by Universal TV.

KATE McSHANE CBS

10 SEPTEMBER 1975–12 NOVEMBER 1975   An early fatality of the 1975–1976 season, *Kate McShane* perished opposite ABC's *Starsky and Hutch.* It starred Anne Meara as Kate McShane, a gutsy lawyer; Sean McClory as Pat McShane, her father, an ex-cop who worked as Kate's investigator; and Charles Haid as Edmond McShane, her brother, a Jesuit priest who doubled as a law professor. E. Jack Neuman, who created the series, was its executive producer; Robert Stambler and Robert Foster produced it. The pilot was televised 11 April 1975.

THE KATE SMITH HOUR NBC
25 SEPTEMBER 1950–18 JUNE 1954
THE KATE SMITH EVENING HOUR NBC
19 SEPTEMBER 1951–11 JUNE 1952
THE KATE SMITH SHOW CBS
25 JANUARY 1960–18 JULY 1960   Kate Smith, the solid singer who was the butt of countless "fat" jokes throughout her show business career, hosted several radio programs from 1930 through 1951. Her first, and most successful, television program—*The Kate Smith Hour*—premiered in 1950 and ran four years in a late afternoon slot,

Mondays through Fridays. Appearing with her was her long-time manager, Ted Collins, who also produced the show with Barry Wood. The show was usually divided into discrete fifteen-minute segments, the composition of which changed over the years. Typical segments included "The Cracker Barrel," in which guests were interviewed; "America Sings," in which Smith and her guests performed musical numbers; "The House in the Garden," a continuing drama which was an outgrowth of *Fairmeadows, U.S.A.* (see also that title); "The World of Mr. Sweeney," a continuing comedy which later became a separate series (see also that title); "Ethel and Albert," a domestic comedy which also became a separate series (see also that title); and "The Story Princess," with Alene Dalton narrating stories for children. Kate Smith also hosted two prime-time series. The first, entitled *The Kate Smith Evening Hour,* was seen on Wednesdays during the 1951–1952 season; like the daytime show, it was directed by Greg Garrison, who later produced *The Dean Martin Show.* In 1960 she hosted a half-hour variety series on CBS, which also featured the Harry Simeone Chorus. After that she made a few guest appearances. She attracted attention in 1976 when she sang "God Bless America" at the Philadelphia Flyers' ice hockey games.

THE KATHI NORRIS SHOW NBC
1 MAY 1950–9 OCTOBER 1951   Daytime talk show, primarily for women, hosted by Kathi Norris.

THE KATHRYN KUHLMAN SHOW
See I BELIEVE IN MIRACLES

KAY KYSER'S KOLLEGE OF MUSICAL KNOWLEDGE
See COLLEGE OF MUSICAL KNOWLEDGE

KAY O'BRIEN CBS
25 SEPTEMBER 1986–13 NOVEMBER 1986   Life at New York's Manhattan General Hospital was depicted on this hour medical drama. With Patricia Kalember as Dr. Kay "Kayo" O'Brien, surgical resident; Brian Benben as Dr. Mark Doyle, her sexist rival; Keone Young as Dr. Michael Kwan; Lane Smith as Dr. Robert Moffitt, Kayo's mentor; Tony Soper as intern Cliff Margolis; Jan Rubes as Dr. Josef Wallach, chief of surgery; and Priscilla Lopez as E/R nurse Rosa Villanueva. *Kay O'Brien* was filmed in Toronto, partly at a real hospital. The series was briefly alluded to in NBC's rival medical drama, *St. Elsewhere*; in a fall 1986 episode, one *St. Elsewhere* physician mentioned to another that "O'Brien" had gone to New York, whereupon the other slyly retorted, "I'll bet she won't last thirteen weeks." He was right.

KAZ CBS
10 SEPTEMBER 1978–19 AUGUST 1979   An hour crime show set in Los Angeles, starring Ron Leibman as Martin Kazinski, a lawyer who earned his degree the hard way—while serving time in prison. Also featured were Patrick O'Neal as Samuel Bennett, the successful attorney who agreed to hire Kaz; Mark Withers as Peter Colcourt, a junior partner at Bennett's firm; Edith Atwater as Mrs. Fogel, the firm's chief secretary; Linda Carlson as Kaz's friend, newspaper reporter Katie McKenna; Dick O'Neill as Malloy, Kaz's streetwise friend; Gloria LeRoy as Mary Parnell, owner of the Starting Gate, a nightspot where Kaz relaxed by playing the drums; and George Wyner as Frank Revko, an assistant district attorney. Ron Leibman and Don Carlos Dunaway created the series; Lee Rich and Marc Merson were the executive producers for Lorimar Productions.

THE KEANE BROTHERS SHOW CBS
12 AUGUST 1977–2 SEPTEMBER 1977   Four-week half-hour musical variety series, aimed principally at young viewers. Its hosts, brothers Tom and John Keane, aged thirteen and twelve, were reportedly the youngest people ever to host a prime-time series; both were talented musicians and singers. Also on hand were the Anita Mann Dancers. Pierre Cossette was the series' executive producer, Darryl Hickman its

producer. The show was created by Woody Kling and developed by Don Kirshner with Norman Lear.

THE KEEFE BRASSELLE SHOW   CBS
25 JUNE 1963–17 SEPTEMBER 1963   Keefe Brasselle hosted this variety hour, a summer replacement for *The Garry Moore Show*. Regulars included Ann B. Davis, French singer Noelle Adam, former boxer Rocky Graziano, the Bill Foster Dancers, and Charles Sanford's Orchestra. Brasselle later developed three series for CBS in 1964 (*The Baileys of Balboa, The Cara Williams Show,* and *The Reporter*) before retiring from show business.

KEEP IT IN THE FAMILY   ABC
12 OCTOBER 1957–8 FEBRUARY 1958   Each week on this Saturday-night quiz show, two five-member families competed against each other. Keefe Brasselle was the first host but was succeeded by Bill Nimmo.

KEEP ON CRUISIN'   CBS
9 JANUARY 1987–5 JUNE 1987   Another of CBS's sporadic attempts to devise a late-night Friday variety show, this one presented music and comedy from various Southern California locales. Rock-and-roller Stephen Bishop and comic Sinbad hosted until April, when comic Jimmy Aleck replaced Bishop.

KEEP ON TRUCKIN'   ABC
12 JULY 1975–2 AUGUST 1975   Four-week summer comedy-variety series hosted by impressionist Fred Travalena and featuring a group of newcomers: Franklin Ajaye, Rhonda Bates, Kathrine Baumann, Jeannine Burnier, Didi Conn, Charles Fleischer, Wayland Flowers, Larry Ragland, Marion Ramsey, Rhilo, Jack Riley (he played Mr. Carlin on *The Bob Newhart Show*), Gailard Sartain, and Richard Lee Sung. Frank Peppiatt and John Aylesworth produced the series.

KEEP POSTED   DUMONT
9 OCTOBER 1951–18 JANUARY 1954   Topical issues were debated on this half-hour public affairs program, which was developed by Lawrence Spivak and moderated by Martha Rountree. The show was titled *Keep Posted* for its first two seasons, when it was sponsored by the *Saturday Evening Post* magazine. In May of 1953, after the *Post* dropped its sponsorship, the show was retitled *The Big Issue*.

KEEP TALKING   CBS/ABC
8 JULY 1958–24 JUNE 1959 (CBS); 29 OCTOBER 1959–3 MAY 1960 (ABC)   This prime-time game show featured two teams of celebrities; each team was provided with a secret phrase that was supposed to be inserted into a dialogue improvised by the competitors. At the end of each round, each team tried to identify the secret phrase given to the opponents. Monty Hall was the first host of the series; he was succeeded late in 1958 by Carl Reiner, who was in turn succeeded by Merv Griffin when the show switched networks. Often seen on the celebrity panel were Morey Amsterdam, Joey Bishop, Peggy Cass, Pat Carroll, Ilka Chase, and Danny Dayton.

THE KELLY MONTEITH SHOW   CBS
16 JUNE 1976–7 JULY 1976   Four-week half-hour variety series hosted by comedian Kelly Monteith, also featuring Nellie Bellflower and Harry Corden. Executive producer: Robert Tamplin. Producer: Ed Simmons.

KEN BERRY'S WOW   ABC
15 JULY 1972–12 AUGUST 1972   Five-week summer variety hour showcasing the singing and dancing talents of Ken Berry, former star of *Mayberry R.F.D.* Other regulars included Teri Garr, Billy Van, Laura Lacey, Don Lane, Steve Martin, the New Seekers, the Jaime Rogers Dancers, and the Jimmy Dale Orchestra. Allan Blye and Chris Bearde, producers of *The Sonny and Cher Comedy Hour,* created the show.

THE KEN MURRAY SHOW   CBS
15 APRIL 1950–7 JUNE 1952; 8 FEBRUARY 1953–14 JUNE 1953   Vaudevillian Ken Murray hosted an hour-long variety show on Saturday nights for two seasons; early in 1953 he returned to host a half-hour show on Sundays, which alternated with *The Alan Young Show*. Also on hand were comedienne Laurie Anders ("Ah love the wide open spaces!"), Darla Hood (1950–1951, former star of the "Our Gang" comedies), Anita Gordon (1951–1952), Art Lund, Johnny Johnston, and the Glamourlovelies.

KENTUCKY JONES   NBC
19 SEPTEMBER 1964–11 SEPTEMBER 1965   Dennis Weaver left the *Gunsmoke* fold to star in this comedy-drama; he played Kentucky Jones, a widowed veterinarian who became the guardian of a ten-year-old Chinese orphan. Also featured were Ricky Der as his ward, Dwight Eisenhower (Ike) Wong; Harry Morgan as Seldom Jackson, a former jockey who assisted Dr. Jones on his ranch; Cherylene Lee as Annie Ng, Ike's friend; Arthur Wong as Mr. Ng, her father; Keye Luke as Mr. Wong, a friend of Dr. Jones; and Nancy Rennick as Miss Thorncroft, Ike's teacher.

KEY TO THE AGES   DUMONT
27 FEBRUARY 1955–22 MAY 1955   Half-hour cultural show hosted by Dr. Theodore Low. Broadcast from Baltimore, the show received much help from the Walters Art Gallery and the Enoch Pratt Free Library.

KEY TO THE MISSING   DUMONT
4 JULY 1948–23 SEPTEMBER 1949   Archdale Jones, "the finder of lost persons," hosted this half-hour documentary series, on which he interviewed people who were searching for long-lost friends and relatives.

KEY WEST   FOX
19 JANUARY 1993–16 MARCH 1993   Hour dramatic series about a New Jersey man who won the lottery and moved to Key West to write. With Fisher Stevens as writer Seamus O'Neill; Ivory Ocean as blind newspaper editor King Cole; Jennifer Tilly as Savannah, a prostitute with a heart of gold; T. C. Carson as Jo-Jo, a free-spirited, dreadlocked local; Leland Crooke as Gumbo, owner of Gumbo's Bar & Grill; Denise Crosby as Chaucy Caldwell, who waged a campaign for mayor; Lara Piper as Rikki; Brian Thompson as Cody Jefferson, the sheriff; Nicolas Surovy as Mayor Boone Penbroke, a gay man; Nita Whitaker as Mamie, a dolphin researcher; and Geno Silva as Julio, who worked at the newspaper.

KEYHOLE   SYNDICATED
1961   A series of half-hour documentaries and pseudo-documentaries filmed all over the world, produced and narrated by Jack Douglas. Distributed by Ziv TV.

KHAN!   CBS
7 FEBRUARY 1975–28 FEBRUARY 1975   This hour-long crime show lasted only four weeks. It featured Khigh Dhiegh (who had played Wo Fat, Steve McGarrett's archenemy, on *Hawaii Five-O*) as Khan, a private detective in San Francisco's Chinatown; Vic Tayback as Lieutenant Gubbins of the San Francisco police; Irene Yah-Ling Sun as Khan's daughter, Anna, a biophysics student at San Francisco State; and Evan Kim as Kim, Khan's son. Laurence Heath produced the series.

KID GLOVES   CBS
24 FEBRUARY 1951–18 AUGUST 1951   Broadcast from Philadelphia, *Kid Gloves* was a boxing show for very young boxers. Each week boys aged three and up fought each other in abbreviated three-round contests (each round lasted only thirty seconds). Bill Sears and John "Ox" Da Groza hosted the series, which was produced and directed by Alan Bergman.

KID 'N PLAY   NBC

8 SEPTEMBER 1990–7 SEPTEMBER 1991   Black rap artists Kid 'n Play, who had been featured in the 1989 film *House Party,* were the central characters in this half-hour Saturday-morning cartoon show. The animated pair was assisted by Herbie, their manager, and three female dancers: Lela, Play's sister, Marika, and Downtown Patty. The duo (whose real names, Christopher Martin and Christopher Reid, were not divulged in the program credits) also appeared in taped wraparounds at the beginning and end of each show.

KID POWER   ABC

16 SEPTEMBER 1972–1 SEPTEMBER 1974   Cartoon series based on the comic strip *Wee Pals*. The show was seen Saturday mornings during the 1972–1973 season, and reruns were broadcast Sunday mornings during the 1973–1974 season.

THE KID SUPER POWER HOUR WITH SHAZAM   NBC

12 SEPTEMBER 1981–11 SEPTEMBER 1982   Live action and cartoons were combined in this Saturday morning children's show, hosted by a seven-member rock band. Each member of the band was also represented by a cartoon character. The rockers included John Berwick as Rex Ruthless; Jere Fields as Misty Magic; Jim Greenleaf as Weatherman; Christopher Hensel as Captain California; Maylo McCaslin as Dirty Trixie; Becky Perle as Gorgeous Gal; and Johnny Venocour as Punk Rock. The cartoon segments included "Hero High" and "Shazam." Arthur H. Nadel produced the series.

KIDD VIDEO   NBC/CBS

15 SEPTEMBER 1984–4 APRIL 1987 (NBC); 19 SEPTEMBER 1987–26 DECEMBER 1987 (CBS)   This Saturday-morning kids' show was an imaginative blend of live action, cartoons, and rock videos. The story line centered around a four-piece rock band that was seized by the evil Master Blaster (assisted by the Copy Cats) and taken to the "flipside," where they became cartoon characters. The live performers included Gabriele Bennett as Carla; Robbie Rist as Whiz; Steve Alterman as Ash; and Bryan Scott as Kidd.

KIDS AND COMPANY   DUMONT

1 SEPTEMBER 1951–1 JUNE 1952   Saturday-morning kids' show cohosted by Johnny Olson (who was also hosting *Johnny Olson's Rumpus Room* five days a week) and cartoonist Ham Fisher, creator of *Joe Palooka*.

KIDS ARE PEOPLE TOO   ABC/SYNDICATED

10 SEPTEMBER 1978–7 NOVEMBER 1982 (ABC); 1986 (SYNDICATED)   Sunday-morning magazine series for children. It was hosted by Bob McAllister until January 1979, when Michael Young took over. Randy Hamilton succeeded Young in 1981, but Young returned to host the syndicated version in 1986.

THE KIDS FROM C.A.P.E.R.   NBC

11 SEPTEMBER 1976–3 SEPTEMBER 1977   Live-action Saturday kids' show about the four young operatives of C.A.P.E.R. (Civilian Authority for the Protection of Everyone Regardless). With John Lansing as Doc; Steve Bonino as P. T.; Cosie Costa as Bugs; and Biff Warren as Doomsday. Don Kirshner and Alan Landsburg produced the series.

THE KIDS IN THE HALL   HBO/CBS

21 JULY 1989–17 JANUARY 1990; 21 DECEMBER 1990–29 NOVEMBER 1992 (HBO); 18 SEPTEMBER 1992–6 JANUARY 1995 (CBS)   Half-hour series of comedy sketches, presented by the Canadian improvisational group The Kids in the Hall: Bruce McCulloch, Kevin McDonald, Dave Foley, Scott Thompson, and Mark McKinney. The Kids had previously starred in a comedy special, telecast on HBO in October 1988. The series was rerun on the Comedy Channel cable network beginning in 1991.

The CBS version, which was usually shown in a late-night time slot on Fridays, was comprised of edited portions of the HBO series, together with some new material.

KIDSWORLD   SYNDICATED
1976–1982   A half-hour magazine series for children, produced by the Behrens Company.

KIERNAN'S CORNER   ABC
16 AUGUST 1948–25 APRIL 1949   Half-hour interview show hosted by Walter Kiernan.

THE KILLY CHALLENGE   SYNDICATED
1969–1970   On this filmed sports series, former Olympic skiing champion Jean-Claude Killy faced challengers in head-to-head races for prizes of $10,000.

KIMBA THE WHITE LION   SYNDICATED
1966   Japanese-produced cartoon series about a white lion, Kimba, benevolent ruler of an African kingdom.

THE KING FAMILY SHOW   ABC
23 JANUARY 1965–8 JANUARY 1966; 12 MARCH 1969–10 SEPTEMBER 1969   This wholesome musical show featured the several dozen members of the King clan, none of whom was named King—all were descended from William King Driggs, who organized a family musical group in the 1930s. Three of his daughters—Maxine, Alyce, and Luise—later toured professionally as the King Sisters. After regrouping at a family reunion, the clan put on a show at Brigham Young University, which eventually led to an appearance on *The Hollywood Palace* and, later, to the first *King Family Show,* an hour-long series that replaced *The Outer Limits* early in 1965. The show was revived in 1969, this time in a half-hour version, to replace *Turn-On;* by that time thirty-six Kings appeared on camera, and one member—Tina Cole—was also a regular on *My Three Sons.*

KING KONG   ABC
10 SEPTEMBER 1966–31 AUGUST 1969   Saturday-morning cartoon series in which the giant ape was friendly and battled evil together with Professor Bond and his children; reruns were shown on Sunday mornings during the 1968–1969 season. Another segment was "Tom of T.H.U.M.B.," the adventures of a miniature secret agent (Tom) who was employed by the Tiny Humans Underground Military Bureau.

KING LEONARDO   NBC
15 OCTOBER 1960–28 SEPTEMBER 1963   Saturday-morning cartoon series about King Leonardo, beneficent leonine ruler of Bongoland, a peaceable African kingdom, and his pal, Odie Cologne, a skunk; together they battled two sinister villains, Biggy Rat and Itchy Brother. For part of its network run the show was titled *King Leonardo and His Short Subjects,* and in syndication it was known as *The King and Odie.*

KING OF DIAMONDS   SYNDICATED
1961   Half-hour adventure series from Ziv TV, starring Broderick Crawford as Johnny King, chief of security for the diamond industry. Also featured was Ray Hamilton as his right-hand man, Casey O'Brien.

KING OF KENSINGTON   SYNDICATED
1976   Canadian sitcom, presumably inspired by *All in the Family.* With Al Waxman as Larry King, typical blue-collar worker; Fiona Reid as Kathy, his wife; and Helene Winston as Gladys, Larry's live-in mother. Created and developed by Perry Rosemond.

KINGDOM OF THE SEA   SYNDICATED
1957   Half-hour documentaries about marine life, narrated by Robert Stevenson and John D. Craig.

KING'S CROSSING   ABC
16 JANUARY 1982–27 FEBRUARY 1982   This short-lived prime-time serial told the story of the Hollister family, who had returned to this small California town after a ten-year absence. The cast included: Mary Frann as Nan Hollister; Bradford Dillman as her alcoholic husband, Paul Hollister, a teacher and playwright; Linda Hamilton as their older daughter, Lauren, an accomplished pianist; Marilyn Jones as Carey, their younger daughter; Beatrice Straight as Nan's Aunt Louisa, who resented the Hollisters' return; Doran Clark as Cousin Jillian; and Daniel Zippi as Billy McCall, Louisa's horse trainer. The hour series was produced by Lorimar and bore a passing resemblance to two other Lorimar serials: *Secrets of Midland Heights,* its 1980 serial, which had featured Clark, Hamilton, and Zippi and was also set in a small town; and *Falcon Crest,* its 1981 serial in which a family had returned to its homestead against the wishes of a domineering matriarchal figure.

KING'S CROSSROADS   ABC
10 OCTOBER 1951–5 OCTOBER 1952   Film shorts, hosted by Carl King.

KING'S ROW   ABC
13 SEPTEMBER 1955–17 JANUARY 1956   *King's Row* was one segment of *Warner Brothers Presents,* which with *Casablanca* and *Cheyenne,* heralded Warner Brothers' entry into TV series production; only *Cheyenne* survived the first season. *King's Row,* set in a town of that name at the turn of the century, starred twenty-eight-year-old Jack Kelly (later star of *Maverick*) as Dr. Parris Mitchell, a psychiatrist. Also featured were Victor Jory as his mentor, Dr. Tower; Robert Horton as Drake; and Nan Leslie as Randy. Only seven or eight episodes were aired.

KINGSTON: CONFIDENTIAL   NBC
23 MARCH 1977–10 AUGUST 1977   Hour-long adventure series starring Raymond Burr as R. B. Kingston, a senior journalist for the Frazier News Group, a San Francisco-based consortium of newspapers and broadcasters. With Art Hindle as Tony Marino, a young reporter; Pamela Hensley as Beth Kelly, another young reporter; and Linda Galloway as Linda, Kingston's secretary. Executive producer: David Victor.

THE KIRBY STONE QUINTET   CBS
9 NOVEMBER 1949–23 JUNE 1950   Instrumental selections were played by the Kirby Stone Quintet on this fifteen-minute series that was seen several times a week at 7 P.M.

KIRK   WB
23 AUGUST 1995–   Half-hour sitcom starring Kirk Cameron as Kirk Hartman, a twenty-four-year-old who moved to New York City, hoping to find work as an illustrator. Instead, he got a job painting billboards and became the guardian of his three younger siblings (their parents had died sometime earlier, and the children's aunt had unexpectedly left town). Chelsea Noble, Cameron's wife, costarred as Kirk's romantic interest, Dr. Elizabeth Waters, an intern who lived in the apartment across the hall. Also featured were Louis Vanaria as Eddie, Kirk's former college roommate and current neighbor; Will Estes as Kirk's brother Corey; Taylor Fry as Kirk's sister, Phoebe; Courtland Mead as Kirk's brother Russell; and Debra Mooney as Sally the landlady.

KISSYFUR   NBC
13 SEPTEMBER 1986–5 SEPTEMBER 1987; 10 SEPTEMBER 1988–25 AUGUST 1990 Saturday-morning cartoon show about a young circus bear, Kissyfur, and his father, Gus, who settled in Paddlecab County, a swampy place where they made friends with

the other residents; Gus operated a ferry boat. The program was introduced in 1985 as a series of specials.

KIT CARSON (THE ADVENTURES OF KIT CARSON)   SYNDICATED
1951–1955   Bill Williams starred as Kit Carson, the famous scout, in this half-hour western from Revue Productions; Don Diamond costarred as his sidekick, El Toro. The series was directed by Richard Irving and Norman Lloyd.

KITTY FOYLE   NBC
13 JANUARY 1958–27 JUNE 1958   Daytime serial about an Irish secretary from Philadelphia who fell for a wealthy fellow; the series started on radio in 1942. On TV Kathleen Murray starred as Kitty Foyle. Also featured were Judy Lewis (as her friend, Molly Scharf), Billy Redfield, Ralph Dunne (as Kitty's father), Ginger MacManus, Marie Worsham, Lee Bergere, and eleven-year-old Patty Duke. Both the radio and TV versions were derived from the story by Christopher Morley.

KLONDIKE   NBC
10 OCTOBER 1960–13 FEBRUARY 1961   Low-budget adventure series set in Skagway, Alaska, during the Gold Rush of 1898. With Ralph Taeger as Mike Halliday, a young adventurer; Mari Blanchard as Kathy O'Hara, hotel owner; James Coburn as Jeff Durain, a fast-talking adventurer; and Joi Lansing as Goldie. In midseason the format was drastically changed—Taeger and Coburn were retained but were moved up to the twentieth century and south to Mexico: see *Acapulco*. William Conrad produced the series.

KNIGHT & DAYE   NBC
8 JULY 1989–14 AUGUST 1989   Short-lived summer sitcom about a pair of former radio stars who were reunited on a San Diego radio show, and promptly continued their feuding. With Jack Warden as Hank Knight; Mason Adams as Everett Daye; Hope Lange as Gloria, Everett's wife; Julia Campbell as station manager Janet Glickman; and Lela Ivey as Ellie, Everett's daughter.

KNIGHT RIDER   NBC
26 SEPTEMBER 1982–8 AUGUST 1986   This hour adventure series starred David Hasselhoff (formerly of *The Young and the Restless*) as Michael Long, an undercover cop who was killed; brought back to life by a mysterious millionaire, Wilton Knight, he was given a new identity—Michael Knight—and a specially equipped automobile, a Pontiac Trans Am with a talking computer. Known as KITT (Knight Industries Two Thousand), the car helped Knight on his various missions—aiding the unfortunate, tracking down crooks, and so on. Also featured were Edward Mulhare as Devon Miles, aide to the now-deceased millionaire; Patricia McPherson (1982–1983; 1984–1986) as mechanic Bonnie Barstow; Rebecca Holden (1983–1984) as April Curtis; and William Daniels as the voice of KITT's computer. Peter Parros was added in 1985 as Reginald Cornelius III ("RC3"), who drove the specially equipped truck that hauled KITT from adventure to adventure. The series was originally scheduled on Fridays at 9:00 p.m. and was the first NBC program in several years to hold its own against CBS's *Dallas*. It was moved to a Sunday time slot in its second and third seasons, and back to Fridays in 1985. Ninety episodes were produced.

Hasselhoff returned to the controls in a TV-movie, "Knight Rider 2000" (19 May 1991, NBC); this time he piloted an even fancier vehicle, the Knight 4000.

KNIGHTWATCH   ABC
10 NOVEMBER 1988–19 JANUARY 1989   The exploits of a community watch group, known as the Knights of the City, were chronicled on this hour crime show. The large cast included Benjamin Bratt as Tony Maldonado; Don Franklin as Calvin; Joshua Cadman as Condo; Ava Haddad as Casey; Calvin Levels as Burn; Ian Tracey as John O'Neill; Paris Vaughn as Leslie; Harley Kozak as Babs; Samantha Mathis as Jake; and Tim Guinee as Kurt. The low-rated series (116th out of 125 for the season) had the misfortune of premiering opposite the birth of Sondra's twins on NBC's jugger-

naut, *The Cosby Show*. Series regulars Bratt and Franklin were teamed up a year later on *Nasty Boys*.

KNOCKOUT   NBC
3 OCTOBER 1977–21 APRIL 1978   Daytime game show hosted by Arte Johnson and featuring three contestants. The object of the game was to score the word "Knockout" by winning the eight letters one or two at a time. A player earned one letter by identifying the one item among four which did not belong with the others; the player could then earn additional letters by identifying the common feature of the items or by successfully challenging another player to do so. The winning contestant then played a bonus round for a top prize of $5,000. The show was a Ralph Edwards Production.

KNOTS LANDING   CBS
27 DECEMBER 1979–13 MAY 1993   Second only to *Gunsmoke* as television's longest-running prime time dramatic series, *Knots Landing* was spun off from the hugely popular *Dallas*. As the hour serial unfolded, Gary Ewing, the middle brother of the *Dallas* Ewings, left Texas and bought a house on a cul-de-sac in Knots Landing, California. Featured were Ted Shackelford as Gary Ewing, an alcoholic; Joan Van Ark as his wife, Valene Ewing, who had remarried him; Michele Lee as their neighbor, Karen Fairgate; Don Murray (1979–1981) as Karen's husband, Sid Fairgate, owner of Knots Landing Motors (Sid was trapped in a car hurtling off a cliff at the end of the 1980–1981 season; when Don Murray demanded more money, Sid's accident was arranged to be fatal); Claudia Lonow (1979–1984) as their daughter, Diana; Pat Petersen (1979–1991) as their son Michael; Steve Shaw (1979–1987 and 1989–1990) as their son Eric; James Houghton (1979–1983) as neighbor Kenny Ward, a recording executive; Kim Lankford (1979–1983) as his wife, Ginger Ward; John Pleshette (1979–1983) as neighbor Richard Avery, an unscrupulous attorney; Constance McCashin (1979–1987) as his wife, Laura Avery; Donna Mills (1980–1989) as Sid Fairgate's sister, Abby Cunningham, a homewrecker who had affairs with most of the men and broke up the marriage of Gary and Valene; Bobby Jacoby (1980–1985) and Brian Greene (1986–1989) as Abby's son, Brian; Tonya Crowe as Abby's daughter, Olivia; Julie Harris (1981–1987) as Valene's mother, Lilimae Clements; Stephen Macht (1981–1983) as Joe Cooper; Lisa Hartman (1982–1983) as singer Ciji Dunne, who was murdered (Hartman returned the next season as Ciji's lookalike, waitress Cathy Geary); Michael Sabatino (1982–1983) as publicist Chip Roberts, Ciji's killer; Kevin Dobson (1982–1993) as attorney M. Patrick (Mack) MacKenzie, who married Karen Fairgate in January 1983; Douglas Sheehan (1983–1987) as Ben Gibson, who married Valene Ewing after her divorce from Gary; William Devane (1983–1993) as politician Gregory Sumner, who married Laura Avery; Danielle Brisebois (1983–1984) as his daughter, Mary-Frances; Alec Baldwin (1984–1985) as preacher Joshua Rush, Valene's half-brother; Howard Duff (1984–1985) as Paul Galveston, Greg Sumner's father; Ava Gardner (spring 1985, in a rare TV appearance) as Paul's widow, Ruth Galveston; Hunt Block (1985–1987) as senatorial candidate Peter Hollister, who was murdered; Leslie Hope (1985–1986) as Linda Martin; Teri Austin (1985–1989) as Jill Bennett; Nicollette Sheridan (1986–1993) as Mack's illegitimate daughter, Paige Matheson; Michelle Phillips (1987–1993) as Paige's mother, Anne Winston Matheson (a former member of the Mamas and the Papas, Phillips sang "Dedicated to the One I Love" to Kevin Dobson [Mack] on a March 1987 episode); Wendy Fulton (1986–1987) as Jean Hackney; Harry Townes (1986–1987) as Russell Winston; Red Buttons (1987–1988) as Al Baker; Lynne Moody (1988–1990) as Patricia Williams, a new resident of the cul-de-sac; Larry Riley (1988–1992) as her husband, Frank Williams; Kent Masters-King (1988–1992) as their daughter, Julie (the Williamses were participants in a federal witness relocation program); Peter Reckell (1988–1989) as Johnny Rourke; Sam Behrens (1989–1990) as Danny Waleska, who was briefly married to Valene; Paul Carafotes (1988–1989) as Harold Dyer, who married Olivia Cunningham; Melinda Culea (1989–1990) as Paula Vertosick; Robert Desiderio (1989–1990) as Ted Melcher; Betsy Palmer (1989–1990) as Virginia Bullock; Penny Peyser (1989–1990) as Amanda Michaels;

Lar Park-Lincoln (1989–1992) as Linda Fairgate; Kathleen Noone (1990–1993) as Greg's sister, Claudia Whittaker; Stacy Galina (1990–1993) as her daughter, Kate Whittaker (Galina had played her cousin, Mary-Frances, briefly during the previous season); Thomas Wilson Brown (1990–1992) as Jason Lochner; Guy Boyd (1990–1991) as Dick Lochner; Lance Guest (1990–1991) as photographer Steve Brewer; Tracy Reed (1990–1991) as Charlotte Anderson; Joseph Gian (1989–1993) as Tom Ryan; Lorenzo Caccialanza (1990–1993) as Nick Schillace; Felicity Waterman (1991–1993) as Vanessa Hunt; Boyd Kestner (1991–1992) as Alex Barth; Bruce Greenwood (1991–1992) as Pierce Lawton; Halle Berry (1991–1992) as Debbie; Stuart Pankin (1991–1992) as Benny; Mark Soper (1991–1992) as Joseph Barringer; Michelle Joyner (1991–1992) as Lynette; Marcia Cross (1991–1992) as Victoria; Maree Cheatham (1992–1993) as Mary Robeson, who was murdered; David James Elliott (1992–1993) as Bill; Tara Marchant (1992–1993) as Toni; Karen Ludwig (1992–1993) as Dr. Stren; Lance Slaughter (1992–1993) as Darryn Flint; and Daniel Gerroll (1992–1993) as Treadwell, a gangster. Claudia Lonow returned to the series briefly in the spring of 1993, and Donna Mills returned for *Knots Landing*'s final episode on 13 May 1993. The two-hour finale was preceded by the "Knots Landing Block Party," a one-hour special on which cast members reminisced about the series.

David Jacobs created the durable series. Unlike most of the other prime-time serials, *Knots Landing* was not overpopulated with larger-than-life characters. It more closely resembled the daytime serials with its emphasis on generally believable storylines and development of three-dimensional characters.

KOBBS CORNER   CBS
22 SEPTEMBER 1948–15 JUNE 1949   Wednesday-night half-hour variety series set at a general store, run by host Hope Emerson. In its earliest weeks the show was titled *Korn Kobblers*.

KODIAK   ABC
13 SEPTEMBER 1974–11 OCTOBER 1974   One of the first casualties of the 1974–1975 season, *Kodiak* was clobbered in the ratings by *Sanford and Son*. It starred Clint Walker (seldom seen on TV since his days as Cheyenne) as Cal McKay, an Alaskan cop nicknamed "Kodiak." Also featured were Abner Biberman as Abraham Lincoln Imhook, his Eskimo partner; Maggie Blye as Mandy, the dispatcher. Stan Shpetner, who created the series with Anthony Lawrence, was the producer.

KOJAK   CBS/ABC
24 OCTOBER 1973–15 APRIL 1978 (CBS); 4 NOVEMBER 1989–30 JUNE 1990 (ABC)   An internationally popular crime show, *Kojak* starred Telly Savalas as Lieutenant Theo Kojak, a savvy but incorruptible cop assigned to Manhattan South. Savalas first played the role in a 1973 TV-movie, "The Marcus-Nelson Murders," written by Abby Mann; the movie was based on the Wylie-Hoffert murders, which occurred in 1963. Savalas, who had often played heavies before landing the Kojak role, first appeared on television in an episode of the *Armstrong Circle Theater* in 1959; before that he had worked as a producer at WABC in New York, and had also assisted casting directors in locating foreign-speaking performers. Though he had much television and film experience (including an Academy Award nomination as Best Supporting Actor in *The Bird Man of Alcatraz*), it was not until his role as the Tootsie Pop-sucking Kojak that he became a superstar. Other regulars on the series included Kevin Dobson as Detective Bobby Crocker, Kojak's earnest right-hand man; Dan Frazer as Detective Captain Frank McNeil, his weary boss; George Savalas (Telly's brother) as Detective Stavros (George was billed as Demosthenes—his middle name—during the first two seasons); Mark Russell as Detective Saperstein; Vince Conti as Detective Rizzo; and Borah Silver as Detective Prince. Matthew Rapf was the executive producer and Jack Laird the supervising producer for Universal Television. One hundred eighteen episodes were made.

Kojak returned to television in a TV-movie, "Kojak: The Belarus File," shown 16 February 1985 on CBS. It featured Telly Savalas, George Savalas, and Dan Frazer from the old cast. A second TV-movie, "Kojak: The Price of Justice," was televised

21 February 1987. In the fall of 1989 Kojak again returned to series television, this time as one segment of *The ABC Saturday Mystery Movie*. Kojak was now an inspector. Other regulars included Andre Braugher as Detective Blake; Kario Salem as unorthodox young cop Paco Montana; and Candace Savalas as Pamela. Kevin Dobson, who had costarred in the original series and was now a regular on *Knots Landing*, returned in one episode as Bobby Crocker, who had become a prosecutor.

KOLCHAK: THE NIGHT STALKER
See THE NIGHT STALKER

THE KOPYKATS
See THE ABC COMEDY HOUR

KORG: 70,000 B.C. ABC
7 SEPTEMBER 1974–31 AUGUST 1975   Essentially a Neanderthal version of *The Waltons, Korg: 70,000 B.C.* was a live-action Saturday-morning show from Hanna-Barbera Productions about a Stone Age family of modest means. With Jim Malinda as Korg; Bill Ewing as Bok; Naomi Pollack as Mara; Christopher Man as Tane; Charles Morteo as Tor; and Janelle Pransky as Ree. Burgess Meredith narrated.

THE KRAFT MUSIC HALL NBC
8 OCTOBER 1958–20 MAY 1959; 13 SEPTEMBER 1967–12 MAY 1971   Kraft Foods sponsored this musical variety program. During the 1958–1959 season it was a half-hour show, hosted by Milton Berle. From 1959 until 1963 Kraft continued to sponsor musical variety shows, but they were known more commonly by other titles: see *The Dave King Show* and *The Perry Como Show*. The 1967 version of *The Kraft Music Hall* was an hour show, which lasted four seasons. It was hosted by a guest celebrity each week, except during the summer of 1969, when Tony Sandler and Ralph Young cohosted it; Judy Carne was also featured on that summer series. Don Ho hosted the show during the latter weeks of the summer of 1969.

KRAFT SUSPENSE THEATRE NBC
10 OCTOBER 1963–9 SEPTEMBER 1965   Hour-long mystery anthology series, sponsored by Kraft Foods. Katharine Ross made her TV dramatic debut in one episode, "Are There Any More Out There Like You?" (7 November 1963).

KRAFT TELEVISION THEATRE NBC/ABC
7 MAY 1947–1 OCTOBER 1958 (NBC); 15 OCTOBER 1953–6 JANUARY 1955 (ABC) *Kraft Television Theatre* best epitomizes television's Golden Age, an era when live, often original dramas were the rule, not the exception. The principal reason for the growth of original drama on TV was the unavailability of most plays—the major motion picture studios owned the rights to most plays not in the public domain and steadfastly refused to permit those works to be aired over a potentially competitive medium. Thus, the path was open for young writers to submit original scripts to the producers of TV's dramatic anthology series, and writers such as Rod Serling, Paddy Chayefsky, Reginald Rose, and Tad Mosel (to name only a few) immediately began to fill the void. Similarly, there was a need for directors, too; newcomers such as George Roy Hill, John Frankenheimer, and Fielder Cook (again, to name only a few) were soon directing telecasts regularly. Finally, there arose a need for talented performers—men and women who could learn their lines quickly, take direction, and perform their roles in a small, hot studio before an audience of machines and technicians. A small sample of the 650 plays presented on *Kraft* (summer reruns were unknown) indicates the large number of stars who appeared, many in their first starring role on television: "Double Door," with John Baragrey (7 May 1947); "Feathers in a Gale," with George Reeves (9 August 1950); "A Play for Mary," with Bramwell Fletcher (23 May 1951); "Ben Franklin," with Jocelyn Brando (30 May 1951); "The Easy Mark," with Jack Lemmon (5 September 1951); "Six by Six," with George Reeves (6 August 1952); "Duet," with Jack Lemmon (28 January 1953); "Snooksie," with Jack Lemmon (18 February 1953); "Double in Ivory," with Beverly

Whitney and Lee Remick (in her first major TV appearance, 9 September 1953); "To Live in Peace," with Anne Bancroft (her first major TV role, 16 December 1953); "The Missing Years," with Mary Astor and Tony Perkins (their first major TV roles, 3 February 1954); "Alice in Wonderland," with Robin Morgan as Alice, accompanied by Edgar Bergen and Charlie McCarthy, Art Carney (as The Mad Hatter), Ernest Truex (The White Knight), and Blanche Yurka (Queen of Hearts) (5 May 1954); "Romeo and Juliet," with Liam Sullivan and sixteen-year-old Susan Strasberg (9 June 1954); "A Connecticut Yankee in King Arthur's Court," with Edgar Bergen and Victor Jory (8 July 1954); "Strangers in Hiding," with Bradford Dillman (his first starring role, 29 December 1954); Rod Serling's "Patterns," with Ed Begley, Richard Kiley, and Everett Sloane (first telecast 12 January 1955, the drama was so highly acclaimed that it was repeated—live—four weeks later); "The Emperor Jones," with Ossie Davis, Everett Sloane, and Rex Ingram (23 February 1955); "The Diamond as Big as the Ritz," with Lee Remick, Elizabeth Montgomery, Signe Hasso, and George Macready (aired 28 September 1955, marking *Kraft*'s five-hundredth broadcast); "A Profile in Courage," with James Whitmore (16 May 1956; the drama was introduced by then Senator John F. Kennedy, from whose book the story was adapted); "Flying Object at Three O'Clock High," with George Peppard (20 June 1956, his first major TV role); "The Singin' Idol," with Tommy Sands and Fred Clark (30 January 1957); "Night of the Plague," with Maggie Smith (20 March 1957, her first American TV role); "Drummer Man," with Sal Mineo (1 May 1957); "The Curly-Headed Kid," with Warren Beatty (26 June 1957, his first major TV role); "The Big Heist," with Patty Duke (her first major role, 13 November 1957); and "The Sea Is Boiling Hot," with Sessue Hayakawa and Earl Holliman (12 March 1958). *Kraft Television Theatre* was actually introduced briefly in New York in 1940; it came to network television in 1947, where it was seen on Wednesdays for eleven seasons on NBC; Kraft also sponsored a second hour, under the same title, over ABC for a season and a half on Thursdays beginning in 1953.

THE KREISLER BANDSTAND   ABC
21 MARCH 1951–20 JUNE 1951   A half-hour musical series hosted by Fred Robbins and sponsored by the Jacques Kreisler Manufacturing Company, makers of watchbands. Benny Goodman's orchestra appeared on the premiere. Dick Gordon and George Foley produced the show, and Perry Lafferty directed it.

THE KROFFT SUPERSHOW   ABC
11 SEPTEMBER 1976–2 SEPTEMBER 1978
THE KROFFT SUPERSTAR HOUR   NBC
9 SEPTEMBER 1978–28 OCTOBER 1978   *The Krofft Supershow* began as a ninety-minute program, but was trimmed to sixty minutes in December of 1976. It was hosted by a rock band assembled for the show, Kaptain Kool and the Kongs: Michael Lembeck as Kaptain Kool, Debbie Clinger as Superchick, Mickey McMell as Turkey, and Louise Duart as Nashville. The foursome introduced the several segments that comprised the series. During the 1976–1977 season the segments included: "Electra-Woman and Dynagirl," the adventures of two female reporters who could turn into superheroes, with Deidre Hall as Mara/Electra-Woman, Judy Strangis as Lori/Dynagirl, and Norman Alden as Frank; "Wonderbug," the adventures of a fantastic automobile, with John Anthony Bailey, David Levy, and Carol Anne Sefflinger; "Dr. Shrinker," the adventures of a group of miniaturized humans, with Jay Robinson as Dr. Shrinker, Billy Barty as Hugo, Ted Eccles, Jeff McKay, and Susan Lawrence; and "The Lost Saucer," a 1975–1976 series that was reedited for the Krofft show (the latter segment was dropped in December 1976). For the 1977–1978 season the "Wonderbug" segment was retained, and two new ones were added: "Magic Mongo," the adventures of an inept genie; and "Bigfoot and Wildboy," the adventures of an apelike creature and a human teenager. In the fall of 1978 *The Krofft Superstar Hour* appeared on NBC; the hour musical and variety show was hosted by the Bay City Rollers, a popular recording group from Scotland. Late in October that series left the air, though the Bay City Rollers continued in a show of their own: see *The Bay City Rollers Show*. The Krofft shows were produced by Sid and Marty

Krofft, two brothers who started out as puppeteers, and who had previously produced several TV shows, including *H. R. Pufnstuf, Lidsville,* and *Far Out Space Nuts.*

THE KRYPTON FACTOR   ABC
7 AUGUST 1981–4 SEPTEMBER 1981   Dick Clark hosted this prime-time game show, on which four contestants competed in arithmetical exercises, on an obstacle course, in a memory test, and in a general knowledge quiz. The winner earned $5,000, and the four weekly winners battled each other on the finale for a grand prize of $50,000.

THE KUDA BUX SHOW   CBS
25 MARCH 1950–24 JUNE 1950   Saturday-night show starring Kuda Bux, the mysterious Hindu wizard who could perform wondrous feats while blindfolded. Also featured were Janet Tyler and announcer Rex Marshall.

KUKLA, FRAN AND OLLIE   NBC/ABC/PBS
29 NOVEMBER 1948–13 JUNE 1954 (NBC); 6 SEPTEMBER 1954–30 AUGUST 1957 (ABC); 25 SEPTEMBER 1961–22 JUNE 1962 (NBC); 1969–1971 (PBS)   A long-running children's series that was equally popular with adults, *Kukla, Fran and Ollie* featured the puppets of Burr Tillstrom and their human friend, Fran Allison. Tillstrom began creating his characters in the 1930s; one of the first puppets he crafted was Kukla (the Russian word for "doll"), a bald puppet with a big nose and a high voice. Before long an entire troupe of Kuklapolitans was in existence; the group included Ollie (short for Oliver J. Dragon), a kindly dragon with one tooth, Fletcher Rabbit, Cecil Bill, Buelah the Witch, Colonel Crackie, Madame Ooglepuss, Dolores Dragon, and many others. The Kuklapolitans appeared on television as early as 1939, and by 1947 they were regularly featured on local TV in Chicago. Late in 1948 *Kukla, Fran and Ollie* (Fran Allison, who continued to work with *Don McNeill's Breakfast Club* radio show, had been added) began over NBC's Midwest network; the show was first seen in the East on 12 January 1949, after the completion of New York-to-Chicago transmission lines. The show was seen daily for several seasons before switching to Sunday afternoons. From 1954 to 1957 it was again broadcast daily over ABC. In the fall of 1961 the puppets again appeared, this time in a five-minute daily show; the series, which did not include Fran Allison, was titled *Burr Tillstrom's Kukla and Ollie.* Finally, the show was revived (with Fran Allison) over educational television, where it ran for two seasons. Most of the shows were done without scripts, except for a number of fairly elaborate productions, such as a puppet version of "The Mikado." Tillstrom himself provided the voices of Kukla and Ollie. Beulah Zachary, after whom Buelah the Witch was named, produced the first NBC version and the ABC version of the show.

KUNG FU   ABC
1 OCTOBER 1972–28 JUNE 1975   Highly stylized western starring David Carradine as Kwai Chang Caine, a soft-spoken drifter who eschewed violence, but when given no other choice utilized his prodigious talents in the martial arts. Caine, who was half Chinese, had studied to become a Shaolin priest in China but was forced to leave China after killing a man there. The series was notable for its use of slow motion, especially in fight sequences, and flashbacks showing the young Caine learning the discipline required by the martial arts. The flashback sequences featured Keye Luke as Master Po; Philip Ahn as Master Kan; and Radames Pera as the young Caine (known affectionately to Master Po as "Grasshopper"). The series was created by Ed Spielman and developed by Herman Miller, who produced it with Alex Beaton; Jerry Thorpe was executive producer. On 1 February 1986 a TV-movie sequel was broadcast on CBS. "Kung Fu: The Movie" featured David Carradine and Keye Luke from the series, and introduced Brandon Lee (son of the late martial arts film star Bruce Lee) as Caine's son. The pilot for the original series was televised 22 February 1972. In 1993 a sequel series appeared: see below.

KUNG FU: THE LEGEND CONTINUES   SYNDICATED

1993–   This sequel to *Kung Fu* again starred David Carradine as Kwai Chang Caine; this Caine, however, was the grandson of the original series' central character. The sequel was set in a large city during the present time, where Caine was reunited with his son, whom he thought had perished in a fire as a child. Also featured were Chris Potter as the son, Peter Caine, a cop; Robert Lansing (1993–1994) as Captain Paul Blaisdell; Kim Chan as The Ancient, a Shaolin priest who ran a local apothecary; William Dunlop as Frank Strenlich; and Nathaniel Moreau as the young Peter, who appeared in flashback sequences. Ernest Abuba was occasionally featured as Tan, a former Shaolin monk and enemy of the elder Caine who was now the city's crime boss. The hour series was filmed in Toronto.

KUP'S SHOW   SYNDICATED/PBS

1962–1975 (SYNDICATED); 1975–1986 (PBS)   Chicago newspaper columnist Irv Kupcinet was seen on local television as early as 1952; by 1958 he was host of an open-ended talk show in Chicago. It was trimmed to an hour when it went into national syndication in 1962; thirteen years later the show was picked up by PBS. Paul Frumkin produced the show for many seasons.

THE KWICKY KOALA SHOW   CBS

12 SEPTEMBER 1981–28 AUGUST 1982   This Hanna-Barbera Saturday morning cartoon show consisted of three cartoon segments. The title character, Kwicky Koala, had been created by veteran animator Tex Avery shortly before his death; Kwicky was a clever marsupial who was constantly pursued by Wilfred Wolf. Rounding out the half hour were "Dirty Dog," a mutt who, with his pal Ratso, battled Officer Bullhorn, and "Crazy Claws," a wildcat whose adversaries were Rawhide Clyde and his faithful canine companion, Bristletooth.

THE KYLE MacDONNELL SHOW
See GIRL ABOUT TOWN

L.A. LAW   NBC

15 SEPTEMBER 1986–19 MAY 1994   A Los Angeles law firm was the setting of this hour dramatic series created by Steven Bochco and Terry Louise Fisher. Bochco had developed *Hill Street Blues* while Fisher, herself an attorney, had produced *Cagney and Lacey.* The series used several of the stylistic devices popularized on *Hill Street*: an ensemble cast, a standard opening scene (the squad room at *Hill Street,* the conference room at *L.A. Law*), a theme and score by Mike Post, and multiple story lines, some of which carried over from week to week. The firm's cases ranged from the thought-provoking to the trivial, enabling the program to mix seriousness with humor. Refreshingly, *L.A. Law*'s litigators, like those in real life, managed to lose a case from time to time.

   The cast included: Richard Dysart as Leland McKenzie, senior partner of McKenzie, Brackman, Chaney & Kuzak; Alan Rachins as managing partner Douglas Brackman, Jr., whose father had founded the firm with McKenzie; Harry Hamlin (1986–1991) as litigation partner Michael Kuzak; Corbin Bernsen as domestic relations partner Arnie Becker; Jill Eikenberry as litigation partner Ann Kelsey; Michael Tucker as tax partner Stuart Markowitz; Jimmy Smits (1986–1991) as associate Victor Sifuentes, the firm's sole Hispanic attorney; Michele Greene (1986–1992) as associate Abby Perkins; Susan Dey (1986–1992) as assistant district attorney Grace Van Owen; and Susan Ruttan (1986–1993) as Becker's secretary, Roxanne Melman. The firm's fourth "name" partner, Chaney, was found dead, slumped over a law book in the opening scene of the first episode.

   Relationships developed: Kuzak fell for Van Owen, they broke up, and got back together; Markowitz and Kelsey became serious, were married on 7 January 1988 (in real life Jill Eikenberry and Michael Tucker were already married), and, after unsuccessful efforts to adopt a child, had a son; Arnie Becker chased almost anyone in a skirt, including some of his own clients; Roxanne Melman, who carried a torch for

Becker, was briefly married to Dave Meyer, a terminally boring direct mail entrepreneur (brilliantly played by Dann Florek).

The law firm changed, too. Blair Underwood joined the cast in 1987 as hotshot young associate Jonathan Rollins, the firm's first black lawyer. Larry Drake also joined as the mentally retarded office boy, Benny Stulwicz (Drake won an Emmy for his portrayal). After learning that she wasn't on the partnership track, Abby Perkins left the firm to open her own practice, but later returned. Arnie Becker had his name added to the firm's masthead as office politics reared its head in the 1989–1990 season. Diana Muldaur (1989–1991) came aboard that season as Rosalind Shays, a high-powered attorney who maneuvered herself into the top position at the firm, but who was forced to resign in a climactic power struggle headed up by McKenzie (she was killed in a fall down an elevator shaft in a March 1991 episode). Grace Van Owen left the D.A.'s office for a superior court judgeship during the 1989–1990 season, but was dissatisfied, and joined the firm after Shays's departure. Joining the cast during the 1990–1991 season were Amanda Donohoe (1990–1992) as attorney C. J. Lamb; John Spencer (1990–1994) as attorney Tommy Mullaney; and Cecil Hoffmann (1991–1992) as assistant district attorney Zoey Clemmons, Tommy's ex-wife.

More cast changes occurred during *L.A. Law*'s last three seasons, as its ratings began to slide downward. Hamlin and Smits left in the spring of 1991, and five new lawyers were added during the 1991–1992 season: Michael Cumpsty (1991–1992) as Frank Kittredge; Conchata Ferrell (1991–1992) as brassy entertainment lawyer Susan Bloom; Tom Verica (1991–1992) as Billy Castroverti; Anthony DeSando (1991–1992) as Alex DePalma; and Sheila Kelley (1991–1993) as Gwen Taylor. In the fall of 1992 A Martinez joined the cast as Daniel Morales (Martinez had appeared in another role two seasons earlier, in which his character was executed), and Lisa Zane was added later that season as associate Melina Paros. William Finkelstein returned to the series as executive producer in the spring of 1993.

For the series' eighth and final season, long-time regulars Bernsen, Drake, Dysart, Eikenberry, Rachins, Spencer, Tucker, and Underwood all returned, as three new regulars were added. Two of them—Alan Rosenberg as Eli Levinson and Debi Mazar as secretary Denise Iannello—had appeared in the recently canceled ABC lawyer series *Civil Wars* (it was explained that Levinson was Stuart Markowitz's cousin). The third new regular was Alexandra Powers as Jane Halliday, who was one of TV's smallest minority groups, a deeply religious person.

Real life imitated art. Applications to law schools surged, and some ascribed the increase to the show's popularity. Late in 1987, cocreators Fisher and Bochco had a less-than-amiable parting of the ways, which resulted in Fisher's filing a $50 million lawsuit against her former partner; the case was settled in 1988.

LADIES BE SEATED   ABC
22 APRIL 1949–17 JUNE 1949   This half-hour prime-time game show featured female contestants, who competed in dance contests and in question-and-answer segments. It was hosted by Tom Moore and Phil Patton, and produced by Greg Garrison and Phil Patton. A primordial incarnation of the show, with Johnny Olson hosting, was aired on ABC's Schenectady, N.Y., station in 1945.

LADIES BEFORE GENTLEMEN   DUMONT
28 FEBRUARY 1951–2 MAY 1951   This prime-time panel show was the converse of *Leave It to the Girls:* Each week a panel of male celebrities confronted a lone female guest, whose task was to defend the feminine point of view on the subjects discussed. Ken Roberts hosted the series, and Henry Misrock produced it.

LADIES' CHOICE   NBC
8 JUNE 1953–25 SEPTEMBER 1953   Johnny Dugan hosted this late-afternoon half-hour variety series, on which guest performers were selected by women's organizations.

LADIES' DATE   DUMONT
13 OCTOBER 1952–31 JULY 1953   Bruce Mayer hosted this afternoon audience-participation and variety show. Mayer had hosted a similar program on local television in Detroit before moving to New York for a network tryout.

LADIES' MAN   CBS
27 OCTOBER 1980–21 FEBRUARY 1981   Lawrence Pressman starred in this half-hour sitcom as Alan Thackeray, a divorced father who landed a job at *Women's Life* magazine, where he was the only male writer. Also featured were Louise Sorel as Elaine Holstein, the managing editor; Simone Griffeth as Gretchen, a researcher; Allison Argo as Susan, a writer; Betty Kennedy as Andrea, another writer; Karen Morrow as Alan's neighbor, Betty Brill; Natasha Ryan as Amy, Alan's eight-year-old daughter; and Herb Edelman as Reggie, the magazine's accountant.

LADY BLUE   ABC
15 SEPTEMBER 1985–25 JANUARY 1986   Jamie Rose starred in this hour crime show as Detective Katy Mahoney, a tough Chicago cop who toted a .357 Magnum and wasn't afraid to use it (some critics dubbed the character "Dirty Harriet," comparing her to Clint Eastwood's movie cop character *Dirty Harry*). Other regulars were Danny Aiello as her boss, Lieutenant Terry McNichols; Ron Dean as Sergeant Gianelli; and Bruce A. Young (who had played a Chicago cop on *E/R*) as Cassidy. The pilot for the series was telecast 15 April 1985. In November the National Coalition on Television Violence cited *Lady Blue* as the most violent program on the air, averaging fifty violent acts per hour.

LAMB CHOP'S PLAY-ALONG   PBS
13 JANUARY 1992–   Veteran kids' show personality Shari Lewis returned to entertain a new generation of youngsters in this daily half-hour show, assisted by her puppets Lamb Chop, Charlie Horse, and Hush Puppy.

THE LAMBS GAMBOL   NBC
27 FEBRUARY 1949–22 MAY 1949   This half-hour variety series featured performances by members of the Lambs Club, a show business fraternal order, as well as by other guest stars. It was produced by Herb Leder and directed by Tom McDermott.

LAMP UNTO MY FEET   CBS
21 NOVEMBER 1948–21 JANUARY 1979   This Sunday-morning religious program, one of TV's longest-running network shows, featured programs on cultural as well as religious themes. In its early years it was aimed at children and was produced by Isabelle Redman of CBS Public Affairs. It was later produced by Pamela Ilott for CBS News.

LANCELOT LINK, SECRET CHIMP   ABC
12 SEPTEMBER 1970–2 SEPTEMBER 1972   Saturday-morning filmed series about a group of simian secret agents; human voices were dubbed over. Lancelot Link was the principal primate, though a rock band known as the Evolution Revolution was also featured. Other regular characters included Mata Hairi, Darwin (the head of A.P.E.), Creto, Dr. Strangemind, Wang Fu, and the Baron (boss of C.H.U.M.P.). The series was shown in an hour format during its first season, and in a half-hour format during the second season.

LANCER   CBS
24 SEPTEMBER 1968–23 JUNE 1970   This hour-long western was an imitation of *Bonanza*. It starred Andrew Duggan as Murdoch Lancer, twice-widowed California rancher; James Stacy as Johnny Lancer, his hot-headed son; Wayne Maunder as Scott Lancer, his college-educated son, Johnny's half brother; Elizabeth Baur as Teresa O'Brien, Murdoch's ward (daughter of his late foreman); and Paul Brinegar as Jelly Hoskins, the current foreman. Samuel Peeples created the series, which was pro-

duced by Alan A. Armer for 20th Century-Fox. Reruns were broadcast during the summer of 1971.

LAND OF THE GIANTS ABC

22 SEPTEMBER 1968–6 SEPTEMBER 1970   Science fiction series about a group of Earthlings aboard the *Spindrift*, on a flight from Los Angeles to London on June 12, 1983. The aircraft crash lands in a strange world where everything is a dozen times larger than on Earth, and the survivors found themselves hunted by giants. With Gary Conway as Captain Steve Burton; Don Marshall as copilot Dan Erickson; Deanna Lund as Valerie Scott; Don Matheson as the wealthy Mark Wilson; Heather Young as flight attendant Betty Hamilton; Kurt Kasznar as the unscrupulous Alexander Fitzhugh; Stefan Arngrim as youngster Barry Lockridge; and Kevin Hagen as Inspector Kobick, the giant in charge of apprehending the little people. Irwin Allen was executive producer of the series, which was reportedly budgeted at the then astronomical figure of $250,000 per episode.

LAND OF THE LOST NBC/CBS/ABC

7 SEPTEMBER 1974–20 NOVEMBER 1976 (NBC); 4 FEBRUARY 1978–2 SEPTEMBER 1978 (NBC); 22 JUNE 1985–28 DECEMBER 1985 (CBS); 20 JUNE 1987–5 SEPTEMBER 1987 (CBS); 7 SEPTEMBER 1991–3 SEPTEMBER 1994 (ABC)   Innovative, live-action Saturday-morning show about a forest ranger and his two children who, caught in a time warp, found themselves in a prehistoric world. With Spencer Milligan as ranger Rick Marshall; Wesley Eure as Will, his son; Kathy Coleman as Holly, his daughter; Philip Paley as Cha-Ka, one of the Pakuni people, an apelike race discovered by the visitors; Sharon Baird and Joe Giamalva as other Pakunis; and Dave Greenwood, Bill Laimbeer, and John Lambert as Sleestacks, a race of reptilian creatures. Sid and Marty Krofft produced the series, which returned several times.

When the series returned in 1991, it was again seen Saturday mornings, but with a new cast and on a new network. This time three members of the Porter family ended up in a prehistoric world. The new cast included Timothy Bottoms as Tom Porter; Jennifer Drugan as daughter Annie; Robert Gavin as son Kevin; Ed Gale as Tasha, their pet reptile (Danny Mann provided Tasha's voice); Bobby Porter as Stink, a monkey-like creature who befriended them; and Shannon Day as Christa, a mysterious girl whom they met.

LAND'S END SYNDICATED

1995–   Hour crime show filmed on location at Cabo San Lucas in Baja California. With Fred Dryer as Mike Land, a former Los Angeles cop who moved south and became a private eye; Geoffrey Lewis as Mike's partner in the business and lifelong friend, Willis P. Dunleevy; Pamela Bowen as Courtney Sanders, security manager at the Westin Hotel; and Tim Thomerson as Dave, who ran a local charter boat service.

LANIGAN'S RABBI NBC

30 JANUARY 1977–3 JULY 1977   This crime show surfaced irregularly in 1977. Based on Harry Kemelman's novel, *Friday the Rabbi Slept Late*, it featured Art Carney as Paul Lanigan, big city police chief; Bruce Solomon as Rabbi David Small, Lanigan's occasional partner and consultant; Janis Paige as Kate Lanigan, Paul's wife; Janet Margolin as Miriam Small, the Rabbi's wife; Barbara Carney as Bobbie Whittaker; and Robert Doyle as Osgood. The pilot for the series was telecast 17 June 1976. Leonard B. Stern was executive producer.

THE LANNY ROSS SHOW NBC

1 APRIL 1948–4 AUGUST 1949   Lanny Ross, who had been featured on such radio series as *The Maxwell House Show Boat* and *Your Hit Parade,* hosted one of television's first network variety shows. Sponsored by Swift, the half-hour series was also known as *The Swift Show.* Martha Logan and Sandra Gahle were also featured; Lee Cooley was the producer.

THE LARAINE DAY SHOW   ABC
5 MAY 1951–18 AUGUST 1951
DAYDREAMING WITH LARAINE   ABC
17 MAY 1951–19 JULY 1951   Laraine Day hosted two interview shows in 1951. The
first, titled *The Laraine Day Show,* was a half-hour series broadcast on Saturday
afternoons; it featured Ruth Woodner and the Bill Harrington Trio. The second
series, *Daydreaming with Laraine,* was a fifteen-minute show aired on Thursday
evenings; it featured interviews with sports personalities (at the time Day was married to Leo Durocher, then manager of the New York Giants baseball team). *The
Laraine Day Show* was produced by Ted Kneeland, while *Daydreaming with Laraine*
was produced by Ward Byron.

LARAMIE   NBC
15 SEPTEMBER 1959–17 SEPTEMBER 1963   Hour-long western set in Laramie, Wyoming. With John Smith as Slim Sherman and Robert Fuller as Jess Harper, partners
in a ranch who supplemented their income by operating a stagecoach station on the
premises. Also featured were Hoagy Carmichael (1959–1960) as Jonesy, their chief
ranch hand; Bobby Crawford, Jr. (older brother of *The Rifleman*'s Johnny Crawford)
as Andy Sherman, Slim's brother; Don Durant (1960–1963) as Gandy, a ranch hand;
Arch Johnson (1960–1963) as Wellman, another ranch hand; Dennis Holmes (1961–
1963) as Mike, a young orphan who moved in; and Spring Byington (1961–1963) as
Daisy Cooper, the housekeeper.

LAREDO   NBC
16 SEPTEMBER 1965–1 SEPTEMBER 1967   Light western about a group of Texas Rangers who spent as much time fighting among themselves as they did fighting desperadoes. With Neville Brand as Reese Bennett; Peter Brown (formerly of *The Lawman*)
as Chad Cooper; William Smith as Joe Riley; Philip Carey as Captain Parmalee, their
harried commanding officer; and Robert Wolders (1966–1967) as rookie ranger Erik
Hunter. The series was produced by Universal TV.

THE LARRY KANE SHOW   SYNDICATED
1971   Rock-and-roll performers guest starred on this hour program hosted by
Philadelphia disc jockey Larry Kane.

THE LARRY KING SHOW (LARRY KING LIVE)   SYNDICATED/CNN
13 MARCH 1983–10 JULY 1983 (SYNDICATED); 3 JUNE 1985–   (CNN)   Larry
King, whose all-night radio talk show was nationally syndicated, tried to bring his
show to television, but met with unspectacular results at first. The ninety-minute
show was broadcast live on Sunday nights from Washington, D.C., and featured a
telephone hookup that enabled viewers to talk directly to King and his guests. King's
second television effort was far more successful: *Larry King Live!* premiered on CNN
3 June 1985; on this hour weeknight show, also broadcast from Washington, King
interviewed newsmakers, authors, celebrities, and government officials. The show
again featured a telephone line so that viewers could talk with King's guests. *Larry
King Live* celebrated its tenth anniversary during the week of 5–9 June 1995 with an
impressive array of guests: President Bill Clinton, singer Barbra Streisand, media
mogul (and CNN owner) Ted Turner, PLO leader Yasir Arafat, and late-night talk
show host David Letterman.

THE LARRY SANDERS SHOW   HBO
15 AUGUST 1992–   The world of the late-night talk show was the subject of this
innovative sitcom created by Garry Shandling and Dennis Klein. Having served as
frequent guest host on *The Tonight Show Starring Johnny Carson* and been considered as a possible successor to David Letterman on *Late Night,* Shandling was
familiar with the territory. He played Larry Sanders, the self-obsessed, never-
satisfied host of "The Larry Sanders Show," a popular late night talk show. Also
featured were Jeffrey Tambor as his obsequious sidekick, Hank ("Hey now!") Kingsley; Rip Torn as his Machiavellian producer, Artie; Megan Gallagher (1992–1993) as

his wife, Jeannie Sanders; Janeane Garofalo as Paula, the talent booker; Linda Doucett (1992–1995) as Darlene, Hank's assistant; Jeremy Piven (1992–1994) as the head writer, Jerry; Wallace Langham as Phil, the young writer; Penny Johnson as Beverly, Larry's assistant. As the second season unfolded in 1993, Jeannie had left Larry, and Larry's ex-wife had reappeared; Kathryn Harrold (1993–1994) joined the cast as Francine, the ex. Scott Thompson was added in 1995 as Hank's efficient assistant, Brian, a gay man. The talk-show segments were taped before a live studio audience, and featured real-life guests such as Roseanne, Sharon Stone, and Peter Falk. The behind-the-scenes scenes were aired without a laugh track and with plenty of four-letter words.

THE LARRY STORCH SHOW   CBS
11 JULY 1953–12 SEPTEMBER 1953   Larry Storch hosted this variety hour, which was a summer replacement for *The Jackie Gleason Show*. Like Gleason, Storch had earlier hosted *Cavalcade of Stars* on the DuMont network. He would become better known as corporal Agarn on *F Troop*.

LAS VEGAS GAMBIT
See GAMBIT

THE LAS VEGAS SHOW   SYNDICATED
1967   *The Las Vegas Show*, a nightly two-hour talkfest broadcast live from Las Vegas, premiered 1 May 1967, and was supposed to be the cornerstone of a "fourth network," The United Network. Hosted by Bill Dana, the show disappeared after a few weeks, together with the plans for the new network.

LASH OF THE WEST   ABC
4 JANUARY 1953–9 MAY 1953   Fifteen-minute series on which western star Lash LaRue demonstrated skills such as using the bullwhip (LaRue's trademark).

LASSIE   CBS/SYNDICATED
12 SEPTEMBER 1954–12 SEPTEMBER 1971 (CBS); 1971–1974 (SYNDICATED)
Lassie, the daring and resourceful collie owned and trained by Rudd Weatherwax, had starred both in films and on radio before coming to TV in 1954. Over the next two decades the dog survived many changes in format and cast and never seemed to age; actually, over the years Lassie was played by at least six different dogs, all of them males, and other Lassies were used for special shots or difficult stunts. For her first three seasons Lassie lived on the Miller farm near the town of Calverton; the cast then included Tommy Rettig as Jeff Miller; Jan Clayton as Ellen Miller, his widowed mother; George Cleveland as Gramps (George Miller), Jeff's granddad; Donald Keeler (nephew of actress Ruby Keeler) as Jeff's best friend, Porky Brockway; and Paul Maxey as Matt Brockway, Porky's father. By 1957 young Rettig had outgrown the role—that fall the Millers suddenly moved to the city and entrusted Lassie to the care of a young orphan, recently adopted by a Calverton couple. The new cast included Jon Provost as Timmy Martin; Cloris Leachman as his mother, Ruth Martin; Jon Shepodd as Paul Martin, his father; and George Chandler as Uncle Petrie. Leachman and Shepodd lasted only one season as Timmy's parents; they were replaced in 1958 by June Lockhart and Hugh Reilly (again as Ruth and Paul Martin). Other regulars included Todd Ferrell as Boomer Bates, Timmy's pal; Andy Clyde as oldtimer Cully, also a friend of Timmy's. By 1964 the show's owners—The Wrather Corporation—had decided on another change; it was explained that the Martins had decided to move to Australia, and since dogs entering that country had to be quarantined for six months, Lassie would be better off with a new owner. Robert Bray stepped in as Corey Stewart, a forest ranger (Bray had actually been introduced in a five-parter during the 1963–1964 season to test audience reaction). Freed from the farm format, Lassie could now become involved in a wider variety of outdoor adventures. Bray departed in 1968, and Lassie hooked up with a pair of forest rangers (Jed Allan as Scott Turner, and Jack de Mave as Bob) for two seasons. Neither of the rangers was seen in every episode, as Lassie began to become a freelance trou-

bleshooter. During the 1970–1971 and 1971–1972 seasons—the last on CBS and the first on syndication—there were no human regulars. For the final two years of syndication, Lassie returned to a farm (a ranch, actually), run by Keith Holden (played by Larry Wilcox). A cartoon version of the show was also seen during the 1973 and 1974 seasons: see *Lassie's Rescue Rangers*. The earlier versions of the series were syndicated under different titles: the episodes starring Tommy Rettig were titled *Jeff's Collie*, and those with Jon Provost were titled *Timmy and Lassie*. See also *The New Lassie*. A theatrical film appeared in 1994.

LASSIE'S RESCUE RANGERS   ABC
8 SEPTEMBER 1973–31 AUGUST 1975   Ecology-oriented weekend cartoon series based, of course, on *Lassie*. The cartoon Lassie was the boss of a group of animals dedicated to saving the environment. Norm Prescott and Lou Scheimer produced the series.

LAST CALL   SYNDICATED
1994–1995   Created by Brandon Tartikoff and intended for late-night time slots, this half-hour daily series began as a freewheeling discussion of topical events by a panel of five pundits: Terry McDonell (former editor of *Esquire*), Elvis Mitchell, Sue Ellicott (a correspondent for the London *Sunday Times*), Brianne Leary, and Tad Low. After a few weeks, Leary left the studio and was made the show's "road correspondent," reporting from various locations. After a few more weeks McDonell, Mitchell, and Low had departed. Joining Ellicott and guests in the studio was John "Stuttering John" Melendez, a veteran of Howard Stern's popular morning radio show. After a few more weeks the show was canceled.

LAST CHANCE GARAGE   PBS
1982–1985   Half-hour instructional series on do-it-yourself auto repair, hosted by Brad Sears.

THE LAST OF THE MOHICANS
See HAWKEYE

LAST OF THE WILD (LORNE GREENE'S LAST OF THE WILD)   SYNDICATED
1974   Half-hour documentaries about wildlife, narrated by Lorne Greene. From Ivan Tors Productions. See also *Lorne Greene's New Wilderness*.

THE LAST PRECINCT   NBC
11 APRIL 1986–30 MAY 1986   Stephen Cannell's hour cop show was played mostly for laughs. It was set at the 56th Precinct in Los Angeles, where the malcontents and troublemakers from the city's other precincts were all transferred. The large cast included Adam West as Captain Rick Wright; Jonathan Perpich as Sergeant Price Pascall; Randi Brooks as Officer Mel Brubaker, a transsexual; Rick Ducommun as Officer "Raid" Raider; Ernie Hudson as Sergeant Night Train Lane; Lucy Lee Flippin as Officer Tina Starland; Vijay Amritraj as Alphabet, an "exchange" cop from India; Pete Willcox as The King, an Elvis impersonator; Keenan Wynn as Butch; Hank Rolike as Sundance; Wings Hauser as Lieutenant Hobbs of the L.A. Sheriff's Department; and Yana Nirvana as Sergeant Martha Haggerty, Hobbs's assistant. The pilot for the series was telecast 26 January 1986, immediately following Super Bowl XX; seven regular episodes were aired beginning in April.

THE LAST RESORT   CBS
19 SEPTEMBER 1979–17 MARCH 1980   Half-hour sitcom about a group of college kids working at a resort hotel. With Larry Breeding as Michael Lerner, premed student; Stephanie Faracy as Gail Collins, the pastry chef; Zane Lasky as Duane Kaminsky; Walter Olkewicz as Zach Comstock; John Fujioka as Kevin, the cook; Ray Underwood as rich kid Jeffrey Barron; Robert Costanzo as Murray, the maitre d'; and Dorothy Konrad as Mrs. Trilling, one of the guests. Gary David Goldberg created

and produced the show, which got off to a slow start and was pulled from the schedule after three weeks; it returned in December.

THE LAST WORD   CBS

6 JANUARY 1957–18 OCTOBER 1959   The English language was the topic of discussion on this Sunday-afternoon panel show. Each week a panel of three celebrities or authorities discussed questions submitted by viewers about the language. Fred Freed produced the highbrow half hour, and John Mason Brown was featured as a permanent panelist. Dr. Bergen Evans was the moderator.

THE LAST WORD   ABC

26 OCTOBER 1982–22 APRIL 1983   An hour news analysis program, *The Last Word* was broadcast weeknights at midnight, immediately following *ABC News Nightline*. Greg Jackson and Phil Donahue were the cohosts. When *Nightline* was expanded to sixty minutes, *The Last Word* was dropped, though Jackson continued to host an interview show (see *One on One*).

THE LATE LATE SHOW WITH TOM SNYDER   CBS

9 JANUARY 1995–   CBS's entry into late-late night talk show programming was accomplished with Tom Snyder, who had inaugurated the concept as host of the *Tomorrow* show on NBC from 1973 to 1982. In 1982 Snyder's show had been replaced by *Late Night with David Letterman,* so it was only fitting that his 1995 show followed Letterman's at 12:35 A.M. The hour program, which dispensed with a studio audience, was broadcast from Los Angeles live to the East Coast, and was simulcast on radio to other time zones; it featured an 800 telephone number by which viewers and listeners could ask questions of Snyder's guests.

LATE NIGHT WITH CONAN O'BRIEN   NBC

13 SEPTEMBER 1993–   The long search for a successor to David Letterman as host of NBC's post-*Tonight* show talk program began early in 1993, as soon as Letterman announced his upcoming move to CBS. NBC hired *Saturday Night Live* executive producer Lorne Michaels to oversee the new program, and to help find a replacement host. *Saturday Night Live* regular Dana Carvey had been under consideration, but he declined the offer, as did Garry Shandling. The search ended with Conan O'Brien. A tall young man with very little previous on-camera experience, O'Brien had been a writer for *The Wilton North Report, Saturday Night Live* and *The Simpsons.* After several test shows, and a summer of Letterman reruns, O'Brien took over on 13 September. Andy Richter was O'Brien's sidekick, and drummer Max Weinberg led the band.

LATE NIGHT WITH DAVID LETTERMAN   NBC

1 FEBRUARY 1982–10 SEPTEMBER 1993   Comedian David Letterman hosted this late-night (12:30 A.M.) talk show, which replaced *Tomorrow Coast to Coast.* The series was originally aired Mondays through Thursdays, and expanded to Fridays on 12 June 1987. A native of Indianapolis, Letterman moved to Los Angeles in the mid-1970s to do standup comedy. He was a regular on two short-lived variety shows (*The Starland Vocal Band Show* and *Mary,* the 1978 debacle that starred Mary Tyler Moore). After guest-hosting for Johnny Carson on the *Tonight* show, he was given his own daytime show in 1980 (see *The David Letterman Show*). Although the daytime show lasted only four months, the network wisely kept Letterman under contract. The late-night show was launched in early 1982, with the blessing of Johnny Carson. Carson's production company did not own the new show, but wielded some influence over it. Letterman acceded to the Carson requests that the band be no larger than four pieces, and that the bandleader not sit with the host on stage. A request that Letterman perform no opening monologue was gradually ignored as the show became successful.

    The show quickly attracted a loyal following, especially among the 18-to-34 age group, as Letterman's quick wit, irreverence, and unpredictability endeared him to his audience. The influence of older TV iconoclasts Ernie Kovacs and Steve Allen was evidenced by Letterman's willingness to stretch the boundaries of the traditional talk show. (Letterman's studio announcer, Bill Wendell, had worked with Kovacs). Over the years viewers were treated not only to offbeat guests, but also to elevator races, hidden cameras in other NBC offices, "top ten" lists, "stupid pet tricks," and even a guided tour of Letterman's eclectic record collection. On one show the studio camera made a complete 360-degree revolution during the hour (thus showing the host and his guests upside down for part of the broadcast); on another Letterman wore a Velcro suit and threw himself against a wall (he stuck). Letterman even did one show from his Connecticut home, waiting for the cable television installer to arrive. An especially memorable incident occurred on a 1986 program, as Letterman strode to the headquarters of NBC's new owner, General Electric, with a fruit basket for GE executives; he was rebuffed by the corporate security chief, who even refused to shake Letterman's hand. Letterman also hosted several annual prime-time anniversary shows, presenting highlights from the past year's programs.

Also featured on the show were musician Paul Shaffer (formerly of *Saturday Night Live*) and the World's Most Dangerous Band, the inimitable Calvert DeForest (better known as Larry "Bud" Melman), and show writer Chris Elliott (who appeared in various roles, including The Guy Who Lives Under the Seats; he is the son of Bob Elliott). Meg Parsont, a Simon & Schuster publicist, became a minor celebrity on the program; her office building was located directly across the street from the studio, and Letterman occasionally trained a camera through her high-rise office window as he telephoned her from the set.

In 1992 Letterman's future with NBC became cloudy after the network announced that Jay Leno would succeed Johnny Carson as host of the *Tonight* show. Letterman, who had long coveted an earlier time slot, eventually negotiated a lucrative deal with CBS, announced early in 1993, under which he would go head-to-head with Leno at 11:35 P.M. (see *Late Show with David Letterman*). Letterman continued to host his NBC show through September 1993 (the last first-run program aired on 25 June, with special musical guest Bruce Springsteen); in promoting the show during its last few months, NBC referred to it only as *Late Night*. Letterman's successor as host of *Late Night* was the relatively unknown Conan O'Brien (see *Late Night with Conan O'Brien*).

THE LATE SHOW STARRING JOAN RIVERS FOX
9 OCTOBER 1986–21 MAY 1987
THE LATE SHOW FOX
22 MAY 1987–10 DECEMBER 1987; 14 JANUARY 1988–14 OCTOBER 1988   Joan Rivers was the first performer signed to the fledgling Fox network, which had high hopes that a late-night talk show hosted by the quick-witted comedienne would prove to be an auspicious inaugural series. Alas, it was not to be, as Rivers's show was canceled after just seven months. Fox's choice of Rivers seemed to make sense; she had been "permanent guest host" of *The Tonight Show Starring Johnny Carson* since 1983, and that show's ratings had held their own (and sometimes improved) during her guest tenures. Fox executives scheduled a major press conference early in 1986 to announce her arrival; unfortunately, Rivers was unable to notify Johnny Carson beforehand of her new assignment, and the resulting flap upset her considerably.

Nevertheless, plans for *The Late Show Starring Joan Rivers* got underway. Edgar Rosenberg, Rivers's husband, and Bill Sammeth were the executive producers; a $2 million, 420-seat studio was built to Rivers's specifications; musician Mark Hudson was hired as bandleader. It was decided that the show would be broadcast live to the East Coast. Sammeth tried to attract guests who appealed to a younger audience than that of the Carson show. For the premiere telecast, which went out to ninety-five stations, he booked Cher, Elton John, David Lee Roth, and Pee-wee Herman. The initial ratings were encouraging, but by the end of October they had dropped sharply; Fox had promised advertisers a rating of 5, but the show was now averaging less than half of that, which meant that Fox would have to offer "makegoods," or subsequent free spots, to its sponsors.

Relations between Rivers's staff and network executives quickly deteriorated; there were constant battles over expenses, how many guests should be booked on each program, whether the stage crew should be fed, and even over a Pepsi machine installed at the studio. In February 1987 Fox effectively took control of the show, and coexecutive producer Rosenberg was made to feel unwelcome. Ratings remained low, and in April 1987 Fox announced that it was pulling the plug on the show. Rivers's last show aired 15 May 1987, followed by four nights of reruns. Edgar Rosenberg, who had been in poor health, committed suicide in August of that year, while on a business trip to Philadelphia.

After Rivers's departure, Fox briefly experimented with having a different guest host each night; that idea soon proved unworkable, and various celebrities then took longer turns. Among the brightest was a young black comic named Arsenio Hall, under whose stewardship ratings actually improved slightly. By that time, however, Fox was already committed to a replacement series, *The Wilton North Report*. When that disastrous show was axed after less than a month, back came reruns of *The Late Show,* including some programs which Rivers had hosted. A new version of *The Late Show* surfaced on 10 March 1988. Ross Shafer became its permanent host in April; Shafer had previously hosted a local talk show in Seattle, *Almost Live with Ross Shafer,* for four years. After six months Fox shelved the entire idea of a late-night talk show. Three months later Arsenio Hall, whom Fox probably could have signed earlier, premiered his hit syndicated talk show; see *The Arsenio Hall Show.* Fox again tried a late-night talk show—again unsuccessfully—in 1993: see *The Chevy Chase Show.*

LATE SHOW WITH DAVID LETTERMAN CBS

30 AUGUST 1993–   After numerous attempts to compete with NBC's *Tonight* show (and later with *ABC News Nightline*), CBS finally succeeded in 1993 when David Letterman accepted its multi-multi-million dollar offer. As host of NBC's *Late Night with David Letterman* since 1982, Letterman already had years of expèrience in the late-night talk show format. He had hoped to be able to succeed Johnny Carson as host of the *Tonight* show, and was extremely disappointed when NBC announced in mid-1991 that Jay Leno would succeed Carson in May 1992. NBC hoped that Letterman would be content to remain in the *Late Night* spot; he wasn't.

In the fall of 1992 NBC gave Letterman permission to negotiate with other broadcasters, in exchange for Letterman's extending his contract with NBC through June of 1993. NBC also retained the right to match any offer made by a competitor. ABC, CBS, Fox, and several syndicators immediately expressed interest in Letterman's services. CBS and Fox soon emerged as the two most serious contenders; Letterman preferred the prestige and relative stability of a network over the vagaries of syndication, and ABC was not pursued because it could not promise Letterman an 11:30 P.M. time slot due to its commitment to *ABC News Nightline.* By December of 1992 CBS had made Letterman an extraordinary offer: a three-year deal with a base annual salary of $12.5 million (with another $2 million in bonuses if certain ratings marks were achieved), $82 million in production costs, and $7.2 million for several prime-time specials. More importantly, the deal gave Letterman ownership of the show and control over filling the 12:30 A.M. time slot following his show.

The next thirty days were difficult ones for NBC, CBS, David Letterman, and Jay Leno. NBC executives endlessly debated whether to keep or to dump Leno. In early January 1993 NBC made an oral offer to Letterman; it did not match CBS's, but it did promise him the *Tonight* show by May of 1994. Before receiving a definitive answer from Letterman the network withdrew the proposal, and Letterman accepted the CBS deal.

To accommodate the new show CBS refurbished the Ed Sullivan Theater in Manhattan (Letterman preferred that it be a chilly 58 degrees during tapings). *Late Show with David Letterman* premiered on 30 August 1993; Bill Murray, who had been the inaugural guest on *Late Night* in 1982, was the first guest on the new show. Letterman brought much of the old show with him, although NBC had threatened to preclude him from doing so. Bandleader Paul Shaffer came along, although the band was no longer known as the World's Most Dangerous Band, but rather the CBS Orchestra. The nightly "Top Ten" lists were also brought along, and were now introduced with fancier graphics (the feature proved so popular that it was syndicated to radio stations in mid-1994). Letterman himself now appeared in suits, rather than in blazers, and delivered longer monologues. In short, he succeeded in broadening the appeal of his show. Fortunately, some of the quirkiness of the old show remained. Mujibur Rahman and Sirajul Islam, two Bangladeshi immigrants who ran a nearby souvenir store, became semi-regulars on the show as Letterman sent camera crews into their shop and followed them on a cross-country journey. When the show was broadcast from London for a week in May 1995, novelist-in-hiding Salman Rushdie showed up to deliver one evening's Top Ten list to Letterman.

CBS's expensive gamble paid off handsomely, as *Late Show with David Letterman* enjoyed high ratings from the outset. *Late Show* became the first program in thirty-nine years to present a serious challenge to the *Tonight* show at 11:30 P.M. Letterman consistently outdrew Leno, especially in the demographically desirable group of young adult viewers, for the first two years. Leno's overall ratings, however, began to surpass Letterman's in late 1995.

THE LATE SUMMER, EARLY FALL BERT CONVY SHOW CBS
25 AUGUST 1976–15 SEPTEMBER 1976   Four-week half-hour summer variety series hosted by Bert Convy, with Henry Polic II, Sallie James, Lenny Schultz (as "The Bionic Chicken"), Marty Barris, and Donna Ponterotto. Executive producer: Howard Hinderstein.

LATER WITH BOB COSTAS NBC
22 AUGUST 1988–25 FEBRUARY 1994
LATER WITH GREG KINNEAR
28 FEBRUARY 1994–   This half-hour talk show was designed to follow *Late Night with David Letterman* at 1:30 A.M., Mondays through Thursdays. The host was NBC's versatile sportscaster Bob Costas from 1988 to early 1994, when Greg Kinnear (of the E! channel's *Talk Soup*) took over.

LAUGH LINE NBC
16 APRIL 1959–11 JUNE 1959   On this Thursday-night game show hosted by Dick Van Dyke, celebrity panelists were required to supply captions to cartoons. Panelists over the several weeks included Dorothy Loudon, Mike Nichols and Elaine May, Pat Harrington, Jr. (as Guido Panzini), Shelley Berman, Roger Price, and Orson Bean.

LAUGH TRAX SYNDICATED
1982   A half-hour series of rock music, interspersed with comedy sketches. Jim Staahl hosted the show, with assistance from Gail Matthius and Lucy Webb.

LAUGH-IN NBC
22 JANUARY 1968–14 MAY 1973   Hosted by the comedy duo of Dan Rowan and Dick Martin (the show's official title was *Rowan and Martin's Laugh-In*), *Laugh-In* was a fast-moving hour of sight gags, one-liners, short skits, and blackouts. The show was an immediate hit and did much to speed up the pace of TV comedy shows. It relied little on the talents of guest stars, though many celebrities made cameo appearances (including Richard Nixon, who uttered "Sock it to me?" in a 1968 show); instead, a large company of regulars, including many who were new to television, carried the show, and above all, kept it moving. The program seemed to operate on the premise that if enough gags could be crammed into an hour, only a small proportion needed to be genuinely funny for the show to succeed, and at the very least, the viewers could not complain of boredom. Thanks to *Laugh-In*, such phrases as "Ring my chimes," "Look that up in your Funk & Wagnall's," and "You bet your bippy" joined the American vocabulary, at least temporarily. Among the many regulars on the show were Dennis Allen, Chelsea Brown, Ruth Buzzi, Johnny Brown, Judy Carne, Ann Elder, Byron Gilliam, Henry Gibson, Richard Dawson, Teresa Graves, Larry Hovis, Arte Johnson, Goldie Hawn, Jeremy Lloyd, Gary Owens, Dave Madden, Lily Tomlin, Nancie Phillips, Pamela Rodgers, Alan Sues, Barbara Sharma, and Jo Anne Worley. In 1972 several new faces were added, including Patti Deutsch, Sarah Kennedy, Donna Jean Young, Jud Strunk, Brian Bessler, Todd Bass, Willie Tyler, and the

Burbank Quickies. George Schlatter and Ed Friendly were the executive producers until 1971 when Paul Keyes succeeded them. In the fall of 1977 *Laugh-In* (minus hosts Rowan and Martin) returned to NBC as a series of specials, headlined by guest stars. A twenty-fifth anniversary retrospective aired on NBC 7 February 1993. Another special aired 14 February 1994.

LAUGHS FOR SALE   ABC
20 OCTOBER 1963–22 DECEMBER 1963   On this half-hour series a panel of comedians performed material submitted by aspiring comedy writers, after which the material was discussed and evaluated. Hal March hosted the show, which was hastily scheduled to replace *100 Grand,* a game show axed after only three weeks.

LAUREN HUTTON AND . . .   SYNDICATED
1995–   Host Lauren Hutton interviewed a single guest on each half-hour program of this five-day-a-week series.

LAURIE HILL   ABC
30 SEPTEMBER 1992–28 OCTOBER 1992   Half-hour sitcom about a physician and her family. With DeLane Matthews as Dr. Laurie Hill; Robert Clohessy as her husband, Jeff, a writer; Eric Lloyd as their precocious five-year-old, Leo; Kurt Fuller as one of Laurie's medical partners, Dr. Spencer Kramer; Joseph Maher as the other partner, Dr. Walter Weisman; Ellen DeGeneres as Nancy, the nurse; and Doris Belack as Beverly, the receptionist. Neal Marlens and Carol Black created the series.

LAVERNE AND SHIRLEY   ABC
27 JANUARY 1976–10 MAY 1983   Spun off from *Happy Days, Laverne and Shirley* was a rare example of a spinoff that proved as popular (and almost as durable) as the parent series. It was an instant hit, as its premiere topped the weekly ratings and the series finished second in the 1975–1976 annual ratings. *Laverne and Shirley* again placed second (this time to *Happy Days*) in the 1976–1977 race and finished first the following season (with *Happy Days* second). During the 1978–1979 season it again placed second.

Like *Happy Days, Laverne and Shirley* was set in Milwaukee during the late 1950s. Its emphasis was on physical comedy, and its two central characters were a pair of young women who worked together at a brewery and lived together in a basement apartment. It starred Penny Marshall (sister of co-creator Garry Marshall) as Laverne DeFazio and Cindy Williams as Shirley Feeney. Also featured were Phil Foster as Laverne's father, Frank DeFazio, owner of a local pizzeria; David L. Lander as Andrew "Squiggy" Squigman, their dimwitted friend and co-worker; Michael McKean as another friend and co-worker, Lenny Kowznovski, Squiggy's inseparable pal; Betty Garrett (fall 1976–1983) as the landlady, Edna Babish, who married Frank in 1979; and Eddie Mekka as macho Carmine Ragusa, Shirley's on-again, off-again boyfriend.

After a big drop in the ratings during the 1979–1980 season, *Laverne and Shirley* left Wisconsin for Southern California as the sixth season began. Frank and Edna went first, to open a new restaurant, Cowboy Bill's. Laverne and Shirley followed, as their assembly-line jobs at the brewery had been automated; they found an apartment in California and landed jobs at Bardwell's Department Store. Lenny, Squiggy, and Carmine also decided to head West. Joining the cast were Ed Marinaro (1980–1981) as Laverne and Shirley's apartment manager, Sonny St. Jacques, a part-time stuntman; and Leslie Easterbrook (1980–1983) as Rhonda Lee, a conceited but untalented model and actress.

Trouble erupted in the summer of 1982, as production got under way for what would be *Laverne and Shirley*'s last season. Cindy Williams, who was pregnant, chafed at working fourteen-hour days and demanded that her hours be specified in writing. When her demands were not resolved to her satisfaction, she walked off the set and refused to continue working; she also filed suit against Paramount Studios, alleging that Paramount reneged on an agreement to let her work reduced hours. Williams did not return to work and consequently appeared in very few episodes of the 1982–1983 season; her character was married to a medic, Walter Meaney, at a veterans' hospital on 28 September 1982. Over the series' seven and a half seasons, 178 episodes were produced.

LAVERNE & SHIRLEY   ABC
10 OCTOBER 1981–18 SEPTEMBER 1982   This Saturday-morning cartoon version of the prime-time sitcom found Laverne and Shirley in the Army. Sergeant Turnbuckle was their original drill sergeant, but he was succeeded by Sergeant Squealy. In the fall of 1982 the show was incorporated in *The Mork & Mindy/ Laverne & Shirley/Fonz Hour.*

THE LAW AND HARRY McGRAW   CBS
27 SEPTEMBER 1987–10 FEBRUARY 1988   Jerry Orbach starred in this hour crime show as Harry McGraw, a semi-seedy private eye who worked in Boston. Across the hall from McGraw's rundown office were the law offices of Maginnis & Maginnis, now occupied by only one Magginis, the widowed, and very prim and proper, Ellie Maginnis (played by Barbara Babcock). Although they had little in common, the two hit it off. Other regulars included Juli Donald as Harry's niece and secretary, E. J. Brunson; Shea Farrell as Ellie's nephew, tax attorney Steve Lacey; Peter Haskell as assistant district attorney Tyler Chase, who also pursued Ellie; and Marty Davis as Cookie, the bartender at Harry's favorite watering hole, Gilhooley's. Orbach had originally played the character on *Murder, She Wrote.*

THE LAW AND MR. JONES   ABC
7 OCTOBER 1960–22 SEPTEMBER 1961   Half-hour crime show starring James Whitmore as idealistic attorney Abraham Lincoln Jones. With Janet DeGore as his secretary, Marsha Spear; Conlan Carter as his law clerk, C. E. Carruthers. Sy Gomberg created and produced the series.

LAW & ORDER   NBC
13 SEPTEMBER 1990–   Filmed on location in New York, this hour crime show borrowed its format from a 1963 ABC series, *Arrest and Trial.* On the first half of the show a team of detectives apprehended criminals, and on the second half a team of prosecutors attempted to convict them. With George Dzundza (1990–1991) as Det. Sgt. Max Greevey; Chris Noth (1990–1995) as his partner, Detective Mike Logan; Dann Florek (1990–1993) as their boss, Captain John Cragen; Michael Moriarty (1990–1994) as assistant district attorney Ben Stone; Richard Brooks (1990–1993) as assistant D.A. Paul Robinette; Steven Hill as the district attorney, Adam Schiff; Paul Sorvino (1991–1992) as Detective Phil Cerretta (Sorvino left the series after one season to study opera); Jerry Orbach (1992–   ) as Detective Lennie Briscoe; Jill Hennessy as assistant district attorney Claire Kincaid; S. Epatha Merkerson as Lieutenant Anita Van Buren; and Sam Waterston (1994–   ) as assistant district attorney Jack McCoy. Benjamin Bratt was added in the fall of 1995 as Detective Rey Curtis. Of the several actors' departures on the series, Michael Moriarty's was the noisiest; he left the series after complaining about Attorney General Janet Reno's criticism of TV violence. Labeling those who threatened censorship as "liberal fascists," he criticized NBC News for its failure to give him adequate time to air his views. Later in 1994 he announced on CNBC's *Talk Live* that he intended to run for President, but withdrew two days later.

THE LAW OF THE PLAINSMAN   NBC
1 OCTOBER 1959–22 SEPTEMBER 1960   Michael Ansara, who had played an Indian on *Broken Arrow,* again played an Indian on this half-hour western. This time Ansara starred as Sam Buckheart, an Apache who (as a result of befriending a Cavalry officer as a youth) had been educated at Harvard. Buckheart returned to Santa Fe, New Mexico Territory, and became a deputy U.S. marshal there. Also featured were Dayton Lummis as his boss, Marshal Morrison; Robert Harland as fellow deputy Billy Lordan; Gina Gillespie as an orphan, Tess Logan, who was "adopted" by Sam; and Nora Marlowe as Martha, owner of the boarding house where Sam and Tess

lived. Peter Packer produced the program. The pilot for the series was televised 17 February 1959 as an episode of *The Rifleman,* titled "The Indian."

THE LAWBREAKERS   SYNDICATED
1963   Documentary series about real-life criminals, narrated by Lee Marvin.

THE LAWLESS YEARS   NBC
16 APRIL 1959–3 SEPTEMBER 1959; 12 MAY 1961–22 SEPTEMBER 1961   *The Lawless Years* was the first crime show set in the 1920s, antedating *The Untouchables* by a half season. James Gregory starred as Barney Ruditsky, a New York police detective; Robert Karnes was featured as Max, his sidekick. Jack Chertok was the producer.

THE LAWMAN   ABC
5 OCTOBER 1958–9 OCTOBER 1962   Half-hour western from Warner Brothers starring John Russell as Marshal Dan Troop of Laramie, Wyoming; Peter Brown as his deputy, Johnnie McKay; Bek Nelson (1958–1959) as Dru Lemp, owner of the Blue Bonnet Cafe; Barbara Long (1959) as Julie Tate, editor of the Laramie newspaper, and Peggie Castle (1959–1962) as Lily Merrill, proprietor of the Birdcage Saloon.

THE LAWRENCE WELK SHOW   ABC/SYNDICATED
2 JULY 1955–4 SEPTEMBER 1971 (ABC); 1971–1982 (SYNDICATED)
LAWRENCE WELK'S TOP TUNES AND NEW TALENT   ABC
8 OCTOBER 1956–2 JUNE 1958
THE PLYMOUTH SHOW STARRING LAWRENCE WELK   ABC
(LAWRENCE WELK'S LITTLE BAND)
10 SEPTEMBER 1958–27 MAY 1959   One of TV's most durable musical series, *The Lawrence Welk Show* presented middle-of-the-road music ("champagne music," in Welk's words) for almost three decades. It was also one of the few series to be aired on more stations in its syndicated form than when it ran on the ABC network. Welk, an accordionist and bandleader, kept the format simple and predictable—lots of music, a little dancing, and a few guest stars. Numbers were performed by the members of Welk's television family. That large group included the Lennon Sisters (Dianne, Peggy, Kathy, and Janet), Alice Lon, Norma Zimmer, Tanya Falan, Arthur Duncan, Joe Feeney, Guy Hovis, Jim Roberts, Ralna English, Larry Hooper, Jerry Burke, and former Mouseketeer Bobby Burgess. A fixture on ABC's Saturday-night schedule for sixteen seasons, the show was known as *The Dodge Dancing Party* in its first years. From 1956 to 1959 Welk was seen twice a week on ABC; *Lawrence Welk's Top Tunes and New Talent* ran on Monday nights for two seasons, and *The Plymouth Show Starring Lawrence Welk*—which featured a ten-piece orchestra comprised of children, known as Lawrence Welk's Little Band—was seen on Wednesdays during the 1958–1959 season.

THE LAZARUS SYNDROME   ABC
4 SEPTEMBER 1979–16 OCTOBER 1979   Hour medical drama starring Louis Gossett, Jr., as Dr. Macarthur (Mac) St. Clair, a cardiologist and chief of staff at Webster Memorial Hospital; Ronald Hunter as Joe Hamill, an ex-reporter who became the hospital's administrator; Sheila Frazier as Gloria St. Clair, Mac's wife; and Peggy McCay as Stacy, Hamill's secretary. Created by William Blinn (who served as executive producer with Jerry Thorpe), the series was pulled from ABC's schedule in October 1979 for "retooling," and was set to return later in the season. The term "Lazarus syndrome" refers to the belief by patients that physicians are capable of solving all the patients' problems.

LAZER TAG ACADEMY   NBC
13 SEPTEMBER 1986–5 SEPTEMBER 1987   Saturday-morning cartoon series about a teenager, Jamie Jaren, who traveled back in time from the year 3010 to the present day and battled the evil Silas Mayhem.

A LEAGUE OF THEIR OWN   CBS

10 APRIL 1993–24 APRIL 1993; 13 AUGUST 1993   Half-hour sitcom derived from the hit movie about the Rockford Peaches, a team of female baseball players organized during World War II. With Sam McMurray as Jimmy Dugan, the manager; Carey Lowell as star player Dottie Hinson; Christine Elise as Dottie's sister, Kit Keller; Tracy Nelson as Evelyn; Megan Cavanagh as Marla Hooch; Tracy Reiner as Betty, a war widow; Wendy Makkena as Mae; Katie Rich as Doris; Matthew Howard as Stillwell, Evelyn's obnoxious son; Jon Lovitz as Ernie "Cappy" Capadino, a former scout who now worked for the league; and Garry Marshall as league president Walter Harvey. Cavanaugh, Reiner, Lovitz, and Marshall were reprising their movie roles. Introduced in April 1993, the series was placed on hiatus after just three outings; two additional episodes were shown 13 August.

LEAVE IT TO BEAVER   CBS/ABC

4 OCTOBER 1957–17 SEPTEMBER 1958 (CBS); 2 OCTOBER 1958–12 SEPTEMBER 1963 (ABC)   This family sitcom centered around the Cleaver family of Mayfield. With Hugh Beaumont as Ward Cleaver, an accountant and a patient, understanding father; Barbara Billingsley as June Cleaver, a well-dressed housewife and a patient, understanding mother; Tony Dow as their older son, Wally, an all-American kid; and Jerry Mathers as their younger son, Theodore, better known as The Beaver. In almost all of the 234 half-hours Beaver's well-intentioned efforts to do good managed to backfire, landing him in some kind of trouble; Mathers's cuteness (particularly in the early seasons) and his natural acting style helped distinguish the show from other 1950s family sitcoms. Also featured were Ken Osmond as Wally's crafty friend, Eddie Haskell, whose obsequious attitude toward Mr. and Mrs. Cleaver belied his contempt of them (and Beaver); Frank Bank as Wally's chunky friend, Clarence "Lumpy" Rutherford; Richard Deacon as Lumpy's father, Fred Rutherford, Ward's boss; Diane Brewster as Miss Canfield, Beaver's second-grade teacher at the Grant Avenue Elementary School; Sue Randall as Miss Landers, Beaver's third-grade teacher; Doris Packer as Mrs. Cornelia Rayburn, the school principal; Rusty Stevens as Larry Mondello, one of Beaver's friends; Madge Blake as Mrs. Mondello, Larry's mom; and Burt Mustin as Gus, the oldtimer at the fire station. Other friends of Beaver's over the years included Stanley Fafara as Whitey Whitney; Stephen Talbot as Gilbert Bates; Richard Correll as Richard Rickover; Tiger Fafara as Tooey; Buddy Hart as Chester; Jeri Weil as Judy Hensler, Beaver's nemesis at school; and Pamela Beaird as Mary Ellen Rogers, Wally's girlfriend. The series was created, written, and produced by Joe Connelly and Bob Mosher, who had written for *Amos and Andy*. (Richard Correll, who played Beaver's pal Richard in the latter seasons, was the son of Charles Correll, co-creator of *Amos and Andy*).

Leave It to Beaver remained popular in reruns after leaving the network in 1963; by the 1980s it had achieved cult status, perhaps because of its stereotypical depiction of American family life. On 19 March 1983 CBS televised a made-for-TV movie sequel, "Still the Beaver," in which Beaver returned to Mayfield with *his* two young sons after his wife left him. Several members of the original cast were reunited, including Jerry Mathers, Tony Dow, Barbara Billingsley (Hugh Beaumont had died a year earlier), Richard Deacon, Ken Osmond (who had left showbiz to become a police officer), Rusty Stevens, and Richard Correll. On 4 October 1987, cable superstation WTBS celebrated the thirtieth anniversary of the series' premiere by televising the 1957 pilot for the show, "It's a Small World," featuring Mathers, Billingsley, Casey Adams (as Ward), and Paul Sullivan (as Wally). See also *The New Leave It to Beaver*.

LEAVE IT TO LARRY   CBS

14 OCTOBER 1952–23 DECEMBER 1952   Eddie Albert starred in this half-hour sitcom as Larry, a bumbling shoe salesman who worked in his father-in-law's store. Ed Begley appeared as his boss and father-in-law, and Katharine Bard was featured as his wife. Leo Solomon produced the series, and Mervyn Nelson and Allen Reisner directed it. The show was little noted and certainly little watched, for it was scheduled opposite Milton Berle's *The Texaco Star Theater* on Tuesdays.

LEAVE IT TO THE GIRLS   NBC/ABC/SYNDICATED

27 APRIL 1949–30 DECEMBER 1951 (NBC); 3 OCTOBER 1953–27 MARCH 1954 (ABC); 1962–1963 (SYNDICATED)   This early talk show began on radio in 1945. Each week a panel of female celebrities met to air the women's point of view on a certain subject (usually one of a romantic nature). Also on hand was a lone male guest, whose job it was to defend the men's point of view. Maggi McNellis hosted the show for most of its run, and Martha Rountree, who also produced *Meet the Press,* produced it. The syndicated version was a Monday-through-Friday program, also hosted by McNellis.

LEAVE IT TO THE WOMEN   SYNDICATED

1981   Stephanie Edwards moderated this panel show, a modern reincarnation of the old panel show *Leave It to the Girls,* on which a panel of women grilled a male guest.

LEE TREVINO'S GOLF FOR SWINGERS   SYNDICATED

1972   Half-hour game show on which celebrities played three holes with golf pro Lee Trevino.

LEEZA (JOHN & LEEZA)   NBC

14 JUNE 1993–   This hour daytime magazine show began life in 1993 as *John & Leeza,* when it was cohosted by *Entertainment Tonight* veterans John Tesh and Leeza Gibbons. Tesh left on 14 January 1994, and the show carried on thereafter as *Leeza,* with Gibbons as sole host.

THE LEFTOVER REVUE   NBC

17 SEPTEMBER 1951–9 NOVEMBER 1951   Half-hour daytime variety series hosted by Wayne Howell.

LEG WORK   CBS

3 OCTOBER 1987–7 NOVEMBER 1987   Margaret Colin, who had played Alex Harrigan, a Manhattan assistant district attorney in *Foley Square* in 1986, returned in this series as Claire McCarron, a *former* Manhattan assistant district attorney who had become a private eye. With her were Patrick James Clarke as her brother, Lieutenant Fred McCarron of the N.Y.P.D. public information office, and Frances McDormand as Willie Pipal, Claire's contact in the D.A.'s office. Only six episodes were shown; they were filmed on location in New York.

LEGEND   UPN

18 APRIL 1995–22 AUGUST 1995   This hour western owed a tip of the cowboy hat to *The Wild, Wild West.* Richard Dean Anderson starred as Ernest Pratt, a dime novelist with a fondness for alcohol; Pratt, who had written a series of popular novels about a contemporary western hero named Nicodemus Legend, was sometimes forced by his publisher to make public appearances as Legend. He found himself in Sheridan, Colorado, where he hooked up with a scientist who was developing newfangled electric and mechanical devices which they put to use to catch bad guys. Also featured were John deLancie as the inventor, Janos Bartok; Mark Adair Ross as Bartok's Harvard-educated assistant, Ramos; and Jarrad Paul as Skeeter, a wildhaired young man who did odd jobs for Pratt and Bartok.

THE LEGEND OF CUSTER
See CUSTER

THE LEGEND OF JESSE JAMES   ABC

13 SEPTEMBER 1965–5 SEPTEMBER 1966   Jesse James, the notorious frontier outlaw, was portrayed as a nineteenth-century Robin Hood in this unsuccessful half-hour western; according to the series, Jesse and his brother Frank robbed trains only to repay local folks whose property had been confiscated by the railroad barons, who had even hassled their mother when she balked at turning over her ranch. The show

featured Chris Jones as Jesse James; Allen Case as his brother, Frank; Ann Doran as their mother, Mrs. James; and Robert J. Wilke as Marshal Sam Corbett, the lawman who vainly pursued them. The series was produced by 20th Century-Fox TV.

THE LEGEND OF WILLIAM TELL
See WILLIAM TELL (1991)

LEGMEN NBC
20 JANUARY 1984–16 MARCH 1984   Hour crime show about two college students working their way through school as "legmen" for a private investigator. With Bruce Greenwood as Jack Gage; J. T. Terlesky as his roommate, David Taylor; and Don Calfa as their original employer, Oscar Armismendi, proprietor of the Tri-Star Bail Bonds Agency; Claude Akins succeeded him as their new boss, Tom Bannon.

LENNY CBS
10 SEPTEMBER 1990–3 OCTOBER 1990; 15 DECEMBER 1990–9 MARCH 1991   Half-hour sitcom about a blue-collar Irish Catholic Boston family. With Lenny Clarke (a standup comic from Boston) as Lenny Callahan; Lee Garlington as his wife, Shelly; Jenna Von Oy as their daughter Kelly, thirteen; Alexis Caldwell as their daughter Tracy, ten; the Hall Twins (pilot only) and the Farmer Twins as baby Elizabeth; Peter Dobson as Lenny's lazy brother, Eddie Callahan; Eugene Roche as their father, Pat; and Alice Drummond as their mother, Mary. The series' theme was sung by Dion.

LEO & LIZ IN BEVERLY HILLS CBS
25 APRIL 1986–6 JUNE 1986   Half-hour sitcom about an upscale couple from New Jersey who moved into Beverly Hills. With Harvey Korman as Leo Green; Valerie Perrine as Liz Green; Deborah Harmon as their new next-door neighbor, Diane Fedderson; Ken Kimmins as her husband, Jerry Fedderson; Sue Ball as Mitzi, Liz's daughter; Julie Payne as Lucille Trombly, the maid; Michael J. Pollard as Leonard, the houseman; and Peter Aykroyd as Bucky Winthrop, Mitzi's husband. The series was developed from "The Couch," a half-hour comedy which was presented on *George Burns Comedy Week* 16 October 1985.

LEROY JENKINS
See REVIVAL OF AMERICA CRUSADE

THE LES BROWN SHOW SYNDICATED
1993–1994   Short-lived hour daytime talk show, hosted by black motivational speaker Les Brown.

THE LES CRANE SHOW ABC
9 NOVEMBER 1964–5 MARCH 1965   ABC's first attempt at a late-night talk show was hosted by Les Crane; the show featured a "shotgun" microphone which enabled members of the studio audience to talk to Crane's guests. After four months the network decided to go with a series of guest hosts, and the show was retitled *Nightlife*.

THE LESLIE UGGAMS SHOW CBS
26 SEPTEMBER 1969–14 DECEMBER 1969   Leslie Uggams, who had previously been featured on *Sing Along with Mitch,* became the first black woman since Hazel Scott to host a network variety series. It fared poorly against NBC's *Bonanza,* as did most of the CBS shows scheduled in that time slot during the 1960s. Other regulars included Johnny Brown, Alison Mills, Lillian Hayman, and Lincoln Kilpatrick; a regular feature was "Sugar Hill," a running sketch about a poor black family. Saul Ilson and Ernest Chambers, who had previously produced *The Smothers Brothers Comedy Hour,* produced the series.

LET THERE BE STARS ABC
16 OCTOBER 1949–27 NOVEMBER 1949   A half-hour revue from Hollywood, produced by Leighton Brill and William Trinz. Among the many regulars who appeared was a

young singer-comedian named Peter Marshall, who would become the host of *Hollywood Squares* in 1966.

LET'S DANCE   ABC
18 SEPTEMBER 1954–16 OCTOBER 1954   Ballroom dancing was featured on this musical hour, broadcast live from both New York and Chicago, with music supplied by guest bands. Ralph Mooney hosted the New York portion, Art Mooney the Chicago segment.

LET'S MAKE A DEAL   NBC/ABC/SYNDICATED
30 DECEMBER 1963–27 DECEMBER 1968 (NBC); 30 DECEMBER 1968–9 JULY 1976 (ABC); 1971–1976; 1980; 1984–1985 (SYNDICATED); 9 JULY 1990–11 JANUARY 1991 (NBC)   One of TV's best-known game shows, *Let's Make a Deal* required no skill, no dexterity, and no knowledge of its contestants. Each day, thirty-one members of the studio audience (many of whom were dressed in ridiculous outfits) were selected to sit in the "trading area" up front; some of those people then had the chance to "make a deal" with "TV's big dealer," host Monty Hall. Theoretically, the traders were supposed to have brought something of their own to trade, but over the years even this requirement was virtually abandoned. If selected by Hall, each trader was presented with a choice—whether to take one prize or another. Sometimes one prize would be described fully while the other remained hidden inside a box or behind a door; sometimes neither prize would be described; sometimes cash (in stated or unstated amounts) would be offered against a merchandise prize; and sometimes one of the prizes would be worthless—they were known as "zonks." And there lay the show's appeal. A player could be given, for example, $1,000 in cash, trade the money for what proved to be a mink coat, and decide to trade the coat—only to end up with a wheelbarrow. At the end of each show the two players who had won the most were given the chance to trade their winnings for the day's "Big Deal." Each player selected one of three doors and won what was behind it; there were no "zonks" at this level, and the Big Deal, concealed behind one of the doors, was usually worth at least $10,000. Monty Hall, who developed and produced the show with his partner, Stefan Hatos, was the perfect host for the show. Monty kept the show moving while he treated the outrageously garbed and occasionally greedy contestants courteously; it is hard to imagine anyone else but Hall working the trading area as skillfully. Hall was assisted by announcer Jay Stewart and model Carol Merrill. More than 3,800 network shows were done over a thirteen-year span; at the final show, taped in Nevada shortly before Christmas 1976, there were no zonks. The short-lived 1980 version was produced in Vancouver for syndication. The series was produced again for syndication in 1984, again with Hall. In 1990 it returned to its original daytime home, NBC; produced at the Disney/MGM Studios in Florida, the newest incarnation was hosted by Bob Hilton.

LET'S PLAY POST OFFICE   NBC
27 SEPTEMBER 1965–1 JULY 1966   Don Morrow hosted this daytime game show on which contestants tried to identify the "authors" of fictitious letters read aloud a line at a time.

LET'S SEE   ABC
14 JULY 1955–1 SEPTEMBER 1955   John Reed King hosted this summertime panel show.

LET'S TAKE A TRIP   CBS
17 APRIL 1955–23 FEBRUARY 1958   Sunday series for children on which Sonny Fox and two children paid visits to interesting places. Fox was assisted first by youngsters Pud Flanagan and Ginger MacManus; in 1957 they were succeeded by Joan Terrace and Jimmy Walsh. Jim Colligan succeeded Steve Fleischman as producer of the New York-based series.

A LETTER TO LORETTA
See THE LORETTA YOUNG SHOW

LETTERS TO LAUGH-IN   NBC
29 SEPTEMBER 1969–26 DECEMBER 1969   This daytime game show was an unusual
spinoff from *Laugh-In*. Host Gary Owens, the announcer of *Laugh-In*, presided over
the program on which a panel of four guest celebrities read jokes submitted to
Laugh-In by home viewers; judges from the studio audience then rated the jokes.

LEWIS & CLARK   NBC
29 OCTOBER 1981–9 JANUARY 1982; 2 JULY 1982–30 JULY 1982   Gabe Kaplan created
and starred in the half-hour sitcom as Stewart Lewis, a New Yorker who bought a
saloon in Luckenbach, Texas, and headed there with his family. Also featured were
Guich Koock as Roscoe Clark, the manager of the saloon (which Lewis renamed the
Nassau County Cafe); Ilene Graff as Alicia Lewis, Stew's wife; Amy Linker as Kelly,
their daughter; David Hollander as Keith, their son; Clifton James as regular customer Silas Jones; Wendy Holcombe as Wendy, the waitress; and Michael McManus
as John.

LEWISOHN STADIUM CONCERT   ABC
26 JUNE 1950–7 AUGUST 1950   A summer replacement for *Robert Montgomery
Presents* featuring the New York Philharmonic Symphony Orchestra in concert with
guest artists. Ben Grauer was the announcer.

LIARS CLUB   SYNDICATED
1969; 1976–1977; 1988   Game show featuring two contestants, four celebrities, and
a group of unusual objects. Three of the four celebrities suggested a false definition
or description of the object, while the fourth described it correctly. The contestants
tried to figure out who was telling the truth. Rod Serling hosted the 1969 version; Bill
Armstrong was the first host of the mid-1970's version and was succeeded by Allen
Ludden. Eric Boardman emceed the 1988 version, which featured four contestants.
The show was a Ralph Andrews Production.

THE LIBERACE SHOW   NBC/SYNDICATED/ABC/CBS
1 JULY 1952–28 AUGUST 1952 (NBC); 1953–1955 (SYNDICATED); 13 OCTOBER
1958–10 APRIL 1959 (ABC); 15 JULY 1969–16 SEPTEMBER 1969 (CBS)   Liberace,
the flamboyant pianist best remembered for his sequined wardrobe and the can-
delabra atop his instrument, hosted several television programs. The first was a
fifteen-minute series which replaced *The Dinah Shore Show* on Tuesdays and Thursdays during the summer of 1952. It was well enough received so that Liberace
decided to try a syndicated, half-hour show, which proved to be enormously popular; both of the early series also featured Liberace's brother, George, as violinist
and orchestra leader. Illness forced him to curtail his schedule in 1955, but he
returned to television in 1958 to host a half-hour daytime show on ABC; it featured
Joan O'Brien, Erin O'Brien, Dick Roman, Steve Dunne, and the Gordon Robinson Orchestra. Liberace hosted a British series in 1960, and his 1969 summer series,
shown in this country, was produced in London; the hour show featured Richard
Wattis and Georgina Moon. Born Wladziu Valentino Liberace, he preferred to use
just one name.

LIDSVILLE   ABC
11 SEPTEMBER 1971–1 SEPTEMBER 1973   Sid and Marty Krofft were the executive
producers of this Saturday-morning live-action kids' show. It starred Butch Patrick as
Mark, a youngster who found himself in Lidsville, a mysterious world of hats. Also
featured were Charles Nelson Reilly as the evil Whoo Doo, and Billie Hayes as the
good Weenie the Genie.

LIE DETECTOR   SYNDICATED

1983   Flamboyant attorney F. Lee Bailey hosted this half-hour program, on which persons underwent polygraph examinations to help prove that they were telling the truth about a matter in controversy. Polygraph expert Ed Gelb administered the examinations, the results of which suggested that some guests were telling the truth—such as President Reagan's barber, who swore that he did not dye the President's hair—and that others were not—such as Melvin Dummar, who claimed that reclusive billionaire Howard Hughes had left him a share of his estate.

THE LIEUTENANT   NBC

14 SEPTEMBER 1963–5 SEPTEMBER 1964   Hour-long dramatic series set at Camp Pendleton in California. With Gary Lockwood as Lieutenant William Rice, U.S.M.C.; Robert Vaughn as his commanding officer, Captain Raymond Rambridge; Steve Franken as Lieutenant Sam Panosian; Carmen Phillips as Lily, Rambridge's secretary; Henry Beckman as Barker; Richard Anderson as Hiland; John Milford as Kagey; and Don Penny as Harris. Norman Felton was the executive producer of the series, which was created and produced by Gene Roddenberry, who later created *Star Trek*.

THE LIFE AND ADVENTURES OF NICHOLAS NICKLEBY
See NICHOLAS NICKLEBY

THE LIFE AND LEGEND OF WYATT EARP
See WYATT EARP

LIFE AND TIMES OF EDDIE ROBERTS   SYNDICATED

1980   Half-hour comedy serial in the *Mary Hartman, Mary Hartman* vein. With Renny Temple as Eddie Roberts, a professor scrambling for tenure at Cranepool University; Udana Power as his wife, Dolores, an aspiring major-league ball player; Allison Balson as their young daughter, Chrissy; Stephen Parr as faculty colleague Tony Cranepool; Allen Case as Dean Knitzer; Joan Hotchkis as Lydia; Loyita Chapel as Vivian Blankett; Jon Lormer as Boggs; and Daryl Roach as Turner Lequatro. Ann and Ellis Marcus created and wrote the series.

THE LIFE AND TIMES OF GRIZZLY ADAMS   NBC

9 FEBRUARY 1977–26 JULY 1978   Set in the nineteenth century, *The Life and Times of Grizzly Adams* was an hour-long adventure series aimed principally at children. It starred Dan Haggerty as James (Grizzly) Adams; accused of a crime he never committed, Adams escaped to the northwest wilderness to live by himself, in harmony with nature. He fished, but did not hunt, and wore only cloth garments. His best friend was a large grizzly bear called Ben (played by a real bear known as Bozo). Adams also had one or two human acquaintances—Denver Pyle as Mad Jack, who also served as the show's narrator, and Don Shanks as Nakuma, Adams's Indian blood brother. Charles E. Sellier, Jr., was the executive producer of the series, which was produced by Leonard B. Kaufman and Jim Simmons. The TV show was based on the film of the same title, which had starred Haggerty and been produced by Sellier. The character returned in a made-for-TV movie "The Capture of Grizzly Adams," broadcast 21 February 1982 on NBC.

LIFE AROUND US   SYNDICATED

1971   A series of half-hour documentaries on biology from Time-Life Films.

LIFE BEGINS AT EIGHTY   NBC/ABC/DUMONT

13 JANUARY 1950–25 AUGUST 1950 (NBC); 3 OCTOBER 1950–10 MARCH 1952 (ABC); 21 MARCH 1952–24 JULY 1955 (DUMONT); 31 JULY 1955–25 FEBRUARY 1956 (ABC) Produced and hosted by Jack Barry, this panel show was the converse of Barry's previous effort, *Juvenile Jury;* a panel of octogenarians dispensed advice on topics submitted by viewers. Regular panelists included Fred Stein and Georgiana Carhart, who had also been featured on the radio version.

LIFE CHOICES   SYNDICATED

1994–   Half-hour weekly informational series on health, diet, and lifestyle issues, coanchored by Erie Chapman and Kathleen Sullivan.

LIFE GOES ON   ABC

12 SEPTEMBER 1989–29 AUGUST 1993   The first prime-time series to feature a regular with Down's syndrome, this hour family drama aired in the "family viewing hour," 7 P.M. on Sundays. With Bill Smitrovich as Drew Thacher; Patti LuPone as his working wife, Libby; Christopher Burke as their eighteen-year-old ninth grader with Down's syndrome, Charles "Corky" Thacher; Kellie Martin as their younger daughter, Becca, who was embarrased at being in the same grade as her brother; and Monique Lanier (1989–1990) as Paige, Drew's older daughter from a prior marriage. During the show's first season Drew quit his job as a construction foreman and opened a restaurant. David Byrd was later added as his chef, Hans. Occasionally featured were Ray Buktenica (1989–1992) as Libby's boss, Jerry Berkson; Tommy Puett (1989–1992) as Becca's sometime boyfriend, Tyler Benchfield, who was killed in an auto accident; Tanya Fenmore as Becca's friend, Maxie; and Al Ruscio and Penny Santon as Libby's parents, Sal and Teresa Giordano. As the show's second season unfolded, daughter Paige had moved out of the house (and Tracey Needham replaced Monique Lanier as Paige, who no longer appeared regularly), and Libby found herself pregnant at age forty-one. Libby's younger sister, Gina (played by Mary Page Keller) and her daughter, Zoe (Leigh Ann Orsi), arrived in midseason to help run the house. Keller and Orsi departed at the end of the 1990–1991 season. In the fall of 1991 the Thachers welcomed their baby, Nick, and Chad Lowe joined the cast as high school transfer student Jesse McKenna, who was HIV-positive and would develop AIDS by the spring of 1993; Jesse and Becca became very close friends. In the spring of 1992 Paige made plans to marry Kenny Stollmark, Jr. (played by Steven Eckholdt), and in the fall of 1992 Corky eloped with Amanda Swanson (played by Andrea Friedman, who also had Down's syndrome).

LIFE IS WORTH LIVING   DUMONT
12 FEBRUARY 1952–26 APRIL 1955
MISSION TO THE WORLD   ABC
13 OCTOBER 1955–8 APRIL 1957
THE BEST OF BISHOP SHEEN   SYNDICATED
1958–1962   *Life Is Worth Living* and *Mission to the World* were the titles of the two network shows hosted by Bishop Fulton J. Sheen; they were among the few religious shows ever aired during prime time. *Life is Worth Living* was scheduled opposite Milton Berle's *The Texaco Star Theater,* but, unlike most of Berle's competition, managed to attract enough viewers to warrant its continuation. Frank Bunetta, who later directed *The Jackie Gleason Show,* directed *Life Is Worth Living.* Reruns of the network program, together with some newly-taped talks, were syndicated as *The Best of Bishop Sheen.*

THE LIFE OF LEONARDO DA VINCI   CBS/PBS
13 AUGUST 1972–10 SEPTEMBER 1972 (CBS); 20 NOVEMBER 1974–18 DECEMBER 1974 (PBS)   Five-part miniseries on the life of Leonardo Da Vinci. Produced by RAI, Italy's state-owned network, it starred Phillipe Leroy as Leonardo, Alberto Fiorini and Arduino Paolini as the younger Leonardo, and Bruno Cirino as Michelangelo. Giulio Bosetti served as the guide and narrator for the series, and Ben Gazzara introduced the episodes on PBS.

THE LIFE OF RILEY   NBC
4 OCTOBER 1949–28 MARCH 1950; 2 JANUARY 1953–22 AUGUST 1958   This family sitcom began on radio in 1944 and twice came to television. More than any other comedy of the 1950s, it resembled *All in the Family,* as both shows centered around a blue-collar husband and father who frequently found life a bit too perplexing (or, as Riley put it, "What a revoltin' development this is!"). The first, and less well known, TV version starred Jackie Gleason as Chester A. Riley, a riveter at Stevenson Air-

craft in Los Angeles; Rosemary DeCamp as his wife, Peg; Gloria Winters as their daughter, Babs; Lanny Rees as their son, Chester A. Riley, Jr. (Junior); Sid Tomack as Riley's friend and coworker, Jim Gillis; and John Brown as the neighborhood undertaker, Digby "Digger" O'Dell. The series was produced by Irving Brecher, Reuben Ship, and Alan Lipscot, and directed by Herbert I. Leeds. Though the show won an Emmy, it was dropped after twenty-six weeks. Early in 1953 it returned, however, and stayed for more than five years. The second version starred William Bendix (who had played the part on radio) as Chester A. Riley; Marjorie Reynolds as wife, Peg; Lugene Sanders as daughter Babs; Wesley Morgan as Junior; Tom D'Andrea as Gillis; Gloria Blondell as Gillis's wife, Honeybee; Gregory Marshall as Egbert Gillis, son of Jim and Honeybee; Henry Kulky as Riley's friend and co-worker, dimwitted Otto Schmidlap; Emory Parnell as Riley's foreman, Hank Hawkins; and Sterling Holloway as Riley's eccentric friend, Waldo Binney, an amateur inventor. In the fall of 1955 the Gillises, who had lived in the Rileys' next-door cottage, were dropped from the series, as Tom D'Andrea had signed to appear in a new sitcom, *The Soldiers*. George O'Hanlon and Florence Sundstrom joined the cast as their new neighbors, Calvin and Belle Dudley. They in turn were dropped after the 1955–1956 season as D'Andrea and Blondell returned. Tom McKnight produced the second television version.

LIFE ON EARTH   PBS
12 JANUARY 1982–6 APRIL 1982   Naturalist David Attenborough created and narrated this engrossing series on biology and evolution.

LIFE WITH BUSTER KEATON   SYNDICATED
1951   Buster Keaton, star of many silent film comedies, filmed this half-hour series when he was in his late fifties; in most of the stories he appeared as a clerk in a sporting goods shop.

LIFE WITH ELIZABETH   SYNDICATED
1953–1954   Domestic sitcom starring Betty White and Del Moore as newlyweds Elizabeth and Alvin White. Don Fedderson produced the series in association with Guild Films. Each program consisted of three short vignettes.

LIFE WITH FATHER   CBS
22 NOVEMBER 1953–5 JULY 1955   *Life with Father* began as a series of essays by Clarence Day, Jr., which appeared in *Harper's Magazine* and later in *The New Yorker*. A best-selling book ensued, followed shortly by a tremendously successful Broadway play which ran for eight years; a motion picture was made in 1947. The TV version of the comedy was not especially popular, however. Set at the turn of the century, it starred Leon Ames as Clarence Day, Sr., a prosperous banker and an old-fashioned patriarch, and Lurene Tuttle as his wife, Vinnie. Eight actors played the four Day sons during the show's two-year run: Ralph Reed and Steven Terrell as eldest son, Clarence, Jr.; Freddie Leiston and Malcolm Cassell as second son, John; Ronald Keith, B. G. Norman, and Freddy Ridgeway as third son, Whitney; and Harvey Grant as youngest son, Harlan. Also featured was Dorothy Bernard (the only member of the cast who had been in the play) as Margaret, the maid. Ezra Stone, who had played Henry Aldrich on radio, produced the half-hour series. At the insistence of Mrs. Clarence Day, Jr., who served as a special consultant to the show, all of the members of the television Day family had to have red hair (as they had had in real life), even though the show was broadcast in black and white.

LIFE WITH LINKLETTER   ABC/NBC
6 OCTOBER 1950–25 APRIL 1952 (ABC); 29 DECEMBER 1969–25 SEPTEMBER 1970 (NBC)
Art Linkletter's first television series, *Life with Linkletter*, was a prime-time version of *Art Linkletter's House Party*, which began on radio in 1945 and came to TV in 1952; like *House Party*, it featured audience participation games and interviews with schoolchildren. It was produced by John Guedel and directed by Stuart Phelps. In

1969, after *House Party* had left the air, Linkletter and his son cohosted a daytime show on NBC, also entitled *Life with Linkletter.*

LIFE WITH LOUIE   FOX
9 SEPTEMBER 1995–   Saturday morning cartoon show based on the not-especially-happy childhood of comic Louie Anderson. Anderson's own adult voice provided the voice of eight-year-old Louie, who lived with his mom, dad, and little brother, Tommy. Anderson also appeared in filmed sequences to introduce each program.

LIFE WITH LUCY   ABC
20 SEPTEMBER 1986–15 NOVEMBER 1986   Lucille Ball's much-heralded return to weekly television proved to be a disaster. The half-hour sitcom was created by Madelyn Pugh Davis and Bob Carroll, Jr., two of the writers from *I Love Lucy*; Lucy's husband, Gary Morton, was executive producer, together with Aaron Spelling and Douglas S. Cramer. Spelling agreed to give Lucy total creative control, and ABC committed itself to twenty-two episodes. Unfortunately, the combination never jelled, and the series was lifted after only eight weeks. Lucy's physical comedy style just didn't work for a seventy-five-year-old woman.
　　The series was set in South Pasadena, where Lucille Ball played the recently widowed Lucy Barker, who moved in with her daughter's family; Lucy's late husband had left her half of the family hardware store. Gale Gordon (Ball's longtime comic foil) played her business partner, Curtis McGibbon, whose son was married to Lucy's daughter and who also lived in their household. Also appearing were Larry Anderson as Curtis's son, law student Ted McGibbon; Ann Dusenberry as Ted's wife (and Lucy's daughter), Margo McGibbon; Jenny Lewis as their daughter, Becky; Philip J. Amelio II as their son, Kevin; and Donovan Scott as Leonard Stoner, Lucy and Curtis's employee.

LIFE WITH LUIGI   CBS
22 SEPTEMBER 1952–29 DECEMBER 1952; 9 APRIL 1953–4 JUNE 1953   This ethnic sitcom began on radio in 1948. Set in Chicago, it starred J. Carrol Naish as Luigi Basco, an Italian immigrant who opened a small antique store and hoped to become an American citizen; Alan Reed as Luigi's sponsor, Pasquale, proprietor of Pasquale's Spaghetti Palace; Jody Gilbert as Rosa, Pasquale's portly daughter, whom Pasquale hoped would marry Luigi; Mary Shipp as Miss Spalding, Luigi's night-school teacher; Ken Peters as Olson, one of Luigi's classmates; Joe Forte as Horowitz, another classmate; and Sig Ruman as Schultz, another classmate. Except for Sig Ruman, all the cast members had played the roles on radio. Dropped in midseason, the show reappeared briefly in the spring of 1953 with different principals: Vito Scotti as Luigi, Thomas Gomez as Pasquale, and Muriel Landers as Rosa. Produced by Cy Howard, the show was directed by Mac Benoff.

LIFELINE   NBC
7 SEPTEMBER 1978–30 DECEMBER 1978   One of the most unusual prime-time shows of the decade, *Lifeline* was an hour documentary series about the medical profession. Each week the cameras followed a doctor around; much of the action took place in operating rooms. Thomas Moore and Robert Fuisz, M.D., were the executive producers, Jackson Beck the narrator. The series was rerun on PBS during the summer of 1983.

LIFE'S MOST EMBARRASSING MOMENTS   ABC
2 AUGUST 1985–10 SEPTEMBER 1985   Like *TV's Bloopers & Practical Jokes*, this hour show presented outtakes from movies, television programs, and the like. Steve Allen presided over the hijinks, which were originally broadcast as occasional specials and were packaged together for a regular run during the summer of 1985.

481

LIFESTORIES   NBC
20 AUGUST 1990–2 DECEMBER 1990   This hour medical anthology series presented its stories from the patients' point of view. The series was narrated by Robert Prosky, who was credited as the Storyteller.

LIFESTYLES OF THE RICH AND FAMOUS   SYNDICATED/ABC
1984–   (SYNDICATED); *Daytime:* 7 APRIL 1986–5 SEPTEMBER 1986 (ABC); *Nighttime:* 21 JULY 1986–19 SEPTEMBER 1986 (ABC)   Visits to celebrity homes have long been a staple of television, dating back to *Person to Person* in the 1950s and *Here's Hollywood* in the early 1960s. Former *Entertainment Tonight* reporter Robin Leach revived the format in the 1980s with spectacular results. The emphasis was on glitz: the more ostentatious the star's home, the more Leach seemed to revel. The host's loud voice, and his incessant use of superlatives, were frequently lampooned on comedy shows. But the British-born Leach had the last laugh. His show, which began in syndication in 1984, was run on ABC during 1986 in both a daytime and a late-night slot, and was so successful that it spawned a pair of Leach-hosted spinoffs: see *Fame, Fortune & Romance* and *Runaway with the Rich and Famous.* In 1994 several changes occurred: Leach acquired a cohost, Shari Belafonte, and the show was retitled *Lifestyles with Robin Leach and Shari Belafonte.* Somewhat less attention was now paid to affluence and opulence, as the show focused more on persons with interesting lifestyles. Also appearing were Niki Taylor, Katie Wagner, and Mary Major.

LIGHTS, CAMERA, ACTION!   NBC
4 JULY 1950–20 AUGUST 1950   Half-hour talent show, hosted by Walter Wolfe King.

LIGHTS OUT   NBC
12 JULY 1949–29 SEPTEMBER 1952   This anthology series of thriller and suspense dramas ran for three years on television, considerably less than the twelve-year run enjoyed by the radio version under the supervision of Wyllis Cooper and, later, Arch Oboler. Jack LaRue was the first TV host; he was succeeded by Frank Gallop. A sampling of the half-hour presentations includes: "Faithful Heart," with Anne Francis (10 April 1950); "Beware this Woman," with Veronica Lake (4 December 1950); "The House of Dust," with Anthony Quinn and Nina Foch (5 February 1951); and "The Hollow Man," with William Bendix (29 September 1952).

LIKELY SUSPECTS   FOX
11 SEPTEMBER 1992–29 JANUARY 1993   This half-hour series reached back through forty-five years of television for its inspiration. Like the old TV cop show *The Plainclothesman,* the "star" of *Likely Suspects* was the viewer, who was addressed as a rookie cop accompanying a veteran officer to the scene of the crime, shown the clues, introduced to the panoply of perpetrators, and asked to solve the mystery at the end of the episode. Sam McMurray costarred as the senior officer, Detective Lieutenant Marshak, and Jason Schombing appeared as Detective Harry Spinoza.

LILIAS, YOGA AND YOU   PBS
1974–1977   Half-hour physical-and-mental exercise program, hosted by Lilias Folan and produced by WCET-TV, Cincinnati.

THE LILLI PALMER SHOW   CBS
29 MARCH 1951–28 JUNE 1951   Lilli Palmer interviewed celebrities on this fifteen-minute show, seen Thursdays.

LILLI PALMER THEATRE   SYNDICATED
1955–1956   Half-hour dramatic anthology series hosted by actress Lilli Palmer.

LIME STREET   ABC
21 SEPTEMBER 1985–26 OCTOBER 1985   This hour adventure series came to an unexpected, and tragic, end after just five episodes. It starred Robert Wagner as James

Greyson "Grey" Culver, an investigator for the London Insurance Company who lived on a horse farm in Virginia with his two daughters. Featured were John Standing as Edward Wingate, Grey's London-based partner; Samantha Smith as Grey's daughter Elizabeth; Maia Brewton as Grey's daughter Margaret Ann; Julie Fulton as Grey's assistant in Washington, D.C., Celia Westfall; Anne Harvey as Evelyn, the housekeeper; and Lew Ayres as Henry Wade Culver, Grey's father. Young costar Samantha Smith had achieved fame not as an actress, but rather as the schoolgirl who wrote to Soviet leader Yuri Andropov urging peace and who had been invited to visit the U.S.S.R. Sadly, after four episodes of *Lime Street* had been filmed, Samantha and her father were killed in a plane crash on their way home to Maine. The producers decided not to recast her role, but to stop production of the series.

THE LINEUP   CBS
1 OCTOBER 1954–20 JANUARY 1960   Crime show filmed partly on location in San Francisco and later syndicated under the title *San Francisco Beat*. With Warner Anderson as Lieutenant Ben Guthrie; Tom Tully as Inspector Matt Grebb; they were later joined by Marshall Reed as Inspector Fred Asher. In the fall of 1959 major changes took place. Tully and Reed left the series (though Tully returned for two episodes), which expanded to one hour, and four new regulars were added: Rachel Ames as policewoman Sandy McAllister; Tod Burton as Inspector Charlie Summers; William Leslie as Inspector Dan Delaney; and Skip Ward as Officer Pete Larkins. The series was a Desilu production.

LINUS THE LIONHEARTED   CBS
26 SEPTEMBER 1964–3 SEPTEMBER 1966   Saturday-morning cartoon show set in Africa. Voices included those of Sheldon Leonard as Linus, the king; Carl Reiner as Sascha Grouse and Dinny Kangaroo; Jonathan Winters as The Giant; and Ed Graham (the series' producer) as The Mockingbird. Other characters included Rory Raccoon, So-Hi, Billie Bird, and Lovable Truly. The series was rerun by ABC on Sunday mornings between 1966 and 1969.

THE LION KING'S TIMON & PUMBAA
See TIMON & PUMBAA

LITTLE CLOWNS OF HAPPYTOWN   ABC
26 SEPTEMBER 1987–16 JULY 1988   This Saturday-morning cartoon show was set in Itty Bitty City, a municipality in which all the residents were clowns. Norman Cousins was a consultant to the series, which tried to emphasize the importance of developing positive emotions.

LITTLE HOUSE ON THE PRAIRIE   NBC
11 SEPTEMBER 1974–20 SEPTEMBER 1982
LITTLE HOUSE: A NEW BEGINNING   NBC
27 SEPTEMBER 1982–5 SEPTEMBER 1983   Laura Ingalls Wilder's *Little House* books formed the basis for this hour family drama set during the 1870s. One of NBC's few mainstays of the 1970s, *Little House* was under the almost total control of Michael Landon, who was not only the star and executive producer, but also a frequent writer and director. For its first four seasons, *Little House* was set in Walnut Grove, Minnesota. The cast included: Michael Landon as the father, farmer Charles Ingalls; Karen Grassle as the mother, Caroline Ingalls; Melissa Sue Anderson as their eldest daughter, Mary; Melissa Gilbert as their second daughter, Laura, from whose point of view the stories were told; twins Lindsay and Sidney Greenbush as the third daughter, Carrie (a fourth daughter, Grace, was born in 1977 and was played by twins Wendi and Brenda Turnbeaugh); Victor French (1974–1977; spring 1982–1983) as Isaiah Edwards; Bonnie Bartlett (1974–1977) as his wife, Grace Edwards; Richard Bull as storekeeper Nels Oleson; Katherine MacGregor as his haughty wife, Harriet Oleson; Jonathan Gilbert (1975–1983, Melissa Gilbert's real-life brother) as their son, Willie; Alison Arngrim (1974–1981) as their nasty daughter, Nellie; Charlotte Stewart (1974–1977) as Miss Beadle, the schoolteacher; Dabbs Greer as Reverend Robert

Alden; Ted Gehring (1975–1976) as banker Ebenezer Sprague; Kevin Hagen as Doc Baker; Tracie Savage as Laura's friend, Christy; Merlin Olsen (1977–1981) as Jonathan Garvey; Hersha Parady (1977–1980) as his wife, Alice; and Patrick Laborteaux (1977–1981) as their son, Andy.

At the end of the 1977–1978 season Mary, the eldest Ingalls daughter, went blind as the result of a progressive disease (the same incident occurred in Laura Ingalls Wilder's book). Linwood Boomer joined the cast as Mary's teacher, Adam Kendall, who was also blind (he later regained his sight). Mary accepted Adam's offer to help him teach at a school for blind children in the Dakota Territory. At the outset of the 1978–1979 season the entire Ingalls family then left Walnut Grove for Winoka, Dakota. By a strange coincidence the Oleson and Garvey families also decided to relocate in Winoka; later that season, by an equally strange coincidence, everyone decided to move back to good old Walnut Grove. Joining the cast in 1978 was Matthew Laborteaux (foster brother of Patrick) as Albert, a street urchin who was adopted by the Ingallses.

In the fall of 1979 two new cast members were added: Dean Butler as Almanzo Wilder, Laura's future husband; and Lucy Lee Flippin as Eliza Jane Wilder, a schoolteacher (Laura Ingalls was also teaching by this time). During the 1980–1981 season Laura and Almanzo were married, and Nellie Oleson also found a husband, Percival Dalton (played by Steve Tracy). More changes took place at the outset of the 1981–1982 season: Nellie and Percival had moved back East to New York, as had Mary and Adam (Adam, who had regained his sight, had become a lawyer). The Ingalls family adopted two more kids: Cassandra (played by Missy Francis) and James (Jason Bateman). The Olesons also adopted a child, Nancy (Allison Balson), who was as much of a brat as Nellie had been.

Little House underwent even more changes in its ninth, and final, season. Michael Landon ceased to appear regularly, though he continued to produce the series. The show's title was changed to *Little House: A New Beginning,* as Charles and Caroline Ingalls sold their farm to the Carter family and moved to Iowa with younger daughters Carrie and Grace; Laura and Almanzo remained in Walnut Grove and became the central characters. Victor French, who had played Isaiah Edwards from 1974 to 1977, returned at the end of the 1981–1982 season and stayed on. Other new regulars included: Stan Ivar as blacksmith John Carter; Pamela Roylance as his wife, Sarah Carter; Lindsay Kennedy as their son Jeb; David Friedman as their son Jason; Shannen Doherty as Jenny, Almanzo Wilder's niece, who came to live with Laura and Almanzo; and Leslie Landon (daughter of Michael Landon) as the new schoolteacher, Etta Plum.

Three two-hour specials were planned for the 1983–1984 season. The first of these, "Little House: Look Back to Yesterday," was broadcast 12 December 1983.

THE LITTLE MERMAID   CBS
12 SEPTEMBER 1992–2 SEPTEMBER 1995   This half-hour Saturday morning cartoon series from Disney Studios was intended to be a "prequel" to Disney's popular 1989 motion picture of the same title. Ariel, the daughter of King Triton, was a teen mermaid who embarked on adventures with her pals Sebastian and Flounder.

THE LITTLE PEOPLE (THE BRIAN KEITH SHOW)   NBC
15 SEPTEMBER 1972–30 AUGUST 1974   Forgettable sitcom about a pediatrician in Hawaii. With Brian Keith as Dr. Sean Jamison; Shelley Fabares as his daughter and partner, Dr. Anne Jamison; Victoria Young (Brian Keith's wife) as Puni, their nurse; Michael Gray as Ronnie Collins, a student doctor working with them; Stephen Hague as Alfred, a pesky neighborhood youngster; Sean Tyler Hall as Stewart, a friend of Alfred's; and Moe Keale as Officer O'Shaughnessy. In the fall of 1973 the title was changed from *The Little People* to *The Brian Keith Show,* and two new cast members were added: Nancy Kulp as Mrs. Millard Gruber, the landlady; Roger Bowen as Dr. Spencer Chaffee, an allergist. Bruce Johnson produced the series.

THE LITTLE RASCALS/RICHIE RICH SHOW ABC

10 SEPTEMBER 1983–1 SEPTEMBER 1984   On this half-hour cartoon series, segments of "Richie Rich," starring the world's wealthiest youngster and his pals, alternated with "The Little Rascals," an updated, animated version of the Hal Roach short films of the 1930s. Richie Rich had been introduced in 1980 on *The Richie Rich/Scooby Doo Show* (see also that title) and had joined forces with the Little Rascals in 1982 (see *The Pac-Man/Little Rascals/Richie Rich Show*).

THE LITTLE REVUE ABC

4 SEPTEMBER 1949–11 DECEMBER 1949; 17 MARCH 1950–28 APRIL 1950   Half-hour musical variety show, featuring Bill Sherry, Gloria Van, Nancy Evans, and Dick Larkin. The series was seen Sundays in 1949 and Fridays in 1950. It was one of the few variety shows of the era on which there was no studio audience.

LITTLE ROSEY ABC

8 SEPTEMBER 1990–31 AUGUST 1991   Saturday-morning cartoon show inspired by the hit sitcom *Roseanne*. The animated program depicted the childhood adventures of Roseanne Barr, her pal Buddy, her sister Tess, and her brother Tater. Kathleen Laskey supplied the voice of the title character.

LITTLE SHOP FOX

7 SEPTEMBER 1991–29 AUGUST 1992   Saturday morning cartoon show based on the musical stage and screen versions of the original 1960 horror-comedy film, *Little Shop of Horrors*. Here, a teenage Seymour Krelborn embarked upon adventures with Junior, the rap-talking carnivorous plant.

THE LITTLE SHOW NBC/ABC

27 JUNE 1950–22 NOVEMBER 1951 (NCB); 3 APRIL 1953–19 JUNE 1953 (ABC) Fifteen-minute musical show hosted by John Conte; it was seen Tuesdays and Thursdays before the network news on NBC, Friday nights over ABC.

LITTLE VIC SYNDICATED

1977   Six-part miniseries about a horse (Little Vic) and the orphaned black teenager who trained and rode him. With Joey Green as Gilly Walker; the series was produced by Linda Marmelstein.

THE LITTLE WIZARDS ABC

26 SEPTEMBER 1987–3 SEPTEMBER 1988   Young Prince Dexter struggled to regain his throne from his evil uncle on this Saturday-morning cartoon show. The prince was aided by a trio of little wizards, Winkle, Boo, and Gump.

LITTLE WOMEN SYNDICATED

1972   Louisa May Alcott's classic book became a nine-part miniseries, televised as part of *Family Classics Theatre*. Produced in England, it featured Stephanie Bidmead as Mrs. March; Sara Craze as Beth; Angela Down as Jo; Janina Faye as Amy; and Jo Rowbottom as Meg.

LITTLE WOMEN NBC

8 FEBRUARY 1979–8 MARCH 1979   Hour dramatic series which began where Louisa May Alcott's classic novel left off. With Jessica Harper as Jo March; Eve Plumb as Lissa; Ann Dusenberry as Amy; Susan Walden as Meg; Dorothy McGuire as Marmee; William Schallert as Reverend March; Richard Gilliland as Laurie; Virginia Gregg as Hannah; David Ackroyd as Friedrich Bhaer, Jo's fiancé; Mildred Natwick as Aunt March; and Robert Young as Mr. Laurence. Executive producer: David Victor for Universal TV. The series was intended as a sequel to a two-part adaptation of the novel which NBC had telecast 2 and 3 October 1978.

THE LITTLES

ABC

10 SEPTEMBER 1983–6 SEPTEMBER 1986   The central characters in this Saturday-morning cartoon show were a group of six-inch-tall humanoids (they resembled people, except for their tails) who live in various places in a large city. Two of the Littles committed a major offense when they revealed the group's existence to teenager Henry Bigg, in the walls of whose house they dwelt. Bigg spent most of his time protecting the group from discovery by prodding scientists.

THE LITTLEST HOBO

SYNDICATED

1963; 1982   This Canadian-produced series was one of few shows without a human regular. The Littlest Hobo was a German shepherd named London who wandered about and helped out people with problems.

LIVE! DICK CLARK PRESENTS

CBS

14 SEPTEMBER 1988–22 OCTOBER 1988   Dick Clark hosted this hour variety show, which was hastily concocted to fill a gap in CBS's prime-time schedule caused by the 1988 writers' strike. The first three programs were televised live on Wednesdays; the remaining three were aired on tape on Saturdays.

LIVE LIKE A MILLIONAIRE

CBS/ABC

5 JANUARY 1951–14 MARCH 1952 (CBS); 25 OCTOBER 1952–7 FEBRUARY 1953 (ABC)
On this prime-time talent show all the acts were parents, who were introduced by their children. Jack McCoy and John Nelson hosted the series. Winning contestants earned the right to "live like a millionaire" only in a technical sense; in addition to merchandise prizes, they actually were awarded a week's worth of the *interest* on a million dollars, which amounted to less than $1000 at then prevailing interest rates.

LIVE SHOT

UPN

29 AUGUST 1995–10 JANUARY 1996   The hectic news room at Los Angeles's channel 3 was the setting for this hour drama. With David Birney as pompous Harry Chandler Moore, co-anchor of the Re-Action News evening broadcast, and whose sobriquet was "The Beacon of Truth"; Rebecca Staab as the Harry's co-anchor, Sherry Beck; Sam Anderson as ultraconservative commentator Marvin Seaborn; Tom Byrd as sportscaster Lou Waller; Jeff Yagher as the newly named (and newly separated) news director, Alex Rydell; Michael Watson as video photographer Fast Eddie Santini; Hill Harper as soundman Tommy Greer; Eddie Velez as Ricardo Sandoval, anchor of the noon newscast and evening reporter; Bruce McGill as Joe Vitale, producer of the early evening newscast; Cheryl Pollak as Nancy Lockridge, producer of the late evening newscast; Antonia Jones as intern Peggy Trainor; Wanda De Jesus as reporter Liz Vega; David Coburn as assignment editor Rick Evers; Karen Austin as the station's new general manager, Helen Forbes; and Spencer Klein as Sean, Alex's young son.

LIVE WITH REGIS AND KATHIE LEE

SYNDICATED

1989–   Five-day-a-week hour magazine-talk show, made available live to local stations. Regis Philbin and Kathie Lee Gifford cohosted, although Philbin's wife, Joy Philbin, filled in for Gifford when the latter left to have a baby in the spring of 1990. Virtually alone among daytime talk shows of the 1990s, the series managed to hold a large audience without resorting to sensational or confrontational topics.

LIVE-IN

CBS

20 MARCH 1989–5 JUNE 1989   Half-hour sitcom about a working couple who hired a beautiful live-in babysitter from Australia for their infant daughter, much to the delight of their two teenage sons. With Lisa Patrick as Lisa Wells, the live-in; Hugh Maguire as the father, Ed Matthews; Kimberly Farr as the mother, Sarah Matthews; Chris Young as elder son Danny; David Moscow as younger son Peter; and Lightfield Lewis as their pal Gator.

THE LIVELY ONES   NBC
26 JULY 1962–13 SEPTEMBER 1962; 25 JULY 1963–12 SEPTEMBER 1963   Hosted by Vic
Damone, this half-hour musical variety show was a summer replacement for *Hazel*
for two seasons. Produced by Barry Shear, the show also featured Joan Staley and
Shirley Yelm as Damone's "constant dates," Tiger and Charley, in 1962; Quinn
O'Hara and Gloria Neil were Damone's 1963 dates, Smitty and Melvin. Music was
provided by Jerry Fielding's orchestra. Many of the segments were taped on location
at unusual sites throughout the country.

LIVING DOLLS   ABC
26 SEPTEMBER 1989–30 DECEMBER 1989   Half-hour sitcom about four teenage models
in New York. With Michael Learned as Trish Carlin, who ran the modeling agency
and was housemother to the girls; Leah Remini as Charlie; Alison Elliott as Martha;
Deborah Tucker as Caroline; Halle Berry as Emily; David Moscow as Rick, Trish's
teenage son; and Marion Ross as Trish's sister, Marion. The series had been spun off
from *Who's the Boss?*

LIVING EASY WITH DR. JOYCE BROTHERS
See DR. JOYCE BROTHERS

THE LIVING PLANET: A PORTRAIT OF THE EARTH   PBS
3 FEBRUARY 1985–21 APRIL 1985   On this twelve-part sequel to his 1982 series, *Life
on Earth*, host David Attenborough examined the planet's ecosystems.

LIVING SINGLE   FOX
22 AUGUST 1993–   Half-hour sitcom about four black career women who shared a
Brooklyn apartment. With Queen Latifah as Khadijah James, editor of *Flavor* magazine, a periodical aimed at black women; Kim Coles as her cousin and office manager, Synclaire James; Erika Alexander as divorce lawyer Max Shaw (who later
moved into her own apartment); Kim Fields as Regine Hunter, who worked in a
boutique; T. C. Carson as their neighbor, Kyle Barker, who became Max's boyfriend; John Henton as Overton Wakefield Jones, the building superintendent, who
became Synclaire's boyfriend; and Cress Williams as Scooter, Khadijah's boyfriend.

THE LLOYD BRIDGES SHOW   CBS
11 SEPTEMBER 1962–3 SEPTEMBER 1963   Half-hour dramatic anthology series hosted
by former *Sea Hunt* star Lloyd Bridges, who portrayed writer Adam Shepherd from
September until January. Each week Shepherd was transformed into the main character of the story. In January the show became a straightforward anthology series
hosted by Bridges. His two sons, Beau and Jeff, appeared occasionally on the show.
Aaron Spelling was the producer.

THE LLOYD THAXTON SHOW   SYNDICATED
1964   An hour of rock music, hosted by disc jockey Lloyd Thaxton.

LOBO
See THE MISADVENTURES OF SHERIFF LOBO

LOCK UP   SYNDICATED
1959–1960   Low-budget crime show from Ziv TV, with Macdonald Carey as defense attorney Herbert L. Maris and John Doucette as his legman, Weston. Olive
Carey (no relation to Macdonald) was added for the second season of 39 episodes as
the secretary, Casey, who was always trying to fix Herb up with a date. The series was
based on the real-life Herbert L. Maris, a Philadelphia attorney who sought to free
persons wrongly convicted of crimes.

LOGAN'S RUN   CBS
16 SEPTEMBER 1977–16 JANUARY 1978   This science fiction series was based on the
movie of the same title. It starred Gregory Harrison as Logan 5, a young man who

chose to escape from the Domed City, a futuristic society in which life was pleasurable, but in which all inhabitants were "terminated" when they reached age thirty. Also featured were Heather Menzies as Jessica 6, a young woman who escaped with him; Donald Moffat as Rem, their android companion; and Randy Powell as Francis 7, the man sent to apprehend them (he was promised a seat on the secret council of elders, a group of persons who were permitted to live beyond thirty and who, unknown to the rest of the populace, actually ran the Domed City). Despite the enormous popularity of contemporaneous sci-fi films like *Star Wars* and *Close Encounters of the Third Kind*, *Logan's Run* ended in midseason after only a few episodes. Ivan Goff and Ben Roberts were the executive producers; Leonard Katzman was the producer.

LOIS & CLARK: THE NEW ADVENTURES OF SUPERMAN ABC

12 SEPTEMBER 1993–   This hour prime-time series was much more lavish than the original TV incarnation of *Superman,* which had aired forty years earlier. It focused on the Man of Steel's early adult years in Metropolis, where, disguised as Clark Kent, he found work as a reporter; there he met fellow reporter Lois Lane, who only had eyes for Superman and spurned Clark's efforts at establishing a relationship. The cast included Dean Cain as Clark Kent/Superman; Teri Hatcher as Lois Lane; Michael Landes (1993–1994) and Justin Whalin (1994–   ) as cub reporter Jimmy Olsen; Lane Smith as editor Perry White; Tracy Scoggins (1993–1994) as society columnist Catherine "Cat" Grant; and John Shea as archvillain Lex Luthor, who was thought to have been killed off at the end of the first season, but reappeared sporadically thereafter. Occasionally featured were K Callan and Eddie Jones as Superman's adoptive parents, Martha and Jonathan Kent. In a salute to the older version of the series, Phyllis Coates guest starred as Lois's mother, Ellen Lane, on 8 May 1994; Coates had been the original Lois in the first *Superman* series. The romantic aspect of the show received greater emphasis as the series progressed. By the end of the second season Lois had finally realized that Clark Kent was indeed Superman, and thus was not surprised when he finally revealed his true identity to her—and proposed marriage. They had fallen in love.

THE LONE RANGER ABC

15 SEPTEMBER 1949–12 SEPTEMBER 1957   One of television's most popular westerns, *The Lone Ranger* was created for radio in 1933 by George W. Trendle. Clayton Moore starred in most of the 221 half hours as the Lone Ranger, though John Hart played the part in at least twenty-six episodes filmed between 1951 and 1953. Jay Silverheels costarred as Tonto, his faithful Indian companion. At least once each year the "original" episode was telecast, which explained the origins of the character. In brief, the Lone Ranger was really a Texas Ranger named John Reid, who was the only survivor of an ambush by Butch Cavendish's Hole in the Wall Gang. Nursed back to health by Tonto (coincidentally, the two had been childhood friends), he vowed to help bring justice to the West and donned a mask (originally, to fool the Cavendish gang). Armed with silver bullets, he shot only to wound, not to kill. In the later episodes Chuck Courtney was also featured as the Lone Ranger's nephew, Dan Reid; on his horse, Victor, he sometimes rode with his uncle (astride Silver) and Tonto (on Scout). Faithful viewers never seemed to mind that, wherever they traveled throughout the West, the Lone Ranger and Tonto always seemed to camp near the same set of rocks, "just outside of town." From their campground Tonto might venture into town, posing as an ignorant Redskin in order to overhear the bad guys, or the Lone Ranger might don one of his several disguises (which, of course, enabled him to shed his mask): The Oldtimer, a Swedish immigrant; José, a bandito; Don Pedro O'Sullivan, a Mexican Irishman; or "Professor" Horatio Tucker, seller of patent medicines. The show is still seen in syndication in many local areas. A cartoon version also appeared (see below). *The Lone Ranger*'s classic introduction ("A fiery horse with the speed of light. . .") was read by announcer Fred Foy to the strains of Rossini's "William Tell Overture." Clayton Moore continued to make public appearances as the Lone Ranger for many years, but in 1979 Lone Ranger Television, Inc., a subsidiary of the Wrather Corporation, obtained a court injunction prohibiting

Moore from wearing his mask in public. The Wrather Corporation had recently made a Lone Ranger feature film with an actor other than Moore. In 1985 Moore won back the right to wear the mask. The character reappeared on Saturday mornings in 1980 (see *The Tarzan/Lone Ranger Adventure Hour*).

THE LONE RANGER CBS
10 SEPTEMBER 1966–6 SEPTEMBER 1969 This cartoon version of the long-running western was seen on Saturday mornings for three seasons.

THE LONE WOLF (STREETS OF DANGER) SYNDICATED
1955 Half-hour adventure series starring Louis Hayward as Mike Lanyard (The Lone Wolf), globe-trotting private eye. Based on the stories by Louis Joseph Vance, the show had been featured on radio in 1948.

THE LONER CBS
18 SEPTEMBER 1965–30 APRIL 1966 Created and produced by Rod Serling, this half-hour western starred Lloyd Bridges as William Colton, a Union soldier disillusioned by the Civil War who decided to head West after Appomattox and who helped out people along the way.

LONESOME DOVE CBS
5 FEBRUARY 1989–8 FEBRUARY 1989 This handsome, sprawling western, a four-part adaptation of Larry McMurtry's novel about a cattle drive, was by far the top-rated miniseries of the 1988–1989 season (and the highest-rated miniseries since *North and South* in 1985). Principal players included Robert Duvall as Augustus McCrae; Tommy Lee Jones as Woodrow Call; Robert Urich as Jake Spoon; Danny Glover as Joshua Deets; Diane Lane as Lorena Wood; Ricky Schroder as Newt Dobbs; Anjelica Huston as Clara Allen; and Frederic Forrest as Blue Duck. Simon Wincer directed. The miniseries won a Peabody Award in 1989. A three-part sequel, "Return to Lonesome Dove," aired on CBS 14, 16, and 18 November 1993. The seven-hour story starred Rick Schroder, Louis Gossett Jr., Jon Voight, Oliver Reed, William Petersen and Reese Witherspoon. A nationally syndicated weekly series surfaced in 1994: see below.

LONESOME DOVE: THE SERIES SYNDICATED
1994– The success of the 1989 miniseries *Lonesome Dove* and its sequel, *Return to Lonesome Dove,* led to this hour weekly series, which continued the story. The central character was Newt Call (formerly known as Newt Dobbs, he took his real father's last name after Woodrow Call acknowledged paternity), who settled in the small Montana town of Curtis Wells and soon found love. The cast included Scott Bairstow as Newt Call; Christianne Hirt as Hannah Peale, who married him; Paul Le Mat as her father, newspaper publisher Josiah Peale; Eric McCormack as Colonel Francis Clay Mosby, a former Confederate officer who became obsessed with Hannah; Diahann Carroll as Ida Grayson, a black woman who bought the local hotel and renamed it "The Lonesome Dove"; and Paul Johansson as Hannah's brother, Austin Peale. Each episode began with a scene set in 1925, as an unseen elderly man took a book from a shelf and began narrating the episode. The series was filmed on location in Alberta, and in its second season was entitled *Lonesome Dove: The Outlaw Years*.

LONG AGO & FAR AWAY PBS
1989–1991 James Earl Jones hosted this anthology series for children. Most of the stories were produced overseas; some were adaptations of children's classics, while others were original stories. Some were animated, others featured puppets, and a few employed real actors.

THE LONG HOT SUMMER ABC
16 SEPTEMBER 1965–13 JULY 1966 After ABC introduced a successful prime-time serial—*Peyton Place*—in 1964, it followed suit a year later with *The Long Hot Summer*. The hour-long show was based on the film of the same title, which in turn

was based on William Faulkner's *The Hamlet.* Set in the Southern town of Frenchman's Bend, it told the story of Ben Quick, a drifter who returned to the town and found it was run by one man, Will Varner; Quick fell in love with Varner's daughter and attempted to clear the good name of his late father, who was suspected of murder. Principal characters included: Roy Thinnes as Ben Quick; Edmond O'Brien (to January 1966) and Dan O'Herlihy (after January) as Will Varner; Nancy Malone as Clara Varner, Will's daughter; Lana Wood as Eula Varner, Clara's younger sister; Paul Geary as Jody Varner, their brother; Paul Bryar as Sheriff Harve Anders; John Kerr as Duane Galloway; Ruth Roman as Minnie, Will Varner's lady friend; Harold Gould as Bo Chamberlain; Wayne Rogers as Curley; Josie Lloyd as Agnes; Tish Sterling as Susan; Charles Lampkin as Andrew; Jason Wingreen as Dr. Clark; William Mims as Ruddabaw; and Warren Kemmerling as Lucas Taney. Frank Glicksman produced the series for 20th Century-Fox TV.

LONG JOHN SILVER   SYNDICATED
1955   Robert Newton recreated the role of Long John Silver, goodhearted pirate, which he had first played in the 1950 film, *Treasure Island.* Set during the 1700s on the island of Porto Bello, the half-hour series was filmed in Sydney, Australia. Also featured were Kit Taylor as young Jim Hawkins, his unofficial ward; Connie Gilchrist as Purity, the proprietor of Long John's favorite pub.

LONGSTREET   ABC
16 SEPTEMBER 1971–10 AUGUST 1972   This hour-long crime show starred James Franciscus as Michael Longstreet, a New Orleans insurance investigator who was blinded in an attempt on his life in which his wife was killed. Seeking no sympathy from anyone, Longstreet, with a little help from his friends and his seeing-eye dog, Pax, a white German shepherd, continued at his job, solving mysteries week after week. Also featured were Marlyn Mason as Nikki Bell, his Braille instructor and companion; Peter Mark Richman (formerly known as Mark Richman) as Duke Paige of the Great Pacific Casualty Company, Longstreet's employer; and Ann Doran as Mrs. Kingston, Longstreet's housekeeper. Stirling Silliphant was the executive producer for Paramount TV.

LOOK AT US   SYNDICATED
1981   Half-hour magazine show, hosted by Richard Crenna.

LOOK HERE   NBC
15 SEPTEMBER 1957–4 MAY 1958   NBC correspondent Martin Agronsky interviewed newsmakers on this live public affairs program, aired Sunday afternoons. Agronsky's first guest was Secretary of State John Foster Dulles.

LOOK UP AND LIVE   CBS
3 JANUARY 1954–21 JANUARY 1979   This long-running religious show was a Sunday-morning fixture for two dozen years. In the early years, the Reverend Lawrence McMaster frequently appeared, and Merv Griffin hosted the show briefly in 1955. In later years, however, there was no fixed format, since different religious and cultural themes were explored. Pamela Ilott, director of religious programming for CBS News, was executive producer.

THE LORENZO AND HENRIETTA MUSIC SHOW   SYNDICATED
1976   Short-lived talk show cohosted by Lorenzo Music (producer and voice of Carlton on *Rhoda*) and his wife, Henrietta Music.

THE LORETTA YOUNG SHOW (A LETTER TO LORETTA)   NBC
20 SEPTEMBER 1953–10 SEPTEMBER 1961   Hosted by, and frequently starring, Loretta Young, this half-hour dramatic anthology series was seen Sunday nights at 10:00 p.m. It is probably best remembered for Young's fashions, and her swirling entrance through a door at the beginning of each episode. During its first season the show was titled *A Letter to Loretta;* Young read a letter supposedly written by a viewer which

served as an introduction to the evening's presentation. In 1954 that device was dropped. It was reported in 1972 that Young had been awarded $559,000 in a suit against NBC for the network's violation of her contract in permitting syndicated reruns of the series to be shown with her outdated fashions and hairstyles. John Newland, who later hosted *One Step Beyond*, appeared many times, and also directed several shows.

LORNE GREENE'S NEW WILDERNESS   SYNDICATED
1982–1986   Lorne Greene hosted this, his second series of half-hour nature films (see also *Last of the Wild*).

LOST CIVILIZATIONS   NBC
25 JUNE 1995–3 SEPTEMBER 1995   Ten-week hour series, sponsored by Time-Life, about civilizations and cultures of the past. Sam Waterston hosted the series, which blended documentary film with dramatic reenactments.

LOST IN SPACE   CBS
15 SEPTEMBER 1965–11 SEPTEMBER 1968   Science fiction series about the Space Family Robinson. Dispatched by the United States government in 1997 to colonize a planet in Alpha Centauri, the Robinsons' spacecraft was thrown hopelessly off course by a stowaway. With Guy Williams as Dr. John Robinson, astrophysicist; June Lockhart as Maureen Robinson, his wife; Marta Kristen as Judy, their elder daughter; Billy Mumy as Will, their son; Angela Cartwright as Penny, their younger daughter; Mark Goddard as Don West, the pilot; Jonathan Harris as the stowaway, Dr. Zachary Smith, an enemy agent who was to have sabotaged the craft on the launching pad; and Bob May as The Robot. Irwin Allen created the series and was also its executive producer; eighty-three hour episodes were filmed.

THE LOST SAUCER   ABC
6 SEPTEMBER 1975–4 SEPTEMBER 1976   Live-action Saturday-morning show about two extraplanetary creatures who inadvertently pick up a boy and his babysitter while visiting Earth. With Ruth Buzzi as Fi; Jim Nabors as Fum; Alice Playten as Alice, the babysitter; and Jarrod Johnson as Jerry, the boy. Produced by Sid and Marty Krofft, the series was later shown as one segment of *The Krofft Supershow*.

LOTSA LUCK   NBC
10 SEPTEMBER 1973–24 MAY 1974   Blue-collar sitcom based on the British series, *On the Buses*. With Dom DeLuise as Stanley Belmont, lost-and-found clerk for a New York bus company; Kathleen Freeman as his mother, Iris Belmont; Beverly Sanders as his sister, Olive Swan; Wynn Irwin as Olive's unemployed husband, Arthur Swan; and Jack Knight as the Belmonts' neighbor, Bummy Pfitzer, a bus driver. The show was created by three alumni of *The Dick Van Dyke Show:* Carl Reiner, Bill Persky, and Sam Denoff.

LOTTERY$ ABC
9 SEPTEMBER 1983–12 JULY 1984   This hour series closely resembled two earlier shows, *The Millionaire* and *Sweepstakes*, which focused on persons who won, or were given, large sums of money. *Lottery$* dealt, logically enough, with the winners of the Intersweep Lottery, a big-money sweepstakes game. It starred Ben Murphy as Patrick Sean Flaherty, employed by the Intersweep Bank, whose job was to notify the winners and give them the proceeds; and Marshall Colt as Eric Rush, an IRS agent whose job was to make sure the winners paid all necessary federal taxes. Each episode of *Lottery$* featured three stories; unlike *The Millionaire*, which followed the recipients *after* they had been given the cashier's check, *Lottery$* focused more on finding the persons, verifying their tickets, and presenting the winnings (*Lottery$*'s episodes did close with a short epilogue, showing the winners "one year later"). Rick Rosner created the series.

LOU GRANT   CBS

20 SEPTEMBER 1977–13 SEPTEMBER 1982   In this hour-long series Edward Asner continued to play the part he had created on *The Mary Tyler Moore Show*—Lou Grant, who, having lost his job at WJM in Minneapolis, moved to Los Angeles and got a new job as city editor of the Los Angeles *Tribune*. While it is not uncommon for characters to be spun off from one series to another, this appears to have been the first instance in which a character left a situation comedy to headline a dramatic series. Also featured were Mason Adams as managing editor Charlie Hume, an old friend of Lou's; Nancy Marchand as Margaret Pynchon, owner and publisher of the *Tribune;* Jack Bannon as Art Donovan, assistant city editor; Robert Walden as scrappy young reporter Joe Rossi; and Daryl Anderson as photographer Dennis (Animal) Price. In the earliest episodes Rebecca Balding appeared as another young reporter, Carla Mardigian, but she was replaced by Linda Kelsey as reporter Billie Newman, who maintained a rivalry with Rossi. Allen Williams joined the cast in 1978 as reporter Adam Wilson, and Emilio Delgado was added in 1980 as reporter Reuben Castillo. In the fall of 1981 Billie married Ted McCovey, a former baseball player.

   Lou Grant tackled many controversial issues during its five-year run, including child abuse, gun control, survivalism, the plight of Vietnamese refugees, and even Mrs. Pynchon's stroke. It was canceled in 1982 as its ratings slipped, amid reports that the network had become uneasy about star Ed Asner's outspoken support of various liberal causes.

LOUIS RUKEYSER'S BUSINESS JOURNAL   SYNDICATED

1981   Louis (*Wall $treet Week*) Rukeyser hosted this half-hour informational series on business and economic issues.

LOVE, AMERICAN STYLE   ABC

29 SEPTEMBER 1969–11 JANUARY 1974; 23 DECEMBER 1985–15 AUGUST 1986   A rarity in television programming, *Love, American Style* was a comedy anthology series about love and romance; each week two or three stories of mixed lengths were televised, and short blackouts were aired between them. The group which performed the blackouts usually numbered about eight, and from time to time included Bill Callaway, Buzz Cooper, Phyllis Elizabeth Davis, Jaki DeMar, Mary Grover, James Hampton, Stuart Margolin, Lynne Marta, Barbara Minkus, Bernie Kopell, Tracy Reed, and Richard Williams. Arnold Margolin and Jim Parker were the show's executive producers for most of its run. Writers included Frank Buxton, Jerry Rannow, Greg Strangis, Ed Scharlach, and Doug Tibbles. The show was broadcast in an hour-long format except during the 1970–1971 season, when it was a half hour. Late in 1985 ABC revived the series (now titled *New Love, American Style*) for its daytime lineup.

LOVE AND MARRIAGE   NBC

21 SEPTEMBER 1959–25 JANUARY 1960   Featured in this half-hour sitcom were William Demarest as Bill Harris, owner of a music publishing company in shaky financial condition; Stubby Kaye as Stubby Wilson, his promo man; Kay Armen as Sophie, the secretary; Jeanne Bal as Pat Baker, Bill's daughter, who tried to bring new talent to the firm; Murray Hamilton as her husband, Steve Baker, a lawyer; Susan Reilly as their daughter, Susan; and Jeannie Lynn as their daughter, Jenny.

LOVE AND WAR   CBS

21 SEPTEMBER 1992–1 FEBRUARY 1995; 18 AUGUST 1995   Half-hour sitcom set in New York, where a newly divorced woman, having lost her trendy restaurant in the divorce, impulsively purchased a corner bar. With Susan Dey (1992–1993) as Wallis "Wally" Porter, who stopped by the Blue Shamrock for a stiff drink after the divorce hearing and ended up buying the place; Jay Thomas as bar regular Jack Stein, an opinionated newspaper columnist who quickly became Wally's new love interest (wasting little time, the couple had slept together by the second episode); John Hancock (fall 1992) as Ike Johnson, the former owner of the bar who agreed to stay

on; Joel Murray as bar regular Ray Litvak, a sanitation worker; Michael Nouri (1992–1993) as Kip Zakaris, Wally's ex; and Suzie Plakson as bar regular Mary Margaret "Meg" Tynan, a sportswriter. John Hancock died unexpectedly after a few episodes had been completed; after his death Charlie Robinson joined the cast as Ike's brother Abe; Joanna Gleason was added later in the first season as waitress Nadine Berkus. Susan Dey left the series after the initial season (it was explained that Wally had gone to Paris), and was replaced by Annie Potts as chef Dana Palladino, who became the new love interest for Jack. Created by Diane English, *Love and War* was the highest rated new series of the 1992–1993 season, ranking 13th for the year.

THE LOVE BOAT
ABC

24 SEPTEMBER 1977–5 SEPTEMBER 1986   One of the most popular new shows of the 1977–1978 season, *The Love Boat* followed the format of *Love, American Style,* featuring guest stars in comedy vignettes; unlike *Love, American Style,* the stories were intertwined rather than telecast consecutively. All the action took place aboard *The Pacific Princess,* a cruise ship. The ship's crew, who were the only regulars on the series, included Gavin MacLeod as Captain Merrill Stubing; Bernie Kopell as Doc (Adam Bricker), the ship's doctor; Fred Grandy as Burl (Gopher) Smith, assistant purser; Ted Lange as Isaac Washington, the bartender; and Lauren Tewes (1977–1984) as Julie McCoy, social director. In the fall of 1979 Jill Whelan was added as Vicki, Stubing's illegitimate daughter. Pat Klous joined the cast in the fall of 1984 as social director Judy McCoy, replacing Lauren Tewes, who candidly admitted that drug abuse led to her departure from the series; Tewes returned as guest star on the episode of 30 November 1985. Ted McGinley also signed on in 1984 as photographer Ashley Covington "Ace" Evans. In the fall of 1985 *The Pacific Princess* was upgraded to *The Royal Princess,* and the Love Boat Mermaids, a team of eight singer-dancers, were added. On 24 May 1986 Captain Stubing married Emily Haywood (played by Marion Ross). *The Love Boat* ended its nine-season regular run in September of that year, but returned in three two-hour specials broadcast during the 1986–1987 season. By that time, former regular Fred Grandy had been elected to Congress from Iowa. Several of the other regulars (MacLeod, Lange, Kopell, and Whelan) were reunited for "The Love Boat: A Valentine Voyage," which aired 12 February 1990 on CBS. Aaron Spelling and Douglas S. Cramer were the executive producers. Many episodes were directed by Richard Kinon, who succinctly described *The Love Boat*'s format as "romance and pap."

LOVE CONNECTION
SYNDICATED

1983–1993   Chuck Woolery hosted this updated version of *The Dating Game,* on which single people selected dates through videotaped interviews; after their initial date, the couple came back to the show and reported the outcome of their first encounter.

THE LOVE EXPERTS
SYNDICATED

1978   A game show not unlike *The Amateur's Guide to Love,* this series featured a panel of four celebrities who gave advice to contestants on matters of love and romance. At the end of each show the panel selected the contestant who had posed the most interesting "love problem"; the lucky player then won a prize. Bill Cullen hosted the half-hour show.

LOVE IS A MANY SPLENDORED THING
CBS

18 SEPTEMBER 1967–23 MARCH 1973   Another of the daytime serials developed by Irna Phillips, *Love Is a Many Splendored Thing* was intended to be a continuation of the 1955 film, which had starred William Holden and Jennifer Jones. Its central theme at first involved interracial romance; when the network insisted that that theme be dropped, Phillips quit. Under new writers, story lines veered toward political intrigue. Principal players included Nancy Hsueh as Mia Elliott, the daughter of an American father and an Asian mother who, as the series began, came to San Francisco to study medicine; Nicholas Pryor as Paul Bradley, Mia's first romantic interest; Robert Milli and Ron Hale as Dr. Jim Abbott, Mia's second romantic

interest; Sam Wade, David Birney, Michael Hawkins, Vincent Cannon, and Tom Fuccello as Mark Elliott, Mia's cousin; Grace Albertson and Gloria Hoye as Mark's mother, Helen Elliott; Leslie Charleson and Bibi Besch as Iris Donnelly, Mark's girlfriend; Robert Burr and Albert Stratton as Lieutenant Tom Donnelly, Iris's brother; Shawn Campbell as Ricky Donnelly, Tom's son; Beverlee McKinsey as Martha Donnelly, Tom's estranged wife (who was also known as Julie Richards); Berkeley Harris as Jim Whitman, Martha's boyfriend; Donna Mills, Velekka Gray, and Barbara Stanger as Laura Donnelly, sister of Iris and Tom, who eventually married Mark Elliott; Judson Laire as Dr. Will Donnelly, father of Iris, Tom, and Laura; Ed Power and Brett Halsey as Spence Garrison, an aspiring politician who became involved with Iris; Susan Browning as Nancy Garrison, Spence's wife; Don Gantry as Senator Alfred E. Preston; John Carpenter as millionaire Walter Travis, Preston's backer; Leon Russom as Joe Taylor, a former employee of Travis; Andrea Marcovicci as Betsy Chernak, who married Joe Taylor; Vincent Baggetta as Dr. Peter Chernak, Betsy's brother; and Diana Douglas as Lily Chernak, widowed mother of Peter and Betsy, who eventually married Dr. Will Donnelly.

LOVE OF LIFE   CBS

24 SEPTEMBER 1951–1 FEBRUARY 1980   A durable daytime serial, *Love of Life* enjoyed a run of twenty-eight years. It was created by John Hess for The Biow Company but was sold to CBS in the early 1960s. Roy Winsor was its first executive producer, Charles Schenck its first producer. In recent years Darryl Hickman (a former child actor and brother of Dwayne Hickman) was the executive producer, with Jean Arley the producer. Larry Auerbach was the director from the beginning (though Jerry Evans and John Desmond codirected with him during the 1970s). Later head writers included Claire Labine and Paul Avila Mayer (who subsequently created *Ryan's Hope*), Margaret DePriest, Paul Schneider, and Gabrielle Upton.

Love of Life premiered as a fifteen-minute show and was then set in the town of Barrowsville. It was expanded to thirty minutes on 14 April 1958, and was trimmed to a twenty-five-minute format in 1962. Over the years, the action shifted away from Barrowsville to the nearby town of Rosehill. The story originally centered around two sisters—noble, long-suffering Vanessa Dale and amoral, opportunistic Margaret (Meg) Dale. After Meg was written out of the story in the late 1950s, the story lines diffused as younger characters were introduced; Meg was brought back, however, late in 1973 by then head writers Labine and Mayer. The large cast has included: Peggy McCay (1951–1955), Bonnie Bartlett (1955–1959), and Audrey Peters as Vanessa Dale; Jean McBride (1951–1956) and Tudi Wiggins (who joined the cast in 1973, when the role was revived after a seventeen-year absence) as Margaret Dale Harper Aleata; Jane Rose (1951–1956) and Joanna Roos (who took the role in 1968, when the character returned after a long absence) as Sarah Dale, mother of Van and Meg; Ed Jerome as Will Dale, father of Van and Meg; Paul Potter as Charles Harper, Meg's first husband; Dennis Parnell (1951–1957), Tommy White (1957–1958), Christopher Reeve (1968–1976), and Chandler Hill Harben (1976–1980) as Benno, the son of Meg and Charles Harper, who was known as "Beanie" in his youth and, when he returned to the show after some ten years, as "Ben"; Joe Allen, Jr., as Miles Pardee, an unsavory boyfriend of Meg's who was found murdered; Ronald Long as lawyer Evans Baker; Richard Coogan as lawyer Paul Raven, who married Van in 1954 and was reported killed in 1958 (actually, Paul lived, though he was stricken with amnesia: played by Robert Burr, he showed up in 1971 under the name of Matt Corby; he was later jailed and died); Bonnie Bartlett (1951) and Hildy Parks (1951–1956) as Van's roommate, Ellie Crown (Bartlett later played Van herself); Marie Kenney as Mrs. Rivers; Joanna Roos as Althea Raven, Paul's mother (Roos returned to the show as Sarah Dale); Virginia Robinson as Judith Lodge Raven, Paul's first wife; Steven Gethers as casino owner Hal Craig; Donald Symington as Jack Andrews, Meg's second husband; Lauren Gilbert as Tom Craythorne, Meg's third husband; Ann Loring as actress Tammy Forrest; Gene Peterson as Noel Penn; Ron Tomme (1959–1980) as Bruce Sterling, who married Van, divorced her, and married her again in 1972; Jimmy Bayer, Dan Ferrone (to 1966), Dennis Cooney (1966–1969), and John Fink (1969–1970) as Alan Sterling, Bruce's son by a former marriage; Nina Reader (to 1961), Lee Lawson (1961–1965), and Zina Bethune as Barbara Sterling, Bruce's daughter by a former marriage; Helene Dumas (1959–1977) as Vivian Carlson, mother of Bruce's former wife; Tom Shirley (1959–1961) and Jack Stamberger (1961–1970) as Henry Carlson, father of Bruce's former wife and head of a paper company; Ron Jackson as Dr. Tony Vento, Barbara Sterling's first husband; Kimetha Laurie as Cindy Craythorne, Tom Craythorne's daughter; Gene Pelligrini as Link Porter; Joan Copeland as Link's wife, Maggie Porter, and her twin, Kay Logan; John Straub as Guy Latimer; Paul Savior (1961–1966), Michael Ebert, Edward Moore, and Jerry Lacy (1971–1978) as his son, Rick Latimer, who became Barbara Sterling's second husband; Fred Stewart (1966–1971) and Charles White (1971–1973) as Alex Caldwell, who married Sarah Dale after Will Dale died; Eileen Letchworth as Sharon Ferris; Marie Masters as Hester Ferris, her daughter; Robert Alda as Jason Ferris, Sharon's husband; Stan Watt and Jonathan Moore as bookdealer Charles Lamont, next-door neighbor of Van and Bruce Sterling; Diane Rousseau as Diana Lamont, his wife (and ex-wife); Gene Bua as Bill Prentiss, son of Charles Lamont, who died in 1972 of a blood disease; Toni Bull as Tess Krakauer, Bill's wife; Frances Sternhagen and Jocelyn Brando as Mrs. Krakauer, Tess's mother; Alan York as Mickey Krakauer; Byron Sanders as John Randolph, who was married briefly to Tess and turned up murdered in 1970; Lawrence Weber as Richard Rollins, Randolph's killer; Renée Roy as Clair Bridgeman; Cathy Bacon as Sally Bridgeman, her daughter; Lincoln Kilpatrick as Joe Bond; Darlene Cotton as his wife, Rita Bond (the Bonds were the first black couple on *Love of Life*); Leonie Norton and Sally Stark as singer Kate Swanson; Drew Snyder as Dr. Dan Phillips, who married Kate and was later killed in a crash; Keith Charles as Kate's next husband, Dr. Ted Chandler, who ran a sex clinic; Michael Glaser and Tony LoBianco as Dr. Joe Corelli (Glaser, later known as Paul Michael Glaser, starred in *Starsky and Hutch*); Paul McGrath as Larry Andrews; Roy Scheider, Ben Piazza, and Roy Shuman as Jonas Falk; Bonnie Bedelia as Sandy Porter; Jessica Walter as Julia Moreno; David Rounds as Philip Holden; John Gabriel and George Kane as Link Morrison; Nancy Marchand as Vinnie Phillips; Douglass Watson as Lloyd Phillips; Polly Rowles as Helen Hunt; Shirley Blanc as Dr. Lederer; David Sabin as Dr. Peck; Carl Betz as Collie Jordan; Shari Freels as Daisy Allen; Ja'net DuBois as Loretta Allen; Joe Silver as Larry Prince; Brian Brownlee as Jack Bendarik; Phil Sterling as Dr. Westheimer; Cindy Grover as Stacy Corby, daughter of Matt Corby (Matt was really Van's long-lost husband, Paul Raven); Don Warfield and Ray Wise as Jamie Rollins, a lawyer who married Diana Lamont; Deborah Courtney (1973–1977) and Roxanne Gregory (1977–1978) as Caroline (Cal) Aleata, daughter of Meg Dale Aleata; Charles Baxter as Jeff Hart, the corrupt mayor of Rosehill who married Meg Dale Aleata after her return; Brian Farrell as David Hart, his son; Elizabeth Kemp as Betsy Crawford, who married Ben Harper after his return; Birgitta Tolksdorf (1974–1980) as Arlene Lovett, Ben's previous wife; Peg Murray as Carrie Lovett, her mother; Leon B. Stevens as Dr. Kreisinger; Nancy MacKay and Season Hubley as nurse Candy Lowe; Richard Cox as Bobby Mackey, who tried to defraud Tess and was murdered; Richard McKenzie as Walter Morgan, Bobby's partner and killer; Michael Fairman as Phil Waterman; Ed Crowley as Howie Howells; John Aniston as Edouard Aleata; Pamela Lincoln as Felicia Fleming, who married Charles Lamont (in real life, Pamela Lincoln was married to *Love of Life*'s executive producer, Darryl Hickman); David Carlton Stambaugh as Hank Latimer, son of Rick and Barbara Latimer; Oren Jay, Raymond Cass, and Trip Randall as Johnny Prentiss, son of Bill and Tess Prentiss; Romola Robb Allrud as Linda Crawford; Kenneth McMillan as James Crawford; Chris Chase as Connie Loomis; Earle Hyman as Dr. Paul Bryson; Marsha Mason as Judith Cole; Natalie Schafer as Augusta Rolland; Geraldine Brooks as Arden Delecort; Renne Jarrett as Eileen McCallion; Stephen Elliott as Paul Ailey; Bert Convy as Gene Hamilton; Lloyd Battista as Roy Slater; Peter Brouwer as Joe Cusack; Michael Allinson as Ian Russell; Amy Gibson as Lynn Henderson; Velekka Gray as Mia Marriott; Ron Harper as Andrew Marriott; Richard Council as Michael Blake; Corinne Neuchateau as Mary Owens; Elaine Grove as Wendy Hayes; Sherry Rooney as Dory Patton; Danielle Cusson as Susie Ryker; Robert McCone as Danny Ryker; Michael Kennedy as Kevin Patten; Jessica Rooney as Kirsten Patten; Jack

Marks as Leon Matthews; Donald Warfield (again) as Bert; Martin Zurla as T. J. Brogger; Gretchen Walther as Faith Manning; Elizabeth Stack as Cherie Manning; Ted Leplat as Elliott Lang; Chris Marlowe as Andrew Marriott, Jr.; Richard Fasciano as Dr. Paul Graham; Peter Gatto as Tony Alphonso; Ann Spangler McCarthy as Bambi Brewster; Margo McKenna as Elizabeth Lang; Shepperd Strudwick as Timothy McCauley; Jake Turner as Zachary Bly; Richard K. Weber and Mark Pinter as Dr. Tom Crawford.

In addition, according to Ron Lackmann's book, *TV Soap Opera Almanac,* other roles have been played by such notables as Martin Balsam, Warren Beatty, Damon Evans, Peter Falk, and Anne Jackson.

LOVE ON A ROOFTOP ABC
13 SEPTEMBER 1966–31 AUGUST 1967 Domestic sitcom about two newlyweds who moved into a tiny top-floor apartment in San Francisco. With Judy Carne as Julie Willis, an art student; Peter Deuel (he later shortened his last name to Duel) as her husband, Dave Willis, an architect; Rich Little as their neighbor, Stan Parker; Barbara Bostock as Carol Parker, Stan's wife; Herb Voland as Julie's father, Fred Hammond, owner of a string of used car lots; Edith Atwater as Julie's mother, Phyllis Hammond; and Lillian Adams as the Willises' landlady, Mrs. Lewis. E. W. Swackhamer produced and directed the series, which was rerun on ABC during the summer of 1971.

THE LOVE REPORT ABC
2 APRIL 1984–6 APRIL 1984; 18 JUNE 1984–27 JULY 1984 Chuck Henry and Tawny Schneider cohosted this daytime magazine series which purported to focus on love, sexuality, and romance. Celebrity interviews as well as documentary segments were featured.

LOVE, SIDNEY NBC
28 OCTOBER 1981–25 DECEMBER 1982; 28 MARCH 1983–29 AUGUST 1983 Tony Randall starred in this sitcom as lonely Sidney Shorr, a commercial artist who decided to share his New York apartment with a struggling actress and her young daughter. Also featured were Swoosie Kurtz as actress Laurie Morgan, who soon landed the role of Gloria Trinnell on the soap opera "As Thus We Are"; and Kaleena Kiff as Patti, Laurie's daughter. The series was produced in New York for most of its first season, but the cast was forced to head West in 1982 when *Sesame Street* preempted their New York facilities. Joining the show in the fall of 1982 were Chip Zien as ad executive Jason Stoller, for whom Sidney did assignments; and Barbara Bryne as Mrs. Gaffney, the wife of the building superintendent. *Love, Sidney* was derived from the 1981 made-for-TV movie "Sidney Shorr" (which had starred Randall, Kiff, and Lorna Patterson), with one significant difference: in the movie Sidney had been homosexual, but in the series (according to the network, if not to the show's writers) he was not.

LOVE STORIES SYNDICATED
1991 Daytime soap star Kristian Alfonso hosted this half-hour series about relationships. Each program focused on two couples who had fallen in love and had gone to the brink of breakup; each partner was separately interviewed, and excerpts of the interviews were telecast. At the end of the program Alfonso revealed which one of the two couples had gotten back together.

LOVE STORY DUMONT
20 APRIL 1954–29 JUNE 1954 Half-hour dramatic anthology series, produced by David Lowe.

LOVE STORY CBS
31 OCTOBER 1955–30 MARCH 1956 Jack Smith, assisted by Pat Meikle, hosted this daytime game show on which newlyweds or to-be-weds competed in a quiz segment for the chance to win a trip to Paris. Smith and Meikle had previously worked

together on *Welcome Travelers,* a human interest show which had occupied the same time slot.

LOVE STORY   NBC
3 OCTOBER 1973–2 JANUARY 1974   This dramatic anthology series died in midseason, having been slotted opposite *Kojak.*

LOVE THAT BOB   NBC/CBS
2 JANUARY 1955–25 SEPTEMBER 1955 (NBC); 1 SEPTEMBER 1955–19 SEPTEMBER 1957 (CBS); 24 SEPTEMBER 1957–15 SEPTEMBER 1959 (NBC)   Popular half-hour sitcom starring Bob Cummings as Bob Collins, a girl-crazy photographer ("Hold it—I think you're gonna like this picture!"). With Ann B. Davis as his gal Friday, Schultzy (short for Charmaine Schultz); Rosemary DeCamp as Margaret MacDonald, Bob's widowed sister; Dwayne Hickman as Chuck MacDonald, her teenage son; Joi Lansing as Shirley Swanson, the buxom model who chased after Bob; Nancy Kulp as Pamela Livingstone, a local birdwatcher; King Donovan as Harvey Helm, Bob's Air Force buddy; Mary Lawrence as Harvey's wife, Ruth; Charles Herbert as Tommy Helm, their son; and Marjorie Bennett as Mrs. Neemeyer, a neighbor.

LOVE THAT JILL   ABC
20 JANUARY 1958–28 APRIL 1958   Half-hour sitcom starring Anne Jeffreys as Jill Johnson and Robert Sterling as Jack Gibson, owners of rival modeling agencies in New York. The two had previously worked together in *Topper.* Also featured on *Love That Jill* were Barbara Nichols as Ginger, one of Jill's models, and James Lydon as Richard, Jill's secretary. Alex Gottlieb produced the series.

LOVE THY NEIGHBOR   ABC
15 JUNE 1973–19 SEPTEMBER 1973   Predictable ethnic sitcom about a white-collar black couple who moved in next door to a blue-collar white couple. With Harrison Page and Janet MacLachlan as Ferguson and Jackie Bruce, the black couple; Ron Masak and Joyce Bulifant as Charlie and Peggy Wilson; and Milt Kamen as Murray Bronson, another employee at Turner Electronics, where Ferguson and Charlie both worked.

LOVERS AND FRIENDS   NBC
3 JANUARY 1977–6 MAY 1977   Created by Harding Lemay, this short-lived daytime serial was set in Point Clair, a fashionable suburb of Chicago, where dwelt two families: the Cushings, an aristocratic family who had lived there for generations, and the Saxtons, a family of humbler origins who had just moved in from a less prestigious suburb. The cast included: Ron Randell as Richard Cushing, a wealthy stockbroker; Nancy Marchand as his wife, Edith Slocum Cushing; Rod Arrants as their son, Austin, a dropout; Patricia Estrin as Megan Cushing, their daughter; Dianne Harper as Laurie Brewster, Austin's girlfriend; David Knapp as Desmond Hamilton, Megan's fiancé; John Heffernan as Lester Saxton, a reformed alcoholic; Patricia Englund as his wife, Josie; Flora Plumb as Eleanor Saxton Kimball, their elder daughter; Bob Purvey as Rhett Saxton, their eldest son, who fell in love with Megan Cushing; Richard Backus as Jason Saxton, their second eldest son; David Abbott as Bentley Saxton, their youngest son; Vicky Dawson as Tessa Saxton, their younger daughter; Stephen Joyce as lawyer George Kimball, husband of Eleanor; Christine Jones as Amy Gifford, cousin of the Saxton kids; Margaret Barker as Sophia Slocum, mother of Edith Cushing; Karen Philipp as Barbara Manners, an employee and afterhours companion of Richard Cushing; and Susan Foster as Connie Ferguson, sometime girlfriend of Rhett Saxton. Paul Rauch, a former daytime programming executive at CBS, was executive producer of the series. Late in 1977 a revamped version of the serial reappeared on NBC: see *For Richer, for Poorer.*

LOVES ME, LOVES ME NOT   CBS
20 MARCH 1977–27 APRIL 1977   Courtship was the theme of this sitcom which starred Kenneth Gilman and Susan Dey as Dick Phillips and Jane Benson. Also featured

were Art Metrano as Tom, Dick's boss (Dick was a reporter); Phyllis Glick as Sue, Jane's friend. Created by Susan Harris, the show was produced by Paul Younger Witt and Tony Thomas.

LOVING (THE CITY)   ABC
27 JUNE 1983–   This half-hour daytime serial was created by two soap opera veterans: Agnes Nixon (who had created or cocreated *All My Children, As the World Turns, One Life to Live,* and *Search for Tomorrow*) and Douglas Marland (who had written for *Another World, The Doctors,* and *The Guiding Light,* among others). The program is set at Alden University in the town of Corinth. The cast has included: John Shearin and Peter Brown as Roger Forbes, a former ambassador, Alden's president, thought to have perished in an air crash; Shannon Eubanks and Callan White as Ann (Alden) Forbes, his wife; Perry Stephens and Christopher Cass as Jack, Roger's son; Susan Walters and O'Hara Parker as Lorna, Roger's daughter; Wesley Addy as Cabot Alden, Ann's father; Patricia Kalember as Merrill Vochek, anchorwoman at the local TV station; Marilyn McIntyre and Elizabeth Barr as Merrill's sister, Noreen Donovan, a nurse; James Kiberd as Noreen's husband, Mike Donovan, a cop; Lauren-Marie Taylor as Mike's sister, Stacy Donovan (the last remaining member of *Loving*'s original cast, Taylor left the series in mid-1995); Teri Keane and Dorothy Stinette as Rose Donovan; Noah Keen and George Smith as Patrick Donovan; John Cunningham as Dean Garth Slater, who had been passed over for the presidency of the university; Jennifer Ashe and Britt Helfer as Lily Slater; Ann Williams as June Slater; Tom Ligon as Billy Bristow, the athletics director; Pamela Blair as his wife, Rita Mae Bristow; Christopher Marcantel, Linden Ashby, Burke Moses, Stan Albers, Patrick Johnson, Michael Lord, and Christopher Marcantel (again) as Curtis Alden; Peter Davies as Father Jim Vochek; Meg Mundy, Augusta Dabney, Celeste Holm, and Patricia Barry as Isabelle Alden; Willie Carpenter as Dr. Ron Turner; Peter Radon and Richard McWilliams as Tony Perili; Susan Keith as Shana Sloane; Anthony Herrera as Dane Hammond; Leslie Vogel as Edie Lester; Bryan Cranston as Douglas Donovan; W. T. Martin as Warren Hodges; Ed Moore as Harry Sowalsky; John O'Hurley as Jonathan Matalaine; Patty Lotz, Roya Megnot, and Lisa Peluso as Ava Rescott; Nada Rowand as Kate Rescott; Christine Tudor (also known as Christine Tudor-Newman) and Elizabeth Savage as Gwyneth Alden; Noelle Beck as Trisha Alden, Gwyneth's daughter; John R. Johnston as Steve Sowolsky, who married Trisha and was killed in a bank robbery; Colleen Dion as Cecilia Thompson, who had previously been married to Steve; Judith Hoag as Lotty Bates, who married Curtis Alden in 1987; John Gabriel as lawyer Zack Conway; Jeff Gendelman as casino owner Nick Dinatos; Phil MacGregor and Brian Robert Taylor as Linc Beecham; Neil Zevnik as Judd Beecham; Deborah Allison as Jane Kincaid; Corey Mall as Tony Benedict; James Horan, Larkin Malloy, and Dennis Parlato as Clay Alden; Randolph Mantooth and Robert Dubac as Alex Masters; Luke Perry as Ned Bates; Isabel Glasser as Marty Edison; Teri Polo as Kristin Larsen; Alexandra Wilson and Marisol Massey as April Hathaway; Jacqueline Courtney as Diane Winston; Matthew Cowles as Eban Japes; Kathleen Fisk as Kelly Conway; Ron Nummi and Brian Fitzpatrick as Rick Stewart Alden; Mark Pinter as Dan Hollister; Deborah H. Quail as Carrie Davis; Scott Freaco, Michael Maguire, and Richard Steinmetz as Jeff Hartman, who married Trisha Alden in 1989; Linda Cook as Egypt Masters; Louise Stubbs as Minnie Madden; Ron Harper as Charles Hartman; Todd McDurmont as Todd, Egypt's brother; Rena Sofer as Amelia "Rocky" McKenzie Domecq; Robert Tyler as Trucker McKenzie; Kathryn Meisle as Juliette; Bernard Barrow and Jack Davidson as Louie Slavinski; George Wilson Loomis, Noah Sagan, and Geoffrey Wigdor as J.J. Forbes, son of Jack and Stacy; Rick Telles as Rio Domecq; Lonnie Price as assistant district attorney Howie Miller; Ira Hawkins, John Danelle, and Herb Downer as Lieutenant Hindman; Patrick O'Connell as attorney Archie Knapp; Mark Hofmaier as Professor Brad Spencer; Joseph Breen as Paul Slavinski; Will Osborne as Robert; and Colleen Quinn as Carly Rescott.

Subsequent cast changes included Laura Sisk as Alison (Ally) Rescott; Lisby Larson as Bonnie Rescott, Ally's mother; Jessica Collins and Elizabeth Mitchell as Dinah Lee Mayberry; Rebecca Gayheart as her sister, Hannah Mayberry; Keith Pruitt as Flynn Riley; Lauren Woods and Gerry Bamman as Reverend Ford; Jacqueline Knapp as Mrs. Ford; Eric Woodall as their son, Matthew Ford; Richard Cox as deranged art historian Giff Bowman; Paul Anthony Stewart as Casey Bowman; Alexander Kniffen as Michael Slavinsky; Keith Grumet as Arthur Davis; Eden Atwood as Staige Prince; John Schneider as Larry Lamont; Roger Howarth as Kent Winslow; Michael Weatherly as Cooper Alden, Isabella's grandnephew; Melba Moore as Dr. Burkhardt; Jeffrey Sams as Dr. Turner; Susan Cameron as Selena; James Carroll as Leo Burnell; Michael Gallardi as Armand Rosario; Jon Manfrelotti as Manny; Jean LeClerc as Jeremy Hunter (LeClerc had played the same role on *All My Children;* he also played a second role, Gilbert, on *Loving*); Faith Prince as Dianne; Simon Jones as Mr. Butler; Chris Waddell as Noah; Philip Brown as Buck Huston; Donna McKechnie as Margie; Forrest Compton as Dr. Daly; Catherine Hickland as Tess Wilder; Alice Hirson as Lisa Helman; Anders Hove as Cesar Faison; Alexander and Britton Steele and Gavin Lieb as Chris McKenzie, son of Trucker; Tony Musante as Mac, Trucker's father; Debbi Morgan as Dr. Angie Hubbard; Alimi Ballard as Frankie Hubbard, her son; Lee Chamberlin as Pat Baxter (the latter three characters had also been on *All My Children*); Dominic Cuskern as Ned Delaney; Jacob Penn as Sandy Masters, son of Ava and Alex; Krista Bonura as Alexis Masters; Thom Christopher as Dante Partou; Geoffrey C. Ewing as Charles Harrison; Nancy Addison Altman as Deborah Brewster; Robert Lupone as Leonard Brill; Simon Prebble as Lenox, Clay Alden's butler; Marian Seldes as Denise Nostrand; Darnell Williams as Jacob Johnson; Larry Haines as Neal Warren; Meta Golding as Brianna; Maggie Rush as Lorraine, Brianna's mother; and Halle Hirsh as Heather Forbes.

Like *Capitol*, CBS's 1982 soap, *Loving* was introduced in prime time; a two-hour movie version was telecast on 26 June 1983, the day before the daytime premiere. The series never achieved ratings success; after the demise of *Santa Barbara* in early 1993, *Loving* was consistently the lowest rated of the ten network daytime soaps. In late 1995 the series underwent a radical change. Eight major characters were written out; six of them were dispatched by a serial killer, who then killed herself. Most of the survivors relocated from sleepy Corinth to New York, where Morgan Fairchild joined the cast as media baroness Sydney Chase, and *Loving* was reborn as *The City* 13 November 1995.

LUCAN   ABC

12 SEPTEMBER 1977–4 DECEMBER 1978   An irregularly scheduled adventure series starring Kevin Brophy as Lucan, a boy who had lived with wolves in the woods of Minnesota until he was ten, and who, as a teenager, searched for his real identity. Also featured were John Randolph as Dr. Hoagland, a research scientist at the university to which the boy had been taken for study, and from which he escaped, and Don Gordon as Prentiss, a modern-day bounty hunter hired by the university to find the boy.

LUCAS TANNER   NBC

11 SEPTEMBER 1974–20 AUGUST 1975   Family drama starring David Hartman as Lucas Tanner, a sportswriter who decided to become a schoolteacher after his wife and son were killed in an automobile accident; Tanner managed to find a position in the English department at Harry S. Truman Memorial High School in Webster Groves, Missouri. Also featured were Rosemary Murphy (to January 1975) as Mrs. Margaret Blumenthal, the principal; John Randolph (from January 1975) as John Hamilton, the new principal; Robbie Rist as Glendon, the youngster who lived next door to Tanner; Alan Abelew as Jaytee, one of Tanner's students; Trish Soodik as Cindy, another student; Kimberly Beck as Terry, a student; and Michael Dwight-Smith as Wally, a student. David Victor was executive producer of the series, which was produced by Jay Benson.

THE LUCIE ARNAZ SHOW   CBS

2 APRIL 1985–30 APRIL 1985; 4 JUNE 1985–11 JUNE 1985   Lucie Arnaz, the daughter of Lucille Ball and Desi Arnaz, starred in her own sitcom as Jane Lucas, a psychologist who cohosted a popular radio talk program, "The Love and Lucas Show," on

WPLE in New York. Also featured were Karen Jablons-Alexander as her secretary, Loretta; Lee Bryant as Jill, Jane's sister; Todd Waring as her cohost, Larry Love; and Tony Roberts as station manager Jim Gordon.

LUCKY PAIR
SYNDICATED

1969   Celebrities and studio contestants teamed up on this game show hosted by Richard Dawson.

LUCKY PARTNERS
NBC

30 JUNE 1958–22 AUGUST 1958   On this little-known daytime game show, hosted by Carl Cordell, members of the studio audience tried to match serial numbers on dollar bills with those of on-stage contestants. Home viewers could also participate. The show was bumped from NBC's schedule after only a few weeks to make room for another game show, *Concentration*.

LUCKY PUP (THE ADVENTURES OF LUCKY PUP)
CBS

23 AUGUST 1948–23 JUNE 1951   This fifteen-minute puppet show was seen early weekday evenings for most of its run. It featured Doris Brown and the puppets of Hope and Morey Bunin. Two of the puppets, Pinhead and Foodini, later had their own series: see *Foodini the Great*.

LUCKY STRIKE THEATER
See ROBERT MONTGOMERY PRESENTS

THE LUCY SHOW
CBS

1 OCTOBER 1962–16 SEPTEMBER 1968   Lucille Ball returned to the air, without her ex-husband Desi Arnaz, in this half-hour sitcom. She remained on the air for the next twelve seasons (the last six were as star of *Here's Lucy*). On *The Lucy Show* she played Lucy Carmichael, a recently widowed bank secretary. Originally she worked at the First National Bank in Danfield, Connecticut, and the show also featured Vivian Vance (her crony from *I Love Lucy*) as her pal and cotenant, Vivian Bagley; Jimmy Garrett as Lucy's son, Jerry; Candy Moore as Lucy's daughter, Chris; Ralph Hart as Vivian's son, Sherman; Dick Martin as Lucy's friend, Harry; and Charles Lane as cantankerous Mr. Barnsdahl, Lucy's boss. In the fall of 1963 Gale Gordon replaced Lane as Lucy's new, but equally cantankerous, boss, Theodore J. Mooney. In the fall of 1965 all the supporting players (except for Gordon) were dropped, and the new format found Lucy as a bank secretary in San Francisco. Joining the cast were Roy Roberts as bank president Harrison Cheever, and Mary Jane Croft as Lucy's friend, Mary Jane Lewis.

LUX PLAYHOUSE
CBS

3 OCTOBER 1958–18 SEPTEMBER 1959   This half-hour dramatic anthology series shared a time slot with *Schlitz Playhouse of Stars* for one season.

THE LUX SHOW STARRING ROSEMARY CLOONEY
NBC

26 SEPTEMBER 1957–19 JUNE 1958   After sponsoring a dramatic series for seven seasons, the makers of Lux detergent decided to sponsor a musical variety show. Pop singer Rosemary Clooney, who had previously hosted her own syndicated show, headlined the half hour, which also featured the Modernaires and the Frank DeVol Orchestra. Rosemary Clooney's theme song was "Tenderly," composed by Lloyd Gross.

LUX VIDEO THEATRE
CBS/NBC

2 OCTOBER 1950–24 JUNE 1954 (CBS); 26 AUGUST 1954–12 SEPTEMBER 1957 (NBC) This dramatic anthology series was the television counterpart of *Lux Radio Theatre*, the popular radio anthology series which began in 1934. During the 1954–1955 season it was hosted by James Mason, who was succeeded by Otto Kruger and Gordon MacRae. Notable guest appearances included those by Robert Stack (in "Inside Story," one of his earliest TV roles, 18 June 1951), Peter Lorre ("The Taste,"

his first major TV role, 31 March 1952), Grace Kelly ("A Message for Janice," 29 September 1952), Edward G. Robinson ("Witness for the Prosecution," his TV dramatic debut, 17 September 1953), Barbara Rush ("Gavin's Darling," her first major role, 22 April 1954), James Arness ("The Chase," his first major TV role, 30 December 1954), and Esther Williams ("The Armed Venus," a rare TV appearance, 23 May 1957). The show was seen in a half-hour format on CBS, and in a one-hour format on NBC.

M.A.N.T.I.S. FOX

26 AUGUST 1994–3 MARCH 1995   Hour adventure series about a black superhero, starring Carl Lumbly as Dr. Miles Hawkins. Paralyzed as a result of a shooting, Hawkins developed a artificial exo-skeleton known as MANTIS (Mechanically Augmented Neurotransmitter Interactive System) which, when worn, made him extremely strong. Also featured were Roger Rees as John Stonebrake, Hawkins's former college roommate and scientific partner; Christopher Gartin as Taylor Savidge, a young bicycle messenger who joined forces with them; Gayln Görg as Lieutenant Leora Maxwell of the Port Columbia Police Department; and Lorena Gale as Lynette, Hawkins's housekeeper. Created by Sam Raimi and Sam Hamm, the character was introduced in a made-for-TV movie, also titled "M.A.N.T.I.S.," telecast on Fox 24 January 1994.

M*A*S*H CBS

17 SEPTEMBER 1972–19 SEPTEMBER 1983   One of television's most popular programs, M*A*S*H was based on Robert Altman's 1970 film (which in turn was based on Richard Hooker's novel). It was set at the 4077th M*A*S*H (Mobile Army Surgical Hospital) Unit, located just a few miles from the front lines in wartime Korea. Although the Korean War lasted only three years, M*A*S*H lasted eleven.

The cast included: Alan Alda as Captain Benjamin Franklin (Hawkeye) Pierce, a surgeon from Crabapple Cove, Maine, whose disdain for Army rules and regulations was matched by his skill with a scalpel, his quick wit, and his compassion; Wayne Rogers (1972–1975) as Captain John F. X. (Trapper John) McIntire, Hawkeye's tentmate, who was also a skilled surgeon and was every bit as rambunctious as Pierce; McLean Stevenson (1972–1975) as Lieutenant Colonel Henry Blake, the easygoing commanding officer who preferred to avoid exercising authority; Loretta Swit as Major Margaret (Hot Lips) Houlihan, the misunderstood commanding officer of the nurses; Larry Linville (1972–1977) as Major Frank Burns, a by-the-book zealot who was the butt of many Pierce-McIntire practical jokes; Gary Burghoff (1972–1979) as Corporal Walter (Radar) O'Reilly, the naive but efficient company clerk; William Christopher as Father Francis Mulcahy, the kindly chaplain; and Jamie Farr as Corporal Max Klinger, an enlisted man desperate to get out of the Army. Of that group only Burghoff had been featured in the movie. In the earliest episodes a few other regulars were also featured, but most had been phased out by the end of the first season: Tim Brown (who had also appeared in the movie) as Spearchucker Jones, a football star who was also a doctor; Odessa Cleveland as Lieutenant Ginger Ballis, a nurse; Karen Philipp as Lieutenant Maggie Dish, a nurse; Patrick Adiarte as Ho Jon, Trapper and Hawkeye's houseboy; John Orchard as Ugly John; and G. Wood as General Hammond.

M*A*S*H premiered in a Sunday time slot, and barely escaped cancellation after its first season. In the fall of 1973, however, it was moved to Saturday night, where it inherited one of the best time slots in television history, the 8:30 "hammock" between two established CBS sitcoms, *All in the Family* and *The Mary Tyler Moore Show*. There it zoomed to fourth in the 1973–1974 seasonal ratings, and remained a Top Ten show for all but one of the next nine seasons.

At the end of the third season McLean Stevenson and Wayne Rogers left the show. Stevenson's character, Colonel Blake, was killed in a plane crash on the final episode of the 1974–1975 season. In the fall of 1975 two new regulars were added: Harry Morgan as Colonel Sherman Potter, the new commanding officer, a surprisingly tolerant career man (Morgan had previously guested on M*A*S*H as a demented general); and Mike Farrell as Captain B. J. Hunnicutt, Trapper's replacement, who turned out to be another gifted surgeon who loved practical jokes. At the end of the 1976–1977 season Major Houlihan, who had had a not-so-secret affair with Major Burns for the past five seasons, finally got married—to Lieutenant Colonel Donald Penobscot (played by Beeson Carroll), who was stationed at headquarters (they were later divorced). Larry Linville, who played Burns, left in 1977 and was succeeded by David Ogden Stiers as Major Charles Emerson Winchester, a stuffy but skillful Boston-bred surgeon. Gary Burghoff left at the beginning of the 1979–1980 season; his character, Radar, was succeeded as company clerk by Corporal Klinger (by this time, Klinger had resigned himself to staying in the Army; he no longer wore dresses in an effort to have himself classified as psychologically unfit).

Other regulars (in smaller roles) included: Allan Arbus as Dr. Sidney Freedman, a psychiatrist; Loudon Wainwright III (1974–1975) as Captain Calvin Spaulding; Kellye Nakahara as Lieutenant Kellye Nakahara, a nurse; Jeff Maxwell (1976–1983) as Igor Straminsky, the cook; Johnny Haymer (1977–1979) as Sergeant Zale; and G. W. Bailey (1980–1983) as Sergeant Luther Rizzo.

During its eleven seasons *M*A*S*H* was able to experiment in some of its episodes. Among the most memorable of these were a "documentary," filmed in black and white, in which an American television reporter (Clete Roberts) interviewed the crew; a "first person" story, in which the camera was a wounded soldier; and a "real time" episode, in which all the action took place in just thirty minutes. Alan Alda also became increasingly involved with the series, writing and directing a number of episodes (he is the only person to have won Emmys for acting, writing, and directing). He took over as the principal creative force after the departure of Gene Reynolds and Larry Gelbart, who had produced the show during its first few seasons; Burt Metcalfe produced the show during the latter seasons.

Wisely, the people behind *M*A*S*H* decided to end the series while it was still popular. The final first-run episode, a two-and-a-half-hour special titled "Goodbye, Farewell and Amen" (28 February 1983), was the most widely watched television program of all time. It posted a 60.3 rating and a 77 share (meaning that 77 percent of all people watching TV were tuned to *M*A*S*H*). In its eleven seasons and 251 episodes, *M*A*S*H* succeeded in depicting the horror and futility of war. CBS aired a series retrospective, "Memories of M*A*S*H," on 25 November 1991. See also *AfterMASH*.

M.A.S.K. SYNDICATED
1985   Another of the many cartoon sci-fi series based on toys, M.A.S.K. stood for Mobil Armored Strike Kommand, a line of action figures produced by Kenner Toys.

THE M & M CANDY CARNIVAL CBS
6 JANUARY 1952–28 JUNE 1953   Gene Crane hosted this Sunday-afternoon talent contest, broadcast from Philadelphia and sponsored by the manufacturers of M & M candy. In 1954 Crane returned as host of a similar program: see *Contest Carnival*.

M-G-M PARADE ABC
14 SEPTEMBER 1955–2 MAY 1956   ABC, which had succeeded in persuading Disney and Warner Brothers to produce TV series by 1955 (see *Warner Brothers Presents*), also succeeded in landing a second major film studio—Metro-Goldwyn-Mayer. George Murphy hosted the half-hour series that presented clips from vintage films, biographies of stars, and previews of upcoming motion pictures.

M SQUAD NBC
20 SEPTEMBER 1957–13 SEPTEMBER 1960   Half-hour crime show starring Lee Marvin (who also owned a 50 percent interest in the show) as Lieutenant Frank Ballinger, a Chicago plainclothesman assigned to M Squad, a unit that mainly investigated homicides. Paul Newlan was also featured as his superior, Captain Grey. Burt Reynolds played one of his first major TV roles in one episode, "The Teacher," aired 2 January 1959. The *M Squad* theme was composed by Count Basie.

MTV UNPLUGGED   ·   MTV
21 JANUARY 1990–   A semi-regular musical series, *MTV Unplugged* gave rock artists the opportunity to perform before a small studio audience and without the tons of electronic equipment ordinarily required for a rock concert. Some artists performed using only acoustic equipment, while others appeared with stripped-down, low-wattage electric gear. The results were generally impressive, as the musicality of the performer was the focus of each event. Among the many artists featured on the show have been Paul McCartney, Eric Clapton, Sting, Mariah Carey, Nirvana, Elton John, Bruce Springsteen, Tony Bennett, and Hole. Jules Shear hosted the first few broadcasts.

M. V. P. SYNDICATED
1971   Sports-oriented talk show hosted by Cincinnati Reds' catcher Johnny Bench, who was named the National League's M.V.P. (Most Valuable Player) in 1972.

THE MAC DAVIS SHOW NBC
11 JULY 1974–29 AUGUST 1974; 19 DECEMBER 1974–22 MAY 1975; 18 MARCH 1976–17 JUNE 1976   Singer Mac Davis hosted three hour variety shows. The first one was a summer replacement for *The Flip Wilson Show;* the second one was activated to replace *Sierra* late in 1974. Sandy Gallin was its executive producer, and Arnie Rosen and Bob Ellison produced it. Davis's third show appeared in the spring of the following season, with Gary Smith and Dwight Hemion as executive producers, and Mike Post and Steve Binder as producers. Regulars included mimes Shields and Yarnell, who later hosted their own variety series (see also *Shields and Yarnell*).

MacGRUDER AND LOUD ABC
20 JANUARY 1985–30 APRIL 1985; 11 JUNE 1985–3 SEPTEMBER 1985   Aaron Spelling and Douglas Cramer produced this hour crime show in which the two principal cops—MacGruder and Loud—were partners both on and off duty; unfortunately, marriage was against department policy, so MacGrudger and Loud tried to hide that fact. Featured were John Getz as Officer Malcolm MacGruder; Kathryn Harrold as Officer Jenny Loud; Ted Ross as Detective Don Debbin; Frank McCarthy as Sergeant Bob Myhrum; Lee De Broux as Sergeant Hansen; and Gail Grate as Naomi, Malcolm and Jenny's friend. The officers worked for an unnamed big city police force; their shoulder patches read "L.S.P.D." The series premiered on ABC immediately following the network's telecast of Super Bowl XIX before settling into a Tuesday night slot.

MacGYVER ABC
29 SEPTEMBER 1985–8 AUGUST 1992   Hour adventure series starring Richard Dean Anderson as MacGyver, a resourceful agent for the Phoenix Foundation, an organization that undertook various secret missions for the government and others. MacGyver carried no weapons, preferring to use whatever materials he had on hand to solve whatever problems he might encounter. Also on hand were Dana Elcar as Peter Thornton, his boss; Bruce McGill (1987–1989) as fellow agent Jack Dalton; and Elyssa Davalos (1987–1989) as lawyer Nikki Carpenter. The series was created by Henry Winkler and John Rich. In the pilot episode, MacGyver was referred to as "Stace" and "Bud" by his grandfather, but Winkler and Rich subsequently decided to omit any references to the character's first name until 1991, when it was revealed (during a dream) to be Angus. Production moved from Hollywood to Vancouver in the fall of 1987. By 1991 Elcar had begun to lose his sight because of glaucoma; his character, Peter Thornton, also began to suffer vision difficulties. Michael Des Barres appeared in a few later episodes as MacGyver's archenemy, Murdoc. Following the series's cancellation, MacGyver showed up in two 1994 TV-movies on ABC: "MacGyver: Lost Treasure of Atlantis" (14 May) and "MacGyver: Trail to Doomsday" (24 November).

THE MacKENZIES OF PARADISE COVE ABC
27 MARCH 1979–18 MAY 1979   Irregularly scheduled hour series about five orphans who hooked up with an adventurer in Hawaii. With Clu Gulager as Cuda Webber,

the orphans' adopted guardian; Lory Walsh as Bridget MacKenzie; Shawn Stevens as Kevin MacKenzie, her twin brother; Sean Marshall as Michael MacKenzie; Randi Kiger as Celia MacKenzie; Keith Mitchell as Timothy MacKenzie; Harry Chang as Barney, a friend of Cuda's; Moe Keale as Big Ben, another pal of Cuda's. Jerry Thorpe and William Blinn were the producers.

MACKENZIE'S RAIDERS   SYNDICATED
1958   Half-hour western starring Richard Carlson as Colonel Ranald Mackenzie, a cavalry officer who headed an outfit that operated along the Mexican border during the 1870s.

THE MacNEIL-LEHRER REPORT   PBS
5 JANUARY 1976–2 SEPTEMBER 1983
THE MacNEIL-LEHRER NEWSHOUR   PBS
5 SEPTEMBER 1983–   PBS's nightly news analysis series began in 1975 as *The Robert MacNeil Report*, a local program in New York. Its host was Robert MacNeil, a native Canadian who had worked for CBC (the Canadian Broadcasting Corporation), BBC, NBC, and the Reuters News Agency. In the fall of 1976 MacNeil was joined by Jim Lehrer, who had worked as a reporter at the PBS station in Dallas (MacNeil and Lehrer had previously teamed up to cover the 1973 Senate Watergate hearings for PBS). *The MacNeil-Lehrer Report* covered a single topic each night and was widely praised for its depth and objectivity. The half-hour program was televised each weeknight; MacNeil was based in New York, Lehrer in Washington. Early in 1978 Charlayne Hunter-Gault was added as a third reporter, and former NBC newswoman Judy Woodruff joined the staff in August 1983.
    In the fall of 1983 the program was expanded to an hour and was transformed into a newscast, TV's first regularly scheduled daily hour news show. A fifth correspondent was added at that time: Kwame Holman, who reported from Denver. By the end of the decade, Holman had left and Hunter-Gault had become chiefly a field reporter. Woodruff was the principal backup anchor, and Roger Mudd also appeared regularly. By the mid-1990s Woodruff and Mudd had departed, and Hunter-Gault remained as national correspondent; a number of other reporters were regular contributors. In early 1995 Robert MacNeil announced his decision to retire later in the year. Following his departure in October 1995, the program carried on as *The Newshour with Jim Lehrer*.

MAD ABOUT YOU   NBC
23 SEPTEMBER 1992–   Standup comic Paul Reiser was co-creator, co-executive producer (with Danny Jacobson), and costar of this sitcom about a young married couple. Reiser played Paul Buchman, and Helen Hunt played his wife, Jamie Buchman. As the series got underway, Paul and Jamie were newlyweds living in a downtown Manhattan apartment with their dog, Murray; Paul was a documentary filmmaker who later went to work for a cable television network, Jamie a public relations executive (she later quit her job, went back to school, and worked freelance before opening her own firm). A large cast of regulars and semiregulars were also on hand, including Tommy Hinkley (1992–1993) as Paul's friend Selby; Anne Ramsay as Jamie's younger sister, Lisa; Leila Kenzle as Jamie's friend and later business partner Fran; Richard Kind (1992–1993) as Fran's husband (and subsequent ex-husband) Mark; John Pankow as Paul's divorced cousin Ira, who ran the family sporting goods store; Jerry Adler as Wicker, the building superintendent; Judy Geeson as Maggie Conway, the Buchmans' snooty British neighbor; Paxton Whitehead and Jim Piddock as Maggie's husband, Hal; Nancy Dussault and Penny Fuller as Jamie's mother, Theresa; Paul Dooley and John Karlen as Jamie's father; Louis Zorich as Paul's father, Burt; Cynthia Harris as Paul's mother, Sylvia; Lisa Kudrow (1993–   ) as Ursula, the ditzy waitress at the Buchmans' favorite restaurant (in 1994 Kudrow became a regular on NBC's new sitcom, *Friends;* her character was Ursula's twin sister); Steven Wright (1993) as Warren, Paul's laconic camera operator; Anne Bobby (1994–   ) as Jamie's childhood pal, Susannah; and Meg Wyllie as Aunt Lolly. The series finished in a mediocre 59th place after its first season, but was renewed.

504

During its second season it rose to a respectable 31st place finish, and achieved genuine hit status during its third season, finishing in eleventh place.

MAD MOVIES WITH THE L.A. CONNECTION   SYNDICATED
1985   Old movies and TV shows were shown with a twist on this comedy series — new dialogue was dubbed by the L.A. Connection, a comedy troupe. A similar format had been attempted in 1963: see *Fractured Flickers*.

MAD TV   FOX
14 OCTOBER 1995–   An hour comedy sketch show inspired by *Mad* magazine and broadcast at 11 P.M. on Saturdays to compete with NBC's *Saturday Night Live*. The series' cast included Bryan Callan, David Herman, Orlando Jones, Phil Lamarr, Artie Lange, Mary Scheer, Nicole Sullivan, and Debra Wilson. In addition to the sketches, the show featured animated segments based on *Mad*'s venerable Don Martin and "Spy vs. Spy" cartoons.

MADAME'S PLACE   SYNDICATED
1982   Wayland Flowers's garrulous puppet, Madame, headlined this half-hour comedy series. The puppet played herself, the host of a TV talk show. The human regulars included Johnny Haymer (as Madame's butler, Walter Pinkerton), Judy Landers (as her niece, Sara Joy), and Susan Tolsky.

MADE IN AMERICA   CBS
5 APRIL 1964–3 MAY 1964   Robert Maxwell hosted this prime-time game show on which a celebrity panel tried to figure out the identities of guests, all of whom were self-made millionaires. The short-lived series replaced half of *The Judy Garland Show* and was in turn replaced by reruns of *Brenner*.

MADIGAN   NBC
20 SEPTEMBER 1972–22 AUGUST 1973   This ninety-minute crime show was one segment of *The NBC Wednesday Mystery Movie* and alternated with *Banacek* and *Cool Million*. It starred Richard Widmark, a major film star whose television appearances have been extremely infrequent, as Sergeant Dan Madigan, a typically tough New York cop. Dean Hargrove and Roland Kibbee produced the series for Universal Television.

MADMAN OF THE PEOPLE   NBC
22 SEPTEMBER 1994–26 JANUARY 1995; 10 JUNE 1995–24 JUNE 1995   Dabney Coleman, who had played irascible characters in previous short-lived sitcoms such as *Buffalo Bill, The 'Slap' Maxwell Story,* and *Drexell's Class,* did it again in this one. Here he played irascible Jack "Madman" Buckner, the outspoken columnist for *Your Times* magazine, whose daughter was named the magazine's new publisher. Joining him were Cynthia Gibb as Meg, his daughter and new boss; Concetta Tomei as Delia, his wife; John Ales as Dylan, his lazy son; Ashley Gardner as Caroline, Jack and Delia's other daughter; and Robert Pierce as Caroline's husband, Kenny, who ran a kennel. Added during the season were Craig Bierko as B. J., a reporter for the magazine who became Meg's boyfriend, and Amy Aquino as Sasha, Jack's assistant. *Madman of the People* was the highest-rated show of the 1994–1995 season to be canceled; although it ranked twelfth for the season, its performance was considered a disappointment because it had been scheduled in a highly favorable time slot on Thursdays.

MAGGIE   ABC
24 OCTOBER 1981–14 NOVEMBER 1981; 30 APRIL 1982–21 MAY 1982   Syndicated columnist Erma Bombeck created this sitcom about domestic life. Featured were Miriam Flynn as housewife Maggie Weston; James Hampton as her husband, Len Weston; Billy Jacoby as their twelve-year-old son, Mark; Christian Jacobs as their eight-year-old son, Bruce (the Westons also had a sixteen-year-old son, L. J., who was never seen); Doris Roberts as Maggie's friend and neighbor, Loretta, a beautician; Marga-

ret Impert as her friend, Chris, a manicurist; and Judith-Marie Bergan as insufferable Buffy Croft, a realtor. *Maggie* was the first new show of the 1981–1982 season to leave the air, although it returned five months later for a short run.

MAGGIE AND THE BEAUTIFUL MACHINE   PBS
1972–1975   Half-hour exercise program hosted by Maggie Lettwin. The show was seen locally on WGBH-TV, Boston, for three seasons before going network in 1972.

MAGGIE BRIGGS   CBS
4 MARCH 1984–15 APRIL 1984   Suzanne Pleshette had star billing in this half-hour sitcom, the full title of which was *Suzanne Pleshette Is Maggie Briggs*. Pleshette played a veteran newspaperwoman for the *New York Examiner* who was suddenly forced to write for the paper's new "Modern Living" section. Also on hand were Kenneth McMillan as Maggie's crony, Walter Holden; John Getz as Geoff Bennett, the new editor of the Modern Living section; Stephen Lee as food critic Sherman Milslagle; and Shera Danese as Maggie's best friend, Connie Piscopoli, a lingerie model.

MAGGI'S PRIVATE WIRE   NBC
12 APRIL 1949–2 JULY 1949   Fifteen-minute interview show, hosted by Maggi McNellis.

MAGIC CIRCUS   SYNDICATED
1972   An hour of magic, sponsored by Pillsbury, starring Mark Wilson, Nani Darnell, and Rebo the Clown. The trio had previously been featured on Wilson's network magic show, *The Magic Land of Allakazam*.

THE MAGIC CLOWN   NBC
11 SEPTEMBER 1949–27 JUNE 1954   This fifteen-minute kids' show was seen on Sunday mornings and starred a magician known as Zovella. The series was written and produced by Al Garry.

THE MAGIC COTTAGE   DUMONT
18 JULY 1949–12 SEPTEMBER 1952   Pat Meikle hosted this Monday-through-Friday kids' show.

THE MAGIC EYE   SYNDICATED
1959   Scientific topics were explored on this educational show for children.

THE MAGIC LAND OF ALLAKAZAM   CBS/ABC
1 OCTOBER 1960–22 SEPTEMBER 1962 (CBS); 29 SEPTEMBER 1962–28 DECEMBER 1963 (ABC); 25 APRIL 1964–12 DECEMBER 1964 (ABC)   Magician Mark Wilson hosted this Saturday kids' show, which blended magic tricks and illusions with a fantasy story line. Wilson's wife, Nani Darnell, and their son Mike, who was seven when the show began, were also featured, as were Rebo the Clown (played by Bev Bergeron) and the King of Allakazam (played by Bob Towner). Wilson himself was the executive producer of the series, and Dan Whitman was its producer. Many of the principals later appeared in Wilson's 1972 syndicated show, *Magic Circus*.

MAGIC MIDWAY   NBC
22 SEPTEMBER 1962–16 MARCH 1963   Claude Kirchner, who had hosted *Super Circus* for several years during the 1950s, returned as ringmaster of this Saturday-morning circus show for children. Also featured were Bonnie Lee and Lou Stein. The show was sponsored by Marx Toys.

THE MAGIC OF MARK WILSON   SYNDICATED
1978   Half-hour magic show, with illusionist Mark Wilson (formerly host of *The Magic Land of Allakazam*), Nani Darnell, and Greg Wilson, Mark's son.

THE MAGIC RANCH   ABC
30 SEPTEMBER 1961–17 DECEMBER 1961   Don Alan hosted this Saturday-morning kids' show, which was set at a dude ranch. Alan's guests included not only professional magicians, but also talented junior illusionists. George B. Anderson produced the series that was telecast from Chicago.

THE MAGIC SCHOOL BUS   PBS
11 SEPTEMBER 1994–   The first fully animated series produced by PBS, *The Magic School Bus* was based on the books written by Joanna Cole and illustrated by Bruce Degen. Each week on the show, an elementary school science teacher, Ms. Frizzle, led her class aboard the Magic School Bus. The vehicle could miniaturize, enabling Ms. Frizzle to show her class the world of nature and science from a different perspective. Lily Tomlin provided the voice of Ms. Frizzle, and Little Richard performed the series theme song.

THE MAGIC SLATE   NBC
2 JUNE 1950–25 AUGUST 1950; 21 JANUARY 1951–24 JUNE 1951   Plays for children were presented on this half-hour series shown on alternate Fridays in 1950, and alternate Sunday afternoons in 1951.

THE MAGICIAN   NBC
2 OCTOBER 1973–20 MAY 1974   Bill Bixby starred in this nonviolent crime show as Anthony Blake, a wealthy nightclub magician who used his talents offstage to solve crimes. Also featured were Keene Curtis as Max Pomeroy, his manager; Todd Crespi as Dennis, Max's young son; and Jim Watkins as Jerry Anderson, pilot of Blake's full-size jet plane. Bixby, who performed his own tricks on the show, was coached by illusionist Mark Wilson (star of *The Magic Land of Allakazam*). The series was produced by Paramount TV.

THE MAGILLA GORILLA SHOW   SYNDICATED/ABC
1964–1965 (SYNDICATED); 1 JANUARY 1966–2 SEPTEMBER 1967 (ABC) Principal characters on this half-hour cartoon show from Hanna-Barbera Productions were Magilla Gorilla, an enormous ape who lived in Peebles' Pet Shop, Mr. Peebles, and Ogee, a little girl. Additional segments included "Ricochet Rabbit and Droopalong Coyote," "Mushmouse and Punkin' Puss," and "Breezly and Sneezly," a polar bear and seal duo.

MAGNAVOX THEATER   CBS
15 SEPTEMBER 1950–15 DECEMBER 1950   Friday-night hour-long dramatic anthology series.

THE MAGNIFICENT MARBLE MACHINE   NBC
7 JULY 1975–11 JUNE 1976   A daytime game show that tried to capitalize on the pinball-machine craze. Art James hosted the show on which celebrity-and-contestant pairs played a word game with the winning pair earning the opportunity to play a giant pinball machine for prizes. In January 1976 the format was changed to include only celebrity players. Robert Noah was executive producer of the series for Heatter-Quigley Productions.

MAGNUM, P.I.   CBS
11 DECEMBER 1980–12 SEPTEMBER 1988   This hour crime show starred rugged Tom Selleck as Thomas Sullivan Magnum, a Vietnam veteran who left the Navy and became a private investigator in Hawaii; hired by a wealthy mystery writer, Robin Masters, to test the security systems at Masters's estate, Magnum gained entry to the property and was rewarded by being invited to live in the guest house (Masters himself was seldom at home and never seen on camera; Orson Welles supplied Masters's voice from 1981 to 1985). Other cast members included Jonathan Hillerman as Masters's stuffy major domo, Jonathan Quayle Higgins III, a former sergeant major in the British Army who barely tolerated Magnum's presence and his informal style and who

tended Masters's two Dobermans, Zeus and Apollo; Roger E. Mosley as Magnum's Navy buddy, T. C. (the initials stood for Theodore Calvin), who now ran a helicopter charter service, Island Hoppers; and Larry Manetti as another Navy buddy, Orville "Rick" Wright, proprietor of the King Kamehameha Club. Occasionally featured over the years were Jeff MacKay as Navy buddy Mac Reynolds; Gillian Dobb (1982–1988) as Agatha Chumley, a British woman who was wild about Higgins; Jean Bruce Scott (1982–1984; 1986–1988) as Navy Lieutenant Maggie Poole; Kwan Hi Lim as police lieutenant Tanaka; Kathleen Lloyd (1983–1988) as assistant district attorney Carol Baldwin; and Elisha Cook, Jr., as "Ice Pick," a shady character.

At the end of the 1986–1987 season Magnum was shot, apparently killed, and ascended into heaven. To the producers' surprise, the series was renewed for an eighth season, so it was explained in the fall 1987 opener that Magnum had only dreamed his demise. A final "finale" was telecast 1 May 1988, in which Magnum decided to rejoin the Navy and it was suggested that Higgins was really Robin Masters.

Although the series was able to land many guest stars, including Frank Sinatra (who played a retired New York cop in a February 1987 episode), it was never able to land Jack Lord, who had starred in *Hawaii Five-O* for twelve years (and whose character, Steve McGarrett, was often referred to on the show).

Magnum's powerful hard-rock musical theme, used in all but the earliest episodes, was composed by Mike Post and Pete Carpenter.

THE MAIL STORY   ABC
7 OCTOBER 1954–30 DECEMBER 1954   Half-hour dramatic anthology series about the United States Post Office. Postmaster General Arthur Summerfield introduced the premiere telecast. The show was also seen under the title *Handle with Care*.

THE MAIN EVENT   SYNDICATED
1961   Former heavyweight champion Rocky Marciano introduced film clips of classic fights and interviewed boxing greats on this half-hour sports series.

MAJOR ADAMS
See WAGON TRAIN

MAJOR DAD   CBS
18 SEPTEMBER 1989–13 SEPTEMBER 1993   Half-hour sitcom about a widowed liberal reporter from a small-town paper who interviewed a gung-ho, spit-and-polish Marine, and married him. With Gerald McRaney as the Marine, Major J. D. "Mac" MacGillis; Shanna Reed as the reporter, Polly Cooper; Marisa Ryan as her daughter Elizabeth, thirteen; Nicole Dubuc as daughter Robin, eleven; Chelsea Hertford as daughter Casey, six; Matt Mulhern as Lieutenant Gene Holowachuk, Mac's aide; Marlon Archey (1989–1990) as Sergeant Byron James; and Whitney Kershaw (1989–1990) as Mac's secretary, Merilee. In the fall of 1990 Mac and family moved to a new post, Camp Hollister in Virginia, where Mac became staff secretary to General Marcus Craig (played by Jon Cypher). Also added to the cast were Beverly Archer as Gunnery Sergeant Alva "Gunny" Bricker; and Chance Michael Corbitt as the general's grandson, Jeffrey. Vice President Dan Quayle appeared in a November 1990 episode commemorating the 215th anniversary of the Marine Corps. The series took note of the events in the Persian Gulf during its second season; the episode of 4 February 1991 involved Mac's request for a transfer to Saudi Arabia after he learned of the outbreak of war.

MAJOR DEL CONWAY OF THE FLYING TIGERS   DUMONT
14 APRIL 1951–26 MAY 1951; 29 JULY 1951–2 MARCH 1952   Eric Fleming first starred as Major Del Conway, an American agent whose cover was that of a pilot for the Flying Tigers Airline. When the show returned in July 1951, Ed Peck was the new Major Conway. Bern Hoffman was also featured in the half-hour series. In real life, the Flying Tigers Airline was a cargo airline founded by General Claire L. Chennault during the late 1940s.

MAJORITY RULES   ABC
2 SEPTEMBER 1949–30 JULY 1950   Hosted by Ed Prentiss, this prime-time game show featured a panel of three contestants. When the panel was asked a question, at least two panelists had to agree on an answer.

MAKE A FACE   ABC
2 OCTOBER 1961–30 MARCH 1962; 29 SEPTEMBER 1962–22 DECEMBER 1962   Bob Clayton hosted this game show on which contestants were required to assemble pictures of famous persons; the pictures had been cut up and placed on moving belts in front of the contestants. Art Baer produced the series, which was first seen Mondays through Fridays; in the fall of 1962 a children's version was seen Saturdays.

MAKE A WISH   ABC
12 SEPTEMBER 1971–5 SEPTEMBER 1976   Tom Chapin hosted this highly acclaimed Sunday-morning educational series for children. During the early seasons two themes were explored each week through songs, films, and interviews. During the final season the nation's bicentennial observance was emphasized, and songs were provided by Harry Chapin (Tom's brother). Lester Cooper was the executive producer, director, and head writer of the series.

MAKE ME LAUGH   ABC/SYNDICATED
20 MARCH 1958–12 JUNE 1958 (ABC); 1979 (SYNDICATED)   Robert Q. Lewis hosted the network version of this unusual game show on which contestants earned money by keeping a straight face. Each week three comedians were on hand, each of whom was given one minute to try to break up the contestant; a contestant won one dollar for each second of non-smiling. Johnny Stearns produced and directed the prime-time series, and Renny Peterson escorted the contestants. *TV Guide* reported in 1958 that some comedians were reluctant to appear on the show because they felt their popularity might suffer if the contestants succeeded in remaining stonefaced. Twenty-one years later a syndicated version of *Make Me Laugh* surfaced, with Bobby Van as host.

MAKE MINE MUSIC   CBS
13 DECEMBER 1948–19 MAY 1949   Carole Coleman, Bill Skipper, and Larry Douglas were featured on this fifteen-minute musical show, which was seen after the network news on certain weeknights.

MAKE ROOM FOR DADDY (THE DANNY THOMAS SHOW)   ABC/CBS
29 SEPTEMBER 1953–18 JULY 1957 (ABC); 7 OCTOBER 1957–14 SEPTEMBER 1964 (CBS)
One of the few situation comedies to last more than a decade, *Make Room for Daddy* starred Danny Thomas, a nightclub singer and comedian, as Danny Williams, a nightclub singer and comedian. During the show's first three seasons, Danny was married and had two children. Jean Hagen played his wife, Margaret, with Sherry Jackson as eleven-year-old Terry and Rusty Hamer as seven-year-old Rusty. Also featured were Amanda Randolph as Louise, the housekeeper; Horace McMahon (1953–1954) as Danny's agent, Phil Arnold; Jesse White (1954–1957) as his agent, Jesse Leeds; Sid Melton as Charlie Halper, owner of the Copa Club; Ben Lessy as Ben, Danny's pianist; Mary Wickes as Liz O'Neal, Danny's publicist; Hans Conried as Uncle Tonoose, Danny's wacky Lebanese relation; and Nan Bryant (1955–1956) as Danny's mother-in-law. Jean Hagen left the series at the end of the 1955–1956 season, and in the fall of 1956 the title was changed to *The Danny Thomas Show*. Danny was a widower during the 1956–1957 season, but in the spring of 1957 Marjorie Lord was introduced as Kathy O'Hara, a widowed nurse who came to take care of Rusty when he contracted the measles; Danny and Kathy were married at the end of the season. Lelani Sorenson was also introduced as Patty, Kathy's six-year-old daughter. When the show switched networks in the fall of 1957, Angela Cartwright had been added as Kathy's daughter Linda, replacing Lelani Sorenson. Also joining the cast were Sheldon Leonard as Phil Arnold, Danny's agent; Pat Harrington, Jr., as Pat Hannigan, Terry's boyfriend and eventual husband; and Pat Carroll (1961–1964) as

Bunny Halper, Charlie's wife. In 1960 Penney Parker replaced Sherry Jackson as daughter Terry. Many of the principals were reunited in two specials aired in 1967 and 1969, and in 1970 the crew reappeared in a new sitcom: see *Make Room for Granddaddy*. The show's original title, *Make Room for Daddy,* was inspired by the actual goings-on in Danny Thomas's household. As explained in a 1954 *TV Guide* feature, whenever Thomas was on the road, one of his daughters (Margaret, later known as Marlo, or Teresa) moved in to the master bedroom with his wife, Rosemary. When he came back home, Rosemary reminded the girl to leave, explaining that "We must make room for daddy."

MAKE ROOM FOR GRANDDADDY   ABC

23 SEPTEMBER 1970–2 SEPTEMBER 1971   A sequel to *Make Room for Daddy,* this half-hour sitcom again featured Danny Thomas as Danny Williams, who had become a grandfather sometime between the two series. Many of the old *Make Room for Daddy* troupe were also on hand: Marjorie Lord as Danny's wife, Kathy; Rusty Hamer as Rusty, now a med student; Angela Cartwright as Linda, now at boarding school; Sid Melton as Charlie Halper, now Danny's agent; and Hans Conried as the still-wacky Uncle Tonoose. Sherry Jackson was seen in the premiere episode as Danny's older daughter, Terry Johnson, who wanted to leave her young son with Danny and Kathy while she visited her serviceman-husband in Japan. Other regulars included Michael Hughes as Michael, Terry's son; Rosey Grier as Rosey Robbins, Danny's pianist; and Stanley Myron Handelman as Henry, the elevator operator in Danny's apartment building. Jana Taylor was occasionally featured as Rusty's wife, Susan. Richard Crenna, former star of *The Real McCoys,* produced the show.

MAKE THAT SPARE   ABC

15 OCTOBER 1960–11 SEPTEMBER 1964   A bowling series of variable length, *Make That Spare* was seen immediately following *The Fight of the Week; Make That Spare* filled out the hour time slot and began whenever the boxing match ended. Johnny Johnston hosted the series except during the 1961–1962 season, when Win Elliott took over. After a twenty-four-year hiatus, *Make That Spare* returned to ABC for a one-shot telecast on 12 March 1988, with Chris Schenkel and Nelson Burton, Jr., immediately preceding the network's long-running Saturday afternoon *Pro Bowlers' Tour.*

MAKE THE CONNECTION   NBC

7 JULY 1955–29 SEPTEMBER 1955   Mark Goodson and Bill Todman produced this prime-time game show on which a celebrity panel tried to figure out how the lives of two contestants had crossed. Jim McKay, in his first network appearance, hosted the series in its early weeks; he was succeeded by Gene Rayburn. The celebrity panelists were Betty White, Gene Glavan, Eddie Bracken, and a guest celebrity.

MAKE YOUR OWN KIND OF MUSIC   NBC

20 JULY 1971–7 SEPTEMBER 1971   This summer variety hour was hosted by the Carpenters—sister Karen and brother Richard—and also featured trumpeter Al Hirt, singer Mark Lindsay (formerly of Paul Revere and the Raiders), comics (Tom) Patchett and (Jay) Tarses (who later became the executive producers of *The Bob Newhart Show*) and the New Doodletown Pipers.

MAKIN' IT   ABC

1 FEBRUARY 1979–16 MARCH 1979   Half-hour sitcom with a disco flavor, set in Passaic, New Jersey. With David Naughton as college student Billy Manucci; Greg Antonacci as his older brother, Tony Manucci, star dancer at the Inferno, Passaic's hottest disco; Ellen Travolta as their mother, Dorothy Manucci; Lou Antonio as their father, Joseph Manucci; Denise Miller as their younger sister, Tina Manucci; Rebecca Balding as Corky Crandall, Billy's girlfriend, a receptionist at the William Morris Agency; Ralph Seymour as Billy's pal, Kingfish; Gary Prendergast as Billy's pal, Bernard; Wendy Hoffman as Suzanne, Bernard's girlfriend; Diane Robin as Felice, Kingfish's girlfriend; and Jennifer Perrito as Ivy, a waitress at the ice cream

store where Billy worked part time. The show was created by Mark Rothman, Lowell Ganz and Garry Marshall.

MAKING A LIVING
See IT'S A LIVING

THE MAKING OF A CONTINENT   PBS
3 NOVEMBER 1986–8 DECEMBER 1986   A six-part study of North American geology. The series grew out of a two-part documentary broadcast in November 1983.

MAKING THE GRADE   CBS
5 APRIL 1982–10 MAY 1982   Half-hour sitcom set at Franklin High School in St. Louis. With James Naughton as Harry Barnes, the compassionate dean of boys; Graham Jarvis as bureaucrat Jack Felspar, the assistant principal; Steven Peterman as Jeffrey Kelton, a new substitute teacher; George Wendt as gym teacher Gus Bertoya; Alley Mills as Sara, the drama teacher; Philip Charles MacKenzie as chemistry teacher Dave Wasserman; and Zane Lasky as Anton Zemetkis. Gary David Goldberg created the series and was its executive producer.

MAKING THINGS GROW   PBS
1970–1975   Half-hour series for indoor and outdoor gardeners, hosted by Thalassa Cruso and produced at WGBH-TV, Boston.

MALIBU RUN   CBS
1 MARCH 1961–27 SEPTEMBER 1961   Produced by Ivan Tors, *Malibu Run* was a revamped version of *The Aquanauts*. It starred Jeremy Slate as Larry Lahr and Ron Ely as Mike Madison; both had been featured in *The Aquanauts,* but on *Malibu Run* they seemed to spend a little more time on land trying to solve crimes.

MALIBU U.   ABC
21 JULY 1967–1 SEPTEMBER 1967   Rick Nelson hosted this half-hour summer musical series; Nelson was the "dean" of a "college" located on the beach at Malibu. Other regulars included Australian singer Robie Porter and the Bob Banas Dancers.

MAMA   CBS
1 JULY 1949–27 JULY 1956; 16 DECEMBER 1956–17 MARCH 1957   One of TV's first popular sitcoms, *Mama* was based on John Van Druten's play, *I Remember Mama,* which was in turn derived from Kathryn Forbes's book, *Mama's Bank Account.* The series told the story of the Hansens, a closely knit Norwegian family living on San Francisco's Steiner Street in 1917. Featured were Peggy Wood as Marta (Mama) Hansen; Judson Laire as Lars (Papa) Hansen, a carpenter; Rosemary Rice as elder daughter Katrin, whose off-screen voice introduced each episode; Dick Van Patten as son Nels; Iris Mann (1949–1950) and Robin Morgan (1950–1956) as younger daughter Dagmar; Ruth Gates as Aunt Jenny, Mama's older sister; Malcolm Keen as Uncle Chris; Carl Frank as Uncle Gunnar; Alice Frost as Aunt Trina, Mama's younger sister; Patty McCormack (1953–1956) as Ingeborg; and Kevin Coughlin (1954–1957) as T. R. Ryan. From 1949 through the summer of 1956, the show was done live. After its cancellation in 1956, public demand prompted CBS to revive the series that winter. The second version was filmed and lasted only thirteen weeks. By that time daughter Katrin had become a secretary, and son Nels had become a medical student. Toni Campbell joined the cast as daughter Dagmar, replacing Robin Morgan (who had been featured on *The Quiz Kids* and later became active in the women's movement). The half-hour series was originally produced and directed by Ralph Nelson and was later produced by Carol Irwin.

MAMA MALONE   CBS
7 MARCH 1984–21 JULY 1984   Originally produced for the 1982–1983 season, *Mama Malone* remained on the CBS shelf for a year and a half. The half-hour sitcom starred Lila Kaye as Renata Malone, the Italian widow of an Irish cop who hosted a cooking

show over cable TV from her Brooklyn apartment. Also featured were Randee Heller as her daughter, Connie Karamacopolous, a waitress; Evan Richards as Frankie, Connie's son; Don Amendolia as Mama's brother, Dino Forresti, a lounge singer; Richard Yñiguez as Father Jose Silva, the new local priest; Ralph Manza as Padre Guardino, the old priest; Sam Anderson as Stanley; and Raymond Singer as the floor director of the cooking show.

MAMA'S BOY   NBC
19 SEPTEMBER 1987–6 AUGUST 1988   *Mama's Boy,* together with *Beverly Hills Buntz,* was intended by NBC as a "designated hitter" series, to be shown once a month until a suitable place emerged for it on the network's schedule. The show's premiere telecast ranked fourth for the week, but network executives were not impressed with previews of the next five episodes. The series' cancellation was announced in October, and the remaining programs were aired sporadically during the remainder of the season. Bruce Weitz (late of *Hill Street Blues*) starred as Manhattan newspaper columnist Jake McCaskey, whose widowed mother moved in with him. Nancy Walker played his meddlesome mom, Molly, and Dan Hedaya was Jake's friend Mickey.

MAMA'S FAMILY   NBC
22 JANUARY 1983–4 JUNE 1983; 11 AUGUST 1983–15 SEPTEMBER 1984; 1 JUNE 1985–17 AUGUST 1985 (NBC); 1986–1990 (SYNDICATED)   This half-hour sitcom was essentially an expanded version of the sketches that had been regularly featured on *The Carol Burnett Show* in the mid-1970s. Set in the Southern hamlet of Raytown, it starred Vicki Lawrence (who was in her early thirties) as Thelma Harper, a cantankerous, crotchety old lady who always found something to complain about. Also featured were Ken Berry as her son, Vint, a recently divorced locksmith who moved back in with her; Eric Brown as Vint's teenage son, Buzz; Karin Argoud as Vint's teenage daughter, Sonia; Dorothy Lyman as their neighbor, Naomi Oates, who fell for Vint and later married him; Rue McClanahan as Thelma's sister, Fran, who wrote for the Raytown paper; Betty White as Ellen, Thelma's daughter; and Harvey Korman as urbane Alistair Quince, who introduced each episode. Korman also appeared occasionally as Ed, Thelma's long-suffering son-in-law, and Carol Burnett sometimes appeared as Ed's wife (and Thelma's daughter), Eunice. The series returned in syndication in 1986, with Lawrence, Lyman, and Berry from the old cast. Two new regulars were added: Alan Payser as Bubba Higgins, son of Ed and Eunice, who moved in with Thelma; and Beverly Archer as next-door neighbor Iola Boylen, who lusted for Vint.

MAN AGAINST CRIME   CBS/DUMONT/NBC
7 OCTOBER 1949–2 OCTOBER 1953 (CBS); 11 OCTOBER 1953–4 APRIL 1954 (DUMONT); 18 OCTOBER 1953–4 JULY 1954 (NBC); 1 JULY 1956–26 AUGUST 1956 (NBC)   Ralph Bellamy originally starred in this half-hour crime show as Mike Barnett, a New York City private eye who didn't use a gun. When Bellamy took a vacation during the summer of 1951, Robert Preston filled in for him, playing Mike's brother, Pat. During the 1953–1954 season both NBC and DuMont carried the series. In 1956 NBC briefly revived the series as a live summer replacement for *The Loretta Young Show.* This version starred Frank Lovejoy as Mike Barnett, who was no longer unarmed. The Bellamy episodes were widely syndicated under the title *Follow That Man.* Larry Klee created the series.

THE MAN AND THE CHALLENGE   NBC
12 SEPTEMBER 1959–3 SEPTEMBER 1960   Ivan Tors produced this half-hour adventure series, starring George Nader as Dr. Glenn Barton, a research scientist for the Institute of Human Factors, an agency that conducted experiments designed to measure human endurance.

THE MAN AND THE CITY   ABC
15 SEPTEMBER 1971–5 JANUARY 1972   An unsuccessful hour-long dramatic series that starred Anthony Quinn as Thomas Jefferson Alcala, a widower, mayor of a South-

western city. Also featured were Mike Farrell as Andy Hays, his aide, and Mala Powers as Marian Crane, his secretary. The show was produced by Universal TV.

THE MAN BEHIND THE BADGE   CBS/SYNDICATED
11 OCTOBER 1953–3 OCTOBER 1954 (CBS); 1955 (SYNDICATED)   The stories on this half-hour anthology series were based on the exploits of real-life law enforcement officers. The CBS version, hosted by Norman Rose, was broadcast live. Another thirty-nine episodes were produced on film in 1955 for first-run syndication, with Charles Bickford hosting. Jerry Robinson was the producer.

A MAN CALLED HAWK   ABC
28 JANUARY 1989–6 MAY 1989; 1 JULY 1989–31 AUGUST 1989   In this violent hour crime show, spun off from *Spenser: For Hire,* Avery Brooks starred as Spenser's mysterious associate, Hawk, who moved from Boston back to his hometown, Washington, D.C., where he became a one-man truth-and-justice squad. Moses Gunn was occasionally featured as Old Man, a streetwise acquaintance of Hawk's.

A MAN CALLED SHENANDOAH   ABC
13 SEPTEMBER 1965–5 SEPTEMBER 1966   Robert Horton starred in this half-hour western as an amnesiac who called himself Shenandoah. Nursed back to health after having been shot, Shenandoah wandered around the West trying to get his head together. E. Jack Neuman created the series and was its executive producer; Fred Freiberger produced it for M-G-M TV.

A MAN CALLED SLOANE   NBC
22 SEPTEMBER 1979–22 DECEMBER 1979   Hour adventure series starring Robert Conrad as counterintelligence agent Thomas Remington Sloane III, an employee of UNIT. With Ji-Tu Cumbuka as his aide, Torque, who was conveniently equipped with a metal right hand; Dan O'Herlihy as The Director; Karen Purcill as Kelly, another UNIT employee; and Michele Carey as the voice of Effie, the UNIT computer. Cliff Gould created the show for QM Productions.

THE MAN CALLED X   SYNDICATED
1956   Barry Sullivan starred as Ken Thurston, a globe-trotting United States intelligence agent whose code name was "X." The series, which began on radio in 1944, was produced and directed by Eddie Davis. Ladislas Farago, a real-life intelligence agent and successful author, was technical supervisor.

THE MAN FROM ATLANTIS   NBC
22 SEPTEMBER 1977–2 MAY 1978   Apparently undaunted by the failure of *The Invisible Man* in 1975 and the failure of *Gemini Man* in 1976, NBC made a third attempt to introduce an hour-long adventure series featuring a man with super-human powers; like its predecessors, *The Man from Atlantis* sank in midseason, though it resurfaced briefly later in 1978. It starred Patrick Duffy as Mark Harris, an unusual fellow who was apparently a survivor of the lost continent of Atlantis. Equipped with webbed hands and feet, and with the ability to breathe underwater, Harris worked with the Foundation for Oceanic Research. Also featured were Belinda J. Montgomery as Dr. Elizabeth Merrill, a Foundation scientist; Alan Fudge as C. W. Crawford, another Foundation employee; and Victor Buono as Mr. Schubert, the archvillain whose schemes were thwarted by Harris. As Harris, Patrick Duffy wore latex webbing and full-eye green contact lenses in order to look authentically Atlantean. Herbert F. Solow was the executive producer of the series, and Herman Miller the producer. After its undistinguished network run in this country, *The Man from Atlantis* became the first American television series to be purchased by the People's Republic of China.

THE MAN FROM BLACKHAWK   ABC

9 OCTOBER 1959–23 SEPTEMBER 1960   Robert Rockwell (formerly of *Our Miss Brooks*) starred in this half-hour western as Sam Logan, an investigator for the Blackhawk Insurance Company, which was headquartered in Chicago.

MAN FROM INTERPOL   NBC

30 JANUARY 1960–22 OCTOBER 1960   Filmed in Europe, this half-hour crime show starred Richard Wyler as Anthony Smith, a special agent assigned to Interpol, the international police organization. John Longden was also featured as Superintendent Mercer. Edward and Harry Danziger produced the series, which was a midseason replacement for *It Could Be You.*

THE MAN FROM U.N.C.L.E.   NBC

22 SEPTEMBER 1964–15 JANUARY 1968   This lighthearted hour-long spy show was inspired by the James Bond stories. Bond's creator, Ian Fleming, had been consulted by Norman Felton, the series' executive producer, and had agreed to let Felton use the name of a character who had appeared in *Goldfinger* (Fleming had little else to do with the show, as he died of a heart attack in 1964). The character, Napoleon Solo, was an underworld chieftain who had been killed off in the book, but on television Solo was a stalwart secret agent. Robert Vaughn starred as Napoleon Solo, and David McCallum costarred as his partner, Illya Kuryakin; Leo G. Carroll rounded out the cast as Alexander Waverly, head of U.N.C.L.E. (the United Network Command for Law and Enforcement), an international crime-fighting organization based in New York. Most of the episodes were titled "The _____ Affair," and the recurring theme of the stories was that the U.N.C.L.E. agents required the help of an ordinary citizen each week. A spinoff, *The Girl from U.N.C.L.E.,* was introduced in 1966 and lasted one season (see also that title). Though *The Man from U.N.C.L.E.* lasted four seasons and is widely remembered today, it is surprising to note that it cracked Nielsen's Top Twenty only in its second season. It should also be noted that the show was scheduled in a different time slot each autumn. A total of 132 episodes were filmed. Vaughn and McCallum were reunited in their roles in a made-for-TV movie "The Return of the Man from U.N.C.L.E," broadcast 5 April 1983 on CBS.

MAN IN A SUITCASE   ABC

3 MAY 1968–20 SEPTEMBER 1968   Filmed in England, this hour-long adventure show starred Richard Bradford as John McGill, an American adventurer for hire.

THE MAN IN THE FAMILY   ABC

19 JUNE 1991–31 JULY 1991   Half-hour sitcom about a man who moved from Las Vegas back home to Brooklyn to manage the family business, Carmine's Deli, after his father's death. With Ray Sharkey as the son, Sal Bavasso; Anne De Salvo as his divorced sister, Annie; Leah Remini as his younger sister, Tina; Billy L. Sullivan as Annie's son, Robby; Louis Guss as Uncle Bennie; Don Stark as Cha Cha, Sal's nerdy pal; and Julie Bovasso as Sal's mom, Angie Bavasso.

MAN OF THE PEOPLE   NBC

15 SEPTEMBER 1991–26 OCTOBER 1991; 6 DECEMBER 1991   James Garner starred in this half-hour sitcom as Jim Doyle, who was appointed 7th District Councilman in the city of Long View, California, after the death of his wife, who had held the seat. It featured Corinne Bohrer as Constance Leroy, Jim's assistant; Kate Mulgrew as Lisbeth Chardin, the scheming mayor who had appointed Jim; Taylor Nichols as Richard Lawrence; George Wyner as Art Lurie; and Romy Walthall as Rita, Jim's secretary.

MAN OF THE WEEK   CBS

26 AUGUST 1951–10 OCTOBER 1954   On this Sunday-afternoon public affairs program a different male guest was interviewed each week. Vice President Alben W. Barkley was the guest on the premiere. The series was the antecedent of CBS's long-running interview show, *Face the Nation.*

MAN OF THE WORLD   SYNDICATED
1962   Produced in England and distributed by ITC, *Man of the World* was an adventure series, starring Craig Stevens (late of *Peter Gunn*) as Michael Strait, an American freelance writer.

THE MAN WHO NEVER WAS   ABC
7 SEPTEMBER 1966–4 JANUARY 1967   Half-hour spy show about a secret agent who masqueraded through Europe under the identity of a multimillionaire. Robert Lansing starred as Peter Murphy, an American agent who had escaped from East Berlin with the East German authorities hot on his trail. Murphy stumbled onto the estate of wealthy Mark Wainwright, who turned out to be Murphy's exact double. When Wainwright was killed by the East Germans, Murphy, with the cooperation of Wainwright's widow, assumed his identity. Also featured were Dana Wynter as Eva Wainwright, Mark's widow; Alex Davion as Roger Berry, Mark's suspicious half-brother; Murray Hamilton as Jack Forbes, Murphy's commanding officer; and Paul Stewart as Grant, another American agent. The series was filmed on location; John Newland was the executive producer.

MAN WITH A CAMERA   ABC
10 OCTOBER 1958–29 FEBRUARY 1960   Essentially an updated version of *Casey, Crime Photographer,* this half-hour crime show starred Charles Bronson as Mike Kovac, a freelance photographer who helped the cops solve crimes. James Flavin was also featured as Lieutenant Donovan, Kovac's contact on the New York City police force.

MAN WITHOUT A GUN   SYNDICATED
1959   Half-hour western from 20th Century-Fox, starring Rex Reason as crusading newspaper editor Adam MacLean, a man hoping to prove the supremacy of the pen over the sword in the Old West. Also on hand was Mort Mills as Marshal Frank Tallman, in case things got out of hand. Created by Peter Packer, the series was set in Yellowstone, Dakota Territory.

MANAGING OUR MIRACLES: HEALTH CARE IN AMERICA   PBS
30 SEPTEMBER 1986–2 DECEMBER 1986   A ten-week series of panel discussions on medical ethics, moderated by Fred W. Friendly.

THE MANCINI GENERATION   SYNDICATED
1972   Half-hour musical show with Henry Mancini and his orchestra. A gifted composer and arranger, Mancini wrote the theme to *Peter Gunn* and to films such as *The Pink Panther* and *Breakfast at Tiffany's.*

MANCUSO F.B.I.   NBC
13 OCTOBER 1989–18 MAY 1990   Robert Loggia starred in this hour crime show as Nick Mancuso, a career F.B.I. agent who was asked by the President not to retire; Loggia had first played the role in the 1988 miniseries *Favorite Son.* Also featured were Randi Brazen as his secretary, Jean St. John; Lindsay Frost as Department of Justice lawyer Kristen Carter, Mancuso's sometime colleague; Frederic Lehne as his young boss, Eddie McMasters; and Charles Siebert as Dr. Paul Summers. Drew Pillsbury appeared occasionally as Jean's ex-husband, Matt, who was later murdered. NBC reran the series during the summer of 1993.

MANHATTAN HONEYMOON   ABC
22 FEBRUARY 1954–30 APRIL 1954   Neva Patterson hosted this daytime game show on which the winning couple was awarded a trip to New York.

MANHATTAN SHOWCASE   CBS
28 FEBRUARY 1949–16 JUNE 1949   This fifteen-minute talent show was hosted by Johnny Downs and Helen Gallagher, and featured the music of the Tony Mottola Trio. The thrice-weekly show had previously been known as *Places, Please,* when it was hosted by Barry Wood (see also that title).

MANHATTAN SPOTLIGHT   DUMONT
17 JANUARY 1949–20 APRIL 1951   Fifteen-minute Monday-through-Friday interview
show hosted by Charles Tranum.

THE MANHATTAN TRANSFER   CBS
10 AUGUST 1975–31 AUGUST 1975   Four-week summer variety hour showcasing the
Manhattan Transfer, a slick vocal group whose musical tastes ranged from the harmo-
nies of the 1940s to the heavy hits of the present day. The foursome consisted of Alan
Paul, Janis Siegel, Tim Hauser, and Laurel Masse. Archie Hahn was also featured on
the series.

MANHUNT   SYNDICATED
1959   Half-hour crime show with Victor Jory as Lieutenant Howard Finucane of the
San Diego Police Department and Patrick McVey as police reporter Ben Andrews.
The show was a Screen Gems production.

THE MANHUNTER   CBS
11 SEPTEMBER 1974–9 APRIL 1975   Hour-long crime show set in Idaho during the
1930s, with Ken Howard as Dave Barrett, amateur crime-fighter and non-amateur
farmer. Also seen were Hilary Thompson as Elizabeth Barrett, his sister; Robert
Hogan as Sheriff Paul Tate; Ford Rainey as James Barrett, Dave's father; and Claudia Bryar as Mary Barrett, Dave's mother. Quinn Martin was the executive producer.

MANIMAL   NBC
30 SEPTEMBER 1983–31 DECEMBER 1983   In this fanciful hour crime show, an animal
behaviorist possessed the power to transform himself at will into any species of
animal; electing to use his power for noble purposes, he signed on as a consultant to a
special investigative unit of the New York Police Department. Featured were Simon
MacCorkindale as the scientist, Professor Jonathan Chase, who had learned "the
secrets that divide man from animal" from his late father; Melody Anderson as
Detective Brooke McKenzie, who knew of Chase's extraordinary ability; Glynn
Turman (in the pilot only) and Michael D. Roberts as Chase's assistant, Tyrone C.
Earl; and Reni Santoni as Lieutenant Nick Rivera, head of the investigative unit.
Glen Larson and Donald Boyle created the series, and William Conrad provided the
narration.

MANN & MACHINE   NBC
5 APRIL 1992–14 JULY 1992   Hour crime show, set in Los Angeles, about a male cop
who was teamed up with a crime-fighting female robot. Featured were Yancy Butler
as the robot, Sergeant Eve Edison; David Andrews as her partner, Detective Bobby
Mann; and S. Epatha Merkerson as the boss, Lieutenant Claghorn.

MANNIX   CBS
16 SEPTEMBER 1967–27 AUGUST 1975   This popular hour-long crime show starred
Mike Connors as Joe Mannix, Los Angeles private eye. During the first season
Mannix worked for Intertect, an ultramodern, computerized organization, and Joe
Campanella was featured as Lew Wickersham, his boss. As the second season began,
however, Mannix had left Intertect and set up his own shop at 17 Paseo Verdes in
West Los Angeles. Gail Fisher joined the cast as Peggy Fair, his black secretary.
Occasionally featured were Robert Reed as Lieutenant Adam Tobias and Ward
Wood as Lieutenant Art Malcolm. Bruce Geller was the executive producer for
Paramount TV.

MAN'S HERITAGE   SYNDICATED
1956   Raymond Massey recited Bible stories on this half-hour series.

MANTRAP   SYNDICATED
1971   A reworking of the 1950s panel show *Leave It to the Girls*, *Mantrap* featured a
panel of three female celebrities who grilled a male guest each week. Al Hamel was

the moderator of the series and frequent panelists included Chelsea Brown, Selma Diamond, Margot Kidder, Phyllis Kirk, Sue Lyon, Meredith MacRae, Jaye P. Morgan, Jan Sterling, Jacqueline Susann, and Carol Wayne.

MANY HAPPY RETURNS
CBS

21 SEPTEMBER 1964–12 APRIL 1965   Half-hour sitcom set at Krockmeyer's Department Store in Los Angeles. With John McGiver as Walter Burnley, manager of the complaint department; Russell Collins as store manager Owen Sharp; Elinor Donahue as Burnley's daughter, Joan Randall; Mark Goddard as Bob, Joan's husband; Elena Verdugo as store worker Lynn Hall; Mickey Manners as employee Joe Foley; Jesslyn Fax as employee Wilma Fritter; Richard Collier as Harry; Arte Johnson as Virgil Slamm; and Jerome Cowan as store owner J. L. Fox.

MAPLE TOWN
SYNDICATED

1987   The cartoon adventures of the animal residents of Maple Town were depicted on this half-hour series. Each cartoon was introduced by Mrs. Maple (played by Janice Adams).

MARBLEHEAD MANOR
SYNDICATED

1987   Half-hour sitcom that focused on the antics of the household staff at Marblehead Manor, an estate owned by the Stonehills. With Paxton Whitehead as Alfred Dudley, the butler; Phil Morris as Jerry Stockton, the chauffeur; Rodney Scott as Jerry's brother, Dwayne, the handyman; Dyana Ortelli as Lupe, the cook; Humberto Ortiz as Elvis, Lupe's young son (Ortiz was Ortelli's son in real life as well); Michael Richards as Rick, the gardener; Bob Fraser as Randolph Stonehill; and Linda Thorson as Hilary Stonehill, his wife.

THE MARCH OF TIME THROUGH THE YEARS
ABC

23 FEBRUARY 1951–27 AUGUST 1951; 8 OCTOBER 1952–10 DECEMBER 1952   *March of Time,* which ran on radio from 1931 to 1945, was revived for television in 1951. John Daly hosted the series that year, introducing not only vintage newsreels and other documentary film footage, but also live guests. Westbrook Van Voorhis, who had narrated the show through most of its radio run, was the host in 1952. Arthur Tourtellot and Dick Krolik produced the half-hour series, and Fred Feldkamp directed it.

MARCO POLO
NBC

16 MAY 1982–19 MAY 1982   This ten-hour miniseries about the thirteenth-century Italian traveler was produced by RAI, the Italian television network. Directed by Giuliano Montaldo, it was filmed in four countries (Italy, Morocco, Mongolia, and China), utilizing 217 scenes, 180 speaking parts, and some 5,000 extras. Principal players included: Ken Marshall as Marco Polo, who accompanied his father and uncle on a trip across Asia and who became a favorite of Kubla Khan; Denholm Elliott as Marco's father, Niccolo Polo; Tony Vogel as Marco's uncle, Matteo Polo; John Gielgud as The Doge; Burt Lancaster as Teobaldo Visconti/Pope Gregory X; Ying Ruocheng as Kubla Khan; Beulah Quo as Chabi; Junichi Ishida as Chinkin; Tony Lo Bianco as Brother Nicholas; Leonard Nimoy as Achmet; James Hong as Phags-Pa; and Kathryn Dowling as Monica. Ennio Morricone composed the score.

MARCUS WELBY, M.D.
ABC

23 SEPTEMBER 1969–11 MAY 1976   A popular medical show, starring Robert Young as Dr. Marcus Welby, Southern California's kindliest physician. Welby, whose very name ("well-be") suggested good health, had offices at his house in Santa Monica and also became associated with the Family Practice Center at Lang Memorial Hospital. Also featured were James Brolin as Dr. Steven Kiley, Welby's young associate who made his house calls by motorcycle; Elena Verdugo as Consuelo Lopez, their receptionist and nurse; Sharon Gless (1974– 1975) as Kathleen Faverty, a nurse; and Pamela Hensley (1975–1976) as Janet Blake, the hospital public relations director who married Kiley in October 1975. David Victor was executive producer of the

series for Universal. In its second year (1970–1971) *Marcus Welby* became the first ABC series to top the seasonal Nielsen ratings. On 16 May 1984 ABC telecast a made-for-TV movie "The Return of Marcus Welby, M.D.," which featured Young and Verdugo. A second TV-movie, "Marcus Welby, M.D.: A Holiday Affair," with Young, surfaced on NBC 19 December 1988.

THE MARGE AND GOWER CHAMPION SHOW NBC

31 MARCH 1957–9 JUNE 1957   Marge and Gower Champion, a popular husband-and-wife dance team during the 1950s, played themselves in this half-hour sitcom, which blended song and dance into a story line. Also featured were Jack Whiting as Marge's father, the couple's agent; drummer Buddy Rich as Cozy, a drummer; and Peg LaCentra as Amanda, a singer.

MARGE AND JEFF DUMONT

21 SEPTEMBER 1953–24 SEPTEMBER 1954   This fifteen-minute domestic sitcom was seen weekday evenings at 7:15. It starred Marge Greene and Jess Cain as Manhattan newlyweds Marge and Jeff Green. Marge Greene also wrote the series, which was produced by Ernest Walling and directed by Leonard Valenta.

MARGIE ABC

12 OCTOBER 1961–31 AUGUST 1962   One of the three series set in the 1920s or 1930s that ran on ABC during the 1961–1962 season (the other two were *The Roaring Twenties* and *The Untouchables*), *Margie* was a half-hour sitcom about a teenage girl growing up in New England. With Cynthia Pepper as Margie Clayton, student at Madison High; Dave Willock as her father, banker Harvey Clayton; Wesley Tackitt as her mother, Nora Clayton; Hollis Irving as Aunt Phoebe; Billy Hummert and Johnny Bangert as her brother, Cornell; Tommy Ivo as her boyfriend, Heywood Botts; Dick Gering as her occasional boyfriend, Johnny Green; and Penney Parker as her best friend, Maybelle Jackson.

MARIAH ABC

1 APRIL 1987–13 MAY 1987   Although a couple of sitcoms had been set at prisons (e.g., *On the Rocks*, *Stir Crazy*), *Mariah* was the first network dramatic series to be set at a correctional facility. Included in the ensemble cast were Philip Baker Hall as James Malone, superintendent of Mariah State Penitentiary; John Getz as deputy superintendent Ned Sheffield; Tovah Feldshuh as psychiatrist Deena Hertz; Kathleen Layman as Brandis Lasalle, a wealthy woman from Mariah village who volunteered at the prison; Wanda De Jesus as Officer Leda Cervantes; Renee Lippin as Mrs. Linda Grincato, who taught the female inmates; William Allan Young as chaplain Howard Bouchard; and Chris Wiggins as Father Timothy Quinlan. Seven episodes were shown.

MARIE NBC

12 DECEMBER 1980–26 SEPTEMBER 1981   Wholesome Marie Osmond, who had previously cohosted *Donny and Marie* with her brother, headlined her own variety series. The hour show was intermittently scheduled in several different time slots during its nine-month run.

MARILU SYNDICATED

1994–1995   Hour daytime talk show hosted by actress Marilu Henner.

THE MARILYN McCOO & BILLY DAVIS, JR. SHOW CBS

15 JUNE 1977–20 JULY 1977   Six-week summer variety series hosted by singers Marilyn McCoo and Billy Davis, Jr. Both McCoo and Davis, who were married to each other, had sung with the Fifth Dimension. Dick Broder was the executive producer.

MARINE BOY SYNDICATED

1966   Japanese-produced cartoon series about Marine Boy, a diminutive agent for the Ocean Patrol who helped save the world from sea monsters.

MARK SABER ABC/NBC

5 OCTOBER 1951–30 JUNE 1954 (ABC); 16 MARCH 1957–23 SEPTEMBER 1961 (NBC) Mark Saber was the central character in two quite different series. In the first series, Tom Conway starred as Inspector Mark Saber of the New York City Homicide Squad, and James Burke costarred as Sergeant Tim Maloney. Produced by Roland Reed Productions, the half-hour filmed series was shown under several titles during its three-year run, including *Mark Saber Mystery Theatre, Inspector Mark Saber,* and *Homicide Squad.* The second *Mark Saber* series was produced in England by Edward J. Danziger and Harry Lee Danziger, and starred a one-armed actor, Donald Gray, as Mark Saber; in this version Saber was a former chief inspector at Scotland Yard who had become a private detective. Also featured were Michael Balfour as Barney O'Keefe; Diana Decker as Stephanie Ames; Colin Tapley as Inspector Parker; Neil McCallum as Pete Paulson; Garry Thorne as Eddie Wells; and Robert Arden as Bob Page. The series ran for four years in a Saturday-afternoon slot on NBC under the title *Detective's Diary,* and also surfaced in prime-time slots on NBC between 1957 and 1960. (It should be noted that the final episodes of *Detective's Diary* were reruns of *Man from Interpol,* starring Richard Wyler.)

MARK WALBERG SYNDICATED

1995–1996   Hour daytime talk show hosted by Mark Walberg (who should not be confused with Mark Wahlberg, better known as pop/rap star Marky Mark).

MARKER UPN

17 JANUARY 1995–16 AUGUST 1995   Hour dramatic series starring Richard Grieco as Richard DeMorra, a New Jersey man who went to Hawaii to attend the funeral of his estranged father. Upon his arrival he learned that his father had had the unusual sideline of giving special tokens, or "markers," to persons who were in need of help, and had told the recipients to redeem the markers when the need arose. Richard decided to remain in Hawaii, to the consternation of his father's widow, to honor his father's practice. Also featured were Gates McFadden as Kimba, Richard's father's widow; Andy Bumatai as Danny "Pipeline" Kahala, a local man who became Richard's friend; Keone Young as Moch, a trusted confidante of the father's. Nicolas Ramos appeared in flashback sequences as the young Richard. Stephen J. Cannell created the series, which was filmed on location.

MARKHAM CBS

2 MAY 1959–22 SEPTEMBER 1960   Half-hour crime show starring Ray Milland as Roy Markham, a combination lawyer and private eye, with Simon Scott as John Riggs, his boss. Joe Sistrom and Warren Duff were the producers.

MARLO AND THE MAGIC MOVIE MACHINE SYNDICATED

1977–1979   Kids' show hosted by Laurie Faso as Marlo, operator of the Magic Movie Machine, a talking computer that could be programmed to show old newsreels and film shorts as well as baby pictures of celebrities. Taped at WFSB-TV in Hartford, the show was first seen in an hour-long format, but was later trimmed to a half hour. Mert Koplin provided the voice of the Machine.

THE MARRIAGE NBC

1 JULY 1954–19 AUGUST 1954   One of the first prime-time programs broadcast in color, *The Marriage* was a half-hour comedy-drama starring Hume Cronyn and Jessica Tandy (who were husband and wife in real life) as Ben and Liz Marriott. Ben was a lawyer, and he and Liz lived in New York with their two children, Emily (played by Susan Strasberg and Natalie Trundy) and Pete (Malcolm Broderick). William Redfield also appeared as Emily's boyfriend, Bobby Logan.

MARRIED PEOPLE ABC

18 SEPTEMBER 1990–11 SEPTEMBER 1991   Half-hour sitcom about three married couples who lived in a Manhattan brownstone. With Ray Aranha and Barbara Montgomery as Nick and Olivia Williams, the long-married owners (the house was located in Harlem, but the neighborhood had been renamed Central Park North in order to attract upscale tenants); Jay Thomas and Bess Armstrong as the second-floor tenants, yuppies Russell and Elizabeth Myers, a writer and lawyer, respectively; and Megan Gallivan and Chris Young as the top-floor occupants, newlyweds Cindy and Allen Campbell, a waitress and Columbia student. Robert Sternin and Prudence Fraser created the series.

MARRIED: THE FIRST YEAR CBS

28 FEBRUARY 1979–21 MARCH 1979   Hour dramatic series about the trials and tribulations of a young married couple. With Leigh McCloskey as Billy Baker; Cindy Grover as his wife, Joanna Huffman; K Callan as Cathy; Claudette Nevins as Barbara; Christine Belford as Aunt Emily; Stepfanie Kramer as Sharon; Gigi Vorgan as Cookie; Stephen Manley as Donny; Jennifer McAllister as Millie; and Stanley Grover as Bert.

MARRIED . . . WITH CHILDREN FOX

5 APRIL 1987–   After a slow start, this delightfully raunchy sitcom became the most popular series on the Fox network. It was developed by Ron Leavitt and Michael Moye, who had written for *The Jeffersons*, and who were given the green light from Fox to create a series that would not be mistaken for any of the standard sitcom fare offered by ABC, CBS, or NBC. Leavitt and Moye happily obliged; as Leavitt said to Alex Ben Block, author of *Outfoxed*, "We'd always hated the typical family on television. It just makes us sick, basically." Their creation resembled a sexually charged version of the old radio comedy *The Bickersons* more than it did any TV sitcom. The two stars were Ed O'Neill and Katey Sagal, as Al and Peg Bundy (Leavitt and Moye chose the name Bundy after one of their favorite pro wrestlers, King Kong Bundy). Al was a hapless Chicago shoe salesman with bad breath, armpit stains, and smelly feet. Peg wore lots of spandex and teased hair, and loathed housework and cooking. Most of their home life was spent making wisecracks about their sex life (or lack thereof). The rest of the cast included Christina Applegate as their teenage daughter Kelly, a sexy airhead; David Faustino as their teenage son Bud, a budding young con man; and David Garrison and Amanda Bearse as wholesome next-door neighbors Steve and Marcy Rhoades, who became separated during the 1988–1989 season (it was explained that Steve left home to be a park ranger after losing his job; the plot device was developed to permit David Garrison to appear in a play). Ted McGinley joined the cast early in 1991 as Marcy's new husband, Jefferson D'Arcy. Ritch Shydner appeared occasionally during the early weeks as Al's horny coworker, Luke Ventura. The Bundy family pet was a shaggy dog named Buck.

Married . . . with Children's ratings grew steadily on Sunday nights, and actually improved during the 1988 writers' strike as audiences left the big three networks to sample other program offerings. Nevertheless, Fox refused to air the fall 1988 premiere episode, originally titled "A Period Piece," in which the Bundys and the Rhoadses went camping together and all three women started their menstrual periods; after many changes, it ran later in the season, in a later time slot, under the title "The Camping Show." Another episode later that season, in which Al and Peg were videotaped having sex at a sleazy motel, was killed and has never been televised. The episode of 27 November 1988 was the first Fox show to achieve a Nielsen rating in double digits—a perfect 10. Ratings received another unexpected boost later that season, when Michigan housewife Terry Rakolta (incensed by the 15 January 1989 show, in which Peg shopped for a new bra) tried to organize an advertiser boycott to protest the show's offensiveness; the result was that even more people tuned in to see what all the fuss was about.

In the fall of 1991 both Peg and Marcy were pregnant; in real life, Katey Sagal was pregnant, too. Unfortunately Sagal suffered a miscarriage late in the pregnancy; the producers extricated the characters from the situation by turning their pregnancies into a dream of Peg's. A new character was added in the fall of 1992, as Shane Sweet appeared in several episodes as Seven, the young son of Peg's cousins who came to live with the Bundys; the effort was unsuccessful, and the character was quietly dropped in 1993. Bud, finally out of school, landed a job at the state registry of motor vehicles. In the fall of 1995 Buck the dog died (the real-life canine who played him simply retired), and was reincarnated as Lucky, a cocker spaniel. By 1994 *Married . . . with Children* was the longest currently running sitcom on network TV; the series celebrated its 200th episode in February 1995.

MARSHA WARFIELD
NBC

26 MARCH 1990–25 JANUARY 1991   Half-hour daytime talk show, hosted by *Night Court* regular and former standup comic, Marsha Warfield. The set resembled the interior of an apartment.

THE MARSHAL
ABC

31 JANUARY 1995–25 DECEMBER 1995   Hour crime show starring Jeff Fahey as Deputy U.S. Marshal Winston MacBride, a modern-day law enforcement officer whose specialty was tracking down fugitives.

MARSHAL DILLON
See GUNSMOKE

THE MARSHAL OF GUNSIGHT PASS
ABC

12 MARCH 1950–30 SEPTEMBER 1950   Half-hour western for children starring Russell Hayden.

THE MARSHALL CHRONICLES
ABC

4 APRIL 1990–2 MAY 1990   This half-hour sitcom could have been subtitled "Woody Allen Goes to High School." Its central character was a New York City teenager who resembled a young Allen, trying to get through high school and sharing his observations with the camera. The cast included twenty-four-year-old Joshua Rifkind (who was actually from Beverly Hills) as seventeen-year-old Marshall Brightman; Gabriel Bologna as Johnny, the class thug; Bradley Gregg as Sean, Marshall's best friend; Nile Lanning as Melissa, the girl of Marshall's dreams, who, inexplicably, dated Johnny; Meredith Scott Lynn as the hyper Leslie; Jennifer Salt as Cynthia, Marshall's level-headed mom; and Steven Anderson as Mike, Marshall's soft-spoken dad, a doctor. Richard Rosenstock created the series. After the series' limited run during the spring of 1990, a final episode was broadcast 22 July.

MARSHALL EFRON'S ILLUSTRATED, SIMPLIFIED AND PAINLESS SUNDAY SCHOOL
CBS

9 DECEMBER 1973–28 AUGUST 1977   Marshall Efron, formerly a regular on PBS's *The Great American Dream Machine,* hosted a multipart religious series for young children, which CBS broadcast on Sunday mornings from time to time between 1973 and 1977. Pamela Ilott was the executive producer, Ted Holmes the director.

THE MARSHALL PLAN IN ACTION
ABC

23 JULY 1950–30 DECEMBER 1951   One of the first documentary series filmed especially for television, *The Marshall Plan in Action* was filmed largely in Europe, showing the results of the $12 billion postwar reconstruction program developed by Secretary of State George C. Marshall. The series was developed by Robert Saudek, who would later help develop *Omnibus* for the Ford Foundation.

MARSUPILAMI
CBS

18 SEPTEMBER 1993–27 AUGUST 1994   Introduced a season earlier on *Disney's Raw Toonage,* Marsupilami headlined his own series in 1993. Each program contained two episodes featuring Marsupilami, a spotted yellow creature with a long tail, and one

episode (on alternate weeks) of Sebastian the Crab or Shnookums and Meat, a cat and dog duo.

THE MARTHA RAYE SHOW   NBC

20 MARCH 1954–29 MAY 1956   Comedienne Martha Raye began appearing regularly on television in 1951 as occasional host of *All-Star Revue*. By the fall of 1953, when *All-Star Revue* had become a once-a-month replacement for Sid Caesar's *Your Show of Shows,* Raye was its regular host; in March of 1954 that show's title was officially changed to *The Martha Raye Show*. During the 1954– 1955 and 1955–1956 seasons, her show was seen Tuesday nights as a monthly replacement for *The Milton Berle Show*. Raye's sidekick on most of the shows was former boxer Rocky Graziano.

MARTHA STEWART LIVING TELEVISION   SYNDICATED

1993–   Half-hour weekly informational series hosted by Martha Stewart, offering tips on such topics as gardening, cooking, housekeeping, decoration, and home renovation. Stewart's highly successful 1982 book, *Entertaining,* led to a veritable cottage industry of books, home videos, and a magazine, also entitled *Martha Stewart Living*.

THE MARTHA WRIGHT SHOW
See THE PACKARD SHOWROOM

MARTIN   FOX

27 AUGUST 1992–   Half-hour sitcom with a mostly black cast, starring standup comic Martin Lawrence as Martin Payne, host of a talk show on Detroit radio station WZUP, with Tisha Campbell as his girlfriend, Gina Waters; Carl Anthony Payne as his pal Cole; Thomas Mikal Ford as his pal Tommy; Tichina Arnold as Pam, who was Tommy's girlfriend, Gina's friend, and the butt of many of Martin's jokes; Jonathan Gries (1992–1994) as station engineer Sean McDermott; Garrett Morris (1992–1994) as station manager Stan Kemrite; and LaWanda Page (1992–1994) as Evelyn. Lawrence also appeared from time to time in two other roles: as his mother and as Sheneneh, a dimwitted female neighbor. In the fall of 1994 Martin moved from local radio to local TV to host a talk show. Martin and Gina were married in the spring of 1995.

MARTIN AGRONSKY: EVENING EDITION   PBS

1971–1976   Half-hour nightly news analysis program hosted by Martin Agronsky, produced at WETA-TV, Washington, D.C. See also *Agronsky & Co.*

THE MARTIN BLOCK SHOW   ABC

17 SEPTEMBER 1956–31 DECEMBER 1957   A half-hour daytime variety series, hosted by New York disc jockey Martin Block.

MARTIN KANE, PRIVATE EYE   NBC/SYNDICATED

1 SEPTEMBER 1949–17 JUNE 1954 (NBC); 1958 (SYNDICATED)   One of the first fictional detectives to move from radio to television, *Martin Kane* was played by four actors on the latter medium. William Gargan was the first Martin Kane, a tough private eye who worked in New York; Gargan had been a private investigator before turning to show business and had played the role on radio. After two seasons Gargan had decided to become a producer and left the series. Lloyd Nolan took over the role on 30 August 1951, and played it for one season; Lee Tracy succeeded him in 1952. During its first four seasons the show was done live, and the commercial—for a cigarette manufacturer—was worked into the story: Kane, for example, would stop at his favorite newsstand (it was usually operated by Horace McMahon) and ask for the sponsor's brand. In the fall of 1953, a filmed version of the series, entitled *The New Adventures of Martin Kane,* appeared, with Mark Stevens in the title role; the show was filmed in Europe and lasted a single season. In 1958 Gargan again played Kane in a second series filmed in Europe (from United Artists), entitled *The Return of Martin Kane.*

THE MARTIN SHORT SHOW NBC
15 SEPTEMBER 1994–27 SEPTEMBER 1994 This troubled program was bounced after only three telecasts. Using a show-within-a-show format, the sitcom starred Martin Short as Martin Short, a family man who was also the star of a TV comedy show. Also featured were Jan Hooks as Meg Harper Short, wife of the sitcom Martin and costar of his comedy show; Andrea Martin as Alice Manoogian, the other costar of the comedy show; Noley Thornton and Zack Duhame as Caroline and Charlie, the sitcom children of Martin and Meg; and Brian Doyle-Murray as Gary, the comedy show makeup artist. Short and Hooks later appeared in the season on a ninety-minute pastiche of sketches, "The Show Formerly Known as the Martin Short Show," which aired 20 May 1995 in the *Saturday Night Live* time slot.

THE MARTY FELDMAN COMEDY MACHINE ABC
12 APRIL 1972–23 AUGUST 1972 Segments of this comedy show were taped in England and edited into half hours for American viewing. Marty Feldman, pop-eyed British comedian, was the host and star of the series. Animations were done by Terry Gilliam of *Monty Python's Flying Circus*.

MARTY ROBBINS' SPOTLIGHT SYNDICATED
1977 Taped in Nashville, this half-hour series was essentially a version of *This Is Your Life* for stars of country music. Singer Marty Robbins hosted the show.

MARVEL SUPERHEROES SYNDICATED
1966 Five characters from the Marvel comic books made the transition to television in this crudely drawn, low-budget cartoon series. Each half-hour program featured an adventure starring one of the five superheroes: Captain America, The Incredible Hulk, Iron Man, Mighty Thor, or Sub-Mariner. One of them, of course, would later come to prime-time TV (see *The Incredible Hulk*).

MARY CBS
24 SEPTEMBER 1978–8 OCTOBER 1978 An hour variety show starring Mary Tyler Moore, *Mary* opened to lackluster ratings and dismal reviews, and was abruptly pulled off the air after only three showings (several more shows had already been taped, but were never broadcast). Also featured on the series were Dick Shawn, Jim Hampton, Judy Kahan, Michael Keaton, Swoosie Kurtz, and David Letterman; Tom Patchett and Jay Tarses were the producers for MTM Enterprises. Following the show's cancellation, a new producer (Perry Lafferty) was brought in, and a new Mary Tyler Moore series was introduced in midseason: see *The Mary Tyler Moore Hour*.

MARY CBS
11 DECEMBER 1985–8 APRIL 1986 Another of Mary Tyler Moore's unsuccessful efforts to find a suitable TV vehicle after the demise of her 1970–1977 sitcom. In this one she starred as Mary Brenner, who lost her job at *Woman's Digest* when the publication folded, and landed a new job as the consumer helpline columnist at the *Chicago Eagle*, a tabloid newspaper. Also aboard were James Farentino as managing editor Frank DeMarco; John Astin as theater critic Ed La Salle; Katey Sagal as chain-smoking Jo Tucker, author of the "Mainline Chicago" column; David Byrd as Vincent Tully, the legally blind copy editor; Carlene Watkins as Mary's neighbor, city planner Susan Wilcox; and James Tolkan as Susan's fiancé, mobster Lester Mintz. Ken Levine and David Isaacs created the series.

THE MARY HARTLINE CHILDREN'S SHOW ABC
12 FEBRUARY 1951–15 JUNE 1951 Mary Hartline, who was also seen on *Super Circus,* hosted this half-hour kids' show, which was seen Monday through Friday at 5 P.M.

MARY HARTMAN, MARY HARTMAN SYNDICATED
1976–1977 Developed by Norman Lear, this half-hour serial was part parody and part soap opera. Set in Fernwood, Ohio, the first season began with a mass murder

and culminated with the heroine's crackup on a television talk show. Louise Lasser starred as Mary Hartman, the pigtailed, gingham-frocked Ohio housewife who lived in a world where television commercials were as meaningful as personal experiences, and who tried to remain calm while her daughter was held hostage by a mass murderer, her husband was impotent, her father disappeared, and her best friend was paralyzed. Other principals included Greg Mullavey as her husband, Tom Hartman, an assembly-line worker whose emotional development was arrested during adolescence; Dody Goodman as Martha Shumway, Mary's addled mother; Philip Bruns as George Shumway, Mary's father; Debralee Scott as Cathy Shumway, Mary's active younger sister; Claudia Lamb as Heather Hartman, Tom and Mary's sullen daughter; Victor Kilian as Mary's grandfather, Raymond Larkin, the "Fernwood Flasher"; Bruce Solomon as Sergeant Dennis Foley, the Fernwood cop who eventually convinced Mary to have an affair with him; Mary Kay Place as Mary's best friend, Loretta Haggers, an aspiring country-and-western singer; Graham Jarvis as Charlie Haggers, Loretta's husband and Tom's co-worker; Sparky Marcus as eight-year-old Jimmy Joe Jeeter, a child evangelist who was electrocuted when a TV set fell into his bathtub; Dabney Coleman as Merle Jeeter, Jimmy Joe's father; and Marian Mercer as Wanda Rittenhouse, wife of a Fernwood politician. After 325 episodes Louise Lasser decided to leave the show; after a summer hiatus (during which *Fernwood 2-Night,* a TV talk show spoof, was telecast), production resumed with most of the other principals under the title *Forever Fernwood. Mary Hartman, Mary Hartman* was created by Gail Parent, Ann Marcus, Jerry Adelman, and Daniel Gregory Browne.

MARY KAY AND JOHNNY   DUMONT/NBC/CBS
18 NOVEMBER 1947–24 AUGUST 1948 (DUMONT); 10 OCTOBER 1948–13 FEBRUARY 1949 (NBC); 23 FEBRUARY 1949–1 JUNE 1949 (CBS); 13 JUNE 1949–11 MARCH 1950 (NBC)   One of TV's first domestic sitcoms, *Mary Kay and Johnny* starred Mary Kay and Johnny Stearns as themselves. Broadcast live from Philadelphia, and later from New York, the series was shown in a fifteen-minute weekly format on the DuMont network, and then in a half-hour weekly format except during the summer of 1949, when it was seen for fifteen minutes five nights a week.

THE MARY MARGARET McBRIDE SHOW   NBC
21 SEPTEMBER 1948–14 DECEMBER 1948   One of radio's best-known female interviewers and saleswomen, Mary Margaret McBride also hosted her own half-hour television interview show for thirteen weeks.

THE MARY TYLER MOORE HOUR   CBS
4 MARCH 1979–6 MAY 1979   An hour comedy-variety series which surfaced in midseason, following the demise of Mary Tyler Moore's ill-fated fall effort, *Mary.* In the new show Mary Tyler Moore starred as Mary McKinnon, star of her own variety show. Also featured were Michael Keaton as Kenneth Christy, the studio gofer; Michael Lombard as Mary's producer, Harry Sinclair; Ron Rifkin as her director, Artie Miller; and Joyce Van Patten as Mary's secretary and assistant, Iris Chapman. Perry Lafferty produced the series for MTM Enterprises.

THE MARY TYLER MOORE SHOW   CBS
19 SEPTEMBER 1970–3 SEPTEMBER 1977   This highly successful sitcom starred Mary Tyler Moore, who was well known to television audiences as Laura Petrie on *The Dick Van Dyke Show.* Here she played Mary Richards, a single woman of thirty or so who settled in Minneapolis after calling it quits with her boyfriend (as originally conceived, Mary was to have been a divorcée, but this idea was abandoned). Mary landed a job as associate producer of the evening news at WJM-TV, Channel 12, Minneapolis's lowest-rated station, and found herself a small apartment. In most of the 168 episodes Mary Richards was the center of the storm, the calm, level-headed professional with whom an assortment of zany characters (all played by gifted performers) interacted. That group originally included Edward Asner (whose previous TV roles had largely been limited to heavies) as gruff Lou Grant, Mary's boss, the

producer of the news show; Gavin MacLeod as Murray Slaughter, the quick-witted news writer; Ted Knight as Ted Baxter, the dense and self-centered anchorman; Valerie Harper (1970–1974) as Mary's upstairs neighbor, Rhoda Morgenstern, a window dresser; and Cloris Leachman as Mary's high-strung landlady, Phyllis Lindstrom. Occasionally featured were John Amos (1970–1973) as Gordy Howard, the weatherman; Lisa Gerritsen (1970–1974) as Phyllis's daughter, Bess; Nancy Walker (1970–1974) as Rhoda's undersized but overbearing mother, Ida Morgenstern; and Harold Gould (1970–1974) as Rhoda's father, Martin Morgenstern. In the fall of 1973 Georgia Engel joined the cast as Georgette Franklin, Ted Baxter's naive girlfriend; in the fall of 1975 she and Ted were married, and in the fall of 1976 they had a baby, Mary Lou. In the fall of 1974 Betty White was added as Sue Ann Nivens, the man-hungry "Happy Homemaker" of Channel 12; Sheree North was also seen occasionally that season as Charlene McGuire, Lou Grant's girlfriend (Lou's wife had left him earlier). In the fall of 1975 Mary Richards moved from her old apartment to a high rise; her former landlady had left for San Francisco and a show of her own.

In its seven-year run *The Mary Tyler Moore Show* spawned two spinoffs, *Rhoda* and *Phyllis,* and when production ceased in 1977, many of the remaining regulars found work that fall in new series: Betty White and Georgia Engel on *The Betty White Show,* Edward Asner on *Lou Grant,* and Gavin MacLeod as the skipper of *The Love Boat.* All of those series, except for *The Love Boat,* were produced by MTM Enterprises, the production company established by Mary Tyler Moore and her husband, Grant Tinker. James L. Brooks and Allan Burns were the executive producers of *The Mary Tyler Moore Show,* Ed. Weinberger and Stan Daniels the producers. The show's theme song, "Love Is All Around," was composed and sung by Sonny Curtis. On 18 February 1991 CBS aired a ninety-minute retrospective of the series.

In 1993 *Entertainment Weekly* ranked *The Mary Tyler Moore Show* Number One in its list of the "101 most important prime-time TV shows of the past."

MASADA   ABC
5 APRIL 1981–8 APRIL 1981   The story of the siege of Masada by the Roman Tenth Legion in 72–73 A.D. was told in this four-part, eight-hour miniseries. Principal players included: Peter Strauss as Eleazar ben Yair, leader of the Jewish Zealots, who ultimately convinced his compatriots to commit mass suicide rather than face capture; Peter O'Toole as Eleazar's adversary, Cornelius Flavius Silva, commander of the Roman legions; Richard Pierson as Ephraim, a Zealot; David Opatoshu as Shimon, a rabbi; Denis Quilley as Quadratus; Anthony Quayle as Gallus; Barbara Carrera as Sheva, Silva's concubine; Giulia Pagano as Miriam; David Warner as Falco; and Timothy West as the Roman emperor, Vespasian. Based on the novel *The Antagonists* by Ernest K. Gann, the series was written by Joel Oliansky and directed by Boris Sagal. Although the program did well in the ratings when it was originally televised, its reruns were a disaster—*Variety* noted that ABC's weekly rating for the week of 9 July 1983 (when the *Masada* reruns anchored its prime-time lineup) was the lowest in "modern television history."

THE MASK   ABC
10 JANUARY 1954–16 MAY 1954   An hour-long crime show starring Gary Merrill and William Prince as brothers Walter and Peter Guilfoyle, attorneys at law. Paul Newman guest starred in one episode, "The Party Night," 11 April. Both Merrill and Prince were again featured as attorneys in *Justice,* an NBC series.

THE MASK   CBS
12 AUGUST 1995–   Saturday morning cartoon show based on the hit movie which had starred Jim Carrey (Carrey, however, had nothing to do with the TV series). The central character was Stanley Ipkiss, who became extra-human whenever he donned an eleventh-century mask. Assisted by his friend Peggy, Stanley battled the evil Pretorius.

MASKED RIDER

FOX

16 SEPTEMBER 1995–   Live-action Saturday morning hour series about a prince who left his home planet and fled to Earth, where he was taken in by a multi-ethnic American family and began protecting the planet from an evil invader. With T. J. Roberts as the prince, Dex, whose home planet, Edenoi, was threatened and who could transform himself into the super-human Masked Rider; David Stenstrom as Hal Stuart, the father of Dex's Earth family; Candace Camille Bender as Hal's Asian-American wife, Barbara; Rheannon J. Slover as their adopted Caucasian daughter, Molly; Ashton McArn II as their adopted African-American son, Albee; Ken Ring as Dex's uncle, the evil Count Dregon; Jennifer Tung as Dregon's chief henchperson, Nefaria; Libby Letlow as Patsy, Molly's classmate at Leawood High School; and Matt Bates as Herbie. Dex was accompanied to Earth by a fuzzy pet named Ferbus, which had to be hidden from Hal Stuart who was allergic to fur.

THE MASLAND AT HOME SHOW

CBS/ABC

14 SEPTEMBER 1949–7 JUNE 1950 (CBS); 30 AUGUST 1951–21 FEBRUARY 1952 (ABC) Masland Carpets sponsored this fifteen-minute musical series, which featured vocalist Earl Wrightson and the Norman Paris Trio. It was seen Wednesdays after the news on CBS and Thursday nights over ABC.

MASQUERADE

ABC

15 DECEMBER 1983–27 APRIL 1984   This hour adventure series mixed elements of *Mission: Impossible* with *The Man from U.N.C.L.E.* It starred Rod Taylor as Lavender, an agent of NIA (the National Intelligence Agency); Lavender's bright idea was for the NIA to employ American tourists to assist in its operations abroad. Lavender reasoned that these "ordinary Americans" would be eager to serve their country, would be unknown to foreign agents, and could perform specific tasks for the Agency without costly training. Also accompanying Lavender on his capers were a pair of rookie agents—Greg Evigan as Danny and Kirstie Alley as Casey.

MASQUERADE PARTY

NBC/CBS/ABC/SYNDICATED

14 JULY 1952–25 AUGUST 1952 (NBC); 22 JUNE 1953–14 SEPTEMBER 1953 (CBS); 21 JUNE 1954–27 SEPTEMBER 1954 (CBS); 29 SEPTEMBER 1954–29 DECEMBER 1956 (ABC); 6 MARCH 1957–4 SEPTEMBER 1957 (NBC); 4 AUGUST 1958–15 SEPTEMBER 1958 (CBS); 2 OCTOBER 1958–24 SEPTEMBER 1959 (NBC); 26 OCTOBER 1959–18 JANUARY 1960 (CBS); 29 JANUARY 1960–23 SEPTEMBER 1960 (NBC); 1974 (SYNDICATED)   This durable game show was seen throughout the 1950s, most frequently as a summer replacement. The object of the game was for a panel of celebrities to guess the identity of guest celebrities, who always appeared in elaborate costumes and heavy makeup. The show had several hosts through the years, including Bud Collyer (1952), Douglas Edwards (1953), Peter Donald (1954–1956), Eddie Bracken (1957), Robert Q. Lewis (1958), and Bert Parks (the 1958–1959 and 1960 NBC shows). After a fourteen-year absence *Masquerade Party* reappeared briefly as a syndicated offering in 1974; Stefan Hatos and Monty Hall were the executive producers, Richard Dawson was the host, and the celebrity panel included Bill Bixby, Nipsey Russell, and Lee Meriwether. On the syndicated version two members of the studio audience were also given the chance to guess the identity of the mystery guests.

THE MASTER

NBC

20 JANUARY 1984–31 AUGUST 1984   Veteran character actor Lee Van Cleef, perhaps best known as the star of several Italian western films (and as the villain in hundreds of TV westerns), starred in this hour adventure series as a martial arts expert known simply as The Master (or, to outsiders, as John Peter McAlister). Searching for his daughter and pursued by members of the ninja, The Master teamed up with a young drifter and agreed to instruct him in the martial arts. Timothy Van Patten costarred as the protegé, Max Keller; also featured was Sho Kusugi as Okasa, The Master's chief pursuer.

MASTERPIECE PLAYHOUSE   NBC

23 JULY 1950–3 SEPTEMBER 1950   A summer replacement for *Philco Television Playhouse, Masterpiece Playhouse* presented hour-long versions of well-known dramatic works such as "Hedda Gabler," with Jessica Tandy and Walter Abel (23 July); "Richard III," with William Windom and Blanche Yurka (30 July); "Six Characters in Search of an Author," with Joseph Schildkraut and Betty Field (13 August); and "Uncle Vanya," with Walter Abel, Eva Gabor, and Boris Karloff (3 September).

MASTERPIECE THEATRE   PBS

10 JANUARY 1971–   *Masterpiece Theatre* has been one of public television's most popular dramatic anthology series; most of its presentations have been multipart serializations, adapted from literary works or from original screenplays. Funded by a grant from Mobil Oil, the show was hosted by Alistair Cooke through November 1992. Russell Baker took over as host in October 1993. Virtually all of the presentations are produced in Great Britain, most of them by the BBC. During the first season presentations included: "The First Churchills," a twelve-part adaptation of Sir Winston Churchill's *Marlborough, His Life and Times,* with John Neville, Susan Hampshire, John Westbrook, James Villiers, and Moira Redmond; Henry James's "The Spoils of Poynton," a four-parter with Pauline Jameson, Ian Ogilvy, and Diane Fletcher; Dostoevsky's "The Possessed," in six parts, with Keith Bell, Rosalie Crutchley, Joseph O'Conor, and Anne Stallybrass; a four-part adaptation of Balzac's "Pere Goriot," with Andrew Keir, David Dundas, Michael Goodliffe, and June Ritchie.

Seven offerings were telecast during the 1971–1972 season: Thomas Hardy's "Jude the Obscure," in six parts, with Robert Powell, Fiona Walker, Alex Marshall, and Daphne Heard; a two-part adaptation of Dostoevsky's "The Gambler," with Dame Edith Evans; Tolstoy's "Resurrection," in four parts, with Alan Dobie, Bridget Turner, and Clifford Parrish; a one-part, two-hour telecast of Stella Gibson's "Cold Comfort Farm," with Sarah Badel, Alistair Sim, and Rosalie Crutchley; "The Six Wives of Henry VIII," a repeat of the six-part miniseries originally broadcast on CBS (see also that title); "Elizabeth R," a six-parter starring Glenda Jackson as Queen Elizabeth I; an eight-part adaptation of James Fenimore Cooper's "The Last of the Mohicans," with Andrew Crawford, Kenneth Ives, Patricia Maynard, Richard Warwick, and Philip Madoc.

Six novels were serialized during the 1972–1973 season: Thackeray's "Vanity Fair," in five parts, with Susan Hampshire, Dyson Lovell, Barbara Cooper, and John Moffatt; Balzac's "Cousin Bette," in five parts, with Margaret Tyzack, Colin Baker, Thorley Walters and Helen Mirren; Wilkie Collins's "The Moonstone," in five parts, with Vivien Heilbron, Robin Ellis, Martin Jarvis, and Peter Sallis; Thomas Hughes's "Tom Brown's Schooldays," in five parts, with Simon Turner, Anthony Murphy, Gerald Flood, John Paul, and Valerie Holliman; Aldous Huxley's "Point Counter Point," in five parts, with Lyndon Brook, Tristam Jellinek, Valerie Gearon, and David Graham; Henry James's "The Golden Bowl," in six parts, with Barry Morse, Jill Townsend, Daniel Massey, and Gayle Hunnicutt.

During the 1973–1974 season five dramas were introduced, including "Upstairs Downstairs," the longest-running and most popular drama in the *Masterpiece Theatre* repertoire. The season's first four presentations included: Dorothy Sayers's "Clouds of Witness," in five parts, with Ian Carmichael, Glyn Houston, and Rachel Herbert; N. J. Crisp's "The Man Who Was Hunting Himself," in three parts, with Donald Burton, Carol Austin, David Savile, and Conrad Phillips; Sayers's "The Unpleasantness at the Bellona Club," in four parts, with Ian Carmichael, Derek Newark, and John Quentin; and a one-shot presentation of H. E. Bates's "The Little Farm," with Bryan Marshall, Barbara Ewing, and Michael Elphick. On 6 January 1974 the first of the season's thirteen episodes of "Upstairs Downstairs" premiered. Created by Jean Marsh and Eileen Atkins, the series was produced by London Weekend Television. It told the story of the members of a wealthy London family and their several servants; between 1974 and 1977 some fifty-five episodes were telecast on *Masterpiece Theatre,* spanning the first three decades of the twentieth century (ten earlier episodes, covering the late 1890s, were never shown in America). Principal players included: David Langton as Richard Bellamy, head of the clan, member of Parliament; Simon Williams as his son, James; Meg Wynn Owen as Hazel, James's wife; Lesley-Anne Down as Georgina Worsley, Richard Bellamy's ward; Gordon Jackson as Hudson, the dutiful butler; Jean Marsh as Rose, the maid; Angela Baddeley as Mrs. Bridges, the cook; Christopher Beeny as Edward, the footman; Jenny Tomasin as Ruby, the scullery maid; and Jacqueline Tong as Daisy, the maid.

On the fifth season of *Masterpiece Theatre* (1974–1975) five selections were presented: Dorothy Sayers's "Murder Must Advertise," in four parts, with Ian Carmichael, Rachel Herbert, Mark Eden, and Bridget Armstrong; thirteen more episodes of "Upstairs Downstairs"; "Country Matters," a miniseries of four one-episode playlets; a six-part miniseries, "Vienna 1900: Games with Love and Death," in which five stories by Arthur Schnitzler were adapted; Dorothy Sayers's "The Nine Tailors," in four parts, with Ian Carmichael, Glyn Houston, Donald Eccles, and Keith Drinkel.

Another five presentations made up the 1975–1976 season: the six-part "Shoulder to Shoulder," with Sian Phillips, Patricia Quinn, Angela Down, and Georgia Brown; "Notorious Woman," a seven-part dramatization of the life of George Sand, with Rosemary Harris and George Chakiris; another thirteen episodes of "Upstairs Downstairs"; a three-part adaptation of Somerset Maugham's "Cakes and Ale," with Judy Cornwell, Michael Hordern, and Mike Pratt; a six-part adaptation of Lewis Grassic Gibbon's "Sunset Song," with Vivien Heilbron, Andrew Keir, Edith Macarthur, and James Grant.

Presentations in the 1976–1977 season included: Gustave Flaubert's "Madame Bovary," in four parts, with Francesca Annis and Tom Conti; Richard Llewellyn's "How Green Was My Valley," in six parts, with Stanley Baker, Sian Phillips, and Nerys Hughes; Dorothy Sayers's "Five Red Herrings," in four parts, with Ian Carmichael, Glyn Houston, John Junkin, and Ian Ireland; the final sixteen episodes of "Upstairs Downstairs"; the sixteen-part "Poldark," adapted from Winston Graham's novels, with Robin Ellis, Clive Francis, Norma Streader, and Angharad Rees.

The 1977–1978 season began early (28 August) with the ten-part "Dickens of London," from Yorkshire Television, with Roy Dotrice, Diana Coupland, Karen Dotrice, and Richard Leech. Later presentations included: the thirteen-part "I, Claudius," adapted from Robert Graves's historical novels, with Derek Jacobi, Sian Phillips, Brian Blessed, and John Paul; a ten-part adaptation of Tolstoy's "Anna Karenina," with Nicola Pagett, Stuart Wilson, Davyd Harries, and Robert Swan; and Dickens's "Our Mutual Friend," with Andrew Ray, Jack Wild, Lesley Dunlop, and Duncan Lamont.

The 1978–1979 season led off with a seven-part adaptation of Thomas Hardy's "The Mayor of Casterbridge," with Alan Bates. Subsequent presentations included fifteen segments of "The Duchess of Duke Street," with Gemma Jones; "Country Matters," in four parts, with Meg Owens; and thirteen episodes of "Lillie," starring Francesca Annis as actress Lillie Langtry.

Scheduled for the 1979–1980 season were: "Kean," a two-parter with Anthony Hopkins as actor Edmund Kean; twelve episodes of "Love for Lydia," starring Mel Martin; "Prince Regent"; fifteen more episodes of "The Duchess of Duke Street"; "Disraeli, Portrait of a Romantic"; and "Lillie."

Only four new productions were televised during the 1980–1981 season: a five-part adaptation of Jane Austen's *Pride and Prejudice,* adapted by Fay Weldon, with David Rintoul and Elizabeth Garvie; "Testament of Youth," a five-part adaptation of British feminist Vera Brittain's autobiography, starring Cheryl Campbell; "Danger UXB," a thirteen-part dramatization of a World War II bomb squad in London, starring Anthony Andrews; and Emile Zola's "Thérèse Raquin," in three parts, starring Kate Nelligan.

The 1981–1982 season led off with the very popular "A Town Like Alice," a six-part story set in Malaya during World War II. Following "Alice" were: a rerun of "Edward & Mrs. Simpson" (see that title); "The Flame Trees of Thika," a seven-parter set in Africa, with Hayley Mills; "I Remember Nelson," a four-part biography of the British admiral, with Kenneth Colley and Geraldine James; "Love in a Cold Climate," an eight-part adaptation of Nancy Mitford's novel about the British aristocracy; and "Flickers," a rare comedy (in six installments) about the early days of the British film industry.

The 1982–1983 season presented "To Serve Them All My Days," a thirteen-part adaptation of R. F. Delderfield's novel of life at an English boys' school; "The Good Soldier," a rare one-parter; "Winston Churchill: The Wilderness Years," an eight-part look at Churchill's life from 1929 to 1939, starring Robert Hardy; two more one-parters, "On Approval" and "Drake's Venture"; another comedy, "Private Schulz," starring Michael Elphick as a would-be counterfeiter; and a seven-part adaptation of D. H. Lawrence's "Sons and Lovers."

Scheduled for the 1983–1984 season were: "Pictures," a seven-parter about a British film starlet of the 1920s; "The Citadel," a ten-week story of a London doctor, starring Ben Cross; "The Irish R.M.," a comedy in six parts with Peter Bowles; "The Tale of Beatrix Potter," a two-part biography of the children's writer; and "Nancy Astor," the eight-part story of Great Britain's first female M.P., with Lisa Harrow.

The 1984–1985 season led off with a seven-part adaptation of Anthony Trollope's "Barchester Chronicles," with Donald Pleasence, Angela Pleasence, Janet Maw, and David Gwillim; next came the highly acclaimed fourteen-part "The Jewel in the Crown," adapted from Paul Scott's *The Raj Quartet,* with Peggy Ashcroft, Susan Wooldridge, Art Malik, and Tim Piggott-Smith; an anthology of five single plays, shown under the umbrella title "All for Love"; and, lastly, C. P. Snow's "Strangers and Brothers," in seven installments, with Shaughan Seymour, Sheila Ruskin, Martyn Jacobs, and Carmen du Sautoy.

Presented during the 1985–1986 season were: "The Last Place on Earth," a six-part dramatization of the Scott and Amundsen efforts to reach the South Pole, with Martin Shaw, Sverre Anker Ousdal, Max von Sydow, and Susan Wooldridge; Dickens's "Bleak House," in eight parts, with Denholm Elliott, Diana Rigg, Philip Franks, and Lucy Hornak; "Lord Mountbatten: The Last Viceroy," in six parts, with Nicol Williamson and Janet Suzman; a fifteenth-anniversary retrospective; "By the Sword Divided," a nine-parter set in seventeenth-century England, with Julian Glover, Lucy Aston, and Sharon Mughan; and a six-part sequel to "The Irish R. M." with Peter Bowles.

Seven new presentations graced the 1986–1987 season: John Mortimer's "Paradise Postponed," in eleven parts, with Michael Hordern, Peter Egan, David Threlfall, and Annette Crosbie; "Goodbye Mr. Chips," in three parts, starring Roy Marsden; J. B. Priestley's "Lost Empires," in seven segments, with Colin Firth and John Castle; Ben Kingsley in "Silas Marner"; five Noel Coward stories, telecast under the umbrella title "Star Quality"; "The Death of the Heart," with Jojo Cole; and "Love Song," a two-parter with Michael Kitchen and Diana Hardcastle.

The following season brought "The Bretts," and eight-parter set in the theater during the 1920s, with Barbara Murray and Norman Rodway; Jane Austen's comedy, "Northanger Abbey," with Katharine Schlesinger; a five-part adaptation of Warwick Deeping's "Sorrell and Son," with Richard Pasco and Paul Critchley; "Fortunes of War," in seven parts, adapted from Olivia Manning's trilogies set during World War II, with Kenneth Branagh and Emma Thompson; "Day after the Fair," based on Thomas Hardy's short story, with Hannah Gordon; and a five-part staging of "David Copperfield," with David Dexter, Francesca Hall, and Jenny McCracken.

The 1988–1989 season brought John le Carre's seven-part "A Perfect Spy," with Peter Egan and Ray McAnally; "Heaven on Earth," a CBC-BBC coproduction with Huw Davies, Sian Leisa Davies, and Amos Crawley; "A Wreath of Roses," with Joanna McCallum and Trevor Eve; "A Very British Coup," in two parts, with Ray McAnally; the three-part "All Passion Spent," with Wendy Hiller; "Talking Heads: Bed Among the Lentils," starring Maggie Smith; "Christabel," in four parts, with Elizabeth Hurley and Stephen Dillon; the six-part "The Charmer," with Nigel Havers; and six new episodes of "The Bretts."

Televised in 1989–1990 were: "And a Nightingale Sang," with Joan Plowright, Tom Watt, Phyllis Logan, and John Woodvine; "Precious Bane," a two-parter with Janet McTeer and Clive Owen set in the nineteenth century; "Glory Enough for All," in two parts, with R. H. Thomson and Robert Wisden as the discoverers of insulin; a four-part adapatation of Dickens's "A Tale of Two Cities," with Jean-Pierre Aumont, Serena Gordon, and John Mills; "The Yellow Wallpaper," with Julia Watson and Stephen Dillon; the ten-part "After the War," with Adrian Lukis, Serena Gordon, and Anton Rodgers; "The Real Charlotte," in three parts, with Jeananne Crowley and Joanna Roth; "The Dressmaker," a two-hour play with Joan Plowright, Billie Whitelaw, Tim Ransom, and Jane Horrocks; a modern thriller, "Traffik," a five-part look at the narcotics business, with Bill Paterson, Tilo Pruckner, Fritz Muller-Scherz, and Peter Lakenmacher; and a rare first-run summer presentation, "Piece of Cake," a six-parter about the RAF in WWII, with Tim Woodward and Tom Burlinson.

The 1990–1991 season led off with "The Heat of the Day," an adaptation by Harold Pinter of the Elizabeth Bowen novel, with Patricia Hodge, Michael York, Michael Gambon, and Grant Parsons; it was followed by "The Ginger Tree," a four-parter set in Asia with Samantha Bond, Adrian Rawlins, and Daisuke Ryu; "Jeeves and Wooster," a five-parter based on the P. G. Wodehouse stories, with Stephen Fry and Hugh Laurie; the four-part "House of Cards"; a fond look back at the highlights of *Masterpiece Theatre*'s first twenty seasons; and John Mortimer's four-part "Summer's Lease," with John Gielgud, Susan Fleetwood, and Michael Pennington.

The 1991–1992 season began with "A Matter of Quality," a two-part spy drama, with Denholm Elliott (as George Smiley) and Glenda Jackson. It continued with "Sleepers," a four-part spy drama with Warren Clarke and Nigel Havers; "She's Been Away," a 1989 theatrical film starring Peggy Ashcroft; "Parnell and the English-woman," in four parts, with Trevor Eve (as Irish nationalist Charles Stewart Parnell) and Francesca Annis; "Titmuss Regained," a three-part sequel to the 1986 presentation "Paradise Postponed"; a two-part adaptation of Eliot's "Adam Bede," with Iain Glen, Patsy Kensit, and James Wilby; Ibsen's "A Doll's House," with Juliet Stevenson; "Clarissa," a three-part adaptation of Samuel Richardson's 1748 novel, with Sarah Wickham and Sean Bean; "A Perfect Hero," in four parts, with Nigel Havers as an RAF pilot; and the three-part "Portrait of a Marriage," with Janet McTeer (as Vita Sackville-West), David Haig, and Cathryn Harrison.

Twelve presentations comprised the 1992–1993 season: "A Question of Attribution," with James Fox; "The Best of Friends," with John Gielgud, Patrick McGoohan, and Wendy Hiller; "Memento Mori," in two parts, with Maggie Smith and Michael Hordern; "The Secret Agent," in three parts, with David Suchet (at the conclusion of which Alistair Cooke bid farewell after twenty-one years as host); additional "Jeeves and Wooster" stories; "The Countess Alice," with Wendy Hiller; "The Blackheath Poisonings," in three parts, with Judy Parfitt and James Faulkner; "Hedda Gabler," with Fiona Shaw and Stephen Rea; "The Black Velvet Gown," in two parts, with Bob Peck and Janet McTeer; the three-part "Calling the Shots," with Lynn Redgrave; and the six-part "Doctor Finlay," with David Rintoul.

The 1993–1994 season introduced Russell Baker as host, who in turn introduced "Selected Exits," with Anthony Hopkins; more "Jeeves and Wooster" stories; "Where Angels Fear to Tread," a 1991 motion picture based on the E. M. Forster novel; "Sharpe's Rifles" and "Sharpe's Eagle," each in two parts, with Sean Bean as a nineteenth-century military officer; "To Play the King," in four parts, a sequel to 1991's "House of Cards"; "Body and Soul," in four parts, with Kristin Scott Thomas; a six-part adaptation of Eliot's "Middlemarch," with Juliet Aubrey and Patrick Mala-hide; "A Foreign Field," a 1993 motion picture with Alec Guinness and Lauren Bacall; and "The Best Intentions," a three-parter written by Ingmar Bergman and directed by Bille August.

The 1994–1995 season included "The Blue Boy," starring Emma Thompson, Adrain Dunbar, and Joanna Roth; "The Rector's Wife," in three parts, with Lindsay Duncan; "Dandelion Dead," a two-parter based on an actual crime, with Michael Kitchen and Sarah Miles; "Doctor Finlay II," in six parts, with David Rintoul; "Impromptu," a 1991 motion picture with Judy Davis and Hugh Grant (as George Sand and Fredric Chopin); still more of "Jeeves and Wooster"; "The Cinder Path," in three parts, with Lloyd Owen; "Charles Dickens' 'Martin Chuzzlewit,' " in five parts, starring Paul Scofield; Dickens' "Hard Times," with Alan Bates and Bob Peck; "Much Ado About Nothing," the 1993 film starring Kenneth Branagh and Emma Thompson; and three more "Sharpe" tales, with Sean Bean.

MASTERS OF MAGIC   CBS

16 FEBRUARY 1949–11 MAY 1949   One of TV's first magic shows, *Masters of Magic* was a fifteen-minute show seen on Wednesdays after the network news. Originally titled *Now You See It,* the show was emceed by Andre Baruch and produced by Sherman H. Dreyer Productions.

THE MATCH GAME   NBC/CBS/SYNDICATED/ABC

31 DECEMBER 1962–20 SEPTEMBER 1969 (NBC); 2 JULY 1973–20 APRIL 1979 (CBS); 1975–1981 (SYNDICATED); 1985 (SYNDICATED); 16 JULY 1990–29 MARCH 1992 (ABC)   Most of the incarnations of this Goodson-Todman game show have been hosted by Gene Rayburn. On the NBC version, entitled simply *The Match Game,* two three-member teams, each consisting of a celebrity and two contestants, competed; the object of the game was to fill in the blank in a sentence read by the host, and contestants who matched answers with their teammates won money. On the CBS version, which added the last two digits of the year to the title (*Match Game '73,* etc.), and on the syndicated version (titled *Match Game PM*), two contestants played with a panel of six celebrities, and contestants won points for each celebrity whose answer matched theirs. The ABC daytime revival was hosted by Ross Shafer and featured Charles Nelson Reilly as a permanent panelist. See also *The Match Game/ Hollywood Squares Hour.*

THE MATCH GAME/HOLLYWOOD SQUARES HOUR   NBC

31 OCTOBER 1983–27 JULY 1984   Television history was made on this hour daytime series, the first program to combine two game shows into a single package. For the first half hour, three contestants played *The Match Game;* the two top scorers then competed at *The Hollywood Squares* during the second half hour. Gene Rayburn hosted the *Match Game* portion, Jon Bauman (formerly of Sha Na Na) the *Hollywood Squares* segment. Rayburn was also a regular panelist on the *Hollywood Squares* portion, while Bauman reciprocated on the *Match Game* component.

MATINEE IN NEW YORK   NBC

9 JUNE 1952–5 SEPTEMBER 1952   A summer replacement for *The Kate Smith Hour,* this daytime variety program featured Robin Chandler and Bill Goodwin. A regular feature was a game-show segment, "Winner Take All," hosted by Bill Cullen. See also *Winner Take All.*

MATINEE THEATER   NBC

31 OCTOBER 1955–27 JUNE 1958   John Conte hosted this ambitious anthology series—each weekday afternoon a new drama was presented live and in color. Some 7,000 actors were used in some 650 productions, but the series never attracted large audiences. Albert McCleery was the producer.

MATLOCK   NBC/ABC

20 SEPTEMBER 1986–11 SEPTEMBER 1992 (NBC); 5 NOVEMBER 1992–7 SEPTEMBER 1995 (ABC)   Hour crime show starring Andy Griffith as Benjamin Matlock, an Atlanta-based criminal defense attorney whose down-home folksiness masked his wily courtroom manner. With Linda Purl (1986–1987) as his daughter (and junior partner), Charlene Matlock; Kene Holliday (1986–1989) as his investigator, Tyler Hudson; Nancy Stafford (1987–1992) as new junior partner Michelle Thomas; Kari Lizer (1987–1988) as office manager Cassie Phillips (Lizer had actually played other roles on two episodes during the first season); Julie Sommars (1987–1992) as assistant district attorney (and Matlock's sometime romantic interest) Julie Marsh; and Clarence Gilyard, Jr. (1989–1993) as investigator Conrad McMasters. Don Knotts, Griffith's costar in the old *Andy Griffith Show,* joined up in the fall of 1988 as Matlock's neighbor, Les "Ace" Calhoun. An unusual gimmick was employed in the 16 February 1988 episode: viewers could call in on a 900 telephone number to pick the guilty party. The producers had filmed three different endings, in which Matlock announced the name of a different suspect. Thus it was possible that a different killer could have been chosen in different time zones. Dropped by NBC in 1992, *Matlock*

moved to ABC that fall. The first ABC presentation was a two-hour movie, and the series found a weekly berth in January 1993. Griffith and Gilyard remained as regulars, and three new cast members were added: Brynn Thayer as Matlock's daughter, Leanne, also an attorney; Warren Frost as Billy Lewis, an old friend of Ben's; and Daniel Roebuck as Ben's son, Cliff, a young attorney. Gilyard left at the end of the 1992–1993 season, Thayer at the end of the 1993–1994 season. *Matlock* was scheduled as a backup series for the 1994–1995 season, and was pressed into service in October, replacing the short-lived *McKenna*. Carol Huston joined for the ninth and final season as Matlock's new investigator, Jerri Stone. The series came about after NBC Entertainment chief Brandon Tartikoff spotted Griffith as the prosecuting attorney in the 1984 miniseries *Fatal Vision*. Tartikoff suggested the possibility of a series to producer Fred Silverman (for whom Tartikoff had previously worked at ABC and NBC). A pilot film, "Diary of a Perfect Murder," was produced, which aired 3 March 1986 on NBC.

THE MATT DENNIS SHOW NBC
27 JUNE 1955–29 AUGUST 1955   Pianist Matt Dennis hosted this fifteen-minute summer musical series.

MATT HELM ABC
20 SEPTEMBER 1975–3 JANUARY 1976   Uninspired hour-long crime show, starring Tony Franciosa as Matt Helm, a high-living former government agent who became a private detective in Los Angeles. Also featured were Laraine Stephens as his friend, Claire Kronski, a lawyer; Gene Evans as Sergeant Hanrahan of the L.A. police; and Jeff Donnell (seldom seen on TV since her days on *The George Gobel Show*) as Ethel, operator of Helm's answering service. Charles FitzSimmons and Ken Pettus produced the series. The character was created by Donald Hamilton and played by Dean Martin in several films during the 1960s.

MATT HOUSTON ABC
26 SEPTEMBER 1982–19 JULY 1985   Lee Horsley starred in this hour crime show as Matt Houston, an incredibly wealthy Texan who dabbled in crime-solving while in California supervising offshore drilling projects undertaken by his oil company. Featured during the first season were Pamela Hensley as lawyer C. J. Parsons, Matt's close friend; John Aprea as Lieutenant Vince Novelli of the Los Angeles Police Department; Dennis Fimple as Bo, one of Houston's ranch hands; Paul Brinegar as Lamar, another ranch hand; and Penny Santon as Mrs. Novelli, Vince's mother. For the show's second season, it was decided that Houston would forgo his many business interests and would concentrate instead on detective work. All of the regulars except for Horsley and Hensley were dropped, and Lincoln Kilpatrick joined the cast as Lieutenant Hoyt. Buddy Ebsen joined the cast for the series' final season as Matt's uncle, Roy Houston, a retired p.i. who helped out his nephew; Ebsen, of course, is better known for another TV detective role, Barnaby Jones.

MATT LINCOLN ABC
24 SEPTEMBER 1970–14 JANUARY 1971   Vincent Edwards, who had played a neurosurgeon on *Ben Casey,* returned to television as Matt Lincoln, a community psychiatrist, in this forgettable hour series. Also featured were Chelsea Brown as Tag, Michael Larrain as Kevin, June Harding as Ann, and Felton Perry as Jimmy.

MATTY'S FUNDAY FUNNIES ABC
11 OCTOBER 1959–30 DECEMBER 1961   A half-hour cartoon series sponsored by Mattel Toys, *Matty's Funday Funnies* was seen on Sunday afternoons during the 1959–1960 season, and on Friday nights during the 1960–1961 season. The cartoons were from Harvey Films, and segments included "Casper the Friendly Ghost," "Little Audrey," and "Baby Huey." Hosting the show were two animated characters known as Matty and Sisterbelle. In the fall of 1961 the series shifted to early Saturday evenings, and early in 1962 a new set of cartoons was introduced: see *Time for Beany*.

MAUDE CBS

12 SEPTEMBER 1972–29 APRIL 1978   First introduced on *All in the Family* as Edith
Bunker's cousin, Maude Findlay proved herself every bit as vocal and opinionated—
on the liberal side—as her reactionary in-law. Beatrice Arthur starred as Maude
Findlay, a loud, liberal, middle-aged woman living with her fourth husband in subur-
ban Tuckahoe. Also featured were Bill Macy as Walter Findlay, her current husband,
owner of Findlay's Friendly Appliances; Adrienne Barbeau as Carol Traynor,
Maude's divorced daughter (by one of her previous marriages), who lived with the
Findlays; Conrad Bain as their conservative neighbor, Dr. Arthur Harmon; Rue
McClanahan (1973–1978) as Arthur's wife, Vivian Harmon, Maude's best friend;
Brian Morrison (1972–1977) and Kraig Metzinger (1977–1978) as Philip, Carol's son;
Esther Rolle (1972–1974) as Florida Evans, Maude's black maid; and John Amos
(1972–1974) as James Evans, Florida's husband. Rolle and Amos left the series in
January of 1974 to star in their own series, *Good Times.* Hermione Baddeley then
joined the cast as Mrs. Nell Naugatuck, an English maid. J. Pat O'Malley was added
in 1975 as gravedigger Bert Beasley, who courted Mrs. Naugatuck (a widow) and
married her in 1977. In the fall of 1977, Marlene Warfield joined the series as
Maude's third maid, Victoria Butterfield, a Caribbean native. Created by Norman
Lear, the series fared well, cracking Nielsen's Top Ten in each of its first four seasons.
But ratings had slipped drastically by the 1977–1978 season, and in March of 1978
Beatrice Arthur announced she would be leaving the show. Rod Parker, who pro-
duced the show for several seasons, became executive producer in 1975, succeeding
Norman Lear. In 1977 Parker was coexecutive producer with Hal Cooper, and Char-
lie Hauck was the producer. The show's theme, "And Then There's Maude," com-
posed by Marilyn Bergman, Alan Bergman, and Dave Grusin, was sung by Donny
Hathaway. One hundred forty-one episodes were produced.

MAURICE WOODRUFF PREDICTS SYNDICATED

1969   Hour-long talk show hosted by seer Maurice Woodruff.

THE MAURY POVICH SHOW SYNDICATED

1991–   Successful hour daytime talk show, hosted by Maury Povich. The son of a
Washington, D. C., sportswriter, Povich had previously anchored the tabloid investigative series, *A Current Affair.* Among the topics covered during April and May 1995
were "Men Who Flirt with Teenage Girls," "Phone Sex," "Female Impersonators,"
"Mothers Who Dislike Their Daughters," and "Sexy Bartenders."

MAVERICK ABC

22 SEPTEMBER 1957–8 JULY 1962   This popular hour-long western originally starred
James Garner as Bret Maverick, an unconventional western hero who preferred
chicanery to combat and a card table to a covered wagon. Garner was to have been
the only star, but when it became obvious to the show's executives after a few weeks
that production was hopelessly behind schedule, a second Maverick was introduced:
Jack Kelly as Bret's equally devious brother, Bart Maverick. Kelly first appeared on
10 November 1957, and starred in about one third of that season's episodes (the Kelly
episodes were produced by a separate production crew). By 1960 Kelly and Garner
were featured more or less equally, and in some episodes they appeared together.
Garner left the series after the 1960–1961 season, and Kelly starred in virtually all of
the final season's shows. Occasionally featured were Roger Moore (1960–1962) as
Beau Maverick, their English cousin; Robert Colbert (1961–1962) as brother Brent
Maverick; and Diane Brewster as their friend, Samantha Crawford, an accomplished
swindler in her own right. *Maverick* is best remembered for its light touch, and for its
parodies of other westerns, such as "Gunshy," a lampoon of *Gunsmoke,* and "Three
Queens Full," a takeoff on *Bonanza.* William L. Stewart produced the series for
Warner Brothers. See also *Bret Maverick; Young Maverick.*

In 1994 a theatrical movie based on the series was produced, starring Mel Gibson
as Bret Maverick; James Garner costarred as lawman Zane Cooper.

MAX HEADROOM   CINEMAX

1 AUGUST 1986–19 DECEMBER 1986; 23 JULY 1987–9 OCTOBER 1987   One of television's most innovative creations, Max Headroom came to American TV screens in
two formats. Both starred Canadian actor Matt Frewer in the title role; through the
use of makeup and elaborate production techniques, Max Headroom was made to
appear as a computer-generated image. The character was originally created on
England's Channel 4 to host a music video show, sometimes interrupting the video
clips with irreverent commentary. By 1985 Headroom had begun to interview celebrities as well. As interest in the character grew, a one-hour special was produced,
which explained Headroom's background. Titled "Rebus: The Max Headroom
Story," it served as the foundation for the science fiction series subsequently broadcast on ABC (see below).

Cinemax aired "Rebus" in 1985 and picked up the British series in the fall of 1986.
The 1987 version of the talk show was produced in New York, and was titled *Original
Max Headroom* to differentiate it from the ABC sci-fi series, which was airing
simultaneously.

MAX HEADROOM   ABC

31 MARCH 1987–5 MAY 1987; 14 AUGUST 1987–16 OCTOBER 1987   An imaginative sci-fi
series, the second series titled *Max Headroom* was set sometime in the future, in a
world where TV sets couldn't be turned off, where fierce competition existed among
a host of television networks, and where ratings (which were available on a second-
by-second basis) ruled supreme. Matt Frewer starred as Edison Carter, a reporter for
Network 23 who was almost killed in a motorcycle accident; while Carter fought for
his life, the network's youthful research chief, Bryce Lynch (played by Chris Young)
managed to create Carter's computerized alter ego, Max Headroom (named for the
last words Carter saw, on a warning sign just before his accident). Carter recovered,
and roamed about the postmodern city; among the stories he investigated was a
hush-hush plan among the networks to compress commercials into ultra-short spots
known as "blipverts." Max, meanwhile, could show up on TV screens as he chose,
insulting viewers at will. Other regulars included Amanda Pays as Theora Jones,
Carter's assistant; Jeffrey Tambor as Murray, the news producer; George Coe as Ben
Cheviot, president of Network 23; and William Morgan Sheppard as heavily ear-
ringed Blank Reg, who ran an underground TV channel.

MAX MONROE: LOOSE CANNON   CBS

5 JANUARY 1990–26 JANUARY 1990; 5 APRIL 1990–19 APRIL 1990   Short-lived crime
show, with former disc jockey and game show panelist Shadoe Stevens as Max
Monroe, a hip, wisecracking, chess-playing L.A. cop; Bruce A. Young as his black
partner, Charlie; and Arnetia Walker as Charlie's wife, Loretta. Dean Hargrove and
Joel Steiger created the series.

MAYA   NBC

16 SEPTEMBER 1967–10 FEBRUARY 1968   Hour-long adventure series about an American boy searching for his missing father, a big game hunter, in the jungles of India.
With Jay North as Terry Bowen; Sajid Khan as Raji, a native lad who joined up with
Terry; and Maya, Raji's pet elephant. Frank King was executive producer of the
series, which was filmed entirely on location.

MAYBE THIS TIME   ABC

15 SEPTEMBER 1995–17 FEBRUARY 1996   Trite sitcom about three generations of
women living together. With Marie Osmond as divorcee Julia Wallace; Betty White
as her mother, Shirley, who ran a coffee store with her daughter; Ashley Johnson as
Julia's eleven-year-old daughter, Gracie; Amy Hill as Kay Ohara, who owned a
nearby pawn shop; and Craig Ferguson as the cook, Logan, a Scotsman.

MAYBERRY, R.F.D.   CBS

23 SEPTEMBER 1968–6 SEPTEMBER 1971   This half-hour sitcom was the direct successor of *The Andy Griffith Show*. With Ken Berry as Sam Jones, farmer and town

councillor in Mayberry, North Carolina; Buddy Foster as his son, Mike; Frances Bavier (1968–1970) as Aunt Bee Taylor, their housekeeper; Alice Ghostley (1970–1971) as Alice, the housekeeper; Arlene Golonka as Millie Swanson, girlfriend of widower Sam; George Lindsey as Goober Pyle, slow-witted gas pump jockey; Paul Hartman as Emmett Clark, owner of the town repair shop; Mary Lansing as Martha Clark, Emmett's wife; and Jack Dodson as Howard Sprague, the county clerk. Andy Griffith and Richard O. Linke were the executive producers of the series; seventy-eight episodes were made.

MAYOR OF HOLLYWOOD   NBC
29 JUNE 1952–18 SEPTEMBER 1952   Walter O'Keefe interviewed celebrity guests in Hollywood on this twice-weekly half-hour summer series.

MAYOR OF THE TOWN   SYNDICATED
1954   Thomas Mitchell starred as Mayor Russell of Springdale in this short-lived television version of the series that ran on radio from 1942 to 1949. Also featured were Kathleen Freeman as his housekeeper, Marilly, and David Saber as his ward, Butch.

McCLAIN'S LAW   NBC
20 NOVEMBER 1981–24 AUGUST 1982   After twenty years on *Gunsmoke* (and one or two on *How the West Was Won*), James Arness returned as Jim McClain, a retired cop who returned to the San Pedro (California) police force after the murder of a friend. Marshall Colt costarred as his new partner, Harry Gates, whose modern approach to police work irritated the no-nonsense McClain. Also featured were George DiCenzo as their boss, Lieutenant DeNisco; Conchata Ferrell as McClain's friend Vangie, who ran a bar; and Carl Franklin as Cross. The hour series was created by Eric Bercovici.

McCLOUD   NBC
16 SEPTEMBER 1970–28 AUGUST 1977   This crime show began in 1970 as one segment of NBC's *Four-In-One*. In the fall of 1971 it expanded from an hour to ninety minutes and was featured as one segment of *The NBC Mystery Movie* on Wednesdays. The following year it moved to Sunday, as one segment of *The NBC Sunday Mystery Movie,* where it remained for the next five years; some features were two hours, others ninety minutes. Dennis Weaver starred as Sam McCloud, a deputy marshal from Taos, New Mexico, on assignment in New York to learn sophisticated crimefighting techniques. Also featured were J. D. Cannon as the Chief of Detectives, Peter B. Clifford; Terry Carter as Sergeant Joe Broadhurst; Ken Lynch as gravel-voiced Sergeant Grover; and Diana Muldaur as Chris Coughlin, McCloud's female friend. The pilot for the series, "McCloud: Who Killed Miss U.S.A.?" was televised 17 February 1970. Glen A. Larson was executive producer of the series for Universal Television. Weaver returned to the role in a TV-movie, "The Return of Sam McCloud," broadcast on CBS 12 NOVEMBER 1989, also featuring J. D. Cannon; by then, McCloud had become a U.S. senator.

McCOY   NBC
5 OCTOBER 1975–28 MARCH 1976   One segment of *The NBC Sunday Mystery Movie,* *McCoy* shared a slot with *McCloud, Columbo,* and *McMillan and Wife.* Created by Roland Kibbee and Dean Hargrove, it starred Tony Curtis as McCoy, a con artist with a heart of gold, and Roscoe Lee Browne as his associate, Gideon Gibbs.

McDUFF, THE TALKING DOG   NBC
11 SEPTEMBER 1976–20 NOVEMBER 1976   Abysmal live-action Saturday-morning series about a ghostly English sheepdog (McDuff) and a veterinarian, the only person who could see or communicate with him. The human roles were played by Walter Willison as veterinarian Calvin Campbell; Gordon Jump as next-door neighbor Amos Ferguson; Monty Margetts as Mrs. Osgood, Calvin's nurse and housekeeper; Johnnie Collins III as Ferguson's nephew, Squeaky; and Michelle Stacy as Kimmy.

The voice of McDuff was supplied by Jack Lester. William Raynor and Myles Wilder created, produced, and wrote the half-hour series.

McHALE'S NAVY   ABC
11 OCTOBER 1962–30 AUGUST 1966   This popular service sitcom was set on a South Pacific island during World War II for its first three seasons. It featured Ernest Borgnine as Lieutenant Commander Quinton McHale, skipper of PT73 and commanding officer of a squadron of goof-offs, gamblers, and nincompoops; Joe Flynn as blustery Captain Wallace Binghamton, McHale's meddlesome superior; Tim Conway as Ensign Chuck Parker, the bumbling klutz whom Binghamton assigned to the squadron in the vain hope that he could whip it into shape. The rest of the crew included Carl Ballantine as Lester Gruber; Gary Vinson as "Christy" Christopher; Bob Hastings as Lieutenant Carpenter, Binghamton's aide; Billy Sands as "Tinker" Bell; Gavin MacLeod (1962–1964) as Happy Haines; Edson Stroll as Virgil Edwards; John Wright as Willy Moss; and Yoshio Yoda as Fuji, a Japanese POW who served as the squadron's cook. Occasionally seen were Roy Roberts as Admiral Rogers; Jacques Aubuchon as Tali Urulu, the local chieftain; Jane Dulo (1962–1964) as Nurse Molly Turner. At the outset of the fourth season Binghamton, McHale and company (including Fuji) were transferred to Italy and assigned to duty near the town of Voltafiore. Joining the cast were Henry Beckman as Colonel Harrigan; Simon Scott as General Bronson; Jay Novello as Mayor Lugatto; and Dick Wilson as Dino Barone, one of the locals. One of TV's longer-lasting military comedies, with 130 episodes, *McHale's Navy* is still widely seen in syndication.

McKEEVER AND THE COLONEL   NBC
23 SEPTEMBER 1962–16 JUNE 1963   Half-hour sitcom set at Westfield Academy, a boys' military school. With Scott Lane as Cadet Gary McKeever, a fun-loving youngster; Allyn Joslyn as Colonel Harvey T. Blackwell, the head of the academy; Jackie Coogan as Sergeant Barnes; Elisabeth Fraser as Mrs. Warner, the academy dietician; Johnny Eimen as Monk, one of McKeever's pals; and Keith Taylor as Tubby, another of McKeever's pals. R. Allen Saffian and Harvey Bullock created the series, and Billy Friedberg produced it.

McKENNA   ABC
15 SEPTEMBER 1994–29 SEPTEMBER 1994; 13 JULY 1995–20 JULY 1995   An early fatality of the 1994 fall season, *McKenna* was lifted after just three telecasts (though it returned for two more the next July). It told the short saga of the McKenna family, who ran McKenna Wilderness Outfitters in Bend, Oregon. The cast included Chad Everett as the patriarch, Jack McKenna; Eric Close as the rebellious son, Brick, a stock car mechanic who came home after the death of his brother, Guy (Brick also narrated the series); Shawn Huff as Guy's widow, Leigh; Vanessa Shaw (premiere episode) and Jennifer Love Hewitt as daughter Cassidy; Jacob Loyst as Leigh's young son, Harry; Ashlee Lauren as Leigh's young daughter, Rose; Rick Peters as local cop Dale Goodwin; and Jack Kehler as townsman Walter Maddock.

THE McLEAN STEVENSON SHOW   NBC
1 DECEMBER 1976–9 MARCH 1977   Half-hour sitcom with McLean Stevenson as Max Ferguson, a Chicago hardware dealer; Barbara Stuart as Peggy Ferguson, his wife; Steve Nevil as Chris, their live-at-home son in his twenties; Ayn Ruymen as Janet, their recently divorced daughter; David Hollander as Janet's son David; Jason Whitney as Janet's son Jason; Madge West as Grandma ("Gram"); Andrew Parks as Allan; and Sandra Kerns as Susan. Monty Hall was the executive producer of the series, and Paul Williams composed the show's theme music.

THE McLAUGHLIN GROUP   SYNDICATED
1982–   Faced paced half-hour weekly news analysis show, with a distinctly conservative viewpoint. John McLaughlin created the show and serves as its producer and moderator. His stable of regular analysts has included Robert Novak, Patrick Bu-

chanan, Morton Kondracke, Jack Germond, Fred Barnes, and Christopher Matthews. The series is shown on many public television stations.

McMILLAN AND WIFE
NBC

29 SEPTEMBER 1971–21 AUGUST 1977   *McMillan and Wife* premiered in 1971 as one segment of *The NBC Mystery Movie* on Wednesdays. In 1972 it moved to Sundays and was featured as one segment of *The NBC Sunday Mystery Movie* for the next five years. It starred Rock Hudson in his first dramatic role on television as Stewart McMillan, Commissioner of Police in San Francisco. Susan Saint James costarred as his wife, Sally McMillan, who usually became involved in her husband's cases. Also featured during the first five seasons were John Schuck as Sergeant Charles Enright, McMillan's chief aide, and Nancy Walker as Mildred, the McMillans' housekeeper. At the end of the 1975–1976 season St. James, Schuck, and Walker all left the series (Schuck to star in *Holmes and Yoyo,* Walker to star in *The Nancy Walker Show*). For the final season, the title was shortened to *McMillan,* and McMillan was now a widower. Martha Raye joined the cast as Agatha, McMillan's new housekeeper, and Richard Gilliland was featured as his aide, Sergeant DiMaggio. The pilot for the series, "Once upon a Dead Man," was telecast 17 September 1971. Leonard B. Stern was executive producer of the series for Universal Television.

ME AND MAXX
NBC

22 MARCH 1980–12 SEPTEMBER 1980   Half-hour sitcom about a divorced father whose precocious eleven-year-old daughter came to live with him in his New York apartment. With Joe Santos as Norman Davis, owner of the Empire Ticket Agency; Melissa Michaelsen as his daughter, Maxx; Jenny Sullivan as Barbara, Norman's friend and employee; Jim Weston as Mitch Russell, Norman's neighbor; and Denny Evans as Gary, the elevator operator. James Komack created the show.

ME & MOM
ABC

5 APRIL 1985–17 MAY 1985   Morgan, Garfield & Hunnicutt was the name of the San Francisco private detective agency in this light hour show, with Lisa Eilbacher as Kate Morgan; Holland Taylor as her wealthy mother, Zena Hunnicutt, who bankrolled the operation; James Earl Jones as their partner, Lou Garfield, a former cop; and Henry Darrow as Lieutenant Rojas of the San Francisco Police Department.

ME & MRS. C
NBC

21 JUNE 1986–26 JULY 1986; 11 APRIL 1987–4 JULY 1987   Half-hour sitcom about a widowed white matron who took in a black ex-con boarder. With Peg Murray as the widow, Ethel Conklin; Misha McK as the ex-con, Gerri Kilgore; Gary Bayer as Ethel's son, Ethan, A C.P.A.; and Ellen Regan as Kathleen, Ethan's wife. Scoey Mitchlll created the series, which had a brief summer run in 1986 before returning with new episodes the following spring.

ME AND THE BOYS
ABC

20 SEPTEMBER 1994–28 FEBRUARY 1995; 3 JUNE 1995–2 AUGUST 1995   *My Three Sons* with a black cast, this sitcom starred standup comic Steve Harvey as video store owner Steve Tower, widowed father of three boys. Also aboard were Chaz Lamar Shepherd as son Artis, 16; Wayne Collins as son William, 13; Benjamin LeVert as son Andrew, 10; Madge Sinclair as Steve's mother-in-law, Mary Cook, who moved in with him to help take care of the boys; and Wendy Raquel Robinson as Steve's girlfriend, Amelia.

ME AND THE CHIMP
CBS

13 JANUARY 1972–18 MAY 1972   One of the most dismal failures of the 1971–1972 season, *Me and the Chimp* somehow limped through nineteen weeks before its well-deserved cancellation. Created by Garry Marshall and Tom Miller (who later worked together on *Happy Days* and *Laverne and Shirley*), it told the story of a dentist who was persuaded by his two children to take in a runaway chimpanzee. With Ted Bessell as dentist Mike Reynolds; Anita Gillette as his wife, Liz; Scott Kolden as

their son, Scott; and Kami Cotler (who landed a role on *The Waltons* a few months later) as their daughter, Kitty. Buttons, the chimp, was played by a three-and-a-half-year-old primate named Jackie.

MEATBALLS AND SPAGHETTI CBS

18 SEPTEMBER 1982–10 SEPTEMBER 1983   Half-hour Saturday cartoon series about a fat musician (Meatballs), his thin wife (Spaghetti), and their dog (Woofer).

MEDALLION THEATRE CBS

11 JULY 1953–3 APRIL 1954   This half-hour dramatic anthology series was seen on Saturday nights. Presentations included: "The Decision at Arrowsmith," with Henry Fonda (his first major TV dramatic role, 11 July); "The Grand Cross of the Crescent," with Jack Lemmon (25 July); "The Man Who Liked Dickens," with Claude Rains (his first major TV dramatic role, 1 August); "Dear Cynthia," with Janet Gaynor (her first major TV dramatic role, 28 November); and "A Day in Town," with Charlton Heston (12 December).

MEDIA PROBES PBS

1982   A series of eight half-hour programs, each of which examined a different facet of modern communications. Among the hosts were John Cameron Swayze (for the segment on television news), Cheryl Tiegs (on photography), Ruth Warrick (on soap operas), and Bill Blass (on design).

MEDIC NBC

13 SEPTEMBER 1954–19 NOVEMBER 1956   One of TV's first medical anthology shows, *Medic* was created by James Moser (who later worked on *Ben Casey*) and produced by Worthington Miner (who formerly produced *Studio One*). As Dr. Konrad Styner, Richard Boone hosted the series and starred in many of the stories. Filmed in cooperation with the Los Angeles County Medical Association, *Medic* presented both historical and contemporary medical dramas; it was the first television series to show the birth of a baby (26 September and 3 October 1955). Among the guest stars who played some of their earliest TV roles on the show were Dennis Hopper ("Boy in the Storm," 3 January 1955), John Saxon ("Walk with Lions," 12 September 1955), and Robert Vaughn ("Black Friday," 21 November 1955).

MEDICAL CENTER CBS

24 SEPTEMBER 1969–6 SEPTEMBER 1976   Hardy hour-long medical drama, with James Daly as Dr. Paul Lochner, chief of staff at the University Medical Center in Los Angeles; Chad Everett as Dr. Joe Gannon, his young colleague, a skilled surgeon and accurate diagnostician. Occasionally featured were Jayne Meadows as Nurse Chambers; Audrey Totter (1972–1976) as Nurse Wilcox; Chris Hutson (1973–1975) as Nurse Courtland; and Barbara Baldavin (1973–1975) as Nurse Holmby. O. J. Simpson and Cicely Tyson guest-starred in the premiere telecast, "The Last Ten Yards." Frank Glicksman and Al C. Ward were the executive producers.

MEDICAL HORIZONS ABC

12 SEPTEMBER 1955–9 JUNE 1957   Don Goddard hosted this half-hour documentary series on medical technology and health care.

MEDICAL STORY NBC

4 SEPTEMBER 1975–8 JANUARY 1976   Short-lived hour-long medical anthology series. Abby Mann was the executive producer, Christopher Morgan the producer.

MEDICINE BALL FOX

13 MARCH 1995–29 MAY 1995   The popularity of medical dramas such as *ER* and *Chicago Hope* prompted Fox to develop its own, which focused on a multi-ethnic group of new residents at Seattle's Bayview Medical Center. The cast included Jensen Daggett as Katie Cooper; Darryl Fong as Max Chang; Donal Logue as Danny Macklin; Harrison Pruett as Harley Spencer; Jeffrey D. Sams as senior resident Clate

Baker; Kai Soremekun as Elizabeth Vasquez; Vincent Ventresca as Tom Powell; and Sam McMurray as Dr. Douglas McGill, director of the residency program.

MEDIX   SYNDICATED
1971–1978   Half-hour public affairs program on health care, hosted by Mario Machado (1971–1977) and Stephanie Edwards (1977–1978). Distributed by Dave Bell Ax Associates, the series was produced in cooperation with the Los Angeles County Medical Association.

MEET BETTY FURNESS   CBS
2 JANUARY 1953–3 JULY 1953   Betty Furness hosted this fifteen-minute talk show, which was seen Friday mornings. Set in a living room and kitchen, the show was produced by Lester Lewis.

MEET CORLISS ARCHER   CBS/SYNDICATED
13 JULY 1951–10 AUGUST 1951 (CBS); 26 JANUARY 1952–29 MARCH 1952 (CBS); 1954 (SYNDICATED)   Neither of the TV versions of this adolescent sitcom were as successful as the radio version, which ran from 1943 to 1955, and was based on F. Hugh Herbert's play, *Kiss and Tell*. The show surfaced on television briefly in 1951, in what was apparently a trial run, and was revived early in 1952. It starred Lugene Sanders as Corliss Archer, a headstrong teenager (Sanders played the part on radio for a time and later played Babs on *The Life of Riley*). Also featured were Fred Shields as her father, Harry Archer, an insurance agent; Frieda Inescort (1951) and Irene Tedrow (1952) as her mother, Janet Archer; and Bobby Ellis as Dexter Franklin, Corliss's boyfriend. When the series resurfaced in 1954, only Bobby Ellis remained from the first TV cast. Ann Baker was now seen as Corliss, with John Eldredge as Harry and Mary Brian as Janet. Also featured was Ken Christy as Dexter's father, Mr. Franklin. The 1954 series, which featured offscreen narration and still cartoons, was filmed and was widely syndicated during the 1950s.

MEET McGRAW   NBC
2 JULY 1957–24 JUNE 1958   This half-hour crime show starred Frank Lovejoy as McGraw, a private eye with no first name; as Lovejoy put it at the beginning of each episode, "This is McGraw, just McGraw. It's enough of a name for a man like McGraw." Lovejoy first played the part on an episode of *Four Star Playhouse*, "Meet McGraw," aired 25 February 1954. Angie Dickinson guest-starred on one of the early episodes, broadcast 9 July 1957. The series was rerun on ABC during part of the 1958–1959 season. The show's theme, "One for My Baby," was written by Harold Arlen and Johnny Mercer.

MEET ME AT THE ZOO   CBS
10 JANUARY 1953–30 MAY 1953   This half-hour educational series for children was broadcast from the Philadelphia Zoo. Each week host Jack Whitaker (who later became a CBS sportscaster) brought three young visitors along to chat with zoo director Freeman Shelly and meet the zoo's residents. Glen Bernard directed the show, which was aired Saturdays.

MEET MILLIE   CBS
25 OCTOBER 1952–28 FEBRUARY 1956   The misadventures of a Manhattan secretary were the subject of this half-hour sitcom. With Elena Verdugo as Millie Bronson; Florence Halop as her widowed mother, Mrs. Bronson, eager to find a husband for her daughter; Ross Ford as J. R. (Johnny) Boone, Jr., the boss's son, Millie's occasional romantic interest; Earl Ross and Roland Winters as J. R. Boone, Sr., Millie's boss; Marvin Kaplan as Alfred, the young man who lived next door; and Ray Montgomery (1955–1956) as Jack. Though *Meet Millie* was set in New York, it was one of the first series broadcast from CBS's Television City facility in Hollywood.

MEET MR. McNULTY/MEET MR. McNUTLEY
See THE RAY MILLAND SHOW

MEET THE BOSS   DUMONT
10 JUNE 1952–12 MAY 1953   Leaders of American industry were profiled on this
half-hour series. Bill Cunningham, the first host, was succeeded by Robert Sullivan.

MEET THE CHAMPIONS   NBC
7 JULY 1956–12 JANUARY 1957   Jack Lescoulie interviewed athletes on this fifteen-
minute Saturday-evening series.

MEET THE MASTERS   NBC
24 FEBRUARY 1952–4 MAY 1952   This half-hour series of classical music was seen on
alternate Sunday afternoons. Violinist Jascha Heifetz was the guest on the premiere.

MEET THE PRESS   NBC
6 NOVEMBER 1947–   Network television's oldest program has changed little since
its inception: Each week a well-known guest, usually a political figure, is grilled by
four journalists. The show was created by Martha Rountree, who brought it to radio
in 1945; Lawrence E. Spivak, then editor of *American Mercury* magazine, was a
permanent panelist from the earliest days, and producer Rountree also served as
moderator. In 1953 Spivak bought out Rountree's interest in the show, and Ned
Brooks succeeded her as moderator. By the early 1960s Spivak himself had become
moderator and remained there until 1975. Spivak decided to retire from the show in
November of that year, and the guest on Spivak's last regular show (an hour-long
special aired 9 November, commemorating the series' twenty-eighth anniversary on
television) was President Gerald Ford; it was the first time that an incumbent President had appeared on the program. NBC newsman Bill Monroe was the moderator
from 1975 to 1984; Marvin Kalb subsequently took over as moderator and Monroe
became a permanent panelist. Chris Wallace succeeded Marvin Kalb as moderator in
1987 and was in turn succeeded by Garrick Utley in 1988. Tim Russert took over as
moderator in December 1991. On 20 September 1992 the series expanded to a full
hour. As of January 1995 *Meet the Press*'s most frequent guest was Senator Robert
Dole of Kansas, who had appeared more than fifty times.

MEET THE PROFESSOR   ABC
5 FEBRUARY 1961–14 MAY 1961; 7 JANUARY 1962–1 JULY 1962; 11 NOVEMBER 1962–9
JUNE 1963   A Sunday-afternoon show with an academic flavor. Each week Dr.
Harold Taylor, former president of Sarah Lawrence College, interviewed a guest
from the world of education. When the series returned in 1962, there was no regular
host.

MEET THE VEEP   NBC
1 FEBRUARY 1953–1 SEPTEMBER 1953   Alben W. Barkley, former Vice President
under Harry S Truman, chatted with Earl Goodwin on this public affairs program. It
began as a half-hour show on Sundays and later switched to fifteen minutes on
Fridays, then Tuesdays.

MEET YOUR CONGRESS   NBC/DUMONT
1 JULY 1949–12 NOVEMBER 1949 (NBC); 8 JULY 1953–4 JULY 1954 (DUMONT) Broadcast from Washington, this public affairs program was moderated by Blair Moody;
each week four Congressional representatives, two from each party, discussed topical
issues. Charles Christiansen produced the half-hour series.

MEET YOUR COVER GIRL   CBS
24 OCTOBER 1950–1 NOVEMBER 1951   Robin Chandler interviewed guest models on
this half-hour daytime series.

MEET YOUR MATCH   NBC
25 AUGUST 1952–5 SEPTEMBER 1952   This prime time audience participation quiz
show was hosted by Jan Murray. The fifteen-minute series was telecast only six times,
while the stars of *Those Two,* the series whose time slot it occupied, were on vacation.

MEETING OF MINDS PBS

1977–1981   An unusual talk show created and hosted by versatile Steve Allen, *Meeting of Minds* featured guests not from the present, but from the past. Each week four or five historical figures (played by actors) got together and discussed matters past, present, and future. Steve Allen's "guests" on the premiere included Cleopatra (played by Jayne Meadows, Allen's wife), Thomas Aquinas (Peter Bromilow), Thomas Paine (Joe Sirola), and Theodore Roosevelt (Joe Earley). The hour series won a Peabody Award for the year 1977.

MEL & SUSAN TOGETHER ABC

22 APRIL 1978–13 MAY 1978   Four-week variety show hosted by country and western singer Mel Tillis and former Miss California Susan Anton. The executive producers of the half-hour series were Merrill and Alan Osmond, and the show was taped at the Osmonds' production facilities in Orem, Utah.

THE MEL MARTIN SHOW

See BREAKFAST PARTY

THE MEL TORMÉ SHOW CBS

17 SEPTEMBER 1951–21 AUGUST 1952   One of the first shows to be broadcast in color, *The Mel Tormé Show* was a half-hour daytime musical variety show. Assisting Tormé were singers Ellen Martin and Peggy King, comedienne Kaye Ballard, Haitian dancer Jean Leon Dustine, and a French sketch artist known as Monsieur Crayon.

MELBA CBS

28 JANUARY 1986; 2 AUGUST 1986–13 SEPTEMBER 1986   Melba Moore starred in this ill-fated sitcom as single mother Melba Patterson, who ran the Manhattan Visitors' Center in New York. The series premiered on 28 January 1986, the day of the Challenger space shuttle explosion, and was lifted from CBS's schedule after a single airing until August, when the remaining episodes were played. As *TV Guide* noted, its return on Saturday, August 2, contributed to CBS's lowest-rated prime-time evening in the network's history. Other regulars included Barbara Meek as Melba's mom, Rose; Jamila Perry as Melba's young daughter, Tracy; Gracie Harrison as Melba's lifelong friend, Susan Slater; and Lou Jacobi and Evan Mirand as Jack and Gil, two of Melba's coworkers.

THE MELBA MOORE-CLIFTON DAVIS SHOW CBS

7 JUNE 1972–5 JULY 1972   A five-week summer replacement for *The Carol Burnett Show,* this musical variety hour was cohosted by Melba Moore and her husband, Clifton Davis. Also on hand were Timmie Rogers, Ron Carey, Dick Libertini, and Liz Torres.

MELODY, HARMONY & RHYTHM NBC

13 DECEMBER 1949–16 FEBRUARY 1950   Broadcast from Philadelphia on Tuesdays and Thursdays before the network news, this fifteen-minute show featured the music of the Tony DeSimone Trio and singers Carol Reed and Lynne Barrett.

MELODY STREET DUMONT

23 SEPTEMBER 1953–5 FEBRUARY 1954   Half-hour musical variety series hosted by Elliott Lawrence.

MELODY TOUR ABC

8 JULY 1954–30 SEPTEMBER 1954   This half-hour musical revue was set in a different locale each week. It featured pianist Stan Freeman, soprano Nancy Kenyon, baritones Norman Scott and Robert Rounseville, dancers Nellie Fisher, Jonathan Lucas, and Peter Gladke, and comedienne Jorie Remes.

MELROSE PLACE

FOX

8 JULY 1992–   Spun off from *Beverly Hills 90210,* this hour serial examined the lives of several young adults, most of whom lived in a Los Angeles apartment building. The original cast included Grant Show as Jake Hanson (the character was introduced on *90210* as an old friend of Dylan's); Andrew Shue as writer Billy Campbell; Courtney Thorne-Smith as Alison Parker; Doug Savant as gay social worker Matt Fielding; Amy Locane as Sandy Louise Harling; Vanessa Williams as aerobics instructor Rhonda Blair; Thomas Calabro as medical intern Michael Mancini, who was also the building manager; and Josie Bissett as Michael's wife, Jane Mancini, a designer. Locane and Williams were gone by the end of the first season, as two new characters were added in midseason: Daphne Zuniga as photographer Jo Beth Reynolds; and Heather Locklear as scheming Amanda Woodward, who was Alison's boss at an advertising agency. Locklear was originally signed for only four episodes, but her character was so popular with viewers that she was made a permanent cast member; by the end of the season, Amanda had bought the apartment house.

Marcia Cross joined the cast at the end of the 1992–1993 season as Dr. Kimberly Shaw, and Laura Leighton joined in the fall of 1993 as Jane's younger sister, Sydney Andrews. By the end of the second season, Michael had divorced Jane and had married Sydney. Occasionally featured during the 1993–1994 season were William R. Moses as Keith; Parker Stevenson as Steve; Beata Pozniak as Katya; Kristian Alfonso as Lauren; Mara Wilson as Nikki; Wayne Tippit as Palmer Woodward; Jason Beghe as Jeffrey; James Wilder as Reed; and Linda Gray as Hillary Michaels (Hillary was spun off into her own series, *Models Inc.,* in the summer of 1994). Tippit and Beghe also appeared occasionally during the 1994–1995 season, as did Tracy Nelson as Meredith Parker, Alison's sister; Andrew Williams as Chris; Cheryl Pollak as Susan; Jasmine Guy as Caitlin; Jack Wagner as Dr. Peter Burns; David James Elliott as Terry; Traci Lords as Rikki; Kristin Davis as Brooke Armstrong, who married Billy; and Dan Cortese as Jess. The 1994–1995 season ended with a bang, as Kimberly blew up the apartment building. Antonio Sabato, Jr., joined the cast briefly in the fall of 1995 as Jack Parezi, Amanda's ex-husband.

MEMORIES . . . THEN AND NOW

SYNDICATED

1990–1991   Half-hour syndicated look back at events and personalities of the past, incorporating newsreel footage, celebrity biographies, and present-day interviews. Chuck Scarborough and Kathryn Kinley cohosted.

THE MEN

ABC

21 SEPTEMBER 1972–1 SEPTEMBER 1973   *The Men* was the umbrella title for three alternating hour-long adventure series: see *Assignment: Vienna, The Delphi Bureau,* and *Jigsaw.*

MEN

ABC

25 MARCH 1989–22 APRIL 1989   This five-episode dramatic series was reminiscent of the 1982 film *Diner.* Like *Diner,* it was set in Baltimore, and traced the lives of four men who became friends in high school and who continued to get together for a weekly poker game. Unlike *Diner, Men* was set in the present, not in the 1950s. Appearing as the four pals were Ted Wass as Steven Ratajkowski, a surgeon; Ving Rhames as Charlie Hazard, a lawyer; Saul Rubinek as Paul Armas, a reporter; and Tom O'Brien as Danny McDaniel, a cop. *Men* finished at the bottom of the 1988–1989 ratings heap, tied for 125th out of 126 prime-time series.

MEN AT LAW

See THE STOREFRONT LAWYERS

MEN IN CRISIS

SYNDICATED

1965   Edmond O'Brien narrated this half-hour biographical series, which focused on great decision makers. The show was produced and directed by Alan Landsburg.

MEN INTO SPACE   CBS

30 SEPTEMBER 1959–7 SEPTEMBER 1960   The first of the post-Sputnik space shows, *Men into Space* was filmed with the cooperation of the Department of Defense, which retained script approval. Thus, the show dealt with space travel in a fairly plausible fashion and avoided the use of aliens, monsters, and secret weapons. Thirty-eight half-hour episodes were filmed, with William Lundigan as Colonel Ed McCauley, American space pioneer. Occasionally featured were Joyce Taylor as his wife, Mary, and Tyler McVey as General Norgath. Lewis Rachmil produced the series.

MEN OF ANNAPOLIS   SYNDICATED

1957   Produced by Ziv TV, *Men of Annapolis* was a companion piece to Ziv's 1956 service academy show, *West Point*. The half-hour anthology series was filmed largely on location at the United States Naval Academy in Annapolis, Maryland.

MENASHA THE MAGNIFICENT   NBC

3 JULY 1950–11 SEPTEMBER 1950   Half-hour sitcom starring Menasha Skulnik as a restaurant manager. Skulnik had previously played Uncle David on the radio version of *The Goldbergs* and joined the television cast of that series in 1953. Produced by Martin Goodman, the show was given a weekly slot some months after the pilot, "Magnificent Menasha," was telecast on 20 February 1950.

THE MEREDITH WILLSON SHOW   NBC

31 JULY 1949–21 AUGUST 1949   Half-hour musical variety series hosted by bandleader-composer Meredith Willson. Also featured were the Talking People, a five-member vocal group. Bill Brown produced and directed the series.

THE MERV GRIFFIN SHOW   NBC/SYNDICATED/CBS

1 OCTOBER 1962–29 MARCH 1963 (NBC); 1965–1969 (SYNDICATED); 18 AUGUST 1969–11 FEBRUARY 1972 (CBS); 1972–1986 (SYNDICATED)   Merv Griffin hosted talk shows almost continuously from 1962 to 1986. Before that he had been featured on several series, first as a singer, later as a game show host (*The Freddy Martin Show, Going Places, Keep Talking, Play Your Hunch, The Robert Q. Lewis Show,* and *Song Snapshots on a Summer Holiday*). On 1 October 1962, the day that Johnny Carson took over as host of the *Tonight* show, Griffin began hosting an afternoon talk show on NBC; the fifty-five-minute daily show lasted twenty-six weeks. After developing two game shows—*Jeopardy* and *Word for Word* (he also emceed the latter)—Griffin again hosted a talk show. This effort, syndicated by Westinghouse, was seen on weekday afternoons in most markets and fared well enough to attract the attention of CBS. At that time CBS, which had not previously aired a late-night talk show, was interested in finding someone to challenge Johnny Carson at 11:30 p.m. The network signed Griffin to a lucrative contract and renovated the Cort Theater in New York especially for the new show. Griffin's guests on the 1969 premiere included Woody Allen, Hedy Lamarr, Moms Mabley, Ted Sorensen, and Leslie Uggams. Also on hand were announcer Arthur Treacher and the Mort Lindsey Orchestra, both of whom had been with Griffin on the Westinghouse show. In March of 1970 antiwar activist Abbie Hoffman came on the show wearing a red, white, and blue shirt that resembled the American flag. The network, skittish about possible political repercussions, decided to air the tape, but arranged to have Hoffman's image electronically obscured; when the program was broadcast, Griffin and his other guests could be seen clearly, while Hoffman's voice emanated from within a jumble of lines. Although the incident attracted some controversy, it did little to bolster the show's ratings; the network continued to have difficulty in lining up enough affiliates to mount a serious challenge to Carson (many local stations found that running old movies against the *Tonight* show was more profitable). In September of 1970, the show moved from New York to Los Angeles, but to no avail. Griffin and CBS called it quits early in 1972; later that year, after negotiating again with Westinghouse, Griffin signed with Metromedia and began hosting his second syndicated talk show. That show, like the Westinghouse show, was seen on weekday afternoons in most

markets. Directed by Dick Carson, brother of Johnny Carson (and former director of the *Tonight* show), it proved to be Griffin's most successful effort, lasting fourteen years. On the evening of the show's final telecast, 5 September 1986, Griffin was a guest, for the first time, on *The Tonight Show Starring Johnny Carson*. By then, thanks to his prowess at developing game shows (*Jeopardy* and *Wheel of Fortune* being the most successful of his efforts), Griffin had become one of the wealthiest people in show business.

METROPOLITAN OPERA AUDITIONS ON THE AIR ABC
15 JANUARY 1952–1 APRIL 1952   Viewers had the rare opportunity to watch auditions for the Metropolitan Opera Company on this prime-time half-hour series. Milton Cross, "the voice of the Met," hosted the show.

MIAMI UNDERCOVER SYNDICATED
1961   Low-budget half-hour crime show starring Lee Bowman as Jeff Thompson, a private eye employed by the Miami Hotel Owners Association, and Rocky Graziano as his partner, Rocky.

MIAMI VICE NBC
16 SEPTEMBER 1984–26 JULY 1989   This was the series that most captured the style of the 1980s, as *The Man from UNCLE* had reflected the style of its time twenty years earlier. On one level *Miami Vice* was a straightforward cop show, with its two protagonists—one white, one black—battling the usual parade of bad guys each week. But on another level it was a treat for the senses because of its meticulous attention to form, color, and sound.

The genesis of the series was a two-word notation made by NBC Entertainment President Brandon Tartikoff: "MTV cops." Tartikoff had in mind an action show that would incorporate the bold, fast-paced visual style of the music videos popularized by MTV. Anthony Yerkovich, who had written for and produced *Hill Street Blues,* wrote the pilot script. Michael Mann, who had previous experience in TV and film, was hired as executive producer. After briefly considering New York City, they decided to set the new series in Miami. Some local resistance was encountered at first, as officials feared that the city would be portrayed unflatteringly; most of those concerns evaporated after the show went on the air. The opening title sequence, reminiscent of *Hawaii Five-O*'s, was virtually a tourism ad for the city.

Although other crime shows had been set there (e.g., *Miami Undercover, SurfSide 6, Michael Shayne,* and *Caribe*), this was the first to make Miami itself an integral part of the show; the city's splashy architecture was fully exploited. The show's production staff chose buildings and exterior locations with great care; one of the early "rules" was that there be no brick, no reds, and no browns.

Pulsating under the titles and through the stories was Jan Hammer's theme and score (Tim Truman scored the show during its final season, though Hammer's theme was retained). A native of Czechoslovakia with a rock and jazz background, Hammer linked music to story as effectively as Henry Mancini had done in *Peter Gunn* a generation earlier. Contemporary rock music, performed by the original artists, was also liberally employed, at a cost of up to $50,000 per episode. Hammer's theme reached Number One on the pop music charts, and two successful *Miami Vice* LP's (featuring Hammer's music and songs by other artists) were released.

The casting, for the regulars and the guest stars, was offbeat. None of the regulars was a household name in 1984. Don Johnson had made a handful of films and five unsuccessful TV pilots before signing on as Detective James "Sonny" Crockett, an undercover cop who (as high-roller Sonny Burnett) drove a Ferrari and lived on a boat with a pet alligator named Elvis. Philip Michael Thomas, who had some stage and screen experience, costarred as his hip partner, Detective Ricardo Tubbs, newly arrived from New York (originally to investigate the death of his brother), who cruised around town in a vintage Cadillac. Tubbs was given an urban look, with double-breasted jackets, ties and silk shirts, while Crockett was given an ultra-casual look, with European jackets thrown over T-shirts and baggy pants, with neither belts nor socks. Crockett even sported an unshaven look for the first season, but, fortunately, the stubble look never really caught on with male viewers.

Rounding out the cast were Edward James Olmos as Lieutenant Martin Castillo, the unsmiling, laconic head of the Organized Crime Bureau (Olmos replaced Gregory Sierra, who had played Lieutenant Lou Rodriguez and was killed off in the fourth episode); Saundra Santiago as Detective Gina Calabrese; Olivia Brown as Detective Trudy Joplin (Gina and Trudy often seemed to go undercover as hookers); Michael Talbott as Detective Stanley Switek; and John Diehl as Switek's partner, Detective Larry Zito, who was killed off in a two-parter in December 1986. Martin Ferrero was frequently seen as hapless hustler Izzy Moreno.

Many of the show's guest stars were persons who were seldom, if ever, seen on dramatic TV: rockers Phil Collins, Ted Nugent, and Glenn Frey (who recorded "Smuggler's Blues" and "You Belong to the City" for the show), jazzman Miles Davis, singer/poet Leonard Cohen, Watergate figure G. Gordon Liddy, boxer Roberto Duran, socialite Bianca Jagger, auto magnate Lee Iacocca, and stage actor Julian Beck. Another notable guest was Melanie Griffith, Don Johnson's ex-wife, who played a madam in an 1987 episode directed by Johnson. As a result of their onscreen reacquaintance, their offscreen relationship was rekindled.

Originally scheduled Fridays at 10 P.M., *Miami Vice* did well in the ratings, finishing ninth in its second season. In June 1986 the show was moved back an hour, to go head to head with CBS's *Dallas,* which was going into its tenth season. The show also changed its "look," consciously adopting darker tones. The combination backfired, as *Miami Vice* slipped to 23rd place in 1986–1987, and 36th in 1987–1988. Singer Sheena Easton joined the cast in the fall of 1987 as rocker Caitlin Davies, who married Crockett; their wedding episode, telecast 20 November 1987, was the first to top *Dallas* in the ratings. Caitlin was killed off later in the season.

Executive producer Mann decided that the fifth season would be the series' last. The chief reason for this decision was financial; *Miami Vice* ran consistently over its budget, and the show needed to be sold into syndication in order for Universal Studios to recoup its investment. A move back to 10 P.M. for the final season was ineffective, as the series finished in 53rd place. On the two-hour "finale," aired 21 May 1989, Crockett and Tubbs left the force. The series was sold to the USA Cable Network, which began running it in the fall of 1989. The package included one episode, "Too Much Too Late," which never ran on NBC; the story, involving a mother who sold her daughter for sex in order to buy cocaine, was considered too objectionable by the network.

MICHAEL NESMITH IN TELEVISON PARTS   NBC

14 JUNE 1985–27 JULY 1985   Following the cancellation of *The Monkees* in 1968 and the breakup of the group, Michael Nesmith remained active in music as a songwriter and as a solo artist. By the end of the 1970s he had begun producing videos for himself and for other artists. His 1982 effort, "Elephant Parts," won the first Grammy award given for a video. On 7 March 1985 he hosted a comedy special on NBC, with guests Martin Mull and Garry Shandling. Three months later his series was given a brief run. The half hour was a potpourri of videos and comedy skits, emceed by Nesmith. Four of the seven programs were shown in prime time on Fridays; the last three were pieced together as a late-night special on Saturday, 27 July.

MICHAEL SHAYNE   NBC

30 SEPTEMBER 1960–22 SEPTEMBER 1961   Michael Shayne, the private eye created by Brett Halliday (the pen name of Davis Dresser), first appeared on radio in 1944. The television series, which ran a full hour, was set in Miami Beach and featured Richard Denning as Michael Shayne; Jerry Paris as reporter Tim O'Rourke; Patricia Donahue and Margie Regan as Shayne's secretary, Lucy Hamilton; Gary Clarke as Dick, Lucy's younger brother; and Herbert Rudley as Lieutenant Gentry, Miami Beach cop.

THE MICHAELS IN AFRICA SYNDICATED
1960   A series of documentaries filmed in Africa, hosted by George and Marjorie Michael.

MICHELOB PRESENTS NIGHT MUSIC
See NIGHT MUSIC

MICKEY ABC
16 SEPTEMBER 1964–13 JANUARY 1965   Unsuccessful half-hour sitcom starring Mickey Rooney as Mickey Grady, a midwestern businessman who inherited a hotel in Newport Beach, California, from his late uncle. With Emmaline Henry as his wife, Nora; Timmy Rooney (Mickey's real-life son) as their son Tim; Brian Nash as their son Buddy; Sammee Tong as Sammy Ling, manager of the hotel; and Alan Reed as Mr. Swidler, owner of a nearby gas station.

THE MICKEY MOUSE CLUB ABC
3 OCTOBER 1955–24 SEPTEMBER 1959
THE NEW MICKEY MOUSE CLUB SYNDICATED
1977
MICKEY MOUSE CLUB DISNEY
1989–1994   The second television series from Walt Disney Studios, *The Mickey Mouse Club* was introduced as a Monday-through-Friday show a year after *Disneyland* premiered. The filmed show was seen for an hour a day during its first two seasons and was trimmed to a half-hour in the fall of 1957. Unlike other popular children's shows of the day, *The Mickey Mouse Club* did not use a studio audience, and, instead of a sole adult host (such as Pinky Lee or Buffalo Bob Smith), it employed a group of child performers; the T-shirted, mouse-hatted company was known, of course, as the Mouseketeers.

Though the format of each day's show was approximately the same (a typical hour usually consisted of a newsreel or other short documentary film, a production number or sketch, an episode of a filmed serial, and a Disney cartoon), the show for each day of the week was constructed around a general theme. Monday was "Fun with Music Day," on which original musical numbers were performed; Tuesday was "Guest Star Day," featuring appearances by celebrities; Wednesday was "Anything Can Happen Day," on which a potpourri of features was presented; Thursday was "Circus Day," which featured a cartoon appearance by Jiminy Cricket followed by stunts and games involving the Mouseketeers; Friday was "Talent Roundup Day," on which talented youngsters performed and were then made "Honorary Mouseketeers." During the show's first two seasons, a short, child-oriented newsreel was shown three times a week.

The thread that held the show together was the Mouseketeers, who sang, danced, starred in the filmed serials, introduced the cartoons, and provided an audience for the guest stars and talent acts. Twenty-four youngsters were featured regularly during the first season: Nancy Abbate, Sharon Baird, Billie Jean Beanblossom, Bobby Burgess, Lonnie Burr, Tommy Cole, Johnny Crawford, Dennis Day, Dickie Dodd, Mary Espinosa, Annette Funicello, Darlene Gillespie, Judy Harriet, John Lee Johann, Bonni Lou Kern, Carl "Cubby" O'Brien, Karen Pendleton, Mary Sartori, Bronson Scott, Michael Smith, Ronnie Steiner, Mark Sutherland, Doreen Tracey, and Don Underhill. Three other youngsters were featured on the earliest shows, but left after only a few weeks: Paul Petersen (who later was featured on *The Donna Reed Show*), and Tim and Mickey Rooney, Jr. (sons of actor Mickey Rooney). Two adults, similarly hatted and shirted, rounded out the cast: Jimmie Dodd, an actor and songwriter who was, in effect, the show's host and Roy Williams ("The Big Mooseketeer"), a veteran Disney writer and animator; it was Williams who designed the Club hat.

Only ten of the first two dozen Mouseketeers returned for the 1956–1957 season: Sharon, Bobby, Lonnie, Tommy, Dennis, Annette, Darlene, Cubby, Karen, and Doreen. Seven new Mouseketeers were added: Sherry Allen, Eileen Diamond, Cheryl Holdridge, Charley Laney, Larry Larsen, Jay-Jay Solari, and Margene

Storey. Again, ten of that group returned for the remaining seasons (the shows seen during the fourth season were actually produced in 1958): Sharon, Bobby, Lonnie, Tommy, Annette, Darlene, Cubby, Karen, Doreen, and Cheryl. Four newcomers were added: Don Agrati (later known as Don Grady when he was featured on *My Three Sons*), Bonnie Lynn Fields, Linda Hughes, and Lynn Ready. Other youngsters were featured as Mouseketeers from time to time, especially those who appeared in the serials.

The Mickey Mouse Club was one of the few children's shows that presented made-for-TV serials. Several features were produced, most of which consisted of fifteen to thirty episodes. Among the more popular cliff-hangers were: "Corky and White Shadow," with Darlene Gillespie, Buddy Ebsen, and Lloyd Corrigan; "The Hardy Boys: The Mystery of the Applegate Treasure," with Tim Considine, Tommy Kirk, and Florenz Ames (a sequel, "The Hardy Boys: The Mystery of Ghost Farm," was also produced); "Clint and Mac," with Neil Wolfe and Jonathan Bailey; "Annette," with Annette Funicello, Tim Considine, and Roberta Shore. The most popular of the serials, however, was "The Adventures of Spin and Marty," the story of two boys at the Triple R Ranch, a western summer camp; it featured Tim Considine (as Spin Evans), David Stollery (as Marty Markham), J. Pat O'Malley, and Roy Barcroft. "Spin and Marty" was introduced during the 1955–1956 season, and two sequels were produced.

Produced by Bill Walsh, the series left ABC in the fall of 1959 after a four-year run. Reruns were syndicated in 1962 and again in 1975. In the fall of 1976 the series was revived, as production began on *The New Mickey Mouse Club*. This version was a half-hour series, and was videotaped. A new group of Mouseketeers (that included black and Asian-American faces) was formed, which included: Pop Attmore, Scott Craig, Nita DiGiampaolo, Mindy Feldman, Angelo Florez, Allison Fonte, Shawnte Northcutte, Kelly Parsons, Julie Piekarski, Todd Turquand, Lisa Whelchel, and Curtis Wong. Ron Miller was the executive producer.

A new *Mickey Mouse Club* set sail on The Disney Channel in April 1989, with a decidedly modern look: no mouse ears and no uniforms for the new multi-ethnic band of Mouseketeers. Rap music and computer graphics also helped update the show. Fred Newman and Mowava Pryor were the adult cohosts. It remained in production for more than five years.

THE MICKEY ROONEY SHOW NBC
28 AUGUST 1954–4 JUNE 1955 Also seen under the title *Hey Mulligan,* this half-hour filmed sitcom starred Mickey Rooney as Mickey Mulligan, a TV studio page, aspiring to become a performer. Also featured were Regis Toomey as his father, Joe Mulligan, a cop; Claire Carleton as his mother, Nell Mulligan, a former burlesque queen; Carla Belenda as Pat Harding, his girlfriend; Joey Forman as his pal Freddie; John Hubbard as his boss, Mr. Brown, the program director; and Alan Mowbray as Mickey's drama coach, Mr. Swift. Blake Edwards and Richard Quine created the series.

MICKEY SPILLANE'S MIKE HAMMER
See MIKE HAMMER

MICKIE FINN'S NBC
21 APRIL 1966–1 SEPTEMBER 1966 Half-hour musical variety series cohosted by Fred Finn and his wife, Mickie Finn. The show, which had a gay nineties flavor, was taped at a replica of the Finns' San Diego nightclub, where Fred led the band while Mickie played the banjo.

MIDDLE AGES CBS
3 SEPTEMBER 1992–1 OCTOBER 1992 Hour continuing drama about a group of friends in suburban Chicago who were about to turn 40. With Peter Riegert as salesman Walter Cooper, whose job was in jeopardy; Ashley Crow as his wife, Cindy; William Russ as Walter's friend, Terry; Michael O'Keefe as Walter's friend, Ron Steffey; James Gammon as Dave Nelson, Walter's father-in-law; Kyle Secor as Walter's hard-

driving boss, Brian Conover; Lisa Zane as Nora, Brian's wife; Maria Pitillo as Brian's secretary, Robin; Ryan McWhorter as Walter and Cindy's son, Carson; Alex McKenna as Walter and Cindy's daughter, Hilary; and Ruby Dee as cleaning woman Estelle Williams. One of the series's story lines concerned the efforts of Walter, Terry, and Ron to reform the Deacons, the rock band they had had years earlier until their female singer had died. Amy Brenneman was featured as their new singer, Blanche, while Holly Gagnier appeared in flashbacks and dream sequences as the old singer, Jill Peabody. Stan Rogow and John Byrum created the series.

MIDDLETOWN
PBS
24 MARCH 1982–21 APRIL 1982   In 1929 sociologists Helen and Robert Lynd wrote a book, *Middletown,* a study of Muncie, Indiana, a town they had selected as "typically American." In 1981 producer Peter Davis revisited Muncie and filmed this documentary series. Although six programs were filmed, complaints from students, parents, and the series' underwriter (Xerox) forced one segment to be withdrawn before its scheduled broadcast; one reason for the complaints was that Davis had filmed several high-schoolers smoking marijuana.

MIDNIGHT CALLER
NBC
25 OCTOBER 1988–2 AUGUST 1991   An atmospheric hour dramatic series, starring Gary Cole as Jack "Nighthawk" Killian, a San Fransisco cop who left the force after accidentally killing his partner and became the host of a late-night radio talk show. With Wendy Kilbourne (1988–1990) as Devon King, owner of the station (KJCM); Arthur Taxier as Lieutenant Carl Zymak of the S.F.P.D.; Dennis Dun as Jack's producer and engineer, Billy Po; and Mykel T. Williamson (1989–1991) as investigative reporter Deacon Bridges. Lisa Eilbacher joined the cast in the fall of 1990 as Nicky Molloy, Jack's new boss, as did Steven Anthony Jones as Inspector Martin Slocum. One first-season episode, "After It Happened," generated controversy because of its AIDS-related story line. According to AIDS activists, an early draft of the script called for a woman to shoot the bisexual man who had infected her and others; the ending was modified before the show aired. For the sequel, televised during the second season, the show's producers invited some of the protesting groups to advise them on the script.

THE MIDNIGHT HOUR
CBS
23 JULY 1990–14 SEPTEMBER 1990   Broadcast live from Hollywood, this hour late-night (12:40 A.M.) talk show featured a different guest host each week; Joy Behar led off, followed by Peter Tilden. Jennifer Martin was the announcer, Patrice Rushen the bandleader. The show featured an 800 telephone number on which viewers could talk to the guest host or the guests.

THE MIDNIGHT SPECIAL
NBC
2 FEBRUARY 1973–1 MAY 1981   Network television's first regularly scheduled attempt at late-late night programming, *The Midnight Special* was a ninety-minute rock music show, which ran from 1:00 A.M. to 2:30 A.M. on Fridays. Helen Reddy hosted the premiere telecast and also served as regular host from 1975 to 1977. America's legendary disc jockey Wolfman Jack was the announcer. Burt Sugarman was the executive producer.

MIDWEST HAYRIDE
SYNDICATED/NBC/ABC
1951–1961   *Midwest Hayride,* also known as *Midwestern Hayride,* was a long-running country and western music show that was filmed (and later taped) on location throughout the nation. It was hosted by Willie Thall (1951–1955), Hugh Cherry (1955–1956), and Paul Dixon (1957–1961). The syndicated show was occasionally picked up by one of the major networks as a summer replacement; it was seen on NBC during the summers of 1951, 1952, 1954, 1955, and 1959, and on ABC during the summers of 1957 and 1958. NBC also carried the show during the 1955–1956 season.

MIGHTY HEROES   CBS

29 OCTOBER 1966–2 SEPTEMBER 1967   This half-hour cartoon series, which replaced *Mighty Mouse Playhouse* on CBS's Saturday-morning schedule, featured an odd quintet of superheroes, led by a powerful baby named Diaper Man. The deep-voiced infant and his four cohorts—Tornado Man, Strong Man, Rope Man, and Cuckoo Man—battled an assortment of villains each week. Produced by Terrytoons, the series was directed by Ralph Bakshi, who would later direct such innovative animated films as *Fritz the Cat* and *Lord of the Rings.*

MIGHTY MORPHIN POWER RANGERS   FOX

28 AUGUST 1993–   Daily half-hour live-action kids show about a group of teenagers who could "morph," or transform themselves into the Power Rangers, a spandex-clad and helmeted crew who fought various extraterrestial villains. The show was derived from a Japanese television series, *Zyu Rangers,* with a similar format. American producer Haim Saban hired American actors to play the teens, then spliced in the Japanese action sequences with the Americans' voices; as the Power Rangers were all helmeted, the faces of the Japanese performers could not be seen. The cast included Amy Jo Johnson as Kimberly, who became the Pink Ranger; David Yost as Billy, the Blue Ranger; Walter Jones (1993–1994) as Zack, the Black Ranger; Austin St. John (1993–1994) as Jason, the Red Ranger; Thuy Trang (1993–1994) as Trini, the Yellow Ranger; Jason Frank (added early in the first season) as Tommy, the Green Ranger (he became the White Ranger for the second season); Steve Cardenas (1994–   ) as Rocky, the Red Ranger; Karan Ashley (1994–   ) as Aisha, the Yellow Ranger; Johnny Yong Bosch (1994–   ) as Adam, the Black Ranger; and Paul Schrier and Jason Narvy as Bulk and Skull, two bullies who hassled the teens. As the Power Rangers, the teens battled Rita Repulsa and Zordon; they could also summon the Dino Zords, a group of robotized dinosaurs who could meld together into a giant Mega-Zord.

The series became an immediate hit with young viewers, and millions of dollars of Power Ranger merchandise was sold in 1993 and 1994. A feature film was released in mid-1995. The series was retitled *Power Rangers Zeo* in April 1996.

THE MIGHTY MOUSE PLAYHOUSE   CBS

10 DECEMBER 1955–22 OCTOBER 1966   The star of this long-running Saturday-morning cartoon show was Mighty Mouse, a caped crimefighter who was the rodent equivalent of Superman. Although other segments were also telecast on the series, such as "The Adventures of Gandy Goose," the Mighty Mouse episodes are the best remembered, primarily because of their operatic style. See also *The New Adventures of Mighty Mouse and Heckle and Jeckle,* and *Mighty Mouse: The New Adventures.*

MIGHTY MOUSE: THE NEW ADVENTUES   CBS

19 SEPTEMBER 1987–2 SEPTEMBER 1989   Mighty Mouse returned to television in a new series of Saturday-morning cartoons, produced by veteran animator Ralph Bakshi. Surprisingly, the series managed to attract some controversy because of a brief scene in one program showing Mighty Mouse sniffing a handful of crushed flowers; media watchdog Reverend Donald Wildmon claimed that the famed rodent was actually sniffing cocaine. Though CBS and Bakshi denied the assertion, the offending scene was cut when the episode was rerun.

THE MIGHTY ORBOTS   ABC

8 SEPTEMBER 1984–31 AUGUST 1985   The main characters on this Saturday-morning cartoon show were five twenty-third-century robots who could combine themselves into a single synergistic robot.

MIKE AND BUFF   CBS

20 AUGUST 1951–27 FEBRUARY 1953   Mike Wallace and Buff Cobb, who was Wallace's wife at the time, cohosted one of CBS's first color shows in 1951. The experimental telecasts were conducted weekday mornings, and in its earliest days their show was called *Two Sleepy People.* By November of 1951, the show had been

retitled *Mike and Buff* and was seen—in black and white—on weekday afternoons, where it remained for the next fifteen months.

MIKE & MATY   ABC
11 APRIL 1994–   This hour daytime magazine series replaced *The Home Show*. Its coanchors were Michael Burger, a former standup comic, and Maty Monfort, who had hosted several Spanish language series in Miami. Joining them in the summer of 1994 as special correspondent was ten-year-old Michael Kearney, America's youngest college graduate.

THE MIKE DOUGLAS SHOW   SYNDICATED
1963–1982   One of television's durable talk-show hosts, Mike Douglas started out as a singer and was a featured vocalist on such shows as *College of Musical Knowledge* and *Club 60*. From 1953 to 1955 he hosted his own daytime variety program in Chicago, *Hi Ladies*. In 1961 he started hosting a daily ninety-minute talk show in Cleveland. That program was nationally syndicated by 1963, and two years later Douglas's operation moved to Philadelphia, where it remained for thirteen years; during that time it was the only major national series to originate from that city. Each week Douglas was joined by a celebrity cohost (the first was Carmel Quinn); most of Douglas's guests came from New York, a two-hour limousine drive from Philadelphia. In 1978, however, Douglas left Philadelphia for Los Angeles, primarily because of the comparative ease of booking guests on the West Coast. Douglas's first producer was Woody Fraser; subsequent producers included Jack Reilly, Brad Lachman, Vince Calandra, and E. V. DiMassa. In 1967 *The Mike Douglas Show* became the first syndicated talk show to win an Emmy. After almost two decades, Douglas's distributor, Group W, dropped the show in mid-1980, and hired John Davidson to host a new talk show. Douglas carried on for two more years with another distributor; during its final months the show was titled *The Mike Douglas Entertainment Hour*.

MIKE HAMMER   SYNDICATED
1958   Mike Hammer, the gritty private eye created by Mickey Spillane, was played by Darren McGavin in this half-hour show. Seventy-eight episodes were filmed. The character returned in a made-for-TV movie with one of the longest titles ever: "Mickey Spillane's Mike Hammer: 'Murder Me, Murder You.'" Broadcast by CBS on 9 April 1983, it starred Stacy Keach, Lisa Blount, and Tanya Roberts.

MIKE HAMMER   CBS
26 JANUARY 1984–14 APRIL 1984; 30 AUGUST 1984–18 JANUARY 1985; 4 MAY 1985–6 JUNE 1985; 22 APRIL 1986–6 MAY 1986; 20 SEPTEMBER 1986–9 SEPTEMBER 1987   The second TV incarnation of Mickey Spillane's ultra-macho private eye became a weekly series after two made-for-TV movies had been televised (the second of the two, "More Than Murder," actually led off the series). Stacy Keach starred as Mike Hammer, the brawling, womanizing, chain-smoking New York detective. Also featured were Don Stroud as Hammer's friend, Captain Pat Chambers of the N.Y.P.D.; Kent Williams as Hammer's humorless nemesis, Assistant District Attorney Barrington; Lindsay Bloom as Hammer's shapely secretary, Velda; and Danny Goldman (1984–1985) as Ozzie the Answer, one of Hammer's street sources. Also featured was a mysterious woman (credited only as "The Face") who made a brief appearance in each episode. The role was played by Donna Denton. Lee Benton appeared as Jenny, the bartender at Mike's favorite watering hole.

Before he agreed to let the series be produced, Hammer's creator, Mickey Spillane, made three demands: that it be filmed in New York, that Hammer be "surrounded" by beautiful women, and that Hammer carry a .45 automatic rather than the less macho .38. Executive producer Jay Bernstein and the network acceded to all three demands.

Unfortunately, production of the show's second season was interrupted when Stacy Keach encountered his own legal troubles. On 4 April 1984 he was arrested in England for possession of cocaine, and subsequently served a jail term there. After his release a new TV-movie, "The Return of Mickey Spillane's Mike Hammer," was broadcast, and in the fall of 1986 *The New Mike Hammer* found a place on CBS's schedule. The "new" Hammer may have been less sexist, but he remained every bit as violent as the "old" Hammer. In May 1987 Hammer finally came face to face with The Face, and learned that she was a mystery writer. On 21 May 1989 a TV-movie sequel was aired on CBS: "Mickey Spillane's Mike Hammer: Winner Takes All" found Hammer in Las Vegas. Hammer again returned in the clumsily titled TV-movie, "Come Die with Me: A Mickey Spillane's Mike Hammer Mystery" (6 December 1994, CBS). Rob Estes starred as Hammer, and Pamela Anderson filled the role of Velda.

THE MIKE WALLACE INTERVIEW ABC
28 APRIL 1957–14 SEPTEMBER 1958   Mike Wallace interviewed a single guest each week on this half-hour series. Though Wallace is best known today as one of *60 Minutes'* hard-hitting reporters, his earliest TV appearances were as an actor (see *Stand By for Crime*), as the cohost of a daytime variety show (see *Mike and Buff*), and as emcee of a game show (see *The Big Surprise*). He honed his interviewing techniques during the mid-1950s on a local show in New York, *Nightbeat,* which led to this nationally televised series.

MILLER'S COURT SYNDICATED
1982–1985   Topical legal issues were dramatized in a courtroom setting and then discussed by the studio audience, in this half-hour informational series. Harvard law professor Arthur Miller was the host, and he was joined each week by prominent lawyers.

THE MILLION DOLLAR VIDEO CHALLENGE SYNDICATED
1990–1991   One of several programs attempting to capitalize on the popularity of home videos, this one was hosted by Steve Kelley. Each week a celebrity panel judged videos submitted by viewers in four categories: music, children, comedy, and real-life.

THE MILLIONAIRE CBS
19 JANUARY 1955–28 SEPTEMBER 1960   Essentially an anthology series, *The Millionaire* starred Marvin Miller as Michael Anthony, executive secretary to a reclusive multibillionaire whose hobby was giving away a million dollars to persons he had never met. Typically, the show began with Anthony being summoned to the study of his employer, John Beresford Tipton, at "Silverstone," Tipton's 60,000-acre estate. After a brief conversation, Tipton (whose face was never shown to viewers) gave Anthony a cashier's check together with instructions on its delivery. Anthony would track down the donee and present the check, explaining to the recipient that the million dollars was tax free, the donor wished to remain anonymous, and the donee merely had to agree never to divulge the exact amount of the check or the circumstances under which it was received (except to his or her spouse, if the donee should marry). Anthony then disappeared, leaving the recipient richer, if not wiser. The voice of the benevolent Mr. Tipton was supplied by Paul Frees. Don Fedderson, the producer of the series, disclosed in a 1955 *TV Guide* interview that Tipton's name was "a composite of Fedderson's home town, his wife's home town, and his lawyer's first name." Fedderson also managed to include his wife, Tido Fedderson, as an uncredited extra in almost every episode. *TV Guide* later reported that Marvin Miller regularly received requests from people who wanted their own check for a million dollars. Miller's customary reply was to send each person a "check" for "a million dollars' worth of good luck." The half-hour series was syndicated under the title *If You Had a Million.* On 19 December 1978 CBS televised a two-hour made-for-TV movie based on the series; titled "The Millionaire," it featured Robert Quarry as Michael Anthony.

THE MILTON BERLE SHOW (THE TEXACO STAR THEATER) NBC
21 SEPTEMBER 1948–9 JUNE 1953

THE BUICK-BERLE SHOW   NBC

29 SEPTEMBER 1953–14 JUNE 1955

THE MILTON BERLE SHOW   NBC

27 SEPTEMBER 1955–5 JUNE 1956

THE KRAFT MUSIC HALL   NBC

8 OCTOBER 1958–13 MAY 1959

THE MILTON BERLE SHOW   ABC

9 SEPTEMBER 1966–6 JANUARY 1967   Milton Berle was television's first superstar. His first series, *The Texaco Star Theater,* was the most popular variety show in video history; its phenomenal success proved that TV was more than a toy and that it could (and would) compete effectively with stage and screen as an entertainment medium. Berle's sobriquet, "Mr. Television," was fully deserved.

Though he is remembered today chiefly as a television entertainer, Berle had an extensive background in vaudeville, films, and radio; he was five years old when he first appeared on stage. He was also one of the first persons to appear on television, having participated in some experimental broadcasts in 1929 and 1933. During the 1940s Berle hosted several radio shows, the last of which were *The Philip Morris Playhouse,* a 1947 anthology series of comedies, and *The Texaco Star Theater,* a comedy-variety show. Among the writers on the latter show were Nat Hiken, Aaron Ruben, and brothers Danny and Neil Simon.

By the spring of 1948 Texaco had become interested in sponsoring a variety show on television. Several prospective hosts, including Berle, "auditioned" on Tuesday nights during the summer of 1948; Berle first hosted the program on 8 June, with guests Pearl Bailey, Harry Richman, Bill "Bojangles" Robinson, and Señor Wences. Pleased with Berle's performance, Texaco chose him as permanent host of the show. Berle's guests on the fall premiere (21 September) included Phil Silvers, Evelyn Knight, Stan Fisher, Smith and Dale, Park and Clifford, and the Four Carters.

The new show was an immediate smash, scoring ratings as high as eighty during its first season. Theater and nightclub attendance dwindled on Tuesdays, as people gathered at the homes of friends who owned television sets. Many of those people soon bought sets of their own—set ownership passed the million mark early in 1949 and doubled later that year. The millions who tuned in on Tuesdays saw broad comedy; Berle, who was actively involved with every aspect of the show's production, capitalized on the visual impact of the medium, relying heavily on outlandish costumes (many of which were designed by his sister, Rosalind) and sight gags. Laughter from the studio audience was further guaranteed by the presence of Berle's mother at almost every telecast. Guest stars were featured each week, and most programs concluded with a musical sketch. Woody Kling and Buddy Arnold, who wrote the show's theme, "We're the Men from Texaco," composed hundreds of numbers for the program. Also featured from the earliest days was vaudevillian Sid Stone, who, as a pitchman, delivered the commercials through 1951.

Berle continued to do the radio version during the 1948–1949 season and also found time to host the first telethon on 4 April 1949, for the Damon Runyon Cancer Fund. After a summer's rest he returned to TV (but not to radio) in the fall of 1949. The show continued to top the ratings and again dominated Tuesday-night viewing. Ad-libbing at the end of one show that season, Berle referred to himself as "Uncle Miltie," a nickname that endeared him to younger viewers. *The Texaco Star Theater* continued as TV's number-one show in its third season (1950–1951), though the margin between it and its competition was lessening. In 1951 Berle signed a thirty-year contract with NBC, which guaranteed him an annual income of $200,000 whether he worked or not.

In the fall of 1951, as *Texaco's* fourth season began, Berle cut back his schedule, hosting the show three out of every four weeks. The show was finally surpassed in the ratings (by Arthur Godfrey's *Talent Scouts*); Berle attributed the decline to the fact that he was appearing less regularly, but in all probability the show's popularity would have tapered off anyway. In the fall of 1952, Berle's last show with Texaco as his sponsor, several changes were made. Veteran radio writer Goodman Ace was brought in as head writer, and several new writers were added, including Selma Diamond, George Foster, Mort Greene, and Jay Burton. Greg Garrison, a young director with several years' experience in the medium, was also hired. A new "show-within-a-show" format was introduced—Berle played himself, the star of a TV variety show, and was joined by a group of regulars: Ruth Gilbert as his secretary, Max, Fred Clark as his agent, and Arnold Stang as Francis the stagehand. Ventriloquist Jimmy Nelson as his dummy, Danny O'Day, handled the commercials.

In spite of all the changes, the show's ratings continued to slip (*Texaco Star Theater* finished fifth that year), and Texaco dropped its sponsorship of the Berle show at the end of the 1952–1953 season (Texaco sponsored a Saturday-night show in the fall of 1953 on NBC, with Jimmy Durante and Donald O'Connor alternating as hosts). Buick, however, picked up the Tuesday-night slot in the fall of 1953; *The Buick-Berle Show* ran for two seasons, continuing with the same format that had been introduced in the fall of 1952. Singers Charlie Applewhite and Connie Russell also joined the cast.

Buick decided to switch its allegiance to CBS—and Jackie Gleason—in 1955. Berle moved his operation from New York to Hollywood that summer and hosted an hour show on Tuesdays—*The Milton Berle Show*—for one more season. It was one of the first color variety shows broadcast from the West Coast. One of the guests on the final telecast in 1956 was Elvis Presley. Though Berle's Tuesday-night shows came to an end in 1956, he continued to be seen throughout the next decade. In the fall of 1958 he hosted *The Kraft Music Hall*, a half-hour variety show on Wednesday nights (see also that title). In the fall of 1960 he hosted an unsuccessful sports show, *Jackpot Bowling Starring Milton Berle* (see that title). In 1965 Berle renegotiated his thirty-year contract with NBC; annual payments were reduced to $120,000, and Berle received the right to appear on other networks. In the fall of 1966 Berle hosted a Friday-night variety hour on ABC, which was canceled in midseason. Produced by Bill Dana, the show also featured Donna Loren, Bobby Rydell, and Irving Benson as an offstage heckler. Berle has also made several dramatic appearances in such series as *The Mod Squad, Mannix,* and *Batman* (as Louie the Lilac), and has guest-starred on dozens of variety shows. On 26 March 1978, almost thirty years after he first stepped into thousands of television homes, Milton Berle was honored in a celebrity-studded, televised special, "A Tribute to Milton Berle"; he was also given a special award at the 1978–1979 Emmy Awards show.

MILTON THE MONSTER ABC
9 OCTOBER 1965–8 SEPTEMBER 1968 Saturday-morning cartoon show starring Milton the Monster, a lovable denizen of Transylvania's Horrible Hill.

THE MIND PBS
12 OCTOBER 1988–14 DECEMBER 1988 On this nine-part sequel to the 1984 series *The Brain,* host George Paige explored "what the brain does." Among the many topics examined were memory, aging, autism, and language.

MIND YOUR MANNERS NBC
24 JUNE 1951–2 MARCH 1952 Allen Ludden, who would later host such shows as *College Bowl* and *Password,* was the moderator of this Sunday-afternoon public affairs program on which teenaged panelists discussed current events.

MINDREADERS NBC
13 AUGUST 1979–11 JANUARY 1980 Dick Martin presided over this daytime game show of "hunch and ESP." The game involved a team of four women and a team of four men, each captained by a celebrity; each of the several rounds required the players to predict how their teammates, or a panel of studio audience members, would respond to a personal or hypothetical question.

MINOR ADJUSTMENTS NBC/UPN
16 SEPTEMBER 1995–19 NOVEMBER 1995 (NBC); 23 JANUARY 1996– (UPN) Half-hour sitcom about an African-American child psychologist and his home life. With standup comedian Rondell Sheridan as Dr. Ron Aimes; Wendy Raquel Robinson as his wife, Rachel; Bobby E. McAdams II as their ten-year-old son, Trevor; Camille

Winbush as their young daughter, Emma; Mitchell Whitfield as Dr. Bruce Hampton, an orthodontist who shared offices with Ron; Linda Kash as Dr. Francine Bailey, a pediatrician who also shared offices; and Sara Rue as Bruce's niece, Darby, their dimwitted receptionist.

MIRROR THEATER (REVLON MIRROR THEATER) NBC/CBS
23 JUNE 1953–1 SEPTEMBER 1953 (NBC); 19 SEPTEMBER 1953–5 DECEMBER 1953 (CBS)   Sponsored by Revlon, this half-hour dramatic anthology series was hosted by Robin Chandler. It was seen Tuesdays on NBC during the summer of 1953, then shifted to Saturdays on CBS that fall. Presentations included: "The Little Wife," with Eddie Albert (23 June); "Salt of the Earth," with Richard Kiley (30 June); "Because I Love Him," with Joan Crawford (her first major TV role, 19 September); and "Uncle Jack," with Jack Haley (28 November). Donald Davis and Dorothy Mathews produced the series, and Daniel Petrie directed it. The NBC version was broadcast live from New York; the CBS version was on film from Hollywood.

THE MISADVENTURES OF SHERIFF LOBO NBC
18 SEPTEMBER 1979–2 SEPTEMBER 1980
LOBO NBC
30 DECEMBER 1980–25 AUGUST 1981   This hour comedy-adventure series, spun off from *BJ and the Bear,* starred Claude Akins as the slightly corrupt sheriff of Orly County, Elroy S. Lobo. Also featured during the 1979–1980 season were Mills Watson as bumbling Deputy Perkins, who was also Lobo's brother-in-law; Brian Kerwin as Deputy Birdie Hawkins; Leann Hunley as hotelkeeper Sarah Cumberland; Cyd Crampton as Lobo's sister (and Perkins's wife), Rose; and Janet Lynn Curtis as Margaret Ellen. When the series returned for its second season, it was retitled *Lobo.* Lobo and his deputies had been invited to Atlanta, where they became special cops. Joining Akins, Watson, and Kerwin as regulars were Nicolas Coster as their new boss, Chief J. C. Carson; Nell Carter as Sergeant Hildy Jones; and Tara Buckman and Amy Botwinick as Brandy and Peaches, a pair of undercover cops. Glen Larson was the executive producer.

MISERY LOVES COMPANY FOX
30 SEPTEMBER 1995–22 OCTOBER 1995   Half-hour sitcom about four men who hung out together in New York City. With Dennis Boutsikaris as film professor Joe DeMarco, recently divorced after twelve years of marriage, who moved in with his single younger brother; Christopher Meloni as his brother, Mitch; Julius Carry as their divorced pal, Perry; Stephen Furst as their unhappily married pal, Lewis, a dentist; Wesley Jonathan as Connor, Perry's teenage son; Nikki Deloach as Tracy, Lewis's teenage daughter; and Kathe Mazur as Nicky St. Hubbin, proprietor of Nicky St. Hubbin's, the guys' favorite hangout.

MISFITS OF SCIENCE NBC
4 OCTOBER 1985–21 FEBRUARY 1986   Three young adults with unusual powers were melded into a crimefighting unit on this Friday night adventure hour. Featured were Dean Paul Martin as Dr. Billy Hayes, a scientist with the Humanidyne Institute, who organized the unit; Kevin Peter Hall (variously billed as seven-foot-two or seven-foot-four, certainly the tallest person ever to be a TV series regular) as Dr. Elvin "El" Lincoln, who could shrink himself to a size of six inches for up to fifteen minutes an hour; Mark Thomas Miller as Johnny "Johnny B" Bukowski, a former rock star who had been electrocuted at a concert and could now unlease powerful bolts of current through his fingertips; Courteney Cox as seventeen-year-old Gloria Dinallo, a juvenile delinquent who possessed telekinetic powers; Jennifer Holmes as Jane Miller, Gloria's probation officer; Max Wright as Dick Stetmeyer, director of the institute; and Diane Civita as Miss Nance, the receptionist. A fourth misfit, Arnold Biefneiter (played by Mickey Jones), who could freeze anything, was featured on the pilot episode.

MISS SUSAN   NBC

12 MARCH 1951–28 DECEMBER 1951   This unusual soap opera starred Susan Peters, an actress who was paralyzed from the waist down as the result of a hunting accident in 1945. On the show she appeared as Susan Martin, a wheelchair-bound lawyer who had just moved back to her hometown, Martinsville, Ohio. Also featured on the series were Mark Roberts, Robert McQueeney, Katharine Grill, Natalie Priest, and Jon Lormer. The daily, fifteen-minute show was broadcast live from Philadelphia, where it was written by William Kendal Clarke and produced and directed by Kenneth Buckridge.

MISS WINSLOW & SON   CBS

28 MARCH 1979–2 MAY 1979   Half-hour sitcom based on the British series *Miss Jones & Son*. With Darleen Carr as artist Susan Winslow, mother of a son by a man with whom she had lived for two years but who left her for South America (she named the baby Edmund Hillary Winslow, after the man who first scaled Mount Everest); Roscoe Lee Browne as Harold Neistadter, her neighbor; Elliott Reid as her father, Warren Winslow, a pharmacist; Sarah Marshall as her mother, Evelyn Winslow; William Bogert as Mr. Callahan, her boss. Ted Bergmann and Don Taffner were the executive producers for T.T.C. Productions.

MISSING LINKS   NBC/ABC

9 SEPTEMBER 1963–27 MARCH 1964 (NBC); 30 MARCH 1964–25 DECEMBER 1964 (ABC) Daytime game show on which contestants tried to predict the ability of celebrity guests to supply the missing words to a story previously read aloud. The show, a Mark Goodson-Bill Todman Production, was hosted by Ed McMahon on NBC and Dick Clark on ABC.

MISSING PERSONS   ABC

30 AUGUST 1993–17 FEBRUARY 1994   Set in Chicago, this hour cop show centered on the Department of Missing Persons. Daniel J. Travanti played Lieutenant Ray McAuliffe, head of the unit. With him were Erik King as Bobby Davidson; Fred Weller as Johnny Sandowski; Jorjan Fox as Connie Karadzik; Bob Swan as Dan Manaher; Juan Ramirez as Carlos Marrone; and Paty Lombard as Ray's wife, Barbara.

MISSING/REWARD   SYNDICATED

1989–1991   Half-hour informational series, hosted by Stacy Keach, which offered rewards for the recovery of stolen goods or the apprehension of wanted fugitives; a few "rewards" were offered by collectors of various goods looking for additional items for their collections. Like *America's Most Wanted* and other similar shows, the series presented dramatizations of crimes and interviews with law enforcement personnel. Unlike *America's Most Wanted,* with its toll-free 800 number for viewers to call, *Missing/Reward* featured a 900 number for which users were charged. Most of the rewards were offered by private sources; some seemed unlikely to be collected, such as the $2,000,000 bounty posted for the return of any living American MIA from Southeast Asia, or a reward offered for the return of a set of rare coins last seen in 1906.

MISSION: IMPOSSIBLE   CBS

17 SEPTEMBER 1966–8 SEPTEMBER 1973   Bruce Geller was the executive producer of this durable hour-long adventure series, which depicted the exploits of the I.M.F. (Impossible Missions Force), a government agency that undertook extremely hazardous or intricate espionage missions. Typically, the I.M.F. leader received his instructions on a miniature tape recorder ("Your mission, Jim, should you decide to accept it"), which self-destructed after its message had been conveyed. After assembling his crew of experts, the leader explained to them the nature of the project, usually with the help of films or photos. The first head of the I.M.F. was Dan Briggs, played by Steven Hill. He was replaced, however, after one season, ostensibly because of the difficulty of accommodating the show's production schedule to the preferences of

Hill, an Orthodox Jew, who declined to work after sundown Fridays and on Saturdays. The new leader of the I.M.F. was Jim Phelps, played by Peter Graves, who remained with the show for the rest of its run. The rest of the I.M.F. crew included: Martin Landau (1966–1969) as Rollin Hand, an expert at disguises; Barbara Bain (1966–1969) as Cinnamon Carter, who could turn on the charm when needed; Greg Morris as Barney Collier, ace mechanic and electronics technician; and Peter Lupus as hefty Willy Armitage, resident strong man. Landau and Bain (who was married to Landau) quit the show after three seasons in a dispute over budget cuts. Leonard Nimoy was added in the fall of 1969 as Paris, the new master of disguise; Nimoy left the show after two seasons. Other additions to the crew included: Lesley Warren (1970–1971) as Dana Lambert; Sam Elliott (1970–1971) as Doug; Lynda Day George (1971–1972) as Casey; and Barbara Anderson (1972–1973) as Mimi Davis. The voice on the tape recordings was supplied by Bob Johnson.

In 1988 the series was revived: see below.

MISSION IMPOSSIBLE ABC
23 OCTOBER 1988–24 FEBRUARY 1990; 26 MAY 1990–9 JUNE 1990   This remake of the classic 1966–1973 series was hastily put together to fill some gaps in ABC's schedule caused by the 1988 writers' strike. It was produced in Australia, and used some of the scripts from the earlier series. Peter Graves returned as Jim Phelps, head of the Impossible Missions Force (this was Graves's second Australia-based series; he'd done *Whiplash* in 1961). His new crew included Phil Morris (son of Greg Morris) as technical ace Grant Collier, son of Barney Collier; Tony Hamilton as muscleman Max Harte; Thaao Penghlis as actor Nicholas Black; Terry Markwell (1988–1989) as Casey Randall; and Jane Badler (spring 1989–1990) as athlete Shannon Reed. Technological change even came to the series' opening sequence: instead of the old self-destructing audio tape, the new version featured a self-destructing laser disc.

MISSION: MAGIC! ABC
8 SEPTEMBER 1973–31 AUGUST 1974   Saturday-morning cartoon show about a group of six high school students and their teacher, who traveled together through time. They were assisted in their weekly journeys by the cartoon form of Australian singer Rick Springfield, who performed a song each week. Springfield went on to greater fame on *General Hospital,* from which he was able to relaunch his musical career.

MISSION TO THE WORLD
See LIFE IS WORTH LIVING

THE MISSISSIPPI CBS
25 MARCH 1983–6 MAY 1983; 27 SEPTEMBER 1983–13 MARCH 1984   This hour dramatic series starred Ralph Waite as Ben Walker, a big-city criminal attorney who suddenly left the city to realize his lifelong dream of running a riverboat on the Mississippi River; Walker was still able to use his lawyering skills, however, as his travels brought him in contact with people who needed legal help. Also on board were Linda G. Miller (the daughter of Jackie Gleason) as Stella McMullen, a former client of Walker's who was now studying law; and Stan Shaw as Walker's pilot, Lafayette "Lafe" Tate. The series was filmed on location.

MISSUS GOES A-SHOPPING CBS
19 NOVEMBER 1947–12 JANUARY 1949   CBS's first commercial daytime series was an audience participation show, broadcast live from various Manhattan supermarkets. John Reed King was the original host. Toward the end of its run the show was retitled *This Is the Missus* and was hosted by Bud Collyer.

MR. ADAMS AND EVE CBS
4 JANUARY 1957–23 SEPTEMBER 1958   Half-hour sitcom with Howard Duff as film star Howard Adams and Ida Lupino as his wife, film star Eve Adams (known professionally as Eve Drake). Also featured were Hayden Rorke as Steve, their agent; Olive Carey as Elsie, their housekeeper; Alan Reed as J. B. Hafter, the head of the

studio; and Larry Dobkin as their director. Sixty-eight episodes were produced. Collier Young, former husband of Ida Lupino, was the executive producer.

MR. AND MRS. JIMMY CARROLL   DUMONT
18 OCTOBER 1950–13 APRIL 1951   Fifteen-minute twice-weekly variety program, cohosted by Jimmy and Rita Carroll.

MR. AND MRS. NORTH   CBS/NBC
3 OCTOBER 1952–25 SEPTEMBER 1953 (CBS); 26 JANUARY 1954–20 JULY 1954 (NBC) *Mr. and Mrs. North* began on radio as a situation comedy, but by 1942 it had shifted to a lighthearted murder mystery show. A "pilot" program was telecast 4 July 1949, starring Joseph Allen, Jr. and Mary Lou Taylor, but it was not until 1952 that production of a TV series got underway. Produced by John W. Loveton and directed by Ralph Murphy, the filmed, half-hour series starred Richard Denning as Jerry North, a publisher, and Barbara Britton as his wife, Pamela North, a New York couple who seemed to stumble on an unsolved murder every week. Also featured was Francis DeSales as Lieutenant Bill Weigand. Both the radio and the television series were based on the stories written by Richard and Frances Lockridge.

MR. ARSENIC   ABC
8 MAY 1952–26 JUNE 1952   Half-hour mystery anthology series hosted by Burton Turkus, author of *Murder, Inc.*

MR. BELVEDERE   ABC
15 MARCH 1985–26 APRIL 1985; 16 AUGUST 1985–11 SEPTEMBER 1987; 30 OCTOBER 1987–16 DECEMBER 1989; 1 JULY 1990–8 JULY 1990   A resilient sitcom about the sarcastic, and "veddy British" male housekeeper for a Pittsburgh sportswriter and his family, starring Christopher Hewett as Lynn Belvedere; onetime major leaguer Bob Uecker as his employer, George Owens; Ilene Graff as George's wife, Marsha, a law student; Rob Stone as teenage son Kevin; Tracy Wells as teenage daughter Heather; and Brice Beckham as younger son Wesley. At the end of almost every episode, Mr. Belvedere wrote the "lesson" of the evening's story in his diary. The series was actually canceled at the end of the 1986–1987 season, but was hastily ordered back into production to replace the sagging *Max Headroom* in October 1987. When the series was lifted in December 1989, ten completed episodes had yet to air.

The character was made famous by Clifton Webb in three movies made between 1948 and 1951. A TV series had been proposed as early as 1959, with Hans Conried as Belvedere, but never materialized.

MR. BLACK   ABC
19 SEPTEMBER 1949–7 NOVEMBER 1949   This Monday-night mystery anthology series was hosted by Anthony Christopher as Mr. Black, a mysterious soul who was seen each week in his cobweb-shrouded study. Broadcast from Chicago, the half-hour series was written by Bill Ballanger and directed by Tony Rizzo.

MR. BROADWAY   CBS
26 SEPTEMBER 1964–26 DECEMBER 1964   Garson Kanin created this unsuccessful hour-long adventure series, which starred Craig Stevens as New York public relations man Mike Bell. Also featured were Lani Miyazaki as Toki, his assistant; Horace McMahon as Hank McClure, his contact at the police department. David Susskind and Daniel Melnick produced the series, and Dave Brubeck supplied music. The thirteen episodes included rare guest appearances by Liza Minnelli (in her first TV dramatic role, "Nightingale for Sale," 24 October), Sandy Dennis ("Don't Mention My Name in Sheboygan," 7 November), and Lauren Bacall ("Something to Sing About," 19 December).

MR. CHIPS   SYNDICATED
1976   Bill Brown and Don McGowan cohosted this series aimed at the do-it-yourselfer.

MR. CITIZEN   ABC

20 APRIL 1955–20 JULY 1955   Allyn Edwards hosted this unusual anthology series, which depicted real-life incidents in which ordinary citizens had come to the assistance of those in need. A prominent American presented the "Mister Citizen Award" each week to the person whose efforts had been cited.

MR. DEEDS GOES TO TOWN   ABC

26 SEPTEMBER 1969–16 JANUARY 1970   The television adaptation of Frank Capra's 1936 film starred Monte Markham as Longfellow Deeds, a newspaper publisher from the small town of Mandrake Falls who inherited a huge corporation from his late uncle. Also on hand were Pat Harrington, Jr., as Tony Lawrence, his aide; Ivor Barry as George the butler; and Herb Voland as Henry Masterson, chairman of the board of Deeds Enterprises. The half-hour sitcom was pounded by *Hogan's Heroes* and *The Name of the Game* and was dropped at midseason.

MR. DISTRICT ATTORNEY   ABC/SYNDICATED

1 OCTOBER 1951–23 JUNE 1952 (ABC); 1954 (SYNDICATED)   Created by Ed Byron, *Mr. District Attorney* began on radio in 1939 and twice came to television. Jay Jostyn, who had taken over the role on radio in 1940, was the first D.A. and was known simply as "The D.A." or "Chief." (Thomas E. Dewey, New York's district attorney during the 1930s, and presidential contender in 1948, was reported to have been the model for the role.) Also featured were Vicki Vola as Miss Miller, the D.A.'s secretary, and Len Doyle as Detective Harrington, an investigator for the D.A.'s office. In 1954 Ziv TV revived the series with David Brian in the lead role; by this time the D.A. had a name— Paul Garrett. Jackie Loughery now played his secretary, Miss Miller. The 1951–1952 series, which was seen on alternate Mondays, was produced and directed by Ed Byron.

MISTER ED   SYNDICATED/CBS

1961 (SYNDICATED); 1 OCTOBER 1961–4 SEPTEMBER 1966 (CBS)   Half-hour sitcom about a talking horse. With Alan Young as Wilbur Post, an architect who discovered the horse, Mister Ed, in the barn of their new house and also discovered that he was the only person to whom the horse deigned to talk; Connie Hines as Carol Post, Wilbur's wife; Larry Keating (1961–1964) as next-door neighbor Roger Addison; Edna Skinner (1961–1964) as Roger's wife, Kay Addison; Leon Ames (1964–1966) as next-door neighbor Gordon Kirkwood; and Florence MacMichael (1964–1966) as Gordon's wife, Winnie Kirkwood. The voice of Ed was provided by former western star Allan "Rocky" Lane. Al Simon was executive producer of the series, and Arthur Lubin the producer-director.

MR. EXECUTIVE   SYNDICATED

1954   Host Westbrook Van Voorhis interviewed leading American industrialists on this half-hour documentary series.

MR. GARLUND   CBS

7 OCTOBER 1960–13 JANUARY 1961   This light adventure series starred Charles Quinlivan as Frank Garlund, a young tycoon whose origins were uncertain. Also featured were Kam Tong as Kam Chang, his foster brother, and Philip Ahn as Po Chang, the Chinese businessman who raised Garlund. In November of 1960 the show's title was changed to *The Garlund Touch,* but under either title the show proved weak competition for *77 Sunset Strip* and *The Bell Telephone Hour.*

MR. I. MAGINATION   CBS

29 MAY 1949–28 JUNE 1952   This half-hour children's show was partly educational and partly fantasy. As Mr. I. Magination, Paul Tripp hosted the series, which was set in Imagination Town, a place where any child's wish could come true. Also featured was Tripp's wife, Ruth Enders. The show, which featured much original music, was produced by Worthington Miner, Irving Pincus, and Norman Pincus.

MR. LUCKY   CBS

24 OCTOBER 1959–3 SEPTEMBER 1960   This half-hour adventure series was based on the 1943 film that had starred Cary Grant. On TV John Vivyan starred as Mr. Lucky, owner of the *Fortuna,* a casino ship moored off the California coast. Ross Martin costarred as Andamo, Lucky's man Friday, and Pippa Scott played Lucky's girlfriend, Maggie Shank-Rutherford. The show was a Blake Edwards production, and music was supplied by Henry Mancini. By midseason the show's sponsor, Lever Brothers, demanded that gambling be deemphasized on the series; accordingly, the *Fortuna* became a floating restaurant and nightclub.

MR. MAGOO   SYNDICATED/NBC/CBS

1960–1962 (SYNDICATED); 19 SEPTEMBER 1964–21 AUGUST 1965 (NBC); 10 SEPTEMBER 1977–9 SEPTEMBER 1979 (CBS)   Quincy Magoo, the myopic star of hundreds of theatrical cartoons (the first of which was made in 1949), first came to television in a syndicated series. He is better known as the star of a prime-time series on NBC, which lasted one season. Officially titled *The Famous Adventures of Mr. Magoo,* the series cast Magoo in a different role each week, usually a historical figure. Magoo returned to TV in 1977 on a half-hour weekend cartoon show, *What's New, Mister Magoo?,* in which he was teamed up with McBaker, a nearsighted dog. Jim Backus supplied Magoo's distinctive voice.

MISTER MAYOR   CBS

26 SEPTEMBER 1964–18 SEPTEMBER 1965   This Saturday-morning kids' show featured Bob Keeshan (who played Captain Kangaroo weekday mornings) as Mister Mayor, Jane Connell as Aunt Maud and Miss Melissa, and Rollo the hippopotamus.

MR. MERLIN   CBS

7 OCTOBER 1981–15 SEPTEMBER 1982   Barnard Hughes starred in this half-hour sitcom as Merlin, the 1600-year-old wizard who had once worked for King Arthur; now known as Max Merlin, he opened an auto repair shop in San Francisco, where he hoped to find an apprentice. Also featured were Clark Brandon as Zac Rogers, the young man chosen to be the apprentice; Jonathan Prince as Zac's pal, Leo Samuels; and Elaine Joyce as the mysterious Alexandria, Merlin's friend and contemporary.

MR. NOVAK   NBC

24 SEPTEMBER 1963–31 AUGUST 1965   Hour-long dramatic series set at Jefferson High School in Los Angeles. With James Franciscus as John Novak, English teacher; Dean Jagger (to December 1964) as Albert Vane, the principal; Burgess Meredith as Martin Woodridge, Vane's successor as principal; Steve Franken (1963–1964) as Mr. Allen, French teacher; Jeanne Bal (1963–1964) as Jean Pagano, assistant vice principal; Donald Barry (1963–1964) as Mr. Gallo; Marian Collier as Miss Scott; Vince Howard as Pete Butler; André Phillippe as Mr. Johns; Stephen Roberts as Mr. Peeples; Kathleen Ellis as Mrs. Floyd; Marjorie Corley as Miss Dorsey; Phyllis Avery (1964–1965) as Ruth Wilkinson, girls' vice principal; Bill Zuckert (1964–1965) as Mr. Bradwell; David Sheiner (1964–1965) as Paul Webb; Peter Hansen (1964–1965) as Mr. Parkson; and Irene Tedrow (1965) as Mrs. Ring. E. Jack Neuman was executive producer for M-G-M.

MR. PEEPERS   NBC

3 JULY 1952–12 JUNE 1955   Broadcast live from New York, this low-key situation comedy starred a young comedian named Wally Cox as Robinson J. Peepers, a mild-mannered science teacher at Jefferson Junior High. The talented cast also included Tony Randall as Peepers's pal, English teacher Harvey Weskitt; Georgann Johnson as Marge Weskitt, Harvey's wife; Patricia Benoit as Nancy Remington, the school nurse who married Peepers on 23 May 1954; Marion Lorne as Mrs. Gurney, Peepers's daffy landlady; Reta Shaw as Aunt Lil; Jack Warden as Coach; Ernest Truex as Mr. Remington, Nancy's father; and Sylvia Field as Mrs. Remington, Nancy's mother. The half-hour series was created especially for Cox by David Swift in association with producer Fred Coe. Originally sponsored by Ford Motor Company, the

show was introduced in 1952 as a summer replacement for *Ford Theater*. The series earned rave reviews, and *Mr. Peepers* was brought back by NBC in the fall of 1952 with a new sponsor—Reynolds Aluminum—after a Sunday-night sitcom, *Doc Corkle,* bombed. Reviewing the series in 1954, *TV Guide* opined that *Mr. Peepers* "comes close to being the perfect TV show."

MR. PIPER   SYNDICATED
1962   This children's show was hosted by Alan Crofoot as Mr. Piper; produced in England, it was distributed by ITC.

MR. PRESIDENT   FOX
3 MAY 1987–2 APRIL 1988   The American presidency was the subject of two sitcoms during the Reagan years. The first, *Hail to the Chief,* had starred Patty Duke as the first woman chief executive. This one starred George C. Scott (in his first series role since *East Side, West Side* left the air in 1964) as President Samuel Arthur Tresch, a former governor of Wisconsin; Carlin Glynn as First Lady Meg Tresch; Andre Gower as their twelve-year-old son, Nick; Maddie Corman as their sixteen-year-old daughter, Cynthia; Susan Wheeler Duff as their married daughter, Jennifer Hayes; Daniel McDonald as her husband, Fred Hayes; Conrad Bain as presidential aide Charley Ross; Allen Williams as staffer Daniel Cummings; and Earl Boen as staffer Dave. In the fall of 1987 Carlin Clynn left the show, and Madeline Kahn joined the cast as Meg's sister, Lois Gullickson, who assumed the duties of First Lady.

MR. ROBERTS   NBC
17 SEPTEMBER 1965–2 SEPTEMBER 1966   The remake of the 1955 film starred Roger Smith as Lieutenant Douglas Roberts, a Naval officer assigned to duty in the South Pacific aboard the *Reluctant,* a cargo ship. Desperate to be transferred to a ship that would see some action, Mr. Roberts found his efforts thwarted by the captain. Also featured were Richard X. Slattery as Captain John Morton; Steve Harmon as Ensign Frank Pulver; George Ives as Doc; Ronald Starr as Seaman Mannion; Richard Sinatra as Seaman D'Angelo; Ray Reese as Seaman Reber; and John McCook as Seaman Stefanowski. James Komack produced the half-hour comedy.

MISTER ROGERS' NEIGHBORHOOD   PBS
1968–   Public television's longest-running children's program is hosted by Fred Rogers, a Presbyterian minister from Pittsburgh. Rogers had previously worked on a 1955 network kids' show, *The Children's Corner,* but is best known as the host of this series of half hours. Through the use of puppets, guests, and musical numbers, Rogers and his crew have gently taught young viewers to handle problems such as divorce, impatience and anger, and minor crises such as the death of a pet. Other regulars on the show have included Betty Aberlin, Betsy Nadas, Joe Negri, David Newell, Don Brockett, François Clemmons, Robert Trow, Audrey Roth, Elsie Neal, and Yoshi Ito. The show was televised in Canada, in a fifteen-minute format, from 1963 to 1967, when it was first shown on a group of NET stations in this country. It has been produced at WQED-TV in Pittsburgh, and Rogers has been the executive producer. In its early years the title was spelled *MisteRogers' Neigborhood.* Production ceased in 1975, but resumed in 1979; each year a few new programs were produced, and were blended in with older shows. PBS honored Rogers in March 1990 with a prime-time retrospective, "Our Neighbor, Fred Rogers."

MR. SMITH   NBC
23 SEPTEMBER 1983–16 DECEMBER 1983   The title character in this series was an orangutan who accidentally swallowed a chemical concoction that transformed him into a talking ape with an IQ of 256. Now known as Mr. Smith, the anthropoid went to work for a Washington, D.C., government consulting firm. He continued to live with his former trainer, Tommy Atwood (played by Tim Dunigan), and the trainer's little sister, Ellie (Laura Jacoby). Also featured were Leonard Frey as Raymond Holyoke, a government official assigned to be Mr. Smith's liaison man; Terri Garber as Judy Tyson, one of Smith's coworkers; and Stuart Margolin as Dr. Kline, a top-

sider at the consulting outfit. The ape was played by a real orangutan, C. J., who had extensive showbiz experience, having costarred with Clint Eastwood in the film *Any Which Way You Can,* and with Bo Derek in *Tarzan.* The voice of Mr. Smith was supplied by Ed. Weinberger, who created the series with Stan Daniels. The third TV sitcom to feature a monkey in a leading role (see also *The Hathaways* and *Me and the Chimp*), *Mr. Smith* got off to a slow start on NBC's low-rated Friday-night lineup.

MR. SMITH GOES TO WASHINGTON ABC
29 SEPTEMBER 1962–30 MARCH 1963   Half-hour sitcom based on the 1939 film that starred James Stewart. On TV Fess Parker starred as Eugene Smith, an honest but unsophisticated politician from a rural state who was elected to a Senate vacancy following the death of the incumbent. Also featured were Sandra Warner as Pat Smith, his wife; Red Foley as the Senator's Uncle Cooter; Rita Lynn as his secretary, Miss Kelly; and Stan Irwin as the chauffeur, Arnie.

MR. SUNSHINE ABC
28 MARCH 1986–3 SEPTEMBER 1986   Jeffrey Tambor starred in this unusual half-hour sitcom as Paul Stark, a fiercely independent blind college professor who moved into an attic apartment after separating from his wife. Other regulars included Nan Martin as Grace D'Angelo, his typist; Cecilia Hart as Janice Hall, his on-again, off-again female friend; Barbara Babcock as June Swinford, his landlady; and Leonard Frey as Stark's colleague, drama professor Leon Walters.

MISTER T NBC
17 SEPTEMBER 1983–6 SEPTEMBER 1986   The sudden popularity of *The A Team,* the prime-time NBC series that debuted in January 1983, prompted the network to commission a Saturday-morning cartoon show built around one of *The A Team's* stars, Mr. T. On this series, T ran a gymnasium, and he and a group of teenaged pals became involved in various adventures. The bejeweled, spangled, Mandinka-coiffed Mr. T appeared in filmed inserts at the beginning and end of each program, to explain the social message of the day's adventure, and he also provided the voice of his cartoon character. Joe Ruby and Ken Spears were the executive producers for Ruby-Spears Enterprises.

MR. T AND TINA ABC
25 SEPTEMBER 1976–30 OCTOBER 1976   This half-hour sitcom was one of the first casualties of the 1976–1977 season: only five episodes were shown. Produced by James Komack, the show starred Pat Morita as Taro Takahashi, a widowed Japanese inventor who moved to Chicago with his children; Susan Blanchard as Tina Kelly, a young woman from Nebraska hired by Mr. T as governess for the children; Pat Suzuki as Michi, Mr. T's sister-in-law; Jerry Fujikawa as Uncle Matsu; June Angela as Sachi, Mr. T's young daughter; Eugene Profanato as Aki, Mr. T's young son; Ted Lange as Mr. Harvard, the handyman; and Miriam Byrd-Nethery as Miss Llewellyn, the landlady.

MR. TERRIFIC CBS
9 JANUARY 1967–28 AUGUST 1967   This insignificant half-hour sitcom, an imitation *Batman,* featured Stephen Strimpell as Stanley Beamish, the owner of a service station in Washington, D.C., who was on call as an agent for the Bureau of Special Projects. Beamish could take a pill developed by the Bureau, which gave him an hour's worth of super powers and turned him into Mr. Terrific, a caped crusader. Also on hand were Dick Gautier as Hal, Beamish's friend; John McGiver as Barton J. Reed, director of the Bureau; and Paul Smith as Harley Trent, another Bureau agent. Jack Arnold produced the series, which should not be confused with *Captain Nice,* a similar spoof that ran on NBC at the same time (Strimpell had tested for *Captain Nice* before landing the role on *Mr. Terrific*).

MR. WIZARD (WATCH MR. WIZARD) NBC/NICK

3 MARCH 1951–4 JULY 1965; 11 SEPTEMBER 1971–2 SEPTEMBER 1972 (NBC); 1983– (NICK) On this long-running educational series for children, Don Herbert (as Mr. Wizard) explained the principles of science and showed how to perform various experiments. Each week a dutifully amazed boy or girl was on hand to marvel at Mr. Wizard's revelations. The series ran continuously for fourteen years and returned six years later for one season. Broadcast from Chicago, it was produced by Jules Pewowar. Don Herbert returned in 1983 to host *Mr. Wizard's World* on the Nickelodeon cable TV channel. The series ceased production in 1990, but continued to be shown in reruns.

MRS. COLUMBO

See KATE LOVES A MYSTERY

MRS. G GOES TO COLLEGE CBS

4 OCTOBER 1961–5 APRIL 1962 This half-hour sitcom starred Gertrude Berg, the creator and star of *The Goldbergs,* as Sarah Green, a widow who decided to go to college. Also featured were Sir Cedric Hardwicke as Professor Crayton; Skip Ward as freshman Joe Caldwell; Marion Ross (later to star in *Happy Days*) as Sarah's daughter, Susan; Leo Penn as Sarah's son-in-law, Jerry; Mary Wickes as Maxfield, Sarah's landlady; Paul Smith as George Howell; Aneta Corsaut as Irma Howell; and Karyn Kupcinet as Carol. Though the show's title was changed in January to *The Gertrude Berg Show* (as Sarah bought a half interest in Maxfield's rooming house), the ratings did not improve. Hy Averback produced the series. Costar Hardwicke explained the motivation for taking his role in a 1962 interview in *TV Guide:* "If you're going to work in rubbish, you might as well get paid for it."

MRS. ROOSEVELT MEETS THE PUBLIC NBC

12 FEBRUARY 1950–15 JULY 1951 Sunday-afternoon panel discussion show moderated by Eleanor Roosevelt. Produced by Roger Muir, the series was originally titled *Today with Mrs. Roosevelt.*

MIXED DOUBLES NBC

5 AUGUST 1949–12 NOVEMBER 1949 Carleton E. Morse produced, wrote, and directed this half-hour sitcom about two newlywed couples who lived next door to each other in a New York apartment building. The cast included Billy Idelson, Ada Friedman, Eddy Firestone, and Rhoda Williams.

MOBILE ONE ABC

12 SEPTEMBER 1975–29 DECEMBER 1975 Hour-long adventure series with Jackie Cooper as Peter Campbell, news reporter for KONE-TV, a West Coast station; Julie Gregg as Maggie Spencer, the producer; and Mark Wheeler as Doug McKnight, Campbell's camera operator. Jack Webb was the executive producer of the series, which was created by James M. Miller.

MOBY DICK AND THE MIGHTY MIGHTOR CBS

9 SEPTEMBER 1967–6 SEPTEMBER 1969 Saturday-morning cartoon show from Hanna-Barbera Productions. The two segments depicted the adventures of Moby Dick, a great white whale whose pals were a pair of boys named Tom and Tub, and The Mighty Mightor, the super-powered alter ego of a cave boy named Tor.

THE MOD SQUAD ABC

24 SEPTEMBER 1968–23 AUGUST 1973 Hour-long crime show about three young people who comprised the Mod Squad, an undercover unit of the Los Angeles Police Department. With Michael Cole as Pete Cochrane; Clarence Williams III as Linc Hayes; Peggy Lipton as Julie Barnes; and Tige Andrews as Captain Adam Greer, their boss, the only other officer who knew of their identities. Aaron Spelling was the producer. The four principals were reunited in a two-hour made-for-TV movie, "The Return of Mod Squad," broadcast 18 May 1979 on ABC.

MODELS INC. FOX

29 JUNE 1994–6 MARCH 1995   An hour dramatic serial spun off from *Melrose Place* (which in turn was spun off from *Beverly Hills 90210*), *Models Inc.* was set at an elite Los Angeles modeling agency. The cast included Linda Gray as the agency owner, Hillary Michaels; Brian Gaskill as her son, David, who schemed to open his own agency; Cameron Daddo as photographer Brian Petersen; Teresa Hill as model Linda Holden; David Goldsmith as Linda's boyfriend, Eric Dearborn; Carrie-Anne Moss as model Carrie Spencer; Cassidy Rae as model Sarah Owens; Stephanie Romanov as Carrie's younger sister, model Teri Spencer, who was murdered in the first episode but continued to appear in flashback sequences (Romanov later played new model Monique); Kylie Travis as Australian model Julie Dante; Heather Medway as Stephanie, the receptionist; Robert Beltran as Lieutenant Louis Soto, who investigated Teri's murder; Garcelle Beavais (July 1994–1995) as model Cynthia; James Wilder (September 1994–1995) as Adam Louder; Emma Samms (September 1994–1995) as his estranged wife, Gayson Louder; Nancy Lee Grahn as Detective Beverly Towers; Don Michael Paul (October 1994–1995) as Craig; William Katt as Paul Carson; Leann Hunley as his wife, Marcia; John Haymes Newton as Mark; and Harley Venton as Dr. Heller.

MODERN ROMANCES NBC

4 OCTOBER 1954–19 SEPTEMBER 1958   A new five-part story was introduced each week on this fifteen-minute weekday series. Martha Scott was originally the host and narrator; Mel Brandt succeeded her, and later guest celebrities took over the duties. The stories were all adapted from those appearing in *Modern Romances* magazine.

THE MOHAWK SHOWROOM

See THE MORTON DOWNEY SHOW; THE ROBERTA QUINLAN SHOW

MOLLOY FOX

25 JULY 1990–15 AUGUST 1990   Half-hour sitcom about a thirteen-year-old girl who moved in with her father and his family in Beverly Hills after her mother's death. With Mayim Bialik as Molloy Martin, a performer on *Wonderland,* a children's TV show; Kevin Scannell as her father, Paul, program director at a radio station; Pamela Brull as her stepmother, Lynn, a designer; Jennifer Aniston as her self-absorbed older stepsister, Courtney; Luke Edwards as her younger stepbrother, Jason; I. M. Hobson as Simon, one of the adult performers on *Wonderland*; Ashley Maw as Sara, one of the teen performers; Bumper Robinson as Lewis Jackson, another of the teens; and Terri Hoyos as Marguerita, the maid. George Beckerman created the series.

THE MOLLY PICON SHOW ABC

1 MARCH 1949–12 APRIL 1949   Half-hour variety series hosted by Yiddish actress Molly Picon.

MOMENT OF FEAR NBC

1 JULY 1960–23 SEPTEMBER 1960   First seen during the summer of 1960, this half-hour anthology of thrillers was broadcast live. NBC also televised reruns of other anthology series under the title *Moment of Fear* during the summers of 1964 and 1965.

MOMENT OF TRUTH NBC

4 JANUARY 1965–5 NOVEMBER 1965   This half-hour daytime serial was produced in Toronto and was set in an Ontario college town. Principal players included: Douglass Watson as Dr. Bob Wallace, a psychologist; Louise King as his wife, Nancy Wallace; Sandra Scott as Lila, Nancy's sister; Robert Goodier as Walter Leeds; Lynne Gorman as his wife, Wilma Leeds; Stephen Levy as Jack Williams; Barbara Pierce as Sheila; Michael Dodds as Johnny; Toby Tarnow as Carol; Lucy Warner as Helen Gould; Mira Pawluk as Barbara Harris; Peter Donat as Vince Conway; Ann Campbell as Diane; Alan Bly as Arthur; John Bethune as Dr. Gil Bennett; Ivor Barry as

Dr. Russell Wingate; Fernande Giroux as Monique; John Horton as Eric; Chris Wiggins as Dexter; and Anne Collings as Kathy. After a ten-month run the half-hour series was replaced by *Days of Our Lives*.

MOMENTS OF MUSIC   ABC
24 JULY 1951–11 SEPTEMBER 1951   A fifteen-minute filmed musical interlude.

THE MOMMIES   NBC
18 SEPTEMBER 1993–10 SEPTEMBER 1994; 2 JANUARY 1995–3 APRIL 1995; 10 JUNE 1995   Half-hour sitcom based on the standup comedy routines of housewives Marilyn Kentz and Caryl Kristensen, who joked about the topics they knew best: domestic life and motherhood. Kentz and Kristensen appeared as Marilyn Larson and Caryl Kellogg, next-door neighbors and best friends. Joining them were David Dukes as Marilyn's husband, Jack, an accountant; Robin Thomas (1993–1994) as Caryl's husband, Paul, a computer troubleshooter; Ashley Peldon as Casey, Jack and Marilyn's young daughter; Shiloh Strong as Adam, Jack and Marilyn's teenage son; Sam Gifaldi as Danny, Caryl and Paul's older son; Ryan Merriman as Blake, Caryl and Paul's younger son (a third son, Zack, was born during the 1993–1994 season); and Jennifer Blanc as Tiffany, Adam's dimwitted girlfriend. Over the course of the next season and a half, several changes occurred, most of them involving the addition of adult characters and the de-emphasis of the children. Julia Duffy was added in the late fall of 1993 as neighbor Barb Ballantine, who ran the perfect household to the chagrin of Caryl and Marilyn; Taylor Nix was featured as Barb's son, Christopher. In March 1994 Jere Burns (late of *Dear John*) joined as neighbor Tom Booker, a stay-at-home husband who learned the fine points of domestic life from his female cohorts while his wife worked overseas. Also added were Justin Berfield and Courtney Peldon (sister of Ashley Peldon) as Tom's kids, Jason and Beth. The series did not appear on NBC's fall 1994 schedule, but resurfaced in January 1995. Now known as *Mommies,* it featured Kristensen, Kentz, Duffy, and Burns as returning adult regulars, with Lane Davies replacing Robin Thomas as Paul Kellogg. Courtney Peldon and Justin Berfield also appeared, but the other children were rarely seen; David Dukes was no longer a regular, but did appear in some episodes.

MONA McCLUSKEY   NBC
16 SEPTEMBER 1965–14 APRIL 1966   Half-hour sitcom about a glamorous movie star struggling to make ends meet on the salary of her serviceman husband. With Juliet Prowse as Mona Carroll McCluskey (known professionally as Mona Jackson); Denny Miller as her husband, Sergeant Mike McCluskey of the U.S. Air Force; Herbert Rudley as General Crone; Bartlett Robinson as Mr. Caldwell, Mona's producer; Robert Strauss as Sergeant Stan Gruzewsky, a friend of Mike's; Elena Verdugo as Alice, Stan's girlfriend; and Frank Wilcox as General Somers. George Burns produced the series.

MONCHHICHIS   ABC
10 SEPTEMBER 1983–1 SEPTEMBER 1984   The central characters on this Saturday-morning cartoon series were the Monchhichis, a group of happy little humanoids who lived in the treetops of Monchhia, a land ruled by a kind wizard. Their idyllic existence was threatened by the gloomy Grumplins of nearby Grumplor.

THE MONEY MAZE   ABC
23 DECEMBER 1974–4 JULY 1975   On this daytime game show, hosted by Nick Clooney, contestants first answered questions; the winning contestant then tried to guide his or her spouse through a maze for prizes. Don Lipp was the producer.

MONITOR (FIRST CAMERA)   NBC
12 MARCH 1983–1 APRIL 1984   Another attempt by NBC to launch a viable television newsmagazine series, *Monitor* was introduced some seven months after the demise of its predecessor, *NBC Magazine*. The title *Monitor* was borrowed from the network's long-running weekend radio service. The hour series premiered in March 1983 in one

of NBC's weakest time slots, Saturdays at 10:00 p.m. (*NBC Magazine with David Brinkley* had foundered there during the 1980–1981 season), and despite critical praise, consistently finished at the bottom of the ratings heap. Its hosts were Lloyd Dobyns, Steve Delaney, and Rebecca Sobel. In the fall of 1983, the network revamped the program; the new show sported a new title—*First Camera*—a new set, new music, and a new reporter (Mark Nykanen). It also received a new time slot: Sundays at 7:00 p.m., directly opposite CBS's eminently successful newsmagazine show *60 Minutes*. This bold scheduling move was viewed as suicidal by some NBC affiliates; nine percent of the NBC stations declined to carry the program. This low "clearance rate" (the lowest of NBC's prime-time shows that season) further helped to guarantee continued low ratings for *First Camera*.

THE MONKEES   NBC
12 SEPTEMBER 1966–19 AUGUST 1968   This half-hour comedy featured a rock-and-roll group that was supposed to be the American version of the Beatles (even the names of the two groups were similar plays on words); the loosely structured show was obviously inspired by the Beatles' films *A Hard Day's Night* and *Help*. Open auditions were held for the four roles, and more than 400 actors were tested by producers Bert Schneider and Robert Rafelson. Four young men were finally selected: Mickey Dolenz, Davy Jones, Mike Nesmith, and Peter Tork. Dolenz had had prior television experience: he had starred in *Circus Boy* (under the name of Mickey Braddock). Nesmith and Tork had had prior musical experience, while Jones had been a jockey in England, his native country. The four spent most of the summer of 1966 learning improvisational acting techniques (the producers wanted spontaneity) and had little time to learn to play music together. Their first records, which they lip-synched on the show, were produced by Don Kirshner, and, except for some of the vocal parts, were actually performed by studio sidemen. Nevertheless, because of the weekly exposure given the group, the early records were tremendously popular: more than eight million Monkees albums had been sold by the end of 1966. By 1967, however, Dolenz, Jones, Nesmith, and Tork, after a heated meeting with Kirshner, secured the right to perform their own music. Their third album, "Headquarters," produced without Kirshner, also proved successful. Their TV series, though popular with younger viewers, was hurt by competition from *Gunsmoke* in its second season and was dropped in 1968; reruns were shown Saturdays on CBS and later on ABC. Mike Nesmith remained in the music business, primarily as a songwriter (he wrote "Different Drum" for Linda Ronstadt and the Stone Poneys) and video producer. Davy Jones and Mickey Dolenz teamed up in 1975 with Tommy Boyce and Bobby Hart (who had written such Monkees's hits as "Last Train to Clarksville"), but the group went nowhere. In the late 1980s three of the original group—Jones, Dolenz, and Tork—teamed up for a successful reunion tour, and were even joined by Nesmith on a few dates; the original series enjoyed a renaissance on MTV. Unfortunately, overeager producers couldn't leave well enough alone, and a new version of the series was trotted out, to disastrous results, in 1987: see *The New Monkees*.

MONOPOLY   ABC
16 JUNE 1990–1 SEPTEMBER 1990   A rare prime-time game show, hosted by Mike Reilly (himself a former *Jeopardy* contestant). Three players competed, standing before a giant Monopoly board; the players worked their way around the board, earning properties and money by answering questions correctly. Each set of properties of the same color was awarded to a single player. In the second round, the players spent some of their money to improve the properties, and traveled around the board a second time. The player with the most amount of money at the end of the game played a bonus round for a possible top prize of $50,000 Kathy Davis rolled the dice for the contestants.

THE MONROES   ABC
7 SEPTEMBER 1966–30 AUGUST 1967   Hour-long western about a pioneer family headed for Wyoming; when the parents drowned in the first episode, the children decided to go on and set up a homestead on the land their father had marked out

years earlier. With Michael Anderson, Jr., as Clayt Monroe, the eldest; Barbara Hershey as Kathy Monroe; Keith Schultz as Jefferson (Big Twin) Monroe; Kevin Schultz as Fenimore (Little Twin) Monroe; Tammy Locke as Amy Monroe, the youngest; Ron Soble as Jim, an Indian whom the Monroes befriended; Liam Sullivan as Major Mapoy, an evil land dealer; Jim Westmoreland as Ruel; and Ben Johnson as Sleeve.

THE MONROES ABC
12 SEPTEMBER 1995–19 OCTOBER 1995   Hour prime time serial, set in Maryland, home state of the politically ambitious Monroe clan. With William Devane as the patriarch, John Monroe, newly announced candidate for governor; Susan Sullivan as his wife, Kathryn Monroe; David Andrews as son Billy, a Congressman; Steven Eckholdt as son James, an astronaut; Cecil Hoffmann as daughter Greer, a lawyer; Tracy Griffith as daughter Ruby, recently (but unhappily) married; Tristan Tait as son Gabriel, who attended Georgetown University; Darryl Theirse as Michael Bradley, a lawyer and trusted family adviser; and Lynn Clark as Anne.

MONSTER SQUAD NBC
11 SEPTEMBER 1976–3 SEPTEMBER 1977   Live-action Saturday-morning kids' show about a night watchman in a wax museum who could summon the resident monsters to help him fight crimes. With Fred Grandy as Walter, the watchman; Henry Polic II as Dracula; Buck Kartalian as Wolfman; and Michael Lane as Frankenstein.

THE MONTE CARLO SHOW SYNDICATED
1980   Patrick Wayne was the host of this hour variety series, taped on location at the Sporting Club in Monte Carlo, Monaco.

THE MONTEFUSCOS NBC
4 SEPTEMBER 1975–23 OCTOBER 1975   Together with *Fay,* another ill-fated Thursday-night sitcom, *The Montefuscos* was the first casualty of the 1975–1976 season. The story of a big Italian-American family living in Connecticut, it featured Joe Sirola as Tony (Papa) Montefusco; Naomi Stevens as Rose (Mama) Montefusco; Ron Carey as their son, Frank, a dentist; Phoebe Dorin as Frank's wife, Theresa; Sal Viscuso as their son, Nunzio, an actor; John Aprea as their son, Joey, a priest; Linda Dano as Angelina, their daughter; Bill Cort as Jim Cooney, Angie's husband; Damon Raskin as Anthony Patrick Cooney, Jim and Angie's son; Dominique Pinassi as Gina, Frank and Theresa's daughter; Jeff Palladini as Anthony Carmine, Frank and Theresa's son; and Robby Paris as Jerome, Frank and Theresa's second son. Bill Persky and Sam Denoff created the show and were its executive producers; Don Van Atta and Bill Idelson produced it.

THE MONTEL WILLIAMS SHOW SYNDICATED
1991–   Hour daytime talk show, hosted by Montel Williams. A former naval intelligence officer, Williams had begun counseling the wives and families of fellow servicemen during his tour of duty. After leaving the Navy he became a motivational speaker. His series was test marketed in several cities in the middle of 1991 before being offered nationally that fall.

MONTY FOX
11 JANUARY 1994–15 FEBRUARY 1994   Ten years after he last played Fonzie on *Happy Days,* Henry Winkler returned to series TV as Monty Richardson, the conservative host of "Rightspeak," a Long Island cable television program, who, when he wasn't battling liberals on the air, battled with his family at home. Also featured were Kate Burton as his wife, Fran, a schoolteacher; David Krumholtz as their fourteen-year-old, David; David Schwimmer as their older son, Greg, a college grad who returned home with his new girlfriend; China Kantner (daughter of Jefferson Airplane members Grace Slick and Paul Kantner) as the girlfriend, Geena, whose nontraditional ways irked Monty; Joyce Guy as Monty's African-American producer, Rita Simon; and Tom McGowan as Monty's announcer, Clifford Walker.

MONTY NASH   SYNDICATED

1971   Half-hour crime show starring Harry Guardino as government investigator Monty Nash.

MONTY PYTHON'S FLYING CIRCUS   PBS

1969–1974   Produced for the BBC and aired in Great Britain from 1969 to 1974, *Monty Python's Flying Circus* was not made available in the United States until 1974. The half-hour series consisted of skits (some filmed, some videotaped), blackouts, and animated sequences, vaguely unified by a common comic thread. Though the show was sometimes uneven, its best moments were probably those which satirized television programming—boring talk shows and pretentious documentaries were favorite targets of the Python troupe. Six young men comprised the group, though only five—Graham Chapman, John Cleese, Eric Idle, Terry Jones, and Michael Palin—appeared on camera regularly. The sixth member and the sole American, Terry Gilliam, designed the animated sequences. Ian MacNaughton produced the show. Only forty-five shows were made (Cleese did not appear in the final half-dozen). Following the series, the troupe reassembled for three movies (*Monty Python and the Holy Grail, Life of Brian,* and *Monty Python's The Meaning of Life*) and a 1982 performance film, *Monty Python Live at the Hollywood Bowl,* and embarked on a number of solo projects in film and television. See also *Fawlty Towers.*

MOON OVER MIAMI   ABC

15 SEPTEMBER 1993–22 DECEMBER 1993   A clone of *Moonlighting,* this hour private eye show starred Bill Campbell and Ally Walker as Walter Tatum and Gwen Cross. Walter, a Miami Beach private detective, ended up with Gwen as his partner after her father hired him to investigate her jumping from a yacht at her wedding. Also featured were Agustin Rodriquez as Tito, and Marlo Marron as Billie, who helped out the principals.

MOONLIGHTING   ABC

3 MARCH 1985–2 APRIL 1985; 6 AUGUST 1985–14 MAY 1989   Described by its creator as "the show that knows it's on television," *Moonlighting* was a witty, fast-paced detective show beset by production problems that hastened its cancellation. The series' first two seasons went fairly smoothly, but a bungled story line, unavailable stars, and behind-the-scenes personality conflicts all contributed to a rocky final two seasons.

Inspired by the 1940 film *His Girl Friday,* starring Cary Grant and Rosalind Russell, Glenn Gordon Caron sold ABC on the idea of a series about a former high-fashion model who discovered that her business manager had embezzled most of her fortune. One of the remaining assets was the Blue Moon Detective Agency, with a fast-talking male private eye who was able to persuade her to keep the business. Caron envisioned a series with rapid, overlapping dialogue and with sexual chemistry between the two stars. Cybill Shepherd, herself a former high-fashion model, agreed to play the female lead, Maddie Hayes. Bruce Willis, a virtual unknown, was selected as the male lead, David Addison. The chemistry was there: Shepherd played the icy Maddie to the hilt, deftly turning away David's incessant amorous advances. Allyce Beasley played the third regular, secretary Agnes Dipesto.

The writers had fun, churning out pages of dialog for David and Maddie full of rhymes, puns, in-jokes, and double entendres. Sometimes, the characters commented on the plot or talked directly to the camera. A 1985 episode was produced in black and white. One 1986 program was a full-dress version of Shakespeare's *The Taming of the Shrew,* while another referred slyly to the show's having won only one Emmy out of the sixteen for which it had been nominated. Unfortunately, the elaborate productions led to production delays and cost overruns. Only twenty episodes were produced during the 1985–1986 season, at least two short of the expected number. One episode ran short of the usual forty-eight minutes; Willis and Shepherd simply talked to the camera to fill the gap. Some shows were not delivered until a day or two before airtime, which prevented them from being promoted. In other cases, reruns had to be substituted at the last moment. One reason for the delay was the length of the scripts; there was so much dialogue between David and Maddie that scripts were 50 percent longer than those of other hour series. Another reason for the delay was Shepherd's dissatisfaction with many of the scripts; she felt that her character was becoming too bitchy and had grown weary of the "screaming Maddie" formulas. Another new cast member was hired in the fall of 1986: Curtis Armstrong as Herbert Viola, who was hired by Maddie as a temporary accountant but who chose to stay on as an apprentice detective. Secretary Dipesto fell for him.

Nevertheless, the series enjoyed high ratings, finishing in a tie for 20th place in 1985–1986. Ratings improved over the following season, as *Moonlighting* rose to ninth place. The series culminated in March of 1987 with Maddie and David, after two years of foreplay, finally making love. The story line, however, was almost certainly mishandled, as Maddie also made love with another suitor, Sam Crawford (played by Mark Harmon), and eventually married a third man whom she met on a train (the marriage was later annulled); many viewers were turned off by the character's apparent promiscuity.

In real life, complications arose when Cybill Shepherd announced her pregnancy (with twins) in February 1987. When Shepherd was available to film new episodes in June 1987, Willis was away making a movie; when Willis returned, Shepherd was unavailable for medical reasons. She did not return to the set until January 1988 (and when she did, she was upset with all the lines of apology that had been written for Maddie). The result was that only fourteen new episodes were made during the chaotic 1987–1988 season, few of which featured Willis and Shepherd together; one program starred supporting players Beasley and Armstrong. On the show, Maddie Hayes became pregnant as well, but suffered a miscarriage. *Moonlighting* lost about 20 percent of its audience that season, but still managed to finish twelfth in the ratings race.

Tensions escalated before the 1988–1989 season got underway. A power struggle between Caron and Shepherd resulted in Caron's departure from the series; three of the show's writers also left. Jay Daniels took over as executive producer, and the series finished its run with a disappointing 41st-place finish, following several changes of time slot.

MORECAMBE AND WISE   SYNDICATED
1980   Half-hour comedy series hosted by the British comedy duo Eric Morecambe and Ernie Wise.

THE MOREY AMSTERDAM SHOW   CBS/DUMONT
17 DECEMBER 1948–7 MARCH 1949 (CBS); 21 APRIL 1949–12 OCTOBER 1950 (DUMONT)   Morey Amsterdam, the cello-stroking comic with a joke on any subject, hosted a half-hour comedy-variety series which began on CBS and later moved to the DuMont network. The CBS version was set at a nightspot known as the Golden Goose Café and featured Art Carney (in one of his earliest TV roles) as Charlie the doorman and Jacqueline Susann (who would later write several best-selling novels) as Lola the cigarette girl. Susann's husband, Irving Mansfield, produced and directed the show. The DuMont version was set at the Silver Swan Café and featured Art Carney as Newton the waiter and singer Vic Damone. Amsterdam later cohosted *Broadway Open House* and appeared on *The Dick Van Dyke Show*.

MORK & MINDY   ABC
14 SEPTEMBER 1978–12 AUGUST 1982   A sitcom about an alien visiting Earth, *Mork & Mindy* was the most popular new series of the 1978–1979 season. Unfortunately, personnel and time-slot changes proved disastrous, and *Mork & Mindy* was never able to win back its large first-season following. The show starred Robin Williams, a brilliant improvisational comedian with almost no television experience, as Mork, a free-spirited humanoid who was an outcast on his native planet, Ork, where emotions had been bred out of the citizenry. Dispatched to Earth to learn more about its backward ways, Mork's eggshaped space capsule landed in Boulder, Colorado. There Mork met a young woman, Mindy, and persuaded her to let him stay in her apartment while he studied human civilization; gradually, they fell in love. Pam Dawber costarred as Mindy McConnell, who introduced Mork to a world of emotions and educated him about human behavior.

Also featured during the first season were: Conrad Janis as Mindy's square father, Fred McConnell, who owned a music store; Elizabeth Kerr as Mindy's hip grandmother, Cora Hudson; and Jeffrey Jacquet as Eugene, a black youngster who frequented the store. By the end of the season two other regulars had been added: Tom Poston as the downcast downstairs neighbor, Franklin Bickley, who designed greeting cards; and Robert Donner as Exidor, a demented Earthling who was convinced that the Venusians were coming.

Scheduled on Thursdays during its first season, *Mork & Mindy* was a smash hit, finishing third in the annual ratings; some of Mork's sayings, such as "Na-noo, na-noo" (Orkan for "hello") and "Shazbat!" ("drat!") crept into the American vocabulary. Curiously, the network decided to move the show to Sundays for the following season, assuming that its audience would follow. It didn't—ratings plummeted, and *Mork & Mindy* was moved back to Thursdays in January 1980. But even there, the show failed to perform as well as it had a year earlier. It ended the season at 26th in the ratings. Another reason for this drop in popularity may have been the departure of three regulars: Janis, Kerr, and Jacquet. It was explained that Fred McConnell had been hired as a trombonist with the Salt Lake City Orchestra. Three new regulars were added in 1979: Jim Staahl as Mindy's boorish cousin, Nelson Flavor; Jay Thomas as Remo DaVinci, who moved to Boulder from New York to open the New York Delicatessen there; and Gina Hecht as Remo's sister, Jean DaVinci, a med student. Conrad Janis was rehired (and given a substantial raise) for the 1980–1981 season, and Elizabeth Kerr also reappeared occasionally. Crissy Wilzak joined the cast as Glenda Comstock, an obnoxious neighbor. By this time, Mindy had landed a job at a TV station; Foster Brooks appeared as Mr. Sternhagen, the station manager, and Pat Cranshaw played camera operator Jake Loomis.

In a final effort to revitalize the show, which had dropped to 49th in the ratings, veteran improvisationist Jonathan Winters was hired for the 1981–1982 season. Winters was Robin Williams's comedic idol, and it was hoped that the chemistry between the two would lift the show to new heights. To incorporate Winters as a character, Mork proposed to Mindy and married her on 15 October 1981. They then hatched a son, Mearth, who was played by Winters (on Ork, children were born full grown in body but not in mind, from giant eggs). The results were disappointing, as *Mork & Mindy* concluded its run that year, 60th in the ratings. The series lasted four seasons, one longer than the previous alien-visits-Earth sitcom, *My Favorite Martian*.

The half-hour series was created by Garry Marshall, Joe Glauberg, and Dale McRaven. The character first appeared on an episode of *Happy Days,* another popular Marshall sitcom. Ralph James provided the voice of Orson, Mork's Orkan superior, to whom Mork dutifully reported at the end of each of the 95 episodes. In 1982 a cartoon version appeared (see following).

THE MORK & MINDY/LAVERNE & SHIRLEY/FONZ HOUR ABC
25 SEPTEMBER 1982–3 SEPTEMBER 1983   This Saturday-morning cartoon show consisted of two segments. "Mork & Mindy," based on the prime-time series that had been canceled a month earlier, found a teenaged Mork attending high school, and living with Mindy and her father; Mork's six-legged dog, Doyng, also hung around, as did their young black friend, Eugene. Robin Williams and Pam Dawber supplied their own voices for the series. In "Laverne & Shirley," also based on the prime-time series, the two women were in the Army, stationed at Camp Fillmore, where their friend Fonz (and his dog, Mr. Cool) was assigned to the motor pool. Both "Laverne & Shirley" and "Fonz" had been the central characters in other cartoon series (see also *The Fonz and the Happy Days Gang; Laverne & Shirley*).

MORNING
See CBS MORNING NEWS

MORNING COURT ABC
10 OCTOBER 1960–12 MAY 1961   This half-hour daytime entry presented simulated court cases and was a companion to ABC's longer-running courtroom show, *Day in Court.* William Gwinn and Georgianna Hardy presided over the morning sessions.

THE MORNING PROGRAM
See CBS MORNING NEWS

THE MORNING SHOW CBS
15 MARCH 1954–5 APRIL 1957 An unsuccessful attempt to compete with NBC's *Today* show, *The Morning Show* went through several changes of personnel during its three low-rated years. CBS newsman Walter Cronkite, who was then hosting *You Are There*, was the first host; Charles Collingwood read the news, and other features were handled by Estelle Parsons, Jack Lyman, and the Bil and Cora Baird Puppets. Cronkite had left by the summer of 1954, and on 16 August, Jack Paar replaced him. Paar had previously hosted a weekly daytime show, and he brought with him most of the regulars from that series: pianist Jose Melis, Pupi Campo and his Orchestra, and singer Edie Adams. Betty Clooney and Charlie Applewhite also joined *The Morning Show* when Paar took over, and Charles Collingwood and the Baird Puppets also remained. By November of 1954, the Baird Puppets were gone, and when Paar took a brief vacation that winter, a young comedian named Johnny Carson filled in. Paar lasted until June 1955, and was succeeded briefly by John Henry Faulk, the folksy humorist who was blacklisted a few months later (and who subsequently won a libel suit against his accusers). Faulk was succeeded late in 1955 by Dick Van Dyke. Van Dyke's regulars included singers Merv Griffin and Sandy Stewart. Ginger Stanley was the weather forecaster; as a stunt, for one three-week period in 1956 she was forced to do the weather chores while immersed in a tank of water. Will Rogers, Jr., was the last host of the series, and when he took over on 20 February 1956, the show's title was changed to *Good Morning*. Before the show left the air fourteen months later, its title was again changed to *The Will Rogers, Jr. Show.* The network later introduced *The Jimmy Dean Show* at the same hour (7 a.m.) as *The Morning Show,* but shifted Dean to a later time slot after a few weeks. The idea of a morning show was shelved until 1963, when *The CBS Morning News* was introduced. *The Morning Show* began as a two-hour program and was reduced to one hour on 3 October 1955, when *Captain Kangaroo* premiered in the 8 a.m. slot. Among the writers for *The Morning Show* was Barbara Walters, who would later cohost *Today*.

MORNING STAR NBC
27 SEPTEMBER 1965–1 JULY 1966 This daytime serial starred Elizabeth Perry and Shary Marshall as Katy Elliott, a fashion designer who moved to New York from New England after her fiancé had been killed. Also featured were Adrienne Ellis as her younger sister Jan; Nina Roman as Liz; Olive Dunbar as Ann Burton; Edward Mallory as Bill Porter; Ed Prentiss as Uncle Ed; Sheila Bromley as Aunt Milly; and Burt Douglas as Gregory Ross.

MORNING STRETCH SYNDICATED
1981 Half-hour exercise show hosted by Joanie Greggains. The series had begun as a local program on San Francisco's KPIX-TV in 1980.

MORNINGSTAR/EVENINGSTAR CBS
25 MARCH 1986–6 MAY 1986 Earl (*The Waltons*) Hamner developed this sappy dramatic series about a group of orphans who moved into an old folks' home (Eveningstar) after a fire destroyed the orphanage (Morningstar); the idea was that the two generations would learn from each other. Appearing as the seniors were: Mason Adams as Gordon Blair; Jeff Corey as Bill MacGregor; Scatman Crothers as Excell Dennis; Ketty Lester as Nora Blake; Kate Reid as Martha Cameron; Sylvia Sidney as Binnie Baylor; Elizabeth Wilson as Kathy Kelly; and Teresa Wright as Alice Blair, Gordon's wife. Sherry Hursey and Darrell Larson played Debbie Flynn and Bob Lane, the two social workers who concocted the idea, and who themselves were lovers. The youngsters were played by Missy Francis as Sarah Bishop; David Goldsmith as Martin Palmer; Chris Peters as Kevin Murphy; Leaf Phoenix as Doug Roberts; Ebonie Smith as Eugenia Waters; and Fred Savage as Sarah's mute brother, Alan Bishop.

MORTON & HAYES   CBS

24 JULY 1991–28 AUGUST 1991   Rob Reiner paid an affectionate tribute to the slapstick comedy film shorts of the 1930s and 1940s in this offbeat comedy series. Reiner, who created the show with Phil Mishkin, served as the "host" of the program, introducing the supposedly long-lost black and white short films of comedy duo Morton and Hayes; in reality, of course, the shorts were filmed in 1991 specifically for the series. Kevin Pollak and Bob Amaral starred as comics Chick Morton and Eddie Hayes, an Abbott-and-Costello-esque pair.

THE MORTON DOWNEY SHOW   NBC

2 MAY 1949–9 DECEMBER 1949   Irish tenor Morton Downey hosted his own fifteen-minute musical show three nights a week; it was officially titled *Mohawk Showroom* and featured Carmen Mastren's Orchestra and announcer Bob Stanton. See also *The Roberta Quinlan Show*.

THE MORTON DOWNEY, JR., SHOW   SYNDICATED

30 MAY 1988–8 SEPTEMBER 1989   Morton Downey, Jr.'s show was much different from his father's. It was a throwback to the confrontational talk shows pioneered by Joe Pyne and Alan Burke in the late 1960s. *The Morton Downey, Jr., Show* began on 12 October 1987 as a live evening talk show on New York–New Jersey superstation WWOR; the patriotic, chain-smoking host quickly acquired a cult following, especially among young men, for his loud, abrasive style and his penchant for insulting his guests; on one January 1988 show Downey wrapped an American flag around his bottom and told his Iranian guest to kiss it. In May 1988 the show was nationally syndicated and enjoyed a brief reign of popularity. The series' opening featured Downey heading onstage from a corridor to the cheers of his devout audience. On one of the more notorious shows a fight broke out between black activist Roy Innis (who was also involved in an altercation on *Geraldo*) and outspoken black minister Al Sharpton. Another bizarre incident occurred offstage in 1989, when Downey claimed to have been attacked and beaten by skinheads in the San Francisco airport; no corroborating evidence was ever adduced. Inevitably, audiences soon tired of the style, and the show vanished quietly fourteen months after its national premiere.

MOSES THE LAWGIVER   CBS

21 JUNE 1975–2 AUGUST 1975   This six-part miniseries about the life of Moses was filmed in Israel. An Italian-English production, it featured Burt Lancaster as Moses, Irene Papas as Zipporah, Anthony Quayle as Aaron, and Laurent Terzieff as Pharaoh.

THE MOST DEADLY GAME   ABC

10 OCTOBER 1970–16 JANUARY 1971   Hour-long crime show with three ace criminologists: Ralph Bellamy as Ethan Arcane; Yvette Mimieux as Vanessa Smith; and George Maharis as Jonathan Croft. The series was produced by Mort Fine, David Friedkin, and Joan Harrison and was developed by Aaron Spelling.

MOST WANTED   ABC

16 OCTOBER 1976–20 AUGUST 1977   Hour-long crime show about a special unit of the Los Angeles Police Department that went after the big crooks. With Robert Stack as Captain Link Evers; Shelly Novack as Charlie Benson; and Jo Ann Harris as Kate Manners. Quinn Martin, John Wilder, and Paul King were the executive producers.

MOTHER GOOSE AND GRIMM   CBS

14 SEPTEMBER 1991–13 MARCH 1993   Saturday morning animated version of the Mike Peters comic strip about Mother Goose and her madcap mutt, Grimm. During the 1992–1993 season the series was titled *Grimmy*.

MOTHER'S DAY   ABC

13 OCTOBER 1958–2 JANUARY 1959   Dick Van Dyke hosted this daytime game show; each day three mothers competed at household tasks for the chance to win prizes.

MOTHER'S DAY   LIFETIME

1983–1989   Daytime talk show aimed at mothers with young children, hosted by busy Joan Lunden, who was simultaneously cohosting ABC's *Good Morning America*.

THE MOTHERS-IN-LAW   NBC

10 SEPTEMBER 1967–7 SEPTEMBER 1969   Half-hour sitcom about two next-door neighbors whose children intermarried. With Eve Arden as Eve Hubbard; Herbert Rudley as her husband, Herb Hubbard, a lawyer; Roger C. Carmel (1967–1968) and Richard Deacon (1968–1969) as Roger Buell, a TV writer; Kaye Ballard as his wife, Kaye Buell; Jerry Fogel as Roger and Kaye's son, Jerry Buell; and Deborah Walley as Eve and Herb's daughter, Suzie, who married Jerry and lived with him in the Hubbard garage. Desi Arnaz, the executive producer of the series, also appeared occasionally as bullfighter Raphael del Gado.

MOTORMOUSE   ABC

12 SEPTEMBER 1970–4 SEPTEMBER 1971   Formerly featured on *Cattanooga Cats*, Motormouse headlined his own show for one season. The Saturday-morning cartoon show was a Hanna-Barbera production.

THE MOTOROLA TV HOUR   ABC

3 NOVEMBER 1953–18 MAY 1954   Sponsored by Motorola, this hour-long dramatic anthology series alternated on Tuesdays with *The U.S. Steel Hour*. Presentations included: "Outlaw's Reckoning," with Eddie Albert and Jane Wyatt (3 November); "Westward the Sun," with Brian Keith (in his first major TV role, 17 November); "The Brandenburg Gate," with Jack Palance and Maria Riva (1 December); "The Thirteen Clocks," with John Raitt (29 December); and "Love Song," with Oscar Homolka and Lisa Kirk (4 May).

MOTORWEEK   PBS/SYNDICATED

1982–   (PBS); 1993–   (SYNDICATED)   Half-hour weekly informational series on cars — how to purchase them, how to test them, how to drive them, and how to repair them. John Davis hosted, with help from Pat Goss on repair, and Craig Singhaus and Lisa Barrow on other topics. Produced by Maryland Public Television, the series ran on public TV for eleven years before being offered in national syndication in 1993.

THE MOTOWN REVIEW   NBC

9 AUGUST 1985–13 SEPTEMBER 1985   Six-week summer variety hour, hosted by singer-songwriter William "Smokey" Robinson, one of the best-known artists who recorded for Motown Records, the seminal "soul" label founded in Detroit by Berry Gordy, Jr. Other regulars were comedians Arsenio Hall, Cheryl Roads, George Solomon, and Douglas Wood, and The Hitsville Gang Dancers.

THE MOUSE FACTORY   SYNDICATED

1972   Old Walt Disney cartoons and film clips were presented on this half-hour series aimed principally at children. Each show was hosted and narrated by a guest celebrity.

THE MOVIE GAME   SYNDICATED

1969–1970   Films were the subject of this game show. First hosted by Sonny Fox, it featured two three-member teams, each consisting of two stars and one contestant. When Larry Blyden succeeded Fox as host, the format was changed slightly—to two panels of three stars each, playing for a home viewer. Hollywood columnist Army Archerd was also featured on both versions.

MOVIELAND QUIZ   ABC

19 AUGUST 1948–26 OCTOBER 1948   The questions on this half-hour prime-time game show were based on film clips from old movies that were shown to the show's contestants. Arthur Q. Bryan, the first emcee, was succeeded by Ralph Dumke.

MOVIN' ON   NBC

12 SEPTEMBER 1974–14 SEPTEMBER 1976   Hour-long adventure series about a couple of truckers: Claude Akins as gritty Sonny Pruett, and Frank Converse as Will Chandler, an idealistic fellow who had attended law school. During the second season a second pair of truckers was added: Rosey Grier as Benjy and Art Metrano as Moose. Like *Route 66*, a highway adventure show of the 1960s, *Movin' On* was filmed on location all over the United States. Philip D'Antoni and Barry Weitz were the executive producers.

MOYERS: IN SEARCH OF THE CONSTITUTION   PBS

19 APRIL 1987–21 JUNE 1987   Bill Moyers helped celebrate the 200th anniversary of the United States Constitution with this ten-part series, which consisted mainly of interviews with constitutional scholars and with Supreme Court Justices Brennan, Blackmun, and O'Connor.

MOYERS: THE POWER OF THE WORD   PBS

15 SEPTEMBER 1989–20 OCTOBER 1989   Contemporary American poets read from their works and discussed them with host Bill Moyers on this six-part series.

MOYERS: THE PUBLIC MIND   PBS

8 NOVEMBER 1989–29 NOVEMBER 1989   Bill Moyers probed the effects on the American public of public relations, advertising, and political reportage in this thought-provoking four-part series.

MUDDLING THROUGH   CBS

9 JULY 1994–7 SEPTEMBER 1994   Dark sitcom about a woman, recently paroled after shooting her husband, who returned to the family coffee shop, Drego's Oasis. With Stephanie Hodge as the parolee, Connie Drego; Jennifer Aniston as her older daughter, Madeline; Aimee Brooks as her younger daughter, Kerri, a tenth-grader; Scott Waara as Duane Sawyer, the state trooper who had arrested Connie and who was now married to Madeline; D. David Morin as Sonny, Connie's husband; and Hal Landon, Jr., and Hank Underwood as the cafe's two elderly regulars, Gidney and Lyle. Barton Dean created the series.

MUGGSY   NBC

11 SEPTEMBER 1976–2 APRIL 1977   Taped in Bridgeport, Connecticut, this half-hour Saturday-morning children's show starred Sarah McDonnell as Muggsy, a teenager. Also featured were Ben Masters as Nick, her half-brother; Star-Shemah as Clytemnestra, her friend; Donny Cooper as T. P.; Paul Michael as Gus; and Jimmy McCann as Li'l Man. George A. Heinemann was the executive producer, and Joseph F. Callo the producer.

MULLIGAN'S STEW   NBC

25 OCTOBER 1977–13 DECEMBER 1977   The story of "nine people and two bathrooms," *Mulligan's Stew* was a short-lived family drama. Mr. and Mrs. Mulligan had not only their own three kids to care for, but also four nieces and nephews whose parents had been killed in a plane crash in Hawaii. With Lawrence Pressman as Mike Mulligan, a high school teacher and football coach; Elinor Donahue as Jane Mulligan, his wife; Johnny Doran as Mark, their elder son; Julie Anne Haddock as their daughter, Melinda; K. C. Martel as Jimmy, their younger son; Christopher Ciampa as Adam (Moose) Friedman, their nephew; Suzanne Crough as Stevie Friedman, their niece; Lory Kochheim as Polly Friedman, their niece; and Sunshine Lee as Kimmy Nguyen Friedman, their youngest niece, a Vietnamese orphan whom the Friedmans had adopted. Joanna Lee produced the hour series. The show finished dead last—109th—in the 1977–1978 prime-time seasonal ratings race.

THE MUNSTERS   CBS

24 SEPTEMBER 1964–1 SEPTEMBER 1966   Like *The Addams Family,* which premiered on ABC in 1964 and ran for two seasons, *The Munsters* was a half-hour sitcom about

a motley family of misfits. With Fred Gwynne as Herman Munster, a six-foot ten-inch funeral director who resembled Frankenstein's monster; Yvonne DeCarlo as his vampirish wife, Lily Munster; Beverly Owen (to December 1964) and Pat Priest (from January 1965) as their attractive niece, Marilyn Munster, considered by the rest of the clan to be the abnormal one; Al Lewis as Lily's ancient father, Grandpa; and Butch Patrick as Edward Wolfgang (Eddie) Munster, Herman and Lily's lycanthropic young son. Joe Connelly and Bob Mosher, who had worked together on *Leave It to Beaver,* created the series for Universal Television. Three members of the original cast—Gwynne, DeCarlo, and Lewis—were reunited for "The Munsters' Revenge," an NBC made-for-TV movie broadcast 27 February 1981. K. C. Martel played Eddie, and Jo McDonnell played Marilyn. The series was remade in 1988: see *The Munsters Today.*

THE MUNSTERS TODAY SYNDICATED
1988–1990   An updated version of *The Munsters,* completely recast and shot in color on videotape. With John Schuck as Herman Munster; Lee Meriwether as Lily Munster; Howard Morton as Grandpa; Jason Marsden as Eddie; and Hilary Van Dyke as Marilyn. The premise was the Grandpa had accidentally frozen the family back in 1966, and they thawed out twenty-two years later.

MUPPET BABIES CBS
15 SEPTEMBER 1984–5 SEPTEMBER 1992   This Saturday-morning series placed Jim Henson's Muppet characters, famous from *Sesame Street* and *The Muppet Show,* back in time to their early childhood, where they all lived together in a nursery. The Muppet Babies were seen in cartoon form, but the series imaginatively mixed in live-action footage, music, and guest appearances by real-life showbiz people. The series began in 1984 as a thirty-minute show, and expanded to a full hour in 1985, with the title *Jim Henson's Muppets, Babies & Monsters* (in May of 1986 it reverted to *Jim Henson's Muppet Babies*). In the fall of 1987 it was hastily expanded to ninety minutes in order to fill the gap caused by the cancellation of *Garbage Pail Kids,* a controversial cartoon show that never aired. In the fall of 1988 it went back to an hour.

THE MUPPET SHOW SYNDICATED
1976–1981   The Muppets, the lovable puppets created by Jim Henson and company, starred in their own half-hour comedy-variety show. Each week a guest celebrity was also on hand to assist master of ceremonies Kermit the Frog. At one time ABC could have picked up the program, but the network let its option lapse because it did not think that adults would watch the show. Henson then accepted an offer to produce the series in England. It went on to become the most popular first-run syndicated series in TV history, reaching hundreds of millions of viewers in more than one hundred countries.

MURDER ONE ABC
19 SEPTEMBER 1995–   The most highly acclaimed new series of the 1995–1996 season, *Murder One* was created by Steven Bochco. A continuing drama, it presented a first degree murder case, from the crime scene to the jury's verdict, over the course of the season. The series opened with the discovery of the body of a fifteen-year-old girl; charged with murder was a prominent philanthropist who was having an affair with the victim's older sister. The cast included Daniel Benzali as lead defense attorney Teddy Hoffman; Mary McCormack as his associate, Justine Appleton; Michael Hayden as associate Chris Docknovich; Grace Phillips as associate Lisa Gillespie; J. C. Mackenzie as associate Arnold Spivak; Stanley Tucci as the original prime suspect, Richard Cross; Dylan Baker as police detective Arthur Polson; Vanessa Williams as Hoffman's receptionist, Lila Marquette; John Fleck as Hoffman's administrative assistant, Lewis Heinsbergen; Barbara Bosson as prosecutor Miriam Grasso; Kevin Tighe as David Blalock, who was killed off early in the season; Patricia Clarkson as Hoffman's wife, Georgia; and Jason Gedrick as actor Neil Avedon who became the chief suspect and defendant.

MURDER, SHE WROTE   CBS

30 SEPTEMBER 1984–   One of the few series in television history in which the sole
lead character was a woman, *Murder, She Wrote* was one of the most popular series
of the decade. A formulaic whodunnit created by Richard Levinson, William Link,
and Peter S. Fischer, it was reminiscent of their earlier series, *Columbo* and *Ellery
Queen*. It starred Angela Lansbury as Jessica Fletcher, a widowed mystery writer
living in Cabot Cove, Maine, who was often called upon to solve real crimes. Supporting players included Tom Bosley (1984–1988) as Sheriff Amos Tupper; William
Windom (1985–) as Dr. Seth Hazlitt (Windom described his role to a Canadian
reporter as "the eunuch doctor of Cabot Cove with a crusty New England bedside
manner"); Michael Horton (1985–1988) as Jessica's nephew, accountant Grady
Fletcher; and Ron Masak (1988–) as the new sheriff, Mort Metzger, a former New
York cop. One unusual episode, "Strangest of Bargains," was broadcast 3 May 1987;
it reunited Harry Morgan, Jeffrey Lynn, and Martha Scott, three of the stars of the
1949 film *Strange Bargain*. By the 1989–1990 season, Lansbury's role was reduced so
that she was no longer required to star in each episode; on several shows she appeared only at the beginning, to introduce the evening's "guest sleuth." In the fall of
1991 Lansbury returned to the show full-time, as Jessica split her time between Cabot
Cove and New York, where she had taken a teaching job. In subsequent seasons,
Fletcher spent even less time in Cabot Cove, traveling all over the country and the
world to solve crimes. By 1994 *Murder, She Wrote* was the longest currently running
drama on network television, and had consistently placed in the top ten of the annual
Nielsen rankings.

MURPHY BROWN   CBS

14 NOVEMBER 1988–   Half-hour sitcom set in Washington, D.C., at the offices of
F.Y.I., a fictitious TV newsmagazine show. With Candice Bergen as Murphy Brown,
high-strung reporter who gave up booze and cigarettes after a stay at the Betty Ford
Clinic; Grant Shaud as her new, twenty-five-year-old producer, Miles Silverberg;
Faith Ford as empty-headed reporter, and former Miss America, Corky Sherwood;
Joe Regalbuto as intense reporter Frank Fontana; Charles Kimbrough as the stuffy
anchor, Jim Dial; Pat Corley as Phil, owner of Phil's Place, the local watering hole;
and Robert Pastorelli (1988–fall 1994) as Eldin Bernecky, the world's slowest
painter, hired by Murphy to redo her apartment. Occasionally featured over the
several years were Colleen Dewhurst (1988–1991) as Murphy's mother Avery
Brown; John Hostetter as John, the stage manager; Scott Bryce (1989–1993) as Will
Forrest, who married Corky (thereby giving her the name of Corky Sherwood Forrest; they eventually divorced); Alan Oppenheimer (1990–1992) as network executive Gene Kinsella; Julius Carry (1992–fall 1993) as network executive Mitchell
Baldwin; Jane Leeves (1992–fall 1993) as Miles's girlfriend, Audrey; Scott Bakula
(1993–) as reporter Peter Hunt; Garry Marshall (spring 1994–) as network executive Stan Lansing; and Paula Korologos (1995–) as young reporter McGovern. One
of the series's running gags was Murphy's inability to find a suitable secretary; on
almost every episode a new candidate was tried out and was quickly dismissed.
Among the more notable hopefuls were Carol Kester (played by Marcia Wallace,
who had originated the role on *The Bob Newhart Show*) and Stan Lansing's nerdy
nephew (played by Paul Reubens who became a semi-regular) Andrew Lansing;
young Lansing later became a network executive.
    During the 1990–1991 season Murphy had a relationship with Jerry Gold (played
by Jay Thomas), and a brief fling with ex-husband Jake Lowenstein (played by Robin
Thomas; they'd once been married for five days). In the fall of 1991 she learned that
she was pregnant with Jake's baby. She decided to have the child, and to raise it by
herself; the baby was born on the final episode of the season. The event attracted
little attention until Vice President Dan Quayle, in a May 1992 speech addressing the
"poverty of values" in America, criticized the fictional character's decision to bear a
child out of wedlock. The controversy raged during the summer, and propelled
Murphy Brown's fall 1992 premiere to the top of the ratings. Murphy did not refer to
the issue during that episode on which she decided to name her baby Avery, but a
subsequent episode did address the uproar.

Just as she was unable to keep a secretary at work, Murphy was unable to keep a nanny for the baby. Eventually, Eldin (still at work painting her place) agreed to do the job. However, Eldin left in the fall of 1994 to study art (in real life, Robert Pastorelli left for his own sitcom, *Double Rush*). By that time, young Avery was played by Dyllan Christopher. Meanwhile, Miles had begun a relationship with Corky (the two impulsively got married in 1995 but quickly regretted it), and Murphy had embarked on one with Peter Hunt. Christopher Rich was added in 1995 as anchorman Miller Redfield.

One of the few TV series of the 1980s and 1990s to remain in a stable time slot, *Murphy Brown* was a fixture on Mondays at 9 P.M. It cracked Nielsen's Top Ten in the 1991–1992 season, finishing third, and again the following season, finishing fourth. It won a Peabody Award in 1991. Diane English and Joel Shukovsky created the series.

MURPHY'S LAW   ABC
2 NOVEMBER 1988; 3 DECEMBER 1988–18 MARCH 1989   There were two new series in the fall of 1988 with the word *Murphy* in their titles; only one succeeded. *Murphy's Law* was George Segal's second flop series in as many years (see also *Take Five*). Here he played Daedalus Patrick Murphy, an insurance investigator recovering from alcoholism. Maggie Han played model Kimiko Fannuchi, who shared an apartment with Murphy and who sometimes worked as his assistant, and Josh Mostel played Murphy's boss, Wesley Hardin.

MUSCLE   WB
11 JANUARY 1995–24 MAY 1995   One of the first series on the new Warner Bros. Network, this was a half-hour sitcom which, like *Soap*, featured a continuing story line. Set mostly at the Survival Gym, a posh Manhattan health club, the program featured Wendy Benson as Cleo, an aspiring actress; Michael Boatman as Garnett, a media-savvy lawyer; Nestor Carbonell as Johnny, a gigolo; Dan Gauthier as Kent Atkinson, son of the club's late owner; Stephan "Tower" Henneberry as bodybuilder Sam Pippin; Shannon Kenny as Jane Atkinson, widow of the club's owner; Jerry Levine as Robert Bingham, a recently paroled white collar criminal; Amy Pietz as Kent's cousin, Bronwyn Jones, a gay TV anchorwoman; Alan Ruck as Dr. Marshall Gold, a gossipy psychiatrist; T. E. Russell as Victor; and Michole White as Angela.

MUSIC BINGO   NBC/ABC
29 MAY 1958–11 SEPTEMBER 1958 (NBC); 5 DECEMBER 1958–1 JANUARY 1960 (ABC) Two contestants played a version of bingo on this game show. By correctly identifying a song, a contestant won a square on a giant bingo board. Johnny Gilbert hosted the series, which was introduced as a prime-time show over NBC and moved to a daytime slot when it switched networks.

MUSIC COUNTRY   NBC
26 JULY 1973–6 SEPTEMBER 1973; 17 JANUARY 1974–16 MAY 1974   Taped in Nashville, *Music Country* was an hour of country music, all performed by guest artists. The show's official title was *Dean Martin Presents Music Country*.

MUSIC '55   CBS
12 JULY 1955–13 SEPTEMBER 1955   Bandleader Stan Kenton hosted this half-hour musical variety series.

MUSIC FOR A SPRING NIGHT
See MUSIC FOR A SUMMER NIGHT

MUSIC FOR A SUMMER NIGHT   ABC
3 JUNE 1959–21 SEPTEMBER 1959; 2 MARCH 1960–21 SEPTEMBER 1960   This musical variety show featured guest artists and the music of Glenn Osser's Orchestra. From March to May of 1960 it was titled *Music for a Spring Night*.

MUSIC FROM CEDAR GROVE   ABC
23 MAY 1953–26 DECEMBER 1953; 26 JANUARY 1956–19 APRIL 1956   This hour-long musical variety series was broadcast from Frank Dailey's Meadowbrook in Cedar Grove, New Jersey (the show was also titled *Music from Meadowbrook*). In 1953 Jimmy Blaine was the emcee, and music was provided by Ralph Marterie's Orchestra. Singer Bill Williams was also a regular in 1953. When the series returned in 1956, it was in a half-hour format, with Blaine as emcee and Ralph Flanagan's Orchestra; Hannah Flanagan was a regular guest.

MUSIC FROM CHICAGO   DUMONT
15 APRIL 1951–17 JUNE 1951   Another of the several Chicago-based music and variety shows, this one was broadcast on Sundays over the DuMont network. See also *Chicago Jazz; Chicago Symphony Chamber Orchestra; Concert Tonight; The Music Room; Music in Velvet; Sing-Co-Pation;* and *Vaudeo Varieties*.

MUSIC HALL AMERICA   SYNDICATED
1976   Hour-long country music series, taped in Nashville.

MUSIC IN VELVET   ABC
16 JANUARY 1949–17 APRIL 1949; 15 JULY 1951–28 OCTOBER 1951   Broadcast from Chicago, *Music in Velvet* was first seen in the Midwest in 1948 and was one of the first shows to be televised live in the East after coaxial cable facilities linking Chicago and New York became operational early in 1949. Don Lindley and the Velveteers were featured on the 1949 version, which was produced and directed by Ed Skotch. Rex Maupin and his orchestra were featured on the 1951 version of the half-hour show.

MUSIC ON ICE   NBC
8 MAY 1960–11 SEPTEMBER 1960   This frosty summer variety show, taped somewhere in Brooklyn, was hosted by singer Johnny Desmond and featured skater Jacqueline du Bief, the singing Skip-Jacks, the dancing Blades, and the Bob Boucher Orchestra.

THE MUSIC SCENE   ABC
22 SEPTEMBER 1969–12 JANUARY 1970   This popular music series featured appearances by guest artists from the rock and folk scene. The forty-five-minute series preceded *The New People*, another forty-five-minute series, on Monday nights. It was hosted by comedian David Steinberg, and the resident troupe of performers included Chris Bokeno, Larry Hankin, Paul Reid Roman, Christopher Ross, and Lily Tomlin (who joined *Laugh-In* shortly after the series folded). Stan Harris and Ken Fritz were the producers.

THE MUSIC SHOP   NBC
11 JANUARY 1959–8 MARCH 1959   Half-hour musical variety show, hosted by bandleader Buddy Bregman. Rock-and-roller Ritchie Valens made a rare TV appearance on the premiere, just three weeks before his death in a plane crash.

THE MUSIC SHOW   DUMONT
19 MAY 1953–17 OCTOBER 1954   Broadcast from Chicago, this half-hour series presented light classical and popular selections without commercial interruptions. Robert Trendler conducted the orchestra, and vocalists included Mike Douglas, Henri Noel, Jackie Van, and Eleanore Warner. J. E. Faraghan produced the series and Barry McKinley directed it.

MUSICAL CHAIRS   NBC
9 JULY 1955–17 SEPTEMBER 1955   The first of the two programs by this title was a prime-time game show hosted by Bill Leyden (*It Could Be You*), who quizzed a celebrity panel on musical subjects. The panel included Mel Blanc, singer Peggy King, lyricist Johnny Mercer, and trumpeter Bobby Troup.

MUSICAL CHAIRS   CBS

16 JUNE 1975–31 OCTOBER 1975   The second of the two shows titled *Musical Chairs* was a daytime game show hosted by singer Adam Wade. Contestants listened to songs and then tried to select the next line of the song from three choices shown to them. Produced by Bill W. Chastain, Jr., *Musical Chairs* is notable in that it was the first game show emceed by a black performer.

MUSICAL COMEDY TIME   NBC

2 OCTOBER 1950–19 MARCH 1951   This Monday-night anthology series shared a time slot with *Robert Montgomery Presents*. Presentations included: "Anything Goes," with Martha Raye (2 October); "Babes in Toyland," with Dennis King (25 December); "No No Nanette," with Jackie Gleason and Ann Crowley (5 March); and "Flying High," with Bert Lahr (19 March).

MUSICAL MERRY-GO-ROUND   NBC

2 OCTOBER 1947–25 MARCH 1949   Twenty-minute musical variety show hosted by Jack Kilty.

MUSICAL MINIATURES   NBC

10 MAY 1948–12 JANUARY 1949   A twenty-minute musical series with no regulars, broadcast two or three times a week before the evening newsreel. The show was also aired under the titles *Topical Tunes* and *Musical Almanac*. It was also seen irregularly later in 1949.

MY FAVORITE HUSBAND   CBS

12 SEPTEMBER 1953–27 DECEMBER 1955   This domestic sitcom, starring Lucille Ball, came to radio in 1948 and lasted three seasons there. It was resurrected for TV in 1953. Because Lucille Ball was then starring in *I Love Lucy,* Joan Caulfield was chosen for the part of Liz Cooper, the scatterbrained wife of George Cooper, a Manhattan banker; Barry Nelson costarred as George. Also featured were Alix Talton as neighbor Myra Cobb and Bob Sweeney as her husband, Gilmore Cobb. In the fall of 1955 Vanessa Brown replaced Joan Caulfield as Liz Cooper, and Alix Talton was seen as neighbor Myra Shepard; Bob Sweeney also left the series and Dan Tobin joined the TV cast as Myra's husband, Oliver Shepard. The half-hour show was directed by George Cahan, who was the husband of costar Talton. The latter episodes were rerun on CBS during the summer of 1957.

MY FAVORITE MARTIAN   CBS

29 SEPTEMBER 1963–4 SEPTEMBER 1966   Half-hour sitcom about a Martian whose spaceship crash landed on Earth and who moved in with the reporter who witnessed the crash landing. With Bill Bixby as Tim O'Hara, reporter for the Los Angeles *Sun;* Ray Walston as the Martian, who took the name Martin O'Hara (Tim's uncle) when he settled in; Pamela Britton as Mrs. Lorelei Brown, Tim's befuddled landlady; and Alan Hewitt as Bill Brennan, a Los Angeles cop. Jack Chertok produced the series, of which 107 episodes were made. See also *My Favorite Martians*.

MY FAVORITE MARTIANS   CBS

8 SEPTEMBER 1973–30 AUGUST 1975   This Saturday-morning cartoon show was derived from the 1963 sitcom, *My Favorite Martian*. In the cartoon version, there were three Martians who were discovered by two Earthlings. Norm Prescott and Lou Scheimer produced the series.

MY FAVORITE STORY   SYNDICATED

1953–1954   This half-hour filmed dramatic anthology series was hosted by Adolphe Menjou.

MY FRIEND FLICKA   CBS

10 FEBRUARY 1956–1 FEBRUARY 1957   *My Friend Flicka,* a half-hour western based on Mary O'Hara's book (and a 1943 movie), was the first filmed series from 20th

Century-Fox. Set at the Goose Bar Ranch in Montana at the turn of the century, it featured Johnny Washbrook as Ken McLaughlin; Gene Evans as his father, Rob McLaughlin; Anita Louise as his mother, Nell McLaughlin; and Frank Ferguson as Gus the ranch hand. Flicka, Ken's equine companion, was played by an Arabian sorrel named Wahama. The thirty-nine half-hour episodes were filmed in color.

MY FRIEND IRMA
CBS

8 JANUARY 1952–25 JUNE 1954   Created by Cy Howard, *My Friend Irma* began on radio in 1947 and ran for seven years. The television adaptation was less successful, even though most of the members of the radio cast recreated their roles for TV. The half-hour sitcom starred Marie Wilson as Irma Peterson, a not-too-bright legal secretary living in a New York boardinghouse; Cathy Lewis (1952–1953) as her roommate, Jane Stacey, a level-headed young woman who, like George Burns on *The Burns and Allen Show,* addressed the viewing audience directly from time to time during the show; Sid Tomack (1952–1953) as Al, Irma's boyfriend, a scheming con man; Brooks West as Richard Rhinelander III, Jane's wealthy boyfriend; Gloria Gordon as Mrs. O'Reilly, proprietor of the boardinghouse; Donald McBride as Mr. Clyde, Irma's boss; and Richard Eyer as Bobby, Irma's young nephew. In the fall of 1953 Mary Shipp succeeded Cathy Lewis as Irma's new roommate, newspaper reporter Kay Foster, and Hal March replaced Sid Tomack as Irma's new boyfriend, Joe. The series was produced by Nat Perrin and directed by Richard Whorf; in the fall of 1952 it became the first series to be broadcast from CBS's Television City facility in Hollywood.

MY FRIEND TONY
NBC

5 JANUARY 1969–31 AUGUST 1969   Hour-long crime show with James Whitmore as Professor John Woodruff, teacher of criminology and private detective, and Enzo Cerusico as Tony Novello, Woodruff's partner, an Italian whom Woodruff had met during World War II. Sheldon Leonard created the series and was its executive producer.

MY HERO
NBC

8 NOVEMBER 1952–1 AUGUST 1953   Half-hour sitcom starring Bob Cummings as Bob Beanblossom, an inept real estate salesman; John Litel as Mr. Thackery, his boss; and Julie Bishop as Thackery's secretary and Beanblossom's girlfriend, Julie Marshall. Produced by Mort Green for Don Sharpe Enterprises, *My Hero* was the first of several sitcoms for Cummings: see also *The Bob Cummings Show, Love That Bob,* and *My Living Doll.*

MY LIFE AND TIMES
ABC

24 APRIL 1991–30 MAY 1991   Ron Koslow created this hour series, set in a retirement home in the year 2035, from which an 85-year-old man looked back at events in his life. It featured Tom Irwin as retired writer Ben Miller (Irwin appeared as a younger man in the flashbacks); Helen Hunt as his wife, Rebecca Eastman Miller; and Megan Mullally as Susan, who worked at the retirement home.

MY LITTLE MARGIE
CBS/NBC

16 JUNE 1952–30 JULY 1953 (CBS); 2 SEPTEMBER 1953–24 AUGUST 1955 (NBC)   Half-hour sitcom about a womanizing widower and his meddlesome daughter. With Gale Storm as Margie Albright; Charles Farrell as her father, investment counselor Vern Albright; Don Hayden as Margie's boyfriend, Freddie Wilson; Clarence Kolb as Vern's boss, George Honeywell, president of Honeywell & Todd; Hillary Brooke (1952–1954) as Vern's frequent girlfriend, Roberta Townsend; Gertrude Hoffman as their kindly old neighbor, Mrs. Odetts; and Willie Best as Charlie, the elevator operator in their New York apartment house. Produced by Hal Roach, Jr., and Roland Reed, the series was first introduced as a summer replacement for *I Love Lucy* and found a place on CBS's fall schedule for one season before shifting networks. A radio version was also introduced in 1952. The 126 TV episodes were widely syndicated throughout the 1950s and 1960s.

MY LITTLE PONY AND FRIENDS   SYNDICATED

1986–1990   Half-hour cartoon series featuring the "My Little Pony" characters, based on the popular line of kids' toys, and introducing "The Glo Friends," "The Moondreamers," and "The Potato Head Kids."

MY LIVING DOLL   CBS

27 SEPTEMBER 1964–8 SEPTEMBER 1965   Half-hour sitcom about a psychiatrist and his live-in patient, a female robot. With Bob Cummings as Dr. Bob McDonald; Julie Newmar as Rhoda, the government-built robot (Project AF709); Jack Mullaney as Dr. Peter Robinson, a colleague of McDonald's; Doris Dowling as Irene McDonald, Bob's sister, who also lived at home with Bob and Rhoda; and Nora Marlowe as Mrs. Moffat. Bob Cummings quit the series after twenty-one episodes, and Dr. Robinson became Rhoda's caretaker for the remaining shows (it was explained that Dr. Mc-Donald had been sent to Pakistan).

MY MOTHER THE CAR   NBC

14 SEPTEMBER 1965–6 SEPTEMBER 1966   Universally blasted as one of the feeblest sitcoms of the decade, *My Mother the Car* told the story of a man who heard his late mother's voice emanating from a 1928 Porter. With Jerry Van Dyke as lawyer Dave Crabtree; Maggie Pierce as his wife, Barbara Crabtree; Cindy Eilbacher as their daughter, Cindy; Randy Whipple as their son, Randy; Avery Schreiber as the evil Captain Manzini, an antique automobile collector desperate to add the 1928 Porter to his collection; and Ann Sothern as the voice of Dave's mother, Gladys. Created by Allan Burns and Chris Hayward, the half-hour series was produced by Rod Amateau.

MY PARTNER THE GHOST   SYNDICATED

1973   Produced in England, where it was titled *Randall & Hopkirk (Deceased)*, this lighthearted crime show featured Mike Pratt as private eye Jeff Randall; Kenneth Cope as Marty Hopkirk, Jeff's former partner who was killed on the job but who returned as a ghost (visible only to Randall) to help his associate; and Annette Andre as Marty's widow, Jean Hopkirk, who worked as Randall's secretary.

MY PET MONSTER   ABC

12 SEPTEMBER 1987–3 SEPTEMBER 1988   Saturday-morning cartoon series based on the stuffed toy; in the TV series the toy, who belonged to a boy named Max, could turn into a friendly six-foot-tall monster.

MY SECRET IDENTITY   SYNDICATED

1988–1991   Half-hour syndicated sitcom, produced in Canada, about a teenage boy who became endowed with superpowers after his accidental exposure to a scientific experiment. With Jerry O'Connell as the teenager, Andrew Clements; Derek Mc-Grath as the scientist, Dr. Jeffcoat, Andrew's next-door neighbor; Wanda Cannon as Jerry's mother, Stephanie; and Marsha Moreau as Jerry's kid sister, Erin.

MY SISTER EILEEN   CBS

5 OCTOBER 1960–12 APRIL 1961   Ruth McKinney's book was the subject of two movies and this half-hour comedy series. With Elaine Stritch as Ruth Sherwood, magazine writer; Shirley Bonne as her sister, Eileen Sherwood, an actress; Leon Belasco as Mr. Appopolous, their Greenwich Village landlord; Rose Marie as Bertha, a friend of theirs; Jack Weston as Chick Adams, a reporter; Stubby Kaye as Marty, Eileen's agent; and Raymond Bailey as Mr. D. X. Beaumont, Ruth's boss.

MY SISTER SAM   CBS

6 OCTOBER 1986–7 NOVEMBER 1987; 22 MARCH 1988–12 APRIL 1988   Half-hour sitcom about a San Francisco photographer whose kid sister moved in with her. With Pam Dawber as Samantha (Sam) Russell; Rebecca Schaeffer as Patti, her sixteen-year-old sister, a sophomore at Fillmore High; Jenny O'Hara as Dixie Randazzo, Sam's assistant; Joel Brooks as J. D. Lucas, Sam's agent; and David Naughton as Jack

Kincaid, a photojournalist who lived across the hall from Sam and Patti. Diane English was executive producer. The show fared well in its first season, ranking 21st in the prime-time ratings; a shift to a Saturday time slot in the fall of 1987 proved disastrous, as the series slipped to 84th place and was lifted in November; a few more episodes surfaced in the spring of 1988. In July 1989 twenty-one-year-old Rebecca Schaeffer was shot and killed outside her West Hollywood apartment by an obsessed fan.

MY SO-CALLED LIFE ABC
25 AUGUST 1994–26 JANUARY 1995   Created by Marshall Herskovitz and Edward Zwick, the duo responsible for *thirtysomething*, this hour dramatic series was set in suburban Pittsburgh, and examined life from a tenth grader's point of view. It starred Claire Danes as frequently confused fifteen-year-old Angela Chase, and featured Bess Armstrong and Tom Irwin as her parents, Patty and Graham, who ran a printing business; Lisa Wilhoit as her younger sister, Danielle; A. J. Langer as Angela's flaky new pal, Rayanne Graf; Wilson Cruz as gay teen Rickie Vasquez; Jared Leto as teen hunk Jordan Catalano; Devon Odessa as Sharon; and Devon Gummersall as nerdy neighbor Brian Krakow. Occasionally featured were: Patti D'Arbanville-Quinn as Amber, Rayanne's mom; Mary Kay Place as Camille, Sharon's mom; May Quigley as Ms. Lerner; and Lisa Waltz as Hallie Lowenthal. Although praised by the critics and popular with teens, *My So-Called Life* failed to attract a large enough audience and was dropped, amid protests, in midseason. MTV picked up the reruns in April 1995.

MY SON JEEP NBC
4 JULY 1953–22 SEPTEMBER 1953   Half-hour sitcom about a widower and his young son. With Jeffrey Lynn as Doc Allison; Martin Huston as his son, Jeep; Anne Sargent as Barbara, Doc's receptionist and secretary; Betty Lou Keim as Jeep's older sister, Peggy; and Leona Powers as the housekeeper. Though regular broadcasting of the series did not begin until July, a "sneak preview" was telecast 3 June 1953.

MY TALK SHOW SYNDICATED
1990   Like *Fernwood 2-Night* of the late 1970s, *My Talk Show* attempted to parody the talk show format. It was set in the living room of a Derby, Wisconsin, homemaker. Cynthia Stevenson played the host, Jennifer Bass, and Stephanie Hodge played Jennifer's next-door neighbor and cohost, Angela Davenport. Before the end of the series's brief run, Stevenson had been replaced by Debra McGrath, as Anne Marie Snelling, from whose living room the show was now broadcast. Like *Fernwood 2-Night*, the show's guests included both real-life celebrities and fictional guests played by actors.

MY THREE SONS ABC/CBS
29 SEPTEMBER 1960–2 SEPTEMBER 1965 (ABC); 16 SEPTEMBER 1965–24 AUGUST 1972 (CBS)   Second only to *Ozzie and Harriet* as network television's longest-running situation comedy, *My Three Sons* starred Fred MacMurray as widower Steve Douglas, a West Coast aerodynamics engineer trying to raise three boys. His first "three sons" were played by Tim Considine as Mike, the eldest; Don Grady (a onetime Mouseketeer) as Robbie; and Stanley Livingston as Chip, the youngest. Also featured was William Frawley as the boys' grandfather, "Bub" O'Casey, who also resided in the Douglas household. In the fall of 1963 Meredith MacRae joined the cast as Mike's girlfriend, Sally Morrison. Midway through the 1964–1965 season William Frawley left the series for health reasons, and William Demarest was brought in as Charley O'Casey, the boys' live-in uncle. Several more changes took place in the fall of 1965 as *My Three Sons* shifted networks: eldest son Mike married Sally, and the two were written out of the series; a new "son" joined the household: Ernie, a bespectacled orphan, was adopted by Steve. The role was played by Barry Livingston, younger brother of costar Stanley Livingston. Tina Cole joined the crew a year later as Robbie's girlfriend, Katie Miller; she and Robbie subsequently got married, continued to live at home, and eventually had triplets. The three youngest Douglases—Charlie, Steve,

and Robbie, Jr.— were played by Michael, Daniel, and Joseph Todd. In the fall of 1969 Steve Douglas remarried. His new wife, Barbara Harper (played by Beverly Garland), had been one of Ernie's high school teachers; Barbara was a widow and the mother of a small daughter, Dodie (played by Dawn Lyn). In the fall of 1970 Ronnie Troup joined the cast as Polly Williams, a college classmate of Chip (the original youngest son); she and Chip were married that year. Don Fedderson was the executive producer of the series.

MY TRUE STORY   ABC
5 MAY 1950–22 SEPTEMBER 1950   Produced in cooperation with *True Story* magazine, this half-hour dramatic anthology series presented stories based on the ostensibly true accounts from the periodical. The television show was not nearly as successful as the radio adaptation, which ran from 1943 to 1961. Charles Powers was the producer and director of the television version.

MY TWO DADS   NBC
20 SEPTEMBER 1987–28 FEBRUARY 1988; 5 JUNE 1988–29 JULY 1988; 11 JANUARY 1989– 10 JANUARY 1990; 5 MARCH 1990–30 APRIL 1990; 2 JUNE 1990–16 JUNE 1990   A premise for a TV series that would have been inconceivable a generation earlier was calmly accepted in this sitcom. A single mother died, leaving her twelve-year-old daughter to the two men she had loved thirteen years ago, either of whom could be her father. The two men, whose lifestyles were vastly different, accepted the assignment, moving in together to help raise the child. The cast included: Paul Reiser as financial analyst Michael Taylor; Greg Evigan as artist Joey Harris; Staci Keanan as the girl, Nicole Bradford; Florence Stanley as Judge Wilbur, who oversaw the unusual arrangement; Dick Butkus (1987–1989) as Ed Klawicki, who owned a nearby diner; Vonni Ribisi as Nicole's boyfriend, Cory Kupkus; Amy Hathaway as her friend, Shelby Haskell; Chad Allen (1988–1990) as her old boyfriend Zach; and Don Yesso (1989–1990) as Justin, the new chef at the diner.

MY WILDEST DREAMS   FOX
28 MAY 1995–25 JUNE 1995   Half-hour sitcom starring standup comic Lisa Ann Walter as Lisa McGinnis, a wisecracking woman who put her dreams of being a rock star on hold while coping with a husband and two kids. Also featured were John Posey as her husband, Jack; Evan Bonifant as their son, Danny (Lisa and Jack also had a baby daughter, Delilah); Kelly Bishop as Lisa's mother, Gloria; Mary Jo Keenen as Lisa's sister, Stephanie; and Miguel A. Nunez, Jr., as Chandler Trapp, owner of Mound of Sound, the recording studio where Lisa worked.

MY WORLD AND WELCOME TO IT   NBC
15 SEPTEMBER 1969–7 SEPTEMBER 1970   This whimsical sitcom was based loosely on the life and writings of humorist James Thurber. It starred William Windom as John Monroe, a writer and cartoonist for *Manhattanite* magazine who, like Walter Mitty, frequently fantasized about what life could be like; animated sequences were regularly employed to depict Monroe's daydreams and other diversions. Also featured were Joan Hotchkis as Monroe's wife, Ellen; Lisa Gerritsen as their daughter, Lydia; and Harold J. Stone as Monroe's boss, Hamilton Greeley. Henry Morgan was occasionally featured as Monroe's colleague, Phil Jensen (the character was reportedly inspired by that of Robert Benchley). Sheldon Leonard was the executive producer of the half-hour series, and Danny Arnold produced it.

MYSTERIES OF CHINATOWN   ABC
4 DECEMBER 1949–23 OCTOBER 1950   One of the first ABC shows telecast from Hollywood, *Mysteries of Chinatown* was a half-hour crime show set in San Francisco's Chinatown. The cast included Robert Bice, Spencer Chan, Herb Ellis, and Cy Kendall. Ray Buffum produced the series and Richard Goggin directed it.

MYSTERY!

5 FEBRUARY 1980–   Most of the presentations on this mystery anthology series were made in England. Among the highlights have been John Mortimer's "Rumpole of the Bailey," a series of several mysteries starring Leo McKern as barrister Horace Rumpole; "Malice Aforethought," a four-parter with Hywel Bennett and Judy Parfitt; and "Sergeant Cribb," another recurring series, with Alan Dobie. The highlight of the 1984–1985 season was the first of several Sherlock Holmes stories. Unlike the Basil Rathbone–Nigel Bruce movies of the 1940s, these stories were true to Arthur Conan Doyle's original tales, and were set in the late nineteenth century. Jeremy Brett played Holmes brilliantly, ably complemented by David Burke as trusty Doctor Watson. Later highlights included a series of mysteries with David Suchet as Hercule Poirot, a series with Michael Gambon as Chief Inspector Maigret, another with Patrick Malahide as Inspector Alleyn, and still another with Derek Jacobi as Brother Cadfael, a twelfth-century sleuth. The most highly acclaimed of *Mystery!*'s many presentations, however, were the several "Prime Suspect" mysteries, first shown here in January 1992, starring Helen Mirren as Deputy Chief Inspector Jane Tennison. Gene Shalit hosted the series during the 1980 season; Vincent Price succeeded him in 1981. Diana Rigg took over as host in 1989.

THE MYSTERY CHEF NBC

1 MARCH 1949–29 JUNE 1949   One of NBC's first daytime programs, this cooking show was broadcast from Philadelphia, where it was hosted by John MacPherson, the "Mystery Chef." First seen on Tuesday and Thursday afternoons, the show later shifted to Wednesdays.

MYSTERY SCIENCE THEATER 3000 COM

18 NOVEMBER 1989–   An offbeat comedy series in which a janitor and two robots were blasted into space by a team of mad scientists and forced to watch bad movies. The trio, who appeared silhouetted at the bottom of the movie image, proceeded to wisecrack their way through an array of some of the worst motion pictures ever made, such as *Godzilla vs. Megalon*, *Girls Town*, *Invasion U.S.A.*, and *The Slime People*, to name just a few. The series was the brainchild of Joel Hodgson, a former standup comic who sold the idea to a local station in Minneapolis in 1988; a year later it was picked up by the fledgling Comedy Channel, which merged with Ha! into Comedy Central in 1991. Hodgson played Joel Robinson, and series writers Kevin Murphy and Trace Beaulieu provided the voices of the two robots, Tom Servo and Crow. Mike Nelson (who was head writer and had previously played various roles on the show) succeeded Hodgson as the robots' human companion in October 1993. The series, which usually featured hundreds of pop-culture-laden asides from the trio during each telecast, quickly acquired cult status, and won a Peabody Award in 1993.

NBA INSIDE STUFF NBC

27 OCTOBER 1990–   Pro basketball and its players were the subjects of this half-hour Saturday-afternoon series, cohosted by Ahmad Rashad and Julie Moran. Willow Bay succeeded Moran as cohost in 1991.

THE NBC COMEDY HOUR NBC

8 JANUARY 1956–10 JUNE 1956   The successor to *The Colgate Comedy Hour*, *The NBC Comedy Hour* was a Sunday-night variety show hosted by a different guest star each week, except during the spring of 1956, when Gale Storm was the permanent host.

NBC DRAMATIC THEATRE NBC

17 APRIL 1949–10 JULY 1949   Also known as *NBC Repertory Theatre,* this hour anthology series was a temporary replacement for *Philco Television Playhouse.* Vaughn Taylor starred in the premiere telecast, "Mr. Mergenthwirker's Lobblies."

NBC FOLLIES NBC

13 SEPTEMBER 1973–27 DECEMBER 1973   Thursday-night variety hour, hosted by Sammy Davis, Jr. Mickey Rooney was featured in most of the shows.

THE NBC FRIDAY NIGHT MYSTERY NBC

22 OCTOBER 1993–13 MAY 1994   The umbrella title for various two-hour made-for-TV movies. Among the presentations were two "Perry Mason" features, four "Hart to Hart" films (reuniting Robert Wagner and Stefanie Powers), two "MacShane" movies (starring Kenny Rogers), and several one-shot films.

NBC MAGAZINE WITH DAVID BRINKLEY NBC

26 SEPTEMBER 1980–18 SEPTEMBER 1981

NBC MAGAZINE NBC

25 SEPTEMBER 1981–31 JULY 1982   This hour magazine show was hosted during its first season by veteran NBC newsman David Brinkley; regular contributors included Betsy Aaron, Douglas Kiker, Jack Perkins, and Garrick Utley. The series presented both hard and soft features, anchored by Brinkley's wry commentary, and was critically praised. Unfortunately, it was originally scheduled on Fridays opposite *Dallas* on CBS, and finished at the bottom of the ratings heap almost every week. A midseason shift of time slots to Saturdays at 10:00 P.M., a chronic weak spot for NBC, helped little. *NBC Magazine with David Brinkley* finished 97th—out of 97 series—in the 1980–1981 Nielsen ratings; nevertheless, it was renewed for another season. In the fall of 1981 the show suffered an even greater setback: the loss of David Brinkley, who ended a thirty-eight-year career with NBC and signed with ABC. The show carried on with an abbreviated title (*NBC Magazine* was doubtlessly a wiser choice than *NBC Magazine without David Brinkley*) in another luckless time slot, opposite *The Dukes of Hazzard* on CBS. With or without Brinkley, *NBC Magazine* marked the network's fifth attempt since 1969 to establish a successful magazine series (see also *First Tuesday, Chronolog, Weekend,* and *Prime Time Sunday*); undaunted, NBC tried again in 1983 with a new effort, *Monitor*.

THE NBC MYSTERY MOVIE/THE NBC SUNDAY MYSTERY MOVIE/
THE NBC WEDNESDAY MYSTERY MOVIE NBC

These were the umbrella titles for the several multipart series that ran on NBC between 1971 and 1977. The composition changed slightly each year. In the fall of 1971 *The NBC Mystery Movie* included *Columbo, McCloud,* and *McMillan and Wife.* Two umbrella series were featured in the fall of 1972: *The NBC Sunday Mystery Movie* (*Columbo, McCloud, McMillan and Wife,* and *Hec Ramsey*) and *The NBC Wednesday Mystery Movie,* which introduced three new crime shows: *Banacek, Cool Million,* and *Madigan.* The composition of *The NBC Sunday Mystery Movie* remained intact during the 1973–1974 season, but *The NBC Wednesday Movie* presented *Banacek* and three newcomers: *Faraday and Company, The Snoop Sisters,* and *Tenafly.* By the fall of 1974 *The NBC Wednesday Movie* was gone entirely, but *The NBC Sunday Mystery Movie* carried on for three more seasons. *Columbo, McCloud,* and *McMillan and Wife* shared space with a new fourth member each season—*Amy Prentiss* in 1974–1975, *McCoy* in 1975–1976, and *Quincy* in 1976–1977 (*Quincy* was given its own regular slot partway through the 1976–1977 season). See individual titles for details.

NBC NEWS NBC

16 FEBRUARY 1948–   Nightly newscasts on the NBC television network began in February 1948 with *The Camel Newsreel Theatre,* a ten-minute Fox Movietone Newsreel sponsored by Camel Cigarettes; earlier, the network had experimented with a fifteen-minute weekly newscast, *NBC Television Newsroom* (also known as *The Esso Newsreel*). *The Camel Newsreel Theatre* lasted a year; on 14 February 1949 John Cameron Swayze took the helm of *The Camel News Caravan,* a nightly fifteen-minute broadcast. Like most of television's early newscasters, Swayze had worked in radio for several years before switching to the new medium. He had appeared on

local television in Kansas City as early as 1937. There was little on-the-spot reportage on *The Camel News Caravan;* the newscasts consisted mainly of Swayze reading the evening's news. Swayze anchored the Monday-through-Friday broadcasts for more than seven and one-half years (during the 1949–1950 season NBC also carried a Saturday-evening newscast, anchored by Leon Pearson); he later hosted a game show (*Chance for Romance*) and served as commercial spokesman for Timex watches. In 1954 *The Camel News Caravan* became the first network news show to be broadcast in color (though regular colorcasting did not begin until 15 November 1965).

On 29 October 1956 *The Camel News Caravan* was succeeded by *The Huntley-Brinkley Report,* a fifteen-minute newscast coanchored by Chet Huntley and David Brinkley, two NBC newsmen who had been paired up that summer to host the network's coverage of the political conventions. Huntley, a westerner, had worked for several radio stations before joining CBS News in 1939. From 1951 to 1955 he worked for ABC News, earning a Peabody Award in 1953 for his radio reporting; in 1955 he joined NBC. Brinkley, a southerner, joined NBC News in 1943 after a stint with the United Press, and served as a local reporter in Washington during the early 1950s. *The Huntley-Brinkley Report* soon became television's top-rated news show, and remained in that position for most of its fourteen-year run. Huntley and Brinkley complemented each other almost perfectly, with Huntley's no-nonsense toughness neatly offset by Brinkley's dry and wry wit. Their familiar closing exchange— "Good night, Chet/Good night, David"—was suggested by producer Reuven Frank in order to provide a touch of warmth to the newscast. In real life, however, the two saw little of each other, for Huntley was usually based in New York while Brinkley generally broadcast from Washington. NBC followed CBS's lead in expanding its newscasts from fifteen to thirty minutes in 1963; NBC's initial half-hour show was on 9 September, just a week after CBS's. In 1970 Huntley announced his retirement, and the final *Huntley-Brinkley Report* was broadcast 31 July 1970. Huntley died in 1974.

After Huntley's departure, the newscast was retitled *NBC Nightly News,* and seven-nights-a-week broadcasts were inaugurated. The weeknight newscasts were first anchored solely by David Brinkley, but in August of 1971 John Chancellor became the new anchorman. Chancellor, who joined NBC News in 1950, had been a floor correspondent at the 1956 political conventions (when Huntley and Brinkley were upstairs), and later served as a correspondent in Vienna, London, and Moscow before succeeding Dave Garroway as host of the *Today* show in 1961; in 1964 Chancellor took a leave of absence from NBC to head the Voice of America. Throughout the 1970s Brinkley and Chancellor were teamed together, though Brinkley's role has fluctuated between coanchor and commentator. In October 1979 Brinkley left the coanchor position, and no longer appeared regularly. He moved to ABC in 1981.

John Chancellor remained as the sole anchor until the spring of 1982. NBC reintroduced a dual anchor on 5 April of that year, as Tom Brokaw and Roger Mudd took over. (Chancellor continued to do editorial commentaries on the newscast until his retirement in July 1993). Brokaw had been an NBC news correspondent for many years and had most recently hosted the *Today* show. Mudd had been a CBS correspondent for many years and had moved to NBC shortly after Dan Rather had been named to replace Walter Cronkite as anchor of *The CBS Evening News.* Mudd and Brokaw were unable to improve NBC's news ratings substantially, and Mudd quit the anchor desk on 2 September 1983, leaving Brokaw as sole anchor. Though the newscast often finished in third place in the hotly contested evening news ratings game, *NBC Nightly News* achieved some major successes during the late 1980s, including an exclusive interview in 1986 (by Henry Champ) with Abul Abbas of the Palestine Liberation Front and an exclusive interview (by Brokaw) in November 1987 with Soviet leader Mikhail Gorbachev. By lucky coincidence, Brokaw happened to be on assignment in West Germany in the fall of 1989 when the Berlin Wall was opened; Brokaw was the first of the network anchormen to be on the scene for the event. By 1993 *NBC Nightly News*'s ratings had climbed, and the newscast usually finished second in the ratings, behind ABC. In 1993 Brokaw began cohosting a weekly newsmagazine series: see *Now.*

NBC NEWS AT SUNRISE   NBC

1 AUGUST 1983–   This early-morning news show was the successor to *Early Today*.
It was first anchored by Connie Chung, a former CBS news reporter who had left that
network to anchor a local news broadcast in Los Angeles. Chung anchored the
broadcast until March 1986 and returned to CBS News a month later. Bob Jamieson
took over for her and remained there until January 1987, when Deborah Norville
succeeded him. In September 1989 Norville was moved up to the *Today* show, as John
Palmer (who had read the news on *Today*) was moved back to replace her on the
early broadcast. Faith Daniels, who had previously anchored the early morning news
on CBS, succeeded Palmer in June 1990. She was succeeded by Ann Curry in 1991.

NBC NEWS OVERNIGHT   NBC

5 JULY 1982–2 DECEMBER 1983   The success of *ABC News Nightline* led NBC to
introduce its own late-late news program. Broadcast Monday through Thursday
nights from 1:30 to 2:30 A.M., and Friday nights from 2:00 to 3:00 A.M., the show was
originally coanchored by Lloyd Dobyns and Linda Ellerbee. Dobyns left the show in
November of 1982 (he subsequently turned up on *Monitor* and *First Camera*), and
was succeeded by Bill Schechner. After seventeen months of low ratings and meager
advertising revenues, *NBC News Overnight* was laid to rest. The concept was revived
in 1991: see *Nightside*.

NBC NOVELS FOR TELEVISION   NBC

14 FEBRUARY 1979–21 MARCH 1979   An umbrella title for a group of miniseries, each
of which was based on a best-selling novel. The show led off with "From Here to
Eternity," an adaptation of James Jones's novel, set in Hawaii in 1941. The three-
parter featured William Devane as Sergeant Milt Warden; Roy Thinnes as his commanding officer, Captain Holmes; Natalie Wood as Karen Holmes, his wife; Steve
Railsback as Private Robert E. Lee Prewitt; Kim Basinger as Lorene, a prostitute;
and Peter Boyle as Fatso Judson. The second miniseries was "Studs Lonigan," a
three-parter based on James T. Farrell's trilogy chronicling the coming of age of a
tough young man in Chicago during the 1920s. Featured were Dan Shor and Harry
Hamlin as Studs Lonigan; Charles Durning as his father; Colleen Dewhurst as his
mother; and Lisa Pelikan as Lucy, his girlfriend.

NBC REPORTS   NBC

12 SEPTEMBER 1972–4 SEPTEMBER 1973   A series of news documentaries, *NBC Reports* shared a time slot on Tuesdays with *First Tuesday* and *America*.

NBC SPORTS IN ACTION   NBC

17 JANUARY 1965–5 JUNE 1966   This sports anthology series, hosted by Jim Simpson,
was seen both on Sunday afternoons and in prime time.

N.E.T. FESTIVAL   NET/PBS

6 DECEMBER 1967–29 SEPTEMBER 1970   Umbrella title for a series of American- and
foreign-produced hour-long programs devoted to the arts.

N.E.T. JOURNAL   NET/PBS

1966–1970   Umbrella title for a series of documentaries.

N.E.T. PLAYHOUSE   NET/PBS

9 OCTOBER 1966–24 JANUARY 1972   Dramatic anthology series. The premiere telecast was "Ten Blocks on the Camino Real" by Tennessee Williams.

N.F.L. MONDAY NIGHT FOOTBALL   ABC

21 SEPTEMBER 1970–   ABC took a gamble in 1970 when it chose to experiment
with coverage of a professional football game on Monday nights during the fall;
professional football had not been played regularly on that night previously. It was
reported that the network paid $8 million for the Monday-night rights, but the
gamble paid off. For most seasons a trio of broadcasters has handled the games, but

occasionally a duo or quartet has been used. Keith Jackson, Don Meredith, and ABC's ubiquitous sportscaster, Howard Cosell, handled the chores during the 1970–1971 season. In the fall of 1971 former New York Giants running back Frank Gifford replaced Jackson, joining Meredith and Cosell; that group stayed together for two more seasons. In the fall of 1974 Meredith left to try his hand at acting and was replaced by former defensive back Fred Williamson; Williamson was replaced later that season by Alex Karras, an ex-lineman for the Detroit Lions. Karras, Gifford, and Cosell were featured during the 1975 and 1976 seasons as well. In the fall of 1977, however, Don Meredith returned, replacing Karras. Fran Tarkenton was added in the fall of 1979 and stayed for two seasons. In 1983 former Buffalo Bills running back O. J. Simpson joined Meredith, Cosell, and Gifford. Cosell retired after the 1983 season, but did not fade quietly away. In his 1985 autobiography, *I Never Played the Game,* he managed to criticize most of his broadcasting compatriots (citing Gifford's propensity for on-the-air gaffes, Meredith's lack of preparation, and Simpson's insecurity) while gloating over the fact that the show's ratings slipped the year after he departed ("the telecasts were dreadful," he observed). Another book disclosed that Cosell's off-the-air nicknames for Gifford and Meredith were "The Mannequin" and "The Imbecile."

Simpson, Meredith, and Gifford carried on for the 1984 season, after which Meredith left. Former New York Jets quarterback Joe Namath joined Simpson and Gifford for the 1985 season. In 1986 the network experimented with a duo in the broadcast booth—Frank Gifford (who now did the color commentary) and Al Michaels (doing the play-by-play). For the 1987 season former St. Louis Cardinal lineman Dan Dierdorf joined them; that trio remained together through the end of the decade, and into the 1990s, becoming a quartet during the 1988 season when ex-Pittsburgh Steeler receiver Lynn Swann was added.

N.O.P.D.   SYNDICATED

1956   *N.O.P.D.* stood for the New Orleans Police Department in this low-budget crime show, starring Stacy Harris as Detective Beaujac and Lou Sirgo as Detective Conroy, who was on leave from the department. Frank Phares produced the series, which was filmed on location; thirty-nine episodes were made.

N.Y.P.D.   ABC

5 SEPTEMBER 1967–16 SEPTEMBER 1969   Filmed on location in New York, *N.Y.P.D.* was produced by Talent Associates and was filmed with the cooperation of the real N.Y.P.D., the New York Police Department. Most of the filming was done with 16-millimeter cameras. The half-hour show starred Jack Warden as Detective Lieutenant Mike Haines; Frank Converse as Detective Johnny Corso; and Robert Hooks as Detective Jeff Ward.

NYPD BLUE   ABC

21 SEPTEMBER 1993–   Steven Bochco's police drama attracted controversy even before it premiered, as word leaked out of its steamy sex scenes and coarse language. Some fifty-seven ABC affiliates initially declined to carry the show, though eighteen relented during the first season. The series was highly acclaimed and proved popular, finishing a surprisingly high nineteenth in the Nielsen ratings after its first season, despite the lack of nationwide clearance. Set in New York, the hour drama starred David Caruso as Detective John Kelly, a troubled hero, and Dennis Franz as his older partner, Detective Andy Sipowicz, who battled his own demons, including alcohol. Caruso quickly became a major star, but left the series early in its second season after his demands for a hefty salary increase were not met. He was replaced in November 1994 by Jimmy Smits as Sipowicz's new partner, Detective Bobby Simone, who had previously worked on the police commissioner's personal staff. Also featured were James McDaniel as the boss, Lieutenant Arthur Fancy; Sherry Stringfield (1993–1994) as Kelly's ex-wife, Laura Hughes Kelly, a lawyer; Amy Brenneman (1993–fall 1994) as rookie Officer Janice Licalsi, who had an affair with Kelly and was later convicted of homicide; Nicholas Turturro as young detective James Martinez; Sharon Lawrence as assistant district attorney Sylvia Costas, who became involved with

Sipowicz and married him in the spring of 1995 (in an early episode, before their romance, Sipowicz had called her a "pissy little bitch"); Gail O'Grady as administrative assistant Donna Abandando; Gordon Clapp as Detective Greg Medavoy; Wendy Makkena as Detective Sharon LaSalle; Justine Micelli as Detective Adrienne Lesniak; Debra Messing (1994–) as Donna's sister, Dana Abandando; Kim Delaney (1995–) as Detective Diane Russell; and Bill Brochtrup (1995–) as receptionist John Irvin.

Caruso's departure did not hurt *NYPD Blue*'s ratings, which rose to seventh place during its second season. The series was nominated for 26 Emmys in 1994, a record for a first-year program.

NAKED CITY ABC
30 SEPTEMBER 1958–29 SEPTEMBER 1959; 12 OCTOBER 1960–11 SEPTEMBER 1963
Filmed entirely on location in New York, this popular crime show began as a half-hour series in 1958 and ran for one season. It returned after a season's absence in an hour-long format, which ran for three seasons. The first cast included James Franciscus as Detective Jim Halloran of the Sixty-fifth Precinct; John McIntire as Lieutenant Dan Muldoon, his superior; and Harry Bellaver as Sergeant Frank Arcaro. Suzanne Storrs was occasionally featured as Halloran's wife, Janet. McIntire left the series in March of 1959 and was replaced by Horace McMahon as Lieutenant Mike Parker. When *Naked City* returned in the fall of 1960, Bellaver and McMahon returned with it, Paul Burke was introduced as Detective Adam Flint, and Nancy Malone was featured as Flint's girlfriend, Libby. *Naked City*'s famous tag line ("There are eight million stories in the naked city; this has been one of them") was first used in the 1948 film from which the series was derived. The title of the film and the series was taken from a book of photographs published by Arthur H. Fellig, better known as "Weegee." Herbert B. Leonard was the executive producer of the series, and some of the many guest stars who appeared were Robert Redford ("Tombstone for a Derelict," 5 April 1961), Dustin Hoffman ("Sweet Prince of Delancey Street," 7 June 1961, his first major TV role), Peter Fonda ("The Night the Saints Lost Their Halos," 17 January 1962, his first major TV role), Sandy Dennis ("Idylls of a Running Back," 26 September 1962, her first major TV role), and Jon Voight ("Alive and Still a Second Lieutenant," 6 March 1963, his first major TV role).

NAKED HOLLYWOOD A&E
28 JULY 1991–1 SEPTEMBER 1991   An unflattering six-part documentary series on the entertainment industry's movers and shakers, produced by the British Broadcasting Company. Portions of one BBC segment, focusing on film producers Don Simpson and Jerry Bruckheimer, were not televised in the A&E version.

THE NAKED TRUTH ABC
13 SEPTEMBER 1995–   Half-hour sitcom starring Tea Leoni as Nora Wilde, who spurned a lucrative divorce settlement and found work as a photographer for a tabloid newspaper. Also featured were Holland Taylor as her boss, Camilla Dane, editor of The Comet; Jonathan Penner as fellow photographer Nicky Columbus; Amy Ryan as Chloe, the adult daughter of Nora's ex-husband; and Jack Blessing as Nora's landlord, Earl Donner.

NAKIA ABC
21 SEPTEMBER 1974–28 DECEMBER 1974   Hour-long crime show starring Robert Forster as Nakia Parker, a Navajo who was a deputy sheriff in New Mexico. With Arthur Kennedy as Sheriff Sam Jericho; Taylor Lacher as Hubbell Martin, another deputy; and Gloria DeHaven as Irene James, also a deputy. Charles Larson was executive producer of the series, which was filmed largely on location.

THE NAME DROPPERS NBC
29 SEPTEMBER 1969–27 MARCH 1970   Daytime game show cohosted by Los Angeles disc jockeys Al Lohman and Roger Barkley. The object of the game was for selected members of the studio audience to determine which of the three celebrity guest

panelists was related to the "name dropper," a guest who described his or her relationship to the celebrity (without, of course, divulging which of the celebs was the "correct" relative).

THE NAME OF THE GAME   NBC

20 SEPTEMBER 1968–10 SEPTEMBER 1971   This ninety-minute crime show was a tripartite series: Each of the three stars appeared every third week. It starred Gene Barry as Glenn Howard, publisher of *Crime* magazine; Tony Franciosa as investigative correspondent Jeff Dillon; Robert Stack as senior editor Dan Farrell, a former FBI agent. Also featured were Susan Saint James as Peggy Maxwell, their research assistant; Ben Murphy (1968–1970) as Dan's assistant, Joe Sample; Cliff Potter as Andy Hill, a young correspondent; and Mark Miller as reporter Ross Craig. Each of the three costars selected his own producer: Richard Irving produced the Barry episodes, E. Jack Neuman (and, later, Leslie Stevens) the Franciosa episodes, and David Victor the Stack episodes. In a 1969 article *TV Guide* reported that the series was the most expensive in the history of television, budgeted at $400,000 per episode. The pilot for the series, "Fame Is the Name of the Game," starring Tony Franciosa and Susan Saint James, was telecast 26 November 1966.

NAME THAT TUNE   NBC/CBS/SYNDICATED

6 JULY 1953–14 JUNE 1954 (NBC); 2 SEPTEMBER 1954–19 OCTOBER 1959 (CBS); 1970 (SYNDICATED); 29 JULY 1974–3 JANUARY 1975 (NBC); 1974–1980 (SYNDICATED); 3 JANUARY 1977–10 JUNE 1977 (NBC)   The best known of the musical identification game shows, *Name That Tune* has been presented in several different formats over the years. Created by Harry Salter, the show first appeared as a prime-time series in the summer of 1953, with Red Benson as host. When it switched networks the following season, Bill Cullen became the host; he was succeeded in 1955 by George DeWitt. At that time the show featured two contestants, who stood at one side of the stage while the orchestra played a musical selection; the contestant who could identify it then raced across the stage and rang a bell (female contestants were placed closer to the bell than male contestants). The winner of that round then tried to identify several songs within a specified time period. After an eleven-year absence a syndicated version of the show appeared in 1970 with Richard Hayes as host. In 1974 both a new network and a new syndicated version appeared. The network version was a daytime show, hosted by Dennis James; the syndicated show was emceed by Tom Kennedy. Both versions added two new features: the "Bid-a-Note" round, in which the contestants challenged each other to identify a song from as few notes as possible, and the "Golden Medley," in which the winning contestant tried to identify seven songs in thirty seconds. In 1976 the syndicated version was retitled *The $100,000 Name That Tune*—a contestant who won the "Golden Medley" could return to try to identify a "mystery tune" for a grand prize of $10,000 a year for the next ten years. When the series was revived for network television again in 1977, Tom Kennedy hosted; top prize on that daytime effort was $25,000. In the fall of 1977 vocalist Kathie Lee Johnson was added to the syndicated version and a playoff system was devised to award the grand prize. Ralph Edwards was the executive producer of the 1970s versions.

NAME YOUR ADVENTURE   NBC

12 SEPTEMBER 1992–2 SEPTEMBER 1995   This Saturday morning series gave youngsters who wrote in to the show the opportunity to live out their fantasies, which might include meeting famous persons or going on an adventure. Mario Lopez and Jordan Brady were the cohosts.

THE NAME'S THE SAME   ABC

5 DECEMBER 1951–7 OCTOBER 1955   On this prime-time game show a celebrity panel tried to discern the names of the contestants; each contestant's name was the same as that of a well-known personality or famous event. The show was first hosted by Robert Q. Lewis, and then by Dennis James, Clifton Fadiman, and finally by Bob (Elliott) and Ray (Goulding).

NANCY   NBC

17 SEPTEMBER 1970–7 JANUARY 1971   Insipid sitcom about the daughter of the President, who, while vacationing in Iowa, met and married a Center City veterinarian. With Renne Jarrett as Nancy Smith; John Fink as Adam Hudson, the vet; Celeste Holm as Abby Townsend, Nancy's official chaperone (and the press secretary of the President's wife); Robert F. Simon as Adam's Uncle Everett; William Bassett as Agent Turner of the Secret Service; Ernesto Macias as Agent Rodriquez; and Eddie Applegate as Willie, a local reporter. Sidney Sheldon created and produced the half-hour series.

NANCY DREW MYSTERIES
See THE HARDY BOYS/NANCY DREW MYSTERIES

THE NANCY WALKER SHOW   ABC

30 SEPTEMBER 1976–23 DECEMBER 1976   Half-hour sitcom starring Nancy Walker as Nancy Kitteridge, a Hollywood talent agent. Also featured were William Daniels as her husband, Kenneth Kitteridge, a Merchant Marine commander who had just retired after being at sea for most of their twenty-nine years of marriage; Beverly Archer as their forlorn daughter, Loraine; and Ken Olfson as Terry Folsom, their gay boarder, a struggling actor. Produced by Norman Lear's T.A.T. Communications, the series was canceled in midseason. Walker returned a few weeks later in a new (and equally unsuccessful) sitcom, *Blansky's Beauties*.

THE NANNY   CBS

3 NOVEMBER 1993–   Fran Drescher starred in this half-hour sitcom as native New Yorker Fran Fine, who lost her job at a Flushing bridal shop and found work as a nanny for a wealthy Manhattan widower. Also featured were Charles Shaughnessy as her boss, Maxwell Sheffield; Lauren Lane as Maxwell's lusty business associate, Cece Babcock; Daniel Davis as Niles the butler; Nicholle Tom as older daughter, Maggie; Benjamin Salisbury as son, Brighton; Madeline Zima as younger daughter, Gracie; and Ann Guilbert (1994–) as Fran's grandmother, Yetta. Guilbert is best known for her role as Millie Helper on *The Dick Van Dyke Show* (when she went by Ann Morgan Guilbert). Occasionally featured were Renee Taylor (1994–) as Fran's mother Sylvia; and Rachel Chagall (1995–) as Fran's pal, Val.

NANNY AND THE PROFESSOR   ABC

21 JANUARY 1970–27 DECEMBER 1971   Half-hour sitcom starring Juliet Mills as Phoebe Figalilly, better known as Nanny, housekeeper and governess to a widowed professor and his three children. Gifted with mysterious powers, Nanny attributed her abilities to "a little bit of faith and lots of love." Also featured were Richard Long as Professor Howard Everett; David Doremus as son Hal; Trent Lehman as son Butch; and Kim Richards as daughter Prudence. Elsa Lanchester joined the cast in the fall of 1971 as Nanny's Aunt Henrietta. Charles B. FitzSimmons produced the series.

NASHVILLE 99   CBS

1 APRIL 1977–22 APRIL 1977   Hour-long crime show starring Claude Akins as Lieutenant Stoney Huff of the Nashville Police Department. With Jerry Reed as his sidekick, Detective Trace Mayne; Lucille Benson as Stoney's mother, Birdie Huff. Ernie Frankel created the miniseries and was its executive producer.

NASHVILLE ON THE ROAD   SYNDICATED

1976   Country-and-western music show, taped on location around the country.

NASHVILLE PALACE   NBC

24 OCTOBER 1981–28 NOVEMBER 1981; 3 JULY 1982–7 AUGUST 1982   This hour variety show, consisting mostly of country-and-western music and comedy skits, was taped at the Nashville Palace Theater; inexplicably, it was scheduled on Saturdays at 9:00 p.m., immediately following NBC's other hour of country-and-western music and

comedy, *Barbara Mandrell and the Mandrell Sisters*. Viewers seemed to have tired quickly of the format, as *Nashville Palace* was the first announced cancellation of the 1981–1982 season. Featured were Slim Pickens, Lynn Hancock, Chuck Bulot, Terri Gardner, Harry Murphy, Kent Perkins, Donna Siegel, Wendy Suits, and the Dixie Dozen Dancers.

NASTY BOYS NBC
19 FEBRUARY 1990–22 JULY 1990   The title characters of this hour crime show comprised a special undercover unit of the North Las Vegas Narcotics Bureau (such a unit actually existed). The Boys wore ninja hoods while in action to aviod identification, and the unit was permitted to keep one half of all assets seized for use in subsequent operations. With Jeff Kaake as Paul Morrisey; Benjamin Bratt as Officer Eduardo Cruz; Don Franklin as Officer Alex Wheeler; Craig Hurley as Officer Danny Larsen; James Pax as Officer Jimmy Kee; Dennis Franz as the boss, Lieutenant Stan Krieger; Nia Peeples as Eduardo's wife, Serena Cruz; and Sandy McPeak as Chief Bradley.

THE NAT KING COLE SHOW NBC
5 NOVEMBER 1956–24 JUNE 1957; 2 JULY 1957–17 DECEMBER 1957   Nat King Cole, the popular black pianist and singer, appeared frequently as a guest star on variety shows during the 1950s. In the fall of 1956 he was given his own fifteen-minute show, broadcast on Mondays before the network news. In the summer of 1957 he was shifted to a half-hour slot on Tuesdays at 10:00 P.M., and in September he was given the 7:30 P.M. slot that night. The Nelson Riddle Orchestra and the Randy Van Horne Singers were featured on all three shows. Sadly, Cole's show failed to attract a nationwide sponsor and was dropped in midseason. Though it was reported that potential sponsors feared a southern boycott, it should be noted that several NBC affiliates in the North as well as the South declined to carry the show. Cole's show is sometimes described as the first network variety program hosted by a black performer, but in fact Cole was preceded by Hazel Scott and Billy Daniels. In any event, it was not until 1966 that a black performer—Sammy Davis, Jr.—again hosted a network variety series.

NATIONAL BARN DANCE ABC
21 FEBRUARY 1949–7 NOVEMBER 1949   Also known as *ABC Barn Dance,* this half-hour musical series was the television version of the long-running radio series that began locally in Chicago in 1924 and was broadcast nationally beginning in 1933. John Dolce hosted most of the television broadcasts.

NATIONAL BOWLING CHAMPIONS NBC
8 APRIL 1956–24 MARCH 1957   Late-night series of head-to-head bowling matches between two professionals. Broadcast from Chicago, the show was hosted by "Whispering Joe" Wilson. See also *Bowling Stars.*

NATIONAL GEOGRAPHIC EXPLORER NICKELODEON/WTBS
7 APRIL 1985–11 JANUARY 1986 (NICKELODEON); 2 FEBRUARY 1986–   Magazine show produced by *National Geographic* magazine. The series was originally seen in a three-hour format on Nickelodeon and was reduced first to two hours, and later to one hour, when it switched to WTBS.

NATIONAL GEOGRAPHIC SPECIALS CBS/ABC/PBS
1964–1973 (CBS); 1973–1975 (ABC); 1975– (PBS)   Produced in cooperation with the National Geographic Society, this long-running series of specials on biological, historical, and cultural subjects was first produced by Wolper Productions, later by Metromedia, and again by Wolper. Approximately four new specials are produced each year. Joseph Campanella narrated many of the specials on CBS, and E. G. Marshall has narrated most of those on PBS.

NATIONAL VELVET   NBC
18 SEPTEMBER 1960–10 SEPTEMBER 1962   Based on the 1944 film (which had starred Elizabeth Taylor) about a young girl who trained her horse for the Grand National Steeplechase, this half-hour dramatic series starred Lori Martin as Velvet Brown; Arthur Space as her father, Herbert Brown; Ann Doran as her mother, Martha Brown; James McCallion as Mi Taylor, the Browns' handyman; Carole Wells as Edwina, Velvet's sister; and Joey Scott as Donald, Velvet's brother. Rudy Abel produced the series.

THE NATION'S FUTURE   NBC
12 NOVEMBER 1960–16 SEPTEMBER 1961   John K. M. McCaffery was the moderator of this Saturday-night public affairs program, which presented debates on topical issues. Edwin Newman succeeded McCaffery as moderator in June 1961. Irving Gitlin was the producer.

NATURE   PBS
10 OCTOBER 1982–   An hour series of documentaries on biological subjects. The series led off with the three-part "Flight of the Condor," a lyrical look at the great bird's travels through the South American continent.

THE NATURE OF THINGS   NBC
5 FEBRUARY 1948–29 MARCH 1954   One of television's first science shows, this fifteen-minute series was hosted by astronomer Dr. Roy K. Marshall, director of the Fels Planetarium at Philadelphia's Franklin Institute.

NAVY LOG   CBS/ABC
20 SEPTEMBER 1955–25 SEPTEMBER 1956 (CBS); 17 OCTOBER 1956–25 SEPTEMBER 1958 (ABC)   A half-hour anthology series about Navy life, *Navy Log* was produced by Simeon G. Gallu, Jr. The show's opening, in which 2,000 sailors formed the words "Navy Log," was filmed aboard the U.S.S. *Hancock*. James Cagney made a very rare TV appearance as host of one episode, "The Lonely Watch," aired 9 January 1958; the episode starred Clint Eastwood, in one of his first television roles.

NEARLY DEPARTED   NBC
10 APRIL 1989–8 MAY 1989   Former Monty Python trouper Eric Idle stepped down to the world of the mundane sitcom in this update of *Topper.* Idle and Caroline McWilliams played Grant and Claire Pritchard, a deceased couple who continued to inhabit their old house and made life difficult for the new owners, the Dooleys. Also featured were Stuart Pankin as Mike Dooley; Wendy Schaal as Liz Dooley; Jay Lambert as their son, Derek; and Henderson Forsythe as Grampa, the only person who could see or hear the two ghosts.

NED AND STACEY   FOX
11 SEPTEMBER 1995–   An updated version of 1966's *Occasional Wife, Ned and Stacey* was a half-hour sitcom about an ambitious New York ad executive who won a promotion by telling his boss he was getting married; he then found someone who agreed to marry him so that she could have a place to live. The cast included Thomas Haden Church (late of *Wings*) as adman Ned Dorsey; Debra Messing as his new wife, Stacey Colbert, a reporter for the Village Voice; Greg Germann and Nadia Dajani as Ned's friends Eric and Amanda Moyer; Harry Goz as Stacey's dad, Saul Colbert; Dori Brenner as Stacey's mom, Ellen Colbert; and Alan Oppenheimer as Ned's boss, Spencer Haywood.

NED BLESSING: THE STORY OF MY LIFE & TIMES   CBS
18 AUGUST 1993–15 SEPTEMBER 1993   Atmospheric western, narrated by the elderly title character who looked back on his days as a lawman while he awaited his execution. With Brad Johnson as Ned Blessing, who had returned to the town of Plum Creek to care for his father; Tim Scott as the deputy, Sticks Packwood; Luis Avalos as Crescencio Salas; Bill McKinney as bad guy Verlon Borgers, who was struck deaf

and blind; Rob Campbell as his son, Roby; Brenda Bakke as Wren; Richard Riehle as Judge Longley; Rusty Schwimmer as Big Emma; and Wes Studi as One Horse, the Native American. The title character had been introduced in a TV-movie, "Ned Blessing" (14 April 1992, CBS), which starred Daniel Baldwin and was based on the Larry McMurtry novel.

NEEDLES AND PINS   NBC
21 SEPTEMBER 1973–28 DECEMBER 1973   Half-hour sitcom set in New York's garment district. With Deirdre Lenihan (a newcomer to television) as Wendy Nelson, a designer from Nebraska who got a job at Lorelei Fashions; Norman Fell as her boss, Nathan Davidson; Louis Nye as Davidson's dilettante brother-in-law, Harry Karp; Sandra Deel as Sonia Baker, the bookkeeper; Bernie Kopell as Charlie Miller, the salesman; Larry Gelman as Max Popkin, the cutter; Alex Henteloff as Myron, the patternmaker; and Milton Selzer as Singer, Davidson's chief competitor. David Gerber was executive producer of the series, and Hy Averback produced and directed it.

THE NEIGHBORS   ABC
29 DECEMBER 1975–9 APRIL 1976   Silly game show on which five neighbors exchanged gossip about each other for the chance to win prizes. Regis Philbin, assisted by Jane Nelson, was the host, and Bill Carruthers the executive producer of this short-lived daytime show.

NERO WOLFE   NBC
16 JANUARY 1981–25 AUGUST 1981   Rex Stout's reclusive detective came to television in this hour series. It featured William Conrad as Nero Wolfe, the epicurean private eye who preferred to stay put in his West 35th Street townhouse; Lee Horsley as his energetic legman, Archie Goodwin; George Voskovec as the butler, Fritz Brenner; Robert Coote as horticulturist Theodore Horstman, who helped Wolfe tend his orchid collection; George Wyner as Wolfe's investigator, Saul Panzer; and Allan Miller as Inspector Cramer of the New York Police Department. Ivan Goff and Ben Roberts were the executive producers for Paramount TV.

NEVER TOO YOUNG   ABC
27 SEPTEMBER 1965–24 JUNE 1966   This daytime serial focused on a group of active teenagers and their harried parents. Set at Malibu Beach, the cast included: Michael Blodgett as Tad; Cindy Carol as Susan; Pat Connolly as Barbara; Tony Dow (late of *Leave It to Beaver*) as Chet; Robin Grace as Joy; John Lupton as Frank; Tommy Rettig (formerly of *Lassie*) as JoJo; David Watson as Alfie; and Patrice Wymore as Rhoda. Though *Never Too Young* failed in its attempt to attract teenaged viewers to a continuing drama, its successor in the late-afternoon time slot—*Dark Shadows*—performed admirably.

THE NEW ADAM 12   SYNDICATED
1990–1991   A new version of the 1968–1975 crime show, with Peter Parros as Officer Gus Grant and Ethan Wayne as his partner, Officer Matt Doyle, two uniformed members of the Los Angeles Police Department who shared a patrol car. Also featured was Miguel Fernandes as Sergeant Harry Santos.

THE NEW ADVENTURES OF BEANS BAXTER   FOX
18 JULY 1987–9 APRIL 1988   Half-hour comedy-adventure series about a Kansas family who moved to Washington, D.C., where the teenage son became an afterschool spy in order to find his father, a top-secret intelligence courier who had been kidnapped by subversives. With Jonathan Ward as Benjamin (Beans) Baxter, Jr.; Elinor Donahue as his mother, Susan Baxter; Scott Bremner as his little brother, Scooter; Jerry Wasserman as Number Two, Beans's boss at The Network; Karen Mistal as Cake Lase, Beans's would-be girlfriend; Stuart Fratkin as Woodshop, Beans's school pal; and Kurtwood Smith as Mr. Sue, leader of U.G.L.I., the group that had kidnapped Beans's father.

THE NEW ADVENTURES OF CHARLIE CHAN
See CHARLIE CHAN

THE NEW ADVENTURES OF CHINA SMITH
See CHINA SMITH

THE NEW ADVENTURES OF GILLIGAN   ABC
7 SEPTEMBER 1974–4 SEPTEMBER 1977   Saturday-morning cartoon show based on the
1964 sitcom, *Gilligan's Island* (see also that title). Five members of the *Gilligan's
Island* cast—Bob Denver, Alan Hale, Jr., Jim Backus, Natalie Schafer, and Russell
Johnson—lent their voices to the animated production, and two new voices—those
of Jane Webb and Jane Edwards—were added. Norm Prescott and Lou Scheimer
were the executive producers. See also *Gilligan's Planet.*

THE NEW ADVENTURES OF HUCKLEBERRY FINN   NBC
15 SEPTEMBER 1968–7 SEPTEMBER 1969   This half-hour Sunday-night series bore
almost no resemblance to Mark Twain's classic. The series combined live action with
animated sequences, and its premise was that Huck, Tom, Becky, and Joe had been
caught in a time warp and were trying to find their way through time and space back
to Missouri. With Kevin Schultz as Tom Sawyer; Michael Shea as Huck Finn; Lu Ann
Haslam as Becky Thatcher; and Ted Cassidy as Injun Joe. The show was a Hanna-
Barbera production.

THE NEW ADVENTURES OF MADELINE   ABC
9 SEPTEMBER 1995–21 OCTOBER 1995   Short-lived half-hour Saturday morning cartoon show based on the characters created by author Ludwig Bemelman: French
schoolgirl Madeline, her eleven schoolmates, and the little boy who lived next door,
Pepito (son of the Spanish ambassador). Christopher Plummer narrated.

**THE NEW ADVENTURES OF MIGHTY MOUSE AND HECKLE AND
JECKLE**   CBS
8 SEPTEMBER 1979–12 SEPTEMBER 1982   Mighty Mouse, the caped rodent who left
network TV in 1967, returned in a series of new cartoon adventures, in which he
battled his nemesis, Oilcan Harry, to save the honor of Pearl Pureheart. Other
segments on the Saturday-morning series included new adventures of Heckle and
Jeckle, the mischievous crows, and Quacula, a vampirish duck. See also *Heckle and
Jeckle; The Mighty Mouse Playhouse.*

THE NEW ADVENTURES OF WINNIE THE POOH   ABC
10 SEPTEMBER 1988–2 SEPTEMBER 1989; 8 SEPTEMBER 1990–23 JANUARY 1993
Saturday-morning cartoon series from Disney Studios, featuring the characterrs from
the A. A. Milne books: Winnie the Pooh, Piglet, Owl, Kanga and Roo, Rabbit,
Eeyore, and Tigger. Jim Cummings supplied the voice of Pooh, and Paul Winchell
(one of TV's early stars) that of Tigger. The series had been broadcast on The Disney
Channel before coming to ABC in 1988. During the 1989–1990 season it merged with
a second Disney series: see *The Gummi Bears.*

THE NEW ANDY GRIFFITH SHOW   CBS
8 JANUARY 1971–21 MAY 1971   *The New Andy Griffith Show* was the title given to
the series that began in the fall of 1970 as *Headmaster* and changed formats in
midseason. Griffith had played an educator on *Headmaster;* in the new format he
played a role more similar to that he'd played on *The Andy Griffith Show*—the
mayor of a small town in North Carolina. Featured were Andy Griffith as Andy
Sawyer; Lee Meriwether as his wife, Lee Sawyer; Marty McCall as their son, T. J.;
Lori Ann Rutherford as their daughter, Lori; Glen Ash as town councilman Buff
McKnight; and Ann Morgan Guilbert as Nora, Lee's unmarried sister.

THE NEW ARCHIE SABRINA HOUR
See THE ARCHIE SHOW

NEW ATTITUDE ABC

8 AUGUST 1990–1 SEPTEMBER 1990　Black sitcom set at a beauty salon. With Sheryl Lee Ralph and Phyllis Yvonne Stickney as the co-owners, sisters Vicy and Yvonne St. James; Ja'net DuBois as Irma; Morris Day as flamboyant hair stylist Lamarr, hoping to become a singer; and Earl Billings as Leon.

THE NEW AVENGERS

See THE AVENGERS

THE NEW BILL COSBY SHOW CBS

11 SEPTEMBER 1972–7 MAY 1973　Hour-long variety show hosted by comedian Bill Cosby and featuring Lola Falana, Foster Brooks, Oscar deGruy, and Susan Tolsky. Quincy Jones conducted the orchestra, and the Donald McKayle Dancers were also featured.

THE NEW BREED ABC

3 OCTOBER 1961–25 SEPTEMBER 1962　The heroes of this hour-long crime show were the men of Los Angeles's Metropolitan Squad: Leslie Nielsen as Lieutenant Price Adams, the squad leader; Greg Roman as Officer Pete Garcia; John Clarke as Officer Joe Huddleston; John Beradino as Sergeant Vince Cavelli; and Byron Morrow as Captain Gregory, Adams's commanding officer.

THE NEW CANDID CAMERA

See CANDID CAMERA

THE NEW CHRISTY MINSTRELS SHOW NBC

6 AUGUST 1964–10 SEPTEMBER 1964　A summer replacement for *Hazel,* this half-hour musical variety show featured the New Christy Minstrels, a wholesome folk troupe organized in 1962 by Randy Sparks; the name was taken from the Christy Minstrels, a nineteenth-century American singing group founded by Edwin P. Christy. In 1964 the New Christy Minstrels included: Karen Gunderson, Barry Kane, Barry McGuire, Art Podell, Paul Potash, Larry Ramos, Clarence Treat, Ann White, and Nick Woods. Gary Smith produced the five-week series, and Al deCaprio directed it.

THE NEW DATING GAME

See THE DATING GAME

THE NEW DENNIS THE MENACE CBS

18 SEPTEMBER 1993–10 SEPTEMBER 1994　Half-hour Saturday-morning cartoon series, featuring Hank Ketcham's comic strip characters.

THE NEW DICK VAN DYKE SHOW CBS

18 SEPTEMBER 1971–2 SEPTEMBER 1974　Created by Carl Reiner (the man responsible for *The Dick Van Dyke Show*), this half-hour sitcom went through two formats in its three seasons. In both formats Dick Van Dyke starred as Dick Preston and Hope Lange costarred as his wife, Jenny Preston; Angela Powell was also featured as their daughter, Annie. For the first two seasons the show was set in Phoenix (and was actually produced there), where Dick Preston was host of a local television talk show. The cast also included Marty Brill as Dick's manager, Bernie Davis; Nancy Dussault as Bernie's wife, Carol Davis; Fannie Flagg as Mike, Dick's sister and secretary; David Doyle as Ted Atwater, the station manager; and Michael Shea as Lucas Preston, Dick and Jenny's college-age son. In the fall of 1973 the Prestons moved to Hollywood, where Dick landed a role as Dr. Brad Fairmont on a soap opera entitled "Those Who Care." The new cast included: Richard Dawson as their neighbor, Richard Richardson, a television star; Chita Rivera as his wife, Connie Richardson; Dick Van Patten as Max, producer of "Those Who Care"; Henry Darrow as Alex, the stage manager; Barry Gordon as Dennis Whitehead, one of the writers; and Barbara Rush as Dick's costar on "Those Who Care," Margot Brighton.

THE NEW DRAGNET   SYNDICATED

1990–1991   An undistinguished update of one of TV's classic crime shows. This version—*Dragnet*'s third TV incarnation—starred Jeff Osterhage as Sergeant Vic Daniels, Bernard White as his partner, Sergeant Carl Molina, Thalmus Rasulala as Captain Boltz, and Don Stroud as Captain Lussen.

THE NEW FRED AND BARNEY SHOW
See THE FLINTSTONES

THE NEW GIDGET   SYNDICATED

1986–1989   In this updated sequel to the 1965 TV series, Gidget had grown up, gotten married, and started her own busienss. With Caryn Richman as Frances "Gidget" Griffin, who ran a travel agency; Dean Butler as her husband, Jeff "Moondoggie" Griffin, a city planner; Sydney Penny as Gidget's teenage niece, Danni Collins, who lived with the Griffins while her parents were in Europe; William Schallert as Gidget's father, Russ Lawrence; Jill Jacobson (1986–1987) as Gidget's lifelong chum, Larue Wilson, now an ardent environmentalist; and Lili Haydn as Gail Baker, Danni's best friend.

THE NEW HIGH ROLLERS
See HIGH ROLLERS

THE NEW JOEY BISHOP SHOW
See THE JOEY BISHOP SHOW

NEW KIDS ON THE BLOCK   ABC

8 SEPTEMBER 1990–27 JULY 1991   The phenomenally popular teen singing group came to Saturday-morning television in this show, which blended bits of live action and concert footage into a mostly animated story line. The five New Kids—Donnie Wahlberg, Jordan Knight, Jonathan Knight, Joe McIntyre, and Danny Wood— appeared as themselves. See also *Guys Next Door*.

A NEW KIND OF FAMILY   ABC

16 SEPTEMBER 1979–21 OCTOBER 1979   One of the first casualties of the 1979– 1980 season, this was a half-hour comedy about two families—a widow with three kids, and a divorcée with one child—who ended up renting the same house. With Eileen Brennan as Kit Flanagan, the widow, who moved west from New York; Gwynne Gilford as Abby Stone, the divorcée, who was starting law school; David Hollander as Andy Flanagan; Lauri Hendler as Hillary Flanagan; Rob Lowe as Tony Flanagan; Connie Ann Hearn as Jill Stone; and Chuck McCann as next-door neighbor Harold Zimmerman. Margie Gordon and Jane Eisner created the series and were its executive producers. A few episodes were later shown, with Telma Hopkins (replacing Gilford) as Jessie Ashton, and Janet Jackson as her daughter, JoJo.

THE NEW LAND   ABC

14 SEPTEMBER 1974–19 OCTOBER 1974   This hour-long family drama, set in Minnesota in 1858, collapsed early in the season under competition from CBS's *All in the Family* and NBC's *Emergency!* It featured Scott Thomas as Christian Larsen, the head of a family of Swedish immigrants; Bonnie Bedelia as his wife, Anna Larsen; Todd Lookinland as their son, Tuliff; Debbie Lytton as their daughter, Annaliese; Kurt Russell as Christian's brother, Bo Larsen; Donald Moffat as Lundstrom; Gwen Arner as Molly, Lundstrom's wife; and Lew Frizzell as Murdock. William Blinn was the executive producer and Philip Leacock the producer for Warner Brothers Television.

THE NEW LASSIE   SYNDICATED

1989–1991   After a fifteen-year hiatus, television's favorite collie returned to the screen in a series of new adventures. This time Lassie lived in the suburbs with the McCulloch family. The human cast included Will Nipper as Lassie's ten-year-old master, Will; Christopher Stone as his father, Chris; Dee Wallace Stone (Christopher

Stone's real-life wife) as his mother, Dee; Wendy Cox as his sister, Megan; and Jon Provost (who, of course, had played Timmy in the old *Lassie* series) as Uncle Steve.

THE NEW LEAVE IT TO BEAVER   DISNEY/WTBS
1985–1986 (DISNEY); 1986–1989 (WTBS)   The success of the 1983 TV-movie *Still the Beaver* led to this revival of the classic family sitcom *Leave It to Beaver,* which featured several members of the original cast. The new series starred Jerry Mathers as Theodore "Beaver" Cleaver, now divorced with two sons of his own and living (temporarily) at home; Tony Dow as Wally Cleaver, now a successful attorney, married to his high school sweetheart; Barbara Billingsley as their mother, June Cleaver, now a widow; Kipp Marcus as Ward "Kip" Cleaver, Beaver's older son; John Snee as Oliver Cleaver, Beaver's younger son; Janice Kent as Mary Ellen Rogers Cleaver, Wally's wife; Kaleena Kiff as their daughter, Kelly Cleaver; Troy Davidson (1987–1989) as their young son, Kevin Cleaver; Ken Osmond as Beaver's old nemesis, Eddie Haskell, still sleazy, now a contractor; Ellen Maxted as Eddie's wife, Gert; Eric Osmond (Ken Osmond's real-life son) as Eddie's son Freddie Haskell (known as Eddie Jr. during the first season); Christian Osmond (also Ken Osmond's real-life son) as Eddie's son Bomber Haskell; and Frank Bank as Clarence "Lumpy" Rutherford. The series was titled *Still the Beaver* on The Disney Channel.

Like most sequels and remakes, *The New Leave It to Beaver* pales in comparison to the original.

THE NEW LORETTA YOUNG SHOW   CBS
24 SEPTEMBER 1962–18 MARCH 1963   Loretta Young starred in this continuing comedy-drama as Christine Massey, a recently widowed writer with seven children who got a job with a New York magazine; in the last episode Christine married her editor. Also featured were James Philbrook as Paul Belzer, the editor; Celia Kaye as Marnie, the oldest child; Dack Rambo as Peter; Dirk Rambo as Peter's twin brother, Paul; Beverly Washburn as Vickie; Carol Sydes as Binkie; Sandy Descher as Judy; and Tracy Stratford as Maria, the youngest.

THE NEW LOVE, AMERICAN STYLE
See LOVE, AMERICAN STYLE

THE NEW MICKEY MOUSE CLUB
See THE MICKEY MOUSE CLUB

THE NEW MONKEES   SYNDICATED
1987   A short-lived, unsuccessful remake of the 1966 series. As before, a nation-wide search was undertaken to find the four "New Monkees": Marty Ross, Dino Kovas, Larry Saltis, and Jared Chandler were ultimately selected. The new group lived in a mansion, with a butler named Manford (Gordon Oas-Heim), and ate at a nearby diner, with a waitress named Rita (Bess Motta). Also featured on the series was Helen, a disembodied pair of lips that appeared on video screens throughout the mansion; Lynne Godfrey provided the voice.

THE NEW ODD COUPLE   ABC
29 OCTOBER 1982–25 FEBRUARY 1983; 13 MAY 1983–16 JUNE 1983   This half-hour sitcom was, of course, a remake of *The Odd Couple,* the popular 1970s comedy about two divorced men sharing a New York apartment. This time around, however, the principal players were black: Ron Glass as fashion photographer Felix Unger; De-mond Wilson as sportswriter Oscar Madison; and Sheila Anderson and Ronalda Douglas as their neighbors, sisters Cecily and Gwendolyn Pigeon. John Schuck (who is white) was also featured as their friend, police officer Murray Greshler. Unfortu-nately, though the cast of *The New Odd Couple* may have been "new," the stories were not: the show's producer conceded in November of 1982 that seven of the series' first thirteen scripts had been recycled from the original *Odd Couple.*

THE NEW PEOPLE   ABC

22 SEPTEMBER 1969–12 JANUARY 1970   This forty-five-minute continuing drama was
the companion to *The Music Scene,* a forty-five-minute variety series that preceded it
on Mondays. *The New People* told the implausible story of a planeload of American
young people who crash landed on a remote Pacific island; the island was conveniently outfitted with structures, supplies, and provisions, because it had been designated as a nuclear test site but abandoned before any tests were ever made. The cast
included: Peter Ratray as George Potter, the group's unofficial leader; Tiffany
Bolling as Susan Bradley; Zooey Hall as Bob Lee; Jill Jaress as Ginny Loomis; David
Moses as Gene Washington; Dennis Olivieri as Stanley Gabriel; Clive Clerk as Jack;
and Donna Bacalla as Wendy. Though the youngsters were supposedly isolated from
the rest of the world, guest stars managed to appear almost every week; one of them
was Richard Dreyfuss, who was featured in the 29 September episode. Aaron Spelling and Harold Gast were the producers.

THE NEW PERRY MASON   CBS

16 SEPTEMBER 1973–27 JANUARY 1974   An unsuccessful remake of television's most
famous courtroom show, *The New Perry Mason* lasted about one-twentieth as long as
the old *Perry Mason.* The new cast included Monte Markham as Perry Mason;
Sharon Acker as his secretary, Della Street; Albert Stratton as investigator Paul
Drake; Harry Guardino as prosecutor Hamilton Burger; Dane Clark as Lieutenant
Arthur Tragg; and Brett Somers as Perry's receptionist, Gertie. Ernie Frankel and
Art Seid, who had both been associated with the old *Perry Mason,* were the produc-
ers of the new version for 20th Century-Fox Television.

THE NEW PHIL SILVERS SHOW   CBS

28 SEPTEMBER 1963–27 JUNE 1964   Phil Silvers's "new" show was a lot like his "old"
show, *You'll Never Get Rich.* In this half-hour sitcom he played Harry Grafton, a
plant foreman for a large corporation. Always on the lookout for a get-rich-quick
scheme, Grafton and his crew of stooges never seemed to find the elusive pot of gold.
The cast also included: Stafford Repp as Grafton's boss, Mr. Brink; Jim Shane as
Lester; Herbie Faye (who had also played one of the enlistees on *You'll Never Get
Rich*) as Waluska; Steve Mitchell as Starkey; Bob Williams as Bob; Buddy Lester as
Nick; Pat Renella as Roxy; and Norm Grabowski as Grabowski. In February of 1964
three new cast members were added as Grafton moved in with his widowed sister:
Elena Verdugo as his sister, Audrey; Sandy Descher as her daughter, Susan; and
Ronnie Dapo as Andy, Audrey's son.

THE NEW SHMOO   NBC

22 SEPTEMBER 1979–1 DECEMBER 1979   Al Capp's amorphous cartoon creation came
to Saturday-morning television in this half-hour cartoon series. The Shmoo assisted
three teenage journalists who investigated phenomena for Mighty Mysteries Comics.
In December 1979 the show became part of the ninety-minute *Fred and Barney Meet
the Shmoo.*

THE NEW SHOW   NBC

6 JANUARY 1984–23 MARCH 1984   Lorne Michaels, the first producer of *NBC's
Saturday Night Live,* brought this disappointing comedy-variety show to prime time.
Valri Bromfield, Buck Henry, and Dave Thomas were the principal regulars.

THE NEW TEMPERATURES RISING SHOW
See TEMPERATURES RISING

THE NEW THREE STOOGES   SYNDICATED

1965   The cartoon adventures of the Three Stooges—Moe, Larry, and Curly. Moe
Howard, Larry Fine, and Curly Joe DeRita provided the voices and appeared in live-
action sequences as well. See also *The Skatebirds; The Three Robonic Stooges.*

THE NEW TIC TAC DOUGH
See TIC TAC DOUGH

THE NEW TREASURE HUNT
See TREASURE HUNT

THE NEW TRUTH OR CONSEQUENCES
See TRUTH OR CONSEQUENCES

THE NEW WKRP IN CINCINNATI   SYNDICATED
1991–1993 The syndicated remake of the 1978–1982 network series *WKRP in Cincinnati* brought back three of the original cast: Gordon Jump as station manager Arthur Carlson; Frank Bonner as salesman Herb Tarlek; and Richard Sanders as newsman Les Nessman (other original cast members Howard Hesseman and Loni Anderson made guest appearances). Rounding out the cast were Mykelti Williamson (formerly known as Mykel T. Williamson) as program director Donovan Aderhold; Michael Des Barres (1991–1992) and Kathleen Garrett (1991–1992) as morning drive-time deejays Jack Allen and Dana Burns, who were divorced from each other; Hope Alexander-Willis as traffic manager Claire Hartline; Wendy Davis (1991–1992) as receptionist Ronnie Lee; Marla Jeanette Rubinoff (1992–1993) as receptionist Nancy Braithwaite; John Chappell as station engineer Buddy Dornster; Lightfield Lewis as rookie salesman Arthur Carlson, Jr.; Tawny Kitaen as late-night deejay Mona Loveland; and Mark Roberts as Dirk, the security guard.

NEW YORK CONFIDENTIAL   SYNDICATED
1959   Half-hour crime show starring Lee Tracy as crimefighting reporter Lee Cochran.

NEW YORK NEWS   CBS
28 SEPTEMBER 1995–14 DECEMBER 1995   A New York newspaper was the center of this hour drama, which featured Mary Tyler Moore as Louise Felcott, editor-in-chief of the *New York Reporter*; Gregory Harrison as columnist Jack Reilly; Melina Kanakaredes as reporter Angela Villanova; Joe Morton as managing editor Mitch Cotter; Anthony DeSando as reporter Anthony Amato; Kelli Williams as intern Ellie Molanski; Kevin Chamberlin as Victor the office boy; and Madeline Kahn as gossip columnist Nan Chase.

THE NEW YORK TIMES YOUTH FORUM   DUMONT
14 SEPTEMBER 1952–14 JUNE 1953   This Sunday-evening public affairs program for young people was produced by Al Hollander and moderated by Dorothy Gordon.

NEW YORK UNDERCOVER   FOX
8 SEPTEMBER 1994–   Hour crime show set in New York City's Fourth Precinct, with Malik Yoba as Detective J. C. Williams, Michael DeLorenzo as his partner, Detective Eddie Torres, and Patti D'Arbanville-Quinn as the boss, Lieutenant Virginia Cooper. Lauren Velez joined in the fall of 1995 as Detective Nina Moreno. Created by Dick Wolf and Kevin Arkadie, the series was filmed on location.

THE NEW YOU ASKED FOR IT   SYNDICATED
1981–1982   This half-hour series was a remake of the 1950s show *You Asked for It*, which answered viewers' requests to see the unusual. Rich Little, better known as an impressionist than as an emcee, hosted the new series during its first season; Jack Smith, who had been the second host of the original show, also appeared on the remake to introduce clips from the old show. In the fall of 1982 he succeeded Little as host of the new series. *The New You Asked for It* also featured a staff of female correspondents, who included Georgette D'Aruba, Adrienne Allyn, Suzanne Childs, Kathy Cronkite (daughter of CBS newsman Walter Cronkite), Alanna Davis, Delaney Delvaney, Leah Erickson, Danielle Folquet, Desiree Goyette, Dale Harimoto, Janet Langhart, Laura Louise, Mattie Majors, and Toni Thomas.

NEW ZOO REVUE SYNDICATED

1972–1975 This half-hour children's show was seen daily in most markets. Created by Barbara Atlas and Douglas Momary (who also appeared as Doug), it introduced viewers to cultural and educational themes principally through musical numbers. Other cast members included Emily Peden as Emily Jo; Yanco Inone as Freddie the Frog; Larri Thomas as Henrietta the Hippo; and former Mouseketeer Sharon Baird as Charlie the Owl. Stephen W. Jahn was the executive producer.

THE NEWCOMERS CBS

12 JULY 1971–6 SEPTEMBER 1971 A summer replacement for *The Carol Burnett Show,* this lackluster variety hour was hosted by Dave Garroway and featured a group of young professionals: singers David Arlen, Cynthia Clawson, Raul Perez, Gay Perkins, Peggy Sears, and the Californians; comics Joey Garza, Rodney Winfield, and the Good Humor Company.

NEWHART CBS

25 OCTOBER 1982–31 AUGUST 1990 Four years after leaving *The Bob Newhart Show,* comedian Bob Newhart returned to star in another sitcom. This time he played Dick Loudon, a history buff and the author of several successful "how to" books. He and his wife, Joanna, decided to move to New England; they bought the Stratford Inn in Stratford, Vermont. Also featured were Mary Frann as Dick's wife, Joanna Loudon; Tom Poston as George Utley, the slow-moving, slow-thinking caretaker of the inn; Steven Kampmann (1982–1984) as Kirk Devane, the compulsive liar who ran a cafe-cum-souvenir shop next door; Jennifer Holmes (1982–1983) as Leslie Vanderkellen, a preppy-type who signed on as the maid at the inn; and Julia Duffy (1983–1990) as Stephanie Vanderkellen, Leslie's self-infatuated cousin, who succeeded her as the maid.

Several changes took place in the show's third season (1984–1985): Dick started hosting a talk show on the local television station. Peter Scolari joined the cast as Michael Harris, the trendy young producer of Dick's show, *Vermont Today;* Michael and Stephanie soon became an item, and were married in November 1987 (their baby, little Stephanie, was born during the show's final season). The Minute Man Cafe changed hands in 1984 also. Its new owners were a bizarre trio of backwoods brothers who had previously appeared only briefly: William Sanderson played Larry, the spokesman of the group; Tony Papenfuss played his brother Darryl, and John Volstad played his other brother Darryl. With such a large cast of regulars, most of the stories soon centered around them; the Stratford Inn seldom seemed to have any guests.

The series' final first-run episode (21 May 1990) yielded several surprises. Alone among the townsfolk, Dick and Joanna refused to sell out to a Japanese developer intent on turning Stratford into a golf course. Five years later the townsfolk returned to Stratford for a reunion; Larry and his brothers had married chatterboxes, and the two Darryls finally uttered their only line of the entire series: "Quiet!" Dick was hit in the head by an errant golf ball and woke up in bed—as Bob Hartley, his character from *The Bob Newhart Show.* Next to him was his wife Emily Hartley (played by Suzanne Pleshette), also, of course, from the old show—suggesting that the entire *Newhart* series had simply been a dream of Bob Hartley's.

Newhart was videotaped during its first season and switched to film thereafter. Henry Mancini composed the show's theme. The actual Vermont inn used for the exteriors was The Waybury Inn in East Middlebury.

THE NEWLYWED GAME ABC/SYNDICATED

11 JULY 1966–20 DECEMBER 1974 (ABC); 1977–1980 (SYNDICATED); 13 FEBRUARY 1984–17 FEBRUARY 1984 (ABC); 1985–1990 (SYNDICATED) Bob Eubanks hosted this tasteless but highly successful game show on which four newly married couples compete for prizes. One set of spouses was sent offstage while the remaining set was asked questions and predicted the responses that the offstage spouses would make when asked the same question. Couples whose answers matched won points. The durable series, which ran for eight years in a daytime slot, was also seen in prime

time on occasion between 1967 and 1971. The show was created by Chuck Barris, the man responsible for *The Dating Game* and *The Gong Show*. Sometimes Eubanks took the show on the road, staging it at shopping malls all around the country. In 1985 the series turned up again, titled *The New Newlywed Game*. Eubanks continued as host until 1989, when Paul Rodriguez took over. Reviewing the series in 1987, *TV Guide* dubbed it "the worst piece of sleaze on television today."

THE NEWS AND ITS MEANING CBS
27 AUGUST 1950–24 SEPTEMBER 1950   Five-week, Sunday-night news analysis series hosted by John Daly, who later became head of ABC's news division.

THE NEWS IS THE NEWS NBC
15 JUNE 1983–20 JULY 1983   A feeble attempt at satirizing news shows. Regulars included Michael Davis, Simon Jones, Charlotte Moore, Lynne Thigpen, and Trey Wilson. The half-hour show was broadcast live from New York.

NEWSGAL
See BYLINE

NEWSRADIO NBC
21 MARCH 1995–9 MAY 1995; 3 AUGUST 1995–   Half-hour sitcom set at WNYX, an all-news radio station in New York. With Dave Foley as the new news director, Dave Nelson; Phil Hartman as the vain news anchor, Bill McNeal; Stephen Root as station owner Jimmy James; Andy Dick as Matthew, the insecure reporter; Maura Tierney as news writer Lisa Miller; Vicki Lewis as Beth, the secretary; Khandi Alexander as Catherine Duke, Bill's coanchor; and Joe Rogan as Joe, the engineer. Paul Simms created the series.

NEWSWEEK VIEWS THE NEWS DUMONT
7 NOVEMBER 1948–22 MAY 1950   On this prime-time public affairs program, members of the board of editors of *Newsweek* magazine met to discuss the views and to interview guests. Ernest K. Lindley was the moderator. The show was originally titled *Newsweek Analysis*.

NEWTON'S APPLE PBS
1983–   Principles of science were explained to viewers in this series, produced by KTCA-TV in Minneapolis. The program was first hosted by Ira Flatow, with occasional assistance from his skeleton sidekick, Dead Ernest. David Heil, associate director of The Oregon Museum of Science and Industry, became the host in 1989.

THE NEWZ SYNDICATED
1994–1995   Half-hour daily comedy sketch series, inspired mainly by current events, and performed by Tommy Blaze, Deborah Magdalena, Dan O'Connor, Stan Quash, Brad Sherwood, Nancy Sullivan, Shawn Alex Thompson, and Lou Thornton. Financial difficulties forced the discontinuation of the series early in 1995.

THE NEXT PRESIDENT SYNDICATED
1987–1988   David Frost conducted interviews with the 1988 presidential aspirants on this public affairs series.

THE NEXT STEP BEYOND SYNDICATED
1978   A revival of *One Step Beyond*, ABC's 1960s anthology series, *The Next Step Beyond* dwelt on the occult and the supernatural. John Newland returned as host and director, with Collier Young the executive producer, Alan J. Factor producer, and Merwin Gerard writer.

NICHOLAS NICKLEBY SYNDICATED
10 JANUARY 1983–13 JANUARY 1983   The Royal Shakespeare Company's adaptation of Charles Dickens's classic novel was presented on television as a four-part, nine-

hour miniseries, produced by the Mobil Showcase Network. The TV version was based directly on the RSC's 1980 stage version, which had been written by David Edgar and directed by Trevor Nunn and John Caird. The RSC's thirty-nine performers played more than 150 roles; as Nicholas, Roger Rees was the only actor to play a single part.

NICHOLS NBC
16 SEPTEMBER 1971–1 AUGUST 1972   Set in Nichols, Arizona, in 1914, this light-hearted western starred James Garner as Nichols, a drifter who returned to his hometown and reluctantly became the sheriff; on the last first-run episode, Nichols was killed, but was replaced by his twin brother. Also featured were Neva Patterson as Ma Ketcham; Margot Kidder as Ruth, the barmaid; John Beck as Ketcham, Ma's son, Ruth's boyfriend; Stuart Margolin as Mitchell, Nichols's deputy; and Paul Hampton as Johnson. Produced by Garner's company, Cherokee Productions, the show was officially titled *James Garner as Nichols* after October 1971.

NICK AND HILLARY
See TATTINGER'S

THE NICK KENNY SHOW NBC
18 JULY 1951–1 JANUARY 1952   Nick Kenny, radio editor for the New York *Mirror,* hosted a late-night, fifteen-minute series on which he read poetry, sang a few songs, and interviewed guests.

NIGHT COURT SYNDICATED
1958   Half-hour courtroom drama show, with Jay Jostyn as the presiding judge of a big-city night court session.

NIGHT COURT NBC
4 JANUARY 1984–17 SEPTEMBER 1992   What started out as a *Barney Miller*–type sitcom set in an urban courtroom, peopled by an endless parade of defendants, litigants, and lawyers, gradually turned into one of TV's bawdiest shows as the stories began to focus on the show's regular characters, most of whom were unmarried. The original cast included Harry Anderson as Judge Harry T. Stone, the young, unorthodox jurist who presided over the night sessions in Manhattan's district court; Karen Austin (spring 1984) as his clerk, Lana Wagner; Paula Kelly (spring 1984) as public defender Liz Williams; John Larroquette as libidinous prosecutor Dan Fielding; Richard Moll as the tall and thick court officer Bull Shannon; and Selma Diamond (1984–1985) as short and acerbic court officer Selma Hacker. In the fall of 1984 Ellen Foley succeeded Kelly as public defender Billie Young (Shelley Hack had originally been hired as the new p.d., but was dropped); Foley in turn was succeeded in 1985 by Markie Post, as public defender Christine Sullivan. Charles Robinson was also added in the fall of 1984, as court clerk Mac Robinson. Selma Diamond died in 1985, and Florence Halop appeared during the 1985–1986 season as Court Officer Florence Kleiner. Halop died in 1986, and Marsha Warfield stepped in as new court officer Roz Russell. Occasionally featured as courtroom regulars were Terry Kiser (1984) as reporter Al Craven; William Utay (1985–1986, 1989–1992) as Phil the derelict; and Bumper Robinson (1985–1986) as Leon the runaway. Rounding out the cast were Mike Finneran as Art, the courthouse's hapless janitor, Denice Kumagai as Quon Le, Mac's wife, John Astin (1990–1992) as Harry's flaky father, Buddy Ryan, and Jolene Lutz (1990–1992) as Lisette Hocheiser, the court reporter. Singer Mel Tormé showed up on a few shows, as himself; in real life he and Harry Anderson were close friends. In February 1990 Christine Sullivan married police officer Tony Giuliano (played by Ray Abruzzo); they later divorced.

NIGHT EDITOR DUMONT
14 MARCH 1954–8 SEPTEMBER 1954   An unusual fifteen-minute show, *Night Editor* was a series of dramas written, narrated, and starring Hal Burdick. Burdick appeared as the night editor of a newspaper, and began to tell the evening's story; as the tale

progressed, Burdick himself then acted out some of the segments as he narrated. Ward Byron produced the show, and Dick Sandwick directed it.

NIGHT GALLERY   NBC

16 DECEMBER 1970–14 JANUARY 1973   This anthology series of supernatural tales was introduced in 1970 as one segment of NBC's *Four-in-One*. In the fall of 1971 it was given its own slot. Rod Serling hosted the show from an art-gallery setting. In the fall of 1972 the show was cut back from sixty to thirty minutes, and *Night Gallery* vanished in the middle of its third season. Among the many directors who worked on the show was twenty-one-year-old Steven Spielberg, who later directed such colossal films as *Jaws* and *Close Encounters of the Third Kind*. Spielberg's first major TV work was directing one of three segments of the "Night Gallery" made-for-TV movie, which aired 8 November 1969.

NIGHT GAMES   CBS

14 OCTOBER 1991–12 JUNE 1992   A late-night game show introduced by CBS in 1991 (see also *Personals*), this one was emceed by Jeff Marder, with help from Luann Lee. A panel of three men and three women evaluated each other in various categories, and the couple with the most points won a date together.

NIGHT HEAT   CBS

31 JANUARY 1985–13 SEPTEMBER 1991   The longest-running of CBS's several late-night action series of the late 1980s, *Night Heat* was an atmospheric crime show, filmed largely on location in Toronto, and, appropriately, largely at night. In its original plans for the late-night slot, CBS had considered following real New York City police officers around (an idea subsequently employed on Fox's *Cops*), but ultimately agreed to the more traditional fiction format proposed by producers Sonny Grosso (himself a former New York cop) and Larry Jacobson. To help achieve a gritty look, and to keep expenses down, the producers used sixteen-millimeter film and relied heavily on hand-held camera techniques. The series was jointly financed by CBS, the Canadian network CTV, and the Canadian government; CTV aired it in prime time. CBS also gave the series brief exposure in prime time, airing it at 10 P.M. on Tuesdays from 4 August to 8 September 1987. A total of ninety-six episodes were produced.

Night Heat's principal characters were two big-city cops assigned to the Major Case Squad of the Mid-South Precinct, and the journalist who wrote about them in his "Night Heat" column for the city paper. Scott Hylands played veteran detective Kevin O'Brien; Jeff Wincott was his young partner, Detective Frank Giambone; and Allan Royal was the reporter, Tom Kirkwood, who also did the voiceover at the end of each episode. Other regulars included Susan Hogan as Nicole Rimbaud, Kevin's girlfriend; Sean McCann as the boss, Lieutenant Jim Hogan; Wendy Crewson (1985) as prosecutor Dorothy Fredericks; Lynda Mason Green (1985) as Detective Fleece Toland; Louise Vallance (1985–1986) as Detective Stevie Brodie; Deborah Grover as prosecutor Elaine Jeffers; Laura Robinson (1985–1988) as Detective Christine Meadows; Eugene Clark as Detective Colby Burns; Stephen Mendel as Detective Freddie Carson; and Tony Rosato as snitch Whitey Low.

NIGHT MUSIC   SYNDICATED

1987–1990   An hour musical series, intended for late-night time slots on Sunday evenings. The emphasis was truly on music, as the series showcased many serious musicians from the worlds of jazz and rock in live performance; some vintage clips were also telecast. The show was originally cohosted by jazz saxophonist David Sanborn and rocker Jools Holland; Sanborn later became the sole host. Lorne Michaels (of *Saturday Night Live*) was executive producer. The series was officially titled *Michelob Presents Sunday Night* during its first season and *Michelob Presents Night Music* thereafter.

THE NIGHT STALKER   ABC

13 SEPTEMBER 1974–30 AUGUST 1975   This hour-long fantasy series starred Darren McGavin as Carl Kolchak, a gritty reporter for the Independent News Service who stalked a new and mysterious murderer each week, whether it be Jack the Ripper, a swamp monster, a vampire, a werewolf, or an invisible force. Also featured were Simon Oakland as Kolchak's disbelieving boss, Tony Vincenzo; Jack Grinnage as Ron Updyke, another reporter for I.N.S.; Ruth McDevitt as Emily Cowles, author of the advice-to-the-lovelorn column; John Fiedler as Gordy Spangler; and Carol Ann Susi as Monique Marmelstein. The series was ordered into production after two successful made-for-TV movies, "The Night Stalker" (17 March 1972) and "The Night Strangler" (16 January 1973). Twenty one-hour episodes were filmed; Darren McGavin was executive producer, and Paul Playdon and Cy Chermak the producers.

NIGHT STAND WITH DICK DIETRICK   SYNDICATED

1995–   TV's sleazy talk shows were long overdue for a spoof, which was accomplished by this weekly series. Timothy Stack played Dick Dietrick, the not-too-bright host of his own talk show, *Night Stand with Dick Dietrick*. The show's guests were played by actors, as were the audience members who asked questions of them. Each hour show was comprised of two half-hour spoofs.

NIGHTINGALES   NBC

21 JANUARY 1989–26 APRIL 1989   An hour medical series from Aaron Spelling and Douglas S. Cramer about five student nurses. With Suzanne Pleshette as Chris Broderick, director of student nursing at Wilshire Community Hospital; Barry Newman as Dr. Garrett Braden, the chief of staff; Susan Walters as Bridget Loring, who entered the program as part of a witness protection program; Kristy Swanson as Rebecca, fresh from Missouri; Chelsea Field as Samantha, a recovering alcoholic; Roxann Biggs as Yolanda Puente; Kim Ulrich as Allyson; and Fran Bennett as Head Nurse Ritt. Gil Gerard appeared occasionally as Chris's ex-husband, Paul Petrillo. The five nursing students—Bridget, Rebecca, Samantha, Yolanda, and Allyson— resided at the Nightingale Residence Hall, where they seemed to do a lot of aerobics and clothing changes. Professional nursing organizations sharply criticized the show for its *Charlie's Angels*–type excesses. The pilot for the series was a two-hour TV-movie broadcast 27 June 1988.

NIGHTLIFE   ABC

8 MARCH 1965–12 NOVEMBER 1965   This late-night talk show was the successor to *The Les Crane Show*, ABC's first attempt to compete with NBC's Johnny Carson. The show featured a different guest host each week for the first few months, but by late June Les Crane was back in the host's chair, assisted by Nipsey Russell and the Elliott Lawrence Orchestra.

NIGHTLIFE   SYNDICATED

8 SEPTEMBER 1986–4 SEPTEMBER 1987   Half-hour weeknight talk show hosted by comedian David Brenner. Billy Preston led the band.

NIGHTLINE

See ABC NEWS NIGHTLINE

THE NIGHTLY BUSINESS REPORT   PBS

1981–   Half-hour daily summary of economic and business news, produced by WPBT-TV in Miami, Florida. Recent anchors have included Jim Wicks, Linda O'Bryon, Paul Kangas, and Cassie Seifert.

NIGHTMARE CAFE   NBC

29 JANUARY 1992; 28 FEBRUARY 1992–3 APRIL 1992   An hour fantasy series, created by Wes Craven and Thomas Braun. Each episode centered on a person who had been selected by a "higher authority" to have the chance to relive a crucial moment in his or her life. The situation was explained to the selectees at the All-Night Cafe, a

mysterious bistro whose neon sign was then transformed into the Nightmare Cafe. The regulars included Robert Englund (the star of Craven's numerous *Nightmare on Elm Street* films) as Blackie, the apparent proprietor of the cafe, and Jack Coleman and Lindsay Frost as Frank Nolan and Fay Fiernovic, the central characters in the premiere telecast who then stayed on at the café.

NIGHTSIDE   NBC
3 NOVEMBER 1991–   NBC, which had pioneered the concept of the post-midnight newscast in 1982 with *NBC News Overnight*, revived it nine years later under this title. The program was produced in Charlotte, North Carolina.

NIGHTTALK WITH JANE WHITNEY
See THE JANE WHITNEY SHOW

9 TO 5   ABC/SYNDICATED
25 MARCH 1982–15 APRIL 1982; 28 SEPTEMBER 1982–27 OCTOBER 1983 (ABC); 1986–1988 (SYNDICATED)   This half-hour sitcom was based on the 1980 film about three working women trapped in go-nowhere careers at a large conglomerate. It featured Rita Moreno as Violet Newstead, a section supervisor at Consolidated Companies; Valerie Curtin as Judy Bernley, a new employee; Rachel Dennison as Doralee Rose, a curvaceous but crafty secretary (Dennison's more famous sister, Dolly Parton, had played the role in the film); Jeffrey Tambor (spring 1982) and Peter Bonerz (fall 1982–1983) as their boss, chauvinistic Franklin Hart. Supporting players included Suzanne Stone as Roberta; Mary Farrell as Denise, the receptionist; Peggy Pope as Betty; Ann Weldon as Clair; Peter Hobbs as Mr. O'Malley, an executive vice-president; and Herb Edelman (fall 1982–1983) as salesman Harry Pearlman. During the 1982–1983 season *9 to 5* deemphasized the feminist overtones that had been integral to the film, and the series became indistinguishable from other office sitcoms. At the end of the season executive producers Bruce Gilbert and Jane Fonda (who had also made a rare on-camera appearance in one episode as a night watchperson) left the show; they were succeeded by veteran producer James Komack (who also appeared as a high-level executive). Valerie Curtin also left the show, and several new regulars were added: Leah Ayres as new employee Linda Bowman; George Deloy as handsome salesman Michael Henderson; and Tony La Torre as Violet's young son, Tommy. The changes of personnel went in vain, and *9 to 5* was cancelled after just four episodes of the new season. Dolly Parton wrote and sang the show's theme, except during the spring 1982 tryout, when Phoebe Snow sang it.
    20th Century-Fox TV produced new episodes for syndication starting in 1986. Set at a new conglomerate, Barkley Foods International, it brought back Valerie Curtin and Rachel Dennison from the old cast. Joining them were Sally Struthers as divorced secretary Marsha MacMurray Shrimpton; Edward Winter as Doralee's boss, Bud Coleman; Peter Evans as Judy's boss, Russ Merman; Dorian Lopinto (1986–1987) as Marsha's first boss, Charmin Cunningham; and Fred Applegate (1987–1988) as Marsha's new boss, E. Nelson Felb.

1986   NBC
10 JUNE 1986–30 DECEMBER 1986   Another in NBC's seemingly endless parade of attempts to establish a prime-time newsmagazine series, *1986* was coanchored by Roger Mudd and Connie Chung. Like its predecessors, it failed to catch on.

90 BRISTOL COURT   NBC
5 OCTOBER 1964–4 JANUARY 1965   *90 Bristol Court* was the umbrella title for three half-hour situation comedies, all set at the same apartment complex in Southern California, and all aired back-to-back on Mondays: *Karen; Tom, Dick and Mary;* and *Harris Against the World*. Guy Raymond was featured on all three shows as Cliff Murdock, the handyman. Produced by Revue Studios, it is probably not coincidental that the initials of the umbrella series were NBC. See also *Karen; Tom, Dick and Mary;* and *Harris Against the World*.

NO HOLDS BARRED   CBS

12 SEPTEMBER 1980–3 OCTOBER 1980   Apparently intended as CBS's answer to
NBC's *Saturday Night Live* and ABC's *Fridays, No Holds Barred* arrived with little
fanfare and vanished before many viewers had had a chance to see it. Kelly Monteith
hosted the seventy-minute series, which was aired at 11:30 P.M. on Fridays and
consisted of comedy, music, and filmed segments of unusual people.

NO SOAP, RADIO   ABC

15 APRIL 1982–13 MAY 1982   This offbeat sitcom may have been inspired by *Monty
Python's Flying Circus*—each episode's storyline was periodically interrupted by
seemingly irrelevant blackouts. The half-hour series was set at the Hotel Pelican, and
the cast included Steve Guttenberg as Roger, the manager; Hillary Bailey as his
assistant, Karen (Brianne Leary had played Sharon the assistant in the first episode);
Bill Dana as Mr. Plitzky, a guest; Fran Ryan as Mrs. Belmont, another guest; Jerry
Maren as Morris, the bellhop; and Stuart Pankin as Tuttle. Edie McClurg and Joe
Baker were also featured in various roles.

NO TIME FOR SERGEANTS   ABC

14 SEPTEMBER 1964–6 SEPTEMBER 1965   *No Time for Sergeants* was a half-hour sitcom
based on the movie of the same title, which was based on the play of the same title,
which was based on the television show of the same title broadcast on *The U.S. Steel
Hour* 15 March 1955 (it starred Andy Griffith, who repeated his role on stage and on
film). The television series starred Sammy Jackson as Private Will Stockdale, a
southern lad assigned to Andrews Air Force Base. Also featured were Kevin O'Neal
as Private Ben Whitledge; Harry Hickox as Sergeant King; Hayden Rorke as Colonel
Farnsworth; Paul Smith as Captain Martin; Laurie Sibbald as Milly Anderson,
Stockdale's girlfriend; Andy Clyde as Grandpa Jim Anderson, Milly's grandfather;
Michael McDonald as Private Langdon; George Murdock as Captain Krupnick;
Greg Benedict as Private Blanchard; and Joey Tata as Private Neddick. The Warner
Brothers series, as well as the film, the play, and the original telecast, were all based
on Mac Hyman's story.

NO WARNING!   NBC

6 APRIL 1958–7 SEPTEMBER 1958   *No Warning!* was the title given to this series of
half-hour suspense dramas produced by Al Simon. Simon had produced a similar
series the preceding season, entitled *Panic!,* and nine *Panic!* episodes were rerun on
No Warning! along with fourteen originals. Westbrook Van Voorhis returned as host
and narrator.

NOAH'S ARK   NBC

18 SEPTEMBER 1956–26 FEBRUARY 1957   Jack Webb produced this half-hour dramatic
series about a pair of veterinarians. It featured Paul Burke as young Dr. Noah
McCann; Vic Rodman as Dr. Sam Rinehart, Noah's mentor, who was confined to a
wheelchair; and May Winn as their receptionist and nurse, Liz Clark. The series was
filmed in color.

NOBLE HOUSE (JAMES CLAVELL'S NOBLE HOUSE)   NBC

21 FEBRUARY 1988–24 FEBRUARY 1988   This four-part miniseries, adapted from
Clavell's novel about the warring Hong Kong business dynasties, was filmed partly
on location. Principal players included Pierce Brosnan as Ian Dunross, "tai-pan," or
supreme leader, of Struan and Company, a leading trading company; John Rhys-
Davies as Quillan Gornt, his chief rival; Ben Masters as corporate raider Linc Bart-
lett; Deborah Raffin as Casey Tcholok; Julia Nickson as Orlanda Ramos; Khigh
Dhiegh as drug lord Four Finger Wu; Tia Carrere as Wu's mistress, Venus Poon; and
Gordon Jackson as Superintendent Armstrong.

NOBODY'S PERFECT   ABC

26 JUNE 1980–28 AUGUST 1980   Half-hour sitcom starring Ron Moody as Inspector
Roger Hart, a bumbling detective from Scotland Yard who was assigned to San

Francisco's 22nd Precinct. Also featured were Cassie Yates as Hart's partner, Detective Jennifer Dempsey; Michael Durrell as the commanding officer, Lieutenant De Gennaro; Renny Roker as Ramsey; Tom Williams as Grauer; and Victor Brandt as Jacobi.

THE NOEL EDMONDS SHOW   ABC
23 JUNE 1986–27 JULY 1986   In another of ABC's occasional efforts to develop a late-night series to follow *Nightline,* BBC Television personality Noel Edmonds was given a one-week tryout in an hour talk show format.

NON FICTION TELEVISION   PBS
4 APRIL 1980–2 JULY 1980   A thirteen-week series of documentaries produced by independent filmmakers.

NORBY   NBC
5 JANUARY 1955–6 APRIL 1955   This half-hour sitcom starred David Wayne as Pearson Norby, vice president of the First National Bank in Pearl River, New York. Also featured were Joan Lorring as his wife, Helen Norby; Susan Hallaran as their daughter, Diane; Evan Elliott as their son, Hank; Paul Ford as the bank president; Ralph Dunn as Mr. Rudge, another vice president; Janice Mars as Wahleen Johnson, the switchboard operator; and Carol Veazie as Maude Endless. Created by David Swift, the series was the first television show sponsored by Eastman Kodak. It was filmed in color, and exteriors were actually shot in Pearl River, New York. The show's time slot (Wednesdays at 7 p.m., a slot which relatively few network affiliates made available for network broadcasts) was probably the chief factor behind its early cancellation.

NORMAL LIFE   CBS
21 MARCH 1990–25 APRIL 1990; 30 MAY 1990–18 JULY 1990   Considering the fact that this series was created for Dweezil and Moon Unit Zappa, two of the children of iconoclastic musician Frank Zappa, *Normal Life* proved to be a disappointingly trite, and mercifully short-lived, sitcom. The cast included Max Gail as the father, Max Harlow; Cindy Williams as the mother, Anne Harlow; Moon Unit Zappa as daughter Tess, twenty-two; Dweezil Zappa as son Jake, nineteen; Josh Williams as son Ben, thirteen; Bess Meyer as Tess's crony, Prima; Adam Jeffries as Ben's buddy, Raffie; and Jim Staahl as the next-door neighbor, Dr. Bob.

NORMAN CORWIN PRESENTS   SYNDICATED
1971   Half-hour dramatic anthology series produced and hosted by Norman Corwin, one of radio's most prolific writers and directors.

NORTH AND SOUTH   ABC
3 NOVEMBER 1985–10 NOVEMBER 1985   The top-rated miniseries of the season, *North and South* was a six-part, twelve-hour, $25 million adaptation of John Jakes's novel of the tensions leading up to the Civil War. The story focused on two familes, the Mains of South Carolina and the Hazards of Pennsylvania. Principal players included Patrick Swayze as Orry Main; James Read as George Hazard; Lesley-Anne Down as Madeline; Robert Guillaume as Frederick Douglass; Inga Swenson as Maude Hazard; Jonathan Frakes as Stanley Hazard; David Carradine as Justin LaMotte; Jean Simmons as Clarissa Main; Genie Francis as Brett Main; Terri Garber as Ashton Main; Kirstic Alley as Virgilia; and (in a small role) Elizabeth Taylor as Mme. Conti, a madam. David L. Wolper was executive producer. A sequel aired in the spring of 1986: see below.

NORTH AND SOUTH, BOOK II   ABC
4 MAY 1986–11 MAY 1986   The six-part sequel to *North and South,* based on John Jakes's novel *Love and War,* was played out largely on the battlefields of the Civil War. Many of the *North and South* cast were again featured—Patrick Swayze, James Read, Lesley-Anne Down, Terri Garber, Genie Francis, Jean Simmons, and Kirstie Alley—together with others, including Hal Holbrook as Abraham Lincoln, Lloyd

Bridges as Jefferson Davis, James Stewart as Miles Colbert, Morgan Fairchild as Burdetta Halloran, and Nancy Marchand as Dorothea Dix.

NORTHERN EXPOSURE CBS

12 JULY 1990–30 AUGUST 1990; 8 APRIL 1991–9 AUGUST 1995   Refreshing hour comedy-drama about a young New York City physician who found himself assigned to a tiny, remote village in Alaska. With Rob Morrow (1990–1995) as Dr. Joel Fleischman, the only doctor in the town of Cicely; Janine Turner as bush pilot Maggie O'Connell, Joel's landlady and possible romantic interest; Barry Corbin as former astronaut Maurice Minnifield, Cicely's principal businessman; Darren E. Burrows as Ed Chigliak, a young Native American who was an expert on contemporary pop culture; John Cullum as the mayor and bar owner, Holling Vincoeur; John Corbett as Chris Stevens, deejay on KBHR, Cicely's radio station; Cynthia Geary as Shelly Tambo, Holling's waitress and girlfriend; Elaine Miles as Marilyn Whirlwind, Joel's phlegmatic, self-appointed assistant; and Peg Phillips as Ruth-Anne Miller, proprietor of the general store. Occasionally featured were Adam Arkin as Adam, the fierce individualist who sometimes cooked at Holling's cafe, the Brick; Valerie Mahaffey as his hypochondriac wife, Eve; and Doug Ballard and Don R. McManus as Ron Bance and Erick Hillman, a gay couple who were married in May 1994.

After three years of kindling, the romantic relationship between Fleischman and O'Connell was finally consummated in February 1993. By the fall of 1994 Rob Morrow had announced his intention to leave the series, and did so in February 1995. By that time Paul Provenza had joined the cast as Cicely's new doctor, Phillip Capra, and Teri Polo had been added as his wife, Michelle Capra.

Much of *Northern Exposure*'s charm was due to the fact that it was filmed on location in Washington. Most exterior shots were filmed in the tiny town of Roslyn, which itself soon became a tourist attraction. Joshua Brand and John Falsey, who had created *St. Elsewhere,* created the series.

NORTHWEST PASSAGE NBC

14 SEPTEMBER 1958–8 SEPTEMBER 1959   This half-hour adventure series told the story of Rogers' Rangers during the French and Indian War. Set in upstate (or upcolony) New York in 1754, it starred Keith Larsen as Major Robert Rogers; Buddy Ebsen as Sergeant Hunk Marriner; and Don Burnett as Ensign Towne. The show was produced by M-G-M TV.

NOT FOR HIRE SYNDICATED

1959   Set in Hawaii, this half-hour crime show starred Ralph Meeker as Sergeant Steve Dekker, a criminal investigator for the United States Army. Also featured were Norman Alden, Ken Drake, and Herb Ellis. John Florea produced and directed.

NOT FOR PUBLICATION DUMONT

27 APRIL 1951–27 AUGUST 1951; 21 DECEMBER 1951–27 MAY 1952   William Adler first starred in this dramatic series as Collins, an investigative reporter for the New York *Ledger.* When the show began in April of 1951, it was a fifteen-minute series, but it returned to the air in December in a half-hour format, with Jerome Cowan as Collins.

NOT FOR WOMEN ONLY SYNDICATED

1971–1979   Half-hour daytime talk show. First hosted by Barbara Walters, the show began as a local show in New York, titled *For Women Only.* Hugh Downs later became cohost, and in 1976 Polly Bergen and Frank Field took over as cohosts.

NOT JUST NEWS SYNDICATED

1993–   Half-hour informational series for children, hosted by Steve Doocy (1993–1994) and Marty Putz (1994–).

NOT NECESSARILY THE NEWS HBO

8 JANUARY 1983–26 AUGUST 1990   Like *That Was the Week That Was, Not Necessarily the News* lampooned current events, often using actual newsreel footage. Among the

show's regular "reporters" have been Stuart Pankin, Anne Bloom, Danny Breen, Mitchell Laurance, Lucy Webb, Rich Hall, Audrie Neenan, Tom Parks, and Annabelle Gurwitch. The series was produced by John Moffitt and was inspired by the British series *Not the Nine O'Clock News*.

NOTHING BUT THE BEST   NBC
7 JULY 1953–13 SEPTEMBER 1953   Eddie Albert hosted this half-hour summer variety series.

NOTHING IN COMMON   NBC
2 APRIL 1987–3 JUNE 1987   A Chicago ad agency was the setting of this half-hour sitcom, based on the 1986 film that had starred Jackie Gleason and Tom Hanks. In the TV version Todd Waring starred as young David Basner, head of David Basner & Associates; Bill Macy costarred as his happy-go-lucky father, Max. Other regulars included Wendy Kilbourne as researcher Jacqueline North; Elizabeth Bennett as Victoria Upton-Smythe; Mona Lyden as copywriter Norma Starr; Bill Applebaum as copywriter Mark Glick; Billy Wirth as cameraman Joey D.; Patrick Richwood as student gofer Myron Nipper; Allan Kent as Wally; and Julie Paris as Autumn.

NOTHING IS EASY
See TOGETHER WE STAND

NOTRE DAME FOOTBALL   ABC
27 SEPTEMBER 1953–29 NOVEMBER 1953   Broadcast Sunday nights, this seventy-five-minute series consisted of films of the previous day's football game between Notre Dame and its opponent. Harry Wismer did the play-by-play.

NOVA   PBS
3 MARCH 1974–   High-quality series of filmed documentaries on scientific subjects. Produced at WGBH-TV, Boston, the show receives the cooperation of the American Association for the Advancement of Science. Most programs are sixty minutes, though some ninety-minute shows have been aired. A small sample of the series' presentations would include: "How to Create a Junk Food" (26 January 1987); "Can We Make a Better Doctor?" (13 December 1988); "Can You Believe TV Ratings?" (18 February 1992); "Sex and the Single Rhino" (29 December 1992); "The Secrets of the Psychics," with James Randi (19 October 1993); "Little Creatures Who Run the World," with Edward O. Wilson (31 January 1995); and "Mystery of the Senses," with Diane Ackerman (19–22 February 1995).

NOW   ABC
23 MARCH 1970–14 SEPTEMBER 1970   A half-hour informational series from ABC News. The first three programs, for example, focused on taxes and were cohosted by financial columnist Sylvia Porter and ABC's economics editor, Louis Rukeyser.

NOW   NBC
18 AUGUST 1993–7 SEPTEMBER 1994   Prime-time newsmagazine anchored by Tom Brokaw and Katie Couric. Bob Costas also contributed celebrity interviews.

NOW AND THEN   CBS
1 AUGUST 1954–5 SEPTEMBER 1954; 16 JANUARY 1955–26 JUNE 1955   Dr. Frank Baxter, professor of English literature at the University of Southern California, hosted this half-hour Sunday afternoon series of lectures on literature. The show was first televised locally in Los Angeles, and at that time USC offered college credit for the televised course. Dr. Baxter later hosted many television documentaries, including the highly acclaimed "Bell Science Series."

NOW IT CAN BE TOLD   SYNDICATED
1991–1992   In addition to hosting a popular daytime talk show, Geraldo Rivera anchored a daily half-hour investigative series for one season. Among the reporters on this program was Geraldo's brother, Craig Rivera.

NOW YOU SEE IT   CBS
1 APRIL 1974–13 JUNE 1975; 3 APRIL 1989–14 JULY 1989   On this daytime game show contestants tried to find words hidden within a grid of letters. Jack Narz hosted the first version, Chuck Henry the second.

NOWHERE MAN   UPN
28 AUGUST 1995–   Reminiscent of *The Fugitive*, this hour series starred Bruce Greenwood as Thomas Veil, who suddenly found his life turned upside down. A photojournalist, Veil slipped out of an exhibition of his work to a restaurant for a quiet dinner with his wife; returning from the restroom, he found his wife gone and their table occupied by another couple. At home, he found his wife was married to another man. Back at the exhibition, he found that one of his photos, "Hidden Agenda," which showed an execution in a foreign country, was also missing. Gradually, Veil became aware that he was a target of a powerful conspiracy and hit the road, trying to uncover the plot while eluding his pursuers.

NUMBER 96   NBC
10 DECEMBER 1980–2 JANUARY 1981   Sex was the main theme of this hour sitcom, set at 96 Pacific Way, a Southern California apartment complex that catered to singles and swingers. The large cast included: James Murtaugh as recently divorced Roger Busky, a new tenant; Barney Martin as retired navy officer Horace Batterson; John Reilly as the manager, Chick Walden, who was also a two-bit filmmaker; Randee Heller as pianist Marion Quintzel; Greg Mullavey as her husband, architect Max Quintzel (the Quintzels were experimenting with an open marriage); Todd Susman as Nathan Sugarman, a cop; Rosina Widdowson-Reynolds as Nathan's wife, Anthea Bryan, who was trying to dump him; Howard McGillin as baseball player Mark Keaton; Sherry Hursey as his naive wife, Jill Keaton; Jill Choder as nurse Sandy Galloway; Betsy Palmer as Sandy's recently widowed mother, Maureen Galloway; Hilarie Thompson as actress Sharon St. Clair; Maria O'Brien as Sharon's roommate, Ginny Ramirez, a Puerto Rican comic; William Bryan Curran as Dr. Robert Leon, a psychologist who hosted a popular radio program and was a transvestite at home; Christine Jones as Lisa Brendon; Charles Bloom as Lyle the maintenance man; Eddie Barth as Nathan's brother, bartender Lou Sugarman; and Ellen Travolta as Rita, Lou's wife. The show was based on the Australian series of the same title, which had created much controversy because of its use of nudity. The tamer American version didn't last long enough to generate controversy.

NUMBER PLEASE   ABC
31 JANUARY 1961–29 DECEMBER 1961   Hosted by Bud Collyer, this daytime game show was similar to the word game, Hangman. The show was a Goodson-Todman production.

NURSE   CBS
2 APRIL 1981–7 MAY 1981; 11 NOVEMBER 1981–21 MAY 1982   Michael Learned starred in this hour dramatic series as Mary Benjamin, who returned to her former job as a nurse at Grant Memorial Hospital following the death of her husband. Also featured were Robert Reed as Dr. Adam Rose, her friend and colleague; Christopher Marcantel as Mary's son, Chip, who attended Dartmouth; Hattie Winston as Nurse Toni Gillette; Hortensia Colorado as Nurse Betty La Sada; and Bonnie Hellman as Penny, also a nurse. In the fall of 1981 Dennis Boutsikaris joined the cast as Mary's neighbor, Calvo, a lawyer. Filmed on location in New York, the series was based on the made-for-TV movie "Nurse," which aired 9 April 1980.

THE NURSES   CBS

27 SEPTEMBER 1962–7 SEPTEMBER 1965   This hour-long medical drama was produced in New York by Herbert Brodkin. It starred Shirl Conway as Nurse Liz Thorpe, a supervising nurse at Alden Hospital; Zina Bethune as Nurse Gail Lucas, new to the job; Edward Binns as Dr. Kiley; and Stephen Brooks as Dr. Lowry. In the fall of 1964 two new male leads were signed to beef up the show, and the show's title was changed to *The Doctors and the Nurses*. Joining the cast were Michael Tolan as Dr. Alexander Tazinski and Joseph Campanella as Dr. Ted Steffen. Alan Alda made a rare guest appearance on the series ("Many a Sullivan," 17 January 1963), as did Dustin Hoffman ("The Heroine," 4 May 1965). A daytime serial based on the show ran on ABC beginning in 1965 (see below).

THE NURSES   ABC

27 SEPTEMBER 1965–31 MARCH 1967   This half-hour daytime serial was based on the prime-time series of the same title. The cast included: Mary Fickett as Nurse Liz Thorpe; Melinda Plank as Nurse Gail Lucas; Carol Gainer as Donna; Patricia Hyland as Brenda; Judson Laire as Jaimie MacLeod; Mimi Turque as Sandy Feigin; Polly Rowles as Mrs. Grossberg; Darryl Wells as Mike; Arthur Franz as Hugh; Nicholas Pryor as Ken; Dick McMurray as Jake; Sally Gracie as Pat; Joan Wetmore as Martha; and Nat Polen as Dr. Crager.

NURSES   NBC

14 SEPTEMBER 1991–2 JULY 1994   The Third Floor West nurses' station at Miami's Community Medical Center was the setting for this unimaginative sitcom. The cast included Stephanie Hodge (1991–1993) as acerbic nurse Sandy Miller, who was divorced; Mary Jo Keenen as phobic nurse Julie Milbury, new on the job; Jeff Altman (1991–1992) as nurse Greg Vincent; Arnetia Walker as head nurse Annie Rollin; Ada Maris as nurse Gina Cuevas, who had immigrated from a Latin American country; Kenneth David Gilman as Dr. Hank Kaplan; Carlos LaCamara as orderly Paco Ortiz; Markus Flanagan (1992–1993) as nurse Luke; David Rasche (1992–1994) as Jack Trenton, a convicted white-collar criminal who was performing his community service obligation by volunteering at the hospital; and Loni Anderson (1993–1994) as hospital administrator Casey MacAfee.

THE NUTT HOUSE   NBC

20 SEPTEMBER 1989–1 NOVEMBER 1989   Mel Brooks and Alan Spencer created this farcical sitcom, set at a seedy New York Hotel. With Harvey Korman as Reginald Tarkington, manager of the Nutt House; Cloris Leachman (in two roles) as the Teutonic head housekeeper Ms. Frick, and as dotty Mrs. Nutt, the hotel's elderly owner; Mark Blankfield as Freddy, the nearsighted elevator operator; Molly Hagan as Sally Lonnaneck, Mrs. Nutt's secretary; and Brian McNamara as Charles Nutt III, Mrs. Nutt's playboy grandson.

THE O. HENRY PLAYHOUSE   SYNDICATED

1957   The works of O. Henry (the pen name of William Sidney Porter) were the subjects of this half-hour dramatic anthology series, hosted by Thomas Mitchell.

O.K. CRACKERBY!   ABC

16 SEPTEMBER 1965–6 JANUARY 1966   Created by Cleveland Amory and Abe Burrows, this half-hour sitcom starred Burl Ives as O.K. Crackerby, a folksy Oklahoman who happened to be the richest man in the world. Also featured were Hal Buckley as St. John Quincy, the Harvard-educated tutor to widower Crackerby's children; Joel Davison as O.K.'s son Hobart; Brooke Adams as O.K.'s daughter Cynthia; Brian Corcoran as O. K., Jr.; Laraine Stephens as Susan Wentworth; and Dick Foran as Slim.

O.S.S.   ABC

26 SEPTEMBER 1957–17 MARCH 1958   Stories on this half-hour spy series were gleaned from the files of the O.S.S. (Office of Strategic Services), the American intelligence

unit active during World War II. Produced in England by former O.S.S. officer William Eliscu, the half-hour series starred Ron Randell as Captain Frank Hawthorn and Lionel Murton as The Chief.

THE OBJECT IS ABC
30 DECEMBER 1963–27 MARCH 1964   Dick Clark hosted this daytime game show on which a panel of six, including three celebrities and three studio contestants, tried to identify the names of famous personalities from "object" clues.

OCCASIONAL WIFE NBC
13 SEPTEMBER 1966–29 AUGUST 1967   Half-hour sitcom from Screen Gems about a young bachelor who landed a job with a company that hired only married men; to overcome the obstacle, he arranged with another tenant in his apartment building, a female art student, to pose as his wife when needed. With Michael Callan as Peter Christopher; Patricia Harty as Greta Patterson; Jack Collins as Peter's boss, Mr. Brahms, president of Brahms Baby Food Company; Joan Tompkins as Mrs. Brahms; and Bryan O'Byrne as Man-in-Middle, the unlucky tenant whose apartment was between Peter's seventh-floor place and Greta's ninth-floor pad. Sara Seegar was occasionally featured as Peter's mother, and Vince Scully narrated the episodes. In real life, Callan and Harty fell in love and were married during the show's run. They were subsequently divorced. In 1983 they were recast in an unsuccessful sitcom pilot, "Young Hearts," as parents.

AN OCEAN APART PBS
16 MAY 1988–27 JUNE 1988   British journalist David Dimbleby examined British-American relations on this seven-part program.

OCEANQUEST NBC
18 AUGUST 1985–15 SEPTMBER 1985   Al Giddings produced and directed this unusual five-part documentary series filmed in all the oceans of the world. Giddings and partner Peter Guber chose to present *OceanQuest* through the eyes of someone who had never dived before; ultimately they selected former Miss Universe Shawn Weatherly. Giddings taught her to dive, and they spent almost a year aboard the *Oz*, logging nearly 150,000 miles, exploring coral reefs, polar ice caps, shipwrecks, and all kinds of marine life.

THE ODD COUPLE ABC
24 SEPTEMBER 1970–4 JULY 1975   Based on Neil Simon's play, this half-hour sitcom told the story of a fastidious photographer who shared an apartment with a sloppy sportswriter; the two men had been childhood friends and had renewed their acquaintance after their respective divorces. It starred Tony Randall as tidy Felix Unger and Jack Klugman as messy Oscar Madison. The only other regular who remained with the show for its entire run was Al Molinaro as one of their poker-playing pals, Murray Greshler, a New York cop. Others who came and went included Garry Walberg, Ryan MacDonald, and Larry Gelman as poker pals Speed, Roy, and Vinnie; Monica Evans and Carole Shelley as Cecily and Gwen Pigeon, their daffy neighbors for the first half of the first season (Evans and Shelley had also played the roles in the 1968 motion picture); Joan Hotchkis as Oscar's first female friend, Dr. Nancy Cunningham; Elinor Donahue (1972–1975) as Miriam Welby, their neighbor and Felix's female friend; Penny Marshall (1973–1975) as Myrna Turner, Oscar's secretary; Brett Somers (Jack Klugman's real-life wife) as Blanche, Oscar's ex-wife; and Janis Hansen as Gloria, Felix's ex-wife. Garry Marshall and Sheldon Keller were the executive producers of the series for Paramount Television. In his book celebrating *The Odd Couple*'s twenty-fifth anniversary, author Edward Gross notes that the producers of the series had wanted Art Carney and Martin Balsam as the leads, and that ABC had hoped to land Tony Randall and Mickey Rooney. A cartoon version of the show also ran for one season (see *The Oddball Couple*) and in 1982 the series was remade with black principals (see *The New Odd Couple*).

Klugman, Randall, Marshall, and Walberg returned to their roles in "The Odd

Couple: Together Again" (24 September 1993, CBS), a two-hour telefilm in which Felix moved back in with Oscar, who was recovering from throat cancer surgery (in real life, Klugman had been stricken with throat cancer).

THE ODDBALL COUPLE ABC
6 SEPTEMBER 1975–3 SEPTEMBER 1977   This Saturday-morning cartoon show was inspired by *The Odd Couple;* its central characters were Spiffy, a neat cat, and Fleabag, a messy dog, who shared an office as reporters. Produced by David H. DePatie and Friz Freleng, the show consisted entirely of reruns during its second season.

ODYSSEY CBS
6 JANUARY 1957–2 JUNE 1957   This half-hour educational series for children was seen Sunday afternoons. Hosted by CBS newsman Charles Collingwood, it was filmed on location throughout the country and was produced in cooperation with local museums and historical societies; the premiere telecast, for example, was based in Virginia City, Nevada, and told the story of the Comstock Lode. Irving Gitlin was the executive producer, and Fred Freed was script editor for most of the show's run.

ODYSSEY PBS
1980–1981   An hour series of anthropological documentaries.

OF ALL THINGS CBS
23 JULY 1956–24 AUGUST 1956   This daytime variety show was a summer replacement for *The Garry Moore Show.* It was hosted by Faye Emerson and featured singers Ilene Woods and Jack Haskell.

OF LANDS AND SEAS SYNDICATED
1965–1970   Travelogue, hosted by Colonel John D. Craig.

OF MANY THINGS ABC
5 OCTOBER 1953–11 JANUARY 1954   Half-hour panel discussion show hosted by Dr. Bergen Evans. The series was not carried regularly by ABC's New York affiliate.

OFF THE RACK ABC
15 MARCH 1985–26 APRIL 1985; 9 AUGUST 1985–6 SEPTEMBER 1985   Half-hour sitcom set at a garment factory in Los Angeles. With Edward Asner as Sam Waltman, co-owner of H & W Garments; Eileen Brennan as Kate Halloran, who became Sam's new partner after the death of her husband; Pamela Brull as employee Brenda Patagorski; Dennis Haysbert as employee Cletus Maxwell; Sandy Simpson as designer Skip Wagner; Claudia Wells as Kate's daughter, Shannon, and Cory Yothers as Kate's son, Timothy.

OFF TO SEE THE WIZARD ABC
8 SEPTEMBER 1967–20 SEPTEMBER 1968   This prime-time hour was an anthology series of films for children. It was hosted by cartoon characters from *The Wizard of Oz.* Though the series only lasted a year, ABC revived the concept of a children's anthology show in the 1970s when it introduced *The ABC Afterschool Special.*

THE OFFICE CBS
11 MARCH 1995–15 APRIL 1995   Trite sitcom set at the main offices of a package design company, with Valerie Harper as administrative assistant Rita Stone; Andrea Abbate as Mae, a temporary worker who was hired full-time; Kevin Conroy as Steve Gilman; Lisa Darr as executive Natalie Stanton; Kristin Dattilo-Hayward as Deborah, a naive MBA candidate working as a secretary; Gary Dourdan as designer Bobby Harold; Dakin Matthews as the boss, Frank Gerard; and Debra Jo Rupp as Beth, the constantly harried secretary who was also juggling motherhood.

OFFICIAL DETECTIVE SYNDICATED

1957   Produced in cooperation with *Official Detective* magazine, this half-hour crime show was based on the radio series that began in 1946. Everett Sloane hosted the anthology show on television.

OH, BOY! ABC

16 JULY 1959–3 SEPTEMBER 1959   This British pop music show was imported by ABC for a brief summer run. Regularly featured were such early British rockers as Cliff Richard and Marty Wilde, and one of the 1959 guest stars was Tony Sheridan, who subsequently recorded several sides with the Beatles. Tony Hall hosted the series, and music was supplied by the house band, Lord Rockingham's XI, under the direction of Harry Robinson. The half-hour series was produced by Jack Good, who later helped develop ABC's American rock series, *Shindig.* Apparently, *Oh, Boy!* was something less than a smash in this country; reviewing it for the New York *Herald Tribune,* critic Sid Bakal described it as "an appalling piece of trash."

OH, KAY! ABC

24 FEBRUARY 1951–18 AUGUST 1951   This half-hour variety show was broadcast live from Chicago on Saturday mornings. It was hosted by Kay Westfall and featured Jim Dimitri and David LeWinter. Dan Schuffman produced and directed it.

OH MADELINE ABC

27 SEPTEMBER 1983–15 MAY 1984   Madeline Kahn starred in this half-hour domestic sitcom as Madeline Wayne, a trendy housewife who dabbled in one recreational activity after another. Also featured were James Sloyan as her husband, Charlie Wayne, who wrote romance novels under the pseudonym "Crystal Love"; Louis Giambalvo as Charlie's best friend, Robert, a travel agent; Jesse Welles as Madeline's best friend, Doris, Robert's ex-wife; and Francine Tacker as Annie, Charlie's amorous editor. The series was adapted from a British sitcom, *Pig in the Middle.*

OH! SUSANNA CBS/ABC

29 SEPTEMBER 1956–11 APRIL 1959 (CBS); 1 OCTOBER 1959–24 MARCH 1960 (ABC)   Half-hour sitcom starring Gale Storm as Susanna Pomeroy, social director of the S.S. *Ocean Queen,* a cruise ship. Also featured were ZaSu Pitts as her cohort, Elvira (Nugey) Nugent, the ship's beautician; Roy Roberts as Captain Huxley; James Fairfax as Cedric, the first mate; Ray Montgomery as the ship's doctor, Dr. Jones; and Joe Cranston as the purser. Created by Lee Karson, the series was produced by Hal Roach, Jr. The series was titled *Oh! Susanna* during its first two seasons on CBS; in the fall of 1958 it was retitled *The Gale Storm Show.* Ninety-nine episodes were shown on CBS between 1956 and 1959; in the spring of 1959 ABC acquired the rights to the show and began showing reruns in the daytime; an additional twenty-six first-run episodes were telecast in prime time on ABC during the 1959–1960 season.

OH, THOSE BELLS! CBS

8 MARCH 1962–31 MAY 1962   This half-hour sitcom starred the Wiere brothers (Herbert, Harry, and Sylvester), a German-born comedy trio, as Herbert, Harry, and Sylvester Bell, three employees at a Hollywood theatrical supply house. Also featured were Henry Norell as their boss, Mr. Slocum; Carol Byron as Kitty, the secretary; and Reta Shaw as the Bells' landlady. Ben Brady produced the series of thirteen episodes, which were filmed in 1960.

OHARA ABC

17 JANUARY 1987–30 MAY 1987; 3 OCTOBER 1987–6 AUGUST 1988   This Ohara (no first name) was not Irish, but Japanese-American, and was played by Pat Morita. As the series started, Ohara was a Zen-practicing lieutenant in the Los Angeles Police Department who preferred to use intelligence and intuition to solve his cases (ABC's ads called him the "un-cop"). Other regulars in the hour crime show included Richard Yniguez as Detective Jesse Guerrera; Kevin Conroy as Captain Lloyd Hamilton; Madge Sinclair as Gussie Lemmons; Catherine Keener as Lieutenant Cricket Sideris;

and Jon Polito (March–May 1987) as Captain Ross. When the series returned in the fall of 1987 Ohara was assigned to a Federal crime task force. All the old regulars had been jettisoned, Rachel Ticotin joined the cast as assistant district attorney Teresa Storm, and Robert Clohessy became Ohara's new partner, Lieutenant George Shaver. Bruce Beatty appeared as Grillo, and Meagen Fay played Roxy. In March of 1988 yet another format was attempted, as Ohara and Shaver left cop work to become private eyes.

O'HARA, UNITED STATES TREASURY CBS

17 SEPTEMBER 1971–8 SEPTEMBER 1972   Jack Webb produced this hour-long crime show, which starred David Janssen as Treasury Agent Jim O'Hara.

OIL PBS

5 OCTOBER 1987–23 NOVEMBER 1987   The world's petroleum industry was the subject of this eight-part documentary series (coincidentally, the original title of *Dynasty* was to have been *Oil*).

OKAY MOTHER DUMONT

1 NOVEMBER 1948–6 JULY 1951   One of TV's first daytime shows, *Okay Mother* was an audience participation and variety show hosted by Dennis James.

THE OLD AMERICAN BARN DANCE DUMONT

5 JULY 1953–13 SEPTEMBER 1953   Bill Bailey hosted this half-hour country-and-western music show. Among the regulars were Pee Wee King and Tennessee Ernie Ford (who was billed merely as Tennessee Ernie).

OLD FASHIONED MEETING ABC

8 OCTOBER 1950–1 APRIL 1951   Half-hour Sunday-night religious series.

THE OLDEST ROOKIE CBS

16 SEPTEMBER 1987–6 JANUARY 1988   Hour police drama, with Paul Sorvino as Ike Porter, fifty, who decided to give up his career as deputy chief of public affairs to become a detective with the force; D. W. Moffett as Ike's young partner, Detective Tony Jonas; Raymond J. Barry as their commanding officer, Lieutenant Marco Zaga; Marshall Bell as Detective Gordon Lane; and Patrick Cronin as Chief Black.

OLDSMOBILE MUSIC THEATRE NBC

26 MARCH 1959–7 MAY 1959   Bill Hayes and Florence Henderson cohosted this live, half-hour anthology series. Most presentations were musicals.

THE OLDSMOBILE SHOW
See THE PATTI PAGE SHOW

THE OLD-TIME GOSPEL HOUR
See JERRY FALWELL

OMNI: THE NEW FRONTIER SYNDICATED

1981   Half-hour magazine show on science and technology, hosted by Peter Ustinov.

OMNIBUS CBS/ABC/NBC

9 NOVEMBER 1952–1 APRIL 1956 (CBS); 7 OCTOBER 1956–31 MARCH 1957 (ABC); 20 OCTOBER 1957–10 MAY 1959 (NBC)   *Omnibus* was the first major television project underwritten by the Ford Foundation, which in turn offered the show to commercial advertisers. During its seven-year run it was carried by each of the three main commercial networks and was usually telecast Sunday afternoons. Hosted by Alistair Cooke, British by birth but American by choice, the aptly titled series presented everything from dramas to musicals to documentaries; each program usually contained several segments. Presentations during the first season included James Agee's

"Mr. Lincoln," a continuing story that starred Royal Dano as Abraham Lincoln; three Maxwell Anderson plays; Chekhov's "The Bear," with June Havoc and Michael Redgrave (4 January); "Die Fledermaus," with Eugene Ormandy conducting the Metropolitan Opera Orchestra (1 February); Agnes DeMille's ballet, "Three Virgins and the Devil" (broadcast 22 March, the title was changed, at network insistence, to "Three Maidens and the Devil"); and Shaw's "Arms and the Man," with Nanette Fabray and Jean-Pierre Aumont (3 May). A small sample of highlights from later seasons would include selections from the Broadway hit "Oklahoma!" by the original cast (4 October 1953); "King Lear," with Orson Welles in his television dramatic debut (18 October 1953); concerts conducted by Leonard Bernstein (frequent throughout the 1954–1955 and 1955–1956 seasons); documentary films from undersea explorer Jacques Cousteau (featured during the 1956–1957 season); "Oedipus Rex," with Christopher Plummer (6 January 1957); "The Empty Chair," with George C. Scott and Peter Ustinov (7 December 1958); and Gilbert and Sullivan's "H.M.S. Pinafore," with Cyril Ritchard (10 May 1959). *Omnibus* was first produced by Robert Saudek and was later produced by Fred Rickey. A few additional programs were televised on NBC during the 1960–1961 season on an irregular basis. The program was revived in 1980 as a series of irregularly scheduled specials on ABC; Hal Holbrook hosted one such program on 15 June 1980.

ON BROADWAY TONIGHT   CBS
8 JULY 1964–16 SEPTEMBER 1964; 1 JANUARY 1965–12 MARCH 1965   Hour-long variety show hosted by Rudy Vallee; promising young professionals were regularly featured. Irving Mansfield produced the series, which was introduced as a summer replacement for *The Danny Kaye Show.*

ON GUARD   ABC
28 APRIL 1952–29 MAY 1954   A series of half-hour documentary films on America's armed forces, *On Guard* was one of several "filler" shows scheduled by ABC during the 1950s. Few of the network's affiliates bothered to carry such dry programming, opting instead to carry a syndicated or locally produced show during the time slot when series like *On Guard* were offered.

ON OUR OWN   CBS
9 OCTOBER 1977–20 AUGUST 1978   Half-hour sitcom about two young women who shared an apartment and worked at a Manhattan advertising agency. With Lynnie Greene as Maria Teresa Bonino; Bess Armstrong as her co-worker and roommate, Julia Peters; Gretchen Wyler as their boss at Bedford Advertising, Toni McBain; Dixie Carter as copywriter April Baxter; Dan Resin as salesman Craig Boatwright; and John Christopher Jones as producer Eddie Barnes. David Susskind was the executive producer of the series, which was created by Bob Randall and produced by Sam Denoff. *On Our Own* was the only primetime dramatic series produced in New York during the 1977–1978 season.

ON OUR OWN   ABC
13 SEPTEMBER 1994–28 DECEMBER 1994; 3 MARCH 1995–14 APRIL 1995   Half-hour sitcom built around the six real-life siblings of the Smollett family. Set in St. Louis, it told the story of a group of seven orphaned black children who sought to stay together by outwitting the Department of Children's Services. The cast included Ralph Louis Harris as the eldest sibling, restaurant manager Josh Jerrico, who masqueraded whenever necessary as the kids' guardian, Aunt Jelcinda; JoJo Smollett as Jimi Jerrico; Jazz Smollett as Jai Jerrico; Jussie Smollett as Jesse Jerrico; Jurnee Smollett as Jordee Jerrico; Jake Smollett as Joc Jerrico; Jocqui Smollett as baby Jarreau Jerrico; Kimberley Kates as social worker Alana Michaels, who knew of the kids' scam; Roger Aaron Brown as Alana's officious boss, Gordon Ormsby, who was smitten with Jelcinda; and Rae'ven Kelly as Hannah. When the series returned in March 1995, Josh was finally granted custody of the Jerrico brood, and learned that he was the half-brother of the other six. The household gained another member when

T'Keyah "Crystal" Keymah joined the cast as Scotti, a contractor who lived in the house while repairing it.

ON PARADE   NBC
24 JULY 1964–18 SEPTEMBER 1964   This half-hour variety series, which had no regulars, was produced in Canada by Norman Sawdawie.

ON STAGE   SYNDICATED
1970–1972   This Canadian-produced hour-long anthology series was also seen in the United States; some shows were aired on NBC as specials.

ON STAGE AMERICA   SYNDICATED
1984   A two-hour syndicated magazine show consisting of celebrity interviews, home visits, and performance clips, reported by Susie Bono, Todd Christensen, Steve Edwards, and Randi Oakes.

ON THE AIR   ABC
20 JUNE 1992–4 JULY 1992   Short-lived half-hour sitcom set in 1957 at the Zoblotnick Broadcasting Company in New York, home of a fictitious TV variety program, "The Lester Guy Show," on which everything usually went wrong. With Miguel Ferrer as network president Buddy Budwaller; Ian Buchanan as star Lester Guy; David L. Lander as the director, Valdja Gochktch; Marla Jeanette Rubinoff as Lester's costar, Betty Hudson; Gary Grossman as Lester's second banana, Bert Schein; Nancye Ferguson as Vladja's assistant, Ruth Trueworthy; Mel Johnson, Jr., as Mickey; Marvin Kaplan as the producer, Mr. McGonigle; Kim McGuire as Buddy's assistant, Nicole; and Tracey Walter as Blinky Watts, a technician with a visual disorder. Mark Frost and David Lynch, who had collaborated on *Twin Peaks*, created the series.

ON THE BOARDWALK   ABC
30 MAY 1954–1 AUGUST 1954   Broadcast from Steel Pier in Atlantic City, New Jersey, this talent show was hosted by bandleader Paul Whiteman.

ON THE GO   CBS
27 APRIL 1959–8 JULY 1960   Jack Linkletter, son of Art Linkletter, hosted this daytime variety show from locations throughout the country. The videotaped half-hour series was produced by William Kayden.

ON THE LINE WITH CONSIDINE
See THE BOB CONSIDINE SHOW

ON THE MONEY   PBS
11 OCTOBER 1984–17 JANUARY 1985   Thirteen-part self-help series on personal finance.

ON THE ROAD WITH CHARLES KURALT   CBS
26 JUNE 1983–23 AUGUST 1983   CBS News correspondent Charles Kuralt hosted this delightful series of vignettes from the back roads and small towns of America. Kuralt's travels took him to such places as Marlboro, South Carolina (to tour a tiny bottling plant), Sharon, Pennsylvania (to watch a shoe salesman at work), and Louisburg, North Carolina (to cover a whistlers' convention). Kuralt began his "On the Road" essays on *The CBS Evening News* in 1967.

ON THE ROCKS   ABC
11 SEPTEMBER 1975–17 MAY 1976   Based on a British sitcom entitled *Porridge*, this half-hour series was set at Alamesa Prison. The show stirred some controversy late in 1975, when the National Association for Justice asked ABC to cancel the series on the grounds that it painted too rosy a picture of prison life. The network refused to cancel the program at that time, and it was later reported that the show was a hit at

many real-life prisons. The show starred José Perez as inmate Hector Fuentes; Bobby Sandler as Nicky Palik; Hal Williams as DeMott; Rick Hurst as Cleaver; Jack Grimes as Baxter; Mel Stewart as Mr. Gibson, one of the officers; Tom Poston as Mr. Sullivan, another officer; and Logan Ramsey as The Warden. Created by Dick Clement and Ian La Frenais, the series was produced by John Rich.

ON TRIAL ABC
22 NOVEMBER 1948–1 JULY 1952   On the first of the three series titled *On Trial*, issues of public importance were formally debated each week.

ON TRIAL NBC
14 SEPTEMBER 1956–13 SEPTEMBER 1957   The second of the three series titled *On Trial* was an anthology series of courtroom dramas, hosted by (and occasionally starring) Joseph Cotten. In March 1957 the series was retitled *The Joseph Cotten Show*.

ON TRIAL SYNDICATED
1988   Another of the several "courtroom" shows of the late 1980s. *On Trial* was more realistic than the others: it presented actual taped excerpts from real trials. Nick Clooney was the host.

ON YOUR ACCOUNT NBC/CBS
8 JUNE 1953–2 JULY 1954 (NBC); 5 JULY 1954–30 MARCH 1956 (CBS)   This daytime game show was similar to *Strike It Rich* and *Queen for a Day:* Contestants related their hard-luck stories to a panel, which selected the most deserving candidate at the end of the show. The contestants also earned money by answering questions. The half-hour series was hosted by Eddie Albert (1953), Win Elliot (1953–1954), and Dennis James (1954–1956).

ON YOUR MARK ABC
23 SEPTEMBER 1961–30 DECEMBER 1961   This Saturday-morning game show for children was hosted by Sonny Fox, with help from Johnny Olson. Lloyd Gross produced and directed it. Each week a group of nine-to-thirteen-year-olds were quizzed about their future career hopes.

ON YOUR WAY DUMONT/ABC
9 SEPTEMBER 1953–20 JANUARY 1954 (DUMONT); 23 JANUARY 1954–17 APRIL 1954 (ABC)   This nighttime game show began as a quiz show and was first hosted by Bud Collyer. The premise of the show was that the contestants were trying to go somewhere; the contestant who answered the most questions correctly won a trip to his or her destination. When the show switched networks in 1954, it also changed formats and hosts: John Reed King and Kathy Godfrey (sister of Arthur Godfrey) cohosted the show on ABC, and the quiz format was scrapped in favor of a talent contest.

ONCE A HERO ABC
19 SEPTEMBER 1987–3 OCTOBER 1987   Only three episodes of this hour comedy-adventure series were shown. Its premise was interesting—a comic book superhero decides to cross the "Forbidden Zone" into the real world after realizing that people weren't reading his comics anymore. Featured were Jeff Lester as Captain Justice (the Crimson Crusader), who learned to his surprise after crossing the zone that he had no superpowers in the real world; Robert Forster as Gumshoe, the private eye who accompanied Justice from the comic book world; Milo O'Shea as cartoonist Abner Bevis, their creator; Caitlin Clarke as nosy reporter Emma Greely; Josh Blake as Emma's young son, Woody; and Dianne Kay as Captain Justice's girlfriend, Rachel Kirk, who also crossed the Forbidden Zone. Dusty Kay created the series.

ONCE UPON A CLASSIC   PBS

9 OCTOBER 1976–5 MAY 1979   Half-hour dramatic anthology series for children, which has presented original stories as well as adaptations of classic tales.

ONCE UPON A TUNE   DUMONT

6 MARCH 1951–15 MAY 1951   This hour-long series presented original musicals. Bob Loewi was the producer and Sid Frank the writer.

ONE BIG FAMILY   SYNDICATED

1986   Half-hour sitcom starring Danny Thomas as Jake Hatton, an ex-vaudevillian who decided to help raise the five children of his late brother and sister-in-law. Also featured were Anthony Starke as the eldest, twenty-three-year-old Don; Kim Gillingham as Don's wife, Jan; Anastasia Fielding as nineteen-year-old Marianne; Michael DeLuise as seventeen-year-old Brian; Alison McMillan as 14-year-old Kate; and Gabriel Damon as eight-year-old Roger.

ONE DAY AT A TIME   CBS

16 DECEMBER 1975–2 SEPTEMBER 1984   This half-hour sitcom began as the story of a divorced mother trying to raise her two teenage daughters; as the kids grew up, the storylines broadened. Bonnie Franklin starred as the divorcée, Ann Romano, who, as the series began, had moved with her two daughters into an apartment in Indianapolis. Mackenzie Phillips and Valerie Bertinelli costarred as the daughters, Julie and Barbara Cooper. Julie, the older one, was headstrong and rebellious, while Barbara was generally well-behaved and popular. Pat Harrington also costarred as the building superintendent, macho Dwayne Schneider, who wore his tool belt like a holster and fancied himself an experienced man of the world. Other regulars included: Richard Masur (1975–November 1976) as neighbor David Kane, a lawyer who was Ann's boyfriend (David landed a job in Los Angeles and asked Ann to marry him, but she refused); Mary Louise Wilson (1976–1977) as neighbor Ginny Wrobliki, a brassy cocktail waitress; John Hillerman and Charles Siebert (both of whom appeared occasionally) as Claude Connors and Jerry Davenport, the principals of Connors & Davenport, an ad agency where Ann found a job; John Putch as Bob Morton, Barbara's loyal boyfriend; and Nanette Fabray as Ann's mother, Katherine Romano (Fabray appeared occasionally until 1979, when she became a regular).

In 1979 Julie Cooper met and married Max Horvath (played by Michael Lembeck), a flight attendant (he would later become a writer). A year later Mackenzie Phillips, who played Julie, was dropped from the show because of her cocaine addiction (she kicked the habit and returned to the show in the fall of 1981; on the show, Max and Julie moved away to Houston during Phillips' absence). In 1980 Ann quit her job at Connors & Davenport to open her own agency; she soon found a partner, Nick Handris (played by Ron Rifkin). Glenn Scarpelli also joined the cast in 1980 as Nick's ten-year-old son, Alex. Rifkin left after one season, but Scarpelli stayed until 1983. In the fall of 1981 it was explained that Nick had been killed in an auto accident, as Alex moved in with Ann and Barbara (super Schneider enlarged the apartment by closing off a room from a vacant adjoining apartment). Ann took in a new partner, Francine Webster (played by Shelley Fabares), who had previously been her rival at Connors & Davenport.

Barbara also found a partner in the fall of 1981, when Boyd Gaines joined the show as dental student Mark Royer. He and Barbara were married in 1982 and later shared a house with Max and Julie (who had moved back to Indianapolis) and their baby daughter, Annie (first played by twins J. C. and R. J. Dilley, later by Lauren and Paige Maloney). Meanwhile, Ann Romano fell in love with her son-in-law's father and married him in the spring of 1983; Howard Hesseman played Mark's father, architect Sam Royer. In the fall of 1983 Mackenzie Phillips was again written out of the show for health reasons; on camera, it was explained simply that Julie had walked out on her husband and young daughter. *One Day at a Time* was created by Whitney Blake (who had been a regular on *Hazel*) and Allan Manings, and developed by Norman Lear. Jeff Barry and Nancy Barry composed the show's theme.

THE $1.98 BEAUTY CONTEST
See THE $1.98 BEAUTY CONTEST under *Dollar*

ONE HAPPY FAMILY NBC
13 JANUARY 1961–15 SEPTEMBER 1961   Half-hour sitcom about three generations living under one roof. With Dick Sargent and Jody Warner as newlyweds Dick and Penny Cooper; Chick Chandler and Elisabeth Fraser as Penny's parents, Barney and Mildred Hogan; and Jack Kirkwood and Cheerio Meredith as Charley and Lovey Hackett, Penny's grandparents.

100 GRAND ABC
15 SEPTEMBER 1963–29 SEPTEMBER 1963   One of the shortest-lived game shows in TV history, *100 Grand* was axed after only three airings. Jack Clark hosted the big money, prime-time show, on which an amateur faced a panel of experts and tried to answer questions posed by them.

THE 100 LIVES OF BLACK JACK SAVAGE NBC
31 MARCH 1991–26 MAY 1991   A joint venture of Stephen J. Cannell Productions and Walt Disney Television, this Sunday-night adventure series was set on a Caribbean island. A 300-year-old pirate, having taken a hundred lives, needed to save a hundred lives to escape eternal damnation; he joined forces with a white collar criminal—a financial pirate—who had fled to the island to escape prosecution. With Daniel Hugh-Kelly as the new arrival, Barry Tarberry; Stoney Jackson (premiere telecast only) and Steven Williams as the pirate, Black Jack Savage; Bert Rosario as Governor General Vasquez, dictator of the island, San Pietro; Roma Downey as Danielle St. Clair, a crusader who tried to thwart Vasquez's misrule; and Steve Hytner as Logan "F.X." Murphy, the inventor of a speedboat used by Tarberry and Savage.

THE $100,000 BIG SURPRISE
See THE BIG SURPRISE

THE $100,000 NAME THAT TUNE
See NAME THAT TUNE

THE $128,000 QUESTION SYNDICATED
1976–1978   *The $128,000 Question* was a remake of the big-money game show of the 1950s, *The $64,000 Question,* presumably adjusted for inflation. Like the old show, the new version featured contestants who were experts in a particular field of knowledge. Contestants started at the $64 level, and by answering successive questions correctly, could double their money up to $512. The next question was worth $1,000, and the values of the remaining questions again doubled, up to the limit of $128,000. Mike Darrow hosted the show during its first season and was succeeded by Alex Trebek in 1977. Steve Carlin was the executive producer. See also *The $64,000 Question.*

ONE IN A MILLION ABC
3 APRIL 1967–16 JUNE 1967   Danny O'Neil hosted this short-lived daytime game show on which contestants tried to guess the unusual secrets held in common by a guest panel.

ONE IN A MILLION ABC
8 JANUARY 1980–23 JUNE 1980   Half-hour sitcom about a Los Angeles cabbie who inherited the chairmanship and controlling financial interest in Grayson Enterprises, a huge conglomerate. With Shirley Hemphill as cabbie-cum-chairperson Shirley Simmons; Richard Paul as Mr. Stone, another Grayson executive; Carl Ballantine as Max, proprietor of Shirley's favorite restaurant; Dorothy Fielding as Nancy, Shirley's secretary; Ralph Wilcox as Duke, a neighborhood street vendor; Keene Curtis as Mr.

Cushing, Grayson's vice chairman and Shirley's chief rival; Mel Stewart as Raymond Simmons, Shirley's father; and Ann Weldon as Edna Simmons, Shirley's stepmother. Alan W. Livingston created the show, and Saul Turteltaub and Bernie Orenstein developed it.

ONE LIFE TO LIVE   **ABC**
15 JULY 1968–   This daytime serial was created by Agnes Nixon, who served her apprenticeship on Irna Phillips's *The Guiding Light* and *As the World Turns,* and who later created *All My Children.* Set in the suburban town of Llanview, *One Life to Live* stressed ethnic situations from the beginning— Jews, WASP's, Poles, and blacks are all well represented. One story line was taped on location at New York's Odyssey House, a drug rehabilitation center. Sold by Nixon to ABC, *One Life to Live* has been produced by Doris Quinlan, Joseph Stuart, Jean Arley, Paul Rauch, Linda Gottlieb, and Susan Bedsow Morgan. The show expanded from thirty to forty-five minutes on 26 July 1976 and expanded again to sixty minutes on 16 January 1978.

The cast has included: Ernest Graves, Shepperd Strudwick, and Tom O'Rourke as widower Victor Lord, a newspaper publisher; Gillian Spencer, Christine Jones, and Erika Slezak as his daughter, Victoria Lord (Viki was a split personality for a while; her *alter ego* was Niki Smith); Trish Van Devere and Lynn Benesch as his daughter, Meredith Lord, who died after being surprised by a burglar; Lee Patterson as reporter Joe Riley, who married Vicki (they were divorced and remarried); Patricia Rose and Alice Hirson as Eileen Riley Siegel, Joe's sister; Allan Miller as lawyer Dave Siegel, Eileen's husband, who died of a heart attack; Lee Warrick and Leonie Norton as their daughter, Julie Siegel (Eileen and Julie left Llanview for Florida); Bill Fowler, William Cox, and Tom Berenger as Eileen and Dave's son, Timmy, who died in a fall; David Snell and Jack Ryland as Julie's boyfriend, Jack Lawson; Doris Belack, Kathleen Maguire, and Phyllis Behar as Anna Wolek; Antony Ponzini, Jordan Charney, and Michael Ingram as Anna's brother, Vince Wolek; Paul Tulley; James Storm, and Michael Storm (brother of James) as Anna's brother, Dr. Larry Wolek, whose second wife was Meredith Lord; Niki Flacks, Kathryn Breech, and Judith Light as nurse Karen Martin, Larry's first wife (they later remarried); Terry Logan as murder victim Dr. Ted Hale; Joe Gallison as Tom Edwards; Jan Chasmar as Amy, an orphan; Justin McDonough as District Attorney Bill Kimbrough; Donald Moffat, Norman Rose, and James Douglas as Dr. Marcus Polk, who cured Vicki Lord's personality disorder; Ellen Holly as Carla Gray, a light-skinned black who tried to pass for white (calling herself Carla Benari), but who later married a black cop; Lillian Hayman as Sadie Gray, Carla's mother; Thurman Scott and Peter DeAnda as Dr. Pryce Trainor, a black physician who was interested in Carla; Robert Milli and Nat Polen as Dr. James Craig, a white physician who was also interested in Carla, but later married Anna Wolek; Cathy Burns, Amy Levitt, Jane Alice Brandon, Dorrie Kavanaugh, and Jennifer Harmon as Cathy Craig, daughter of James, who became involved with drugs; John Cullum as Artie Duncan, murdered by a drug-crazed Cathy; Bernie Grant as Steve Burke, who married Vicki Lord Riley (Viki thought Joe Riley had been killed in a car crash, but he turned up alive and remarried her); Millee Taggart as Millie Parks; Francesca James as murder victim Marcy Wade; Lon Sutton and Jack Crowder as Lieutenant Jack Neal; Tommy Lee Jones as Dr. Mark Toland, who married Julie Siegel, and was later shot; Marilyn Chris, Lee Lawson, and Marilyn Chris (again) as waitress Wanda Webb, who wed Vince Wolek; Katherine Glass and Brynn Thayer as Jenny Martin, a novitiate nun who left her order to marry Timmy Siegel just before his death; Nancy Pinkerton, Claire Malis, Robin Strasser, and Elaine Princi as Dr. Dorian Cramer, who married Victor Lord; Al Freeman, Jr., and David Pendleton as Lieutenant Ed Hall, who married Carla Gray (Ed later became involved in politics); Laurence Fishburne and Todd Davis as Joshua West, a youngster adopted by Ed and Carla; George Reinholt, Philip MacHale, and Chip Lucia as Victor Lord's long-lost illegitimate son, Tony Harris; Jacquie Courtney as Pat Ashley (Kendall) Brewster, who married Tony Lord; Stephen Austin as Brian Kendall, illegitimate son of Tony and Pat; Neail Holland, Eddie Moran, Tim Waldrip (later known as Timothy Owen), Steven Culp, Ted Demers, Josh Cox, and Michael Palance as young Danny Wolek, son of Larry and

Meredith; Lisa Richards as Susan Barry; Donald Madden as John Douglas; Rod Browning as Ben Farmer; Lani Miyazaki as Michiko; Wayne Jones and Herb Davis as Bert Skelly; Christine Jones as Sheila Rafferty; Patricia Pearcy, Jane Badler, and Sharon Gabet as Melinda Cramer; Jeffrey Pomerantz, Robert Burton, and Denny Albee as Dr. Peter Janssen; Farley Granger, Bernie McInerney, and Anthony George as Dr. Will Vernon; Teri Keane as Naomi Vernon; Jameson Parker, Steve Fletcher (later known as Steve Blizzard), and Ted Leplat as Brad Vernon, who married Jenny Siegel (they were later divorced); Julie Montgomery, Susan Keith, and Dorian Lopinto as Brad's sister, Samantha Vernon; Vance Jeffries as Matthew McAlister; Morgan Melis, Chris Cunningham, Ryan Janis, Matthew Vipond, Joey Thrower, Kirk Geiger, Jack Armstrong, and Ken Kenitzer as Kevin Riley, son of Joe and Viki Riley; Roger Rathburn as Alan Bennett; Jackie Zeman as Lana McLain; Gerald Anthony as Marco Dane; Kathleen Devine as Pamela Shepard; Tom Fuccello as Paul Kendall; Stuart Germain as Ethan Allen Bottomly; Sally Gracie as Ina Hopkins; Margaret Klenck as Edwina Lewis; Luke Reilly, Keith Langsdale, Jeffrey Byron, and Robert Gribbon as Richard Abbott; Jill Voight and Mary Gordon Murray as singer Rebecca Lee Hunt, who married Marco Dane; Marshall Borden as Luke Jackson; Arthur Burghardt as Dr. Jack Scott; Byron Sanders as Talbot Huddleston; Andrea Evans, Kelli Maroney, Marsha Clark, Karen Witter, and Krista Tesreau as Tina Clayton (one of soapdom's most hapless characters, Tina suffered the indignity of having two of her weddings interrupted at the altar before falling over a waterfall in Argentina while pregnant; she showed up alive to interrupt another wedding with a baby she said was the groom's [it wasn't]); Stephen Bolster as Roger Landover; Joan Copeland as Gwendolyn Abbott; Linda Dano as Gretel Cummings; Paul Joynt as Greg Huddleston; Lori March as Adele Huddleston; John Mansfield as Adam Brewster; Nancy Snyder as Katrina Karr; A. C. Weary as Dick Grant; Jeremy Slate as Chuck Wilson; and William Mooney as Paul Martin.

Other regulars have included: Anthony Call as Herb Callison, who married Dorian Cramer; Cusi Cram, Ava Haddad, Holly Gagnier, and Laura Bonarrigo as Cassie Callison; Peter Coleman as Kyle Dickenson; Jeff Fahey as Marco Dane's brother, Gary Corelli; Diedra Buonaro and Regan McManus as Mary Vernon, Katrina's daughter, who was actually raised by Jenny; Ken Meeker as Rafe Garretson; Matthew Ashford and Keith Bogart as Drew Ralston; Shelly Burch as Delilah Ralston; Grayson Hall as Euphemia Ralston; Phil Carey as wealthy Asa Buchanan; Clint Ritchie as Asa's son, Clint Buchanan; Robert S. Woods as Bo (Ralston) Buchanan, who was raised as Asa's son; Taina Elg as Olympia Buchanan, Bo's mother; Dick Carbellas as Lou Cardoza; Wayne Massey as Johnny Drummond; Kim Zimmer as Echo DiSavoy; Robert Gentry as Giles Morgan; Jim McDonnell as Mick Gordon; Kristen Meadows as Mimi King; James Chesson as Lloyd Dieter; Keith Charles and Mark Goddard as Ted Clayton; Stephen Schnetzer as Marcello Salta; Barbara Britton and Willie Burke as Frances Gordon; Craig Sheffer as Ian Hayden; Suzanne Leuffen as Shelley Johnson; Ryan Morris, John Learn, Christopher McKenna, and Nathan Fillion as Joey Riley, son of Joe and Vicki Riley; Michael Zaslow as David Reynolds; Phylicia Ayers-Allen as Courtney Wright; Roger Hill as Alec Lowndes; Richard K. Weber and Robert Desiderio as Steve Piermont; Arlene Dahl as Lucinda Schneck; Nicolas Coster as Anthony Makana; Tim Hart as Simon Warfield; Kristen Vigard and JulieAnn Johnson as Joy O'Neill; Liz Keifer as Connie O'Neill; Arlen Dean Snyder and Frank Converse as Harry O'Neill; Nancy Barrett as Rachel Wilson and as District Attorney Debra Van Druten; Barbara Treutelaar as Didi O'Neill; and Brian Davies (husband of Erika Slezak) as Scott Edgar.

Also: Janice Lynde as Laurel Chapin; David Beecroft as Trent Chapin; Christine Ebersole as Maxie McDermont; Michael Billington and Peter Brown as Charles Sanders; BarBara Luna as Maria Roberts; Christine Jones (in her second role) as Pamela Buchanan, who was married to Asa on the mysterious island of Malekava; John Loprieno as Cord Roberts, who married Tina Clayton (after she had interrupted an earlier wedding of his) in 1988; Jonathan Martin as John Russell; Barbara Garrick as Allison Perkins; Lee Patterson (in his second role) as Tom Dennison; Louise Sorel as Judith Sanders; Mary B. Ward as Diane Bristol; Jim O'Sullivan as Pete O'Neill; Richard Grieco as Rick Gardner; Marcia Cross as Kate Sanders; Cain

Devore as Chip Cooper; Terry Donahoe as Connie Vernon; Russ Anderson as Steve Holden; James DePaiva and Nicholas Walker as Max Holden; Fiona Hutchinson as Gabriella Medina; Laura Carrington as Lisa Baron; Guy Davis as Josh Hall; Mark Philpott as Jamie Sanders; Cynthia Vance as Cindy; Janet Zarish as Lee Halpern, who married Charles Sanders in 1987; John Fiedler as gardener Gilbert Lange; Don Fisher as Geoffrey McGrath; Jeff Gendelman as Frank Montaigne; Judith Chapman as Sandra Montaigne; Phyllis Newman and Patricia Elliott as former madam Renee Divine, who married Asa Buchanan in 1988; Stephen Meadows as Patrick London; Doug Wert as Wade Coleman; Lisa Peluso as Billie Giordano; Bonnie Burroughs as Stacy Giordano; Jensen Buchanan and Grace Phillips as Sarah Gordon; Blair Underwood as Bobby Blue; Tammy Amerson as Mari Lynn Dennison; Ted Marcoux and Mark Arnold as Rob Coronal; Roma Downey as Joanna Leighton, who married Rob in 1988; Jared Martin as Donald LaMarr; Antony Ponzini (in his second role) as Charlie Smith; Braeden Danner as young Buddy McGillis; Brenda Brock as Brenda McGillis; Richard Burgi as Randy Stone; Alan Coates as Garth Buckley; Jessica Tuck as Megan Gordon, one of the stars of "Fraternity Row," *One Life To Live*'s soap-within-a-soap; Fia Porter as Audrey Ames, another of "Fraternity Row's" stars; Henry Darrow as Dante Wolff; Susan Floyd as Christine Cromwell; Alan Scarfe as Leo Cromwell; Steve Flynn as Neil Delaney; Mary Gordon Murray as Becky Lee; Larry Pine as environmentalist Roger Gordon; Lois Kibbee as Elizabeth Sanders; Dennis Parlato as developer Michael Grande; Marcia McCabe as Alicia Grande; Jim Wlcek as Jack Gibson; Richard Merrell as Herron; David Gautreaux as Austin Buchanan, Asa's nephew; Jill Larson as Ursula Blackwell; Jeff Bankert as Tyler McGillis; Bronwen Booth and Wendee Pratt as Andrea Harrison; Lucinda Fisher as Debra Medina; Joe Lando as Jake Harrison; Danielle Harris as Sammi Garretson; Linda Thorson as Julia Medina; Lorraine Toussaint as Vera Williams; John Viscardi as Tony Vallone; Robert Westenberg as Prince Raymond; Thom Christopher as Carlo Hesser; Audrey Landers as Charlotte Hesser; Valarie Pettiford and Stephanie Williams as Sheila Price; Vanita Harbour as Rika Price; David Purdham as Fred Porter; Danielle DuClos as Lisa Porter, Fred's daughter; Leonard Stabb as filmmaker Hunter Guthrie; Alexandra Smith and Erin Torpey as Jessica Ann Buchanan, Vicki's daughter; Terry Alexander as Troy Nichols; Anna Guarduno as Gloria Mundy; Neith Hunter as Laura Jean Ellis; Jonas Khaka as Yusef; Allan Dean Moore as Kerry Nichols; Dex Sanders as Miles; Robert Sedgwick as Greg Ellis; Brian Tarantina as Lucky Lippmann; and Tonja Walker as Alex Olanov Hesser.

Among the many new faces of the 1990s were: Yasmine Bleeth as Lee Ann Demarest; Ann Flood as Mrs. Guthrie; Kelly Eviston as Blaine Adams; Christiaan Mills and Robyn Griggs as Stephanie Hobart; John Martin as Jonathan Russell; Christopher Cousins as actor Cain Rogan; Mark Brettschneider as Jason Webb; Susan Batten as Luna Moody; Casper Van Dien as Luna's brother Ty Moody; Christopher Douglas as Luna's brother Dylan Moody; Wortham Krimmer as Andrew Carpenter; Carole Shelley as Babs Bartlett; Mia Korf and Kassie Wesley as Blair Daimler Buchanan; Ryan and Sean Buckley, Evan Bonifant, and Michael Roman as Al Holden; Paul Bartel as O.W. McDermott; Pamela Payton-Wright as Addie; Ryan Murphy and Tyler Noyes as C.J. Roberts; Nathan Purdee as district attorney Gannon; Ellen Bethea as Rachel Gannon; Susan Haskell as Marty Saybrooke; LaTanya Richardson and Cynthia Martells as Rodi; Yvette Lawrence and Mari Morrow as Maggie Vega; Roy Thinnes as Sloan Carpenter; Bruce McCarty as Jonathan Michaelson; Eileen Heckart as Wilma Burr; Hillary Bailey Smith as Nora Gannon; Joe Fiske as Rick Mitchell; Sean Moynihan as Powell Lord III; Susan Diol as Angela Holloway; Kevin Garvanne as Joe Shelby; Reiko Ayelsworth as Rebecca Lewis; Shirley Stoler as Gert Mulligan; J. Smith-Cameron as assistant district attorney Kate Noonan; Nick Wyman as Peter Manning; Matt Servitto as Nick Manzo; James Villemaire as Bobby Ever; Charles Malik Whitfield and Peter Parros as Dr. Ben Price; Bethel Leslie as Ethel Crawford; Roger Howarth as Todd Manning; Tuc Watkins as David Vickers; Peter Bartlett as Nigel, Asa Buchanan's butler; Oni Faida Lampley as Hallie Mitchell; David Ledingham as Suede Pruitt; Courtney Chase and Hayden Panettiere as Sarah Roberts; Gina Tognoni as Kelly Cramer Gannon; Patricia Mauceri as Carlotta Vega; Yorlin Madera as Carlotta's son, Cristian Vega; Dorothy Barton as Beth; Wai Ching Ho as Kim; Kelly Waymire as Emily; Burke Moses as Bulge; Erin O'Brien as Alice Henson; and Timothy D. Stickney as Jimmy Glover.

Guest stars on *One Life* have included Dr. Joyce Brothers (as herself), Walter Slezak (as Laszlo Braedeker, godfather of Viki Lord, played by his real-life daughter), John Beradino (repeating his *General Hospital* role as Dr. Steve Hardy), William Mooney (repeating his *All My Children* role as lawyer Paul Martin), and Sammy Davis, Jr. (as Chip Warren). Sharp-eyed viewers could also have spotted Donna Rice (former companion of Senator Gary Hart) in 1985, as Jeannie, a friend of Niki Smith's. Former *Search for Tomorrow* star Mary Stuart also made an appearance on *One Life to Live,* as the judge presiding over a murder trial in 1988.

The series received mixed reviews for its tendency to use extended fantasy storylines during the late 1980s. Viewers were treated to such unusual happenings as Vicki Lord Buchanan's out-of-body experiences as she lay on an operating table, Clint Buchanan's time travel to the Wild West of 1888, and the discovery of the lost city of Eterna near Llanview.

ONE MAN'S EXPERIENCE   DUMONT
6 OCTOBER 1952–10 APRIL 1953   Literary classics—those that depicted the struggles of men—were serialized each week on this fifteen-minute daytime show. When the series began in 1952, it was telecast back to back with a female-oriented series, *One Woman's Experience.* Early in 1953 the title was changed to *One Man's Story,* and the series was seen on an alternating basis with *One Woman's Story.*

ONE MAN'S FAMILY   NBC
4 NOVEMBER 1949–21 JUNE 1952; 1 MARCH 1954–1 APRIL 1955   Created by Carleton E. Morse, *One Man's Family* was one of radio's most popular continuing dramas; its twenty-seven-year run began in 1932. The show twice came to television, but neither version was particularly popular. The first version was a prime-time show; the cast included Bert Lytell as Henry Barbour, head of the clan, a wealthy stockbroker who lived in San Francisco's Sea Cliff area; Marjorie Gateson as his wife, Frances (Fanny) Barbour; Russell Thorsen as Paul, the eldest of their five children, a writer and aviator; Patricia Robbins and Lillian Schaaf as their daughter Hazel; Nancy Franklin and Eva Marie Saint as their daughter Claudia; Billy Idelson and James Lee as their son Clifford, Claudia's twin; Arthur Casell and Robert Wigginton as their son Jack; Walter Brooke as Hazel's husband, Bill Herbert; Susan Shaw as Beth Holly, Paul's female friend; Madeline Belgard as Teddy Lawton, Paul's adopted daughter; Tony Randall as Mac; Nancy Franklin (in her second role) as Ann Waite; Jim Boles as Joe. In the fall of 1951 at least one member of the Barbour clan was shown pregnant; this pregnancy, which predated Lucy Ricardo's on *I Love Lucy,* was probably the first involving a continuing character on a prime-time television series. The show, which was done live, was also the first NBC series to use rear-screen projection. In the spring of 1954 the show returned to TV as a daily fifteen-minute serial. At that time the cast included Theodore van Eltz as Henry; Mary Adams as Fanny; Linda Leighton as Hazel; Anne Whitfield as Claudia; Martin Dean as Jack; Jack Edwards as Johnny Roberts, Claudia's boyfriend; Lois Hall as Beth Holly; Glen Vernon as Johnny MacPherson; and Emerson Treacy as Dr. Thompson. Curiously, both of the TV versions of *One Man's Family* started where the radio program had in 1932, and thus were twenty years behind the radio show. Anne Whitfield, for example, appeared on the second TV version as Claudia, but simultaneously played Claudia's daughter, Penelope, on radio.

THE $1,000,000 CHANCE OF A LIFETIME   SYNDICATED
1985   Jim Lange hosted this game show on which two couples competed, trying to identify words as the letters appeared one at a time. Couples who won multiple games had a chance at a super jackpot worth up to one millon dollars.

ONE MINUTE PLEASE   DUMONT
6 JULY 1954–17 FEBRUARY 1955   John K. M. McCaffery first hosted this prime-time game show, based on a British series, on which celebrity panelists were required to

extemporize for sixty seconds on a given subject. Allyn Edwards succeeded McCaffery in November 1954.

ONE OF A KIND   CBS
12 JANUARY 1964–29 MARCH 1964   Harry Reasoner hosted this Sunday-afternoon series of twelve filmed documentaries on subjects of general interest.

ONE OF THE BOYS   NBC
23 JANUARY 1982–20 MARCH 1982; 6 AUGUST 1982–20 AUGUST 1982   Mickey Rooney starred in this sitcom as 66-year-old Oliver Nugent, who impulsively decided to leave the Bayview Retirement Home and move in with his college-age grandson. Other regulars included Dana Carvey as the grandson, Adam, who attended Sheffield University; Nathan Lane as Jonathan, Adam's roommate; Francine Beers as the landlady, Mrs. Green; and Scatman Crothers as Bernard Soloman, who became Oliver's partner in a song-and-dance act.

ONE OF THE BOYS   NBC
15 APRIL 1989–20 MAY 1989   Sitcom about a waitress who decided to work for a construction company, fell in love with the owner and, by the end of the series' brief run, married him. With Maria Conchita Alonso as Maria Navarro; Robert Clohessy as the boss, Mike Lukowski, owner of Lukowski Construction; Michael DeLuise as Mike's son Luke; Billy Morrissette as Mike's son Steve; Justin Whalin as Mike's son Nick; Amy Aquino as Bernice; and Dan Hedaya as Ernie, the foreman.

ONE ON ONE   ABC
25 APRIL 1983–28 JULY 1983   Greg Jackson interviewed newsmakers on this late-night series, broadcast after *ABC News Nightline*. The distinctive feature of the program was that Jackson was seated just off camera, so that the cameras concentrated on the interviewee. Jackson had used the technique previously on his *Signature* series, which had aired on the short-lived CBS Cable Channel.

ONE ON ONE WITH JOHN TESH   NBC
9 JANUARY 1991–12 JUNE 1992   Half-hour daytime interview series hosted by *Entertainment Tonight* coanchor John Tesh, with correspondents Sandie Newton, Jill Rappaport, and Jennifer Valoppi. Tesh would cohost a similar series a year later: see *Leeza*.

ONE STEP BEYOND   ABC
20 JANUARY 1959–3 OCTOBER 1961   John Newland directed and hosted this anthology series of tales of the occult and supernatural; the stories were said to have been based on true incidents. Sponsored by Alcoa, the series was also titled *Alcoa Presents*. A total of ninety-four half-hour episodes were filmed, with Collier Young as producer. Merwin Gerard created the series. In 1978 Newland, Young, and Gerard again combined forces to produce a syndicated successor: see *The Next Step Beyond*.

1,2,3—GO!   NBC
8 OCTOBER 1961–27 MAY 1962   This educational series for children was seen early on Sunday evenings. Each week cohosts Jack Lescoulie and ten-year-old Richard Thomas (who would star in *The Waltons* eleven years later) explored subjects of interest to young people. Jack Kuney produced the half-hour series.

ONE WEST WAIKIKI   CBS/SYNDICATED
4 AUGUST 1994–8 SEPTEMBER 1994 (CBS); 1995– (SYNDICATED)   Cheryl Ladd starred in this hour crime show as Dr. Dawn "Holli" Holliday. A female *Quincy*, Holliday was a medical examiner from Los Angeles who had been called in on a case while attending a conference in Hawaii, and decided to stay there. Also featured were Richard Burgi as Lieutenant Mack Wolfe, a cop who was just back from a suspension; Paul Gleason as Captain David Herzog; Elsie Sniffen as Holli's investiga-

tor, Nui Shaw; and Ogie Zulueta as Wolfe's partner, Kimo. Glen A. Larson created the series.

ONE WOMAN'S EXPERIENCE DUMONT
6 OCTOBER 1952–3 APRIL 1953   This fifteen-minute daytime show serialized classics from literature that emphasized the stories of women. It was introduced in 1952 together with its counterpart, *One Man's Experience;* early in 1953 the shows' titles were changed to *One Man's Story* and *One Woman's Story,* and the two were seen on an alternating basis.

THE O'NEILLS DUMONT
6 SEPTEMBER 1949–10 JANUARY 1950   A once-a-week serial, *The O'Neills* was a short-lived TV version of the radio soap opera that ran from 1934 to 1943. It featured Vera Allen as Peggy O'Neill, a widow; Ian Martin as Uncle Bill; Janice Gilbert as Mrs. O'Neill's daughter, Peggy; Michael Lauson as son Danny O'Neill; Ben Fishbein as family friend Morris Levy, a hardware dealer in the town of Royalton; and Celia Budkin as his wife, Trudy Levy.

ONLY ONE EARTH PBS
7 SEPTEMBER 1987–29 NOVEMBER 1987   A series of documentaries on ecology, narrated by Julian Pettifer.

OPEN ALL NIGHT ABC
28 NOVEMBER 1981–9 JANUARY 1982   This sitcom was set at a "364 Store," a convenience store that was open twenty-four hours a day, 364 days a year, and was patronized by an assortment of zany customers. The cast included George Dzundza as Gordon Feester, the harried manager; Susan Tyrrell as his wife, Gretchen Feester; Sam Whipple as Susan's son, Terry; Jay Tarses (who created the series with Tom Patchett) as Steve, a neighborhood cop; Bever-Leigh Banfield as his partner, Edie; and Bubba Smith as Robbin, the store's night manager.

OPEN END
See THE DAVID SUSSKIND SHOW

OPEN HEARING ABC
1 FEBRUARY 1954–1 JULY 1954; 3 FEBRUARY 1957–4 SEPTEMBER 1960   John Secondari was the host and moderator of this half-hour public affairs program; it was seen on Sunday afternoons during most of its run, though it surfaced in prime time during the 1957–1958 season.

OPEN HOUSE FOX
27 AUGUST 1989–21 JULY 1990   This half-hour sitcom, the successor to *Duet,* was set at the Juan Verde Real Estate office in southern California. Alison LaPlaca and Mary Page Keller repeated their *Duet* roles as Linda Phillips and Laura Kelly, both of whom were now real estate brokers. Chris Lemmon appeared occasionally as Linda's husband, Richard, but the couple separated in the middle of the season. New cast members included Philip Charles MacKenzie as Ted Nichols, Linda's rival at the agency; Nick Tate as the boss, Roger McSwain; impressionist Danny Gans as Scott Babylon, the many-voiced broker; and Ellen DeGeneres as Margo van Meter, the dotty receptionist.

OPERA CAMEOS DUMONT
8 NOVEMBER 1953–9 JANUARY 1955   Excerpts from operas were presented on this half-hour series. Giovanni Martinelli was the host and narrator of the series, which began as a local show in New York in 1950.

OPERA VS. JAZZ ABC
25 MAY 1953–21 SEPTEMBER 1953   Though billed as a "symposium," this half-hour series featured little in the way of debate or discussion on jazz or classical music, but

instead presented selections from the two genres. Nancy Kenyon was the host, or "moderator," of the series, and Alan Dale and Jan Peerce were regularly featured. Fred Heider produced the series, and Charles Dubin directed it.

OPERATION ENTERTAINMENT ABC

5 JANUARY 1968–26 APRIL 1968; 27 SEPTEMBER 1968–31 JANUARY 1969   This hour-long variety show was staged at a different military base each week and was hosted by a guest star. Regulars included Jim Lange, the Operation Entertainment Girls, and the Terry Gibbs Band. Chuck Barris produced the series.

OPERATION INFORMATION DUMONT

17 JULY 1952–18 SEPTEMBER 1952   This public service series sought to inform veterans of their rights. See also *Operation Success* (1948–1949 version).

OPERATION NEPTUNE NBC

28 JUNE 1953–16 AUGUST 1953   Created by Maurice Brockhausen, this Sunday-evening children's adventure series starred Tod Griffin as Commander Bill Hollister, skipper of an American submarine, who battled deep-sea evildoers. Richard Holland costarred as Dink.

OPERATION PETTICOAT ABC

17 SEPTEMBER 1977–26 OCTOBER 1978   The story of a group of Army nurses stationed aboard a pink submarine during World War II, *Operation Petticoat* was based on the 1959 film of the same title. During the 1977–1978 season the large cast included: John Astin as Lieutenant Commander Matthew Sherman, skipper of the *Sea Tiger;* Richard Gilliland as Lieutenant Nick Holden, the crafty supply officer; Yvonne Wilder as Major Barbara Hayward, chief of the nurses; Melinda Naud as Lieutenant Dolores Crandall; Dorrie Thomson as Lieutenant Colfax; Jamie Lee Curtis as Lieutenant Barbara Duran; Bond Gideon as Lieutenant Claire Reid; Richard Brestoff as Yeoman Hunkle; Christopher J. Brown as Ensign Stovall; Kraig Cassity as Seaman Dooley; Wayne Long as Chief Herbert Molumphrey; Richard Marion as Williams; Michael Mazes as Chief Sam Gossett; Jack Murdock as Tostin; Peter Schuck as Seaman Horwich; Raymond Singer as Watson; Jim Varney as Seaman "Doom and Gloom" Broom; and Jesse Dizon as Ramon Galardo. Leonard B. Stern was the executive producer, David J. O'Connell and Si Rose the producers for Universal. When the show returned for its abortive second season, it featured new producers (Jeff Harris and Bernie Kukoff were the new executive producers, Michael Rhodes the new producer) and an almost entirely new cast. Only Melinda Naud, Richard Brestoff, and Jim Varney remained from the first season, and the new faces included: Robert Hogan as the new skipper, Commander Haller; Randolph Mantooth as Lieutenant Bender, the executive officer; Jo Ann Pflug as Lieutenant O'Hara; Hilary Thompson as Lieutenant Wheeler; Warren Berlinger as Stanley Dobritch; Fred Kareman as Doplos; and Scott McGinnis as Dixon.

OPERATION: RUNAWAY

See THE RUNAWAYS

OPERATION SUCCESS DUMONT

21 SEPTEMBER 1948–19 OCTOBER 1948; 27 JANUARY 1949–16 JUNE 1949   A public service show in the truest sense of the term, *Operation Success* was produced by the DuMont network in cooperation with the Veterans Administration. Its goal was to find jobs for disabled veterans. Veterans, doctors, training officers, and guidance officers all appeared on the show, and employers were asked to telephone in with job offers. Apparently, *Operation Success* was a success—late in 1948 a spokesman for the VA noted that, as a result of the first series, requests for disabled veterans' services had "almost doubled."

OPERATION SUCCESS   SYNDICATED

1955   Quentin Reynolds interviewed successful business executives on this half-hour public affairs program.

THE OPRAH WINFREY SHOW   SYNDICATED

8 SEPTEMBER 1986–   The first black woman to host a successful daytime talk show, Oprah Winfrey became one of the most popular, and wealthiest, performers of the 1980s. At age nineteen, she had been a news anchor in Nashville. She later cohosted a local talk show in Baltimore, and moved from there to Chicago, where early in 1984 she became host of another local talk show, *A.M. Chicago.* Within two months her show had overtaken *Donahue* (which then also originated from Chicago) in the local ratings. In the fall of 1986 her show was syndicated nationally and proved highly popular. In 1988 Winfrey acquired ownership of her show and purchased a production studio in Chicago. In 1989 *TV Guide* named her the richest woman on television.

Like most of the other daytime talk shows, *The Oprah Winfrey Show* concentrates on a single topic each day and is taped before a studio audience, which is encouraged to ask questions. In the words of producer Debra DiMaio, the show is "emotionally oriented." Winfrey frequently hugs her guests and has been known to cry with them, too. Winfrey has also bared much of her personal life on the show, admitting on one program that she had been sexually abused as a child, towing a wagon filled with sixty-seven pounds of animal fat (indicating the amount of weight she had lost) on another, and admitting to past drug abuse on a third. Other shows have tackled serious topics; one memorable 1987 show, focusing on racial prejudice, was taped in virtually all-white Forsyth County, Georgia, site of several anti-integration demonstrations.

In addition to her hour show, Winfrey has also actively pursued other projects. She was nominated for an Academy Award for her first motion picture role, in *The Color Purple* (1985). In 1987 she taped a sitcom pilot, in which she played a talk show host, but shelved the idea. She was the executive producer and star of the two-part TV-movie "The Women of Brewster Place (19–20 March, ABC), which was made into a limited-run series in which she also starred, *Brewster Place,* in 1990.

The Oprah Winfrey Show maintained its ratings dominance through the mid-1990s, and survived the departure of several longtime staffers, including producer DiMaio, in 1994.

ORAL ROBERTS   SYNDICATED

1954–1967; 1969–   Television's best-known Pentecostal evangelist and faith healer, Oral Roberts has been on the air almost continously since 1954, when his show was first telecast on sixteen stations. A year later he began broadcasting from a large tent. Roberts shut down his TV operations in 1967, returning to the air two years later with a revamped program, *Oral Roberts and You,* which originated first from NBC studios in Burbank and later from Roberts's own facilities in Tulsa, Oklahoma. The latter program also featured his son, Richard Roberts. Though Roberts was unaffected by the scandals that ruined fellow televangelists Jim Bakker and Jimmy Swaggart, he managed to raise a few eyebrows in March 1987 with his pronouncement that God intended to call him "back to Heaven" unless his ministry received an urgently needed $8 million in contributions. When the pledges failed to materialize as hoped, Roberts scaled back his demand and managed to remain on Earth.

THE ORCHID AWARD   ABC

24 MAY 1953–24 JANUARY 1954   Each week on this fifteen-minute series a celebrity guest was honored. Ronald Reagan hosted the premiere telecast from Hollywood, presenting the "Orchid Award" to Rosemary Clooney. Thereafter the show was broadcast from New York, with Bert Lytell as host, until July, when Donald Woods became the New York host and Ronald Reagan the Los Angeles host. Harold Romm produced the series and Robert Finkel directed it. *Variety* noted in 1953 that *The Orchid Award* was the first show under ABC's new corporate structure to have been fully sold to sponsors before its premiere.

THE OREGON TRAIL   NBC
21 SEPTEMBER 1977–30 NOVEMBER 1977   Only six episodes of this hour-long western
were telecast. Set along the Oregon Trail in 1842, it starred Rod Taylor as widower
Evan Thorpe, a member of the wagon party who became the leader in the first
episode. Also featured were Andrew Stevens as Andrew, his seventeen-year-old son;
Tony Becker as William, his twelve-year-old son; Gina Marie Smika as Rachel, his
seven-year-old daughter; Darleen Carr as Margaret Devlin, one of the passengers;
and Charles Napier as Luther Sprague, the scout recruited by Thorpe in the first
episode. Michael Gleason was the executive producer, Richard Collins the supervising producer, and Carl Vitale the producer for Universal. The pilot for the series was
telecast 10 January 1976.

ORIENT EXPRESS   SYNDICATED
1953   Most of the stories on this half-hour filmed dramatic anthology series were set
in Europe.

THE OSMOND FAMILY SHOW   ABC
28 JANUARY 1979–27 MAY 1979   An hour variety show, the successor to *Donny and
Marie, The Osmond Family Show* featured the performing members of the Osmond
clan: Donny, Marie, Alan, Wayne, Jay, Merrill, and Jimmy. See also *Marie*.

THE OSMONDS   ABC
9 SEPTEMBER 1972–1 SEPTEMBER 1974   Saturday-morning cartoon show inspired by
the real-life singing group, The Osmond Brothers. The animated series told the story
of a globe-trotting musical group, who were goodwill ambassadors for the United
States. The voices of the several Osmond Brothers—Merrill, Wayne, Alan, Jay,
Donny, and Jimmy—were used. Reruns were shown Sunday mornings during the
second season.

OSSIE AND RUBY!   PBS
1980–1981   Ossie Davis and his wife, Ruby Dee, presented the works of black
artists on this half-hour magazine series.

OTHER PEOPLE OTHER PLACES   SYNDICATED
1974   Travelogue, hosted by Peter Graves.

THE OTHER SIDE   NBC
17 OCTOBER 1994–13 OCTOBER 1995   Hour daytime talk show hosted by psychologist
Dr. Will Miller. The programs focused on persons who had had paranormal experiences such as encounters with ghosts or space aliens, and similar phenomena. Miller
was dropped as host in mid-May 1995, and reruns were aired until mid-1995, when
Dana Fleming was named host.

OTHERWORLD   CBS
26 JANUARY 1985–16 MARCH 1985   An interesting sci-fi series, *Otherworld* told the
story of a normal American family who, while touring the Egyptian pyramids, were
drawn through a "mysterious vortex" into the "otherworld," a universe of alternate
realities in which things were not as they seemed. During their eight-episode journey
they searched for a way to return home, but never found it. Featured were Sam
Groom as Hal Sterling; Gretchen Corbett as June Sterling; Tony O'Dell as their elder
son, Trace; Jonna Lee as their daughter, Gina; Brandon Crane and Chris Hebert as
their younger son, Smith; and Jonathan Banks as evil Commander Kroll, who pursued the Sterlings through the otherworld.

OUR AMERICAN HERITAGE   NBC
1959–1961   Broadcast as a series of specials, this American historical anthology
series was produced by Mildred Freed Alberg in cooperation with *American Heritage*
magazine.

OUR FAMILY HONOR   ABC

17 SEPTEMBER 1985–3 JANUARY 1986   Set in New York City, this prime-time serial told the tale, in the words of the series' introductory narration, of "two families on opposite sides of the law, struggling for power and survival." Principal players included Kenneth McMillan as police commissioner Patrick McKay; Georgann Johnson as his wife, Katherine; Eli Wallach as mob boss Vincent Danzig; Barbara Stuart as his wife, Marianne; Tom Mason as Patrick's son, Frank, a cop who had a vendetta with the Danzigs, believing them responsible for his brother's death; Daphne Ashbrook as Frank's niece, Liz, also a cop; Michael Woods as Vincent's good son, lawyer Jerry Cole, who had a romance with Liz; Michael Madsen as Vincent's bad son, mobster Augie Danzig; Sheree J. North as Augie's wife, Rita; and Ron Karabatsos as the Danzigs' assistant, George Bennett.

OUR FIVE DAUGHTERS   NBC

2 JANUARY 1962–28 SEPTEMBER 1962   This short-lived daytime serial centered on the lives of the five girls in the Lee family. Featured were Esther Ralston as Helen Lee, their mother; Michael Keene as Jim Lee, their father; Patricia Allison as daughter Barbara; Iris Joyce as daughter Marjorie; Nuella Dierking as daughter Jane; Wynne Miller as daughter Mary; Jacquie Courtney as daughter Ann; and Robert W. Stewart as Uncle Charlie.

OUR GOODLY HERITAGE   CBS

16 NOVEMBER 1952–26 JANUARY 1958   Williams Rush Baer of New York University hosted this Sunday-morning Bible study show.

OUR HOUSE   NBC

11 SEPTEMBER 1986–26 JUNE 1988   NBC had reasonable success in the Sunday "family viewing hour" (7 P.M.) with this wholesome drama about a widow and her three children who moved from Fort Wayne, Indiana, to California to live with her curmudgeonly father-in-law. With Wilford Brimley as Gus Witherspoon; Deidre Hall as Jessie Witherspoon; Shannen Doherty as fifteen-year-old Kris; Chad Allen as twelve-year-old David; Keri Houlihan as eight-year-old Molly; and Gerald S. O'Loughlin as Gus's equally curmudgeonly pal, Joe Kaplan.

OUR MAN HIGGINS   ABC

3 OCTOBER 1962–11 SEPTEMBER 1963   Half-hour sitcom about a British butler inherited by the American branch of the MacRobert clan. With Stanley Holloway as Higgins; Frank Maxwell as Duncan MacRobert; Audrey Totter as his wife, Alice MacRobert; Rickey Kelman as their son, Tommy; K. C. Butts as their son, Dinghy; and Regina Groves as their daughter, Joannie.

OUR MISS BROOKS   CBS

3 OCTOBER 1952–21 SEPTEMBER 1956   *Our Miss Brooks,* a situation comedy about a high school English teacher, began on radio in 1948; when it moved to television in 1952, most of the radio cast came with it: Eve Arden as Connie Brooks, Madison High's favorite educator; Gale Gordon as blustery Osgood Conklin, the principal; Richard Crenna as high-voiced Walter Denton, the student who usually drove Miss Brooks to school; Gloria McMillan as Walter's girlfriend, Harriet Conklin, the principal's daughter; and Jane Morgan as Miss Brooks's landlady, Mrs. Margaret Davis. Robert Rockwell, the only regular who had not been one of the original radio cast, was seen as biology teacher Philip Boynton, Miss Brooks's shy and elusive quarry. In the fall of 1955 the show's format changed slightly—Madison High was torn down to make room for a new highway, and Miss Brooks and Mr. Conklin found jobs at a private elementary school (on the radio version of the show, everyone remained at Madison High through the season). Eve Arden, Gale Gordon, and Jane Morgan remained from the old cast, and several newcomers were added: Nana Bryant as Mrs. Nestor, owner of Mrs. Nestor's School; Bob Sweeney as Oliver Munsey, Mrs. Nestor's brother; Ricky Vera as Benny Romero, a troublesome ten-year-old. Gene Barry was seen during the first half of the 1955–1956 season as Gene Talbot, the physical education teacher, one

of Miss Brooks's romantic interests, but he was replaced in midseason when Robert Rockwell returned as Mr. Boynton. William Ching also appeared that season as athletic director Clint Albright, another romantic interest. In midseason, Isabel Randolph, as Mrs. Nestor's sister-in-law, also named Mrs. Nestor, succeeded Nana Bryant and took over as owner of the school. The half-hour series was produced by Larry Berns and directed by Al Lewis. In a 1992 interview with a Toronto newspaper, Eve Arden, herself only a high school graduate, reminisced about the inspiration for her role: "I wasn't as smart as Connie Brooks to be a teacher. I played Connie as I remembered my third grade teacher, Miss Waterman."

OUR PLACE   CBS
2 JULY 1967–3 SEPTEMBER 1967   A summer replacement for *The Smothers Brothers Comedy Hour, Our Place* was actually hosted by Rowlf the Muppet, one of puppeteer Jim Henson's first creations (Rowlf had previously been featured on *The Jimmy Dean Show*). The comedy duo of Jack Burns and Avery Schreiber provided human company for Rowlf, and the Doodletown Pipers were also featured. Bill Angelos and Buz Kohan wrote and produced the hour series.

OUR PRIVATE WORLD   CBS
5 MAY 1965–10 SEPTEMBER 1965   To compete with ABC's popular prime-time soap opera *Peyton Place,* CBS attempted a spinoff from its popular daytime serial, *As the World Turns. Our Private World* was seen on Wednesday and Friday nights. As the show opened, Lisa Hughes (played by Eileen Fulton for several years on *As the World Turns*) moved to Chicago after a divorce. Other members of the evening cast included Sandra Smith as Sandy, who was facing a trial for murder as the series closed; Julienne Marie as Eve; Robert Drivas as Brad, Eve's boyfriend; Geraldine Fitzgerald as Helen; Pamela Murphy as Franny; Sam Groom as Tom; David O'Brien as Dr. Tony Larson; Nicolas Coster as John; Ken Tobey as Dick; Cathy Dunn as Pat; and Michael Strong as Sergeant Clark.

OUR SECRET WEAPON: THE TRUTH   DUMONT
22 OCTOBER 1950–17 APRIL 1951   Half-hour panel discussion show which focused on exposing Communist propaganda. The discussions were usually moderated by Ralph De Toledano and Leo Cherne.

OUR TIME   NBC
27 JULY 1985–7 SEPTEMBER 1985   Lots of baby-boom nostalgia was crammed into this half-hour variety show, hosted by perky Karen Valentine, and featuring vintage film and video clips as well as present-day guest appearances by stars of yesterday and today. Guests on the premiere included Frankie Avalon, Rick Nelson and the Jordanaires, Paul Revere and the Raiders, Adam West, Ed Begley, Jr., Jay North, Edd Byrnes, Joe Penny, Richard Kline, Morgan Brittany, William Christopher, Telma Hopkins, and Stanley and Barry Livingston.

OUR TIMES WITH BILL MOYERS   CBS
26 JUNE 1983–23 AUGUST 1983   Bill Moyers hosted this wide-ranging half-hour documentary series. Among the topics covered were the anti-nuclear debate, unemployment, marriage, and the production of a Chinese version of Arthur Miller's play *Death of a Salesman.*

OUR WORLD   ABC
25 SEPTEMBER 1986–3 SEPTEMBER1987   ABC developed this low-rated but critically acclaimed documentary hour to go up against NBC's *The Cosby Show* on Thursdays. Despite its low ratings, *Our World* made programming sense for the network, because it was relatively inexpensive to produce. Each week cohosts Linda Ellerbee and Ray Gandolf looked back at a recent time in history—a single event, a weekend, or an entire year—using film and video clips, music, and guest appearances by the then newsmakers.

OUT ALL NIGHT   NBC
19 SEPTEMBER 1992–12 FEBRUARY 1993; 25 JUNE 1993–9 JULY 1993   Half-hour sitcom
starring pop/soul singer Patti LaBelle as pop/soul singer Chelsea Paige, who owned a
Los Angeles nightspot, Club Chelsea. With Morris Chestnut as Jeff Carswell, a
graduate of NYU who was hired by Chelsea as a manager trainee and given an
apartment in a building owned by her; Vivica A. Fox as Chelsea's daughter,
Charisse, a fashion stylist; Duane Martin as Jeff's friend and roommate, Vidal
Thomas; Simon O'Brien as their Scottish neighbor, Angus McEwen; and Tahj
Mowry as Shavon, a youngster to whom Vidal served as a Big Brother. The nightclub
setting enabled various real-life musical acts to appear on the program.

OUT OF THE BLUE   ABC
9 SEPTEMBER 1979–21 OCTOBER 1979   Half-hour sitcom about a probationary angel
who was sent to Earth to help out a family of five orphaned kids in Chicago. With
Jimmy Brogan as Random, the angel who lived in a vacant room in the household
and found a job as a high-school science teacher; Dixie Carter as Marion McLemore,
the aunt of the five orphans who was taking care of them; Tammy Lauren as orphan
Stacey Richards; Jason Keller as Jason Richards; Shane Keller (twin brother of Jason
Keller) as Shane Richards; and Eileen Heckart as The Boss Angel, Random's supervisor. Thomas L. Miller and Robert L. Boyett created the series, which perished
after a few weeks along with *A New Kind of Family*. Austin Kalish and Irma Kalish
were the executive producers.

OUT OF THE FIERY FURNACE   PBS
5 OCTOBER 1986–16 NOVEMBER 1986   Only on PBS could one find a series such as this
one—a seven-part look at metallurgy.

OUT OF THE FOG   ABC
7 APRIL 1952–22 SEPTEMBER 1952   Half-hour filmed mystery anthology series.

OUT OF THIS WORLD   SYNDICATED
1959   Half-hour series of lectures and experiments on scientific topics. Host Dr.
Daniel Q. Posin was occasionally assisted by his cat, Minerva.

OUT OF THIS WORLD   SYNDICATED
1987–1990   Low-budget syndicated sci-fi sitcom about a California teenager, the
daughter of an Earthling and an alien, who possessed extranormal powers. With
Maureen Flannigan as Evie Garland; Donna Pescow as her Earthling mother, Donna
Garland; Burt Reynolds as the voice of her alien father, Troy; Doug McClure as Kyle
Applegate, mayor of the town (Marlowe, California); Joe Alaskey as Donna's
brother, Beano Froelich; and Buzz Belmondo as Buzz. Former astronaut Scott Carpenter served as technical adviser.

OUT ON THE FARM   NBC
11 JULY 1954–21 NOVEMBER 1954   This half-hour documentary series examined life
on an American farm. Televised Sunday afternoons, the show was filmed at the
Wilbert Landmeier farm near Cloverdale, Illinois. Eddy Arnold was the host.

OUT THERE   CBS
28 OCTOBER 1951–13 JANUARY 1952   One of TV's first science fiction anthology
series, *Out There* was also one of the first shows to mix filmed special effects with live
action. The half-hour series, seen Sunday evenings, was produced by John Haggodd;
Donald Davis was executive producer.

THE OUTCASTS   ABC
23 SEPTEMBER 1968–15 SEPTEMBER 1969   Hour-long western about two bounty hunt-
ers, one black and one white, who joined forces after the Civil War. With Don
Murray as Earl Corey, a former slaveowner; Otis Young as Jemal David, a former

slave. Hugh Benson was the executive producer of the series, and Jon Epstein the producer for Screen Gems.

OUTDOORS WITH KEN CALLAWAY   SYNDICATED
1975   Half-hour series for hunters and fishermen, hosted by Ken Callaway.

THE OUTER LIMITS   ABC/SHO
16 SEPTEMBER 1963–16 JANUARY 1965 (ABC); 26 MARCH 1995– (SHO)   Leslie Stevens was the creator and executive producer of this hour-long science fiction anthology series. Most of the forty-nine filmed episodes involved contact with extraterrestial life forms. Joseph Stefano produced the show during the first season and Ben Brady during the second. Vic Perrin provided the famous voiceovers for the introduction and conclusion of the show: "There is nothing wrong with your television set. . . ." A new series of 44 episodes was produced for the Showtime cable network in 1995.

THE OUTLAWS   NBC
29 SEPTEMBER 1960–13 SEPTEMBER 1962   Set in Stillwater, Oklahoma Territory, this hour-long western starred Barton MacLane as Marshal Frank Caine. Also featured were Don Collier as Deputy Will Foreman; Jock Gaynor as Deputy Heck Martin; Bruce Yarnell (1961–1962) as Deputy Chalk Breeson; Judy Lewis (daughter of Loretta Young) (1961–1962) as Connie, Will's girlfriend; and Slim Pickens (1961–1962) as Slim.

OUTLAWS   CBS
28 DECEMBER 1986–30 MAY 1987   The second western with this title had a more unusual premise: it started out in 1899, with a sheriff pursuing a gang of four outlaws. The five were caught in a strange electrical storm and were transported ahead in time, to the Houston of 1986, where they bought a ranch and opened the Double Eagle Detective Agency using the loot from the 1899 robbery. Featured were Rod Taylor as Sheriff Jonathan Grail; William Lucking as Harland Pike; Richard Roundtree as Isaiah McAdame; Charles Napier as Wolf Lucas; Patrick Houser as Harland's younger brother, Billy Pike; and Christine Belford as Maggie Randall, a modern-day deputy sheriff and neighbor.

OUTLOOK   NBC
1 APRIL 1956–19 OCTOBER 1958   Half-hour news analysis show, hosted by Chet Huntley. In the fall of 1958 the series, which was seen on Sunday afternoons or evenings, was retitled *Chet Huntley Reporting* (see also that title).

OUTRAGEOUS OPINIONS   SYNDICATED
1967   Half-hour talk show hosted by Helen Gurley Brown, editor of *Cosmopolitan* magazine.

OUTSIDE THE U.S.A.   ABC
1 SEPTEMBER 1955–3 JUNE 1956   Travelogue, hosted by Quincy Howe.

THE OUTSIDER   NBC
18 SEPTEMBER 1968–3 SEPTEMBER 1969   Hour-long crime show starring Darren McGavin as David Ross, an unarmed private detective recently released from prison (he'd killed a man, but it wasn't his fault). Roy Huggins was executive producer of the series.

THE OUTSIDERS   FOX
25 MARCH 1990–26 AUGUST 1990   Francis Ford Coppola and Fred Ross were the executive producers of this hour dramatic series intended as a sequel to Coppola's 1983 film of the same name, which was based on S. E. Hinton's novel. Set in Oklahoma in 1966, its central characters were three orphaned brothers, living under the custody of the oldest boy. Featured were Jay R. Ferguson as the youngest brother

(and narrator), fifteen-year-old Pony Boy Curtis, who attended Walker Ridge High School where he and his "greaser" buddies battled the preppy "socs;" Rodney Harvey as the middle brother, Soda Pop Curtis; Boyd Kestner as the oldest brother, Darrel Curtis, a roofer; David Arquette as Two Bit; Harold P. Pruett as Steve; Scott Coffee as Randy; Robert Rusler as Tim Shepard; Kim Walker as Cherry; and Heather McComb as Scout.

OVER EASY   PBS
1977–1983   Produced under a grant from the United States Department of Health, Education and Welfare, *Over Easy* was a daily, half-hour public affairs program for older Americans. Hugh Downs was the original host of the series. He was joined in 1980 by Frank Blair (the two had previously worked together on the *Today* show). Mary Martin and Jim Hartz (another former *Today* regular) took over as cohosts in 1981.

OVER MY DEAD BODY   CBS
26 OCTOBER 1990–21 DECEMBER 1990; 6 JUNE 1991–20 JUNE 1991   Light hour crime show about a former Scotland Yard inspector who became a mystery writer and settled in San Francisco, where he reluctantly teamed up with an obituary writer to solve crimes. With Edward Woodward as the writer, Maxwell Beckett (*Over My Dead Body* was the title of one of his novels); Jessica Lundy as Nikki Page, obit writer for the San Francisco *Union;* Gregory Itzin as Cosby, Nikki's co-worker and would-be boyfriend; and Jill Tracy as Nikki's assistant, Wendy. William Link and David Chisholm created the series.

OVERLAND TRAIL   NBC
7 FEBRUARY 1960–11 SEPTEMBER 1960   Hour-long western starring William Bendix as Fred Kelly, superintendent of the Overland Stage Company, and Doug McClure as "Flip" Flippen, his sidekick. The series should not be confused with ABC's 1960 effort, *Stagecoach West.*

OVERSEAS PRESS CLUB   CBS
2 OCTOBER 1949–25 JUNE 1950   This Sunday-afternoon public affairs program featured panel discussions by members of the Overseas Press Club of America.

OVERTIME . . . WITH PAT O'BRIEN   CBS
10 AUGUST 1990–24 AUGUST 1990   CBS sportscaster Pat O'Brien was given a three-week tryout as host of a live, sixty-minute talk show, scheduled Fridays at 11:30 P.M.

OWEN MARSHALL: COUNSELOR AT LAW   ABC
16 SEPTEMBER 1971–24 AUGUST 1974   This hour-long dramatic show starred Arthur Hill as Owen Marshall, a widowed attorney who practiced in Santa Barbara. Also featured were Lee Majors (1971–1973) as his associate, Jess Brandon; Joan Darling as his secretary, Frieda Krause; Christine Matchett as his twelve-year-old daughter, Melissa; Reni Santoni (fall 1973–January 1974) as his new associate, Danny Paterno; and David Soul (January 1974–August 1974) as his newest associate, Ted Warrick. David Victor was executive producer for Universal Television.

OWL/TV   PBS
3 NOVEMBER 1985–5 JANUARY 1986; 19 OCTOBER 1986–4 JANUARY 1987   A science show for kids, starring Anais Granofsky, Robin Sandler, and Nigmendra Narain as "The Mighty Mites," a trio of youngsters who could shrink to microscopic size to explore things.

OZARK JUBILEE   ABC
22 JANUARY 1955–21 NOVEMBER 1961   Red Foley hosted this country and western music show, which originated from Springfield, Missouri, for most of its run. Among the many regulars over the years were Smiley Burnette, Bobby Lord, Wanda Jackson, and Brenda Lee (who was only ten years old when she became a regular in

1956), Webb Pierce, Suzi Arden, Uncle Cyp and Aunt Sap Brasfield, The Tall Timber Trio, and The Promenaders. Hank Garland composed the show's theme song, "Sugarfoot Rag." The show was titled *Country Music Jubilee* during the 1957–1958 season, and *Jubilee U.S.A.* thereafter; in the fall of 1959 it was reduced from one hour to thirty minutes. The show left ABC's regular schedule in the spring of 1960, but returned later as a replacement series.

OZMOE ABC
6 MARCH 1951–12 APRIL 1951   Principal characters on this twice-weekly puppet show included a monkey named Ozmoe, a leprechaun named Rhoderick Dhon't, a mermaid known as Misty Waters, Poe the Crow, Sam the Clam, Throckmorton the sea serpent, and Horatio, a caterpillar. The several puppets were made of latex and were operated by gears; they were created by Henry Banks, who produced the show, and Skip Weshner, who wrote it.

OZZIE AND HARRIET ABC
3 OCTOBER 1952–3 SEPTEMBER 1966   Television's longest-running situation comedy was a family affair—Ozzie Nelson created it, directed it, wrote it (together with his brother Don Nelson, Bill Davenport, and Ben Gershman), and starred in it with his wife and two sons. Nelson had graduated from Rutgers with a law degree, but his first love was music; he led a popular dance band in the early 1930s, and in 1935 he married Harriet Hilliard, the band's singer. Harriet Hilliard, born Peggy Lou Snyder, had grown up in show business. In 1944 they introduced a radio sitcom, *The Adventures of Ozzie and Harriet,* in which they played themselves. On the show, and in real life, they had two young sons, David and Ricky (born Eric), but the boys' parts were played by child actors during the show's first five seasons; in February 1949 David and Ricky began playing themselves. The four Nelsons also starred in a 1950 film, *Here Come the Nelsons.* The radio show lasted until 1954.

The television series was also officially titled *The Adventures of Ozzie and Harriet,* but the title seems a misnomer. It is hard to imagine a series less adventuresome than *Ozzie and Harriet*—Ozzie seemed to spend all his time at home or in his yard (he was never at work and his occupation on the show—if he had one—was never revealed, much less the subject of an episode), and Harriet could usually be found in the kitchen. The Nelsons' TV home—a two-story Colonial at 822 Sycamore Road in the town of Hillsdale—was an exact replica of their real home in Hollywood. The show's real drawing cards were the boys, especially Ricky, who was able to capitalize on weekly television exposure to become one of rock-and-roll's biggest stars. Rick (as he preferred to be called in his teens) first sang on 10 April 1957, in an episode titled "Rick the Drummer." He performed Fats Domino's "I'm Walkin'," which became his first record for the Verve label. Rick's singing career really took off in the fall of 1957, when "Be-Bop Baby," his first record on the Imperial label, topped the million mark. Thereafter he performed regularly on *Ozzie and Harriet;* his backup musicians included guitarist James Burton, pianist Ray Johnson, bassists James Kirkland and Joe Osborne, and drummer Richie Frost.

Of course, not all of the action centered around young Rick. A small host of friends and neighbors was around throughout the years to give Ozzie an occasional hand, whether it involved planning a fishing trip or mowing the lawn. The supporting cast included: Don DeFore (1952–1956) as "Thorny" Thornberry; Parley Baer as Herb Darby; Lyle Talbot as Joe Randolph; Mary Jane Croft as Joe's wife, Clara Randolph; and Frank Cady as Doc Williams. Sons David and Rick also acquired a number of friends, particularly after they started attending college in the late 1950s (on the show, both David and Rick became lawyers). Among them were: Skip Young as Wally Plumstead (Young's real name was Ronald Plumstead); Charlene Salerno as Wally's girlfriend, Ginger; Connie Harper (who later married Don Nelson) as David and Rick's secretary, Miss Edwards; Sean Morgan as Sean (he also played a friend named Bruce); Greg Dawson as Greg; Karl George (known earlier as Karl Kindberg) as Dink; Jack Wagner as Jack; James Stacy as Fred; Kent McWhirter as Kent (McWhirter was later known as Kent McCord when he starred on *Adam-12*); Tracy Stratford as Betty; Ivan Bonar as Dean Hopkins, the college dean; and Melinda Plowman as

Melinda. Finally, David and Rick's real-life wives also joined the cast. June Blair, who married David in 1961, joined the cast that year (though she played David's girlfriend for one season), and Rick's wife, Kris (Harmon) Nelson, joined in 1963.

After thirteen seasons in black and white, *Ozzie and Harriet* was filmed in color for the 1965–1966 season. It left the air in 1966 after a fourteen-year, 435-episode TV run; the Nelsons made few television appearances after that, until 1973 when Ozzie and Harriet starred in a syndicated sitcom, *Ozzie's Girls* (see below). David, who had long been interested in behind-the-scenes work, produced the show. Rick continued his musical career, and in 1972 released a bittersweet song, "Garden Party," in which he expressed a desire not to be trapped forever in the past; he also made a few guest appearances in dramatic series such as *Owen Marshall: Counselor at Law* and *McCloud*. He died in a plane crash 31 December 1985.

OZZIE'S GIRLS   SYNDICATED
1973   On this limp sequel to *Ozzie and Harriet,* the elder Nelsons decided to rent out the boys' old room to two college girls. Ozzie and Harriet Nelson played themselves, and Susan Sennett and Brenda Sykes played the two coeds, Susie Hamilton and Brenda MacKenzie (Brenda was known as Jennifer for some reason in the first episodes). David Nelson produced the half-hour series.

PBL   NET
5 NOVEMBER 1967–25 MAY 1969   An ambitious Sunday-evening magazine series, *PBL* stood for "Public Broadcasting Laboratory," and was chiefly funded by the Ford Foundation. Edward F. Morgan was the chief correspondent for the series, which was scheduled biweekly during the 1967–1968 season and weekly during the 1968–1969 season; most shows were two hours long.

PBS LATENIGHT   PBS
1982–1984   Dennis Wholey hosted this late-evening interview program, broadcast live from the studios of WTVS in Detroit.

P.D.Q.   SYNDICATED
1965–1969   On this game show two two-member teams competed; one member of the team was placed in an isolation booth and tried to identify a word or phrase as his partner placed letters from the word or phrase on a rack. The show was hosted by Dennis James and later by Bill Cullen. A network version of the show appeared in 1973: see *Baffle*.

P.M. EAST—P.M. WEST   SYNDICATED
1961–1962   This ninety-minute nightly talk show was videotaped in New York and San Francisco. The first hour, from New York, was cohosted by Mike Wallace and Joyce Davidson, and the last half hour, from San Francisco, was emceed by Terrence O'Flaherty.

P.M. MAGAZINE   SYNDICATED
1978–1990   This half-hour weeknight magazine show was designed for the "access" period—the half-hour slot (7:30 to 8:00 P.M. in the East) preceding the networks' prime-time offerings. The program originated in 1976 at KPIX, the Group W (Westinghouse) outlet in San Francisco; it was subsequently carried by all Group W stations, and was then syndicated nationally (the Group W stations used the title *Evening Magazine* rather than *P.M. Magazine*). The series was produced cooperatively; each station supplied its own host or cohosts, but obtained most (if not all) of the features from a central pool. The Group W stations each produced five features a week for the central pool, while other stations were required to produce only one story a week. After Group W ceased supplying the central pool in 1990, most stations abandoned the concept; the last station to do so was KYW in Philadelphia, which ceased its version in September 1992. Perhaps the best-known personality on the series was the gregarious Chef Tell, whose full name is Friedemann Tell Erhardt.

P.M. PLAYHOUSE
See THE PHILIP MORRIS PLAYHOUSE

P.O.V.   PBS
9 JULY 1988–   A wide-ranging series of independently produced documentaries
was presented on this summer series. "P.O.V." stands for "point of view"; according
to executive producer Marc N. Weiss, his was "the only documentary series on
television that admits that it has a point of view." The works selected for broadcast
were not commissioned, but rather were selected in a competition. A small sampling
of the fare included "Who Killed Vincent Chin?" an examination of a homicide;
"Through the Wire," a report on a maximum security prison unit for female offend-
ers; "Tongues Untied," a look at black gay life; and "Rate It 'X'," a study of pornogra-
phy. Other presentations were less controversial, such as a behind-the-scenes look at
Jeopardy's "Tournament of Champions," or "On Ice," a short film about cryogenics.

P.S. I. LUV U   CBS
15 SEPTEMBER 1991–2 JANUARY 1992   A light adventure hour about a New York cop
and his informant who, posing as a married couple, escaped to Palm Springs and
went to work for P.S.I.—Palm Security Investigations. With Greg Evigan as the cop,
Joey Paciorek, now known as Cody Powell; Connie Sellecca as the informant, Wanda
Talbert, now known as Danielle Powell; and Earl Holliman as the boss, Matthew
Durning. P. S. I.'s telephone number was 774–5888 (PSI–LUVU).

THE P.T.L. CLUB   SYNDICATED
1976–1987   "P.T.L." stood for "Praise the Lord"and for "People That Love,"
according to its founder, Jim Bakker, who would become television's most infamous
evangelist. A minister of the Pentecostal Assemblies of God church, Bakker had
dropped out of Bible school to marry Tamara (Tammy) Faye LaValley. Together they
traveled through the South for several years as itinerant evangelists before landing a
children's religious program in 1964 on a UHF station in Portsmouth, Virginia; there
Jim served as the show's host and Tammy as the puppeteer. Their little show caught
the attention of the station's owner, Pat Robertson, who asked them to join his
fledgling religious broadcasting service, the Christian Broadcasting Network. In 1966
they began hosting the first version of *The 700 Club,* a late-night religious talk show
on which Jim interviewed guests and Tammy sang. The Bakkers left CBN in 1972
(Roberstson took over *The 700 Club*). In 1975 they relocated in Charlotte, North
Carolina, and set up *The P.T.L. Club* a year later.
   The Bakkers again adopted a talk-show format; Jim eschewed sermonizing for
guest interviews and chats with Tammy (Bakker stated in 1979 that "my specific
calling from God is to be a television talk-show host"). Indeed, if there was any true
theological message to the show (other than Jim's usual end-of-show benediction,
"God loves you, He really, really does"), it was that it was all right to be prosperous.
The P.T.L. Network (as the Bakkers referred to their operation) soon became one of
the nation's three richest TV ministries (together with those of Jimmy Swaggart and
Pat Robertson). By 1984 revenues had reached $66 million a year.
   The Bakkers took the prosperity message to heart. Jim's basic annual salary of
$250,000 did not include the bonuses, houses, and cars that he regularly awarded
himself. Tammy, whose facial makeup became more bizarre over the years, went on
innumerable shopping binges, especially for clothes. The two once chartered a jet, at
a cost of $100,000, simply to fly their clothes from North Carolina to California.
Tammy also bought gifts for her husband, of course; she announced on the air in 1987
that her birthday present to Jim would be a pair of giraffes.
   Jim Bakker also went ahead with his grandiose plan to construct Heritage USA, a
religious-based theme park near Charlotte. To help finance it, he offered "lifetime
partnerships" on the air; a contribution of $1000 or more would entitle the donor to
three nights' annual accommodation at the park forever. Bakker sold more than
100,000 such partnerships.
   In 1986 Bakker's chief evangelical rival, Jimmy Swaggart, began publicly criticiz-
ing *The P.T.L. Club* for its excesses and for its promotion of material values. Fearful

that Swaggart might make public the news of his sexual liaison with P.T.L. secretary Jessica Hahn, and that Swaggart might try to take over the P.T.L. organization, Jim Bakker abruptly resigned from his ministry in March 1987. He appointed a fundamentalist Baptist televangelist, Jerry Falwell, to run P.T.L. News of the Hahn affair (and of subsequent payments to her of "hush money") soon became public anyway. Falwell immediately audited the P.T.L. books and discovered massive irregularities, which he promptly publicized, together with reports of other sexual activity of Jim Bakker's. Accused of bilking his followers of some $158 million, Bakker was convicted in federal court in October 1989 of twenty-four counts of fraud and conspiracy, mainly in connection with the sale of "lifetime partnerships." Originally sentenced to forty-five years in prison, he was released in 1994. Tammy had previously divorced him.

PABST BLUE RIBBON BOUTS   CBS
28 OCTOBER 1948–25 MAY 1955   CBS's weekly boxing series was seen on Wednesday nights and was sponsored by Pabst Breweries for most of its run. Russ Hodges was the ringside announcer for several seasons, and Bill Nimmo was the commercial spokesman.

PACIFIC STATION   NBC
15 SEPTEMBER 1991–26 OCTOBER 1991; 20 DECEMBER 1991–3 JANUARY 1992   Half-hour sitcom set at the Venice, California, police station. With Robert Guillaume as Detective Bob Ballard; Richard Libertini as his first partner, Detective Richard Capparelli, a touchy-feely guy; Joel Murray as Captain Kenny Epstein; Ron Leibman as sex-obsessed Detective Al Burkhardt; John Hancock as Deputy Commissioner Hank Bishop, a compulsive eater; and Megan Gallagher (October 1991–1992) as Bob's new partner, Detective Sandy Calloway.

THE PACKARD SHOWROOM   ABC
18 APRIL 1954–5 DECEMBER 1954   Sponsored by Packard automobiles, this fifteen-minute Sunday-night musical series was hosted by Martha Wright and featured trumpeter Bobby Hackett.

PAC-MAN   ABC
25 SEPTEMBER 1982–SEPTEMBER 1984
THE PAC-MAN/LITTLE RASCALS/RICHIE RICH SHOW   ABC
5 SEPTEMBER 1982–3 SEPTEMBER 1983   Pac-Man, the omnivorous little hero of the popular video arcade game, came to Saturday-morning TV as the star of not one, but two, cartoon shows, broadcast back to back. *Pac-Man* was a half-hour series featuring Pac-Man, his wife (Ms. Pac-Man), and their child (Pac-Baby). *The Pac-Man/Little Rascals/Richie Rich Show,* which preceded *Pac-Man,* was an hour program containing three separate cartoon segments: "Pac-Man," "The Little Rascals" (based on the theatrical shorts produced by Hal Roach in the 1930s), and "Richie Rich" (the world's wealthiest youngster, who had been introduced in 1980 on *The Richie Rich/Scooby Doo Show*). After one season, the trio separated: *Pac-Man* continued as a half-hour series, and *The Little Rascals/Richie Rich Show* carried on in a half-hour format. The voice of Pac-Man was provided by Marty Ingels.

PADDY THE PELICAN   ABC
11 SEPTEMBER 1950–13 OCTOBER 1950   Broadcast from Chicago on weekday afternoons, this fifteen-minute children's show starred a pelican named Paddy, who appeared both in animated form and as a puppet. Mary Frances Desmond was also featured as Pam.

PALACE GUARD   CBS
18 OCTOBER 1991–1 NOVEMBER 1991   Short-lived hour adventure series about a former thief who was hired as special head of security of the Palace Hotels, the chain which he used to rob. With D. W. Moffett as the ex-thief, Tommy Logan; Marcy Walker as his boss, Christy Cooper, a former actress who was head of publicity and

public relations; Tony LoBianco as Arturo Taft, the founder and president (Tommy, who had been raised in an orphanage, was Arturo's illegitimate son, although Arturo did not reveal it to him); and Noelle Parker as Melissa Taft, Arturo's estranged daughter (and Tommy's half-sister).

THE PALLISERS   **PBS**
31 JANUARY 1977–27 JUNE 1977   A twenty-two-part adaptation of six novels by Anthony Trollope, *The Pallisers* concerned a wealthy English family living in the Victorian era. Principal players included: Susan Hampshire as Lady Glencora Palliser; Philip Latham as her husband, Plantagenet Palliser, M.P.; Barry Justice as Burgo Fitzgerald, for whom Glencora developed a penchant; Donal McCann as Phineas Finn, an ambitious Irish M.P.; Roland Culver as The Duke of Omnium; Caroline Mortimer as Alice Vavasor; Gary Watson as George Vavasor; Anna Massey as Lady Laura Standish; Fabia Drake as Countess Midlothian; and Rachel Herbert as Lady Dumbello. The series was jointly produced by the BBC and Time-Life Television; Sir John Gielgud introduced the episodes.

PALMERSTOWN U.S.A.   **CBS**
10 MARCH 1980–1 MAY 1980; 17 MARCH 1981–9 JUNE 1981   This hour dramatic series was set in 1934 in a small Southern town. It was created by author Alex Haley (who drew on his own childhood in Henning, Tennessee) and developed by producer Norman Lear. The central characters were two young boys—one black, one white—who were best friends. The cast included Jermain H. Johnson as Booker T. Freeman; Brian G. Wilson as David Hall; Bill Duke as Booker's father, Luther Freeman, a blacksmith; Jonelle Allen as Booker's mother, Bessie Freeman; Star-Shemah Bobatoon as Booker's sister, Diana; Beeson Carroll as David's father, W. D. Hall, a grocer; Janice St. John as David's mother, Coralee Hall; and Michael Fox as David's brother, Willie-Joe (Fox would soon become better known as Michael J. Fox of *Family Ties*). When the series returned in the spring of 1981 it was titled *Palmerstown*.

THE PAMELA MASON SHOW   **SYNDICATED**
1965   Talk show hosted by Pamela Mason, former wife of James Mason.

PANDAMONIUM   **CBS**
18 SEPTEMBER 1982–10 SEPTEMBER 1983   Saturday-morning cartoon series about a trio of talking pandas who accompanied a group of teenagers on a quest to find the pieces of a magic pyramid.

PANHANDLE PETE AND JENNIFER   **NBC**
18 SEPTEMBER 1950–28 JUNE 1951   This late-afternoon children's show was set at a western ranch; featured were Panhandle Pete, a dummy operated by Jennifer Holt, and Johnny Coons (who later hosted his own kids' show). The fifteen-minute series was originally seen Mondays through Fridays but was later cut back to Tuesdays and Thursdays.

PANIC!   **NBC**
5 MARCH 1957–17 SEPTEMBER 1957   Westbrook Van Voorhis hosted this half-hour anthology series of suspenseful dramas. Al Simon was the producer. See also *No Warning!*

PANTOMIME QUIZ (STUMP THE STARS)   **CBS/NBC/DUMONT/ABC/SYNDICATED**
4 OCTOBER 1949–20 AUGUST 1951 (CBS); 2 JANUARY 1952–26 MARCH 1952 (NBC); 4 JULY 1952–28 AUGUST 1953 (CBS); 20 OCTOBER 1953–13 APRIL 1954 (DUMONT); 9 JULY 1954–27 AUGUST 1954 (CBS); 22 JANUARY 1955–6 MARCH 1955 (ABC); 8 JULY 1955–6 SEPTEMBER 1957 (CBS); 8 APRIL 1958–9 OCTOBER 1959 (ABC); 17 SEPTEMBER 1962–16 SEPTEMBER 1963 (CBS); 1968–1970 (SYNDICATED)   One of television's most durable prime-time game shows, *Pantomime Quiz* began as a local show in Los Angeles in 1948 and won an Emmy that season (a prehistoric version of the show was briefly telecast there in 1939). A year later the series went nationwide. The format

was simple: two teams, each with four celebrities, played charades. One member of the team acted out the charade (all of which were suggested by home viewers) and the other three teammates were required to guess it within two minutes; the team with the lower total elapsed time was the winner. Mike Stokey produced and hosted the half-hour show, which was often scheduled as a midseason or summer replacement throughout the 1950s. In 1958 the celebrity teams consisted of Howard Morris, Carol Burnett, Milt Kamen, and a guest versus Stubby Kaye, Denise Darcel, Tom Poston, and a guest. A daytime version of the show, also hosted by Stokey, ran from 11 May to 9 October 1959. In 1962 the show returned, after a three-year absence, in the same format but with a new title: *Stump the Stars*. It also featured—briefly—a new host: Pat Harrington, Jr., who emceed for thirteen weeks, after which Mike Stokey returned. Regular panelists at that time included Sebastian Cabot, Robert Clary, Hans Conried, Beverly Garland, Stubby Kaye, Ruta Lee, Richard Long, Ross Martin, and Tommy Noonan. On the syndicated version, also titled *Stump the Stars,* regulars included Sebastian Cabot, Roger C. Carmel, Beverly Garland, Stubby Kaye, Deanna Lund, Ross Martin, and Dick Patterson.

THE PAPER CHASE   CBS/SHOWTIME
19 SEPTEMBER 1978–17 JULY 1979 (CBS); 15 APRIL 1983–9 AUGUST 1986 (SHOWTIME)   Hour dramatic series based on John Jay Osborn, Jr.'s novel (which was made into a movie in 1973), *The Paper Chase* was highly acclaimed but little watched. Set at a prestigious but unnamed Eastern law school, it starred John Houseman (repeating his film role) as the awesomely autocratic Professor Charles W. Kingsfield, Jr., who strove to make his students think like lawyers in his contracts class, and James Stephens as James T. Hart, a first-year student from the Midwest who strove to learn all he could from the course. Hart's classmates were played by Tom Fitzsimmons as Franklin Ford, son of a prominent lawyer; Robert Ginty as Thomas Anderson; James Keane as Willis Bell; Jonathan Segal (to January 1979) as Jonathan Brooks, who left school after a cheating incident; and Francine Tacker as Elizabeth Logan. Deka Beaudine was also featured in the first episode (and credited for many weeks) as Asheley, Brooks's wife. Occasionally featured were Betty Harford as Mrs. Nottingham, Kingsfield's officious secretary, and Charles Hallahan as Ernie, proprietor of the pizza joint where Hart worked part time. The series was developed for television by James Bridges; Robert C. Thompson was the executive producer for 20th Century-Fox TV. In 1983 *The Paper Chase* became network TV's first dramatic series to move to cable, as the Showtime cable network introduced new episodes; titled *The Paper Chase: The Second Year,* the new programs featured Houseman, Stephens, Keane, and Fitzsimmons from the old crew, and Jane Kaczmarek as Hart's girlfriend, first-year student Connie Lehman. *The Paper Chase: The Third Year* got underway in May 1985, adding Lainie Kazan as new student Rose Samuels and Claire Kirkconnel as Rita Harriman. The last of the thirty-six new Showtime episodes, "The Graduation," aired 9 August 1986, a scant eight years after the eager students had begun their studies on CBS.

PAPER DOLLS   ABC
23 SEPTEMBER 1984–25 DECEMBER 1984   Derived from the 1982 TV-movie, this hour prime-time serial was set amidst the modeling business in New York City. The large cast included Lloyd Bridges as tycoon Grant Harper; Morgan Fairchild as bitchy Racine, owner of a modeling agency; Nicollette Sheridan as sixteen-year-old Taryn Blake, top model; Terry Farrell as new teen model Laurie Caswell; Jennifer Warren as Laurie's mother, Dinah Caswell; Mimi Rogers as Grant's daughter, Blair Fenton, also a model; Richard Beymer as Blair's husband, David Fenton, sportswear executive; Dack Rambo as Wesley Harper, Grant's son, head of a cosmetics company; Brenda Vaccaro as Taryn's mother, Julia Blake; and Anne Schedeen as assistant district attorney Sara Frank.

PAPER MOON   ABC
12 SEPTEMBER 1974–2 JANUARY 1975   Based on Peter Bogdanovich's 1973 film, this half-hour sitcom starred Chris Connelly as Moze Pray, an itinerant con artist who

worked the Midwest during the 1930s, and Jodie Foster as Addie Pray, an eleven-year-old waif who, convinced that Moze was her father, teamed up with him. Anthony Wilson was the executive producer and Robert Stambler the producer for Paramount Television.

PARADISE (GUNS OF PARADISE) CBS
27 OCTOBER 1988–1 SEPTEMBER 1990; 4 JANUARY 1991–14 JUNE 1991   The first TV western to be renewed for a second season since the demise of *Gunsmoke, Paradise* starred Lee Horsley as Ethan Allen Cord, a former gunslinger living in the mining town of Paradise, California, who inherited four young children from his deceased sister (who had mistakenly believed that her brother was a storekeeper). Also featured were Jenny Beck as the oldest kid, Claire Carroll, thirteen; Matthew Newmark as Joseph, eleven; Brian Lando as Benjamin, eight; Michael Patrick Carter as George, five; Sigrid Thornton as the British owner of the local bank, Amelia Lawson, who took a liking to Cord and his brood; Dehl Berti as John Taylor, Ethan's Native American friend; Mack Dryden (1988–1990) as Scotty; and Benjamin Lum (1988–1990) as Mr. Lee. The series paid homage to the westerns of TV's bygone days: Hugh O'Brian and Gene Barry reprised their roles as Wyatt Earp and Bat Masterson in a two-part episode at the start of the second season, and *The Rifleman*'s Chuck Connors and Johnny Crawford were reunited (in different roles) in a 1990 episode. The series was not on CBS's fall 1990 schedule, but reappeared in midseason with a new title, *Guns of Paradise,* and with Cord serving as the town's new marshal. John Terlesky joined the cast as Dakota, Cord's gambler pal.

PARADISE BAY NBC
27 SEPTEMBER 1965–1 JULY 1966   Set in Paradise Bay, California, this half-hour daytime serial featured Keith Andes as Jeff Morgan, manager of a radio station; Marion Ross as Mary Morgan, his wife; Heather North as their daughter, Kitty; Walter Brooke as newspaper editor Walter Montgomery; Paulle Clark as Charlotte Baxter; Dennis Cole as Duke Spalding; and Steven Mines as Fred.

PARADISE ISLAND SYNDICATED
1949   Starring Danny O'Neil and Anne Sterling, this fifteen-minute variety show was filmed at Churubusco Studios in Mexico City by Jerry Fairbanks Productions; the series, which featured the music of Everett Hoagland and his orchestra, was produced in Mexico to reduce costs and to circumvent regulations imposed on domestic productions by the American Federation of Musicians.

THE PARENT GAME SYNDICATED
1972   Clark Race hosted this game show on which three married couples were asked questions about child behavior and tried to select the response that a child psychologist had determined was the correct one.

THE PARENT 'HOOD WB
18 JANUARY 1995–   One of the first series offered by the new Warner Bros. network, this was a sitcom about a black family. With Robert Townsend as Robert Peterson, a college professor; Suzzanne Douglas as his wife Jerri Peterson, a law student; Kenny Blank as older son Michael; Reagan Gomez-Preston as older daughter Zaria; Curtis Williams as younger son Nicholas; Ashli Adams as younger daughter CeCe; Derek Sawyer (premiere telecast only) and Bobby McGee as neighbor Derek; and Carol Woods as Mrs. Wilcox.

PARENTHOOD NBC
20 AUGUST 1990–16 DECEMBER 1990   Half-hour sitcom based on the 1989 movie about the trials and tribulations of contemporary family life. With Ed Begley, Jr., as Gil Buckman; Jayne Atkinson as his wife, Karen; Max Elliott Slade as their angst-ridden ten-year-old, Kevin; Thora as their eight-year-old daughter, Taylor; Zachary LaVoy as their anxiety-producing four-year-old, Justin; Maryedith Burrell as Gil's divorced sister, Helen; Leonardo DiCaprio as her thirteen-year-old son, Garry; Bess

Meyer as her teenage daughter, Julie; David Arquette as Julie's new husband, Tod Hawks, a housepainter; Susan Norman as Gil's other sister, Susan Buckman-Merrick; Ken Ober as her husband, Nathan Merrick; Ivyann Schwan as their four-year-old daugher, Patty, whom Nathan is trying to nurture into a genius; William Windom as Gil's father, Frank; Sheila MacRae as Gil's mother, Marilyn; and Mary Jackson as Marilyn's mother, Great Grandma Greenwell. Three of the children—Slade, LaVoy, and Schwan—had also appeared in the film. A lone first-run episode was televised 11 August 1991.

PARIS   CBS
29 SEPTEMBER 1979–15 JANUARY 1980   Hour crime show starring James Earl Jones as Los Angeles police detective, Captain Woodrow "Woody" Paris, with Lee Chamberlin as his wife, Barbara, a nurse; Hank Garrett as Deputy Chief Jerome Bench; Cecilia Hart as Sergeant Stacy Erickson; Jake Mitchell as Charlie Bogart; Frank Ramirez as Ernesto; and Michael Warren as Willie Miller. Steven Bochco created the series and was the executive producer for MTM Enterprises.

PARIS CAVALCADE OF FASHIONS   NBC
11 NOVEMBER 1948–6 JANUARY 1949   One of TV's first fashion series, this fifteen-minute show was hosted first by Faye Emerson, later by Julie Gibson.

PARIS PRECINCT   SYNDICATED
1955   Filmed in Paris, this half-hour crime show was based on the files of Sûreté, the French national police agency. Featured were Louis Jourdan as Inspector Beaumont and Claude Dauphin as Inspector Bolbec.

PARIS 7000   ABC
22 JANUARY 1970–4 JUNE 1970   When *The Survivors,* ABC's ambitious and costly attempt to serialize a novel, failed in midseason, George Hamilton, who had starred in *The Survivors,* was inserted into a new, hastily concocted format. On *Paris 7000* Hamilton played Jack Brennan, an employee of the United States Department of State assigned to the American consulate in Paris. Also featured were Jacques Aubuchon as Jules Maurois, head of Sûreté, the French national police agency, and Gene Raymond as Robert Stevens, Brennan's occasional sidekick.

PARK PLACE   CBS
9 APRIL 1981–30 APRIL 1981   This half-hour sitcom was reminiscent of *Barney Miller.* It was set at the Legal Assistance Bureau in downtown Manhattan, where the pace was hectic and the clientele bizarre. Featured were Harold Gould as David Ross, the director; David Clennon as lawyer Jeff O'Neill; Don Calfa as lawyer Howie Beech, who was perpetually waiting for the "big case"; Cal Gibson as receptionist Ernie Rice; Alice Drummond as Frances Heine, the devoutly religious secretary; Lionel Smith as wheelchair-using Mac MacRae; Mary Elaine Monti as lawyer Jo Keene; and James Widdoes as lawyer Brad Lincoln.

PARKER LEWIS CAN'T LOSE   FOX
2 SEPTEMBER 1990–27 SEPTEMBER 1992; 21 MARCH 1993–22 AUGUST 1993   Half-hour sitcom which, like NBC's *Ferris Bueller,* chronicled the exploits of a well-connected student at suburban Santo Domingo High School. Featured were Corin Nemec as Parker Lewis; William Jayne as his "best bud," Mikey Randall; Troy Slaten as Parker's nerdy freshman sycophant, Jerry Steiner; Maia Brewton as Parker's kid sister, Shelly; Melanie Chartoff as the principal, Ms. Grace Musso; Abraham Benrubi as the big dumb jock, Larry Kubiac; Taj Johnson as Ms. Musso's student protege, Frank Lemmer; Timothy Stack as Parker's father, Marty Lewis; Anne Bloom (1990–1991) and Mary Ellen Trainor (1991–1993) as Parker's mother, Judy Lewis; Paul Johansson (1991–1993) as Nick Comstock, proprietor of the Atlas Diner; Harold Pruett (1991–1993) as Brad; and John Pinette (1991–1993) as Coach Kohler. When the show returned to Fox's schedule in 1993 its title was shortened to *Parker Lewis.*

PAROLE   SYNDICATED
1958   Actual parole hearings, filmed at American prisons, were presented on this half-hour documentary series, produced and directed by Fred Becker.

THE PARTNERS   NBC
18 SEPTEMBER 1971–8 JANUARY 1972   Slated opposite CBS's *All in the Family,* this half-hour sitcom about two wacky detectives was canceled in midseason (a few reruns were shown during the summer of 1972). It starred Don Adams as Detective Sergeant Lenny Crooke; Rupert Crosse as his black partner, Detective Sergeant George Robinson; John Doucette as their commanding officer, Captain Andrews; and Dick Van Patten as Sergeant Higgenbottom.

PARTNERS   FOX
11 SEPTEMBER 1995–   Half-hour sitcom about a pair of San Francisco architects, one of whom becomes engaged to be married. With Jon Cryer as Bob; Tate Donovan as his best friend, Owen; Maria Pitillo as Alicia, Owen's fiancee; and Catherine Lloyd Burns as Heather Pond, Bob and Owen's office person.

PARTNERS IN CRIME   NBC
22 SEPTEMBER 1984–29 DECEMBER 1984   A lighthearted crime show about a private eye (Raymond Dashiell Caulfield) who died, leaving his San Francisco mansion and his detective agency to his two ex-wives. With Lynda Carter as freelance photographer Carole Stanwyck and Loni Anderson as bass violinist Sydney Kovack, the two exes; Walter Olkewicz as Harmon Shane, their assistant; Leo Rossi as Lieutenant Vronsky of the San Francisco P. D.; and Eileen Heckart as Raymond's mother, Jeanine, who owned a mystery bookstore.

THE PARTRIDGE FAMILY   ABC
25 SEPTEMBER 1970–31 AUGUST 1974   Popular with younger viewers, *The Partridge Family* was a half-hour sitcom about a fatherless family of six who decided to become a rock-and-roll band. Featured were Shirley Jones as Shirley Partridge; David Cassidy as Keith; Susan Dey as Laurie; Danny Bonaduce as Danny; Jeremy Gelbwaks (1970–1971) and Brian Forster (1971–1974) as Chris; Suzanne Crough as Tracy; and Dave Madden as their manager, Reuben Kincaid. In the fall of 1973 the show was moved from its Friday slot to Saturdays, opposite *All in the Family* and *Emergency!,* where its ratings sagged quickly. Two youngsters were added to the cast that season: Ricky Segall as Ricky Stevens, the little boy who lived next door; Alan Bursky as Alan, Reuben's nephew. *The Partridge Family* helped establish David Cassidy (stepson of Shirley Jones) as a teen idol, and millions of Partridge Family records were sold. On record, however, only the voices of Jones and Cassidy from the TV cast were used, with the rest of the vocals supplied by studio musicians. Bob Claver was executive producer of the series. Ninety-six episodes were made. See also *Partridge Family: 2200 A.D.*

PARTRIDGE FAMILY: 2200 A.D.   CBS
7 SEPTEMBER 1974–8 MARCH 1975   A cartoon sequel to *The Partridge Family,* this Saturday-morning show found the rock-and-rolling Partridges in space. The voices of Susan Dey, Danny Bonaduce, Brian Forster, Suzanne Crough, and Dave Madden from the prime-time show were used. Iwao Takamoto was the producer for Hanna-Barbera Productions.

THE PARTY MACHINE WITH NIA PEEPLES   SYNDICATED
1991   Half-hour late-night music and dance program, hosted by Nia Peeples.

PARTY OF FIVE   FOX
12 SEPTEMBER 1994–15 MARCH 1995; 7 JUNE 1995–   Hour dramatic series about a family of five children trying to cope after the death of their parents in an auto accident six months earlier. With Matthew Fox as eldest son Charlie Salinger, 24, who tended bar at Salinger's, the restaurant owned by his late father; Scott Wolf as

second son Bailey, 16; Neve Campbell as daughter Julia, 15, a high school student; Lacey Chabert as daughter Claudia, 11, an accomplished violinist; Brandon and Taylor Porter as infant son Owen; Paula Devicq as Kirsten Bennett, a graduate student in child psychology who was hired as the nanny; Jennifer Blanc as Kate, Bailey's girlfriend; Megan Ward as Jill; Mitchell Anderson as Ross, Claudia's violin teacher; Michael Shulman as Artie; Michael Goorjian as Justin, Julia's boyfriend; and Tom Mason as Joe, the restaurant manager. Christopher Keyser and Amy Lippman created the series, which, despite low ratings in its first season was renewed.

PARTY TIME AT CLUB ROMA   NBC
14 OCTOBER 1950–6 JANUARY 1951   A Saturday-night audience-participation show, this series was hosted by Ben Alexander (who later costarred with Jack Webb on *Dragnet*). It started out as a quiz and stunt show before shifting formats to a talent contest.

PASS THE BUCK   CBS
3 APRIL 1978–30 JUNE 1978   Bill Cullen hosted this daytime game show on which four contestants competed. During the first round each contestant was required to supply an answer to a general question (e.g., name a word that rhymes with "blink"), and contestants who failed to make a timely response were exiled to the "bullpen" until only one contestant remained. The survivor then played a second round, alone, in which the top prize was $5,000. The executive producer of the short-lived series was Bob Stewart.

PASSPORT TO DANGER   SYNDICATED
1954–1955   Half-hour adventure series starring Cesar Romero as Steve McQuinn, a diplomatic courier. Hal Roach, Jr., produced the show.

PASSWORD   CBS/SYNDICATED/ABC/NBC
2 OCTOBER 1961–15 SEPTEMBER 1967 (CBS); 1967–1969 (SYNDICATED); 5 APRIL 1971–27 JUNE 1975 (ABC); 8 JANUARY 1979–26 MARCH 1982 (NBC); 24 SEPTEMBER 1984–24 MARCH 1989 (NBC)   A durable game show, *Password* was long hosted by Allen Ludden and has appeared in several different formats. Originally the game was played by two two-member teams; one member of each team was shown the "password," and sought to have her or his partner guess the password by providing one-word clues. If the password was guessed after the first clue, the successful team was awarded ten points; if the word was guessed after two clues, the team was given nine points, and so on. The first team to score twenty-five points won the game and proceeded to the "lightning round," where a player won $50 for each of five words that she or he could identify within sixty seconds. A Mark Goodson-Bill Todman Production, *Password* enjoyed a six-year daytime run on CBS, and was seen in prime time as well, usually surfacing as a midseason replacement. Late in 1974, during *Password*'s daytime run on ABC, the show was retitled *Password Allstars* and featured six celebrities instead of the celebrity-and-contestant pairs previously used. In January of 1979 the series appeared on NBC's daytime schedule; titled *Password Plus,* it again featured two celebrity-and-contestant teams. The teams no longer played for points, however; players won money not by guessing the passwords, but rather by guessing a second word or phrase suggested by each series of passwords. Allen Ludden hosted *Password Plus* until October 1980, when he was sidelined by a heart attack (he died in 1981). Tom Kennedy succeeded him as host. In 1984 the series returned to NBC's daytime schedule, titled *Super Password,* hosted by Bert Convy, and substantially identical in format to *Password Plus.* One unlucky contestant was arrested after winning $58,600, having been spotted by a home viewer as a fugitive in an insurance fraud case.

THE PASTOR   SYNDICATED
1955   This religious anthology series was hosted by Dr. Robert E. Goodrich, Jr., of the First Methodist Church in Dallas. Each show was a drama depicting the life of a minister.

THE PAT BOONE SHOW   ABC/NBC/SYNDICATED

3 OCTOBER 1957–23 JUNE 1960 (ABC); 17 OCTOBER 1966–30 JUNE 1967 (NBC); 1969
(SYNDICATED)   Pat Boone, the cleancut singer who became a regular on Arthur
Godfrey's *Talent Scouts* in 1954, hosted three shows of his own. The first, on ABC,
was a prime-time half-hour variety series and featured the McGuire Sisters and the
Mort Lindsey Orchestra. The second was a daytime half-hour variety and talk show
on NBC and featured the Paul Smith Orchestra. The third, a ninety-minute talk
show, was titled *Pat Boone in Hollywood*.

PAT PAULSEN'S HALF A COMEDY HOUR   ABC

22 JANUARY 1970–16 APRIL 1970   Pat Paulsen, the deadpan comedian who had been
featured on *The Smothers Brothers Comedy Hour,* hosted his own half-hour comedy
series, which also featured Pepe Brown, Bob Einstein, Sherry Miles, Vanetta Rogers, George Spell, and the Denny Vaughn Orchestra. Former vice president Hubert
Humphrey guested on the premiere.

THE PAT SAJAK SHOW   CBS

9 JANUARY 1989–13 APRIL 1990   Seventeen years after *The Merv Griffin Show* left
CBS, the network decided to give the late-night talk show format another try. Pat
Sajak, who had hosted the higly successful game show *Wheel of Fortune* (also a Merv
Griffin production) for seven years, was selected. The show bore deep resemblances
to *The Tonight Show Starring Johnny Carson*—a similar set, an opening monologue,
a sidekick (Dan Miller) and a bandleader (Tom Scott)—but never seriously threat-
ened the ratings of the Carson show. Moreover, competition from a new syndicated
talk show—*The Arsenio Hall Show*—siphoned away younger viewers. *The Pat Sajak
Show* began as a ninety-minute effort. It was cut back to an hour on 30 October 1989.
A new set was introduced early in 1990, together with the use of guest hosts on
Fridays, but all to no avail. After a fifteen-month run it was canceled.

THE PATRICE MUNSEL SHOW   ABC

18 OCTOBER 1957–13 JUNE 1958   Opera star Patrice Munsel turned to popular music
in her half-hour variety show. Also featured were the Martin Quartet and the Charles
Sanford Orchestra. Munsel's husband, Bob Schuler, was the executive producer, and
the show's theme, "Breezy and Easy," was composed by Hugh Martin.

THE PATRICIA BOWMAN SHOW   CBS

11 AUGUST 1951–3 NOVEMBER 1951   Fifteen-minute Saturday-evening variety show
hosted by dancer Patricia Bowman.

PATROL CAR   SYNDICATED

See FABIAN OF SCOTLAND YARD.

THE PATTI PAGE SHOW   SYNDICATED/NBC/ABC

1955–1956 (SYNDICATED); 16 JUNE 1956–7 JULY 1956 (NBC); 24 SEPTEMBER 1958–
16 MARCH 1959 (ABC)   Patti Page, born Clara Ann Fowler, began making records
in 1948 and became one of the biggest pop singers of the 1950s. She hosted several
television scries during that decade, beginning in 1952 with *The Scott Music Hall* (see
that title). In 1955 she began a fifteen-minute musical series, which was widely
syndicated, featuring the Page Five Singers and the Jack Rael Orchestra (Rael was
her longtime musical director). In the summer of 1956 she hosted a four-week summer replacement for *The Perry Como Show;* the hour series, broadcast in color,
featured the Jack Rael Orchestra and the Spellbinders. During the 1957–1958 season
she hosted *The Big Record,* a series designed to compete with *Your Hit Parade* (see
also those titles). In the fall of 1958 she hosted a half-hour variety series, also known
as *The Oldsmobile Show,* which featured Rocky Cole, The Jerry Packer Singers, and
the Vic Schoen Orchestra. The latter series was produced by Ted Mills.

THE PATTY DUKE SHOW   ABC

18 SEPTEMBER 1963–31 AUGUST 1966   When Patty Duke was given her own series in 1963 at the age of seventeen, she was the youngest person in television history to have a prime-time series named after herself. Before that, however, she had had considerable experience in both television (as a guest star and as a regular, on *Kitty Foyle*) and on stage (most notably in *The Miracle Worker* on Broadway). In the series she played identical cousins, Patty and Cathy Lane; Patty was a typically outgoing American teenager, and Cathy, who was living with Patty's family while her father was overseas, was a reserved and artistic English lass. Both attended Brooklyn Heights High School. Also featured were William Schallert as Patty's father, Martin Lane, a magazine editor; Jean Byron as Patty's mother, Natalie Lane; Paul O'Keefe as Patty's younger brother, Ross; and Eddie Applegate as Richard Harrison, Patty's boyfriend. Occasionally seen were John McGiver (1963–1964) as Martin's boss, J. R. Castle; Kitty Sullivan as Patty's archrival, Sue Ellen Turner; Skip Hinnant as Ted, Cathy's sometime boyfriend; Alberta Grant as Maggie; Robyn Miller as Roz; and Kelly Wood as Gloria.

THE PAUL ARNOLD SHOW   CBS

24 OCTOBER 1949–23 JUNE 1950   This fifteen-minute musical series, hosted by singer Paul Arnold, was seen several nights a week before CBS's evening newscast.

THE PAUL DIXON SHOW   ABC/DUMONT/SYNDICATED

8 AUGUST 1951–24 SEPTEMBER 1952 (ABC); 29 SEPTEMBER 1952–8 APRIL 1955 (DU-MONT); 1973 (SYNDICATED)   Paul Dixon, a popular television personality in Cincinnati, hosted four nationally distributed programs. The first two were on ABC: a prime time variety hour and, briefly in 1952, a daytime half-hour. On both, Dixon and Dotty Mack pantomimed routines to popular recordings (Dotty Mack later did the same thing on her own ABC series). Other regulars included Wanda Lewis and Len Goorian. Jack Taylor produced the series, and Lee Hornback directed it. In the fall of 1952 Dixon hosted a daytime series on the DuMont network, which became one of that network's longest-running daytime shows; it again featured Wanda Lewis and Dotty Mack and was produced by Dick Perry. After a long absence from national television, Dixon returned in 1973 as host of a half-hour variety show that also featured Coleen Sharp and Bonnie Lou.

THE PAUL HARTMAN SHOW
See PRIDE OF THE FAMILY

THE PAUL LYNDE SHOW   ABC

13 SEPTEMBER 1972–8 SEPTEMBER 1973   Half-hour sitcom starring Paul Lynde as high-strung lawyer Paul Simms, with Elizabeth Allen as his wife, Martha Simms; Jane Actman as their daughter, Barbara; John Calvin as Barbara's husband, Howie Dickerson, an obnoxious genius who was unemployed and lived with the elder Simmses; Pamelyn Ferdin as Sally, Paul and Martha's younger daughter; Herb Voland as T. J. McNish, Paul's law partner; James Gregory as T. R. Scott, another law partner; and Allison McKay as Alice, Paul's secretary. William Asher was executive producer of the series.

PAUL SAND IN FRIENDS AND LOVERS
See FRIENDS AND LOVERS

THE PAUL WHITEMAN CLUB
See TV TEEN CLUB

THE PAUL WHITEMAN REVUE   ABC

6 NOVEMBER 1949–30 MARCH 1952   Bandleader Paul Whiteman hosted this half-hour musical variety show for three seasons; Linda Romay and Joe Young were also on hand. While Whiteman vacationed during the summer of 1951, Earl Wrightson and Maureen Cannon filled in (the series was then titled *Paul Whiteman's Goodyear*

Summertime Revue). Whiteman also hosted several other series: see *America's Greatest Bands, On the Boardwalk,* and *TV Teen Club*.

PAUL WINCHELL AND JERRY MAHONEY   NBC/ABC/SYNDICATED
18 SEPTEMBER 1950–23 MAY 1954; 20 NOVEMBER 1954–25 FEBRUARY 1956 (NBC); 29 SEPTEMBER 1957–2 APRIL 1961 (ABC); 1965 (SYNDICATED)   Ventriloquist Paul Winchell constructed his most famous dummy, Jerry Mahoney, when he was a teenager. The two appeared on radio, first on *Major Bowes' Original Amateur Hour,* and later on their own short-lived series in 1943. Winchell and Mahoney began appearing regularly on TV as early as 1947, and in 1948 Winchell cohosted a prime-time series known as *The Bigelow Show* (see also that title) with mentalist Dunninger (the two had previously worked together on stage). In the fall of 1950 Winchell and Mahoney were given their own prime-time series, which ran for four years on NBC. For the first two seasons the show was titled *The Speidel Show* and was essentially a comedy-variety series that also featured Knucklehead Smiff (a dim-witted dummy created by Winchell), Dorothy Claire, Hilda Vaughn, and Jimmy Blaine. Other segments were also incorporated, including dramatic scenes and a quiz. Titled "What's My Name?" and hosted by Ted Brown, the latter segment required contestants to try to identify a famous person from clues suggested by Winchell and his crew. "What's My Name?" was also featured during the series' fourth season, when the show shifted to a Sunday-evening time slot. In the fall of 1954 Winchell and Mahoney moved from prime time to Saturday mornings on NBC, where their half-hour show featured a live audience and Mary Ellen Terry; occasionally seen in 1956 was a young comedienne named Carol Burnett, in her earliest TV appearances. In the fall of 1956 Winchell and company moved to ABC, where they hosted *Circus Time* for one season (see also that title), before beginning *The Paul Winchell Show* in the fall of 1957; *The Paul Winchell Show* was aimed principally at younger viewers and was usually seen Sunday afternoons. It featured Frank Fontaine and the Milton DeLugg Orchestra. After that show left the air in 1961, Winchell was seen less frequently on TV, though he did host a Saturday-morning cartoon show in 1963 (see *Cartoonies*), an hour syndicated show in 1965 titled *Winchell and Mahoney Time,* and a children's game show in 1972 (see *Runaround*). Winchell had studied medicine intermittently, and in 1962 he developed a blood storage system and followed that a year later with an artificial heart; since that time Winchell's primary interest has been medical technology rather than show business.

THE PAULA POUNDSTONE SHOW   ABC
30 OCTOBER 1993–6 NOVEMBER 1993   One of the biggest flops of the 1993–1994 season, this was a free-form variety hour, hosted by standup comic Paula Poundstone. It combined musical performances, comedy sketches, and offbeat interviews (for example, a panel of economists was quizzed while riding in teacups at an amusement park). Nils Lofgren served as music director of the ill-fated program, which was axed after two telecasts.

PAULINE FREDERICK'S GUEST BOOK   ABC
15 AUGUST 1948–30 MARCH 1949   A fifteen-minute interview series hosted by Pauline Frederick, who later became the United Nations correspondent for NBC News.

PAY CARDS   SYNDICATED
1968   On this game show, hosted by Art James, three players attempted to build poker hands by acquiring cards from a twenty-card board.

A PEACEABLE KINGDOM   CBS
20 SEPTEMBER 1989–15 NOVEMBER 1989   The Los Angeles Zoo was the setting of this hour dramatic series, one of the early fatalities of the 1989–1990 season. With Lindsay Wagner as Rebecca Cafferty, managing director; Michael Manasseri as her teenage son, Dean; Melissa Clatyon as her twelve-year-old daughter, Courtney; Victor DiMattia as her six-year-old son, Sam; Tom Wopat as her brother, Dr. Jed McFadden,

a zoo veterinarian; David Renan as Ridge, the groundskeeper; and David Ackroyd as the pompous research director, Dr. Bart Langley.

THE PEARL BAILEY SHOW ABC
23 JANUARY 1971–8 MAY 1971   ABC had high hopes for this hour-long variety show, hosted by the incomparable Pearl Bailey, but even against unimpressive competition the show failed to catch on. Taped at the Hollywood Palace, the show was produced by Bob Finkel and featured the Allan Davies Singers, the Robert Sidney Dancers, and the orchestra of Louis Bellson (Bailey's husband).

PEBBLES AND BAMM BAMM CBS
11 SEPTEMBER 1971–4 SEPTEMBER 1976   Spun off from *The Flintstones, Pebbles and Bamm Bamm* was seen as a separate series during the 1971–1972 season and again from 1974 to 1976; from 1972 to 1974 it was part of *The Flintstones Comedy Hour.* The title characters and their cohorts attended Bedrock High School. Sally Struthers and Mickey Stevens supplied the voice of Pebbles, while Jay North supplied that of Bamm Bamm. See also *The Flintstones.*

PECK'S BAD GIRL CBS
5 MAY 1959–4 AUGUST 1959   Patty McCormack, who had made a big splash in *The Bad Seed* on stage and on film, played a mischievous twelve-year-old named Torey Peck in this half-hour sitcom. Also featured were Wendell Corey as her father, attorney Steven Peck; Marsha Hunt as her mother, Jennifer Peck; Roy Ferrell as her little brother, Roger; and Reba Waters as her friend, Francesca. Norman Felton was the executive producer of the series and Stanley Rubin the producer. The show was rerun on CBS during the summer of 1960.

THE PEE WEE KING SHOW ABC
23 MAY 1955–5 SEPTEMBER 1955   Regulars on this Cincinnati-based half-hour country-and-western music show included Pee Wee King, Redd Stewart, Little Eller Long, Neal Burris, Bonnie Sloan, Mitchell Torok, and Lulabelle and Scotty.

PEE-WEE'S PLAYHOUSE CBS
13 SEPTEMBER 1986–27 JULY 1991   This surreal live-action Saturday-morning kids' show quickly achieved cult status. Pee-wee Herman, the high-voiced, bow-tied character created by actor Paul Reubens, presided over a playhouse peopled by talking furniture, puppets, and a robot. The program combined live action, special effects, celebrity visits, and the occasional vintage cartoon. Assisting Pee-wee were Lynne Stewart as Miss Yvonne, Johann Carlo as Dixie, Gilbert Lewis and William Marshall as King Cartoon; Gregory Harrison as Conky the Robot, S. Epatha Merkerson as Reba, John Paragon as Jambi (the disembodied genie head), Shawn Weiss as Elvis, Diane Yang as Cher, Natasha Lyonne as Opal. Wayne White, George Michael Mc-Grath, Larry Fishburne, Suzanne Kent, Alison Mork, and Ric Heitzman were also seen and/or heard. Following Reubens's arrest for indecent exposure at a Florida adult cinema, CBS hastily yanked the series.

PENNY TO A MILLION ABC
4 MAY 1955–19 OCTOBER 1955   Bill Goodwin hosted this prime-time game show, which featured two teams of five; any panelist who answered a question incorrectly was eliminated, until only one panelist from each side remained. Those two players then had the chance to go for the show's top prize of $10,000 (a million cents). Herb Wolf produced the show.

PENTAGON DUMONT
6 MAY 1951–24 NOVEMBER 1952   The progress of the Korean War was the principal subject of discussion on this half-hour public affairs show, DuMont's counterpart of NBC's *Battle Report.*

PENTAGON U.S.A. CBS

6 AUGUST 1953–1 OCTOBER 1953   A half-hour crime show depicting the exploits of the officers of the Criminal Investigation Division of the United States Army, starring Addison Richards, and later, Robert Pastene (as The Colonel). The series was to have been titled *Corridor D. Pentagon;* that title was changed to *Pentagon Confidential,* which was in turn changed to *Pentagon U.S.A.* just before the show premiered. William Dozier was the executive producer, Alex March the producer.

PENTHOUSE PARTY ABC

15 SEPTEMBER 1950–8 JUNE 1951   Betty Furness hosted this half-hour variety show, which also featured Don Cherry.

PENTHOUSE PLAYERS ABC

20 MARCH 1949–23 OCTOBER 1949   Half-hour Sunday-night dramatic anthology series.

PEOPLE NBC

21 AUGUST 1955–9 OCTOBER 1955   Morgan Beatty narrated this Sunday-afternoon series of live and filmed human interest segments.

PEOPLE CBS

18 SEPTEMBER 1978–11 NOVEMBER 1978   A half-hour magazine series, based on *People* magazine. The segments, almost all of which were three minutes or less, included peeks at celebrities and a few human interest features. Phyllis George, Miss America of 1971, was the host; some interviews were handled by correspondent Mark Shaw. David Susskind was executive producer for Time-Life TV.

PEOPLE ARE FUNNY NBC

19 SEPTEMBER 1954–2 APRIL 1961; 24 MARCH 1984–21 JULY 1984   Art Linkletter first hosted this half-hour show, which combined stunts and audience participation features. A regular feature for several seasons was a Univac computer, which tried to match eligible young men and women. Reruns were shown after 1958. Flip Wilson hosted the short-lived 1984 revival.

PEOPLE DO THE CRAZIEST THINGS ABC

20 SEPTEMBER 1984–11 OCTOBER 1984; 31 MAY 1985–2 AUGUST 1985   Bert Convy hosted this *Candid Camera* clone, on which people were the unsuspecting victims of various stunts. It was the lowest-rated show of the 1984–1985 prime-time season, ranking 97th.

THE PEOPLE NEXT DOOR CBS

18 SEPTEMBER 1989–16 OCTOBER 1989   Only four episodes of this fantasy sitcom were shown. It starred Jeffrey Jones as widower Walter Kellogg, a cartoonist (creator of the strip "The People Next Door") who could imagine things into existence. Walter's young son Matthew (played by Chance Quinn) and daughter Aurora (Jaclyn Bernstein) were used to seeing figments of his imagination, but Walter's new wife, psychotherapist Abigail MacIntyre (Mary Gross) was not. Also featured were Christina Pickles as Abigail's sister, Cissy, a beautician, and Leslie Jordan as Truman Fipps, the mailman in Covington, Ohio, where Walter and the kids had relocated upon Walter's remarriage. Among the real-life celebrities who strolled in to appear as themselves were Dick Clark, Dr. Joyce Brothers, Henny Youngman, and Casey Kasem. Wes Craven (director of the film *A Nightmare on Elm Street*) was cocreator of the series.

PEOPLE WILL TALK NBC

1 JULY 1963–27 DECEMBER 1963   The format of this daytime game show, hosted by Dennis James, was not unlike that of *The Celebrity Game*—contestants tried to predict how members of a studio audience panel would respond to yes-or-no questions. The show was a Merrill Heatter-Bob Quigley Production.

THE PEOPLE'S CHOICE   NBC
6 OCTOBER 1955–25 SEPTEMBER 1958   Jackie Cooper starred in this half-hour sitcom as Socrates (Sock) Miller, a government naturalist who became a city councillor in New City, Oklahoma, and sold houses in a real estate development there. Also featured were Pat Breslin as Amanda (Mandy) Peoples, Sock's girlfriend (and later his wife); Paul Maxey as New City's mayor and Mandy's corpulent father, John Peoples; Margaret Irving as Sock's Aunt Gus; Leonid Kinskey as Pierre, an artist pal of Sock's; and Dick Wesson (1957–1958) as Rollo, another friend of Sock's. The "gimmick" on the show was a talking basset hound named Cleo, who made droll comments (with the help of Mary Jane Croft, who provided the voice) from time to time during each episode.

THE PEOPLE'S COURT   SYNDICATED
1981–1993   On this unusual half-hour series, real-life small claims cases were litigated by the actual plaintiffs and defendants before a real judge (Joseph A. Wapner, a retired judge of the California Superior Court). The parties who appeared on the program agreed to be bound by Wapner's rulings; a successful plaintiff could recover up to $1,500 (with the defendant receiving $25), and a successful defendant would split $500 with the plaintiff. The show's production staff looked for offbeat cases, such as a complaint involving a strip-teaser who failed to disrobe completely, or one involving a babysitter who wasn't paid. Doug Llewelyn hosted the show, and interviewed the litigants after the verdicts were announced; Rusty Burrell served as the bailiff. In later years the series went on the road occasionally, broadcasting from cities all over the country.

PEOPLE'S PLATFORM   CBS
17 AUGUST 1948–18 AUGUST 1950   Charles Collingwood was the moderator of this early public affairs program. The show, which originated on radio in 1938, featured a panel of experts discussing a topical subject.

PEPSI-COLA PLAYHOUSE   ABC
2 OCTOBER 1953–26 JUNE 1955   This half-hour dramatic anthology series was filmed at Revue Studios. Arlene Dahl was the first host of the series; she was succeeded by Anita Colby and later by Polly Bergen. Robert G. Walker was the director.

THE PERFECT MATCH   SYNDICATED
1967   Dick Enberg hosted this game show, which was similar in format to *The Dating Game:* three women and three men participated, and a computer had previously matched up the three couples. Those who chose their computer-assigned matches won a cash prize.

A PERFECT SCORE   CBS
19 JUNE 1992–18 SEPTEMBER 1992   Jeff Marder hosted this late-late-night game show which combined *The Dating Game* with *Love Connection*. Each program introduced a single contestant and three of his or her best friends; the three friends then interviewed a group of three potential dates, and selected one for the contestant. In a follow-up segment, taped after the date, the participants revealed how the date had gone.

PERFECT STRANGERS   ABC
25 MARCH 1986–29 APRIL 1986; 6 AUGUST 1986–11 SEPTEMBER 1992; 9 JULY 1993–6 AUGUST 1993   In this "buddy" sitcom a European shepherd came to America to live with his cousin in Chicago. It starred Mark Linn-Baker as Larry Appleton, the level-headed American cousin, and Bronson Pinchot as Balki Bartokomous, the naive immigrant from Mypos who was amazed and sometimes bewildered by American life and language. When the series began, Larry was working at the Ritz Discount Store, but in the fall of 1987 he and Balki got jobs at the Chicago *Chronicle*—Larry a reporter, Balki in the mailroom. Other regulars included Ernie Sabella (1986–1987) as Larry's boss at the store, Donald "Twinkie" Twinkacetti; Belita Moreno (1986–

1987) as his wife, Edwina; Lise Cutter (1986) as neighbor Susan Campbell; Melanie Wilson (fall 1986–1993) and Rebeca Arthur (1986–1993) as new neighbors Jennifer Lyon and Mary Anne (originally they were aerobics instructors, but later they became flight attendants); Sam Anderson (1987–1993) as Mr. Gorpley, Balki's boss at the mailroom; Belita Moreno (1987–1993, in her second role on the series) as Lydia Markham, the advice columnist; and JoMarie Payton-France (1987–1989) as Harriette Winslow, the *Chronicle*'s elevator operator. In the fall of 1989 Payton-France departed for her own series: see *Family Matters*. Alisan Porter came aboard for the 1990–1991 season as Larry and Balki's seven-year-old neighbor, Tess Holland. In the fall of 1991 Larry and Jennifer were married and moved into a house, where Balki and Mary Anne joined them. *Perfect Strangers* did not appear on ABC's 1992 fall schedule; the last batch of new episodes was aired during the summer of 1993. By that time, Balki and Mary Anne were also married, and both wives were pregnant. Larry and Jennifer's baby was born on the final program.

THE PERILS OF PENELOPE PITSTOP CBS
13 SEPTEMBER 1969–5 SEPTEMBER 1971   A female auto racer named Penelope Pitstop was the central character in this Saturday-morning cartoon show from Hanna-Barbera Productions. The series was spun off from a 1968 CBS cartoon show, *Wacky Races*.

THE PERRY COMO SHOW NBC/CBS
(THE CHESTERFIELD SUPPER CLUB) (THE KRAFT MUSIC HALL)
24 DECEMBER 1948–4 JUNE 1950 (NBC); 2 OCTOBER 1950–24 JUNE 1955 (CBS); 17 SEPTEMBER 1955–12 JUNE 1963 (NBC)   Perry Como was a barber before he began singing professionally in 1933. In 1944, the year his first record was released, he appeared on radio in *The Chesterfield Supper Club;* when that show came to television late in 1948, Como came with it and has remained on television for more than four decades. *The Chesterfield Supper Club,* which also featured the Mitchell Ayres Orchestra and the Fontane Sisters, was originally seen on Friday nights but soon shifted to a half-hour slot on Sundays, opposite Ed Sullivan's *Toast of the Town.* In the fall of 1950 Como shifted to CBS, where he hosted his own show for the next five seasons; the fifteen-minute program was seen Mondays, Wednesdays, and Fridays following the network news. Also featured were the Mitchell Ayres Orchestra and the Fontane Sisters, together with announcer Frank Gallop. In the fall of 1955 Como returned to NBC, where he hosted a weekly hour show for the next eight years; from 1955 to 1959 it was seen Saturdays and was titled *The Perry Como Show.* From 1959 to 1963 it was seen Wednesdays and was titled *The Kraft Music Hall* (*The Kraft Music Hall* had previously been hosted by Milton Berle, and the series returned in 1967; see also that title). The Mitchell Ayres Orchestra and Frank Gallop were again featured, along with the Ray Charles Singers and the Louis DaPron Dancers (later, the Peter Gennaro Dancers). The Como Music Hall Players included Don Adams, Kaye Ballard, Jack Duffy, Paul Lynde, and Sandy Stewart. Como's theme song, "Dream Along with Me," was composed by Carl Sigman. For several seasons the show was produced by Bob Finkel, directed by Grey Lockwood, with Goodman Ace as head writer. Though he has not hosted a weekly series since 1963, Como has regularly appeared in specials since then.

PERRY MASON CBS
21 SEPTEMBER 1957–4 SEPTEMBER 1966   Perry Mason, one of fiction's most successful criminal lawyers, was created by Erle Stanley Gardner (who was himself an attorney) in 1933. Though the character was featured in dozens of novels, several films, a radio serial that ran for twelve years, and two television series, Raymond Burr's portrayal of the Los Angeles lawyer in the nine-year run of the first *Perry Mason* TV series overshadows all the others.

After the radio series left the air in 1955, Gardner formed a partnership— Paisano Productions—with his agent, Cornwall Jackson; Jackson's wife, Gail Patrick Jackson, a former actress who had attended law school, was hired as executive producer, and Ben Brady, who was also an attorney, was hired as producer. Though Gardner did no writing for the show, he exercised script approval and helped insure that the quality of the show met his expectations.

Several actors were considered for the leading role before Raymond Burr was chosen. Among the also-rans were William Hopper, Richard Carlson, Fred MacMurray, and Efrem Zimbalist, Jr. Burr, who had starred in the movie *Godzilla* and had played heavies in several other films, originally tested for the role of prosecuting attorney Hamilton Burger. Burr's Mason was an aggressive advocate blessed with superb powers of deductive reasoning. Usually it took no more than a quick pause and a short breath for Burr's Mason to piece together an intricate sequence of events from a few sketchy facts. Typically, Mason's clients found themselves linked by a chain of circumstantial evidence to a murder ("But, Mr. Mason, he was dead when I got there!"). Some hapless clients were even convinced that they had, in fact, committed the crime; all, however, were grateful for Mason's uncanny ability to secure an in-court confession (usually on the witness stand, but occasionally from the spectators' area) from the real culprit.

Perry Mason first cracked Nielsen's Top Twenty series in its second season, when it ranked nineteenth. It climbed as high as fifth in 1961–1962 before the ratings began to taper off. The demands on Raymond Burr were so great that, by the series's third season, it was impossible for him to memorize all of his lines. Instead, he regularly read his lines off a TelePrompTer located just off-camera. As veteran character actor Dabbs Greer (who appeared in eight episodes) recalled in a 1994 interview, "If you were playing a scene with Ray, he was looking over your shoulder at the TelePrompTer, or he was looking at the floor. You got no eye contact. You learned not to play to him, but to play either just off the TelePrompTer or off of his face, because it would distract you if you saw his eyes reading. But he was a master [of the technique]; I've never seen anybody master it as well."

Not all of the credit for the series' success belongs to Burr; a popular and talented supporting cast was an integral part of the show. Though four other regulars were featured in most episodes, only two of them were featured continuously through the nine-year run: Barbara Hale as Della Street, Mason's cool and efficient private secretary, and William Hopper (son of Hollywood columnist Hedda Hopper) as private detective Paul Drake, Mason's tireless investigator. William Talman, as prosecutor Hamilton Burger, was Mason's usual courtroom foe, but was not featured continuously: Talman had been arrested at a wild Hollywood party early in 1960 and was seen only occasionally during the 1960–1961 season. Mason also handled cases outside the Los Angeles area from time to time, which, of course, pitted him against other prosecutors; all of them, however, were as unsuccessful as Burger in obtaining convictions against Mason's clients. Rounding out the long-term supporting cast was veteran character actor Raymond Collins, who played Lieutenant Arthur Tragg, the grim homicide officer from the Los Angeles Police Department from 1957 to 1964; Collins died in 1965. A few other players were also featured occasionally: Wesley Lau (1961–1965) as Lieutenant Anderson, a colleague of Tragg's; Richard Anderson (1965–1966) as Lieutenant Steve Drumm, Tragg's successor; Lee Miller (1965–1966) as Lieutenant Brice; Carl Held (1961–1962) as David Gideon, an associate of Paul Drake's; and Connie Cezon as the rarely seen Gertie, Mason's switchboard operator and receptionist. Even Burr himself was not featured in every show; during a three-week period early in 1963, when Burr was recuperating from minor surgery, Bette Davis, Hugh O'Brian, and Walter Pidgeon filled in for him as "guest attorneys." Mike Connors also filled in for Burr, as attorney Joe Kelly, on 5 November 1964.

Almost all of the episodes followed the same format. Most featured alliterative titles (such as the premiere, "The Case of the Restless Redhead"; "The Case of the Treacherous Toupee," with Robert Redford, 17 September 1960; and "The Case of the Bountiful Beauty," with Ryan O'Neal, 6 February 1964). The action was usually confined to the first thirty minutes (the identity of the killer was never divulged to the viewers), and the courtroom segment comprised the second half hour. Strictly speaking, few of the courtroom proceedings were actually trials. Most were styled as "evidentiary hearings"; by using that technique, the producers saved the expense of hiring twelve extras to play jurors. Though Mason seemed to elicit a confession from the guilty party week after week, it is probably not accurate to say that he won every case; in at least one episode, "The Case of the Deadly Verdict," telecast during the fall of 1963, a jury returned a guilty verdict.

Approximately 271 hour episodes were produced between 1957 and 1966. On the last first-run episode, "The Case of the Final Fade-Out" (telecast 22 May 1966), Mason's creator, Erle Stanley Gardner, appeared as the judge. The *Perry Mason* theme music, one of TV's best remembered signatures, was composed by Fred Steiner. Reruns of the series were widely syndicated after 1966, and by 1973 CBS was interested in reviving the series. The new version, titled *The New Perry Mason*, was gone in fourteen weeks (see also that title).

Burr revived the character in a two-hour TV-movie, "Perry Mason Returns," broadcast on NBC 1 December 1985. Mason left the appellate bench to defend Della Street, who had been framed for a murder she hadn't committed. Joining Burr were Barbara Hale, William Katt (Hale's real-life son, who played Paul Drake, Jr.) and Richard Anderson (who had played a cop during *Perry Mason*'s final season, but who played the murderer here). The film was the second-highest-rated TV-movie of the season and was the springboard for Burr's continued appearances as Mason in three or four such films during each successive season. Burr died in 1993. The last of his *Perry Mason* TV-movies, "The Case of the Killer Kiss," was broadcast 29 November 1993. The *Perry Mason* title continued to be used for various NBC mystery movies (such as "A Perry Mason Mystery: The Case of the Grimacing Governor," 9 November 1994); although the Mason character did not appear, some scenes were shot at his office, and references were made to his working on other cases.

PERRY PRESENTS NBC

13 JUNE 1959–5 SEPTEMBER 1959   A summer replacement for *The Perry Como Show,* this hour-long musical show was broadcast in color and was hosted by singers Tony Bennett, Teresa Brewer, and Jaye P. Morgan. Other regulars included the Four Lads, the Modernaires, the Louis DaPron Dancers, and the Mitchell Ayres Orchestra.

PERSON TO PERSON CBS

2 OCTOBER 1953–23 SEPTEMBER 1960; 23 JUNE 1961–15 SEPTEMBER 1961   *Person to Person,* a prime-time interview show, made effective use of television's technological advances. Thanks to coast-to-coast coaxial cable, celebrities and newsmakers could be interviewed—live—almost anywhere in North America. Each week on *Person to Person* two interviews were conducted; the interviewees were usually seen in their homes, while the host (Edward R. Murrow from 1953 to 1959, then Charles Collingwood) remained in a studio in New York, watching the guests on a monitor. On the 1953 premiere Murrow first "visited" Leopold Stokowski and Gloria Vanderbilt, and then dropped in on Brooklyn Dodgers' catcher Roy Campanella. Among the most famous of those interviewed was Marilyn Monroe, whose television appearances were indeed infrequent; Monroe was interviewed at the home of friends in Connecticut on 8 April 1955. For most of its run *Person to Person* was produced by Edward R. Murrow, Jesse Zousmer, and John Aaron.

PERSONAL & CONFIDENTIAL NBC

1 AUGUST 1983–5 AUGUST 1983   Steve Edwards and Christine Belford cohosted this daytime hour magazine series, which was given a one-week tryout in the summer of 1983.

PERSONAL APPEARANCE THEATER ABC

27 OCTOBER 1951–23 MAY 1952   Half-hour dramatic anthology series.

PERSONALITIES SYNDICATED

3 SEPTEMBER 1990–25 OCTOBER 1991   Half-hour daily informational series, consisting mainly of interviews with celebrities and newsmakers, hosted first by Charlie Rose. Bill Sternoff succeeded Rose in October 1990, and Janet Zappala became his cohost. In July the show was retitled *E.D.J.* (for Entertainment Daily Journal), and was hosted by Zappala and Jim Moret.

PERSONALITY   NBC

30 JULY 1967–26 SEPTEMBER 1969   A panel of three celebrities was featured on this daytime game show hosted by Larry Blyden. The game was played in three rounds, during which the celebs tried to determine (a) how the other two celebs responded to various personal and topical questions, (b) how members of the public had predicted that the celebrity himself or herself would answer, and (c) how another celebrity (who appeared in a prerecorded sequence) responded to each of three questions. Bob Stewart created and produced the series.

PERSONALITY PUZZLE   ABC

19 MARCH 1953–25 JUNE 1953   A biweekly prime-time game show, *Personality Puzzle* was similar to *What's My Line?* A celebrity panel tried to guess the identity of a guest celebrity from articles of the guest's clothing or from other props associated with the person. Robert Alda was the host.

PERSONALS   CBS

16 SEPTEMBER 1991–23 DECEMBER 1992   CBS inaugurated its late-late-night game show sequence (see also *Night Games*) with this program. Hosted by Michael Berger, it was taped in the lounge of the Sheraton Los Angeles Airport Hotel, at which a contestant met three potential dates (who were selected by the show's staff from ads and videos solicited by the show), and won a date with the person who best guessed how the contestant had answered certain questions. Home viewers could also leave messages for contestants by calling a special 900 number.

PERSPECTIVE   ABC

6 NOVEMBER 1952–6 APRIL 1953   Produced by the ABC Public Affairs Department in cooperation with the New York Bar Association, this prime-time public affairs program had no moderator. Featured on the premiere were Lester B. Pearson and Dean Rusk (then president of the Rockefeller Foundation). The half-hour series was directed by Edward Nugent.

THE PERSUADERS   ABC

18 SEPTEMBER 1971–14 JUNE 1972   This hour-long adventure series, produced in Europe by England's Associated Television Corporation (ATV), starred Tony Curtis and Roger Moore as two wealthy playboys, Danny Wilde and Lord Brett Sinclair. According to the story line, they were sent to investigate various matters at the behest of Judge Fulton, a retired jurist (played by Laurence Naismith). The show's Saturday-night slot probably helped to keep the ratings down, and it vanished after only one season. Robert S. Baker was the creator and producer for ATV.

THE PET SET   SYNDICATED

1971   Betty White hosted this half-hour series on which celebrities dropped by with their pets.

THE PET SHOP   DUMONT

1 DECEMBER 1951–14 MARCH 1953   Gail Compton hosted this prime-time series on pets and pet care, with help from his eight-year-old daughter, Gay.

PETE AND GLADYS   CBS

19 SEPTEMBER 1960–10 SEPTEMBER 1962   Parke Levy was the executive producer of this half-hour sitcom, a spinoff from *December Bride*. It starred Harry Morgan as wisecracking insurance agent Pete Porter and Cara Williams as his daffy wife, Gladys Porter; Morgan had played Pete on *December Bride* but his wife Gladys had never been seen on that series. Also featured were Verna Felton, who repeated her *December Bride* role as Hilda Crocker; Alvy Moore as Howie, Pete and Gladys's friend and neighbor; Barbara Stuart as Howie's wife, Alice; Peter Leeds as neighbor George Colton; Shirley Mitchell as his wife, Janet; Ernest Truex as Pop, Gladys's father; Barry Kelley as Pete's boss, Mr. Slocum; Helen Kleeb and Lurene Tuttle as his wife,

Mrs. Slocum; Gale Gordon (1961–1962) as Pete's Uncle Paul; Joe Mantell (1961–1962) as neighbor Ernie Briggs; and Mina Kolb (1961–1962) as his wife, Peggy.

PETE KELLY'S BLUES   NBC
31 MARCH 1959–4 SEPTEMBER 1959   A half-hour crime show set in Kansas City during the 1920s, starring William Reynolds as Pete Kelly, a cornetist and bandleader at a local speakeasy who also found time to help people in distress. Also featured were Fred Eisley (later known as Anthony Eisley) as Johnny Cassiano, a tough Kansas City cop; Connee Boswell as Savannah Brown, singer at the club; and Phil Gordon as George Lupo, owner of the club. Jack Webb, who had starred in the 1951 radio series and the 1955 film on which the TV series was based, produced and directed the show. Webb was himself a jazz fan and employed an eight-piece band, headed by Dick Cathcart, to provide the music for the series.

PETER GUNN   NBC/ABC
22 SEPTEMBER 1958–26 SEPTEMBER 1960 (NBC); 3 OCTOBER 1960–25 SEPTEMBER 1961 (ABC)   This half-hour crime show is probably best remembered for its driving jazz theme, composed by Henry Mancini. It starred Craig Stevens as Peter Gunn, a smooth private eye who sported a brush cut and hung out at a nightspot known as Mother's. Also featured were Herschel Bernardi as Lieutenant Jacoby; Lola Albright as Gunn's romantic interest, Edie Hart, the singer at Mother's; and Hope Emerson (1958–1959) and Minerva Urecal (1959–1960) as Mother, the clubowner. For its third season, *Peter Gunn* moved to ABC; Edie finally opened her own nightspot, Edie's, and two new regulars were added: James Lamphier as Leslie, the maitre d'; and Bill Chadney as Emmett. Blake Edwards produced the series. Edwards also wrote and directed a TV-movie, "Peter Gunn," starring Peter Strauss and Peter Jurasik, which was broadcast on ABC 23 April 1989.

THE PETER LIND HAYES SHOW   NBC/ABC
23 NOVEMBER 1950–29 MARCH 1951 (NBC); 13 OCTOBER 1958–10 APRIL 1959 (ABC)
Peter Lind Hayes, together with his wife, Mary Healy, hosted two variety shows. The first was a prime-time show, seen Thursday nights during the 1950–1951 season. The second was a half-hour daytime series that also featured Anita Bryant, Don Cherry, and the Four Voices. Hayes and Healy later costarred in a situation comedy: see *Peter Loves Mary.*

PETER LOVES MARY   NBC
12 OCTOBER 1960–31 MAY 1961   This half-hour sitcom starred Peter Lind Hayes and Mary Healy (who were married in real life) as Peter and Mary Lindsey, a showbiz couple living in suburban Oakdell, Connecticut. Also featured were Merry Martin as their daughter, Leslie; Gil Smith as their son, Steve; and Bea Benaderet as their housekeeper, Wilma.

THE PETER MARSHALL VARIETY SHOW   SYNDICATED
1976   Peter Marshall, better known as host of *Hollywood Squares,* also hosted his own ninety-minute variety series, which also featured Rod Gist and Denny Evans and Chapter 5. David Salzman was the executive producer of the show, which was distributed by Westinghouse Broadcasting.

PETER PAN & THE PIRATES   FOX
8 SEPTEMBER 1990–11 SEPTEMBER 1992   James M. Barrie's characters came to television in animated form in this half-hour series, which had a special premiere on Fox's Saturday morning lineup and moved to a daytime spot a week later.

THE PETER POTAMUS SHOW   SYNDICATED/ABC
1964–1965 (SYNDICATED); 2 JANUARY 1966–24 JANUARY 1967 (ABC)   The star of this cartoon series was Peter Potamus, a purple hippo who traveled through history in a giant balloon, accompanied by his trusty ape, So So. Other segments included "Breezly and Sneezly," the adventures of a polar bear and a seal, and "Yippee, Yappee

and Yahooey," a trio of canine musketeers. After a year and a half in syndication, the series was picked up by ABC for its Sunday-morning cartoon schedule.

PETER POTTER'S JUKE BOX JURY
See JUKEBOX JURY

PETER THE GREAT   NBC
2 FEBRUARY 1986–5 FEBRUARY 1986   The life of Russian tsar Peter I was dramatized in this four-part, eight-hour, $26 million miniseries, filmed largely in the Soviet Union. With Jan Niklas and Maximilian Schell as Peter; Vanessa Redgrave as his half-sister Sophia; Omar Sharif as Prince Romodanovsky; Helmut Griem as Alexander Menshikov; Boris Plotnikov as Peter's son, Alexis; and Hanna Schygulla as Empress Catherine. Laurence Olivier and Trevor Howard appeared in small roles as England's King William and Sir Isaac Newton, although there is no historical evidence that Peter ever met either of them.

PETROCELLI   NBC
11 SEPTEMBER 1974–3 MARCH 1976   This hour-long crime show starred Barry Newman as Anthony Petrocelli, a criminal lawyer who gave up his big-city practice to settle in the southwestern town of San Remo. Susan Howard costarred as his wife, Maggie Petrocelli, and Albert Salmi was seen as his right-hand man, Pete Ritter. Thomas L. Miller and Edward K. Milkis were the executive producers of the show, which was filmed in Tucson, Arizona.

PETTICOAT JUNCTION   CBS
24 SEPTEMBER 1963–12 SEPTEMBER 1970   CBS introduced this rural sitcom one year after *The Beverly Hillbillies,* which had been the number one show of the 1962–1963 season; *Petticoat Junction* proved to be the most popular new show of the 1963–1964 season, ranking fourth that year. Though its ratings declined sharply after the first year, the show enjoyed a seven-year run and was one of CBS's mainstays during the decade. Paul Henning, who had created *The Beverly Hillbillies,* was also the creator and executive producer of *Petticoat Junction;* the half-hour series was produced by Dick Wesson. The large cast included: Bea Benaderet (1963–1968) as Kate Bradley, the widowed owner of the Shady Rest Hotel in Hooterville, terminus of the Cannonball, an ancient steam train; Edgar Buchanan as Joseph P. (Uncle Joe) Carson, the uncle of Kate's three eligible daughters; Linda Kaye as daughter Betty Jo (Kaye, the boss's daughter, was also known as Linda Kaye Henning later in the series); Pat Woodell (1963–1965) and Lori Saunders (1965–1970) as daughter Bobbie Jo; Jeannine Riley (1963–1965), Gunilla Hutton (1965–1966), and Meredith MacRae (1966–1970) as daughter Billie Jo; Charles Lane as Homer Bedloe, the railroad man who schemed to scrap the Cannonball; Smiley Burnette as engineer Charley Pratt; Rufe Davis as engineer Floyd Smoot; Byron Foulger as engineer Wendell Gibbs; Regis Toomey as Doc Stuart; Mike Minor (1966–1970) as Steve Elliott, Betty Jo's boyfriend and eventual husband; Elvia Allman (1966–1970) as Selma Plout, the woman who hoped to wrest Steve Elliott away from Betty Jo for her own daughter; Lynette Winter (1966–1970) as Selma's daughter, Henrietta Plout; June Lockhart (1968–1970) as Dr. Janet Craig, a physician (in essence, Lockhart replaced Bea Benaderet, who had died in 1968); and Jonathan Daly (1969–1970) as game warden Orrin Pike, Bobbie Jo's boyfriend. Other regulars included members of the cast of *Green Acres,* another Paul Henning series which was also set in Hooterville (see also that title).

PEYTON PLACE   ABC
15 SEPTEMBER 1964–2 JUNE 1969   *Peyton Place* was television's first prime-time serial since its earliest days and was the first successful prime-time soap opera in the medium's history. Based on Grace Metalious's enormously popular novel, which had been made into a movie in 1957, it premiered in 1964 amid much fanfare. It was telecast twice a week during the 1964–1965 season, and both segments cracked Nielsen's Top Twenty that year; as the 1965–1966 season began, telecasts were pushed up to three times weekly, but the show's ratings had already begun to fade.

The show was reduced to twice a week thereafter and lasted three more seasons. The basic theme of the show involved sexual goings-on in the lives of the residents of Peyton Place, a small New England town. The huge cast included: Mia Farrow as Allison MacKenzie; Ryan O'Neal as Rodney Harrington; Dorothy Malone as Constance MacKenzie Carson; Tim O'Connor as Elliott Carson; Frank Ferguson as Eli Carson; Steven Oliver as Lee Webber; Chris Connelly as Norman Harrington; Pat Morrow as Rita Jacks; Barbara Parkins as Betty Anderson; John Kerr as Fowler; George Macready as Martin Peyton; Ruth Warrick as Hannah Cord; James Douglas as Steven Cord; Leigh Taylor-Young as Rachel Welles; Lana Wood as Sandy Webber; Ed Nelson as Dr. Michael Rossi; Dan Duryea as Eddie; Gena Rowlands as Adrienne; Paul Langton as Leslie Harrington; Joyce Jillson as Jill; Warner Anderson as Matthew Swain; Heather Angel as Mrs. Dowell; Ruby Dee as Alma Miles; Lee Grant as Stella; Diana Hyland as Susan Winter; Kent Smith as Dr. Morton; and Mariette Hartley as Clair. Paul Monash produced the series for 20th Century-Fox Television. In 1972 a daytime version was introduced: see *Return to Peyton Place*.

Members of the cast were reunited for two made-for-TV movie sequels. The first, "Murder in Peyton Place" (NBC, 3 October 1977), investigated the deaths of Rodney Harrington and Alison MacKenzie, and featured Christopher Connelly, Dorothy Malone, Ed Nelson, Tim O'Connor, and Joyce Jillson. The second, "Peyton Place: The Next Generation" (NBC, 13 May 1985), featured Connelly, Malone, Nelson, O'Connor, Barbara Parkins, Pat Morrow, Evelyn Scott, Ruth Warrick, and James Douglas.

PHENOM   ABC

14 SEPTEMBER 1993–31 AUGUST 1994   Half-hour sitcom about a "phenom," a fifteen-year-old tennis champ, and her home life. With Angela Goethals as the phenom, Angela Doolan; Judith Light as her divorced mother, Dianne Doolan, a shorthand reporter; Todd Louiso as Angela's brother, Brian; Ashley Johnson as Angela's sister, Mary Margaret; Jennifer Lien as Brian's girlfriend, Roanne; Gina Hecht as Dianne's boss, Lori; and William Devane as Angela's new coach, Lou Del La Rosa, who tried to ingratiate himself with Dianne.

PHIL DONAHUE EXAMINES THE HUMAN ANIMAL   NBC

11 AUGUST 1986–15 AUGUST 1986   Phil Donahue hosted this week-long prime-time documentary series, which examined various aspects of the human condition: love and sexuality, heredity and environment, war and violence, men and women, and family and survival.

THE PHIL DONAHUE SHOW   SYNDICATED

1970–1996   Phil Donahue began hosting a local talk show in Dayton, Ohio, in 1967; by 1970 it was syndicated nationally, and the number of stations carrying the show increased steadily through the 1970s. By 1977 Donahue had shifted his base of operations to Chicago and the show became known simply as *Donahue*. His hour-long show is usually devoted to a single topic and features an active studio audience, skillfully worked by Donahue. In January 1985 the show again moved its base of operations, this time to New York. Shortly after the move a team of pranksters victimized Donahue by staging a mass fainting in the studio audience during the taping of one show. Later in 1985 Donahue orchestrated a "Citizens Summit" program, on which studio audiences in the U. S. and the U. S. S. R. were able to quiz each other. Early in 1987 he taped a week's worth of shows in the Soviet Union. Not all of his programs have been as noble, however: for one 1988 program, focusing on men who liked to wear women's clothing, Donahue wore a skirt, and on another 1988 show, on male baldness, he sported a flesh-colored skullcap. During the summer of 1992 some programs were produced even while the host was on vacation. Donahue pre-taped the introductions and other inserts, but unseen production staffers held the microphones used by the studio audience to ask questions of the guests.

By the early 1990s *Donahue*'s ratings had been eclipsed by *The Oprah Winfrey Show*; other daytime talkers also made a dent in viewership. Donahue tried to one-up his competitors in May 1994 by bidding to televise the execution of condemned

North Carolina murderer David Lawson; his request was turned down by the authorities. A sample of topics covered during April and May 1995 disclosed the following: "Country Music Female Impersonators," "Husbands Learn How to Become Exotic Dancers," "Multiple Personalities," "Penthouse Pets," and "Teen Prostitutes." Ratings continued to decline in 1995, as the show was no longer carried in New York City, the nation's largest TV market and the site of the show's taping. Early in 1996, Donahue announced that he would cease production of the program.

THE PHIL SILVERS SHOW
See THE ARROW SHOW; THE NEW PHIL SILVERS SHOW

THE PHIL SILVERS SHOW   CBS
20 SEPTEMBER 1955–11 SEPTEMBER 1959   One of the favorite sitcoms of the 1950s, *The Phil Silvers Show* was created by Nat Hiken and starred Phil Silvers as Master Sergeant Ernie Bilko, a conniving con man with a heart of gold, whose unceasing efforts to raise money almost never paid off. The half-hour series was originally titled *You'll Never Get Rich*, but after a few weeks became *The Phil Silvers Show;* in syndication, the reruns were titled *Sergeant Bilko*. The show was set at Fort Baxter, located near Roseville, Kansas. Over the years a large number of regulars appeared, but the long-term supporting cast included: Harvey Lembeck and Allan Melvin as Bilko's two main henchmen, Corporal Rocco Barbella and Corporal Henshaw; Paul Ford as Bilko's short-tempered commanding officer, Colonel John Hall; Elisabeth Fraser as Bilko's occasional girlfriend, Sergeant Joan Hogan; Maurice Gosfield as Private Duane Doberman, the fattest and most hapless member of Bilko's motley platoon; Herbie Faye as Private Sam Fender; Billy Sands as Private Dino Paparelli; Mickey Freeman as Private Zimmerman; Hope Sansberry as the colonel's wife, Nell Hall, an easy mark for Bilko's flattery; Joe E. Ross as Sergeant Rupert Ridzik; Jimmy Little as Sergeant Francis Grover (also known, inexplicably, as Steve Grover); Beatrice Pons as Ridzik's nagging wife, Emma Ridzik; and Nicholas Saunders as Colonel Hall's adjutant, Captain Barker. Others who came and went included Tige Andrews as Private Gander; P. Jay Sidney as Private Palmer; Walter Cartier as Private Dillingham; Jack Healy as Private Mullen; Bernie Fein as Private Gomez; Maurice Brenner as Private Fleishman; Terry Carter as Private Sugarman; Ned Glass as Sergeant Andy Pendleton; and Gary Clarke as Sergeant Stanley Zewicki. *The Phil Silvers Show* was one of the few shows of the 1950s to feature black performers—Bilko's platoon almost always included at least one black. Among those who made guest appearances on the show were Fred Gwynne ("The Eating Contest," 15 November 1955), Dody Goodman ("The Rich Kid," 27 December 1955), Margaret Hamilton ("The Merry Widow," 17 September 1957), Dick Van Dyke ("Bilko's Cousin," 28 January 1958), Alan Alda (in his first major TV role, "Bilko, the Art Lover," 7 March 1958), and Dick Cavett, in an uncredited appearance as an extra sometime in 1959. For its final season Bilko and all of his cohorts moved from Fort Baxter to Camp Fremont in California. Bilko had discovered a map of an abandoned gold mine, located within Camp Fremont, and persuaded Colonel Hall and his command to relocate. Sharp-eyed viewers may have noticed other, more subtle, changes during the show's run; for example, when Schick became a sponsor, the platoon members ceased shaving by razors and lather and switched to electric shavers (which, not coincidentally, Schick manufactured). Likewise, the men no longer lit their cigarettes with matches, but began using lighters (also manufactured by Schick). Two of the show's regulars, Joe E. Ross and Beatrice Pons, later appeared on Nat Hiken's next show, *Car 54, Where Are You?*

PHILCO TELEVISION PLAYHOUSE   NBC
3 OCTOBER 1948–2 OCTOBER 1955   One of the best known of the several dramatic anthology series that comprised television's so-called "Golden Age," *Philco Television Playhouse* was produced by Fred Coe, who was twenty-nine when the series began in 1948. Like the other dramatic shows, *Philco* was a training ground for young writers and directors as well as for performers. *Philco* held down a Sunday slot for its entire seven-year run; from 1951 to 1955 it shared sponsorship with Goodyear on a

biweekly basis (both shows were produced by Coe). A representative selection of offerings illustrates the variety of material presented on *Philco:* "Dinner at Eight," with Peggy Wood, Dennis King, Mary Boland, and Vicki Cummings (3 October 1948); "The Late Christopher Bean," with Lillian Gish (in her TV debut, 6 February 1949); "The Story of Mary Surratt," with Dorothy Gish (in her TV debut, 13 February 1949); "Ann Rutledge," with Grace Kelly (12 February 1950); "Nocturne," with Cloris Leachman (2 April 1950); "Leaf Out of a Book," with Grace Kelly (31 December 1950); "No Medals on Pop," with Brandon DeWilde (in his first major TV role, 11 March 1951); "The Basket Weaver," with Walter Matthau (in his first major TV role, 20 April 1952); "A Little Something in Reserve," with Tony Randall (10 May 1953); "The Way of the Eagle," with Grace Kelly (in her last dramatic appearance on TV, 7 June 1953); "Statute of Limitations," with Barbara Baxley and Martin Balsam (in his first major TV role, 21 February 1954); "The Dancers," with Joanne Woodward (7 March 1954); "Run Like a Thief," with James Dean, Kurt Kasznar, Gusti Huber, and Barbara O'Neill (5 September 1954); Robert Alan Aurthur's "Shadow of the Champ," with Eli Wallach, Jack Warden, and Lee Grant (20 March 1955); and Robert Alan Aurthur's "A Man Is Ten Feet Tall," with Sidney Poitier (in a rare television appearance, 2 October 1955). See also *Goodyear Playhouse.*

PHILIP MARLOWE ABC
29 SEPTEMBER 1959–29 MARCH 1960   Raymond Chandler's fictional sleuth, Philip Marlowe, was played by Philip Carey on this half-hour crime show. The character reappeared in 1983 in a five-part miniseries on the HBO cable network, *Philip Marlowe—Private Eye.* Powers Boothe played the title role. Six new episodes were shown on HBO in 1986.

THE PHILIP MORRIS PLAYHOUSE CBS
8 OCTOBER 1953–4 MARCH 1954   This half-hour filmed dramatic anthology series was hastily ordered by sponsor Philip Morris after its first offering in that time slot, *Pentagon Confidential,* was blasted by the critics. Kent Smith hosted the series, which was also known as *P.M. Playhouse.*

THE PHOENIX ABC
26 MARCH 1982–16 APRIL 1982   Judson Scott starred in this hour fantasy series as Bennu, a mysterious being from another world who had been sent to Earth centuries previously; released from his sarcophagus, he searched (in the words of the show's promotional announcements) "for the one woman who can save him and the Earth." Also featured were Richard Lynch as Preminger, a government agent who pursued Bennu, believing him to be an ancient astronaut, and E. G. Marshall as Dr. Frazier, a research scientist. Introduced in the spring of 1982, the four-week series was rerun that summer.

PHOTOCRIME ABC
21 SEPTEMBER 1949–28 DECEMBER 1949   Inspector Cobb (played by Chuck Webster) was the chief character on this half-hour Wednesday-night crime show.

PHOTOPLAY TIME
See THE WENDY BARRIE SHOW

PHYL AND MIKHY CBS
26 MAY 1980–30 JUNE 1980   Half-hour sitcom about an American runner and the Russian athlete who defected to marry her. With Murphy Cross as Phyllis Wilson, a track star at Pacific Western University; Rick Lohman as Soviet decathloner Mikhail Orlov; Larry Haines as Phyllis's father, Max Wilson, the college track coach, with whom Phyl and Mikhy lived; Michael Pataki as Vladimir Jimenko, a Soviet consular official; and Jack Dodson as Truck Morley, head of the college's alumni association.

PHYLLIS CBS

8 SEPTEMBER 1975–30 AUGUST 1977   In this spinoff from *The Mary Tyler Moore Show,* Cloris Leachman starred as Phyllis Lindstrom; as her own series began, Phyllis had just been widowed and had left Minneapolis with her daughter for San Francisco, where she moved in with her late husband's mother and *her* second husband. The original cast also included Jane Rose as Phyllis's mother-in-law, Audrey Dexter; Henry Jones as Audrey's husband, Judge Jonathan Dexter; Lisa Gerritsen as Phyllis's teenage daughter, Bess; Barbara Colby (who was found murdered after three episodes had been filmed) and Liz Torres as Julie Erskine, the owner of a photography studio where Phyllis found work as a secretary; and Richard Schaal as Leo Heatherton, a photographer who worked at the studio. Judith Lowry became a regular during the first season as Jonathan's crusty and outspoken eighty-seven-year-old mother, Sally (Mother) Dexter. Liz Torres and Richard Schaal left the cast after one season, as Phyllis got a new job as a secretary at the San Francisco Board of Supervisors. Joining the cast were Carmine Caridi as supervisor Dan Valenti; John Lawlor as supervisor Leonard Marsh; and Garn Stephens as fellow secretary Harriet Hastings. In the fall of 1976 Mother Dexter married eighty-nine-year-old Arthur Lanson, played by Burt Mustin (Judith Lowry, who played Mother Dexter, had died two weeks before the episode was telecast). In the spring of 1977 Phyllis's daughter Bess married Dan Valenti's nephew, Mark (played by Craig Wasson). Ed. Weinberger and Stan Daniels were the executive producers of the half-hour series for MTM Enterprises.

THE PHYLLIS DILLER SHOW
See THE BEAUTIFUL PHYLLIS DILLER SHOW;
THE PRUITTS OF SOUTHAMPTON

PICCADILLY CIRCUS PBS

19 JANUARY 1976–11 SEPTEMBER 1977   Telecast monthly, *Piccadilly Circus* was the umbrella title for a potpourri of programs from Great Britain: dramas, comedies, and documentaries were all presented. The series was funded by a grant from Mobil Oil.

PICCADILLY PALACE ABC

20 MAY 1967–9 SEPTEMBER 1967   A summer replacement for *The Hollywood Palace,* this hour-long variety series was taped at London's Piccadilly Palace and hosted by Millicent Martin. Other regulars included comics Eric Morecambe and Ernie Wise, The Paddy Stone Dancers, and The Michael Sammes Singers. Colin Clews produced the series and directed it with Philip Casson.

PICK AND PAT ABC

20 JANUARY 1949–17 MARCH 1949   This short-lived variety hour was no doubt the only TV series that regularly featured minstrel acts. Guest minstrels joined regulars Pick and Pat each week; also on hand were comedian and host Jack Carter and singer Mary Small. Ed Wolfe produced the show and Fred Carr directed it. By the end of the show's run, Jack Carter had begun hosting his own variety show: see *Jack Carter and Company.*

PICKET FENCES CBS

18 SEPTEMBER 1992–   David E. Kelley was the executive producer, and frequent writer, of this hour dramatic series set in Rome, Wisconsin. The small Midwestern town was anything but placid, serving as a backdrop for such issues as euthanasia, bigamy, religious expression, forced school busing, and plain old murder. The cast included Tom Skerritt as Sheriff Jimmy Brock; Kathy Baker as his wife, Dr. Jill Brock; Holly Marie Combs as Jimmy's teenage daughter, Kimberly; Justin Shenkarow as Jimmy and Jill's elder son, Matthew; Adam Wylie as their younger son, Zack; Costas Mandylor as Deputy Kenny Latkos; Lauren Holly as Deputy Maxine Stewart; Fyvush Finkel as lawyer Douglas Wambaugh, indefatigable advocate of unpopular causes; Ray Walston as wise Judge Henry Bone; Zelda Rubinstein (1992–1994) as police

dispatcher Ginny Weedon; Kelly Connell as medical examiner Carter Pike; Dabbs Greer as Reverend Henry Novotny; Michael Keenan (1992–fall 1993) as Mayor Bill Pugen, who died by spontaneous combustion; Leigh Taylor-Young (1993–) as Mayor Rachel Harris; and Don Cheadle (1993–) as district attorney John Littleton; Amy Aquino (1995–) as Dr. Joey Diamond; and Marlee Matlin (1995–) as Rome's new mayor, Laurie Bey.

PICTURE THIS   CBS
25 JUNE 1963–17 SEPTEMBER 1963   This prime-time game show, a summer replace-ment for *The Jack Benny Program,* was hosted by Jerry Van Dyke. It featured two teams, each consisting of a celebrity and a contestant; one member of the team tried to get the other to identify a secret phrase by suggesting that his or her teammate draw clues.

PIG STY   UPN
23 JANUARY 1995–24 JULY 1995   Five guys shared a Manhattan apartment on this half-hour sitcom, one of the first offerings of the United Paramount Network. With David Arnott as ad executive Cal Evans; Matt Borlenghi as Johnny, a young attor-ney; Timothy Fall as P. J.; Brian McNamara as Randy, a writer and bartender; Sean O'Bryan as Joe "Iowa" Dantley, a doctor doing his residency at a New York hospital; and Liz Vassey as the attractive building manager, Tess Galloway, an aspiring actress.

PIGGSBURG PIGS!   FOX
15 SEPTEMBER 1990–31 AUGUST 1991   This animated series was set in Piggsburg, a city populated by porkers, located just behind the world's largest pig farm. The Bacon Brothers—Bo, Portley, and Pighead—did battle with Rembrandt Proupork.

PINK LADY   NBC
1 MARCH 1980–11 APRIL 1980   Hour variety series starring Japan's popular rock-and-roll duo Pink Lady—Mitsuyo (Mie) Nemoto and Keko (Kei) Masuda—and Ameri-can comedian Jeff Altman. The series lasted only a few weeks, in part, no doubt, because neither Mie nor Kei spoke English.

THE PINK PANTHER AND SONS   NBC/ABC
15 SEPTEMBER 1984–7 SEPTEMBER 1985 (NBC); 1 MARCH 1986–6 SEPTEMBER 1986 (ABC)   A somewhat more mature Pink Panther returned to Saturday morning television in this new cartoon series. Here, he had to keep an eye on his two mischie-vous sons, Pinky and Panky.

THE PINK PANTHER SHOW   NBC/ABC/SYNDICATED
6 SEPTEMBER 1969–2 SEPTEMBER 1978 (NBC); 9 SEPTEMBER 1978–1 SEPTEMBER 1979 (ABC); 1993–1994 (SYNDICATED)   Created for the title sequences of the 1964 film "The Pink Panther," the suave but silent pink feline began to appear in his own theatrical cartoons later that year. In 1969 he came to television in what would become one of NBC's longest-running Saturday-morning series. The first incarna-tion, *The Pink Panther Show*, ran for two seasons and was hosted by comedian Lenny Schultz and the Paul and Mary Ritts Puppets. The Pink Panther appeared in his own cartoons; a second animated segment starred The Inspector, a bumbling detective inspired by Peter Sellers's character in the Pink Panther films. In 1971 the live action segments were jettisoned, and the show was titled *The New Pink Panther Show*. Other cartoon segments included "The Ant and the Aardvark" (the voice of the aardvark was provided by Jackie Mason). In the fall of 1976 the show was expanded to ninety minutes and was retitled *The Pink Panther Laugh & 1/2 Hour & 1/2 Show*. Two new cartoons were added: "The Texas Toads" and "Misterjaws." After one season in that format, it reverted back to thirty minutes in 1977 under the title *The Think Pink Panther Show*. In 1978, after nine years on NBC, the show shifted to ABC, and was known as *The All-New Pink Panther Show*. The second cartoon component of that program was Crazylegs Crane, a wacky bird. The title character returned to television in 1984 (see *The Pink Panther and Sons*). In the fall of 1993

new episodes were produced for first-run syndication. In the latter cartoons the title character finally had a voice; it was supplied by Matt Frewer.

PINKY & THE BRAIN   WB
Daytime: 9 SEPTEMBER 1995–   *Prime time*: 10 SEPTEMBER 1995–   The title characters of this half-hour cartoon series were two laboratory mice who plotted—always unsuccessfully—to take over the world. The pair originally appeared on *Animaniacs*. The series was seen on Saturday mornings and in prime time on Sundays.

THE PINKY LEE SHOW   NBC
19 APRIL 1950–9 NOVEMBER 1950; 4 JANUARY 1954–11 MAY 1956   Though he is best remembered as the host of a daily children's show, Pinky Lee's first TV series was a prime-time variety show telecast in 1950. A year later he cohosted *Those Two,* a fifteen-minute musical variety series that lasted a year and a half. His most successful show began early in 1954, and, in most areas, was broadcast immediately preceding *Howdy Doody* (during the 1955–1956 season it was also seen Saturday mornings). On the half-hour show Lee, in hat and checkered coat, sang, danced, and told stories. Also featured were Roberta Shore, Mel Koontz, Barbara Luke, Jimmy Brown, and Jane Howard. After the show left the air in 1956, Lee was rarely seen on national television, though he hosted local shows in Los Angeles in 1964 and 1966.

PIP THE PIPER   ABC/NBC
25 DECEMBER 1960–28 MAY 1961 (ABC); 24 JUNE 1961–22 SEPTEMBER 1962 (NBC) This children's fantasy series was set in Pipertown, a city in the clouds where musical instruments grew on trees. Featured were Jack Spear as Pip the Piper; Phyllis Spear as Miss Merry Note; and Lucian Kaminsky as The Leader (and other roles). The show was seen first on Saturdays and later on Sundays during its ABC run and exclusively on Saturdays during its NBC run.

PIRATES OF DARK WATER   ABC
7 SEPTEMBER 1991–5 SEPTEMBER 1992   Saturday-morning cartoon show about the efforts of a young man named Ren to save his home planet, Mer, from the evil Dark Water force.

PISTOLS 'N' PETTICOATS   CBS
17 SEPTEMBER 1966–26 AUGUST 1967   One of the first CBS shows regularly broadcast in color, *Pistols 'n' Petticoats* was a half-hour comedy western. Set in Wretched, Colorado, it featured Ann Sheridan as gun-toting widow Henrietta Hanks; Ruth McDevitt as gun-toting Grandma Hanks, her mother; Douglas V. Fowley as Andrew (Grandpa) Hanks, her father; Carole Wells as Henrietta's daughter, Lucy Hanks; and Gary Vinson as Wretched's bumbling sheriff, Harold Sikes. Occasionally featured were Robert Lowery as land baron Buss Courtney; Lon Chaney, Jr., as Chief Eagle Shadow; Marc Cavell as Gray Hawk; Alex Henteloff as Little Bear; and Bowser, the Hanks' pet wolf. Joe Connelly produced the series.

PLACE THE FACE   NBC/CBS
2 JULY 1953–20 AUGUST 1953 (NBC); 27 AUGUST 1953–26 AUGUST 1954 (CBS); 25 SEPTEMBER 1954–25 DECEMBER 1954 (NBC); 28 JUNE 1955–13 SEPTEMBER 1955 (NBC) On this prime-time game show contestants tried to identify persons from their past who were brought to the studio and seated opposite them. Jack Smith was the first host of the series and was succeeded by Bill Cullen, who went on to emcee many more game shows.

PLACES, PLEASE   CBS
5 JULY 1948–25 FEBRUARY 1949   Barry Wood produced and hosted this early-evening talent show, which was broadcast two or three times a week. When Wood left in February of 1949, the show was retitled *Manhattan Showcase* (see also that title).

THE PLAINCLOTHESMAN   DUMONT

12 OCTOBER 1949–12 SEPTEMBER 1954   One of the longer-running shows on the DuMont network, *The Plainclothesman* was a half-hour crime show that starred Ken Lynch as The Lieutenant; Lynch's face was not seen on camera, as the show employed the subjective camera technique. Jack Orrison was also featured (and was seen as well) as Sergeant Brady, as was Helen Gillette as Annie the waitress, and Betty Beuhler as Dottie. The viewer-as-character technique was employed again in 1992. See *Likely Suspects*.

PLANET EARTH   PBS

22 JANUARY 1986–5 MARCH 1986   A seven-part study of the Earth and its geology, oceanography, and climate, narrated by Richard Kiley.

PLANET OF THE APES   CBS

13 SEPTEMBER 1974–27 DECEMBER 1974   Based on the movie of the same title, this hour-long sci-fi series chronicled the adventures of two American astronauts who stumbled into a time warp and were hurtled 2,000 years into the future, where they found the Earth ruled by English-speaking apes, who treated the planet's humans as chattel. With Ron Harper as astronaut Alan Virdon; James Naughton as astronaut Pete Burke; Roddy McDowall as Galen, an inquisitive ape who befriended the visitors; Booth Colman as Zaius, leader of the apes; and Mark Lenard as Urko, Zaius's right-hand simian. Herbert Hirschman was the executive producer, and Stan Hough the producer for 20th Century-Fox Television. See also *Return to the Planet of the Apes*.

THE PLASTICMAN COMEDY/ADVENTURE SHOW   ABC/CBS

15 SEPTEMBER 1979–5 SEPTEMBER 1981 (ABC); 12 NOVEMBER 1983–4 FEBRUARY 1984 (CBS)   Segments on this two-hour Saturday-morning cartoon show included "Plasticman," the adventures of the "superfantastic highly elastic" superhero and his pals Penny and Hulahula; "Mighty Man and Yukk," the adventures of the world's smallest superhero and the world's ugliest dog; "Rickety Rocket," a talking spaceship and four teenage detectives; and "Fangface and Fangpuss" (*Fangface* had been a separate series during the 1978–1979 season). The series was trimmed to ninety minutes in the middle of the 1979–1980 season, dropping the "Rickety Rocket" segment. In the fall of 1980 it was cut to thirty minutes and retitled *The Plasticman-Baby Plas Super Comedy*. By this time, Plasticman had married Penny and they had had a child, Baby Plas, who was every bit as elastic as his dad.

PLATYPUS MAN   UPN

23 JANUARY 1995–24 JULY 1995   Another in the wave of sitcoms starring standup comics, this one starred Richard Jeni as single guy Richard Jeni, the host of a TV cooking show. Joining him were Ron Orbach as his pal Lou Golembiewski; Denise Miller as his pal Paige McAlistair; and David Dundara as his dumb brother, Tommy, who owned a bar where the other three frequently hung out. Jeni, who had starred in a January 1993 HBO comedy special also titled "Platypus Man," explained the relevance of the title to *TV Guide*: the platypus, an egg-laying mammal, "lives alone, is short-legged, and tries to mate frequently but can't."

THE PLAY OF THE WEEK   SYNDICATED

1959–1961   *The Play of the Week* was a New York-based dramatic anthology series that relied heavily on talent from Broadway. Among the presentations were: Graham Greene's "The Power and the Glory," John Steinbeck's "Burning Bright," Jean Anouilh's "The Waltz of the Toreadors," "Black Monday," with Robert Redford, Eugene O'Neill's "The Iceman Cometh" (also with Redford), and "The Closing Door," with George Segal (in one of his earliest television appearances). Underwritten by Standard Oil of New Jersey, the series' executive producer was David Susskind.

PLAY THE PERCENTAGES   SYNDICATED

1980   Geoff Edwards hosted this game show, on which two married couples competed. Each couple tried to predict what percentage of persons previously surveyed
had provided the correct answer to a given question. The couple with the more
accurate prediction won points, and could win additional points by providing the
correct answer to the question. The first couple to score 300 points won the game and
a chance at the bonus round for a possible jackpot of $25,000 or more. The half-hour
show was a Jack Barry & Dan Enright Production.

PLAY YOUR HUNCH   CBS/ABC/NBC

30 JUNE 1958–2 JANUARY 1959 (CBS); 5 JANUARY 1959–8 MAY 1959 (ABC); 7 DECEM-
BER 1959–26 SEPTEMBER 1963 (NBC)   One of the few game shows to have been aired
by all three networks, *Play Your Hunch* was somewhat similar to *To Tell the Truth:*
contestants tried to guess which of three objects or situations (labeled X, Y, and Z)
was the real one. The show was seen during the daytime on all three networks and
was also seen at night in 1960 and 1962 on NBC. It was hosted by Richard Hayes,
Gene Rayburn, Merv Griffin, and Robert Q. Lewis. Among the contestants was a
young actor named Robert Redford, who appeared in 1959.

PLAYBOY AFTER DARK   SYNDICATED

1969   The second of the two variety shows hosted by Hugh Hefner, publisher of
Playboy magazine, *Playboy After Dark* was set at a party—Hefner contrived to
bump into his guests and always managed to persuade them to sing a number or tell a
few jokes. The Checkmates and several Playboy Bunnies were regularly featured.
See also *Playboy's Penthouse*.

PLAYBOY'S PENTHOUSE   SYNDICATED

1959–1960   Hugh Hefner, publisher of *Playboy* magazine, tried his hand at hosting
a variety show in 1959 (ten years before *Penthouse* magazine first appeared on the
newsstand). Taped at WBKB-TV in Chicago, it was set at a party. Ten years later
Hefner again tried a TV show: see *Playboy After Dark*.

PLAYHOUSE 90   CBS

4 OCTOBER 1956–18 MAY 1960   Generally regarded as the most ambitious of television's dramatic anthology series, *Playhouse 90* presented a ninety-minute drama each
week during its first three seasons. It was broadcast as a series of specials during the
1959–1960 season, and reruns were aired in 1961. More than one hundred plays were
presented, many of them live, including some of TV's best-known original works,
such as "Requiem for a Heavyweight" and "The Miracle Worker." With Martin
Manulis as its first producer, *Playhouse 90* premiered in 1956 with a Rod Serling
screenplay, "Forbidden Area," featuring Charlton Heston, Tab Hunter, Diana Lynn,
Vincent Price, and Jackie Coogan. The following week it presented the widely acclaimed "Requiem for a Heavyweight"; written by Serling and directed by Ralph
Nelson, it starred Jack Palance as Mountain McClintock, a broken-down boxer,
Keenan Wynn (as his manager), Kim Hunter, and Ed Wynn. "Requiem" won an
Emmy for best single program of the season, and Palance also won an Emmy for his
performance (*Playhouse 90* itself also won, as best new series). Several more top-
notch plays were broadcast that season, including: "Eloise," with Evelyn Rudie,
Ethel Barrymore, Louis Jourdan, and Kay Thompson (22 November); "So Soon to
Die," with Richard Basehart (in his first dramatic role on TV, 17 January); "The
Miracle Worker," with Patty McCormack, Teresa Wright, and Burl Ives (written by
William Gibson, directed by Arthur Penn, and televised 7 February, it subsequently
ran on Broadway, and a filmed version was made in 1962); "Charley's Aunt," with
Jeanette MacDonald (in a rare television appearance) and Art Carney (28 March);
"Three Men on a Horse," with Carol Channing (in a rare TV dramatic appearance)
and Johnny Carson (in his first TV dramatic role, 18 April); "Child of Trouble," with
Lillian Roth (in a rare TV appearance, 2 May); "Without Incident," with Errol Flynn
(also making a rare appearance, 6 June). The quality of the presentations remained
high through the rest of *Playhouse 90*'s run. A representative sampling would include

the following from the 1957–1958 season: "The Dark Side of the Earth," with Earl Holliman, Kim Hunter, and Dean Jagger (19 September); "The 80 Yard Run," with Paul Newman (in his last TV dramatic role) and Joanne Woodward (16 January); "No Time at All," with Jack Haley (13 February); "The Male Animal," with Andy Griffith (13 March). From the 1958–1959 season: "The Days of Wine and Roses," with Charles Bickford, Piper Laurie, and Cliff Robertson (2 October); Joseph Conrad's "Heart of Darkness," with Oscar Homolka and Eartha Kitt (6 November); "Face of a Hero," with Jack Lemmon (in his last TV dramatic role until 1976; 1 January); "Child of Our Time," with Maximilian Schell and Bobby Crawford, Jr. (5 February); Ernest Hemingway's "For Whom the Bell Tolls," with Jason Robards, Jr., Maria Schell, Nehemiah Persoff, Maureen Stapleton, Steven Hill, and Eli Wallach (adapted by A. E. Hotchner and directed by John Frankenheimer, it was broadcast in two parts on 12 March and 19 March); Abby Mann's "Judgment at Nuremburg," with Claude Rains, Melvyn Douglas, and Maximilian Schell (16 April). From the 1959–1960 season: "Misalliance," with Claire Bloom (29 October); "Alas, Babylon," with Dana Andrews, Don Murray, Kim Hunter, Barbara Rush, and Burt Reynolds (David Shaw adapted it from Pat Frank's novel, and Robert Stevens directed; it was aired 3 April); "Journey to the Day," with Mike Nichols (22 April); "In the Presence of Mine Enemies," with Charles Laughton, Arthur Kennedy, and Robert Redford (18 May).

THE PLAY'S THE THING   CBS
17 MARCH 1950–30 JUNE 1950   This Friday-night dramatic anthology hour replaced another anthology series, *Theatre Hour.*

PLAYWRIGHTS '56   NBC
4 OCTOBER 1955–19 JUNE 1956   Fred Coe produced this dramatic anthology hour, which shared a slot on Tuesdays with *Armstrong Circle Theater;* it was also known as *The Playwright Hour.* Presentations included: "The Battler," with Phyllis Kirk and Paul Newman (18 October); "Lost," with Steven Hill (17 January); and "Flight," with Kim Stanley (28 February).

PLEASE DON'T EAT THE DAISIES   NBC
14 SEPTEMBER 1965–2 SEPTEMBER 1967   Based on Jean Kerr's book (which was made into a movie in 1960, starring Doris Day), this half-hour sitcom was set in the town of Ridgemont. It featured Patricia Crowley as freelance writer Joan Nash, suburban wife and mother of four boys; Mark Miller as her husband, Jim Nash, a professor at Ridgemont College; Kim Tyler as their son Kyle; Brian Nash as their son Joel; Jeff and Joe Fithian as their twin sons Trevor and Tracy; Harry Hickox (1965–1966) and King Donovan (1966–1967) as neighbor Herb Thornton, a lawyer; Shirley Mitchell as his wife, Marge Thornton; Bill Quinn (1966–1967) as Dean Carter; Melinda Plowman as Jim's secretary, Terry; and Lord Nelson as the Nash family sheepdog, Ladadog. Paul West produced the series for M-G-M.

PLEASE STAND BY   SYNDICATED
1978   Half-hour sitcom about an oil executive who quit his job to run a small television station in the boondocks. With Richard Schaal as Frank Lambert; Elinor Donahue as his wife, Carol Lambert; Bryan Scott as their son, Rocky; Marcie Barkin as Vicki James; Stephen Michael Schwartz as David; and Darian Mathias as Susan. Bob Banner and Ed Warren were the executive producers.

THE PLUCKY DUCK SHOW   FOX
19 SEPTEMBER 1992–7 NOVEMBER 1992   Introduced on the syndicated cartoon series *Tiny Toon Adventures,* Plucky Duck starred in his own Saturday-morning cartoon show for eight weeks in the fall of 1992. On 14 November 1992 Fox retitled the series *Tiny Toon Adventures.*

PLYMOUTH PLAYHOUSE
See ABC ALBUM

POINTMAN SYNDICATED

1995 Light hour adventure series starring Jack Scalia as Connie Harper, a onetime Wall Street wheeler-dealer who'd been sent to prison on trumped-up charges. Upon his release Connie took over a beachfront restaurant and provided assistance to those who sought his help. The show was filmed on location in Jacksonville, Florida.

POLE POSITION CBS

15 SEPTEMBER 1984–30 AUGUST 1986 Saturday-morning cartoon series based on the popular video game. The principal characters were Wheels and Roadie, two specially equipped "vehicles of justice."

POLICE CALL SYNDICATED

1955 An undistinguished anthology series of twenty-six half-hour crime shows, *Police Call* was distributed by MCA-TV.

POLICE SQUAD! ABC

4 MARCH 1982–25 MARCH 1982; 1 JULY 1982–2 SEPTEMBER 1982 TV's innumerable police dramas were satirized on this half-hour comedy series, which focused on the Police Squad, an elite unit of a big-city police force. Featured were Leslie Nielsen as Frank Drebin, whose rank varied from Sergeant to Lieutenant; Alan North as his boss, Captain Ed Hocken; Ed Williams as Ted Olson, the demented lab man; Peter Lupus as Norberg; and William Duell as Johnny, the omniscient shoeshine boy. One reason for the show's cancellation, according to ABC programming executive Tony Thomopolous, was that the program required "too much attention" from the viewer; presumably, he was referring to the abundance of sight gags in the series, such as the recurring one in which the title of the episode as announced by the narrator was different from that shown on the screen. Nielsen went on to star in the highly popular "Naked Gun" film comedies based on the series. CBS aired the TV show reruns during the summer of 1991.

POLICE STORY CBS

4 APRIL 1952–26 SEPTEMBER 1952 This early police anthology series, which premiered more than twenty years before Joseph Wambaugh's *Police Story* (see below), was a half-hour show that dramatized incidents taken from police files throughout the nation. Norman Rose narrated the series, Jerome Robinson produced it, and David Rich directed.

POLICE STORY NBC/ABC

2 OCTOBER 1973–23 AUGUST 1977 (NBC); 29 OCTOBER 1988–3 DECEMBER 1988 (ABC) One of the few successful anthology series of the 1970s, *Police Story* was created by Joseph Wambaugh, a Los Angeles police officer who wrote such police novels as *The New Centurions* and *Black Marble*. As production consultant for the series, Wambaugh tried to insure that it depicted police life more realistically than most other crime shows. Stanley Kallis was the first executive producer of the series and was succeeded in 1976 by David Gerber; Christopher Morgan was the producer until 1975, when he was succeeded by Liam O'Brien and Carl Pingitore. The pilots for two other police shows were televised on *Police Story: Joe Forrester* and *Police Woman*. Though *Police Story* ceased to be seen as a weekly series in the summer of 1977, a few new episodes were shown as specials during the 1977–1978 season. A handful of newly produced episodes, based on stories from the original series, ran on ABC during the fall of 1988 to fill a programming gap caused by the writers' strike.

POLICE SURGEON SYNDICATED

1972–1973 On this half-hour crime show, Sam Groom again played Dr. Simon Locke; Groom had played the part a season earlier on *Doctor Simon Locke,* in which the title character was a small-town physician. In this series Locke had become a surgeon with the medical unit of a big-city police department. Also featured was Larry D. Mann as Lieutenant Jack Gordon. Wilton Schiller was the executive producer, and Chester Krumholz the producer of the series, which was filmed in Toronto.

POLICE WOMAN NBC

13 SEPTEMBER 1974–30 AUGUST 1978   This hour-long crime show starred Angie Dickinson as Sergeant Pepper Anderson, an attractive divorcée who was an under-cover officer for the criminal conspiracy division of the Los Angeles Police Department. Also featured were Earl Holliman as her frequent companion (both on and off duty), Sergeant Bill Crowley; Charles Dierkop as Detective Pete Royster; and Ed Bernard as Detective Joe Styles. David Gerber was the executive producer and Douglas Benton was the producer. The pilot for the series, entitled "The Gamble," was televised on *Police Story* on 26 March 1974; it featured Dickinson as Lisa Beaumont and Bert Convy as Crowley, with Dierkop and Bernard in their later roles.

POLITICALLY INCORRECT COM

25 JULY 1993–   Comedian Bill Maher hosted this half-hour panel discussion show, which took a humorous look at politics and the news. Each program usually featured four guests, chosen from the worlds of show business and politics. The series premiered as a weekly program; it moved to late night on weeknights in January 1994, and to weeknight prime time in October 1994.

POLITICS ON TRIAL ABC

11 SEPTEMBER 1952–30 OCTOBER 1952   Issues relating to the 1952 presidential campaign were debated in a mock courtroom setting by opposing sides on this half-hour prime-time show.

POLKA-GO-ROUND ABC

23 JUNE 1958–28 SEPTEMBER 1959   ABC's second attempt at a polka series (the first was *It's Polka Time*) was hosted by Bob Lewandowski and broadcast from Chicago. Other regulars included Carolyn DeZurik (who had also been featured on *It's Polka Time*), Lou Prohut, Georgia Drake, Tom Fouts and the Singing Waiters, the Polka Rounders, and the Chaine Dancers. The show was seen Monday nights in both hour and half-hour versions.

THE POLLY BERGEN SHOW NBC

21 SEPTEMBER 1957–31 MAY 1958   Polly Bergen hosted her own variety series for one season; the half-hour show alternated biweekly with *Club Oasis* and featured the orchestra of Luther Henderson, Jr., and the Peter Gennaro Dancers. The show's theme song, "The Party's Over," was composed by Jule Styne.

PONDEROSA
See BONANZA

POND'S THEATER ABC

13 JANUARY 1955–7 JULY 1955   *Pond's Theater* was the new title for the Thursday-night dramatic anthology series sponsored by Kraft Foods from October 1953 to 6 January 1955 (Kraft continued to sponsor *Kraft Television Theatre* on NBC, however). Sidney Poitier played his first major dramatic role on television in one episode of *Pond's Theater,* "The Fascinating Stranger," broadcast 23 June; Booth Tarkington's story was adapted by Elizabeth Hart. Paul Lammers produced and directed the hour series.

PONY EXPRESS SYNDICATED

1959   Half-hour western with Grant Sullivan as Brett Clark, roving investigator for the Pony Express; Bill Cord as Tom Clyde; and Don Dorell as Donovan. See also *The Young Riders*.

POP! GOES THE COUNTRY SYNDICATED

1974–1983   Ralph Emery was the first host, Tom T. Hall the second, of this half-hour country-and-western music show. Bill Graham was the executive producer and J. Reginald Dunlap the producer.

THE POP 'N' ROCKER GAME   SYNDICATED

1983   Jon "Bowzer" Bauman, formerly of Sha Na Na, hosted this half-hour game show, which combined a quiz on modern music with guest appearances by rock-and-roll acts.

THE POPCORN KID   CBS

23 MARCH 1987–24 APRIL 1987   A little-heralded sitcom about four Kansas City teens who worked at the concession stand at the Majestic Cinema. With Bruce Norris as Scott Creasman; Faith Ford as his unrequited romantic interest, Lynn Holly Brickhouse; Jeffrey Joseph as Willie Dawson; Penelope Ann Miller as Gwen Stottlemeyer; Raye Birk as Leonard Brown, theater manager; and John Christopher Jones as the projectionist, Marlin Bond.

POPEYE   SYNDICATED
1958–1963
THE ALL-NEW POPEYE HOUR   CBS

9 SEPTEMBER 1978–10 SEPTEMBER 1983   *Popeye,* the spinach-eating sailor created by Max Fleischer in the 1930s, starred in more than 250 cartoons made for theatrical release; in most of them he tangled with the villain Bluto to save his girlfriend Olive Oyl. Between 1961 and 1963 an additional 200 cartoons were produced, in many of which Popeye faced a villain named Brutus, who closely resembled Bluto. The cartoons were shown individually by some stations, as part of a local cartoon show, or were strung together to comprise a full half-hour. In the fall of 1978 Popeye came to network television for the first time in *The All-New Popeye Hour.* The latter series originally included such segments as "The Adventures of Popeye," "Popeye's Treasure Hunt," and "Dinky Dog," the adventures of an oversized puppy. In 1979 "Popeye's Sports Parade" was added. In 1981 the show was trimmed from sixty to thirty minutes, and new segments were introduced, in which Popeye was a caveman and Olive an army private.

POPEYE AND SON   CBS

19 SEPTEMBER 1987–3 SEPTEMBER 1988   In this updated Saturday-morning cartoon series, Popeye and Olive Oyl had finally tied the knot, and were the proud parents of a nine-year-old son, Popeye Jr., who hated spinach. Popeye's nemesis, Bluto, and his wife, Lizzie, also had a son, Tank.

POPI   CBS

20 JANUARY 1976–24 AUGUST 1976   This half-hour sitcom about a Puerto Rican widower and his two sons was a midseason replacement for *Joe and Sons,* a half-hour sitcom about an Italian widower and his two sons. *Popi* featured Hector Elizondo as Abraham (Popi) Rodriguez, a widowed handyman who lived in New York with his two boys; Anthony Perez as Junior, the older son; Dennis Vasquez as Luis, the younger son; Edith Diaz as Lupe, their neighbor; and Lou Criscuolo as Mr. Maggio. Created by Tina Pine and Lester Pine, the series was based on the 1969 film of the same title; the pilot was shown on CBS 2 May 1975. Herbert B. Leonard was the executive producer, and Don Van Atta was the producer.

THE POPSICLE PARADE OF STARS   CBS

15 MAY 1950–17 JULY 1950   This fifteen-minute Monday-evening variety show was hosted by a different guest star each week. Among the headliners were Paul Winchell (22 May), Arthur Godfrey (29 May), Martha Raye (3 July), and Groucho Marx (17 July).

THE PORKY PIG SHOW   ABC

20 SEPTEMBER 1964–2 SEPTEMBER 1967   Porky Pig, Warner Brothers' stuttering swine, had his own weekend cartoon show for two seasons. The half-hour series also featured other Warner Brothers cartoons, such as "Bugs Bunny," "Daffy Duck," and "Sylvester and Tweety."

THE PORTER WAGONER SHOW   SYNDICATED

1960–1979   One of TV's longest-running country-and-western music shows, this half-hour show was hosted by singer Porter Wagoner for almost two decades. Bill Graham was the executive producer and J. Reginald Dunlap the producer.

PORTIA FACES LIFE   CBS

5 APRIL 1954–1 JULY 1955   *Portia Faces Life* began on radio in 1940 and came to television fourteen years later. The fifteen-minute daily serial starred Frances Reid and Fran Carlon as Portia Blake Manning, a successful attorney. Also featured were Karl Swenson and Donald Woods as her husband, Walter Manning; Charles Taylor as their son, Dick; Ginger MacManus and Renne Jarrett as their daughter, Shirley; and Patrick O'Neal as Portia's brother, Carl. The serial was also seen under the title *The Inner Flame*.

PORTRAIT   CBS

9 AUGUST 1963–13 SEPTEMBER 1963   CBS newsman Charles Collingwood interviewed celebrities and newsmakers on this Friday-night half-hour series, which replaced *Eyewitness*. Peter Sellers was the guest on the premiere.

PORTRAIT OF A LEGEND   SYNDICATED

1981   James Darren hosted this biographical series, on which stars from the music business were profiled.

POUND PUPPIES   ABC

13 SEPTEMBER 1986–3 SEPTEMBER 1988   Saturday-morning cartoon series whose main characters, the wrinkled Pound Puppies, were inspired by the popular line of stuffed toys. Here, the Pound Puppies lived at the pound, but could get out through a secret tunnel. Assisted by their human friend Holly, they tried to outwit Holly's evil guardian, Katrina Stoneheart, and her spoiled daughter, Brattina. During its second season the show was titled *All New Pound Puppies*.

THE POWER OF WOMEN   DUMONT

1 JULY 1952–11 NOVEMBER 1952   Half-hour public affairs discussion program for women, moderated first by Vivien Kellems, later by Mrs. John G. Lee.

THE POWERS OF MATTHEW STAR   NBC

17 SEPTEMBER 1982–11 SEPTEMBER 1983   Peter Barton starred in this hour sci-fi series as Matthew Star, a youth who fled his native planet, Quadris, as it was being conquered, and came to Earth; equipped with nascent powers of telekinesis and ESP, he tried to fit in as a high school student. Louis Gossett, Jr., costarred as Walt Shepherd, Matthew's guardian and mentor, who signed on as a science teacher at Crestridge. Amy Steel was also featured as Matthew's classmate, Pam Elliot. In midseason the series underwent a change of producers and of format—Matthew and Walter left school (and Steele left the cast) and were recruited by the U.S. government. James Karen was added as Wymore, the government agent who gave them their assignments. Matthew also found himself endowed with even greater powers, such as astral projection. The series was originally scheduled for the fall of 1981 (and was to have been shown under the title *The Powers of Daniel Star*), but production was halted after Barton was badly burned when he fell on a magnesium flare during shooting (Gossett was also injured in the accident).

THE POWERS THAT BE   NBC

7 MARCH 1992–18 APRIL 1992; 22 AUGUST 1992–5 SEPTEMBER 1992; 7 NOVEMBER 1992–2 JANUARY 1993; 5 JUNE 1993–19 JUNE 1993   Half-hour sitcom, created by Marta Kauffman and David Crane and produced by Norman Lear, about a dimwitted United States senator. With John Forsythe as amiable but empty-headed Senator William Powers; Holland Taylor as his wife, Margaret; Eve Gordon as his mistress and chief administrative assistant, Jordan Miller; Peter MacNicol as his press secretary, Bradley Grist; Valerie Mahaffey as Powers's neurotic daughter, Caitlyn; David

Hyde Pierce as her depressed husband, Congressman Theodore Van Horn; Joseph Gordon-Levitt as their son, Pierce; Elizabeth Berridge as the Powers's hapless maid, Charlotte; and Robin Bartlett as Sophia Lipkin, who claimed to be Powers's illegitimate daughter.

THE PRACTICE   NBC
30 JANUARY 1976–26 JANUARY 1977   Half-hour sitcom starring Danny Thomas as Dr. Jules Bedford, a crusty but compassionate physician practicing on New York's West Side. Also featured were David Spielberg as Dr. David Bedford, his less idealistic son; Dena Dietrich as Nurse Molly Gibbons; Shelley Fabares as Jenny Bedford, David's wife; Didi Conn as Helen, the receptionist; Allen Price as Paul, David and Jenny's son; Damon Raskin as Tony, David and Jenny's other son; Sam Laws as Nate; John Byner (spring 1976) as Dr. Roland Caine; and Mike Evans (fall 1976) as Lenny. Produced by Danny Thomas Productions in association with M-G-M and NBC, the series' executive producer was Paul Younger Witt, and its supervising producer was Tony Thomas.

THE PRACTICE TEE   NBC
5 AUGUST 1949–9 SEPTEMBER 1949   Broadcast from Cleveland, this fifteen-minute Friday-night show was hosted by William P. Barbour, resident pro at the Sleepy Hollow Country Club, who showed golfers at home how to improve their games.

PRESENTING SUSAN ANTON   NBC
26 APRIL 1979–17 MAY 1979   Four-week musical variety hour starring Susan Anton, with Jack Fletcher and Jack Knight. Jack Stein was the executive producer, Ernest Chambers the producer.

PRESIDENTIAL TIMBER   CBS
4 APRIL 1952–27 JUNE 1952   On this Friday-night public affairs program, air time was made available to any announced candidate for the Presidency. Robert Trout moderated the series, which was produced by David Zellman and directed by Don Hewitt (who later became the executive producer of CBS's *60 Minutes*).

PRESS CONFERENCE   ABC/NBC
2 FEBRUARY 1955–11 SEPTEMBER 1955 (ABC); 4 JULY 1956–26 SEPTEMBER 1956 (NBC); 28 OCTOBER 1956–15 JULY 1957 (ABC)   The 1955 version of this public affairs program presented filmed coverage of President Eisenhower's news conferences. The 1956 and 1957 versions were panel shows on which guest journalists grilled newsmakers. Martha Rountree, who had previously produced NBC's *Meet the Press*, was the moderator of the latter versions.

PRESS CORRESPONDENTS PANEL   CBS
10 APRIL 1949–22 MAY 1949   Current events were discussed by groups of journalists on this half-hour Sunday-evening program.

PRESS YOUR LUCK   CBS
19 SEPTEMBER 1983–26 SEPTEMBER 1986   Peter Tomarken hosted this daytime game show, on which three players competed by answering questions correctly. Each correct answer earned the player a "spin" on the game board; each spin could prove to be worth cash, or could turn up a "whammy," in which case the player lost all of his or her accumulated earnings. In June 1984 a contestant pressed his luck to win $110,237 in cash and trips, a TV game show record for single-sitting earnings. After carefully analyzing videotapes of the program, Paul Michael Larson determined that the whammies appeared in predictable patterns. Following his remarkable feat (which was aired in two parts), the producers randomized the game board sequence.

THE PRESTON EPISODES   FOX
9 SEPTEMBER 1995–28 OCTOBER 1995   Half-hour sitcom starring David Alan Grier as David Preston, a newly divorced English professor who quit his academic post to

become a writer; he landed a job writing for "Stuff," a New York gossip magazine which consisted mainly of photos. Also featured were Judith Scott as coworker Kelly Freeman; Tommy Hinkley as Preston's strange neighbor, Derek; Matthew Walker as Adam Green, head of personnel; Brent Hinkley as coworker Harlow; and Clive Revill as Larry Dunhill, the editor. Deborah Lacey appeared occasionally as Mary Ann, Preston's ex.

PREVIEW   CBS
7 MARCH 1949–5 SEPTEMBER 1949   *Preview* was a Monday-night potpourri of features, hosted by the husband-and-wife team of Tex McCrary and Jinx Falkenburg.

PREVIEW—THE BEST OF THE NEW   SYNDICATED
1990   Half-hour daily magazine show, hosted by Chuck Henry. Regular contributors included Robin Leach (on living), Marilyn McCoo (music), Paula McClure (television), Bobbie Brown (fashion), Dana Hersey (films), and Rona Elliot (celebrity news). The series was abruptly canceled after thirteen weeks.

THE PRICE IS RIGHT   NBC/ABC/SYNDICATED/CBS
26 NOVEMBER 1956–6 SEPTEMBER 1963 (NBC); 9 SEPTEMBER 1963–3 SEPTEMBER 1965 (ABC); 1972–1974 (SYNDICATED); 4 SEPTEMBER 1972– (CBS); 1985 (SYNDICATED); 1994 (SYNDICATED)   More merchandise has been given away on this game show than on any other show. The series, a Mark Goodson-Bill Todman production, has been seen in several different formats, on network and in syndication, in prime time and in the daytime. In the fall of 1956 the show began a nine-year daytime run, with Bill Cullen as host. The format was fairly rigid then; each day four contestants were featured, all seated behind "tote" machines (manufactured by the American Totalizator Corporation). After being shown an item of merchandise, the contestants bid on it, and the prize was awarded to the contestant who had bid the highest without going over the manufacturer's suggested list price. For most items, each contestant's bid had to be higher than the previous contestant's, and the players were constantly exhorted from the studio audience to stop bidding, or "freeze." Occasionally, an item would be a "one-bid" item, in which the contestants could bid just once, and, in some cases, each successive bid had to be a certain dollar amount higher than the preceding bid. The show ran for seven years on NBC and was also seen during prime time from 1957 to 1963; in the fall of 1963 it moved to ABC, where it ran for two more years in a daytime slot and was also seen briefly in prime time. Announcer Don Pardo was also on hand to introduce the host and to describe the wares. After a seven-year hiatus two versions of the show resurfaced in 1972; both were known briefly as *The New Price Is Right*. A syndicated version, hosted by Dennis James, was seen in prime time in most markets; the network version, broadcast daily, is hosted by Bob Barker, and in November 1975 it became the first regularly scheduled daytime game show to expand to an hour. On both of the latter versions the format was less rigid; several different price-guessing games were employed, rather than the single form of bidding formerly used. Although most of the show's contestants were ordinary citizens, a few famous or later-to-be-famous people have appeared; among them was Vanna White, who was a contestant in 1980. Within two years she was a fixture on another popular game show, *Wheel of Fortune*.

As the daytime *Price Is Right* rolled through the 1980s and into 1990, it became television's longest-running daily game show, eclipsing *Truth or Consequences* (which, coincidentally, Bob Barker had also hosted for much of its 1956–1974 run). Barker also became one of TV's first game show hosts to let his hair turn naturally gray-white; the decision was approved by the network in 1987 and met with the overwhelming approval of the home audiences. Johnny ("Come on down!") Olson was the series' announcer until his death in 1985; Rod Roddy succeeded him. The show has employed a number of models to show off the merchandise, but three of the longest-serving were Holly Hallstrom, Dian Parkinson, and Janice Pennington. After leaving the show, Parkinson filed suit against Bob Barker, alleging sexual harassment; the case was dropped in 1995.

A prime-time version of *The Price Is Right,* also hosted by Barker, turned up briefly on CBS between 14 August and 18 September 1986, and a new syndicated version, with Tom Kennedy as emcee, was produced in 1985. Another syndicated version was produced briefly in 1994. Hosted by Doug Davidson, the half-hour daily show featured models Ferrari Ferris, Julie Cialini, and Lisa Stahl.

PRIDE & JOY   NBC
21 MARCH 1995–2 MAY 1995; 20 JUNE 1995–11 JULY 1995   Half-hour sitcom about two young families who were neighbors in a New York apartment building. With Julie Warner as Amy Sherman, new mother; Caroline Rhea as her friend, Carol Green, a mother of two (Carol and Amy also worked together at an ad agency); Craig Bierko as Amy's husband, Greg, a freelance writer; Jeremy Piven as Carol's husband, Nathan, an unemployed stockbroker; and Natasha Pavlovic as Katya, the Shermans's nanny.

PRIDE OF PLACE   PBS
24 MARCH 1986–12 MAY 1986   An eight-part look at American architecture, with host Robert A. M. Stern.

PRIDE OF THE FAMILY   ABC
2 OCTOBER 1953–24 SEPTEMBER 1954   Half-hour sitcom starring Paul Hartman as Albie Morrison, head of the advertising department of the local paper. With Fay Wray as his wife, Catherine Morrison; Natalie Wood as their teenage daughter, Ann; and Bobby Hyatt as their son, Junior. Bob Finkel directed the series for Revue Productions.

PRIME TIME PETS   CBS
9 JULY 1990–31 AUGUST 1990   This half-hour summer show was an animal version of *America's Funniest Home Videos,* relying heavily on footage from viewers of pets doing tricks. Wil Shriner hosted the show, which, like *America's Funniest,* employed a living room set and a studio audience; Shriner also supplied supposedly witty commentary as the home videos rolled. Also featured was Dorothy Lucey as the show's roving reporter.

PRIME TIME SUNDAY (PRIME TIME SATURDAY)   NBC
24 JUNE 1979–5 JULY 1980   A weekly magazine series, *Prime Time Sunday* was the successor to *Weekend.* Tom Snyder, host of NBC's *Tomorrow,* was the host of the hour show, which was broadcast live with taped segments. Jack Perkins was a regular contributor. Paul Friedman had left his job as executive producer of the *Today* show to head up the production team for *Prime Time Sunday.* In December 1979 the show moved to Saturday and was suitably retitled.

PRIMETIME LIVE   ABC
3 AUGUST 1989–   A live hour weekly newsmagazine coanchored by ABC's former White House reporter Sam Donaldson and Diane Sawyer, newly arrived from CBS. As originally conceived, the program would originate from New York with a studio audience, would rely little on previously taped pieces, and would emphasize its "liveness" by featuring live reports from ABC correspondents and unscripted dialogue between Sawyer and Donaldson. The premiere program featured three live interviews. The studio audience was quickly dropped, however, and the show began to rely more heavily on previously taped investigative reports and interviews. On 21 September 1989 Donaldson and Sawyer hosted a live visit with President and Mrs. Bush at the White House. The hoped-for chemistry between the two anchors never materialized; by mid-1990 Donaldson had relocated to Washington, and he and Sawyer no longer appeared together in the studio. Regular correspondents have included Chris Wallace, Sylvia Chase, John Quinones, Judd Rose, and Jay Schadler. By early 1994 Diane Sawyer was appearing on two other ABC newsmagazine programs as well: see *Day One* and *Turning Point. PrimeTime Live* scored big ratings for its program of 14 June 1995, when Diane Sawyer conducted a live interview with reclusive pop star Michael Jackson and his wife, Lisa Marie Presley.

PRIMUS   SYNDICATED

1971   Essentially an updated version of *Sea Hunt, Primus* starred Robert Brown as oceanographer Carter Primus, with Will Kuluva as his assistant, Charlie Kingman, and Eva Renzi as assistant Toni Hyden. Primus and his cohorts floated about in such craft as *Big Kate,* a sort of underwater robot, and *Pegasus,* a smaller craft used for underwater photography.

PRINCE PLANET   SYNDICATED

1966   Another of the several Japanese-produced cartoon series of the late 1960s, Prince Planet was a young lad from another galaxy who came to Earth to fight wrongdoers.

PRINCESSES   CBS

27 SEPTEMBER 1991–25 OCTOBER 1991   Half-hour sitcom about three young women sharing a rent-free Manhattan penthouse. With Julie Hagerty as Tracy Dillon, who taught English to adults; Fran Drescher as Melissa Kirshner, who worked at a department store; and Twiggy Lawson as Georgy Delarue, a real princess (of Scilly), who had been Melissa's college roommate. The apartment had been given to Tracy as a wedding gift by a friend of Tracy's fiance, and Tracy stayed on even after the wedding plans fell through; the same friend had also promised the place to Georgy. Princesses was placed on hiatus after Hagerty quit the show in October 1991, but it never returned to the air.

PRINCETON '55   NBC

2 JANUARY 1955–27 MARCH 1955   This Sunday-afternoon public affairs program was produced at Princeton University; it began as a local show the previous year (when it was titled *Princeton '54*), before going network in January. The 1955 premiere show was titled "Communists and Who They Are," while Robert Frost was featured the following week, on "Enjoyment of Poetry." Steve Krantz was the executive producer, and Harry Olesker was the producer.

THE PRISONER   CBS

1 JUNE 1968–21 SEPTEMBER 1968; 29 MAY 1969–11 SEPTEMBER 1969   Regarded by many buffs as the finest dramatic series ever broadcast, *The Prisoner* was certainly one of the most imaginative and enigmatic shows in TV history. The hour series was the brainchild of Patrick McGoohan, who was its star and executive producer, as well as the writer and director of several episodes. As *The Prisoner* unfolded, McGoohan, who had previously played John Drake on *Secret Agent,* found himself living in a mysterious, self-contained cosmopolitan community known simply as "the village." Most of the village's inhabitants were known merely by numbers—McGoohan was Number 6, and in the opening episode he met Number 2, who explained to him that he had been transported to the village because the information stored in his head had made him too valuable "outside" (McGoohan denied that his character was John Drake, though it appeared from the opening sequence that Number 6 was a secret agent who, for one reason or another, had left the intelligence service). Thus Number 6 gradually realized that he was a prisoner, though his prison was an idyllic place with plenty of green fields and parks, recreational activities, and even a butler (the mute manservant was played by Angelo Muscat). Nevertheless, Number 6 was determined to preserve his individuality, and through most of the seventeen episodes, he either tried to escape from the village or to learn the identity of Number 1, the person assumed to run the village. His attempts to escape were always thwarted by large white balloonlike spheres, known as "rovers." In the final episode, "Fall Out" (written by McGoohan), Number 6 ultimately earned the right not to be called by a number and learned that *he* had been Number 1; as the episode closed, he was seen driving away from the village toward London. In real life, "the village," where almost all of the action took place, was a resort in North Wales called the Hotel Portmeirion, designed by Sir Clough Williams-Ellis.

PRISONER: CELL BLOCK H SYNDICATED

1980   Imported from Australia, this half-hour serial was set at a women's prison, which housed a motley crew of murderers, drug dealers, thieves, and terrorists. The cast included: Patsy King as the warden (or "governor"), Erica Davidson; Gerard Maguire as Jim Fletcher, the deputy governor; Fiona Spence as sadistic guard Vera Bennett; Val Lehman as inmate boss "Queen Bea" Smith, serving a life sentence for killing her husband; Carol Burns as lesbian inmate Franky Doyle; Kerry Armstrong as new arrival Lynn Warner; Pieta Tommano as Lynn's former lover, Karen Travers; Mary Ward as Mum Brooks; Monica Maughan as Pat O'Connell; and Barry Quin as Greg Miller, the prison doctor. The series was an instant hit in Australia, where it premiered in February of 1979; it was introduced in Los Angeles in August of that year and proved popular there, thus paving the way for national syndication. However, because of its graphic violence, most American stations scheduled the series late at night, and the show did not attract large audiences.

PRIVATE BENJAMIN CBS

6 APRIL 1981–27 APRIL 1981; 12 OCTOBER 1981–10 JANUARY 1983; 9 MAY 1983–5 SEPTEMBER 1983   This half-hour sitcom, about a spoiled young woman who enlisted in "Today's Army," was based on the hit movie. The series featured Lorna Patterson as Private Judy Benjamin, who gamely struggled through basic training at Fort Bradley; Eileen Brennan as her frustrated commanding officer, Captain Doreen Lewis; Hal Williams as the drill instructor, Sergeant Ted Ross; Joyce Little as Private White; Joan Roberts as Private Glass; Lisa Raggio as Private Maria Gianelli; and Ann Ryerson as gung-ho Private Carol Winter (Brennan and Williams had also appeared in the movie). The show's spring 1981 tryout was a ratings smash; *Private Benjamin* ranked fifth in the 1980–1981 seasonal Nielsens, and the network quickly renewed the series. When it returned to the air in the fall of 1981, Little and Roberts had left the cast, and Private Benjamin found herself with three new platoon mates: Lucy Webb as naive Private Lou Ann Hubble; Francesca Roberts as Private Dorsey; and Damita Jo Freeman as Private Jackie Simms. Benjamin and her cohorts eventually completed basic training, and Captain Lewis won her coveted promotion to the position of Inspector General; unfortunately, Private Benjamin was assigned to be her administrative assistant. In the fall of 1982 Captain Lewis became the post's public affairs officer, and Benjamin continued to be her assistant. Webb and Francesca Roberts were dropped, and Wendie Jo Sperber joined the cast as Private Stacy Kouchalakas. Robert Mandan, who had appeared occasionally as post commander Colonel Fielding, also became a regular. Polly Holliday was featured in the final episodes as Major Allen—Holliday had been signed to fill in for Eileen Brennan, who had been seriously injured in an automobile accident.

PRIVATE EYE NBC

13 SEPTEMBER 1987–8 JANUARY 1988   Anthony Yerkovich, who created *Miami Vice* in 1984, paid homage to the 1950s in this hour crime show. Set in Los Angeles in the mid-1950s, against a backdrop of muscle cars and nascent rock and roll, it starred Michael Woods as Jack Cleary, an ex-cop who took over his murdered brother's private detective business. Other regulars were Josh Brolin as greaser Johnny Betts, who sometimes helped Cleary; Bill Sadler as Lieutenant Charlie Fontana, Cleary's ex-partner; and Lisa Jane Persky as Dottie, Cleary's secretary. NBC announced in October that the series would be "lightened," i.e., that subsequent episodes would contain more humor and less violence. However, ratings did not improve, and the series was dropped in midseason.

PRIVATE SECRETARY CBS/NBC

1 FEBRUARY 1953–10 SEPTEMBER 1957 (CBS); 20 JUNE 1953–5 SEPTEMBER 1953 (NBC); 26 JUNE 1954–4 SEPTEMBER 1954 (NBC)   Half-hour sitcom starring Ann Sothern as brassy Susie MacNamara, a private secretary. With Don Porter as her boss, theatrical agent Peter Sands; Ann Tyrrell as Susie's confidante, switchboard operator Violet Praskins; Jesse White as rival agent Cagey Calhoun; and Joan Banks as Susie's friend Sylvia. In the later seasons Louis Nye and Ken Berry appeared as Delbert and

Woody. Jack Chertok produced the series and Christian Nyby directed it. On CBS *Private Secretary* alternated biweekly with *The Jack Benny Program;* during the summers of 1953 and 1954 NBC carried reruns of *Private Secretary* as a replacement for *Your Hit Parade.* The series was syndicated under the title *Susie.*

PRIZE PARTY   CBS
6 DECEMBER 1948–17 JUNE 1949   Bill Slater hosted this Friday-night game show on which the contestants performed stunts. Its full title was *The Messing Prize Party,* as its sponsor was Messing Bakeries.

PRIZE PERFORMANCE   CBS
3 JULY 1950–12 SEPTEMBER 1950   This summer replacement show was a talent showcase for aspiring young performers. Arlene Francis was the host, and Cedric Adams and Peter Donald were regular panelists.

PRO BOWLERS' TOUR   ABC
6 JANUARY 1962   Long-running sports show, usually seen Saturday afternoons; each week a bowling tournament was telecast live. Chris Schenkel, the anchor, has been assisted by Jack Buck (1962–1964), Billy Welu (1964–1974) and Nelson Burton, Jr. (1975–).

PRO FOOTBALL HIGHLIGHTS   ABC/DUMONT
15 SEPTEMBER 1950–8 DECEMBER 1950 (ABC); 24 SEPTEMBER 1952–17 DECEMBER 1952; 1 OCTOBER 1953–17 DECEMBER 1953 (DUMONT)   Half-hour wrap-up of pro football news. Because the show was broadcast from New York, much of the show centered around the local eleven, the New York Giants. Joe Hasel hosted the show in 1950, and was succeeded by Steve Owen (the Giants' coach) in 1952 and 1953.

PROBE   ABC
7 MARCH 1988–29 JUNE 1988   Hour crime show, filmed in Phoenix, starring Parker Stevenson as genius Austin James, who worked for a think-tank and solved crimes in his spare time using the latest in computers and technology, and Ashley Crow as his assistant, Mickey Castle. Writer Isaac Asimov created the series with Michael Wagner.

PRODUCERS' SHOWCASE   NBC
18 OCTOBER 1954–24 JUNE 1957   One of the most costly of the several high-quality dramatic anthology series, *Producers' Showcase,* under the supervision of Fred Coe, was seen approximately once a month. Some of television's most notable single programs were presented on the highly acclaimed series. Among them were: "Tonight at 8:30," with Trevor Howard and Ginger Rogers (both making their TV dramatic debuts, 18 October 1954); "State of the Union," with Nina Foch, Joseph Cotten, and Margaret Sullavan (directed by Arthur Penn, it was aired 15 November 1954); the extraordinarily popular telecast of "Peter Pan," with Mary Martin and Cyril Ritchard (directed by Jerome Robbins, it was first aired 7 March 1955, and was restaged 9 January 1956); Sidney Kingsley's "Darkness at Noon," with Joseph Wiseman, Lee J. Cobb, Nehemiah Persoff, and Ruth Roman (directed by Delbert Mann, it was broadcast 2 May 1955); Robert Sherwood's "The Petrified Forest," with Humphrey Bogart (in his only dramatic appearance on television, recreating the role of Duke Mantee, which he had played on stage and on film), Henry Fonda, Lauren Bacall, Jack Klugman, and Richard Jacckel (30 May 1955); a musical version of Thornton Wilder's "Our Town," with Paul Newman and Frank Sinatra (19 September 1955); "The Barretts of Wimpole Street," with Katharine Cornell (in her TV debut), Anthony Quayle, and Nancy Coleman (2 April 1956); Sidney Howard's "Dodsworth," with Fredric March, Florence Eldridge, and Claire Trevor (30 April 1956); "The Lord Don't Play Favorites," with Louis Armstrong, Buster Keaton, Kay Starr, and Dick Haymes (17 September 1956); "Jack and the Beanstalk," with Joel Grey, Celeste Holm, Cyril Ritchard, and Peggy King (12 November 1956); Anatole Litvak's "Mayerling," with Audrey Hepburn, Mel Ferrer, Raymond Massey, Diana Wynyard, Judith Evelyn, Basil Sydney, Nehemiah Persoff, Lorne Greene, Nancy

Marchand, Monique Van Vooren, Sorrell Booke, and Suzy Parker (4 February 1957); "The Great Sebastians," starring Alfred Lunt and Lynn Fontanne in their television debut (1 April 1957). *Producers' Showcase* almost succeeded in landing Marilyn Monroe, who, had she taken the part, would have made her TV dramatic debut in "Lysistrata" sometime in 1956; after much consideration, she turned down the offer and never appeared in a dramatic role on television.

PRODUCTION FOR FREEDOM ABC
22 JUNE 1952–21 SEPTEMBER 1952   Sunday-night series of films about American industry. See also *Enterprise U.S.A.; Industry on Parade.*

PROFESSIONAL FATHER CBS
8 JANUARY 1955–2 JULY 1955   Half-hour sitcom starring Steve Dunne as Dr. Tom Wilson, a child psychologist who has trouble raising his own kids at home; Barbara Billingsley as his wife, Helen Wilson; Ted Marc as their son, Twig; Beverly Washburn as their daughter, Kit; Phyllis Coates as their neighbor, Madge; Joseph Kearns as Madge's husband, Fred; Ann O'Neal as the Wilsons' housekeeper, Nana; and Arthur Q. Bryan as Mr. Boggs, the neighborhood handyman. Harry Kronman produced the series, and Sherman Marks directed it.

PROFILES IN COURAGE NBC
8 NOVEMBER 1964–9 MAY 1965   An anthology series based on John F. Kennedy's 1956 book about American political leaders who faced difficult decisions. Robert Saudek was executive producer of the half-hour series, and Theodore H. Sorensen and Allan Nevins served as special consultants.

PROGRAM PLAYHOUSE DUMONT
22 JUNE 1949–14 SEPTEMBER 1949   James L. Caddigan produced this live half-hour anthology series. The premiere telecast, "The Timid Soul," was based on H. T. Webster's comic strip and starred Ernest Truex as Caspar Milquetoast.

PROJECT U.F.O. NBC
19 FEBRUARY 1978–4 JANUARY 1979   On this hour-long science fiction series a team of Air Force investigators tracked down reports of sightings of unidentified flying objects and of contact with alien beings. Featured were William Jordan as Major Jake Gatlin; Caskey Swaim as Staff Sergeant Harry Fitz; and Aldine King as Libby. Jack Webb, the executive producer and narrator of the series, obtained information from the United States government on nearly 13,000 sightings of unidentified flying objects, some of which were used as the bases for the episodes. William T. Coleman, who headed an Air Force investigation project in the early 1960s, was the producer. In the fall of 1978 Edward Winter joined the cast as Captain Ben Ryan, replacing William Jordan.

PROS & CONS ABC
26 SEPTEMBER 1991–2 JANUARY 1992   This light crime show was the successor to the 1990–1991 series *Gabriel's Fire*, which had starred James Earl Jones. Jones continued to play Gabriel Bird, but the character had moved from Chicago to Los Angeles, where he teamed up with a local private detective. Richard Crenna costarred as Bird's new partner, Mitch O'Hannon, and Madge Sinclair continued her role from *Gabriel's Fire* as "Empress" Josephine Austin, who became Bird's wife in October. Like most efforts to retool TV series after launching, this one proved unsuccessful.

PROSTARS NBC
14 SEPTEMBER 1991–25 JUNE 1992   Three top professional athletes — hockey player Wayne Gretzky, basketball player Michael Jordan, and baseball/football player Bo Jackson—joined forces on this Saturday morning cartoon series. The three stars were usually accompanied by a female character named Denise. The animated segments were introduced by live–action clips of Gretzky, Jordan, and Jackson.

THE PROTECTORS   SYNDICATED

1972–1974   Filmed in Europe, this widely syndicated half-hour adventure series followed the activities of the Protectors, an elite crew of private eyes. Featured were Robert Vaughn as Harry Rule; Nyree Dawn Porter as Contessa Caroline di Contini; and Tony Anholt as Paul Buchet.

PRUDENTIAL FAMILY THEATER   CBS

10 OCTOBER 1950–27 MARCH 1951   This hour-long dramatic anthology series was seen on Tuesday nights, opposite Milton Berle's *The Texaco Star Theater,* where it alternated biweekly with *Sure As Fate.* Presentations included: "The Barretts of Wimpole Street," with Helen Hayes and Bethel Leslie (5 December); "Over 21," with Ruth Gordon (19 December); "Burlesque," with Bert Lahr (2 January); "Berkeley Square," with Richard Greene and Grace Kelly (13 February); and "Ruggles of Red Gap," with Cyril Ritchard, Glenda Farrell, and Walter Abel (27 February).

THE PRUITTS OF SOUTHAMPTON   ABC

6 SEPTEMBER 1966–1 SEPTEMBER 1967   Phyllis Diller's attempt at a situation comedy was unsuccessful. She starred as Phyllis Pruitt, a Long Island socialite who had to make a rapid transition from luxury to poverty when she learned she owed millions in back taxes. Also featured were Reginald Gardiner as eighty-one-year-old Uncle Ned; Grady Sutton as Sturgis, the butler; Pam Freeman as her daughter, Stephanie; Lisa Loring as her daughter, Suzy; and Richard Deacon as Mr. Baldwin, the Internal Revenue Service agent. In midseason the format was changed slightly, and the show was retitled; on 13 January *The Phyllis Diller Show* premiered, and the Pruitts' mansion was now a boardinghouse. Added to the cast were three new regulars: John Astin as Rudy Pruitt; Marty Ingels as Norman Krump; and Gypsy Rose Lee as Regina. David Levy was the executive producer of the series for Filmways.

PRYOR'S PLACE   CBS

22 SEPTEMBER 1984–15 JUNE 1985   Inventive funnyman Richard Pryor brought his considerable talents to Saturday-morning television in this live-action series produced by Sid and Marty Krofft. The setting was an urban neighborhood, with Pryor reminiscing about his childhood to a group of local kids; he then played various characters in the ensuing stories. Also appearing were Akili Prince as Little Richie, the childhood Pryor; Cliffy Magee as Wally; Danny Nucci as Freddy; Tony Cox as Allen; Keland Love as Meatrack; and (in various capacities) the Krofft Puppets. Ray Parker, Jr., sang the series' theme.

THE PSYCHIATRIST   NBC

3 FEBRUARY 1971–1 SEPTEMBER 1971   The concluding segment of NBC's *Fourin-One, The Psychiatrist* starred Roy Thinnes as Dr. James Whitman, a Los Angeles analyst, and Luther Adler as his colleague, Dr. Bernard Altman.

PUBLIC DEFENDER   CBS

11 MARCH 1954–23 JUNE 1955   This half-hour crime show starred Reed Hadley (formerly the star of *Racket Squad*) as public defender Bart Matthews.

PUBLIC PROSECUTOR   SYNDICATED/DUMONT

1947–1948 (SYNDICATED); 6 SEPTEMBER 1951–28 FEBRUARY 1952 (DUMONT)   The first filmed series made especially for television, *Public Prosecutor* was a series of twenty-six 17½-minute mysteries starring John Howard as a prosecuting attorney, Stephen Allen, with Anne Gwynne as his secretary, Patricia Kelly, and Walter Sande as a police lieutenant. When the DuMont network obtained the series in 1951, it turned the program into a panel show in order to fill a thirty-minute time slot. Each week three guest panelists—mystery buffs or amateur sleuths—watched an episode (along with the home audience), which was halted just before the climax; each panelist then tried to guess the identity of the guilty party. Warren Hull served as the host of the DuMont version of the show. Other local stations which bought *Public Prosecutor* rarely bothered to employ a panel or a host, preferring instead to pad the rest of the half-hour slot with extra commercials. *Public Prosecutor* was produced by Jerry Fairbanks for Jerry Fairbanks Productions.

PUD'S PRIZE PARTY ABC
21 JUNE 1952–13 DECEMBER 1952   Fifteen-minute, Saturday-morning, audience participation show for kids. Broadcast from Philadelphia, it was hosted by Todd Russell.

PULITZER PRIZE PLAYHOUSE ABC
6 OCTOBER 1950–29 JUNE 1951; 2 JANUARY 1952–4 JUNE 1952   Presentations on this hour-long dramatic anthology series were adapted from Pulitzer Prize-winning stories. Included were: Emlyn Williams's "The Late Christopher Bean," with Helen Hayes (in her TV debut) and Charles Dingle (27 October 1950); "The Magnificent Ambersons" (based on the novel by Booth Tarkington), with Ruth Hussey (3 November 1950); Sidney Howard's "The Silver Cord," with Joanne Dru and Dame Judith Anderson (26 January 1951); and "The Happy Journey," with Jack Lemmon (4 May 1951).

PULSE OF THE CITY DUMONT
15 SEPTEMBER 1953–9 MARCH 1954   Fifteen-minute dramatic anthology series.

PUNKY BREWSTER NBC/SYNDICATED
16 SEPTEMBER 1984–7 SEPTEMBER 1986 (NBC); 1987–1988 (SYNDICATED)   The title character of this half-hour sitcom, aired on NBC during the Sunday "family viewing hour" (7–8 P.M.), was a seven-year-old girl whose father had walked out and whose mother abandoned her in Chicago; the little girl found shelter in a vacant apartment, and was soon discovered by the building manager, who arranged to be her guardian. Featured were Soleil Moon Frye (sister of child actor Meeno Peluce) as Punky Brewster; George Gaynes as building manager Henry Warnimont, a photographer; Susie Garrett as Mrs. Betty Johnson, a neighbor; Cherie Johnson as her granddaughter, Cherie; Eddie Deezen as Eddie, the building handyman; Dody Goodman (1984–1985) as Punky's teacher, Mrs. Morton; T. K. Carter (1985–1986) as Punky's teacher, Mr. Fulton; Ami Foster as classmate Margaux Kramer; and Casey Ellison as Punky's pal Allen Anderson. The name Punky Brewster was supplied by NBC Entertainment executive Brandon Tartikoff, who had known a real Punky Brewster when he attended The Lawrenceville School in New Jersey; the real Punky Brewster was tracked down for the series and received a royalty for the use of her name. The TV Punky kept Tartikoff's name alive: her dog was named Brandon. After two seasons on the network, more first-run episodes were produced for syndication in the fall of 1987, to be added to the reruns. In the fall of 1985 NBC introduced a cartoon version of the show on Saturday mornings: see *It's Punky Brewster.*

A PUP NAMED SCOOBY DOO ABC
10 SEPTEMBER 1988–31 AUGUST 1991   Saturday-morning cartoon series depicting the early years of that durable canine sleuth, Scooby Doo, and his cohorts Shaggy, Daphne, Freddie, and Velma. Two earlier animated series—*The Flintstone Kids* and *Muppet Babies*—had utilized the same idea.

THE PUPPY'S FURTHER ADVENTURES ABC/CBS
10 SEPTEMBER 1983–10 NOVEMBER 1984 (ABC); 13 SEPTEMBER 1986–8 NOVEMBER 1986 (CBS)   Petey the Puppy, a lost dog searching for his family, was the main character on this Saturday-morning cartoon series. Petey had been introduced during the 1981–1982 season on *The ABC Weekend Special* and was a featured segment on *Scooby & Scrappy Doo/The Puppy's New Adventures* during the 1982–1983 season. The series was retitled *The Puppy's Great Adventures* in the fall of 1984.

PURSUIT CBS
22 OCTOBER 1958–14 JANUARY 1959   This hour-long anthology series of thrillers should not be confused with any of the other similarly titled suspense anthologies of the period, such as *Climax, Moment of Fear, Panic!,* and *Suspicion.*

PURSUIT OF HAPPINESS ABC

30 OCTOBER 1987–8 JANUARY 1988   Half-hour sitcom set at a Philadelphia college campus. With Paul Provenza as history teacher David Hanley, who had just returned to academia after spending several years traveling around the country; Brian Keith as Professor Roland Duncan, Hanley's mentor, who turned out to be far more jaded and worldy than Hanley had imagined him to be; Judie Aronson as Sara, Duncan's daughter, Wendel Meldrum as Professor Margaret Callahan, an Egyptologist; and Wesley Thompson as Vernon Morris, Hanley's old college roommate. Also making frequent cameo appearances were Los Angeles Laker Magic Johnson (as himself) and Kevin Scannell as Thomas Jefferson, both of whom popped onscreen from time to time to advise Hanley. The series was a replacement for *Max Headroom*.

THE PURSUIT OF HAPPINESS NBC

19 SEPTEMBER 1995–7 NOVEMBER 1995   Half-hour sitcom with Tom Amandes as Chicago lawyer Steve Rutledge; Melinda McGraw as his wife, Macenzie (Mac) Rutledge; Brad Garrett as his best friend and law partner, Alex Chosik, who announced he was gay in the premiere episode; Maxine Stuart as Gram, Steve's grandmother, who lived in a nursing home; Meredith Scott Lynn as Jean, Steve and Alex's secretary; and Larry Miller as Mac's obnoxious brother, Larry.

PUTTIN' ON THE HITS SYNDICATED

1985   Contestants lip-synched to rock records, and were judged on their performances, on this game show hosted by Allen Fawcett.

THE PUZZLE PLACE PBS

16 JANUARY 1995–   Half-hour weekday series for children, designed to teach respect for others, and hosted by a multicultural Muppet sextet: Ben, Leon, Julie, Skye, Jody, and Kiki.

Q. E. D. ABC

3 APRIL 1951–25 SEPTEMBER 1951   Fred Uttal hosted this prime-time game show on which a celebrity panel tried to solve mystery stories submitted by home viewers.

Q. E. D. CBS

23 MARCH 1982–27 APRIL 1982   Set in 1912, this hour adventure series starred Sam Waterston as Quentin Everhart Deverill, a brash young science professor who left the Harvard faculty for England, where he dabbled in sleuthing. Also on hand were A. C. Weary as Charlie Andrews, an American reporter; Sarah Berger as Betsy Stevens, Q.E.D.'s first client; Julian Glover as Q.E.D.'s nemesis, Dr. Stefan Kilkiss, a mad scientist; George Innes as Phipps; and Caroline Langrishe as Jenny.

QUADRANGLE CBS

14 MARCH 1949–22 APRIL 1949   Ralph Levy produced and directed this fifteen-minute talent show, which was set at a campus drugstore.

QUANTUM LEAP NBC

26 MARCH 1989–15 AUGUST 1993   Hour fantasy series, starring Scott Bakula as Sam Beckett, the unfortunate subject of a time-travel experiment gone awry; unable to return to the present, Beckett could travel backward about thirty years, assuming the identities of other people, young or old, male or female. Dean Stockwell costarred as Beckett's holographic advisor known first as The Observer, and later as just Al, who was visible only to Sam. Al provided Sam with some details of his new identities and gave him guidance on the people around him whose lives could be affected by his presence; Al never seemed to be able to give Sam all the information he needed, however, forcing Sam to improvise his way through each new identity.

QUARK NBC

24 FEBRUARY 1978–14 APRIL 1978   This half-hour science fiction comedy show starred Richard Benjamin as Adam Quark, commander of a garbage scow for the

United Galaxy Sanitation Patrol. The cast also included: Timothy Thomerson as Gene Jean, his androgynous assistant; Richard Kelton as Ficus, a boring but talkative plant; twins Tricia and Cyb Barnstable as Betty I and Betty II (Betty II was cloned from Betty I); Conrad Janis as Otto Palindrome, Quark's boss back at Perma One, the space center; Alan Caillou as The Head, Palindrome's boss; and Bobby Porter as Andy, the cowardly robot aboard Quark's ship. David Gerber was the executive producer for Columbia Pictures TV, with Mace Neufeld the coexecutive producer and Bruce Johnson the producer.

THE QUEEN AND I   CBS
16 JANUARY 1969–1 MAY 1969   Situation comedy set aboard the *Amsterdam Queen,* an ocean liner that had seen better days. Featured were Larry Storch as opportunistic Mr. Duffy, the first mate; Billy DeWolfe as First Officer Nelson; Carl Ballantine as Seaman Becker; Pat Morita as Barney Cook; Dave Willock as Ozzie; Barbara Stuart as Wilma; Dave Morick as Max Kowalski; Liam Dunn as Captain Washburn; and Reginald Owen as the ship's owner, Commodore Dodds.

QUEEN FOR A DAY   NBC/ABC/SYNDICATED
3 JANUARY 1956–2 SEPTEMBER 1960 (NBC); 28 SEPTEMBER 1960–2 OCTOBER 1964 (ABC); 1970 (SYNDICATED)   Possibly the most maudlin game show ever broadcast, *Queen for a Day* awarded merchandise prizes to the contestant who could evoke the most sympathy from the studio audience. The show began on radio in 1945 (as *Queen for Today*), and when Jack Bailey became its host later that year, the show settled into a format that changed little over the next nineteen years. Each day four or five women were chosen from the studio audience to appear on stage; one by one each contestant then stated what she most needed and why she needed it. At the end of the show the studio audience then voted, by its applause, who should become that day's "queen." The winner was crowned and throned and given her desired prize, as well as other merchandise. Though not all of the contestants told sob stories (one contestant merely wanted to trade places with emcee Jack Bailey for a day, and another wanted her nails filed by Bailey), a tear-jerking narrative was most likely to reap lots of applause. *Queen for a Day* came to daytime TV in 1956 and soon became the top-rated daytime show; in July of 1956 it was expanded from a half hour to forty-five minutes (in 1958 it reverted to a half hour). The show was based in Hollywood, though Bailey also took the show on the road from time to time; Jeanne Cagney was also featured as the show's fashion commentator. In 1970 the series was revived briefly for syndication with Dick Curtis as host.

THE QUEST   NBC
22 SEPTEMBER 1976–29 DECEMBER 1976   One of the few westerns introduced during the 1970s, *The Quest* starred Kurt Russell and Tim Matheson as brothers Morgan and Quentin Beaudine; the two had been separated at an early age—Morgan had been captured by Indians and raised by the Cheyennes, while Quentin was raised by an aunt and attended medical school. Finally reunited, they joined forces to search for their younger sister, who they believed was still a captive of the Cheyennes. Unfortunately, the series never really got off the ground, for it was scheduled opposite *Charlie's Angels* and vanished in midseason. Tracy Keenan Wynn created the series; David Gerber was the executive producer and Mark Rodgers and James H. Brown the producers. The pilot for the series, titled "Quest," was aired 13 May 1976.

THE QUEST   ABC
22 OCTOBER 1982–19 NOVEMBER 1982   One of the early fatalities of the 1982–1983 season, this hour adventure show was apparently inspired by the film *Raiders of the Lost Ark.* It told the tale of four Americans, each of whom was a possible heir to the throne of a European kingdom, and all of whom were dispatched on a quest—a series of adventures to determine which of the four was the most worthy person to inherit the kingdom. Featured were Perry King as Dan Underwood, a photojournalist; Ray Vitte as Cody Johnson, a con artist; Karen Austin as Carrie, an assistant shoe buyer for a department store; Noah Beery, Jr., as Art, a retired cop; Ralph Michael as Charles

Phillipe, the present King of Glendora; John Rhys Davies as Sir Edward, the king's aide; and Michael Billington as the exiled Count Louis Dardinay, who plotted to thwart the Americans' efforts.

QUEST FOR ADVENTURE ABC
22 JULY 1957–2 SEPTEMBER 1957   A summer series of assorted human interest and informational films.

QUEST FOR THE KILLERS PBS
8 SEPTEMBER 1985–7 OCTOBER 1985   The careers of physicians, epidemiologists, and scientists who have battled to eradicate communicable diseases were profiled on this five-part documentary series, based on the book by June Goodfield.

QUICK AS A FLASH ABC
12 MARCH 1953–25 FEBRUARY 1954   Bobby Sherwood hosted this prime-time game show. A panel of two men faced a panel of two women; the object of the game was to guess a phrase or personality suggested by a specially prepared film clip. Charles B. Moss and Dick Lewis were the producers. The radio version of the series, which used a different format, ran from 1944 to 1951.

QUICK ON THE DRAW DUMONT
8 JANUARY 1952–9 DECEMBER 1952   On this prime-time game show contestants tried to guess phrases suggested by drawings. Robin Chandler hosted the series and Bob Dunn did the sketching. *Quick on the Draw* should not be confused with other cartoon-oriented game shows of TV's early days, such as *Draw Me a Laugh* and *Draw to Win*. The show premiered locally in New York on 27 May 1950.

QUICKDRAW McGRAW SYNDICATED
1959–1962   Segments featured on this widely syndicated Hanna-Barbera cartoon series included "Quickdraw McGraw," the adventures of a bumbling equine marshal; "Snooper and Blabb," a cat-and-mouse detective duo, and "Augie Doggie and Doggie Daddy," father-and-son canines. The series was rerun on CBS's Saturday-morning schedule from 1963 to 1966.

QUINCY, M.E. NBC
3 OCTOBER 1976–5 SEPTEMBER 1983   *Quincy, M.E.,* a medically oriented crime show, began as one segment of *The NBC Sunday Mystery Movie* and became a weekly series early in 1977. Jack Klugman starred as Dr. Quincy, a medical examiner for the Los Angeles County Coroner's Office. Quincy's intense curiosity about his cases often led him to discount his initial impressions. After ordering additional tests and doing some independent investigative work, he was able to shed new light on matters. Featured were John S. Ragin as Dr. Robert J. Asten, the coroner; Garry Walberg as Lieutenant Frank Monahan, police liaison; Robert Ito as Sam Fujiyama, one of Quincy's assistants; Val Bisoglio as Danny Tovo, another assistant; Joseph Roman as Sergeant Brill; and Lynnette Mettey (1976–1977) as Quincy's female companion, Lee Potter. Glen Larson, the executive producer, created the series with Robert F. O'Neill, the supervising producer. Late in 1977 Jack Klugman caused a minor stir among television writers when he complained publicly of the dearth of high-quality scripts (Klugman himself had done some writing for TV, which included at least one episode of *Kraft Television Theatre*). During the show's latter years, Quincy became involved with a number of issues, such as illiteracy, that had little to do with forensic medicine; every program seemed designed to give Quincy the opportunity to crusade against some societal evil. For the series's final season, Quincy found a new romantic interest. Anita Gillette joined the cast as Dr. W. Emily Hanover, a psychiatrist; she and Quincy were married on 23 February 1983 (Gillette had played Quincy's first wife in a 1979 flashback episode). Though Quincy's first name was never divulged on the show, a closeup of his business card in one episode revealed that his first initial was "R."

THE QUIZ KIDS   NBC/CBS

6 JULY 1949–2 NOVEMBER 1951 (NBC); 7 JULY 1952–18 AUGUST 1952 (NBC); 17
JANUARY 1953–8 NOVEMBER 1953 (CBS); 12 JANUARY 1956–27 SEPTEMBER 1956 (CBS)
The Quiz Kids began on radio in 1940 and ran for thirteen years. Originating from
Chicago, it featured a panel of five child prodigies who fielded questions submitted
by viewers; the ages of the panelists usually ranged from six to sixteen, and three or
four youngsters generally stayed on the show for weeks or months (the fifth seat was
occupied by a guest child). Joe Kelly, who hosted the radio version, was also the first
host on television; he was succeeded by Clifton Fadiman. Packaged by Lou Cowan,
the prime-time game show was produced by Rachael Stevenson.

THE QUIZ KIDS CHALLENGE   SYNDICATED

1990–1991   Jonathan Prince hosted this daily game show on which teams of three
youngsters faced a squad of three adults, competing for cash by answering questions
in various categories.

QUIZZING THE NEWS   ABC

11 AUGUST 1948–5 MARCH 1949   One of ABC's first network programs, *Quizzing the
News* was a prime-time game show on which a celebrity panel tried to guess a topical
news story from cartoons. Allen Prescott was the host and Robert Brenner the
producer.

THE RCA VICTOR SHOW

See THE DENNIS DAY SHOW; THE EZIO PINZA SHOW

R.C.M.P.   SYNDICATED

1960   This Canadian crime show centered on the Royal Canadian Mounted Police.
Featured were Gilles Pelletier as Corporal Jacques Gagnier; Don Francks as Constable Bill Mitchell; and John Perkins as Constable Frank Scott. The action took place
in the community of Shamattawa somewhere in the Canadian Northwest. The show's
producers proudly boasted that the series was actually endorsed by the real R.C.M.P.

R.F.D. AMERICA   NBC

26 MAY 1949–15 SEPTEMBER 1949   Chicago-based educational series on farming and
gardening, hosted by Bob Murphy.

THE RACERS   SYNDICATED

1976–1977   Half-hour filmed series on auto racing, narrated by Curt Gowdy.

RACHEL GUNN, R. N.   FOX

28 JUNE 1992–4 SEPTEMBER 1992   Half-hour sitcom set at a Nebraska hospital. With
Christine Ebersole as acid-tongued head nurse Rachel Gunn; Kevin Conroy as Dr.
David Dunkel, a newly divorced numbskull who rented out half of Rachel's duplex;
Megan Mullally as nurse Becky Jo; Bryan Brightcloud as nurse Zac, a Native American; Lois Foraker as Jeanette, a dietician with a fondness for snacks; Dan Tullis, Jr.,
as orderly Dane Grey; and Kathleen Mitchell as Sister Joan, a nun who volunteered
at the hospital. Katherine Green created the series.

RACKET SQUAD   SYNDICATED/CBS

1950 (SYNDICATED); 7 JUNE 1951–28 SEPTEMBER 1953 (CBS)   One of television's
first classic crime shows, *Racket Squad* starred Reed Hadley as Captain John
Braddock, tireless investigator for San Francisco's Racket Squad, who tracked down
a wide variety of flimflammers and con artists. The half-hour show was produced by
Hal Roach, Jr., and Carroll Case and directed by Jim Tinling.

RAFFERTY   CBS

5 SEPTEMBER 1977–28 NOVEMBER 1977   One of the early casualties of the 1977–1978
season, *Rafferty* was an hour-long medical drama starring Patrick McGoohan as
flinty Dr. Sidney Rafferty, a general practitioner with a gift for diagnosis. Also

featured were Millie Slavin as Vera Wales, his receptionist; John Getz as Dr. Daniel Gentry, his young associate. Created by James Lee, the show was produced by Norman S. Powell and Robert Van Scoyk; Jerry Thorpe was executive producer.

RAGS TO RICHES   NBC
9 MARCH 1987–15 JANUARY 1988; 3 JULY 1988–11 SEPTEMBER 1988   An unusual comedy-drama with music, *Rags to Riches* was set in 1961. It told the tale of a swinging millionaire who, eager to impress a client, took in a group of orphaned girls. The cast included Joseph Bologna as wealthy Nick Foley; Kimiko Gelman as Rose, the Asian girl; Tisha Campbell as Marva, the black girl; Bridget Michele as Diane, the blonde girl; Blanca DeGarr as Patti, the tomboy; Heidi Zeigler as Mickey, the little one; and Douglas Seale as Nick's British butler, John Clapper. Most episodes featured elaborate musical numbers, with contemporary lyrics added to classic sixties rock melodies.

RAISING MIRANDA   CBS
5 NOVEMBER 1988–31 DECEMBER 1988   Racine, Wisconsin, was the scene of this domestic sitcom. With James Naughton as contractor Donald Marshak, whose wife had walked out after attending a self-improvement class, leaving him to care for their teenage daughter; Royana Black as the daughter, Miranda Marshak; Steve Vinovich and Miriam Flynn as neighbors Bob and Joan Hoodenpyle; Bryan Cranston as unemployed Uncle Russell; and Amy Lynne as Marcine, Miranda's best friend. Curiously, CBS had introduced another sitcom, *First Impressions,* earlier in the fall on the same evening (Saturday), with an almost identical format.

RAMAR OF THE JUNGLE   SYNDICATED
1952–1953   Jon Hall starred in this widely syndicated children's adventure series as Dr. Tom Reynolds, a physician and scientist who worked in the "jungles" of Kenya and India, where he was known to the local folk as "Ramar." Also featured were Ray Montgomery as his colleague, Professor Howard Ogden; James Fairfax; and M'Lisa McClure. Victor Millan appeared as Zahir, Ramar's guide while in India. Harry S. Rothschild and Leon Fromkess produced the series.

RAMBO   SYNDICATED
1986   Half-hour cartoon series based on the character created by Sylvester Stallone in the 1982 movie *First Blood* and two sequels.

THE RAMONA STORIES   PBS
10 SEPTEMBER 1988–21 JANUARY 1989   Half-hour comedy-drama series for children, based on the popular books by Beverly Cleary about an eight-year-old girl and her family. With Sarah Polley as Ramona Quimby; Lori Chodos as her older sister, Beatrice ("Beezus"); Barry Flatman as their father, Bob; and Lynda Mason Green as their mother, Dory.

RANCH PARTY   SYNDICATED
1958   Regulars on this half-hour country-and-western music series included host Tex Ritter, Bonnie Guitar, Johnny Cash, Tex Williams, Bobby Helms, Ray Price, and Smiley Burnette.

THE RANGE RIDER   SYNDICATED
1951–1953   Aimed principally at children, this half-hour western starred Jock Mahoney as The Range Rider, a wandering good guy, and Dick Jones as his youthful sidekick, Dick West. The series was produced by Louis Gray for Gene Autry's Flying A Productions.

RANGO   ABC
13 JANUARY 1967–1 SEPTEMBER 1967   Comedy-western with Tim Conway as Rango, an inept Texas Ranger; Norman Alden as Captain Horton, his commanding officer; and Guy Marks as Pink Cloud, his Indian scout.

THE RANSOM SHERMAN SHOW   NBC
3 JULY 1950–25 AUGUST 1950   A summer replacement for *Kukla, Fran and Ollie*, this half-hour musical variety show was hosted by Ransom Sherman and featured singers Nancy Wright and Johnny Bradford.

THE RAT PATROL   ABC
12 SEPTEMBER 1966–16 SEPTEMBER 1968   One of the several World War II dramas of the 1960s, *The Rat Patrol* lasted two seasons. Created by Tom Gries, the series was based on the exploits of a British armored car outfit known as the Long Range Desert Group, which harassed Rommel's Afrika Korps during the war. On television, the unit became an American squad, featuring Christopher George as Sergeant Sam Troy; Gary Raymond as Sergeant Jack Moffitt; Lawrence Casey as Private Mark Hitchcock; Justin Tarr as Private Tully Pettigrew; and Hans Gudegast as Captain Hans Dietrich of the Afrika Korps (Gudegast later changed his name to Eric Braeden). The first few episodes were filmed in Spain; despite production difficulties, the show was one of the more popular new series of the 1966–1967 season and was renewed. Stanley Shpetner was the first producer of the half-hour series but was replaced by Lee Rich.

RAVEN   CBS
24 JUNE 1992–3 OCTOBER 1992; 2 JANUARY 1993–17 APRIL 1993   Hour adventure series about a former ninja fighter who teamed up with a former special forces agent. With Jeffrey Meek as Jonathon Raven, a westerner who had grown up in Japan and was now being chased by the Black Dragons while he searched for his missing son; Lee Majors as Herman "Ski" Jablonski, who had served with Raven in the U. S. Army Special Forces and who was now a private eye; and Andy Bumatai as their assistant, B. K.

RAWHIDE   CBS
9 JANUARY 1959–4 JANUARY 1966   *Rawhide*, like *Wagon Train*, was a western on the move; *Rawhide's* passengers, however, were cattle, as the theme of the show was the long drive from North Texas to Sedalia, Kansas. Featured on the hour show were: Eric Fleming (1959–1965) as Gil Favor, the trail boss; Clint Eastwood as Rowdy Yates, the ramrod (Eastwood, one of the few regulars to remain with the show for its entire run, became the trail boss in the fall of 1965 when Fleming left the show); Jim Murdock (1959–1965) as Mushy; Paul Brinegar as Wishbone, the cook; Steve Raines as Quince; Rocky Shahan (1959–1965) as Joe Scarlett; Sheb Wooley (1961–1965) as scout Pete Nolan; Robert Cabal (1962–1965) as Hey Soos (pronounced and spelled "Hey Soos," the character's Spanish name was undoubtedly Jesus); John Ireland (1965–1966) as Jed Colby; David Watson (1965–1966) as Ian Cabot; Raymond St. Jacques (1965–1966) as Simon Blake (St. Jacques thereby became the first black actor to be regularly featured on a western series). *Rawhide's* producers and executive producers seemed to change even more often than the cast. The succession of executives included Charles Marquis Warren, who created the series, and was succeeded in 1961 by Endre Bohem; Bohem was replaced a year later by Vincent Fennelly, who was subsequently replaced by Bernard Kowalski and Bruce Geller. Endre Bohem then returned, only to be succeeded by Ben Brady.

THE RAY ANTHONY SHOW   SYNDICATED/ABC
1956 (SYNDICATED); 12 OCTOBER 1956–3 MAY 1957 (ABC); 1969 (SYNDICATED)
Bandleader Ray Anthony formed his own group in the mid-1940s and made records throughout the 1950s. His first television program was a summer replacement for *The Perry Como Show:* see *TV's Top Tunes.* In 1956 he hosted his own syndicated series, which was later picked up by ABC; it featured the Four Freshmen, Don Durant, Med Flory, and football coach Frank Leahy. Anthony's then wife, actress Mamie Van Doren, also appeared occasionally. In 1969 he hosted a second musical variety series, also titled *The Ray Anthony Show.* It featured singer Vikki Carr.

THE RAY BRADBURY THEATER   HBO/USA

1985–1987 (HBO); 17 OCTOBER 1987–11 SEPTEMBER 1992 (USA)   Half-hour sci-fi anthology series, hosted by science fiction writer Ray Bradbury. Many of the episodes were adaptations of Bradbury stories.

THE RAY BOLGER SHOW   ABC

8 OCTOBER 1953–10 JUNE 1955   *The Ray Bolger Show*, which was originally entitled *Where's Raymond*, was a situation comedy with plenty of song and dance thrown in; this format enabled Ray Bolger to play himself—Bolger starred as Ray Wallace, a Broadway star living in suburbia. The 1953–1954 cast included Richard Erdman as Pete Morrisey, his landlord, along with Allyn Joslyn, Claire Dubrey, Frances Karath, and Betty Lynn. The 1954–1955 cast included Richard Erdman and several new faces: Marjie Millar as Susan, an aspiring writer from Iowa who became Ray's girlfriend; Charles Cantor as Ray's pal Artie Herman; Christine Nelson as Katy Jones; Sylvia Lewis; and Maureen Stephenson. Jerry Bresler produced the series, and Marc Daniels directed it.

THE RAY MILLAND SHOW   CBS

17 SEPTEMBER 1953–30 SEPTEMBER 1955   This half-hour sitcom premiered in the fall of 1953 under the title *Meet Mr. McNutley;* it starred Ray Milland as Ray McNutley, eccentric professor at Lynnhaven, a women's college, and Phyllis Avery as Peggy McNutley, his down-to-earth wife. Also featured were Minerva Urecal as Dean Bradley, Lynnhaven's formidable head; Gordon Jones as Pete Thompson; and Jacqueline DeWitt as Pete's wife, Ruth Thompson. After a summer hiatus, the show returned with a slightly changed format and a new title: *The Ray Milland Show.* Milland now played Ray McNulty, a somewhat less eccentric professor who taught at Comstock College (the show was subtitled *Meet Mr. McNulty*). Phyllis Avery was again featured as his wife, Peggy McNulty, but her character became more wacky to counterbalance Ray's shift in character. Lloyd Corrigan rounded out the cast as Dean Dodsworth, Comstock's head. A total of eighty half-hours were filmed for Revue Studios; Joe Connelly and Bob Mosher wrote and produced the series.

THE RAY STEVENS SHOW   NBC

20 JUNE 1970–8 AUGUST 1970   A summer replacement for *The Andy Williams Show,* this hour-long musical variety series was taped in Toronto and hosted by Ray Stevens, who during the 1960s, had recorded several popular novelty records, such as "Ahab the Arab," "Harry the Hairy Ape," and "Gitarzan." Also on hand were British pop star Lulu, American singer Cass Elliott (formerly of The Mamas and the Papas), Steve Martin, Billy Van, Dick Curtis, Carol Robinson, and Solari & Carr.

REACH FOR THE STARS   NBC

2 JANUARY 1967–31 MARCH 1967   Bill Mazer hosted this short-lived daytime game show, on which contestants were required to answer questions and to perform stunts.

READING OUT LOUD   SYNDICATED

1960   Famous people read literature to children on this Westinghouse series.

READING RAINBOW   PBS

1983–   LeVar Burton hosted this half-hour educational series, which was designed to encourage children to read more. The show consisted of stories adapted from books written for children, book reports (delivered by youngsters), and filmed inserts.

READING ROOM   CBS

22 SEPTEMBER 1962–16 MARCH 1963   Saturday-afternoon educational show for children, on which a panel of youngsters each week discussed a book with its author. Ned Hoopes was the host and moderator.

THE REAL GHOSTBUSTERS   ABC

13 SEPTEMBER 1986–3 SEPTEMBER 1988

SLIMER! AND THE REAL GHOSTBUSTERS   ABC

10 SEPTEMBER 1988–5 SEPTEMBER 1992   A popular Saturday-morning cartoon show
from Columbia Pictures, based on the characters from the blockbuster 1984 film,
Ghostbusters. The main characters—Peter, Ray, Egon, and Winston—and their ecto-
plasmic pet, Slimer, did battle against all sorts of mysterious apparitions. After two
seasons in a half-hour format, the show expanded to a full hour and Slimer sometimes
starred in separate stories. In 1991 the show reverted to a half-hour format. The series
should not be confused with another 1986 cartoon series titled *Ghostbusters* (see also
that title).

REAL LIFE WITH JANE PAULEY   NBC

17 JULY 1990–4 SEPTEMBER 1990; 6 JANUARY 1991–1 NOVEMBER 1991   Seven months
after leaving the *Today* show, Jane Pauley hosted her first regular series of prime-time
programs. The limited run summer series focused on American lifestyles. In addition
to Pauley, contributors included Boyd Matson (who filed reports from the road),
Marjorie Margolis, Keith Morrison, Ann Rubenstein, and Bill Schechner. The series
was seen in an hour format during its summer 1990 tryout. When it returned to
NBC's schedule in 1991, it was broadcast in a half-hour format most weeks; approximately once a month it expanded to an hour, filling the half-hour usually occupied by
Exposé, NBC's new news program.

THE REAL McCOYS   ABC/CBS

3 OCTOBER 1957–20 SEPTEMBER 1962 (ABC); 30 SEPTEMBER 1962–22 SEPTEMBER 1963
(CBS)   *The Real McCoys* was TV's first successful rural sitcom, antedating *The
Andy Griffith Show* and *The Beverly Hillbillies* by several seasons; during its five
seasons on ABC it was one of the network's most popular programs, ranking as high
as fifth in the Nielsen seasonal averages for the 1960–1961 season. Featured were:
Walter Brennan as Grandpa Amos McCoy, the head of the family, all of whom lived
in rural northern California; Richard Crenna as his grandson, Luke McCoy; Kathy
Nolan (1957–1962) as Luke's wife, Kate (called "Sugar Babe" by Luke); Michael
Winkelman as Little Luke McCoy, an orphaned grandson of Amos; Lydia Reed as
Hassie, Little Luke's older sister; Tony Martinez as Pepino Garcia, the McCoys'
hired hand; Andy Clyde as George MacMichael, Amos's sometime friend and occa-
sional enemy; and Madge Blake as Flora MacMichael, George's sister. Kathy Nolan
left the series at the end of the 1961–1962 season. *The Real McCoys* moved from
ABC to CBS for the following season, during which Luke McCoy was a widower.
Janet DeGore joined the cast in January 1963 as the McCoys' neighbor, a young
widow named Louise Howard, and Butch Patrick appeared as her son, Greg. Joan
Blondell joined a month later as Louise's aunt, Winifred Jordan, who tried to match
Luke up with Louise. Irving Pincus was the executive producer of the series, and
Danny Arnold was the producer.

REAL PEOPLE   NBC

18 APRIL 1979–23 MAY 1979; 25 JULY 1979–4 JULY 1984   Introduced as a short-flight
series in the spring of 1979, *Real People* earned a place on NBC's fall schedule. The
hour show was part live and part videotape and emphasized light features on non-
celebrities. The original hosts included Fred Willard, Sarah Purcell, John Barbour,
Skip Stephenson, and Bill Rafferty. In the fall of 1979 the group included Purcell,
Barbour, Stephenson, Rafferty, and Byron Allen. Byron Allen ceased appearing as a
regular from 1981 to 1983 though he was featured as an occasional correspondent.
John Barbour left the show in the spring of 1982. Fred Willard returned for the 1981–
1982 and 1982–1983 seasons. Newcomer Peter Billingsley was added in the fall of
1981, Kerry Millerick in the fall of 1982, and David Ruprecht in the fall of 1983.
George Schlatter was the executive producer. Purcell and Willard cohosted "Real
People Reunion" (1 October 1991, NBC), a one-hour combination of highlights and
new features.

REAL STORIES OF THE HIGHWAY PATROL SYNDICATED
1993–   Not to be confused with *Highway Patrol*, the fictional syndicated staple of 1950s television, this half-hour daily series was a reality-based program depicting the work of highway patrol officers. Hosted by California Highway Commissioner Maury Hannigan, the series used videotapes of actual incidents as well as re-enactments.

THE REAL WORLD MTV
21 MAY 1992–   An unusual reality series reminiscent of PBS's *An American Family*, *The Real World* took a group of seven young adults, gave them a place to live, videotaped their interactions, and televised the edited results in thirteen-week segments. Each season focused on a new group (selected from among thousands of hopefuls), housed in a new city. The 1992 crew lived in a Manhattan loft, and the seven residents were known only by their first names: Julie, 19, a dancer; Eric, 20, a model; Kevin, 25, a writer; Rebecca, 24, a singer; Norman, 24, an artist; Andre, 21, a rocker; and Heather, 21, a rapper. Eric remained at MTV that fall. Now using his full name—Eric Nies—he hosted a dance series, *The Grind*.
   The Real World of 1993 housed its group at the beach in Venice, California: Beth S., an actress; Dominic, from Ireland; Irene, a deputy marshal; Jon, a virgin from Kentucky; Tami, a singer; Aaron, a surfer; and Dave, a comic who was ejected from the house (and the series) after pulling a blanket off a half-naked Tami. After Dave's departure Glen moved in, as did Beth A.
   The 1994 edition of the series placed its unusually diverse septet in San Francisco: Cory Murphy, Judd Winick, Mohammed Bilal, Pam Ling, Pedro Zamora, David Rainey (better known as Puck), and Rachel Campos. The hygienically challenged Puck, who worked as a bicycle messenger, so alienated his housemates that they voted to eject him after a few weeks. He was replaced by Joanna Rhodes, who had formerly lived in England. Zamora, who had revealed to the others that he was HIV-positive, died of AIDS in November 1994, a few days after the last telecast of that season's programs.
   The 1995 edition brought an international group together in a large house in London: Kat, a nineteen-year-old American fencer; Jay, a playwright, also a nineteen-year-old American; Mike, a twenty-one-year-old American who liked to race autos; Sharon, a twenty-year-old English singer and songwriter; Neil, a twenty-four-year-old English rocker; Jacinda, a twenty-two-year-old Australian model; and Lars, a twenty-four-year-old German, an aspiring deejay.
   The series was created by Mary-Ellis Bunim and Jon Murray.

REALITIES PBS
5 OCTOBER 1970–20 SEPTEMBER 1971   Umbrella title for a series of independently produced documentaries.

REALLY WILD ANIMALS CBS
16 SEPTEMBER 1995–   Half-hour Saturday series of wildlife films, produced by National Geographic. The show was hosted and narrated by an animated globe named Spin, whose voice was supplied by Dudley Moore.

REASONABLE DOUBTS NBC
26 SEPTEMBER 1991–31 JULY 1993   Marlee Matlin made history as the first deaf performer to star in a television series. She played Tess Kaufman, a Chicago assistant district attorney. Mark Harmon costarred as Detective Richard "Dicky" Cobb, who was her investigator and (because he knew American Sign Language) translator. Also featured were Nancy Everhard as Dicky's girlfriend, Kay Lockman; William Converse-Roberts as Tess's boss, division chief Arthur Gold; Tim Grimm (1991–1992) as Tess's estranged husband, Bruce; Kay Lenz (1992–1993) as attorney Maggie Zombro; Vanessa Angel (1992–1993) as Officer Peggy Eliot; and Jim Pirri (1992–1993) as Tess's boyfriend, Asher. Robert Singer created the series.

THE REASONER REPORT   ABC

24 FEBRUARY 1973–28 JUNE 1975   ABC newsman Harry Reasoner hosted this news analysis and commentary program, seen on weekends. Albert T. Primo was executive producer for ABC News.

THE REBEL   ABC

4 OCTOBER 1959–17 SEPTEMBER 1961   This half-hour western was billed as more cerebral than most, but whether it really was more intellectual was a matter of opinion. Nick Adams starred as Johnny Yuma, a former Confederate soldier who "roamed through the West," presumably searching for an inner peace. *The Rebel*'s familiar theme song was sung by Johnny Cash. The show was produced by Goodson-Todman Productions (one of the few nongame shows produced by that outfit) in association with Celestial Productions and Fen-Ker-Ada Productions.

REBOOT   ABC

10 SEPTEMBER 1994–   Innovative Saturday morning cartoon series which utilized computer-generated animation techniques. The series was set inside a computer, where the hero, Bob, and his pals Enzo and Dot, battled the evil virus MegaByte and his sidekicks Hack and Slash. The series expanded from thirty to sixty minutes for a few weeks during the summer of 1995.

REBOP   PBS

1976–1979   A half-hour series aimed at preteenagers, *Rebop* consisted mainly of filmed segments about children of many different cultural and ethnic backgrounds. Topper Carew was executive producer for WGBH-TV, Boston. LeVar Burton, star of *Roots*, became the host in the fall of 1978.

REBOUND   ABC/DUMONT

8 FEBRUARY 1952–30 MAY 1952 (ABC); 5 DECEMBER 1952–16 JANUARY 1953 (DUMONT)   An undistinguished half-hour dramatic anthology series. Lee Marvin played his first major TV dramatic role on one episode, "The Mine," aired 29 February.

THE REBUS GAME   ABC

29 MARCH 1965–24 SEPTEMBER 1965   Jack Linkletter hosted this daytime game show, which featured two two-member teams. The object of the game was for one player to guess a word or phrase from drawings sketched by his or her partner.

REBUTTAL   CBS

12 JUNE 1960–4 SEPTEMBER 1960   Sunday-afternoon series of debates between teams from colleges and universities, moderated by Jack Kennedy.

RED BARBER'S CLUB HOUSE   CBS

2 JULY 1949–18 FEBRUARY 1950; 12 SEPTEMBER 1953–12 DECEMBER 1953   This Saturday-evening sports show was hosted by veteran sportscaster Red Barber; produced by John Peyser and John Derr, the show was simulcast on radio in 1950. The 1953 show, titled *Peak of the Sports News,* was seen Saturday evenings.

THE RED BUTTONS SHOW   CBS/NBC

14 OCTOBER 1952–14 JUNE 1954 (CBS); 1 OCTOBER 1954–27 MAY 1955 (NBC) Though it is scarcely recalled today, *The Red Buttons Show* was hailed almost universally as the most promising new show of the 1952–1953 season (Buttons even appeared on the cover of *Time* magazine that season). But by the end of its second season, after several changes in format and writers, the show's popularity had sagged considerably, and it was dropped by CBS. NBC picked up the show for the 1954–1955 season (where it was slated on Friday nights, with *The Jack Carson Show* occupying the slot approximately every fourth week), but it did even less well. Buttons had had considerable experience as a burlesque comedian, and his show began as a comedy-variety show; it was introduced by his familiar theme song, "The Ho Ho Song." The half-

hour series was produced by Jess Kimmell and directed by Peter Kass. Other regulars included Dorothy Joliffe (who often played his wife in sketches), Joe Silver, Jeanne Carson, Sara Seegar, Jimmy Little, Ralph Stanley, Sammy Birch, and the Elliott Lawrence Orchestra. By the end of the 1953–1954 season, however, the show had become a situation comedy and remained a sitcom when it switched networks that fall. In the new format Buttons played himself, a television comedian, and Phyllis Kirk played his wife; Paul Lynde, a newcomer to TV, was also featured as a network vice president. After the demise of his series, Buttons continued to appear in dramatic roles on television and on film, winning an Academy Award in 1957 for his performance in *Sayonara*. Buttons later starred in a 1966 sitcom: see *The Double Life of Henry Phyfe*.

THE RED HAND GANG NBC
10 SEPTEMBER 1977–21 JANUARY 1978   Five juvenile detectives were the central characters in this live-action Saturday-morning show. Featured were Matthew Laborteaux as Frankie; J. R. Miller as J. R.; Jolie Newman as Joanne; James Bond as Doc; and Johnny Brogna as Li'l Bill.

THE RED ROWE SHOW CBS
16 NOVEMBER 1959–8 JULY 1960   Red Rowe hosted a daytime variety series of little note, which featured Bill Cunningham and Peggy Taylor.

RED SHOE DIARIES SHO
27 JUNE 1992–   Erotic tales, many directed by Zalman King, were the grist of this occasionally scheduled anthology series. The series was preceded by a made-for-TV movie of the same title, which aired on Showtime 16 May 1992.

THE RED SKELTON SHOW NBC/CBS
30 SEPTEMBER 1951–21 JUNE 1953 (NBC); 22 SEPTEMBER 1953–23 JUNE 1970 (CBS); 14 SEPTEMBER 1970–29 AUGUST 1971 (NBC)   One of television's most popular comedians, Red Skelton hosted his own series for twenty years, seventeen of them on CBS. Active in show business from boyhood, Skelton had extensive experience in vaudeville before he began his own radio series in 1941. On that show, which lasted until 1953, Skelton developed most of the characters that he would later bring to television— Junior (the Mean Widdle Kid), Freddie the Freeloader, Clem Kadiddlehopper, George Appleby, Sheriff Deadeye, Willy Lump Lump, Cauliflower McPugg, Cookie the Sailor, San Fernando Red, Bolivar Shagnasty, and others. As Skelton's real comedic talents were in the realm of pantomime, pratfalls, and sight gags, his television series proved to be even more popular than the radio show had been—unlike many other radio comedians, Skelton was able to bring something more to television than his voice. Skelton's first NBC series, which he produced with Freeman Keyes, was a half-hour program seen on Sunday evenings; it also featured Lucy Knoch, and ranked fourth overall that year, just behind *I Love Lucy*. In the fall of 1953 Skelton moved to a Tuesday-night slot on CBS, where he remained until 1970. The CBS show, which expanded to an hour in the fall of 1962, cracked Nielsen's Top Twenty in its third season and remained there until its cancellation (*The Red Skelton Hour* ranked seventh in its final year on CBS, but, because of rising production costs, had become only marginally profitable to the network). One of Skelton's writers in the early seasons on CBS was Johnny Carson; Carson unexpectedly got a big break one day in 1954, when he was summoned on a few hours' notice to fill in for Skelton, who had knocked himself unconscious during rehearsal. Carson, whose previous on-camera experience had been limited to a local show and a summertime game show, performed admirably and was given his own show by CBS in 1955. Skelton, an inveterate ad-libber, delighted in breaking up his guest stars, and very few comedy sketches appeared to have been performed precisely as written. Musical groups were also featured on the series; the Rolling Stones made one of their earliest American television appearances on 22 September 1964. Skelton's final series, on NBC, was a half-hour comedy-variety show with a large cast of regulars, including Jan Arvan, Elsie Baker, Jackson Bostwick, Yvonne Ewald, Chanin Hale, Dorothy Love, John Magruder, Ida Mae McKenzie,

Janos Prohaska, Peggy Rea, Mike Wagner, and the Burgundy Street Singers. The David Rose Orchestra was long associated with Skelton's shows. Vice President Spiro Agnew appeared on the 1970 premiere of the series.

THE REDD FOXX COMEDY HOUR   ABC
15 SEPTEMBER 1977–26 JANUARY 1978   Redd Foxx left *Sanford and Son* to star in his own hour comedy-variety show. The series had a few bright moments but was generally uneven and was dropped in midseason. Regulars included Slappy White, Damita Jo, LaWanda Page, Hal Smith, Billy Barty, Bill Saluga (as Raymond J. Johnson), and "Iron Jaw" Wilson. Redd Foxx was the executive producer, Allan Blye and Bob Einstein the producers.

THE REDD FOXX SHOW   ABC
18 JANUARY 1986–19 APRIL 1986   This half-hour sitcom changed formats slightly during its twelve-episode run. It starred Redd Foxx as Al Hughes, who ran a coffee shop/newsstand in New York City. (Foxx, who chose characters' names from his own past in his TV series, selected the name of an uncle this time.) Originally, Hughes was a widower who agreed to become a foster parent to a teenaged white girl. Pamela Segall played his ward, Toni Rutledge. After a few weeks, however, Hughes suddenly acquired an ex-wife, and his foster daughter was dropped from the cast. (ABC claimed that research studies showed that Foxx's fans "preferred him grumpier"). Beverly Todd joined the cast in March as Felicia, Al's ex, as did Sinbad as Al's son, Byron. Other regulars were Rosana DeSoto as waitress Diana Olmos; Barry Van Dyke as Sergeant Dwight Stryker, a cop; Nathaniel Taylor and Teddy Wilson as Jim-Jam; and Ursaline Bryant as Darice.

REDIGO
See EMPIRE

THE REEL GAME   ABC
18 JANUARY 1971–3 MAY 1971   Jack Barry hosted this prime-time game show on which three contestants competed. The questions concerned famous people and events, and the answers were "verified" by showing newsreel or other documentary film footage.

REGGIE   ABC
2 AUGUST 1983–1 SEPTEMBER 1983   This half-hour sitcom was based on a British series, *The Fall and Rise of Reginald Perrin*. The American version starred Richard Mulligan as Reggie Potter, an advertising executive at a dessert company who tried to cope with middle age. Other regulars included Barbara Barrie as his patient wife, Elizabeth; Timothy Busfield as their son, Mark, an aspiring actor; Dianne Kay as their daughter, Linda; Timothy Stack as Linda's boring husband, Tom; Jean Smart as Reggie's secretary, Joan; and Chip Zien as Reggie's high-powered young boss, C. J. The show made frequent use of intercuts in which Reggie acted out his fantasies.

THE REGIS PHILBIN SHOW   SYNDICATED
1964–1965   Regis Philbin succeeded Steve Allen as host of Westinghouse's syndicated ninety-minute talk show. Philbin had earlier hosted *Philbin's People,* a talk show telecast in New York and Los Angeles, and later became Joey Bishop's sidekick on *The Joey Bishop Show.*

THE REGIS PHILBIN SHOW   NBC
30 NOVEMBER 1981–9 APRIL 1982   Half-hour daytime talk show, hosted by Regis Philbin; Philbin was joined by a celebrity cohost each week until late fall, when Mary Hart became the permanent cohost.

REGIS PHILBIN'S LIFESTYLES   LIFETIME
1982–1988   Weekday talk show hosted by Regis Philbin. Known in its early years as *Health Styles,* it featured segments on health, fitness, and cooking.

THE RELUCTANT DRAGON AND MR. TOAD   ABC

12 SEPTEMBER 1970–17 SEPTEMBER 1972   Weekend cartoon series based loosely on
The Wind in the Willows. The Reluctant Dragon was named Tobias and was featured
in one segment, while Mr. Toad was the main character in his own segment. Both
creatures were originally featured in stories by Kenneth Grahame.

REMEMBER THIS DATE   NBC

14 NOVEMBER 1950–28 JUNE 1951   Bill Stern hosted this audience participation game
show, which was seen Tuesday and Thursday afternoons.

REMINGTON STEELE   NBC

1 OCTOBER 1982–2 AUGUST 1986; 5 JANUARY 1987–9 MARCH 1987   Stephanie
Zimbalist (daughter of Efrem Zimbalist, Jr.) starred in this hour crime show as Laura
Holt, a private detective who had attracted very little business operating under her
own name; things began to improve after she set up an agency under the name
Remington Steele (Holt was always able to convince clients that the fictitious Steele
was out of the office or on assignment). Shortly thereafter, a mysterious man showed
up, claiming to be the real Remington Steele, and the two joined forces. Pierce
Brosnan costarred as the debonair Steele. Also featured during the first season were
James Read as Holt's assistant, Murphy Michaels, and Janet DeMay as the secretary,
Bernice Fox. Read and DeMay were dropped in 1983, and Doris Roberts joined the
cast as Mildred Krebs, an IRS agent who was trailing Steele but who later decided to
work for Steele and Holt. Meanwhile, over the course of the series' run, Holt and
Steele found themselves attracted to each other and gradually fell in love. Holt
married Steele at the end of the 1985–1986 season in order to keep him from being
deported, and the two finally consummated their relationship during the show's all
too brief final season, which consisted of only five telecasts: two two-hour movies, a
third movie shown in two weekly installments, and a rerun.

REMOTE CONTROL   MTV/SYNDICATED

7 DECEMBER 1987–2 MARCH 1990 (MTV); 1989–1990 (SYNDICATED)   An irreverent game show, *Remote Control* started on MTV before being offered in national
syndication. It was a quiz show for the young; almost all of the questions were about
television and pop music. Ken Ober was the host, Colin Quinn his not-so-genial
sidekick; Marisol Massey (1987–1988), Kari Wuhrer, and Steve Trecasse also helped
out. The show's set was the basement of Ober's parents' house at 72 Whooping
Cough Lane in suburbia. Each day three contestants competed, securely strapped
into naugahyde chairs with bowls of popcorn in front of them. Losers were unceremoniously whisked offstage while still in their chairs.

THE REN & STIMPY SHOW   NICK

11 AUGUST 1991–   Ostensibly intended for children, this cartoon series soon found
its audience among young adults. The title characters were a chihuahua named Ren
and a cat named Stimpy, whose interest in matters crude and scatalogical was rivaled
only by that of Beavis and Butt-head. John Kricfalusi created the series and served as
its first producer; he was demoted to creative consultant in 1992 because of delays in
the production of new episodes.

RENDEZVOUS   ABC

13 FEBRUARY 1952–5 MARCH 1952   Ilona Massey starred in this half-hour adventure
series as the owner of a nightclub in Nazi-occupied Paris during World War II.

RENDEZVOUS   SYNDICATED

1958   Charles Drake hosted this half-hour dramatic anthology series.

RENDEZVOUS WITH MUSIC   NBC

11 JULY 1950–8 AUGUST 1950   Half-hour musical series featuring Carol Reed, Don
Gallagher, and the Tony DeSimone Trio. See also *Melody, Harmony & Rhythm*.

RENEGADE   SYNDICATED

1992–   This hour adventure series from Stephen J. Cannell Productions starred
Lorenzo Lamas as Reno Raines, a police officer who was framed for murder after
uncovering corruption in the force; now on the run, he helped out people in distress
while trying to clear his name and nail his framers. Also featured were Branscombe
Richmond as Bobby Sixkiller and Kathleen Kinmont as Bobby's stepsister, Cheyenne Phillips, who had been dispatched to kill Raines but eventually joined forces
with him. Stephen J. Cannell appeared occasionally as Lieutenant Donald "Dutch"
Dickerson, the bad cop who was trying to catch Raines. Lorenzo Lamas was married
to costar Kathleen Kinmont when production began in 1992; they continued to work
together even after their marriage ended.

THE RENEGADES   ABC

4 MARCH 1983–8 APRIL 1983   Based on a 1982 made-for-TV movie, this hour crime
show was reminiscent of *The Mod Squad*. Here, the members of a youth gang agreed
to become "special deputies" to assist the Los Angeles Police. With Patrick Swayze
as Bandit; Randy Brooks as Eagle; Paul Mones as J.T.; Tracy Scoggins as Tracy;
Robert Thaler as Dancer; Brian Tochi as Dragon; Fausto Bara as Gaucho; Kurtwood
Smith as Captain Sheridan; and James Luisi as their liaison, Lieutenant Marciano.
The Renegades was the lowest-rated prime-time dramatic series of the 1982–1983
season; only NBC's newsmagazine show, *Monitor,* finished lower.

REPORT CARD FOR PARENTS   DUMONT

1 DECEMBER 1952–2 FEBRUARY 1953   Half-hour prime-time discussion show on child
behavior and education.

REPORT TO MURPHY   CBS

5 APRIL 1982–31 MAY 1982   Half-hour sitcom starring Michael Keaton as Eddie
Murphy, an idealistic young parole officer working in a large city. Joining him were
Olivia Cole as his supervisor, Blanche; Donna Ponterotto as Lucy; Donnelly Rhodes
as Charlie; and Peter Jurasik as Vernon Culley, an officer from the Internal Affairs
Department who usually hassled Murphy.

THE REPORTER   CBS

25 SEPTEMBER 1964–18 DECEMBER 1964   The *New York Globe* was the setting for this
hour-long dramatic series. Featured were Harry Guardino as reporter Danny Taylor;
Gary Merrill as city editor Lou Sheldon; George O'Hanlon as Danny's pal, cabbie
Artie Burns; and Remo Pisani as bartender Ike Dawson. Created by Jerome
Weidman, the series was developed by Keefe Brasselle.

THE REPORTERS   FOX

30 JULY 1988–31 MARCH 1990   Hour newsmagazine show, featuring investigative
reports and "dramatic recreations" of events. The original reporters were Rafael
Abramovitz, Krista Bradford, Steve Dunleavy, and Steve Dunlop; Abramovitz and
Dunlop were succeeded by Jim Paymar and Steve Wilson; Kristin Altman and Bob
Drury were later added. Celebrity guest reporters were also featured during the
second season.

RESCUE 8   SYNDICATED

1958   This half-hour series about a pair of rescue workers was the antecedent of
NBC's *Emergency!* It starred Jim Davis as Wes Cameron and Lang Jeffries as Skip
Johnson.

RESCUE 911   CBS

5 SEPTEMBER 1989–13 SEPTEMBER 1995; 1 FEBRUARY 1996–   An hour "actuality"
series, hosted by William Shatner, which employed newsreel footage, interviews, and
dramatic recreations of all kinds of rescue situations involving firefighters, paramedics, police officers, and ordinary citizens. Relatively inexpensive to produce and
surprisingly durable, *Rescue 911* was especially popular with children; some of the

young viewers were able to apply what they learned to rescue family members from life-threatening situations.

THE RESTLESS GUN   NBC
23 SEPTEMBER 1957–14 SEPTEMBER 1959   This half-hour western from Revue Studios starred John Payne as Vint Bonner, a Civil War veteran who roamed the West. Dan Blocker, who later starred in *Bonanza,* made his first TV appearance in a 1957 episode, "The Child" (23 December), and James Coburn played his first major role in a 1958 show, "Take Me Home" (29 December). Bonner's mount, Scar, was played by a horse named John Henry.

RETURN TO PEYTON PLACE   NBC
3 APRIL 1972–4 JANUARY 1974   This half-hour daytime serial picked up where *Peyton Place,* ABC's prime-time soap opera, had left off three years earlier. Though *Peyton Place* had been popular with viewers, *Return to Peyton Place* never really caught on; one reason for its lack of success may have been that viewers had identified too strongly with the stars of *Peyton Place* (such as Mia Farrow, Ryan O'Neal, and Ed Nelson), none of whom appeared on the daytime sequel. Principal players on the daytime version included: Kathy Glass as Allison MacKenzie; Bettye Ackerman and Susan Brown as her mother, Constance MacKenzie Carson; Warren Stevens as Elliot Carson, her husband; Guy Stockwell as Dr. Michael Rossi; Joe Gallison as Steven Cord; Mary K. Wells as Hannah Cord; Lawrence Casey and Yale Summers as Rodney Harrington; Ron Russell as Norman Harrington; Patricia Morrow as Rita Jacks Harrington; Julie Parrish and Lynn Loring as Betty Anderson Harrington; Evelyn Scott as Ada Jacks; John Levin as young Matthew Carson; John Hoyt as Martin Peyton; Frank Ferguson as Eli Carson; Dino Fantini as Gino Panzini; and Ben Andrews as Benny Tate.

RETURN TO THE PLANET OF THE APES   NBC
6 SEPTEMBER 1975–4 SEPTEMBER 1976   This Saturday-morning cartoon show was based on the *Planet of the Apes* films and television series. David H. DePatie and Friz Freleng were the producers.

REVIVAL OF AMERICA CRUSADE   SYNDICATED
1975–1979   Half-hour religious show, with evangelist and faith healer LeRoy Jenkins. Jenkins, who once described himself as "the nation's most controversial evangelist," had previously conducted services in Columbus, Ohio, calling his congregation "The Church of What's Happening Now." Comedian Flip Wilson, who created a Reverend Leroy character in his 1970 variety show, used the same name for his congregation.

THE REVLON REVUE   CBS
28 JANUARY 1960–16 JUNE 1960   *The Revlon Revue* was the scaled-down successor to *The Big Party,* CBS's lavish ninety-minute variety series that was dropped in midseason. *The Revlon Revue* was an hour show and had no regulars; Mickey Rooney, Dick Shawn, Patachou, Joey Forman, and Bob Crewe appeared on the premiere, and Maurice Chevalier was the guest star on the second show. The last several shows were titled *The Revlon Spring Music Festival.* Abe Burrows was the executive producer.

REX HUMBARD   SYNDICATED
1952–1983   One of America's best known evangelists, Rex Humbard began his television broadcasts in Akron in 1952; by the early 1970s his program was seen on approximately 350 stations. In later years the show was titled *The Rex Humbard World Outreach Ministry* and was taped at the Cathedral of Tomorrow in Cuyahoga Falls, Ohio. Regulars included the Rex Humbard Family Singers, with Maude Aimee Humbard (Rex's wife) and Elizabeth Humbard (his daughter) featured as soloists. The show's executive producer was Rex Humbard, Jr.

RHODA   CBS

9 SEPTEMBER 1974–9 DECEMBER 1978   Valerie Harper starred in this spinoff from *The Mary Tyler Moore Show* as Rhoda Morgenstern. On her own show, Rhoda returned to her native New York from Minneapolis, got a job, and finally found a fella. David Groh costarred as her new boyfriend, Joe Gerard, owner of the New York Wrecking Company, a demolition outfit; Joe had previously been married and was the father of a ten-year-old son. Rhoda and Joe were married in the series' eighth episode and lived in the same apartment building as Rhoda's younger sister, Brenda (played by Julie Kavner), a bank teller. Also featured during the first season were Nancy Walker as Rhoda's meddlesome mother, Ida Morgenstern; Harold Gould as Rhoda's father, Martin Morgenstern; Lorenzo Music (*Rhoda*'s coproducer) as the heard-but-not seen Carlton the Doorman. Rhoda and Joe stayed married through the series' second season, as a few new regulars began to be seen: Richard Masur as Brenda's sometime boyfriend, Nick Lobo, a thick-headed accordionist; Wes Stern as Brenda's friend Lenny Fiedler; Barbara Sharma as Rhoda's high school classmate Myrna Morgenstein, who became Rhoda's employee in her freelance window-dressing business; and Scoey Mitchlll as Joe's employee, Justin Culp. By the beginning of the third season, however, it was decided that Rhoda and Joe should separate, and early in the fall of 1976 the two agreed to a trial separation. Joe moved out, and Rhoda moved to a smaller apartment in the same building; Nancy Walker (who was then starring in her own series, *The Nancy Walker Show*) and Harold Gould were gone from the series (it was explained that Rhoda's folks had decided to take a motor trip around the country), and Masur, Stern, Sharma, and Mitchlll were no longer seen as regulars. More new faces were added, however: Ron Silver as Gary Levy, an aggressive young schlep who ran a boutique and who agreed to swap apartments with Rhoda; Anne Meara as Rhoda's friend, Sally Gallagher, an airline stewardess; Michael DeLano as Johnny Venture, a minimally talented but very macho lounge singer newly arrived from Las Vegas, who fell for Rhoda. More changes took place at the outset of the fourth season, as Rhoda and Joe were finally divorced. David Groh, who had appeared infrequently during the 1976–1977 season, was dropped entirely; Nancy Walker returned after a season's absence; Rhoda got a new job, with a theatrical costume supply house; and three new players were added, joining Harper, Kavner, Music, Silver, and DeLano: Kenneth McMillan as Rhoda's gruff boss, Jack Doyle; Rafael Campos as Doyle's other employee, Ramón Diaz; and Ray Buktenica as Brenda's boyfriend, Benny Goodwin. DeLano, Silver and Campos left the show at the end of the 1977–1978 season, and, as the 1978–1979 season began, Rhoda's mother, Ida Morgenstern, was suddenly single: her husband had left her. Nancy Lane also joined the cast in the fall of 1978 as Tina Molinari, Jack Doyle's third employee. James L. Brooks and Allan Burns were the executive producers of *Rhoda* from 1974 until 1978, when Charlotte Brown became the new executive producer for MTM Enterprises.

RHYME AND REASON   ABC

7 JULY 1975–9 JULY 1976   Hosted by Bob Eubanks, this daytime game show was essentially a poetic version of *The Match Game*—two contestants tried to guess which word would be rhymed to an open-ended couplet by the panel of six celebrities. Steven Friedman was the executive producer for W. T. Naud Productions, Inc.

RHYTHM & BLUES   NBC

24 SEPTEMBER 1992–22 OCTOBER 1992; 12 FEBRUARY 1993   Half-hour sitcom set at a black radio station in Detroit. With Roger Kabler as Bobby Soul, a white deejay mistakenly hired by the station; Anna Maria Horsford as Veronica Washington, the widowed owner of WBLZ; Ron Glass as Don Philips; Troy Curvey, Jr., as deejay "Love Man"; Vanessa Bell Calloway as program director Colette Hawkins; Christopher Babers as Earl; and Miguel A. Nunez, Jr., as deejay "Jammin'."

RHYTHM RODEO   DUMONT

30 JULY 1950–31 DECEMBER 1950   Half-hour musical series, hosted by Art Jarrett.

THE RICH LITTLE SHOW   NBC

2 FEBRUARY 1976–19 JULY 1976   Impressionist Rich Little hosted his own hour-long comedy-variety series. Other regulars included Charlotte Rae, R. G. Brown, Julie McWhirter, Joe Baker, and Mel Bishop. Jerry Goldstein was executive producer for Little's production company, Dudley Enterprises (Dudley, Little's English sheepdog, appeared at the show's conclusion).

RICH MAN, POOR MAN   ABC

1 FEBRUARY 1976–15 MARCH 1976; 21 SEPTEMBER 1976–8 MARCH 1977   *Rich Man, Poor Man* was introduced early in 1976 as a twelve-hour serialization of Irwin Shaw's novel, which chronicled the lives of the Jordache family from 1945 to 1965. The series was a smash hit, ranking third in the seasonal Nielsens and reaping twenty-three Emmy nominations. In the fall of 1976 ABC introduced *Rich Man, Poor Man—Book II,* a twenty-one-part continuation of the Shaw novel (Shaw himself had virtually nothing to do with *Book II*), which fared less well. The cast of *Book I* (as the original twelve-hour adaptation came to be called when it was rerun in May and June of 1977) included: Peter Strauss as Rudy Jordache; Nick Nolte as Tom Jordache, his brother; Edward Asner as Axel Jordache, their father; Dorothy McGuire as Mary Jordache, their mother; Susan Blakely as Julie Prescott; Bill Bixby as Willie Abbott; Robert Reed as Teddy Boylan; Ray Milland as Duncan Calderwood; Kim Darby as Virginia Calderwood; Talia Shire as Teresa Santoro; Lawrence Pressman as Bill Benton; and Kay Lenz as Kate. The cast of *Book II* included only a few of the principals from *Book I*—Peter Strauss as Rudy, Kay Lenz as Kate, and (in the first episode only) Susan Blakely as Julie. The remainder of the *Book II* cast included: Gregg Henry as Wesley Jordache, Tom's son; James Carroll Jordan as Billy Abbott, Julie's son; Susan Sullivan as Maggie Porter; William Smith as Anthony Falconetti; Dimitra Arliss as Marie Falconetti; Sorrell Booke as Phil Greeneberg; Peter Haskell as Charles Estep; Laraine Stephens as Claire Estep; Penny Peyser as Ramona Scott; John Anderson as Scotty; Peter Donat as Arthur Raymond; Cassie Yates as Annie Adams; Barry Sullivan as Senator Paxton; G. D. Spradlin as Senator Dillon; and Philip Abbott as John Franklin. Harve Bennett was the executive producer and Jon Epstein the producer of *Book I;* Michael Gleason was executive producer and Epstein the producer of *Book II.* Both books were produced for Universal Television. In sum, the phenomenal success of *Book I* led to a boom in the programming of serialized novels and other stories on prime-time network television.

RICHARD BEY   SYNDICATED

1995–   Hour daytime talk show, hosted by Richard Bey.

THE RICHARD BOONE SHOW   NBC

24 SEPTEMBER 1963–15 SEPTEMBER 1964   This hour program was a television rarity—a dramatic anthology series with an in-house repertory company. Richard Boone, formerly of *Have Gun Will Travel,* was both host and performer. The rest of the company included Robert Blake, Lloyd Bochner, Laura Devon, June Harding, Bethel Leslie, Harry Morgan, Jeanette Nolan, Ford Rainey, Warren Stevens, and Guy Stockwell. The show was a Goodson-Todman Production in association with Classic Films and NBC.

RICHARD DIAMOND, PRIVATE DETECTIVE   CBS/NBC

1 JULY 1957–30 SEPTEMBER 1957; 2 JANUARY 1958–25 SEPTEMBER 1958; 15 FEBRUARY 1959–20 SEPTEMBER 1959 (CBS); 5 OCTOBER 1959–6 SEPTEMBER 1960 (NBC)   *Richard Diamond, Private Detective* was first a radio series; introduced in 1949, it starred Dick Powell. The TV version, which bore little resemblance to the radio show, was produced by Four Star Films and starred unsmiling David Janssen as Richard Diamond. Originally, Diamond worked in New York, and Regis Toomey costarred as Lieutenant McGough. When the series returned to the air in February, 1959, however, Diamond had relocated to Los Angeles, where he became one of TV's first characters to have a car phone, which he used to check in with Sam, the woman who ran his answering service. Sam's face never appeared on camera, but her legs were

displayed prominently. Joining the cast were Barbara Bain (in her first major TV role) as Diamond's girlfriend, Karen Wells (Bain was featured only in the first few 1959 episodes); Mary Tyler Moore (then billed as Mary Moore) as Sam (Roxanne Brooks took over the role in May 1959); and Russ Conway as Lieutenant Pete Kile. The half-hour series was first introduced as a summer replacement for *December Bride;* in 1958 it returned as a midseason replacement for *Harbourmaster,* and in 1959 it took over the slot formerly occupied by *The $64,000 Challenge.* In syndication the show was titled *Call Mr. D.*

THE RICHARD HARKNESS SHOW   NBC
7 JANUARY 1948–5 JANUARY 1949   Richard Harkness interviewed newsmakers on this fifteen-minute public affairs series.

THE RICHARD PRYOR SHOW   NBC
13 SEPTEMBER 1977–20 OCTOBER 1977   *The Richard Pryor Show,* which could have been one of the brightest spots of the 1977–1978 season, never really got off the ground for a number of reasons. It starred Richard Pryor, a gifted actor and an inventive but unorthodox comedian; Pryor's humor was unmistakably aimed at adult audiences, yet the show was broadcast during the so-called family hour (8 p.m. to 9 p.m. on the East Coast). Even worse, NBC scheduled it opposite ABC's *Happy Days* and *Laverne and Shirley,* two of the top-rated shows of the previous season. Finally, Pryor became involved with the network in a dispute involving censorship; a sequence showing Pryor apparently nude and emasculated (he was wearing a body stocking), while explaining that he had relinquished nothing to get his own series, was ordered deleted by the network. Pryor himself decided to halt production of the series shortly after the incident, and only five shows (including a rerun of his spring 1977 special) were broadcast. Other regulars on the short-lived series included Allegra Allison, Sandra Bernhard, Victor Delapp, Argus Hamilton, Jimmy Martinez, Paul Mooney, Tim Reid, Marsha Warfield, Robin Williams, and "Detroit" John Witherspoon. Burt Sugarman was the executive producer and Rocco Urbisci and John Moffitt the producers.

THE RICHARD SIMMONS SHOW   SYNDICATED
1980–1984   Peripatetic Richard Simmons hosted this popular half-hour physical fitness series, aimed principally at women. Simmons, who himself slimmed down from 268 to 137 pounds, led his studio audience through exercises and introduced recipes for nutritious dishes. Before getting his own show in 1980, Simmons had appeared as himself on *General Hospital,* where he ran an exercise salon.

THE RICHARD WILLIS SHOW   NBC
8 OCTOBER 1951–15 FEBRUARY 1957   Makeup artist Richard Willis dispensed advice on beauty and grooming to women on this daytime series, which was originally titled *Here's Looking at You.*

RICHIE BROCKELMAN, PRIVATE EYE   NBC
17 MARCH 1978–14 APRIL 1978   This hour-long crime show was a five-week replacement for *The Rockford Files.* Featured were Dennis Dugan as Richie Brockelman, a private eye in his early twenties; Robert Hogan as Sergeant Ted Coppersmith, his police contact; Barbara Bosson as Sharon Deterson, Brockelman's female friend and assistant. The character was first introduced in a 1976 made-for-TV movie, "Richie Brockelman: The Missing 24 Hours," and was again introduced on an episode of *The Rockford Files* broadcast 10 March 1978. Stephen J. Cannell and Steven Bochco created the series and were its executive producers; Peter S. Fischer was the producer. Reruns were shown during the summer of 1978.

THE RICHIE RICH/SCOOBY-DOO SHOW   ABC/CBS
8 NOVEMBER 1980–18 SEPTEMBER 1982 (ABC); 11 JANUARY 1986–30 AUGUST 1986 (CBS); 15 NOVEMBER 1986–27 DECEMBER 1986 (CBS)   The "Scooby-Doo" cartoon series, which began on TV in 1969, alternated with "Richie Rich" cartoons in this

hour Saturday-morning series. Based on the comic book character, Richie Rich was the world's wealthiest youngster; assisted by his pals, Gloria and Freckles, his dog Dollar, his butler Cadbury, and his robot maid Irona, Richie roamed the world on various adventures. In 1982 Richie and Scooby-Doo split up, each remaining on ABC's Saturday lineup (see *The Pac-Man/Little Rascals/Richie Rich Show; Scooby & Scrappy Doo/The Puppy's New Adventures*). Richie Rich reruns later surfaced on CBS's Saturday morning lineup.

RICKI LAKE SYNDICATED
1993– Hour daytime talk show hosted by Ricki Lake. Lake had been an unknown until 1988, when the overweight teenager was discovered by film director John Waters and cast in the movie *Hairspray*. Later she was a regular for one season on *China Beach*. By the time she began hosting her talk show she had lost 125 pounds. The program quickly became popular with young adult females. Typical discussion topics (as telecast during April and May 1995) included "Mothers and Daughters Who Fight," "Jilted People," "Promiscuous Teens," "Sexy-Man Search," and "Upsets Over Mothers' Boyfriends."

RIDERS IN THE SKY CBS
14 SEPTEMBER 1991–5 SEPTEMBER 1992 Saturday-morning kids' show set at the Harmony Ranch, where three live-action characters—Woody Paul, Ranger Doug, and Too Slim—introduced animated segments, puppets, and clay animation sequences. Paul Chrisman played Paul, Douglas Green was Doug, and Fred LaBour was Too Slim.

RIDDLE ME THIS CBS
5 DECEMBER 1948–13 MARCH 1949 Conrad Nagel hosted this Sunday-night game show, the subject of which was riddles. Celebrity panelists included John Daly and Ilka Chase. See also *Celebrity Time*.

THE RIFLEMAN ABC
30 SEPTEMBER 1958–1 JULY 1963 Chuck Connors starred in this half-hour western as Lucas McCain, a widower trying to raise his young son on a ranch outside North Fork, New Mexico; unfortunately, McCain had little time to concentrate on ranching, as he was constantly called on to use his prowess with a .44 Winchester rifle to rid North Fork of assorted undesirables. Also featured were Johnny Crawford as his son, Mark; Paul Fix as North Fork's ineffective marshal, Micah Torrance; Bill Quinn as Sweeney, the bartender; Hope Summers as storekeeper Hattie Denton; Joan Taylor as Millie Scott, proprietor of the general store; and Pat Blair (1962–1963) as Lou Mallory, the hotelkeeper. *The Rifleman* was the most popular new series of the 1958–1959 season, ranking fourth overall in the seasonal Nielsens; though it lasted four more years, it never equalled the success of the first season. With its dark lighting and somber musical underscore, *The Rifleman* seems, in retrospect, more grim than most of the other westerns of the time; star Chuck Connors maintained, however, that it was a wholesome family drama in which violence was kept to a minimum. Arthur Gardner, Arnold Laven, and Jules Levy produced the show's 168 episodes for Four Star Films. Chuck Connors and Johnny Crawford were reunited in 1990 in an episode of *Paradise,* another TV western.

THE RIGHTEOUS APPLES PBS
1981 Half-hour comedy-drama about three inner-city youngsters who started a rock band. With Kutee as Gloretta; Mykel T. Williamson as Big Neck; and Joey Camen as D.C.

RIKER CBS
14 MARCH 1981–11 APRIL 1981 Josh Taylor starred as Frank Riker in this hour crime show. Riker, a cop who was implicated in a departmental scandal, was convinced by Deputy Attorney General Bryce Landis (played by Michael Shannon) to resign from the force rather than prove his innocence, and to work for the D.A. as an undercover

agent. The series was CBS's lowest-rated show of the 1980–1981 season, ranking 95th out of 97 programs.

RIN TIN TIN   ABC

15 OCTOBER 1954–28 AUGUST 1959   "Rin Tin Tin," TV's best-known German shepherd, was the star of this half-hour western. The dog and his young master, a boy named Rusty, were the only survivors of an Indian raid on a wagon train and were taken in by the members of the 101st Cavalry. The humans in the cast included: Lee Aaker as Rusty, who was commissioned a corporal in the first episode (Rin Tin Tin was made a private); Jim L. Brown as Lieutenant Ripley (Rip) Masters; Joe Sawyer as Sergeant Biff O'Hara; and Rand Brooks as Corporal Boone. Herbert B. Leonard produced the series, and William Beaudine directed it; the 164 episodes were filmed at Crash Corrigan's movie ranch in California. The original Rin Tin Tin was a veteran of the German Army in World War I and had starred in several silent films during the 1920s; *Rin Tin Tin* had also been a radio series (once in 1930 and again in 1955). The TV Rin Tin Tin was owned by Lee Duncan. The dog reappeared thirty years later in a more modern format: see below.

RIN TIN TIN K-9 COP   FAM

17 SEPTEMBER 1988–19 SEPTEMBER 1993   On this series the brave German shepherd no longer served in the nineteenth-century cavalry, but in a twentieth-century police department. The human cast included Jesse Collins as Officer Hank Katts, Rinty's master; Sharon Acker as Alice; Ken Pogue as Captain Cullen Murdoch; and Andrew Bednarski as Stevie Katts, son of Hank's late brother, whom Hank was raising. The half-hour series was produced in Canada and was televised there beginning in 1987, under the title *Katts and Dog*.

THE RING OF TRUTH   PBS

20 OCTOBER 1987–24 NOVEMBER 1987   Tools were the subject of this six-part documentary series, hosted by Philip Morrison of the Massachusetts Institute of Technology.

RIPCORD   SYNDICATED

1962   The central characters in this half-hour adventure series were a pair of parachutists who operated Ripcord, Inc., a skydiving school. Larry Pennell and Ken Curtis starred as partners Ted McKeever and Jim Buckley. Maurice Unger and Leon Benson produced the series for United Artists.

RIPLEY'S BELIEVE IT OR NOT   ABC

26 SEPTEMBER 1982–4 SEPTEMBER 1986   "Ripley's Believe It or Not," the popular comic strip created by Robert L. Ripley, was the basis of this hour "reality show." Each week various amazing but true stories, or incredible but true facts, were depicted, usually on film. Jack Palance hosted the show; his first cohost, Catherine Shirriff, was succeeded early in 1983 by Holly Palance, who (in a less than amazing coincidence) happened to be Jack's daughter. Marie Osmond was Jack Palance's cohost for the show's fourth, and final, season. *Ripley's Believe It or Not* is the second television series taken from the comic strip; Ripley himself had hosted the first version, *Believe It or Not,* in 1949 (see also that title).

RIPTIDE   NBC

3 JANUARY 1984–18 APRIL 1986   An hour crime show about two private eyes and their pal, a computer whiz, who operated out of a boat docked at a Southern California harbor. With Perry King as Cody Allen; Joe Penny as his partner, Nick Ryder; Thom Bray as Murray "Boz" Bozinsky, the klutzy computer and electronics genius; Jack Ging (1984–1985) as Lieutenant Ted Quinlan, the cop who had little tolerance for any of them; Gianni Russo as Straightaway, a local restaurateur; Anne Francis (1984) as Mama Jo, skipper of a charter boat with an all-female crew; Ken Orlandt as Kirk "The Dool" Dooley, their part-time assistant; and June Chadwick (1985–1986) as Lieutenant Joanna Parisi. The series was a Stephen J. Cannell Production.

RITUALS   SYNDICATED

1984–1985   Half-hour syndicated soap opera, taped in Hollywood, and set in fictional Wingfield, Virginia, a college town near Washington, D.C. With Christine Jones as Christine Robertson, dean of women at Haddon Hall; Monte Markham as her husband, Carter Robertson, a former executive of Chapin Industries; George Lazenby as playwright Logan Williams; Philece Sampler as Lacey Jarrett, dorm proctor; Kin Shriner as her beau, art teacher Mike Gallagher; Andrea Moar as Julia Chapin Field; Dennis Patrick as Patrick Chapin; Jo Ann Pflug and Tina Louise as Taylor Chapin Field von Platen; Claire Yarlett and Mary Beth Evans as Dakota Lane; Gina Gallego as Diandra Santiago; Patti Davis (daughter of Ronald Reagan) and Janice Heiden as Marissa Mallory. Jorn Winther was the producer, Gene Palumbo the head writer.

RIVERBOAT   NBC

13 SEPTEMBER 1959–16 JANUARY 1961   This hour-long adventure series starred Darren McGavin as Grey Holden, captain of the *Enterprise,* a riverboat which plied the Mississippi River during the 1840s. Also on board were Burt Reynolds (1959–1960, in his first continuing role) as pilot Ben Frazer; Noah Beery (1960–1961) as pilot Bill Blake; Dick Wessel as Carney; Jack Lambert as Joshua; Mike McGreevey as Chip; John Mitchum as Pickalong; and Bart Patton as Terry. A total of forty-four episodes were produced.

THE ROAD   SYNDICATED

1994   Hour variety series which followed country and western acts as they traveled across America. There was no regular host.

THE ROAD HOME   CBS

5 MARCH 1994–16 APRIL 1994   Hour dramatic series about a family who took a vacation trip to visit the folks in North Carolina and decided to stay there. With Karen Allen as Alison Matson; Terence Knox as her husband, Jack Matson; Ed Flanders as her father, Walter Babineaux; Frances Sternhagen as her mother, Charlotte Babineaux; Jessica Bowman as Alison and Jack's teen daughter, Darcy; Cecilley Carroll as their younger daughter, Jinx; Christopher Masterson as their older son, Sawyer; Gregg Perrelli as their younger son, Calvin; Alex McArthur as Alison's brother, Dickie; and Bobby Fain as teenage neighbor Arthur Dumas, who took a liking to Darcy. John Tinker and Bruce Paltrow created the series.

ROAD OF LIFE   CBS

13 DECEMBER 1954–1 JULY 1955   One of radio's most popular serials, *Road of Life* was created by Irna Phillips in 1937 and lasted until 1959; the television version was far less successful. It starred Don MacLaughlin as Dr. Jim Brent, a surgeon. Also featured in the TV cast were Barbara Becker as Sybill Fuller; Virginia Dwyer as Jocelyn Brent; Harry Holcombe as Malcolm Overton; Charles Dingle as Conrad Overton; Elizabeth Lawrence as Francie Brent; Bill Lipton as John Brent; John Larkin as Frank Dana; and Dorothy Sands as Aunt Reggie. Nelson Case was the narrator, and John Egan was the producer.

THE ROAD RUNNER SHOW   CBS/ABC

10 SEPTEMBER 1966–7 SEPTEMBER 1968 (CBS); 11 SEPTEMBER 1971–2 SEPTEMBER 1972 (ABC)   The Road Runner, the resourceful bird who constantly outwitted his pursuer, Wile E. Coyote, had his own Saturday-morning cartoon show for three seasons. At other times he has shared a show with Bugs Bunny, which has usually been titled *The Bugs Bunny/Road Runner Hour.* See also *Bugs Bunny.*

THE ROAD TO LOS ANGELES   SYNDICATED

1982–1984   The aspirations of American amateur athletes, all hoping to compete in the 1984 Olympic Games in Los Angeles, were chronicled in this half-hour series.

ROAD TO REALITY   ABC
17 OCTOBER 1960–31 MARCH 1961   A therapy group was the setting of this half-hour daytime serial, ABC's first, which starred John Beal as psychoanalyst Dr. Lewis.

THE ROAD WEST   NBC
12 SEPTEMBER 1966–28 AUGUST 1967   An undistinguished hour-long western from Universal Television, *The Road West* was the story of a pioneer family who settled in Kansas. Featured were Barry Sullivan as Ben Pride; Kathryn Hays as Elizabeth Pride, his wife; Andrew Prine as their son, Tim; Brenda Scott as their daughter, Midge (Prine and Scott had been married in 1965 but were divorced when production of the series began); Kelly Corcoran as their son, Kip; Glenn Corbett as Chance Reynolds, Elizabeth's brother; and Charles Seel as Tom (Grandpa) Pride, Ben's father.

ROALD DAHL'S TALES OF THE UNEXPECTED   SYNDICATED
1979–1981   Most of the presentations on this British-produced anthology series were written by Roald Dahl. In 1981 the program was retitled *Tales of the Unexpected* (however, the series should not be confused with the 1977 NBC series of the same title), and John Houseman became the host.

ROAR OF THE RAILS   CBS
26 OCTOBER 1948–14 DECEMBER 1948; 24 OCTOBER 1949–12 DECEMBER 1949   A fifteen-minute series on railroading, sponsored by the A. C. Gilbert Company. See also *Tales of the Red Caboose.*

THE ROARING TWENTIES   ABC
15 OCTOBER 1960–21 SEPTEMBER 1962   Set in New York during the 1920s, this hour-long adventure series tried to capitalize on the success of *The Untouchables,* which was also set in the Prohibition era. *The Roaring Twenties,* however, was considerably less violent and considerably less popular. Featured were Dorothy Provine as Pinky Pinkham, singer at the Charleston Club; Donald May as Pat Garrison, reporter for the New York *Record;* Rex Reason as Scott Norris, also a *Record* reporter; John Dehner as reporter Duke Williams; Mike Road as Lieutenant Joe Switoski, New York cop; Gary Vinson as Chris Higby, the *Record*'s copy-boy; and James Flavin as Howard.

THE ROBBINS NEST   ABC
29 SEPTEMBER 1950–22 DECEMBER 1950   Fifteen-minute Friday-night variety show, hosted by Fred Robbins.

THE ROBERT GUILLAUME SHOW   ABC
5 APRIL 1989–9 AUGUST 1989   Half-hour sitcom starring Robert Guillaume as Edward Sawyer, a divorced marriage counselor; Hank Rolike as his father, Henry Sawyer; Kelsey Scott as his daughter, Pamela; Marc Joseph as his son, William; and Wendy Phillips as Ann Sheer, Sawyer's secretary, with whom Edward had a romantic (and interracial) relationship.

ROBERT HERRIDGE THEATRE   SYNDICATED
1961   This half-hour dramatic anthology series was seen on many educational stations.

ROBERT MONTGOMERY PRESENTS   NBC
30 JANUARY 1950–24 JUNE 1957   Another of television's high-quality dramatic anthology series, this hour show was produced and hosted by actor Robert Montgomery, who occasionally starred in the presentations. A sampling of the shows broadcast would include: "Victoria Regina," with Helen Hayes (30 January 1950); "Arrowsmith," with Van Heflin (9 October 1950); "The Philadelphia Story," with Barbara Bel Geddes (4 December 1950); "Rise Up and Walk," with Kim Hunter (4 February 1952); "Penny," with Joanne Woodward (in her first major TV role, 9 June 1952);

"Dinah, Kip, and Mr. Barlow," with Jack Lemmon (23 February 1953); "Harvest," with Ed Begley, Dorothy Gish, Vaughn Taylor, and James Dean (23 November 1953); "Wages of Fear," with Louis Jourdan (3 May 1954); "The Great Gatsby," with Phyllis Kirk, John Newland, and Gena Rowlands (11 April 1955); "Soldier from the Wars Returning," with James Cagney (in the first of his few television appearances, 10 September 1956); "Return Visit," with Peter Falk (in his first major TV role, 13 May 1957). In its first seasons *Robert Montgomery Presents* was also known as *Lucky Strike Theater.* During the summer months between seasons, Montgomery introduced a repertory company, whose productions were presented under titles such as *Montgomery's Summer Stock* or *The Robert Montgomery Summer Theater.* A regular performer in these companies was Montgomery's daughter, Elizabeth Montgomery, who had made her TV debut in a 1951 episode of *Robert Montgomery Presents,* "Top Secret" (broadcast 3 December). In the summer of 1954 the company consisted of Elizabeth Montgomery, Jan Miner (better known in later years as Madge, the manicurist in Palmolive commercials), John Newland, Anne Seymour, Cliff Robertson, and Vaughn Taylor. In the summer of 1956 the group included Elizabeth Montgomery, John Gibson, Tom Middleton, and Mary K. Wells. Robert Montgomery became a media consultant for President Eisenhower during the 1950s and in 1969 became president of the Lincoln Center Repertory Theater.

THE ROBERT Q. LEWIS SHOW   CBS
16 JULY 1950–7 JANUARY 1951; 16 OCTOBER 1950–19 JANUARY 1951; 11 JANUARY 1954– 25 MAY 1956   Robert Q. Lewis, frequently seen during the 1950s as a game-show host and substitute emcee, hosted a prime-time show and two daytime variety series of his own. The prime-time show was a fifteen-minute interview program seen Sundays. The first daytime series, titled *Robert Q's Matinee,* was a forty-five-minute daily show that ran only fourteen weeks. The second, titled *The Robert Q. Lewis Show,* was much more successful, lasting more than two years. Among the many regulars on the half-hour show were Jaye P. Morgan, Jan Arden, Betty Clooney, Jane Wilson, Lois Hunt and Earl Wrightson, Merv Griffin, Julann Wright (who later married Griffin), The Chordettes, dancer-choreographer Don Liberto, and announcer Lee Vines.

THE ROBERT RIPLEY SHOW
See BELIEVE IT OR NOT

ROBERT TAYLOR'S DETECTIVES
See THE DETECTIVES

THE ROBERTA QUINLAN SHOW   NBC
3 MAY 1949–23 NOVEMBER 1951   Singer Roberta Quinlan hosted her own fifteen-minute musical series of two and a half years; it was seen two or three nights a week before the evening news. In 1949 her show, telecast Tuesdays and Thursdays, was actually part of *The Mohawk Showroom*—singer Morton Downey hosted the series on the other three weeknights.

ROBIN HOOD   CBS
26 SEPTEMBER 1955–22 SEPTEMBER 1958   Officially titled *The Adventures of Robin Hood,* this British import told the story of the legendary twelfth-century hero who, together with his band of men, stole from the rich and gave to the poor; on TV most of Robin's exploits involved attempts to oust Prince John, the hated ruler of Nottingham. The half-hour series starred Richard Greene as Robin Hood and featured Alexander Gauge as Friar Tuck; Archie Duncan and Rufus Cruikshank as Little John; Bernadette O'Farrell (1955–1957) and Patricia Driscoll (1957–1958) as Maid Marian, Robin's apparent romantic interest; Paul Eddington and John Dearth as Will Scarlett; Alan Wheatley as the hapless Sheriff of Nottingham; and Donald Pleasence as Prince John. In 1967 an updated cartoon version appeared: see *Rocket Robin Hood.* In 1975 a prime-time sitcom also appeared: see *When Things Were Rotten.*

ROBIN OF SHERWOOD   SHOWTIME
17 DECEMBER 1984–19 JANUARY 1985; 23 NOVEMBER 1985–22 MARCH 1986   A remake
of the Robin Hood legend, this one starred Michael Praed (1984–1985) as the first
Robin Hood, who was killed off, and Jason Connery (1985–1986) as Robert of
Nottingham, who became the new Robin Hood. Also on hand were Nickolas Grace
was the Sheriff of Nottingham; Philip David as King John; and Judi Trott as Maid
Marian. The series premiered with a made-for-TV movie, *Robin Hood: The Swords
of Wayland.*

ROBIN'S HOODS   SYNDICATED
1994   Hour adventure series starring Linda Purl as Brett Robin. A former prosecutor, Robin took over the ownership of her late husband's nightclub, Robin's Nest,
and tried to find his killer. Assisting her were five parolees who had been hired by the
husband to work at the club. Also featured were David Gail as Eddie Bartlett; Julie
McCullough as Stacey Wright; Jennifer Campbell as Anastasia (Annie) Beckett;
Mayte Vilan as Maria Alvarez; and Claire Yarlett as MacKenzie (Mac) Magnuson.

ROBOCOP   SYNDICATED
1994–1995   Hour crime show set in the "near future" and based on the 1987 movie.
The TV version starred Richard Eden as Alex Murphy, a slain police officer whose
human remains had been implanted in a super-high-tech cyborg body known as
RoboCop; he patrolled Delta City, a dangerous metropolis adjacent to Old Detroit.
Also featured were Yvette Nipar as his human partner, Lisa Madigan; Blu Mankuma
as the boss, Sergeant Stan Parks; Andrea Roth as Diana Powers, a secretary whose
brain had been stolen by a mad scientist and who now "existed" inside a mainframe
computer, from which she assisted RoboCop; David Gardner as The Chairman, head
of the evil conglomerate Omni Consumer Products; Sarah Campbell as Gadget, a
young orphan; Dan Duran and Erica Ehm as Bo Harlan and Rocky Crenshaw, coanchors of a three-minute news program, "Media Break"; Jennifer Griffin as Nancy
Murphy, who believed that her husband (Alex) was dead; Peter Costigan as Jimmy,
Nancy and Alex's thirteen-year-old; Cliff DeYoung as the mad scientist, Dr. Cray Z.
Mallardo; John Rubinstein as Chip Chaykin; and James Kidnie as villain Pudface
Morgan, who had been disfigured by toxic waste.

ROC   FOX
24 AUGUST 1991–30 AUGUST 1994   Half-hour sitcom, set in Baltimore, about a black
garbage collector and his family. With Charles S. Dutton as Roc Emerson; Ella Joyce
as his wife, Eleanor, a nurse; Rocky Carroll as his live-in brother, Joey, an unemployed musician; and Carl Gordon as his father, Andrew "Pop" Emerson. During its
second season *Roc* was broadcast live, becoming the first sitcom to do so since 1959.
For the series' third season two new regulars were added: Alexis Fields as Sheila
Hendricks, the young daughter of a friend of Roc's who had been imprisoned; and
Jamie Foxx as George, a not-too-bright regular at Roc's favorite bar. Also featured
was Clifton Powell as Andre, a local drug dealer. Roc and Eleanor had a baby,
Marcus, during the show's final season.

ROCK & ROLL   PBS
24 SEPTEMBER 1995–28 SEPTEMBER 1995   Five-night, ten-hour survey of rock and roll
music, narrated by Liev Schreiber.

THE ROCK & ROLL EVENING NEWS   SYNDICATED
1986   An hour weekly effort, consisting of news, interviews, and performances
from the world of rock-and-roll. Steve Kmetko was the host. Regular contributors
included Bob Hilburn, Richard Blade, Marjorie Wallace, Nelson George, and Eleanor Mondale (daughter of the former vice president).

ROCK-N-AMERICA   SYNDICATED
1984   Rock videos were sandwiched in around talk and comedy sketches on this
low-budget syndicated show. Frazer Smith hosted, assisted by Russ Parr as Magic.

ROCK 'N' ROLL SUMMER ACTION   ABC
17 JULY 1985–28 AUGUST 1985   Hour prime-time summer pop music series, hosted
by Christopher Atkins, with guest appearances by rock stars of today and yesterday.

ROCK 'N' ROLL TONITE   SYNDICATED
1983   A series of ninety-minute rock concerts, taped specifically for television at a
California soundstage. The sound was simulcast in stereo over FM stations in many
local markets.

ROCKET ROBIN HOOD   SYNDICATED
1967   In this futuristic cartoon version of the Robin Hood legend, Rocket Robin
Hood and his band of spacemen were stationed aboard Sherwood Asteroid in the
thirtieth century.

THE ROCKFORD FILES   NBC
13 SEPTEMBER 1974–25 JULY 1980   James Garner starred in this hour-long crime
show as Jim Rockford, a private eye recently released from prison (for a crime he
never committed) who lived in a trailer in Malibu. Also featured were Noah Beery as
Joe Rockford, his semiretired father; Joe Santos as Sergeant Dennis Becker of the
Los Angeles Police; Gretchen Corbett (1974–1978) as defense attorney Beth Davenport; and Stuart Margolin as Angel Martin. Bo Hopkins was featured during the
1978–1979 season as disbarred attorney John Cooper. Created by Roy Huggins and
Stephen J. Cannell, the series' executive producer was Meta Rosenberg. Garner,
Margolin and Santos were reunited for a two-hour sequel, "The Rockford Files: I
Still Love L.A." (27 November 1994, CBS).

ROCKSCHOOL   PBS
1985   An eight-part instructional series on the fundamentals of rock-and-roll music,
hosted by musician Herbie Hancock.

ROCKWORLD   SYNDICATED
1980   Another of the many series featuring performances by rock-and-roll acts.

ROCKY AND HIS FRIENDS   ABC
19 NOVEMBER 1959–23 SEPTEMBER 1961   Jay Ward created this popular cartoon
series, whose stars were a flying squirrel, Rocky (short for Rocket J. Squirrel) and a
dim-witted moose, Bullwinkle. The two battled Mr. Big and his henchpeople, Boris
Badenov and Natasha, in a series of adventures. Other segments on the half-hour
series included "Fractured Fairy Tales," narrated by Edward Everett Horton,
"Bullwinkle's Corner," a poetry segment, and the adventures of Sherman and Mr.
Peabody, a boy and a pedantic dog who traveled through time via Peabody's invention, the Wayback Machine. Ward's show attracted a cult following, as had his earlier
cartoon series, *Crusader Rabbit* (which also featured a diminutive hero and a not-too-
bright sidekick). Ward later created *George of the Jungle* for Saturday morning
consumption. See also *The Bullwinkle Show.* On 17 April 1992 the Showtime cable
network aired a live-action film, "Boris and Natasha," starring Dave Thomas and
Sally Kellerman, with a cameo appearance by June Foray, who had supplied the
voice of Rocky. The movie had been made for theatrical release, but never made it to
the big screen. Rocky and Bullwinkle were seen again in 1993, in a series of commercials for Taco Bell.

ROCKY JONES, SPACE RANGER   SYNDICATED
1954   One of the few "space shows" of the 1950s to be produced on film, rather
than live, *Rocky Jones, Space Ranger* was created and produced by Roland Reed.
The cast included Richard Crane as Rocky Jones, who commanded a spaceship, the
Orbit Jet, for the Space Rangers, who worked for the United Worlds; Sally Mansfield
as Vena Ray, his navigator; Scotty Becket (early episodes) as Winky; James Lydon as
Biffen Cardoza, a ranger from the planet Herculon; Maurice Cass (early episodes) as
Professor Newton; Robert Lyden as Bobby, Newton's young ward, who traveled with

the crew; Reginald Sheffield (later episodes) as Professor Mayberry; Charles Meredith as Secretary Drake, head of the Space Rangers; and Ann Robinson as Juliandra, ruler of Herculon. Thirty-nine episodes were made; almost all of the stories were in three parts.

ROCKY KING, DETECTIVE DUMONT
14 JANUARY 1950–26 DECEMBER 1954   This early crime show starred Roscoe Karns as Rocky King, a hardworking New York City police inspector; Earl Hammond (1950–1953) as Sergeant Lane; and Todd Karns (Roscoe's son, 1953–1954) as Detective Hart. Rocky's wife, Mabel, was also a regular, though she was never seen. Grace Carney provided her voice. The half-hour series was produced by Lawrence Menkin and Charles Spear and was originally titled *Rocky King, Inside Detective*.

ROD BROWN OF THE ROCKET RANGERS CBS
10 APRIL 1953–29 MAY 1954   This Saturday-morning space opera was notable mainly because it starred Cliff Robertson (in one of his earliest television roles) as Rod Brown, a member of the Rocket Rangers, one of the several interplanetary defense organizations featured on shows of the genre. Also featured were John Boruff as Commander Swift, Bruce Hall as Ranger Frank Boyle, and Jack Weston as Ranger Wilbur "Wormsey" Wormser. Rod and his twenty-second-century colleagues were stationed at Omega Base and traveled through space aboard the *Beta*. William Dozier produced the half-hour series; he and Robertson would later be reunited on Dozier's 1966 series *Batman*, when Robertson appeared as guest villain Shame.

THE ROGER MILLER SHOW NBC
12 SEPTEMBER 1966–26 DECEMBER 1966   Country and western singer Roger Miller ("King of the Road," "Chug-a-Lug," etc.) hosted his own half-hour musical variety series; music was provided by the Eddie Karam Orchestra.

ROGER RAMJET SYNDICATED
1965   Cartoon series about a research scientist (Roger Ramjet), who developed a "proton pill" that endowed him with great strength for limited periods of time.

ROGGIN'S HEROES SYNDICATED
1991–   Half-hour roundup of video clips of unusual moments in sports—professional and amateur—many of which were submitted by viewers. Los Angeles sportscaster Fred Roggin hosted.

THE ROGUES NBC
13 SEPTEMBER 1964–5 SEPTEMBER 1965   The central characters in this light adventure hour were a family of fair-minded felons whose specialty was swindling swindlers and conning con artists. The concept had been used before on television, in *Colonel Humphrey Flack*, and was later employed on such series as *Switch* and *The Feather and Father Gang*. *The Rogues* was a product of Four Star Television and featured David Niven as Alexander (Alec) Fleming; Charles Boyer as Marcel St. Clair, Alec's French cousin; Gig Young as Tony Fleming, Alec's American cousin; Gladys Cooper as Auntie Margaret, Alec's aunt; and Robert Coote as Timmy Fleming, an English cousin. John Williams was occasionally seen as Inspector Briscoe of Scotland Yard.

ROLL OUT! CBS
5 OCTOBER 1973–4 JANUARY 1974   *Roll Out!* was a short-lived service sitcom about a predominantly black supply outfit (the 5050th) headquartered in France during World War II. The cast included: Stu Gilliam as Corporal Sweet Williams; Hilly Hicks as Private Jed Brooks; Val Bisoglio as Captain Rocco Calvelli; Ed Begley, Jr., as Lieutenant Robert Chapman; Mel Stewart as Sergeant B. J. Bryant; Penny Santon as Madame Delacourt, a restaurateur; Garrett Morris (later to join *NBC's Saturday Night Live*) as Wheels; Darrow Igus as Jersey; Rod Gist as Phone Booth; and Theodore Wilson as High Strung.

ROLLERGAMES   SYNDICATED
1989–1990   An updated version of the perennial low-budget TV staple of yesteryear, *Roller Derby.* For the new series, six new teams were concocted—Violators,
Maniacs, Rockets, Bad Attitude, Hot Flash, and T-Birds—as well as a new obstacle,
the Alligator Pit.

ROLLERGIRLS   NBC
24 APRIL 1978–10 MAY 1978   Created by James Komack, this half-hour sitcom, four
episodes of which were shown, dwelt on a women's roller skating team, the Pittsburgh Pitts. Featured were Rhonda Bates as Mongo Sue Lampert; Candy Ann
Brown as J. B. Johnson; Marcy Hanson as Honey Bee Novak; Marilyn Tokuda as
Pipeline Akira; Terry Kiser as their hustling manager, Don Mitchell; and James
Murtaugh as the team's radio announcer, Howie.

ROLLIN' ON THE RIVER   SYNDICATED
1971–1973   This half-hour musical variety series was hosted by singer Kenny Rogers and his group, the First Edition. In the fall of 1972 the show's title was changed to
Rollin' with Kenny Rogers and the First Edition; both versions of the show were set
aboard a riverboat.

ROLONDA   SYNDICATED
1994–   Hour daytime talk show hosted by Rolonda Watts. Before hosting her
own program, Watts had been a weekend news anchor in New York and a reporter on
Inside Edition.

ROMAN HOLIDAYS   NBC
9 SEPTEMBER 1972–1 SEPTEMBER 1973   This Hanna-Barbera cartoon show was set
about halfway between two of Hanna-Barbera's best known shows, *The Flintstones*
(set in the Stone Age) and *The Jetsons* (set in the twenty-first century); *Roman
Holidays* was set in first-century Rome, and its central characters were the Holiday
family—father Gus, mother Laurie, daughter Precocia, son Happius, and pet lion
Brutus—who frequently battled their landlord, Mr. Evictus.

ROMANCE   CBS
3 NOVEMBER 1949–12 JANUARY 1950   Also known as *Theater of Romance,* this half-
hour anthology series of romantic stories alternated on Thursday nights with *Inside
U.S.A.,* replacing *Sugar Hill Times,* a short-lived all-black variety show. Robert
Stevens produced and directed.

ROMANCE THEATRE   SYNDICATED
1982   Half-hour anthology series of romantic stories, hosted by Louis Jourdan.
Each story was in five parts and was written by a member of the Romance Writers of
America Guild.

ROMPER ROOM   SYNDICATED
1954–1994   Like *Bozo the Clown, Romper Room* was really a franchised children's
program, rather than a syndicated one: local stations were free to use their hosts. The
idea was developed by Bert Claster and his wife, Nancy, who originated the show in
Baltimore in 1953. As the show grew more popular, the Clasters offered to train the
local *Romper Room* teachers. By the late 1950s more than 100 stations aired the
show, most of which employed their own teachers. The program consisted of songs,
games, and educational activities for young viewers. The teacher had a studio audience of children to work with, but could also hold up her "Magic Mirror" and
pretend to see kids watching the show from home. In 1977 *Variety* noted that *Romper
Room* was televised in forty-six American markets, twenty-nine of which used Chicago's Miss Sally as host; in real life Miss Sally was Sally Claster Gelbard, the
daughter of Bert and Nancy Claster.

THE RON REAGAN SHOW   SYNDICATED

1991   Presidential son Ron Reagan hosted this hour talk show, which focused on a single topic each night. Introduced in August 1991, the series was placed on hiatus after thirteen weeks. In 1992 Reagan hosted a series of documentaries on the E! cable network, and in 1993 he became a correspondent on the Fox series *The Front Page*.

THE ROOKIES   ABC

11 SEPTEMBER 1972–29 JUNE 1976   Straightforward crime show about three young police recruits. Featured were Gerald S. O'Loughlin as Lieutenant Ed Ryker, the commanding officer; Michael Ontkean (1972–1974) as Willie Gillis; Georg Stanford Brown as Terry Webster; Sam Melville as Mike Danko; Kate Jackson as nurse Jill Danko, Mike's wife; and Bruce Fairbairn (1974–1976) as Chris Owens. The executive producers of the hour series were Aaron Spelling and Leonard Goldberg; Spelling and Goldberg had previously produced a successful crime show about three young plainclothes officers, *The Mod Squad,* and later produced a very successful crime show about three female private eyes, *Charlie's Angels.* The pilot for the series was telecast 7 March 1972.

ROOM FOR ONE MORE   ABC

27 JANUARY 1962–22 SEPTEMBER 1962   Half-hour sitcom about a family with four children—two natural and two foster. With Andrew Duggan as George Rose; Peggy McCay as his wife, Anna Rose; Anna Capri as daughter Mary, age sixteen; Timothy Rooney as son Jeff, age fourteen; Carol Nicholson as daughter Laurie, age ten; Ronnie Dapo as son Flip, age nine; Jack Albertson as neighbor Walter Burton; and Maxine Stuart as his wife, Ruth Burton. Ed Jurist produced the series.

ROOM FOR ROMANCE   CBS

27 JULY 1990–24 AUGUST 1990   An unusual anthology series which explored the love lives of the residents of a Manhattan apartment building. Two or three stories were threaded together each week. The regulars were Dom Irrera as concierge Roman Carciofi (who sometimes commented on the proceedings to the camera), Rebecca Harrell as ten-year-old tenant Caroline Gidot, and Sumant as Vikram Seth, the doorman. Don Novello succeeded Irrera as Aldo the concierge. Robin Green created the series.

ROOM FOR TWO   ABC

24 MARCH 1992–29 APRIL 1992; 3 SEPTEMBER 1992–17 DECEMBER 1992; 8 JUNE 1993–6 JULY 1993   Half-hour sitcom about a widow from Ohio who visited her daughter in New York and became a regular on "Wake Up, New York," a local TV talk show produced by the latter. The cast included Linda Lavin as the widow, Edie Kurland, who also moved in with her daughter; Patricia Heaton as the daughter, Jill Kurland; Peter Michael Goetz as mail-order catalog salesman Ken Kazurinsky, their neighbor; John Putch as Jill's boyfriend, Matt; Jeff Yagher as Keith; Bess Meyer as Diahnn; and Ron Rifkin (1993) as Edie's new boyfriend, Jack.

ROOM 222   ABC

17 SEPTEMBER 1969–11 JANUARY 1974   *Room 222* was a half-hour comedy-drama set at Walt Whitman High School, an integrated school in Los Angeles (exteriors for the series were actually shot at Los Angeles High). The cast included: Lloyd Haynes (who had been a production assistant for the Heatter-Quigley game shows before landing acting jobs) as Pete Dixon, black American history teacher; Karen Valentine as chipper Alice Johnson, a student teacher in the English department; Michael Constantine as Seymour Kaufman, Walt Whitman's good-natured principal; and Denise Nicholas as Liz McIntyre, a black guidance counselor, and Dixon's female friend. Regular students included: Howard Rice as Richie Lane; Ta-Tanisha (1969–1972) as Pam; Heshimu as Jason Allen; Judy Strangis as Helen Loomis; David Joliffe as Bernie; Carol Green as Kim; and Ty Henderson as Cleon. James L. Brooks created the series, which was produced and directed by Gene Reynolds.

ROOMIES   NBC

19 MARCH 1987–15 MAY 1987   Half-hour sitcom about two unlikely roommates
matched up at Saginaw University: a forty-two-year-old ex-Marine and a fourteen-
year-old child prodigy. With Burt Young as the ex-Marine, Nick Chase; Corey Haim
as the prodigy, Matthew Wiggins; Jane Daly as Ms. Adler, the dorm mother; Sean
Gregory Sullivan as Carl; and Joshua Nelson as Sheldon. Reruns popped up on
NBC's Saturday morning schedule during the summer of 1991.

ROOTIE KAZOOTIE   NBC/ABC

9 DECEMBER 1950–1 NOVEMBER 1952 (NBC); 22 DECEMBER 1952–7 MAY 1954 (ABC)
Todd Russell hosted this half-hour children's show, set at the Rootie Kazootie Club.
The show featured puppets (such as Rootie Kazootie, Gala Poochie, Polka Dottie, El
Squeako, and Poison Zoomack), along with games and prizes for the studio audi-
ence. John Vee was also featured on the series, and the puppets were handled by Paul
Ashley and Frank Milano. The show was seen Saturdays over NBC, and weekday
evenings over ABC; the latter version was written and produced by Steve Carlin.

ROOTS   ABC

23 JANUARY 1977–30 JANUARY 1977   One of the most remarkable achievements in
television history, *Roots* was a twelve-hour adaptation, telecast on eight consecutive
nights, of Alex Haley's moving story about his search for his African ancestors. *Roots*
was the highest-rated series of all time—all eight telecasts ranked among the thirteen
highest-rated single programs of all time, and the final segment topped all shows with
a 51.1 rating and a 71 share. The A. C. Nielsen Company estimated that some 130
million viewers watched at least part of *Roots*. The adaptation of Haley's story was
simple and straightforward—it began with the capture of Kunta Kinte in West Africa
by slave traders and ended a century and a half later in Tennessee. Principal players
in the large cast included: LeVar Burton (a college student appearing in his first
television role) as Kunta Kinte; John Amos as Toby, as Kunta Kinte came to be called
in later life; Louis Gossett, Jr., as Fiddler; Leslie Uggams as Kizzy; Ben Vereen as
Chicken George; Cicely Tyson as Binta; Edward Asner as Captain Davies; Ralph
Waite as Slater; Lorne Greene as John Reynolds; Lynda Day George as Mrs. Reyn-
olds; Robert Reed as William Reynolds; Chuck Connors as Tom Moore; John
Schuck as Ordell; George Hamilton as Stephen Bennett; Lloyd Bridges as Evan
Brent; Scatman Crothers as Mingo; Lillian Randolph as Sister Sara; Richard
Roundtree as Sam Bennett; Georg Stanford Brown as Tom; and Hilly Hicks as
Lewis. David L. Wolper was the executive producer of *Roots*, which was nominated
for some three dozen Emmys. Stan Margulies was the producer; Marvin Chomsky,
John Erman, David Greene, and Gilbert Moses directed it. William Blinn was the
script supervisor, and Alex Haley served as consultant. Series stars Gossett and
Burton reprised their roles in a two-hour TV-movie, "Roots: The Gift," televised 11
December 1988 on ABC.

ROOTS: THE NEXT GENERATIONS   ABC

18 FEBRUARY 1979–25 FEBRUARY 1979   A seven-night, twelve-hour, $18-million-
sequel to *Roots, Roots: The Next Generations* (commonly known as *Roots II*) chronicled the saga of author Alex Haley's ancestors from 1882 to 1967. Although *Roots II*
did not utterly dominate the ratings as had *Roots I,* the miniseries proved highly
popular—the seven telecasts all ranked within the week's top eleven programs.
Principal players included: Avon Long as Chicken George Moore (Ben Vereen had
played the role in *Roots I*); Georg Stanford Brown as Tom Harvey (repeating his
Roots I role); Lynne Moody as his wife, Irene Harvey (also repeating from *Roots I*);
Henry Fonda as Colonel Warner, the local political boss; Richard Thomas as his son,
Jim Warner, who was disowned when he married a black woman; Marc Singer as
Andy Warner, who succeeded his father as the political boss; Olivia de Havilland as
Mrs. Warner, the Colonel's wife; Paul Koslo as Earl Crowther, Andy's hatchet man;
Bever-Leigh Banfield and Beah Richards as Cynthia Harvey, daughter of Tom and
Irene; Stan Shaw as Will Palmer, who married Cynthia (Will and Cynthia were Alex
Haley's grandparents); Harry Morgan as Bob Campbell, Will's employer; Irene Cara

as Bertha Palmer, daughter of Will and Cynthia; Dorian Harewood as Simon Haley, who married Bertha; Ruby Dee as Queen Haley, Simon's mother; Paul Winfield as Dr. Huguley, dean of the college where Simon Haley landed a teaching job; Christoff St. John, Damon Evans, and James Earl Jones as Alex Haley, son of Simon and Bertha; Debbie Allen as Nan, Haley's wife; Al Freeman, Jr., as Malcolm X, the charismatic Black Muslim whose autobiography was "told to" Haley; Marlon Brando (in his first TV dramatic role in thirty years) as George Lincoln Rockwell, leader of the American Nazi Party, whom Haley interviewed for *Playboy* magazine. The miniseries culminated with Haley's trip to West Africa, where a *griot*, or oral historian, told him of the disappearance of Kunta Kinte some 200 years before. *Roots: The Next Generations* was produced by Stan Margulies; David L. Wolper was the executive producer.

THE ROPERS   ABC
13 MARCH 1979–17 APRIL 1979; 15 SEPTEMBER 1979–22 MAY 1980   A spinoff from *Three's Company, The Ropers* starred Audra Lindley and Norman Fell as Helen and Stanley Roper, who moved into a condominium development. Also featured were Jeffrey Tambor as their new neighbor, Jeffrey P. Brookes III; Patricia McCormack as his wife, Anne Brookes; Evan Cohen as their young son, David; Louise Vallance (January 1980–May 1980) as Jenny Ballinger, the Ropers' boarder. Don Nicholl, Michael Ross, and Bernie West were the executive producers.

ROSEANNE   ABC
18 OCTOBER 1988–   One of the most influential series of its time, *Roseanne* was a sitcom about working class Americans whose star was herself a member of the working class. Known simply as Roseanne by 1994, she was born Roseanne Barr in 1952 and grew up in Salt Lake City. Married to Bill Pentland in the early 1970s, she was living in suburban Denver in 1978 and raising three young children (a fourth child, born to Roseanne in 1971 before her marriage, was given up for adoption). While working as a waitress she began writing comedy material for herself and appearing in local comedy clubs.

In 1985 she made her first appearance on the *Tonight* show (chewing gum during her act, she described herself as a "domestic goddess"), and in 1987 headlined her own comedy special on HBO. A year later she signed with producers Marcy Carsey and Tom Werner, who had produced the hit sitcoms *The Cosby Show* and *A Different World*, to star in a sitcom. The series, which was to have been titled *Life and Stuff*, had not been created specifically for her, but Roseanne made it uniquely her own. It was set in Lanford, Illinois, and starred Roseanne Barr (as she was then still known) as Roseanne Conner, a wife and mother of three who worked in a plastics factory. John Goodman costarred as her husband, Dan, a building contractor. Roseanne and Dan were overweight. Though they were the parents of three kids, they didn't have all the answers; often, neither mother nor father knew best. Rounding out the original cast were Lecy Goranson as elder daughter Becky (Goranson was succeeded by Sarah Chalke in 1993); Sara Gilbert as younger daughter Darlene; Michael Fishman as son D. J.; Laurie Metcalf as Roseanne's unhappy sister, Jackie Harris, a police officer; Natalie West as Roseanne's thrice-married coworker, Crystal Anderson; and George Clooney (1988–1989) as supervisor Booker Brooks.

Roseanne was an immediate success. It finished second in the annual Nielsen ratings during its first season, and finished in the top five for each of its first six seasons. With success, however, came controversy and disagreements. Never one to shy away from confrontation, Roseanne clashed with her producers and writers, and eventually with members of her own family. Series creator Matt Williams and director Ellen Falcon left the show by the middle of the first season, and executive producers Carsey and Werner absented themselves from the set. Roseanne's marriage to Bill Pentland ended in divorce, and in 1990 she married standup comedian Tom Arnold; Arnold appeared occasionally on the show as Dan's pal Arnie (the character was originally known as Arnie Merchant, and later as Arnie Thomas). After her remarriage Roseanne continued to make headlines when she accused her parents of abusing her as a child. In 1991 Roseanne Barr became known professionally as Roseanne Arnold.

The series evolved over the years as its characters, like many working class Americans, lost their jobs and found new ones. As the second season opened, Roseanne no longer worked at Wellman Plastics. After a stint at a beauty salon, she became a waitress. By 1991 she was working at Rodbell's Coffee Shop in a shopping mall. Martin Mull joined the cast as her gay boss, Leon Carp. Occasionally featured were Michael Des Barres as Leon's companion, Jerry, and Bonnie Sheridan (formerly known as Bonnie Bramlett when she was a rock and roll singer) as fellow waitress Bonnie. In 1991 Dan opened his own motorcycle business, Lanford Custom Cycles. Daughter Becky found a boyfriend, Mark Healy (played by Glenn Quinn), with whom she eloped in 1992. Daughter Darlene, like many teenagers, became more and more morose at home, spending much of her time in her room. She, too, acquired a boyfriend, David (played by Johnny Galecki). Dan's pal Arnie got married. Sandra Bernhard appeared occasionally as his wife, Nancy; unfortunately for Arnie, Nancy left him—for another woman. Roseanne's sister, Jackie, left the police force and became a long distance trucker. Estelle Parsons appeared occasionally as Roseanne and Jackie's troublesome mother, Bev.

In the fall of 1992 Dan's motorcycle business had folded, and the Conner family faced financial difficulties; their electricity was briefly shut off. Eventually, Dan landed a municipal job, and Roseanne and Jackie (with financial help from their mother) opened the Lanford Lunch Box. After years of unhappy relationships, Jackie had a baby and got married in 1994; Michael O'Keefe played her husband, Fred. Darlene ended her relationship with David, and went to Chicago to study art (David moved into the Conners' basement, however; in real life, Sara Gilbert started college at Yale, and taped her scenes in New York).

A Saturday-morning cartoon show based on a younger version of Roseanne's character appeared in 1990 (see *Little Rosey*). In the spring of 1993 Roseanne and Tom Arnold launched *The Jackie Thomas Show*, a sitcom starring Tom Arnold. Despite good ratings, it was not renewed, and Roseanne briefly threatened to take her series off the air in retaliation. The threat did not materialize, and in the spring of 1994 Roseanne filed for divorce.

As the seventh season premiered in 1994, the star was known no longer as Roseanne Arnold, but simply as Roseanne (the change was noted in the premiere episode's closing credits, as all cast and crew members were listed only by their first names). Early in 1995 Roseanne married Ben Thomas, who had been hired by Tom Arnold as their bodyguard and chauffeur; she was pregnant, through in-vitro fertilization, with Thomas's child. On the series, Roseanne was also pregnant. Roseanne's first husband, Bill Pentland, appeared briefly in one 1995 episode. Lecy Goranson returned as Becky in the fall of 1995, replacing Sarah Chalke (the two appeared together in the season premiere's closing credits, and Chalke also showed up in the 1995 Halloween episode). The Conners' baby was born on 31 October 1995, and was named Jerry Garcia Conner (although the new arrival had been announced as a girl during the previous season, Roseanne explained that she changed her mind and wanted it to be the same sex as her real-life son, Buck).

The success of *Roseanne* no doubt led to a proliferation of sitcoms starring standup comedians. Several of them, including *Seinfeld*, *Home Improvement*, *Grace Under Fire*, and *Ellen*, became major hits. Despite *Roseanne*'s huge popularity, it was snubbed at the Emmy awards. During its first six seasons the series was never nominated for Outstanding Comedy Series, and Roseanne herself was not nominated for Outstanding Lead Actress in a Comedy Series until the show's fourth season (she did not win until the following season). The series did win a prestigious Peabody Award in 1993, however (it was cited for having "the courage to look unflinchingly at contemporary family life"). By 1995 Roseanne had become the most powerful woman in domestic television. Earning an estimated $1 million per episode, she also had negotiated commitments to produce four new television series for ABC. One of them was expected to be an adaptation of the British sitcom, *Absolutely Fabulous*, to which Roseanne had obtained the American rights.

THE ROSEMARY CLOONEY SHOW   SYNDICATED

1956–1957   Rosemary Clooney, pop singer of the 1950s, hosted this series of thirty-nine half-hour variety shows, which also featured the Hi-Lo's (Bob Morse, Clark Burrows, Gene Puerling, and Bob Strasen) and Nelson Riddle's orchestra. In the fall of 1957 Clooney hosted her own network series: see *The Lux Show Starring Rosemary Clooney.*

ROSETTI AND RYAN   NBC

22 SEPTEMBER 1977–10 NOVEMBER 1977   This hour-long crime show vanished early in the 1977–1978 season. It featured Tony Roberts as lawyer Joe Rosetti, the dashing half of a successful defense team; Squire Fridell as his more serious partner, Frank Ryan, a former cop; Jane Elliott as Assistant District Attorney Jessica Hornesby; Ruth Manning as Emma; Randi Oakes as Georgia; and Dick O'Neill as Judge Praetor D. Hardcastle. Leonard B. Stern was the executive producer, Don M. Mankiewicz and Gordon Cotler the supervising producers, and Jerry Davis the producer for Universal Television. The series pilot was televised 23 May 1977.

THE ROSEY GRIER SHOW   SYNDICATED

1969   Former professional football star Roosevelt Grier hosted his own half-hour talk show for a brief time.

ROUGH GUIDE   PBS

1993–1994   Produced by the BBC, this travel series based on a popular series of travel books presented an un-whitewashed view of the selected destinations. Aired on PBS during the summertime, it was hosted by Magenta DeVine, Rajan Datar, and Sankha Guha in 1993, and by DeVine and Datar in 1994.

ROUGH RIDERS   ABC

2 OCTOBER 1958–24 SEPTEMBER 1959   An implausible western about three Civil War veterans—two Union soldiers and one Confederate soldier—who teamed up after the war. With Kent Taylor as Captain Flagg; Jan Merlin (the ex-Confederate) as Lieutenant Kirby; and Peter Whitney as Sergeant Sinclair. Kirby wore his guns backward in the holster, permitting him to "cross-draw."

THE ROUND TABLE   NBC

18 SEPTEMBER 1992–16 OCTOBER 1992   Hour continuing drama set in Washington, D.C., where the regulars congregated after work at a bar known as the Round Table. With Stacy Haiduk as Rhea McPherson, a former reporter trying to get a job with the FBI; Jessica Walter as her mother, Anne, a publisher; Roxann Biggs as Rhea's roommate, Jennifer Clemente, a federal prosecutor; David Gail as bartender Danny Burke; Thomas Breznahan as Mitchell Clark, who worked with Jennifer; David Ackroyd as Senator Jack Reed; Pepper Sweeney as Secret Service agent Devereaux Jones; Erik King as Wade Carter, a cop; and Alex Wilson as Rhea's cousin, Kaitlin Cavanaugh.

THE ROUNDERS   ABC

6 SEPTEMBER 1966–3 JANUARY 1967   Short-lived sitcom about a couple of cowpokes at a Texas cattle ranch. With Ron Hayes as Ben Jones; Patrick Wayne (son of John Wayne) as Howdy Lewis; Chill Wills as Jim Ed Love, owner of the J. L. Ranch; Janis Hansen as Sally, Ben's girlfriend; Bobbi Jordan as Ada, Howdy's girlfriend; Jason Wingreen as Shorty; James Bowen Brown as Luke; and Walker Edmiston as Regan. Ed Adamson produced the half-hour series for M-G-M.

THE ROUSTERS   NBC

1 OCTOBER 1983–26 DECEMBER 1983; 9 JUNE 1984–21 JULY 1984   Stephen J. Cannell created this hour light adventure series, which was set at the Sladetown Carnival in Southern California. The cast included Chad Everett as Wyatt Earp III (great-grandson of the legendary lawman), the carnival's chief roustabout and peacekeeper; Jim Varney as Evan Earp, Wyatt's con-artist brother; Mimi Rodgers as Ellen Slade,

daughter of the carnival owner, who taught the carnival youngsters and worked with the animals; Maxine Stuart as Wyatt's mother, Amanda Earp, a would-be bounty hunter; Timothy Gibbs as Michael, Wyatt's teenage son; and Hoyt Axton as the carnival owner, Cactus Jack Slade.

ROUTE 66   CBS
7 OCTOBER 1960–18 SEPTEMBER 1964   *Route 66,* an hour-long adventure series about two guys tooling around the country in a 1960 Corvette, was filmed on location throughout America. Featured were Martin Milner as Tod Stiles, a Yale grad, and George Maharis (1960–1962) as Buzz Murdock, a streetwise New Yorker; in the spring of 1963 Glenn Corbett succeeded Maharis as Tod's partner, Lincoln Case. Notable guest appearances on the series included those by Alan Alda ("Soda Pop and Paper Flags," 31 May 1963); Joey Heatherton (in her first TV dramatic role, "Three Sides," 18 November 1960); Robert Redford ("First Class Mouliak," 20 October 1961); Rod Steiger ("Welcome to the Wedding," 8 November 1963), and Ethel Waters ("Goodnight Sweet Blues," 6 October 1961; Waters's performance earned her an Emmy nomination, the first such nomination for a black actress). Herbert B. Leonard was the executive producer of the series for Screen Gems. Nelson Riddle's brilliant theme was a minor hit record in 1962. A new version of the series surfaced briefly in 1993: see below.

ROUTE 66   NBC
8 JUNE 1993–6 JULY 1993   The short-lived revival of the 1960-1963 series marked the 66th anniversary of the opening of the real U.S. Route 66. It starred James Wilder as Nick Lewis, the son of Buz Murdock from the old series, who had inherited his father's 1961 Corvette, and Dan Cortese as Arthur Clark, a hitchhiker picked up by Lewis.

THE ROWAN AND MARTIN SHOW   NBC
16 JUNE 1966–8 SEPTEMBER 1966   A summer replacement for *The Dean Martin Show, The Rowan and Martin Show* was an hour-long variety series cohosted by comedians Dan Rowan and Dick Martin. Also on hand were Lainie Kazan, Frankie Randall, Judi Rolin, Dom DeLuise, the Wisa D'Orso Dancers, and Les Brown and his band. Rowan and Martin are, of course, better known as the hosts of *Laugh-In* (see also that title).

ROXIE   CBS
1 APRIL 1987–8 APRIL 1987   One of the shortest-lived prime-time series in history, *Roxie* lasted only two episodes (as did *Take Five,* the unfortunate program which premiered immediately after it). It was set at the studios of WNYV, a tiny UHF television station in Manhattan. The cast included Andrea Martin as Roxie Brinkerhoff, the program director; Jack Riley as Leon Buchanan, the manager; Teresa Ganzel as Marcie McKinley, the secretary; Mitchell Laurance as Roxie's husband, Michael, a teacher; Ernie Sabella as Vito Carteri, the engineer; and Jerry Pavlon as Randy Grant, the gofer.

THE ROY DOTY SHOW   DUMONT
10 MAY 1953–4 OCTOBER 1953   Sunday-morning children's show, hosted by Roy Doty, who drew sketches and told stories.

THE ROY ROGERS AND DALE EVANS SHOW   ABC
29 SEPTEMBER 1962–22 DECEMBER 1963   Roy Rogers and Dale Evans, who had previously starred in a western, *The Roy Rogers Show,* cohosted this Saturday-night variety hour. Also featured were Cliff Arquette, Pat Brady, Cathie Taylor, and the Sons of the Pioneers.

THE ROY ROGERS SHOW   NBC
30 DECEMBER 1951–23 JUNE 1957   One of the most popular of TV's early westerns, especially with younger viewers, this half-hour show, set in the present, starred Roy

Rogers and his wife, Dale Evans, as themselves. Pat Brady was featured as Rogers's jeep-driving sidekick (the jeep was named Nellybelle), and the Sons of the Pioneers, the singing group with which Rogers (then known as Leonard Slye) broke into show business, were also on hand. Rogers rode Trigger, a trained horse (which Rogers had stuffed after its death), while Evans rode Buttermilk; rounding out the animal cast was Bullet, a German shepherd. Some 101 episodes were produced by Rogers' own company, Roy Rogers Productions.

THE ROYAL FAMILY   CBS

18 SEPTEMBER 1991–27 NOVEMBER 1991; 8 APRIL 1992–13 MAY 1992   Redd Foxx's last sitcom was this one, on which he played Al Royal, an Atlanta letter carrier whose imminent plans for a peaceful retirement with his wife were spoiled by the arrival back home of their adult daughter and her three kids. Joining Foxx were Della Reese as Al's wife, Victoria; Mariann Aalda as their newly divorced daughter, Elizabeth; Sylver Gregory as Elizabeth's sixteen-year-old, Kim; Larenz Tate as Elizabeth's fifteen-year-old, Curtis; and Naya Rivera as Elizabeth's four-year-old, Hillary. Eddie Murphy created the series, and Foxx tested CBS's censors by coining the catchphrase "Motherfather!" which Al uttered whenever he became exasperated.

On October 11, 1991, after seven episodes had been completed, Foxx collapsed on the set and died of a heart attack. Jackee then joined the series for several episodes as Ruth, Victoria's half-sister, who moved into the household. When the show returned in April 1992, Jackee was reintroduced as a new character, Coco, Victoria's elder daughter.

ROYAL PLAYHOUSE   DUMONT

12 APRIL 1951–12 JULY 1951; 3 APRIL 1952–26 JUNE 1952   This half-hour dramatic anthology series was seen on Thursday nights.

RUBIK THE AMAZING CUBE   ABC

10 SEPTEMBER 1983–1 SEPTEMBER 1984; 4 MAY 1985–31 AUGUST 1985   The central figure in this Saturday-morning cartoon show was Rubik, an animated version of the Rubik's Cube puzzle. The cartoon Rubik paled around with three kids, Renaldo, Carlos, and Lisa. Rubik was powerless when his colored sides were unaligned, but when his six faces were correctly positioned he wielded an array of superpowers. Ron Palillo (formerly of *Welcome Back, Kotter*) provided the voice of Rubik, which was electronically speeded up for television. During the 1983–1984 season the series was shown as the second portion of *The Pac-Man/Rubik the Amazing Cube Hour*. A few reruns popped up on ABC a season later.

RUDE DOG AND THE DWEEBS   CBS

16 SEPTEMBER 1989–1 SEPTEMBER 1990   Saturday morning cartoon show starring Rude Dog, a cool canine who operated a delivery service and drove a pink 1956 Cadillac, and his puppy pals.

RUFF AND REDDY   NBC

14 DECEMBER 1957–8 OCTOBER 1960; 29 SEPTEMBER 1962–26 SEPTEMBER 1964   *Ruff and Reddy* was the first network television series from Hanna-Barbera Productions. William Hanna and Joseph Barbera, who had created the *Tom and Jerry* cartoons early in the 1940s, formed their television partnership in 1957 and went on to produce some 100 series, most of which were animated. *Ruff and Reddy* was a Saturday-morning half-hour show and featured the adventures of a cat (Ruff) and dog (Reddy) team. Don Messick supplied Ruff's voice, Daws Butler supplied Reddy's. Other theatrical cartoons were also shown. The show was first hosted by Jimmy Blaine and later by Bob Cottle. The success of *Ruff and Reddy* soon led to such well-known Hanna-Barbera shows as *The Flintstones, Huckleberry Hound, The Jetsons,* and *Quickdraw McGraw*.

THE RUGGLES   ABC
3 NOVEMBER 1949–19 JUNE 1952   Kinescoped in Hollywood, this half-hour sitcom
starred Charles Ruggles as himself, Erin O'Brien Moore and Ruth Tedrow as his
wife, Margaret, and Margaret Kerry as their daughter. Robert Raisbeck was the
producer.

RUGRATS   NICK
11 AUGUST 1991–   Half-hour cartoon series on which life was examined from the
point of view of a group of toddlers—Tommy Pickles, twins Phil and Lil, Tommy's
cousin Angelica, and Spike the dog.

RUN, BUDDY, RUN   CBS
12 SEPTEMBER 1966–2 JANUARY 1967   Jack Sheldon starred in this half-hour sitcom as
Buddy Overstreet, a mild-mannered accountant who was forced to flee his pursuers
from The Syndicate after he overheard mobsters discussing "Chicken Little" in a
steam room. Also featured were Bruce Gordon as Mr. Devere, syndicate chieftain;
Jim Connell as Junior, Devere's son; Nick Georgiade as Wendell, one of Devere's
henchmen; and Gregg Palmer as Harry, another henchman.

RUN FOR YOUR LIFE   NBC
13 SEPTEMBER 1965–11 SEPTEMBER 1968   Roy Huggins, who developed *The Fugitive,*
also developed and produced this hour series about a man on the run. It starred
Ben Gazzara as Paul Bryan, a lawyer who learned that he had no more than two
years to live and decided to spend his remaining time traveling around and assisting
others. Though Bryan was told in the initial episode that he had only two years, the
series managed to stay on the air for three. The producers searched carefully for a
noncontagious, incurable disease which would enable Bryan to remain active; they
settled on chronic myelocytic leukemia, an illness which apparently has no debilitating symptoms.

RUN, JOE, RUN   NBC
7 SEPTEMBER 1974–4 SEPTEMBER 1976   This unusual live-action Saturday-morning
series combined *Lassie* with *The Fugitive.* Its central character was a German shepherd named Joe, who, while undergoing training for the Army K-9 Corps, was
wrongly accused of attacking his master and ran away; each week Joe found time to
help out someone in distress. During the first season Arch Whiting was featured as
Joe's master, Sergeant William Corey, who vainly pursued Joe to let him know that
he had been exonerated. During the second season Joe teamed up with a young hiker
named Josh McCoy (played by Chad States). Joe was played by Heinrich of Midvale.
The half-hour series was produced by Robert Williams and Bill Schwartz the first
season, and by Dick O'Connor the second season for William P. D'Angelo Productions, Inc.

RUNAROUND   NBC
9 SEPTEMBER 1972–1 SEPTEMBER 1973   Paul Winchell hosted this Saturday-morning
game show for children, on which nine youngsters competed; when questions were
asked, the players were supposed to run to certain squares onstage, which represented possible answers to the questions.

RUNAWAY WITH THE RICH AND FAMOUS   SYNDICATED
1987–1994   The third of Robin Leach's trilogy of celebrity-fawning shows (see also
Lifestyles of the Rich and Famous and *Fame, Fortune and Romance*), this one offered
the lure of first-class transportation and accommodations, plus spending money, to
celebs who were willing to have a camera crew accompany them on their "dream
vacations."

THE RUNAWAYS (OPERATION: RUNAWAY)   NBC
27 APRIL 1978–18 MAY 1978; 29 MAY 1979–4 SEPTEMBER 1979   An hour dramatic
series about a psychologist whose specialty was tracking down runaways and convinc-

ing them to return home, the show premiered in 1978 as a short-run series, titled *Operation: Runaway*. It starred Robert Reed as psychologist David McKay, with Karen Machon as his friend Karen Wingate, dean of women at the college where McKay's office was located; Michael Biehn as Mark Johnson, David's ward; and Ruth Cox as Susan. The show had been scheduled for NBC's fall 1978 schedule, but was yanked in August of 1978; it finally reappeared in May of 1979 entitled *The Runaways* and starring Alan Feinstein as psychologist Steve Arizzio. Karen Machon and Michael Biehn were retained from the 1978 cast, and two new faces were added: James Callahan as Sergeant Hal Grady, and Patti Cohoon as Debbie Shaw. The series was a QM Production.

RUNNING THE HALLS   NBC
11 SEPTEMBER 1993–3 SEPTEMBER 1994   A companion program to *Saved by the Bell*, this Saturday-morning live-action show was set at a private school, Middlefield Academy, where hijinks prevailed. With Richard Hayes as Andy McBain; Trevor Lissauer as Reese; Senta Moses as Nikki; Laurie Fortier as Holiday; Lackey Bevis as Molloy Simpson; Richard Speight, Jr., as Shark; Craig Kirkwood as Taylor; Mike Sabatino as Ferris Bachman; and Pamela Bowen as Miss Gilman.

RUSH LIMBAUGH, THE TELEVISION SHOW   SYNDICATED
1992–   Conservative Rush Limbaugh was already well known before inaugurating his television program in 1992. After a career as a disc jockey in the 1970s, he became host of a nationally syndicated talk radio show in 1988; the three-hour daytime radio broadcast became highly popular, and was syndicated to some 500 stations within four years. For television, Limbaugh distilled his presentation to a daily half hour of Limbaugh himself. The show featured no guests or callers, relying instead on the host's verbal skills to skewer liberals, gays, feminists, and other un-American undesirables. Limbaugh managed to hold his diatribes together with a sense of humor, and came across as articulate and affable. He held forth from behind a desk in a wood-paneled set which resembled a den, with its bookshelves lined with multiple copies of the host's two best-selling books. His studio audience was well dressed, with most men sporting coats and ties. Limbaugh succinctly explained himself to *Time* magazine in a 1995 interview: "I'm an entertainer with a conservative agenda." Roger Ailes, who had assisted the Reagan and Bush administrations in television strategy, was the executive producer.

RUSS HODGES' SCOREBOARD   DUMONT
14 APRIL 1948–22 APRIL 1949   Fifteen-minute nightly sports report by veteran sportscaster Russ Hodges.

THE RUSS MORGAN SHOW   CBS
7 JULY 1956–1 SEPTEMBER 1956   This Saturday-night half-hour musical variety series was hosted by bandleader Russ Morgan and featured singer Helen O'Connell.

RUTH LYONS' 50 CLUB   NBC
1 OCTOBER 1951–5 SEPTEMBER 1952   Broadcast from Cincinnati, this half-hour daytime variety show was hosted by Ruth Lyons and featured singers Bill Thall and Dick Noel.

RUTHIE ON THE TELEPHONE   CBS
7 AUGUST 1949–5 NOVEMBER 1949   A five-minute filmed comedy series, *Ruthie on the Telephone* starred Ruth Gilbert as Ruthie and Philip Reed as the unwilling recipient of her telephone calls. The show was seen five nights a week at 7:55.

RYAN'S FOUR   ABC
5 APRIL 1983–27 APRIL 1983   Hour medical drama about a physician supervising four interns. With Tom Skerritt as Dr. Thomas Ryan, who agreed to become director of interns at Wilshire Memorial Hospital after the suicide of his son, who had been an intern there; Albert Hall as intern Dr. Terence Wilson, a former cop; Timothy Daly

as Dr. Gillian; Dirk Blocker as Dr. Norman Rostov; Lisa Eilbacher as Dr. Ingrid Sorenson; and Nicolas Coster as Dr. Morris Whitford, the hospital director. David Victor created the series, and served as executive producer with Henry Winkler.

RYAN'S HOPE   ABC

7 JULY 1975–13 JANUARY 1989   One of the few daytime serials to be set in a large metropolis, Ryan's Hope was named after a fictional tavern located on Manhattan's West Side; most of the action took place there or at Riverside Hospital, to which most of the show's medical people were affiliated. The half-hour show was created by Claire Labine and Paul Avila Mayer. The original cast included: Faith Catlin as Dr. Faith Coleridge; Justin Deas as Dr. Bucky Carter; Bernard Barrow as Johnny Ryan, founder of Ryan's Hope; Helen Gallagher as his wife, Maeve Ryan; Michael Hawkins as Frank Ryan, their eldest son; Ilene Kristen as Delia Ryan, Frank's wife; Malcolm Groome as Dr. Pat Ryan, Johnny and Maeve's younger son; Kate Mulgrew as Mary Ryan, Johnny and Maeve's daughter; Diana Van Der Vlis as Dr. Nell Beaulac; John Gabriel as her husband, Seneca Beaulac; Frank Latimore as Dr. Ed Coleridge, Faith's father, an old friend of Johnny Ryan; Nancy Addison (later known as Nancy Addison Altman) as Jillian Coleridge, Ed's adopted daughter, who married and divorced Seneca Beaulac; Ronald Hale as Ed's son, Dr. Roger Coleridge, who had an affair with Delia Ryan and eventually married her; Michael Levin as reporter Jack Fenelli, who fell for Mary Ryan and married her; Michael Fairman as unscrupulous Nick Szabo; Earl Hindman as Delia's brother, Bob Reid; Hannibal Penney, Jr., as Clem Moultrie; and Rosalinda Guerra as Ramona Gonzalez.

Subsequent additions to the cast have included: Nancy Barrett (who replaced Faith Catlin), Catherine Hicks, and Karen Ann Morris (later known as Karen Morris-Gowdy) as Dr. Faith Coleridge; Andrew Robinson (who replaced Michael Hawkins), Daniel Hugh-Kelly, Geoffrey Pierson and John Sanderford as Frank Ryan; Robyn Millan, Randall Edwards, Ilene Kristen (again), Robin Mattson and Kristen (yet again) as Delia; Mary Carney (who replaced Kate Mulgrew), Kathleen Tolan, and Nicolette Goulet as Mary Ryan Fenelli, who was killed by mobsters (Mulgrew subsequently played the part in fantasy sequences); Tom MacGreevey as Tom Desmond, who married Faith; Julia Barr as Renie Szabo; Dennis Jay Higgins as Sam Crowell; John Perkins as Father McShane; Rosetta LeNoire as Miriam George; Jose Aleman as Angel Nieves; Ana Alicia Ortiz (later known as Ana Alicia) as Alicia Nieves; Louise Shaffer as Rae Woodard; Jadrien Steele and Jason Adams as Little John Ryan; Fat Thomas as Jumbo Marino; Lisa Sutton, Megan McCracken, and Nana Tucker (later known as Nana Visitor) as Nancy Feldman; John Blazo (who replaced Malcolm Groome), Robert Finoccoli, Patrick James Clarke, and Malcolm Groome (again) as Dr. Pat Ryan; Sarah Felder, Ann Gillespie, Marg Helgenberger, Carrell Myers, and Barbara Blackburn as Siobhan Ryan, another of Johnny and Maeve's children (Johnny and Maeve also had a fifth child, Kathleen Ryan [played by Nancy Reardon], who was occasionally glimpsed on the program); Pauline Flanagan as Annie Colleary; and Patrick Horgan as Thatcher Ross.

Also, Maureen Garrett as Elizabeth Jean Ryan, Johnny's niece; Will Patton as Ox Knowles, her husband; Richard Backus as Barry Ryan, Johnny's nephew; Richard Muenz, Roscoe Born, Michael Hennessy, Walt Willey, and Born (again) as ex-gangster Joe Novak, who married Siobhan Ryan; Kelli Maroney as Kimberly Harris, Rae Woodard's unstable daughter; Peter Haskell as Hollis Kirkland III, Kim's father; Christine Jones as Catsy Kirkland, Hollis's wife; Felicity LaFortune as Leigh Kirkland; Mary Page Keller and Ariane Munker as Amanda Kirkland; Stan Birnbaum (later known as Sam Behrens) as Dr. Adam Cohen; James Sloyan as Mitch Bronsky; Donald Vanhorn as Prince Albert, an ape who (in a *King Kong* story line) ran off with poor Delia; Michael Corbett as Michael Pavel; Trent Jones as Ken George Jones; Rose Alaio as Rose Melina; Christine Ebersole and Kathryn Dowling as Lilly Darnell; Nell Carter as Ethel Green; David Clarke as mobster Tizo Novotny; Kay de Lancey as Amy Morris; Charles Cioffi as Claudius Church; Joe Silver as Eliot; Kerry MacNamara, Jenny Rebecca Dweir, and Yasmine Bleeth as Ryan Fenelli, daughter of Jack and Mary Fenelli; Malachy McCourt as Kevin MacGuinness; Judith Chapman as Charlotte Greer MacCurtain; Roy Poole as Neil Greer MacCurtain; David Sederholm as Bill

Hyde; Kathleen Widdoes as Una MacCurtain; Gloria DeHaven as Bess Shelby; Robin Greer as Sidney Price; Cali Timmins as Maggie Shelby; Gerit Quealy as Jacqueline Novak; Daniel Pilon as Max Dubujak; Scott Holmes as David Greenberg; Corbin Bernsen as Kenny Graham; Fred Burnstein as Laslo Novotny; Lauren O'Bryan and Julia Campbell as Katie, daughter of the seldom-seen Kathleen; Traci Lin as Pru Shepherd; Herb Anderson as Jeremy Winthrop; Harve Presnell as Matthew Crane; Duncan Gamble as Tiger Bennett; Marisa Pavan as Chantal Dubujak; Susan Scannell as Gabrielle Dubujak/Chessy Blake; Christian Slater as D. J. LaSalle; Franc Luz as Stephen Latham; David O'Brien as Charles Whitehall; Nancy Valen as Melinda Weaver, who married Pat Ryan; Grant Show as Rick Hyde, who eloped with Ryan Fenelli; Tracey Ross as Diana Douglas; Leslie Easterbrook as Devlin Kowalski; Christopher Durham as fisherman Dakota Smith, who took in an amnesiac Jillian; Jack Palmer as Sam Banachek; Tichina Arnold as Zena Brown; Lois Robbins as Concetta D'Angelo, who also married Pat Ryan; Cynthia Dozier as Emily Hall; Jim Wlcek as Ben Shelby; Catherine Larson as Lizzie Ransome, who married young John Ryan; Lewis Arlt as Richard Rowan; Maria Pitillo as Nancy Don Louis; Diana Van Der Vlis (who had played Nell Beaulac in the original cast) as Sherry Rowan; Regis Philbin as Malachy Malone; Brian McGovern as Chaz; Lydia Hannibal as Chris Hannold; Irving Allen Lee as Evan Cooper; Cesare Danova as Silvio Conti; Michael Palance as Robert Rowan; Steve Fletcher as Matthew Strand; and Sylvia Sidney, Nancy Coleman, Natalie Priest, Jacqueline Brookes, Pauline Flanagan, and Rosemary Prinz as Sister Mary Joel, who ultimately turned out to be Jack Fenelli's mother.

During *Ryan's Hope*'s first years, Claire Labine and Paul Avila Mayer were the executive producers and the head writers. Labine and Mayer left the show, but returned briefly as head writers in 1983. Labine returned again in 1988, but by that time the series was in serious trouble. It had been moved to a late morning time slot, and a number of network affiliates were no longer carrying it; as a result it had sunk to the bottom of the daytime ratings. *Ryan's Hope* breathed its last in January 1989, with Maeve Ryan singing "Danny Boy" at the tavern.

SCTV NETWORK   NBC

15 MAY 1981–24 JUNE 1983   Television itself was satirized on this innovative and often hilarious late-night show. Aired at 12:30 A.M. on Friday nights, it replaced NBC's *Midnight Special* in the spring of 1981. *SCTV* was a longer and more expensive version of *Second City TV,* a half-hour syndicated series which ran from 1977 to 1980. It featured members of the Second City comedy troupe, most of whom came along to the network version: John Candy, Joe Flaherty, Eugene Levy, Andrea Martin, Rick Moranis, Catherine O'Hara, and Dave Thomas (Martin Short joined the group in 1982). Celebrity guests and rock bands also appeared regularly. Like *Second City TV, SCTV* was produced in Canada; facilities in Edmonton, Alberta, and Scarborough, Ontario, were used.

In the series "SCTV" was the call letters of the only television station in Melonville. The station was owned by Guy Caballero (Flaherty), a tasteless clod who cared only about making money, and run by Edith Prickley, an obnoxious administrator. Practically everything on commercial television was lampooned, from Perry Como to promotional spots to public service announcements. Among the station's many semi-regular offerings were such shows as "The Sammy Maudlin Show," a soap opera called "Days of the Week," and the ever-popular "The Fracases, America's Nastiest Couple."

An unexpectedly popular feature was "The Great White North." The segment was prepared in order to satisfy a Canadian regulatory requirement that programs produced there have at least some intrinsically Canadian content. Rick Moranis and Dave Thomas concocted a pair of stereotypical Canadians— the work-shirted, wool-capped, beer-guzzling brothers Bob and Doug McKenzie. As the co-hosts of "The Great White North," Bob and Doug spent most of their time talking aimlessly ("eh?"), opening six-packs, and "hosing" each other with suds. Nevertheless, the characters caught on with both Canadian and American audiences; the "McKenzies" released a popular record album and headlined a 1983 film, aptly titled *Strange Brew.*

The series went through three titles in its two-year run; it premiered as *SCTV*

Network 90, but switched to *SCTV Comedy Network* in the fall of 1981. A year later the title was shortened to *SCTV Network.* After two years in a late-night slot, the show's producers and cast turned down NBC's offer to move to prime time. The proffered slot was Sundays at 7:00 P.M., which was not only opposite CBS's formidable *60 Minutes,* but which also would have necessitated more family-oriented content. Instead, *SCTV* moved to the Cinemax cable network, where it surfaced late in 1983 as a twice-monthly, forty-five-minute show. Four of the network regulars were featured: Andrea Martin, Joe Flaherty, Eugene Levy, and Martin Short.

S.S. TELECRUISE ABC

28 APRIL 1951–2 JUNE 1951   This two-hour Saturday-morning variety show began locally in Philadelphia before going network for a few weeks in 1951. Hosted by "Cap'n" Jack Steck, it featured the Dave Appell Trio, baritone Eddie Roecker, Bon Bon, and Carol Wynne. The show's musical numbers were performed in front of photographs of exotic places.

S.W.A.T. ABC

24 FEBRUARY 1975–29 JUNE 1976   Generally criticized as one of the most violent shows of the decade, *S.W.A.T.* was the story of the Special Weapons and Tactics team, an elite unit of police officers stationed somewhere in California. Featured were Steve Forrest as Lieutenant Dan "Hondo" Harrelson, the leader; Rod Perry as Sergeant David "Deacon" Kay, second in command; Robert Urich as Officer James Street; Mark Shera as Officer Dominic Luca; and James Coleman as Officer T. J. McCabe. Created by Robert Hamner, *S.W.A.T.*'s executive producers were Aaron Spelling and Leonard Goldberg; the pilot for the series was telecast 17 February 1975, as one episode of *The Rookies,* another Spelling-Goldberg Production.

SABER OF LONDON
See MARK SABER

SABLE ABC

7 NOVEMBER 1987–2 JANUARY 1988   Seven-episode crime show based on a comic book, starring Lewis Van Bergen as Nicholas Flemming, mild-mannered author of children's books by day, and as Jon Sable, black-clad, striped-faced crimefighter by night. With Rene Russo as Nicholas's agent, Eden Kendall; Ken Page as Cheesecake, a black and blind computer whiz, the only person who knew of Flemming's dual identity; Holly Fulger as Myke Blackman, Flemming's illustrator; and Marge Kotlisky as Cynthia, his secretary. Dick Rosetti was executive producer.

SABRINA, THE TEENAGE WITCH CBS

12 SEPTEMBER 1970–31 AUGUST 1974   Sabrina, a teenage witch, was first introduced on *The Archie Show,* but in the fall of 1970 she was given her own hour cartoon series; that season the show was titled *Sabrina and the Groovie Goolies.* In the fall of 1971 the show was reduced to thirty minutes and retitled *Sabrina, the Teenage Witch* (*The Groovie Goolies* were given their own series that year, too). Sabrina was later reunited with Archie and Company on *The Archie Comedy Hour* and *The New Archie Sabrina Hour.* In the fall of 1977 she was again featured on her own series: see *Super Witch.* See also *The Archie Show; The Groovie Goolies.*

SAFARI TO ADVENTURE SYNDICATED

1971–1973   Bill Burrud served as host and narrator of this half-hour series of nature films.

SAFARILAND SYNDICATED

1963   Half-hour African travelogue, narrated by Jim Stewart.

SAILOR OF FORTUNE SYNDICATED

1957   Lorne Greene starred in this Canadian-produced half-hour adventure series as freighter captain Grant (Mitch) Mitchell.

THE SAINT   SYNDICATED/NBC/CBS

1963–1966 (SYNDICATED); 21 MAY 1967–3 SEPTEMBER 1967; 17 FEBRUARY 1968–14
SEPTEMBER 1968; 18 APRIL 1969–12 SEPTEMBER 1969 (NBC); 21 DECEMBER 1979–15
AUGUST 1980 (CBS)   The Saint, as fictional detective Simon Templar was sometimes
known, was created by Leslie Charteris in a series of novels. The first television
version, which starred Roger Moore as Simon Templar, was produced in England by
ITC. Also featured were Winsley Pithey, Norman Pitt, and Ivor Dean as Inspector
Claude Teal of Scotland Yard. The CBS version, titled *Return of the Saint*, starred Ian
Ogilvy.

ST. ELSEWHERE   NBC

26 OCTOBER 1982–25 MAY 1988   This hour medical drama was set at St. Eligius, a
city-run hospital in Boston. The hospital was derisively known as "St. Elsewhere"
because of its reputation as a "dumping ground." The series was described by some
critics (and advertised by the network) as "*Hill Street Blues* set in a hospital." There
were several similarities: both series were supplied by MTM Enterprises, both employed large casts, and both used continuing storylines. Also, both shows premiered
to critical praise but low ratings. Miraculously, *St. Elsewhere* was renewed for a
second season even though it wound up in 86th place out of 98 prime-time series (it
was, by far, the season's lowest-rated entertainment series to be renewed).

The large cast of regulars included: Ed Flanders (1982–fall 1987) as Dr. Donald
Westphall, St. Eligius's caring and well-respected chief of staff, a widower who lived
with his teenage daughter and autistic son; William Daniels as Dr. Mark Craig, the
abrasive but highly capable chief of surgery; Ed Begley, Jr., as Dr. Victor Ehrlich,
the klutzy resident who worshipped Dr. Craig; David Morse as long-suffering Dr.
Jack Morrison, who was put through as many travails as the writers could devise;
Howie Mandel as Dr. Wayne Fiscus, specialist in emergency medicine; Christina
Pickles as oft-married nurse Helen Rosenthal; Denzel Washington as Dr. Philip
Chandler; Norman Lloyd as hospital administrator Dr. Daniel Auschlander, a liver
specialist who battled his own liver cancer; David Birney (1982–1983) as libidinous
surgeon Dr. Ben Samuels; G. W. Bailey (1982–1983) as psychiatrist Dr. Hugh Beale;
Kavi Raz (1982–1984) as anesthesiologist Dr. V. J. Kochar; Cynthia Sikes (1982–
1985) as Dr. Annie Cavanero; Barbara Whinnery (1982–1985) as pathologist Dr.
Cathy Martin, who was raped; Terence Knox (1982–1985) as Dr. Peter White, the
rapist; Ellen Bry (1983–1985) as Nurse Shirley Daniels, who shot and killed White;
Nancy Stafford (1983–1985) as city health advisor Joan Halloran; Kim Miyori (1983–
1984) as Dr. Wendy Armstrong, who committed suicide; Paul Sand (1983–1984) as
psychologist Dr. Michael Ridley; Stephen Furst (1983–1988) as anxiety-filled Dr.
Elliot Axelrod; Sagan Lewis (1983–1988) as surgeon Dr. Jacqueline Wade; Mark
Harmon (1983–1986) as sexually active surgeon Dr. Bob Calswell, who developed
AIDS; Eric Laneuville as Luther Hawkins, an orderly who became an emergency
medical technician; Byron Stewart as orderly Warren Coolidge (the same role he'd
played on *The White Shadw*) Florence Halop (1984–1985) as the chronically pesky
patient Mrs. Hufnagel; Cindy Pickett (1985–1988) as Carol Novino, a nurse who
became a physician; Alfre Woodard (1985–1987) as obstetrician-gynecologist Dr.
Roxanne Turner, who had a romance with Chandler; Jennifer Savidge as Nurse Lucy
Papandreou, who had a torrid afair with Ehrlich and eventually married him; Bruce
Greenwood (1986–1988) as manipulative Dr. Seth Griffin; and France Nuyen (1986–
1988) as surgeon Dr. Paulette Kiem.

Occasionally featured over the years were Bonnie Bartlett as Ellen Craig, David's
patient wife (Bartlett and Daniels were married in real life, and Bartlett became a
full-fledged regular during the later seasons); Dana Short as Lizzie, Westphall's
daughter; Chad Allen as Tommy, Westphall's autistic son; Patricia Wettig (1986–
1988) as Joanne McFadden, Dr. Morrison's second wife; and Karen Landry (1982–
1984) as Myra White, Peter's wife.

In the fall of 1987, St. Eligius was sold to Ecumena, a private health care corporation determined to run the hospital at a profit. Ronny Cox joined the cast as the new
administrator, Dr. John Gideon, who soon was at odds with Drs. Auschlander and
Westphall. Ed Flanders (as Westphall) left after the first three episodes of the season,

departing in the now-famous program of 30 September, "Moon for the Misbegotten," on which Westphall dropped his trousers and "mooned" Gideon. Westphall returned for the series' concluding episode, "The Last One," telecast 25 May 1988; in the final scene, young Tommy is seen playing at home with a miniature St. Eligius snow globe, which is taken from his hands by Donald Westphall, who is not a doctor. The suggestion, of course, was that the entire series had been nothing more than a figment of the imagination.

The series' producers and writers used their imaginations to stretch the series beyond the confines of the ordinary medical drama. References were often made to other TV shows and to films; the hospital's public address system frequently paged other TV doctors, such as "Dr. Morton Chegley" from *Julia*. Jack Riley, who played the troubled Mr. Carlin on *The Bob Newhart Show* in the 1970s, showed up in the psycho ward on one episode; the name of an NBC executive was given to a cadaver on one show. Other episodes pushed further, introducing rock videos in a dream sequence, taking Dr. Fiscus to Heaven, and flashing back to the origins of St. Eligius fifty years earlier (with many of the older regulars playing younger versions of themselves). Joshua Brand and John Falsey created the series.

SAINTS AND SINNERS   NBC
17 SEPTEMBER 1962–28 JANUARY 1963   This hour-long dramatic series was set at a newspaper, the New York *Record* (the same paper had been featured in *The Roaring Twenties*). It starred Nick Adams as Nick Alexander, a reporter, and featured John Larkin as city editor Mark Grainger; Richard Erdman as Klugie, the photographer; Robert F. Simon as copy editor Dave Tobiak; and Barbara Rush as Washington correspondent Liz Hogan.

SALE OF THE CENTURY   NBC/SYNDICATED
29 SEPTEMBER 1969–13 JULY 1973 (NBC); 1973 (SYNDICATED); 3 JANUARY 1983–24 MARCH 1989 (NBC); 1985 (SYNDICATED)   On this merchandise giveaway show, contestants won the right to "buy" proffered prizes at very low prices by answering simple questions. Jack Kelly hosted the series from 1969 to 1971, when affable Joe Garagiola succeeded him. After the series ended its original run here in 1973, it was bought by Australian producer Reg Grundy. Grundy succeeded in turning the show into a hugely popular hit Down Under and was able to interest NBC in a new American version. When the show reappeared here in 1983, Jim Perry was its new host. Sally Julian was his original assistant; she was replaced by Lee Menning in March 1983. Top prize on the new version was a possible jackpot of $310,000.

SALLY   NBC
15 SEPTEMBER 1957–30 MARCH 1958   *Sally* was a half-hour sitcom about a former salesclerk who was invited to accompany a slightly daffy widow on a trip around the world. It starred Joan Caulfield as Sally Truesdale and Marion Lorne as her patron, Myrtle Banford. By February of 1958, the two had returned home, and Sally went back to her job at the Banford and Bleacher Department Store. Three new regulars were added for the last few episodes: Gale Gordon as Bascomb Bleacher, Sr., manager of the store; Johnny Desmond as Jim Kendall; and Arte Johnson as Junior Bleacher. *Sally* was the first filmed series produced by Paramount Television.

SALLY JESSY RAPHAEL   SYNDICATED
1985–   Daytime talk show, hosted by former radio talk show host Sally Jessy Raphael. Like her competitors, Raphael's show employed a studio audience and frequently presented shows on titillating topics. Also like some of her competitors, the show fell prey to impostors: one man who claimed to be an impotent husband on her show also appeared as an unmarried virgin on *Geraldo,* while a woman masquerading as a surrogate sex partner had been a "wife who hated sex" on *The Oprah Winfrey Show*. A sampling of topics from shows aired during April and May 1995 would include "Overweight People's Fashion Blunders," "Female Teenage Bullies," "Girls Embarrassed by Their Mothers' Sexy Styles," "Videotaped Indiscretions," and "Teens Who Flaunt Their Sexuality."

SALTY   SYNDICATED

1974   An innocuous half-hour adventure series about two boys and Salty, their pet sea lion. With Mark Slade and Johnny Doran as brothers Taylor and Tim Reed, who were rescued in the hurricane that claimed their parents' lives; Julius Harris as Clancy Ames, their rescuer, owner of the Cove Marina; and Vincent Dale as Tim's pal, Rod Porterfield. Filmed in the Bahamas, the series was produced by Kobi Jaeger.

SALVAGE 1   ABC

29 JANUARY 1979–11 NOVEMBER 1979   Hour adventure series starring Andy Griffith as Harry Broderick, a junk dealer with high aspirations; each week he and his crew embarked on a salvage expedition of epic proportions (in the pilot film, for example, they built a rocket and flew to the moon to retrieve the debris left behind by the astronauts). Also featured were Joel Higgins as Skip Carmichael, a former astronaut; Trish Stewart as Melanie Slozar, a fuel expert; J. Jay Saunders as Mack; and Richard Jaeckel as Jack Klinger, a federal agent who kept an eye on Broderick. Executive producers: Harve Bennett and Harris Katleman for Bennett-Katleman Productions in association with Columbia Pictures TV. Though the show did not appear on ABC's schedule for the fall of 1979, it resurfaced as a replacement series for *Out of the Blue* and *A New Kind of Family.*

SAM   CBS

14 MARCH 1978–18 APRIL 1978   Sam was a Labrador retriever assigned to the Los Angeles Police Department in this half-hour crime show from Jack Webb's Mark VII Ltd. Also featured were Mark Harmon as Officer Mike Breen and Len Wayland as Officer Clagett. The pilot for the series was aired 24 May 1977.

SAM BENEDICT   NBC

15 SEPTEMBER 1962–7 SEPTEMBER 1963   An hour-long crime show about a San Francisco defense attorney. With Edmond O'Brien as Sam Benedict; Richard Rust as his young associate, Hank Tabor; and Joan Tompkins as his secretary, Trudy Warner. William Froug produced the series for MGM. The character was loosely based on real-life San Francisco defense attorney Jake Ehrlich.

THE SAM LEVENSON SHOW   CBS

27 JANUARY 1951–30 JUNE 1951; 10 FEBRUARY 1952–10 JUNE 1952; 27 APRIL 1959–25 SEPTEMBER 1959   Humorist Sam Levenson hosted three shows of his own. On the first, which was seen on Saturday nights, celebrity guests appeared with their children and discussed the trials and tribulations of child raising. The second *Sam Levenson Show* was a half-hour variety series, which began on Sunday nights but later shifted to Tuesdays. Levenson's third series was a daytime show which replaced *Arthur Godfrey Time* when Godfrey had to undergo surgery; this half-hour series was produced by Charles Andrews.

SAMMY AND COMPANY   SYNDICATED

1975–1977   Sammy Davis, Jr., hosted this ninety-minute variety series; other regulars included Johnny Brown, Kay Dingle, Joyce Jillson, Avery Schreiber, and announcer William B. Williams. Pierre Cossette was executive producer of the series, which was taped in New York, Las Vegas, and Los Angeles.

THE SAMMY DAVIS, JR. SHOW   NBC

7 JANUARY 1966–22 APRIL 1966   The first variety show of the decade to be hosted by a black performer, *The Sammy Davis, Jr. Show* unfortunately inherited the Friday slot formerly occupied by *Convoy* and, despite an impressive guest list (Richard Burton and Elizabeth Taylor on the premiere, Judy Garland on two other shows), failed to attract decent ratings. Also featured were the Lester Wilson Dancers and the George Rhodes Orchestra. One reason for the show's failure was that, because of contractual commitments to ABC, Davis himself was unable to appear on the program after the premiere until 11 February. Another reason was that it was scheduled opposite two popular sitcoms on CBS, *Hogan's Heroes* and *Gomer Pyle.*

THE SAMMY KAYE SHOW   CBS/NBC/ABC

28 JULY 1951–19 JULY 1952 (CBS); 8 AUGUST 1953–5 SEPTEMBER 1953 (NBC); 20 SEPTEMBER 1958–13 JUNE 1959 (ABC)   Bandleader Sammy Kaye hosted three Saturday-night musical programs. All were half-hour shows; the first was an early evening show on CBS; the second, on NBC, was seen at 8 P.M.; and the third, originally titled *Sammy Kaye's Music from Manhattan,* was scheduled at 10 P.M. on ABC. The latter show also featured singers Ray Michaels, Lynn Roberts, Larry Ellis, and Hank Kanui, plus Kaye's seventeen-piece band. Kaye also hosted a musical game show: see *So You Want to Lead a Band.*

SAMSON AND GOLIATH   NBC

9 SEPTEMBER 1967–31 AUGUST 1968   On this Saturday-morning cartoon show from Hanna-Barbera Productions, a boy named Samson and his dog, Goliath, could, when the need arose, transform themselves into a superhero and a lion, respectively. The series was retitled *Young Samson* in April 1968.

SAN FRANCISCO BEAT

See THE LINEUP

SAN FRANCISCO INTERNATIONAL AIRPORT   NBC

28 OCTOBER 1970–25 AUGUST 1971   The second segment of NBC's *Four-in-One* umbrella program, this hour show was, obviously, set at a big-city airport. Featured were Lloyd Bridges as Jim Conrad, the manager; Clu Gulager as security chief Bob Hatten; Barbara Siegel as Suzie, Jim's daughter; and Barbara Werle as Jim's secretary, June.

SAN FRANCISCO MIX   PBS

6 OCTOBER 1970–29 JUNE 1971   Each program of this twenty-six-week series focused on a single topic or theme. Richard Moore was the producer, and the regulars included Taula Lawrence, Tom Dahlgren, John Sharp, Victor Wong, and Virginia Anderson.

THE SAN PEDRO BEACH BUMS   ABC

19 SEPTEMBER 1977–19 DECEMBER 1977   An unsuccessful attempt at an hour sitcom, *The San Pedro Beach Bums* were a group of five guys who lived on an old boat in the San Pedro (Calif.) harbor: Chris Murney as Buddy Binder; Stuart Pankin as Stuf; John Mark Robinson as Dancer (Ed McClory); Darryl McCullough as Moose; and Christopher DeRose as Boychick. Also featured were Christoff St. John as Ralphie; Susan Mullen as Suzy; and Lisa Reeves as Margo. Aaron Spelling and Douglas S. Cramer were the executive producers; the pilot for the series, "The San Pedro Bums," was telecast 13 May 1977.

SANDY DREAMS   ABC

7 OCTOBER 1950–2 DECEMBER 1950   The principal character in this Saturday-evening children's show was a girl named Sandy, who was transported to the fantasy land of her dreams each week.

THE SANDY DUNCAN SHOW   CBS

17 SEPTEMBER 1972–31 DECEMBER 1972   Sandy Duncan, who had formerly been featured in *Funny Face,* returned in this half-hour sitcom with a faintly different format. Duncan starred as Sandy Stockton, a U.C.L.A. student, a part-time secretary, and an occasional star of commercials. Also featured were Marian Mercer as Kay Fox, her neighbor; Tom Bosley as Bert Quinn, her boss at the Quinn and Cohen Advertising Agency; Pam Zarit as Hilary, the receptionist; Eric Christmas as Ben Hampton, the handyman in Sandy's apartment building; and M. Emmet Walsh as Alex Lembeck, a motorcycle cop who was a neighbor of Sandy's.

SANFORD   NBC

15 MARCH 1980–10 SEPTEMBER 1980; 29 MAY 1981–14 AUGUST 1981   After a three-year absence, Redd Foxx returned as junk dealer Fred Sanford in this short-lived sequel to *Sanford and Son*. Also featured were Dennis Burkley as Fred's hefty white partner, Cal Petty; Marguerite Rae as a wealthy Beverly Hills widow, Evelyn (Eve) Lewis, Sanford's romantic interest; Suzanne Stone as Cissy, Eve's daughter; Cathy Cooper as Clara, Eve's maid; Percy Rodriguez as Winston, Eve's stuffy butler; Nathaniel Taylor as Sanford's pal, Raoul "Rollo" Larson; and Clinton Derricks-Carroll as Cliff, Sanford's nephew.

SANFORD AND SON   NBC

14 JANUARY 1972–2 SEPTEMBER 1977   *Sanford and Son*, the second TV series developed by then partners Norman Lear and Bud Yorkin, was NBC's most popular prime-time series for four seasons (1972–1973 through 1975–1976). Lear and Yorkin acquired the rights to a British series, *Steptoe and Son*, and Americanized it by casting it with black performers. The half-hour sitcom starred veteran comedian Redd Foxx as cantankerous Fred Sanford, a widowed junk dealer living in Los Angeles (Foxx, whose real name was John Sanford, had seldom been seen on television before the series), and Demond Wilson as his devoted but restless son, Lamont Sanford. Foxx also brought in some of his contemporaries to work on the show, such as Whitman Mayo, who appeared as Grady Wilson (and later received his own show, *Grady*), Slappy White, who played Melvin, and LaWanda Page, who played Aunt Esther, the sister of Fred's late wife Elizabeth and the butt of many of Fred's jokes. Also featured were Gregory Sierra (1972–1974) as Julio, a friend of Lamont's; Nathaniel Taylor as Rollo; Raymond Allen as Uncle Woody; Don Bexley as Bubba Hoover; Lynn Hamilton as Donna Harris, Fred's female friend; Howard Platt as Hoppy, a local police officer; Hal Williams as Smitty, another cop; Pat Morita (1975–1976) as Ah Chew; Marlene Clark as Janet; and Edward Crawford as Roger. By the end of the 1976–1977 season, both Foxx and Wilson had decided to leave the series—Foxx signed with ABC and hosted his own variety show (see *The Redd Foxx Comedy Hour*) and Wilson turned up in a midseason sitcom (see *Baby, I'm Back*). NBC, however, decided to salvage what it could from the old show and introduced *Sanford Arms* in the fall of 1977 (see below). Bud Yorkin was the executive producer of *Sanford and Son* and Aaron Ruben was its first producer; Ruben was succeeded by coproducers Saul Turteltaub and Bernie Orenstein.

SANFORD ARMS   NBC

16 SEPTEMBER 1977–14 OCTOBER 1977   *Sanford Arms*, NBC's attempt to keep *Sanford and Son* going after the departures of Redd Foxx and Demond Wilson, proved to be one of the first cancellations of the 1977–1978 season. As *Sanford Arms* opened, it was explained that Fred and Lamont Sanford had moved to Phoenix, and that their house and the place next door had been bought. Featured were Teddy Wilson as Phil Wheeler, the new purchaser, who planned to convert the place next door to a rooming house and to use the Sanford place as his home and office; Tina Andrews as Angie Wheeler, Phil's twenty-year-old daughter; John Earl as Nat Wheeler, Phil's twelve-year-old son; Bebe Drake-Hooks as Jeannie, Phil's girlfriend; Don Bexley as Bubba Hoover; LaWanda Page as Esther, who collected the mortgage payments for Fred Sanford; and Whitman Mayo as Grady Wilson. Bud Yorkin, Bernie Orenstein, and Saul Turteltaub (all of whom had worked on *Sanford and Son*) were the executive producers of *Sanford Arms* and Woody Kling was its producer.

SANTA BARBARA   NBC

30 JULY 1984–15 JANUARY 1993   An hour daytime serial, *Santa Barbara* was created by Bridget and Jerome Dobson, who had previously served as head writers for *General Hospital*, *Guiding Light*, and *As the World Turns*. The Dobsons sold the show to New World Television in 1985; battles over "creative control" ensued, and the Dobsons' connections to the series were severed for a time. Anne Howard Bailey succeeded the Dobsons as head writer; Bailey was replaced by Charles Pratt, Jr., late in 1988. The Dobsons regained control of the series in 1991.

Santa Barbara never achieved ratings success, though it did win Emmys for outstanding daytime drama series in 1987–1988 and in 1988–1989. It was generally considered TV's wittiest soap opera. Originally, its central characters were the members of two wealthy families—the Capwells and the Lockridges—who were neighbors in Santa Barbara, California (their mansions were even connected by a secret tunnel). Most of the Lockridges had been written out by the end of the 1980s, and the lower-class Castillos, DiNapolis, and Donnellys had become prominent.

The cast included: Dame Judith Anderson and Janis Paige as Minx Lockridge, grand dame of the clan; Nicolas Coster as her son, Lionel Lockridge; Louise Sorel as Lionel's wife, Augusta Lockridge; Julie Ronnie, Susan Marie Snyder, and Shell Danielson as their daughter, Laken Lockridge; John Allen Nelson, Scott Jenkins, and Jack Wagner as their son, Warren Lockridge; Peter Mark Richman, Paul Burke, Charles Bateman, and Jed Allan as Channing Creighton (C. C.) Capwell, head of the Capwell clan; Shirley Ann Field and Marj Dusay as his first wife, Pamela; Judith McConnell as his second wife, Sophia Wayne, a former actress; Lane Davies, Terry Lester, and Gordon Thomson as Mason Capwell, son of C. C. and Pamela (Davies also played Mason's alter ego, Sonny Sprockett); Robin Wright, Kimberly MacArthur, Carrington Garland, and Eileen Davidson as Kelly Capwell, daughter of C. C. and Sophia; Marcy Walker as Eden Capwell, daughter of C. C. and Sophia (one of daytime's longest-suffering characters, Eden was hospitalized seven times in the show's first three years; later in the series she split into four personalities, one of them male); Todd McKee and Michael Brainard as Ted Capwell, son of C. C. and Sophia; Robert Wilson as Channing Capwell, Jr., who was actually the son of Lionel Lockridge and Sophia, and who was accidentally killed by Sophia; A Martinez as Cruz Castillo, whose romance with Eden lasted for several years (and innumerable crises) until they finally made it to the altar in 1988 (their honeymoon involved a trip back to the 1960s); Linda Gibboney and Robin Mattson as bitchy Gina Demott, who would become C. C. Capwell's third (and fourth) wife; Scott Curtis, Brandon Call, and Justin Gocke as her adopted son, Brandon Demott; Dane Witherspoon, Mark Arnold, and Andrew Masset as Joe Perkins; Melissa Brennan as teen Jade Perkins; Valorie Armstrong as Marisa Perkins; Robert Alan Browne as John Perkins; Ava Lazar, Margaret Michaels, Gina Gallego, and Wanda De Jesus as Santana Andrade; Rupert Ravens as Danny Andrade; Margarita Cordova as Rosa Andrade; Ismael Carlo as Ruben Andrade; Stephen Meadows as Peter Flint, the "Carnation Killer"; Nancy Grahn as lawyer Julia Wainwright; Paula Kelly as Ginger Jones; Richard Eden as Brick Wallace, son of Sophia and Lionel; Wolf Muser as Marcello Armanti; Suzanne Marshall as Maggie Gillis; Tricia Cast as Christy Duvall; Harley Kozak as Mary Duvall (unfortunately killed, when the "C" from the Capwell Hotel sign fell on her); Joel Bailey as Lindsay Smith; Carmen Zapata, Marisol Rodriguez, and Karmin Murcelo as Cruz's mother, Carmen Castillo; Lenore Kasdorf as Caroline Wilson; Jane Sibbett as her daughter, split personality Jane Wilson/Roxanne; Robert Thaler as Pearl Bradford; Stacy Edwards as Hayley Benson, who married Ted Capwell; Lynn Clark and Paula Irvine as Lily Light, daughter of Gina; Justin Deas and John Novak as district attorney Keith Timmons, who married Gina; David Haskell as Nick Hartley; Page Moseley as his brother, Dylan Hartley; Kristen Meadows as Tori Lane, ex-lover of Cruz, who married Mason Capwell; Joseph Bottoms as evil Kirk Cranston; Kyle Secor as Brian Bradford; Marie-Alise Recasner as Alice Jackson; Julia Campbell as Courtney Capwell, C. C.'s niece; Stoney Jackson as cop Phil Whitney; Ross Kettle as Jeffrey Conrad; Michael Durrell as Dr. Alex Nikolas; Sherilyn Wolter as Elena Nikolas, who threw poor Eden off a cliff; Scott Jaeck as Cain Garver, the mountain man who rescued Eden; David Fonteno as Gus Jackson; Rick Edwards as Jake Morton; Chip Mayer as T. J. Daniels; Vincent Irrizarry as Dr. Scott Clark; James Luisi as Frank Clark; Ally Walker as Andrea Bedford; Eva LaRue as Margot; Warren Burton as Major Philip Hamilton; Jane Rogers as Heather Donnelly; Frank Runyeon as Father Michael Donnelly; Jon Cypher as Dr. Arthur Donnelly; Deborah Pollack as Sister Agatha; Phyllis Frelich as Sister Sarah; Tamlyn Tomita as Ming Li; Leigh McCloskey as rapist Zach Kelton (McCloskey returned to play a second role, district attorney Ethan Asher); Jeanna Michaels as Lydia Saunders; Joe Marinelli as transvestite Bunny Tagliari; Russell Curry as Lieutenant Boswell; Signy Coleman as

Crystal/Celeste; Julie Condra as Celeste's sister, Emily DiNapoli; Tawny Kitaen as Lisa DiNapoli; Denise Gentile as Vanessa; Meg Bennett as Megan Richardson; Paul Johannson as Greg Richardson; Christopher Norris as Laura Asher; Kelly Ann Conn as Wanda Berkowski; John Considine as Grant Capwell, C. C.'s brother; Kayla Savage as Anisa; Peter Love as Cruz's brother, Ricardo Castillo; Elizabeth Storm as Hollis Castillo, Ric's wife; Nathan Purdee as Jed; Roscoe Born as Robert Barr; Steve Carlson as Sean Morrissey; Miranda Wilson as Sandra Mills; Steve Bond as Mack Blake; James Healey as Derek Griffin; Constance Marie as Nikki; Michelle Nicastro as Sasha; John O'Hurley as Stephen Slade; Stella Stevens as Phyllis; Karen Moncrieff as Cassandra Benedict; Roberta Bizeau and Marguerite Hickey as split personality Debra/Flame; Jenny Lester McKeon and Rosalind Allen as Gretchen Richards; Allan Miller as Harland Richards, Gretchen's husband; Timothy Gibbs as Dash Nichols; Linden Chiles as Edward Nichols, Dash's dad; Robert Mandan as Maxwell; William Schallert as Roger Wainwright; Kai Wulff as Andre; John Callahan as Craig Hunt; Jennifer Hale as Melanie; Rawley Valverde as Amado Alvarez; Maria Ellingsen as East German immigrant Katrina Braun; John Beck as Judge David Raymond; Nina Arvesen as his wife, Angela Raymond; Terri Garber as Suzanne Collier; Henry Darrow and Castulo Guerra as Rafael Castillo; Alan Feinstein as Jim Sanders; Jack Bannon as Nathaniel Marley; Earl Boen as Judge Cauldwell; Kenny Johnson as Ray Minotta; Kim Zimmer as Jodie Walker; Forry Smith as Jodie's husband, Reese Walker; Eric Close as Sawyer Walker; Robert Fontaine as Rafe Castillo, Cruz's half-brother; Thaao Penghlis as Marcus Disgrazia; Lonnie Quinn as Richard Landers; Stephen Nichols as Skylar; Krista Tesreau as Andie; Charles Grant as Connor McCabe; former Olympic champion Florence Griffith Joyner as photographer Terry Holloway; Manuela Metrix Campanero as Countess Carla Rinaldi; Mitchell Laurance and Matthew Laurance (Mitchell's twin brother) as district attorney Ben Arnold; and Susan Ventulett as Gracie.

SANTO BUGITO   CBS
16 SEPTEMBER 1995–   The setting of this Saturday-morning cartoon series was Carmen's, a cafe along the Mexican border owned by a pair of insects, Carmen and Paco de la Antchez, and which attracted a buggy clientele.

SARA   CBS
13 FEBRUARY 1976–30 JULY 1976   Based on a novel by Marian Cockrell, *Sara* was an hour-long western about an Eastern schoolteacher who came to Independence, Colorado, in the 1870s. The cast included Brenda Vaccaro as Sara Yarnell; Bert Kramer as Emmet Ferguson, a townsman who was also a member of the school board; Albert Stratton as Martin Pope, newspaper publisher; William Wintersole as banker George Bailey, another school board member; Mariclare Costello as Julia Bailey, his wife; Louise Latham as Sara's landlady, Martha Higgins; William Phipps as Claude Barstow, the third member of the school board; Kraig Metzinger as Georgie Bailey, son of George and Julia, one of Sara's students; Debbie Lytton as Debbie Higgins, Martha's daughter, another student; and Hallie Morgan as Emma Higgins, Debbie's sister, another student. George Eckstein was the executive producer and Richard Collins the producer, for Universal Television.

SARA   NBC
23 JANUARY 1985–8 MAY 1985   Gary David Goldberg and Ruth Bennett created this half-hour sitcom, set at the Bay Area Law Offices in San Francisco. With Geena Davis as attorney Sara McKenna; Alfre Woodard as her best friend, attorney Roz Dupree; Bill Maher as wisecracking attorney Marty Lang; Bronson Pinchot as gay attorney Dennis Kemper; Ronnie Claire Edwards as receptionist Helen Newcomb; Mark Hudson as Sara's neighbor, Stewart Webber, a teacher; and Matthew Lawrence as Jesse, Stewart's four-year-old son. NBC reran the series during the summer of 1988; by that time Geena Davis and Alfre Woodard had become major film stars, and Bronson Pinchot was established as the star of *Perfect Strangers* on ABC.

THE SARAH CHURCHILL SHOW CBS

7 OCTOBER 1951–30 DECEMBER 1951   Fifteen-minute interview show hosted by Sarah Churchill and sponsored by Hallmark Cards. Early in 1952 Hallmark and Churchill moved to NBC, as Churchill became the first host of *Hallmark Hall of Fame.*

SARGE NBC

21 SEPTEMBER 1971–11 JANUARY 1972   George Kennedy starred in this hour dramatic series as Samuel Patrick ("Sarge") Cavanaugh, a former police officer who decided to become a Catholic priest after his wife was murdered; he was assigned to a parish in San Diego. Also featured were Sallie Shockley as Valerie, his secretary; Ramon Bieri as Lieutenant Barney Varick; and Harold Sakata (better remembered as Oddjob in the movie *Goldfinger*) as Kenji Takichi, the volunteer athletic director for the parish youth. The pilot for the series, "Sarge: The Badge or the Cross," was televised 22 February 1971.

SATELLITE POLICE
See SPACE PATROL

SATURDAY MORNING VIDEOS NBC

8 SEPTEMBER 1990–29 AUGUST 1992   NBC, which had brought *Friday Night Videos* to its late-night schedule seven years earlier, introduced this show into its Saturday morning lineup. Each week the program, which consisted of rock videos, was emceed by different guest hosts.

SATURDAY NIGHT AT THE GARDEN DUMONT

7 OCTOBER 1950–31 MARCH 1951   Live coverage of events at New York's Madison Square Garden was offered on this Saturday-night series.

SATURDAY NIGHT DANCE PARTY NBC

7 JUNE 1952–30 AUGUST 1952   Jerry Lester, formerly the host of *Broadway Open House,* emceed this variety hour, a summer replacement for Sid Caesar's *Your Show of Shows.*

THE SATURDAY NIGHT FIGHTS
See THE FIGHT OF THE WEEK

SATURDAY NIGHT JAMBOREE NBC

4 DECEMBER 1948–2 JULY 1949   Country-and-western music, broadcast from New York.

SATURDAY NIGHT LIVE NBC

11 OCTOBER 1975–   NBC introduced this freewheeling ninety-minute comedy-variety show into what appeared to be an unpromising time slot—11:30 P.M. on Saturdays (the slot had previously been occupied by reruns of *The Tonight Show*). To the surprise of almost everyone, the show took off, and in some ways it represented the boldest leap in television comedy since Sid Caesar's *Your Show of Shows,* which had held down an earlier slot on Saturdays two decades before. One of the few live network entertainment programs of any kind, the show is presented on three Saturdays a month. Each week a guest host emcees the show, backed up by a stock company of regulars. Originally billed as Not Ready for Prime Time Players, this group first included Chevy Chase, Dan Aykroyd, John Belushi, Jane Curtin, Garrett Morris, Laraine Newman, and Gilda Radner (Chase left the series in the fall of 1976 and was later replaced by Bill Murray; Aykroyd and Belushi left after the 1978–1979 season). The members of this talented group were virtual newcomers to television (though Chase had been featured on *The Great American Dream Machine* and Morris had appeared regularly on a 1973 sitcom, *Roll Out!*). Several of the others, along with a number of the show's writers, had been featured in various productions under the auspices of *National Lampoon* magazine. George Carlin was the first guest host, but the show has not always relied on show business regulars for its hosts—among the

more unusual emcees have been Presidential press secretary Ron Nessen (17 April 1976), consumer advocate Ralph Nader (15 January 1977), Georgia legislator Julian Bond (9 April 1977), and even NBC Entertainment president Brandon Tartikoff (9 November 1985). Regular segments have included "Weekend Update," a news satire first presented by Chevy Chase, later by Jane Curtin and Dan Aykroyd; "The Coneheads," the story of a family from another planet trying to blend inconspicuously into American society; "Samurai Warrior," the adventures of an Oriental swordsman (played by John Belushi). Some of the comedy presented on the show has been criticized as being in poor taste, but that criticism can be made of almost any variety series in television history (Arthur Godfrey was regularly condemned in the late 1940s for his "blue" material). *NBC's Saturday Night Live* was developed by network vice president Dick Ebersol, who was its executive producer during the 1975–1976 season. Lorne Michaels, who began his career as a writer on *Laugh-In,* was the producer. The show was originally titled *NBC's Saturday Night*—the word *Live* was officially added in May of 1977; *NBC's* was later discarded. The stable of writers has included Aykroyd, Belushi, Chase, Morris, and Murray, together with Anne Beatts, Tom Davis, Al Franken, producer Michaels, Marilyn Suzanne Miller, Michael O'Donoghue, Herb Sargent, Tom Schiller, Rosie Shuster, and Alan Zweibel. The show's announcer is Don Pardo, whose mellifluous voice is most closely associated with game shows. In the fall of 1979 the series came to prime time; beginning 24 October, edited reruns were shown Wednesdays at 10 p.m. as *The Best of Saturday Night Live.* The show's early seasons also featured short films from Albert Brooks and Gary Weiss, and (in the earliest programs) a special puppet segment created by Jim Henson. The Not Ready for Prime Time Players also performed seventeen skits as The Killer Bees, a routine that John Belushi found particularly loathsome.

Major changes took place in 1980, as producer Lorne Michaels departed, together with most of the writers and all of the regulars—Jane Curtin, Garrett Morris, Laraine Newman, Gilda Radner, Bill Murray, and Don Novello (who had appeared regularly as Father Guido Sarducci for two seasons). Jean Doumanian was named the new producer, and put together a new company of performers: Gilbert Gottfried, Charles Rocket, Joe Piscopo, Denny Dillon, Ann Risley, and Gail Matthius. A young and very talented black performer, Eddie Murphy, also appared occasionally that season; not technically a regular, he was billed as a "featured" player. The results were disappointing. Ratings sagged as internal problems mounted, and Doumanian was dismissed in the spring of 1981. Dick Ebersol, who had put the show on the air in 1975, succeeded her as producer, and was able to put one show on the air in April 1981 before a writers' strike shut down production for the remainder of the season. Retaining only Piscopo and Murphy from the Doumanian crew, Ebersol assembled his own group of regulars: Robin Duke (1981–1984), Christine Ebersole (1981–1982), Mary Gross (1981–1985), Tim Kazurinsky (1981–1984), Tony Rosato (1981–1982), and Brian Doyle-Murray (1981–1982). Added in 1982 were Julia Louis-Dreyfus, Brad Hall, and Gary Kroeger (announcer Don Pardo also returned that year). Louis-Dreyfus and Kroeger stayed for three seasons, Hall for two. Jim Belushi, brother of John Belushi (who had died of a drug overdose in 1982), joined the group in the fall of 1983. The new crew succeeded in turning the show around, as *Saturday Night Live* began to recapture its audience. Joe Piscopo and Eddie Murphy emerged as the most popular members of this crew. Piscopo was able to impersonate such diverse personalities as Frank Sinatra and Ted Koppel, while Murphy's repertoire extended from Stevie Wonder to Buckwheat to his own invention, militant film critic Raheem Abdul Muhammad. Murphy also went on to enjoy success in films, with starring roles in *48 Hrs.* and *Trading Places* (in which he costarred with *SNL* alumnus Dan Aykroyd).

In the fall a half-dozen new regulars joined Gross, Louis-Dreyfus, Kroeger, and Jim Belushi, giving the series its largest annual stable of performers. The new faces were Billy Crystal, Martin Short, Rich Hall, Christopher Guest, Harry Shearer, and Pamela Stephenson. Crystal's "Fernando" talk-show host ("you look mahvelous!") and Short's hyper-nerdy Ed Grimley were probably the most popular bits of the season.

After five years away from the show, Lorne Michaels returned as producer in the spring of 1985. The following fall he introduced an all-new cast, just as his successor Jean Doumanian had done in 1980. The 1985–1986 troupe was comprised of Joan Cusack, Robert Downey, Jr., Nora Dunn, Anthony Michael Hall, Jon Lovitz, Randy Quaid, Terry Sweeney, and Danitra Vance, with A. Whitney Brown, Don Novello (again), and Damon Wayans as featured performers. The season was not particularly successful, and another overhaul took place in the fall of 1986. Joining Dunn and Lovitz were newcomers Dana Carvey, Phil Hartman, Jan Hooks, Victoria Jackson, and Dennis Miller; Kevin Nealon, a featured player that season, became a regular the following season. This unit managed to stay intact through the 1989–1990 season, and developed its own set of memorable characters: Carvey's "Church Lady" and impersonations of George Bush, Dunn's talk-show hostess "Pat Stevens," Miller's "Weekend Update," and Lovitz's "Master Thespian," to name a few. A. Whitney Brown remained a featured player, usually doing commentary on the Weekend Update segment, and writer Al Franken returned in 1987 as a featured player. Mike Myers was featured in 1988 and in 1989, Ben Stiller in 1988.

Nora Dunn boycotted the final show of the 1989–1990 season, which was hosted by controversial comedian Andrew Dice Clay (scheduled music guest Sinead O'Connor also boycotted). Shortly afterward both Dunn and Jon Lovitz announced that they would not be returning to the series for the 1990–1991 season. They were succeeded by new regulars Chris Rock and Chris Farley. The 1991–1992 troupe included Dana Carvey, Chris Farley, Phil Hartman, Victoria Jackson, Mike Myers, Kevin Nealon (who succeeded Dennis Miller as "Weekend Update" anchor), Chris Rock, Rob Schneider, David Spade, Julia Sweeney, Ellen Cleghorne, Tim Meadows, Adam Sandler, and Siobhan Fallon. Most of the group, except for Jackson and Fallon, returned for the 1992–1993 season, together with newcomer Melanie Hutsell. Dana Carvey departed in the spring of 1993 (by that time, Phil Hartman had taken over the presidential impersonation chores, as Bill Clinton). Norm McDonald became a regular in 1993, and eventually succeeded Nealon as "Weekend Update" anchor. Michael McKean was added in the spring of 1994. A major shakeup occurred at the end of the 1993–1994 season, as Hartman, Hutsell, Schneider, and Sweeney all left. Joining returnees Cleghorne, Farley, McDonald, McKean, Meadows, Myers, Nealon, Sandler, and Spade in the fall of 1994 were Chris Elliott and Janeane Garofalo; Garofalo left in midseason and was succeeded by Morwenna Banks and Molly Shannon. By the end of its twentieth season the series was criticized for a decline in its writing quality, and further changes materialized for the 1995–1996 season. McDonald, Mark McKinney (who had joined in the middle of the previous season), Meadows, Shannon, and Spade returned, and six newcomers were introduced: Jim Breuer, Will Ferrell, Darrell Hammond, David Koechner, Cheri Oteri, and Nancy Walls.

A number of *SNL* sketches were transformed into motion pictures over the years, with varying success. The Mike Myers-Dana Carvey "Wayne's World" sketches, set in a teenager's basement cable-TV local access show in Aurora, Illinois, spawned a hugely successful feature film in 1992 and a moderately successful sequel the following year. "Coneheads," starring Dan Aykroyd and Jane Curtin, proved to be a moderate hit as a 1993 film, while "It's Pat," starring Julia Sweeney in the gender-unspecified title role, was released in only a tiny handful of cinemas before vanishing completely.

Rock and roll music has been a central part of *Saturday Night Live* from its inception. Each week a musical guest has performed—live. The roster of acts has been impressive, ranging from the Rolling Stones to Roy Orbison, Devo to Tracy Chapman, and Living Color to Kate Bush. The show has also had its own band, which was originally led by Howard Shore; Paul Shaffer succeeded Shore and remained with the show for several seasons (occasionally appearing in other roles as well, such as concert promoter Don Kirshner) before leaving to become musical director of *Late Night with David Letterman*. Guitarist G. E. Smith later became the house bandleader.

Saturday Night Live celebrated its fifteenth anniversary with a prime-time retrospective on 24 September 1989; the festivities were actually held a year early, as the series had only been on the air for fourteen years at the time.

See also *Fridays; The New Show; No Holds Barred.*

SATURDAY NIGHT LIVE WITH HOWARD COSELL ABC
20 SEPTEMBER 1975–17 JANUARY 1976 Not to be confused with *NBC's Saturday Night Live,* which also premiered in the fall of 1975, this hour-long variety show was seen in prime time and was hosted by ABC sportscaster Howard Cosell. The show originated from New York, with pickups from other parts of the country. Roone Arledge was the executive producer, and Rupert Hitzig was the producer. Among Cosell's regulars was Bill Murray, who later turned up on *NBC's Saturday Night Live.*

THE SATURDAY NIGHT REVUE NBC
6 JUNE 1953–5 SEPTEMBER 1953; 12 JUNE 1954–18 SEPTEMBER 1954 *The Saturday Night Revue* was twice a summer replacement for Sid Caesar's *Your Show of Shows.* Hoagy Carmichael was the host in 1953 and Eddie Albert in 1954, with Alan Young and Ben Blue alternating biweekly as guest stars. The latter version also featured Pat Carroll and the Sauter-Finnegan Band and was produced by Ernie Glucksman.

SATURDAY NIGHT WITH CONNIE CHUNG CBS
23 SEPTEMBER 1989–2 JUNE 1990 This self-titled hour news magazine show was the successor to *West 57th.* Before joining CBS News, Chung had been a correspondent and weekend anchor at NBC News and a local anchorwoman in Los Angeles. The new show received some criticism for its use of "dramatic reenactments" of some events. The series earned low ratings in its Saturday slot, and seemed destined for cancellation until it was given two Monday airings in May 1990, which achieved much larger numbers. As a result, the show was permanently moved to Mondays in July, with an emphasis on celebrity interviews, and given a new title: see *Face to Face with Connie Chung.*

SATURDAY PROM NBC
15 OCTOBER 1960–1 APRIL 1961 Merv Griffin hosted this half-hour music show for teens, which was telecast early on Saturday evenings.

SATURDAY ROUNDUP NBC
16 JUNE 1951–1 SEPTEMBER 1951 Kermit Maynard, younger brother of Ken Maynard, starred in this unusual western series. Maynard did not play a continuing character, but rather a different character each week.

SATURDAY SPORTS MIRROR CBS
14 JULY 1956–15 SEPTEMBER 1956 Cohosts Jack Drees and Bill Hickey presented news from the world of sports and interviews with athletes on this half-hour Saturday-evening series.

SATURDAY SQUARE NBC
7 JANUARY 1950–18 FEBRUARY 1950 This short-lived prime-time variety series, broadcast from Chicago, was produced by Ted Mills and Norman Felton. The setting was a city block in downtown Chicago.

SATURDAY SUPERCADE CBS
17 SEPTEMBER 1983–24 AUGUST 1985 Several cartoon segments, all inspired by popular video arcade games, were presented on this hour Saturday morning series: "Donkey Kong," the adventures of a gorilla who escaped from a circus and is pursued by his trainer and the trainer's assistant; "Donkey Kong, Junior," the adventures of Donkey Kong's young son, who was also looking for his famous father; "Frogger," the story of an investigative reporter for the *Swamp Gazette;* "Pitfall," the escapades of Pitfall Harry, a treasure hunter; and "Q*Bert," the tale of a teenager named Q*Bert living in a town named Q*Bert (the latter two segments were telecast

on alternate weeks). For the show's second season the segments included "Q*Bert" and "Donkey Kong" from before, and two new features, "Kangaroo" and "Space Ace."

SATURDAY TODAY NBC

1 AUGUST 1992–   In the first change in Saturday-morning network programming in decades, NBC scrapped two hours of kids' shows to make room for a Saturday edition of the *Today* show (a Sunday version had been launched in 1987). It was hosted first by Jackie Nespral and Scott Simon; Mike Schneider replaced Simon in June 1993; Schneider and Nespral hosted until the end of 1994, when Nespral departed. She was succeeded by Giselle Fernandez. Jack Ford succeeded Mike Schneider in May 1995.

SAVED BY THE BELL NBC

20 AUGUST 1989–4 SEPTEMBER 1993   Live-action Saturday morning comedy set at Bayside High School in Palisades, California. With Mark-Paul Gosselaar as girl-crazy teenager Zack Morris who, like TV's *Dobie Gillis,* addressed the camera directly; Mario Lopez as his pal, A. C. Slater; Tiffani-Amber Thiessen as Kelly Kapowski; Elizabeth Berkley as Jessie Spano; Lark Voorhies as Lisa Turtle; Dustin Diamond as Screech Powers, the nerd; Ed Alonzo as Max, who worked at the nearby soda fountain; Leanna Creel (1992–1993) as Tory; and Dennis Haskins as the principal, Richard Belding. In an effort to build an audience the series was given two prime-time airings before settling on the Saturday morning schedule in September 1989. Two prime-time specials aired on NBC during the 1992–1993 season: "Saved by the Bell—Hawaiian Style" (27 November 1992), and "Saved by the Bell Goes to College" (22 May 1993). The latter telecast led to the shift of the series itself to prime time in the fall of 1993 (see *Saved by the Bell: The College Years*), while a new cast was assembled for a continuation of the Saturday-morning show (see *Saved by the Bell: The New Class*).

SAVED BY THE BELL: THE COLLEGE YEARS NBC

14 SEPTEMBER 1993–8 FEBRUARY 1994   *Saved by the Bell,* the popular Saturday-morning kids' sitcom, made a brief attempt at prime time here, as four of the gang headed for college at California University: Mark-Paul Gosselaar as Zach Morris; Mario Lopez as A.C. Slater; Dustin Diamond as Samuel "Screech" Powers; and Tiffani-Amber Thiessen as Kelly Kapowski. The four pals shared a dorm suite with two newcomers: Anne Tremko as Leslie Burke, and Kiersten Warren as Alex, a drama major. Rounding out the cast were former pro footballer Bob Golic as former pro footballer Mike Rogers, who had gone back to obtain his degree; and Roger Kabler as anthropology professor Jeremiah Lasky.

SAVED BY THE BELL: THE NEW CLASS NBC

11 SEPTEMBER 1993–   As the original *Saved by the Bell* crew headed to college, and prime time, in the fall of 1993 (see *Saved by the Bell: The College Years*), a new cast was introduced on the Saturday-morning show, now retitled *Saved by the Bell: The New Class*. Dennis Haskins was the only holdover, continuing his role as Bayside High's much put-upon principal, Richard Belding. Joining him were David Byrd (1993–1994) as Hammersmith; Jonathan Angel as tough guy "Tommy Dee" Deluca; Isaac Lidsky (1993–1994) as nerd Weasel; Natalie Cigliuti as Lindsay Warner; Bianca Lawson (1993–1995) as Meghan; Bonnie Russavage (1993–1994) as Vicki; and Ryan Hurst (1993–1995) as Crunch Grabowski, captain of the football team. In the fall of 1994 Dustin Diamond of the original *Saved by the Bell* cast returned to the show; his character, Samuel "Screech" Powers, was now Belding's administrative assistant. Also added were Christian Oliver (1994–1995) as Brian Keller; Sarah Lancaster as Rachel Myers; and Spankee Rogers (1994–1995) as Bobby Wilson. Three new cast members were added in the fall of 1995: Richard Lee Jackson as Ryan Parker; Salim Grant as R. J. "Hollywood" Collins; and Samantha Becker as Maria Lopez. All were transfer students from Valley High.

SAWYER VIEWS HOLLYWOOD   ABC
14 APRIL 1951–31 AUGUST 1951   Hal Sawyer hosted this half-hour variety and interview program.

SAY IT WITH ACTING   NBC/ABC
14 AUGUST 1949–24 SEPTEMBER 1950 (NBC); 7 SEPTEMBER 1951–22 FEBRUARY 1952 (ABC)   Ben Grauer hosted this game show, on which teams from Broadway shows played charades. See also *Act It Out.*

SAY WHAT?   CBS
26 JUNE 1992–10 JULY 1992   Limited-run comedy series, hosted by Bill Maher, on which wacky dialogue was added to newsreel footage and other video clips.

SAY WHEN   NBC
2 JANUARY 1961–26 MARCH 1965   This merchandise giveaway show from Goodson-Todman Productions was similar in format to *The Price Is Right*— contestants could choose items of merchandise, and the object of the game was to choose a set of items that totaled closest to a preset dollar amount. The player whose bid was closer won whatever he or she had chosen. Art James hosted the series and was assisted by Ruth Hasely.

SCARECROW AND MRS. KING   CBS
3 OCTOBER 1983–10 SEPTEMBER 1987   In this hour adventure series a government agent teamed up with a suburban housewife. Featured were Bruce Boxleitner as Lee Stetson, a government agent whose code name was "Scarecrow"; pursued by enemy agents in a train station, he handed a mysterious package to a woman standing on the platform. Kate Jackson played the recipient, recently divorced housewife Amanda King, who decided that she liked being a part-time, unofficial agent. Also on hand were Beverly Garland as Amanda's mother, Dotty West; Paul Stout as Amanda's son Philip; Greg Morton as Amanda's son Jamie; Mel Stewart as Scarecrow's section chief, Billy Melrose; and Martha Smith as Billy's assistant, Francine Desmond. In one 1985 episode Mr. King finally showed up; he was played by Sam Melville, who had played Kate Jackson's husband on *The Rookies.* Several changes occurred for the series' final season, as Amanda became a trainee agent at "the Agency," and she and Scarecrow were finally married in February 1987. Raleigh Bond and Myron Natwick also became regulars that season, as informant T. P. Aquinas and Agency boss Dr. Smyth, respectively. The series was filmed in Washington, D. C.

THE SCARLET LETTER   PBS
2 APRIL 1979–5 APRIL 1979   A meticulous but labored adaptation of Nathaniel Hawthorne's 1850 novel, *The Scarlet Letter* was telecast in four consecutive hour installments. Principal players included Meg Foster as Hester Prynne, the convicted adulteress who was condemned to wear the letter A on her dress forever (inexplicably, the letter used on the series was gold, not scarlet); John Heard as her lover, the Reverend Arthur Dimmesdale; Kevin Conway as Hester's husband, Roger Chillingworth. Herbert Hirschman was the executive producer of the series, which was filmed largely in Rhode Island. Rick Hauser produced and directed.

THE SCARLET PIMPERNEL   SYNDICATED
1958   This half-hour adventure series, a European import, was based on Baroness Orczy's novel and starred Marius Goring as The Scarlet Pimpernel, hero of the French Revolution.

SCARLETT   CBS
13 NOVEMBER 1994–17 NOVEMBER 1994   Alexandra Ripley's 1991 novel, the bestselling sequel to *Gone with the Wind,* came to television as a four-night, eight-hour miniseries, following Scarlett O'Hara and Rhett Butler from America to Ireland and England. Produced by Robert Halmi, Sr., and directed by John Erman, the series cost a reported $45 million. The cast included Joanne Whalley-Kilmer as Scarlett

O'Hara; Timothy Dalton as Rhett Butler; Stephen Collins as Ashley Wilkes; Julie Harris as Eleanor Butler; Annabeth Gish as Anne Hampton; John Gielgud as Pierre Robillard; George Grizzard as Henry Hamilton; Ann-Margret as Belle Watling; Melissa Leo as Scarlett's sister, Suellen; Sean Bean as Lord Fenton; Colm Meaney as Father Colum O'Hara; and Brian Bedford as Sir John Morland.

SCATTERGORIES   NBC
18 JANUARY 1993–11 JUNE 1993   Daytime game show, hosted by Dick Clark, based on the popular home game. Two four-person teams competed in an effort to supply answers beginning with a designated letter to various questions. Each team won or lost points as their answers were compared with those given by a panel of celebrities in pre-taped interviews.

SCENE OF THE CRIME   NBC
14 APRIL 1985–26 MAY 1985   NBC almost literally pasted this hour series together, and put it on with little fanfare. Orson Welles hosted the series, which consisted of two separate half-hour mysteries.

SCENE OF THE CRIME   CBS
3 APRIL 1991–24 AUGUST 1994   A television rarity, *Scene of the Crime* was a late-night mystery series presented by a repertory company. One segment of CBS's *Crime Time After Prime Time,* it was hosted by one of TV's most prolific writers and producers, Stephen J. Cannell. The series, a Canadian-French co-production, was filmed in Vancouver and Paris, and featured an international cast: Canadians Maxine Miller, Robert Paisley, and Barbara Parkins, Americans George Touliatos, Stephen McHattie, and Teri Austin, and French actors Lisa Houle, Olivier Pierre, and Francois Montagut. Two episodes were specially scheduled in prime time on 31 August 1991. *Scene of the Crime* was scheduled regularly through the spring of 1992, later popping up in reruns through 1994.

SCENE 70   SYNDICATED
1969   Jay Reynolds hosted this hour-long rock music show.

THE SCHAEFER CENTURY THEATRE   SYNDICATED
1952   Filmed half-hour dramatic anthology series. Natalie Wood made her first major TV appearance on one episode, "Playmates."

SCHLITZ PLAYHOUSE OF STARS   CBS
5 OCTOBER 1951–27 MARCH 1959   This long-running half-hour dramatic anthology series was hosted for several seasons by Irene Dunne and later by Robert Paige. A sampling of presentations would include: "Not a Chance," with Helen Hayes (5 October 1951); "Never Wave at a WAC," with Rosalind Russell (19 October 1951); "Dark Fleece," with Anthony Quinn (21 December 1951); "Double Exposure," with Amanda Blake (in her first major TV role, 15 August 1952); "Four Things He'd Do," with Lee Van Cleef (in his first major TV role, 5 February 1954); "The Long Trail," with Anthony Quinn (19 November 1954); "The Unlighted Road," with James Dean (in his last dramatic appearance on television, 6 May 1955); "Bandit's Hideout," with Anthony Quinn (in his last TV appearance until 1971, 7 October 1955); "The Life You Save," with Gene Kelly (in his TV dramatic debut, 1 March 1957); "Carriage from Britain," with Janet Leigh (her first dramatic role on American television, 8 March 1957); "The Restless Gun," with John Payne (telecast 29 March 1957, this was the pilot for the series of the same title); and "Old Spanish Custom," with Dolores Del Rio (7 June 1957).

THE SCHOOL HOUSE   DUMONT
18 JANUARY 1949–12 APRIL 1949   This Tuesday-night revue featured Kenny Delmar and Arnold Stang.

SCIENCE ALL-STARS ABC

12 JANUARY 1964–26 APRIL 1964; 10 JANUARY 1965–25 APRIL 1965   Don Morrow hosted this Sunday-afternoon show on which youngsters demonstrated their own science projects and talked with guest scientists.

SCIENCE CIRCUS ABC

4 JULY 1949–12 SEPTEMBER 1949   A half-hour of scientific experiments, hosted by Bob Brown.

SCIENCE FICTION THEATER SYNDICATED

1955–1956   Truman Bradley hosted this science fiction anthology show. The half-hour series was one of the first shows produced by Ivan Tors, who later developed *Sea Hunt, Flipper,* and other such shows.

SCOOBY-DOO CBS/ABC

13 SEPTEMBER 1969–7 AUGUST 1976 (CBS); 11 SEPTEMBER 1976–6 SEPTEMBER 1986 (ABC)   This Saturday-morning cartoon show from Hanna-Barbera Productions about a cowardly Great Dane (Scooby-Doo) and four teenage sleuths (Daphne, Freddy, Shaggy, and Velma) has been seen in several different formats over the years. It premiered in 1969 as a half-hour series, *Scooby-Doo, Where Are You?,* which ran for three years. In the fall of 1972 it expanded to an hour and was titled *The New Scooby-Doo Movies.* In the fall of 1974 reruns of *Scooby-Doo, Where Are You?* were shown under the latter title. The series switched networks in 1976 and became known as *The Scooby-Doo/Dynomutt Hour,* as a new segment was added: the adventures of Dynomutt, bionic dog who battled crime together with the Blue Falcon. In the fall of 1977 the series expanded to two hours, and several cartoon segments were shown under the title *Scooby's All-Star Laff-A-Lympics.* In the fall of 1978 Scooby starred in two Saturday cartoon shows on ABC: the half-hour *Scooby-Doo, Where Are You?,* followed later in the morning by the ninety-minute *Scooby's All-Stars,* the new title for the *Laff-A-Lympics.* In the fall of 1979 Scooby returned to a single program, teaming up with his feisty nephew in *Scooby and Scrappy-Doo.* In the summer of 1980 reruns were shown as *Scooby's Laff-a-Lympics.* In 1980 Scooby took second billing for the first time in his career on *The Richie Rich/Scooby-Doo Show* (see also that title). Another set of reruns popped up briefly in September 1981, when an animators' strike delayed many cartoon premieres; these were titled *Scooby-Doo Classics.* Scooby regained top billing in the fall of 1982 on an hour series, *Scooby & Scrappy-Doo/The Puppy's New Adventures.* A year later Scooby and The Puppy went their separate ways: The Puppy headlined his own show (see *The Puppy's Further Adventures*), while Scooby could be seen on not one but *two* Saturday-morning cartoon shows: *The Best of Scooby-Doo* (reruns) and *The New Scooby & Scrappy-Doo* (fresh fare). During the 1984–1985 season two more Scooby shows graced the airwaves: *The New Scooby-Doo Mysteries* and *Scary Scooby Funnies.* For the 1985–1986 season Scooby was carried on *The 13 Ghosts of Scooby-Doo* and *Scooby's Mystery Funhouse;* the latter series was replaced by reruns of *Laff-a-Lympics* in March 1986. In 1988 another incarnation of the Great Dane appeared: see *A Pup Named Scooby Doo.* The name of the title character was suggested by CBS programming chief Fred Silverman after hearing Frank Sinatra singing the phrase "scooby-dooby-doo" in "Strangers in the Night."

SCORCH CBS

28 FEBRUARY 1992–13 MARCH 1992   Asinine sitcom about a wisecracking 1,300-year-old dragon who fell out of the sky and befriended an actor in New Haven, Connecticut. With Jonathan Walker as the actor, Brian Stevens, who then got a job as a TV weather forecaster using Scorch as his puppet; Rhea Silver-Smith as his young daughter, Jessica; Rose Marie as the landlady, Mrs. Bracken; John O'Hurley as news anchor Howard Gurman; Brenda Strong as coanchor Allison King; and Todd Susman as station manager Jack Fletcher. *Scorch* was scheduled Fridays with another new entry, *Fish Police;* both shows were yanked after three showings.

SCOTLAND YARD ABC

17 NOVEMBER 1957–3 OCTOBER 1958   Produced in England, this half-hour filmed series was based on case histories from Scotland Yard and was hosted by British author and criminologist Edgar Lustgarten.

SCOTT ISLAND

See HARBOURMASTER

THE SCOTT MUSIC HALL NBC

8 OCTOBER 1952–26 AUGUST 1953   Scott Paper Company sponsored this biweekly half-hour musical variety series, hosted by Patti Page and featuring Frank Fontaine and Mary Ellen Terry.

SCRABBLE NBC

2 JULY 1984–23 MARCH 1990; 18 JANUARY 1993–11 JUNE 1993   Chuck Woolery hosted this daytime game show, based loosely on the popular word game. Two contestants competed one at a time, trying to identify words from clues read by Woolery and by guessing whether certain letters appeared in the word. Winning contestants could play for a top prize of $40,000. A "900" number was later introduced to permit home viewers to play a version of the game as well.

SCREEN DIRECTORS PLAYHOUSE NBC

5 OCTOBER 1955–26 SEPTEMBER 1956   Members of the Screen Directors Guild directed the presentations on this half-hour dramatic anthology series. Among the major stars who appeared on the series were John Wayne (in "Rookie of the Year," 7 December, his only real dramatic role on TV), Robert Ryan (in "Lincoln's Doctor's Bag," 14 December, his first TV dramatic role), Jeanette MacDonald (in "The Prima Donna," 1 February, a rare television appearance), Buster Keaton (in "The Silent Partner," 21 March), and Errol Flynn (in "The Sword of Villon," 4 April, his first TV dramatic role).

SEA HUNT SYNDICATED

1957–1961; 1987   Lloyd Bridges starred as underwater adventurer Mike Nelson in this half-hour series, one of the most widely syndicated shows of its time. Ivan Tors produced the series. The short-lived 1987 syndicated revival starred Ron Ely (formerly TV's Tarzan) as Mike Nelson, and Kimberly Sissons as his daughter, Jennifer Nelson, a college student.

SEALAB 2020 NBC

9 SEPTEMBER 1972–1 SEPTEMBER 1973   Half-hour Saturday-morning cartoon series from Hanna-Barbera Productions about a group of oceanauts led by Dr. Paul Williams.

SEAQUEST DSV (SEAQUEST 2032) NBC

12 SEPTEMBER 1993–27 DECEMBER 1995   Reportedly the most expensive regular series in television history (at $2 million per episode), this hour show was produced by Steven Spielberg's Amblin Entertainment. It was set in the year 2018 aboard the *SeaQuest,* a 1000-foot research submarine, or "DSV"—Deep Submergence Vehicle. The cast included Roy Scheider as Captain Nathan Bridger; Stephanie Beacham as chief science officer Dr. Kristin Westphalen; Don Franklin as Commander Jonathan Ford; Stacy Haiduk as Lieutenant Commander Katherine Hitchcock; Jonathan Brandis as kid computer genius Lucas Wolenczak; Royce D. Applegate as Chief Manilow Crocker; John D'Aquino as supply officer Benjamin King; and Ted Raimi as O'Neill. The ship's human crew was assisted by a talking bottlenose dolphin named Darwin. Several changes occurred after the first season. The original *SeaQuest* was destroyed and was replaced by a smaller vehicle with a different design; production shifted from California to Orlando; and Beacham, Haiduk, Applegate, and D'Aquino left the series. Joining the cast were Edward Kerr as Lieutenant Brody, an expert on armaments; Rosalind Allen as Dr. Smith, a biologist with

ESP; Michael DeLuise as Tony Piccolo; Peter DeLuise as Dagwood, the janitor; Mario Sanchez as Ortiz; and Kathy Evison as Ensign Henderson.

In the fall of 1995 the series acquired a new title and more new cast members. Now known as *SeaQuest 2032*, it had jumped several decades into the future. Scheider, Allen, and Sanchez were gone, and the ship had a new commanding officer: Michael Ironside as Captain Oliver Hudson. Also featured was Michael York as Alexander Bourne, the evil dictator of the nation of Macronesia.

THE SEARCH   CBS
17 OCTOBER 1954–27 SEPTEMBER 1955   Charles Romine hosted this Sunday afternoon public affairs program; most of the shows were filmed at American colleges and universities. Irv Gitlin produced the series, which resurfaced briefly in the summers of 1957 and 1958 with Eric Sevareid as host.

SEARCH   NBC
13 SEPTEMBER 1972–29 AUGUST 1973   An hour-long adventure series about three agents for Probe, a division of World Securities Corporation, a Washington-based outfit. The Probe agents, equipped with ultramodern scientific gadgets (such as miniaturized receivers implanted in their ears), could be hired to search for anything. The principals included Hugh O'Brian as Hugh Lockwood; Tony Franciosa as Nick Bianco; Doug McClure as C. R. Grover; Burgess Meredith as B. C. Cameron, head of the Probe unit; and Ford Rainey as Dr. Barnett, the research director. The three stars seldom appeared together—O'Brian was featured in about half of the episodes, and Franciosa and McClure split up the remaining half. Among the lesser Probe agents who were occasionally featured were Angel Tompkins as Gloria Harding; Byron Chung as Kuroda; Albert Popwell as Griffin; Ron Castro as Carlos; and Cheryl Stoppelmoor (later known as Cheryl Ladd of *Charlie's Angels* fame) as Amy. Leslie Stevens was the executive producer.

SEARCH AND RESCUE: THE ALPHA TEAM   NBC
10 SEPTEMBER 1977–28 JANUARY 1978   The Alpha Ranch, a wildlife preserve, was the setting for this Saturday-morning series about a pair of young rescuers. Featured were: Michael J. Reynolds as Bob; Donann Cavin as Katy; and Michael Kane as Uncle Jack. Levy Lehman produced the half-hour series.

THE SEARCH FOR BEAUTY   NBC
26 SEPTEMBER 1955–9 DECEMBER 1955   Makeup consultant Ern Westmore interviewed celebrity guests and dispensed advice on beauty to members of the studio audience on this half-hour daytime show. Late in the summer Westmore had become the host of a daytime show called *Hollywood Backstage,* and this series continued in that time slot.

SEARCH FOR THE NILE   NBC
25 JANUARY 1972–29 FEBRUARY 1972   This six-hour dramatization of the efforts by members of the Royal Geographic Society to discover the source of the Nile was produced by the BBC and filmed in Africa; it was run by NBC as a five-part miniseries. James Mason narrated the show, and the principal cast included: Kenneth Haigh as Sir Richard Burton; John Quentin as John Hanning Speke; Ian McCulloch as Captain James Grant; Norman Rossington as Samuel Baker; Catherine Schell as Florence Baker; Keith Buckley as Henry Morgan Stanley; and Michael Gough as David Livingstone.

SEARCH FOR TOMORROW   CBS/NBC
3 SEPTEMBER 1951–26 MARCH 1982 (CBS); 29 MARCH 1982–26 DECEMBER 1986 (NBC)   Before its cancellation in 1986 after a remarkable thirty-five-year run, *Search for Tomorrow* could claim several TV records for longevity, with more than 9,000 episodes telecast. However, most of those records were soon eclipsed by *The Guiding Light,* which came to TV nine months after *Search,* and ultimately outlasted it. *Search for Tomorrow* was created by Roy Winsor, who also served as its first execu-

tive producer; Charles Irving was the first producer and director. Subsequent producers have included Frank Dodge, Bernie Sofronski, Mary-Ellis Bunim, Joanna Lee, Ellen Barrett, and John Whitesell. Agnes Nixon was the first head writer, but was succeeded late in 1951 by Irving Vendig. Later head writers have included, among others, Ann Marcus, Peggy O'Shea, Joyce and John William Corrington, and Gary Tomlin. Like most soaps of the 1950s, *Search* began as a fifteen-minute program. It was one of the last to expand to thirty minutes, doing so in September 1968, when it also shifted from live to videotaped performances. In 1983 one of the tapes was lost, so the episode of 4 August 1983 was done live; because of advance publicity, ratings were higher than usual that day. In 1982 *Search* became only the second daytime serial to switch networks (*The Edge of Night* was first).

Search for Tomorrow was set in the town of Henderson, and its central character was Joanne Gardner Barron Tate Vincente Tourneur, a considerate and compassionate woman who was married four times and widowed three times; the part was played by Mary Stuart for the show's entire run. Other principal players over the many years included: Johnny Sylvester as Joanne's first husband, Keith Barron, who died in a car crash (Johnny Sylvester was later known as John Sylvester White and was featured on *Welcome Back, Kotter*); Lynn Loring (1951–1961), Nancy Pinkerton (1961), Abigail Kellogg (1961–1964); Patricia Harty (1964–1965), Trish Van Devere (briefly in 1965), Gretchen Walther (1965–1966), Melissa Murphy (1966–1967), Melinda Plank (1967–1969), Leigh Lassen (1969–1974), Tina Sloan (1976), and Jacqueline Schultz (1985–1986) as their daughter, Patti Barron; Cliff Hall as Victor Barron, Keith's father; Bess Johnson as Irene Barron, Keith's mother; Harry Holcombe and Eric Dressler as Frank Gardner, Joanne's father; Melba Rae (1951–1971) as Joanne's best friend, Marge Bergman; Larry Haines as Marge's husband, Stu Bergman; Ellen Spencer, Sandy Robinson (to 1961), Fran Sharon (1961–1966), Nancy Franklin, Marian Hailey, and Millee Taggart (who would later become the head writer of another daytime serial, *Loving*) as their daughter, Janet Bergman, Patti Barron's best friend; Peter Broderick, Ray Bellaran, John James, Mitch Litrofsky, and Robert LuPone as their son, Tommy Bergman; Joanna Roos and Nydia Westman as Jessie Bergman; Peter Lazar as Jimmy Bergman; Coe Norton as Dr. Ned Hilton, who befriended Joanne after her first husband's death; Terry O'Sullivan (1955–1966) and Karl Weber (briefly in 1956) as Arthur Tate, who became Joanne's second husband on 18 May 1955, and died of a heart attack in 1966; Mary Patton as Sue, who masqueraded as her twin sister, Hazel Tate, Arthur Tate's ex-wife; Jeffrey Krolik (son of Mary Stuart in real life) as Duncan Eric Tate, the son of Joanne and Arthur Tate who died in infancy; George Petrie, Richard Derr, Mark Lenard, and Frank Overton as lawyer Nathan Walsh; Lee Grant, Nita Talbot, and Constance Ford as Rose Peabody; Don Knotts as Rose's mute brother, Wilbur Peabody; Marion Brash and Ann Williams as Eunice, Joanne's widowed sister; Larry Hugo as Rex Twining, who married Eunice; Doris Dalton as Cornelia Simmons, Arthur Tate's aunt; Vicki Vola as Harriet Baxter, Cornelia's housekeeper; Nina Reader and Ann Pearson as Allison Simmons, Cornelia's sister; Tom Carlin, Donald Madden, and David O'Brien as Fred Metcalf, who married Allison; Katherine Meskill as Agnes Metcalf, Fred's mother; Tony Ray, Anthony Cannon, and George Maharis as Joanne's nephew, Bud Gardner, who married Janet Bergman; Martin Brooks, Philip Abbott, and Ron Husmann as Dr. Dan Walton, who also married Janet; Denise Nickerson, Kathy Beller, Meg Bennett, Hope Busby, Sherry Mathis, and Louan Gideon as Liza Walton, daughter of Dan and Janet Walton; Robert Mandan, George Gaynes, and Roy Shuman as Sam Reynolds, who romanced Joanne for several years after Arthur Tate's death but never married her; Virginia Gilmore, Lesley Woods, and Joan Copeland as Andrea Whiting, Sam's ex-wife; Dino Narizzano, Jeff Pomerantz, and Dino Narizzano (again) as Len Whiting, son of Sam and Andrea, who married Patti Barron; Freida Altman as Mrs. Miller; Carl Low as Dr. Bob Rogers; Pamela Murphy, Louise Shaffer, and Kathryn Walker as Emily Rogers, Bob's daughter; Burr De Benning, Stephen Joyce, Terry Logan, and Ken Kercheval as Nick Hunter, who married Emily; Ken Harvey as lawyer Doug Martin, who married Eunice; John Napier and Michael Wagner as Cliff Williams; Martin Brooks as Dr. Everett Moore; Lenka Peterson as Isabelle Kittridge Moore; Geoffrey Lumb as Geoffrey Crane;

Selena Longo as Tracy Ellen; Jill Clayburgh as Grace Bolton, who died of a brain tumor; Kelly Wood as Lauri Leshinsky; Christopher Lowe as Erik, Lauri's son; Peter Simon and Peter Ratray as Scott Phillips, who married Lauri; Lilia Skala as Magda Leshinsky, Lauri's mother; Nicolette Goulet and Courtney Sherman as Kathy Parker, who later married Scott Phillips; John Cunningham as Dr. Wade Collins, a psychiatrist who married Janet Bergman Gardner Walton; Natalie Schafer as Helen Collins; Ralph Clanton as William Collins; Brett Halsey as Clay Collins; Val Dufour as lawyer John Wyatt, who married Eunice Martin; Pat Stanley as Marion Malin, Wyatt's secretary; Kipp Osborne as George, and Susan Sarandon as Sarah, a pair of drifters who murdered Sam Reynolds; Lawrence Weber, Robert Loggia, and Anthony George as Dr. Tony Vincente, who became Joanne's third husband and died of a heart attack in 1975; Jeannie Carson as Marcy Vincente, Tony's ex-wife; Hal Linden as Larry Carter; Michael Shannon as Jim McCarren; Frank Schofield and Stephen Elliott as John Austin; Billie Lou Watt as Ellie Harper, housekeeper for widower Stu Bergman, and eventually married him in 1976; Linda Bove as Melissa Hayley, a deaf woman taken in by Joanne and Tony (Bove herself was a member of the National Theater of the Deaf); Robert Phelps as Dr. Matt Weldon, who married Melissa; Robin Eisenmann and Morgan Fairchild as Jennifer Phillips, Scott Phillips's ex-wife; Tommy Norden, John Driver, Richard Lohman, Robert Bannard, and Stephen Burleigh as Gary Walton, son of Janet and Dan Walton; Anne Revere as Agnes Lake; Michael Nouri as Steve Kaslo, who moved in with Liza Walton; Pamela Miller and Anne Wyndham as Steve's sister, Amy Kaslo; Mike Durrell as Mike Kaslo; Tom Ewell as Bill Lang; Wayne Rogers as Slim Davis; Byron Sanders as Dr. Walter Osmond; Joe Morton as Dr. James Foster; Gene Fanning as Dr. Lew Brown; Barbara Monte-Britton as Dr. Maria Pettit; Camille Yarbrough as Terry Benjamin; James Hainesworth as Jay Benjamin; Robby Benson, Michael Maitland, Gary Tomlin, Steve Nisbet, and Joel Higgins as Bruce Carson; Robert Burr as Mr. McCrady; Dale Robinette as Dave Wilkins; Andrea McArdle (who left the show to star in the musical *Annie*) and Lisa Peluso as Wendy Wilkins; Maree Cheatham and Louise Shaffer as Wendy's mother, Stephanie Wilkins Wyatt, a nurse; Katherine Squire as Raney Wesner; Kathleen Dezina as Karen Dehner; Virginia Martin as Connie Schultz; Vera Allen as Ida Weston; Sharon Spelman as Paula Markham; Delphi Harrington as Leslie Halliday; Stephen Joyce as Sam Hunter; Vince O'Brien as Hal Conrad; Lewis Arlt as United States Marshal David Sutton (also known as David Sloane); Lane Binkley as Robin Kennemer; Gayle Pines and Marilyn McIntyre as Caroline Hanley Walton; Allison Argo as Cindy French; Kevin Kline as Woody Reed; Bob Rockwell as Dr. Greg Hartford; Tina Orr as Meredith Hartford; James O'Sullivan and Drew Snyder as Ralph Heywood; Michael Sivy as Howard Horton; Robert Heitman as William Mandell; Dana Ivey as Maria Thompson; Kristan Carl, Amy Arutt, Stacy Moran, Cynthia Gibb, Elizabeth Swackhamer, and Teri Eoff as Suzie Martin Wyatt, daughter of Eunice and Doug Martin; Lenka Peterson (in her second role) as Evelyn Reedy; Leslie Ann Ray as Donna Davis; Neil Billingsley, Cain DeVore, and John Loprieno as Danny Walton, son of Dan and Janet Walton; Lisa Buck as Kylie Halliday; George Shannon as Chance Halliday; Jack Ryland as Lonnie Garrison; Chris Loomis as Buck Peterson; Verna Pierce as Sharon Peterson; Vincent Stewart as Jackie Peterson; John Aniston as Martin Tourneur, who became Joann Gardner Vincente's fourth husband; Rod Arrants as Travis Sentell, who married Liza Walton; Doug Stevenson as Lee Sentell, Travis's cousin; David Gayle as Rusty Sentell; Megan Bagot as Laine Adamson; Chris Goutman as Marc D'Antoni; Marcia McCabe as Sunny McClure Adamson; William Robertson as Roger Tourneur; and Tucker Smallwood as Bobby Stuart.

Later additions to the cast included: Susan Scannell as Kristin Carter; Michael Corbett as Warren Carter, Kristin's brother; Tom Wright as Kristin's husband, Detective John "Colt" Colton; Robert Desiderio as Prince Tony; Sonia Petrovna as Princess Renata Sutton; Patsy Pease as Cissy Mitchell; Gregory Sutton as Simon D'Antoni; Nicholas Cortland as Dr. Winston Kyle; George Bamford as Cliff; Danny Goldring as Beau Mitchell; Brian Krulish and Gordon Novod as Doug Phillips; Biff McGuire as Sergeant McKay; Ralph Byers as Jim Ramsey; Don Chastain as Dr. Max Taper; Debbie McLeod as Marlena; Linda Gibboney as Jenny Deacon; Jerry Lanning as Nick D'Antoni; Patricia Estrin as Dr. Jamie Larsen; Pat Dixon as Claire Johnson; Marcus Smythe as Dane Taylor; Susan Monts as Aja Doyan; Craig Augustine as Keith McNeil, who married Wendy Wilkins; Stacy Glick as Andrea McNeil, Keith's sister; Timothy Patrick Murphy as Spencer Langley; Paul Joynt, Larry Joshua, Gene Pietragallo, and Jay Acovone as blinded boxer Brian Emerson, Wendy's half-brother; Malachi Throne and Wayne Tippit as Ted Adamson, Sunny's father; Larry Fleischman as Ringo Altman; Lezlie Dalton as Helena St. John; Peter Haskell and Joe Lambie as Lloyd Kendall, who married Liza Sentell; Michelle Phillips as Ruby Ashford; Philip Brown as Steve Kendall; Olympia Dukakis as Barbara Moreno; Josh Freund and Damion Scheller as Josh Moreno; Tina Johnson as Rhonda Sue Huckaby; Tom Sullivan as singer Michael Kendall; Jennifer Gatti as Angela Moreno; Sheryl Lee Ralph as Laura McCarthy; Jo Henderson and Maeve McGuire as Kate McCleary; Matthew Ashford as Cagney McCleary; Page Hannah and Susan Carey-Lamm as Adair McCleary; Leslie Stevens as Justine Calvert; Patrick James Clarke as Jack Benton; Jane Krakowski as Rebecca "T. R." Kendall; Kevin Conroy as Chase Kendall; Robert Curtis Brown as Alec Kendall; David Gautreaux as Garth Taper; Will Patton as Kentucky Bluebird; Adam Storke as Andrew Ryder; Paul Espel and Lee Godart as Bela; Mary Jo Keenen as Kat; Ann Flood as Ella Hobbs; Tim Loughlin as Jerry Henderson; William Prince as Judge Henderson; Patrick Novatt as Malcolm McCleary; David Forsyth as newspaperman Hogan McCleary; Domini Blythe as Estelle Kendall; Rosemary Joyce as Daphne Draper; Jack Betts as David Glenn; and Anita Gillette as Wilma.

After its switch to NBC in 1982 the series never fared well; some critics believed that the de-emphasis of Mary Stuart's character harmed the show. John Whitesell took over as the series' last executive producer, but was unable to salvage it from the bottom of the daytime ratings heap. The ambitious story line of flooding the town of Henderson failed to lift the ratings, and *Search for Tomorrow* ended just after Christmas 1986, some three months after its special thirty-fifth anniversary telecast, which contained flashbacks of notable events on the show. On the finale, Patty married Hogan McCleary, and in the last scene Jo Tourneur looked up at the night sky, turned to her longtime friend and neighbor Stu Bergman, and said: "Tomorrow, I can't wait!"

SEAWAY   SYNDICATED
1965   Produced in Canada in 1965 but not made available in the United States until later, this hour adventure series starred Stephen Young as Nick King, a security agent working along the St. Lawrence Seaway, and Austin Willis as Admiral Fox, his boss, the head of the Ship Owners Association.

SECOND CHANCE   ABC
7 MARCH 1977–15 JULY 1977   Jim Peck hosted this daytime game show on which three contestants competed; after writing down their answers to various questions, contestants were shown three possible answers (including the correct one) and were permitted to change their answer. After each round the contestants took a spin at the prize board, where they could win cash and prizes or lose everything. Bill Carruthers, who created the series with Jan McCormack, was the executive producer.

SECOND CHANCE   FOX
26 SEPTEMBER 1987–2 JULY 1988   From September until January, this half-hour sitcom was titled *Second Chance,* and starred Kiel Martin (fresh from *Hill Street Blues*) as Charles Russell, who died in the year 2011, but was sent back to Earth by St. Peter to earn a "second chance" to enter heaven. Charles returned to Venice, California, in 1987, rented a room above his garage, and tried to advise his teenaged self on matters of life and love. Other regulars were Matthew Perry as fifteen-year-old Charles "Chazz" Russell; Randee Heller as his divorced mother, Helen; William Gallo as Chazz's pal Booch; Demian Slade as Chazz's pal Eugene; and Joseph Maher as St. Peter.

On 16 January the series changed formats and titles, dropping Martin and Maher. Now known as *Boys Will Be Boys,* it featured Perry, Gallo and Slade as teen pals,

Heller as the now-widowed Helen, and added Terri Ivens as Chazz's girlfriend, Debbie Miller.

SECOND CHANCES   CBS
2 DECEMBER 1993–27 JANUARY 1994   Ill-fated continuing drama set in Santa Rita, California. With Connie Sellecca as Dianne Benedict, who was running for a judgeship; Justin Lazard as law student Kevin Cook; Jennifer Lopez as Kevin's fiancee, Melinda Lopez; Megan Porter Follows as Dianne's sister, Kate; Matt Salinger as Mike; Pepe Serna as Melinda's father, Sal Lopez; Ronny Cox as Kevin's father, George Cook; Ray Wise as Judge Stinson, Dianne's political opponent; Michelle Phillips as Joanna; Ramy Zada as Detective Kuntz; and Stephen Nichols as Tommy. The series's production facilities were badly damaged by the Northridge earthquake in January 1994, and production was halted; the series resurfaced briefly on CBS's late-night schedule in February 1994. Lopez and Serna received a second chance to repeat their roles, however, on a subsequent CBS offering: see *Hotel Malibu*.

SECOND CITY T.V.   SYNDICATED
1977–1980   This half-hour videotaped series satirized television. Featured were: John Candy, Joe Flaherty, Eugene Levy, Andrea Martin, Catherine O'Hara, Harold Ramis, and Dave Thomas. Bernard Sahlins was the producer. By the end of its syndicated run the show was known as *SCTV Television Network*. In 1981 most of the crew moved to network television (see *SCTV Network*).

THE SECOND HALF   NBC
7 SEPTEMBER 1993–14 DECEMBER 1993; 22 MARCH 1994–12 APRIL 1994   Standup comic John Mendoza headlined this sitcom as John Palmaro, a newly divorced 42-year-old sportswriter for the *Chicago Daily Post*. Also on hand were Jessica Lundy as his sister, Denise, who lived in the same apartment building; Ellen Blain as his fourteen-year-old, Cathy; Brooke Stanley as his nine-year-old, Ruth; Joe Guzaldo as his pal and coworker, David; Wayne Knight as Robert Piccolo, his editor; and Kimberley Kates as John's dog-walking neighbor, Gloria.

THE SECOND HUNDRED YEARS   ABC
6 SEPTEMBER 1967–19 SEPTEMBER 1968   Monte Markham played dual roles in this half-hour sitcom—Luke Carpenter, a gold prospector who was frozen in an avalanche in 1900 and who miraculously thawed out, unharmed, after a second avalanche in 1967, and Ken Carpenter, Luke's thirty-three-year-old grandson, who looked exactly like him. Arthur O'Connell costarred as sixty-seven-year-old Edwin Carpenter, Luke's son and Ken's father. Luke came to live with Edwin and Ken, while the Army, for security reasons, struggled to keep secret the fact of Luke's discovery. Also featured were Frank Maxwell as Colonel Garroway and Bridget Hanley as Nurse Anderson; Karen Black, in one of her first TV roles, appeared occasionally as Garroway's hippie daughter, Marcia. Harry Ackerman was the executive producer and Bob Claver the producer for Screen Gems.

SECRET AGENT   CBS
5 APRIL 1961–13 SEPTEMBER 1961; 3 APRIL 1965–11 SEPTEMBER 1965; 4 DECEMBER 1965–10 SEPTEMBER 1966   Patrick McGoohan starred in this adventure series as John Drake, a comparatively moral intelligence agent who refused to carry a gun and who avoided violence when possible. The series was produced in England by ATV; thirty-nine half-hour episodes were filmed in 1961, and the series was televised there and here as *Danger Man,* in which Drake was a NATO agent. The series was revived in 1965 in an hour format, under the title *Secret Agent,* with Drake now working for British intelligence. The show's theme, "Secret Agent Man," was composed by P. F. Sloan and Steve Barri, and sung by Johnny Rivers.

SECRET FILE, U.S.A. SYNDICATED

1955 Filmed principally in Amsterdam, this half-hour Cold War spy show starred Robert Alda as Major William Morgan of Army Intelligence and Lois Hensen as Colonel Custer.

THE SECRET LIVES OF WALDO KITTY NBC

6 SEPTEMBER 1975–4 SEPTEMBER 1976 This live and animated Saturday-morning series was inspired by the *Walter Mitty* stories. Waldo Kitty was a daydreaming cat who fantasized about saving his girlfriend, Felicia, from the clutches of his nemesis, Tyrone the bulldog. Howard Morris was the voice of Waldo, Jane Webb that of Felicia, and Allan Melvin that of Tyrone. Lou Scheimer and Norm Prescott were the executive producers.

SECRET SERVICE NBC

16 AUGUST 1992–23 JUNE 1993 Re-enactments of great moments in the history of the Secret Service, the federal agency in charge of protecting the president and tracking down counterfeiters, were presented on this reality-based show, hosted by actor Steven Ford. As the son of former president Gerald Ford, Steven Ford had first-hand knowledge of the work of the organization.

SECRET SQUIRREL NBC

2 OCTOBER 1965–2 SEPTEMBER 1967 Secret Squirrel, a Hanna-Barbera cartoon character, had his own Saturday-morning series for two seasons before joining forces with Atom Ant in the fall of 1967. Secret Squirrel was accompanied on his missions by Morocco Mole; other animated segments included "Winnie Witch" and "Squiddly Diddly," a squid who habitually escaped from his aquarium. See also *Atom Ant*.

THE SECRET STORM CBS

1 FEBRUARY 1954–8 FEBRUARY 1974 *The Secret Storm* was created by Roy Winsor, who had previously developed *Search for Tomorrow*. For many years it was produced by Gloria Monty; Joe Manetta produced it during the later seasons. The story lines centered on the comings and goings of the Ames family of Woodbridge until the late 1960s, when the show was sold by American Home Products to CBS; successive sets of writers managed to kill off almost all of the Ameses, and *The Secret Storm,* which had been television's most popular daytime serial at one time, left the air in 1974 after a run of twenty years and a week. It had begun as a fifteen-minute show and had expanded to thirty minutes in June 1962. Principal players included: Peter Hobbs (1954–1960), Cec Linder (1960–1964), Ward Costello (1964–1966), and Lawrence Weber (1966–1968) as Peter Ames, a father of three who was widowed during the first week of the story when his wife, Ellen, was hit by a car; Jean Mowry, Rachel Taylor, Mary Foskett, and Judy Lewis as Susan Ames, his elder daughter; Robert Morse, Warren Berlinger, Wayne Tippit, Peter White, and Stephen Bolster as Jerry Ames, his son; Jada Rowland, Beverly Lunsford, and Lynne Adams as Amy Ames, his younger daughter (Rowland played the role from 1954 until 1974, but not continuously); Russell Hicks as Judge J. T. Tyrell, father of the late Ellen Ames; Marjorie Gateson and Eleanor Phelps as Grace Tyrell, Ellen's mother; Haila Stoddard as Pauline, Ellen's sister; Virginia Dwyer as Jane Edwards, the Ames' housekeeper; Ed Bryce as Bruce Edwards, her estranged husband; James Vickery (1957–1965) as Alan Dunbar, who married Susan Ames and later bought the town newspaper; Donny Melvin as Peter Dunbar; Joan Hotchkis and June Graham as Myra Lake, one of Amy's schoolteachers, who married Peter Ames in 1959; Carl King as Bryan Fuller, who married Pauline and later divorced her; Frank Sutton as reporter Joe Sullivan; Jane McArthur as Nancy Hewlett; Jim Pritchett as Jeff Nichols; Don Galloway, David O'Brien, and Ed Griffith as Kip Rysdale, a boyfriend of Amy's; John Baragrey as Arthur Rysdale, Kip's father; Polly Childs as Kate Lodge, who married Jerry Ames and was later found murdered; Pamela Raymond as Hope, who later married Jerry; Lori March as Valerie Hill, who married Peter Ames; Bibi Besch as Janet Hill, Valerie's daughter; Roy Scheider, Justin McDonough, and Ed Winter as Bob Hill, Valerie's son; Diana Muldaur as Ann Wicker; Nick Coster, Jed Allan, Ed

Kemmer, Ryan MacDonald, Conrad Fowkes, and Linden Chiles as Paul Britton, who married Amy Ames; Julie Wilson as Brooke Lawrence, who was accidentally killed by Valerie; Jane Rose as Aggie Parsons; Jacqueline Brookes as Ursula Winthrop; Robert Sherwood as Doug Winthrop; Jack Ryland, Robert Loggia, and Laurence Luckinbill as Frank Carver, who married Susan Ames Dunbar; Keith Charles as Nick Kane; Christina Crawford (daughter of Joan Crawford) as Joann Kane; Jeffrey Lynn as Charlie Clemens; Marla Adams as Belle Clemens, who married Paul Britton; Diane Dell, Terry Falis, and Judy Safran as Lisa Britton, daughter of Paul and Amy Britton; Bernie Barrow as Dan Kincaid, who married Belle Clemens; David Ackroyd and Dennis Cooney as Kevin Kincaid, Dan's son; Barbara Rodell as Jill Stevens Clayborne; Peter MacLean as her husband, Hugh Clayborne, who was killed with her in a plane crash; Joel Crothers as Ken Stevens, Jill's brother; James Grover as Clay Stevens, his son; Stephanie Braxton as Lauri Reddin; David Gale as Mark Reddin, who left the priesthood to marry Lauri, but later returned to it while Lauri married Ken Stevens; Frances Sternhagen as Jesse Reddin; Gary Sandy as Stacey Reddin; Troy Donahue (seldom seen on TV since he starred in *SurfSide 6*) as Keefer, a drug dealer; Jennifer Darling as Iris Sims, Keefer's girlfriend; Gordon Rigsby and Alexander Scourby as Dr. Ian Northcote, who married Valerie Hill Ames; Terry Kiser as Cory Boucher; James Storm as Sean Childers, Jr.; Jeff Pomerantz and Keith Charles as Dr. Brian Neeves; Audre Johnston as nurse Martha Ann Ashley; Dan Hamilton as Robert Landers, son of Dan Kincaid; Ellen Barber and Audrey Landers as Joanna Morrison; Sidney Walker as Monsignor Quinn; Joe Ponazecki as Reilly; Patrick Fox as Phil; Madeline Sherwood as Carmen; Richard Venture as Tom Gregory; Sue Ann Gifillan as Lurene Post; Roberta Royce as Freddie; Susan Sudert as Charlotte; Philip Bruns as Julius Klepner; Mary K. Wells as Nola Hallister; Diane Ladd as Kitty Styles; Scott Medford as Jonathan Styles; and Nicholas Lewis as Tim Brannigan.

THE SECRETS OF ISIS
See ISIS

THE SECRETS OF LAKE SUCCESS
See GREAT ESCAPES

SECRETS OF MIDLAND HEIGHTS   CBS
6 DECEMBER 1980–24 JANUARY 1981   An hour prime-time serial, set in a Midwestern college town. The cast included Bibi Besch as Dorothy Wheeler; Linda Grovenor (in the first episode) and Nancy Jones as her daughter, Holly Wheeler; Jordan Christopher as scheming Guy Millington; Doran Clark as Guy's niece, Ann Dulles; Martha Scott as Guy's mother, Margaret Millington, the grand dame of Midland Heights; Robert Hogan as Professor Nathan Welsh, a widower who had an affair with Dorothy; Daniel Zippi as Nathan's son, Teddy Welsh; Stephen Manley as Nathan's son, Danny Welsh; Mark Pinter as Calvin Richardson; Lorenzo Lamas as Burt Carroll; Linda Hamilton as Burt's girlfriend, Lisa Rogers; Jim Youngs as gas jockey John Gray; Melora Hardin as Micky Carroll; and Jenny O'Hara as Lucy Dexter. Although the series was canceled after only eight weeks, several of the show's regulars showed up in *King's Crossing,* which aired during the 1981–1982 season on ABC. Both were produced by Lorimar Productions, which dominated the prime-time serial field during the early 1980s.

SECRETS OF THE DEEP   SYNDICATED
1974   Former astronaut Scott Carpenter hosted this half-hour documentary series about oceans and marine life.

SEE IT NOW   CBS
18 NOVEMBER 1951–7 JULY 1958   Though it was not television's first public affairs program, *See It Now* was surely its most significant. Through careful preparation, thoughtful production, and skillful editing, it demonstrated that television could present to the viewer something more, something deeper, than a mere interview or

newsreel. As Alexander Kendrick noted in his book, *Prime Time: The Life of Edward R. Murrow, See It Now* was the first public affairs show to use its own film footage instead of newsreel or file footage; no interview was rehearsed and nothing was dubbed.

See It Now also pioneered the use of field producers, who supervised the filming on location. *See It Now* was jointly produced by Edward R. Murrow (who also hosted the series) and Fred W. Friendly. The two had previously collaborated on two projects: "I Can Hear It Now," a series of three record albums, narrated by Murrow, of "aural history" from 1919 to 1949, and *Hear It Now,* a CBS radio news analysis show. Murrow and Friendly were deeply committed to a high-quality television program; though Murrow continued to do a nightly news show on CBS radio, *See It Now's* weekly schedule gave Murrow and Friendly time to assemble material and to focus the presentation. The producers hoped that *See It Now* would not only show a news event but would explain to the viewer why it happened. Though a sponsor—Alcoa— had been acquired, the advertising fees paid for only a small fraction of the show's cost; the remainder was absorbed by the network.

The show premiered 18 November 1951; the opening showed, on a split screen, San Francisco's Golden Gate Bridge and New York's Brooklyn Bridge, in the first live commercial coast-to-coast broadcast (the first coast-to-coast broadcast had been on 4 September, when President Truman addressed the Japanese Peace Treaty Conference in San Francisco). Many of the early shows focused on the Korean War, but few stirred any real controversy. It was during *See It Now's* third season, as the series began to examine the anti-Communist fervor of the time, that the program grew to full maturity. The first notable broadcast of the season took place on 20 October 1953, with the telecast of "The Case Against Milo Radulovich, AO589839." Radulovich, an Air Force lieutenant, had been ordered dismissed from the service because his father, a Serbian immigrant, and sister were said to be Communist sympathizers; following the broadcast, Secretary of the Air Force Harold E. Talbott reviewed the case and ordered Radulovich reinstated. The program was widely hailed as the best single program of the year, and Murrow won an Emmy as most outstanding personality of 1953. Though CBS never pressured Friendly or Murrow to refrain from airing the program, neither the network nor the sponsor would agree to advertise it; Murrow and Friendly put up $1,500 of their own money to purchase an ad in the *New York Times.*

Another significant broadcast from 1953 was titled "Argument in Indianapolis." Shown on 24 November, it examined the refusal by the Indianapolis chapter of the American Legion to permit its meeting hall to be used by the American Civil Liberties Union. The single most important show of the season, however, was shown on 9 March 1954; the untitled half hour, which had been months in preparation, was a series of film clips of Senator Joseph McCarthy, the bombastic demagogue who most embodied the anti-Communist hysteria. The clips showed McCarthy as a shallow and callous man whose stock in trade included conflicting statements, misstatements, and half-truths. The following week's program showed a second half hour of McCarthy, principally of his recent questioning of Annie Lee Moss, an alleged subversive who was employed by the State Department. On 6 April McCarthy accepted Murrow's offer of equal time; McCarthy's appearance on that show probably did as much to weaken his own credibility as the two earlier shows. McCarthy concluded his rebuttal with these remarks: "Now ordinarily I would not take time out from the important work at hand to answer Murrow. However, in this case I feel justified in doing so because Murrow is a symbol, the leader and cleverest of the jackal pack which is always found at the throat of anyone who dares to expose individual Communists and traitors." At a subsequent press conference Murrow uttered his now-famous response: "Who has helped the Communist cause and who has served his country better, Senator McCarthy or I? I would like to be remembered by the answer to that question." After the broadcasts, opposition to McCarthy strengthened; though McCarthy's subcommittee conducted several more weeks of investigations (which ABC and DuMont covered live), McCarthy was censured by the Senate late in 1954, and his influence diminished rapidly.

During the 1954–1955 season *See It Now* presented several noteworthy programs, including a report on *Brown* v. *Board of Education,* the Supreme Court's historic school desegregation decision; stories on the changing face of Africa and the Middle East; "A Conversation with J. Robert Oppenheimer," who had previously been labeled a security risk; and a two-part series on tobacco and lung cancer (Murrow, a chain smoker, lost a lung to cancer and died of a brain tumor in 1965). At the end of the season, *See It Now* lost both its sponsor and its prime-time slot; the reasons for the losses are not entirely clear, but it has been suggested that Alcoa withdrew its sponsorship as a result of pressure following a May 1955 report on a small Texas newspaper that had uncovered a major land scandal (Alcoa was then expanding its Texas operations). The loss of the time slot was principally due to the introduction of *The $64,000 Question* into the preceding half hour on 7 June 1955; network executives no doubt felt that a runaway hit such as that could serve as an effective lead-in to a more popular type of show.

From the fall of 1955 until the summer of 1958, *See It Now* was broadcast as a series of specials, most of which were in a sixty-minute format; some CBS insiders by that time referred to the show as "See It Now and Then." This latter group of broadcasts ranged from "The Secret Life of Danny Kaye" to an interview with Chinese premier Chou En-Lai (filmed in Rangoon, the meeting was arranged by Burma's premier, U Nu). The final telecast, on 7 July 1958, was a report on postwar Germany, entitled "Watch on the Ruhr."

Though *See It Now* left the air in 1958, its legacy has survived. In 1959 the network introduced *CBS Reports;* though not always a regularly scheduled program, it has presented a number of hard-hitting news documentaries. In 1968 CBS introduced *60 Minutes,* which gradually built up a large audience; its executive producer is Don Hewitt, who directed *See It Now* for several years, and one of its principal producers is Joe Wershba, who was a staff reporter on *See It Now.*

SEE THE PROS   SYNDICATED
1958   Former West Point football star Glenn Davis interviewed professional footballers on this half-hour series.

THE SEEKING HEART   CBS
5 JULY 1954–10 DECEMBER 1954   A medically oriented soap opera. The cast of the fifteen-minute daily serial included Judith Braun, Flora Campbell, Scott Forbes (who later turned up in *Jim Bowie*), Dorothy Lovett, and James Yarborough. *Road of Life* replaced *The Seeking Heart* in December of 1954.

SEINFELD   NBC
31 MAY 1990–21 JUNE 1990; 23 JANUARY 1991–   Standup comic Jerry Seinfeld brought his unique perspective on everyday life to this sitcom, which he created with former standup comic Larry David. Jerry Seinfeld starred as himself, a standup comic (and neatness fanatic) who lived in an apartment on Manhattan's Upper West Side; when Seinfeld was not at home, he could often be seen doing a brief standup routine at a local club. Unlike other sitcoms, however, the central characters were neither coworkers nor related to one another. Instead, three friends of the fictional Seinfeld were the other regulars: Jason Alexander as hapless George Costanza, who was a realtor as the series began but later bumbled through other jobs; Julia Louis-Dreyfus as Jerry's ex-girlfriend Elaine Benes, who worked for a publisher; and Michael Richards as Jerry's oddball neighbor Kramer (his first name was revealed to be Cosmo in a 1995 episode). Occasionally featured were Wayne Knight as Newman, Estelle Harris and Jerry Stiller as George's overbearing parents, and Elizabeth Sheridan and Barney Martin as Jerry's parents.

The insignificant aspects of everyday life formed the grist for most programs; not since *The Adventures of Ozzie and Harriet* has a sitcom been less truly plot-driven. As Seinfeld succinctly explained his show to *TV Guide:* "It's micro-concept TV." Co-creator Larry David elaborated slightly on the concept to *Entertainment Weekly:* "No hugging. No kissing." The carefully crafted scripts explored such details of life as forgetting a date's name, waiting in line at the bank, finding a parking space, and even the etiquette of "double dipping"—putting a potato chip back in the dip after having already taken a bite. Bodily functions were also fair game for examination; in one well-known show, "The Contest," Jerry, George, Kramer, and Elaine tried to see who could last the longest without masturbating (the episode won a writing Emmy).

The series was not an immediate hit. Introduced in a four-week trial run in 1990 (a quasi-pilot, "The Seinfeld Chronicles," had aired on NBC 5 July 1989), *Seinfeld* attracted chiefly a cult audience until early 1993, when it was moved from Wednesday nights to Thursdays, immediately after *Cheers*. In the fall of 1993 it replaced *Cheers* as NBC's Thursday night anchor show, and rose to third place in the seasonal Nielsens; it topped the ratings the following season. *Seinfeld* also won a prestigious Peabody Award in 1992.

SEMINAR ABC

11 OCTOBER 1952–3 JANUARY 1953   In this early experiment in educational television, the camera sat in on an actual course in American civilization, taught at Columbia University by Professor Donald Bigelow. Erik Barnouw, Jack Pacey, and Dorothy Oshlag produced the Saturday-evening series, and Alex Segal directed it.

SEMI-TOUGH ABC

29 MAY 1980–19 JUNE 1980   This half-hour sitcom was based on the movie of the same title (which was in turn based on Dan Jenkins' novel). It starred Bruce McGill and David Hasselhoff as Billy Clyde Puckett and Shake Tiller, two stars of the New York Bulls professional football team, and Markie Post as their roommate, writer Barbara Jane Bookman (the relationship among the three was purely platonic). Also featured were Ed Peck as Coach Cooper; Bubba Smith (who had played pro ball in real life) as teammate Puddin'; Freeman King as teammate Story Time; and Carlos Brown as teammate T. J.

SERGEANT PRESTON OF THE YUKON CBS/SYNDICATED

29 SEPTEMBER 1955–25 SEPTEMBER 1958 (CBS); 1958 (SYNDICATED)   This half-hour adventure series, which ran on radio from 1947 to 1955, starred Richard Simmons as Sergeant Preston of the Royal Northwest Mounted Police; astride his horse, Rex, and accompanied by his faithful canine companion, King, Preston seemed to spend most of his time by himself, trudging through the snow to apprehend fugitives. The character was created by George W. Trendle, who had previously conceived *The Lone Ranger* and *The Green Hornet*. The series was filmed in color, principally at Ashcroft, Colorado, and was produced by the Wrather Corporation; Von Reznicek's "Donna Diana Overture" was used as the theme music. An additional twenty-six episodes were produced for first-run syndication after the show concluded its network prime-time run in 1958. Richard Simmons, the star of the show, later revealed in an interview that Sergeant Preston's first name was Frank, though he added that the first name was never used on the air.

SERPICO NBC

24 SEPTEMBER 1976–28 JANUARY 1977   This unsuccessful hour-long crime show was based on Peter Maas's biography of Frank Serpico, an unorthodox New York cop (the book had been made into a movie in 1974, starring Al Pacino). On TV David Birney starred as the uncorruptible Frank Serpico, with Tom Atkins as Lieutenant Tom Sullivan. Emmet G. Lavery was executive producer for Emmet G. Lavery Productions in association with Paramount Television and NBC-TV.

SESAME STREET NET-PBS

10 NOVEMBER 1969–   The most important children's show in the history of television, *Sesame Street* proved to be not only informative, but also phenomenally successful. It was developed by Joan Ganz Cooney, executive director of the Children's Television Workshop, a company established in 1967 to produce the series with financial support from the United States Office of Education, the Ford Foundation, and the Carnegie Corporation. The show is set along a city street because it was primarily targeted at inner-city preschoolers (fortunately, *Sesame Street* proved popular with children of all backgrounds). Through a skillful blending of skits, songs, puppetry, and animation, *Sesame Street* has managed to teach letters, numbers, and

grammatical concepts in a totally entertaining fashion. Most shows are "sponsored" by particular letters or numbers, which are presented as "commercials." *Sesame Street*'s human performers have included: Loretta Long as Susan; Matt Robinson and Roscoe Orman as Gordon; Bob McGrath as Bob; Will Lee as Mr. Hooper; Northern J. Calloway as David; Emilio Delgado as Luis; and Sonia Manzano as Maria. Equally important are the Muppets, the talented group of expressive puppets created by Jim Henson: Ernie, Bert, Grover, Oscar the Grouch, The Cookie Monster, and Big Bird (who is not really a puppet, but rather a life-size figure played by Frank Oz and later by Carroll Spinney). Songs for the series have been composed by Jeff Moss and Joe Raposo. Other versions of *Sesame Street* have been produced in countries throughout the world. The series has managed to confront life and death during its run. When Will Lee (Mr. Hooper) died, the series chose not to replace him, but to deal with the character's departure in a sensitive program in which Big Bird learns of the death. On 13 May 1988 audiences celebrated the TV wedding of Luis and Maria. A network prime-time special, telecast 7 April 1989 on NBC, hosted by Bill Cosby, commemorated the series' twentieth anniversary. A second special, on 18 May 1994 on ABC, saluted its twenty-fifth anniversary.

In the fall of 1992 a new opening sequence was created, replacing the original one. Steve Whitmire became the new puppeteer and voice of Ernie, following Jim Henson's sudden death earlier that year. In the fall of 1993, as *Sesame Street* embarked on its twenty-fifth season, a new, larger set was introduced. It included the Furry Arms Hotel and the Finders Keepers thrift shop (operated by Ruth Buzzi); Tarah Lynne Schaeffer joined the cast as Tarah, a nine-year-old with a disability. Hillary Rodham Clinton made a guest appearance on the show 22 November 1993.

SEVEN AT ELEVEN   NBC

28 MAY 1951–27 JUNE 1951   Broadcast Mondays and Wednesdays at 11:00 P.M., *Seven at Eleven* alternated with *Broadway Open House,* which was cut back from five nights a week to three after Jerry Lester left the show. The seven regulars were host George DeWitt, singers Denise Lor, Betty Luster, and Jack Stanton, bandleader Milton DeLugg, comic Sid Gould, and the show's unidentified floor manager.

SEVEN BRIDES FOR SEVEN BROTHERS   CBS

19 SEPTEMBER 1982–2 JULY 1983   This hour dramatic series was based on the 1954 musical film. Featured were Richard Dean Anderson as Adam McFadden, the eldest of seven orphaned brothers; Terri Treas as his new wife, Hannah Moss, who came home with Adam to find six more McFaddens living on the ranch; Drake Hogestyn as Brian; Peter Horton as Crane; Roger Wilson as Daniel; Tim Topper as Evan; Bryan Utman as Ford; and River Phoenix as Guthrie (conveniently, the brothers had been named in alphabetical order). The ambitious series featured original music by Jim Webb, but failed to catch on with family audiences.

THE 700 CLUB   SYNDICATED/FAM

1976–   Based in Virginia Beach, this syndicated daily religious talk show is hosted by Pat Robertson, president of the Christian Broadcasting Network. Robertson got his start in television in October 1961, when he put back on the air a foundering UHF outlet in Virginia that he had recently purchased. In 1963 he asked for 700 viewers to pledge ten dollars a month to keep the station afloat. In 1966, when Robertson staffer Jim Bakker started hosting a talk show, the name *700 Club* was suggested. Bakker hosted the program for six years, until he and his wife, Tammy, left Robertson's employ (the Bakkers, of course, would later set up *The P. T. L. Club*). Robertson himself then took over as host of *The 700 Club*. The program was distributed nationally beginning in 1976. It became one of the cornerstones of Robertson's cable service, the Christian Broadcasting Network (later known as the Family Channel), which he established in 1977. Robertson temporarily resigned as host in 1986 in order to pursue his quest for the 1988 Republican presidential nomination; his son, Tim Robertson, took over. The senior Robertson returned to the anchor desk in 1988. By the mid-1990s the nightly hour broadcast was divided into two segments, both hosted by Robertson, his longtime sidekick Ben Kinchlow, and former Miss America Terry

Meeuwsen. The first segment was a newsmagazine, with topical stories filed by contributing reporters; the second segment focused on religious topics, and featured guests and a live studio audience.

SEVEN KEYS   ABC
3 APRIL 1961–27 MARCH 1964   Jack Narz hosted this daytime game show on which two contestants attempted to advance along a board of squares by identifying pictures on the squares. The winner of the game won one of seven keys. One of the seven was the key to the prize for which the contestant was playing; thus, a player who won seven games was certain to win the desired prize.

SEVEN LEAGUE BOOTS   SYNDICATED
1959   Another of the several documentary series hosted by Jack Douglas, this one presented adventurers from all over the world.

THE SEVEN LIVELY ARTS   CBS
3 NOVEMBER 1957–16 FEBRUARY 1958   This ambitious Sunday-afternoon show was supposed to compete with *Omnibus* (which had left CBS in 1956), but never did; thanks to a disastrous premiere, the show never really had a chance to get off the ground. John Crosby, television critic for the New York *Herald Tribune*, was the host of the series. Among the varied presentations were: "The Changing Ways of Love," by S. J. Perelman, with Perelman, Piper Laurie, Jason Robards, Jr., Rip Torn, Mike Wallace, and Dick York (3 November); "The World of Nick Adams," adapted by A. E. Hotchner from Hemingway's stories, with Steven Hill, William Marshall, and Eli Wallach (10 November); "Here Is New York" narrated by E. G. Marshall (15 December); "Hollywood Around the World," a look at the film industry (29 December). Blues singer Billie Holiday also made a rare television appearance on the series (8 December). The executive producer of the hour show was John Houseman.

704 HAUSER   CBS
11 APRIL 1994–9 MAY 1994   One of TV's better-known addresses, 704 Hauser Street in Queens had been Archie and Edith Bunker's home on creator Norman Lear's landmark sitcom, *All in the Family*. By 1994, however, the house had passed into the hands of a black family. Featured were John Amos as Ernest Cumberbatch, an auto mechanic; Lynnie Godfrey as his wife, Rose; T. E. Russell as their son, business school student Thurgood Marshall ("Goodie") Cumberbatch, whose conservatism baffled his father; Maura Tierney as Goodie's white girlfrend, Cherlyn Markowitz; and Casey Siemaszko as Joey Stivic, the Bunkers' grandson.

THE SEVENTH SENSE   SYNDICATED
1978   Jim Peck hosted this interview series, which attempted to probe the subconscious minds of those interviewed through the use of hypnosis. Elroy Schwartz, a hypnotist, was the producer.

77 SUNSET STRIP   ABC
10 OCTOBER 1958–9 SEPTEMBER 1964   Warner Brothers' best-known detective show starred Efrem Zimbalist, Jr., and Roger Smith as Stu Bailey and Jeff Spencer, two private eyes whose offices were located at 77 Sunset Strip in Hollywood; Zimbalist had first played his role in an episode of Warner Brothers' anthology show, *Conflict*, titled "Anything for Money" (aired 23 July 1957). Edd Byrnes costarred in *77 Sunset Strip* as Gerald Lloyd Kookson III, better known as Kookie; the character, a hip-talking parking lot attendant at Dino's Lodge next door, was not intended to be a recurring one, but public reaction (chiefly from teenage girls) was so strong that Byrnes was given a regular role. Byrnes capitalized on the character in 1959 with a hit record, "Kookie, Kookie (Lend Me Your Comb)," recorded with Connie Stevens (soon to appear on Warner Brothers' *Hawaiian Eye*). Because of a contract dispute, Byrnes did not appear on the series during most of the 1959–1960 season; shortly after his return (in May of 1960), however, Kookie became a private eye, working with Bailey and Spencer (in Byrnes's absence, Troy Donahue had played the parking

lot attendant in several 1959 episodes; Donahue later starred in *SurfSide 6*). Also featured were Jacqueline Beer (Miss France of 1954) as Suzanne Fabray, the receptionist and switchboard operator; Louis Quinn as Roscoe (introduced in the third episode), a horse-playing contact man who hung out at the office; and Byron Keith as Lieutenant Gilmore of the Los Angeles police. In 1960 Richard Long joined the cast as detective Rex Randolph (Long had played the same part a year earlier on Warner Brothers' *Bourbon Street Beat*), and in 1961 Robert Logan was added as J. R. Hale, the new parking lot attendant who usually spoke in abbreviations. Major changes took place in the fall of 1963 as all the regulars except for Zimbalist were dropped; Zimbalist continued as Stu Bailey, but his offices were no longer at 77 Sunset Strip; Joan Staley was added as his secretary, Hannah. The series even acquired a new theme, Bob Thomson's "New Sunset," which replaced the familiar finger-snapping "77 Sunset Strip" written by Mack David and Jerry Livingston. The series left the air for a few weeks in February 1964 but returned (in reruns) in April of that year. Production was handled first by Roy Huggins, later by Howie Horwitz, and finally by William Conrad (who later starred in *Cannon*). The success of *77 Sunset Strip* spawned several other Warner Brothers hours (*Bourbon Street Beat* and *Hawaiian Eye* in 1959, *SurfSide 6* in 1960), but none of them was as popular as the first of the line.

77TH BENGAL LANCERS NBC
21 OCTOBER 1956–2 JUNE 1957   This half-hour adventure series was set in India at Fort Oghora, headquarters of the Seventy-seventh Bengal Lancers during the late nineteenth century. The show, a Screen Gems production, featured Warren Stevens as Lieutenant Rhodes; Philip Carey as Lieutenant Storm; and John Sutton and Patrick Whyte as Colonel Standish.

SHA NA NA SYNDICATED
1977–1981   A successful half-hour musical series, *Sha Na Na* was named for its hosts, a ten-member aggregation dedicated to reviving interest in the music of the 1950s, the Golden Era of rock and roll. The group was founded at Columbia University in 1968, when the members of the Kingsmen, a campus singing group, began to include hits of the fifties in their repertoire; the name "Sha Na Na" was taken from the background chant of the Silhouettes' 1958 classic, "Get a Job." By 1977 the group included Lenny Baker, Johnny Contardo, Denny Greene, Jocko Marcellino, Danny (Dirty Dan) McBride, Chico Ryan, (Screamin') Scott Simon, Scott Powell (also known as Tony Santini), Don York, and muscle-flexing Jon (Bowzer) Bauman, the unofficial leader of the gang (Denny, Jocko, Tony, and Don were original members). Among those featured on the show were Jane Dulo, Pamela Myers, Avery Schreiber (1977–1978), Kenneth Mars, and Soupy Sales (1978–1981). Pierre Cossette was the executive producer, and Bernard Rothman and Jack Wohl were the producers.

SHADOW CHASERS ABC
14 NOVEMBER 1985–16 JANUARY 1986   A tongue-in-cheek adventure series about a tabloid newspaper reporter and an anthropologist who teamed up to investigate reports of paranormal phenomena and other strange stuff. With Dennis Dugan as Edgar "Benny" Benedek, reporter for the National Register; Trevor Eve as Professor Jonathan MacKensie; and Nina Foch as Dr. Julianne Moorhouse, who directed the boys' investigations.

SHADOW OF THE CLOAK DUMONT
6 JUNE 1951–20 MARCH 1952   This half-hour spy show starred Helmut Dantine as Peter House, an agent for International Security Intelligence. Roger Gerry produced the series.

SHADOW THEATER USA
1 APRIL 1990–22 JULY 1990   Half-hour magazine show on horror films, hosted by Robert Englund, who is perhaps better known as Freddy of the *Nightmare on Elm Street* movies.

SHAFT   CBS

9 OCTOBER 1973–20 AUGUST 1974   This ninety-minute crime show shared a Tuesday slot with *Hawkins* and with *The New CBS Tuesday Movie*. Richard Roundtree starred as John Shaft, a slick and successful black private eye who worked in New York, and Ed Barth costarred as Lieutenant Al Rossi. The TV series was considerably less violent than the 1971 film (which had also starred Roundtree) on which it was based. Allan Balter and William Read Woodfield produced the series for M-G-M.

SHAKESPEARE ON TV   SYNDICATED

1954   This lecture series was presented by Dr. Frank Baxter of the University of Southern California.

THE SHAKESPEARE PLAYS   PBS

14 FEBRUARY 1979–31 MAY 1985   One of the most ambitious projects in broadcasting history, *The Shakespeare Plays* was a six-year effort by the BBC (with financial assistance from Exxon, Morgan Guaranty Trust Company and Metropolitan Life Insurance) to produce all thirty-seven of William Shakespeare's plays. *Julius Caesar* was the first of the works to be broadcast (the plays were not produced in chronological order). The series concluded in 1985 with *Love's Labour's Lost*.

SHAKY GROUND   FOX

13 DECEMBER 1992–4 JULY 1993   Domestic sitcom about a wacky but lovable dad and his family. With Matt Frewer as Bob Moody, who worked at United General Technologies, a Southern California aerospace company; Robin Riker as his wife, Helen; Matthew Brooks as teen son Carter; Love Hewitt as teen daughter Bernadette; Bradley Pierce as preteen son Dylan; Harold Sylvester as Bob's coworker, Russell; Alex Nevil as Arthur Dannenberg, a younger coworker who had nudged out Bob for a promotion; Stephen Elliott as Helen's father, Heywood; and Gloria Dorson as Helen's mother, Beverly.

SHANE   ABC

10 SEPTEMBER 1966–31 DECEMBER 1966   Based on the 1953 film, this hour-long western starred David Carradine as Shane, a drifting gunman who signed on as a hired hand with the Starrett family and helped them save their farm from the clutches of an evil land baron. Also featured were Jill Ireland as widow Marian Starrett, owner of the place; Chris Shea as her young son, Joey; Tom Tully as Tom Starrett, her father-in-law; Bert Freed as Rufe Ryker, the land baron; and Sam Gilman as Grafton, Ryker's henchman. Herbert Brodkin was the executive producer.

SHANNON   SYNDICATED

1961   George Nader starred in this half-hour crime show as Joe Shannon, insurance investigator for the Transport Bonding & Surety Company; Regis Toomey was featured as his boss, Bill Cochran. Shannon drove an ultramodern 1961 Buick, equipped with cameras, a dictating machine, tape recorders, and weapons. Jerry Briskin produced the series for Screen Gems.

SHANNON   CBS

11 NOVEMBER 1981–2 DECEMBER 1981; 17 MARCH 1982–7 APRIL 1982   Kevin Dobson starred in this hour crime show as Jack Shannon, a tough New York cop who moved to San Francisco after the death of his wife. Also featured were Michael Durrell as his new boss, Lieutenant Moraga; Charlie Fields as John, Shannon's ten-year-old son; Al Ruscio as Paul Lobatelli, Shannon's father-in-law, a fisherman; Karen Kondazian as Irene, Shannon's mother-in-law; and Bruce Kirby as Officer Schmidt, one of Shannon's colleagues.

SHANNON'S DEAL   NBC

13 APRIL 1990–16 MAY 1990; 10 AUGUST 1990–17 AUGUST 1990; 23 MARCH 1991–21 MAY 1991   Filmmaker John Sayles created this hour series about a Philadelphia lawyer who left his job with a big firm and opened his own office after piling up heavy

gambling debts and destroying his marriage. Featured were Jamey Sheridan as Jack Shannon; Jenny Lewis as his teenage daughter, Neala; Elizabeth Peña as his secretary, Lucy Acosta; Martin Ferrero as lawyer Lou Gondolph, whose office was in the same building as Shannnon's; and Richard Edson as Wilmer Slade, the legbreaker sent to collect Shannon's outstanding gambling loans. The series featured an excellent score by trumpeter Wynton Marsalis. The pilot, a two-hour TV-movie, was aired on NBC 4 June 1989.

THE SHAPE OF THINGS NBC
6 APRIL 1982–27 APRIL 1982   This hour comedy-variety show was described in ads as "a hilarious view of today's world through women's eyes!" Not only was it not hilarious, but its executive producer (George Schlatter), its producer (Bob Wynn), and most of its writers and crew were men. On-camera regulars included Dottie Archibald, Rhonda Bates, Elaine Boosler, Judy Carter, Alvernette Jiminez, Maureen Murphy, Howie Mandel, David Ruprecht, comedy duo Monteith & Rand, and the Chippendale Dancers.

SHAPING UP ABC
20 MARCH 1984–17 APRIL 1984   This witless sitcom was set at a Santa Monica health club. Featured were Leslie Nielsen as the owner, Buddy Fox, who had been married eight times (he wanted to have a child, but had had a vasectomy somewhere along the way); Michael Fontaine as Ben, the manager; Jennifer Tilly as Shannon, one of the instructors, an aspiring actress; Shawn Weatherly as Melissa, another instructor, studying for her master's degree; Cathy Shirriff as Zoya Antonova; and Judy Pioli as Shirley.

THE SHARI LEWIS SHOW NBC
1 OCTOBER 1960–28 SEPTEMBER 1963   Saturday-morning puppet show hosted by Shari Lewis and her puppets, Lamb Chop, Hush Puppy, and Charlie Horse. Also featured were Jackie Warner as Jum-Pup, Ronald Radd as Mr. Goodfellow, and Clive Russell. Robert Scherer was the producer.

THE SHARI SHOW SYNDICATED
1975   Half-hour puppet show hosted by Shari Lewis. See also *The Shari Lewis Show.*

SHAZAM! CBS
7 SEPTEMBER 1974–3 SEPTEMBER 1977   Based on the Marvel Comics character, this live-action Saturday-morning series featured Michael Gray as Billy Batson, a young man who could transform himself into Captain Marvel, the World's Mightiest Mortal, by uttering the word "Shazam!" (Shazam was an acronym for the six immortal elders—Solomon, Hercules, Atlas, Zeus, Achilles, and Mercury—who selected Batson and chose to endow him with rare powers). Also featured were Les Tremayne as Mentor, Batson's traveling companion; John Davey (1974–1976) and Jackson Bostwick (1976–1977) as Captain Marvel. Lou Scheimer and Norm Prescott were the executive producers of the half-hour series; during its last two seasons *Shazam!* was one-half of *The Shazam!/Isis Hour* (see also *Isis*). *Shazam!* was rerun on CBS in 1980.

SHAZZAN! CBS
9 SEPTEMBER 1967–6 SEPTEMBER 1969   Not to be confused with *Shazam!*, this half-hour cartoon show from Hanna-Barbera Productions featured a pair of twins (Chuck and Nancy) who were transported back to the time of the Arabian Nights. Shazzan was a giant genie at their disposal.

SHE TV ABC
16 AUGUST 1994–13 SEPTEMBER 1994   Hour sketch comedy series, performed by a mostly female company and occasional guest stars. The regular performers included Jennifer Coolidge, Linda Kash, Simbi Khali, Becky Thyre, Linda Wallem, Nick

Bakay, Carl Banks, Elon Gold, and Henriette Mantel. Music was provided by the She TV All Girl She Band.

SHEBANG   SYNDICATED
1965   Another of the several rock-and-roll shows that followed in the wake of *Hullabaloo* and *Shindig*.

SHEENA, QUEEN OF THE JUNGLE   SYNDICATED
1955   Based on the comic strip, this half-hour children's adventure series starred Irish McCalla as Sheena, the leopard-tunicked jungle denizen who was the female counterpart of Tarzan. Christian Drake was also featured as her friend Bob, a trader, and Chim the chimpanzee was on hand to keep Sheena company. The twenty-six episodes were filmed in Mexico by Nassour Studios. The character returned in a 1984 theatrical film, *Sheena,* starring Tanya Roberts.

THE SHEILA MacRAE SHOW   SYNDICATED
1971   Half-hour talk show hosted by Sheila MacRae, with help from her daughters Meredith and Heather MacRae.

THE SHEILAH GRAHAM SHOW   NBC
20 JANUARY 1951–14 JULY 1951   Hollywood gossip columnist Sheilah Graham hosted her own fifteen-minute show on Saturday nights. In 1955 she hosted a daytime show: see *Hollywood Today.*

SHELL GAME   CBS
8 JANUARY 1987–12 FEBRUARY 1987   Hour adventure series about a couple of former con artists who got back together after their divorce to work as producers on a consumer affairs TV show at KJME, channel six in Santa Ana, California. With James Read as John Reid; Margot Kidder as Jennie Jerome, his ex; Chip Zien as reporter Bert Luna; Rod McCary as Bill Bauer, coanchor of the show, called "Solutions"; Marg Helgenberger as the other coanchor, Natalie Thayer; and Fred McCarren as the boss, Vince Vanneman.

SHELL'S WONDERFUL WORLD OF GOLF   NBC
20 JANUARY 1963–28 FEBRUARY 1970   Weekend series of golf matches filmed at courses throughout the world. Sponsored by Shell Oil, the show was hosted by Gene Sarazen and George Rogers.

SHENANIGANS   ABC
26 SEPTEMBER 1964–20 MARCH 1965   A Saturday-morning game show for kids, hosted by Stubby Kaye.

SHE-RA: PRINCESS OF POWER   SYNDICATED
1985   Half-hour daily cartoon series starring She-Ra, the twin sister of He-Man (from whose series, *He-Man and the Masters of the Universe,* she was spun off). The characters were based on the line of Mattel toys.

SHERIFF OF COCHISE (U.S. MARSHAL)   SYNDICATED
1956–1958   John Bromfield starred in both of these half-hour crime shows as modern-day law enforcement officer Frank Morgan. In the first thirty-nine episodes, syndicated as *Sheriff of Cochise* or *Man from Cochise,* Morgan was the sheriff of Cochise County, Arizona. In the latter thirty-nine shows, syndicated as *U.S. Marshal,* Morgan was a federal marshal working in Arizona. Stan Jones was also featured as Deputy Olson. Mort Briskin was the producer and writer.

SHERLOCK HOLMES   SYNDICATED
1954   Ronald Howard starred as Sherlock Holmes, fiction's most famous sleuth, in this series of thirty-nine half hours. Also featured were H. Marion-Crawford as his faithful companion, Dr. John H. Watson, and Archie Duncan as Inspector Lestrade.

The series was filmed in France and produced by Sheldon Reynolds, who also directed most of the episodes; some of the stories were based on Arthur Conan Doyle's works, and others were newly written.

SHE'S THE SHERIFF   SYNDICATED
1987–1988   Half-hour sitcom starring Suzanne Somers as Hildy Granger, a widow who took over her late husband's job as sheriff of Lakes County, Nevada. Also on board were George Wyner as Deputy Max Rubin; Pat Carroll as Hildy's mother, Gussie Holt; Nicky Rose as Hildy's daughter, Allison; Taliesin Jaffe as Hildy's son, Kenny; Lou Richards as Deputy Dennis Putnam; Guich Koock (who had played a similar role in *Carter County* a decade earlier) as Deputy Hugh Mulcahy; and Leonard Lightfoot as Deputy Alvin Wiggins. A pilot for this series was made for CBS in 1983, but was never picked up by the network.

SHIELDS AND YARNELL   CBS
13 JUNE 1977–25 JULY 1977; 31 JANUARY 1978–28 MARCH 1978   This half-hour variety series was cohosted by Robert Shields and Lorene Yarnell, a husband-and-wife mime team who had previously worked as street performers in San Francisco. Other regulars included Ted Zeigler and Joanna Cassidy in 1977, and Gailard Sartain and John Bloom in 1978. Shields and Yarnell's best-known sketch was "The Clinkers," an inept bionic couple. Steve Binder was the executive producer and director, Frank Peppiatt and John Aylesworth the producers.

SHINDIG   ABC
16 SEPTEMBER 1964–8 JANUARY 1966   West Coast disc jockey Jimmy O'Neill was the host of this prime-time rock-and-roll show, which predated NBC's *Hullabaloo* by a few months and spawned a host of syndicated competitors. *Shindig* was probably a cut above the rest, if for no other reason than that it was broadcast live (usually) and the acts actually performed on stage, rather than lip-synching to a recording. Several acts were regularly featured on *Shindig,* such as Bobby Sherman, The Righteous Brothers (Bill Medley and Bob Hatfield, who weren't brothers at all), The Wellingtons, The Blossoms (featuring Darlene Love and Fanita James), Glen Campbell, and Donna Loren. The composition of the house combo, the Shindogs, changed periodically but included James Burton, Delaney Bramlett, Chuck Blackwell, Joey Cooper, Glen Hardin, Don Preston, and Leon Russell. The Ray Pohlman Band was also featured, as were the Shindigger Dancers, choreographed by Andre Tayir. Several shows were produced in England, including one with the Beatles (telecast 7 October 1964). The lineup on the 1965 fall premiere (16 September) included the Rolling Stones, the Kinks, the Byrds, and the Everly Brothers; the Who made their American TV debut on the show later that year (2 October). *Shindig* was introduced as a half-hour show in the fall of 1964 and expanded to an hour in January 1965. In the fall of 1965 it was broken into two half hours, scheduled Thursdays and Saturdays, and was bumped in midseason to make room for *Batman. Shindig* was developed by Jack Good, a British producer who had put together several such shows in England (one of which, *Oh, Boy!,* was carried briefly by ABC). Leon I. Mirell was the executive producer and Dean Whitmore the producer.

SHINING TIME STATION   PBS
1989–   Half-hour children's series set at a magical train depot, with Didi Conn as Stacy Jones, the station manager; Brian O'Connor as Schemer; Leonard Jackson as Harry, the engineer; Nicole Leach as Tanya; Jason Woliner as Matt; and Ringo Starr as Mr. Conductor, an eighteen-inch-tall character who appeared and disappeared in a cloud of magic dust. George Carlin succeeded Starr as Mr. Conductor in 1992. The series grew out of a five-minute British kids' show, *Thomas the Tank Engine and Friends,* first produced in 1982, for which Starr had done the narration. Segments of *Thomas* were used on the American series.

SHIRLEY NBC

26 OCTOBER 1979–25 JANUARY 1980   Hour comedy-drama about a widow and her children who moved from New York City to Lake Tahoe, starring Shirley Jones as Shirley Miller, with Patrick Wayne as her friend Lew; Peter Barton as Shirley's stepson, Bill; Rosanna Arquette as her daughter Debra; Bret Shryer as her son, Hemm; Tracey Gold as her daughter Michelle; John McIntire as Dutch McHenry, a crusty local character; Ann Doran as Charlotte McHenry, Dutch's ex-wife, the Millers' housekeeper; Cynthia Eilbacher as Tracy, Debra's friend; and Oregano, the family dog.

SHIRLEY TEMPLE'S STORYBOOK NBC/ABC

12 JANUARY 1958–21 DECEMBER 1958 (NBC); 12 JANUARY 1959–21 DECEMBER 1959 (ABC)

SHIRLEY TEMPLE THEATRE NBC

18 SEPTEMBER 1960–10 SEPTEMBER 1961   Shirley Temple, who has appeared rarely on television, served as host, narrator, and occasional star of these children's anthology series. Presentations included: "Beauty and the Beast," with Charlton Heston (12 January 1958); "Rumpelstiltskin," with Kurt Kasznar (2 February 1958); "Rapunzel," with Carol Lynley and Agnes Moorehead (27 October 1958); "Mother Goose," with Elsa Lanchester (21 December 1958); "The Land of Oz," with Shirley Temple (as Princess Ozma) and Jonathan Winters (18 September 1960); "Babes in Toyland," with Jonathan Winters (25 December 1960). *Shirley Temple's Storybook*, introduced on NBC, was broadcast as a series of specials, usually on Sundays; reruns were shown on ABC in 1959, when the show was seen on occasional Mondays. *Shirley Temple Theatre* was a weekly series, scheduled on Sundays; William H. Brown, Jr., was its executive producer, and William Asher produced it.

SHIRLEY'S WORLD ABC

15 SEPTEMBER 1971–5 JANUARY 1972   Another example of an unsuccessful TV series featuring a major film star, *Shirley's World* was an expensive half-hour situation comedy, produced in England (by ITC) and filmed on location around the world. It starred Shirley MacLaine as photojournalist Shirley Logan, on assignment for *World Illustrated* magazine, and featured John Gregson as her editor, Dennis Croft. Sheldon Leonard was the producer.

SHIRT TALES NBC/CBS

18 SEPTEMBER 1982–8 SEPTEMBER 1984 (NBC); 15 SEPTEMBER 1984–23 MARCH 1985 (CBS)   A half-hour Saturday-morning cartoon series from Hanna-Barbera Productions, *Shirt Tales* was inspired by a popular line of greeting cards which depicted a group of cuddly animals. Five such creatures originally comprised the TV Shirt Tales; Rick (a raccoon), Pammy (a panda), Digger (a mole), Bogey (a monkey), and Tyg (a tiger). A sixth animal (and second female), a kangaroo named Kit, subsequently joined. All of the animals wore shirts on which words from the show's dialogue appeared and lived in a city park. Occasionally assisted by Mr. Dinkle, the park superintendent, the Shirt Tales became involved in assorted adventures.

SHIVAREE SYNDICATED

1965   Gene Weed hosted this half-hour rock-and-roll show, an imitation *Shindig* or *Hullabaloo*.

THE SHOCK OF THE NEW PBS

1981   An eight-part look at modern art, hosted by Robert Hughes, art critic for *Time* magazine. The series was coproduced by the BBC and Time-Life Productions.

SHŌGUN NBC

15 SEPTEMBER 1980–19 SEPTEMBER 1980   James Clavell's epic novel was made into a five-part, twelve-hour miniseries. Set in feudal Japan in the early 1600s, it starred Richard Chamberlain as John Blackthorne, the English pilot of a Dutch ship which was wrecked off the Japanese coast. Toshiro Mifune costarred as Toranaga, a power-

ful warlord with whom Blackthorne allied, and Yoko Shimada costarred as Lady Mariko, the interpreter with whom Blackthorne fell in love. Also featured were John Rhys-Davies as Rodrigues, a Portuguese emissary; Damien Thomas as Father Alvito, a Portuguese missionary; Frankie Sabai as Yabu; Nobuo Kaneko as Ishido, Toranaga's enemy; and Alan Badel as Dell'Aqua. The series was written for television and produced by Eric Bercovici, and directed by Jerry London. Filmed on location, it made extensive use of Japanese dialogue; when the miniseries was rerun in 1983, additional narration (by Orson Welles) was added to further explicate these passages.

SHOOT FOR THE STARS   NBC
3 JANUARY 1977–30 SEPTEMBER 1977   Geoff Edwards hosted this daytime game show, a phrase identification game that was played similarly to *The $20,000 Pyramid* and featured two celebrity-and-contestant teams. Bob Stewart was the executive producer.

SHORT SHORT DRAMAS   NBC
30 SEPTEMBER 1952–9 APRIL 1953   Ruth Woods hosted this fifteen-minute anthology series, seen Tuesday and Thursday evenings at 7:15.

SHOTGUN SLADE   SYNDICATED
1959–1960   Scott Brady starred in this half-hour western as Shotgun Slade, who was apparently intended to be a nineteenth-century Peter Gunn. To the accompaniment of a jazz score by Gerald Fried, Slade wandered the west as a detective on horseback. In case of trouble, Slade could rely on his specially designed double-barreled shotgun. The lower barrel fired a 12-gauge shotgun shell, while the upper one discharged a .32 caliber rifle bullet.

THE SHOW   PBS
11 JANUARY 1970–12 JULY 1970   Variety series for young people hosted by Bob Walsh (who also produced it) and singer Donal Leace. Each week a studio audience of about twenty-five young people was on hand to talk with the performing guests.

SHOW BUSINESS, INC.   NBC
10 MARCH 1949–4 SEPTEMBER 1949   This half-hour variety show was first hosted by New York *News* columnist Danton Walker; Dick Kollmar took over as emcee in June, and the show was later titled *Broadway Scrapbook* and *Broadway Spotlight*.

THE SHOW GOES ON   CBS
19 JANUARY 1950–23 FEBRUARY 1952   Robert Q. Lewis hosted this prime-time talent show, on which talent buyers—agents, producers, and stars—dropped by to audition and hire promising young hopefuls. Lester Gottlieb produced the half-hour series, and Alex Leftwich directed it.

SHOW STREET   SYNDICATED
1964   Phyllis Diller hosted this half-hour talent show.

SHOW WAGON   NBC
8 JANUARY 1955–1 OCTOBER 1955   Officially known as *The Swift Show Wagon,* this variety show featured Horace Heidt and the American Way and was presented from a different American city each week, utilizing local talent. Jerry Brown produced the half-hour series.

SHOWCASE '68   NBC
11 JUNE 1968–3 SEPTEMBER 1968   Disc jockey Lloyd Thaxton hosted this half-hour variety series that featured new professional talent. Most shows were taped at American colleges and universities, and the ten weekly winners (who included Julie Budd, Andrea Marcovicci, the Chambers Brothers, Sly and the Family Stone, and the American Breed) competed on the finale at the Ohio State Fair in Columbus.

SHOWDOWN NBC
4 JULY 1966–14 OCTOBER 1966   The only interesting feature of this daytime game show, hosted by Joe Pyne, was that it featured breakaway seats, so that contestants who missed a question would fall to the floor. Two three-member teams competed.

SHOWER OF STARS CBS
30 SEPTEMBER 1954–17 APRIL 1958   *Shower of Stars,* a once-a-month replacement for *Climax* on Thursdays, was the catchall title for a wide variety of presentations. Most shows were variety spectaculars, such as the 1954 premiere, which featured Betty Grable, Mario Lanza, and bandleader Harry James (Grable's husband), though some dramatic shows were aired, such as Dickens's "A Christmas Carol," with Fredric March (3 December 1954). William Lundigan, who also hosted *Climax,* was the first master of ceremonies and was succeeded by Jack Benny.

SHOWOFFS ABC
30 JUNE 1975–26 DECEMBER 1975   On this daytime game show from Goodson-Todman Productions, teams consisting of two celebrities and a contestant tried to pantomime words to one another. Larry Blyden was to have hosted the series, but he died just before production; Bobby Van was selected to replace him.

SHOWTIME CBS
11 JUNE 1968–17 SEPTEMBER 1968   Produced in England, this hour-long variety series was hosted by a guest celebrity each week; the show was a summer replacement for *The Red Skelton Hour.*

SHOWTIME U.S.A. ABC
1 OCTOBER 1950–24 JUNE 1951   Vinton Freedley was the usual host of this half-hour series, on which scenes from current Broadway plays were performed by the cast members.

SIBS ABC
17 SEPTEMBER 1991–30 OCTOBER 1991; 15 APRIL 1992–29 APRIL 1992   Half-hour sitcom about a middle-aged woman whose two single sisters moved in just as she and her husband sent their child off to college. With Marsha Mason as the eldest sister, Nora Ruscio; Margaret Colin as middle sister Audie, a recovering alcoholic and realtor; Jami Gertz as youngest sister Lily; Alex Rocco as Nora's husband, Howie, an eighth grade teacher; and Dan Castellaneta as Warren Morris, Nora's boss at the business management firm of Morris & Morris. Heide Perlman created the series.

SID CAESAR INVITES YOU ABC
26 JANUARY 1958–25 MAY 1958   This half-hour comedy show briefly reunited Sid Caesar and Imogene Coca, who had worked together on *Your Show of Shows.* Paul Reed, Milt Kamen, Carl Reiner, and Howard Morris were also on hand, but the Sunday-night show failed to catch on.

SID CAESAR PRESENTS NBC
4 JULY 1955–12 SEPTEMBER 1955   A summer replacement for *Caesar's Hour,* this hour-long variety show was produced by Sid Caesar and directed by Carl Reiner. Among the regulars were Sid Gould, Barbara Nichols, Sandra Deel, Phil Foster, Bill Hayes, and Cliff Norton.

THE SID CAESAR SHOW ABC
19 SEPTEMBER 1963–12 MARCH 1964   The last of the several comedy-variety shows hosted by Sid Caesar, this series was a half-hour program that alternated biweekly with *Here's Edie.* Other regulars included Gisele MacKenzie, Joey Forman, and Charlotte Rae. See also *Caesar's Hour; Sid Caesar Invites You;* and *Your Show of Shows.*

SIDEKICKS   ABC

19 SEPTEMBER 1986–14 MARCH 1987; 6 JUNE 1987–27 JUNE 1987   *Sidekicks* was a rarity in late-80s prime-time TV: a half-hour dramatic series. It was derived from "The Last Electric Knight," a 1986 presentation on *The Disney Sunday Movie.* The series starred Gil Gerard as Sergeant Jake Rizzo, bachelor cop; Ernie Reyes, Jr., as Ernie Lee, an Asian youngster and martial arts expert. Ernie and his dying grandfather had recently arrived from Patasan, and his grandfather's last mission was to find a suitable guardian for Ernie; reluctantly, Rizzo agreed to the idea. Also featured were Keye Luke as the grandfather, Sabasan, who appeared in flashbacks (a technique used in the 1970s martial arts series *Kung Fu,* also featuring Luke); Nancy Stafford as social worker Patricia Blake; Frank Bonner as Detective R. T. Mooney, a colleague of Rizzo's; and Vinny Argiro as Captain Blanks. In real life, Ernie Reyes, Jr., was a martial arts expert; his younger brother Lee Reyes sometimes appeared in the flashback sequences as young Ernie.

SIERRA   NBC

12 SEPTEMBER 1974–12 DECEMBER 1974   This hour-long adventure series from Jack Webb's Mark VII, Ltd., was set at Sierra National Park and told the story of a dedicated group of park rangers; like the members of the *Emergency!* team, they seemed to spend most of their time rescuing people. Featured were James C. Richardson as Tim Cassidy; Ernest Thompson as Matt Harper; Susan Foster as Julie Beck; Mike Warren as P. J. Lewis; and Jack Hogan as Jack Moore, the chief ranger. Scheduled on Thursdays, *Sierra* proved to be no match for CBS's *The Waltons* and was gone in thirteen weeks. Robert A. Cinader was the executive producer, Bruce Johnson the producer.

SIGHTINGS   FOX/SYNDICATED

17 APRIL 1992–23 JULY 1993 (FOX); 1994–   (SYNDICATED)   One of several "documentary" series about paranormal subjects (ghosts, alien encounters, near-death experiences), this one was hosted by Tim White. After a moderately successful run on the Fox network, it was offered in first-run weekly syndication in 1994.

SIGHTSEEING WITH THE SWAYZES
See VACATIONLAND AMERICA

SIGMUND AND THE SEA MONSTERS   NBC

8 SEPTEMBER 1973–18 OCTOBER 1975   On this live-action Saturday-morning series two brothers took in a refugee sea monster (Sigmund) and helped him elude the other members of his monstrous family. With Billy Barty as Sigmund Ooz; Johnny Whitaker as Johnny Stuart; Scott Kolden as Scott Stuart; Mary Wickes as Zelda, the Stuart family's housekeeper; Rip Taylor as Sheldon the Sea Genie; Fran Ryan as Gertrude; and Sparky Marcus as Shelby. Si Rose was the executive producer for Sid and Marty Krofft Productions.

THE SILENT FORCE   ABC

21 SEPTEMBER 1970–11 JANUARY 1971   Bruce Geller was the executive producer of this half-hour crime show about a trio of federal undercover agents. With Ed Nelson as Ward Fuller; Lynda Day (later known as Lynda Day George after her marriage to Chris George) as Amelia Cole; and Percy Rodriguez as Jason Hart.

THE SILENT SERVICE   SYNDICATED

1957   This half-hour anthology series about submarine warfare was hosted by Rear Admiral (Ret.) Thomas M. Dykers.

SILENTS PLEASE   ABC/SYNDICATED

4 AUGUST 1960–5 OCTOBER 1961 (ABC); 1962 (SYNDICATED)   Host Ernie Kovacs introduced clips from vintage silent movies on this half-hour documentary series.

THE SILK ROAD SYNDICATED

1991   42-part documentary series on the history of China.

SILK STALKINGS CBS/USA

7 NOVEMBER 1991–4 NOVEMBER 1993 (CBS); 10 NOVEMBER 1991– (USA) Jointly financed by a broadcast and a cable network, *Silk Stalkings* premiered as part of CBS's late-night umbrella, *Crime Time After Prime Time*. Each episode was rerun on the USA cable network, in prime time, a few days later. The hour series was set in Palm Beach, Florida, and starred Rob Estes and Mitzi Kapture as homicide detectives Chris Lorenzo and Rita Lee Lance, whose cases often involved sex crimes among the wealthy; Ben Vereen costarred as the boss, Captain Hutch Hutchinson. Rita also served as the series narrator; she had a brain aneurysm, but declined to undergo surgery for it because of the dangers posed by such an operation. The long-simmering romantic relationship between Chris and Rita matured into marriage in the fall of 1995, following which Chris departed (Rob Estes had long planned to leave the series, and Mitzi Kapture had also announced her intention to quit). Two new cast members were introduced: Nick Kokotakis as Detective Michael Price and Tyler Layton as Detective Holly Rawlins.

SILVER SPOONS NBC/SYNDICATED

25 SEPTEMBER 1982–7 SEPTEMBER 1986 (NBC); 1986–1987 (SYNDICATED)   Half-hour sitcom about wealthy, but immature, divorcée whose son came to live with him. With Joel Higgins as Edward Stratton III, a tycoon who spent most of his time playing with his toys; Ricky Schroder as his sensible son, Ricky, who left military school to live with his father, and helped the elder Stratton to grow up; Erin Gray as Edward's secretary, Kate Summers, who married him in February 1985; Leonard Lightfoot (1982–1983) as Edward's lawyer, Leonard Rollins; Franklyn Seales (1983–1987) as Edward's business manager, Dexter Stuffins; Alfonso Ribeiro (1984–1987) as Dexter's nephew, Alfonso Speers, who was adopted by Dexter and became Ricky's best friend; Jason Bateman (1982–1984) as Ricky's conniving pal, Derek Taylor; and Corky Pigeon (1983–1985) as Ricky's nerdy pal, Freddy Lippin-cottleman. Ray Walston appeared during the 1985–1986 season as Kate's uncle, Harry Summers. John Houseman also appeared from time to time as Edward's imperious father, Edward Stratton II. The series lasted four years on NBC, after which another twenty-two episodes were made for first-run syndication.

THE SILVER SWAN CAFE

See THE MOREY AMSTERDAM SHOW

SILVER THEATER CBS

3 OCTOBER 1949–10 JULY 1950   This dramatic anthology series, sponsored by the International Silver Company, began on radio in 1938; Conrad Nagel hosted the half-hour television version, which ran on Monday nights. Representative presentations included: "Farewell Supper," with Charles Korvin (31 October); "The First Show of 1950," with George Reeves (2 January); "My Brother's Keeper," with Ward Bond and Glenn Corbett (20 February); "Minor Incident," with Nancy Kelly (10 April); "Papa Romani," with William Frawley, Margaret Hamilton, and Chico Marx (15 May); and "My Heart's in the Highlands," with Howard Da Silva (12 June). Although most presentations were live, several were filmed using the "Multicam" process, by which the action was filmed by three motion picture cameras. A similar technique was later used on *I Love Lucy*.

SIMON WB

10 SEPTEMBER 1995–   Half-hour sitcom about a pair of white brothers who found a cheap apartment in Harlem. With Harland Williams as Simon Himple, a Forrest Gump-type who stumbled into a job at a cable TV network; Jason Bateman as his brother, Carl Himple, an MBA who had trouble finding work; Paxton Whitehead as Duke Stone, owner of Vintage Television, the rerun network where Simon was hired; Patrick Breen as Duke's nephew, Mitch Lowin, who battled Simon at the

office; Andrea Bendewald as Libby, another Vintage exec; and Clifton Powell as the Himples' ex-con neighbor, John Doe.

SIMON & SIMON — CBS

24 NOVEMBER 1981–8 SEPTEMBER 1987; 3 DECEMBER 1987–11 AUGUST 1988; 8 OCTOBER 1988–31 DECEMBER 1988   This hour crime show starred Jameson Parker and Gerald McRaney as brothers A. J. and Rick Simon, a pair of none-too-prosperous private eyes; A. J. was a suave college man, while Rick was a laid-back Vietnam veteran. The genesis of the series was a 1980 made-for-TV movie "Pirate's Key," which had been filmed in Florida. By the time a series had been ordered, the locale had shifted to San Diego. Also featured were Eddie Barth (1981–1983) as Myron Fowler, owner of the rival Peerless Detective Agency; Jeannie Wilson (1981–1983) as Myron's daughter, Janet Fowler, who worked for her father during the first season, and was an assistant district attorney the second; Mary Carver as Cecilia Simon, A. J. and Rick's mother; and Tim Reid (1983–1987) as Downtown Brown, an undercover cop. Joan McMurtrey joined the cast in the fall of 1987 as Lieutenant Abby Marsh. *Simon & Simon* performed marginally but unspectacularly during its first season; in 1982 it changed producers and theme music (an instrumental theme by Barry DeVorzon replaced the country-flavored "Best of Friends," sung by the Thrasher Brothers), and zoomed into Nielsen's top ten on Thursday nights, following *Magnum, P.I.* The series was virtually indestructible during the 1980s. Canceled at the end of the 1986–1987 season, it remained in production as a backup series and returned in December 1987. Another batch of episodes popped up in the fall of 1988. The characters returned in a TV-movie, "Simon & Simon: In Trouble Again" (23 February 1995, CBS).

THE SIMPSONS — FOX

14 JANUARY 1990–   A prime-time cartoon show, *The Simpsons* was Fox's top-rated series of the 1989–1990 season, ranking 30th among all prime-time programs. The series quickly became a cult favorite. *The Simpsons* was created by Matt Groening, who had achieved fame for his "Life in Hell" comic strip. Groening's TV family—father Homer, who worked at a nuclear power plant; blue-haired mother Marge; proud underachiever Bart, a fourth-grader; brainy goody two-shoes Lisa, a second-grader; and pacifier-sucking baby Maggie—originally appeared as a brief but regular feature of *The Tracey Ullman Show.* A thirty-minute *Simpsons* holiday special was telecast 23 December 1989. Voices: Nancy Cartwright (Bart), Dan Castellaneta (Homer), Julie Kavner (Marge), Yeardley Smith (Lisa), and Harry Shearer (others). It is probably not coincidental that Groening's own parents were named Homer and Margaret, and that his two sisters were named Lisa and Maggie. Among the many celebrities who lent their voices to the show were Michael Jackson (as a mental patient who thought he was Michael Jackson), Elizabeth Taylor (who uttered baby Maggie's first word, "Dad-dee"), Bob Hope, Dustin Hoffman, Ringo Starr, Kathleen Turner, Michelle Pfeiffer, and Johnny Carson.

Consistently well written, *The Simpsons* examined "family values" in its own unique way, against a backdrop of cynicism and greed in their hometown of Springfield. More importantly, it was the first TV cartoon series since *The Flintstones* (which premiered a generation earlier) to appeal successfully to an adult audience. It opened the door for subsequent animated series such as *The Ren and Stimpy Show* and *Beavis and Butt-head.*

THE SINBAD SHOW — FOX

16 SEPTEMBER 1993–28 JULY 1994   Standup comic Sinbad, who had previously appeared on *A Different World,* was given his own half-hour sitcom in 1993. Sinbad (whose real name was David Adkins) played David Brian, owner of a computer graphics company whose life changed when he took in two foster children. Also featured were Erin Davis and Willie Norwood as two kids, Zana and Little John (L.J.) Beckley; T. K. Carter as David's pal Clarence, who worked at a clothing store; Salma Hayek as Gloria, the daughter of David's landlady; and Hal Williams as David's father, Rudy Brian.

SING ALONG CBS

4 JUNE 1958–9 JULY 1958   This short-lived half-hour musical series predated *Sing Along with Mitch* by some three years. As on *Sing Along with Mitch,* the lyrics to the songs performed on stage were shown at the bottom of viewers' home screens so that everyone could sing along. Jim Lowe hosted the series and featured vocalists included Tina Robin, Florence Henderson, and Somethin' Smith and the Redheads.

SING ALONG WITH MITCH NBC

27 JANUARY 1961–21 APRIL 1961; 28 SEPTEMBER 1961–21 SEPTEMBER 1964   Home viewers were able to participate in this hour-long musical series, as the lyrics to the songs were superimposed at the bottom of their screens; viewers were invited to "follow the bouncing ball" as it moved from one lyric to the next. Goateed composer-arranger Mitch Miller led the Sing-Along Gang, an on-stage aggregation of about two dozen. Among the featured vocalists were Leslie Uggams, Diana Trask, Barbara McNair, and Gloria Lambert. *Sing Along with Mitch* was introduced on *Ford Startime* in 1960 and had a limited run in the spring of 1961, alternating with *The Bell Telephone Hour,* before going weekly in the fall of that year. Reruns were exhumed in the spring of 1966 to replace the faltering *Sammy Davis, Jr. Show.* Bill Hobin produced and directed the series.

SING IT AGAIN CBS

7 OCTOBER 1950–23 JUNE 1951   *Sing It Again* ran on CBS radio for two years before coming to television. The Saturday-night game show featured contestants from the studio audience who tried to identify songs from a few notes; phone calls were also placed to home viewers, who were given the chance to identify a "mystery voice." Dan Seymour hosted the hour show until February, when Jan Murray took over.

SING-CO-PATION ABC

23 JANUARY 1949–30 OCTOBER 1949   Fifteen-minute musical-variety program, broadcast on Sunday night from Chicago. Subsequently titled *Serenade,* the show was hosted first by Dolores Marshall, later by Joanelle James.

SINGER & SONS NBC

9 JUNE 1990–27 JUNE 1990   Half-hour sitcom about a widowed New York deli owner with no sons of his own who decided to turn the business over to the sons of his black housekeeper. With Harold Gould as Nathan Singer; Esther Rolle as his long-time housekeeper, Mrs. Patterson; Bobby Hosea as her elder son, Mitchell, who was college educated and divorced; Tommy Ford as her younger son, Reggie, who was streetwise; Fred Stoller as Nathan's meek nephew, Sheldon, who worked at the deli; Arnetia Walker as Claudia, the black waitress at the deli; Phil Leeds as Lou Gold, a regular patron; and Brooke Fontaine as Deanna, Mitchell's young daughter. Michael Jacobs and Bob Young created the series.

THE SINGING LADY ABC

12 AUGUST 1948–6 AUGUST 1950; 27 SEPTEMBER 1953–21 MARCH 1954   "The Singing Lady" was Ireene Wicker, who began this children's series on radio in 1931; the Suzarri Marionettes were also featured. The 1948–1950 series was seen Sunday evenings; the 1953–1954 series, titled *Ireene Wicker Storytime,* was seen Sunday mornings.

THE SINGLE GUY NBC

21 SEPTEMBER 1995–   Half-hour sitcom about a single guy (what else?) and his four married pals. With Jonathan Silverman as title character Jonathan Eliot, a novelist; Jessica Hecht as Janeane Percy-Parker; Mark Moses as Janeane's husband, Matt Parker; Joey Slotnick as Jonathan's best friend, Sam Sloane, who worked at a recording studio; Ming-Na Wen as Sam's wife, Trudy; and Ernest Borgnine as Manny, the doorman of Jonathan's New York apartment building.

SIR FRANCIS DRAKE   NBC

24 JUNE 1962–9 SEPTEMBER 1962   Produced in Great Britain, this half-hour adventure series starred Terence Morgan as Sir Francis Drake, commander of *The Golden Hind.* Also featured were Milton Reid as Diego; Roger Delgado as Mendoza, the Spanish ambassador; Peter Diamond as Bosun; Patrick McLoughlin as Richard Trevelyan; Howard Lang as Grenville; Michael Crawford as John Drake; and Jean Kent as Queen Elizabeth I.

SIR LANCELOT   NBC

24 SEPTEMBER 1956–24 JUNE 1957   This British import followed *Robin Hood* one season later. Featured were William Russell as Sir Lancelot; Ronald Leigh-Hunt as King Arthur; Jane Hylton as Queen Guinevere; Cyril Smith as Merlin; and Bobby Scroggins as Brian the Squire. Scheduled opposite *The Burns and Allen Show* and *The Danny Thomas Show,* the half-hour swashbuckler was dropped after one season. Dallas Bower produced the series.

SIRENS   ABC/SYNDICATED

10 MARCH 1993–28 APRIL 1993; 12 JUNE 1993–18 AUGUST 1993 (ABC); 1994–1995 (SYNDICATED)   Hour crime show focusing on three new female members of the Pittsburgh Police Department. The ABC version featured Adrienne-Joi Johnson as Officer Lynn Stanton, recently divorced; Liza Snyder as Officer Molly Whelan, daughter of a police commander; Jayne Brook as Officer Sarah Berkezchuk, a former teacher's aide; Deirdre O'Connell as Heidi Schiller, Molly's partner; Tim Thomerson as Buddy Zunder, Lynn's partner; John Terlesky as Dan Kelly, Sarah's partner; John Speredakos as Sarah's husband, Cary; and Jesse Goins as the desk sergeant. In 1994 new episodes were produced for first-run syndication. Johnson, Snyder, and Thomerson remained from the network cast, and were joined by Jayne Heitmeyer as Officer Jessie Jaworski; Ellen Cohen as Amy Shapiro, Molly's new partner; D. Christopher Judge as Richie Styles, Jessie's partner; and Joel Wyner as Detective Springer. Ann Lewis Hamilton created the series.

SIROTA'S COURT   NBC

1 DECEMBER 1976–20 APRIL 1977   This half-hour sitcom came and went almost unnoticed, as it was scheduled irregularly during the middle of the 1976–1977 season. Featured were Michael Constantine as Judge Matthew J. Sirota, magistrate of a big city night court; Cynthia Harris as Maureen O'Connor, the court clerk; Kathleen Miller as public defender Gail Goodman; Ted Ross as defense attorney Sawyer Dabney; Fred Willard as assistant district attorney H. R. Nugent; and Owen Bush as John Belson, the bailiff. Harvey Miller and Peter Engel were the producers.

SISKEL & EBERT   SYNDICATED

1986–   Originally titled *Siskel & Ebert & the Movies,* this was the third series of film reviews cohosted by Chicago film critics Roger Ebert and Gene Siskel. See also *Sneak Previews* and *At the Movies.* On 21 May 1990 the two critics hosted their first network prime-time special on CBS.

SISTER KATE   NBC

16 SEPTEMBER 1989–21 JANUARY 1990; 16 JULY 1990–1 SEPTEMBER 1990   Stephanie Beacham, late of *The Colbys,* had the title role in this insipid sitcom about a nun who was dispatched to Redemption House, a big-city orphanage, where she was put in charge of seven delightfully delinquent youngsters. Appearing as her charges were Harley Cross as eleven-year-old Eugene Colodner; Erin Reed as teenager April Newberry; Jason Priestley as teenager Todd Mahaffey; Penina Segall as twelve-year-old Hilary Logan; Hannah Cutrona as teenager Fredddy Marasco; Joel Robinson as seven-year-old Neville Williams; and Alexaundria Simmons as nine-year-old Violet Johnson.

SISTER, SISTER
ABC/WB

1 APRIL 1994–20 MAY 1994; 28 JUNE 1994–6 SEPTEMBER 1994; 16 NOVEMBER 1994–28 APRIL 1995 (ABC); 2 AUGUST 1995–   (WB)   Set in Detroit, this sitcom told the story of twin sisters who had been adopted by separate families at birth; as ninth graders they were accidentally reunited and tried to get their now-single parents to get together. With real-life twins Tia Mowry and Tamera Mowry as Tia Landry and Tamera Campbell; Tim Reid as Tamera's adoptive father, Ray Campbell, a level-headed man who owned a limosine service; Jackée Harry as Tia's adoptive mother, the impulsive Lisa Landry; and Marques Houston as Roger, Tamera's neighbor, who had a crush on her.

SISTERS
NBC

11 MAY 1991–4 MAY 1996   Hour dramatic series about the lives of four sisters who were reunited in their hometown (Winnetka, Illinois) following the death of their father. Introduced in the spring of 1991 for a seven-episode test run, the series was renewed and performed surprisingly well over the next several seasons in a 10 P.M. time slot on Saturday nights. The very first scene of the premiere episode, with the four siblings sitting in a steam room discussing orgasms, was not televised by NBC (it was included in the off-network rerun package, however). The series deftly blended serious topics such as cancer, career changes, and crime with lighter ones, such as an attempt to make a TV-movie about the characters. It also incorporated fantasy sequences in which the adult sisters meet with their childhood selves. The large cast has included: Swoosie Kurtz as eldest sister Alex Halsey, who was married to a physician as the show began; Patricia Kalember as sister Georgie Whitsig; Sela Ward as sister Teddy Reed; Julianne Phillips (1991–February 1995) as youngest sister Frankie Reed; Elizabeth Hoffman as their mother, Beatrice Reed; David Dukes as Alex's husband, Wade Halsey (they divorced in 1991, although the character appeared in subsequent episodes); Kathy Wagner (spring 1991), Ashley Judd (fall 1991–1995), and Noelle Parker (1995–1996) as their daughter, Reed; Garrett M. Brown as Georgie's husband, John Whitsig (he filed for divorce in 1995); Dustin Berkovitz as their son Evan; Ryan Francis as their son Trevor; Ed Marinaro (1991–1994) as Mitch Margolis, who had been married to Teddy, and later married (and separated from) Frankie; Heather McAdam as Cat Margolis, daughter of Teddy and Mitch; Philip Sterling (1991–1995) as Judge Truman Ventnor, who married Beatrice in the fall of 1992 (later stricken with Alzheimer's disease, Truman asked Alex to assist him in dying); David Gianopoulos (1991–1992) as Victor; Mary Donnelly (1991–1992) as Fern Neuswanger; Paul Rudd (1992–1996) as Kirby, Reed's boyfriend; Mark Frankel (1992–1994) as Simon; George Clooney (1993–1994) as Detective James Falconer, who married Teddy and was murdered; Nora Dunn (1993–1996) as Norma Lear, a gay TV producer who convinced Alex to host a talk show; Robert Klein (1993–1996) as Big Al Barker, a discount store magnate who married Alex, was sent to prison, and became mayor; Jo Anderson (spring 1994–1995) and Sheila Kelley (1995–1996) as Dr. Charley Bennett, who turned out to be the sisters' half-sister (their late father had had an affair years earlier); John Wesley Shipp (1994–1996) as boxer Lucky Williams, who helped Teddy search for Falconer's killer; Daniel Gerroll (1994–1996) as therapist Dr. David Caspian, who seduced Georgie (Gerroll was the husband of Patricia Kalember in real life); Gregory Harrison (1994–1996) as Daniel Albright; and Stephen Collins as Dr. Gabriel Sorenson.

SIT OR MISS
ABC

6 AUGUST 1950–29 OCTOBER 1950   Half-hour game show on which five contestants played a form of musical chairs, with quizzes and stunts thrown in as well. Kay Westfall and George Sotos cohosted the series, which offered a top prize of $75.

THE SIX MILLION DOLLAR MAN
ABC

20 OCTOBER 1973–6 MARCH 1978   *The Six Million Dollar Man* was introduced as a monthly feature on *The ABC Suspense Movie* before becoming a weekly series in January of 1974. It starred Lee Majors as Steve Austin, an American astronaut who was severely injured in a training mishap and who was rebuilt (at a cost of $6 million)

by the Office of Strategic Information, a government agency. Equipped with two bionic legs, a bionic arm, and a bionic eye, Austin was far stronger than any mere mortal and was employed by the O.S.I. to undertake an assortment of delicate missions. Also featured were Richard Anderson as Oscar Goldman, an O.S.I. topsider; Alan Oppenheimer and Martin E. Brooks as Dr. Rudy Wells, an O.S.I. physician. The series was very popular with younger viewers, and a spinoff was introduced in January of 1976; see *The Bionic Woman*. The pilot for *The Six Million Dollar Man* was telecast 7 March 1973, and was based on *Cyborg*, a novel by Martin Caidin. Harve Bennett was executive producer of the series for Harve Bennett Productions in association with Universal Television. Lee Majors and Lindsay Wagner were reunited in several made-for-TV sequels: "The Return of the Six Million Dollar Man and the Bionic Woman" (17 May 1987, NBC), which also featured Richard Anderson, "Bionic Showdown: The Six Million Dollar Man and the Bionic Woman" (30 April 1989, NBC), with Anderson and Martin E. Brooks, and "Bionic Ever After?" (29 November 1994, CBS), also with Anderson and Brooks.

SIX O'CLOCK FOLLIES   NBC
24 APRIL 1980–26 APRIL 1980; 2 AUGUST 1980–13 SEPTEMBER 1980   The Vietnam War was the unlikely setting for this half-hour sitcom, five episodes of which were sporadically televised by NBC. Featured were A. C. Weary as Specialist Sam Page and Larry Fishburne as Corporal Don "Robby" Robinson, two former Chicago newscasters who were reunited in Saigon, where they were assigned to the Army news broadcast, nicknamed "The Six O'Clock Follies." Also on board were Philip Charles MacKenzie as Midas Metkovich, proprietor of a Saigon bar where the crew hung out; Randall Carver as stick-in-the-mud Lieutenant Beuhler; David Hubbard as Specialist Percy Wiggins; Aarika Wells as Candi, the weather forecaster; Joby Baker as Colonel Marvin; and George Kee Cheung as Ho, a civilian employee. Although the success of *M*A*S*H* had demonstrated that audiences could appreciate an antiwar comedy, the memory of the Vietnam debacle was too fresh for a comedy set there to have even a chance to succeed.

THE SIX WIVES OF HENRY VIII   CBS
1 AUGUST 1971–5 SEPTEMBER 1971   CBS imported this six-part historical miniseries from England. Each of the six 90-minute stories centered on one of King Henry's marriages. Keith Michell starred as Henry VIII. His wives were played by: Annette Crosbie as Catherine of Aragon, whom Henry divorced; Dorothy Tutin as Anne Boleyn, who was beheaded; Anne Stallybrass as Jane Seymour, who died after giving birth to Henry's long awaited male heir; Elvi Hale as Anne of Cleves, whom Henry divorced; Angela Pleasence as Catherine Howard, who was also beheaded; and Rosalie Crutchley as Catherine Parr, who survived Henry. Anthony Quayle narrated the series when it was telecast on CBS; the show was rerun on PBS's *Masterpiece Theatre* in 1972.

THE SIXTH SENSE   ABC
15 JANUARY 1972–30 DECEMBER 1972   This hour-long dramatic series purported to examine the occult and the supernatural. It starred Gary Collins as Dr. Michael Rhodes, a trained parapsychologist, researcher, and college instructor; also featured was Catherine Ferrar as his assistant, Nancy Murphy. Stan Shpetner was the producer.

60 MINUTES   CBS
24 SEPTEMBER 1968–   An hour newsmagazine with a strong emphasis on investigative reporting, *60 Minutes* began in 1968 as a biweekly show, alternating on Tuesdays with *CBS Reports*. In the fall of 1971 it shifted to Sunday evenings but was often preempted by professional football games and was later seen only during the winter and spring. In the fall of 1975 it finally became a weekly series, and its ratings have steadily improved to the point where *60 Minutes* is the highest-rated public affairs program in television history. A typical show consists of two or three features, each separately produced but put together under the careful supervision of executive producer Don Hewitt. From 1968 until 1970 the show was cohosted by veteran CBS

newsmen Mike Wallace and Harry Reasoner; when Reasoner left CBS for ABC, he was replaced by Morley Safer, a Canadian-born CBS correspondent who had been its bureau chief in Saigon and in London. In the fall of 1975 Dan Rather, who had been the network's White House correspondent, joined Wallace and Safer. Another regular feature of *60 Minutes* was "Point/Counterpoint," a segment on which liberal and conservative viewpoints on topical issues were vocally, if not intensively, exchanged; conservative columnist James J. Kilpatrick originally did battle with liberal Nicholas von Hoffman and jousted with Shana Alexander until 1979, when the feature was dropped. Among the best-known stories covered by *60 Minutes* were those concerning ITT lobbyist Dita Beard, Howard Hughes's supposed biographer Clifford Irving, and Colonel Anthony Herbert, whose claims that certain Vietnam war atrocities had been covered up were disputed by other officers. Herbert's libel suit went all the way to the Supreme Court, which ruled in 1979 that Herbert was entitled to question *60 Minutes'* producers as to their state of mind and motives in presenting the story. Mike Wallace also did two one-hour interviews with former Nixon aide H. R. Haldeman (these were technically broadcast as specials, but were scheduled in *60 Minutes'* time slot); Wallace and his producers were criticized when it was learned that Haldeman had been paid (some estimates ranged as high as $100,000) for the appearances. In the fall of 1978, Harry Reasoner returned to CBS News and rejoined *60 Minutes;* a new regular feature, "A Few Minutes with Andy Rooney," was also added. Dan Rather left the show in 1981, when he was named to succeed Walter Cronkite as host of *The CBS Evening News.* Ed Bradley took Rather's place on *60 Minutes.* Diane Sawyer became a regular correspondent in the fall of 1984.

In the 1979–1980 season *60 Minutes* was the highest-rated prime-time series, the first public affairs program ever to top the ratings. After running second to *Dallas* for the next two seasons, it again topped the Nielsens during the 1982–1983 season, and remained in Nielsen's top ten for the remainder of the decade. *60 Minutes* celebrated its twentieth anniversary with a two-part retrospective on 10 and 17 October 1988. In the fall of 1989 Diane Sawyer moved to ABC to cohost her own prime-time news magazine series, *PrimeTime Live.* She was replaced by Meredith Vieira and Steve Kroft, both of whom had previously worked on CBS's trendier magazine series, *West 57th.* Andy Rooney was briefly suspended from the broadcast in 1990 as a result of his remarks during a December 1989 CBS News special citing (among other things) "homosexual unions" as a cause of "self-induced" death among Americans. Though his suspension was to have been for three months, it was lifted after just three weeks; perhaps it was only coincidental that *60 Minutes'* ratings had slipped during that three-week period.

Meredith Vieira left early in 1991, and Harry Reasoner retired at the end of the 1990–1991 season. Lesley Stahl was added in the fall of 1991, joining Wallace, Safer, Bradley, and Kroft as regular correspondents, with Rooney continuing to provide commentary. *60 Minutes* remained virtually invincible, returning to the number one spot in the ratings during the 1991–1992 and 1992–1993 seasons. It won a prestigious Peabody Award in 1991 for its "Friendly Fire" segment, which investigated a Gulf War friendly fire incident; it helped boost Bill Clinton's candidacy in January 1992 when he and Hillary Rodham Clinton were interviewed by Steve Kroft about their marriage and about Clinton's alleged affair with Gennifer Flowers. The series celebrated its twenty-fifth anniversary with a two-hour retrospective on 14 November 1993; by that time it had become the second longest-running prime time series in TV history, trailing only the several incarnations of *Walt Disney.*

THE $64,000 CHALLENGE   CBS
8 APRIL 1956–14 SEPTEMBER 1958   The first TV game show spun off from another TV game show, *The $64,000 Challenge* offered alumni of *The $64,000 Question* the chance to win even more money; contestants who had won at least $8,000 on *Question* were eligible to compete on *Challenge,* where they faced two challengers in their chosen field of knowledge. Big winners included Myrt Power, Leonard Ross, Dr. Joyce Brothers, Billy Pearson, Gino Prato, Teddy Nadler, and Michael Della-Rocca. Sonny Fox was the first host of *Challenge,* but he was abruptly replaced by Ralph Story in September of 1956. Among the young women who escorted the contestants

on and off stage (such assistants were known as "elbow grabbers") were Doris Wiss, Lisa Laughlin, and Pat Donovan. Along with most of television's big money prime-time game shows, *The $64,000 Challenge* was canceled in September of 1958 as the heat of the game show scandals intensified; the show had been scheduled to shift to NBC beginning 18 September 1958, but it never reached the air.

THE $64,000 QUESTION   CBS

7 JUNE 1955–9 NOVEMBER 1958   The first of prime-time television's big money game shows, *The $64,000 Question* premiered in the summer of 1955 and became an instant hit; three years later it passed away unceremoniously amidst the quiz show scandals of 1958. The object of the game was for contestants, each of whom was an expert in a particular field of knowledge, to double their money each time they answered a question correctly; the questions, of course, became increasingly harder as the stakes grew larger, and an incorrect answer at any point ended the game. The first question was worth a dollar, and the stakes doubled up to the tenth question, worth $512. The next question was worth an even $1,000, and the stakes again began to double progressively. To heighten the suspense at the higher levels, players were placed in isolation booths onstage for the question-and-answer sessions, and, if they answered correctly, returned the following week to compete at the next level (a player could always elect to stop after any level, but few of them chose to do so). Thus, on any given show, some contestants would be starting out at the lowest levels while others were announcing their decisions to return the following week to try for more big money. A player who chose to try for the $64,000 question was permitted to bring an expert along, but if neither the player nor the expert answered the question correctly, the player left the show with $4,000. Hal March was the host of the series and was assisted by Lynn Dollar, who escorted the contestants into the isolation booth (Pat Donovan succeeded her in 1958). Dr. Bergen Evans compiled the questions and served as the judge. The first $64,000 winner was a captain in the Marines, Richard S. McCutchen; his area of expertise was gastronomy. Dr. Joyce Brothers, a psychologist who later hosted several TV shows of her own, was the second big winner; her category was boxing. Actress Barbara Feldon, later seen on *Get Smart,* won the top prize for her knowledge of Shakespeare, and dancer-choreographer Geoffrey Holder won $16,000 on the show. Other well-known winners included ten-year-old Rob Strom (science), Myrt Power (baseball), Dr. Alexander Sas-Jaworsky (history), jockey Billy Pearson (art), Gloria Lockerman (spelling), Gino Prato (opera), police officer Redmond O'Hanlon (Shakespeare), and Teddy Nadler, one of the biggest money winners in television history; after his appearances on *The $64,000 Question*'s sister show, *The $64,000 Challenge* (see also that title), Nadler had won $264,000. As a gag, Jack Benny once appeared on the show but elected to quit after winning the first dollar. *The $64,000 Question* was packaged by Louis G. Cowan, who sold out his interest in the show shortly after it began and later became a CBS executive; Revlon sponsored the series, and Steve Carlin produced it. Though no specific allegations against *The $64,000 Question* were ever substantiated during the game show investigations of 1958 and 1959, the series was dropped along with almost all other prime-time game shows. In 1976 a syndicated version, adjusted for inflation, reappeared: see *The $128,000 Question.*

SKAG   NBC

6 JANUARY 1980–21 FEBRUARY 1980   Hour family drama starring Karl Malden as Pete "Skag" Skagska, a foreman at a Pittsburgh steel mill. With Piper Laurie as wife Jo; Craig Wasson as son David; Peter Gallagher as son John; Leslie Ackerman as daughter Barbara; and Kitty Holcomb as daughter Patricia. Abby Mann created the series.

THE SKATEBIRDS   CBS

10 SEPTEMBER 1977–21 JANUARY 1978   Three skateboarding birds (played by actors) were the hosts of this Saturday-morning hour. The Skatebirds introduced three cartoon segments ("The Robonic Stooges," "Wonder Wheels," and "Woofer and Wimper") and a live-action segment ("Mystery Island"). Trimmed to a half hour in

midseason, the series continued under the title *The Three Robonic Stooges. The Skatebirds* was rerun on CBS's Sunday-morning cartoon schedule between September 1979 and January 1981.

SKELETON WARRIORS CBS
1 OCTOBER 1994–2 SEPTEMBER 1995   Good battled evil on this half-hour Saturday-morning cartoon series. The kingdom of Luminicity was threatened by the evil Baron Dark, who had acquired half of a magic crystal and had assembled his Skeleton Warriors. They were opposed by three siblings—Prince Justin, Prince Joshua, and Princess Jennifer—who were transformed into Prince Lightstar, Grimskull, and Talon, respectively. The trio was assisted by their wise uncle, Guardian.

THE SKIP FARRELL SHOW ABC
17 JANUARY 1949–28 AUGUST 1949   Half-hour variety series hosted by Skip Farrell and featuring Joanelle James.

SKIPPY SYNDICATED
1969   A kangaroo named Skippy was the marsupial star of this Australian import; Skippy, wounded and apparently orphaned, had been taken in by a park ranger and his two sons. The human roles were played by Ed Deveraux as Matt Hammond; Garry Pankhurst as Sonny; Ken James as Mark; and Liza Goddard as Clancy, a young woman who boarded with the Goddards. Officially titled *Skippy the Bush Kangaroo,* the half hour series was filmed on location in Australia's Waratah National Park and was sponsored in this country by Kellogg cereals.

SKY HAWKS ABC
6 SEPTEMBER 1969–4 SEPTEMBER 1971   Saturday-morning cartoon series about the members of the Wilson family, who ran Sky Hawks, Incorporated, an all-purpose air service.

SKY KING NBC/ABC
16 SEPTEMBER 1951–26 OCTOBER 1952 (NBC); 8 NOVEMBER 1952–12 SEPTEMBER 1954 (ABC)   Kirby Grant starred in this half-hour adventure series for children as Schuyler J. (Sky) King, the airborne owner of the Flying Crown Ranch; King used his plane, *The Songbird,* not only to patrol his spread but also to rescue the trapped and to capture fugitives. Also featured were Gloria Winters as Penny, King's niece; Ron Hagerthy as Clipper, King's nephew; Ewing Mitchell as Mitch, the local sheriff; Norman Ollstead as Bob Carey; and Gary Hunley as Mickey. The series began on radio in 1947, and the TV version was rerun on CBS after its initial run on NBC and ABC. It was supplied by Jack Chertok Productions.

THE SKY'S THE LIMIT NBC
1 NOVEMBER 1954–1 JUNE 1956   A daytime game show, *The Sky's the Limit* was hosted first by Gene Rayburn and later by Monty Hall; Hope Lange and Marilyn Cantor were on hand as assistants. The show, which involved both stunts and quizzes, began as a fifteen-minute series but expanded to thirty minutes in the summer of 1955.

THE "SLAP" MAXWELL STORY ABC
23 SEPTEMBER 1987–16 MARCH 1988; 30 APRIL 1988–14 SEPTEMBER 1988   One of several so-called "dramadies" on the 1987–1988 schedule (see also *Frank's Place, Hooperman,* and *The Days and Nights of Molly Dodd*), *The "Slap" Maxwell Story* starred Dabney Coleman as "Slap" Maxwell, an egotistical sportswriter for a Midwest newspaper, *The Ledger,* whose column ("Slap Shots") provoked anger and frequent lawsuits from those who were its subjects. Slap's personal life was a mess as well: he had a rocky relationship with his girlfriend and his ex-wife also hung around. Other regulars included Megan Gallagher as Slap's girlfriend, Judy Ralston, a *Ledger* secretary; Susan Anspach as his ex-wife, Annie; Brian Smiar as the editor, Nelson Kruger; Bill Calvert as copyboy Charlie Wilson; and Bill Cobbs as The Dutchman,

the barkeep at Slap's favorite watering hole. Joseph Brutsman was occasionally seen as Eliot, Slap's estranged son. The series was crated by Jay Tarses, who had previously created *Buffalo Bill,* an iconoclastic sitcom also starring Dabney Coleman.

SLATTERY'S PEOPLE CBS

21 SEPTEMBER 1964–26 NOVEMBER 1965   Richard Crenna starred in this hour-long dramatic series as Slattery, the idealistic leader of the minority party in the legislature of an unnamed state. Also featured during the first season were Paul Geary as his aide, Johnny Ramos; Maxine Stuart as B. J. Clawson, Slattery's secretary; Ed Asner as Frank Radcliff, veteran political reporter for the *Times-Chronicle;* and Tol Avery as Bert Metcalf, the speaker of the state house of representatives. For the show's abortive second season Slattery acquired not only a new supporting cast but also a first name—Jim. New regulars included: Alejandro Rey as aide Mike Valera; Francine York as secretary Wendy Wendowski; and Kathie Browne as TV newscaster Liz Andrews, Slattery's romantic interest. James Moser created the series, and Matthew Rapf produced it, for Bing Crosby Productions. Some of the show's exteriors were filmed on location in Sacramento.

SLEDGE HAMMER! ABC

23 SEPTEMBER 1986–3 MARCH 1988; 16 JUNE 1988–30 JUNE 1988   Offbeat sitcom about a cop whose best friend and confidant was his gun, a .44 Magnum called "Gun." With David Rasche as Inspector Sledge Hammer; Anne Marie Martin as his partner, Sergeant Dori Doreau; Harrison Page as beleaguered Captain Trunk; Leslie Morris as Officer Mayjoy; Patti Tippo (1987–1988) as Officer Daley; and Kurt Paul (1987–1988) as Coroner Norman Blates (a takeoff on the lead character from the movie *Psycho,* Norman Bates). In the final episode of the 1986–1987 season Sledge was apparently blown to smithereens while attempting to dismantle a nuclear device; the show's producers had not expected the series to be renewed. When the green light was given for a second season, Sledge showed up alive and well.

SLEEPY JOE ABC/SYNDICATED

3 OCTOBER 1949–28 OCTOBER 1949 (ABC); 1951 (SYNDICATED)   Originally a radio series, *Sleepy Joe* was created by Jimmy Scribner, the dialectician who had created *The Johnson Family* on radio in 1934. *Sleepy Joe* first came to television as a local series over KTSL-TV in Los Angeles. On that version Scribner appeared in blackface as Sleepy Joe, an Uncle Remus-type character who spun yarns at the request of a little girl named Gayle (played by Gayle Scribner, Jimmy's daughter). The ABC and syndicated versions of the show were filmed puppet programs, however, with voices supplied by Scribner.

SLIDERS FOX

22 MARCH 1995–17 MAY 1995; 25 JUNE 1995–27 AUGUST 1995; 1 MARCH 1996–   Hour sci-fi series in which a quartet of people slid each week through a "wormhole" into alternate worlds. Each world they encountered had the same geographic setting—San Francisco—but different historical events had created a separate reality; on one program, for example, the sliders found themselves in a Communist Bay Area, while on another they encountered an ultra-Conservative scene. With Jerry O'Connell as grad student Quinn Mallory, who discovered the way to reach those parallel worlds while working in his basement; John Rhys-Davies as his physics professor, Maximilian Arturo; Sabrina Lloyd as his girlfriend, Wade Wells; and Cleavant Derricks as washed-up soul singer Rembrandt "Crying Man" Brown, who accidentally got mixed up with the others during their first adventure.

SLIMER! AND THE REAL GHOSTBUSTERS
See THE REAL GHOSTBUSTERS

SMALL & FRYE CBS

7 MARCH 1983–21 MARCH 1983; 1 JUNE 1983–15 JUNE 1983   Half-hour sitcom about a pair of private eyes, one of whom had the power to shrink in size. With Darren

McGavin as Nick Small, the tall one; Jack Blessing as Chip Frye, the shrinkable one; Bill Daily as Dr. Hanratty; and Debbie Zipp as Phoebe, Nick's daughter. This series, which came from Walt Disney Productions, was not the first to feature miniature detectives (see also *Inch High, Private Eye* and *The World of Giants*).

SMALL FRY CLUB   DUMONT
11 MARCH 1947–15 JUNE 1951   Network television's first successful children's program, *Small Fry Club* was broadcast every weekday evening for most of its run. "Big Brother" Bob Emery hosted the program, which employed most of the devices featured in subsequent kids' shows—cartoons, silent films, puppets, skits, songs, and demonstrations.

SMALL TALK   CBS
4 MAY 1990–25 MAY 1990   This half-hour prime-time series combined equal parts of *America's Funniest Home Videos, Candid Camera* and *Art Linkletter's House Party* to present a look at things through the eyes of children. Roger Rose hosted the show, which featured a studio audience, vidoes of kids submitted by viewers, and prerecorded and onstage interviews with precocious young moppets.

SMALL WONDER   SYNDICATED
1985–1989   Low-budget half-hour sitcom about a scientist who built a robot that looked like a ten-year-old girl. With Dick Christie as Ted Lawson, who worked at United Robotronics; Tiffany Brissette as the robot, Vicki (an acronym for Voice Input Child Identicant), who came home to live with Ted and his family; Marla Pennington as Ted's wife, Joan; Jerry Supiran as their son, Jamie; Emily Schulman as nosy Harriet Brindle, the girl who lived next door and had a crush on Jamie; Edie McClurg (1985–1986) as Harriet's nosy mother, Bonnie; William Bogert (1986–1989) as Harriet's father, and Ted's boss, Brandon Brindle; Lihann Jones (1986–1989) as Jessica, Jamie's girlfriend; and Daryl T. Bartley (1986–1987) as Jamie's classmate, Warren. Howard Leeds created the series for Metromedia Video Productions.

SMALL WORLD   CBS
12 OCTOBER 1958–5 APRIL 1959   On this Sunday-afternoon public affairs program, host Edward R. Murrow conversed with three guests; the show was not unlike *Person to Person,* as Murrow remained in New York while his guests were filmed on location throughout the world. On the premiere Murrow chatted with Indian premier Jawaharlal Nehru, former governor Thomas E. Dewey, and Aldous Huxley. Other guest threesomes included Hyman Rickover, Rebecca West, and Mark Van Doren (2 November), and Noel Coward, James Thurber, and Siobhan McKenna (29 March). Murrow produced the show with Fred W. Friendly and had planned to have Eric Sevareid host it; the network, however, insisted that Murrow take the job. The show was broadcast during the 1959–1960 season as a series of specials.

SMILIN' ED'S GANG   NBC/CBS/ABC
26 AUGUST 1950–19 MAY 1951 (NBC); 11 AUGUST 1951–11 APRIL 1953 (CBS); 22 AUGUST 1953–16 APRIL 1955 (ABC); 23 APRIL 1955–13 AUGUST 1955 (NBC)   Smilin' Ed McConnell began this popular children's show on radio in 1943 and brought it to television seven years later; the show was a mixture of stories, filmed segments and onstage antics with McConnell and his unpredictable puppets: Midnight the Cat, Squeaky the Mouse, and Froggy the Gremlin. Some of the voices were supplied by June Foray, who later provided the voice of Rocky the Flying Squirrel. Frank Ferrin produced and directed the series, which was produced in Hollywood and sponsored by Buster Brown Shoes (it was originally titled *The Buster Brown TV Show With Smilin' Ed McConnell and the Buster Brown Gang*). When McConnell died in 1955, Andy Devine took over as host, and the show was retitled *Andy's Gang* (see also that title).

SMITH & JONES   CBS

16 SEPTEMBER 1991–10 OCTOBER 1991   British comedy duo Mel Smith and Griff Rhys Jones cohosted this comedy series, which ran weeknights at 1 A.M. for four weeks. The twenty half-hours were edited from the pair's long-running BBC series.

THE SMITH FAMILY   ABC

20 JANUARY 1971–5 JANUARY 1972; 12 APRIL 1972–14 JUNE 1972   Half-hour comedy-drama about a Los Angeles police officer and his family. With Henry Fonda as Detective Sergeant Chad Smith, a twenty-five-year veteran; Janet Blair as his wife, Betty Smith; Darleen Carr as their elder daughter, Cindy, a college student; Ronny Howard as their teenage son, Bob; and Michael-James Wixted as their younger son, Brian (who inexplicably spoke with a British accent). Don Fedderson was the executive producer of the series.

THE SMITHSONIAN   NBC

15 OCTOBER 1966–8 APRIL 1967   Bill Ryan hosted this Saturday afternoon informational series for children, which was filmed at the Smithsonian Institution in Washington, D.C., and on location.

SMITHSONIAN WORLD   PBS

1984–1991   Wide-ranging hour documentary series, produced in cooperation with the Smithsonian Institution.

THE SMOKEY BEAR SHOW   ABC

6 SEPTEMBER 1969–12 SEPTEMBER 1971   Weekend cartoon series starring Smokey the Bear, the animated version of the real Smokey, who had been saved from a forest fire as a cub and spent the rest of his days in the National Zoo in Washington. One of the first of the conservation-oriented cartoon shows, *The Smokey Bear Show* was seen Saturdays during its first season; reruns were shown Sundays the following year.

THE SMOTHERS BROTHERS COMEDY HOUR   CBS

5 FEBRUARY 1967–8 JUNE 1969

THE SMOTHERS BROTHERS SUMMER SHOW   ABC

15 JULY 1970–16 SEPTEMBER 1970

TOM SMOTHERS' ORGANIC PRIME TIME SPACE RIDE   SYNDICATED

1971

THE SMOTHERS BROTHERS SHOW   NBC

13 JANUARY 1975–26 MAY 1975   Brothers Tom and Dick Smothers, who cohosted *The Smothers Brothers Comedy Hour* on CBS, battled the network over the program content for two years, and finally lost their show. Though the series was planned to appeal to the under-thirty generation, its open criticism of the Vietnam War and the Johnson administration created a dilemma for an understandably sensitive network; the dilemma was solved by canceling the show less than 100 days into the Nixon administration. To most of its audience, *The Smothers Brothers Comedy Hour* was a breath of fresh air, but to CBS the Smothers Brothers seemed to be in the wrong place at the wrong time with the wrong things to say.

The brothers were singing together at San Jose State College as early as 1959, and made their network TV debut on Jack Paar's *Tonight* show. In 1965 they were involved in a trivial sitcom (see *The Smothers Brothers Show* below); though their first series was unsuccessful, CBS did not lose interest. When network research suggested that a variety show with appeal to the fifteen-to-thirty age group could compete with NBC's *Bonanza* on Sundays (previous CBS casualties in the 9 p.m. slot included *The Judy Garland Show, My Living Doll, The Joey Bishop Show, Perry Mason,* and *The Garry Moore Show*), CBS executives contacted Tom Smothers, who negotiated a twenty-six-week contract for a variety series. *The Smothers Brothers Comedy Hour* premiered in February 1967 and ranked a surprising sixteenth over the remainder of the season (during the 1967–1968 season the show slipped to eighteenth but succeeded in toppling *Bonanza* from first to sixth).

On camera, Tom Smothers, the funny one (and the older one), seemed to be an inarticulate bumbler. Off camera, though, Tom was keenly involved with almost every aspect of the production; the show went through several producers (including Saul Ilson, Ernie Chambers, and Allan Blye) and at least six directors. More importantly, it was Tom who sought to use the show not only to introduce little-known performers to national audiences but also to provide a forum for the expression of political and critical viewpoints seldom expressed on a variety show. Though brother Dick shared Tom's sentiments, he preferred to let Tom take charge; Dick was less interested in show business and the media than Tom; he spent as much time as he could pursuing his real passions—automobile collecting and racing.

Censorship problems arose almost immediately and persisted throughout the Smothers' seventy-one-show run on CBS. Unlike most disputes between performers and networks over program material, the Smothers' disputes usually involved neither lines nor words (though the use of the word "mindblowing" was forbidden), but entire segments. Among the battles which the brothers lost and won were: a skit on film censorship with Tom Smothers and Elaine May, deleted; Pete Seeger's performance on the fall 1967 premiere of "Waist Deep in the Big Muddy," a song with antiwar overtones, deleted (the appearance marked Seeger's return to network television after being blacklisted in the 1950s; Seeger was permitted to perform the number on a later show); a special 1968 Mother's Day message (which concluded with the words, "Please talk peace"), deleted; Harry Belafonte singing in front of a filmed montage of disturbances at the 1968 Democratic convention in Chicago, deleted; an interview with Dr. Benjamin Spock, who had been convicted of aiding draft evaders, deleted. The Smothers Brothers also received a lot of hate mail, particularly for their frequent use of black performers on the show.

After the telecast of 27 October 1968 (from which a David Steinberg "sermonette" had generated much critical mail), CBS took the then unusual step of demanding that a tape of each upcoming show be prescreened for network affiliates by closed circuit. When Tom Smothers failed to deliver one tape until a day before air time, CBS yanked the show and did not broadcast it until three weeks later (on that show, Joan Baez dedicated a song to her husband, David Harris, then serving a jail sentence for draft evasion).

In spite of the constant conflicts, CBS announced its decision to renew *The Smothers Brothers Comedy Hour* on 14 March 1969. Less than two weeks later Tom Smothers attended the National Broadcasters Association convention in Washington, where he sought support from liberal Congressmen and other officials, such as FCC Commissioner Nicholas Johnson. Undoubtedly, Smothers's appearance in Washington worried the network, which would hardly have welcomed any government investigation. On 3 April 1969, Bob Wood, president of CBS Television, telegraphed Smothers that the show was canceled; ostensibly, the reason was that Smothers had failed to deliver a tape on time, though Smothers insisted that timely delivery had been made (the Smothers' guests on that show were David Steinberg, Dan Rowan, and Nancy Wilson). *TV Guide* ran a special editorial in its 19 April issue, characterizing CBS's decision to axe the show "wise, determined, and wholly justified," and citing the network's responsibility to the American public.

Neither ABC nor NBC expressed interest in signing the Smothers Brothers immediately after their cancellation, and *The Smothers Brothers Comedy Hour* left the air quietly in June 1969; it was replaced by *Hee Haw.* ABC signed the two for a summer series a year later; *The Smothers Brothers Summer Show* was a toned-down variety hour and attracted little, if any, controversy. Tom Smothers later starred in an ill-conceived comedy half hour known as *Tom Smothers' Organic Prime Time Space Ride,* which also featured comics Hudson and Landry. In 1975 Tom and Dick returned to network TV as hosts of *The Smothers Brothers Show,* a toothless effort; Joe Hamilton was the executive producer of the variety hour.

Many of the regulars on the Smothers Brothers' shows have become major stars. Among the more successful from *The Smothers Brothers Comedy Hour* crew were comedian Pat Paulsen (who campaigned for the Presidency in 1968), singers Glen Campbell and John Hartford, writer-composer Mason Williams, Bob Einstein (who often appeared as Officer Judy, the humorless cop, and later produced *The Redd Foxx Comedy Hour* with Allan Blye), and Steve Martin (who began as a writer for the show, but occasionally appeared on camera). Other regulars included Leigh French, Jennifer Warren (later known as Jennifer Warnes), and Don Wyatt. Regulars on the Smothers' 1970 summer series included Spencer Quinn and Sally Struthers, who later starred in *All in the Family*. Regulars on the 1975 show included Pat Paulsen, Bob Einstein, and Don Novello.

THE SMOTHERS BROTHERS COMEDY HOUR   CBS
30 MARCH 1988–25 MAY 1988; 28 JANUARY 1989–18 FEBRUARY 1989; 2 AUGUST 1989–23 AUGUST 1989   On 3 February 1988 CBS welcomed back Tom and Dick Smothers with "The Smothers Brothers Comedy Hour 20th Reunion," which featured guests Pat Paulsen, Bob Einstein, Leigh French, Jennifer Warnes, Steve Martin, John Hartford, Glen Campbell, and Mason Williams. A few weeks later the Brothers returned on a regular basis, with regulars Pat Paulsen and Jim Stafford. The look and format of the show were much the same as they had been twenty years previously, but the sharp, irreverent edge was no longer there. The show popped up in various niches on CBS's prime-time schedule during the next eighteen months, and was occasionally seen as a one-shot telecast at times other than those listed above.

THE SMOTHERS BROTHERS SHOW   CBS
17 SEPTEMBER 1965–9 SEPTEMBER 1966   This first of the several series starring brothers Tom and Dick Smothers was a half-hour situation comedy in which they played themselves. Tom Smothers was a probationary angel assigned to return to Earth and help people there, while Dick Smothers was a publishing executive who was forced to share his apartment with his late sibling. Also featured were Roland Winters as Dick's boss, Leonard J. Costello; Harriet MacGibbon as Mrs. Costello; Marilyn Scott as their daughter, Diane Costello; and Ann Elder as Janet, Dick's girlfriend. Neither of the Smothers Brothers was happy with the show; both felt that the situation comedy format was not the right showcase for their talents. The filmed series was originally produced by Phil Sharp for Four Star Films. See also *The Smothers Brothers Comedy Hour*.

SMURFS   NBC
12 SEPTEMBER 1981–25 AUGUST 1990   The smash hit of the 1981–1982 Saturday-morning season, *Smurfs* was an hour series chronicling the adventures of a lovable group of little blue humanoids living peacefully in the forest; their enemy, the evil Gargamel, tried in vain to capture them. The characters were created in 1957 by Belgian cartoonist Peyo Culliford, and various Smurf toys were licensed in the United States in the late 1970s. After seeing his young daughter playing with a Smurf doll, Fred Silverman (then president of NBC Television) ordered the cartoon series. His decision proved to be a wise one, as *Smurfs* helped NBC to dominate the Saturday-morning ratings race. *Smurfs* expanded to ninety minutes in 1982 and inspired several imitations (see also *The Littles, Monchhichis, Shirt Tales,* and *Trollkins*). New characters were introduced over the years, such as Smurfette (the only female Smurf), Grandpa Smurf, and the evil Scruple. In the fall of 1988 the show returned to an hour format.

SNAP JUDGMENT   NBC
3 APRIL 1967–28 MARCH 1969   This Goodson-Todman daytime game show was similar in format to *Password*; Ed McMahon was the first host, and was succeeded by Gene Rayburn.

SNARKY PARKER   CBS
9 JANUARY 1950–29 SEPTEMBER 1950   The Bil and Cora Baird Puppets were the stars of this fifteen-minute children's serial with a western setting. Snarky Parker and his horse, Heathcliffe, were the principal characters. Officially titled *Life with Snarky Parker,* and usually broadcast four evenings a week, the show was directed by Yul Brynner, whose stage and film career took off after *Snarky Parker* left the air.

SNEAK PREVIEWS   PBS/LIFETIME

1978–1987 (PBS); 1987–1988 (LIFETIME); 1988–   (PBS)   Movies are the subject
of this half-hour series. Each week cohosts Roger Ebert (film critic for the *Chicago
Sun-Times*) and Gene Siskel (film critic for the *Chicago Tribune*) introduced clips
from four or five new releases, then discussed and rated the films. Occasional programs were dedicated not to current films, but to some other aspect of the medium.
By 1982 *Sneak Previews* had become the highest-rated regular series in PBS history,
but Siskel and Ebert elected to move to commercial television (see *At the Movies*).
Sneak Previews carried on with new critics Jeffrey Lyons and Neal Gabler. Michael
Medved replaced Gabler in the fall of 1985.

   After nine seasons on PBS, the series moved to the Lifetime cable network for one
season, returning to PBS in the fall of 1988. In the fall of 1989 the series changed
formats and titles. Now known as *Sneak Previews Goes Video,* it concentrated not on
motion pictures newly released to theaters, but rather on films and other subjects
recently made available on the home video market. In 1991 the series reverted to its
original title.

THE SNOOKY LANSON SHOW   NBC

17 JULY 1956–13 SEPTEMBER 1956   Snooky Lanson, who was regularly featured on
Your Hit Parade, hosted this summer replacement for the *Dinah Shore Show.* The
fifteen-minute musical series was officially titled *Chevrolet on Broadway* and also
featured the Mello-Larks.

THE SNOOP SISTERS   NBC

19 DECEMBER 1973–20 AUGUST 1974   One segment of *The NBC Wednesday Movie,*
The Snoop Sisters starred Helen Hayes and Mildred Natwick as sisters Ernesta and
Gwendolin Snoop, who wrote mystery stories and solved real mysteries as well. Also
featured were Lou Antonio as their friend Barney, an ex-con; Bert Convy as their
nephew, Lieutenant Steve Ostrowski, a New York cop. Six episodes were filmed.

SNOOPS   CBS

22 SEPTEMBER 1989–8 DECEMBER 1989; 22 JUNE 1990–6 JULY 1990   Tim Reid and his
wife, Daphne Maxwell Reid, appeared in their third series together, this time as a
sophisticated Washington, D.C., couple who solved crimes in their spare time. Tim
Reid played Chance Dennis, a professor of criminology at Georgetown; Daphne
Maxwell Reid played Micki Dennis, a protocol aide at the State Department; John
Karlen was Lieutenant Sam Akers, Chance and Micki's police contact; and Troy
Curvey, Jr., was Hugo, a State Department driver. Tim Reid and Sam Egan created
the series and were its executive producers.

SNORKS   NBC

15 SEPTEMBER 1984–6 SEPTEMBER 1986   The title characters in this Saturday-morning
cartoon show were a tribe of multi-colored submarine creatures with long snorkels.

SO THIS IS HOLLYWOOD   NBC

1 JANUARY 1955–19 AUGUST 1955   Half-hour sitcom about two young women trying
to make it in show business. With Mitzi Green as Queenie Dugan, an aspiring stunt
woman; Virginia Gibson as Kim Tracey, an aspiring actress; Jimmy Lydon as Kim's
agent and boyfriend, Andy Boone; Gordon Jones as Queenie's boyfriend, stunt man
Hubie Dodd; and Peggy Knudsen as April Adams, the actress for whom Queenie
became a stand-in. The filmed series was produced by Ed Beloin and directed by
Richard Bare.

SO YOU THINK YOU GOT TROUBLES?!   SYNDICATED

1982   Ventriloquist Jay Johnston and his dummy, Bob, hosted this contrived game
show. Persons with unusual problems appeared as contestants, and discussed their
problems with Johnston and the wisecracking Bob. A panel of three experts then
gave advice as to how the contestant might solve the problem; the contestant then

tried to guess which expert's advice had impressed the largest segment of the studio audience.

SO YOU WANT TO LEAD A BAND
ABC

5 AUGUST 1954–27 JANUARY 1955   Bandleader Sammy Kaye hosted this half-hour musical series, on which members of the studio audience were given a chance to conduct the band; the audience selected the winning amateur conductor by its applause, and the lucky contestant won a prize. Featured vocalists included Barbara Benson and Jeffrey Clay.

SOAP
ABC

13 SEPTEMBER 1977–20 APRIL 1981   This prime-time comedy serial barely made it to the air because of protests lodged before its premiere by an assortment of religious and ethnic groups; ABC's excessive and exaggerated publicity doubtless precipitated the onslaught of complaints, most of which died down after the show came to the air. Though the plot dealt with impotence, transsexualism, extramarital affairs, and organized crime, *Soap* was no more sensational than Norman Lear's pioneer serial, *Mary Hartman, Mary Hartman*. Set in Dunn's River, Connecticut, it told the story of the wealthy Tate family and the middle-class Campbell family. Principal players included Katherine Helmond as Jessica Tate, a free-thinking socialite who was convicted of murder during the first season; Robert Mandan as Chester Tate, her philandering husband; Jennifer Salt as their daughter Eunice; Diana Canova as their daughter Corinne; Jimmy Baio as their son, Billy; Robert Guillaume (1977–1979) as Benson, the family's cook; Cathryn Damon as Mary Campbell, Jessica's sister; Richard Mulligan as Burt Campbell, her second husband; Ted Wass as Mary's macho son, Danny, who became involved with organized crime; Billy Crystal as Mary's son, Jodie Dallas, who intended to change his gender; Richard Libertini as The Godfather; Katherine Reynolds as Claire; Robert Urich (1977–1978) as Peter; Arthur Peterson as Grandpa Tate, a veteran who was unaware that the war is over; Roscoe Lee Browne (March 1980–1981) as Saunders, the new butler; and Jay Johnston as Chuck. Rod Roddy was the announcer. Susan Harris created, produced, and wrote the half-hour series. See also *Benson*.

SOAP BOX THEATER
ABC

1 JULY 1950–3 DECEMBER 1950   Half-hour dramatic anthology series.

THE SOAP FACTORY
SYNDICATED

1978   A half hour of disco dancing, taped at the Soap Factory in Palisades Park, New Jersey. Paul Harriss was the host of the series, and David Bergman the executive producer.

SOAP WORLD
SYNDICATED

1982   The growing popularity of TV's serials spawned this half-hour magazine show. Host Michael Young spent most of the time interviewing the stars of the several soap operas.

SOLDIER PARADE
ABC

14 JULY 1954–8 SEPTEMBER 1955   This Army talent show was hosted at various times by Gisele MacKenzie, Arlene Francis, and Martha Wright. Richard Hayes, then an Army private, was the cohost. The half-hour show grew out of an earlier military talent show, *Talent Patrol* (see also that title).

THE SOLDIERS
NBC

25 JUNE 1955–3 SEPTEMBER 1955   Half-hour sitcom starring Hal March and Tom D'Andrea as a couple of Army privates. Bud Yorkin produced and directed. March and D'Andrea had previously played the characters on several variety shows, such as *The Colgate Comedy Hour*.

SOLDIERS OF FORTUNE SYNDICATED

1955 Half-hour adventure series with John Russell as Tim Kelly and Chick Chandler as Toubo Smith, a pair of freewheeling troubleshooters. The show was produced at Revue Studios.

SOLID GOLD SYNDICATED

1980–1988 This hour variety series highlighted the week's top records, with personal appearances or video clips of the featured recording artists. Also on hand were a bevy of briefly attired dancers. Dionne Warwick hosted the series during the first season, joined each week by a celebrity guest host. Andy Gibb (whose three older brothers were the Bee Gees) and Marilyn McCoo (formerly of the Fifth Dimension) took over as cohosts for the 1981–1982 season. In the fall of 1982 Rex Smith succeeded Gibb as McCoo's cohost. Marilyn McCoo was the sole host for the 1983–1984 season. In the fall of 1984 disc jockey Rick Dees became the sole host. He lasted a season, and was replaced by Dionne Warwick in the fall of 1985. Warwick was in turn succeeded by McCoo in the fall of 1986. In the fall of 1987 the series was titled *Solid Gold in Concert,* in an attempt to call attention to the fact that many of the artists who appeared were performing live.

In June 1984 a second version of the series surfaced briefly; titled *Solid Gold Hits,* it was broadcast daily in a half-hour format, hosted by Grant Goodeve.

SOMEONE LIKE ME NBC

14 MARCH 1994–25 APRIL 1994 Half–hour sitcom whose central character was an eleven-year-old girl living in St. Louis. With Gaby Hoffmann as Gaby Stepjak; Patricia Heaton as her mother, Jean; Anthony Tyler Quinn as her stepfather, Steven, an optician; Nikki Cox as her older sister, Sam; Joseph Tello as her younger half-brother, Evan; and Raegan Kotz as her pal, Jane Schmidt.

SOMERSET NBC

30 MARCH 1970–31 DECEMBER 1976 Though *Somerset* was the first serial spinoff from another serial, it had little in common with its parent, *Another World,* even though it was titled *Another World/Somerset* at first. Though some of the characters from *Another World* traveled back and forth from Bay City to Somerset, *Somerset's* principal characters were developed independently. While *Another World's* story lines centered on psychological and romantic themes, *Somerset's* emphasized crime and intrigue; the principal reason for the difference was that *Somerset's* first head writer was Henry Slesar, who had previously worked on *The Edge of Night* (all three soaps were owned by Procter and Gamble). Subsequent head writers included Roy Winsor and Russell Kubec.

The two main characters who emigrated from Bay City to Somerset (a town of 25,000) as the series premiered were lawyer Sam Lucas (played by Jordan Charney) and his wife, Lahoma Vane Lucas (played by Ann Wedgeworth); Missy Matthews (played by Carol Roux), another Bay City resident, was also featured in the early months. Other members of the cast included: Ed Kemmer as Ben Grant, Sam's law partner, who died in a plane crash; Georgann Johnson as his wife, Ellen Bishop Grant, who later fell for a much younger man; Ralph Clanton as Jasper Delaney, owner of Delaney Brands, a major industry in Somerset; Len Gochman as his son, Peter Delaney; Nick Coster as his son, Robert Delaney; Dorothy Stinette as his daughter, Laura Delaney Cooper; Marie Wallace as Robert's wife, India Delaney; Paul Sparer as Laura's husband, Rex Cooper; Doug Chapin, Ernest Thompson, and Barry Jenner as Laura's son, Tony Cooper; Fred J. Scollay as Ike Harding (also known as Harry Wilson), Tony's real father, and the murderer of Jasper Delaney; Susan MacDonald as Jill Grant, daughter of Ben and Ellen Grant; Ron Martin and Tom Calloway as David Grant, Jill's twin brother; Dick Shoberg as Mitch Farmer, who married Jill and later died; Alan Gifford as Judge Brad Bishop, Ellen Grant's father; Phil Sterling as Rafe Carter; Walter Matthews as Gerald Davis; Alice Hirson as Marsha Davis; Wynne Miller as nightclub singer Jessica Buchanan; Gary Sandy as Randy Buchanan; Gene Fanning and George Coe as Leo Kurtz, who became the owner of Delaney Brands; Michael Lipton as Leo's brother, Dr. Stanley Kurtz;

Renne Jarrett, Meg Wittner, and Fawne Harriman as Leo's daughter, Ginger Kurtz, who married Tony Cooper; Lois Smith as the deranged Zoe Cannel; Joel Crothers as her husband, Julian Cannel; Harriet Hall as Andrea Moore, whom Zoe tried to poison; Chris Pennock as Andrea's brother, Dana Moore; Lois Kibbee as their mother, Emily Moore; Frank Schofield as Zoe's father, Philip Matson, who married Emily Moore; Jay Gregory as Zoe's brother, Carter Matson, whom Zoe murdered; Diahn Williams as Chrystal Ames, also killed by Zoe; Marc Alaimo as Virgil Paris, plant manager at Delaney Brands; Bibi Besch as Eve Lawrence, fiancée of Judge Bishop; Audrey Landers as Eve's daughter, Heather Lawrence Kane; James O'Sullivan as Dr. Jerry Kane, Heather's husband; Gary Swanson as reporter Greg Mercer, Heather's half brother; Stanley Grover as Mark Mercer; Judith Searle as Edith Mercer, Mark's wife; Joseph Julian as Vic Kirby; Ed Winter as Chuck Hillman; Melinda Plank as Danny Cotsworth; Dortha Duckworth as Rowena Standish; Peter MacLean as Scott MacKensie; Glenn Zachar as Skipper MacKensie; Bill Hunt as Bill Greeley; Polly Rowles as Freida Lang; Tina Sloan as Kate Cannel, who became the second wife of Julian Cannel; Eugene Smith as Lieutenant Will Price; Michael Nouri and Ted Danson as lawyer Tom Conway; James Congdon as Ned Paisley; Velekka Gray as Ned's sister, Victoria Paisley; Gloria Hoye as Dr. Teri Martin, who married Stanley Kurtz; Sean Ward as Joey Cooper; Bernard Grant as Dan Briskin; Molly Picon as Sarah Briskin; Nancy Pinkerton as Karen MacMillan; Abby Lewis as Lena Andrews; Elizabeth Lowry as Marge; Helen Funai as Lyling Sun; Jane Rose as Becky Winkler; Ellen Barber as Marion Parker; Bruce Gray as Warren Parker; Matthew Greene as Bobby Hansen; Lou Jacobi as Mac Wells; Jameson Parker as Dale Robinson, the younger man who became involved with widow Ellen Grant; Sigourney Weaver as Avis Ryan; and Gene Bua as Steve Slade.

SOMERSET MAUGHAM THEATRE   CBS/NBC
18 OCTOBER 1950–28 MARCH 1951 (CBS); 2 APRIL 1951–10 DECEMBER 1951 (NBC)   W. Somerset Maugham hosted this anthology series of adaptations of Maugham stories. The show began on CBS as a half-hour series and was kinescoped for presentation on those CBS affiliates that did not have direct transmission lines to the New York station from which the program originated; when it shifted networks in April of 1951 it expanded to an hour, was seen biweekly (alternating with *Robert Montgomery Presents*), and was presented only in live form. The latter change enabled several more Maugham stories to be presented on television, since, in the absence of a kinescope transcription, there was no longer any legal dispute with the owners of the film rights to those stories. Among the stories presented were: "The Dream," with Joan Bennett (14 February 1951); "The Moon and Sixpence," with Lee J. Cobb (30 April 1951); and "Cakes and Ale," with June Havoc (28 May 1951). The CBS version of the series was also titled *Teller of Tales*.

SOMETHING ELSE   SYNDICATED
1970   Half-hour musical variety show, hosted by John Byner and later by John Hartford.

SOMETHING IS OUT THERE   NBC
21 OCTOBER 1988–9 DECEMBER 1988   Hour sci-fi series, derived from the two-part TV-movie of the same name broadcast 8 and 9 May 1988. The series starred Joe Cortese as Los Angeles cop Jack Breslin and Maryam D'Abo as Ta'ra, a mind-reading alien, who teamed up to track down a "xenomorph," an evil creature from Ta'ra's spacecraft that could assume human form. Ta'ra and Jack became interested in one another, although Ta'ra was satisfied merely to look at Jack's hands, as the hands were considered the most attractive body part on Ta'ra's planet. Also featured was Gregory Sierra as Captain Victor Maldonado. Frank Lupo and John Ashley were executive producers.

SOMETHING WILDER   NBC
1 OCTOBER 1994–22 OCTOBER 1994; 6 DECEMBER 1994–14 MARCH 1995; 6 JUNE 1995–13 JUNE 1995   Half-hour sitcom set in Stockbridge, Massachusetts, where an older

father and his wife were raising their four-year-old twins. With Gene Wilder as Gene Bergman, who owned Berkshire Hills Advertising; Hillary B. Smith as his wife, Annie; Carl Michael Lindner as son Sam; Ian Bottiglieri as son Gabe; Jake Weber as Gene's brother-in-law, Richie, who worked at the ad agency; and Gregory Itzin as Jack Travis, who also worked at the ad agency.

SONG AND DANCE   NBC
7 JANUARY 1949–14 JUNE 1949   Irregularly scheduled prime-time musical series, hosted by Roberta Quinlan.

SONG AT TWILIGHT   NBC
3 JULY 1951–31 AUGUST 1951   This fifteen-minute musical series was hosted by Bob Carroll, then by Buddy Greco, and finally by Johnny Andrews. A summer replacement for John Conte's *The Little Show* and *The Roberta Quinlan Show,* the Monday-through-Friday program was produced by Richard Schneider. It was originally titled *Songs at Twilight.*

SONG SNAPSHOTS ON A SUMMER HOLIDAY   CBS
24 JUNE 1954–9 SEPTEMBER 1954   A summer replacement for *The Jane Froman Show,* this fifteen-minute musical series was cohosted by Merv Griffin and Betty Ann Grove.

SONGS FOR SALE   CBS
4 JULY 1950–1 SEPTEMBER 1950; 30 JUNE 1951–28 JUNE 1952   On this hour-long musical show compositions by amateur songwriters were performed by guest vocalists and were then judged by a panel of music business professionals. The series, which also ran on radio, was hosted by Jan Murray in 1950; Steve Allen was the host when the show returned to TV in the summer of 1951. Al Span was the producer, Bob Bleyer the director.

SONGTIME   ABC
6 OCTOBER 1951–17 MAY 1952   Jack Wyrtzen sang religious songs on this weekly show, broadcast Saturdays at 11:00 P.M.

SONIC THE HEDGEHOG   ABC
18 SEPTEMBER 1993–3 JUNE 1995   Half-hour Saturday-morning cartoon series derived from the popular video game. Set in the Great Forest, its chief characters were Sonic and his animal pals Nicole, Sally, and Rotor. Jaleel White (better known as Urkel on *Family Matters*) provided the voice of the title character.

THE SONNY AND CHER COMEDY HOUR   CBS
1 AUGUST 1971–5 SEPTEMBER 1971; 27 DECEMBER 1971–29 MAY 1974
THE SONNY AND CHER SHOW   CBS
1 FEBRUARY 1976–29 AUGUST 1977   *The Sonny and Cher Comedy Hour* was introduced as a summer variety show and found a place in the network's schedule in midseason. By the 1973–1974 season it was television's top-rated variety series. Unfortunately, after nine years of marriage, Sonny (born Salvatore Bono) and Cher (born Cherilyn LaPiere) were divorced in 1974, and the show came to an end. Each of them later hosted their own variety series (*The Sonny Comedy Revue* and *Cher*), neither of which was particularly successful; finally, in 1976, they were reunited, at least on camera, in *The Sonny and Cher Show,* and became the first divorced couple to cohost a variety series. The two had met in the mid-1960s, when Sonny was an occasional songwriter and studio musician (he played percussion at many of Phil Spector's recording sessions) and Cher was an aspiring singer. Their first records, released under the name Caesar and Cleo, went nowhere, but in 1965 "I Got You Babe," released under their own names, was a smash (and subsequently became their theme song on their TV shows). After a few years of relative obscurity in the late 1960s, Sonny persevered in getting them their summer show; its freshness and slick production insured its chances of renewal. The show was produced by Chris

Bearde and Allan Blye, and Cher's elaborate costumes were designed by Bob Mackie. The show also made effective use of such videotape tricks as chroma-key, a process by which one image can be superimposed upon another. Other regulars on *The Sonny and Cher Comedy Hour* included their daughter Chastity Bono, Peter Cullen, Freeman King, Teri Garr, Ted Zeigler, Billy Van, and Murray Langston (who later appeared as "The Unknown Comic" on *The Gong Show*). Nick Vanoff was the executive producer of *The Sonny and Cher Show,* and Frank Peppiatt and Phil Hahn were the producers. Regulars on that show included Ted Zeigler, the mime team of Shields and Yarnell (who later cohosted their own show), Billy Van, and Gailard Sartain. See also *Cher; The Sonny Comedy Revue.*

THE SONNY COMEDY REVUE   ABC
22 SEPTEMBER 1974–29 DECEMBER 1974   Following the breakup of his marriage to Cher, and the cancellation of *The Sonny and Cher Comedy Hour* on CBS, Sonny Bono tried to go it alone as host of a comedy hour on ABC. The effort, produced by Allan Blye and Chris Bearde (who had worked on *The Sonny and Cher Comedy Hour*), was unsuccessful. Other regulars included Freeman King, Billy Van, Ted Zeigler, Peter Cullen, Murray Langston, and Teri Garr. Sonny and Cher were later reunited on *The Sonny and Cher Show.*

THE SONNY KENDIS SHOW   CBS
18 APRIL 1949–6 JANUARY 1950   Sonny Kendis hosted this musical series, seen once or twice a week before or after the evening news. It was seen in both a ten-minute and fifteen-minute format. Gigi Durston was the featured vocalist.

SONNY SPOON   NBC
12 FEBRUARY 1988–25 MARCH 1988; 27 MAY 1988–15 JULY 1988; 7 OCTOBER 1988–16 DECEMBER 1988   Mario Van Peebles had the title role in this hour crime show, playing Sonny Spoon, a fast-talking black private eye who was a master of disguise. Other regulars included Terry Donahoe as assistant district attorney Carolyn Gilder; Joe Shea as newsstand operator Lucius DeLuce; Jordana Capra as Monique the hooker; and Bob Wieland as Johnny Skates, the skateboarding amputee. In the fall of 1988 Van Peebles's father, actor/director Melvin Van Peebles, joined the cast as Sonny's father, Mel.

SONS AND DAUGHTERS   CBS
11 SEPTEMBER 1974–6 NOVEMBER 1974   A high school drama set at Southwest High in Stockton, California, during the 1950s, *Sons and Daughters* was presumably inspired by the 1973 film *American Graffiti.* The hour series featured Gary Frank as Jeff Reed, all-American boy; Glynnis O'Connor as Anita Cramer, all-American girl, Jeff's girlfriend; Jay W. MacIntosh as Lucille Reed, Jeff's recently widowed mother; John S. Ragin as Walter Cramer, Anita's father; Jan Shutan as Ruth Cramer, Anita's mother; Michael Morgan as Danny Reed, Jeff's younger brother; Debralee Scott as Evie; Laura Siegel as Mary Anne; Scott Colomby as Stash; Barry Livingston as Moose; Lionel Johnston as Charlie; and Christopher Nelson as Cody. David Levinson was the executive producer, and Michael Gleason the producer, for Universal Television.

SONS AND DAUGHTERS   CBS
4 JANUARY 1991–1 MARCH 1991   The second series of this title was an hour comedy-drama which told the stories of the Hammersmith family of Portland, Oregon. The cast included: Lucie Arnaz as Tess Hammersmith; Michelle Wong as her adopted daughter, Astrid; Peggy Smithhart as Tess's sister, Patty Lincoln; Rick Rossovich as her husband, Spud Lincoln, a high-school coach; Paul Scherrer as their sixteen-year-old, Rocky; Kamaron Harper as their fourteen-year-old, Paulette; Billy O'Sullivan as their seven-year-old, Ike; Scott Plank as Tess's brother, Gary Hammersmith; Stacy Edwards as Gary's wife, Lindy; Don Murray as Tess's father, Bing Hammersmith; Lisa Blount as Bing's wife, Mary Ruth; Aaron Brownstein as Bing and Mary's four-year-old, Bing Jr.; and George D. Wallace as Grandpa Hank.

SOUL!   PBS

1970–1975   An hour-long variety series featuring black musicians, singers, and dancers; produced at WNET-TV, New York.

SOUL TRAIN   SYNDICATED

1971–   Essentially the black counterpart of *American Bandstand, Soul Train* features a group of about seventy teenagers who dance to the music and listen to assorted recording artists who drop by to lip-synch their newest hits. The hour series was created and is produced and hosted by Don Cornelius. The show began in 1970 as a local series in Chicago and later moved to Hollywood. Cornelius relinquished the hosting chores in 1993, appearing only to introduce each program's guest host.

SOUND-OFF TIME   NBC

14 OCTOBER 1951–6 JANUARY 1952   Half-hour comedy-variety show, with three rotating hosts: Bob Hope, Jerry Lester, and Fred Allen.

SOUNDSTAGE   PBS

1974–1981   A series of hour concerts by popular musical acts, produced at WTTW-TV, Chicago.

THE SOUPY SALES SHOW   ABC/SYNDICATED

4 JULY 1955–26 AUGUST 1955 (ABC); 3 OCTOBER 1959–25 JUNE 1960 (ABC); 3 DECEMBER 1960–25 MARCH 1961 (ABC); 26 JANUARY 1962–13 APRIL 1962 (ABC); 1965–1967 (SYNDICATED); 1979 (SYNDICATED)   Soupy Sales has hosted a plethora of children's shows, both local and national. His first effort was *Soupy's On,* a local show in Detroit that began in 1953; the show caught ABC's attention, and in 1955 Sales hosted his first network program, *The Soupy Sales Show.* It originated from Detroit and was seen weekday evenings for eight weeks. Sales then headed to Los Angeles and hosted a local show there for several years before returning to network TV in the fall of 1959 with a Saturday-morning show, which lasted until 1961 (with one six-month interruption). Early in 1962 Sales hosted a Friday evening show on ABC, and in 1964 he began a daily local show in New York, which was offered in syndication a year later. In 1979 Sales again hosted a syndicated half-hour show, produced in Hollywood. All of his shows have incorporated a combination of features—jokes, puns, songs, silent films, and sketches with an assortment of puppets, including White Fang, Black Tooth, Marilyn MonWolf, Herman the Flea, and Pookie the Lion. Pie-throwing was also a regular feature—Sales no doubt holds the world's record for receiving pies in the face. Sales's offbeat humor occasionally got him in trouble; *The New York Times* reported in January 1965 that Sales had been suspended for one week by WNEW-TV after asking his young viewers to go to their parents' wallets and send him "those little green pieces of paper." It was noted that although the incident had been intended as a joke, it could have been misinterpreted by certain members of Sales's audience.

SOUTH AMERICAN JOURNEY   PBS

30 JUNE 1987–18 AUGUST 1987   An eight-week series filmed on location throughout South America, hosted by Australian TV reporter Jack Pizzey.

SOUTH BEACH   NBC

6 JUNE 1993–6 JULY 1993   Miami's South Beach was the setting for this hour crime show, on which a con artist helped a government agent nail the bad guys. With Yancy Butler as the con artist, Kate Patrick; John Glover as the g-man, Roberts; Eagle-Eye Cherry as Kate's partner, Vernon; and Patti D'Arbanville as Roxanne, a former federal agent who now ran an inn.

SOUTH CENTRAL   FOX

5 APRIL 1994–30 AUGUST 1994   Gritty comedy-drama about a black single parent household trying to cope in Los Angeles's sprawling South Central district. With Tina Lifford as Joan Mosley, a divorcee who lost her job and found work as assistant

manager of a food co-op; Larenz Tate as her teenage son, Andre (an older son had been killed by gang warfare); Tasha Scott as her preteen daughter, Tasha; Keith Mbulo as her troubled foster son, Deion, who would not speak; Clifton Powell as her patronizing boss, Bobby Deavers; Jennifer Lopez as coworker Lucille; Earl Billings as coworker Mayo Bonner; and Paula Kelly as Joan's friend, Sweets. The critically acclaimed, but little watched, series was created by Michael J. Weithorn and Ralph Farquar.

SOUTH OF SUNSET   CBS
27 OCTOBER 1993 *South of Sunset* was a member of one of TV's most exclusive clubs—series canceled after one episode. Glenn Frey (better known as a rocker than an actor) starred as Los Angeles private eye Cody McMahon, with Aries Spears as his partner, an ex-thief named Ziggy Duane, and Maria Pitillo as their secretary, an aspiring actress named Gina. The premiere (and finale) notched an anemic 6.1 rating/9 share, a figure believed to be the lowest ever achieved by a major network fall premiere.

THE SOUTHERNAIRES   ABC
19 SEPTEMBER 1948–21 NOVEMBER 1948 Half-hour prime-time musical series starring a vocal quartet known as the Southernaires.

SPACE   CBS
14 APRIL 1985–18 APRIL 1985 A thirteen-hour, five-part adaptation of James A. Michener's epic novel chronicling the American efforts to explore space from 1946 to a late-1960s mission to the dark side of the moon. Principal players included James Garner as Senator Norman Grant; Harry Hamlin as astronaut John Pope; David Dukes as Martin Scorcella; Bruce Dern as Stanley Mott; Michael York as scientist Dieter Kolff; Blair Brown as Penny Pope; Susan Anspach as Elinor Grant; Melinda Dillon as Rachel Mott; Beau Bridges as Randy Clagget; and Maggie Han as Cindy Rhee. Laurence Luckinbill narrated. The series was rerun, in edited form, on CBS during the summer of 1987; the ratings were disastrous.

SPACE: ABOVE AND BEYOND   FOX
24 SEPTEMBER 1995– This sci-fi series drew on *Combat* for its inspiration. The hour show was set in 2063 A.D., when a peaceful Earth had begun to colonize other planets. Discovering that one such colony had been annihilated, a squadron of United States Marine space warriors was deployed to battle the unknown enemy. The cast included Morgan Weisser as Lieutenant Nathan West, who was convinced that his girlfriend (who had been dispatched to the colony) had escaped death and was determined to find her; Kristen Cloke as Lieutenant Shane Vansen; Rodney Rowland as Lieutenant Cooper Hawkes, an "In Vitro," or second-class citizen born without parents; Lanei Chapman as Lieutenant Vanessa Damphousse; Joel de la Fuente as Lieutenant Paul Wang; and James Morrison as their commanding officer, Colonel McQueen, who was also an In Vitro.

SPACE ACADEMY   CBS
10 SEPTEMBER 1977–1 SEPTEMBER 1979 This half-hour Saturday-morning series was set at the Space Academy, an artificial planetoid founded in Star Year 3732 as a training school for young space explorers. Featured were Jonathan Harris as Commander Gampu, the three-hundred-year-old head of the Academy; Pamelyn Ferdin as Laura; Ty Henderson as Paul; Ric Carrott as Chris; Pam Cooper as Adrian; Brian Tochi as Tee Gai; Eric Greene as Loki, the junior cadet; and Peepo the robot. Norm Prescott and Lou Scheimer were the executive producers.

SPACE CADET
See TOM CORBETT, SPACE CADET

SPACE GHOST AND DINO BOY   CBS/NBC

10 SEPTEMBER 1966–7 SEPTEMBER 1968 (CBS); 27 NOVEMBER 1976–3 SEPTEMBER 1977 (NBC)   Half-hour Saturday-morning cartoon series from Hanna-Barbera Productions about a galactic hero whose magic belt rendered him invisible. Space Ghost was assisted in his exploits by two teenagers, Jan and Jayce. Gary Owens provided the voice of Space Ghost. The second segment, "Dino Boy," featured the adventures of a young man who had parachuted into a prehistoric world. The series ran for two seasons on CBS and returned in the fall of 1976 on NBC to replace *Land of the Lost*, where it was shown under the title *Space Ghost/Frankenstein Jr.*, and included segments of *Frankenstein Jr. and the Impossibles*, another 1966 cartoon series from Hanna-Barbera. In April 1994 Space Ghost reappeared on cable television, in a totally new format: as the thickheaded host of a talk show. *Space Ghost: Coast to Coast* aired on the Cartoon Network. The host was in animated format, and his human guests appeared in TV monitors.

SPACE KIDETTES   NBC

10 SEPTEMBER 1966–2 SEPTEMBER 1967   Another cartoon series from Hanna-Barbera Productions, *Space Kidettes* featured a group of preteen space rangers.

SPACE: 1999   SYNDICATED

1975–1977   Produced in England, this hour-long science fiction series told the story of the 311 inhabitants of Moonbase Alpha, a lunar space colony. As the result of a tremendous nuclear explosion (caused by the storage of radioactive wastes on the dark side of the moon), the moon—with the surprised colonists aboard—was sent out of its orbit and careening into space. Featured were Martin Landau as Commander John Koenig; Barbara Bain as Dr. Helena Russell, research scientist; Barry Morse (1975–1976) as Professor Victor Bergman; Roy Dotrice as Commissioner Simmonds, Koenig's commanding officer, who was visiting Moonbase Alpha when the explosion occurred; Nick Tate as First Lieutenant Alan Carter; Zienia Merton as communications officer Sandra Benes; Anton Phillips as medical officer Dr. Bob Mathias; Clifton Jones (1975–1976) as David Kano; and Prentis Hancock (1975–1976) as Paul Morrow. In the fall of 1976 Catherine Schell joined the cast as Moonbase Alpha's scientific officer and resident alien, Maya, who could transform herself into any kind of creature at will; Tony Anholt also joined the cast as First Officer Tony Verdeschi. Gerry Anderson (who had previously worked on such series as *Fireball XL-5* and *Thunderbirds*) was the executive producer. Sylvia Anderson, his wife, was producer during the first season, and Fred Freiberger (who had worked on *Star Trek*) was producer during the second season.

SPACE PATROL   ABC

11 SEPTEMBER 1950–26 FEBRUARY 1955   One of the longer-running children's space shows of the early 1950s, *Space Patrol* was set in the thirtieth century. It featured Ed Kemmer as Commander Buzz Corry; Lyn Osborn as his assistant, Cadet Happy; Ken Mayer as Major Robbie Robertson; Paul Cavanaugh as Colonel Henderson, the Secretary General of the United Planets; Virginia Hewitt as Carol, the Secretary General's daughter; Nina Bara as Tonga, a onetime enemy who became an ally. *Space Patrol* began as a fifteen-minute daily series but shifted to a once-a-week, half-hour format late in 1951. Jack Narz, who later hosted several game shows, was the announcer. Mike Moser produced the series, and Dik Darley directed.

SPACE PRECINCT   SYNDICATED

1994–1995   Created by Gerry Anderson and filmed in England, this hour cop show was set in the year 2040 in the City of Demeter on the planet Altor, where the law enforcement community battled all sorts of evil life forms. Featured were Ted Shackelford as Lt. Patrick Brogan, a former New York City cop; Rob Youngblood as Officer Jack Haldane; Simone Bendix as Officer Jane Castle; Nancy Paul as Patrick's wife, Sally Brogan; Nic Klein as their son, Matt; and Megan Olive as their daughter, Liz.

SPACE RANGERS   CBS

6 JANUARY 1993–27 JANUARY 1993   Short-lived sci-fi hour set in 2104 A.D. on the planet Avalon, headquarters of a planetary police force. With Jeff Kaake as Captain John Boon; Jack McGee as Doc; Marjorie Monaghan as JoJo; Cary-Hiroyuki Tagawa as Zylyn; Linda Hunt as Commander Chennault; Danny Quinn as Kincaid; and Gottfried John as Colonel Weiss.

SPACE SENTINELS

See THE YOUNG SENTINELS

SPACE STARS   NBC

12 SEPTEMBER 1981–11 SEPTEMBER 1982   This Saturday-morning cartoon consisted of four segments, all supplied by Hanna-Barbera Studios. Two were reruns—"Space Ghost" and "The Herculoids"—and two were new—"Teen Force" and "Astro and the Space Mutts."

SPACE STRIKERS   UPN

10 SEPTEMBER 1995–   An updated version of Jules Verne's *20,000 Leagues Under the Sea,* this Sunday-morning cartoon series found Captain Nemo skippering the starship Nautilus for the Earthside Military Command, and battling the evil Master Phantom.

SPACECATS   NBC

14 SEPTEMBER 1991–25 JULY 1992   Half-hour Saturday-morning kids show which mixed live action and animated segments to depict the adventures of a group of feline-like visitors from another galaxy. Led by Captain Catgut, the Spacecats received their orders from DORC—the Disembodied Omnipotent Ruler of Cats—who was played by Charles Nelson Reilly.

SPARRING PARTNERS   ABC

8 APRIL 1949–13 MAY 1949   Prime-time game show hosted by Walter Kiernan, on which three men competed against three women in a question-and-answer format.

SPEAK UP AMERICA   NBC

1 AUGUST 1980–10 OCTOBER 1980   This ill-conceived series, billed as "the *Time* magazine of the airwaves," was little more than a pastiche of audience and person-on-the-street reactions to various topical questions. Former child evangelist Marjoe Gortner was the principal host of the show, assisted by Jayne Kennedy and by stentorian Rhonda Bates. Blasted by the critics, detested by the network's top executives, and ignored by the public, the program was abruptly cancelled after two months. It ranked second to last in the 1980–1981 seasonal ratings.

SPEAKEASY   SYNDICATED

1964   Host Chip Monck rapped with rock stars on this hour series.

SPECIAL AGENT 7   SYNDICATED

1958   Half-hour crime show starring Lloyd Nolan as Conroy, an agent for the Treasury Department.

SPECIAL EDITION   SYNDICATED

1977   Barbara Feldon hosted this documentary series, the segments of which were filmed versions of various nonfiction magazine articles. Alan Sloan produced the series.

THE SPECTACULAR WORLD OF GUINNESS RECORDS   SYNDICATED

1987   The second television series inpsired by the popular *Guinness Book of World Records* (see also *The Guinness Game*), this one was cohosted by David Frost and Shawn Southwick. It featured stories about present record holders as well as attempts to break existing records.

SPEED BUGGY   CBS/ABC/NBC
8 SEPTEMBER 1973–30 AUGUST 1975 (CBS); 6 SEPTEMBER 1975–4 SEPTEMBER 1976
(ABC); 27 NOVEMBER 1976–3 SEPTEMBER 1977 (NBC); 28 JANUARY 1978–2 SEPTEMBER
1978 (CBS); 18 SEPTEMBER 1982–29 JANUARY 1983 (CBS)   A seemingly indestructible cartoon series from Hanna-Barbera Productions, Speed Buggy was a flying car
that carried three teenage passengers: Debbie, Mark, and Tinker. Mel Blanc provided the voice of Speed Buggy.

SPEED RACER   SYNDICATED
1967; 1993   Japanese-produced cartoon series about a race-car driver, Speed Racer.

THE SPEIDEL SHOW
See PAUL WINCHELL AND JERRY MAHONEY

SPENCER (UNDER ONE ROOF)   NBC
1 DECEMBER 1984–12 JANUARY 1985; 23 MARCH 1985–11 MAY 1985; 14 JUNE 1985–5
JULY 1985   This half-hour sitcom about the trials and tribulations of a high school
student went through its own trials and tribulations during its brief run. It started out
as *Spencer,* with Chad Lowe (younger brother of Rob Lowe) in the title role as
sixteen-year-old Spencer Winger; Mimi Kennedy as his mother, Doris; Ronny Cox as
his father, George; Amy Locane as his younger sister, Andrea; Grant Heslov as his
pal Wayne; Dean Cameron as his pal Herbie Bailey; Richard Sanders as the guidance
counselor, Mr. Benjamin Beanley; and Beverly Archer as the English teacher, Miss
Spier. Production was halted after just five episodes, when Chad Lowe quit the series
after his demands for above-the-title billing and creative control were turned down.
The role was eventually recast, and the series returned to the air in March with a new
title, *Under One Roof,* and a new star, Ross Harris as Spencer Winger. The other
regulars from *Spencer* remained, except for Ronny Cox (it was explained that George
had run off with a younger woman), and Harold Gould and Frances Sternhagen
joined the cast as Doris's parents, Ben and Millie Sprague, who moved into the
Winger household. Guidance counselor Beanley was now the principal of Spencer's
high school, and Miss Spier was teaching Spanish. After *Under One Roof* left the air
in May 1985, reruns of the original *Spencer* series popped up on NBC's Friday
schedule for four weeks in June and July.

SPENCER'S PILOTS   CBS
17 SEPTEMBER 1976–19 NOVEMBER 1976   An unimpressive adventure series about
charter pilots working for Spencer Aviation. *Spencer's Pilots* was scheduled Fridays
at 8 P.M., a slot which CBS found difficult to fill successfully for most of the 1970s.
Only six episodes were televised. Featured were Gene Evans as Spencer Parish;
Christopher Stone as Cass Garrett; Todd Susman as Stan Lewis; Margaret Impert as
Linda Dann, a pilot and secretary; and Britt Leach as Mickey "Wig" Wiggins, the
mechanic. The hour series was created and produced by Larry Rosen; Bob Sweeney
and Edward H. Feldman were the executive producers for CBS Television.

SPENSER: FOR HIRE   ABC
20 SEPTEMBER 1985–3 SEPTEMBER 1988   This modestly successful crime show, inspired by Robert B. Parker's books, was filmed on location in Boston. It starred
Robert Urich as Spenser, the one-named, quotation-spouting, principled private eye,
and featured Avery Brooks as Hawk, Spenser's black, semi-malevolent, Magnum-
toting street source; Barbara Stock as Spenser's lady friend, guidance counselor
Susan Silverman (ousted after the first season due to a change in producers, Stock
was brought back for the series' third, and final, year); Carolyn McCormick (1986–
1987) as assistant district attorney Rita Fiore, Spenser's second-season romantic
interest; Richard Jaeckel (1985–1987) as Lieutenant Martin Quirk; and Ron McLarty
as Sergeant Frank Belson. The character returned in several TV-movies aired on the
Lifetime cable network beginning in 1993. See also *A Man Called Hawk.*

SPIDER-MAN   ABC

9 SEPTEMBER 1967–30 AUGUST 1969; 22 MARCH 1970–6 SEPTEMBER 1970

SPIDER-MAN AND HIS AMAZING FRIENDS   NBC

12 SEPTEMBER 1981–11 SEPTEMBER 1982; 15 SEPTEMBER 1984–6 SEPTEMBER 1986

THE INCREDIBLE HULK AND THE AMAZING SPIDER-MAN   NBC

18 SEPTEMBER 1982–10 SEPTEMBER 1983

THE AMAZING SPIDER-MAN AND THE INCREDIBLE HULK   NBC

17 SEPTEMBER 1983–8 SEPTEMBER 1984

SPIDER-MAN   FOX

4 FEBRUARY 1995–   *Spider-Man* first came to Saturday-morning television in 1967, as the star of a half-hour cartoon series; the character had first appeared in Marvel Comics in 1962. In real life, Spider-Man was none other than Peter Parker, who had been bitten by a radioactive spider as a college freshman and had acquired the power to spin webs and to walk on walls. The first TV version of *Spider-Man* remained on Saturday mornings for two seasons; reruns were seen on Sunday mornings in 1970. The character reappeared in a new series in 1981; in *Spider-Man and His Amazing Friends,* Spider-Man attended college with two other unusual superheroes, Iceman and Firestar. In 1982 Spider-Man teamed up with a cartoon version of The Incredible Hulk, and nobly gave the latter top billing; The Hulk graciously returned the favor the following season. Reruns of *Spider-Man and His Amazing Friends* were carried on NBC's Saturday morning lineup (usually under that title) for two more seasons. The character returned to Saturday morning, in new episodes, on the Fox network in 1995.

SPIDER-WOMAN   ABC

22 SEPTEMBER 1979–1 MARCH 1980   Saturday-morning cartoon show starring Jessica Drew, editor-publisher of *Justice* magazine, who had been bitten by a poisonous spider as a child and had been treated with an experimental serum that endowed her with arachnid powers.

SPIES   CBS

3 MARCH 1987–14 APRIL 1987   A short-lived comedy-adventure series about a veteran spy assigned to train a new agent. With George Hamilton as the senior snoop, Ian Stone; Gary Kroeger as his protegé, Ben Smythe; and Barry Corbin as Thomas Brady, the boss.

THE SPIKE JONES SHOW   NBC/CBS

2 JANUARY 1954–8 MAY 1954 (NBC); 2 APRIL 1957–27 AUGUST 1957 (CBS); 1 AUGUST 1960–19 SEPTEMBER 1960 (CBS); 17 JULY 1961–25 SEPTEMBER 1961 (CBS)   Bandleader Spike Jones hosted several half-hour comedy-variety shows; all of them featured Jones, singer Helen Grayco (his wife), and Jones's band, The City Slickers. Born Lindley Armstrong Jones, the gum-chewing, loud-suited bandleader injected a great deal of humor and slapstick into his shows—unusual musical instruments and pies in the face were commonplace. Jones is perhaps best remembered for his recording of "Der Führer's Face," popular during World War II.

SPIN THE PICTURE   DUMONT

25 JUNE 1949–4 FEBRUARY 1950   Kathi Norris hosted this early game show on which telephone calls were placed to home viewers, who were then given the opportunity to identify a celebrity from a rapidly revolving photograph. The hour series replaced a similar game show called *Cut.*

SPIN-OFF   CBS

16 JUNE 1975–5 SEPTEMBER 1975   Jim Lange was the host of this short-lived daytime game show, on which the contestants played an automated version of poker. Nick Nicholson and E. Roger Muir were the executive producers.

780

SPLIT PERSONALITY   NBC
28 SEPTEMBER 1959–5 FEBRUARY 1960   Tom Poston hosted this daytime game show from Goodson-Todman Productions. Contestants attempted to identify celebrities from clues read by the host.

SPLIT SECOND   ABC/SYNDICATED
20 MARCH 1972–27 JUNE 1975 (ABC); 1987 (SYNDICATED)   Tom Kennedy first hosted this fast-moving daytime quiz show. Each day three contestants competed for money; a player won a greater sum if he or she was the only person to answer a particular question correctly. At the end of the show the top money winner chose one of five automobiles that were on display; if the car started (only one of them did), the contestant won it. If not, the contestant returned the following day to compete again (if the same contestant won the second day, one of the five cars would be eliminated; thus, a contestant who won five shows automatically received a car). Stu Billet was the executive producer for Stefan Hatos–Monty Hall Productions. Monty Hall hosted the short-lived syndicated remake, which surfaced in 1987.

THE SPORTING LIFE   PBS
16 APRIL 1985–18 JUNE 1985   Half-hour series of interviews with athletes and other notables from the sports world, hosted by the former Baltimore Orioles pitcher Jim Palmer.

SPORTS ALBUM   SYNDICATED
1949   One of the first series made especially for television syndication, *Sports Album* was a package of sports newsreels distributed by Ziv TV, one of the industry's pioneers in the field of syndication.

THE SPORTS CAMERA   ABC
12 SEPTEMBER 1950–14 JUNE 1952   Half-hour series of sports films.

SPORTS CHALLENGE   SYNDICATED
1971–1973   Dick Enberg hosted this sports quiz show, which featured two three-member teams composed of athletes.

SPORTS CLUB   SYNDICATED
1958   Sports interview show hosted by former pro football star Elroy "Crazy Legs" Hirsch.

SPORTS FOCUS   ABC
3 JUNE 1957–12 SEPTEMBER 1958   Monday-through-Friday sports commentary show, hosted by Howard Cosell.

SPORTSBEAT   ABC
16 AUGUST 1981–15; DECEMBER 1985   Veteran ABC sportscaster Howard Cosell hosted this half-hour weekend afternoon series, which usually investigated a behind-the-scenes sports story. The program was originally televised once a month, but went weekly early in 1982.

SPORTSMEN'S QUIZ   CBS
26 APRIL 1948–2 MAY 1949   This five-minute, once-a-week sports quiz was sponsored by *Sports Afield* magazine.

SPORTSWOMAN OF THE WEEK
See GIRL OF THE WEEK

SPORTSWORLD   NBC
22 JANUARY 1978–   *Sportsworld* is the umbrella title for NBC's weekend sports anthology series, similar in concept to *ABC's Wide World of Sports*. The series celebrated its tenth anniversary with a prime-time special on 19 August 1988.

SPOTLIGHT   CBS
4 JULY 1967–29 AUGUST 1967   This Tuesday-night summer variety hour had no
regulars, other than the Lionel Blair Dancers and the Jack Parnell Orchestra. It was
taped in London and produced and directed by Jon Scoffield.

SPOTLIGHT ON SPORTS   NBC
8 JULY 1950–3 SEPTEMBER 1950   Bill Stern hosted this half-hour prime-time sports-
interview show. During its later weeks the show was titled *The Bill Stern Show.*

SQUARE ONE TV   PBS
26 JANUARY 1987–7 OCTOBER 1994   Produced by The Children's Television Workshop, *Square One TV* was an ambitious effort, intended to promote an interest in
mathematics among third- to sixth-graders, using songs, skits, and guest celebrities.

SQUARE PEGS   CBS
27 SEPTEMBER 1982–12 SEPTEMBER 1983   Anne Beatts, a former writer for *NBC's
Saturday Night Live,* created this offbeat sitcom. Set at suburban Weemawee High
School, its central characters were two klutzy girls—one tall with glasses, the other
short with braces—who were never able to penetrate the ranks of the "in" crowd.
Featured were Sarah Jessica Parker as Patty Greene (the tall one); Amy Linker as
Lauren Hutchison (the short one); Merrit Butrick as John "Johnny Slash" Ulasewicz,
the punk rocker; John Femia as Marshall Blechtman, would-be comic; Tracy Nelson
(daughter of actor-singer Rick Nelson) as empty-headed valley girl Jennifer DeNuccio;
Jami Gertz as Muffy Tepperman, captain of the Pep Squad; Claudette Wells as
LaDonna Fredericks, the token black; Jon Caliri as heartthrob Vinnie Pasetta; Catlin
Adams as Ms. Loomis, one of the teachers; Basil Hoffman as Mr. Dingleman, the
principal; and Steven Peterman as Rob Donovan, the political science teacher. The
series' New Wave theme song was composed and sung by the Waitresses.

THE SQUARE WORLD OF ED BUTLER   SYNDICATED
1970   Half-hour talk show hosted by Ed Butler.

STACCATO   NBC/ABC
10 SEPTEMBER 1959–24 MARCH 1960 (NBC); 27 MARCH 1960–25 SEPTEMBER 1960 (ABC)
John Cassavetes starred in this half-hour crime show as New York private eye Johnny
Staccato, a former jazz pianist. Also featured was Eduardo Ciannelli as Waldo,
owner of Waldo's, the MacDougal Street club where Staccato usually hung out.
Despite an excellent jazz score by Elmer Bernstein, *Staccato* was panned by most
critics as an imitation *Peter Gunn* (with a touch of *Pete Kelly's Blues* thrown in), and
was dropped in midseason by NBC; ABC picked up the reruns for another twenty-six
weeks.

STAGE A NUMBER   DUMONT
10 SEPTEMBER 1952–20 MAY 1953   This prime-time talent program showcased not
only aspiring performers, but also fledgling writers, directors, choreographers, and
other backstage people. The two best presentations, as selected by a celebrity panel,
were invited to return to the show the following week. Bill Wendell hosted the series,
and Roger Gerry produced it.

STAGE DOOR   CBS
7 FEBRUARY 1950–28 MARCH 1950   This short-lived Tuesday-night half-hour series
starred Louise Allbritton as Celia Knox, an aspiring actress, and also featured Scott
McKay and Tom Pedi. It was produced by Carol Irwin and directed by Barry
Kroeger.

STAGE ENTRANCE   DUMONT
2 MAY 1951–2 MARCH 1952   Columnist Earl Wilson hosted this fifteen-minute variety
and interview series; it was produced by Tod Hammerstein and directed by Bill
Seaman.

STAGE 7   CBS

30 JANUARY 1955–25 SEPTEMBER 1955   An undistinguished half-hour dramatic anthology series. Don Rickles played his first TV dramatic role on one show, "A Note of Fear," broadcast 15 May. Warren Lewis produced the series.

STAGE SHOW   CBS

3 JULY 1954–18 SEPTEMBER 1954; 1 OCTOBER 1955–22 SEPTEMBER 1956   *Stage Show* was a musical variety series cohosted by bandleaders Tommy and Jimmy Dorsey. It was introduced, in an hour format, in 1954 as a summer replacement for *The Jackie Gleason Show* (Gleason was its executive producer). Gleason resurrected the show in the fall of 1955, trimmed it to thirty minutes, and scheduled it immediately preceding his own show on Saturdays (Gleason, too, cut back to a half-hour format that season, as he had decided to do only *The Honeymooners,* instead of a full-hour variety show). Jack Carter, who guested frequently on the show, became the permanent emcee early in 1956 in an effort to boost ratings. It was on *Stage Show* that Elvis Presley, barely twenty-one, made his first national television appearances. Elvis first appeared on the show 28 January 1956, performing "Shake, Rattle and Roll," "Flip, Flop and Fly" and "I Got a Woman"; public reaction was strong, and Presley made five more appearances on *Stage Show* over the following eight weeks. Bobby Darin also made his national TV debut on the show that spring, singing "Rock Island Line."

STAGE 13   CBS

19 APRIL 1950–28 JUNE 1950   Wyllis Cooper produced and directed this suspense anthology series.

STAGE TWO REVUE   ABC

30 JULY 1950–24 SEPTEMBER 1950   Half-hour Sunday-night variety series, hosted by Georgia Lee.

STAGECOACH WEST   ABC

4 OCTOBER 1960–26 SEPTEMBER 1961   This hour-long western borrowed heavily from *Wagon Train* and *Overland Trail.* It featured Wayne Rogers as stagecoach driver Luke Perry; Robert Bray as driver Simon Kane; and Richard Eyer as Simon's young son, Davey.

STAINED GLASS WINDOWS   ABC

26 SEPTEMBER 1948–2 OCTOBER 1949   ABC's first religious program, *Stained Glass Windows* was a filmed-series broadcast for fifteen or thirty minutes on Sunday evenings.

THE STAND (STEPHEN KING'S THE STAND)   ABC

8 MAY 1994–12 MAY 1994   Four-night, eight-hour miniseries adapted by Stephen King from his apocalyptic 600-page 1978 novel (which he expanded to 1100 pages in 1990). It pitted good against evil, in the conflict between two groups of people who survived the outbreak of a viral infection which killed most of the world's population. The large cast included Jamey Sheridan as Randall Flagg, satanic leader of the evil group, which was headquartered in Las Vegas; Ruby Dee as Mother Abigail, saintly leader of the good group, which formed in Nebraska; Gary Sinise as Stu Redman; Ray Walston as Professor Glen Bateman; Rob Lowe as Nick Andros; Miguel Ferrer as Lloyd Henreid; Kathy Bates as Rae Flowers; Molly Ringwald as Fran Goldsmith; Corin Nemec as Harold Lauder; Laura San Giacomo as Nadine Cross; and Adam Storke as Larry Underwood. King himself had a small role, as trucker Teddy Weizak.

STAND BY FOR CRIME   ABC

22 JANUARY 1949–27 AUGUST 1949   Thirty-minute murder mysteries were presented on this series; at the climax of the show a guest "detective" tried to guess the identity of the killer. Telephone calls from home viewers were also aired during the show. The series was produced in Chicago by Greg Garrison. In May of 1949 Myron Wallace

was added as Lieutenant Kidd, Chief of Homicide, who showed the solution to the crime through the use of flashbacks. Wallace went on to greater fame, not as an actor but as a newsman—Mike Wallace.

STAND BY YOUR MAN   FOX
5 APRIL 1992–9 APRIL 1992   Half-hour sitcom about two New Jersey sisters who moved in together after their husbands were imprisoned for bank robbery. With Melissa Gilbert-Brinkman as Rochelle Dunphy, the wealthy sister; Rosie O'Donnell as Lorraine Popowski, who moved out of a trailer and into Rochelle's fancy house; Sam McMurray as Rochelle's husband, Roger Dunphy; Rick Hall as Lorraine's husband, Artie Popowski; Don Gibb as Scab; and Miriam Flynn as Adrienne, the sisters' neighbor. The series was based on the British sitcom *Birds of a Feather*.

STAND UP AND BE COUNTED   CBS
28 MAY 1956–6 SEPTEMBER 1957   On this unusual daytime audience participation show, preselected guests appeared and related a problem to the studio audience. Possible solutions to the problem were then suggested by members of the studio audience, who strode to the "rail of justice" to air their views. The entire audience then voted on the best solution propounded by the panel. One of television's few twenty-minute series, *Stand Up and Be Counted* was hosted by Bob Russell.

STAND UP AND CHEER   SYNDICATED
1971   On this half-hour musical series host Johnny Mann, together with the Johnny Mann Singers and assorted guests, sang the praises of the good old U.S.A.

STANDBY . . . LIGHTS! CAMERA! ACTION!   NICKELODEON
9 APRIL 1983–4 OCTOBER 1986   Leonard Nimoy hosted this children's show, which provided a behind-the-scenes look at movies and movie-making, as well as clips from newly released films.

STANLEY   NBC
24 SEPTEMBER 1956–11 MARCH 1957   Buddy Hackett starred in this half-hour sitcom as Stanley Peck, manager of a newsstand and ticket agency at a New York hotel. Also featured were Carol Burnett as Celia, his girlfriend; Frederic Tozere as Mr. Phillips, manager of the hotel; Tom Pedi; and Danny Dayton. Produced and directed by Max Liebman, the show was broadcast live from New York; the premiere episode was written by Billy Friedberg and Neil Simon.

STAR BLAZER   SYNDICATED
1979   A fifty-two-part series of half-hour cartoon shows made in Japan and set in outer space. The series was shown in Japan under the title *Space Cruiser Yamato*.

STAR GAMES   SYNDICATED
1985   Bruce Jenner and Pamela Sue Martin cohosted this hour sports show, on which cast members of two television series battled one another in various athletic endeavors. Dick Butkus refereed.

STAR NIGHT   NBC
25 FEBRUARY 1951–2 SEPTEMBER 1951   Bill Stern and Candy Jones cohosted this half-hour audience participation and variety series.

STAR OF THE FAMILY   CBS
22 SEPTEMBER 1950–26 JUNE 1952   The celebrity guests who appeared on this half-hour variety show were supposedly "nominated" by letters submitted by members of their families. Morton Downey hosted the series during the 1950–1951 season, and Peter Lind Hayes and Mary Healy were the cohosts during the 1951–1952 season.

STAR OF THE FAMILY   ABC

30 SEPTEMBER 1982–23 DECEMBER 1982   Half-hour sitcom about a crusty but lovable firefighter and his teenage daughter, a promising singer. With Brian Dennehy as Leslie "Buddy" Krebs, Captain of Engine Company 64; Kathy Maisnik as his sixteen-year-old daughter, Jennie; Michael Dudikoff as his thick son, Douggie; Todd Susman as firefighter Leo Feldman; George Deloy as firefighter Francis Rosetti; Danny Mora as firefighter Max; and Judy Pioli as Jennie's hefty road manager, Moose. Rick Mitz, author of *The Great TV Sitcom Book*, created the series with Stu Silver.

STAR SEARCH   SYNDICATED

1983–   Ed McMahon hosted this talent contest for hopeful singers, dancers, actors, and comics. Competition was held in eight categories: male actor, female actor, male vocalist, female vocalist, vocal group, dancer, comic, and model/spokesperson. Each week seven pairs of contestants competed in seven of those categories. The winning contestant, determined by a panel of judges, returned the following week to face a new challenger in that category. The longest-reigning champions in each of the eight categories were to return in the spring for the final competition to select the Best New Star of the year. In the fall of 1992 a five-day-a-week version of *Star Search* was introduced; it lasted only a few months, while the weekly series continued. By the mid-1990s, production had shifted to the Disney-MGM Studios in Orlando. In the fall of 1994 the program, now officially titled *Ed McMahon's Star Search*, added a male spokesmodel category. Former MTV vee-jay Martha Quinn emceed the vocal competition segments.

STAR STAGE   NBC

8 SEPTEMBER 1955–7 SEPTEMBER 1956   A Friday-night half-hour filmed dramatic anthology series of little note. Louise Beavers and Betty Grable costarred in one presentation, "Cleopatra Collins," broadcast 9 March.

STAR TIME   DUMONT

5 SEPTEMBER 1950–27 FEBRUARY 1951   An hour-long variety series cohosted by Frances Langford and Don Ameche, also featuring the Benny Goodman Sextet and Lew Parker.

STAR TONIGHT   ABC

3 FEBRUARY 1955–9 AUGUST 1956   The format of this half-hour dramatic anthology series was similar to that of *Hollywood Screen Test*—each week an unknown actor was teamed up with established professionals. Jacqueline Holt, for example, was showcased on the premiere. The series was produced by Harry Herrmann and was broadcast live from New York in 1955; by 1956 the series was filmed.

STAR TREK   NBC

8 SEPTEMBER 1966–2 SEPTEMBER 1969   One of the few series to prove more popular in reruns than in its three-year network run, *Star Trek* acquired a fiercely loyal cult following. Its devoted fans were almost certainly responsible for securing the show's renewal for a third season on NBC, having written more than one million letters to the network protesting its threatened cancellation. Surprisingly, the fans (commonly known as "Trekkers") remained loyal as the reruns went into syndication; several fans' conventions have been held, and more *Star Trek* merchandise was sold during the 1970s than during the late 1960s. For these reasons, *Star Trek* should probably be considered television's most popular adult science fiction series. Set in the twenty-third century aboard the starship *Enterprise*, *Star Trek*'s voyagers were commissioned by the United Federation of Planets to embark on a five-year mission to "seek out new life and new civilizations." Many of the seventy-nine episodes stressed the differences between humankind, an obviously imperfect but essentially noble species, and the other life forms, which ranged from gaseous beings to remarkably similar humanoids.

Though the *Enterprise* was designed to be staffed by a crew of 400, there were only eight principals in the cast: William Shatner as Captain James Kirk; Leonard Nimoy as Science Officer Spock, an extremely intelligent but coldly unemotional creature born of a Vulcan father and an Earthling mother; DeForest Kelley as Dr. Leonard "Bones" McCoy, the medical officer; James Doohan as Montgomery Scott (Scotty), the chief engineer; Nichelle Nichols as Lieutenant Uhura, the communications officer; George Takei as Mr. Sulu, the helmsman; Majel Barrett as Christine Chapel, chief nurse; and Walter Koenig (1967–1969) as Ensign Pavel Chekov, the navigator. During the first season Grace Lee Whitney was occasionally featured as Yeoman Janice Rand. *Star Trek* was created by Gene Roddenberry, who also served as executive producer. Gene Coon was the first producer and was succeeded by John Meredyth Lucas and Fred Freiberger. Special effects (which Roddenberry wisely refrained from overemphasizing) were created by the Howard Anderson Company, Film Effects of Hollywood, Jim Rugg, and the Westheimer Company. The pilot for the series (which starred Jeffrey Hunter as Captain Pike) was never televised in its entirety, though footage from it was used on a two-part episode, "The Menagerie." In 1973 an animated version of the series was introduced: see below. The series also spawned seven motion pictures made between 1979 and 1993, and a second TV series: see *Star Trek: The Next Generation*.

STAR TREK   NBC
8 SEPTEMBER 1973–30 AUGUST 1975   The Saturday-morning cartoon version of the 1966–1969 science fiction series (see above) featured the voices of seven of *Star Trek*'s principals: William Shatner, Leonard Nimoy, DeForest Kelley, Nichelle Nichols, George Takei, Majel Barrett, and James Doohan. Many of the episodes were based on stories originally televised on the prime-time show. Norm Prescott and Lou Scheimer produced the half-hour series.

STAR TREK: DEEP SPACE NINE   SYNDICATED
1993–   Spun off from *Star Trek: The Next Generation,* this hour sci-fi series was set far off in space, at a rundown space station orbiting the planet Bajor, which had been used for mining; it was also conveniently located near a "wormhole," a shortcut to unexplored parts of the galaxy. The cast included Avery Brooks as Commander Benjamin Sisko; Nana Visitor as the First Officer, Major Kira Nerys; Armin Shimerman as Quark, who ran the concessions; Siddig El Fadil as Doctor Julian Bashir (El Fadil changed his name to Alexander Siddig in 1995); Colm Meaney (formerly of *Star Trek: The Next Generation*) as Miles O'Brien, chief of operations; Rene Auberjonois as the security officer, Odo, a shape-shifting alien; Terry Farrell as Lieutenant Jadzia Dax, chief science officer, a "trill" whose human body was inhabited by a 300-year-old being; Cirroc Lofton as Jake Sisko, Benjamin's young son; and Rosalind Chao as Keiko O'Brien, wife of Miles. Michael Dorn joined the cast in the fall of 1995 as Worf, a Klingon (he'd played the same role on *Star Trek: The Next Generation*).

STAR TREK: THE NEXT GENERATION   SYNDICATED
1987–1994   The continuing popularity of the parent series in reruns, coupled with the success of the five *Star Trek* Motion pictures, led to the creation of this sequel series in 1987. Gene Roddenberry, who had created the original series, was the executive producer. The new series was set in the early twenty-fourth century, about eighty years after the prior series, aboard a new, and larger, starship *Enterprise*. The new cast included: Patrick Stewart as Captain Jean-Luc Picard; Jonathan Frakes as Commander William Riker; LeVar Burton as Lieutenant Geordi LaForge, the blind flight controller (and later chief engineer) who wore a special sensor which enabled him to "see" (the character was named to honor a real-life "Trekker," George La Forge, a handicapped fan who died in 1975); Denise Crosby (1987–1988) as security chief Tasha Yar; Gates McFadden (1987–1988; 1989–1994) as medical officer Dr. Beverly Crusher; Marina Sirtis as half-alien Starfleet Counselor Deanna Troi; Brent Spiner as Lieutenant Commander Data, an android; Michael Dorn as Lieutenant Worf, a Klingon; Wil Wheaton (1987–1990) as Beverly's son, Wesley, who became a crew member in the second season; Colm Meaney (1987–1992) as Transporter Chief

Miles O'Brien; Diana Muldaur (1988–1989) as medical officer Dr. Kate Pulaski; and Whoopi Goldberg (1988–1994, appearing occasionally) as Guinan, hostess of the Enterprise's lounge. One of the original *Star Trek* cast members, Majel Barrett (who was married to Gene Roddenberry), appeared occasionally as Deanna's mother, Lwaxana Troi (Barrett also supplied the voice of the *Enterprise*'s computer). Other notable guest stars included John de Lancie as the villainous Q, member of a super-race which despised humans; Leonard Nimoy (who guested as Spock in a two-part 1991 episode); Mae Jemison, America's first black female astronaut (who appeared in a 1993 episode; Jemison credited *Star Trek*'s Nichelle Nichols with inspiring her career); and physicist Stephen Hawking, who also appeared in a 1993 episode (playing a cosmic game of poker with Data, Albert Einstein, and Isaac Newton).

Star Trek: The Next Generation is a rare example of a sequel series which was more popular than its progenitor. *STTNG* spawned a spinoff in 1993 (series regular Colm Meaney joined it; see *Star Trek: Deep Space Nine*), and a successor series in 1995 (see *Star Trek: Voyager*). *STTNG*'s two-hour finale, televised in May 1994, was the highest rated syndicated program of the season. A feature film, *Star Trek Generations,* was released in 1994. It starred most of the cast of *The Next Generation,* as well as William Shatner as Captain Kirk.

STAR TREK: VOYAGER   UPN
16 JANUARY 1995–   Third of the *Star Trek* progeny, *Star Trek: Voyager* was the first series aired on the United Paramount Network (and the only one of the fledgling network's first offerings to be renewed for a second season). It was also the first of the *Star Trek* group in which the regular commanding officer was a woman. Its premise paid tribute to *Lost in Space,* as its central characters—the crew of the U.S.S. Voyager, a starship smaller than the Enterprise—took a cosmic wrong turn while pursuing the rebel Maquis; the two crews realized that they had to join forces in order to get themselves back to the right side of the galaxy. The cast included Kate Mulgrew as the commander, Captain Kathryn Janeway (Genevieve Bujold had originally been cast but quit after a few days); Robert Beltran as the new First Officer, the Native American Chakotay, who had been the Maquis leader; Roxann Biggs-Dawson as Chief Engineer B'Elanna Torres, who was half human and half Klingon; Robert Duncan McNeill as Lieutenant Tom Paris, the womanizing pilot; Tim Russ as the Vulcan security officer, Tuvok; Ethan Phillips as Neelix, the Talaxian cook; Jennifer Lien as Neelix's love interest, Kes, a one-year-old Ocampan (Ocampans had a life span of only nine years); Robert Picardo as the holographic Doc Zimmerman; and Garrett Wang as the communication officer, Ensign Harry Kim.

STARCADE   SYNDICATED
1983   Calling itself "TV's first video game arcade show," this half-hour series was hosted by Geoff Edwards. Each week two youngsters (or, occasionally, two parent-child teams) competed at various video arcade games for the chance to win prizes such as home computers or the games themselves.

STARCOM   SYNDICATED
1987   Cartoon series set in space, on which the good guys of Starcom battled the evil Emperor Dark.

THE STARLAND VOCAL BAND SHOW   CBS
31 JULY 1977–2 SEPTEMBER 1977   A limited-run half-hour variety series hosted by the Starland Vocal Band (Bill Danoff, Taffy Danoff, Jon Carroll, and Margot Chapman) and taped on location at several sites, including Washington, D.C. Additional regulars included Phil Proctor and Peter Bergman (formerly of the Firesign Theater), Washington satirist Mark Russell, Jeff Altman, and Dave Letterman. The Starland Vocal Band was given the summer series primarily on the strong showing of one hit record, "Afternoon Delight." Jerry Weintraub was the executive producer, and Al Rogers was the producer.

STARLIGHT THEATER CBS
2 APRIL 1950–4 OCTOBER 1951   A half-hour dramatic anthology series produced by Robert Stevens and directed by John Peyser. During the 1950–1951 season it alternated biweekly with *The Burns and Allen Show*.

STARLIT TIME DUMONT
9 APRIL 1950–19 NOVEMBER 1950   This Sunday-night musical revue was the successor to *Front Row Center* and retained many of its regulars. *Starlit Time* featured Phil Hanna, Bill Williams, Allen Prescott, Gordon Dillworth, Bibi Osterwald, Holly Harris, and the Cy Coleman Trio. Bela Lugosi made a very rare guest appearance on the show (21 May).

STARLOST SYNDICATED
1973   Created by Harlan Ellison and produced in Canada, this hour-long science fiction series was set in the twenty-eighth century. Traveling through space in a large spacecraft were the three principals: Keir Dullea as Devon, Gay Rowan as Rachel (Devon's beloved), and Robin Ward as Garth (the man who had intended to marry Rachel). Disappointed with the results, Ellison had his name removed from the credits (the pseudonym of Cordwainer Bird was given for the creator).

STARMAN ABC
19 SEPTEMBER 1986–4 SEPTEMBER 1987   Hour sci-fi series derived from the 1984 motion picture. Robert Hays starred as Starman, a creature from another planet who had visited Earth and fathered a son fourteen years earlier; he returned to Earth to rescue his now-orphaned son (whose stepparents had died) and to look for the boy's mother, Jenny. Upon his return, Starman assumed the identity of photographer Paul Forrester, who had been killed in a helicopter crash. Also featured were C. B. Barnes as the son, Scott Hayden, who helped his father learn about Earth customs; and Michael Cavanaugh as George Fox of the Federal Security Agency, who pursued Starman. In a two-part finale (4 and 11 April) Paul and Scott found Jenny (played by Erin Gray) in Arizona.

STARRING BORIS KARLOFF ABC
22 SEPTEMBER 1949–15 DECEMBER 1949   Boris Karloff hosted and occasionally starred in this half-hour mystery anthology series, which was directed by Alex Segal.

STARS IN KHAKI AND BLUE NBC
13 SEPTEMBER 1952–27 SEPTEMBER 1952   Wendy Barrie hosted this prime-time talent show for members of the Armed Forces. Craig G. Allen directed the half-hour series.

STARS OF JAZZ ABC
18 APRIL 1958–30 NOVEMBER 1958   Half-hour musical series, hosted by trumpeter Bobby Troup, and featuring guest artists from the world of jazz.

STARS ON PARADE DUMONT
4 NOVEMBER 1953–30 JUNE 1954   Half-hour prime-time variety show featuring talent from the armed forces, as well as civilian acts. Don Russell was the first host of the show, but was succeeded by Bobby Sherwood on the third telecast.

STARS OVER HOLLYWOOD NBC
6 SEPTEMBER 1950–29 AUGUST 1951   This half-hour filmed dramatic anthology series was seen on Wednesday nights. One 1950 program, "Grady Everett for the People," was the first script written by Rod Serling; it was bought for $100.

STARSKY AND HUTCH ABC
10 SEPTEMBER 1975–21 AUGUST 1979   A popular, and comparatively violent, hour-long crime show about a pair of undercover cops. With Paul Michael Glaser as Dave Starsky; David Soul as his partner, Ken Hutchinson; Bernie Hamilton as their com-

manding officer, Captain Harold Dobey; and Antonio Fargas as their street contact, Huggy Bear. William Blinn created the series, and Aaron Spelling and Leonard Goldberg were the executive producers.

THE START OF SOMETHING BIG SYNDICATED
1985–1986   Hour documentary series hosted by Steve Allen (whose many musical compositions included "This Could Be the Start of Something Big"), consisting of interviews with celebrities about their origins in showbiz and segments explaining the origins of various products.

STARTING FROM SCRATCH SYNDICATED
1988–1989   Predictable half-hour sitcom starring Bill Daily as James Shepherd, a divorced veterinarian raising two teenagers, and Connie Stevens as Helen, his meddlesome ex-wife. With Heidi Helmer as daughter Kate; Jason Marin as son Robbie; and Nita Talbot as Rose, James's assistant.

STAT ABC
16 APRIL 1991–21 MAY 1991   Created by Danny Arnold and reminiscent of his 1978 series, *A.E.S. Hudson Street,* this was a medical sitcom set at Hudson Memorial Hospital in New York. It featured Dennis Boutsikaris as senior resident Tony Menzies; Alison LaPlaca as first-year resident Elizabeth Newberry; Alix Elias as Jeanette Lemp; Casey Biggs as Dr. Lewis "Cowboy" Doniger; Ron Canada as Nurse Anderson "Mary" Roche; Dannel Arnold as Dr. Werner; Julio Oscar Mechoso as orderly Julio Oscar; and Wren T. Brown as Dr. Ron Murphy. Costars Boutsikaris and LaPlaca would later work together on *The Jackie Thomas Show.*

STATE TROOPER SYNDICATED
1957   Half-hour crime show starring Rod Cameron as Nevada State Trooper Rod Blake. Much of the series was filmed in Las Vegas.

STEP BY STEP ABC
20 SEPTEMBER 1991–   This sitcom borrowed its premise from *The Brady Bunch:* two single parents, each with three kids, get married and blend themselves into one happy family. Set in Port Washington, Wisconsin, it featured Patrick Duffy as divorced contractor Frank Lambert; Suzanne Somers as widow Carol Foster, who operated a beauty shop with her mother and sister; Staci Keanan as Dana Foster; Angela Watson as Karen Foster; Brandon Call as J. T. Lambert; Christine Lakin as Alicia "Al" Lambert; Josh Byrne as Brendan Lambert; Christopher Castile as Mark Foster; Patrika Darbo as Carol's sister, Penny Williams; and Peggy Rea as Carol's mother, Ivy Williams. Sasha Mitchell joined the cast later in the fall of 1991 as Frank's nephew, Cody.

STEP THIS WAY ABC/SYNDICATED
9 JULY 1955–14 APRIL 1956 (ABC); 1966 (SYNDICATED)   *Step This Way* was a half-hour dance contest. The 1955 version was hosted by Bobby Sherwood and featured the Nat Brandwynne Orchestra. The 1966 version was hosted by Gretchen Wyler and featured singer Jim Lucas; music was supplied by Warren Covington and his band, and later by Ray McKinley and his band.

THE STEPHANIE MILLER SHOW SYNDICATED
1995   Although several new syndicated daytime talk shows were introduced in 1995, *The Stephanie Miller Show* was aimed at late-night viewers. Hosted by former disc jockey Stephanie Miller, the short-lived hour show was comprised of celebrity interviews and comedy sketches. Fellow talker Danny Bonaduce filled in for Miller during the series' final week.

STEPHEN KING'S GOLDEN YEARS
See GOLDEN YEARS

STEPHEN KING'S THE STAND
See THE STAND

STEVE ALLEN PRESENTS STEVE LAWRENCE AND EYDIE GORMÉ   NBC
13 JULY 1958–31 AUGUST 1958   Steve Lawrence and Eydie Gormé, who had been featured vocalists on Steve Allen's *Tonight* show, were given their own series in 1958, a summer replacement for Steve Allen's Sunday-night variety show. Also featured were Gene Rayburn, the Artie Malvin Singers, and the Jack Kane Orchestra.

THE STEVE ALLEN SHOW   CBS/NBC/ABC/SYNDICATED
25 DECEMBER 1950–22 FEBRUARY 1952 (CBS); 17 JULY 1952–28 AUGUST 1952 (CBS); 24 JUNE 1956–6 JUNE 1960 (NBC); 27 SEPTEMBER 1961–27 DECEMBER 1961 (ABC); 1962–1964 (SYNDICATED); 14 JUNE 1967–16 AUGUST 1967 (CBS); 1967–1969 (SYNDICATED); 1976 (SYNDICATED)   Steve Allen is not only one of the busiest performers in television, but he is also one of the most versatile people in show business. In addition to hosting several TV series, he has also starred in films (*The Benny Goodman Story*), on Broadway (*The Pink Elephant*), and in summer stock (*The Fourposter*), has written at least a dozen books and several television scripts, has composed hundreds of songs (to win a bet with singer Frankie Laine, he once "composed" 350 songs in one week), has played several musical instruments, and has had time left over to deliver an occasional lecture or do a little sculpture.

In 1948 Allen was working at KNX radio in Los Angeles, where his late-night radio show began to attract a studio audience and unscheduled visits by celebrities; it was here that Allen first began to interview members of the studio audience, a device he has continued to use effectively in most of his TV shows. Allen also hosted a radio giveaway show, *Earn Your Vacation* (Johnny Carson would later emcee the TV version). In 1950 he was brought East to New York for the first of his TV shows. *The Steve Allen Show* began as an evening show, broadcast Mondays through Fridays at 7:00 P.M. After thirteen weeks he moved to a daytime slot, and the show remained on the air for another year; the show was directed by Fred Kelly, and in 1952 featured singer Peggy Lee, announcer Bern Bennett, and a llama named Llemuel. By the time the daytime show left the air, Allen had substituted for Arthur Godfrey on *Talent Scouts* and had hosted a prime-time musical show, *Songs for Sale*. During the summer of 1952 he hosted a prime-time half-hour show on alternate Thursdays. In 1953 he hosted *Talent Patrol* on ABC and later began a local late-night talk show; in the summer of 1954 Allen's local show went network, and the *Tonight* show was born.

The nightly pace of the *Tonight* show did not seem to slow Allen down, however. In the summer of 1956 he agreed to host a variety show opposite *The Ed Sullivan Show* on Sunday nights. The second *Steve Allen Show* premiered on 24 June, with guests Kim Novak, Sammy Davis, Jr., Dane Clark, Wally Cox, Vincent Price, and Bambi Linn and Rod Alexander. Elvis Presley also appeared that summer, and Allen's use of big name guest stars provoked a long-running feud between Sullivan and Allen. Though both shows were variety hours, the difference between them was considerable, as Allen's hour emphasized humor. Allen assembled a talented group of young funny men, who appeared in the well-remembered "Man in the Street" sequences and in the other comedy sketches. Over the years the group included Don Knotts, Tom Poston, Louis Nye, Gabe Dell, Pat Harrington, Jr., Dayton Allen, Cal Howard, and Bill Dana. Allen's writers at the time included Leonard Stern, Stan Burns, Herb Sargent, Bill Dana, Don Hinkley, Arne Sultan, and Marvin Worth.

Though the Sunday-night show rarely outdrew Sullivan's show on a weekly basis, it did succeed in making a significant dent in Sullivan's ratings; *The Ed Sullivan Show* slipped from the second top-rated show during the 1956–1957 season to the nineteenth during the next season. Allen, who gave up his *Tonight* show hosting chores early in 1957, later took his variety show to the West Coast; during the 1959–1960 season the show was seen on Monday nights.

After a season's absence Allen returned to TV, this time on ABC. *The New Steve Allen Show* was a lot like the old Steve Allen show and featured Louis Nye, Don Knotts, Pat Harrington, Jr., Gabe Dell, and Dayton Allen; slotted on Wednesdays opposite *Wagon Train,* it was gone in thirteen weeks. A year later Allen returned to the talk-show format, hosting a daily ninety-minute show for Westinghouse; in many markets the show was scheduled opposite the *Tonight* show that Allen had started eight years earlier (Johnny Carson had since taken over as host). Allen later hosted *I've Got A Secret* for three seasons, and in the summer of 1967 he emceed *The Steve Allen Comedy Hour;* that series featured Jayne Meadows (Steve's wife), Louis Nye, Ruth Buzzi, John Byner, Ron Carey, and the Terry Gibbs Band. Toward the end of 1967 he again hosted a syndicated, ninety-minute talk show. He later hosted a series of musical performances for educational television, *The Sounds of Summer,* and in 1972 he presided over the short-lived syndicated revival of *I've Got a Secret.* In 1976 he again returned to the syndication arena as the host of *Steve Allen's Laughback;* on that ninety-minute show Allen, Jayne Meadows, and guests reminisced over kinescopes and film clips of Allen's old shows. Allen also wrote and hosted a series for PBS, *Meeting of Minds,* a kind of historical talk show on which actors, appearing as historical figures from different eras, discussed issues. See also *I've Got A Secret; Songs for Sale; Talent Patrol; Tonight;* and *What's My Line?*

STEVE CANYON   NBC
13 SEPTEMBER 1958–8 SEPTEMBER 1959   Steve Canyon, the fearless Air Force pilot created by cartoonist Milton Caniff in 1948, came to life for one season. Produced by David Haft and Michael Meshekoff, the half-hour series was set at Big Thunder Air Force Base and starred Dean Fredericks (who actually resembled the cartoon prototype) as Lieutenant Colonel Stevenson B. Canyon. Jerry Paris was occasionally seen as Major Willie Williston, and Abel Fernandez appeared as Police Chief Hagedorn.

STEVE DONOVAN, WESTERN MARSHAL   SYNDICATED
1955   Half-hour western set in Wyoming during the 1870s, with Doug Kennedy as Marshal Steve Donovan and Eddy Waller as his sidekick, Rusty Lee. The series was also shown under the title *Western Marshal.*

THE STEVE LAWRENCE AND EYDIE GORMÉ SHOW
See STEVE ALLEN PRESENTS STEVE LAWRENCE AND EYDIE GORMÉ

THE STEVE LAWRENCE SHOW   CBS
13 SEPTEMBER 1965–13 DECEMBER 1965   Steve Lawrence's Monday-night variety hour lasted only thirteen weeks. Other regulars included comics Charles Nelson Reilly and Betty Walker, the Pussycat Dancers, the Dick Williams Singers, and the Joe Guercio Orchestra. The series was taped principally in New York.

THE STEVEN BANKS SHOW   PBS
1994   A rarity for public television, *The Steven Banks Show* was an American-produced comedy program. Comedian/musician Steven Banks starred, playing himself, a single guy in his thirties who lived in a cluttered apartment. The other regulars were Teresa Parente and Michael Kostroff, who played several different characters during the series' thirteen-episode run.

STILL THE BEAVER
See THE NEW LEAVE IT TO BEAVER

STINGRAY   SYNDICATED
1965   Stingray was another of the half-hour puppet adventure shows produced in England by Gerry and Sylvia Anderson (creators of *Fireball XL-5, Supercar,* and *Thunderbirds*); all utilized a process known as Supermarionation. *Stingray* was set aboard a futuristic submarine, whose crew battled the usual assortment of wrongdoers, despots, and invaders.

STINGRAY   NBC
4 MARCH 1986–22 AUGUST 1986; 9 JANUARY 1987–31 JULY 1987   Although television has had its share of heroes with only one name (Paladin, Columbo, Quincy, and Spenser, to cite a few), creator Stephen J. Cannell invented a protagonist with no

name at all for this hour action series. The solitary hero, played by Nick Mancuso, was known only by the car he drove: a 1965 Corvette Stingray. He tooled around, stopping to help people in distress; Stingray asked for no money in return, but reserved the right to request a return favor from those he helped. One of the most interesting features of the show was its closing credits, which showed members of the series' crew at work, setting up shots from that evening's episode. The pilot for the series was telecast 14 July 1985.

STIR CRAZY   CBS
18 SEPTEMBER 1985–23 OCTOBER 1985; 17 DECEMBER 1985–7 JANUARY 1986   A short-lived comedy-adventure series inspired by the 1980 movie. Joe Guzaldo and Larry Riley starred as Skip Harrington and Harry Fletcher, two pals (one white, one black) who were wrongly imprisoned for murder in Texas, escaped from a chain gang, and set out to find the real killer, the tattooed Crawford (played by Marc Silver). Chasing them was Captain Betty Phillips (played by Jeannie Wilson).

STOCK CAR DERBY   NBC
28 JANUARY 1950–11 MARCH 1950   This late-night series offered coverage of the races from the Kingsbridge Armory in the Bronx; Herb Sheldon provided the commentary.

THE STOCKARD CHANNING SHOW   CBS
24 MARCH 1980–28 JUNE 1980   Stockard Channing starred in this half-hour series, her second sitcom in as many years (she had headlined in *Just Friends* in 1979). Here she appeared as Susan Goodenow, a single woman who landed a job at a TV station assisting its consumer advocate. Also featured were Jack Somack as Mr. Kramer, Susan's landlord; Ron Silver as egotistical Brad Gabriel, the consumer advocate; Max Showalter as Gus Kline, the station manager; and Sydney Goldsmith as her neighbor and coworker, Earlene Cunningham.

STONE   ABC
14 JANUARY 1980–17 MARCH 1980   Hour crime show starring Dennis Weaver as Sergeant Daniel Ellis Stone, a cop and a writer, with Bobby Weaver (his real-life son) as his young partner, Buck Rogers.

STONEY BURKE   ABC
1 OCTOBER 1962–2 SEPTEMBER 1963   One of two modern-day westerns introduced in 1962 (*Wide Country* was the other), *Stoney Burke* starred Jack Lord in the title role as a rodeo performer. Also featured were Bruce Dern as E. J. Stocker; Bill Hart as Red; Warren Oates as Ves Painter; and Robert Dowdell as Cody Bristol. Leslie Stevens produced the hour-long series for Daystar Productions.

STOP ME IF YOU'VE HEARD THIS ONE   NBC
5 MARCH 1948–22 APRIL 1949   Half-hour game show, based on the radio program, on which celebrity panelists tried to supply punch lines to jokes submitted by home viewers. Ira Skutch produced the show, which was hosted first by Ted Brown, and later by Leon Janney. Panelists included Lew Lahr, Morey Amsterdam, Cal Tinney, Mae Questel, and Benny Rubin.

STOP THE MUSIC   ABC
5 MAY 1949–24 APRIL 1952; 7 SEPTEMBER 1954–14 JUNE 1956   A prime-time game show, *Stop the Music* came to television a year after it began on radio. For most of its run it was hosted by Bert Parks, though Dennis James filled in occasionally. The game involved identification of songs by members of the studio audience and by home viewers, who were telephoned during the broadcast. Featured vocalists over the years included Kay Armen, Jimmy Blaine, Betty Ann Grove, Estelle Loring, Jaye P. Morgan, and June Valli; rounding out the group of regulars were dancers Sonja and Courtney Van Horne, cartoonist Chuck Luchsinger, and the orchestra of

Harry Salter. Louis G. Cowan, who later developed *The $64,000 Question,* packaged the half-hour series.

THE STOREFRONT LAWYERS (MEN AT LAW)   CBS
16 SEPTEMBER 1970–1 SEPTEMBER 1971   This hour-long dramatic series began with three stars: Robert Foxworth as David Hanson, Sheila Larken as Deborah Sullivan, and David Arkin as Gabe Kaye. The three were members of a Los Angeles law firm but also operated Neighborhood Legal Services, a nonprofit law clinic. In midseason the format was changed slightly, the show was retitled *Men at Law,* and Gerald S. O'Loughlin was added as attorney Devlin McNeil, a senior partner at Horton, Troy, McNeil, and Carroll. Leonard Freeman was the executive producer.

STORIES OF THE CENTURY   SYNDICATED
1954   Half-hour western about a pair of detectives for the Southwestern Railroad. With Jim Davis as Matt Clark; Mary Castle as his first partner, Frankie Adams; Kristine Miller as his second partner, Jonesy. *Stories of the Century* was one of the first syndicated series to win a major Emmy award; it was named the best western or adventure series of 1954.

THE STORK CLUB   CBS/ABC
7 JULY 1950–31 OCTOBER 1953 (CBS); 11 SEPTEMBER 1954–24 JULY 1955 (ABC) Sherman Billingsley hosted this variety show, telecast from the fourth floor of The Stork Club, a Manhattan night club which Billingsley had opened in 1934. Peter Lind Hayes and Mary Healy were also featured in the early weeks. *The Stork Club* began as a fifteen-minute show and was first telecast five nights a week. In January 1951 it was cut back to twice weekly, and in the fall of 1952 it became a once-a-week, half-hour show.

STORY FOR AMERICANS   CBS
6 JULY 1952–2 NOVEMBER 1952   A Sunday-afternoon anthology series that dramatized incidents from American history.

THE STORY OF . . .   SYNDICATED
1962   A half-hour anthology series from David Wolper Productions and United Artists, *The Story Of* . . . was advertised as a "semidocumentary." John Willis narrated the filmed series.

THE STORY OF ENGLISH   PBS
15 SEPTEMBER 1986–10 NOVEMBER 1986   Highly acclaimed nine-part documentary series on the English language—its origins, evolution, usage, and popularity—hosted by Robert MacNeil.

STORY THEATER   DUMONT/NBC
24 NOVEMBER 1950–11 MAY 1951 (DUMONT); 24 JUNE 1951–17 SEPTEMBER 1951 (NBC)   Half-hour filmed dramatic anthology series.

STORY THEATRE   SYNDICATED
1971   *Story Theatre* was an unusual anthology series, based on the Broadway show of the same title. The half-hour show featured a large repertory company, the members of which acted out various fables, parables, and other stories. Paul Sills directed both the stage and the television versions; the series was taped in British Columbia. Among the members of the repertory company were Peter Bonerz, Paul Sand, Richard Schaal, Bob Dishy, Hamilton Camp, Melinda Dillon, Richard Libertini, Eugene Troobnick, and Severn Darden.

THE STORYBOOK SQUARES   NBC
4 JANUARY 1969–30 AUGUST 1969   *The Storybook Squares* was a children's edition of *The Hollywood Squares;* the Saturday-morning show was hosted by Peter Marshall.

The principal difference was that the nine celebrity panelists were costumed on *The Storybook Squares*.

STRAIGHTAWAY ABC

6 OCTOBER 1961–4 JULY 1962   This half-hour adventure series starred Brian Kelly as Scott Ross and John Ashley as Clipper Hamilton, the partners who ran the Straight-away Garage, an exclusive garage for race car drivers and other exciting people. The series was beset with production problems, having gone through three producers before the first episode was televised; Joe Shaftel was the fourth producer. It was to have been titled *The Racers,* with Autolite Spark Plugs as its sponsor. In the summer of 1961 Autolite was absorbed by the Ford Motor Company, which then insisted that the racing angle be deemphasized. Maynard Ferguson composed the music for the series.

STRANGE LUCK FOX

15 SEPTEMBER 1995–   Offbeat hour series starring D. B. Sweeney as Chance Harper. As a young child, Harper had been the only survivor of a plane crash; as an adult, he discovered that luck—good and bad—seemed to follow him. He embarked upon a career as a photojournalist, because of his propensity to be present where unusual events occurred. He also discovered that he had an older brother who had not been killed in the air crash, and set out to find him. Also featured were Pamela Gidley as Audrey Westin, Harper's ex-girlfriend, who was the photo editor of a newspaper and often gave him assignments; Cynthia Martells as Dr. Richter, a police psychiatrist who befriended Harper; and Frances Fisher as Angie, the waitress at Harper's favorite hangout, the Blue Plate Cafe.

STRANGE PARADISE SYNDICATED

1969   One of television's few syndicated serials, *Strange Paradise* was an imitation of *Dark Shadows.* Set at Maljardin Island, a mysterious Caribbean isle, its story lines dealt with voodoo, communication with spirits, and family curses. The cast included: Colin Fox as Jean Paul Desmond, owner of Desmond Hall, and as Jacques Eloi Des Mondes, an ancestor; Tudi Wiggins as his wife, Erica Desmond, who died—once—and returned to life; Dawn Greenhalgh as Erica's sister, Dr. Alison Carr, a visitor to Maljardin; Jon Granik as Dan Forrest; Bruce Gray as artist Tim Stanton; Sylvia Feigel as Holly Marshall; Paisley Maxwell as Holly's mother, Elizabeth Marshall; Dan MacDonald as Reverend Matt Dawson; Costee Lee as Raxl, an island priestess; Kurt Schiegl as Quito; Patricia Collins as Huaco; Peg Dixon as Ada; Pat Moffat as Irene; Jack Creley as Laslo; Lucy Warner as Emily; David Wells as Cort; and Neil Dainard as Philip. Videotaped in color, the half-hour series was produced in Canada.

STRANGE REPORT NBC

8 JANUARY 1971–10 SEPTEMBER 1971   British import about a trio of criminologists, with Anthony Quayle as widower Adam Strange; Kaz Garas as Ham Gynt; and Anneke Wills as Evelyn McClain. The hour series was a midseason replacement for *Bracken's World.*

STRANGE STORIES SYNDICATED

1956   Edward Arnold hosted this half-hour anthology series of supernatural tales.

THE STRANGER DUMONT

25 JUNE 1954–11 FEBRUARY 1955   Frank Telford produced and directed this half-hour series, which is reminiscent of *The Millionaire.* It starred Bob Carroll as The Stranger, a mysterious individual who appeared each week to help someone in distress.

THE STRAUSS FAMILY ABC

5 MAY 1973–16 JUNE 1973   ABC imported this seven-part series from England. It traced the lives of the famous composers over a seventy-five-year period. Principal players included: Eric Woolfe as Johann Strauss, Sr.; Anne Stallybrass as Anna, his

wife; Stuart Wilson as Johann Strauss, Jr.; Barbara Ferris as Emilie; Derek Jacobi as Lanner; Lynn Farleigh as Adele; and Tony Anholt as Eduard.

STRAWHAT MATINEE NBC
25 JUNE 1951–7 SEPTEMBER 1951   A summer replacement for *The Kate Smith Show, Strawhat Matinee* was broadcast from Cincinnati and featured country-and-western music. Principal vocalists included Mel Martin, Rosemary Olberding, and Dick and Pat.

THE STRAWHATTERS DUMONT
27 MAY 1953–9 SEPTEMBER 1953; 23 JUNE 1954–8 SEPTEMBER 1954   Johnny Olson hosted this summer variety show, broadcast from Palisades Park, New Jersey. The half-hour series was produced by Roger Gerry and directed by Frank Bunetta.

THE STREET SYNDICATED
1988   An unusual half-hour crime show, produced on location in Newark, N.J., *The Street* used a video verité style (and lots of four-letter words) as it focused on the lives of four police officers. Appearing were Bruce MacVittie as Bud Peluso; Stanley Tucci as Arthur Scolari, his partner on the night shift; Ron J. Ryan as Jack Runyon; and Michael Beach as Shepard Scott, his partner on the graveyard shift.

STREET HAWK ABC
4 JANUARY 1985–8 MARCH 1985; 2 MAY 1985–16 MAY 1985   Hour crime show, with an emphasis on vehicular hardware. The series starred Rex Smith as Jesse Mach, an ex-motorcycle cop who was recruited by the government for special missions and rode the Street Hawk, a super-powered cycle: it could travel at speeds up to 300 m.p.h., it could go on any terrain, it had a .50 caliber machine gun and a special "blue ray" particle beam weapon. Mach kept his cover as a public relations officer with the police department. Also featured were Joe Regalbuto as Norman Tuttle, inventor of the Street Hawk, the only person who knew of Mach's dual role; Richard Venture as Commander Leo Altobelli, Mach's boss on the police force, who wanted to apprehend Street Hawk; and Jeannie Wilson as Officer Rachel Adams.

STREET JUSTICE SYNDICATED
1991–1993   Hour crime show, filmed in Vancouver, with Carl Weathers as Sergeant Adam Beaudreaux; Charlene Fernetz as Malloy, who co-owned a local bar with Beaudreaux; Bryan Genesse as Grady Jamieson, who worked at the bar and lived with Beaudreaux; and Leam Blackwood as Beaudreaux's boss, Lieutenant Charles Pine.

STREET MATCH ABC
28 JULY 1993–1 SEPTEMBER 1993   This unusual prime time series was a revamped version of *The Dating Game.* Host Ricky Paull Goldin roamed the streets of various cities, introducing strangers to each other, and accompanying them on their first dates.

STREET PEOPLE SYNDICATED
1971   A half-hour series with almost no format—host Mal Sharpe merely interviewed people, or asked them to tell jokes or sing or whatever; the show was filmed on location throughout the United States.

STREET STORIES CBS
9 JANUARY 1992–6 AUGUST 1993   Hour investigative series, hosted by Ed Bradley, with regular contributors Harold Dow, Bob McKeown, Bernard Goldberg, and Victoria Corderi.

STREETS OF DANGER
See THE LONE WOLF

THE STREETS OF SAN FRANCISCO   ABC

16 SEPTEMBER 1972–23 JUNE 1977   This hour-long crime show was filmed entirely on location in San Francisco. It starred Karl Malden as Detective Lieutenant Mike Stone, a streetwise veteran; Michael Douglas as his young partner, Inspector Steve Keller; and Lee Harris as Lieutenant Lessing. Michael Douglas left the show at the outset of the 1976–1977 season (it was explained that he had decided to pursue a teaching career), and Richard Hatch was added in the fall of 1976 as Stone's new partner, Inspector Dan Robbins. The series was developed by Edward Hume and was based on a novel by Carolyn Weston. Quinn Martin was the executive producer. On 27 January 1992 NBC aired a two-hour telefilm, "Back to the Streets of San Francisco," starring Malden as Stone, investigating Keller's disappearance.

STRIKE FORCE   ABC

13 NOVEMBER 1981–23 APRIL 1982   Hour crime show starring Robert Stack as Captain Frank Murphy, head of the Strike Force, an elite unit of the Los Angeles Police Department. Also on hand were Richard Romanus as Charlie Gunzer; Trisha Noble as Rosie; Dorian Harewood as Paul; Michael Goodwin as Mark Osborn; and Herb Edelman as Murphy's commanding officer, Detective Commander Herb Klein.

STRIKE IT RICH   CBS

7 MAY 1951–3 JANUARY 1958   *Strike It Rich*, which began on radio in 1947, was a game show not unlike *Queen for a Day*. Each day a succession of needy people came on; whoever told the most woeful story (as determined by the studio audience) was the day's winner. The show also featured a perfunctory quiz segment, and the "Heart Line," where viewers could call in with offers of aid for any of the contestants. The show aroused the wrath of the New York City Welfare Department early in 1954, when it was disclosed that in 1953 some fifty-five families had come to New York, hoping to get on the show, and had remained in New York and gone on welfare. *Strike It Rich* was hosted by Warren Hull; the daytime version of the half-hour series ran from May 1951 to January 1958, while a nighttime version was broadcast between July 1951 and January 1955. Walt Framer was the producer.

STRIKE IT RICH   SYNDICATED

1986   This game show bore no resemblance to the 1950s series of the same title. Joe Garagiola hosted the show, on which two couples competed, moving across a series of arches onstage by answering multiple choice questions correctly.

STRUCK BY LIGHTNING   CBS

19 SEPTEMBER 1979–3 OCTOBER 1979   A short-lived sitcom that was pulled from the air after only three showings, *Struck By Lightning* was set at the Brightwater Inn in Maine, where Frankenstein's monster worked as the handyman. The half-hour series featured Jeffrey Kramer as Ted Stein, a science teacher from Boston who inherited the inn from his late grandfather and subsequently learned that he was a descendant of *the* Frankensteins; Jack Elam as Frank, the 231-year-old monster; Millie Slavin as Nora, who worked at the inn and had expected to inherit it; Bill Erwin as Glenn, one of the inn's guests; Jeff Cotler as Brian, Nora's young son; and Richard Stahl as Walt Calvin, the local realtor. Arthur Fellows and Terry Keegan were the executive producers.

THE STRUGGLE FOR DEMOCRACY   PBS

11 JULY 1989–12 SEPTEMBER 1989   A timely look at the evolution of the democratic form of government. The series' host, Canadian journalist Patrick Watson, visited thirty nations for the ten-part series.

STRYKER OF SCOTLAND YARD   SYNDICATED

1957   Half-hour crime show from England, starring Clifford Evans as Inspector Robert Stryker of Scotland Yard.

THE STU ERWIN SHOW   ABC

21 OCTOBER 1950–13 APRIL 1955   One of TV's first filmed sitcoms, *The Stu Erwin Show* helped set the pace for dozens of comedies to come—it featured a bumbling father, his loving and level-headed wife, and two irrepressible kids. Stu Erwin (playing himself) starred as the principal of Hamilton High School. Also on hand were June Collyer (Erwin's real-life wife and Bud Collyer's sister) as his wife, June Erwin; Ann Todd and Merry Anders as their older daughter, Joyce; Sheila James as their younger daughter, Jackie; Martin Milner as Joyce's boyfriend (and husband in the final season), Jimmy Clark; and Willie Best as Willie, the Erwins' handyman. Produced by Hal Roach, Jr., the half-hour series was aired under several other titles during its network run and later in syndication—*Life with the Erwins, The New Stu Erwin Show,* and *The Trouble with Father.*

STUDIO 59

See INTO THE NIGHT STARRING RICK DEES

STUDIO 57   DUMONT/SYNDICATED

21 SEPTEMBER 1954–26 JULY 1955 (DUMONT); 1955–1956 (SYNDICATED) A half-hour dramatic anthology series from Revue Studios, sponsored by Heinz 57 Varieties.

STUDIO 5B   ABC

24 JANUARY 1989–5 FEBRUARY 1989   Only three episodes of this hour dramatic series were televised. It was supposed to provide a behind-the-scenes look at a fictional popular network morning television show, *Studio 5B*. Its dismal ratings (the series finished in a tie for last place among all prime-time shows for the season) suggested that American viewers are not really interested in what happens behind the screen. The cast included Wendy Crewson as producer Gail Browning; Kerrie Keane as anchor Carla Montgomery; Kim Myers as rookie production assistant Samantha Hurley; Justin Deas as Carla's ex-boyfriend, Jake; Jeffrey Tambor as Lionel, the executive producer; Kenneth David Gilman as David, the senior producer; Kate Zentell as Rosemary; George Grizzard as Douglas Hayward; and William Thomas, Jr., as Woody.

STUDIO ONE   CBS

7 NOVEMBER 1948–29 SEPTEMBER 1958   *Studio One* was one of the oldest, and most highly acclaimed, of the several dramatic anthology series that comprised television's "Golden Age." The hour-long series was produced by Worthington "Tony" Miner from 1948 until 1952, and was later produced by Herbert Brodkin. Many directors worked on *Studio One* at one time or another, but Franklin Schaffner and Paul Nickell, who alternated biweekly during part of the show's ten-year-run, were especially closely associated with it. Other prominent directors who were involved with *Studio One* included Yul Brynner, George Roy Hill, Sidney Lumet, and Robert Mulligan. *Studio One* was broadcast live from New York until January of 1958, when production shifted to the West Coast (and the show was retitled *Studio One in Hollywood*); the show left the air a few months later. A sampling of the many presentations from *Studio One* would include: "The Storm," with Margaret Sullavan (7 November 1948); a 1949 production of "Mary Poppins," with Mary Wickes, E. G. Marshall, and Valerie Cossart; "Of Human Bondage," with Charlton Heston and Felicia Montealegre (Maugham's story was adapted by Sumner Locke Elliott, and broadcast 21 November 1949); "The Rockingham Tea Set," with Grace Kelly (23 January 1950); "The Taming of the Shrew," with Charlton Heston and Lisa Kirk (5 June 1950); "Macbeth," with Charlton Heston and Judith Evelyn (22 October 1951); "The Kill," with Grace Kelly (22 September 1952); "The Laugh Maker," with Jackie Gleason (18 May 1953, in a rare dramatic appearance); "Sentence of Death," with James Dean (in one of his first major TV roles, broadcast 17 August 1953 on *Summer Studio One*); "A Handful of Diamonds," with Lorne Greene (in his first major TV role, 19 April 1954); "Sue Ellen," with Inger Stevens (in her first major TV role, 9 August 1954); Reginald Rose's "Twelve Angry Men," with Edward Arnold, John Beal, Walter Abel, Bart Burns, Robert Cummings, Paul Hartman, Lee Philips,

Joseph Sweeney, Franchot Tone, George Voskovec, and Will West (broadcast 20 September 1954, the drama was later made into a movie); "A Picture in the Paper," with Jason Robards, Jr. (in his first major TV role, 9 May 1955); "For the Defense," with Mike Wallace (in a rare dramatic role, 27 June 1955); "Dino," with Sal Mineo (written by Reginald Rose, broadcast 2 January 1956); Reginald Rose's "The Defender," with Ralph Bellamy, William Shatner, and Steve McQueen (broadcast in two parts on 25 February and 4 March 1957, the drama was the basis for *The Defenders,* a 1961 series); "The Mother Bit," with Peter Falk (10 June 1957); and "The Night America Trembled," with Warren Beatty (in a rare TV appearance, 9 September 1957).

STUDIO SEE   PBS
25 JANUARY 1977–3 AUGUST 1979   Half-hour magazine series aimed principally at young people between ten and fifteen; filmed on location, the show included poetry readings, original animation, and filmed segments. Jayne Adair created the show.

STUDS   SYNDICATED
1991–1993   Prurient game show featuring a panel of two men and three women; the guys, each of whom had dated all three of the women, attempted to match the gals' double-entendre-laden responses to various questions about the date. Mark DeCarlo hosted the festivities.

STUDS' PLACE   NBC/ABC
26 NOVEMBER 1949–24 AUGUST 1950 (NBC); 13 OCTOBER 1950–24 DECEMBER 1951 (ABC)   This half-hour comedy was set at Studs' Place, a corner bar and grille in a Chicago neighborhood. Most of the dialogue was improvised by the regulars: Studs Terkel as the owner, Beverly Younger as Grace the waitress, Win Stracke, Chet Roble, and Philip Lord. Developed by Charles Andrews, the show was produced and directed in Chicago by Ben Park and Dan Petrie.

STUMP THE AUTHORS   ABC
15 JANUARY 1949–2 APRIL 1949   Another of the several Chicago-based shows that were broadcast back East after the opening of the coaxial cable in 1949, *Stump the Authors* was a Saturday-night panel series on which professional writers tried to extemporize on various subjects.

STUMP THE STARS
See PANTOMIME QUIZ

STUMPERS   NBC
4 OCTOBER 1976–31 DECEMBER 1976   Allen Ludden hosted this daytime game show that was quite similar to *Password,* which Ludden had also hosted. Two teams, each with a celebrity and a contestant, competed, trying to identify words from various three-word clues supplied by their partner. The winning team then had the chance to identify ten words within one minute for a large cash prize. Lin Bolen, former chief of daytime programming for NBC-TV, was the executive producer.

SUGAR AND SPICE   CBS
30 MARCH 1990–11 MAY 1990   Half-hour sitcom about two black sisters who lived together with their niece in Ponca City, Oklahoma. With Loretta Devine as the sensible Loretta, a cafe hostess; Vickilyn Reynolds as the carefree Vickilyn, a shopkeeper; LaVerne Anderson as their teenage niece, Toby; Dana Hill as Toby's friend, Ginger; Stephanie Hodge as neighbor Bonnie Buttram; Gerrit Graham as Bonnie's husband, Cliff, a trucker; Troy Searcy as Toby's schoolmate, Ralph; Bumper Robinson as schoolmate Brian Cooper; and Leslie Jordan as diminutive Jacques, manager of the restaurant where Loretta worked.

SUGAR RAY LEONARD'S GOLDEN GLOVES SYNDICATED

1982   A series of boxing matches, hosted by former lightweight champion Sugar Ray Leonard.

SUGAR TIME! ABC

13 AUGUST 1977–29 MAY 1978   Half-hour sitcom about a female rock-and-roll trio known as "Sugar." With Barbi Benton as Maxx; Marianne Black as Maggie Barton; Didi Carr as Diane; Wynn Irwin as Al Marks; Mark Winkworth as Paul Landson; and Charles Fleischer as Lightnin' Jack Rappaport. Created by James Komack and developed by Hank Bradford, the series had a four-week run in the summer of 1977 and was seen irregularly thereafter. Komack was the executive producer; Bradford and Martin Cohan were the producers. Paul Williams supervised the music.

SUGARFOOT ABC

17 SEPTEMBER 1957–20 SEPTEMBER 1960   An hour western from Warner Brothers starring Will Hutchins as Tom (Sugarfoot) Brewster, a naive, sarsaparilla-drinking Easterner who headed West, intending to become a lawyer. Introduced in the fall of 1957, *Sugarfoot* alternated with *Cheyenne* for its first two seasons, then alternated with *Bronco* for one season; a few more *Sugarfoot* episodes were telecast under the *Cheyenne* title during the 1960–1961 season. See also *Bronco; Cheyenne*. William T. Orr was the executive producer, and Carroll Case the producer.

THE SULLIVANS SYNDICATED

1980   This Australian serial premiered there in 1976, and was exported to the United States four years later (a second Australian soap opera, *Prisoner: Cell Block H,* was also syndicated that year). Set in Melbourne in 1939, its central characters were, of course, the members of the Sullivan family. The cast included Paul Cronin as David Sullivan; Lorraine Bayly as his wife, Grace Sullivan; Andrew McFarlane as their son John, a pacifist medical student who reluctantly joined the army; Steven Tandy as their son Tom; Richard Morgan as their son Terry; Susan Hannaford as their daughter, Kitty (in real life, Hannaford was 24, though her character was supposed to be only 13); and Ingrid Mason as John's girlfriend, Anna Kauffman.

THE SUMMER BROTHERS SMOTHERS SHOW
See THE GLEN CAMPBELL GOODTIME HOUR

SUMMER CAMP SYNDICATED

1977   Half-hour educational series for children, emphasizing instruction in arts and crafts, produced by the YMCA.

SUMMER SCHOOL CBS

6 JULY 1953–4 SEPTEMBER 1953   Monday-through-Friday educational series for young children. Broadcast from Philadelphia every afternoon at 4:00, the half-hour show featured guest teachers rather than regular instructors.

SUMMER SHOWCASE NBC

28 JUNE 1988–30 AUGUST 1988   Tuesday-night series of documentaries, hosted by various NBC News correspondents.

SUMMER SUNDAY U.S.A. NBC

1 JULY 1984–7 SEPTEMBER 1984   One of NBC's least successful attempts at a prime-time newsmagazine, *Summer Sunday U.S.A.* was telecast opposite *60 Minutes* on CBS. Cohosted by Andrea Mitchell and Linda Ellerbee, it was broadcast live from various locations around the country. One regular feature of the series was a segment called "Trading Places," in which newsmakers were given the opportunity to grill reporters. Because of the show's low clearance rate, and frequent technical glitches, one NBC executive later described the show as "one of the most screwed-up programs in history."

SUMMERTIME U.S.A. CBS

7 JULY 1953–27 AUGUST 1953   A summer replacement for *The Jane Froman Show, Summertime U.S.A.* was a twice-weekly, fifteen-minute musical series cohosted by Teresa Brewer and Mel Tormé.

SUNDAY NBC

27 OCTOBER 1963–11 JULY 1965   *Sunday* was a Sunday-afternoon newsmagazine hosted by Frank Blair. Regular contributors included Joe Garagiola (sports), Ray Scherer (politics), Richard Schickel (books), and William K. Zinsser (films).

SUNDAY AT HOME NBC

10 JULY 1949–31 JULY 1949   The several members of the Pickard Family were the stars of this fifteen-minute musical show, one of the first Hollywood-based programs to be kinescoped for broadcast in the East.

SUNDAY AT THE BRONX ZOO ABC

11 JUNE 1950–17 SEPTEMBER 1950   This self-explanatory children's show was hosted by William Bridges, with assistance from Durward Kirby.

SUNDAY BEST NBC

3 FEBRUARY 1991–24 FEBRUARY 1991   This hour show, scheduled at 7 P.M. on Sundays, took a lighthearted look at television. Carl Reiner hosted the show, which featured highlights of NBC's shows from the preceding week, clips from vintage TV series, and other light fare. Regular contributors included Harry Shearer, Linda Ellerbee (who had appeared seven years earlier in the same time slot on *Summer Sunday U.S.A.*), Merrill Markoe, and Jeff Cesario.

THE SUNDAY COMICS

See COMIC STRIP LIVE

SUNDAY DATE NBC

21 AUGUST 1949–9 OCTOBER 1949   Hosted by Helen Lee, this fifteen-minute Sunday musical series was set at a café.

SUNDAY DINNER CBS

2 JUNE 1991–7 JULY 1991   Producer Norman Lear based this sitcom on his own life: after his divorce from Frances Lear, he married a much younger woman. The series, set in Great Neck, New York, featured a 56-year-old man who became engaged to a 30-year-old woman, much to the chagrin of his grown children. The cast included Robert Loggia as Ben Benedict; Teri Hatcher as his fiancee, lawyer Thelma Todd (TT) Fagori, who talked directly to God; Kari Lizer as Ben's 30-year-old daughter, Diana; Martha Gehman as Ben's divorced daughter, Vicki, a scientist; Patrick Breen as Ben's son, Kenneth, a realtor; Shiri Appleby as Vicki's young daughter, Rachel; and Marian Mercer as Ben's sister, Martha.

THE SUNDAY MYSTERY HOUR NBC

29 MAY 1960–25 SEPTEMBER 1960; 2 JULY 1961–17 SEPTEMBER 1961   This summer anthology hour was hosted by Walter Slezak. The show was presented live and in color during the summer of 1960, but the 1961 fare consisted of reruns. Among the presentations were "Murder Me Nicely," with Everett Sloane (3 July 1960), and "Trial by Fury," with Agnes Moorehead (7 August 1960).

SUNDAY NIGHT

See NIGHT MUSIC

SUNDAY TODAY NBC

20 SEPTEMBER 1987–   Almost nine years after CBS expanded its morning news show to Sundays, NBC followed suit with this version of the *Today* show. The ninety-minute program was originally cohosted by Boyd Matson and Maria Shriver. Garrick

Utley replaced Matson as cohost in 1988 and became sole host after Shriver's departure in 1989. Utley was later joined by Mary Alice Williams. They were succeeded by Jackie Nespral and Scott Simon in August 1992; Nespral and Simon were also the anchors of NBC's new venture, *Saturday Today.* In September 1992 the Sunday broadcast was reduced to sixty minutes. Mike Schneider succeeded Simon as cohost in June 1993, and Giselle Fernandez succeeded Nespral in January 1995. Jack Ford succeeded Mike Schneider in May 1995.

SUNRISE SEMESTER   CBS
1963–1980   An early-morning educational series, *Sunrise Semester* was CBS's answer to NBC's *Continental Classroom.* It began in 1957 as a local show in New York and went network six years later. Each year several college-level courses were presented by members of the faculty of New York University. The half-hour show was produced by Roy Allen for WCBS-TV, New York. During the summers, courses were offered under the title *Summer Semester.*

SUNSET BEAT   ABC
21 APRIL 1990–28 APRIL 1990   Only two episodes of this Saturday night cop show were televised. It followed the exploits of an experimental unit of undercover Los Angeles cops who posed as bikers. With George Clooney as Chic Chesbro, who moonlighted as a guitarist in a rock and roll band; Michael DeLuise as Tim Kelly, a med school dropout; Markus Flanagan as Bradley Coolidge; Erik King as Tucson Smith; and James Tolkan as the boss, Captain Ray Parker.

SUNSHINE   NBC
6 MARCH 1975–19 JUNE 1975   Offbeat sitcom about a recently widowed young musician, trying to raise his young stepdaughter in Vancouver. Featured were Cliff DeYoung as Sam Hayden; Elizabeth Cheshire as his stepdaughter, Jill Hayden; Bill Mumy as Sam's musician friend, Weaver; Corey Fischer as Givits, another musician who formed a trio with Sam and Weaver; and Meg Foster as their friend, Nora. The half-hour series was based on a journal excerpted in the Los Angeles *Times,* which was made into a TV-movie shown on CBS on 9 November 1973, with De Young, Mumy, Fischer, and Foster. A TV-movie sequel, "Sunshine Christmas" (12 December 1977, NBC), was also produced, with De Young, Mumy, Foster, and Cheshire. The series was produced by George Eckstein for Universal Television.

THE SUPER   ABC
21 JUNE 1972–23 AUGUST 1972   Half-hour summer sitcom starring Richard S. Castellano as Joe Girelli, the harried superintendent of a New York City apartment building. Also featured were Ardell Sheridan as his wife, Francesca Girelli; B. Kirby, Jr., as their son, Anthony; Margaret E. Castellano (Richard's daughter) as their daughter, Joanne; Ed Peck as Officer Clark, a tenant; Virginia Vincent as his wife, Dottie Clark; Janet Brandt as Mrs. Stein; and Louis Basile as Louie. The series was created by Rob Reiner and Phil Mishkin (who appeared as Joe's brother, Frankie), and produced and directed by Alan Rafkin.

SUPER CIRCUS   ABC
16 JANUARY 1949–3 JUNE 1956   This long-running circus show was aimed principally at children. It was broadcast from Chicago from 1949 to 1955, where it was hosted by ringmaster Claude Kirchner and his assistant, Mary Hartline. Also on hand were three clowns: Cliffy Sobier as Cliffy, Bardy Patton and Sandy Dobritch as Scampy, and Nicky Francis as Nicky. In 1955 the show moved to New York, and Jerry Colonna took over as ringmaster, assisted by baton twirler Sandy Wirth. Jack Gibney produced the series.

SUPER DAVE   SHOWTIME/USA
21 NOVEMBER 1987–12 MAY 1993 (SHOWTIME); 7 JANUARY 1995–19 FEBRUARY 1995 (USA)   Half-hour comedy show, spun off from *Bizarre,* starring Bob Einstein as bumbling stuntman Super Dave Osborne. On the short-lived USA Cable Network

sitcom, titled *Super Dave's Vegas Spectacular,* Dave operated a Las Vegas hotel. Assisting him were Art Irizawa as Fuji and Jennifer Grant as Sandi.

SUPER DAVE   FOX
12 SEPTEMBER 1992–21 AUGUST 1993   The animated version of the comedy series featured live-action wraparounds by Bob Einstein. Following a special premiere on 9 September, it settled into a Saturday morning slot.

SUPER FRIENDS   ABC
8 SEPTEMBER 1973–30 AUGUST 1975; 21 FEBRUARY 1976–4 SEPTEMBER 1976; 4 DECEMBER 1976–3 SEPTEMBER 1983; 8 SEPTEMBER 1984–31 AUGUST 1985   *Super Friends,* a Hanna-Barbera cartoon series, depicted the adventures of the members of the Justice League of America—Superman, Batman and Robin, Aquaman, Wonder Woman, Marvin and Wendy, and Wonder Dog. Several of the group had previously been seen in other series, such as *The Superman/Aquaman Hour* or *The Batman/Tarzan Adventure Hour.* In the fall of 1977 the show expanded from thirty to sixty minutes and was retitled *The All-New Superfriends Hour.* The Wondertwins, Zan and Jayna, were added, along with their monkey Gleek. In the fall of 1978 it continued under a new title, *Challenge of the Superfriends,* as the members of the Justice League of America battled emissaries of the Legion of Doom. In 1979 it continued as *The World's Greatest Superfriends.*

SUPER GHOSTS   NBC
27 JULY 1952–21 SEPTEMBER 1952; 19 JULY 1953–6 SEPTEMBER 1953   Hosted by Dr. Bergen Evans, this prime-time summer game show was broadcast from Chicago. The game was similar to Hangman—each successive panelist named a letter of the alphabet, and the object of the game was to avoid completing a word. The 1952 panel included Dr. Irving Lee of Northwestern University, former drama critic Robert Pollak, housewife Shirl Stern, and a guest panelist.

THE SUPER GLOBETROTTERS   NBC
8 SEPTEMBER 1979–1 DECEMBER 1979; 12 APRIL 1980–3 MAY 1980   Saturday-morning cartoon series featuring the animated antics of the Harlem Globetrotters. See also *The Harlem Globetrotters; The Godzilla Power Hour.*

SUPER JEOPARDY!
See JEOPARDY!

THE SUPER MARIO BROS. SUPER SHOW   SYNDICATED
1989–1991   Half-hour daily cartoon series featuring the two heroes of the popular Nintendo series of video games, plumbers Mario and Luigi. Wrapped around the cartoons was a live-action segment, starring professional wrestling personality Captain Lou Albano as Mario and Danny Wells as Luigi. See also *Captain N: The Game Master.*

SUPER POWERS TEAM: GALACTIC GUARDIANS   ABC
7 SEPTEMBER 1985–6 SEPTEMBER 1986   Saturday morning cartoon series on which Cyborg, "a black bionic wonder," teamed up with Superman, Batman and Robin, and Wonder Woman, to protect the galaxy from evil.

SUPER PRESIDENT AND SPY SHADOW   NBC
9 SEPTEMBER 1967–28 DECEMBER 1968   The central character in this half-hour Saturday cartoon show was James Norcross, President of the United States, who possessed the ability to transform himself into almost anything. The second segment of the show, "Spy Shadow," featured a private eye whose shadow had a mind of its own.

THE SUPER 6   NBC
10 SEPTEMBER 1966–31 AUGUST 1969   Half-hour cartoon show about a half-dozen crimefighters.

SUPER WITCH NBC

19 NOVEMBER 1977–28 JANUARY 1978   *Super Witch* was the title given to the episodes of *Sabrina the Teenage Witch* when *The New Archie-Sabrina Hour* was broken up in midseason. See also *The Archie Show; The Groovie Goolies;* and *Sabrina, the Teenage Witch.*

SUPERBOY SYNDICATED

1988–1991   This half-hour sci-fi series focused on the life of superhero Superman when he was a college lad. Filmed in Florida, it featured John Haymes Newton (1988–1989) and Gerard Christopher (1989–1991) as the young man of steel, attending college as journalism major Clark Kent; Jim Calvert (1988–1989) as Clark's pal T. J. White (son of Perry White, editor of the *Daily Planet*); Ilan Mitchell-Smith (1989–1991) as Clark's roommate, Andy McAllister; Stacy Haiduk as Clark's girlfriend, Lana Lang; Robert Levine (1990–1991) as C. Dennis Jackson, head of the Bureau for Extranormal Matters, for which Clark and Lana worked as interns; and Peter Jay Fernandez (1990–1991) as Bureau field officer Matt Ritter. Scott Wells and Sherman Howard appeared occasionally as young Lex Luthor, Superboy's nemesis.

SUPERCAR SYNDICATED

1961   One of the first children's series developed by Gerry and Sylvia Anderson, *Supercar* was a marionette show which centered on Mike Mercury, driver of Supercar, a very versatile vehicle. Other characters included Dr. Beeker, Professor Popkiss, Jimmy, and Mitch the Monkey. The Andersons later refined their technique in such series as *Fireball XL-5, Stingray,* and *Thunderbirds.*

SUPERCARRIER ABC

6 MARCH 1988–24 APRIL 1988; 2 JULY 1988–27 AUGUST 1988   Life aboard the *Georgetown,* a giant aircraft carrier, was depicted on this hour dramatic series. With Robert Hooks as Captain Jim Coleman, supervisor of the carrier's team of pilots; Dale Dye as Captain Henry Madigan, the ship's commanding officer; Richard Jaeckel as Master Chief Sam Rivers; Ken Olandt as Lietenant Jack "Sierra" DiPalma, a pilot; Cec Verrell as Lieutenant Commander Ruth "Bee Bee" Rutkowski, a pilot; John David Bland as Lieutenant Doyle "Anzac" Sampson, a pilot; Gerardo Mejia as Master-at-Arms; Luis Cruz, an m.p.; Matthew Walker as Seaman Raymond Lafitte; Michael Sharrett as Ocean Specialist Donald Willoughby; Tasia Valenza as Yeoman Rosie Henriques; and Marie Windsor as Billie Costello, proprietor of a nearby bar.

SUPERHUMAN SAMURAI SYBER-SQUAD SYNDICATED

1994–   No doubt inspired by the success of *The Mighty Morphin Power Rangers,* this daily half-hour live action kids' adventure series featured a quartet of high school students who could transform themselves into the Superhuman Samurai Syber-Squad. They then battled the evil Kilokahn, a dragon-like virus which dwelled in computer circuits but was capable of unleashing other monsters. The four SSSS members were played by Matthew Lawrence as Sam Collins (known as Servo when he was in uniform); Troy Slaten as Amp; Kevin Castro as Tank; and Robin Mary Florence as Sidney. Also featured were Glen Beaudin as Malcolm, a teenager who assisted Kilokahn; Jayme Betcher as Jennifer, Sam's girlfriend; Diana Bellamy as Mrs. Starkey, the cafeteria lady; and Tim Curry as the voice of Kilokahn.

SUPERIOR COURT SYNDICATED

1986–1990   One of the several courtroom dramas of the late 1980s, this one starred a former judge, William E. Burns, as the first season's presiding judge. For the second and third seasons various actors played the judge, and in 1989 Raymond St. Jacques took over the role.

SUPERMAN SYNDICATED

1951–1957   One of fiction's best known heroes, *Superman* was created by Jerry Siegel and Joe Shuster and first appeared in the June 1938 issue of "Action Comics." This humanlike creature had been sent to Earth as an infant by his parents, who discovered that their native planet, Krypton, was about to be destroyed. The boy was raised in a small town by the Kent family and took the name Clark Kent. He soon discovered that he possessed "powers and abilities far beyond those of mortal men." His senses of sight and hearing were extraordinarily acute, he was incredibly strong, and best of all, he was virtually indestructible (certain particles of Kryptonite, which apparently reached Earth from the exploding planet, could render Superman ineffective, however). Fortunately, he vowed to use his gifts for the good of humanity, fighting "a never-ending battle for truth, justice, and the American way." When he grew up, he moved to Metropolis and got a job as a reporter for the *Daily Planet*. As a reporter, Kent was in a position to learn immediately of impending catastrophes, major crimes, and other compelling situations in which the presence of Superman might be needed.

The Superman character appeared not only in comic books, but also in a radio series beginning in 1940 (on which Bud Collyer played the lead), in a series of feature-length cartoons produced between 1941 and 1943, in two 15-chapter movie serials made in 1948 and 1950 (both of which starred Kirk Alyn), and in a full-length film, *Superman and the Mole Men*, made in 1951 (a second, lavishly produced picture was released late in 1978). Aside from the comic books, the character is most closely associated with the 104 half-hour television episodes, produced between 1951 and 1957, starring George Reeves (Reeves had played Superman in the 1951 motion picture; the film was later edited into a two-part TV story). Still widely syndicated today, *Superman*'s reruns are rivaled in popularity only by those of *I Love Lucy*.

As production of the first twenty-six episodes began in the summer of 1951, the cast included (in addition to Reeves) Phyllis Coates as Lois Lane, another *Daily Planet* reporter, who was infatuated with Superman but cared little for Kent (none of the show's principals ever realized that the two were one and the same, though in one 1955 episode, "The Wedding of Superman," Lois dreamed not only that she married Superman, but also that Kent revealed his true identity to her); Jack Larson as the *Planet*'s cub reporter, Jimmy Olsen; John Hamilton as the *Planet*'s apoplectic editor, Perry White; and Robert Shayne as Inspector William Henderson of the Metropolis police. The 1951 episodes were produced by Robert Maxwell and Bernard Luber, and directed by Lee Sholem and Tommy Carr; though they were somewhat more violent than the remaining episodes (the only on-screen murders were committed during the first twenty-six shows), they set the tone for the run of the series—a low budget, a hectic production schedule, a small guest cast, and lots of stock footage. In spite of the cost cutting, the stock sequences of Superman in flight (production of which was supervised by Thol "Si" Simonson) and the other frequently used special effects, such as Superman crashing through a brick wall (he rarely used the door), were quite effective for the time. Because of the production schedule, parts of several episodes were filmed at the same time (*Superman* was one of the first TV shows to employ this technique); this explains the fact that Clark, Lois, Jimmy, and Perry often seemed to wear the same set of clothes week after week.

Though twenty-six episodes had been completed by the end of 1951, the series was not made available to any broadcasting stations until early in 1953. By that time Kellogg's Cereals had agreed to sponsor the series. Production of *Superman* resumed in May 1953, and a second set of twenty-six episodes was filmed. Whitney Ellsworth was now the producer (and would remain so) and, as Phyllis Coates had accepted other offers, Noel Neill was signed to play Lois Lane (Neill had previously played the part in the fifteen-chapter serials). These episodes were directed by Tommy Carr and George Blair. By now the character had become extremely popular, and all kinds of Superman merchandise flooded the market; Reeves himself did several successful promotional tours.

Production slowed down to a more leisurely pace in 1954, as only thirteen new episodes were produced (this schedule continued for the next three years); the most significant change was that the show was now being filmed in color. The majority of the final fifty-two episodes were directed by Harry Gerstad, Phil Ford, and George Blair, though Reeves himself directed three shows. In one of the 1957 episodes, "The Big Forget," Clark Kent actually did reveal his identity to Lois, Perry, and Jimmy, but thanks to an antimemory vapor developed by eccentric Professor Pepperwinkle (played by Phillips Tead), the three immediately forgot what they had witnessed.

In June of 1959, two years after production ceased, George Reeves shot and killed himself; he left no note, and the reasons for his death remain conjectural. Because of his close identity with the Superman character, Reeves did have trouble finding suitable work after 1957, but, according to Gary Grossman's book, *Superman—Serial to Cereal,* Reeves had several offers pending at the time of his death. Another possible explanation is that Reeves, who had been in a serious auto accident two weeks earlier, may have taken his life while under the influence of alcohol and pain killers. Sadly, Reeves, who often lamented that he wished he'd had a few adult fans among the *Superman* viewers, did not live long enough to watch his audiences grow up.

Though no major guest stars appeared on *Superman,* several struggling young performers played some of their first television roles on the series. Among them were: Claude Akins ("Peril By Sea," 1955), Hugh Beaumont ("The Big Squeeze," 1953), John Beradino ("The Unlucky Number," 1955), Paul Burke ("My Friend Superman," 1953, and "The Phantom Ring," 1955), Chuck Connors ("Flight to the North," 1954), and Joi Lansing ("Superman's Wife," 1957). In 1966 an animated version of *Superman* first appeared on television: see below. In 1988 a new live-action series appeared: see *Superboy.* In 1993 the characters came to network prime-time: see *Lois & Clark: The New Adventures of Superman.*

SUPERMAN CBS

10 SEPTEMBER 1966–7 SEPTEMBER 1968; 17 SEPTEMBER 1988–9 SEPTEMBER 1989 *Superman* first appeared in a Saturday-morning cartoon series in the fall of 1966—the show, produced by Allen Ducovny, was titled *The New Adventures of Superman* during the 1966–1967 season. The half-hour show featured "Superman" and "Superboy" cartoon segments. In the fall of 1967, Superman shared an hour program with Aquaman, but retained top billing as the show was titled *The Superman Aquaman Hour.* Superman continued to be seen on Saturday mornings after 1968 but no longer commanded top billing: see *The Batman-Superman Hour* and *Super Friends.* A new series of cartoons was made for CBS's 1988–1989 Saturday morning slate; in addition to the usual adventures, the show also presented a "family album" segment, focusing on the Man of Steel's early years.

SUPERMARKET SWEEP ABC/LIFETIME

20 DECEMBER 1965–14 JULY 1967 (ABC); 5 FEBRUARY 1990– (LIFETIME) A daytime game show taped at supermarkets throughout the country, *Supermarket Sweep* gave contestant couples the chance to load their shopping carts with merchandise for a limited period of time; the couple whose total was the highest was declared the winner and got to keep the goods and return the next day. Bill Malone hosted the half-hour show on ABC. David Ruprecht emceed the 1990 revival on the Lifetime Cable channel.

SUPERSONIC SYNDICATED

1976 Half-hour series of performances by rock stars.

THE SUPERSTARS ABC

27 JANUARY 1974–3 MARCH 1974; 5 JANUARY 1975–23 MARCH 1975; 11 JANUARY 1976–4 APRIL 1976; 2 JANUARY 1977–27 MARCH 1977; 8 JANUARY 1978–26 MARCH 1978; 14 JANUARY 1979–1 APRIL 1979; 20 JANUARY 1980–30 MARCH 1980; 25 JANUARY 1981–29 MARCH 1981; 24 JANUARY 1982–28 MARCH 1982; 6 FEBRUARY 1983–20 FEBRUARY 1983 A Sunday-afternoon sports show, *The Superstars* featured professional athletes, who competed against each other in a variety of athletic endeavors (no competitor was permitted to participate in the sport of his or her profession, however). On some shows teams of athletes competed, and these programs were broadcast under the title *The Superteams.* Keith Jackson was the principal commentator, but he was assisted from time to time by Al Michaels, Donna De Varona, O. J. Simpson, Reggie Jack-

son, Billie Jean King, Bruce Jenner, Hilary Hilton, Andrea Kirby, and Frank Gifford. *The Superstars* proved surprisingly popular with viewers and spawned a host of similar shows—specials such as "Battle of the Network Stars" and "Us vs. the World," and series such as *The Challenge of the Sexes* and *Celebrity Challenge of the Sexes;* the term "trashsport" was coined to describe the genre.

SUPERSTARS OF ROCK SYNDICATED
1973 Wolfman Jack interviewed rock stars on this half-hour series.

SUPERTRAIN NBC
7 FEBRUARY 1979–28 JULY 1979 An anthology series set aboard an atomic-powered train which traveled from coast to coast in 36 hours, *Supertrain* was an expensive flop. Its lavish set (one of the most expensive ever produced for television) failed to captivate viewers, and its uncertain vacillation between comedy and adventure also seemed to discourage large audiences. The Supertrain itself featured a disco, gymnasium, and swimming pool. The original train crew included: Edward Andrews as Harry Flood, the conductor; Patrick Collins as Dave Noonan, the passenger relations officer; Robert Alda as Dr. Lewis; Nita Talbot as Rose Casey; Harrison Page as porter George Boone; Michael DeLano as bartender Lou Atkins; Charlie Brill as Robert the hairdresser; Aarika Wells as exercise attendant Gilda; William Nuckols as exercise attendant Wally; Anthony Palmer as T. C., the chief engineer. Dan Curtis, *Supertrain*'s first executive producer, was replaced by Robert Stambler in March 1979, and *Supertrain* left the air for a few weeks for retooling. It returned with a slimmed-down cast: from the original cast only Andrews, Page, and Alda remained, and Ilene Graff was added as social director Penny Whitaker, along with Joey Aresco as executive operations officer Wayne Randall. The changes were of no avail.

SURE AS FATE CBS
4 JULY 1950–3 APRIL 1951 Half-hour mystery anthology series, narrated by Paul Lukas.

SURF'S UP SYNDICATED
1966 Stan Richards hosted this half-hour documentary series, which presented color film footage of surfing and skateboarding activities at the nation's beaches.

SURFSIDE 6 ABC
3 OCTOBER 1960–24 SEPTEMBER 1962 This Warner Brothers detective series was set in Miami Beach; except for its locale, it was virtually identical to Warners' other hour-long detective shows, *77 Sunset Strip* and *Hawaiian Eye*. SurfSide 6 was the address of a trio of private eyes, whose houseboat was anchored next to a Miami Beach hotel. Featured were Troy Donahue as Sandy Winfield II; Van Williams as Ken Madison; Lee Patterson as Dave Thorne; Diane McBain as their friend, Daphne Dutton; Margarita Sierra as nightclub singer Cha Cha O'Brien; Donald Barry (1960–1961) as Lieutenant Snedigar; Richard Crane (1961–1962) as Lieutenant Plehn; and Mousie Garner as Mousie.

SURVIVAL SYNDICATED
1964 *Survival* was a series of thirty-eight half-hours, mostly containing documentary film footage on famous disasters. James Whitmore narrated the series, and Sherman Grinberg produced it.

THE SURVIVORS ABC
29 SEPTEMBER 1969–12 JANUARY 1970 One of the biggest flops of the decade, *The Survivors* was an expensive hour series created by novelist Harold Robbins. Shot on location around the world, it told a seamy tale of sex, wealth, and power for its fifteen-week run. The series was a success only for Robbins, who had wisely insisted on a guarantee of $500,000 regardless of the show's duration. The cast included: Ralph Bellamy as Baylor Carlyle, wealthy investor; George Hamilton as his son, Duncan Carlyle; Lana Turner as his daughter, Tracy Hastings; Kevin McCarthy as

Philip Hastings, Tracy's husband; Rossano Brazzi as Riakos; Robert Viharo as Miguel Santerra, a South American revolutionary; Jan-Michael Vincent as Jeffrey, Tracy's son; Diana Muldaur as Belle, Baylor's secretary; Louise Sorel as Jean Vale; Kathy Cannon as Sheila; Donna Bacalla as Marguerita, Miguel's sister; Robert Lipton as Tom; Clu Gulager as Senator Jennings; and Louis Hayward as Jonathan. After the show was dropped in midseason, Universal Television, which produced the series, developed a new show for George Hamilton, which premiered in a new time slot shortly afterward. See *Paris 7000*. Reruns of *The Survivors* were shown in that time slot during the summer of 1970.

THE SUSAN POWTER SHOW   SYNDICATED
1994–1995   Half-hour daily talk show hosted by Susan Powter, the crewcut nutrition and fitness guru whose book *Stop the Insanity!* was a best seller.

THE SUSAN RAYE SHOW   DUMONT
2 OCTOBER 1950–20 NOVEMBER 1950   Fifteen-minute musical show hosted by Susan Raye.

SUSAN'S SHOW   CBS
4 MAY 1957–18 JANUARY 1958   Twelve-year-old Susan Heinkel hosted her own children's show on Saturday mornings; it was set in a fantasy land known as Wonderville, to which Susan and her dog Rusty were transported by means of a magic chair in Susan's kitchen. Wonderville was populated by stuffed animals, led by Caesar P. Penguin, and a flying, talking table named Mr. Pegasus. The half-hour program was produced by Paul Frumkin in Chicago, where it had premiered locally in 1956.

SUSIE
See PRIVATE SECRETARY

SUSPENSE   CBS
1 MARCH 1949–17 AUGUST 1954; 25 MARCH 1964–9 SEPTEMBER 1964   *Suspense* was a half-hour anthology series of thrillers, based on the radio series that ran from 1942 to 1962. The TV series aroused some controversy late in 1949, when an episode showing a woman drinking blood precipitated an outcry over violence and gore on television. Bela Lugosi made a rare television appearance in one episode (11 October 1949), and Boris Karloff starred in an early adaptation of "The Monkey's Paw" the same year (17 May). Other unusual guest appearances included those by Jacqueline Susann ("Pigeons in the Cave," 21 July 1953) and Mike Wallace (7 July 1953). One of the earliest televised Sherlock Holmes stories was presented on *Suspense*. "The Adventure of the Black Baronet," written by Adrian Conan Doyle and John Dickson Carr, starring Basil Rathbone and Martyn Green, was broadcast 26 May 1953. Bob Stevens produced and directed the first incarnation of *Suspense*. Sebastian Cabot hosted the 1964 version, which replaced *Tell It to the Camera*.

SUSPICION   NBC
30 SEPTEMBER 1957–22 SEPTEMBER 1958   An hour-long suspense anthology series of little note, *Suspicion* was hosted first by Dennis O'Keefe, and later by Walter Abel. Reruns were shown on NBC during the summer of 1959.

SUZANNE PLESHETTE IS MAGGIE BRIGGS
See MAGGIE BRIGGS

THE SUZANNE SOMERS SHOW   SYNDICATED
1994–1995   Unsuccessful talk show hosted by Suzanne Somers. Each program usually featured a celebrity guest and a non-celebrity expert on a particular topic.

SWAMP THING   USA
27 JUNE 1990–25 OCTOBER 1992   Half-hour adventure series based on the DC Comic character. It starred Dick Durock as Swamp Thing, who lived in the Louisiana bayou

country; formerly a human (Dr. Alec Holland), the plant-like swamp denizen emerged after Holland had ingested a secret formula. Also featured were Jesse Zeigler (1990–1991) as Swamp Thing's young friend, Jimmy Kipp; Carrell Myers as Jimmy's mother, Tressa; Mark Lindsay Chapman as Swamp Thing's enemy, Dr. Anton Arcane; Scott Garrison (1991–1992) as Jimmy's half-brother, Will; and Kari Wuhrer as Abigail. Swamp Thing had previously inspired a 1982 movie and its 1989 sequel, *The Return of Swamp Thing*. An animated version of the series was also produced: see below.

SWAMP THING   FOX
20 APRIL 1991–3 AUGUST 1991   The animated version of the live-action series ran for half a season on Fox's Saturday-morning schedule.

SWANS CROSSING   SYNDICATED
1992   This short-lived daily soap opera was aimed at a teen audience. Set in the town of Swans Crossing somewhere along the Eastern seaboard, its main characters were a group of wealthy young people. The cast included Kristy Barbera as Nancy Robbins; Tom Carroll as J. T. Adams; Carisa Dahlbo as Glory Booth; Brittany Daniel as Mila Rosnovsky; Devin Doherty as Jimmy Clayton; Evan Ferrante as Owen Fowler; Sarah Michelle Gellar as Sydney Rutledge; Kristen Mahon as Sandy Swan; Shane McDermott as Glory's brother, Garrett Booth; Stacey Moseley as Callie Walker; Eddie Tyclus Robinson as Neil Atwater; and Alex Tanaka as Saja Decastro.

SWEATING BULLETS   CBS/SYNDICATED
8 APRIL 1991–2 JANUARY 1995 (CBS); 1992–1993 (SYNDICATED)   Part of CBS's late-night *Crime Time After Prime Time, Sweating Bullets* was a light hour crime show set at Key Mariah in the Florida Keys. Featured were Rob Stewart as private eye Nick Slaughter, a former DEA agent; Carolyn Dunn as Sylvie Girard, a former travel agent who became Slaughter's business partner; John David Bland as Nick's buddy Ian Stewart, a British former rock star who now ran a dive shop and bar; and Pedro Armendariz as the local police chief, Lieutenant Carrillo. Slaughter and Girard were reminiscent of *Moonlighting*'s Addison and Hayes—the sexual tension was rife and the dialogue was laced with double entendres. During its first season, the series was a joint production of Canadian and Mexican concerns and was filmed in Puerto Vallarta, Mexico. During the second season it was a Canadian-Israeli venture, as production shifted to Elat, Israel.

SWEEPSTAKE$ NBC
26 JANUARY 1979–30 MARCH 1979   An hour anthology series focusing on several of the finalists in a state lottery with the grand prize of a million dollars. Edd Byrnes appeared as the sweepstakes emcee. Executive producer: Robert Dozier for Miller-Milkis Productions in association with Paramount TV.

SWEET JUSTICE   NBC
15 SEPTEMBER 1994–22 APRIL 1995   Hour dramatic series about a lawyer who left New York for her Southern hometown, where she joined the law firm of her father's rival. With Melissa Gilbert as Kate Delacroy; Cicely Tyson as Kate's new boss, Carrie Grace Battle, a progressive black attorney; Ronny Cox as Kate's father, James Lee Delacroy; Greg Germann as Andy, a young associate in Carrie's firm; Jim Antonio as Ross, an older attorney in the firm; and Cree Summer as Reese Dawkins, another new lawyer in the firm.

SWEET SURRENDER   NBC
18 APRIL 1987–16 MAY 1987   Short-lived sitcom about an earnest yuppie couple trying to raise two small children. With Dana Delany as Georgia Holden, who quit work to be with the kids; Mark Blum as her husband, Ken Holden; David Doyle as Georgia's divorced father, Francis Macklin; Marjorie Lord as Ken's mother, Joyce Holden; Edan Gross as Georgia and Ken's kindergartener, Bart; Rebecca and Sarah

Simms as their baby, Lynnie; Thom Sharp as neighbor Marty Gafney; Louise Williams as Lyla Gafney; Victor DiMattia as Taylor Gafney; Christopher Rich as swinging bachelor Vaughn Parker; Damon Wayans as Ray; and Viveka Davis as the Holdens' punk babysitter, Cak. Five episodes were shown in a Saturday night time slot in the spring of 1987, temporarily replacing *227*. A sixth episode was run on 8 July. Dana Delany went on to bigger fame a year later in an altogether different series, *China Beach*.

SWEET VALLEY HIGH   SYNDICATED
1994–   Half-hour dramatic series for teens and preteens, based on the popular series of books created by Francine Pascal. With twins Cynthia Daniel and Brittany Daniel as 16-year-old twins Elizabeth and Jessica Wakefield (Elizabeth was the shy one, Jessica the flirt); Amarilis as Patty; Ryan James Bittle as Todd Wilkins; Brock Burnett as Bruce; Amy Danles as Enid, Elizabeth's pal; Bridget Flanery as Lila Fowler, Jessica's pal; and Michael Perl as nerdy Winston Egbert.

SWEETHEARTS   SYNDICATED
1988   Charles Nelson Reilly hosted this game show, which was reminiscent of *To Tell the Truth:* a panel of three celebs tried to ascertain which of three pairs of purported sweethearts were real lovers.

THE SWIFT SHOW WAGON
See SHOW WAGON

SWINGIN' COUNTRY   NBC
4 JULY 1966–30 DECEMBER 1966   Regulars on this twenty-five minute daytime country-and-western music show included Rusty Draper, Roy Clark, and Molly Bee.

SWISS FAMILY ROBINSON   ABC
14 SEPTEMBER 1975–11 APRIL 1976   Based on Johann Wyss's novel, this hour-long adventure series told the story of a family marooned on a tropic isle. With Martin Milner as Karl Robinson; Pat Delany as his wife, Lotte Robinson; Willie Aames as their son Fred; Eric Olson as their son Ernie; Cameron Mitchell as Jeremiah Worth, a shipwrecked sea captain; and Helen Hunt as Helga Wagner, a teenager adopted by the Robinsons. Irwin Allen produced the series.

THE SWISS FAMILY ROBINSON   SYNDICATED
1976   This Canadian import was similar to the 1975 network show, except that it was a half-hour series. Featured were Chris Wiggins as Johann Robinson; Diana Leblanc as his wife, Elizabeth Robinson; Ricky O'Neill as their son, Franz; Heather Graham as their daughter, Marie; Michael Duhig as their son, Ernest; and Bruno, the dog. Gerald Mayer produced the series.

SWITCH   CBS
9 SEPTEMBER 1975–3 SEPTEMBER 1978   An hour-long adventure series about an ex-cop and an ex-con who teamed up as private investigators; their specialty, like that of *The Rogues,* was fleecing the fleecers and outconning the con artists. The show starred Eddie Albert as Frank MacBride, the ex-cop, and Robert Wagner as Peterson T. (Pete) Ryan, the ex-con. Also featured were Sharon Gless as their receptionist and assistant, Maggie; Charlie Callas as Malcolm Argos, an occasional helper; William Bryant (1976–1978) as Lieutenant Shilton; and James Hong (1977–1978) as Wang, Malcolm's cook. Glen A. Larson was the executive producer during the first season, Matthew Rapf during the second, and Jon Epstein during the third, for Glen Larson Productions in association with Universal Television.

THE SWORD OF FREEDOM   SYNDICATED
1957   Half-hour adventure series imported from Europe and set during the Italian Renaissance. Edmund Purdom starred as Marco del Monte, a painter and freedom

fighter who battled the Medici family. Also featured were Martin Benson as the Duke de' Medici, Adrienne Corri as Angelica; Kenneth Hyde as Machiavelli.

SWORD OF JUSTICE   NBC
9 SEPTEMBER 1978–31 DECEMBER 1978   An hour-long crime show starring Dack Rambo as Jack Cole, a man who served three years in prison on a trumped-up embezzlement charge after his father's death and who vowed upon his release to go after those wrongdoers whom the law couldn't touch; while in prison Cole learned all he could about such subjects as lock-picking and bugging in order to facilitate his crimefighting career. Also featured were Bert Rosario as Hector Ramirez, Cole's former cellmate and present partner, and Alex Courtney as Arthur Woods, the federal agent who was always a step or two behind Cole and Ramirez. Glen A. Larson was the executive producer.

SYDNEY   CBS
21 MARCH 1990–6 AUGUST 1990   Half-hour sitcom about a female private eye in Los Angeles. With Valerie Bertinelli as Sydney Kells; Craig Bierko as Matt Keating, the lawyer who hired her; Matthew Perry as Sydney's brother, Bill Kells; Rebeccah Bush as Sydney's best friend, Jill; Barney Martin as Ray, owner of the Blue Collar, Sydney's favorite hangout; Daniel Baldwin as Chester "Cheezy" Chadwell, the womanizing regular at the bar; and Perry Anzilotti as Perry the snitch.

SYLVANIAN FAMILIES   SYNDICATED
1987   Cartoon series, inspired by the toy line, in which the animal residents of an enchanted forest worked together to make a child's wish come true.

SYLVESTER AND TWEETY   CBS
11 SEPTEMBER 1976–3 SEPTEMBER 1977   Though Warner Brothers' most famous cat-and-bird twosome had been featured on several earlier cartoon shows, it was not until 1976 that Sylvester ("Thufferin' thuckotash!") and Tweety ("I taut I taw a puddy tat!") starred in a series of their own. Mel Blanc provided the voices of the two characters in the half-hour Saturday-morning show.

THE SYLVESTER & TWEETY MOVIES   WB
9 SEPTEMBER 1995–   The venerable Warner Bros. cat and bird duo appeared in a set of new cartoons on this Saturday-morning series, in which they teamed up with Granny and Hector the bulldog to solve mysteries all over the world.

SZYSZNYK   CBS
1 AUGUST 1977–29 AUGUST 1977; 7 DECEMBER 1977–25 JANUARY 1978   *Szysznyk* starred Ned Beatty as Nick Szysznyk, a twenty-seven-year Marine Corps veteran who became the supervisor of the Northeast Community Center in Washington, D.C. The half-hour sitcom also featured Leonard Barr as Leonard Kriegler, the custodian; Olivia Cole as Ms. Harrison, the district supervisor; Susan Lanier (summer 1977) as Sandi Chandler, the nursery school instructor; Thomas Carter as Ray Gun; Scott Colomby as Tony; Barry Miller as Fortwengler; and Jarrod Johnson as Ralph. Jerry Weintraub was the executive producer, Rich Eustis and Michael Elias the producers. Writers Jim Mulligan and Ron Landry created the series, which languished at the bottom of the ratings when it returned in December of 1977.

T AND T   SYNDICATED
1988–1989   Half-hour crime show starring the inimitable Mr. T as T. S. Turner, an ex-con who became a private investigator for a female attorney after she sprung him from imprisonment for a crime he hadn't committed. Alex Amini played his partner, lawyer Amanda Taler, during the first season; Kristina Nicoll took over in 1989 as lawyer Terri Taylor. Also on hand were Jackie Richardson as Turner's Aunt Martha, with whom he lived; Rachael Crawford as her daughter, Renee; David Nerman as Dick Decker, owner of the gym where Turner (who was also a former boxer) worked out; Ken James as Detective Ted Jones; and Catherine Disher as Sophie, Amanda's

secretary. The series was filmed in Toronto. In an attempt to get it off to a popular start, the producers reportedly offered ABC $1 million to air the premiere episode immediately after the Super Bowl in January 1988, but were turned down by the network.

T.H.E. CAT NBC
16 SEPTEMBER 1966–1 SEPTEMBER 1967   Half-hour adventure series starring Robert Loggia as T.H.E. (Thomas Hewitt Edward) Cat, a former cat burglar who turned to crimefighting. Also on hand were R. G. Armstrong as Captain McAllister, and Robert Carricart as Pepe, proprietor of the Casa del Gato (House of the Cat), the club where Cat's services could be obtained. Robert Loggia had played another catlike character previously on *Walt Disney Presents,* when he played western hero Elfego Baca, "the man with nine lives." *T.H.E. Cat* was produced by Boris Sagal.

T. J. HOOKER ABC/CBS
13 MARCH 1982–10 APRIL 1982; 4 SEPTEMBER 1982–7 SEPTEMBER 1985 (ABC); 25 SEPTEMBER 1985–17 SEPTEMBER 1987 (CBS)   William Shatner starred in this hour cop show as Sergeant T. J. Hooker, a hard-nosed veteran police officer. When the show was introduced in the spring of 1982, Hooker was assigned mainly to the police academy to train new recruits. The cast included Adrian Zmed as Officer Vince Romano, a trainee assigned to Hooker; April Clough as Vicki, a recruit; Richard Herd as Captain Sheridan, Hooker's superior; and Lee Bryant as Fran, Hooker's ex-wife. When the series returned in the fall of 1982, Hooker had more general responsibilities, and Clough and Bryant had been dropped. Heather Locklear joined the force as Stacy Sheridan (the Captain's daughter), a new officer, and early in 1983 James Darren began to appear regularly as Officer Jim Corrigan, Stacy's partner. The series left ABC's prime-time scheule in the fall of 1985 and was picked up by CBS for a weekly late-night slot. Seventeen new episodes were filmed during the 1985–1986 season, with Shatner, Darren, and Locklear (Adrian Zmed quit, as he was unwilling to take a pay cut). CBS reran the series during the 1986–1987 season, again in a late-night slot.

TV AUCTION ABC
10 JULY 1954–28 AUGUST 1954   Sid Stone hosted this fifteen-minute series on which viewers were invited to submit bids on merchandise featured on stage.

TV GENERAL STORE ABC
14 JUNE 1953–12 JULY 1953   On this Sunday-morning hour series, cohosts Dave and Judy Clark offered merchandise for sale to viewers.

TV HOUR
See THE MOTOROLA TV HOUR

TV NATION NBC/FOX
19 JULY 1994–30 AUGUST 1994; 28 DECEMBER 1994 (NBC); 21 JULY 1995–8 SEPTEMBER 1995 (FOX)   Michael Moore's idiosyncratic documentary series came to prime time television in the summer of 1994. Moore, who made the 1989 film "Roger & Me," described the series as a "nonfiction, comedic newsmagazine with a point of view." The description was apt; Moore's point of view was decidedly liberal, and his main targets were corporations and government agencies. Among the features Moore presented were a real estate agent who sold properties at Love Canal in New York, a fully staffed prison with no inmates, and efforts to persuade American businesses to relocate to Mexico. Moore even challenged several corporate chiefs to demonstrate their companies' products; the CEO of Ford Motor Company obliged by changing the oil on one of Ford's automobiles. Wearing his trademark baseball cap, Moore himself handled most of the on-camera reporting, although Merrill Markoe and Rusty Cundieff were also regular contributors on the NBC version. When the series shifted to Fox in the summer of 1995, Janeane Garofalo joined Cundieff as a regular correspondent. Karen Duffy and Louis Theroux also contributed.

TV 101   CBS

29 NOVEMBER 1988–25 MARCH 1989   An offbeat hour series about a high school journalism teacher who returned to his alma mater, where he had edited the school paper, and motivated his students to produce a video news show instead of a newspaper. With Sam Robards as teacher Kevin Keegan; Leon Russom as the principal of Roosevelt High, Edward Steadman; Brynn Thayer as the department head (and Kevin's former teacher), Emilie Walker; Andrew White as Vance Checker; Mary B. Ward as Penny; Teri Polo as Amanda; Andrew Cassese as Sherman Fischer; Alex Desert as Holden Hines; Matthew LeBlanc as Chuck; Stacey Dash as Monique; and Stewart Goddard as Marty Voight. The series ranked 120th out of 126 prime-time series for the 1988–1989 season.

TV READERS DIGEST   ABC

17 JANUARY 1955–9 JULY 1956   The presentations on this filmed half-hour dramatic anthology series were adapted from stories appearing in *Readers Digest* magazine. The series was produced by Chester Erskine, directed by William Beaudine, and hosted first by Hugh Reilly, then by Gene Raymond.

TV SCREEN MAGAZINE   NBC

8 JANUARY 1948–30 APRIL 1949   One of television's first magazine shows, *TV Screen Magazine* was a potpourri of features, including interviews, musical numbers, and fashion shows. It was originally hosted by John K. M. McCaffery (editor of *American Mercury*) and Millicent Fenwick (an editor of *Vogue;* later, of course, she became a Congresswoman). Ray Forrest, who had been the announcer on the early shows, later took over as host.

TV SHOPPER   DUMONT

1 NOVEMBER 1948–1 DECEMBER 1950   Kathi Norris, who hosted this early daytime series for most of its run, dispensed shopping hints to housewives.

TV SOUNDSTAGE   NBC

10 JULY 1953–3 SEPTEMBER 1954   Half-hour dramatic anthology series. James Dean appeared in one program, "Life Sentence," broadcast 16 October 1953.

TV TEEN CLUB   ABC

2 APRIL 1949–28 MARCH 1954   One of the first network musical shows aimed at teenagers, *TV Teen Club* was the brainchild of bandleader Paul Whiteman. It was an outgrowth of a series of Saturday-night teen dances Whiteman had staged in his home town, Lambertville, New Jersey, in a successful effort to combat juvenile delinquency. The TV verson, broadcast live from Philadelphia, was primarily a talent contest for youngsters. Regulars included cohosts Margo Whiteman (1949–1950; she was Paul's daughter) and Nancy Lewis (1950–1953; she was a high school student when she began the job), singers Junie Keegan and Andrea McLaughlin (who was only three and a half when she began appearing on the show), and accordionist Stan Klet. Among the contestants was Leslie Uggams, who sang on the show in 1950 at age seven. The show, which was also titled *Paul Whiteman's TV Teen Club,* was produced by Jack Steck and directed by Herb Horton.

TV TWIN DOUBLE   SYNDICATED

1977   George DeWitt hosted this syndicated game show on which home viewers could win prizes based on the results of previously filmed horse races. Local sponsors who purchased the series arranged to distribute the race tickets required for viewer participation. Jack O'Hara announced the races and Laura Lane assisted George DeWitt.

TV'S BLOOPERS & PRACTICAL JOKES   NBC

9 JANUARY 1984–24 FEBRUARY 1986; 20 MAY 1988–2 SEPTEMBER 1988   Dick Clark and Ed McMahon were the cohosts of this hour series. Clark and McMahon introduced clips of "outtakes"—fluffs and miscues from TV shows and movies—commercials

from yesteryear, and videotaped "practical jokes" played on unsuspecting celebrities. The genesis of the weekly series was a group of popular specials on "bloopers" and commercials which had been hosted separately by Clark and McMahon. See also *Foul-Ups, Bleeps & Blunders.* Additional programs popped up sporadically during subsequent seasons under the title *Super Bloopers.*

TV'S TOP TUNES   CBS
2 JULY 1951–17 AUGUST 1951; 29 JUNE 1953–21 AUGUST 1953; 28 JUNE 1954–20 AUGUST 1954; 9 JULY 1955–3 SEPTEMBER 1955   *TV's Top Tunes* was a frequent summer replacement series. In 1951, 1953, and 1954 it was seen Mondays, Wednesdays, and Fridays in a fifteen-minute format as a replacement for *The Perry Como Show;* it was hosted by Peggy Lee and Mel Tormé in 1951, Helen O'Connell and Bob Eberle in 1953, and Ray Anthony in 1954. The 1955 version was a half-hour series, shown on Saturdays; produced and directed by Lee Cooley, it was hosted by Julius LaRosa and featured the Mitchell Ayres Orchestra.

THE TAB HUNTER SHOW   NBC
18 SEPTEMBER 1960–10 SEPTEMBER 1961   Tab Hunter starred as fun-loving cartoonist Paul Morgan, creator of the *Bachelor at Large* strip, in this half-hour sitcom. Also featured were Richard Erdman as his bachelor pal Peter Fairfield and Jerome Cowan as Paul's publisher, John Larsen.

TABITHA   ABC
10 SEPTEMBER 1977–25 AUGUST 1978   This irregularly scheduled comedy series was a sequel to *Bewitched,* and starred Lisa Hartman as Tabitha Stevens, the now grown daughter of *Bewitched*'s Samantha Stevens. Also featured were David Ankrum as Tabitha's mortal brother, Adam; Robert Urich as Paul Thurston, star of the TV talk show for which Tabitha worked as a production assistant; and Mel Stewart as Marvin, Thurston's producer. Jerry Mayer was the executive producer and Bob Stambler the producer.

TAG THE GAG   NBC
13 AUGUST 1951–27 AUGUST 1951   Hal Block hosted this short-lived prime-time game show on which guest panelists tried to supply the punch lines to jokes acted out in charade form.

TAKE A CHANCE   NBC
1 OCTOBER 1950–24 DECEMBER 1950   Don Ameche hosted this prime-time half-hour quiz show.

TAKE A GIANT STEP   NBC
11 SEPTEMBER 1971–2 SEPTEMBER 1972
TALKING WITH A GIANT   NBC
9 SEPTEMBER 1972–1 SEPTEMBER 1973   *Take a Giant Step* was an unusual Saturday-morning show. Developed by George Heinemann, NBC's vice president for children's programming, the hour series featured a group of seven- to fourteen-year-olds who, with the help of staff researchers, put together a program that centered on a particular theme each week. In 1972 the concept was revised, but the new version, titled *Talking with a Giant,* was equally ignored by young viewers; the half-hour show featured a guest celebrity who was interviewed by a panel of youngsters. Gloria Peropat and Giovanna Nigro produced and directed *Take a Giant Step.*

TAKE A GOOD LOOK   ABC
22 OCTOBER 1959–16 MARCH 1961   Ernie Kovacs hosted this half-hour prime-time game show. At the beginning of the first season, the show involved two contestants, who tried to identify famous newsmakers from documentary clues. By early 1960, a panel format had been substituted and three celebrities tried to identify a celebrity guest from clues suggested in a skit performed by Kovacs, Bobby Lauher, and Peggy Connelly. Frequent panelists included Edie Adams, Hans Conried, Ben Alexander,

Cesar Romero, and Carl Reiner. As with any show involving a comic genius like Ernie Kovacs, the emphasis was on comedy rather than on the game itself.

TAKE A GUESS CBS

11 JUNE 1953–10 SEPTEMBER 1953   A summer replacement for *The Burns and Allen Show*, *Take A Guess* was a half-hour game show emceed by John K. M. McCaffery. Contestants tried to identify a secret phrase, with help from a celebrity panel that consisted of John Crawford, Dorothy Hart, Ernie Kovacs, and Margaret Lindsay.

TAKE CHARGE! PBS

1988   Thirteen-part series on personal finance, hosted by Jane Bryant Quinn.

TAKE FIVE CBS

1 APRIL 1987–8 APRIL 1987   *Take Five* premiered the same evening as CBS's other short-lived 1987 sitcom, *Roxie;* both were dropped after only two outings. This one starred George Segal as Andy Kooper, a recently divorced man who landed a job as operations manager at a San Francisco public relations agency; in his spare time Kooper played banjo in a dixieland band. Also featured were Jim Haynie as clarinetist Lenny Goodman, leader of the band (the Lenny Goodman Quartet); Derek McGrath as Al, the pianist; Bruce Jarchow as drummer Monty, Kooper's best friend; Todd Field as Kevin Davis, Kooper's boss at Davis & Son; Eugene Roche as Kevin's retired father, Max; Melanie Chartoff as Laraine McDermott, Kooper's in-house rival for his job; and Severn Darden as Kooper's shrink, Dr. Noah Wolf.

TAKE IT FROM ME

See THE JEAN CARROLL SHOW

TAKE MY ADVICE NBC

5 JANUARY 1976–11 JUNE 1976   Kelly Lange hosted this daytime series on which celebrities and their spouses suggested answers to problems submitted by viewers. The twenty-five-minute show was produced by Mark Massari for Burt Sugarman Productions.

TAKE TWO ABC

5 MAY 1963–11 AUGUST 1963   Don McNeill hosted this Sunday-afternoon game show on which celebrities were paired with noncelebrity contestants. The object of the game was to determine the common feature of two photographs from an array of four photos.

TAKING ADVANTAGE SYNDICATED

1983   Matters relating to personal finance were discussed on this half-hour informational series, cohosted by Jerry Graham and Sybil Robson. The show was produced by the same company that developed *Entertainment Tonight*.

TALE SPIN SYNDICATED

1990–1994   One component of the two-hour cartoon block *Disney Afternoon*, this one was based on Disney's *Jungle Book*. Set in the town of Cape Suzette, its main characters were Baloo the Bear (now a cargo pilot), King Louie the Ape, and the tiger Shere Khan.

TALENT JACKPOT DUMONT

19 JULY 1949–23 AUGUST 1949   Vinton Freedley and Bud Collyer cohosted this five-week prime-time talent show on which five acts competed. Each act could win a "jackpot" of as much as $250, based on the amount of applause the act received from the studio audience. The evening's top winner received not only his or her own jackpot, but whatever was left in the other acts' jackpots.

TALENT PATROL   ABC
19 JANUARY 1953–28 JUNE 1954   Contestants on this half-hour talent show were
selected from the nation's armed forces. Steve Allen was the first host of the series
and was succeeded by Arlene Francis. See also *Soldier Parade*.

TALENT SCOUTS   CBS
6 DECEMBER 1948–28 JULY 1958; 1 AUGUST 1960–26 SEPTEMBER 1960; 3 JULY 1962–11
SEPTEMBER 1962; 2 JULY 1963–17 SEPTEMBER 1963; 22 JUNE 1965–7 SEPTEMBER 1965; 20
DECEMBER 1965–5 SEPTEMBER 1966   This long-running prime-time talent show, on
which celebrity guests introduced amateur or young professional talent, was hosted
first by Arthur Godfrey, who began the show on radio in 1946. From 1948 to 1958 it
was a weekly show; when Godfrey was unavailable due to illness or other commitments, substitute hosts such as Steve Allen or Robert Q. Lewis filled in. Beginning in
1960 it was seen as a summer replacement series for several years and was titled
Celebrity Talent Scouts or *Hollywood Talent Scouts;* Sam Levenson hosted it in 1960,
Jim Backus in 1962, Merv Griffin in 1963, and Art Linkletter in 1965. Linkletter also
hosted the show when it was revived later in 1965 as a midseason replacement.
Among the many future stars who were introduced on *Talent Scouts* were Pat Boone,
Shari Lewis, the McGuire Sisters, Carmel Quinn, and June Valli. One of the many
performers who flunked the audition was Elvis Presley.

TALENT SEARCH   NBC
15 FEBRUARY 1950–6 SEPTEMBER 1951   Skitch Henderson hosted this half-hour talent
show.

THE TALENT SHOP   DUMONT
13 OCTOBER 1951–29 MARCH 1952   A half-hour talent show for young people, *The
Talent Shop* was set at a New York City drugstore and was hosted by Fred Robbins
and Pat Adair.

TALENT VARIETIES   ABC
28 JUNE 1955–1 NOVEMBER 1955   Slim Wilson hosted this country-and-western talent
show. Broadcast from Springfield, Missouri, the half-hour series was produced and
directed by Bill Ring.

TALES FROM THE CRYPT   HBO
10 JUNE 1989–3 JANUARY 1996   Horror anthology series, based on stories that originally appeared in the 1950s magazine of the same name. Several of the early segments were directed by such Hollywood luminaries as Richard Donner, Robert
Zemeckis, and Walter Hill. The finale of the 1994–1995 season (first aired 15 February 1995), "You, Murderer," directed by Zemeckis, starred Isabella Rossellini, John
Lithgow, and Sherilyn Fenn. It also featured, through computerized wizardry, images of Humphrey Bogart (colorized from several of his films) as narrator.
    Edited versions of episodes were syndicated in 1993, and were picked up by the
Fox network beginning in January 1994. A Saturday-morning cartoon series debuted
in 1993: see below.

TALES FROM THE CRYPTKEEPER   ABC
18 SEPTEMBER 1993–15 JULY 1995   Saturday-morning cartoon series loosely derived
from the series *Tales from the Crypt*. The tales on the cartoon show were considerably tamer than those on the live action show.

TALES FROM THE DARKSIDE   SYNDICATED
1984–1987   Half-hour horror anthology series, including some with humorous endings. The series was produced by George Romero, who is perhaps best known for his
1968 low-budget horror classic, *Night of the Living Dead*. A feature film consisting of
four gruesome stories was released in 1990.

TALES OF THE BLACK CAT   SYNDICATED

1950   Half-hour filmed suspense anthology series, hosted by James Monks and his cat, Thanatopsis.

TALES OF THE CITY   CBS

25 JUNE 1953–17 SEPTEMBER 1953   A summer replacement for *Four Star Playhouse,* this half-hour dramatic anthology series was hosted by Ben Hecht and was officially titled *Willys Theatre Presenting Ben Hecht's Tales of the City.*

TALES OF THE GOLD MONKEY   ABC

22 SEPTEMBER 1982–3 AUGUST 1983   This hour adventure series, set on the South Pacific island of Boragora in 1938, starred Stephen Collins as local cargo pilot Jake Cutter; Cutter's travels brought him in contact with an assortment of people searching for the "Gold Monkey," a thousand-year-old relic made of an alloy believed to be heat resistant. Also featured were Jeff MacKay as Corky, Jake's mechanic; Caitlin O'Heaney as Sarah White, an American spy masquerading as a singer; Ron Moody (in the premiere) and Roddy McDowall as Bon Chance Louie, co-owner of the Monkey Bar, a popular watering hole in Boragora; Marta DuBois as the evil Princess Kogi; John Fujioka as Todo, leader of Kogi's private army; John Calvin as Tenboom, a German spy masquerading as a Dutch priest; Les Jankey as Gushie, Louie's partner; and Leo as Jack, Cutter's one-eyed mutt. Of the three 1982 series that appeared to have been inspired by the film *Raiders of the Lost Ark* (see also *Bring 'Em Back Alive* and *The Quest*), *Tales of the Gold Monkey* seemed to be the closest clone. The series' creator and producer, Don Bellisario, maintained, however, that he took his idea not from *Raiders,* but rather from the 1938 film *Only Angels Have Wings.*

TALES OF THE RED CABOOSE   ABC

22 OCTOBER 1948–14 JANUARY 1949   Fifteen-minute prime-time series, sponsored by Lionel Trains, which consisted of films of model railroads. Dan Magee was the host. See also *Roar of the Rails.*

TALES OF THE SEVENTY-SEVENTH BENGAL LANCERS
See 77TH BENGAL LANCERS

TALES OF THE TEXAS RANGERS   CBS

3 SEPTEMBER 1955–25 MAY 1957   This half-hour western from Screen Gems starred Willard Parker as Jace Pearson and Harry Lauter as Clay Morgan, a pair of Texas Rangers. The most interesting feature of the show was that the stories were not confined to any one era of Texas history; Pearson and Morgan could be seen battling villains from the 1850s one week and tracking down desperadoes from the 1950s the following week. The series, which was seen Saturday mornings on CBS, was later rerun on ABC.

TALES OF THE UNEXPECTED   NBC

2 FEBRUARY 1977–24 AUGUST 1977   This hour-long suspense anthology series was first slated opposite ABC's *Charlie's Angels* and was later seen on an irregular basis. Narrated by William Conrad, the series was produced by John Wilder for Quinn Martin Productions. See also *Roald Dahl's Tales of the Unexpected.*

TALES OF THE VIKINGS
See THE VIKINGS

TALES OF TOMORROW   ABC

3 AUGUST 1951–12 JUNE 1953   Science fiction and supernatural tales were presented on this half-hour anthology series. A sample of presentations would include: "The Last Man on Earth," with Cloris Leachman (31 August 1951); "Frankenstein," with Lon Chaney, Jr. (18 January 1952); "Memento," with Boris Karloff (22 February 1952); "Flight Overdue," with Veronica Lake (28 March 1952); "Black Planet," with

Leslie Nielsen (16 May 1952); and "Two-Faced," with Richard Kiley (31 January 1953).

TALES OF WELLS FARGO
See WELLS FARGO

TALK SOUP   E!
26 DECEMBER 1991–   This offbeat but entertaining series provided a daily recap of highlights from TV's stable of talk shows, with dry commentary from host Greg Kinnear, who was succeeded by John Henson in Janary 1995. After two years, some talk shows (such as *Geraldo, Sally Jessy Raphael,* and *The Oprah Winfrey Show,* among others) declined to make clips available to *Talk Soup. TV Guide* quoted a Warner Bros. executive, who asserted that *Talk Soup* "degrades our shows and makes fools of the guests."

TALKABOUT   SYNDICATED
1989   Wayne Cox hosted this game show on which two teams of two persons competed. While one team was offstage, the other had to "talk about" a given subject for a period of time, trying to name words from a hidden list as they did so; words named were removed from the list. The other team then returned onstage, and tried to guess the topic from the list of words remaining.

TALKING WITH A GIANT
See TAKE A GIANT STEP

TALL HOPES   CBS
25 AUGUST 1993–8 SEPTEMBER 1993   Short-lived sitcom about a black family living in Philadelphia. With George Wallace as George Harris, a cop; Anna Maria Horsford as his wife, Lainie; Terrence Dashon Howard as their older son, Chet, a top high school basketball player; Kenny Blank as their younger son, Ernest, who shot videos at home; and Karla Green as their young daughter, Dee Dee. Michael Elias and Rich Eustis created the series.

THE TALL MAN   NBC
10 SEPTEMBER 1960–1 SEPTEMBER 1962   This fanciful western starred Barry Sullivan as New Mexico Deputy Sheriff Pat Garrett and Clu Gulager as William H. Bonney, better known as Billy the Kid; on the series Billy was not depicted as a sadistic murderer, but rather as a misguided chap who occasionally helped out Garrett. The half-hour show was created and produced by Samuel Peeples.

TALL TALES   SHOWTIME
20 DECEMBER 1985–23 MAY 1988   Shelley Duvall followed up her successful *Faerie Tale Theatre* with this anthology series. Officially titled *Shelley Duvall's Tall Tales and Legends,* it presented adaptations of famliar stories from American folklore. Among the presentations were "Annie Oakley," with Jamie Lee Curtis (20 December 1985); "Darlin' Clementine," with Duvall (30 December 1987); and "John Henry," with Danny Glover (22 April 1988).

TALLAHASSEE 7000   SYNDICATED
1961   Walter Matthau starred in this half-hour crime show as Lex Rogers, special agent for the Florida Sheriffs Bureau. The twenty-six episodes were filmed on location in Florida.

TAMMY   ABC
17 SEPTEMBER 1965–15 JULY 1966   This half-hour sitcom was based on the *Tammy* films, and starred Debbie Watson as Tammy Tarleton, a young Southern lass who left her family's houseboat to become private secretary to a wealthy plantation owner. Also featured were Frank McGrath as Uncle Lucius Tarleton; Denver Pyle as Grandpa (Mordecai) Tarleton; Dennis Robertson as Cousin Cletus; Donald Woods

as her employer, John Brent; Doris Packer as Mrs. Brent; Jay Sheffield as Steven Brent, John's son; George Furth as Dwayne Witt; Dorothy Green as Lavinia Tate, a local widow who had hoped to have her daughter hired for Tammy's job; Linda Marshall as Gloria Tate, Lavinia's daughter, and David Macklin as Peter Tate, Lavinia's son.

THE TAMMY GRIMES SHOW   ABC
8 SEPTEMBER 1966–29 SEPTEMBER 1966   The first fatality of the 1966–1967 season, *The Tammy Grimes Show* was an ill-conceived half-hour sitcom that starred musical comedy star Tammy Grimes as Tamantha Ward, a madcap heiress. Also featured were Dick Sargent as her parsimonious twin brother, Terence Ward; Hiram Sherman as their thrifty Uncle Simon, a banker; and Maudie Prickett as Mrs. Ratchett, the housekeeper. The series was canceled after four episodes had been televised, though ten shows had actually been completed by that time. William Dozier was the executive producer for Greenway Productions in association with 20th Century-Fox; Richard Whorf and Alex Gottlieb were the producers.

TANNER '88   HBO
15 FEBRUARY 1988–27 AUGUST 1988   Garry Trudeau, creator of the *Doonesbury* comic strip, teamed up with director Robert Altman on this satirical look at an American presidential campaign. Michael Murphy starred as hopeful Democratic nominee Jack Tanner. Also featured were Cynthia Nixon as Alex Tanner, and Pamela Reed as T. J. Cavanaugh. Some real-life political figures also made cameo appearances on the twelve-part series, including Bruce Babbitt and Kitty Dukakis.

TARGET   SYNDICATED
1958   Adolphe Menjou hosted, and occasionally starred in, this series of half-hour dramas from Ziv TV.

TARGET: THE CORRUPTORS   ABC
29 SEPTEMBER 1961–21 SEPTEMBER 1962   Stephen McNally starred in this hour crime show as crusading newspaper columnist Paul Marino, who tracked down and exposed racketeers; Robert Harland costarred as his investigator, Jack Flood. Leonard Ackerman and John Burrows produced the series, and Gene Roddenberry (who later created *Star Trek*) supplied at least one script.

TARZAN   NBC
8 SEPTEMBER 1966–13 SEPTEMBER 1968   Edgar Rice Burroughs's famous jungle character, who had been featured in films for decades, finally came to television (without Jane) in 1966. The hour adventure series starred Ron Ely as Tarzan, who was born Lord Greystoke, but who preferred jungle life. Also featured were Manuel Padilla, Jr., as young Jai, who, like Tarzan, was a jungle orphan; Alan Caillou as Jason Flood, Jai's tutor; and Rockne Tarkington as Rao, a veterinarian. Filmed on location in Brazil and Mexico, the show was produced by Banner Productions.

TARZAN   SYNDICATED
1991–1992   TV's second live-action version of the adventure series starred Wolf Larson as Tarzan, who lived in an elaborate treehouse, sported long blond hair, and spoke in more than monosyllables. Also featured were Lydie Denier as environmentalist Jane Porter; Sean Roberge as her young assistant, Roger Taft Jr.; and Malick Bowens as Simon, a native. A chimp named Cheetah was also on hand. Though set in Africa, the thirty-minute syndicated program was filmed in Yucatan.

TARZAN, LORD OF THE JUNGLE   CBS
11 SEPTEMBER 1976–3 SEPTEMBER 1977; 11 FEBRUARY 1984–8 SEPTEMBER 1984
TARZAN AND THE SUPER 7   CBS
9 SEPTEMBER 1978–30 AUGUST 1980
THE TARZAN/LONE RANGER ADVENTURE HOUR   CBS
13 SEPTEMBER 1980–5 SEPTEMBER 1981

THE TARZAN/LONE RANGER/ZORRO ADVENTURE HOUR   CBS

12 SEPTEMBER 1981–11 SEPTEMBER 1982   Edgar Rice Burroughs's character was featured not only in a live-action prime-time series (see above), but also in cartoon form on Saturday mornings. *Tarzan, Lord of the Jungle* was a half-hour show, which ran for one season. In the fall of 1977 Tarzan teamed up with Batman in *The Batman/ Tarzan Adventure Hour* (see that title), and in the fall of 1978 Tarzan regained top billing in *Tarzan and the Super 7,* a ninety-minute show with seven segments: "Tarzan," "Batman and Robin," "The Freedom Force" (a group of superheroes including Hercules, Isis, Super Samurai, Merlin, and Sinbad), "Superstretch and Microwoman" (a husband-and-wife team), "Moray & Manta" (a pair of underwater crimefighters), "Web Woman," and "Jason of Star Command." The latter segment was a live-action feature set in outer space with Craig Littler as Jason, a young trainee with Star Command, a galactic police force; Sid Haig as Dragos, the archvillain; Susan O'Hanlon; Charlie Dell; and James Doohan. Norm Prescott and Lou Scheimer are the executive producers of both *Tarzan, Lord of the Jungle* and *Tarzan and the Super 7. Jason of Star Command* became a separate series in 1979 (see also that title), while *Tarzan and the Super 7* carried on for another season in an hour format. In 1980 "Tarzan" segments were mixed with "Lone Ranger" cartoons on *The Tarzan/Lone Ranger Adventure Hour.* A third hero, Zorro, joined them in 1981 for *The Tarzan/ Lone Ranger/Zorro Adventure Hour.* Norm Prescott and Lou Scheimer produced the several incarnations of the series.

TATE   NBC

8 JUNE 1960–28 SEPTEMBER 1960   This summer western starred David McLean as Tate, a one-armed gunslinger (his bad arm was encased in leather). Robert Redford made two guest appearances on the half-hour show, in "The Bounty Hunter" (22 June) and "Comanche Scalps" (10 August).

TATTINGER'S (NICK AND HILLARY)   NBC

26 OCTOBER 1988–11 JANUARY 1989; 20 APRIL 1989–26 APRIL 1989   *Tattinger's* was an unsuccessful hour comedy-drama from the *St. Elsewhere* creative crew. Set at an elegant Manhattan restaurant, it featured Stephen Collins as Nick Tattinger, the former owner of Tattinger's who returned from Paris to New York and again became involved with the restaurant; Blythe Danner as his ex-wife, Hillary, the owner; Patrice Colihan as their older daughter, Nina; Chay Lentin as their younger daughter, Winnifred; Jerry Stiller as Sid, the assistant manager; Mary Beth Hurt as the new chef, Sheila Bradley; Yusef Bulos as the old chef, Alphonse; Sue Francis Pai as Billie; Robert Clohessy as bartender Tom Smaraldo; Rob Morrow as bartender Marco; Zach Grenier as drug dealer Sonny Franks; and Simon Jones as Norman, Hillary's new beau. Each episode featured cameo appearances by showbiz or sports celebrities, as guests at the restaurant.

Tattinger's left the air in January 1989 after nine episodes for "retooling." It returned three months later, considerably retooled: in a new time slot, in a half-hour format, as a sitcom, with a new title, *Nick and Hillary.* This time, Nick had again returned from a trip (this time to Brazil), only to find that Hillary had completely transformed the restaurant into an ultra-trendy nightspot in his absence. Most of the former cast returned. Jessica Prunell replaced Chay Lentin as Winnifred, and two new characters were introduced: Spin and Marti. Chris Elliott (son of Bob Elliott of Bob and Ray fame) was Spin, the ultra-hip maitre d' hired by Hillary to insure the proper atmosphere for the new venture, and Anna Levine was Marti, a waitress. *Nick and Hillary* proved even less popular than *Tattinger's,* and vanished after only two showings.

TATTLETALES   CBS/SYNDICATED

18 FEBRUARY 1974–31 MARCH 1978 (CBS); 1977 (SYNDICATED); 18 JANUARY 1982– 1 JUNE 1984 (CBS); 1983–1985 (SYNDICATED)   Bert Convy hosted this game show on which three celebrity couples competed, each playing for one-third of the studio audience; the spouses were separated while one set of partners is asked

questions. Couples won points by matching responses correctly. *Tattletales* was a Mark Goodson-Bill Todman Production.

TAXI
ABC/NBC

12 SEPTEMBER 1978–10 JUNE 1982 (ABC); 30 SEPTEMBER 1982–20 JULY 1983 (NBC) A half-hour sitcom set at the Sunshine Cab Company in New York, *Taxi* was created by four former *Mary Tyler Moore Show* staffers—Ed. Weinberger, David Davis, Stan Daniels, and James L. Brooks. Like *Mary Tyler Moore*, *Taxi* was an ensemble comedy set around a workplace. The cast included: Judd Hirsch as Alex Reiger, a career cabbie; Jeff Conaway (1978–1981) as Bobby Wheeler, a struggling actor; Tony Danza as Tony Banta, a struggling boxer; Randall Carver (1978–1979) as John Burns; Marilu Henner as Elaine Nardo, an aspiring art dealer; Danny DeVito as Louie DiPalma, the sadistic dispatcher; and Andy Kaufman as mechanic Latka Gravas, a befuddled immigrant. Subsequently added were: Christopher Lloyd (1979–1983) as "Reverend" Jim Ignatowski, a burned-out survivor of the psychedelic sixties (Lloyd had played the character in one episode of the first season); J. Alan Thomas (1980–1983) as Jeff Bennett, the assistant dispatcher; and Carol Kane (1982–1983) as Latka's wife, Simka, who was also from "the old country." *Taxi* finished in Nielsen's Top Ten at the end of its first season and won the first of its three consecutive Emmys as Outstanding Comedy Series. Nevertheless, ratings dipped slightly during the second season and dropped significantly thereafter. ABC canceled the series after four seasons, and NBC quickly picked it up. Unfortunately, the ratings failed to improve, and NBC dropped *Taxi* after a single season. Andy Kaufman died of lung cancer in May 1984 at the age of thirty-six. A ninety-minute series retrospective, "The Best of Taxi," aired on CBS 19 December 1994.

TAZ-MANIA
FOX

7 SEPTEMBER 1991–3 SEPTEMBER 1994   Half-hour cartoon series starring the hyperkinetic and perpetually hungry creature from Australia, the Tasmanian Devil. Following a prime-time premiere on 1 September 1991 the series was aired on Saturday mornings for three seasons.

TEACHERS ONLY
NBC

14 APRIL 1982–23 SEPTEMBER 1982; 12 FEBRUARY 1983–21 MAY 1983   The central characters in this half-hour sitcom were the faculty and staff at Millard Fillmore High School, an inner-city institution. The 1982 cast included Lynn Redgrave (late of *House Calls*) as teacher Diana Swanson, who took an active interest in the problems of her students and colleagues; Norman Fell as the phlegmatic principal, Ben Cooper; Adam Arkin as Michael Dreyfuss, the biology teacher; Norman Bartold as Mr. Brody, the assistant principal; Van Nessa Clarke as Gwen Edwards; Richard Karron as Pafko, the janitor; and Kit McDonough as Lois, the nosy clerk. When the series returned in 1983 as a midseason replacement, Fillmore High was firmly located in Brooklyn, and Diana Swanson had become the school's guidance counselor. Only Redgrave and Fell remained from the 1982 cast. New regulars included Jean Smart as Shari, Cooper's earthy secretary; Joel Brooks as Barney; Tim Reid as Michael; and Teresa Ganzel as Sam, Diana's best friend, an English teacher. Aaron Ruben created the series.

THE TED KNIGHT SHOW
CBS

8 APRIL 1978–13 MAY 1978   Disappointing sitcom starring Ted Knight as Roger Dennis, operator of a New York City escort service. His employees included: Fawne Harriman as Honey; Cissy Colpitts as Graziella; Tanya Boyd as Phil; Janice Kent as Cheryl; Ellen Regan as Irma; Deborah Harmon as Joy; and Iris Adrian as Dottie, Roger's salty secretary. Also featured were Normann Burton as Roger's brother, Burt, and Thomas Leopold as Roger's son, Winston. The series was created by Lowell Ganz and Mark Rothman, who also served as its executive producers; Martin Cohan and David W. Duclon were the producers. The pilot for the half-hour series was televised on *Busting Loose*. The program should not be confused with *The Ted*

Knight Show of 1986, which was the short-lived successor to *Too Close for Comfort* (see also that title).

TED MACK'S FAMILY HOUR ABC
7 JANUARY 1951–25 NOVEMBER 1951 Ted Mack hosted this Sunday-evening variety half hour, which also featured singer Andy Roberts and announcer Dennis James.

TED MACK'S MATINEE NBC
4 APRIL 1955–28 OCTOBER 1955 This half-hour daytime variety show was hosted by Ted Mack and featured Elise Rhodes, Beth Parks, Dick Lee, and the Honey Dreamers. A regular feature of the program awarded prizes to wives who wrote in to praise their husbands. Louis Graham produced the series.

TED MACK'S ORIGINAL AMATEUR HOUR DUMONT/NBC/ABC/CBS
18 JANUARY 1948–25 SEPTEMBER 1949 (DUMONT); 4 OCTOBER 1949–11 SEPTEMBER 1954 (NBC); 30 OCTOBER 1955–23 JUNE 1957 (ABC); 1 JULY 1957–4 OCTOBER 1958 (NBC); 1 MAY 1959–9 OCTOBER 1959 (CBS); 7 MARCH 1960–26 SEPTEMBER 1960 (ABC); 2 OCTOBER 1960–27 SEPTEMBER 1970 (CBS) Television's most famous talent show was a direct descendant of radio's best-known talent show, *Major Bowes' Original Amateur Hour,* which began in 1934; Major Edward Bowes hosted the radio program from 1934 until his death in 1946. A year later Ted Mack, who had directed the auditions for the Bowes show, took over as host and brought the show to television (the radio version lasted until 1952). The show, which was originally titled *Major Bowes' Original Amateur Hour* even on TV, was seen sporadically in 1947, with regularly scheduled broadcasts beginning in 1948. It was one of the few programs to have been broadcast on all four commercial networks. For most of its long run it was a half-hour series; it was a prime-time show from 1948 until 1960, when it began a lengthy Sunday-afternoon run on CBS. The format of the show was simple and straightforward, changing little over the years: each week a number of amateur performers displayed their talents, and the viewing audience was invited to vote—by postcard—for their favorite act.

THE TED STEELE SHOW NBC/DUMONT/CBS
29 SEPTEMBER 1948–29 OCTOBER 1948 (NBC); 27 FEBRUARY 1949–12 JULY 1949 (DUMONT); 6 JUNE 1949–8 JULY 1949 (CBS); 10 OCTOBER 1949–28 APRIL 1950 (CBS) Singer Ted Steele hosted several musical variety shows. He first hosted a prime-time show on NBC. His DuMont series was seen in both daytime and prime-time versions, and before it was over he had begun a daytime show on CBS. In the fall of 1949 his CBS daytime series was seen Mondays through Fridays at 5:00 P.M.

TEECH CBS
18 SEPTEMBER 1991–16 OCTOBER 1991 This half-hour sitcom may have been inspired by the film "Dead Poets' Society." It starred Phill Lewis as music teacher "Teech" Gibson, who was furloughed from a Philadelphia public school job and landed a position at a private school, Winthrop Academy, where he was the sole black faculty member. Also featured were Maggie Han as Cassie Lee, the assistant headmistress; Steven Gilborn as Alfred Litton, the stuffy headmaster who disapproved of Teech's unorthodox efforts to educate his students; Curnal Achilles Aulisio as George Dubcek, the dumb jock; Joshua Hoffman as Kenny Freedman, the smart kid; Ken Lawrence Johnston as Boyd Askew, the rich kid; Jack Noseworthy as Adrian Peterman, the nerd; and Jason Kristofer as boisterous Albie Nichols. Music for the show was provided by B. B. King, who guested on one episode as Teech's uncle.

TEEN TIME TUNES DUMONT
7 MARCH 1949–15 JULY 1949 Fifteen-minute Monday-through-Friday-evening musical show, featuring the music of the Alan Logan Trio.

TEEN WOLF   CBS

13 SEPTEMBER 1986–27 AUGUST 1988; 29 OCTOBER 1988–2 SEPTEMBER 1989   Saturday morning cartoon series based on the 1985 film about a teenager who discovered that he was a werewolf.

TEENAGE BOOK CLUB   ABC

13 AUGUST 1948–29 OCTOBER 1948   Half-hour panel show featuring discussions on current books of interest to teenagers.

TEENAGE MUTANT NINJA TURTLES   SYNDICATED/CBS

1987 (SYNDICATED); 8 SEPTEMBER 1990– (CBS)   First came the comic book in 1984, a black and white effort created by two young men from Massachusetts, Kevin Eastman and Peter Laird, and produced for $1200. It told the tale of a quartet of turtles who lived in the New York City sewer system, where they were exposed to a radioactive substance, mutagen, that transformed them into pizza-craving, half-turtle, half-human creatures—"heroes on the halfshell." Each took a classical Italian name and a favorite weapon—Leonardo (a ninja sword), Michelangelo (nunchucks), Donatello (a bow or staff) and Raphael (a scythe). Assisted by their comrade Splinter, a sushi-eating rat who taught them the martial arts, and by a TV news reporter, April O'Neil, they battled the evil Shredder.

   This half-hour syndicated cartoon series followed in 1987. A 1990 motion picture, with live-action characters, boosted their popularity tremendously, prompting CBS to announce the addition of a new *Teenage Mutant Ninja Turtles* cartoon series to its Saturday morning schedule in the fall of 1990. A Japanese network also purchased the show in 1990, planning to retitle it *Teenage Mutant Hero Turtles*.

TEKNOMAN   UPN

10 SEPTEMBER 1995–   Sunday-morning cartoon series set in the year 2087, pitting the hero, Teknoman, in a battle against the evil Dakon for control of the world.

TELECOMICS   SYNDICATED/NBC

1949 (SYNDICATED); 18 SEPTEMBER 1950–30 MARCH 1951 (NBC)   Produced by Vallee Video, *Telecomics* included some of the first cartoons made especially for television. Among the first segments were: "Brother Goose," "Joey and Jug," "Rick Rack, Special Agent," and "Sa-Lih." When the series was picked up by NBC (and broadcast under the title *NBC Comics*) segments included "Danny March," "Johnny and Mr. Do-Right," "Kid Champion," and "Space Barton."

TELEDRAMA   SYNDICATED

1952   Half-hour dramatic anthology series.

TELEPHONE TIME   CBS/ABC

8 APRIL 1956–31 MARCH 1957 (CBS); 4 JUNE 1957–1 APRIL 1958 (ABC)   The stories on this half-hour filmed dramatic anthology series were based on true incidents. Jerry Stagg produced the series, which was hosted by John Nesbitt on CBS and by Dr. Frank Baxter on ABC.

TELESPORTS DIGEST   SYNDICATED

1953   Harry Wismer hosted this sports series, on which films of the past week's top athletic events were shown.

TELE-THEATRE   NBC

27 SEPTEMBER 1948–26 JUNE 1950   A half-hour dramatic anthology series, *Tele-Theatre* was sponsored by Chevrolet and was titled *Chevrolet on Broadway* in its early weeks. Vic McLeod was the producer.

TELEVISION   PBS

25 JANUARY 1988–7 MARCH 1988   Edwin Newman hosted this eight-part examination of television itself, which focused principally on the medium's history and its effect

on American society. The series was an edited version of an eleven-part series produced in England by Granada Television.

TELEVISION: INSIDE & OUT   NBC
5 DECEMBER 1981–2 JANUARY 1982   This prime-time Saturday series took a superficial look at television and other entertainment media. Gossip columnist Rona Barrett was the host, assisted by Chicago TV critic Gary Deeb, comic Wil Shriner, and Sylvester "Pat" Weaver, NBC's visionary programmer of the 1950s.

TELEVISION RECITAL HALL   NBC
1 JULY 1951–21 AUGUST 1953; 9 AUGUST 1954–6 SEPTEMBER 1954   This highbrow musical series, on which classical performers appeared, began as a summer replacement for *The Colgate Comedy Hour* and later shifted to Sunday afternoons. During the summer of 1954 it was seen in prime time. Charles Polacheck produced the series.

TELL IT TO GROUCHO   CBS
11 JANUARY 1962–31 MAY 1962   *Tell It to Groucho,* a half-hour midseason replacement series, was similar in format to *You Bet Your Life,* except that the quiz segment was emphasized even less. Two contestants appeared and were perfectly free to state their problems or air their gripes during the interview with host Groucho Marx. A top prize of $500 was available in the quiz segment to a contestant who could identify a photograph of a celebrity that appeared for a split second. Jack Wheeler and Patty Harmon served as Groucho's assistants and George Fenneman was the announcer; Bernie Smith produced the show. See also *Tell It to the Camera; You Bet Your Life.*

TELL IT TO THE CAMERA   CBS
25 DECEMBER 1963–18 MARCH 1964   *Tell It to the Camera* was hastily devised as a midseason replacement for *Glynis* on Wednesdays. People on the street were invited to state their opinions, thoughts, or complaints to the camera. Red Rowe hosted the half-hour series, which was taped on location throughout the United States; Allen Funt was the producer.

TELL ME, DR. BROTHERS
See DR. JOYCE BROTHERS

TELLER OF TALES
See SOMERSET MAUGHAM THEATRE

THE TELLTALE CLUE   CBS
8 JULY 1954–23 SEPTEMBER 1954   Half-hour crime show starring Anthony Ross as Detective Richard Hale of the New York Police Department.

TEMPERATURES RISING   ABC
12 SEPTEMBER 1972–8 JANUARY 1974   Half-hour sitcom set at Capitol General Hospital in Washington, D.C. During the 1972–1973 season the cast included: Cleavon Little as Dr. Jerry Noland; James Whitmore as Dr. Vincent Campanelli; Joan Van Ark as Nurse Annie Carlisle; Reva Rose as Nurse Mildred MacInerney; and Nancy Fox as Nurse Ellen Turner. In the fall of 1973 the show was retitled *The New Temperatures Rising Show;* only Cleavon Little was retained from the previous cast. The new regulars included: Paul Lynde as Dr. Paul Mercy, the hospital administrator; Sudie Bond as Agatha, Paul's mother, owner of the hospital; Alice Ghostley as Edwina, Paul's sister; Jeff Morrow as Dr. Lloyd Axton; Barbara Cason as Nurse Tillis; Jennifer Darling as Nurse Winchester; and John Dehner as Dr. Claver. William Asher was the executive producer of the series.

TEMPESTT   SYNDICATED
1995–   Hour daytime talk show hosted by Tempestt Bledsoe, best known to television viewers as daughter Vanessa on *The Cosby Show.*

TEMPLE HOUSTON   NBC

19 SEPTEMBER 1963–10 SEPTEMBER 1964   This hour western starred Jeffrey Hunter as lawyer Temple Houston, son of Sam Houston. Jack Elam played his sidekick, George Taggart, a former gunslinger. Also featured were Mary Wickes as Ida Goff; Frank Ferguson as Judge Gurney; Chubby Johnson as Concho; and James Best as Gotch.

TEMPTATION   ABC

4 DECEMBER 1967–1 MARCH 1968   Art James hosted this daytime game show, which combined a question-and-answer segment with a merchandise-swapping segment.

THE $10,000 PYRAMID (THE $20,000 PYRAMID)   CBS/ABC/SYNDICATED
(THE $25,000 PYRAMID) (THE $50,000 PYRAMID) (THE $100,000 PYRAMID)

26 MARCH 1973–29 MARCH 1974 (CBS); 6 MAY 1974–27 JUNE 1980 (ABC) 1974–1979 (SYNDICATED); 1981 (SYNDICATED); 20 SEPTEMBER 1982–1 JULY 1988 (CBS); 1985–1989; 1991 (SYNDICATED)   On this half-hour game show from Bob Stewart Productions, two teams, each with a celebrity and a contestant, competed in a two-part word game. In the first part players tried to get their partners to identify a list of words in a given category by supplying definitions to those words. The team with the higher score after three rounds then progressed to the second part of the game, where the procedure was reversed: by naming elements of a listed category, one player tried to get the other to identify the category; the top prize at the second level was originally $10,000 on the network version, but was increased to $20,000 on 19 January 1976, as the show was retitled *The $20,000 Pyramid*. The top prize on the 1974–1979 syndicated version remained steady at $25,000. A new syndicated version was introduced early in 1981 with a top prize of $50,000 (and the show was retitled accordingly), but the figure was scaled down again to $25,000 when the series returned to CBS's daytime schedule in the fall of 1982. The 1985 and 1991 syndicated versions offered a potential grand prize of $100,000. Except for the first syndicated version, which was emceed by Bill Cullen, and the 1991 syndicated version, which John Davidson emceed, all versions of the show were hosted by Dick Clark.

TEN WHO DARED   SYNDICATED

1977   Ten-part historical documentary series on great explorers. Produced by the BBC in cooperation with Time-Life Films, the hour series was sponsored by Mobil Oil. Among the explorers whose lives were dramatized were Columbus, Pizarro, Cook, von Humboldt, Jedediah Smith, Mary Kingsley, and Roald Amundsen. Anthony Quinn was the host and narrator.

TENAFLY   NBC

10 OCTOBER 1973–6 AUGUST 1974   One segment of *The NBC Wednesday Movie*, *Tenafly* alternated for one season with *Banacek, Faraday and Company,* and *The Snoop Sisters*. It starred James McEachin as Harry Tenafly, a decidedly unflashy black private eye who worked in Los Angeles. Also featured were Lillian Lehman as his wife, Ruth Tenafly; David Huddleston as Lieutenant Church; Rosanna Huffman as his secretary, Lorrie; and Paul Jackson as his son, Herb.

THE TENNESSEE ERNIE FORD SHOW   NBC/ABC

3 JANUARY 1955–28 JUNE 1957 (NBC); 4 OCTOBER 1956–29 JUNE 1961 (NBC); 2 APRIL 1962–26 MARCH 1965 (ABC)   Tennessee Ernie Ford, best known as a country-and-western singer and folksy humorist, was actually born in Tennessee; by the early 1950s, however, he had moved West and was hosting a local show in Los Angeles called *Hometown Jamboree*. In 1954 he emceed a revival of Kay Kyser's *College of Musical Knowledge,* and a few months later he began hosting the first of his three network variety shows. The first was a half-hour daytime series, which also featured Molly Bee. The second, which started in the fall of 1956, was a Thursday-night half-hour series (when it was sponsored by the Ford Motor Company, it was known simply as *The Ford Show*); it featured the Top Twenty, Harry Geller's Orchestra, and the Voices of Walter Schumann. Ford's third series was a half-hour daytime show on ABC, which featured Dick Noel and Anita Gordon. His NBC shows were produced

and directed by Bud Yorkin, who later teamed up with Norman Lear on *All in the Family*. Ford's ABC show was produced and directed by William Burch.

TENNESSEE TUXEDO   CBS
28 SEPTEMBER 1963–3 SEPTEMBER 1966   Segments on this Saturday-morning cartoon show included "Tennessee Tuxedo," a penguin, "The Hunter," the story of a beagle tracking a fox, "Tutor the Turtle," and "The World of Commander McBragg."

TENSPEED AND BROWN SHOE   ABC
27 JANUARY 1980–27 JUNE 1980   Hour adventure series about a black con artist and a white stockbroker who teamed up as private investigators. With Ben Vereen as E. L. "Tenspeed" Turner and Jeff Goldblum as Lionel "Brown Shoe" Whitney. The series was a Stephen J. Cannell production. Vereen later appeared as Tenspeed on the last few episodes of another Cannell venture, *J. J. Starbuck*.

TEQUILA AND BONETTI   CBS
17 JANUARY 1992–18 APRIL 1992   Based loosely on the film "Turner & Hooch," this light hour crime show featured Jack Scalia as Nico Bonetti, a New York cop who moved to South Coast, California, after accidentally killing a younsgter, and found himself teamed up with a drooling French mastiff named Tequila. Also featured were Charles Rocket as Captain Midian Knight, an aspiring writer; Mariska Hargitay as Officer Angela Garcia, a widow; Terry Funk as Officer Nuzo; Joe Vita as Officer Vita; Noley Thornton as Angela's young daughter, Teresa; and Brad Sanders as the voice of Tequila, whose observations were communicated to the viewing audience.

TERRAHAWKS   SYNDICATED
1985–1986   The stars of this cartoon series, set in 2020, were the Terrahawks, a band of warriors defending the Earth from alien invaders.

TERRY AND THE PIRATES   SYNDICATED
1952   This half-hour adventure series, based on the comic strip, starred John Baer as Terry Lee, an American adventurer/pilot in the Far East; also featured were Gloria Saunders as his nemesis, The Dragon Lady, Mari Blanchard and Sandra Spence as Burma, Jack Reitzen as Chopstick Joe, owner of Air Cathay, and William Tracy as Hotshot Charlie. The series was produced by Don Sharpe Enterprises.

THE TEX AND JINX SHOW   NBC
18 FEBRUARY 1957–31 JANUARY 1958   This half-hour daytime interview show was hosted by the husband-and-wife team of Tex McCrary and Jinx Falkenburg. Broadcast from New York, the show was originally titled *Closeup*.

THE TEXAN   CBS
29 SEPTEMBER 1958–12 SEPTEMBER 1960   This half-hour western starred Rory Calhoun as Bill Longley, a fast-drawing drifter. Calhoun and Vic Orsatti were the executive producers, and Jerry Stagg was the producer.

TEXAS   NBC
4 AUGUST 1980–31 DECEMBER 1982   The phenomenal popularity of the prime-time serial *Dallas* led to the creation of this daytime soap opera. The hour series was set in Houston, where (according to NBC's ads) "living is fast, loving is free, and rules are meant to be broken." To help *Texas* acquire an audience, two popular performers from the NBC serial *Another World*— Beverlee McKinsey (who received star billing in the credits) and Jim Poyner— were cast as central characters. Nevertheless, *Texas* failed to attract a large audience, principally because it was scheduled at 3:00 P.M., opposite ABC's *General Hospital,* then enjoying a strong ascendancy in the ratings race. The network changed *Texas*'s time slot on 26 April 1982, but the new hour— mornings at 11:00—proved even worse for the show, and *Texas* bit the dust after a twenty-nine-month run.

Principal players included: Beverlee McKinsey as Iris (Cory) (Carrington) (Delaney) Bancroft, who left *Another World*'s Bay City to join her son in Houston; Jim Poyner (who had also emigrated from Bay City) as her son, Dennis Carrington; Bert Kramer as Alex Wheeler, an old flame of Iris's, who (unknown to himself and to Dennis) was really Dennis's father; Donald May as Grant Wheeler, the head of World Oil; Sharon Acker as his wife, Judith Wheeler; Michael Woods as their son, Mark Wheeler, World Oil's president; Harley Kozak as their daughter, Brett Wheeler; Gretchen Oehler as Vivian Gorrow (who had also appeared on *Another World*), the Wheelers' maid; David Forsyth as lawyer Thomas Jefferson (T. J.) Canfield; Larry Weber as his father, Burton Canfield; Lori March as his mother, Mildred Canfield; Josephine Nichols as Kate Marshall; Jerry Lanning as her son, Justin Marshall, head of Marshall Oil; Lisby Larson as her daughter, Paige Marshall; Pamela Long as Justin's wife, Ashley Marshall (Long, also known as Pamela Long Hammer, became a writer for *Texas* and would later become the head writer of *Guiding Light*); Damian Scheler as Gregory Marshall, son of Ashley by T. J.; Terri Garber as Allison Linden, Ashley's sister; Robert Gerringer as Striker Bellman; Elizabeth Allen as TV executive Victoria Bellman, Striker's ex-wife; Carla Borelli as Reena Cook Dekker, Striker's daughter; Randy Hamilton as Rikki Dekker; Caryn Richman as Elena Dekker; Shirley Slater as Maggie Dekker; Shanna Reed as Terry Dekker; Chandler Hill Harben and Jay Hammer as Max Dekker; Barbara Rucker as Ginny Connor; John McCafferty as TV star Billy Joe Wright; Dianne Neil as his sister, Ruby Wright; Joel Colodner as Dr. Bart Walker; Ann McCarthy as Samantha Walker; Charlie Hill as Joel Walker; Cathy Hickland as Dr. Courtney Marshall; Dana Kimmel as Dawn Marshall; Lee Patterson as Kevin Cook; Scott Stevenson as unsavory Clipper Curtis; Tina Johnson as Lurlene Harper; Michael Longfield as Hunt Weston; Chris Goutman as George St. John; Ellen Maxted as Anita Wright; Phil Clark as Ryan Connor; Gregory Sutton as Ginny's son, Steve Marshall; Kin Shriner (who left *General Hospital* and returned to it after *Texas* folded) as Jeb Richmond; Philip English as Miles Renquist; Maher Boutros as Colonel Hassein; and Donna Cyrus as Princess Jasmine of Tanquir. In the fall of 1983, *Texas* achieved a minor distinction when it became one of the few soap operas to be rerun; Procter and Gamble, which owned the serial, sold the reruns (beginning with episode #104) to WTBS, the Atlanta "superstation" whose programs were carried by many cable systems throughout the country.

TEXAS RODEO NBC
30 APRIL 1959–2 JULY 1959 Half-hour rodeo show videotaped in Houston. L. N. Sikes and Bob Gray were the producers.

THE TEXAS WHEELERS ABC
13 SEPTEMBER 1974–4 OCTOBER 1974; 26 JUNE 1975–31 JULY 1975 *The Texas Wheelers* was the first casualty of the 1974–1975 season, axed after only four episodes (though a few additional shows were broadcast during the summer of 1975). The half-hour comedy starred Jack Elam as Zack Wheeler, a lazy opportunist who hoped to live off his four children. Also featured were Gary Busey as his oldest son, Truckie; Mark Hamill as second son Doobie; Karen Oberdiear as daughter Boo; Tony Decker as youngest son T. J.; Lisa Eilbacher as Boo's friend, Sally; Bill Burton as Bud; and Dennis Burkley as Herb. Dale McRaven was the executive producer and Chris Hayward the producer for MTM Enterprises.

THAT GIRL ABC
8 SEPTEMBER 1966–10 SEPTEMBER 1971 Marlo Thomas, daughter of Danny Thomas, starred in this half-hour sitcom as Ann Marie, an aspiring young actress living in New York; Ted Bessell costarred as her boyfriend, Don Hollinger, a writer for *Newsview* magazine (the two were finally engaged in the fall of 1970). Also featured were Lew Parker as Ann's father, Lew Marie, who owned a French restaurant in Brewster, New York, and Rosemary DeCamp as Ann's mother, Helen Marie. A considerable number of performers appeared from time to time on the show, including: Bonnie Scott as Ann's neighbor, Judy Bessemer; Dabney Coleman as Judy's husband, Leon Bessemer, an obstetrician; George Carlin (1966–1967) as Ann's agent, George Lester; Ronnie Schell (1967–1968) as agent Harvey Peck; Morty Gunty as agent Sandy

Stone; Billy DeWolfe (1966–1968) as Ann's acting coach, Jules Benedict; Bernie Kopell as Don's pal, Jerry Meyer (Kopell later played pal Jerry Bauman); Alice Borden as Ruth Bauman, Jerry's wife; Reva Rose as Ann's friend, Marcy; Frank Faylen as Don's father, Bert Hollinger; and Mabel Albertson as Don's mother, Mildred Hollinger. *That Girl* was created by Bill Persky and Sam Denoff, who had both previously written for *The Dick Van Dyke Show*.

THAT GOOD OLE NASHVILLE MUSIC SYNDICATED
1972   Half-hour country-and-western music show.

THAT REMINDS ME ABC
13 AUGUST 1948–1 OCTOBER 1948   Half-hour Friday-night talk show with Walter Kiernan and Harold Hoffman, former governor of New Jersey (Hoffman was later one of the original panelists on *What's My Line?*).

THAT SHOW
See THE JOAN RIVERS SHOW

THAT WAS THE WEEK THAT WAS NBC
10 JANUARY 1964–4 MAY 1965   *That Was the Week That Was,* commonly abbreviated to *TW3,* was based on a British series created by Ned Sherrin. The half-hour series satirized current events, but the American version was never as well received as its British counterpart. Among the regulars on the American version were David Frost, Elliott Reid, Alan Alda, Henry Morgan, Phyllis Newman, Buck Henry, Pat Englund, Doro Merande, Burr Tillstrom's puppets, Skitch Henderson's Orchestra, and vocalist Nancy Ames. Leland Hayward was the executive producer, and Marshall Jamison was the producer; among the writers were Saul Turteltaub, Robert Emmett, and Gerald Gardner. The show was first introduced as a special in November 1963 and became a weekly series in January, replacing *Harry's Girls.* ABC aired a one-hour "That Was the Week That Was" special on 21 April 1985, hosted by David Frost.

THAT WONDERFUL GUY ABC
4 JANUARY 1950–28 APRIL 1950   This early musical comedy series starred Jack Lemmon as Harold, a young songwriter-actor who got a job as the manservant of a crotchety drama critic; Neil Hamilton played the drama critic and Cynthia Stone (whom Lemmon later married) played Harold's girlfriend. Bernard Green's orchestra was also featured. Broadcast live, the half-hour series was produced by Charles Irving and directed by Babette Henry.

THAT'S AMORE SYNDICATED
1992   This American version of the game show which originated in Italy in 1989 was hosted by Luca Barbareschi, and featured married couples who were feuding or quarreling. The studio audience selected the most deserving couple, who were then sent on a second honeymoon.

THAT'S HOLLYWOOD! SYNDICATED
1977–1980   This half-hour documentary series consisted of film clips from the archives of 20th Century-Fox. Jack Haley, Jr. (who put together the nostalgic film, *That's Entertainment*) was the executive producer, Draper Lewis the writer and producer, and Tom Bosley the narrator.

THAT'S INCREDIBLE! ABC
3 MARCH 1980–30 APRIL 1984   *That's Incredible!* was ABC's response to NBC's popular "reality show," *Real People.* The hour prime-time series was hosted by John Davidson, Cathy Lee Crosby, and former footballer Fran Tarkenton. Many of the incredible features presented on the show were staged specifically for the program. Some of the stunts proved too dangerous for those who attempted them. Stan Krumi, for example, was badly burned as he ran through a "tunnel of fire"; his "fireproof" gloves melted in the 1800-degree heat. Other features turned out to be bogus, such as

an inventor's claim that he had found an easy way to make hydrogen fuel by using mass-produced solar cells; the claimant was later convicted on ten counts of fraud. Still other segments were just plain silly, such as one about a Frenchman who ate a ten-speed bicycle. See also *Incredible Sunday*.

THAT'S LIFE ABC

24 SEPTEMBER 1968–20 MAY 1969   One of television's few musical comedy series, *That's Life* starred Robert Morse as Robert Dickson and E. J. (short for Edra Jeanne) Peaker as Gloria Quigley, who, as the show progressed, got married and had a child. Also featured were Shelley Berman as Gloria's father, Mr. Quigley, and Kay Medford as her mother, Mrs. Quigley. Liza Minnelli made a rare guest appearance on 17 December.

THAT'S MY BOY CBS

10 APRIL 1954–1 JANUARY 1955   Half-hour sitcom starring Eddie Mayehoff as Jarrin' Jack Jackson, a former college football star; Rochelle Hudson as his wife, Alice Jackson; and Gil Stratton, Jr., as their son, Junior, a bookish lad who tried to resist his father's continual efforts to interest him in athletics. The series was based on the motion picture of the same title, in which Mayehoff had starred with Dean Martin and Jerry Lewis.

THAT'S MY LINE CBS

9 AUGUST 1980–23 AUGUST 1980; 3 FEBRUARY 1981–11 APRIL 1981   Bob Barker hosted this hour "reality show," which focused on people with unusual occupations. Assisting him were reporters Tiiu Leek, Suzanne Childs, and (in the spring of 1981) Kerry Millerick. The show was supplied by Goodson-Todman Productions; its founders, Mark Goodson and Bill Todman, had created the classic game show *What's My Line?* some thirty years earlier.

THAT'S MY MAMA ABC

4 SEPTEMBER 1974–24 DECEMBER 1975   Set in Washington, D.C., *That's My Mama* told the story of a black family and their friends. Featured were Theresa Merritt as Eloise (Mama) Curtis, a widow; Clifton Davis as her bachelor son, Clifton Curtis, operator of a barber shop; Lynne Moody (1974–spring 1975) and Joan Pringle (fall 1975) as her daughter, Tracy; Lisle Wilson as Tracy's husband, Leonard Taylor; Theodore Wilson as Earl Chambers, the local mail carrier; Jester Hairston as Wildcat, a jive-talking dude; Ted Lange as Clifton's friend, Junior; and DeForest Covan as Josh. Created by Dan T. Bradley and Allan Rice, the half-hour sitcom was a Blye-Beard Production.

THAT'S O'TOOLE ABC

13 MARCH 1949–5 JUNE 1949   Broadcast from Chicago, this half-hour show was aimed at the do-it-yourselfer and featured Arthur Peterson as handyman Tinker O'Toole and Norma Ransome as his wife.

THEA ABC

8 SEPTEMBER 1993–23 FEBRUARY 1994   Half-hour family sitcom starring standup comic Thea Vidale as Thea Turrell, a widow with four children, who worked in a market days and ran a beauty shop from her home at night. Also on hand were Adam Jeffries as sixteen-year-old Jarvis, Jr.; Jason Weaver as fourteen-year-old Jerome; Brandy Norwood as thirteen-year-old Danesha; Brenden Jefferson as youngest son James; Yvette Wilson as Thea's sister, Lynette; and Cleavant Derricks as Lynette's husband, Charles.

THEATER IN AMERICA PBS

1974–1977   A dramatic anthology series of variable length, *Theater in America* presented fourteen to twenty-two plays per season, which were performed by several repertory companies. The series was produced by WNET-TV, New York.

THEATER OF ROMANCE
See ROMANCE

THEATER OF THE MIND   NBC
14 JULY 1949–15 SEPTEMBER 1949   *Theater of the Mind* was a half-hour anthology
series of psychological dramas. Each story was followed by a discussion with a panel
of three experts, moderated by Dr. Houston Peterson. The series was produced and
written by Ann Marlowe.

THEATRE HOUR   CBS
7 OCTOBER 1949–10 MARCH 1950   This hour-long dramatic anthology series was seen
on Friday nights.

THEN CAME BRONSON   NBC
17 SEPTEMBER 1969–9 SEPTEMBER 1970   Michael Parks starred in this hour adventure
series as Jim Bronson, a disillusioned young man riding around the country on his
motorcycle. The series was produced by M-G-M TV.

THERE'S ONE IN EVERY FAMILY   CBS
29 SEPTEMBER 1952–12 JUNE 1953   John Reed King and, later, Dean Miller, hosted
this daytime game show that featured contestants who possessed unusual abilities.
Richard Levine produced the show, and James Sheldon directed it.

THESE ARE MY CHILDREN   NBC
31 JANUARY 1949–4 MARCH 1949   One of TV's first daytime serials, *These Are My
Children* was created by Irna Phillips, who later achieved success with *The Guiding
Light, As the World Turns,* and *Another World.* Directed by Norman Felton, the
fifteen-minute show was broadcast live from Chicago. The cast included Alma Platts
as Mrs. Henehan, a widow who ran a boardinghouse; Jane Brooksmith as her daughter Patricia; Martha McClain as her daughter Penny; George Kluge as her son, John;
Joan Arlt as John's wife, Jean; Eloise Kummer as Kay Carter; and Margaret
Heneghan as Aunt Kitty.

THESE ARE THE DAYS   ABC
7 SEPTEMBER 1974–5 SEPTEMBER 1976   This Hanna-Barbera cartoon series capitalized on the popularity of *The Waltons.* Set in a small town at the turn of the century, it
depicted the lives of the members of the Day family and their friends and neighbors.
The show was seen Saturday mornings during its first season; reruns were shown
Sunday mornings during the second season.

THESE FRIENDS OF MINE
See ELLEN

THEY STAND ACCUSED   DUMONT
11 SEPTEMBER 1949–5 OCTOBER 1952; 9 SEPTEMBER 1954–30 DECEMBER 1954   On this
hour-long anthology series fictional court cases were dramatized. Broadcast live from
Chicago, the show featured Chicago attorney Charles Johnston as the judge and
Harry Creighton as the announcer. The jurors were chosen from the studio audience,
and the verdict was theirs alone. Originally titled *Cross Question,* the show was
directed by Sheldon Cooper and written by William C. Wines, an Illinois assistant
attorney general.

THEY'RE OFF   DUMONT
7 JULY 1949–18 AUGUST 1949   Prime-time game show modeled after a horse race.

THICKE OF THE NIGHT   SYNDICATED
5 SEPTEMBER 1983–15 JUNE 1984   This ninety-minute late-night talk show was designed to compete with *The Tonight Show Starring Johnny Carson* and was scheduled
opposite that show in most areas where it was carried. The program was hosted by

Alan Thicke, a singer-comedian who had hosted a popular daytime series in Canada. The show also featured a resident company of comic actors, who appeared in various sketches and ad-lib with Thicke: Richard Belzer, Chloe Webb, Isabel Grandin, Gilbert Gottfried, Mike McManus, and Charles Fleischer. The show opened to mediocre reviews and low ratings, and within five weeks it had taken on a new producer, a new director, and new sets. Reruns were aired through the summer of 1984.

THICKER THAN WATER ABC
13 JUNE 1973–8 AUGUST 1973   Based on the British series, *Nearest and Dearest,* this half-hour sitcom told the story of a squabbling brother and sister who were each promised a $75,000 inheritance if they agreed to run the family pickle factory for five years. With Julie Harris as Nellie Paine; Richard Long as Ernie Paine; Malcolm Atterbury as their father, Jonas Paine, who believed that his demise was imminent; Jessica Myerson as Cousin Lily; Lou Fant as Cousin Walter; and Pat Cranshaw as longtime employee Bert Taylor.

THE THIN MAN NBC
20 SEPTEMBER 1957–26 JUNE 1959   Half-hour crime show based on the Dashiell Hammett novel and the film series. With Peter Lawford as New York publisher Nick Charles, a former private eye who dabbled in sleuthing for the fun of it; Phyllis Kirk as his wife and frequent partner in crime-solving, Nora Charles; Jack Albertson as Lieutenant Evans; and Asta as Asta, the Charles' pet terrier. The series was produced by M-G-M TV.

THINK FAST ABC
26 MARCH 1949–8 OCTOBER 1950   Celebrity panelists tried to outtalk each other on this prime-time game show by extemporizing on subjects suggested by the host. Mason Gross was the first emcee and was succeeded by Gypsy Rose Lee. Robert Kennings produced the half-hour series.

THE THINK PINK PANTHER SHOW
See THE PINK PANTHER SHOW

THINK TWICE PBS
1994–1995   The first adult game show produced by PBS, *Think Twice* was hosted by Monteria Ivey. Pairs of contestants competed in quiz and story-building segments; the winning team was awarded a small investment portfolio instead of cash.

3RD DEGREE! SYNDICATED
1989–1990   A syndicated game show, hosted by Bert Convy, on which two pairs of celebrities (one female, one male) tried to determine what relationship or bond a panel of three contestants had in common. The celebs were permitted to ask yes or no questions of the panel.

THE THIRD MAN SYNDICATED
1959–1960   Graham Greene's adventure novel was made into a movie in 1949 and a radio series in 1950. Almost a decade later it came to television, where Michael Rennie starred as Harry Lime, international trouble-shooter (James Mason had previously been considered for the part); Jonathan Harris was also featured as Lime's assistant, Bradford Webster. Vernon Burns was executive producer of the half-hour series, filmed both in Hollywood and on location in Europe.

13 EAST NBC
29 JULY 1989–2 SEPTEMBER 1989; 14 APRIL 1990–25 AUGUST 1990   An unfunny sitcom centering on a group of nurses at a large hospital. With Diana Bellamy as nursing supervisor Maggie Poole; Jan Cobler as nurse Monique Roberts; Barbra Isenberg (1989) as Kelly; Ellen Regan (1989) as Janet Tom; Timothy Wade (1989) as Dr. Warren Newman; Rosemarie Jackson (1990) as A. J.; Eric Glenn (1990) as Sidney; and Wayne Powers (1990) as Mr. Frazier, the administrator. Scoey Mitchlll was the

executive producer of the show, which was taped not in Hollywood or New York, but in Irving, Texas.

13 QUEENS BLVD. ABC

20 MARCH 1979–17 APRIL 1979; 10 JULY 1979–24 JULY 1979 An adult sitcom set in a Queens apartment building. The spring cast included Eileen Brennan as Felicia Winters; Jerry Van Dyke as her husband, Steven Winters; Marcia Rodd as her divorced friend and neighbor, Elaine Dowling; Helen Page Camp as her widowed friend and neighbor, Millie Capestro; and Louise Williams as Millie's daughter, Jill Capestro. The summer cast included Brennan, Camp, and Williams, along with Frances Lee McCain as Lois, Felicia's sister-in-law, and Karen Rushmore as Camille. Richard Baer created the half-hour show, which was developed by Bud Yorkin, Bernie Orenstein, and Saul Turteltaub.

30 MINUTES CBS

16 SEPTEMBER 1978–28 AUGUST 1982 A junior edition of *60 Minutes,* this Saturday-afternoon newsmagazine for young people was first cohosted by Betsy Aaron and Christopher Glenn, and later by Glenn and Betty Ann Bowser.

THIRTY MINUTES WITH PBS

12 JANUARY 1971–21 MAY 1973 Half-hour interview show, hosted by Washington political analyst Elizabeth Drew.

thirtysomething ABC

29 SEPTEMBER 1987–28 MAY 1991; 23 JULY 1991–3 SEPTEMBER 1991 An hour dramatic series for baby-boomers, about baby-boomers, *thirtysomething* was created by two baby-boomers, Ed Zwick and Marshall Herskovitz, who had previously written for the 1970s drama *Family.* Asked by MGM/UA to develop a series, Zwick and Herskovitz drew from their own experiences as husbands and fathers, and created a series not unlike *Family,* which explored the everyday details of contemporary urban domestic life.

Instead of focusing on one household as *Family* had done, *thirtysomething* looked at the interwoven lives of seven adults, all in their thirties, living in Philadelphia (Zwick and Herskovitz both hailed from the area). The seven were longtime friends: two couples were married as the show got underway, and three persons were single. The cast included: Mel Harris as Hope Murdoch, a wife and mother who placed her career as a freelance writer on hold to raise a child; Ken Olin as Hope's husband, Michael Steadman, an advertising executive; Timothy Busfield as Elliot Weston, Mike's business partner; Patricia Wettig (who was married to Ken Olin in real life) as Elliot's wife, Nancy; Polly Draper as Hope's best friend, Ellyn Warren, an administrator at City Hall; Melanie Mayron as Michael's cousin, Melissa Steadman, a photographer; Peter Horton as Gary Shepherd, a college teacher; Jade Mortimer (1987) and Brittany and Lacey Craven (1988–1991) as Jane, Hope and Michael's young daughter; Luke Rossi as Ethan, Elliot and Nancy's son; and Jordana "Bink" Shapiro (1987–fall 1990) and Lindsay Riddell (1990–1991) as Brittany, Elliot and Nancy's daughter. Hope and Michael had a second child, Leo, in 1990.

The series was generally well received by the critics, and would win a Peabody Award in 1988. It promptly attracted a modest-sized, but very loyal audience. Indeed, the show evoked strong reactions from most viewers, who either adored it or loathed it for its talky, self-analytical style. Those in the former category were soon immersed in *thirtysomething*'s emotional plot developments: the breakup of Elliot and Nancy's marriage, the unexpected collapse of Elliot and Michael's business, Michael's coping with his father's death, Ellyn and Melissa's concerns about staying single, Nancy's battle with ovarian cancer, and the unexpected death of Gary, who was killed in a car accident while on his way to visit Nancy in the hospital. Not all of the episodes dealt with such serious matters, however; some dealt humorously with such mundane matters as Hope and Michael's attempt to go out for an evening by themselves, while others drifted into fantasy. Part of one program was a black-and-white recreation of *The Dick Van Dyke Show.*

David Clennon joined the cast in the spring of 1989 as overbearing Miles Drentell, head of the ad agency where Michael and Elliot found jobs after their shop foundered. Also featured were Patricia Kalember (1988–1991) as Susannah Hart, Gary's love interest (they were later married); Terry Kinney (1987–1988) as Steve Woodman, Ellyn's boss and erstwhile lover; Richard Gilliland (1988–1989) as Jeffrey Milgrom, Ellyn's love interest; Erich Anderson (1990–1991) as Billy Sidel, who married Ellyn; and Corey Parker (1989–1990) as Lee Owens, Melissa's younger boyfriend. The series' acoustic guitar score was composed by Snuffy Walden and Stewart Levin.

THIS COULD BE YOU
See THE BILL GWINN SHOW

THIS IS ALICE   SYNDICATED
1958   Half-hour family sitcom. With Patty Ann Gerrity as nine-year-old Alice Holliday; Tom Farrell as her father; Phyllis Coates as her mother; Stephen Wootton as her brother; and Leigh Snowden as her friend, Betty Lou. Set in Atlanta, the series was produced and directed by Sidney Salkow.

THIS IS AMERICA, CHARLIE BROWN   CBS
21 OCTOBER 1988–11 NOVEMBER 1988; 10 FEBRUARY 1989–10 MARCH 1989; 19 APRIL 1989–29 MAY 1989; 30 MAY 1990–25 JULY 1990   Although Charles Schulz's "Peanuts" characters had appeared in many TV specials since 1965, this was their first regular prime-time series. On each half-hour animated program, Charlie Brown and his friends re-enacted various events from American history. In the premiere, for example, they found themselves aboard the *Mayflower* in 1620. The voice of Charlie Brown was supplied by a fourteen-year-old girl, Erin Chase.

THIS IS CHARLES LAUGHTON   SYNDICATED
1953   A series of dramatic readings by British actor Charles Laughton; the series marked his American TV debut.

THIS IS GALEN DRAKE   ABC
12 JANUARY 1957–11 MAY 1957   Half-hour variety show for children hosted by Galen Drake.

THIS IS MUSIC   DUMONT/ABC
29 NOVEMBER 1951–9 OCTOBER 1952 (DUMONT); 6 JUNE 1958–21 MAY 1959 (ABC)
On this half-hour musical series the show's regulars pantomimed to popular musical recordings. Regulars on the DuMont version of the series, which was broadcast from Chicago, included Alexander Gray and Colin Male. Regulars on the ABC version included Ramona Burnett, Bob Shreve, Gail Johnson, and Bob Smith.

THIS IS SHOW BUSINESS   CBS/NBC
15 JULY 1949–9 MARCH 1954 (CBS); 26 JUNE 1956–11 SEPTEMBER 1956 (NBC) On this half-hour variety show guest celebrities dropped by to visit a celebrity panel; in theory, anyway, the guests were supposed to present a problem to the panelists, who could then offer their advice on solving it. By the fall of 1953, however, this requirement had been abandoned. Clifton Fadiman hosted the series, and the CBS panel regularly included Sam Levenson, Abe Burrows, and George S. Kaufman, who was suspended from the show as the result of viewer complaints after he remarked on the broadcast of 21 December 1952, "Let's make this one program on which no one sings 'Silent Night'!" In 1956, when the series was revived on NBC, the panel included Abe Burrows, Walter Slezak, and Jacqueline Susann. Irving Mansfield (Susann's husband) produced the series, and Byron Paul directed it. In late September 1951 *This is Show Business* was the first CBS regular series to be televised live from coast to coast.

THIS IS THE ANSWER SYNDICATED

1956–1961   Religious program produced by the Southern Baptist Convention. It is believed to be the first television religious show to be filmed in color.

THIS IS THE LIFE SYNDICATED

1952–1988   This long-running religious show presented dramas dealing with contemporary problems. In the early seasons it centered on the Fisher family of Middleburg, and the regular cast included Forrest Taylor, Onslow Stevens, Nan Boardman, Randy Stuart, Michael Hall, and David Kasday. In later years, however, it relied on guest stars. The show was produced by the International Lutheran Laymen's League, an auxiliary of the Lutheran Church, Missouri Synod. The half-hour series was also carried by ABC and DuMont in 1952 and 1953.

THIS IS TOM JONES ABC

7 FEBRUARY 1969–15 JANUARY 1971   Welsh singer Tom Jones hosted his own musical variety hour, which also featured Big Jim Sullivan, The Ace Trucking Company, the Norman Maen Dancers, and the Johnnie Spence Orchestra.

THIS IS YOUR LIFE NBC/SYNDICATED

1 OCTOBER 1952–10 SEPTEMBER 1961 (NBC); 1970 (SYNDICATED); 1983 (SYNDICATED)   Ralph Edwards hosted this sentimental human interest show, which he began on radio in 1948. Each week a special guest was lured to the studio by a ruse, and then surprised as Edwards announced, "This is your life!" Long-lost friends and relatives materialized during the ensuing half hour to relive long-forgotten incidents in the past. Most of Edwards's guests were celebrities, but some of his most effective shows centered on ordinary people. One program featured a rare television appearance by Stan Laurel and Oliver Hardy; another, honoring educator Laurence C. Jones, generated more than $700,000 in contributions toward the endowment of Piney Woods (Miss.) College, after Edwards suggested that viewers send Dr. Jones a dollar for the fund. One of the very few guests who was not pleasantly surprised by the evening's festivities was Lowell Thomas, who said, "This is a sinister conspiracy!" and refused to crack a smile during the whole show.

NBC televised a special "30th Anniversary Show," cohosted by Edwards and David Frost, on 26 February 1981. In the fall of 1983 a second syndicated version appeared, which combined a few reruns from the old series with a group of new programs; Joseph Campanella was the host. NBC also televised two "This Is Your Life" specials in 1987, both hosted by Ralph Edwards. The first (19 April) honored Betty White and Dick Van Dyke, and the second (26 November) saluted Tim Conway and Barbara Mandrell. On another NBC special, aired 26 November 1993, Edwards handed the hosting duties over to Pat Sajak, who proceeded to salute Kathie Lee Gifford and Roy Scheider (Angie Dickinson had been one of the intended recipients, but refused to participate).

THIS IS YOUR MUSIC SYNDICATED

1955   Half-hour variety show, featuring Joan Weldon and Byron Palmer, among others.

THIS MAN DAWSON SYNDICATED

1959   Half-hour crime show starring Keith Andes as Colonel Frank Dawson, a former Marine officer who took over a big city police department. William Conrad and Elliott Lewis produced the show for Ziv TV.

THIS MORNING

See THE DICK CAVETT SHOW

THIS OLD HOUSE PBS

1979–   Bob Vila hosted this informative series on home repair and construction. Among the projects undertaken on the series have been a modest city house (1979), a stately home (1980), a suburban ranch house (1981), and a Greek revival farmhouse

(1982). An even bolder undertaking was made in 1983: *The All New This Old House* showed the construction of a house from scratch. By the mid-1980s master carpenter Norm Abram had become a regular. Vila was fired as host in the spring of 1989 because of the various products he had endorsed in commercials. He was succeeded by Steve Thomas. Vila later developed a similar show: see *Home Again with Bob Vila*.

THIS WEEK   PBS
6 OCTOBER 1971–26 JUNE 1972   Half-hour show, with no fixed format, hosted by Bill Moyers. See also *Bill Moyers' Journal*.

THIS WEEK IN SPORTS   CBS
20 SEPTEMBER 1949–13 DECEMBER 1949   Fifteen-minute sports newsreel.

THIS WEEK WITH DAVID BRINKLEY   ABC
15 NOVEMBER 1981–   Shortly after he severed his thirty-eight-year association with NBC, veteran newsman David Brinkley was given his own hour newsmagazine show on ABC's Sunday morning schedule; the program replaced *Issues and Answers*. Among the commentators regularly featured on *This Week* have been George Will, Ben Bradlee, Karen Elliott House, Hodding Carter, James Wooten, and ABC correspondents Sam Donaldson, Brit Hume, and Cokie Roberts.

THIS WEEK'S MUSIC   SYNDICATED
1984   Basically a clone of *American Bandstand, This Week's Music* was hosted by Livingston Taylor and featured a live audience dancing to recorded music and appearances by contemporary rock artists. The show was taped in New York.

THE THORN BIRDS   ABC
27 MARCH 1983–30 MARCH 1983   A four-night, ten-hour adaptation of Colleen McCullough's best-selling novel *The Thorn Birds* proved enormously popular on TV. It ranked as the second highest-rated miniseries ever televised (*Roots* was the top-ranked), with its latter three installments ranking among the ten most widely watched programs of all time. The sprawling epic, set in Australia between 1920 and 1962, starred Richard Chamberlain as Ralph de Bricassart, a Roman Catholic priest torn between his desire for advancement within the priesthood and his love for a woman. Rachel Ward costarred as his love, Meggie Carson (Sydney Penny played the character as a child). Other major performers included Barbara Stanwyck as Meggie's imperious grandmother Mary Carson; Jean Simmons as Fee Cleary; Richard Kiley as Paddy Cleary; Christopher Plummer as Archbishop Contini-Verchese; Bryan Brown as Luke O'Neill; Mare Winningham as Meggie's daughter, Justine; and Philip Anglim as Meggie's son, Dane. ABC rebroadcast the miniseries in July 1993.

THE THORNS   ABC
15 JANUARY 1988–11 MARCH 1988   Mike Nichols was the executive producer, and Allan Leicht the creator, of this unfunny sitcom about an obnoxious Manhattan yuppie family. With Tony Roberts as Sloan Thorn, public relations executive; Kelly Bishop as his wife, Ginger; Adam Biesk as their elder son, Chad; Lisa Rieffel as their daughter, Joey; Jesse Tendler as their younger son, Edmund; Marilyn Cooper as Sloan's live-in mother, Rose; Lori Petty as Cricket, the mother's helper; Mary Louise Wilson as Toinette, the maid; Maureen Stapleton as Mrs. Hamilton, a wealthy widowed neighbor, and as Mrs. Hamilton's maid, Peggy; and Kathryn Marcopulos as neighbor Katina Pappas.

THOSE AMAZING ANIMALS   ABC
24 AUGUST 1980–23 AUGUST 1981   Broadcast Sunday evenings at 7:00 P.M., this "reality hour" was aimed principally at younger viewers. It focused, of course, on animals, some of which appeared on stage, others of which were featured in filmed segments. The principal humans on the hour series were Burgess Meredith (who may have qualified for the position because he had played The Penguin on *Batman*),

834

Priscilla Presley, and Jim Stafford. Joan Embry, a naturalist at the San Diego Zoo, oceanographer Jacques-Yves Cousteau, and underwater photographers Ron and Valerie Taylor also appeared regularly.

THOSE ENDEARING YOUNG CHARMS   NBC
30 DECEMBER 1951–26 JUNE 1952   A comedy series, *Those Endearing Young Charms* told the story of the Charms, a family living in a small New England town. Featured were Maurice Copeland and Betty Arnold as Mr. and Mrs. Charm, Clarence Hartzell as the eccentric uncle, Gerald Garvey as the son, and Pat Matthews as the daughter. Ben Park produced and directed the half-hour show, broadcast live from Chicago.

THOSE TWO   NBC
26 NOVEMBER 1951–24 APRIL 1953   Pinky Lee cohosted this musical variety show with Vivian Blaine until May 1952, when Martha Stewart succeeded her. The fifteen-minute show was seen Mondays, Wednesdays, and Fridays before the evening news.

THOSE WHITING GIRLS   CBS
4 JULY 1955–26 SEPTEMBER 1955; 1 JULY 1957–30 SEPTEMBER 1957   This half-hour sitcom was twice a summer replacement for *I Love Lucy;* it was created by two of *Lucy*'s writers, Madelyn Pugh and Bob Carroll, Jr. Sisters Barbara and Margaret Whiting played themselves, Barbara an actress and Margaret a singer. Also featured were Mabel Albertson as their mother, Mrs. Whiting; Jerry Paris as Margaret's accompanist Artie; Beverly Long as their friend, Olive; and Kathy Nolan (1957) as their friend, Penny.

THREE ABOUT TOWN   ABC
11 AUGUST 1948–20 OCTOBER 1948   One of ABC's first network programs, this fifteen-minute musical series was hosted by singer Betsi Allison.

THE THREE FLAMES SHOW   NBC
13 JUNE 1949–20 AUGUST 1949   This summer musical series starred the Three Flames, a black trio. The group had previously been featured on a daytime show seen locally in New York, and later appeared on *Washington Square*.

3 FOR THE MONEY   NBC
29 SEPTEMBER 1975–28 NOVEMBER 1975   Two 3-member teams matched wits on this daytime game show; each was composed of a celebrity captain and two contestants. A Stefan Hatos-Monty Hall Production, the show was hosted by Dick Enberg.

THREE FOR THE ROAD   CBS
14 SEPTEMBER 1975–30 NOVEMBER 1975   A Sunday-evening family drama about a widowed photographer and his two sons who traveled around the country in their camper, the "Zebec." With Alex Rocco as Pete Karras; Vincent Van Patten as son John; Leif Garrett as son Endy (short for Endicott). Jerry McNeely was the executive producer for MTM Enterprises.

3 GIRLS 3   NBC
30 MARCH 1977–29 JUNE 1977   *3 Girls 3,* an imaginative variety hour that introduced three unknowns, was highly acclaimed but suffered from a lack of publicity and poor scheduling—one hour was shown in March, the remaining three in June. Gary Smith and Dwight Hemion were the executive producers, and the three stars were Debbie Allen, Ellen Foley, and Mimi Kennedy.

THE THREE MUSKETEERS   SYNDICATED
1956   Half-hour adventure series produced in Europe, based on Alexandre Dumas's classic novel. With Jeff Stone as D'Artagnan; Paul Campbell as Aramis; Peter Trent as Porthos; Alan Furlan as Sasquinet; and Sebastian Cabot as the Count de Brisemont.

THREE ON A MATCH   NBC
2 AUGUST 1971–28 JUNE 1974   Bill Cullen hosted this daytime game show on which three contestants competed for money by answering true-false questions, then got to spend it on the prize board.

THE THREE ROBONIC STOOGES   CBS
28 JANUARY 1978–2 SEPTEMBER 1978   Half-hour cartoon series which began as one segment of *The Skatebirds*. On this series, Moe, Curly, and Larry were mechanical superheroes. The show was rerun on Sunday mornings between 1979 and 1981.

THREE STEPS TO HEAVEN   NBC
3 AUGUST 1953–31 DECEMBER 1954   Daytime serial about a young woman who left the small town where she grew up to become a model in New York City. With Kathleen Maguire, Phyllis Hill, and Diana Douglas as model Poco Thurmond; Gene Blakely and Mark Roberts as Poco's boyfriend, Bill Morgan; Lori March as Jennifer Alden; Ginger MacManus as Angela; Laurie Vendig as Alice Trent; John Marley as Vince Bannister; Beth Douglas as Nan Waring; Madeline Belgard as Beth; Harriet MacGibbon as Mrs. Montgomery; Lauren Gilbert as Jason Cleve; and Walter Brooke and Joe Brown, Jr. Adrian Samish was the producer, Irving Vendig the writer.

3-2-1 CONTACT   PBS
1980–1992   A science series for children, featuring Liz Moses, Ginny Ortiz, and Leon W. Grant, produced by Kathy Mendoza for the Children's Television Workshop.

THREE'S A CROWD   SYNDICATED
1979   Half-hour game show from Chuck Barris Productions which sought to answer the age-old question: Who knows a man better, his wife or his secretary? First, three husbands were asked a series of questions; their secretaries then came onstage and were asked the same questions. Finally the three wives were brought on and asked the questions. If the three secretaries scored more matches, they split $1000; if the three wives had more matches, they divided up the prize. Jim Peck was the host.

THREE'S A CROWD   ABC
25 SEPTEMBER 1984–10 SEPTEMBER 1985   This was the sequel to the popular sitcom *Three's Company,* in which Jack Tripper (played by John Ritter) moved in with his girlfriend, flight attendant Vicky Bradford (Mary Cadorette), at her insistence. They lived together in an apartment above his restaurant, Jack's Bistro. Robert Mandan played Vicky's meddlesome father, James Bradford, who bought the building. Alan Campbell played E. Z. Taylor, Jack's assistant chef. Like most sequels, *Three's a Crowd* never equalled the popularity of the parent show, and was canceled after a single season.

THREE'S COMPANY   CBS
18 MAY 1950–29 SEPTEMBER 1950   This fifteen-minute musical series, seen Tuesdays and Thursdays following the network news, featured Cy Walters, Stan Freeman, and Judy Lynn.

THREE'S COMPANY   ABC
15 MARCH 1977–21 APRIL 1977; 11 AUGUST 1977–18 SEPTEMBER 1984   This sex comedy, based on a British show called *Man About the House,* was introduced as a limited series in the spring of 1977 and returned to stay a few months later; it wound up as the third top-rated show for the 1977–1978 season. Set in Los Angeles, it told the tale of a young man sharing an apartment with two young women; the landlord, mistakenly believing the man to be homosexual, permitted the arrangement. Created and produced by Don Nicholl, Michael Ross, and Bernie West, the half-hour series featured: John Ritter as Jack Tripper, a self-employed caterer who later opened up his own restaurant, The Little Bistro; Joyce DeWitt as Janet Wood, Jack's sensible roommate, a florist; Suzanne Somers (1977–1981) as Chrissy Snow, Jack's daffy

roommate, a secretary; Norman Fell (1977–1979) as the apparently impotent landlord, Stanley Roper; Audra Lindley (1977–1979) as his sex-starved wife, Helen Roper; and Richard Kline (1978–1984) as Larry Dallas, Jack's best friend. Fell and Lindley left the series in 1979 to star in a spinoff (see *The Ropers*), and Don Knotts was added in the fall of 1979 as the new landlord, Ralph Furley. Ann Wedgeworth also appeared during the 1979–1980 season as neighbor Lana Shields, a buyer for a department store.

In the summer of 1980 Suzanne Somers asked for a fivefold salary increase—from $30,000 to $150,000 per show—and a share of the profits. *Three's Company*'s producers did not renegotiate and held Somers to her contract for a final year. During the 1980–1981 season she appeared only in one-minute inserts at the end of each show, in which her character, Chrissy, spoke with one of the other regulars by telephone from Fresno (where Chrissy was visiting relatives); these sequences were taped separately on a closed set. Jennilee Harrison was added in the fall of 1980 as Chrissy's cousin, Cindy Snow, who moved into the apartment with Jack and Janet. After one season Cindy moved out, to study veterinary medicine at U.C.L.A. (Harrison stayed on as a regular for the 1981–1982 season, however). Priscilla Barnes joined the cast in the fall of 1981 as the new roommate, nurse Terri Alden. Major changes took place in the spring of 1984, as Jack and Janet each met the loves of their lives and plans were made for a sequel series, *Three's a Crowd*, which would focus on Jack and his love, Vicky Bradford (played by Mary Cadorette).

THRILL HUNTERS   SYNDICATED
1966   A series of half-hour films about people with exciting occupations or hobbies, *Thrill Hunters* was hosted by Bill Burrud, and was thus distinguishable from such shows as *Danger Is My Business* and *The Thrillseekers*.

THRILLER   NBC
13 SEPTEMBER 1960–9 JULY 1962   Boris Karloff was the host and occasional star in this anthology series of crime and horror stories. Hubbell Robinson was the executive producer of the hour show for Revue Studios. Fletcher Markle, the original producer, and James P. Cavanaugh, the story editor, were replaced after eight episodes by producers Maxwell Shane and William Frye. A total of sixty-seven episodes were produced.

THE THRILLSEEKERS   SYNDICATED
1973   Chuck Connors hosted this half-hour series, which profiled persons with dangerous occupations and interests.

THROB   SYNDICATED
1986–1988   Half-hour sitcom about a divorced woman who moved from Buffalo to New York, where she landed a job with Throb Records, a small punk label. Featured were Diana Canova as Sandy Beatty; Paul W. Walker (1986–1987) and Sean de Veritch (1987–1988) as her son, Jeremy; Maryedith Burrell as Meredith, Sandy's neighbor; Jonathan Prince as Zach Armstrong, the head of the label; Jane Leeves as Blue, the talent handler, who moved in with Sandy during the second season; and Richard Cummings, Jr., as Phil, who also worked for the record company.

THROUGH THE CRYSTAL BALL   CBS
18 APRIL 1949–4 JULY 1949   Pantomime and ballet were prominently featured on this offbeat half-hour prime-time series. The premiere telecast was a version of "Robinson Crusoe," while the second program, "Cinderella," featured choreography by George Balanchine. Mime Jimmy Savo hosted and starred for the first few weeks. Paul Belanger produced and directed.

THROUGH THE CURTAIN   ABC
21 OCTOBER 1953–24 FEBRUARY 1954   This fifteen-minute prime-time public affairs program was hosted by George Hamilton Combs. It consisted of interviews with

people who had been behind the Iron Curtain and digests of press reports from Communist news agencies.

THROUGH WENDY'S WINDOW
See THE WENDY BARRIE SHOW

THUNDARR THE BARBARIAN ABC/NBC
4 OCTOBER 1980–18 SEPTEMBER 1982 (ABC); 9 APRIL 1983–8 SEPTEMBER 1984 (NBC)
This Saturday-morning cartoon series was set in the future, some two thousand years after the destruction of civilization in 1994 (when a comet passed too close to Earth). Thundarr was a slave who was set free by Princess Ariel, stepdaughter of Sabian, an evil wizard. Together with Ookla the Mok, a semi-human creature, Thundarr and Ariel roamed the ravaged planet fighting for the rights of the enslaved against an assortment of wizards, mutants, and monsters. Joe Ruby and Ken Spears were the executive producers for Ruby-Spears Enterprises.

THUNDER NBC
10 SEPTEMBER 1977–2 SEPTEMBER 1978   The central character in this live-action Saturday-morning show was a wild black stallion named Thunder, the equine equivalent of Lassie. The human roles were filled by: Clint Ritchie as rancher Bill Williams; Melissa Converse as his wife, Anne Williams, a veterinarian; Melora Hardin as their daughter, Cindy; Justin Randi as their son, Willie. Thunder and Cupcake, the mule ridden by Cindy and Willie, were owned by Bobby Davenport. The half-hour series was created and produced by Irving Cummings and Charles Marion for Charles Fries Productions.

THUNDER ALLEY ABC
9 MARCH 1994–4 MAY 1994; 10 AUGUST 1994–2 NOVEMBER 1994; 7 MARCH 1995–25 JULY 1995   Half-hour sitcom about a retired race car driver whose daughter and grandchildren moved in with him. With Edward Asner as gruff but lovable Gil Jones, who owned Thunder Alley, a garage; Diane Venora (spring 1994) and Robin Riker (fall 1994–1995) as his daughter, Bobbi Turner; Kelly Vint as eleven-year-old Claudine; Lindsay Felton as eight-year-old Jenny; Haley Joel Osment as five-year-old Harry; and Jim Beaver as Leland, Gil's employee at the garage.

THUNDER IN PARADISE SYNDICATED
1994–1995   This hour adventure series, set in Florida, starred pro wrestler Terry "Hulk" Hogan as ex-Navy Seal R. J. "Hurricane" Spencer, who owned a super-powered speedboat known as Thunder; the 43-foot craft was able to reach speeds of 500 miles per hour. With Chris Lemmon as Thunder's builder, Martin "Bru" Brubaker, who had worked with Spencer in the Navy Seals; Carol Alt as Kelly La Rew, a part-time sculptress and manager of the Scuttlebutt Beach Bar; Ashley Gorrell as R. J.'s nine-year-old adoptive daughter, Jessica Whitaker; and Patrick Macnee as Jessica's grandfather, Edward Whitaker, former British intelligence agent and owner of the Paradise Beach Hotel.

THUNDERBIRDS SYNDICATED
1967   Another of the marionette adventure series developed in England by Gerry Anderson, *Thunderbirds* was the most highly sophisticated of Anderson's efforts. Anderson had by now refined the technique of Supermarionation, a process using wires and electric devices to manipulate the marionettes, which he had previously used on such shows as *Fireball XL-5* and *Supercar. Thunderbirds,* produced in hour-long form, told the story of a group of twenty-first-century space heroes. Edited and redubbed reruns appeared on the Fox network's Saturday morning schedule briefly during the summer of 1994.

THUNDERCATS   SYNDICATED

1983; 1985   Another of the several cartoon shows of the mid-1980s inspired by a line of toys, *ThunderCats* told the tale of a band of catlike creatures led by Lion-O, who battled the Mutants.

TIC TAC DOUGH   NBC

30 JULY 1956–30 OCTOBER 1959

THE NEW TIC TAC DOUGH   CBS/SYNDICATED

3 JULY 1978–1 SEPTEMBER 1978 (CBS); 1978–1986; 1990 (SYNDICATED)   Two contestants played tic-tac-toe on this game show. The game board was divided into nine categories; one of the players selected a category, and a question was read. Whoever answered correctly won the square, and then selected another category; the winner of the game then faced a new challenger. *Tic Tac Dough* was seen in both daytime and prime-time versions; the latter ran from September 1957 to December 1958, and was hosted for most of its run by Jay Jackson. The daytime version, which ran for more than three years, was hosted by Jack Barry, Gene Rayburn, and Bill Wendell. Nineteen years later two versions of *The New Tic Tac Dough* surfaced, both hosted by Wink Martindale. The network version was seen during the daytime on CBS, while the syndicated version was shown evenings in most markets. Both reincarnations were basically similar to the original version of the show. One contestant on the syndicated version, Navy lieutenant Thom McKee, became the biggest money winner in game-show history. Over a span of several weeks, McKee amassed $307,400 in cash and prizes, including eight automobiles. Patrick Wayne hosted the 1990 version.

THE TICK   FOX

10 SEPTEMBER 1994–   Half-hour cartoon series based on the cartoon characters created by Ben Edlund. The Tick was a bumbling 400-pound superhero who took a bus to The City, intending to save it from evildoers. There he teamed up with Arthur, a mild-mannered accountant who dressed as an oversized moth to assist the Tick.

TIGHTROPE!   CBS

8 SEPTEMBER 1959–13 SEPTEMBER 1960   Half-hour crime show starring Michael Connors as an undercover police agent who hid his gun in the small of his back. In the earliest episodes Connors's character had no name, but by late autumn the character was christened Nick Stone. Clarence Greene and Russell Rouse produced the series.

THE TIM CONWAY COMEDY HOUR   CBS

20 SEPTEMBER 1970–13 DECEMBER 1970   Tim Conway's second 1970 show was a variety hour, but it was even less successful than his previous effort. Conway did, however, line up an impressive list of regulars: McLean Stevenson, Sally Struthers, Art Metrano, Bonnie Boland, singers Belland and Somerville (during the 1950s Bruce Belland had sung with the Four Preps and Dave Somerville with the Diamonds), the Tom Hansen Dancers, the Jimmy Joyce Singers, and announcer Ernie Anderson.

THE TIM CONWAY SHOW   CBS

30 JANUARY 1970–19 JUNE 1970   The first of Tim Conway's two 1970 series was a half-hour sitcom in which he was reunited with his *McHale's Navy* costar, Joe Flynn. They played Tim "Spud" Barrett and Herb Kenworth, owners and crew of the one-plane Anytime Anyplace Airlines. Also aboard were Anne Seymour as Mrs. Crawford, owner of the local airport; Johnnie Collins III as her son, Ronnie; Fabian Dean as Harry, operator of the airport burger stand; and Emily Banks as Becky, a Crawford employee and Spud's romantic interest.

THE TIM CONWAY SHOW   CBS

22 MARCH 1980–17 MAY 1980; 30 AUGUST 1980–7 MARCH 1981   Comedian Tim Conway was given yet another shot at a series in this, his second variety show (see also *The Tim Conway Comedy Hour*). Conway's cohorts on the show included Dick

Orkin, Bert Berdis, Jack Riley, Maggie Roswell, Miriam Flynn, Eric Boardman, and the Don Crichton Dancers, a talented group of child hoofers. The show started out in an hour format, but when it returned in August 1980 it had been trimmed to thirty minutes, and Jack Riley and Eric Boardman had left. Early in 1981 Harvey Korman, Conway's former foil on *The Carol Burnett Show,* became a regular, and Dick Orkin and Bert Berdis were dropped. Like all of Conway's starring ventures, this one failed to last more than a year; undaunted, he returned in 1983 in still another show (see *Ace Crawford, Private Eye*).

TIM CONWAY'S FUNNY AMERICA ABC

29 JULY 1990–2 SEPTEMBER 1990   This half-hour series borrowed heavily from *Candid Camera.* A hidden camera recorded Tim Conway, in various guises, playing jokes on unsuspecting passers-by. Conway then showed the results to a studio audience.

TIME EXPRESS CBS

26 APRIL 1979–17 MAY 1979   Four-week fantasy series set aboard a mysterious train on which passengers personally selected by "the head of the line" were given the opportunity to return to an incident from their past. With Vincent Price as Jason Winters and Coral Brown as Margaret Winters, the on-board hosts; Woodrow Parfrey as the Ticket Agent; William Edward Phipps as E. Patrick Callahan, the engineer; James Reynolds as Robert Jefferson (R.J.) Walker, the conductor. Ivan Goff and Ben Roberts created the series and were the executive producers; Leonard B. Kaufman was the producer.

TIME FOR BEANY SYNDICATED
1950–1955
THE BEANY AND CECIL SHOW ABC
6 JANUARY 1962–3 SEPTEMBER 1967
BEANY AND CECIL ABC
10 SEPTEMBER 1988–15 OCTOBER 1988   Beany and Cecil, two characters created by Bob Clampett, first appeared nationally in a fifteen-minute puppet show broadcast from Hollywood. Beany was a little boy who sailed the high seas aboard the *Leakin' Lena* with his uncle, Captain Horatio K. Huffenpuff; Cecil was a sea serpent (and a seasick one at that) who was, at first, visible only to Beany, but who later revealed himself to the Captain as well. In their travels the trio encountered a host of unusual characters, such as Tearalong the Dotted Lion and The Staring Herring, but their most persistent nemesis was Dishonest John. The creator of the series, Bob Clampett, was an animator for Warner Brothers who dabbled in puppetry. Cecil, whom Clampett had created several years earlier, was introduced on a local show in Los Angeles in 1948; the show soon acquired a sizable audience and attracted the attention of Paramount Television, which offered it nationwide in 1950. Stan Freberg provided the voice of the Captain; Daws Butler (later the voice of Huckleberry Hound, Quickdraw McGraw, and Yogi Bear) that of Beany; and Clampett himself that of Cecil. Clampett's characters later appeared in a half-hour cartoon series which was carried by ABC for several years. Originally sponsored by Mattel Toys, the latter series was titled *Matty's Funnies with Beany and Cecil* in its early weeks. A new cartoon series surfaced briefly on ABC's Saturday morning lineup in 1988.

TIME FOR REFLECTION DUMONT
30 APRIL 1950–14 JANUARY 1951   David Ross read poetry on this fifteen-minute Sunday-evening show.

A TIME FOR US ABC
28 DECEMBER 1964–16 DECEMBER 1966   This half-hour daytime serial premiered in 1964 under the title *Flame in the Wind* and was renamed in June of 1965. Set in the town of Havilland, its stories centered on young people. The cast included: Beverly Hayes as Jane Driscoll; Joanna Miles as her sister, Linda Driscoll, an aspiring actress; Ray Poole as their father, Al Driscoll, a contractor; Lenka Peterson as their mother, Martha Driscoll; Gordon Gray and Tom Fielding as Steve Reynolds, the romantic

interest of both Jane and Linda; Maggie Hayes as Roxanne Reynolds; Walter Coy as Roxanne's father, Jason Farrell; Ian Berger as Doug Colton; Morgan Sterne as Tony Gray; Josephine Nichols as Louise; Conrad Fowkes as Paul; Elaine Hyman as Fran; Terry Logan as Dave, a medical student; Lesley Woods as Miriam Bentley; Kathleen Maguire as Kate Austin, a widow; Richard Thomas as her son, Chris; and Jacqueline Brookes as Flora Perkins.

TIME MACHINE   NBC
7 JANUARY 1985–26 APRIL 1985   Contestants' knowledge of nostalgia and recent events was tested on this daytime game show, hosted by John Davidson. Most questions put to the three daily competitors involved matching events with the correct years in which they occurred, or guessing whether an event happened before or after a given date.

A TIME TO LIVE   NBC
5 JULY 1954–31 DECEMBER 1954   This fifteen-minute daytime serial starred Pat Sully and Larry Kerr as journalists Kathy Byron and Don Riker. Also featured were Barbara Foley as Lenore Eustice; Len Wayland as Chick Buchanan, Kathy's boyfriend (they were married on the final episode); Jeanne Jerrems and Zora Alton as Greta Powers; and Muriel Monsel as Doanna Sims. The program was broadcast from Chicago.

TIME TO REMEMBER   SYNDICATED
1963   Half-hour filmed documentary series on great historical events of the twentieth century.

TIME TRAX   SYNDICATED
1993–1994   High-tech crime show about a 22nd-century cop who traveled back to the present time to catch a mad scientist who had escaped through time. "Trax" was an acronym for Trans-Time Research and Experimentation. With Dale Midkiff as the cop, Darien Lambert; Peter Donat as the villain, Dr. Mordicai Sahmbi; Elizabeth Alexander as Selma, a holographic computer image ("Selma" was an acronym for Specified Encapsulated Limited Memory Archive); Henry Darrow as Darien's boss, the Chief; and Mia Sara as Elissa. The hour series was produced at Warner Bros. facilities in Australia.

THE TIME TUNNEL   ABC
9 SEPTEMBER 1966–1 SEPTEMBER 1967   Hour-long science fiction series about two research scientists who, working on a government-sponsored project, developed a time machine by which they could be transported into the past or the future. With James Darren as Dr. Tony Newman; Robert Colbert as Dr. Doug Phillips; Whit Bissell as Lieutenant General Heywood Kirk, project supervisor; John Zaremba as Dr. Raymond Swain; Lee Meriwether as Dr. Ann MacGregor; and Wesley Lau as Master Sergeant Jiggs, the security officer. The series was created by Irwin Allen, who was also its executive producer (Allen also developed *Land of the Giants, Lost in Space,* and *Voyage to the Bottom of the Sea*). Special effects were supervised by Bill Abbott, who won an Emmy for his services.

TIME WILL TELL   DUMONT
27 AUGUST 1954–15 OCTOBER 1954   Ernie Kovacs hosted this short-lived prime-time game show.

TIMON & PUMBAA   CBS
16 SEPTEMBER 1995–   The title characters of this Saturday-morning cartoon series—Pumbaa the warthog and Timon the meerkat—had originally appeared in the Disney motion picture "The Lion King." The pair were assisted by their pals Rafiki the baboon, Ned the elephant, and Speedy the snail.

TIN PAN ALLEY TV ABC

28 APRIL 1950–29 SEPTEMBER 1950   Each week this half-hour variety show featured the music of a guest composer. Regulars included Johnny Desmond, Gloria Van, Chet Roble, Montero and Yvonne, the Visionaires, and the Rex Maupin Orchestra. Broadcast from Chicago, the show was produced by Fred Kilian and Tim Morrow.

TINY TOON ADVENTURES SYNDICATED/FOX

1990–1992 (SYNDICATED); 14 NOVEMBER 1992–   (FOX)   Younger versions of classic Warner Bros. cartoon characters were the stars of this all-new daily animated series, set at Acme Acres. Among the animated headliners were Buster and Babs Bunny, Plucky Duck, a pig named Hamton, ornery Montana Max, Dizzy Devil, Furrball, and Snazzer. The series premiered as a half-hour prime time special on CBS, 14 September 1990. See also *The Plucky Duck Show.*

TO ROME WITH LOVE CBS

28 SEPTEMBER 1969–1 SEPTEMBER 1971   Half-hour sitcom about a widowed professor and his three daughters, all of whom moved to Rome when he was hired to teach at an American school there. With John Forsythe as Professor Mike Endicott; Joyce Menges as daughter Alison; Susan Neher as daughter Penny; Melanie Fullerton as daughter Pokey; Kay Medford (1969–1970) as Aunt Harriet; Walter Brennan (1970–1971) as Andy Pruitt, the girls' maternal grandfather; Peggy Mondo as Mama Vitale, the landlady; Vito Scotti as cabbie Gino Mancini; and Gerald Michenaud as Penny's pal, Nico. Don Fedderson was the executive producer.

TO SAY THE LEAST NBC

3 OCTOBER 1977–21 APRIL 1978   Daytime game show hosted by Tom Kennedy on which two 2-member teams (each with a celebrity and a player) played a word game. The half-hour show was from Heatter-Quigley Productions.

TO TELL THE TRUTH CBS/SYNDICATED/NBC

Nighttime: 18 DECEMBER 1956–5 SEPTEMBER 1966 (CBS); 12 DECEMBER 1966–22 MAY 1967 (CBS); *Daytime:* 18 JUNE 1962–6 SEPTEMBER 1968 (CBS); 1969–1977 (SYNDICATED); 1980 (SYNDICATED); 3 SEPTEMBER 1990–31 MAY 1991 (NBC)   One of TV's most popular game shows, *To Tell the Truth* was developed by Mark Goodson and Bill Todman, who also put together *What's My Line?, I've Got a Secret, The Match Game,* and a host of other game shows. The format was simple—a panel of four celebrities tried to determine which of three guests, each claiming to be the same person, was telling the truth. The three guests stood at center stage while an affidavit, reciting the story of the real claimant, was read aloud; the guests were then seated, and the panelists took turns questioning them. The two impostors were free to lie, but the real claimant was sworn to tell the truth. At the conclusion of the questioning each panelist voted separately, and the identity of the claimant was revealed ("Will the real _____ please stand up?"). The three guests then split a cash award, calculated on the number of incorrect votes. Because the identity of the real claimant was not revealed to the viewing audience until the end of the questioning, viewers were able to play the game along with the panelists. *To Tell the Truth* began in 1956 as a prime-time show. The title was changed shortly before the premiere from *Nothing But the Truth.* The celebrity panel on the premiere included Polly Bergen, Dick Van Dyke, Hildy Parks, and John Cameron Swayze. Other panelists who appeared frequently on the network versions were Tom Poston, Kitty Carlisle, Peggy Cass, Orson Bean, and Phyllis Newman. Bud Collyer hosted both the prime-time and the daytime versions on CBS. The syndicated version, which began in 1969, was hosted by Garry Moore until 1977, when Joe Garagiola took over for the last few shows; the celebrity regulars on that version were Kitty Carlisle, Peggy Cass, and Bill Cullen, plus a guest celeb. Robin Ward hosted the 1980 syndicated version, on which Peggy Cass was a regular panelist. Gordon Elliott hosted the 1990 daytime revival until February 1991, when Alex Trebek took over (Richard Kline hosted the premiere telecast, when NBC mistakenly ran the pilot for the series).

TO THE QUEEN'S TASTE
See DIONE LUCAS' COOKING SHOW

TOAST OF THE TOWN
See THE ED SULLIVAN SHOW

TODAY NBC

14 JANUARY 1952– Network television's first early-morning program, *Today* survived a shaky start to become one of the most profitable shows in history. Not only is it network television's longest-running daytime series, but also because of its two-hours-per-weekday slot it has occupied more total air time—some 24,000 hours—than any other single show. In its early years, *Today* was actually telecast for three hours a day, though only two hours were carried by any affiliate; the show's first hour was seen from 7:00 to 8:00 A.M. only in the East, and was recreated—live—for the Midwest after the second East Coast hour (by late 1958, when high-quality videotape had become available, the show was broadcast to other parts of the country on a delayed basis, and the extra hour was no longer necessary).

The show was the brainchild of Sylvester "Pat" Weaver, one of the most creative executives in the history of broadcasting. Weaver realized that television was more than radio with pictures and sought to develop new kinds of programs to capitalize on television's unique qualities. One of his first concepts was the Saturday-night comedy program which became *Your Show of Shows*. He is also credited with developing the special entertainment broadcast, which he called the "spectacular." In addition to the *Today* show, Weaver also developed *Home, Tonight,* and *Wide Wide World.*

Weaver saw the *Today* show as a program that few people would watch from beginning to end; instead, it was to be designed so that viewers could eat breakfast and get ready for school or work without devoting all of their time and attention to the television set. A news summary was given every half hour, and the other segments (chiefly consisting of sports, weather, interviews, and features) were kept short. As early-morning broadcasting was then virtually unknown (even daytime broadcasting was a rarity in some parts of the country), Weaver sought to make the show attractive to local stations by offering them a share of *Today*'s network advertising revenues plus several minutes of commercial time each hour (the latter feature soon became standardized, as most affiliates "cut away" for a five-minute local newscast at twenty-five minutes past each hour).

The man chosen to host the show was Dave Garroway. Though he started out as a radio newscaster in Pittsburgh, he did not attract attention until he began hosting a variety series, *Garroway at Large,* over WMAQ-TV in Chicago. Garroway was not Weaver's first choice for the *Today* job, but his relaxed, conversational manner on camera convinced Weaver that he would be just right for a waking audience. Chosen to assist Garroway were Jack Lescoulie, to handle sports and light features, and Jim Fleming, to read the news.

The show premiered on 14 January 1952, a week behind schedule, in its own studio on the ground floor of the RCA Exhibition Hall on West Forty-ninth Street in New York. A large plate-glass window enabled passersby to see the show and to be seen as the cameras periodically panned it (President Harry S Truman, who liked to take a morning walk wherever he stayed, was once maneuvered into camera range for an abortive interview). Teletape machines, telephones, and a row of clocks showing the time in selected cities throughout the world dominated the set. The show opened with just one sponsor (the Kiplinger Newsletter), thirty-one affiliates, and poor reviews—most of the critics thought that the show was poorly paced and that its human performers seemed overwhelmed by its gadgetry. These early problems were gradually worked out, and the use of electronics was deemphasized; Garroway, Lescoulie, and company even began to appear in skits to help give the show a lighter touch. By the end of 1952 *Today* had managed to pick up a few new sponsors and a few more affiliates.

The year 1953 proved to be a signal year for *Today,* as it attracted large audiences and began to make money. One reason for its change of fortune was an aggressive sales staff, but an equally important factor in boosting ratings was a chimpanzee named J. Fred Muggs, whose antics helped lure hundreds of thousands of children, and their parents, to the screen. Owned by trainer Buddy Menella and Roy Waldron, Muggs was ten months old when he came to the show early in 1953; he soon became one of America's most popular animal celebrities and went on several personal appearance tours (he was especially in demand to dedicate supermarkets). Muggs was never popular with the show's staff, but the same could be said of several of *Today*'s human regulars. Having become increasingly hard to handle, Muggs was dropped after four years (the press release announcing his departure stated that he was leaving to "extend his personal horizons"). He was briefly succeeded by another chimp named Mr. Kokomo.

Shortly after Muggs's arrival in 1953, newscaster Jim Fleming announced his departure; he was replaced by Frank Blair, who remained with *Today* for twenty-two years, longer than anyone else connected with the show. It was also in 1953 that *Today* began to feature a woman regularly. The "Today Girl," as she was called for many years, originally had few responsibilities, but the role gradually expanded so that by 1974 Barbara Walters, the incumbent, had become a full-fledged cohost. The first "Today Girls," however, were shapely young women who were featured just for the day. The first permanent "Today Girl" was a program staffer whose duties included reading the temperature and a one-word description of the weather in America's major cities; she left the show in 1954 for a more promising career on stage and in films. Her name was Estelle Parsons. Among the other women who appeared during Garroway's tenure were Lee Ann Meriwether (Miss America of 1955), who left the show late in 1956, singer Helen O'Connell (1956–1958), game show panelist Betsy Palmer (1958–1959), actress Florence Henderson (1959–1960), former Miss Rheingold Robbin Bain (1960), journalist Beryl Pfizer (1960–1961), and actress Anita Colby (1961). Physical fitness expert Bonnie Prudden and learned Charles Van Doren (a big winner on *Twenty-One*) also appeared regularly during the late 1950s.

In 1958, partly to accommodate Dave Garroway's busy schedule (he was hosting *Wide Wide World* on TV and doing several NBC radio broadcasts), the *Today* show began to be taped a day in advance (the news segments, of course, continued to be done live), a practice that continued on and off for the next four years. Despite the change of schedule, Garroway became more difficult to work with, and after the death of his second wife in April of 1961, he decided to leave the show. In July of that year, after more than nine years as host of *Today* (which was by then titled *The Dave Garroway Today Show*), Garroway closed the show for the last time with his familiar "Peace" signoff, to the accompaniment of Lionel Hampton's version of "Sentimental Journey." Garroway made few appearances on network TV thereafter; he was a guest on *Today*'s fifteenth and twenty-fifth anniversary shows, and also hosted *The Newcomers* in 1971 on CBS (he committed suicide in 1982). Following Garroway's departure, *Today* turned more stolid under new host John Chancellor. A veteran newsman, Chancellor never really felt at home in the role, and lasted only fourteen months. Garroway's second banana, Jack Lescoulie, had also left the show, and Chancellor's regulars included Edwin Newman, who was brought in to read the news, Louise King, the new "Today Girl," and a disgruntled Frank Blair, who found himself in the unwanted role of sidekick (the four even appeared in skits from time to time, an idea revived to make the show less wooden).

Chancellor's successor was Hugh Downs, who took over in October 1962; Downs thus became the only person to have been a regular on all three of Pat Weaver's weekday programming concepts, *Home, Tonight,* and *Today.* Downs also continued to host a daytime game show, *Concentration,* for the first few years of his *Today* tenure. Frank Blair returned to the news desk; Jack Lescoulie also came back to the show that year, but left within twelve months. Though Downs and his producer, Al Morgan, feuded from 1962 to 1968 (when Morgan was dropped at Downs's insistence), *Today*'s ratings remained steady. During this time the show often originated in places other than New York (the practice had actually started with Garroway), and, with the advent of communications satellites, telecasts from Europe were introduced. It was also during Downs's term as host that Barbara Walters began appearing regularly. Walters had previously worked for CBS's *The Morning Show,* an ineffective competitor of *Today,* and was hired as a freelance writer by *Today*'s then producer, Fred Freed, in 1961. She was pressed into on-camera service for the funeral of President John Kennedy in November 1963, and thereafter was used regularly on the show. Finally, in 1964 she was selected to succeed actress Maureen O'Sullivan as the next in the series of "Today Girls." O'Sullivan, who had replaced Pat Fontaine, found it difficult to work with Downs and was dropped after only a few months. Walters soon established herself as a first-rate interviewer; always well prepared, she sometimes joined Downs in questioning guests. *Variety* later hailed her presence on the show as "a victory of brains over mannequin beauty." In 1964 Judith Crist and Aline Saarinen also began to appear regularly, reviewing films and art respectively. By 1967 Joe Garagiola had also signed on as a regular. A onetime second-string catcher for the St. Louis Cardinals, the affable Garagiola had been an NBC sportscaster; his quick wit helped offset Downs's tendency toward longwindedness.

Having outlasted producer Morgan, Downs departed from *Today* on 11 October 1971, concluding a reign only slightly shorter than Garroway's. Downs's successor, Frank McGee, signaled another shift toward the stolid. McGee was a tough, well respected newsman who had worked in Oklahoma City, Montgomery, Washington, and New York. McGee was not well liked by the *Today* staff. Though he and Barbara Walters appeared to get along on camera, relations between the two were strained— McGee insisted on opening and closing the show himself and also reserved the right to ask the first question of any guest slated to be interviewed by Walters. Whether the rift between the two would have widened will never be known, however, as McGee died of bone cancer in April of 1974, after only two and one-half years on the job.

McGee's replacement, chosen with Barbara Walters's approval, was Jim Hartz. Like McGee, Hartz hailed from Oklahoma (he had delivered the eulogy at McGee's funeral); Hartz had hosted a local newscast in New York beginning in 1965, when he was just twenty-four. Apparently Hartz was never very popular with viewers, for *Today*'s ratings began to decline appreciably during his brief tenure. When Barbara Walters, who was now the official cohost of the show, left the show in June of 1976 for ABC, Hartz too was dropped. It was during Hartz's short stay that Frank Blair left the show; his last newscast was on 14 March 1975, and he was succeeded by Lew Wood. Joe Garagiola had also left the show by this time and was succeeded by bushy-haired Gene Shalit. A former publicity agent, Shalit had originally reviewed films for *Today,* but by 1974 he was the new number two.

Jim Hartz was succeeded by Tom Brokaw on 29 August 1976; like Chancellor and McGee, Brokaw was an experienced newsman who had worked in Omaha, Atlanta, Los Angeles, and at the White House during the final days of the Nixon administration. Brokaw, however, was not as humorless as his newsmen predecessors. Shortly before Brokaw's arrival, Floyd Kalber was hired to read the news (Lew Wood stayed with the show, but did only the weather; Wood left in the spring of 1978 and was succeeded by Bob Ryan).

An intensive search was undertaken to fill the void left by Barbara Walters. Six women were tested on the air for the job—Cassie Mackin, Betty Rollin, Linda Ellerbee, Kelly Lange, Betty Furness, and Jane Pauley. Pauley was finally selected. Born in 1950, Pauley was barely older than the show itself; she had previously worked in Indianapolis and at WMAQ-TV in Chicago (the same station that Garroway had worked for almost thirty years before). By the end of 1977, *Today*'s ratings, which had deteriorated for several years (due in part to competition from ABC's *Good Morning, America*) finally turned around. Tom Brokaw, Jane Pauley, Gene Shalit, Floyd Kalber, and Bob Ryan comprised the show's regular crew; several other people also appeared occasionally, including Betty Furness (reporting on consumer affairs), Dr. Art Ulene (health care), and Edwin Newman (language). In May of 1979 talkshow host Phil Donahue became a regular contributor to the show. Floyd Kalber left during the summer of 1979 and was succeeded by Tony Guida; in the fall of 1979 Guida began to do assignment reporting, and Brokaw and Pauley read the news. Jovial Willard Scott succeeded Bob Ryan as the weather man in March of 1980.

The Brokaw-Pauley-Scott team remained intact for almost two years. Tom Brokaw left at the end of 1981, a few months before he was to begin coanchoring NBC's evening newscast. On 4 January 1982 two new hosts appeared: former NBC sportscaster Bryant Gumbel (who had been contributing sports stories to the show since the fall of 1980) and NBC News correspondent Chris Wallace (son of CBS newsman Mike Wallace). By this time, however, *Today*'s dominance of the early-morning ratings had finally come to an end; ABC's *Good Morning America*, which had first topped *Today* for a couple of weeks in 1979, overtook its rival consistently during 1982 and 1983 (*Today* even slipped to third, for the first time in its thirty-odd year run, during one week in August 1983, as *The CBS Morning News* edged it out for second place). Late in September 1982 Chris Wallace was reassigned, and John Palmer was brought in to read the news. Jane Pauley went on maternity leave late in 1983 but returned early in 1984.

The Gumbel-Pauley-Scott team carried on through the 1980s. Gene Shalit continued to review films, and Linda Ellerbee anchored a popular weekly essay titled "T.G.I.F." until her departure for ABC in the fall of 1986. A prime-time special was televised 26 August 1985, and the series celebrated its thirty-fifth anniversary with a second special on 1 February 1987. *Today* fared well against *Good Morning America* during the latter half of the decade, until a series of events unfolded that sent the series into a decline. The first volley was heard in February 1989, when an internal memo from Gumbel to his superiors was leaked to the press; the memo was extremely critical of Scott and Shalit, and caused Gumbel much embarrassment. The next volley came in the fall of 1989, when NBC Sports executive Dick Ebersol, who had recently been placed in charge of *Today,* decided to bring Deborah Norville aboard to read the news, and to move John Palmer back to Norville's old beat, *NBC News at Sunrise.* Ebersol also decided that Norville's role should be greater than Palmer's had been. Though he insisted that he was not trying to oust Jane Pauley, that was exactly what happened; shortly after Norville's arrival Pauley announced her departure, and bade farewell to *Today* on 28 December 1989 (Pauley remained with NBC News, of course, filling in for Tom Brokaw on *The NBC Nightly News* and hosting her own prime-time magazine series, *Real Life with Jane Pauley,* in the summer of 1990).

By the spring of 1990 *Today*'s ratings were down by 15%, and the show was again running second to *Good Morning America.* Bryant Gumbel had begun hosting some network golf tournaments, and missed several Mondays as a result. Willard Scott seldom appeared in the New York studios, delivering the weathercast either from Washington, D.C., or from a remote location. In June 1990 Joe Garagiola was rehired, and Faith Daniels, who had previously anchored or coanchored *The CBS Early Morning News* for several years, was signed to read the news. Dick Ebersol severed his ties with *Today* and moved back to NBC Sports. In April 1991 Katie Couric succeeded Deborah Norville as cohost. *Today*'s ratings began to rise almost immediately. Couric had been a local reporter in Miami and Washington, D.C., before joining NBC News as deputy Penatagon correspondent in the mid-1980s. In 1990 she joined the *Today* show as national correspondent, and filled in for Norville during the latter's maternity leave in early 1991. Gumbel and Couric were later joined by Matt Lauer, who read the news.

Today marked its fortieth anniversary with a prime time retropsective on 14 January 1992. In June 1994 it moved to a new studio; its ground floor location was a throwback to the program's earliest days (except that the glass was now bulletproof).

See also *Early Today; NBC News at Sunrise; Saturday Today; Sunday Today.*

TODAY IS OURS   NBC
30 JUNE 1958–26 DECEMBER 1958   Half-hour daytime serial about a divorced woman. With Patricia Benoit as Laura Manning, assistant principal of Bolton Central High School; Peter Lazar as her young son, Nicky; Patrick O'Neal as architect Glenn Turner, who fell for Laura; and Joyce Lear as Glenn's wife. When *Today Is Ours* left the air after six months, its central characters were blended into the opening story line of its successor, *Young Dr. Malone.*

TODAY ON THE FARM   NBC
1 OCTOBER 1960–11 MARCH 1961   Broadcast live at 7:00 A.M. on Saturday mornings, this half-hour show was geared toward the American farmer. Eddy Arnold hosted

the show, and other regulars included Mal Hansen (agricultural news), Carmelita Pope (women's features), and Joe Slattery (weather).

TODAY WITH MRS. ROOSEVELT
See MRS. ROOSEVELT MEETS THE PUBLIC

TODAY'S BLACK WOMAN   SYNDICATED
1981   Half-hour magazine series for black females, hosted by singer Freda Payne.

TODAY'S F.B.I.   ABC
25 OCTOBER 1981–14 AUGUST 1982   This hour crime show seemed to have two things going for it, at least on paper: It was a remake of TV's second-longest-running crime show, *The F.B.I.*, and it starred Mike Connors, who had played the title role in *Mannix* for eight seasons. However, like almost all TV sequels, *Today's F.B.I.* proved much less popular than yesterday's. Connors portrayed FBI agent Ben Slater, a twenty-year Bureau veteran who supervised four young agents—Joseph Cali as Nick Frazier, who frequently went undercover; Carol Potter as Maggie Clinton, expert psychologist and markswoman; Rick Hill as Al Gordean, skilled climber and daredevil; and Harold Sylvester as Dwayne Thompson, a former Marine intelligence officer.

TOGETHER WE STAND (NOTHING IS EASY)   CBS
22 SEPTEMBER 1986–29 OCTOBER 1986; 8 FEBRUARY 1987–24 APRIL 1987   Half-hour sitcom about a multi-ethnic family. The series started out in the fall of 1986 as *Together We Stand*, and starred Elliott Gould as David Randall, a former coach of the Portland Trail Blazers who now owned a sporting goods store in Portland, and Dee Wallace Stone as his wife, Lori. David and Lori had four children, three of whom were adopted: fifteen-year-old Amy (played by Katie O'Neill), twelve-year-old Scott, their natural son (Scott Grimes); fourteen-year-old Sam, who was Asian (Ke Huy Quan); and six-year-old Sally, who was black (Natasha Bobo). After five episodes (in three different time slots), *Together We Stand* left the air in October. It returned early in Febrauary with a new title, *Nothing Is Easy*, and without Elliott Gould. Lori Randall was now a widow, and was studying to become a court reporter. Julia Migenes joined the cast as neighbor Marion Simmons, a divorcée.

TOM   CBS
2 MARCH 1994–27 APRIL 1994; 6 JUNE 1994–13 JUNE 1994   A year after the rise and fall of his first sitcom, *The Jackie Thomas Show,* Tom Arnold returned with a new vehicle on a new network. Again, his series failed to catch on. This time Arnold starred as Tom Graham, a welder who, with his wife and five kids, decided to build his dream house on land next to a city dump near Topeka, Kansas; the brood lived in a trailer while Tom worked on the house. Also featured were Alison LaPlaca (who had costarred on *The Jackie Thomas Show*) as his wife, Dorothy; Jason Marsden as son Mike; Josh Stoppelworth as son Trevor; Tiffany Lubran and Kathryn Lubran as twin daughters Emily and Charlotte; Andrew Lawrence as son Donnie; Colleen Camp as Tom's sister, Kara; and Danton Stone as Kara's husband, Rodney. Tom and Roseanne Arnold, who created the series together with Steve Pepoon, were the executive producers.

TOM AND JERRY   CBS/ABC
25 SEPTEMBER 1965–17 SEPTEMBER 1972 (CBS); 6 SEPTEMBER 1975–3 SEPTEMBER 1978 (ABC); 6 SEPTEMBER 1980–4 SEPTEMBER 1982 (CBS)   Tom and Jerry, the cat and mouse cartoon characters created by William Hanna and Joseph Barbera in the 1940s, came to television in 1965; this CBS Saturday-morning show included new episodes as well as some of the theatrical releases. In 1975 Tom and Jerry showed up on ABC's Saturday-morning schedule, sharing an hour with a thirty-foot purple gorilla in *The New Tom and Jerry/Grape Ape Show.* In 1976 a dog was added and the show was retitled *The Tom and Jerry/Grape Ape/Mumbly Show.* The ape departed in December 1976, and Tom and Jerry continued in the half-hour *Tom and Jerry/*

Mumbly Show. Reruns were shown Sunday mornings under the *The Great Grape Ape* title during the 1977–1978 season. In 1980 Tom and Jerry popped up again on Saturday mornings as the stars of CBS's *The Tom and Jerry Comedy Show,* which lasted two seasons.

TOM & JERRY KIDS SHOW   FOX

8 SEPTEMBER 1990–2 OCTOBER 1993   On this Saturday morning animated series from Hanna-Barbera Productions, younger versions of classic M-G-M cartoon characters starred. The cartoon segments included "Tom and Jerry," the cat-and-mouse duo originally drawn for M-G-M by Bill Hanna and Joe Barbera, and two father-and-son dog teams, "Spike and Tike" and "Droopy and Drippy."

TOM CORBETT, SPACE CADET   CBS/ABC/NBC/DUMONT

2 OCTOBER 1950–29 DECEMBER 1950 (CBS); 1 JANUARY 1951–26 SEPTEMBER 1952 (ABC); 7 JULY 1951–8 SEPTEMBER 1951 (NBC); 29 AUGUST 1953–22 MAY 1954 (DU-MONT); 11 DECEMBER 1954–25 JUNE 1955 (NBC)   This durable space opera was not only one of the few shows to have run on all four commercial networks, but it was also one of the very few shows to have run on two networks simultaneously; this occurred in 1951, when the show was seen Saturday mornings on NBC and three weekday evenings on ABC. Set during the 2350s at the Space Academy, a training school for Solar Guards, the show starred Frankie Thomas as Tom Corbett, a hopeful cadet. Also on hand were Edward Bryce as Captain Steve Strong; Jan Merlin as Cadet Roger Manning; Jack Grimes as Cadet T. J. Thistle; Patricia Ferris and Margaret Garland as Dr. Joan Dale; John Fiedler as Cadet Alfie Higgins; Frank Sutton as Cadet Rattison; Denise Alexander as Tom's sister, Betty Corbett; Norma Clarke as Cadet Jo Spencer; and Al Markim as Astro, a Venusian crewman aboard the *Polaris,* the Academy's training ship. The series premiered as a fifteen-minute, thrice-weekly show on CBS, and continued in that format on ABC; the NBC and DuMont versions were half-hour shows, telecast on Saturday mornings.

TOM COTTLE: UP CLOSE.   SYNDICATED

1982   Boston psychologist Tom Cottle interviewed a single guest on each program of this half-hour talk show.

TOM, DICK AND MARY   NBC

5 OCTOBER 1964–4 JANUARY 1965   The third segment of *90 Bristol Court,* NBC's unsuccessful attempt to set three sitcoms at the same California apartment complex, *Tom, Dick and Mary* told the story of a young married couple who moved in with a swinging bachelor. With Don Galloway as Tom Gentry, an intern; Joyce Bulifant as his wife, Mary Gentry; Steve Franken as their roommate, Dick Moran, also an intern; John Hoyt as Dr. Krevoy, chief of staff at the hospital; J. Edward McKinley as Horace; and Guy Raymond as Cliff Murdock, the handyman. See also *Harris Against the World; Karen.*

THE TOM EWELL SHOW   CBS

27 SEPTEMBER 1960–18 JULY 1961   Tom Ewell, who had costarred with Marilyn Monroe in *The Seven Year Itch,* starred in this half-hour sitcom as Tom Potter, a real estate agent who was surrounded by women at home. Also featured were Marilyn Erskine as his wife, Fran; Mabel Albertson as Fran's mother, Irene (Grandma); Cindy Robbins as Tom and Fran's daughter, Carol; Sherry Alberoni as daughter Debbie; and Eileen Chesis as daughter Cissy.

THE TOM JONES SHOW

See THIS IS TOM JONES

THE TOM KENNEDY SHOW   SYNDICATED

1970   Though Tom Kennedy is best known as a game-show host (*Big Game, Name That Tune, Split Second, You Don't Say,* etc.), he also hosted this short-lived hour talk show; its official title was *The Real Tom Kennedy Show,* and it also featured comic Foster Brooks.

TOM TERRIFIC
See CAPTAIN KANGAROO

TOMA ABC
4 OCTOBER 1973–6 SEPTEMBER 1974 *Toma* was an hour-long crime show based on the adventures of David Toma, a real-life detective for the Newark Police Department who relied on the art of disguise to apprehend his prey. The series starred Tony Musante as David Toma; Susan Strasberg as his wife, Patty Toma; Simon Oakland as Toma's supervisor, Inspector Spooner; Sean Manning as David and Patty's son, Jimmy; Michelle Livingston as their daughter, Donna; David Toma himself also appeared in several episodes, usually in disguise. Roy Huggins was the executive producer for Universal Television. Though *Toma* was renewed by ABC for a second season, Tony Musante surprised everyone by announcing his intention not to continue with the show. To fill the void, Universal Television signed Robert Blake and developed an hour crime show for him: see *Baretta.*

TOMAHAWK SYNDICATED
1957 Produced in Canada, this little-known western starred Jacques Godet as Pierre Radisson and Rene Caron as Medard, a pair of scouts.

TOMBSTONE TERRITORY ABC/SYNDICATED
16 OCTOBER 1957–17 SEPTEMBER 1958; 13 MARCH 1959–9 OCTOBER 1959 (ABC); 1959 (SYNDICATED) Half-hour western from Ziv TV, starring Pat Conway as Sheriff Clay Hollister and Richard Eastham as Harris Claibourne, the editor of the Tombstone (Ariz. Terr.) *Epitaph.* The series' theme song ("Whistle me up a memory. . .") was composed by William M. Backer. The show ran for one season on ABC and was recalled in March of 1959 to replace *Man with a Camera.* Following the network run another 26 episodes were produced for first-run syndication.

TOMFOOLERY NBC
12 SEPTEMBER 1970–4 SEPTEMBER 1971 The segments on this Saturday-morning cartoon show were based on stories from children's literary classics.

TOMORROW ABC
26 MARCH 1955–29 MAY 1956 This public affairs program was produced by Johns Hopkins University and moderated by Lynn Poole. It was originally a discussion program, but in September of 1955 it changed its title to *Tomorrow's Careers* and focused on presenting profiles of various occupations to young people.

TOMORROW NBC
15 OCTOBER 1973–28 JANUARY 1982 Network television's first entry into late-late-night programming on weeknights (NBC had introduced *The Midnight Special* on Fridays some months earlier), *Tomorrow* was scheduled at 1:00 A.M., immediately following the *Tonight* show. The hour-long talk show was hosted by Tom Snyder; it was originally broadcast from NBC studios in Burbank, but moved to New York in December 1974. In June 1977 the show returned to Burbank until 1979, when Snyder headed back to New York. On 16 September 1980, when the *Tonight* show was shortened to sixty minutes, the *Tomorrow* show was lengthened to ninety minutes nightly. A month later Hollywood gossip columnist Rona Barrett was added to the show. After numerous squabbles and changes of production executives, Barrett was granted equal billing as the series' West Coast cohost. As of 12 January 1981 the show was retitled *Tomorrow Coast to Coast.* Rona Barrett left the show in the spring of 1981.

Early in 1982, NBC replaced *Tomorrow Coast to Coast* with a new talk show (see *Late Night with David Letterman*).

THE TONI TENNILLE SHOW   SYNDICATED

1980   Singer Toni Tennille hosted this daytime talk show, aimed principally at women between the ages of 30 and 39.

TONI TWIN TIME   CBS

5 APRIL 1950–20 SEPTEMBER 1950   Jack Lemmon hosted this Wednesday-night talent show, which alternated with *What's My Line?* The half-hour series was sponsored by Toni home permanents; each week a pair of twins was featured, one of whom sported a Toni permanent. The show was written and produced by Sherman Marks.

TONIGHT ON BROADWAY   CBS

6 APRIL 1948–23 MAY 1948; 2 OCTOBER 1949–18 DECEMBER 1949   Scenes from current Broadway plays were enacted on this half-hour anthology series. Martin Gosch hosted the show in 1948, John Mason Brown in 1949.

THE TONIGHT SHOW   NBC

27 SEPTEMBER 1954–   NBC's late-night talk show is television's most profitable series. Though it was not the first late-night network series (*Broadway Open House* holds that distinction), it is by far the most successful. Until 1993 it was never seriously challenged in its time slot by any other late-night series, network or syndicated. The chief reason for the show's profitability is that production costs are relatively low and that revenues are high; because of its time slot, the show carries more minutes of commercials than do prime-time programs. *The Tonight Show* has remained popular with viewers because it has kept a predominantly light touch, steering a middle course between brainless burlesque and wordy tedium.

Like most of NBC's innovative programs of the 1950s, *The Tonight Show* was the brainchild of Sylvester "Pat" Weaver, the network executive who also conceived the *Today* show, *Home, Wide Wide World,* and *Your Show of Shows.* Though *Tonight's* predecessor, *Broadway Open House,* perished after a fifteen-month run, it had demonstrated to Weaver that late-night television was a viable concept. Weaver abandoned the idea of a slapstick show in favor of a more relaxed, conversational program; his intuition proved right, as *The Tonight Show* has remained on the air for more than thirty years. *The Tonight Show* was based in New York from 1954 until May of 1972, when it moved to Los Angeles. It has had four principal hosts (and a host of guest hosts) over the years. The first three hosts—Steve Allen, Jack Paar, and Johnny Carson—came to the series from similar backgrounds: all were born in the Midwest, all had brief but unspectacular careers in radio, and all had had considerable experience in television, hosting game shows and variety shows of their own, before taking their seat behind the desk of *The Tonight Show.* The fourth host, Jay Leno, was born and raised in New England, and had twenty years experience doing standup comedy before taking on the job (he had also been the program's permanent guest host for several years). All four are quick-witted people who can keep a conversation going and who can ad-lib skillfully.

As a matter of convenience, the several eras of *The Tonight Show* (all of which have borne slightly different titles) are discussed individually.

I. Steve Allen—*Tonight!* (27 September 1954–25 January 1957)

The first host of *The Tonight Show* (which was then titled *Tonight!*), Steve Allen began his broadcasting career as a disc jockey. In 1950 he came to New York, where he hosted a number of TV series during the next three years (see *Songs for Sale; The Steve Allen Show; Talent Patrol*). On 27 July 1953, Allen began hosting a local show over WNBC-TV in New York. Allen's show, which ran from 11:20 P.M. to midnight, Mondays through Fridays, had been developed by station executive Ted Cott to lure a potential sponsor, Ruppert Breweries, away from a late-night show on New York's Channel 7 (that show, *Talk of the Town,* was hosted by Louis Nye, who would later be featured on Steve Allen's variety shows). After a successful fourteen-month run, *The Steve Allen Show* became a network show; beginning 27 September 1954, the show (retitled *Tonight!*) was offered to NBC affiliates as far west as Omaha, and was expanded to 105 minutes nightly. Ruppert Breweries, the original sponsor, insisted on the unusual length; though few affiliates ever carried the first fifteen minutes, it was not until the late 1960s, at Johnny Carson's insistence, that the show was shortened to ninety minutes.

The basic format of *The Tonight Show* was established during Allen's tenure: an opening monologue, a segment involving the studio audience (through interviews or games such as "Stump the Band"), and a simple set (a desk and chair for the host, a couch for the guests), were all trademarks of the Allen era. Allen inaugurated the out-of-town broadcast (the first was done from Miami), the one-guest show (Carl Sandburg was the first solo guest), and the one-topic show (entire programs were devoted to such subjects as narcotics, civil rights, and black music). Allen also established the practice of paying his guests only "scale," the minimum fee required by union-network contract (this practice led to a highly publicized feud between Steve Allen and Ed Sullivan, and later between Jack Paar and Ed Sullivan, as Sullivan paid top dollar for his guests).

Though Allen's *Tonight!* show closely resembled the shows of his successors, Jack Paar and Johnny Carson, it was a more musical show; Allen himself was an accomplished musician and composer (he wrote his theme, "This Could Be the Start of Something"), and he employed a nucleus of musical regulars on his show. In addition to announcer-sidekick Gene Rayburn, the show featured singers Steve Lawrence (who was only seventeen when he began singing on Allen's local show), Eydie Gormé (who subsequently married Steve Lawrence), Andy Williams (who later hosted several series of his own), and Pat Marshall (who was succeeded by Pat Kirby). Skitch Henderson led the orchestra. The show was produced by Bill Harbach and Nick Vanoff, and directed by Dwight Hemion; Harbach and Vanoff later produced *The Hollywood Palace,* and Hemion has produced and directed a number of award-winning variety series and specials.

Allen introduced audiences to several new comedians, including Mort Sahl, Lenny Bruce, and Shelley Berman. Other, more unusual guests also appeared, such as Joe Interleggi ("the human termite"), Ben Belefonte ("the rhyming inventor"), and upstate farmer John Schafer (who delivered terse film reviews). Two other people were also part of the show, though they sat in the audience: Mrs. Sterling and Miss Dorothy Miller, both of whom were frequently interviewed by Allen. Finally, there was Allen himself, who used his wide-ranging improvisational skills. Sometimes he might dash out of the studio to stop traffic; sometimes he would deliver an extemporaneous narration to a street scene broadcast from a remote camera; sometimes he would compose a melody on the piano, using notes suggested by the audience. Above all, he kept the show moving.

In the summer of 1956 Allen began a Sunday-night variety hour, which NBC had devised to dent the ratings of *The Ed Sullivan Show* on CBS. To ease the strain on Allen (who obviously could not maintain a six-nights-a-week schedule for long), in the fall of 1956 Ernie Kovacs was brought in to host the *Tonight!* show on Mondays and Tuesdays. By the end of the year the network, intent on battling Ed Sullivan on Sundays, ordered Allen to drop his *Tonight!* show chores altogether and to concentrate instead on the Sunday variety show. On 25 January 1957, Allen hosted his last *Tonight!* show, as the series' first era came to a close.

II. The First Interregnum—*Tonight: America After Dark* (28 January 1957–26 July 1957)

Tonight: America After Dark was a disaster. An ill-conceived, diffuse program, it was more of a magazine show than a variety or talk show. There was no central figure around whom the show revolved: though Jack Lescoulie (who had been with the *Today* show) was nominally the host, the show featured a group of correspondents, from different cities, who reported nightly. The original lineup included Hy Gardner, Bob Considine, and Earl Wilson in New York; Irv Kupcinet in Chicago; and Paul Coates and Vernon Scott in Los Angeles. Music was provided by the Lou Stein Trio. Designed to resemble the *Today* show, *Tonight: America After Dark* was supposed to provide a window on American nightlife; mobile units were dispatched to cover celebrity-studded parties, motion picture premieres, nightclub shows, and other "special events" such as a tribute to the ninety-sixth anniversary of the statehood of

Kansas, which was a highlight of the show's premiere broadcast. The show was also supposed to provide hard news coverage as well. *Tonight: America After Dark* opened to poor reviews and low ratings, as affiliates began to drop the show in favor of more profitable local programs. NBC executives began tinkering with the show: Vernon Scott was replaced by Lee Giroux; singer Judy Johnson joined in March; the Mort Lindsey Quartet replaced the Lou Stein Trio, and was in turn replaced by the Johnny Guarnieri Quartet; in June, Al "Jazzbo" Collins became the new host, broadcasting from a set called the Purple Grotto. All of these efforts proved fruitless; when *Tonight: America After Dark* ended its run after twenty-six weeks, only five dozen NBC affiliates carried the show.

III. *The Jack Paar Tonight Show* (29 July 1957–30 March 1962)

As soon as it became apparent that no amount of tinkering could salvage *Tonight: America After Dark*, NBC executives began looking for someone to host its successor. Jack Paar was one of the first people contacted and was eager to take the job. A high school dropout, Paar had entertained servicemen during World War II (where his irreverence toward military brass made him a favorite of enlisted men), and had hosted several TV shows during the early 1950s, including *Bank on the Stars* and *Up to Paar* (both game shows), *The Morning Show* (CBS's abortive attempt to compete with *Today*), and the *Jack Paar Show* (which was first a morning variety show, and later an afternoon show).

With Paar at the helm, the new version of NBC's late-night show set sail on 29 July 1957; it was originally titled *Tonight* (without the exclamation point of Steve Allen's era), but was later officially retitled *The Jack Paar Tonight Show*. Paar's first task was to win back the network affiliates that had dropped his predecessor during the first half of 1957. He succeeded; within eighteen months, Paar's lineup grew from sixty-two stations and two sponsors to 115 stations and full sponsorship. Paar, unlike Allen or Carson, was not a standup comic who could also conduct a conversation; rather, he was a conversationalist who could also deliver a joke. To lure and retain viewers, his show relied more on conversation—and controversy—than on humor. Audiences came to expect the unexpected on Paar's shows; sparks could fly at any time between the host and his guests. A mercurial and petulant person who was surrounded by conflict and controversy (though he professed to detest it), Paar became enmeshed in a series of feuds with other show business luminaries, such as Steve Allen, Dorothy Kilgallen, Walter Winchell, and Ed Sullivan.

Paar began his show with a crew of regulars, but only two stayed with him for the entire run: announcer-sidekick Hugh Downs and bandleader José Melis, a former Army buddy. Others who came and went included Dody Goodman, "weather girl" Tedi Thurman, singer Betty Johnson, and the Bil and Cora Baird Puppets. Another group of people could be classified as semiregulars; all were good talkers who dropped by frequently to chat with the host. This group included, among others, Washington hostess Elsa Maxwell, British humorist Alexander King, French chanteuse Genevieve, writer Jack Douglas (and his Japanese wife, Reiko), Zsa Zsa Gabor, Hans Conried, Peggy Cass, Cliff (Charley Weaver) Arquette, and Mary Margaret McBride. Among the most famous guests who appeared were Robert Kennedy (then counsel to a Senate committee investigating racketeers, Kennedy appeared 22 February 1959), John Kennedy, Richard Nixon (who appeared, separately, during the 1960 Presidential campaign), and Barbra Streisand (who made her network TV debut on 5 April 1961, when Orson Bean was the guest host).

By 1960 the popularity of *The Jack Paar Tonight Show* was assured. The show was videotaped in the early evening, which enabled Paar, like most of his viewers, to watch the show in bed. Paar was able to cut his own appearances on the show back to three nights a week (Paar worked some Monday nights, but most Mondays featured either Hugh Downs or a guest host, and all Friday shows were reruns). Most importantly, from the network's point of view, the show was a huge moneymaker and was carried by 158 affiliates. Commercial success, however, did little to ease Paar's tensions. As early as 1958 Paar had talked publicly about leaving the show, and in February 1960 he made good on his promise. The incident that precipitated Paar's celebrated walkout was the "W.C. Joke." It was a shaggy-dog story about an Englishwoman who planned to travel abroad and wrote her host to inquire if her accommodations included a w.c., her abbreviation for water closet. Her host, who was not fluent in English, was baffled by the term; after some thought he concluded that w.c. stood for wayside chapel, and wrote back to the woman extolling in detail the sumptuousness of the nearby w.c., but cautioning her that it was likely to be crowded on the two days a week that it was open. By today's standards, the story would hardly raise an eyebrow, but in 1960 it was unacceptable, at least to NBC censors. The network deleted the entire story from the show, without advising Paar of its decision. The following night (11 February 1960) a furious Paar walked on stage, announced his displeasure with NBC's unilateral action and his weariness at being a constant center of controversy, and bade an emotional farewell to the audience. His sudden departure left a startled Hugh Downs to entertain the evening's guests, Orson Bean and Shelley Berman. Paar returned to his desk a month later, but the storm of controversy never abated; shortly after his return Paar reignited his feuds with Walter Winchell and Ed Sullivan (Jack Benny finally helped to mediate the Paar-Sullivan tiff).

The most serious incident occurred when Paar took himself, Peggy Cass, and a film crew to West Berlin in September of 1961, less than a month after the erection of the Berlin Wall. In one segment of the film, a detachment of American troops was deployed to stand in the background as Paar stood in the foreground near the Brandenburg Gate. The incident spurred a Defense Department inquiry and the censure of the U.S. Commander in West Berlin. Paar was excoriated in the press for the militaristic overtones of the Berlin broadcast; Paar blamed the press for the brouhaha, insisting that his visit had actually helped ease East-West tensions. Shortly afterward, however, Paar again announced that he would leave the show; this time he gave advance notice and remained firm in his decision to leave at the end of March 1962. His last first-run show was shown 29 March 1962 (the final show on 30 March was a rerun), as dozens of celebrities dropped by or sent film clips wishing him a fond farewell. Though Paar left his late-night show in March, he returned to NBC that fall to host a prime-time variety hour, which ran for three seasons (see *The Jack Paar Show*); in 1973 he again tried a late-night show, this time on ABC (see *Jack Paar Tonite*), which made no waves.

IV. The Second Interregnum (2 April 1962–28 September 1962)
Because of his previous contract, Jack Paar's successor, Johnny Carson, was unable to take over the show until October 1962. The twenty-six-week gap was filled by a succession of guest hosts, most of whom stayed for a week at a time. The parade included, among others, Mort Sahl, Soupy Sales, Art Linkletter, Groucho Marx, Merv Griffin, Jerry Lewis, and Arlene Francis (the first woman to guest-host the show). Hugh Downs stayed on as the announcer until August, when he succeeded John Chancellor as host of the *Today* show; Ed Herlihy replaced Downs on *Tonight*. Skitch Henderson led the band during the transition period. Though the six-month hiatus was uneventful, it was by no means a ratings disaster as *Tonight: America After Dark* had been.

V. *The Tonight Show Starring Johnny Carson* (1 October 1962–22 May 1992)
Johnny Carson had originally turned down NBC's offer to host *The Tonight Show*. Having substituted for Jack Paar, he was familiar with the job and initially felt that it would be too much of a grind (Carson told an interviewer in 1961 that the average life expectancy of a TV comic was about five years). Ultimately, Carson reconsidered and stayed with the show to become one of the most popular entertainers in show business history. His thirty-year stewardship of the show was five times the combined tenure of Allen and Paar. He has hosted more total hours of network programming than anyone.

Born in Corning, Iowa, and raised in Norfolk, Nebraska, Carson made a little money as a teenager doing magic tricks (as "The Great Carsoni"), and developed a ventriloquist act in the Navy. He attended the University of Nebraska, where he wrote his senior thesis on comedy. After a brief stint with radio station WOW in Omaha, he headed for Los Angeles and soon got his own local TV show, a half-hour

Sunday program called *Carson's Cellar*. He later wrote for *The Red Skelton Show,* hosted a summer game show (*Earn Your Vacation*), and finally got his own prime-time variety show (*The Johnny Carson Show*), which lasted thirty-nine weeks. In 1956 he hosted a daytime variety show, and a year later he began his second game show, *Who Do You Trust?* It was on this five-day-a-week program that Carson honed his interviewing and ad-libbing skills, for the quiz portion of *Who Do You Trust?* was clearly secondary to the conversational portion. When Carson left the show five years later (executive producer Don Fedderson refused to release him from his contract before it expired in September 1962), it was TV's top-rated daytime series.

Carson brought with him his sidekick from *Who Do You Trust?*, Ed McMahon, as well as producer Art Stark, who became the producer of *The Tonight Show;* Carson's brother, Dick Carson, was the director, and Skitch Henderson, who had led the band since Paar's departure, stayed on. Carson's guests on the 1962 premiere included Rudy Vallee, Joan Crawford, Mel Brooks, and Tony Bennett. The show opened to good reviews, and the ratings, which were fairly strong to start with, improved over the next few months.

Above all, Carson sought to entertain viewers. A keen student of comedy (and of television in general), Carson intentionally discouraged direct confrontation on his show in order to appeal to the broadest possible public. Though he was criticized for his failure to take sides on controversial issues, he defended the show's middle course ("It's not my job to deliver opinions," he once told an interviewer), while pointing out that the show has had its share of "serious" guests, such as Robert Kennedy, Barry Goldwater, Hubert Humphrey, Martin Luther King, Jr., and Carl Sagan.

Among the more celebrated incidents in the long history of *The Tonight Show Starring Johnny Carson* were: Carson's "first-person adventures," a series of filmed segments showing Carson pitching to members of the New York Yankees, flying with the Navy Thunderbirds, or skydiving; Carson's escorting an incoherent and physically exhausted Peter O'Toole offstage during a commercial break on a 1963 program (a sleepless O'Toole had flown to the show directly from the set of *Lord Jim*); guest Ed Ames's demonstration of tomahawk-throwing on a 1964 show, in which he hit a cardboard dummy directly in the crotch (thereby triggering one of the longest bursts of sustained laughter in TV history); a rare TV appearance by John Lennon and Paul McCartney in the spring of 1968 (announcing the formation of Apple Records to guest host Joe Garagiola); the wedding of singer Tiny Tim to Victoria May Budinger on 17 December 1969; Carson's joking reference in a 1973 monologue to a possible toilet paper shortage, which led to mass hoarding of toilet tissue by American consumers; and author Alex Haley's presentation (to a surprised Carson) of the latter's genealogical charts on a 1977 show.

Carson's most serious dispute with NBC arose in 1967, when Carson honored a strike by members of AFTRA, a performers' trade union. During the strike NBC aired reruns of Carson's shows, without his consent, in apparent violation of Carson's contract. Carson rescinded his contract and refused to return to the *Tonight* show after the AFTRA strike was settled until a new contract was negotiated. From that point on Carson became more actively involved in the financial arrangements and in the production details of the show. Art Stark, Carson's first producer, left the show in 1967 and was replaced by Stan Irwin (Irwin was succeeded by Rudy Tellez, who was in turn succeeded by Fred DeCordova, who had previously worked with Jack Benny). Carson's brother and director, Dick Carson, left in 1968 and was succeeded by Bob Quinn; Dick Carson later went to work for Merv Griffin, directing the latter's talk show. In 1969 Johnny Carson formed Raritan Enterprises with business partner Sonny Werblin; Raritan took over the actual production of *The Tonight Show Starring Johnny Carson* and also served as a vehicle for other ventures, such as television specials, an abortive fast-food restaurant chain, and the successful Johnny Carson Apparel, Inc.

Skitch Henderson, the show's bandleader, left in 1966 and was succeeded briefly by Milton DeLugg. In 1967 trumpet player Carl "Doc" Severinsen took over as bandleader; Severinsen's outlandish stage clothes inspired many a one-liner in Carson's nightly monologue. Through it all, Ed McMahon remained with Carson. A onetime boardwalk pitchman at Atlantic City, and a former all-purpose on-camera performer at a Philadelphia TV station, McMahon hooked up with Carson on *Who Do You Trust?* and stayed with him. McMahon's services as audience warm-up man, announcer, and commercial spokesman were fully appreciated, and he is surely television's best-known second banana. McMahon's famous introduction ("Heerre's . . . Johnny!") was intoned to the strains of "Johnny's Theme," which was composed by Carson and Paul Anka.

In 1972 the show moved from New York to Los Angeles (the show had been broadcast from the West Coast on a periodic basis before then). In 1977 Carson negotiated a new contract with NBC, which not only gave him a lot of money (the exact figure was not divulged, but was said to be well above $2 million a year), but also a lot of time off; his schedule called for about twenty-five 3-show weeks and twelve 4-show weeks, with fifteen weeks' vacation. Carson's work weeks were made even shorter on 16 September 1980, when the *Tonight* show was trimmed (at Carson's request) from ninety to sixty minutes. Carson also acquired ownership of the program in 1980.

In 1983 comedienne Joan Rivers was named as Carson's permanent substitute host. Rivers's association with the show was terminated abruptly in the spring of 1986 when she announced that she would be hosting her own late-night talk show on the fledgling Fox Network (see *The Late Show Starring Joan Rivers*). Garry Shandling appeared frequently as guest host from 1986 to 1988, when standup comic Jay Leno took over the assignment.

Through the years *The Tonight Show Starring Johnny Carson* was almost impervious to competition. ABC scheduled *The Les Crane Show, The Joey Bishop Show,* and *The Dick Cavett Show* before "counterprogramming" with *Nightline,* a news show that attracted a different audience. CBS introduced *The Merv Griffin Show* and *The Pat Sajak Show,* both without success; Rivers's *The Late Show* was a ratings disaster. Syndicated efforts such as David Brenner's *Nightlife* were unimpressive. *The Arsenio Hall Show* was the only talk show to hold its own against Carson's, and it did so not by siphoning away Carson viewers, but by attracting a younger audience.

Carson's production company (appropriately named Carson Productions) has produced a number of series and specials for NBC, such as "Johnny Carson's Greatest Practical Jokes" (28 November 1983), several retrospectives on TV commercials, and *Amen,* among others.

As the 1990s dawned, there was speculation about how long Carson would remain as host. NBC executives expressed no public concern about the matter, as Carson's ratings remained high; however, it was also apparent to the network that Carson was attracting an ever-aging audience, and that younger viewers were likely to be watching competition such as *The Arsenio Hall Show*. Carson himself put the rumors to rest in May 1991 at a meeting of network affiliates in New York, where he stunned the audience by announcing that he would leave the show in May 1992 (Carson repeated the news that night when he appeared on *Late Night with David Letterman*).

Although NBC had no advance knowledge of Carson's announcement, it had already selected his successor: Jay Leno, who had served as the show's permanent guest host since the late 1980s. The network was anxious to keep Leno and, to keep him from going to CBS, had negotiated a contract with him days earlier under which Leno was promised the *Tonight* show upon Carson's departure. Not until later did the network learn of David Letterman's burning desire to host the program, and of his deep hurt about not being considered for it.

Carson's thirtieth and final season went smoothly, as a more emotional side of him was revealed to audiences. In July 1991 Carson delivered a deeply moving tribute to his son Richard, who had been killed in an auto accident four weeks earlier. In September 1991 the starting time of the program was moved to 11:35 P.M., which allowed local stations to sell more commercial time during their eleven o'clock newscasts. During the show's final weeks a steady stream of celebrities dropped by to express their appreciation, including Bob Hope, Clint Eastwood, Roseanne Arnold, Elizabeth Taylor, Steve Martin, James Stewart, and David Letterman (who thanked Carson "for my career"). Curiously, Jay Leno was not booked on the program. Robin Williams and Bette Midler were Carson's final guests (both appeared 21 May 1992); the very last program featured no guests, as Carson, McMahon and Severinsen reminisced and showed clips from previous shows. The last show reached an audience estimated at 50 million, the largest ever for a late-night program.

VI. *The Tonight Show with Jay Leno* (25 May 1992–   )

Born in New Rochelle, New York, and raised in Andover, Massachusetts, Jay Leno began doing standup comedy while still a student at Emerson College in Boston. In 1974 he moved to Los Angeles and quickly became a headliner at local comedy clubs; by the end of the decade he was traveling all over the country, making a good living doing more than 200 one-night comedy shows a year. He made his first appearance on the *Tonight* show 12 March 1977; he appeared three more times during the next several months. After his fourth appearance eight years elapsed before he returned to the *Tonight* show. By 1988, however, he had been named permanent guest host, and in 1991, shortly before Carson announced his upcoming departure, Leno signed a contract with NBC which provided that he would succeed Carson as host. Under the terms of Leno's contract, NBC reacquired ownership of the *Tonight* show, and Leno's longtime manager, Helen Kushnick, became the show's executive producer.

The Tonight Show with Jay Leno premiered 25 May 1992. At Kushnick's insistence, Leno made no mention of Carson on his first program. The Leno show looked much like the Carson show, although there were a few changes. Leno had no sidekick; announcer Edd Hall rarely appeared onstage. The new band, led by jazz trumpeter Branford Marsalis, veered away from a big band sound and toward a funky, progressive sound. Billy Crystal was Leno's first guest.

The first months of Leno's tenure were rocky. Kushnick, who had had no experience in producing a television show, soon engaged in bitter wars with the two syndicated talk shows which she perceived as Leno's main competition, *The Arsenio Hall Show* and *The Dennis Miller Show*. Guests of the Leno show were strongly discouraged from appearing on the rival programs, and those who did sometimes found it impossible to book a subsequent appearance on the Leno show. Kushnick also canceled the taping of an August 1992 program after learning that NBC's coverage of the Republican Convention would run late that evening; the network had only a few minutes to find a Leno show to rebroadcast. In mid-September Kushnick was fired. [Leno would later stipulate that the Kushnick-produced programs were never to be rerun.]

Kushnick's departure did not herald the end of Leno's troubles, however. NBC was anxious to keep both Leno and David Letterman, but Letterman had made known his desire to host the *Tonight* show. In December 1992 Letterman received an extraordinarily lucrative offer from CBS to host a late-night show; under the terms of his contract with NBC, the network had thirty days to match it. Leno waged an all-out campaign to keep his job, garnering support from NBC local affiliate managers and from friends in the press. Ultimately, he succeeded; though NBC did make an oral counter-proposal to Letterman, it withdrew the offer in early January, freeing Letterman to accept the CBS bid.

For the first eight months of 1993 *The Tonight Show with Jay Leno* fared well. *The Dennis Miller Show* had expired in the fall of 1992, and *The Arsenio Hall Show*'s ratings were already beginning to decline. The show's set was redesigned and new theme music was added. The real test came on 30 August 1993, when *Late Show with David Letterman* premiered on CBS. Letterman's show, which was a ratings success from the outset, proved to be the first serious competitor to the *Tonight* show. After thirty-nine years, the *Tonight* show's monopoly of late-night talk had finally come to an end.

Although Letterman's program consistently outdrew Leno's, the *Tonight* show has remained highly profitable. After taking the show to New York for a week in May 1994, Leno again had the set redesigned so that he would be much closer to the studio audience. It now more closely resembled a comedy club, an environment in which Leno felt at home. By 1995 Leno had begun to narrow the ratings gap between his show and Letterman's.

The new set also moved the band closer to the host's desk. Bandleader Branford

Marsalis took a leave of absence in January 1995; his replacement, guitarist Kevin Eubanks, was named permanent bandleader in April.

A full account of the events of 1992 and 1993 involving Jay Leno and David Letterman may be found in Bill Carter's 1994 book, *The Late Shift*.

THE TONY BENNETT SHOW   NBC
11 AUGUST 1956–8 SEPTEMBER 1956   Singer Tony Bennett hosted a summer replacement for *The Perry Como Show*. An hour series, it also featured the Spellbinders. In 1959 Bennett again replaced Como for the summer: see *Perry Presents*.

TONY BROWN'S JOURNAL   SYNDICATED/PBS
1976–1981 (SYNDICATED); 1982– (PBS)   Tony Brown, who had been the host and executive producer of PBS's *Black Journal,* brought his show to commercial television in 1976. The half-hour weekly series was sponsored by Pepsi-Cola. Each show was devoted to a single topic of interest to black Americans. In 1982 Brown returned to public television.

THE TONY MARTIN SHOW   NBC
26 APRIL 1954–27 FEBRUARY 1956   Singer-actor Tony Martin hosted his own fifteen-minute musical show on Monday nights before the network news; also on hand were the Interludes.

TONY ORLANDO AND DAWN   CBS
3 JULY 1974–24 JULY 1974; 4 DECEMBER 1974–28 DECEMBER 1976   After a short recording career in 1961 (during which he recorded "Bless You" and "Halfway to Paradise"), Tony Orlando became a record producer and promoter. In 1970, as a favor for a friend, he added the lead vocal to a demonstration record, "Candida"; as the background vocals had already been recorded, Orlando did not meet the other singers—Telma Hopkins and Joyce Vincent Wilson, who called themselves Dawn—until after the record became a national hit. The three recorded several more hits, including "Knock Three Times" and "Tie a Yellow Ribbon," the biggest record of 1973. In 1974 they hosted a four-week summer replacement for *The Sonny and Cher Comedy Hour;* the series resurfaced later that year in the Wednesday slot previously occupied by *Sons and Daughters*. During the 1975–1976 season regulars included Alice Nunn, Lonnie Schorr, and Lynn Stuart. In the fall of 1976 the show was retitled *Tony Orlando and Dawn Rainbow Hour;* the regulars included George Carlin, Susan Lanier, Bob Holt, Edie McClurg, Adam Wade, and Nancy Steen. Saul Ilson and Ernest Chambers were the producers.

THE TONY RANDALL SHOW   ABC/CBS
23 SEPTEMBER 1976–10 MARCH 1977 (ABC); 24 SEPTEMBER 1977–25 MARCH 1978 (CBS) Half-hour sitcom starring Tony Randall as Judge Walter Franklin, a widowed Superior Court judge who lived and worked in Philadelphia. Also featured were Devon Scott (1976–1977) and Penny Peyser (1977–1978) as his daughter, Roberta (Bobby); Brad Savage as his son, Oliver; Rachel Roberts as the housekeeper, Bonnie McClellan; Allyn Ann McLerie as his prim and proper secretary, Janet Reubner; Barney Martin as court stenographer Jack Terwilliger, an ex-cop; Zane Lasky as the aggressive but addled Mario Lanza, who worked as a law clerk during the first season and as a prosecutor during the second. In the fall of 1977 Hans Conried was added as Walter's father, Ryan Franklin, and Diana Muldaur was seen as Walter's romantic interest, Judge Eleanor Hooper. Tom Patchett and Jay Tarses produced the series for MTM Enterprises.

TOO CLOSE FOR COMFORT   ABC/SYNDICATED
11 NOVEMBER 1980–15 SEPTEMBER 1983 (ABC); 1984–1986 (SYNDICATED) Ted Knight starred in this half-hour sitcom as cartoonist Henry Rush, creator of the "Cosmic Cow" comic strip; Nancy Dussault costarred as his wife, Muriel Rush, a photographer. The Rushes owned a two-family home in San Francisco; after the

death of their downstairs tenant (who, it was discovered, had been a transvestite), Henry and Muriel agreed to let their two grown daughters move into the apartment. Also featured were Deborah Van Valkenburgh as the older daughter, Jackie, a brunette who worked in a bank; Lydia Cornell as the younger daughter, Sarah, a blonde who attended San Francisco State; Hamilton Camp (spring 1981) as Henry's publisher, Arthur Wainwright; Jm J. Bullock as Sarah's befuddled college friend, Munroe Ficus; Deena Freeman (1981–1982) as Henry's niece April, an aspiring songwriter; and Audrey Meadows (1982–1983) as Muriel's mother, Iris Martin. During the 1981–1982 season Henry and Muriel learned that they were going to be parents again, after an eighteen-year hiatus; their baby son, Andrew, was born in the fall of 1982 (twins Jason and Eric Willis played the part during the 1982–1983 season; William and Michael Cannon played the role in 1983–1984).

Too Close for Comfort was based on a British series, Keep It in the Family, created by Brian Cooke. Too Close made history in 1983; after its cancellation by ABC, the supplier (Don-El Productions, headed by D. L. Taffner) and the syndicator (Metromedia) announced that new episodes would be produced in 1984, to be shown by individual stations on a syndicated basis. The principal reason for this decision was to make more episodes available by the time reruns were sold to local stations; only sixty-three half-hours had been produced for ABC, a quantity regarded as too small to assure success in syndication. Too Close for Comfort thus became one of only a handful of series to remain in production after cancellation by the network. The first-run episodes starred Knight, Dussault, Van Valkenburgh, Cornell, and Bullock from the old series. The part of Andrew was now played by Joshua Goodwin. Van Valkenburgh and Cornell left after the first forty-two syndicated episodes had been produced. The series carried on for another twenty-two episodes (until Knight's death in 1986) under a new title, The Ted Knight Show. In this batch, Henry, Muriel, and Andrew moved across the bay to Marin County, as Henry bought into a weekly paper, The Marin Bugler. Joining the cast were Pat Carroll as Henry's new partner, Hope Stinson, and Lisa Antille as Lisa Flores, the Rushs' housekeeper.

One of the series' visual gimmicks was Henry Rush's habit of wearing a different college sweatshirt for each episode.

TOO SOMETHING   FOX
1 OCTOBER 1995–29 OCTOBER 1995   Another of the several "buddy" sitcoms of the 1995 fall season, this one starred Donal Lardner Ward as Donny Reeves and Eric Schaeffer as Eric MacDougal. Donny, a frustrated photographer, and Eric, a frustrated writer, shared a New York apartment and worked together in the mailroom of Crown, Fink & Wagner, an investment brokerage firm. Also on hand were Lisa Gerstein as their pal, Evelyn, who worked in a boutique; Portia De Rossi as Maria Hunter, a new executive at the firm who became interested in Eric; Mindy Seeger as Daisy, who rented a room from the lads and made her living as a dog-walker; and Charlie Schlatter as Jeffrey Crown, Donny and Eric's insufferable young boss. The series was lifted from Fox's schedule for retooling in October, and the network announced a contest to rename it.

TOO YOUNG TO GO STEADY   NBC
14 MAY 1959–25 JUNE 1959   Half-hour sitcom starring Brigid Bazlen as fourteen-year-old Pam Blake, boy-crazy teenager; Donald Cook as her father, attorney Tom Blake; Joan Bennett as her mother, Mary Blake; and Martin Huston as her brother, seventeen-year-old John Blake. David Susskind was executive producer of the series, which was broadcast live from New York.

TOON NIGHT   CBS
17 APRIL 1991–3 JULY 1991   A rarity in prime time television, Toon Night was an animated anthology series that presented a mixture of new and vintage cartoons during its brief run. On some weeks two half-hour programs were televised back to back.

TOOTSIE HIPPODROME ABC

3 FEBRUARY 1952–30 JANUARY 1954   This half-hour children's show consisted of variety acts and games for the kids in the studio audience. John Reed King was the first host but was succeeded by Whitey Carson and His Musical Ranch Hands; Mary Reynolds also appeared as Whitey's assistant, Judy Ann. The show began on Sunday mornings and shifted to Saturdays in August of 1953.

TOP CAT ABC

27 SEPTEMBER 1961–26 SEPTEMBER 1962   First introduced as a prime-time series a year after *The Flintstones,* this cartoon series lasted a season in prime time before reverting to Saturday mornings, where reruns were shown for several years. A Hanna-Barbera production, the series was inspired by *The Phil Silvers Show*; its central character, Top Cat, was a scheming feline who lived in a Manhattan trash can. Arnold Stang provided his voice. The voices of T. C.'s henchcats were supplied by Marvin Kaplan as Choo-Choo, Maurice Gosfield (better known as Doberman on *The Phil Silvers Show*) as Benny the Ball, Leo DeLyon as Spook and as The Brain, and John Stephenson as Fancy-Fancy.

TOP COPS CBS

18 JULY 1990–27 AUGUST 1993   An unusual series, *Top Cops* presented dramatic recreations of actual events in the lives of real police officers. Each story was introduced and narrated by the real-life officer whose story was depicted. Among them was officer Ken Osmond of the Los Angeles Police Department, who is better known as Eddie Haskell on *Leave It to Beaver.* The series was produced by Sonny Grosso (himself a former New York cop) and Larry Jacobson, who had previously produced *Night Heat. Top Cops* premiered as an hour series, was trimmed to a half hour in the fall of 1990, and expanded again to an hour early in 1991. Two additional programs were telecast in the fall of 1993 after the series' cancellation.

TOP DOLLAR CBS

Nighttime: 29 MARCH 1958–30 AUGUST 1958; *Daytime:* 18 AUGUST 1958–23 OCTOBER 1959   Contestants played a word game similar to "ghosts" on this game show, hosted first by Toby Reed, later by Jack Narz. Home viewers who owned dollar bills with serial numbers that matched numbers announced on the show could also win cash by sending the matching bills in to the show.

TOP OF THE HEAP FOX

14 APRIL 1991–21 JULY 1991   Half-hour sitcom set in Chicago. With Joseph Bologna as building superintendent Charlie Verducci; Matt LeBlanc as his son, Vinnie, who landed a job at a country club; Joey Adams as sixteen-year-old Mona Mullins, who lived in the building and adored Vinnie; and Rita Moreno as Vinnie's boss, Alixandra Stone. Charlie Verducci had been introduced on Fox's popular sitcom *Married with Children* as Al Bundy's lifelong friend. Following *Top of the Heap*'s demise, LeBlanc reprised the role of Vinnie in 1992's *Vinnie and Bobby*.

TOP OF THE HILL CBS

21 SEPTEMBER 1989–7 DECEMBER 1989   Hour dramatic series about an idealistic young Congressman. With William Katt as Thomas Bell, who won a special election to fill the seat vacated by his ailing father; Dick O'Neill as his father, Pat Bell; and Jordan Baker, Tony Edwards, and Robby Weaver as Thomas's aides, Susan Pengilly, Link, and Mickey. The series was a Stephen J. Cannell Production.

TOP OF THE POPS CBS

25 SEPTEMBER 1987–25 MARCH 1988   Another of CBS's attempts to create a late-night Friday series, *Top of the Pops* was an hour rock music series divided into two segments. The London segment was hosted by Gary Davies, the Los Angeles segment by Nia Peeples. The series, coproduced by The Entertainment Network, the BBC, and Lionheart Television International, was based on the long-running British series

of the same name; reruns of that series, repackaged and introduced by former rocker Dave Clark, popped up on the Disney Channel late in 1989.

TOP OF THE WORLD   PBS
17 JANUARY 1982–11 APRIL 1982   British TV personality Eamonn Andrews hosted this unusual quiz show. Each week three contestants competed—one from the United States, one from England, and one from Australia. Each player remained in his or her home country, and the proceedings were broadcast simultaneously by satellite. On the final program the top point-scorers from each nation played for the grand prize, a 1924 Rolls-Royce.

TOP PRO GOLF   ABC
6 APRIL 1959–28 SEPTEMBER 1959   Network television's only prime-time golf series, *Top Pro Golf* presented filmed coverage of eighteen-hole head-to-head matches.

TOP SECRET   SYNDICATED
1955   Half-hour adventure series starring Paul Stewart as Professor Brand, an agent for the Bureau of Science Information.

TOP VIEWS IN SPORTS   NBC
5 OCTOBER 1949–21 DECEMBER 1949   Fifteen-minute sports newsreel.

TOPPER   CBS
9 OCTOBER 1953–30 SEPTEMBER 1955   This sitcom, based on Thorne Smith's novel (which was made into a film in 1937) starred Leo G. Carroll as Cosmo Topper, a staid banker who moved into a new home, only to discover that it was haunted by the ghosts of its previous owners. Also featured were Anne Jeffreys as Marion Kerby, "the ghostess with the mostest," and Robert Sterling as her husband, George Kerby, "that most sporting spirit"; the Kerbys had been killed in a skiing accident while celebrating their fifth anniversary, and their spirits returned to their former home together with that of Neil, the alcoholic St. Bernard who also perished trying to rescue the Kerbys (Neil was played by Buck). The three ghosts could be seen and heard only by Topper, much to the consternation of Topper's wife and his employer. Rounding out the cast were Lee Patrick as Henrietta Topper, Cosmo's wife; Thurston Hall as Topper's officious boss, Mr. Schuyler; Edna Skinner (1953–1954) as the Toppers' maid, Maggie; and Kathleen Freeman (1954–1955) as their maid, Katy. The half-hour series was produced by John W. Loveton and Bernard L. Schubert; it made effective use of trick photography by making the ghosts appear transparent in scenes in which Topper was present with other mortals.

THE TORKELSONS   NBC
21 SEPTEMBER 1991–22 MARCH 1992; 2 MAY 1992–20 JUNE 1992   Half-hour sitcom about a single mother raising her five kids in Pyramid Corners, Oklahoma. With Connie Ray as Millicent Torkelson; Olivia Burnette as the oldest kid, fourteen-year-old Dorothy Jane; Elizabeth Poyer (pilot episode) and Anna Slotky as Ruth Ann; Benj Thall (pilot) and Aaron Metchik as Steven Floyd; Lee Norris as Chuckie Lee; Rachel Duncan as the youngest kid, Mary Sue; and William Schallert as kindly Wesley Hodges, who rented a basement room from Millicent. Four members of the cast returned in a revamped sitcom in 1993: see *Almost Home*.

THE TORTELLIS   NBC
22 JANUARY 1987–12 MAY 1987   This half-hour sitcom was spun off from *Cheers*. It starred Dan Hedaya as TV repairman Nick Tortelli (ex-husband of Cheers' barmaid Carla) who married an ex-showgirl and moved to Las Vegas. Also featured were Jean Kasem as Nick's statuesque but dippy wife, Loretta; Carlene Watkins as Loretta's pragmatic sister, Charlotte Cooper, who lived with them; Timothy Williams as Nick's son, Anthony; Mandy Ingber as Anthony's wife, Annie (Anthony and Annie also lived with Nick and Loretta); and Aaron Moffatt as Charlotte's young son, Mark.

TOTALLY HIDDEN VIDEO   FOX

9 JULY 1989–7 AUGUST 1992   Steve Skrovan hosted this prime-time series, which in its early months was little more than a clone of *Candid Camera:* unsuspecting people, lured into participating in various staged stunts, were taped by a hidden camera. Subsequently, the series borrowed from *America's Funniest Home Videos,* and solicited submissions from home viewers. The show received much publicity in advance of its premiere when word leaked out that some segments of the pilot had featured actors, rather than innocent citizens; the pilot was subsequently reshot. Skrovan left the series in mid-1990. The show employed guest hosts until January 1991, when Mark Pitta took over as permanent host.

A TOUCH OF GRACE   ABC

20 JANUARY 1973–16 JUNE 1973   Based on the British series, *For the Love of Ada,* this half-hour sitcom starred Shirley Booth as widow Grace Simpson; J. Pat O'Malley as Grace's boyfriend, gravedigger Herbert Morrison; Marian Mercer as Grace's daughter, Myra Bradley; and Warren Berlinger as Myra's husband, Walter Bradley (Grace lived with her daughter and son-in-law). The series was written and produced by Saul Turteltaub and Bernie Orenstein.

TOUCHED BY AN ANGEL   CBS

21 SEPTEMBER 1994–25 DECEMBER 1994; 25 FEBRUARY 1995–4 MARCH 1995; 3 JUNE 1995–   Reminiscent of *Highway to Heaven*, this hour dramatic series starred Roma Downey as Monica and Della Reese as Tess; both were angels, Monica had just been promoted from "search and rescue" to "case worker," and Tess was her supervisor who guided her in her efforts to help mortals deal with problems.

TOUGH COOKIES   CBS

5 MARCH 1986–23 APRIL 1986   Six-episode half-hour comedy-drama about a Chicago cop assigned to patrol his old neighborhood. With Robby Benson as Detective Cliff Brady; Lainie Kazan as Rita, who owned the Windbreaker bar; Art Metrano as Lieutenant Liverson, his commanding officer; Adam Arkin as local bookie Dan Polchek; Matt Craven as Richie the bartender; Alan North as Father McCaskey; and Elizabeth Peña as Detective Connie Rivera.

TOUR OF DUTY   CBS

24 SEPTEMBER 1987–27 AUGUST 1988; 3 JANUARY 1989–25 AUGUST 1990   The first network TV dramatic series set during the Vietnam War, *Tour of Duty* followed the men of Bravo Company beginning in 1967. The cast included Terence Knox as Sergeant Zeke Anderson; Stephen Caffrey as newly arrived Lieutenant Myron Goldman; Tony Becker as Corporal Danny Percell; Ramon Franco as Private Alberto Ruiz; Stan Foster (1987–1990) as Private (later Sergeant) Marvin Johnson; Joshua Maurer (1987–1988) as Private Roger Horn; Kevin Conroy (1987–1988) as Captain Rusty Wallace; Miguel A. Nunez, Jr. as Private Marcus Taylor; Steve Akahoshi (1987–1988) as the medic, "Doc" Matsuda; and Eric Bruskotter (1987–1988) as Private Baker. The first season's episodes were filmed in Hawaii, and Bravo Company was in the field much of the time. For the second season, production was shifted to California, and Bravo Company was reassigned closer to Saigon; the latter move made it easier to add more women to the cast, both as regulars and as guest stars (by that time, a second Vietnam series, *China Beach,* had premiered). New faces for 1988 included Dan Gauthier as helicopter pilot Lieutenant Johnny McKay; Kim Delaney as reporter Alex Devlin; and Betsy Brantley as Jennifer Seymour, a psychiatrist who took an interest in Zeke. In the fall of 1989 three new regulars joined: John Dye as the new medic, "Doc" Hock; Kyle Chandler as Griner; and Carl Weathers as Colonel Carl Brewster. Lee Majors signed on in the spring of 1990 as Pop, the weary veteran soldier who had seen it all.

TOWARDS THE YEAR 2000   SYNDICATED

1971   Half-hour documentary series on ecology and the future.

TOWN HALL
See AMERICAN RELIGIOUS TOWN HALL

TOWNSEND TELEVISION   FOX
12 SEPTEMBER 1993–26 DECEMBER 1993   Hour Sunday-night comedy-variety series, with Robert Townsend, John Witherspoon, Barry Diamond, Roxanne Beckford, and Paula Jai Parker.

THE TRACER   SYNDICATED
1957   Jim Chandler starred in this half-hour series as Regan, the Tracer. The thirty-nine episodes were drawn from the files of the Tracers Company, an organization founded in 1924 by Dan Eisenberg to locate lost heirs and missing beneficiaries. At the end of each show, a list of those persons was broadcast, and several viewers were pleasantly surprised to find themselves on it. The series was produced in New Orleans.

THE TRACEY ULLMAN SHOW   FOX
5 APRIL 1987–1 SEPTEMBER 1990   One of the first series on the Fox network, *The Tracey Ullman Show* was one of its best. Using a sketch format, it showcased the many talents of its star, Tracey Ullman, a British performer who could act, sing, dance and, above all, be funny. Little known in the U. S. before her television show, Ullman had appeared in a few films (including *Plenty* and *Give My Regards to Broad Street*) and had recorded a top ten single ("They Don't Know" in 1984). Her series, produced by James L. Brooks (whose TV credits include *The Mary Tyler Moore Show*), consisted of sketches, usually two or three per half-hour show. Not all were comedic, and many incorporated a rock and roll musical number; Paula Abdul was the choreographer, and funkmaster George Clinton composed the show's theme music. Guest stars sometimes appeared, but most of the load was borne by Ullman and her supporting players: Julie Kavner, Dan Castellaneta, Joe Malone, and Sam McMurray. A master of dialects, Ullman was able to play an exceptionally wide variety of characters; some of her recurring portrayals were Kay, the boring secretary; Francesca, the teenager being raised by her gay father and his lover; and Tina, the New York postal worker.
    Between the sketches were short animated pieces, created by Matt Groening, author of the "Life in Hell" comics. Groening soon settled on the animated antics of an offbeat family known as the Simpsons. In 1990 *The Simpsons* became a separate series (see also that title). In 1988 Tracey Ullman won the first Emmy for the Fox network.

TRACKDOWN   CBS
4 OCTOBER 1957–23 SEPTEMBER 1959   Half-hour western starring Robert Culp as Hoby Gilman, a Texas Ranger. Vincent Fennelly produced the series for Four Star Films; several episodes were written by Culp.

TRADE WINDS
See GREAT ESCAPES

TRAFFIC COURT   ABC
18 JUNE 1958–30 MARCH 1959; 11 SEPTEMBER 1959–2 OCTOBER 1959   Traffic court cases were reenacted on this half-hour prime-time series. Edgar Allan Jones, Jr., played the judge (Jones also presided over ABC's daytime show, *Day in Court*), Frank Chandler McClure the bailiff, and Samuel Whitson the chief clerk.

TRAINING DOGS THE WOODHOUSE WAY   SYNDICATED
1980   An instructional series on training one's dog would hardly seem likely to be a hit show, but that's exactly what happened in England, where this BBC-produced program zoomed to the top of the ratings. The low-budget show was hosted by trainer Barbara Woodhouse and filmed at Campions, her Hertfordshire home. Each week Woodhouse worked her magic on a group of seemingly incorrigible dogs and

their baffled owners. Woodhouse spent almost as much time instructing the humans as she did the canines; "the main thing is to get the owner right for the dog," she explained.

TRANSFORMERS   SYNDICATED

1985   Half-hour sci-fi cartoon series, starring the Transformers, robot-like creatures who could transform into various vehicles or weapons (and vice versa), whose long-waged battle with the evil Decepticons was now being fought on Earth. Production of the series was subsidized by Hasbro Toys, which manufactured the Transformers toy line.

THE TRAP   CBS

29 APRIL 1950–24 JUNE 1950   Half-hour suspense anthology series produced by Franklin Heller.

TRAPPER JOHN, M.D.   CBS

23 SEPTEMBER 1979–4 SEPTEMBER 1986   On this hour medical drama Pernell Roberts starred as Dr. John (Trapper) McIntyre, who worked at San Francisco Memorial Hospital; the character had been featured in *M*A*S*H*, the sitcom set during the Korean War some twenty-seven years earlier. Also featured were Gregory Harrison as Dr. G. Alonzo (Gonzo) Gates, a brash young physician who had spent three years in a Vietnam MASH unit and who had heard of the legendary Trapper John during his tour of duty; Mary McCarty (1979–1980) as Nurse Clara "Starch" Willoughby; Charles Siebert as Dr. Stanley Riverside II, chief of emergency services; Christopher Norris (1979–1985) as Nurse Gloria "Ripples" Brancusi (after the first few seasons, the nickname was dropped); Brian Mitchell as Dr. Justin "Jackpot" Jackson; and Simon Scott (1979–1985) as administrator Arnold Slocum. Mary McCarty died after the first season; on the show it was explained that she had gotten married and left the hospital. Madge Sinclair joined the cast as Nurse Ernestine Shoop, a health nut. Marcia Rodd was added in 1982 as a dentist, Dr. E. J. Willoughby, who married Dr. Riverside. Also featured occasionally was Jessica Walter as Trapper John's ex-wife, Melanie McIntyre. Timothy Busfield joined the cast in the fall of 1984 as Trapper John's son, J. T., a doctor who was interning at his father's hospital. Three additional regulars were added in the fall of 1985: Lorna Luft as Nurse Libby Kegler, Janis Paige as administrator Catherine Hackett, and Beau Gravitte as surgeon Andy Pagano. Gregory Harrison left the show during the 1985–1986 season; his character, Gonzo, had suffered a stroke, terminating his surgical career. Gonzo met and married Fran Brennan (played by Andrea Marcovicci), a patient with multiple sclerosis. Frank Glicksman and Don Brinkley, who developed the series, served as its respective executive producer and producer.

TRAPS   CBS

31 MARCH 1994–27 APRIL 1994   Although father-and-son teams have shown up in TV crime shows before, *Traps* skipped a generation, teaming up a grandfather and grandson as the crimefighting good guys. The hour series featured George C. Scott as Joe Trapchek, retired chief of homicide for the Seattle police department, whose son, also a cop, had been killed in the line of duty; Dan Cortese as his grandson, Chris Trapchek, a young cop who often sought the old man's advice on cases; Bill Nunn as Lieutenant Jack Cloud, Chris's partner (he'd also been Chris's dad's partner); Piper Laurie as Joe's wife, Cora Trapchek, who was beginning to suffer from Alzheimer's Disease; and Lindsay Crouse as Commander Laura Parkhurst, the current homicide chief. Filmed in Vancouver, the series was created by Stephen J. Cannell.

TRASH OR TREASURE?   DUMONT

1 OCTOBER 1952–27 SEPTEMBER 1953   A panel show similar to *What's It Worth?*, this half-hour show was hosted by Sigmund Rothschild and Nelson Case, later by Rothschild and Bill Wendell. Each week people brought various antiques to the show for Rothschild's expert appraisal. The show's title changed to *Treasure Hunt* in April.

TRAUMA CENTER   ABC

22 SEPTEMBER 1983–8 DECEMBER 1983   This hour medical drama was reminiscent of *Emergency!*, which had been a hit series a decade earlier. The "trauma center" was the Medstar Unit of McKee General Hospital, a facility specially designed to treat accident victims during the so-called "golden hour" immediately following the trauma, when the victim's chances of recovery are usually the highest. The cast included James Naughton as Dr. Michael "Cutter" Royce, a surgeon; Wendie Malick as Dr. Brigette Blaine, a surgeon; Dorian Harewood as Dr. Nate "Skate" Baylor, also a surgeon; Jack Bannon as Buck Williams, the helicopter pilot; Lou Ferrigno (late of *The Incredible Hulk*) as paramedic John Six; Alfie Wise as Six's partner, paramedic Sidney "Hatter" Patelli; Eileen Heckart as Nurse Decker, the head nurse; Bill Randolph as Dr. "Beaver" Bouvier; Jayne Modean as Nurse Hooter; and Arlen Dean Snyder as Dr. Charles Sternhauser, the hospital administrator.

TRAUMA CENTER   SYNDICATED

1994–   The second series with this title was a weekly half-hour documentary series taped at various hospital emergency rooms and similar facilities.

TRAVELS   PBS

2 OCTOBER 1989–18 DECEMBER 1989   The series' title succinctly described it: a twelve-week anthology of travels. On the premiere, John Heminway journeyed to the South Atlantic island of Tristan da Cunha, the world's most remote inhabited place.

THE TRAVELS OF JAIMIE McPHEETERS   ABC

15 SEPTEMBER 1963–15 MARCH 1964   Based on the novel by Robert Lewis Taylor, this hour-long western told the story of a twelve-year-old boy from Kentucky who joined a wagon train with his father in 1849. Featured were Kurt Russell as Jaimie McPheeters; Dan O'Herlihy as his father, Doc Sardius McPheeters; Michael Witney as Coulter, the wagonmaster; Donna Anderson as Jenny; James Westerfield as Murrel; Charles Bronson as Murdock; Mark Allen as Matt Kissel; Meg Wyllie as Mrs. Kissel; the singing Osmond Brothers as The Kissel Boys; Sandy Kenyon as Baggott; Hedley Mattingly as Coe; and Vernett Allen as Othello.

TREASURE   SYNDICATED

1958   Bill Burrud hosted this half-hour documentary series, presenting films about buried treasure, lost artifacts, and assorted searches for riches.

TREASURE HUNT   ABC/NBC/SYNDICATED

7 SEPTEMBER 1956–24 MAY 1957 (ABC); 12 AUGUST 1957–4 DECEMBER 1959 (NBC); 1974–1977 (SYNDICATED)   The network versions of this half-hour game show were hosted by Jan Murray. Each day two contestants competed in a question-and-answer segment; the winner then chose one of thirty numbered "treasure boxes," and took home the contents. The show began on ABC as a prime-time series before moving to NBC, where it enjoyed a two-year daytime run as well as a brief prime-time run early in 1958. In 1974 *The New Treasure Hunt* emerged, hosted by Geoff Edwards; this slow-moving and sometimes cruelly suspenseful version (a Chuck Barris Production) eliminated the quiz portion and featured two treasure-box give-away segments, with a top prize of $25,000.

TREASURE ISLE   ABC

18 DECEMBER 1967–27 DECEMBER 1968   This elaborate daytime game show was played on a specially constructed lagoon at the Colonnades Beach Hotel in Palm Beach Shores, Florida. In the first round of the game, married couples paddled around in rafts, picking up pieces of a giant jigsaw puzzle floating off "Puzzle Isle." After putting together the puzzle, the couples deciphered the clue contained in the puzzle and proceeded to Treasure Isle, where they searched for buried treasure. John Bartholomew Tucker hosted the half-hour show, which was produced and directed by Paul Alter for John D. MacArthur, the Florida millionaire who owned the Colonnades Beach Hotel and built the lagoon.

TREASURE QUEST ABC

24 APRIL 1949–26 AUGUST 1949   John Weigel hosted this half-hour game show on which contestants could win a trip by answering questions about geography.

TREASURY MEN IN ACTION ABC/NBC

11 SEPTEMBER 1950–4 DECEMBER 1950 (ABC); 5 APRIL 1951–1 APRIL 1954 (NBC); 7 OCTOBER 1954–30 SEPTEMBER 1955 (ABC)   Half-hour crime show that chronicled the exploits of agents for the United States Treasury Department, starring Walter Greaza as The Chief. Everett Rosenthal produced the series, and David Pressman directed it for Prokter Television Enterprises.

TRIAL AND ERROR CBS

15 MARCH 1988–29 MARCH 1988   This sitcom about two Chicano roommates living in Los Angeles was gone after only three episodes. Featured were Eddie Velez as lawyer John Hernandez, the only Hispanic at his law firm; Paul Rodriguez as T-shirt salesman Tony Rivera; Stephen Elliott as John's boss, Edmund Kittle; Debbie Shapiro as John's secretary, Rhonda; John deLancie as one of John's co-workers, Bob Adams; and Susan Saldivar as Lisa.

TRIAL BY JURY SYNDICATED

1989–1990   Half-hour daily courtroom drama series, hosted by Raymond Burr, who played TV's most famous lawyer, Perry Mason. The series' executive producer was Dick Clark, who played the guilty party on the last episode of the old *Perry Mason* series, "The Case of the Final Fade-Out."

TRIALS OF O'BRIEN CBS

18 SEPTEMBER 1965–27 MAY 1966   Peter Falk starred in this hour-long dramatic series as New York lawyer Daniel J. O'Brien, a shrewd defense attorney. Also featured were Joanna Barnes as O'Brien's ex-wife, Katie; Elaine Stritch as Miss G., O'Brien's secretary; Ilka Chase as Margaret, Katie's mother; Dolph Sweet as Lieutenant Garrison; David Burns as The Great McGonigle, a legendary con man who was a crony of O'Brien's. Richard Alan Simmons was executive producer of the series for Filmways. Among the guest stars who appeared were: Alan Alda ("Picture Me a Murder," 27 November), Faye Dunaway (in her first major TV role, "The 10-Foot, 6-Inch Pole," 14 January), Frank Langella ("How Do You Get to Carnegie Hall," 13 November), and Tony Roberts ("Charlie Has All the Luck," 20 November).

THE TRIALS OF ROSIE O'NEILL CBS

17 SEPTEMBER 1990–9 MAY 1992   Barney Rosenzweig, the guiding light of *Cagney & Lacey,* developed this series for *Cagney & Lacey* costar Sharon Gless. Here, Gless played Fiona "Rosie" O'Neill, a Beverly Hills attorney who, on the heels of a painful divorce, quit her job to go to work for the Los Angeles Public Defenders. Also featured were Dorian Harewood as Hank Mitchell, her openly cynical officemate; Ron Rifkin as Ben Meyer, their supervisor; Georgann Johnson as Rosie's mother, Charlotte O'Neill; Lisa Banes as Rosie's married sister, Doreen Morrison; Lisa Rieffel as Kim Ginty, daughter of her ex-husband; Bridget Gless (the star's niece) as office aide Barbara Navis; and Elaine Kagan as the receptionist, Carole Kravitz. Ed Asner joined the cast in the fall of 1991 as politically conservative investigator Walter Kovatch. Each episode opened with Rosie in the office of her psychiatrist (played by Rosenzweig; he and Gless were married in 1991). Rosie's first line on the premiere was one of television's most memorable openings: "I'm thinking about maybe having my tits done."

TRIALWATCH NBC

28 JANUARY 1991–26 JULY 1991   The American legal system was the focus of this half-hour daytime series, which presented excerpts from actual trials, together with interviews of attorneys, litigants, and witnesses. Robb Weller and attorney Lisa Specht coanchored.

TRIBECA   FOX

23 MARCH 1993–4 MAY 1993; 25 JULY 1993–5 SEPTEMBER 1993   Stylish hour dramatic anthology series set in the lower Manhattan neighborhood of Tribeca. Providing continuity from hour to hour were two regulars: Philip Bosco as cafe owner Harry Yeshosky, and Joe Morton as mounted policeman Carlton Thomas. The series's executive producers were David J. Burke, Jane Rosenthal, and Robert DeNiro.

TRIPLE THREAT   SYNDICATED

1988   Jim Lange hosted this game show on which two three-member teams competed in a pop music quiz. Each team was comprised of a contestant, a celebrity, and the celebrity's child.

TRIVIA TRAP   ABC

8 OCTOBER 1984–5 APRIL 1985   Bob Eubanks hosted this daytime game show on which two three-person teams competed by answering various multiple-choice general knowledge questions. On each show the members of one team were over thirty years of age, and the members of the other team were under thirty.

TROLLKINS   CBS

12 SEPTEMBER 1981–4 SEPTEMBER 1982   Half-hour Saturday-morning cartoon series about a bunch of dwarflike creatures who lived in Trolltown, a city in the woods. *Trollkins* should not be confused with *Smurfs,* NBC's 1981 cartoon series about a group of small sylvan souls.

THE TROUBLE WITH FATHER
See THE STU ERWIN SHOW

THE TROUBLE WITH LARRY   CBS

25 AUGUST 1993–8 SEPTEMBER 1993   Fresh from *Perfect Strangers,* Bronson Pinchot stumbled into this ill-conceived sitcom which lasted only three episodes. He starred as Larry Burton, who'd suffered the misfortune of being dragged off by a troupe of baboons on his wedding night; he returned home ten years later to find that his wife was happily remarried. Also featured were Shanna Reed as his wife, Sally Flatt; Perry King as her current husband, Boyd Flatt; Courteney Cox as Sally's sister, Gabriella Easden, who ran an art gallery with Sally; and Alex McKenna as Sally's daughter, Lindsay (Larry was actually her father). The show was the first fatality of the 1993–1994 season.

TROUBLESHOOTERS   NBC

11 SEPTEMBER 1959–17 JUNE 1960   Half-hour adventure series starring Keenan Wynn as Kodiak and former Olympic decathlon champion Bob Mathias as Dugan, a pair of construction engineers who traveled the world troubleshooting problems for their company. Also featured were Bob Fortier as Scotty; Carey Loftin as Skinner; Chet Allen as Slats; and Bob Harris as Jim. The series was the first network show supplied by United Artists.

TRUE BLUE   NBC

3 DECEMBER 1989–19 JANUARY 1990; 28 JUNE 1991–5 JULY 1991   Hour cop show focusing on the members of the New York Police Department's Emergency Services Unit. With Joe Lisi as Captain Motta; Leo Burmester as Red Tollin; Grant Show as Casey Pierce; Timothy Van Patten as Wojeski; Eddie Velez as Avila; Darnell Williams as Odom; Nestor Serrano as Geno; Dick Latessa as Mike; John Bolger as Bobby; Ally Walker as Jessy; and Elya Baskin as Yuri, a Russian cabbie. Filmed on location, the series was one of two midseason shows dealing with the N.Y.P.D.: see also *H.E.L.P.* The two-hour TV-movie pilot was rerun on 22 April 1990.

TRUE COLORS   FOX

2 SEPTEMBER 1990–23 AUGUST 1992   Half-hour sitcom about a white woman and a black man, each with children, who married each other. With Stephanie Faracy as

Ellen Freeman, a kindergarten teacher; Frankie R. Faison (1990–1991) and Cleavon Little (1991–1992) as her husband, Ron Freeman, a dentist; Claude Brooks as Ron's son Terry; Adam Jeffries as Ron's son Lester; Brigid Conley Walsh as Ellen's daughter, Katie Davis; and Nancy Walker as Ellen's mother, Sara Bower, who didn't approve of the marriage. The series was set in Baltimore, Maryland.

TRUE CONFESSIONS   SYNDICATED
1986   The stories on this five-day-a-week half-hour dramatic anthology series were drawn from those appearing in *True Confessions* magazine. Bill Bixby hosted the series.

TRUE DETECTIVES   CBS
29 MARCH 1991–12 JULY 1991   Gregory Harrison hosted this prime time series, on which the exploits of real and amateur detectives were re-created. The program, which was introduced as a special on 28 December 1990, was aired in both a thirty- and sixty-minute format.

TRUE STORY   NBC
16 MARCH 1957–9 SEPTEMBER 1961   Kathi Norris hosted this half-hour anthology series consisting of stories ostensibly based on actual incidents. Broadcast at noon on Saturdays, the show was originally aired live and later shifted to videotape.

TRUMP CARD   SYNDICATED
1990–1991   Half-hour daily game show, taped at the Trump Castle Casino Resort in Atlantic City, New Jersey. Former pro footballer and sportscaster Jimmy Cefalo was the host of the series, on which three contestants competed in a bingo-type game by answering questions.

TRUTH OR CONSEQUENCES   CBS/NBC/SYNDICATED
7 SEPTEMBER 1950–7 JUNE 1951 (CBS); 14 JANUARY 1952–16 MAY 1952 (NBC); 18 MAY 1954–28 SEPTEMBER 1956 (NBC); 31 DECEMBER 1956–24 SEPTEMBER 1965 (NBC); 1966–1974 (SYNDICATED)
THE NEW TRUTH OR CONSEQUENCES   SYNDICATED
1977   One of broadcasting's most durable programs, *Truth or Consequences* ran seventeen years on radio and (with some interruptions) twenty-seven years on TV. The raucous half-hour game show was created by Ralph Edwards in 1940 and was based on a parlor game: contestants who failed to answer a question before the buzzer sounded (the buzzer, nicknamed Beulah, usually went off a fraction of a second after the question was asked) were forced to pay the consequences. Most consequences involved the performance of stunts of all description, much to the delight of the studio audiences. Edwards, who later created *This Is Your Life,* hosted the radio version for several years as well as the first TV versions of *Truth or Consequences.* The very first TV version of the show was introduced briefly in New York in 1941. Nine years later the network version came along. It was first seen Thursday nights on CBS for one season, and in 1952, it was a daytime entry on NBC, where it was also known as *The Ralph Edwards Show.* When the show returned to NBC's schedule in 1954, as a prime-time series, Jack Bailey was the host. Bob Barker succeeded him at the end of 1956, when the show began a nine-year daytime run on NBC (a nighttime version also popped up on NBC early in 1958, hosted by Steve Dunne); Barker continued to host the show during its eight-year syndicated run, which began in 1966. The series was revived in 1977 and was shown under the title *The New Truth or Consequences,* with Bob Hilton as host.

TRYING TIMES   PBS
19 OCTOBER 1987–7 DECEMBER 1987; 12 OCTOBER 1989–19 FEBRUARY 1990   A half-hour comedy anthology series.

TUCKER'S WITCH CBS

6 OCTOBER 1982–10 NOVEMBER 1982; 31 MARCH 1983–8 AUGUST 1983   An hour crime show with a twist, *Tucker's Witch* starred Tim Matheson and Catherine Hicks as Rick and Amanda Tucker, a husband-and-wife detective team. The twist was that Amanda was a witch, whose clairvoyant and telekinetic powers were impressive but not infallible. Also featured were Alfre Woodard as Marsha, their secretary; Barbara Barrie as Ellen Hobbes, Amanda's live-in mother; Bill Morey as Lieutenant Fisk of the Los Angeles Police Department; and Dickens, Amanda's cat. The show was to have been titled *The Good Witch of Laurel Canyon,* and the pilot was filmed with Kim Cattrall and Art Hindle in the starring roles; the network was dissatisfied, and both performers were replaced.

TUGBOAT ANNIE SYNDICATED

1958   Half-hour sitcom starring Minerva Urecal as Annie Brennan, skipper of a tug in the Northwest; Walter Sande costarred as Captain Horatio Bullwinkle, Annie's boss.

TURBO-TEEN ABC

8 SEPTEMBER 1984–31 AUGUST 1985   Saturday morning cartoon show about a teenager, Bret Matthews, who turned into an automobile when he became hot. Bret and his pals, Alex and Patty, worked for Dr. Chase.

TURN TO A FRIEND ABC

5 OCTOBER 1953–31 DECEMBER 1953   Cast from the same mold as *Queen for a Day* and *Strike It Rich, Turn to a Friend* was a half-hour game show on which contestants related heart-breaking tales of woe and misfortune; at the end of the show, the studio audience selected the most deserving recipient, who was then showered with gifts. Dennis James hosted the half-hour show.

TURNABOUT NBC

26 JANUARY 1979–30 MARCH 1979   Half-hour sitcom about a husband and wife who woke up one morning to find themselves occupying each other's bodies. With John Schuck as Sam Alston, a sportswriter; Sharon Gless as Penny Alston, vice-president of a cosmetics firm; Richard Stahl and Bobbi Jordan as neighbors Jack and Judy Overmeyer; James Sikking as Penny's boss, Geoffrey St. James; and Bruce Kirby as Al Brennan, Sam's boss. Executive producer: Sam Denoff for Universal TV.

TURNING POINT ABC

9 MARCH 1994–28 DECEMBER 1994   Hour prime-time newsmagazine anchored (separately) by Diane Sawyer, Peter Jennings, and Barbara Walters. Sawyer interviewed mass murderer Charles Manson and two of his accomplices on the premiere in March. The series was preceded by a "Turning Point" special on 27 July 1993, and resurfaced as specials beginning in May 1995.

TURN-ON ABC

5 FEBRUARY 1969   Television's most notorious flop, *Turn-On* was canceled after one outing. Produced by George Schlatter and Ed Friendly, the producers of *Laugh-In,* and by Digby Wolfe, a *Laugh-In* production executive, it was a half-hour of skits and blackouts, bridged together not by a host or narrator, but by electronic music. Most of the skits were overly suggestive (at least by 1969 standards)—one featured a vending machine that dispensed birth control pills, and the longest segment consisted of the word "SEX" flashing on the screen while Tim Conway and Bonnie Boland mugged beneath. The pilot for the show had been developed in 1968; both CBS and NBC turned it down, but ABC picked it up, scheduling it to replace the Wednesday broadcast of *Peyton Place.* Before the first *Turn-On* was over, however, most ABC affiliates had been swamped with telephone calls, virtually all of them negative. By February 7, seventy-five affiliates had dropped the show, and by the end of the week *Turn-On* had been turned off by the network. The cast on the lone broadcast included, in addition to Tim Conway (the guest star) and Bonnie Boland, Hamilton

Camp, Teresa Graves, Ken Greenwald, Maxine Greene, Debbie Macomber, Maura McGiveney, Chuck McCann, Carlo Manteca, Alma Murphy, Cecile Ozorio, Bob Staats, Mel Stuart, and Carol Wayne. Mark Warren directed the show, and Bill Melendez Associates provided the animation.

TWELVE O'CLOCK HIGH ABC
18 SEPTEMBER 1964–13 JANUARY 1967   Another of the several World War II shows of the mid-1960s, this one told the stories of the 918th Flyer Squadron based in England. Featured were Robert Lansing (1964–1965) as Brigadier General Frank Savage, who was killed off after the first season (it was reported that Lansing was upset by the network's decision to change the show's time slot and to lessen his role); Lew Gallo (1964–1965) as Major Joe Cobb; Paul Burke as Colonel Joseph Gallagher; Frank Overton as Major Harvey Stovall; Barney Phillips as Major Doc Kaiser; Chris Robinson (1965–1967) as Sergeant Komansky; Andrew Duggan (1965–1967) as Brigadier General Edward Britt; John Larkin (1964–1965) as Major General Wiley Crowe; and Larry Gates as Johnny. The hour series, adapted from the 1949 film, was a Quinn Martin Production.

THE TWENTIETH CENTURY CBS
20 OCTOBER 1957–7 SEPTEMBER 1969   Walter Cronkite hosted this Sunday-evening documentary series, which presented filmed reports on a wide variety of historical and scientific subjects. In January of 1967 the show's title was changed to *The Twenty-First Century.*

THE 20TH CENTURY-FOX HOUR CBS
5 OCTOBER 1955–18 SEPTEMBER 1957   One of the first television ventures by 20th Century-Fox, this hour dramatic anthology series alternated on Wednesdays with *The U.S. Steel Hour* for two seasons. Peter Packer produced the series, and Joseph Cotten hosted it during the first season.

TWENTY QUESTIONS NBC/ABC/DUMONT
26 NOVEMBER 1949–24 DECEMBER 1949 (NBC); 17 MARCH 1950–29 JUNE 1951 (ABC); 6 JULY 1951–5 APRIL 1954 (DUMONT); 6 JULY 1954–3 MAY 1955 (ABC)   A game show based on the old parlor game, *Twenty Questions* began on radio in 1946 and first came to TV three years later. The object of the game was for a celebrity panel to identify an object by asking up to twenty questions about it; the only clue given to the panel was whether the object was "animal, vegetable, or mineral." Bill Slater hosted the NBC and DuMont versions of the show, Jay Jackson the ABC version. Regular panelists included Fred Van Deventer, Florence Rinard (Van Deventer's wife), Herb Polesie, and Johnny McPhee.

THE $20,000 PYRAMID
See THE $10,000 PYRAMID

20/20 ABC
6 JUNE 1978–   An hour newsmagazine, *20/20* is ABC's answer to CBS's *60 Minutes.* Poorly organized, it got off to a rocky start—the original hosts, TV newcomers Harold Hayes and Robert Hughes, were axed after the first show, and Hugh Downs was brought in the following week. After the first show, an uneven blend of investigative reports and humorous features, interspersed with definitions of polysyllabic words, *20/20* settled down under Downs to a more straightforward presentation of investigative and background reports. The show was scheduled weekly during the summer of 1978 and switched to a monthly slot in the fall before returning to a weekly berth. Barbara Walters became Downs's coanchor in the fall of 1984. Regular contributors have included Tom Jarriel, Sylvia Chase, Geraldo Rivera, Thomas Hoving, Bob Brown, John Stossel, Lynn Sherr, and Stone Phillips. Rivera resigned from ABC News in 1986 in protest over the network's decision to kill a 1985 story (by another reporter) on Marilyn Monroe's love life. *20/20* settled into a Friday night time slot in 1987, and its popularity began to grow. It televised footage of an exorcism

in the spring of 1991, and cracked Nielsen's top twenty for the first time the following season (its fourteenth), finishing 20th.

THE $25,000 PYRAMID
See THE $10,000 PYRAMID

TWENTY-ONE   NBC
12 SEPTEMBER 1956–16 OCTOBER 1958   One of TV's most famous big-money, prime-time game shows, *Twenty-One* was NBC's answer to CBS's *The $64,000 Question*. It was hosted by Jack Barry, who created the series with his longtime partner, Dan Enright. Each week two contestants competed; the object of the game was to score twenty-one points as quickly as possible. Each contestant was placed in an isolation booth on stage and could choose a question from an announced category; within the category the questions were rated for difficulty from one to eleven points. Thus, a contestant who correctly answered a ten-point and an eleven-point question in succession was assured of at least a tie. The money was big—Charles Van Doren, who defeated Herbert Stempel in 1957, won $129,000 in fourteen appearances (Van Doren was beaten by Vivian Nearing). The biggest winner of all was Elfreda Von Nardroff, who went home with $253,500 after twenty-one appearances. Contestant Stempel may have had the last laugh, however, as it was he who revealed that Van Doren had been given some of the answers before air time (it was reported that Stempel was an unpopular contestant). Stempel's allegations, together with charges concerning other game shows, precipitated the cancellation of *Twenty-One, Dotto, The $64,000 Challenge,* and *The $64,000 Question*—all in the fall of 1958. Jack Barry, *Twenty-One*'s host and creator, did not work again in national television for a decade. The rigging scandal was the subhect of the 1994 motion picture "Quiz Show."

21 BEACON STREET   NBC/ABC
2 JULY 1959–24 SEPTEMBER 1959 (NBC); 27 DECEMBER 1959–20 MARCH 1960 (ABC) Set in Boston, this half-hour crime show starred Dennis Morgan as private eye Dennis Chase; Joanna Barnes as Lola, his confederate; Brian Kelly as Brian, their legman, a recent law school graduate; James Maloney as Jim, an expert machinist who worked with them. More than most of the detective shows of the late 1950s, *21 Beacon Street* emphasized gadgetry. The series was introduced as a summer replacement for *The Tennessee Ernie Ford Show* on NBC, and later turned up on ABC.

21 JUMP STREET   FOX/SYNDICATED
12 APRIL 1987–17 SEPTEMBER 1990 (FOX); 1990–1991 (SYNDICATED)   An up-dated version of *The Mod Squad, 21 Jump Street* epitomized the Fox network's strategy of attracting younger viewers. It featured a youthful group of big-city cops who could pass as high school (or later as college) students. With teen heartthrob Johnny Depp as Tommy Hanson; Holly Robinson as Judy Hoffs; Dustin Nguyen as H. T. (for Harry Truman) Ioki; Peter DeLuise as Doug Penhall; Frederic Forrest (1987) as the boss, Captain Jenko; and Steven Williams (1987–) as the new boss, Captain Adam Fuller. In the fall of 1988 Richard Grieco joined the cast as the new member, Dennis Booker; a year later he was given his own series (see *Booker*). Jeff Yagher had originally been cast as Hanson, but just before production got underway he was replaced by Depp. *21 Jump Street* holds the distinction of being the first series on the Fox network ever to beat an ABC, CBS or NBC series in its time slot; this achievement occurred on 23 August 1987, when the series finished third. After three and one-half seasons on Fox, the series moved into first-run syndication in 1990, with DeLuise, Robinson and Williams from the old cast, joined by Michael DeLuise (Peter's brother) as Joey Penhall (Doug's brother), Michael Bendetti as Mac McCann, David Barry Gray as Garrett, and Alexandra Powers as Kati Rocky.

26 MEN   SYNDICATED
1957   Half-hour western about the Arizona Rangers, a group of law officers whose membership was limited to twenty-six. Featured were Tris Coffin as Captain Tom

Rynning; Kelo Henderson as Ranger Clint Travis. Russell Hayden produced the series. The force was established in 1901 by the Arizona Territorial Legislature.

THE TWILIGHT ZONE   CBS
2 OCTOBER 1959–14 SEPTEMBER 1962; 3 JANUARY 1963–18 SEPTEMBER 1964   Television's most popular science fiction anthology series was created and hosted by Rod Serling. One of the medium's most gifted writers, Serling had previously won Emmys for "Patterns," broadcast on *Kraft Television Theatre* in 1955, and "Requiem for a Heavyweight," shown on *Playhouse 90* in 1956. On *The Twilight Zone,* Serling introduced his audiences to "a fifth dimension, beyond that which is known to man." [Serling stated that he had made up the term "twilight zone," and had later learned that the phrase had an aeronautical connotation—referring to the moment when an aircraft descending on its final landing approach loses sight of the horizon. The term also had a legal connotation, having been used in arguments before the U.S. Supreme Court as early as 1911.] The trademarks of the series were Serling's introductions (usually given about a minute into each episode) and surprise endings. Serling himself wrote eighty-nine of the 151 shows; Charles Beaumont and Richard Matheson also wrote several each, and seven were contributed by Earl Hamner, creator of *The Waltons.* All of the shows were filmed in black and white. *The Twilight Zone* began as a half-hour series and was dropped after three seasons; it was brought back by popular demand early in 1963, but in an hour format. The eighteen hour episodes were not as well liked, and the show reverted to a half hour for its final season. Among the best-known episodes were: "Where Is Everybody?" with Earl Holliman (2 October 1959); "People Are Alike All Over," with Roddy McDowall (25 March 1960); "The Mighty Casey," with Jack Warden (17 June 1960); "The Hitch-Hiker," with Inger Stevens (12 August 1960); "The Silence," with Franchot Tone (25 April 1961); "Nothing in the Dark," with Gladys Cooper and Robert Redford (5 January 1962); and "The Dummy," with Cliff Robertson (4 May 1962).

Serling continued to write occasional works for television, and in 1970 he returned as the host of *Night Gallery.* In 1975 Serling died at the age of 50. *The Twilight Zone* continued to prosper in reruns, achieving cult status by the end of the 1970s. A theatrical film version was released in 1983. Titled *Twilight Zone—The Movie,* it comprised four stories (each done by a different director). Three of the four were remakes of TV episodes—"Kick the Can" (directed by Steven Spielberg), "It's a Good Life" (directed by Joe Dante), and "Nightmare at 20,000 Feet" (directed by George Miller)—while the fourth, directed by John Landis, was based on the TV episode "A Quality of Mercy."

On 19 May 1994 CBS televised two previously-unseen Serling stories as "Twilight Zone: Rod Serling's Lost Classics." One, "The Theater," was based on a Serling treatment, and starred Amy Irving and Gary Cole. The other, "Where the Dead Are," featured a Serling script and starred Jack Palance, Patrick Bergin, and Jenna Stern.

THE TWILIGHT ZONE   CBS/SYNDICATED
27 SEPTEMBER 1985–18 OCTOBER 1986; 4 DECEMBER 1986–18 DECEMBER 1986; 10 JULY 1987–31 JULY 1987 (CBS); 1988 (SYNDICATED)   After an absence of two decades, a new version of *The Twilight Zone* came to CBS in the fall of 1985. The series was now in an hour format, and of course in color; new theme music was supplied by the Grateful Dead. Philip DeGuere was executive producer, and sci-fi author Harlan Ellison served as creative consultant. Each hour consisted of two or three separate stories of varying lengths; there were no remakes of old *Twilight Zone* stories. There was no on-screen host, although Charles Aidman (who had starred in two of the old *Twilight Zone* episodes) was the narrator. The show performed reasonably well in its first four or five outings (perhaps as baby-boomers sampled the new show), but then went into a ratings decline from which it never recovered. Network interference also affected the show; creative consultant Ellison quit when the network refused to air "Nackles," a dark Christmas tale. The series was renewed for a second season, but left the air in October of 1986. It returned briefly in December of that year, trimmed to a half-hour, and surfaced briefly again, as an hour show, in July of 1987. In 1988

CBS, which owned the series, entered into a joint venture with MGM/UA to produce thirty new half-hour episodes which, when added to the 1985–1987 package, would provide enough shows for syndication. The thirty new programs were filmed in Toronto. Robin Ward was the narrator, and his voice was dubbed over Aidman's when the 1985–1987 episodes were edited for inclusion in the new package.

TWIN PEAKS   ABC
8 APRIL 1990–23 MAY 1990; 11 AUGUST 1990–16 FEBRUARY 1991; 28 MARCH 1991–18 APRIL 1991 The heavily hyped prime-time serial created by David Lynch and Mark Frost became an instant cult show. It was set in Twin Peaks, a logging town in the Pacific Northwest where a teenage girl had been murdered. Who killed Laura Palmer? That was the question that F.B.I. agent Dale Cooper (and the viewing audience) tried to answer. During the course of the first eight episodes, Cooper gradually learned that much was lurking beneath the placid exterior of Twin Peaks: sex and violence, of course, but also dreams and screams, llamas and log ladies, coffee and doughnuts.

Twin Peaks was the first TV venture for David Lynch, who had made his mark in such films as *Eraserhead* and *Blue Velvet,* in which he explored the darker side of human nature. Mark Frost, his coexecutive producer, had previously worked on *Hill Street Blues.* Lynch directed the two-hour premiere and one other early episode, establishing the series' cinematic look, with its sepia tones, unusual closeups, and distinctive score (by Angelo Badalamenti); allusions to other films also permeated the episodes.

The cast included some newcomers and several others who rarely appeared on television: Kyle MacLachlan (who had starred in *Blue Velvet*) as Dale Cooper, the clairvoyant, coffee-swigging F.B.I. agent who dictated his thoughts into a hand-held microcassette recorder; Michael Ontkean (of *The Rookies*) as Harry S Truman, Twin Peaks' sheriff; Madchen Amick as Shelly Johnson, the abused wife of a trucker; Dana Ashbrook as high school student Bobby Briggs, Laura's boyfriend; Richard Beymer as Benjamin Horne, owner of the Great Northern Hotel (and much of the rest of the town); Sherilyn Fenn as his manipulative daughter, Audrey; Warren Frost as kindly Dr. Hayward; Lara Flynn Boyle as his daughter, Donna, Laura's best friend; Peggy Lipton (of *Mod Squad* fame) as Norma Jennings, who ran the Double R Diner; James Marshall as James Hurley; Everett McGill as his uncle, Ed Hurley, who ran a gas station; Ray Wise as Leland Palmer, Laura's father; Eric Da Re as the trucker Leo Johnson; Joan Chen as widow Jocelyn "Josie" Packard, who owned a half interest in the local sawmill; Piper Laurie as her sister-in-law, Catherine Martell, who owned the other half interest; Russ Tamblyn as psychiatrist Dr. Lawrence Jacoby; Kimmy Robertson as Lucy Moran, dispatcher at the sheriff's office; Harry Goaz as lachrymose deputy sheriff Andy Brennan; Michael Horse as deputy Tommy "Hawk" Hill; and Sheryl Lee as Laura Palmer (who appeared in dream sequences and flashbacks) and as her cousin, Madeleine.

The two-hour premiere episode was released as a theatrical film overseas, with an eighteen-minute ending tacked on which attempted to resolve the mystery. In the U.S., the premiere rated well, but each succeeding episode generally fared worse than its predecessor. Nevertheless, ABC announced in May 1990 that it would renew the series. *Twin Peaks* moved to Saturday nights in the fall of 1990. The Laura Palmer mystery was finally resolved when it was revealed that Laura's killer was her own father, who turned into a homicidal maniac when possessed by an evil spirit known as Bob (Bob was played by a *Twin Peaks* crew member, Frank Silva). After steadily declining ratings, the series faded away quietly in April 1991. A two-hour "finale" aired on 10 June 1991. In 1992 a theatrical film was released. "Twin Peaks: Fire Walk with Me" was intended as a prequel to the TV series, focusing on Laura Palmer's last weeks.

THE TWISTED TALES OF FELIX THE CAT   CBS
16 SEPTEMBER 1995–   Half-hour Saturday-morning animated series starring the venerable feline in newly produced cartoons. Other segments featured such characters as Bag-O-Tricks, Fats Holler, and Sheba Beboporeba.

TWO FACES WEST   SYNDICATED

1961   In this half-hour western, star Charles Bateman played two roles—Ben January, the marshal, and Rick January, his twin brother, a doctor. Matthew Rapf produced the show, which was set in the town of Gunnison.

TWO FOR THE MONEY   NBC/CBS

30 SEPTEMBER 1952–11 AUGUST 1953 (NBC); 15 AUGUST 1953–22 SEPTEMBER 1956 (CBS); 23 MARCH 1957–7 SEPTEMBER 1957 (CBS)   This prime-time general knowledge quiz show was a Goodson-Todman Production. A pilot was made in 1952 with Fred Allen as host, but Allen became ill and was unable to assume the hosting chores when the show was picked up. Herb Shriner, the Hoosier humorist, took over as emcee and hosted the show for most of its run; Walter O'Keefe substituted for Shriner during the summer of 1954, and Dennis James and Sam Levenson later hosted the show.

240-ROBERT   ABC

28 AUGUST 1979–10 DECEMBER 1979; 31 MAY 1980–23 AUGUST 1980; 7 MARCH 1981–21 MARCH 1981; 5 SEPTEMBER 1981–19 SEPTEMBER 1981   This hour adventure series focused on the exploits of the Emergency Services Unit of the Los Angeles County Sheriff's Department. Featured were: Mark Harmon (1979–1980) as Deputy Dwayne "Thib" Thibideaux; John Bennett Perry as Deputy T. R. "Trap" Applegate; Joanna Cassidy (1979–1980) as helicopter pilot Morgan Wainwright; Lew Saunders (1979–1980) as C. B.; Joe Al Nicassio (1979–1980) as Roverino; Thomas Babson (1979–1980) as Terry; and Steve Tannen as Kestenbaum. When the show returned briefly in 1981, Perry and Tannen were joined by two newcomers: Stephan Burns as Brett Cueva, Trap's rookie partner, and Pamela Hensley as helicopter pilot Sandy Harper. Rick Rosner created the show and was its executive producer.

TWO GIRLS NAMED SMITH   ABC

20 JANUARY 1951–13 OCTOBER 1951   Broadcast Saturdays at noon, this half-hour sitcom told the story of two cousins trying to become fashion models in New York. With Peggy French as Frances Smith; Peggy Ann Garner as Babs Smith; Joseph Buloff, as their elderly neighbor, Mr. Basmany; Richard Hayes as Babs's boyfriend, and Nina Foch.

2 HIP 4 TV   NBC

10 SEPTEMBER 1988–22 OCTOBER 1988   This live-action hour Saturday morning series was set in a teenager's basement, which was magically transformed into a television studio. Ahmet Zappa, youngest child of musician Frank Zappa, was the teenager; Colin Quinn was his sidekick. Celebrity impersonators dropped by each week, as did real-life rock and roll stars.

TWO IN LOVE   CBS

19 JUNE 1954–11 SEPTEMBER 1954   Bert Parks hosted this Saturday-night game show on which engaged couples competed. In the first round, relatives and friends of each couple were asked questions about the couple. In the second round, the couples themselves participated in a quiz segment.

TWO MARRIAGES   ABC

23 AUGUST 1983–14 SEPTEMBER 1983; 8 MARCH 1984–26 APRIL 1984   Hour dramatic series about two suburban families—the happily married Daleys and the troubled Armstrongs—who lived next door to one another. With Tom Mason as Jim Daley, who operated a dairy farm with his father; Karen Carlson as his wife, Ann Daley, a construction engineer; Tiffany Toyoshima as Kim, Jim's daughter by a previous marriage; C. Thomas Howell as Scott Morgan, Ann's son by a previous marriage; Ian Fried as Willy, Jim and Ann's son (the Daleys had a baby, Elizabeth, at the end of the show's brief 1984 run); John McLiam as Woody Daley, Jim's father; Michael Murphy as Art Armstrong, a surgeon; Janet Eilber as his wife, Nancy Armstrong, a

housewife; Louanne as their daughter, Shelby; and Kirk Cameron as their son, Eric. The show was produced by Carroll Newman.

THE TWO OF US   CBS
6 APRIL 1981–27 APRIL 1981; 14 SEPTEMBER 1981–24 FEBRUARY 1982   Half-hour sitcom about a prim and proper British butler who went to work for a New York divorcée in her New York City townhouse, which needed all the domestic help it could get. Featured were Peter Cook as the butler, Robert Brentwood; Mimi Kennedy as his employer, Nan Gallagher, the co-host of "Midmorning Manhattan," a TV talk show; Dana Hill as Nan's teenage daughter, Gabrielle; and Oliver Clark as Nan's agent, Cubby Roy. When the show returned as a midseason replacement in 1981, two new regulars were added: Tim Thomerson as Nan's obnoxious cohost, Reggie Cavanaugh; and Candice Azzara as Shirley Havilmeyer.

2000 MALIBU ROAD   CBS
23 AUGUST 1992–9 SEPTEMBER 1992   Short-lived continuing drama set at 2000 Malibu Road, where a retiring prostitute took in three female tenants; murder and corporate intrigue soon followed. With Lisa Hartman Black as the former hooker, Jade O'Keefe; Jennifer Beals as tenant Perry Quinn, a lawyer who fell in love with an accused rapist whom she represented; Drew Barrymore as tenant Lindsay Rule, an actress; Tuesday Knight as tenant Joy Rule, Lindsay's scheming sister; Brian Bloom as screenwriter Eric Adler; Scott Bryce as television executive Scott Sterling; Michael T. Weiss as the accused rapist, Roger Tabor; and Ron Marquette as police officer Joe Munoz. Created by Terry Louise Fisher, the series was put on hiatus after four telecasts and never returned.

227   NBC
14 SEPTEMBER 1985–28 JULY 1990   Half-hour sitcom named for the Washington, D.C., tenement in which its principals lived. The mostly black ensemble cast included Marla Gibbs as Mary Jenkins; Hal Williams as her husband, Lester, a contractor; Regina King as Brenda, their teenage daughter; Alaina Reed (later known as Alaina Reed-Hall) as the landlady, Rose Lee Holloway; Kia Goodwin as Rose's daughter, Tiffany (who was seldom seen after the first season); Jackee Harry (later known as Jackée) as manhungry Sandra Clark; Curtis Baldwin as Calvin Dobbs, Brenda's boyfriend; Helen Martin as Calvin's grandmother, Pearl Shay; Countess Vaughn (1988–1989) as Alexandria, a precocious young student who lived with the Jenkins family for a year; Paul Winfield (1989–1990) as the building owner, Julian Barlow; Barry Sobel (spring 1989–1990) as Brenda's history teacher, Dylan McMillan, who became the only white tenant in the building; and Stoney Jackson (1989–1990) as Dylan's roommate, Travis Filmore. The series was based on a play, *227,* by Christine Houston, which had been presented at Marla Gibbs's Crossroads Theatre and Arts Academy in Los Angeles.

THE TYCOON   ABC
15 SEPTEMBER 1964–7 SEPTEMBER 1965   A season after *The Real McCoys* left the air, Walter Brennan returned to star in this unsuccessful sitcom. Brennan played Walter Andrews, a crusty widower who was chairman of the board of Thunder Corporation, a huge California conglomerate. Also featured were Van Williams as Pat Burns, Walter's personal assistant; Jerome Cowan as Herbert Wilson, president of Thunder Corporation; Pat McNulty as Martha, Walter's granddaughter; George Lindsey as Martha's husband, Tom Keane, a naval officer; Janet Lake as Betty Franklin, Walter's secretary; Monty Margetts as Una Fields, Walter's housekeeper; and Grace Albertson as Louise Wilson, Herbert's wife.

UFO   SYNDICATED
1972   This hour science fiction series, produced in England by Gerry and Sylvia Anderson, was set in the 1980s at SHADO (Supreme Headquarters, Alien Defense Organization), a top-secret agency which monitored an ever-increasing number of civilization-threatening UFOs. SHADO's cover operation was the Harlington-

Straker Film Studios in London. One reason for the series' lack of success was that many of the shows seemed incomprehensible to American viewers. Featured were Ed Bishop as Commander Edward Straker, SHADO chief; George Sewell as Colonel Alec Freeman; Michael Billington as Colonel Paul Foster; Peter Gordeno as Captain Peter Carlin; and Gabrielle Drake as Lieutenant Gay Ellis.

U.N. CASEBOOK CBS
19 SEPTEMBER 1948–6 MARCH 1949   Half-hour discussion show about the work of the United Nations. See also *The U.N. in Action* and *United Or Not?*

THE U.N. IN ACTION CBS
2 OCTOBER 1955–18 DECEMBER 1955; 11 NOVEMBER 1956–2 JUNE 1957; 8 SEPTEMBER 1957–23 FEBRUARY 1958; 7 SEPTEMBER 1958–21 DECEMBER 1958; 13 SEPTEMBER 1959–27 DECEMBER 1959; 18 SEPTEMBER 1960–25 DECEMBER 1960   Larry LeSueur hosted this Sunday-morning public affairs program that examined the work of the United Nations. The half-hour series shared a time slot with *Eye on New York* during most of its run. In 1960 Stuart Novins succeeded Larry LeSueur as host.

U.S.A. CANTEEN
See JANE FROMAN'S U.S.A. CANTEEN

USam SYNDICATED
1981–1982   Produced by the Christian Broadcasting Network and broadcast at 6:00 A.M., this informational hour show was cohosted first by Ross Bagley and former Miss America Terry Meeuwsen, later by Brian Christie and Meeuwsen. Terry Casey read the news, Tom Mahoney gave the weather, and Scott Hatch reported on sports.

USA TODAY: THE TELEVISION SHOW SYNDICATED
12 SEPTEMBER 1988–5 JANUARY 1990   A half-hour daily news magazine show, modeled after the national newspaper *USA Today*. Like its print counterpart, the TV show was broken up into four "sections," each with its own anchor: USA (with Edie Magnus), Money (Kenneth Walker), Sports (Bill Macatee) and Life (Robin Young). It boasted a fast-paced format with splashy graphics and a set laden with monitors and large video screens. The much-ballyhooed show was produced by GTG Entertainment, a partnership between former NBC head Grant Tinker and the Gannett Company, which owned *USA Today;* Steve Friedman, who had produced the *Today* show for seven years, was hired as executive producer. Intended for an early evening time slot, the series premiered in September 1988 on 155 stations; it was an almost instant ratings flop. Many stations moved the show to a less vulnerable time slot, usually after 11:00 P.M. Despite numerous efforts at retinkering the show—including changing the title to *USA Today: on TV,* and hiring Jim Bellows (formerly of *Entertainment Tonight*) as managing editor—the show never lived up to its hype and expired after sixteen months.

USA TONIGHT
See I.N.N. NEWS.

U.S.A. vs. THE WORLD ABC
31 JANUARY 1982–25 APRIL 1982   On this twelve-week Sunday-afternoon series, teams of American amateurs competed against foreign squads in various Olympic events.

U.S. BORDER PATROL
See BORDER PATROL

U.S. CUSTOMS CLASSIFIED SYNDICATED
1995–   Hour weekly reality series based on the files of the United States Customs service. Hosted by prolific TV producer/writer Stephen J. Cannell, the series used dramatic recreations of events and actual surveillance footage.

THE U.S. MARINE BAND   NBC

9 JULY 1949–20 AUGUST 1949   Broadcast from Washington, D.C., on Saturday nights, this half-hour series featured the music of the U.S. Marine Band. The band was also seen on many local stations, as a film of the band playing the national anthem was made available to any station, free of charge, for use as its sign-off.

U.S. MARSHAL

See SHERIFF OF COCHISE

U.S. OF ARCHIE

See THE ARCHIE SHOW

U.S. ROYAL SHOWCASE   NBC

13 JANUARY 1952–29 JUNE 1952   Half-hour comedy-variety show, sponsored by the United States Rubber Company. George Abbott was the first host of the Sunday-night show; Jack Carson succeeded him.

THE U.S. STEEL HOUR   ABC/CBS

27 OCTOBER 1953–21 JUNE 1955 (ABC); 6 JULY 1955–12 JUNE 1963 (CBS)   Another of television's high-quality dramatic anthology series, *The U.S. Steel Hour* was sponsored by United States Steel and produced under the auspices of the Theatre Guild, a group of show business people that was organized in the 1920s and which brought a radio show, *The Theatre Guild on the Air* (also sponsored by U.S. Steel), to the airwaves in 1945. The television version of the show began eight years later, in the heyday of TV's "Golden Age," and lasted ten years. Broadcast live from New York, the hour show was seen biweekly, alternating with *The Motorola TV Hour* and *The Elgin TV Hour* on ABC, and with *Armstrong Circle Theater* and *The 20th Century-Fox Hour on CBS*. A small sample of its presentations includes: "P.O.W.," with Richard Kiley, Phyllis Kirk, Gary Merrill, and Sally Forrest (27 October 1953); "No Time for Sergeants," with Andy Griffith (in his TV debut), Harry Clark, and Eddie LeRoy (15 March 1955; directed by Alex Segal, it was later a Broadway play, a motion picture, and a TV sitcom); "The Rack," with Keenan Wynn (12 April 1955); "The Outcast," with Lillian Roth (9 November 1955); "The Old Lady Shows Her Medals," with Gracie Fields (in her first dramatic role on American TV) and Alfred Lunt (23 May 1956); "Bang the Drum Slowly," with Paul Newman (26 September 1956); "A Drum Is a Woman," a musical fantasy composed and narrated by Duke Ellington, with dialogue written by Will Lorin (8 May 1957); "Beaver Patrol," a rare comedy presentation, starring Walter Slezak (9 April 1958); "Little Tin God," with Gene Hackman (in his first major TV role, 22 April 1959); "Queen of the Orange Bowl," with Anne Francis and Johnny Carson (making a rare TV dramatic appearance, 13 January 1960); "Girl in the Gold Bathtub," with Johnny Carson (in another rare TV dramatic appearance, 4 May 1960); "Brandenburg Gate," with Richard Kiley and Gene Hackman (4 October 1961).

THE UGLIEST GIRL IN TOWN   ABC

26 SEPTEMBER 1968–30 JANUARY 1969   Asinine sitcom about a Hollywood talent agent who disguised himself as a hip female fashion model in order to be closer to his girlfriend, an actress who had returned home to England; much to his chagrin, he discovered that, as a model, he was suddenly a mod sensation. With Peter Kastner as Tim Blair, the agent, and as Timmy Blair, the model; Patricia Brake as his girlfriend, Julia Renfield; Nicholas Parsons as Mr. Courtney, boss of a London modeling agency; and Gary Marshall as Tim's brother, Gene Blair, a photographer.

UKULELE IKE

See THE CLIFF EDWARDS SHOW

THE ULTIMATE CHALLENGE   FOX

13 SEPTEMBER 1991–1 NOVEMBER 1991   Hour reality program showcasing the exploits of stuntpeople, auto racers and assorted daredevils. Mike Adamle, Larry Hoff, John

Long, Spanky Spangler, Greg Stump, and Heather Thomas were on hand to hype the presentations.

ULTRAMAN   SYNDICATED
1966   Japanese-produced science fiction series about Iota, who came to Earth from another civilization and, as Ultraman, battled alien invaders. The live-action, half-hour series was created by Eiji Tsuburaya, who had created Godzilla for the movie of the same name.

THE UNCLE AL SHOW   ABC
18 OCTOBER 1958–19 SEPTEMBER 1959   Saturday-morning variety show for children, hosted by Al Lewis, with Wanda Lewis (as Captain Windy), Janet Greene (as Cinderella), Roger the Robot, and puppeteer Larry Smith. The hour show was broadcast from Cincinnati.

UNCLE BUCK   CBS
10 SEPTEMBER 1990–23 NOVEMBER 1990; 26 JANUARY 1991–6 APRIL 1991   Sitcom based on the 1989 movie about a bachelor slob who inherited a family. Featured were Kevin Meaney as Buck Russell, who came to care for his two nieces and nephew after the deaths of his brother and sister-in-law (in the movie, the children's parents had only gone on vacation); Dah-ve Chodan as teenage niece Tia; Jacob Gelman as nephew Miles; Sarah Martineck as younger niece Maizy; Audrey Meadows as the kids' maternal grandmother, Mrs. Hogoboom; Dennis Cockrum as Buck's pal Skank; and Thomas Mikal Ford as Buck's buddy Rafer Freeman.

UNCLE CROC'S BLOCK   ABC
6 SEPTEMBER 1975–14 FEBRUARY 1976   This Saturday-morning children's show was intended to be a spoof of Saturday-morning children's shows—its host constantly bantered with his assistant and his director and occasionally found the time to introduce a few cartoons. With Charles Nelson Reilly as Uncle Croc, the host; Alfie Wise as Mr. Rabbit Ears, his assistant; and Jonathan Harris as Mr. Bitterbottom, the director. Produced by Mack Bing and Don Christensen for Filmation Productions, the show was trimmed from sixty to thirty minutes late in October. Regular cartoon segments included "Fraidy Cat," "M*U*S*H" (an animal version of *M*A*S*H*), and "Wacky and Packy."

UNCLE JOHNNY COONS   CBS/NBC
19 FEBRUARY 1955–3 DECEMBER 1955 (CBS); 3 MARCH 1956–24 NOVEMBER 1956 (NBC)   On this Chicago-based Saturday show for children, ventriloquist Johnny Coons introduced silent films and traded quips with his wooden partner, George Dummy, and his invisible dog, Blackie.

UNCOMMON VALOR   SYNDICATED
1955   A series of twenty-six half-hour documentaries about the United States Marines narrated by Daniel Riss and featuring General Holland M. (Howlin' Mad) Smith. Cliff Karling and William Karn produced the series.

UNDER COVER   ABC
7 JANUARY 1991–16 FEBRUARY 1991   This hour adventure series starred Anthony John Denison and Linda Purl as Dylan and Kate Del'Amico, a husband-and-wife spy team for the National Intelligence Agency. Also on hand were John Rhys-Davies as fellow spy Flynn; Josef Sommer as their boss, Stuart Merriman; G. W. Bailey as the agency director, Mr. Waugh; John Slattery as Graham Parker, a duty officer; Kasi Lemmons as Alex Robbins, a duty officer; Arlene Taylor as Dylan's daughter (from a prior marriage), Megan; Joshua South (pilot program) and Adam Ryen as Dylan and Kate's son, Marlon; and Sumer Stamper (pilot) and Marne Patterson as Dylan and Kate's daughter, Emily. The series premiered only days before the outbreak of war in the Persian Gulf; one episode was hastily pulled from ABC's schedule, as it dealt

with Middle East terrorists. It surfaced in July, when ABC cobbled together two two-hour TV-movies from unaired programs and a rerun of the premiere episode.

UNDER ONE ROOF
See SPENCER

UNDER ONE ROOF   CBS
14 MARCH 1995–18 APRIL 1995   A rarity in series programming, *Under One Roof* was an hour dramatic series about a black family. It starred James Earl Jones as patriarch Neb Langston, a widower who lived in a two-family house in Seattle with his adult daughter and his foster son (Neb's son and his family lived downstairs). Also featured were Joe Morton as Neb's son, Ron Langston, who had just opened a hardware store; Vanessa Bell Calloway as Ron's wife, Maggie; Essence Atkins as Charlie, Ron and Maggie's fifteen-year-old daughter; Ronald Joshua Scott as Derrick, Ron and Maggie's ten-year-old son, a diabetic; Monique Ridge as Ayesha, Neb's daughter; Merlin Santana as Marcus, Neb's troubled foster son; and Terence Knox as Siggy Sigelos, Ron's partner in the hardware store.

UNDER SUSPICION   CBS
16 SEPTEMBER 1994–10 MARCH 1995; 11 JUNE 1995–9 AUGUST 1995   Atmospheric crime show set in the Pacific Northwest, featuring a cop who juggled her roles as the city's only female detective and as the police department's Women's Coordinator. With Karen Sillas as Detective Rose "Phil" Phillips; Philip Casnoff as Sergeant James Vitelli of the Internal Affairs division; Seymour Cassel as veteran officer Mickey Schwartz, captain of the detectives; Paul McCrane as Detective James Clarke; Anthony DeSando as Detective Costa Papadakos; Richard Foronjy as Detective Lou Barbini; Michael Beach as Detective Desmond Beck; Brian McNamara as Detective Farnsworth; Raymond Baker as the Chief; and Arabella Fried as Phil's friend and therapist, Patsi Moosekian. The hour series was filmed on location in Portland, Oregon.

UNDERDOG   NBC/CBS
3 OCTOBER 1964–3 SEPTEMBER 1966 (NBC); 10 SEPTEMBER 1966–1 SEPTEMBER 1968 (CBS); 7 SEPTEMBER 1968–5 SEPTEMBER 1970 (NBC); 9 SEPTEMBER 1972–1 SEPTEMBER 1973 (NBC)   This durable weekend cartoon series featured the voice of Wally Cox as that of Underdog, a canine superhero whose alter ego was Shoeshine Boy.

THE UNEXPECTED   SYNDICATED
1952   Half-hour suspense anthology series from Ziv TV, hosted by Herbert Marshall.

UNHAPPILY EVER AFTER   WB
11 JANUARY 1995–   Ron Leavitt, who had created *Married. . . . With Children* with Michael Moye, co-created this sitcom with Arthur Silver. Best described as *Unmarried . . . with Children,* it told the story of a recently divorced couple and their three kids; the parents constantly bickered with each other, while the kids paid no attention. With Geoff Pierson as used car salesman Jack Malloy; Stephanie Hodge as his ex-wife, Jennie Malloy; Kevin Connolly as older son Ryan; Nikki Cox as daughter Tiffany; Justin Berfield as younger son Ross; and Joyce Van Patten as Jennie's meddlesome mother, Maureen Slattery. As the series got underway, Jack had moved into an apartment; young Ross had given Jack his stuffed bunny to keep him company, and, to his amazement, Jack discovered that the creature, Mr. Floppy, could talk and move, but only when Jack was alone. Bobcat Goldthwait provided the voice of Mr. Floppy; Alan Trautman was the puppeteer. In the fall of 1995 Jack moved back into the basement of his old house.

UNION PACIFIC   SYNDICATED
1958   Half-hour western, set along the right of way of the Union Pacific Railroad. With Jeff Morrow as Bart McClelland, district supervisor; Judd Pratt as surveyor Bill

Kinkaid; and Susan Cummings as Georgia, the operator of the Golden Nugget Saloon, which was conveniently located in a railroad car that traveled with the train crew.

UNITED OR NOT? ABC
2 JULY 1951–27 OCTOBER 1952   Half-hour discussion series about the United Nations, hosted by John MacVane.

UNITED STATES NBC
11 MARCH 1980–29 APRIL 1980   Larry Gelbart, the cocreator of *M*A*S*H*, was given *carte blanche* by NBC in developing this half-hour comedy-drama; intended to be a contemporary look at marriage, it starred Beau Bridges and Helen Shaver as Richard and Libby Chapin, with Rossie Harris and Justin Dana as their sons, Dylan and Nicky. Taped with no laugh track, no theme music, and handwritten credits, the much ballyhooed program was dropped after just seven weeks. It ended up as NBC's lowest-rated prime-time series of the 1979–1980 season, finishing 102nd out of 105 shows.

THE UNITED STATES STEEL HOUR
See THE U.S. STEEL HOUR

UNIVERSE (WALTER CRONKITE'S UNIVERSE) CBS
12 JULY 1980–2 AUGUST 1980; 23 JUNE 1981–8 SEPTEMBER 1981; 8 JUNE 1982–31 AUGUST 1982   Following his departure from *The CBS Evening News*, Walter Cronkite returned to TV to host this prime-time science series. In 1980 it was seen in an hour format and was titled *Universe*. In 1981 and 1982 it was known as *Walter Cronkite's Universe* and was aired in a half-hour format.

UNIVERSITY HOSPITAL SYNDICATED
1995–   Hour dramatic series about four student nurses who roomed together and worked at a Seattle hospital. With Tonya Pinkins as nurse Mary Jenkins, their instructor; Hillary Danner as nurse Jamie Fuller, who had recently left an abusive relationship; Rebecca Cross as nurse Megan Peterson, originally from Montana; Hudson Leick as nurse Tracy Stone, the sexpot; and Alexandra Wilson as fourth generation nurse Samantha (Sam) McCormack. Also featured were Nancy Sivak as Nurse Shane and Liza Huget as Nurse Astor. Aaron Spelling and E. Duke Vincent were the executive producers.

UNSOLVED MYSTERIES NBC
14 SEPTEMBER 1988–   Hour non-fiction series, hosted by Robert Stack, which frequently focused on such topics as missing persons, unsolved murders, and unclaimed estates. The series followed a number of specials which had been televised during the previous two seasons, and had been hosted by Raymond Burr and Karl Malden. Like other shows of its ilk (*America's Most Wanted, Missing/Reward,* etc.), *Unsolved Mysteries* used interviews with concerned parties and law enforcement officials as well as dramatic recreations of actual events. Some of the mysteries presented on the show were solved. In the spring of 1988, for example, Jerry Strickland, wanted for homicide, was apprehended the day after he was featured on the show. Strickland had seen the program, agreed to tape an interview for an upcoming program, and told the producers that *Unsolved Mysteries* was still his favorite show. John Cosgrove and Terry Dunn Meurer created the series. A spinoff series of sorts aired briefly in the fall of 1992: see *Final Appeal: From the Files of Unsolved Mysteries*.

UNSUB NBC
3 FEBRUARY 1989–14 APRIL 1989   An hour crime show about the Behavioral Sciences Unit of the Department of Justice, which employed the latest methods of scientific and intuitive discovery to hunt down the "unknown subjects" (hence the series' title) suspected of perpetrating various gruesome crimes. With David Soul as Wes Grayson; M. Emmet Walsh as Ned; Joe Maruzzo as Tony; and Jennifer Hetrick as Ann.

THE UNTAMED WORLD   SYNDICATED/NBC

1968 (SYNDICATED); 11 JANUARY 1969–30 AUGUST 1969 (NBC)   Half-hour series
of natural history films, narrated by Phil Carey.

THE UNTOUCHABLES   ABC

15 OCTOBER 1959–10 SEPTEMBER 1963   This hour-long crime show, set in Chicago
during the 1930s was based on the real-life exploits of Eliot Ness and his squad of
Treasury agents, nicknamed "The Untouchables." One of TV's most consistently
violent series, *The Untouchables* received much criticism during its four-season run,
especially from Italian-American civic groups, who objected to the show's repetitive
use of Italian-surnamed gangsters in its early seasons. Their efforts led to a diversifica-
tion of villains, and by 1963 virtually every ethnic group had been represented (even
Russians could not claim to have been slighted, as one hood was named Joe Vodka).
More criticism came from the U.S. Bureau of Prisons, which strongly objected to the
portrayal of prison officials in certain episodes involving Al Capone. The series was
produced by Quinn Martin for Desilu and was narrated by Walter Winchell (Martin
would later use offscreen narration in several of his hit series, such as *The Fugitive*
and *The Invaders*). Featured on-screen were: Robert Stack as Eliot Ness (the part
had been offered to Van Johnson and Van Heflin, but both had turned it down); Jerry
Paris (1959–1960) as Martin Flaherty; Nicholas Georgiade as Rico Rossi; Anthony
George (spring 1960) as Cam Allison; Abel Fernandez as William Youngfellow; Paul
Picerni (1960–1963) as Lee Hobson; and Steve London (1960–1963) as Rossman.
Guest villains included: Neville Brand as Al Capone; Bruce Gordon as Frank Nitti;
and Clu Gulager as "Mad Dog" Coll. James Caan played his first major TV role on
one episode, "A Fist of Five" (4 December 1962), and Robert Redford appeared in
"Snowball" (15 January 1963). The pilot for the series was televised as a two-part
presentation on *Desilu Playhouse,* 20 and 27 April 1959. In 1987 a successful motion
picture was released, based loosely on the series, starring Kevin Costner as Ness.
Stack returned to the role in a TV-movie, "The Return of Eliot Ness," broadcast 10
November 1991 on NBC. In 1993 a new version of the series appeared: see below.

THE UNTOUCHABLES   SYNDICATED

1993–1994   The remake of the 1959–1963 series (see above) was filmed on location
in Chicago. It featured Tom Amandes as Eliot Ness; Michael Horse as wiretap expert
George Steelman; John Haymes Newton as driver Tony Pagano; David James Elliott
(spring 1993) as Paul Robbins; John Rhys-Davies as honest Chicago cop Mike Malone; Nancy Everhard as Ness's first wife, Catherine; William Forsythe as Al Capone; Paul Regina as Frank Nitti; George Carson as Ness's friend Louis Basile;
Hynden Walch as Mae Capone, Al's wife; Jack Thibeau as Bugs Moran; and Byrne
Piven as John Torrio.

UP AND COMING   PBS

1980   Half-hour comedy-drama about a middle-class black family living in San
Francisco. Featured were Yule Caise as Marcus Wilson, the youngest child; Cindy
Herron as his sister, Valerie; L. Wolfe Perry, Jr., as his brother, Kevin; Robert
DoQui as their father, Frank, who ran a construction company; and Gamy L. Taylor
as their mother, Joyce.

UP TO PAAR   NBC

28 JULY 1952–26 SEPTEMBER 1952   In his first national television assignment, Jack
Paar hosted this current events quiz, which was also known as *I've Got News for You.*
The half-hour show was seen Monday, Wednesday, and Friday evenings.

UP TO THE MINUTE   CBS

28 SEPTEMBER 1981–15 JANUARY 1982   This half-hour daytime newsmagazine series
marked CBS's attempt to introduce network programming into its 4:00 P.M. time
slot, which for many years had been the private domain of its local affiliates. Relatively few stations were willing to relinquish the time slot for the network offering,

and *Up to the Minute* perished after sixteen weeks. The series had no permanent host—a different CBS journalist hosted the show each week.

UP TO THE MINUTE   CBS
29 MARCH 1992–   The second CBS news program with this title was used for its late-late-night news service, which had been inaugurated in 1982 as *CBS News Nightwatch*. Revamped in 1992, the new broadcast was originally coanchored by Monica Gayle and Russ Mitchell.

UPBEAT   CBS
5 JULY 1955–22 SEPTEMBER 1955   This fifteen-minute, twice-weekly summer musical series featured the Russ Case Orchestra, the Tommy Morton Dancers, and guests. Jerome Shaw produced and directed.

UPBEAT   SYNDICATED
1966–1971   A Cleveland-based rock music show, hosted by Don Webster. Frequent guests on the hour series included Jeff Kutash and the GTOs.

UPDATE   NBC
16 SEPTEMBER 1961-2 JUNE 1963   A weekend newsmagazine for teenagers, hosted by Robert Abernethy.

UPTOWN JUBILEE   CBS
13 SEPTEMBER 1949–20 OCTOBER 1949   This short-lived all-black variety show was hosted by Willie Bryant. Regulars included Timmie Rogers and Harry Belafonte. The show was later titled *Sugar Hill Times*.

URBAN ANGEL   CBS
29 OCTOBER 1991–18 FEBRUARY 1992; 30 AUGUST 1993–10 SEPTEMBER 1993   Part of CBS's late-night *Crime Time After Prime Time*, this hour series was filmed in Montreal. It starred Justin Louis as Victor Torres, an ex-con who became a reporter for the *Tribune*; Dorothy Berryman as the managing editor, Francine Primeau; and Jack Langedijk as the city editor, Bob Vanverdan.

V   NBC
26 OCTOBER 1984–22 MARCH 1985; 17 MAY 1985–5 JULY 1985   The television series with the shortest title was the sequel to two science fiction miniseries: *V* (1 and 2 May 1983) and *V: The Final Battle* (6–8 May 1984). They told the saga of the Visitors, lizard-like aliens from another planet who came to Earth and assumed human form; the Visitors shrewdly masked their plan to take over the planet, but were eventually thwarted by a group of Los Angeles-based "resistance fighters." The parallels to the Nazi takeover of much of Europe were intentional. The latter miniseries was rerun in mid-October 1984, and the weekly series picked up the story a year later. Principal players included: Jane Badler as Diana, leader of the Visitors, who was kidnapped by an American industrialist on the eve of her trial for crimes against humanity; Marc Singer as resistance leader Mike Donovan, a television newscaster; Faye Grant as resistance scientist Julie Parish; Lane Smith as Nathan Bates, Diana's kidnapper and collaborator; Jeff Yagher as Nathan's son, Kyle, who sided with the resistance; Blair Tefkin as Robin Maxwell, who had had an affair with an alien; Jenny Beck and Jennifer Cooke as Robin's half-human, half-alien daughter, Elizabeth; Robert Englund as Willie, a Visitor who defected to the resistance; June Chadwick as Lydia, a Visitor who was Diana's chief rival; Duncan Regehr as Charles, a Visitor who forced Diana to marry him and died shortly thereafter; Nicky Katt as Mike's young son, Sam Donovan; and Howard K. Smith as himself, a newscaster who introduced most of the episodes. In the final episode (22 March) the Visitors' leader traveled to Earth to negotiate a lasting peace. The series was not without flashes of humor. On the episode of 1 February, when Charles and Diana were married, Diana was shown luxuriating in a bath—of live eels..

VR.5   FOX

10 MARCH 1995–12 MAY 1995   "Virtual reality is real" was the catchphrase uttered on this sci-fi series. Lori Singer starred as Sydney Bloom, a telephone employee technician who, while using her homebuilt computer, accidentally stumbled into the fifth level of virtual reality; at that level, in which all five senses were involved, Bloom learned that she could create the setting and could bring others into it, but she could not control the outcome. Trying to learn what had become of her father, a prominent scientist who had supposedly drowned, she came in contact with a mysterious organization known as the Committee. Also featured were Michael Easton as Sydney's slacker neighbor, Duncan; Will Patton as Dr. Frank Morgan, one of the pioneers of virtual reality technology, who worked for the Committee; David McCallum as Sydney's father, Dr. Joseph Bloom, who appeared in flashbacks and in VR sequences; and Louise Fletcher as Nora Bloom, Sydney's mother, who appeared in flashbacks and in the present time, where she resided in a nursing home.

VACATIONLAND AMERICA   NBC

29 MARCH 1953–28 JUNE 1953   Also known as *Sightseeing with the Swayzes,* this fifteen-minute travelogue was hosted by NBC newscaster John Cameron Swayze and members of his family.

THE VAL DOONICAN SHOW   ABC

5 JUNE 1971–14 AUGUST 1971   Hour-long musical show hosted by Irish folksinger Val Doonican.

VALENTINE'S DAY   ABC

18 SEPTEMBER 1964–10 SEPTEMBER 1965   Half-hour sitcom starring Tony Franciosa as Valentine Farrow, a swinging New York publishing executive. Also on hand were Jack Soo as Rockwell (Rocky) Sin, Val's valet; Janet Waldo as Libby, his secretary; Mimi Dillard as Molly; Eddie Quillan as Fipple, the custodian in Val's apartment house; and Jerry Hausner as Mr. Dunstall, Val's boss.

VALENTINO   ABC

18 DECEMBER 1952–5 MARCH 1953   ABC's answer to CBS's *The Continental, Valentino* was a half-hour series on which singer Barry Valentino tried to woo the female viewers at home.

VALERIE (VALERIE'S FAMILY)

See THE HOGAN FAMILY

VALIANT LADY   CBS

12 OCTOBER 1953–16 AUGUST 1957   A daytime serial, *Valiant Lady* was created by Frank and Ann Hummert and ran on radio from 1938 to 1952. The TV version starred Nancy Coleman and Flora Campbell as Helen Emerson; Jerome Cowan as her husband, Frank, who died; James Kirkwood, Jr., as their son, Mickey; Anne Pearson, Dolores Sutton, Sue Randall, and Leila Martin as their daughter, Diane; Lydia Reed (who later appeared on *The Real McCoys*) and Bonnie Sawyer as their younger daughter, Kim; Terry O'Sullivan as Elliott Norris; Martin Balsam as Joey Gordon; and Frances Helm as Linda Kendall. The fifteen-minute show, broadcast live from New York, was produced by Carl Green, written by Charles Elwyn, and directed by Herb Kenwith.

VALLEY OF THE DINOSAURS   CBS

7 SEPTEMBER 1974–4 SEPTEMBER 1976   Saturday-morning cartoon series from Hanna-Barbera Productions about the Butler family, who found themselves trapped in a prehistoric world. Though the show ran for two seasons, the second season consisted entirely of reruns.

VAN DYKE AND COMPANY   NBC
20 SEPTEMBER 1976–30 DECEMBER 1976   An unsuccessful variety hour hosted by Dick Van Dyke. Other regulars included Andy Kaufman, Pat Proft, Marilyn Sokol, and the Los Angeles Mime Company. Allan Blye and Bob Einstein were the producers.

THE VAN DYKE SHOW   CBS
26 OCTOBER 1988–7 DECEMBER 1988   Dick Van Dyke and Mary Tyler Moore each returned to CBS in back-to-back Wednesday night sitcoms in the fall of 1988; both were unsuccessful. *The Van Dyke Show* starred Dick Van Dyke as Dick Burgess, a veteran Broadway star who decided to help out his son, who ran a small regional theater company. Van Dyke's real-life son Barry Van Dyke co-starred as the son, Matt Burgess. Also aboard were Kari Lizer as Chris, Matt's wife; Billy O'Sullivan as their son, Noah; Whitman Mayo as Doc, the ancient stage manager; and Maura Tierney as Jillian, the all-purpose assistant.

VANISHING SON   SYNDICATED
1995–   Hour adventure series starring Russell Wong as Jian Wa Chang, a martial artist and musician falsely accused of killing two federal agents; Chang tried to find the people who had framed him as he eluded his pursuers. Also featured were Jason Adams as Immigration & Naturalization Service agent Dan Standler, who had organized the Asian Crime Task Force in an effort to get Chang; and Stephanie Niznik as INS agent Judith Phillips, Standler's newly assigned partner, who had doubts about Chang's guilt. The hour series had been preceded in 1994 by a syndicated made-for-TV movie.

VANITY FAIR   CBS
12 OCTOBER 1948–2 NOVEMBER 1951   One of CBS's first daytime shows, *Vanity Fair* began as a twice-weekly show, but by January of 1949 it was broadcast five days a week. Hosted by Robin Chandler and by Dorothy Doan, it presented features of interest to housewives. In 1949 it was produced and directed by Frances Buss, and in 1951 it was written and produced by Virginia Schone and directed by Dan Levin.

VAUDEO VARIETIES   ABC
14 JANUARY 1949–15 APRIL 1949   One of the first Chicago-based programs to be broadcast in the East following the opening of the coaxial cables between New York and Chicago, *Vaudeo Varieties* presented five acts each week. Eddie Hubbard hosted the hour show.

VAUDEVILLE   SYNDICATED
1974   A variety hour with no regulars (except Donna Jean Young, the cardholder), *Vaudeville* consisted of assorted vaudeville acts, introduced by celebrity guest hosts. Burt Rosen was the executive producer for Metromedia.

VAUDEVILLE SHOW   ABC
9 DECEMBER 1953–30 DECEMBER 1953   Five vaudeville acts were presented each week on this short-lived variety show.

THE VAUGHN MONROE SHOW   NBC
31 AUGUST 1954–30 SEPTEMBER 1954; 28 JUNE 1955–8 SEPTEMBER 1955   Bandleader-singer Vaughn Monroe twice hosted a summer replacement for *The Dinah Shore Show;* the fifteen-minute series was seen twice a week. See also *Camel Caravan.*

VEGA$ ABC
20 SEPTEMBER 1978–16 SEPTEMBER 1981   Glittery Las Vegas was the setting of this hour crime show, which starred Robert Urich as private eye Dan Tanna, who drove around town in a red 1957 Thunderbird convertible. Also featured were Phyllis Davis as his woman Friday, Beatrice Travis; Bart Braverman as his inept assistant, Binzer; Naomi Stevens (1978–1979) as Sergeant Bella Archer of the Las Vegas Police Department; Judy Landers (1978–1979) as Angie Turner, a chorus girl who sometimes took

messages for Tanna; and Greg Morris (1979–1981) as Lieutenant Dave Nelson. Tony Curtis appeared occasionally as Roth, a Vegas hotelier who sometimes hired Tanna. Aaron Spelling and Douglas S. Cramer were the executive producers.

VEGETABLE SOUP SYNDICATED
1975   An ambitious magazine show for children, *Vegetable Soup* featured such guest hosts as Bette Midler and James Earl Jones, who introduced live and animated segments. Yanna Kroyt Brandt was the executive producer for the New York State Department of Education. The show was seen in most areas in half-hour form, though it could be adapted into a fifteen-minute format.

VERDICT CBS
21 JUNE 1991–5 SEPTEMBER 1991   This prime time reality series covered trials. Each program was hosted by a CBS News correspondent, who introduced the case and showed edited footage from the trial.

THE VERDICT IS YOURS CBS
2 SEPTEMBER 1957–28 SEPTEMBER 1962   This popular courtroom drama began as a daytime show; it also enjoyed a prime-time run on CBS during the summer of 1958. The series was done without scripts; the show's writers prepared an outline for each case, which served as the starting point for the performers. Professional actors played the litigants and witnesses, while real attorneys played the lawyers and judges. Jurors were chosen from the studio audience. Jim McKay, *Verdict*'s first "court reporter," was succeeded by Bill Stout in July 1960. Stout was succeeded by Jack Whitaker in June 1962. The half-hour show was produced by Eugene Burr.

VERSATILE VARIETIES NBC/CBS/ABC
26 AUGUST 1949–19 JANUARY 1951 (NBC); 28 JANUARY 1951–22 JULY 1951 (CBS); 21 SEPTEMBER 1951–14 DECEMBER 1951 (ABC)   *Versatile Varieties* premiered as a prime-time variety revue in 1949, hosted by George Givot and Bob Russell. Produced by Charles Basch and Frances Scott, and directed by Jay Strong, it was officially titled *The Bonny Maid Versatile Variety Show;* commercials were handled by an eighteen-year-old model named Anne Francis. When the show switched networks in January 1951, it retained little else but its title, as it moved from prime time to Sunday mornings and became a children's show. Lady Iris Mountbatten was the new host, telling stories and singing songs. In the fall of 1951 *Versatile Varieties* again shifted networks.

THE VIC DAMONE SHOW CBS/NBC
2 JULY 1956–24 SEPTEMBER 1956 (CBS); 3 JULY 1957–11 SEPTEMBER 1957 (CBS); 22 JUNE 1967–7 SEPTEMBER 1967 (NBC)   Born Vito Farinola, singer Vic Damone appeared on the radio version of Arthur Godfrey's *Talent Scouts,* and began making records in 1947. He hosted the first of his TV shows in 1956, a summer replacement for *December Bride.* In 1957 he hosted an hour series, a summer replacement for *Arthur Godfrey and His Friends,* which featured Peggy King and the Spellbinders. After hosting *The Lively Ones* for two summers (see that title), he filled in for *The Dean Martin Show* during the summer of 1967; other regulars on that series included Gail Martin (Dean's daughter) and Carol Lawrence; the latter series was rerun on NBC during the summer of 1971.

VICKI! SYNDICATED
1992–1994   Hour daytime talk show, hosted by actress and singer Vicki Lawrence, and produced by Group W Productions.

THE VICTOR BORGE SHOW NBC
3 FEBRUARY 1951–30 JUNE 1951   A Danish pianist with a sense of humor, Victor Borge hosted his own half-hour comedy-variety series on Saturday evenings.

VICTORY AT SEA   NBC
26 OCTOBER 1952–26 APRIL 1953   A documentary series of twenty-six half hours on naval warfare during World War II, *Victory at Sea* was produced by Henry Salomon and narrated by Leonard Graves. Richard Rodgers composed a special score for the program.

VICTORY GARDEN   PBS
1976–   Aimed primarily at the urban gardener, this half-hour show was first hosted by James Underwood Crockett and titled *Crockett's Victory Garden*. Much of the program was taped at the garden constructed outside the studio of Boston's WGBH-TV. After Crockett's death in 1979, Bob Thomson took over as host, and in 1981 the title was shortened to *Victory Garden*. Following Thomson's departure in 1990, the show experimented with three regional hosts—Jim Wilson, Bob Smaus, and Roger Swain—before Swain took over as national host.

VIDEO VILLAGE   CBS
Nighttime: 1 JULY 1960–16 SEPTEMBER 1960; *Daytime*: 11 JULY 1960–15 JUNE 1962
On this half-hour game show two couples competed. One spouse rolled a giant die inside a cage, after which his or her spouse advanced along a life-sized game board according to the roll of the die. Jack Narz was the first host, Monty Hall the second; they were assisted by Joanna Copeland and Eileen Barton; Merrill Heatter and Bob Quigley were the producers. See also *Video Village Junior*.

VIDEO VILLAGE JUNIOR   CBS
30 SEPTEMBER 1961-16 JUNE 1962   This Saturday-morning children's version of *Video Village* was hosted by Monty Hall, with assistance from Eileen Barton.

VIETNAM: A TELEVISION HISTORY   PBS
4 OCTOBER 1983–20 DECEMBER 1983   This compelling but objectively presented thirteen-part chronicle of Vietnam centered on the American involvement in the war, though it also examined the French involvement in the first half of the twentieth century. The program made extensive use of news film and of contemporary interviews with most of the surviving principals, both Vietnamese and American. (According to executive producer Richard Ellison, only two people declined to cooperate with the project: former Defense Secretary Robert MacNamara and former South Vietnam President Nguyen Van Thieu). Will Lyman narrated the series, and Mickey Hart and Billy Kreutzmann (both of the Grateful Dead) composed the theme.

VIETNAM WAR STORY   HBO
29 AUGUST 1987–20 SEPTEMBER 1987; 20 JULY 1988–7 DECEMBER 1988   The experiences of American soldiers in Vietnam were depicted on this gripping anthology series.

THE VIKINGS   SYNDICATED
1960   Officially titled *Tales of the Vikings*, this half-hour medieval adventure series starred Jerome Courtland as Leif Ericson, Norse explorer. Also on hand were Walter Barnes as Finn, Stefan Schnabel as Firebeard, and Buddy Baer. The show was produced by Brynapod Productions, a company owned by Kirk Douglas, and was filmed on location in Europe using sets, costumes, and ships left over from the motion picture, *The Vikings*, in which Douglas had starred.

VILLA ALEGRE   PBS
1974–1979   Half-hour daytime series for children, presented in Spanish and English ("Villa Alegre" is Spanish for "Happy Village"), geared to Spanish-speaking preschool children. Claudio Guzman was the executive producer, and the show's regulars included Nono Arsu, Linda Dangcil, Sam Edwards, Maria Grimm, Darryl Henriquez, Julio Medina, Federico Roberto, Wilfredo H. Rodriquez, Hal Smith, Catana Tully, and Carmen Zapata.

THE VILLAGE BARN NBC

17 MAY 1948–4 JULY 1949; 16 JANUARY 1950–29 MAY 1950   Square dancing from New York's Greenwich Village.

THE VIN SCULLY SHOW CBS

15 JANUARY 1973–23 MARCH 1973   Short-lived half-hour daytime variety series, hosted by Vin Scully.

THE VINCENT LOPEZ SHOW DUMONT/CBS

7 MARCH 1949–30 MARCH 1950 (DUMONT); 13 JUNE 1951–11 JULY 1951 (DU-MONT); 9 FEBRUARY 1957–9 MARCH 1957 (CBS)   Orchestra leader Vincent Lopez hosted three eponymous programs. The first was a fifteen-minute show, seen Mondays, Wednesdays, and Fridays. The second was a half-hour show on Wednesday nights, with Barry Valentino and Ann Warren. The third was a Saturday-evening half hour on CBS, with Judy Lynn, Johnny Amorosa, Johnny Messner, Teddy Norman, Eddie O'Connor, and the Lopezians. See also *Dinner Date*.

VINNIE & BOBBY FOX

30 MAY 1992–5 SEPTEMBER 1992   This half-hour sitcom rose from the ashes of Fox's 1991 sitcom *Top of the Heap*, as Matt LeBlanc returned in the role of Vinnie Verducci. Robert Torti costarred as Vinnie's pal from childhood, Bobby Grazzo; the two shared a Chicago apartment (though Bobby neglected to help out with the rent) and were employed as construction workers slowly building a house for a yuppie couple. Also featured were John Pinette and Ron Taylor as their pals Bill and Stanley, who roomed together, and Joey Adams, also reprising her *Top of the Heap* role, as seventeen-year-old Mona Mullins, who still had the hots for Vinnie.

VIPER NBC

2 JANUARY 1994–1 APRIL 1994   The central character on this hour crime show was not a human being, but rather a super-powered Viper automobile used by the Metro Police in California. The human roles were filled by James McCaffrey as Joe Astor, a former mobster who had been reprogrammed as a cop; Dorian Harewood as the car's designer, Julian Wilkes, who used a wheelchair; Joe Nipote as the motor pool supervisor, Frankie Waters; Faye Hauser as Mara; and Dawn Lyne Gardner as Ronnie.

THE VIRGINIA GRAHAM SHOW SYNDICATED

1970–1972   Hour-long talk show hosted by Virginia Graham, veteran of two previous talk shows (*Food for Thought* and *Girl Talk*). Phil Mayer was the producer.

THE VIRGINIAN NBC

19 SEPTEMBER 1962–9 SEPTEMBER 1970
THE MEN FROM SHILOH NBC

16 SEPTEMBER 1970–8 SEPTEMBER 1971   Television's first ninety-minute western series, *The Virginian* was based on Owen Wister's novel, which had been filmed at least three times. Set at the sprawling Shiloh Ranch in Medicine Bow, Wyoming, its central character was a taciturn foreman known simply as the Virginian, a man trying to come to grips with the inexorable westward advance of technology, culture, and civilization. The only members of the cast who remained with the show for its entire run were James Drury as the Virginian and Doug McClure as Trampas, the headstrong assistant foreman. Other players included: Lee J. Cobb (1962–1966) as Judge Henry Garth, first owner of the Shiloh Ranch; Roberta Shore (1962–1965) as Betsy Garth, his daughter; Pippa Scott (1962–1964) as newspaper publisher Molly Wood; Gary Clarke (1962–1964) as Steve, a ranch hand; Randy Boone (1963–1966) as Randy Garth, Judge Garth's son; L. Q. Jones (1964–1967) as Belden, a ranch hand; Harlan Warde (1964–1966) as Sheriff Brannon; Clu Gulager (1964–1968) as Deputy Ryker; Diane Roter (1965–1966) as Jennifer, Judge Garth's niece; John Dehner (1965–1966) as Starr, a ranch hand; Charles Bickford (1966–November 1967) as John Grainger, second owner of the Shiloh Ranch; Don Quine (1966–1968) as his grandson, Stacy Grainger; Sara Lane (1966–1970) as his granddaughter, Elizabeth Grainger; Ross Elliott (1966–1970)

as Sheriff Abbott; John McIntire (November 1967–1970) as his brother, Clay Grainger, who became the third owner of the ranch; Jeanette Nolan (1968–1970) as Holly Grainger, Clay's wife; David Hartman (1968–1969) as David Sutton, a ranch hand; Tim Matheson (1969–1970) as Jim Horn, a ranch hand. In the fall of 1970 the series was retitled *The Men from Shiloh,* and continued for one final season. Ownership of the Shiloh Ranch again changed hands, as Stewart Granger joined the cast as new owner Colonel Alan MacKenzie, an Englishman. James Drury and Doug McClure remained with the show, and Lee Majors signed on as hired hand Roy Tate. *The Virginian* and *The Men from Shiloh* were produced by Universal Television.

THE VISE ABC
1 OCTOBER 1954–5 JULY 1957   Half-hour dramatic anthology series, produced in England, and hosted by Ron Randell during the first season. Some telecasts were from the series *Mark Saber* (see also that title).

VISION ON SYNDICATED
1972   An inventive British children's series, *Vision On* was developed to aid children with hearing problems. A total of seventy-four half-hour programs were produced by BBC-TV, with Tony Hart as host (Hart also designed the animated sequences).

VISIONS PBS
1976–1978   An ambitious anthology series, *Visions* provided a showcase for young American playwrights. Funded by several grants, it was produced by Barbara Schultz at KCET-TV, Los Angeles.

VISIT WITH THE ARMED FORCES DUMONT
3 JULY 1950–22 JANUARY 1951   Half-hour public service series of films about the armed forces. See also *The Armed Forces Hour.*

THE VISUAL GIRL SYNDICATED
1971   Ron Russell hosted this half-hour series, which focused on beauty care.

VIVA VALDEZ ABC
31 MAY 1976–6 SEPTEMBER 1976   Half-hour sitcom about a Chicano family living in East Los Angeles. With Carmen Zapata as Sophia Valdez; Rodolfo Hoyos as her husband, Luis Valdez, owner of a plumbing business; Nelson D. Cuevas as Ernesto, their eldest son, Lisa Mordente as daughter Connie; Claudio Martinez as Pepe, the youngest son; Maria O'Brien as Connie's friend Inez; Jorge Cervera, Jr., as the Valdez' cousin, Jerry Ramirez, newly arrived in the United States. The series was created by Bernard Rothman, Stan Jacobson, and Jack Wohl, who were also its executive producers.

VOICE OF FIRESTONE NBC/ABC
5 SEPTEMBER 1949–7 JUNE 1954 (NBC); 14 JUNE 1954–16 JUNE 1963 (ABC)   *Voice of Firestone,* which began on radio in 1928, was a Monday-night perennial for more than two decades before coming to television in 1949; for the next five years it was simulcast on NBC radio and television, until a dispute between the sponsor and the network over the Monday time slot led Firestone to shift the program to ABC. The half-hour musical series presented all kinds of music, but emphasized classical and semiclassical selections. Each week a guest celebrity was featured, and for many years the principal guests came from the Metropolitan Opera Company. The Firestone Orchestra was conducted by Howard Barlow, and the show was hosted by John Daly during its years on ABC; Hugh James was the announcer. *Voice of Firestone* was seen as a series of specials from 1959 until 1962; it returned as a weekly series in the fall of 1962 for a final season.

VOICES AND VISIONS PBS

30 JANUARY 1988–23 APRIL 1988   The lives of notable American poets were chronicled on this thirteen-week series. Each program was devoted to a single poet. Among those profiled were Robert Frost, Langston Hughes, Walt Whitman, Emily Dickinson, T. S. Eliot, Wallace Stevens, and Sylvia Plath.

VOLTRON, DEFENDER OF THE UNIVERSE SYNDICATED

1985   An English language version of the long-running Japanese cartoon series about Voltron, the Ultimate Super-Robot.

VOLUME ONE ABC

16 JUNE 1949–21 JULY 1949   Wyllis Cooper wrote and produced the six programs telecast on this half-hour anthology series; the programs were titled "Volume One, Number One," "Volume One, Number Two," etc. Jack Lescoulie and Nancy Sheridan starred in the premiere, a story about a couple who robbed a bank and became trapped in their hotel room.

THE VOYAGE OF CHARLES DARWIN PBS

1980   This seven-part biography of the nineteenth-century British naturalist starred Malcolm Stoddard in the title role.

THE VOYAGE OF THE MIMI PBS

10 SEPTEMBER 1984–15 OCTOBER 1984   A series designed to interest youngsters in marine life, *The Voyage of the Mimi* was filmed aboard the *Mimi* off the Maine seacoast. The vessel was skippered by Clement Granville, with a crew of three teenagers.

VOYAGE TO THE BOTTOM OF THE SEA ABC

14 SEPTEMBER 1964–15 SEPTEMBER 1968   Hour-long science fiction series set aboard the *Seaview,* an American research submarine whose crew came in contact with a never-ending parade of aliens, monsters, and maniacs. Based on the film of the same name, the series featured Richard Basehart as Admiral Harriman Nelson; David Hedison as Captain Lee Crane; Bob Dowdell as Lieutenant Commander Chip Morton; Henry Kulky (1964–1965) as CPO Curley Jones; Terry Becker (1965–1968) as CPO Sharkey; Del Monroe as Kowalski; and Paul Trinka as Patterson. Irwin Allen created the series and was its executive producer. Some 110 episodes were made.

VOYAGERS! NBC

3 OCTOBER 1982–31 JULY 1983   This hour fantasy series starred Jon-Erik Hexum as Phineas Bogg, a "Traveler," a mysterious but not too bright fellow whose job was travel back in time and, when necessary, set straight the course of history. While traveling through the present, Bogg crashed into an apartment window, where he bumped into young Jeffrey Jones (played by Meeno Peluce), an orphan living unhappily with his aunt and uncle. Jeffrey then decided to accompany Bogg on his journeys, which was fortunate for Bogg, because Jeffrey knew his history cold. Their travels were accomplished by means of Bogg's Omni, an egg-shaped device whose controls could be set for any time and place in the past; when its red light was lit, Bogg and Jeffrey were alerted that the projected course of history was wrong.

W.E.B. NBC

13 SEPTEMBER 1978–5 OCTOBER 1978   The first dramatic series concerning the television industry, *W.E.B.* was the first fatality of the 1978–1979 season, lasting only five shows. It was inspired by the movie *Network* and was set at Trans American Broadcasting, a network staffed by a motley crew of lechers and cutthroats. Featured were Pamela Bellwood as Ellen Cunningham, a twenty-nine-year-old programming executive trying to make it in the male-dominated corporate structure; Alex Cord as Jack Kiley, the venal chief of programming; Richard Basehart as news director Gus Dunlap; Andrew Prine as the alcoholic sales chief, Dan Costello; Howard Witt as Walter Matthews, director of operations; Lee Wilkof as Harvey Pearlstein, head of research;

Tisch Raye as Christine Nichols; Peter Coffield as Kevin; and Stephen McNally as the Chairman of the Board. The executive producer of the hour show was Lin Bolen, former vice president in charge of daytime programming for NBC; Bolen was reported to have been the model for Faye Dunaway's character in *Network*.

WIOU   CBS
24 OCTOBER 1990–9 JANUARY 1991; 4 MARCH 1991–20 MARCH 1991   Hour dramatic series set at the newsroom of WNDY-TV, nicknamed WIOU by its staffers because of its precarious financial condition. The ensemble cast included: John Shea as Hank Zaret, the newly hired news director; Harris Yulin as the highly paid, skirt-chasing anchorman, Neal Frazier; Dick Van Patten as weatherman Floyd Graham; Phil Morris as ambitious reporter Eddie Bock; Wallace Langham as intern Willis Teitelbaum; Jayne Brook as field producer Ann Hudson; Joe Grifasi as public relations man Tony Pro; Mariette Hartley as the executive producer of the newcast, Liz McVay; Helen Shaver as Hank's old flame, reporter (and new coanchor) Kelby Robinson; Kate McNeil as new reporter Taylor Young, freshly arrived from Tampa; Scott Harlan as Ralph, the floor director; and Robin Gammell as station manager Kevin Doherty. Rosie Perez appeared in four episodes as sportscaster Lucy Hernandez. John Eisendrath and Kathryn Pratt created the series.

WKRP IN CINCINNATI   CBS
18 SEPTEMBER 1978–20 SEPTEMBER 1982   Half-hour sitcom set at WKRP, a moribund radio station in Cincinnati (coincidentally or not, Cincinnati has a real-life radio station with the call letters WKRC). With Gary Sandy as Andy Travis, the new program director hired to turn the station around, and who turned it into a rock and roll station; Gordon Jump as Arthur Carlson, the cautious station manager; Loni Anderson as Jennifer Marlowe, Carlson's gorgeous and intelligent secretary; Richard Sanders as Les Nessman, the station's news, weather, and agricultural department (Les was especially proud of his Silver Sow Award for agricultural reportage); Frank Bonner as Herb Tarlek, the self-infatuated sales manager; Jan Smithers as program assistant Bailey Quarters; Howard Hesseman as disc jockey Johnny Caravella, whose on-the-air nom de plume was Dr. Johnny Fever; and Tim Reid as Gordon Sims (better known as Venus Flytrap), a flamboyant black DJ brought in by Travis. Occasionally featured was Arthur Carlson's mother, who owned the station; Sylvia Sidney and Carol Bruce played Mama Carlson. Hugh Wilson created the series for MTM Enterprises. During its four years on CBS, the show underwent no less than seven time-slot changes.
   In 1991 the series was revived for first-run syndication: see *The New WKRP in Cincinnati*.

THE WACKIEST SHIP IN THE ARMY   NBC
19 SEPTEMBER 1965–4 SEPTEMBER 1966   Hour sitcom set during World War II aboard the *Kiwi,* a decrepit schooner built in 1871 and pressed into service by Army intelligence for use in the South Pacific. With Jack Warden as Major Simon Butcher; Gary Collins as Lieutenant Rip Riddle; Mike Kellin as Chief Miller; Rudy Solari as Nagurski; Mark Slade as Hollis; Don Penny as Tyler; Fred Smoot as Trivers; Duke Hobbie as Finch; William Zuckert as General Cross; and Charles Irving as Admiral Beckett. Based on the 1960 motion picture, the series was produced by Screen Gems.

WACKO   CBS
17 SEPTEMBER 1977–3 SEPTEMBER 1978   Half-hour weekend variety series for children, featuring musical numbers, skits, and blackouts. The Sylvers and Rip Taylor were frequent guests.

THE WACKY RACES   CBS
14 SEPTEMBER 1968–5 SEPTEMBER 1970   Saturday-morning cartoon series about a transcontinental automobile race. Spinoffs included *Dastardly and Muttley* and *The Perils of Penelope Pitstop*.

THE WACKY WORLD OF JONATHAN WINTERS   SYNDICATED

1972   Half-hour comedy series starring improvisational comedian Jonathan Winters and featuring Marian Mercer and the Soul Sisters. See also *The Jonathan Winters Show*.

WACKY WORLD OF SPORTS   SYNDICATED

1986   Bloopers from sports were the centerpiece of this syndicated series, hosted by the ubiquitous Bob Uecker, himself a former major league baseballer.

WAGON TRAIN   NBC/ABC

18 SEPTEMBER 1957–12 SEPTEMBER 1962 (NBC); 19 SEPTEMBER 1962–5 SEPTEMBER 1965 (ABC)   One of television's most popular westerns, *Wagon Train* was the number-two rated series for three seasons (1958–1959 through 1960–1961) before rising to the number-one spot in 1961–1962. It lost ground after switching networks in 1962 and an attempt to expand it from sixty to ninety minutes (emulating *The Virginian*) in the fall of 1963 was unsuccessful. *Wagon Train* was, of course, set aboard a wagon train along the trail from Missouri to California. To a greater extent than most westerns it relied on guest stars—each episode was entitled "The _____ Story," and was named after that week's guest character. Ward Bond (who had starred in *Wagonmaster,* the 1950 film on which the series was based) starred as the wagonmaster, Major Seth Adams, from 1957 until his death late in 1960. On 15 March 1961, John McIntire was introduced as the new wagonmaster, Chris Hale; McIntire remained with the show until the end. Also featured were Robert Horton (1957–1960 and 1961–1962) as scout Flint McCullough; Frank McGrath as Charlie Wooster, the cook; Terry Wilson as Bill Hawks; Denny (Scott) Miller (spring 1961–1963) as scout Duke Shannon; Michael Burns (spring 1963–1965) as Barnaby West, a teenager; Robert Fuller (1963–1965) as Cooper, *Wagon Train*'s last scout. Howard Christie produced the show for Revue Studios.

WAIT 'TIL YOUR FATHER GETS HOME   SYNDICATED

1972   This Hanna-Barbera cartoon series was aimed at an adult audience and was strongly reminiscent of *All in the Family*. Voices included those of Tom Bosley as Harry Boyle, the father; Joan Gerber as wife Irma; Kristina Holland as daughter Alice; David Hayward as son Chet; Jackie Haley as son Jamie; and Jack Burns as neighbor Ralph.

WAKE RATTLE & ROLL   SYNDICATED

1990–1991   This half-hour daily kids' show from Hanna-Barbera Productions was intended for early morning time slots. It was set in the basement of the Baxter household, where teenage son Sam (played by R. J. Williams) hung out with a robot known as DECKS, and watched cartoons. Tim Lawrence performed as DECKS, while Rob Paulsen provided the voice. Also appearing were Avery Schreiber as Grandpa Quirk, Ebonie Smith as K. C., and Terri Ivens as Sam's older sister, Debbie.

A WALK THROUGH THE 20TH CENTURY WITH BILL MOYERS   PBS

11 JANUARY 1984–27 JUNE 1984   TV journalist Bill Moyers sought to depict the "vivacity of the past" on this wide-ranging, nineteen-week documentary series.

WALKER, TEXAS RANGER   CBS

22 APRIL 1993–1 MAY 1993; 25 SEPTEMBER 1993–   Chuck Norris, star of numerous action films, literally headlined this hour crime show: Its official title was *Chuck Norris Is Walker, Texas Ranger*. Norris played Cordell Walker, a modern day Texas Ranger who relied heavily on his fists and his martial arts skills. Also featured were Clarence Gilyard as his new partner, Jimmy Trivette, who preferred to use scientific methods to solve crimes; Gailard Sartain (spring 1993) and Noble Willingham (fall 1993–   ) as Walker's pal, C. D. Parker, a retired Ranger; Sheree J. Wilson as prosecutor Alex Cahill; and Floyd Red Crow Westerman as Uncle Ray, the wise Native American who raised the half-Indian Walker after his father had died.

Walker's original production company, Cannon Pictures, ceased production after making only four episodes because of financial difficulties; CBS Entertainment then agreed to provide financing, and production was able to continue.

WALKING TALL   NBC
17 JANUARY 1981–6 JUNE 1981   This violent hour crime show was based on the 1973 film and its three sequels (two theatrical films and a 1978 TV-movie, "A Real American Hero"), which in turn were based on a real-life character, Tennessee sheriff Buford Pusser, whose wife was killed in an attempt on his life. The TV series starred Bo Svenson (who had appeared in the theatrical sequels) as Pusser, the club-wielding sheriff of lawless McNeil County. With him were Walter Barnes as his father, Carl Pusser; Harold Sylvester as Deputy Aaron Fairfax; Jeff Lester as Deputy Grady Spooner; Courtney Pledger as Deputy Joan Litton; Rad Daly as Mike, Pusser's teenage son; and Heather McAdam as Dwana, Pusser's preteen daughter.

WALL $TREET WEEK WITH LOUIS RUKEYSER   PBS
7 JANUARY 1972–   Long-running weekly public affairs program, focusing on the American economy, the stock market, and personal investing. Louis Rukeyser is the host and moderator.

WALLY GATOR   SYNDICATED
1963   Hanna-Barbera cartoon series about an alligator who wouldn't stay in the zoo, much to the chargin of Mr. Tuiddles, his keeper.

WALLY'S WORKSHOP   SYNDICATED
1971–1977   Half-hour home improvement show, hosted by Wally Bruner, with help from his wife, Natalie Bruner.

WALT DISNEY   ABC/NBC/CBS
27 OCTOBER 1954–17 SEPTEMBER 1961 (ABC); 24 SEPTEMBER 1961–13 SEPTEMBER 1981 (NBC); 26 SEPTEMBER 1981–24 SEPTEMBER 1983 (CBS); 2 FEBRUARY 1986–11 SEPTEMBER 1988 (ABC); 9 OCTOBER 1988–9 SEPTEMBER 1990 (NBC)   Though Walt Disney is remembered chiefly for his films, his television series was one of the most successful, and remarkable, in the history of broadcasting. It was aired on all three commercial networks under several different titles, but it was really one continuous series; as such, it was TV's longest-running prime-time series, lasting twenty-nine consecutive seasons. *Disneyland* was the first ABC series to crack Nielsen's Top Twenty (this was no mean achievement, because for many years ABC had far fewer affiliates than CBS or NBC). It was also the first prime-time anthology series for children, and the first to incorporate miniseries (though the term itself was not used until much later). It even survived the death of its host and creator.

Walter Elias Disney was born in Chicago in 1901, and began making cartoons in Kansas City in the 1920s. In 1926 he moved to Los Angeles and formed a production company with his older brother, Roy Disney. In 1928 Disney's most famous cartoon character, Mickey Mouse, first came to the screen (Disney himself supplied Mickey's voice). Disney also made some of the first sound cartoons that year, and in 1932 produced the first film in full technicolor. Two years later Disney's second most famous cartoon star, Donald Duck, appeared. By the end of the decade Disney had produced the first feature length animated film, *Snow White and the Seven Dwarfs*. Other features, such *Fantasia, Dumbo,* and *Bambi* followed soon thereafter. By the end of the 1940s he had begun his famous nature documentaries, *True Life Adventures,* and had also started producing live-action (or combination live and animated) films, such as *Song of the South*.

Though Disney produced one or two television specials early in the 1950s, it was not until 1954 that he seriously pursued the idea of a weekly show. By this time he had also laid the plans for his real-life "Magic Kingdom," Disneyland, a year-round amusement park divided into four areas—Frontierland, Adventureland, Fantasyland, and Tomorrowland. The ABC network, which had merged with United Paramount Theaters in 1953, agreed to invest in the venture and to carry the proposed series. Disney was thus able to use the show, which was titled *Disneyland* from 1954 to 1958, not only to promote the park but also to publicize upcoming theatrical features from Disney Studios (a year later, ABC managed to interest two other film studios in similar promotional shows; see *M-G-M Parade* and *Warner Brothers Presents*). The series' premiere telecast, "The Disneyland Story," showed the construction of the park and whetted the curiosity of countless young viewers. Over the succeeding years, several shows were devoted to Disneyland.

In general, the mixture of programs during the first year was typical of the subsequent seasons: edited versions of previously released theatrical features, coupled with a number of original productions (teasers for forthcoming releases were also featured in later seasons). The original shows included documentaries on natural history, behind-the-scenes broadcasts from Disney Studios, and several dramatic shows. The most popular programs of the first season (and perhaps of the entire series) fell into the latter category: the three Davy Crockett segments. These shows (together with two more that were televised the following season) may properly be considered as television's first miniseries. All of them starred Fess Parker as American folk hero Davy Crockett, and they included: "Davy Crockett, Indian Fighter" (15 December 1954), "Davy Crockett Goes to Congress" (26 January 1955), "Davy Crockett at the Alamo" (23 February 1955), "Davy Crockett's Keelboat Race" (16 November 1955), and "Davy Crockett and the River Pirates" (14 December 1955). Disney later admitted that the enormous popularity of the first three segments (especially "Davy Crockett at the Alamo") caught everyone at Disney Studios by surprise; fortunately, however, Disney was quick to capitalize on the hit show by licensing the distribution and sale of all kinds of Davy Crockett paraphernalia; hundreds of thousands of "coonskin" caps and bubble gum cards were quickly bought by young fans.

The Disney people tried hard for the next several years to develop a character as popular as Davy Crockett. Several miniseries were launched hopefully between 1957 and 1960, but none of them came close to eclipsing the Crockett stories. Among the also-rans were: "The Saga of Andy Burnett," starring Jerome Courtland as Andy Burnett, a pioneer who traveled from Pittsburgh to the Rockies (the first of the six stories was introduced 2 October 1957; they were written by Tom Blackburn, and were based on the novels by Stewart Edward White); "The Nine Lives of Elfego Baca," starring Robert Loggia as Elfego Baca, a peace-loving New Mexico lawman (introduced 3 October 1958, six episodes were shown during the 1958–1959 season, and more were shown during the following season); "Tales of Texas John Slaughter," starring Tom Tryon as Texas Ranger John Slaughter (at least thirteen segments were shown, beginning 31 October 1958); "The Swamp Fox," starring Leslie Nielsen as General Francis Marion, the Revolutionary War hero of the Carolinas (six episodes were shown during the 1959–1960 season, beginning 23 October, and more were shown during the 1960–1961 season; General Marion even sported a foxtail on his three-cornered hat, but the headpiece failed to capture the public fancy as the Crockett cap had).

In the fall of 1958 the title of Disney's series was changed to *Walt Disney Presents*. Later that season a Disney experiment produced one of the first stereophonic broadcasts of a television program; on 30 January 1959, "The Peter Tchaikovsky Story" was telecast, and in certain cities the audio portion of the broadcast was transmitted by two radio stations—an AM station carried one channel, while an FM outlet carried the other (FM multiplex stereo was still a phenomenon of the future).

After seven seasons on ABC, Disney switched to NBC in the fall of 1961; the new network affiliation gave Disney the opportunity to broadcast in color, and the show was thus retitled *Walt Disney's Wonderful World of Color*. On the 1961 premiere (24 September), Disney introduced his first major new cartoon character in years, the highly knowledgeable Professor Ludwig von Drake, in "An Adventure in Color, Mathmagic Land." It was the first of several educational shows hosted by von Drake, who was an uncle of Donald Duck (some of the shows were cohosted by Disney himself). The first few seasons of *Wonderful World of Color* consisted mainly of new features, such as the three-part "The Prince and the Pauper," or the two-part "The Mooncussers." The miniseries idea was revived briefly in 1964, with "The Adventures of Gallagher," starring Roger Mobley as Gallagher, a nineteenth-century boy reporter. By the late 1960s, however, more and more of the programs consisted of reruns of Disney films and cartoons. In 1969, almost three years after Disney's death, the show was retitled *The Wonderful World of Disney*. In the fall of 1978 the show celebrated the beginning of its twenty-fifth year on television with a two-part retrospective. The show was retitled *Disney's Wonderful World* in the fall of 1979.

In 1981 the series ended its twenty-year affiliation with NBC and moved to CBS, where it ran another two seasons. In 1983 a cable service was established; The Disney Channel presented entertainment for children, culled from the TV series *Zorro* (Disney's 1957 series) and other Disney films and cartoons.

After a two-and-one-half-year absence from network television, Disney-produced product returned in February 1986, back again on ABC. *The Disney Sunday Movie* ran for two and one half years, in a two-hour format from 1986 until September 1987, when it was trimmed to an hour. The series was hosted by Michael Eisner, the head of Disney Studios, and consisted of reruns of classic Disney theatrical films and first-run made-for-TV movies.

In the fall of 1988 the series again switched networks and titles, moving to NBC as *The Magical World of Disney*. Again hosted by Eisner, the series presented some recurring programs, such as "Parent Trap III," with Hayley Mills (who had starred in the 1961 Disney film *The Parent Trap*), Barry Bostwick, and the Creel Triplets (Joy, Leanna and Monica), "The Absent-Minded Professor," starring Harry Anderson, and "A Brand New Life," starring Barbara Eden. On 20 November 1988 an updated Davy Crockett story was telecast; "Davy Crockett: Rainbow in the Thunder" starred Tim Dunigan as Crockett and Gary Grubbs as Georgie Russell.

WALTER & EMILY NBC
16 NOVEMBER 1991–22 FEBRUARY 1992   Half-hour sitcom about two grandparents who, when not bickering with each other, helped their grown son raise his own son. The cast included Brian Keith as the grandfather, Walter Collins, a retired salesman; Cloris Leachman as the grandmother, Emily; Christopher McDonald as their son, Matt, a divorced San Francisco sportswriter whose job often took him away from home; Matthew Lawrence as their grandson, eleven-year-old Zack; and Edan Gross as Zack's pal, Hartley. Occasionally featured were Sandy Baron and Shelley Berman as Walter's cronies, Stan and Albert, who were also retired salesmen.

WALTER CRONKITE'S UNIVERSE
See UNIVERSE

THE WALTER WINCHELL SHOW ABC/NBC
5 OCTOBER 1952–26 JUNE 1955 (ABC); 5 OCTOBER 1956–28 DECEMBER 1956 (NBC); 2 OCTOBER 1960–6 NOVEMBER 1960 (ABC)
THE WALTER WINCHELL FILE ABC/SYNDICATED
2 OCTOBER 1957–28 MARCH 1958 (ABC); 1958 (SYNDICATED)   Syndicated newspaper columnist Walter Winchell tried several formats on television, but none was particularly successful (Winchell, who died in 1972, is probably best remembered by TV audiences as the narrator of *The Untouchables*). His first series was a fifteen-minute Sunday-night newscast, which lasted three seasons. In 1956, and again in 1960, he was the host of a half-hour variety show; both series were dropped in midseason. In 1957 he was the host and narrator of *The Walter Winchell File,* a half-hour series of crime dramas produced by Mort Briskin. Twenty-six programs were shown on ABC during the 1957–1958 season, and an additional thirteen were added to the first twenty-six when the series went into syndication.

THE WALTONS CBS
14 SEPTEMBER 1972–20 AUGUST 1981   An unpretentious, low-key dramatic series, *The Waltons* told the story of a close-knit family living in rural Virginia during the Depression years. Its creator, Earl Hamner, Jr., based the show largely on his own experiences. One of eight children, Hamner grew up near Schuyler, Virginia, and left home in the late 1930s to become a professional writer. Hamner's first effort at

dramatizing his boyhood ended up as a film, *Spencer's Mountain,* set in Wyoming, and starring Henry Fonda, Maureen O'Hara, and James MacArthur as Clay-Boy.

The genesis of the TV series was a Christmas special, "The Homecoming" (19 December 1971), written by Hamner; the telecast was not intended to be a pilot for a series, but it attracted such favorable public reaction that CBS decided to build a series around the Walton family that Hamner had created. The roles of three of the four Walton adults were recast for the series, but the roles of the seven Walton children were filled by those who had appeared in "The Homecoming": Richard Thomas as John (John-Boy) Walton, Jr.; the eldest; Jon Walmsley as Jason; Judy Norton as Mary Ellen; Eric Scott as Ben; Mary Elizabeth McDonough as Erin; David W. Harper as James Robert (Jim-Bob); and Kami Cotler as Elizabeth. The adult roles on the series were played by: Michael Learned as Olivia Walton, the mother; Ralph Waite as John Walton, the father; Will Geer as Zeb Walton, the grandfather; Ellen Corby as Esther Walton, the grandmother (in "The Homecoming," those parts were played by Patricia Neal, Andrew Duggan, Edgar Bergen, and Ellen Corby).

As a series, *The Waltons* was given little chance to succeed in 1972 when CBS scheduled it on Thursdays opposite *The Flip Wilson Show* on NBC. However, the show attracted not only good reviews (and several Emmys), but also a large enough audience to warrant its renewal (it finished twentieth its first season); in its second season it toppled Flip Wilson, finishing second to *All in the Family* in the seasonal Nielsens. Its popularity remained fairly steady through the 1970s. One reason for its endurance was that, as the show evolved in time (between 1972 and 1980, it moved from 1933 to 1943), its characters were allowed to mature and develop. A second reason may be that the large Walton family was complemented by a small host of supporting characters. Principal members of the latter category included: Joe Conley as Ike Godsey, proprietor of the general store in Walton's Mountain, the tiny Jefferson County hamlet where most of the action took place; Helen Kleeb and Mary Jackson as sisters Mamie and Emily Baldwin, a pair of spinsters who innocently brewed moonshine in their stately home; John Crawford as Sheriff Ep Bridges; Mariclare Costello (1972–1975) as Emily Hunter, the schoolteacher; John Ritter (1973–1975) as Reverend Fordwick, who married Miss Hunter; Ronnie Claire Edwards (January 1975–1981) as John's distant cousin, Cora Beth, a frustrated socialite who married Ike Godsey; and Rachel Longaker (1976–1979) as Aimée, a little girl adopted by Ike and Cora Beth.

Life did not remain static for the several members of the Walton clan. John-Boy, an aspiring writer (like his creator, Earl Hamner, Jr.), graduated from high school, attended Boatwright University, started a local newspaper, finally left Walton's Mountain for New York, and later became a war correspondent in London (in real life, Richard Thomas decided to leave *The Waltons* in 1977 after five seasons, though he returned afterward for guest appearances); Jason, a musician, also finished high school and got a job playing piano in a roadhouse in order to pay for further studies; Mary Ellen became a nurse, got married (Tom Bower joined the cast in November 1976 as her husband, Dr. Curtis Willard), and had a baby, John Curtis (in real life, Judy Norton was married in 1976, and was billed as Judy Norton-Taylor afterward; John Curtis was played by Marshall and Michael Reed); Ben helped out John-Boy on the newspaper, and later worked for the family lumber business; and Erin found secretarial work.

Other changes affected the Walton adults. Ellen Corby, who played Grandma, suffered a stroke in the fall of 1976 and was absent from the series for a year and a half, returning at the end of the 1977–1978 season. Before production resumed for the 1978–1979 season, Will Geer (Grandpa) died. He was not replaced, and the opening show of the seventh season concerned the family's adjustment to Grandpa Walton's death. During the 1978–1979 season an episode was televised in which Mary Ellen's husband, Dr. Curtis Willard, was killed at Pearl Harbor. Later that season, Olivia Walton learned that she had tuberculosis and left Walton's Mountain for a sanitarium (in real life, Michael Learned's contract with the show's production company expired late in 1978, and she announced her intention to cease appearing as a regular). In the spring of 1979 Leslie Winston joined the cast as Cindy, Ben's wife, and in the fall of that year more changes occurred. Ellen Corby did not return to the series, but Michael Learned agreed to make a number of appearances. Three new regulars were also added: Peggy Rea as Olivia's cousin, Rose Burton, who came with her two grandchildren to take care of the Walton household; Martha Nix as Rose's granddaughter, Serena; and Keith Mitchell as her grandson, Jeffrey. Robert Wightman appeared as John-Boy in the 1979 Thanksgiving episode. Later that season Ben and Cindy's daughter, Virginia, was born. Lewis Arquette was also featured as Erin's employer, J. D. Pickett.

More changes occurred in the fall of 1980. All four Walton boys had left home—John-Boy was writing for *Stars and Stripes* in Paris, Jason was also stationed in France, Ben had joined the Seabees and was sent to the South Pacific, and Jim-Bob was being trained at Fort Langley, Virginia. Jeffrey and Serena Burton had gone off to live with their father and his new wife. Mary Ellen's husband, Curtis Willard, thought to have been killed at Pearl Harbor, turned up alive—but not well—in Florida. Rendered impotent by an injury, he refused to return to her.

The Waltons left the weekly schedule in 1981. A few specials were subsequently televised on NBC, such as "A Wedding on Walton's Mountain" (in which Erin got married; 22 February 1982), "Mother's Day on Walton's Mountain" (9 May 1982), and "A Day for Thanks on Walton's Mountain" (22 November 1982). The surviving members of the clan returned to CBS for "A Walton Thanksgiving Reunion" (21 November 1993), which was set at the time of President Kennedy's assassination in 1963, and for "A Walton Wedding" (12 February 1995), when John-Boy tied the knot.

The Waltons was the first family dramatic series of the 1970s; its success led to a proliferation of similar efforts, such as *Apple's Way, Eight Is Enough, Family, The Family Holvak, The Fitzpatricks, Little House on the Prairie, Mulligan's Stew,* and *The New Land.* It was also the first series from Lorimar Productions, a company founded in 1968 by Lee Rich and Merv Adelson (*Apple's Way* and *Eight Is Enough* were also from Lorimar). Lee Rich and Earl Hamner were the executive producers of *The Waltons.*

WANTED   CBS
20 OCTOBER 1955–12 JANUARY 1956   Fugitives from justice were the quarry on this half-hour documentary series hosted by Walter McGraw. Dossiers of wanted criminals were presented, along with interviews with law enforcement officials and relatives of those wanted.

WANTED—DEAD OR ALIVE   CBS
6 SEPTEMBER 1958–29 MARCH 1961   Western starring Steve McQueen as bounty hunter Josh Randall, who toted an 1892 44/40 center-fire Winchester carbine that he affectionately referred to as his "Mare's Laig." In the spring of 1960, Wright King was featured as Jason Nichols, a deputy sheriff who teamed up with Randall. A total of 94 half-hour episodes were filmed, with Vincent Fennelly the executive producer for Four Star Films. The pilot for the series, "The Bounty Hunter," was aired on *Trackdown* on 7 March 1958. In 1987 a theatrical film was released: *Wanted: Dead or Alive* starred Rutger Hauer as Nick Randall, grandson of Josh.

WAR: A COMMENTARY BY GWYNNE DYER   PBS
1 OCTOBER 1985–19 NOVEMBER 1985   British military historian Gwynne Dyer hosted the first seven programs in this eight-part examination of war and warfare, historical and contemporary. The eighth program, "War: The Knife Edge of Deterrence," was moderated by Edwin Newman, and featured Secretary of Defense Caspar Weinberger and three former secretaries of defense.

WAR AND PEACE   PBS
20 NOVEMBER 1973–15 JANUARY 1974   The fourteen-and-a-half-hour adaptation of Tolstoy's novel by the BBC was shown on American television in nine parts. Principal players included: Anthony Hopkins as Pierre; David Swift as Napoleon; Morag Hood as Natasha; Alan Dobie as Andrei; and Anthony Jacobs as Prince Nikolai.

WAR AND PEACE IN THE NUCLEAR AGE   PBS
23 JANUARY 1989–17 APRIL 1989   The development and proliferation of atomic weapons were chronicled in this thirteen-week documentary series.

WAR AND REMEMBRANCE   ABC
13 NOVEMBER 1988–23 NOVEMBER 1988; 7 MAY 1989–14 MAY 1989   The thirty-hour sequel to the 1983 miniseries *The Winds of War, War and Remembrance* was based on Herman Wouk's novel about World War II, and was written for television by Wouk, Dan Curtis and Earl W. Wallace. Curtis also served as executive producer and director. It was filmed in ten countries, using 757 sets; some of the concentration camp scenes were filmed on location at Auschwitz in Poland. The November portion of the miniseries, shown in seven installments, went from 1941 to 1943, while the May airing, in five parts, ran from 1943 to the end of the war in 1945. Principal players included: Robert Mitchum as American naval officer Victor "Pug" Henry; Polly Bergen as his wife, Rhoda Henry; Victoria Tennant as Pamela Tudsbury; Jane Seymour as Natalie Jastrow; Hart Bochner as Byron Henry; Michael Woods as Warren Henry; Sir John Gielgud as Aaron Jastrow; Peter Graves as Palmer Kirby; Robert Hardy as Winston Churchill; and Steven Berkoff as Adolf Hitler. Some of the combat footage consisted of outtakes from a 1941 motion picture, *Dive Bombers*. Because of the huge expense of the production (estimated at $110 million), and the mediocre ratings it garnered, ABC is believed to have lost at least $20 million on the telecast. The era of the long-form miniseries had, unfortunately, already begun its eclipse.

WAR OF THE WORLDS   SYNDICATED
1988–1990   This hour sci-fi series was set in the present time, thirty-five years after the 1953 film version of H. G. Wells's novel. At the end of the film, the alien invaders had supposedly been neutralized by bacteria. As the TV series opened, however, it turned out that the aliens had not been killed, but had reawakened from their underground disposal sites. They now had the power to take over a human body. Fighting the new menace was a team of four: Dr. Harrison Blackwood (played by Jared Martin), computer scientist Norton Drake (Philip Akin), microbiologist Suzanne McCullough (Lynda Mason Green), and Lieutenant Colonel Paul Ironhorse (Richard Chaves). During the show's second season another group of aliens, known as the Morthrens, came to Earth, making life even more difficult for the home team. Also featured were Rachel Blanchard as Suzanne's daughter, Debi; Adrian Paul as good guy John Kincaid; Catherine Disher as alien leader Mana; and Denis Forest as alien leader Malzor. Greg Strangis created the TV series.

WARNER BROTHERS PRESENTS   ABC
13 SEPTEMBER 1955–4 SEPTEMBER 1956   This hour umbrella series, which heralded Warner Brothers' entry into television series production, was hosted by Gig Young. During the season three series were regularly shown in the time slot, together with occasional hour dramas. All three shows were based on popular Warner Brothers films: *Casablanca, Cheyenne,* and *King's Row. Cheyenne* was the only one of the trio to be renewed for a second season. See individual titles for details.

WASHINGTON: BEHIND CLOSED DOORS   ABC
6 SEPTEMBER 1977–11 SEPTEMBER 1977   Six-part miniseries adapted from John Ehrlichman's novel, *The Company*. Principal players included: Jason Robards as President Richard Monckton; Cliff Robertson as William Martin, director of the CIA; Lois Nettleton as Linda Martin; Stefanie Powers as Sally Whalen; Andy Griffith as Esker Anderson, Monckton's predecessor in office; Robert Vaughn as Frank Flaherty, Monckton's brusque chief of staff; Barry Nelson as Bob Bailey; Harold Gould as Carl Tessler; Tony Bill as Adam Gardiner; Nicholas Pryor as Hank Ferris, press secretary; John Houseman as Myron Dunn; and Skip Homeier as Lars Haglund. Stan Kallis was the executive producer for Paramount TV; David Rintels and Eric Bercovici wrote the script.

WASHINGTON CONVERSATION   CBS
26 FEBRUARY 1961–16 SEPTEMBER 1962   Paul Niven interviewed a single guest each week on this Sunday-afternoon public affairs program.

WASHINGTON EXCLUSIVE   DUMONT
21 JUNE 1953–1 NOVEMBER 1953   Sunday-evening public affairs program, moderated by Frank McNaughton, featuring a panel of former senators.

WASHINGTON MERRY-GO-ROUND   SYNDICATED
1954–1957   Fifteen minutes of commentary on political goings-on by Drew Pearson, whose syndicated newspaper column bore the same title.

WASHINGTON REPORT   DUMONT
22 MAY 1951–31 AUGUST 1951   Tris Coffin hosted this twice-weekly fifteen-minute interview series, broadcast from Washington, D.C.

WASHINGTON REPORT   CBS
23 SEPTEMBER 1962–8 SEPTEMBER 1963   Sunday afternoon news analysis series, hosted by CBS News correspondent David Schoenbrun.

WASHINGTON SPOTLIGHT   SYNDICATED
1953   Marquis Childs interviewed newsmakers on this filmed series.

WASHINGTON SQUARE   NBC
21 OCTOBER 1956–13 JUNE 1957   This hour-long musical comedy series was scheduled approximately every other week. It was originally seen on Sunday afternoons, but later shifted to various time slots throughout the week. Its star, Ray Bolger, played himself, and Elaine Stritch costarred as the operator of the Greenwich Village Inn. Other regulars included Daniza Ilitsch, Jo Wilder, Kay Armen, Rusty Draper, Arnold Stang, the Three Flames, the Martins, and the Bil and Cora Baird Puppets.

WASHINGTON WEEK IN REVIEW   NET-PBS
22 FEBRUARY 1967–   Half-hour public affairs discussion program on current events. Each week a panel of four journalists discussed selected topics with a moderator. Peter Lisagor served as moderator until 1976, when Paul Duke took over. Duke continued as moderator until March 1994, when Ken Bode succeeded him. On Duke's next-to-last program he interviewed President Bill Clinton at the White House.

WATCH MR. WIZARD
See MR. WIZARD

WATCH THE WORLD   NBC
23 APRIL 1950–20 AUGUST 1950   John Cameron Swayze first hosted this Sunday afternoon show, presenting film features of interest to children. Frank McCall produced the half-hour show. Don Goddard succeeded Swayze.

THE WATCHER   UPN
17 JANUARY 1995–11 APRIL 1995   This unusual hour anthology series was set in Las Vegas, where the week's story was observed and narrated by a man known simply as the Watcher. A security executive at the Desert Flower Casino in the Riviera Hotel, the omniscient observer did his watching on a bank of video screens. Rapper Sir Mix-a-Lot starred as the Watcher. Christopher Crowe created the series.

WATER WORLD   SYNDICATED
1972–1975   Half-hour documentary series on the oceans and marine world, narrated first by Lloyd Bridges, later by James Franciscus.

WATERFRONT   SYNDICATED
1954–1956   Half-hour adventure series, set principally aboard the *Cheryl Ann,* a tugboat in the San Pedro (Calif.) harbor. With Preston Foster as Captain John Herrick; Lois Moran as his wife, May Herrick; Pinky Tomlin as Tip Hubbard; Douglas Dick as Carl, the Herricks' son, who worked aboard the tug. Ben Fox created and produced the show, which was filmed at Hal Roach Studios. The *Cheryl Ann* was really the *Milton S. Patrick,* an honest-to-goodness tug which plied the San Pedro harbor.

THE WAVERLY WONDERS   NBC
22 SEPTEMBER 1978–6 OCTOBER 1978   An early fatality of the 1978–1979 season, *The Waverly Wonders* was dropped after only three airings. The half-hour sitcom, apparently inspired by the movie *The Bad News Bears,* starred Joe Namath as Joe Casey, the newly arrived coach of the hapless basketball team at Waverly High School. Also on hand were Gwynne Gilford as the principal; James Staley as faculty member Alan Kerner; Ben Piazza as faculty member George Benton; Joshua Grenrock as Faguzzi; Kim Lankford as Connie Rafkin; Tierre Turner as Hasty; and Charles Bloom as Johnny Tate. The show was created by William Bickley and Michael Warren, and produced by Steve Zacharias and Bruce Kane; Lee Rich and Marc Merson were the executive producers for Lorimar Productions.

THE WAY   SYNDICATED
1955–1957   Half-hour series of religious dramas, produced under the auspices of the Methodist Church.

THE WAY IT WAS   PBS
3 OCTOBER 1974–14 MAY 1977   Curt Gowdy hosted this sports nostalgia show, on which he and guest athletes viewed film clips of famous sporting events and reminisced.

WAY OF THE WORLD   NBC
3 JANUARY 1955–7 OCTOBER 1955   Daytime dramatic series; some presentations lasted only one day, while others ran a week or two. Stories were introduced by Gloria Louis, who appeared as Linda Porter.

WAY OUT   CBS
31 MARCH 1961–14 JULY 1961   Half-hour science fiction anthology series hosted by writer Roald Dahl.

WAY OUT GAMES   CBS
11 SEPTEMBER 1976–4 SEPTEMBER 1977   CBS's answer to ABC's *Junior Almost Anything Goes, Way Out Games* was a weekend athletic contest for teams of teenagers representing the states. Produced by Jack Barry and Dan Enright, the half-hour show was hosted by Sonny Fox.

WAY TO GO   SYNDICATED
1980   Half-hour informational series for children, hosted by Peter Kastner (former star of *The Ugliest Girl in Town*). One regular segment was a game called "Word Watchers," hosted by Bill Armstrong, in which two contestants attempted to make words from the letters contained in a larger word.

THE WAYANS BROS.   WB
11 JANUARY 1995–   The first program broadcast on the WB Network, this sitcom starred brothers Marlon Wayans and Shawn Wayans as brothers Marlon and Shawn Williams, two guys who were always looking for a money-making opportunity. The series costarred John Witherspoon as their father, Pop, who owned a restaurant, and Lela Rochon as Shawn's girlfriend, Lisa.

WAYNE & SHUSTER   SYNDICATED
1980   Half-hour comedy-variety show hosted by comedy duo Johnny Wayne and Frank Shuster.

WAYNE AND SHUSTER TAKE AN AFFECTIONATE LOOK AT . . .   CBS
17 JUNE 1966–29 JULY 1966   Canadian comics Johnny Wayne and Frank Shuster hosted this semidocumentary series. Each show focused on a particular aspect of comedy; one show, for example, was a tribute to Jack Benny and incorporated clips from Benny's films and TV series.

WE GOT IT MADE   NBC/SYNDICATED
8 SEPTEMBER 1983–30 MARCH 1984 (NBC); 1987–1988 (SYNDICATED)   Half-hour sitcom about two Manhattan bachelors who hired a gorgeous live-in housekeeper, much to the consternation of their girlfriends. With Teri Copley as the naive house-keeper, Mickey Mackenzie, a Marilyn Monroe clone; Matt McCoy as natty lawyer David Tucker; Tom Villard as his unkempt New Wave roommate, Jay Bostwick, an importer of marginally useful merchandise; Bonnie Urseth as Jay's girlfriend, Beth, a kindergarten teacher; and Stepfanie Kramer as David's girlfriend, Claudia. Gordon Farr and Lynne Farr Brao created the series; Fred Silverman (former NBC president) was the executive producer. Writing in the *Boston Globe,* critic Jack Thomas proclaimed *We Got It Made* as "This year's absolutely, positively unchallenged, worst new show." Nevertheless, the series' premiere telecast ranked second for the week. In 1987 MGM/UA produced new episodes for syndication. Copley and Villard returned from the original cast. John Hillner replaced Matt McCoy as David Tucker, and Ron Karabatsos and Lance Wilson-White appeared as neighbors Max Papavasilios Sr. and Jr.

WE TAKE YOUR WORD   CBS
1 APRIL 1950–23 JANUARY 1951; 9 MARCH 1951–1 JUNE 1951   John K. M. McCaffery hosted this prime-time game show on which a celebrity panel tried to supply the definitions and derivations of words suggested by home viewers. Ilka Chase and Abe Burrows were regular panelists.

WE, THE PEOPLE   CBS/NBC
1 JUNE 1948–25 OCTOBER 1949 (CBS); 4 NOVEMBER 1949–26 SEPTEMBER 1952 (NBC)
This early interview series began on radio in 1936. When it came to television in 1948, Dwight Weist was the host, but in 1949 Dan Seymour replaced him. The show combined celebrity interviews with human interest stories.

WE THE PEOPLE   PBS
22 SEPTEMBER 1987–13 OCTOBER 1987   ABC news anchor Peter Jennings hosted this four-part study of the impact of the United States Constitution on modern society. President Ronald Reagan introduced the series, which examined the following topics: "Free to Believe," "What Price Equality?" "Law and Order," and "Who's in Charge?"

THE WEAKER (?) SEX   SYNDICATED
1968   Pamela Mason interviewed female guests on this half-hour talk show.

THE WEB   CBS/NBC
4 JULY 1950–26 SEPTEMBER 1954 (CBS); 7 JULY 1957–6 OCTOBER 1957 (NBC);   A half-hour dramatic anthology series, *The Web* specialized in stories about people who created the very crises in which they became involved. Jonathan Blake hosted. Frank Heller, and then Vincent McConnor, produced the show for Goodson-Todman Productions. After a four-year run on CBS *The Web* surfaced on NBC as a summer replacement for *The Loretta Young Show.* William Bryant narrated.

THE WEBB PIERCE SHOW   SYNDICATED

1955   Webb Pierce hosted this half-hour country-and-western-music show, broadcast from Nashville.

WEBSTER   ABC/SYNDICATED

16 SEPTEMBER 1983–11 SEPTEMBER 1987 (ABC); 1987–1988 (SYNDICATED)   This half-hour sitcom bore a passing resemblance to NBC's *Diff'rent Strokes*—here, a white couple become the guardians of a diminutive black child who had recently been orphaned. Featured were Alex Karras as George Papadopolis, an ex-pro football player who had promised a black teammate that he would, if necessary, look after his young son; Susan Clark (Karras's real-life wife) as George's wife, Katherine Calder-Young, an ombudsperson for the city of Chicago; Emmanuel Lewis as the orphan, seven-year-old Webster Long (Lewis was actually twelve, but only three feet, four inches tall); and Henry Polic II as Katherine's secretary, Jerry Silver. In the fall of 1984 three new cast members were added, as Webster and his family moved out of their apartment and into a Victorian house. Eugene Roche and Cathryn Damon played Bill and Cassie Parker, owners (and renovators) of the house; Ben Vereen appeared as Webster's uncle, Phillip Long, who tried to win custody of the child. Vereen left after one season, Roche and Damon after two, when George and Katherine bought the house from the Parkers, who moved to Florida. Corky Nemec was added for the show's final season, as George's nephew Nicky, who lived with them while his parents were overseas.

   The genesis of the series came from two sources: ABC programming chief Lew Erlicht had spotted Emmanuel Lewis in a Burger King commercial, and wanted to build a series around him. At the same time, producer Stu Silver had wanted to create a sitcom with characters modeled after those played by Spencer Tracy and Katharine Hepburn in the 1942 film *Woman of the Year*.

WEDDING DAY   NBC

8 JUNE 1981–12 JUNE 1981   A throwback to *Bride and Groom,* this half-hour daytime series featured a wedding—and a wedding party—every day during its one-week tryout. The ratings were disappointing, and the series was not picked up. Mary Ann Mobley and Huell Howser were the cohosts.

WEDDING PARTY   ABC

1 APRIL 1968–12 JULY 1968   Al Hamel hosted this daytime game show on which prospective brides and grooms could win prizes if their selections matched.

THE WEDNESDAY NIGHT FIGHTS
See THE FIGHT OF THE WEEK

THE WEEK IN RELIGION   DUMONT

16 MARCH 1952–28 SEPTEMBER 1952; 28 JUNE 1953–3 OCTOBER 1953   Sunday-evening panel show with Rabbi William S. Rosenbloom, Reverend Robbins Wolcott Barstow, Reverend Joseph N. Moody, and guests.

THE WEEK IN REVIEW   CBS

20 JULY 1947–13 JANUARY 1951   One of television's first news shows, *The Week in Review* was a fifteen-minute wrapup of the week's top news stories.

WEEKEND   NBC

20 OCTOBER 1974–22 APRIL 1979   A monthly series, *Weekend* evolved from two previous NBC magazine shows, *First Tuesday* and *Chronolog.* Hosted by Lloyd Dobyns, it aimed at a younger audience than CBS's *60 Minutes.* From 1974 until 1978 it was a ninety-minute show, usually scheduled on the first Saturday of the month; in the fall of 1978 it was trimmed to an hour and moved to prime time (Sundays at 10:00 P.M., again once a month). Linda Ellerbee joined Lloyd Dobyns as cohost that season. Reuven Frank was the executive producer.

WEEKEND HEROES   SYNDICATED
1981   Former pro footballer Paul Hornung and Jayne Kennedy hosted this half-hour series, which presented biographies and interviews with famous gridiron stars.

WELCOME ABOARD   NBC
3 OCTOBER 1948–20 FEBRUARY 1949   Half-hour musical variety show, hosted by a guest celebrity each week. The Russ Morgan Orchestra was featured during the early weeks, the Vincent Lopez Orchestra during the latter weeks.

WELCOME BACK, KOTTER   ABC
9 SEPTEMBER 1975–3 AUGUST 1979   Half-hour sitcom about a high school teacher who returns to his alma mater, James Buchanan High in Brooklyn, to teach the "sweathogs," a supposedly untrainable group of hard-core underachievers. With Gabriel Kaplan as Gabe Kotter; Marcia Strassman as his wife, Julie Kotter; John Travolta (who would later skyrocket to superstardom in *Saturday Night Fever*) as Vinnie Barbarino; Robert Hegyes as Juan Epstein; Ron Palillo as Arnold Horshack; Lawrence Hilton-Jacobs as Freddie "Boom-Boom" Washington; John Sylvester White as Michael Woodman, the vice principal; and James Wood as Alex Welles, another teacher. In the fall of 1977 Julie Kotter gave birth to twin girls, and in January 1978 Melonie Haller joined the cast as Angie Globagoski, a female sweathog. In the fall of 1978, as John Travolta's contract permitted him to appear less frequently, a new sweathog was added: Stephen Shortridge as Beau De Labarre, an experienced high schooler with seven expulsions to his credit. James Komack was the executive producer of the show, and its theme song, "Welcome Back," was sung by John Sebastian.

WELCOME TRAVELERS   NBC/CBS
8 SEPTEMBER 1952–2 JULY 1954 (NBC); 5 JULY 1954–28 OCTOBER 1955 (CBS) Broadcast from Chicago, this daytime show was created by Tommy Bartlett, who brought it to radio in 1947. Travelers to Chicago were invited to come to the show, where they talked with Bartlett and were presented with gifts. When the show came to TV, Bartlett added a cohost, Bob Cunningham; Jack Smith and Pat Meikle later took over as hosts. The set for the TV version was made to look like the Porterhouse Room of the College Inn, the site of the radio version.

WE'LL GET BY   CBS
14 MARCH 1975–30 MAY 1975   Alan Alda created this family sitcom, set in suburban New Jersey. With Paul Sorvino as lawyer George Platt; Mitzi Hoag as his wife, Liz Platt; Jerry Houser as son Muff; Devon Scott as daughter Andrea; and Willie Aames as son Kenny.

WELLS FARGO   NBC
18 MARCH 1957–8 SEPTEMBER 1962   Officially titled *Tales of Wells Fargo,* this western starred Dale Robertson as Jim Hardie, an agent for the transport company. When the show expanded from thirty to sixty minutes in the fall of 1961, Hardie had bought a ranch, and the cast was also expanded; newcomers included Jack Ging as Beau McCloud, another Wells Fargo agent; Virginia Christine as Ovie, a widow who owned a nearby ranch; Lory Patrick as Ovie's daughter, Tina, the schoolteacher; Mary Jane Saunders as Ovie's daughter, Mary Gee; and William Demarest as Hardie's ranch foreman, Jeb Gaine. The show was first produced by Earle Lyon for Overland Productions and Universal Television, and later by Nat Holt for Juggernaut Productions and Universal. Jack Nicholson appeared in one of his first major TV roles in one episode, "The Washburn Girl," aired 13 February 1961.

WENDY AND ME   ABC
14 SEPTEMBER 1964–6 SEPTEMBER 1965   Half-hour sitcom about an airline pilot and his wife, who move into an apartment building where George Burns (who appeared as himself, and addressed the camera as he did in *The Burns and Allen Show*) was the landlord. With Ron Harper as pilot Jeff Conway; Connie Stevens as his wife, Wendy

Conway; James Callahan as Jeff's friend and copilot, bachelor Danny Adams; J. Pat O'Malley as Mr. Bundy, the handyman; and Bartlett Robinson as Willard Norton, Jeff's boss.

THE WENDY BARRIE SHOW   NBC/DUMONT/ABC

10 NOVEMBER 1948–2 FEBRUARY 1949 (NBC); 17 JANUARY 1949–4 MARCH 1949 (DU-MONT); 7 MARCH 1949–13 JULY 1949 (DUMONT); 26 SEPTEMBER 1949–16 FEBRUARY 1950 (ABC); 21 FEBRUARY 1950–27 SEPTEMBER 1950 (NBC)   One of TV's first popular female personalities, Wendy Barrie had several shows of her own in the medium's early days. The first was a ten-minute prime-time show on NBC, titled *Picture This;* it featured guest cartoonists who drew sketches. Early in 1949, while *Picture This* was still running on NBC, she started a daytime show on DuMont; in March of 1949 she moved to prime time on DuMont, with a half-hour interview show sponsored by *Photoplay* magazine. That show shifted to ABC in the fall of 1949, and in February of 1950 Barrie returned to NBC with a twice-weekly fifteen-minute show. Toward the end of its run this series was titled *Through Wendy's Window.*

WE'RE MOVIN'   SYNDICATED

1981   Half-hour magazine show for teenagers. Scott Baio (of *Happy Days*) was the original host of the series; he was succeeded by Willie Aames (late of *Eight Is Enough*) early in 1982.

WEREWOLF   FOX

11 JULY 1987–21 AUGUST 1988   Frank Lupo created this stylish series about a young man searching for a 1600-year-old werewolf. Featured were John York as Eric Cord, who had been bitten by a werewolf himself (and killed that werewolf in self-defense) and now had to find "the source of the bloodline" in order to rid himself of the werewolf curse; Chuck Connors as the 1600-year-old fishing boat captain Janos Skorzeny, now a diabolical killer; and Lance LeGault as Alamo Joe, a bounty hunter who was after Cord for the apparent "murder" he had committed. In a two-part finale, broadcast in February 1988, Cord finally tracked down Skorzeny and killed him, only to discover that the real "source of the bloodline" was an even more ancient werewolf, Nicholas Remy (played by Brian Thompson). Unfortunately for Cord, the series went into reruns shortly thereafter. John Ashley, who was coexecutive producer with series creator Frank Lupo, cheerfully admitted borrowing the character name of Janos Skorzeny from the 1972 TV-movie "The Night Stalker," as a tribute to the show, which was the first pilot for the series of the same name. The TV-movie had featured Barry Atwater as a vampire named Janos Skorzeny.

WESLEY   CBS

8 MAY 1949–30 AUGUST 1949   Half-hour sitcom about a precocious twelve-year-old and his family. With Donald Devlin and Johnny Stewart as Wesley; Frank Thomas as his father; Mona Thomas (the real-life wife of Frank Thomas) as his mother; Joe Sweeney as his grandfather; Joy Reese as his sister; Jack Ayers as the sister's boy-friend; and Billy Nevard as Wesley's pal. The show was produced by Worthington Miner, directed by Franklin Schaffner, and written by Samuel Taylor.

WEST 57TH   CBS

13 AUGUST 1985–17 SEPTEMBER 1985; 30 APRIL 1986–23 JULY 1986; 6 APRIL 1987–9 SEPTEMBER 1989   A prime-time newsmagazine show, *West 57th* symbolized the changing of the guard at CBS News, spearheaded by CBS News President Van Gordon Sauter and his successors, Ed Joyce and Howard Stringer. It was designed to be hipper and faster-paced than CBS's long-running *60 Minutes;* more significantly, all of its correspondents would be under age thirty-five. Though *60 Minutes* was highly popular through the early 1980's (ranking among the top four series every season between 1980 and 1985), many of the "new guard" at CBS News believed that it was showing its age (seventeen seasons as of 1985) and that its ratings would soon erode. *West 57th* was intentionally promoted as a series that would, in effect, compete with *60 Minutes* and (it was hoped) eventually replace it.

West 57th was given a trial run in the late summer of 1985. It was produced by Andrew Lack, who had previously produced documentaries for *CBS Reports*. Some of the show's support staff came from within the ranks of CBS News; others had been hired away from MTV and *Entertainment Tonight*. *West 57th* was named for the Manhattan street on which the offices of CBS News were located. According to one writer, Lack's choice of the title was inspired by such contemporary dramatic programs as *St. Elsewhere* and *Hill Street Blues*, which bore the titles of the workplaces at which they were set. *West 57th*'s fast-paced opening title sequence showed the four correspondents—John Ferrugia, Bob Sirott, Meredith Vieira and Jane Wallace—walking the halls, grabbing coffee, talking on the phone and meeting with each other, all to a musical score. While the show's basic format was similar to that other news magazine program, *West 57th* usually presented five stories each week, two more than did *60 Minutes*. Show business figures, especially rock and roll stars, were regularly profiled; there were a large number of investigative reports as well, including reports on drugs, right-to-lifers, and the Nicaraguan contras. In spite of their youth, three of the four correspondents had network news experience; Sirott, the sole exception, had been a "lifestyle and entertainment editor" at a Chicago station.

Reviews were generally unimpressive, especially from past and present CBS News staffers. CBS reporter Bill Moyers (whose 1983 show, *Our Times*, had been produced by Andrew Lack) hated it. *60 Minutes* executive producer Don Hewitt called it "light summer fare." Correspondent Andy Rooney even prepared an eight-minute parody of the new show for *60 Minutes*, but CBS News president Ed Joyce refused to let it be broadcast. Despite the internal turmoil, the network was determined to give *West 57th* a fair shot. The series returned during the summer of 1986, and returned again in April 1987; in June of that year it moved to Saturdays at 10:00 P.M., and would remain there for two more years. Of the original four correspondents, only Ferrugia and Vieira remained for the entire run. Steve Kroft was added as a fifth correspondent in April 1987. Jane Wallace left in December 1987, and was succeeded by Karen Burnes. Bob Sirott left in 1988. Selina Scott joined the show as a contributor in 1987, and Stephen Schiff also became a contributor in 1988.

West 57th was succeeded in August 1989 by another newsmagazine show, *Saturday Night with Connie Chung*. Meanwhile, *60 Minutes*, the prime-time dinosaur, continued to do well in the ratings, never ranking below eighth. Don Hewitt, its executive producer, hired Meredith Vieira and Steve Kroft in the fall of 1989 to replace Diane Sawyer, who had defected to ABC and her own series, *PrimeTime Live*.

THE WEST OF THE IMAGINATION   PBS
22 SEPTEMBER 1986–26 OCTOBER 1986   A six-part look at the American west, as seen through the eyes of artists, photographers, and filmmakers. James Whitmore was the narrator.

WEST POINT   CBS/ABC
5 OCTOBER 1956–27 SEPTEMBER 1957 (CBS); 8 OCTOBER 1957–1 JULY 1958 (ABC)   Half-hour anthology series about life at the United States Military Academy, produced by Maurice Unger for Ziv TV. The show was hosted by Donald May, who appeared as Cadet Charles C. Thompson. Among the notable guest stars who appeared were Barbara Eden ("Decision," 23 November 1956, her first major TV role), Leonard Nimoy ("His Brother's Fist," 16 November 1956, his first major TV role), and Clint Eastwood ("White Fury," 4 February 1958). The show's theme music, "West Point March," was composed by Philip Egner and Alfred Parham.

WESTBROOK HOSPITAL
See FAITH FOR TODAY

WESTERN MARSHAL
See STEVE DONOVAN, WESTERN MARSHAL

THE WESTERNER NBC

30 SEPTEMBER 1960–30 DECEMBER 1960   Short-lived half-hour western starring Brian Keith as drifter Dave Blasingame and John Dehner as his occasional companion, Burgundy Smith. Sam Peckinpah, who created, produced, and directed the show, blamed its failure on the fact that it was "too adult."

WESTINGHOUSE PLAYHOUSE NBC

6 JANUARY 1961–7 JULY 1961   Sponsored by Westinghouse, this half-hour domestic sitcom was also known as *The Nanette Fabray Show* or *Yes Yes Nanette*. It starred Nanette Fabray as Nan McGovern, an actress who married a writer with two children from a former marriage. The story line closely paralleled Fabray's life, as she married writer Ranald MacDougall and inherited three children by MacDougall's former marriage in 1957. (MacDougall created the show for Fabray.) Also featured on the series were Wendell Corey as Nan's husband, widower Dan McGovern, a Hollywood writer; Jacklyn O'Donnell as Dan's daughter, Nancy; Bobby Diamond (late of *Fury*) as Dan's son, Buddy; Doris Kemper as the housekeeper, Mrs. Harper; and Mimi Gibson as Barby.

WESTSIDE MEDICAL ABC

15 MARCH 1977–25 AUGUST 1977   Hour-long dramatic series about three young physicians operating a medical clinic. With James Sloyan as Dr. Sam Lanagan; Linda Carlson as Dr. Janet Cottrell; Ernest Thompson as Dr. Phil Parker; and Alice Nunn as Carrie. Martin Starger was the executive producer.

WESTWIND NBC

6 SEPTEMBER 1975–4 SEPTEMBER 1976   Live-action Saturday-morning show about a family sailing aboard the *Westwind* off the coast of Hawaii. With Van Williams as underwater photographer Steve Andrews; Niki Dantine as his wife, marine biologist Kate Andrews; Kimberly Beck as their daughter, Robin; and Steve Burns as their son, Tom. William P. D'Angelo was the executive producer.

WE'VE GOT EACH OTHER CBS

1 OCTOBER 1977–7 JANUARY 1978   Half-hour domestic sitcom. With Oliver Clark as Stuart Hibbard, who took care of the apartment and wrote copy for the Herman Gutman Mail Order Catalog; Beverly Archer as his wife, Judy Hibbard, office manager for a photographer; Tom Poston as Damon Jerome, Judy's befuddled boss; Joan Van Ark as Dee Dee, Jerome's main model; Ren Woods as Donna, Jerome's secretary; and Martin Kove as the Hibbards' neighbor, Ken, a swimming pool contractor. The series was created by Tom Patchett and Jay Tarses, the executive producers of *The Bob Newhart Show*.

WHAT A COUNTRY! SYNDICATED

1986–1987   TV's most ethnically diverse sitcom was set in Los Angeles at a citizenship class for newly arrived immigrants. Featured were Garrett M. Brown as Taylor Brown, the teacher; Gail Strickland (1986) as the first principal, Miss Joan Courtney; Don Knotts (1987) as the next principal, Bud McPherson; Yakov Smirnoff (himself a Russian emigre) as Nicolai Rostopovich; Vijay Amritraj as Ali Nadeem, a Pakistani; George Murdock as Laszlo Garbo, a Hungarian; Julian Reyes as Victor Ortega, a Hispanic; Ada Maris as Maria Conchita Lopez; another Hispanic; Leila Hee Olsen as Yung Hee, an Asian; and Harry Waters, Jr., as Robert Moboto, an African.

WHAT-A-MESS ABC

9 SEPTEMBER 1995–   This half-hour Saturday-morning cartoon series starred a clumsy but lovable dog whose given name was Prince, but who was nicknamed What-A-Mess by his family.

WHAT DO YOU HAVE IN COMMON
CBS

1 JULY 1954–23 SEPTEMBER 1954   Ralph Story hosted this prime-time game show on which teams of three specially selected contestants were given three minutes to figure out what they had in common.

WHAT DO YOU THINK?
ABC

17 JANUARY 1949–14 FEBRUARY 1949   Chicago-based panel-discussion series.

WHAT EVERY BABY KNOWS
LIFETIME

1984–   Half-hour daytime show on infant care and parenting, hosted by pediatrician Dr. T. Berry Brazelton.

WHAT EVERY WOMAN WANTS TO KNOW
SYNDICATED

1972   Half-hour talk show hosted by Bess Myerson.

WHAT HAPPENED?
NBC

25 SEPTEMBER 1992–9 OCTOBER 1992   Short-lived prime time show, hosted by Ken Howard, which attempted to show viewers "what happened" by taking them behind the scenes of various accidents and other disasters. Dramatizations of events were sometimes used. Although the series was canceled after only three outings, single programs popped up on NBC's schedule in March and April of 1993.

WHAT IN THE WORLD
CBS

7 OCTOBER 1951–2 APRIL 1955   Perhaps the most erudite game show in television history, *What in the World* was hosted for most of its run by Dr. Froelich Rainey. Each week a panel of experts tried to identify archaeological artifacts. Regular panelists included Dr. Carlton Coon and Dr. Alfred Kidder. The show was broadcast from Philadelphia, where it began as a local show.

WHAT REALLY HAPPENED TO THE CLASS OF '65?
NBC

8 DECEMBER 1977–27 JULY 1978   An hour anthology series, inspired by the book of the same title by Michael Medved and David Wallechinsky, two graduates of the class of 1965, Palisades High School, Los Angeles, who tracked down several members of their class eleven years later and wrote about them. The TV series was entirely fictional; set at Bret Harte High School, it was hosted by Tony Bill as Sam, a member of the class of 1965 who returned to teach at his alma mater. Richard Irving was the executive producer.

WHAT'S GOING ON?
ABC

28 NOVEMBER 1954–26 DECEMBER 1954   Prime-time game show from Goodson-Todman Productions, hosted by Lee Bowman. Each week six celebrity panelists were divided into groups of three, the "ins" and the "outs." By watching the monitors, the "ins," who remained in the studio, had to guess where the "outs" were headed and what they were doing.

WHAT'S HAPPENING!!
ABC/SYNDICATED

5 AUGUST 1976–26 AUGUST 1976; 13 NOVEMBER 1976–28 APRIL 1979 (ABC); 1985–1988 (SYNDICATED)   Based on the film *Cooley High*, this half-hour sitcom told the story of three black high school students in Los Angeles. Introduced for a four-week trial run in the summer of 1976, it returned to the network schedule that fall. With Ernest Thomas as Roger "Raj" Thomas; Haywood Nelson, Jr., as his friend Dwayne; Fred Berry as their rotund friend Rerun (Freddie Stubbs); Mabel King (1976–1978) as Mama, Roger's mother; Danielle Spencer as Dee, Roger's sassy sister; and Shirley Hemphill as Shirley, the surly waitress at the boys' favorite hangout, Rob's. In the fall of 1978 Roger and Dwayne started college, and moved to an apartment of their own. Added to the cast were: John Welsh as their neighbor, Big Earl, a cop; David Hollander as his son, Little Earl; and Leland Smith as Roger and Dwayne's friend Snake. Bud Yorkin, Saul Turteltaub, and Bernie Orenstein were the executive producers.

Most of the original cast was reassembled for the 1985 syndicated revival of the sitcom, titled *What's Happening Now!!* Ernest Thomas played Raj, now married; Haywood Nelson, Jr., was Dwayne, now a computer programmer; Fred Berry was Rerun, a used-car salesman who roomed with Dwayne; Shirley Hemphill was Shirley, who now ran Rob's; and Danielle Spencer was Dee, now a college student. Added to the cast were Anne-Marie Johnson as Raj's wife, Nadine, and Reina King (1985–1986) as Carolyn, a foster child they took in. Fred Berry was dropped in 1986 after a salary dispute with the producers. In the fall of 1987 two more regulars were added: Martin Lawrence as Maurice, a busboy at Rob's, and Ken Sagoes as Darryl, Maurice's pal.

WHAT'S IN A WORD   CBS
22 JULY 1954–9 SEPTEMBER 1954   Clifton Fadiman hosted this prime-time game show, on which a celebrity panel had to guess a pair of rhyming words from clues supplied by the host. The panel included Audrey Meadows, Faye Emerson, Mike Wallace, and Jim Moran.

WHAT'S IT ALL ABOUT, WORLD?   ABC
6 FEBRUARY 1969–1 MAY 1969   *What's It All About, World?* started out as an hour of satire, hosted by Dean Jones. It proved to be a feeble effort; late in March the first format was scrapped and the show became a straightforward variety series, *The Dean Jones Variety Hour.* The second attempt was as unsuccessful as the first, and the show departed after thirteen uneventful weeks. Other regulars included Dennis Allen, Maureen Arthur, Dick Clair and Jenna McMahon, Scoey Mitchlll, Gerri Granger, Ron Prince, and Bayn Johnson (as Happy Hollywood). Writer Harlan Ellison, reviewing the series in 1969 for the *Los Angeles Free Press,* characterized it as "a horror of right-wing imbecility."

WHAT'S IT FOR?   NBC
12 OCTOBER 1957–4 JANUARY 1958   Prime-time game show, hosted by Hal March, on which a celebrity panel tried to guess the purpose of new or unusual inventions. Panelists included Abe Burrows, Hans Conried, Betsy Palmer, and Cornelia Otis Skinner.

WHAT'S IT WORTH?   CBS
21 MAY 1948–28 APRIL 1949   Prime-time show on which professional art restorer Sigmund Rothschild evaluated heirlooms and art objects, answered inquiries from viewers, and interviewed guest appraisers. Rothschild was assisted by Gil Fates, who later became the executive producer of *What's My Line?* See also *Trash or Treasure?*

WHAT'S MY LINE?   CBS/SYNDICATED
2 FEBRUARY 1950–3 SEPTEMBER 1967 (CBS); 1968–1975 (SYNDICATED) Television's longest-running prime-time game show involved a simple format—a panel of four celebrities tried to guess the occupations of the contestants. The panelists were permitted to ask yes-or-no questions, and the contestant was awarded $5 each time a "no" answer was given; if ten "no" answers were given, the game ended and the contestant won the top prize of $50. Each week a mystery guest also dropped by, and the panelists (who were blindfolded for this segment) tried to guess his or her identity. The show was a Mark Goodson-Bill Todman Production; Goodson and Todman were responsible for several other of TV's best known and most successful game shows, such as *I've Got a Secret, To Tell the Truth,* and *Match Game,* but *What's My Line?* was their first hit show. The show was hosted for its entire seventeen-year network run by John Daly (during many of those years Daly anchored the evening newscasts on ABC as well). The first panel included syndicated columnist Dorothy Kilgallen, Louis Untermeyer, Governor Harold Hoffman (of New Jersey), and psychiatrist Dr. Richard Hoffman. Phil Rizzuto of the New York Yankees was the first mystery guest. Kilgallen remained with the show until her death in 1965, but the other original panelists did not last long. Fred Allen, Hal Block, and Steve Allen (who coined the famous question, "Is it bigger than a breadbox?") were frequently

featured during the early 1950s, but by the end of the decade the regular panel consisted of Kilgallen, Arlene Francis, Bennett Cerf, and a guest celebrity. Among the most notable of the hundreds of mystery guests were Warren Beatty (11 September 1965), James Cagney (15 May 1960), Ty Cobb (31 July 1955), Bette Davis (5 October 1952), Walt Disney (11 November 1956), Howdy Doody (15 August 1954), Judy Garland (5 March 1967), Alfred Hitchcock (12 September 1954), Buster Keaton (2 September 1951), Harold Lloyd (26 April 1953), Jayne Mansfield (12 February 1956), Ronald Reagan (19 July 1953; he later appeared as a guest panelist), Edward G. Robinson (11 October 1953), Carl Sandburg (11 September 1960), Frank Sinatra (27 November 1966; he appeared as a panelist the following week), Barbra Streisand (12 April 1964), and Elizabeth Taylor (14 November 1954). Jimmy Carter also appeared, when he was governor of Georgia, as a contestant. The syndicated version of the show was played the same way. The latter version was hosted by Wally Bruner from 1968 until 1972, when Larry Blyden took over; Blyden died in 1975 from injuries sustained in a car crash in Morocco, and production was discontinued. Arlene Francis and Soupy Sales were regular panelists on the syndicated version. See also *That's My Line.*

WHAT'S NEW MISTER MAGOO
See MR. MAGOO

WHAT'S ON YOUR MIND?   ABC
24 JULY 1951–10 MARCH 1952   Panel show, on which psychiatry was discussed in terms comprehensible to lay people. Isabel Leighton was the moderator. The show was retitled *How Did They Get That Way?*

WHAT'S THE STORY   DUMONT
25 JULY 1951–23 SEPTEMBER 1955   On this prime-time game show a panel of journalists tried to identify famous events from sketches performed on stage. Walter Kiernan was the first host; John K. M. McCaffery succeeded him.

WHAT'S THIS SONG   NBC
26 OCTOBER 1964–24 SEPTEMBER 1965   Wink Martindale hosted this daytime game show on which two 2-member teams (each with a celebrity and a contestant) tried to identify songs and sing their lyrics.

WHAT'S YOUR BID   ABC/DUMONT
14 FEBRUARY 1953–11 APRIL 1953 (ABC); 3 MAY 1953–28 JUNE 1953 (DUMONT) On this prime-time game show merchandise was auctioned off to members of the studio audience; all proceeds were donated to charities. The ABC version was hosted by John Reed King, the DuMont version by Robert Alda. Leonard "Liberal Bill" Rosen was the auctioneer.

WHAT'S YOUR TROUBLE   SYNDICATED
1952–1953   Half-hour series on which Dr. and Mrs. Norman Vincent Peale dispensed advice on coping with life's problems.

WHEEL OF FORTUNE   CBS
3 OCTOBER 1952–25 DECEMBER 1953   The first of the two series of this title was hosted by Todd Russell. It was a human interest show similar to *Mr. Citizen* and *The Girl in My Life*—persons who had done good deeds were rewarded. The half-hour show was introduced as a Friday-morning replacement for *Arthur Godfrey Time,* and a prime-time version was shown during the summer of 1953.

WHEEL OF FORTUNE   NBC/CBS/SYNDICATED
6 JANUARY 1975–30 JUNE 1989 (NBC); 17 JULY 1989–11 JANUARY 1991 (CBS); 14 JANUARY 1991–13 SEPTEMBER 1991 (NBC); 1983– (SYNDICATED)   The second show with this title is a daytime game show on which three contestants take turns spinning a large wheel for the chance to guess the letters of a mystery word or phrase.

Chuck Woolery hosted the show from 1975 to 1982, when Pat Sajak took over. Susan Stafford assisted until the fall of 1982, when she was succeeded by Vanna White. In 1983 a syndicated version of the show was introduced, also hosted by Sajak. It soon became the highest-rated daily syndicated series in television history. Even though she said little on camera, Vanna White became a major celebrity; her autobiography, *Vanna Speaks!,* made the best seller lists.

Sajak hosted the network version until 6 January 1989, shortly before he moved to CBS for his attempt at a late-night talk show (he continued to host the syndicated version, however). Former pro football placekicker Rolf Benirschke took over on 9 January, and lasted until 30 June. When the show shifted networks that summer, Bob Goen became the new host. Early in 1991, the series moved back to NBC, its original home. The syndicated version continued to thrive after the show left NBC's daytime schedule in September 1991.

WHEELIE AND THE CHOPPER BUNCH   NBC
7 SEPTEMBER 1974–30 AUGUST 1975   Saturday-morning cartoon series from Hanna-Barbera Productions about a heroic Volkswagen (Wheelie) who battled a bunch of motorcycles.

WHEN HAVOC STRUCK   SYNDICATED
1978   A series of twelve half-hour films on notable disasters, narrated by Glenn Ford.

WHEN THE WHISTLE BLOWS   ABC
14 MARCH 1980–27 JULY 1980   Construction workers are the central characters of this sitcom. With Dolph Sweet as Norm Jenkins; Doug Barr as Buzz Dillard; Susan Buckner as Lucy; Philip Brown as Randy; Tim Rossovich as Hunk; Sue Ane Langdon as Darlene; Gary Allen as Hanrahan; Alice Hirson as Dottie Jenkins, Norm's wife; and Noble Willingham as Bulldog. Chuck Gordon and Tom Kardozian created the show.

WHEN THINGS WERE ROTTEN   ABC
10 SEPTEMBER 1975–24 DECEMBER 1975   This half-hour sitcom was supposed to be a satire of the Robin Hood legend. Featured were Dick Gautier as Robin Hood; Misty Rowe as Maid Marian; Dick Van Patten as Friar Tuck; Henry Polic II as the Sheriff of Nottingham; Ron Rifkin as Prince John; Richard Dimitri as twins Bertram and Renaldo; David Sabin as Little John; Bernie Kopell as Alan-A-Dale; and Jane Johnston as Princess Isabelle. Mel Brooks, John Boni, and Norman Stiles created the series, and Norman Steinberg produced it for Paramount Television. Brooks exhumed the idea for his 1993 film, "Robin Hood: Men in Tights."

WHERE I LIVE   ABC
5 MARCH 1993–14 MAY 1993; 3 AUGUST 1993–20 NOVEMBER 1993   Critically acclaimed sitcom about life in Harlem, told from the point of view of a seventeen-year-old. With Doug E. Doug as high school senior Douglas St. Martin; Yunoka Doyle as his fourteen-year-old sister, Sharon; Sullivan Walker as his father, James; Lorraine Toussaint as his mother, Marie; Flex as his best friend, Reggie Coltrane; Shaun Baker as his friend Malcolm; and Jason Bose Smith as Kwanzi, a neighborhood youngster. When the series returned in the fall of 1993 Douglas had started junior college.

WHERE IN THE WORLD IS CARMEN SANDIEGO?   PBS
30 SEPTEMBER 1991–   Weekday game show for kids, based on the popular computer game ostensibly intended to teach children about world geography. Greg Lee was the host, Lynne Thigpen appeared as The Chief who gave out clues to the contestants, and a singing group called Rockapella provided the music. See also *Where on Earth Is Carmen Sandiego?*

WHERE ON EARTH IS CARMEN SANDIEGO? FOX
5 FEBRUARY 1994–   One of two series based on the computer game (see also *Where in the World Is Carmen Sandiego?*), this one was a Saturday-morning cartoon show which took place inside a home computer, where a pair of teen detectives—Ivy and Zack—chased classy thief Carmen Sandiego around the world; Ms. Sandiego thoughtfully left clues for her pursuers. Rita Moreno provided the voice of the title character.

WHERE THE ACTION IS ABC
27 JUNE 1965–31 MARCH 1967   Half-hour musical show for teenagers. The daytime show was hosted by Dick Clark, and the regular performers included Paul Revere and the Raiders, Steve Alaimo, and Linda Scott. Among the many guests were Sonny and Cher, who made one of their first TV appearances on 30 July 1965.

WHERE THE HEART IS CBS
8 SEPTEMBER 1969–23 MARCH 1973   This half-hour daytime serial, set in the town of Northcross, a suburb of New York City, concerned the sexual goings-on of the members of two families, the Hathaways and the Prescotts. Principal players included: James Mitchell as Julian Hathaway, a widowed English professor; Diana Walker as Mary Hathaway, Julian's second wife; Gregory Abels as Julian's son (by his first marriage), Michael Hathaway, who fell for his stepmother; Robyn Millan and Lisa Richards as Vicky Lucas, who married Mike and later divorced him; Diana Van Der Vlis as Julian's sister, Kate Hathaway; Laurence Luckinbill and Ron Harper as Steve Prescott, who married Kate; Zohra Lampert as Ellie Jardin, who was murdered; Michael Bersell as Ellie's mute son, Peter, who was taken in by Kate and Steve; Tracy Brooks Swope as Liz Rainey, who became Mike Hathaway's second wife; Bill Post, Jr., as Dr. Joe Prescott; Katherine Meskill as Nancy Prescott; Ted Leplat as Terry Prescott; Peter MacLean as John Rainey; David Cryer as Dr. Hugh Jessup; Louise Shaffer as Allison Jessup; Clarice Blackburn as Amy Snowden; Rue McClanahan as Margaret Jardin; and Alice Drummond as Loretta Jardin. After a three-and-a-half-year run, *Where the Heart Is* was replaced by *The Young and the Restless*.

WHERE WAS I DUMONT
2 SEPTEMBER 1952–6 OCTOBER 1953   Dan Seymour first hosted this prime-time game show, which went through at least two formats. In one format, a celebrity panel tried to guess where the contestant had been at a certain time, and in a second format, a celebrity panel tried to guess the nature of photographs shown to viewers, but hidden from the panelists' view. Regular panelists included Peter Donald, Nancy Guild, and David Ross. John Reed King became the host late in 1952.

WHERE'S HUDDLES CBS
1 JULY 1970–9 SEPTEMBER 1970   A prime-time cartoon show from Hanna-Barbera Productions, *Where's Huddles* centered around a football team. Featured voices included Cliff Norton as Ed Huddles, the quarterback; Mel Blanc as Bubba McCoy, the center; Paul Lynde as Pertwee; Jean van der Pyl as Marge Huddles, Ed's wife; Herb Jeffries as Freight Train; Marie Wilson as Penny McCoy, Bubba's wife; and Alan Reed as Coach. The series was rerun during the summer of 1971.

WHERE'S RAYMOND?
See THE RAY BOLGER SHOW

WHERE'S WALDO? CBS
14 SEPTEMBER 1991–5 SEPTEMBER 1992   Saturday-morning cartoon show based on the best-selling books by Martin Handford in which the title character was hidden within detailed drawings. On TV Waldo was a wandering backpacker who was accompanied by his girlfriend, Wilma, and his dog, Woof. On each program an off-screen voice challenged viewers to find certain objects in Waldo's upcoming adventure.

WHEW! CBS

23 APRIL 1979–30 MAY 1980   A fast-paced daytime game show hosted by Tom Kennedy, *Whew!* involved two contestants, each of whom tried to block the other's progress along a six-level game board. Contestants were given one minute to go from the first level up to the sixth and had to negotiate their way around "blocks" strategically hidden on the board by their opponents. The show was retitled *Celebrity Whew!* in November 1979.

WHIPLASH SYNDICATED

1961   Half-hour "western," starring Peter Graves as Chris Cobb, an American who founded a stagecoach line in Australia. The series was filmed on location.

THE WHIRLYBIRDS SYNDICATED

1957   Half-hour adventure series about a couple of helicopter pilots who worked for Whirlybird Service, an outfit based at Longwood Field. With Kenneth Tobey as Chuck Martin; Craig Hill as P. T. Moore. The show was produced by Desilu.

WHISPERING SMITH NBC

15 MAY 1961–18 SEPTEMBER 1961   Half-hour western, much criticized during its short run for its excessive violence. Set in Denver during the 1870s, it starred Guy Mitchell as Detective George Romack, Audie Murphy as Tom "Whispering" Smith, and Sam Buffington as Chief John Richards. Richard Lewis was the producer. Filming of the twenty-six episodes began in 1959, but the series did not find a place on NBC's schedule until 1961.

WHISTLE STOP U.S.A. CBS

7 SEPTEMBER 1952–2 NOVEMBER 1952   Sunday-afternoon news show that focused on the 1952 Presidential election. Charles Collingwood was the host.

THE WHISTLER SYNDICATED

1954   Half-hour suspense anthology series, based on the radio program that began in 1942. The show was narrated by an unseen voice, known only as "The Whistler," whose distinctive musical theme preceded his comments. Bill Forman provided the voice.

THE WHISTLING WIZARD CBS

3 NOVEMBER 1951–20 SEPTEMBER 1952   Saturday-morning puppet show, featuring the puppets of Bil and Cora Baird. The story line concerned a child, J.P., who was transported to a fantasy land to search for the Whistling Wizard.

WHITE HUNTER SYNDICATED

1959   Half-hour adventure series set in Africa, starring Rhodes Reason as John Hunter, guide and game hunter.

THE WHITE SHADOW CBS

27 NOVEMBER 1978–12 AUGUST 1981   Hour dramatic series about a basketball star who, after an injury that curtailed his professional career, accepted an offer to coach at Carver High School in Los Angeles. With Ken Howard as coach Ken Reeves; Ed Bernard as the principal, Jim Willis, a former college teammate of Reeves's; Joan Pringle as vice-principal Sybil Buchanon; Robin Rose as Ken's sister, Katie Donahue; Jerry Fogel as her husband, Bill Donahue; Kevin Hooks as Morris Thorpe; Eric Kilpatrick as Curtis Jackson; Byron Stewart as Warren Coolidge; Thomas Carter as James Hayward; Nathan Cook as Milton Reese; Timothy Van Patten as Mario (Salami) Petrino; Ken Michelman as Abner Goldstein; and Ira Angustain as Ricardo Gomez. In the fall of 1979 John Mengatti joined the squad as Nick Vitaglia, Salami's cousin, and Russell Phillip Robinson appeared as the team manager, Phil Jeffers. In a moving episode at the end of the 1979–1980 season, Curtis Jackson, an innocent bystander at a liquor store holdup, was shot to death.

The tone of the show was decidedly lighter for its third, and final, season. Bernard,

Rose, Fogel, Kilpatrick, Carter, Cook, Michelman, and Angustain all left the series. Sybil Buchanon had been promoted to principal, and several new regulars joined: Larry Flash Jenkins as Wardell Stone; Wolfe Perry as Teddy Rutherford; Stoney Jackson as Jesse B. Mitchell; John Laughlin as Patrick Falahey; Art Holliday as Eddie Franklin; and Rosey Grier as the wrestling coach, Ezra Davis.

Bruce Paltrow was the executive producer, Mark Tinker the producer, for MTM Enterprises.

WHIZ KIDS   CBS

5 OCTOBER 1983–2 JUNE 1984   An hour prime-time adventure series about a teenage computer genius, his talking computer, and his pals. Featured were Matthew Laborteaux as the genius, Richie Adler, who operated RALF out of his bedroom; Todd Porter as Ham Parker; Jeffrey Jacquet as Jeremy Saldino; Andrea Elson as Alice Tucker; Melanie Gaffin as Richie's little sister, Cheryl; Madelyn Cain as Richie's mother, Irene Adler; Max Gail as reporter Lew Farley, a friend of Richie's who provided adult assistance when needed; A Martinez as Lieutenant Quinn of the Los Angeles Police Department; and Dan O'Herlihy (spring 1984) as intelligence agent Carson Marsh.

WHO DO YOU TRUST?   CBS/ABC

3 JANUARY 1956–26 MARCH 1957 (CBS); 30 SEPTEMBER 1957–27 DECEMBER 1963 (ABC) A popular game show, this series began as a prime-time show on CBS in 1956 under the title *Do You Trust Your Wife?* Hosted by Edgar Bergen, it featured two married couples who competed in a quiz segment; the husbands could choose to answer the questions themselves, or they could "trust" their wives to answer. In the fall of 1957 the show moved to ABC, where it became a daytime show and was hosted by Johnny Carson. Carson spent more of his time interviewing the couples than asking them questions. In July of 1958 the show adopted a less chauvinistic title, *Who Do You Trust?* but continued with the same format. In the fall of 1958 Carson was teamed up for the first time with a new announcer, Ed McMahon, who commuted from Philadelphia to do the show (McMahon succeeded Bill Nimmo). It was the start of a long association, as Carson took McMahon with him when he left *Who Do You Trust?* in 1962 to host the *Tonight* show. Carson was succeeded as host of *Who Do You Trust?* (which by then was actually titled *Whom Do You Trust?* as a concession to grammatical accuracy) by Woody Woodbury. The series was produced by Don Fedderson.

WHO IN THE WORLD   CBS

24 JUNE 1962–16 SEPTEMBER 1962   Prime-time half-hour talk show hosted by Warren Hull.

WHO PAYS   NBC

2 JULY 1959–24 SEPTEMBER 1959   Mike Wallace hosted this prime-time game show. Each contestant was employed by a famous person, and the object of the game was for a celebrity panel to ascertain who the well-known employers were; the employers themselves then appeared and chatted with the panel. See also *Who's the Boss.*

WHO SAID THAT?   NBC/ABC

9 DECEMBER 1948–18 FEBRUARY 1951 (NBC); 5 APRIL 1952–26 APRIL 1952 (NBC); 13 APRIL 1953–5 JULY 1954 (NBC); 2 FEBRUARY 1955–26 JULY 1955 (ABC)   This prime-time game show began on radio in 1948 and featured a panel of celebrities who tried to identify the sources of quotations taken from recent news events. Robert Trout was the first host and was succeeded by Walter Kiernan. Frequent panelists included June Lockhart, Morey Amsterdam, and H. V. Kaltenborn.

WHO, WHAT OR WHERE   NBC

29 DECEMBER 1969–4 JANUARY 1974   Art James hosted this daytime game show on which three contestants competed in a question-and-answer format. Each player was given a stake of $125 and could wager up to $50 on a single question. At the beginning of each round the name of a category was revealed; each category con-

tained three questions—one "Who," one "What," and one "Where." Some questions were more difficult than others and were given higher odds. The player who wagered the most on a single question won the right to answer it, and the player's winnings were increased or depleted by the amount of the wager (or by the odds, if the question was worth more than even money). If two players bid the same amount on a question, an auction was conducted. At the end of the game, players could wager any amount, up to their entire winnings, on the final round.

WHODUNNIT? NBC

12 APRIL 1979–10 MAY 1979   One of the few prime-time game shows since the 1950s, *Whodunnit?* gave three contestants the chance to match wits with a trio of experts in attempting to solve a dramatized crime. Approximately halfway through the dramatization, contestants were given the opportunity to guess the culprit for the show's top prize of $10,000. Contestants who chose not to hazard a guess at that time could then wait to hear the panel of experts announce their guess as to the culprit (the experts were also permitted to interrogate the several suspects); a contestant who then chose the real culprit won either $2500 (if any of the experts had made the same choice) or $5000 (if none of the experts had chosen correctly). Ed McMahon hosted the half-hour show, which was created by Jeremy Lloyd and Lance Percival. Though *Whodunnit?* billed itself as television's first mystery game show, it was not. A similar format had been employed thirty years earlier in CBS's *Armchair Detective* and was again used in the DuMont version of *Public Prosecutor.*

A WHOLE NEW BALLGAME ABC

9 JANUARY 1995–13 MARCH 1995   Created by the producers of *Blue Skies*, this half-hour sitcom starred Corbin Bernsen as Brett Sooner, a Milwaukee Brewer baseball star who, while on strike, signed on as a sportscaster at WPLP, a local television station. Also featured were Julia Campbell as the general manager of the station, Meg O'Donnell, who attracted Brett's interest; Richard Kind as sales manager Dwight King; John O'Hurley as news anchor Tad Sherman; Kari Coleman as Meg's assistant, Libby DeSoto; Stephen Tobolowsky as weatherman Dr. Warner Brakefield; Peter Jason as station owner Vernon Redfield; and Shashawnee Hall as Mickey, owner of Spitter's Sports Bar. Campbell, Kind, and Tobolowsky had all been regulars on *Blue Skies*, and thus became eligible to join the small group of performers who have appeared in two flop shows during the same season.

WHOOPI SYNDICATED

1992–1993   Half-hour talk show on which host Whoopi Goldberg interviewed a single guest. There was no studio audience.

WHO'S THE BOSS ABC

19 FEBRUARY 1954–20 AUGUST 1954   A prime-time game show on which a celebrity panel tried to guess the identities of the famous employers of the show's contestants. Walter Kiernan was the first host of the show and was succeeded by Mike Wallace. Wallace hosted the 1959 version of the show, which was titled *Who Pays.* See also that title.

WHO'S THE BOSS ABC

20 SEPTEMBER 1984–10 SEPTEMBER 1992   Durable sitcom about a widower who left New York City with his younger daughter to become the housekeeper for a divorced woman and her young son in Connecticut; over the course of the seasons, the adults' relationship gradually inched its way toward love. With Tony Danza (late of *Taxi*) as Tony Micelli; Judith Light (late of *One Life to Live*) as Angela Bower, who worked for an ad agency (in the fall of 1986 she opened her own agency); Alyssa Milano as Tony's daughter, Samantha; Danny Pintauro as Angela's son, Jonathan; and Katherine Helmond as Angela's mother, Mona Robinson. Jonathon Halyalkar signed for the 1990–1991 season as Billy, a five-year-old taken in by Tony when the lad's grandmother became too ill to care for him. During the 1991–1992 season Nicole Eggert was seen as Samantha's best friend, Marci, and Curnal Aulisio played Sam's

boyfriend, Hank. Although the series toyed with the idea of a marriage betwen Tony and Angela, it wrapped up—refreshingly—without a wedding as Tony finished college.

WHO'S THERE CBS
14 JULY 1952–15 SEPTEMBER 1952   Arlene Francis hosted this prime-time game show on which a celebrity panel tried to identify guest celebrities from physical clues associated with those celebs. The format was later used in a 1953 game show, *Personality Puzzle.*

WHO'S WATCHING THE KIDS NBC
22 SEPTEMBER 1978–15 DECEMBER 1978   Set in Las Vegas, *Who's Watching the Kids* was a distant cousin of *Blansky's Beauties,* the 1977 sitcom that starred Nancy Walker; the two shared the same producers, and a few cast members, but *Who's Watching the Kids* emphasized the younger regulars rather than the chorus girls. Featured were Caren Kaye as chorus girl Stacy Turner; Lynda Goodfriend as Stacy's roommate and partner, Angie Vitola; Marcia Lewis as their landlady, Mitzi Logan, who was also the emcee at the Club Sand Pile, where Stacy and Angie performed; Scott Baio as Angie's fifteen-year-old live-in brother, Frankie Vitola, who was sent West from South Philadelphia by his folks in the hopes that he could improve his grades; Tammy Lauren as Stacy's nine-year-old live-in sister, Melissa Turner; Larry Breeding as their neighbor, newscaster Larry Parnell; Jim Belushi (brother of John Belushi of *NBC's Saturday Night Live*) as Bert Gunkle, Larry's camera operator; Lorrie Mahaffey as Memphis; Elaine Bolton as Bridget; and Shirley Kirkes as Cochise. Garry K. Marshall, Tony Marshall, and Don Silverman were the executive producers for Henderson Productions in association with Paramount TV.

WHO'S WHO CBS
4 JANUARY 1977–26 JUNE 1977   An hour-long newsmagazine with a lighter touch than *60 Minutes.* On *Who's Who* the emphasis was on people. Dan Rather was the "chief reporter," and Barbara Howar and Charles Kuralt (reporting "on the road") were regular contributors.

WHOSE SIDE ARE YOU ON? CBS
19 JULY 1991–2 AUGUST 1991   Brief Friday-night fill-in series, hosted by various CBS News correspondents, which examined both sides of a controversial topic each week.

WHY? ABC
29 DECEMBER 1952–20 APRIL 1953   Comedy quiz show, hosted by John Reed King, on which the contestants were told the "Who, What, Where, and When" of an event and were required to supply the "Why." The prime-time show was seen on Monday nights. King cohosted the show with Bill Cullen, who also served as the show's producer.

WICHITA TOWN NBC
30 SEPTEMBER 1959–23 SEPTEMBER 1960   Half-hour western starring Joel McCrea as Marshal Mike Dunbar of Wichita, Kansas, and Jody McCrea (Joel's son) as Ben Matheson, his deputy. Also featured were Carlos Romero as Rico and George Neise as Doc. The series was based on *Wichita,* the 1955 film which had starred the elder McCrea.

WIDE COUNTRY NBC
20 SEPTEMBER 1962–12 SEPTEMBER 1963   *Wide Country* was one of a pair of 1962 series set along the professional rodeo circuit (*Stoney Burke* was the other). The hour show starred Earl Holliman as Mitch Guthrie and Andrew Prine as his younger brother, Andy Guthrie.

WIDE WIDE WORLD   NBC
16 OCTOBER 1955–8 JUNE 1958   Another manifestation of Sylvester "Pat" Weaver's fertile imagination, *Wide Wide World* was a Sunday-afternoon documentary series. Most of the ninety-minute shows focused on a single topic and featured live reports from locations throughout North America (filmed segments from other parts of the world were also used). Dave Garroway, whom Weaver had chosen to host the *Today* show three years before, was the "guide" of *Wide Wide World*. The show was first introduced on 27 June 1955, as part of *Producers' Showcase,* but regular Sunday broadcasts did not begin until the fall. On the October 1955 premiere the topic was "A Sunday in Autumn," and reports were made from Lake Mead, the Grand Canyon, Weeki Wachee (Fla.), Dallas, San Francisco, St. Louis, Gloucester (Mass.), Cleveland, Omaha, and New York City. Barry Wood was the executive producer, Herbert Sussan the producer.

WIDE WORLD OF SPORTS
See ABC'S WIDE WORLD OF SPORTS

THE WIL SHRINER SHOW   SYNDICATED
1987–1988   A five-day-a-week, sixty-minute daytime talk show, hosted by Wil Shriner (son of humorist Herb Shriner, a TV personality of the 1950s).

THE WILBURN BROTHERS SHOW   SYNDICATED
1963–1969   Country-and-western music series, hosted by Ted and Doyle Wilburn.

WILD AMERICA   PBS
1982   A half-hour series of nature films, produced, photographed, and narrated by Marty Stouffer.

WILD BILL HICKOK   SYNDICATED
1951–1958   Half-hour western starring Guy Madison as U.S. Marshal James Butler (Wild Bill) Hickok, and Andy Devine as his sidekick, Jingles B. Jones ("Wait fer me, Wild Bill!"). Devine's inimitably gravelly voice was the result of a childhood accident, in which he fell with a stick in his mouth. A total of 112 episodes were filmed. Madison and Devine also played the same roles on the radio version of the series, which began in 1951 and ran through 1956.

WILD CARGO   SYNDICATED
1963   Half-hour documentary series on capturing wild animals for zoos. Arthur Jones was the host.

WILD KINGDOM   NBC/SYNDICATED
6 JANUARY 1963–11 APRIL 1971 (NBC); 1971–1988 (SYNDICATED)   Perhaps the best known, and certainly the longest running of the several documentary series about animal life, *Wild Kingdom* was sponsored by Mutual of Omaha and was hosted for most of its run by Marlin Perkins (formerly the host of *Zoo Parade*). Other hosts or cohosts have included Jim Fowler, Tom Allen, Stan Brock and Peter Eros.

WILD OATS   FOX
4 SEPTEMBER 1994–25 SEPTEMBER 1994   An early casualty of the 1994–1995 season, this sitcom was set in Chicago, and told the tale of a sex-obsessed photographer and his level-headed roommate. With Tim Conlon as the hormone-enhanced Jack Slayton; Paul Rudd as the roommate, Brian Grant, a social worker; Paula Marshall as Jack's ex-girlfriend, Shelly Thomas, a teacher; Jana Marie Hupp as Shelly's pal, Liz, a hairstylist; and Christine Cavanaugh as Kathee, the barmaid at the gang's favorite watering hole.

WILD PALMS   ABC
16 MAY 1993–19 MAY 1993   Heavily hyped four-night, six-hour miniseries set in Los Angeles in the year 2007, at the launching of a new television network incorporating

virtual reality into its programming. The cast included James Belushi as lawyer Harry Wyckoff; Dana Delany as his wife, Grace; Kim Cattrall as his ex-girlfriend, Paige Katz; Robert Loggia as Senator Anton Kreutzer; Angie Dickinson as his evil assistant, Josie Ito; Ernie Hudson as Tommy Lazlo; Bebe Neuwirth as Tabba Schwartzkopf; and Ben Savage as Cody Wyckoff. Derived from a comic strip in *Details* magazine, the series was created by Bruce Wagner, who was co-executive producer with Oliver Stone.

THE WILD WEST C.O.W. BOYS OF MOO MESA   ABC
12 SEPTEMBER 1992–3 SEPTEMBER 1994   Saturday-morning cartoon series about a trio of law-enforcing cattle—Marshal Moo Montana, the Cowlorado Kid, and Dakota Dude—who observed the "C.O.W." (Code of the West) and battled the evil Wild West Bullies.

THE WILD, WILD WEST   CBS
17 SEPTEMBER 1965–19 SEPTEMBER 1969   A fantasy western, *The Wild, Wild West* combined *The Man from U.N.C.L.E.* with *Maverick*. It starred Robert Conrad as James West, a special agent assigned to the frontier by President Ulysses S. Grant. Ross Martin costarred as his associate, Artemus Gordon. The two battled the usual assortment of mad scientists and crazed outlaws, using fanciful gadgets to thwart their adversaries. Occasionally appearing were Michael Dunn as Dr. Miguelito Loveless, West's diminutive archenemy; James Gregory as President Grant; and Charles Aidman as Jeremy, who filled in for Artemus Gordon when Ross Martin was sidelined with a mild heart attack. The hour show was created by Michael Garrison for Bruce Lansbury Productions. It was rerun on CBS during the summer of 1970. On 9 May 1979 Conrad and Martin were reunited in a made-for-TV movie, "The Wild, Wild West Revisited." A second sequel, "More Wild, Wild West," was televised on 7 and 8 October 1980.

WILD, WILD WORLD OF ANIMALS   SYNDICATED
1973–1976   Half-hour documentary series on animal life, from Time-Life Films, narrated by William Conrad.

WILD C.A.T.S   CBS
1 OCTOBER 1994–2 SEPTEMBER 1995   Saturday-morning cartoon show about a group of alien heroes stranded on Earth. The six—Grifter, Maul, Zealot, WarBlade, Spartan, and Voodoo—were brought together by Jacob Marlowe, who assembled them into a C.A.T., or Covert Action Team.

WILDCAT
See THE TROUBLESHOOTERS

WILDFIRE   CBS
13 SEPTEMBER 1986–5 SEPTEMBER 1987   This Saturday morning cartoon series chronicled the efforts of a young princess, Sara, with the assistance of a superpowered stallion (Wildfire), to wrest the throne of her homeland from the evil witch Diabolyn who had deposed her twelve years earlier.

WILDSIDE   ABC
21 MARCH 1985–25 APRIL 1985   This short-lived Western chronicled the exploits of the five self-appointed members of the "Chamber of Commerce of Wildside," a rough-and-tumble county in northern California: Brodie Hollister (played by William Smith), the shootist with twenty-nine notches on his gun, who had recently returned from the East; Sutton Hollister (J. Eddie Peck), his son; Bannister Sparks (Howard E. Rollins, Jr.), the card sharp and demolition ace who ran Bannister's Emporium & Trading Company; huge Prometheus Jones (Terry Funk), a wizard with rope; and Varges De La Cosa (John Di Aquino), a knife expert who owned the local gun store. Other regulars included Sandy McPeak as Governor J. W. Summerhayes; Meg Ryan as Cally Oaks, owner of the newspaper (the *Daily Flash*); Jason Hervey as

young Zeke; and Tommy Lamey as Parks Ritche, a rival of Sutton's. Tom Greene created the series.

WILL THE REAL JERRY LEWIS PLEASE SIT DOWN   ABC

12 SEPTEMBER 1970–2 SEPTEMBER 1972   Half-hour Saturday-morning cartoon show created by Jerry Lewis.

WILLIAM TELL   SYNDICATED

1958   Officially titled *The Adventures of William Tell*, this half-hour adventure series was filmed in Switzerland and produced by National Telefilm Associates. It starred Conrad Phillips as William Tell, the legendary Swiss freedom fighter; Jennifer Jayne as Hedda Tell; Richard Rogers as Walter Tell; and Willoughby Goddard as Gessler, Tell's nemesis.

WILLIAM TELL   SYNDICATED

1991   The second TV version was officially titled *The Legend of William Tell*. Filmed in Europe, the half-hour series starred Will Lyman as William Tell, who was searching for his wife and son, and Jeremy Clyde as Gessler.

WILLY   CBS

18 SEPTEMBER 1954–7 JULY 1955   Half-hour sitcom starring June Havoc as Willa (Willy) Dodger, a lawyer in a small New Hampshire town. Other regulars included Lloyd Corrigan as Papa; Mary Treen as Willy's sister, Emily; Danny Richards, Jr., as her nephew, Franklin; Whitfield Connor as Willy's boyfriend, veterinarian Charlie Bush; and Aaron Spelling (who would achieve far greater fame as a producer) as Homer. In March of 1955 Willy left New England for New York City, where she landed a job as counsel to a vaudeville organization. Added were Hal Peary as her new employer, Mr. Bannister, and Sterling Holloway as Harvey Evelyn, manager of a repertory company. Filmed at Desilu Studios, the series was produced by June Havoc's husband, Bill Spier.

THE WILTON NORTH REPORT   FOX

11 DECEMBER 1987–8 JANUARY 1988   An unusual, unsuccessful, and generally unfunny attempt to fill the late-night slot in Fox's schedule previously occupied by *The Late Show, The Wilton North Report* was a pastiche of comedy skits, serious news items, celebrity interviews, and odd bits of news. A young comedy duo, Phil Cowan and Paul Robins, served as coanchors. Barry Sand, late of *Late Night with David Letterman,* was the producer. After four weeks, the series was replaced with reruns of *The Late Show.*

WIN, LOSE OR DRAW   NBC/SYNDICATED

7 SEPTEMBER 1987–1 SEPTEMBER 1989 (NBC); 1987–1990 (SYNDICATED)   Two versions of this popular game show, which resembled the home game of Pictionary, surfaced in the fall of 1987. On each one, two three-member teams, each consisting of two celebrities and a contestant, competed; one player was given a word or phrase, and had to get a teammate to guess it by drawing pictures on a large sketch pad. The daytime version ran for two years on NBC, and was one of the few game shows to be hosted by a woman: Vicki Lawrence (later known as Vicki Lawrence Schultz). The syndicated version was hosted first by Bert Convy (who was executive producer with Burt Reynolds), later by Robb Weller. A juvenile version, titled *Teen Win, Lose or Draw,* surfaced on the Disney Channel in 1989, hosted by Marc Price.

WIN WITH A WINNER   NBC

24 JUNE 1958–9 SEPTEMBER 1958   Also known as *Winners Circle*, this prime-time game show was hosted by Sandy Becker and involved five players who, like horses in a race, moved along a track as they answered questions. Home viewers could also participate by sending in postcards predicting the players' exact order of finish.

WIN WITH THE STARS   SYNDICATED

1968   Allen Ludden hosted this game show on which teams made up of celebrities and contestants competed in a song-identification game.

WINDOW ON MAIN STREET   CBS

2 OCTOBER 1961–12 SEPTEMBER 1962   Robert Young, fresh from *Father Knows Best,* starred in this comedy-drama as Cameron Garrett Brooks, a widowed novelist who returned to his hometown, Millsburg, to write about the people there. Also featured were Ford Rainey as Lloyd Ramsey, editor of the town paper; Constance Moore as widow Chris Logan, who worked on the paper; Brad Berwick as Arny Logan, Chris's young son; Warner Jones as Harry McGil, desk clerk at the Majestic Hotel; James Davidson as Wally Evans, owner of the hotel; Carol Byron as Wally's wife, Peggy Evans; Marilyn Harvey as Mrs. Miller; Tim Matheson as her son, Roddy Miller; Coleen Gray as Miss Wycliffe; William Cort as Dick Aldrich; and Richard Wyler as Phil Rowan. The half-hour show was created and owned by Robert Young and Eugene B. Rodney, who had owned *Father Knows Best;* the two were given a free hand by CBS in developing this show.

WINDOW ON THE WORLD   DUMONT

27 JANUARY 1949–14 APRIL 1949   Half-hour variety show hosted by Gil Lamb.

WINDOW ON WASHINGTON   NBC

4 JANUARY 1953–12 JULY 1953   Fifteen-minute Sunday-afternoon public affairs program, hosted by Bill Henry and produced by Julian Goodman.

WINDOW SHOPPING   ABC

2 APRIL 1962–29 JUNE 1962   Bob Kennedy hosted this short-lived daytime game show, on which three contestants studied a picture for a few seconds and could then win points by recalling details about it. Professor William Wood of the Columbia University School of Journalism was the judge. The half-hour series was produced by Alan Gilbert for Wolf Productions.

WINDOWS   CBS

8 JULY 1955–26 AUGUST 1955   A live half-hour dramatic anthology series, *Windows* was produced by Mort Abrahams. Four directors shared the assignments: Jack Garfein, José Quintero, John Stix, and Leonard Valenta.

THE WINDS OF WAR   ABC

6 FEBRUARY 1983–13 FEBRUARY 1983   Herman Wouk adapted his mammoth novel for this expensive and lengthy limited series. Almost everything about the project was mammoth—its length (seven nights, eighteen hours), its cost ($40 million), its 962-page script, its 1785 scenes (filmed in 267 locations in six countries over a fourteen-month span). The action spanned the earliest years of World War II, from the Nazi blitzkrieg of Poland in 1939 to the Japanese attack on Pearl Harbor in 1941. The central character was American naval officer Victor "Pug" Henry, whose assignments during those years took him all over the world; the part was played by Robert Mitchum, appearing in his second dramatic role on TV (the first, in the made-for-TV movie "One Shoe Makes It Murder," was televised a few months earlier, though it had actually been filmed after production on *Winds* had been completed). Other key roles were played by Polly Bergen as Pug's wife, Rhoda Henry; Ben Murphy as their older son, Warren; Jan-Michael Vincent as their younger son, Byron; Lisa Eilbacher as their daughter, Madeline; Ali MacGraw (in a rare TV appearance) as Natalie Jastrow, a European Jew who eventually married Byron; John Houseman as Natalie's uncle, Aaron Jastrow; David Dukes as American diplomatic officer Leslie Slote; Victoria Tennant as Pamela Tudsbury, a British woman with whom Pug had an affair; Peter Graves as Palmer Kirby; Ralph Bellamy as Franklin D. Roosevelt; Howard Lang as Winston Churchill; Gunter Meisner as Adolf Hitler; and Jeremy Kemp as German General Von Roon. Dan Curtis, who had previously produced *Dark Shad-*

ows, produced the series. In mid-1984 plans were announced for a sequel, *War and Remembrance* (see also that title).

WINDY CITY JAMBOREE DUMONT
26 MARCH 1950–18 JUNE 1950   An hour-long musical show, broadcast from the Rainbow Gardens in Chicago. Featured were Danny O'Neil, Gloria Van, Jane Brockman and Bud Tygett, Jimmy McPartland, Dick Edwards, "WooWoo" Stephens, Paula Raye, John Dalce, and the Julian Stockdale Orchestra.

WINGO CBS
1 APRIL 1958–6 MAY 1958   A prime-time game show, *Wingo* pitted a champion against a challenger in a question-and-answer format. A contestant won $1,000 each time his or her opponent was defeated, plus the chance to compete for the show's top prize of $250,000. Bob Kennedy was the host.

WINGS NBC
19 APRIL 1990–24 MAY 1990; 6 SEPTEMBER 1990–   Nantucket Island was the setting for this half-hour sitcom about two estranged brothers who were reunited after their father's death. With Timothy Daly as the serious brother Joe Hackett, owner of Sandpiper Air, a one-plane airline; Steven Weber as the happy-go-lucky brother, Brian Hackett; Crystal Bernard as Helen Chappel, waitress at the airline terminal; Thomas Haden Church (1990–1995) as Lowell Mather, Joe's free-spirited maintenance worker; David Schramm as Roy Biggins, owner of Aeromass, the rival air carrier; Rebecca Schull as Faye Evelyn Cochran, the cheery terminal announcer at Tom Nevers Field; Tony Shalhoub (1992–   ) as Antonio the cabbie; Farrah Forke (1992–1994) as Brian's girlfriend, Alex, a helicopter pilot; and Amy Yasbeck (1994–   ) as Helen's younger sister, Casey Davenport. Joe and Helen got married at the end of the 1994–1995 season.

WINKY-DINK AND YOU CBS
10 OCTOBER 1953–27 APRIL 1957   Television's first interactive show, *Winky-Dink and You* was a Saturday morning children's series hosted by Jack Barry. It featured skits and cartoons (Winky-Dink, a gender-neutral pixie-like creature, was the star of many of the cartoons). The gimmick for which the show is best remembered was the Winky-Dink Kit, which could be bought by mail; it consisted of a piece of plastic that could be placed over a television screen, some crayons, and a cloth to wipe clean the plastic. The kit enabled viewers to participate in Winky's adventures by drawing props as suggested by Jack Barry. It also enabled viewers to transcribe a secret message, which was broadcast bit by bit at the end of the day's cartoon adventures. Also featured on the half-hour show was Dayton Allen, who played Barry's inept assistant, Mr. Bungle. Mae Questel provided the voice of Winky. Other cartoon characters included Mike McBean, Dusty Dan, and Mysto the Magician.

The show was an immediate hit with youngsters. From 1954 to 1955 it was also televised on Sunday mornings, and by 1955 more than two million Winky-Dink kits had been sold through the mail. The series was revived briefly for syndication in 1969, with some sixty-four new five-minute cartoons, but without a human host; in this version Winky-Dink was a male character.

WINNER TAKE ALL CBS/NBC
15 JUNE 1948–3 OCTOBER 1950; 12 FEBRUARY 1951–20 APRIL 1951 (CBS); 25 FEBRUARY 1952–2 MAY 1952 (NBC)   One of the first game shows developed by Mark Goodson and Bill Todman, *Winner Take All* began on radio in 1946 and came to television two years later; from 1948 to 1950 it was a prime-time series, and in 1951 and 1952 it was a daytime show. The prime-time version involved a straight question-and-answer format. On the daytime version two contestants competed, answering questions about skits performed on stage by a group of players. Bud Collyer was the prime-time host; the CBS daytime version was hosted by Barry Gray, the NBC version by Bill Cullen. Gil Fates was the producer. During the summer of 1952 "Winner Take All" was a featured segment of the NBC daytime variety series *Matinee in New York.*

WINNETKA ROAD   NBC

12 MARCH 1994–16 APRIL 1994   Hour continuing drama set in the Chicago suburb of
Oak Bluff. With Ed Begley, Jr., as Glenn Barker, who left his wife and kids for a
shapely aerobics instructor; Josh Brolin as cop Jack Passion; Richard M. Tyson as
Duane Serling, who ran a landscaping business; Kristen Cloke as Maybeth Serling,
his wife; Kurt Deutsch as newly unemployed Kevin Page; Paige Turco as actress
Terry Mears, Jack's former girlfriend, who recently returned home to Oak Bluff;
Meg Tilly as George, a mysterious artist; Catherine Hicks as Jeannie; and Megan
Ward as stockbroker Nicole Manning, Jack's current girlfriend. Aaron Spelling and
E. Duke Vincent were the executive producers.

WINNING STREAK   NBC

1 JULY 1974–3 JANUARY 1975   Daytime game show hosted by Bill Cullen on which
contestants answered questions to win letters of the alphabet, which they could then
use to assemble words. The show was a Bob Stewart Production.

WINSTON CHURCHILL—THE VALIANT YEARS   ABC

27 NOVEMBER 1960–11 JUNE 1961   A highly acclaimed series of twenty-six half-hour
segments that focused on Churchill's leadership during World War II. The series was
produced by Robert D. Graff and Ben Feiner, Jr. It was narrated by Gary Merrill,
and selections from Churchill's memoirs were read by Richard Burton. The series
was rerun on ABC in 1962 and 1963. Richard Rodgers composed the score.

WIRE SERVICE   ABC

4 OCTOBER 1956–23 SEPTEMBER 1957   Hour-long adventure series about three reporters for the Trans Globe News Service; the three stars—Mercedes McCambridge as
Kate Wells, Dane Clark as Dan Miller, and George Brent as Dean Evans—appeared
on a rotating basis. Sharp-eyed viewers could have noticed Michael Landon in one
episode, "High Adventure," playing his first major TV role (20 December). Don
Sharpe and Warren Lewis produced the series.

WISDOM OF THE AGES   DUMONT

16 DECEMBER 1952–30 JUNE 1953   On this prime-time panel show, Jack Barry combined features of two of his earlier shows, *Juvenile Jury* and *Life Begins at Eighty*,
both of which he created with his longtime partner, Dan Enright. *Wisdom of the Ages*
featured five panelists—one under twenty, one between twenty-one and forty, one
between forty-one and sixty, one between sixty-one and eighty, and one over
eighty—who dispensed advice on problems suggested by viewers.

THE WISDOM SERIES   NBC

13 OCTOBER 1957–6 APRIL 1958   A Sunday-afternoon series of filmed interviews with
some of the world's greatest figures, *The Wisdom Series* was produced by Robert D.
Graff. Like many of NBC's highly praised programming ideas of the decade, it was
conceived by Sylvester "Pat" Weaver. Though the series did not reach the air until
1957, filming had begun as early as 1952. As a rule, subjects had to be over sixty-five
years of age in order to be eligible for consideration. Among those who participated in
the series were Bertrand Russell, Jawaharlal Nehru, Carl Sandburg, Sean O'Casey,
Herbert Hoover, Edward Steichen, Pablo Casals, Wanda Landowska, Igor
Stravinsky, Edith Hamilton, and Frank Lloyd Wright. The show was rerun in 1959.

WISEGUY   CBS

16 SEPTEMBER 1987–19 JULY 1990; 10 NOVEMBER 1990–8 DECEMBER 1990   Hour crime
show from Stephen J. Cannell Productions, starring Ken Wahl as Vinnie Terranova,
an undercover agent for the Federal Organized Crime Bureau, Jonathan Banks as his
hard-driving boss, Frank McPike, and Jim Byrnes as Lifeguard, the communications
expert who provided Vinnie's sole link to the O.C.B. when on assignment. In order
to establish his credibility with the underworld, Terranova had served eighteen
months in prison.

The producers decided to run the stories in "arcs"—each story spanned from five to ten episodes. This innovative idea was a welcome change from the usual "crook of the week" format of most crime shows. Two main stories were presented during the 1987–1988 season: the first starred Ray Sharkey as Atlantic City mobster Sonny Steelgrave, and the second starred Kevin Spacey and Joan Severance as deranged brother-sister duo Mel and Susan Profitt, with William Russ as fellow "wiseguy" Roger LoCocco. The second season began with the death of Vinnie's brother, Peter (played by Gerald Anthony, and occasionally featured during the previous season), drawing Vinnie into investigating a white supremacist group led by Knox Pooley (played by Fred Dalton Thompson). From there Terranova checked out the garment industry in an arc featuring Jerry Lewis and Ron Silver as Eli and David Sternberg; Anthony Denison appeared as federal agent John Raglin, filling in for an injured Terranova (in real life Ken Wahl's foot had been injured after a camera dolly twice ran over it). After a brief hospital stay in which the image of Steelgrave appeared to the heavily drugged Vinnie, Terranova investigated the record industry; real-life rockers Deborah Harry, Glenn Frey, and Mick Fleetwood all appeared in that arc. During the third season Vinnie infiltrated the highest levels of the New York mob (in an arc with Patti D'Arbanville and George Petrie), exposed a foreign counterfeiting operation (with Kim Greist, Norman Lloyd, and Ford Rainey), and flipped out while tracking down a homicidal maniac in a small town (in an arc with Steve Ryan, David Strathairn, and William Russ, who returned as Roger LoCocco).

Filmed on location in Vancouver, the series returned briefly, without Wahl, during the 1990–1991 season. Steven Bauer starred as the new wiseguy, Michael Santana, in the final five-episode arc; his quarry was a villain named Guzman, played by Maximilian Schell.

WISH YOU WERE HERE   CBS
20 JULY 1990–24 AUGUST 1990   An offbeat comedy series, starring Lew Schneider as Donny Cogswell, who quit his job as a New York stockbroker and headed off to Europe, where he made first-person videos and sent them back to his ex-girlfriend, family, and friends. Cogswell's journeys were filmed entirely on location using a lightweight video camera, and were deliberately intended to look homemade, with out-of-focus shots, slanted angles, and sudden cuts.

WISHBONE   PBS
9 OCTOBER 1995–   The title character in this weekday children's series was a Jack Russell terrier, who, with the help of elaborate costumes and props, enacted scenes chosen from children's literary classics. Wishbone was played by Soccer.

WISHKID STARRING MACAULAY CULKIN   NBC
14 SEPTEMBER 1991–5 SEPTEMBER 1992   Popular child actor Macaulay Culkin received title billing in this half-hour Saturday-morning cartoon show. Culkin introduced the animated features, and provided the voice of the lead character, Nick McClary, a youngster whose wishes came true when he punched his baseball glove. Other characters included Nick's sister, Katie, his dog, Slobber, and his pal, Darryl Singletary.

WITH THIS RING   DUMONT
21 JANUARY 1951–11 MARCH 1951   Prime-time panel show on which engaged couples discussed marriage and marital problems. Bill Slater hosted the show for the first few weeks and was succeeded by Martin Gabel.

THE WITNESS   CBS
29 SEPTEMBER 1960–26 JANUARY 1961   This unusual anthology series was cloaked in pseudo-documentary trappings. Each show was set at a Congressional hearing room, where suspected racketeers were grilled by a panel of investigators. Some of the characters who appeared were entirely fictional, while others were based on real people; Telly Savalas guest starred on the premiere as Lucky Luciano. Paul McGrath appeared as the chairman of the investigating panel, and other members of the body

were played by Charles Haydon, Frank Milan, and William Smithers. Vern Collett played the stenographic reporter.

THE WIZARD   CBS
9 SEPTEMBER 1986–30 APRIL 1987; 9 JUNE 1987–7 JULY 1987   An hour adventure series, starring three-foot, eleven-inch David Rappaport as Simon McKay, a toymaker and inventor who was recruited by the government to help out on various missions. Doug Barr was Alex Jagger, the agent who worked with McKay; Fran Ryan was McKay's housekeeper, Tillie Russell. Occasionally featured was Roy Dotrice as Troyan, McKay's nemesis. Rappaport committed suicide in May 1990.

THE WIZARD OF ODDS   NBC
17 JULY 1973–28 JUNE 1974   Alex Trebek hosted this daytime game show, which replaced *Sale of the Century*. Members of the studio audience competed in a number of rounds, most of which required answering statistical questions posed by the host.

THE WIZARD OF OZ   ABC
8 SEPTEMBER 1990–31 AUGUST 1991   In the first TV animated version of the classic children's story, Dorothy and friends returned to the Land of Oz after learning that the Wicked Witch had come back to life.

WIZARDS AND WARRIORS   CBS
26 FEBRUARY 1983–14 MAY 1983   This tongue-in-cheek fantasy series was set in a mythical medieval kingdom. Featured were Jeff Conaway as the dashing Prince Erik Greystone; Walter Olkewicz as his manservant, Marko; Duncan Regehr as the villainous Prince Dirk Blackpool; Julia Duffy as empty-headed Princess Ariel; Clive Revill as the wizard Vector; and Randi Brooks as Bethel the sorceress.

WOLF   CBS
19 SEPTEMBER 1989–14 NOVEMBER 1989; 21 JUNE 1990–28 JUNE 1990; 18 JULY 1990–12 SEPTEMBER 1990   Jack Scalia appeared in his fifth flop series of the decade, starring in this hour crime show as Tony Wolf, a San Francisco cop who was framed and had to leave the force. Now living aboard a boat, the *Sea Wolf*, in the harbor, he was planning to be a fisherman, but found himself acting as a private investigator instead. Also on board were Joseph Sirola as his father, Sal Lupo; Nicolas Surovy as his former adversary, attorney Dylan Elliott, who now doubted Wolf's guilt; Mimi Kuzyk as his high school sweetheart (and now platonic friend), Connie Bacarri, who ran a restaurant; and J. C. Brandy as Connie's teenage daughter, Angeline. The series joined CBS's late-night lineup in July 1990.

WOLF ROCK TV   ABC
8 SEPTEMBER 1984–24 NOVEMBER 1984   Rock videos were blended into this Saturday morning cartoon series on which Wolfman Jack and a gang of teenagers tried to save an ailing TV station. Disc jockey Wolfman Jack provided his own voice.

THE WOLFMAN JACK SHOW   SYNDICATED
1974   Half-hour talk show on which Wolfman Jack, legendary disc jockey of the 1950s, rapped with rock stars.

WOMAN   SYNDICATED
1971   Half-hour talk show for women, hosted by Sherrye Henry.

WOMAN   PBS
1973–1977   Half-hour public affairs program on topics of interest to women, produced and hosted by Sandra Elkin for WNED-TV, Buffalo.

A WOMAN TO REMEMBER   DUMONT
21 FEBRUARY 1949–15 JULY 1949   One of television's first serials, *A Woman to Remember* began as a daytime show and shifted to an early evening slot after a few

weeks. Its format was that of a serial within a serial, as it dealt with the interaction between the cast and crew of a mythical radio soap opera. The fifteen-minute show featured Patricia Wheel as Christine Baker, the leading lady of the radio soap; Joan Catlin as its villain, Carol Winstead; John Raby as its director, Steve Hammond; Frank Thomas, Jr., as its sound man, Charley Anderson; and Ruth McDevitt as Bessie Thatcher.

WOMAN TO WOMAN   SYNDICATED
1983   Pat Mitchell (formerly of *Hour Magazine*) was the moderator of this discussion show, aimed at women viewers. Each day focused on a single topic, and featured an all-female studio audience. The series was made available to local stations in both an hour and a half-hour format.

WOMAN WITH A PAST   CBS
1 FEBRUARY 1954–2 JULY 1954   This daytime serial premiered on the same day as *The Secret Storm,* but lasted one-sixtieth as long. It starred Constance Ford as Lynn Sherwood, a dress designer.

WOMEN IN PRISON   FOX
11 OCTOBER 1987–2 APRIL 1988   Cellblock J at Bass Women's Prison in Wisconsin was the locale of this half-hour sitcom. With Julia Campbell as Vicki Springer, a young socialite framed for shoplifting; Peggy Cass as veteran con Eve Shipley; C. C. H. Pounder as husband-murderer Dawn Murphy; Wendie Jo Sperber as Pam; Antoinette Byron as Bonnie Murphy; Denny Dillon as Meg Bando, the guard; and Blake Clark as Clint Rafferty, the warden.

WOMEN OF THE HOUSE   CBS
4 JANUARY 1995–20 MARCH 1995; 18 AUGUST 1995   Although Delta Burke had left the popular *Designing Women* after a disagreement with the producers, the fences were eventually mended. Burke again played her *Designing Women* character, Suzanne Sugarbaker, whose fifth husband, a Georgia Congressman, had just died; Suzanne took his seat in Washington. Joining her were Teri Garr as the hard-drinking press secretary, Sissy Emerson; Patricia Heaton as aide Natalie Hollingsworth; Valerie Mahaffey (first four episodes) and Julie Hagerty as eager-to-please receptionist Jennifer Malone; Jonathan Banks as Jim, Suzanne's dimwitted brother; and Brittany Parkyn as Desiree, Suzanne's young daughter.

WONDER WOMAN   ABC/CBS
18 DECEMBER 1976–30 JULY 1977 (ABC); 16 SEPTEMBER 1977–11 SEPTEMBER 1979 (CBS)   An hour adventure series based on the comic book character created by Charles Moulton, *Wonder Woman* was first introduced to television audiences in a 1974 made-for-TV movie, which starred Cathy Lee Crosby. The character reappeared in three specials aired during the 1975–1976 season, all of which starred Lynda Carter— "The New, Original Wonder Woman," "Fausta, the Nazi Wonder Woman," and "Wonder Woman Meets Baroness Von Gunter." Regularly scheduled broadcasts began the following season, again starring Lynda Carter in the title role. A resident of mysterious Paradise Island, the powerfully endowed Wonder Woman helped the Americans fight the Nazis; she took the name Diana Prince as her cover. Also featured on the ABC version of the series were Lyle Waggoner as Major Steve Trevor, Diana's romantic interest; Richard Eastham as General Blankenship; and Beatrice Colen as Corporal Etta Candy. Debra Winger was seen occasionally as Diana's younger sister, Drusilla (or Wonder Girl). When the series moved to CBS in the fall of 1977, it was updated to the present time; Lynda Carter continued as Diana Prince, and Lyle Waggoner returned as Steve Trevor, Jr. (the son of the major), a government agent. Normann Burton joined the cast as Joe Atkinson, their boss at IADC, the Inter-Agency Defense Command. The CBS version was officially titled *The New Adventures of Wonder Woman.* Douglas S. Cramer was the executive producer.

THE WONDER YEARS   ABC

31 JANUARY 1988; 15 MARCH 1988–19 APRIL 1988; 26 OCTOBER 1988–1 SEPTEMBER 1993
Creators Carol Black and Neal Marlens looked back twenty years to suburban life in
1968 in this highly acclaimed half-hour comedy-drama. Fred Savage starred as the
central character, twelve-year-old Kevin Arnold, who was just about to start school
at John F. Kennedy Junior High as the series got underway; Daniel Stern provided
the voice of the adult Kevin, narrating each episode. Also featured were Jason
Hervey as his older brother, Wayne, who delighted in teasing him; Olivia d'Abo
(daughter of sixties rock musician Michael d'Abo) as his hippie older sister, Karen;
Dan Lauria as his gruff father, Jack; Alley Mills as his mother, Norma; Danica
McKellar as his neighbor and sometime girlfriend, Gwendolyn (Winnie) Cooper;
Josh Saviano as his nerdy friend, Paul Pfeiffer; Ben Stein as science teacher Mr.
Cantwell; and Robert Picardo as the fearsome gym teacher, Coach Ed Cutlip. The
series had a special preview in January 1988, immediately following ABC's Super
Bowl telecast. It then surfaced for a limited run that spring, before resuming full-time
production in the fall. By the fall of 1990 Karen had moved out of the Arnold
household and in with her boyfriend, Michael (David Schwimmer); they eventually
married. In the fall of 1991 Kevin and his pals left junior high and started at Mc-
Kinley High.

WONDERFUL JOHN ACTON   NBC

12 JULY 1953–6 OCTOBER 1953   Half-hour sitcom set in 1919 in a small Kentucky
town on the banks of the Ohio River. With Harry Holcombe as John Acton, the court
clerk and town storekeeper; Virginia Dwyer as Julia, John's widowed daughter;
Ronnie Walken as Kevin Acton, John's twelve-year-old son; Ian Martin as Uncle
Terence; Jane Rose as John's sister, Bessie; and Pat Harrington as Peter Bodkin, Jr.
Edward A. Byron was the producer, Grey Lockwood the director. The show was
seen Sundays over most NBC outlets; in New York, however, it was shown Mondays.

WONDERFUL TOWN, U.S.A.
See FAYE EMERSON'S WONDERFUL TOWN

WONDERS OF THE WORLD   SYNDICATED

1958   Travelogue, hosted and narrated by the Linker family.

WONDERWORKS   PBS

1984–1994   An anthology series aimed at preteen children. Most of the presentations were adaptations of children's books, but some were original stories. The series'
most noteworthy presentation was probably the four-part "Anne of Green Gables,"
starring Megan Follows, which won a Peabody Award in 1986.

THE WOODY WOODBURY SHOW   SYNDICATED

1967   Ninety-minute talk show, hosted by Woody Woodbury.

THE WOODY WOODPECKER SHOW   ABC/NBC

3 OCTOBER 1957–25 SEPTEMBER 1958 (ABC); 12 SEPTEMBER 1970–2 SEPTEMBER 1972
(NBC); 11 SEPTEMBER 1976–3 SEPTEMBER 1977 (NBC)   Woody Woodpecker, the
cartoon character created in the 1930s by Walter Lantz, first came to network TV in
1957 in a half-hour series that was carried by ABC on Thursday afternoons. The
cartoon segments included not only Woody Woodpecker, but also Gabby Gator,
Andy Panda, and others. Lantz himself hosted the series and showed viewers the
basics of animation. NBC later carried the cartoons on Saturday mornings. Woody
Woodpecker's voice, and his distinctive laugh, were supplied by Lantz's wife, Gracie
Lantz.

WOOPS!   FOX

27 SEPTEMBER 1992–6 DECEMBER 1992   Perhaps best summarized as a post-
apocalyptic *Gilligan's Island*, *Woops!* was a sitcom about six survivors of a nuclear war
who gathered at a Midwestern farmhouse. With Meagen Fay as Alice McConnell, a

feminist who had run a bookstore; Fred Applegate as Jack Connors, who had been homeless; Evan Handler as Mark Braddock, who had been a teacher; Lane Davies as Curtis Thorpe, who had been a stock analyst; Cleavant Derricks as Frederick Ross, who had been a pathologist; and Marita Geraghty as Suzane Skilman, who had been a manicurist.

WORD FOR WORD   NBC
30 SEPTEMBER 1963–23 OCTOBER 1964   Merv Griffin hosted this daytime game show on which contestants tried to make three- and four-letter words from larger ones, and then tried to unscramble words flashed on a screen.

WORDPLAY   NBC
29 DECEMBER 1986–4 SEPTEMBER 1987   This daytime game show replaced the long-running serial *Search for Tomorrow*. Two contestants competed, trying to guess the correct definitions of words from among possible answers given by a panel of three celebrities. Winning contestants could play a bonus round for a large cash prize. Tom Kennedy hosted.

WORDS AND MUSIC   NBC
2 AUGUST 1949–8 SEPTEMBER 1949   Fifteen-minute twice-weekly musical show, with Barbara Marshall and the Jerry Jerome Trio. Duane McKinney produced and directed.

WORDS AND MUSIC   NBC
28 SEPTEMBER 1970–12 FEBRUARY 1971   Daytime game show hosted by Wink Martindale, on which contestants tried to find word "clues" hidden in the lyrics of songs, which were sung by the show's regulars—Katie Gran, Bob Marlo, Pat Henderson, and Don Minter.

WORKING GIRL   NBC
16 APRIL 1990–14 MAY 1990; 16 JULY 1990–30 JULY 1990   Half-hour sitcom based on the 1988 film. With Sandra Bullock as Tess McGill, a secretary at New York's Trask Industries who landed a position as a junior executive in the marketing department; Nana Visitor as her boss, Bryn Newhouse; George Newbern as her chief rival, Everett Rutledge; Judy Prescott as Lana, a secretary, one of Tess's old cohorts; Edye Byrde as Libby Wentworth, Bryn's secretary; Tom O'Rourke as A. J. Trask, head of the company; B. J. Ward as Tess's mother, Fran McGill; and David Schramm as Tess's father, Joe McGill.

WORKING IT OUT   NBC
22 AUGUST 1990–12 DECEMBER 1990   Half-hour romantic sitcom about two divorcées who met at a cooking class. With Jane Curtin as Sarah Marshall; Stephen Collins as David Stuart; Kyndra Joy Casper as Molly, Sarah's nine-year-old daughter; Mary Beth Hurt as Sarah's friend, Andy; Chevi Colton as Sophie; and David Garrison as David's confidante, Stan.

WORKING STIFFS   CBS
15 SEPTEMBER 1979–6 OCTOBER 1979   Short-lived Saturday-night sitcom starring Jim Belushi as Ernie O'Rourke and Michael Keaton as his brother, Mike O'Rourke, who worked as janitors at the O'Rourke Building in Chicago. Also featured were Val Bisoglio as Al Steckler, the building manager; Phil Rubinstein as Falzone; Allan Arbus as Mitch; and Lorna Patterson as Nikki. Arthur Silver and Bob Brunner were the executive producers for Paramount TV-Frog Productions-Huk, Inc.

WORKING WOMAN   SYNDICATED
1992–   Half-hour weekly magazine series, hosted by Kathleen Matthews.

WORLD   PBS

5 FEBRUARY 1978–12 MAY 1980   Umbrella title for a series of documentaries produced at home and abroad. The premiere telecast, "The Clouded Window," which
examined America's TV news industry, was hosted by Daniel Schorr. The most
controversial program was "Death of a Princess," broadcast 12 May 1980. It was a
dramatization of British journalist Antony Thomas's investigation into the public
executions of a Saudi-Arabian princess and her lover in 1977; the program, which
was shown over the protests of the Saudi-Arabian government, attracted one of the
largest audiences ever to watch a PBS offering. Five *World* specials were aired during
the 1980–1981 season.

A WORLD APART   ABC

30 MARCH 1970–25 JUNE 1971   This half-hour daytime serial premiered on the same
day as two other soap operas, *The Best of Everything* and *Somerset*. Written by
Kathryn Phillips, the daughter of Irna Phillips, it told the stories of a brother and
sister, the adopted children of a television writer. Principal players included: Augusta
Dabney and Elizabeth Lawrence as Betty Kahlman, the writer; Susan Sarandon as
Patrice Kahlman, her daughter; Matthew Cowles as Chris Kahlman, her son; William Prince as Russell Barry, whom Betty eventually married; Robert Gentry as Dr.
John Carr; Tom Ligon as P. D. Drinkard; Rosetta LeNoire as Matilda; James Noble
as Ed Sims; Erin Connor as Becky Sims; Kathleen Maguire as Adrian Sims; William
Tynan as Bill Sims; Stephen Elliott as Jack Condon; Susan Sullivan as Nancy
Condon; Nicolas Surovy as Fred Turner; Carol Willard as Louise Turner; John Dev-
lin as Dr. Nathaniel Fuller; Anna Minot as Meg Johns; Kevin Conway as Bud Whitman; Clifton Davis as Matt Hampton; Jane White as Olivia Hampton; Heather
MacRae as Linda Peters; and Albert Paulsen as Dr. Neil Stevens.

THE WORLD AT WAR   SYNDICATED

1974   An hour documentary series on World War II, *The World at War* was produced in Great Britain and narrated by Sir Laurence Olivier.

WORLD CHAMPIONSHIP GOLF   NBC

18 OCTOBER 1959–26 JUNE 1960   This Sunday afternoon sports series was NBC's
answer to ABC's rival program, *All-Star Golf*. Here, thirty-two top professional
golfers competed in match play elimination rounds. Mike Souchak and Cary Middlecoff emerged as the two finalists. Bob Crosby was the commentator.

WORLD MONITOR   DISCOVERY

12 SEPTEMBER 1988–3 JANUARY 1992   Half-hour nightly news roundup produced by
the highly respected newspaper *The Christian Science Monitor*. Former NBC newsman John Hart was the anchor, former CBS News veteran Sanford Socolow the
executive producer.

THE WORLD OF GIANTS   SYNDICATED

1960   Half-hour adventure series starring Marshall Thompson as Mel Hunter, a six-
inch-tall secret agent, and Arthur Franz as Bill Winters, his normal-sized partner.
Hunter usually traveled by briefcase. The show was produced by William Alland for
CBS Syndication. The thirteen episodes were filmed in England.

THE WORLD OF IDEAS   CBS

18 JANUARY 1959–3 MAY 1959   Sunday-afternoon discussion series, moderated by
Dr. Charles Frankel, chairman of the philosophy department at Columbia University.

THE WORLD OF LOWELL THOMAS   SYNDICATED

1966   Travelogue, hosted by veteran broadcaster Lowell Thomas.

THE WORLD OF MR. SWEENEY   NBC

30 JUNE 1954–31 DECEMBER 1955   This fifteen-minute comedy series began as a
feature on *The Kate Smith Hour* before getting its own slot in the summer of 1954.

Set in the small town of Mapleton, it starred Charles Ruggles as Cicero P. Sweeney, proprietor of the general store and teller of tales. Also featured were Helen Wagner as Marge, his daughter; Glenn Walken as Kippie, his young grandson; Harrison Dowd as Harvey; and Nell Harris as Hannah.

THE WORLD OF PEOPLE   SYNDICATED
1980   Half-hour magazine show about people—the famous and the not-so-famous. Among the several hosts were Steve Edelman, Jane D'Atri, and Sarah Edwards.

THE WORLD OF SPORTS ILLUSTRATED   SYNDICATED/CBS
1971–1972 (SYNDICATED); 28 JANUARY 1973–9 SEPTEMBER 1973 (CBS)   This half-hour sports magazine began as a syndicated effort; when it was picked up by CBS in 1973, its title was changed to *CBS Sports Illustrated;* Jack Whitaker was the host.

THE WORLD OF SURVIVAL   SYNDICATED
1971–1977   Half-hour documentary series on animal life, narrated by John Forsythe. Aubrey Buxton was the executive producer for Anglia, Ltd., in association with the World Wildlife Fund.

WORLD OF TALENT
See DICK CLARK'S WORLD OF TALENT

WORLD WAR ONE   CBS
22 SEPTEMBER 1964–5 SEPTEMBER 1965   A prime-time half-hour documentary series on World War I, narrated by Robert Ryan.

WORLD WAR II: G.I. DIARY   SYNDICATED
1978   Narrated by Lloyd Bridges, this series of twenty-five half-hour documentaries looked at World War II from the point of view of the American soldier. Arthur Holch was the executive producer for Time–Life TV.

WORLD WIDE 60   NBC
23 JANUARY 1960–10 SEPTEMBER 1960   A prime-time hour-long documentary series on current events, *World Wide 60* was hosted by NBC newsmen Chet Huntley and Frank McGee.

THE WORLD'S GREATEST SUPERFRIENDS
See SUPER FRIENDS

WRANGLER   NBC
7 JULY 1960–15 SEPTEMBER 1960   A summer replacement for *The Tennessee Ernie Ford Show, Wrangler* was a half-hour western starring Jason Evers as Pitcairn, an occasionally philosophical cowboy who roamed the West.

THE WREN'S NEST   ABC
13 JANUARY 1949–30 APRIL 1949   A thrice-weekly, fifteen-minute comedy serial about a New York City family, *The Wren's Nest* starred Virginia Sale and Sam Wren (who were married in real life) and their twelve-year-old twins. Tom DeHuff directed.

THE WRIGHT VERDICTS   CBS
31 MARCH 1995–14 APRIL 1995; 4 JUNE 1995—11 JUNE 1995   Dick Wolf created this hour crime show starring Tom Conti as Charles Wright, an English-born criminal defense attorney who worked in New York. Also aboard were Margaret Colin as Sandy, Wright's investigator, and Aida Turturro as Lydia, his secretary.

WUZZLES   CBS/ABC
14 SEPTEMBER 1985–6 SEPTEMBER 1986 (CBS); 13 SEPTEMBER 1986–5 SEPTEMBER 1987 (ABC)   This Saturday morning cartoon show was set on the Isle of Wuz, where lived the Wuzzles, each of whom was a combination of two different animals.

WYATT EARP   ABC

6 SEPTEMBER 1955–26 SEPTEMBER 1961   Officially titled *The Life and Legend of Wyatt Earp,* this half-hour series, together with *Gunsmoke* and *Cheyenne,* marked the beginning of the so-called "adult western." The concept gained popularity over the next few seasons, and by the fall of 1959 there were no fewer than twenty-seven westerns scheduled in prime time. This one was based loosely on fact and starred Hugh O'Brian as Wyatt Earp; for the show's first four seasons Earp was the marshal of Dodge City, Kansas (*Gunsmoke*'s Matt Dillon was also the marshal of Dodge City, but the two lawmen never met, as their shows were on different networks). Also featured were Douglas Fowley and Myron Healey as Doc Holliday and Morgan Woodward as Shotgun Gibbs, Earp's deputy. In the fall of 1959 the show shifted its locale to Tombstone, Arizona (the real Earp had done the same thing), and Earp became the marshal there. Joining the cast were Randy Stuart as saloonkeeper Nellie Cashman; Damian O'Flynn as Doc Goodfellow; Lash LaRue (fall 1959) and Steve Brodie (1959–1961) as Johnny Behan, Tombstone's corrupt sheriff; and Trevor Bardette (1959–1961) as Clanton, the area crime boss. Robert F. Sisk produced the series.

Hugh O'Brian returned as Earp in a two-hour TV movie, "Wyatt Earp: Return to Tombstone" (2 July 1994, CBS), which featured colorized clips from the old series and newly-filmed footage.

THE X-FILES   FOX

10 SEPTEMBER 1993–   On this stylish hour series a pair of FBI agents teamed up to investigate cases classified as "X-Files"—unexplained phenomena. It starred David Duchovny as Fox Mulder, an Oxford-educated psychologist who believed that his sister had been abducted by aliens as a child, and Gillian Anderson as Dana Scully, who had been recruited from medical school and who took a scientific approach to the cases. Together they encountered a bizarre assortment of cases ranging from encounters with aliens to possession by spirits. Created by Chris Carter, the series quickly acquired a large cult following. Refreshingly, not every mystery was resolved by the end of the episode.

X-MEN   FOX

31 OCTOBER 1992–   Half-hour cartoon series based on the Marvel comic books about eight youngsters who attended a school for mutants. Taught by Professor Charles Xavier and known as X-Men, the octet—The Beast, Cyclops, Gambit, Jean Grey, Jubilee, Rogue, Storm, and Wolverine—battled the archvillain Magneto. The popularity of the series led to a 49% increase in the ratings of the Fox Children's Network during the 1992–1993 season.

THE XAVIER CUGAT SHOW   NBC

27 FEBRUARY 1957–24 MAY 1957   A twice-weekly, fifteen-minute musical series, *The Xavier Cugat Show* replaced Eddie Fisher's *Coke Time* on Wednesdays and Fridays. Bandleader Xavier Cugat and his orchestra supplied the music, and vocals were performed by Abbe Lane, Cugat's then wife.

XENA: WARRIOR PRINCESS   SYNDICATED

1995–   Spun off from the syndicated action series *Hercules—The Legendary Journeys,* this hour weekly program was also set in ancient times. Lucy Lawless starred as Xena, who decided to relinquish her warlike past and help the oppressed and needy. Renee O'Connor costarred as Gabrielle, a village lass who decided to accompany Xena.

XUXA   SYNDICATED

1993–1995 An Americanized version of the highly popular Latin American children's program, in which host Xuxa (pronounced *shoo-sha*) led youngsters in songs, dances, and games. Born Maria da Graca Meneghel in Brazil, Xuxa had been a model before turning to children's television.

YANCY DERRINGER CBS

2 OCTOBER 1958–24 SEPTEMBER 1959   Half-hour western set in New Orleans after the Civil War. With Jock Mahoney as Yancy Derringer, a suave and stylishly dressed bon vivant who carried the pistol for which he was known in his hat; X Brands as Pahoo, Yancy's silent and unsmiling Indian companion, who always kept a knife in his headdress (Pahoo's full name, Pahoo Ka-Ta-Wah, was Pawnee for "Wolf who stands in water"); Kevin Hagen as John Colton, the beleaguered city administrator of New Orleans; Frances Bergen as Madame Francine, one of Yancy's female friends. The series was created by Mary Loos and Richard Sale, who owned the show together with executive producers Warren Lewis and Don Sharpe.

A YEAR AT THE TOP CBS

5 AUGUST 1977–4 SEPTEMBER 1977   Comedy-fantasy about a pair of songwriters who sold their souls to the devil for a year at the top of their profession. With Greg Evigan as Greg; Paul Shaffer as his partner, Paul Durban; Gabe Dell as their agent, Frederick Hanover, the son of the devil; Nedra Volz as Belle, Paul's grandmother; Priscilla Morrill as Miss Worley, Hanover's secretary; and Julie Cobb as Trish. The pilot for the series, "Hereafter," was shown on NBC 27 November 1975. The series was created by Woody Kling, and developed by Don Kirshner in association with Norman Lear. Darryl Hickman was the producer.

A YEAR IN THE LIFE NBC

24 AUGUST 1987–20 APRIL 1988   Joshua Brand and John Falsey, who had created *St. Elsewhere,* created this hour dramatic series, which grew out of a three-part NBC miniseries televised on 15–17 December 1986. Loved by the critics ("remarkable television entertainment," wrote Don Merrill in *TV Guide*), it never attracted an audience, and vanished after an eight-month run. The series focused on the members of the Gardner family of Seattle: Joe Gardner (Richard Kiley), a plastics manufacturer who was widowed in the miniseries; eldest child Anne Maxwell (Wendy Phillips), twice divorced; daughter Lindley Eisenberg (Jayne Atkinson), who worked for her father; prodigal son Jack (Morgan Stevens); youngest child Sam (David Oliver), who also worked for his father; Lindley's husband, attorney Jim Eisenberg (Adam Arkin); Sam's wife, Kay (Sarah Jessica Parker); Anne's son from her first marriage, David Sisk (Trey Ames); Anne's daughter, Sunny Sisk (Amanda Peterson); little Ruthie, Lindley and Jim's daughter (Melissa and Erin Leonard); Dr. Alice Foley (Diana Muldaur), who was interested in Joe; and Max the dog (Beau).

YEARBOOK FOX

7 MARCH 1991–6 JULY 1991   Half-hour documentary series chronicling senior year at Glenbard West High School in suburban Chicago. Ken Dashow narrated.

THE YELLOW ROSE NBC

2 OCTOBER 1983–12 MAY 1984   A sprawling Texas cattle ranch known as the Yellow Rose was the setting of this hour prime-time serial. Principal players included: Cybill Shepherd as Colleen Champion, the young widow of Wade Champion, who founded the Yellow Rose; David Soul as Roy Champion, Wade's son by a former marriage; Edward Albert as Quisto, Roy's son, a lawyer; Tom Schanley as Whit, Roy's son; Susan Anspach as Grace McKenzie, the kitchen boss (dissatisfied with her role, Anspach left after the first nine episodes); Sam Elliott as Chance, a newly hired ranch hand who bore a strong resemblance to Wade; Chuck Connors as Jeb Hollister, the previous owner of the ranch; Noah Beery, Jr., as Luther Dillard, a ranch hand; Kerrie Keane as Caryn Cabrerra; and Ken Curtis as Hoyt Coryell, a ranch hand. Jane Russell joined the cast briefly in midseason as Jeb's sister, Rose Hollister, for whom the ranch had been named. NBC reran the series during the summer of 1990.

YESTERDAY, TODAY & TOMORROW NBC

2 AUGUST 1989–28 NOVEMBER 1989   Yet another of NBC's seemingly endless attempts to establish a prime-time news show, this one boasted three hosts—Maria Shriver, Chuck Scarborough and Mary Alice Williams—and was supposed to exam-

ine topics from the past, present and future, using interviews, newsreel footage and, when necessary, "dramatic recreations" of events. It was televised monthly, with the hope that it could go into a weekly slot in midseason, but the series vanished after only four outings.

YESTERDAY'S NEWSREEL   SYNDICATED
1948   Vintage theatrical newsreels were repackaged for local television stations on this series, which was the first program offered by Ziv TV. Ziv would become one of the industry's leading suppliers of syndicated programs during the 1950s.

YO! MTV RAPS   MTV
6 AUGUST 1988–   MTV's first effort at showcasing rap music, *Yo! MTV* Raps was cohosted by rappers Ed Lover and Dr. Dre.

YOGI BEAR   SYNDICATED
1961–1963
YOGI'S GANG   ABC
8 SEPTEMBER 1973–30 AUGUST 1975
YOGI'S SPACE RACE   NBC
9 SEPTEMBER 1978–3 MARCH 1979
YO, YOGI!   NBC
14 SEPTEMBER 1991–25 JULY 1992   *Yogi Bear,* one of the most famous cartoon creations from Hanna-Barbera Productions, first appeared in 1958 on *Huckleberry Hound* and two years later was given his own series. At that time he was a resident of Jellystone National Park, where he spent his days devising ways of pilfering picnic baskets, together with his diminutive companion, Boo Boo. Daws Butler provided the voice of Yogi, while Boo Boo's was supplied by Don Messick. Other segments included "Snagglepuss," a lisping lion, and "Yakky Doodle," a duck. After a season or two, Yogi acquired a girlfriend, Cindy Bear. By 1964 the character had become popular enough to warrant a full-length theatrical film, "Hey There, It's Yogi Bear." By the 1970s, however, Yogi and his pals had long since left Jellystone Park. In *Yogi's Gang,* an hour show, they battled environmental enemies like Mr. Pollution. The "Gang" included many other Hanna-Barbera characters, such as Huckleberry Hound, Wally Gator, and Magilla Gorilla, among others. In the fall of 1978 Yogi and his friends left the planet to star in a ninety-minute show, *Yogi's Space Race.* This series consisted of several segments: "Space Race," in which characters such as Yogi, Huckleberry Hound, Jabberjaw, the Phantom Phink, and Rita and Wendy piloted their respective vehicles through the solar system; "The Buford Files," starring a slow-witted bloodhound who lived in a swamp; "Galaxy Goof-Ups," starring Yogi, Huck, and others; and "The Galloping Ghost," the adventures of a fast-moving spirit. In November of 1978 *Yogi's Space Race* was trimmed to sixty minutes, and *The Galaxy Goof-Ups* became a separate half-hour series. Early in 1979 the show was trimmed to thirty minutes, as *Buford* became a separate series. After a twelve-year absence Yogi returned to network television in 1991. *Yo, Yogi!* found the bear and his pals hanging out at a shopping mall.

YOU AGAIN?   NBC
27 FEBRUARY 1986–7 JANUARY 1987   Half-hour sitcom based on the British series *Home to Roost.* With Jack Klugman as divorcé Henry Willows, a buyer for Global Markets, a grocery chain; John Stamos as his seventeen-year-old son Matt, who left his mother and stepfather to move in with Henry (Henry and Matt hadn't seen each other in seven years); Elizabeth Bennett as Henry's English housekeeper, Enid Tompkins (Bennett played the same role simultaneously on the British series); Valerie Landsburg (fall 1986–1987) as Henry's secretary, Pam; and Barbara Rhoades (fall 1986–1987) as Maggie Davis, who also worked for Global.

YOU ARE AN ARTIST   NBC
1 NOVEMBER 1946–17 JANUARY 1950   One of television's earliest instructional shows, *You Are an Artist* was hosted by Jon Gnagy, who showed viewers how to draw.

YOU ARE THERE   CBS

1 FEBRUARY 1953–13 OCTOBER 1957; 11 SEPTEMBER 1971–2 SEPTEMBER 1972   An unusual public affairs series, *You Are There* began in 1947 as a radio show (it was originally titled *CBS Was There*). Each week a well-known historical event was recreated, and the leading figures in each drama were interviewed by CBS news correspondents (the correspondents always appeared in modern-day dress, regardless of the setting of the story). The television version ran from 1953 to 1957 on Sunday afternoons, and was revived in 1971 as a Saturday-afternoon show, aimed principally at children. Walter Cronkite was the chief correspondent on both TV versions. Paul Newman guest-starred on one program, as Nathan Hale (30 August 1953); and the 1971 premiere, "The Mystery of Amelia Earhart," featured Geraldine Brooks and Richard Dreyfuss.

YOU ASKED FOR IT   DUMONT/ABC/SYNDICATED

29 DECEMBER 1950–7 DECEMBER 1951 (DUMONT); 10 DECEMBER 1951–27 SEPTEMBER 1959 (ABC); 1972 (SYNDICATED)   A half-hour human-interest series, *You Asked for It* answered viewers' requests for unusual acrobatic or magic acts, trained animals, good Samaritans, or whatever. On the network versions of the show, the viewer's letter was read before the act or feature was introduced, while a picture of the viewer was superimposed on a jar of the sponsor's product, Skippy Peanut Butter. Kindly Art Baker hosted the show from 1950 until early 1958, when Jack Smith took over; Smith also hosted the 1972 syndicated version. Another syndicated version appeared in 1981 (see *The New You Asked for It*).

YOU BET YOUR LIFE   NBC/SYNDICATED

5 OCTOBER 1950–21 SEPTEMBER 1961 (NBC); 1980 (SYNDICATED); 1992 (SYNDICATED)   Television's funniest game show was emceed by "The One, the Only"— Groucho Marx. The game was simple enough—a pair of players tried to answer a few questions in a category of their choice (the exact procedure varied somewhat from year to year)—but it took a back seat to the freewheeling interviews conducted by Groucho. The show's production staff was constantly on the lookout for unusual guests and managed to find quite a few. Some stood on their heads, some danced, and some had funny stories to tell, but all provided targets for Groucho's verbal salvos. Most guests were nonprofessionals, but a few—like Richard Rodgers and Oscar Hammerstein—were well known; others, such as Phyllis Diller, Candice Bergen (who appeared with her father, Edgar Bergen), and William Peter Blatty (who wrote *The Exorcist*), later became celebrities. Contestants could win money not only by answering questions, but also if they managed "to say the secret word"—at the outset of each show, an everyday word was selected, then attached to a toy duck that was raised above the stage. If one of the contestants uttered the preselected word, the duck dropped down, and the couple split an extra $50; occasionally, model Marilyn Burtis came down instead of the duck, and on one show Groucho's brother, Harpo Marx, descended. Groucho's longtime sidekick was George Fenneman, who did the announcing, carried in the questions, and kept score; the two began working together when *You Bet Your Life* began on radio in 1947. The television version was produced by John Guedel and was one of the few game shows to be filmed (because the interviews with the contestants ran overtime and had to be edited). A revival of the series was attempted in 1980; the short-lived show was hosted by Buddy Hackett, with Ron Husmann as the announcer. A second revival surfaced in 1992, with host Bill Cosby and sidekick Robbi Chong. It too was unsuccessful.

YOU CAN'T TAKE IT WITH YOU   SYNDICATED

1987   A half-hour syndicated sitcom, based on the popular Moss Hart–George S. Kaufman play. Set on Staten Island in the early 1900s, it featured Harry Morgan as Martin Vanderhof; Lois Nettleton as his daughter, Penny Sycamore; Richard Sanders as her husband, Paul; Heather Blodgett as their daughter Essie; Lisa Aliff as their daughter Alice; and Theodore Wilson as neighbor Darwood Pinner.

YOU DON'T SAY NBC/ABC/SYNDICATED

1 APRIL 1963–26 SEPTEMBER 1969 (NBC); 7 JULY 1975–26 NOVEMBER 1975 (ABC); 1978 (SYNDICATED)   This durable game show involved both contestants and celebrities, who tried to get each other to say the name of a famous person or place by suggesting sentences with blanks in them. Tom Kennedy hosted the show. The NBC version enjoyed a six-year daytime run and also popped up on the prime-time schedule early in 1964. The ABC version was seen only as a daytime program. The half-hour show was a Ralph Andrews Production.

YOU TAKE THE KIDS CBS

15 DECEMBER 1990–12 JANUARY 1991   Domestic sitcom set in Pittsburgh, with Nell Carter (late of *Gimme a Break*) as Nell Kirkland, wife, mother of four, and part-time piano teacher; Roger E. Mosley (late of *Magnum P.I.*) as her husband, Michael Kirkland, a school bus driver; Caryn Ward as their teen daughter, Lorette; Dante Bezé as eldest son Raymond; Marlon Taylor as middle son Peter; Trent Cameron as youngest son Nathaniel; and Leila Danette as Nell's feisty mother, Helen.

YOU WRITE THE SONGS SYNDICATED

1986   An updated version of the 1950–1952 series, *Songs for Sale, You Write the Songs* was a competition for amateur songwriters. Successful submissions were performed by the show's resident singers—a troupe known as the New Song Singers, and individual songsters Monica Page, Catte Adams, and Kenny James—and were then rated by a panel of celebrity judges. Ben Vereen was the host.

YOUNG AND GAY CBS

1 JANUARY 1950–26 MARCH 1950   Also known as *The Girls,* this half-hour sitcom was based loosely on two real characters, Cornelia Otis Skinner and Emily Kimbrough. It starred Bethel Leslie as Beth Skinner; Mary Malone as Mary Kimbrough; and Kenneth Forbes as Tod Hunter. Other in the cast included Harry Bannister, John Campbell, Audrey Christie, Alexander Ivo, and Agnes Young. Carol Irwin was the producer, David Rich the director.

THE YOUNG AND THE RESTLESS CBS

26 MARCH 1973–   A stylish daytime serial, *The Young and the Restless* replaced *Where the Heart Is* in 1973. Specifically aimed at a younger audience than most soaps, the series is generally considered to be TV's most artistic serial. It was created by William Bell and Lee Phillip Bell. John Conboy was its first executive producer. When Conboy left in 1982 for a new serial, *Capitol,* William Bell and H. Wesley Kenney took over as executive producers. Edward Scott was executive producer in 1989, while Bell held the title of senior executive producer (at the same time Bell was guiding a second CBS daytime drama, *The Bold and the Beautiful*). The series won the Emmy for outstanding daytime drama series in its third season (1974–1975), and would win again three times during the 1980s, and once again in 1992–1993. Its popularity climbed steadily; for most of the 1980s it ranked second behind *General Hospital.* By 1988 it had eclipsed *GH* for the top spot, and remained there through the mid-1990s.

Set in the medium-sized town of Genoa City, its storylines revolved around the several members of the Brooks family—Stuart, Jennifer, and their four daughters—and the Fosters—Liz, her two sons and daughter. By the early 1980s, however, almost all the Brookses and Fosters had been written out, and the main storylines centered around the members of the Abbott and Williams families. The cast has included: Robert Colbert (1973–1983) as Stuart Brooks, owner of the Genoa City *Chronicle;* Dorothy Green as his wife, Jennifer Brooks; Trish Stewart and Lynne Richter (also known as Lynne Topping) as daughter Chris; Janice Lynde (1973–1977) and Victoria Mallory (1977–1982) as daughter Leslie; Jaime Lyn Bauer (1973–1982) as daughter Lauralee (Lori); Pamela Peters (also known as Pamela Peters Solow) and Patricia Everly as daughter Peggy; Julianna McCarthy as Liz Foster (McCarthy was the only original cast member still on board as of 1984); James Houghton (1973–1976), Brian Kerwin (1976–1977), Wings Hauser (1977–1981; also known as J. D.

Hauser), and Howard McGillin as Liz's son, Greg Foster, a lawyer who married Chris Brooks; William Gray Espy (1973–1975) and David Hasselhoff (1975–1982) as Liz's son, Bill "Snapper" Foster, who had previously been married to Chris; Brenda Dickson, Bond Gideon, Deborah Adair, Brenda Dickson (again), and Jess Walton as Liz's daughter, Jill Foster, a hairdresser who was hired as a personal assistant to a wealthy matron; Lee Crawford as Sally McGuire, who had an affair with Snapper before his marriage; Tom Hallick as Brad Eliot, a former surgeon who married Leslie Brooks; Robert Clary as Pierre Rouland, a nightclub owner who married Sally and was later murdered; Lilyan Chauvin as Pierre's sister, Marianna Rouland; Jeanne Cooper as Kay Chancellor, the woman who hired Jill Foster (Kay Chancellor became one of the series' major characters, as she coped with alcoholism and a fondness for younger men; when actress Cooper underwent a facelift, scenes from the operation were shown on the air); John Considine and Donnelly Rhodes as Kay's husband, Philip Chancellor, who fell for Jill and married her just before his death; Robert Clarke and Paul Stevens as Dr. Bruce Henderson, an old boyfriend of Jennifer's who fell for her again; Steve Carlson as Bruce's son, Mark Henderson, who fell for Peggy Brooks (Jennifer later confessed to Peggy that Bruce Henderson, not Stuart Brooks, was her real father); Beau Kazer as Brock Reynolds, son of Kay Chancellor; Anthony Herrera as Jack Curtis (or Curtzynski), a college teacher who fell for Peggy; Kay Heberle as Jack's wife, Joann Curtis; John McCook and Dennis Cole as Lance Prentiss, who fell for Lori Brooks; Deidre Hall as Barbara Anderson; Jennifer Leak as Gwen Sherman; Charles Gray as Bill Foster, Sr.; Barry Cahill as Sam Powers; Tom Selleck as Jed Andrews; Jordeann Russo as Regina Henderson; Cathy Carricaburu as Nancy Becker; Dick DeCoit as Ron Becker; K. T. Stevens as Vanessa Prentiss; Joe LaDue as Derek Thurston; Tom Ligon as Lucas Prentiss, who married Leslie Brooks; Brandi Tucker as Karen Becker; Cynthia Harris as Heather Lowe; Karl Bruck as Maestro Fausch; Gary Giem as Larry Larkin; Susan Walden as Linda Larkin; Erica Hope and Melody Thomas (later known as Melody Thomas Scott) as ex-stripper Nikki Reed; Carol Jones as Patty Minter; and Roberta Leighton as Dr. Casey Reed.

Also, Brett Halsey and Jerry Douglas as John Abbott, head of Jabot Cosmetics, who married Jill Foster; Terry Lester and Peter Bergman as Jack Abbott, John's son; Eileen Davidson and Brenda Epperson (also known as Brenda Epperson-Doumani) as Ashley Abbot, John's daughter; Beth Maitland as Tracy Abbott, John's daughter; Tammy Taylor, Lilibet Stern, and Andrea Evans-Massey as Jack's wife, Patty Abbott; Doug Davidson as Patty's brother, Paul Williams; Brett Hadley as their father, Carl Williams, a cop; Carolyn Conwell as their mother, Mary Williams; David Winn as Steve Williams; Meg Bennett as Julia Newman (after her character was written out of the show, Meg Bennett became one of the writers; later, Julia was written back into the program, and Bennett became one of the few persons to hold the dual daytime job of actor and writer); Janet Wood and Cindy Eilbacher (later known as Cynthia Jordan) as April and Jody Stevens; Melinda Cordell as Dorothy Stevens; Jeanna Michaels as Karen Richards; Steve Ford (son of the former President) as her husband, Andy Richards; Mark Roberts as Dr. Young; Jerry Lacy as Jonas; Alex Rebar as Vince; Margaret Mason as Eve Howard; Cindy Fisher as Rebecca; Loyita Chapel as Judy Wilson; Victor Mohica as Felipe Ramirez, who rescued Kay Chancellor from an auto wreck; William H. Bassett as Pete Walker; Ben Hammer as Alex Morgan, a cop; Peter Brown as lawyer Robert Lawrence; Ellen Weston as Suzanne Lynch; Edgar Daniels as Dr. Sebastian Crown; Chris Holder as Kevin Bancroft, who married Nikki Reed; Mark Tapscott as Kevin's father, Earl Bancroft; Lynn Wood as Kevin's mother, Alison Bancroft; Eric Braeden as Victor Newman; Liz Keifer as Robert Lawrence's daughter, Angela Lawrence; Suzanne Zenor as Robert's unstable wife, Claire Lawrence; Michael Damian as singer Danny Romalotti; Michael Evans as Douglas Austin; John Denos as photographer Joe Blair; Alex Donnelly and Devon Pierce as Diane Jenkins; Jay Kerr as Brian Forbes; Ashley Nicole Millan and Heather Tom as Victoria Bancroft Newman, daughter of Victor and Nikki; Brock Peters as Frank Lewis; Marguerite Ray and Veronica Redd (also known as Veronica Redd-Forrest) as Mamie Johnson; Deanna Robbins as Cindy Lake; Joseph Taylor as Tony DiSalvo; Patty Weaver as Gina Roma; Stephanie Williams as Amy Peters;

Marla Adams as Dina Abbott; Tracey E. Bregman (later known as Tracey Bregman Recht) and Caryn Richman as Lauren Fenimore; Glenn Corbett as James Lake; Velekka Gray as Sharon Reaves and as Ruby the manicurist (a rare instance in which a performer simultaneously appeared as two characters who were neither related nor lookalikes); Fawne Harriman as Margaret Lake; Randy Holland as Rick Daros; Brian Matthews as Eric Garrison; Carl Strano as Max; Jon St. Elwood as Jazz Jackson; Scott Palmer as Professor Sullivan; Christopher Templeton as Carol Robbins; Jim Storm as Neil Fenimore; Lauren Koslow as Lindsay Welles; Frank M. Benard as Marc Mergeron; and Jack Wells as Dr. Alan Jacobs.

Subsequent additions have included: Lauralee Bell (daughter of the boss) as Christine "Cricket" Blair; Joy Garrett as Boobsie Caswell; Susan Seaforth Hayes as Jo-Anna Manning; Don Diamont as Brad Carlton, who married Traci in 1986; Darlene Conley as Rose DeVille; Jennifer Karr as Ellen Winters; Lee Nicholl as Sven; Colby Chester as lawyer Michael Crawford; Robert Parucha as Matt Miller; Fay Hauser as Salena Wiley; John Shearin as Evan Sanderson; Kate Linder as Esther Valentine, Kay Chancellor's maid; Rod Arrants as Dr. Steve Lassiter, who married Ashley Abbott in 1988 (Arrants had previously played Jeff the stableboy in 1974); Tricia Cast as Nina Webster; Nathan Purdee, Randy Brooks, and Adam Lazarre White as Nathan Hastings; Colleen Casey as Faren Richards, who married Andy Richard in 1986; Phillip Morris as Tyrone Jackson (a black actor, Morris also played Jackson's white alter ego, Robert Tyrone); Michael Corbett as David Kimball; Quinn Redeker as Rex Sterling, who married Kay Chancellor in 1988; Barbara Crampton as deranged Leanna Randolph, who married Victor Newman in 1988; Rebecca Street as Jessica Blair; Nicholas Walker as Jason Monroe; Jonathan Farwell as George Rawlins; Nina Arvesen as Cassandra Hall; Stephen Gregory as Chase Benson; Peter Barton as Scott Granger; John Philip Law and John O'Hurley as Dr. James Granger; Todd Curtis as Skip Evans; Melissa Morgan as Brittany Norman; Sal Landi and James Michael Gregory as Clint Radisson; Ken Olandt as Daryl Stuart; Laura Bryan Birn as Lynne Bassett; John Castellanos as John Silva; Scott Palmer as Tim Sullivan; Anthony Pena as Miguel Rodriguez; William Wintersole as Mitchell Sherman; Ryan McDonald as Robert Haskell; Ruth Silvera as Shirley Haskell; Mary Sheldon as Nan; Doug Wert as Jeff; Tonya Lee Williams as Olivia Barber; Victoria Rowell as her sister, Drucilla; Norma Donaldson as their mother, Lilliebelle; Michael Barrak as Marc Wagner; Harry G. Sanders as Walter, Lilliebelle's husband; and Kristoff St. John as Neil Winters.

Also, Scott Reeves as Ryan McNeil; Devon Pierce as Diane Westin; Kari Kupcinet as Julie Sanderson; Christian J. LeBlanc as Michael Baldwin; Sharon Farrell as Florence Webster; Michael Tylo as Alex "Blade" Bladeson; Kelly Garrison as Hilary Lancaster; Kimberlin Brown as Sheila Carter Grainger (the character later moved to *The Bold and the Beautiful*); Greg Wrangler as Steve Connelly; Marilyn Alex as Molly Carter; Terrence McNally as Robert Lynch; Parley Baer as Miles Dugan; Maxine Stuart as Margaret Anderson; Signy Coleman as Hope Adams, who was blind; Paul Walker as Brandon Collins; J. Eddie Peck as Cole Howard; Pamela Bach and Diana Barton as Marilyn Mason; Heidi Mark and Sharon Case as Sharon Collins; Victoria Ann-Lewis and Karen Hensel as Doris Collins, Sharon's mother; Robin Scott and Julianne Morris as Amy Wilson; Shemar Moore as Malcolm Winters; Michelle Stafford as Phyllis Romalotti; Josh Taylor as Jed Sanders; Phillip Moon as Keemo Volien; Elizabeth Sung as Luan Volien; Marianne Rees as Mai Volien; John Nelson Alden and Joshua Morrow as Nicholas Newman; Christine McCall as Jeri Paulsen; Freeman Michaels as Drake Belson; Mark Haining as Norman Peterson; David Cowgill as Cliff Wilson; Alex Demir as Wes O'Connell; Abby Dalton as Lydia Summers; Doug Davidson as Paul Williams; and Courtland R. Mead as Philip Chancellor III.

The Young and the Restless was a half-hour serial until 4 February 1980, when it expanded to a full hour. Its theme music, popularly known as "Nadia's Theme," is no doubt the best-recognized theme from any soap opera. The song was composed by Barry DeVorzon and Perry Botkin, Jr., for the 1971 film *Bless the Beasts and the Children,* and was then titled "Cotton's Theme." Subsequently, it was used for several years on *The Young and the Restless,* but achieved much greater recognition when it was chosen as performance music for Romanian gymnast Nadia Comaneci during the 1976 Olympics. In 1983 a California jury awarded DeVorzon $241,000 in damages against A&M Records, because of the latter's failure to list DeVorzon as the co-composer on the first pressings of the "Nadia's Theme" record it released in 1976.

YOUNG DAN'L BOONE   CBS
12 SEPTEMBER 1977–4 OCTOBER 1977   The first casualty of the 1977–1978 season, *Young Dan'l Boone* vanished after four episodes. Not to be confused with *Daniel Boone,* a popular show which lasted six seasons, this one starred Rick Moses as Dan'l Boone, who seemed to be in his mid-twenties; Devon Ericson as his intended, Rebecca Bryan; Ji-Tu Cumbuka as his friend, Hawk, a former slave; John Joseph Thomas as Peter, a twelve-year-old companion of Boone's. Ernie Frankel was the executive producer, and Jimmy Sangster the producer, of the hour show.

YOUNG DR. KILDARE   SYNDICATED
1972   A remake of *Dr. Kildare,* the popular medical show of the early 1960s, *Young Dr. Kildare* starred Mark Jenkins as the intern, Dr. James Kildare, and Gary Merrill as his guiding light, Dr. Leonard Gillespie. The half-hour series was videotaped; Joseph Gantman was the executive producer.

YOUNG DR. MALONE   NBC
29 DECEMBER 1958–29 MARCH 1963   A daytime serial, *Young Dr. Malone* enjoyed a lengthy radio run (from 1939 to 1960) as well as a moderately successful television run. The TV version replaced another serial, *Today Is Ours,* and six characters from that show were worked into the story lines of the new soap opera. Set at Valley Hospital in the town of Three Oaks, *Young Dr. Malone* involved two generations of the Malone family. The cast included: William Prince as Dr. Jerry Malone, chief of staff at the hospital; Virginia Dwyer and Augusta Dabney as Jerry's wife, Tracey Malone (William Prince and Augusta Dabney later married in real life); John Connell as their adopted son, Dr. David Malone, a young physician; Kathleen Widdoes, Freda Holloway and Sarah Hardy as Tracey and Jerry's daughter, Jill Malone; Emily McLaughlin as David's romantic interest, Dr. Eileen Seaton; Peter Brandon as Dr. Tad Powell; Lesley Woods as Clare Bannister; Martin Blaine as Lionel Steele; Zina Bethune, Michele Tuttle, Susan Hallaran and Patty McCormack as Lisha Steele; and Diana Hyland as Gig Houseman.

THE YOUNG INDIANA JONES CHRONICLES   ABC
4 MARCH 1992–7 SEPTEMBER 1992; 13 MARCH 1993–17 APRIL 1993; 5 JUNE 1993–23 JULY 1993   Producer George Lucas intended this expensive adventure series to be a prequel to his "Indiana Jones" movies. On TV, a younger Indy travelled with his father, a Princeton professor who lectured internationally, and became involved in adventures all over the world during the early decades of the twentieth century. The episodes were recounted by the elderly Indy in the present day. The title character, Henry "Indiana" Jones, Jr., was played by three actors: Sean Patrick Flannery was the teenage Indy, Corey Carrier was the ten-year-old Indy, and George Hall was Old Indy, the narrator. Also appearing were Ronny Coutteure as Remy, a pal of the teenage Indy, and Margaret Tyzack as Miss Helen Seymour, tutor of the ten-year-old Indy. Among the historical characters encountered by Indy were Pablo Picasso, T. E. Lawrence, Teddy Roosevelt, and Sigmund Freud. Harrison Ford, who played the adult Indy in the movies, appeared in the episode of 13 March 1993.

Following the series' departure from ABC, the first of several planned TV-movies, "Young Indiana Jones and the Hollywood Follies," aired on the Family Channel 15 October 1994.

THE YOUNG LAWYERS   ABC
21 SEPTEMBER 1970–5 MAY 1971   An hour-long dramatic series set at the Neighborhood Law Office in Boston, where law students handled cases under the supervision of a senior attorney. With Lee J. Cobb as David Barrett, a private practitioner who oversaw the operation; Zalman King as law student Aaron Silverman; Judy Pace as

law student Pat Walters; and Phillip Clark (January 1971–May 1971) as law student Chris Blake. Matthew Rapf produced the show for Paramount TV.

THE YOUNG MARRIEDS   ABC
5 OCTOBER 1964–25 MARCH 1966   A late-afternoon serial aimed at a younger audience than most soaps, *The Young Marrieds* told the stories of several young couples who lived in a suburban town. The cast included: Paul Picerni as Dr. Dan Garrett; Peggy McCay as Susan Garrett; Mike Mikler as Walter Reynolds; Susan Brown as Ann Reynolds; Floy Dean as Liz Forsythe; Constance Moore as Liz's mother, Irene Forsythe; Norma Connolly as Lena Karr Gilroy; Barry Russo as Roy Gilroy; Betty Connor and Brenda Benet as model Jill McComb; Scott Graham and Charles Grodin as Matt Crane; Les Brown, Jr., as Buzz Korman; Frank Maxwell as Mr. Korman; Maxine Stuart as Mrs. Korman; Pat Rossen as Jerry; Irene Tedrow as Aunt Alex; Frank Marvel as Mr. Coleman; Ken Metcalfe as Jimmy; Michael Stefani as Paul; Maria Palmer as Mady; Don Randolph as Theo; Robert Hogan as Gillespie; Ben Astar as Mr. Killeran; and Susan Seaforth as Carol West.

YOUNG MAVERICK   CBS
28 NOVEMBER 1979–16 JANUARY 1980   A sequel to *Maverick,* one of TV's more popular westerns, *Young Maverick* starred Charles Frank as Harvard-educated Ben Maverick, a younger cousin of Bart and Bret, who shared the family's aversion to violence. Also featured were Susan Blanchard as Ben's friend, Nell McGarrahan, and John Dehner as grim Marshal Edge Troy, the Idaho Territory lawman who tried to keep a watchful eye on young Maverick. Executive producer: Robert Van Scoyk for Warner Brothers TV. See also *Bret Maverick.*

YOUNG MR. BOBBIN   NBC
26 AUGUST 1951–18 MAY 1952   Half-hour sitcom starring Jackie Kelk as Alexander Bobbin, a young man working at his first job, and Jane Seymour and Nydia Westman as his two spinster aunts, Aunt Clara and Aunt Bertie. Patricia Hosley was featured as Bobbin's girlfriend, Nancy.

THE YOUNG REBELS   ABC
20 SEPTEMBER 1970–3 JANUARY 1971   A historical adventure series, *The Young Rebels* was set in Chester, Pennsylvania, in 1777, and chronicled the exploits of the members of the Yankee Doodle Society, a group of young guerrilla fighters. With Rick Ely as Jeremy Larkin, son of the mayor; Lou Gossett as Isak Poole, a blacksmith and freeman; Alex Henteloff as the scientifically inclined Henry Abington, a young Ben Franklin; Hilarie Thompson as Elizabeth Coates; and Philippe Fourquet as the young General Lafayette, one of the few outsiders who knew this group's identities. The hour series was a Screen Gems production.

THE YOUNG RIDERS   ABC
20 SEPTEMBER 1989–25 JANUARY 1992; 21 MAY 1992–23 JULY 1992   Ed Spielman created this hour western about six young recruits for the Pony Express. With Anthony Zerbe as the boss, Teaspoon Hunter; Ty Miller as The Kid; Stephen Baldwin as Billy Cody; Josh Brolin as Jimmy Hickok; Travis Fine (1989–1991) as Ike McSwain; Gregg Rainwater as Buck Cross; Yvonne Suhor as Lou McCloud, who disguised herself as a man in order to get the job; Melissa Leo (1989–1990) as Emma Shannon, the cook; Brett Cullen (1989–1990) as Marshal Sam Cain, the local lawman; Clare Wren (1990–1992) as Rachel; and Don Franklin (1990–1992) as Noah Dixon. Apparently, The Kid, Cody and Hickok were all supposed to be the younger incarnations of the future Western notables Billy the Kid, Buffalo Bill, and Wild Bill Hickok, respectively. In the fall of 1991 the action shifted from Sweetwater, Wyoming, to Cross Creek, Nebraska, and Christopher Pettiet signed on as young Jesse James.

THE YOUNG SENTINELS   NBC
10 SEPTEMBER 1977–2 SEPTEMBER 1978   This Saturday-morning cartoon show was set in outer space and changed its name to *Space Sentinels* in midseason. Its central

characters were three youngsters who had been endowed with super powers by Sentinel One, a creature from another galaxy, and who were sent back to Earth to help humanity.

THE YOUNG SET
ABC

6 SEPTEMBER 1965–17 DECEMBER 1965   An hour daytime talk show, hosted by Phyllis Kirk and a weekly celebrity cohost.

YOUR ALL-AMERICAN COLLEGE SHOW
SYNDICATED

1968–1970   Half-hour talent show featuring college-age acts, hosted first by Dennis James and later by Rich Little and Arthur Godfrey.

YOUR BIG MOMENT
DUMONT

19 MAY 1953–2 JUNE 1953   Melvyn Douglas hosted this prime-time program, on which viewers who had written to the show requesting blind dates had the chance to meet the person of their dreams. Ken Roberts and the Ray Bloch Orchestra were also featured on the half-hour series, which was retitled *Blind Date* when Jan Murray succeeded Douglas on 9 June (see also that title).

YOUR FIRST IMPRESSION
NBC

2 JANUARY 1962–26 JUNE 1964   On this daytime game show a panel of three celebrities tried to guess the identity of mystery guests from clues supplied by the host. Bill Leyden emceed, and Dennis James was a regular panelist. Monty Hall was the executive producer.

YOUR FUNNY, FUNNY FILMS
ABC

8 JULY 1963–9 SEPTEMBER 1963   Amateur filmmakers had a rare chance to show their stuff on network television on this half-hour show, hosted by George Fenneman. The accent was on comedy rather than artistry. See also *America's Funniest Home Videos.*

YOUR HIT PARADE
NBC/CBS

7 OCTOBER 1950–7 JUNE 1958 (NBC); 10 OCTOBER 1958–24 APRIL 1959 (CBS); 2 AUGUST 1974–30 AUGUST 1974 (CBS)   *Your Hit Parade* began on radio in 1935 and came to television fifteen years later (four trial telecasts were aired during the summer of 1950, though regular broadcasts did not begin until the fall). For its first eight years on TV, the show was a Saturday-night fixture on NBC; on each show the top musical hits of the week were performed by the show's regulars. Because some songs remained popular week after week, imaginative production sequences were designed to help sustain viewer interest; some of the medium's best-known choreographers— such as Tony Charmoli, Ernie Flatt, and Peter Gennaro—started out on *Your Hit Parade,* and one of its featured dancers was Bob Fosse, who later directed *Cabaret.* The show's early regulars included Dorothy Collins, Eileen Wilson, Snooky Lanson, and Sue Bennett; Russell Arms, June Valli, and bandleader Ray Scott were all aboard by 1952, though June Valli was succeeded by Gisele MacKenzie in 1953. In the fall of 1957 (the series' last season on NBC) the show was overhauled completely, and four new regulars were brought in: Tommy Leonetti, Jill Corey, Alan Copeland, and Virginia Gibson. A year later *Your Hit Parade* switched to CBS and was again overhauled, but the show failed to generate much interest; Dorothy Collins returned to costar with Johnny Desmond for one season. The show was moved to a Tuesday spot, and later to Fridays, before leaving the air in April 1959. *Your Hit Parade* was revived in the summer of 1974, but again failed to catch hold; the regulars at that time included Chuck Woolery, Kelly Garrett, and Sheralee.

YOUR LUCKY CLUE
CBS

13 JULY 1952–31 AUGUST 1952   A summer replacement for *This Is Show Business,* this half-hour game show was hosted by Basil Rathbone. Four contestants competed as two twosomes, and tried to solve criminal cases enacted before them by a group of regular performers.

YOUR NEW DAY   SYNDICATED

1980   Designer Vidal Sassoon hosted this half-hour informational series for women, which focused on health, fashion, and self-improvement.

YOUR NUMBER'S UP   NBC

23 SEPTEMBER 1985–20 DECEMBER 1985   Nipsey Russell hosted this daytime game show, on which three contestants tried to identify, from their initial letters, missing words in selected phrases. Each time a correct answer was given, a one-digit number was posted on a board. Members of the studio audience also had the opportunity to play along; each member had a card with the last four digits of his or her home telephone number; anyone whose card matched the list of posted numbers could come onstage, and select one of the three contestants. If that contestant won the day's game, the audience member also won a prize.

YOUR PET PARADE   ABC

18 MARCH 1951–2 SEPTEMBER 1951   A Sunday-afternoon show on pets and pet care, *Your Pet Parade* was hosted by Jack Gregson; Billy Barty was featured as Billy Bitesize, the commercial spokesman for the sponsor, Ralston Purina. Music was supplied by Ivan Ditmars, and the half-hour show was produced by John Nelson.

YOUR PLAY TIME   CBS/NBC

14 JUNE 1953–6 SEPTEMBER 1953 (CBS); 13 JUNE 1954–5 SEPTEMBER 1954 (CBS); 18 JUNE 1955–3 SEPTEMBER 1955 (NBC)   A half-hour dramatic anthology series of little note, *Your Play Time* popped up three times as a summer replacement series.

YOUR PRIZE STORY   NBC

2 APRIL 1952–28 MAY 1952   The stories on this half-hour dramatic anthology series were submitted by viewers. Any aspiring author whose script was accepted for adaptation by story editor Margaret Sangster won $1,000.

YOUR SHOW OF SHOWS   NBC

25 FEBRUARY 1950–5 JUNE 1954   A ninety-minute variety series, *Your Show of Shows* was a Saturday-night fixture for four years. It was a showcase not for guest stars, but for the comedic talents of its star, Sid Caesar, and his costar, Imogene Coca, who were backed up by two talented supporting players, Carl Reiner and Howard Morris. Most shows followed the same pattern: Sid Caesar introduced the evening's guest host (who usually played a comparatively minor role on the show), then appeared in a sketch with Imogene Coca. After a couple of production numbers and another sketch or two came the main segment—a satire of a popular film. After that, Caesar did a monologue or pantomime, and the entire company then participated in the final production number.

   Your Show of Shows was produced by Max Liebman, who had worked with Caesar and Coca previously in theatrical revues he had staged in the Catskills and in Florida. Liebman first brought the revue idea to television in 1949 on *The Admiral Broadway Revue* (see also that title), an hour show that lasted seventeen weeks. In 1950, at the request of NBC programming chief Sylvester "Pat" Weaver, Liebman agreed to do a ninety-minute revue on Saturday nights; he brought with him most of the people who had been featured on *The Admiral Broadway Revue:* Caesar, Coca, Howard Morris, writers Mel Tolkin and Lucille Kallen, choreographer James Starbuck, set designer Frederick Fox, and conductor Charles Sanford. Other regulars on the first season of *Your Show of Shows* included Tom Avera, dancers Mata and Hari, Nellie Fisher and Jerry Ross, the Hamilton Trio (Bob Hamilton, Pat Horn, and Gloria Stevens), operatic singers Marguerite Piazza and Robert Merrill, pop singers Bill Hayes and Jack Russell, and the Billy Williams Quartet. Tom Avera left after the first season and was replaced by Carl Reiner. Jack Russell also left the show after a short time, and Judy Johnson became Bill Hayes's singing partner. Dancers Fisher and Ross left after the 1951–1952 season and were succeeded by Bambi Linn and Rod Alexander.

   In addition to writers Mel Tolkin and Lucille Kallen, several other talented comedy writers worked for the show, including Mel Brooks, Larry Gelbart (*M*A*S*H*),

Bill Persky and Sam Denoff (who later worked with Carl Reiner on *The Dick Van Dyke Show*), Neil Simon, and Woody Allen.

A melancholy man offstage, Sid Caesar brought his own unique style to the show; notorious for his deviations from the scripts, Caesar was a skilled mime, a gifted dialectician, an inimitable monologist, and a superb comic actor, especially when he was paired with Imogene Coca. Coca, who was born into a showbiz family, was a talented singer and dancer as well as a natural comedienne, who brought several years of professional experience to the show. The most famous characters that they portrayed on the show were Charlie and Doris Hickenlooper, a hopelessly mismatched married couple. In the solo spots, Caesar played hundreds of characters, but the best known include jazz musicians Progress Hornsby and Cool Cees (in real life, Caesar played the saxophone and had been in several bands), storyteller Somerset Winterset, and Italian film authority Giuseppe Marinara. Among the dozens of motion pictures that were lampooned were *From Here to Eternity* (which came out as "From Here to Obscurity") and *Shane* ("Strange").

Your Show of Shows was seen every Saturday night (with a hiatus each summer) from 1950 until the spring of 1953. In its last season it was seen three of every four weeks and left the air in June of 1954, after some 160 telecasts— all of them live. In the fall of 1954 Caesar and Coca went their separate ways; Caesar to *Caesar's Hour,* a comedy-variety show which lasted three seasons, and Coca to *The Imogene Coca Show,* a half-hour effort that lasted one season. The two were reunited in 1958 on *Sid Caesar Invites You,* but the magic had gone. In 1973 Max Liebman packaged a number of outstanding segments from *Your Show of Shows* into a theatrical release, *Ten From Your Show of Shows.*

YOUR SHOW TIME NBC
21 JANUARY 1949–15 JULY 1949   This filmed dramatic anthology series was hosted by Arthur Shields. The half-hour show was a Marshall Grant-Realm Production.

YOUR SURPRISE PACKAGE CBS
13 MARCH 1961–23 FEBRUARY 1962   A daytime game show hosted by George Fenneman (formerly the assistant on *You Bet Your Life*) on which contestants competed in a quiz segment for the chance to identify and win a "surprise package" of merchandise.

YOUR SURPRISE STORE CBS
12 MAY 1952–27 JUNE 1952   Lew Parker and Jacqueline Susann cohosted this daytime merchandise giveaway show.

YOUR WITNESS ABC
17 OCTOBER 1949–26 SEPTEMBER 1950   Another of TV's early courtroom drama shows, *Your Witness* should not be confused with its contemporaries, such as *Famous Jury Trials* and *They Stand Accused,* or with its successors, such as *Day in Court, Divorce Court, Traffic Court,* or *The Verdict Is Yours.*

YOU'RE IN THE PICTURE CBS
20 JANUARY 1961–27 JANUARY 1961   One of TV's biggest flops, *You're in the Picture* was a prime-time game show hosted by Jackie Gleason. Celebrities would drop by and stick their heads through holes in life-sized tableaux. From clues supplied by Gleason, the celebs (who could not see the scene of which they were part) tried to guess what picture they were in. Gleason abandoned the game show format after one week; on the second show he appeared alone, apologizing to viewers for "that bomb" and turned the show into a half-hour talk show for the remaining weeks (its title was then changed to *The Jackie Gleason Show*).

YOU'RE ON YOUR OWN CBS
22 DECEMBER 1956–16 MARCH 1957   A prime-time game show hosted by Steve Dunne, *You're On Your Own* began as a quiz show on which contestants were given time to answer the questions (they were free to use any reference source to obtain the

answers). By the end of its short run, however, it had devolved into a stunt show, on which contestants who gave incorrect answers to general knowledge questions had to pay the consequences.

YOU'RE PUTTING ME ON   NBC
30 MAY 1969–26 DECEMBER 1969   This daytime game show involved six celebrities, divided into three teams. One member of each team assumed the identity of a famous person (real or fictional), and the other member tried to guess who was being depicted. Bill Leyden hosted the show until late September, when Larry Blyden succeeded him.

YOURS FOR A SONG   ABC
Nighttime: 14 NOVEMBER 1961–18 SEPTEMBER 1962; *Daytime:* 4 DECEMBER 1961–29 MARCH 1963   Bert Parks hosted this half-hour game show, on which contestants won money by supplying the missing words in lyrics sung to them. Bob Russell created the show.

YOUTH ON THE MARCH   ABC/DUMONT
9 OCTOBER 1949–25 MAY 1952 (ABC); 5 OCTOBER 1952–7 JUNE 1953 (DUMONT) Sunday-evening religious show with the Reverend Percy Crawford and his Glee Club. Aired live from Philadelphia, the show also featured Crawford's wife, Ruth Duval Crawford, and their five children: Don, Dick, Dan, Dean, and Donna Lee.

YOUTH TAKES A STAND   CBS
18 AUGUST 1953–28 MARCH 1954   One of several Sunday-afternoon public affairs programs on which a group of young people questioned a newsmaker, *Youth Takes a Stand* was moderated by Marc Cramer.

YOUTH WANTS TO KNOW   NBC
8 SEPTEMBER 1951–1 JUNE 1958   Like *Youth Takes a Stand, Youth Wants to Know* was a Sunday show on which a team of youngsters interviewed newsmakers. Theodore Granik was the original moderator of the series; Granik had produced and moderated the adult version of the series, *American Forum of the Air.* Stephen McCormick succeeded Granik as moderator.

ZANE GREY THEATER   CBS
5 OCTOBER 1956–20 SEPTEMBER 1962   Like *Death Valley Days* and *Frontier, Zane Grey Theater* was a western anthology series. It was hosted by Dick Powell and was officially titled *Dick Powell's Zane Grey Theater;* Powell occasionally starred in an episode. Some of the stories were based on those written by Zane Grey, but most were original teleplays. Among the guest stars who appeared were Hedy Lamarr (in her only TV dramatic appearance, "Proud Woman," 25 October 1957), Jack Lemmon ("The Three Graves," 4 January 1957), Ginger Rogers (in a rare TV appearance, "Never Too Late," 4 February 1960), Claudette Colbert (in her last TV dramatic appearance to date, "So Young the Savage Land," 10 November 1960), and Esther Williams (in her last TV dramatic appearance until 1987, "The Black Wagon," 1 December 1960). Hal Hudson was the first producer of the half-hour show, which was supplied by Four Star Films, Zane Grey, and Pamric Productions.

ZAZOO U.   FOX
8 SEPTEMBER 1990–19 JANUARY 1991   Half-hour Saturday morning cartoon show set at a school attended by animals. The principal characters were Boink, Tess, Grizzle, and Bully.

THE ZOO GANG   NBC
16 JULY 1975–6 AUGUST 1975   A three-hour miniseries, *The Zoo Gang* was shown in six parts by NBC during the summer of 1975. It told the story of four freedom fighters who worked together during World War II and reunited almost thirty years later to continue their adventures. With Brian Keith as Stephen Halliday (The Fox);

John Mills as Captain Tommy Devon (The Elephant); Lilli Palmer as Manouche Roget (The Leopard); and Barry Morse as Alec Marlowe (The Tiger). Filmed in Europe, the series was developed by Reginald Rose and produced by Herbert Hirschman for ATV-ITC Productions. Theme music was composed by Paul and Linda McCartney.

ZOO PARADE   NBC
28 MAY 1950–1 SEPTEMBER 1957   This half-hour Sunday-afternoon series on animals and animal behavior was cohosted by Marlin Perkins and Jim Hurlbut. It was broadcast from Chicago's Lincoln Park Zoo until 1955; for the show's last two seasons, Perkins and Hurlbut traveled to zoos throughout the country.

ZOOBILEE ZOO   SYNDICATED
1986   Ben Vereen, who was also hosting the syndicated music show *You Write the Songs,* starred in the children's music and variety series on which the actors all appeared as animals; Vereen played a leopard, Mayor Ben, the leader of the Zoobles.

ZOOM   PBS
1972–1979   A half-hour potpourri of features for children, *Zoom* was hosted by a group of seven children, whose membership changed periodically. Many of the presentations were games, stunts, or filmed segments suggested by the show's legions of young viewers. The show was produced at WGBH-TV, Boston.

ZOORAMA   CBS
25 APRIL 1965–26 SEPTEMBER 1965   Not to be confused with *Zoo Parade,* this half-hour animalogue was hosted by Bob Dale at the San Diego Zoo.

ZORRO   ABC
10 OCTOBER 1957–24 SEPTEMBER 1959   *Zorro,* the masked Spanish swordsman of California, was created by author Johnston McCulley in 1919, and was the hero of several motion pictures before this Walt Disney TV series came to the air in 1957. The character was essentially the Batman of the 1820s (*Zorro* is the Spanish word for "fox"); his real identity was Don Diego de la Vega, a young Spanish nobleman who was summoned to California by his father to help fight the region's despotic commandant. On his way to North America Don Diego decided that he would purport to be a timid fop, so that no one would believe him to be the real "Zorro," defender of the people. The half-hour TV series starred Guy Williams as Don Diego/Zorro; George J. Lewis as his father, Don Alejandro de la Vega; Gene Sheldon as Bernardo, Don Diego's mute manservant, the only person who knew of his dual identity at first (Don Alejandro later learned of the fact); Henry Calvin as portly Sergeant Garcia, Zorro's hapless pursuer; Britt Lomond as Garcia's superior, Captain Monastario; Don Diamond as Corporal Reyes, Garcia's lackey; and Jolene Brand (1958–1959) as Anna Maria, Don Diego's sometime girlfriend. Walt Disney was executive producer of the series, William H. Anderson producer. In 1974 the character reappeared in a made-for-TV movie, "The Mark of Zorro," starring Frank Langella (29 October 1974). A second TV series surfaced in 1983 (see *Zorro and Son*), and a third in 1990 (see below).

ZORRO   FAM
5 JANUARY 1990–21 AUGUST 1993   The second remake of the 1957 TV series was filmed in Spain, and starred Duncan Regehr as Zorro/Don Diego de la Vega, Patrice Camhi as Victoria, and Efrem Zimbalist, Jr., (1990) as Zorro's father, Don Alejandro.

ZORRO AND SON   CBS
6 APRIL 1983–1 JUNE 1983   This sequel to *Zorro* was played for laughs. Set in California a generation later than the original, it starred Henry Darrow as the aging Don Diego/Zorro; realizing that he wasn't getting any younger, and finding it increas-

ingly difficult to swing from chandeliers, Don Diego revealed his identity to his son, Don Carlos, and enlisted his help in protecting the citizenry from the military governors. Also featured were Paul Regina as the son, Don Carlos; Bill Dana as their servant, Bernardo; Gregory Sierra as the officious Captain Paco Pico; Richard Beauchamp as Sergeant Sepulveda; fast-talking John Moschitta, Jr. (better known for his Federal Express commercials), as Corporal Cassette, the human dictaphone; and Barney Martin as two local churchmen, Brother Napa and Brother Sonoma. The half-hour show was supplied by Walt Disney Productions, which had produced the original series.

★★★ PART II

SPECIAL OCCASIONS

1948

2 NOVEMBER	Election coverage (all four networks)
29 NOVEMBER	Live coverage at the New York Metropolitan Opera (ABC)

1949

11 JANUARY	East-to-Midwest coaxial cable opening (all four networks)
20 JANUARY	Inauguration of President Truman (all four networks)
4 MARCH	Golden Gloves boxing championship (CBS)
26 MARCH	"The NBC Symphony" (NBC)—classical music, conducted by Arturo Toscanini
4 APRIL	Signing of the NATO Pact by President Truman (all four networks)
9 APRIL	"Damon Runyon Memorial Fund" (NBC)—Milton Berle anchors the first telethon for charity
14 MAY	The Preakness (CBS)—live coverage of the horse race from Pimlico

1950

29 APRIL	"Damon Runyon Memorial Fund" (NBC)—second annual telethon, hosted by Milton Berle
11 MAY	The Four Freedoms Award (CBS)—presentations by Eleanor Roosevelt
3 SEPTEMBER	"Miss Television U.S.A. Contest" (DUMONT)— beauty pageant, won by Edie Adams
28 OCTOBER	"The Jack Benny Show" (CBS)—Jack Benny's first TV program, with guest Ken Murray
6 NOVEMBER	Opening night at the Metropolitan Opera (ABC)— Verdi's *Don Carlo,* with Robert Merrill
25 DECEMBER	"One Hour in Wonderland" (NBC)—Walt Disney's first TV production, with Edgar Bergen and Charlie McCarthy, and previews of the new Disney film, *Alice in Wonderland*

1951

28 JANUARY	"The Jack Benny Show" (CBS)—comedy with Jack Benny and guests Frank Sinatra and Faye Emerson
4 MARCH	"Richard Rodgers' Jubilee Show" (NBC)—tribute to composer Richard Rodgers, with Mary Martin, Celeste Holm, and Patrice Munsel
14 MAY et seq.	Kefauver Crime Commission Hearings (live coverage by CBS and NBC)
25 JUNE	First regularly scheduled intercity colorcasting (CBS, for its East Coast affiliates)
4 SEPTEMBER	First regular coast-to-coast telecast: President Truman's address at the opening of the Japanese Peace Treaty Conference in San Francisco (live coverage by all four networks)
12 SEPTEMBER	"Irving Berlin: Salute to America" (NBC)—music with Irving Berlin and guests Tony Martin, Dinah Shore, and Margaret Truman
23 DECEMBER	National Football League Championship Game (DUMONT)—first network coverage of an NFL championship game
24 DECEMBER	"Amahl and the Night Visitors" (NBC)—first production of Gian Carlo Menotti's Christmas opera

1952

27 JANUARY	Address by former President Herbert Hoover (CBS)
27 JANUARY	"The Jack Benny Show" (CBS)—comedy with Jack Benny and guest Barbara Stanwyck (in her TV debut)
3 MAY	Kentucky Derby (CBS)—first live coverage of the horse race
11 MAY	"President Truman: Tour of the White House" (CBS)—a filmed tour of the newly refurbished White House conducted by President Truman
22 JUNE	Telethon for the United States Olympic Team (NBC)—hosted by Bob Hope and Bing Crosby
7–11 JULY	Republican National Convention (live coverage by all four networks)
21–24 JULY	Democratic National Convention (live coverage by all four networks)
23 SEPTEMBER	Richard Nixon's "Checkers" speech (CBS and NBC)
19 OCTOBER	"Billy Budd," *NBC Opera Theatre* (NBC)—first of several opera specials, with Theodor Uppman starring in Benjamin Britten's opera
16 NOVEMBER	"Trouble in Tahiti," *NBC Opera Theatre* (NBC)—opera by Leonard Bernstein, with Beverly Wolff and David Atkinson

1953

8 FEBRUARY	"A Visit with Carl Sandburg" (NBC)—Sunday-afternoon interview
1 MARCH	"Answer the Call" (ABC and CBS)—special appeal by the American Red Cross, with President Eisenhower and several celebrity guests
19 MARCH	The Academy Awards (NBC)—first coast-to-coast Oscar telecast, with host Bob Hope
19 APRIL	"And It Came to Pass" (NBC)—a tribute to the fifth anniversary of Israel, with Ezio Pinza, Melvyn Douglas, and Jennie Tourel
17 MAY	"A Conversation with Frank Lloyd Wright" (NBC)— Sunday afternoon interview with the architect
2 JUNE	Coronation of Queen Elizabeth II (CBS and NBC)— filmed coverage
15 JUNE	"The Ford Fiftieth Anniversary Show" (CBS and NBC)—variety tribute, highlighted by the duet of Mary Martin and Ethel Merman, with appearances by Marian Anderson, Oscar Hammerstein II, Eddie Fisher, Frank Sinatra, Lowell Thomas, and Rudy Vallee (produced by Leland Hayward)
23 AUGUST	Arrival of POWs from Korea at San Francisco (NBC)
25 OCTOBER	"Wanda Landowska at Home" (NBC)—Sunday afternoon interview with the harpsichordist
15 NOVEMBER	"Television City" (CBS)—a tour of CBS's new West Coast production facility with Edward R. Murrow

1954

3 JANUARY	"The Bing Crosby Show" (CBS)—Bing Crosby's first variety special, with guest Jack Benny
10 JANUARY	"Resources of Freedom" (CBS)—Edward R. Murrow and a panel of experts discuss a Presidential commission report on technological resources
7 FEBRUARY	"Back to God" (CBS)—interdenominational religious program with President Eisenhower and American religious leaders
14 FEBRUARY	"Guatemala" (NBC)—documentary on Communist influence in Guatemala with Marshall Bannell
28 MARCH	"The General Foods Anniversary Show" (all four networks)—variety, with Richard Rodgers and Oscar Hammerstein II, Mary Martin, Jack Benny, Ezio Pinza, Groucho Marx, John Raitt, Tony

	Martin, Rosemary Clooney, Ed Sullivan, Yul Brynner, and Gordon MacRae
22 APRIL et seq.	The Army-McCarthy Hearings (live coverage by ABC and DuMont)
25 APRIL	"230,000 Will Die" (NBC)—documentary on cancer, narrated by Dr. Charles Cameron of the American Cancer Society
9 MAY	First of three filmed lectures by Bernard Baruch (NBC)
27 JUNE	"The Road to Spandau" (NBC)—documentary on seven convicted Nazi war criminals, narrated by Joseph C. Harsch
11 SEPTEMBER	Miss America Beauty Pageant (ABC)—first coast-to-coast telecast
12 SEPTEMBER	"Satins and Spurs," *Max Liebman Presents* (NBC)— lavish color musical, with Betty Hutton (in her TV debut), Kevin McCarthy, and Genevieve
13 SEPTEMBER	"Three Two One Zero" (NBC)—documentary on atomic power, produced by Henry Salomon
10 OCTOBER	"Sunday in Town" (NBC)—revue with Judy Holliday, Steve Allen, and Dick Shawn
24 OCTOBER	"Light's Diamond Jubilee" (all four networks)—commemoration of the seventy-fifth anniversary of electric light, with appearances by Helen Hayes, George Gobel, and Kim Novak
5 DECEMBER	"Spotlight" (NBC)—revue on ice, with Sonja Henie, Jimmy Durante, Jack Buchanan, Jeannie Carson, and Pat Carroll
18 DECEMBER	"Babes in Toyland" (NBC)—musical with Wally Cox, Jack E. Leonard, and Dave Garroway

1955

7 MARCH	Seventh annual Emmy Awards (NBC)—first coast-to-coast telecast, hosted by Steve Allen
12 MARCH	"A Connecticut Yankee," *Max Liebman Presents* (NBC)—musical with Eddie Albert, Janet Blair, Boris Karloff, and Gale Sherwood
9 APRIL	"The Merry Widow," *Max Liebman Presents* (NBC)— operetta with Anne Jeffreys, John Conte, Brian Sullivan, and Edward Everett Horton
4 JUNE	"The Chocolate Soldier," *Max Liebman Presents* (NBC)—musical adaptation of Shaw's *Arms and the Man,* with Rise Stevens, Eddie Albert, and Akim Tamiroff
7 JUNE	Address by President Eisenhower to the graduates of West Point (NBC)—first colorcast of Eisenhower
22 JUNE	"Three for Tonight" (CBS)—revue with Marge and Gower Champion and Harry Belafonte
30 JULY	"Svengali and the Blonde" (NBC)—musical with Carol Channing and Basil Rathbone
27 AUGUST	"One Touch of Venus" (NBC)—musical with Janet Blair and Russell Nype (broadcast live from Dallas)
11 SEPTEMBER	"The Skin of Our Teeth," *Color Spread* (NBC)— Thornton Wilder's comedy, with Helen Hayes, Mary Martin, and George Abbott
1 OCTOBER	"Heidi" (NBC)—children's drama, with Natalie Wood, Wally Cox, and Jeannie Carson
5 NOVEMBER	"The Great Waltz" (NBC)—musical with Bert Lahr
26 NOVEMBER	"Dearest Enemy" (NBC)—drama with Cornelia Otis Skinner and Robert Sterling
4 DECEMBER	"The Maurice Chevalier Show" (NBC)—variety with Maurice Chevalier, Marcel Marceau, Jeannie Carson, and Pat Carroll

1956

21 JANUARY	"Paris in the Springtime," *Max Liebman Presents* (NBC)—musical with Dan Dailey, Gale Sherwood, and Helen Gallagher
14 MARCH	"The Twisted Cross," *Project 20* (NBC)—documentary on the rise and fall of Adolf Hitler, narrated by Alexander Scourby

14 APRIL	"Marco Polo" (NBC)—musical (cowritten by Neil Simon) with Alfred Drake, Doretta Morrow, and Beatrice Kraft
27 MAY	"Antarctica—the Third World" (NBC)—documentary on Operation Deepfreeze, narrated by Bill Hartigan
9 JUNE	"Holiday" (NBC)—musical with Kitty Carlisle and Tammy Grimes
15 JULY	"The Bachelor," *Sunday Spectacular* (NBC)—musical (with songs by Steve Allen) with Hal March, Jayne Mansfield, and Carol Haney
27 OCTOBER	"Manhattan Tower," *Saturday Spectacular* (NBC)— musical with Peter Marshall, Helen O'Connell, Phil Harris, Ethel Waters, and Edward Everett Horton
19 NOVEMBER	"Our Mr. Sun," *Bell Science Series* (CBS)—first of a series of science documentaries hosted by Dr. Frank Baxter ("Our Mr. Sun" was produced and directed by Frank Capra)
24 NOVEMBER	"High Button Shoes" (NBC)—musical with Nanette Fabray, Hal March, and Don Ameche
30 NOVEMBER	First videotaped news broadcast (CBS to its West Coast outlets)
6 DECEMBER	"The Jazz Age," *Project 20* (NBC)—documentary on American life during the 1920s, narrated by Fred Allen
11 DECEMBER	"The Victor Borge Show" (CBS)—one-man show by the Danish pianist
22 DECEMBER	"Holiday on Ice," *Saturday Spectacular* (NBC)—revue with Sonja Henie, Hayes Alan Jenkins, Julius LaRosa, Ernie Kovacs, and Jaye P. Morgan

1957

19 JANUARY	"The Jerry Lewis Show" (NBC)—Jerry Lewis's first variety special since splitting up with Dean Martin
19 JANUARY	"The Ernie Kovacs Show" (NBC)—Ernie Kovacs in a half-hour comedy special without words
6 MARCH	"Maurice Chevalier's Paris" (NBC)—documentary on modern Paris hosted by Maurice Chevalier
20 MARCH	"Hemo the Magnificent," *Bell Science Series* (NBC)— documentary on blood, with Dr. Frank Baxter (as Dr. Research) and Richard Carlson (produced and directed by Frank Capra)
24 MARCH	"The Black Star Rises" (CBS)—documentary on Vice President Nixon's trip to Africa
31 MARCH	"Cinderella" (CBS)—original musical by Rodgers and Hammerstein, with Julie Andrews, Jon Cypher, Howard Lindsay, and Ilka Chase
13 APRIL	"Salute to Baseball" (NBC)—variety special hosted by Gene Kelly with Paul Winchell, Tony Bennett, Robert Alda, Mickey Mantle, Stan Musial, and Ted Williams
4, 11 MAY	"Rock 'n' Roll Show" (ABC)—first prime-time network special devoted to rock music, hosted by Alan Freed, with Sal Mineo, Guy Mitchell, June Valli, Martha Carson, the Clovers, Screamin' Jay Hawkins, and the Del-Vikings
11 MAY	"Mr. Broadway" (NBC)—musical with Mickey Rooney (as George M. Cohan), Gloria DeHaven, June Havoc, and Garry Moore
19 MAY	"This Is Defense" (CBS)—one-hour demonstration of American military might from Andrews Air Force Base
19 MAY	"The Rebels of Sierra Maestra—Cuba's Jungle Fighters" (CBS)— news documentary on Cuban guerrillas, with an interview of leader Fidel Castro
8 JUNE	"The Jerry Lewis Show" (NBC)—Jerry Lewis's second variety special, with guests Eydie Gormé and Dan Rowan and Dick Martin
4 AUGUST	"As Others See Us" (NBC)—documentary exploring perceptions of America by foreigners
5 SEPTEMBER	"The Dean Martin Show" (NBC)—Dean Martin's first variety spe-

cial since splitting up with Jerry Lewis, with guests James Mason, Louis Prima, and Keely Smith

13 OCTOBER   "Pinocchio" (NBC)—musical with Mickey Rooney and Fran Allison (simulcast on radio and television)

12 NOVEMBER   "High Adventure" (CBS)—first of a series of travel documentaries hosted by Lowell Thomas

16 NOVEMBER   "Holiday in Las Vegas" (NBC)—variety show from Las Vegas, with Ann Sothern, Jayne Mansfield, Mickey Hargitay, Sammy Davis, Jr., Tony Randall, and Vic Damone

17 NOVEMBER   "General Motors Fiftieth Anniversary Show" (NBC)—variety tribute hosted by Kirk Douglas, with appearances by Ernest Borgnine, Cyril Ritchard, Claudette Colbert, Helen Hayes, Pat Boone, Dean Martin, Carol Burnett, June Allyson, and Steve Lawrence

26 NOVEMBER   "The Pied Piper of Hamelin" (NBC)—musical with Van Johnson, Claude Rains, and Kay Starr

27 NOVEMBER   "Annie Get Your Gun" (NBC)—musical with Mary Martin, John Raitt, and William O'Neal

8 DECEMBER   "A Day Called X" (CBS)—documentary examining the civil defense system of Portland, Oregon, in response to a simulated nuclear attack

30 DECEMBER   "All Star Jazz" (NBC)—musical program hosted by Steve Allen, with Louis Armstrong, Dave Brubeck, Paul Desmond, Duke Ellington, Woody Herman, Gene Krupa, Carmen McRae, and Charlie Ventura

30 DECEMBER   "The Lady from Philadelphia: Through Asia with Marian Anderson," *See It Now* (CBS)—documentary on Marian Anderson's goodwill tour of Asia sponsored by the U.S. State Department

1958

1 FEBRUARY   "Young People's Concert" (CBS)—second musical special hosted by Leonard Bernstein, with guest Aaron Copland

1 FEBRUARY   "The Dean Martin Show" (NBC)—variety, with Dean Martin and guests Frank Sinatra, Danny Thomas, and Barbara Perry

23 FEBRUARY   "Education for What?" *The Great Challenge* (CBS)— first of a series of symposiums on contemporary issues, moderated by Howard K. Smith

2 MARCH   "Statehood for Alaska and Hawaii?" *See It Now* (CBS)—news documentary hosted by Edward R. Murrow

30 MARCH   "Radiation and Fallout," *See It Now* (CBS)—investigative documentary narrated by Edward R. Murrow

15 APRIL   "The Jerry Lewis Show" (NBC)—variety with Jerry Lewis and guests Everett Sloane and Helen Traubel

27 APRIL   "Hansel and Gretel" (NBC)—musical with Red Buttons, Barbara Cook, Rise Stevens, and Rudy Vallee

19 SEPTEMBER   "Roberta" (NBC)—musical with Bob Hope, Anna Maria Alberghetti, Howard Keel, and Janis Paige

10 OCTOBER   "The Bing Crosby Show" (ABC)—variety with Bing Crosby and guests Patti Page, Dean Martin, and Mahalia Jackson

12 OCTOBER   "Swiss Family Robinson" (NBC)—adventure with Walter Pidgeon and Laraine Day

15 OCTOBER   "Dead of Noon" (CBS)—drama with Richard Boone as western outlaw John Wesley Hardin

15 OCTOBER   "Ginger Rogers" (CBS)—variety with Ginger Rogers and guests Ray Bolger and the Ritz Brothers

16 OCTOBER   "Little Women" (NBC)—drama with Zina Bethune, Jeannie Carson, Florence Henderson, Margaret O'Brien, Rise Stevens, and Joel Grey

17 OCTOBER   "An Evening with Fred Astaire" (NBC)—Fred Astaire's first vari-

ety special, with Barrie Chase (produced by Bud Yorkin and choreographed by Hermes Pan)

26 OCTOBER   "United Nations Day Concert," *The U.N. in Action* (CBS)—concert by cellist Pablo Casals

10 NOVEMBER   "All-Star Jazz" (CBS)—music with Louis Armstrong, Gene Krupa, Lionel Hampton, Les Brown, Bob Crosby's Bobcats, and Jane Morgan

30 NOVEMBER   "Wonderful Town" (CBS)—musical with Rosalind Russell, Jacquelyn McKeever, and Sydney Chaplin

30 NOVEMBER   "Art Carney Meets Peter and the Wolf" (ABC)—musical with Art Carney and the puppets of Bil and Cora Baird

9 DECEMBER   "The Gift of the Magi" (CBS)—musical adaptation of O. Henry's story, with Gordon MacRae, Sally Ann Howes, and Bea Arthur

28 DECEMBER   "The Face of Red China" (CBS)—documentary using film shot by a German journalist

1959

7 JANUARY   "The Golden Age of Jazz" (CBS)—musical hour hosted by Jackie Gleason, with guests Louis Armstrong, Duke Ellington, Dizzy Gillespie, Gene Krupa, and George Shearing

18 JANUARY   "Ten Little Indians" (NBC)—Agatha Christie mystery, with Nina Foch, Kenneth Haigh, and Barry Jones

21 JANUARY   "The Lost Class of '59" (CBS)—news documentary hosted by Edward R. Murrow on the closing of six Norfolk high schools to forestall federally ordered desegregation

26 JANUARY   "The Alphabet Conspiracy," *Bell Science Series* (NBC)—fantasy on language, with Dr. Frank Baxter (as Dr. Linguistics) and Hans Conried

11 FEBRUARY   "Meet Mr. Lincoln," *Project 20* (NBC)—photographs and drawings of Abraham Lincoln with narration by Alexander Scourby

28 FEBRUARY   "Accent on Love" (NBC)—musical revue with Ginger Rogers, Louis Jourdan, Mike Nichols and Elaine May, Marge and Gower Champion, and Jaye P. Morgan

29 MARCH   "Magic with Mary Martin" and "Music with Mary Martin" (NBC)—two Easter Sunday programs (one afternoon, one evening) with Mary Martin

24 APRIL   "The Gene Kelly Show" (CBS)—variety with Gene Kelly and guests Liza Minnelli (then age thirteen) and Carl Sandburg

26 APRIL   "Meet Me in St. Louis" (CBS)—musical with Jane Powell, Tab Hunter, Myrna Loy, Walter Pidgeon, Ed Wynn, and Patty Duke

8 MAY   "Why Berlin?" (NBC)—news documentary narrated by Chet Huntley

28 JUNE   "The Record Years" (ABC)—tribute to the recording industry hosted by Dick Clark, with guests Johnny Mathis, Fabian, the McGuire Sisters, Les Paul and Mary Ford, Fats Domino, and Stan Freberg

20 SEPTEMBER   "People Kill People Sometimes," *Sunday Showcase* (NBC)—drama with George C. Scott, Geraldine Page, and Jason Robards, Jr.

27 SEPTEMBER, 4 OCTOBER   "What Makes Sammy Run?" *Sunday Showcase (NBC)*—drama with Larry Blyden, Barbara Rush, and John Forsythe

27 OCTOBER   "The Bells of St. Mary's" (CBS)—musical with Claudette Colbert (in a rare TV appearance) and Robert Preston

30 OCTOBER   "The Moon and Sixpence" (NBC)—drama adapted by S. Lee Pogostin and directed by Robert Mulligan, with Laurence Olivier (in his American TV debut), Judith Anderson, Hume Cronyn, Jessica Tandy, and Geraldine Fitzgerald

7 DECEMBER   "The Philadelphia Story" (NBC)—drama with Christopher Plummer and Gig Young

| 10 DECEMBER | "Tonight with Belafonte" (CBS)—music with Harry Belafonte |
| 18 DECEMBER | "Iran: Brittle Ally," *CBS Reports* (CBS)—news documentary narrated by Edward R. Murrow and Winston Burdett |

1960

7 JANUARY	"Mrs. Miniver" (CBS)—drama with Maureen O'Hara, Leo Genn, and Cathleen Nesbitt
29 JANUARY	"The Fifth Column" (CBS)—drama with Richard Burton
31 JANUARY	"The Fabulous Fifties" (CBS)—retrospective, produced by Leland Hayward, hosted by Henry Fonda, with appearances by Rex Harrison, Julie Andrews, Dick Van Dyke, Mike Nichols and Elaine May, Betty Comden and Adolph Green, Shelley Berman, Suzy Parker, Jackie Gleason, and Eric Sevareid
14 FEBRUARY	"The Devil and Daniel Webster" (NBC)—drama with Edward G. Robinson and David Wayne
24 FEBRUARY	"Four for Tonight," *Star Parade* (NBC)—live and taped variety, with Cyril Ritchard, Beatrice Lillie, Tony Randall, and Tammy Grimes
25 MARCH	"The Snows of Kilimanjaro" (CBS)—adaptation of Hemingway's story, with Robert Ryan, Janice Rule, and Ann Todd
31 MARCH	"The Bat," *The Dow Hour of Great Mysteries* (NBC)—drama with Helen Hayes, Jason Robards, Jr., and Margaret Hamilton (first of a series of specials, hosted by Joseph N. Welch)
20 APRIL	"Ninotchka," *Special Tonight* (ABC)—comedy, with Maria Schell, Gig Young, Zsa Zsa Gabor, and Anne Meara
7 MAY	"The Slowest Gun in the West" (CBS)—comedy-western with Jack Benny and Phil Silvers
3 AND 10 JUNE	"The Sacco-Vanzetti Story" (NBC)—docu-drama written by Reginald Rose and directed by Sidney Lumet, with Martin Balsam (as Sacco), Steven Hill (Vanzetti), E. G. Marshall, and Peter Falk
7 JULY	"Lippmann on Leadership," *CBS Reports* (CBS)—political observer Walter Lippmann interviewed by Howard K. Smith
26 AUGUST– 12 SEPTEMBER	Summer Olympics from Rome (coverage by CBS)
26 SEPTEMBER	First of the Kennedy-Nixon Debates (coverage by all three networks)
28 SEPTEMBER	"Astaire Time" (NBC)—variety, with Fred Astaire and Barrie Chase
25 OCTOBER	"John Brown's Raid" (NBC)—drama with James Mason, Robert Duvall, and Ossie Davis
30 OCTOBER	"Danny Kaye" (CBS)—Danny Kaye's first variety special, with guest Louis Armstrong
1 NOVEMBER	"Dean Martin" (NBC)—variety with Dean Martin and guests Frank Sinatra, Dorothy Provine, and Don Knotts
14 NOVEMBER	"The Spirit of the Alamo" (ABC)—tour of the Alamo and promotion of the film *The Alamo,* hosted by John Wayne
30 NOVEMBER	"The Three Musketeers," *Family Classics* (CBS)—adventure with Maximilian Schell, John Colicos, Barry Morse, Tim O'Connor, and Vincent Price
8 DECEMBER	"Peter Pan" (NBC)—restaged version, with Mary Martin, Cyril Ritchard, and Maureen Bailey
20 DECEMBER	"Sit-In," *NBC White Paper* (NBC)—documentary on desegregation in Nashville
21 DECEMBER	"The Coming of Christ," *Project 20* (NBC)—art documentary narrated by Alexander Scourby

1961

| 15 JANUARY | "The Gershwin Years" (CBS)—music, with Ethel Merman |

22 JANUARY	"The Red and the Black," *Closeup* (ABC)—documentary produced by Helen Jean Rogers on Soviet influence in Africa
25 JANUARY	President Kennedy's first press conference (coverage by all three networks; first live telecast of a Presidential news conference)
7 FEBRUARY	"A String of Beads" (NBC)—drama with Jane Fonda (her first dramatic appearance on American TV)
12 FEBRUARY	"Aaron Copland's Birthday Party," *Young People's Concert* (CBS)—music with Leonard Bernstein and the New York Philharmonic
13 FEBRUARY	"The Heiress," *Family Classics* (CBS)—adaptation of the play based on Henry James's *Washington Square,* with Julie Harris, Farley Granger, and Barry Morse
14 FEBRUARY	"Panama—Danger Zone," *NBC White Paper* (NBC)—documentary on the Canal Zone and Panamanian nationalism, narrated by Chet Huntley
5 MARCH	"Fierce, Funny and Far Out," *Omnibus* (NBC)—a look at contemporary drama with William Saroyan and scenes from four recent plays
9 MARCH	"Mother and Daughter," *Purex Special for Women* (NBC)—daytime drama with Patricia Neal, Lynn Loring, and Arthur Hill
20 MARCH	"Twenty-Four Hours in a Woman's Life" (CBS)— drama with Ingrid Bergman and Rip Torn
29 MARCH	"The Real West," *Project 20* (NBC)—cultural documentary narrated by Gary Cooper
18 APRIL	"90 Miles to Communism," *Closeup* (ABC)—documentary on Cuba's political climate
27 APRIL	"Jane Eyre," *Family Classics* (CBS)—live drama, with Sally Ann Howes, Zachary Scott, and Fritz Weaver
9 AUGUST	"The Jimmy Durante Show" (NBC)—comedy on the modern American husband, with Jimmy Durante and guests Bob Hope, Garry Moore, and Janice Rule
23, 30 SEPTEMBER	"The Assassination Plot at Teheran" (ABC)—two-part drama on a supposed German plot to kill Stalin, Churchill, and Roosevelt, with John Larch, Oscar Homolka, and Hermione Gingold
4 OCTOBER	"The Spiral Staircase," *Theatre 62* (NBC)—live drama with Gig Young, Elizabeth Montgomery, and Eddie Albert
12 OCTOBER	"Eisenhower on the Presidency" (CBS)—first of three interviews conducted by Walter Cronkite
29 OCTOBER	"The Power and the Glory" (CBS)—drama with George C. Scott, Laurence Olivier, Patty Duke, and Keenan Wynn
16 NOVEMBER	"The Glamor Trap," *Purex Special for Women* (NBC)—daytime documentary on the beauty and cosmetics industries
17 NOVEMBER	"Vincent Van Gogh: A Self-Portrait" (NBC)—art documentary narrated by Martin Gabel, with Lee J. Cobb reading from Van Gogh's letters
23 DECEMBER	"The Enchanted Nutcracker," *Westinghouse Presents* (ABC)—adaptation of the Tchaikovsky ballet, with Carol Lawrence, Robert Goulet, and Linda Canby
26 DECEMBER	"Khrushchev and Berlin," *NBC White Paper* (NBC)— news documentary (first NBC documentary produced by Fred Freed)

1962

14 JANUARY	"John Brown's Body" (CBS)—adaptation of Benet's poem, narrated by Richard Boone
14 JANUARY	"The Farmer's Daughter," *Theater 62* (NBC)—live comedy, with Lee Remick, Peter Lawford, Charles Bickford, and Cornelia Otis Skinner
28 JANUARY	"The Battle of Newburgh," *NBC White Paper* (NBC)—investigative

documentary on the effect of a tightening of the welfare code in Newburgh, New York

14 FEBRUARY	"A Tour of the White House with Mrs. John F. Kennedy" (CBS and NBC)—deftly directed by Franklin Schaffner
20 FEBRUARY	Orbital space flight of Lieutenant Colonel John Glenn (coverage by all three networks)
9 MARCH	"The Milton Berle Show" (NBC)—variety, with Milton Berle and guests Jack Benny, Lena Horne, Janis Paige, and Laurence Harvey
24 MARCH	"Tonight in Samarkand," *Breck Golden Showcase* (CBS)—drama with Janice Rule and James Mason
29 MARCH	"U.S. Route #1: An American Profile" (NBC)—a trip down the East Coast, narrated by Van Heflin
1 APRIL	"Jacqueline Kennedy's Journey" (NBC)—coverage of the First Lady's trip to India and Pakistan
6 APRIL	"The Vanishing 400" (NBC)—a look at high society, narrated by Walter Pidgeon with commentary by Cleveland Amory
25 MAY	"Robert Ruark's Africa" (NBC)—documentary filmed in Kenya, with Robert Ruark defending colonialism
11 JUNE	"Julie and Carol at Carnegie Hall" (CBS)—music and comedy with Julie Andrews and Carol Burnett
14 JUNE	"Noah and the Flood" (CBS)—world premiere of Igor Stravinsky's ballet, choreographed by George Balanchine
10 JULY	First transmission from the Telstar satellite (coverage by all three networks)
27 JULY	"The World of Sophia Loren" (NBC)—profile of the Italian actress, with appearances by Vittorio DeSica, Anatole Litvak, Anthony Perkins, and Art Buchwald
14 AUGUST	"Shelley Berman: A Personal Appearance" (ABC)—one-man show
16 AUGUST	"Americans: A Portrait in Verses" (CBS)—a series of sketches set to poems by Poe, Emerson, Cummings, and Ginsberg, with Alexander Scourby, Peggy Wood, Kim Hunter, and James Whitmore
28 SEPTEMBER	"Meet Comrade Student" (ABC)—investigative documentary on the Soviet educational system
28 OCTOBER	"The River Nile" (NBC)—documentary narrated by James Mason
11 NOVEMBER	"The Danny Kaye Show" (NBC)—variety with Danny Kaye and guest Lucille Ball
10 DECEMBER	"The Tunnel" (NBC)—documentary on the construction of a tunnel underneath the Berlin Wall by a group of West Germans, narrated by Piers Anderton (who cowrote the show with Reuven Frank)
21 DECEMBER	"What Is a Melody?" *Young People's Concert* (CBS)—musical education with Leonard Bernstein and the New York Philharmonic

1963

24 JANUARY	"The World of Benny Goodman" (NBC)—profile of the jazz clarinetist, narrated by Alexander Scourby
3 FEBRUARY	"The Rise of Khrushchev," *NBC White Paper* (NBC)—documentary produced by Fred Freed and narrated by Chet Huntley
11 FEBRUARY	"Eisenhower on Lincoln" (NBC)—Ike talks with Bruce Catton
17 FEBRUARY	"A Look at Monaco" (CBS)—a guided tour with Princess Grace (CBS's only colorcast of the 1962–1963 season)
22 FEBRUARY	"World of Chevalier" (NBC)—portrait of Maurice Chevalier
19 MARCH	"Judy Garland" (CBS)—variety with Judy Garland and guests Phil Silvers and Robert Goulet
21 MAY	"The Kremlin" (NBC)—a tour with Frank Bourgholtzer
6 AUGUST	"Picture of a Cuban," *Focus on America* (ABC)— documentary about a Cuban family that relocated in Miami

11 AUGUST	"The Crucial Summer" (ABC)—first of five half-hour reports on civil rights
22 AUGUST	"The Voice of the Desert," *Summer Special* (NBC)— documentary on Arizona's Sonora Desert with naturalist Joseph Wood Krutch
28 AUGUST	Civil Rights March on Washington (live coverage by NBC)
2 SEPTEMBER	"The American Revolution of '63" (NBC)—three-hour documentary on the struggle for civil rights
9 SEPTEMBER	"What Happened to Royalty?" (ABC)—profiles of Europe's remaining monarchs, produced by Warren Wallace
11 SEPTEMBER	"Athens, Where the Theater Began," *The Roots of Freedom* (CBS)—cultural documentary with Alfred Lunt and Lynn Fontanne
20 SEPTEMBER	"Hedda Gabler" (CBS)—drama, with Ingrid Bergman (in a rare TV appearance), Trevor Howard, Ralph Richardson, and Michael Redgrave
6 OCTOBER	"Elizabeth Taylor in London" (CBS)—cultural documentary hosted by Elizabeth Taylor (in a rare TV appearance)
6 OCTOBER	"A Man Named Mays" (NBC)—profile of baseball great Willie Mays, written and narrated by Charles Einstein
21 OCTOBER	"Crisis—Behind a Presidential Commitment (ABC)—documentary on the June 1963 integration crisis at the University of Alabama
25 OCTOBER	"The World's Girls" (ABC)—documentary on feminism, with appearances by Simone de Beauvoir, Simone Signoret, and Betty Friedan
10 NOVEMBER	"That Was the Week That Was" (NBC)—satire, with Henry Morgan, Charlie Manna, and Nancy Ames (later a series)
22–25 NOVEMBER	Coverage by all three networks of the events following the assassination of President John F. Kennedy
1 DECEMBER	"The Greatest Showman" (NBC)—profile of Cecil B. DeMille, with appearances by Bob Hope, Charlton Heston, Gloria Swanson, Yul Brynner, Betty Hutton, and Billy Graham
10 DECEMBER	"The Soviet Woman" (ABC)—documentary hosted by John Secondari
25 DECEMBER	"Amahl and the Night Visitors" (NBC)—new version of the Menotti opera, with Kurt Yaghjian and Martha King
29 DECEMBER	"The Making of the President 1960" (ABC)—documentary on the Nixon-Kennedy campaign, narrated by Martin Gabel with commentary by author Theodore H. White

1964

7 JANUARY	"The Orient Express" (NBC)—documentary with Edwin Newman aboard
12 JANUARY	"Birth Control: How?" (NBC)—documentary hosted by David Brinkley
24 JANUARY	"The Restless Sea," *Bell Science Series* (NBC)—documentary from Disney Studios on marine life
4, 9 FEBRUARY	*NBC White Paper* (NBC)—two-part examination of Cuba (I—"The Bay of Pigs," II—"The Missile Crisis")
15 FEBRUARY	"Robin Hood," *NBC Children's Theatre* (NBC)—adventure with Dan Ferrone, Lynda Day, and Sorrell Booke
1 APRIL	"Vietnam: The Deadly Decision" (CBS)—examination of America's increasing involvement, anchored by Charles Collingwood
28 APRIL	"Boxing's Last Round" (NBC)—documentary on the decline in boxing's popularity, hosted by David Brinkley
29 APRIL, 6 MAY	"DeGaulle: Roots of Power," *CBS Reports* (CBS)— biography
27 MAY	"Town Meeting of the World" (CBS)—one of several such broadcasts made possible by satellite technology, this one featured Richard Nixon, J. William Fulbright, Harold Wilson, and Maurice Schumann, with host Eric Sevareid

3 JUNE	"Once upon a Mattress" (CBS)—musical, with Carol Burnett
5 JUNE	"D-Day Plus 20 Years: Eisenhower Returns to Normandy," *CBS Reports* (CBS)—retrospective, with Ike and Walter Cronkite
29 AUGUST	"The King Family" (ABC)—their first TV special
1 SEPTEMBER	"Civil War Portraits" (NBC)—profiles of U.S. Grant and Robert E. Lee, introduced by Hugh Downs
10 SEPTEMBER	"Letters from Viet Nam" (ABC)—profile of an American helicopter squadron, produced by Gregory Shuker
16 OCTOBER	"Have Girls—Will Travel" (NBC)—comedy, with Bob Hope, Rhonda Fleming, Jill St. John, and Marilyn Maxwell
12 NOVEMBER	"Sophia Loren in Rome" (ABC)—tour of Rome with Sophia Loren and her guest, Marcello Mastroianni
15 NOVEMBER	"Around the Beatles" (ABC)—musical special, taped in London in May 1964, with the Beatles and guests Cilla Black, P. J. Proby, and Millie Small
17 NOVEMBER	"The Louvre" (NBC)—cultural documentary produced by Lucy Jarvis and narrated by Charles Boyer
16 DECEMBER	"Casals at Eighty-eight" (CBS)—profile of cellist Pablo Casals
28 DECEMBER	"Carol for Another Christmas" (ABC)—drama, with Peter Sellers (in his American TV dramatic debut), Ben Gazzara, Sterling Hayden, Steve Lawrence, and Eva Marie Saint

1965

25 JANUARY	"The Stately Ghosts of England" (NBC)—lighthearted documentary hosted by Margaret Rutherford
15 FEBRUARY	"Dinah Shore" (ABC)—a tribute to the Peace Corps, with guests Harry Belafonte and Sargent Shriver
22 FEBRUARY	"Cinderella" (CBS)—restaged version of the Rodgers and Hammerstein musical, with Lesley Ann Warren, Stuart Damon, Ginger Rogers, Jo Van Fleet, Walter Pidgeon, and Celeste Holm
23 FEBRUARY	"I, Leonardo da Vinci," *Saga of Western Man* (ABC)—historical documentary produced by John Secondari and Helen Jean Rogers
23 FEBRUARY	"The Journals of Lewis and Clark," *NBC News Special* (NBC)—historical documentary, narrated by Lorne Greene
1 MARCH	"T-Minus 4 Years, 9 Months and 30 Days" (CBS)—documentary examining whether the United States will reach its goal of landing a man on the moon by 1970
28 APRIL	"My Name is Barbra" (CBS)—Barbra Streisand's first TV special
24 MAY	"The National Driver's Test," *CBS News Special* (CBS)—an audience-participation special hosted by Mike Wallace
1 JUNE	"A Journey with Joseph Wood Krutch" (NBC)—a trip through the Grand Canyon with naturalist Joseph Wood Krutch
18 JUNE	"Everybody's Got a System" (ABC)—Terry-Thomas takes a look at gambling
25 AUGUST	"The Agony of Vietnam" (ABC)—documentary focusing on the impact of the war on the Vietnamese people
7 SEPTEMBER	"American White Paper: United States Foreign Policy" (NBC)—three-and-a-half-hour examination of American foreign policy
10 SEPTEMBER	"Americans on Everest," *National Geographic Special* (CBS)—chronicle of the 1963 U.S. expedition, narrated by Orson Welles (first of the *National Geographic Specials*)
29 SEPTEMBER	"Bob Hope" (NBC)—variety with Bob Hope and guests Beatrice Lillie, Douglas Fairbanks, Jr., Dinah Shore, and Andy Williams
5 OCTOBER	"Henry Moore: Man of Form," *CBS News Special* (CBS)—profile of the sculptor
24 NOVEMBER	"Frank Sinatra: A Man and His Music" (NBC)—a one-man show, produced by Dwight Hemion
28 NOVEMBER	"The Dangerous Christmas of Red Riding Hood" (ABC)—musical

with Liza Minnelli (as Lillian Hood), Cyril Ritchard (as Lone T. Wolf), Vic Damone, and the Animals

9 DECEMBER	"A Charlie Brown Christmas" (CBS)—the first of the *Peanuts* specials, based on Charles Schulz's comic strip
20 DECEMBER	"Vietnam: December, 1965," *NBC News Special* (NBC)—documentary produced by Chet Hagan, hosted by Chet Huntley and Frank McGee
21 DECEMBER	"The Nutcracker" (CBS)—ballet with Edward Villella, Patricia McBride, and the New York City Ballet

1966

23, 30 JANUARY	"The Ages of Man" (CBS)—readings from Shakespeare by John Gielgud
18 FEBRUARY	"An Evening with Carol Channing" (CBS)—Carol Channing's first variety special, with guests George Burns and David McCallum
30 MARCH	"Alice in Wonderland, or What's a Nice Girl Like You Doing in a Place Like This?" (ABC)—cartoon, with the voices of Sammy Davis, Jr., Hedda Hopper, Zsa Zsa Gabor, and Harvey Korman
30 MARCH	"Color Me Barbra" (CBS)—Barbra Streisand's second TV special, a one-woman show directed by Dwight Hemion
17 APRIL	"Countdown to Zero," *NBC White Paper* (NBC)— news documentary on the proliferation of nuclear weapons, produced by Fred Freed
22 APRIL	"The Poppy Is Also a Flower" (ABC)—one of a series of dramas depicting some of the work of the United Nations; introduced by Princess Grace of Monaco, with a star-studded cast including E. G. Marshall, Trevor Howard, Angie Dickinson, Eli Wallach, Yul Brynner, Stephen Boyd, Rita Hayworth (in her only TV dramatic appearance), Jack Hawkins, Marcello Mastroianni, and Omar Sharif
1 MAY	"Mississippi: A Self-Portrait," *NBC News Special* (NBC)—documentary produced and directed by Frank DeFelitta
3 MAY	"Stravinsky," *CBS News Special* (CBS)—profile, narrated by Charles Kuralt
8 MAY	"Death of a Salesman" (CBS)—new version of Arthur Miller's play, with Lee J. Cobb, Mildred Dunnock, George Segal, and James Farentino (directed by Alex Segal)
9 MAY	"LBJ's Texas" (NBC)—a tour of the hill country with President Johnson, accompanied by Ray Scherer
12 JUNE	"Politics: The Outer Fringe," *NBC News Special* (NBC)—documentary on the John Birch Society, the Minute Men, the American Nazi Party, and the Ku Klux Klan
15 JUNE	"The Undeclared War," *NBC News Special* (NBC)— documentary on guerrilla activities in Guatemala
16 JUNE	"The Baffling World of ESP" (ABC)—documentary narrated by Basil Rathbone
20 JULY	"Siberia: A Day in Irkutsk," *NBC News Special* (NBC)—documentary narrated by Kenneth Bernstein
6 AUGUST	Wedding of Luci Baines Johnson and Patrick J. Nugent at the White House (coverage by all three networks)
16 AUGUST	"The Angry Voices of Watts," *NBC News Special* (NBC)—black writers and poets present their works at the writers' workshop established in Watts by Budd Schulberg
25 AUGUST	"American White Paper: Organized Crime in America" (NBC)—three-and-a-half-hour examination of organized crime, narrated by Frank McGee
15 OCTOBER	"Brigadoon" (ABC)—musical, with Robert Goulet, Sally Ann Howes, Edward Villella, and Peter Falk
6 NOVEMBER	"Alice Through the Looking Glass" (NBC)—musical, with Judi

Robin (as Alice), Nanette Fabray, Jimmy Durante, Tom and Dick Smothers, Agnes Moorehead, Jack Palance, Ricardo Montalban, and Richard Denning

22 NOVEMBER	"Inside Red China," *CBS Reports* (CBS)—film shot by a German camera crew hired by CBS News
24 NOVEMBER	"Smokey the Bear" (NBC)—children's musical with animated puppets, narrated by James Cagney
6 DECEMBER	"The Legacy of Rome," *Saga of Western Man* (ABC)—historical documentary narrated by Fredric March
7 DECEMBER	"Frank Sinatra: A Man and His Music—Part II" (CBS)—a sequel to Sinatra's 1965 special
8 DECEMBER	"The Glass Menagerie" (CBS)—new version of Tennessee Williams's play, with Shirley Booth, Barbara Loden, Pat Hingle, and Hal Holbrook
13 DECEMBER	"The Long Childhood of Timmy" (ABC)—profile of a retarded child, narrated by E. G. Marshall
18 DECEMBER	"How the Grinch Stole Christmas" (CBS)—cartoon, based on the Dr. Seuss story, narrated by Boris Karloff (animation by Chuck Jones)
27 DECEMBER	*CBS News Special* (CBS)—Charles Collingwood and Morley Safer interview General William Westmoreland in Saigon

1967

10 JANUARY	"The Beatles at Shea Stadium" (ABC)—film of the Beatles' 1965 New York concert
15 JANUARY	Super Bowl I (CBS and NBC)—Green Bay versus Kansas City
26 FEBRUARY	"Jack and the Beanstalk" (NBC)—fantasy, produced by Hanna-Barbera, hosted by Gene Kelly (first TV special to combine live action with animation)
5 MARCH	"Good Day," *Experiment in Television* (NBC)—drama with Jo Van Fleet and Frank Langella
6 MARCH	"Mark Twain Tonight!" (CBS)—one-man show with Hal Holbrook
19 MARCH	"The Medium Is the Message," *Experiment in Television* (NBC)—documentary on Marshall McLuhan
19 MARCH	"Annie Get Your Gun" (NBC)—musical with Ethel Merman
4 MAY	"The Crucible" (CBS)—drama by Arthur Miller, with George C. Scott, Colleen Dewhurst, Fritz Weaver, and Tuesday Weld
7 MAY	"Carousel" (ABC)—musical with Robert Goulet and Mary Grover
30 MAY	"Ivanov" (CBS)—drama by Chekhov, with Claire Bloom and John Gielgud
6 JUNE	"Gauguin in Tahiti: The Search for Paradise," *CBS News Special* (CBS)—documentary, with Michael Redgrave reading from Gauguin's journals
25 JUNE	"Our World" (NET)—first live worldwide broadcast, transmitted by four satellites to thirty countries, with appearances by Franco Zeffirelli, Joan Miro, Marc Chagall, Van Cliburn, and the Beatles
11 JULY	"Khrushchev in Exile," *NBC News Special* (NBC)—documentary produced by Lucy Jarvis and narrated by Edwin Newman
9 SEPTEMBER	"Rowan and Martin's Laugh-In Special" (NBC)—comedy with Dan Rowan and Dick Martin (later a series)
10 SEPTEMBER	"Africa" (ABC)—four-hour news and cultural special on Africa, hosted by Gregory Peck
15 SEPTEMBER	"Summer '67: What We Learned," *NBC News Special* (NBC)—news documentary
11 OCTOBER	"Belle of 14th Street" (CBS)—musical with Barbra Streisand, Jason Robards, and John Bubbles
17 OCTOBER	"Do Not Go Gentle into That Good Night," *CBS Playhouse*

	(CBS)—drama with Melvyn Douglas, Shirley Booth, and Claudia McNeil
24 OCTOBER	"Kismet" (ABC)—musical with Anna Maria Alberghetti, George Chakiris, and José Ferrer
13 NOVEMBER	"Frank Sinatra" (NBC)—music with Frank Sinatra and guests Ella Fitzgerald and Antonio Carlos Jobim
15 NOVEMBER	"Dial M for Murder" (ABC)—drama with Laurence Harvey, Hugh O'Brian, and Diane Cilento
15 NOVEMBER	"Androcles and the Lion" (NBC)—musical with Noel Coward and Norman Wisdom
26 NOVEMBER	"The Diary of Anne Frank" (ABC)—drama with Diane Davila (as Anne Frank), Peter Beiger, Viveca Lindfors, Theodore Bikel, Donald Pleasence, Marisa Pavan, and Max von Sydow
1 DECEMBER	"Ten Days That Shook the World" (NBC)—documentary on the Russian Revolution, narrated by Orson Welles
17 DECEMBER	"Among the Paths to Eden" (ABC)—drama by Truman Capote, with Maureen Stapleton and Martin Balsam

1968

7 JANUARY	"Dr. Jekyll and Mr. Hyde" (ABC)—new version, with Jack Palance
8 JANUARY	"Sharks," *The Undersea World of Jacques Cousteau* (ABC)—first of the Cousteau specials for ABC
24 JANUARY	"Laura" (ABC)—drama with Lee Bouvier and Farley Granger
26 JANUARY	"Flesh and Blood" (NBC)—drama with Edmond O'Brien, Kim Stanley, E. G. Marshall, Suzanne Pleshette, Kim Darby, and Robert Duvall
31 JANUARY	"Of Mice and Men" (ABC)—adaptation of Steinbeck's novel, with Will Geer, Joey Heatherton, and Nicol Williamson
7 FEBRUARY	"The Fred Astaire Show" (NBC)—variety with Fred Astaire and guests Barrie Chase and Simon and Garfunkel
11 FEBRUARY	"A Case of Libel" (ABC)—adaptation of the Broadway play, with Lloyd Bridges, Van Heflin, and Angie Dickinson
18 FEBRUARY	"The Legend of Robin Hood" (NBC)—adventure with David Watson (as Robin Hood), Victor Buono, Walter Slezak, and Noel Harrison
27 FEBRUARY	"Walter Cronkite in Vietnam," *CBS News Special* (CBS)—firsthand reporting by Walter Cronkite
3 MARCH	"A Hatful of Rain" (ABC)—adaptation of the Broadway play, with Sandy Dennis, Peter Falk, Michael Parks, and Don Stroud
6 MARCH	"Tour of Monaco" (ABC)—documentary hosted by Princess Grace (the former Grace Kelly), with appearances by Terry-Thomas and Françoise Hardy
6, 8, 9 MARCH	"The Rise and Fall of the Third Reich" (ABC)—historical documentary narrated by Richard Basehart
17 MARCH	"Travels with Charley" (NBC)—adaptation of Steinbeck's book, narrated by Henry Fonda
18 MARCH	"The Bill Cosby Special" (NBC)—his first variety show
25 MARCH	"Kiss Me Kate" (ABC)—musical, with Robert Goulet, Carol Lawrence, and Jessica Walter
4, 9 APRIL	Special coverage of the Martin Luther King, Jr., assassination and aftermath (CBS)
27 JUNE	"Bias and the Media" (ABC)—first of six hour-long specials on racism
26–29 AUGUST	Coverage of the Democratic National Convention in Chicago (all three commercial networks)
8 SEPTEMBER	"Around the World of Mike Todd" (ABC)—retrospective narrated by Orson Welles, with appearances by Elizabeth Taylor, Gypsy Rose Lee, and Ethel Merman

12 SEPTEMBER	"Certain Honorable Men," *Prudential's On Stage* (NBC)—drama by Rod Serling, with Van Heflin and Peter Fonda
15 OCTOBER	"The People Next Door," *CBS Playhouse* (CBS)— drama by J. P. Miller, with Lloyd Bridges, Kim Hunter, and Deborah Winters
23 OCTOBER	"Sophia" (ABC)—profile of Sophia Loren
17 NOVEMBER	"Heidi" (NBC)—adapted for television by Earl Hamner, with Jennifer Edwards (as Heidi), Michael Redgrave, Jean Simmons, and Walter Slezak (NBC incurred the wrath of many viewers by interrupting the end of a pro football game to start the broadcast of "Heidi" on time)
3 DECEMBER	"Brigitte Bardot" (NBC)—a partially censored variety hour
3 DECEMBER	"Elvis" (NBC)—Elvis Presley's first major TV appearance in several years
3 DECEMBER	"Justice Black and the Bill of Rights," *CBS News Special* (CBS)—the eighty-two-year-old Supreme Court Justice reminisces
5 DECEMBER	"The Secret of Michelangelo: Every Man's Dream" (ABC)—art documentary, narrated by Christopher Plummer and Zoe Caldwell

1969

3 JANUARY	"Male of the Species," *Prudential's On Stage* (NBC)—dramatic vignettes, with host and narrator Laurence Olivier, guest appearances by Sean Connery, Paul Scofield, and Michael Caine
13 JANUARY	"To Love a Child," *ABC News Special* (ABC)—a report on a couple adopting a child
13 JANUARY	"Jean-Claude Killy" (ABC)—a profile of the skier
7 FEBRUARY	"This Is Sholom Aleichem," *Experiment in Television* (NBC)—biographical profile written by David Steinberg, with Jack Gilford (as Aleichem)
9 FEBRUARY	"A Midsummer Night's Dream" (CBS)—filmed performance by the Royal Shakespeare Company
2 APRIL	"Arsenic and Old Lace" (ABC)—new version, with Lillian Gish, Helen Hayes, Fred Gwynne, Sue Lyon, and Bob Crane
11 APRIL	"Fellini: A Director's Notebook," *Experiment in Television* (NBC)—profile, narrated in part by Federico Fellini
21 APRIL	"Francis Albert Sinatra Does His Thing" (CBS)—music with Frank Sinatra, Diahann Carroll, and the 5th Dimension (satisfied with the dress rehearsal tape, Sinatra elected not to do a final taping)
18 MAY	"Pogo" (NBC)—musical cartoon based on Walt Kelly's comic strip (animation by Chuck Jones)
5 JUNE	"Abortion," *Summer Focus* (ABC)—investigative report narrated by Frank Reynolds
1 JULY	Investiture of the Prince of Wales (satellite coverage carried by all three commercial networks)
20–21 JULY	Landing of Apollo 11 on the moon (coverage by all three commercial networks)
25 JULY	Senator Ted Kennedy obtains air time to explain the Chappaquiddick incident (ABC/NBC/CBS)
9 SEPTEMBER	"The Making of the President: 1968," *CBS News Special* (CBS)—documentary narrated by Joseph Campanella, with commentary by author Theodore H. White
12 SEPTEMBER	"Who Killed Lake Erie?" *NBC News Special* (NBC)— documentary on pollution, produced by Fred Freed
21 SEPTEMBER	"Woody Allen" (CBS)—comedy with Woody Allen and guests Candice Bergen and Billy Graham
7 OCTOBER	"From Here to the Seventies," *NBC News Special* (NBC)—two-and-a-half-hour special hosted by Paul Newman, with essays by twelve NBC correspondents

28 OCTOBER	"The Desert Whales," *The Undersea World of Jacques Cousteau* (ABC)—documentary
5 NOVEMBER	"Sinatra" (CBS)—a one-man musical show
9 NOVEMBER	"An Evening with Julie Andrews and Harry Belafonte" (NBC)—music
12 NOVEMBER	"Johnny Carson's Repertory Company" (NBC)—comedy with Johnny Carson, George C. Scott, Maureen Stapleton, and Marian Mercer
12 NOVEMBER	"Hey, Hey, Hey—It's Fat Albert" (NBC)—animated feature based on Bill Cosby's stories
13 NOVEMBER	Coverage by all networks of Vice President Agnew's Iowa speech attacking news commentaries
30 NOVEMBER	"Songs of America" (CBS)—music with Simon and Garfunkel
13 DECEMBER	"J. T.," *CBS Children's Hour* (CBS)—drama set in Harlem with Kevin Hooks and Ja'Net DuBois (later repeated in prime time)

1970

20 JANUARY	"My Sweet Charlie" (NBC)—drama with Patty Duke and Al Freeman, Jr.
18 FEBRUARY	"Annie, the Women in the Life of a Man" (CBS)—Anne Bancroft in a series of vignettes
15 MARCH	"David Copperfield" (NBC)—new version, produced in England, with Alastair Mackenzie and Robin Phillips (as David Copperfield), Laurence Olivier, Michael Redgrave, and Ralph Richardson
22 MARCH	"Harry and Lena" (ABC)—music with Harry Belafonte and Lena Horne
28 MARCH	"The Water Planet," *The Undersea World of Jacques Cousteau* (ABC)—Cousteau expounds on his philosophy
6 APRIL	"This Land Is Mine," *ABC News Special* (ABC)—a look at the American landscape, narrated by Robert Culp, featuring Kim Novak (in a rare TV appearance)
10 APRIL	"Tales from Muppetland" (ABC)—fantasy directed by Jim Henson, with Belinda Montgomery and Robin Ward
26 APRIL	"Raquel" (NBC)—variety with Raquel Welch and guests Bob Hope, John Wayne, and Tom Jones
5 MAY	"Once Before I Die" (NBC)—documentary on mountain climbing in Afghanistan filmed by Michael (*Woodstock*) Wadleigh
5 MAY	"California Impressions by Henri Cartier-Bresson," *CBS News Special* (CBS)—Cartier-Bresson's filmed impressions of life in the U.S.
8 SEPTEMBER	"A Day in the Life of the United States," *CBS News Special* (CBS)—a look at what was happening on 20 July 1969, the day of the moon landing
12 SEPTEMBER	"George M!" (NBC)—musical with Joel Grey (as George M. Cohan), Bernadette Peters and Red Buttons
13 OCTOBER	"The Old Man Who Cried Wolf," *ABC Movie of the Week* (ABC)—drama with Edward G. Robinson, Martin Balsam, and Diane Baker
29 NOVEMBER	"Swing Out, Sweet Land" (NBC)—a look at American history, with John Wayne and two dozen guest stars
18 DECEMBER	"The Smokey Robinson Show" (ABC)—music from Motown, with Smokey Robinson and the Miracles, the Temptations, the Supremes, Stevie Wonder, and Fran Jeffries
22 DECEMBER	"A World of Love" (CBS)—a salute to children, produced in conjunction with UNICEF, hosted by Bill Cosby and Shirley MacLaine, with guests Julie Andrews, Richard Burton, Audrey Hepburn, Barbra Streisand, and Harry Belafonte
31 DECEMBER	"Courts, Warts and All" (PBS)—Walter Cronkite, interviewed by Kevin O'Donnell, speaks on TV coverage of trials

1971

2 FEBRUARY	"The Point," *ABC Tuesday Movie of the Week* (ABC)—animated film (by Fred Wolf) based on Harry Nilsson's story, narrated by Dustin Hoffman
15 FEBRUARY	"Goldie Hawn" (NBC)—variety, with Goldie Hawn and guests Ruth Buzzi, Bob Dishy and Kermit the Frog
23 FEBRUARY	"The Selling of the Pentagon," *CBS Reports* (CBS)— investigative documentary
8–9 MARCH	"Vanished" (NBC)—drama with Arthur Hill, Richard Widmark, and Eleanor Parker
24 MARCH	"Jane Eyre" (NBC)—new version, directed by Delbert Mann, with Susannah York, George C. Scott, Nyree Dawn Porter, and Jack Hawkins
27 MARCH	"Bill Cosby Talks with Children About Drugs," *NBC Children's Theatre* (NBC)—informational special
6 APRIL	"The American Revolution: 1770–1783—A Conversation with Lord North," *CBS News Special* (CBS)—"interview" by Eric Sevareid of Lord North (played by Peter Ustinov)
18 APRIL	"Once Upon a Wheel" (ABC)—documentary on auto racing, narrated by Paul Newman
18 APRIL	"Diana!" (ABC)—music with Diana Ross and guests Bill Cosby, Danny Thomas, and the Jackson 5
2 MAY	"NBC White Paper: This Child Is Rated X" (NBC)—documentary on the criminal justice system and juveniles
21 MAY	"Venice Be Damned!" *NBC News Special* (NBC)—documentary on modern-day Venice narrated by José Ferrer
23 JUNE	Walter Cronkite interviews Daniel Ellsberg about the Pentagon Papers, *CBS News Special* (CBS)
30 JUNE	"June 30, 1971, a Day for History: The Supreme Court and the Pentagon Papers" (NBC)—news documentary
21 AUGUST	"Heroes and Heroin," *ABC News Special* (ABC)—investigative documentary on drug use among U.S. servicemen
11 OCTOBER	"Hogan's Goat" (PBS)—drama with Faye Dunaway (repeating her stage role) and Robert Foxworth
13 OCTOBER	First World Series night game (NBC)—record audience for a World Series telecast
15 OCTOBER	"Marriage: Year One" (NBC)—drama with Sally Field, Robert Pratt, William Windom, and Cicely Tyson
22 OCTOBER	"Good-bye, Raggedy Ann" (CBS)—drama with Mia Farrow and Hal Holbrook
31 OCTOBER	"Aesop's Fables" (CBS)—live-and-animated fantasy written by Earl Hamner, with Bill Cosby as Aesop
13 NOVEMBER	"Duel," *ABC Movie of the Weekend* (ABC)—drama, directed by Steven Spielberg, with Dennis Weaver
29 NOVEMBER	"Home" (PBS)—abridged version of the play, with John Gielgud and Ralph Richardson
30 NOVEMBER	"Brian's Song," *ABC Movie of the Week* (ABC)—biographical drama (later released theatrically) with James Caan (as Chicago Bears halfback and cancer victim Brian Piccolo) and Billy Dee Williams (Gale Sayers)
5 DECEMBER	"The American West of John Ford" (CBS)—a nostalgic look at the West and westerns, with John Wayne, Henry Fonda, and James Stewart
7 DECEMBER	"Julie and Carol at Lincoln Center" (CBS)—musical variety with Julie Andrews and Carol Burnett
19 DECEMBER	"The Homecoming" (CBS)—Christmas drama, written by Earl Hamner, with Patricia Neal, William Windom, and Ellen Corby

1972

17 JANUARY	"Jack Lemmon in 'S Wonderful, 'S Marvelous, 'S Gershwin" (NBC)—a salute to George and Ira Gershwin, hosted by Jack Lemmon, with guests Fred Astaire, Ethel Merman, and Leslie Uggams
27 JANUARY	"LBJ: Lyndon Johnson Talks Politics" (CBS)—interview with Walter Cronkite
12 FEBRUARY	"The Hound of the Baskervilles" (ABC)—new version, with Stewart Granger (as Sherlock Holmes) and Bernard Fox (Watson)
14 FEBRUARY	"The Trial of Mary Lincoln," *NET Opera Theater* (PBS)—original opera by composer Thomas Pasatieri and librettist Anne Howard Bailey
17 FEBRUARY et seq.	Coverage of President Nixon's trip to China (all networks)
21 FEBRUARY	"The Politics—and Comedy—of Woody Allen" (PBS)—Woody Allen in an original work followed by an interview
31 MARCH	"The Crucifixion of Jesus," *Appointment with Destiny* (CBS)—docu-drama filmed on location, narrated by John Huston, with Ron Greenblatt as Jesus (the print of the film was tinted gold)
16 APRIL et seq.	Coverage of the Apollo 16 voyage to the moon (all networks)
24 JULY	"The American Indian: This Was His Land," *ABC News Inquiry* (ABC)—documentary, narrated by Frank Reynolds
12–15 AUGUST	*War and Peace* (ABC)—the six-and-a-half-hour Russian film was shown in four parts
26 AUGUST– 10 SEPTEMBER	Coverage of the Olympic Games from Munich (ABC)
10 SEPTEMBER	"Singer Presents Liza with a 'Z' " (NBC)—variety special with Liza Minnelli
10 SEPTEMBER	"The Cave People of the Philippines," *NBC Reports* (NBC)—documentary on the gentle Tasaday people
24 OCTOBER	"Of Thee I Sing" (CBS)—adaptation of George S. Kaufman's comedy, with Carroll O'Connor and Cloris Leachman
1 NOVEMBER	"That Certain Summer" (ABC)—drama about a homosexual father and his son, with Hal Holbrook, Martin Sheen, and Scott Jacoby
12 NOVEMBER	"The Trouble with People" (NBC)—five sketches written by Neil Simon, with George C. Scott, Gene Wilder, Renée Taylor, Alan Arkin, and Valerie Harper
24 NOVEMBER	"In Concert" (ABC)—the first of ABC's late night rock music specials; Alice Cooper's act causes ABC's Cincinnati affiliate to drop the show in midperformance
3 DECEMBER	"The House Without a Christmas Tree" (CBS)— drama with Mildred Natwick, Jason Robards, and Lisa Lucas
12 DECEMBER	"Once upon a Mattress" (CBS)—restaged version of the musical comedy, with Carol Burnett, Ken Berry, Jack Gilford, and Wally Cox
15 DECEMBER	"John Lennon and Yoko Ono: In Concert" (ABC)— benefit performance for the Willowbrook Home for Retarded Children
17 DECEMBER	"Portrait: The Woman I Love" (NBC)—biographical drama with Richard Chamberlain (as Edward VIII) and Faye Dunaway (as Wallis Warfield)
17 DECEMBER	"Sleeping Beauty" (PBS)—ballet, with Rudolf Nureyev, Veronica Tennant, and the National Ballet of Canada

1973

23 JANUARY	"The Incredible Flight of the Snow Geese" (NBC)— nature documentary filmed by Des and Jan Bartlett, narrated by Glen Campbell
1 FEBRUARY	"The Last King of America" (CBS)—drama with Peter Ustinov as King George III, interviewed by Eric Sevareid

11 FEBRUARY	"Duke Ellington . . . We Love You Madly" (CBS)— an all-star tribute to Duke Ellington, with guests Count Basie, Ray Charles, Roberta Flack, Sammy Davis, Jr., Peggy Lee, and Sarah Vaughan
20 FEBRUARY	"A Brand New Life," *Tuesday Movie of the Week* (ABC)—drama with Cloris Leachman and Martin Balsam as a couple who have their first child after eighteen years of marriage
7 MARCH	"Dr. Jekyll and Mr. Hyde" (NBC)—musical version, with Kirk Douglas (in a rare TV appearance), Susan Hampshire, Michael Redgrave, Susan George, and Donald Pleasence
8 MARCH	"The Marcus-Nelson Murders" (CBS)—the pilot for *Kojak*
10 MARCH	"Long Day's Journey into Night" (ABC)—drama with Laurence Olivier and Constance Cummings
15 MARCH	"Applause" (CBS)—adaptation of the Broadway hit, with Lauren Bacall
16 MARCH	"Acts of Love—and Other Comedies" (ABC)—short sketches written by Renée Taylor and Joseph Bologna, with Marlo Thomas, Art Garfunkel, and Gene Wilder
16 MARCH	"Lily Tomlin" (CBS)—comedy with Lily Tomlin and guests Richard Crenna and Richard Pryor
29 MARCH	"Pueblo," *ABC Theatre* (ABC)—docu-drama with Hal Holbrook
4 APRIL	"Elvis: Aloha from Hawaii" (NBC)—musical special taped in Honolulu with Elvis Presley
22 APRIL	"Portrait: A Man Whose Name Was John" (ABC)— biographical drama with Raymond Burr (as Pope John XXIII)
23 APRIL	"Adventures of Don Quixote" (CBS)—drama with Rex Harrison
24 APRIL	"The Lie," *Playhouse 90* (CBS)—drama written by Ingmar Bergman, with George Segal and Shirley Knight Hopkins
17 MAY–15 NOVEMBER	Watergate coverage; the three commercial networks form a pool, with one network broadcasting live coverage of the hearings of the Senate Select Committee, and PBS broadcasting taped highlights each evening
5 JULY	"The First and Essential Freedom," *ABC News Special* (ABC)— documentary on the First Amendment and a free press
27 JULY	"POWs: The Black Homecoming," *ABC News Special* (ABC)— documentary on the adjustment of black POWs returned to the United States
17 AUGUST	"Sticks and Bones" (CBS)—controversial drama about a blinded Vietnam veteran, originally scheduled for March, with Cliff DeYoung, Tom Aldredge, Asa Gim, and Anne Jackson
20 SEPTEMBER	Tennis—Billie Jean King versus Bobby Riggs (ABC)— live
12 OCTOBER	"Dracula" (CBS)—drama with Jack Palance
2 NOVEMBER	"Barbra Streisand . . . and Other Musical Instruments" (CBS)— music with Barbra Streisand and guest Ray Charles
29 NOVEMBER	"Catholics," *Playhouse 90* (CBS)—drama with Trevor Howard and Martin Sheen
30 NOVEMBER– 1 DECEMBER	"Frankenstein: The True Story" (NBC)—drama with Michael Sarrazin (as the creature), Leonard Whiting, and James Mason
16 DECEMBER	"A Child's Christmas in Wales" (CBS)—with narrator Michael Redgrave and the National Theatre of the Deaf
16 DECEMBER	"The Glass Menagerie" (ABC)—drama with Katharine Hepburn (in her TV dramatic debut) and Joanna Miles

1974

31 JANUARY	"The Autobiography of Miss Jane Pittman" (CBS)— biographical drama with Cicely Tyson
11 MARCH	"Marlo Thomas and Friends in Free to Be . . . You and Me" (ABC)—consciousness-raising special for adults and children

13 MARCH	"The Execution of Private Slovik," *NBC Wednesday Night at the Movies* (NBC)—docu-drama with Martin Sheen
17 MARCH	"6 Rms Riv Vu" (CBS)—drama with Alan Alda and Carol Burnett
29–30 APRIL	"QB VII," *ABC Theatre* (ABC)—adaptation of Leon Uris's book, with Ben Gazzara, Anthony Hopkins, Leslie Caron, Lee Remick, and Jack Hawkins
24 JUNE	"Solzhenitsyn," *CBS News Special* (CBS)—interview
24–30 JULY	Coverage by all networks of the House Judiciary Committee debate on the impeachment of President Nixon
8 AUGUST	President Nixon's resignation speech (all networks)
4 SEPTEMBER	"IBM Presents Clarence Darrow" (NBC)—drama with Henry Fonda
6 SEPTEMBER	"Mrs. Lincoln's Husband" (NBC)—first of the six-part *Sandburg's Lincoln* series, with Hal Holbrook and Sada Thompson
17 OCTOBER	"Rubinstein," *Great Performances* (PBS)—musical special
22 OCTOBER	"The Law," *NBC World Premiere Movie* (NBC)— drama with Judd Hirsch as a New York public defender (later a three-part miniseries)
29 OCTOBER	"The Mark of Zorro," *The ABC Tuesday Movie of the Week* (ABC)—drama with Frank Langella and Ricardo Montalban
28 NOVEMBER	"Shirley MacLaine: If They Could See Me Now" (CBS)—music and variety with Shirley MacLaine and guest Carol Burnett
18 DECEMBER	"The Missiles of October," *ABC Theatre* (ABC)— docu-drama with William Devane (as John Kennedy), Martin Sheen (Robert Kennedy), Howard Da Silva (Nikita Khrushchev), and Ralph Bellamy (Adlai Stevenson)

1975

12 JANUARY	"Judgment: The Court-Martial of Lieutenant William Calley," *ABC Theatre* (ABC)—docu-drama with Tony Musante (as Calley), Richard Basehart, and Bo Hopkins
14 JANUARY	"Satan's Triangle," *Tuesday Movie of the Week* (ABC)—drama with Kim Novak (in a rare TV appearance) and Doug McClure
10 FEBRUARY	"The Legend of Lizzie Borden," *ABC Monday Night Movie* (ABC)—drama, with Elizabeth Montgomery
11 FEBRUARY	"Sara T.—Portrait of a Teenage Alcoholic," *NBC World Premiere Movie* (NBC)—drama with Linda Blair
12 FEBRUARY	"Sad Figure, Laughing" (NBC)—second in the *Sandburg's Lincoln* series
13 FEBRUARY	"Queen of the Stardust Ballroom" (CBS)—drama with Maureen Stapleton and Charles Durning
22 FEBRUARY	"Hustling," *The ABC Saturday Night Movie* (ABC)— drama with Lee Remick and Jill Clayburgh
27 FEBRUARY	"In This House of Brede," *General Electric Theater* (CBS)—drama with Diana Rigg
6 MARCH	"Love Among the Ruins," *ABC Theatre* (ABC)— drama with Laurence Olivier and Katharine Hepburn
7 APRIL	"Prairie Lawyer"—third of the *Sandburg's Lincoln* series
14 APRIL	"I Will Fight No More Forever," *ABC Theatre* (ABC)—drama about the Nez Perce Indians, with James Whitmore and Ned Romero
29 APRIL	"7,382 Days in Vietnam," *NBC News Special* (NBC)— retrospective
27 MAY	"A Moon for the Misbegotten," *ABC Theatre* (ABC)—adaptation of Eugene O'Neill's play, with Jason Robards and Colleen Dewhurst
25 JULY	"Lily Tomlin" (ABC)—comedy special
3 SEPTEMBER	"The Unwilling Warrior" (NBC)—fourth of the *Sandburg's Lincoln* series
2 OCTOBER	"Fear on Trial" (CBS)—biographical drama with William Devane

	(as blacklisted broadcaster John Henry Faulk) and George C. Scott (as attorney Louis Nizer)
23 OCTOBER	"Babe" (CBS)—biographical drama with Susan Clark (as athlete Mildred Zaharias) and Alex Karras
28 OCTOBER	"The Incredible Machine" (PBS)—special about the human body, narrated by E. G. Marshall

1976

11–12 JANUARY	"Eleanor and Franklin," *ABC Theatre* (ABC)—biographical drama with Jane Alexander and Edward Herrmann as Eleanor and Franklin Roosevelt (a sequel aired in 1977)
12 JANUARY	"Crossing Fox River" (NBC)—fifth in the *Sandburg's Lincoln* series
26 FEBRUARY	"The Lindbergh Kidnapping Case," *NBC Thursday Night at the Movies* (NBC)—docu-drama with Cliff DeYoung (as Charles Lindbergh), Anthony Hopkins (Bruno Hauptmann), Joseph Cotten, and Walter Pidgeon
10 MARCH	"The Entertainer" (NBC)—drama with music, with Jack Lemmon, Ray Bolger, and Sada Thompson
1–2 APRIL	"Helter Skelter" (CBS)—four-hour adaptation of prosecutor Vincent Bugliosi's book about the Charles Manson case, with George DiCenzo (Bugliosi) and Steve Railsback (Manson)
14 APRIL	"The Last Days" (NBC)—sixth and final telecast of the *Sandburg's Lincoln* series
22 APRIL	"Judge Horton and the Scottsboro Boys," *NBC World Premiere Movie* (NBC)—drama based on a 1931 rape trial, with Arthur Hill and Vera Miles
4 JULY	"In Celebration of US" (CBS)—sixteen-hour coverage of America's bicentennial celebrations, plus satellite transmission from England (with Alistair Cooke)
23 SEPTEMBER	The Ford-Carter Debate (all networks)—the first of three debates, broadcast live from Philadelphia
25 OCTOBER	"Amelia Earhart," *NBC Monday Night at the Movies* (NBC)—biographical drama, with Susan Clark
7–8 NOVEMBER	"Gone with the Wind" (NBC)—first television broadcast of the movie (highest-rated movie in TV history)
12 NOVEMBER	"The Boy in the Plastic Bubble," *The ABC Friday Night Movie* (ABC)—drama, with John Travolta, Diana Hyland, and Glynnis O'Connor
14–15 NOVEMBER	"Sybil," *The Big Event* (NBC)—drama based on a true case history of a multiple personality, with Sally Field (as Sybil) and Joanne Woodward
25 NOVEMBER	"Sills and Burnett at the Met" (CBS)—music, with Beverly Sills and Carol Burnett
6 DECEMBER	"Cat on a Hot Tin Roof," *NBC Monday Night at the Movies* (NBC)—new production, with Laurence Olivier, Natalie Wood, Robert Wagner, and Maureen Stapleton
9 DECEMBER	"America Salutes Richard Rodgers: The Sound of His Music" (CBS)—musical variety hosted by Gene Kelly (as Oscar Hammerstein II) and Henry Winkler (Lorenz Hart)
13 DECEMBER	"Victory at Entebbe" (ABC)—three-hour special based on the rescue of a hijacked airliner by Israeli commandos, with Burt Lancaster, Anthony Hopkins, Helen Hayes, Elizabeth Taylor, Linda Blair, Kirk Douglas, and Richard Dreyfuss
14 DECEMBER	Barbara Walters's first special (ABC)—interviews with Jimmy and Rosalynn Carter, and Barbra Streisand and Jon Peters
29 DECEMBER	"The Belle of Amherst" (PBS)—one-woman show by Julie Harris (as Emily Dickinson)

1977

9 JANUARY — "Raid on Entebbe," *The Big Event* (NBC)—dramatization of the raid by Israeli commandos on a hijacked airliner, with Charles Bronson, Peter Finch, and Yaphet Kotto

16 JANUARY — "Little Ladies of the Night," *The ABC Sunday Night Movie* (ABC)—drama on teenage prostitution (one of the highest-rated made-for-TV movies in history), with David Soul, Lou Gossett, and Linda Purl

19 JANUARY — "Inaugural Eve Gala Performance" (CBS)—variety from Washington, D.C., with an all-star cast (including Freddie Prinze, who died ten days later)

6 FEBRUARY — "Tail Gunner Joe," *The Big Event* (NBC)—biographical drama with Peter Boyle (as Senator Joseph McCarthy), Burgess Meredith, and Patricia Neal

13 MARCH — "Eleanor and Franklin: The White House Years," *ABC Theatre* (ABC)—sequel to "Eleanor and Franklin," with Jane Alexander and Edward Herrmann

22 MARCH — "The Fire Next Door," *CBS Reports* (CBS)—documentary on arson in the South Bronx, with Bill Moyers

13–14 APRIL — "The Amazing Howard Hughes" (CBS)—biographical drama with Tommy Lee Jones, Ed Flanders, and Tovah Feldshuh

21 APRIL — "Sinatra and Friends" (ABC)—music, with Frank Sinatra, Tony Bennett, Natalie Cole, and John Denver

5 MAY — "The Richard Pryor Special?" (NBC)—Richard Pryor's first comedy special, with guests John Belushi, Maya Angelou, and Mike Evans

26 SEPTEMBER — "In the Matter of Karen Ann Quinlan," *NBC World Premiere Movie* (NBC)—docu-drama with Brian Keith and Piper Laurie

30 SEPTEMBER, 2 OCTOBER — "The Trial of Lee Harvey Oswald" (ABC)—drama speculating on what might have happened if Lee Harvey Oswald had lived, with John Pleshette (as Oswald), Ben Gazzara, and Lorne Greene

19 NOVEMBER — "Contract on Cherry Street," *Saturday Night at the Movies* (NBC)—drama with Frank Sinatra as a vigilante cop

24 NOVEMBER — "The Happy World of Hanna-Barbera" (CBS)— prime-time retrospective of Hanna-Barbera Studios, one of TV's major suppliers of animated features

25 NOVEMBER — "Rolling Stone: The Tenth Anniversary" (CBS)—celebrating a decade of *Rolling Stone* magazine, with guests such as Bette Midler, Steve Martin, Sissy Spacek, and Martin Sheen

27 NOVEMBER — "Doonesbury" (NBC)—animated special based on the Pulitzer-Prize-winning comic strip drawn by Garry Trudeau (animation for TV done by Faith and John Hubley)

7 DECEMBER — "Bette Midler" (NBC)—music with Bette Midler and guests Dustin Hoffman and Emmett Kelly

20 DECEMBER — "Greenpeace: Voyages to Save the Whale" (PBS)— documentary on the conservation efforts of the Greenpeace Foundation

1978

1 FEBRUARY — "See How She Runs," *General Electric Theater* (CBS)—drama with Joanne Woodward as a forty-year-old marathoner

5 FEBRUARY — "ABC's Silver Anniversary Celebration" (ABC)—a retrospective

12–14 FEBRUARY — "King" (NBC)—biographical drama with Paul Winfield (as Martin Luther King, Jr.) and Cicely Tyson (as Coretta King)

2 MARCH — "Ben Vereen: Showcase for a Man of Many Talents" (ABC)—variety with Ben Vereen and guests Cheryl Ladd and Louis Gossett, Jr.

5 MARCH — "TV: The Fabulous Fifties" (NBC)—another retrospective

6 MARCH — "The Body Human" (CBS)—science documentary

13 MARCH — "Gene Kelly: An American in Pasadena" (CBS)— variety with

	Gene Kelly and guests Frank Sinatra, Cyd Charisse, Cindy Williams, Lucille Ball, and Liza Minnelli
26 MARCH–1 APRIL	"CBS: On the Air" (CBS)—a nine-and-one-half-hour retrospective spread out over seven nights
26 MARCH	"Tribute to 'Mr. Television,' Milton Berle" (NBC)— clips of Berle's shows, plus appearances by Frank Sinatra, Johnny Carson, Bob Hope, and Lucille Ball
9 APRIL	"A Family Upside Down" (NBC)—drama with Fred Astaire, Helen Hayes, and Patty Duke Astin
21 MAY	"Ziegfeld: The Man and His Women" (NBC)—biographical drama with Paul Shenar, Samantha Eggar, Barbara Parkins, Valerie Perrine, and Pamela Peadon
MAY	"The Bastard" or "The Kent Family Chronicles" (SYNDICATED)—a two-part adaptation of John Jakes's novel, with Andrew Stevens and Buddy Ebsen
25 JUNE	"The Last Tenant," *ABC Theatre* (ABC)—drama, with Lee Strasberg (in a rare TV appearance) and Tony LoBianco
28 JUNE	"Youth Terror: The View from Behind the Gun," *ABC News Closeup* (ABC)—a cinema-verité look at urban street gangs
14 JULY	"Evening of French Television" (PBS)—a three-hour sampler
22 AUGUST	"Steve and Eydie Celebrate Irving Berlin" (NBC)—a tribute to Irving Berlin on his ninetieth birthday, with Steve Lawrence, Eydie Gormé, Carol Burnett, and Sammy Davis, Jr.
24 SEPTEMBER	"Horowitz—Live!" (NBC)—Vladimir Horowitz and the New York Philharmonic from Lincoln Center
26 SEPTEMBER	"One in a Million: The Ron LeFlore Story" (CBS)— biographical drama with LeVar Burton (as Ron LeFlore, who went from prison to professional baseball), Paul Benjamin, Larry B. Scott, and Billy Martin (as himself)
8 NOVEMBER	"First You Cry" (CBS)—biographical drama with Mary Tyler Moore (as breast cancer victim Betty Rollin), Anthony Perkins, and Richard Crenna
11–12 DECEMBER	"A Woman Called Moses," *NBC World Premiere Movie* (NBC)— biographical drama with Cicely Tyson (as ex-slave Harriet Tubman)
14 DECEMBER	"Rockette: A Holiday Tribute to the Radio City Music Hall" (NBC)—variety-drama, with host Gregory Peck (in a rare TV appearance), Ann-Margret, and Ben Vereen

1979

10 JANUARY	"A Gift of Song" (NBC)—a musical benefit for UNICEF, hosted by David Frost, with the Bee Gees, John Denver, Elton John, and Rod Stewart
28 JANUARY	" . . . And Your Name Is Jonah" (CBS)—drama starring Sally Struthers and James Woods as parents and Jeffrey Bravin as their deaf son
29 JANUARY	"The Corn Is Green" (CBS)—drama starring Katharine Hepburn as a Welsh schoolteacher
9 FEBRUARY	"Heroes of Rock 'n' Roll" (ABC)—musical retrospective hosted by Jeff Bridges
11 FEBRUARY	"Elvis" (ABC)—three-hour biographical drama starring Kurt Russell as Elvis Presley
14 FEBRUARY	"Dolly and Carol in Nashville" (CBS)—variety, with Dolly Parton and Carol Burnett
3 MARCH	"Live from the Grand Ole Opry" (PBS)—six-hour fund raiser, with a host of country-and-western music stars
4 MARCH	"The Ordeal of Patty Hearst" (ABC)—docu-drama starring Lisa Eilbacher as kidnap victim Patty Hearst

12 MARCH	"The American Film Institute Salute to Alfred Hitchcock" (CBS)—tribute to director Alfred Hitchcock, hosted by Ingrid Bergman
13 MARCH	"Einstein's Universe" (PBS)—two-hour documentary hosted by Peter Ustinov (televised on the eve of the one-hundredth anniversary of Einstein's birth)
1, 2, 3, 8 APRIL	"Jesus of Nazareth" (NBC)—an expanded version of Franco Zeffirelli's film, previously shown in 1977
15 APRIL	"Baryshnikov at the White House" (PBS)—excerpts from ballet dancer Mikhail Baryshnikov's February recital at the White House
22 APRIL	"Friendly Fire," ABC Theatre (ABC)—an adaptation of C. D. B. Bryan's book about the efforts of an Iowa couple to learn the truth of their son's death in Vietnam, starring Carol Burnett and Ned Beatty as Peg and Gene Mullen
28 APRIL	"I Know Why the Caged Bird Sings" (CBS)—an adaptation of Maya Angelou's book about growing up in Arkansas, starring Constance Good and Esther Rolle
14 MAY	"The Television Annual 1978/79" (ABC)—a two-hour retrospective of the 1978–1979 TV season
22 MAY	"The Helen Reddy Special" (ABC)—variety, with Helen Reddy and guests Jane Fonda and Elliott Gould (the special had originally been sold to NBC, but was bought back from that network by the producers following a dispute over the air date)
8 JUNE	"The Shooting of Big Man: Anatomy of a Criminal Case," ABC News Closeup (ABC)—documentary detailing the investigation and trial of a criminal case in Seattle
24–25 JULY	"Blacks in America: With All Deliberate Speed?" CBS Reports (CBS)—an examination of 25 years of desegregation, hosted by Ed Bradley
11 SEPTEMBER	"Can You Hear the Laughter? The Story of Freddie Prinze" (CBS)—biographical drama starring Ira Angustain as the late comedian
16 SEPTEMBER	"The Road to China" (NBC)—three-hour variety special starring Bob Hope, produced on location in China
1 OCTOBER et seq.	Coverage by all three commercial networks of the visit of Pope John Paul II to the United States
1 OCTOBER	"The Tonight Show Starring Johnny Carson" (NBC)—the seventeenth-anniversary show, broadcast live in prime time
8 OCTOBER	"Paul Robeson" (PBS)—one-man show starring James Earl Jones
8 OCTOBER	"When Hell Was in Session," NBC Theatre (NBC)— docu-drama starring Hal Holbrook as Admiral Jeremiah Denton, an American POW in North Vietnam
14 OCTOBER	"The Miracle Worker," NBC Theatre (NBC)—drama with Patty Duke Astin (who had played Helen Keller in the Broadway and film versions twenty years earlier) as Annie Sullivan and Melissa Gilbert as Helen Keller
29, 31 OCTOBER	"Freedom Road" (NBC)—four-hour historical drama starring Muhammad Ali as Gideon Jackson, a former slave who became a U.S. senator
12 NOVEMBER	"Jane Fonda" (PBS)—biography of the activist actress, filmed by the BBC in 1977
17 NOVEMBER	"Puff the Magic Dragon" (CBS)—animated fantasy for children, narrated by Burgess Meredith
7 DECEMBER	"Valentine" (ABC)—made-for-TV movie starring Mary Martin (in a rare TV dramatic role) and Jack Albertson as septuagenarians who fall in love
16 DECEMBER	"An American Christmas Carol" (ABC)—an updated version of the Dickens story, starring Henry Winkler as Benedict Slade
18 DECEMBER	"Homosexuals," ABC News Closeup (ABC)—cinema verité study of urban homosexual lifestyles

| 28–29 DECEMBER | "American Dream, American Nightmare" (CBS)—retrospective of the 1970s |

1980

9 JANUARY	"The Lathe of Heaven" (PBS)—science-fiction drama starring Bruce Davison and Kevin Conway
9 JANUARY	"Live from Studio 8H" (NBC)—first of a series of cultural specials, featuring a tribute to conductor Arturo Toscanini
27–29 JANUARY	"The Martian Chronicles" (NBC)—six-hour adaptation of Ray Bradbury's science-fiction story, with Rock Hudson, Gayle Hunnicutt, and Darren McGavin
16 MARCH	"Gala of Stars" (PBS)—classical music from the Metropolitan Opera House, with Plácido Domingo and Isaac Stern
7 APRIL	"The Oldest Living Graduate" (NBC)—live dramatic show, with Henry Fonda, George Grizzard, and Cloris Leachman (broadcast from Southern Methodist University in Dallas, it was NBC's first live prime-time dramatic program in eighteen years)
8 APRIL	"Kenny Rogers as the Gambler" (CBS)—made-for-TV movie with Kenny Rogers, Christine Belford, Harold Gould, and Clu Gulager
15–16 APRIL	"Guyana Tragedy: The Story of Jim Jones" (CBS)— docu-drama, with Powers Boothe, Veronica Cartwright, Randy Quaid, Meg Foster, James Earl Jones, and Ned Beatty
24 APRIL	"Baryshnikov on Broadway" (ABC)—dance fantasy, with Mikhail Baryshnikov, and Liza Minnelli (choreographed by Ron Field)
26 APRIL	"Gay Power, Gay Politics," *CBS Reports* (CBS)—investigative report on San Francisco politics
30 APRIL	"Gideon's Trumpet," *Hallmark Hall of Fame* (CBS)— docu-drama about the U.S. Supreme Court case, with Henry Fonda, Jose Ferrer, and John Houseman
14 MAY	"Haywire" (CBS)—biographical drama, with Lee Remick, Jason Robards, and Deborah Raffin
18–20 MAY	"Moviola" (NBC)—three dramas, based on Garson Kanin's novel: "This Year's Blonde," with Constance Forslund as Marilyn Monroe; "The Scarlett O'Hara War," with Morgan Brittany as Vivien Leigh; and "The Silent Lovers," with Barry Bostwick and Kristina Wayborn as John Gilbert and Greta Garbo
27 MAY	"Front Line" (PBS)—a personal memoir of Vietnam by Australian photographer Neil Davis
2 JUNE	"Picasso—a Painter's Diary" (PBS)—a look at the artist's life, based on his paintings and his writings
12 JUNE	"To Die for Ireland," *ABC News Closeup* (ABC)— documentary, filmed on location by Alan and Susan Raymond
14 SEPTEMBER	"The Women's Room" (ABC)—adaptation of Marilyn French's novel, with Lee Remick, Colleen Dewhurst, and Patty Duke Astin
24–25 SEPTEMBER	"A Rumor of War" (CBS)—made-for-TV movie, with Brad Davis as an American soldier in Vietnam
30 SEPTEMBER	"Playing for Time" (CBS)—docu-drama adapted by Arthur Miller from Fania Fenelon's account of her life at Auschwitz; the program generated controversy when Vanessa Redgrave, an outspoken anti-Zionist, was cast in the lead role.
7 OCTOBER	"The Body Human: The Facts for Girls" (CBS)—afternoon special on female sexuality, hosted by Marlo Thomas
26 OCTOBER	"Sophia Loren—Her Own Story" (NBC)—biographical drama, with Sophia Loren as herself and as her mother, also with Rip Torn, John Gavin, and Armand Assante
6 NOVEMBER	"The Body Human: The Facts for Boys" (CBS)—afternoon special on male sexuality, hosted by Ken Howard

17 NOVEMBER	"The Diary of Anne Frank" (NBC)—TV version of the play and film, with Melissa Gilbert

1981

27 JANUARY	"The Bunker" (CBS)—docu-drama on the last days of Adolf Hitler, with Anthony Hopkins, Susan Blakely, and Richard Jordan
4 FEBRUARY	"Kitty: Return to Auschwitz" (PBS)—Kitty Felix Hart, a concentration camp survivor, returns to the site with her son (an edited version was later shown on *ABC News Closeup*)
4 FEBRUARY	"Crisis at Central High" (CBS)—docu-drama on desegregation in Little Rock, Arkansas, with Joanne Woodward
8 FEBRUARY	"Kent State" (NBC)—docu-drama on the 1970 killing of four students, with Jane Fleiss, Talia Balsam, and Keith Gordon
8, 9, 11 FEBRUARY	"East of Eden" (ABC)—eight-hour miniseries based on John Steinbeck's novel, with Jane Seymour, Timothy Bottoms, Warren Oates, and Bruce Boxleitner
23–24 FEBRUARY	"Evita Peron" (NBC)—biography, starring Faye Dunaway, in a rare TV appearance
24 FEBRUARY	"Fallen Angel" (CBS)—made-for-TV movie about child pornography, with Dana Hill and Richard Masur
30 MARCH	Coverage of the assassination attempt on President Reagan (all three networks)
15 MAY	"TV's Censored Bloopers" (NBC)—the first of several retrospectives of clips of various outtakes and on-camera miscues
17 MAY	"Escape from Iran: The Canadian Caper" (CBS)— docu-drama on the escape of a number of Americans from Iran following the embassy takeover, with Gordon Pinsent, Robert Joy, and Matsu Anderson
20 MAY	"Live from Lincoln Center" (PBS)—featuring the American Ballet Theatre, with Mikhail Baryshnikov and Natalia Makarova
14–18 JUNE	"CBS Reports: The Defense of the United States" (CBS)—in-depth examination of American defense systems, anchored by Dan Rather
29 JULY	Coverage by all three commercial networks of the wedding of Prince Charles and Lady Diana Spencer at St. Paul's Cathedral
26 AUGUST	"The Best Little Statehouse in Texas," *CBS Reports* (CBS)—a look at Texas politics, hosted by Larry L. King (author of *The Best Little Whorehouse in Texas*)
16 SEPTEMBER	"Model" (PBS)—documentary by Frederick Wiseman on the modeling business
20 SEPTEMBER	"Please Don't Hit Me, Mom" (ABC)—made-for-TV movie on child abuse, with Patty Duke Astin and Sean Astin
20 SEPTEMBER	"Get High on Yourself" (NBC)—anti-drug variety program, put together by Robert Evans in order to satisfy a condition of his probation on drug charges
29 SEPTEMBER– 1 OCTOBER	"The Sophisticated Gents" (NBC)—four-hour made-for-TV movie (filmed in 1979) about a reunion of the membership of a black sports club, with Melvin Van Peebles (who wrote the screenplay), Ron O'Neal, Thalmus Rasulala, Bernie Casey, Paul Winfield, and Raymond St. Jacques
6 OCTOBER	Coverage by all three commercial networks of the events following the shooting of Egyptian president Anwar Sadat
14 OCTOBER	"Jacqueline Bouvier Kennedy" (ABC)—biography, with Jaclyn Smith and James Franciscus
14 OCTOBER	"Just Another Missing Kid" (PBS)—documentary on the efforts of an Ottawa family to trace the whereabouts of their missing son and to find his killers
7 NOVEMBER	"Skokie" (CBS)—docu-drama on the attempt by a group of Ameri-

can Nazis to march in Skokie, Illinois, with Danny Kaye, Kim Hunter, and Eli Wallach

22 NOVEMBER	"Sinatra: The Man and His Music" (NBC)—variety show, headlining Frank Sinatra
26 NOVEMBER	Barbara Walters interviews President Reagan (ABC)
21 DECEMBER	"All the Way Home" (NBC)—live adaptation of James Agee's novel, with Sally Field, William Hurt, and Ned Beatty
22 DECEMBER	"Bill" (CBS)—fact-based story of a retarded adult released from an institution, with Mickey Rooney, Randy Quaid, and Largo Woodruff
30 DECEMBER	"Summer Solstice" (ABC)—hour drama starring Henry Fonda and Myrna Loy (the program was bought from an ABC affiliate, WCVB-TV in Boston)

1982

4 JANUARY	"The Elephant Man" (ABC)—an adaptation of the play about a hideously deformed man, with Philip Anglim and Kevin Conway repeating their Broadway roles
10 JANUARY	"Will: G. Gordon Liddy" (NBC)—biographical made-for-TV movie, with Robert Conrad in the title role
23 JANUARY	CBS Reports: "The Uncounted Enemy: A Vietnam Deception" (CBS)—controversial documentary alleging the existence of a conspiracy to falsify intelligence on events leading to the 1968 Tet Offensive in Vietnam (the program led to the filing of a $120 million libel suit against CBS by former General William Westmoreland)
29 JANUARY	"FDR," ABC News Special (ABC)—documentary on Franklin Delano Roosevelt, commemorating the centennial of his birth, and featuring Presidents Nixon, Ford, Carter, and Reagan
3 FEBRUARY	"A Piano for Mrs. Cimino" (CBS)—made-for-TV movie starring Bette Davis as a widow living in a nursing home
16 FEBRUARY	"The Wall" (CBS)—docu-drama based on John Hersey's novel about the 1943 uprising in the Warsaw ghetto, with Tom Conti, Eli Wallach, and Rosanna Arquette
8 MARCH	"Night of 100 Stars" (ABC)—benefit for the Actors' Fund, taped at Radio City Music Hall, with a huge roster of stars, including: Lauren Bacall, Harry Belafonte, James Cagney, Carol Channing, Bette Davis, Sammy Davis, Jr., Robert DeNiro, Douglas Fairbanks, Jr., Jane Fonda, Lillian Gish, Joel Grey, Helen Hayes, James Earl Jones, Diane Keaton, Gene Kelly, Burt Lancaster, Liza Minnelli, Gregory Peck, Jane Powell, Anthony Quinn, Ginger Rogers, Lee Strasberg, Elizabeth Taylor, Ben Vereen, and Orson Welles
20 MARCH	CBS News Special: "Central America in Revolt" (CBS)—investigative documentary
21 MARCH	"I Love Liberty" (ABC)—variety program saluting America, produced by Norman Lear, with Jane Fonda, Barry Goldwater, Burt Lancaster, Mary Tyler Moore, Martin Sheen, and Barbra Streisand
29 MARCH	"Pavarotti & Friends" (ABC)—musical special, with Luciano Pavarotti, Jacqueline Bisset, John McEnroe, Richard Thomas, and John Williams
12 APRIL	"My Body, My Child" (ABC)—drama about a woman facing an abortion, with Vanessa Redgrave and Joseph Campanella
20 APRIL	"Pleasure Drugs: The Great American High," NBC White Paper (NBC)—documentary on recreational drug use, hosted by Edwin Newman
21 APRIL	"Baryshnikov in Hollywood" (CBS)—variety special, with Mikhail Baryshnikov, Gene Wilder, Dom DeLuise, and Bernadette Peters
26 APRIL	"Ian McKellen Acting Shakespeare" (PBS)—a one-man show

APRIL	"A Woman Called Golda" (SYNDICATED)—four-hour biographical drama, with Ingrid Bergman in what turned out to be her last role, as Golda Meir
9–10 MAY	"Inside the Third Reich" (ABC)—docu-drama based on Albert Speer's memoirs, with Rutger Hauer (as Speer), Derek Jacobi (Adolf Hitler), Blythe Danner, and John Gielgud
22 MAY	"Horowitz in London: A Royal Concert" (PBS)—musical special with pianist Vladimir Horowitz
25 MAY	"Television's Greatest Commercials" (NBC)—the first of several retrospectives on TV advertising, hosted by Ed McMahon and Tim Conway
31 MAY	"Benny's Place" (ABC)—drama, with Louis Gossett, Jr., as a mechanic in a steel mill, and Cicely Tyson
7 JUNE	"Sister, Sister" (NBC)—drama written by Maya Angelou, with Diahann Carroll, Rosalind Cash, Irene Cara, Paul Winfield, and Dick Anthony Williams
21 JUNE	"Ain't Misbehavin' " (NBC)—adaptation of the Broadway tribute to composer Fats Waller, with Nell Carter, Andre De Shields, and Charlaine Woodard
11 SEPTEMBER	"Texaco Star Theater" (NBC)—a salute to musicals, with Sammy Davis, Jr., Carol Burnett, Donald O'Connor, Ethel Merman, and Robert Guillaume (curiously, Milton Berle, who had starred in TV's original *Texaco Star Theater,* was not invited to appear)
29 SEPTEMBER	"Life of the Party: The Story of Beatrice" (CBS)— drama, with Carol Burnett as an alcoholic
14, 16, 17 NOVEMBER	"The Blue and the Gray" (CBS)—eight-hour miniseries set during the Civil War, with John Hammond, Stacy Keach, Sterling Hayden (as John Brown), Gregory Peck (Abraham Lincoln), Lloyd Bridges, Colleen Dewhurst, Paul Winfield, and Robert Vaughn
28–29 NOVEMBER	"The Executioner's Song" (NBC)—biographical drama with Tommy Lee Jones as convicted killer Gary Gilmore, Rosanna Arquette, Eli Wallach, and Christine Lahti
20 DECEMBER	"The Member of the Wedding" (NBC)—live version of Carson McCullers's play, with Dana Hill, Pearl Bailey, and Howard E. Rollins, Jr.
23 DECEMBER	"Don't Touch That Dial!" *CBS Reports* (CBS)—a look at the television industry itself, hosted by Morley Safer

1983

2 FEBRUARY	"The Scarlet and the Black" (CBS)—docu-drama with Gregory Peck as an Irish priest who helped Allied prisoners escape during World War II
14 FEBRUARY	"Who Will Love My Children?" (ABC)—fact-based drama about a dying woman who found homes for her ten children, with Ann-Margret (in her TV dramatic debut) and Frederic Forrest
21 FEBRUARY	"Grace Kelly" (ABC)—biographical drama of the late Princess Grace (begun with her cooperation), starring Cheryl Ladd
23 FEBRUARY	"The Operation" (PBS)—live telecast of actual open-heart surgery
27 FEBRUARY	"Cocaine: One Man's Seduction" (NBC)—drama, with Dennis Weaver as an executive who became hooked on cocaine
9 MARCH	"Svengali" (CBS)—an updated remake of the drama, with Peter O'Toole and Jodie Foster
30 MARCH	"American Journey" (PBS)—Richard Reeves recreates the journey of nineteenth century observer Alexis de Tocqueville
26 APRIL	"Crime and Insanity," *NBC White Paper* (NBC)—investigation into the use of the insanity defense in criminal trials, hosted by Edwin Newman
APRIL	"Blood Feud" (SYNDICATED)—docu-drama with Robert Blake

	(as former Teamsters boss Jimmy Hoffa) and Cotter Smith (as his inquisitor, Attorney General Robert Kennedy)
1–2 MAY	"V" (NBC)—expensive science fiction made-for-TV movie, with Marc Singer, Faye Grant, and Richard Herd
16 MAY	"Motown 25" (NBC)—musical special celebrating the twenty-fifth anniversary of Motown Records, with Diana Ross and the Supremes, Smokey Robinson and the Miracles, Michael Jackson, The Jackson Five, The Four Tops, The Temptations, Linda Ronstadt, and Stevie Wonder
22 MAY	"Jacobo Timerman: Prisoner Without a Name, Cell Without a Number" (NBC)—biographical drama, with Roy Scheider (as Argentinian political prisoner Jacobo Timerman) and Liv Ullmann
23 MAY	"Happy Birthday, Bob" (NBC)—variety special honoring Bob Hope on his 80th birthday, with President Reagan, Lucille Ball, George Burns, George C. Scott, and Flip Wilson
29 MAY	"Big Bird in China" (NBC)—children's variety special, taped on location in China, with Big Bird and Barkley, and Ou-yang Lientzee
16 JUNE	Live coverage (by ABC and NBC) of Pope John Paul II's arrival in his native Poland (CBS News, hampered by budget cuts, airs *The Price Is Right*)
27 JULY	"Summer of Judgment" (PBS)—two-hour retrospective on the Watergate hearings
27–29 SEPTEMBER	"Live . . . and in Person" (NBC)—three-part live variety special, hosted by Sandy Gallin, with Neil Diamond, Linda Ronstadt, the cast of *A Chorus Line,* and many others
10 OCTOBER	"Adam" (NBC)—fact-based made-for-TV movie, starring Daniel J. Travanti and JoBeth Williams as the parents of a missing child (after the broadcast, a number of missing children were actually reunited with their families, and a Florida prison inmate confessed to the murder of young Adam Walsh, about whose disappearance the film was based)
22 OCTOBER	"Live from the Met" (PBS)—celebration of the one hundredth anniversary of New York's Metropolitan Opera, hosted by Alexander Scourby, with more than seventy operatic stars
2, 9 NOVEMBER	"The Chemical People" (PBS)—two-part "outreach" program on drug and alcohol abuse among young people, hosted by Nancy Reagan
20 NOVEMBER	"The Day After" (ABC)—controversial made-for-TV movie about the effects of nuclear war, which graphically simulated the destruction of Lawrence, Kansas; directed by Nicholas Meyer, featuring Jason Robards, JoBeth Williams, and John Cullum
20–22 NOVEMBER	"Kennedy" (NBC)—seven-hour miniseries on John F. Kennedy's presidency, with Martin Sheen (JFK), Blair Brown (Jacqueline Kennedy), John Shea (Robert Kennedy), and Vincent Gardenia (J. Edgar Hoover)
NOVEMBER	"Sadat" (SYNDICATED)—biography of the late Egyptian president Anwar Sadat, with Louis Gossett, Jr., in the title role

1984

9 JANUARY	"Something About Amelia" (ABC)—made-for-TV movie about incest, with Ted Danson, Glenn Close, and Roxana Zal
24 JANUARY	"The Lost Honor of Kathryn Beck" (CBS)—made-for-TV movie starring Marlo Thomas as a woman hounded by the police and the press
12–14 FEBRUARY	"Celebrity" (NBC)—three-part adaptation of Thomas Thompson's novel about three high school chums and their dark secret, with Michael Beck, Joseph Bottoms, and Ben Masters
19–21 FEBRUARY	"Master of the Game" (CBS)—three-part adaptation of Sidney

	Sheldon's novel of "power, lust, romance, revenge, and obsession," with Dyan Cannon, Ian Charleson, Johnny Sekka, and Jean Marsh
27 MARCH	"Terrible Joe Moran" (CBS)—made-for-TV movie starring James Cagney (in a rare TV appearance) and Art Carney
8, 10, 11 APRIL	"George Washington" (CBS)—eight-hour miniseries tracing Washington's life through the end of the Revolutionary War, with Barry Bostwick, Patty Duke Astin, Jaclyn Smith, and David Dukes
6–8 MAY	"V: The Final Battle" (NBC)—three-part sequel to the 1983 science-fiction miniseries, with Marc Singer, Richard Herd, and Faye Grant
6–8 MAY	"The Last Days of Pompeii" (ABC)—historical miniseries, with Duncan Regehr, Linda Purl, and Ned Beatty
13 MAY	"The Dollmaker" (ABC)—made-for-TV movie starring Jane Fonda as a Kentucky mother trying to keep her family together in Detroit during the Depression
20–21 MAY	"The Mystic Warrior" (ABC)—made-for-TV movie about the Mahto band of Oglala Dakota (Sioux) Indians, with Robert Beltran, Doug Toby, and Ron Soble (beset with production problems, the film took some five years to reach the screen)
20–21 MAY	"The First Olympics—Athens 1896" (NBC)—made-for-TV movie chronicling the efforts of the American athletes at the first modern Olympiad, with Louis Jourdan (as the organizer, Baron Pierre de Coubertin) and David Ogden Stiers
16 AUGUST	"Andrea Doria: The Final Chapter" (SYNDICATED)—George Plimpton hosted the opening of a safe salvaged from the 1956 shipwreck
4 SEPTEMBER	"To Save Our Schools, to Save Our Children" (ABC)—three-hour report on American education
24–26 SEPTEMBER	"Mistral's Daughter" (CBS)—miniseries based on Judith Krantz's novel, with Stacy Keach, Stefanie Powers, Lee Remick and Philippine Leroy Beaulieu
28 SEPTEMBER	"On Television: The Violence Factor" (PBS)—documentary on TV violence
30 SEPTEMBER	"Heartsounds" (ABC)—fact-based TV-movie about a terminally ill physician and his caring wife, with James Garner and Mary Tyler Moore
8 OCTOBER	"The Burning Bed" (NBC)—fact-based TV-movie starring Farrah Fawcett as a woman who killed her abusive husband (highest-rated single entertainment program of 1984–1985 season)
11, 13, 14 NOVEMBER	"Ellis Island" (CBS)—three-part miniseries about American immigrants, with Richard Burton, Faye Dunaway, Ann Jillian, Ben Vereen and Kate Burton
12 NOVEMBER	"Victims for Victims: The Theresa Saldana Story" (NBC)—actress Theresa Saldana, victim of a stabbing incident in 1982, reenacted her story
18–19 NOVEMBER	"Fatal Vision" (NBC)—two-part TV-movie based on Joe McGinniss's book on convicted murderer Jeffrey MacDonald, with Gary Cole, Karl Malden, Eva Marie Saint, Barry Newman, and Andy Griffith
17 DECEMBER	"A Christmas Carol" (CBS)—a new version of Dickens's holiday classic, starring George C. Scott

1985

27–29 JANUARY	"Robert Kennedy and His Times" (CBS)—biographical miniseries, starring Brad Davis, Veronica Cartwright, Trey Wilson and Cliff DeYoung
10, 12 FEBRUARY	"The Atlanta Child Murders" (CBS)—two-part fact-based TV-

	movie, narrated by Morgan Freeman, starring James Earl Jones, Gloria Foster and Calvin Levels
17–19 FEBRUARY	"Hollywood Wives" (ABC)—three-part adaptation of Jackie Collins's novel, with Angie Dickinson, Candice Bergen, Mary Crosby, Stefanie Powers, Robert Stack, Rod Steiger and Anthony Hopkins (top-rated miniseries of 1984–1985 season)
24–26 FEBRUARY	"Evergreen" (NBC)—three-part saga of three generations of an American Jewish family, based on Belva Plain's novel, with Ian McShane, Lesley Ann Warren and Armand Assante
16 MARCH	"Spitting Image," *Cinemax Comedy Experiment* (CINEMAX)—satirical puppet show, based on the popular British series
20 MARCH	"Rodgers and Hammerstein: The Sound of American Music" (PBS)—two-hour musical tribute to Richard Rodgers and Oscar Hammerstein II
1 APRIL	"The Laundromat" (HBO)—one-hour drama, directed by Robert Altman, starring Carol Burnett and Amy Madigan
8–9 APRIL	"Wallenberg: A Hero's Story" (NBC)—fact-based two-part biographical drama of World War II civilian hero Raoul Wallenberg, starring Richard Chamberlain
12 APRIL	"Avoiding Nuclear War" (CNN)—roundtable discussion, with Jimmy Carter, Gerald Ford, Robert MacFarlane, and Anatoly Dobrynin
13 APRIL	"The Second City 25th Anniversary Special" (HBO)—all-star tribute to the Chicago-based comedy troupe
11 MAY	"Saturday Night's Main Event" (NBC)—professional wrestling returns to network television
12 MAY	"Malice in Wonderland" (CBS)—TV-movie starring Elizabeth Taylor and Jane Alexander as feuding Hollywood gossip columnists Louella Parsons and Hedda Hopper
12–13 MAY	"A Death in California" (ABC)—fact-based TV-movie starring Cheryl Ladd as a woman who became involved with her boyfriend's killer (played by Sam Elliott)
19–20 MAY	"Christopher Columbus" (CBS)—biographical drama, with Gabriel Byrne, Faye Dunaway, Oliver Reed and Max von Sydow
21 MAY	"Do You Remember Love" (CBS)—TV-movie with Joanne Woodward as a victim of Alzheimer's disease, and Richard Kiley
27 MAY	"The Rape of Richard Beck" (ABC)—TV-movie starring Richard Crenna as a police officer who is the victim of a sexual assault
4 JUNE	"The History of White People in America, Part I," *Cinemax Comedy Experiment* (CINEMAX)—satirical comedy special, starring Martin Mull
13 JULY	"Live Aid" (MTV, ABC & SYNDICATED)—seventeen-hour rock and roll extravaganza from Philadelphia and London, for African famine relief
AUGUST	"High on the Job" (SYNDICATED)—documentary on drug abuse in the workplace, hosted by Stacy Keach
15 SEPTEMBER	"Death of a Salesman" (CBS)—new version of Arthur Miller's play, from the 1984 Broadway production, with Dustin Hoffman, Kate Reid, John Malkovich, and Stephen Lang
18 SEPTEMBER	"45/85" (ABC)—three-hour examination of American foreign policy since 1945, with Peter Jennings and Ted Koppel
22 SEPTEMBER	"Farm Aid" (TNN & SYNDICATED)—twelve-hour country and rock benefit concert for American farmers
23 SEPTEMBER	"Izzy and Moe" (CBS)—TV-movie reuniting Jackie Gleason and Art Carney as Prohibition agents
6–7 OCTOBER	"The Long Hot Summer" (NBC)—steamy adaptation of William Faulkner's stories, with Don Johnson, Cybill Shepherd, Jason Robards and Ava Gardner

5 NOVEMBER	"Stone Pillow" (CBS)—TV-movie starring Lucille Ball as a homeless woman in New York City
11 NOVEMBER	"An Early Frost" (NBC)—first TV-movie on AIDS, starring Aidan Quinn, Gena Rowlands and Ben Gazzara
17–19 NOVEMBER	"Kane and Abel" (CBS)—seven-hour adaptation of Jeffrey Archer's novel, with Sam Neill and Peter Strauss
17 NOVEMBER	"The Execution of Raymond Graham," *ABC Theater* (ABC)—live drama about the last hours of a convicted killer, starring Jeff Fahey
24–26 NOVEMBER	"Mussolini: The Untold Story" (NBC)—historical drama, starring George C. Scott and Lee Grant
2 DECEMBER	"John and Yoko: A Love Story" (NBC)—fact-based TV-movie starring Mark McGann and Kim Miyori as John Lennon and Yoko Ono (McGann got the role after it was learned that the real name of the actor originally cast was Mark Chapman, the same name as the man who assassinated Lennon in 1980)
9–10 DECEMBER	"Alice in Wonderland" (CBS)—star-studded musical adaptation of Lewis Carroll's fantasy, with Natalie Gregory (as Alice), Sammy Davis Jr., Telly Savalas, Jayne Meadows, Sid Caesar, Shelley Winters, Karl Malden and Carol Channing

1986

5 JANUARY	"A Rockabilly Session—Carl Perkins and Friends" (CINEMAX)—rock and roll with Carl Perkins, Eric Clapton, George Harrison and Ringo Starr
5 JANUARY	"The Defiant Ones" (ABC)—remake of the 1958 film, starring Robert Urich and Carl Weathers
19 JANUARY	"Mafia Princess" (NBC)—TV-movie starring Susan Lucci (in a rare prime-time appearance) as a mobster's daughter, and Tony Curtis
2–4 FEBRUARY	"Sins" (CBS)—three-part adaptation of Judith Gould's novel, starring Joan Collins
23–25 FEBRUARY	"Crossings" (ABC)—three-part adaptation of Danielle Steel's novel, with Jane Seymour, Lee Horsley, Cheryl Ladd and Christopher Plummer
9–10 MARCH	"Dress Gray" (NBC)—fact-based TV-movie adapted by Gore Vidal about a murder at West Point, with Hal Holbrook, Lloyd Bridges and Alec Baldwin
16–18 MARCH	"If Tomorrow Comes" (CBS)—three-part adaptation of Sidney Sheldon's novel, with Madolyn Smith, Tom Berenger and Richard Kiley
29 MARCH	"Comic Relief" (HBO)—live three-hour benefit for the homeless, with Billy Crystal, Whoopi Goldberg and Robin Williams hosting
30 MARCH	"Mrs. Delafield Wants to Marry" (CBS)—TV-movie with Katharine Hepburn and Harold Gould as a WASP and Jew who fall in love
6 APRIL	"Nobody's Child" (CBS)—fact-based TV-movie starring Marlo Thomas as Marie Balter, who overcame mental illness
7 APRIL	"My Two Loves" (ABC)—TV-movie starring Mariette Hartley as a widow who became romantically attracted to a man (played by Barry Newman) and a woman (Lynn Redgrave)
13–15 APRIL	"Dreams West" (CBS)—seven-hour saga of American explorer John C. Fremont, starring Richard Chamberlain
21 APRIL	"Alex: The Life of a Child" (ABC)—fact-based TV-movie taken from Frank Deford's book about his young daughter's death, with Craig T. Nelson, Bonnie Bedelia and Gennie James
21 APRIL	"The Mystery of Al Capone's Vaults" (SYNDICATED)—live two-hour coverage of the opening of a sealed underground room thought to have been controlled by Al Capone; nothing of interest was unearthed, much to the disappointment of host Geraldo Rivera

26 APRIL	"A Prairie Home Companion" (PBS)—Garrison Keillor brought his radio show to TV for the first time, from St. Paul, Minnesota
4–5 MAY	"The Deliberate Stranger" (NBC)—fact-based two-part TV-movie starring Mark Harmon as serial killer Ted Bundy
13 MAY	"Second Serve" (CBS)—biographical drama, with Vanessa Redgrave as transsexual Renee Richards
22 JUNE	"Drinking in America," *Cinemax Comedy Experiment* (CINEMAX)—one-man show, with Eric Bogosian
2–6 JULY	"Liberty Weekend" (ABC)—coverage of the 100th anniversary of the Statue of Liberty
9 JULY	"The Burger Years" (CBS)—Bill Moyers interviewed retiring Chief Justice Warren Burger
30 JULY	"After the Sexual Revolution," *ABC News Closeup* (ABC)—documentary on changing American sexual mores
2 SEPTEMBER	"48 Hours on Crack Street," *CBS News Special*—gripping two-hour examination of the drug problem in the New York City area
3 SEPTEMBER	"At a Loss for Words . . . Illiterate in America," *ABC News Closeup* (ABC)—Peter Jennings examined adult illiteracy
5 SEPTEMBER	"Cocaine Country," *NBC News Special* (NBC)—documentary on America's cocaine epidemic
14 SEPTEMBER	"The Last Days of Patton" (CBS)—George C. Scott starred in a sequel to his 1970 film
29 SEPTEMBER	"Adam: His Song Continues" (NBC)—sequel to the 1983 TV-movie, with JoBeth Williams and Daniel J. Travanti
21–22 NOVEMBER	"On Trial: Lee Harvey Oswald" (SHOWTIME)—imaginary "trial" of alleged assassin Oswald, with Vincent Bugliosi as the prosecutor and Gerry Spence as the defense attorney (and a 900 telephone number for viewers to call with their votes)
23 NOVEMBER	"Nazi Hunter: The Beate Klarsfeld Story" (ABC)—biographical drama starring Farrah Fawcett
2 DECEMBER	"American Vice: The Doping of a Nation" (SYNDICATED)—live special with Geraldo Rivera accompanying police on a drug bust
22 DECEMBER	"Christmas Eve" (NBC)—TV-movie with Loretta Young (in a rare TV appearance) as a widow trying to locate her three grandchildren

1987

11 JANUARY	"Mercy or Murder?" (NBC)—fact-based TV-movie with Robert Young as a man who killed his wife, who was a victim of Alzheimer's disease
18–19 JANUARY	"Out on a Limb" (ABC)—Shirley MacLaine starred in a two-part, five-hour adaptation of her book about her quest for spiritual answers
1 FEBRUARY	"LBJ: The Early Years" (NBC)—biographical drama tracing Lyndon Johnson's early political career, starring Randy Quaid
3 FEBRUARY	"Guilty of Innocence: The Lenell Geter Story" (CBS)—fact-based TV-movie developed from the *60 Minutes* story of a man wrongly convicted of a crime, starring Dorian Harewood and Dabney Coleman
8–9 FEBRUARY	"The Two Mrs. Grenvilles" (NBC)—Two-part adaptation of Dominick Dunne's novel, starring Ann-Margret and Claudette Colbert
23 FEBRUARY	"Love Among Thieves" (ABC)—comedy-mystery starring Audrey Hepburn (in her TV-movie debut) and Robert Wagner
22–24 MARCH	"Nutcracker: Money, Madness, Murder" (NBC)—miniseries based on Shana Alexander's account of a 1978 murder in Utah, with Lee Remick, Tate Donovan and Tony Musante
8 APRIL	"Lyndon Johnson" (PBS)—Laurence Luckinbill's one-man show
12 APRIL	"Escape from Sobibor" (CBS)—docu-drama about an escape from

a World War II prison camp, with Alan Arkin, Rutger Hauer and Joanna Pacula

21 APRIL "Carnegie Hall: The Grand Reopening" (CBS)—musical tribute, with Leonard Bernstein, Frank Sinatra, Zubin Mehta, Yo-Yo Ma, and Lena Horne

5 MAY First day of Iran-Contra hearings (ABC, CBS, CNN, NBC)

9 MAY "Uptown Comedy Express" (HBO)—comedy special with Marsha Warfield, Robert Townsend, Arsenio Hall and Chris Rock

20 MAY "Red Hot Rhythm and Blues" (ABC)—musical tribute, with Diana Ross, Billy Dee Williams, Etta James, Little Richard, and Bernadette Peters

6 JUNE "Prayer for World Peace" (SYNDICATED)—live hour prayer service led by Pope John Paul II

24 JUNE "Seven Days in the Soviet Union," *CBS News Special* (CBS)—a look at everyday life in the U.S.S.R.

16 AUGUST "Elvis '56" (CINEMAX)—a look at Elvis Presley's first big year, narrated by Levon Helm

31 AUGUST "Michael Jackson: The Magic Returns" (CBS)—broadcast premiere of Michael Jackson's "Bad" video

13 SEPTEMBER "Bluffing It" (ABC)—TV-movie about adult illiteracy, starring Dennis Weaver

16 SEPTEMBER "The Blessings of Liberty" (ABC)—three-hour salute to the bicentennial of the U.S. Constitution, hosted by Peter Jennings, Ted Koppel and David Brinkley

20 SEPTEMBER "Mandela" (HBO)—biography, starring Danny Glover and Alfre Woodard

5–6 OCTOBER "Intimate Contact" (HBO)—TV-movie about the effect of AIDS on a British couple, starring Claire Bloom and Daniel Massey

12 OCTOBER "Right to Die" (NBC)—TV-movie starring Raquel Welch as a victim of Lou Gehrig's Disease (ALS)

18 OCTOBER Rescue of baby Jessica McClure from a well in Taxas (ABC, CBS, CNN and NBC)

28 OCTOBER "Return to the Titanic—Live" (SYNDICATED)—live opening of a safe hoisted from the 1912 shipwreck, hosted by Telly Savalas (nothing of value was discovered)

6 NOVEMBER "AIDS: Changing the Rules" (PBS)—informational special, hosted by Ron Reagan, Ruben Blades and Beverly Johnson

8–9 NOVEMBER "Billionaire Boys Club" (NBC)—fact-based TV-movie starring Judd Nelson as a preppie murderer

10–12 NOVEMBER "Napoleon and Josephine: A Love Story" (ABC)—biographical drama, with Armand Assante and Jacqueline Bisset

16–18 NOVEMBER "Poor Little Rich Girl: The Barbara Hutton Story" (NBC)—biographical drama, starring Farrah Fawcett and James Read

24 NOVEMBER "Rolling Stone Magazine's First 20 Years" (ABC)—a compendium of interviews and performance clips of rockers, hosted by Dennis Hopper

1988

3 JANUARY "Roy Orbison & Friends: A Black and White Night" (CINEMAX)—musical special, with veteran rocker Roy Orbison and many others, including Bruce Springsteen, Elvis Costello, k.d. lang and Bonnie Raitt

4 JANUARY "The Ann Jillian Story" (NBC)—autobiographical account of the actress' battle with breast cancer, starring Ann Jillian, Tony LoBianco and Viveca Lindfors

9, 16, 23 JANUARY "The Singing Detective" (PBS)—surreal British miniseries, starring Michael Gambon as mystery writer Philip Marlowe

12 JANUARY	"The Sword of Islam" (PBS)—1987 British-made documentary on the rise of Islam worldwide
24, 26 JANUARY	"The Murder of Mary Phagan" (NBC)—fact-based drama based on a 1913 murder, with Jack Lemmon, Peter Gallagher and Richard Jordan
5 FEBRUARY	"The Main Event" (NBC)—first prime-time network wrestling since 1955, broadcast live from Indianapolis, with Hulk Hogan vs. Andre the Giant
6 FEBRUARY	"The World According to Me" (HBO)—adaptation of Jackie Mason's one-man Broadway show
7–8 FEBRUARY	"Elvis and Me" (ABC)—biographical drama, based on Priscilla Presley's account of her courtship and marriage, with Dale Midkiff and Susan Walters (top-rated TV-movie of 1987–1988 season)
7 MARCH	"Laura Lansing Slept Here" (NBC)—TV-movie starring Katharine Hepburn as a writer who decided to live with a Typical American Family
27–28 MARCH	"Gore Vidal's Lincoln" (NBC)—biographical drama, starring Mary Tyler Moore and Sam Waterston
3 APRIL	"The Woman He Loved" (CBS)—biographical drama starring Anthony Andrews and Jane Seymour as the Duke and Duchess of Windsor
3 APRIL	"Dear America: Letters Home from Vietnam" (HBO)—excerpts from letters sent by American G.I.s stationed in Vietnam, read off-camera by actors against images of the war and other film clips
10 APRIL	"Red River" (CBS)—remake of the 1948 motion picture, with James Arness, Bruce Boxleitner, Gregory Harrison (and, in cameos, TV western stars Ty Hardin, John Lupton, Guy Madison, and Robert Horton)
13 APRIL	"Murder: Live from Death Row" (SYNDICATED)—live special hosted by Geraldo Rivera, featuring a previously taped interview with convicted murderer Charles Manson
16 APRIL	"Conversations with the Presidents" (ABC)—schoolchildren interview President Reagan and former Presidents Carter and Ford
2 MAY	"The Taking of Flight 847: The Uli Derickson Story" (NBC)—docu-drama starring Lindsay Wagner as heroic flight attendant Derickson
14 MAY	"Atlantic Records 40th Anniversary" (HBO)—star-studded musical tribute (highlights telecast on ABC 26 June)
22–23 MAY	"Baby M" (ABC)—docu-drama of the famous surrogate mother case, starring JoBeth Williams, John Shea and Robin Strasser
23 MAY	"Execution: 14 Days in May," *America Undercover* (HBO)—documentary on the final days of convicted murderer Edward Earl Johnson
27 MAY	"Irving Berlin's 100th Birthday Celebration" (CBS)—tribute to songwriter Irving Berlin, with Shirley MacLaine, Nell Carter, Rosemary Clooney and Tony Bennett
MAY	"Hemingway" (SYNDICATED)—biographical drama starring Stacy Keach as Ernest Hemingway
13 SEPTEMBER	"The Koppel Report: A National Town Meeting on the Legalization of Drugs" (ABC)—debate
21, 23 OCTOBER	"Jack the Ripper" (CBS)—allegedly fact-based TV-movie, starring Michael Caine, Jane Seymour and Armand Assante
25 OCTOBER	"Devil Worship: Exposing Satan's Underground" (NBC)—lurid two-hour examination of Satanism, hosted by Geraldo Rivera (NBC's highest-rated special of the 1988–1989 season)
26 OCTOBER	"The Secret Identity of Jack the Ripper" (SYNDICATED)—live documentary, hosted by Peter Ustinov
30–31 OCTOBER,	"Favorite Son" (NBC)—steamy miniseries set against a back-

1 NOVEMBER	ground of Washington politics, with Harry Hamlin, Robert Loggia and Linda Kozlowski
30–31 OCTOBER	"Dadah Is Death" (CBS)—fact-based TV-movie about drug smugglers sentenced to death in Malaysia, starring Julie Christie, John Polson and Hugo Weaving
2 NOVEMBER	"American Expose: Who Murdered J.F.K.?" (SYNDICATED)—two-hour live rehash of conspiracy theories, hosted by Jack Anderson
6–7 NOVEMBER	"The Great Escape II: The Untold Story" (NBC)—sequel to the 1963 motion picture, with Christopher Reeve, Ian McShane, Judd Hirsch, Charles Haid and Anthony Denison
20 NOVEMBER	"Goddess of Love" (NBC)—TV-movie starring Vanna White as Venus in her ill-fated prime-time debut
21 NOVEMBER	"Inside the Sexes" (CBS)—explicit documentary (not aired by all CBS affiliates)
22 NOVEMBER	"The JFK Assassination: As It Happened" (A & E)—six-hour and five-minute rebroadcast of NBC's coverage of the events of 22 November 1963
29 NOVEMBER	"Barbara Walters' 50th Special" (ABC)—highlights from Walters' previous 49 interview specials

1989

1 JANUARY	"The Karen Carpenter Story" (CBS)—biographical drama of the pop singer, with Cynthia Gibb and Mitchell Anderson
16 JANUARY	"The Ryan White Story" (ABC)—biographical drama of a child AIDS victim, with Lukas Haas and Judith Light
25 FEBRUARY	"Chasing a Rainbow: The Life of Josephine Baker" (PBS)—documentary on the life of the singer-dancer
27 FEBRUARY	"What's Alan Watching?" (CBS)—offbeat comedy special, produced by Eddie Murphy, starring Corky Nemec
24 MARCH	"Peter Pan" (NBC)—rerun of the 1960 telecast
2 APRIL	"The Case of the Hillside Stranglers" (NBC)—fact-based crime drama, starring Richard Crenna
9 APRIL	"Bridge to Silence" (CBS)—TV-movie with Marlee Matlin as a young widow, and Lee Remick
23 APRIL	"Murderers Among Us: The Simon Wiesenthal Story" (HBO)—TV-movie biography of Nazi hunter Wiesenthal, starring Ben Kingsley
15 MAY	"Roe vs. Wade" (NBC)—fact-based TV-movie about the U.S. Supreme Court's 1973 abortion case, starring Holly Hunter
21 MAY	"Everybody's Baby: The Rescue of Jessica McClure" (ABC)—fact-based TV-movie about the toddler rescued from a Texas well, starring Patty Duke and Beau Bridges
22–23 MAY	"I Know My First Name Is Steven" (NBC)—fact-based story of a youngster abducted by a sex offender and held captive for seven years, starring Corky Nemec and Arliss Howard (part 2 was the top-rated TV-movie of 1988–1989 season)
17 JULY	"Hanna-Barbera's 50th Anniversary" (TNT)—celebration of the careers of animator-producers William Hanna and Joseph Barbera
19 JULY	"The Other Side of the Moon" (PBS)—documentary commemorating the 20th anniversary of the Moon landing
26 JULY	"Halftime" (PBS)—documentary examining the lives of five Yale graduates returning to New Haven for their 25th reunion
5–6 SEPTEMBER	*NBC News Special,* "The R.A.C.E." (NBC)—two-part look at race relations, using the "Racial Attitudes and Consciousness Exam"
6 SEPTEMBER	"The 1989 MTV Music Awards" (MTV)—live awards show, highlighted by comedian Andrew Dice Clay's foul-mouthed performance
24 SEPTEMBER	"The Preppie Murder" (ABC)—fact-based TV-movie based on the

	1986 Central Park murder case, with William Baldwin, Danny Aiello, and Joanna Kerns
1 OCTOBER	"Tennessee Williams' Sweet Bird of Youth" (NBC)—new presentation of the 1959 play, with Elizabeth Taylor and Mark Harmon
16 OCTOBER	"Cold Sassy Tree" (TNT)—TV-movie with Faye Dunaway and Richard Widmark as lovers
17 OCTOBER	Coverage of the San Francisco earthquake (ABC, CBS, CNN and NBC)
29 OCTOBER	"The Final Days" (ABC)—dramatization of President Nixon's last days in office, starring Lane Smith
29 OCTOBER	"The Strange Case of Dr. Jekyll and Mr. Hyde," *Nightmare Classics* (SHOWTIME)—TV-movie starring Anthony Andrews
5–6 NOVEMBER	"Cross of Fire" (NBC)—fact-based TV-movie about the Ku Klux Klan, with John Heard and Mel Harris
10 NOVEMBER	"Thunder and Mud" (PPV)—women's mud wrestling, hosted by Jessica Hahn
12, 14 NOVEMBER	"Small Sacrifices" (ABC)—fact-based drama about a woman convicted of killing her cildren, with Farrah Fawcett, Ryan O'Neal and John Shea
13 DECEMBER	"Julie and Carol: Together Again" (ABC)—musical special, with Julie Andrews and Carol Burnett
19 DECEMBER	Rolling Stones concert (PPV)—live from Atlantic City
28 DECEMBER	"A Year with Andy Rooney: 1989" (NBC)—Rooney's retrospective led to his suspension from CBS News, caused in part by his remarks about AIDS

1990

7–9 JANUARY	"Drug Wars: The Camarena Story" (NBC)—fact-based miniseries on the death of a DEA agent in Mexico, starring Steven Bauer, Treat Williams and Craig T. Nelson
8 JANUARY	"Rock Hudson" (ABC)—TV-movie biography of the actor who died of AIDS, starring Thomas Ian Griffith
21 JANUARY	"Jekyll and Hyde" (ABC)—TV-movie starring Michael Caine and Cheryl Ladd
22 JANUARY	"Treasure Island" (TNT)—TV-movie starring Charlton Heston, Fraser Heston and Christopher Lee
29 JANUARY	"Where Pigeons Go to Die" (NBC)—TV-movie starring Michael Landon and Art Carney
4 FEBRUARY	"Sammy Davis Jr.'s 60th Anniversary Celebration" (ABC)—tribute to entertainer Sammy Davis Jr. (who died later in 1990), with Eddie Murphy, Michael Jackson, Frank Sinatra, and Shirley MacLaine
5 FEBRUARY	"Murder in Mississippi" (NBC)—TV-movie based on the 1964 murders of three civil rights workers, with Tom Hulce, Blair Underwood and Jennifer Grey
11, 13 FEBRUARY	"Blind Faith" (NBC)—TV-movie adaptation of Joe McGinniss' book about a New Jersey man who murdered his wife, starring Robert Urich and Joanna Kerns
18, 19, 21 FEBRUARY	"The Kennedys of Massachusetts" (ABC)—biographical miniseries, starring William Petersen, Charles Durning, Annette O'Toole, Steven Weber and Campbell Scott
25 FEBRUARY	"Challenger" (ABC)—TV-movie chronicling the ill-fated 1986 space shuttle launch, with Karen Allen, Barry Bostwick, Brian Kerwin, Keone Young, Julie Fulton, Richard Jenkins and Joe Morton
18–19 MARCH	"The Phantom of the Opera" (NBC)—non-musical adaptation of the 1911 novel, with Charles Dance, Teri Polo, Burt Lancaster and Ian Richardson
25, 27 MARCH	"Common Ground" (CBS)—TV-movie based on J. Anthony

Lukas's book about the desegregation of Boston's schools, starring Richard Thomas, Jane Curtin, C. C. H. Pounder and James Farentino

21 APRIL "Cartoon All-Stars to the Rescue" (ABC, BET, CBS, FOX, NBC, NIK and USA)—half-hour Saturday morning cartoon special about drug abuse, with "guest appearances" by many animated stars

4 MAY "Richard Nixon Reflects," *American Interests* (PBS)—interview with the former president by Morton Kondracke

10–12 JUNE "World without Walls" (PBS)—panel discussion on the post-Cold War world, moderated by Ted Koppel

25 JUNE "A Conversation with Fidel Castro" (CNN)—the Cuban leader was interviewed by Ted Turner

16 JULY "Guns: A Day in the Death of America" (HBO)—documentary examining the deaths of sixty-one persons by handguns on 16 July 1989

6 AUGUST "Hiroshima: Out of the Ashes" (NBC)—fact-based TV-movie, with Max von Sydow, Judd Nelson, Mako, and Pat Morita

5 SEPTEMBER "Learning in America: Schools That Work" (PBS)—documentary hosted by Roger Mudd

6 SEPTEMBER "America's Toughest Assignment: Solving the Education Crisis," *CBS News Special Report* (CBS)—two-hour special hosted by Charles Kuralt

7 OCTOBER "When You Remember Me" (ABC)—TV-movie, with Fred Savage, Kevin Spacey, and Ellen Burstyn

22 OCTOBER "Extreme Close-up" (NBC)—TV-movie, with Blair Brown, Morgan Weisser, and Craig T. Nelson (directed by Peter Horton)

28 OCTOBER "Sunday Night with Larry King" (NBC)—hour variety special, with guests Sylvester Stallone, David Letterman, Bart Simpson, and magicians Siegfried & Roy

9 NOVEMBER "Two Decades and a Wake-up" (PBS)—documentary examining the lives of eight Vietnam veterans with posttraumatic stress disorder

10 NOVEMBER "Psycho IV: The Beginning" (SHO)—a flashback to Norman Bates's origins, starring Anthony Perkins, Henry Thomas, Olivia Hussey, and C. C. H. Pounder

11 NOVEMBER "Call Me Anna" (ABC)—autobiographical TV-movie, starring Patty Duke

20 NOVEMBER "Bobby Kennedy: In His Own Words" (HBO)—documentary on the life of Robert Kennedy

21 NOVEMBER "The Muppets Celebrate Jim Henson" (CBS)—a poignant tribute to the late puppeteer

21 NOVEMBER "After the Warming" (PBS)—James Burke traveled to the year 2150 to look at the effects of global warming

1 DECEMBER "Red, Hot & Blue" (ABC)—AIDS benefit, with rock and roll stars singing Cole Porter songs

16 DECEMBER "Sinatra 75: The Best Is Yet to Come" (CBS)—two-hour tribute to Frank Sinatra on his 75th birthday

19 DECEMBER "Sex in the Soviet Union," *The Koppel Report* (ABC)—documentary on changing mores in the Soviet Union (some material from Russian television had to be censored for American audiences)

1991

16–17 JANUARY Coverage of the war in the Persian Gulf (ABC, CBS, CNN & NBC)

26 JANUARY *ABC News Special* (ABC)—Peter Jennings anchored a 90-minute special on Saturday morning to explain the events in the Persian Gulf to youngsters

3–4 FEBRUARY "Son of the Morning Star" (ABC)—two-part drama on the life of General George Armstrong Custer, starring Gary Cole

12 FEBRUARY	"Doing Time" (HBO)—Alan and Susan Raymond examined life at the maximum-security Federal prison in Lewisburg, PA
17 FEBRUARY	"What Ever Happened to Baby Jane" (ABC)—remake of the 1962 film, with Vanessa Redgrave and Lynn Redgrave (working together for the first time)
17–18 FEBRUARY	"Love, Lies and Murder" (NBC)—fact-based made-for-TV movie, with Sheryl Lee, Moira Kelly, and Clancy Brown
16 MARCH	"The Josephine Baker Story" (HBO)—TV-movie biography of the African-American entertainer, starring Lynn Whitfield
7–8 APRIL	"Separate But Equal" (ABC)—TV-movie biography starring Sidney Poitier as Thurgood Marshall
20 APRIL	"Paris Trout" (SHO)—TV-movie with Dennis Hopper, Barbara Hershey, and Ed Harris, based on the novel by Pete Dexter
5 MAY	"Carnegie Hall: Live at 100!" (PBS)—salute to the centennial of the New York performance theater
4 JULY	"Bob Simon: Back to Baghdad," *CBS News Special* (CBS)—news reporter Bob Simon, who had been detained in Iraq during the Gulf War, revisited the country
14 AUGUST	"The Elvis Files" (SYNDICATED)—exploration of the question whether Elvis Presley really died in 1977
15 AUGUST	"Born at the Right Time" (HBO)—Paul Simon in live concert from New York's Central Park
20 SEPTEMBER	"Us" (CBS)—TV-movie written, produced, directed by and starring Michael Landon (in his last TV appearance)
6–9 OCTOBER	"Columbus and the Age of Discovery" (PBS)—seven-hour documentary commemorating the 499th anniversary of Columbus's voyages to the New World
6 OCTOBER	"Ray Charles: 50 Years in Music" (FOX)—musical celebration of Ray Charles's career
11–14 OCTOBER	Confirmation hearings of Supreme Court nominee Clarence Thomas (ABC, CBS, NBC, and CNN)
29 OCTOBER	"Losing It All: The Reality of Alzheimer's Disease" (HBO)—documentary
14 NOVEMBER	"Black or White" (BET, FOX, MTV, VH-1)—premiere of Michael Jackson's latest video
17, 19 NOVEMBER	"In a Child's Name" (CBS)—two-part fact-based TV-movie starring Valerie Bertinelli, Michael Ontkean, and Karla Tamburelli (part 2 was the highest rated TV-movie of the 1991–1992 season)
27 NOVEMBER	"MTV 10" (ABC)—tenth-anniversary tribute to the music cable channel, starring Madonna and Michael Jackson
30 NOVEMBER	"Dame Edna's Hollywood" (NBC)—first of several comedy specials starring Barry Humphries as celebrity interviewer Edna Everage
4 DECEMBER	"The Judds' Farewell Concert" (PPV)—live performance by Naomi and Wynonna Judd
7 DECEMBER	"Remember Pearl Harbor," CBS News Special (CBS)—joint production with Tokyo Broadcasting System marking the fiftieth anniversary of the Pearl Harbor bombing, anchored by Charles Kuralt and H. Norman Schwarzkopf
9 DECEMBER	"The Story Lady" (NBC)—TV-movie starring Jessica Tandy
15 DECEMBER	"Christmas on Division Street" (CBS)—TV-movie starring Hume Cronyn

1992

| 17 JANUARY | "This Is Garth Brooks" (NBC)—first network special starring the popular country and western singer |
| 2 FEBRUARY | "Growing Up in the Age of AIDS: An ABC News Town Meeting for the Family" (ABC)—early-evening documentary, aimed at children and adults, moderated by Peter Jennings |

8 FEBRUARY	"NBA All-Star Stay in School Jam" (BET, NBC, NICK, and TNT)—daytime special, encouraging youngsters to stay in school
16 MARCH	"Doing Time on Maple Drive" (FOX)—TV-movie about a dysfunctional family, with James B. Sikking, Bibi Besch, and Jim Carrey
25 MARCH	"A Conversation with Magic" (NICK)—Linda Ellerbee moderating a panel discussion between Magic Johnson and a group of youngsters
21 AUGUST	"Driving Miss Daisy" (CBS)—unsuccessful pilot for a sitcom, starring Robert Guillaume, Joan Plowright, and Saul Rubinek
22 AUGUST	"Citizen Cohn" (HBO)—TV-movie biography of Roy Cohn, starring James Woods
4 SEPTEMBER	"Age Seven in America" (CBS)—a documentary looking at the lives of several seven-year-olds, hosted by Meryl Streep
4 SEPTEMBER	"Scared Silent" (CBS, NBC, and PBS)—documentary on child abuse, hosted by Oprah Winfrey (also televised by ABC on 6 September)
28 SEPTEMBER	"Fergie & Andrew: Behind the Palace Doors" (NBC)—TV-movie based on the British royal couple, starring Pippa Hinchley and Sam Miller
8 OCTOBER	"Total Exposure: Privacy and the Press," *First Person with Maria Shriver* (NBC)—news special on the extent of media coverage of newsmakers' private lives
10 OCTOBER	"Michael Jackson: In Concert in Bucharest" (HBO)—Michael Jackson concert, taped in Romania
17 OCTOBER	"The Missiles of October: What the World Didn't Know," *ABC News Special* (ABC)—documentary on the 1962 Cuban missile crisis
26 OCTOBER	"In the Deep Woods" (NBC)—TV-movie starring Rosanna Arquette and Anthony Perkins (in his last film role)
8, 10 NOVEMBER	"Sinatra" (CBS)—five-hour TV-movie biography of Frank Sinatra, starring Philip Casnoff
15, 18 NOVEMBER	"The Jacksons—An American Dream" (ABC)—five-hour TV-movie biography of the childhood and family life of pop star Michael Jackson, with Alex Burrall, Jason Weaver, and Wylie Draper as Michael Jackson (highest rated TV-movie of the 1992–1993 season)
13 DECEMBER	"Charles and Diana: Unhappily Ever After" (ABC)—TV-movie based on the marital troubles of Prince Charles and Princess Diana, starring Roger Rees and Catherine Oxenberg
26–27 DECEMBER	"Lincoln" (ABC)—a two-part photographic biography of Abraham Lincoln
28 DECEMBER	"Amy Fisher: My Story" (NBC)—the first of the three TV-movies based on the true story of the Long Island teenager who attempted to kill the wife of the man she was sexually involved with, starring Noelle Parker as Fisher

1993

3 JANUARY	"The Amy Fisher Story" (ABC)—the second of the three TV-movies, starring Drew Barrymore as Fisher
3 JANUARY	"Casualties of Love: The 'Long Island Lolita' Story" (CBS)—the third of the three TV-movies, starring Alyssa Milano as Fisher
22 JANUARY	"Who Killed Martin Luther King?" (FOX)—documentary examining the 1968 assassination of the civil rights leader, hosted by Larry Fishburne
10 FEBRUARY	Oprah Winfrey interviews Michael Jackson (ABC)—ninety-minute interview (top-rated special of the 1992–1993 season)
20 FEBRUARY	"President Clinton: Answering Children's Questions," *ABC News Special* (ABC)—ninety-minute Saturday morning special
20 MARCH	"Barbarians at the Gate" (HBO)—TV-movie, starring James Garner (later rebroadcast on NBC)
10 APRIL	"The Positively True Adventures of the Alleged Texas Cheerleader-

	Murdering Mom" (HBO)—TV-movie, based loosely on fact, starring Holly Hunter and Beau Bridges
9–10 MAY	"Stephen King's 'The Tommyknockers' " (ABC)—two-part adaptation of the book, starring Marg Helgenberger and Jimmy Smits
14 MAY	"Bob Hope: The First 90 Years" (NBC)—three-hour tribute to Bob Hope
16–17 MAY	"Woman on the Run: The Lawrencia Bembeneck Story" (NBC)—fact based TV-movie, starring Tatum O'Neal
23 MAY	"In the Line of Duty: Ambush in Waco" (NBC)—hastily-produced TV-movie based on the federal raid of David Koresh's headquarters in April 1993, starring Timothy Daly as Koresh
15 JUNE	"Blockbuster Video Presents Paul McCartney Live in the New World" (FOX)—live concert from Charlotte, North Carolina (time constraints necessitate the cutting of "Hey Jude" in mid-song)
27 JUNE	"The Wonderful World of Dung" (DSC)—documentary exploring excrement
1 JULY	"The Broadcast Tapes of Dr. Peter" (HBO)—documentary chronicling Canadian physician Peter Jepson-Young's battle with AIDS
18 JULY	"Chantilly Lace" (SHO)—TV-movie, filmed in a largely improvisational style, with Lindsay Crouse, Jill Eikenberry, Martha Plimpton, Ally Sheedy, Talia Shire, Helen Slater, and JoBeth Williams, directed by Linda Yellen
11 SEPTEMBER	"And the Band Played On" (HBO)—TV-movie based on Randy Shilts's book about the AIDS epidemic in the 1980s (rebroadcast on NBC 28 March 1994)
11 DECEMBER	"Attack of the 50 Ft. Woman" (HBO)—remake of the low-budget horror film, starring Daryl Hannah
12 DECEMBER	"Gypsy" (CBS)—remake of the musical, starring Bette Midler and Cynthia Gibb
31 DECEMBER	Howard Stern's New Year's Celebration (PPV)

1994

16 JANUARY	"Out of Darkness" (ABC)—TV-movie starring Diana Ross as a woman suffering from mental illness
13 FEBRUARY	"Witness to the Execution" (NBC)—TV-movie about a prisoner who wants his execution to be broadcast, starring Timothy Daly and Sean Young
19 MARCH	"The Birds II" (SHO)—sequel to the 1963 Hitchcock film, starring Tippi Hedren
10 APRIL	"David's Mother" (CBS)—TV-movie starring Kirstie Alley as the mother of an autistic child
24 APRIL	"Bedtime with Barney: Imagination Island" (NBC)—the purple dinosaur's commercial television debut
26 APRIL	"Kids Killing Kids" (CBS and FOX)—documentary on teen violence, moderated by Malcolm-Jamal Warner
30 APRIL	"Tonya and Nancy: The Inside Story" (NBC)—TV-movie based on the infamous ice-skating rivalry, starring Heather Langenkamp and Alexandra Powers
1, 3 MAY	"Oldest Living Confederate Widow Tells All" (CBS)—TV-movie based on the popular novel, starring Diane Lane and Donald Sutherland
17 JUNE	Live coverage of the Los Angeles police pursuit of O. J. Simpson's white Bronco (ABC, CBS, and NBC)
2 AUGUST	"Gang War: Bangin' in Little Rock" (HBO)—documentary on urban violence
13–14 AUGUST	"Woodstock '94" (MTV and PPV)—coverage of the musical festival
21 AUGUST	"Barbra Streisand: The Concert" (HBO)—The singer's first public concert appearance in twenty-seven years

2 OCTOBER	"For the Love of Nancy" (ABC)—TV-movie about anorexia, starring Tracey Gold (who had been anorexic in real life)
26 OCTOBER	"Gary Larson's Tales from the Far Side" (CBS)—animated special based on the popular comic strip
31 OCTOBER	"Roseanne and Tom: Behind the Scenes" (NBC)—TV-movie biography of Roseanne and Tom Arnold, starring Patrika Darbo and Stephen Lee
4 DECEMBER	"The Return of the Native" (CBS)—TV-movie adaptation of Thomas Hardy's novel, starring Catherine Zeta Jones
15 DECEMBER	"Wuthering Heights" (TNT)—TV-movie adaptation of the Bronte novel, starring Ralph Fiennes
18 DECEMBER	"Don't Drink the Water" (ABC)—remake of the theatrical film, starring Woody Allen (who also wrote and directed), Julie Kavner, Mayim Bialik, and Michael J. Fox

1995

1 FEBRUARY	"Boys and Girls Are Different: Men, Women and the Sex Differences," *ABC News Special* (ABC)—documentary on gender-based differences, hosted by John Stossel
6 FEBRUARY	"Serving in Silence: The Margarethe Cammermeyer Story" (NBC)—fact-based TV-movie, starring Glenn Close as an Army officer discharged for being a lesbian
19, 20, 22 FEBRUARY	"A Woman of Independent Means" (NBC)—three-part miniseries based on the 1978 novel, starring Sally Field as Bess Alcott
16 MARCH	"Peter Jennings Reports: In the Name of God" (ABC)—a look at religion in contemporary America
20–21 APRIL, 27–28 MAY	"500 Nations" (CBS)—four-part, eight-hour documentary on Native American cultures, hosted by Kevin Costner
14–15 MAY	"Naomi & Wynonna: Love Can Build a Bridge" (NBC)—two-part TV-movie based on the lives of Naomi and Wynonna Judd, starring Cari Shayne and Viveka Davis
14–15 MAY	"Stephen King's 'The Langoliers' " (ABC)—two-part adaptation of King's novella, starring Patricia Wettig, Dean Stockwell, Bronson Pinchot, and David Morse
20 MAY	"Indictment: The McMartin Trial" (HBO)—fact-based TV-movie about California day-care operators accused of child molesting, starring James Woods, Mercedes Ruehl, and Sada Thompson
28 JUNE	"Common Sense with John Stossel," ABC News Special (ABC)—a look at handling everyday problems
29 JUNE	"Before Your Eyes" (CBS)—documentary about a Florida child with AIDS, narrated by Julia Roberts
27 JULY	"Hiroshima: Why the Bomb Was Dropped," Peter Jennings Reporting (ABC)—a re-examination of the decision to drop the atomic bomb in 1945
6 AUGUST	"Hiroshima" (SHO)—made-for-TV movie on the dropping of the atomic bomb, starring Kenneth Welsh as President Truman
12 AUGUST	"20 Years of Comedy on HBO" (HBO)—retrospective, hosted by George Carlin
19 AUGUST	Mike Tyson (boxing for the first time in four years) vs. Peter McNeeley (PPV)—the fight lasted less than two minutes
27 AUGUST	"Brian Wilson: I Just Wasn't Made for These Times" (DISNEY)—documentary on the life of Beach Boy Brian Wilson
2 SEPTEMBER	"Concert for the Rock and Roll Hall of Fame" (HBO)—live six-hour rock concert from Cleveland, with Chuck Berry, Little Richard, Bruce Springsteen, and many others
3 OCTOBER	The verdict (not guilty) in the trial of O. J. Simpson (ABC, CBS, CNN, Court TV, NBC)

★★★ **PART III**

PRIME TIMES

Explanatory notes: The following charts show the prime-time fall schedules for each of the major commercial networks. The times shown are the times when the network broadcast the program (eastern standard time), rather than when a local affiliate broadcast it; in most cases, however, the New York City network affiliates (particularly those of CBS and NBC) carried network programs at the same time as the network.

Series that appear in boldface are new for that season; a series is considered "new" if it premiered after 1 June in a given year. Series that are shaded are those which were canceled that season. A series is deemed canceled if it did not appear on a regularly scheduled first-run basis on a network schedule for the following fall season. Examples: *Father Knows Best* is deemed canceled during the 1959–1960 season, though it was rerun in prime time the following season. *The Twilight Zone* is deemed canceled during the 1961–1962 season, though it returned the following midseason. *Police Story* is deemed canceled during the 1976–1977 season, though a few *Police Story* specials were broadcast during the following season.

The numbers that appear at the right of the boxes indicate the age of the series in seasons.

Motion pictures are not considered "series" for the purposes of renewal or cancellation. The titles of some series have been abbreviated as a matter of convenience.

KEY TO NETWORK-SCHEDULE CHARTS

*	**New Network affiliation**
†	**Reruns**
‡	**Once a month**
§	**Every fourth week**
‖	**Alternating every fourth week**
#	**Concurrently running on two networks**
**	**From 6:30 P.M.**
††	**To 11:30 P.M.**
‡‡	**From late afternoon**

1948–1949

Day	Net	7	7:30	8	8:30	9	9:30	10	10:30	11 PM
SUN	ABC	LOCAL		HOLLYWOOD SCREEN TEST	ACTORS' STUDIO	LOCAL				ABC
	CBS	WEEK IN REVIEW 2	FILM	PAULINE FREDERICK / FORD THEATER	RIDDLE ME THIS	THE ED SULLIVAN SHOW		NEWS-REEL		CBS
	NBC		NEWS	AUTHOR MEETS THE CRITICS 2	MEET THE PRESS 2	PHILCO TELEVISION PLAYHOUSE				NBC
MON	ABC	MARY KAY & JOHNNY	KIERNAN'S CORNER	QUIZZING THE NEWS	FILM	LOCAL				ABC
	CBS		NEWS	FACE THE MUSIC 2	PRIZE PARTY	TALENT SCOUTS	SPORTING EVENT			CBS
	NBC		MUSICAL MINIATURES 2	NEWS	TELE-THEATRE	BEN GRAUER'S AMERICANA 2	NEWS-REEL / BOXING			NBC
TUE	ABC	CHILD'S WORLD		LOCAL	AMERICA'S TOWN MEETING					ABC
	CBS		NEWS	FACE THE MUSIC 2	FILM	WE THE PEOPLE	PEOPLE'S PLATFORM	NEWS-REEL		CBS
	NBC	AMERICAN SONG 2	NEWS	THE MILTON BERLE SHOW		M.M. McBRIDE	WRESTLING			NBC
WED	ABC	BUZZY WUZZY	FILM	CLUB SEVEN	QUIZZING THE NEWS	WRESTLING				ABC
	CBS		NEWS	FACE THE MUSIC 2	KOBBS KORNER	WINNER TAKE ALL	BOXING (PABST BLUE RIBBON BOUTS)			CBS
	NBC	YOU ARE AN ARTIST 3	NEWS	GIRL ABOUT TOWN 2 / FILM	RICHARD HARKNESS 2	KRAFT TELEVISION THEATER		NEWS-REEL 3	THE VILLAGE BARN 2	NBC
THU	ABC	LOCAL		FASHION STORY	CRITIC AT LARGE	LOCAL		NEWS-REEL		ABC
	CBS		NEWS	MUSICAL MINIATURES 2	DIONE LUCAS COOKING SHOW 2	FILMS				CBS
	NBC		MUSICAL MINIATURES 2	NEWS	FILM / NATURE OF THGS. 2	LANNY ROSS 2	GULF ROAD SHOW 2	BIGELOW SHOW		NBC
FRI	ABC	RED CABOOSE	FILM	CANDID MICROPHONE	GAY NINETIES REVUE	BREAK THE BANK	LOCAL			ABC
	CBS		NEWS	FACE THE MUSIC 2	WHAT'S IT WORTH?	CAPT. BILLY'S MUSIC HALL	FILM	LOCAL		CBS
	NBC		MUSICAL MERRYGRD. 2	NEWS	FILM	STOP ME IF YOU HEARD THIS ONE 2	I'D LIKE TO SEE 2	BOXING (GILLETTE CAVALCADE OF SPORTS)		NBC
SAT	ABC	ABC SPORTS	FILM	LOCAL	PROGRAM PREVIEW	LOCAL	LOCAL			ABC
	CBS					SPORTING EVENT				CBS
	NBC		FILMS		TV SCREEN MAGAZINE 3	FILMS				NBC

NOTES: 1Girl of the Week (7:45)   2Sportsmen's Quiz (8:00)

1949–1950

Day	Net	7	7:30	8	8:30	9	9:30	10	10:30	11 PM
SUN	ABC	PAUL WHITEMAN REVUE	PENTHOUSE PLAYERS 2	THINK FAST	LITTLE REVUE 2	LET THERE BE STARS		CELEBRITY TIME	YOUTH ON THE MARCH 2	
	CBS	TONIGHT ON BROADWAY 2	THIS IS SHOW BUSINESS 2	THE ED SULLIVAN SHOW		THE FRED WARING SHOW 2		WEEK IN REVIEW 3	LOCAL	
	NBC	LEAVE IT TO THE GIRLS 2	ALDRICH FAMILY	PERRY COMO 2	COLGATE THEATRE 2	PHILCO TELEVISION PLAYHOUSE 2		GARROWAY AT LARGE 2		
MON	ABC		LOCAL	LOCAL	AUTHOR MEETS THE CRITICS *3	MR. BLACK	WRESTLING			
	CBS		NEWS / SONNY KENDIS' 2	SILVER THEATER 2	TALENT SCOUTS 2	CANDID CAMERA *2	GOLDBERGS 2	STUDIO ONE 2		2
	NBC		MORTON DOWNEY 2 / NEWS	TELE-THEATRE 2	VOICE OF FIRESTONE 2	LIGHTS OUT	BAND OF AMERICA	QUIZ KIDS		
TUE	ABC		LOCAL	LOCAL		LOCAL		BOXING 2		
	CBS		NEWS / SONNY KENDIS' 2	FILM 2		ACTORS' STUDIO *2	SUSPENSE *2	THIS WK. IN SPTS. 2 / BLUES BY BARGY	PANTOMIME QUIZ	
	NBC		ROBERTA QUINLAN 2 / NEWS	THE MILTON BERLE SHOW		FIRESIDE THEATER 2	LIFE OF RILEY 2	TED MACK'S AMATEUR HOUR	*3	
WED	ABC		LOCAL	PHOTOPLAY TIME	PHOTOCRIME	FILM	WRESTLING			
	CBS		NEWS / MASLAND AT HOME	ARTHUR GODFREY & HIS FRIENDS	THE CLOCK 2	BIGELOW SHOW 2	BOXING (PABST BLUE RIBBON BOUTS) *2	BREAK THE BANK 4	2	
	NBC		MORTON DOWNEY 2 / NEWS	CRISIS 2		KRAFT TELEVISION THEATER 2			TOP VIEW IN SPORT / LOCAL *2	
THU	ABC	LONE RANGER		STOP THE MUSIC	INSIDE U.S.A. ROMANCE	CRUSADE IN EUROPE 2	STARRING BORIS KARLOFF	ROLLER DERBY		
	CBS		NEWS / SONNY KENDIS' 2	THE FRONT PAGE 2		ED WYNN SHOW	FILM		BLUES BY BARGY 2 / NEWS-REEL	
	NBC		ROBERTA QUINLAN 2 / NEWS	SPECIALS	MARY KAY & JOHNNY 2	FIREBALL FUN FOR ALL	FUN FOR THE MONEY	MARTIN KANE	LOCAL	
FRI	ABC	FILM		MAJORITY RULES	BLIND DATE 2	AUCTION-AIRE 2	FUN FOR THE MONEY	ROLLER DERBY		
	CBS		NEWS / AMAZING POLGAR 1	MAMA	MAN AGAINST CRIME	FORD THEATER 54TH ST. REVUE 2 / THEATER HOUR		PEOPLE'S PLATFORM	CAPITOL CLOAKROOM 2	
	NBC		MORTON DOWNEY 2 / NEWS	ONE MAN'S FAMILY	WE THE PEOPLE *2	VERSATILE VARIETIES	BIG STORY	BOXING (GILLETTE CAVALCADE OF SPORTS)	2	
SAT	ABC	HOLLYWOOD SCREEN TEST	TV TEEN CLUB			FILM 2				
	CBS		IN THE 1ST POSITION 2 / BLUES BY BARGY 2	WINNER TAKE ALL	FILMS 2					
	NBC	NATURE OF THGS. 2 / NEWS	MEET YOUR CONGRESS		MIXED DOUBLES 2	WHO SAID THAT 2	MEET THE PRESS 2	FILM 3		

NOTE: 1*Ruthie on the Telephone* (7:55 p.m.)

1950–1951

Day	Net	7:00	7:30	8:00	8:30	9:00	9:30	10:00	10:30
SUN	ABC	PAUL WHITEMAN REVUE (2)	SHOWTIME USA	HOLLYWOOD THEATER TIME	SIT OR MISS	MARSHALL PLAN IN ACTION	LOCAL	OLD FASHIONED MEETING	YOUTH ON THE MARCH (2)
SUN	CBS	GENE AUTRY (2)	THIS IS SHOW BUSINESS (2)	THE ED SULLIVAN SHOW		THE FRED WARING SHOW (3)		CELEBRITY TIME (3)	WHAT'S MY LINE (3)
SUN	NBC	LEAVE IT TO THE GIRLS (3)	ALDRICH FAMILY (2)	THE COLGATE COMEDY HOUR		PHILCO TELEVISION PLAYHOUSE (3)		GARROWAY AT LARGE (3)	TAKE A CHANCE (2)
MON	ABC		HOLLYWOOD SCREEN TEST	TREASURY MEN IN ACTION (3)	DICK TRACY	COLLEGE BOWL (CHICO MARX)	ON TRIAL (3)	FILM (3)	
MON	CBS		NEWS / PERRY COMO (3)	LUX VIDEO THEATRE	TALENT SCOUTS	HORACE HEIDT (3)		STUDIO ONE (3)	
MON	NBC		ROBERTA QUINLAN / NEWS (3)	PAUL WINCHELL	VOICE OF FIRESTONE	LIGHTS OUT (2)	ROBERT MONTGOMERY PRESENTS / MUSICAL COMEDY TIME (2)		TALENT SEARCH (2)
TUE	ABC		BEULAH	FOOTBALL FILMS	BUCK ROGERS	BILLY ROSE'S PLAYBILL (2)	CAN YOU TOP THIS	LIFE BEGINS AT EIGHTY	ROLLER DERBY (*2)
TUE	CBS		NEWS / FAYE EMERSON (2)	SURE AS FATE / PRUDENTIAL FAMILY THEATER (2)		CAMEL CARAVAN (2)	SUSPENSE	DANGER (3)	WE TAKE YOUR WORD (2)
TUE	NBC		LITTLE SHOW / NEWS	THE MILTON BERLE SHOW		FIRESIDE THEATER (3)	ARMSTRONG CIRCLE TH. (3)	TED MACK'S AMATEUR HOUR (2)	
WED	ABC		CHANCE OF A LIFETIME	FILM	ARTHUR GODFREY & HIS FRIENDS	DON McNEILL'S TV CLUB		WRESTLING	
WED	CBS		NEWS / PERRY COMO (3)			SOMERSET MAUGHAM THEATER	THE WEB	PABST BLUE RIBBON BOUTS (3)	
WED	NBC		NEWS / ROBERTA QUINLAN (3)	FOUR STAR REVUE		KRAFT TELEVISION THEATER		BREAK THE BANK (5)	STARS OVER HOLLYWOOD (3)
THU	ABC		LONE RANGER	STOP THE MUSIC		HOLIDAY HOTEL (3)	BLIND DATE (2)	I COVER TIMES SQUARE (3)	ROLLER DERBY
THU	CBS		NEWS / FAYE EMERSON (2)	STARLIGHT TH. (2) / THE SHOW GOES ON	BURNS & ALLEN (2)	ALAN YOUNG SHOW	BIG TOWN (2)	TRUTH OR CONSEQUENCES	AIRFLYTE THEATRE
THU	NBC		LITTLE SHOW / NEWS	YOU BET YOUR LIFE	PETER LIND HAYES SHOW	COLLEGE OF MUSICAL KNOWLEDGE (2)		MARTIN KANE (2)	QUICK ON THE DRAW (2)
FRI	ABC		LIFE WITH LINKLETTER	SOAP BOX THEATER	PRO FOOTBALL HIGHLIGHTS	PULITZER PRIZE PLAYHOUSE	FORD THEATER	PENTHOUSE PARTY	STUDS' PLACE (*2)
FRI	CBS		NEWS / PERRY COMO (3)	MAMA (2)	MAN AGAINST CRIME (2)	MAGNAVOX THEATER	VERSATILE VARIETIES (2)	STAR OF THE FAMILY (3)	BEAT THE CLOCK (2)
FRI	NBC		ROBERTA QUINLAN / NEWS (3)	QUIZ KIDS	WE THE PEOPLE (*2)	THE CLOCK (3)	BIG STORY (2)	GILLETTE CAVALCADE OF SPORTS (3)	
SAT	ABC		STU ERWIN SHOW	TV TEEN CLUB		ROLLER DERBY (3)			
SAT	CBS		WEEK IN REVIEW (4) / FAYE EMERSON (2)	THE KEN MURRAY SHOW		THE FRANK SINATRA SHOW (2)		SING IT AGAIN	
SAT	NBC		ONE MAN'S FAMILY (2)	ALL-STAR REVUE		YOUR SHOW OF SHOWS (2)			YOUR HIT PARADE (2)

1951–1952

Day	Net	7	7:30	8	8:30	9	9:30	10	10:30	11 PM
SUN	ABC	PAUL WHITEMAN REVUE (3)	BY-LINE	MOVIE			LOCAL	BILLY GRAHAM	YOUTH ON THE MARCH (3)	ABC
	CBS	GENE AUTRY (2)	THIS IS SHOW BUSINESS (3)	THE ED SULLIVAN SHOW (3)		THE FRED WARING SHOW (4)		CELEBRITY TIME (4)	WHAT'S MY LINE (4)	CBS 3
	NBC	SOUND-OFF TIME	YOUNG MR. BOBBIN	THE COLGATE COMEDY HOUR		PHILCO TELEVISION PLAYHOUSE (4) / GOODYEAR TELEVISION PLAYHOUSE (2)		RED SKELTON (4)	LEAVE IT TO THE GIRLS (4)	NBC 4
MON	ABC		HOLLYWOOD SCREEN TEST (4)	THE AMAZING MR. MALONE	LIFE BEGINS AT EIGHTY (3)	FILM (3)		BILL GWINN SHOW (2)	STUDS' PLACE (3)	ABC 3
	CBS		NEWS / PERRY COMO (4)	LUX VIDEO THEATRE (4)	TALENT SCOUTS (2)	I LOVE LUCY (4)	IT'S NEWS TO ME (2)	STUDIO ONE (2)		CBS 4
	NBC		THOSE TWO / NEWS	PAUL WINCHELL	VOICE OF FIRESTONE	LIGHTS OUT (3)	ROBERT MONTGOMERY PRESENTS / SOMERSET MAUGHAM THEATRE (*2)		LOCAL	NBC
TUE	ABC		BEULAH (2)	CHARLIE WILD (*2)	HOW DID THEY GET THAT WAY (2)	UNITED OR NOT (4)	ON TRIAL (4)	LOCAL	ACTORS HOTEL	ABC
	CBS		NEWS / STORK CLUB (2)	THE FRANK SINATRA SHOW		CRIME SYNDICATED (2)	SUSPENSE (4)	DANGER (4)	LOCAL (2)	CBS
	NBC		DINAH SHORE / NEWS	THE MILTON BERLE SHOW		FIRESIDE THEATER (4)	ARMSTRONG CIRCLE TH. (4)	TED MACK'S AMATEUR HOUR (3)		NBC 5
WED	ABC		CHANCE OF A LIFETIME (2)	THE PAUL DIXON SHOW		A. MURRAY / DON McNEILL (2)	THE CLOCK (2)	CELANESE THEATER (*4) / KING'S CROSSROADS		ABC
	CBS		NEWS / PERRY COMO (4)	ARTHUR GODFREY & HIS FRIENDS		STRIKE IT RICH (4)	THE WEB	PABST BLUE RIBBON BOUTS (4)		CBS
	NBC		THOSE TWO / NEWS	THE KATE SMITH EVENING HOUR		KRAFT TELEVISION THEATER		BREAK THE BANK (6)	FREDDY MARTIN (4)	NBC 4
THU	ABC		LONE RANGER (3)	STOP THE MUSIC (3)		HERB SHRINER (4)	GRUEN GUILD PLAYHOUSE	PAUL DIXON SHOW	MASLAND AT HOME / CARMEL MYERS	ABC
	CBS		NEWS / STORK CLUB (2)	BURNS & ALLEN (2) / STAR OF FAMILY (2)	AMOS & ANDY (2)	ALAN YOUNG (2)	BIG TOWN (2)	RACKET SQUAD (2)	CRIME PHOTOG. (2)	CBS 2
	NBC		DINAH SHORE / NEWS	YOU BET YOUR LIFE (2)	TREASURY MEN IN ACTION (*2)	FORD FESTIVAL (2)		MARTIN KANE (2)	LOCAL (3)	NBC 2
FRI	ABC		LIFE W/LINKL'R (*2) / SAY IT W/ACT. (*2)	MARK SABER (2)		CRIME WITH FATHER (2)	VERSATILE VAR / TALES OF TOMORROW	LOCAL (*3)		ABC
	CBS		NEWS / PERRY COMO (*2)	MAMA (3)	MAN AGAINST CRIME (3)	SCHLITZ PLAYHOUSE OF STARS (3)		LIVE LIKE A MILLIONAIRE (2)	HOLLYWOOD OPENING NIGHT (2)	CBS
	NBC		THOSE TWO / NEWS	RCA VICTOR SHOW (EZIO PINZA) (3)	WE THE PEOPLE (4)	BIG STORY (4)	ALDRICH FAMILY (3)	GILLETTE CAVALCADE OF SPORTS (3)		NBC 4
SAT	ABC		LOCAL	TV TEEN CLUB		LOCAL (4)				ABC
	CBS		BEAT THE CLOCK (3)	THE KEN MURRAY SHOW (3)		FAYE EMERSON'S WONDERFUL TOWN (3)	THE SHOW GOES ON (3)	SONGS FOR SALE (3)		CBS 2
	NBC		ONE MAN'S FAMILY (3)	ALL-STAR REVUE (3)		YOUR SHOW OF SHOWS (3)			YOUR HIT PARADE (3)	NBC 2

1952–1953

Day	Network	7	7:30	8	8:30	9	9:30	10	10:30	11 PM
SUN	ABC	YOU ASKED FOR IT •3	LOCAL •3	ALL-STAR NEWS		FILM	THIS IS THE LIFE	BILLY GRAHAM 2	LOCAL 2	ANYWHERE USA
SUN	CBS	GENE AUTRY	THIS IS SHOWBIZ 3 / JACK BENNY 4	THE ED SULLIVAN SHOW		THE FRED WARING SHOW 5	BREAK THE BANK 5	THE WEB 3	WHAT'S MY LINE 3	CBS 4
SUN	NBC	RED SKELTON	DOC CORKLE 2	THE COLGATE COMEDY HOUR		PHILCO TELEVISION PLAYHOUSE 3 / GOODYEAR TELEVISION PLAYHOUSE 2		THE DOCTOR 2	LOCAL	NBC 5
MON	ABC		HOLLYWOOD SCREEN TEST	MARK SABER 5	THE HOT SEAT 2	ALL-STAR NEWS 2		LOCAL		ABC
MON	CBS		NEWS / PERRY COMO 5	LUX VIDEO THEATRE 5	TALENT SCOUTS 3	I LOVE LUCY 5	LIFE WITH LUIGI 2	STUDIO ONE		CBS -5
MON	NBC		THOSE TWO 2 / NEWS 2	PAUL WINCHELL 3	VOICE OF FIRESTONE 3	HOLLYWOOD OPEN. NIGHT 4	ROBERT MONTGOMERY PRESENTS •2		WHO SAID THAT? 4	NBC 5
TUE	ABC		BEULAH 3	LOCAL 3		LOCAL		LOCAL	LOCAL	ABC
TUE	CBS		NEWS / HEAVEN FOR BETSY	LEAVE IT TO LARRY	RED BUTTONS	CRIME SYND. CITY HOSPITAL 2	SUSPENSE 2	DANGER 5	LOCAL 3	CBS
TUE	NBC		DINAH SHORE 2 / NEWS	THE MILTON BERLE SHOW	THE BUICK CIRCUS HOUR	FIRESIDE THEATER 5	ARMSTRONG CIRCLE TH. 5	TWO FOR THE MONEY 4	BOB & RAY / BOB CONSIDINE 3	NBC
WED	ABC		THE NAME'S THE SAME	ALL-STAR NEWS 2		ELLERY QUEEN •2	MARCH OF TIME 2	WRESTLING 2		ABC
WED	CBS		NEWS / PERRY COMO 2	ARTHUR GODFREY & HIS FRIENDS		STRIKE IT RICH 5	MAN AGAINST CRIME 2	PABST BLUE RIBBON BOUTS 4		CBS 5
WED	NBC		THOSE TWO 2 / NEWS 2	I MARRIED JOAN	CAVALCADE OF AMERICA / SCOTT MUSIC HALL	KRAFT TELEVISION THEATER		THIS IS YOUR LIFE 7		NBC
THU	ABC		LONE RANGER 4	CHANCE OF A LIFETIME 3		PERSPECTIVE 3	ON GUARD	LOCAL 2	LOCAL	ABC
THU	CBS		NEWS / HEAVEN FOR BETSY	BURNS & ALLEN	AMOS & ANDY / FOUR STAR PLAYHOUSE 2	BIFF BAKER USA 2	BIG TOWN	RACKET SQUAD 3	I'VE GOT A SECRET 2	CBS
THU	NBC		DINAH SHORE 2 / NEWS	YOU BET YOUR LIFE	TREASURY MEN IN ACTION 3	DRAGNET / GANGBUSTERS 3	FORD THEATER 2	MARTIN KANE •4	LOCAL 4	NBC
FRI	ABC		STU ERWIN SHOW 3	OZZIE & HARRIET	ALL-STAR NEWS	TALES OF TOMORROW		LOCAL	LOCAL	ABC
FRI	CBS		NEWS / PERRY COMO 5	MAMA	MY FRIEND IRMA 4	SCHLITZ PLAYHOUSE 2	OUR MISS BROOKS 2	MR. & MRS. NORTH	LOCAL	CBS
FRI	NBC		THOSE TWO 2 / NEWS 2	RCA VICTOR SHOW (DENNIS DAY)	GULF PLAYHOUSE 2	BIG STORY 4	ALDRICH FAMILY 4	GILLETTE CAVALCADE OF SPORTS		NBC 5
SAT	ABC		LIVE LIKE A MILLIONAIRE •3	FILM •3		LOCAL		LOCAL		ABC
SAT	CBS		BEAT THE CLOCK 4	THE JACKIE GLEASON SHOW		JANE FROMAN'S USA CANTEEN	MEET MILLIE	BALANCE YOUR BUDGET	BATTLE OF THE AGES •2	CBS •2
SAT	NBC		MY HERO	ALL-STAR REVUE		YOUR SHOW OF SHOWS 4			YOUR HIT PARADE 4	NBC 3

1953–1954

Day	Net	7:00	7:30	8:00	8:30	9:00	9:30	10:00	10:30	11 PM
SUN	ABC	YOU ASKED FOR IT	FRANK LEAHY (4)	NOTRE DAME FOOTBALL	NOTRE DAME FOOTBALL		JUKEBOX JURY	JUKEBOX JURY	BILLY GRAHAM (3) / LOCAL	ABC
	CBS	LIFE WITH FATHER	JACK BENNY (2) / PRIVATE SECY. (2)	THE ED SULLIVAN SHOW	THE ED SULLIVAN SHOW	WALTER WINCHELL (2) / ORCHID AWARD (2)		THE WEB	WHAT'S MY LINE (5)	CBS
	NBC	PAUL WINCHELL (4)	MR. PEEPERS (2)	THE COLGATE COMEDY HOUR	THE COLGATE COMEDY HOUR	FRED WARING (6) / G.E. THEATER (2)	PHILCO TELEVISION PLAYHOUSE (3) / GOODYEAR TELEVISION PLAYHOUSE (3)	THE MAN BEHIND THE BADGE (6) / LORETTA YOUNG (A LETTER TO …) (3)	MAN AGAINST CRIME * (5)	NBC
MON	ABC			JAMIE	OF MANY THINGS †	JUNIOR PRESS CONFERENCE (2)	BIG PICTURE (3)	RACKET SQUAD †	LOCAL	ABC
	CBS		NEWS / PERRY COMO (6)	SKY KING †	BURNS & ALLEN (6) / TALENT SCOUTS (4)	I LOVE LUCY (6)	RED BUTTONS (3)	STUDIO ONE		CBS
	NBC		NEWS / ARTHUR MURRAY • (4)	NAME THAT TUNE	VOICE OF FIRESTONE	DENNIS DAY (5)	ROBERT MONTGOMERY PRESENTS		WHO SAID THAT (5)	NBC
TUE	ABC		NEWS	CAVALCADE OF AMERICA • (2)	LOCAL	MAKE ROOM FOR DADDY	THE U.S. STEEL HOUR / THE MOTOROLA TV HOUR	THE U.S. STEEL HOUR / THE MOTOROLA TV HOUR	THE NAME'S THE SAME (3)	ABC
	CBS		NEWS (2)	GENE AUTRY (4)	RED SKELTON	THIS IS SHOW BUSINESS • (3)	SUSPENSE (6)	DANGER (6)	SEE IT NOW (3)	CBS
	NBC		DINAH SHORE (3) / NEWS	THE MILTON BERLE SHOW / THE BOB HOPE SHOW	THE MILTON BERLE SHOW / THE BOB HOPE SHOW	FIRESIDE THEATER (6)	ARMSTRONG CIRCLE TH. (6)	JUDGE FOR YOURSELF (5)	BOB CONSIDINE / I.H.I.S.¹ (4)	NBC
WED	ABC		MARK SABER	AT ISSUE / THRU THE CURTAIN	ANSWERS FOR AMERICANS	JEAN CARROLL	DOCTOR I.Q.	WRESTLING		ABC
	CBS		NEWS / PERRY COMO (6)	ARTHUR GODFREY & HIS FRIENDS	ARTHUR GODFREY & HIS FRIENDS	STRIKE IT RICH (6)	I'VE GOT A SECRET (3)	PABST BLUE RIBBON BOUTS (2)		CBS
	NBC		COKE TIME (2) / NEWS (2)	I MARRIED JOAN (2)	MY LITTLE MARGIE (2)	KRAFT TELEVISION THEATER • (2)	KRAFT TELEVISION THEATER • (2)	THIS IS YOUR LIFE # 8	LOCAL (2)	NBC
THU	ABC		LONE RANGER (5)	QUICK AS A FLASH (2)	RAY BOLGER	BACK THAT FACT	KRAFT TELEVISION THEATER # 8	KRAFT TELEVISION THEATER # 8	PLACE THE FACE / LOCAL	ABC
	CBS		NEWS / JANE FROMAN (2)	RAY MILLAND	FOUR STAR PLAYHOUSE	LUX VIDEO THEATRE	BIG TOWN (4)	PHILIP MORRIS PLAYHOUSE (4)		CBS
	NBC		DINAH SHORE (3) / NEWS (3)	YOU BET YOUR LIFE	TREASURY MEN IN ACTION (4)	DRAGNET	FORD THEATER (3)	MARTIN KANE (4)		NBC
FRI	ABC		STU ERWIN SHOW (4)	OZZIE AND HARRIET (4)	PEPSI-COLA PLAYHOUSE (2)	PRIDE OF THE FAMILY	COMEBACK STORY	CHEVROLET SHOWROOM	LOCAL (5)	ABC
	CBS		NEWS / PERRY COMO (6)	MAMA (5)	TOPPER (2)	SCHLITZ PLAYHOUSE	OUR MISS BROOKS (3)	MY FRIEND IRMA (2)	PERSON TO PERSON (3)	CBS
	NBC		COKE TIME (2) / NEWS (2)	DAVE GARROWAY	LIFE OF RILEY	BIG STORY (2)	TV SOUNDSTAGE (5)	GILLETTE CAVALCADE OF SPORTS	LOCAL (6)	NBC
SAT	ABC		LEAVE IT TO THE GIRLS • (5)	TALENT PATROL (5)	MUSIC FROM MEADOWBRK.	SATURDAY NIGHT FIGHTS (2)	SATURDAY NIGHT FIGHTS (2)	LOCAL (2)		ABC
	CBS		BEAT THE CLOCK (5)	THE JACKIE GLEASON SHOW	THE JACKIE GLEASON SHOW	TWO FOR THE MONEY (2)	MY FAVORITE HUSBAND • (2)	MEDALLION THEATER	MIRROR THEATER *	CBS
	NBC		ETHEL AND ALBERT (2)	BONINO (2)	TED MACK'S AMATEUR HOUR (7)	YOUR SHOW OF SHOWS / ALL-STAR REVUE	YOUR SHOW OF SHOWS / ALL-STAR REVUE	YOUR SHOW OF SHOWS	YOUR HIT PARADE (4)	NBC

NOTE: '¹It Happened in Sports (Tues. 10:45).'

1954–1955

Day	Net	7:00	7:30	8:00	8:30	9:00	9:30	10:00	10:30
SUN	ABC	YOU ASKED FOR IT	PEPSI-COLA PLAYHOUSE	FLIGHT NO. 7	BIG PICTURE	WALTER WINCHELL / PACKARD SHOWRM	WHAT'S GOING ON	BREAK THE BANK	*7 LOCAL
	CBS	LASSIE	JACK BENNY / PRIVATE SECY.	THE ED SULLIVAN SHOW		G.E. THEATER	HONESTLY, CELESTE!	FATHER KNOWS BEST	WHAT'S MY LINE
	NBC	PEOPLE ARE FUNNY	MR. PEEPERS	THE COLGATE COMEDY HOUR		PHILCO TELEVISION PLAYHOUSE / GOODYEAR TELEVISION PLAYHOUSE		LORETTA YOUNG	THE HUNTER
MON	ABC		THE NAME'S THE SAME	COME CLOSER	VOICE OF FIRESTONE	COLLEGE PRESS CONFERENCE			
	CBS		NEWS / PERRY COMO	BURNS & ALLEN	TALENT SCOUTS	I LOVE LUCY	DECEMBER BRIDE	STUDIO ONE	
	NBC		TONY MARTIN / NEWS	CAESAR'S HOUR		BOXING	ROBERT MONTGOMERY PRESENTS		LOCAL
TUE	ABC		LOCAL	CAVALCADE OF AMERICA	TWENTY QUESTIONS	MAKE ROOM FOR DADDY	THE U.S. STEEL HOUR / THE ELGIN TV HOUR		STOP THE MUSIC
	CBS		JO STAFFORD / NEWS	RED SKELTON	HALLS OF IVY	MEET MILLIE	DANGER	LIFE WITH FATHER	SEE IT NOW
	NBC		DINAH SHORE / NEWS	THE MILTON BERLE SHOW		FIRESIDE THEATER	ARMSTRONG CIRCLE THEATER	TRUTH OR CONSEQUENCES	IT'S A GREAT LIFE
WED	ABC		DISNEYLAND		STU ERWIN SHOW	MASQUERADE PARTY	ENTERPRISE U.S.A.	LOCAL	LOCAL
	CBS		NEWS / PERRY COMO	ARTHUR GODFREY & HIS FRIENDS		STRIKE IT RICH	I'VE GOT A SECRET	PABST BLUE RIBBON BOUTS / THE BEST OF BROADWAY	
	NBC		COKE TIME / NEWS	I MARRIED JOAN	MY LITTLE MARGIE	KRAFT TELEVISION THEATER		THIS IS YOUR LIFE	BIG TOWN
THU	ABC		LONE RANGER	THE MAIL STORY	TREASURY MEN IN ACTION	SO YOU WANT TO LEAD A BAND	KRAFT TELEVISION THEATER		LOCAL
	CBS		JANE FROMAN / NEWS	RAY MILLAND	CLIMAX! / SHOWER OF STARS		FOUR STAR PLAYHOUSE	PUBLIC DEFENDER	NAME THAT TUNE
	NBC		DINAH SHORE / NEWS	YOU BET YOUR LIFE	JUSTICE	DRAGNET	FORD THEATER	LUX VIDEO THEATRE	
FRI	ABC		RIN TIN TIN	OZZIE AND HARRIET	RAY BOLGER	DOLLAR A SECOND	THE VISE	LOCAL	LOCAL
	CBS		NEWS / PERRY COMO	MAMA	TOPPER	SCHLITZ PLAYHOUSE	OUR MISS BROOKS	THE LINEUP	PERSON TO PERSON
	NBC		COKE TIME / NEWS	RED BUTTONS / JACK CARSON	LIFE OF RILEY	BIG STORY	DEAR PHOEBE	GILLETTE CAVALCADE OF SPORTS	
SAT	ABC		COMPASS	THE DOTTY MACK SHOW		SATURDAY NIGHT FIGHTS		STORK CLUB	LOCAL
	CBS		BEAT THE CLOCK	THE JACKIE GLEASON SHOW		TWO FOR THE MONEY	MY FAVORITE HUSBAND	THAT'S MY BOY	WILLY
	NBC		ETHEL AND ALBERT	MICKEY ROONEY	PLACE THE FACE	IMOGENE COCA	JIMMY DURANTE / DONALD O'CONNOR	GEORGE GOBEL	YOUR HIT PARADE

1955–1956

Day	Net	7	7:30	8	8:30	9	9:30	10	10:30	11 PM
SUN	ABC	YOU ASKED FOR IT	MOVIE			CHANCE OF A LIFETIME	TED MACK'S AMATEUR HR.	LIFE BEGINS AT EIGHTY	LOCAL	LOCAL
	CBS	LASSIE	JACK BENNY / PRIVATE SECY.	THE ED SULLIVAN SHOW		G.E. THEATER	ALFRED HITCHCOCK	APPT. WITH ADVENTURE	WHAT'S MY LINE	WHAT'S MY LINE
	NBC	IT'S A GREAT LIFE	FRONTIER	THE COLGATE VARIETY HOUR		GOODYEAR PLAYHOUSE / THE ALCOA HOUR		LORETTA YOUNG	JUSTICE	JUSTICE
MON	ABC			TV READERS' DIGEST	VOICE OF FIRESTONE	DOTTY MACK	MEDICAL HORIZONS	BIG PICTURE	LOCAL	LOCAL
	CBS		ROBIN HOOD	BURNS & ALLEN	TALENT SCOUTS	I LOVE LUCY	DECEMBER BRIDE	STUDIO ONE		
	NBC		TONY MARTIN / NEWS	CAESAR'S HOUR		MEDIC	ROBERT MONTGOMERY PRESENTS		LOCAL	
TUE	ABC		WARNER BROTHERS PRESENTS		WYATT EARP	MAKE ROOM FOR DADDY	CAVALCADE THEATER	TALENT VARIETIES	LOCAL	LOCAL
	CBS		NAME THAT TUNE	NAVY LOG	YOU'LL NEVER GET RICH	MEET MILLIE	RED SKELTON	THE $64,000 QUESTION	MY FAVORITE HUSBAND	MY FAVORITE HUSBAND
	NBC		DINAH SHORE / NEWS	MILTON BERLE / BOB HOPE / MARTHA RAYE / GUEST HOSTS		JANE WYMAN PRESENTS	ARMSTRONG CIRCLE THEATER / PLAYWRIGHTS '56		BIG TOWN	BIG TOWN
WED	ABC		DISNEYLAND		M-G-M PARADE	MASQUERADE PARTY	BREAK THE BANK	WEDNESDAY NIGHT FIGHTS		
	CBS		BRAVE EAGLE / NEWS	ARTHUR GODFREY & HIS FRIENDS		THE MILLIONAIRE	I'VE GOT A SECRET	THE U.S. STEEL HOUR / 20TH CENTURY-FOX HOUR		
	NBC		COKE TIME / NEWS	SCREEN DIRECTORS PLAYHOUSE	FATHER KNOWS BEST	KRAFT TELEVISION THEATER		THIS IS YOUR LIFE / MIDWEST HAYRIDE		
THU	ABC		LONE RANGER	BISHOP SHEEN (MISSION...)	STOP THE MUSIC	STAR TONIGHT	DOWN YOU GO	OUTSIDE U.S.A.	LOCAL	LOCAL
	CBS		SGT. PRESTON	BOB CUMMINGS (LOVE THAT BOB)	CLIMAX! / SHOWER OF STARS		FOUR STAR PLAYHOUSE	JOHNNY CARSON	WANTED	WANTED
	NBC		DINAH SHORE / NEWS	YOU BET YOUR LIFE	PEOPLE'S CHOICE	DRAGNET	FORD THEATER	LUX VIDEO THEATRE		
FRI	ABC		RIN TIN TIN	ADVENTURES OF CHAMPION	OZZIE AND HARRIET	DOLLAR A SECOND	THE VISE	ETHEL AND ALBERT	LOCAL	
	CBS			MAMA	OUR MISS BROOKS	CROSSROADS	THE CRUSADER	SCHLITZ PLAYHOUSE / THE LINEUP	PERSON TO PERSON	PERSON TO PERSON
	NBC		COKE TIME / NEWS	TRUTH OR CONSEQUENCES	LIFE OF RILEY	BIG STORY	STAR STAGE	GILLETTE CAVALCADE OF SPORTS		
SAT	ABC		OZARK JUBILEE / GRAND OLE OPRY			THE LAWRENCE WELK SHOW		TOMORROW	LOCAL	LOCAL
	CBS		BEAT THE CLOCK	STAGE SHOW	HONEYMOONERS (J. GLEASON)	TWO FOR THE MONEY	IT'S ALWAYS JAN	GUNSMOKE	DAMON RUNYON THEATER	DAMON RUNYON THEATER
	NBC		BIG SURPRISE	THE PERRY COMO SHOW		PEOPLE ARE FUNNY	JIMMY DURANTE	GEORGE GOBEL	YOUR HIT PARADE	YOUR HIT PARADE

1956–1957

Day	Network	7	7:30	8	8:30	9	9:30	10	10:30	11 PM
SUN	ABC	YOU ASKED FOR IT	7 TED MACK'S AMATEUR HOUR		10 PRESS CONFERENCE	OMNIBUS			*5 LOCAL	
SUN	CBS	3 LASSIE	JACK BENNY 5 / PRIVATE SECY. 5	THE ED SULLIVAN SHOW		9 G.E. THEATER	5 ALFRED HITCHCOCK	2 THE $64,000 CHALLENGE	2 WHAT'S MY LINE	8
SUN	NBC	77TH BENGAL LANCERS	CIRCUS BOY	THE STEVE ALLEN SHOW		GOODYEAR PLAYHOUSE / THE ALCOA HOUR		6 LORETTA YOUNG	4 NATIONAL BOWLING CHAMPS	2
MON	ABC		BOLD JOURNEY	4 MAKE ROOM FOR DADDY	VOICE OF FIRESTONE	8 BISHOP SHEEN	5 LAWRENCE WELK'S TOP TUNES AND NEW TALENT		LOCAL	
MON	CBS		ROBIN HOOD	2 BURNS & ALLEN	7 TALENT SCOUTS	9 I LOVE LUCY	6 DECEMBER BRIDE	3 STUDIO ONE		9
MON	NBC		NAT KING COLE / NEWS	SIR LANCELOT	STANLEY	MEDIC	3 ROBERT MONTGOMERY PRESENTS		8 LOCAL	
TUE	ABC		CHEYENNE¹ / CONFLICT	2 WYATT EARP		2 BROKEN ARROW	CAVALCADE THEATER	5 IT'S POLKA TIME	LOCAL	
TUE	CBS		4 NAME THAT TUNE	YOU'LL NEVER GET RICH	2 THE BROTHERS	HERB SHRINER	6 RED SKELTON	THE $64,000 QUESTION	2 DO YOU TRUST YOUR WIFE?	2
TUE	NBC		JONATHAN WINTERS / NEWS	2 BIG SURPRISE	2 NOAH'S ARK	JANE WYMAN THEATER	ARMSTRONG CIRCLE THEATER / KAISER ALUMINUM HOUR 2	8	BREAK THE $250,000 BANK *9	
WED	ABC		DISNEYLAND		3 NAVY LOG	OZZIE AND HARRIET *2	5 FORD THEATER	*7 WEDNESDAY NIGHT FIGHTS		2
WED	CBS		GIANT STEP	2 THE ARTHUR GODFREY SHOW		9 MILLIONAIRE	3 I'VE GOT A SECRET	5 THE U.S. STEEL HOUR / 20TH CENTURY-FOX HOUR		4
WED	NBC		COKE TIME 5 / NEWS	HIRAM HOLLIDAY	FATHER KNOWS BEST	3 KRAFT TELEVISION THEATER		11 THIS IS YOUR LIFE	5 TWENTY-ONE	2
THU	ABC		8 LONE RANGER	CIRCUS TIME		WIRE SERVICE		OZARK JUBILEE		3
THU	CBS		SGT. PRESTON	2 LOVE THAT BOB	3 CLIMAX! / SHOWER OF STARS	3 PLAYHOUSE 90 §3				
THU	NBC		DINAH SHORE 6 / NEWS	2 YOU BET YOUR LIFE	7 DRAGNET	6 PEOPLES' CHOICE	2 TENNESSEE ERNIE FORD	LUX VIDEO THEATRE		7
FRI	ABC		3 RIN TIN TIN	3 JIM BOWIE	CROSSROADS	2 TREASURE HUNT	THE VISE	3 RAY ANTHONY		
FRI	CBS		2 MY FRIEND FLICKA	WEST POINT	ZANE GREY THEATER	2 THE CRUSADER	2 SCHLITZ PLAYHOUSE	6 THE LINEUP	3 PERSON TO PERSON	4
FRI	NBC		COKE TIME 5 / NEWS	LIFE OF RILEY	5 WALTER WINCHELL	ON TRIAL	BIG STORY	8 GILLETTE CAVALCADE OF SPORTS		9
SAT	ABC		MOVIE			THE LAWRENCE WELK SHOW		2 MASQUERADE PARTY	5 LOCAL	3
SAT	CBS		THE BUCCANEERS	THE JACKIE GLEASON SHOW		5 OH! SUSANNA	HEY JEANNIE	GUNSMOKE	2 HIGH FINANCE	2
SAT	NBC		3 PEOPLE ARE FUNNY	THE PERRY COMO SHOW		2 CAESAR'S HOUR		3 GEORGE GOBEL	3 YOUR HIT PARADE	7

NOTE: ¹Formerly one segment of *Warner Brothers Presents*

1957–1958

Day	Net	7	7:30	8	8:30	9	9:30	10	10:30
SUN	ABC	YOU ASKED FOR IT	MAVERICK		BOWLING STARS	OPEN HEARING	FOOTBALL FILMS	SCOTLAND YARD	LOCAL
	CBS	LASSIE	JACK BENNY / BACHELOR FATHER	THE ED SULLIVAN SHOW		G.E. THEATER	ALFRED HITCHCOCK	THE $64,000 CHALLENGE	WHAT'S MY LINE
	NBC	TED MACK'S AMATEUR HR. *11	SALLY	THE STEVE ALLEN SHOW		THE DINAH SHORE CHEVY SHOW		LAWRENCE WELK'S TOP TUNES AND NEW TALENT / LORETTA YOUNG	LOCAL
MON	ABC		AMERICAN BANDSTAND	GUY MITCHELL	BOLD JOURNEY	VOICE OF FIRESTONE		LAWRENCE WELK'S TOP TUNES	LOCAL
	CBS		ROBIN HOOD	BURNS & ALLEN	TALENT SCOUTS	DANNY THOMAS'	DECEMBER BRIDE	STUDIO ONE	LOCAL
	NBC		PRICE IS RIGHT	RESTLESS GUN	WELLS FARGO	TWENTY-ONE	GOODYEAR TH. / ALCOA TH.	SUSPICION	
TUE	ABC		CHEYENNE / SUGARFOOT		WYATT EARP	BROKEN ARROW	TELEPHONE TIME	WEST POINT	LOCAL
	CBS		NAME THAT TUNE	YOU'LL NEVER GET RICH	EVE ARDEN SHOW	TO TELL THE TRUTH	RED SKELTON	THE $64,000 QUESTION	ASSIGNMENT: FOREIGN LEGION
	NBC		NAT KING COLE	THE GEORGE GOBEL SHOW / THE EDDIE FISHER SHOW		MEET McGRAW	LOVE THAT BOB	CALIFORNIANS	LOCAL
WED	ABC		DISNEYLAND		TOMBSTONE TERRITORY	OZZIE AND HARRIET	WALTER WINCHELL FILE	WEDNESDAY NIGHT FIGHTS	
	CBS		I LOVE LUCY	THE BIG RECORD †		MILLIONAIRE	I'VE GOT A SECRET	ARMSTRONG CIRCLE THEATER / THE U.S. STEEL HOUR	LOCAL
	NBC		WAGON TRAIN		FATHER KNOWS BEST	KRAFT TELEVISION THEATER		THIS IS YOUR LIFE	LOCAL
THU	ABC		CIRCUS BOY	ZORRO	REAL McCOYS	PAT BOONE SHOW	O.S.S.	NAVY LOG	LOCAL
	CBS		SGT. PRESTON	HARBOURMASTER	CLIMAX! / SHOWER OF STARS		PLAYHOUSE 90		LOCAL
	NBC		TIC TAC DOUGH	YOU BET YOUR LIFE	DRAGNET	PEOPLES' CHOICE	TENNESSEE ERNIE FORD	THE LUX SHOW (R. CLOONEY)	JANE WYMAN THEATER
FRI	ABC		RIN TIN TIN	JIM BOWIE	PATRICE MUNSEL	FRANK SINATRA	DATE WITH THE ANGELS	COLT .45	LOCAL
	CBS		LEAVE IT TO BEAVER	TRACKDOWN	ZANE GREY THEATER	MR. ADAMS AND EVE	SCHLITZ PLAYHOUSE	THE LINEUP	PERSON TO PERSON
	NBC		SABER OF LONDON	COURT OF LAST RESORT	LIFE OF RILEY	M SQUAD	THE THIN MAN		GILLETTE CAVALCADE OF SPORTS
SAT	ABC		KEEP IT IN THE FAMILY	OZARK (COUNTRY MUSIC) JUBILEE		THE LAWRENCE WELK SHOW		MIKE WALLACE INTERVIEW	LOCAL
	CBS		PERRY MASON		DICK AND THE DUCHESS	OH! SUSANNA	HAVE GUN WILL TRAVEL	GUNSMOKE	LOCAL
	NBC		PEOPLE ARE FUNNY	THE PERRY COMO SHOW		POLLY BERGEN / CLUB OASIS	GISELE MacKENZIE	WHAT'S IT FOR	YOUR HIT PARADE

NOTE: *Formerly Make Room for Daddy

1958–1959

Day	Net	7:00	7:30	8:00	8:30	9:00	9:30	10:00	10:30	11 PM
SUN	ABC	You Asked For It	Maverick	The Lawman		Colt .45	Encounter		Local	ABC
	CBS	Lassie	Jack Benny / Bachelor Father	The Ed Sullivan Show		G.E. Theater	Alfred Hitchcock	The $64,000 Question	What's My Line	CBS (10)
	NBC	Saber of London	Northwest Passage	The Steve Allen Show		The Dinah Shore Chevy Show		Loretta Young	Local	NBC
MON	ABC		Polka-Go-Round	Bold Journey		Voice of Firestone	Anybody Can Play	This Is Music	News	ABC
	CBS		Name That Tune	The Texan	Father Knows Best	Danny Thomas	Ann Sothern	Desilu Playhouse		CBS
	NBC		Tic Tac Dough	Restless Gun	Wells Fargo	Peter Gunn	Goodyear Th. / Alcoa Th.	Arthur Murray	Local	NBC
TUE	ABC		Cheyenne¹ / Sugarfoot		Wyatt Earp	The Rifleman	Naked City	Confession	News	ABC
	CBS		Burns & Allen	Keep Talking	To Tell the Truth	Arthur Godfrey	Red Skelton	The Garry Moore Show		CBS (3)
	NBC		Dragnet	The George Gobel Show / The Eddie Fisher Show		George Burns	Bob Cummings	Californians	Local	NBC
WED	ABC		Lawrence Welk's Little Band		Ozzie and Harriet	Donna Reed Show	Patti Page (Oldsmobile)	Wednesday Night Fights		ABC (4)
	CBS		Twilight Theater	Pursuit		Millionaire	I've Got a Secret	Armstrong Circle Theater / The U.S. Steel Hour		CBS (10/6)
	NBC		Wagon Train		Price Is Right	Milton Berle (Kraft Music H.)	Bat Masterson	This Is Your Life	Local	NBC
THU	ABC		Leave It to Beaver	Zorro	Real McCoys	Pat Boone	Rough Riders	Traffic Court	News	ABC
	CBS		I Love Lucy	December Bride	Yancy Derringer	Zane Grey Theater	Playhouse 90	DuPont Show of the Month		CBS
	NBC		Jefferson Drum	Ed Wynn Show	Twenty-One	Behind Closed Doors	Tennessee Ernie Ford	You Bet Your Life	Masquerade Party	NBC (7)
FRI	ABC		Rin Tin Tin	Walt Disney Presents²		Man with a Camera	77 Sunset Strip		News	ABC
	CBS		Your Hit Parade	Trackdown	Jackie Gleason	You'll Never Get Rich	Schlitz Playh. / Lux Playhouse	The Lineup	Person to Person	CBS (6)
	NBC		Buckskin	Ellery Queen		M Squad	The Thin Man	Gillette Cavalcade of Sports		NBC (11)
SAT	ABC		Dick Clark	Jubilee U.S.A.³		Lawrence Welk		Sammy Kaye's Music...	Local	ABC
	CBS		Perry Mason		Wanted: Dead or Alive	OH! Susanna	Have Gun Will Travel	Gunsmoke	Local	CBS
	NBC		People Are Funny	The Perry Como Show		Steve Canyon	Cimarron City		Brains and Brawn	NBC

NOTES: ¹Bronco episodes shown under Cheyenne title during 1958–1959 season   ²Formerly Disneyland   ³Formerly Ozark Jubilee

1959–1960

Day		7	7:30	8	8:30	9	9:30	10	10:30	11 PM
SUN	ABC	COLT .45 (3)	MAVERICK		THE LAWMAN (3)	THE REBEL (2)	THE ALASKANS		DICK CLARK'S WORLD OF TALENT	ABC
	CBS	LASSIE (6)	DENNIS THE MENACE	THE ED SULLIVAN SHOW		G.E. THEATER (12)	ALFRED HITCHCOCK (8)	JACK BENNY / GEO GOBEL (5)	WHAT'S MY LINE (*8)	11 — CBS
	NBC	RIVERBOAT		SPECIALS	THE CHEVY SHOW (DINAH SHORE AND GUEST HOSTS)			LORETTA YOUNG (3)	LOCAL (7)	NBC
MON	ABC		CHEYENNE		BOURBON STREET BEAT (5)		ADVENTURES IN PARADISE		MAN WITH A CAMERA (2)	2 — ABC
	CBS		MASQUERADE PARTY (*8)	THE TEXAN	FATHER KNOWS BEST (2)	DANNY THOMAS (6)	ANN SOTHERN (7)	HENNESEY (2)	JUNE ALLYSON	CBS
	NBC		RICHARD DIAMOND (*3)	LOVE & MARRIAGE (*3)	WELLS FARGO (4)	PETER GUNN (4)	GOODYEAR TH. / ALCOA TH. (9 / 4)	THE STEVE ALLEN SHOW		4 — NBC
TUE	ABC		SUGARFOOT BRONCO (3)		WYATT EARP (3)	THE RIFLEMAN (5)	PHILIP MARLOWE (2)	ONE STEP BEYOND (2)	KEEP TALKING (*2)	2 — ABC
	CBS		LOCAL	DENNIS O'KEEFE	DOBIE GILLIS	TIGHTROPE! (8)	RED SKELTON	THE GARRY MOORE SHOW (9)		2 — CBS
	NBC		LARAMIE		FIBBER McGEE AND MOLLY	ARTHUR MURRAY (10)	FORD STARTIME		LOCAL	NBC
WED	ABC		COURT OF LAST RESORT (*†)	CHARLEY WEAVER'S HOBBY LOBBY	OZZIE AND HARRIET (6)	HAWAIIAN EYE (8)	WEDNESDAY NIGHT FIGHTS		(5)	5 — ABC
	CBS		THE LINEUP		MEN INTO SPACE (3)	MILLIONAIRE	I'VE GOT A SECRET (8)	THE U.S. STEEL HOUR (8)	ARMSTRONG CIRCLE THEATER (7)	11 — CBS
	NBC		WAGON TRAIN		PRICE IS RIGHT (3)	THE PERRY COMO SHOW (THE KRAFT MUSIC HALL) (3)		THIS IS YOUR LIFE (5)	WICHITA TOWN (8)	NBC
THU	ABC		GALE STORM (OH! SUSANNA) (*4)		REAL McCOYS (2)	PAT BOONE (3)	THE UNTOUCHABLES (3)	TAKE A GOOD LOOK		ABC
	CBS		TO TELL THE TRUTH (4)	BETTY HUTTON	DONNA REED (2)	ZANE GREY THEATER	PLAYHOUSE 90 / THE BIG PARTY (4)			4 — CBS
	NBC		LAW OF THE PLAINSMAN (*3)	BAT MASTERSON (2)	STACCATO	BACHELOR FATHER (*3)	TENNESSEE ERNIE FORD (4)	YOU BET YOUR LIFE (2)	LAWLESS YEARS (10)	2 — NBC
FRI	ABC		WALT DISNEY PRESENTS (6)		MAN FROM BLACKHAWK (2)	77 SUNSET STRIP	THE DETECTIVES (2)		BLACK SADDLE (*2)	2 — ABC
	CBS		RAWHIDE (2)		HOTEL DE PAREE (2)	DESILU PLAYHOUSE		TWILIGHT ZONE (2)	PERSON TO PERSON (7)	7 — CBS
	NBC		PEOPLE ARE FUNNY (6)	TROUBLE-SHOOTERS	BELL TELEPHONE HOUR / SPECIALS (2)		M SQUAD (2)	GILLETTE CAVALCADE OF SPORTS (3)	(10)	12 — NBC
SAT	ABC		DICK CLARK (3)	HIGH ROAD (3)	LEAVE IT TO BEAVER (3)	THE LAWRENCE WELK SHOW (3)		JUBILEE U.S.A. (5)		6 — ABC
	CBS		PERRY MASON		WANTED: DEAD OR ALIVE (2)	MR. LUCKY (3)	HAVE GUN WILL TRAVEL	GUNSMOKE (3)	MARKHAM (5)	2 — CBS
	NBC		BONANZA		THE MAN AND THE CHALLENGE (3)	THE DEPUTY	FIVE FINGERS		IT COULD BE YOU (5)	2 — NBC

1960–1961

Day	Net	7	7:30	8	8:30	9	9:30	10	10:30	11 PM
SUN	ABC	WALT DISNEY PRESENTS	MAVERICK ••7		THE LAWMAN 4	THE REBEL 3	THE ISLANDERS 2		THE WALTER WINCHELL SHOW	ABC
SUN	CBS	LASSIE 7	DENNIS THE MENACE	THE ED SULLIVAN SHOW 7		G.E. THEATER 13	JACK BENNY 9	CANDID CAMERA 9	WHAT'S MY LINE 12	CBS
SUN	NBC	SHIRLEY TEMPLE THEATRE		NATIONAL VELVET	THE TAB HUNTER SHOW	THE DINAH SHORE CHEVY SHOW		LORETTA YOUNG 4	THIS IS YOUR LIFE 9	NBC
MON	ABC		CHEYENNE¹		SURFSIDE 6 — 6		ADVENTURES IN PARADISE 2		PETER GUNN * 3	ABC
MON	CBS		TO TELL THE TRUTH 5	PETE & GLADYS	BRINGING UP BUDDY 6	DANNY THOMAS 8	ANDY GRIFFITH	HENNESEY	FACE THE NATION 7	CBS
MON	NBC		RIVERBOAT 2		WELLS FARGO 2	KLONDIKE 5	DANTE	BARBARA STANWYCK SHOW	JACKPOT BOWLING (MILTON BERLE)	NBC
TUE	ABC		BUGS BUNNY	THE RIFLEMAN 3	WYATT EARP 3	STAGECOACH WEST 6		ONE STEP BEYOND 3	LOCAL	ABC
TUE	CBS		LOCAL	FATHER KNOWS BEST	DOBIE GILLIS 7	TOM EWELL SHOW 2	RED SKELTON	THE GARRY MOORE SHOW 10	— 3	CBS
TUE	NBC		LARAMIE 2		ALFRED HITCHCOCK 2	THRILLER • 6		SPECIALS³	— 3	NBC
WED	ABC		HONG KONG		OZZIE AND HARRIET 2	HAWAIIAN EYE 9		NAKED CITY 2	— 2	ABC
WED	CBS		THE AQUANAUTS		WANTED: DEAD OR ALIVE 3	MY SISTER EILEEN 3	I'VE GOT A SECRET	ARMSTRONG CIRCLE THEATER / THE U.S. STEEL HOUR 9	— 12 / 8	CBS
WED	NBC		WAGON TRAIN 4		PRICE IS RIGHT 4	THE PERRY COMO SHOW (THE KRAFT MUSIC HALL) 4		PETER LOVES MARY 6	LOCAL	NBC
THU	ABC		GUESTWARD HO! 3	DONNA REED 3	REAL McCOYS 3	MY THREE SONS 4	THE UNTOUCHABLES		TAKE A GOOD LOOK 2	ABC
THU	CBS		THE WITNESS		ZANE GREY THEATER	ANGEL 5	ANN SOTHERN 3	PERSON TO PERSON	JUNE ALLYSON 2	CBS
THU	NBC		THE OUTLAWS		BAT MASTERSON 3	BACHELOR FATHER 3	TENNESSEE ERNIE FORD 4	YOU BET YOUR LIFE 5	LOCAL 11	NBC
FRI	ABC		MATTY'S FUNDAY FUNNIES 2	HARRIGAN & SON 2	FLINTSTONES 3	77 SUNSET STRIP 4		THE DETECTIVES 3	THE LAW AND MR. JONES 2	ABC
FRI	CBS		RAWHIDE 3		ROUTE 66 3		MR. GARLUND 3	TWILIGHT ZONE 3	EYEWITNESS TO HISTORY 2	CBS
FRI	NBC		DAN RAVEN		THE WESTERNER 3	THE BELL TELEPHONE HOUR / SPECIALS		MICHAEL SHAYNE		NBC
SAT	ABC		THE ROARING TWENTIES		LEAVE IT TO BEAVER 4	THE LAWRENCE WELK SHOW 4		THE FIGHT OF THE WEEK³ 6		ABC
SAT	CBS		PERRY MASON		CHECKMATE 4		HAVE GUN WILL TRAVEL 4	GUNSMOKE 4	LOCAL 6	CBS
SAT	NBC		BONANZA 2		THE TALL MAN 2	THE DEPUTY 2		THE NATION'S FUTURE 2	LOCAL	NBC

NOTES: ¹Including episodes of *Bronco* and *Sugarfoot* ²Including *The Dow Hour of Great Mysteries* and NBC news specials ³Followed by *Make That Spare*

1961–1962

SUNDAY

Net	7:00	7:30	8:00	8:30	9:00	9:30	10:00	10:30	11 PM
ABC	MAVERICK	FOLLOW THE SUN ** 5		THE LAWMAN	BUS STOP 4		ADVENTURES IN PARADISE		3
CBS	LASSIE 8	DENNIS THE MENACE 8	THE ED SULLIVAN SHOW 3		G.E. THEATER 14	JACK BENNY 10	CANDID CAMERA 10	WHAT'S MY LINE 2	13
NBC	BULLWINKLE SHOW	WALT DISNEY'S WONDERFUL WORLD OF COLOR[1] * 8		CAR 54, WHERE ARE YOU * 8	BONANZA		THE DUPONT SHOW OF THE WEEK 3		2

MONDAY

Net	7:30	8:00	8:30	9:00	9:30	10:00	10:30	11 PM
ABC	CHEYENNE[2]		THE RIFLEMAN 7	SURFSIDE 6 4		BEN CASEY 2		3
CBS	TO TELL THE TRUTH 6	PETE & GLADYS 6	WINDOW ON MAIN STREET 2	DANNY THOMAS 9	ANDY GRIFFITH 2	HENNESEY 3	I'VE GOT A SECRET	10
NBC	LOCAL	NATIONAL VELVET 2	PRICE IS RIGHT 5	87TH PRECINCT		THRILLER		2

TUESDAY

Net	7:30	8:00	8:30	9:00	9:30	10:00	10:30	11 PM
ABC	BUGS BUNNY 2	BACHELOR FATHER	CALVIN AND THE COLONEL * 5	THE NEW BREED		ALCOA PREMIERE		3
CBS	MARSHAL DILLON ‡	DICK VAN DYKE ‡	DOBIE GILLIS 3	RED SKELTON 11	ICHABOD AND ME	THE GARRY MOORE SHOW 4		4
NBC	LARAMIE 3		ALFRED HITCHCOCK	THE DICK POWELL SHOW 7		CAIN'S HUNDRED		2

WEDNESDAY

Net	7:30	8:00	8:30	9:00	9:30	10:00	10:30	11 PM
ABC	THE NEW STEVE ALLEN SHOW		TOP CAT 3	HAWAIIAN EYE		NAKED CITY 3		3
CBS	THE ALVIN SHOW	FATHER KNOWS BEST ‡	CHECKMATE ‡		MRS. G. GOES TO COLLEGE 2	ARMSTRONG CIRCLE THEATER / THE U.S. STEEL HOUR		13 / 9
NBC	WAGON TRAIN		JOEY BISHOP 5	THE PERRY COMO SHOW (THE KRAFT MUSIC HALL)		BOB NEWHART 7	DAVID BRINKLEY'S JOURNAL	2

THURSDAY

Net	7:30	8:00	8:30	9:00	9:30	10:00	10:30	11 PM
ABC	OZZIE AND HARRIET 10		REAL McCOYS 4	MY THREE SONS 5	MARGIE 2	THE UNTOUCHABLES		3
CBS	FRONTIER CIRCUS		BOB CUMMINGS 2	THE INVESTIGATORS		CBS REPORTS		3
NBC	THE OUTLAWS		DOCTOR KILDARE 2		HAZEL	SING ALONG WITH MITCH		2

FRIDAY

Net	7:30	8:00	8:30	9:00	9:30	10:00	10:30	11 PM
ABC	STRAIGHTAWAY	THE HATHAWAYS	FLINTSTONES 4	77 SUNSET STRIP 2		TARGET: THE CORRUPTORS		4
CBS	RAWHIDE		ROUTE 66 4		FATHER OF THE BRIDE 2	TWILIGHT ZONE	EYEWITNESS TO HISTORY 3	2
NBC	INTERNATIONAL SHOWTIME		ROBERT TAYLOR'S DETECTIVES[3] 3		THE DINAH SHORE SHOW / THE BELL TELEPHONE HOUR * 3	FRANK McGEE: HERE AND NOW		5 / 4

SATURDAY

Net	7:30	8:00	8:30	9:00	9:30	10:00	10:30	11 PM
ABC	THE ROARING TWENTIES		LEAVE IT TO BEAVER 2	THE LAWRENCE WELK SHOW 5		THE FIGHT OF THE WEEK[4] 7		2
CBS	PERRY MASON		THE DEFENDERS 5		HAVE GUN WILL TRAVEL	GUNSMOKE 5		7
NBC	WELLS FARGO		THE TALL MAN 6	MOVIE 2				

NOTES: [1]Formerly *Walt Disney Presents* [2]Including episodes of *Bronco* [3]Formerly *The Detectives* [4]Followed by *Make That Spare*

1962–1963

Day		7	7:30	8	8:30	9	9:30	10	10:30	11 PM
SUN	ABC	FATHER KNOWS BEST	THE JETSONS *1	MOVIE				VOICE OF FIRESTONE	HOWARD K. SMITH 14	2
	CBS	LASSIE 9	DENNIS THE MENACE 4	THE ED SULLIVAN SHOW		REAL McCOYS 15	G.E. TRUE *6	CANDID CAMERA	WHAT'S MY LINE 3	14
	NBC	ENSIGN O'TOOLE		WALT DISNEY'S WONDERFUL WORLD OF COLOR 9	CAR 54, WHERE ARE YOU 2	BONANZA		THE DUPONT SHOW OF THE WEEK 4		2
MON	ABC		CHEYENNE 8		THE RIFLEMAN 5	STONEY BURKE		BEN CASEY		2
	CBS		TO TELL THE TRUTH 7	I'VE GOT A SECRET 11	THE LUCY SHOW	DANNY THOMAS 10	ANDY GRIFFITH 3	THE NEW LORETTA YOUNG SHOW	STUMP THE STARS	CBS
	NBC		IT'S A MAN'S WORLD		SAINTS AND SINNERS	PRICE IS RIGHT 6		DAVID BRINKLEY'S JOURNAL 2	LOCAL	NBC
TUE	ABC		COMBAT		HAWAIIAN EYE		THE UNTOUCHABLES		SPECIALS2 4	ABC
	CBS		MARSHAL DILLON *1	LLOYD BRIDGES	THE RED SKELTON SHOW	JACK BENNY 12		THE GARRY MOORE SHOW 11		5
	NBC		LARAMIE		EMPIRE 4		THE DICK POWELL SHOW	CHET HUNTLEY REPORTING 2		5
WED	ABC		WAGON TRAIN		GOING MY WAY *6		OUR MAN HIGGINS	NAKED CITY		4
	CBS		CBS REPORTS		DOBIE GILLIS 4	THE BEVERLY HILLBILLIES	DICK VAN DYKE 2	ARMSTRONG CIRCLE THEATER / THE U.S. STEEL HOUR		14 / 10
	NBC		THE VIRGINIAN			THE PERRY COMO SHOW (THE KRAFT MUSIC HALL)		THE ELEVENTH HOUR 8		NBC
THU	ABC		OZZIE AND HARRIET 11	DONNA REED 5	LEAVE IT TO BEAVER 5	MY THREE SONS 6	McHALE'S NAVY 3	ALCOA PREMIERE		2
	CBS		MISTER ED *3	PERRY MASON 3		THE NURSES		ALFRED HITCHCOCK		*8
	NBC		WIDE COUNTRY		DOCTOR KILDARE		HAZEL 2	THE ANDY WILLIAMS SHOW 2		NBC
FRI	ABC		THE GALLANT MEN		FLINTSTONES	I'M DICKENS, HE'S FENSTER 3	77 SUNSET STRIP		LOCAL 5	ABC
	CBS		RAWHIDE		ROUTE 66 5		FAIR EXCHANGE 3		EYEWITNESS	3
	NBC		INTERNATIONAL SHOWTIME		SING ALONG WITH MITCH 2		DON'T-CALL ME CHARLIE	THE JACK PAAR PROGRAM		NBC
SAT	ABC		ROY ROGERS & DALE EVANS SHOW			MR. SMITH GOES TO WASHINGTON	THE LAWRENCE WELK SHOW	THE FIGHT OF THE WEEK4 8		3
	CBS		JACKIE GLEASON'S AMERICAN SCENE MAGAZINE		THE DEFENDERS		HAVE GUN WILL TRAVEL 2	GUNSMOKE 6		8
	NBC		SAM BENEDICT		JOEY BISHOP 2	MOVIE				NBC

NOTES: 1Reruns of *Gunsmoke*. 2Including *Close-Up, Here's Edie* and *As Caesar Sees It*. 3Including one season in syndication. 4Followed by *Make That Spare*

1963–1964

Day	Net	7	7:30	8	8:30	9	9:30	10	10:30	11 PM
SUN	ABC	LOCAL	TRAVELS OF JAIMIE McPHEETERS		ARREST AND TRIAL			100 GRAND	ABC NEWS REPORT	
SUN	CBS	LASSIE 10	MY FAVORITE MARTIAN	THE ED SULLIVAN SHOW		THE JUDY GARLAND SHOW 16			CANDID CAMERA 4 / WHAT'S MY LINE	15
SUN	NBC	BILL DANA SHOW	WALT DISNEY'S WONDERFUL WORLD OF COLOR 10		GRINDL	BONANZA		THE DUPONT SHOW OF THE WEEK 5		3
MON	ABC		THE OUTER LIMITS		WAGON TRAIN		BREAKING POINT 7			
MON	CBS		TO TELL THE TRUTH 8	I'VE GOT A SECRET 12	THE LUCY SHOW 2	DANNY THOMAS	ANDY GRIFFITH 11	EAST SIDE, WEST SIDE 4		
MON	NBC		MOVIE			HOLLYWOOD AND THE STARS	SING ALONG WITH MITCH 4			
TUE	ABC		COMBAT		McHALE'S NAVY 2	THE GREATEST SHOW ON EARTH 2		THE FUGITIVE		
TUE	CBS		MARSHAL DILLON	THE RED SKELTON SHOW		PETTICOAT JUNCTION 13	JACK BENNY	THE GARRY MOORE SHOW 12		6
TUE	NBC		MR. NOVAK		REDIGO 2	THE RICHARD BOONE SHOW 2		THE BELL TELEPHONE HOUR 6 / THE ANDY WILLIAMS SHOW		2
WED	ABC		OZZIE AND HARRIET	PATTY DUKE SHOW 12	PRICE IS RIGHT *7	BEN CASEY		CHANNING 3		
WED	CBS		CBS REPORTS / CHRONICLE 5		GLYNIS	THE BEVERLY HILLBILLIES	DICK VAN DYKE 2	THE DANNY KAYE SHOW 3		
WED	NBC		THE VIRGINIAN			ESPIONAGE 2		THE ELEVENTH HOUR		2
THU	ABC		FLINTSTONES	DONNA REED 4	MY THREE SONS 6	THE JIMMY DEAN SHOW 4		SID CAESAR / HERE'S EDIE	LOCAL	
THU	CBS		PASSWORD 3	RAWHIDE		PERRY MASON 6		THE NURSES 7		2
THU	NBC		TEMPLE HOUSTON		DOCTOR KILDARE		HAZEL 3	KRAFT SUSPENSE THEATRE³ 3		
FRI	ABC		77 SUNSET STRIP		BURKE'S LAW 6		THE FARMER'S DAUGHTER 3	THE FIGHT OF THE WEEK⁴		4
FRI	CBS		THE GREAT ADVENTURE		ROUTE 66		TWILIGHT ZONE 4	ALFRED HITCHCOCK 5		9
FRI	NBC		INTERNATIONAL SHOWTIME		BOB HOPE PRESENTS THE CHRYSLER THEATER 3		HARRY'S GIRLS	THE JACK PAAR PROGRAM		2
SAT	ABC		HOOTENANNY		THE LAWRENCE WELK SHOW 2		THE JERRY LEWIS SHOW 9			‡
SAT	CBS		JACKIE GLEASON'S AMERICAN SCENE MAGAZINE		THE NEW PHIL SILVERS SHOW 2	THE DEFENDERS		GUNSMOKE 3		9
SAT	NBC		THE LIEUTENANT		JOEY BISHOP 3	MOVIE				

NOTES: ¹Reruns of *Gunsmoke* ²Formerly *Empire* ³*Kraft Music Hall* (Perry Como) every fourth week ⁴Followed by *Make That Spare*

1964–1965

Day	Net	7:00	7:30	8:00	8:30	9:00	9:30	10:00	10:30	11 PM
SUN	ABC	LOCAL	WAGON TRAIN		BROADSIDE (8)	MOVIE				ABC
SUN	CBS	LASSIE (11)	MY FAVORITE MARTIAN (17)	THE ED SULLIVAN SHOW (2)		MY LIVING DOLL	JOEY BISHOP	CANDID CAMERA (*4)	WHAT'S MY LINE (5)	CBS (16)
SUN	NBC	PROFILES IN COURAGE	WALT DISNEY'S WONDERFUL WORLD OF COLOR (**)		BILL DANA SHOW (11)	BONANZA (2)		THE ROGUES (6)		NBC
MON	ABC		VOYAGE TO THE BOTTOM OF THE SEA		NO TIME FOR SERGEANTS	WENDY AND ME	BING CROSBY	BEN CASEY (4)		ABC
MON	CBS		TO TELL THE TRUTH	I'VE GOT A SECRET (9)	ANDY GRIFFITH (13)	THE LUCY SHOW (5)	MANY HAPPY RETURNS (3)	SLATTERY'S PEOPLE		CBS
MON	NBC		90 BRISTOL COURT (KAREN; HARRIS AGAINST THE WORLD; TOM, DICK & MARY)			THE ANDY WILLIAMS SHOW² (*10)		ALFRED HITCHCOCK (3)		NBC
TUE	ABC		COMBAT (3)		McHALE'S NAVY (3)	THE TYCOON	PEYTON PLACE (I)	THE FUGITIVE (2)		ABC (2)
TUE	CBS		MARSHAL DILLON⁴	WORLD WAR ONE	THE RED SKELTON SHOW		PETTICOAT JUNCTION (14)	THE DOCTORS AND THE NURSES¹ (2)		CBS (3)
TUE	NBC		MR. NOVAK		THE MAN FROM U.N.C.L.E.		THAT WAS THE WK. THAT WAS (2)	THE BELL TELEPHONE HOUR / SPECIALS (2)		NBC (7)
WED	ABC		OZZIE AND HARRIET	PATTY DUKE SHOW (13)	SHINDIG (2)	MICKEY (2)	BURKE'S LAW		ABC SCOPE (2)	ABC
WED	CBS		CBS REPORTS		THE BEVERLY HILLBILLIES (6)	DICK VAN DYKE (3)	CARA WILLIAMS (4)	THE DANNY KAYE SHOW (2)		CBS (2)
WED	NBC		THE VIRGINIAN			MOVIE (3)				NBC
THU	ABC		FLINTSTONES (7)	DONNA REED (5)	MY THREE SONS	BEWITCHED (5)	PEYTON PLACE (II)	THE JIMMY DEAN SHOW		ABC (2)
THU	CBS		THE MUNSTERS	PERRY MASON		PASSWORD (8)	THE BAILEYS OF BALBOA (4)	THE DEFENDERS		CBS (4)
THU	NBC		DANIEL BOONE		DOCTOR KILDARE		HAZEL (4)	KRAFT SUSPENSE THEATRE³ (4)		NBC (2)
FRI	ABC		JONNY QUEST	THE FARMER'S DAUGHTER (2)	ADDAMS FAMILY (2)	VALENTINE'S DAY	TWELVE O'CLOCK HIGH (4)		LOCAL	ABC
FRI	CBS		RAWHIDE		THE ENTERTAINERS (7)	GOMER PYLE (10)	THE REPORTER			CBS
FRI	NBC		INTERNATIONAL SHOWTIME		BOB HOPE PRESENTS THE CHRYSLER THEATER (4)		JACK BENNY (*13)	THE JACK PAAR PROGRAM		NBC (3)
SAT	ABC		THE OUTER LIMITS		THE LAWRENCE WELK SHOW (2)		THE HOLLYWOOD PALACE (10)		LOCAL (2)	ABC (3)
SAT	CBS		JACKIE GLEASON'S AMERICAN SCENE MAGAZINE		GILLIGAN'S ISLAND (3)	MR. BROADWAY		GUNSMOKE		CBS (10)
SAT	NBC		FLIPPER	MR. MAGOO	KENTUCKY JONES	MOVIE				NBC

NOTES: ¹Formerly *The Nurses* ²Jonathan Winters specials once a month ³Kraft Music Hall (Perry Como) every fourth week ⁴Reruns of *Gunsmoke*

1965–1966

Day	Net	7:30	8:00	8:30	9:00	9:30	10:00	10:30	11 PM
SUN	ABC	VOYAGE TO THE BOTTOM OF THE SEA		THE F.B.I. 2	MOVIE				ABC
SUN	CBS	LASSIE 12	MY FAVORITE MARTIAN	THE ED SULLIVAN SHOW 3	PERRY MASON 18		CANDID CAMERA 9	WHAT'S MY LINE 6	CBS 17
SUN	NBC	BELL TEL. HR. **8 / SPECIALS	WALT DISNEY'S WONDERFUL WORLD OF COLOR 12	BRANDED 2	BONANZA 2		THE WACKIEST SHIP IN THE ARMY 7		NBC
MON	ABC	TWELVE O'CLOCK HIGH		THE LEGEND OF JESSE JAMES 2	A MAN CALLED SHENANDOAH	THE FARMER'S DAUGHTER 3	BEN CASEY 3		ABC 5
MON	CBS	TO TELL THE TRUTH 10	I'VE GOT A SECRET	THE LUCY SHOW 14	ANDY GRIFFITH 4	HAZEL 6	THE STEVE LAWRENCE SHOW *5		CBS
MON	NBC	HULLABALOO	JOHN FORSYTHE 2	DR. KILDARE (I)	THE ANDY WILLIAMS SHOW' 5		RUN FOR YOUR LIFE 4		NBC
TUE	ABC		COMBAT 4	McHALE'S NAVY 4	F TROOP 4	PEYTON PLACE (I)	THE FUGITIVE 2		ABC 3
TUE	CBS		RAWHIDE	THE RED SKELTON SHOW 8		PETTICOAT JUNCTION 15	CBS REPORTS / SPECIALS 3		CBS 7
TUE	NBC	MY MOTHER THE CAR	PLEASE DON'T EAT THE DAISIES	DR. KILDARE (II)	MOVIE 5				NBC
WED	ABC	OZZIE AND HARRIET	PATTY DUKE 14	GIDGET 3	THE BIG VALLEY		AMOS BURKE, SECRET AGENT 2		ABC 3
WED	CBS	LOST IN SPACE	THE BEVERLY HILLBILLIES 4	GREEN ACRES 4	DICK VAN DYKE	THE DANNY KAYE SHOW 5		CBS 3
WED	NBC	THE VIRGINIAN		BOB HOPE PRESENTS THE CHRYSLER THEATER 4		I SPY 3		NBC
THU	ABC	SHINDIG (I) 2	DONNA REED 8	O.K. CRACKERBY 8	BEWITCHED	PEYTON PLACE (II) 2	THE LONG HOT SUMMER 2		ABC
THU	CBS	THE MUNSTERS 2	GILLIGAN'S ISLAND 2	MY THREE SONS 2	MOVIE *6				CBS
THU	NBC	DANIEL BOONE	LAREDO 2						NBC
FRI	ABC	FLINTSTONES 6	TAMMY	ADDAMS FAMILY 2	HONEY WEST 2	MONA McCLUSKEY / PEYTON PLACE (III)	THE DEAN MARTIN SHOW		ABC 3
FRI	CBS	THE WILD, WILD WEST	HOGAN'S HEROES	GOMER PYLE 2	SLATTERY'S PEOPLE / THE SMOTHERS BROTHERS SHOW 2	THE JIMMY DEAN SHOW 2		CBS 2
FRI	NBC	CAMP RUNAMUCK	HANK	CONVOY	MR. ROBERTS	THE MAN FROM U.N.C.L.E.		NBC 2
SAT	ABC	SHINDIG (II) 2	KING FAMILY 2		THE LAWRENCE WELK SHOW 2	THE HOLLYWOOD PALACE 11	ABC SCOPE 3		ABC 2
SAT	CBS	THE JACKIE GLEASON SHOW 4		TRIALS OF O'BRIEN		GUNSMOKE	THE LONER		CBS 11
SAT	NBC	FLIPPER 2	I DREAM OF JEANNIE 2	GET SMART	MOVIE				NBC

NOTES: ¹Perry Como special every fourth week   ²Formerly *Burke's Law*

1966–1967

Day	Net	7:30	8:00	8:30	9:00	9:30	10:00	10:30	11 PM
SUN	ABC	VOYAGE TO THE BOTTOM OF THE SEA	THE F.B.I.		MOVIE				ABC
	CBS	LASSIE	IT'S ABOUT TIME	THE ED SULLIVAN SHOW	THE GARRY MOORE SHOW		CANDID CAMERA	WHAT'S MY LINE	CBS 18
	NBC	BELL TEL. HR. / SPECIALS	WALT DISNEY'S WONDERFUL WORLD OF COLOR	HEY LANDLORD	BONANZA		THE ANDY WILLIAMS SHOW		NBC 5
MON	ABC	IRON HORSE		RAT PATROL	FELONY SQUAD	PEYTON PLACE (I)	THE BIG VALLEY		ABC 2
	CBS	GILLIGAN'S ISLAND	RUN BUDDY RUN	THE LUCY SHOW	ANDY GRIFFITH	FAMILY AFFAIR	JEAN ARTHUR	I'VE GOT A SECRET	CBS 15
	NBC	THE MONKEES	I DREAM OF JEANNIE	ROGER MILLER	THE ROAD WEST		RUN FOR YOUR LIFE		NBC 2
TUE	ABC	COMBAT		THE ROUNDERS	THE PRUITTS OF SOUTHAMPTON	LOVE ON A ROOFTOP	THE FUGITIVE		ABC 4
	CBS	DAKTARI		THE RED SKELTON SHOW		PETTICOAT JUNCTION	CBS REPORTS / SPECIALS		CBS 8
	NBC	THE GIRL FROM U.N.C.L.E.		OCCASIONAL WIFE	MOVIE				NBC
WED	ABC	BATMAN (I)	THE MONROES		THE MAN WHO NEVER WAS	PEYTON PLACE (II)	ABC STAGE '67		ABC 4
	CBS	LOST IN SPACE		THE BEVERLY HILLBILLIES	GREEN ACRES	GOMER PYLE	THE DANNY KAYE SHOW		CBS 4
	NBC	THE VIRGINIAN			BOB HOPE PRESENTS THE CHRYSLER THEATER		I SPY		NBC 2
THU	ABC	BATMAN (II)	F TROOP	TAMMY GRIMES	BEWITCHED	THAT GIRL	HAWK		ABC
	CBS	JERICHO		MY THREE SONS	MOVIE				CBS
	NBC	DANIEL BOONE		STAR TREK		THE HERO	THE DEAN MARTIN SHOW		NBC 2
FRI	ABC	GREEN HORNET	THE TIME TUNNEL		THE MILTON BERLE SHOW		TWELVE O'CLOCK HIGH		ABC 3
	CBS	THE WILD, WILD WEST		HOGAN'S HEROES	MOVIE				CBS
	NBC	TARZAN		THE MAN FROM U.N.C.L.E.		T.H.E. CAT	LAREDO		NBC 2
SAT	ABC	SHANE		THE LAWRENCE WELK SHOW		THE HOLLYWOOD PALACE		ABC SCOPE	ABC 3
	CBS	THE JACKIE GLEASON SHOW		PISTOLS 'N' PETTICOATS	MISSION: IMPOSSIBLE		GUNSMOKE		CBS 12
	NBC	FLIPPER	PLS. DON'T EAT THE DAISIES	GET SMART	MOVIE				NBC

1967–1968

Day	Network	7	7:30	8	8:30	9	9:30	10	10:30	11 PM
SUN	ABC		VOYAGE TO THE BOTTOM OF THE SEA	THE F.B.I. 4		MOVIE 3				
SUN	CBS	LASSIE 14	GENTLE BEN	THE ED SULLIVAN SHOW		THE SMOTHERS BROTHERS 20		MISSION: IMPOSSIBLE 2		
SUN	NBC	AFL FOOTBALL 11	WALT DISNEY'S WONDERFUL WORLD OF COLOR		MOTHERS-IN-LAW 14	BONANZA		THE HIGH CHAPARRAL 9		
MON	ABC		COWBOY IN AFRICA		RAT PATROL 2	FELONY SQUAD 2	PEYTON PLACE (I)	THE BIG VALLEY 4		
MON	CBS		GUNSMOKE		THE LUCY SHOW 13	ANDY GRIFFITH 8	FAMILY AFFAIR 2	THE CAROL BURNETT SHOW 2		
MON	NBC		THE MONKEES 2	THE MAN FROM U.N.C.L.E.		THE DANNY THOMAS HOUR 4		I SPY 3		
TUE	ABC		GARRISON'S GORILLAS		THE INVADERS		N.Y.P.D. 2	THE HOLLYWOOD PALACE 5		
TUE	CBS		DAKTARI		THE RED SKELTON SHOW 3		GOOD MORNING WORLD 17	CBS REPORTS SPECIALS 9		
TUE	NBC		I DREAM OF JEANNIE	THE JERRY LEWIS SHOW 3		MOVIE				
WED	ABC		CUSTER		THE SECOND HUNDRED YEARS	MOVIE				
WED	CBS		LOST IN SPACE		THE BEVERLY HILLBILLIES 3	GREEN ACRES 5	HE & SHE 3	DUNDEE AND THE CULHANE		
WED	NBC		THE VIRGINIAN			THE KRAFT MUSIC HALL 6		RUN FOR YOUR LIFE 3		
THU	ABC			BATMAN 3	THE FLYING NUN 3	BEWITCHED 4	THAT GIRL 2	PEYTON PLACE (II) 2	GOOD COMPANY 4 / LOCAL	
THU	CBS		CIMARRON STRIP			MOVIE				
THU	NBC		DANIEL BOONE		IRONSIDE 4		DRAGNET 2	THE DEAN MARTIN SHOW 3		
FRI	ABC		OFF TO SEE THE WIZARD		HONDO		THE GUNS OF WILL SONNETT	JUDD FOR THE DEFENSE		
FRI	CBS		THE WILD WILD WEST		GOMER PYLE 3	MOVIE 4				
FRI	NBC		TARZAN		STAR TREK 2	ACCIDENTAL FAMILY 2		THE BELL TELEPHONE HOUR SPECIALS 10		
SAT	ABC		DATING GAME 2	NEWLYWED GAME 2	THE LAWRENCE WELK SHOW 2	IRON HORSE 13			ABC SCOPE 2	
SAT	CBS		THE JACKIE GLEASON SHOW		MY THREE SONS 6	HOGAN'S HEROES 8	PETTICOAT JUNCTION 3	MANNIX 5		
SAT	NBC		MAYA		GET SMART 3	MOVIE 3				

1968–1969

Day	7	7:30	8	8:30	9	9:30	10	10:30	11 PM	Net
SUN	LAND OF THE GIANTS		THE F.B.I.		MOVIE 4					ABC
	LASSIE 15	GENTLE BEN 2	THE ED SULLIVAN SHOW		THE SMOTHERS BROTHERS 21		MISSION: IMPOSSIBLE 3			CBS
	NEW ADVENTURES OF HUCK FINN	WALT DISNEY'S WONDERFUL WORLD OF COLOR		MOTHERS-IN-LAW 15	BONANZA 2		BEAUTIFUL PHYLLIS DILLER SHOW 10			NBC
MON		THE AVENGERS		PEYTON PLACE (I) 4	THE OUTCASTS 5		THE BIG VALLEY 4			ABC
		GUNSMOKE		HERE'S LUCY 14	MAYBERRY RFD 5	FAMILY AFFAIR 3	THE CAROL BURNETT SHOW 2			CBS
		I DREAM OF JEANNIE	LAUGH-IN 4		MOVIE 2					NBC
TUE		THE MOD SQUAD		IT TAKES A THIEF		N.Y.P.D. 2	THAT'S LIFE 2			ABC
		LANCER		THE RED SKELTON SHOW		DORIS DAY SHOW 18	60 MINUTES SPECIALS			CBS
		THE JERRY LEWIS SHOW	JULIA 2		MOVIE					NBC
WED		HERE COME THE BRIDES		PEYTON PLACE (II) 5	MOVIE 5					ABC
		DAKTARI		THE GOOD GUYS 4	THE BEVERLY HILLBILLIES	GREEN ACRES 4	THE JONATHAN WINTERS SHOW 2			CBS
		THE VIRGINIAN			THE KRAFT MUSIC HALL 7		THE OUTSIDER 2			NBC
THU		THE UGLIEST GIRL IN TOWN	THE FLYING NUN 2	BEWITCHED 5	THAT GIRL 5	JOURNEY TO THE UNKNOWN 3		LOCAL		ABC
		BLONDIE	HAWAII FIVE-O		MOVIE					CBS
		DANIEL BOONE	IRONSIDE 5		DRAGNET 2		THE DEAN MARTIN SHOW 3			NBC
FRI		OPERATION: ENTERTAINMENT		FELONY SQUAD 2	DON RICKLES 3	THE GUNS OF WILL SONNETT	JUDD FOR THE DEFENSE 2			ABC
		THE WILD WILD WEST		GOMER PYLE 4	MOVIE 5					CBS
		THE HIGH CHAPARRAL		THE NAME OF THE GAME 2			STAR TREK 3			NBC
SAT		DATING GAME 3	NEWLYWED GAME 3	THE LAWRENCE WELK SHOW 3		THE HOLLYWOOD PALACE 14		LOCAL 6		ABC
		THE JACKIE GLEASON SHOW	MY THREE SONS 7	HOGAN'S HEROES 9		PETTICOAT JUNCTION 4	MANNIX 6 2			CBS
		ADAM-12	GET SMART 4	THE GHOST & MRS. MUIR 4	MOVIE					NBC

1969–1970

Day	7	7:30	8	8:30	9	9:30	10	10:30	11 PM
SUN	LAND OF THE GIANTS		2 THE F.B.I.		5 MOVIE				ABC
	LASSIE 16	TO ROME WITH LOVE	THE ED SULLIVAN SHOW	22 THE LESLIE UGGAMS SHOW			MISSION: IMPOSSIBLE		4 CBS
	WILD KINGDOM 8	THE WONDERFUL WORLD OF DISNEY¹		16 BILL COSBY	BONANZA		11 THE BOLD ONES		NBC
MON			THE MUSIC SCENE	THE NEW PEOPLE				LOVE, AMERICAN STYLE	ABC
		GUNSMOKE		15 HERE'S LUCY	2 MAYBERRY RFD	2 DORIS DAY SHOW	THE CAROL BURNETT SHOW		3 CBS
		MY WORLD AND WELCOME TO IT	LAUGH-IN		3 MOVIE				NBC
TUE		THE MOD SQUAD		2 MOVIE			MARCUS WELBY, M.D.		ABC
		LANCER		2 THE RED SKELTON SHOW		19 THE GOVERNOR AND J.J.	60 MINUTES / SPECIALS		2 CBS
		I DREAM OF JEANNIE	5 THE DEBBIE REYNOLDS SHOW	JULIA	2 MOVIE: FIRST TUESDAY				1 2 NBC
WED		THE FLYING NUN	3 THE COURTSHIP OF EDDIE'S FATHER	ROOM 222	MOVIE				ABC
		THE GLEN CAMPBELL GOODTIME HOUR		2 THE BEVERLY HILLBILLIES	8 MEDICAL CENTER		HAWAII FIVE-O		2 CBS
		THE VIRGINIAN			8 THE KRAFT MUSIC HALL		3 THEN CAME BRONSON		NBC
THU			*2 THE GHOST & MRS. MUIR	4 THAT GIRL	4 BEWITCHED	6 THIS IS TOM JONES	2 IT TAKES A THIEF		3 ABC
			4 FAMILY AFFAIR	THE JIM NABORS HOUR	MOVIE				CBS
		DANIEL BOONE		6 IRONSIDE		3 DRAGNET	4 THE DEAN MARTIN SHOW		5 NBC
FRI		LET'S MAKE A DEAL	3 THE BRADY BUNCH	MR. DEEDS GOES TO TOWN		15 HERE COME THE BRIDES	2 JIMMY DURANTE PRESENTS THE LENNON SISTERS HOUR		ABC
		*5 GET SMART	2 THE GOOD GUYS	2 HOGAN'S HEROES	5 MOVIE				CBS
		THE HIGH CHAPARRAL		3 THE NAME OF THE GAME			2 BRACKEN'S WORLD		NBC
SAT		4 DATING GAME	4 NEWLYWED GAME		15 THE LAWRENCE WELK SHOW		15 THE HOLLYWOOD PALACE	7 LOCAL	ABC
		THE JACKIE GLEASON SHOW		8 MY THREE SONS	10 GREEN ACRES	5 PETTICOAT JUNCTION		7 MANNIX	3 CBS
		THE ANDY WILLIAMS SHOW		ADAM-12	2 MOVIE				NBC

NOTE: ¹Formerly *Walt Disney's Wonderful World of Color*

1970–1971

TV Prime-Time Network Schedule

Day	Net	7:00	7:30	8:00	8:30	9:00	9:30	10:00	10:30	11 PM
SUN	ABC	THE YOUNG REBELS		THE F.B.I.		MOVIE (6)			THE TIM CONWAY COMEDY HOUR	ABC
	CBS	LASSIE (17)	HOGAN'S HEROES (6)	THE ED SULLIVAN SHOW		GLEN CAMPBELL GOODTIME HOUR (23)		THE TIM CONWAY COMEDY HOUR (2)		CBS
	NBC	WILD KINGDOM (9)	THE WONDERFUL WORLD OF DISNEY (17)		BILL COSBY	BONANZA (2)		THE BOLD ONES (12)		NBC
MON	ABC		THE YOUNG LAWYERS		SILENT FORCE	NFL MONDAY NIGHT FOOTBALL				ABC
	CBS		GUNSMOKE (16)		HERE'S LUCY (16)	MAYBERRY RFD (3)	DORIS DAY SHOW (3)	THE CAROL BURNETT SHOW (3)		CBS
	NBC		RED SKELTON (*20)	LAUGH-IN		MOVIE (4)				NBC
TUE	ABC		THE MOD SQUAD		MOVIE (3)			MARCUS WELBY, M.D. (2)		ABC
	CBS		THE BEVERLY HILLBILLIES (9)	GREEN ACRES (9)	HEE HAW (6)	TO ROME WITH LOVE		60 MINUTES (3) / SPECIALS (2)		CBS
	NBC		THE DON KNOTTS SHOW		JULIA (3)	MOVIE / FIRST TUESDAY (3)				NBC
WED	ABC		THE COURTSHIP OF EDDIE'S FATHER	MAKE ROOM FOR GRANDDADDY (2)	ROOM 222 (2)	THE JOHNNY CASH SHOW (2)		DAN AUGUST† (2)		ABC
	CBS		THE STOREFRONT LAWYERS		THE GOVERNOR AND J.J. (2)	MEDICAL CENTER (2)		HAWAII FIVE-0 (2)		CBS
	NBC		THE MEN FROM SHILOH†			THE KRAFT MUSIC HALL (9)		FOUR-IN-ONE (McCLOUD / NIGHT GALLERY / PSYCHIATRIST / S.F. AIRPORT) (4)		NBC
THU	ABC		MATT LINCOLN		BEWITCHED (7)	BAREFOOT IN THE PARK	THE ODD COUPLE	THE IMMORTAL		ABC
	CBS		FAMILY AFFAIR (5)	THE JIM NABORS HOUR		MOVIE (2)				CBS
	NBC		THE FLIP WILSON SHOW		IRONSIDE		NANCY (4)	THE DEAN MARTIN SHOW (6)		NBC
FRI	ABC		THE BRADY BUNCH	NANNY AND THE PROFESSOR (2)	THE PARTRIDGE FAMILY	THAT GIRL	LOVE, AMERICAN STYLE (5)	THIS IS TOM JONES (2)		ABC
	CBS		THE INTERNS		HEADMASTER	MOVIE				CBS
	NBC		THE HIGH CHAPARRAL		THE NAME OF THE GAME (4)			BRACKEN'S WORLD (3)		NBC
SAT	ABC		LET'S MAKE A DEAL (4)	NEWLYWED GAME (4)	THE LAWRENCE WELK SHOW (5)		THE MOST DEADLY GAME (16)		LOCAL	ABC
	CBS		MISSION: IMPOSSIBLE		MY THREE SONS (5)	ARNIE (11)	THE MARY TYLER MOORE SHOW (16)	MANNIX (4)		CBS
	NBC		THE ANDY WILLIAMS SHOW (3)		ADAM-12 (2)	MOVIE (3)				NBC

NOTE: *Formerly The Virginian

1971–1972

Day	Network	7:00	7:30	8:00	8:30	9:00	9:30	10:00	10:30	11 PM
SUN	ABC	LOCAL	LOCAL	THE F.B.I.		MOVIE				7
	CBS	LOCAL	MOVIE	CADE'S COUNTY				LOCAL		
	NBC	LOCAL	THE WONDERFUL WORLD OF DISNEY	THE JIMMY STEWART SHOW (18)		BONANZA		THE BOLD ONES (13)		3
MON	ABC	LOCAL		NANNY AND THE PROFESSOR (3)	LOCAL	NFL MONDAY NIGHT FOOTBALL				2
	CBS	LOCAL		GUNSMOKE		HERE'S LUCY (17)	DORIS DAY SHOW (4)	MY THREE SONS (4)	ARNIE (12)	2
	NBC	LOCAL		LAUGH-IN		MOVIE (5)				
TUE	ABC	LOCAL	THE MOD SQUAD	MOVIE (4)				MARCUS WELBY, M.D.		3
	CBS	LOCAL	GLEN CAMPBELL GOODTIME HOUR	HAWAII FIVE-0 (3)		CANNON (4)			LOCAL	
	NBC	LOCAL	IRONSIDE	SARGE (5)		THE FUNNY SIDE			LOCAL	
WED	ABC	LOCAL		BEWITCHED	THE COURTSHIP OF EDDIE'S FATHER (8)	SMITH FAMILY (3)	SHIRLEY'S WORLD (2)	THE MAN AND THE CITY		
	CBS	LOCAL		THE CAROL BURNETT SHOW		MEDICAL CENTER (5)		MANNIX (3)		5
	NBC	LOCAL		ADAM-12	THE NBC MYSTERY MOVIE (McCLOUD[2]; COLUMBO; McMILLAN AND WIFE) (4)			NIGHT GALLERY[1]		2
THU	ABC	LOCAL		ALIAS SMITH AND JONES		LONGSTREET (2)		OWEN MARSHALL: COUNSELOR AT LAW		
	CBS	LOCAL		BEARCATS!		MOVIE	CBS REPORTS			‡
	NBC	LOCAL		THE FLIP WILSON SHOW		NICHOLS (2)		THE DEAN MARTIN SHOW		7
FRI	ABC	LOCAL		BRADY BUNCH (3)	THE PARTRIDGE FAMILY (3)	ROOM 222 (2)	THE ODD COUPLE (3)	LOVE, AMERICAN STYLE (2)		3
	CBS	LOCAL		THE CHICAGO TEDDY BEARS		O'HARA, UNITED STATES TREASURY		MOVIE		
	NBC	LOCAL		THE D.A.	MOVIE CHRONOLOG				LOCAL	
SAT	ABC	LOCAL		GETTING TOGETHER	MOVIE			THE PERSUADERS	‡	
	CBS	LOCAL		ALL IN THE FAMILY (2)	FUNNY FACE (2)	THE NEW DICK VAN DYKE SHOW	THE MARY TYLER MOORE SHOW (2)	MISSION: IMPOSSIBLE		6
	NBC	LOCAL		THE PARTNERS (2)	THE GOOD LIFE	MOVIE				

NOTE: ¹Formerly one segment of *Four-in-One*

Day	Net	7	7:30	8	8:30	9	9:30	10	10:30	11 PM
SUN	ABC	LOCAL	LOCAL	THE F.B.I.		8 MOVIE				ABC
	CBS	LOCAL	ANNA & THE KING	M*A*S*H	SANDY DUNCAN	THE NEW DICK VAN DYKE SHOW 2	MANNIX		6 LOCAL	CBS
	NBC	LOCAL	THE WONDERFUL WORLD OF DISNEY	THE NBC SUNDAY MYSTERY MOVIE (McCLOUD [3]; COLUMBO [2]; McMILLAN AND WIFE [2] & HEC RAMSEY) 19				NIGHT GALLERY	3 LOCAL	NBC
MON	ABC			THE ROOKIES		NFL MONDAY NIGHT FOOTBALL				3 ABC
	CBS			GUNSMOKE		18 HERE'S LUCY	5 DORIS DAY SHOW	5 THE NEW BILL COSBY SHOW		CBS
	NBC			LAUGH-IN		6 MOVIE				NBC
TUE	ABC			TEMPERATURES RISING	MOVIE			MARCUS WELBY, M.D.		4 ABC
	CBS			MAUDE	HAWAII FIVE-0		5 MOVIE			CBS
	NBC			BONANZA		14 THE BOLD ONES		4 NBC REPORTS[1] / AMERICA		NBC
WED	ABC			PAUL LYNDE SHOW	MOVIE			THE JULIE ANDREWS HOUR		ABC
	CBS			THE CAROL BURNETT SHOW		6 MEDICAL CENTER		4 CANNON		2 CBS
	NBC			ADAM-12	5 THE NBC WEDNESDAY MYSTERY MOVIE (BANACEK; COOL MILLION; MADIGAN)			SEARCH		NBC
THU	ABC			THE MOD SQUAD		5 THE MEN (ASSIGNMENT: VIENNA; THE DELPHI BUREAU; JIGSAW)		OWEN MARSHALL: COUNSELOR AT LAW		2 ABC
	CBS			THE WALTONS		MOVIE				CBS
	NBC			THE FLIP WILSON SHOW		3 IRONSIDE		6 THE DEAN MARTIN SHOW		8 NBC
FRI	ABC			BRADY BUNCH	4 THE PARTRIDGE FAMILY	3 ROOM 222	4 THE ODD COUPLE	3 LOVE, AMERICAN STYLE		4 ABC
	CBS			THE SONNY AND CHER COMEDY HOUR		2 MOVIE				CBS
	NBC			SANFORD & SON	2 THE LITTLE PEOPLE	GHOST STORY		BANYON		NBC
SAT	ABC			ALIAS SMITH AND JONES		3 THE STREETS OF SAN FRANCISCO		THE SIXTH SENSE		2 ABC
	CBS			ALL IN THE FAMILY	3 BRIDGET LOVES BERNIE	3 THE MARY TYLER MOORE SHOW	3 BOB NEWHART	MISSION: IMPOSSIBLE		7 CBS
	NBC			EMERGENCY!		2 MOVIE				NBC

KUNG FU

NOTE: *First Tuesday once a month*

1973–1974

Day	Net	7	7:30	8	8:30	9	9:30	10	10:30	11 PM
SUN	ABC	LOCAL	THE F.B.I.	MOVIE					LOCAL	ABC
	CBS	LOCAL	THE NEW PERRY MASON	MANNIX		BARNABY JONES			LOCAL	CBS
	NBC	LOCAL	THE WONDERFUL WORLD OF DISNEY	THE NBC SUNDAY MYSTERY MOVIE (McCLOUD [4]; COLUMBO [3]; McMILLAN AND WIFE [3]; HEC RAMSEY [2])					LOCAL	NBC
MON	ABC			THE ROOKIES		NFL MONDAY NIGHT FOOTBALL				ABC
	CBS			GUNSMOKE		HERE'S LUCY	THE NEW DICK VAN DYKE SHOW	MEDICAL CENTER		CBS
	NBC			LOTSA LUCK	DIANA	MOVIE				NBC
TUE	ABC			THE NEW TEMPERATURES RISING¹	MOVIE			MARCUS WELBY, M.D.		ABC
	CBS			MAUDE	HAWAII FIVE-O	MOVIE		HAWKINS / SHAFT		CBS
	NBC			CHASE		THE MAGICIAN		POLICE STORY		NBC
WED	ABC			BOB & CAROL & TED & ALICE	MOVIE			OWEN MARSHALL, COUNSELOR AT LAW / DOC ELLIOT		ABC
	CBS			THE SONNY AND CHER COMEDY HOUR		CANNON		KOJAK		CBS
	NBC			ADAM-12	THE NBC WEDNESDAY MYSTERY MOVIE (BANACEK [2]; FARADAY AND CO.; THE SNOOP SISTERS; TENAFLY)			LOVE STORY		NBC
THU	ABC			TOMA		KUNG FU		THE STREETS OF SAN FRANCISCO		ABC
	CBS			THE WALTONS		MOVIE				CBS
	NBC			THE FLIP WILSON SHOW		IRONSIDE		NBC FOLLIES		NBC
FRI	ABC			THE BRADY BUNCH	THE ODD COUPLE	ROOM 222	ADAM'S RIB	LOVE, AMERICAN STYLE		ABC
	CBS			CALUCCI'S DEPT.	ROLL OUT!	MOVIE				CBS
	NBC			SANFORD & SON	THE GIRL WITH SOMETHING EXTRA	NEEDLES AND PINS	BRIAN KEITH²	THE DEAN MARTIN COMEDY HOUR		NBC
SAT	ABC			THE PARTRIDGE FAMILY	MOVIE	THE SIX MILLION DOLLAR MAN		GRIFF		ABC
	CBS			ALL IN THE FAMILY	M*A*S*H	THE MARY TYLER MOORE SHOW	BOB NEWHART	THE CAROL BURNETT SHOW		CBS
	NBC			EMERGENCY!		MOVIE				NBC

NOTES: ¹Formerly *Temperatures Rising* ²Formerly *The Little People*

1974–1975

Day	Net	7	7:30	8	8:30	9	9:30	10	10:30	11 PM
SUN	ABC	LOCAL	LOCAL	THE SONNY COMEDY REVUE		MOVIE				ABC
	CBS	LOCAL	APPLE'S WAY	2 KOJAK		2 MANNIX			8 LOCAL	CBS
	NBC	LOCAL	THE WONDERFUL WORLD OF DISNEY	THE NBC SUNDAY MYSTERY MOVIE (McCloud [5]: COLUMBO [4]; McMILLAN AND WIFE [4]; AMY PRENTISS) 21					LOCAL	NBC
MON	ABC			THE ROOKIES		3 NFL MONDAY NIGHT FOOTBALL				5 ABC
	CBS			GUNSMOKE 20		MAUDE 3	RHODA	MEDICAL CENTER		6 CBS
	NBC			BORN FREE		MOVIE				NBC
TUE	ABC			HAPPY DAYS 2	MOVIE			MARCUS WE..BY, M.D.		6 ABC
	CBS			GOOD TIMES 2	M*A*S*H	3 HAWAII FIVE-0		7 BARNABY JONES		3 CBS
	NBC			ADAM-12 7	MOVIE			POLICE STORY		2 NBC
WED	ABC			THAT'S MY MAMA	MOVIE			GET CHRISTIE LOVE!		ABC
	CBS			SONS AND DAUGHTERS		CANNON		4 THE MANHUNTER		CBS
	NBC			LITTLE HOUSE ON THE PRAIRIE		LUCAS TANNER		PETROCELLI		NBC
THU	ABC			THE ODD COUPLE	5 PAPER MOON	THE STREETS OF SAN FRANCISCO		3 HARRY O		ABC
	CBS			THE WALTONS		3 MOVIE				CBS
	NBC			SIERRA		IRONSIDE		8 MOVIN' ON		NBC
FRI	ABC			KODIAK	THE SIX MILLION DOLLAR MAN		2 TEXAS WHEELERS	THE NIGHT STALKER		ABC
	CBS			PLANET OF THE APES		MOVIE				CBS
	NBC			SANFORD & SON	4 CHICO & THE MAN	THE ROCKFORD FILES		POLICE WOMAN		NBC
SAT	ABC			THE NEW LAND		KUNG FU		3 NAKIA		ABC
	CBS			ALL IN THE FAMILY	5 FRIENDS AND LOVERS	THE MARY TYLER MOORE SHOW	5 BOB NEWHART	3 THE CAROL BURNETT SHOW		8 CBS
	NBC			EMERGENCY!		4 MOVIE				NBC

1975–1976

Day	Net	7:00	7:30	8:00	8:30	9:00	9:30	10:00	10:30	11 PM
SUN	ABC	SWISS FAMILY ROBINSON		THE SIX MILLION DOLLAR MAN		MOVIE (3)				ABC
SUN	CBS	THREE FOR THE ROAD		CHER		KOJAK (2)		BRONK (2)		CBS
SUN	NBC	THE WONDERFUL WORLD OF DISNEY (22)		THE FAMILY HOLVAK		THE NBC SUNDAY MYSTERY MOVIE (McCLOUD [6]; COLUMBO [5]; McMILLAN AND WIFE [5]; McCOY)				NBC (6)
MON	ABC			BARBARY COAST		NFL MONDAY NIGHT FOOTBALL				ABC (6)
MON	CBS			RHODA (2)	PHYLLIS	ALL IN THE FAMILY	MAUDE (6)	MEDICAL CENTER (4)		CBS (7)
MON	NBC			THE INVISIBLE MAN		MOVIE				NBC
TUE	ABC			HAPPY DAYS (3)	WELCOME BACK, KOTTER	THE ROOKIES		MARCUS WELBY, M.D. (4)		ABC (7)
TUE	CBS			GOOD TIMES (3)	JOE AND SONS	SWITCH (2)		BEACON HILL		CBS
TUE	NBC			MOVIN' ON		POLICE STORY (2)		JOE FORRESTER (3)		NBC
WED	ABC			WHEN THINGS WERE ROTTEN	THAT'S MY MAMA	BARETTA (2)		STARSKY AND HUTCH (2)		ABC
WED	CBS			TONY ORLANDO AND DAWN		CANNON (2)		KATE McSHANE (5)		CBS
WED	NBC			LITTLE HOUSE ON THE PRAIRIE		DOCTORS HOSPITAL (2)		PETROCELLI		NBC (2)
THU	ABC			BARNEY MILLER (2)	ON THE ROCKS	THE STREETS OF SAN FRANCISCO		HARRY O (4)		ABC (2)
THU	CBS			THE WALTONS		MOVIE (4)				CBS
THU	NBC			THE MONTEFUSCOS	FAY	ELLERY QUEEN		MEDICAL STORY		NBC
FRI	ABC			MOBILE ONE		MOVIE		BARNABY JONES (8)		ABC
FRI	CBS			BIG EDDIE	M*A*S*H (4)	HAWAII FIVE-O (4)		BARNABY JONES (8)		CBS (4)
FRI	NBC			SANFORD & SON	CHICO & THE MAN (5)	THE ROCKFORD FILES (2)		POLICE WOMAN (2)		NBC (2)
SAT	ABC			SATURDAY NIGHT LIVE		S.W.A.T.		MATT HELM (2)		ABC (2)
SAT	CBS			THE JEFFERSONS	DOC (2)	THE MARY TYLER MOORE SHOW	BOB NEWHART (6)	THE CAROL BURNETT SHOW (4)		CBS (9)
SAT	NBC			EMERGENCY!		MOVIE (5)				NBC

1976–1977

Day	Net	7	7:30	8	8:30	9	9:30	10	10:30	11 PM
SUN	ABC	COS		THE SIX MILLION DOLLAR MAN		4 MOVIE			3 DELVECCHIO	ABC
	CBS	9 60 MINUTES		THE SONNY AND CHER SHOW		2 KOJAK				CBS
	NBC	THE WONDERFUL WORLD OF DISNEY		23 THE NBC SUNDAY MYSTERY MOVIE (McCLOUD [7]; COLUMBO [6]; McMILLAN¹ [8]; QUINCY)			THE BIG EVENT			NBC
MON	ABC			THE CAPTAIN & TENNILLE		NFL MONDAY NIGHT FOOTBALL				7 ABC
	CBS			RHODA	3 PHYLLIS	2 MAUDE	5 ALL'S FAIR	EXECUTIVE SUITE		CBS
	NBC			LITTLE HOUSE ON THE PRAIRIE		3 MOVIE				NBC
TUE	ABC			HAPPY DAYS	4 LAVERNE AND SHIRLEY	2 RICH MAN, POOR MAN—BOOK II		2 FAMILY		ABC
	CBS			TONY ORLANDO AND DAWN RAINBOW HOUR		3 M*A*S*H	5 ONE DAY AT A TIME	2 SWITCH		CBS
	NBC			BAA BAA BLACK SHEEP		3 POLICE WOMAN		POLICE STORY		4 NBC
WED	ABC			THE BIONIC WOMAN		2 BARETTA		3 CHARLIE'S ANGELS		ABC
	CBS			GOOD TIMES	4 BALL FOUR	ALL IN THE FAMILY	7 ALICE	THE BLUE KNIGHT		2 CBS
	NBC			THE PRACTICE	2 MOVIE			THE QUEST		NBC
THU	ABC			WELCOME BACK, KOTTER	2 BARNEY MILLER	3 TONY RANDALL	NANCY WALKER	THE STREETS OF SAN FRANCISCO		6 ABC
	CBS			THE WALTONS		5 HAWAII FIVE-O		9 BARNABY JONES		5 CBS
	NBC			GEMINI MAN		BEST SELLERS		VAN DYKE AND COMPANY		NBC
FRI	ABC			DONNY AND MARIE		2 MOVIE				ABC
	CBS			SPENCER'S PILOTS		MOVIE				CBS
	NBC			SANFORD & SON	6 CHICO & THE MAN	3 THE ROCKFORD FILES		3 SERPICO		NBC
SAT	ABC			HOLMES & YOYO	MR. T AND TINA	STARSKY AND HUTCH		2 MOST WANTED		ABC
	CBS			THE JEFFERSONS	3 DOC	2 THE MARY TYLER MOORE SHOW	7 BOB NEWHART	5 THE CAROL BURNETT SHOW		10 CBS
	NBC			EMERGENCY!		6 MOVIE				NBC

NOTE: ¹Formerly *McMillan and Wife*

1977–1978

Day	Network	7:00	7:30	8:00	8:30	9:00	9:30	10:00	10:30
SUN	ABC	THE HARDY BOYS/ NANCY DREW MYSTERIES		THE SIX MILLION DOLLAR MAN		MOVIE			
SUN	CBS	60 MINUTES		RHODA	ON OUR OWN	ALL IN THE FAMILY	ALICE	KOJAK	
SUN	NBC	THE WONDERFUL WORLD OF DISNEY		THE BIG EVENT					
MON	ABC			THE SAN PEDRO BEACH BUMS		NFL MONDAY NIGHT FOOTBALL			
MON	CBS			YOUNG DAN'L BOONE		BETTY WHITE	MAUDE	RAFFERTY	
MON	NBC			LITTLE HOUSE ON THE PRAIRIE		MOVIE			
TUE	ABC			HAPPY DAYS	LAVERNE AND SHIRLEY	THREE'S COMPANY	SOAP	FAMILY	
TUE	CBS			THE FITZPATRICKS		M*A*S*H	ONE DAY AT A TIME	LOU GRANT	
TUE	NBC			THE RICHARD PRYOR SHOW		MULLIGAN'S STEW		POLICE WOMAN	
WED	ABC			EIGHT IS ENOUGH		CHARLIE'S ANGELS		BARETTA	
WED	CBS			GOOD TIMES	BUSTING LOOSE	MOVIE			
WED	NBC			THE LIFE AND TIMES OF GRIZZLY ADAMS		THE OREGON TRAIL		BIG HAWAII	
THU	ABC			WELCOME BACK, KOTTER	WHAT'S HAPPENING!!	BARNEY MILLER	CARTER COUNTRY	THE REDD FOXX COMEDY HOUR	
THU	CBS			THE WALTONS		HAWAII FIVE-0		BARNABY JONES	
THU	NBC			CHIPS		THE MAN FROM ATLANTIS		ROSETTI AND RYAN	
FRI	ABC			DONNY AND MARIE		MOVIE			
FRI	CBS			WONDER WOMAN		LOGAN'S RUN		SWITCH	
FRI	NBC			SANFORD ARMS	CHICO & THE MAN	THE ROCKFORD FILES		QUINCY	
SAT	ABC			FISH	OPERATION PETTICOAT	STARSKY AND HUTCH		THE LOVE BOAT	
SAT	CBS			BOB NEWHART	WE'VE GOT EACH OTHER	THE JEFFERSONS	TONY RANDALL	THE CAROL BURNETT SHOW	
SAT	NBC			THE BIONIC WOMAN		MOVIE			

1978–1979

		7	7:30	8	8:30	9	9:30	10	10:30	11 PM
SUN	ABC	THE HARDY BOYS MYSTERIES		3 BATTLESTAR GALACTICA		MOVIE		3 KAZ		9 ABC
	CBS	60 MINUTES		11 MARY		ALL IN THE FAMILY	9 ALICE			9 CBS
	NBC	THE WONDERFUL WORLD OF DISNEY		25 THE BIG EVENT (I)				2 LIFELINE		2 NBC
MON	ABC			WELCOME BACK, KOTTER	4 OPERATION PETTICOAT	2 NFL MONDAY NIGHT FOOTBALL				9 ABC
	CBS			WKRP IN CINCINNATI	PEOPLE	M*A*S*H	7 ONE DAY AT A TIME	4 LOU GRANT		2 CBS
	NBC			LITTLE HOUSE ON THE PRAIRIE		5 MOVIE				NBC
TUE	ABC			HAPPY DAYS	6 LAVERNE AND SHIRLEY	THREE'S COMPANY	3 TAXI	4 STARSKY AND HUTCH		4 ABC
	CBS			THE PAPER CHASE		MOVIE				CBS
	NBC			GRANDPA GOES TO WASHINGTON		THE BIG EVENT (II)				2 NBC
WED	ABC			EIGHT IS ENOUGH		3 CHARLIE'S ANGELS		3 VEGAS		ABC
	CBS			THE JEFFERSONS	5 IN THE BEGINNING	MOVIE				CBS
	NBC			DICK CLARK'S LIVE WEDNESDAY		MOVIE				NBC
THU	ABC			MORK & MINDY	WHAT'S HAPPENING!!	3 BARNEY MILLER	5 SOAP	2 FAMILY		4 ABC
	CBS			THE WALTONS		7 HAWAII FIVE-0		11 BARNABY JONES		7 CBS
	NBC			PROJECT U.F.O.		2 QUINCY		3 W.E.B.		NBC
FRI	ABC			DONNY AND MARIE		4 MOVIE		2 FLYING HIGH		ABC
	CBS			WONDER WOMAN		3 THE INCREDIBLE HULK		5 THE EDDIE CAPRA MYSTERIES		CBS
	NBC			THE WAVERLY WONDERS	WHO'S WATCHING THE KIDS	THE ROCKFORD FILES				NBC
SAT	ABC			CARTER COUNTRY	2 APPLE PIE	THE LOVE BOAT		2 FANTASY ISLAND		2 ABC
	CBS			RHODA	5 GOOD TIMES	6 THE AMERICAN GIRLS		DALLAS		2 CBS
	NBC			CHIPS		2 SPECIALS		SWORD OF JUSTICE		NBC

1979–1980

Day	Net	7:00	7:30	8:00	8:30	9:00	9:30	10:00	10:30	11 PM
SUN	ABC	OUT OF THE BLUE	A NEW KIND OF FAMILY	MORK & MINDY (2)	THE ASSOCIATES (2)	MOVIE				
SUN	CBS	60 MINUTES		ARCHIE BUNKER'S PLACE¹ (12)	ONE DAY AT A TIME (10)	ALICE (5)	THE JEFFERSONS (4)	TRAPPER JOHN, M.D. (6)		
SUN	NBC		DISNEY'S WONDERFUL WORLD	THE BIG EVENT (26)				PRIME TIME SUNDAY (3)		
MON	ABC			NFL MONDAY NIGHT FOOTBALL						10
MON	CBS			240-ROBERT	THE WHITE SHADOW	M*A*S*H (2)	WKRP IN CINCINNATI (8)	LOU GRANT (2)		3
MON	NBC			LITTLE HOUSE ON THE PRAIRIE		MOVIE (6)				
TUE	ABC			HAPPY DAYS (7)	ANGIE (7)	THREE'S COMPANY (2)	TAXI (4)	THE LAZARUS SYNDROME (2)		
TUE	CBS			CALIFORNIA FEVER		MOVIE				
TUE	NBC			THE MISADVENTURES OF SHERIFF LOBO		MOVIE				
WED	ABC			EIGHT IS ENOUGH		CHARLIE'S ANGELS (4)		VEGA$ (4)		2
WED	CBS			THE LAST RESORT	STRUCK BY LIGHTNING	MOVIE				
WED	NBC			REAL PEOPLE (2)		DIFF'RENT STROKES (2)	HELLO, LARRY (2)	THE BEST OF SATURDAY NIGHT LIVE² (2)		
THU	ABC			LAVERNE AND SHIRLEY	BENSON (5)	BARNEY MILLER (6)	SOAP (3)	20/20 (3)		2
THU	CBS			THE WALTONS		HAWAII FIVE-O (8)		BARNABY JONES (12)		8
THU	NBC			BUCK ROGERS IN THE 25TH CENTURY		QUINCY (8)		KATE LOVES A MYSTERY (4)		2
FRI	ABC			FANTASY ISLAND		MOVIE (3)				
FRI	CBS			THE INCREDIBLE HULK		THE DUKES OF HAZZARD (3)		DALLAS (2)		3
FRI	NBC			SHIRLEY		THE ROCKFORD FILES		EISCHIED (6)		
SAT	ABC			THE ROPERS (2)	DETECTIVE SCHOOL (2)	THE LOVE BOAT		HART TO HART (3)		
SAT	CBS			WORKING STIFFS (2)	THE BAD NEWS BEARS	BIG SHAMUS, LITTLE SHAMUS (2)		PARIS		
SAT	NBC			CHIPS		BJ AND THE BEAR (3)		A MAN CALLED SLOANE (2)		

NOTES: ¹Formerly All in the Family ²Reruns of NBC's Saturday Night Live

1980–1981

Day	Net	7	7:30	8	8:30	9	9:30	10	10:30	11 PM
SUN	ABC 4	THOSE AMAZING ANIMALS		CHARLIE'S ANGELS 13		MOVIE 5				
SUN	CBS 2		60 MINUTES	ARCHIE BUNKER'S PLACE 11	ONE DAY AT A TIME	ALICE 6	JEFFERSONS 5	TRAPPER JOHN, M.D. 7		
SUN	NBC		DISNEY'S WONDERFUL WORLD 27			THE BIG EVENT 4				
MON	ABC 11			THAT'S INCREDIBLE 2		NFL MONDAY NIGHT FOOTBALL				
MON	CBS 4			FLO 2	LADIES' MAN	M*A*S*H 9	HOUSE CALLS 2	LOU GRANT 4		
MON	NBC			LITTLE HOUSE ON THE PRAIRIE 7		MOVIE				
TUE	ABC 2			HAPPY DAYS 8	LAVERNE & SHIRLEY	THREE'S COMPANY 6	TOO CLOSE FOR COMFORT 5	HART TO HART		
TUE	CBS			THE WHITE SHADOW 3		MOVIE 3				
TUE	NBC			LOBO [1] 2		BJ AND THE BEAR 2		FLAMINGO ROAD 3		
WED	ABC 3			EIGHT IS ENOUGH 5		TAXI 5	SOAP 3	VEGA$ 4		
WED	CBS			ENOS		MOVIE				
WED	NBC 5			REAL PEOPLE 3		DIFF'RENT STROKES 3	THE FACTS OF LIFE 3	QUINCY 2		
THU	ABC 3			MORK & MINDY 3	BOSOM BUDDIES	BARNEY MILLER 7	IT'S A LIVING	20/20		
THU	CBS 2			THE WALTONS		MAGNUM, P.I. 9		KNOTS LANDING		
THU	NBC			BUCK ROGERS		MOVIE 2				
FRI	ABC 4			BENSON 2	I'M A BIG GIRL NOW	MOVIE				
FRI	CBS			THE INCREDIBLE HULK		THE DUKES OF HAZZARD 4		DALLAS 3		
FRI	NBC			HARPER VALLEY PTA	SANFORD	NERO WOLFE 2		NBC MAGAZINE		
SAT	ABC 4			BREAKING AWAY		THE LOVE BOAT		FANTASY ISLAND 4		
SAT	CBS			WKRP IN CINCINNATI 3	THE TIM CONWAY SHOW	FREEBIE AND THE BEAN 2		SECRETS OF MIDLAND HTS.		
SAT	NBC			BARBARA MANDRELL & THE MANDRELL SISTERS		WALKING TALL		HILL STREET BLUES		

NOTES: 1 Formerly *The Misadventures of Sheriff Lobo.*

Special Note: A strike by the Screen Actors Guild forced the postponement of many series; some shows did not begin until early in 1981

1981–1982

Day	Net	7:00	7:30	8:00	8:30	9:00	9:30	10:00	10:30	11 PM
SUN	ABC	CODE RED		TODAY'S FBI		MOVIE				ABC
	CBS	60 MINUTES 14		ARCHIE BUNKER'S PLACE 12	ONE DAY AT A TIME	ALICE 7	JEFFERSONS 6	TRAPPER JOHN, M.D. 8		CBS 3
	NBC	FLINTSTONES	HERE'S BOOMER 3	CHiPs 5		MOVIE				NBC
MON	ABC		SPECIALS	THAT'S INCREDIBLE 3		NFL MONDAY NIGHT FOOTBALL 3				ABC 12
	CBS			PRIVATE BENJAMIN 2	THE TWO OF US	M*A*S*H 2	HOUSE CALLS 10	LOU GRANT 3		CBS 5
	NBC			LITTLE HOUSE ON THE PRAIRIE 8		MOVIE				NBC
TUE	ABC			HAPPY DAYS 9	LAVERNE & SHIRLEY	THREE'S COMPANY 7	TOO CLOSE FOR COMFORT 6	HART TO HART 2		ABC 3
	CBS			SIMON & SIMON		MOVIE				CBS
	NBC			FATHER MURPHY		BRET MAVERICK 2		FLAMINGO ROAD		NBC 2
WED	ABC			GREATEST AMERICAN HERO 2		THE FALL GUY		DYNASTY		ABC 2
	CBS			MR. MERLIN 4	WKRP IN CINCINNATI	NURSE 4		SHANNON 2		CBS
	NBC			REAL PEOPLE 4		THE FACTS OF LIFE 4	LOVE, SIDNEY 3	QUINCY		NBC 6
THU	ABC			MORK & MINDY 4	BEST OF THE WEST	BARNEY MILLER 8	TAXI 3	20/20 4		ABC 4
	CBS			MAGNUM, P.I.		KNOTS LANDING 2		JESSICA NOVAK 3		CBS
	NBC			HARPER VALLEY 1	LEWIS & CLARK 2	DIFF'RENT STROKES 2	GIMME A BREAK 4	HILL STREET BLUES 3		NBC 2
FRI	ABC			BENSON 3	BOSOM BUDDIES	DARKROOM 2		STRIKE FORCE		ABC
	CBS			THE DUKES OF HAZZARD		DALLAS 4		FALCON CREST 5		CBS
	NBC			NBC MAGAZINE 2		McCLAIN'S LAW 2		SPECIALS / CASSIE & CO. 5		NBC
SAT	ABC			MAGGIE 3	MAKING A LIVING 2	THE LOVE BOAT 2		FANTASY ISLAND 5		ABC 5
	CBS			WALT DISNEY 3		MOVIE 28				CBS
	NBC			BARBARA MANDRELL & THE MANDRELL SISTERS 2		THE NASHVILLE PALACE 2		FITZ & BONES	BILLY CRYSTAL: TELEVISION: INSIDE AND OUT	NBC

NOTES: 1 Formerly Harper Valley P.T.A. 2 Formerly It's a Living. 3 Formerly Disney's Wonderful World.

1982–1983

Day	Net	7:30	8	8:30	9	9:30	10	10:30	11 PM
SUN	ABC	RIPLEY'S BELIEVE IT OR NOT	MATT HOUSTON		MOVIE				
	CBS	60 MINUTES 15	ARCHIE BUNKER'S PLACE 13	GLORIA	JEFFERSONS 9	ONE DAY AT A TIME	TRAPPER JOHN, M.D. 8		4
	NBC	VOYAGERS!	CHiPs 6		MOVIE				
MON	ABC		THAT'S INCREDIBLE 4		NFL MONDAY NIGHT FOOTBALL				13
	CBS		SQUARE PEGS 3	PRIVATE BENJAMIN 11	M*A*S*H	NEWHART	CAGNEY & LACEY		2
	NBC		LITTLE HOUSE: A NEW BEGINNING 1 9		MOVIE				
TUE	ABC		HAPPY DAYS 10	LAVERNE & SHIRLEY	THREE'S COMPANY 8	9 TO 5 7	HART TO HART 2		4
	CBS		BRING 'EM BACK ALIVE		MOVIE				
	NBC		FATHER MURPHY		GAVILAN 2				
WED	ABC		TALES OF THE GOLD MONKEY		THE FALL GUY		DYNASTY 2		3
	CBS		SEVEN BRIDES FOR SEVEN BROTHERS		ALICE 5	FILTHY RICH 7	TUCKER'S WITCH		CBS
	NBC		REAL PEOPLE		THE FACTS OF LIFE 5	FAMILY TIES 4	QUINCY		7
THU	ABC		JOANIE LOVES CHACHI 2	STAR OF THE FAMILY	TOO CLOSE FOR COMFORT 3	IT TAKES TWO 3	20/20		5
	CBS		MAGNUM, P.I.		SIMON & SIMON 3		KNOTS LANDING 2		4
	NBC		FAME		CHEERS 2	TAXI*	HILL STREET BLUES 5		3
FRI	ABC		BENSON 4	THE NEW ODD COUPLE	GREATEST AMERICAN HERO		THE QUEST 3		ABC
	CBS		THE DUKES OF HAZZARD		DALLAS 5		FALCON CREST 6		2
	NBC		THE POWERS OF MATTHEW STAR		KNIGHT RIDER		REMINGTON STEELE		NBC
SAT	ABC		T.J. HOOKER		THE LOVE BOAT 2		FANTASY ISLAND 6		6
	CBS		WALT DISNEY 29		MOVIE				CBS
	NBC		DIFF'RENT STROKES	SILVER SPOONS 5	GIMME A BREAK	LOVE, SIDNEY 2	THE DEVLIN CONNECTION		NBC

NOTES: 1 Formerly *Little House on the Prairie*.

1983–1984

Day	Net	7	7:30	8	8:30	9	9:30	10	10:30	11 PM
SUN	ABC	RIPLEY'S BELIEVE IT OR NOT (2)		HARDCASTLE & McCORMICK (2)		MOVIE				ABC
	CBS	60 MINUTES		ALICE (16)	ONE DAY AT A TIME (8)	JEFFERSONS (9)	GOODNIGHT BEANTOWN (10)	TRAPPER JOHN, M.D. (2)		(5) CBS
	NBC	FIRST CAMERA (1)		KNIGHT RIDER (2)		MOVIE (2)				NBC
MON	ABC			THAT'S INCREDIBLE (5)		NFL MONDAY NIGHT FOOTBALL				ABC
	CBS			SCARECROW & MRS. KING		AFTERMASH (2)	NEWHART	EMERALD POINT N.A.S. (2)		CBS
	NBC			BOONE		MOVIE				NBC
TUE	ABC			JUST OUR LUCK (11)	HAPPY DAYS	THREE'S COMPANY (8)	OH MADELINE	HART TO HART (2)		(5) ABC
	CBS			THE MISSISSIPPI (2)		MOVIE				CBS
	NBC			THE A TEAM (2)		REMINGTON STEELE (2)		BAY CITY BLUES		NBC
WED	ABC			THE FALL GUY (3)		DYNASTY (3)		HOTEL (4)		ABC
	CBS			WHIZ KIDS		MOVIE				CBS
	NBC			REAL PEOPLE (6)		THE FACTS OF LIFE (6)	FAMILY TIES (5)	ST. ELSEWHERE (2)		(2) NBC
THU	ABC			TRAUMA CENTER (3)		9 TO 5 (3)	IT'S NOT EASY	20/20		(6) ABC
	CBS			MAGNUM, P.I. (4)		SIMON & SIMON		KNOTS LANDING (3)		(5) CBS
	NBC			GIMME A BREAK (3)	MAMA'S FAMILY (2)	WE GOT IT MADE (2)	CHEERS	HILL STREET BLUES (2)		(4) NBC
FRI	ABC			BENSON (5)	WEBSTER	LOTTERY (2)		MATT HOUSTON		(2) ABC
	CBS			THE DUKES OF HAZZARD		DALLAS (6)		FALCON CREST (7)		(3) CBS
	NBC			MR. SMITH	JENNIFER SLEPT HERE	MANIMAL		FOR LOVE AND HONOR		NBC
SAT	ABC			T.J. HOOKER		THE LOVE BOAT (3)		FANTASY ISLAND (7)		(7) ABC
	CBS			CUTTER TO HOUSTON		MOVIE				CBS
	NBC			DIFF'RENT STROKES (6)	SILVER SPOONS (3)	THE ROUSTERS (3)		THE YELLOW ROSE		NBC

NOTES: 1 Formerly *Monitor.*

1984–1985

Day	7	7:30	8	8:30	9	9:30	10	10:30	11 PM	Net
SUN	RIPLEY'S BELIEVE IT OR NOT 3		HARDCASTLE & McCORMICK 2		MOVIE 2					ABC
SUN	60 MINUTES 17		MURDER, SHE WROTE		JEFFERSONS 11	ALICE	TRAPPER JOHN, M.D. 9		6	CBS
SUN	SILVER SPOONS 3	PUNKY BREWSTER	KNIGHT RIDER 3		MOVIE					NBC
MON			CALL TO GLORY		NFL MONDAY NIGHT FOOTBALL				15	ABC
MON			SCARECROW & MRS. KING		KATE & ALLIE 2	NEWHART 3	CAGNEY & LACEY		4	CBS
MON			TV'S BLOOPERS & PRACTICAL JOKES		MOVIE 2					NBC
TUE			FOUL-UPS, BLEEPS & 2	THREE'S A CROWD	PAPER DOLLS		JESSIE			ABC
TUE			AFTERMASH 2	E/R	MOVIE					CBS
TUE			A-TEAM 3		RIPTIDE 3		REMINGTON STEELE 2			NBC
WED			FALL GUY 4		DYNASTY		HOTEL 5			ABC
WED			CHARLES IN CHARGE	DREAMS	MOVIE					CBS
WED			HIGHWAY TO HEAVEN		FACTS OF LIFE 6	IT'S YOUR MOVE	ST. ELSEWHERE 3			NBC
THU			PEOPLE DO THE CRAZIEST THINGS	WHO'S THE BOSS	GLITTER		20/20 7			ABC
THU			MAGNUM, P.I. 5		SIMON & SIMON 4		KNOTS LANDING 6			CBS
THU			COSBY	FAMILY TIES	CHEERS 3	NIGHT COURT 2	HILL STREET BLUES 5			NBC
FRI			BENSON 6	WEBSTER 2	HAWAIIAN HEAT		MATT HOUSTON 3			ABC
FRI			DUKES OF HAZZARD 7		DALLAS 8		FALCON CREST 4			CBS
FRI			>	V	HUNTER 4		MIAMI VICE			NBC
SAT			T.J. HOOKER 4		LOVE BOAT 8		FINDER OF LOST LOVES 8			ABC
SAT			AIRWOLF 2		MIKE HAMMER 2		COVER UP 2			CBS
SAT			DIFFRENT STROKES 7	GIMME A BREAK 4	PARTNERS IN CRIME 4		HOT PURSUIT			NBC

	7	7:30	8	8:30	9	9:30	10	10:30	11 PM	
SUN	RIPLEY'S BELIEVE IT OR NOT	4	**MacGYVER**		MOVIE					ABC
	60 MINUTES	18	MURDER, SHE WROTE	2	CRAZY LIKE A FOX	2	TRAPPER JOHN, M.D.	7		CBS
	PUNKY BREWSTER 2	SILVER SPOONS 4	**AMAZING STORIES**	**ALFRED HITCHCOCK**	MOVIE					NBC
MON			HARDCASTLE & McCORMICK	3	NFL MONDAY NIGHT FOOTBALL			16		ABC
			SCARECROW & MRS. KING	3	KATE & ALLIE 3	NEWHART 4	CAGNEY & LACEY	5		CBS
			TV'S BLOOPERS & PRACTICAL JOKES	3	MOVIE					NBC
TUE			WHO'S THE BOSS 2	**GROWING PAINS**	MOONLIGHTING	2	**OUR FAMILY HONOR**			ABC
			HOMETOWN	2	MOVIE					CBS
			A-TEAM	4	RIPTIDE	3	REMINGTON STEELE	4		NBC
WED			**INSIDERS**		DYNASTY	6	HOTEL	3		ABC
			STIR CRAZY		**CHARLIE & CO.**	**GEORGE BURNS COMEDY WEEK**	**EQUALIZER**			CBS
			HIGHWAY TO HEAVEN	2	**HELL TOWN**		ST. ELSEWHERE	4		NBC
THU			FALL GUY	5	**LADY BLUE** / **COLBYS**		20/20	8		ABC
			MAGNUM, P.I.	6	SIMON & SIMON	5	KNOTS LANDING	7		CBS
			COSBY 2	FAMILY TIES 4	CHEERS 4	NIGHT COURT 3	HILL STREET BLUES	6		NBC
FRI			WEBSTER 3	MR. BELVEDERE 2	DIFF'RENT STROKES *8	BENSON 7	**SPENSER: FOR HIRE**			ABC
			TWILIGHT ZONE		DALLAS	9	FALCON CREST	5		CBS
			KNIGHT RIDER	4	**MISFITS OF SCIENCE**		MIAMI VICE	2		NBC
SAT			**HOLLYWOOD BEAT**		**LIME STREET**		LOVE BOAT	9		ABC
			AIRWOLF	3	MOVIE					CBS
			GIMME A BREAK 5	FACTS OF LIFE 7	**GOLDEN GIRLS**	227	HUNTER	2		NBC

1985–1986

1986–1987

Day	Net	7	7:30	8	8:30	9	9:30	10	10:30	11 PM
SUN	ABC	DISNEY SUNDAY MOVIE*				MOVIE 31				ABC
	CBS	60 MINUTES 19		MURDER, SHE WROTE		MOVIE 3				CBS
	NBC	OUR HOUSE		EASY STREET	VALERIE	MOVIE 2				NBC
MON	ABC			MacGYVER		NFL MONDAY NIGHT FOOTBALL				17 ABC
	CBS			KATE & ALLIE 4	MY SISTER SAM	NEWHART 5	DESIGNING WOMEN	CAGNEY & LACEY		6 CBS
	NBC			ALF	AMAZING STORIES 2	MOVIE				NBC
TUE	ABC			WHO'S THE BOSS 3	GROWING PAINS	MOONLIGHTING 2		JACK AND MIKE 3		ABC
	CBS			THE WIZARD		MOVIE				CBS
	NBC			MATLOCK		CRIME STORY		1986		2 NBC
WED	ABC			PERFECT STRANGERS 2	HEAD OF THE CLASS	DYNASTY		HOTEL 7		4 ABC
	CBS			TOGETHER WE STAND	BETTER DAYS	MAGNUM, P.I.		EQUALIZER 7		2 CBS
	NBC			HIGHWAY TO HEAVEN		GIMME A BREAK 3	YOU AGAIN 6	ST. ELSEWHERE 2		5 NBC
THU	ABC			OUR WORLD		THE COLBYS		20/20 2		9 ABC
	CBS			SIMON & SIMON		KNOTS LANDING 6		KAY O'BRIEN 8		CBS
	NBC			COSBY 3	FAMILY TIES	CHEERS 5	NIGHT COURT 5	HILL STREET BLUES 4		7 NBC
FRI	ABC			WEBSTER 4	MR BELVEDERE	SIDEKICKS 3	SLEDGE HAMMER	STARMAN		ABC
	CBS			SCARECROW & MRS KING		DALLAS 4		FALCON CREST 10		6 CBS
	NBC			A-TEAM		MIAMI VICE 5		L.A. LAW 3		NBC
SAT	ABC			LIFE WITH LUCY	ELLEN BURSTYN	HEART OF THE CITY		SPENSER FOR HIRE		2 ABC
	CBS			DOWNTOWN		MIKE HAMMER		TWILIGHT ZONE 4		2 CBS
	NBC			FACTS OF LIFE 8	227	GOLDEN GIRLS 2	AMEN	HUNTER		3 NBC

1987–1988

Day	Net	7	7:30	8	8:30	9	9:30	10	10:30	11 PM
SUN	ABC	DISNEY HOUR (32)		SPENSER: FOR HIRE (20)		DOLLY (3)		BUCK JAMES		ABC
	CBS	60 MINUTES		MURDER, SHE WROTE		MOVIE (4)				CBS
	FOX	21 JUMP STREET (2)		WEREWOLF	MARRIED ... WITH CHILDREN (2)	TRACEY ULLMAN (2)	DUET	LOCAL (2)		FOX
	NBC	OUR HOUSE (2)		FAMILY TIES (6)	MY TWO DADS	MOVIE (3)				NBC
MON	ABC			MacGYVER (3)		NFL MONDAY NIGHT FOOTBALL				ABC (18)
	CBS			FRANK'S PLACE	KATE & ALLIE (5)	NEWHART	DESIGNING WOMEN (6)	CAGNEY & LACEY (2)		CBS (7)
	NBC			ALF (2)	VALERIE'S FAMILY[1] (3)	MOVIE				NBC
TUE	ABC			WHO'S THE BOSS (2)	GROWING PAINS (4)	MOONLIGHTING (3)		THIRTYSOMETHING (4)		ABC
	CBS			HOUSTON KNIGHTS (2)		JAKE & THE FATMAN (2)		THE LAW & HARRY McGRAW		CBS (2)
	NBC			MATLOCK (2)		J.J. STARBUCK (2)		CRIME STORY		NBC
WED	ABC			PERFECT STRANGERS (3)	HEAD OF THE CLASS (2)	HOOPERMAN	"SLAP" MAXWELL STORY (3)	DYNASTY (8)		ABC (8)
	CBS			THE OLDEST ROOKIE		MAGNUM, P.I.		EQUALIZER (3)		CBS (3)
	NBC			HIGHWAY TO HEAVEN (4)		A YEAR IN THE LIFE		ST. ELSEWHERE (6)		NBC (6)
THU	ABC			SLEDGE HAMMER (2)	CHARMINGS' (2)	MOVIE (2)				ABC
	CBS			TOUR OF DUTY		WISEGUY		KNOTS LANDING		CBS (9)
	NBC			COSBY (4)	DIFFERENT WORLD	CHEERS (6)	NIGHT COURT (6)	L.A. LAW (5)		NBC (2)
FRI	ABC			FULL HOUSE	I MARRIED DORA	MAX HEADROOM		20/20 (2)		ABC (10)
	CBS			BEAUTY AND THE BEAST		DALLAS		FALCON CREST (11)		CBS (7)
	NBC			RAGS TO RICHES (2)		MIAMI VICE		OHARA (2)		NBC
SAT	ABC			ONCE A HERO (2)		LEG WORK		PRIVATE EYE (2)		ABC (5)
	CBS			MY SISTER SAM (2)	EVERYTHING'S RELATIVE (2)	BEANS BAXTER (2)		HOTEL (2)	WEST 57TH	CBS (2)
	FOX			MR. PRESIDENT (2)	WOMEN IN PRISON (2)	GOLDEN GIRLS (3)	SECOND CHANCE	LOCAL		FOX
	NBC			FACTS OF LIFE (9)	227 (3)		AMEN (3)	HUNTER (2)		NBC (4)

NOTE: [1] Formerly *Valerie*.

1988–1989

Day	Network	7	7:30	8	8:30	9	9:30	10	10:30	11 PM
SUN	ABC	INCREDIBLE SUNDAY				MOVIE				ABC
SUN	CBS	60 MINUTES 21		MURDER, SHE WROTE 5		MOVIE 5				CBS
SUN	FOX	21 JUMP STREET 3		AMERICA'S MOST WANTED 2	MARRIED...WITH CHILDREN 3	IT'S GARRY SHANDLING'S	TRACEY ULLMAN 2	DUET 3	LOCAL 3	FOX
SUN	NBC	MAGICAL WORLD OF DISNEY *33		FAMILY TIES 7	DAY BY DAY 2	MOVIE 2				NBC
MON	ABC			MacGYVER 4		NFL MONDAY NIGHT FOOTBALL				ABC 19
MON	CBS			NEWHART 7	COMING OF AGE 2	MURPHY BROWN 2	DESIGNING WOMEN 3	ALMOST GROWN		CBS 3
MON	NBC			ALF 3	HOGAN FAMILY[1] 4	MOVIE 4				NBC
TUE	ABC			WHO'S THE BOSS 5	ROSEANNE 2	MOONLIGHTING		THIRTYSOMETHING 5		ABC 2
TUE	CBS			TV 101		MOVIE				CBS
TUE	NBC			MATLOCK 3		IN THE HEAT OF THE NIGHT 3		MIDNIGHT CALLER 2		NBC 2
WED	ABC			GROWING PAINS 4	HEAD OF THE CLASS 3	WONDER YEARS 2	HOOPERMAN 2	CHINA BEACH 2		ABC 2
WED	CBS			VAN DYKE SHOW	ANNIE McGUIRE	EQUALIZER 4		WISEGUY 2		CBS 2
WED	NBC			UNSOLVED MYSTERIES		NIGHT COURT 2	BABY BOOM 6	TATTINGER'S 9		NBC
THU	ABC			KNIGHTWATCH		DYNASTY 2		HEARTBEAT 9		ABC 2
THU	CBS			48 HOURS 2		PARADISE 2		KNOTS LANDING		CBS 10
THU	NBC			COSBY 5	DIFFERENT WORLD 2	CHEERS 7	DEAR JOHN 5	L.A. LAW		NBC 3
FRI	ABC			PERFECT STRANGERS 4	FULL HOUSE 2	MR BELVEDERE 2	JUST THE TEN OF US 2	20/20		ABC 11
FRI	CBS			BEAUTY AND THE BEAST 2		DALLAS 2		FALCON CREST 12		CBS 8
FRI	NBC			SONNY SPOON 2		SOMETHING IS OUT THERE 2		MIAMI VICE		NBC 5
SAT	ABC			MURPHY'S LAW		MOVIE				ABC
SAT	CBS			DIRTY DANCING	RAISING MIRANDA	TOUR OF DUTY 2		WEST 57TH		CBS 3
SAT	FOX			THE REPORTERS		BEYOND TOMORROW 4		LOCAL		FOX
SAT	NBC			227 4	AMEN 4	GOLDEN GIRLS 3	EMPTY NEST 4	HUNTER 5		NBC

NOTE: [1] Formerly *Valerie's Family*.

1989–1990

Day	Network	7	7:30	8	8:30	9	9:30	10	10:30	11 PM
SUN	ABC	LIFE GOES ON		FREE SPIRIT	HOMEROOM	MOVIE				
SUN	CBS	60 MINUTES (22)		MURDER, SHE WROTE (6)		MOVIE				
SUN	FOX	BOOKER		AMERICA'S MOST WANTED (3)	TOTALLY HIDDEN VIDEO (3)	MARRIED . . . WITH CHILDREN (4)	OPEN HOUSE[1] (4)	TRACEY ULLMAN (4)	IT'S GARRY SHANDLING'S (3)	
SUN	NBC	MAGICAL WORLD OF DISNEY (34)		SISTER KATE	MY TWO DADS (3)	MOVIE (5)				
MON	ABC			MacGYVER (5)		NFL MONDAY NIGHT FOOTBALL (20)				
MON	CBS			MAJOR DAD	THE PEOPLE NEXT DOOR	MURPHY BROWN (2)	FAMOUS TEDDY Z	DESIGNING WOMEN	NEWHART (4)	(6)
MON	FOX			21 JUMP STREET (4)		ALIEN NATION		LOCAL		
MON	NBC			ALF (4)	HOGAN FAMILY (5)	MOVIE				
TUE	ABC			WHO'S THE BOSS (6)	WONDER YEARS (6)	ROSEANNE (3)	CHICKEN SOUP (2)	THIRTYSOMETHING (3)		
TUE	CBS			RESCUE 911		WOLF		ISLAND SON		
TUE	NBC			MATLOCK		IN THE HEAT OF THE NIGHT (4)		MIDNIGHT CALLER (3)		(2)
WED	ABC			GROWING PAINS (5)	HEAD OF THE CLASS	ANYTHING BUT LOVE (4)	DOOGIE HOWSER, M.D. (2)	CHINA BEACH (3)		(3)
WED	CBS			PEACEABLE KINGDOM		JAKE & THE FATMAN		WISEGUY (3)		(3)
WED	NBC			UNSOLVED MYSTERIES (3)		NIGHT COURT (3)	NUTT HOUSE (7)	QUANTUM LEAP		(2)
THU	ABC			MISSION: IMPOSSIBLE		YOUNG RIDERS (2)		PRIME TIME LIVE		
THU	CBS			48 HOURS (3)		TOP OF THE HILL (3)		KNOTS LANDING		(11)
THU	NBC			COSBY (6)	DIFFERENT WORLD (3)	CHEERS (8)	DEAR JOHN (2)	L.A. LAW		(4)
FRI	ABC			FULL HOUSE (3)	FAMILY MATTERS	PERFECT STRANGERS	JUST THE TEN OF US (5)	20/20 (3)		(12)
FRI	CBS			SNOOPS		DALLAS (13)		FALCON CREST (9)		
FRI	NBC			BAYWATCH		HARDBALL		MANCUSO F.B.I.		
SAT	ABC			MR. BELVEDERE (6)	LIVING DOLLS	ABC SATURDAY MYSTERY				(2)
SAT	CBS			PARADISE		TOUR OF DUTY (2)		SATURDAY NIGHT W/CONNIE CHUNG (3)		(2)
SAT	FOX			COPS (2)	THE REPORTERS (2)		BEYOND TOMORROW (2)	COMIC STRIP LIVE (2)		
SAT	NBC			227 (5)	AMEN (5)	GOLDEN GIRLS (4)	EMPTY NEST (5)	HUNTER (2)		(6)

NOTE: [1] Formerly *Duet*.

1990–1991

Day	Net	7	7:30	8	8:30	9	9:30	10	10:30	11 PM
SUN	ABC	LIFE GOES ON		AMERICA'S FUNNIEST VIDEOS 2	AMERICA'S FUNNIEST PEOPLE 2	MOVIE				ABC
SUN	CBS	60 MINUTES		MURDER, SHE WROTE 23		MOVIE 7				CBS
SUN	FOX	TRUE COLORS	PARKER LEWIS CAN'T LOSE	IN LIVING COLOR 2	GET A LIFE 2	MARRIED... WITH CHILDREN 5	GOOD GRIEF	AGAINST THE LAW		FOX
SUN	NBC	HULL HIGH		LIFESTORIES		MOVIE				NBC
MON	ABC			MacGYVER 6		NFL MONDAY NIGHT FOOTBALL 21				ABC 21
MON	CBS			UNCLE BUCK 2	MAJOR DAD 2	MURPHY BROWN 3	DESIGNING WOMEN 5	TRIALS OF ROSIE O'NEILL		CBS
MON	FOX			MOVIE				LOCAL		FOX
MON	NBC			FRESH PRINCE OF BEL-AIR	FERRIS BUELLER	MOVIE				NBC
TUE	ABC			WHO'S THE BOSS 7	HEAD OF THE CLASS 5	ROSEANNE 3	COACH 3	THIRTYSOMETHING 4		ABC 4
TUE	CBS			RESCUE 911		MOVIE 2				CBS
TUE	NBC			MATLOCK 5		IN THE HEAT OF THE NIGHT 5		LAW & ORDER 4		NBC
WED	ABC			WONDER YEARS 4	GROWING PAINS 6	DOOGIE HOWSER, M.D. 2	MARRIED PEOPLE	COP ROCK		ABC
WED	CBS			LENNY	DOCTOR, DOCTOR 2	JAKE & THE FATMAN 4		WIOU 4		CBS
WED	NBC			UNSOLVED MYSTERIES 4		FANELLI BOYS 4	DEAR JOHN 3	HUNTER 3		NBC 7
THU	ABC			FATHER DOWLING MYSTERIES 3		GABRIEL'S FIRE 3		PRIME TIME LIVE 2		ABC 2
THU	CBS			THE FLASH		SONS AND DAUGHTERS		KNOTS LANDING 12		CBS 12
THU	FOX			SIMPSONS 2	BABES 2	BEVERLY HILLS 90210		LOCAL		FOX
THU	NBC			COSBY 7	DIFFERENT WORLD 4	CHEERS 9	GRAND 2	L.A. LAW 5		NBC 5
FRI	ABC			FULL HOUSE 4	FAMILY MATTERS 2	PERFECT STRANGERS 6	GOING PLACES	20/20 13		ABC 13
FRI	CBS			EVENING SHADE 2	BAGDAD CAFE 2	OVER MY DEAD BODY 2		DALLAS 14		CBS 14
FRI	FOX			AMERICA'S MOST WANTED 4		DEA 4		LOCAL		FOX
FRI	NBC			QUANTUM LEAP 2		NIGHT COURT 3	WINGS 8	MIDNIGHT CALLER 3		NBC 3
SAT	ABC			YOUNG RIDERS 2		CHINA BEACH 2		TWIN PEAKS 4		ABC 2
SAT	CBS			FAMILY MAN 6	HOGAN FAMILY*	E.A.R.T.H. FORCE 6		48 HOURS 4		CBS 4
SAT	FOX			TOTALLY HIDDEN VIDEO 2	HAYWIRE 2	COPS 3	AMERICAN CHRONICLES 3	COMIC STRIP LIVE 2		FOX 2
SAT	NBC			PARENTHOOD	WORKING IT OUT	GOLDEN GIRLS 6	EMPTY NEST 6	CAROL & COMPANY 3	AMERICAN DREAMER 2	NBC

1991–1992

Day	Net	7	7:30	8	8:30	9	9:30	10	10:30	11 PM
SUN	ABC	LIFE GOES ON (3)		AMERICA'S FUNNIEST HOME VIDEOS (3)	AMERICA'S FUNNIEST PEOPLE (3)	MOVIE				
	CBS	60 MINUTES (24)		MURDER, SHE WROTE		MOVIE				
	FOX	TRUE COLORS (2)	PARKER LEWIS (2)	IN LIVING COLOR (3)	ROC (3)	MARRIED...WITH CHILDREN (6)	HERMAN'S HEAD	THE SUNDAY COMICS		(2)
	NBC	MARK & BRIAN	EERIE INDIANA	MAN OF THE PEOPLE	PACIFIC STATION	MOVIE				
MON	ABC			MacGYVER (7)		NFL MONDAY NIGHT FOOTBALL				(22)
	CBS			EVENING SHADE (2)	MAJOR DAD (2)	MURPHY BROWN (4)	DESIGNING WOMEN (3)	NORTHERN EXPOSURE (6)		(2)
	FOX			MOVIE				LOCAL		
	NBC			FRESH PRINCE OF BEL-AIR (2)	BLOSSOM (2)	MOVIE				
TUE	ABC			FULL HOUSE (5)	HOME IMPROVEMENT	ROSEANNE (4)	COACH (4)	HOMEFRONT (4)		
	CBS			RESCUE 911 (3)		MOVIE				
	NBC			I'LL FLY AWAY		IN THE HEAT OF THE NIGHT (5)		LAW & ORDER (5)		(2)
WED	ABC			DINOSAURS (2)	WONDER YEARS (5)	DOOGIE HOWSER M.D. (3)	SIBS (3)	ANYTHING BUT LOVE (5)	GOOD & EVIL (4)	(2)
	CBS			ROYAL FAMILY	TEECH	JAKE & THE FATMAN (5)		48 HOURS (5)		(5)
	NBC			UNSOLVED MYSTERIES		NIGHT COURT (5)	SEINFELD (9)	QUANTUM LEAP (3)		(4)
THU	ABC			PROS & CONS		FBI: UNTOLD (2)	AMERICAN DETECTIVE (2)	PRIMETIME LIVE (3)		(3)
	CBS			TOP COPS		TRIALS OF ROSIE O'NEILL (2)		KNOTS LANDING (2)		(13)
	FOX			SIMPSONS (3)	DREXELL'S CLASS (3)	BEVERLY HILLS 90210		LOCAL (2)		
	NBC			COSBY (8)	DIFFERENT WORLD (5)	CHEERS (10)	WINGS (3)	L.A. LAW (3)		(6)
FRI	ABC			FAMILY MATTERS (3)	STEP BY STEP	PERFECT STRANGERS (7)	BABY TALK (7)	20/20 (2)		(14)
	CBS			PRINCESSES	BROOKLYN BRIDGE	CAROL BURNETT SHOW (5)		PALACE GUARD		
	FOX			AMERICA'S MOST WANTED		LOCAL (5)				
	NBC			REAL LIFE (2)	EXPOSE (2)	DEAR JOHN (4)	FLESH 'N' BLOOD (4)	REASONABLE DOUBTS		(3)
SAT	ABC			WHO'S THE BOSS (8)	GROWING PAINS (7)	YOUNG RIDERS (7)		THE COMMISH (3)		
	CBS			MOVIE				P.S. I LUV U		
	FOX			COPS (4)	COPS (4)	TOTALLY HIDDEN VIDEO (4)	GET A LIFE (3)	LOCAL (2)		
	NBC			GOLDEN GIRLS (7)	TORKELSONS	EMPTY NEST (4)	NURSES (4)	SISTERS		(2)

1992–1993

Day	Net	7:00	7:30	8:00	8:30	9:00	9:30	10:00	10:30
SUN	ABC	LIFE GOES ON		AMERICA'S FUNNIEST VIDEOS	AMERICA'S FUNNIEST PEOPLE	MOVIE			
SUN	CBS	60 MINUTES		MURDER, SHE WROTE		MOVIE			
SUN	FOX	GREAT SCOTT	BEN STILLER SHOW	IN LIVING COLOR	ROC	MARRIED... WITH CHILDREN	HERMAN'S HEAD	FLYING BLIND	WOOPS!
SUN	NBC	SECRET SERVICE		I WITNESS VIDEO		MOVIE			
MON	ABC			YOUNG INDIANA JONES CHRONICLES		NFL MONDAY NIGHT FOOTBALL			
MON	CBS			EVENING SHADE	HEARTS AFIRE	MURPHY BROWN	LOVE & WAR	NORTHERN EXPOSURE	
MON	FOX			MOVIE				LOCAL	
MON	NBC			FRESH PRINCE OF BEL-AIR	BLOSSOM	MOVIE			
TUE	ABC			FULL HOUSE	HANGIN' WITH MR. COOPER	ROSEANNE	COACH	GOING TO EXTREMES	
TUE	CBS			RESCUE 911		MOVIE			
TUE	FOX			CLASS OF '96		KEY WEST		LOCAL	
TUE	NBC			QUANTUM LEAP		REASONABLE DOUBTS		DATELINE NBC	
WED	ABC			WONDER YEARS	DOOGIE HOWSER M.D.	HOME IMPROVEMENT	LAURIE HILL	CIVIL WARS	
WED	CBS			THE HAT SQUAD		IN THE HEAT OF THE NIGHT"		48 HOURS	
WED	FOX			BEVERLY HILLS 90210		MELROSE PLACE		LOCAL	
WED	NBC			UNSOLVED MYSTERIES		SEINFELD	MAD ABOUT YOU	LAW & ORDER	
THU	ABC			DELTA	ROOM FOR TWO	HOMEFRONT		PRIMETIME LIVE	
THU	CBS			TOP COPS		STREET STORIES		KNOTS LANDING	
THU	FOX			SIMPSONS	MARTIN	THE HEIGHTS		LOCAL	
THU	NBC			DIFFERENT WORLD	RHYTHM & BLUES	CHEERS	WINGS	L.A. LAW	
FRI	ABC			FAMILY MATTERS	STEP BY STEP	DINOSAURS	CAMP WILDER	20/20	
FRI	CBS			GOLDEN PALACE	MAJOR DAD	DESIGNING WOMEN	BOB	PICKET FENCES	
FRI	FOX			AMERICA'S MOST WANTED		SIGHTINGS		LOCAL	
FRI	NBC			FINAL APPEAL	WHAT HAPPENED	THE ROUND TABLE	LIKELY SUSPECTS	I'LL FLY AWAY	
SAT	ABC			COVINGTON CROSS		CROSSROADS		THE COMMISH	
SAT	CBS			FRANNIE'S TURN	BROOKLYN BRIDGE	RAVEN		ANGEL STREET	
SAT	FOX			COPS	COPS	CODE 3	THE EDGE	LOCAL	
SAT	NBC			HERE & NOW	OUT ALL NIGHT	EMPTY NEST	NURSES	SISTERS	

1993–1994

Day	Net	7:00	7:30	8:00	8:30	9:00	9:30	10:00	10:30
SUN	ABC	America's Funniest Videos	America's Funniest People (5)	Lois & Clark (4)		Movie			
SUN	CBS	60 Minutes		Murder, She Wrote		Movie (10)			
SUN	FOX		Townsend Television (26)	Martin (2)	Living Single	Married... With Children (8)	Daddy Dearest	Local	
SUN	NBC	I Witness Video (2)		SeaQuest DSV		Movie			
MON	ABC			Day One (2)		NFL Monday Night Football (24)			
MON	CBS			Evening Shade (4)	Dave's World	Murphy Brown (6)	Love & War (2)	Northern Exposure (4)	
MON	FOX			Movie				Local	
MON	NBC			Fresh Prince of Bel-Air (4)	Blossom	Movie		Local	
TUE	ABC			Full House	Phenom (7)	Roseanne (6)	Coach	NYPD Blue (6)	
TUE	CBS			Rescue 911		Movie (5)			
TUE	FOX			Roc (3)	Bakersfield P.D.	America's Most Wanted (7)		Local	
TUE	NBC			Saved by the Bell	Getting By* (2)	John Larroquette	Second Half	Dateline NBC (3)	
WED	ABC			Thea	Joe's Life (3)	Grace Under Fire		Moon Over Miami	
WED	CBS			The Trouble with Larry	The Nanny (7)	South of Sunset		48 Hours (7)	
WED	FOX			Beverly Hills 90210 (4)		Melrose Place (2)		Local	
WED	NBC			Unsolved Mysteries		Now (7)		Law & Order (4)	
THU	ABC			Missing Persons (5)		Matlock (7)		Primetime Live (5)	
THU	CBS			In the Heat of the Night		Eye to Eye with Connie Chung (7)		Angel Falls (8)	
THU	FOX			Simpsons (5)	Sinbad	In Living Color (5)	Herman's Head	Local (3)	
THU	NBC			Mad About You (2)	Wings	Seinfeld (5)	Frasier	L.A. Law (8)	
FRI	ABC			Family Matters (5)	Boy Meets World	Step by Step (3)	Hangin' with Mr. Cooper	20/20 (16)	
FRI	CBS			It Had to Be You	Family Album	Good Advice (2)	Bob	Picket Fences (2)	
FRI	FOX			Adventures of Brisco County Jr		The X-Files		Local	
FRI	NBC			Against the Grain		NBC Friday Night Mystery			
SAT	ABC			George (2)	Where I Live	The Paula Poundstone Show		The Commish (3)	
SAT	CBS			Dr. Quinn, Medicine Woman (2)		Harts of the West		Walker, Texas Ranger (2)	
SAT	FOX			Cops (6)	Cops	Front Page (6)		Local	
SAT	NBC			The Mommies	Cafe American	Empty Nest	Nurses (6)	Sisters (3) (4)	

1994–1995

Day	Net	7:00	7:30	8:00	8:30	9:00	9:30	10:00	10:30
SUN	ABC	AMERICA'S FUNNIEST VIDEOS (6)	ON OUR OWN (6)	LOIS & CLARK (2)		MOVIE (2)			
	CBS	60 MINUTES (27)		MURDER, SHE WROTE (11)		MOVIE			
	FOX	FORTUNE HUNTER		SIMPSONS (6)	HARDBALL	MARRIED . . . WITH CHILDREN (9)	WILD OATS	LOCAL	
	NBC	EARTH 2		SEAQUEST DSV (2)		MOVIE (2)			
MON	ABC			COACH (7)	BLUE SKIES (25)	NFL MONDAY NIGHT FOOTBALL			
	CBS			THE NANNY (2)	DAVE'S WORLD (2)	MURPHY BROWN (7)	LOVE & WAR (3)	NORTHERN EXPOSURE (5)	
	FOX			MELROSE PLACE (3)		PARTY OF FIVE		LOCAL	
	NBC			FRESH PRINCE OF BEL-AIR (5)	BLOSSOM (3)	MOVIE (5)			
TUE	ABC			FULL HOUSE (8)	ME & THE BOYS	HOME IMPROVEMENT (4)	GRACE UNDER FIRE (2)	NYPD BLUE (2)	
	CBS			RESCUE 911 (6)		MOVIE			
	FOX			MOVIE				LOCAL	
	NBC			WINGS (6)	MARTIN SHORT	FRASIER (2)	JOHN LARROQUETTE (2)	DATELINE NBC (4)	
WED	ABC			THUNDER ALLEY (2)	ALL-AMERICAN GIRL	ROSEANNE (7)	ELLEN	TURNING P3INT (2)	
	CBS			THE BOYS ARE BACK	DADDY'S GIRLS	TOUCHED BY AN ANGEL		48 HOURS (8)	
	FOX			BEVERLY HILLS 90210 (5)		MODELS INC. (5)		LOCAL	
	NBC			THE COSBY MYSTERIES		DATELINE NBC (4)		LAW & ORDER (5)	
THU	ABC			MY SO-CALLED LIFE		McKENNA		PRIMETIME LIVE (6)	
	CBS			DUE SOUTH		EYE TO EYE WITH CONNIE CHUNG		CHICAGO HOPE (2)	
	FOX			MARTIN (3)	LIVING SINGLE (2)	NEW YORK UNDERCOVER		LOCAL	
	NBC			MAD ABOUT YOU (3)	FRIENDS	SEINFELD (6)	MADMAN OF THE PEOPLE	ER	
FRI	ABC			FAMILY MATTERS (6)	BOY MEETS WORLD (2)	STEP BY STEP (4)	HANGIN' WITH MR. COOPER (3)	20/20 (17)	
	CBS			DIAGNOSIS MURDER		UNDER SUSPICION (2)		PICKET FENCES (3)	
	FOX			M.A.N.T.I.S. (2)		THE X-FILES (2)		LOCAL	
	NBC			UNSOLVED MYSTERIES (8)		DATELINE NBC (4)		HOMICIDE: LIFE ON THE STREET (3)	
SAT	ABC			THE ABC FAMILY MOVIE				THE COMMISH (4)	
	CBS			DR. QUINN, MEDICINE WOMAN (3)		THE FIVE MRS. BUCHANANS	HEARTS AFIRE (3)	WALKER, TEXAS RANGER (3)	
	FOX			COPS (7)	COPS	AMERICA'S MOST WANTED (7)		LOCAL (8)	
	NBC			SOMETHING WILDER	EMPTY NEST (7)	SWEET JUSTICE (7)		SISTERS (5)	

1995–1996

SUNDAY

Net	7:00	7:30	8:00	8:30	9:00	9:30	10:00	10:30	11 PM
ABC	America's Funniest Videos		Lois & Clark (7)		Movie (3)				ABC
CBS	60 Minutes (28)		Cybill (2)	Almost Perfect (2)	Movie				CBS
FOX	Space: Above and Beyond		Simpsons (7)	Too Something (7)	Married...With Children (10)	Misery Loves Company	Local		FOX
NBC	Brotherly Love	Minor Adjust.	Mad About You (4)	Hope & Gloria (2)	Movie (2)		Local		NBC
WB	Pinky & Brain	Sister, Sister	Kirk (2)	Simon (2)	Cleghorne! (2)	First Time Out	Local		WB

MONDAY

Net	8:00	8:30	9:00	9:30	10:00	10:30	11 PM
ABC	The Marshal (2)		NFL Monday Night Football				ABC (26)
CBS	The Nanny (3)	Can't Hurry Love (3)	Murphy Brown (8)	If Not For You (8)	Chicago Hope		CBS (2)
FOX	Melrose Place (4)		Partners	Ned & Stacey	Local		FOX
NBC	Fresh Prince of Bel-Air (6)	In the House (6)	Movie (2)		Local		NBC
UPN	Star Trek: Voyager (2)		Nowhere Man (2)		Local		UPN

TUESDAY

Net	8:00	8:30	9:00	9:30	10:00	10:30	11 PM
ABC	Roseanne (8)	Hudson Street (8)	Home Improvement (5)	Coach (5)	NYPD Blue (8)		ABC (3)
CBS	The Client		Movie				CBS
FOX	Movie				Local		FOX
NBC	Wings (7)	News Radio (7)	Frasier (2)	Pursuit of Happiness (3)	Dateline NBC		NBC (5)
UPN	Deadly Games		Live Shot		Local		UPN

WEDNESDAY

Net	8:00	8:30	9:00	9:30	10:00	10:30	11 PM
ABC	Ellen (3)	The Drew Carey Show (3)	Grace Under Fire (3)	Naked Truth (3)	Primetime Live		ABC (7)
CBS	Bless This House	Dave's World (3)	Central Park West (3)		Courthouse (2)		CBS
FOX	Beverly Hills 90210 (6)		Party of Five (2)		Local		FOX
NBC	Seaquest 2032 (3)		Dateline NBC (3)		Law & Order (5)		NBC (6)
WB	Sister, Sister (2)	Parent 'Hood (2)	Wayans Bros (2)	Unhappily Ever After	Local (2)		WB

THURSDAY

Net	8:00	8:30	9:00	9:30	10:00	10:30	11 PM
ABC	Charlie Grace		The Monroes		Murder One		ABC (9)
CBS	Murder, She Wrote (12)		New York News (12)		48 Hours		CBS
FOX	Living Single (3)	The Crew (3)	New York Undercover (2)		Local (2)		FOX
NBC	Friends (2)	Single Guy (2)	Seinfeld (7)	Caroline in the City (7)	ER (2)		NBC (2)

FRIDAY

Net	8:00	8:30	9:00	9:30	10:00	10:30	11 PM
ABC	Family Matters (7)	Boy Meets World (5)	Step by Step (5)	Hangin' with Mr. Cooper (5)	20/20 (4)		ABC (18)
CBS	Dweebs	Bonnie Hunt	Picket Fences (4)		American Gothic (4)		CBS
FOX	Strange Luck		The X-Files (3)		Local		FOX
NBC	Unsolved Mysteries		Dateline NBC (9)		Homicide: Life on the Street (5)		NBC (4)

SATURDAY

Net	8:00	8:30	9:00	9:30	10:00	10:30	11 PM
ABC	Jeff Foxworthy (4)	Maybe This Time (4)	Movie				ABC
CBS	Dr. Quinn, Medicine Woman (4)		Touched by an Angel (4)		Walker, Texas Ranger (2)		CBS (4)
FOX	Martin (4)	Preston Episodes (4)	Cops (8)	America's Most Wanted (8)	Local		FOX

★★★ PART IV

THE ENVELOPES,
PLEASE

Television's best-known awards, the Emmys were first presented in January 1949 in Hollywood by the newly formed Academy of Television Arts and Sciences. The awards bore a distinctly local flavor for the first few years, but by 1955 (the year of the first coast-to-coast Emmy telecast, honoring achievements for 1954) they had acquired a truly national character. In 1957 the National Academy of Television Arts and Sciences was formed, which administered the awards exclusively from that year through 1976. In 1977 tension between the Hollywood and New York chapters of the National Academy led to the secession of the Hollywood group, which was reborn as the Academy of Television Arts and Sciences. Lawsuits and countersuits concerning the right to confer the Emmy statuette ensued; eventually a compromise was struck, permitting the Hollywood-based Academy of Television Arts and Sciences to administer the Emmys for prime-time entertainment programs and the New York-based National Academy of Television Arts and Sciences to award Emmys for daytime, sports, and local shows (the National Academy was also authorized to present awards for news programs, but the news divisions of the three commercial networks for several years declined to participate in the Emmys).

Despite a troubled history of internecine warfare, boycotts and frequently boring awards telecasts, the Emmys remain popular. Presented here are all the winners of Emmy awards from 1948 through 1953; from 1954 on, as the number of award categories began to proliferate, the list has been edited. Included are all awards given to series and individual programs, all awards given to actors, performers, directors, writers, and any noteworthy engineering and special awards. Not included are awards in the technical craft areas (such as cinematography, film and tape editing, sound mixing and editing, lighting, costume design, makeup, choreography, and musical direction). The awards for each year are not listed in the order in which they were presented, but rather have been grouped together insofar as practicable so that awards to programs are listed first, awards to actors and performers second, and awards for directing, writing and other achievements third. The titles of some award categories have been abridged slightly. Though separate awards for daytime shows were first presented in 1974, the daytime Emmys have been integrated with the prime-time Emmys through 1975–1976. Beginning with the 1976–1977 awards—the first to be separately administered by the two Television Academies—the daytime Emmys are listed separately. It should also be noted that for the years 1948 through 1957 the Emmys were presented on a calendar year basis. Beginning in 1958, however, the awards were given on a seasonal basis; the 1958–1959 Emmy season covers a fourteen-month period, and later awards cover a twelve-to-thirteen-month period which usually runs from March to March or April to April. The term "Emmy" is derived from "Immy," a nickname for the image orthicon camera tube developed during the late 1940s.

1948

MOST POPULAR TELEVISION PROGRAM: *Pantomime Quiz Time,* KTLA
BEST FILM MADE FOR TELEVISION: "The Necklace," *Your Show Time*
MOST OUTSTANDING TELEVISION PERSONALITY: Shirley Dinsdale and her puppet, Judy Splinters, KTLA
TECHNICAL AWARD: Charles Mesak, Don Lee Television, for the phase-finder
STATION AWARD: KTLA, Los Angeles
SPECIAL AWARD: Louis McManus, "for his original design of the Emmy"

1949

BEST LIVE SHOW: *The Ed Wynn Show,* KTTV (CBS)
BEST KINESCOPE SHOW: *The Texaco Star Theater,* KNBH (NBC)
BEST FILM MADE FOR, AND VIEWED ON TELEVISION: *The Life of Riley,* KNBH (NBC)
BEST PUBLIC SERVICE, CULTURAL, OR EDUCATIONAL PROGRAM: *Crusade in Europe,* KECA-TV and KTTV (ABC)
BEST CHILDREN'S SHOW: *Time for Beany,* KTLA
MOST OUTSTANDING LIVE PERSONALITY: Ed Wynn
MOST OUTSTANDING KINESCOPE PERSONALITY: Milton Berle
BEST SPORTS COVERAGE: Wrestling, KTLA
STATION ACHIEVEMENT: KTLA, Los Angeles (Honorable mention: KECA-TV)
BEST COMMERCIAL MADE FOR TELEVISION: Lucky Strike, N. W. Ayer & Son, Inc., for the American Tobacco Company
TECHNICAL AWARD: Harold W. Jury, KTSL, Los Angeles, for the synchronizing coordinator

1950

BEST VARIETY SHOW: *The Alan Young Show,* KTTV (CBS)
BEST DRAMATIC SHOW: *Pulitzer Prize Playhouse,* KECA-TV (ABC)
BEST GAME AND AUDIENCE PARTICIPATION SHOW: *Truth or Consequences,* KTTV (CBS)
BEST CHILDREN'S SHOW: *Time for Beany,* KTLA
BEST EDUCATIONAL SHOW: *KFI University,* KFI-TV
BEST CULTURAL SHOW: *Campus Chorus and Orchestra,* KTSL
BEST PUBLIC SERVICE: *City at Night,* KTLA
BEST SPORTS COVERAGE: *Rams Football,* KNBH
BEST NEWS PROGRAM: *KTLA Newsreel,* KTLA
SPECIAL EVENTS: "Departure of Marines for Korea," KFMB-TV and KTLA
MOST OUTSTANDING PERSONALITY: Groucho Marx, KNBH (NBC)
BEST ACTOR: Alan Young, KTTV (CBS)
BEST ACTRESS: Gertrude Berg, KTTV (CBS)
STATION ACHIEVEMENT: KTLA, Los Angeles
TECHNICAL ACHIEVEMENT: KNBH (NBC), for the Orthogram TV Amplifier

1951

BEST VARIETY SHOW: *Your Show of Shows* (NBC)
BEST COMEDY SHOW: *The Red Skelton Show* (NBC)
BEST DRAMATIC SHOW: *Studio One* (CBS)
BEST ACTOR: Sid Caesar (NBC)
BEST ACTRESS: Imogene Coca (NBC)
BEST COMEDIAN OR COMEDIENNE: Red Skelton (NBC)
SPECIAL ACHIEVEMENT AWARD: Senator Estes Kefauver, "for outstanding public service on television"

1952

BEST VARIETY PROGRAM: *Your Show of Shows* (NBC)
BEST SITUATION COMEDY: *I Love Lucy* (CBS)
BEST DRAMATIC PROGRAM: *Robert Montgomery Presents* (NBC)
BEST MYSTERY, ACTION, OR ADVENTURE PROGRAM: *Dragnet* (NBC)
BEST PUBLIC AFFAIRS PROGRAM: *See It Now* (CBS)
BEST AUDIENCE PARTICIPATION, QUIZ, OR PANEL PROGRAM: *What's My Line?* (CBS)
BEST CHILDREN'S PROGRAM: *Time for Beany* (SYNDICATED)
MOST OUTSTANDING PERSONALITY: Bishop Fulton J. Sheen (DUMONT)

BEST ACTOR: Thomas Mitchell
BEST ACTRESS: Helen Hayes
BEST COMEDIAN: Jimmy Durante (NBC)
BEST COMEDIENNE: Lucille Ball (CBS)

1953

BEST NEW PROGRAMS: *Make Room for Daddy* (ABC); *The U.S. Steel Hour* (ABC)
BEST VARIETY PROGRAM: *Omnibus* (CBS)
BEST SITUATION COMEDY: *I Love Lucy* (CBS)
BEST DRAMATIC PROGRAM: *The U.S. Steel Hour* (ABC)
BEST MYSTERY, ACTION, OR ADVENTURE PROGRAM: *Dragnet* (NBC)
BEST PUBLIC AFFAIRS PROGRAM: *Victory at Sea* (NBC)
BEST PROGRAM OF NEWS OR SPORTS: *See It Now* (CBS)
BEST AUDIENCE PARTICIPATION, QUIZ, OR PANEL PROGRAMS: *This Is Your Life* (NBC);
   What's My Line? (CBS)
BEST CHILDREN'S PROGRAM: *Kukla, Fran and Ollie* (NBC)
MOST OUTSTANDING PERSONALITY: Edward R. Murrow (CBS)
BEST MALE STAR OF REGULAR SERIES: Donald O'Connor, *The Colgate Comedy Hour*
   (NBC)
BEST FEMALE STAR OF REGULAR SERIES: Eve Arden, *Our Miss Brooks* (CBS)
BEST SERIES SUPPORTING ACTOR: Art Carney, *The Jackie Gleason Show* (CBS)
BEST SERIES SUPPORTING ACTRESS: Vivian Vance, *I Love Lucy* (CBS)

1954

BEST VARIETY SERIES, INCLUDING MUSICAL VARIETIES: *Disneyland* (ABC)
BEST SITUATION COMEDY SERIES: *Make Room for Daddy* (ABC)
BEST DRAMATIC SERIES: *The U.S. Steel Hour* (ABC)
BEST MYSTERY OR INTRIGUE SERIES: *Dragnet* (NBC)
BEST WESTERN OR ADVENTURE SERIES: *Stories of the Century* (SYNDICATED)
BEST CULTURAL, RELIGIOUS, OR EDUCATIONAL PROGRAM: *Omnibus* (CBS)
BEST SPORTS PROGRAM: *Gillette Cavalcade of Sports* (NBC)
BEST AUDIENCE, GUEST PARTICIPATION, OR PANEL PROGRAM: *This Is Your Life* (NBC)
BEST DAYTIME PROGRAM: *Art Linkletter's House Party* (CBS)
BEST CHILDREN'S PROGRAM: *Lassie* (CBS)
BEST INDIVIDUAL PROGRAM OF THE YEAR: "Operation Undersea," *Disneyland* (ABC)
MOST OUTSTANDING NEW PERSONALITY: George Gobel (NBC)
BEST ACTOR STARRING IN A REGULAR SERIES: Danny Thomas, *Make Room for Daddy*
   (ABC)
BEST ACTRESS STARRING IN A REGULAR SERIES: Loretta Young, *The Loretta Young Show*
   (NBC)
BEST ACTOR IN A SINGLE PERFORMANCE: Robert Cummings, "Twelve Angry Men,"
   Studio One (CBS)
BEST ACTRESS IN A SINGLE PERFORMANCE: Judith Anderson, "Macbeth," *Hallmark Hall
   of Fame* (NBC)
BEST SUPPORTING ACTOR IN A REGULAR SERIES: Art Carney, *The Jackie Gleason Show*
   (CBS)
BEST SUPPORTING ACTRESS IN A REGULAR SERIES: Audrey Meadows, *The Jackie Gleason
   Show* (CBS)
BEST MALE SINGER: Perry Como (CBS)
BEST FEMALE SINGER: Dinah Shore (NBC)
BEST NEWS REPORTER OR COMMENTATOR: John Daly (ABC)
BEST DIRECTION: Franklin Schaffner, "Twelve Angry Men," *Studio One* (CBS)
BEST WRITTEN DRAMATIC MATERIAL: Reginald Rose, "Twelve Angry Men," *Studio One*
   (CBS)

BEST WRITTEN COMEDY MATERIAL: James Allardice, Jack Douglas, Hal Kanter, Harry Winkler, *The George Gobel Show* (NBC)

BEST TECHNICAL ACHIEVEMENT: John West, Color TV Policy and Burbank Color (NBC)

1955

BEST VARIETY SERIES: *The Ed Sullivan Show* (CBS)

BEST COMEDY SERIES: *You'll Never Get Rich* (CBS)

BEST DRAMATIC SERIES: *Producers' Showcase* (NBC)

BEST ACTION OR ADVENTURE SERIES: *Disneyland* (ABC)

BEST MUSIC SERIES: *Your Hit Parade* (NBC)

BEST DOCUMENTARY (RELIGIOUS, EDUCATIONAL OR INTERVIEW PROGRAM): *Omnibus* (CBS)

BEST AUDIENCE PARTICIPATION SERIES: *The $64,000 Question* (CBS)

BEST CONTRIBUTION TO DAYTIME PROGRAMMING: *Matinee Theater* (NBC)

BEST CHILDREN'S SERIES: *Lassie* (CBS)

BEST SINGLE PROGRAM OF THE YEAR: "Peter Pan," *Producers' Showcase* (NBC)

BEST SPECIAL EVENT OR NEWS PROGRAM: A-Bomb Coverage (CBS)

BEST ACTOR IN A CONTINUING PERFORMANCE: Phil Silvers, *You'll Never Get Rich* (CBS)

BEST ACTRESS IN A CONTINUING PERFORMANCE: Lucille Ball, *I Love Lucy* (CBS)

BEST ACTOR IN A SINGLE PERFORMANCE: Lloyd Nolan, "The Caine Mutiny Court Martial," *Ford Star Jubilee* (CBS)

BEST ACTRESS IN A SINGLE PERFORMANCE: Mary Martin, "Peter Pan," *Producers' Showcase* (NBC)

BEST ACTOR IN A SUPPORTING ROLE: Art Carney, *The Honeymooners* (CBS)

BEST ACTRESS IN A SUPPORTING ROLE: Nanette Fabray, *Caesar's Hour* (NBC)

BEST EMCEE OR PROGRAM HOST: Perry Como (NBC)

BEST COMEDIAN: Phil Silvers (CBS)

BEST COMEDIENNE: Nanette Fabray (NBC)

BEST MALE SINGER: Perry Como (NBC)

BEST FEMALE SINGER: Dinah Shore (NBC)

BEST NEWS COMMENTATOR OR REPORTER: Edward R. Murrow (CBS)

BEST SPECIALTY ACT: Marcel Marceau (NBC)

BEST PRODUCER (LIVE SERIES): Fred Coe, *Producers' Showcase* (NBC)

BEST PRODUCER (FILM SERIES): Walt Disney, *Disneyland* (ABC)

BEST DIRECTOR (LIVE SERIES): Franklin Schaffner, "The Caine Mutiny Court Martial," *Ford Star Jubilee* (CBS)

BEST DIRECTOR (FILM SERIES): Nat Hiken, *You'll Never Get Rich* (CBS)

BEST ORIGINAL TELEPLAY WRITING: Rod Serling, "Patterns," *Kraft Television Theatre* (NBC)

BEST TELEVISION ADAPTATION: Paul Gregory and Franklin Schaffner, "The Caine Mutiny Court Martial," *Ford Star Jubilee* (CBS)

BEST COMEDY WRITING: Nat Hiken, Barry Blitser, Arnold Auerbach, Harvey Orkin, Vincent Bogert, Arnie Rosen, Coleman Jacoby, Tony Webster, and Harry Ryan, *You'll Never Get Rich* (CBS)

1956

BEST SERIES (HALF HOUR OR LESS): *You'll Never Get Rich* (CBS)

BEST SERIES (ONE HOUR OR MORE): *Caesar's Hour* (NBC)

BEST NEW PROGRAM SERIES: *Playhouse 90* (CBS)

BEST PUBLIC SERVICE SERIES: *See It Now* (CBS)

BEST SINGLE PROGRAM OF THE YEAR: "Requiem for a Heavyweight," *Playhouse 90* (CBS)

BEST COVERAGE OF A NEWSWORTHY EVENT: "Years of Crisis," Edward R. Murrow and correspondents (CBS)

BEST CONTINUING PERFORMANCE IN A DRAMATIC SERIES (ACTOR): Robert Young, *Father Knows Best* (NBC)

BEST CONTINUING PERFORMANCE IN A DRAMATIC SERIES (ACTRESS): Loretta Young, *The Loretta Young Show* (NBC)

BEST SINGLE PERFORMANCE (ACTOR): Jack Palance, "Requiem for a Heavyweight," *Playhouse 90* (CBS)

BEST SINGLE PERFORMANCE (ACTRESS): Claire Trevor, "Dodsworth," *Producers' Showcase* (NBC)

BEST MALE PERSONALITY (CONTINUING PERFORMANCE): Perry Como (NBC)

BEST FEMALE PERSONALITY (CONTINUING PERFORMANCE): Dinah Shore (NBC)

BEST CONTINUING PERFORMANCE BY A COMEDIAN IN A SERIES: Sid Caesar, *Caesar's Hour* (NBC)

BEST CONTINUING PERFORMANCE BY A COMEDIENNE IN A SERIES: Nanette Fabray, *Caesar's Hour* (NBC)

BEST SUPPORTING PERFORMANCE (ACTOR): Carl Reiner, *Caesar's Hour* (NBC)

BEST SUPPORTING PERFORMANCE (ACTRESS): Pat Carroll, *Caesar's Hour* (NBC)

BEST NEWS COMMENTATOR: Edward R. Murrow (CBS)

BEST DIRECTION (HALF HOUR OR LESS): Sheldon Leonard, "Danny's Comeback," *The Danny Thomas Show* (ABC)

BEST DIRECTION (ONE HOUR OR MORE): Ralph Nelson, "Requiem for a Heavyweight," *Playhouse 90* (CBS)

BEST TELEPLAY WRITING (HALF HOUR OR LESS): James P. Cavanaugh, "Fog Closing in," *Alfred Hitchcock Presents* (CBS)

BEST TELEPLAY WRITING (ONE HOUR OR MORE): Rod Serling, "Requiem for a Heavyweight," *Playhouse 90* (CBS)

BEST COMEDY WRITING: *You'll Never Get Rich* (CBS)

BEST ENGINEERING OR TECHNICAL ACHIEVEMENT: Ampex and CBS, for videotape development

1957

BEST MUSICAL, VARIETY, AUDIENCE PARTICIPATION, OR QUIZ SERIES: *The Dinah Shore Show* (NBC)

BEST COMEDY SERIES: *The Phil Silvers Show* (*You'll Never Get Rich*) (CBS)

BEST DRAMATIC SERIES WITH CONTINUING CHARACTERS: *Gunsmoke* (CBS)

BEST DRAMATIC ANTHOLOGY SERIES: *Playhouse 90* (CBS)

BEST NEW PROGRAM SERIES: *The Seven Lively Arts* (CBS)

BEST PUBLIC SERVICE PROGRAM OR SERIES: *Omnibus* (ABC and NBC)

BEST SINGLE PROGRAM OF THE YEAR: "The Comedian," *Playhouse 90* (CBS)

BEST CONTINUING PERFORMANCE BY AN ACTOR IN A LEADING ROLE IN A DRAMATIC OR COMEDY SERIES: Robert Young, *Father Knows Best* (NBC)

BEST CONTINUING PERFORMANCE BY AN ACTRESS IN A LEADING ROLE IN A DRAMATIC OR COMEDY SERIES: Jane Wyatt, *Father Knows Best* (NBC)

BEST SINGLE PERFORMANCE BY AN ACTOR: Peter Ustinov, "Life of Samuel Johnson," *Omnibus* (NBC)

BEST SINGLE PERFORMANCE BY AN ACTRESS: Polly Bergen, "The Helen Morgan Story," *Playhouse 90* (CBS)

BEST CONTINUING PERFORMANCE BY A MALE WHO PLAYS HIMSELF: Jack Benny, *The Jack Benny Show* (CBS)

BEST CONTINUING PERFORMANCE BY A FEMALE WHO PLAYS HERSELF: Dinah Shore, *The Dinah Shore Show* (NBC)

BEST CONTINUING SUPPORTING PERFORMANCE BY AN ACTOR IN A DRAMATIC OR COMEDY SERIES: Carl Reiner, *Caesar's Hour* (NBC)

BEST CONTINUING SUPPORTING PERFORMANCE BY AN ACTRESS IN A DRAMATIC OR COMEDY SERIES: Ann B. Davis, *The Bob Cummings Show* (CBS and NBC)

BEST NEWS COMMENTARY: Edward R. Murrow, *See It Now* (CBS)

BEST DIRECTION (HALF HOUR OR LESS): Robert Stevens, "The Glass Eye," *Alfred Hitchcock Presents* (CBS)

BEST DIRECTION (ONE HOUR OR MORE): Bob Banner, *The Dinah Shore Show* (NBC)
BEST TELEPLAY WRITING (HALF HOUR OR LESS): Paul Monash, "The Lonely Wizard," *Schlitz Playhouse of Stars* (CBS)
BEST TELEPLAY WRITING (HOUR OR MORE): Rod Serling, "The Comedian," *Playhouse 90* (CBS)
BEST COMEDY WRITING: Nat Hiken, Billy Friedberg, Phil Sharp, Terry Ryan, Coleman Jacoby, Arnold Rosen, Sidney Zelinka, A. J. Russell, and Tony Webster, *The Phil Silvers Show* (*You'll Never Get Rich*) (CBS)
BEST ENGINEERING OR TECHNICAL ACHIEVEMENT: *Wide, Wide World* (NBC)

1958–1959   (1 JANUARY 1958–28 FEBRUARY 1959)

BEST MUSICAL OR VARIETY SERIES: *The Dinah Shore Chevy Show* (NBC)
BEST COMEDY SERIES: *The Jack Benny Show* (CBS)
BEST DRAMATIC SERIES (LESS THAN ONE HOUR): *Alcoa-Goodyear Theatre* (NBC)
BEST DRAMATIC SERIES (ONE HOUR OR LONGER): *Playhouse 90* (CBS)
BEST WESTERN SERIES: *Maverick* (ABC)
BEST NEWS REPORTING SERIES: *The Huntley-Brinkley Report* (NBC)
BEST PUBLIC SERVICE PROGRAM OR SERIES: *Omnibus* (NBC)
BEST PANEL, QUIZ, OR AUDIENCE PARTICIPATION SERIES: *What's My Line?* (CBS)
MOST OUTSTANDING SINGLE PROGRAM OF THE YEAR: "An Evening with Fred Astaire" (NBC)
BEST SPECIAL MUSICAL OR VARIETY PROGRAM: "An Evening with Fred Astaire" (NBC)
BEST SPECIAL DRAMATIC PROGRAM: "Little Moon of Alban," *Hallmark Hall of Fame* (NBC)
BEST SPECIAL NEWS PROGRAM: "Face of Red China" (CBS)
BEST ACTOR IN A LEADING ROLE IN A DRAMATIC SERIES: Raymond Burr, *Perry Mason* (CBS)
BEST ACTRESS IN A LEADING ROLE IN A DRAMATIC SERIES: Loretta Young, *The Loretta Young Show* (NBC)
BEST ACTOR IN A LEADING ROLE IN A COMEDY SERIES: Jack Benny, *The Jack Benny Show* (CBS)
BEST ACTRESS IN A LEADING ROLE IN A COMEDY SERIES: Jane Wyatt, *Father Knows Best* (NBC and CBS)
BEST PERFORMANCE BY AN ACTOR IN A MUSICAL OR VARIETY SERIES: Perry Como, *The Perry Como Show* (NBC)
BEST PERFORMANCE BY AN ACTRESS IN A MUSICAL OR VARIETY SERIES: Dinah Shore, *The Dinah Shore Chevy Show* (NBC)
BEST SINGLE PERFORMANCE BY AN ACTOR: Fred Astaire, "An Evening with Fred Astaire," (NBC)
BEST SINGLE PERFORMANCE BY AN ACTRESS: Julie Harris, "Little Moon of Alban," *Hallmark Hall of Fame* (NBC)
BEST SUPPORTING ACTOR IN A DRAMATIC SERIES: Dennis Weaver, *Gunsmoke* (CBS)
BEST SUPPORTING ACTRESS IN A DRAMATIC SERIES: Barbara Hale, *Perry Mason* (CBS)
BEST SUPPORTING ACTOR IN A COMEDY SERIES: Tom Poston, *The Steve Allen Show* (NBC)
BEST SUPPORTING ACTRESS IN A COMEDY SERIES: Ann B. Davis, *The Bob Cummings Show* (NBC)
BEST NEWS COMMENTATOR OR ANALYST: Edward R. Murrow (CBS)
BEST DIRECTION OF A SINGLE PROGRAM OF A DRAMATIC SERIES (LESS THAN ONE HOUR): Jack Smight, "Eddie," *Alcoa-Goodyear Theatre* (NBC)
BEST DIRECTION OF A SINGLE PROGRAM OF A DRAMATIC SERIES (ONE HOUR OR LONGER): George Schaefer, "Little Moon of Alban," *Hallmark Hall of Fame* (NBC)
BEST DIRECTION OF A SINGLE MUSICAL OR VARIETY PROGRAM: Bud Yorkin, "An Evening with Fred Astaire" (NBC)
BEST DIRECTION OF A SINGLE PROGRAM OF A COMEDY SERIES: Peter Tewksbury, "A Medal for Margaret," *Father Knows Best* (CBS)
BEST WRITING OF A SINGLE PROGRAM OF A DRAMATIC SERIES (LESS THAN ONE HOUR): Alfred Brenner and Ken Hughes, "Eddie," *Alcoa-Goodyear Theatre* (NBC)

BEST WRITING OF A SINGLE PROGRAM OF A DRAMATIC SERIES (ONE HOUR OR LONGER): James Costigan, "Little Moon of Alban," *Hallmark Hall of Fame* (NBC)

BEST WRITING OF A SINGLE MUSICAL OR VARIETY PROGRAM: Bud Yorkin and Herbert Baker, "An Evening with Fred Astaire" (NBC)

BEST WRITING OF A SINGLE PROGRAM OF A COMEDY SERIES: Sam Perrin, George Balzer, Hal Goodman, and Al Gordon, "The Jack Benny Show with Ernie Kovacs," *The Jack Benny Show* (CBS)

BEST ON-THE-SPOT COVERAGE OF A NEWS EVENT: CBS, for coverage of the Cuban Revolution

BEST ENGINEERING OR TECHNICAL ACHIEVEMENT: "Industry-wide improvement of editing videotape as exemplified by ABC, CBS, NBC"

TRUSTEES' AWARD: Bob Hope

1959–1960   (1 MARCH 1959–31 MARCH 1960)

OUTSTANDING PROGRAM ACHIEVEMENT IN THE FIELD OF VARIETY: "The Fabulous Fifties" (CBS)

OUTSTANDING PROGRAM ACHIEVEMENT IN THE FIELD OF HUMOR: "Art Carney Special" ("Very Important People") (NBC)

OUTSTANDING PROGRAM ACHIEVEMENT IN THE FIELD OF DRAMA: *Playhouse 90* (CBS)

OUTSTANDING ACHIEVEMENT IN THE FIELD OF MUSIC: "Leonard Bernstein and the New York Philharmonic" (CBS)

OUTSTANDING PROGRAM ACHIEVEMENT IN THE FIELD OF NEWS: *The Huntley-Brinkley Report* (NBC)

OUTSTANDING PROGRAM ACHIEVEMENT IN THE FIELD OF PUBLIC AFFAIRS AND EDUCATION: *The Twentieth Century* (CBS)

OUTSTANDING PROGRAM ACHIEVEMENT IN THE FIELD OF CHILDREN'S PROGRAMMING: *Huckleberry Hound* (SYNDICATED)

OUTSTANDING PERFORMANCE BY AN ACTOR IN A SERIES: Robert Stack, *The Untouchables* (ABC)

OUTSTANDING PERFORMANCE BY AN ACTRESS IN A SERIES: Jane Wyatt, *Father Knows Best* (CBS)

OUTSTANDING SINGLE PERFORMANCE BY AN ACTOR: Laurence Olivier, "The Moon and Sixpence" (NBC)

OUTSTANDING SINGLE PERFORMANCE BY AN ACTRESS: Ingrid Bergman, "The Turn of the Screw," *Ford Startime* (NBC)

OUTSTANDING PERFORMANCE IN A VARIETY OR MUSICAL PROGRAM OR SERIES: Harry Belafonte, "Tonight with Belafonte," *The Revlon Revue* (CBS)

OUTSTANDING DIRECTORIAL ACHIEVEMENT IN DRAMA: Robert Mulligan, "The Moon and Sixpence" (NBC)

OUTSTANDING DIRECTORIAL ACHIEVEMENT IN COMEDY: Ralph Levy, for the Jack Benny hour specials (CBS)

OUTSTANDING WRITING ACHIEVEMENT IN DRAMA: Rod Serling, *The Twilight Zone* (CBS)

OUTSTANDING WRITING ACHIEVEMENT IN COMEDY: Al Gordon and Hal Goldman, *The Jack Benny Show* (CBS)

OUTSTANDING WRITING ACHIEVEMENT IN THE DOCUMENTARY FIELD: Howard K. Smith and Av Westin, "The Population Explosion" (CBS)

TRUSTEES' AWARD: Dr. Frank Stanton, president of CBS, Inc., "for outstanding service to television"

1960–1961   (1 APRIL 1960–15 APRIL 1961)

OUTSTANDING PROGRAM ACHIEVEMENT IN THE FIELD OF VARIETY: "Astaire Time" (NBC)

OUTSTANDING PROGRAM ACHIEVEMENT IN THE FIELD OF HUMOR: *The Jack Benny Show* (CBS)

OUTSTANDING PROGRAM ACHIEVEMENT IN THE FIELD OF DRAMA: "Macbeth," *Hallmark Hall of Fame* (NBC)

OUTSTANDING PROGRAM ACHIEVEMENT IN THE FIELD OF NEWS: *The Huntley-Brinkley Report* (NBC)

OUTSTANDING PROGRAM ACHIEVEMENT IN THE FIELD OF PUBLIC AFFAIRS AND EDUCATION: *The Twentieth Century* (CBS)

OUTSTANDING ACHIEVEMENT IN THE FIELD OF CHILDREN'S PROGRAMMING: "Aaron Copland's Birthday Party," *Young People's Concert* (CBS)

OUTSTANDING ACHIEVEMENT IN THE FIELD OF MUSIC FOR TELEVISION: "Leonard Bernstein and the New York Philharmonic" (CBS)

PROGRAM OF THE YEAR: "Macbeth," *Hallmark Hall of Fame* (NBC)

OUTSTANDING PERFORMANCE BY AN ACTOR IN A SERIES: Raymond Burr, *Perry Mason* (CBS)

OUTSTANDING PERFORMANCE BY AN ACTRESS IN A SERIES: Barbara Stanwyck, *The Barbara Stanwyck Show* (NBC)

OUTSTANDING SINGLE PERFORMANCE BY AN ACTOR IN A LEADING ROLE: Maurice Evans, "Macbeth," *Hallmark Hall of Fame* (NBC)

OUTSTANDING SINGLE PERFORMANCE BY AN ACTRESS IN A LEADING ROLE: Judith Anderson, "Macbeth," *Hallmark Hall of Fame* (NBC)

OUTSTANDING PERFORMANCE IN A VARIETY OR MUSICAL PROGRAM OR SERIES: Fred Astaire, "Astaire Time" (NBC)

OUTSTANDING PERFORMANCE IN A SUPPORTING ROLE BY AN ACTOR OR ACTRESS IN A SERIES: Don Knotts, *The Andy Griffith Show* (CBS)

OUTSTANDING PERFORMANCE IN A SUPPORTING ROLE BY AN ACTOR OR ACTRESS IN A SINGLE PROGRAM: Roddy McDowall, "Not Without Honor," *Our American Heritage* (NBC)

OUTSTANDING DIRECTORIAL ACHIEVEMENT IN DRAMA: George Schaefer, "Macbeth," *Hallmark Hall of Fame* (NBC)

OUTSTANDING DIRECTORIAL ACHIEVEMENT IN COMEDY: Sheldon Leonard, *The Danny Thomas Show* (CBS)

OUTSTANDING WRITING ACHIEVEMENT IN DRAMA: Rod Serling, *The Twilight Zone* (CBS)

OUTSTANDING WRITING ACHIEVEMENT IN COMEDY: Sherwood Schwartz, Dave O'Brien, Al Schwartz, Martin Ragaway, and Red Skelton, *The Red Skelton Show* (CBS)

OUTSTANDING WRITING ACHIEVEMENT IN THE DOCUMENTARY FIELD: Victor Wolfson, *Winston Churchill—The Valiant Years* (ABC)

TRUSTEES' AWARDS: (1) National Educational Television and Radio Center and its affiliated stations; and (2) Joyce C. Hall, president of Hallmark Cards, Inc. (sponsor of *Hallmark Hall of Fame*)

1961–1962   (16 APRIL 1961–14 APRIL 1962)

OUTSTANDING PROGRAM ACHIEVEMENT IN THE FIELD OF VARIETY: *The Garry Moore Show* (CBS)

OUTSTANDING PROGRAM ACHIEVEMENT IN THE FIELD OF HUMOR: *The Bob Newhart Show* (NBC)

OUTSTANDING PROGRAM ACHIEVEMENT IN THE FIELD OF DRAMA: *The Defenders* (CBS)

OUTSTANDING PROGRAM ACHIEVEMENT IN THE FIELD OF MUSIC: "Leonard Bernstein and the New York Philharmonic in Japan" (CBS)

OUTSTANDING PROGRAM ACHIEVEMENT IN THE FIELD OF NEWS: *The Huntley-Brinkley Report* (NBC)

OUTSTANDING PROGRAM ACHIEVEMENT IN THE FIELDS OF EDUCATIONAL AND PUBLIC AFFAIRS PROGRAMMING: *David Brinkley's Journal* (NBC)

OUTSTANDING PROGRAM ACHIEVEMENT IN THE FIELD OF CHILDREN'S PROGRAMMING: "New York Philharmonic Young People's Concert with Leonard Bernstein" (CBS)

OUTSTANDING DAYTIME PROGRAM: "Purex Specials for Women" (NBC)

PROGRAM OF THE YEAR: "Victoria Regina," *Hallmark Hall of Fame* (NBC)

OUTSTANDING CONTINUED PERFORMANCE BY AN ACTOR IN A SERIES: E. G. Marshall, *The Defenders* (CBS)

OUTSTANDING CONTINUED PERFORMANCE BY AN ACTRESS IN A SERIES: Shirley Booth, *Hazel* (NBC)

OUTSTANDING SINGLE PERFORMANCE BY AN ACTOR IN A LEADING ROLE: Peter Falk, "Price of Tomatoes," *Dick Powell Theatre* (NBC)

OUTSTANDING SINGLE PERFORMANCE BY AN ACTRESS IN A LEADING ROLE: Julie Harris, "Victoria Regina," *Hallmark Hall of Fame* (NBC)

OUTSTANDING PERFORMANCE IN A VARIETY OR MUSICAL PROGRAM OR SERIES: Carol Burnett, *The Garry Moore Show* (CBS)

OUTSTANDING PERFORMANCE IN A SUPPORTING ROLE BY AN ACTOR: Don Knotts, *The Andy Griffith Show* (CBS)

OUTSTANDING PERFORMANCE IN A SUPPORTING ROLE BY AN ACTRESS: Pamela Brown, "Victoria Regina," *Hallmark Hall of Fame* (NBC)

OUTSTANDING DIRECTORIAL ACHIEVEMENT IN DRAMA: Franklin Schaffner, *The Defenders* (various episodes) (CBS)

OUTSTANDING DIRECTORIAL ACHIEVEMENT IN COMEDY: Nat Hiken, *Car 54, Where Are You?* (NBC)

OUTSTANDING WRITING ACHIEVEMENT IN DRAMA: Reginald Rose, *The Defenders* (various episodes) (CBS)

OUTSTANDING WRITING ACHIEVEMENT IN COMEDY: Carl Reiner, *The Dick Van Dyke Show* (CBS)

OUTSTANDING WRITING ACHIEVEMENT IN THE DOCUMENTARY FIELD: Lou Hazam, "Vincent Van Gogh: A Self-Portrait" (NBC)

SPECIAL TRUSTEE AWARDS: (1) CBS, "A Tour of the White House with Mrs. Jacqueline Kennedy"; (2) Mrs. Jacqueline Kennedy; (3) The news departments of ABC, CBS, and NBC for coverage of Colonel John Glenn's orbital flight; and (4) Brigadier General David Sarnoff, chairman of the board, RCA

1962–1963   (15 APRIL 1962–14 APRIL 1963)

OUTSTANDING ACHIEVEMENT IN THE FIELD OF VARIETY: *The Andy Williams Show* (NBC)

OUTSTANDING PROGRAM ACHIEVEMENT IN THE FIELD OF HUMOR: *The Dick Van Dyke Show* (CBS)

OUTSTANDING PROGRAM ACHIEVEMENT IN THE FIELD OF DRAMA: *The Defenders* (CBS)

OUTSTANDING ACHIEVEMENT IN THE FIELD OF NEWS: *The Huntley-Brinkley Report* (NBC)

OUTSTANDING PROGRAM ACHIEVEMENT IN THE FIELD OF NEWS COMMENTARY OR PUBLIC AFFAIRS: *David Brinkley's Journal* (NBC)

OUTSTANDING ACHIEVEMENT IN THE FIELD OF DOCUMENTARY PROGRAMS: "The Tunnel," Reuven Frank, producer (NBC)

OUTSTANDING PROGRAM ACHIEVEMENT IN THE FIELD OF PANEL, QUIZ, OR AUDIENCE PARTICIPATION: *G-E College Bowl* (CBS)

OUTSTANDING PROGRAM ACHIEVEMENT IN THE FIELD OF MUSIC: "Julie and Carol at Carnegie Hall" (CBS)

OUTSTANDING PROGRAM ACHIEVEMENT IN THE FIELD OF CHILDREN'S PROGRAMMING: *Walt Disney's Wonderful World of Color* (NBC)

PROGRAM OF THE YEAR: "The Tunnel" (NBC)

OUTSTANDING CONTINUED PERFORMANCE BY AN ACTOR IN A SERIES: E. G. Marshall, *The Defenders* (CBS)

OUTSTANDING CONTINUED PERFORMANCE BY AN ACTRESS IN A SERIES: Shirley Booth, *Hazel* (NBC)

OUTSTANDING PERFORMANCE IN A VARIETY OR MUSICAL PROGRAM OR SERIES: Carol Burnett, "Julie and Carol at Carnegie Hall" and "Carol and Company" (CBS)

OUTSTANDING SINGLE PERFORMANCE BY AN ACTOR IN A LEADING ROLE: Trevor Howard, "The Invincible Mr. Disraeli," *Hallmark Hall of Fame* (NBC)

OUTSTANDING SINGLE PERFORMANCE BY AN ACTRESS IN A LEADING ROLE: Kim Stanley, "A Cardinal Act of Mercy," *Ben Casey* (ABC)

OUTSTANDING PERFORMANCE IN A SUPPORTING ROLE BY AN ACTOR: Don Knotts, *The Andy Griffith Show* (CBS)

OUTSTANDING PERFORMANCE IN A SUPPORTING ROLE BY AN ACTRESS: Glenda Farrell, "A Cardinal Act of Mercy," *Ben Casey* (ABC)

OUTSTANDING ACHIEVEMENT IN INTERNATIONAL REPORTING OR COMMENTARY: Piers Anderton, "The Tunnel" (NBC)

OUTSTANDING DIRECTORIAL ACHIEVEMENT IN DRAMA: Stuart Rosenberg, "The Madman," *The Defenders* (CBS)

OUTSTANDING DIRECTORIAL ACHIEVEMENT IN COMEDY: John Rich, *The Dick Van Dyke Show* (CBS)

OUTSTANDING WRITING ACHIEVEMENT IN DRAMA: Robert Thom and Reginald Rose, "The Madman," *The Defenders* (CBS)

OUTSTANDING WRITING ACHIEVEMENT IN COMEDY: Carl Reiner, *The Dick Van Dyke Show* (CBS)

TRUSTEES' AWARDS: (1) American Telephone and Telegraph Company (for Telstar I and II); (2) Dick Powell (in memoriam)

TRUSTEES' CITATION: To the President of the United States

1963–1964   (15 APRIL 1963–12 APRIL 1964)

OUTSTANDING PROGRAM ACHIEVEMENT IN THE FIELD OF VARIETY: *The Danny Kaye Show* (CBS)

OUTSTANDING PROGRAM ACHIEVEMENT IN THE FIELD OF COMEDY: *The Dick Van Dyke Show* (CBS)

OUTSTANDING PROGRAM ACHIEVEMENT IN THE FIELD OF DRAMA: *The Defenders* (CBS)

OUTSTANDING PROGRAM ACHIEVEMENT IN THE FIELD OF NEWS REPORTS: *The Huntley-Brinkley Report* (NBC)

OUTSTANDING PROGRAM ACHIEVEMENT IN THE FIELD OF NEWS COMMENTARY OR PUBLIC AFFAIRS: "Cuba: Parts I and II—The Bay of Pigs and the Missile Crisis," *NBC White Paper* (NBC)

OUTSTANDING ACHIEVEMENT IN THE FIELD OF DOCUMENTARY PROGRAMS: "The Making of the President 1960" (ABC)

OUTSTANDING PROGRAM ACHIEVEMENT IN THE FIELD OF MUSIC: *The Bell Telephone Hour* (NBC)

OUTSTANDING PROGRAM ACHIEVEMENT IN THE FIELD OF CHILDREN'S PROGRAMMING: *Discovery '63–'64* (ABC)

PROGRAM OF THE YEAR: "The Making of the President 1960" (ABC)

OUTSTANDING CONTINUED PERFORMANCE BY AN ACTOR IN A SERIES: Dick Van Dyke, *The Dick Van Dyke Show* (CBS)

OUTSTANDING CONTINUED PERFORMANCE BY AN ACTRESS IN A SERIES: Mary Tyler Moore, *The Dick Van Dyke Show* (CBS)

OUTSTANDING SINGLE PERFORMANCE BY AN ACTOR IN A LEADING ROLE: Jack Klugman, "Blacklist," *The Defenders* (CBS)

OUTSTANDING SINGLE PERFORMANCE BY AN ACTRESS IN A LEADING ROLE: Shelley Winters, "Two Is the Number," *Bob Hope Presents the Chrysler Theatre* (NBC)

OUTSTANDING PERFORMANCE IN A VARIETY PROGRAM OR SERIES: Danny Kaye, *The Danny Kaye Show* (CBS)

OUTSTANDING PERFORMANCE IN A SUPPORTING ROLE BY AN ACTOR: Albert Paulsen, "One Day in the Life of Ivan Denisovich," *Bob Hope Presents the Chrysler Theatre* (NBC)

OUTSTANDING PERFORMANCE IN A SUPPORTING ROLE BY AN ACTRESS: Ruth White, "Little Moon of Alban," *Hallmark Hall of Fame* (NBC)

OUTSTANDING DIRECTORIAL ACHIEVEMENT IN DRAMA: Tom Gries, "Who Do You Kill?" *East Side, West Side* (CBS)

OUTSTANDING DIRECTORIAL ACHIEVEMENT IN COMEDY: Jerry Paris, *The Dick Van Dyke Show* (CBS)

OUTSTANDING DIRECTORIAL ACHIEVEMENT IN VARIETY OR MUSIC: Robert Scherer, *The Danny Kaye Show* (CBS)

OUTSTANDING WRITING ACHIEVEMENT IN DRAMA (ORIGINAL WORK): Ernest Kinoy, "Blacklist," *The Defenders* (CBS)

OUTSTANDING WRITING ACHIEVEMENT IN DRAMA (ADAPTATION): Rod Serling, "It's Mental Work," *Bob Hope Presents the Chrysler Theatre* (NBC)

OUTSTANDING WRITING ACHIEVEMENT IN COMEDY OR VARIETY: Carl Reiner, Sam Denoff, and Bill Persky, *The Dick Van Dyke Show* (CBS)

1964–1965 (13 APRIL 1964–30 APRIL 1965)

OUTSTANDING PROGRAM ACHIEVEMENTS IN ENTERTAINMENT: (1) *The Dick Van Dyke Show* (CBS); Carl Reiner, producer; (2) "The Magnificent Yankee," *Hallmark Hall of Fame* (NBC); George Schaefer, producer; (3) "My Name is Barbra" (CBS); Richard Lewine, producer; and (4) "What Is Sonata Form?" *New York Philharmonic Young People's Concerts with Leonard Bernstein* (CBS); Roger Englander, producer

OUTSTANDING PROGRAM ACHIEVEMENTS IN NEWS, DOCUMENTARIES, INFORMATION, AND SPORTS: (1) "I, Leonardo da Vinci," *Saga of Western Man* (ABC); John H. Secondari and Helen Jean Rogers, producers; and (2) "The Louvre" (NBC); Lucy Jarvis, producer; John J. Sughrue, coproducer

OUTSTANDING INDIVIDUAL ACHIEVEMENTS IN ENTERTAINMENT (ACTORS AND PERFORMERS): (1) Dick Van Dyke, *The Dick Van Dyke Show* (CBS); (2) Alfred Lunt, "The Magnificent Yankee," *Hallmark Hall of Fame* (NBC); (3) Lynn Fontanne, "The Magnificent Yankee," *Hallmark Hall of Fame* (NBC); (4) Barbra Streisand, "My Name is Barbra" (CBS); and (5) Leonard Bernstein, *New York Philharmonic Young People's Concerts with Leonard Bernstein* (CBS)

OUTSTANDING INDIVIDUAL ACHIEVEMENTS IN ENTERTAINMENT (DIRECTORS AND WRITERS): (1) Paul Bogart (director), "The 700-Year-Old Gang," *The Defenders* (CBS); (2) David Karp (writer), "The 700-Year-Old Gang," *The Defenders* (CBS)

OUTSTANDING INDIVIDUAL ACHIEVEMENTS IN NEWS, DOCUMENTARIES, INFORMATION, AND SPORTS: (1) John J. Sughrue (director), "The Louvre" (NBC); and (2) Sidney Carroll (writer), "The Louvre" (NBC)

1965–1966 (1 MAY 1965–10 APRIL 1966)

OUTSTANDING VARIETY SERIES: *The Andy Williams Show* (NBC); Bob Finkel, producer

OUTSTANDING COMEDY SERIES: *The Dick Van Dyke Show* (CBS); Carl Reiner, producer

OUTSTANDING DRAMATIC SERIES: *The Fugitive* (ABC); Alan Armer, producer

OUTSTANDING VARIETY SPECIAL: "Chrysler Presents the Bob Hope Christmas Special" (NBC); Bob Hope, executive producer

OUTSTANDING DRAMATIC PROGRAM: "Ages of Man" (CBS); David Susskind and Daniel Melnick, producers

OUTSTANDING MUSICAL PROGRAM: "Frank Sinatra: A Man and His Music" (NBC); Dwight Hemion, producer

OUTSTANDING CHILDREN'S PROGRAM: "A Charlie Brown Christmas" (CBS); Lee Mendelson and Bill Melendez, producers

ACHIEVEMENTS IN NEWS AND DOCUMENTARIES—PROGRAMS: (1) "American White Paper: United States Foreign Policy" (NBC); Fred Freed, producer; (2) "KKK—The Invisible Empire," *CBS Reports* (CBS); David Lowe, producer; (3) "Senate Hearings on Vietnam" (NBC); Chet Hagan, producer

ACHIEVEMENTS IN DAYTIME PROGRAMMING: (1) *Camera Three* (CBS); Dan Gallagher, producer; and (2) *Mutual of Omaha's Wild Kingdom* (NBC); Don Meier, producer

ACHIEVEMENTS IN SPORTS (PROGRAMS): (1) *ABC's Wide World of Sports* (ABC); Roone Arledge, executive producer; (2) "CBS Golf Classic" (CBS); Frank Chirkinian, producer; and (3) *Shell's Wonderful World of Golf* (NBC); Fred Raphael, producer

OUTSTANDING CONTINUED PERFORMANCE BY AN ACTOR IN A LEADING ROLE IN A DRAMATIC SERIES: Bill Cosby, *I Spy* (NBC)

OUTSTANDING CONTINUED PERFORMANCE BY AN ACTRESS IN A LEADING ROLE IN A DRAMATIC SERIES: Barbara Stanwyck, *The Big Valley* (ABC)

OUTSTANDING CONTINUED PERFORMANCE BY AN ACTOR IN A LEADING ROLE IN A COMEDY SERIES: Dick Van Dyke, *The Dick Van Dyke Show* (CBS)

OUTSTANDING CONTINUED PERFORMANCE BY AN ACTRESS IN A LEADING ROLE IN A COMEDY SERIES: Mary Tyler Moore, *The Dick Van Dyke Show* (CBS)

OUTSTANDING SINGLE PERFORMANCE BY AN ACTOR IN A LEADING ROLE IN A DRAMA: Cliff Robertson, "The Game," *Bob Hope Presents the Chrysler Theatre* (NBC)

OUTSTANDING SINGLE PERFORMANCE BY AN ACTRESS IN A LEADING ROLE IN A DRAMA: Simone Signoret, "A Small Rebellion," *Bob Hope Presents the Chrysler Theatre* (NBC)

OUTSTANDING PERFORMANCE BY AN ACTOR IN A SUPPORTING ROLE IN A DRAMA: James Daly, "Eagle in a Cage," *Hallmark Hall of Fame* (NBC)

OUTSTANDING PERFORMANCE BY AN ACTRESS IN A SUPPORTING ROLE IN A DRAMA: Lee Grant, *Peyton Place* (ABC)

OUTSTANDING PERFORMANCE BY AN ACTOR IN A SUPPORTING ROLE IN A COMEDY: Don Knotts, "The Return of Barney Fife," *The Andy Griffith Show* (CBS)

OUTSTANDING PERFORMANCE BY AN ACTRESS IN A SUPPORTING ROLE IN A COMEDY: Alice Pearce, *Bewitched* (ABC)

ACHIEVEMENT IN EDUCATIONAL TELEVISION (INDIVIDUAL): Julia Child, *The French Chef* (NET)

OUTSTANDING DIRECTORIAL ACHIEVEMENT IN DRAMA: Sidney Pollack, "The Game," *Bob Hope Presents the Chrysler Theatre* (NBC)

OUTSTANDING DIRECTORIAL ACHIEVEMENT IN COMEDY: William Asher, *Bewitched* (ABC)

OUTSTANDING DIRECTORIAL ACHIEVEMENT IN VARIETY OR MUSIC: Alan Handley, "The Julie Andrews Show" (NBC)

OUTSTANDING WRITING ACHIEVEMENT IN DRAMA: Millard Lampell, "Eagle in a Cage," *Hallmark Hall of Fame* (NBC)

OUTSTANDING WRITING ACHIEVEMENT IN COMEDY: Bill Persky and Sam Denoff, "Coast to Coast Big Mouth," *The Dick Van Dyke Show* (CBS)

OUTSTANDING WRITING ACHIEVEMENT IN VARIETY: Al Gordon, Hal Goldman, and Sheldon Keller, "An Evening with Carol Channing" (CBS)

SPECIAL CLASSIFICATIONS OF INDIVIDUAL ACHIEVEMENTS: Burr Tillstrom, *That Was the Week That Was* (NBC), "for his 'Berlin Wall' hand ballet"

TRUSTEES' AWARDS: (1) Edward R. Murrow; and (2) Xerox Corporation

1966–1967   (25 MARCH 1966–16 APRIL 1967)

OUTSTANDING VARIETY SERIES: *The Andy Williams Show* (NBC); Edward Stephenson and Bob Finkel, producers

OUTSTANDING COMEDY SERIES: *The Monkees* (NBC); Bert Schneider and Bob Rafelson, producers

OUTSTANDING DRAMATIC SERIES: *Mission: Impossible* (CBS); Joseph Gantman and Bruce Geller, producers

OUTSTANDING VARIETY SPECIAL: "The Sid Caesar, Imogene Coca, Carl Reiner, Howard Morris Special" (CBS); Jack Arnold, producer

OUTSTANDING DRAMATIC PROGRAM: "Death of a Salesman" (CBS); David Susskind and Daniel Melnick, producers

OUTSTANDING MUSICAL PROGRAM: "Brigadoon" (ABC); Fielder Cook, producer

OUTSTANDING CHILDREN'S PROGRAM: "Jack and the Beanstalk" (NBC); Gene Kelly, producer

ACHIEVEMENTS IN NEWS AND DOCUMENTARIES—PROGRAMS: (1) "China: The Roots of Madness" (SYNDICATED); Mel Stuart, producer; (2) "Hall of Kings" (ABC); Harry Rasky, producer; and (3) "The Italians" (CBS); Bernard Birnbaum, producer

ACHIEVEMENTS IN NEWS AND DOCUMENTARIES—INDIVIDUAL: Theodore H. White, writer of "China: The Roots of Madness" (SYNDICATED)

ACHIEVEMENTS IN DAYTIME PROGRAMMING—PROGRAMS: *Mutual of Omaha's Wild Kingdom* (NBC); Don Meier, producer

ACHIEVEMENTS IN DAYTIME PROGRAMMING—INDIVIDUAL: Mike Douglas, *The Mike Douglas Show* (SYNDICATED)

ACHIEVEMENTS IN SPORTS—PROGRAMS: *ABC's Wide World of Sports* (ABC); Roone Arledge, executive producer

OUTSTANDING CONTINUED PERFORMANCE BY AN ACTOR IN A LEADING ROLE IN A DRAMATIC SERIES: Bill Cosby, *I Spy* (NBC)

OUTSTANDING CONTINUED PERFORMANCE BY AN ACTRESS IN A LEADING ROLE IN A DRAMATIC SERIES: Barbara Bain, *Mission: Impossible* (CBS)

OUTSTANDING CONTINUED PERFORMANCE BY AN ACTOR IN A LEADING ROLE IN A COMEDY SERIES: Don Adams, *Get Smart* (NBC)

OUTSTANDING CONTINUED PERFORMANCE BY AN ACTRESS IN A LEADING ROLE IN A COMEDY SERIES: Lucille Ball, *The Lucy Show* (CBS)

OUTSTANDING SINGLE PERFORMANCE BY AN ACTOR IN A LEADING ROLE IN A DRAMA: Peter Ustinov, "Barefoot in Athens," *Hallmark Hall of Fame* (NBC)

OUTSTANDING SINGLE PERFORMANCE BY AN ACTRESS IN A LEADING ROLE IN A DRAMA: Geraldine Page, "A Christmas Memory," *ABC Stage 67* (ABC)

OUTSTANDING PERFORMANCE BY AN ACTOR IN A SUPPORTING ROLE IN A DRAMA: Eli Wallach, "The Poppy Is also a Flower" (ABC)

OUTSTANDING PERFORMANCE BY AN ACTRESS IN A SUPPORTING ROLE IN A DRAMA: Agnes Moorehead, "Night of the Vicious Valentine," *The Wild, Wild West* (CBS)

OUTSTANDING PERFORMANCE BY AN ACTOR IN A SUPPORTING ROLE IN A COMEDY: Don Knotts, "Barney Comes to Mayberry," *The Andy Griffith Show* (CBS)

OUTSTANDING PERFORMANCE BY AN ACTRESS IN A SUPPORTING ROLE IN A COMEDY: Frances Bavier, *The Andy Griffith Show* (CBS)

OUTSTANDING DIRECTORIAL ACHIEVEMENT IN DRAMA: Alex Segal, "Death of a Salesman" (CBS)

OUTSTANDING DIRECTORIAL ACHIEVEMENT IN COMEDY: James Frawley, "Royal Flush," *The Monkees* (NBC)

OUTSTANDING DIRECTORIAL ACHIEVEMENT IN VARIETY OR MUSIC: Fielder Cook, "Brigadoon" (ABC)

OUTSTANDING WRITING ACHIEVEMENT IN DRAMA: Bruce Geller, *Mission: Impossible* (CBS)

OUTSTANDING WRITING ACHIEVEMENT IN COMEDY: Buck Henry and Leonard Stern, "Ship of Spies," *Get Smart* (NBC)

OUTSTANDING WRITING ACHIEVEMENT IN VARIETY: Mel Brooks, Sam Denoff, Bill Persky, Carl Reiner, and Mel Tolkin, "The Sid Caesar, Imogene Coca, Carl Reiner, Howard Morris Special" (CBS)

SPECIAL CLASSIFICATIONS OF INDIVIDUAL ACHIEVEMENTS: (1) Art Carney, *The Jackie Gleason Show* (CBS); (2) Truman Capote and Eleanor Perry, for the adaptation of "A Christmas Memory," *ABC Stage 67* (ABC); and (3) Arthur Miller, for the adaptation of "Death of a Salesman" (CBS)

TRUSTEES' AWARD: Sylvester L. "Pat" Weaver, Jr.

1967–1968   (27 MARCH 1967–6 MARCH 1968)

OUTSTANDING MUSICAL OR VARIETY SERIES: *Rowan and Martin's Laugh-In* (NBC); George Schlatter, producer

OUTSTANDING COMEDY SERIES: *Get Smart* (NBC); Burt Nodella, producer

OUTSTANDING DRAMATIC SERIES: *Mission: Impossible* (CBS); Joseph E. Gantman, producer

OUTSTANDING MUSICAL OR VARIETY PROGRAM: "Rowan and Martin's Laugh-In Special" (NBC); George Schlatter, producer

OUTSTANDING DRAMATIC PROGRAM: "Elizabeth the Queen," *Hallmark Hall of Fame* (NBC); George Schaefer, producer

OUTSTANDING ACHIEVEMENT IN CULTURAL DOCUMENTARIES: (1) "Eric Hoffer, the Passionate State of Mind," Jack Beck, producer, *The CBS News Hour* (CBS); (2) "Gauguin in Tahiti: The Search for Paradise," Martin Carr, producer, *The CBS News Hour* (CBS); (3) "John Steinbeck's 'America and Americans'" (NBC); Lee Mendelson, producer; (4) "Dylan Thomas: The World I Breathe," Perry Miller Adato, producer, *NET Festival* (NET); (5) Nathaniel Dorsky, art photographer, "Gauguin in Tahiti: The Search for Paradise," *The CBS News Hour* (CBS); (6) Harry Morgan, writer, "The Wyeth Phenomenon, on Who, What, When, Where,

Why with Harry Reasoner," *The CBS News Hour* (CBS); and (7) Thomas A. Priestley, director of photography, and Robert Loweree, film editor, "John Steinbeck's 'America and Americans'" (NBC)

OUTSTANDING ACHIEVEMENT IN NEWS DOCUMENTARIES: (1) "Africa" (ABC); James Fleming, executive producer; (2) "Summer '67: What We Learned" (NBC); Fred Freed, producer; (3) "CBS Reports: What About Ronald Reagan?" *The CBS News Hour* (CBS); Harry Reasoner, writer; and (4) "Same Mud, Same Blood" (NBC); Vo Huynh, cameraman

OUTSTANDING ACHIEVEMENT WITHIN REGULARLY SCHEDULED NEWS PROGRAMS: (1) "1st Cavalry, Con Thien" and other segments, *The CBS Evening News with Walter Cronkite* (CBS); John Laurence, correspondent; Keith Kay, cameraman; and (2) "Crisis in the Cities," *PBL* (NET); Av Westin, executive producer

OUTSTANDING ACHIEVEMENT IN COVERAGE OF SPECIAL EVENTS (NEWS ANALYSIS): (1) "State of the Union/68" (NET); Jim Karayn, executive producer; and (2) Satellite coverage of Adenauer's funeral (NBC); Frank McGee, commentator

OTHER OUTSTANDING NEWS AND DOCUMENTARY ACHIEVEMENTS: (1) *The Twenty-First Century* (CBS); Isaac Kleinerman, producer; (2) "Science and Religion: Who Will Play God?" *CBS News Special* (CBS); Ben Flynn, producer; and (3) George Delerue, composer, "Our World" (NET)

OUTSTANDING ACHIEVEMENT IN DAYTIME PROGRAMMING: *Today* (NBC); Al Morgan, producer

OUTSTANDING ACHIEVEMENTS IN SPORTS PROGRAMMING: (1) *ABC's Wide World of Sports* (ABC); Roone Arledge, executive producer; and (2) Jim McKay, commentator, *ABC's Wide World of Sports* (ABC)

OUTSTANDING CONTINUED PERFORMANCE BY AN ACTOR IN A LEADING ROLE IN A DRAMATIC SERIES: Bill Cosby, *I Spy* (NBC)

OUTSTANDING CONTINUED PERFORMANCE BY AN ACTRESS IN A LEADING ROLE IN A DRAMATIC SERIES: Barbara Bain, *Mission: Impossible* (CBS)

OUTSTANDING CONTINUED PERFORMANCE BY AN ACTOR IN A LEADING ROLE IN A COMEDY SERIES: Don Adams, *Get Smart* (NBC)

OUTSTANDING CONTINUED PERFORMANCE BY AN ACTRESS IN A LEADING ROLE IN A COMEDY SERIES: Lucille Ball, *The Lucy Show* (CBS)

OUTSTANDING SINGLE PERFORMANCE BY AN ACTOR IN A LEADING ROLE IN A DRAMA: Melvyn Douglas, "Do Not Go Gentle into That Good Night," *CBS Playhouse* (CBS)

OUTSTANDING SINGLE PERFORMANCE BY AN ACTRESS IN A LEADING ROLE IN A DRAMA: Maureen Stapleton, "Among the Paths to Eden," *Xerox Special Event* (ABC)

OUTSTANDING PERFORMANCE BY AN ACTOR IN A SUPPORTING ROLE IN A DRAMA: Milburn Stone, *Gunsmoke* (CBS)

OUTSTANDING PERFORMANCE BY AN ACTRESS IN A SUPPORTING ROLE IN A DRAMA: Barbara Anderson, *Ironside* (NBC)

OUTSTANDING PERFORMANCE BY AN ACTOR IN A SUPPORTING ROLE IN A COMEDY: Werner Klemperer, *Hogan's Heroes* (CBS)

OUTSTANDING PERFORMANCE BY AN ACTRESS IN A SUPPORTING ROLE IN A COMEDY: Marion Lorne, *Bewitched* (ABC)

SPECIAL CLASSIFICATIONS OF OUTSTANDING INDIVIDUAL ACHIEVEMENT: (1) Art Carney, *The Jackie Gleason Show* (CBS); and (2) Pat Paulsen, *The Smothers Brothers Comedy Hour* (CBS)

OUTSTANDING DIRECTORIAL ACHIEVEMENT IN DRAMA: Paul Bogart, "Dear Friends," *CBS Playhouse* (CBS)

OUTSTANDING DIRECTORIAL ACHIEVEMENT IN COMEDY: Bruce Bilson, "Maxwell Smart, Private Eye," *Get Smart* (NBC)

OUTSTANDING DIRECTORIAL ACHIEVEMENT IN MUSIC OR VARIETY: Jack Haley, Jr., "Movin' with Nancy" (NBC)

OUTSTANDING WRITING ACHIEVEMENT IN DRAMA: Loring Mandel, "Do Not Go Gentle into That Good Night," *CBS Playhouse* (CBS)

OUTSTANDING WRITING ACHIEVEMENT IN COMEDY: Allan Burns and Chris Hayward, "The Coming-Out Party," *He & She* (CBS)

OUTSTANDING WRITING ACHIEVEMENT IN MUSIC OR VARIETY: Paul Keyes, Hugh Wedlock,

Allan Manings, Chris Bearde, David Panich, Phil Hahn, Jack Hanrahan, Coslough Johnson, Marc London, and Digby Wolfe, *Rowan and Martin's Laugh-In* (NBC)

TRUSTEES' AWARD: Donald H. McGannon, president and chairman of the board of directors of Group W (Westinghouse Broadcasting Company)

1968–1969   (7 MARCH 1968–16 MARCH 1969)

OUTSTANDING MUSICAL OR VARIETY SERIES: *Rowan and Martin's Laugh-In* (NBC); George Schlatter, executive producer; Paul W. Keyes and Carolyn Raskin, producers; Dan Rowan and Dick Martin, stars

OUTSTANDING COMEDY SERIES: *Get Smart* (NBC); Arne Sultan, executive producer; Burt Nodella, producer

OUTSTANDING DRAMATIC SERIES: *NET Playhouse* (NET); Curtis Davis, executive producer

OUTSTANDING VARIETY OR MUSICAL PROGRAM: "The Bill Cosby Special" (NBC); Roy Silver, executive producer; Bill Hobin, Bill Persky, and Sam Denoff, producers; Bill Cosby, star

OUTSTANDING DRAMATIC PROGRAM: "Teacher, Teacher," *Hallmark Hall of Fame* (NBC); Henry Jaffe, executive producer; George Lefferts, producer

OUTSTANDING CULTURAL DOCUMENTARY AND MAGAZINE-TYPE PROGRAM OR SERIES ACHIEVEMENT (PROGRAMS AND INDIVIDUALS): (1) "Don't Count the Candles," William K. McClure, producer, *The CBS News Hour* (CBS); (2) "Justice Black and the Bill of Rights," Burton Benjamin, producer, *CBS News Special* (CBS); (3) "Man Who Dances: Edward Villella," Robert Drew and Mike Jackson, producers, *The Bell Telephone Hour* (NBC); and (4) "The Great American Novel," Arthur Barron, producer, *The CBS News Hour* (CBS); (5) Walter Dombrow and Jerry Sims, cinematographers, "The Great American Novel," *The CBS News Hour* (CBS); (6) Tom Pettit, producer, "CBW: The Secrets of Secrecy," *First Tuesday* (NBC); and (7) Lord Snowdon, cinematographer, "Don't Count the Candles," *The CBS News Hour* (CBS)

OUTSTANDING NEWS DOCUMENTARY PROGRAM ACHIEVEMENT (PROGRAMS AND INDIVIDUALS): (1) "Hunger in America," Martin Carr, producer, *The CBS News Hour* (CBS); (2) "Law and Order," Frederick Wiseman, producer, *PBL* (NET); and (3) Perry Wolff and Andrew A. Rooney, writers, "Black History: Lost, Stolen or Strayed—Of Black America," *The CBS News Hour* (CBS)

OUTSTANDING ACHIEVEMENT WITHIN REGULARLY SCHEDULED NEWS PROGRAMS: (1) Coverage of hunger in the United States, Wallace Westfeldt, executive producer, *The Huntley-Brinkley Report* (NBC); (2) "On the Road," *The CBS Evening News with Walter Cronkite* (CBS); Charles Kuralt, correspondent; James Wilson, cameraman; Robert Funk, soundman; and (3) "Police after Chicago," *The CBS Evening News with Walter Cronkite* (CBS); John Laurence, correspondent

OUTSTANDING ACHIEVEMENT IN COVERAGE OF SPECIAL EVENTS: "Coverage of Martin Luther King Assassination and Aftermath," *CBS News Special Reports and Special Broadcasts* (CBS); Robert Wussler, Ernest Leiser, Don Hewitt, and Burton Benjamin, executive producers

OUTSTANDING ACHIEVEMENT IN DAYTIME PROGRAMMING: *The Dick Cavett Show* (ABC); Don Silverman, producer

OUTSTANDING ACHIEVEMENT IN SPORTS PROGRAMMING: "19th Summer Olympic Games" (ABC); Roone P. Arledge, executive producer; Bill Bennington, Mike Freedman, Mac Hemion, Robert Riger, Marv Schlenker, Andy Sidaris, Lou Volpicelli and Doug Wilson, directors

OUTSTANDING PROGRAM ACHIEVEMENT, SPECIAL CLASSIFICATION: (1) *Firing Line with William F. Buckley, Jr.* (SYNDICATED); Warren Steibel, producer; and (2) *Mutual of Omaha's Wild Kingdom* (NBC); Don Meier, producer

OUTSTANDING CONTINUED PERFORMANCE BY AN ACTOR IN A LEADING ROLE IN A DRAMATIC SERIES: Carl Betz, *Judd for the Defense* (ABC)

OUTSTANDING CONTINUED PERFORMANCE BY AN ACTRESS IN A LEADING ROLE IN A DRAMATIC SERIES: Barbara Bain, *Mission: Impossible* (CBS)

OUTSTANDING CONTINUED PERFORMANCE BY AN ACTOR IN A LEADING ROLE IN A COMEDY SERIES: Don Adams, *Get Smart* (NBC)

OUTSTANDING CONTINUED PERFORMANCE BY AN ACTRESS IN A LEADING ROLE IN A COMEDY SERIES: Hope Lange, *The Ghost and Mrs. Muir* (NBC)

OUTSTANDING SINGLE PERFORMANCE BY AN ACTOR IN A LEADING ROLE: Paul Scofield, "Male of the Species," *Prudential's On Stage* (NBC)

OUTSTANDING SINGLE PERFORMANCE BY AN ACTRESS IN A LEADING ROLE: Geraldine Page, "The Thanksgiving Visitor" (ABC)

OUTSTANDING CONTINUED PERFORMANCE BY AN ACTOR IN A SUPPORTING ROLE IN A SERIES: Werner Klemperer, *Hogan's Heroes* (CBS)

OUTSTANDING CONTINUED PERFORMANCE BY AN ACTRESS IN A SUPPORTING ROLE IN A SERIES: Susan Saint James, *The Name of the Game* (NBC)

OUTSTANDING SINGLE PERFORMANCE BY AN ACTRESS IN A SUPPORTING ROLE: Anna Calder-Marshall, "Male of the Species," *Prudential's On Stage* (NBC)

OUTSTANDING INDIVIDUAL ACHIEVEMENT, SPECIAL CLASSIFICATION: (1) Arte Johnson, *Rowan and Martin's Laugh-In* (NBC); and (2) Harvey Korman, *The Carol Burnett Show* (CBS)

OUTSTANDING DIRECTORIAL ACHIEVEMENT IN DRAMA: David Greene, "The People Next Door," *CBS Playhouse* (CBS)

OUTSTANDING WRITING ACHIEVEMENT IN DRAMA: J. P. Miller, "The People Next Door," *CBS Playhouse* (CBS)

OUTSTANDING WRITING ACHIEVEMENT IN COMEDY, VARIETY, OR MUSIC: Allan Blye, Bob Einstein, Murray Roman, Carl Gottlieb, Jerry Music, Steve Martin, Cecil Tuck, Paul Wayne, Cy Howard, and Mason Williams, *The Smothers Brothers Comedy Hour* (CBS)

TRUSTEES' AWARDS: (1) William R. McAndrew, NBC News; and (2) Apollo VII, VIII, IX and X Space Missions; Apollo VII astronauts Walter Schirra, Don Eisele, and Walter Cunningham; Apollo VIII astronauts Frank Borman, James A. Lovell, Jr., and William A. Anders; Apollo IX astronauts James A. McDivitt, David R. Scott, and Russell L. Schweickart; Apollo X astronauts Thomas B. Stafford, Eugene A. Cernan, and John W. Young

1969–1970   (17 MARCH 1969–15 MARCH 1970)

OUTSTANDING VARIETY OR MUSICAL SERIES: *The David Frost Show* (SYNDICATED); Peter Baker, producer; David Frost, star

OUTSTANDING COMEDY SERIES: *My World and Welcome to It* (NBC); Sheldon Leonard, executive producer; Danny Arnold, producer

OUTSTANDING DRAMATIC SERIES: *Marcus Welby, M.D.* (ABC); David Victor, executive producer; David J. O'Connell, producer

OUTSTANDING NEW SERIES: *Room 222* (ABC); Gene Reynolds, producer

OUTSTANDING DRAMATIC PROGRAM: "A Storm in Summer," *Hallmark Hall of Fame* (NBC); M. J. Rifkin, executive producer; Alan Landsburg, producer

OUTSTANDING VARIETY OR MUSICAL PROGRAMS: (1) (Classical music) "Cinderella" (National Ballet of Canada), *NET Festival* (NET); John Barnes and Curtis Davis, executive producers; Norman Campbell, producer; and (2) (Variety and popular music) "Annie, the Women in the Life of a Man" (CBS); Joseph Cates, executive producer; Martin Charnin, producer; Anne Bancroft, star

OUTSTANDING ACHIEVEMENT IN CHILDREN'S PROGRAMMING: *Sesame Street* (NET); David D. Connell, executive producer; Sam Gibson, Jon Stone, and Lutrelle Horne, producers; Jon Stone, Jeffrey Moss, Ray Sipherd; Jerry Juhl, Dan Wilcox, Dave Connell, Bruce Hart, Carole Hart, and Virginia Schone, writers, for "Sally Sees Sesame Street"

OUTSTANDING ACHIEVEMENT IN DAYTIME PROGRAMMING: *Today* (NBC); Stuart Schulberg, producer

OUTSTANDING ACHIEVEMENT IN SPORTS PROGRAMMING: (1) *ABC's Wide World of Sports*

(ABC); Roone P. Arledge, executive producer; and (2) *The NFL Games* (CBS); William Fitts, executive producer

SPECIAL CLASSIFICATION OF OUTSTANDING PROGRAM AND INDIVIDUAL ACHIEVEMENT: *Mutual of Omaha's Wild Kingdom* (NBC); Don Meier, producer

OUTSTANDING ACHIEVEMENT IN "MAGAZINE TYPE" PROGRAMMING: (1) *Black Journal* (NET); William Greaves, executive producer; and (2) Tom Pettit, reporter and writer, "Some Footnotes to 25 Nuclear Years," *First Tuesday* (NBC)

OUTSTANDING ACHIEVEMENT IN NEWS DOCUMENTARY PROGRAMMING: (1) "Hospital," Frederick Wiseman, producer, *NET Journal* (NET); and (2) "The Making of the President, 1968" (CBS); M. J. Rifkin, executive producer; Mel Stuart, producer

OUTSTANDING ACHIEVEMENT WITHIN REGULARLY SCHEDULED NEWS PROGRAMS: (1) "An Investigation of Teenage Drug Addiction—Odyssey House," Wallace Westfeldt, executive producer, Les Crystal, producer, *The Huntley-Brinkley Report* (NBC); and (2) "Can the World Be Saved?" Ronald Bonn, producer, *The CBS Evening News with Walter Cronkite* (CBS)

OUTSTANDING ACHIEVEMENT IN CULTURAL DOCUMENTARY PROGRAMMING: (1) "Artur Rubinstein" (NBC); George A. Vicas, producer; (2) Artur Rubinstein, commentator, "Artur Rubinstein" (NBC); (3) "Fathers and Sons," Ernest Leiser, executive producer, Harry Morgan, producer, *The CBS News Hour* (CBS); (4) "The Japanese," Perry Wolff, executive producer, Igor Oganesoff, producer, *The CBS News Hour* (CBS); and (5) Edwin O. Reischauer, commentator, "The Japanese," *The CBS News Hour* (CBS)

OUTSTANDING ACHIEVEMENT IN COVERAGE OF SPECIAL EVENTS: (1) "Apollo: A Journey to the Moon (Apollo X, XI, XII)" (NBC); James W. Kitchell, executive producer; (2) "Solar Eclipse: A Darkness at Noon" (NBC); Robert Northshield, executive producer; Walter Kravetz, producer; and (3) Walter Cronkite, reporter, "Man on the Moon: The Epic Journey of Apollo XI" (CBS)

OUTSTANDING CONTINUED PERFORMANCE BY AN ACTOR IN A LEADING ROLE IN A DRAMATIC SERIES: Robert Young, *Marcus Welby, M.D.* (ABC)

OUTSTANDING CONTINUED PERFORMANCE BY AN ACTRESS IN A LEADING ROLE IN A DRAMATIC SERIES: Susan Hampshire, *The Forsyte Saga* (NET)

OUTSTANDING CONTINUED PERFORMANCE BY AN ACTOR IN A LEADING ROLE IN A COMEDY SERIES: William Windom, *My World and Welcome to It* (NBC)

OUTSTANDING CONTINUED PERFORMANCE BY AN ACTRESS IN A LEADING ROLE IN A COMEDY SERIES: Hope Lange, *The Ghost and Mrs. Muir* (ABC)

OUTSTANDING SINGLE PERFORMANCE BY AN ACTOR IN A LEADING ROLE: Peter Ustinov, "A Storm in Summer," *Hallmark Hall of Fame* (NBC)

OUTSTANDING SINGLE PERFORMANCE BY AN ACTRESS IN A LEADING ROLE: Patty Duke, "My Sweet Charlie" (NBC)

OUTSTANDING PERFORMANCE BY AN ACTOR IN A SUPPORTING ROLE IN A DRAMA: James Brolin, *Marcus Welby, M.D.* (ABC)

OUTSTANDING PERFORMANCE BY AN ACTRESS IN A SUPPORTING ROLE IN A DRAMA: Gail Fisher, *Mannix* (CBS)

OUTSTANDING PERFORMANCE BY AN ACTOR IN A SUPPORTING ROLE IN A COMEDY: Michael Constantine, *Room 222* (ABC)

OUTSTANDING PERFORMANCE BY AN ACTRESS IN A SUPPORTING ROLE IN A COMEDY: Karen Valentine, *Room 222* (ABC)

OUTSTANDING DIRECTORIAL ACHIEVEMENT IN DRAMA: Paul Bogart, "Shadow Game," *CBS Playhouse* (CBS)

OUTSTANDING DIRECTORIAL ACHIEVEMENT IN COMEDY, VARIETY, OR MUSIC: Dwight A. Hemion, "The Sound of Burt Bacharach," *Kraft Music Hall* (NBC)

OUTSTANDING WRITING ACHIEVEMENT IN DRAMA: Richard Levinson and William Link, "My Sweet Charlie" (NBC)

OUTSTANDING WRITING ACHIEVEMENT IN COMEDY, VARIETY, OR MUSIC: Gary Belkin, Peter Bellwood, Herb Sargent, Thomas Meehan, and Judith Viorst, "Annie, the Women in the Life of a Man" (CBS)

OUTSTANDING ACHIEVEMENT IN ENGINEERING DEVELOPMENT: "Apollo Color Television from Space"—Video Communications Division of NASA; Westinghouse Electric Corporation, and Ampex Corporation

1970–1971

OUTSTANDING COMEDY SERIES: *All in the Family* (CBS); Norman Lear, producer

OUTSTANDING DRAMATIC SERIES: *The Senator* (segment), *The Bold Ones* (NBC); David Levinson, producer

OUTSTANDING VARIETY MUSICAL SERIES: *The Flip Wilson Show* (NBC); Monte Kay, executive producer; Bob Henry, producer; Flip Wilson, star

OUTSTANDING VARIETY SERIES—TALK: *The David Frost Show* (SYNDICATED); Peter Baker, producer; David Frost, star

OUTSTANDING NEW SERIES: *All in the Family* (CBS); Norman Lear, producer

OUTSTANDING SINGLE PROGRAM: "The Andersonville Trial," *Hollywood Television Theatre* (PBS); Lewis Freedman, producer

OUTSTANDING VARIETY OR MUSICAL PROGRAMS: (1) (Classical music) "Leopold Stokowski," *NET Festival* (PBS); Curtis W. Davis, executive producer; Thomas Slevin, producer; Leopold Stokowski, star; and (2) (Variety and popular music) "Singer Presents Burt Bacharach" (NBC); Gary Smith and Dwight Hemion, producers; Burt Bacharach, star

OUTSTANDING ACHIEVEMENT IN CHILDREN'S PROGRAMMING: (1) Burr Tillstrom, *Kukla, Fran and Ollie* (PBS); and (2) *Sesame Street* (PBS); David Connell, executive producer; Jon Stone and Lutrelle Horn, producers; Jeffrey Moss, Ray Sipherd, Jerry Juhl, Dan Wilcox, Dave Connell, Bruce Hart, Carole Hart, and Virginia Schone, writers

OUTSTANDING ACHIEVEMENT IN DAYTIME PROGRAMMING: *Today* (NBC); Stuart Schulberg, producer

OUTSTANDING ACHIEVEMENT IN SPORTS PROGRAMMING: (1) *ABC's Wide World of Sports* (ABC); Roone P. Arledge, executive producer; (2) Jim McKay, commentator, *ABC's Wide World of Sports* (ABC); and (3) Don Meredith, commentator, *NFL Monday Night Football* (ABC)

OUTSTANDING ACHIEVEMENT IN MAGAZINE-TYPE PROGRAMMING: (1) Gulf of Tonkin segment, Joseph Wershba, producer, *60 Minutes* (CBS); and (2) *The Great American Dream Machine* (PBS); A. H. Perlmutter and Jack Willis, executive producers

OUTSTANDING ACHIEVEMENT IN CULTURAL DOCUMENTARY PROGRAMMING: (1) "The Everglades" (NBC); Craig Fisher, producer; (2) "The Making of Butch Cassidy and the Sundance Kid" (NBC); Ronald Reissman, producer; and (3) "Arthur Penn, 1922– : Themes and Variants" (PBS); Robert Hughes, producer

OUTSTANDING ACHIEVEMENT IN NEWS DOCUMENTARY PROGRAMMING: (1) "The Selling of the Pentagon" (CBS); Perry Wolff, executive producer; Peter Davis, producer; (2) "The World of Charlie Company" (CBS); Ernest Leiser, executive producer; Russ Bensley, producer; and (3) "NBC White Paper: Pollution Is a Matter of Choice" (NBC); Fred Freed, producer

OUTSTANDING ACHIEVEMENT WITHIN REGULARLY SCHEDULED NEWS PROGRAMS: (1) Five-part investigation of welfare, Wallace Westfeldt, executive producer, *The Huntley-Brinkley Report* (NBC); and (2) Bruce Morton, correspondent, reporting from the trial of Lieutenant Calley, *The CBS Evening News with Walter Cronkite* (CBS)

OUTSTANDING ACHIEVEMENT IN COVERAGE OF SPECIAL EVENTS: CBS News, for its space coverage in 1970–1971

OUTSTANDING CONTINUED PERFORMANCE BY AN ACTOR IN A LEADING ROLE IN A DRAMATIC SERIES: Hal Holbrook, *The Senator* (segment), *The Bold Ones* (NBC)

OUTSTANDING CONTINUED PERFORMANCE BY AN ACTRESS IN A LEADING ROLE IN A DRAMATIC SERIES: Susan Hampshire, *The First Churchills* (PBS)

OUTSTANDING CONTINUED PERFORMANCE BY AN ACTOR IN A LEADING ROLE IN A COMEDY SERIES: Jack Klugman, *The Odd Couple* (ABC)

OUTSTANDING CONTINUED PERFORMANCE BY AN ACTRESS IN A LEADING ROLE IN A COMEDY SERIES: Jean Stapleton, *All in the Family* (CBS)

OUTSTANDING SINGLE PERFORMANCE BY AN ACTOR IN A LEADING ROLE: George C. Scott, "The Price," *Hallmark Hall of Fame* (NBC)

OUTSTANDING SINGLE PERFORMANCE BY AN ACTRESS IN A LEADING ROLE: Lee Grant, "The Neon Ceiling," *NBC Monday Night at the Movies* (NBC)

OUTSTANDING PERFORMANCE BY AN ACTOR IN A SUPPORTING ROLE IN A DRAMA: David Burns, "The Price," *Hallmark Hall of Fame* (NBC)

OUTSTANDING PERFORMANCE BY AN ACTRESS IN A SUPPORTING ROLE IN A DRAMA: Margaret Leighton, "Hamlet," *Hallmark Hall of Fame* (NBC)

OUTSTANDING PERFORMANCE BY AN ACTOR IN A SUPPORTING ROLE IN A COMEDY: Edward Asner, *The Mary Tyler Moore Show* (CBS)

OUTSTANDING PERFORMANCE BY AN ACTRESS IN A SUPPORTING ROLE IN A COMEDY: Valerie Harper, *The Mary Tyler Moore Show* (CBS)

OUTSTANDING PROGRAM AND INDIVIDUAL ACHIEVEMENT, SPECIAL CLASSIFICATION: Harvey Korman, *The Carol Burnett Show* (CBS)

OUTSTANDING DIRECTORIAL ACHIEVEMENT IN DRAMA, SINGLE PROGRAM OF CONTINUING SERIES: Daryl Duke, "The Day the Lion Died," *The Senator* (segment), *The Bold Ones* (NBC)

OUTSTANDING DIRECTORIAL ACHIEVEMENT IN DRAMA, SINGLE PROGRAM: Fielder Cook, "The Price," *Hallmark Hall of Fame* (NBC)

OUTSTANDING DIRECTORIAL ACHIEVEMENT IN COMEDY, SINGLE PROGRAM OF CONTINUING SERIES: Jay Sandrich, "Toulouse Lautrec Is One of My Favorite Artists," *The Mary Tyler Moore Show* (CBS)

OUTSTANDING DIRECTORIAL ACHIEVEMENT IN VARIETY OR MUSIC, SINGLE PROGRAM OF A SERIES: Mark Warren, *Rowan and Martin's Laugh-In* (NBC)

OUTSTANDING DIRECTORIAL ACHIEVEMENT IN COMEDY, VARIETY, OR MUSIC, SPECIAL PROGRAM: Sterling Johnson, "Timex Presents Peggy Fleming at Sun Valley" (NBC)

OUTSTANDING WRITING ACHIEVEMENT IN DRAMA, SINGLE PROGRAM OF CONTINUING SERIES: Joel Oliansky, "To Taste of Death but Once," *The Senator* (segment), *The Bold Ones* (NBC)

OUTSTANDING WRITING ACHIEVEMENT IN DRAMA, ORIGINAL TELEPLAY, SINGLE PROGRAM: Tracy Keenan Wynn and Marvin Schwartz, "Tribes," *ABC Movie of the Week* (ABC)

OUTSTANDING WRITING ACHIEVEMENT IN DRAMA, ADAPTATION, SINGLE PROGRAM: Saul Levitt, "The Andersonville Trial," *Hollywood Television Theatre* (PBS)

OUTSTANDING WRITING ACHIEVEMENT IN COMEDY, SINGLE PROGRAM OF CONTINUING SERIES: James L. Brooks and Allan Burns, "Support Your Local Mother," *The Mary Tyler Moore Show* (CBS)

OUTSTANDING WRITING ACHIEVEMENT IN VARIETY OR MUSIC, SINGLE PROGRAM OF A SERIES: Herbert Baker, Hal Goodman, Larry Klein, Bob Weiskopf, Bob Schiller, Norman Steinberg, and Flip Wilson, *The Flip Wilson Show* (NBC)

OUTSTANDING WRITING ACHIEVEMENT IN COMEDY, VARIETY, OR MUSIC, SPECIAL PROGRAM: Bob Ellison and Marty Farrell, "Singer Presents Burt Bacharach" (NBC)

TRUSTEES' AWARD: Ed Sullivan

1971–1972

OUTSTANDING COMEDY SERIES: *All in the Family* (CBS); Norman Lear, producer

OUTSTANDING DRAMATIC SERIES: "Elizabeth R.," *Masterpiece Theatre* (PBS); Christopher Sarson, executive producer; Roderick Graham, producer

OUTSTANDING VARIETY MUSICAL SERIES: *The Carol Burnett Show* (CBS); Joe Hamilton, executive producer; Arnie Rosen, producer; Carol Burnett, star

OUTSTANDING VARIETY SERIES—TALK: *The Dick Cavett Show* (ABC); John Gilroy, producer; Dick Cavett, star

OUTSTANDING NEW SERIES: "Elizabeth R.," *Masterpiece Theatre* (PBS); Christopher Sarson, executive producer; Roderick Graham, producer

OUTSTANDING SINGLE PROGRAM: "Brian's Song," Paul Younger Witt, producer, *ABC Movie of the Week* (ABC)

OUTSTANDING VARIETY OR MUSICAL PROGRAM: (1) (Classical music) "Beethoven's Birthday: A Celebration in Vienna with Leonard Bernstein" (CBS); James Krayer, executive producer; Humphrey Burton, producer; Leonard Bernstein, star; and (2) (Variety and popular music) "Jack Lemmon in 'S Wonderful, 'S Marvelous, 'S Gershwin," *Bell System Family Theatre* (NBC); Joseph Cates, executive producer; Martin Charnin, producer; Jack Lemmon, star

OUTSTANDING ACHIEVEMENT IN CHILDREN'S PROGRAMMING: *Sesame Street* (PBS); David D. Connell, executive producer; Jon Stone, producer

OUTSTANDING ACHIEVEMENT IN DAYTIME PROGRAMMING: *The Doctors* (NBC); Allen Potter, producer

OUTSTANDING ACHIEVEMENT IN SPORTS PROGRAMMING: (1) *ABC's Wide World of Sports* (ABC); Roone Arledge, executive producer; and (2) "AFC Championship Game" (NBC); William P. Kelley, technical director

OUTSTANDING ACHIEVEMENT IN MAGAZINE-TYPE PROGRAMMING: (1) *Chronolog* (NBC); Eliot Frankel, executive producer; (2) *The Great American Dream Machine* (PBS); A. H. Perlmutter, executive producer; (3) Mike Wallace, correspondent, *60 Minutes* (CBS)

OUTSTANDING ACHIEVEMENT IN CULTURAL DOCUMENTARY PROGRAMMING: (1) "Hollywood: The Dream Factory" (ABC); Nicolas Noxon, executive producer; Irwin Rosten and Bud Friedgen, producers; and (2) "A Sound of Dolphins," *The Undersea World of Jacques Cousteau* (ABC); Jacques Cousteau and Marshall Flaum, executive producers; Andy White, producer; (3) "The Unsinkable Sea Otter," *The Undersea World of Jacques Cousteau* (ABC); Jacques Cousteau and Marshall Flaum, executive producers; Andy White, producer; (4) Louis J. Hazam, writer, "Venice Be Damned!" (NBC); and (5) Robert Northshield, writer, "Suffer the Little Children—An NBC News White Paper on Northern Ireland" (NBC)

OUTSTANDING ACHIEVEMENT IN NEWS DOCUMENTARY PROGRAMMING: (1) "A Night in Jail, a Day in Court," Burton Benjamin, executive producer, John Sharnik, producer, *CBS Reports* (CBS); and (2) "This Child Is Rated X: An NBC White Paper on Juvenile Justice" (NBC); Martin Carr, producer

OUTSTANDING ACHIEVEMENT WITHIN REGULARLY SCHEDULED NEWS PROGRAMS: (1) Defeat of Dacca, Wallace Westfeldt, executive producer, Robert Mulholland and David Teitelbaum, producers, *The NBC Nightly News* (NBC); (2) Phil Brady, reporter, Defeat of Dacca, *The NBC Nightly News* (NBC); and (3) Bob Schieffer, Phil Jones, Don Webster, and Bill Plante, correspondents, covering "The Air War," *CBS Evening News* (CBS)

OUTSTANDING ACHIEVEMENT IN COVERAGE OF SPECIAL EVENTS: (1) "The China Trip" (ABC); Av Westin and Wally Pfister, executive producers; Bill Lord, producer; (2) "June 30, 1971, A Day for History: The Supreme Court and the Pentagon Papers" (NBC); Lawrence E. Spivak, executive producer; and (3) "A Ride on the Moon: The Flight of Apollo 15" (CBS); Robert Wussler, executive producer; Joan Richman, producer

SPECIAL CLASSIFICATIONS OF OUTSTANDING PROGRAM AND INDIVIDUAL ACHIEVEMENT: (1) (general programming) "The Pentagon Papers: PBS Special" (PBS); David Prowitt, executive producer; Martin Clancy, producer; (2) (docu-drama) *The Search for the Nile* (parts I–VI) (NBC); Christopher Ralling, producer; and (3) (individuals) Michael Hastings and Derek Marlowe, writers, *The Search for the Nile* (parts I-VI) (NBC)

OUTSTANDING CONTINUED PERFORMANCE BY AN ACTOR IN A LEADING ROLE IN A DRAMATIC SERIES: Peter Falk, *Columbo* (NBC)

OUTSTANDING CONTINUED PERFORMANCE BY AN ACTRESS IN A LEADING ROLE IN A DRAMATIC SERIES: Glenda Jackson, "Elizabeth R.," *Masterpiece Theatre* (PBS)

OUTSTANDING CONTINUED PERFORMANCE BY AN ACTOR IN A LEADING ROLE IN A COMEDY SERIES: Carroll O'Connor, *All in the Family* (CBS)

OUTSTANDING CONTINUED PERFORMANCE BY AN ACTRESS IN A LEADING ROLE IN A COMEDY SERIES: Jean Stapleton, *All in the Family* (CBS)

OUTSTANDING ACHIEVEMENT BY A PERFORMER IN MUSIC OR VARIETY: Harvey Korman, *The Carol Burnett Show* (CBS)

OUTSTANDING SINGLE PERFORMANCE BY AN ACTOR IN A LEADING ROLE: Keith Michell, "Catherine Howard," *The Six Wives of Henry VIII* (CBS)

OUTSTANDING SINGLE PERFORMANCE BY AN ACTRESS IN A LEADING ROLE: Glenda Jackson, "Shadow in the Sun," "Elizabeth R.," *Masterpiece Theatre* (PBS)

OUTSTANDING PERFORMANCE BY AN ACTOR IN A SUPPORTING ROLE IN A DRAMA: Jack Warden, "Brian's Song," *ABC Movie of the Week* (ABC)

OUTSTANDING PERFORMANCE BY AN ACTRESS IN A SUPPORTING ROLE IN A DRAMA: Jenny Agutter, "The Snow Goose," *Hallmark Hall of Fame* (NBC)

OUTSTANDING PERFORMANCE BY AN ACTOR IN A SUPPORTING ROLE IN A COMEDY: Edward Asner, *The Mary Tyler Moore Show* (CBS)

OUTSTANDING PERFORMANCE BY AN ACTRESS IN A SUPPORTING ROLE IN A COMEDY: (1) Valerie Harper, *The Mary Tyler Moore Show* (CBS); and (2) Sally Struthers, *All in the Family* (CBS)

OUTSTANDING DIRECTORIAL ACHIEVEMENT IN DRAMA, SINGLE PROGRAM OF CONTINUING SERIES: Alexander Singer, "The Invasion of Kevin Ireland," *The Lawyers* (*The Bold Ones*) (NBC)

OUTSTANDING DIRECTORIAL ACHIEVEMENT IN DRAMA, SINGLE PROGRAM: Tom Gries, "The Glass House," *The New CBS Friday Night Movies* (CBS)

OUTSTANDING DIRECTORIAL ACHIEVEMENT IN COMEDY, SINGLE PROGRAM OF CONTINUING SERIES: John Rich, "Sammy's Visit," *All in the Family* (CBS)

OUTSTANDING DIRECTORIAL ACHIEVEMENT IN VARIETY OR MUSIC, SINGLE PROGRAM OF A SERIES: Art Fisher, *The Sonny and Cher Comedy Hour* (program of 31 January 1972, with guest star Tony Randall) (CBS)

OUTSTANDING DIRECTORIAL ACHIEVEMENT IN COMEDY, VARIETY, OR MUSIC, SPECIAL PROGRAM: Walter C. Miller and Martin Charnin, "Jack Lemmon in 'S Wonderful, 'S Marvelous, 'S Gershwin," *Bell System Family Theatre* (NBC)

OUTSTANDING WRITING ACHIEVEMENT IN DRAMA, SINGLE PROGRAM OF CONTINUING SERIES: Richard L. Levinson and William Link, "Death Lends a Hand," *Columbo* (NBC)

OUTSTANDING WRITING ACHIEVEMENT IN DRAMA, ORIGINAL TELEPLAY, SINGLE PROGRAM: Allan Sloane, "To All My Friends on Shore" (CBS)

OUTSTANDING WRITING ACHIEVEMENT IN DRAMA, ADAPTATION, SINGLE PROGRAM: William Blinn, "Brian's Song," *ABC Movie of the Week* (ABC)

OUTSTANDING WRITING ACHIEVEMENT IN COMEDY, SINGLE PROGRAM OF CONTINUING SERIES: Burt Styler, "Edith's Problem," *All in the Family* (CBS)

OUTSTANDING WRITING ACHIEVEMENT IN VARIETY OR MUSIC, SINGLE PROGRAM OF SERIES: Don Hinkley, Stan Hart, Larry Siegel, Woody Kling, Roger Beatty, Art Baer, Ben Joelson, Stan Burns, Mike Marmer, and Arnie Rosen, *The Carol Burnett Show* (program of 26 January 1972, with guests Tim Conway and Ray Charles) (CBS)

OUTSTANDING WRITING ACHIEVEMENT IN COMEDY, VARIETY, OR MUSIC, SPECIAL PROGRAM: Anne Howard Bailey, "The Trial of Mary Lincoln," *NET Opera Theatre* (PBS)

TRUSTEES' AWARDS: (1) Bill Lawrence; and (2) Dr. Frank Stanton

1972–1973

OUTSTANDING COMEDY SERIES: *All in the Family* (CBS); Norman Lear, executive producer; John Rich, producer

OUTSTANDING DRAMA SERIES (CONTINUING): *The Waltons* (CBS); Lee Rich, executive producer; Robert L. Jacks, producer

OUTSTANDING DRAMA OR COMEDY (LIMITED EPISODES): "Tom Brown's Schooldays" (*Masterpiece Theatre*) (PBS); John McRae, producer

OUTSTANDING VARIETY MUSICAL SERIES: *The Julie Andrews Hour* (ABC); Nick Vanoff, producer; Julie Andrews, star

OUTSTANDING NEW SERIES: *America* (NBC); Michael Gill, producer

OUTSTANDING SINGLE PROGRAM, DRAMA OR COMEDY: "A War of Children," Roger Gimbel, executive producer, George Schaefer, producer, *The New CBS Tuesday Night Movies* (CBS)

OUTSTANDING SINGLE PROGRAM, CLASSICAL MUSIC: "The Sleeping Beauty" (PBS); J. W. Barnes and Robert Kotlowitz, executive producers; Norman Campbell, producer

OUTSTANDING SINGLE PROGRAM, VARIETY OR MUSICAL: "Singer Presents Liza with a 'Z'" (NBC); Bob Fosse and Fred Ebb, producers; Liza Minnelli, star

OUTSTANDING ACHIEVEMENT IN CHILDREN'S PROGRAMMING (PROGRAMS AND INDIVIDUAL ACHIEVEMENTS): Entertainment and fictional—(1) *Sesame Street* (PBS); Jon Stone, executive producer; Bob Cuniff, producer; (2) *Zoom* (PBS); Christopher Sarson, producer; and (3) Tom Whedon, John Boni, Sara Compton, Tom Dunsmuir, Thad Mumford, Jeremy Stevens, and Jim Thurman, writers, *The Electric Company* (PBS). Information and factual—(1) "Last of the Curlews," William Hanna and Joseph Barbera, producers, *The ABC Afterschool Special* (ABC); and (2) Shari Lewis, performer, "A Picture of Us," *NBC Children's Theatre* (NBC)

OUTSTANDING ACHIEVEMENT IN SPORTS PROGRAMMING: (1) *ABC's Wide World of Sports* (ABC); Roone Arledge, executive producer; (2) "1972 Summer Olympic Games" (ABC); Roone Arledge, executive producer; (3) Jim McKay, commentator, "1972 Summer Olympic Games" (ABC); and (4) John Croak, Charles Gardner, Jakob Hierl, Conrad Kraus, Edward McCarthy, Nick Mazur, Alex Moskovic, James Parker, Louis Rende, Ross Skipper, Robert Steinback, John DeLisa, George Boettcher, Merrit Roesser, Leo Scharf, Randy Cohen, Vito Gerardi, Harold Byers, Winfield Gross, Paul Scoskie, Peter Fritz, Leo Stephan, Gerber McBeath, Louis Torino, Michael Wenig, Tom Wight, and James Kelley, videotape editors, "1972 Summer Olympic Games" (ABC)

OUTSTANDING PROGRAM ACHIEVEMENT IN DAYTIME: *Dinah's Place* (NBC); Henry Jaffe, executive producer; Fred Tatashore, producer; Dinah Shore, star

OUTSTANDING PROGRAM ACHIEVEMENT IN DAYTIME DRAMA: *The Edge of Night* (CBS); Erwin Nicholson, producer

OUTSTANDING ACHIEVEMENT FOR REGULARLY SCHEDULED MAGAZINE-TYPE PROGRAMS (PROGRAMS AND INDIVIDUALS): (1) "Poppy Fields of Turkey—The Heroin Labs of Marseilles—The New York Connection," Don Hewitt, executive producer, William McClure, John Tiffin, and Philip Scheffler, producers, *60 Minutes* (CBS); (2) "The Selling of Colonel Herbert," Don Hewitt, executive producer, Barry Lando, producer, *60 Minutes* (CBS); (3) *60 Minutes* (CBS); Don Hewitt, executive producer; (4) Mike Wallace, correspondent, "The Selling of Colonel Herbert," *60 Minutes* (CBS); (5) Mike Wallace, correspondent, *60 Minutes* (CBS)

OUTSTANDING DOCUMENTARY PROGRAM ACHIEVEMENT—CULTURAL (PROGRAMS AND INDIVIDUALS): (1) *America* (NBC); Michael Gill, executive producer; (2) "Jane Goodall and the World of Animal Behavior—The Wild Dogs of Africa" (ABC); Marshall Flaum, executive producer; Hugo Van Lawick, Bill Travers, and James Hill, producers; (3) Alistair Cooke, narrator, *America* (NBC); (4) Alistair Cooke, writer, "A Fireball in the Night," *America* (NBC); (5) Hugo Van Lawick, director, "Jane Goodall and the World of Animal Behavior—The Wild Dogs of Africa" (ABC)

OUTSTANDING DOCUMENTARY PROGRAM ACHIEVEMENT—CURRENT EVENTS: (1) "The Blue Collar Trap," Fred Freed, producer, *NBC News White Paper* (NBC); (2) "The Mexican Connection," Burton Benjamin, executive producer, Jay McMullen, producer, *CBS Reports* (CBS); (3) "One Billion Dollar Weapon and Now the War is Over—The American Military in the 1970s," Fred Freed, executive producer, Al Davis, producer, *NBC Reports* (NBC)

OUTSTANDING ACHIEVEMENT WITHIN REGULARLY SCHEDULED NEWS PROGRAMS (PROGRAMS AND INDIVIDUALS): (1) "The U.S./Soviet Wheat Deal: Is There a Scandal?" Paul Greenberg and Russ Bensley, executive producers, Stanhope Gould and Linda Mason, producers, *The CBS Evening News with Walter Cronkite* (CBS); (2) Walter Cronkite, Dan Rather, Daniel Schorr, and Joel Blocker, correspondents, "The Watergate Affair," *The CBS Evening News with Walter Cronkite* (CBS); (3) David Dick, Dan Rather, Roger Mudd, and Walter Cronkite, correspondents, "Coverage of the Shooting of Governor Wallace," *The CBS Evening News with Walter*

Cronkite (CBS); (4) Eric Sevareid, correspondent, "LBJ—The Man and the President," *The CBS Evening News with Walter Cronkite* (CBS)

SPECIAL CLASSIFICATION OF OUTSTANDING PROGRAM AND INDIVIDUAL ACHIEVEMENT: (1) *The Advocates* (PBS); Greg Harney, executive producer; Tom Burrows, Russ Morash, and Peter McGhee, producers; (2) "VD Blues," *The Special of the Week* (PBS), Don Fouser, producer

OUTSTANDING PERFORMANCE BY AN ACTOR IN A LEADING ROLE IN A DRAMA SERIES (CONTINUING): Richard Thomas, *The Waltons* (CBS)

OUTSTANDING PERFORMANCE BY AN ACTRESS IN A LEADING ROLE IN A DRAMA SERIES (CONTINUING): Michael Learned, *The Waltons* (CBS)

OUTSTANDING PERFORMANCE BY AN ACTOR IN A LEADING ROLE IN A DRAMA OR COMEDY (LIMITED EPISODES): Anthony Murphy, "Tom Brown's Schooldays," (*Masterpiece Theatre*) (PBS)

OUTSTANDING PERFORMANCE BY AN ACTRESS IN A LEADING ROLE IN A DRAMA OR COMEDY (LIMITED EPISODES): Susan Hampshire, "Vanity Fair," *Masterpiece Theatre* (PBS)

OUTSTANDING CONTINUED PERFORMANCE BY AN ACTOR IN A LEADING ROLE IN A COMEDY SERIES: Jack Klugman, *The Odd Couple* (ABC)

OUTSTANDING CONTINUED PERFORMANCE BY AN ACTRESS IN A LEADING ROLE IN A COMEDY SERIES: Mary Tyler Moore, *The Mary Tyler Moore Show* (CBS)

OUTSTANDING SINGLE PERFORMANCE BY AN ACTOR IN A LEADING ROLE: Laurence Olivier, "Long Day's Journey into Night" (ABC)

OUTSTANDING SINGLE PERFORMANCE BY AN ACTRESS IN A LEADING ROLE: Cloris Leachman, "A Brand New Life," *Tuesday Movie of the Week* (ABC)

OUTSTANDING PERFORMANCE BY AN ACTOR IN A SUPPORTING ROLE IN DRAMA, A CONTINUING OR ONE-TIME APPEARANCE IN A SERIES, OR FOR A SPECIAL PROGRAM: Scott Jacoby, "That Certain Summer," *Wednesday Movie of the Week* (ABC)

OUTSTANDING PERFORMANCE BY AN ACTRESS IN A SUPPORTING ROLE IN DRAMA, A CONTINUING OR ONE-TIME APPEARANCE IN A SERIES, OR FOR A SPECIAL PROGRAM: Ellen Corby, *The Waltons* (CBS)

OUTSTANDING PERFORMANCE BY AN ACTOR IN A SUPPORTING ROLE IN COMEDY, A CONTINUING OR ONE-TIME APPEARANCE IN A SERIES, OR FOR A SPECIAL PROGRAM: Ted Knight, *The Mary Tyler Moore Show* (CBS)

OUTSTANDING PERFORMANCE BY AN ACTRESS IN A SUPPORTING ROLE IN COMEDY, A CONTINUING OR ONE-TIME APPEARANCE IN A SERIES, OR FOR A SPECIAL PROGRAM: Valerie Harper, *The Mary Tyler Moore Show* (CBS)

OUTSTANDING ACHIEVEMENT BY A SUPPORTING PERFORMER IN MUSIC OR VARIETY, A CONTINUING OR ONE-TIME APPEARANCE IN A SERIES, OR FOR A SPECIAL PROGRAM: Tim Conway, *The Carol Burnett Show* (program of 17 February 1973) (CBS)

OUTSTANDING ACHIEVEMENT BY AN INDIVIDUAL IN DAYTIME DRAMA: Mary Fickett, *All My Children* (ABC)

OUTSTANDING DIRECTORIAL ACHIEVEMENT IN DRAMA, A SINGLE PROGRAM OF A SERIES WITH CONTINUING CHARACTERS AND/OR THEME: Jerry Thorpe, "An Eye for an Eye," *Kung Fu* (ABC)

OUTSTANDING DIRECTORIAL ACHIEVEMENT IN DRAMA, A SINGLE PROGRAM: Joseph Sargent, "The Marcus-Nelson Murders," *The CBS Thursday Night Movies* (CBS)

OUTSTANDING DIRECTORIAL ACHIEVEMENT IN COMEDY, A SINGLE PROGRAM OF A SERIES WITH CONTINUING CHARACTERS AND/OR THEME: Jay Sandrich, "It's Whether You Win or Lose," *The Mary Tyler Moore Show* (CBS)

OUTSTANDING DIRECTORIAL ACHIEVEMENT IN VARIETY OR MUSIC, A SINGLE PROGRAM OF A SERIES: Bill Davis, *The Julie Andrews Hour* (program of 13 September 1972) (ABC)

OUTSTANDING DIRECTORIAL ACHIEVEMENT IN COMEDY, VARIETY, OR MUSIC, A SPECIAL PROGRAM: Bob Fosse, "Singer Presents Liza with a 'Z'" (NBC)

OUTSTANDING WRITING ACHIEVEMENT IN DRAMA, A SINGLE PROGRAM OF A SERIES WITH CONTINUING CHARACTERS AND/OR THEME: John McGreevey, "The Scholar," *The Waltons* (CBS)

OUTSTANDING WRITING ACHIEVEMENT IN DRAMA, ORIGINAL TELEPLAY, A SINGLE PROGRAM: Abby Mann, "The Marcus-Nelson Murders," *The CBS Thursday Night Movies* (CBS)

OUTSTANDING WRITING ACHIEVEMENT IN DRAMA, ADAPTATION, A SINGLE PROGRAM: Eleanor Perry, "The House without a Christmas Tree" (CBS)

OUTSTANDING WRITING ACHIEVEMENT IN COMEDY, A SINGLE PROGRAM OF A SERIES WITH CONTINUING CHARACTERS AND/OR THEME: Michael Ross, Bernie West, and Lee Kalcheim, "The Bunkers and the Swingers," *All in the Family* (CBS)

OUTSTANDING WRITING ACHIEVEMENT IN VARIETY OR MUSIC, A SINGLE PROGRAM OF A SERIES: Stan Hart, Larry Siegel, Gail Parent, Woody Kling, Roger Beatty, Tom Patchett, Jay Tarses, Robert Hillard, Arnie Kogen, Bill Angelos, and Buz Kohan, *The Carol Burnett Show* (program of 8 November 1972) (CBS)

OUTSTANDING WRITING ACHIEVEMENT IN COMEDY, VARIETY, OR MUSIC, A SPECIAL PROGRAM: Renee Taylor and Joseph Bologna, "Acts of Love—and Other Comedies" (ABC)

1973–1974

OUTSTANDING COMEDY SERIES: *M*A*S*H* (CBS); Gene Reynolds and Larry Gelbart, producers

OUTSTANDING DRAMA SERIES: "Upstairs, Downstairs," *Masterpiece Theatre* (PBS); Rex Firkin, executive producer; John Hawkesworth, producer

OUTSTANDING LIMITED SERIES: *Columbo* (NBC); Dean Hargrove and Roland Kibbee, executive producers; Douglas Benton, Robert F. O'Neill, and Edward K. Dodds, producers

OUTSTANDING MUSIC-VARIETY SERIES: *The Carol Burnett Show* (CBS); Joe Hamilton, executive producer; Ed Simmons, producer; Carol Burnett, star

OUTSTANDING SPECIAL, COMEDY, OR DRAMA: "The Autobiography of Miss Jane Pittman" (CBS); Robert Christiansen and Rick Rosenberg, producers

OUTSTANDING COMEDY-VARIETY, VARIETY OR MUSIC SPECIAL: "Lily" (CBS); Irene Pinn, executive producer; Herb Sargent and Jerry McPhie, producers; Lily Tomlin, star

OUTSTANDING CHILDREN'S SPECIAL (BROADCAST DURING THE EVENING): "Marlo Thomas and Friends in Free to Be . . . You and Me" (ABC); Marlo Thomas and Carole Hart, producers; Marlo Thomas, star

OUTSTANDING ACHIEVEMENT IN SPORTS PROGRAMMING: (1) *ABC's Wide World of Sports* (ABC); Roone Arledge, executive producer; Dennis Lewin, producer; and (2) Jim McKay, host, *ABC's Wide World of Sports* (ABC)

OUTSTANDING DRAMA SERIES (DAYTIME): *The Doctors* (NBC); Joseph Stuart, producer

OUTSTANDING TALK, SERVICE OR VARIETY SERIES (DAYTIME): *The Merv Griffin Show* (SYNDICATED); Bob Murphy, producer

OUTSTANDING GAME SHOW (DAYTIME): *Password* (ABC); Frank Wayne, executive producer; Howard Felsher, producer

OUTSTANDING DRAMA SPECIAL (DAYTIME): "The Other Woman," *ABC Matinee Today* (ABC); John Conboy, producer

OUTSTANDING ENTERTAINMENT CHILDREN'S SERIES (DAYTIME): *Zoom* (PBS); Jim Crum and Christopher Sarson, producers

OUTSTANDING INFORMATIONAL CHILDREN'S SERIES: *Make a Wish* (ABC); Lester Cooper, executive producer; Tom Bywaters, producer

OUTSTANDING INSTRUCTIONAL CHILDREN'S PROGRAMMING: *Inside/Out* (SYNDICATED); Larry Walcoff, executive producer

OUTSTANDING ENTERTAINMENT CHILDREN'S SPECIAL (DAYTIME): "Rookie of the Year," Dan Wilson, producer, *The ABC Afterschool Special* (ABC)

OUTSTANDING INFORMATIONAL CHILDREN'S SPECIAL: "The Runaways" (ABC); Joseph Barbera and William Hanna, executive producers; Bill Schwartz, producer

OUTSTANDING DOCUMENTARY PROGRAM ACHIEVEMENTS, PROGRAMS DEALING WITH EVENTS OR MATTERS OF CURRENT SIGNIFICANCE: (1) "Fire!" *ABC News Close-Up* (ABC); Pamela Hill, producer; Jules Bergman, correspondent/narrator; and (2) "CBS News Special Report: The Senate and the Watergate Affair" (CBS); Leslie Midgley, executive producer; Hal Haley, Bernard Birnbaum and David Browning, producers; Dan Rather, Roger Mudd, Daniel Schorr and Fred Graham, correspondents

OUTSTANDING DOCUMENTARY PROGRAM ACHIEVEMENTS, PROGRAMS DEALING WITH ARTISTIC, HISTORICAL OR CULTURAL SUBJECTS: (1) "Journey to the Outer Limits," *National Geographic Society Specials* (ABC); Nicholas Clapp and Dennis Kane, executive producers; Alex Grasshoff, producer; (2) *The World at War* (SYNDICATED); Jeremy Isaacs, producer; and (3) "CBS Reports: The Rockefellers" (CBS); Burton Benjamin, executive producer; Howard Stringer, producer; Walter Cronkite, correspondent

OUTSTANDING ACHIEVEMENT FOR REGULARLY SCHEDULED MAGAZINE-TYPE PROGRAMS (FOR PROGRAM SEGMENTS): (1) "America's Nerve Gas Arsenal," Eliot Frankel, executive producer, William B. Hill and Anthony Potter, producers, Tom Pettit, correspondent, *First Tuesday* (NBC); (2) "The Adversaries," Carey Winfrey, executive producer, Peter Forbath, producer/reporter, Brendan Gill, host/moderator, *Behind the Lines* (PBS); and (3) "A Question of Impeachment," Jerome Toobin, executive producer, Martin Clancy, producer, Bill Moyers, broadcaster, *Bill Moyers' Journal* (PBS)

OUTSTANDING INTERVIEW PROGRAM (PUBLIC AFFAIRS, SINGLE PROGRAM): (1) "Solzhenitsyn," *CBS News Special* (CBS); Burton Benjamin, producer; Walter Cronkite, correspondent; and (2) "Henry Steele Commager," Jerome Toobin, executive producer, Jack Sameth, producer, Bill Moyers, broadcaster, *Bill Moyers' Journal* (PBS)

OUTSTANDING ACHIEVEMENT WITHIN REGULARLY SCHEDULED NEWS PROGRAMS: (1) Coverage of the October War from Israel's Northern Front, *CBS Evening News with Walter Cronkite* (CBS); John Laurence, correspondent; (2) The Agnew Resignation, *CBS Evening News with Walter Cronkite* (CBS); Paul Greenberg, executive producer; Ron Bonn, Ed Fouhy, John Lane, Don Bowers, John Armstrong and Robert Mead, producers; Walter Cronkite, Robert Schakne, Fred Graham, Robert Pierpoint, Roger Mudd, Dan Rather, John Hart, and Eric Sevareid, correspondents; (3) The Key Biscayne Bank Charter Struggle, *CBS Evening News with Walter Cronkite* (CBS); Ed Fouhy, producer; Robert Pierpoint, correspondent; and (4) Reports on World Hunger, *The NBC Nightly News* (NBC); Lester M. Crystal, executive producer; Richard Fischer, Joseph Angotti and Fred Flamenhaft, producers; Tom Streithorst, Phil Brady, John Palmer and Liz Trotta, correspondents

OUTSTANDING ACHIEVEMENT IN COVERAGE OF SPECIAL EVENTS: (1) "Watergate: The White House Transcripts" (CBS); Russ Bensley, executive producer; Sylvia Westerman, Barry Jagoda, Mark Harrington and Jack Kelly, producers; Walter Cronkite, Dan Rather, Barry Serafin, Bob Schieffer, Daniel Schorr, Nelson Benton, Bruce Morton, Roger Mudd and Fred Graham, correspondents; and (2) Watergate Coverage (17 May through 15 November 1973) (PBS); Martin Clancy, executive producer; the NPACT Staff, producers; Jim Lehrer, Peter Kaye and Robert MacNeil, reporters

SPECIAL CLASSIFICATION OF OUTSTANDING PROGRAM AND INDIVIDUAL ACHIEVEMENT: (1) *The Dick Cavett Show* (ABC); John Gilroy, producer; Dick Cavett, star; and (2) Tom Snyder, host, *Tomorrow* (NBC)

ACTOR OF THE YEAR (SERIES): Alan Alda, *M*A*S*H* (CBS)

ACTRESS OF THE YEAR (SERIES): Mary Tyler Moore, *The Mary Tyler Moore Show* (CBS)

ACTOR OF THE YEAR (SPECIAL): Hal Holbrook, "Pueblo," *ABC Theatre* (ABC)

ACTRESS OF THE YEAR (SPECIAL): Cicely Tyson, "The Autobiography of Miss Jane Pittman" (CBS)

SUPPORTING ACTOR OF THE YEAR: Michael Moriarty, "The Glass Menagerie" (ABC)

SUPPORTING ACTRESS OF THE YEAR: Joanna Miles, "The Glass Menagerie" (ABC)

BEST LEAD ACTOR IN A DRAMA SERIES: Telly Savalas, *Kojak* (CBS)

BEST LEAD ACTRESS IN A DRAMA SERIES: Michael Learned, *The Waltons* (CBS)

BEST LEAD ACTOR IN A LIMITED SERIES: William Holden, *The Blue Knight* (NBC)

BEST LEAD ACTRESS IN A LIMITED SERIES: Mildred Natwick, *The Snoop Sisters* (NBC)

BEST LEAD ACTOR IN A COMEDY SERIES: Alan Alda, *M*A*S*H* (CBS)

BEST LEAD ACTRESS IN A COMEDY SERIES: Mary Tyler Moore, *The Mary Tyler Moore Show* (CBS)

BEST LEAD ACTOR IN A DRAMA (SPECIAL PROGRAM OR SINGLE APPEARANCE IN A DRAMA OR COMEDY SERIES): Hal Holbrook, "Pueblo," *ABC Theatre* (ABC)

BEST LEAD ACTRESS IN A DRAMA (SPECIAL PROGRAM OR SINGLE APPEARANCE IN A DRAMA OR COMEDY SERIES): Cicely Tyson, "The Autobiography of Miss Jane Pittman" (CBS)

BEST SUPPORTING ACTOR IN DRAMA (SPECIAL PROGRAM, ONE-TIME APPEARANCE, OR CONTINUING ROLE): Michael Moriarty, "The Glass Menagerie" (ABC)

BEST SUPPORTING ACTRESS IN DRAMA (SPECIAL PROGRAM, ONE-TIME APPEARANCE, OR CONTINUING ROLE): Joanna Miles, "The Glass Menagerie" (ABC)

BEST SUPPORTING ACTOR IN COMEDY (SPECIAL PROGRAM, ONE-TIME APPEARANCE, OR CONTINUING ROLE): Rob Reiner, *All in the Family* (CBS)

BEST SUPPORTING ACTRESS IN COMEDY (SPECIAL PROGRAM, ONE-TIME APPEARANCE, OR CONTINUING ROLE): Cloris Leachman, "The Lars Affair," *The Mary Tyler Moore Show* (CBS)

BEST SUPPORTING ACTOR IN COMEDY-VARIETY, VARIETY OR MUSIC (SPECIAL PROGRAM, ONE-TIME APPEARANCE, OR CONTINUING ROLE): Harvey Korman, *The Carol Burnett Show* (CBS)

BEST SUPPORTING ACTRESS IN COMEDY-VARIETY, VARIETY OR MUSIC (SPECIAL PROGRAM, ONE-TIME APPEARANCE, OR CONTINUING ROLE): Brenda Vaccaro, "The Shape of Things" (CBS)

DAYTIME ACTOR OF THE YEAR: Pat O'Brien, "The Other Woman," *ABC Matinee Today* (ABC)

DAYTIME ACTRESS OF THE YEAR: Cathleen Nesbitt, "The Mask of Love," *ABC Matinee Today* (ABC)

DAYTIME HOST OF THE YEAR: Peter Marshall, *The Hollywood Squares* (NBC)

BEST ACTOR IN DAYTIME DRAMA (SERIES): Macdonald Carey, *Days of Our Lives* (NBC)

BEST ACTRESS IN DAYTIME DRAMA (SERIES): Elizabeth Hubbard, *The Doctors* (NBC)

BEST ACTOR IN DAYTIME DRAMA (SPECIAL PROGRAM): Pat O'Brien, "The Other Woman," *ABC Matinee Today* (ABC)

BEST ACTRESS IN DAYTIME DRAMA (SPECIAL PROGRAM): Cathleen Nesbitt, "The Mask of Love," *ABC Matinee Today* (ABC)

BEST HOST OR HOSTESS IN A GAME SHOW (DAYTIME): Peter Marshall, *The Hollywood Squares* (NBC)

BEST HOST OR HOSTESS IN A TALK, SERVICE, OR VARIETY SERIES (DAYTIME): Dinah Shore, *Dinah's Place* (NBC)

OUTSTANDING TELEVISION NEWS BROADCASTER: (1) Harry Reasoner, *ABC News* (ABC); and (2) Bill Moyers, "Essay on Watergate," *Bill Moyers' Journal* (PBS)

DIRECTOR OF THE YEAR (SERIES): Robert Butler, *The Blue Knight* (part III) (NBC)

DIRECTOR OF THE YEAR (SPECIAL): Dwight Hemion, "Barbra Streisand . . . And Other Musical Instruments" (CBS)

WRITER OF THE YEAR (SERIES): Treva Silverman, "The Lou and Edie Story," *The Mary Tyler Moore Show* (CBS)

WRITER OF THE YEAR (SPECIAL): Fay Kanin, "Tell Me Where It Hurts," *G-E Theater* (CBS)

BEST DIRECTING IN DRAMA, SINGLE PROGRAM OF A SERIES WITH CONTINUING CHARACTERS AND/OR THEME: Robert Butler, *The Blue Knight* (part III) (NBC)

BEST DIRECTING IN DRAMA, SINGLE PROGRAM, COMEDY, OR DRAMA: John Korty, "The Autobiography of Miss Jane Pittman" (CBS)

BEST DIRECTING IN COMEDY, SINGLE PROGRAM OF A SERIES WITH CONTINUING CHARACTERS AND/OR THEME: Jackie Cooper, "Carry On, Hawkeye," *M*A*S*H* (CBS)

BEST DIRECTING IN VARIETY OR MUSIC, SINGLE PROGRAM OF A SERIES: Dave Powers, "The Australia Show," *The Carol Burnett Show* (CBS)

BEST DIRECTING IN COMEDY-VARIETY, VARIETY OR MUSIC, A SPECIAL PROGRAM: Dwight Hemion, "Barbra Streisand . . . And Other Musical Instruments" (CBS)

DAYTIME DIRECTOR OF THE YEAR: H. Wesley Kenney, "Miss Kline, We Love You," *ABC Afternoon Playbreak* (ABC)

BEST INDIVIDUAL DIRECTOR FOR A DRAMA SERIES (DAYTIME): H. Wesley Kenney, *Days of Our Lives* (NBC)

BEST INDIVIDUAL DIRECTOR FOR A SPECIAL PROGRAM (DAYTIME): H. Wesley Kenney, "Miss Kline, We Love You," *ABC Afternoon Playbreak* (ABC)

BEST INDIVIDUAL DIRECTOR FOR A TALK, SERVICE, OR VARIETY PROGRAM (DAYTIME): Dick

Carson, *The Merv Griffin Show* (program with guests Rosemary Clooney, Helen O'Connell, Fran Warren, and Kay Starr) (SYNDICATED)

BEST INDIVIDUAL DIRECTOR FOR A GAME SHOW (DAYTIME): Mike Gargiulo, *Jackpot!* (NBC)

OUTSTANDING ACHIEVEMENT IN NEWS AND DOCUMENTARY DIRECTING: Pamela Hill, "Fire!" *ABC News Close-Up* (ABC)

BEST WRITING IN DRAMA, SINGLE PROGRAM OF A SERIES WITH CONTINUING CHARACTERS AND/OR THEME: Joanna Lee, "The Thanksgiving Story," *The Waltons* (CBS)

BEST WRITING IN DRAMA, ORIGINAL TELEPLAY (SINGLE PROGRAM, COMEDY OR DRAMA): Fay Kanin, "Tell Me Where It Hurts," *G-E Theater* (CBS)

BEST WRITING IN DRAMA, ADAPTATION (SINGLE PROGRAM, COMEDY OR DRAMA): Tracy Keenan Wynn, "The Autobiography of Miss Jane Pittman" (CBS)

BEST WRITING IN COMEDY, SINGLE PROGRAM OF A SERIES WITH CONTINUING CHARACTERS AND/OR THEME: Treva Silverman, "The Lou and Edie Story," *The Mary Tyler Moore Show* (CBS)

BEST WRITING IN VARIETY OR MUSIC, SINGLE PROGRAM OF A SERIES: Ed Simmons, Gary Belkin, Roger Beatty, Arnie Kogen, Bill Richmond, Gene Perret, Rudy DeLuca, Barry Levinson, Dick Clair, Jenna McMahon and Barry Harman, *The Carol Burnett Show* (program of 16 February 1974) (CBS)

BEST WRITING IN COMEDY-VARIETY, VARIETY OR MUSIC, SPECIAL PROGRAM: Herb Sargent, Rosalyn Drexler, Lorne Michaels, Richard Pryor, Jim Rusk, James R. Stein, Robert Illes, Lily Tomlin, George Yanok, Jane Wagner, Rod Warren, Ann Elder and Karyl Geld, "Lily" (CBS)

DAYTIME WRITER OF THE YEAR: Lila Garrett and Sandy Krinski, "Mother of the Bride," *ABC Afternoon Playbreak* (ABC)

BEST WRITING FOR A DRAMA SERIES (DAYTIME): Henry Slesar, *The Edge of Night* (CBS)

BEST WRITING FOR A SPECIAL PROGRAM (DAYTIME): Lila Garrett and Sandy Krinski, "Mother of the Bride," *ABC Afternoon Playbreak* (ABC)

BEST WRITING FOR A TALK, SERVICE OR VARIETY PROGRAM (DAYTIME): Tony Garafalo, Bob Murphy and Merv Griffin, *The Merv Griffin Show* (program with guests Billie Jean King, Mark Spitz, Hank Aaron, and Johnny Unitas) (SYNDICATED)

BEST WRITING FOR A GAME SHOW (DAYTIME): Jay Redack, Harry Friedman, Harold Schneider, Gary Johnson, Steve Levitch, Rick Kellard, and Rowby Goren, *The Hollywood Squares* (NBC)

OUTSTANDING INDIVIDUAL ACHIEVEMENTS IN CHILDREN'S PROGRAMMING: (1) Charles M. Schulz, writer, "A Charlie Brown Thanksgiving" (CBS); (2) William Zaharuk, art director; Peter Razmofski, set decorator, "The Borrowers," *Hallmark Hall of Fame* (NBC); (3) Ronald Baldwin, art director; Nat Mongioli, set director, *The Electric Company* (program of 19 February 1974) (PBS); (4) The Muppets, *Sesame Street* (PBS); Jim Henson, Frank Oz, Carroll Spinney, Jerry Nelson, Richard Hunt, and Fran Brill, performers; and (5) Jon Stone, Joseph A. Bailey; Jerry Juhl, Emily Perl Kingsley, Jeffrey Moss, Ray Sipherd, and Norman Stiles, writers, *Sesame Street* (program of 19 November 1973)

1974–1975

OUTSTANDING COMEDY SERIES: *The Mary Tyler Moore Show* (CBS); James L. Brooks and Allan Burns, executive producers; Ed. Weinberger and Stan Daniels, producers

OUTSTANDING DRAMA SERIES: "Upstairs, Downstairs," *Masterpiece Theatre* (PBS); Rex Firkin, executive producer; John Hawkesworth, producer

OUTSTANDING LIMITED SERIES: "Benjamin Franklin" (CBS); Lewis Freedman, executive producer; George Lefferts and Glenn Jordan, producers

OUTSTANDING COMEDY-VARIETY OR MUSIC SERIES: *The Carol Burnett Show* (CBS); Joe Hamilton, executive producer; Ed Simmons, producer; Carol Burnett, star

OUTSTANDING SPECIAL, DRAMA OR COMEDY: "The Law," *NBC World Premiere Movie* (NBC); William Sackheim, producer

OUTSTANDING SPECIAL, COMEDY-VARIETY OR MUSIC: "An Evening with John Denver"

(ABC); Jerry Weintraub, executive producer; Al Rogers and Rich Eustis, producers; John Denver, star

OUTSTANDING CLASSICAL MUSIC PROGRAM: "Profile in Music: Beverly Sills" (PBS); Patricia Foy, producer; Beverly Sills, star

OUTSTANDING CHILDREN'S SPECIAL (BROADCAST DURING THE EVENING): "Yes, Virginia, There Is a Santa Claus" (ABC); Burt Rosen, executive producer; Bill Melendez and Mort Green, producers

OUTSTANDING SPORTS PROGRAM (PROGRAM CONTAINING EDITED SEGMENTS): *ABC's Wide World of Sports* (program of 14 April 1974) (ABC); Roone Arledge, executive producer; Doug Wilson, Ned Steckel, Dennis Lewin, John Martin and Chet Forte, producers

OUTSTANDING SPORTS EVENT (BROADCAST UNEDITED): "Jimmy Connors vs. Rod Laver Tennis Challenge" (CBS); Frank Chirkinian, executive producer

OUTSTANDING DAYTIME DRAMA SERIES: *The Young and the Restless* (CBS); John J. Conboy, producer; William J. Bell and Lee Phillip Bell, creators

OUTSTANDING TALK, SERVICE, OR VARIETY SERIES (DAYTIME): *Dinah!* (SYNDICATED); Henry Jaffe and Carolyn Raskin, executive producers; Fred Tatashore, producer

OUTSTANDING GAME OR AUDIENCE PARTICIPATION SHOW (DAYTIME): *The Hollywood Squares* (NBC); Merrill Heatter and Bob Quigley, executive producers; Jay Redack, producer

OUTSTANDING DAYTIME DRAMA SPECIAL: "The Girl Who Couldn't Lose," *ABC Afternoon Playbreak* (ABC); Ira Barmak, executive producer; Lila Garrett, producer

OUTSTANDING ENTERTAINMENT CHILDREN'S SERIES (DAYTIME): *Star Trek* (NBC); Lou Scheimer and Norm Prescott, producers

OUTSTANDING ENTERTAINMENT CHILDREN'S SPECIAL (DAYTIME): "Harlequin," *The CBS Festival of Lively Arts for Young People* (CBS); Edward Villella, executive producer; Gardner Compton, producer

SPECIAL CLASSIFICATION OF OUTSTANDING PROGRAM AND INDIVIDUAL ACHIEVEMENT: (1) "The American Film Institute Salute to James Cagney" (CBS); George Stevens, Jr., executive producer; Paul W. Keyes, producer; and (2) Alistair Cooke, host, *Masterpiece Theatre* (PBS)

OUTSTANDING LEAD ACTOR IN A DRAMA SERIES: Robert Blake, *Baretta* (ABC)

OUTSTANDING LEAD ACTRESS IN A DRAMA SERIES: Jean Marsh, "Upstairs, Downstairs," *Masterpiece Theatre* (PBS)

OUTSTANDING LEAD ACTOR IN A LIMITED SERIES: Peter Falk, *Columbo* (NBC)

OUTSTANDING LEAD ACTRESS IN A LIMITED SERIES: Jessica Walter, *Amy Prentiss* (NBC)

OUTSTANDING LEAD ACTOR IN A COMEDY SERIES: Tony Randall, *The Odd Couple* (ABC)

OUTSTANDING LEAD ACTRESS IN A COMEDY SERIES: Valerie Harper, *Rhoda* (CBS)

OUTSTANDING LEAD ACTOR IN A SPECIAL PROGRAM (DRAMA OR COMEDY): Laurence Olivier, "Love Among the Ruins," *ABC Theatre* (ABC)

OUTSTANDING LEAD ACTRESS IN A SPECIAL PROGRAM (DRAMA OR COMEDY): Katharine Hepburn, "Love Among the Ruins," *ABC Theatre* (ABC)

OUTSTANDING CONTINUING PERFORMANCE BY A SUPPORTING ACTOR IN A DRAMA SERIES: Will Geer, *The Waltons* (CBS)

OUTSTANDING CONTINUING PERFORMANCE BY A SUPPORTING ACTRESS IN A DRAMA SERIES: Ellen Corby, *The Waltons* (CBS)

OUTSTANDING CONTINUING PERFORMANCE BY A SUPPORTING ACTOR IN A COMEDY SERIES: Ed Asner, *The Mary Tyler Moore Show* (CBS)

OUTSTANDING CONTINUING PERFORMANCE BY A SUPPORTING ACTRESS IN A COMEDY SERIES: Betty White, *The Mary Tyler Moore Show* (CBS)

OUTSTANDING CONTINUING OR SINGLE PERFORMANCE BY A SUPPORTING ACTOR IN VARIETY OR MUSIC: Jack Albertson, *Cher* (program of 2 March 1975) (CBS)

OUTSTANDING CONTINUING OR SINGLE PERFORMANCE BY A SUPPORTING ACTRESS IN VARIETY OR MUSIC: Cloris Leachman, *Cher* (program of 2 March 1975) (CBS)

OUTSTANDING SINGLE PERFORMANCE BY A SUPPORTING ACTOR IN A COMEDY OR DRAMA SERIES: Patrick McGoohan, "By Dawn's Early Light," *Columbo* (NBC)

OUTSTANDING SINGLE PERFORMANCE BY A SUPPORTING ACTRESS IN A COMEDY OR DRAMA SERIES: Cloris Leachman, "Phyllis Whips Inflation," *The Mary Tyler Moore Show* (CBS)

OUTSTANDING SINGLE PERFORMANCE BY A SUPPORTING ACTOR IN A COMEDY OR DRAMA SPECIAL: Anthony Quayle, "QB VII" (parts 1 and 2), *ABC Movie Special* (ABC)

OUTSTANDING SINGLE PERFORMANCE BY A SUPPORTING ACTRESS IN A COMEDY OR DRAMA SPECIAL: Juliet Mills, "QB VII" (parts 1 and 2), *ABC Movie Special* (ABC)

OUTSTANDING SPORTS BROADCASTER: Jim McKay, *ABC's Wide World of Sports* (ABC)

OUTSTANDING ACTOR IN A DAYTIME DRAMA SERIES: Macdonald Carey, *Days of Our Lives* (NBC)

OUTSTANDING ACTRESS IN A DAYTIME DRAMA SERIES: Susan Flannery, *Days of Our Lives* (NBC)

OUTSTANDING ACTOR IN A DAYTIME DRAMA SPECIAL: Bradford Dillman, "The Last Bride of Salem," *ABC Afternoon Playbreak* (ABC)

OUTSTANDING ACTRESS IN A DAYTIME DRAMA SPECIAL: Kay Lenz, "Heart in Hiding," *ABC Afternoon Playbreak* (ABC)

OUTSTANDING HOST OR HOSTESS IN A TALK, SERVICE, OR VARIETY SERIES (DAYTIME): Barbara Walters, *Today* (NBC)

OUTSTANDING HOST IN A GAME OR AUDIENCE PARTICIPATION SHOW (DAYTIME): Peter Marshall, *The Hollywood Squares* (NBC)

OUTSTANDING INDIVIDUAL ACHIEVEMENT IN DAYTIME PROGRAMMING: Paul Lynde, performer, *The Hollywood Squares* (NBC)

OUTSTANDING DIRECTING IN A DRAMA SERIES (SINGLE EPISODE): Bill Bain, "A Sudden Storm," "Upstairs, Downstairs," *Masterpiece Theatre* (PBS)

OUTSTANDING DIRECTING IN A COMEDY SERIES (SINGLE EPISODE): Gene Reynolds, "O.R.," *M*A*S*H* (CBS)

OUTSTANDING DIRECTING IN A SPECIAL PROGRAM, DRAMA OR COMEDY: George Cukor, "Love Among the Ruins," *ABC Theatre* (ABC)

OUTSTANDING DIRECTING IN A COMEDY-VARIETY OR MUSIC SERIES (SINGLE EPISODE): Dave Powers, *The Carol Burnett Show* (program of 21 December 1974) (CBS)

OUTSTANDING DIRECTING IN A COMEDY-VARIETY OR MUSIC SPECIAL: Bill Davis, "An Evening with John Denver" (ABC)

OUTSTANDING INDIVIDUAL DIRECTOR FOR A DAYTIME DRAMA SERIES (SINGLE EPISODE): Richard Dunlap, *The Young and the Restless* (program of 25 November 1974) (CBS)

OUTSTANDING INDIVIDUAL DIRECTOR FOR A DAYTIME SPECIAL PROGRAM: Mort Lachman, "The Girl Who Couldn't Lose," *ABC Afternoon Playbreak* (ABC)

OUTSTANDING INDIVIDUAL DIRECTOR FOR A DAYTIME VARIETY PROGRAM (SINGLE EPISODE): Glen Swanson, "Dinah Salutes Broadway," *Dinah!* (SYNDICATED)

OUTSTANDING INDIVIDUAL DIRECTOR FOR A GAME OR AUDIENCE PARTICIPATION SHOW (SINGLE EPISODE): Jerome Shaw, *The Hollywood Squares* (program of 28 October 1974) (NBC)

OUTSTANDING WRITING IN A DRAMA SERIES (SINGLE EPISODE): Howard Fast, "The Ambassador," "Benjamin Franklin" (CBS)

OUTSTANDING WRITING IN A SPECIAL PROGRAM (ORIGINAL TELEPLAY, DRAMA OR COMEDY): James Costigan, "Love Among the Ruins," *ABC Theatre* (ABC)

OUTSTANDING WRITING IN A SPECIAL PROGRAM (ADAPTATION, DRAMA, OR COMEDY): David W. Rintels, "IBM Presents Clarence Darrow" (NBC)

OUTSTANDING WRITING IN A COMEDY SERIES (SINGLE EPISODE): Ed. Weinberger and Stan Daniels, "Mary Richards Goes to Jail," *The Mary Tyler Moore Show* (CBS)

OUTSTANDING WRITING IN A COMEDY-VARIETY OR MUSIC SERIES (SINGLE EPISODE): Ed Simmons, Gary Belkin, Roger Beatty, Arnie Kogen, Bill Richmond, Gene Perret, Rudy DeLuca, Barry Levinson, Dick Clair and Jenna McMahon, *The Carol Burnett Show* (program of 21 December 1974) (CBS)

OUTSTANDING WRITING IN A COMEDY-VARIETY OR MUSICAL SPECIAL: Bob Wells, John Bradford and Cy Coleman, "Shirley MacLaine: If They Could See Me Now" (CBS)

OUTSTANDING WRITING FOR A DAYTIME DRAMA SERIES: Harding Lemay, Tom King, Charles Kozloff, Jan Merlin, and Douglas Marland, *Another World* (NBC)

OUTSTANDING WRITING FOR A DAYTIME SPECIAL PROGRAM: Audrey Davis Levin, "Heart in Hiding," *ABC Afternoon Playbreak* (ABC)

TRUSTEES' AWARDS: (1) Elmer Lower, vice president, corporate affairs, American

Broadcasting Companies, Inc.; and (2) Dr. Peter Goldmark, president, Goldmark Laboratories

1975–1976

OUTSTANDING COMEDY SERIES: *The Mary Tyler Moore Show* (CBS); James L. Brooks and Allan Burns, executive producers; Ed. Weinberger and Stan Daniels, producers

OUTSTANDING DRAMA SERIES: *Police Story* (NBC); David Gerber and Stanley Kallis, executive producers; Liam O'Brien and Carl Pingitore, producers

OUTSTANDING LIMITED SERIES: "Upstairs, Downstairs," *Masterpiece Theatre* (PBS); Rex Firkin, executive producer; John Hawkesworth, producer

OUTSTANDING COMEDY-VARIETY OR MUSIC SERIES: *NBC's Saturday Night* (NBC); Lorne Michaels, producer

OUTSTANDING SPECIAL, DRAMA OR COMEDY: "Eleanor and Franklin," *ABC Theatre* (ABC); David Susskind, executive producer; Harry Sherman and Audrey Maas, producers

OUTSTANDING SPECIAL, COMEDY-VARIETY OR MUSIC: "Gypsy in My Soul" (CBS); William O. Harbach, executive producer; Cy Coleman and Fred Ebb, producers; Shirley MacLaine, star

OUTSTANDING CLASSICAL MUSIC PROGRAM: "Bernstein and the New York Philharmonic, Great Performances" (PBS); Klaus Hallig and Harry Kraut, executive producers; David Griffiths, producer; Leonard Bernstein, star

OUTSTANDING CHILDREN'S SPECIAL (BROADCAST DURING THE EVENING): (1) "You're a Good Sport, Charlie Brown" (CBS); Lee Mendelson, executive producer; Bill Melendez, producer; and (2) "Huckleberry Finn" (ABC); Steven North, producer

OUTSTANDING EDITED SPORTS SERIES: *ABC's Wide World of Sports* (ABC); Roone Arledge, executive producer; Doug Wilson, Chet Forte, Ned Steckel, Brice Weisman, Terry Jastrow, Bob Goodrich, John Martin, Dennis Lewin and Don Ohlmeyer, producers

OUTSTANDING LIVE SPORTS SERIES: *NFL Monday Night Football* (ABC); Roone Arledge, executive producer; Don Ohlmeyer, producer

OUTSTANDING EDITED SPORTS SPECIAL: (1) "XII Winter Olympic Games" (ABC); Roone Arledge, executive producer; Chuck Howard, Don Ohlmeyer, Geoff Mason, Chet Forte, Bob Goodrich, Ellie Riger, Brice Weisman, Doug Wilson, and Bob Wilcox, producers; (2) "Triumph and Tragedy . . . The Olympic Experience" (ABC); Roone Arledge, executive producer; Don Ohlmeyer, producer

OUTSTANDING LIVE SPORTS SPECIAL: "1975 World Series" (NBC); Scotty Connal, executive producer; Roy Hammerman, producer

OUTSTANDING DRAMA SERIES (DAYTIME): *Another World* (NBC); Paul Rauch, executive producer; Joe Rothenberger and Mary S. Bonner, producers

OUTSTANDING TALK, SERVICE OR VARIETY SERIES (DAYTIME): *Dinah!* (SYNDICATED); Henry Jaffe and Carolyn Raskin, executive producers; Fred Tatashore, producer

OUTSTANDING GAME OR AUDIENCE PARTICIPATION SHOW (DAYTIME): *The $20,000 Pyramid* (ABC); Bob Stewart, executive producer; Anne Marie Schmitt, producer

OUTSTANDING DRAMA SPECIAL (DAYTIME): "First Ladies' Diaries: Edith Wilson" (NBC); Jeff Young, producer

OUTSTANDING ENTERTAINMENT CHILDREN'S SERIES (DAYTIME): *Big Blue Marble* (SYNDICATED); Henry Fownes, producer

OUTSTANDING INFORMATIONAL CHILDREN'S SERIES (FOR THE PERIOD 1 JULY 1974 TO 15 MARCH 1976): *Go* (NBC); George A. Heinemann, executive producer; Rift Fournier, J. Phillip Miller, William W. Lewis and Joan Bender, producers

OUTSTANDING INSTRUCTIONAL CHILDREN'S PROGRAMMING (SERIES AND SPECIALS): "Grammar Rock" (ABC); Thomas G. Yohe, executive producer; Radford Stone, producer

OUTSTANDING ENTERTAINMENT CHILDREN'S SPECIAL (DAYTIME): "Danny Kaye's Look-In at the Metropolitan Opera," *The CBS Festival of Lively Arts for Young People* (CBS); Sylvia Fine, executive producer; Bernard Rothman, Herbert Bones and Jack Wohl, producers

OUTSTANDING INFORMATIONAL CHILDREN'S SPECIAL (FOR THE PERIOD 1 JULY 1974 TO 15

MARCH 1976): "Happy Anniversary, Charlie Brown" (CBS); Lee Mendelson and Warren Lockhart, producers

SPECIAL CLASSIFICATION OF OUTSTANDING PROGRAM AND INDIVIDUAL ACHIEVEMENT: (1) "Bicentennial Minutes" (CBS); Bob Markel, executive producer; Gareth Davies and Paul Waigner, producers; (2) *The Tonight Show Starring Johnny Carson* (NBC); Fred DeCordova, producer; Johnny Carson, star; (3) Ann Marcus, Jerry Adelman and Daniel Gregory Browne, writers, *Mary Hartman, Mary Hartman* (pilot episode) (SYNDICATED)

OUTSTANDING LEAD ACTOR IN A DRAMA SERIES: Peter Falk, *Columbo* (NBC)

OUTSTANDING LEAD ACTRESS IN A DRAMA SERIES: Michael Learned, *The Waltons* (CBS)

OUTSTANDING LEAD ACTOR IN A LIMITED SERIES: Hal Holbrook, "Sandburg's Lincoln" (NBC)

OUTSTANDING LEAD ACTRESS IN A LIMITED SERIES: Rosemary Harris, "Notorious Woman," *Masterpiece Theatre* (PBS)

OUTSTANDING LEAD ACTOR IN A COMEDY SERIES: Jack Albertson, *Chico and the Man* (NBC)

OUTSTANDING LEAD ACTRESS IN A COMEDY SERIES: Mary Tyler Moore, *The Mary Tyler Moore Show* (CBS)

OUTSTANDING LEAD ACTOR (SINGLE APPEARANCE, DRAMA OR COMEDY SERIES): Edward Asner, *Rich Man, Poor Man* (program of 1 February 1976) (ABC)

OUTSTANDING LEAD ACTRESS (SINGLE APPEARANCE, DRAMA OR COMEDY SERIES): Kathryn Walker, "John Adams, Lawyer," *The Adams Chronicles* (PBS)

OUTSTANDING LEAD ACTOR IN A DRAMA OR COMEDY SPECIAL: Anthony Hopkins, "The Lindbergh Kidnapping Case," *NBC World Premiere Movie* (NBC)

OUTSTANDING LEAD ACTRESS IN A DRAMA OR COMEDY SPECIAL: Susan Clark, "Babe" (CBS)

OUTSTANDING CONTINUING PERFORMANCE BY A SUPPORTING ACTOR IN A DRAMA SERIES (REGULAR OR LIMITED): Anthony Zerbe, *Harry O* (ABC)

OUTSTANDING CONTINUING PERFORMANCE BY A SUPPORTING ACTRESS IN A DRAMA SERIES (REGULAR OR LIMITED): Ellen Corby, *The Waltons* (CBS)

OUTSTANDING CONTINUING PERFORMANCE BY A SUPPORTING ACTOR IN A COMEDY SERIES (REGULAR OR LIMITED): Ted Knight, *The Mary Tyler Moore Show* (CBS)

OUTSTANDING CONTINUING PERFORMANCE BY A SUPPORTING ACTRESS IN A COMEDY SERIES (REGULAR OR LIMITED): Betty White, *The Mary Tyler Moore Show* (CBS)

OUTSTANDING CONTINUING OR SINGLE PERFORMANCE BY A SUPPORTING ACTOR IN VARIETY OR MUSIC (CONTINUING ROLE, ONE-TIME APPEARANCE, OR SPECIAL): Chevy Chase, *NBC's Saturday Night* (program of 17 January 1976) (NBC)

OUTSTANDING CONTINUING OR SINGLE PERFORMANCE BY A SUPPORTING ACTRESS IN VARIETY OR MUSIC (CONTINUING ROLE, ONE-TIME APPEARANCE, OR SPECIAL): Vicki Lawrence, *The Carol Burnett Show* (program of 7 February 1976) (CBS)

OUTSTANDING SINGLE PERFORMANCE BY A SUPPORTING ACTOR IN A COMEDY OR DRAMA SERIES: Gordon Jackson, "The Beastly Hun," "Upstairs, Downstairs," *Masterpiece Theatre* (PBS)

OUTSTANDING SINGLE PERFORMANCE BY A SUPPORTING ACTRESS IN A COMEDY OR DRAMA SERIES: Fionnuala Flanagan, *Rich Man, Poor Man* (program of 2 February 1976) (ABC)

OUTSTANDING SINGLE PERFORMANCE BY A SUPPORTING ACTOR IN A COMEDY OR DRAMA SPECIAL: Ed Flanders, "A Moon for the Misbegotten," *ABC Theatre* (ABC)

OUTSTANDING SINGLE PERFORMANCE BY A SUPPORTING ACTRESS IN A COMEDY OR DRAMA SPECIAL: Rosemary Murphy, "Eleanor and Franklin," *ABC Theatre* (ABC)

OUTSTANDING SPORTS PERSONALITY: Jim McKay, *ABC's Wide World of Sports* and *ABC's XII Winter Olympics* (ABC)

OUTSTANDING ACTOR IN A DAYTIME DRAMA SERIES: Larry Haines, *Search for Tomorrow* (CBS)

OUTSTANDING ACTRESS IN A DAYTIME DRAMA SERIES: Helen Gallagher, *Ryan's Hope* (ABC)

OUTSTANDING ACTOR IN A DAYTIME DRAMA SPECIAL: (1) Gerald Gordon, "First Ladies' Diaries: Rachel Jackson" (NBC); (2) James Luisi, "First Ladies' Diaries: Martha Washington" (NBC)

OUTSTANDING ACTRESS IN A DAYTIME DRAMA SPECIAL: Elizabeth Hubbard, "First Ladies' Diaries: Edith Wilson" (NBC)

OUTSTANDING HOST OR HOSTESS IN A TALK, SERVICE OR VARIETY SERIES (DAYTIME): Dinah Shore, *Dinah!* (SYNDICATED)

OUTSTANDING HOST OR HOSTESS IN A GAME OR AUDIENCE PARTICIPATION SHOW: Allen Ludden, *Password* (ABC)

OUTSTANDING INDIVIDUAL ACHIEVEMENT IN CHILDREN'S PROGRAMMING (SINGLE EPISODE OF A SERIES OR SPECIAL PROGRAM): The Muppets, *Sesame Street* (program of 25 April 1975) (PBS); Jim Henson, Frank Oz, Jerry Nelson, Carroll Spinney and Richard Hunt, performers

OUTSTANDING DIRECTING IN A DRAMA SERIES (SINGLE EPISODE): David Greene, *Rich Man, Poor Man* (program of 15 March 1976) (ABC)

OUTSTANDING DIRECTING IN A COMEDY SERIES (SINGLE EPISODE): Gene Reynolds, "Welcome to Korea," *M*A*S*H* (CBS)

OUTSTANDING DIRECTING IN A COMEDY-VARIETY OR MUSIC SERIES (SINGLE EPISODE): Dave Wilson, *NBC's Saturday Night* (program of 18 October 1975, with host Paul Simon) (NBC)

OUTSTANDING DIRECTING IN A SPECIAL PROGRAM, DRAMA OR COMEDY: Daniel Petrie, "Eleanor and Franklin," *ABC Theatre* (ABC)

OUTSTANDING DIRECTING IN A COMEDY-VARIETY OR MUSIC SPECIAL: Dwight Hemion, "Steve and Eydie: 'Our Love Is Here to Stay'" (CBS)

OUTSTANDING INDIVIDUAL DIRECTOR FOR A DRAMA SERIES (SINGLE EPISODE, DAYTIME SERIES): David Pressman, *One Life to Live* (program of 26 January 1976) (ABC)

OUTSTANDING INDIVIDUAL DIRECTOR FOR A SPECIAL PROGRAM (DAYTIME): Nicholas Havinga, "First Ladies' Diaries: Edith Wilson" (NBC)

OUTSTANDING INDIVIDUAL DIRECTOR FOR A VARIETY PROGRAM (SINGLE EPISODE, DAYTIME SERIES): Glen Swanson, "Dinah Salutes Tony Orlando and Dawn on Their Fifth Anniversary," *Dinah!* (SYNDICATED)

OUTSTANDING INDIVIDUAL DIRECTOR FOR A GAME OR AUDIENCE PARTICIPATION SHOW (SINGLE EPISODE, DAYTIME SERIES): Mike Gargiulo, *The $20,000 Pyramid* (program of 18 February 1976) (ABC)

OUTSTANDING WRITING IN A DRAMA SERIES (SINGLE EPISODE): Sherman Yellen, "John Adams, Lawyer," *The Adams Chronicles* (PBS)

OUTSTANDING WRITING IN A SPECIAL PROGRAM (ORIGINAL TELEPLAY, DRAMA OR COMEDY): James Costigan, "Eleanor and Franklin," *ABC Theatre* (ABC)

OUTSTANDING WRITING IN A SPECIAL PROGRAM (ADAPTATION, DRAMA, OR COMEDY): David W. Rintels, "Fear on Trial" (CBS)

OUTSTANDING WRITING IN A COMEDY SERIES (SINGLE EPISODE): David Lloyd, "Chuckles Bites the Dust," *The Mary Tyler Moore Show* (CBS)

OUTSTANDING WRITING IN A COMEDY-VARIETY OR MUSIC SERIES (SINGLE EPISODE): Anne Beatts, Chevy Chase, Al Franken, Tom Davis, Lorne Michaels, Marilyn Suzanne Miller, Michael O'Donoghue, Herb Sargent, Tom Schiller, Rosie Shuster and Alan Zweibel, *NBC's Saturday Night* (program of 10 January 1976, with host Elliott Gould) (NBC)

OUTSTANDING WRITING IN A COMEDY-VARIETY OR MUSIC SPECIAL: Jane Wagner, Lorne Michaels, Ann Elder, Christopher Guest, Earl Pomerantz, Jim Rusk, Lily Tomlin, Rod Warren and George Yanok, "Lily Tomlin" (ABC)

OUTSTANDING WRITING FOR A DRAMA SERIES (DAYTIME): William J. Bell, Kay Lenard, Pat Falken Smith, Bill Rega, Margaret Stewart, Sheri Anderson, and Wanda Coleman, *Days of Our Lives* (NBC)

OUTSTANDING WRITING FOR A SPECIAL PROGRAM (DAYTIME): Audrey Davis Levin, "First Ladies' Diaries: Edith Wilson" (NBC)

1976–1977

I. PRIME-TIME AWARDS (administered by the Academy of Television Arts and Sciences)

OUTSTANDING COMEDY SERIES: *The Mary Tyler Moore Show* (CBS); Allan Burns and James L. Brooks, executive producers; Ed. Weinberger and Stan Daniels, producers

OUTSTANDING DRAMA SERIES: "Upstairs, Downstairs," *Masterpiece Theatre* (PBS); John Hawkesworth and Joan Sullivan, producers

OUTSTANDING LIMITED SERIES: *Roots* (ABC); David L. Wolper, executive producer; Stan Margulies, producer

OUTSTANDING COMEDY-VARIETY OR MUSIC SERIES: *Van Dyke and Company* (NBC); Byron Paul, executive producer; Allan Blye and Bob Einstein, producers; Dick Van Dyke, star

OUTSTANDING SPECIAL, DRAMA OR COMEDY: (1) "Eleanor and Franklin: The White House Years," *ABC Theatre* (ABC); David Susskind, executive producer; Harry R. Sherman, producer; and (2) "Sybil," *The Big Event* (NBC); Philip Capice and Peter Dunne, executive producers; Jacqueline Babbin, producer

OUTSTANDING SPECIAL, COMEDY-VARIETY OR MUSIC: "The Barry Manilow Special" (ABC); Miles Lourie, executive producer; Steve Binder, producer; Barry Manilow, star

OUTSTANDING CLASSICAL PROGRAM IN THE PERFORMING ARTS (SERIES OR SPECIAL): "American Ballet Theatre: Swan Lake Live from Lincoln Center," *Great Performances* (PBS); John Goberman, producer

OUTSTANDING CHILDREN'S SPECIAL (BROADCAST DURING THE EVENING): "Ballet Shoes" (parts 1 and 2), *Piccadilly Circus* (PBS); John McRae and Joan Sullivan, producers

SPECIAL CLASSIFICATION OF OUTSTANDING PROGRAMMING ACHIEVEMENT: *The Tonight Show Starring Johnny Carson* (NBC); Fred DeCordova, producer; Johnny Carson, star

OUTSTANDING LEAD ACTOR IN A DRAMA SERIES: James Garner, *The Rockford Files* (NBC)

OUTSTANDING LEAD ACTRESS IN A DRAMA SERIES: Lindsay Wagner, *The Bionic Woman* (ABC)

OUTSTANDING LEAD ACTOR IN A LIMITED SERIES: Christopher Plummer, "The Moneychangers," *The Big Event* (NBC)

OUTSTANDING LEAD ACTRESS IN A LIMITED SERIES: Patty Duke Astin, "Captains and the Kings," *Best Sellers* (NBC)

OUTSTANDING LEAD ACTOR IN A COMEDY SERIES: Carroll O'Connor, *All in the Family* (CBS)

OUTSTANDING LEAD ACTRESS IN A COMEDY SERIES: Beatrice Arthur, *Maude* (CBS)

OUTSTANDING LEAD ACTOR FOR A SINGLE APPEARANCE IN A DRAMA OR COMEDY SERIES: Louis Gossett, Jr., *Roots* (part 2) (ABC)

OUTSTANDING LEAD ACTRESS FOR A SINGLE APPEARANCE IN A DRAMA OR COMEDY SERIES: Beulah Bondi, "The Pony Cart," *The Waltons* (CBS)

OUTSTANDING LEAD ACTOR IN A DRAMA OR COMEDY SPECIAL: Ed Flanders, "Harry S Truman: Plain Speaking" (PBS)

OUTSTANDING LEAD ACTRESS IN A DRAMA OR COMEDY SPECIAL: Sally Field, "Sybil," *The Big Event* (NBC)

OUTSTANDING CONTINUING PERFORMANCE BY A SUPPORTING ACTOR IN A DRAMA SERIES: Gary Frank, *Family* (ABC)

OUTSTANDING CONTINUING PERFORMANCE BY A SUPPORTING ACTRESS IN A DRAMA SERIES: Kristy McNichol, *Family* (ABC)

OUTSTANDING CONTINUING PERFORMANCE BY A SUPPORTING ACTOR IN A COMEDY SERIES: Gary Burghoff, *M*A*S*H* (CBS)

OUTSTANDING CONTINUING PERFORMANCE BY A SUPPORTING ACTRESS IN A COMEDY SERIES: Mary Kay Place, *Mary Hartman, Mary Hartman* (SYNDICATED)

OUTSTANDING CONTINUING OR SINGLE PERFORMANCE BY A SUPPORTING ACTOR IN VARIETY OR MUSIC: Tim Conway, *The Carol Burnett Show* (CBS)

OUTSTANDING CONTINUING OR SINGLE PERFORMANCE BY A SUPPORTING ACTRESS IN VARIETY OR MUSIC: Rita Moreno, *The Muppet Show* (SYNDICATED)

OUTSTANDING SINGLE PERFORMANCE BY A SUPPORTING ACTOR IN A COMEDY OR DRAMA SERIES: Edward Asner, *Roots* (part 1) (ABC)

OUTSTANDING SINGLE PERFORMANCE BY A SUPPORTING ACTRESS IN A COMEDY OR DRAMA SERIES: Olivia Cole, *Roots* (part 8) (ABC)

OUTSTANDING PERFORMANCE BY A SUPPORTING ACTOR IN A COMEDY OR DRAMA SPECIAL: Burgess Meredith, "Tail Gunner Joe," *The Big Event* (NBC)

OUTSTANDING PERFORMANCE BY A SUPPORTING ACTRESS IN A COMEDY OR DRAMA SPECIAL: Diana Hyland, "The Boy in the Plastic Bubble," *The ABC Friday Night Movie* (ABC)

OUTSTANDING DIRECTING IN A DRAMA SERIES (SINGLE EPISODE): David Greene, *Roots* (part 1) (ABC)

OUTSTANDING DIRECTING IN A COMEDY SERIES (SINGLE EPISODE): Alan Alda, "Dear Sigmund," *M*A*S*H* (CBS)

OUTSTANDING DIRECTING IN A COMEDY-VARIETY OR MUSIC SERIES (SINGLE EPISODE): Dave Powers, *The Carol Burnett Show* (program of 12 February 1977) (CBS)

OUTSTANDING DIRECTING IN A SPECIAL PROGRAM, DRAMA OR COMEDY: Daniel Petrie, "Eleanor and Franklin: The White House Years," *ABC Theatre* (ABC)

OUTSTANDING DIRECTING IN A COMEDY-VARIETY OR MUSIC SPECIAL: Dwight Hemion, "America Salutes Richard Rodgers: The Sound of His Music" (CBS)

OUTSTANDING WRITING IN A DRAMA SERIES (SINGLE EPISODE): Ernest Kinoy and William Blinn, *Roots* (part 2) (ABC)

OUTSTANDING WRITING IN A SPECIAL PROGRAM (ORIGINAL TELEPLAY, DRAMA OR COMEDY): Lane Slate, "Tail Gunner Joe," *The Big Event* (NBC)

OUTSTANDING WRITING IN A SPECIAL PROGRAM (ADAPTATION, DRAMA OR COMEDY): Stewart Stern, "Sybil," *The Big Event* (NBC)

OUTSTANDING WRITING IN A COMEDY SERIES (SINGLE EPISODE): Allan Burns, James L. Brooks, Ed. Weinberger, Stan Daniels, David Lloyd and Bob Ellison, "The Last Show," *The Mary Tyler Moore Show* (CBS)

OUTSTANDING WRITING IN A COMEDY-VARIETY OR MUSIC SERIES (SINGLE EPISODE): Anne Beatts, Dan Aykroyd, Al Franken, Tom Davis, James Downey, Lorne Michaels, Marilyn Suzanne Miller, Michael O'Donoghue, Herb Sargent, Tom Schiller, Rosie Shuster, Alan Zweibel, John Belushi, and Bill Murray, *NBC's Saturday Night* (program of 12 March 1977, with host Sissy Spacek) (NBC)

OUTSTANDING WRITING IN A COMEDY-VARIETY OR MUSICAL SPECIAL: Alan Buz Kohan and Ted Strauss, "America Salutes Richard Rodgers: The Sound of His Music" (CBS)

II. DAYTIME AWARDS (administered by the National Academy of Television Arts and Sciences)

OUTSTANDING DAYTIME DRAMA SERIES: *Ryan's Hope* (ABC); Paul Avila Mayer and Claire Labine, executive producers; Robert Costello, producer

OUTSTANDING DAYTIME TALK, SERVICE OR VARIETY SERIES: *The Merv Griffin Show* (SYNDICATED); Bob Murphy, producer

OUTSTANDING GAME OR AUDIENCE PARTICIPATION SHOW: *The Family Feud* (ABC); Howard Felsher, producer

OUTSTANDING ENTERTAINMENT CHILDREN'S SERIES: *Zoom* (PBS); Cheryl Susheel Bibbs, executive producer; Monia Joblin and Mary Benjamin Blau, producers

OUTSTANDING INFORMATIONAL CHILDREN'S SERIES: *The Electric Company* (PBS); Samuel Y. Gibbon, Jr., executive producer

OUTSTANDING INSTRUCTIONAL CHILDREN'S PROGRAMMING (SERIES AND SPECIALS): *Sesame Street* (PBS); Jon Stone, executive producer; Dulcy Singer, producer

OUTSTANDING ENTERTAINMENT CHILDREN'S SPECIAL: "Big Henry and the Polka Dot Kid," *Special Treat* (NBC); Linda Gottlieb, producer

OUTSTANDING INFORMATIONAL CHILDREN'S SPECIAL: "My Mom's Having a Baby," *ABC Afterschool Specials* (ABC); David H. DePatie and Friz Freleng, executive producers; Bob Chenault, producer

OUTSTANDING PROGRAM AND INDIVIDUAL ACHIEVEMENT IN DAYTIME DRAMA SPECIALS: (1) "The American Woman: Portraits of Courage" (ABC); Gaby Monet, producer; (2) Lois Nettleton, performer, "The American Woman: Portraits of Courage" (ABC); and (3) Gaby Monet and Anne Grant, writers, "The American Woman: Portraits of Courage" (ABC)

OUTSTANDING ACTOR IN A DAYTIME DRAMA SERIES: Val Dufour, *Search for Tomorrow* (CBS)

OUTSTANDING ACTRESS IN A DAYTIME DRAMA SERIES: Helen Gallagher, *Ryan's Hope* (ABC)

OUTSTANDING HOST OR HOSTESS IN A TALK, SERVICE OR VARIETY SERIES: Phil Donahue, *Donahue* (SYNDICATED)

OUTSTANDING HOST OR HOSTESS IN A GAME OR AUDIENCE PARTICIPATION SHOW: Bert Convy, *Tattletales* (CBS)

OUTSTANDING INDIVIDUAL DIRECTOR FOR A DAYTIME DRAMA SERIES: Lela Swift, *Ryan's Hope* (program of 8 February 1977) (ABC)

OUTSTANDING INDIVIDUAL DIRECTOR FOR A DAYTIME VARIETY PROGRAM (SINGLE EPISODE): Donald R. King, "Mike in Hollywood with Ray Charles and Michel Legrand," *The Mike Douglas Show* (SYNDICATED)

OUTSTANDING INDIVIDUAL DIRECTOR FOR A GAME OR AUDIENCE PARTICIPATION SHOW (SINGLE EPISODE): Mike Gargiulo, *The $20,000 Pyramid* (program of 10 August 1976) (ABC)

OUTSTANDING WRITING FOR A DAYTIME DRAMA SERIES (SINGLE EPISODE OR ENTIRE SERIES): Claire Labine, Paul Avila Mayer and Mary Munisteri, *Ryan's Hope* (ABC)

1977–1978

I. PRIME-TIME AWARDS (administered by the Academy of Television Arts and Sciences)

OUTSTANDING COMEDY SERIES: *All in the Family* (CBS); Mort Lachman, executive producer; Milt Josefsberg, producer

OUTSTANDING DRAMA SERIES: *The Rockford Files* (NBC); Meta Rosenberg, executive producer; Stephen J. Cannell, supervising producer; David Chase and Charles F. Johnson, producers

OUTSTANDING LIMITED SERIES: *Holocaust* (NBC); Herbert Brodkin, executive producer; Robert Berger, producer

OUTSTANDING COMEDY-VARIETY OR MUSIC SERIES: *The Muppet Show* (SYNDICATED); David Lazer, executive producer; Jim Henson, producer; The Muppets—Frank Oz, Jerry Nelson, Richard Hunt, Dave Goelz and Jim Henson, stars

OUTSTANDING INFORMATIONAL SERIES: *The Body Human* (CBS); Thomas W. Moore, executive producer; Alfred R. Kelman, producer

OUTSTANDING SPECIAL, DRAMA OR COMEDY: "The Gathering" (ABC); Joseph Barbera, executive producer; Harry R. Sherman, producer

OUTSTANDING SPECIAL, COMEDY-VARIETY OR MUSIC: "Bette Midler—Ol' Red Hair Is Back" (NBC); Aaron Russo, executive producer; Gary Smith and Dwight Hemion, producers; Bette Midler, star

OUTSTANDING CLASSICAL PROGRAM IN THE PERFORMING ARTS: American Ballet Theatre's "Giselle," *Live from Lincoln Center* (PBS); John Goberman, producer

OUTSTANDING INFORMATIONAL SPECIAL: "The Great Whales," *National Geographic Specials* (PBS); Thomas Skinner and Dennis B. Kane, executive producers; Nicolas Noxon, producer

OUTSTANDING CHILDREN'S SPECIAL (BROADCAST DURING THE EVENING): "Halloween Is Grinch Night" (ABC); David H. DePatie and Friz Freleng, executive producers; Ted Geisel, producer

SPECIAL CLASSIFICATION OF OUTSTANDING PROGRAM ACHIEVEMENT: *The Tonight Show Starring Johnny Carson* (NBC); Fred De Cordova, producer; Johnny Carson, star

OUTSTANDING LEAD ACTOR IN A DRAMA SERIES: Edward Asner, *Lou Grant* (CBS)

OUTSTANDING LEAD ACTRESS IN A DRAMA SERIES: Sada Thompson, *Family* (ABC)

OUTSTANDING LEAD ACTOR IN A LIMITED SERIES: Michael Moriarty, *Holocaust* (NBC)

OUTSTANDING LEAD ACTRESS IN A LIMITED SERIES: Meryl Streep, *Holocaust* (NBC)

OUTSTANDING LEAD ACTOR IN A COMEDY SERIES: Carroll O'Connor, *All in the Family* (CBS)

OUTSTANDING LEAD ACTRESS IN A COMEDY SERIES: Jean Stapleton, *All in the Family* (CBS)

OUTSTANDING LEAD ACTOR FOR A SINGLE APPEARANCE IN A DRAMA OR COMEDY SERIES: Barnard Hughes, "Judge," *Lou Grant* (CBS)

OUTSTANDING LEAD ACTRESS FOR A SINGLE APPEARANCE IN A DRAMA OR COMEDY SERIES: Rita Moreno, "The Paper Palace," *The Rockford Files* (NBC)

OUTSTANDING LEAD ACTOR IN A DRAMA OR COMEDY SPECIAL: Fred Astaire, "A Family Upside Down" (NBC)

OUTSTANDING LEAD ACTRESS IN A DRAMA OR COMEDY SPECIAL: Joanne Woodward, "See How She Runs," *G.E. Theater* (CBS)

OUTSTANDING CONTINUING PERFORMANCE BY A SUPPORTING ACTOR IN A DRAMA SERIES: Robert Vaughn, *Washington: Behind Closed Doors* (ABC)

OUTSTANDING CONTINUING PERFORMANCE BY A SUPPORTING ACTRESS IN A DRAMA SERIES: Nancy Marchand, *Lou Grant* (CBS)

OUTSTANDING CONTINUING PERFORMANCE BY A SUPPORTING ACTOR IN A COMEDY SERIES: Rob Reiner, *All in the Family* (CBS)

OUTSTANDING CONTINUING PERFORMANCE BY A SUPPORTING ACTRESS IN A COMEDY SERIES: Julie Kavner, *Rhoda* (CBS)

OUTSTANDING CONTINUING OR SINGLE PERFORMANCE BY A SUPPORTING ACTOR IN VARIETY OR MUSIC: Tim Conway, *The Carol Burnett Show* (CBS)

OUTSTANDING CONTINUING OR SINGLE PERFORMANCE BY A SUPPORTING ACTRESS IN VARIETY OR MUSIC: Gilda Radner, *NBC's Saturday Night Live* (NBC)

OUTSTANDING SINGLE PERFORMANCE BY A SUPPORTING ACTOR IN A COMEDY OR DRAMA SERIES: Ricardo Montalban, *How the West Was Won* (Part II) ABC

OUTSTANDING SINGLE PERFORMANCE BY A SUPPORTING ACTRESS IN A COMEDY OR DRAMA SERIES: Blanche Baker, *Holocaust* (Part I) (NBC)

OUTSTANDING PERFORMANCE BY A SUPPORTING ACTOR IN A COMEDY OR DRAMA SPECIAL: Howard Da Silva, "Verna: USO Girl," *Great Performances* (PBS)

OUTSTANDING PERFORMANCE BY A SUPPORTING ACTRESS IN A COMEDY OR DRAMA SPECIAL: Eva Le Gallienne, "The Royal Family" (PBS)

OUTSTANDING DIRECTING IN A DRAMA SERIES: Marvin J. Chomsky, *Holocaust* (NBC)

OUTSTANDING DIRECTING IN A COMEDY SERIES: Paul Bogart, "Edith's 50th Birthday," *All in the Family* (CBS)

OUTSTANDING DIRECTING IN A COMEDY-VARIETY OR MUSIC SERIES: Dave Powers, *The Carol Burnett Show* (program of 5 March 1978, with guests Steve Martin and Betty White) (CBS)

OUTSTANDING DIRECTING IN A SPECIAL PROGRAM, DRAMA OR COMEDY: David Lowell Rich, "The Defection of Simas Kudirka" (CBS)

OUTSTANDING DIRECTING IN A COMEDY-VARIETY OR MUSIC SPECIAL: Dwight Hemion, "The Sentry Collection Presents Ben Vereen—His Roots" (ABC)

OUTSTANDING WRITING IN A DRAMA SERIES: Gerald Green, *Holocaust* (NBC)

OUTSTANDING WRITING IN A SPECIAL PROGRAM, DRAMA OR COMEDY (ORIGINAL TELEPLAY): George Rubino, "The Last Tenant" (ABC)

OUTSTANDING WRITING IN A SPECIAL PROGRAM, DRAMA OR COMEDY (ADAPTATION): Caryl Lender, "Mary White" (ABC)

OUTSTANDING WRITING IN A COMEDY SERIES: Bob Weiskopf and Bob Schiller (teleplay), Barry Harman and Harve Brosten (story), "Cousin Liz," *All in the Family* (CBS)

OUTSTANDING WRITING IN A COMEDY-VARIETY OR MUSIC SERIES: Ed Simmons, Roger Beatty, Rick Hawkins, Liz Sage, Robert Illes, James Stein, Franelle Silver, Larry Siegel, Tim Conway, Bill Richmond, Gene Perrett, Dick Clair, and Jenna McMahon, *The Carol Burnett Show* (program of 5 March 1978, with guests Steve Martin and Betty White) (CBS)

FIRST ANNUAL ATAS GOVERNOR'S AWARD: William S. Paley, Chairman of the Board, CBS

II. DAYTIME AWARDS (administered by the National Academy of Television Arts and Sciences)

OUTSTANDING DAYTIME DRAMA SERIES: *Days of Our Lives* (NBC); Betty Corday and Wesley Kenney, executive producers; Jack Herzberg, producer

OUTSTANDING DAYTIME TALK, SERVICE OR VARIETY SERIES: *Donahue* (SYNDICATED); Richard Mincer, executive producer; Patricia McMillen, producer

OUTSTANDING GAME OR AUDIENCE PARTICIPATION SHOW: *The Hollywood Squares* (NBC); Merrill Heatter and Bob Quigley, executive producers; Jay Redack, producer

OUTSTANDING CHILDREN'S ENTERTAINMENT SERIES: *Captain Kangaroo* (CBS); Jim Hirschfeld, producer

OUTSTANDING CHILDREN'S INFORMATION SERIES: *Animals Animals Animals* (ABC); Lester Cooper, executive producer; Peter Weinberg, producer

OUTSTANDING CHILDREN'S INSTRUCTIONAL SERIES: *Schoolhouse Rock* (ABC); Tom Yohe, executive producer; Radford Stone and George Newall, producers

OUTSTANDING CHILDREN'S ENTERTAINMENT SPECIAL: "Hewitt's Just Different," *ABC Afterschool Special* (ABC); Daniel Wilson, executive producer; Fran Sears, producer

OUTSTANDING CHILDREN'S INFORMATION SPECIAL: "Very Good Friends," *ABC Afterschool Special* (ABC); Martin Tahse, producer

OUTSTANDING ACTOR IN A DAYTIME DRAMA SERIES: James Pritchett, *The Doctors* (NBC)

OUTSTANDING ACTRESS IN A DAYTIME DRAMA SERIES: Laurie Heineman, *Another World* (NBC)

OUTSTANDING HOST OR HOSTESS IN A TALK, SERVICE OR VARIETY SERIES: Phil Donahue, *Donahue* (SYNDICATED)

OUTSTANDING HOST OR HOSTESS IN A GAME OR AUDIENCE PARTICIPATION SHOW: Richard Dawson, *The Family Feud* (ABC)

OUTSTANDING INDIVIDUAL DIRECTOR FOR A DAYTIME DRAMA SERIES FOR A SINGLE EPISODE: Richard Dunlap, *The Young and the Restless* (program of 3 March 1978) (CBS)

OUTSTANDING INDIVIDUAL DIRECTOR FOR A VARIETY PROGRAM FOR A SINGLE EPISODE: Martin Haig Mackey, *Over Easy* (program of 20 March 1978) (PBS)

OUTSTANDING INDIVIDUAL DIRECTOR FOR A DAYTIME GAME OR AUDIENCE PARTICIPATION SHOW: Mike Gargiulo, *The $20,000 Pyramid* (program of 20 June 1977) (ABC)

OUTSTANDING WRITING FOR A DAYTIME DRAMA SERIES (SINGLE EPISODE OR ENTIRE SERIES): Claire Labine, Paul Avila Mayer, Mary Munisteri, Allan Leicht and Judith Pinsker, *Ryan's Hope* (ABC)

1978–1979

I. PRIME-TIME AWARDS (administered by the Academy of Television Arts and Sciences)

OUTSTANDING COMEDY SERIES: *Taxi* (ABC); James L. Brooks, Stan Daniels, David Davis, and Ed. Weinberger, executive producers; Glen Charles and Les Charles, producers

OUTSTANDING DRAMA SERIES: *Lou Grant* (CBS); Gene Reynolds, executive producer; Seth Freeman and Gary David Goldberg, producers

OUTSTANDING LIMITED SERIES: *Roots: The Next Generations* (ABC); David L. Wolper, executive producer; Stan Margulies, producer

OUTSTANDING COMEDY-VARIETY OR MUSIC PROGRAM (SPECIAL OR SERIES): "Steve and Eydie Celebrate Irving Berlin" (NBC); Steve Lawrence and Gary Smith, executive producers; Gary Smith and Dwight Hemion, producers; Steve Lawrence and Eydie Gormé, stars

OUTSTANDING INFORMATIONAL PROGRAM (SPECIAL OR SERIES): "Scared Straight!" (SYNDICATED); Arnold Shapiro, producer

OUTSTANDING CLASSICAL PROGRAM IN THE PERFORMING ARTS (SPECIAL OR SERIES): "Balanchine IV," *Great Performances* (PBS); Jac Venza, executive producer; Merrill Brockway, series producer; Emile Ardolino, series coordinating producer; Judy Kinberg, producer

OUTSTANDING CHILDREN'S PROGRAM (SPECIAL OR SERIES): "Christmas Eve on Sesame Street" (PBS); Jon Stone, executive producer; Dulcy Singer, producer

OUTSTANDING ANIMATED PROGRAM (SPECIAL OR SERIES): "The Lion, the Witch and the Wardrobe" (CBS); David Connell, executive producer; Steve Melendez, producer

OUTSTANDING DRAMA OR COMEDY SPECIAL: "Friendly Fire" (ABC); Martin Starger, executive producer; Philip Barry, producer; Fay Kanin, coproducer

OUTSTANDING PROGRAM ACHIEVEMENT—SPECIAL CLASS: (1) *The Tonight Show Starring Johnny Carson* (NBC); Fred DeCordova, producer; Johnny Carson, star; (2) *Lifeline* (NBC); Thomas W. Moore and Robert E. Fuisz, M.D., executive producers; Alfred Kelman, producer; Geof Bartz, coproducer

OUTSTANDING PROGRAM ACHIEVEMENT—SPECIAL EVENTS: (1) "51st Annual Awards Presentation of the Academy of Motion Picture Arts and Sciences" (ABC); Jack Haley, Jr., producer (2) "Baryshnikov at the White House" (PBS); Gerald Slater, executive producer; Hal Hutkoff, producer

OUTSTANDING LEAD ACTOR IN A DRAMA SERIES (CONTINUING OR SINGLE PERFORMANCE): Ron Leibman, *Kaz* (CBS)

OUTSTANDING LEAD ACTRESS IN A DRAMA SERIES (CONTINUING OR SINGLE PERFORMANCE): Mariette Hartley, "Married," *The Incredible Hulk* (CBS)

OUTSTANDING LEAD ACTOR IN A COMEDY SERIES (CONTINUING OR SINGLE PERFORMANCE): Carroll O'Connor, *All in the Family* (CBS)

OUTSTANDING LEAD ACTRESS IN A COMEDY SERIES (CONTINUING OR SINGLE PERFORMANCE): Ruth Gordon, "Sugar Mama," *Taxi* (ABC)

OUTSTANDING LEAD ACTOR IN A LIMITED SERIES OR A SPECIAL (CONTINUING OR SINGLE APPEARANCE): Peter Strauss, "The Jericho Mile" (ABC)

OUTSTANDING LEAD ACTRESS IN A LIMITED SERIES OR A SPECIAL (CONTINUING OR SINGLE APPEARANCE): Bette Davis, "Strangers: The Story of a Mother and Daughter" (CBS)

OUTSTANDING SUPPORTING ACTOR IN A DRAMA SERIES (CONTINUING OR SINGLE PERFORMANCE): Stuart Margolin, *The Rockford Files* (NBC)

OUTSTANDING SUPPORTING ACTRESS IN A DRAMA SERIES (CONTINUING OR SINGLE PERFORMANCE): Kristy McNichol, *Family* (ABC)

OUTSTANDING SUPPORTING ACTOR IN A COMEDY, COMEDY-VARIETY OR MUSIC SERIES (CONTINUING OR SINGLE PERFORMANCE): Robert Guillaume, *Soap* (ABC)

OUTSTANDING SUPPORTING ACTRESS IN A COMEDY, COMEDY-VARIETY OR MUSIC SERIES (CONTINUING OR SINGLE PERFORMANCE): Sally Struthers, "California Here We Are," *All in the Family* (CBS)

OUTSTANDING SUPPORTING ACTOR IN A LIMITED SERIES OR A SPECIAL (CONTINUING OR SINGLE APPEARANCE): Marlon Brando, *Roots: The Next Generations,* episode seven (ABC)

OUTSTANDING SUPPORTING ACTRESS IN A LIMITED SERIES OR A SPECIAL (CONTINUING OR SINGLE APPEARANCE): Esther Rolle, "Summer of My German Soldier" (NBC)

OUTSTANDING INDIVIDUAL ACHIEVEMENT—SPECIAL EVENTS: Mikhail Baryshnikov (as himself), "Baryshnikov at the White House" (PBS)

OUTSTANDING DIRECTING IN A DRAMA SERIES (SINGLE EPISODE): Jackie Cooper, *The White Shadow,* pilot episode (CBS)

OUTSTANDING DIRECTING IN A COMEDY OR COMEDY-VARIETY OR MUSIC SERIES (SINGLE EPISODE): Noam Pitlik, "The Harris Incident," *Barney Miller* (ABC)

OUTSTANDING DIRECTING IN A LIMITED SERIES (SINGLE EPISODE) OR A SPECIAL: David Greene, "Friendly Fire" (ABC)

OUTSTANDING INDIVIDUAL ACHIEVEMENT—INFORMATIONAL PROGRAM: John Korty, director, "Who Are the DeBolts . . . and Where Did They Get 19 Kids?" (ABC)

OUTSTANDING WRITING IN A DRAMA SERIES (SINGLE EPISODE): Michele Gallery, "Dying," *Lou Grant* (CBS)

OUTSTANDING WRITING IN A COMEDY OR COMEDY-VARIETY OR MUSIC SERIES (SINGLE EPISODE): Alan Alda, "Inga," *M*A*S*H* (CBS)

OUTSTANDING WRITING IN A LIMITED SERIES (SINGLE EPISODE) OR A SPECIAL (ORIGINAL TELEPLAY OR ADAPTATION): Patrick Nolan and Michael Mann, "The Jericho Mile" (ABC)

SECOND ANNUAL ATAS GOVERNORS' AWARD: Walter Cronkite, CBS News

SPECIAL PRESENTATION: Milton Berle, "Mr. Television"

II. DAYTIME AWARDS (administered by the National Academy of Television Arts and Sciences)

OUTSTANDING DAYTIME DRAMA SERIES: *Ryan's Hope* (ABC); Claire Labine and Paul Avila Mayer, executive producers; Ellen Barrett and Robert Costello, producers

OUTSTANDING TALK, SERVICE OR VARIETY SERIES: *Donahue* (SYNDICATED); Richard Mincer, executive producer; Patricia McMillen, producer

OUTSTANDING GAME OR AUDIENCE PARTICIPATION SHOW: *The Hollywood Squares* (NBC); Merrill Heatter and Bob Quigley, executive producers; Jay Redack, producer

OUTSTANDING CHILDREN'S ENTERTAINMENT SERIES: *Kids Are People Too* (ABC); Lawrence Einhorn, executive producer; Noreen Conlin, coproducer; Laura Shrock, producer

OUTSTANDING CHILDREN'S INFORMATIONAL SERIES: *Big Blue Marble* (SYNDICATED); Robert Wiemer, executive producer; Richard Berman, producer

OUTSTANDING CHILDREN'S INSTRUCTIONAL SERIES: *Science Rock* (ABC); Tom Yohe, executive producer; George Newall and Radford Stone, producers

OUTSTANDING CHILDREN'S ENTERTAINMENT SPECIAL: "The Tap Dance Kid" (NBC); Linda Gottlieb, executive producer; Evelyn Barron, producer

OUTSTANDING CHILDREN'S INFORMATIONAL SPECIAL: *Razzmatazz* (program of 1 February 1979) (CBS); Joel Heller, executive producer; Vern Diamond, producer

SPECIAL CLASSIFICATION OF OUTSTANDING PROGRAM ACHIEVEMENT: *Camera* (CBS); John Musilli, executive producer; Roger Englander, producer

OUTSTANDING ACHIEVEMENT IN RELIGIOUS PROGRAMMING—SPECIAL: *Marshall Efron's Illustrated, Simplified and Painless Sunday School* (CBS); Pamela Ilott, executive producer; Ted Holmes, producer

OUTSTANDING ACHIEVEMENT IN COVERAGE OF SPECIAL EVENTS—PROGRAMS: (1) "Horowitz: Live!" (NBC); Herbert Kloiber, executive producer; John Goberman, producer (2) "Leontyne Price at the White House" (PBS); Hal Hutkoff, producer

OUTSTANDING ACTOR IN A DAYTIME DRAMA SERIES: Al Freeman, Jr., *One Life to Live* (ABC)

OUTSTANDING ACTRESS IN A DAYTIME DRAMA SERIES: Irene Dailey, *Another World* (NBC)

OUTSTANDING SUPPORTING ACTOR IN A DAYTIME DRAMA SERIES: Peter Hansen, *General Hospital* (ABC)

OUTSTANDING SUPPORTING ACTRESS IN A DAYTIME DRAMA SERIES: Suzanne Rogers, *Days of Our Lives* (NBC)

OUTSTANDING HOST OR HOSTESS IN A TALK, SERVICE OR VARIETY SERIES: Phil Donahue, *Donahue* (SYNDICATED)

OUTSTANDING HOST IN A GAME OR AUDIENCE PARTICIPATION SHOW: Dick Clark, *The $20,000 Pyramid* (ABC)

OUTSTANDING INDIVIDUAL ACHIEVEMENT IN CHILDREN'S PROGRAMMING (PERFORMERS): (1) Geraldine Fitzgerald, "Rodeo Red and the Runaway," *NBC Special Treat* (NBC); (2) Jack Gilford, "Hello in There," *Big Blue Marble* (SYNDICATED); (3) Jim Henson, Frank Oz, Carroll Spinney, Jerry Nelson, and Richard Hunt, "The Muppets of Sesame Street," *Sesame Street* (PBS)

OUTSTANDING INDIVIDUAL ACHIEVEMENT IN RELIGIOUS PROGRAMMING: (1) Rolanda Mendels (performer), "Interrogation in Budapest" (NBC); (2) Martin Hoade (director), "Interrogation in Budapest" (NBC)

OUTSTANDING ACHIEVEMENT IN COVERAGE OF SPECIAL EVENTS—PERFORMERS: (1) Vladimir Horowitz, "Horowitz: Live!" (NBC); (2) Leontyne Price, "Leontyne Price at the White House" (PBS)

SPECIAL CLASSIFICATION OF OUTSTANDING INDIVIDUAL ACHIEVEMENT: (1) Paul Lynde (panelist), *The Hollywood Squares* (program of 18 May 1978) (NBC); (2) Bill Walker, Jay Burton, Tom Perew, Mark Davidson, and Fred Tatashore (writers), *Dinah!* (SYNDICATED)

OUTSTANDING DIRECTION FOR A DAYTIME DRAMA SERIES: Jerry Evans and Lela Swift, *Ryan's Hope* (ABC)

OUTSTANDING INDIVIDUAL DIRECTION FOR A VARIETY PROGRAM: Ron Wiener, "Nazis and the Klan," *Donahue* (SYNDICATED)

OUTSTANDING INDIVIDUAL DIRECTION FOR A GAME OR AUDIENCE PARTICIPATION SHOW: Jerome Shaw, *The Hollywood Squares* (program of 20 June 1978) (NBC)

OUTSTANDING INDIVIDUAL ACHIEVEMENT IN CHILDREN'S PROGRAMMING (DIRECTOR): Larry Elikann, "Mom & Dad Can't Hear Me," *ABC Afterschool Special* (ABC)

OUTSTANDING WRITING FOR A DAYTIME DRAMA SERIES: Claire Labine, Paul Avila Mayer, Mary Munisteri, Judith Pinsker, and Jeffrey Lane, *Ryan's Hope* (ABC)

I. PRIME-TIME AWARDS (administered by the Academy of Television Arts and Sciences)

OUTSTANDING COMEDY SERIES: *Taxi* (ABC); James L. Brooks, Stan Daniels, and Ed. Weinberger, executive producers; Glen Charles and Les Charles, producers

OUTSTANDING DRAMA SERIES: *Lou Grant* (CBS); Gene Reynolds, executive producer; Seth Freeman, producer

OUTSTANDING LIMITED SERIES: *Edward & Mrs. Simpson* (SYNDICATED); Andrew Brown, producer

OUTSTANDING VARIETY OR MUSIC PROGRAM: "IBM Presents Baryshnikov on Broadway" (ABC); Herman Krawitz, executive producer; Gary Smith and Dwight Hemion, producers

OUTSTANDING DRAMA OR COMEDY SPECIAL: "The Miracle Worker" (NBC); Raymond Katz and Sandy Gallin, executive producers; Fred Coe, producer

OUTSTANDING CLASSICAL PROGRAM IN THE PERFORMING ARTS: "Live from Studio 8H: A Tribute to Toscanini" (NBC); Judith de Paul and Alvin Cooperman, producers

OUTSTANDING INFORMATIONAL PROGRAM: "The Body Human: The Magic Sense" (CBS); Thomas W. Moore, executive producer; Alfred R. Kelman and Robert E. Fuisz, M.D., producers; Charles A. Bangert and Vivian R. Moss, coproducers

OUTSTANDING PROGRAM ACHIEVEMENT—SPECIAL EVENTS: "The 34th Annual Tony Awards" (CBS); Alexander H. Cohen, executive producer; Hildy Parks, producer; Roy A. Somlyo, coproducer

OUTSTANDING PROGRAM ACHIEVEMENT—SPECIAL CLASS: "Fred Astaire: Change Partners and Dance" (PBS); George Page and Jac Venza, executive producers; David Heeley, producer

OUTSTANDING ANIMATED PROGRAM: "Carlton Your Doorman" (CBS); Lorenzo Music and Barton Dean, producers

OUTSTANDING LEAD ACTOR IN A DRAMA SERIES: Ed Asner, *Lou Grant* (CBS)

OUTSTANDING LEAD ACTRESS IN A DRAMA SERIES: Barbara Bel Geddes, *Dallas* (CBS)

OUTSTANDING LEAD ACTOR IN A LIMITED SERIES OR A SPECIAL: Powers Boothe, "Guyana Tragedy: The Story of Jim Jones" (CBS)

OUTSTANDING LEAD ACTRESS IN A LIMITED SERIES OR A SPECIAL: Patty Duke Astin, "The Miracle Worker" (NBC)

OUTSTANDING LEAD ACTOR IN A COMEDY SERIES: Richard Mulligan, *Soap* (ABC)

OUTSTANDING LEAD ACTRESS IN A COMEDY SERIES: Cathryn Damon, *Soap* (ABC)

OUTSTANDING SUPPORTING ACTOR IN A DRAMA SERIES: Stuart Margolin, *The Rockford Files* (NBC)

OUTSTANDING SUPPORTING ACTRESS IN A DRAMA SERIES: Nancy Marchand, *Lou Grant* (CBS)

OUTSTANDING SUPPORTING ACTOR IN A LIMITED SERIES OR A SPECIAL: George Grizzard, "The Oldest Living Graduate" (NBC)

OUTSTANDING SUPPORTING ACTRESS IN A LIMITED SERIES OR A SPECIAL: Mare Winningham, "Amber Waves" (ABC)

OUTSTANDING SUPPORTING ACTOR IN A COMEDY OR VARIETY OR MUSIC SERIES: Harry Morgan, *M*A*S*H* (CBS)

OUTSTANDING SUPPORTING ACTRESS IN A COMEDY OR VARIETY OR MUSIC SERIES: Loretta Swit, *M*A*S*H* (CBS)

OUTSTANDING DIRECTING IN A DRAMA SERIES: Roger Young, "Cop," *Lou Grant* (CBS)

OUTSTANDING DIRECTING IN A COMEDY SERIES: James Burrows, "Louie and the Nice Girl," *Taxi* (ABC)

OUTSTANDING DIRECTING IN A LIMITED SERIES OR A SPECIAL: Marvin J. Chomsky, "Attica" (ABC)

OUTSTANDING DIRECTING IN A VARIETY OR MUSIC PROGRAM: Dwight Hemion, "IBM Presents Baryshnikov on Broadway" (ABC)

OUTSTANDING WRITING IN A DRAMA SERIES: Seth Freeman, "Cop," *Lou Grant* (CBS)

OUTSTANDING WRITING IN A COMEDY SERIES: Bob Colleary, "Barney Miller, Photographer," *Barney Miller* (ABC)

OUTSTANDING WRITING IN A LIMITED SERIES OR A SPECIAL: David Chase, "Off the Minnesota Strip" (ABC)

OUTSTANDING WRITING IN A VARIETY OR MUSIC PROGRAM: Buz Kohan, "Shirley MacLaine . . . Every Little Movement" (CBS)

THIRD ANNUAL ATAS GOVERNORS AWARD: Johnny Carson

II. DAYTIME AWARDS (administered by the National Academy of Television Arts and Sciences)

OUTSTANDING DAYTIME DRAMA SERIES: *Guiding Light* (CBS); Allen M. Potter, executive producer; Leslie Kwartin and Joe Willmore, producers

OUTSTANDING TALK, SERVICE OR VARIETY SERIES: *Donahue* (SYNDICATED); Richard Mincer, executive producer; Patricia McMillen, senior producer; Darlene Hayes and Sheri Singer, producers

OUTSTANDING GAME OR AUDIENCE PARTICIPATION SHOW: (1) *The Hollywood Squares* (NBC); Merrill Heatter and Robert Quigley, executive producers; Jay Redack, producer; (2) *The $20,000 Pyramid* (ABC); Bob Stewart, executive producer; Anne Marie Schmitt and Jane Rothchild, producers

OUTSTANDING CHILDREN'S ENTERTAINMENT SERIES: *Hot Hero Sandwich* (NBC); Bruce Hart and Carole Hart, executive producers; Howard G. Malley, producer

OUTSTANDING CHILDREN'S ENTERTAINMENT SPECIAL: "The Late Great Me: Story of a Teenage Alcoholic," *ABC Afterschool Special* (ABC); Daniel Wilson, executive producer; Linda Marmelstein, producer

OUTSTANDING CHILDREN'S ANTHOLOGY/DRAMATIC PROGRAMMING: (1) "Animal Talk," *CBS Library* (CBS); Diane Asselin, executive producer; Paul Asselin, producer; (2) "The Gold Bug," *ABC Weekend Special* (ABC); Linda Gottlieb, executive producer; Doro Bachrach, producer; (3) "Leatherstocking Tales," *Once Upon a Classic* (PBS); Jay Rayvid, executive producer; Bob Walsh, producer; (4) "Once Upon a Midnight Dreary," *CBS Library* (CBS); Diane Asselin and Paul Asselin, producers

OUTSTANDING CHILDREN'S INFORMATIONAL/INSTRUCTIONAL SERIES/SPECIALS: (1) *Sesame Street* (PBS); Al Hyslop, executive producer; Dave Freyss, producer; (2) *30 Minutes* (CBS); Joel Heller, executive producer; Allen Ducovny, Madeline Amgott, Diego Echeverria, Horace Jenkens, Elisabeth Lawrence, Patti Obrow White, Robert Rubin, Susan Mills, Catherine Olian, and Virginia Gray, producers; (3) "Why a Conductor? CBS Festival of Lively Arts for Young People" (CBS): Kirk Browning, executive producer

OUTSTANDING CHILDREN'S INFORMATIONAL/INSTRUCTIONAL PROGRAMMING—SHORT FORMAT: (1) "ABC Schoolhouse Rock" (ABC); Thomas Yohe, executive producer; George Newall and Radford Stone, producers; (2) "Ask NBC News" (NBC); Lester Crystal, senior executive producer; Beryl Pfizer, producer; (3) "H.E.L.P.!!! (Dr. Henry's Emergency Lessons for People)" (ABC); Ken Greengrass and Phil Lawrence, executive producers; Lynn Ahrens, producer; (4) "In the News" (CBS); Joel Heller, executive producer; Walter Lister, producer

OUTSTANDING ACHIEVEMENT IN RELIGIOUS PROGRAMMING—SERIES/SPECIALS: (1) *Directions* (ABC); Sid Darion, executive producer; (2) *For Our Times* (CBS); Pamela Ilott, executive producer; Joseph Clement, Chalmers Dale, Marlene DiDonato, and Ted Holmes, producers

OUTSTANDING ACHIEVEMENT IN COVERAGE OF SPECIAL EVENTS: (1) "La Gioconda" (PBS); Jeanne Mulcahy, executive producer; John Goberman, producer; (2) "Macy's 53rd Annual Thanksgiving Day Parade" (NBC); Dick Schncider, producer

SPECIAL CLASSIFICATION OF OUTSTANDING PROGRAM ACHIEVEMENT: "FYI" (ABC); Yanna Kroyt Brandt, producer

OUTSTANDING ACTOR IN A DAYTIME DRAMA SERIES: Douglass Watson, *Another World* (NBC)

OUTSTANDING ACTRESS IN A DAYTIME DRAMA SERIES: Judith Light, *One Life to Live* (ABC)

OUTSTANDING PERFORMANCE BY AN ACTOR IN A SUPPORTING ROLE FOR A DAYTIME DRAMA SERIES: Warren Burton, *All My Children* (ABC)

OUTSTANDING PERFORMANCE BY AN ACTRESS IN A SUPPORTING ROLE FOR A DAYTIME DRAMA SERIES: Francesca James, *All My Children* (ABC)

OUTSTANDING GUEST/CAMEO APPEARANCE IN A DAYTIME DRAMA SERIES: Hugh McPhillips, *Days of Our Lives* (NBC)

OUTSTANDING HOST OR HOSTESS IN A TALK, SERVICE OR VARIETY SERIES: Phil Donahue, *Donahue* (SYNDICATED)

OUTSTANDING HOST OR HOSTESS IN A GAME OR AUDIENCE PARTICIPATION SHOW: Peter Marshall, *The Hollywood Squares* (NBC)

OUTSTANDING DIRECTION FOR A DAYTIME DRAMA SERIES: Lela Swift and Jerry Evans, *Ryan's Hope* (ABC)

OUTSTANDING INDIVIDUAL DIRECTION FOR A TALK, SERVICE OR VARIETY SERIES: Duke Struck, "Henry Fonda Tribute," *Good Morning America* (ABC)

OUTSTANDING INDIVIDUAL DIRECTION FOR A GAME OR AUDIENCE PARTICIPATION SHOW: Jerome Shaw, *The Hollywood Squares* (program of 14 June 1979) (NBC)

OUTSTANDING WRITING FOR A DAYTIME DRAMA SERIES: Claire Labine, Paul Avila Mayer, Mary Munisteri, Judith Pinsker, and Jeffrey Lane, *Ryan's Hope* (ABC)

OUTSTANDING INDIVIDUAL ACHIEVEMENT IN CHILDREN'S PROGRAMMING: (1) Melissa Sue Anderson, performer, "Which Mother Is Mine?" *ABC Afterschool Special* (ABC); (2) Maia Danziger, performer, "The Late Great Me: Story of a Teenage Alcoholic," *ABC Afterschool Special* (ABC); (3) Butterfly McQueen, performer, "The Seven Wishes of a Rich Kid," *ABC Afterschool Special* (ABC); (4) Fred Rogers, performer, "Mister Rogers Goes to School," *Mister Rogers' Neighborhood* (PBS); (5) Anthony Lover, director, "The Late Great Me: Story of a Teenage Alcoholic," *ABC Afterschool Special* (ABC); (6) Arthur Allan Seidelman, director, "Which Mother Is Mine?" *ABC Afterschool Special* (ABC); (7) David Axlerod, Joseph A. Bailey, Andy Breckman, Richard Camp, Sherry Coben, Bruce Hart, Carole Hart, and Marianne Mayer, writers, *Hot Hero Sandwich* (program of 8 December 1979) (NBC); (8) Jan Hartman, writer, "The Late Great Me: Story of a Teenage Alcoholic," *ABC Afterschool Special* (ABC)

OUTSTANDING INDIVIDUAL ACHIEVEMENT IN RELIGIOUS PROGRAMMING: (1) Dean Jagger, performer, "Independence and 76," *This Is The Life* (SYNDICATED); (2) Richard F. Morean, writer, "If No Birds Sang," *This Is the Life* (SYNDICATED)

OUTSTANDING INDIVIDUAL ACHIEVEMENT IN COVERAGE OF SPECIAL EVENTS: (1) Luciano Pavarotti, performer, "La Gioconda" (PBS); (2) Renata Scotto, performer, "La Gioconda" (PBS); (3) Kirk Browning, director, "La Gioconda" (PBS)

1980–1981

I. PRIME-TIME AWARDS (administered by the Academy of Television Arts and Sciences)

OUTSTANDING COMEDY SERIES: *Taxi* (ABC); James L. Brooks, Stan Daniels, and Ed. Weinberger, executive producers; Glen Charles and Les Charles, producers

OUTSTANDING DRAMA SERIES: *Hill Street Blues* (NBC); Steven Bochco and Michael Kozoll, executive producers; Gregory Hoblit, producer

OUTSTANDING LIMITED SERIES: *Shōgun* (NBC); James Clavell, executive producer; Eric Bercovici, producer

OUTSTANDING VARIETY, MUSIC OR COMEDY PROGRAM: "Lily: Sold Out" (CBS); Lily Tomlin and Jane Wagner, executive producers; Rocco Urbisci, producer; Lily Tomlin, star

OUTSTANDING INFORMATIONAL SERIES: *Steve Allen's Meeting of Minds* (PBS); Loring d'Usseau, producer

OUTSTANDING DRAMA SPECIAL: "Playing for Time" (CBS); Linda Yellen, executive producer and producer; John E. Quill, coproducer

OUTSTANDING INFORMATIONAL SPECIAL: "The Body Human, The Bionic Breakthrough" (CBS); Thomas W. Moore, executive producer; Alfred R. Kelman and Robert E. Fuisz, M.D., producers; Charles A. Bangert and Nancy Smith, coproducers

OUTSTANDING CHILDREN'S PROGRAM: "Donahue and Kids" (NBC); Walter Bartlett, executive producer; Don Mischer, producer; Jan Cornell, coproducer

OUTSTANDING ANIMATED PROGRAM: "Life Is a Circus, Charlie Brown" (CBS); Lee Mendelson, executive producer; Bill Melendez, producer

OUTSTANDING CLASSICAL PROGRAM IN THE PERFORMING ARTS: "Live from Studio 8H: An Evening of Jerome Robbins' Ballets with Members of the New York City Ballet" (NBC); Alvin Cooperman and Judith De Paul, producers

OUTSTANDING LEAD ACTOR IN A DRAMA SERIES: Daniel J. Travanti, *Hill Street Blues* (NBC)

OUTSTANDING LEAD ACTRESS IN A DRAMA SERIES: Barbara Babcock, *Hill Street Blues* (NBC)

OUTSTANDING LEAD ACTOR IN A LIMITED SERIES OR A SPECIAL: Anthony Hopkins, "The Bunker" (CBS)

OUTSTANDING LEAD ACTRESS IN A LIMITED SERIES OR A SPECIAL: Vanessa Redgrave, "Playing for Time" (CBS)

OUTSTANDING LEAD ACTOR IN A COMEDY SERIES: Judd Hirsch, *Taxi* (ABC)

OUTSTANDING LEAD ACTRESS IN A COMEDY SERIES: Isabel Sanford, *The Jeffersons* (CBS)

OUTSTANDING SUPPORTING ACTOR IN A DRAMA SERIES: Michael Conrad, *Hill Street Blues* (NBC)

OUTSTANDING SUPPORTING ACTRESS IN A DRAMA SERIES: Nancy Marchand, *Lou Grant* (CBS)

OUTSTANDING SUPPORTING ACTOR IN A LIMITED SERIES OR A SPECIAL: David Warner, *Masada* (ABC)

OUTSTANDING SUPPORTING ACTRESS IN A LIMITED SERIES OR A SPECIAL: Jane Alexander, "Playing for Time" (CBS)

OUTSTANDING SUPPORTING ACTOR IN A COMEDY OR VARIETY OR MUSIC SERIES: Danny DeVito, *Taxi* (ABC)

OUTSTANDING SUPPORTING ACTRESS IN A COMEDY OR VARIETY OR MUSIC SERIES: Eileen Brennan, *Private Benjamin* (CBS)

OUTSTANDING INDIVIDUAL ACHIEVEMENT—SPECIAL CLASS: Sarah Vaughn, performer, "Rhapsody and Song—A Tribute to George Gershwin" (PBS)

OUTSTANDING DIRECTING IN A DRAMA SERIES: Robert Butler, "Hill Street Station," *Hill Street Blues* (NBC)

OUTSTANDING DIRECTING IN A COMEDY SERIES: James Burrows, "Elaine's Strange Triangle," *Taxi* (ABC)

OUTSTANDING DIRECTING IN A LIMITED SERIES OR A SPECIAL: James Goldstone, "Kent State" (NBC)

OUTSTANDING DIRECTING IN A VARIETY, MUSIC OR COMEDY PROGRAM: Don Mischer, "The Kennedy Center Honors: A National Celebration of the Performing Arts" (PBS)

OUTSTANDING WRITING IN A DRAMA SERIES: Michael Kozoll and Steven Bochco, "Hill Street Station," *Hill Street Blues* (NBC)

OUTSTANDING WRITING IN A COMEDY SERIES: Michael Leeson, "Tony's Sister and Jim," *Taxi* (ABC)

OUTSTANDING WRITING IN A LIMITED SERIES OR A SPECIAL: Arthur Miller, "Playing for Time" (CBS)

OUTSTANDING WRITING IN A VARIETY, MUSIC OR COMEDY PROGRAM: Jerry Juhl, David Odell, Chris Langham, Jim Henson, and Don Hinkley, *The Muppet Show* (program with Carol Burnett) (SYNDICATED)

FOURTH ANNUAL ATAS GOVERNORS AWARD: Elton H. Rule, president, American Broadcasting Company, Inc.

II. DAYTIME AWARDS (administered by the National Academy of Television Arts and Sciences)

OUTSTANDING DAYTIME DRAMA SERIES: *General Hospital* (ABC); Gloria Monty, producer

OUTSTANDING TALK/SERVICE SERIES: *Donahue* (SYNDICATED); Richard Mincer, executive producer; Patricia McMillen, senior producer; Darlene Hayes and Sheri Singer, producers

OUTSTANDING VARIETY SERIES: *The Merv Griffin Show* (SYNDICATED); Peter Barsocchini, producer

OUTSTANDING GAME OR AUDIENCE PARTICIPATION SHOW: *The $20,000 Pyramid* (ABC); Bob Stewart, executive producer; Anne Marie Schmitt and Jane Rothchild, producers

OUTSTANDING CHILDREN'S ENTERTAINMENT SERIES: (1) *Captain Kangaroo* (CBS); Robert Keeshan, executive producer; Joel Kosofsky, producer; (2) "A Tale of Two Cities," *Once Upon a Classic* (PBS); Jay Rayvid, executive producer; James A. DeVinney and Barry Letts, producers; Christine Ochtun, coproducer

OUTSTANDING CHILDREN'S ENTERTAINMENT SPECIAL: "A Matter of Time," *ABC Afterschool Special* (ABC); Martin Tahse, executive producer and producer

OUTSTANDING CHILDREN'S INFORMATIONAL/INSTRUCTIONAL SERIES: *30 Minutes* (CBS); Joel Heller, executive producer; Madeline Amgott, Allen Ducovny, Diego Echeverria, Virginia Gray, Susan Mills, Patti Obrow White, Catherine Olian, Robert Rubin, and Martin Smith, producers

OUTSTANDING CHILDREN'S INFORMATIONAL/INSTRUCTIONAL SPECIAL: "Julie Andrews' Invitation to the Dance with Rudolf Nureyev," *The CBS Festival of Lively Arts for Young People* (CBS); Jack Wohl and Bernard Rothman, producers

OUTSTANDING CHILDREN'S INFORMATIONAL/INSTRUCTIONAL PROGRAMMING—SHORT FORM: "In the News" (CBS); Joel Heller, executive producer; Walter Lister, producer

OUTSTANDING ACHIEVEMENT IN RELIGIOUS PROGRAMMING: (1) *Directions* (ABC); Sid Darion, producer; (2) *Insight* (SYNDICATED); Ellwood E. Kieser, executive producer; Mike Rhodes, producer

SPECIAL CLASSIFICATION OF OUTSTANDING PROGRAM ACHIEVEMENT: "FYI" (ABC); Yanna Kroyt Brandt, producer; Mary Ann Donahue, coordinating producer

OUTSTANDING ACTOR IN A DAYTIME DRAMA SERIES: Douglass Watson, *Another World* (NBC)

OUTSTANDING ACTRESS IN A DAYTIME DRAMA SERIES: Judith Light, *One Life to Live* (ABC)

OUTSTANDING ACTOR IN A SUPPORTING ROLE FOR A DAYTIME DRAMA SERIES: Larry Haines, *Search for Tomorrow* (CBS)

OUTSTANDING ACTRESS IN A SUPPORTING ROLE FOR A DAYTIME DRAMA SERIES: Jane Elliot, *General Hospital* (ABC)

OUTSTANDING HOST OR HOSTESS IN A TALK OR SERVICE SERIES: Hugh Downs, *Over Easy* (PBS)

OUTSTANDING HOST OR HOSTESS IN A VARIETY SERIES: David Letterman, *The David Letterman Show* (NBC)

OUTSTANDING HOST OR HOSTESS IN A GAME OR AUDIENCE PARTICIPATION SHOW: Peter Marshall, *The Hollywood Squares* (NBC)

OUTSTANDING DIRECTION FOR A DAYTIME DRAMA SERIES: Marlena Laird, Alan Pultz, and Phillip Sogard, *General Hospital* (ABC)

OUTSTANDING INDIVIDUAL DIRECTION FOR A TALK OR SERVICE SERIES: Jerry Kupcinet, *The Richard Simmons Show* (program of 13 March 1980) (SYNDICATED)

OUTSTANDING INDIVIDUAL DIRECTION FOR A VARIETY SERIES: Sterling Johnson, "Dinah & Friends in Israel" (SYNDICATED)

OUTSTANDING INDIVIDUAL DIRECTION FOR A GAME OR AUDIENCE PARTICIPATION SHOW: Mike Gargiulo, *The $20,000 Pyramid* (program of 15 May 1980) (ABC)

OUTSTANDING WRITING FOR A DAYTIME DRAMA SERIES: Douglas Marland, Robert Dwyer, Nancy Franklin, and Harding Lemay, *Guiding Light* (CBS)

OUTSTANDING INDIVIDUAL ACHIEVEMENT IN CHILDREN'S PROGRAMMING: (1) Bill Cosby, performer, "The Secret," *The New Fat Albert Show* (CBS); (2) Ken Howard, performer, "The Body Human: The Facts for Boys" (CBS); (3) Marlo Thomas, performer, "The Body Human: The Facts for Girls" (CBS); (4) Danny Aiello, performer, "Family of Strangers," *ABC Afterschool Special* (ABC); (5) John Herzfeld, director, "Stoned," *ABC Afterschool Special* (ABC); (6) Blossom Elfman, writer, "I Think I'm Having a Baby," *The CBS Afternoon Playhouse* (CBS); (7) Robert E. Fuisz, M.D., writer, "The Body Human: The Facts for Girls" (CBS); (8) Mary Munisteri, writer, "Mandy's Grandmother" (SYNDICATED)

SPECIAL CLASSIFICATION OF OUTSTANDING INDIVIDUAL ACHIEVEMENT: Merrill Markoe, Rich Hall, David Letterman, Gerard Mulligan, Paul Raley, and Ron Richards, writers, *The David Letterman Show* (NBC)

I. PRIME-TIME AWARDS (administered by the Academy of Television Arts and Sciences)

OUTSTANDING COMEDY SERIES: *Barney Miller* (ABC); Danny Arnold and Roland Kibbee, executive producers: Frank Dungan and Jeff Stein, producers; Gary Shaw, coproducer

OUTSTANDING DRAMA SERIES: *Hill Street Blues* (NBC); Steven Bochco, executive producer; Gregory Hoblit, supervising producer; David Anspaugh and Anthony Yerkovich, producers

OUTSTANDING LIMITED SERIES: *Marco Polo* (NBC); Vincenzo Labella, producer

OUTSTANDING VARIETY, MUSIC OR COMEDY PROGRAM: "Night of 100 Stars" (ABC); Alexander H. Cohen, executive producer; Hildy Parks, producer; Roy A. Somlyo, coproducer

OUTSTANDING INFORMATIONAL SERIES: *Creativity with Bill Moyers* (PBS); Merton Koplin and Charles Grinker, executive producers; Betsy McCarthy, coordinating producer

OUTSTANDING DRAMA SPECIAL: "A Woman Called Golda" (SYNDICATED); Harve Bennett, executive producer; Gene Corman, producer

OUTSTANDING INFORMATIONAL SPECIAL: "The Making of Raiders of the Lost Ark" (PBS); Sidney Ganis, executive producer; Howard Kazanjian, producer

OUTSTANDING CHILDREN'S PROGRAM: "The Wave" (ABC); Virginia L. Carter, executive producer; Fern Field, producer

OUTSTANDING ANIMATED PROGRAM: "The Grinch Grinches the Cat in the Hat" (ABC); David H. DePatie, executive producer; Ted Geisel and Friz Freleng, producers

OUTSTANDING CLASSICAL PROGRAM IN THE PERFORMING ARTS: "La Boheme," *Live from the Met* (PBS); Michael Bronson, executive producer; Clemente D'Alessio, producer

OUTSTANDING LEAD ACTOR IN A DRAMA SERIES: Daniel J. Travanti, *Hill Street Blues* (NBC)

OUTSTANDING LEAD ACTRESS IN A DRAMA SERIES: Michael Learned, *Nurse* (CBS)

OUTSTANDING LEAD ACTOR IN A LIMITED SERIES OR A SPECIAL: Mickey Rooney, "Bill" (CBS)

OUTSTANDING LEAD ACTRESS IN A LIMITED SERIES OR A SPECIAL: Ingrid Bergman, "A Woman Called Golda" (SYNDICATED)

OUTSTANDING LEAD ACTOR IN A COMEDY SERIES: Alan Alda, *M*A*S*H* (CBS)

OUTSTANDING LEAD ACTRESS IN A COMEDY SERIES: Carol Kane, "Simka Returns," *Taxi* (ABC)

OUTSTANDING SUPPORTING ACTOR IN A DRAMA SERIES: Michael Conrad, *Hill Street Blues* (NBC)

OUTSTANDING SUPPORTING ACTRESS IN A DRAMA SERIES: Nancy Marchand, *Lou Grant* (CBS)

OUTSTANDING SUPPORTING ACTOR IN A LIMITED SERIES OR A SPECIAL: Laurence Olivier, *Brideshead Revisited* (PBS)

OUTSTANDING SUPPORTING ACTRESS IN A LIMITED SERIES OR A SPECIAL: Penny Fuller, "The Elephant Man" (ABC)

OUTSTANDING SUPPORTING ACTOR IN A COMEDY OR VARIETY OR MUSIC SERIES: Christopher Lloyd, *Taxi* (ABC)

OUTSTANDING SUPPORTING ACTRESS IN A COMEDY OR VARIETY OR MUSIC SERIES: Loretta Swit, *M*A*S*H* (CBS)

OUTSTANDING INDIVIDUAL ACHIEVEMENT—SPECIAL CLASS: (1) Nell Carter (performer), "Ain't Misbehavin'" (NBC); (2) Andre De Shields (performer), "Ain't Misbehavin'" (NBC)

OUTSTANDING DIRECTING IN A DRAMA SERIES: Harry Harris, "To Soar and Never Falter," *Fame* (NBC)

OUTSTANDING DIRECTING IN A COMEDY SERIES: Alan Rafkin, "Barbara's Crisis," *One Day at a Time* (CBS)

OUTSTANDING DIRECTING IN A LIMITED SERIES OR A SPECIAL: Marvin J. Chomsky, "Inside the Third Reich" (ABC)

OUTSTANDING DIRECTING IN A VARIETY OR MUSIC PROGRAM: Dwight Hemion, "Goldie and the Kids . . . Listen to Us" (ABC)

OUTSTANDING WRITING IN A DRAMA SERIES: Steven Bochco, Anthony Yerkovich, Jeffrey Lewis, and Michael Wagner, (teleplay), Michael Kozoll and Steven Bochco (story), "Freedom's Last Stand," *Hill Street Blues* (NBC)

OUTSTANDING WRITING IN A LIMITED SERIES OR A SPECIAL: Corey Blechman (teleplay), Barry Morrow (story), "Bill" (CBS)

OUTSTANDING WRITING IN A COMEDY SERIES: Ken Estin, "Elegant Iggy," *Taxi* (ABC)

OUTSTANDING WRITING IN A VARIETY OR MUSIC PROGRAM: John Candy, Joe Flaherty, Eugene Levy, Andrea Martin, Rick Moranis, Catherine O'Hara, Dave Thomas, Dick Blasucci, Paul Flaherty, Bob Dolman, John McAndrew, Doug Steckler, Mert Rich, Jeffrey Barron, Michael Short, Chris Cluess, Stuart Kreisman, and Brian McConnachie, "Moral Majority Show," *SCTV Network* (NBC)

FIFTH ANNUAL ATAS GOVERNORS AWARD: *Hallmark Hall of Fame*

II. DAYTIME AWARDS (administered by the National Academy of Television Arts and Sciences)

OUTSTANDING DAYTIME DRAMA SERIES: *Guiding Light* (CBS); Allen Potter, executive producer; Joe Willmore and Leslie Kwartin, producers

OUTSTANDING TALK OR SERVICE SERIES: *The Richard Simmons Show* (SYNDICATED); Woody Fraser, executive producer; Nora Fraser, producer

OUTSTANDING VARIETY SERIES: *The Regis Philbin Show* (NBC); E. V. DiMassa, Jr., and Fred Tatashore, producers

OUTSTANDING GAME OR AUDIENCE PARTICIPATION SHOW: *Password Plus* (NBC); Robert Sherman, producer

OUTSTANDING CHILDREN'S ENTERTAINMENT SERIES: *Captain Kangaroo* (CBS); Robert Keeshan, executive producer; Joel Kosofsky, producer

OUTSTANDING CHILDREN'S ENTERTAINMENT SPECIAL: "Starstruck," *ABC Afterschool Special* (ABC)

OUTSTANDING CHILDREN'S INFORMATIONAL/INSTRUCTIONAL SERIES: *30 Minutes* (CBS); Joel Heller, executive producer; Madeline Amgott, John Block, Jo Ann Caplin, Vern Diamond, Nancy Duffy, Carolyn Kreskey, Irene Molnar, Susan Mills, Robert Rubin, Martin Smith, and Patti Obrow White, producers

OUTSTANDING INFORMATIONAL/INSTRUCTIONAL PROGRAMMING—SHORT FORMAT: "In the News" (CBS); Joel Heller, executive producer; Walter Lister, producer

OUTSTANDING CHILDREN'S INFORMATIONAL/INSTRUCTIONAL SPECIAL: "Kathy" (PBS); Kier Cline and Barry Teicher, producers

OUTSTANDING ACHIEVEMENT IN RELIGIOUS PROGRAMMING—SERIES: *Insight* (SYNDICATED); Ellwood Kieser, executive producer; Mike Rhodes and Terry Sweeney, producers

SPECIAL CLASSIFICATION OF OUTSTANDING PROGRAM ACHIEVEMENT: "FYI" (ABC); Yanna Kroyt Brandt, producer; Mary Ann Donahue, coproducer

OUTSTANDING LEAD ACTOR IN A DAYTIME DRAMA SERIES: Anthony Geary, *General Hospital* (ABC)

OUTSTANDING LEAD ACTRESS IN A DAYTIME DRAMA SERIES: Robin Strasser, *One Life to Live* (ABC)

OUTSTANDING SUPPORTING ACTOR IN A DAYTIME DRAMA SERIES: David Lewis, *General Hospital* (ABC)

OUTSTANDING SUPPORTING ACTRESS IN A DAYTIME DRAMA SERIES: Dorothy Lyman, *All My Children* (ABC)

OUTSTANDING HOST OR HOSTESS IN A VARIETY SERIES: Merv Griffin, *The Merv Show* (SYNDICATED)

OUTSTANDING HOST OR HOSTESS IN A TALK OR SERVICE SERIES: Phil Donahue, *Donahue* (SYNDICATED)

OUTSTANDING HOST OR HOSTESS IN A GAME OR AUDIENCE PARTICIPATION SHOW: Bob Barker, *The Price Is Right* (CBS)

OUTSTANDING PERFORMER IN CHILDREN'S PROGRAMMING: Bob Keeshan, *Captain Kangaroo* (CBS)

OUTSTANDING DIRECTION OF A DAYTIME DRAMA SERIES: Marlena Laird, Alan Pultz, and Phillip Sogard, *General Hospital* (ABC)

OUTSTANDING DIRECTION OF A VARIETY SERIES: Roy Weiner, *Donahue* (program of 21 January 1982) (SYNDICATED)

OUTSTANDING INDIVIDUAL DIRECTION FOR A VARIETY SERIES: Barry Glazer, *American Bandstand* (program of 18 April 1981) (ABC)

OUTSTANDING INDIVIDUAL DIRECTION OF A GAME SHOW: Paul Alter, *Family Feud* (program of 29 May 1981) (ABC)

OUTSTANDING INDIVIDUAL DIRECTION IN CHILDREN'S PROGRAMMING: Arthur Allan Seidelman, "She Drinks a Little," *ABC Afterschool Special* (ABC)

SPECIAL CLASSIFICATION OF OUTSTANDING INDIVIDUAL ACHIEVEMENT—DIRECTING: Alfred R. Kelman, "The Body Human, The Loving Process—Women" (CBS)

OUTSTANDING WRITING FOR A DAYTIME DRAMA SERIES: Douglas Marland, Nancy Franklin, Patrick Mulcahey, Gene Palumbo, and Frank Salisbury, *Guiding Light* (CBS)

OUTSTANDING WRITING FOR CHILDREN'S PROGRAMMING: Paul W. Cooper, "She Drinks a Little," *ABC Afterschool Special* (ABC)

SPECIAL CLASSIFICATION OF OUTSTANDING INDIVIDUAL ACHIEVEMENT—WRITING: Elaine Meryl Brown, Betty Cornfeld, Mary Ann Donahue, Joe Gustaitis, and Robin Westen, "FYI" (ABC)

1982–1983

I. PRIME-TIME AWARDS (administered by the Academy of Television Arts and Sciences)

OUTSTANDING COMEDY SERIES: *Cheers* (NBC); James Burrows, Glen Charles, and Les Charles, executive producers; Ken Levine and David Isaacs, coproducers

OUTSTANDING DRAMA SERIES: *Hill Street Blues* (NBC); Steven Bochco, executive producer; Gregory Hoblit, co-executive producer; Anthony Yerkovich, supervising producer; David Anspaugh and Scott Brazil, producers

OUTSTANDING LIMITED SERIES: *Nicholas Nickleby* (SYNDICATED); Colin Callender, producer

OUTSTANDING VARIETY, MUSIC, OR COMEDY PROGRAM: "Motown 25: Yesterday, Today, Forever" (NBC); Suzanne de Passe, executive producer; Don Mischer and Buz Kohan, producers; Suzanne Coston, producer for Motown

OUTSTANDING INFORMATIONAL SERIES: "The Barbara Walters Specials" (ABC); Beth Polson, producer; Barbara Walters, host

OUTSTANDING DRAMA SPECIAL: "Special Bulletin" (NBC); Don Ohlmeyer, executive producer; Marshall Herskovitz and Edward Zwick, producers

OUTSTANDING CHILDREN'S PROGRAM: "Big Bird in China" (NBC); Jon Stone, executive producer; David Liu, Kuo Bao-Xiang, and Xu Ja-Cha, producers

OUTSTANDING ANIMATED PROGRAM: "Ziggy's Gift" (ABC); Lena Tabori, executive producer; Richard Williams, Tom Wilson, and Lena Tabori, producers

OUTSTANDING CLASSICAL PROGRAM IN THE PERFORMING ARTS: "Pavarotti in Philadelphia: La Boheme" (PBS); Margarett Anne Everitt, executive producer; Clemente D'Alessio, producer; Luciano Pavarotti, star

OUTSTANDING LEAD ACTOR IN A DRAMA SERIES: Ed Flanders, *St. Elsewhere* (NBC)

OUTSTANDING LEAD ACTRESS IN A DRAMA SERIES: Tyne Daly, *Cagney & Lacey* (CBS)

OUTSTANDING LEAD ACTOR IN A COMEDY SERIES: Judd Hirsch, *Taxi* (NBC)

OUTSTANDING LEAD ACTRESS IN A COMEDY SERIES: Shelley Long, *Cheers* (NBC)

OUTSTANDING LEAD ACTOR IN A LIMITED SERIES OR A SPECIAL: Tommy Lee Jones, "The Executioner's Song" (NBC)

OUTSTANDING LEAD ACTRESS IN A LIMITED SERIES OR A SPECIAL: Barbara Stanwyck, *The Thorn Birds* (Part I) (ABC)

OUTSTANDING SUPPORTING ACTOR IN A DRAMA SERIES: James Coco, "Cora and Arnie," *St. Elsewhere* (NBC)

OUTSTANDING SUPPORTING ACTRESS IN A DRAMA SERIES: Doris Roberts, "Cora and Arnie," *St. Elsewhere* (NBC)

OUTSTANDING SUPPORTING ACTOR IN A COMEDY, VARIETY OR MUSIC SERIES: Christopher Lloyd, *Taxi* (NBC)

OUTSTANDING SUPPORTING ACTRESS IN A COMEDY, VARIETY OR MUSIC SERIES: Carol Kane, *Taxi* (NBC)

OUTSTANDING SUPPORTING ACTOR IN A LIMITED SERIES OR A SPECIAL: Richard Kiley, *The Thorn Birds* (Part I) (ABC)

OUTSTANDING SUPPORTING ACTRESS IN A LIMITED SERIES OR A SPECIAL: Jean Simmons, *The Thorn Birds* (ABC)

OUTSTANDING INDIVIDUAL PERFORMANCE IN A VARIETY OR MUSIC PROGRAM: Leontyne Price, "Live from Lincoln Center, Leontyne Price, Zubin Mehta and the New York Philharmonic" (PBS)

OUTSTANDING DIRECTING IN A DRAMA SERIES: Jeff Bleckner, "Life in the Minors," *Hill Street Blues* (NBC)

OUTSTANDING DIRECTING IN A COMEDY SERIES: James Burrows, "Showdown— Part 2," *Cheers* (NBC)

OUTSTANDING DIRECTING IN A LIMITED SERIES OR A SPECIAL: John Erman, "Who Will Love My Children?" (ABC)

OUTSTANDING DIRECTING IN A VARIETY OR MUSIC PROGRAM: Dwight Hemion, "Sheena Easton . . . Act One" (NBC)

OUTSTANDING WRITING IN A DRAMA SERIES: David Milch, "Trial By Fury," *Hill Street Blues* (NBC)

OUTSTANDING WRITING IN A COMEDY SERIES: Glen Charles and Les Charles, "Give Me a Ring Sometime," *Cheers* (NBC)

OUTSTANDING WRITING IN A VARIETY OR MUSIC SERIES: John Candy, Joe Flaherty, Eugene Levy, Andrea Martin, Martin Short, Dick Blasucci, Paul Flaherty, John McAndrew, Doug Steckler, Bob Dolman, Michael Short, and Mary Charlotte Wilcox, "The Energy Ball/Sweeps Week," *SCTV Network* (NBC)

OUTSTANDING INDIVIDUAL ACHIEVEMENT—INFORMATIONAL PROGRAMMING: (1) Alfred R. Kelman and Charles Bangert, directors, "The Body Human: The Living Code" (CBS); (2) Louis H. Gorfain and Robert E. Fuisz, M.D., writers, "The Body Human: The Living Code" (CBS)

SIXTH ANNUAL ATAS GOVERNORS AWARD: Sylvester L. "Pat" Weaver, Jr.

II. DAYTIME AWARDS (administered by the National Academy of Television Arts and Sciences)

OUTSTANDING DAYTIME DRAMA SERIES: *The Young and the Restless* (CBS); William J. Bell and H. Wesley Kenney, executive producers; Edward Scott, producer

OUTSTANDING TALK/SERVICE SERIES: *This Old House* (PBS); Russell Morash, producer

OUTSTANDING VARIETY SERIES: *The Merv Griffin Show* (SYNDICATED); Peter Barsocchini, producer

OUTSTANDING GAME OR AUDIENCE PARTICIPATION SHOW: *The $25,000 Pyramid* (CBS); Bob Stewart, executive producer; Anne Marie Schmitt and Sande Stewart, producers

OUTSTANDING CHILDREN'S ENTERTAINMENT SERIES: (1) *Captain Kangaroo* (CBS); Robert Keeshan and Jim Hirschfeld, executive producers; (2) *Smurfs* (NBC); William Hanna and Joseph Barbera, executive producers; Gerard Baldwin, producer

OUTSTANDING CHILDREN'S INFORMATIONAL/INSTRUCTIONAL SERIES: *Sesame Street* (PBS); Dulcy Singer, executive producer; Lisa Simon, producer

OUTSTANDING CHILDREN'S ENTERTAINMENT SPECIAL: "The Woman Who Willed a Miracle," *ABC Afterschool Special* (ABC); Dick Clark and Preston Fischer, executive producers; Joanne A. Curley and Sharon Miller, producers

OUTSTANDING CHILDREN'S INFORMATIONAL/INSTRUCTIONAL SPECIAL: "Winners" (SYNDICATED); Tom Robertson, producer

OUTSTANDING ACHIEVEMENT IN RELIGIOUS PROGRAMMING—SERIES: *Insight* (SYNDICATED); Ellwood E. Kieser, executive producer; Mike Rhodes and Terry Sweeney, producers

OUTSTANDING ACHIEVEMENT IN RELIGIOUS PROGRAMMING—SPECIALS: (1) "The Juggler of Notre Dame" (SYNDICATED); Ellwood E. Kieser, executive producer; Mike Rhodes and Terry Sweeney, producers; (2) "Land of Fear, Land of Courage" (NBC); Helen Marmor, executive producer

OUTSTANDING PROGRAM ACHIEVEMENT IN THE PERFORMING ARTS: (1) "Hansel and Gretel: Live from the Met" (PBS); Michael Bronson, executive producer; Clemente D'Alessio, producer; (2) "Zubin and the I.P.O." (NBC); Samuel Elfert, producer

OUTSTANDING ACHIEVEMENT IN THE COVERAGE OF SPECIAL EVENTS: "Macy's Thanksgiving Day Parade" (NBC); Dick Schneider, producer

OUTSTANDING INFORMATIONAL/INSTRUCTIONAL PROGRAMMING—SHORT FORM: "In the News" (CBS); Joel Heller, executive producer; Walter Lister, producer

SPECIAL CLASSIFICATION OF OUTSTANDING PROGRAM ACHIEVEMENT: *American Bandstand* (ABC); Dick Clark, executive producer; Larry Klein, producer; Barry Glazer, coproducer

OUTSTANDING ACTOR IN A DAYTIME DRAMA SERIES: Robert Woods, *One Life to Live* (ABC)

OUTSTANDING ACTRESS IN A DAYTIME DRAMA SERIES: Dorothy Lyman, *All My Children* (ABC)

OUTSTANDING ACTOR IN A SUPPORTING ROLE IN A DAYTIME DRAMA SERIES: Darnell Williams, *All My Children* (ABC)

OUTSTANDING ACTRESS IN A SUPPORTING ROLE IN A DAYTIME DRAMA SERIES: Louise Shaffer, *Ryan's Hope* (ABC)

OUTSTANDING HOST/HOSTESS IN A VARIETY SERIES: Leslie Uggams, *Fantasy* (NBC)

OUTSTANDING HOST/HOSTESS IN A TALK/SERVICE SERIES: Phil Donahue, *Donahue* (SYNDICATED)

OUTSTANDING HOST/HOSTESS IN A GAME OR AUDIENCE PARTICIPATION SHOW: Betty White, *Just Men!* (NBC)

OUTSTANDING PERFORMER IN CHILDREN'S PROGRAMMING: Cloris Leachman, "The Woman Who Willed a Miracle," *ABC Afterschool Special* (ABC)

OUTSTANDING INDIVIDUAL ACHIEVEMENT IN RELIGIOUS PROGRAMMING—PERFORMERS: (1) Lois Nettleton, "A Gun for Mandy," *Insight* (SYNDICATED); (2) Edwin Newman (moderator), "Kids, Drugs and Alcohol" (NBC)

OUTSTANDING INDIVIDUAL ACHIEVEMENT IN THE PERFORMING ARTS—PERFORMERS: Zubin Mehta (symphony conductor), "Zubin and the I.P.O." (NBC)

SPECIAL CLASSIFICATION OF OUTSTANDING INDIVIDUAL ACHIEVEMENT—PERFORMERS: Hal Linden (host), "FYI" (ABC)

OUTSTANDING DIRECTION FOR A DAYTIME DRAMA SERIES (ENTIRE SERIES): Allen Fristoe, Norman Hall, Peter Miner, and David Pressman, *One Life to Live* (ABC)

OUTSTANDING INDIVIDUAL DIRECTION FOR A VARIETY SERIES (SINGLE EPISODE): Dick Carson, *The Merv Griffin Show* (program of 17 September 1982) (SYNDICATED)

OUTSTANDING INDIVIDUAL DIRECTION FOR A TALK/SERVICE SERIES (SINGLE EPISODE): Glen Swanson, *Hour Magazine* (program of 10 November 1982) (SYNDICATED)

OUTSTANDING INDIVIDUAL DIRECTION FOR A GAME OR AUDIENCE PARTICIPATION SHOW (SINGLE EPISODE): Mark Breslow, *The Price Is Right* (program of 30 December 1982) (CBS)

OUTSTANDING INDIVIDUAL ACHIEVEMENT IN CHILDREN'S PROGRAMMING FOR DIRECTING: Sharon Miller, "The Woman Who Willed a Miracle," *ABC Afterschool Special* (ABC)

OUTSTANDING WRITING FOR A DAYTIME DRAMA SERIES: Claire Labine, Paul Avila Mayer, Mary Ryan Munisteri, Eugene Price, Judith Pinsker, Nancy Ford, B. K. Perlman, Rory Metcalf, and Trent Jones, *Ryan's Hope* (ABC)

OUTSTANDING INDIVIDUAL ACHIEVEMENT IN CHILDREN'S PROGRAMMING FOR WRITING: Arthur Heinemann, "The Woman Who Willed a Miracle," *ABC Afterschool Special* (ABC)

TRUSTEES AWARD: Robert E. Short (daytime programmer for Procter and Gamble)

I. PRIME-TIME AWARDS

OUTSTANDING COMEDY SERIES: *Cheers* (NBC); James Burrows, Glen Charles, and Les Charles, producers

OUTSTANDING DRAMA SERIES: *Hill Street Blues* (NBC); Steven Bochco, executive producer; Gregory Hoblit, co-executive producer; Scott Brazil, supervising producer; Jeffrey Lewis, Sascha Schneider, producers; David Latt, coproducer

OUTSTANDING LIMITED SERIES: "Concealed Enemies," *American Playhouse* (PBS); Lindsay Law, David Elstein, executive producers; Peter Cook, producer

OUTSTANDING VARIETY, MUSIC OR COMEDY PROGRAM: "The 6th Annual Kennedy Center Honors: A Celebration of the Performing Arts" (CBS); Nick Vanoff, George Stevens, Jr., producers

OUTSTANDING INFORMATIONAL SERIES: *A Walk Through the 20th Century with Bill Moyers* (PBS); Merton Y. Koplin, senior executive producer; Charles Grinker, Sanford H. Fisher, executive producers; Betsy McCarthy, coordinating producer; David Grubin, Ronald Blumer, producers; Bill Moyers, host

OUTSTANDING DRAMA/COMEDY SPECIAL: "Something About Amelia, An ABC Theatre Presentation" (ABC); Leonard Goldberg, executive producer; Michele Rappaport, producer

OUTSTANDING CHILDREN'S PROGRAM: "He Makes Me Feel Like Dancin' " (NBC); Edgar J. Scherick, Scott Rudin, executive producers; Emile Ardolino, producer; Judy Kinberg, co-producer

OUTSTANDING ANIMATED PROGRAM: "Garfield on the Town" (CBS); Jay Poynor, executive producer; Lee Mendelson, Bill Melendez, producers.

OUTSTANDING INFORMATIONAL SPECIAL: "America Remembers John F. Kennedy" (SYNDICATED); Thomas F. Horton, producer

OUTSTANDING CLASSICAL PROGRAM IN THE PERFORMING ARTS: "Placido Domingo Celebrates Seville," *Great Performances* (PBS); Horant H. Hohlfeld, executive producer; David Griffiths and Thomas Buerger, producers; Placido Domingo, host

OUTSTANDING LEAD ACTOR IN A DRAMA SERIES: Tom Selleck, *Magnum, P. I.* (CBS)

OUTSTANDING LEAD ACTRESS IN A DRAMA SERIES: Tyne Daly, *Cagney & Lacey* (CBS)

OUTSTANDING LEAD ACTOR IN A COMEDY SERIES: John Ritter, *Three's Company* (ABC)

OUTSTANDING LEAD ACTRESS IN A COMEDY SERIES: Jane Curtin, *Kate & Allie* (CBS)

OUTSTANDING LEAD ACTOR IN A LIMITED SERIES OR A SPECIAL: Laurence Olivier, "Laurence Olivier's King Lear" (SYNDICATED)

OUTSTANDING LEAD ACTRESS IN A LIMITED SERIES OR A SPECIAL: Jane Fonda, "The Dollmaker, An ABC Theatre Presentation" (ABC)

OUTSTANDING SUPPORTING ACTOR IN A DRAMA SERIES: Bruce Weitz, *Hill Street Blues* (NBC)

OUTSTANDING SUPPORTING ACTRESS IN A DRAMA SERIES: Alfre Woodard, "Doris in Wonderland," *St. Elsewhere* (NBC)

OUTSTANDING SUPPORTING ACTOR IN A COMEDY SERIES: Pat Harrington, Jr., *One Day at a Time* (CBS)

OUTSTANDING SUPPORTING ACTRESS IN A COMEDY SERIES: Rhea Perlman, *Cheers* (NBC)

OUTSTANDING SUPPORTING ACTOR IN A LIMITED SERIES OR A SPECIAL: Art Carney, "Terrible Joe Moran, An ITT Theatre Special" (CBS)

OUTSTANDING SUPPORTING ACTRESS IN A LIMITED SERIES OR A SPECIAL: Roxana Zal, "Something About Amelia, An ABC Theatre Presentation" (ABC)

OUTSTANDING INDIVIDUAL PERFORMANCE IN A VARIETY OR MUSIC PROGRAM: Cloris Leachman, "Screen Actors Guild 50th Anniversary Celebration" (CBS)

OUTSTANDING DIRECTING IN A DRAMA SERIES: Corey Allen, "Goodbye, Mr. Scripps," *Hill Street Blues* (NBC)

OUTSTANDING DIRECTING IN A COMEDY SERIES: Bill Persky, "A Very Loud Family," *Kate & Allie* (CBS)

OUTSTANDING DIRECTING IN A LIMITED SERIES OR A SPECIAL: Jeff Bleckner, "Concealed Enemies," *American Playhouse,* part 3: Investigation (PBS)

OUTSTANDING DIRECTING IN A VARIETY OR MUSIC PROGRAM: Dwight Hemion, "Here's Television Entertainment" (NBC)

OUTSTANDING WRITING IN A DRAMA SERIES: John Ford Noonan, teleplay; John Masius, Tom Fontana, story, "The Women," *St. Elsewhere* (NBC)

OUTSTANDING WRITING IN A COMEDY SERIES: David Angell, "Old Flames," *Cheers* (NBC)

OUTSTANDING WRITING IN A LIMITED SERIES OR A SPECIAL: William Hanley, "Something About Amelia, An ABC Theatre Presentation" (ABC)

OUTSTANDING WRITING IN A VARIETY OR MUSIC PROGRAM: Steve O'Donnell, Gerard Mulligan, Sanford Frank, Joseph E. Toplyn, Christopher Elliott, Matt Wickline, Jeff Martin, Ted Greenberg, David Yazbek, Merrill Markoe, David Letterman, *Late Night with David Letterman,* Show #312 (NBC)

OUTSTANDING INDIVIDUAL ACHIEVEMENT—ANIMATED PROGRAMMING: R. O. Blechman, director, "The Soldier's Tale" (PBS)

OUTSTANDING INDIVIDUAL ACHIEVEMENT—CLASSICAL MUSIC/DANCE PROGRAMMING: (1) James Levine, performer, "Live from the Met, Centennial Gala, Part 2" (PBS); (2) Leontyne Price, performer, "In Performance at the White House: An Evening of Spirituals and Gospel Music" (PBS); (3) Merrill Brockway, director, "A Song for Dead Warriors, San Francisco Ballet, Dance in America" (PBS)

OUTSTANDING INDIVIDUAL ACHIEVEMENT—INFORMATIONAL PROGRAMMING: (1) Emile Ardolino, director, "He Makes Me Feel Like Dancin' " (NBC); (2) Bill Moyers, writer, "Marshall, Texas. Marshall, Texas" (PBS)

SEVENTH ANNUAL ATAS GOVERNORS AWARD: Bob Hope

SPECIAL RECOGNITION: David L. Wolper

II. DAYTIME PROGRAMMING

OUTSTANDING DAYTIME DRAMA SERIES: *General Hospital* (ABC); Gloria Monty, producer

OUTSTANDING TALK/SERVICE SERIES: *Woman to Woman* (SYNDICATED); Mary Muldoon, producer

OUTSTANDING VARIETY SERIES: *The Merv Griffin Show* (SYNDICATED); Bob Murphy, executive producer; Peter Barsocchini, producer

OUTSTANDING GAME OR AUDIENCE PARTICIPATION SHOW: *The $25,000 Pyramid* (CBS); Bob Stewart, executive producer

OUTSTANDING CHILDREN'S ENTERTAINMENT SERIES: (1) *Captain Kangaroo* (CBS); Bob Keeshan, Jim Hirschfeld, executive producers; Bette Chicon, Ruth Manecke, producers; (2) *Smurfs* (NBC); William Hanna, Joseph Barbera, executive producers; Gerard Baldwin, producer

OUTSTANDING CHILDREN'S INFORMATIONAL/INSTRUCTIONAL SERIES: *ABC Weekend Specials* (ABC); Robert Chenault, executive producer

OUTSTANDING CHILDREN'S ENTERTAINMENT SPECIAL: "The Great Love Experiment," *ABC Afterschool Special;* Jane Startz, executive producer; Doro Bachrach, producer

OUTSTANDING CHILDREN'S INFORMATIONAL/INSTRUCTIONAL SPECIAL: "Dead Wrong: The John Evans Story" (CBS); S. Bryan Hickox, Jay Daniel, executive producers

OUTSTANDING ACHIEVEMENT IN RELIGIOUS PROGRAMMING—SERIES: (1) *Directions* (ABC); Sid Darion, executive producer; (2) *Insight* (SYNDICATED); Ellwood Kieser (Paulist), executive producer; Mike Rhodes, Terry Sweeney, producers

OUTSTANDING ACHIEVEMENT IN RELIGIOUS PROGRAMMING—SPECIAL: "The Last Journey" (CBS); Philip Gittleman, producer

OUTSTANDING PROGRAM ACHIEVEMENT IN THE PERFORMING ARTS: "Live from the Met: Metropolitan Opera Centennial Gala, part 1" (PBS); Michael Bronson, executive producer; Clemente D'Allessio, producer

OUTSTANDING ACHIEVEMENT IN COVERAGE OF SPECIAL EVENTS: "Macy's Thanksgiving Day Parade" (NBC); Dick Schneider, producer

SPECIAL CLASSIFICATION OF OUTSTANDING PROGRAM ACHIEVEMENT: *FYI* (ABC); Yanna Kroyt Brandt, producer; Mary Ann Donahue, coordinating producer

OUTSTANDING ACTOR IN A DAYTIME DRAMA SERIES: Larry Bryggman, *As the World Turns* (CBS)

OUTSTANDING ACTRESS IN A DAYTIME DRAMA SERIES: Erika Slezak, *One Life to Live* (ABC)

OUTSTANDING ACTOR IN A SUPPORTING ROLE IN A DAYTIME DRAMA SERIES: Justin Deas, *As the World Turns* (CBS)

OUTSTANDING ACTRESS IN A SUPPORTING ROLE IN A DAYTIME DRAMA SERIES: Judi Evans, *Guiding Light* (CBS)

OUTSTANDING HOST/HOSTESS IN A TALK/SERVICE SERIES: Gary Collins, *Hour Magazine* (SYNDICATED)

OUTSTANDING HOST/HOSTESS IN A VARIETY SERIES: Merv Griffin, *The Merv Griffin Show* (SYNDICATED)

OUTSTANDING HOST/HOSTESS IN A GAME OR AUDIENCE PARTICIPATION SHOW: Bob Barker, *The Price Is Right* (CBS)

OUTSTANDING PERFORMER IN CHILDREN'S PROGRAMMING: Dick Van Dyke, "The Wrong Way Kid" (CBS)

SPECIAL CLASSIFICATION OF OUTSTANDING INDIVIDUAL ACHIEVEMENT—PERFORMER: Carroll Spinney, *Sesame Street* (PBS)

SPECIAL CLASSIFICATION OF OUTSTANDING INDIVIDUAL ACHIEVEMENT—HOST/HOSTESS: Hal Linden, *FYI* (ABC)

OUTSTANDING INDIVIDUAL ACHIEVEMENT IN THE COVERAGE OF SPECIAL EVENTS—HOST/HOSTESS: Bryant Gumbel, "Macy's Thanksgiving Day Parade" (NBC)

OUTSTANDING INDIVIDUAL ACHIEVEMENT IN THE PERFORMING ARTS—HOST/HOSTESS: Dorothy Hamill, "Romeo and Juliet on Ice" (CBS)

OUTSTANDING DIRECTION FOR A DAYTIME DRAMA SERIES: Larry Auerbach, George Keathley, Peter Miner, David Pressman, *One Life to Live* (ABC)

OUTSTANDING INDIVIDUAL DIRECTION FOR A TALK/SERVICE SERIES: Ron Weiner, *Donahue* (SYNDICATED)

OUTSTANDING INDIVIDUAL DIRECTION FOR A GAME OR AUDIENCE PARTICIPATION SHOW: Marc Breslow, *The Price Is Right* (CBS)

OUTSTANDING INDIVIDUAL ACHIEVEMENT IN CHILDREN'S PROGRAMMING—DIRECTING: Robert Mandel, "Andrea's Story: A Hitchhiking Tragedy," *ABC Afterschool Special* (ABC)

OUTSTANDING INDIVIDUAL ACHIEVEMENT IN RELIGIOUS PROGRAMMING—DIRECTION: Jay Sandrich, "The Day Everything Went Wrong," *Insight* (SYNDICATED)

OUTSTANDING CLASSIFICATION OF OUTSTANDING INDIVIDUAL ACHIEVEMENT—DIRECTING: Mike Gargiulo, *FYI* (ABC)

OUTSTANDING INDIVIDUAL ACHIEVEMENT IN THE COVERAGE OF SPECIAL EVENTS—DIRECTORS: Dick Schneider, "Macy's Thanksgiving Day Parade" (NBC)

OUTSTANDING INDIVIDUAL ACHIEVEMENT IN THE PERFORMING ARTS—DIRECTING: Rob Iscove, "Romeo and Juliet on Ice" (CBS)

OUTSTANDING WRITING FOR A DAYTIME DRAMA SERIES: *Ryan's Hope* (ABC); Claire Labine, Paul Avila Mayer, Mary Ryan Munisteri, Judith Pinsker, Nancy Ford, B. K. Perlman

OUTSTANDING INDIVIDUAL ACHIEVEMENT IN CHILDREN'S PROGRAMMING—WRITING: *Sesame Street* (PBS); Norman Stiles, Gary Belkin, Sara Compton, Tom Dunsmuir, Judy Freudberg, Tony Geiss, Emily Perl Kingsley, David Korr, Sonia Manzano, Jeff Moss, Luis Santeiro

SPECIAL CLASSIFICATION OF OUTSTANDING INDIVIDUAL ACHIEVEMENT—WRITING: Mary Ann Donahue, Joseph Gustaitis, Linda Kline, Robin Westen, Elaine Whitley, *FYI* (ABC)

1984–1985

I. NIGHTTIME PROGRAMMING

OUTSTANDING COMEDY SERIES: *The Cosby Show* (NBC); Marcy Carsey, Tom Werner, executive producers; Earl Pomerantz, Elliot Shoenman, co-executive producers;

John Markus, supervising producer; Caryn Sneider, producer; Jerry Ross, Michael Loman, co-producers

OUTSTANDING DRAMA SERIES: *Cagney & Lacey* (CBS); Barney Rosenzweig, executive producer; Steve Brown, Terry Louise Fisher, Peter Lefcourt, producers

OUTSTANDING LIMITED SERIES: "The Jewel in the Crown," *Masterpiece Theatre* (PBS); Denis Forman, executive producer; Christopher Morahan, producer

OUTSTANDING VARIETY, MUSIC OR COMEDY PROGRAM: "Motown Returns to the Apollo" (NBC); Suzanne de Passe, executive producer; Don Mischer, producer; Suzanne Coston, Michael L. Weisbarth, co-producers

OUTSTANDING INFORMATIONAL SERIES: *The Living Planet: A Portrait of the Earth* (PBS); Richard Brock, executive producer; Adrian Warren, Ned Kelly, Andrew Neal, Richard Brock, producers

OUTSTANDING DRAMA/COMEDY SPECIAL: "Do You Remember Love" (CBS); Dave Bell, executive producer; Marilyn Hall, co-executive producer; Wayne Threm, James E. Thompson, producers; Walter Halsey Davis, co-producer

OUTSTANDING INFORMATIONAL SPECIAL: "Cousteau: Mississippi" (SYNDICATED); Jacques-Yves Cousteau, Jean-Michel Cousteau, executive producers; Andrew Solt, producer; Jacques-Yves Cousteau, host

OUTSTANDING ANIMATED PROGRAM: "Garfield in the Rough" (CBS); Jay Poynor, executive producer; Phil Roman, producer; Jim Davis, writer; Phil Roman, director

OUTSTANDING CLASSICAL PROGRAM IN THE PERFORMING ARTS: "Tosca, Live from the Met" (PBS); Michael Bronson, executive producer; Samuel J. Paul, producer

OUTSTANDING CHILDREN'S PROGRAM: "Displaced Person," *American Playhouse* (PBS); Allison Maher, Barry Solomon, Rick Traum, Patrick Lynch, executive producers; Patrick Drumgoole, supervising executive producer; Barry Levinson, producer

OUTSTANDING LEAD ACTOR IN A DRAMA SERIES: William Daniels, *St. Elsewhere* (NBC)

OUTSTANDING LEAD ACTRESS IN A DRAMA SERIES: Tyne Daly, *Cagney & Lacey* (CBS)

OUTSTANDING LEAD ACTOR IN A COMEDY SERIES: Robert Guillaume, *Benson* (ABC)

OUTSTANDING LEAD ACTRESS IN A COMEDY SERIES: Jane Curtin, *Kate & Allie* (CBS)

OUTSTANDING LEAD ACTOR IN A LIMITED SERIES OR A SPECIAL: Richard Crenna, "The Rape of Richard Beck, An ABC Theatre Presentation" (ABC)

OUTSTANDING LEAD ACTRESS IN A LIMITED SERIES OR A SPECIAL: Joanne Woodward, "Do You Remember Love" (CBS)

OUTSTANDING SUPPORTING ACTOR IN A DRAMA SERIES: Edward James Olmos, *Miami Vice* (NBC)

OUTSTANDING SUPPORTING ACTRESS IN A DRAMA SERIES: Betty Thomas, *Hill Street Blues* (NBC)

OUTSTANDING SUPPORTING ACTOR IN A COMEDY SERIES: John Larroquette, *Night Court* (NBC)

OUTSTANDING SUPPORTING ACTRESS IN A COMEDY SERIES: Rhea Perlman, *Cheers* (NBC)

OUTSTANDING SUPPORTING ACTOR IN A LIMITED SERIES OR A SPECIAL: Karl Malden, "Fatal Vision" (NBC)

OUTSTANDING SUPPORTING ACTRESS IN A LIMITED SERIES OR A SPECIAL: Kim Stanley, "Cat on a Hot Tin Roof," *American Playhouse* (PBS)

OUTSTANDING INDIVIDUAL PERFORMANCE IN A VARIETY OR MUSIC PROGRAM: George Hearn, "Sweeney Todd," *Great Performances* (PBS)

OUTSTANDING INDIVIDUAL ACHIEVEMENT—CLASSICAL MUSIC/DANCE PROGRAMMING—PERFORMING: Luciano Pavarotti, Duke of Mantua, "Rigoletto," *Great Performances* (PBS)

OUTSTANDING DIRECTING IN A DRAMA SERIES: Karen Arthur, "Heat," *Cagney & Lacey* (CBS)

OUTSTANDING DIRECTING IN A COMEDY SERIES: Jay Sandrich, "The Younger Woman," *The Cosby Show* (NBC)

OUTSTANDING DIRECTING IN A VARIETY OR MUSIC PROGRAM: Terry Hughes, "Sweeney Todd," *Great Performances* (PBS)

OUTSTANDING DIRECTING IN A LIMITED SERIES OR A SPECIAL: Lamont Johnson, "Wallenberg: A Hero's Story" (NBC)

OUTSTANDING INDIVIDUAL ACHIEVEMENT—CLASSICAL MUSIC/DANCE PROGRAMMING—DIRECTING: (1) Don Mischer, Twyla Tharp, "Dance in America: Baryshnikov by

Tharp with American Ballet Theatre" (PBS); (2) Franco Zeffirelli, "I Pagliacci," *Great Performances* (PBS)

OUTSTANDING WRITING IN A DRAMA SERIES: Patricia Green, "Who Said It's Fair," *Cagney & Lacey* (CBS)

OUTSTANDING WRITING IN A COMEDY SERIES: Ed. Weinberger, Michael Leeson, premiere episode, *The Cosby Show* (NBC)

OUTSTANDING WRITING IN A VARIETY OR MUSIC PROGRAM: Gerard Mulligan, Sandy Frank, Joe Toplyn, Chris Elliott, Matt Wickline, Jeff Martin, Eddie Gorodetsky, Randy Cohen, Larry Jacobson, Kevin Curran, Fred Graver, Merrill Markoe, David Letterman, "Christmas with the Lettermans," *Late Night with David Letterman* (NBC)

OUTSTANDING WRITING IN A LIMITED SERIES OR A SPECIAL: Vickie Patik, "Do You Remember Love" (CBS)

OUTSTANDING INDIVIDUAL ACHIEVEMENT—CLASSICAL MUSIC/DANCE PROGRAMMING— WRITING: Twyla Tharp, Peter Elbing, "Dance in America: Baryshnikov by Tharp with American Ballet Theatre" (PBS)

EIGHTH ANNUAL ATAS GOVERNORS AWARD: Alistair Cooke

SPECIAL RECOGNITION: National Endowment for the Arts

II. DAYTIME AWARDS

OUTSTANDING DAYTIME DRAMA SERIES: *The Young and the Restless* (CBS); H. Wesley Kenney, William J. Bell, executive producers; Edward Scott, producer

OUTSTANDING TALK OR SERVICE SERIES: *Donahue* (SYNDICATED); Richard Mincer and Patricia McMillen, executive producers; Darlene Hayes, senior producer; Gail Steinberg, Lorri Antosz Benson, Susan Sprecher and Marlaine Selip, producers

OUTSTANDING GAME/AUDIENCE PARTICIPATION SHOW: *The $25,000 Pyramid* (CBS); Bob Stewart, executive producer; Anne Marie Schmitt, producer

OUTSTANDING CHILDREN'S SERIES: *Sesame Street* (PBS); Dulcy Singer, executive producer; Lisa Simon, producer

OUTSTANDING ANIMATED PROGRAM: *Jim Henson's Muppet Babies* (CBS); Margaret Loesch, Lee Gunther, Jim Henson, executive producers; Bob Richardson, producer; Hank Saroyan, John Gibbs, directors; Jeffrey Scott, writer

OUTSTANDING CHILDREN'S SPECIAL: "All the Kids Do It," *CBS Schoolbreak Special* (CBS); Roger Birnbaum, Henry Winkler, executive producers; Edna Hallinan, producer

SPECIAL CLASS PROGRAMS: "To See a World," *For Our Times* (CBS); Pamela Ilott, executive producer; Chalmers Dale, producer

OUTSTANDING ACTOR IN A DAYTIME SERIES: Darnell Williams, *All My Children* (ABC)

OUTSTANDING ACTRESS IN A DAYTIME SERIES: Kim Zimmer, *Guiding Light* (CBS)

OUTSTANDING ACTOR IN A SUPPORTING ROLE IN A DAYTIME DRAMA SERIES: Larry Gates, *Guiding Light* (CBS)

OUTSTANDING ACTRESS IN A SUPPORTING ROLE IN A DAYTIME DRAMA SERIES: Beth Maitland, *The Young and the Restless* (CBS)

OUTSTANDING JUVENILE/YOUNG MAN IN A DRAMA SERIES: Brian Bloom, *As the World Turns* (CBS)

OUTSTANDING INGENUE/WOMAN IN A DRAMA SERIES: Tracey E. Bregman, *The Young and the Restless* (CBS)

OUTSTANDING HOST OR HOSTESS IN A TALK OR SERVICE SERIES: Phil Donahue, *Donahue* (SYNDICATED)

OUTSTANDING HOST IN A GAME SHOW: Dick Clark, *The $25,000 Pyramid* (CBS)

OUTSTANDING PERFORMER IN CHILDREN'S PROGRAMMING: John Carradine, "Umbrella Jack" (SYNDICATED)

OUTSTANDING DIRECTING IN A DRAMA SERIES: *Guiding Light* (CBS); John Whitesell II, Bruce Barry, Matthew Diamond, Irene M. Pace, directors; Robert D. Kochman, Joanne Rivituso, Matthew Diamond, Jo Anne Sedwick, associate directors

OUTSTANDING DIRECTING IN A TALK/SERVICE SHOW: Dick Carson, *The Merv Griffin Show* (SYNDICATED)

OUTSTANDING DIRECTING IN A GAME SHOW: Marc Breslow, *The Price Is Right* (CBS)

OUTSTANDING DIRECTING IN CHILDREN'S PROGRAMMING: Joan Darling, "Mom's on Strike," *ABC Afterschool Special* (ABC)

OUTSTANDING WRITING IN A DRAMA SERIES: *All My Children* (ABC); Agnes Nixon, Lorraine Broderick, Victor Miller, Art Wallace, Jack Wood, Mary K. Wells, Clarice Blackburn, Susan Kirshenbaum, Elizabeth Wallace, Elizabeth Page, Carlina Della Pietra, Wisner Washam

OUTSTANDING CHILDREN'S SERIES WRITING: Fred Rogers, *Mister Rogers' Neighborhood* (PBS)

OUTSTANDING WRITING IN A CHILDREN'S SPECIAL: Charles Purpura, "The Day the Senior Class Got Married," *CBS Schoolbreak Special* (CBS)

SPECIAL RECOGNITION AWARD: Larry Haines, Mary Stuart, Charita Bauer

1985–1986

I. NIGHTTIME AWARDS

OUTSTANDING COMEDY SERIES: *The Golden Girls* (NBC); Paul Junger Witt, Tony Thomas, executive producers; Paul Bogart, supervising producer; Kathy Speer, Terry Grossman, producers; Marsha Posner Williams, coproducer

OUTSTANDING DRAMA SERIES: *Cagney & Lacey* (CBS); Barney Rosenzweig, executive producer; Liz Coe, supervising producer; Ralph Singleton, Patricia Green, Steve Brown, producers; P. K. Knelman, coproducer

OUTSTANDING MINISERIES: *Peter the Great* (NBC); Lawrence Schiller, executive producer; Marvin J. Chomsky, producer; Konstantin Thoeren, line producer

OUTSTANDING VARIETY, MUSIC OR COMEDY PROGRAM: "The Kennedy Center Honors: A Celebration of the Performing Arts" (CBS); Nick Vanoff, George Stevens, Jr., producers

OUTSTANDING INFORMATIONAL SERIES: (1) "Laurence Olivier—A Life," *Great Performances* (PBS); Nick Evans, Nick Elliott, executive producers; Bob Bee, producer. (2) *Planet Earth* (PBS); Thomas Skinner, executive producer; Gregory Andorfer, series producer; Georgann Kane, coordinating producer

OUTSTANDING DRAMA/COMEDY SPECIAL: "Love Is Never Silent," *Hallmark Hall of Fame* (NBC); Marian Rees, executive producer; Julianna Field, co-executive producer; Dorothea G. Petrie, producer

OUTSTANDING CHILDREN'S PROGRAM: "Anne of Green Gables," *Wonderworks* (PBS); Kevin Sullivan, Lee Polk, executive producers; Kevin Sullivan, Ian McDougall, producers

OUTSTANDING ANIMATED PROGRAM: "Garfield's Halloween Adventure" (CBS); Jay Poynor, executive producer; Phil Roman, producer; Jim Davis, writer; Phil Roman, director

OUTSTANDING INFORMATIONAL SPECIAL: "W. C. Fields Straight Up" (PBS); Robert B. Weide, executive producer; Ronald J. Fields, co-producer

OUTSTANDING CLASSICAL PROGRAM IN THE PERFORMING ARTS: "Wolf Trap Presents the Kirov: Swan Lake" (PBS); Michael B. Styer, executive producer; Phillip Byrd, senior producer; John D. Potthast, producer

OUTSTANDING LEAD ACTOR IN A DRAMA SERIES: William Daniels, *St. Elsewhere* (NBC)

OUTSTANDING LEAD ACTRESS IN A DRAMA SERIES: Sharon Gless, *Cagney & Lacey* (CBS)

OUTSTANDING LEAD ACTOR IN A COMEDY SERIES: Michael J. Fox, *Family Ties* (NBC)

OUTSTANDING LEAD ACTRESS IN A COMEDY SERIES: Betty White, *The Golden Girls* (NBC)

OUTSTANDING LEAD ACTOR IN A MINISERIES OR A SPECIAL: Dustin Hoffman, "Death of a Salesman" (CBS)

OUTSTANDING LEAD ACTRESS IN A MINISERIES OR A SPECIAL: Marlo Thomas, "Nobody's Child" (CBS)

OUTSTANDING SUPPORTING ACTOR IN A DRAMA SERIES: John Karlen, *Cagney & Lacey* (CBS)

OUTSTANDING SUPPORTING ACTRESS IN A DRAMA SERIES: Bonnie Bartlett, *St. Elsewhere* (NBC)

OUTSTANDING SUPPORTING ACTOR IN A COMEDY SERIES: John Larroquette, *Night Court* (NBC)

OUTSTANDING SUPPORTING ACTRESS IN A COMEDY SERIES: Rhea Perlman, *Cheers* (NBC)

OUTSTANDING SUPPORTING ACTOR IN A MINISERIES OR A SPECIAL: John Malkovich, "Death of a Salesman" (CBS)

OUTSTANDING SUPPORTING ACTRESS IN A MINISERIES OR A SPECIAL: Colleen Dewhurst, "Between Two Women" (ABC)

OUTSTANDING GUEST PERFORMER IN A DRAMA SERIES: John Lithgow, *Amazing Stories* (NBC)

OUTSTANDING GUEST PERFORMER IN A COMEDY SERIES: Roscoe Lee Browne, *The Cosby Show* (NBC)

OUTSTANDING INDIVIDUAL PERFORMANCE IN A VARIETY OR MUSIC PROGRAM: Whitney Houston, "The 28th Annual Grammy Awards" (CBS)

OUTSTANDING DIRECTING IN A DRAMA SERIES: Georg Stanford Brown, "Parting Shots," *Cagney & Lacey* (CBS)

OUTSTANDING DIRECTING IN A COMEDY SERIES: Jay Sandrich, "Denise's Friend," *The Cosby Show* (NBC)

OUTSTANDING DIRECTING IN A VARIETY OR MUSIC PROGRAM: Waris Hussein, "Copacabana" (CBS)

OUTSTANDING DIRECTING IN A MINISERIES OR A SPECIAL: Joseph Sargent, "Love Is Never Silent," *Hallmark Hall of Fame* (NBC)

OUTSTANDING INDIVIDUAL ACHIEVEMENT—CLASSICAL MUSIC/DANCE PROGRAMMING: Franco Zeffirelli, director, "Cavalleria Rusticana," *Great Performances* (PBS)

OUTSTANDING WRITING IN A DRAMA SERIES: Tom Fontana, John Tinker, John Masius, "Time Heals," *St. Elsewhere* (NBC)

OUTSTANDING WRITING IN A COMEDY SERIES: Barry Fanaro, Mort Nathan, "A Little Romance," *The Golden Girls* (NBC)

OUTSTANDING WRITING IN A VARIETY OR MUSIC PROGRAM: David Letterman, Steve O'Donnell, Sandy Frank, Joe Toplyn, Chris Elliott, Matt Wickline, Jeff Martin, Gerard Mulligan, Randy Cohen, Larry Jacobson, Kevin Curran, Fred Graver, Merrill Markoe, "Fourth Anniversary Special," *Late Night with David Letterman* (NBC)

OUTSTANDING WRITING IN A MINISERIES OR A SPECIAL: Ron Cowen, Daniel Lipman, teleplay; Sherman Yellen, story, "An Early Frost" (NBC)

OUTSTANDING INDIVIDUAL ACHIEVEMENTS—INFORMATIONAL PROGRAMMING: (1) John L. Miller, writer, "The Spencer Tracy Legacy: A Tribute by Katharine Hepburn" (PBS); (2) David Heeley, director, "The Spencer Tracy Legacy: A Tribute by Katharine Hepburn" (PBS)

ATAS GOVERNORS AWARD: Red Skelton

II. DAYTIME AWARDS

OUTSTANDING DRAMA SERIES: *The Young and the Restless* (CBS); William J. Bell, H. Wesley Kenney, executive producers; Edward Scott, Tom Langan, producers

OUTSTANDING TALK/SERVICE PROGRAM: *Donahue* (SYNDICATED); Patricia McMillen, executive producer; Gail Steinberg, senior producer; Lorri Antosz Benson, Janet Harrell, Marlaine Selip, Susan Sprecher, producers

OUTSTANDING GAME/AUDIENCE PARTICIPATION SHOW: *The $25,000 Pyramid* (CBS); Bob Stewart, executive producer; Anne Marie Schmitt, producer

OUTSTANDING CHILDREN'S SERIES: *Sesame Street* (PBS); Dulcy Singer, executive producer; Lisa Simon, producer

OUTSTANDING ANIMATED PROGRAM: *Jim Henson's Muppet Babies* (CBS); Jim Henson, Margaret Loesch, Lee Gunther, executive producers; Bob Richardson, producer; John Gibbs, director; Jeffrey Scott, writer

OUTSTANDING CHILDREN'S SPECIAL: "THE WAR BETWEEN THE CLASSES," *CBS Schoolbreak Special* (CBS); Frank Doelger, Mark Gordon, executive producers; Alan C. Blomquist, producer

SPECIAL CLASS PROGRAM AREA: (1) "Chagall's Journey" (NBC); Helen Marmor, executive producer; Randolph Wands, producer. (2) "Live from Lincoln Center: Chamber Music Society of Lincoln Center with Irene Worth and Horacio Gutierrez" (PBS); John Goberman, producer

OUTSTANDING LEAD ACTOR IN A DRAMA SERIES: David Canary, *All My Children* (ABC)

OUTSTANDING LEAD ACTRESS IN A DRAMA SERIES: Erika Slezak, *One Life to Live* (ABC)

OUTSTANDING SUPPORTING ACTOR IN A DRAMA SERIES: John Wesley Shipp, *As the World Turns* (CBS)

OUTSTANDING SUPPORTING ACTRESS IN A DRAMA SERIES: Leann Hunley, *Days of Our Lives* (NBC)

OUTSTANDING YOUNGER LEADING MAN IN A DRAMA SERIES: Michael E. Knight, *All My Children* (ABC)

OUTSTANDING INGENUE IN A DRAMA SERIES: Ellen Wheeler, *Another World* (NBC)

OUTSTANDING TALK/SERVICE SHOW HOST: Phil Donahue, *Donahue* (SYNDICATED)

OUTSTANDING GAME SHOW HOST: Dick Clark, *The $25,000 Pyramid* (CBS)

OUTSTANDING PERFORMER IN CHILDREN'S PROGRAMMING: Pearl Bailey, "Cindy Eller: A Modern Fairy Tale," *ABC Afterschool Special* (ABC)

OUTSTANDING DRAMA SERIES DIRECTING TEAM: *The Young and the Restless* (CBS); Dennis Steinmetz, Rudy Vejar, Frank Pacelli, directors; Randy Robbins, Betty Rothenberg, associate directors

OUTSTANDING DIRECTING IN A TALK/SERVICE PROGRAM: Russell F. Morash, *This Old House* (PBS)

OUTSTANDING DIRECTING IN A GAME/AUDIENCE PARTICIPATION SHOW: Dick Carson, *Wheel of Fortune* (NBC)

OUTSTANDING DIRECTING IN CHILDREN'S PROGRAMMING: Martin Sheen, "Babies Having Babies," *CBS Schoolbreak Special* (CBS)

OUTSTANDING DRAMA SERIES WRITING TEAM: *Guiding Light* (CBS); Pam Long Hammer, Jeff Ryder, head writers; Addie Walsh, John Kuntz, Christopher Whitesell, breakdown writers; Megan McTavish, Stephen Demorest, Victor Gialalnella, Mary Pat Gleason, Trent Jones, Pete T. Rich, N. Gail Lawrence, Nancy Curlee, associate writers

OUTSTANDING WRITING IN A CHILDREN'S SERIES: *Sesame Street* (PBS); Norman Stiles, Sara Compton, Tom Dunsmuir, Judy Freudberg, Tony Geiss, Emily Kingsley, David Korr, Sonia Manzano, Jeff Moss, Mark Saltzman, Nancy Sans, Luis Santeiro, Cathi Rosenberg Turow

OUTSTANDING WRITING IN A CHILDREN'S SPECIAL: Kathryn Montgomery, Jeffrey Auerbach, "Babies Having Babies," *CBS Schoolbreak Special* (CBS)

SPECIAL CLASS WRITING AREA: Catherine Faulconer, "Chagall's Journey" (NBC)

1986–1987

I. NIGHTTIME PROGRAMMING

OUTSTANDING COMEDY SERIES: *The Golden Girls* (NBC); Paul Junger Witt, Tony Thomas, Susan Harris, executive producers; Kathy Speer, Terry Grossman, producers; Mort Nathan, Barry Fanaro, Winifred Hervey, Marsha Posner Williams, coproducers

OUTSTANDING DRAMA SERIES: *L. A. Law* (NBC); Steven Bochco, executive producer; Gregory Hoblit, co-executive producer; Terry Louise Fisher, supervising producer; Ellen S. Pressman, Scott Goldstein, producers; Phillip M. Goldfarb, coordinating producer

OUTSTANDING MINISERIES: "A Year in the Life" (NBC); Joshua Brand, John Falsey, executive producers; Stephen Cragg, producer

OUTSTANDING VARIETY, MUSIC OR COMEDY PROGRAM: "The 1987 Tony Awards" (CBS); Don Mischer, executive producer; David J. Goldberg, producer

OUTSTANDING INFORMATIONAL SERIES: (1) *Smithsonian World* (PBS); Adrian Malone, executive producer; David Grubin, producer. (2) "Unknown Chaplin," *American Masters* (PBS); Kevin Brownlow, David Gill, producers

OUTSTANDING DRAMA/COMEDY SPECIAL: "Promise," *Hallmark Hall of Fame* (CBS);

Peter K. Duchow, James Garner, executive producers; Glenn Jordan, producer; Richard Friedenberg, co-producer

OUTSTANDING INFORMATIONAL SPECIAL: "Dance in America: Agnes, the Indomitable DeMille," *Great Performances* (PBS); Jac Venza, executive producer; Judy Kinberg, producer

OUTSTANDING CHILDREN'S PROGRAM: "Jim Henson's the Story Teller: Hans My Hedgehog" (NBC); Jim Henson, executive producer; Mark Shivas, producer

OUTSTANDING ANIMATED PROGRAM: "Cathy" (CBS); Lee Mendelson, executive producer; Bill Melendez, producer; Cathy Guisewite, writer; Evert Brown, director

OUTSTANDING CLASSICAL PROGRAM IN THE PERFORMING ARTS: "Vladimir Horowitz: The Last Romantic" (PBS); Peter Gelb, executive producer; Susan Froemke, producer; Vladimir Horowitz, star

OUTSTANDING LEAD ACTOR IN A DRAMA SERIES: Bruce Willis, *Moonlighting* (ABC)

OUTSTANDING LEAD ACTRESS IN A DRAMA SERIES: Sharon Gless, *Cagney & Lacey* (CBS)

OUTSTANDING LEAD ACTOR IN A COMEDY SERIES: Michael J. Fox, *Family Ties* (NBC)

OUTSTANDING LEAD ACTRESS IN A COMEDY SERIES: Rue McClanahan, *The Golden Girls* (NBC)

OUTSTANDING LEAD ACTOR IN A MINISERIES OR A SPECIAL: James Woods, "Promise," *Hallmark Hall of Fame* (CBS)

OUTSTANDING LEAD ACTRESS IN A MINISERIES OR A SPECIAL: Gena Rowlands, "The Betty Ford Story" (ABC)

OUTSTANDING SUPPORTING ACTOR IN A DRAMA SERIES: John Hillerman, *Magnum, P. I.* (CBS)

OUTSTANDING SUPPORTING ACTRESS IN A DRAMA SERIES: Bonnie Bartlett, *St. Elsewhere* (NBC)

OUTSTANDING SUPPORTING ACTOR IN A COMEDY SERIES: John Larroquette, *Night Court* (NBC)

OUTSTANDING SUPPORTING ACTRESS IN A COMEDY SERIES: Jackee Harry, *227* (NBC)

OUTSTANDING SUPPORTING ACTOR IN A MINISERIES OR A SPECIAL: Dabney Coleman, "Sworn to Silence" (ABC)

OUTSTANDING SUPPORTING ACTRESS IN A MINISERIES OR A SPECIAL: Piper Laurie, "Promise," *Hallmark Hall of Fame* (CBS)

OUTSTANDING INDIVIDUAL PERFORMANCE IN A VARIETY OR MUSIC PROGRAM: Robin Williams, "A Carol Burnett Special: Carol, Carl, Whoopi & Robin" (ABC)

OUTSTANDING GUEST PERFORMER IN A DRAMA SERIES: Alfre Woodard, *L. A. Law,* pilot (NBC)

OUTSTANDING GUEST PERFORMER IN A COMEDY SERIES: John Cleese, "Simon Says," *Cheers* (NBC)

OUTSTANDING INDIVIDUAL ACHIEVEMENT—CLASSICAL MUSIC/DANCE PROGRAMMING—PERFORMING: (1) Leonard Bernstein, "Carnegie Hall: The Grand Reopening" (CBS); (2) Isaac Stern, "Carnegie Hall: The Grand Reopening" (CBS)

OUTSTANDING DIRECTING IN A DRAMA SERIES: Gregory Hoblit, *L. A. Law,* pilot (NBC)

OUTSTANDING DIRECTING IN A COMEDY SERIES: Terry Hughes, "Isn't It Romantic," *The Golden Girls* (NBC)

OUTSTANDING DIRECTING IN A MINISERIES OR A SPECIAL: Glenn Jordan, "Promise," *Hallmark Hall of Fame* (CBS)

OUTSTANDING DIRECTING IN A VARIETY OR MUSIC PROGRAM: Don Mischer, "The Kennedy Center Honors: A Celebration of the Performing Arts" (CBS)

OUTSTANDING INDIVIDUAL ACHIEVEMENT—CLASSICAL MUSIC/DANCE PROGRAMMING—DIRECTING: (1) Kirk Browning, "Goya with Placido Domingo," *Great Performances* (PBS); (2) Albert Maysles, David Maysles, "Vladimir Horowitz: The Last Romantic" (PBS)

OUTSTANDING WRITING IN A DRAMA SERIES: Steven Bochco, Terry Louise Fisher, "Venus Butterfly," *L. A. Law* (NBC)

OUTSTANDING WRITING IN A COMEDY SERIES: Gary David Goldberg, Alan Uger, " 'A,' My Name Is Alex," *Family Ties* (NBC)

OUTSTANDING WRITING IN A MINISERIES OR A SPECIAL: Richard Friedenberg, teleplay; Kenneth Blackwell, Tennyson Flowers, Richard Friedenberg, story, "Promise," *Hallmark Hall of Fame* (CBS)

OUTSTANDING WRITING IN A VARIETY OR MUSIC PROGRAM: Steve O'Donnell, Sandy Frank, Joe Toplyn, Chris Elliott, Matt Wickline, Jeff Martin, Gerard Mulligan, Randy Cohen, Larry Jacobson, Kevin Curran, Fred Graver, Adam Resnick, David Letterman, "Fifth Anniversary Special," *Late Night with David Letterman* (NBC)

OUTSTANDING INDIVIDUAL ACHIEVEMENT—INFORMATIONAL PROGRAMMING—WRITING: Robert McCrum, Robert MacNeil, "A Muse of Fire," *The Story of English* (PBS)

TENTH ANNUAL ATAS GOVERNORS AWARD: Grant Tinker

II. DAYTIME AWARDS

OUTSTANDING DRAMA SERIES: *As the World Turns* (CBS); Robert Calhoun, executive producer; Ken Fitts, supervising producer; Michael Laibson, Christine S. Banas, Bonnie Bogard, Lisa Wilson, producers

OUTSTANDING TALK/SERVICE SHOW: *The Oprah Winfrey Show* (SYNDICATED); Debra DiMaio, executive producer; Mary Kay Clinton, Christine Tardio, Dianne Hudson, Ellen Rakieten, producers

OUTSTANDING GAME/AUDIENCE PARTICIPATION SHOW: *The $25,000 Pyramid* (CBS); Bob Stewart, executive producer; Anne Marie Schmitt, supervising producer; David Michaels, Francine Bergman, producers

OUTSTANDING CHILDREN'S SERIES: *Sesame Street* (PBS); Dulcy Singer, executive producer; Lisa Simon, producer

OUTSTANDING ANIMATED PROGRAM: *Jim Henson's Muppet Babies* (CBS); Margaret Loesch, Jim Henson, Lee Gunther, executive producers; Bob Richardson, producer; Bob Shellhorn, supervising director; Jeffrey Scott, writer

OUTSTANDING CHILDREN'S SPECIAL: "Wanted: The Perfect Guy," *ABC Afterschool Special* (ABC); Milton Justice, executive producer; Joseph Feury, producer

OUTSTANDING SPECIAL CLASS PROGRAM AREA: (1) "The Children of Ellis Island," *ABC Notebook* (ABC); Jane Paley, executive producer. (2) "One to Grow On" (NBC); Charles Stepner, producer. (3) "Taking Children Seriously" (NBC); Helen Marmor, executive producer; Patricia Mauger, producer

OUTSTANDING LEAD ACTOR IN A DRAMA SERIES: Larry Bryggman, *As the World Turns* (CBS)

OUTSTANDING LEAD ACTRESS IN A DRAMA SERIES: Kim Zimmer, *Guiding Light* (CBS)

OUTSTANDING SUPPORTING ACTOR IN A DRAMA SERIES: Gregg Mars, *As the World Turns* (CBS)

OUTSTANDING SUPPORTING ACTRESS IN A DRAMA SERIES: Kathleen Noone, *All My Children* (ABC)

OUTSTANDING YOUNGER LEADING MAN IN A DRAMA SERIES: Michael E. Knight, *All My Children* (ABC)

OUTSTANDING INGENUE IN A DRAMA SERIES: Martha Byrne, *As the World Turns* (CBS)

OUTSTANDING GUEST PERFORMER IN A DRAMA SERIES: John Wesley Shipp, *Santa Barbara* (NBC)

OUTSTANDING TALK/SERVICE SHOW HOST: Oprah Winfrey, *The Oprah Winfrey Show* (SYNDICATED)

OUTSTANDING GAME SHOW HOST: Bob Barker, *The Price Is Right* (CBS)

OUTSTANDING PERFORMER IN CHILDREN'S PROGRAMMING: Madeline Kahn, "Wanted: The Perfect Guy," *ABC Afterschool Special* (ABC)

OUTSTANDING DRAMA SERIES DIRECTING TEAM: *The Young and the Restless* (CBS); Frank Pacelli, Rudy Vejar, directors; Betty Rothenberg, Randy Robbins, associate directors

OUTSTANDING DIRECTING IN A TALK/SERVICE SHOW: Jim McPharlin, *The Oprah Winfrey Show* (SYNDICATED)

OUTSTANDING DIRECTING IN A GAME/AUDIENCE PARTICIPATION SHOW: Marc Breslow, *The Price Is Right* (CBS)

OUTSTANDING DIRECTING IN CHILDREN'S PROGRAMMING: Dan F. Smith, *Square One TV* (PBS)

OUTSTANDING ACHIEVEMENT IN DIRECTING—SPECIAL CLASS: Dick Schneider, "Macy's 60th Annual Thanksgiving Day Parade" (NBC)

OUTSTANDING DRAMA SERIES WRITING TEAM: *One Life to Live* (ABC); Peggy O'Shea, head writer; S. Michael Schnessel, Craig Carlson, Lanie Bertram, Ethel M. Brea, Mel Brea, associate head writers; Lloyd Gold, writer

OUTSTANDING WRITING IN A CHILDREN'S SERIES: *Sesame Street* (PBS); Norman Stiles, Cathi Rosenberg-Turow, Jeffrey Moss, Sonia Manzano, Mark Saltzman, Belinda Ward, David Korr, Sara Compton, Tom Dunsmuir, Tony Geiss, Emily Perl Kingsley, Judy Freudberg, Jon Stone, Nancy Sans, Luis Santeiro

OUTSTANDING WRITING IN A CHILDREN'S SPECIAL: Melvin Van Peebles, "The Day They Came to Arrest the Book," *CBS Schoolbreak Special* (CBS)

1987–1988

I. NIGHTTIME PROGRAMMING

OUTSTANDING COMEDY SERIES: *The Wonder Years* (ABC); Carol Black, Neal Marlens, executive producers; Jeff Silver, producer

OUTSTANDING DRAMA SERIES: *thirtysomething* (ABC); Edward Zwick, Marshall Herskovitz, executive producers; Paul Haggis, supervising producer; Edward Zwick, Scott Winant, producers

OUTSTANDING MINISERIES: "The Murder of Mary Phagan" (NBC); George Stevens, Jr., producer

OUTSTANDING VARIETY, MUSIC OR COMEDY PROGRAM: "Irving Berlin's 100th Birthday Celebration" (CBS); Don Mischer, executive producer; Jan Cornell, David J. Goldberg, producers; Sara Lukinson, co-producer

OUTSTANDING INFORMATIONAL SERIES: "Buster Keaton: A Hard Act to Follow," *American Masters* (PBS); Kevin Brownlow, David Gill, producers

OUTSTANDING DRAMA/COMEDY SPECIAL: "Inherit the Wind," *A T & T Presents* (NBC); Peter Douglas, executive producer; Robert A. Papazian, producer

OUTSTANDING INFORMATIONAL SPECIAL: "Dear America: Letters Home from Vietnam" (HBO); Bill Couturie, Thomas Bird, producers

OUTSTANDING CHILDREN'S PROGRAM: "The Secret Garden," *Hallmark Hall of Fame* (CBS); Norman Rosemont, executive producer; Steve Lanning, producer

OUTSTANDING ANIMATED PROGRAM: "A Claymation Christmas Celebration" (CBS); Will Vinton, executive producer; David Altschul, producer; Will Vinton, director; Ralph Liddle, writer

OUTSTANDING CLASSICAL PROGRAM IN THE PERFORMING ARTS: "Nixon in China," *Great Performances* (PBS); Jac Venza, executive producer; David Horn, series producer; Michael Bronson, producer; John Walker, coordinating producer

OUTSTANDING LEAD ACTOR IN A DRAMA SERIES: Richard Kiley, *A Year in the Life* (NBC)

OUTSTANDING LEAD ACTRESS IN A DRAMA SERIES: Tyne Daly, *Cagney & Lacey* (CBS)

OUTSTANDING LEAD ACTOR IN A COMEDY SERIES: Michael J. Fox, *Family Ties* (NBC)

OUTSTANDING LEAD ACTRESS IN A COMEDY SERIES: Beatrice Arthur, *The Golden Girls* (NBC)

OUTSTANDING LEAD ACTOR IN A MINISERIES OR A SPECIAL: Jason Robards, "Inherit the Wind," *A T & T Presents* (NBC)

OUTSTANDING LEAD ACTRESS IN A MINISERIES OR A SPECIAL: Jessica Tandy, "Foxfire," *Hallmark Hall of Fame* (CBS)

OUTSTANDING SUPPORTING ACTOR IN A DRAMA SERIES: Larry Drake, *L. A. Law* (NBC)

OUTSTANDING SUPPORTING ACTRESS IN A DRAMA SERIES: Patricia Wettig, *thirtysomething* (ABC)

OUTSTANDING SUPPORTING ACTOR IN A COMEDY SERIES: John Larroquette, *Night Court* (NBC)

OUTSTANDING SUPPORTING ACTRESS IN A COMEDY SERIES: Estelle Getty, *The Golden Girls* (NBC)

OUTSTANDING SUPPORTING ACTOR IN A MINISERIES OR A SPECIAL: John Shea, "Baby M" (ABC)

OUTSTANDING SUPPORTING ACTRESS IN A MINISERIES OR A SPECIAL: Jane Seymour, "Onassis: The Richest Man in the World" (ABC)

OUTSTANDING INDIVIDUAL PERFORMANCE IN A VARIETY OR MUSIC PROGRAM: Robin Williams, "ABC Presents a Royal Gala" (ABC)

OUTSTANDING GUEST PERFORMER IN A DRAMA SERIES: Shirley Knight, "The Parents Are Coming," *thirtysomething* (ABC)

OUTSTANDING GUEST PERFORMER IN A COMEDY SERIES: Beah Richards, "The Bridge," *Frank's Place* (CBS)

OUTSTANDING DIRECTING IN A DRAMA SEIRES: Mark Tinker, "Weigh In, Weigh Out," *St. Elsewhere* (NBC)

OUTSTANDING DIRECTING IN A COMEDY SERIES: Gregory Hoblit, *Hooperman,* pilot (ABC)

OUTSTANDING DIRECTING IN A MINISERIES OR A SPECIAL: Lamont Johnson, "Gore Vidal's Lincoln" (NBC)

OUTSTANDING DIRECTING IN A VARIETY OR MUSIC SPECIAL: Patricia Birch, Humphrey Burton, "Celebrating Gershwin," *Great Performances* (PBS)

OUTSTANDING WRITING IN A DRAMA SERIES: Paul Haggis, Marshall Herskovitz, "Business As Usual," *thirtysomething* (ABC)

OUTSTANDING WRITING IN A COMEDY SERIES: Hugh Wilson, "The Bridge," *Frank's Place* (CBS)

OUTSTANDING WRITING IN A MINISERIES OR A SPECIAL: William Hanley, "The Attic: The Hiding of Anne Frank" (CBS)

OUTSTANDING WRITING IN A VARIETY OR MUSIC PROGRAM: Jackie Mason, "Jackie Mason on Broadway" (HBO)

II. DAYTIME AWARDS

OUTSTANDING DRAMA SERIES: *Santa Barbara* (NBC); Jill Farren Phelps, Bridget Dobson, executive producers; Steven Kent, supervising producer; Leonard Friedlander, Julie Hanan, producers

OUTSTANDING TALK/SERVICE SHOW: *The Oprah Winfrey Show* (SYNDICATED); Debra DiMaio, executive producer; Mary Kay Clinton, Dianne Atkinson Hudson, Ellen Sue Rakieten, Christine Tardio, producers

OUTSTANDING GAME/AUDIENCE PARTICIPATION SHOW: *The Price Is Right* (CBS); Frank Wayne, executive producer; Phillip Wayne, Roger Dobkowitz, producers

OUTSTANDING CHILDREN'S SERIES: *Sesame Street* (PBS); Dulcy Singer, executive producer; Lisa Simon, supervising producer; Arlene Sherman, coordinating producer

OUTSTANDING ANIMATED PROGRAM: *Jim Henson's Muppet Babies* (CBS); Margaret Ann Loesch, Lee Gunther, Jim Henson, executive producers; Bob Richardson, supervising producer; John Ahern, Bob Shellhorn, producers

OUTSTANDING CHILDREN'S SPECIAL: "Never Say Goodbye," *CBS Schoolbreak Special* (CBS); Michael D. Little, executive producer; Susan Rohrer, producer; Craig S. Cummings, co-producer

OUTSTANDING SPECIAL CLASS PROGRAM AREA: *American Bandstand* (SYNDICATED); Dick Clark, executive producer; Larry Klein, supervising producer; Barry Glazer, producer

OUTSTANDING LEAD ACTOR IN A DRAMA SERIES: David Canary, *All My Children* (ABC)

OUTSTANDING LEAD ACTRESS IN A DRAMA SERIES: Helen Gallagher, *Ryan's Hope* (ABC)

OUTSTANDING SUPPORTING ACTOR IN A DRAMA SERIES: Justin Deas, *Santa Barbara* (NBC)

OUTSTANDING SUPPORTING ACTRESS IN A DRAMA SERIES: Ellen Wheeler, *All My Children* (ABC)

OUTSTANDING YOUNGER LEADING MAN IN A DRAMA SERIES: Billy Warlock, *Days of Our Lives* (NBC)

OUTSTANDING INGENUE IN A DRAMA SERIES: Julianne Moore, *As the World Turns* (CBS)

OUTSTANDING TALK/SERVICE SHOW HOST: Phil Donahue, *Donahue* (SYNDICATED)

OUTSTANDING GAME SHOW HOST: Bob Barker, *The Price Is Right* (CBS)

OUTSTANDING DRAMA SERIES DIRECTING TEAM: *The Young and the Restless* (CBS); Rudolph L. Vejar, Frank Pacelli, Heather Hill, directors; Randy Robbins, Betty Rothenberg, associate directors

OUTSTANDING DIRECTING IN A TALK/SERVICE SHOW: Russell Morash, *This Old House* (PBS)

OUTSTANDING DIRECTING IN A GAME/AUDIENCE PARTICIPATION SHOW: Bruce Burmester, *The $25,000 Pyramid* (CBS)

OUTSTANDING DIRECTING IN CHILDREN'S PROGRAMMING: Jeff Brown, "What If I'm Gay?" *CBS Schoolbreak Special* (CBS)

OUTSTANDING DIRECTING IN SPECIAL CLASS: Dick Schneider, "Macy's 61st Annual Thanksgiving Day Parade" (NBC)

OUTSTANDING DRAMA SERIES WRITING TEAM: *All My Children* (ABC); Agnes Nixon, Clarice Blackburn, Lorraine Broderick, Susan Kirshenbaum, Kathleen Klein, Karen L. Lewis, Victor Miller, Megan McTavish, Elizabeth Page, Peggy Sloane, Gillian Spencer, Elizabeth Wallace, Wisner Washam, Mary K. Wells, Jack Wood

OUTSTANDING WRITING IN A CHILDREN'S SERIES: *Sesame Street* (PBS); Norman Stiles, head writer; Christian Clark, Sara Compton, Judy Freudberg, Tony Geiss, Emily Kingsley, David Korr, Sonia Manzano, Jeff Moss, Cathi Rosenberg-Turow, Mark Saltzman, Nancy Sans, Luis Santeiro, Jocelyn Stevenson, Jon Stone, Belinda Ward, John Weidman, writers

OUTSTANDING WRITING IN A CHILDREN'S SPECIAL: Victoria Hochberg, "Just a Regular Kid: An AIDS Story," *ABC Afterschool Special* (ABC)

OUTSTANDING ACHIEVEMENT IN WRITING—SPECIAL CLASS: David Forman, Barry Adelman, "The 4th Annual Soap Opera Awards" (NBC)

1988–1989

I. NIGHTTIME AWARDS

OUTSTANDING COMEDY SERIES: *Cheers* (NBC); James Burrows, Glen Charles, Les Charles, executive producers; Cheri Eichen, Bill Steinkellner, Peter Casey, David Lee, producers; Tim Berry, Phoef Sutton, co-producers

OUTSTANDING DRAMA SERIES: *L. A. Law* (NBC); Steven Bochco, executive producer; Rick Wallace, co-executive producer; David E. Kelley, supervising producer; Scott Goldstein, Michele Gallery, producers; William M. Finkelstein, Judith Parker, co-producers; Phillip M. Goldfarb, Alice West, coordinating producers

OUTSTANDING MINISERIES: *War and Remembrance* (ABC); Dan Curtis, executive producer; Barbara Steele, producer

OUTSTANDING VARIETY, MUSIC OR COMEDY PROGRAM: *The Tracey Ullman Show* (FOX); James L. Brooks, Jerry Belson, Heide Perlman, Ken Estin, Sam Simon, executive producers; Richard Sakai, Ted Bessell, producers; Marc Flanagan, co-producer; Tracey Ullman, host

OUTSTANDING DRAMA/COMEDY SPECIAL: (1) "Day One," *A T & T Presents* (CBS); Aaron Spelling, E. Duke Vincent, executive producers; David W. Rintels, producer. (2) "Roe vs. Wade" (NBC); Michael Manheim, executive producer; Gregory Hoblit, producer; Alison Cross, co-producer

OUTSTANDING INFORMATIONAL SERIES: *Nature* (PBS); David Heeley, executive producer; Fred Kaufman, series producer

OUTSTANDING INFORMATIONAL SPECIAL: "Lillian Gish: The Actor's Life for Me," *American Masters* (PBS); Freida Lee Mock, executive producer; Terry Sanders, producer; William T. Cartwright, co-producer; Susan Lacy, executive producer

OUTSTANDING CHILDREN'S PROGRAM: "Free to Be . . . a Family" (ABC); Marlo Thomas, Christopher Cerf, executive producers (U.S.A.); Robert Dalrymple, producer (U.S.A.); Leonid Zolotarevsky, executive producer (U.S.S.R.); Igor Menzelintsev, producer (U.S.S.R.); Vern T. Calhoun, coproducer

OUTSTANDING ANIMATED PROGRAM: "Garfield: Babes and Bullets" (CBS); Phil Roman, producer; Jim Davis, writer; Phil Roman, director; John Sparey, Bob Nesler, co-directors

OUTSTANDING SPECIAL EVENTS: (1) "Cirque du Soleil The Magic Circus" (HBO); Helene Dufresne, producer. (2) "The 11th Annual Kennedy Center Honors: A Celebration of the Performing Arts" (CBS); George Stevens, Jr., Nick Vanoff, producers. (3) "The 42nd Annual Tony Awards" (CBS); Don Mischer, executive producer; David J. Goldberg, producer; Jeffrey Lane, co-producer. (4) "The 17th Annual American

Film Institute Film Achievement Award: A Salute to Gregory Peck" (NBC); George Stevens, Jr., producer; Jeffrey Lane, co-producer.

OUTSTANDING CLASSICAL PROGRAM IN THE PERFORMING ARTS: "Bernstein at 70!" *Great Performances* (PBS); Harry Kraut, Klaus Hallig, executive producers; Michael Bronson, Thomas P. Skinner, producers

OUTSTANDING LEAD ACTOR IN A DRAMA SERIES: Carroll O'Connor, *In the Heat of the Night* (NBC)

OUTSTANDING LEAD ACTRESS IN A DRAMA SERIES: Dana Delany, *China Beach* (ABC)

OUTSTANDING LEAD ACTOR IN A COMEDY SERIES: Richard Mulligan, *Empty Nest* (NBC)

OUTSTANDING LEAD ACTRESS IN A COMEDY SERIES: Candice Bergen, *Murphy Brown* (CBS)

OUTSTANDING LEAD ACTOR IN A MINISERIES OR A SPECIAL: James Woods, "My Name Is Bill W.," *Hallmark Hall of Fame* (ABC)

OUTSTANDING LEAD ACTRESS IN A MINISERIES OR A SPECIAL: Holly Hunter, "Roe vs. Wade" (NBC)

OUTSTANDING SUPPORTING ACTOR IN A DRAMA SERIES: Larry Drake, *L. A. Law* (NBC)

OUTSTANDING SUPPORTING ACTRESS IN A DRAMA SERIES: Melanie Mayron, *thirtysomething* (ABC)

OUTSTANDING SUPPORTING ACTOR IN A COMEDY SERIES: Woody Harrelson, *Cheers* (NBC)

OUTSTANDING SUPPORTING ACTRESS IN A COMEDY SERIES: Rhea Perlman, *Cheers* (NBC)

OUTSTANDING SUPPORTING ACTOR IN A MINISERIES OR A SPECIAL: Derek Jacobi, "The Tenth Man," *Hallmark Hall of Fame* (CBS)

OUTSTANDING SUPPORTING ACTRESS IN A MINISERIES OR A SPECIAL: Colleen Dewhurst, "Those She Left Behind" (NBC)

OUTSTANDING GUEST ACTOR IN A DRAMA SERIES: Joe Spano, "The Execution of John Saringo," *Midnight Caller* (NBC)

OUTSTANDING GUEST ACTRESS IN A DRAMA SERIES: Kay Lenz, "After It Happened . . . " *Midnight Caller* (NBC)

OUTSTANDING GUEST ACTOR IN A COMEDY SERIES: Cleavon Little, "Stand By Your Man," *Dear John* (NBC)

OUTSTANDING GUEST ACTRESS IN A COMEDY SERIES: Colleen Dewhurst, "Mama Said," *Murphy Brown* (CBS)

OUTSTANDING INDIVIDUAL PERFORMANCE IN A VARIETY OR MUSIC PROGRAM: Linda Ronstadt, "Canciones de mi Padre," *Great Performances* (PBS)

OUTSTANDING PERFORMANCE IN INFORMATIONAL PROGRAMMING: Hal Holbrook, "Portrait of America: Alaska" (TBS)

OUTSTANDING PERFORMANCE IN SPECIAL EVENTS: Billy Crystal, "The 31st Annual Grammy Awards" (CBS)

OUTSTANDING INDIVIDUAL PERFORMANCE IN CLASSICAL MUSIC/DANCE PROGRAMMING: Mikhail Baryshnikov, "Dance in America: Baryshnikov Dances Balanchine," *Great Performances* (PBS)

OUTSTANDING DIRECTING IN A DRAMA SERIES: Robert Altman, "The Boiler Room," *Tanner '88* (HBO)

OUTSTANDING DIRECTING IN A COMEDY SERIES: Peter Baldwin, "Our Miss White," *The Wonder Years* (ABC)

OUTSTANDING DIRECTING IN A MINISERIES OR A SPECIAL: Simon Wincer, *Lonesome Dove* (CBS)

OUTSTANDING DIRECTING IN A VARIETY OR MUSIC PROGRAM: Jim Henson, "Dog City," *The Jim Henson Hour* (NBC)

OUTSTANDING DIRECTING FOR SPECIAL EVENTS: Dwight Hemion, "The 11th Annual Kennedy Center Honors: A Celebration of the Performing Arts" (CBS)

OUTSTANDING WRITING IN A DRAMA SERIES: Joseph Dougherty, "First Day/Last Day," *thirtysomething* (ABC)

OUTSTANDING WRITING IN A COMEDY SERIES: Diane English, "Respect" (pilot), *Murphy Brown* (CBS)

OUTSTANDING WRITING IN A MINISERIES OR A SPECIAL: Abby Mann, Robin Vote, Ron Hutchinson, "Murderers Among Us: The Simon Wiesenthal Story" (HBO)

OUTSTANDING WRITING IN A VARIETY OR MUSIC PROGRAM: *Saturday Night Live* (NBC); James Downey, head writer; John Bowman, A. Whitney Brown, Gregory Daniels,

Tom Davis, Al Franken, Shannon Gaughan, Jack Handey, Phil Hartman, Lorne Michaels, Mike Myers, Conan O'Brien, Bob Odenkirk, Herb Sargent, Tom Schiller, Robert Smigel, Bonnie Turner, Terry Turner, Christine Zander, writers; George Meyer, additional sketches

OUTSTANDING WRITING IN INFORMATIONAL PROGRAMMING: John Heminway, "Search for Mind," *The Mind* (PBS)

OUTSTANDING WRITING FOR SPECIAL EVENTS: Jeffrey Lane, "The 42nd Annual Tony Awards" (CBS)

GOVERNORS AWARD: Lucille Ball

II. DAYTIME PROGRAMMING

OUTSTANDING DRAMA SERIES: *Santa Barbara* (NBC); Jill Farren Phelps, executive producer; Steven Kent, senior supervising producer; Charlotte Savitz, supervising producer; Julie Hanan Carruthers, Leonard Friedlander, producers

OUTSTANDING TALK/SERVICE PROGRAM: *The Oprah Winfrey Show* (SYNDICATED); Debra DiMaio, executive producer; Oprah Winfrey, supervising producer; Ellen Rakieten, Dianne Hudson, Mary Kay Clinton, Angela Thame, Alice McGee, producers

OUTSTANDING GAME/AUDIENCE PARTICIPATION HOW: *The $25,000 Pyramid* (CBS); Bob Stewart, executive producer; Anne Marie Schmitt, supervising producer; Francine Bergman, David Michaels, producers

OUTSTANDING CHILDREN'S SERIES: *Newton's Apple* (PBS); James Steinbach, executive producer; Lee Carey, Tacy Mangan, supervising producers; Lynne Reeck, producer

OUTSTANDING ANIMATED PROGRAM: *The New Adventures of Winnie the Pooh* (ABC); Karl Geurs, producer/director; Mark Zaslove, story editor/writer; Bruce Talkington, Carter Crocker, writers

OUTSTANDING CHILDREN'S SPECIAL: "Taking a Stand," *ABC Afterschool Special* (ABC); Frank Doelger, executive producer; Roberta Rowe, producer

SPECIAL CLASS PROGRAM AREA: (1) "China: Walls and Bridges" (ABC); Jimmy R. Allen, Richard T. McCartney, executive producers; Robert Thornton, supervising producer and producer. (2) "James Stewart's Wonderful Life" (CINEMAX); Mary Frances Shea, executive producer; Phil Delbourgo, supervising producer; Dan Gurskis, producer

OUTSTANDING LEAD ACTOR IN A DRAMA SERIES: David Canary, *All My Children* (ABC)

OUTSTANDING LEAD ACTRESS IN A DRAMA SERIES: Marcy Walker, *Santa Barbara* (NBC)

OUTSTANDING SUPPORTING ACTOR IN A DRAMA SERIES: (1) Debbi Morgan, *All My Children* (ABC); (2) Nancy Lee Grahn, *Santa Barbara* (NBC)

OUTSTANDING JUVENILE MALE IN A DRAMA SERIES: Justin Gocke, *Santa Barbara* (NBC)

OUTSTANDING JUVENILE FEMALE IN A DRAMA SERIES: Kimberly McCullough, *General Hospital* (ABC)

OUTSTANDING TALK/SERVICE SHOW HOST: Sally Jessy Raphael, *Sally Jessy Raphael* (SYNDICATED)

OUTSTANDING GAME SHOW HOST: Alex Trebek, *Jeopardy!* (SYNDICATED)

OUTSTANDING PERFORMER IN A CHILDREN'S SERIES: Jim Varney, *Hey Vern, It's Ernest!* (CBS)

OUTSTANDING DRAMA SERIES DIRECTING TEAM: *The Young and the Restless* (CBS); Frank Pacelli, Heather Hill, Randy Robbins, Rudy Vejar, directors; Betty Rothenberg, Kathryn Foster, associate directors

OUTSTANDING DIRECTING IN A TALK/SERVICE SHOW: Jim McPharlin, *The Oprah Winfrey Show* (SYNDICATED)

OUTSTANDING DIRECTING IN A GAME/AUDIENCE PARTICIPATION SHOW: Dick Schneider, *Jeopardy!* (SYNDICATED)

OUTSTANDING DIRECTING IN A CHILDREN'S SERIES: (1) Matthew Diamond, *Shining Time Station* (PBS); (2) Ozzie Alfonso, *3-2-1 Contact* (PBS)

OUTSTANDING DRAMA SERIES WRITING TEAM: *Santa Barbara* (NBC); Charles Pratt, Jr., Anne Howard Bailey, head writers; Robert Guza, Jr., Courtney Simon, Lynda Myles, Patrick Mulcahey, Gary Tomlin, script writers; Josh Griffith, Jane Atkins, breakdown/script writer; Don Harary, breakdown writer

OUTSTANDING WRITING IN A CHILDREN'S SERIES: *Sesame Street* (PBS); Norman Stiles, head writer; Nancy Sans, Luis Santeiro, Cathi Rosenberg-Turow, Belinda Ward, Sonia Manzano, Jeff Moss, Sara Compton, Judy Freudberg, David Korr, John Weidman, Tony Geiss, Emily Perl Kingsley, Mark Saltzman, Christian Clark, Jon Stone, writers

1989–1990

I. PRIME TIME AWARDS

OUTSTANDING COMEDY SERIES: *Murphy Brown* (CBS); Diane English, Joel Shukovsky, executive producers; Korby Siamis, consulting producer; Tom Seeley, Norm Gunzenhauser, Russ Woody, Gary Dontzig, Steven Peterman, Barnet Kellman, producers; Deborah Smith, coproducer

OUTSTANDING DRAMA SERIES: *L. A. Law* (NBC); David E. Kelley, executive producer; Rick Wallace, co-executive producer; William M. Finkelstein, supervising producer; Elodie Keene, Michael M. Robin, producers; Alice West, coordinating producer; Robert M. Breech, coproducer

OUTSTANDING MINISERIES: "Drug Wars: The Camarena Story" (NBC); Michael Mann, executive producer; Richard Brams, co-executive producer; Christopher Canaan, Rose Schacht, Ann Powell, supervising producers; Branko Lustig, producer; Mark Allan, co-producer

OUTSTANDING VARIETY, MUSIC OR COMEDY SERIES: *In Living Color* (FOX); Keenen Ivory Wayans, executive producer; Kevin S. Bright, supervising producer; Tamara Rawitt, producer; Michael Petok, coproducer

OUTSTANDING INFORMATIONAL SERIES: *Smithsonian World* (PBS); Adrian Malone, executive producer; Sandra W. Bradley, producer

OUTSTANDING INFORMATIONAL SPECIAL: (1) "Dance in America: Bob Fosse Steam Heat," *Great Performances* (PBS); Jac Venza, executive producer; Judy Kinberg, producer; (2) "Broadway's Dreamers: The Legacy of the Group Theater," *American Masters* (PBS); Jac Venza, Susan Lacy, executive producers; Joan Kramer, David Heeley, producers; Joanne Woodward, host/producer

OUTSTANDING DRAMA/COMEDY SPECIAL: (1) "Caroline?" *Hallmark Hall of Fame* (CBS); Dan Enright, Les Alexander, executive producers; Barbara Hiser, Joseph Broido, coexecutive producers; Dorothea G. Petrie, producer; (2) "The Incident," *AT & T Presents* (CBS); Robert Halmi, executive producer; Bill Brademan, Ed Self, producers

OUTSTANDING VARIETY, MUSIC OR COMEDY SPECIAL: "Sammy Davis Jr.'s 60th Anniversary Celebration" (ABC); George Schlatter, producer; Buz Kohan, Jeff Margolis, Gary Necessary, coproducers

OUTSTANDING CLASSICAL PROGRAM IN THE PERFORMING ARTS: "Aida," *The Metropolitan Opera Presents* (PBS); Peter Gelb, executive producer

OUTSTANDING CHILDREN'S PROGRAM: "A Mother's Courage: The Mary Thomas Story," *The Magical World of Disney* (NBC); Ted Field, Robert W. Cort, executive producers; Patricia Clifford, Kate Wright, co-executive producers; Richard L. O'Connor, producer; Chet Walker, co-producer

OUTSTANDING ANIMATED PROGRAM: *The Simpsons* (FOX); James L. Brooks, Matt Groening, Sam Simon, executive producers; Richard Sakai, producer; Al Jean, Mike Reiss, Larina Jean Adamson, co-producers; Magot Pipkin, animation producer; Gabor Csupo, supervising animation director; David Silverman, director; John Swartzwelder, writer

OUTSTANDING ACTOR IN A DRAMA SERIES: Peter Falk, *Columbo* (ABC)

OUTSTANDING ACTRESS IN A DRAMA SERIES: Patricia Wettig, *thirtysomething* (ABC)

OUTSTANDING ACTOR IN A COMEDY SERIES: Ted Danson, *Cheers* (NBC)

OUTSTANDING ACTRESS IN A COMEDY SERIES: Candice Bergen, *Murphy Brown* (CBS)

OUTSTANDING ACTOR IN A MINISERIES OR A SPECIAL: Hume Cronyn, "Age-Old Friends" (HBO)

OUTSTANDING ACTRESS IN A MINISERIES OR A SPECIAL: Barbara Hershey, "A Killing in a Small Town" (CBS)

OUTSTANDING SUPPORTING ACTOR IN A DRAMA SERIES: Jimmy Smits, *L. A. Law* (NBC)

OUTSTANDING SUPPORTING ACTRESS IN A DRAMA SERIES: Marg Helgenberger, *China Beach* (ABC)

OUTSTANDING SUPPORTING ACTOR IN A COMEDY SERIES: Alex Rocco, *The Famous Teddy Z* (CBS)

OUTSTANDING SUPPORTING ACTRESS IN A COMEDY SERIES: Bebe Neuwirth, *Cheers* (NBC)

OUTSTANDING SUPPORTING ACTOR IN A MINISERIES OR A SPECIAL: Vincent Gardenia, "Age-Old Friends" (HBO)

OUTSTANDING SUPPORTING ACTRESS IN A MINISERIES OR A SPECIAL: Eva Marie Saint, "People Like Us" (NBC)

OUTSTANDING GUEST ACTOR IN A DRAMA SERIES: Patrick McGoohan, "Agenda for Murder," *Columbo* (ABC)

OUTSTANDING GUEST ACTRESS IN A DRAMA SERIES: Viveca Lindfors, "Save the Last Dance for Me," *Life Goes On* (ABC)

OUTSTANDING GUEST ACTOR IN A COMEDY SERIES: Darren McGavin, "Brown Like Me," *Murphy Brown* (CBS)

OUTSTANDING GUEST ACTRESS IN A COMEDY SERIES: Swoosie Kurtz, "Reunion," *Carol & Company* (NBC)

OUTSTANDING INDIVIDUAL PERFORMANCE IN A VARIETY OR MUSIC PROGRAM: Tracey Ullman, "The Best of the Tracey Ullman Show" (FOX)

OUTSTANDING INDIVIDUAL ACHIEVEMENT IN A CLASSICAL MUSIC/DANCE PROGRAM: (1) Katarina Witt, performer, "Carmen on Ice" (HBO); (2) Brian Orser, performer, "Carmen on Ice" (HBO); (3) Brian Boitano, performer, "Carmen on Ice" (HBO); (4) Peter Rosen, director; Alan Skog, director of concert performances, "The Eighth Van Cliburn International Piano Competition: How to Make Music" (PBS)

OUTSTANDING INDIVIDUAL ACHIEVEMENT—INFORMATIONAL PROGRAMMING: (1) George Burns, "A Conversation With . . . " (DISNEY); (2) Gene Lasko, director, "W. Eugene Smith—Photography Made Difficult," *American Masters* (PBS)

OUTSTANDING DIRECTING IN A DRAMA SERIES: (1) Thomas Carter, "Promises to Keep," *Equal Justice* (ABC); (2) Scott Winant, "The Go-Between," *thirtysomething* (ABC)

OUTSTANDING DIRECTING IN A COMEDY SERIES: Michael Dinner, "Goodbye," *The Wonder Years* (ABC)

OUTSTANDING DIRECTING IN A MINISERIES OR A SPECIAL: Joseph Sargent, "Caroline?" *Hallmark Hall of Fame* (CBS)

OUTSTANDING DIRECTING IN A VARIETY OR MUSIC PROGRAM: Dwight Hemion, "The Kennedy Center Honors: A Celebration of the Performing Arts" (CBS)

OUTSTANDING WRITING IN A DRAMA SERIES: David E. Kelley, "Blood, Sweat & Fears," *L. A. Law* (NBC)

OUTSTANDING WRITING IN A COMEDY SERIES: Bob Brush, "Goodbye," *The Wonder Years* (ABC)

OUTSTANDING WRITING IN A MINISERIES OR A SPECIAL: Terrence McNally, "Andre's Mother," *American Playhouse* (PBS)

OUTSTANDING WRITING IN A VARIETY OR MUSIC PROGRAM: (1) Billy Crystal, "Midnight Train to Moscow" (HBO); (2) James L. Brooks, Heide Perlman, Sam Simon, Jerry Belson, Marc Flanagan, Dinah Kirgo, Jay Kogen, Wallace Wolodarsky, Ian Praiser, Marilyn Suzanne Miller, Tracey Ullman, *The Tracey Ullman Show* (FOX)

GOVERNOR'S AWARD: Leonard Goldenson

II. DAYTIME AWARDS

OUTSTANDING DRAMA SERIES: *Santa Barbara* (NBC); John Conboy, senior executive producer; Jill Farren Phelps, executive producer; Steve Kent, senior supervising producer; Charlotte Savitz, supervising producer; Julie Hanan Carruthers, producer

OUTSTANDING TALK/SERVICE SHOW: *Sally Jessy Raphael* (SYNDICATED); Burt

Dubrow, executive producer; Kari Sagin, senior producer; Linda Finnell, Alex Williamson, Donna Benner Ingber, Mary Duffy, producers

OUTSTANDING GAME/AUDIENCE PARTICIPATION SHOW: *Jeopardy!* (SYNDICATED); Merv Griffin, executive producer; George Vosburgh, producer

OUTSTANDING ANIMATED PROGRAM: (1) *Beetlejuice* (ABC); David Geffen, Tim Burton, executive producers; Leonora Hume, supervising producer; Stephen Hodgins, coordinating producer; Michael Hirsh, Patrick Loubert, Clive A. Smith, producers; Robin Budd, director; Patsy Cameron, Tedd Anasti, story editors; (2) *The New Adventures of Winnie the Pooh* (ABC); Ken Kessel, Karl Geurs, producer/directors; Ed Ghertner, producer; Terence Harrison, director; Bruce Talkington, Mark Zaslove, story editor; Carter Crocker, Steven Sustarsic, writers

OUTSTANDING CHILDREN'S SERIES: *Reading Rainbow* (PBS); Twila Liggett, Tony Buttino, executive producers; Cecily Truett, supervising producer/producer; Larry Lancit, supervising producer; Orly Berger, Jill Gluckson, Ronnie Krauss, producers

OUTSTANDING CHILDREN'S SPECIAL: "A Matter of Conscience," *CBS Schoolbreak Special* (CBS); Eve Silverman, executive producer; Susan Aronson, producer

OUTSTANDING LEAD ACTOR IN A DRAMA SERIES: A Martinez, *Santa Barbara* (NBC)

OUTSTANDING LEAD ACTRESS IN A DAYTIME DRAMA: Kim Zimmer, *Guiding Light* (CBS)

OUTSTANDING SUPPORTING ACTOR IN A DRAMA SERIES: Henry Darrow, *Santa Barbara* (NBC)

OUTSTANDING SUPPORTING ACTRESS IN A DRAMA SERIES: Julia Barr, *All My Children* (ABC)

OUTSTANDING JUVENILE MALE IN A DRAMA SERIES: Andrew Kavovit, *As the World Turns,* (CBS)

OUTSTANDING JUVENILE ACTRESS IN A DRAMA SERIES: Cady McClain, *All My Children* (ABC)

OUTSTANDING TALK/SERVICE SHOW HOST: Joan Rivers, *The Joan Rivers Show* (SYNDICATED)

OUTSTANDING GAME SHOW HOST: (1) Alex Trebek, *Jeopardy!* (SYNDICATED); (2) Bob Barker, *The Price Is Right* (CBS)

OUTSTANDING PERFORMER IN A CHILDREN'S SERIES: Kevin Clash, *Sesame Street* (PBS)

OUTSTANDING PERFORMER IN A CHILDREN'S SPECIAL: Gregg Spottiswood, "Looking for Miracles" (DISNEY)

OUTSTANDING DRAMA SERIES DIRECTING TEAM: *Santa Barbara* (NBC); Michael Gliona, Rick Bennewitz, Robert Schiller, directors; Pamela Fryman, Jeanine Guarneri-Frons, associate directors

OUTSTANDING DIRECTING IN A TALK/SERVICE SHOW: Russell Morash, *This Old House* (PBS)

OUTSTANDING DIRECTING IN A GAME/AUDIENCE PARTICIPATION SHOW: Joseph Behar, *Fun House* (SYNDICATED)

OUTSTANDING DIRECTING IN A CHILDREN'S SHOW: Mike Gargiulo, series director, Charles Dubin, series director ("Mathnet"), *Square One TV* (PBS)

OUTSTANDING ACHIEVEMENT IN DIRECTING—SPECIAL CLASS: Victoria Hochberg, "Sweet 15," *Wonderworks* (PBS)

OUTSTANDING DRAMA SERIES WRITING TEAM: *Guiding Light* (CBS); Pamela K. Long, head writer; Nancy Curlee, Trent Jones, associate head writers; Jeff Ryder, story consultant; Stephen Demorest, script editor; Garrett Foster, Peter Brash, Nancy Williams, breakdown writers; Patty Gideon Sloan, Richard Culliton, breakdown/script writers; N. Gail Lawrence, Pete T. Rich, Melissa Salmons, script writers

OUTSTANDING ACHIEVEMENT IN WRITING IN A CHILDREN'S SERIES: *Sesame Street* (PBS); Norman Stiles, series head writer; Judy Freudberg, Cathi Rosenberg-Turow, Nancy Sans, Tony Geiss, Luis Santeiro, Jeff Moss, Sara Compton, Belinda Ward, John Weidman, Josh Selig, Emily Perl Kingsley, David Korr, Sonia Manzano, Mark Saltzman, Jon Stone, series writers

OUTSTANDING ACHIEVEMENT IN WRITING IN A CHILDREN'S SPECIAL: Paul Cooper, "A Matter of Conscience," *CBS Schoolbreak Special* (CBS)

OUTSTANDING ACHIEVEMENT IN WRITING—SPECIAL CLASS: Glenn Kirschbaum, Robert Kirk, "Remembering World War II—Hitler: Man & Myth" (SYNDICATED)

I. PRIME TIME AWARDS

OUTSTANDING COMEDY SERIES: *Cheers* (NBC); Glen Charles, Les Charles, Cheri Eichen, Bill Steinkellner, Phoef Sutton, executive producers; Tim Berry, producer; Andy Ackerman, Brian Pollack, Mert Rich, Dan O'Shannon, Tom Anderson, Larry Balmagia, coproducers

OUTSTANDING DRAMA SERIES: *L. A. Law* (NBC); David E. Kelley, Rick Wallace, executive producers; Patricia Green, supervising producer; Elodie Keene, James C. Hart, Alan Brennert, Robert Breech, John Hill, producers; Alice West, coordinating producer

OUTSTANDING DRAMA/COMEDY SPECIAL OR MINISERIES: "Separate But Equal" (ABC); George Stevens, Jr., Stan Margulies, executive producers

OUTSTANDING VARIETY, MUSIC, OR COMEDY PROGRAM: "The 63rd Annual Academy Awards" (ABC); Gilbert Cates, producer

OUTSTANDING INFORMATIONAL SERIES: *The Civil War* (PBS); Ken Burns, Ric Burns, producers; Stephen Ives, Julie Dunfey, Mike Hill, coproducers; Catherine Eisele, coordinating producer

OUTSTANDING INFORMATIONAL SPECIAL: "Edward R. Murrow: This Reporter," *American Masters* (PBS); Susan Lacy, executive producer; Susan Steinberg, producer; Elizabeth Kreutz, Harlene Freezer, coproducers

OUTSTANDING CHILDREN'S PROGRAM: "You Can't Go Home Again: A 3–2–1 Contact Extra" (PBS); Anne MacLeod, executive producer; Tom Cammisa, producer

OUTSTANDING ANIMATED PROGRAM: *The Simpsons* (FOX); James L. Brooks, Matt Groening, Sam Simon, executive producers; Al Jean, Mike Reiss, supervising producers; Jay Kogen, Wallace Wolodarsky, Richard Sakai, Larina Jean Adamson, producers; George Meyer, coproducer; Gabor Csupo, executive animated producer; Sherry Gunther, animation producer; Steve Pepoon, writer; Rich Moore, director

OUTSTANDING CLASSICAL PROGRAM IN THE PERFORMING ARTS: "Tchaikovsky's 150th Birthday Gala from Leningrad" (PBS); Peter Gelb, executive producer; Helmut Rost, producer; Anne Cauvin, Laura Mitgang, coordinating producers

OUTSTANDING LEAD ACTOR IN A DRAMA SERIES: James Earl Jones, *Gabriel's Fire* (ABC)

OUTSTANDING LEAD ACTRESS IN A DRAMA SERIES: Patricia Wettig, *thirtysomething* (ABC)

OUTSTANDING LEAD ACTOR IN A COMEDY SERIES: Burt Reynolds, *Evening Shade* (CBS)

OUTSTANDING LEAD ACTRESS IN A COMEDY SERIES: Kirstie Alley, *Cheers* (NBC)

OUTSTANDING LEAD ACTOR IN A MINISERIES OR SPECIAL: John Gielgud, "Summer's Lease," *Masterpiece Theatre* (PBS)

OUTSTANDING LEAD ACTRESS IN A MINISERIES OR SPECIAL: Lynn Whitfield, "The Josephine Baker Story" (HBO)

OUTSTANDING SUPPORTING ACTOR IN A DRAMA SERIES: Timothy Busfield, *thirtysomething* (ABC)

OUTSTANDING SUPPORTING ACTRESS IN A DRAMA SERIES: Madge Sinclair, *Gabriel's Fire* (ABC)

OUTSTANDING SUPPORTING ACTOR IN A COMEDY SERIES: Jonathan Winters, *Davis Rules* (ABC)

OUTSTANDING SUPPORTING ACTRESS IN A COMEDY SERIES: Bebe Neuwirth, *Cheers* (NBC)

OUTSTANDING SUPPORTING ACTOR IN A MINISERIES OR SPECIAL: James Earl Jones, "Heat Wave" (TNT)

OUTSTANDING SUPPORTING ACTRESS IN A MINISERIES OR SPECIAL: Ruby Dee, "Decoration Day," *Hallmark Hall of Fame* (NBC)

OUTSTANDING GUEST ACTOR IN A DRAMA SERIES: David Opatoshu, "A Prayer for the Goldsteins," *Gabriel's Fire* (ABC)

OUTSTANDING GUEST ACTRESS IN A DRAMA SERIES: Peggy McCay, "State of Mind," *The Trials of Rosie O'Neill* (CBS)

OUTSTANDING GUEST ACTOR IN A COMEDY SERIES: Jay Thomas, "Gold Rush," *Murphy Brown* (CBS)

OUTSTANDING GUEST ACTRESS IN A COMEDY SERIES: Colleen Dewhurst, "Bob and Murphy and Ted and Avery," *Murphy Brown* (CBS)

OUTSTANDING INDIVIDUAL PERFORMANCE IN A VARIETY OR MUSIC PROGRAM: Billy Crystal, host, "The 63rd Annual Academy Awards" (ABC)

OUTSTANDING INDIVIDUAL ACHIEVEMENT—CLASSICAL MUSIC/DANCE PROGRAMMING: (1) Kurt Moll, performer, "The Ring of Nibelung," *The Metropolitan Opera Presents* (PBS); (2) Yo-Yo Ma, performer, "Tchaikovsky's 150th Birthday Gala from Leningrad" (PBS)

OUTSTANDING DIRECTING IN A DRAMA SERIES: Thomas Carter, "In Confidence," *Equal Justice* (ABC)

OUTSTANDING DIRECTING IN A COMEDY SERIES: James Burrows, "Woody Interruptus," *Cheers* (NBC)

OUTSTANDING DIRECTING IN A MINISERIES OR SPECIAL: Brian Gibson, "The Josephine Baker Story" (HBO)

OUTSTANDING DIRECTING IN A VARIETY OR MUSIC PROGRAM: Hal Gurnee, *Late Night with David Letterman* (show #1425) (NBC)

OUTSTANDING WRITING IN A DRAMA SERIES: David E. Kelley, "On the Toad Again," *L. A. Law* (NBC)

OUTSTANDING WRITING IN A COMEDY SERIES: Gary Dontzig, Steven Peterman, "Jingle Hell, Jingle Hell, Jingle All the Way," *Murphy Brown* (CBS)

OUTSTANDING WRITING IN A MINISERIES OR SPECIAL: Andrew Davies, "House of Cards," *Masterpiece Theatre* (PBS)

OUTSTANDING WRITING IN A VARIETY OR MUSIC PROGRAM: Hal Kanter, Buz Kohan, writers, Billy Crystal, David Steinberg, Bruce Vilanch, Robert Wuhl, special material, "The 63rd Annual Academy Awards" (ABC)

OUTSTANDING INDIVIDUAL ACHIEVEMENT—INFORMATIONAL PROGRAMMING: (1) Geoffrey C. Ward, Ric Burns, Ken Burns, writers, *The Civil War* (PBS); (2) Todd McCarthy, writer, "Preston Sturges: The Rise and Fall of an American Dreamer," *American Masters* (PBS); (3) Peter Gelb, Susan Froemke, Albert Maysles, Bob Eisenhardt, directors, "Soldiers of Music: Rostropovich Returns to Russia" (PBS)

GOVERNORS AWARD: (1) Mobil Oil; (2) *Masterpiece Theatre* (PBS)

II. DAYTIME AWARDS

OUTSTANDING DRAMA SERIES: *As the World Turns* (CBS); Laurence Caso, executive producer; Kenneth L. Fitts, supervising producer; Christine S. Banas, David Domedion, producers; Lisa Anne Wilson, coordinating producer

OUTSTANDING TALK/SERVICE SHOW: *The Oprah Winfrey Show* (SYNDICATED); Debra Di Maio, executive producer; Ray Nunn, senior producer; Oprah Winfrey, supervising producer; David Boul, Mary Kay Clinton, Rudy Guido, Dianne Hudson, Alice McGee, Sally Lou Oaks, Ellen Rakieten, producers

OUTSTANDING GAME/AUDIENCE PARTICIPATION SHOW: *Jeopardy!* (SYNDICATED); Merv Griffin, executive producer; George Vosburgh, producer

OUTSTANDING ANIMATED PROGRAM: *Tiny Toon Adventures* (SYNDICATED); Steven Spielberg, executive producer; Tom Ruegger, producer; Ken Boyer, Art Leonardi, Art Vitello, directors; Paul Dini, story editor; Sherri Stoner, writer

OUTSTANDING CHILDREN'S SERIES: *Sesame Street* (PBS); Dulcy Singer, executive producer; Lisa Simon, producer; Arlene Sherman, coordinating producer

OUTSTANDING CHILDREN'S SPECIAL: "Lost in the Barrens" (DISNEY); Michael MacMillan, Michael Scott, executive producers; Seaton McLean, Derek Mazur, Joan Scott, producers

OUTSTANDING SPECIAL CLASS PROGRAM: "Live from Lincoln Center: Yo-Yo Ma in Concert" (PBS); John Goberman, executive producer; Marc Bauman, coordinating producer; Hugh Downs, host

OUTSTANDING LEAD ACTOR IN A DRAMA SERIES: Peter Bergman, *The Young and the Restless* (CBS)

OUTSTANDING LEAD ACTRESS IN A DRAMA SERIES: Finola Hughes, *General Hospital* (ABC)

OUTSTANDING SUPPORTING ACTOR IN A DRAMA SERIES: Bernie Barrow, *Loving* (ABC)

OUTSTANDING SUPPORTING ACTRESS IN A DRAMA SERIES: Jess Walton, *The Young and the Restless* (CBS)

OUTSTANDING YOUNGER ACTOR IN A DRAMA SERIES: Rick Hearst, *Guiding Light* (CBS)

OUTSTANDING YOUNGER ACTRESS IN A DRAMA SERIES: Anne Heche, *Another World* (NBC)

OUTSTANDING TALK/SERVICE SHOW HOST: Oprah Winfrey, *The Oprah Winfrey Show* (SYNDICATED)

OUTSTANDING GAME SHOW HOST: Bob Barker, *The Price Is Right* (CBS)

OUTSTANDING PERFORMER IN A CHILDREN'S SERIES: Tim Curry (voice), *Peter Pan and the Pirates* (FOX)

OUTSTANDING PERFORMER IN A CHILDREN'S SPECIAL: Joanne Vannicola, "Maggie's Secret," *CBS Schoolbreak Special* (CBS)

OUTSTANDING DRAMA SERIES DIRECTING TEAM: *Santa Barbara* (NBC); Rick Bennewitz, Peter Brinckerhoff, Michael Gliona, Robert Schiller, directors; Jeanine Guarneri-Frons, Pamela Fryman, Robin Raphaelian, associate directors

OUTSTANDING DIRECTING IN A TALK/SERVICE SHOW: Peter Kimball, *The Oprah Winfrey Show* (SYNDICATED)

OUTSTANDING DIRECTING IN A GAME/AUDIENCE PARTICIPATION SHOW: Dick Schneider, *Jeopardy!* (SYNDICATED)

OUTSTANDING DIRECTING IN A CHILDREN'S SERIES: Brian Henson and Michael J. Kerrigan, *Jim Henson's Mother Goose Stories* (DISNEY)

OUTSTANDING ACHIEVEMENT IN DIRECTING—SPECIAL CLASS: Krstoffer Siegel-Tabori, "The Perfect Date," *ABC Afterschool Special* (ABC)

OUTSTANDING DRAMA SERIES WRITING TEAM: *Santa Barbara* (NBC); Chuck Pratt, Jr., head writer; Sheri Anderson, Sam Ratcliffe, Maralyn Thoma, co-head writers; Josh Griffith, Robert Guza, associate head writers; Linda Hamner, breakdown writer; Lynda Myles, Frank Salisbury, script writers; Richard Culliton, script writer/editor

OUTSTANDING WRITING IN A CHILDREN'S SERIES: *Sesame Street* (PBS); Norman Stiles, head writer; Judy Freudberg, Nancy Sans, Tony Geiss, Jeff Moss, Cathi Rosenberg-Turow, David Korr, Belinda Ward, Lou Berger, Sonia Manzano, Josh Selig, Sara Compton, Luis Santeiro, John Weidman, Emily Perl Kingsley, Mark Saltzman, Jon Stone, series writers

OUTSTANDING WRITING IN A CHILDREN'S SPECIAL: Courtney Flavin, Tracey Thompson, Beth Thompson, "A Question About Sex," *ABC Afterschool Special* (ABC)

OUTSTANDING ACHIEVEMENT IN WRITING—SPECIAL CLASS: Harry Eisenberg, Steven Dorfman, Kathy Easterling, Frederik Pohl IV, Steve D. Tamerius, Debbie Griffin, Michele Johnson, Carol Campbell, *Jeopardy!* (SYNDICATED)

1991–1992

I. PRIME TIME AWARDS

OUTSTANDING COMEDY SERIES: *Murphy Brown* (CBS); Diane English, Joel Shukovsky, executive producers; Steven Peterman, Gary Dontzig, supervising producers; Tom Palmer, co-supervising producer; Korby Siamis, consulting producer; Deborah Smith, producer; Peter Tolan, coproducer

OUTSTANDING DRAMA SERIES: *Northern Exposure* (CBS); Joshua Brand, John Falsey, executive producers; Andrew Schneider, co-executive producer; Diane Frolov, Jeff Melvoin, Cheryl Bloch, Robin Green, supervising producers; Matthew Nodella, Rob Thompson, producers

OUTSTANDING MINISERIES: "A Woman Named Jackie" (NBC); Lester Persky, executive producer; Lorin Bennett Salob, producer; Tomlinson Dean, coproducer

OUTSTANDING MADE FOR TELEVISION MOVIE: "Miss Rose White," *Hallmark Hall of Fame* (NBC); Marian Rees, executive producer; Andrea Baynes, Francine Lefrak, co-executive producers; Anne Hopkins, producer

OUTSTANDING VARIETY, MUSIC OR COMEDY PROGRAM (SERIES): *The Tonight Show Starring Johnny Carson* (NBC); Fred DeCordova, Peter Lassally, executive producers; Jeff Sotzing, producer; Jim McCawley, coproducer; Johnny Carson, host

OUTSTANDING VARIETY, MUSIC OR COMEDY PROGRAM (SPECIAL): "Cirque Du Soleil II: A New Experience" (HBO); Helene Dufresne, producer

OUTSTANDING INFORMATIONAL SERIES: *MGM: When the Lion Roars* (TNT); Joni Levin, producer

OUTSTANDING INFORMATIONAL SPECIAL: "Abortion: Desperate Choices" (HBO); Susan Froemke, executive producer

OUTSTANDING CHILDREN'S PROGRAM: "Mark Twain and Me" (DISNEY); Geoffrey Cowan, Julian Fowles, executive producers

OUTSTANDING ANIMATED PROGRAM: "A Claymation Easter" (CBS); Will Vinton, executive producer; Paul Diener, producer; Mark Gustafson, director/writer; Barry Bruce, Ryan Holznagel, writers

OUTSTANDING CLASSICAL PROGRAM IN THE PERFORMING ARTS: "Perlman in Russia" (PBS); Robert Dalrymple, producer; Itzhak Perlman, performer

OUTSTANDING LEAD ACTOR IN A DRAMA SERIES: Christopher Lloyd, *Avonlea* (DISNEY)

OUTSTANDING LEAD ACTRESS IN A DRAMA SERIES: Dana Delany, *China Beach* (ABC)

OUTSTANDING LEAD ACTOR IN A COMEDY SERIES: Craig T. Nelson, *Coach* (ABC)

OUTSTANDING LEAD ACTRESS IN A COMEDY SERIES: Candice Bergen, *Murphy Brown* (CBS)

OUTSTANDING LEAD ACTOR IN A MINISERIES OR SPECIAL: Beau Bridges, "Without Warning: The James Brady Story" (HBO)

OUTSTANDING LEAD ACTRESS IN A MINISERIES OR SPECIAL: Gena Rowlands, "Face of a Stranger" (CBS)

OUTSTANDING SUPPORTING ACTOR IN A DRAMA SERIES: Richard Dysart, *L.A. Law* (NBC)

OUTSTANDING SUPPORTING ACTRESS IN A DRAMA SERIES: Valerie Mahaffey, *Northern Exposure* (CBS)

OUTSTANDING SUPPORTING ACTOR IN A COMEDY SERIES: Michael Jeter, *Evening Shade* (CBS)

OUTSTANDING SUPPORTING ACTRESS IN A COMEDY SERIES: Laurie Metcalf, *Roseanne* (ABC)

OUTSTANDING SUPPORTING ACTOR IN A MINISERIES OR SPECIAL: Hume Cronyn, "Neil Simon's 'Broadway Bound' " (ABC)

OUTSTANDING SUPPORTING ACTRESS IN A MINISERIES OR SPECIAL: Amanda Plummer, "Miss Rose White," *Hallmark Hall of Fame* (NBC)

OUTSTANDING INDIVIDUAL PERFORMANCE IN A VARIETY OR MUSIC PROGRAM: Bette Midler, *The Tonight Show Starring Johnny Carson* (NBC)

OUTSTANDING VOICE-OVER PERFORMANCE: Nancy Cartwright, Jackie Mason, Julie Kavner, Yeardley Smith, Marcia Wallace, Dan Castellaneta, *The Simpsons* (FOX)

OUTSTANDING INDIVIDUAL ACHIEVEMENT IN DIRECTING IN A DRAMA SERIES: Eric Laneuville, "All God's Children," *I'll Fly Away* (NBC)

OUTSTANDING INDIVIDUAL ACHIEVEMENT IN DIRECTING IN A COMEDY SERIES: Barnet Kellman, "Birth 101," *Murphy Brown* (CBS)

OUTSTANDING INDIVIDUAL ACHIEVEMENT IN DIRECTING IN A VARIETY OR MUSICAL PROGRAM: Patricia Birch, "Unforgettable, with Love: Natalie Cole Sings the Songs of Nat King Cole," *Great Performances* (PBS)

OUTSTANDING INDIVIDUAL ACHIEVEMENT IN DIRECTING FOR A MINISERIES OR A SPECIAL: Daniel Petrie, "Mark Twain and Me" (DISNEY)

OUTSTANDING INDIVIDUAL ACHIEVEMENT—INFORMATIONAL PROGRAMMING—DIRECTING: George Hickenlooper, Fax Bahr, Eleanor Coppola, "Hearts of Darkness: A Filmmaker's Apocalypse" (SHOWTIME)

OUTSTANDING INDIVIDUAL ACHIEVEMENT—CLASSICAL MUSIC/DANCE PROGRAMMING—DIRECTING: Brian Large, "The Metropolitan Opera Silver Anniversary Gala" (PBS)

OUTSTANDING INDIVIDUAL ACHIEVEMENT IN WRITING IN A DRAMA SERIES: Andrew Schneider, Diane Frolov, "Seoul Mates," *Northern Exposure* (CBS)

OUTSTANDING INDIVIDUAL ACHIEVEMENT IN WRITING IN A COMEDY SERIES: Elaine Pope, Larry Charles, "The Fix Up," *Seinfeld* (NBC)

OUTSTANDING INDIVIDUAL ACHIEVEMENT IN WRITING IN A VARIETY OR MUSIC PROGRAM: Hal Kanter, Buz Kohan, writers; Billy Crystal, Marc Shaiman, David Steinberg, Robert Wuhl, Bruce Vilanch, writers of special material, "The 64th Annual Academy Awards" (ABC)

OUTSTANDING INDIVIDUAL ACHIEVEMENT IN WRITING FOR A MINISERIES OR SPECIAL: John Falsey, Joshua Brand, *I'll Fly Away* (pilot) (NBC)

OUTSTANDING INDIVIDUAL ACHIEVEMENT—INFORMATIONAL PROGRAMMING—WRITING: Fax Bahr, George Hickenlooper, "Hearts of Darkness: A Filmmaker's Apocalypse" (SHOWTIME)

II. DAYTIME AWARDS

OUTSTANDING DRAMA SERIES: *All My Children* (ABC); Felicia Minei Behr, executive producer; Terry Cacavio, Thomas de Villiers, supervising producers; Nancy Horwich, coordinating producer

OUTSTANDING TALK/SERVICE SHOW: *The Oprah Winfrey Show* (SYNDICATED); Debra DiMaio, executive producer; Oprah Winfrey, supervising producer; Mary Kay Clinton, Ellen Rakieten, David Boul, Dianne Hudson, Rudy Guido, Alice McGee, producers

OUTSTANDING GAME/AUDIENCE PARTICIPATION SHOW: *Jeopardy!* (SYNDICATED); Merv Griffin, executive producer; George Vosburgh, producer

OUTSTANDING CHILDREN'S SERIES: *Sesame Street* (PBS); Dulcy Singer, executive producer; Lisa Simon, producer; Arlene Sherman, coordinating producer

OUTSTANDING CHILDREN'S SPECIAL: "Vincent and Me" (DISNEY); Rock Demers, producer; Daniel Louis, line producer; Claude Nedjar, coproducer

OUTSTANDING ANIMATED PROGRAM: *Rugrats* (NICKELODEON); Vanessa Coffey, Gabor Csupo, Arlene Klasky, executive producers; Paul Germain, creative producer; Mary Harrington, Sherry Gunther, supervising producers; David Blum, producer; Bee Beckman, coproducer; Norton Virgien, Howard Baker, Dan Thompson, directors

OUTSTANDING SPECIAL CLASS PROGRAM: "Spaceship Earth: Our Global Environment" (DISNEY); Kirk Bergstrom, executive producer; Kit Thomas, producer; Khrystyne Haje, host

OUTSTANDING LEAD ACTOR IN A DRAMA SERIES: Peter Bergman, *The Young and the Restless* (CBS)

OUTSTANDING LEAD ACTRESS IN A DRAMA SERIES: Erika Slezak, *One Life to Live* (ABC)

OUTSTANDING SUPPORTING ACTOR IN A DRAMA SERIES: Thom Christopher, *One Life to Live* (ABC)

OUTSTANDING SUPPORTING ACTRESS IN A DRAMA SERIES: Maeve Kinkead, *Guiding Light* (CBS)

OUTSTANDING YOUNGER ACTOR IN A DRAMA SERIES: Kristoff St. John, *The Young and the Restless* (CBS)

OUTSTANDING YOUNGER ACTRESS IN A DRAMA SERIES: Tricia Cast, *The Young and the Restless* (CBS)

OUTSTANDING TALK/SERVICE SHOW HOST: Oprah Winfrey, *The Oprah Winfrey Show* (SYNDICATED)

OUTSTANDING GAME SHOW HOST: Bob Barker, *The Price Is Right* (CBS)

OUTSTANDING PERFORMER IN A CHILDREN'S SERIES: Shari Lewis, *Lamb Chop's Play-Along* (PBS)

OUTSTANDING PERFORMER IN A CHILDREN'S SPECIAL: Josh Hamilton, "Abby, My Love," *CBS Schoolbreak Special* (CBS)

OUTSTANDING DRAMA SERIES DIRECTING TEAM: *Another World* (NBC); Michael Eilbaum, Bob Schwarz, Casey Childs, Susan Strickler, directors; Carol Sedwick, Mary Madeiras, Janet Andrews, associate directors

OUTSTANDING DIRECTING IN A TALK/SERVICE SHOW: Russell Morash, *This Old House* (PBS)

OUTSTANDING DIRECTING IN A GAME/AUDIENCE PARTICIPATION SHOW: Dick Schneider, *Jeopardy!* (SYNDICATED)

OUTSTANDING DIRECTING IN A CHILDREN'S SERIES: Larry Lancit, Ed Wiseman, Mark Mannucci, *Reading Rainbow* (PBS)

OUTSTANDING DIRECTING IN A CHILDREN'S SPECIAL: David Cobham, "Woof!" (DISNEY)

OUTSTANDING ACHIEVEMENT IN DIRECTING—SPECIAL CLASS: Dick Schneider, "Macy's 65th Annual Thanksgiving Day Parade" (NBC)

OUTSTANDING DRAMA SERIES WRITING TEAM: *The Young and the Restless* (CBS); William J. Bell, head writer; Kay Alden, co-head writer; Jerry Birn, John F. Smith, Eric Freiwald, Rex M. Best, Janice Ferri, Frederick Johnson, Jim Houghton, writers

OUTSTANDING WRITING IN A CHILDREN'S SERIES: *Sesame Street* (PBS); Norman Stiles, head writer; Nancy Sans, Judy Freudberg, Tony Geiss, Sonia Manzano, Cathi Rosenberg-Turow, Belinda Ward, Lou Berger, David Korr, Josh Selig, Jeff Moss, John Weidman, Sara Compton, Luis Santeiro, Molly Boylan, Emily Perl Kingsley, Mark Saltzman, Jon Stone, writers

OUTSTANDING WRITING IN A CHILDREN'S SPECIAL: Paul W. Cooper, "Abby, My Love," *CBS Schoolbreak Special* (CBS)

OUTSTANDING WRITING IN AN ANIMATED PROGRAM: Nicholas Hollander and Tom Ruegger, writers, Paul Dini and Sherri Stoner, story editors, *Tiny Toon Adventures* (SYNDICATED)

OUTSTANDING ACHIEVEMENT IN WRITING—SPECIAL CLASS: Kerry Millerick, Julie Engelman, Neal Rogin, "Spaceship Earth: Our Global Environment" (DISNEY)

1992–1993

I. PRIME TIME AWARDS

OUTSTANDING COMEDY SERIES: *Seinfeld* (NBC); Larry David, Andrew Scheinman, George Shapiro, Howard West, executive producers; Larry Charles, Tom Cherones, supervising producers; Jerry Seinfeld, producer; Joan Van Horn, line producer; Tim Kaiser, coordinating producer

OUTSTANDING DRAMA SERIES: *Picket Fences* (CBS); David E. Kelley, executive producer; Michael Pressman, co-executive producer; Alice West, senior producer; Robert Breech, Mark B. Perry, producers; Jonathan Pontell, coproducer

OUTSTANDING VARIETY, MUSIC OR COMEDY SERIES: *Saturday Night Live* (NBC); Lorne Michaels, executive producer; James Downey, Al Franken, producers

OUTSTANDING INFORMATIONAL SERIES: *Healing and the Mind with Bill Moyers* (PBS); David Grubin, executive producer/producer; Alice Markowitz, producer; Bill Moyers, editorial producer/host; Judith Davidson Moyers, editorial producer

OUTSTANDING CHILDREN'S PROGRAM: (1) *Avonlea* (DISNEY); Kevin Sullivan, Trudy Grant, executive producers; Brian Leslie Parker, line producer; (2) "Beethoven Lives Upstairs" (HBO); Terence E. Robinson, executive producer; David Devine, Richard Mozer, producers

OUTSTANDING ANIMATED PROGRAM: *Batman: The Series* (FOX); Jean H. MacCurdy, Tom Ruegger, executive producers; Alan Burnett, Eric Radomski, Bruce W. Timm, producers; Randy Rogel, writer; Dick Sebast, director

OUTSTANDING MINISERIES: "Prime Suspect 2," *Mystery!* (PBS); Sally Head, executive producer; Paul Marcus, producer

OUTSTANDING MADE FOR TELEVISION MOVIE: (1) "Barbarians at the Gate" (HBO); Thomas M. Hammel, Glenn Jordan, executive producers; Ray Stark, producer; Marykay Powell, coproducer; (2) "Stalin" (HBO); Mark Carliner, producer; Don West, line producer; Ilene Kahn, coproducer

OUTSTANDING VARIETY, MUSIC OR COMEDY SPECIAL: "Bob Hope: The First 90 Years" (NBC); Linda Hope, executive producer; Nancy Malone, supervising producer; Don Mischer, producer

OUTSTANDING INFORMATIONAL SPECIAL: "Lucy and Desi: A Home Movie" (NBC); Lucie Arnaz, Laurence Luckinbill, executive producers; Don Buford, producer

OUTSTANDING CLASSICAL PROGRAM IN THE PERFORMING ARTS: "Tosca in the Settings and at the Times of Tosca" (PBS); Rada Rassimov, executive producer; Andrea Andermann, producer; Zubin Mehta, conductor

OUTSTANDING LEAD ACTOR IN A DRAMA SERIES: Tom Skerritt, *Picket Fences* (CBS)

OUTSTANDING LEAD ACTRESS IN A DRAMA SERIES: Kathy Baker, *Picket Fences* (CBS)

OUTSTANDING LEAD ACTOR IN A COMEDY SERIES: Ted Danson, *Cheers* (NBC)

OUTSTANDING LEAD ACTRESS IN A COMEDY SERIES: Roseanne Arnold, *Roseanne* (ABC)

OUTSTANDING LEAD ACTOR IN A MINISERIES OR SPECIAL: Robert Morse, "Tru," *American Playhouse* (PBS)

OUTSTANDING LEAD ACTRESS IN A MINISERIES OR SPECIAL: Holly Hunter, "The Positively True Adventures of the Alleged Texas Cheerleader-Murdering Mom" (HBO)

OUTSTANDING SUPPORTING ACTOR IN A DRAMA SERIES: Chad Lowe, *Life Goes On* (ABC)

OUTSTANDING SUPPORTING ACTRESS IN A DRAMA SERIES: Mary Alice, *I'll Fly Away* (NBC)

OUTSTANDING SUPPORTING ACTOR IN A COMEDY SERIES: Michael Richards, *Seinfeld* (NBC)

OUTSTANDING SUPPORTING ACTRESS IN A COMEDY SERIES: Laurie Metcalf, *Roseanne* (ABC)

OUTSTANDING SUPPORTING ACTOR IN A MINISERIES OR SPECIAL: Beau Bridges, "The Positively True Adventures of the Alleged Texas Cheerleader-Murdering Mom" (HBO)

OUTSTANDING SUPPORTING ACTRESS IN A MINISERIES OR SPECIAL: Mary Tyler Moore, "Stolen Babies" (LIFETIME)

OUTSTANDING GUEST ACTOR IN A DRAMA SERIES: Laurence Fishburne, "The Box," *Tribeca* (FOX)

OUTSTANDING GUEST ACTRESS IN A DRAMA SERIES: Elaine Stritch, "Point of View," *Law & Order* (NBC)

OUTSTANDING GUEST ACTOR IN A COMEDY SERIES: David Clennon, "For Peter's Sake," *Dream On* (HBO)

OUTSTANDING GUEST ACTRESS IN A COMEDY SERIES: Tracey Ullman, "The Prima Dava," *Love and War* (CBS)

OUTSTANDING INDIVIDUAL PERFORMANCE IN A VARIETY OR MUSIC PROGRAM: Dana Carvey, *Saturday Night Live* (NBC)

OUTSTANDING VOICE-OVER PERFORMANCE: Dan Castellaneta, "Mr. Plow," *The Simpsons* (FOX)

OUTSTANDING INDIVIDUAL ACHIEVEMENT IN DIRECTING IN A DRAMA SERIES: Barry Levinson, "Gone for Goode," *Homicide: Life on the Street* (NBC)

OUTSTANDING INDIVIDUAL ACHIEVEMENT IN DIRECTING IN A COMEDY SERIES: Betty Thomas, "For Peter's Sake," *Dream On* (HBO)

OUTSTANDING INDIVIDUAL ACHIEVEMENT IN DIRECTING IN A VARIETY OR MUSIC PROGRAM: Walter C. Miller, "The 1992 Tony Awards" (CBS)

OUTSTANDING INDIVIDUAL ACHIEVEMENT IN DIRECTING FOR A MINISERIES OR A SPECIAL: James Sadwith, "Sinatra" (CBS)

OUTSTANDING INDIVIDUAL ACHIEVEMENT IN WRITING IN A DRAMA SERIES: Tom Fontana, "Three Men and Adena," *Homicide: Life on the Street* (NBC)

OUTSTANDING INDIVIDUAL ACHIEVEMENT IN WRITING IN A COMEDY SERIES: Larry David, "The Contest," *Seinfeld* (NBC)

OUTSTANDING INDIVIDUAL ACHIEVEMENT IN WRITING IN A VARIETY OR MUSIC PROGRAM: Judd Apatow, Robert Cohen, David Cross, Brent Forrester, Jeff Kahn, Bruce Kirschbaum, Bob Odenkirk, Sultan Pepper, Dino Stamatopoulos, Ben Stiller, *The Ben Stiller Show* (FOX)

OUTSTANDING INDIVIDUAL ACHIEVEMENT IN WRITING IN A MINISERIES OR A SPECIAL: Jane Anderson, "The Positively True Adventures of the Alleged Texas Cheerleader-Murdering Mom" (HBO)

OUTSTANDING INDIVIDUAL ACHIEVEMENT—INFORMATIONAL PROGRAMMING: (1) Lee Stanley, director, *Gridiron Gang* (SYNDICATED); (2) Audrey Hepburn, host, "Gardens of the World" (PBS)

OUTSTANDING INDIVIDUAL ACHIEVEMENT—CLASSICAL MUSIC/DANCE PROGRAMMING: (1) Giuseppe Patroni Griffi, Brian Large, directors, "Tosca in the Settings and at the Times of Tosca" (PBS); (2) Catherine Malfitano, performer, "Tosca in the Settings and at the Times of Tosca" (PBS)

OUTSTANDING DRAMA SERIES: *The Young and the Restless* (CBS); William J. Bell, senior executive producer; Edward J. Scott, executive producer; David Shaughnessy, producer; Nancy Bradley Wiard, coordinating producer

OUTSTANDING TALK/SERVICE SHOW: *Good Morning America* (ABC); Jack Reilly, executive producer; Steve Lewis, senior producer; Frederica Gaffney, Kevin Magee, Roni Selig, Bob Reichblum, Roberta Dougherty, producers; Randall Barone, coordinating producer

OUTSTANDING GAME/AUDIENCE PARTICIPATION SHOW: *Jeopardy!* (SYNDICATED); Merv Griffin, executive producer; George Vosburgh, producer

OUTSTANDING ANIMATED CHILDREN'S PROGRAM: *Tiny Toon Adventures* (SYNDICATED); Steven Spielberg, executive producer; Tom Ruegger, senior producer; Sherri Stoner, producer; Rich Arons, Byron Vaughns, Ken Boyer, Alfred Gimeno, and David West, directors

OUTSTANDING CHILDREN'S SERIES: *Reading Rainbow* (PBS); Twila C. Liggett, Tony Buttino, executive producers; Cecily Truett, Larry Lancit, Orly Berger, supervising producers; LeVar Burton, contributing producer; Ronnie Krauss, Jill Gluckson, Kathy Kinsner, producers

OUTSTANDING CHILDREN'S SPECIAL: "Shades of a Single Protein," *ABC Afterschool Special* (ABC); Debra DiMaio, executive producer; Oprah Winfrey, supervising producer; Tod Solomon Lending, coordinating producer; Ray Nunn, senior producer; John Watkin, Eamon Harrington, producers

OUTSTANDING SPECIAL CLASS PROGRAM: "Great Wonders of the World: Wonders of Nature" (DISNEY); Kim Thomas, James R. Conner, Edward J. Murphy, executive producers; Chris Valentini, producer

OUTSTANDING LEAD ACTOR IN A DRAMA SERIES: David Canary, *All My Children* (ABC)

OUTSTANDING LEAD ACTRESS IN A DRAMA SERIES: Linda Dano, *Another World* (NBC)

OUTSTANDING SUPPORTING ACTOR IN A DRAMA SERIES: Gerald Anthony, *General Hospital* (ABC)

OUTSTANDING SUPPORTING ACTRESS IN A DRAMA SERIES: Ellen Parker, *Guiding Light* (CBS)

OUTSTANDING YOUNGER ACTOR IN A DRAMA SERIES: Monti Sharp, *Guiding Light* (CBS)

OUTSTANDING YOUNGER ACTRESS IN A DRAMA SERIES: Heather Tom, *The Young and the Restless* (CBS)

OUTSTANDING TALK/SERVICE SHOW HOST: Oprah Winfrey, *The Oprah Winfrey Show* (SYNDICATED)

OUTSTANDING GAME SHOW HOST: Pat Sajak, *Wheel of Fortune* (SYNDICATED)

OUTSTANDING PERFORMER IN A CHILDREN'S SERIES: Shari Lewis, *Lamb Chop's Play-Along* (PBS)

OUTSTANDING PERFORMER IN A CHILDREN'S SPECIAL: Dina Sbivey, "Public Law 106: The Becky Bell Story" (HBO)

OUTSTANDING DRAMA SERIES DIRECTING TEAM: *As the World Turns* (CBS); Paul Lammers, Maria Wagner, Dan Hamilton, Charles C. Dyer, Larry Carpenter, directors; Joel Aronowitz, Michael Kerner, associate directors

OUTSTANDING DIRECTING IN A TALK/SERVICE SHOW: Bob McKinnon, *Good Morning America* (ABC)

OUTSTANDING DIRECTING IN A GAME/AUDIENCE PARTICIPATION SHOW: Kevin McCarthy and Dick Schneider, *Jeopardy!* (SYNDICATED)

OUTSTANDING DIRECTING IN A CHILDREN'S SERIES: Ed Wiseman and Mark Mannucci, *Reading Rainbow* (PBS)

OUTSTANDING DIRECTING IN A CHILDREN'S SPECIAL: Laszlo Pal, "Journey to Spirit Island" (DISNEY)

OUTSTANDING ACHIEVEMENT IN DIRECTING—SPECIAL CLASS: (1) Michael Gargiulo, "All-American Thanksgiving Parade" (CBS); (2) Russell Morash, *The Victory Garden* (PBS)

OUTSTANDING DRAMA SERIES WRITING TEAM: *Guiding Light* (CBS); Nancy Curlee, Stephen Demorest, Lorraine Broderick, James E. Reilly, head writers; Nancy Williams Watt, associate head writer; Michael Conforti, Bill Elverman, Barbara

Esensten, James Harmon Brown, Trent Jones, N. Gail Lawrence, Pete T. Rich, Sally Mandel, Patrick Mulcahey, Roger Newman, Dorothy Purser, Peggy Schibi, Courtney Simon, Wisner Washam, writers

OUTSTANDING WRITING IN AN ANIMATED PROGRAM: Paul Dini, Martin Pasko, Michael Reaves, story editors, Sean Catherine Derek, writer, *Batman: The Animated Series* (FOX)

OUTSTANDING WRITING IN A CHILDREN'S SERIES: Shari Lewis and Bernard Rothman, *Lamb Chop's Play-Along* (PBS)

OUTSTANDING WRITING IN A CHILDREN'S SPECIAL: Bruce Harmon, "Public Law 106: The Becky Bell Story" (HBO)

OUTSTANDING ACHIEVEMENT IN WRITING—SPECIAL CLASS: Victoria Costello, "This Island Earth" (DISNEY)

1993–1994

I. PRIME TIME AWARDS

OUTSTANDING COMEDY SERIES: *Frasier* (NBC); Peter Casey, David Angell, David Lee, executive producers; Christopher Lloyd, co-executive producer; Denise Moss, Sy Dukane, supervising producers; Maggie Randell, producer; Linda Morris, Vic Rauseo, consulting producers

OUTSTANDING DRAMA SERIES: *Law & Order* (NBC); Dick Wolf, executive producer; Walon Green, Ed Sherin, co-executive producers; Robert Nathan, supervising producer; Jeffrey Hayes, Michael Chernunchin, Arthur Forney, producers; Rene Balcer, Lew Gould, coproducers

OUTSTANDING VARIETY, MUSIC OR COMEDY SERIES: *Late Show with David Letterman* (NBC); Peter Lassally, Robert Morton, executive producers; Hal Gurnee, supervising producer; Jude Brennan, producer; David Letterman, host

OUTSTANDING INFORMATIONAL SERIES: *Later with Bob Costas* (NBC); Lou Del Prete, Matthew McCarthy, executive producers; Fred Rothenberg, Bruce Cornblatt, senior producers; Michael L. Weinberg, producer; Bob Costas, host

OUTSTANDING MINISERIES: "Prime Suspect 3," *Mystery!* (PBS); Sally Head, executive producer; Paul Marcus, producer

OUTSTANDING CHILDREN'S PROGRAM: "Kids Killing Kids/Kids Saving Kids" (CBS/FOX); Arnold Shapiro, executive producer; David J. Eagle, Kerry Neal, producers; Norman Marcus, Michael Killen, coproducers

OUTSTANDING MADE FOR TELEVISION MOVIE: "And the Band Played On" (HBO); Aaron Spelling, E. Duke Vincent, executive producers; Midge Sanford, Sarah Pillsbury, producers

OUTSTANDING VARIETY, MUSIC OR COMEDY SPECIAL: "The Kennedy Center Honors" (CBS); George Stevens, Jr., Don Mischer, producers

OUTSTANDING CULTURAL PROGRAM: "Vladimir Horowitz: A Reminiscence" (PBS); Peter Gelb, executive producer; Pat Jaffe, producer

OUTSTANDING INFORMATIONAL SPECIAL: "I Am a Promise: The Children of Stanton Street Elementary School" (HBO); Alan Raymond, Susan Raymond, producers

OUTSTANDING ANIMATED PROGRAM: "The Roman City" (PBS); Bob Kurtz, producer/director/writer; Mark Olshaker, writer

OUTSTANDING LEAD ACTOR IN A DRAMA SERIES: Dennis Franz, *NYPD Blue* (ABC)

OUTSTANDING LEAD ACTRESS IN A DRAMA SERIES: Sela Ward, *Sisters* (NBC)

OUTSTANDING LEAD ACTOR IN A COMEDY SERIES: Kelsey Grammer, *Frasier* (NBC)

OUTSTANDING LEAD ACTRESS IN A COMEDY SERIES: Candice Bergen, *Murphy Brown* (CBS)

OUTSTANDING LEAD ACTOR IN A MINISERIES OR SPECIAL: Hume Cronyn, "To Dance with the White Dog," *Hallmark Hall of Fame* (CBS)

OUTSTANDING LEAD ACTRESS IN A MINISERIES OR SPECIAL: Kirstie Alley, "David's Mother" (CBS)

OUTSTANDING SUPPORTING ACTOR IN A DRAMA SERIES: Fyvush Finkel, *Picket Fences* (CBS)

OUTSTANDING SUPPORTING ACTRESS IN A DRAMA SERIES: Leigh Taylor-Young, *Picket Fences* (CBS)

OUTSTANDING SUPPORTING ACTOR IN A COMEDY SERIES: Michael Richards, *Seinfeld* (NBC)

OUTSTANDING SUPPORTING ACTRESS IN A COMEDY SERIES: Laurie Metcalf, *Roseanne* (ABC)

OUTSTANDING SUPPORTING ACTOR IN A MINISERIES OR SPECIAL: Michael Goorjian, "David's Mother" (CBS)

OUTSTANDING SUPPORTING ACTRESS IN A MINISERIES OR SPECIAL: Cicely Tyson, "Oldest Living Confederate Widow Tells All," parts 1 and 2 (CBS)

OUTSTANDING GUEST ACTOR IN A DRAMA SERIES: Richard Kiley, "Buried Alive," *Picket Fences* (CBS)

OUTSTANDING GUEST ACTRESS IN A DRAMA SERIES: Faye Dunaway, "It's All in the Game," *Columbo* (ABC)

OUTSTANDING GUEST ACTOR IN A COMEDY SERIES: Martin Sheen, "Angst for the Memories," *Murphy Brown* (CBS)

OUTSTANDING GUEST ACTRESS IN A COMEDY SERIES: Eileen Heckart, "You Make Me Feel So Young," *Love & War* (CBS)

OUTSTANDING INDIVIDUAL PERFORMANCE IN A VARIETY OR MUSIC PROGRAM: Tracey Ullman, "Tracey Ullman — Takes on New York" (HBO)

OUTSTANDING VOICE-OVER PERFORMANCE: Christopher Plummer, narrator, "Madeline" (FAMILY)

OUTSTANDING INDIVIDUAL ACHIEVEMENT—CULTURAL PROGRAMMING: (1) Itzhak Perlman, violinist, "The Dvorak Concert from Prague: A Celebration" (PBS); (2) Seiji Ozawa, conductor, "The Dvorak Concert from Prague: A Celebration" (PBS); (3) Nuala O'Conner, writer, "Irish Music and America . . . A Musical Migration" (DISNEY)

OUTSTANDING INDIVIDUAL ACHIEVEMENT IN DIRECTING IN A DRAMA SERIES: Daniel Sackheim, "Tempest in a C-Cup," *NYPD Blue* (ABC)

OUTSTANDING INDIVIDUAL ACHIEVEMENT IN DIRECTING IN A COMEDY SERIES: James Burrows, "The Good Son," *Frasier* (NBC)

OUTSTANDING INDIVIDUAL ACHIEVEMENT IN DIRECTING FOR A MINISERIES OR A SPECIAL: John Frankenheimer, "Against the Wall" (HBO)

OUTSTANDING INDIVIDUAL ACHIEVEMENT IN DIRECTING IN A VARIETY OR MUSIC PROGRAM: Walter C. Miller, "The Tony Awards" (CBS)

OUTSTANDING INDIVIDUAL ACHIEVEMENT IN WRITING IN A DRAMA SERIES: Ann Biderman, "Steroid Roy," *NYPD Blue* (ABC)

OUTSTANDING INDIVIDUAL ACHIEVEMENT IN WRITING IN A COMEDY SERIES: David Angell, Peter Casey, David Lee, "The Good Son," *Frasier* (NBC)

OUTSTANDING INDIVIDUAL ACHIEVEMENT IN WRITING IN A MINISERIES OR A SPECIAL: Bob Randall, "David's Mother" (CBS)

OUTSTANDING INDIVIDUAL ACHIEVEMENT IN WRITING IN A VARIETY OR MUSIC PROGRAM: Jeff Cesario, Mike Dugan, Eddie Feldmann, Gregory Greenberg, Dennis Miller, Kevin Rooney, *Dennis Miller Live* (HBO)

OUTSTANDING INDIVIDUAL ACHIEVEMENT—INFORMATIONAL PROGRAMMING: (1) Robin Leahman, director, "Cats & Dogs: Dogs Segment" (TBS); (2) George Stevens, Jr., narrator, "George Stevens: D-Day to Berlin" (DISNEY); (3) George Stevens, Jr., writer, "George Stevens: D-Day to Berlin" (DISNEY); (4) Todd Robinson, writer, "The Legend of Billy the Kid" (DISNEY); (5) Dereck Joubert, writer, "Reflections on Elephants" (PBS); (6) Dennis Watlington, writer, "The Untold West: The Black West" (TBS)

II. DAYTIME AWARDS

OUTSTANDING DRAMA SERIES: *All My Children* (ABC); Felicia Minei Behr, executive producer; Terry Cacavio, Thomas De Villiers, supervising producers; Nancy Horwich, coordinating producer

OUTSTANDING TALK SHOW: *The Oprah Winfrey Show* (SYNDICATED); Debra DiMaio, executive producer; Oprah Winfrey, supervising producer; Dianne Hudson, supervising senior producer; Alice McGee, Ellen Rakieten, Mary Kay Clinton, senior producers; David Boul, Legrande Green, Rudy Guido, Dana Newton, producers

OUTSTANDING GAME/AUDIENCE PARTICIPATION SHOW: *Jeopardy!* (SYNDICATED); Merv Griffin, executive producer; George Vosburgh, producer

OUTSTANDING SERVICE SHOW: *This Old House* (PBS); Russell Morash, executive producer; Nina Sing Fialkow, coordinating producer; Bruce Irving, producer

OUTSTANDING CHILDREN'S SERIES: *Sesame Street* (PBS); Michael Loman, executive producer; Lisa Simon, supervising producer; Arlene Sheman, coordinating producer

OUTSTANDING ANIMATED CHILDREN'S PROGRAM: *Rugrats* (NICK); Vanessa Coffey, Gabor Csupo, Arlene Klasky, executive producers; Paul Germain, Charles Swenson, Mary Harrington, supervising producers; Geraldine Clarke, producer; Howard E. Baker, Norton Virgien, Jim Duffy, directors

OUTSTANDING CHILDREN'S SPECIAL: "Dead Drunk: The Kevin Tunell Story" (HBO); Frank Doelger, Howard Meltzer, producers

OUTSTANDING SPECIAL CLASS PROGRAM: "Macy's 67th Annual Thanksgiving Day Parade" (NBC); Dick Schneider, executive producer; Willard Scott and Katie Couric, hosts

OUTSTANDING LEAD ACTOR IN A DRAMA SERIES: Michael Zaslow, *Guiding Light* (CBS)

OUTSTANDING LEAD ACTRESS IN A DRAMA SERIES: Hillary B. Smith, *One Life to Live* (ABC)

OUTSTANDING SUPPORTING ACTOR IN A DRAMA SERIES: Justin Deas, *Guiding Light* (CBS)

OUTSTANDING SUPPORTING ACTRESS IN A DRAMA SERIES: Susan Haskell, *One Life to Live* (ABC)

OUTSTANDING YOUNGER ACTOR IN A DRAMA SERIES: Roger Howarth, *One Life to Live* (ABC)

OUTSTANDING YOUNGER ACTRESS IN A DRAMA SERIES: Melissa Hayden, *Guiding Light* (CBS)

OUTSTANDING TALK SHOW HOST: Oprah Winfrey, *The Oprah Winfrey Show* (SYNDICATED)

OUTSTANDING GAME SHOW HOST: Bob Barker, *The Price Is Right* (CBS)

OUTSTANDING SERVICE SHOW HOST: T. Berry Brazelton, *What Every Baby Knows* (LIF)

OUTSTANDING PERFORMER IN A CHILDREN'S SERIES: Shari Lewis, *Lamb Chop's Play-Along* (PBS)

OUTSTANDING PERFORMER IN A CHILDREN'S SPECIAL: Justin Whalin, "Other Mothers," *CBS Schoolbreak Special* (CBS)

OUTSTANDING DRAMA SERIES DIRECTING TEAM: *Guiding Light* (CBS); Bruce Barry, Jo Anne Sedwick, Irene Pace, Brian Mertes, directors; John O'Connell, Matthew Lagle, Scott Riggs, Lisa Connor, associate directors

OUTSTANDING DIRECTING IN A TALK SHOW: Peter Kimball, Joey Ford, Duke Struck, *The Oprah Winfrey Show* (SYNDICATED)

OUTSTANDING DIRECTING IN A GAME/AUDIENCE PARTICIPATION SHOW: Bob Levy, *American Gladiators* (SYNDICATED)

OUTSTANDING DIRECTING IN A SERVICE SHOW: Russell Morash, *This Old House* (PBS)

OUTSTANDING DIRECTING IN A CHILDREN'S SERIES: Ed Wiseman, Mark Mannucci, *Reading Rainbow* (PBS)

OUTSTANDING DIRECTING IN A CHILDREN'S SPECIAL: Hank Saroyan, "William Saroyan's The Parsley Garden," *ABC Weekend Special* (ABC)

OUTSTANDING ACHIEVEMENT IN DIRECTING—SPECIAL CLASS: Bob McKinnon, *Good Morning America* (ABC)

OUTSTANDING DRAMA SERIES WRITING TEAM: *One Life to Live* (ABC); Michael Malone, Josh Griffith, head writers; Jean Passanante, associate head writer; Susan Bedlow-Hogan, Chris Whitesell, Becky Cole, David Colson, Lloyd Gold, David Smilow, writers

OUTSTANDING WRITING IN A CHILDREN'S SERIES: (1) Daryl Busby and Tom J. Astle, *Adventures in Wonderland* (DISNEY); (2) Norman Stiles, Lou Berger, Molly Boylan, Sara Compton, Judy Freudberg, Tony Geiss, Ian Ellis James, Emily Perl Kingsley, David Korr, Sonia Manzano, Joey Mazzarino, Nancy Sans, Luis Santeiro,

Josh Selig, Jon Stone, Cathi Turow, Belinda Ward, John Weidman, *Sesame Street* (PBS)

OUTSTANDING WRITING IN A CHILDREN'S SPECIAL: Ann Dunkleberger, "Other Mothers," *CBS Schoolbreak Special* (CBS)

OUTSTANDING WRITING IN AN ANIMATED PROGRAM: Ray Bradbury, "Halloween Tree" (SYNDICATED)

OUTSTANDING ACHIEVEMENT IN WRITING—SPECIAL CLASS: Terrence McDonnell, Steven Dorfman, Kathy Easterling, Debbie Griffin, Frederik Pohl IV, Steve D. Tamerius, *Jeopardy!* (SYNDICATED)

1994–1995

I. PRIME TIME AWARDS

OUTSTANDING COMEDY SERIES: *Frasier* (NBC); Peter Casey, David Angell, David Lee, Christopher Lloyd, executive producers; Vic Rauseo and Linda Morris, co-executive producers; Maggie Randell, Elias Davis, David Pollock, producers; Chuck Ranberg, Anne Flett-Giordano, Jo Keenan, coproducers

OUTSTANDING DRAMA SERIES: *NYPD Blue* (ABC); Steven Bochco, David Milch, Gregory Hoblit, Mark Tinker, executive producers; Michael Robin, Walon Green, Charles H. Eglee, Channing Gibson, co-executive producers; Ted Mann, producer; Burton Armus, Gardner Stern, Steven DePaul, coproducers; Robert Doherty, coordinating producer; Bill Clark, consulting producer

OUTSTANDING MINISERIES: *Joseph* (TNT); Gerald Rafshoon, executive producer; Lorenzo Minoli, producer; Laura Fattori, line producer

OUTSTANDING VARIETY, MUSIC OR COMEDY SERIES: *The Tonight Show with Jay Leno* (NBC); Debbie Vickers, executive producer; Patti Grant, supervising producer; Larry Goitia, line producer; Bill Royce, coproducer; Jay Leno, host

OUTSTANDING INFORMATIONAL SERIES: (1) *Baseball* (PBS); Ken Burns, producer/director; Lynn Novick, producer; Geoffrey C. Ward and Ken Burns, writers; John Chancellor, narrator; (2) *TV Nation* (NBC); Michael Moore, executive producer/director/writer/host; Kathleen Glynn, producer; Jerry Kupfer, supervising producer; Eric Zicklin, Stephen Sherrill, Chris Kelly, Randy Cohen, writers

OUTSTANDING MADE FOR TELEVISION MOVIE: "Indictment: The McMartin Trial" (HBO); Oliver Stone, Janet Yang, Abby Mann, executive producers; Diana Pokorny, producer

OUTSTANDING ANIMATED PROGRAM: *The Simpsons* (FOX); David Mirkin, James L. Brooks, Matt Groening, Sam Simon, executive producers; Jace Richdale, George Meyer, J. Michael Mendel, Greg Daniels, Bill Oakley, David Sacks, Josh Weinstein, Jonathan Collier, Richard Raynis, Richard Sakai, Mike Scully, David Silverman, producers; Al Jean and Mike Reiss, consulting producers; Phil Roman, animation executive producer; Bill Schultz and Michael Wolf, animation producers; Greg Daniels, writer; Jim Reardon, director

OUTSTANDING CULTURAL PROGRAM: "Verdi's 'La Traviata' with the New York City Opera," *Live from Lincoln Center* (PBS); John Guberman, producer; Marc Bauman, coordinating producer

OUTSTANDING CHILDREN'S PROGRAM: "The World Wildlife Fund Presents 'Going, Going, Almost Gone! Animals in Danger!' " (HBO); Sheila Nevins, executive producer; Ellen Goosenberg Kent, producer; Carole Rosen, senior producer

OUTSTANDING INFORMATIONAL SPECIAL: (1) "Taxicab Confessions" (HBO); Sheila Nevins, executive producer; Joe Gantz and Harry Gantz, producers/directors; (2) "The United States Holocaust Memorial Museum Presents: One Survivor Remembers" (HBO); Kary Antholis, producer; Sheila Nevins, senior producer; Michael Berenbaum and Raye Farr, coproducers

OUTSTANDING VARIETY, MUSIC OR COMEDY SPECIAL: "Barbra Streisand The Concert" (HBO); Martin Erlichman and Gary Smith, executive producers; Barbra Streisand and Dwight Hemion, producers

OUTSTANDING LEAD ACTOR IN A DRAMA SERIES: Mandy Patinkin, *Chicago Hope* (CBS)

OUTSTANDING LEAD ACTRESS IN A DRAMA SERIES: Kathy Baker, *Picket Fences* (CBS)

OUTSTANDING LEAD ACTOR IN A COMEDY SERIES: Kelsey Grammer, *Frasier* (NBC)

OUTSTANDING LEAD ACTRESS IN A COMEDY SERIES: Candice Bergen, *Murphy Brown* (CBS)

OUTSTANDING LEAD ACTOR IN A MINISERIES OR A SPECIAL: Raul Julia, "The Burning Season" (HBO)

OUTSTANDING LEAD ACTRESS IN A MINISERIES OR A SPECIAL: Glenn Close, "Serving in Silence: The Margarethe Cammermeyer Story" (NBC)

OUTSTANDING SUPPORTING ACTOR IN A DRAMA SERIES: Ray Walston, *Picket Fences* (CBS)

OUTSTANDING SUPPORTING ACTRESS IN A DRAMA SERIES: Julianna Margulies, *ER* (NBC)

OUTSTANDING SUPPORTING ACTOR IN A COMEDY SERIES: David Hyde Pierce, *Frasier* (NBC)

OUTSTANDING SUPPORTING ACTRESS IN A COMEDY SERIES: Christine Baranski, *Cybill* (CBS)

OUTSTANDING SUPPORTING ACTOR IN A MINISERIES OR A SPECIAL: Donald Sutherland, "Citizen X" (HBO)

OUTSTANDING SUPPORTING ACTRESS IN A MINISERIES OR A SPECIAL: (1) Judy Davis, "Serving in Silence: The Margarethe Cammermeyer Story" (NBC); (2) Shirley Knight, "Indictment: The McMartin Trial" (HBO)

OUTSTANDING GUEST ACTOR IN A DRAMA SERIES: Paul Winfield, "Enemy Lines," *Picket Fences* (CBS)

OUTSTANDING GUEST ACTRESS IN A DRAMA SERIES: Shirley Knight, "Large Mouth Bass," *NYPD Blue* (ABC)

OUTSTANDING GUEST ACTOR IN A COMEDY SERIES: Carl Reiner, "The Alan Brady Show," *Mad About You* (NBC)

OUTSTANDING GUEST ACTRESS IN A COMEDY SERIES: Cyndi Lauper, "Money Changes Everything," *Mad About You* (NBC)

OUTSTANDING INDIVIDUAL PERFORMANCE IN A VARIETY OR MUSIC PROGRAM: Barbra Streisand, "Barbra Streisand The Concert" (HBO)

OUTSTANDING VOICE-OVER PERFORMANCE: Jonathan Katz, *Dr. Katz, Professional Therapist* (COM)

OUTSTANDING INDIVIDUAL ACHIEVEMENT IN DIRECTING IN A DRAMA SERIES: Mimi Leder, "Love's Labor Lost," *ER* (NBC)

OUTSTANDING INDIVIDUAL ACHIEVEMENT IN DIRECTING IN A COMEDY SERIES: David Lee, "The Marchmaker," *Frasier* (NBC)

OUTSTANDING INDIVIDUAL ACHIEVEMENT IN DIRECTING FOR A MINISERIES OR A SPECIAL: John Frankenheimer, "The Burning Season" (HBO)

OUTSTANDING INDIVIDUAL ACHIEVEMENT IN DIRECTING IN A VARIETY OR MUSIC PROGRAM: Jeff Margolis, "The 67th Annual Academy Awards" (ABC)

OUTSTANDING INDIVIDUAL ACHIEVEMENT—CULTURAL PROGRAMMING: David Hinton, director, "Two by Dove," *Great Performances/Dance in America* (PBS)

OUTSTANDING INDIVIDUAL ACHIEVEMENT IN WRITING IN A DRAMA SERIES: Lance A. Gentile, "Love's Labor Lost," *ER* (NBC)

OUTSTANDING INDIVIDUAL ACHIEVEMENT IN WRITING IN A COMEDY SERIES: Chuck Ranberg and Annie Flett-Giordano, "An Affair to Forget," *Frasier* (NBC)

OUTSTANDING INDIVIDUAL ACHIEVEMENT IN WRITING IN A MINISERIES OR A SPECIAL: Alison Cross, "Serving in Silence: The Margarethe Cammermeyer Story" (NBC)

OUTSTANDING INDIVIDUAL ACHIEVEMENT IN WRITING IN A VARIETY OR MUSIC PROGRAM: Eddie Feldman, writing supervisor, Jeff Cesario, Ed Driscoll, David Feldman, Gregory Greenberg, Dennis Miller, Kevin Rooney, writers, *Dennis Miller Live* (HBO)

II. DAYTIME AWARDS

OUTSTANDING DRAMA SERIES: *General Hospital* (ABC); Wendy Riche, executive producer; Shelley Curtis and Francesca James, supervising producers; Jerry Balme and Bob Bardo, coordinating producers; Julie Carruthers, producer

OUTSTANDING TALK SHOW: *The Oprah Winfrey Show* (SYNDICATED); Dianne

Atkinson-Hudson, Debra DiMaio, executive producers; Oprah Winfrey, supervising producer; Ellen Rakieten, David Boul, Alice McGee, senior producers; Dana Newton and Legrande Green, producers

OUTSTANDING SERVICE SHOW: *Martha Stewart Living Television* (SYNDICATED); Leslie McNeil, executive producer

OUTSTANDING GAME/AUDIENCE PARTICIPATION SHOW: *Jeopardy!* (SYNDICATED); Merv Griffin, executive producer; George Vosburgh, producer

OUTSTANDING CHILDREN'S SERIES: *Nick News* (SYNDICATED); Linda Ellerbee and Rolfe Tessem, executive producers; Murr Lebey, coordinating producer; Bob Brienza and Mark Lyons, producers

OUTSTANDING PRE-SCHOOL CHILDREN'S SERIES: *Sesame Street* (PBS); Michael Loman, executive producer; Lisa Simon, supervising producer; Arlene Sherman, coordinating producer; Yvonne Hill Ogunkoya, producer

OUTSTANDING ANIMATED CHILDREN'S PROGRAM: *Where on Earth Is Carmen Sandiego?* (FOX); Andy Heyward, Robby London, Michael Maliani, Michael Uslan, Benjamin Melniker, executive producers; Sean Roche, coordinating producer

OUTSTANDING CHILDREN'S SPECIAL: "A Child Betrayed: The Calvin Mire Story," *Lifestories: Families in Crisis* (HBO)

OUSTANDING SPECIAL CLASS PROGRAM: *Talk Soup* (E!); Alex Duda, executive producer; Greg Kinnear, executive producer/host; Angela Gordon, senior producer; Mark Turner and David Bernstein, producers

OUTSTANDING LEAD ACTOR IN A DRAMA SERIES: Justin Deas, *Guiding Light* (CBS)

OUTSTANDING LEAD ACTRESS IN A DRAMA SERIES: Erika Slezak, *One Life to Live* (ABC)

OUTSTANDING SUPPORTING ACTOR IN A DRAMA SERIES: Jerry Ver Dorn, *Guiding Light* (CBS)

OUTSTANDING SUPPORTING ACTRESS IN A DRAMA SERIES: Rena Sofer, *General Hospital* (ABC)

OUTSTANDING YOUNGER ACTOR IN A DRAMA SERIES: Jonathan Jackson, *General Hospital* (ABC)

OUTSTANDING YOUNGER ACTRESS IN A DRAMA SERIES: Sarah Michelle Gellar, *All My Children* (ABC)

OUTSTANDING TALK SHOW HOST: Oprah Winfrey, *The Oprah Winfrey Show* (SYNDICATED)

OUTSTANDING SERVICE SHOW HOST: Martha Stewart, *Martha Stewart Living Television* (SYNDICATED)

OUTSTANDING GAME SHOW HOST: Bob Barker, *The Price Is Right* (CBS)

OUTSTANDING PERFORMER IN A CHILDREN'S SERIES: Shari Lewis, *Lamb Chop's Play-Along* (PBS)

OUTSTANDING PERFORMER IN AN ANIMATED PROGRAM: Lily Tomlin, *The Magic School Bus* (PBS)

OUTSTANDING PERFORMER IN A CHILDREN'S SPECIAL: Hal Linden, "The Writing on the Wall," *CBS Schoolbreak Special* (CBS)

OUTSTANDING DRAMA SERIES DIRECTING TEAM: *All My Children* (ABC); Christopher Goutman, Henry Kaplan, Conal O'Brien, James A. Baffico, directors; Barbara Martin Simmons, Shirley Simmons, Robin Maizes, Sybil Costello, associate directors

OUTSTANDING DIRECTING IN A TALK SHOW: Bryan Russo, *Donahue* (SYNDICATED)

OUTSTANDING DIRECTING IN A SERVICE SHOW: Russell Morash, *This Old House* (PBS)

OUTSTANDING DIRECTING IN A GAME/AUDIENCE PARTICIPATION SHOW: Kevin McCarthy, *Jeopardy!* (SYNDICATED)

OUTSTANDING DIRECTING IN A CHILDREN'S SERIES: Ted May, Jon Stone, Lisa Simon, Emily Squires, *Sesame Street* (PBS)

OUTSTANDING DIRECTING IN A CHILDREN'S SPECIAL: Juan Jose Campanella, "A Child Betrayed: The Calvin Mire Story," *Lifestories: Families in Crisis* (HBO)

OUTSTANDING SPECIAL CLASS DIRECTING: Charles Jarrott, "A Promise Kept: The Oksana Baiul Story" (CBS)

OUTSTANDING DRAMA SERIES WRITING TEAM: *General Hospital* (ABC); Claire Labine, Matthew Labine, Eleanor Mancusi, Ralph Ellis, Meg Bennett, Michele Val Jean, Lewis Arlt, Stephanie Braxton, Karen Harris, Judith Pinsker, writers

OUTSTANDING WRITING IN A CHILDREN'S SERIES: *Sesame Street* (PBS); Norman Stiles, head writer; Lou Berger, Molly Boylan, Sara Compton, Christine Ferraro, Judy Freudberg, Tony Geiss, Ian Ellis James, Emily P. Kingsley, David Korr, Sonia Manzano, Joey Mazzarino, Jeff Moss, Adam Rudman, Nancy Sans, Luis Santeiro, Josh Selig, Jon Stone, Cathi R. Turow, writers

OUTSTANDING WRITING IN A CHILDREN'S SPECIAL: Bruce Harmon, "A Child Betrayed: The Calvin Mire Story," *Lifestories: Families in Crisis* (HBO)

OUTSTANDING SPECIAL CLASS WRITING: Bob Carruthers, "Dinosaurs: Myths & Reality" (DIS)

OUTSTANDING ACHIEVEMENT IN ANIMATION: *The Rugrats* (NIK); Jim Duffy, Steve Socki, Howard E. Baker, directors; Jonathan Greenberg, Peter Gaffney, Rachel Lipman, writers

The George Foster Peabody Broadcasting Awards were established in 1940, and are administered by the Henry W. Grady School of Journalism at the University of Georgia. Awards are given in radio, television and related fields, but only those pertaining to national television are listed here. The award categories have varied from year to year, and in recent years the categories themselves have been abolished.

1948

OUTSTANDING CONTRIBUTION TO THE ART OF TELEVISION: *Actors' Studio* (ABC)
OUTSTANDING CHILDREN'S PROGRAM: *Howdy Doody* (NBC)

1949

ENTERTAINMENT: *The Ed Wynn Show* (CBS)
EDUCATION: *Crusade in Europe* (ABC)
REPORTING AND INTERPRETATION OF THE NEWS: *The United Nations in Action* (CBS)
OUTSTANDING CHILDREN'S PROGRAM: *Kukla, Fran and Ollie* (NBC)

1950

ENTERTAINMENT: Jimmy Durante (NBC)
CHILDREN'S PROGRAMS: (1) *Saturday at the Zoo* (ABC); and (2) *Zoo Parade* (NBC)
SPECIAL AWARD: To ABC (Robert E. Kintner, president, and associates Robert Saudek and Joseph McDonald) "for their courageous stand in resisting organized pressures and their reaffirmation of basic American principles."

1951

ENTERTAINMENT (NONMUSICAL): *Celanese Theatre* (ABC)
ENTERTAINMENT (MUSICAL): Gian Carlo Menotti, "Amahl and the Night Visitors" (NBC)
EDUCATION: *What in the World* (WCAU-TV, Philadelphia)
NEWS AND INTERPRETATION: Edward R. Murrow and *See It Now* (CBS)

1952

ENTERTAINMENT: (1) *Mr. Peepers* (NBC); and (2) *Your Hit Parade* (NBC)
EDUCATION: *The Johns Hopkins Science Review* (DUMONT)
NEWS: *Meet the Press* (NBC)
YOUTH AND CHILDREN'S PROGRAMS: *Ding Dong School* (NBC)
SPECIAL AWARD: *Victory at Sea* (NBC)

1953

ENTERTAINMENT: (1) *(Philco) Television Playhouse* (NBC); and (2) Imogene Coca (*Your Show of Shows*) (NBC)
MUSIC: *NBC Television Opera Theatre* (NBC)

EDUCATION: (1) *Cavalcade of Books* (KNXT-TV, Los Angeles); and (2) *Camera Three* (WCBS-TV, New York)
YOUTH AND CHILDREN'S PROGRAMS: *Mr. Wizard* (NBC)
SPECIAL AWARD: Edward R. Murrow (CBS)
PROMOTION OF INTERNATIONAL UNDERSTANDING THROUGH TELEVISION: British Broadcasting Corporation for coverage of the coronation

1954

ENTERTAINMENT: George Gobel (NBC)
EDUCATION: *Adventure* (CBS)
NEWS (RADIO AND TELEVISION): John Daly (ABC)
YOUTH AND CHILDREN'S PROGRAMS: *Disneyland* (ABC)
SPECIAL AWARDS: (1) *Omnibus* (CBS); and (2) *The Search* (CBS)
NATIONAL PUBLIC SERVICE: *Industry on Parade* (National Association of Manufacturers)

1955

ENTERTAINMENT: (1) Jackie Gleason (CBS); and (2) Perry Como (NBC)
DRAMATIC ENTERTAINMENT: *Producers' Showcase* (NBC)
MUSIC (RADIO AND TELEVISION): *Voice of Firestone* (ABC)
EDUCATION: Dr. Frank Baxter (KNXT-TV, Los Angeles)
NEWS: Douglas Edwards (CBS)
YOUTH AND CHILDREN'S PROGRAMS: *Lassie* (CBS)
PUBLIC SERVICE (RADIO AND TELEVISION): Sylvester L. Weaver, Jr., NBC, "for pioneering program concepts"
PROMOTION OF INTERNATIONAL UNDERSTANDING (RADIO AND TELEVISION): Quincy Howe (ABC)

1956

ENTERTAINMENT: *The Ed Sullivan Show* (CBS)
EDUCATION: *You Are There* (CBS)
NEWS: ABC, John Daly and associates (for convention coverage)
YOUTH AND CHILDREN'S PROGRAMS: *Youth Wants to Know* (NBC)
PUBLIC SERVICE: "World in Crisis" (CBS)
WRITING: Rod Serling
PROMOTION OF INTERNATIONAL UNDERSTANDING: "The Secret Life of Danny Kaye" (UNICEF)
PROMOTION OF INTERNATIONAL UNDERSTANDING (SPECIAL AWARD): United Nations Radio and Television
SPECIAL AWARD: Jack Gould of *The New York Times* (for his writings on radio and television)

1957

ENTERTAINMENT (NONMUSICAL): *Hallmark Hall of Fame* (NBC)
ENTERTAINMENT (MUSICAL): *The Dinah Shore Chevy Show* (NBC)
EDUCATION: *The Heritage Series* (WQED-TV, Pittsburgh)
NEWS: ABC, for "Prologue '58' and other significant news coverage"
NEWS (RADIO AND TELEVISION): CBS, "for depth and range"
YOUTH AND CHILDREN'S PROGRAMS: *Captain Kangaroo* (CBS)
PUBLIC SERVICE: *The Last Word* (CBS)
CONTRIBUTION TO INTERNATIONAL UNDERSTANDING: Bob Hope (NBC)
SPECIAL AWARDS: (1) NBC, for "outstanding contribution to education"; and (2) Wes-

tinghouse Broadcasting Company, Inc., for "its Boston Conference and the high quality of its public service broadcasting"

1958

DRAMATIC ENTERTAINMENT: *Playhouse 90* (CBS)
ENTERTAINMENT WITH HUMOR: *The Steve Allen Show* (NBC)
MUSICAL ENTERTAINMENT: "Lincoln Presents Leonard Bernstein and the New York Philharmonic" (CBS)
EDUCATION: *Continental Classroom* (NBC)
NEWS: *The Huntley-Brinkley Report* (NBC)
PROGRAMS FOR YOUTH: *College News Conference* (ABC)
PUBLIC SERVICE: CBS
WRITING: James Costigan, for "Little Moon of Alban," *Hallmark Hall of Fame* (NBC)
CONTRIBUTION TO INTERNATIONAL UNDERSTANDING: "M.D. International" (NBC)
SPECIAL AWARDS: (1) "An Evening with Fred Astaire" (NBC); and (2) Orson Welles, "Fountain of Youth," *Colgate Theatre* (NBC)

1959

ENTERTAINMENT (NONMUSICAL): (1) *The Play of the Week* (WNTA-TV), Newark); and (2) David Susskind, executive producer, "The Moon and Sixpence" (NBC)
ENTERTAINMENT (MUSICAL): (1) *The Bell Telephone Hour* (NBC); and (2) *Great Music from Chicago* (WGN-TV, Chicago)
EDUCATION: (1) "Decisions" (WGBH-TV, Boston, and the World Affairs Council); and (2) "The Population Explosion" (CBS) ·
NEWS: "Khrushchev Abroad" (ABC)
CONTRIBUTION TO INTERNATIONAL UNDERSTANDING: (1) *The Ed Sullivan Show* (CBS); and (2) *Small World* (CBS)
SPECIAL AWARDS: (1) Dr. Frank Stanton (CBS); and (2) "The Lost Class of '59" (CBS)

1960

ENTERTAINMENT: "The Fabulous Fifties" (CBS)
EDUCATION: *White Paper* series (NBC)
NEWS: *The Texaco Huntley-Brinkley Report* (NBC)
PROGRAMS FOR YOUTH: *G-E College Bowl* (CBS)
PROGRAMS FOR CHILDREN: *The Shari Lewis Show* (NBC)
PUBLIC SERVICE: *CBS Reports* (CBS)
CONTRIBUTION TO INTERNATIONAL UNDERSTANDING: CBS (for its Olympics coverage)
EDUCATION (RADIO AND TELEVISION): Broadcasting and Film Commission, National Council of Churches of Christ in the U.S.A.
SPECIAL AWARD: Dr. Frank Stanton (CBS)

1961

ENTERTAINMENT: *The Bob Newhart Show* (NBC)
EDUCATION: (1) *An Age of Kings* (BBC); and (2) "Vincent Van Gogh: A Self-Portrait" (NBC)
NEWS: *David Brinkley's Journal* (NBC)
YOUTH AND CHILDREN'S PROGRAMS: *Expedition!* (ABC)
CONTRIBUTION TO INTERNATIONAL UNDERSTANDING: Walter Lippmann and CBS
SPECIAL AWARDS: (1) Fred W. Friendly, CBS; (2) Newton N. Minow, chairman, Federal Communications Commission; and (3) Capital Cities Broadcasting Corporation, for "Verdict for Tomorrow: The Eichmann Trial on Television"

1962

ENTERTAINMENT: (1) Carol Burnett (CBS); and (2) *The Dupont Show of the Week* (NBC)

EDUCATION: *Biography* (Official Films, Inc.)

NEWS: Walter Cronkite (CBS)

YOUTH AND CHILDREN'S PROGRAMS: (1) *Exploring* (NBC); and (2) *Walt Disney's Wonderful World of Color* (NBC)

PUBLIC SERVICE: "A Tour of the White House with Mrs. John F. Kennedy" (CBS)

CONTRIBUTION TO INTERNATIONAL UNDERSTANDING: *Adlai Stevenson Reports* (ABC)

SPECIAL AWARDS: (1) William R. McAndrew and NBC News; and (2) Television Information Office of the National Association of Broadcasters (for a study on local children's programming)

1963

ENTERTAINMENT: (1) *The Danny Kaye Show* (CBS); and (2) *Mr. Novak* (NBC)

EDUCATION: (1) "American Revolution '63" (NBC); and (2) "Saga of Western Man" (ABC)

NEWS: Eric Sevareid (CBS)

PUBLIC SERVICE: "Storm over the Supreme Court," *CBS Reports* (CBS)

CONTRIBUTION TO INTERNATIONAL UNDERSTANDING: "Town Meeting of the World" CBS, and Dr. Frank Stanton, president

SPECIAL AWARD: To the broadcasting industry of the United States for its coverage of President John F. Kennedy and related events

1964

AWARDS NOT GIVEN IN SPECIFIC CATEGORIES

(1) Joyce Hall (president, Hallmark Cards, Inc., sponsor of *Hallmark Hall of Fame*); (2) *Profiles in Courage* (NBC); (3) *CBS Reports* (CBS); (4) William H. Lawrence, ABC News; (5) "The Louvre" (NBC); (6) Julia Child, *The French Chef* (WGBH-TV, Boston, and NET); (7) Intertel (International Television Federation); (8) Burr Tillstrom; and (9) The networks and the broadcasting industry, "for inescapably confronting the American public with the realities of racial discontent"

1965

ENTERTAINMENT: (1) "Frank Sinatra—a Man and His Music" (NBC); (2) "The Julie Andrews Show" (NBC); and (3) "My Name is Barbra" (CBS)

EDUCATION: National Educational Television

NEWS: (1) Frank McGee (NBC); (2) Morley Safer (CBS); and (3) KTLA-TV, Los Angeles

YOUTH AND CHILDREN'S PROGRAMS: "A Charlie Brown Christmas" (CBS)

PUBLIC SERVICE: "KKK—The Invisible Empire," *CBS Reports* (CBS)

CONTRIBUTION TO INTERNATIONAL UNDERSTANDING: Xerox Corporation

INNOVATION: "The National Driver's Test" (CBS)

MOST INVENTIVE ART DOCUMENTARY: "The Mystery of Stonehenge" (CBS)

SPECIAL AWARD: "A Visit to Washington with Mrs. Lyndon B. Johnson—On Behalf of a More Beautiful America" (ABC)

1966

ENTERTAINMENT: "A Christmas Memory," *ABC Stage 67* (ABC)

EDUCATION: (1) "American White Paper: Organized Crime in the United States" (NBC); and (2) *National Geographic Specials* (CBS)

NEWS: Harry Reasoner (CBS)

YOUTH AND CHILDREN'S PROGRAMS: "The World of Stuart Little" (NBC)

PROMOTION OF INTERNATIONAL UNDERSTANDING: (1) *ABC's Wide World of Sports* (ABC); and (2) "Siberia: A Day in Irkutsk" (NBC)

LOCAL NEWS AND ENTERTAINMENT: *Kup's Show* (WBKB-TV, Chicago)

SPECIAL AWARDS: (1) *The Bell Telephone Hour* (NBC); (2) Tom John (CBS) (for art direction in "Death of a Salesman," "The Strollin' Twenties," and "Color Me Barbra"); (3) National Educational Television; and (4) "The Poisoned Air," *CBS Reports* (CBS)

1967

ENTERTAINMENT: (1) *CBS Playhouse* (CBS); and (2) "An Evening at Tanglewood" (NBC)

NEWS ANALYSIS AND COMMENTARY (RADIO AND TELEVISION): Eric Sevareid (CBS)

YOUTH OR CHILDREN'S PROGRAMS: *CBS Children's Film Festival* (CBS)

PROMOTION OF INTERNATIONAL UNDERSTANDING: "Africa" (ABC)

SPECIAL AWARDS: (1) *The Ed Sullivan Show* (CBS); (2) Bob Hope (NBC Radio and Television); and (3) Dr. James R. Killian, Jr., Massachusetts Institute of Technology (broadcasting education); and (4) *Meet the Press* (NBC Radio and Television)

1968

ENTERTAINMENT: *Playhouse* (NET)

EDUCATION: (1) Robert Cromie and *Book Beat* (WTTW-TV, Chicago); and (2) ABC, "for its creative 1968 documentaries"

NEWS: Charles Kuralt and "On the Road" (CBS)

YOUTH OR CHILDREN'S PROGRAMS: *Mister Rogers' Neighborhood* (NET)

PUBLIC SERVICE: Westinghouse Broadcasting Company, for "One Nation Indivisible"

PROMOTION OF INTERNATIONAL UNDERSTANDING: ABC, for its coverage of the 1968 Olympic Games

SPECIAL AWARD: "Hunger in America," *CBS Reports* (CBS)

1969

ENTERTAINMENT: (1) "Experiment in Television" (NBC); and (2) Curt Gowdy, sportscaster

EDUCATION: (1) *The Advocates* (WGBH-TV, Boston, and KCET-TV, Los Angeles); and (2) "Who Killed Lake Erie?" (NBC)

NEWS: Frank Reynolds (ABC)

YOUTH OR CHILDREN'S PROGRAMS: *Sesame Street* (Children's Television Workshop)

PUBLIC SERVICE: Tom Pettit (NBC)

PROMOTION OF INTERNATIONAL UNDERSTANDING: "The Japanese" (CBS)

LOCAL PUBLIC SERVICE: "The Negro in Indianapolis" (WFBM-TV, Indianapolis)

SPECIAL AWARDS: (1) Bing Crosby (outstanding service to television); (2) Chet Huntley (contributions to television news); and (3) "J. T.," *CBS Children's Hour* (CBS)

1970

ENTERTAINMENT: (1) "The Andersonville Trial" (PBS and KCET-TV, Los Angeles); (2) *Evening at Pops* (PBS); and (3) *The Flip Wilson Show* (NBC)

EDUCATION: "Eye of the Storm" (ABC)

NEWS: *60 Minutes* (CBS)

YOUTH OR CHILDREN'S PROGRAMS: (1) The "Dr. Seuss" programs (NBC); and (2) *Hot Dog* (NBC)
PUBLIC SERVICE: "Migrant: An NBC White Paper" (NBC)
PROMOTION OF INTERNATIONAL UNDERSTANDING: *Civilisation* (BBC)
SPECIAL AWARD: "The Selling of the Pentagon" (CBS)

1971

ENTERTAINMENT: (1) "The American Revolution: 1770–1783, A Conversation with Lord North" (CBS); (2) "Brian's Song" (ABC and William Blinn); and (3) NBC, for its dramatic programming
NEWS: John Rich (NBC Radio and Television)
YOUTH OR CHILDREN'S PROGRAMS: *Make a Wish* (ABC)
PUBLIC SERVICE: "This Child Is Rated X" (NBC)
PROMOTION OF INTERNATIONAL UNDERSTANDING: "United Nations Day Concert with Pablo Casals" (United Nations Television)
SPECIAL AWARDS: (1) George Heinemann of NBC (for contributions to children's programming); (2) Mississippi Authority for Educational Television and William Smith, executive director; and (3) Dr. Frank Stanton, president, CBS, Inc.

1972

AWARDS NOT GIVEN IN SPECIFIC CATEGORIES

(1) CBS, for *The Waltons* ("A sensitive dramatic interpretation of life during the Depression"); (2) NBC, for "Jack Lemmon in 'S Wonderful, 'S Marvelous, 'S Gershwin," "Singer Presents Liza with a 'Z'," and "The Timex All-Star Swing Festival" ("three special programs devoted to Twentieth Century American music"); (3) BBC and NBC, for *The Search for the Nile* ("outstanding series of documentaries"); (4) NBC, for "Pensions: The Broken Promise" (investigative documentary); (5) Bill Monroe, NBC-TV, Washington editor of *Today* ("excellence in news reporting"); (6) Alistair Cooke ("for a meaningful perspective look at America"); (7) ABC, for ABC Afterschool Specials ("an innovative series for young people"); (8) CBS, for *Captain Kangaroo* ("a long-running show for young children"); (9) WNET, New York, and BBC, for "The Restless Earth" (promotion of international understanding); (10) ABC for "XX Olympiad" (sports coverage)

1973

ENTERTAINMENT: (1) "Myshkin" (WTIU-TV, Bloomington, Ind.); and (2) NBC, ABC, and CBS (joint award for "outstanding contributions to television drama as evidenced by 'The Red Pony' [NBC], 'Pueblo' and 'The Glass Menagerie' [ABC], and 'CBS Playhouse 90: The Catholics' [CBS]")
EDUCATION: (1) ABC ("as evidenced by 'The First and Essential Freedom' and 'Learning Can Be Fun' "); and (2) *Dusty's Treehouse* (KNXT-TV, Los Angeles)
NEWS: *Close-Up* (ABC)
YOUTH AND CHILDREN'S PROGRAMS: (1) "The Borrowers," *Hallmark Hall of Fame* (NBC); and (2) "Street of the Flower Boxes," *NBC Children's Theatre* (NBC)
PUBLIC SERVICE: Pamela Ilott (CBS) (executive producer of *Lamp unto My Feet* and *Look Up and Live*)
SPECIAL AWARDS: (1) "The Energy Crisis . . . An American White Paper" (NBC); (2) Joe Garagiola, for *The Baseball World of Joe Garagiola* (NBC); and (3) Peter Lisagor, *Chicago Daily News* (for contributions to broadcast news)

1974

(1) NBC, for "distinguished . . . dramatic programs, as evidenced by 'The Execution of Private Slovik,' 'The Law' and 'IBM Presents Clarence Darrow' "; (2) CBS, for the "four-part series of dramatic specials based on the life of Benjamin Franklin"; (3) WNET, New York, and PBS, for *Theatre in America;* (4) WGBH-TV, Boston, for *NOVA;* (5) Carl Stern of NBC News, for "exceptional journalistic enterprise during a time of national crisis"; (6) Fred Graham of CBS News, for "thoroughly professional and consistently penetrating reporting during a time of national crisis"; (7) ABC, for "Free to Be . . . You and Me" (excellence in programming for young people); (8) NBC, for *Go!* (excellence in children's programming); (9) ABC, for "Sadat: Action Biography" (news documentary); (10) NBC, for "Tornado! 4:40 P.M., Xenia, Ohio" (news documentary); (11) The National Public Affairs Center for Television (NPACT), for "outstanding overall effort to bring meaningful public affairs programming to the nation"; and (12) Julian Goodman, chairman of the board of NBC, for "outstanding work in the area of first amendment rights and privileges for broadcasting"

1975

(1) CBS, for *M*A*S*H* ("a creative entertainment effort . . . with first-rate humor"); (2) ABC, for *ABC Theatre:* "Love Among the Ruins" ("entertainment programming of the highest order"); (3) CBS News, for "Mr. Rooney Goes to Washington" ("outstanding and meritorious service"); (4) CBS News, for "The American Assassins" (news documentary); (5) NBC, for *Weekend* ("a new and refreshing approach to television programming"); (6) Charles Kuralt, CBS News, for "On the Road to '76" ("a first-rate effort"); (7) ABC, for *The ABC Afterschool Specials* (outstanding children's programming); (8) Group W, for *Call It Macaroni* (outstanding children's programming); (9) Alphaventure, for *Big Blue Marble* (outstanding children's programming); (10) Kaiser Broadcasting, for *Snipets* ("an excellent way in which children can learn from television"); (11) Dr. James Killian, Boston, for "outstanding contributions to educational television"

1976

(1) NBC, for "Sybil" (outstanding dramatic program); (2) ABC, for "Eleanor and Franklin" (outstanding historical drama); (3) KCET/28, Los Angeles, for *Visions* ("for giving extensive new opportunities to writers and independent filmmakers"); (4) WETA-TV, Washington, D.C., for *In Performance at Wolf Trap* ("a superb example of the use of television to expand exponentially the audience for great cultural events"); (5) Perry Como ("with especial reference to . . . 'Perry Como's Christmas in Austria' " [NBC]); (6) Tomorrow Entertainment, Inc., for "Judge Horton and the Scottsboro Boys" ("a program representative of the excellence one has come to expect from Thomas W. Moore and his associates"); (7) CBS News for *60 Minutes* (broadcast journalism); (8) WNET/13, New York, for *The Adams Chronicles* ("an impressive endeavor"); (9) ABC News, for "Suddenly an Eagle" (historical documentary); (10) ABC News, for *Animals Animals Animals* (documentary series); (11) Hughes Rudd and Bruce Morton of *The CBS Morning News* ("for their inventive and creative writing coupled with their reporting of significant and insignificant events"); (12) Sy Pearlman, producer of *Weekend*'s "Sawyer Brothers" segment (NBC) ("an outstanding example of the power of television to investigate and uncover new facts resulting in a reexamination of criminal justice in this case"); (13) CBS News, for "In Celebration of US" (coverage of July 4, 1976): (14) Jim Karayn and the League of Women Voters for " '76 Presidential Debates" ("for persistence against formidable obstacles which resulted in a series of joint appearances"); (15) WETA-TV, Washington, D.C., and WNET/13, New York, for "A Conversation with Jimmy Carter" (demonstrating "the tremendous impact

through which television brought Candidate Jimmy Carter to the attention of the American people"); (16) CBS News for *In the News* (enabling "children to better understand events, people and concepts"); (17) ABC Sports, for its Olympics coverage

1977

(1) David Wolper and ABC-TV, for *Roots* ("for dramatically exposing us to an aspect of our history"); (2) Norman Lear, for *All in the Family* ("for establishing the right to express social comment in a social comedy, for devising the technique of humor as the bridge to better understanding of national issues, for presenting an excellent production in every way, for providing the public with that greatest of all healers, humor"); (3) London Weekend Television, for *Upstairs, Downstairs* ("it has no equal in the level of its intelligence, its humanity, and its performances . . . a model of civilized entertainment"); (4) MTM Productions, for *The Mary Tyler Moore Show* ("for maintaining a consistent high level of characterization and writing . . . and for presenting an affectionate and sympathetic portrayal of the career woman in today's changing society"); (5) WNET/13, New York, and WETA, Arlington, Virginia, for *The MacNeil-Lehrer Report* ("an example of broadcast journalism of the highest order"); (6) WCBS-TV (New York), for *Camera Three* ("its consistently high quality fare has won a remarkably loyal audience"); (7) Steve Allen, for *Meeting of Minds* (an "ingenious re-creation of the essence of historical personages who come alive in a theatrical form rich in philosophical fireworks and engaging wit"); (8) Lorimar Productions, for "Green Eyes" ("a touching, moving treatment of an excellent script—the story of a young, black veteran of the war in Vietnam . . . desperately searching for the child he fathered but left behind"); (9) NBC-TV, Arthur Rankin and Jules Bass, for "The Hobbit" ("a vividly original animated version of J.R.R. Tolkien's classic"); (10) NBC-TV, for "Tut: The Boy King" ("exceptional accomplishment in bringing outstanding cultural treasures to a widespread public with dramatic force"); (11) Metropolitan Opera Association, for "Live from the Met" (for "building an extraordinarily successful bridge between a necessarily limited audience within the Metropolitan Opera House and the vast audience viewing the performance on television")

1978

(1) MTM Enterprises and the CBS Television Network, for *Lou Grant* ("an entertaining yet realistic look at the problems and issues which face those involved in the 'Fourth Estate'"); (2) Four D Productions/Trisene Corporation and the ABC Television Network, for *Barney Miller* ("a prime example of excellence in scripting, the use of humor with a message, and a program which provides Americans with entertainment of value"); (3) CBS News, for *30 Minutes* ("the excellent television magazine for teenagers"); (4) Newsweek Broadcasting, for "Cartoon-A-Torial" ("for successfully translating the editorial cartoon from the newspaper page to the television screen"); (5) KQED-TV, San Francisco, for *Over Easy* (a series which shows how "those of various ages and ethnic backgrounds cope with growing older by living meaningful and rewarding lives"); (6) Titus Productions and NBC Television, for *Holocaust* ("this series has won international acclaim, despite the controversial nature of its subject in some countries of the world"); (7) CBS News, for "The Battle for South Africa" ("an in-depth look at the terrorist war being ravaged against the government in that country"); (8) Survival Anglia Limited/World Wildlife Fund and NBC Television, for "Mysterious Castles of Clay" (a "fascinating story of the life cycle of the energetic African termite"); (9) WQED-TV, Pittsburgh, for "A Connecticut Yankee in King Arthur's Court," from *Once Upon a Classic* [PBS] ("the first fully American production in the *Classic* series," it was done with a "high level of quality"); (10) Tomorrow Entertainment/Medcom Company and the CBS Television Network, for "The Body Human: The Vital Connec-

tion" (a "marvelous and absorbing production," which took "an excursion into the workings of the human brain"); (11) Bob Keeshan, "known to millions as 'Captain Kangaroo'" ("he has not only brought superior entertainment to children of all ages but" has also "promoted quality children's programs on American television"); (12) Richard S. Salant ("in recognition of his leadership at CBS News and also in recognition of his staunch defense of the First Amendment guarantee of a free press"); (13) The Muppets ("for gentle satire, clever characters, genuine good humor and for high standards in family viewing"); (14) The Baptist Radio-TV Commission of Fort Worth, Texas, for "A River to the Sea" ("a fascinating look at English history from the early Roman occupation of Britain to modern times")

1979

(1) CBS News, for *CBS News Sunday Morning,* hosted by Charles Kuralt; (2) Sylvia Fine Kaye, for "Musical Comedy Tonight" ("an entertaining look at American musical comedy through four significant eras"); (3) ABC-TV, for "Valentine" ("a sensitive and sentimental love story of two people in their declining years"); (4) ABC-TV, for "Friendly Fire" ("a powerful dramatization of the human tragedy of an American family's involvement in the Vietnam War"); (5) NBC-TV, for "When Hell Was in Session" ("detailing the true story of Navy Commander Jeremiah Denton, a Vietnam prisoner of war for 7½ years"); (6) NBC-TV, for "Dummy" ("the story of an illiterate black deaf youth, who suffered injustice after his arrest as a murder suspect because of his handicap"); (7) NBC and the BBC, for "Treasures of the British Crown" ("an intriguing look at the priceless paintings and crown jewels of the Royal Collection in Britain, as described by members of the Royal Family"); (8) ABC-TV, for "A Special Gift," *ABC Afterschool Special* ("the fascinating story of a young boy with two talents: ballet and basketball"); (9) Roger Mudd, CBS News, "for his searching questions of Senator Edward Kennedy in the *CBS Reports* program "Teddy"; (10) CBS News, for "The Boston Goes to China" ("coverage of the Boston Symphony Orchestra's trip and the combined concert presented by the Symphony and the Peking Philharmonic"); (11) Robert Trout of ABC News ("for his nearly 50 years of service as a thoroughly knowledgeable and articulate commentator on national and international affairs"); (12) WGBH-TV, Boston, for *World* ("a series of international documentaries on diverse topics")

1980

(1) CBS News, for *Universe* ("a fresh addition to the 1980 summer schedule"); (2) CBS Entertainment, for "Gideon's Trumpet" ("a true and compelling story of a Florida convict who alters the course of legal history . . . a program which went far beyond the realm of entertainment"); (3) NBC and Paramount Television, for *Shōgun* ("the story is told with considerable taste, great excitement, and a marvelous look at the customs of Japan in the 17th century"); (4) ABC, for "IBM Presents Baryshnikov on Broadway" ("a dazzling display of talent . . . excellent family entertainment of the rarest order"); (5) ABC, for "Amber Waves" ("an excellent statement concerning the status of the work ethic in America"); (6) CBS Entertainment, for "Playing for Time" ("a searing indictment of war's inhumanity to the individual"); (7) BBC, for *All Creatures Great and Small* ("few series have achieved the warmth and the charm of this story"); (8) Carroll O'Connor, for "Edith's Death," an episode of *Archie Bunker's Place* ("O'Connor's sensitive reaction to the loss of his beloved Edith is so profound, so moving and so real that it becomes more than a performance; it has all the agony of real grief"); (9) Phil Donahue ("his sensitive yet probing interviews, his ability to ask the tough question without seeming to offend, his knack for getting to the heart of the matter are all important"); (10) Walter Cronkite ("has distinguished himself with a pace-setting career in broadcast journalism, exemplifying dedication and professionalism in bringing journalism to the public with competence and impartiality"); (11)

Sol Taishoff ("a true broadcasting pioneer . . . his fifty years of reporting and interpreting current events in radio and television (and more recently in cable) have earned for him the respect and admiration of the industry"); (12) Robert Geller and PBS, for *The American Short Story* ("an entertaining and finely crafted group of short stories by distinguished American writers"); (13) KCET (Los Angeles), Adrian Malone, and Carl Sagan, for *Cosmos* ("an intriguing, exciting, and exhilarating program"); (14) WQED and National Geographic Society, for "National Geographic Specials" ("four programs . . . were so inherently superior that the Peabody Board chose to recognize them all as a group, terming them 'unsurpassed excellence in documentaries'"); (15) KUED-TV (Salt Lake City) and WNET/13 (New York), for "The MX Debate" ("a special edition of *Bill Moyers' Journal* which dealt totally with the MX controversy")

1981

(1) NBC and MTM Enterprises, for *Hill Street Blues* ("this unique portrayal of police work in a decaying section of a big city has an air of realism that so many similar programs lack"); (2) CBS-TV and Alan Landsburg Productions, for "Bill" ("based on the true story of a mentally retarded adult . . . befriended by a young filmmaker, this gripping human drama brings Bill back into community life and, eventually, into independence"); (3) ABC and T.A.T. Communications, for "The Wave" ("this truly outstanding program . . . demonstrates a remarkable variety of truths, but none more important than it recognizes the ease with which cruelties can be perpetrated in the name of the state"); (4) ABC News, for "Viewpoint," *Nightline,* and "America Held Hostage: The Secret Negotiations" ("ABC News has a cup which almost 'runneth over' . . . a Peabody Award to ABC News for its talents, its abilities, and its excellence"); (5) WGBH, Boston, and Granada-TV, for "The Red Army," *World* (an "incisive analysis of the strengths and weaknesses of the military forces of the Soviet Union"); (6) WNET/13, New York, and PBS, for "Dance in America" ("created an interest in this art form that has never been manifested so strongly before"); (7) The Nebraska Educational Television Network, and The Great Amwell Company, for "The Private History of a Campaign That Failed" ("an instant from Mark Twain's brief stint in the Confederate militia . . . [the program was] a gigantic undertaking crowned with great success"); (8) Home Box Office and *Ms.* Magazine, for "She's Nobody's Baby: The History of American Women in the 20th Century" ("a magnificent and truly outstanding tribute to the forward movement of American women" [the first Peabody Award given to a cable television system]); (9) Bill Leonard, CBS News (he has "maintained high standards of excellence, accuracy and integrity throughout his most distinguished career"); (10) Danny Kaye, for "An Evening with Danny Kaye and the New York Philharmonic; Zubin Mehta, Music Director" and "Skokie" ("for virtuoso performances and versatility as a superb clown and as a sensitive dramatic actor"); (11) KTEH (San Jose, California), for "The Day After Trinity: J. Robert Oppenheimer and the Atomic Bomb" ("a moving drama of moral and historical forces at work, and a program which stands head and shoulders above the usual documentary")

1982

(1) NBC-TV, Margie-Lee Enterprises, and The Blue Marble Company, in association with ITC Productions, for "Skeezer" ("an exceptionally well-written and ably-produced movie-for-television which relates the true story of a dog used by therapists in the treatment of emotionally disturbed children") (2) CBS Entertainment and Cinetex International, for "The Wall" ("this dramatic presentation recreates the heroic Warsaw ghetto uprising during World War II . . . [it] is distinguished by its humanity and its humility"); (3) NBC and Highgate Pictures, for "The Electric Grandmother," *Project Peacock* (the story of a "robot grandmother 'adopted' by a motherless, grieving family . . . teaches that there is room for humanity in the

technological future"); (4) NBC News, for "The Man Who Shot the Pope: A Study in Terrorism," *NBC White Paper* ("this television documentary is an exceptional example of the art that is both comprehensive and compelling, but one that doesn't go beyond the evidence"); (5) ABC News, for *ABC News Closeup*/"Vietnam Requiem" ("this outstanding work personalizes both the issues and the consequences of the United States' involvement in Southeast Asia"); (6) CBS News, for the CBS News Special, "Juilliard and Beyond: A Life in Music" ("a program which examined the classical differences between Greek and Roman education, as exemplified in the Juilliard approach to educational excellence"); (7) Daniel Wilson Productions and Taurus Film, for "Blood and Honor: Youth Under Hitler" ("the drama carefully and dramatically exposes how hate can be taught and nurtured among impressionable minds"); (8) The Television Corporation of America, for "784 Days That Changed America—from Watergate to Resignation" ("the condensing of two years of American history into two great hours of television"); (9) Warner Amex Satellite Entertainment Company, for its overall programming for children and young people on Nickelodeon: The First Channel for Kids ("one of the most outstanding of the new cable programming channels"); (10) Texaco, Inc., the Texaco Foundation, and the Metropolitan Opera Association, for their commitment to both radio and television presentations of great opera ("characterized by continuing excellence and a real dedication to giving the viewer a rich and rewarding experience"); (11) BBC, Paramount Television, and Operation Prime Time, for "Smiley's People" ("an exceptional television experience . . . the traditional obsession of the British to pay close attention to detail brings a realism to the viewer"); (12) WQED, Pittsburgh, for Stravinsky's "Firebird" by the Dance Theater of Harlem ("viewers were treated to a marvelous look at what goes on behind the scenes . . . and . . . the premier performance itself"); (13) KQED-TV, San Francisco, for "Current Affairs/The Case of Dashiell Hammett" ("a compelling biographical sketch of the American mystery writer"); (14) Alistair Cooke, a personal award ("a master communicator in print and in picture")

1983

(1) ABC and Dick Clark Productions, for "The Woman Who Willed a Miracle," *ABC Afterschool Specials* ("a powerful drama . . . communicating to young audiences that no handicap is insurmountable given perseverance and hope"); (2) CBS Entertainment and Mendelson-Melendez Productions, for "What Have We Learned, Charlie Brown?" ("Charlie Brown just simply has that certain something that not only entertains but almost always imparts a message of very real importance"); (3) CBS Entertainment and Smith-Hemion Productions, for "Romeo and Juliet on Ice," *The CBS Festival of Lively Arts for Young People* ("a production that was innovative, was beautifully produced, and was certain to get children interested in learning more"); (4) CBS News for "The Plane That Fell from the Sky" ("Distinguished by its fairness, thorough attention to detail and reliance on the facts of the incident . . . television documentary at its best"); (5) CBS News, for *60 Minutes:* "Lenell Geter's in Jail" ("As a result of its investigation, which produced new witnesses and revealed a number of prosecution errors and omissions, Mr. Geter [who had been convicted of armed robbery and sentenced to life in prison] was granted his release"); (6) NBC and Motown Productions, for "Motown 25: Yesterday, Today, Forever" ("a thoroughly entertaining tribute to a truly unique style of American music"); (7) Chrysalis-Yellen Productions and NBC, for "Prisoner without a Name, Cell without a Number" ("a dramatic recreation of the imprisonment and ultimate release of journalist Jacobo Timerman in Argentina . . . a stunning technical achievement"); (8) NBC and Edgar J. Scherick Associates, for "He Makes Me Feel Like Dancin'" ("When a very talented group undertook to weave together the story of how Jacques d'Amboise—principal dancer with the New York City Ballet—taught children to dance in fourteen New York City area schools the result was sheer magic"); (9) WGBH-TV, Boston; Central Independent TV and Antenne-2, for *Vietnam: A Television History* ("the definitive visual record of the war in Vietnam");

(10) WGBH-TV, Boston, for *NOVA:* "The Miracle of Life" ("an homage to the biological complexity and uniqueness of the human species"); (11) WTTW/Chicago and the BBC, for "The Making of a Continent" ("its vivid imagery recounts geologic and ecological history in a way that could not be matched by textbook or lecture"); (12) WTTW/Chicago, for "The Merry Widow" ("a stirring televised ballet which proves that dance can be effectively presented on the small screen"); (13) Sunbow Productions, New York, for *The Great Space Coaster* ("a mixture of animation, puppets, live action, music, and guest stars that combines to make an appealing and instructive program"); (14) WTBS, Atlanta, for "Portrait of America" ("an ambitious series which attempts to present a rarely seen positive view of our country"); (15) Cable News Network ("for making the concept of continuous television news an influential and respected reality"); (16) Don McGannon ("He piloted his Westinghouse stations through many uncharted waters and he insisted that they be leaders in the communities they served"); (17) The Grand Ole Opry ("the Opry has made an important mark on both music and broadcasting in this country . . . [it] has spawned hundreds of television specials, a number of regularly scheduled radio and television programs, and 1983 saw the beginning of 'The Nashville Channel,' a 24-hour program service from the Opry")

1984

(1) "The Protestant Hour," produced by the Protestant Radio and Television Center, Atlanta ("for forty years of outstanding religious programming to the people of the world"); (2) *ABC Theatre,* for "Heartsounds" ("a sensitive and highly emotional teleplay dramatizing the triumph of love over illness and despair"); (3) WNET/ Thirteen, New York, for *Heritage: Civilization and the Jews* ("9 hours of intelligent and thought-provoking television"); (4) *ABC News Closeup,* for "To Save Our Schools, To Save Our Children" ("a substantial inquiry, in prime viewing time, into problems of education"); (5) *Frontline,* Boston ("for . . . overall excellence"); (6) WNET/Thirteen, New York, for *The Brain* ("a fascinating, instructive, and entertaining trip to the landscape of the mind"); (7) CBS Entertainment, for "George Washington" ("a miniseries of unusual scope, historical insight and intelligence"); (8) NBC and MTM Enterprises, for *St. Elsewhere* ("which examines the medical profession in human terms"); (9) To Central Independent Television of England for "Seeds of Despair" ("an early and exhaustive report on the widespread famine in Ethiopia"); (10) Showtime, for *Faerie Tale Theatre* ("a thoroughly entertaining retelling of classic fairy tales"); (11) Turner Broadcasting System, Atlanta, for "Cousteau/Amazon" ("a series of three documentary programs . . . with one of the world's most authoritative researchers"); (12) Ted Koppel/*Nightline,* New York ("an invaluable source for timely and insightful news commentary"); (13) "The Roger Rosenblatt Essays" as presented on *The MacNeil/Lehrer NewsHour* ("a combination of still and moving images . . . produc[ing] some of television's finest commentary"); (14) *A Walk Through the 20th Century with Bill Moyers,* produced by The Corporation for Entertainment and Learning, New York ("a television series which has brought viewers information coated with excitement"); (15) Granada Television of England, for "The Jewel in the Crown" [*Masterpiece Theatre*] ("a masterwork of extraordinary scope"); (16) Roone Arledge of ABC ("for significant contributions to television news and sports programming")

1985

(1) *The MacNeil/Lehrer NewsHour,* for "Apartheid's People" ("an incisive look at the day-to-day life in South Africa"); (2) NBC News, for "Vietnam: Ten Years After" ("an overall effort to provide the widest possible coverage of the 10th anniversary of the United States' withdrawal from Vietnam"); (3) CBS News, for "Whose America Is It?" ("a timely and revealing report focusing on the . . . conflicts created by America's newest wave of immigrants"); (4) CBS Entertainment and Dave Bell

Productions, for "Do You Remember Love" ("the dramatic story of . . . the agony of Alzheimer's disease"); (5) NBC Television, for "An Early Frost" ("an honest and tender drama dealing with . . . an American family trying to cope with the news that their son is dying of AIDS"); (6) KGO-TV, San Francisco, for "The American West: Steinbeck Country" ("one of a series of compelling programs"); (7) Spinning Reels and Home Box Office, for "Braingames" ("an outstanding series of animated television programs which both entertain and instruct"); (8) "The Final Chapter?" ("a documentary . . . which vividly depicts the chilling prospect of nuclear destruction"); (9) *Frontline,* for "Crisis in Central America" ("an exceptional four-part series"); (10) The Harvey Milk Film Project, Inc., and WNET/Thirteen, for "The Times of Harvey Milk" ("the story of . . . one of the decade's most prominent leaders of the lesbian and gay rights movement"); (11) Lincoln Center for the Performing Arts, New York, for *Live from Lincoln Center* ("ten years of the finest in the performing arts"); (12) Bob Geldof and "Live Aid" ("for his personal commitment to alleviating hunger throughout the world"); (13) Lawrence Fraiberg ("in recognition of his outstanding contributions to broadcasting in the United States"); (14) Johnny Carson, for almost 25 years of late-night humor on NBC's *The Tonight Show Starring Johnny Carson* ("a program which has entertained and amused American television viewers as no other program has")

1986

(1) CBS News, for "Sunday Morning: Vladimir Horowitz," with special reference to the contributions of Robert "Shad" Northshield; (2) MacNeil/Lehrer Productions and the British Broadcasting Corporation, for *The Story of English*; (3) WQED/Pittsburgh, for "Anne of Green Gables"; (4) ABC Entertainment and Churchill Films, for "The Mouse and the Motorcycle"; (5) Thames Television International and D. L. Taffner Ltd., for "Unknown Chaplin" [*American Masters*]; (6) WQED/Pittsburgh and the The National Geographic Society, for "The National Geographic Specials"; (7) CBS News, for "CBS Reports: The Vanishing Family—Crisis in Black America"; (8) The John F. Kennedy Center for the Performing Arts, for "The 1986 Kennedy Center Honors: A Celebration of the Performing Arts"; (9) Thames Television International and WGBH-TV, Boston, for "Paradise Postponed" [*Masterpiece Theatre*]; (10) NBC Entertainment, for *The Cosby Show*; (11) CBS Entertainment and Garner-Duchow Productions, for "Promise" [*Hallmark Hall of Fame*]; (12) Jim Henson and the Muppets, for 30 years of entertainment; (13) ABC News, for *This Week with David Brinkley*

1987

(1) Cable News Network, Atlanta, for live coverage of breaking news stories as evidenced by coverage of the October 1987 stock market crash; (2) *Hallmark Hall of Fame* and CBS-TV, for "Foxfire" and "Pack of Lies"; (3) *The MacNeil/Lehrer NewsHour,* for "Japan Series"; (4) "LBJ: The Early Years," produced by Louis Rudolph Films and Brice Productions in association with Fried Entertainment and NBC-TV; (5) "Corridos! Tales of Passion and Revolution," produced by KQED, San Francisco, in association with El Teatro Campesino; (6) "Mandela," produced by Titus Productions in association with Polymuse, Inc. and Home Box Office, New York; (7) *L. A. Law,* produced by 20th Century Fox Television in association with NBC-TV; (8) *Star Trek: The Next Generation*—"The Big Good-bye," produced by Paramount Pictures Corporation; (9) WNET/Thirteen, New York, for *Nature*—"A Season in the Sun"; (10) Blackside, Inc., Boston, for *Eyes on the Prize: America's Civil Rights Years*; (11) WGBH-TV, Boston, and KCET, Los Angeles, for *Nova*—"Spy Machines"; (12) "America Undercover: Drunk and Deadly," produced by Niemack Productions, Inc., in association with Home Box Office, New York; (13) The Center for New American Media, Inc., for "American Tongues"; (14) "Small Happiness: Women of a Chinese Village," a part of "One

Village in China," produced by Long Bow Group, Inc., New York, in association with PBS; (15) *Shoah*, a Claude Lanzmann film presented by WNET/Thirteen, New York, in association with PBS; (16) Kevin Brownlow and David Gill, as evidenced by "Hollywood," "Unknown Chaplin," and "Buster Keaton: A Hard Act to Follow," produced in association with Thames Television and D. L. Taffner, Ltd. American Media, Inc., for "American Tongues"; (14) "Small Happiness: Women of a Chinese Village," a part of "One Village in China," produced by Long Bow Group, Inc., New York, in association with PBS; (15) *Shoah*, a Claude Lanzmann film presented by WNET/Thirteen, New York, in association with PBS; (16) Kevin Brownlow and David Gill, as evidenced by "Hollywood," "Unknown Chaplin," and "Buster Keaton: A Hard Act to Follow," produced in association with Thames Television and D. L. Taffner, Ltd.

1988

(1) MacNeil/Lehrer Productions, New York, for "The MacNeil/Lehrer NewsHour: Election '88 Coverage" ("a superb comprehensive treatment of the personalities and issues"); (2) Frontline, Boston, for *Frontline*—"The Choice" ("provided viewers with the most extensive background reporting on the 1988 presidential candidates"); (3) CBS News, New York, for "Abortion Battle" and "On Runaway Street," as a part of *48 Hours* ("which typify exceptional handling of issues that are at once complex and often divisive"); (4) CBS Entertainment and Telecom Entertainment in association with Yorkshire Television, for "The Attic: The Hiding of Anne Frank" ("an exceptional television offering of an inspiring story of courage and love"); (5) BBC, London, and WNET/Thirteen, New York, for *The Singing Detective* ("a haunting, humorous and highly unusual film for television"); (6) NBC-TV, for "The Murder of Mary Phagan" ("a gripping account of brutality and prejudice in early twentieth-century America"); (7) ABC Television and The Bedford Falls Company in association with MGM/UA Television, for *thirtysomething* ("marked by vivid writing, fine production and exceptional performances"); (8) The Children's Television Workshop, for "3-2-1 Contact Extra: I Have AIDS, A Teenager's Story" ("a primer on AIDS for children"); (9) South Carolina ETV Network and the Mosaic Group, Inc., for "Children's Express Newsmagazine: Campaign '88" ("a fascinating look at how effectively children can function as news reporters"); (10) Christian Science Monitor Reports, for "Islam in Turmoil" ("a comprehensive examination of the political, cultural and racial strife within one of the world's great religions"); (11) HBO, in association with Pro Image Productions, for "Suzi's Story" ("a tragic but tender and touching account of one woman's struggle against AIDS"); (12) HBO, for "Dear America: Letters Home from Vietnam" ("a poignant documentary that uses personal letters of Vietnam veterans to accompany footage from the war"); (13) Turner Network Television, for "The Making of a Legend: Gone with the Wind" ("a fascinating look at film footage never before seen by the public"); (14) CBS News, for "Mr. Snow Goes to Washington," as a part of *60 Minutes* ("produced significant results by achieving a higher degree of child safety through both increased public awareness and national legislation"); (15) Public Affairs Television, for *Bill Moyers' World of Ideas* ("a series of extraordinary interviews with great thinkers of our time"); (16) Jim McKay, ABC-TV Sports Commentator ("for his pioneering efforts and career accomplishments in the world of televised sports"); (17) Don Hewitt, CBS News ("for exceptional contributions to television news over an important period of American history spanning forty years"); (18) Ambassador Walter Annenberg ("for his philanthropic role in support of the educational uses of radio and television")

1989

(1) Cable News Network's coverage of China ("a series of thorough, dramatic, courageous and internationally important reports of the crisis"); (2) "Cambodia Year

Ten," Central Independent Television, London ("a passionate and strident examination of the plight of the Asian nation"); (3) "Decade," MTV ("a fresh, vibrant, and unique look at the 1980s as seen through the eyes of music performers and newsmakers"); (4) *Lonesome Dove,* CBS Television, Motown Productions, in association with Pangaea Productions and Qintex Entertainment, Inc. ("a compelling drama of the old west which proved that the western is not dead"); (5) *The Wonder Years,* ABC Television and Black/Marlens Company in association with New World Television ("an innovative, humorous and often touching series about adolescence and family life in the tumultuous 1960s"); (6) *China Beach,* "Vets," ABC Television and Sacret, Inc., in association with Warner Bros. Television ("an episode which recounts the experience of American nurses in compelling, chilling and emotional terms"); (7) "Small Sacrifices," ABC Television, Lou Rudolph Films, Inc., and Motown Productions in association with Allarcom, Ltd. and Fried Entertainment, Inc. ("exceptional acting, coupled with a great script . . . provide[d] television that is powerful and emotionally charged"); (8) "The Great Wall of Iron," Beyond International Group, Sydney, Australia ("an unprecedented behind-the-scenes examination of the Chinese People's Liberation Army, completed only weeks before the infamous events in Tiananmen Square"); (9) "Common Threads: Stories from the Quilt," HBO ("a stirring elegy to the victims of AIDS"); (10) *The Public Mind,* Alvin H. Perlmutter, Inc. and Public Affairs Television ("Bill Moyers' critical look at public opinion formation and change in America"); (11) "Who Killed Vincent Chin?" Film News Now, Detroit and WTVS, Detroit, in association with *P. O. V.* ("a penetrating examination of a murder in Detroit revealing the racism, class conflict and media power which permeate modern America"); (12) *Sesame Street,* Children's Television Workshop ("for two decades of innovative and effective education through the medium of television"); (13) "NBC News Special: To Be An American," NBC News ("which sparks pride in what this country stands for and which validates the continuing contributions of an able and dedicated newsman, Tom Brokaw"); (14) David Brinkley, ABC-TV ("attesting to the exceptional contributions he has made to broadcasting during his tenure as one of this country's richest treasures"); (15) J. Leonard Reinsch ("a pioneer in broadcasting, cable and political communication, for a lifetime of outstanding service to his chosen profession")

1990

(1) *Eyes on the Prize II: America at the Racial Crossroads* (*1965–1985*), Blackside, Inc., Boston ("for the second installment of the documentary series which stands as the definitive record of the American civil rights movement"); (2) *The Civil War,* Florentine Films and WETA-TV, Washington, D.C. ("a landmark documentary by Ken Burns which galvanized the nation and redefined the form for television"); (3) "John Hammond: From Bessie Smith to Bruce Springsteen," *American Masters,* CBS Music Video Enterprises and *American Masters* in association with Perry Films ("a stunning television biography of a titanic figure in the evolution of American popular music"); (4) "The Koppel Report: Death of a Dictator," ABC News and Koppel Communications ("a riveting behind-the-scenes report of events in [Eastern Europe]"); (5) *P.O.V.,* "Days of Waiting," Mouchette Films/*P.O.V.* and the National Asian American Telecommunications Association ("a stirring personal account of the tragic and unwarranted treatment of Japanese-Americans during World War II"); (6) "Peter Jennings Reporting: Guns," ABC News/Time ("for presenting a critical issue . . . in a fair, even-handed and timely manner"); (7) "Backhauling," KCTS-TV, Seattle, and *MacNeil/Lehrer NewHour* ("an investigative report on illegal trucking practices which led directly to remedial action in Congress"); (8) Cable News Network ("for its unique 24-hour global coverage from the scene of the Persian Gulf crisis"); (9) *Twin Peaks* (premiere episode), ABC-TV, Lynch-Frost Productions in association with Propaganda Films and Worldvisions Enterprises, Inc. ("which invigorated the television dramatic form with innovation and imagination"); (10) *Saturday Night Live,* NBC Television ("for providing fifteen years of topical entertainment, political satire, and exciting music to the

American viewing public"); (11) *American Playhouse* ("for an outstanding record of achievement over nine seasons"); (12) "Futures," FASE Productions ("a series which demonstrates the power of television to teach math and science without elaborate special effects and visual gadgetry"); (13) "Mother Goose Rock 'N' Rhyme," Think Entertainment on the Disney Channel ("a delightful and whimsical romp through the pages of our favorite book of nursery rhymes"); (14) The John D. and Catherine T. MacArthur Foundation ("for its distinguished record of achievement in support of quality television"); (15) Red Barber ("for his six decades as a broadcaster . . ."); (16) Frederick Wiseman ("whose body of work and personal approach to documentary television have set the standard for generations of film and video producers to follow"); (17) Paul Fine and Holly Fine ("whose signatures of impassioned and personal reporting span two decades of local and network television").

1991

(1) NBC NEWS, for its reports on the B.C.C.I. banking scandal ("investigative reporting of the highest caliber"); (2) CBS NEWS, for *60 Minutes:* "Friendly Fire" ("for the first time in American history a friendly fire accident was taken all the way into the public domain and the individual responsible for the accident was named"); (3) KTLA-TV, Los Angeles, for "Rodney King: Videotaped Beating" ("KTLA has handled the Rodney King incident and related matters with the highest standards of journalistic research and ethics"); (4) CNN, for coverage of the Soviet coup ("CNN continues its tradition of excellence as the international channel of record for breaking news"); (5) *Murphy Brown,* CBS, Shukovsky/English Productions and Warner Brothers Television (it "weaves current issues into its scripts . . . features a strong ensemble cast . . . [and] reveals a personal vision of the world through the exceptional work of its producers and writers"); (6) "When It Was a Game," HBO Sports and Black Canyon Productions ("a lyrical and loving look at our national game"); (7) Brand-Falsey Productions, for *I'll Fly Away* and *Northern Exposure* ("Joshua Brand and John Falsey have brought renewed vigor, innovation, intelligence and a sense of style to one of TV's most moribund forms—evening serial drama"); (8) "Dance in America: Everybody Dance Now!" Thirteen/WNET, New York ("In this exuberant program popular dance is given an historical context and the often overlooked choreographer is paid tribute"); (9) *Late Night with David Letterman,* NBC Productions, in association with Carson Productions and Worldwide Pants Productions ("Together, the 'Late Night' team manages to take one of TV's most conventional and least inventive forms—the talk show—and infuse it with freshness and imagination"); (10) "America Undercover: Heil Hitler! Confessions of a Hitler Youth," HBO (a "chilling and timely reminder of the not-so-distant past"); (11) "Nickelodeon Special Edition: It's Only Television," Lucky Duck Productions and Nickelodeon ("From behind the scenes, television's youngest viewers are taught the critical skills essential for separating fact from fantasy in 'televisionland' "); (12) "Coup d'Etat: The Week That Changed the World," Turner Multimedia ("For providing a model of the implementation of video resources in the classroom and for producing one of the most compelling documentaries of 1991 on events in the former Soviet Union"); (13) "Soviets: Red Hot," Central Independent Television (U.K.) and WETA-TV (Washington, D.C.) ("a compelling documentary of a diverse population awakening politically, socially and spiritually after slumbering under decades of oppression"); (14) "Pearl Harbor: Two Hours That Changed the World," ABC News and NHK (Japan) ("a collaborative effort [that] pays powerful tribute to those who gave their lives"); (15) "People of the Forest: The Chimps of Gombe," The Discovery Channel ("This extraordinary documentary, produced by Hugo van Lawick . . . follows a family of wild chimpanzees over the course of twenty years in their natural habitat"); (16) Armed Forces Radio and Television Service (for providing half a century of a "full and free flow of news and information to American military, civilian and diplomatic personnel overseas"); (17) "The Masters," CBS Sports ("golf's premier event" is turned into "television of high drama in a setting of

exquisite beauty"); (18) Peggy Charren (for 24 years "an advocate of quality children's programming on television, most notably through her formation and leadership of Action for Children's Television").

1992

(1) *Seinfeld,* NBC-TV and Castle Rock Entertainment ("its comedy is universal and instructive in many aspects of everyday life"); (2) "72 Hours to Victory: Behind the Scenes with Bill Clinton," *ABC News Nightline Special,* Capital Cities/ABC, Inc. ("for unusual and important campaign reporting"); (3) "The Donner Party," *The American Experience,* WGBH-TV and Steeplechase Films ("a compelling metaphor for the American expansion westward"); (4) "The Machine That Changed the World," WGBH-TV, BBC-TV, in association with NDR, Hamburg ("this landmark five-hour documentary of the origin and current status of computing raises as many questions as it answers"); (5) "Abortion: Desperate Choices," HBO and Maysles Films, Inc. ("for taking the abortion debate out of the realm of inflammatory rhetoric and reflecting the intensely personal decision it represents"); (6) "Color Adjustment," Signifyin' Works and *P.O.V.,* for PBS ("a revealing examination of the presentation of African-American life on television"); (7) "Moment of Crisis," *ABC News Nightline Special,* Capital Cities/ABC, Inc. ("a detailed, behind-the-scenes account of the hours immediately preceding and following the announcement of the Rodney King verdict on April 29, 1992"); (8) *Reading Rainbow:* "The Wall," GPN/Nebraska ETV Network and WNED-TV in cooperation with Lancit Media Productions, Ltd. (a "stirring episode" in which the "Vietnam Veterans Memorial in Washington, D.C., is explored and interpreted for viewers"); (9) *AIDS,* Channel One/Whittle Communications ("these reports serve to remind us of television's possibilities in our schools, in particular how a specific audience can be presented valuable information in manner which is accessible to them as well as influential in their lives"); (10) *Where in the World Is Carmen Sandiego?* WQED-TV and WGBH-TV, for PBS ("a uniquely creative and influential use of television on a topic of primary importance"); (11) "Rock the Vote," Propaganda Films, for Fox Broadcasting Company ("as a direct result of the 800 number posted during the program, it is estimated that more than a quarter million young people registered to vote"); (12) "The More You Know," NBC (a series of public service announcements designed to "focus attention on the issues affecting education throughout the United States"); (13) "The Health Quarterly: The AIDS Report Series," WGBH-TV ("This series stands out for its reasoned approach and sensitive production"); (14) "Choose or Lose Campaign," MTV ("for enfranchising a previously disenfranchised group"); (15) "Citizen Cohn," HBO ("an outstanding achievement in documenting an important era and in exposing the public and private life of an influential individual from our recent past"); (16) *Roseanne,* ABC-TV and The Carsey-Werner Company ("tough comedy with a heart," it "has the courage to look unflinchingly at contemporary family life"); (17) "Cicely," *Northern Exposure,* CBS-TV, The Finnegan-Pinchuk Company in association with Brand-Falsey Productions ("by the close of the episode, Cicely has been transformed to a place where differences are universally accepted"); (18) "Larry King Live Election Coverage 1992," CNN (King "let the candidates speak for themselves and let his national and international viewers ask the questions that reveal the character of the people who would lead our nation"); (19) "Age Seven in America," CBS-TV and Granada Television ("it encapsulates the contemporary American condition in the words and images of seven-year-olds around the country"); (20) Daniel Schorr ("one of the principal members of a generation of broadcast journalists identified with the highest ideals and integrity in the field"); (21) C-SPAN (it fulfills the promise of television in a democratic society by providing access to information indispensable to an intelligent citizenry"); (22) Fred Rogers ("for teaching us a little about life each day, and for reminding us that the power of television rests not so much in those who produce it as in the impressionable and inquisitive minds and hearts of its smallest consumers").

(1) "Scarred for Life," *Day One,* ABC News (for bringing "the centuries-old ritual of female circumcision . . . to public attention"); (2) "Health and Science Reporting by Robert Bazell," NBC News (exemplifying "the best reporting on science and medicine"); (3) "The New Explorers," WTTW and Kurtis Productions, Ltd. ("an unprecedented initiative, in which over 100,000 students across the country are provided with exceptional science education"); (4) *Steven Spielberg Presents Animaniacs,* Warner Bros. Animation and Amblin Entertainment, for Fox Children's Network ("this series, with appeal to adults as well as children, reminds us of the glory days of Hollywood animation and brings that period up-to-date with sparkling characters, witty dialogue, and stunning production"); (5) "Fox Children's Network: 1993 Public Service Campaign," Churchill Entertainment ("by teaching self-acceptance, racial and gender tolerance, sensitivity and love" it "endeavors to influence the lives of younger viewers"); (6) "I Am a Promise: The Children of Stanton Elementary School," HBO and Video Verite Films ("this insightful documentary filmed at an inner city elementary school . . . reveals the best and worst in or educational system"); (7) "Silverlake Life: The View from Here," *P.O.V.* ("a candid and heart-wrenching documentary on love, commitment, and mortality in the age of AIDS"); (8) "The CIA's Cocaine," *60 Minutes,* CBS News ("by revealing the story of a covert CIA operation in Venezuela that led to an unabated flood of cocaine into this country, *60 Minutes* performs vital public service"); (9) "Katie and Eilish: Siamese Twins," Yorkshire Television, presented on The Discovery Channel ("for providing insightful television without pandering to the sensational"); (10) *Homicide: Life on the Street,* NBC and Baltimore Pictures in association with Reeves Entertainment (an "innovative, quirky, and frequently brilliant combination of style and substance"); (11) "The Ernest Green Story," A.M.L. Productions for The Disney Channel ("a story which reminds adults and teaches children about the courageous steps taken toward the elimination of discrimination in American society"); (12) "Paul Simon: Born at the Right Time," *American Masters* ("transcends the standard rock biography"); (13) *Mystery Science Theater 3000,* Comedy Central and Best Brains, Inc. ("fuses superb, clever writing with wonderfully terrible B-grade movies"); (14) "Prime Suspect," *Mystery!* Granada Television of England in association with WGBH-TV ("for adroitly intertwining emotional, political, and dramatic themes"); (15) *The Larry Sanders Show,* HBO and Brillstein-Grey Entertainment ("a dead-on depiction from the front lines of the late-night wars"); (16) The Discovery Networks ("for providing outstanding public service and for realizing the potential of cable television"); (17) Christiane Amanpour ("a heroic reporter whose balanced and courageous coverage in recent years has brought the impact of numerous world crises to a global audience").

1994

(1) "Break the Silence: Kids Against Child Abuse," Arnold Shapiro Productions & USAA, presented by CBS ("for performing a vital public service in a compelling and accessible way"); (2) "Rush to Read," *PrimeTime Live,* ABC News ("for providing a timely investigation into the shockingly unacceptable error rates of laboratories testing for cervical cancer and for precipitating change"); (3) "CBS Reports: D-Day," CBS News ("for personalizing the heroism of those who risked their lives on the beaches of Normandy and in the liberation of Europe"); (4) "The Battle of the Bulge," *The American Experience,* Lennon Documentary Group ("marked by exceptionally well-researched and restored archival footage, poignant recollections, and the unmatched narration of historian David McCullough . . . [it] remind[s] us of the price paid to preserve democracy"); (5) "The Hunger Inside," *20/20,* ABC News ("reveals how anorexia has been misunderstood and ill-served by traditional medical approaches"); (6) "FDR," *The American Experience,* David Grubin Productions ("a taut and compelling narrative"); (7) "Normandy: The

Great Crusade," Discovery Productions and Koch TV Productions, Inc. ("more than a commemoration of the 50th anniversary of D-Day, this program takes viewers back to the time when every man, woman, and child was mobilized on behalf of the war effort"); (8) "China: Beyond the Clouds," a River Films Production for National Geographic Television in association with Channel 4 Television (London) and Canal Plus (Paris) ("For revealing the heart, soul, and spirit of a nation just now opening itself to the world"); (9) "Malcolm X: Make It Plain," *The American Experience*, Blackside, Inc. and ROJA Productions, for WGBH-TV ("this program examines Malcolm X without the myth-making or derision marked by those who would blindly laud or vilify him"); (10) "National Geographic: Reflections on Elephants," National Geographic Television ("for bringing majesty to the screen with a faithful and touching description of the disappearing natural environment of the wild elephant"); (11) "Nick News," Nickelodeon and Lucky Duck Productions ("for presenting news in a thoughtful and non-condescending manner for both children and adults"); (12) *ER*, NBC, a Constant *c* Production, Amblin Television in association with Warner Bros. Television ("for capturing the drama of contemporary emergency medicine with particular skill"); (13) "Tales of the City," *American Playhouse*, KQED, A Propaganda/Working Title Production for Channel 4 (London) ("a miniseries which moves beyond nostalgia and which stretches the boundaries of television drama"); (14) *Frasier*, NBC, Grub Street Productions in association with Paramount Television ("an ensemble of eccentric and interesting characters marks this breakthrough series"); (15) *MTV Unplugged*, MTV ("by de-electrifying contemporary music [it] has built a bridge across the chasm known as the 'generation gap' "); (16) *Mad About You*, NBC, In Front Productions and Nuance Productions in association with TriStar Television ("this quirky, dead-on depiction of married life in the 1990s offers insight into or everyday experiences even as it makes us laugh"); (17) "Barbra Streisand The Concert," J.E.G. Productions, presented on HBO ("testimony to how great the presentation of music on television can be"); (18) "Moon Shot," Turner Original Productions/Varied Directions ("of the numerous commemorations of the events leading to and following America's successful landing of a man on the moon, this was the most provocative and insightful").

PART V

THE HIT PARADE

Explanatory note: The following lists of top-rated series for each season are based on the rating reports compiled by the A. C. Nielsen Company. The list for the 1949–1950 season is for the month of October 1949, and was supplied by *Variety*.

1949–1950

(1)	Texaco Star Theater	NBC
(2)	Toast of the Town (Ed Sullivan)	CBS
(3)	Arthur Godfrey's Talent Scouts	CBS
(4)	Fireball Fun for All	NBC
(5)	Philco Television Playhouse	NBC
(6)	Fireside Theatre	NBC
(7)	The Goldbergs	CBS
(8)	Suspense	CBS
(9)	Ford Theater	CBS
(10)	Cavalcade of Stars	DUMONT

1950–1951

(1)	Texaco Star Theater	NBC
(2)	Fireside Theatre	NBC
(3)	Your Show of Shows	NBC
(4)	Philco Television Playhouse	NBC
(5)	The Colgate Comedy Hour	NBC
(6)	Gillette Cavalcade of Sports	NBC
(7)	Arthur Godfrey's Talent Scouts	CBS
(8)	Mama	CBS
(9)	Robert Montgomery Presents	NBC
(10)	Martin Kane, Private Eye	NBC
(11)	Man Against Crime	CBS
(12)	Somerset Maugham Theatre	CBS
(13)	Kraft Television Theatre	NBC
(14)	Toast of the Town (Ed Sullivan)	CBS
(15)	The Aldrich Family	NBC
(16)	You Bet Your Life	NBC
(17)	Armstrong Circle Theater	NBC
(18)	Big Town	CBS
(19)	Lights Out	NBC
(20)	The Alan Young Show	CBS

1951–1952

(1)	Arthur Godfrey's Talent Scouts	CBS
(2)	Texaco Star Theater	NBC
(3)	I Love Lucy	CBS
(4)	The Red Skelton Show	NBC
(5)	The Colgate Comedy Hour	NBC
(6)	Fireside Theatre	NBC
(7)	The Jack Benny Program	CBS
(8)	Your Show of Shows	NBC
(9)	You Bet Your Life	NBC

(10)	Arthur Godfrey and His Friends	CBS
(11)	Mama	CBS
(12)	Philco Television Playhouse	NBC
(13)	Amos 'n' Andy	CBS
(14)	Big Town	CBS
(15)	Pabst Blue Ribbon Bouts	CBS
(16)	Gillette Cavalcade of Sports	NBC
(17)	The Alan Young Show	CBS
(18)	All-Star Revue	NBC
(19)	Dragnet	NBC
(20)	Kraft Television Theatre	NBC

1952–1953

(1)	I Love Lucy	CBS
(2)	Arthur Godfrey's Talent Scouts	CBS
(3)	Arthur Godfrey and His Friends	CBS
(4)	Dragnet	NBC
(5)	Texaco Star Theater	NBC
(6)	The Buick Circus Hour	NBC
(7)	The Colgate Comedy Hour	NBC
(8)	Gangbusters	NBC
(9)	You Bet Your Life	NBC
(10)	Fireside Theatre	NBC
(11)	The Red Buttons Show	CBS
(12)	The Jack Benny Program	CBS
(13)	Life with Luigi	CBS
(14)	Pabst Blue Ribbon Bouts	CBS
(15)	Goodyear Television Playhouse	NBC
(16)	The Life of Riley	NBC
(17)	Mama	CBS
(18)	Your Show of Shows	NBC
(19)	What's My Line?	CBS
(20)	Strike It Rich	CBS

1953–1954

(1)	I Love Lucy	CBS
(2)	Dragnet	NBC
(3)	Arthur Godfrey's Talent Scouts	CBS
(4)	You Bet Your Life	NBC
(5)	The Bob Hope Show	NBC
(6)	The Buick-Berle Show	NBC
(7)	Arthur Godfrey and His Friends	CBS
(8)	Ford Theater	NBC
(9)	The Jackie Gleason Show	CBS
(10)	Fireside Theatre	NBC
(11)	The Colgate Comedy Hour	NBC
(12)	This Is Your Life	NBC
(13)	The Red Buttons Show	CBS
(14)	The Life of Riley	NBC
(15)	Our Miss Brooks	CBS
(16)	Treasury Men in Action	NBC
(17)	All-Star Revue (Martha Raye)	NBC
(18)	The Jack Benny Program	CBS
(19)	Gillette Cavalcade of Sports	NBC
(20)	Philco Television Playhouse	NBC

(1)	I Love Lucy	CBS
(2)	The Jackie Gleason Show	CBS
(3)	Dragnet	NBC
(4)	You Bet Your Life	NBC
(5)	Toast of the Town (Ed Sullivan)	CBS
(6)	Disneyland	ABC
(7)	The Bob Hope Show	NBC
(8)	The Jack Benny Program	CBS
(9)	The Martha Raye Show	NBC
(10)	The George Gobel Show	NBC
(11)	Ford Theater	NBC
(12)	December Bride	CBS
(13)	The Buick-Berle Show	NBC
(14)	This Is Your Life	NBC
(15)	I've Got a Secret	CBS
(16)	Two for the Money	CBS
(17)	Your Hit Parade	NBC
(18)	The Millionaire	CBS
(19)	General Electric Theater	CBS
(20)	Arthur Godfrey's Talent Scouts	CBS

1955–1956

(1)	The $64,000 Question	CBS
(2)	I Love Lucy	CBS
(3)	The Ed Sullivan Show	CBS
(4)	Disneyland	ABC
(5)	The Jack Benny Program	CBS
(6)	December Bride	CBS
(7)	You Bet Your Life	NBC
(8)	Dragnet	NBC
(9)	I've Got a Secret	CBS
(10)	General Electric Theater	CBS
(11)	Private Secretary	CBS
(12)	Ford Theater	NBC
(13)	The Red Skelton Show	CBS
(14)	The George Gobel Show	NBC
(15)	The $64,000 Challenge	CBS
(16)	Arthur Godfrey's Talent Scouts	CBS
(17)	The Lineup	CBS
(18)	Shower of Stars	CBS
(19)	The Perry Como Show	NBC
(20)	The Honeymooners (Jackie Gleason)	CBS

1956–1957

(1)	I Love Lucy	CBS
(2)	The Ed Sullivan Show	CBS
(3)	General Electric Theater	CBS
(4)	The $64,000 Question	CBS
(5)	December Bride	CBS
(6)	Alfred Hitchcock Presents	CBS
(7)	I've Got a Secret	CBS
(8)	Gunsmoke	CBS
(9)	The Perry Como Show	NBC

(10)	The Jack Benny Program	CBS
(11)	Dragnet	NBC
(12)	Arthur Godfrey's Talent Scouts	CBS
(13)	The Millionaire	CBS
(14)	Disneyland	ABC
(15)	Shower of Stars	CBS
(16)	The Lineup	CBS
(17)	The Red Skelton Show	CBS
(18)	You Bet Your Life	NBC
(19)	Wyatt Earp	ABC
(20)	Private Secretary	CBS

1957–1958

(1)	Gunsmoke	CBS
(2)	The Danny Thomas Show	CBS
(3)	Tales of Wells Fargo	NBC
(4)	Have Gun, Will Travel	CBS
(5)	I've Got a Secret	CBS
(6)	Wyatt Earp	ABC
(7)	General Electric Theater	CBS
(8)	The Restless Gun	NBC
(9)	December Bride	CBS
(10)	You Bet Your Life	NBC
(11)	Alfred Hitchcock Presents	CBS
(12)	Cheyenne	ABC
(13)	The Tennessee Ernie Ford Show	NBC
(14)	The Red Skelton Show	CBS
(15)	Wagon Train	NBC
(16)	Sugarfoot	ABC
(17)	Father Knows Best	NBC
(18)	Twenty-One	NBC
(19)	The Ed Sullivan Show	CBS
(20)	The Jack Benny Program	CBS

1958–1959

(1)	Gunsmoke	CBS
(2)	Wagon Train	NBC
(3)	Have Gun, Will Travel	CBS
(4)	The Rifleman	ABC
(5)	The Danny Thomas Show	CBS
(6)	Maverick	ABC
(7)	Tales of Wells Fargo	NBC
(8)	The Real McCoys	ABC
(9)	I've Got a Secret	CBS
(10)	Wyatt Earp	ABC
(11)	The Price Is Right	NBC
(12)	The Red Skelton Show	CBS
(13)	Zane Grey Theater	CBS
(14)	Father Knows Best	CBS
(15)	The Texan	CBS
(16)	Wanted: Dead or Alive	CBS
(17)	Peter Gunn	NBC
(18)	Cheyenne	ABC
(19)	Perry Mason	CBS
(20)	The Tennessee Ernie Ford Show	NBC

1959–1960

(1)	Gunsmoke	CBS
(2)	Wagon Train	NBC
(3)	Have Gun, Will Travel	CBS
(4)	The Danny Thomas Show	CBS
(5)	The Red Skelton Show	CBS
(6)	Father Knows Best	CBS
(7)	77 Sunset Strip	ABC
(8)	The Price Is Right	NBC
(9)	Wanted: Dead or Alive	CBS
(10)	Perry Mason	CBS
(11)	The Real McCoys	ABC
(12)	The Ed Sullivan Show	CBS
(13)	Bing Crosby (specials)	ABC
(14)	The Rifleman	ABC
(15)	The Tennessee Ernie Ford Show	NBC
(16)	The Lawman	ABC
(17)	Dennis the Menace	CBS
(18)	Cheyenne	ABC
(19)	Rawhide	CBS
(20)	Maverick	ABC

1960–1961

(1)	Gunsmoke	CBS
(2)	Wagon Train	NBC
(3)	Have Gun, Will Travel	CBS
(4)	The Andy Griffith Show	CBS
(5)	The Real McCoys	ABC
(6)	Rawhide	CBS
(7)	Candid Camera	CBS
(8)	The Untouchables	ABC
(9)	The Price Is Right	NBC
(10)	The Jack Benny Program	CBS
(11)	Dennis the Menace	CBS
(12)	The Danny Thomas Show	CBS
(13)	My Three Sons	ABC
(14)	77 Sunset Strip	ABC
(15)	The Ed Sullivan Show	CBS
(16)	Perry Mason	CBS
(17)	Bonanza	NBC
(18)	The Flintstones	ABC
(19)	The Red Skelton Show	CBS
(20)	Alfred Hitchcock Presents	NBC

1961–1962

(1)	Wagon Train	NBC
(2)	Bonanza	NBC
(3)	Gunsmoke	CBS
(4)	Hazel	NBC
(5)	Perry Mason	CBS
(6)	The Red Skelton Show	CBS
(7)	The Andy Griffith Show	CBS
(8)	The Danny Thomas Show	CBS
(9)	Dr. Kildare	NBC

(10)	Candid Camera	CBS
(11)	My Three Sons	ABC
(12)	The Garry Moore Show	CBS
(13)	Rawhide	CBS
(14)	The Real McCoys	ABC
(15)	Lassie	CBS
(16)	Sing Along with Mitch	NBC
(17)	Dennis the Menace	CBS
(18)	Marshal Dillon (Gunsmoke *reruns*)	CBS
(19)	Ben Casey	ABC
(20)	The Ed Sullivan Show	CBS

1962–1963

(1)	The Beverly Hillbillies	CBS
(2)	Candid Camera	CBS
(3)	The Red Skelton Show	CBS
(4)	Bonanza	NBC
(5)	The Lucy Show	CBS
(6)	The Andy Griffith Show	CBS
(7)	Ben Casey	ABC
(8)	The Danny Thomas Show	CBS
(9)	The Dick Van Dyke Show	CBS
(10)	Gunsmoke	CBS
(11)	Dr. Kildare	NBC
(12)	The Jack Benny Program	CBS
(13)	What's My Line?	CBS
(14)	The Ed Sullivan Show	CBS
(15)	Hazel	NBC
(16)	I've Got a Secret	CBS
(17)	The Jackie Gleason Show	CBS
(18)	The Defenders	CBS
(19)	The Garry Moore Show	CBS
(20)	(tie) Lassie	CBS
(20)	(tie) To Tell the Truth	CBS

1963–1964

(1)	The Beverly Hillbillies	CBS
(2)	Bonanza	NBC
(3)	The Dick Van Dyke Show	CBS
(4)	Petticoat Junction	CBS
(5)	The Andy Griffith Show	CBS
(6)	The Lucy Show	CBS
(7)	Candid Camera	CBS
(8)	The Ed Sullivan Show	CBS
(9)	The Danny Thomas Show	CBS
(10)	My Favorite Martian	CBS
(11)	The Red Skelton Show	CBS
(12)	I've Got a Secret	CBS
(13)	Lassie	CBS
(14)	The Jack Benny Program	CBS
(15)	The Jackie Gleason Show	CBS
(16)	The Donna Reed Show	ABC
(17)	The Virginian	NBC
(18)	The Patty Duke Show	ABC
(19)	Dr. Kildare	NBC
(20)	Gunsmoke	CBS

1964–1965

(1)	Bonanza	NBC
(2)	Bewitched	ABC
(3)	Gomer Pyle, U.S.M.C.	CBS
(4)	The Andy Griffith Show	CBS
(5)	The Fugitive	ABC
(6)	The Red Skelton Hour	CBS
(7)	The Dick Van Dyke Show	CBS
(8)	The Lucy Show	CBS
(9)	Peyton Place (II)	ABC
(10)	Combat	ABC
(11)	Walt Disney's Wonderful World	NBC
(12)	The Beverly Hillbillies	CBS
(13)	My Three Sons	ABC
(14)	Branded	NBC
(15)	Petticoat Junction	CBS
(16)	The Ed Sullivan Show	CBS
(17)	Lassie	CBS
(18)	The Munsters	CBS
(19)	Gilligan's Island	CBS
(20)	Peyton Place (I)	ABC

1965–1966

(1)	Bonanza	NBC
(2)	Gomer Pyle, U.S.M.C.	CBS
(3)	The Lucy Show	CBS
(4)	The Red Skelton Hour	CBS
(5)	Batman (II)	ABC
(6)	The Andy Griffith Show	CBS
(7)	Bewitched	ABC
(8)	The Beverly Hillbillies	CBS
(9)	Hogan's Heroes	CBS
(10)	Batman (I)	ABC
(11)	Green Acres	CBS
(12)	Get Smart	NBC
(13)	The Man from U.N.C.L.E.	NBC
(14)	Daktari	CBS
(15)	My Three Sons	CBS
(16)	The Dick Van Dyke Show	CBS
(17)	Walt Disney's Wonderful World	NBC
(18)	The Ed Sullivan Show	CBS
(19)	The Lawrence Welk Show	ABC
(20)	I've Got a Secret	CBS

1966–1967

(1)	Bonanza	NBC
(2)	The Red Skelton Hour	CBS
(3)	The Andy Griffith Show	CBS
(4)	The Lucy Show	CBS
(5)	The Jackie Gleason Show	CBS
(6)	Green Acres	CBS
(7)	Daktari	CBS
(8)	Bewitched	ABC
(9)	The Beverly Hillbillies	CBS

(10)	Gomer Pyle, U.S.M.C.	CBS
(11)	The Virginian	NBC
(12)	The Lawrence Welk Show	ABC
(13)	The Ed Sullivan Show	CBS
(14)	The Dean Martin Show	NBC
(15)	Family Affair	CBS
(16)	Smothers Brothers Comedy Hour	CBS
(17)	CBS Friday Night Movies	CBS
(18)	Hogan's Heroes	CBS
(19)	Walt Disney's Wonderful World	NBC
(20)	Saturday Night at the Movies	NBC

1967–1968

(1)	The Andy Griffith Show	CBS
(2)	The Lucy Show	CBS
(3)	Gomer Pyle, U.S.M.C.	CBS
(4)	Gunsmoke	CBS
(5)	Family Affair	CBS
(6)	Bonanza	NBC
(7)	The Red Skelton Hour	CBS
(8)	The Dean Martin Show	NBC
(9)	The Jackie Gleason Show	CBS
(10)	Saturday Night at the Movies	NBC
(11)	Bewitched	ABC
(12)	The Beverly Hillbillies	CBS
(13)	The Ed Sullivan Show	CBS
(14)	The Virginian	NBC
(15)	The CBS Friday Night Movie	CBS
(16)	Green Acres	CBS
(17)	The Lawrence Welk Show	ABC
(18)	Smothers Brothers Comedy Hour	CBS
(19)	Gentle Ben	CBS
(20)	Tuesday Night at the Movies	NBC

1968–1969

(1)	Rowan and Martin's Laugh-In	NBC
(2)	Gomer Pyle, U.S.M.C.	CBS
(3)	Bonanza	NBC
(4)	Mayberry R.F.D.	CBS
(5)	Family Affair	CBS
(6)	Gunsmoke	CBS
(7)	Julia	NBC
(8)	The Dean Martin Show	NBC
(9)	Here's Lucy	CBS
(10)	The Beverly Hillbillies	CBS
(11)	Mission: Impossible	CBS
(12)	Bewitched	ABC
(13)	The Red Skelton Hour	CBS
(14)	My Three Sons	CBS
(15)	The Glen Campbell Goodtime Hour	CBS
(16)	Ironside	NBC
(17)	The Virginian	NBC
(18)	The F.B.I.	ABC
(19)	Green Acres	CBS
(20)	Dragnet	NBC

1969–1970

(1)	Rowan and Martin's Laugh-In	NBC
(2)	Gunsmoke	CBS
(3)	Bonanza	NBC
(4)	Mayberry R.F.D.	CBS
(5)	Family Affair	CBS
(6)	Here's Lucy	CBS
(7)	The Red Skelton Hour	CBS
(8)	Marcus Welby, M.D.	ABC
(9)	The Wonderful World of Disney	NBC
(10)	The Doris Day Show	CBS
(11)	The Bill Cosby Show	NBC
(12)	The Jim Nabors Hour	CBS
(13)	The Carol Burnett Show	CBS
(14)	The Dean Martin Show	NBC
(15)	My Three Sons	CBS
(16)	Ironside	NBC
(17)	The Johnny Cash Show	ABC
(18)	The Beverly Hillbillies	CBS
(19)	Hawaii Five-O	CBS
(20)	(tie) Glen Campbell Goodtime Hour	CBS
(20)	(tie) Hee Haw	CBS

1970–1971

(1)	Marcus Welby, M.D.	ABC
(2)	The Flip Wilson Show	NBC
(3)	Here's Lucy	CBS
(4)	Ironside	NBC
(5)	Gunsmoke	CBS
(6)	ABC Movie of the Week	ABC
(7)	Hawaii Five-O	CBS
(8)	Medical Center	CBS
(9)	Bonanza	NBC
(10)	The F.B.I.	ABC
(11)	The Mod Squad	ABC
(12)	Adam-12	NBC
(13)	Rowan and Martin's Laugh-In	NBC
(14)	The Wonderful World of Disney	NBC
(15)	Mayberry R.F.D.	CBS
(16)	Hee Haw	CBS
(17)	Mannix	CBS
(18)	The Men from Shiloh	NBC
(19)	My Three Sons	CBS
(20)	The Doris Day Show	CBS

1971–1972

(1)	All in the Family	CBS
(2)	The Flip Wilson Show	NBC
(3)	Marcus Welby, M.D.	ABC
(4)	Gunsmoke	CBS
(5)	The ABC Movie of the Week	ABC
(6)	Sanford and Son	NBC
(7)	Mannix	CBS
(8)	Funny Face	CBS

(9)	Adam-12	NBC
(10)	The Mary Tyler Moore Show	CBS
(11)	Here's Lucy	CBS
(12)	Hawaii Five-O	CBS
(13)	Medical Center	CBS
(14)	The NBC Mystery Movie	NBC
(15)	Ironside	NBC
(16)	The Partridge Family	ABC
(17)	The F.B.I.	ABC
(18)	The New Dick Van Dyke Show	CBS
(19)	The Wonderful World of Disney	NBC
(20)	Bonanza	NBC

1972–1973

(1)	All in the Family	CBS
(2)	Sanford and Son	NBC
(3)	Hawaii Five-O	CBS
(4)	Maude	CBS
(5)	Bridget Loves Bernie	CBS
(6)	The NBC Sunday Mystery Movie	NBC
(7)	The Mary Tyler Moore Show	CBS
(8)	Gunsmoke	CBS
(9)	The Wonderful World of Disney	NBC
(10)	Ironside	NBC
(11)	Adam-12	NBC
(12)	The Flip Wilson Show	NBC
(13)	Marcus Welby, M.D.	ABC
(14)	Cannon	CBS
(15)	Here's Lucy	CBS
(16)	The Bob Newhart Show	CBS
(17)	ABC Tuesday Movie of the Week	ABC
(18)	NFL Monday Night Football	ABC
(19)	(tie) The Partridge Family	ABC
(19)	(tie) The Waltons	CBS

1973–1974

(1)	All in the Family	CBS
(2)	The Waltons	CBS
(3)	Sanford and Son	NBC
(4)	M*A*S*H	CBS
(5)	Hawaii Five-O	CBS
(6)	Maude	CBS
(7)	Kojak	CBS
(8)	The Sonny and Cher Comedy Hour	CBS
(9)	The Mary Tyler Moore Show	CBS
(10)	Cannon	CBS
(11)	The Six Million Dollar Man	ABC
(12)	The Bob Newhart Show	CBS
(13)	The Wonderful World of Disney	NBC
(14)	The NBC Sunday Mystery Movie	NBC
(15)	Gunsmoke	CBS
(16)	Happy Days	ABC
(17)	Good Times	CBS
(18)	Barnaby Jones	CBS

(19)	(tie) NFL Monday Night Football	ABC
(19)	(tie) The CBS Friday Night Movie	CBS

1974–1975

(1)	All in the Family	CBS
(2)	Sanford and Son	NBC
(3)	Chico and the Man	NBC
(4)	The Jeffersons	CBS
(5)	M*A*S*H	CBS
(6)	Rhoda	CBS
(7)	The Waltons	CBS
(8)	Good Times	CBS
(9)	Maude	CBS
(10)	Hawaii Five-O	CBS
(11)	The Mary Tyler Moore Show	CBS
(12)	The Rockford Files	NBC
(13)	Kojak	CBS
(14)	Little House on the Prairie	NBC
(15)	Police Woman	NBC
(16)	S.W.A.T.	ABC
(17)	The Bob Newhart Show	CBS
(18)	The Wonderful World of Disney	NBC
(19)	Mannix	CBS
(20)	(tie) Cannon	CBS
(20)	(tie) The Rookies	ABC
(20)	(tie) The NBC Sunday Mystery Movie	NBC

1975–1976

(1)	All in the Family	CBS
(2)	Laverne and Shirley	ABC
(3)	Rich Man, Poor Man	ABC
(4)	Maude	CBS
(5)	The Bionic Woman	ABC
(6)	Phyllis	CBS
(7)	The Six Million Dollar Man	ABC
(8)	Sanford and Son	NBC
(9)	Rhoda	CBS
(10)	Happy Days	ABC
(11)	The ABC Monday Movie	ABC
(12)	M*A*S*H	CBS
(13)	One Day at a Time	CBS
(14)	The Waltons	CBS
(15)	Starsky and Hutch	ABC
(16)	Good Heavens	ABC
(17)	Welcome Back, Kotter	ABC
(18)	Kojak	CBS
(19)	The Mary Tyler Moore Show	CBS
(20)	The ABC Sunday Movie	ABC

1976–1977

(1)	Happy Days	ABC
(2)	Laverne and Shirley	ABC
(3)	The ABC Monday Night Movie	ABC

(4)	M*A*S*H	CBS
(5)	Charlie's Angels	ABC
(6)	The Big Event	NBC
(7)	The Six Million Dollar Man	ABC
(8)	The ABC Sunday Night Movie	ABC
(9)	Baretta	ABC
(10)	One Day at a Time	CBS
(11)	Three's Company	ABC
(12)	All in the Family	CBS
(13)	Welcome Back, Kotter	ABC
(14)	The Bionic Woman	ABC
(15)	The Waltons	CBS
(16)	Little House on the Prairie	NBC
(17)	Barney Miller	ABC
(18)	60 Minutes	CBS
(19)	Hawaii Five-O	CBS
(20)	NBC Monday Night at the Movies	NBC

(Note: *Roots* was not considered a regularly scheduled series for ratings purposes.)

1977–1978

(1)	Laverne and Shirley	ABC
(2)	Happy Days	ABC
(3)	Three's Company	ABC
(4)	Charlie's Angels	ABC
(5)	All in the Family	CBS
(6)	(tie) Little House on the Prairie	NBC
(6)	(tie) 60 Minutes	CBS
(8)	(tie) M*A*S*H	CBS
(8)	(tie) One Day at a Time	CBS
(10)	Alice	CBS
(11)	Soap	ABC
(12)	How the West Was Won	ABC
(13)	(tie) Monday Night at the Movies	NBC
(13)	(tie) Eight Is Enough	ABC
(13)	(tie) NFL Monday Night Football	ABC
(13)	(tie) The Love Boat	ABC
(17)	Barney Miller	ABC
(18)	The ABC Sunday Night Movie	ABC
(19)	(tie) Fantasy Island	ABC
(19)	(tie) Project U.F.O.	NBC

1978–1979

(1)	Three's Company	ABC
(2)	Laverne and Shirley	ABC
(3)	Mork & Mindy	ABC
(4)	Happy Days	ABC
(5)	Angie	ABC
(6)	(tie) 60 Minutes	CBS
(6)	(tie) M*A*S*H	CBS
(8)	The Ropers	ABC
(9)	Charlie's Angels	ABC
(10)	(tie) All in the Family	CBS
(10)	(tie) Taxi	ABC

(12)	Eight Is Enough	ABC
(13)	Alice	CBS
(14)	Little House on the Prairie	NBC
(15)	Barney Miller	ABC
(16)	(tie) The ABC Sunday Night Movie	ABC
(16)	(tie) The Love Boat	ABC
(16)	The MacKenzies of Paradise Cove	ABC
(19)	(tie) One Day at a Time	CBS
(19)	(tie) Soap	ABC

1979–1980

(1)	60 Minutes	CBS
(2)	Three's Company	ABC
(3)	M*A*S*II	CBS
(4)	Alice	CBS
(5)	Dallas	CBS
(6)	Flo	CBS
(7)	(tie) The Jeffersons	CBS
(7)	(tie) The Dukes of Hazzard	CBS
(9)	That's Incredible	ABC
(10)	One Day at a Time	CBS
(11)	Archie Bunker's Place	CBS
(12)	Eight Is Enough	ABC
(13)	Taxi	ABC
(14)	House Calls	CBS
(15)	(tie) Real People	NBC
(15)	(tie) Happy Days	ABC
(17)	Little House on the Prairie	NBC
(18)	(tie) CHiPs	NBC
(18)	(tie) Charlie's Angels	ABC
(20)	Trapper John, M.D.	CBS

1980–1981

(1)	Dallas	CBS
(2)	60 Minutes	CBS
(3)	The Dukes of Hazzard	CBS
(4)	The Love Boat	ABC
(5)	Private Benjamin	CBS
(6)	M*A*S*H	CBS
(7)	House Calls	CBS
(8)	The Jeffersons	CBS
(9)	(tie) The Two of Us	CBS
(9)	(tie) Little House on the Prairie	NBC
(11)	Alice	CBS
(12)	Real People	NBC
(13)	(tie) One Day at a Time	CBS
(13)	(tie) The Greatest American Hero	ABC
(15)	Three's Company	ABC
(16)	Magnum, P.I.	CBS
(17)	(tie) Too Close for Comfort	ABC
(17)	(tie) ABC Sunday Movie	ABC
(19)	Diff'rent Strokes	NBC
(20)	Archie Bunker's Place	CBS

1981–1982

(1)	Dallas	CBS
(2)	60 Minutes	CBS
(3)	The Jeffersons	CBS
(4)	(tie) Joanie Loves Chachi	ABC
(4)	(tie) Three's Company	ABC
(6)	Alice	CBS
(7)	(tie) The Dukes of Hazzard	CBS
(7)	(tie) Too Close for Comfort	ABC
(9)	ABC Monday Night Movie	ABC
(10)	M*A*S*H	CBS
(11)	One Day at a Time	CBS
(12)	NFL Monday Night Football	ABC
(13)	Archie Bunker's Place	CBS
(14)	Falcon Crest	CBS
(15)	The Love Boat	ABC
(16)	(tie) Hart to Hart	ABC
(16)	(tie) Trapper John, M.D.	CBS
(18)	Magnum, P.I.	CBS
(19)	Happy Days	ABC
(20)	Dynasty	ABC

1982–1983

(1)	60 Minutes	CBS
(2)	Dallas	CBS
(3)	(tie) M*A*S*H	CBS
(3)	(tie) Magnum, P.I.	CBS
(5)	Dynasty	ABC
(6)	Three's Company	ABC
(7)	Simon & Simon	CBS
(8)	Falcon Crest	CBS
(9)	The Love Boat	ABC
(10)	(tie) The A Team	NBC
(10)	(tie) NFL Monday Night Football	ABC
(12)	(tie) The Jeffersons	CBS
(12)	(tie) Newhart	CBS
(14)	(tie) The Fall Guy	ABC
(14)	(tie) The Mississippi	CBS
(16)	9 to 5	ABC
(17)	One Day at a Time	CBS
(18)	Hart to Hart	ABC
(19)	(tie) Gloria	CBS
(19)	(tie) Trapper John, M.D.	CBS
(19)	(tie) Goodnight, Beantown	CBS

1983–1984

(1)	Dallas	CBS
(2)	60 Minutes	CBS
(3)	Dynasty	ABC
(4)	The A Team	NBC
(5)	Simon & Simon	CBS
(6)	Magnum, P.I.	CBS
(7)	Falcon Crest	CBS
(8)	Kate & Allie	CBS

(9)	Hotel	ABC
(10)	Cagney & Lacey	CBS
(11)	Knots Landing	CBS
(12)	(tie) ABC Sunday Movie	ABC
(12)	(tie) ABC Monday Movie	ABC
(14)	TV's Bloopers & Practical Jokes	NBC
(15)	AfterMASH	CBS
(16)	The Fall Guy	ABC
(17)	The Love Boat	ABC
(18)	Riptide	NBC
(19)	The Jeffersons	CBS
(20)	Scarecrow & Mrs. King	CBS

1984–1985

(1)	Dynasty	ABC
(2)	Dallas	CBS
(3)	The Cosby Show	NBC
(4)	60 Minutes	CBS
(5)	Family Ties	NBC
(6)	The A Team	NBC
(7)	Simon & Simon	CBS
(8)	Murder, She Wrote	CBS
(9)	Knots Landing	CBS
(10)	(tie) Falcon Crest	CBS
(10)	(tie) Crazy Like a Fox	CBS
(12)	(tie) Hotel	ABC
(12)	(tie) Cheers	NBC
(14)	Riptide	NBC
(15)	Magnum, P. I.	CBS
(16)	Newhart	CBS
(17)	Kate & Allie	CBS
(18)	NBC Monday Night Movie	NBC
(19)	Highway to Heaven	NBC
(20)	Night Court	NBC

1985–1986

(1)	The Cosby Show	NBC
(2)	Family Ties	NBC
(3)	Murder, She Wrote	CBS
(4)	60 Minutes	CBS
(5)	Cheers	NBC
(6)	Dallas	CBS
(7)	(tie) Dynasty	ABC
(7)	(tie) The Golden Girls	NBC
(9)	Miami Vice	NBC
(10)	Who's the Boss?	ABC
(11)	Night Court	NBC
(12)	CBS Sunday Night Movie	CBS
(13)	Highway to Heaven	NBC
(14)	Kate & Allie	CBS
(15)	NFL Monday Night Football	ABC
(16)	Newhart	CBS
(17)	(tie) Knots Landing	CBS
(17)	(tie) Growing Pains	ABC

(19)	You Again?	NBC
(20)	227	NBC

1986–1987

(1)	The Cosby Show	NBC
(2)	Family Ties	NBC
(3)	Cheers	NBC
(4)	Murder, She Wrote	CBS
(5)	The Golden Girls	NBC
(6)	60 Minutes	CBS
(7)	Night Court	NBC
(8)	Growing Pains	ABC
(9)	Moonlighting	ABC
(10)	Who's the Boss?	ABC
(11)	Dallas	CBS
(12)	Newhart	CBS
(13)	Amen	NBC
(14)	227	NBC
(15)	(tie) Matlock	NBC
(15)	(tie) CBS Sunday Night Movie	CBS
(15)	(tie) NBC Monday Night Movie	NBC
(18)	NFL Monday Night Football	ABC
(19)	Kate & Allie	CBS
(20)	NBC Sunday Night Movie	NBC

1987–1988

(1)	The Cosby Show	NBC
(2)	A Different World	NBC
(3)	Cheers	NBC
(4)	The Golden Girls	NBC
(5)	Growing Pains	ABC
(6)	Who's the Boss?	ABC
(7)	Night Court	NBC
(8)	60 Minutes	CBS
(9)	Murder, She Wrote	CBS
(10)	(tie) ALF	NBC
(10)	(tie) The Wonder Years	ABC
(12)	(tie) Moonlighting	ABC
(12)	(tie) L. A. Law	NBC
(14)	Matlock	NBC
(15)	Amen	NBC
(16)	NFL Monday Night Football	ABC
(17)	Family Ties	NBC
(18)	CBS Sunday Night Movie	CBS
(19)	In the Heat of the Night	NBC
(20)	(tie) My Two Dads	NBC
(20)	(tie) Valerie's Family	NBC

1988–1989

(1)	The Cosby Show	NBC
(2)	Roseanne	ABC
(3)	A Different World	NBC
(4)	Cheers	NBC

(5)	The Golden Girls	NBC
(6)	Who's the Boss?	ABC
(7)	60 Minutes	CBS
(8)	Murder, She Wrote	CBS
(9)	Empty Nest	NBC
(10)	Anything But Love	ABC
(11)	Dear John	NBC
(12)	(tie) ALF	NBC
(12)	(tie) L. A. Law	NBC
(14)	Matlock	NBC
(15)	(tie) Unsolved Mysteries	NBC
(15)	(tie) In the Heat of the Night	NBC
(17)	Growing Pains	ABC
(18)	Hunter	NBC
(19)	(tie) NFL Monday Night Football	ABC
(19)	(tie) Head of the Class	ABC

1989–1990

(1)	Roseanne	ABC
(2)	The Cosby Show	NBC
(3)	Cheers	NBC
(4)	A Different World	NBC
(5)	America's Funniest Home Videos	ABC
(6)	The Golden Girls	NBC
(7)	60 Minutes	CBS
(8)	The Wonder Years	ABC
(9)	Empty Nest	NBC
(10)	NFL Monday Night Football	ABC
(11)	Unsolved Mysteries	NBC
(12)	Who's the Boss?	ABC
(13)	(tie) Murder, She Wrote	CBS
(13)	(tie) Chicken Soup	ABC
(15)	Grand	NBC
(16)	L. A. Law	NBC
(17)	In the Heat of the Night	NBC
(18)	Dear John	NBC
(19)	Coach	ABC
(20)	Matlock	NBC

1990–1991

(1)	Cheers	NBC
(2)	60 Minutes	CBS
(3)	Roseanne	ABC
(4)	A Different World	NBC
(5)	The Cosby Show	NBC
(6)	Murphy Brown	CBS
(7)	(tie) Empty Nest	NBC
(7)	(tie) America's Funniest Home Videos	ABC
(9)	NFL Monday Night Football	ABC
(10)	The Golden Girls	NBC
(11)	Designing Women	CBS
(12)	Murder, She Wrote	CBS
(13)	America's Funniest People	ABC
(14)	Full House	ABC
(15)	Family Matters	ABC

(16)	Unsolved Mysteries	NBC
(17)	Matlock	NBC
(18)	Coach	ABC
(19)	(tie) Who's the Boss	ABC
(19)	(tie) CBS Sunday Movie	CBS

1991–1992

(1)	60 Minutes	CBS
(2)	Roseanne	ABC
(3)	Murphy Brown	CBS
(4)	Cheers	NBC
(5)	Home Improvement	ABC
(6)	Designing Women	CBS
(7)	Coach	ABC
(8)	Full House	ABC
(9)	Unsolved Mysteries	NBC
(10)	Murder, She Wrote	CBS
(11)	Major Dad	CBS
(12)	NFL Monday Night Football	ABC
(13)	Evening Shade	CBS
(14)	Northern Exposure	CBS
(15)	A Different World	NBC
(16)	The Cosby Show	NBC
(17)	Wings	NBC
(18)	The Fresh Prince of Bel-Air	NBC
(19)	America's Funniest Home Videos	ABC
(20)	20/20	ABC

1992–1993

(1)	60 Minutes	CBS
(2)	Roseanne	ABC
(3)	Home Improvement	ABC
(4)	Murphy Brown	CBS
(5)	Murder, She Wrote	CBS
(6)	Coach	ABC
(7)	NFL Monday Night Football	ABC
(8)	Cheers	NBC
(9)	Full House	ABC
(10)	Northern Exposure	CBS
(11)	20/20	ABC
(12)	Rescue 911	CBS
(13)	Love and War	CBS
(14)	(tie) The Fresh Prince of Bel-Air	NBC
(14)	(tie) Hangin' with Mr. Cooper	ABC
(14)	(tie) The Jackie Thomas Show	ABC
(17)	Evening Shade	CBS
(18)	Unsolved Mysteries	NBC
(19)	Hearts Afire	CBS
(20)	PrimeTime Live	ABC

1993–1994

(1)	Home Improvement	ABC
(2)	60 Minutes	CBS

(3)	Seinfeld	NBC
(4)	Roseanne	ABC
(5)	These Friends of Mine	ABC
(6)	Grace Under Fire	ABC
(7)	Frasier	NBC
(8)	Coach	NBC
(9)	Murder, She Wrote	CBS
(10)	NFL Monday Night Football	ABC
(11)	Murphy Brown	CBS
(12)	Thunder Alley	ABC
(13)	20/20	ABC
(14)	Love and War	CBS
(15)	Wings	NBC
(16)	(tie) Full House	ABC
(16)	(tie) Northern Exposure	CBS
(16)	(tie) PrimeTime Live	ABC
(19)	(tie) Dave's World	CBS
(19)	(tie) Dr. Quinn, Medicine Woman	CBS
(19)	(tic) NYPD Blue	ABC
(19)	(tie) Rescue 911	CBS

1994–1995

(1)	Seinfeld	NBC
(2)	ER	NBC
(3)	Home Improvement	ABC
(4)	Grace Under Fire	ABC
(5)	NFL Monday Night Football	ABC
(6)	60 Minutes	CBS
(7)	NYPD Blue	ABC
(8)	Friends	NBC
(9)	(tie) Roseanne	ABC
(9)	(tie) Murder, She Wrote	CBS
(11)	Mad About You	NBC
(12)	Madman of the People	NBC
(13)	Ellen	ABC
(14)	Hope & Gloria	NBC
(15)	Frasier	NBC
(16)	Murphy Brown	CBS
(17)	20/20	ABC
(18)	CBS Sunday Movie	CBS
(19)	NBC Monday Movie	NBC
(20)	Dave's World	CBS

Baxley, Barbara, 23, 32, 659
Baxter, Anne, 316, 391
Baxter, Billy, 414
Baxter, Carol, 168
Baxter, Charles, 50, 62, 495
Baxter, Frank, 20, 609, 747, 822, 948, 950, 1122
Baxter, Meredith (Meredith Baxter-Birney), 66, 119, 273, 276
Bay City Rollers, 80, 457
Bay, Willow, 336, 583
Bayer, Gary, 337, 537
Bayer, Jimmy, 494
Bayly, Lorraine, 799
Baynes, Andrea, 1108
Bays, Michael, 206
Bazlen, Brigid, 204, 858
Beach Boys, The, 143, 329
Beach, Michael, 795, 878
Beacham, Stephanie, 170, 245, 733, 758
Beaird, Barbara, 284
Beaird, Betty, 442
Beaird, Pamela, 473
Beal, John, 14, 50, 303, 700, 797
Beals, Jennifer, 874
Bean, Orson, 87, 104, 225, 297, 469, 842, 852
Bean, Sean, 530, 731
Bean, Steve, 167
Beanblossom, Billie Jean, 546
Beard, Dita, 761
Beard, James, 425
Bearde, Chris, 108, 157, 180, 334, 397, 448, 773, 774, 1053
Bearse, Amanda, 30, 520
Beasley, Allyce, 567
Beatles, The, 82, 248, 249, 263, 398, 421, 614, 750, 955, 957
Beaton, Alex, 458
Beattie, Bob, 9
Beatts, Anne, 726, 782, 1070, 1072
Beatty, Bruce, 615
Beatty, Morgan, 649
Beatty, Ned, 24, 114, 387, 417, 810, 968, 969, 971, 974
Beatty, Robert, 215
Beatty, Roger, 1059, 1062, 1065, 1067, 1074
Beatty, Warren, 217, 223, 457, 496, 798, 907
Beauchamp, Richard, 135, 941
Beaudin, Glen, 803
Beaudine, Deka, 640
Beaudine, William, 347, 812
Beaulieu, Philippine Leroy, 974
Beaulieu, Trace, 583
Beaumont, Charles, 871
Beaumont, Chris, 374
Beaumont, Hugh, 473, 805
Beavais, Garcelle, 563
Beaver, Jim, 838
Beavers, Louise, 90, 785
Beck, Jack, 1051
Beck, Jackson, 481
Beck, Jenny, 641, 881
Beck, John, 194, 289, 602, 724
Beck, Julian, 545
Beck, Kimberly (Kimberly Beck-Hilton), 142, 317, 499, 904
Beck, Michael, 394, 973
Beck, Noelle, 498
Beck-Hilton, Kimberly. *See* Beck, Kimberly
Beckel, Graham, 136
Becker, Barbara, 699
Becker, Fred, 643
Becker, George, 219
Becker, Samantha, 729
Becker, Sandy, 916

Becker, Terry, 888
Becker, Tony, 295, 629, 861
Becker, Vernon, 429
Beckering, Raymond, 393
Beckerman, George, 563
Becket, Scotty, 703
Beckford, Roxanne, 287, 862
Beckham, Brice, 557
Beckley, Barbara, 206
Beckman, Bee, 1110
Beckman, Claire, 30, 62
Beckman, Harry, 406
Beckman, Henry, 122, 157, 309, 373, 478, 536
Bedard, Rolland, 297
Bedelia, Bonnie, 495, 596, 976
Bedford, Brad, 50
Bedford, Brian, 180, 731
Bedford-Lloyd, John, 387
Bedi, Kabir, 318
Bedlow-Hogan, Susan, 1116
Bednarski, Andrew, 698
Bee, Bob, 1093
Bee Gees, The, 367, 773, 969
Bee, Molly, 432, 809, 824
Beecroft, David, 272, 369, 622
Beecroft, Gregory (Greg), 63, 348
Beeny, Christopher, 528
Beer, Jacqueline, 746
Beers, Francine, 252, 625
Beery, Noah, Jr., 165, 223, 388, 680, 699, 703, 928
Bega, Leslie, 367
Beghe, Jason, 286, 542
Begley, Ed, 457, 473, 701
Begley, Ed, Jr., 631, 641, 704, 718, 919
Behar, Joseph, 1105
Behar, Joy, 548
Behar, Phyllis, 621
Behr, Felicia Minei, 1110, 1115
Behrens, Bernard, 236
Behrens, Sam (Stan Birnbaum), 318, 454, 715
Beiger, Peter, 958
Beir, Fred, 205
Beirne, Jeanne, 50
Bekins, Richard, 50, 64
Bel Geddes, Barbara, 23, 193, 194, 700, 1078
Belack, Doris, 51, 72, 227, 274, 470, 621
Belafonte, Gina, 175
Belafonte, Harry, 316, 392, 767, 881, 947, 951, 955, 960, 971, 1045
Belafonte-Harper, Shari, 392, 482
Belafsky, Marty, 397
Belanger, Paul, 837
Belasco, Leon, 429, 580
Belefonte, Ben, 851
Belenda, Carla, 547
Belford, Christine, 31, 73, 257, 520, 633, 653, 969
Belgard, Madeline, 624, 836
Belkin, Gary, 1055, 1065, 1067, 1090
Bell, Bradley, 109
Bell, Darryl, 218
Bell, Dave, 1091
Bell, Felecea M., 207, 319
Bell, Joy, 53
Bell, Keith, 527
Bell, Lauralee, 933
Bell, Lee Phillip, 109, 931, 1066
Bell, Marshall, 397, 615
Bell, Steve, 9
Bell, Steven, 225
Bell, Vanessa, 30
Bell, William J., 50, 60, 109, 204,

931, 1066, 1070, 1086, 1092, 1094, 1111, 1113
Bellamy, Diana, 803, 830
Bellamy, Ralph, 163, 210, 255, 398, 512, 571, 798, 806, 917, 964
Belland, Bruce, 839
Belland & Somerville, 839
Bellaran, Ray, 735
Bellaver, Harry, 588
Beller, Kathleen (Kathy), 122, 244, 735
Beller, Mary Linn, 119, 199
Bellflower, Nellie, 448
Bellini, Cal, 215
Bellisario, Donald (Don), 21, 816
Bellows, Jim, 875
Bellson, Louis, 648
Bellwood, Pamela, 244, 888
Bellwood, Peter, 1055
Belmondo, Buzz, 632
Belnavis, Christian, 356
Beloin, Ed, 769
Belson, Jerry, 1100, 1104
Beltran, Robert, 563, 787, 974
Belushi, James (Jim), 726, 913, 915, 924
Belushi, John, 211, 725, 726, 913, 966, 1072
Belzer, Richard, 289, 388, 830
Benaderet, Bea, 127, 290, 321, 401, 420, 655, 656
Benard, Frank M., 933
Benard, Maurice, 30, 320, 403
Benben, Brian, 238, 313, 447
Bench, Johnny, 312, 503
Bendall, Robert, 49
Bender, Jim, 277
Bender, Joan, 1068
Bendetti, Michael, 870
Bendewald, Andrea, 756
Bendix, Simone, 777
Bendix, William, 126, 422, 480, 482, 634
Benedict, Amy, 320
Benedict, Dirk, 11, 79, 163
Benedict, Greg, 606
Benedict, Nicholas (Nick), 28, 49, 207
Benedict, Paul, 428
Benesch, Lynn, 621
Benet, Brenda, 205, 935
Beniades, Ted, 45
Benirschke, Rolf, 908
Benjamin, Burton, 1053, 1058, 1060, 1063
Benjamin, Cynthia, 60
Benjamin, Julia, 366
Benjamin, Paul, 967
Benjamin, Richard, 366, 679
Benjamin, Susan, 13
Bennett, Al, 35
Bennett, Bern, 790
Bennett, Donn, 94
Bennett, Elizabeth, 609, 929
Bennett, Fran, 604
Bennett, Gabriele, 450
Bennett, Harve, 40, 100, 315, 412, 695, 720, 760, 1083
Bennett, Hywel, 583
Bennett, Jahary, 387
Bennett, Joan, 20, 87, 198, 772, 858
Bennett, John Aaron, 405
Bennett, Marjorie, 124, 431, 497
Bennett, Meg, 724, 735, 932, 1119
Bennett, Nigel, 298
Bennett, Ruth, 724
Bennett, Sue, 936
Bennett, Sydney, 114

Breech, Kathryn, 621
Breech, Robert M., 1103, 1106, 1111
Breeding, Larry, 465, 913
Breen, Bridget, 227
Breen, Danny, 97, 609
Breen, Joseph (Joe), 64, 348, 498
Breen, Patrick, 96, 755, 800
Breen, Paulette, 29
Breen, Robert, 236
Bregman, Buddy, 250, 577
Bregman, Tracey E. (Tracey Bregman Recht), 205, 933, 1092
Bremner, Scott, 593
Bremseth, Lloyd, 227
Brennan, Eileen, 32, 596, 613, 674, 831, 1081
Brennan, John, 52, 112
Brennan, Jude, 1114
Brennan, Melissa. See Reeves, Melissa
Brennan, Ryan, 207
Brennan, Walter, 350, 686, 842, 874
Brenneman, Amy, 548, 587
Brenner, Alfred, 1044
Brenner, David, 604, 855
Brenner, Dori, 88, 150, 156, 592
Brenner, Lisa D., 31
Brenner, Maurice, 658
Brenner, Robert, 682
Brennert, Alan, 1106
Brent, George, 919
Bresler, Jerry, 423, 685
Breslin, Jimmy, 201, 432
Breslin, Patricia (Pat), 87, 316, 650
Breslow, Marc, 1087, 1090, 1092, 1097
Brestoff, Richard, 627
Brett, Jeremy, 583
Brettschneider, Mark, 623
Breuer, Jim, 727
Brewer, Betty, 98, 382
Brewer, Teresa, 653, 800
Brewster, Diane, 308, 413, 473, 533
Brewster, Jordana, 64
Brewster, Ralph, 170
Brewton, Maia, 483, 642
Breznahan, Thomas (Tom), 353, 710
Brian, David, 558
Brickell, Beth, 321
Bricken, Jules, 296
Bridges, Beau, 258, 355, 363, 776, 879, 980, 985, 1109, 1112
Bridges, James, 640
Bridges, Jeff, 967
Bridges, Lloyd, 97, 141, 363, 434, 487, 489, 607, 640, 707, 721, 733, 897, 926, 958, 959, 972, 976
Bridges, Todd, 218, 219, 288
Bridges, William, 800
Bridgewater, Dee Dee, 49
Brienza, Bob, 1119
Bright, Kevin S., 1103
Bright, Patricia, 416
Brightcloud, Bryan, 682
Briles, Charles, 96
Brill, Charlie, 806
Brill, Fran, 395, 1065
Brill, Leighton, 475
Brill, Marty, 595
Brimley, Wilford, 114, 630
Brinckerhoff, Peter, 1108
Brinegar, Paul, 461, 532, 684
Brinkley, David, 7, 201, 584, 585, 834, 954, 978

Brinkley, Don, 265, 863
Briscoe, Don, 204
Brisebois, Danielle, 27, 454
Briskin, Jerry, 747
Briskin, Mort, 749, 893
Brissette, Tiffany, 765
Britt, May, 197
Brittany, Morgan, 193, 330, 631, 969
Britton, Barbara (Barbara Monte-Britton), 218, 557, 622
Britton, Pamela, 103, 578
Brochtrup, Bill, 588
Brock, Brenda, 623
Brock, Richard, 1091
Brock, Stanley (Stan), 375, 914
Brockett, Don, 560
Brockhausen, Maurice, 627
Brockman, Jane, 918
Brockway, Merrill, 1075, 1089
Broder, Dick, 518
Broderick, Beth, 289, 330, 369
Broderick, James, 118, 273
Broderick, Lorraine, 1093, 1100, 1113
Broderick, Malcolm, 303, 519
Broderick, Matthew, 42
Broderick, Peter, 735
Brodie, Steve, 377, 927
Brodkin, Herbert, 156, 180, 210, 296, 611, 747, 797, 1073
Brody, Adrien, 48
Brogan, Jimmy, 632
Brogna, Johnny, 689
Brogren, Stefan, 210
Broido, Joseph, 1103
Brokaw, Tom, 265, 585, 609, 845, 846
Brokenshire, Norman, 78, 89, 299, 356
Brolin, James, 47, 265, 391, 517, 1055
Brolin, Josh, 674, 919, 935
Bromfield, John, 749
Bromfield, Valri, 88, 201, 339, 598
Bromilow, Peter, 541
Bromka, Elaine, 207
Bromley, Sheila, 403, 570
Bronowski, Jacob, 64
Bronson, Charles, 223, 257, 515, 864, 966
Bronson, Michael, 1083, 1087, 1089, 1091, 1098, 1101
Bronson, Milt, 11
Brook, Jayne, 758, 889
Brook, Lyndon, 527
Brook, M. C., 146
Brook, Pamela, 51
Brooke, Hillary, 11, 579
Brooke, Walter, 344, 624, 641, 836
Brookes, Jacqueline, 51, 420, 716, 740, 841
Brooks, Aimee, 206, 573
Brooks, Albert, 332, 726
Brooks, Anne Rose, 52
Brooks, Avery, 513, 779, 786
Brooks, Claude, 387, 867
Brooks, David, 252
Brooks, Elizabeth, 205
Brooks, Foster, 569, 595, 849
Brooks, Garth, 983
Brooks, Geraldine, 242, 279, 495, 930
Brooks, J. Cynthia, 207
Brooks, James L. (Jim), 65, 306, 525, 694, 706, 820, 862, 1057, 1065, 1068, 1070, 1072, 1075, 1078, 1080, 1100, 1103, 1104, 1106, 1117
Brooks, Jason, 207

Brooks, Joel, 240, 335, 353, 580, 820
Brooks, Martin E., 100, 753, 760
Brooks, Matthew, 275, 747
Brooks, Mel, 324, 611, 854, 908, 937, 1051
Brooks, Ned, 540
Brooks, Rand, 698
Brooks, Randi, 465, 921
Brooks, Randy, 53, 123, 320, 692, 933
Brooks, Richard, 471
Brooks, Roxanne, 696
Brooks, Stephen, 206, 267, 411, 611
Brooks, Tracy, 52
Brookshier, Tom, 151
Brooksmith, Jane, 829
Broomall, Colleen, 63
Brophy, Kevin, 499
Brophy, Sallie, 124, 294
Brosnan, Pierce, 606, 691
Brosten, Harve, 1074
Brothers, Joyce, 225, 624, 649, 761, 762, 764, 765
Brough, Candi, 68
Brough, Randi, 68
Broun, Heywood Hale, 227
Brouwer, Peter, 63, 495
Browder, Ben, 114
Brower, Millicent, 333
Brown, A. Whitney, 727, 1101
Brown, Aaron, 9
Brown, Alli, 206
Brown, Andrew, 1078
Brown, Bill, 557
Brown, Blair, 42, 203, 776, 973, 982
Brown, Bob, 732, 869
Brown, Bobbie, 671
Brown, Brandy, 53
Brown, Bryan, 834
Brown, Candy Ann, 705
Brown, Carlos, 743
Brown, Charles, 373
Brown, Charlotte, 694
Brown, Charnele, 218
Brown, Chelsea, 469, 517, 532
Brown, Cheryl Lynn, 347
Brown, Christopher J., 51, 627
Brown, Clancy, 246, 983
Brown, Coral, 840
Brown, Dave, 424
Brown, Donna, 172
Brown, Doris, 500
Brown, Earl, 197, 219
Brown, Elaine Meryl, 1085
Brown, Eric, 512
Brown, Evert, 1096
Brown, Gail, 51
Brown, Garrett M., 759, 904
Brown, Georg Stanford, 706, 707, 1094
Brown, Georgia, 288, 528
Brown, Graham, 205
Brown, Helen Gurley, 336, 633
Brown, James, 37
Brown, James H., 434, 680
Brown, James Harmon, 1114
Brown, Jeff, 1100
Brown, Jerry, 752
Brown, Jim L., 698
Brown, Jimmy, 662
Brown, Joe E., 125
Brown, Joe, Jr., 836
Brown, John, 127, 480
Brown, John Mason, 188, 466, 850
Brown, Johnny, 324, 337, 469, 475, 720
Brown, Julie, 168, 250
Brown, Kale, 31, 52

Corey, Wendell, 6, 151, 255, 359, 648, 904
Corff, Robert, 263
Corley, Al, 243
Corley, Bob, 90
Corley, Marjorie, 559
Corley, Pat, 79, 304, 375, 575
Corman, Gene, 1083
Corman, Maddie, 6, 32, 560
Cornblatt, Bruce, 1114
Cornelius, Don, 775
Cornell, Jan, 1080, 1098
Cornell, Katharine, 675
Cornell, Lydia, 858
Cornfeld, Betty, 1085
Cornwell, Judy, 528
Correll, Charles, 44, 138, 473
Correll, Richard, 473
Corri, Adrienne, 810
Corrigan, Lloyd, 356, 357, 547, 685, 916
Corrigan, Ray "Crash," 185
Corrington, John William, 142, 320, 735
Corrington, Joyce, 142, 320, 735
Corsaut, Aneta, 46, 393, 562
Cort, Robert W., 1103
Cort, William (Bill), 10, 243, 566, 917
Cortese, Dan, 542, 711, 863
Cortese, Joe, 772
Cortez, Stacey, 319
Cortland, Nicholas, 736
Corwin, Christopher, 51
Corwin, Norman, 607
Cosby, Bill, 45, 97, 144, 180, 255, 280, 404, 744, 930, 960, 961, 1049, 1051, 1052, 1053, 1082
Cosell, Gordon, 263
Cosell, Howard, 9, 395, 587, 728, 781
Cosgrove, John, 879
Cossart, Valerie, 287, 797
Cossette, Pierre, 46, 447, 720, 746
Costa, Cosie, 450
Costa, Mary, 168
Costa, Peter, 181
Costanzo, Robert, 155, 157, 330, 434, 465
Costas, Bob, 469, 609, 1114
Costello, Elvis, 978
Costello, Lou, 11, 399
Costello, Mariclare, 288, 724, 894
Costello, Pat, 11, 399
Costello, Robert, 198, 1072, 1076
Costello, Sybil, 1119
Costello, Victoria, 1114
Costello, Ward, 252, 739
Coster, Nicolas (Nick), 51, 64, 554, 622, 631, 715, 723, 739, 771
Costigan, James, 1045, 1067, 1070, 1123
Costigan, Jeannine, 227
Costigan, Peter, 702
Costner, Kevin, 880, 986
Coston, Suzanne, 1085, 1091
Cote, Suzy, 349
Cothran, John, Jr., 118
Cotler, Jeff, 796
Cotler, Kami, 538, 894
Cott, Ted, 850
Cotten, Joseph, 315, 382, 618, 675, 869, 965
Cottet, Mia, 287
Cottle, Bob, 712
Cottle, Tom, 848
Cotton, Darlene, 495
Couch, Jack, 30

Coufos, Paul, 205
Coughlin, Francis, 236
Coughlin, Kevin, 511
Coulier, David (Dave), 43, 309
Council, Richard, 495
Country Lads, The, 432
Coupland, Diana, 528
Courakos, Irene, 210
Couric, Katie, 609, 846, 1116
Court, Geraldine, 52, 62, 227, 348
Court, Hazel, 216
Courtland, Jerome, 885, 892
Courtleigh, Bob, 66, 287
Courtney, Alex, 810
Courtney, Chuck, 488
Courtney, Deborah, 495
Courtney, Jacqueline (Jacquie), 50, 498, 621, 630
Cousins, Christopher (Chris), 52, 623
Cousins, Norman, 483
Cousteau, Jacques-Yves, 616, 835, 1058, 1091,
Cousteau, Jean-Michel, 1091
Coutteure, Ronny, 934
Couturie, Bill, 1098
Covan, DeForest, 828
Cover, Franklin, 427
Covington, Warren, 789
Cowan, Geoffrey, 1109
Cowan, Jerome, 517, 608, 813, 874, 882
Cowan, Louis G. (Lou), 682, 762, 793
Cowan, Phil, 916
Coward, Noel, 296, 529, 765, 958
Cowen, Ron, 1094
Cowgill, David, 933
Cowles, Matthew, 29, 498, 925
Cowling, Sam, 230
Cox, Courteney, 276, 305, 554, 866
Cox, Dick, 376
Cox, Josh, 621
Cox, Monty, 321
Cox, Nikki, 319, 771, 878
Cox, Richard, 264, 495, 499
Cox, Ronny, 55, 179, 718, 738, 779, 808
Cox, Rosetta, 332
Cox, Ruth, 714
Cox, Tony, 677
Cox, Wally, 314, 380, 384, 559, 790, 947, 962
Cox, Wayne, 817
Cox, Wendy, 597
Cox, William, 621
Coxe, George Harmon, 186
Coy, Walter, 307, 841
Crabb, Cristopher, 196
Crabbe, Buster, 124, 143
Crabbe, Cullen, 143
Crable, Debra, 247
Cragg, Stephen, 1095
Craig, Carolyn, 316
Craig, John D., 196, 265, 403, 452, 613
Craig, L. Michael, 390
Craig, Scott, 547
Craig, Tony, 240, 252
Craig, Yvonne, 77
Cram, Cusi, 622
Cramer, Douglas S., 305, 392, 434, 481, 493, 503, 604, 721, 884, 922
Cramer, Marc, 939
Crampton, Barbara, 206, 348, 933
Crampton, Cyd, 554
Crane, Bob, 106, 231, 381, 959
Crane, Brandon, 629

Crane, Dagne, 62
Crane, David, 305, 669
Crane, Gene, 178, 339, 502
Crane, Les, 436, 475, 604
Crane, Matthew, 52
Crane, Richard, 703, 806
Cranshaw, Pat, 569, 830
Cranston, Bryan, 498, 683
Cranston, Joe, 614
Craven, Brittany, 831
Craven, John, 254
Craven, Lacey, 831
Craven, Matt, 362, 861
Craven, Wes, 604, 649
Crawford, Andrew, 527
Crawford, Bobby, Jr., 463, 665
Crawford, Broderick, 378, 411, 451
Crawford, Christina, 740
Crawford, Edward, 722
Crawford, Joan, 316, 554, 740, 854
Crawford, John, 814, 894
Crawford, Johnny, 546, 641, 697
Crawford, Katherine, 315
Crawford, Lee, 333, 932
Crawford, Michael, 758
Crawford, Percy, 939
Crawford, Rachael, 118, 373, 810
Crawford, Ruth Duval, 939
Crawford-McCullah, Renee, 49
Crawley, Amos, 529
Crayon, Monsieur, 541
Craze, Sara, 485
Crean, Robert, 210
Creasey, John, 76
Creech, Cassandra, 53
Creel, Joy, 895
Creel, Leanna, 729, 895
Creel, Monica, 895
Creighton, Harry, 829
Creley, Jack, 794
Crenna, Richard, 32, 94, 177, 415, 490, 510, 630, 676, 686, 764, 963, 967, 975, 980, 1091
Crespi, Todd, 507
Crewe, Bob, 693
Crewson, Wendy, 359, 603, 797
Crichton, Don, 259, 432, 840
Crichton, Michael, 93, 245
Criscuolo, Lou, 252, 443, 668
Crisp, N. J., 527
Crist, Judith, 845
Cristal, Linda, 319, 376
Critchley, Paul, 529
Crittenden, James, 394
Croak, John, 1060
Crocker, Carter, 1102, 1105
Crocker, Frankie, 304
Crockett, James Underwood, 885
Crockett, Jan, 432
Crofoot, Alan, 560
Croft, Alyson, 105
Croft, Mary Jane, 374, 402, 500, 635, 650
Crombie, Peter, 42
Cromelin, Carey, 349
Cromie, Robert, 111, 1125
Cromwell, James, 247, 390
Cromwell, Rudy, 241
Cronin, Laurel, 442
Cronin, Lois, 408
Cronin, Patrick, 615
Cronin, Paul, 799
Cronin, Terence, 393
Cronkite, Kathy, 599
Cronkite, Walter, 20, 129, 130, 134, 418, 421, 570, 585, 761, 869, 879, 930, 952, 955, 958, 960, 962, 1055, 1060, 1063, 1076, 1124, 1129

Daniels, Billy, 99, 591
Daniels, David Mason, 141
Daniels, Edgar, 932
Daniels, Faith, 129, 133, 586, 846
Daniels, Gregory (Greg), 1101, 1117
Daniels, J. D., 332
Daniels, Jay, 568
Daniels, Marc, 296, 401, 685
Daniels, Mark, 119
Daniels, Penny, 189, 410
Daniels, Stan, 65, 223, 525, 561, 660, 820, 1065, 1067, 1068, 1070, 1072, 1075, 1078, 1080
Daniels, William, 14, 113, 145, 303, 453, 590, 718, 1091, 1093
Danielson, Shell, 319, 723
Daniely, Lisa, 412
Danles, Amy, 809
Dann, Mike, 242
Dann, Roger, 98
Dannay, Frederic, 256
Danner, Blythe, 14, 819, 972
Danner, Braeden, 623
Danner, Hillary, 879
Dano, Linda, 52, 63, 566, 622, 1113
Dano, Royal, 616
Danoff, Bill, 787
Danoff, Taffy, 787
Danova, Cesare, 313, 716
Danson, Ted, 86, 158, 772, 973, 1103, 1112
Dante, Joe, 871
Dante, Michael, 190
Dante, Willie, 87
Dantine, Helmut, 746
Dantine, Niki, 904
D'Antoni, Philip, 573
Danza, Tony, 70, 397, 820, 912
Danzig, Jerry, 187
Danziger, Cory, 83
Danziger, Edward J., 514, 519
Danziger, Harry Lee, 514, 519
Danziger, Maia, 51, 1080
Dapo, Ronnie, 598, 706
DaPron, Louis, 106, 651
D'Aquino, John, 733
D'Arbanville-Quinn, Patti (Patti D'Arbanville), 53, 581, 599, 775, 920
Darbo, Patrika, 789, 986
Darby, Kim, 695, 958
Darcel, Denise, 312, 640
Darcy, Georgine, 361
Darden, Severn, 93, 297, 793, 814
Da Re, Eric, 872
Darin, Bobby, 108, 195, 783
Darion, Sid, 220, 1079, 1082, 1089
Dark, Johnny, 424
Darley, Dik, 777
Darling, Jennifer, 254, 740, 823
Darling, Joan, 634, 1093
Darlow, David, 134
Darnay, Toni, 61, 227
Darnell, Mike, 94
Darnell, Nani, 506
Darr, Lisa, 186, 290, 613
Darren, James, 38, 231, 669, 811, 841
Darrow, Henry, 362, 376, 537, 595, 623, 724, 841, 940, 1105
Darrow, Mike, 238, 620
D'Aruba, Georgette, 599
Das, Alisha, 142
Dash, Stacey, 812
Dashow, Ken, 928
Da Silva, Howard, 296, 755, 964, 1074

Datar, Rajan, 710
D'Atri, Jane, 926
Dattilo, Bryan, 207
Dattilo-Hayward, Kristin, 397, 613
Dauer, John, 64
Daugherty, Allison, 349
Dauphin, Claude, 642
Davalos, Dick, 43
Davalos, Elyssa, 503
Dave Appell Trio, 717
Davenport, Bill, 635
Davenport, Bobby, 838
Davey, John, 748
Davich, Marty, 205
David, Brad, 286
David, Hugh, 123
David, Larry, 305, 742, 1111, 1112
David, Mack, 746
David, Philip, 702
Davidson, Ben, 73, 169
Davidson, Doug, 672, 932, 933
Davidson, Eileen, 121, 207, 723, 932
Davidson, Jack, 498
Davidson, James, 917
Davidson, John, 259, 328, 354, 384, 409, 436, 550, 824, 827, 841
Davidson, Joyce, 636
Davidson, Mark, 1077
Davidson, Suzanne, 61, 395
Davidson, Tommy, 406
Davidson, Troy, 597
Davies, Andrew, 1107
Davies, Blair, 119
Davies, Brian, 622
Davies, Gareth, 303, 1069
Davies, Gary, 859
Davies, Geraint Wyn, 21, 236, 297
Davies, Huw, 529
Davies, Jeffrey, 224
Davies, John Rhys, 681
Davies, Lane, 186, 335, 564, 723, 924
Davies, Peter, 498
Davies, Sian Leisa, 529
Davila, Diane, 958
Davion, Alex, 515
Davis, Al, 1060
Davis, Alanna, 599
Davis, Angela, 101
Davis, Ann B., 115, 116, 436, 448, 497, 1043, 1044
Davis, Bette, 316, 391, 652, 907, 971, 1076
Davis, Bill, 1061, 1067
Davis, Billy, Jr., 518
Davis, Brad, 969, 974
Davis, Clifton, 37, 828, 925
Davis, Curtis W., 1053, 1054, 1056
Davis, Daniel, 590
Davis, David, 107, 820, 1075
Davis, Donald, 554, 632
Davis, Eddie, 113, 513
Davis, Elias, 1117
Davis, Erin, 756
Davis, Fred, 116
Davis, Gail, 49
Davis, Geena, 124, 724
Davis, Glenn, 742
Davis, Guy, 623
Davis, Helen, 297
Davis, Herb, 252, 622
Davis, Janette, 59
Davis, Janie, 408
Davis, Jerry, 179
Davis, Jim, 185, 192, 313, 692, 793, 1091, 1093, 1100
Davis, Jo, 432

Davis, Joan, 403
Davis, John, 572
Davis, Josie, 155
Davis, Judy, 530, 1118
Davis, Kathy, 565
Davis, Kristin, 542
Davis, Mac, 503
Davis, Madelyn Pugh (Madelyn Pugh), 233, 400, 481, 835
Davis, Marty, 471
Davis, Michael, 601
Davis, Miles, 545
Davis, Neil, 969
Davis, Ossie, 68, 167, 210, 263, 457, 629, 951
Davis, Patti, 699
Davis, Peter, 548, 1056
Davis, Phyllis Elizabeth (Phyllis), 492, 883
Davis, Roger, 24, 257, 312
Davis, Rufe, 656
Davis, Sammy, Jr., 6, 316, 584, 591, 624, 720, 790, 949, 956, 963, 967, 971, 972, 976, 981
Davis, Terry, 52, 252
Davis, Todd, 317, 621
Davis, Tom, 726, 1070, 1072, 1102
Davis, Viveka, 809, 986
Davis, Walter Halsey, 1091
Davis, Wendy, 599
Davis-Voss, Sammi, 387
Davison, Bruce, 362, 399, 969
Davison, Joel, 611
Davison, Peter, 226
Dawber, Pam, 568, 569, 580
Dawn, Hazel, Jr., 270
Dawson, Curt, 14, 52, 62, 348
Dawson, Greg, 635
Dawson, Mark, 29
Dawson, Richard, 274, 381, 469, 500, 526, 595, 1075
Dawson, Vicky, 51, 62, 390, 497
Day, Clarence, Jr., 480
Day, Dennis, 211, 420, 546
Day, Doris, 209, 232, 665
Day, James, 202
Day, Laraine, 234, 463, 949
Day, Lynda. See George, Lynda Day
Day, Marilyn, 279
Day, Morris, 595
Day, Mrs. Clarence, Jr., 480
Day, Patrick, 42
Day, Shannon, 462
Dayton, Danny, 27, 448, 784
Dayton, June, 22, 119
Deacon, Richard, 68, 154, 217, 473, 572, 677
Deacon, Ron, 109
Deakins, Lucy, 63
Dean, Barton, 236, 573, 1078
Dean, Fabian, 839
Dean, Floy, 204, 935
Dean, Ivor, 718
Dean, James, 82, 196, 659, 701, 731, 797, 812
Dean, Jimmy, 132, 197, 419, 432
Dean, John, 103
Dean, Martin, 624
Dean, Maureen, 103
Dean, Morton, 403
Dean, Ron, 47, 461
Dean, Suzi, 361
Dean, Tomlinson, 1108
DeAnda, Peter, 621
Deane, Lezlie, 245
Deane, Palmer, 227
DeAngelis, Barbara, 74
Dearden, Robin, 320
Dearring, Mary Lee, 387
Dearth, John, 701

DeWitt, George, 81, 589, 744, 812
DeWitt, Jacqueline, 685
DeWitt, Joyce, 836
DeWolf, Cecilia, 31
DeWolfe, Billy, 209, 232, 336, 680, 827
Dexter, David, 529
Dexter, Pete, 983
Dey, Susan, 256, 334, 459, 492, 497, 643
DeYoung, Cliff, 702, 801, 963, 965, 974
Dezina, Kathleen (Kate), 29, 355, 736
DeZurik, Carolyn, 418, 667
Dhiegh, Khigh, 364, 449, 606
Diamond, Barry, 354, 862
Diamond, Bobby, 310, 904
Diamond, Don, 453, 940
Diamond, Dustin, 729
Diamond, Eileen, 546
Diamond, Jack, 275
Diamond, Janis, 399
Diamond, Matthew, 1092, 1102
Diamond, Neil, 973
Diamond, Peter, 758
Diamond, Reed, 388
Diamond, Robert, 223
Diamond, Selma, 517, 552, 602
Diamond, Vern, 1077, 1084
Diamont, Don, 206, 933
DiAquino, John, 221, 915
Diaz, Edith, 668
Dibbs, Kem, 123
DiBlasio, Raffi, 33
DiBona, Vin, 43
DiCaprio, Leonardo, 345, 641
DiCenzo, George, 259, 435, 535, 965
Dick, Andy, 85, 324, 601
Dick, David, 1060
Dick, Douglas, 898
Dick, Gina, 376
Dickens, Charles, 6, 601
Dickinson, Angie, 150, 539, 667, 833, 915, 956, 958, 975
Dickinson, Emily, 888
Dickson, Brenda, 932
Dickson, Neil, 10
Dicopoulos, Frank, 348
DiDonato, Marlene, 1079
Diehl, John, 545
Diener, Paul, 1109
Dierdorf, Dan, 587
Dierking, Nuella, 630
Dierkop, Charles, 667
Dietrich, Dena, 14, 30, 445, 670
Dietz, Eileen, 318, 348
Diffring, Anton, 65
DiGiampaolo, Nita, 547
DiLello, Richard, 191
Dillard, Mimi, 882
Diller, Phyllis, 82, 677, 752, 930
Dilley, J. C., 619
Dilley, R. J., 619
Dillman, Bradford, 5, 183, 452, 457, 1067
Dillon, Denny, 238, 390, 726, 922
Dillon, Melinda, 776, 793
Dillon, Sean, 421
Dillon, Stephen, 529, 530
Dillworth, Gordon, 788
DiMaio, Debra, 628, 1097, 1099, 1102, 1110, 1113, 1115, 1119
DiMassa, E. V., Jr., 550, 1084
DiMattia, Victor, 647, 809
Dimbleby, David, 612
Dimitri, Jim, 614
Dimitri, Richard, 908
Dimond, Diane, 359
Dinehart, Alan, 427

Dingle, Charles, 678, 699
Dingle, Kay, 720
Dingo, Ernie, 229
Dini, Paul, 1107, 1111, 1114
Dinner, Michael, 1104
Dinsdale, Shirley, 441, 1039
Dinster, Dennis, 317
Diol, Susan, 207, 392, 623
Dion, Colleen, 53, 109, 498
diReda, Joe, 319
DiSante, Joseph, 317
DiSanti, John, 387
Disher, Catherine, 297, 810, 896
Dishy, Bob, 793, 961
Disney, Roy, 891
Disney, Walt, 248, 891, 907, 940, 941, 1042
Ditmars, Ivan, 937
DiTosti, Ben, 205
Dixon, Bob, 382
Dixon, Donna, 87, 112
Dixon, Franklin W. See Stratemeyer, Edward
Dixon, Ivan, 243, 381
Dixon, MacIntyre, 174
Dixon, Pat, 29, 737
Dixon, Paul, 548, 646
Dixon, Peg, 794
Dizon, J. P., 203
Dizon, Jesse, 627
Doan, Dorothy, 883
Dobb, Gillian, 508
Dobie, Alan, 527, 583, 895
Dobkin, Larry, 557
Dobkowitz, Roger, 1099
Dobritch, Sandy, 801
Dobrynin, Anatoly, 975
Dobson, Bridget, 60, 320, 346, 722, 1099
Dobson, Jerome, 60, 320, 341, 722
Dobson, Kevin, 454, 455, 456, 747
Dobson, Peter, 437, 475
Dobson, Tamara, 426
Dobyns, Lloyd, 565, 586, 900
Dodd, Dickie, 546
Dodd, Jimmie, 546
Dodds, Edward K., 1062
Dodds, Michael, 563
Dodge, Frank, 735
Dodson, Jack, 32, 45, 407, 535, 659
Dodson, Rhonda, 371
Doelger, Frank, 1094, 1102, 1116
Doherty, Charla, 204
Doherty, Dan, 135
Doherty, Devin, 808
Doherty, Robert, 1117
Doherty, Shannen, 91, 92, 484, 630
Dohring, Kelsey, 345
Dohring, Kristen, 345
Dolan, Don, 319
Dolan, Ellen, 63, 348
Dolce, John, 591
Dole, Robert, 540
Doleman, Guy, 319
Dolenz, Ami, 6, 283, 319
Dolenz, George, 182
Dolenz, Mickey (Mickey Braddock), 165, 283, 319, 565
Dollar, Lynn, 762
Dolman, Bob, 1084, 1086
Dombrow, Walter, 1053
Domedion, David, 1107
Domergue, Faith, 182
Domingo, Plácido, 969, 1088
Domino, Fats, 950
Don Lindley and the Velveteers, 577
Donahoe, Terry, 623, 774

Donahue, Elinor, 45, 228, 280, 323, 517, 573, 593, 612, 665
Donahue, Mary Ann, 1082, 1084, 1085, 1089, 1090
Donahue, Patricia, 545
Donahue, Phil, 323, 433, 466, 657, 845, 1073, 1075, 1077, 1080, 1084, 1087, 1092, 1095, 1099, 1129
Donahue, Raechel, 353
Donahue, Troy, 364, 740, 745, 806
Donald, Juli, 471
Donald, Peter, 15, 526, 675, 909
Donaldson, Helen, 210
Donaldson, Norma, 933
Donaldson, Sam, 672, 834
Donat, Peter, 119, 563, 695, 841
DonHowe, Gwyda, 264
Donlevy, Brian, 196
Donnell, Jeff, 318, 322, 532
Donnelly, Alex, 932
Donnelly, Mary, 759
Donnelly, Tim, 257
Donner, Richard, 815
Donner, Robert, 569
Donohoe, Amanda, 460
Donohue, Nancy, 227
Donovan, King, 497, 665
Donovan, Pat, 762
Donovan, Tate, 643, 977
Dontzig, Gary, 1103, 1107, 1108
Doocy, Steve, 393, 608
Doohan, James, 109, 426, 786, 819
Dooley, Paul, 174, 229, 258, 339, 504
Doonican, Val, 882
DoQui, Robert, 880
Doran, Ann, 475, 490, 592, 751
Doran, Bobby, 50
Doran, Johnny, 573, 720
Doran, Phil, 149
Dorell, Don, 667
Doremus, David, 590
Dorfman, Sid, 127, 337
Dorfman, Steven, 1108, 1117
Dorin, Phoebe, 61, 566
Dorn, Michael, 135, 786
Dorsey, Jimmy, 783
Dorsey, Tommy, 351, 783
Dorsky, Nathaniel, 1051
D'Orso, Wisa, 711
Dorson, Gloria, 747
Dortort, David, 163, 376
Dotrice, Karen, 528
Dotrice, Roy, 82, 332, 355, 528, 777, 921
Doty, Roy, 711
Doubet, Steve, 205
Doucett, Linda, 464
Doucette, Jeff, 245
Doucette, John, 487, 643
Doug, Doug E., 908
Dougherty, Joseph, 1101
Dougherty, Roberta, 1113
Douglas, Beth, 836
Douglas, Brandon, 166, 272, 283
Douglas, Burt, 205, 251, 317, 570
Douglas, Christopher, 623
Douglas, Diana, 185, 205, 494, 836
Douglas, Donna, 91
Douglas, Harrison, 206
Douglas, Jack, 13, 109, 196, 213, 449, 745, 852, 1042
Douglas, James, 51, 61, 227, 621, 657
Douglas, Jerry, 932
Douglas, Kirk, 885, 949, 963, 965

Fanning, Bill, 432
Fanning, Gene, 736, 771
Fant, Lou, 830
Fantini, Dino, 693
Farabee, Carol, 76
Faracy, Stephanie, 266, 337, 380, 465, 866
Faraghan, J. E., 577
Farago, Joe, 117
Farago, Ladislas, 513
Farber, Burt, 81
Farber, Paul, 59
Farentino, Debrah (Deborah Mullowney), 142, 246, 259, 389
Farentino, James, 105, 110, 179, 210, 244, 442, 523, 956, 982
Fargas, Antonio, 30, 789
Farge, Annie, 47
Fargo, Donna, 231
Farina, Dennis, 186
Farinola, Vito, 884
Farleigh, Lynn, 795
Farley, Chris, 727
Farley, Duke, 146
Farley, Elizabeth, 252
Farley, James A., 391
Farmer, Gary, 298
Farmer Twins, The, 475
Farnsworth, Richard, 114
Farquar, Ralph, 776
Farr, Gordon, 899
Farr, Jamie, 19, 160, 334, 501
Farr, Kimberly, 486
Farr, Lee, 214
Farr, Raye, 1117
Farrel, Brioni, 318
Farrell, Brian, 495
Farrell, Charles (Charlie), 154, 579
Farrell, Glenda, 677, 1047
Farrell, James T., 586
Farrell, Marty, 1057
Farrell, Mary, 605
Farrell, Mike, 204, 411, 501, 513
Farrell, Sharon, 364, 933
Farrell, Shea, 141, 391, 471
Farrell, Skip, 763
Farrell, Terry, 640, 786
Farrell, Tom, 832
Farrell, Tommy, 314
Farrell, Tyra, 165
Farrow, Mia, 657, 693, 961
Farwell, Jonathan, 933
Fasciano, Richard, 496
Faso, Laurie, 406, 519
Fast, Howard, 1067
Fates, Gil, 382, 906, 918
Fattori, Laura, 1117
Faulconer, Catherine, 1095
Faulk, John Henry, 570
Faulkner, Eric, 80
Faulkner, James, 184, 530
Faulkner, William, 490, 975
Faust, Frederick Schiller. *See* Brand, Max
Faustino, David, 400, 520
Fawcett, Allen, 252, 679
Fawcett, Farrah (Fawcett-Majors), 156, 336, 400, 974, 977, 978, 981
Fawcett, William, 310
Fax, Jesslyn, 517
Fay, Meagen, 147, 148, 385, 615, 923
Faye, Herbie, 223, 658
Faye, Janina, 485
Faylen, Carol, 99
Faylen, Frank, 222, 827
Fedderson, Don, 199, 274, 480, 551, 582, 766, 842, 854, 911
Fedderson, Gregg, 274

Fedderson, Tido, 551
Fee, Melinda, 204, 347, 412
Feeney, Joe, 472
Feig, Paul, 336, 423
Feigel, Sylvia, 794
Feiman, Alan, 215
Fein, Bernard (Bernie), 381, 658
Fein, Doren, 369
Feiner, Ben, Jr., 249, 267, 919
Feinstein, Alan, 251, 319, 431, 714, 724
Feist, Felix, 138
Felder, Clarence, 389
Felder, Don, 268
Felder, Sarah, 715
Feldkamp, Fred, 517
Feldman, Corey, 71, 243
Feldman, David, 1118
Feldman, Edward H. (Eddie, Ed), 381, 779, 1118
Feldman, Marty, 332, 523
Feldman, Mindy, 547
Feldmann, Eddie, 1115
Feldner, Sheldon, 335
Feldon, Barbara, 174, 324, 762, 778
Feldshuh, Tovah, 64, 518, 966
Feliciano, José, 161
Fell, Norman, 195, 254, 593, 708, 820, 837
Feller, Howard, 439
Fellig, Arthur H., 588
Fellini, Federico, 959
Fellows, Arthur, 796
Felsher, Howard, 1062, 1072
Felton, Happy, 359, 415
Felton, Lindsay, 838
Felton, Norman, 225, 255, 265, 429, 478, 514, 648, 728, 829
Felton, Verna, 209, 654
Femia, John, 371, 782
Fenady, Andrew, 388
Fenmore, Tanya, 479
Fenn, Sherilyn, 815, 872
Fennell, Albert, 68
Fennelly, Parker, 367
Fennelly, Vincent, 202, 684, 862
Fenneman, George, 53, 237, 823, 930, 936, 938
Fenwick, Millicent, 812
Ferber, Mel, 151
Ferdin, Pamelyn, 104, 189, 436, 646, 776
Ferguson, Bianca, 318
Ferguson, Craig, 534
Ferguson, Frank, 579, 657, 693, 824
Ferguson, Jason, 62
Ferguson, Jay R., 263, 633
Ferguson, Maynard, 794
Ferguson, Nancye, 617
Ferguson, Sandra, 52
Fernandes, Miguel, 593
Fernandez, Abel, 791, 880
Fernandez, Giselle, 129, 729, 801
Fernandez, Peter Jay, 803
Fernetz, Charlene, 795
Ferrante, Evan, 808
Ferrar, Catherine (Cathy), 204, 316, 760
Ferrare, Cristina, 409
Ferraro, Christine, 1120
Ferrell, Conchata, 68, 245, 369, 390, 460, 535
Ferrell, Kristi, 348
Ferrell, Roy, 648
Ferrell, Todd, 464
Ferrell, Will, 727
Ferrer, José, 5, 88, 118, 958, 961, 969
Ferrer, Mel, 84, 271, 675
Ferrer, Miguel, 121, 617, 783

Ferrero, Martin, 545, 748
Ferri, Janice, 1111
Ferrigno, Lou, 408, 864
Ferrin, Frank, 765
Ferris, Barbara, 795
Ferris, Ferrari, 672
Ferris, Irena, 184
Ferris, Jack, 275
Ferris, Patricia, 848
Ferris, Paul, 76
Ferriter, Bill, 30
Ferro, Dan, 272
Ferro, Mathilde, 320
Ferro, Theodore, 320
Ferrone, Dan, 494, 954
Ferrugia, John, 903
Feton, Mary Jean, 49
Feury, Joseph, 1097
Fialkow, Nina Sing, 1116
Fichtner, William, 63
Fickett, Mary, 29, 31, 137, 611, 1061
Fiedler, Arthur, 262
Fiedler, John, 107, 124, 604, 623, 848
Field, Betty, 527
Field, Chelsea, 47, 141, 604
Field, Fern, 1083
Field, Frank, 608
Field, Julianna, 1093
Field, Logan, 199
Field, Ron, 969
Field, Sally, 93, 293, 326, 328, 961, 965, 971, 986, 1071
Field, Shirley Ann, 723
Field, Sylvia, 212, 559
Field, Ted, 1103
Field, Todd, 814
Fielding, Anastasia, 619
Fielding, Dorothy, 227, 620
Fielding, Tom, 840
Fields, Alexis, 702
Fields, Bonnie Lynn, 547
Fields, Charlie, 747
Fields, Chip, 36, 205
Fields, Gracie, 243, 876
Fields, Jere, (Jerrelyn), 189, 450
Fields, Joan, 307
Fields, Kim, 69, 269, 487
Fields, Ronald J., 1093
Fields, Sid, 11
Fields, Thor, 227
Fiennes, Ralph, 986
Fierstein, Harvey, 191
Fifth Dimension, The 771
Figueroa, Ruben, 5
Figuerroa, Efrain, 394
Figus, Lisa, 318
Fillion, Nathan, 622
Fimple, Dennis, 363, 532
Finch, Peter, 966
Fine, Holly, 1136
Fine, Larry, 598
Fine, Mort, 87, 404, 571
Fine, Paul, 1136
Fine, Sylvia, 1068
Fine, Travis, 935
Finefrock, Chris, 203
Fink, John, 494, 590
Finkel, Bob (Robert), 429, 628, 648, 651, 672, 1049, 1050
Finkel, Fyvush, 660, 1114
Finkelstein, William M., 166, 179, 460, 1100, 1103
Finlay-McLennan, Stewart, 164, 245
Finley, Eileen, 252
Finley, Patte (Pat), 107, 306, 310
Finn, Fred, 547
Finn, Michael, 62
Finn, Mickie, 547
Finn, Pat, 322

Forman, Carl, 112
Forman, David, 1100
Forman, Denis, 1091
Forman, Joey, 547, 693, 753
Forney, Arthur, 1114
Foronjy, Richard, 878
Forrest, Frederic, 489, 870, 972
Forrest, Gregg, 71
Forrest, Ray, 812
Forrest, Sally, 876
Forrest, Steve, 76, 194, 717
Forrester, Brent, 1112
Forslund, Constance, 969
Forster, Brian, 334, 643
Forster, E. M., 530
Forster, Robert, 74, 588, 618
Forsyth, David, 52, 63, 737, 826
Forsyth, Elizabeth, 30
Forsyth, Rosemary, 204
Forsythe, Brook, 436
Forsythe, Bruce, 391
Forsythe, Henderson, 61, 255, 306, 592
Forsythe, John, 70, 156, 243, 404, 436, 669, 842, 926, 950
Forsythe, Page, 436
Forsythe, William, 880
Fortas, Daniel, 347
Forte, Chet, 1066, 1068
Forte, Joe, 481
Fortier, Bob, 866
Fortier, Laurie, 714
Fortier, Robert, 309
Foskett, Mary, 739
Fosse, Bob, 284, 936, 1060, 1061
Foster, Ami, 678
Foster, Bill, 448
Foster, Buddy, 388, 535
Foster, Chip, 162
Foster, Donald, 366
Foster, Frances, 30
Foster, Garrett, 1105
Foster, George, 552
Foster, Gloria, 975
Foster, Jodie, 5, 106, 184, 641, 972
Foster, Kathryn, 1102
Foster, Kimberly, 31, 184, 194
Foster, Linda, 356
Foster, Meg, 136, 730, 801, 969
Foster, Pepper, 162
Foster, Phil, 470, 753
Foster, Phillip, 343
Foster, Preston, 350, 898
Foster, Robert, 446
Foster, Ron, 63
Foster, Stan, 861
Foster, Susan, 497, 754
Fouhy, Ed, 1063
Foulger, Byron, 309, 656
Four Carters, The, 552
Four Freshmen, The, 684
Four Lads, The, 653
Four Tops, The, 973
Four Voices, The, 655
Fournier, Rift, 1068
Fourquet, Philippe, 935
Fouser, Don, 1061
Fowkes, Conrad, 61, 251, 376, 740, 841
Fowler, Bill, 621
Fowler, Clara Ann, 645
Fowler, Jim, 914
Fowles, Julian, 1109
Fowley, Douglas V., 214, 662, 927
Fownes, Harry (Henry), 93, 1068
Fox, Ben, 898
Fox, Bernard, 962
Fox, Colin, 376, 794
Fox, Crystal, 407
Fox, Edward, 253

Fox, Frederick, 937
Fox, James, 530
Fox, Jorjan, 555
Fox, Matthew, 304, 643
Fox, Michael, 109, 639
Fox, Michael J., 71, 276, 639, 986, 1093, 1096, 1098
Fox, Nancy, 823
Fox, Patrick, 740
Fox, Peter, 211
Fox, Sonny, 476, 572, 618, 761, 898
Fox, Vivica A., 320, 632
Foxworth, Jaimee, 276
Foxworth, Robert, 271, 793, 961
Foxworthy, Jeff, 427
Foxx, Jamie, 406, 702
Foxx, Redd, 690, 712, 722
Foy, Eddie, Jr., 270
Foy, Fred, 216, 488
Foy, Gina, 347
Foy, Patricia, 1066
Frabotta, Don, 205
Frakes, Jonathan, 74, 227, 607, 786
Framer, Walt, 343, 796
Francine, Anne, 361
Franciosa, Tony, 285, 532, 589, 734, 882
Francis, Angelique, 206
Francis, Anne, 127, 298, 388, 482, 698, 876, 884
Francis, Arlene, 56, 103, 128, 173, 279, 385, 675, 770, 815, 853, 907, 913
Francis, Clive, 528
Francis, Connie, 216, 432
Francis, Elliott, 247
Francis, Genie (Genie Ann), 31, 74, 206, 316, 317, 319, 607
Francis, Ivor, 243
Francis, Missy, 435, 484, 570
Francis, Nicky, 801
Francis, Ryan, 759
Franciscus, James, 223, 398, 412, 490, 559, 588, 897, 970
Francks, Don, 429, 682
Franco, Abel, 339
Franco, Ramon, 377, 861
Frangione, Nancy, 29, 51
Frank, Carl, 251, 511
Frank, Charles, 29, 163, 256, 285, 935
Frank, Gary, 273, 774, 1071
Frank, Jason, 549
Frank, Pat, 665
Frank, Reuven, 585, 900, 953, 1047
Frank, Richard, 54
Frank, Sandy, 1092, 1094, 1097
Frank, Scott, 100
Frank, Sid, 619
Franke, Jay Anthony, 137
Frankel, Charles, 925
Frankel, David, 340
Frankel, Eliot, 287, 1058, 1063
Frankel, Ernie, 590, 598, 934
Frankel, Mark, 298, 759
Frankel, Stanley A., 15
Franken, Al, 726, 727, 1070, 1072, 1102, 1111
Franken, Rose, 167
Franken, Stephen (Steve), 222, 223, 478, 559, 848
Frankenheimer, John, 456, 665, 1115, 1118
Frankfather, William, 47
Franklin, Aretha, 41, 218
Franklin, Bonnie, 619
Franklin, Carl, 147, 278, 535
Franklin, Don, 453, 591, 733, 935

Franklin, Hugh, 28
Franklin, Jeff, 309
Franklin, Nancy, 227, 624, 735, 1082, 1085
Franklyn, Shelley, 253
Franks, Philip, 529
Frann, Mary, 205, 254, 452, 600
Franz, Arthur, 611, 925
Franz, Caroline, 60
Franz, Dennis, 79, 91, 160, 380, 587, 591, 1114
Franz, Eduard, 117
Franz, Elizabeth, 52
Franzblau, Rose, 385
Franzen, Oscar, 47
Fraser, Bob, 517
Fraser, Elisabeth, 283, 536, 620, 658
Fraser, Nora, 1084
Fraser, Prudence, 520
Fraser, Woody, 37, 409, 550, 1084
Frates, Robin, 54
Fratkin, Stuart, 593
Frawley, James, 1051
Frawley, William, 401, 581, 755
Fray, Jacques, 424
Frazee, June, 90
Frazer, Dan, 63, 455
Frazier, Cliff, 286
Frazier, Sheila, 472
Freaco, Scott, 498
Freberg, Stan, 840, 950
Frechette, Peter, 238
Frederick, Hal, 112, 411
Frederick, Pauline, 647
Fredericks, Carlton, 147
Fredericks, Dean (Norman Fredric), 443, 791
Free, Stan, 136
Freebairn-Smith, Thomas, 339
Freed, Alan, 948
Freed, Bert, 172, 747
Freed, Fred, 385, 466, 613, 952, 953, 956, 959, 1049, 1052, 1056, 1060
Freed, Sam, 283, 446
Freedley, Vinton, 753, 814
Freedman, Lewis, 1056, 1065
Freedman, Mike, 1053
Freedman, Winifred, 433
Freels, Shari, 495
Freeman, Al, Jr., 390, 621, 708, 960, 1077
Freeman, Damita Jo, 674
Freeman, Deena, 858
Freeman, J. E., 284
Freeman, J. Paul, 271
Freeman, Joan, 127
Freeman, Jon, 220
Freeman, Kathleen, 231, 309, 416, 491, 535, 860
Freeman, Leonard, 364, 793
Freeman, Mickey, 658
Freeman, Morgan, 52, 166, 255, 975
Freeman, Pam, 677
Freeman, Sandy, 239
Freeman, Seth, 1075, 1078
Freeman, Stan, 541, 836
Freer, Randall, 309
Frees, Paul, 82, 138, 551
Freezer, Harlene, 1106
Freiberger, Fred, 513, 777, 786
Freiwald, Eric, 1111
Freleng, Friz, 72, 278, 613, 693, 1072, 1073, 1083
Frelich, Phyllis, 723
Fremin, Jourdan, 65
Fremont, John C., 976
French, Leigh, 216, 329, 768
French, Marilyn, 969

Goodson, Mark, 82, 128, 138,
163, 230, 233, 306, 366, 427,
441, 510, 555, 842, 906, 918
Goodwin, Bill, 98, 127, 323, 414,
531, 648
Goodwin, Earl, 540
Goodwin, James M., 53, 348
Goodwin, Joshua, 858
Goodwin, Kia, 874
Goodwin, Michael, 51, 295, 355,
796
Goorian, Len, 646
Goorjian, Michael, 644, 1115
Goranson, Lecy, 708, 709
Gorbachev, Mikhail, 585
Gordeno, Peter, 875
Gordon, Al, 420, 1045, 1050
Gordon, Angela, 1119
Gordon, Anita, 449, 824
Gordon, Barry, 28, 230, 275,
288, 336, 420, 595
Gordon, Bruce, 84, 713, 880
Gordon, Carl, 355, 702
Gordon, Charles (Chuck), 444,
908
Gordon, Colin, 76
Gordon, Dick, 457
Gordon, Don, 104, 499
Gordon, Dorothy, 599
Gordon, Eve, 33, 335, 669
Gordon, Gale, 122, 212, 374,
401, 481, 500, 630, 655, 719
Gordon, Gerald, 227, 317, 378,
1069
Gordon, Glen, 224
Gordon, Gloria, 579
Gordon, Gregory, 31
Gordon, Hannah, 529
Gordon, Keith, 970
Gordon, Lawrence, 228, 444
Gordon, Leo V., 258
Gordon, Margie, 596
Gordon, Mark, 1094
Gordon, Phil, 655
Gordon, Richard, 183, 224
Gordon, Ruth, 677, 1076
Gordon, Serena, 530
Gordon-Levitt, Joseph, 198, 670
Gordy, Berry, Jr., 572
Gore, Brent, 137
Goren, Charles, 154
Goren, Rowby, 1065
Gorfain, Louis H., 1086
Görg, Gayln, 501
Goring, Marius, 253, 730
Gorman, Breon, 295
Gorman, Lynne, 563
Gorman, Mari, 361, 375
Gorman, Marvin, 433
Gorman, Robert Hy, 385, 435
Gormé, Eydie, 46, 790, 851, 948,
967, 1075
Gormley, Jim, 146
Gorney, Karen, 29
Gorodetsky, Eddie, 1092
Gorrell, Ashley, 838
Gorshin, Frank, 6, 77
Gortner, Marjoe, 778
Gosch, Martin, 850
Gosden, Freeman, 44, 138
Gosfield, Maurice, 658
Goss, Pat, 572
Gosselaar, Mark-Paul, 116, 729
Gossett, Cindy, 206
Gossett, Louis, Jr. (Lou), 71,
326, 472, 489, 669, 707, 935,
966, 972, 973, 1071
Gothie, Robert, 312
Gottfried, Gilbert, 726, 830
Gottlieb, Alex, 11, 434, 497
Gottlieb, Carl, 1054
Gottlieb, Lester, 752

Gottlieb, Linda, 621, 1072, 1077,
1079
Gottlieb, Stan, 390
Gough, Lloyd, 344
Gough, Michael, 734
Gould, Chester, 217
Gould, Cliff, 513
Gould, Diana, 87
Gould, Elliott, 245, 847, 968,
1070
Gould, Graydon, 297
Gould, Harold, 42, 282, 294,
357, 366, 490, 525, 642, 694,
757, 779, 896, 969, 976
Gould, Jack, 1122
Gould, Judith, 976
Gould, Lew, 1114
Gould, Sandra, 92, 403, 420
Gould, Sid, 744, 753
Gould, Stanhope, 1060
Goulding, Ray, 106, 175, 357,
589
Goulet, Nicolette, 348, 715, 736
Goulet, Robert, 104, 952, 953,
956, 957, 958
Goutman, Christopher (Chris),
736, 826, 1119
Gowdy, Curt, 42, 43, 682, 898,
1125
Gower, Andre, 69, 281, 560
Goyette, Desiree, 599
Goz, Harry, 592
Gozier, Bernie, 110
Grable, Betty, 296, 394, 753, 785
Grabowski, Norm, 598
Grace, Mary, 416
Grace, Nickolas, 341, 702
Grace, Robin, 593
Gracen, Elizabeth, 266
Gracie, Sally, 227, 611, 622
Grade, Lew, 442
Grady, Don (Don Agrati), 547,
581
Graf, David, 375
Graff, Ilene, 477, 557, 806
Graff, Randy, 239
Graff, Robert D., 267, 919
Graham, Bill, 667, 669
Graham, Billy, 99, 954, 959
Graham, David, 527
Graham, Ed, 483
Graham, Elain, 49
Graham, Fred, 1062, 1063, 1127
Graham, Gary, 25
Graham, Gerrit, 187, 443, 798
Graham, Heather, 809
Graham, Jerry, 814
Graham, June, 347, 382, 739
Graham, Louis, 821
Graham, Nancyanne, 385
Graham, Roderick, 1057, 1058
Graham, Ronny, 106, 161, 397
Graham, Samaria, 104
Graham, Scott, 935
Graham, Sheilah, 384, 749
Graham, Virginia, 37, 294, 328,
886
Graham, Winston, 528
Grahame, Kenneth, 691
Grahn, Nancy Lee, 563, 723,
1102
Grammer, Kelsey, 158, 302,
1114, 1118
Gran, Katie, 924
Grandin, Isabel, 371, 830
Grandy, Fred, 493, 566
Granfield, Suzanne, 49
Granger, Farley, 63, 622, 952,
958
Granger, Gerri, 906
Granger, Stewart, 887, 962
Granik, Jon, 794

Granik, Theodore, 40, 939
Granofsky, Anais, 210, 634
Grant, Alberta, 251, 646
Grant, Anne, 1072
Grant, Bernard (Bernie), 347,
621, 772
Grant, Beth, 211
Grant, Brian, 311
Grant, Cary, 559, 567
Grant, Charles (Charles Flohe),
53, 252, 724
Grant, Deborah, 253
Grant, Faye, 343, 881, 973, 974
Grant, Gil, 184
Grant, Harvey, 231, 480
Grant, Hugh, 530
Grant, James, 528
Grant, Jennifer, 802
Grant, Kirby, 763
Grant, Lee, 6, 71, 196, 281, 657,
659, 735, 976, 1050, 1057
Grant, Leon W., 836
Grant, Micki, 51, 252, 348
Grant, Patti, 1117
Grant, Perry, 371
Grant, Rodney A., 365
Grant, Saginaw, 363
Grant, Salim, 729
Grant, Sarina, 271
Grant, Taylor, 6
Grant, Trudy, 1111
Granville, Clement, 888
Grasshoff, Alex, 1063
Grassic, Lewis, 528
Grassle, Karen, 483
Grate, Gail, 503
Grateful Dead, The, 885
Grau, Doris, 187
Graubart, Judy, 174, 255
Grauer, Ben, 85, 96, 416, 477,
730
Graver, Fred, 1092, 1094, 1097
Graves, Ernest, 347, 621
Graves, Karron, 229
Graves, Leonard, 885
Graves, Leslie, 142, 374
Graves, Peter, 99, 183, 310, 351,
556, 629, 896, 910, 917
Graves, Robert, 528
Graves, Teresa, 310, 324, 469, 869
Gravino, Chuckie, 320
Gravino, Kenny, 320
Gravitte, Beau, 224, 863
Gray, Alexander, 832
Gray, Barry, 918
Gray, Billy, 151, 280
Gray, Bob, 826
Gray, Bruce, 29, 252, 320, 376,
772, 794
Gray, Charles, 351, 932
Gray, Coleen, 119, 205, 917
Gray, David Barry, 167, 238, 870
Gray, Dolores, 125
Gray, Donald, 519
Gray, Erin, 124, 755, 788
Gray, Gary, 18, 181
Gray, Gordon, 840
Gray, Janet, 348
Gray, Joan, 347
Gray, Linda, 32, 193, 194, 542,
563
Gray, Louis, 683
Gray, Michael, 484, 748
Gray, Phil, 168
Gray, Robert, 361
Gray, Velekka, 63, 494, 495, 772,
933
Gray, Virginia, 1079, 1082
Grayco, Helen, 168, 780
Graziano, Rocky, 372, 448, 522,
544
Greason, Staci, 207

James, Kenny, 931
James, Olga, 97
James, Peter Francis, 63
James, Ralph, 569
James, Sallie, 469
James, Sheila, 120, 222, 223, 797
James, Stephanie, 442
James, Steven, 29
Jameson, House, 22, 354
Jameson, Joyce, 318
Jameson, Nick, 187
Jameson, Pauline, 527
Jamieson, Bob, 84, 586
Jamison, Breck, 63
Jamison, Julie, 251
Jamison, Marshall, 827
Janis, Conrad, 111, 569, 680
Janis, Ryan, 622
Jankey, Les, 816
Jann, Jerald, 388
Janney, Allison, 349
Janney, Leon, 50, 365, 792
Janssen, Berniece, 308
Janssen, David, 308, 362, 615,
    695
Jarchow, Bruce, 814
Jaress, Jill, 598
Jarkowsky, Andrew, 51
Jarrett, Art, 694
Jarrett, Chris, 252
Jarrett, Gregg, 183
Jarrett, Renne, 251, 495, 590,
    669, 772
Jarriel, Tom, 869
Jarrin, Mauricio, 180
Jarrott, Charles, 1119
Jarvis, Graham, 103, 273, 297,
    347, 511, 524
Jarvis, Lucy, 955, 957, 1049
Jarvis, Martin, 298, 527
Jasmer, Brent, 109
Jason, Harvey, 88, 120
Jason, Peter, 912
Jason, Rick, 173, 197
Jastrow, Terry, 1068
Jay, Oren, 495
Jayne, Jennifer, 916
Jayne, William, 642
Jean, Al, 187, 1103, 1106, 1117
Jefferson, B. J., 53
Jefferson, Brenden, 828
Jefferson, Herb, Jr., 79, 311
Jeffory, Dawn, 318
Jeffreys, Anne, 211, 285, 319,
    497, 860, 947
Jeffries, Adam, 607, 828, 867
Jeffries, Fran, 960
Jeffries, Herb, 909
Jeffries, Lang, 692
Jeffries, Vance, 622
Jellinek, Tristam, 527
Jemison, Mae, 787
Jenesky, George, 206
Jeni, Richard, 663
Jenkens, Horace, 1079
Jenkins, Allen, 241, 375
Jenkins, Carol Mayo, 273
Jenkins, Dan, 743
Jenkins, Daniel, 332
Jenkins, Hayes Alan, 948
Jenkins, Ken, 386
Jenkins, Larry Flash, 80, 285,
    911
Jenkins, Mark, 934
Jenkins, Richard, 981
Jenkins, Sam, 330
Jenkins, Scott, 723
Jenks, Frank, 172
Jenner, Barry, 51, 771
Jenner, Bruce, 37, 135, 336, 784,
    806
Jenner, Chrystie, 336

Jennings, Brent, 53
Jennings, Peter, 7, 868, 899, 975,
    977, 978, 982, 983, 986
Jennings, Waylon, 241
Jenny, Julie, 49
Jensen, Johnny, 317
Jensen, Karen, 114
Jensen, Kristen, 31
Jensen, Maren, 79
Jensen, Sanford, 293, 403
Jepson-Young, Peter, 985
Jerome, Ed, 494
Jerome, Jerry, 924
Jerrems, Jeanne, 841
Jerry Packer Singers, The, 645
Jerry, Tom, 38
Jessel, George, 33, 173, 322
Jessup, Hubert, 79
Jessup, Paul, 70
Jessup, Ryan, 70
Jeter, Felicia, 133
Jeter, Michael, 263, 392, 1109
Jewell, Geri, 269
Jewison, Norman, 441
Jezek, Ken, 206
Jillian, Ann, 48, 366, 415, 428,
    974, 978
Jillson, Joyce, 657, 720
Jiminez, Alvernette, 327, 748
Jimmy Joyce Singers, The, 329
Jo, Damita, 690
Jobim, Antonio Carlos, 958
Joblin, Monia, 1072
Joel, Dennis, 89
Joelson, Ben, 179, 1059
Johann, John Lee, 546
Johannson, Paul, 724
Johansen, David, 146
Johansson, Paul, 489, 642
John, Elton, 159, 467, 503, 967
John, Gottfried, 778
John, Tom, 1125
Johnny Mann Singers, The, 322
Johns, Glynis, 174, 330
Johnson, Adrienne-Joi, 758
Johnson, Alicia, 70
Johnson, Amy Jo, 549
Johnson, Anne-Marie, 407, 906
Johnson, Arch, 64, 139, 463
Johnson, Arte, 72, 85, 231, 312,
    324, 330, 334, 416, 454, 469,
    517, 719, 1054
Johnson, Ashley, 345, 534, 657
Johnson, Bayn, 906
Johnson, Ben, 566
Johnson, Bess, 735
Johnson, Betty, 250, 852
Johnson, Beverly, 978
Johnson, Bob, 556
Johnson, Brad, 49, 183, 592
Johnson, Bruce, 484, 680, 754
Johnson, Cecilia, 70
Johnson, Charles F., 1073
Johnson, Cherie, 678
Johnson, Chic, 285
Johnson, Chubby, 824
Johnson, Clark, 388, 391
Johnson, Coslough, 435, 1053
Johnson, Dean, 387
Johnson, Don, 306, 544, 975
Johnson, Edward Earl, 979
Johnson, Frederick, 1111
Johnson, Gail, 205, 832
Johnson, Gary, 1065
Johnson, Geordie, 236
Johnson, Georgann, 62, 236,
    559, 630, 771, 865
Johnson, Gerry, 290
Johnson, Janet Louise, 68, 360
Johnson, Jarrod, 305, 491, 810
Johnson, Jay, 151
Johnson, Jermain H., 639

Johnson, Joanna, 109
Johnson, Judy, 852, 937
Johnson, JulieAnn, 622
Johnson, June, 285
Johnson, Kathie Lee. See Gif-
    ford, Kathie Lee
Johnson, Kenneth, 100, 168, 409
Johnson, Kenny, 724
Johnson, Lamont, 1091, 1099
Johnson, Laura, 271, 368
Johnson, Lyndon B., 98, 130
Johnson, Magic, 679, 984
Johnson, Mark, 408
Johnson, Mel, Jr., 617
Johnson, Michael, 398
Johnson, Michele, 1108
Johnson, Nicholas, 767
Johnson, Patrick, 498
Johnson, Penny, 387, 464
Johnson, Ray, 635
Johnson, Robin, 170
Johnson, Russell, 101, 327, 594
Johnson, Stephen, 168
Johnson, Sterling, 1057, 1082
Johnson, Taj, 642
Johnson, Tania, 71
Johnson, Timothy, 10, 366, 368
Johnson, Tina, 737, 826
Johnson, Tony T., 321
Johnson, Van, 880, 949
Johnson, Virginia, 37
Johnston, Amy, 123
Johnston, Audre, 740
Johnston, Charles, 829
Johnston, Jane, 908
Johnston, Jay, 769, 770
Johnston, John Dennis, 208
Johnston, John R., 498
Johnston, Johnny, 385, 438, 449,
    510
Johnston, Ken Lawrence, 821
Johnston, Lionel, 51, 774
Johnstone, Jay, 121
Johnstone, William, 62
Joliffe, David, 706
Joliffe, Dorothy, 689
Jolley, Norman, 164
Jolly, Mike, 221
Jonathan, Wesley, 554
Jones, Amanda, 205
Jones, Anissa, 274
Jones, Antonia, 486
Jones, Archdale, 449
Jones, Arthur, 914
Jones, Arthur E., 51
Jones, Barry, 950
Jones, Ben, 241
Jones, Candy, 784
Jones, Carol, 932
Jones, Carolyn, 15, 142
Jones, Catherine Zeta, 986
Jones, Charlie, 33
Jones, Chris, 475
Jones, Christine, 50, 295, 497,
    610, 621, 622, 699, 715
Jones, Chuck, 189, 239, 957, 959
Jones, Clifton, 166, 777
Jones, Daphne Lyn, 387
Jones, Davy, 6, 565
Jones, Dean, 160, 258, 372, 906
Jones, Dick, 124, 683
Jones, Eddie, 488
Jones, Edgar Allan, Jr., 13, 203,
    862
Jones, Gemma, 528
Jones, Ginger, 90
Jones, Gordon, 11, 685, 769
Jones, Griff Rhys, 766
Jones, Henry, 14, 23, 154, 350,
    403, 446, 660
Jones, James, 306, 586
Jones, James Cellan, 298

Kercheval, Ken, 193, 194, 395, 735
Kern, Bonni Lou, 546
Kern, James V., 402
Kerner, Michael, 1113
Kerns, Joanna, 299, 344, 981
Kerns, Sandra, 155, 536
Kerr, Deborah, 355
Kerr, Edward, 733
Kerr, Elaine, 51
Kerr, Elizabeth, 569
Kerr, Graham, 312
Kerr, Jay, 286, 932
Kerr, Jean, 665
Kerr, John, 490, 657
Kerr, Larry, 841
Kerr, Treena, 312
Kerrigan, Michael J., 1108
Kerry, Ann, 52
Kerry, Margaret, 713
Kershaw, Whitney, 508
Kerwin, Brian, 47, 163, 342, 554, 931, 981
Kerwin, Lance, 275, 425
Kessel, Ken, 1105
Kestner, Boyd, 455, 634
Ketcham, Hank, 212, 595
Ketchum, Dave, 139, 324, 406
Kettle, Ross, 723
Kettner, Paige, 207
Kettner, Ryanne, 207
Key, Ted, 366
Keyes, Freeman, 689
Keyes, Joe, 179
Keyes, Paul W., 470, 1052, 1053, 1066
Keymah, T'Keyah "Crystal", 406, 617
Keyser, Christopher, 644
Khaka, Jonas, 623
Khali, Simbi, 748
Khan, Sajid, 534
Khrushchev, Nikita, 202, 269
Kibbee, Lois, 252, 623, 772
Kibbee, Roland, 208, 275, 505, 535, 1062, 1083
Kiberd, James, 31, 53, 498
Kidder, Alfred, 905
Kidder, Margot, 517, 602, 749
Kidnie, James, 702
Kid 'n Play, 450
Kiel, Richard, 74
Kieran, John, 409, 445
Kiernan, Walter, 451, 778, 827, 907, 911, 912
Kieser, Ellwood E., 410, 1082, 1084, 1087, 1089
Kiff, Kaleena, 496, 597
Kiger, Randi, 504
Kiger, Robby, 185
Kiker, Douglas, 584
Kilbourne, Lorelei, 96
Kilbourne, Wendy, 548, 609
Kiley, Richard, 10, 190, 341, 457, 554, 663, 817, 834, 876, 928, 975, 976, 1086, 1098, 1115
Kilgallen, Dorothy, 852, 906
Kilian, Fred, 842
Kilian, Victor, 297, 524
Killen, Michael, 1114
Killiam, Paul, 143
Killian, James R., Jr., 1125, 1127
Killick, Tim, 184
Killmond, Frank, 319
Killum, Guy, 89
Killy, Jean-Claude, 451
Kilman, Peter, 317
Kilner, Kevin, 34
Kilpatrick, Eric, 430, 910
Kilpatrick, James J., 410, 761
Kilpatrick, Lincoln, 301, 475, 495, 532

Kilty, Jack, 578
Kim, Evan, 449
Kimball, Peter, 1108, 1116
Kimbrough, Charles, 575
Kimbrough, Emily, 262
Kimmel, Bruce, 219
Kimmel, Dana, 206, 826
Kimmell, Jess, 689
Kimmins, Ken, 169, 475
Kinberg, Judy, 1075, 1088, 1096, 1103
Kincaid, Jason, 30, 62
Kincannon, Kit, 198
Kinchlow, Ben, 744
Kind, Richard, 105, 147, 148, 504, 912
King, Alan, 6, 88, 180, 419
King, Aldine, 445, 676
King, Alexander, 421, 852
King, B. B., 65, 821
King, Billie Jean, 806, 963, 1065
King, Carl, 452, 739
King, Carole, 6
King, Cynthia Marie, 48
King, Dana, 38, 202, 336
King, Dave, 200
King, David L., 31, 53
King, Dennis, 354, 578, 659
King, Donald R., 1073
King, Erik, 555, 710, 801
King, Evelyn "Champagne", 221
King, Frank, 534
King, Freeman, 195, 743, 774
King, Gayle, 184
King, John Reed, 78, 154, 328, 363, 476, 556, 618, 829, 859, 907, 909, 913
King, Kathi, 208
King, Kathryn, 49
King, Kip, 155
King, Larry, 463
King, Larry L., 970
King, Louise, 563, 844
King, Mabel, 905
King, Martha, 954
King, Martin Luther, Jr., 8, 134, 182, 854
King, Meegan, 205
King, Morgana, 31
King, Pamela, 347
King, Patsy, 674
King, Paul, 571
King, Pee Wee, 615, 648
King, Peggy, 322, 541, 577, 675, 884
King, Perry, 34, 88, 405, 680, 698, 866
King, Regina, 874
King, Reina, 906
King, Rodney, 1137
King Sisters, The, 451
King, Sonny, 421
King, Stephen, 333, 783, 986
King, Tom, 50, 60, 1067
King, Tony, 122
King, Walter Wolfe, 482
King, Wright, 438, 895
King, Zalman, 689, 934
Kingsley, Ben, 529, 980
Kingsley, Emily Perl, 1065, 1090, 1095, 1098, 1100, 1103, 1105, 1108, 1111, 1116, 1120
Kingsley, Sidney, 675
Kingston, Harry, 123
Kinison, Sam, 156
Kinkead, Maeve, 51, 348, 1110
Kinks, The, 750
Kinley, Kathryn, 542
Kinmont, Kathleen, 692
Kinne, Katherine, 385
Kinnear, Greg, 88, 171, 817, 1119

Kinney, Kathy, 239
Kinney, Terry, 832
Kinon, Richard, 493
Kinoy, Ernest, 210, 1048, 1072
Kinskey, Leonid, 650
Kinsley, Michael, 188
Kinsner, Kathy, 1113
Kintner, Robert E., 1121
Kiper, Tammy, 357
Kirby, Andrea, 806
Kirby, B., Jr., 801
Kirby, Bruce, 54, 384, 747, 868
Kirby, Durward, 140, 314, 345, 800
Kirby, George, 6, 45, 354
Kirby, Pat, 851
Kirby, Randy, 328
Kirby Stone Quintet, 452
Kirchenbauer, Bill, 345, 444
Kirchner, Claude, 506, 801
Kirgo, Dinah, 387, 1104
Kirgo, Julie, 387
Kirk, Joe, 11
Kirk, Lisa, 307, 572, 797
Kirk, Phyllis, 517, 665, 689, 701, 830, 876, 936
Kirk, Robert, 1105
Kirk, Tommy, 547
Kirkconnel, Claire, 640
Kirkes, Shirley, 103, 913
Kirkland, James, 635
Kirkland, Pat, 254
Kirksey, Diane, 228
Kirkwood, Craig, 714
Kirkwood, Jack, 620
Kirkwood, James, Jr., 882
Kirkwood, Joe, Jr., 435
Kirsch, Stan, 378
Kirschbaum, Bruce, 1112
Kirschbaum, Glenn, 1105
Kirschner, Jennifer, 347
Kirshenbaum, Susan, 1093, 1100
Kirshner, Don, 230, 448, 450, 565, 727, 928
Kirshner, Mia, 236
Kiser, Terry, 147, 227, 602, 705, 740
Kitaen, Tawny, 43, 599, 724
Kitchell, James W., 1055
Kitchen, Michael, 529, 530
Kitt, Eartha, 77, 665
Kittrell, Kaye, 319
Klaboe, Dana, 52
Klasky, Arlene, 1110, 1116
Klatscher, Laurie, 227
Klee, Larry, 512
Kleeb, Helen, 361, 654, 894
Klein, Dennis, 463
Klein, Kathleen, 1100
Klein, Larry, 1057, 1087, 1099
Klein, Nic, 777
Klein, Robert, 60, 174, 759
Klein, Spencer, 435, 486
Kleinerman, Isaac, 1052
Klemperer, Werner, 381, 1052, 1054
Klenck, Margaret, 64, 622
Klet, Stan, 812
Klick, Mary, 322, 432
Kline, Kevin, 736
Kline, Linda, 1090
Kline, Richard, 380, 631, 837, 842
Kling, Woody, 448, 552, 722, 928, 1059, 1062
Kloiber, Herbert, 1077
Klous, Pat, 34, 293, 493
Kluge, George, 829
Klugman, Jack, 146, 343, 361, 612, 675, 681, 929, 1048, 1057, 1061
Klynn, Herbert, 240

Menzelintsev, Igor, 1100
Menzies, Heather, 488
Merande, Doro, 120, 827
Mercer, Johnny, 539, 577
Mercer, Marian, 208, 229, 294,
    297, 385, 415, 524, 721, 800,
    861, 890, 960
Meredith, Burgess, 77, 96, 264,
    330, 456, 559, 734, 834, 966,
    968, 1071
Meredith, Charles, 704
Meredith, Cheerio, 620
Meredith, Don, 587, 1056
Meredith, Judi, 392
Meredith, Lee, 63
Meriwether, Lee (Lee Ann), 75,
    77, 167, 526, 574, 594, 841,
    844
Merkerson, S. Epatha, 373, 471,
    516, 648
Merlin, Jan, 848, 1067
Merman, Ethel, 77, 441, 946,
    951, 957, 958, 962, 972
Merrell, Richard, 623
Merrick, Dawn, 319
Merrill, Carol, 476
Merrill, Dina, 391
Merrill, Don, 928
Merrill, Gary, 23, 444, 525, 692,
    876, 919, 934
Merrill, Howard, 419
Merrill, Robert, 937, 945
Merriman, Grant, 276
Merriman, Randy, 95
Merriman, Ryan, 564
Merriman, Tyler, 276
Merritt, Theresa, 828
Merson, Marc, 447, 898
Mertes, Brian, 1116
Merton, Zienia, 777
Mesak, Charles, 1039
Meserve, Jeanne, 9
Meshekoff, Michael, 791
Meskill, Katherine, 226, 251,
    735, 909
Messick, Don, 240, 430, 439,
    712, 929
Messing, Debra, 588, 592
Messner, Johnny, 886
Mesta, Perle, 279
Meston, John, 351
Meszaros, Michu, 23
Metalious, Grace, 656
Metcalf, Laurie, 708, 1109, 1112,
    1115
Metcalf, Rory, 1087
Metcalfe, Burt, 281, 357, 502
Metcalfe, Ken, 935
Metchik, Aaron, 860
Metrano, Art, 45, 160, 433, 498,
    573, 839, 861
Mettey, Lynnette, 288, 681
Metz, Robert, 59
Metzinger, Kraig, 533, 724
Metzler, Jim, 88, 190
Meurer, Terry Dunn, 879
Meyer, Anton, 88
Meyer, Bess, 114, 607, 641, 706
Meyer, Breckin, 385, 423
Meyer, George, 1102, 1106, 1117
Meyer, Nicholas, 973
Meyer, Taro, 52
Meyerink, Victoria, 197
Meyers, Ari, 446
Meyers, Nancy, 69
Miano, Robert, 320
Micelli, Justine, 588
Michael, George, 322, 546
Michael, Marjorie, 546
Michael, Ralph, 225, 680
Michaelis, Arnold, 15
Michaels, Al, 587, 805

Michaels, Corinne, 142, 205
Michaels, David, 1097, 1102
Michaels, David Shawn, 437
Michaels, Frankie, 62
Michaels, Freeman, 933
Michaels, Jeanna, 318, 723, 932
Michaels, Lorne, 466, 598, 603,
    726, 727, 1065, 1068, 1070,
    1072, 1102, 1111
Michaels, Margaret, 723
Michaels, Marilyn, 6
Michaels, Nick, 304
Michaels, Ray, 721
Michaels, Tommy J., 31
Michaelsen, Kari, 327
Michaelsen, Melissa, 537
Michaux, Solomon Lightfoot,
    255
Michel, Franny, 55
Michel, Werner, 251
Michele, Bridget, 683
Michele, Michael, 152, 196, 341
Michell, Keith, 760, 1059
Michelman, Ken, 116, 910
Michenaud, Gerald, 842
Michener, James A., 67, 94, 776
Mickey, Patricia, 332
Middendorf, Tracy, 206
Middlecoff, Cary, 925
Middleton, Tom, 701
Midgley, Leslie, 1062
Midkiff, Dale, 195, 238, 841, 979
Midler, Bette, 159, 855, 884,
    966, 985, 1073, 1109
Mifune, Toshiro, 751
Migday, Anita, 150
Migenes, Julia, 847
Mike Curb Congregation, 329
Mikler, Mike, 935
Milan, Frank, 921
Milano, Alyssa, 912, 984
Milano, Frank, 707
Milch, David, 141, 1086, 1117
Miles, Elaine, 608
Miles, Hank, 314
Miles, Joanna, 28, 251, 840, 963,
    1063, 1064
Miles, Richard, 89
Miles, Sarah, 530
Miles, Sherry, 370, 645
Miles, Vera, 965
Milford, John, 258, 478
Milgrim, Lynn, 50, 64
Milian, Tomas, 302
Milkis, Edward K., 103, 656
Millan, Ashley Nicole, 932
Millan, Robyn, 715, 909
Millan, Victor, 683
Milland, Ray, 88, 519, 685, 695
Millar, Marjie, 237, 685
Miller, Alan, 93
Miller, Allan, 10, 311, 319, 395,
    593, 621, 724
Miller, Arthur, 551, 631, 956,
    957, 969, 975, 1051, 1081
Miller, Barry, 259, 434, 810
Miller, Cheryl, 192
Miller, Christa, 239
Miller, Cory, 27
Miller, Dan, 645
Miller, Dean, 163, 209, 374, 829
Miller, Denise, 27, 288, 510, 663
Miller, Dennis, 212, 727, 1115,
    1118
Miller, Denny (Scott), 564, 890
Miller, Dick, 273
Miller, Dorothy, 851
Miller, Gary, 436
Miller, George, 871
Miller, Glenn, 329
Miller, Harvey, 758
Miller, Herman, 458, 513

Miller, Howard, 19, 169, 443
Miller, J. P., 1054
Miller, J. Phillip, 1068
Miller, J. R., 689
Miller, Jack, 55
Miller, James M., 562
Miller, Jeremy, 344
Miller, John L., 1094
Miller, Jonathan, 109, 342
Miller, Kathleen, 758
Miller, Kristine, 793
Miller, Lara Jill, 327
Miller, Larry, 679
Miller, Lee, 159, 652
Miller, Linda G., 556
Miller, Marilyn Suzanne, 726,
    1070, 1072, 1104
Miller, Mark, 119, 205, 317, 346,
    589, 665
Miller, Mark Thomas, 554
Miller, Marvin, 551
Miller, Maxine, 731
Miller, Mitch, 296, 757
Miller, Nolan, 245
Miller, Pamela, 736
Miller, Penelope Ann, 668
Miller, Peter, 318
Miller, Robyn, 646
Miller, Roger, 704
Miller, Ron, 547
Miller, Sam, 984
Miller, Sharon, 1086, 1087
Miller, Stephanie, 789
Miller, Taylor, 29, 51
Miller, Thomas L., 103, 337,
    632, 656
Miller, Tom, 537
Miller, Ty, 392, 935
Miller, Victor, 1093, 1100
Miller, Walter C., 1059, 1112,
    1115
Miller, Will, 629
Miller, Wynne, 630, 771
Millerick, Kerry, 686, 828, 1111
Millhollin, James, 344
Milli, Robert, 30, 50, 347, 493,
    621
Milligan, Patti, 99
Milligan, Spencer, 462
Mills, Alison, 442, 475
Mills, Alley, 65, 511, 923
Mills, Christiaan, 623
Mills, Donna, 335, 437, 454, 494
Mills, Gordon, 258
Mills, Hayley, 528, 893
Mills, John, 242, 530, 940
Mills, Judson, 64
Mills, Juliet, 590, 1067
Mills, Mort, 197, 515
Mills, Susan, 1079, 1082, 1084
Mills, Ted, 313, 645, 728
Millstein, Beth, 204
Milne, A. A., 594
Milner, Martin, 14, 797, 809
Milos, Sofia, 136
Mimieux, Yvette, 87, 571
Mims, William, 317, 490
Mincer, Richard, 1074, 1076,
    1079, 1081, 1092
Mineo, Sal, 457, 798, 948
Miner, Jan, 186, 701
Miner, Peter, 1087, 1090
Miner, Rachel, 349
Miner, Worthington "Tony," 268,
    307, 444, 538, 558, 797, 902
Mines, Steven (Steve), 61, 204,
    641
Minkus, Barbara, 189, 492
Minnelli, Liza, 441, 557, 828,
    950, 956, 962, 967, 969, 971,
    1060
Minnesota Fats, 151

Newmar, Julie, 77, 580
Newmark, Matthew, 641
New Seekers, The, 448
Newsom, David, 387
Newton, Connie. *See* Needham, Connie
Newton, Dana, 1116, 1119
Newton, John, 227
Newton, John Haymes, 563, 803, 880
Newton, Richard, 364
Newton, Robert, 490
Newton, Sandie, 625
Newton, Wayne, 422, 428
New Yorkers, The, 437
Ng, Irene, 31
Nguyen, Dustin, 870
Nguyen Van Thieu, 885
Nicassio, JoeAl, 873
Nicastro, Michelle, 724
Nicholas, Denise, 69, 408, 706
Nicholl, Don, 242, 428, 708, 836
Nicholl, Lee, 933
Nichols, Anthony, 153
Nichols, Barbara, 497, 753
Nichols, Josephine, 826, 841
Nichols, Mike, 243, 273, 469, 665, 834, 950, 951
Nichols, Nichelle, 786, 787
Nichols, Stephen, 206, 258, 724, 738
Nichols, Taylor, 514
Nicholson, Bobby, 350, 396
Nicholson, Carol, 706
Nicholson, Erwin, 251, 1060
Nicholson, Jack, 78, 365, 901
Nicholson, Nick, 780
Nickell, Paul, 797
Nickerson, Charles, 23
Nickerson, Dawn, 362
Nickerson, Denise, 735
Nickerson, J. R., 23
Nickerson, Shane, 348
Nicksay, Lily, 114
Nickson, Julia, 606
Nicola, Nassira, 308
Nicoll, Kristina, 810
Nielsen, Leslie, 71, 110, 115, 333, 338, 595, 666, 748, 817, 892
Nielsen, Tom, 348
Nies, Eric, 687
Nigh, Jane, 96
Nigro, Giovanna, 813
Niklas, Jan, 656
Niles, Wendell, 414
Nilsson, Harry, 961
Nimmo, Bill, 295, 448, 638, 911
Nimoy, Leonard, 179, 407, 517, 556, 784, 786, 787, 903
Nipar, Yvette, 319, 702
Nipote, Joe, 886
Nipper, Will, 596
Nirvana, 503
Nirvana, Yana, 465
Nisbet, Steve, 736
Nissen, Tim, 51
Nite, Norm, 35
Nittoli, Tony Deacon, 264
Niven, David, 22, 202, 299, 704
Niven, Kip, 31
Niven, Paul, 897
Nix, Martha, 205, 895
Nix, Taylor, 564
Nixon, Agnes, 28, 30, 50, 60, 346, 498, 621, 735, 1093, 1100
Nixon, Cynthia, 818
Nixon, President Richard (Dick), 131, 201, 469, 852, 946, 954, 982
Niznik, Stephanie, 883
Noah, Robert, 391, 507

Noble, Chelsea, 345, 452
Noble, James (Jim), 61, 86, 119, 287, 925
Noble, Trisha, 264, 796
Nodella, Burt, 1051, 1053
Nodella, Matthew, 1108
Noel, Dick, 714, 824
Noel, Henri, 577
Nolan, Barry, 359
Nolan, Jeanette, 221, 392, 695, 887
Nolan, Kathy, 120, 425, 686, 835
Nolan, Lloyd, 296, 442, 522, 778, 1042
Nolan, Patrick, 1076
Nolan, Tommy (Tom), 124, 430
Nolin, Gena Lee, 80
Nolte, Nick, 695
Nomkeena, Keena, 116
Noonan, Hugh, 393
Noonan, John Ford, 1089
Noonan, Tommy, 640
Noone, Kathleen, 29, 455, 1097
Norcross, Clayton, 109
Norden, Tommy, 292, 736
Norell, Henry, 614
Norman, B. G., 480
Norman, Cleandre, 321
Norman, Maidie, 205
Norman, Susan, 642
Norman, Teddy, 886
Norrell, Michael, 257
Norris, Bruce, 668
Norris, Christopher, 349, 724, 863
Norris, Chuck, 164, 890
Norris, Jan, 416
Norris, Kathi, 447, 780, 812, 867
Norris, Lee, 34, 114, 860
North, Alan, 274, 666, 861
North, Heather, 204, 641
North, Jay, 212, 534, 631, 648
North, Sheree, 93, 405, 525, 630
North, Steven, 1068
North, Zeme, 234
Northcutte, Shawnte, 547
Northrop, Wayne, 206, 244
Northshield, Robert, 1055, 1058
Norton, Cliff, 200, 310, 313, 416, 753, 909
Norton, Coe, 735
Norton, John K., 53
Norton, Judy (Judy Norton-Taylor), 894
Norton, Leonie, 50, 495, 621
Norville, Deborah, 38, 410, 586, 846
Norwood, Brandy, 828
Norwood, Willie, 756
Noseworthy, Jack, 207, 821
Noseworthy, James, 252
Noteworthies, The, 432
Noth, Chris, 471
Nouri, Michael, 79, 81, 168, 236, 313, 493, 736, 772
Nourse, Allen, 251
Novack, Shelly, 267, 571
Novak, John, 723
Novak, Kim, 272, 790, 947, 960, 964
Novak, Robert, 188, 262, 536
Novatt, Patrick, 737
Novello, Don, 706, 726, 727, 768
Novello, Jay, 536
Novick, Lynn, 1117
Novins, Stuart, 875
Novod, Gordon, 736
Noxon, Nicolas, 1058, 1073
Noyes, Tyler, 623
Nozizwe, Lena, 271
Nucci, Danny, 272, 677
Nuckols, William, 806

Nuemann, Dorothy, 357
Nugent, Edward, 654
Nugent, Ted, 545
Nummi, Ron, 498
Nunez, Miguel A., Jr., 582, 694, 861
Nunn, Alice, 139, 857, 904
Nunn, Bill, 863
Nunn, Ray, 1107, 1113
Nunn, Trevor, 602
Nureyev, Rudolf, 383, 962
Nusser, James, 351
Nuyen, France, 718
Nyby, Christian, 675
Nye, Bill, 98
Nye, Louis, 48, 357, 593, 674, 790, 791, 850
Nykanen, Mark, 565
Nype, Russell, 233, 947

Oakes, Randi, 135, 617
Oakland, Simon, 69, 201, 604, 849
Oakley, Bill, 1117
Oaks, Sally Lou, 1107
Oas-Heim, Gordon, 597
Oates, Warren, 792, 970
Ober, Ken, 642, 691
Oberdiear, Karen, 826
Oberon, Merle, 64
Oboler, Arch, 174, 482
O'Boyle, Maureen, 189, 265
O'Brian, Hugh, 641, 652, 734, 927, 958
O'Brien, Carl "Cubby," 546
O'Brien, Clay, 185
O'Brien, Conal, 1119
O'Brien, Conan, 466, 467, 1102
O'Brien, David (Dave), 52, 227, 631, 716, 735, 739, 1046
O'Brien, Edmond, 438, 490, 542, 720, 958
O'Brien, Erin. *See* Moore, Erin O'Brien
O'Brien, Joan, 106, 477
O'Brien, Liam, 666, 1068
O'Brien, Margaret, 949
O'Brien, Maria, 610, 887
O'Brien, Mary, 317
O'Brien, Pat, 307, 361, 395, 634, 1064
O'Brien, Rory, 279
O'Brien, Simon, 632
O'Brien, Tom, 542
O'Brien, Vince, 736
O'Bryan, Lauren, 716
O'Bryan, Sean, 661
O'Bryon, Linda, 604
O'Byrne, Bryan, 104, 612
O'Casey, Sean, 919
Ocean, Ivory, 449
Ochs, Ace, 268
Ochtun, Christine, 1082
O'Connell, Arthur, 738
O'Connell, David J., 627, 1054
O'Connell, Deirdre, 758
O'Connell, Helen, 370, 374, 714, 813, 844, 948, 1065
O'Connell, Jerry, 139, 580, 764
O'Connell, John, 1116
O'Connell, Kevin, 331
O'Connell, Patrick, 349, 498
O'Connell, Taaffe, 102
O'Conner, Nuala, 1115
O'Connor, Brian, 750
O'Connor, Candace, 376
O'Connor, Carroll, 26, 27, 28, 355, 407, 962, 1058, 1071, 1073, 1076, 1101, 1129
O'Connor, Dan, 601
O'Connor, Des, 213
O'Connor, Dick, 713

Peterson, Gene, 343, 494
Peterson, Gordon, 410
Peterson, Houston, 829
Peterson, James A., 295
Peterson, Jennifer, 205
Peterson, Lenka, 52, 53, 111, 735, 736, 840
Peterson, Maggie, 98
Peterson, Nathanal, 366
Peterson, Renny, 509
Peterson, Robyn, 69, 377, 415
Peterson, Virgilia, 67
Petok, Michael, 1103
Petrie, Daniel (Dan), 264, 798, 1070, 1072, 1109
Petrie, Doris, 376
Petrie, Dorothea G., 1093, 1103
Petrie, George, 61, 735, 920
Petrovna, Sonia, 252, 736
Pettet, Joanna, 88
Pettiet, Christopher, 935
Pettifer, Julian, 626
Pettiford, Valarie, 53, 623
Pettit, Tom, 1053, 1055, 1063, 1125
Pettus, Ken, 532
Petty, Lori, 111, 834
Petty, Ross, 29
Petty, Tom, 417
Pewowar, Jules, 562
Peyser, John, 187, 688, 788
Peyser, Penny, 185, 454, 695, 857
Peyton, K. M., 289
Pfander, Carol, 227
Pfeiffer, Dedee, 191
Pfeiffer, Michelle, 68, 211, 342, 756
Pfenning, Wesley Ann, 50
Pfister, Wally, 1058
Pfizer, Beryl, 844, 1079
Pflug, Jo Ann, 140, 272, 627, 699
Phares, Frank, 587
Phelps, Brian, 18
Phelps, Eleanor, 739
Phelps, Jill Farren, 1099, 1102, 1104
Phelps, Peter, 80
Phelps, Robert, 736
Phelps, Stuart, 480
Philbin, Jack, 423
Philbin, Joy, 486
Philbin, Regis, 33, 436, 486, 593, 690, 716
Philbrick, Herbert A., 400
Philbrook, James, 412, 413, 597
Philipp, Karen, 497, 501
Philips, Julie, 51
Philips, Lee, 256, 797
Philips, Tacey, 170
Phillipe, Ryan, 341
Phillippe, André, 559
Phillips, Anton, 777
Phillips, Barney, 90, 237, 283, 438, 869
Phillips, Britta, 428
Phillips, Carmen, 478
Phillips, Conrad, 527, 916
Phillips, Ethan, 86, 787
Phillips, Grace, 574, 623
Phillips, Irna, 49, 50, 60, 119, 204, 346, 493, 621, 699, 829
Phillips, Jeff, 349
Phillips, Joseph C., 181, 320
Phillips, Julianne, 759
Phillips, Katherine, 60
Phillips, Kathryn, 925
Phillips, Mackenzie, 619
Phillips, Michelle, 392, 454, 737, 738
Phillips, Nancie, 469
Phillips, Peggy, 204, 608

Phillips, Robin, 960
Phillips, Sian, 528
Phillips, Stone, 199, 869
Phillips, Wendy, 250, 264, 272, 387, 700, 928
Phillips, William F., 166
Philpott, John, 125
Philpott, Mark, 623
Phipps, Joey Alan, 252
Phipps, William Edward, 85, 112, 724, 840
Phoenix, Leaf, 570
Phoenix, River, 744
Piazza, Ben, 134, 495, 898
Piazza, Marguerite, 937
Picardo, Robert, 162, 787, 923
Picerni, Paul, 880, 935
Pickard, Jack, 112
Pickard, John, 351
Pickens, James, Jr., 52
Pickens, Jane, 426
Pickens, Slim, 68, 190, 285, 591, 633
Pickering, Robert (Bob), 205, 346
Pickett, Cindy, 44, 138, 348, 718
Pickles, Christina, 51, 347, 649, 718
Picon, Molly, 563, 772
Picotte, Lisa, 380
Pidgeon, Walter, 652, 949, 950, 955, 965
Piekarski, Julie, 269, 547
Pierce, Barbara, 297, 563
Pierce, Bradley, 747
Pierce, David Hyde, 302, 669, 1118
Pierce, Devon, 932, 933
Pierce, Maggie, 580
Pierce, Robert, 505
Pierce, Verna, 736
Pierce, Webb, 635, 900
Pierce, Wendell, 141
Pierpoint, Eric, 25, 273, 391
Pierpoint, Robert, 1063
Pierre, Olivier, 731
Pierson, Geoffrey (Geoff), 53, 715, 878
Pierson, Lin, 347
Pierson, Richard, 525
Pietragallo, Gene, 737
Pietropinto, Angela, 53
Pietz, Amy, 148, 576
Pigeon, Corky, 755
Piggott-Smith, Tim, 529
Pike, James A., 42
Pillar, Gary, 346
Pillot, Judd, 105
Pillsbury, Drew, 515
Pillsbury, Sarah, 1114
Pilon, Daniel, 348, 355, 716
Pinassi, Dominique, 566
Pinchot, Bronson, 36, 321, 650, 724, 866, 986
Pincus, Irving, 256, 558, 686
Pincus, Norman, 256, 558
Pine, Larry, 31, 349, 623
Pine, Lester, 668
Pine, Phillip, 333
Pine, Robert, 87, 109, 135
Pine, Tina, 668
Pines, Gayle, 736
Pinette, John, 642, 886
Pingitore, Carl, 666, 1068
Pinkard, Ron, 257
Pinkerton-Peabody, Nancy (Nancy Pinkerton), 63, 227, 621, 735, 772
Pinkett, Jada, 218
Pinkins, Tonya, 31, 63, 879
Pinn, Irene, 1062
Pinsent, Gordon, 297, 970

Pinsker, Judith, 1075, 1077, 1080, 1087, 1090, 1119
Pintauro, Daniel (Danny), 63, 912
Pinter, Colleen Zenk (Colleen Zenk), 62
Pinter, Harold, 530
Pinter, Mark, 53, 62, 84, 348, 496, 498, 740
Pinto, Johnny, 161
Pinza, Ezio, 33, 111, 267, 946
Pioli, Judy, 748, 785
Piper, Lara, 367, 449
Piper, "Rowdy" Roddy, 379
Pipkin, Magot, 1103
Pirri, Jim, 687
Pisani, Remo, 692
Piscopo, Joe, 726
Pithey, Winsley, 718
Pitillo, Maria, 548, 643, 716, 776
Pitlik, Noam, 107, 406, 1076
Pitoniak, Anne, 19
Pitt, Brad, 330
Pitt, Norman, 718
Pitta, Mark, 861
Pittman, Frank, 77
Pitts, ZaSu, 126, 614
Piven, Byrne, 880
Piven, Jeremy, 147, 255, 464, 672
Pizo, Vince, 434
Pizzey, Jack, 775
Place, Lou, 223
Place, Mary Kay, 297, 524, 581, 1071
Plain, Belva, 975
Plakson, Suzie, 493
Plana, Tony, 73
Plank, Melinda, 611, 735, 772
Plank, Scott, 774
Plante, Bill, 1058
Plante, Carol-Ann, 362
Plantt-Winston, Susan, 29
Plath, Sylvia, 888
Plato, Dana, 218, 219
Platt, Edward (Ed), 316, 324
Platt, Howard, 257, 293, 722
Platt, Louise, 347
Platts, Alma, 829
Playdon, Paul, 604
Player, Gary, 153
Player, Jessica, 245, 275
Playten, Alice, 491
Plaza, Begona, 198
Pleasence, Angela, 529, 760
Pleasence, Donald, 529, 701, 958, 963
Pledger, Courtney, 891
Pleshette, John, 454, 966
Pleshette, Suzanne, 107, 114, 118, 359, 506, 604, 958
Pleven, Katel, 349
Plimpton, George, 343, 974
Plimpton, Martha, 985
Plotnikov, Boris, 656
Plowman, Melinda, 635, 665
Plowright, Joan, 529, 530, 984
Plumb, Eve, 115, 116, 308, 485
Plumb, Flora, 295, 497
Plummer, Amanda, 1109
Plummer, Christopher, 354, 594, 616, 834, 950, 959, 976, 1071, 1115
Podell, Art, 595
Podewell, Cathy, 194
Pogostin, S. Lee, 950
Pogue, Ken, 15, 698
Pohl, Frederick IV, 1110, 1119
Pohle, Robin, 205
Pohlman, Ray, 750
Poindexter, Larry, 240
Poindexter, Ron, 329
Pointer, Priscilla, 194

Serrano, Diego, 53
Serrano, Nestor, 363, 866
Server, Eric, 68, 317
Servitto, Matt, 31, 64, 623
Seton, Bruce, 268
Sevareid, Eric, 43, 90, 130, 142,
  178, 259, 734, 765, 951, 954,
  961, 962, 1061, 1063, 1124,
  1125
Severance, Joan, 920
Severinsen, Carl "Doc", 213, 854
Sewell, Anna, 17
Sewell, George, 875
Sexton, Dee Ann, 52
Seymour, Anne, 257, 701, 839
Seymour, Dan, 264, 349, 757,
  899, 909
Seymour, Jane, 176, 225, 896,
  935, 970, 976, 979, 1098
Seymour, Ralph, 510
Seymour, Shaughan, 529
Sha Na Na, 746
Shabba-Doo, 95
Shackelford, Gary, 194
Shackelford, Michael David, 273
Shackelford, Ted, 51, 454, 777
Shackleford, Lynn, 33
Shadel, Willard (Bill), 7, 142, 293
Shadix, Glenn, 437
Shafer, Ross, 204, 468, 531
Shaffer, Louise, 30, 32, 252, 715,
  735, 736, 909, 1087
Shaffer, Lydia Jean, 265
Shaffer, Paul, 467, 468, 727, 928
Shaftel, Joe, 794
Shahan, Rocky, 684
Shaiman, Marc, 1110
Shakar, Martin, 227
Shakespeare, William, 20, 747
Shakman, Matt, 444
Shaler, Anna, 51
Shalhoub, Tony, 918
Shalit, Gene, 583, 845, 846
Shandling, Garry, 417, 463, 466,
  545, 855
Shane, Jim, 598
Shane, Maxwell, 837
Shanks, Bill, 63
Shanks, Don, 478
Shannon, Del, 187
Shannon, George, 320, 736
Shannon, James, 227
Shannon, Michael, 29, 310, 697,
  736
Shannon, Molly, 727
Shannon, Wanda, 357
Shapiro, Arnold, 1075, 1114
Shapiro, Debbie, 865
Shapiro, Esther, 245, 256
Shapiro, George, 1111
Shapiro, Jordana "Bink," 831
Shapiro, Ken, 340
Shapiro, Richard, 245, 256
Sharif, Omar, 656, 956
Sharkey, Ray, 514, 920
Sharma, Barbara, 330, 469, 694
Sharnik, John, 1058
Sharon, Fran, 50, 251, 735
Sharp, Coleen, 646
Sharp, John, 721
Sharp, Monti, 349, 1113
Sharp, Phil, 768, 1044
Sharp, Thom, 287, 354, 809
Sharpe, Damon, 352
Sharpe, Don, 825, 919, 928
Sharpe, Karen, 438
Sharpe, Mal, 795
Sharpton, Al, 571
Sharrett, Michael, 435, 803
Shatner, William, 74, 210, 296,
  338, 409, 692, 786, 787, 798,
  811

Shatz, Diane, 208
Shaud, Grant, 575
Shaughnessy, Charles, 206, 590
Shaughnessy, David, 1113
Shaughnessy, Mickey, 160
Shaver, Helen, 430, 879, 889
Shaw, David, 665
Shaw, Dee, 408
Shaw, Fiona, 530
Shaw, Gary, 1083
Shaw, Holly, 6
Shaw, Irwin, 695
Shaw, Jerome, 881, 1067, 1077,
  1080
Shaw, Lou, 93
Shaw, Mark, 649
Shaw, Martin, 224, 529
Shaw, Reta, 48, 90, 147, 325,
  404, 559, 614
Shaw, Robert, 123
Shaw, Robert J., 320
Shaw, Roderick, 17
Shaw, Stan, 556, 707
Shaw, Steve, 454
Shaw, Susan, 624
Shaw, Vanessa, 536
Shaw, Victoria, 317
Shawlee, Joan, 11, 89, 217, 282
Shawn, Dick, 144, 523, 693, 947
Shay, Michelle, 52
Shayne, Cari, 319, 986
Shayne, Robert, 804
Shea, Chris, 747
Shea, Eric, 48
Shea, Joe, 774
Shea, John, 488, 889, 973, 979,
  981, 1098
Shea, Mary Frances, 1102
Shea, Michael, 594, 595
Sheafe, Alex, 227
Shear, Barry, 346, 432, 440, 487
Shear, Jules, 503
Shear, Pearl, 107, 174
Shearer, Harry, 283, 726, 756,
  800
Shearin, John, 118, 227, 498, 933
Shearing, George, 950
Sheedy, Ally, 985
Sheehan, David, 37
Sheehan, Douglas (Doug), 203,
  318, 454
Sheehan, Tony, 10
Sheen, Fulton J., 479, 1040
Sheen, Martin, 103, 210, 962, 963,
  964, 966, 971, 973, 1095, 1115
Sheffer, Craig, 355, 622
Sheffield, Jay, 818
Sheffield, Jeanne, 431
Sheffield, Reginald, 704
Sheffield, Sally, 287
Sheiner, David, 215, 559
Sheinkopf, David, 272
Sheldon, Gene, 940
Sheldon, Herb, 792
Sheldon, Jack, 146, 328, 713
Sheldon, James, 829
Sheldon, Lee, 251
Sheldon, Mary, 933
Sheldon, Sidney, 400, 590, 973,
  976
Shelle, Lori, 348
Shelley, Carole, 30, 612, 623
Shelley, Joshua, 68
Shellhorn, Bob, 1097, 1099
Shelly, Freeman, 539
Shelton, Deborah, 194
Shelton, George, 414
Shelton, Marlee, 47
Shelton, Reid, 286
Shelton, Sloane, 295
Sheman, Arlene, 1116
Shenar, Paul, 967

Shenkarow, Justin, 253, 660
Shepard, Kiki, 418
Shepherd, Chaz Lamar, 537
Shepherd, Cybill, 191, 567, 928,
  975
Shepherd, Jean, 427
Shepherd, Sherri, 167
Shepodd, Jon, 464
Sheppard, Sam, 335
Sheppard, William Morgan, 534
Sher, Jack, 384
Shera, Mark, 75, 717
Sheralee, 936
Sheridan, Ann, 51, 297, 662
Sheridan, Ardell, 801
Sheridan, Bonnie (Bonnie
  Bramlett), 709
Sheridan, Elizabeth, 742
Sheridan, Jamey, 160, 748, 783
Sheridan, Liz, 22
Sheridan, Nancy, 294, 888
Sheridan, Nicollette, 454, 640
Sheridan, Rondell, 553
Sheridan, Tony, 614
Sherin, Ed, 1114
Sherman, Allan, 284, 419
Sherman, Arlene, 1099, 1107,
  1110, 1119
Sherman, Bobby, 325, 373, 750
Sherman, Courtney, 64, 736
Sherman, Harry R., 1068, 1071,
  1073
Sherman, Howard, 317
Sherman, Jenny, 205, 317
Sherman, Melissa, 227, 435
Sherman, Ransom, 45, 281, 684
Sherman, Robert, 1084
Sherman, Wayne, 318
Sherr, Lynn, 869
Sherrill, Stephen, 1117
Sherrin, Ned, 827
Sherry, Bill, 485
Sherry, Diane, 99
Sherwood, Anthony, 21
Sherwood, Bobby, 681, 788, 789
Sherwood, Brad, 601
Sherwood, Don, 169
Sherwood, Gale, 947
Sherwood, Jane, 247
Sherwood, Madeline, 293, 347,
  740
Sherwood, Robert, 675, 740
Shield, Bob, 440
Shields & Yarnell, 750, 774
Shields, Arthur, 938
Shields, Fred, 539
Shields, Helen, 176, 306
Shields, Robert, 750
Shilts, Randy, 985
Shimada, Yoko, 752
Shimerman, Armin, 786
Shimoda, Yuki, 438
Shimono, Sab, 350
Ship, Reuben, 480
Shipp, John Wesley, 31, 63, 289,
  348, 759, 1095, 1097
Shipp, Mary, 481, 579
Shire, Talia, 695, 985
Shirley, Tom, 306, 495
Shirriff, Catherine (Cathy), 698,
  748
Shivas, Mark, 1096
Shoberg, Dick (Richard), 29,
  252, 771
Shockley, Sallie, 725
Shockley, William, 225, 335
Shoemaker, Pamela, 252, 253
Shoenman, Elliot, 1090
Sholdar, Mickey, 279
Sholem, Lee, 804
Shor, Dan, 136, 586
Shore, Dinah, 107, 164, 219,

FOR THE BEST IN PAPERBACKS, LOOK FOR THE

In every corner of the world, on every subject under the sun, Penguin represents quality and variety—the very best in publishing today.

For complete information about books available from Penguin—including Penguin Classics, Penguin Compass, and Puffins—and how to order them, write to us at the appropriate address below. Please note that for copyright reasons the selection of books varies from country to country.

In the United States: Please write to *Penguin Group (USA), P.O. Box 12289 Dept. B, Newark, New Jersey 07101-5289* or call *1-800-788-6262*.

In the United Kingdom: Please write to *Dept. EP, Penguin Books Ltd, Bath Road, Harmondsworth, West Drayton, Middlesex UB7 0DA*.

In Canada: Please write to *Penguin Books Canada Ltd, 10 Alcorn Avenue, Suite 300, Toronto, Ontario M4V 3B2*.

In Australia: Please write to *Penguin Books Australia Ltd, P.O. Box 257, Ringwood, Victoria 3134*.

In New Zealand: Please write to *Penguin Books (NZ) Ltd, Private Bag 102902, North Shore Mail Centre, Auckland 10*.

In India: Please write to *Penguin Books India Pvt Ltd, 11 Panchsheel Shopping Centre, Panchsheel Park, New Delhi 110 017*.

In the Netherlands: Please write to *Penguin Books Netherlands bv, Postbus 3507, NL-1001 AH Amsterdam*.

In Germany: Please write to *Penguin Books Deutschland GmbH, Metzlerstrasse 26, 60594 Frankfurt am Main*.

In Spain: Please write to *Penguin Books S. A., Bravo Murillo 19, 1° B, 28015 Madrid*.

In Italy: Please write to *Penguin Italia s.r.l., Via Benedetto Croce 2, 20094 Corsico, Milano*.

In France: Please write to *Penguin France, Le Carré Wilson, 62 rue Benjamin Baillaud, 31500 Toulouse*.

In Japan: Please write to *Penguin Books Japan Ltd, Kaneko Building, 2-3-25 Koraku, Bunkyo-Ku, Tokyo 112*.

In South Africa: Please write to *Penguin Books South Africa (Pty) Ltd, Private Bag X14, Parkview, 2122 Johannesburg*.